BECKETT

Non-Sport ALMANAC

2023 • 9TH EDITION

THE #1 AUTHORITY ON COLLECTIBLES

THE HOBBY'S MOST RELIABLE AND RELIED UPON SOURCE™

Founder: Dr. James Beckett III

Edited By Matt Bible with the staff of Beckett Collectibles

Manufactured in the United States of America | Published by Beckett Collectibles LLC

BECKETT

Beckett Collectibles LLC
2700 Summit Ave, Ste 100
Plano, TX 75074
(866) 287-9383
beckett.com

First Printing
ISBN 978-1-953801-96-8

BECKETT Non-Sport ALMANAC

2023 • 9TH EDITION

EDITORIAL
Mike Payne - **Editorial Director**
Eric Knagg - **Lead Graphic Designer**

COLLECTIBLES DATA PUBLISHING
Brian Fleischer
Manager I Sr. Market Analyst
Daniel Moscoso - **Digital Studio**
Lloyd Almonguera, Ryan Altubar, Matt Bible, Jeff Camay, Steve Dalton, Justin Grunert, Sam Zimmer - **Price Guide Staff**

ADVERTISING
Alex Soriano - **Advertising Sales Executive**
alex@beckett.com 619.392.5299
Mike Garner - **Senior Sales Executive**
mgarner@beckett.com 615.447.5440

BECKETT GRADING SERVICES
2700 Summit Ave, Ste 100, Plano, TX 75074
Grading Sales – 972.448.9188 | grading@beckett.com

BECKETT GRADING SALES/SHOW STAFF
Dallas Office
2700 Summit Ave, Ste 100, Plano, TX 75074
Aram Munoz - **Senior Sales Executive**
amunoz@beckett.com

GRADING AND AUTH CUSTOMER SERVICE
customerservice@beckett.com

New York Office
484 White Plains Rd, 2nd Floor, Eastchester, N.Y. 10709
Charles Stabile - **Northeast Regional Sales Manager**
cstabile@beckett.com
914.268.0533

Asia Office
Seoul, Korea
Dongwoon Lee - **Asia/Pacific Sales Manager**
dongwoonl@beckett.com
Cell +82.10.6826.6868

OPERATIONS
Alberto Chavez - **Sr. Logistics & Facilities Manager**

CUSTOMER SERVICE
Beckett Collectibles LLC
2700 Summit Ave, Ste 100, Plano, TX 75074
Subscriptions, address changes, renewals, missing or damaged copies - 866.287.9383
239.653.0225 Foreign inquires subscriptions@beckett.com

Price Guide Inquiries
customerservice@beckett.com
239.280.2348

Back Issues beckettmedia.com
Books, Merchandise, Reprints 239.280.2380
Dealer Sales 239.280.2380 dealers@beckett.com

BECKETT

Beckett Collectibles LLC
Jeromy Murray - **President/COO**

Table of CONTENTS

Beckett® Almanac of Non-Sport Cards
Card Price Guide

THE WORLD'S MOST-TRUSTED SOURCE IN COLLECTING

Welcome to the 9th Annual Beckett® Almanac of Non-Sport Cards. This new edition has been enhanced and expanded from the previous volume with the addition of new releases, updated prices, and changes to older listings. The Beckett® Non-Sport Almanac will do what no other non-sports publication has done -- give you the most complete and comprehensive listings possible. The prices were added to the card lists just prior to printing and reflect not the author's opinions or desires, but the going retail prices for each card, based on the marketplace such as conventions and shows, hobby shops, online trading, auction results and other firsthand reports of realized sales.

What is the best price guide available on the market today? Of course, sellers will prefer the price guide with the highest prices, while buyers will naturally prefer the one with the lower prices. Accuracy, however, is the true test. Compared to other price guides, The Beckett® Non-Sport Almanac may not always have the highest or lowest values, but the accuracy of both our checklists and pricing – produced with the utmost integrity – will make it the most widely used reference book in the hobby.

LISTINGS AND SECTIONS

Each collection is personal and reflects the individuality of its owner. There are no set rules on how to collect cards. Since card collecting is a hobby or leisure pastime, what you collect, how much you collect, and how much time and money you spend collecting are entirely up to you. The funds you have available for collecting and your own personal taste should determine how you collect.

It is not possible to collect every card ever produced. Therefore, beginners as well as intermediate and advanced collectors usually specialize in some way. One of the reasons this hobby is popular is that individual collectors can define and tailor their collecting methods to match their own tastes.

Many collectors select complete sets from particular years, acquire only certain actors/superheroes, while some collectors are only interested in collecting certain genres or autographs. And still, others collect cards by franchise, such as Marvel or Star Wars.

Remember, this is a hobby, so pick a style of collecting that appeals to you.

WHAT'S LISTED

Products listed in the Price Guide typically:

- Are produced by licensed manufacturers
- Have market activity on single items
- Are widely available
- International releases

HOW IT'S LISTED

Unlike regular Beckett® almanacs, the sort order of this publication is somewhat unique. Like the others, all listings are organized 1) alphabetically then 2) chronologically. However, some exceptions have been made to further accommodate the reader. Some television and movie franchises have been organized into special subsections that are marked with a header. For example, any and all Buffy the Vampire Slayer related sets are listed under a header entitled: Buffy the Vampire Slayer Universe. This is the case for several franchises including but not limited to: Doctor Who, Game of Thrones, Harry Potter, James Bond, and The Walking Dead. While these products are grouped into subsections, they will still maintain the alphabetic integrity of the publication as a whole.

WHAT THE COLUMNS MEAN

The LO and HI columns reflect current retail selling ranges. The HI column on the right generally represents the full retail selling price. The LO column on the left generally represents the lowest price one would expect to find with extensive shopping.

GRADING

All cards in the price guide are based on NrMint to Mint condition. Damaged cards are generally sold for 25 to 75 percent of Mint value. Toy prices are based on Mint condition. Toys that are loose (out-of-package) are generally sold for 50 percent of the listed price, but may list for less/more depending on market sales.

CURRENCY

This price guide is intended to reflect the entire North American market. While not all of the cards are produced in the United States, they will reflect the market value in U.S. dollars.

GLOSSARY/LEGEND

Our glossary defines terms most frequently used in the non-sports card collecting hobby. Some of these terms are common to other types of collecting. Some terms may have several meanings depending on the use and context.

ALB – Album exclusive card. This indicates that a card was only available in a collector album or binder that was devoted to a certain product.

AU – Certified autograph

B&W – Black and White variant - This indicates a color variant of card

BB – Box Bottom - A card or panel of cards on the bottom of a trading card box.

BI – Box-Incentive

BT – Box-Topper - A card, either regulation or jumbo sized, that is inserted in the top of a box of trading cards.

CH – Chase

CI – Case-Incentive or Case Insert - A unique card that is offered as an incentive to purchase a case (or cases) of trading cards.

CL – Checklist card. A card that lists, in order, the cards and players in the set or series.

COA – Certificate of Authenticity - A certificate issued by the manufacturer to insure the product's authenticity.

CON – Convention exclusive - These are cards that were only available, but widely distributed, throughout general non-sport conventions.

COR – Corrected version of an error card

CT – Case-topper exclusive card

EE – Entertainment Earth exclusive - An exclusive that was offered for sale on Entertainment Earth's website.

EL – Extremely Limited

ERR – Error card. A card with erroneous information, spelling or depiction on either side of the card. Most errors are not corrected by the manufacturer.

EXCH – Exchange

FACT – Factory set exclusive

FOIL – Holofoil

GEN – General Distribution

HOLO – Hologram

L – Limited

LE – Limited Edition

LS – Limited Series

MEM – Memorabilia card

NNO – Unnumbered card

NSU – Non-Sport Update exclusive card

NYCC – New York Comic Con

OPC – O-Pee-Chee (a Canadian subsidiary of Topps)

RED – Redemption card

RR – Rittenhouse Reward - A card that was only offered through Rittenhouse's membership reward program.

SDCC – San Diego Comic Con exclusive.

SI – Set-Incentive

SP – Single or Short Print. A short print is a card that was printed in less quantity compared to the other cards in the same series.

UER – Uncorrected error

UNC – Uncut sheet or panel

VAR – Variation card. One of two or more cards from the same series, with the same card number, that differ from one and other in some way. This sometimes occurs when the manufacture notices an error in one or more of the cards, corrects the mistake, and then resumes the printing process. In some cases, one of the variations may be relatively scarce.

VL – Very Limited

As with any new publication, we appreciate reader feedback. If you have any questions, concerns, or suggestions, please contact us at: nonsports@beckett.com

**We are currently editing our non-sport titles to include manufacturer/brand name so many titles may be different than the previous edition; however, they still appear in the same order.

THE HOT LIST >> TOP 10 NON-SPORT PRODUCTS OF THE YEAR

2022 SkyBox Marvel Metal Universe Spider-Man

2022 Fleer Ultra Avengers

2022 Topps Chrome Star Wars Galaxy

2022 Topps Chrome Garbage Pail Kids Series 5

2022 Finest Star Wars

2022 Topps Chrome Garbage Pail Kids Series 4

2022 Topps Garbage Pail Kids Book Worms

2022 Topps Star Wars The Book of Boba Fett

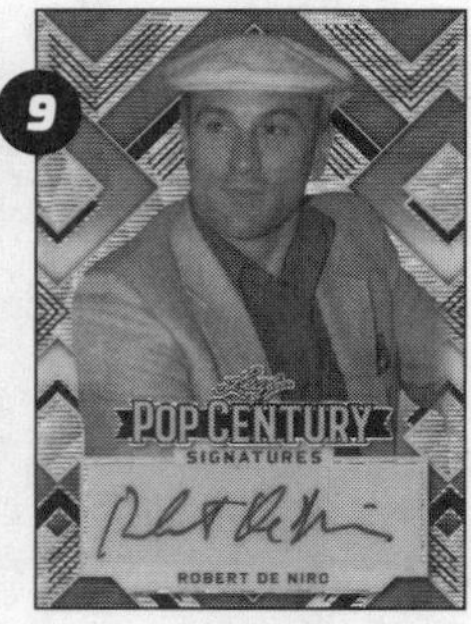

2022 Leaf Pop Century Metal

2022 Topps Chrome Black Star Wars

THE HOT LIST >> TOP 10 NON-SPORT AUTOGRAPHS OF THE YEAR

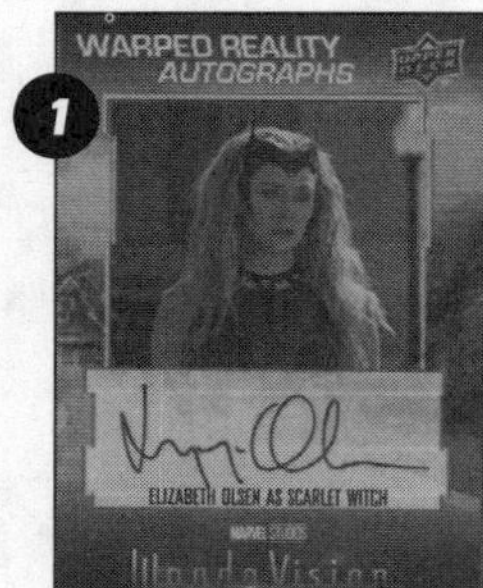

2022 Upper Deck WandaVision Warped Reality Autographs #WRAEO Elizabeth Olsen C

2022 Rittenhouse Game of Thrones The Complete Series Volume 2 Full Bleed Autographs #NNO Emilia Clarke S

2022 CZX Middle-Earth Autographs #IMGG2 Ian McKellen as Gandalf/65

2022 Topps Chrome Star Wars Galaxy #GARD Rosario Dawson

2023 Rittenhouse Doctor Who Series 1-4 Full Bleed Autographs #NNO Andrew Garfield

2022 Upper Deck Spider-Man Into the Spider-Verse Spider-Sigs Portraits #SSPHS2 Hailee Steinfeld D

2022 Upper Deck WandaVision Warped Reality Autographs #WRAKH2 Kathryn Hahn B

2023 Upper Deck Shang-Chi and the Legend of the Ten Rings Autographs #A9 Awkwafina B

2023 Rittenhouse Doctor Who Series 1-4 Full Bleed Autographs #NNO David Tennant

2023 Upper Deck Shang-Chi and the Legend of the Ten Rings Autographs #A5 Simu Liu as Shang-Chi A

THE HOT LIST >> TOP 20 SKETCH ARTISTS

Matt Stewart

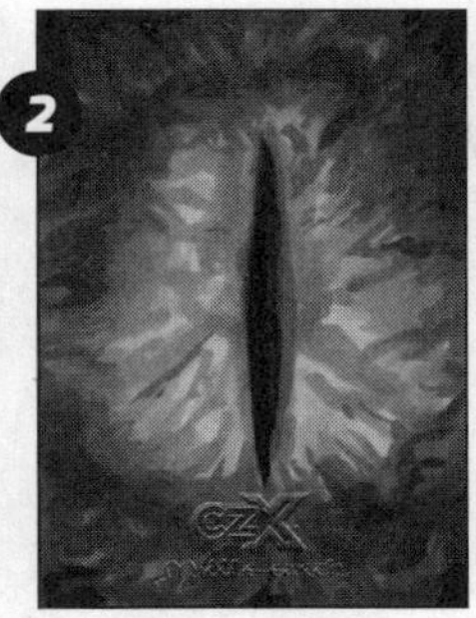

Rich Molinelli

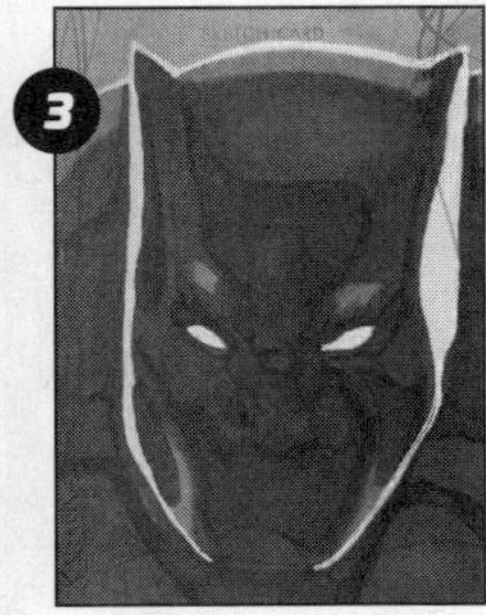

Jason Montoya

Neil Camera

Javier Gonzalez

Rich Hennemann

Darrin Pepe

Huy Truong

Michael Munshaw

Tim Shinn

Jomar Bulda

Chris Foreman

Omar Soto

Leon Braojos

Roy Cover

Chris Meeks

Chenduz

Charles Hall

Joe Simko

Eric Lehtonen

Al Jaffee

Angela Lansbury

Chaim Topol

Coolio

Ivana Trump

James Caan

Jerry Lee Lewis

Jerry Springer

Kevin Conroy

Kirstie Alley

Lance Reddick

Lisa Loring

Loretta Lynn

IN MEMORIAM

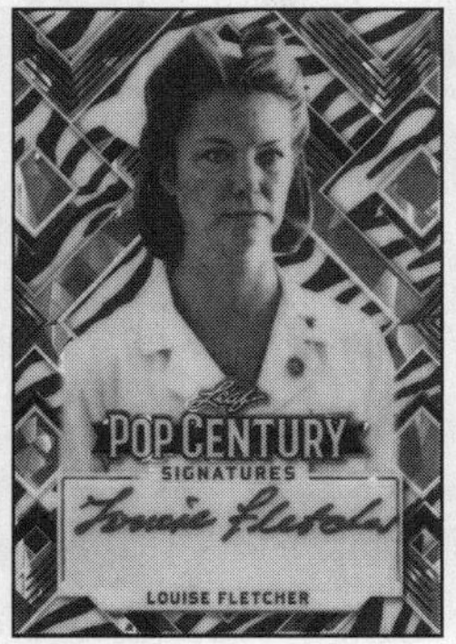

Louise Fletcher

Melinda Dillon

Mikhail Gorbachev

Nichelle Nichols

Olivia Newton-John

Queen Elizabeth II

Paul Sorvino

Pope Benedict XVI

Raquel Welch

Ray Liotta

Robbie Coltrane

Shinzo Abe

Tom Sizemore

Tony Dow

Vintage

VINTAGE

Pre-War

1938 Action Gum R1

COMPLETE SET (96)	900.00	1800.00
COMMON CARD (1-96)	6.00	15.00
4 Night Bombing Attack	8.00	20.00
67 Artillery Moves Up	8.00	20.00

1934 Action Pictures R103

COMPLETE SET (24)	275.00	550.00
COMMON CARD (1-24)	5.00	12.00
8 Football Hero	20.00	50.00
9 Little Black Sambo	25.00	60.00
10 The Battling Champs	15.00	40.00
19 Scooter Boy	20.00	50.00
23 The Dancing Duck	12.00	30.00

1940 World Wide Gum Action Series V350

COMPLETE SET (60)	650.00	1200.00
COMMON CARD (1-60)	6.00	15.00
4 Night Bombing Attack	8.00	20.00

1938 Actors Natural and Character Studies

COMPLETE SET (50)	250.00	500.00
COMMON CARD (1-50)	3.00	8.00

1930 Adventure Pictures R2

COMPLETE SET (10)	450.00	900.00
COMMON CARD (1-10)	30.00	75.00

1936 Adventures of Mickey Mouse ABC Bread Backs

COMPLETE SET (96)	500.00	1000.00
COMMON CARD (1-96)	5.00	12.00

*ASHEVILLE BAKING: SAME VALUE
*BAKE-RITE: SAME VALUE
*BAMBY: SAME VALUE
*BELL: SAME VALUE
*BLANK BACKS: SAME VALUE
*BUTTERFLY: SAME VALUE
*COTE'S: SAME VALUE
*DALE MYER: SAME VALUE
*FREIHOFER: SAME VALUE
*GOLD CUP: SAME VALUE
*HARDIN'S: SAME VALUE
*HECHT'S: SAME VALUE
*HOME SCIENCE: SAME VALUE
*JAEGER'S: SAME VALUE
*KUSS'S: SAME VALUE
*LIBERTY: SAME VALUE
*LONG BUTTER CRUST: SAME VALUE
*M AND M: SAME VALUE
*MAIER'S: SAME VALUE
*MODEL'S: SAME VALUE
*MOTHER'S: SAME VALUE
*PAN DANDY: SAME VALUE
*PETER PAN: SAME VALUE
*PURITAN MAID: SAME VALUE
*SAYLOR'S: SAME VALUE
*STROEHMANN'S: SAME VALUE
*SWAN'S: SAME VALUE
*TAR-HEEL: SAME VALUE
*TRAVIS: SAME VALUE
*WALDENSIAN: SAME VALUE
*WESLEY'S: SAME VALUE
*WOLF'S: SAME VALUE
*YOUTH: SAME VALUE

1930 Adventures of the Army, Navy, and the Marines R3

COMPLETE SET (45)	700.00	1400.00
COMMON CARD	10.00	25.00
A113 Motorcycle Patrol	12.00	30.00
N100 U.S.S. Relief Hospital Ship	12.00	30.00

1932 Aeroplane Series R5

COMPLETE SET (25)	75.00	150.00
COMMON CARD (1-25)	2.00	5.00

1940 Tydol Aeroplanes Series U0-1

COMPLETE SET (40)	250.00	500.00
COMMON CARD (1-40)	4.00	10.00

1935 African Animal Jig R6

COMPLETE SET (24)	375.00	750.00
COMMON CARD (1-24)	10.00	25.00

1938 Air-Raid Precautions

COMPLETE SET (50)	120.00	250.00
COMMON CARD (1-50)	1.50	4.00

1941 Imperial Tobacco Aircraft Spotter Series C271

COMPLETE SET (66)	350.00	700.00
COMMON CARD (1-66)	2.50	6.00

1930 Airplane Pictures

COMPLETE SET (12)	60.00	120.00
COMMON CARD (1-12)	3.00	8.00

1940 Kerr's Butter Scotch Airplane Pictures R9

COMMON CARD (1-23)	10.00	25.00

1941 Richfield Gas Airplanes U02-A

COMPLETE SET W/O ALBUM (12)	60.00	120.00
COMMON CARD (1-12)	3.00	8.00
ALB Richfield Airplanes Album	20.00	50.00

1930 Alice in Wonderland Large

COMPLETE SET (48)	175.00	350.00
COMMON CARD (1-48)	2.50	6.00

1930 Alice in Wonderland Round

COMPLETE SET (48)	175.00	350.00
COMMON CARD (1-48)	2.50	6.00

1930 Alice in Wonderland Square

COMPLETE SET (48)	175.00	350.00
COMMON CARD (1-48)	2.50	6.00

1943 Coca-Cola America's Fighting Planes

COMPLETE SET (20)	190.00	375.00
COMMON CARD	6.00	15.00

1933 American G-Men R13-1

COMPLETE SET (48)	600.00	1200.00
COMMON CARD (101-148)	8.00	20.00

1933 American G-Men R13-2

COMPLETE SET (48)	600.00	1200.00
COMMON CARD (701-748)	8.00	20.00

1930 American Historical Characters R14

COMMON CARD	15.00	40.00

1930 American History R129

COMPLETE SET (48)	225.00	450.00
COMMON CARD (300-347)	3.00	8.00

1933 Animals F55

COMPLETE SET (44)	100.00	200.00
COMMON CARD (1-44)	1.25	3.00
CARD ALBUM	15.00	40.00

1935 Animals R15-1

COMPLETE SET (54)	300.00	600.00
COMMON CARD (1-54)	3.00	8.00

*R15-2: SAME VALUE AS BASIC CARDS

1935 Animals R15-2

COMPLETE SET (54)	300.00	600.00
COMMON CARD (1-54)	3.00	8.00

1930 Animals R159-1

COMPLETE SET (16)	75.00	150.00
COMMON CARD	3.00	8.00

1938 Army Air Corps Insignia R17-1

COMPLETE SET (100)	1250.00	2500.00
COMMON CARD (1-100)	8.00	20.00

1938 Army Air Corps Insignia R17-2

COMPLETE SET (100)	600.00	1200.00
COMMON CARD (1-100)	4.00	10.00

1933 Aviary and Cage Birds

COMPLETE SET (50)	190.00	375.00
COMMON CARD (1-50)	2.50	6.00

1930 Aviation R132

COMPLETE SET (48)	225.00	450.00
COMMON CARD (301-348)	3.00	8.00

1930 Aviation V88

COMPLETE SET (52)	400.00	775.00
COMMON CARD (1-52)	5.00	12.00

1938 Battleship Gum R20

COMPLETE SET (50)	700.00	1300.00
COMMON CARD (1-50)	8.00	20.00

1930 Beautiful Bird Pictures F274-3A

COMPLETE SET (24)	30.00	75.00
COMMON CARD	1.25	3.00

1933 Beautiful Ships R135-1

COMPLETE SET (24)	450.00	900.00
COMMON CARD (1-24)	12.00	30.00

1933 Beautiful Ships R135-2

COMPLETE SET (24)	300.00	600.00
COMMON CARD (1-24)	8.00	20.00

1934 Believe It or Not

COMPLETE SET (50)	450.00	900.00
COMMON CARD (1-50)	6.00	15.00

1937 Believe It or Not R21

COMPLETE SET (48)	1050.00	2100.00
COMMON CARD (1-24)	8.00	20.00
COMMON CARD (25-48)	20.00	50.00

1930 Betholine Animals U062

COMPLETE SET (10)	90.00	175.00
COMMON CARD	6.00	15.00

1939 Big Chief V118

COMPLETE SET (50)	200.00	400.00
COMMON CARD (1-50)	2.50	6.00
5 Geronimo	8.00	20.00
6 Always Riding	3.00	8.00
7 Chief Joseph	3.00	8.00
11 Iron Bull	3.00	8.00
16 British	4.00	10.00
18 Big Snake	3.00	8.00
19 Big Chief	3.00	8.00
22 War Captain	3.00	8.00
27 Wetcunie	3.00	8.00
30 Red Cloud	6.00	15.00
34 Sitting Bull	4.00	10.00
38 Red Bird	3.00	8.00
47 King of the Crows	5.00	12.00
50 True Eagle	3.00	8.00

1940 Chicle Big Chief Wahoo R22-1

COMPLETE SET (9)	120.00	250.00
COMMON CARD (1-9)	8.00	20.00

1937 Big Little Book Series R23

COMPLETE SET (224)	3000.00	7500.00
FLASH GORDON (1-32)	30.00	80.00
DICK TRACY (33-64)	12.00	30.00
POPEYE (65-96)	20.00	50.00
TOM MIX (97-128)	12.00	30.00
G-MAN (129-161)	8.00	20.00
BUCK JONES (162-193)	8.00	20.00
DAN DUNN (194-224)	8.00	20.00

1934 Big Thrill Booklets R24

COMPLETE SET (24)	825.00	1650.00
BUCK JONES (A1-A6)	15.00	40.00
DICK TRACY (B1-B6)	20.00	50.00
TAILSPIN TOMMY (C1-C6)	12.00	30.00
BUCK ROGERS (D1-D6)	50.00	100.00

1933 Boy Scouts R26

COMPLETE SET (48)	350.00	700.00
COMMON CARD (1-48)	5.00	12.00

1937 Boys and Girls of All Nations F275-2

COMPLETE SET (38)	60.00	120.00
COMMON CARD	1.25	3.00

1930 Bridge Favors and Place-Cards T14A

COMPLETE SET (80)	600.00	1200.00
COMMON CARD (1-80)	5.00	12.00
23 James Rennie	8.00	20.00
27 Lina Basquette	6.00	15.00
29 Bernice Claire	12.00	30.00
79 Sleepy-Time Gal	6.00	15.00

1939 British Buildings T46

COMPLETE SET (24)	60.00	120.00
COMMON CARD (UNNUMBERED)	1.50	4.00

1938 British Railways

COMPLETE SET (48)	100.00	200.00
COMMON CARD (1-48)	1.50	4.00

1936 British Sovereigns T47 Finer Backs

COMMON CARD (HT1-HT42)	5.00	12.00

1936 British Sovereigns T47 Firm Backs

COMMON CARD (HT1-HT42)	5.00	12.00

1936 British Sovereigns T47 Lips Backs

COMMON CARD (HT1-HT42)	5.00	12.00

1936 British Sovereigns T47 Lipstick Backs

COMMON CARD (HT1-HT42)	5.00	12.00

1936 British Sovereigns T47 Loose Ends Backs

COMMON CARD (HT1-HT42)	5.00	12.00

1935 Brooksie and Her Pals Cut-Outs

COMPLETE SET (5)	12.00	30.00
COMMON CARD	2.00	5.00

1936 Cartoon Adventures R28

COMPLETE SET (48)	850.00	1700.00
COMMON CARD (401-448)	6.00	15.00
401 Tailspin Tommy	10.00	25.00
402 Tommy Chases a Bandit Plane	8.00	20.00
403 Boy, What a Shot!	10.00	25.00
406 Tommy, here are the stolen jewels	10.00	25.00
407 Tommy Stops the Thieve's Take-Off	8.00	20.00
408 Tommy, Darling! I'm so glad you are safe!	8.00	20.00
409 Tarzan of the Apes	10.00	25.00
410 Tarzan Swings through the Trees	10.00	25.00
411 Tarzan Catches a Crocodile	10.00	25.00
412 Tarzan Slays the Great Bull-Ape	10.00	25.00
413 Tarzan Aids Kala	10.00	25.00
414 Tarzan Eats High in a Tree	15.00	40.00
415 The Monkey-Man Reaches for Tarzan's Knife	10.00	25.00
416 Tarzan Challenges Sheeta	8.00	20.00
417 Broncho Bill	10.00	25.00
418 I'm Gonna Let Them Have It!	10.00	25.00
419 There Are Our Horses!	8.00	20.00
420 Bill Rescues Brent	10.00	25.00
421 I'm Wounded, Sheriff!	8.00	20.00
422 The Spider Traps Bill	10.00	25.00
423 Bill Surprises Peg-Leg	10.00	25.00
424 Run for It, Nell!	8.00	20.00
425 Buck Rogers	10.00	25.00
426 Doctor Huel Tried Desperately to Radio the Earth	10.00	25.00
427 Huel Tells Them Something Has Happened	10.00	25.00
428 Fear Gripped Them	20.00	50.00
429 They Were Afraid	10.00	25.00
430 The Refugeees Leader Showed Them	10.00	25.00
431 The Aeroscout Carried Them Westward	10.00	25.00
432 Within an Hour	10.00	25.00
433 Buck Rogers	10.00	25.00
434 Buck and Wilma Saw Furious Outbreaks	10.00	25.00
435 The Patrol Officer Warns Them	10.00	25.00
436 They had to Protect Themselves	15.00	40.00
437 Refugees Clung to the Doomed Buildings	10.00	25.00
438 A Speed Demon of the Air Carries Them	10.00	25.00
439 The Viewplate Showed the Forthcoming Catastrophe.	15.00	40.00
440 The Heat of Friction with Earth's Atmosphere	15.00	40.00
441 Buck Rogers	25.00	60.00
442 Their Relief Was Cut Short	10.00	25.00
443 The Hooded Figure Was Kane	25.00	60.00
444 Buck and Wilma Hop Off with Their Jumping Belts	10.00	25.00
445 The Comet Pulsed with Blinding Light	20.00	50.00
446 Buck and Wilma Hear a Stupendous Crash	20.00	50.00
447 The Storm Rock Struck the Ship.	10.00	25.00
448 Buck Hid in the Shadows	20.00	50.00

1935 Cartoon Comics R27

COMPLETE SET (48)	500.00	1000.00
DICK TRACY (101-108)	8.00	20.00
ORPHAN ANNIE (109-116)	6.00	15.00
HAROLD TEEN (117-124)	6.00	15.00
MOON MULLINS (125-132)	6.00	15.00
JOE PALOOKA (133-140)	6.00	15.00
TERRY & PIRATES (141-148)	8.00	20.00
111 Watch over her Punjab...	8.00	20.00

1933 Century of Progress Chicago World's Fair R30-1

COMPLETE SET (32)	100.00	200.00
COMMON CARD (1-32)	2.00	5.00

1933 Chicago World's Fair Postcards Rigot

COMPLETE SET (60)	225.00	450.00
COMMON CARD	2.50	6.00

1933 Chicago World's Fair Postcards Shure

COMPLETE SET (50)	150.00	300.00
COMMON CARD (36A1-36A50)	2.00	5.00

1931 Cinema Stars 3rd Series

COMPLETE SET (50)	250.00	500.00
COMMON CARD (1-50)	3.00	8.00
7 Oliver Hardy/Stan Laurel	5.00	12.00
24 Walt Disney/Mickey Mouse	12.00	30.00

1930 Comic Pictures R35

COMPLETE SET (10)	250.00	500.00
COMMON CARD (1-10)	15.00	40.00

1930 Construction of Railway Trains

COMPLETE SET (50)	120.00	250.00
COMMON CARD (1-50)	1.50	4.00

1930 Cops and Robbers R36

COMPLETE SET (35)	400.00	900.00
COMMON CARD (1-35)	8.00	20.00

1930 Cops and Robbers R36 No Tabs

COMPLETE SET (35)	325.00	650.00
COMMON CARD (1-35)	6.00	15.00

1937 Coronation Kensitas

COMPLETE SET (50)	500.00	800.00
COMMON CARD (1-50)	10.00	25.00

1930 Cowboy Series V290

COMPLETE SET (50)	200.00	400.00
COMMON CARD (1-50)	5.00	12.00

1940 W.S. Corp Cowboys and Indians R185

COMPLETE SET (48)	90.00	175.00
COMMON CARD (49-96)	1.25	3.00

1930 Darby's Picture Puzzles R181

COMMON CARD (SKIP NUMBERED)	12.00	30.00

1933 Dare Devils R39

COMPLETE SET (24)	400.00	800.00
COMMON CARD (1-12)	12.00	30.00
COMMON CARD (13-24)	8.00	20.00

1941 W.S. Corps Defending America R40

COMPLETE SET (48)	200.00	400.00
COMMON CARD (201-248)	2.50	6.00

1937 Dick Tracy R41

COMPLETE SET (144)	1000.00	1900.00
COMMON CARD (1-96)	4.00	10.00
COMMON CARD (97-120)	8.00	20.00
COMMON CARD (121-144)	.75	2.00

1935 Dick Tracy R42

COMMON CARD (1-22)	12.00	30.00

1937 Dick Tracy V404

COMPLETE SET (144)	300.00	600.00
COMMON CARD (1-144)	2.00	5.00

1938 Don't Let It Happen over Here R44

COMPLETE SET (24)	800.00	1600.00
COMMON CARD (1-24)	20.00	50.00

1934-35 Famous Airplane Pictures Series 1 F277-2 14735 Backs

COMMON CARD	6.00	15.00

1934-35 Famous Airplane Pictures Series 1 F277-2 27434 Backs

COMMON CARD	6.00	15.00

1934-35 Famous Airplane Pictures Series 1 F277-2 9935 Backs

COMPLETE SET (25)		
COMMON CARD	6.00	15.00

1935-39 Famous Airplane Pictures Series 2 F277-1 0969 Backs

COMMON CARD	5.00	12.00

1935-39 Famous Airplane Pictures Series 2 F277-1 13137 Backs

COMMON CARD	5.00	12.00

1935-39 Famous Airplane Pictures Series 2 F277-1 14636 Backs

COMMON CARD	5.00	12.00

1935-39 Famous Airplane Pictures Series 2 F277-1 22738 Backs

COMMON CARD	5.00	12.00

1935-39 Famous Airplane Pictures Series 2 F277-1 23235 Backs

COMMON CARD	5.00	12.00

1935-39 Famous Airplane Pictures Series 2 F277-1 3238 Backs

COMMON CARD 5.00 12.00

1935-39 Famous Airplane Pictures Series 2 F277-1 9836 Backs

COMMON CARD 5.00 12.00

1935 Famous Airplanes Premium F277-3

COMPLETE SET (4) 60.00 150.00
COMMON CARD (SKIP #'d) 12.00 30.00

1936 Famous Aviators F277-4a

COMMON CARD (1-25) 6.00 15.00
1 Col. Charles A. Lindbergh 20.00 50.00
2 Amelia Earhart 400.00 800.00
5 Laura Ingalls 30.00 75.00
7 Howard Hughes 120.00 250.00
8 Capt. Edwin Musick 30.00 75.00
9 Commander Frank Hawks 150.00 300.00

1937 Famous Aviators Premium F277-5

COMPLETE SET (4) 100.00 200.00
COMMON CARD (SKIP #'d) 15.00 40.00

1935 Famous Film Scenes

COMPLETE SET (48) 175.00 350.00
COMMON CARD (1-48) 2.50 6.00

1933 Famous Film Stars

COMPLETE SET (100) 500.00 1000.00
COMMON CARD (1-100) 3.00 8.00

1935 Famous Film Stars

COMPLETE SET (96) 500.00 1000.00
COMMON CARD (1-96) 3.00 8.00
NO.'s 5, 11, 67, 68, 86, 96 HAVE VARIANTS

1939 Famous Film Stars

COMPLETE SET (54) 250.00 500.00
COMMON CARD (1-54) 3.00 8.00

1930 Famous Trains V48

COMPLETE SET (35) 200.00 500.00
COMMON CARD (1-35) 5.00 12.00

1938 Fighting Planes R47

COMPLETE SET (24) 300.00 600.00
COMMON CARD (1-24) 8.00 20.00

1936 Film Episodes

COMPLETE SET (48) 225.00 450.00
COMMON CARD (1-48) 3.00 8.00

1935 Film Funnies R48-1

COMPLETE SET (24) 120.00 250.00
COMMON CARD (1-24) 8.00 20.00

1935 Film Funnies R48-2

COMPLETE SET (24) 120.00 250.00
COMMON CARD (1-24) 8.00 20.00

1936 Film Stars Desmond

COMPLETE SET (50) 200.00 400.00
COMMON CARD (1-50) 2.50 6.00
3 Fred Astaire 8.00 20.00
22 Shirley Temple 8.00 20.00

1933 Film Stars First Edition Allen's

COMPLETE SET (72) 350.00 700.00
COMMON CARD (1-72) 3.00 8.00

1939 Foreign Legion R54

COMPLETE SET (48) 300.00 600.00
COMMON CARD (325-372) 4.00 10.00

1938 Frank Buck Series R55A

COMPLETE SET (48) 600.00 1200.00
COMMON CARD (1-48) 8.00 20.00

1938 Frank Buck Series R55B

COMPLETE SET (48) 600.00 1200.00
COMMON CARD (1-48) 8.00 20.00

1936 From Screen and Stage

COMPLETE SET (50) 450.00 900.00
COMMON CARD (1-50) 6.00 15.00

1934 Funnies R56

COMPLETE SET (24) 375.00 750.00
COMMON CARD 10.00 25.00

1936 G-Men and Heroes of the Law R60

COMPLETE SET (168) 4900.00 9800.00
COMMON CARD (1-196) 7.50 15.00
COMMON CARD (201-283) 20.00 40.00
COMMON CARD (307-451) 40.00 80.00
1 G-Men Riddle . . . Pretty Boy Floyd 20.00 40.00
10 G-Men Track Down . . . John Dillinger 20.00 40.00
11 G-Men Track . . . Machine Gun Kelly 15.00 30.00
19 Two G-Men . . . Baby Face Nelson 15.00 30.00
28 G-Men Deliver Death SP 60.00 120.00
38 Grapple with Bloody Death SP 60.00 120.00
45 Satan's Disciple SP 120.00 250.00
49 Far Flung Fingers of the Law SP 60.00 120.00
57 Mining for Murder SP 120.00 250.00
64 The Killers in Tunnel 13 SP 120.00 250.00
76 The Trail of the Secret Symbol SP 60.00 120.00
83 A Bullet-Collected Debt SP 60.00 120.00
88 Target of Death! SP 120.00 250.00
94 G-Men Strike in the Dark SP 60.00 120.00
100 The Dragnet Snares It's Prey SP 120.00 250.00
103 G-Men Answer Public Enemy 15.00 30.00
107 Trapping a Cop Killer SP 100.00 200.00
115 Binding the Beast SP 60.00 120.00
121 G-Men Blot Out a Crime Career SP 120.00 250.00
127 The Gallows Prey 15.00 30.00
136 A Bullet Finds and Frees 15.00 30.00
149 A Desperate Crime at Sea 15.00 30.00
156 The Mask of Death 15.00 30.00
169 Death Rewards an Extortionist 15.00 30.00
177 A Boat Betrays Its Killer Crew 30.00 75.00
181 Death Ends a Crimson Trail 15.00 30.00
185 G-Men Discover a Dead Hand's Secret 15.00 30.00
191 Death in a Poison Cup 15.00 30.00
196 Gun Butts and Bullets SP 120.00 250.00
203 A G-Man Finds a Murderer's Mark 25.00 60.00
451 The Voice From the Ether Cone 100.00 200.00

1936 Gallery of 1935

COMMON CARD (1-50) 6.00 15.00
17 Walt Disney 75.00 150.00
26 Shirley Temple 8.00 20.00

1939 Generals and Their Flags R58

COMPLETE SET (24) 150.00 300.00
COMMON CARD (425-448) 4.00 10.00

1930 Golden West R207

COMPLETE SET (18) 225.00 450.00
COMMON CARD (1-18) 8.00 20.00

1930-49 Good Neighbors of the Americas

COMPLETE SET (24) 150.00 300.00
COMMON CARD 4.00 10.00

1936 Government Agents vs. Public Enemies R761

COMPLETE SET (24) 300.00 600.00
COMMON CARD (A201-A224) 8.00 20.00

1940 Augenblick Guardians of America F95

COMPLETE SET (25) 80.00 150.00
COMMON CARD 2.00 5.00

1939 Heroes of the Sea R67

COMPLETE SET (24) 150.00 300.00
COMMON CARD (449-472) 4.00 10.00

1936 History of Aviation R65

COMMON CARD (1-10) 8.00 20.00
1 Howard Hughes 30.00 75.00
2 Capt. Edward V. Rickenbacker 15.00 40.00
3 Wiley Post 25.00 60.00
4 Colonel Charles A. Lindbergh 30.00 75.00
6 Wiley Post's Winnie Mae 15.00 40.00
7 Hughes' Record Smasher 15.00 40.00
8 Lindbergh's Spirit of St. Louis 30.00 75.00
9 Over the North Pole with Byrd 25.00 60.00
10 Wings Over the Pacific 25.00 60.00

1933 Hollywood Picture Star Gum R68

COMPLETE SET (40) 250.00 400.00
COMMON CARD (1-40) 8.00 20.00

1933 Hollywood Picture Star Gum V289

COMPLETE SET (40) 375.00 750.00
COMMON CARD (1-40) 6.00 15.00

1941 O-Pee-Chee Home Defence V277

COMPLETE SET (48) 600.00 1200.00
COMMON CARD (1-48) 8.00 20.00

1938 Horrors of War

COMPLETE SET (288) 7500.00 12000.00
COMMON CARD (1-24) 8.00 20.00
COMMON CARD (25-48) 6.00 15.00
COMMON CARD (49-192) 5.00 12.00
COMMON CARD (193-240) 15.00 40.00
COMMON CARD (241-264) 12.00 30.00
COMMON CARD (265-276) 20.00 50.00
COMMON CARD (277-288) 30.00 80.00
1 Marco Polo Bridge 50.00 100.00
78 River Gate is Death Trap 20.00 50.00
139 Franco Retakes Teruel 12.00 30.00
169 Peiping State Procession 5.00 12.00
240 The Frightful Cost of War 250.00 500.00
277 Hitler's Border Tour 250.00 500.00
283 Hitler Threatens Force 500.00 1000.00
286 Chamberlain Meets Hitler 350.00 700.00
287 Premier Hodza Confers with Army 30.00 80.00
288 Czech President Surrenders 100.00 200.00

1930 Humpty Dumpty Up-to-Date R70

COMPLETE SET (24) 300.00 600.00
COMMON CARD (1-24) 8.00 20.00

1933 Hunted Animals R71

COMPLETE SET (25) 75.00 150.00
COMMON CARD (1-25) 2.00 5.00

1930 I'm Going to Be R72

COMPLETE SET W/O #4 (24) 200.00 425.00
COMPLETE SET W/#4 (25) 1800.00 3000.00
COMPLETE SET W/BOTH #4 VARIANTS (26) 2500.00 4400.00
COMMON CARD (1-25) 5.00 12.00
1 Clown 10.00 25.00
4A Strong Man SP (unmarked) 1200.00 2000.00
4B Strong Man SP (marked void) 500.00 1000.00
19 Baseball Player 10.00 25.00

1930 In History's Spotlight R76

COMPLETE SET (24) 400.00 800.00
COMMON CARD (1-24) 10.00 25.00

1930 Indian Chiefs R184-1

COMPLETE SET (24) 50.00 100.00
COMMON CARD (101-124) 3.00 8.00

1930 Indian Chiefs R184-2

COMPLETE SET (24) 150.00 300.00
COMMON CARD (101-124) 4.00 10.00

1933 Indian Gum R73

SERIES OF 24 COMMONS 40.00 80.00
SERIES OF 48 BLUE COMMONS 10.00 20.00
SERIES OF 48 RED COMMONS (1-24) 7.50 15.00
SERIES OF 48 RED COMMONS (25-48) 15.00 30.00
SERIES OF 48 RED COMMONS (110-152) 40.00 80.00
SERIES OF 48 RED COMMONS (154-209) 20.00 40.00
SERIES OF 96 COMMONS (1-24) 10.00 20.00
SERIES OF 96 COMMONS (25-48) 4.00 8.00
SERIES OF 96 COMMONS (49-72) 3.00 6.00
SERIES OF 192 COMMONS (25-48) 6.00 12.00
SERIES OF 192 COMMONS (25-48) MC 12.50 25.00
SERIES OF 192 COMMONS (73-141) 3.00 6.00
SERIES OF 216 COMMONS 6.00 12.00
SERIES OF 264 COMMONS 10.00 20.00
SERIES OF 288 COMMONS (110-152) 150.00 250.00
SERIES OF 288 COMMONS (154-209) 50.00 100.00
SERIES OF 312 SCENE COMMONS 15.00 30.00
SERIES OF 312 WHITE COMMONS 40.00 80.00

1930 Indians Cowboys Western R75

COMPLETE SET (48) 450.00 900.00
COMMON CARD (UNNUMBERED) 6.00 15.00

1936 Jolly Roger Pirates

COMPLETE SET (48)	125.00	250.00
COMMON CARD (1-48)	1.50	4.00

1933 Jungle Gum R78

COMPLETE SET (48)	250.00	500.00
COMMON CARD (1-24)	2.50	6.00
COMMON CARD (25-71)	4.00	10.00

1940 Trio Gum Know Your Presidents R210

COMPLETE SET (32)	150.00	300.00
COMMON CARD	2.50	6.00
1 George Washington	10.00	25.00
4 James Madison	5.00	12.00
5 James Monroe	3.00	8.00
6 John Quincy Adams	5.00	12.00
7 Andrew Jackson	4.00	10.00
11 James K. Polk	4.00	10.00
13 Millard Fillmore	5.00	12.00
16 Abraham Lincoln	12.00	30.00
18 Ulysses S. Grant	4.00	10.00
19 Rutherford B. Hayes	3.00	8.00
20 James A. Garfield	4.00	10.00

1930 Leader Discs R79

COMPLETE SET (51)	375.00	750.00
COMMON CARD	5.00	12.00

1930 League of Nations R80

COMPLETE SET (50)	650.00	1300.00
COMMON CARD (1-50)	8.00	20.00
50 United States	20.00	50.00

1936 License Plates R19-1

COMPLETE SET (35)	125.00	250.00
COMMON CARD (1-35)	2.50	6.00

1937 License Plates R19-2

COMPLETE SET (67)	175.00	350.00
COMMON CARD (1-67)	1.50	4.00

1938 License Plates R19-3

COMPLETE SET (66)	175.00	350.00
COMMON CARD (1-66)	1.50	4.00

1939 License Plates R19-4

COMPLETE SET (30)	80.00	150.00
COMMON CARD (1-30)	1.50	4.00

1940 Gum Inc. Lone Ranger R83

COMPLETE SET W/SP (48)	2500.00	4000.00
COMMON CARD (1-36)	15.00	40.00
COMMON CARD (37-47)	50.00	120.00
SP (48)	100.00	200.00
1 A Silver Bullet Stops a Hanging	30.00	75.00
48 Silver's Vigil SP	100.00	200.00

1940 Lone Ranger Premium R83A

COMPLETE SET (5)	2050.00	4100.00
COMMON CARD	300.00	600.00
1a Lone Ranger (with mask)	450.00	900.00
1b Lone Ranger (w/o mask)		

1930 Men of the Mounted V102

COMMON CARD (1-40)	15.00	40.00

1935 Mickey Mouse R89

COMPLETE SET (96)	2500.00	4000.00
COMMON TYPE I (1-25)	20.00	40.00
COMMON TYPE II (1-96)	15.00	30.00
1A Let's Make Hoop-Ee! (Type I)	30.00	60.00
1B Let's Make Hoop-Ee! (Type II)	25.00	50.00
21B He's Sure a Handy (Type II)	20.00	30.00
96 Look! Uncle Tom's Crabbin	25.00	50.00

1934 Mickey Mouse Recipes D97 Armstrong Backs

COMPLETE SET (48)	350.00	700.00
COMMON CARD (1-48)	5.00	12.00

1934 Mickey Mouse Recipes D97 Bell Bread White Backs

COMPLETE SET (48)	350.00	700.00
COMMON CARD	5.00	12.00

1934 Mickey Mouse Recipes D97 Bell Bread XL Backs

COMPLETE SET (48)	350.00	700.00
COMMON CARD	5.00	12.00

1934 Mickey Mouse Recipes D97 Diamond White Backs

COMPLETE SET (48)	350.00	700.00
COMMON CARD	5.00	12.00

1934 Mickey Mouse Recipes D97 Home Science Backs

COMPLETE SET (48)	350.00	700.00
COMMON CARD	5.00	12.00

1934 Mickey Mouse Recipes D97 Wesley Backs

COMPLETE SET (48)	350.00	700.00
COMMON CARD	5.00	12.00

1935 Mickey Mouse with the Movie Stars R90

COMPLETE SET (24)	1850.00	3700.00
COMMON CARD (97-120)	50.00	100.00
98 It' an Honor to Have You Play in My	60.00	120.00
101 Am I Right on the Left Page, Mickey?	60.00	120.00
103 Life is Just a Bowl of Chariots	225.00	450.00
106 My Next Picture Will Be Silent, Mickey	60.00	120.00
110 Lip and Let Lip	80.00	150.00
111 A Dime for This? Yes, Ten Cents a Trance	80.00	150.00
116 So You're Putting on the High Hat, Eh?	60.00	120.00
117 Look Out I'm Going to Strike You! Ah!	60.00	120.00
118 Le'slee How Shall We Take This?	60.00	120.00

1931 Military Head-Dress

COMPLETE SET (50)	90.00	175.00
COMMON CARD (1-50)	1.25	3.00

1930 Minute Biographies R91

COMPLETE SET (40)	250.00	450.00
COMMON CARD (1-40)	8.00	20.00
8 Calvin Coolidge	15.00	40.00
15 Franklin Delano Roosevelt	10.00	25.00
18 Guglielmo Marconi	30.00	80.00

1938 Modern Armaments

COMPLETE SET (50)	120.00	250.00
COMMON CARD (1-50)	1.50	4.00

1938 Modern Armaments Unnumbered

COMPLETE SET (50)	150.00	300.00
COMMON CARD (1-50)	2.00	5.00

1934 Motion Picture Stars T84

COMPLETE SET (50)	100.00	200.00
COMMON CARD (1-50)	1.25	3.00
6 Joan Blondell	2.00	5.00
10 James Cagney	3.00	8.00
14 Bette Davis	2.50	6.00
22 Cary Grant	3.00	8.00
25 Buck Jones in "The Red Rider"	2.00	5.00

1933 Movie Gum R97-2

COMPLETE SET (24)	90.00	175.00
COMMON CARD (1-24)	2.50	6.00
13 Clark Gable	15.00	40.00
14 Greta Garbo	10.00	25.00
18 Buster Keaton	10.00	25.00
23 Will Rogers	15.00	40.00

1934 Movie Stars R133

COMPLETE SET (96)	1250.00	2500.00
COMMON CARD (101-196)	8.00	20.00
132 Yakima Canutt	20.00	50.00
171 Charles Laughton	20.00	50.00

1939 My Favourite Part

COMPLETE SET (48)	50.00	100.00
COMMON CARD (1-48)	1.00	2.50
8 Sir C. Hardwicke	2.50	6.00
13 Judy Garland	10.00	25.00

1930 Navy R127

COMPLETE SET (24)	225.00	450.00
COMMON CARD (501-524)	6.00	15.00

1938 Nightmare of Warfare R99

COMPLETE SET (48)	225.00	450.00
COMMON CARD (901-948)	3.00	8.00

1933 Noah's Ark R100

COMPLETE SET (24)	300.00	600.00
COMMON CARD (1-24)	8.00	20.00

1933 Novelties R102

COMPLETE SET (24)	60.00	1200.00
COMMON CARD (1-12; 25-36)	15.00	40.00
CARDS 13 THROUGH 24 DON'T EXIST		

1935 Papoose Animal Gum V255

COMPLETE SET (70)	350.00	700.00
COMMON CARD (1-70)	3.00	8.00

1930 Pee Wee Says R105

COMPLETE SET (24)	112.50	225.00
COMMON CARD (1-24)	3.00	8.00

1930 Pinocchio Circus Performers D64

COMPLETE SET (60)	190.00	375.00
COMMON CARD	2.00	5.00

1930 Pirate Treasure R110-1

COMPLETE SET (48)	250.00	500.00
COMMON CARD (1-48)	3.00	8.00

1930 Pirate Treasure R110-2

COMPLETE SET (18)	100.00	200.00
COMMON CARD (1-18)	3.00	8.00

1930 Pirate Treasure R110-3

COMPLETE SET (18)	100.00	200.00
COMMON CARD (1-18)	3.00	8.00

1936 Pirate's Picture R109

COMPLETE SET (72)	1350.00	2700.00
COMMON CARD (1-72)	10.00	25.00
1 Fighting Aloft	15.00	40.00
9 I Command Surrender	50.00	100.00
34 Left to Their Fate	50.00	100.00
59 Fight at Pirates' Cove SP	120.00	250.00
72 Prepare for Action	6.00	30.00

1940 Kellogg's Plane Spotters

COMPLETE SET (44)	225.00	450.00
COMMON CARD	3.00	8.00

1933 Popeye Comics R113

COMPLETE SET (30)	1200.00	2400.00
COMMON CARD (1-30)	25.00	60.00

1932 Presidents

COMPLETE SET (30)	1350.00	2700.00
COMMON CARD (1-30)	25.00	60.00
18 Abraham Lincoln	75.00	150.00
24 F.D. Roosevelt	75.00	150.00
30 George Washington	120.00	250.00

1936 Presidents R114 Blue

COMPLETE W/O SP (30)	400.00	800.00
COMMON CARD	6.00	15.00
1 George Washington	30.00	75.00
2 John Adams	10.00	25.00
3 Thomas Jefferson	15.00	40.00
4 James Madison	20.00	50.00
5 James Monroe	15.00	40.00
6 John Quincy Adams	8.00	20.00
7 Andrew Jackson	10.00	25.00
8 Martin Van Buren	10.00	25.00
9 William Henry Harrison	10.00	25.00
11 James Knox Polk	8.00	20.00
12 Zachary Taylor	8.00	20.00
14 Franklin Pierce	12.00	30.00

16 Abraham Lincoln	30.00	60.00
18 Ulysses S Grant	25.00	60.00
19 Rutherford B Hayes	10.00	25.00
20 James Abram Garfield	10.00	25.00
21 Chester A Arthur	8.00	20.00
22 Grover Cleveland	12.00	30.00
23 Benjamin Harrison	10.00	25.00
24 William McKinley SP		
25 Theodore Roosevelt	12.00	30.00
26 William Howard Taft	12.00	30.00
27 Woodrow Wilson	10.00	25.00
31 Franklin D Roosevelt	10.00	25.00

1936 Presidents R114 Orange

COMPLETE SET W/O SP (30)	350.00	700.00
COMMON CARD	6.00	15.00
1 George Washington	15.00	40.00
2 John Adams	8.00	20.00
3 Thomas Jefferson	12.00	30.00
5 James Monroe	8.00	20.00
6 John Quincy Adams	10.00	25.00
7 Andrew Jackson	10.00	25.00
11 James Knox Polk	8.00	20.00
14 Franklin Pierce	12.00	30.00
16 Abraham Lincoln	20.00	50.00
18 Ulysses S Grant	12.00	30.00
19 Rutherford B Hayes	8.00	20.00
22 Grover Cleveland	10.00	25.00
23 Benjamin Harrison	8.00	20.00
24 William McKinley SP		
25 Theodore Roosevelt	12.00	30.00
27 Woodrow Wilson	12.00	30.00
31 Franklin D Roosevelt	10.00	25.00

1936 Presidents R114 Red

COMPLETE SET W/O SP (30)	325.00	750.00
COMMON CARD (1-31)	6.00	15.00
1 George Washington	25.00	60.00
2 John Adams	10.00	25.00
3 Thomas Jefferson	10.00	25.00
6 John Quincy Adams	8.00	20.00
7 Andrew Jackson	10.00	25.00
10 John Tyler	8.00	20.00
12 Zachary Taylor	8.00	20.00
16 Abraham Lincoln	20.00	50.00
18 Ulysses S Grant	10.00	25.00
20 James Abram Garfield	10.00	25.00
23 Benjamin Harrison	8.00	20.00
24 William McKinley SP		
25 Theodore Roosevelt	12.00	30.00
27 Woodrow Wilson	8.00	20.00
31 Franklin D Roosevelt	10.00	25.00

1932 Presidents R115

COMPLETE SET (14)	425.00	850.00
COMMON CARD (16-30)	20.00	50.00

1932 Presidents R116

COMMON CARD (1-30)	6.00	15.00

1937 Presidents Play Bucks R118

COMPLETE SET (38)	475.00	950.00
COMMON CARD (1-38)	8.00	20.00

1935 Pulver Pictures R108

COMPLETE SET (30)	1000.00	2000.00
COMMON CARD (100-129)	20.00	50.00

1930 Red Jacket Wrapper Indians V253

COMPLETE SET (50)	190.00	375.00
COMMON CARD (UNNUMBERED)	2.50	6.00

1941 Candyland Remember Pearl Harbor R120

COMPLETE SET (8)	120.00	250.00
COMMON CARD (1-8)	10.00	25.00

1933 Sea Raiders R124

COMPLETE SET (48)	1750.00	3500.00
COMMON CARD (1-24)	15.00	30.00
COMMON CARD (25-48)	40.00	80.00
1 Blackbeard	50.00	100.00
48 A Difference In Weapons	80.00	150.00

1938 Seal Craft Discs R123

COMPLETE SET (241)	600.00	1200.00
COMMON CARD (1-241)	2.00	5.00

1939 The Second World War R126

COMPLETE SET (48)	200.00	400.00
COMMON CARD (125-172)	2.00	5.00
172 Hitler Makes Peace	30.00	80.00

1935 Secret Service Flashes R125

COMPLETE SET (24)	450.00	900.00
COMMON CARD (1-24)	12.00	30.00

1936 Shirley Temple Wheaties

COMPLETE SET (12)	100.00	200.00
COMMON CARD (1-12)	6.00	15.00

1936 Sights of Britain Second Series Printing 1

COMPLETE SET (48)	120.00	250.00
COMMON CARD (1-48)	1.50	4.00

1933-34 Sky Birds R136

COMPLETE SET (132)	2900.00	5800.00
SERIES OF 48 COMMONS (1-36)	8.00	20.00
SERIES OF 48 COMMONS (37-48)	8.00	20.00
SERIES OF 144 COMMONS (25-36)	20.00	50.00
SERIES OF 144 COMMONS (37-48)	10.00	25.00
SERIES OF 144 COMMONS (49-72)	10.00	25.00
SERIES OF 144 COMMONS (73-84)	10.00	25.00
SERIES OF 144 COMMONS (85-96)	25.00	60.00
SERIES OF 144 COMMONS (97-108)	25.00	60.00
1 David Putnam	15.00	40.00
2 Rene Fonck	8.00	20.00
3 Lieut. Thieffry	8.00	20.00
4 Capt. Albert Ball	8.00	20.00
5 J.N. Hall	8.00	20.00
6 Albert Heurteaux	8.00	20.00
7 Rene Dorme	8.00	20.00
8 Major Barracca	8.00	20.00
9 Roland Garros	8.00	20.00
10 Charles Nungesser	8.00	20.00
11 Lt. Norman Prince	8.00	20.00
12 Frank Luke	8.00	20.00
13 Kiffin Rockwell	8.00	20.00
14 Sgt.James McConnell	8.00	20.00
15 Bert Hall	8.00	20.00
16 Max Immelman	8.00	20.00
17 Lt. Douglas Campbell	8.00	20.00
18 Quentin Rossevelt	8.00	20.00
19 Capt. Debeauchamp	8.00	20.00
20 Edward Rickenbacker	15.00	40.00
21 Georges Guynemer	8.00	20.00
22 Maj. Raoul Lufbery	8.00	20.00
23 Baron Von Richthofen	12.00	30.00
24 Lieut. Frank Bylies	8.00	20.00
25A Lt. Joseph Wehner (48)	8.00	20.00
25B Lt. Joseph Wehner (144)	20.00	50.00
26A Col. William A. Bishop (48)	8.00	20.00
26B Col. William A. Bishop (144)	20.00	50.00
27A Col. William Thaw (48)	8.00	20.00
27B Col. William Thaw (144)	20.00	50.00
28A Russell N. Boardman (48)	8.00	20.00
28B Russell N. Boardman (144)	20.00	50.00
29A Floyd Bennett (48)	8.00	20.00
29B Floyd Bennett (144)	20.00	50.00
30A Willy Coppens (48)	8.00	20.00
30B Willy Coppens (144)	20.00	50.00
31A George A. Vaughn Jr (48)	8.00	20.00
31B George A. Vaughn Jr (144)	20.00	50.00
32A Lt. James Doolittle (48)	10.00	25.00
32B Lt. James Doolittle (144)	25.00	60.00
33A C.Kingsford-Smith (48)	8.00	20.00
33B C.Kingsford-Smith (144)	20.00	50.00
34A Frank M. Hawks (48)	8.00	20.00
34B Frank M. Hawks (144)	20.00	50.00
35A Gen. Italo Balbo (48)	8.00	20.00
35B Gen. Italo Balbo (144)	20.00	50.00
36A Charles Lindbergh (48)	25.00	60.00
36B Charles Lindbergh (144)	75.00	150.00
37A Clarence Chamberlin (48)	8.00	20.00
37B Clarence Chamberlin (144)	10.00	25.00
38A James B. McCudden (48)	8.00	20.00
38B James B. McCudden (144)	10.00	25.00
39A Edward A. Stinson (48)	10.00	25.00
39B Edward A. Stinson (144)	10.00	25.00
40A Bernt Balchen (48)	8.00	20.00
40B Bernt Balchen (144)	10.00	25.00
41A Spad (48)	8.00	20.00
41B Spad (144)	10.00	25.00
42A Albatross-Taube 1914 (48)	8.00	20.00
42B Albatross-Taube 1914 (144)	10.00	25.00
43A Juan De La Cierva (48)	8.00	20.00
43B Juan De La Cierva (144)	10.00	25.00
44A Admiral Wm. Moffett (48)	8.00	20.00
44B Admiral Wm. Moffett (144)	10.00	25.00
45A E. Hamilton Lee (48)	8.00	20.00
45B E. Hamilton Lee (144)	10.00	25.00
46A Capt.Oswald Boelcke (48)	8.00	20.00
46B Capt.Oswald Boelcke (144)	10.00	25.00
47A Lt. Edward Parsons (48)	8.00	20.00
47B Lt. Edward Parsons (144)	10.00	25.00
48A Amelia Earhart (48)	30.00	75.00
48B Amelia Earhart (144)	60.00	120.00
49 Orville Wright	15.00	40.00
50 Ruth Nichols	10.00	25.00
51 Lt. Werner Voss	10.00	25.00
52 The Salamander	10.00	25.00
53 Edmond Genet	10.00	25.00
54 Georges Madon	10.00	25.00
55 Maj. Reed G. Landis	10.00	25.00
56 D.H. 10 Bomber	10.00	25.00
57 The Bristol Fighter	10.00	25.00
58 Captain Alcock	10.00	25.00
59 Lt. John A. Macready	10.00	25.00
60 Roald Amundsen	10.00	25.00
61 Gabriel D'Annunzio	10.00	25.00
62 Wiley Post	12.00	30.00
63 Nieuport Triplane	10.00	25.00
64 Deperdussin Monopl.	10.00	25.00
65 Vickers Vampire B.R.2	25.00	60.00
66 Lt. Col. A. Pinsard	10.00	25.00
67 Sidor Malloc Singh	10.00	25.00
68 Fokker Triplane	10.00	25.00
69 Ernst Udet	10.00	25.00
70 Capt. Frank Hunter	10.00	25.00
71 Winnie Mae	10.00	25.00
72 Spirit of St. Louis	12.00	30.00
73 Lt.Paul H. Neibling	10.00	25.00
74 Lt. R. Von Eschwege	10.00	25.00
75 Elliot White Springs	10.00	25.00
76 Capt. Brocard	10.00	25.00
77 Capt. A. Roy Brown	10.00	25.00
78 Maj. Donald McLaren	10.00	25.00
79 German Gotha	15.00	40.00
80 German Junkers	10.00	25.00
81 Macchi	10.00	25.00
82 Parnell Panther	10.00	25.00
83 Albatross D. 1	10.00	25.00
84 Sopwith Camel	10.00	25.00
85 Lt. Alan A. Mcleod	25.00	60.00
86 The Austin Ball	25.00	60.00
87 Eugene Gilbert	25.00	60.00
88 C.B. (Ben) Eielson	25.00	60.00
89 Nieuport Balloon Rocket Ship	25.00	60.00
90 Wild Bill Wellman	25.00	60.00
91 Major Deseversky	25.00	60.00
92 Capt. Francis McCubbin	25.00	60.00
93 Sopwith Tabloid	25.00	60.00
94 Voisin 12 Bn 2	25.00	60.00
95 Buggatti-Spad	25.00	60.00
96 A.E.G. Bomber	25.00	60.00
97 Capt. Thenault	25.00	60.00
98 Elliot Cowdin	25.00	60.00
99 David S. Ingalls	25.00	60.00
100 Maj. David Mck. Peterson	25.00	60.00
101 Harold June	25.00	60.00
102 Lt. Alan F. Winslow	25.00	60.00
103 Spad Herbemont	25.00	60.00
104 Halberstadt	25.00	60.00
105 Sopwith Torpedo Carrier	25.00	60.00
106 Morane Parasol	25.00	60.00
107 Marchetti-Vickers	25.00	60.00
108 Fokker D 8	60.00	120.00

1941 Goudey Sky Birds R137

COMPLETE SET (24)	200.00	400.00
COMMON CARD (1-24)	5.00	12.00
1 U.S.A. Patrol Bomber	10.00	25.00
24 China Northrup	12.00	30.00
China Northrup		

1932 Soldier R139

COMPLETE SET (36)	225.00	450.00
COMMON CARD (1-36)	4.00	10.00

1936 Soldier Boys R142

COMPLETE SET (24)	400.00	800.00
COMMON CARD (1-24)	10.00	25.00

1940 New England Confectionery Strange People of Many Lands E196

COMPLETE SET (24)	150.00	300.00
COMMON CARD	4.00	10.00

1936 Strange True Stories R144

COMPLETE SET (24)	1300.00	2600.00
COMMON CARD (1-24)	30.00	80.00
1 The Malay Boot	60.00	120.00
24 The Bat Man	50.00	100.00

1933 Teepee Gum Series V416

COMPLETE SET (50)	150.00	300.00
COMMON CARD (1-50)	2.00	5.00

1930 Time Marches On R150

COMPLETE SET (48)	350.00	700.00
COMMON CARD (601-648)	5.00	12.00

1934 Tom Mix and Tony R151

COMPLETE SET (48)	1000.00	2000.00
COMMON CARD (1-24)	8.00	20.00
COMMON CARD (25-48)	15.00	40.00

1933 Tootsie Circus R152

COMPLETE SET (25)	400.00	1000.00
COMMON CARD	12.00	30.00

1939 True Spy Stories R156

COMPLETE SET (24)	600.00	1200.00
COMMON CARD (1-24)	15.00	40.00

1941 Gum Inc. Uncle Sam

COMPLETE SET (96)	250.00	500.00
COMMON CARD (1-48)	2.00	5.00
COMMON CARD (49-96)	2.50	6.00

1940 Walter Lowney United Nations Battle Planes V407-3

COMMON CARD	2.50	6.00

1940 Novel Package U.S. Navy Warships R98

COMPLETE SET (8)	100.00	200.00
COMMON CARD (1-8)	8.00	20.00

1933 Useful Birds of America J9-1

COMPLETE SET (15)	25.00	60.00
COMMON CARD (1-15)	1.25	3.00

1933 Useful Birds of America J9-2

COMPLETE SET (15)	25.00	60.00
COMMON CARD (1-15)	1.25	3.00

1934 Useful Birds of America J9-3

COMPLETE SET (15)	25.00	60.00
COMMON CARD (1-15)	1.25	3.00

1936 Useful Birds of America J9-5

COMPLETE SET (15)	25.00	60.00
COMMON CARD (1-15)	1.25	3.00

1938 Useful Birds of America J9-6

COMPLETE SET (15)	25.00	60.00
COMMON CARD (1-15)	1.25	3.00

1941 Gum Inc. War Gum R164

COMPLETE SET (132)	1000.00	2000.00
COMMON CARD (1-84)	4.00	10.00
COMMON CARD (85-132)	6.00	15.00

1939 War News Pictures R165

COMPLETE SET (144)	2450.00	4900.00
COMMON CARD (1-48)	4.00	10.00
COMMON CARD (49-108)	3.00	8.00
COMMON CARD (109-120)	100.00	200.00
COMMON CARD (121-144)	10.00	25.00

1935 Warriors of the World R170

1 United States		
2 United States		
3 British Empire	50.00	100.00
4 France		
5 Italy	60.00	120.00
6 Russia	60.00	120.00
7 China	60.00	120.00
8 Japan		
9 Spain		
10 Roumania	30.00	75.00
11 Sweden		
12 Austria	75.00	150.00
13 Hungary		
14 Belgium	25.00	60.00
15 Greece	60.00	120.00
16 Switzerland	30.00	75.00
17 British East India		
18 Germany	60.00	120.00
20 Bulgaria	25.00	60.00
21 Norway	50.00	100.00
22 Persia		
23 Turkey		
24 Scotland		

1930 Western R130

COMPLETE SET (48)	175.00	350.00
COMMON CARD (301-348)	2.50	6.00

1930 Western R131

COMPLETE SET (48)	175.00	350.00
COMMON CARD (801-848)	2.50	6.00

1933 Western Series R128-1

COMPLETE SET (48)	225.00	450.00
COMMON CARD (1-48)	3.00	8.00
*R128-2: SAME VALUE	3.00	8.00
10 Davy Crockett	5.00	12.00
13 Andy Burnett Shooting Grizzly	6.00	15.00
32 Pawnee Tribe	5.00	12.00
34 Indian Fighting Kit Carson	5.00	12.00

1933 Western Series R128-2

COMPLETE SET (48)	450.00	900.00
COMMON CARD (201-248)	3.00	8.00
201 Buffalo Bill	5.00	12.00
202 Bull Dogging	6.00	15.00
204 Bronco Busting	5.00	12.00
205 Cowboy Whoopee	8.00	20.00
206 Stampede	6.00	15.00
207 Prairie Fire	5.00	12.00
208 Stage Coach	6.00	15.00
209 Custer's Last Stand	10.00	25.00
210 Davy Crockett	15.00	40.00
211 Deadwood Dick	5.00	12.00
213 Andy Burnett Shooting Grizzly	5.00	12.00
214 Early 49'er	5.00	12.00
216 Daniel Boone	12.00	30.00
217 Buffalo Bill	6.00	15.00
218 Joe Logston	15.00	40.00
219 William Penn	10.00	25.00
220 Davy Crockett	6.00	15.00
221 Gen George Crook	10.00	25.00
223 La Salle	8.00	20.00
224 Kit Carson	4.00	10.00
225 Tecumseh	15.00	40.00
226 Pontiac	6.00	15.00
227 Sioux Tribe	6.00	15.00
228 Ogallala Tribe	6.00	15.00
229 The Prophet	5.00	12.00
230 Pot-O-Wat-O-Mies Tribe	5.00	12.00
232 Pawnee Tribe	5.00	12.00
233 Chief Powhattan	5.00	12.00
234 Indian Fighting Kit Carson	5.00	12.00
235 Indians Attacking Train	5.00	12.00
236 Indian Captive Dance	5.00	12.00
237 Apaches Attacking Pioneers	5.00	12.00
238 Indians Attacking Stockade	5.00	12.00
239 Soldiers Shooting Indians	5.00	12.00
240 Bill Cody Fighting Indians	5.00	12.00
241 Red Tomahawk	5.00	12.00
242 Buffalo Bull	5.00	12.00
243 Massasoit	5.00	12.00
244 Spotted Tail	5.00	12.00
246 King Phillip	5.00	12.00
247 Red Jacket	5.00	12.00
248 Sitting Bull	12.00	30.00

1933 Wild West Series R172

COMPLETE SET W/O SP (48)	475.00	950.00
COMMON CARD (1-48)	6.00	15.00
1 Davy Crockett Defending The Alamo	20.00	50.00
14 Custer's Last Stand	12.00	30.00

1937 Wild West Series V306

COMPLETE SET (48)	225.00	450.00
COMMON CARD (1-48)	3.00	8.00

1933 Wonder Cities of the World

COMPLETE SET (25)	80.00	150.00
COMMON CARD (1-25)	2.00	5.00

1939 World in Arms R173

COMPLETE SET (48)	325.00	650.00
COMMON CARD	5.00	12.00
1FA United States 3-inch Anti-aircraft Gun	10.00	25.00

1933 World War Gum R174

COMPLETE SET (96)	600.00	1200.00
COMMON CARD (1-96)	4.00	10.00

Post-War

1976 Monty Gum ABBA

COMPLETE SET (50)	15.00	40.00
COMMON CARD (1-50)	.50	1.25

1976 Tonibell Action Soldiers

COMPLETE SET (12)	4.00	10.00
COMMON CARD (1-12)	.50	1.25

1973 Topps Adam-12 Emergency

COMPLETE SET (50)	4500.00	7500.00
COMMON CARD (1-50)	120.00	200.00

1964 Donruss The Addams Family

COMPLETE SET (66)	200.00	350.00
UNOPENED PACK	300.00	400.00
COMMON CARD (1-66)	2.00	5.00
1 Gomez	5.00	12.00
66 Quit Shaking the Coffin	4.00	10.00

1973 Brooke Bond Adventurers and Explorers

COMPLETE SET (50)	5.00	12.00
COMMON CARD (1-50)	.12	.30

1951 Ziegler Candy Adventures at the Giant Bar Ranch Rustlers

COMPLETE SET (26)	150.00	300.00
COMMON CARD (1-26)	4.00	10.00

1951 Ziegler Candy Adventures at the Giant Bar Ranch Space

COMPLETE SET (27)	150.00	300.00
COMMON CARD (1-27)	4.00	10.00

1952 Granose Foods Adventures of Billy the Buck

COMPLETE SET (48)	15.00	40.00
COMMON CARD (1-48)	.30	.75

1962 Mister Softee Adventures of Captain Chapel

COMPLETE SET (10)	15.00	40.00
COMMON CARD (1-10)	1.25	3.00

1957 Parkhurst Adventures of Radisson

COMPLETE SET (50)	125.00	250.00
COMMON CARD (1-50)	1.50	4.00

1960 Cadet Sweets Adventures of Rin Tin Tin

COMPLETE SET (48)	50.00	100.00
COMMON CARD (1-48)	1.25	3.00
*LARGE: SAME VALUE		

1943 Samuel Eppy Adventures of Smilin' Jack

COMPLETE SET (128)	225.00	450.00
COMMON CARD (1-128)	1.25	3.00

1944 Leaf Card-O Aeroplanes

COMPLETE SET (81)	300.00	600.00
COMMON CARD	2.50	6.00

1964 Brooke Bond African Animals

COMPLETE SET (48)	15.00	40.00
COMMON CARD (1-48)	.30	.75

1962 Brooke Bond African Wild Life

COMPLETE SET (50)	12.00	30.00
COMMON CARD (1-50)	.25	.60

1971 Cadbury Age of the Dinosaur

COMPLETE SET (12)	5.00	12.00
COMMON CARD (1-12)	.60	1.50

1979 Barratt Age of the Dinosaurs

COMPLETE SET (50)	12.00	30.00
COMMON CARD (1-50)	.50	1.25
STATED ODDS 1:1 CANDY CIGARETTE BOX		

1952 Good Luck Margarine Airplanes

COMPLETE SET (32)	175.00	350.00
COMMON CARD (1-32)	3.00	8.00

1959 Sicle Airplanes

COMPLETE SET (76)	190.00	375.00
COMMON CARD (A1-AA76)	1.50	4.00

1959 Sicle Airplanes Aurora Backs

COMPLETE SET (21)	50.00	100.00
COMMON CARD (A1-A21)	1.50	4.00

1979 Topps Alien

COMPLETE SET (84)	12.00	30.00
UNOPENED BOX (36 PACKS)	125.00	250.00
UNOPENED PACK (10 CARDS+1 STICKER)	4.00	8.00
COMMON CARD (1-84)	.30	.75

1979 Topps Alien Stickers

COMPLETE SET (22)	6.00	15.00
COMMON CARD (1-22)	.50	1.25
STATED ODDS 1:1		

1978 Donruss All-Pro Skateboard

COMPLETE SET (42)	10.00	25.00
UNOPENED BOX (36 PACKS)	35.00	50.00
UNOPENED PACK		
COMMON STICKER (1-42)	.40	1.00

1947 Exhibit All-Star Cowboys

COMPLETE SET (32)	200.00	400.00
COMMON CARD (1-32)	4.00	10.00

1945 W.H. Brady Allies in Action

COMPLETE SET (140)	1150.00	2300.00
COMMON CARD (AA71-AA140)	4.00	10.00
COMMON CARD (AA141-AA175)	12.00	30.00

1960 Tip-Top Snack Cakes Alphabet Monster Cards

COMPLETE SET (27)	20.00	50.00
COMMON CARD (1-27)	.60	1.50

1976 Ty-Phoo Tea Amazing World of Doctor Who

COMPLETE SET (12)	10.00	25.00
PRODUCED BY TYPHOO TEA		

1942 W.S. Corps America at War

COMPLETE SET (48)	300.00	600.00
UNOPENED BOX (36 PACKS)		
UNOPENED PACK (12 CARDS)		
COMMON CARD (501-548)	4.00	10.00

1949 Bowman America Salutes the FBI White Backs

COMPLETE SET (36)	600.00	950.00
COMMON CARD (1-36)	8.00	20.00
*GREY BACKS: SAME VALUE AS WHITE		
*BLANK BACKS: SAME VALUE AS WHITE		

1944 Gum Inc. American Beauties

COMPLETE SET (24)	375.00	750.00
COMMON CARD (1-24)	10.00	25.00

1961 Milton Bradley American Heritage Steamboats

COMPLETE SET (40)	100.00	200.00
COMMON CARD (1-40)	1.50	4.00

1976 Scholastic American History

COMPLETE SET (36)	8.00	20.00
COMMON CARD	.30	.75

1954 Red Man American Indian Chiefs

COMPLETE SET (40)	150.00	300.00
COMMON CARD (1-40)	2.50	6.00

1963 Nabisco American Marvels of Nature

COMPLETE SET (10)	90.00	175.00
COMMON CARD	6.00	15.00

1980 Ed-U-Cards American Presidents

COMPLETE SET (39)	30.00	75.00
COMMON CARD	1.00	2.50
NO. 24 DOES NOT EXIST		

1963 Nabisco Sugar Daddy American Zoo Animals

COMPLETE SET (25)	30.00	75.00
COMMON CARD (1-25)	1.00	2.50

1978 Donruss Andy Gibb Posters

COMPLETE SET (42)	25.00	60.00
UNOPENED BOX (36 PACKS)	40.00	50.00
UNOPENED PACK (1 POSTER)	2.00	3.00
COMMON POSTER	.75	2.00

1960 Primrose Andy Pandy

COMPLETE SET (50)	50.00	100.00
COMMON CARD (1-50)	.75	2.00

1950 DCA Food Animal Stories Fun with Pop

COMPLETE SET (24)	25.00	60.00
COMMON CARD (1-24)	.75	2.00

1975 Shell Oil Animals 3-D

COMPLETE SET (16)	12.00	30.00
COMMON CARD (1-16)	1.50	4.00

1965 Nabisco Sugar Daddy Animals and Flags of the World

COMPLETE SET (50)	75.00	150.00
COMMON CARD (1-50)	1.00	2.50

1960 Golden Press Animals

COMPLETE SET (45)	75.00	150.00
COMMON CARD (1-45)	1.25	3.00

1960 Brooke Bond Animals of North America Black Backs

COMPLETE SET (48)	15.00	40.00
COMMON CARD (1-48)	.60	1.50

1960 Brooke Bond Animals of North America Blue Backs

COMPLETE SET (48)	15.00	40.00
COMMON CARD (1-48)	.60	1.50

1960 Ewbanks Animals of the Farmyard

COMPLETE SET (25)	6.00	15.00
COMMON CARD (1-25)	.50	1.25

1951 Topps Animals of the World

COMPLETE SET (100)	250.00	500.00
COMMON CARD (101-200)	1.50	4.00

1960 Oak Manufacturing Animals Premiere

COMPLETE SET (21)	10.00	25.00
COMMON (NNO)	.50	1.25

1953 Signal Oil Antique Auto

COMPLETE SET (64)	300.00	600.00
COMMON CARD	3.00	8.00
NNO 1907 Mitchell	15.00	40.00

1953 Bowman Antique Autos

COMPLETE SET (48)	200.00	400.00
COMMON CARD (1-48)	2.50	6.00
NNO 3-D Glasses	7.50	20.00

1957 Oak Manufacturing Antique Autos Premiere

COMPLETE SET (69)	175.00	350.00
COMMON CARD (1-69)	1.50	4.00

1969 Topps Archie Tattoos

COMPLETE SET (16)	75.00	150.00
COMMON SHEET (1-16)	3.00	8.00

1973 Brooke Bond The Arctic

COMPLETE SET (48)	6.00	15.00
COMMON CARD (1-48)	.20	.50

1961 Cadet Sweets Arms and Armour

COMPLETE SET (25)	8.00	20.00
COMMON CARD (1-25)	.50	1.25

1958 General Mills Cheerios Army Guided Missile

COMPLETE SET (9)	75.00	150.00
COMMON CARD (1-9)	6.00	15.00

1942 W.S. Corps Army Navy and Air Corps

COMPLETE SET (48)	150.00	300.00
COMMON CARD (601-648)	4.00	10.00
615 Prime Minister Of England	8.00	20.00

1945 Mutoscope Artist Pin-Ups

COMPLETE SET (64)	475.00	950.00
COMMON CARD (1-64)	5.00	12.00

1962 Brooke Bond Asian Wild Life

COMPLETE SET (50)	15.00	40.00
COMMON CARD (1-50)	.25	.60

1963 Topps Astronauts

COMPLETE SET (55)	225.00	450.00
COMMON CARD (1-55)	2.50	6.00
55 Checklist	15.00	30.00
NNO 3-D Viewer	8.00	20.00

1963 O'Henry Astronauts

COMPLETE SET (7)	20.00	50.00
COMMON CARD	2.00	5.00

1952 Parkhurst Audubon Society Birds

COMPLETE SET (100)	190.00	375.00
COMMON CARD (1-100)	1.25	3.00

1959 Lyons Tea Australia

COMPLETE SET (48)	15.00	40.00
COMMON CARD (1-48)	.25	.60

1976 Topps Autos of 1977

COMPLETE SET (99)	30.00	80.00
COMPLETE SET W/STICKERS (119)	50.00	100.00
UNOPENED BOX (36 PACKS)	100.00	120.00
UNOPENED PACK	4.00	5.00
COMMON CARD (UNNUMBERED)	.40	1.00

1976 Topps Autos of 1977 Foil Stickers

COMPLETE SET (20)	5.00	12.00
COMMON CARD (UNNUMBERED)	.50	1.25
STATED ODDS 1:1		

1967 Fleer Back Slappers

COMPLETE SET (60)	112.50	225.00
UNOPENED BOX (36 PACKS)	150.00	200.00
UNOPENED PACK		
COMMON CARD (1-60)	1.25	3.00

1960 Goodies Baloney Ads

COMPLETE SET (52)	90.00	175.00
COMMON CARD (1-52)	1.25	3.00

1973 Donruss Baseball Super Freaks Series 1

COMPLETE SET (44)	20.00	50.00
COMMON CARD (1-44)	.60	1.50

1973 Donruss Baseball Super Freaks Series 2

COMPLETE SET (42)	20.00	50.00
COMMON CARD (1-42)	.60	1.50

1965 Topps Battle

COMPLETE SET (66)	500.00	1000.00
COMMON CARD (1-66)	5.00	12.00
66 Battle Checklist	25.00	60.00

1965 Topps Battle Cloth Emblems

COMPLETE SET (24)	400.00	800.00
COMMON CARD (1-24)	10.00	25.00

1965 A&BC Battle

COMPLETE SET (66)	75.00	150.00
COMMON CARD (1-66)	1.25	3.00
1 Fight to the Death	2.00	5.00
73 Battle Checklist	3.00	8.00

1972 Trucards Battle of Britain

COMPLETE SET (30)	5.00	12.00
COMMON CARD (1-30)	.25	.60

1969 A&BC Battle of Britain

COMPLETE SET (66)	120.00	250.00
COMMON CARD (1-66)	1.25	3.00

1969 Scanlens Battle of Britain

COMPLETE SET (66)	120.00	250.00
COMMON CARD (1-66)	1.25	3.00

1968 Topps Batty Book Covers

COMPLETE SET (24)	100.00	200.00
COMMON COVER	3.00	8.00

1973 Topps Batty Buttons

COMPLETE SET (24)	30.00	75.00
UNOPENED PACK (1 BUTTON)	25.00	40.00
COMMON BUTTON	1.50	4.00

1975 Topps Bay City Rollers

COMPLETE SET (66)	25.00	60.00
COMMON CARD (1-66)	.40	1.00
*SCANLENS: SAME VALUE		

1979 Topps Bazooka Gum Scratch-Offs

COMPLETE SET (6)	10.00	25.00
COMMON CARD (UNNUMBERED)	2.00	5.00

1964 Topps The Beatles Black and White

COMPLETE SET (165)	500.00	1000.00
COMPLETE SERIES 1 SET (60)	190.00	375.00
COMPLETE SERIES 2 SET (55)	175.00	350.00
COMPLETE SERIES 3 SET (50)	150.00	300.00
SERIES 1 COMMON (1-60)	2.00	5.00
SERIES 2 COMMON (61-115)	2.00	5.00
SERIES 3 COMMON (116-165)	2.00	5.00
*OPC: SAME VALUE	2.00	5.00
*UK: .5X TO 1.2X BASIC CARDS	2.50	6.00

1964 Topps The Beatles Color

COMPLETE SET (64)	80.00	150.00
COMMON CARD (1-64)	1.50	4.00
*OPC: SAME VALUE		

1964 Topps The Beatles Diary

COMPLETE SET (60)	120.00	250.00
COMMON CARD (1A-60A)	1.25	3.00

1964 Topps The Beatles A Hard Day's Night

COMPLETE SET (55)	150.00	300.00
COMMON CARD (1-55)	1.50	4.00
20 Who is the Man in the Beard?	6.00	15.00
27 Paul,Ringo and George are Getting Ready	5.00	12.00
40 John, Paul, George, and Ringo are Getting	3.00	8.00
49 The Beatles are Actors Now and They	4.00	10.00
52 Paul McCartney Holds a Clapboard On	6.00	15.00
53 In this Scene From a Hard Day's Night	5.00	12.00

1964 Topps The Beatles Plaks

COMPLETE SET (55)	350.00	700.00
COMMON CARD W/PICTURE (1-55)	4.00	10.00
COMMON CARD W/O PICTURE (1-55)	5.00	12.00

1974 Lyons Maid Beautiful Butterflies

COMPLETE SET (12)	8.00	20.00
COMMON CARD (1-12)	1.00	2.50

1985 Fleer Beautiful People

COMPLETE SET (64)	30.00	80.00
UNOPENED BOX (24 PACKS)	100.00	120.00
UNOPENED PACK	5.00	6.00
COMMON CARD	1.00	2.00

1961 Lambert's Tea Before Our Time

COMPLETE SET (25)	8.00	20.00
COMMON CARD (1-25)	.50	1.25

1961 Vita Brits Believe It or Not

COMPLETE SET (30)	10.00	25.00
COMMON CARD (1-30)	.50	1.25

1978 Fleer Best of Cracked Magazine

COMPLETE SET (56)	8.00	20.00
COMPLETE SET W/STICKERS (66)	10.00	25.00
UNOPENED BOX (36 PACKS)	150.00	250.00
UNOPENED PACK (6 CARDS+1 STICKER)	6.00	8.00
COMMON CARD (1-56)	.20	.50

1978 Fleer Best of Cracked Magazine Stickers

COMPLETE SET (10)	1.50	4.00
COMMON CARD (1-10)	.20	.50

1963 Topps Beverly Hillbillies

COMPLETE SET (66)	475.00	850.00
UNOPENED BOX (24 PACKS)		
COMMON CARD (1-66)	4.00	10.00

1976 Sunbeam Bread Bicentennial Daze

COMPLETE SET (24)	6.00	15.00
COMMON CARD (1-24)	.40	1.00

1950 Quaker Big Sports Trophies

COMPLETE SET (9)	60.00	120.00
COMMON CARD (1-9)	5.00	12.00

1976 Donruss Bionic Woman

COMPLETE SET (44)	15.00	30.00
UNOPENED BOX (24 PACKS)	125.00	150.00
UNOPENED PACK	6.00	8.00
COMMON CARD (1-44)	.40	1.00
NNO1 44-Card Base Set Panel	80.00	150.00

1964 Kosto Pudding Birds

COMPLETE SET (48)	90.00	175.00
COMMON CARD (1-48)	1.50	3.00

1976 Church and Dwight Birds of Prey

COMPLETE SET (10)	6.00	15.00
COMMON CARD (1-10)	.75	2.00
*CANADIAN: SAME VALUE AS AMERICAN		

1958 Oak Manufacturing Birds Premiere

COMPLETE SET (42)	75.00	150.00

1977 Kellogg's Birds Stick'R

COMPLETE SET (10)	12.00	30.00
COMMON CARD	1.50	4.00
*CARD ONLY: .2X TO .5X BASIC CARDS	.75	2.00

1979 Topps Black Hole

COMPLETE SET (88)	6.00	15.00
COMMON CARD (1-88)	.15	.40
*UK: SAME VALUE AS USA		

1979 Topps Black Hole Stickers

COMPLETE SET (22)	.75	2.00
COMMON STICKER (1-22)	.05	.15

1963 Philadelphia Gum Blackstone's Magic Tricks

COMPLETE SET (24)	90.00	175.00
COMMON CARD (1-24)	2.50	6.00

1967 Topps Blockheads

COMMON BLOCKHEAD	20.00	50.00

1971 Topps Brady Bunch

COMPLETE SET (88)	600.00	1200.00
UNOPENED PACK	400.00	600.00
COMMON CARD (1-88)	5.00	12.00
1 The Brady Bunch	10.00	25.00
2 The Brady Girls	12.00	30.00
3 The Brady Boys	8.00	20.00
87 Feeling Better Yet?	6.00	15.00
88 Say Cheese!	6.00	15.00

1950 Topps Bring 'Em Back Alive

COMPLETE SET (100)	175.00	350.00
COMMON CARD (1-100)	1.00	2.50

1976 Glengettie Tea British Army 1815 Blue Backs

COMPLETE SET (25)	2.50	6.00
COMMON CARD (1-25)	.20	.50

1961 Lever Brothers British Birds and Their Nests

COMPLETE SET (20)	3.00	8.00
COMMON CARD (1-20)	.25	.60

1963 H.E. Empson and Son British Cavalry Uniforms of the 19th Century

COMPLETE SET (25)	8.00	20.00
COMMON CARD (1-25)	.25	.60

1959 Glengettie Tea British Locomotives

COMPLETE SET (25)	10.00	25.00
COMMON CARD (1-25)	.30	.75

1965 Phillips Choice Tea British Rail

COMPLETE SET (25)	10.00	25.00
COMMON CARD (1-25)	.30	.75

1971 Hitchman's Dairies British Railways

COMPLETE SET (25)	5.00	12.00
COMMON CARD (1-25)	.40	1.00

1962 G.P. Tea British Railways

COMPLETE SET (25)	20.00	50.00
COMMON CARD (1-25)	.60	1.50

1954 Mornflake British Uniforms

COMPLETE SET (25)	15.00	40.00
COMMON CARD (1-25)	.50	1.25

1956 Ewbanks British Uniforms

COMPLETE SET (25)	15.00	40.00
COMMON CARD (1-25)	.50	1.25

1979 Topps Buck Rogers

COMPLETE SET (88)	10.00	25.00
COMPLETE SET W/STICKERS (110)	12.00	30.00
UNOPENED BOX (36 PACKS)	150.00	200.00
UNOPENED PACK (10 CARDS+1 STICKER)	4.00	6.00
COMMON CARD (1-88)	.15	.40
*SCANLENS: SAME VALUE AS TOPPS		

1979 Topps Buck Rogers Stickers

COMPLETE SET (22)	2.50	6.00
COMMON CARD (1-22)	.25	.60
STATED ODDS 1:1		

1964 Primrose Bugs Bunny

COMPLETE SET (50)	50.00	100.00
COMMON CARD (1-50)	1.00	2.50

1970 Topps Bugs Bunny Tattoos

COMPLETE SET (16)	20.00	50.00
COMMON TATTOO	2.50	6.00

1960 Lambert's Tea Butterflies and Moths

COMPLETE SET (25)	6.00	15.00
COMMON CARD (1-25)	.40	1.00

1964 Brooke Bond Butterflies of the World

COMPLETE SET (50)	15.00	40.00
COMMON CARD (1-50)	.25	.60

1961 Lambert's Tea Cacti

COMPLETE SET (25)	4.00	10.00
COMMON CARD (1-25)	.25	.60

1962 Lamberts Tea Cacti

COMPLETE SET (25)	10.00	25.00
COMMON CARD (1-25)	.50	1.25

1967 Topps Captain Nice Test Series

COMMON CARD (1-30)	75.00	150.00

1968 Anglo Confectionery Captain Scarlet and the Mysterons

COMPLETE SET (66)	125.00	250.00
COMMON CARD (1-66)	1.25	3.00

1943 Leaf Card-O Air Squadron Insignia

COMPLETE SET (9)	35.00	90.00
COMMON CARD (1-9)	3.00	8.00

1944 Leaf Card-O Fighters and Bombers

COMPLETE SET (21)	100.00	200.00
COMMON CARD	3.00	8.00

1944 Leaf Card-O U.S. Navy

COMPLETE SET (22)	25.00	60.00
COMMON CARD (1-22)	1.00	2.50

1962 Topps Casey and Kildare

COMPLETE SET (110)	200.00	400.00
UNOPENED BOX		
UNOPENED CELLO PACK	15.00	40.00
COMMON CARD (1-110)	1.50	4.00
1 Vincent Edwards	3.00	8.00

1960 Fleer Casper

COMPLETE SET (66)	200.00	350.00
UNOPENED PACK	120.00	250.00
COMMON CARD (1-66)	1.50	4.00

1971 Lyons Catweazle Magic

COMPLETE SET (16)	30.00	75.00
COMMON CARD (1-16)	2.50	6.00

1978 Donruss CB Convoy Code Stickers

COMPLETE SET (44)	10.00	25.00
UNOPENED BOX (24 PACKS)	40.00	50.00
UNOPENED PACK	2.00	3.00
COMMON CARD (1-44)	.30	.75

1977 Vaughn's CB Jeebies

COMPLETE SET (25)	10.00	25.00
COMMON CARD (1-25)	.60	1.50
*SUNBEAM: SAME VALUE		

1976 Tip-Top Bakery CB Stickers

COMPLETE SET (15)	12.00	30.00
COMMON CARD	1.00	2.50

1977 Fleer CB Talk

COMPLETE SET (60)	6.00	15.00
COMPLETE SET W/STICKERS (68)	10.00	20.00
UNOPENED BOX	50.00	60.00
COMMON CARD (1-60)	.10	.25

1977 Fleer CB Talk Official Truck Stickers

COMPLETE SET (8)	2.00	5.00
COMMON CARD (1-8)	.30	.75
STATED ODDS 1:1		
UNNUMBERED SET		

1950 Quaker Challenge of the Yukon

COMPLETE SET (35)	90.00	175.00
COMMON CARD (1-35)	1.50	4.00

1977 Topps Charlie's Angels

COMPLETE SET W/STICKERS (297)	125.00	250.00
COMP.SER.1 SET W/STICKERS (66)	40.00	100.00
COMP.SER.2 SET W/STICKERS (77)	40.00	100.00
COMP.SER.3 SET W/STICKERS (77)	25.00	60.00
COMP.SER.4 SET W/STICKERS (77)	30.00	80.00
SER.1 BOX (36 PACKS)	400.00	600.00
SER.1 PACK (5 CARDS+1 STICKER)	10.00	15.00
SER.2 BOX (36 PACKS)	400.00	600.00
SER.2 PACK (5 CARDS+1 STICKER)	10.00	15.00
SER.3 BOX (36 PACKS)	200.00	400.00
SER.3 PACK (5 CARDS+1 STICKER)	6.00	12.00
SER.4 BOX (36 PACKS)	65.00	80.00
SER.4 PACK (5 CARDS+1 STICKER)	2.00	3.00
COMMON CARD (1-55)	.30	.75
COMMON CARD (56-121)	.20	.50
COMMON CARD (122-187)	.15	.40
COMMON CARD (188-253)	.10	.25
*OPC: SAME VALUE AS TOPPS		

1977 Topps Charlie's Angels Stickers

COMPLETE SET (44)	4.00	10.00
COMP.SER.1 SET (11)	2.50	6.00
COMP.SER.2 SET (11)	2.00	5.00
COMP.SER.3 SET (11)	1.50	4.00
COMP.SER.4 SET (11)	1.50	4.00
COMMON CARD (1-11)	.30	.75
COMMON CARD (12-22)	.25	.60
COMMON CARD (23-33)	.20	.50
COMMON CARD (34-44)	.20	.50

1979 Donruss CHiPs Stickers

COMPLETE SET (60)	6.00	15.00
UNOPENED BOX (36 PACKS)	125.00	250.00
UNOPENED PACK (4 STICKERS)	3.50	6.00
COMMON CARD (1-60)	.20	.50

1979 Donruss CHiPs Die-Cut Stickers

COMPLETE SET (6)	1.25	3.00
COMMON CARD (1-6)	.30	.75
STATED ODDS 1:1		

1967 Scanlens Chitty Chitty Bang Bang

COMMON CARD (1-66)	5.00	12.00

1972 Donruss Choppers and Hot Bikes

COMPLETE SET (66)	50.00	100.00
UNOPENED BOX	300.00	450.00
UNOPENED PACK	8.00	20.00
COMMON CARD (1-66)	.75	2.00

1962 Topps Civil War News

COMPLETE SET (88)	625.00	1250.00
COMMON CARD (1-88)	3.00	8.00
1 The Angry Man	10.00	25.00
2 President Jeff Davis	5.00	12.00
3 The War Starts	6.00	15.00
7 Death at Sea	5.00	12.00
11 Attack	5.00	12.00
13 Dying Effort	4.00	10.00
15 Nature's Fury	4.00	10.00
18 Death to the Enemy	5.00	12.00
19 Pushed to His Doom	5.00	12.00
21 Painful Death	5.00	12.00
22 Wave of Death	5.00	12.00
23 Crushed by the Wheels	4.00	10.00
24 After the Battle	4.00	10.00
25 Hanging the Spy	6.00	15.00
26 Messenger of Death	5.00	12.00
27 Massacre	6.00	15.00
29 Bridge of Doom	5.00	12.00
32 Death Struggle	5.00	12.00
34 Wall of Corpses	5.00	12.00
35 Gasping for Air	8.00	20.00
37 Death Barges In	8.00	20.00
38 General Grant	4.00	10.00
39 General Lee	6.00	15.00
40 Bullets of Death	4.00	10.00
42 The Battle Continues	5.00	12.00
43 Costly Mistake	6.00	15.00
44 Shot to Death	5.00	12.00
45 The Riverboat Explodes	10.00	25.00
49 The Explosion	4.00	10.00
51 Horse Thieves	5.00	12.00
55 The Silent Drum	4.00	10.00
57 Hand to Hand Combat	4.00	10.00
59 Submarine Attack	4.00	10.00
66 Victim of the War	5.00	12.00
67 Deadly Duel	6.00	15.00
72 The Cannon's Victim	4.00	10.00
73 Through the Swamp	4.00	10.00
76 Blazing Cannon	4.00	10.00
79 Council of War - Lincoln	6.00	15.00
81 Deadly Defense	4.00	10.00
82 Destroying the Rails	4.00	10.00
86 Dynamite Victim	5.00	12.00
87 The War Ends	5.00	12.00
88 Checklist	50.00	100.00

1962 Topps Civil War News Currency

COMPLETE SET (17)	150.00	300.00
COMMON CARD	3.00	8.00
1 $1 Serial #355	12.00	30.00
2 $1 Serial #3691	4.00	10.00
4 $2 Serial #94505	4.00	10.00
7 $5 Serial #138590	10.00	25.00
8 $10 Serial #45956	10.00	25.00
9 $10 Serial #77389	10.00	25.00
10 $20 No Serial Number	12.00	30.00
11 $20 Serial #1372	6.00	15.00
13 $50 Serial #31351	6.00	15.00
14 $50 Serial #59204	5.00	12.00
15 $100 Serial #801	5.00	12.00
16 $500 Serial #33546	6.00	15.00
17 $1000 Serial #176A	8.00	20.00

1965 Bettman Civil War Pictures

COMPLETE SET (55)	250.00	550.00
COMMON CARD (1-55)	3.00	8.00

1944 Leaf Card-O Civilian Planes and Military Trainers

COMPLETE SET (13)	60.00	120.00
COMMON CARD	3.00	8.00

1978 Topps Close Encounters of the Third Kind

COMPLETE SET (66)	5.00	12.00
COMPLETE SET W/STICKERS (77)	8.00	20.00
UNOPENED BOX (36 PACKS)	100.00	150.00
UNOPENED PACK (7 CARDS+1 STICKER)	3.00	4.00
COMMON CARD (1-66)	.08	.20

1978 Topps Close Encounters of the Third Kind Stickers

COMPLETE SET (11)	1.25	3.00
COMMON CARD (1-11)	.12	.30
STATED ODDS 1:1		

1978 Wonder Bread Close Encounters of the Third Kind White

COMPLETE SET (24)	6.00	15.00
COMMON CARD (1-24)	.40	1.00
*YELLOW: SAME VALUE AS WHITE		

1951 Parkhurst Color Comic Cards

COMPLETE SET (39)	190.00	375.00
COMMON CARD	3.00	8.00

1964 Donruss Combat

COMPLETE SET (132)	125.00	250.00
COMPLETE SER.1 SET (66)	100.00	175.00
COMPLETE SER.2 SET (66)	120.00	250.00
UNOPENED SER.1 PACK	30.00	40.00
UNOPENED SER.2 PACK	25.00	30.00
COMMON CARD (1-66)	.75	2.00
COMMON CARD (67-132)	1.25	3.00

1945 W.H. Brady Commando Ranger

COMPLETE SET (70)	500.00	1100.00
COMMON CARD (CR1-CR70)	5.00	12.00

1955 Ty-Phoo Tea Common British Birds

COMPLETE SET (20)	15.00	40.00
COMMON CARD (1-20)	.60	1.50

VINTAGE

1960 Sketchley Cleaners Communications

COMPLETE SET (25)	12.00	30.00
COMMON CARD (1-25)	.75	2.00

1954 General Mills Cheerios Confederate Money

COMPLETE SET (10)	12.00	30.00
COMMON CARD	1.00	2.50
NNO Exclusive Display Album	10.00	25.00

1957 Weetabix Conquest of Space Series A

COMPLETE SET (25)	30.00	75.00
COMMON CARD (1-25)	1.00	2.50

1959 Weetabix Conquest of Space Series B

COMPLETE SET (25)	30.00	75.00
COMMON CARD (1-25)	1.00	2.50

1974 Lyons Maid County Badge Collection

COMPLETE SET (20)	4.00	10.00
COMMON CARD (UNNUMBERED)	.30	.75

1958 Leaf Card-O Cowboys and Indians

COMPLETE SET (15)	30.00	80.00
COMMON CARD (SKIP-NUMBERED)	1.50	4.00

1976 Wonder Bread Crazy Cars

COMPLETE SET (20)	12.00	30.00
COMMON CARD (UNNUMBERED)	1.25	3.00

1961 Topps Crazy Cards

COMPLETE SET (66)	120.00	250.00
COMMON CARD (1-66)	1.25	3.00

1979 Fleer Crazy Labels

COMPLETE SET (64)	10.00	25.00
UNOPENED BOX (36 PACKS)	50.00	60.00
UNOPENED PACK (6 STICKER-CARDS)	2.00	3.00
COMMON CARD (1-64)	.20	.50

1974 Fleer Crazy Magazine Covers Series 1

COMPLETE SET (30)	10.00	20.00
COMMON CARD (1-30)	.40	1.00

1974 Fleer Crazy Magazine Covers Series 2

COMPLETE SET (30)	10.00	20.00
COMMON CARD (1-30)	.40	1.00

1974 Fleer Crazy Magazine Covers Series 3

COMPLETE SET (10)	2.50	6.00
COMMON CARD (1-10)	.40	1.00

1968 Topps Crazy TV

COMPLETE SET (22)	60.00	120.00
COMMON CARD (SKIP-NUMBERED)	3.00	8.00

*TEST: UNPRICED DUE TO SCARCITY

1968 Topps Crazy TV Knock-Knocks

COMPLETE SET (22)	30.00	80.00
COMMON CARD (1-22)	2.50	6.00

1950 Novel Candy Crime Buster Stories

COMMON CARD	120.00	250.00

1961 Bell Brand Crusader Rabbit

COMPLETE SET (12)	750.00	1500.00
COMMON CARD (1-12)	50.00	100.00

1961 Bell Brand Crusader Rabbit Coloring Cards

COMPLETE SET (12)
*COLORING: X TO X BASIC CARDS

1973 Primrose Dad's Army

COMPLETE SET (25)	10.00	25.00
COMMON CARD (1-25)	.50	1.25

1967 Philadelphia Gum Daktari

COMPLETE SET (66)	50.00	100.00
UNOPENED BOX	500.00	800.00
UNOPENED PACK	20.00	50.00
COMMON CARD (1-66)	.40	1.00

1954 Calvert Dan Dare

COMPLETE SET (25)	30.00	80.00
COMMON CARD (1-25)	2.50	6.00

1970 Cadbury Dangerous Animals

COMPLETE SET (48)	12.00	30.00
COMMON CARD (1-48)	.50	1.25

1965 Topps Daniel Boone Test Series

COMMON CARD (1-55)	300.00	550.00

1969 Philadelphia Gum Dark Shadows Giant Pin-Ups

COMPLETE SET (16)	100.00	200.00
UNOPENED PACK	8.00	20.00
COMMON PIN-UP (1-16)	1.50	4.00
1 Reverend Trask	3.00	8.00
2 Quentin Collins (looking to his left)	5.00	12.00
3 Charles Tate	4.00	10.00
5 Judith Collins	4.00	10.00
8 Jamison Collins	8.00	20.00
9 Count Petoji	6.00	15.00
10 Barnabas (finger to chin)	8.00	20.00
15 Angelique	8.00	20.00
16 Magda	6.00	15.00

1969 Philadelphia Gum Dark Shadows Green

COMPLETE SET (66)	150.00	300.00
UNOPENED PACK	65.00	80.00
COMMON CARD (1-66)	1.50	4.00

1968 Philadelphia Gum Dark Shadows Pink

COMPLETE SET (66)	150.00	300.00
UNOPENED PACK	65.00	80.00
COMMON CARD (1-66)	1.50	4.00

1969 Philadelphia Gum Dark Shadows Quentin Postcards

COMPLETE SET (12)	25.00	60.00
UNOPENED BOX (24 PACKS)	250.00	300.00
UNOPENED PACK (3 CARDS)	10.00	12.00
COMMON CARD (1-12)	1.50	4.00

1956 Exhibit Davy Crockett

COMPLETE SET (16)	110.00	225.00
COMMON CARD	5.00	12.00

1956 Topps Davy Crockett Orange Backs

COMPLETE SET (80)	200.00	400.00
COMMON CARD (1-80)	1.50	4.00

1956 Topps Davy Crockett Green Backs

COMPLETE SET (80)	600.00	1200.00
COMMON CARD (1-8) SP	8.00	20.00
COMMON CARD (9-10/20) SP	6.00	15.00
COMMON CARD (40/43-50) SP	6.00	15.00
COMMON CARD (11-80)	4.00	10.00

ALL CARDS ARE #'d WITH AN A SUFFIX

1959 Nabisco Defenders of America

COMPLETE SET (24)	60.00	120.00
COMMON CARD	1.50	4.00

1961 Revell Development of Naval Flight

COMPLETE SET (24)	175.00	350.00
COMMON CARD (1-24)	5.00	12.00

1952 Tip Top Bread Dick Tracy

COMPLETE SET (10)	190.00	375.00
COMMON CARD	12.00	30.00

1961 Nu-Cards Dinosaur Series

COMPLETE SET (80)	250.00	550.00
UNOPENED PACK	25.00	30.00
COMMON CARD (1-80)	2.50	6.00

1961 Golden Press Dinosaurs and Other Prehistoric Animals

COMPLETE SET (45)	55.00	110.00
COMMON CARD (1-45)	.75	2.00

1962 York Peanut Butter Dinosaurs

COMPLETE SET (40)	120.00	250.00
COMMON CARD (1-40)	2.00	5.00

1967 Topps Disgusting Disguises

COMPLETE SET (24)	50.00	100.00
COMPLETE SET W/STICKERS (51)	120.00	250.00
UNOPENED PACK	10.00	25.00
COMMON CARD (1-24)	1.50	4.00

1967 Topps Disgusting Disguises Stickers

COMPLETE SET (27)	50.00	100.00
COMMON CARD (1-27)	1.50	4.00

1970 Topps Ireland Disgusting Disguises

COMPLETE SET (24)	50.00	100.00
COMPLETE SET W/STICKERS (51)	100.00	200.00
UNOPENED PACK	10.00	25.00
COMMON CARD (1-24)	1.50	4.00

PRODUCED BY TOPPS IRELAND

1970 Topps Ireland Disgusting Disguises Stickers

COMPLETE SET (27)	50.00	100.00
COMMON CARD (1-27)	1.50	4.00

1974 Wonder Bread Disney Character Stickers

COMPLETE SET (29)	15.00	40.00
COMMON CARD (UNNUMBERED)	1.00	2.50

1944 General Mills Disney Comics

COMPLETE SET (32)	75.00	150.00
COMMON CARD	1.50	4.00

1974 Wonder Bread Disney Stickers

COMMON CARD	1.25	3.00

1976 Wonder Bread Disney's Crazy College Pennants

COMPLETE SET (25)	20.00	50.00
COMMON CARD (1-25)	1.25	3.00
NNO1 Starting Next Week (CL)	15.00	40.00

1976 Wonder Bread Disney's Crazy License Plate Stickers

COMPLETE SET (25)	15.00	40.00
COMMON STICKER	.75	2.00
STICKER FOLDER	8.00	20.00

25 2-STICKER PANELS; 50 TOTAL STICKERS
INSERTED IN PACKAGES OF WONDER BREAD

1965 Donruss Disneyland Blue Backs

COMPLETE SET (66)	100.00	175.00
UNOPENED BOX	1000.00	1200.00
UNOPENED PACK	50.00	60.00
COMMON CARD (1-66)	.75	2.00

1965 Donruss Disneyland Puzzle Backs

COMPLETE SET (66)	50.00	90.00
COMMON CARD (1-66)	.40	1.00

1952 Dixie Cup Lids

COMPLETE SET (24)	50.00	100.00
COMMON CARD (1-24)	2.50	6.00

1970 Glengettie Tea Do You Know?

COMPLETE SET (25)	12.00	30.00
COMMON CARD (1-25)	.75	2.00

1967 Wall's Ice Cream Doctor Who

COMPLETE SET (36)	60.00	120.00
COMMON CARD (1-36)	2.00	5.00

1948 Kellogg's Dog Pictures

COMPLETE SET (24)
COMMON CARD

1957 Oak Manufacturing Dogs

COMPLETE SET (42)	75.00	150.00
COMMON CARD (1-42)	1.25	3.00

1961 Barber's Tea Dogs

COMPLETE SET (24)	8.00	20.00
COMMON CARD (1-24)	.30	.75

1950 Hood's Ice Cream Dogs

COMPLETE SET (42)	100.00	200.00
COMMON CARD (UNNUMBERED)	1.50	4.00

1961 Horniman's Tea Dogs

COMPLETE SET (48)	8.00	20.00
COMMON CARD (1-48)	.30	.75

1976 Kellogg's Dogs of the World Stick'R

COMPLETE SET (10)	15.00	40.00
COMMON CARD	2.00	5.00
*CARD ONLY: .2X TO .5X BASIC CARDS	1.00	2.50

1967 Topps Dopey Books

COMPLETE SET (42)	120.00	250.00
UNOPENED PACK	40.00	50.00
COMMON CARD (1-42)	1.50	4.00

1967 Post Dr. Dolittle

COMPLETE SET (60)	150.00	300.00
COMMON CARD	1.50	4.00

1964 RCA Dracula's Greatest Hits

COMPLETE SET (15)	30.00	75.00
COMMON CARD (1-15)	2.00	5.00
PAN Uncut 15-card panel	50.00	100.00

1980 Donruss Dukes of Hazzard

COMPLETE SET (66)	12.00	30.00
UNOPENED BOX (36 PACKS)	60.00	100.00
UNOPENED PACK (6 CARDS)	2.00	3.00
COMMON CARD (1-66)	.25	.60

1962 Nabisco Earth-Shaking Events Canadian

COMPLETE SET (24)	15.00	40.00
COMMON CARD (1-24)	.50	1.25

1973 Kellogg's Ecology Stickers

COMMON CARD	1.50	4.00

1980 Warwick District Council England's Historic Heartland

COMPLETE SET (30)	5.00	12.00
COMMON CARD (1-30)	.30	.75

1960 Becker Elephant Jokes

COMPLETE SET (50)	60.00	120.00
COMMON CARD (1-50)	.75	2.00

1978 Donruss Elvis

COMPLETE SET (66)	12.50	30.00
UNOPENED BOX (36 PACKS)	75.00	125.00
UNOPENED PACK	2.00	3.00

1978 Monty Gum Elvis

COMPLETE SET (50)	15.00	40.00
COMMON CARD (1-50)	.75	2.00

1956 Topps Elvis Presley

COMPLETE SET (66)	350.00	700.00
UNOPENED 1 CENT PACK	400.00	600.00
UNOPENED 5 CENT PACK		
COMMON CARD (1-66)	3.00	8.00
2 Elvis Presley Checklist	8.00	20.00

1974 Topps Evel Knievel

COMPLETE SET (60)	300.00	500.00
COMPLETE SET W/STICKERS (82)	120.00	250.00
UNOPENED BOX (48 PACKS)		
UNOPENED PACK (5 CARDS+1 STICKER)	100.00	150.00
COMMON CARD (1-60)	1.25	3.00

1974 Topps Evel Knievel Auto Stickers

COMPLETE SET (22)	15.00	30.00
COMMON CARD (1-22)	.75	2.00

1957 Swettenhams Tea Evolution of the Royal Navy

COMPLETE SET (25)	10.00	25.00
COMMON CARD (1-25)	.30	.75

1959 Cadet Sweets Evolution of the Royal Navy

COMPLETE SET (25)	8.00	20.00
COMMON CARD (1-25)	.25	.60

1960 Nabisco Exciting Scenes in American History

COMPLETE SET (8)	10.00	25.00
COMMON CARD	2.00	5.00
STATED ODDS 1:		

1960 A&BC Exploits of William Tell

COMPLETE SET (36)	150.00	300.00
COMMON CARD (1-36)	6.00	15.00
1 The Arch Enemy	8.00	20.00
36 The Prisoner	8.00	20.00

1959 Topps Fabian

COMPLETE SET (55)	30.00	80.00
COMMON CARD (1-55)	.40	1.00

1973 Donruss Fabulous Odd Rods

COMPLETE SET (66)	50.00	100.00
COMMON STICKER (1-66)	.75	2.00

1968 Topps Fabulous Rock Records

COMPLETE SET (16)	900.00	1700.00
COMMON RECORD	30.00	80.00

1966 ARO Milk Famous Americans

COMPLETE SET (20)	15.00	40.00
COMMON CARD (1-20)	1.25	3.00

1962 Topps Famous Americans Stamps Test Series

COMPLETE SET (80)		
COMMON CARD (1-80)	1.50	4.00

1955 Ty-Phoo Tea Famous Buildings

COMPLETE SET (20)	12.00	30.00
COMMON CARD (1-20)	.50	1.25

1979 William Tell Publishing Famous Civil War Generals

COMPLETE SET (50)	20.00	50.00
COMMON CARD (1-50)	1.25	3.00

1953 Sugar Daddy Famous Comic Characters

COMPLETE SET (50)	120.00	250.00
COMMON CARD (1-50)	1.50	4.00
25 Daddy Warbucks	6.00	15.00
31 Annie	10.00	25.00
36 Sandy	5.00	12.00

1953 Sugar Daddy Famous Comic Characters Welch Backs

COMPLETE SET (50)	120.00	250.00
COMMON CARD (1-50)	1.50	4.00
25 Daddy Warbucks	6.00	15.00
31 Annie	10.00	25.00
36 Sandy	5.00	12.00

1961 Famous Discoveries and Adventures

COMPLETE SET (50)	60.00	120.00
COMMON CARD (1-50)	.75	2.00
48 Einstein	4.00	10.00

1963 Kellogg's Famous Firsts

COMPLETE SET (12)	6.00	15.00
COMMON CARD (1-12)	.40	1.00

1969 Chix Confectionery Famous Last Words

COMPLETE SET (50)	20.00	50.00
COMMON CARD (1-50)	.60	1.50

1964 Lyons Maid Famous Locomotives

COMPLETE SET (40)	30.00	75.00
COMMON CARD (1-40)	.25	.60

1963 Rosan Famous Monsters

COMPLETE SET (64)	120.00	250.00
COMMON CARD (1-64)	1.25	3.00

1969 Brooke Bond Famous People

COMPLETE SET (50)	15.00	40.00
COMMON CARD (1-50)	.25	.60

1972 Trebor Chews Famous Pets

COMPLETE SET (24)	2.00	5.00
COMMON CARD (1-24)	.12	.30

1978 Jacob's Club Famous Pictures from History

COMPLETE SET (32)	5.00	12.00
COMMON CARD (1-32)	.25	.60

1943 Associated Oil Famous War Posters

COMPLETE SET (50)	150.00	300.00
COMMON CARD (1-50)	2.00	5.00

1976 Topps Fancy Pants Test Issue

COMPLETE SET (31)	150.00	300.00
UNOPENED PACK	120.00	150.00
COMMON STICKER	5.00	12.00

1973 Donruss Fantastic Odd Rods 1st Series

COMPLETE SET (66)	.80	150.00
UNOPENED BOX	200.00	250.00
UNOPENED PACK	8.00	10.00
COMMON CARD (67-132)	.75	2.00

1973 Donruss Fantastic Odd Rods 2nd Series

COMPLETE SET (66)	80.00	150.00
UNOPENED BOX	200.00	250.00
UNOPENED PACK	8.00	10.00
COMMON CARD (1-66)	.75	2.00

1970 Donruss Fiends and Machines

COMPLETE SET (66)	150.00	300.00
COMMON CARD (1-66)	2.50	6.00

1979 Kellogg's 50 States Stick'R

COMPLETE SET (50)	25.00	60.00
COMMON CARD	.75	2.00
*CARD ONLY: .2X TO .5X BASIC CARDS	.40	1.00

1953 Topps Fighting Marines

COMPLETE SET (96)	600.00	1200.00
COMMON CARD (1-48)	3.00	8.00
COMMON CARD (49-96)	4.00	10.00

1953 Bowman Firefighters

COMPLETE SET (64)	325.00	650.00
UNOPENED PACK (1 CENT)	300.00	350.00
COMMON CARD (1-64)	3.00	8.00

1954 White Fish Authority The Fish We Eat

COMPLETE SET (25)	10.00	25.00
COMMON CARD (1-25)	.30	.75

1963 Topps Flag Midgee

COMPLETE SET (99)	75.00	150.00
COMMON CARD (1-99)	.50	1.25

1961 Goodies Flags and Emblems

COMPLETE SET (25)	5.00	12.00
COMMON CARD (1-25)	.40	1.00

1967 Brooke Bond Flags and Emblems of the World

COMPLETE SET (50)	5.00	12.00
COMMON CARD (1-50)	.15	.40
1 United Kingdom	.40	1.00
40 U.S.A.	.75	2.00

1949 Topps Flags of All Nations and Soldiers of the World

COMPLETE SET (100)	300.00	600.00
COMMON CARD (1-100)	2.00	5.00

1956 Topps Flags of the World

COMPLETE SET (80)	100.00	200.00
COMMON CARD (1-80)	.75	2.00

1970 Topps Flags of the World

COMPLETE SET (80)	60.00	120.00
COMMON CARD (1-80)	1.25	3.00

1965 Topps Flash Gordon Test Series

COMMON CARD (1-24)	30.00	75.00

1978 Phoenix Candy Flash Gordon Candy Boxes

COMPLETE SET (8)	20.00	50.00
COMMON CARD (1-8)	4.00	10.00

1980 Flash Gordon Cartoon Shrinky-Dinks

COMPLETE SET (8)	6.00	15.00
COMMON CARD	1.25	3.00

1961 Domino Filter Fleurs de Culture

COMPLETE SET (25)	3.00	8.00
COMMON CARD (1-25)	.15	.40

1963 Primrose The Flintstones

COMPLETE SET (50)	120.00	250.00
COMMON CARD (1-50)	1.50	4.00

1967 Nabisco Weeties Flintstones Die-Cut Stand-Ups

COMPLETE SET (40)	200.00	400.00
COMMON CARD (UNNUMBERED)	3.00	8.00

1949 Post Flip Movies

COMPLETE SET (12)	75.00	150.00
COMMON CARD	4.00	10.00

1949 Topps Flip-O-Vision The Movie Maker Bubble Gum

COMPLETE SET (41)	400.00	800.00
COMMON CARD	6.00	15.00
SKIP-NUMBERED SET		

1966 Topps Flipper Test Series

COMMON CARD (1-30)	120.00	250.00

1966 Topps Flipper's Magic Fish

COMPLETE SET (10)	90.00	175.00
COMMON CARD (1-10)	6.00	15.00

1968 Donruss Flower Power

COMPLETE SET (24)	60.00	120.00
COMMON CARD	1.50	4.00

1972 Trucards Flowers

COMPLETE SET (30)	4.00	10.00
COMMON CARD (1-30)	.20	.50

1977 Carreras Flowers All the Year Round

COMPLETE SET (50)	15.00	40.00
COMMON CARD (1-50)	.30	.75

1948 Nabisco Flying Circus

COMPLETE SET (24)	75.00	150.00
COMMON CARD (1-24)	2.00	5.00

1948 Nabisco Flying Circus Aviation Notebook

COMPLETE SET (12)		75.00
COMMON CARD (1A-12A)	2.00	5.00

1968 Donruss Flying Nun

COMPLETE SET (66)	100.00	175.00
UNOPENED BOX (24 PACKS)	350.00	400.00
UNOPENED PACK	15.00	20.00
COMMON CARD (1-66)	.75	2.00

1979 Sanitarium Focus on New Zealand

COMPLETE SET (12)	8.00	20.00
COMMON CARD (1-12)	1.25	3.00

1960 Topps Fold-A-Roos Test Series

COMPLETE SET (24)	400.00	800.00
COMMON CARD (SKIP #'d)	10.00	25.00

1962 Topps Foldees

COMPLETE SET (44)	75.00	150.00
COMMON CARD (1-44)	1.25	3.00

1960 Leaf Foney Ads

COMPLETE SET (72)	120.00	250.00
COMMON CARD (1-72)	2.00	5.00

1974 Donruss Football Super Freaks

COMPLETE SET (42)	15.00	40.00
UNOPENED BOX (24 PACKS)		
UNOPENED PACK		
COMMON CARD (1-42)	.50	1.25

1966 Topps Frankenstein Valentine Stickers

COMPLETE SET (44)	250.00	500.00
COMMON CARD (1-44)	4.00	10.00

1965 Donruss Freddie and the Dreamers

COMPLETE SET (66)	30.00	80.00
UNOPENED PACK (8 CARDS)	30.00	40.00
COMMON CARD (1-66)	.50	1.25

1950 Topps Freedom's War

COMPLETE SET (203)	700.00	1200.00
COMMON CARD (1-96/104-203)	1.50	4.00
COMMON TANK (97-103)	25.00	60.00
*GRAY BACKS: .5X TO 1.2X BASIC CARDS		
183 General George S. Patton Jr.	2.50	6.00
198 Gen. Mark W. Clark	2.50	6.00
199 General James H. Doolittle	2.50	6.00
200 General George C. Marshall	2.50	6.00
201 General Dwight D. Eisenhower	2.50	6.00
202 General Omar N. Bradley	2.50	6.00

1960 Brooke Bond Freshwater Fish

COMPLETE SET (50)	8.00	20.00
COMMON CARD (1-50)	.40	1.00

1953 Bowman Frontier Days

COMPLETE SET (128)	325.00	650.00
COMMON CARD (1-128)	1.50	4.00

1955 Parkhurst Frontier Days

COMPLETE SET (121)	300.00	600.00
COMMON CARD (1-121)	1.50	4.00

1972 Fry's Fun Cards

COMPLETE SET (12)	4.00	10.00
COMMON CARD (1-12)	.50	1.25

1970 Topps Funny Doors

COMPLETE SET (24)	125.00	250.00
COMMON CARD (1-24)	3.00	8.00

1948 Topps Funny Foldees

COMPLETE SET (66)	600.00	1200.00
COMMON CARD (1-66)	6.00	15.00

1955 Topps Funny Foldees

COMPLETE SET (66)	325.00	650.00
COMMON CARD (1-66)	3.00	8.00

1970 Topps Funny Lil' Joke Books

COMPLETE SET (44)	150.00	300.00
COMMON CARD (1-44)	2.50	6.00

1966 Topps Funny Rings

COMPLETE SET (24)	300.00	600.00
COMMON CARD (1-24)	12.00	30.00

1967 Topps Funny Travel Posters

COMPLETE SET (24)	150.00	300.00
COMMON POSTER (1-24)	4.00	10.00

1959 Topps Funny Valentines

COMPLETE SET (66)	100.00	175.00
UNOPENED PACK	35.00	50.00
COMMON CARD (1-66)	.75	2.00

1960 Topps Funny Valentines 'A' Series

COMPLETE SET (66)	70.00	120.00
UNOPENED BOX (24 PACKS)	450.00	500.00
UNOPENED PACK	15.00	20.00
COMMON CARD (1-66)	1.00	2.50

1967 British American Tobacco Gallery of Great Cars

COMPLETE SET (24)	30.00	75.00
COMMON CARD (UNNUMBERED)	1.00	2.50
*TABS: UNPRICED DUE TO SCARCITY		

1967 Leaf Garrison's Gorillas

COMPLETE SET (72)	60.00	120.00
UNOPENED BOX (24 PACKS)	300.00	400.00
UNOPENED PACK	20.00	25.00
COMMON CARD (1-72)	.75	2.00

1950 Quaker Gene Autry Comics

COMPLETE SET (5)	90.00	175.00
COMMON COMIC	12.00	30.00

1966 Topps Get Smart

COMPLETE SET (66)	200.00	400.00
COMMON CARD (1-66)	2.00	5.00
*OPC: SAME VALUE		

1966 Topps Get Smart Secret Agent Kits

COMPLETE SET (16)	200.00	400.00

1971 Topps Getting Together with Bobby Sherman

COMPLETE SET (55)	1500.00	3000.00
COMMON CARD (1-55)	30.00	75.00

1968 Topps Giant Plaks

COMPLETE SET (50)	150.00	300.00
COMMON CARD (1-50)	2.00	5.00

1968 Topps Giant Plaks Test Series

COMPLETE SET (50)	200.00	375.00
COMMON CARD (1-50)	2.50	6.00

1961 Topps Giant Size Funny Valentines

COMPLETE SET (55)	100.00	200.00
COMMON CARD (1-55)	1.25	3.00

1968 Topps Giant Size Funny Valentines

COMPLETE SET (55)	75.00	150.00
UNOPENED BOX (PACKS)		
UNOPENED PACK (CARDS)		
COMMON CARD (1-55)	1.00	2.50

1961 O-Pee-Chee Giant Size Funny Valentines

COMPLETE SET (55)		
*OPC: SAME VALUE AS BASIC CARDS		

1963 Nabisco Giants of Science

COMPLETE SET (18)		
COMMON CARD (1-18)		

1965 Topps Gilligan's Island

COMPLETE SET (55)	700.00	1400.00
UNOPENED PACK		
COMMON CARD (1-55)	10.00	25.00
1 You'll Be Safe Skipper!	15.00	40.00
55 The Castaways	15.00	40.00

1967 A&BC The Girl from U.N.C.L.E.

COMPLETE SET (25)	60.00	120.00
UNOPENED BOX (48 PACKS)	650.00	800.00
COMMON CARD (1-25)	1.50	4.00

1969 Topps Go-Go Buttons

COMPLETE SET (24)	75.00	150.00
UNOPENED BOX		
UNOPENED PACK		
COMMON BUTTON	2.00	5.00

1976 Sharman Golden Age of Flying

COMPLETE SET (24)	6.00	15.00
COMMON CARD (1-24)	.50	1.25

1977 Doncella Golden Age of Flying

COMPLETE SET (24)	6.00	15.00
COMMON CARD (1-24)	.50	1.25

1975 Doncella Golden Age of Motoring

COMPLETE SET (24)	5.00	12.00
COMMON CARD (1-24)	.40	1.00

1978 Doncella Golden Age of Sail

COMPLETE SET (24)	5.00	12.00
COMMON CARD (1-24)	.30	.75

1965 Fleer Gomer Pyle

COMPLETE SET (66)	75.00	80.00

UNOPENED BOX (24 PACKS)

UNOPENED PACK	50.00	60.00
COMMON CARD (1-66)	.40	1.00

1977 Fleer Gong Show

COMPLETE SET (66)	6.00	15.00
COMPLETE SET W/STICKERS (76)	8.00	20.00
UNOPENED BOX (36 PACKS)	100.00	150.00
UNOPENED PACK (7 CARDS+1 STICKER)	3.00	5.00
COMMON CARD (1-66)	.10	.25

1977 Fleer Gong Show Stickers

COMPLETE SET (10)	1.50	4.00
COMMON CARD (1-10)	.15	.40

STATED ODDS 1:1

1966 Leaf Good Guys and Bad Guys

COMPLETE SET (72)	175.00	350.00
UNOPENED PACK	175.00	200.00
COMMON CARD (1-72)	1.50	4.00

CARD NO. 43 NOT ISSUED

1975 Topps Good Times

COMPLETE SET (55)	15.00	40.00
COMPLETE SET W/STICKERS (76)	20.00	50.00
UNOPENED BOX (36 PACKS)	300.00	500.00
UNOPENED PACK (10 CARDS+1 STICKER)	12.00	20.00
COMMON CARD (1-55)	.40	1.00

1975 Good Times Stickers

COMPLETE SET (21)	6.00	15.00
COMMON CARD (1-21)	.40	1.00

1963 Fleer Goofy Gags

COMPLETE SET (55)	300.00	600.00
COMMON CARD	5.00	12.00

1970 Topps Goofy Goggles

COMPLETE SET (12)	75.00	150.00
UNOPENED BOX		
UNOPENED PACK		
COMMON GOGGLES (UNNUMBERED)	6.00	15.00
NNO Come Fly with Me	6.00	15.00
NNO Get Lost	6.00	15.00
NNO Guess Who?	6.00	15.00
NNO Here's My Heart/Here's My Heart	6.00	15.00
NNO I'm Cool	6.00	15.00
NNO I've Got My Eyes on You	6.00	15.00
NNO Kiss Me	6.00	15.00
NNO Let's Have a Ball	6.00	15.00
NNO Please Ignore Me	6.00	15.00
NNO Stop Wasting My Time	6.00	15.00
NNO Stop/Stop	6.00	15.00
NNO What's Cooking?	6.00	15.00

1957 Topps Goofy Postcards

COMPLETE SET (60)	30.00	75.00
COMMON CARD (1-60)	.40	1.00

1957 O-Pee-Chee Goofy Postcards

COMPLETE SET (60)	30.00	75.00
COMMON CARD	.40	1.00

1978 Topps Grease

COMPLETE SET (132)	15.00	40.00
COMPLETE SET W/STICKERS (154)	25.00	60.00
COMPLETE SER.1 SET (66)	10.00	25.00
COMPLETE SER.1 SET W/STICKERS (77)	15.00	40.00
COMPLETE SER.2 SET (66)	10.00	25.00
COMPLETE SER.2 SET W/STICKERS (77)	15.00	40.00
UNOPENED SER.1 BOX (36 PACKS)	100.00	200.00
UNOPENED SER.1 PACK (7 CARDS+1 STICKER)	3.00	5.00
UNOPENED SER.2 BOX (36 PACKS)	150.00	250.00
UNOPENED SER.2 PACK (7 CARDS+1 STICKER)	4.00	6.00
COMMON CARD (1-66)	.10	.25
COMMON CARD (67-132)	.10	.25

*OPC: SAME VALUE

1978 Topps Grease Stickers

COMPLETE SET (22)	6.00	15.00
COMPLETE SERIES 1 SET (11)	4.00	10.00
COMPLETE SERIES 2 SET (11)	4.00	10.00
COMMON SERIES 1 CARD (1-11)	.40	1.00
COMMON SERIES 2 CARD (12-22)	.40	1.00

*OPC: SAME VALUE

1975 Bob's Big Boy A Great American

COMPLETE SET (30)	10.00	25.00
COMMON CARD (1-30)	.60	1.50

1976 Rainbo Bread Great Americans

COMPLETE SET (50)	8.00	20.00
COMMON CARD	.39	.75

1976 Sunbeam Bread Great Americans

COMPLETE SET (50)	8.00	20.00
COMMON CARD (1-50)	.30	.75

1972 Shell Oil Great Britons

COMPLETE SET (20)	6.00	15.00
COMMON CARD (1-20)	.40	1.00

1961 Quaker Great Feats of Building

COMPLETE SET (12)	3.00	8.00
COMMON CARD (1-12)	.40	1.00

1967 Esso Great Moments in American History

COMPLETE SET (24)	50.00	100.00
COMMON CARD (1-24)	1.25	3.00

1966 Philadelphia Gum Green Berets

COMPLETE SET (66)	80.00	150.00
UNOPENED BOX (24 PACKS)	600.00	1000.00
UNOPENED PACK	25.00	40.00
COMMON CARD (1-66)	.75	2.00
1 The Green Berets (JFK)	4.00	10.00
66 Checklist	4.00	10.00

1966 Donruss Green Hornet

COMPLETE SET (44)	125.00	250.00
UNOPENED BOX (24 PACKS)	1500.00	1800.00
UNOPENED PACK	65.00	80.00
COMMON CARD (1-44)	1.50	4.00

1966 Topps Green Hornet Stickers

COMPLETE SET (44)	175.00	350.00
UNOPENED PACK	20.00	30.00
COMMON CARD (1-44)	2.50	6.00

1980 Wonder Bread Guinness World Records

COMPLETE SET (16)	15.00	40.00
COMMON CARD (1-16)	1.25	3.00

1971 Topps Gum Berries Lids

COMPLETE SET (55)	60.00	120.00
COMMON CARD (1-55)	1.25	3.00

1953 Parkhurst Guns and Pistols

COMPLETE SET (50)	120.00	250.00
COMMON CARD (1-50)	1.50	4.00

1974 Wonder Bread Hanna-Barbera Magic Tricks

COMPLETE SET W/CL (26)	50.00	100.00
COMPLETE SET W/O CL (25)	30.00	75.00
COMMON CARD (1-25; CL)	1.50	4.00
CL Checklist	15.00	40.00

1976 Topps Happy Days

COMPLETE SET (44)	8.00	20.00
COMPLETE SET W/STICKERS (55)	12.00	30.00
UNOPENED BOX (36 PACKS)	200.00	350.00
UNOPENED PACK (5 CARDS+1 STICKER)	6.00	10.00
COMMON CARD (1-44)	.20	.50

*OPC: SAME VALUE AS TOPPS

1976 Topps Happy Days Stickers

COMPLETE SET (11)	3.00	8.00
COMMON CARD (1-11)	.40	1.00

1976 Topps Happy Days 'A' Series

COMPLETE SET (44)	15.00	40.00
COMPLETE SET W/STICKER (55)	20.00	50.00
UNOPENED BOX (36 PACKS)	100.00	120.00
UNOPENED PACK (5 CARDS+1 STICKER)	3.00	4.00
COMMON CARD (1A-44A)	.30	.75

*OPC: SAME VALUE AS TOPPS

1976 Topps Happy Days 'A' Series Stickers

COMPLETE SET (11)	2.00	5.00
COMMON CARD (1-11)	.20	.50

STATED ODDS 1:1

1972 Philadelphia Gum Happy Horoscopes

COMPLETE SET (72)	20.00	50.00
UNOPENED PACK	8.00	12.00
COMMON CARD (1-72)	.20	.50

1975 Primrose Happy Howlers

COMPLETE SET (25)	15.00	40.00
COMMON CARD (1-25)	1.25	3.00

1970 Topps Hee Haw Test Series

COMMON CARD (1-55)	120.00	200.00

1942 Candyland Heroes of Pearl Harbor Killed in Action

COMPLETE SET (8)	300.00	650.00
COMMON CARD (1-8)	25.00	60.00

1970 Sharp Hey Presto

COMPLETE SET (25)	10.00	25.00
COMMON CARD (1-25)	.30	.75

1969 A&BC High Chaparral

COMPLETE SET (36)	55.00	110.00
COMMON CARD (1-36)	1.00	2.50

1961 Lambert's Tea Historic East Anglia

COMPLETE SET (25)	12.00	30.00
COMMON CARD (1-25)	.40	1.00

1971 Kraft Historic Military Uniforms

COMPLETE SET (12)	3.00	8.00
COMMON CARD (1-12)	.40	1.00

1967 Quaker Historic Ships

COMPLETE SET (8)	15.00	40.00
COMMON CARD (1-8)	1.50	4.00

1954 E.D.L. Moseley Historical Buildings

COMPLETE SET (25)	12.00	30.00
COMMON CARD (1-25)	.40	1.00

1957 Kane Products Historical Characters

COMPLETE SET (50)	25.00	60.00
COMMON CARD (1-50)	.40	1.00

1964 Ringtons Historical Scenes

COMPLETE SET (25)	8.00	20.00
COMMON CARD (1-25)	.25	.60

1968 Glengettie Tea Historical Scenes

COMPLETE SET (25)	8.00	20.00
COMMON CARD (1-25)	.25	.60

1972 Brooke Bond History of Aviation

COMPLETE SET (50)	15.00	40.00
COMMON CARD (1-50)	.40	1.00

1963 Kellogg's History of British Military Aircraft

COMPLETE SET (16)	15.00	40.00
COMMON CARD (1-16)	.75	2.00

1960 Barratt History of the Air

COMPLETE SET (25)	8.00	20.00
COMMON CARD (1-25)	.50	1.25

1962 CBT-Grayson History of the Blue Lamp Complete Series

COMPLETE SET (50)	15.00	40.00
COMMON CARD (1-50)	.25	.60

1968 Brooke Bond History of the Motor Car

COMPLETE SET (50)	5.00	12.00
COMMON CARD (1-50)	.20	.50

1974 Glengettie Tea History of the Railways

COMPLETE SET (50)	8.00	20.00

COMPLETE SERIES 1 SET (25)	5.00	12.00
COMPLETE SERIES 2 SET (25)	5.00	12.00
COMMON SERIES 1 CARD (1-25)	.25	.60
COMMON SERIES 2 CARD (26-50)	.25	.60

1980 John Player & Sons History of the VC

COMPLETE SET (24)	3.00	8.00
COMMON CARD (1-24)	.25	.60

1957 Topps Hit Stars

COMPLETE SET (88)	900.00	1800.00
COMMON CARD (1-88)	4.00	10.00
1 Clyde McPhatter	10.00	25.00
27 Jerry Lewis	10.00	25.00
34 Nat King Cole DP	6.00	15.00
35 Little Richard	12.00	30.00
50 Fats Domino	12.00	30.00
51 The Crickets (Buddy Holly)	20.00	50.00
53 Jerry Lee Lewis	10.00	25.00
59 Elvis Presley DP	30.00	75.00
63 James Dean DP	20.00	50.00
65 James Dean	10.00	25.00
66 James Dean DP	20.00	50.00
69 Tony Curtis	6.00	15.00
71 James Dean	50.00	100.00
72 Bob Hope	20.00	50.00
77 Gene Kelly DP	6.00	15.00
83 Sammy Davis Jr. DP	8.00	20.00
85 Elizabeth Taylor DP	15.00	40.00
86 Jerry Lewis	10.00	25.00
88 Debbie Reynolds	6.00	15.00

1972 Hitmakers

COMPLETE SET (36)	25.00	60.00
COMMON CARD (1-36)	.75	2.00

1962 Lyons Tea HMS 1902-1962

COMPLETE SET (32)	15.00	40.00
COMMON CARD (1-32)	.40	1.00

1966 Exhibit Hobo the Bum Fortune Teller

COMPLETE SET (16)	15.00	40.00
COMMON CARD (1-16)	.75	2.00

1965 Fleer Hogan's Heroes

COMPLETE SET (66)	600.00	1200.00
UNOPENED PACK	250.00	300.00
COMMON CARD (1-66)	6.00	15.00
1 Lose a Tank Col. Klink?	20.00	50.00
66 He Told Me He Bought It	12.00	30.00

1957 Amalgamated Tobacco Holiday Resorts

COMPLETE SET (25)	15.00	40.00
COMMON CARD (1-25)	.50	1.25

1963 B.T. Limited Holiday Resorts

COMPLETE SET (25)	8.00	20.00
COMMON CARD (1-25)	.30	.75

1951 Post Hopalong Cassidy

COMPLETE SET (36)	175.00	350.00
COMMON CARD (1-36)	3.00	8.00

1950 Topps Hopalong Cassidy

COMPLETE SET (230)	1800.00	2500.00
UNOPENED PACK (1 CENT)	200.00	250.00
UNOPENED PACK (5 CENT)	200.00	250.00
COMMON CARD (1-186)	3.00	8.00
COMMON CARD (187-230)	4.00	10.00

1950 Topps Hopalong Cassidy Foil

COMPLETE SET (8)	500.00	1000.00
COMMON CARD	50.00	100.00
UNNUMBERED SET		

1972 Philadelphia Gum Horrible Horoscopes

COMPLETE SET (72)	30.00	80.00
COMMON CARD (1-72)	.60	1.50

1961 Nu-Cards Horror Monsters

COMPLETE SET (147)	475.00	950.00
COMP.GREEN SET (1-66)	350.00	700.00
COMP.ORANGE SET (67-146)	150.00	300.00
UNOPENED PACK	80.00	100.00
COMMON GREEN (1-66)	3.00	8.00
COMMON ORANGE (67-146)	1.25	3.00
6 Teen Age Werewolf	8.00	20.00
7 The Terror From Beyond Space	8.00	20.00
8 King Kong	12.00	30.00
21 Abbott and Costello Meet Frankenstein	3.00	120.00
26 Creature From The Black Lagoon	12.00	30.00
45 Frankenstein	15.00	40.00
50 The Wolfman	5.00	12.00
57 The She Creature	8.00	20.00
58 Animal Man In Island Of Lost Souls	5.00	12.00
59 Vegetable Man, It Conquered The World	6.00	15.00
60 Hunchback Of Notre Dame	5.00	12.00
61 Skeleton Man	25.00	60.00
102B The Electronic Monster-Bonus Card	60.00	120.00

1948 Gordon's Bread Horses

COMPLETE SET (24)	120.00	250.00
COMMON CARD	3.00	8.00

1976 Kellogg's Horses Stick'R

COMPLETE SET (8)	8.00	20.00
COMMON CARD	1.50	4.00
*CARD ONLY: .2X TO .5X BASIC CARDS	.75	2.00

1969 Cadet Sweets How?

COMPLETE SET (25)	25.00	60.00
COMMON CARD (1-25)	.75	2.00

1942 Nabisco How America Travels

COMPLETE SET (36)	110.00	225.00
COMMON CARD (1-36)	2.00	5.00

1955 Bibby & Sons How What and Why?

COMPLETE SET (25)	25.00	60.00
COMMON CARD (1-25)	.75	2.00

1953 Welch's Howdy Doody Doodyville Village

COMPLETE SET (8)	75.00	150.00
COMMON BOX	6.00	15.00

1968 A&BC Huck Finn

COMPLETE SET (55)	175.00	325.00
COMMON CARD (1-55)	2.00	5.00
*ILAMI: .6X TO 1.5X BASIC CARDS	3.00	8.00

1976 Topps Hysterical History Stickers

COMPLETE SET (66)	15.00	40.00
UNOPENED BOX (36 PACKS)		
UNOPENED PACK		
COMMON STICKER (1-66)	.30	.75
*CARD VERSION: .75X TO 2X BASIC STICKERS		

1970 Kellogg's H.R. Pufnstuf Banners

COMPLETE SET (6)	60.00	120.00
COMMON BANNER	8.00	20.00

1969 Kellogg's H.R. Pufnstuf Stickers

COMPLETE SET (8)	12.00	30.00
COMMON CARD (UNNUMBERED)	1.25	3.00

1960 Priory Tea I-Spy Bridges

COMPLETE SET (24)	12.00	30.00
COMMON CARD (1-24)	.40	1.00

1961 Donruss Idiot Cards

COMPLETE SET (66)	75.00	150.00
COMMON CARD (1-66)	.75	2.00

1950 Novel Candy Indian Chief Stories Boxes

COMPLETE SET (12)	75.00	150.00
COMMON CARD (1-12)	4.00	10.00

1972 Ovaltine Indian Chiefs

COMPLETE SET (6)	6.00	15.00
COMMON CARD (UNNUMBERED)	1.25	3.00

1947 Goudey Indian Gum

COMPLETE SET (96)	700.00	1200.00
COMMON CARD (1-96)	5.00	12.00
1 Shienne Tribe	12.50	30.00
30 Custer's Last Stand	15.00	40.00
96 Sassacus	8.00	20.00

1956 Armour Meats Indian Language

COMMON CARD	6.00	15.00

1959 Fleer Indian Trading Cards

COMPLETE SET (80)	125.00	250.00
COMMON CARD (1-80)	1.00	2.50

1974 Kellogg's Indian World 3-D

COMPLETE SET (16)	30.00	75.00
COMMON CARD (1-16)	2.50	6.00

1974 Brooke Bond Indians of Canada

COMPLETE SET (48)	20.00	50.00
COMMON CARD (1-48)	.75	2.00

1966 Topps Insult Postcards

COMPLETE SET (32)	60.00	120.00
COMMON CARD (1-32)	1.50	4.00

1953 Teddy Bear Lollies Interesting Animals

COMPLETE SET (50)	25.00	60.00
COMMON CARD (1-50)	.40	1.00

1954 Neilson's Interesting Animals

COMPLETE SET (50)	25.00	60.00
COMMON CARD (1-50)	.40	1.00

1959 Mills Interesting Hobbies

COMPLETE SET (25)	12.00	30.00
COMMON CARD (1-25)	.40	1.00

1965 Home Counties Dairies International Air-Liners

COMPLETE SET (25)	10.00	25.00
COMMON CARD (1-25)	.30	.75

1959 Mills Into Space

COMPLETE SET (25)	15.00	40.00
COMMON CARD (1-25)	.50	1.25

1960 A.S. Wilkin Into Space

COMPLETE SET (25)	12.00	30.00
COMMON CARD (1-25)	.40	1.00

1960 Fine Fare Tea Inventions and Discoveries Complete Series

COMPLETE SET (50)	5.00	12.00
COMMON CARD (1-25)	.20	.50
COMMON CARD (26-50)	.20	.50

1963 Tonibell Inventions That Changed the World

COMPLETE SET (25)	12.00	30.00
COMMON CARD (1-25)	.40	1.00

1975 Brooke Bonds Inventors and Inventions

COMPLETE SET (50)	15.00	40.00
COMMON CARD (1-50)	.30	.75

1964 Seymour Mead Island of Ceylon

COMPLETE SET (24)	15.00	40.00
COMMON CARD (1-24)	.50	1.25

1955 Bibby & Sons Isn't It Strange?

COMPLETE SET (25)	20.00	50.00
COMMON CARD (1-25)	1.00	2.50

1957 Topps Isolation Booth

COMPLETE SET (88)	125.00	250.00
COMMON CARD (1-88)	.75	2.00

1973 Weetabix Jackson Five 3-D

COMPLETE SET (5)	8.00	20.00
COMMON CARD (UNNUMBERED)	2.00	5.00
NNO Michael	4.00	10.00

1978 Topps Jaws 2

COMPLETE SET (59)	5.00	12.00
COMPLETE SET W/STICKERS (70)	6.00	15.00
UNOPENED BOX (36 PACKS)	100.00	200.00

UNOPENED PACK (7 CARDS+1 STICKER)	4.00	6.00
COMMON CARD (1-59)	.12	.30

1978 Topps Jaws 2 Stickers

COMPLETE SET (11)	2.50	6.00
COMMON CARD (1-11)	.20	.50
*OPC: SAME VALUE		

1978 O-Pee-Chee Jaws 2

COMPLETE SET (59)	5.00	12.00
COMPLETE SET W/STICKERS (70)	6.00	15.00
UNOPENED BOX (36 PACKS)		
UNOPENED PACK (7 CARDS+1 STICKER)		
COMMON CARD (1-59)	.15	.30

1960 Ching Jersey Past and Present 1st Series

COMPLETE SET (24)	15.00	40.00
COMMON CARD (1-24)	.50	1.25

1963 Ching Jersey Past and Present 3rd Series

COMPLETE SET (24)	15.00	40.00
COMMON CARD (1-24)	.50	1.25

1956 Sunmecta Jet Aircraft of the World

COMPLETE SET (24)	10.00	25.00
COMMON CARD (1-24)	.30	.75

1958 Master Vending Jet Aircraft of the World

COMPLETE SET (100)	125.00	250.00
COMMON CARD (1-100)	.75	2.00

1950 Lever Bros. Jet and Rocket Planes

COMPLETE SET (30)	150.00	300.00
COMMON CARD (1-30)	3.00	8.00

1978 Fleer Jet Set Stickers

COMPLETE SET (40)	15.00	40.00
COMPLETE SET W/POSTCARDS (54)	20.00	50.00
UNOPENED BOX (24 PACKS)		
UNOPENED PACK		
COMMON CARD (1-40)	.50	1.25

1978 Fleer Jet Set Stickers Funny Postcards

COMPLETE SET (14)	5.00	12.00
COMMON CARD (1-14)	.40	1.00

1956 Topps Jets

COMPLETE SET (240)	400.00	800.00
UNOPENED PACK	65.00	80.00
COMMON CARD (1-121)	.75	2.00
COMMON CARD (121-240)	1.25	3.00

1951 Bowman Jets Rockets Spacemen

COMPLETE SET (108)	950.00	1800.00
UNOPENED PACK (1 CENT)	80.00	100.00
COMMON CARD (1-36)	3.00	8.00
COMMON CARD (37-72)	6.00	15.00
COMMON CARD (73-108)	4.00	10.00

1980 Trever & Koch Jets Rockets Spacemen Update Reprints

COMPLETE SET (36)	4.00	10.00
COMMON CARD (145-180)	.20	.50

1961 West London Synagogue Jewish Symbols and Ceremonies Part 1

COMPLETE SET (25)	12.00	30.00
COMMON CARD (1-25)	.40	1.00

1950 Model Airplane Co. Jiggleys Die-Cuts

COMPLETE SET (60)	375.00	750.00
COMMON CIRCUS (1-30)	4.00	10.00
COMMON MILITARY (31-60)	4.00	10.00

1965 Somportex John Drake Danger Man

COMPLETE SET (72)	125.00	250.00
UNOPENED PACK	65.00	80.00
COMMON CARD (1-72)	1.25	3.00

1963 Rosan John F. Kennedy

COMPLETE SET (64)	30.00	80.00
COMMON CARD (1-64)	.40	1.00

1964 Topps John F. Kennedy

COMPLETE SET (77)	100.00	200.00
COMMON CARD (1-77)	.75	2.00

1964 Topps Johnson vs. Goldwater

COMPLETE SET (66)	125.00	250.00
COMMON CARD (1-66)	1.25	3.00

1959 Sweetule Junior Service Quiz

COMPLETE SET (25)	25.00	60.00
COMMON CARD (1-25)	.75	2.00

1959 Kellogg's Fun Cards

COMPLETE SET (16)	20.00	50.00
COMMON CARD	1.00	2.50

1980 Whiteheads Kings and Queens

COMPLETE SET (25)	4.00	10.00
COMMON CARD (1-25)	.30	.75

1977 Carreras Kings and Queens of England

COMPLETE SET (50)	12.00	30.00
COMMON CARD (1-50)	.50	1.25

1977 Mister Softee Kings of the Road

COMPLETE SET (24)	5.00	12.00
COMMON CARD (UNNUMBERED)	.30	.75

1976 Topps King Kong

COMPLETE SET (55)	8.00	20.00
COMPLETE SET W/STICKERS (66)	12.00	30.00
UNOPENED BOX (36 PACKS)	400.00	700.00
UNOPENED PACK (5 CARDS+1 STICKER)	15.00	25.00
COMMON CARD (1-40)	.15	.40
COMMON CARD (41-55)	.20	.50

1976 Topps King Kong Stickers

COMPLETE SET (11)	3.00	8.00
COMMON CARD (1-11)	.40	1.00

1965 Donruss King Kong

COMPLETE SET (55)	350.00	700.00
UNOPENED BOX (24 PACKS)		
UNOPENED PACK	200.00	300.00
COMMON CARD (1-55)	4.00	10.00
1 Okay, So You Won The Tooth Paste Test	8.00	20.00
55 All Right, Knock It Off, You Cats	10.00	25.00

1978 Donruss KISS

COMPLETE SET (132)	40.00	100.00
COMPLETE SERIES 1 SET (66)	20.00	50.00
COMPLETE SERIES 2 SET (66)	25.00	60.00
UNOPENED SERIES 1 BOX (36 PACKS)	175.00	200.00
UNOPENED SERIES 1 PACK (7 CARDS)	5.00	6.00
UNOPENED SERIES 2 BOX (36 PACKS)	500.00	600.00
UNOPENED SERIES 2 PACK (7 CARDS)	12.00	15.00
COMMON CARD (1-66)	.20	.50
COMMON CARD (67-132)	.40	1.00

1976 Colonial Bread Know Your US Presidents

COMPLETE SET (40)	12.00	30.00
COMMON CARD (1-40)	.60	1.50
*KILPATRICK'S: SAME VALUE		
*MANOR: SAME VALUE		
*RAINBOW: SAME VALUE		

1965 Topps Kookie Plaks

COMPLETE SET (88)	225.00	450.00
COMMON CARD (1-88)	1.50	4.00

1968 Topps Kooky Awards

COMPLETE SET (44)	125.00	250.00
UNOPENED PACK	65.00	75.00
COMMON CARD (1-44)	2.00	5.00
*OPC: SAME VALUE		

1968 Topps Kooky Awards Shields

COMPLETE SET (15)	50.00	100.00
COMMON CARD (1-15)	2.00	5.00
*OPC: SAME VALUE		

1967 Topps Krazy Little Comics

COMPLETE SET (16)	250.00	500.00
COMMON CARD (UNNUMBERED)	10.00	25.00

1973 Topps Kung Fu

COMPLETE SET (60)	60.00	120.00
UNOPENED BOX (48 PACKS)		
UNOPENED PACK	12.00	20.00
COMMON CARD (1-60)	.60	1.50

1974 Fleer Kustom Cars Series 1

COMPLETE SET (30)	20.00	50.00
UNOPENED BOX	125.00	150.00
UNOPENED PACK		
COMMON CARD	.75	2.00
*BOX BACKS: SAME VALUE		

1974 Fleer Kustom Cars Series 1 Puzzle

COMPLETE SET (9)	8.00	20.00
COMMON CARD	1.00	2.50
*RED BACKS: SAME VALUE		
STATED ODDS 1:1		

1975 Fleer Kustom Cars Series 2

COMPLETE SET (39)	12.00	30.00
COMPLETE SET W/CARDS (49)	15.00	40.00
COMPLETE SET W/VARIANTS (62)	20.00	50.00
UNOPENED BOX	300.00	350.00
UNOPENED PACK	10.00	12.00
COMMON CARD	.40	1.00

1975 Fleer Kustom Cars Series 2 Puzzle

COMPLETE SET (10)	6.00	15.00
COMPLETE SET W/VARIANTS (23)	12.00	30.00
COMMON CARD	.75	2.00
STATED ODDS 1:1		

1968 Topps Land of the Giants Test Series

COMPLETE SET (55)	1600.00	2800.00
COMMON CARD (1-55)	15.00	40.00

1968 Topps Laugh-In

COMPLETE SET (77)	120.00	200.00
COMMON CARD (1-45)	.75	2.00
COMMON CARD (46-77)	1.50	4.00
*OPC: SAME VALUE		
*SCANLENS: SAME VALUE		

1968 Topps Laugh-In Goldie's Laugh-On Stickers

COMPLETE SET (24)	60.00	120.00
COMMON STICKERS (1-24)	1.50	4.00
*OPC: SAME VALUE		
*SCANLENS: SAME VALUE		

1979 Garo Legends of the West

COMPLETE SET (25)	25.00	60.00
COMMON CARD (1-25)	1.25	3.00

1967 A&BC Legend of Custer

COMPLETE SET (54)	100.00	200.00
COMMON CARD (1-54)	1.25	3.00

1950 Topps License Plates

COMPLETE SET (100)	250.00	500.00
COMMON CARD (1-100)	1.50	4.00

1953 Topps License Plates

COMPLETE SET (75)	137.50	275.00
COMMON CARD (1-75)	1.25	3.00

1979 RNLI Lifeboats

COMPLETE SET (16)	6.00	15.00
COMMON CARD (1-16)	.60	1.50

1959 Lionel's Train Engines

COMPLETE SET (24)	150.00	300.00
COMMON CARD	4.00	10.00

VINTAGE

1961 Sanitarium Living Birds of the World

COMPLETE SET (25)	5.00	12.00
COMMON CARD (1-25)	.25	.60

1979 Bassett Living Creatures of Our World

COMPLETE SET (50)	3.00	8.00
COMMON CARD (1-50)	.10	.30

1950 Ed-U-Cards The Lone Ranger

COMPLETE SET (120)	400.00	800.00
COMMON CARD (1-120)	2.00	5.00

1967 Longleat House

COMPLETE SET (25)	8.00	20.00
COMMON CARD (1-25)	.30	.75

1952 Topps Look 'n See

COMPLETE SET (135)	3500.00	6000.00
COMMON CARD (1-135)	12.00	30.00
COMMON CARD (1-135) DP's	12.00	30.00
COMMON CARD(1-75) SP's	12.00	30.00
COMMON CARD (76-135) SP's	15.00	40.00
DP'S PRINTED AT RATE OF 1.5X		
1 Franklin Roosevelt SP	30.00	60.00
4 Abraham Lincoln SP	20.00	50.00
6 Theodore Roosevelt SP	30.00	60.00
9 George Washington	20.00	50.00
15 Babe Ruth	250.00	500.00
20 Albert Einstein SP	30.00	60.00
30 Charles Lindbergh SP	30.00	60.00
32 Douglas MacArthur SP	30.00	60.00
34 Robert E. Lee	15.00	40.00
41 Dwight Eisenhower	15.00	40.00
42 John Paul Jones SP	15.00	40.00
45 Amelia Earhart SP	40.00	80.00
46 Annie Oakley	20.00	50.00
47 Admiral Robert E. Peary SP	15.00	40.00
51 Christopher Columbus SP	15.00	40.00
56 Geronimo	15.00	40.00
57 Jesse James SP	20.00	50.00
75 Elias Howe SP	30.00	60.00
78 Thomas Paine	30.00	60.00
80 Will Rogers	15.00	40.00
81 Sir Walter Raleigh	15.00	40.00
82 Rembrandt SP	250.00	500.00
84 Julius Caesar SP	15.00	40.00
85 Chiang Kai-Shek	15.00	40.00
88 Roald Amundsen SP	30.00	60.00
92 Louis Daguerre	15.00	40.00
97 Jules Verne	40.00	80.00
98 Adlai Stevenson SP	50.00	100.00
99 Lester B. Pearson DP	40.00	80.00
100 William Beaverbrook DP	15.00	40.00
101 Daniel De Foe SP	40.00	80.00
104 Queen Elizabeth II	15.00	40.00
105 Leonardo Da Vinci	15.00	40.00
106 Machiavelli	20.00	50.00
107 George C. Marshall	15.00	40.00
112 John D. Rockefeller SP	40.00	80.00
113 Sir Walter Scott	15.00	40.00
115 John Philip Sousa	20.00	50.00
116 Robert L. Stevenson	30.00	60.00
117 Arturo Toscanini	20.00	50.00
118 Amerigo Vespucci SP	30.00	60.00
120 Wendell L. Wilkie	15.00	40.00
123 Sir Henry Morgan	20.00	50.00
124 Charles Darwin	15.00	40.00
126 Leif Ericson	20.00	50.00
127 Galileo	20.00	50.00
129 Johannes Gutenberg DP	20.00	50.00
130 Victor Herbert SP	20.00	50.00
131 Henry Hudson	30.00	60.00
132 Henry VIII DP	20.00	50.00
133 Joan of Arc SP	30.00	60.00
135 Dolly Madison	15.00	40.00

1960 Abby Finishing Loony Series

COMPLETE SET (66)	75.00	150.00
COMMON CARD (67-132)	1.50	4.00

1966 Topps Lost in Space

COMPLETE SET (55)	250.00	500.00
UNOPENED BOX	2500.00	4000.00
UNOPENED PACK	120.00	250.00
COMMON CARD (1-55)	3.00	8.00

1976 Topps Mad Ad Foldees

COMPLETE SET (33)	60.00	120.00
COMMON CARD (1-33)	1.25	3.00

1972 Sunicrest Bread Mad Moon Monsters

COMPLETE SET (40)	100.00	175.00
COMMON CARD (1-40)	2.00	5.00

1955 Bowman Magic Pictures

COMPLETE SET (240)	375.00	750.00
UNOPENED 1 CENT PACK	20.00	25.00
COMMON CARD (1-240)	1.00	2.50

1956 Exhibit Magic Tricks

COMPLETE SET (16)	12.00	30.00
COMMON CARD	1.00	2.50

1950 DCA Food Magic Tricks Fun with Pop

COMPLETE SET (24)	25.00	60.00
COMMON CARD (T1-T24)	.75	2.00

1966 Topps Make Your Own Name Stickers

COMPLETE SET (33)	60.00	125.00
COMMON CARD	1.25	3.00

1966 Topps Make Your Own Name Stickers Name Tag Sheets

COMMON SHEET	4.00	10.00

1965 Topps Man from U.N.C.L.E.

COMPLETE SET (55)	80.00	150.00
COMMON CARD (1-55)	1.00	2.50

1966 Cadet Sweets Man from U.N.C.L.E.

COMPLETE SET (50)	60.00	120.00
COMMON CARD (1-50)	.75	2.00

1969 Topps Man on the Moon

COMPLETE SET (55)	50.00	100.00
COMMON CARD (1A-55B)	1.25	3.00
1A Apollo 10 Emblem	1.50	4.00
52B Astronaut Aldrin!	1.50	4.00
55B First Men on the Moon!	1.50	4.00

1969 O-Pee-Chee Man on the Moon

COMPLETE SET (55)	75.00	150.00
COMMON CARD (1-55)	1.00	2.50

1970 Topps Man on the Moon Re-Issue

COMPLETE SET (99)	60.00	120.00
COMMON CARD (1-99)	1.00	2.50

1969 Kellogg's Man-In-Space Patches

COMPLETE SET (20)	30.00	75.00
COMMON PATCH	1.25	3.00

1974 Whitbread Maritime Inn Signs

COMPLETE SET (25)	12.00	30.00
COMMON CARD (1-25)	.60	1.50

1967 Topps Maya

COMPLETE SET (55)	15.00	30.00
UNOPENED PACK	40.00	50.00
COMMON CARD (1-55)	.20	.50

1967 Topps Maya Puzzle

COMPLETE SET (16)	150.00	300.00
COMMON CARD (1-16)	6.00	15.00

1965 Fleer McHale's Navy

COMPLETE SET (66)	60.00	120.00
UNOPENED BOX (24 PACKS)	700.00	800.00
UNOPENED PACK	35.00	40.00
COMMON CARD (1-66)	.75	2.00

1977 Rowntree Merry Monarchs

COMPLETE SET (20)	10.00	25.00
COMMON CARD (1-20)	1.25	3.00

1961 Mills Tobacco Mervailles Modernes

COMPLETE SET (25)	20.00	50.00
COMMON CARD (1-25)	.60	1.50

1966 Nabisco Mickey Mouse and His Pals

COMPLETE SET (25)	100.00	175.00
COMMON CARD (1-25)	2.00	5.00

1958 Nesbitt's Missile and Jet Planes

COMPLETE SET (42)	375.00	750.00
COMMON CARD (1-42)	6.00	15.00

1958 Parkhurst Missiles and Satellites

COMPLETE SET (50)	125.00	250.00
COMMON CARD (1-50)	1.50	4.00

1966 Topps Mod Generation Stickers

COMPLETE SET (55)	400.00	800.00
COMMON CARD (1-55)	5.00	12.00

1969 Topps Mod Squad

COMPLETE SET (55)	100.00	200.00
UNOPENED BOX	650.00	800.00
UNOPENED PACK	50.00	60.00
COMMON CARD (1-55)	1.00	2.50
*OPC: .6X TO 1.5X BASIC CARDS	1.50	4.00

1954 Nabisco Model Sports Cars

COMPLETE SET (5)	60.00	120.00
COMMON CARD	8.00	20.00

1942 Kellogg's Model Warplane Series Set 1

COMPLETE SET (7)	50.00	100.00
COMMON CARD (UNNUMBERED)	5.00	12.00

1942 Kellogg's Model Warplane Series Set 2

COMPLETE SET (7)	50.00	100.00
COMMON CARD (UNNUMBERED)	5.00	12.00

1942 Kellogg's Model Warplane Series Set 3

COMPLETE SET (7)	50.00	100.00
COMMON CARD (UNNUMBERED)	5.00	12.00

1942 Kellogg's Model Warplane Series Set 4

COMPLETE SET (7)	50.00	100.00
COMMON CARD (UNNUMBERED)	5.00	12.00

1954 Sweetule Modern Aircraft

COMPLETE SET (50)	30.00	75.00
COMMON CARD (1-50)	.50	1.25

1942 Kellogg's Modern American Airplanes T87C

COMPLETE SET (50)	190.00	375.00
COMMON CARD	2.50	6.00

1952 Supertest Gas Modern Jet Planes

COMPLETE SET (15)	30.00	80.00
COMMON CARD	2.00	5.00
*FRENCH: SAME VALUE		

1955 Sweetule Modern Transport

COMPLETE SET (25)	12.00	30.00
COMMON CARD (1-25)	.40	1.00

1966 Devlin & Sons Modern Transport

COMPLETE SET (50)	15.00	40.00
COMMON CARD (1-50)	.25	.60

1967 Donruss The Monkees Badges

COMPLETE SET (44)	125.00	250.00
UNOPENED PACK	20.00	30.00
COMMON CARD (1-44)	1.50	4.00

1966 Donruss The Monkees Color Series A

COMPLETE SET (44)	40.00	80.00
COMMON CARD (1-44)	.75	2.00

1966 Donruss The Monkees Color Series B

COMPLETE SET (44)	40.00	80.00
COMMON CARD (1-44)	.75	2.00

1967 Donruss The Monkees Color Series C

COMPLETE SET (44)	40.00	80.00
COMMON CARD (1-44)	.75	2.00

1967 Raybert Productions The Monkees Flip Books

COMPLETE SET (16)	60.00	120.00
COMMON BOOK (1-16)	6.00	15.00

1967 A&BC The Monkees Hit Songs

COMPLETE SET (30)	75.00	150.00
COMMON CARD (1-30)	1.50	4.00

1967 Kellogg's The Monkees Coins

COMPLETE SET (12)	60.00	120.00
COMMON CARD (UNNUMBERED)	6.00	15.00

1966 Donruss The Monkees Sepia

COMPLETE SET (44)	40.00	80.00
COMMON CARD (1-44)	.75	2.00

1950 Exhibit Monkey Shines

COMPLETE SET (32)	30.00	75.00
COMMON CARD	.75	2.00

1970 Monogram Models

COMPLETE SET (23)	175.00	350.00
COMMON CARD (1-23)	5.00	12.00

1965 Rosan Monster Cards

COMPLETE SET (84)	200.00	400.00
COMMON CARD (1-84)	2.50	6.00

1963 Topps Monster Flip Movies

COMPLETE SET (36)	300.00	550.00
COMMON CARD (1-36)	12.00	30.00

1965 Topps Monster Greeting Cards

COMPLETE SET (50)	75.00	150.00
COMMON CARD (1-50)	1.00	2.50

1966 Topps Monster Laffs

COMPLETE SET (66)	30.00	60.00
COMMON CARD (1-66)	.25	.60

1963 Topps Monster Laffs Midgee

COMPLETE SET (153)	125.00	250.00
COMMON CARD (1-108)	.40	1.00
COMMON CARD (109-153)	1.00	2.50

1964 Abby Finishing Monster Magic Action

COMPLETE SET (24)	45.00	90.00
COMMON CARD (1-24)	1.25	3.00
LENS VIEWER 1:1		
NNO Lens Viewer	4.00	10.00

1979 Topps Monstickers

COMPLETE SET (68)	25.00	60.00
UNOPENED PACK	10.00	15.00
COMMON 3-STICKER PANEL	2.00	5.00
ARRANGED IN RANDOM 3-STICKER PANELS		

1967 Wall's Ice Cream Moon Fleet

COMPLETE SET (48)	75.00	150.00
COMMON CARD (1-48)	1.25	3.00

1966 Chix Confectionery Moon Shot

COMPLETE SET (50)	20.00	50.00
COMMON CARD (1-50)	.30	.75

1976 Ralston-Purina Moonstones Cereal Monster Stickers

COMPLETE SET (8)	20.00	50.00
COMMON CARD (1-8)	3.00	8.00

1978 Topps Mork and Mindy

COMPLETE SET (99)	10.00	20.00
COMPLETE SET W/STICKERS (121)	12.00	30.00
UNOPENED BOX (36 PACKS)	125.00	200.00
UNOPENED PACK (10 CARDS+1 STICKER)	3.00	5.00
COMMON CARD (1-99)	.10	.25
*OPC: SAME VALUE		

1978 Topps Mork and Mindy Stickers

COMPLETE SET (22)	3.00	8.00
COMMON CARD (1-22)	.30	.75
*OPC: SAME VALUE		

1949 Kellogg's Motor Cars Black and White

COMPLETE SET (40)	60.00	120.00
COMMON CARD (1-40)	1.00	2.50

1949 Kellogg's Motor Cars Color

COMPLETE SET (40)	60.00	120.00
COMMON CARD (1-40)	1.00	2.50

1949 Bowman Movie Pre-Vue Flipbooks

COMPLETE SET (24)	375.00	750.00
COMMON CARD (1-24)	10.00	25.00

1948 Bowman Movie Stars

COMPLETE SET (36)	175.00	350.00
COMMON CARD (1-36)	3.00	8.00

1953 Mother's Cookies Movie Stars

COMPLETE SET (63)	225.00	450.00
COMMON CARD (1-63)	2.50	6.00
31 Rock Hudson	6.00	15.00
48 John Wayne	12.00	30.00

1950 Novel Candy Mr. Magic Tricks

COMPLETE SET (12)	150.00	300.00
COMMON CARD (1-12)	8.00	20.00

1964 Leaf The Munsters Theatre

COMPLETE SET (72)	375.00	750.00
COMPLETE BOX (24 PACKS)	4000.00	6500.00
UNOPENED PACK		
COMMON CARD (1-72)	3.00	8.00
1 Let Hearse Put You in the Driver's Seat!	4.00	10.00
72 Now I See It	4.00	10.00

1964 Leaf The Munsters Theatre Stickers

COMPLETE SET (16)	325.00	650.00
COMMON CARD (1-16)	12.00	30.00

1979 General Mills Muppet Movie

COMPLETE SET (12)	20.00	50.00
COMMON CARD (1-12)	2.50	6.00

1979 General Mills Muppet Movie Panels

COMPLETE SET (4)	15.00	40.00
COMMON PANEL	5.00	12.00

1967 Topps Nasty Notes

COMPLETE SET (32)	120.00	250.00
COMMON CARD (1-32)	2.50	6.00

1971 Topps Nasty Valentine Notes

COMPLETE SET (30)	15.00	40.00
COMMON CARD (1-30)	.75	2.00

1960 Sweetule A Nature Series

COMPLETE SET (25)	12.00	30.00
COMMON CARD (1-25)	.75	2.00

1971 Glengettie Tea Naval Battles

COMPLETE SET (25)	6.00	15.00
COMMON CARD (1-25)	.40	1.00

1971 Hitchman's Dairies Naval Battles

COMPLETE SET (25)	6.00	15.00
COMMON CARD (1-25)	.40	1.00

1966 Nestle Keen Chiller Club Monsters

COMPLETE SET (50)	450.00	800.00
COMMON CARD (1-50)	8.00	20.00

1971 Topps Nice or Nasty Valentines

COMPLETE SET (33)	25.00	60.00
COMMON CARD	1.25	3.00

1964 Topps Nutty Awards

COMPLETE SET (32)	80.00	150.00
COMMON CARD (1-32)	3.00	8.00

1971 Donruss Odd Rod All-Stars

COMPLETE SET (66)	80.00	150.00
COMMON CARD (1-66)	.75	2.00

1969 Donruss Odd Rods

COMPLETE SET (44)	60.00	120.00
COMMON CARD (1-44)	.75	2.00

1970 Odder Odd Rods

COMPLETE SET (66)	80.00	150.00
COMMON STICKER (1-66)	.75	2.00

1970 Oddest Odd Rods

COMPLETE SET (66)	80.00	150.00
COMMON STICKER (67-132)	.75	2.00

1970 Wendy's Old West

COMPLETE SET (10)	8.00	20.00
COMMON CARD (1-10)	1.25	3.00

1955 Miranda 100 Years of Motoring

COMPLETE SET (50)	25.00	60.00
COMMON CARD (1-50)	.40	1.00

1956 Miranda 150 Years of Locomotives

COMPLETE SET (50)	30.00	75.00
COMMON CARD (1-50)	.50	1.25

1955 Parkhurst Operation Sea Dog

COMPLETE SET (50)	100.00	200.00
COMMON CARD (1-50)	1.50	4.00

1973 Donruss The Osmonds

COMPLETE SET (66)	30.00	80.00
UNOPENED BOX (24 PACKS)	350.00	400.00
UNOPENED PACK (CARDS)	15.00	20.00
COMMON CARD (1-66)	.40	1.00

1961 Weetabix Our Pets

COMPLETE SET (25)	8.00	20.00
COMMON CARD (1-25)	.30	.60

1980 Sanitarium Our Weather

COMPLETE SET (20)	4.00	10.00
COMMON CARD (1-20)	.30	.75

1964 Topps Outer Limits

COMPLETE SET (50)	325.00	650.00
COMMON CARD (1-50)	3.00	8.00
COMMON SP (1-50)	5.00	12.00

1980 Fleer Pac-Man Stickers

COMPLETE SET (54)	20.00	50.00
UNOPENED BOX (36 PACKS)	90.00	110.00
UNOPENED PACK (3 CARDS & 3 STICKERS)	3.00	4.00
COMMON CARD	.50	1.25

1957 Quaker Pack-O-Ten Birds

COMMON CARD (UNNUMBERED)	1.25	3.00

1956 Quaker Pack-O-Ten Braves of Indian Nations

COMPLETE SET (18)	90.00	175.00
COMMON CARD (1-18)	3.00	8.00

1957 Quaker Pack-O-Ten Warplanes

COMPLETE SET (27)	90.00	175.00
COMMON CARD (1-27)	2.00	5.00

1969 Topps Pak-O-Fun

COMPLETE SET (36)	350.00	700.00
UNOPENED PACK		
COMMON CARD (1-12; 25-42)	6.00	15.00
COMMON PANEL (13-24)	8.00	20.00

1950 Topps Parade Flags of the World

COMPLETE SET (100)	60.00	120.00
COMMON CARD (1-100)	1.00	2.50

1971 Topps Partridge Family

COMPLETE SET (55)	40.00	80.00
UNOPENED PACK	40.00	50.00

COMMON CARD (1-55)	.75	2.00
*OPC: SAME VALUE		

1971 Topps Partridge Family Series A

COMPLETE SET (55)	40.00	80.00
COMMON CARD (1-55)	.75	2.00
*OPC: .5X TO 1.2X BASIC CARDS	1.00	2.50

1971 Topps Partridge Family Series B

COMPLETE SET (88)	50.00	100.00
UNOPENED PACK	20.00	25.00
COMMON CARD (1-88)	.75	2.00

1971 Topps Partridge Family Posters

COMPLETE SET (24)	25.00	60.00
COMMON POSTER (1-24)	1.50	4.00

1972 A&BC Partridge Family

COMPLETE SET (55)	30.00	80.00
COMMON CARD (1-55)	.75	2.00

1963 Northern Cooperative Society Passenger Liners

COMPLETE SET (25)	15.00	40.00

1965 Bishops Stortford Dairy Passenger Liners

COMPLETE SET (25)	15.00	40.00

1967 Wilcocks Passenger Liners

COMPLETE SET (25)	15.00	40.00
COMMON CARD (1-25)	.50	1.25

1960 Horniman's Tea Pets

COMPLETE SET (48)	6.00	15.00
COMMON CARD (1-48)	.20	.50

1967 Topps Phoney Records Stickers

COMPLETE SET (40)	250.00	500.00
COMMON CARD (1-40)	8.00	20.00

1967 Topps Phoney Records Stickers Stupid Hit Songs

COMPLETE SET (16)	150.00	300.00
COMMON CARD (1-16)	6.00	15.00

1971 Pigeons

COMPLETE SET (25)	5.00	12.00
COMMON CARD (1-25)	.30	.75

1950 Novel Candy Pirate Adventures

COMPLETE SET (12)	200.00	400.00
COMMON CARD (1-12)	10.00	25.00

1948 Leaf Pirates

COMPLETE SET (49)	300.00	600.00
UNOPENED PACK	250.00	300.00
COMMON CARD	4.00	10.00
SKIP-NUMBERED SET		

1961 Fleer Pirates Bold

COMPLETE SET (66)	200.00	400.00
UNOPENED PACK	400.00	450.00
COMMON CARD (1-66)	2.00	5.00

1961 Fleer Pirates Bold Flags of the Spanish Main Stamps

COMPLETE SET (21)	1250.00	2500.00
COMMON STAMP	50.00	100.00
STATED ODDS 1:1		

1957 Topps Planes Blue Backs

COMPLETE SET (120)	250.00	500.00
COMMON CARD (1-60)	1.25	3.00
COMMON CARD (61-120)	1.50	4.00

1957 Topps Planes Red Backs

COMPLETE SET (120)	250.00	500.00
COMMON CARD (1-60)	1.25	3.00
COMMON CARD (61-120)	2.00	5.00
CL Checklist Card	10.00	25.00

1957 A&BC Planes

COMPLETE SET (120)	300.00	600.00
COMMON CARD (1-120)	1.00	4.00

1955 Exhibit Planes Series 1

COMPLETE SET (64)	112.50	225.00
COMMON CARD (1-64)	1.25	3.00

1955 Exhibit Planes Series 2

COMPLETE SET (64)	112.50	225.00
COMMON CARD (1-64)	1.25	3.00

1958 Leaf Card-O Planes Trains and Ships

COMPLETE SET (20)	50.00	100.00
COMMON CARD (SKIP-NUMBERED)	1.50	4.00

1969 Topps Planet of the Apes

COMPLETE SET (44)	100.00	175.00
UNOPENED BOX (36 PACKS)	600.00	700.00
UNOPENED PACK (CARDS)	15.00	25.00
COMMON CARD (1-44)	1.25	3.00
*A&BC: .75X TO 2X BASIC CARDS	2.50	6.00
*OPC: SAME VALUE		

1969 Topps Planet of the Apes Test Series

COMPLETE SET (44)	1650.00	3300.00
COMMON CARD (1-44)	25.00	60.00

1975 Topps Planet of the Apes

COMPLETE SET (66)	25.00	50.00
UNOPENED BOX (36 PACKS)	250.00	400.00
UNOPENED PACK	10.00	15.00
COMMON CARD (1-66)	.40	1.00

1974 Phoenix Candy Planet of the Apes Candy Boxes

COMPLETE SET (8)	12.00	30.00
COMMON CARD (1-8)	2.00	5.00

1977 Brooke Bond Police File

COMPLETE SET (40)	5.00	12.00
COMMON CARD (1-40)	.20	.50

1967 A.C.W. Francis Pond Life

COMPLETE SET (25)	25.00	60.00
COMMON CARD (1-25)	.75	2.00

1974 Bassett Pop Stars

COMPLETE SET (25)	8.00	20.00
COMMON CARD (1-25)	.50	1.25
*MISTER SOFTEE: SAME VALUE		

1959 Ad-Trix Popeye

COMPLETE SET (66)	125.00	250.00
COMMON CARD (1-66)	1.25	3.00

1959 CHIX Popeye

COMPLETE SET (50)	200.00	400.00
COMMON CARD (1-50)	2.50	6.00

1962 Dynamic Toy Popeye Jumbo

COMPLETE SET (35)	150.00	300.00
COMMON CARD (106-140)	3.00	8.00

1977 Scanlens Popswops

COMPLETE SET (72)	150.00	300.00
COMMON CARD (1-72)	2.00	5.00

1964 Pond Life Lamberts of Norwich Backs

COMPLETE SET (25)	25.00	60.00
COMMON CARD (1-25)	.75	2.00

1946 Kellogg's Portraits of the Presidents

COMPLETE SET (32)	75.00	150.00
COMMON CARD	1.50	4.00

1959 Mills Ports of the World

COMPLETE SET (25)	10.00	25.00
COMMON CARD (1-25)	.30	.75

1954 Bowman Power for Peace

COMPLETE SET (96)	125.00	250.00
COMMON CARD (1-96)	.75	2.00

1972 Brooke Bond Prehistoric Animals

COMPLETE SET (50)	6.00	15.00
COMMON CARD (1-50)	.15	.40

1978 Rowntree Mackintosh Prehistoric Animals

COMPLETE SET (18)	3.00	8.00
COMMON CARD (1-18)	.25	.60

1960 Vita Brits Prehistoric Beasts

COMPLETE SET (36)	10.00	25.00
COMMON CARD (1-36)	.40	1.00

1975 Curly Wurly Prehistoric Monsters

COMPLETE SET (8)	6.00	15.00
COMMON CARD (1-8)	1.00	2.50

1963 General Mills President Portraits

COMPLETE SET (35)		
COMMON CARD	1.00	2.50

1963 General Mills President Portraits Panels

COMPLETE SET (9)	35.00	90.00
COMMON PANEL	3.00	8.00

1980 Kellogg's Presidential Series Stick'R

COMPLETE SET (38)	12.00	30.00
COMMON STICKER-CARD	.75	2.00
*CARD ONLY: .20X TO .50X BASIC CARDS		

1958 Leaf Card-O Presidents

COMPLETE SET (6)	20.00	50.00
COMMON CARD (SKIP-NUMBERED)	2.50	6.00

1960 Golden Press Presidents

COMPLETE SET (33)	60.00	120.00
COMMON CARD (1-33)	1.50	4.00
1 George Washington	3.00	8.00
16 Abraham Lincoln	2.00	5.00

1965 Topps Presidents and Famous Americans

COMPLETE SET (44)	200.00	400.00
COMMON CARD (1-44)	5.00	12.00
1 George Washington	10.00	25.00

1957 Edwards & Sons Products of the World

COMPLETE SET (12)		

1961 Musgrave Brothers Products of the World

COMPLETE SET (25)	8.00	20.00
COMMON CARD (1-25)	.25	.60

1953 Amalgamated Tobacco Propelled Weapons

COMPLETE SET (25)	8.00	20.00
COMMON CARD (1-25)	.25	.60

1968 Topps Put-On Stickers

COMPLETE SET (33)	60.00	120.00
COMMON CARD (1-33)	1.25	3.00

1954 Parkhurst Race Against Time

COMPLETE SET (40)	150.00	300.00
COMMON CARD (1-40)	2.50	6.00

1974 Brooke Bond Race into Space Black Backs

COMPLETE SET (50)	5.00	12.00
COMMON CARD (1-50)	.20	.50

1971 Brooke Bond Race into Space Blue Backs

COMPLETE SET (50)	20.00	50.00
COMMON CARD (1-50)	.50	1.25

1955 Brach's Railroad

COMMON CARD (UNNUMBERED)	3.00	8.00

1955 Topps Rails and Sails

COMPLETE SET (200)	1050.00	2100.00
COMMON CARD (1-80)	1.50	4.00
COMMON CARD (81-130)	5.00	12.00
COMMON CARD (131-150)	1.25	3.00
COMMON CARD (151-200)	5.00	12.00

1 Locomotive 999 2.50 6.00
200 Flat Top 7.50 20.00

1960 Sonny Boy Railway Engines
COMPLETE SET (50) 20.00 50.00
COMMON CARD (1-50) .75 2.00

1958 Barbers Tea Railway Equipment
COMPLETE SET (24) 15.00 40.00
COMMON CARD (1-24) .50 1.25

1960 Sanitarium Rare Animals and Reptiles
COMPLETE SET (25) 6.00 15.00
COMMON CARD (1-25) .40 1.00

1967 Glengettie Tea Rare British Birds
COMPLETE SET (25) 15.00 40.00
COMMON CARD (1-25) .50 1.25

1965 Topps Rat Fink Greeting Cards
COMPLETE SET (40) 125.00 250.00
COMMON CARD (1-40) 2.00 5.00

1966 Topps Rat Patrol
COMPLETE SET (66) 60.00 120.00
UNOPENED PACK 45.00 60.00
COMMON CARD (1-66) .60 1.50

1966 Topps Rat Patrol Insignia Rings
COMPLETE SET (22) 325.00 650.00
COMMON CARD (1-22) 10.00 25.00

1966 O-Pee-Chee Rat Patrol
COMPLETE SET (66) 75.00 120.00
UNOPENED BOX
UNOPENED PACK
COMMON CARD (1-66) .60 1.50

1966 O-Pee-Chee Rat Patrol Insignia Rings
COMPLETE SET (22) 325.00 650.00
COMMON CARD (1-22) 10.00 25.00

1978 Fleer Real Road Signs Stickers
COMPLETE SET (41) 25.00 60.00
COMMON CARD (1-41) .75 2.00

1960 Gaycon Products Red Indians Complete Series
COMPLETE SET (50) 8.00 20.00
COMMON CARD (1-50) .20 .50

1951 Bowman Red Menace White Backs
COMPLETE SET (48) 600.00 1200.00
COMMON CARD (1-48) 8.00 20.00
*GREY BACKS: .30X TO .75X WHITE BACKS

1973 Hitchman's Dairies Regimental Uniforms of the Past
COMPLETE SET (25) 5.00 12.00
COMMON CARD (1-25) .25 .60

1958 Nabisco Rin Tin Tin Patches
COMMON PATCH (UNNUMBERED) 6.00 15.00

1959 Rinso Soap Paladin
COMPLETE SET (24) 1125.00 2250.00
COMMON CARD (1-24) 30.00 75.00

1953 Parkhurst Ripley's Believe It or Not
COMPLETE SET (100) 375.00 750.00
COMMON CARD (1-100) 2.50 6.00

1970 Fleer Ripley's Believe It or Not
COMPLETE SET (84) 80.00 150.00
UNOPENED PACK (5 CARDS) 20.00 25.00
COMMON CARD (1-84) .75 2.00

1968 Philadelphia Gum Robert F. Kennedy
COMPLETE SET (55) 100.00 200.00
UNOPENED BOX (24 PACKS) 450.00 500.00
UNOPENED PACK 30.00 40.00
COMMON CARD (1-55) 1.25 3.00

1957 Topps Robin Hood
COMPLETE SET (60) 175.00 350.00
COMMON CARD (1-60) 1.50 4.00

1958 Band-Aid Robin Hood
COMPLETE SET (20) 100.00 200.00
COMMON CARD (UNNUMBERED) 3.00 8.00

1958 Band-Aid Robin Hood No Tabs
COMPLETE SET (20) 90.00 175.00
COMMON CARD 2.50 6.00

1959 Nu-Cards Rock and Roll
COMPLETE SET (64) 150.00 300.00
COMMON CARD (1-64) 2.00 5.00
37 Elvis Presley 10.00 25.00

1979 Donruss Rock Stars
COMPLETE SET (66) 8.00 20.00
UNOPENED BOX (36 PACKS) 35.00 50.00
UNOPENED PACK (7 CARDS) 1.50 2.00
COMMON CARD (1-66) .20 .50

1979 FTCC Rocketship X-M
COMPLETE SET (50) 6.00 15.00
UNOPENED BOX 80.00 100.00
UNOPENED PACK
COMMON CARD (1-50) .25 .60

1971 Topps Rocks O' Gum Lids
COMPLETE SET (55) 80.00 150.00
COMMON LID (UNNUMBERED) 1.25 3.00

1979 Topps Rocky II
COMPLETE SET (99) 4.00 10.00
COMPLETE SET W/STICKERS (121) 6.00 15.00
UNOPENED BOX (36 PACKS) 250.00 400.00
UNOPENED PACK (10 CARDS+1 STICKER) 8.00 12.00
COMMON CARD (1-99) .10 .25

1979 Topps Rocky II Stickers
COMPLETE SET (22) 1.25 3.00
COMMON CARD (1-22) .06 .15

1980 FTCC Rocky Horror Picture Show
COMPLETE SET (60) .50 12.00
UNOPENED BOX (36 PACKS) 65.00 80.00
UNOPENED PACK 2.50 3.00
COMMON CARD (1-60) .15 .40

1965 A&BC The Rolling Stones
COMPLETE SET (40) 60.00 120.00
COMMON CARD (1-40) 1.00 2.50

1973 Topps The Rookies
COMPLETE SET (44) 1000.00 2000.00
COMMON CARD (1-44) 30.00 75.00

1969 Topps Room 222 Black and White
COMPLETE SET (44) 2750.00 5500.00
COMMON CARD (1-44) 50.00 100.00

1969 Topps Room 222 Color
COMMON CARD (1-44) 60.00 120.00

1956 Topps Round-Up
COMPLETE SET (80) 1000.00 2000.00
UNOPENED PACK (1 CENT) 35.00 50.00
UNOPENED PACK (5 CENTS) 45.00 60.00
COMMON CARD (1-80) 2.50 6.00
COMMON CARD SP (1-80) 3.00 8.00

1958 Kane Products Roy Rogers Color Series
COMPLETE SET (25) 10.00 25.00
COMMON CARD (1-25) .30 .75

1955 Roy Rogers Gum Old Amarillo
COMPLETE SET (24) 25.00 60.00
COMMON CARD (1-24) .75 2.00

1953 Post Roy Rogers Pop-Outs
COMPLETE SET (36) 500.00 1000.00
COMMON CARD (1-36) 8.00 20.00
1 Double-R Bar Ranch 12.00 30.00
15 Trigger, Dale and Roy 10.00 25.00
20 The King and Queen of the West 12.00 30.00
30 Roy Rogers 10.00 25.00
36 Dale Evans 12.00 30.00

1955 Roy Rogers Gum South of Caliente
COMPLETE SET (24) 15.00 40.00
COMMON CARD (1-24) .60 1.50

1973 O-Pee-Chee Royal Canadian Mounted Police Centennial
COMPLETE SET (55) 50.00 100.00
UNOPENED BOX (36 PACKS)
UNOPENED PACK (8 CARDS+1 EMBLEM) 20.00 30.00
COMMON CARD (1-55) 1.00 2.50

1973 O-Pee-Chee Royal Canadian Mounted Police Centennial Emblem
COMPLETE SET (30) 50.00 100.00
COMMON CARD (1-30) 2.00 5.00

1970 Royal Leamington Spa
COMPLETE SET (25) 6.00 15.00
COMMON CARD (1-25) .40 1.00

1952 Royal Desserts Stars of the Sky
COMPLETE SET (24) 112.50 225.00
COMMON CARD 3.00 8.00

1970 Brooke Bond Saga of Ships
COMPLETE SET (50) 6.00 15.00
COMMON CARD (1-50) .25 .60

1978 Donruss Saturday Night Fever
COMPLETE SET (66) 10.00 25.00
UNOPENED BOX (36 PACKS) 50.00 60.00
UNOPENED PACK (6 CARDS) 1.50 2.00
COMMON CARD (1-66) .20 .50
CARD NO. 63 DOESN'T EXIST

1971 Clover Dairies Science in the 20th Century
COMPLETE SET (25) 2.00 5.00
COMMON CARD (1-25) .12 .30

1954 Topps Scoop
COMPLETE SET (156) 1500.00 3000.00
COMMON CARD (1-78) 3.00 8.00
COMMON CARD (79-156) 5.00 12.00
1 San Francisco Earthquake 6.00 15.00
3 Lindbergh Flies Atlantic 6.00 15.00
6 Lincoln Shot 6.00 15.00
12 First Atom Bomb Dropped 6.00 15.00
17 S.S. Titanic Sinks 6.00 15.00
19 Pearl Harbor Attacked 6.00 15.00
20 Dirigible Hindenburg Burns 6.00 15.00
27 Bob Feller Strikeout King 30.00 60.00
31 Roosevelt Wins 4th Term 6.00 15.00
33 MacArthur Returns 6.00 15.00
39 Dempsey Defeats Willard 15.00 30.00
40 Joe Louis New Champ 15.00 30.00
41 Babe Ruth Sets Record 75.00 150.00
45 Custer's Last Stand 6.00 15.00
51 Washington Inaugurated 6.00 15.00
59 Big 3 Meet at Yalta 6.00 15.00
65 Marciano K.O.'s Walcott 15.00 30.00
71 John L. Sullivan Defeated 6.00 15.00
74 Mussolini Dead 6.00 15.00
75 Dillinger Shot 6.00 15.00
110 Notre Dame's Four Horsemen 40.00 80.00
128 Jesse Owens Races Horse 15.00 30.00
129 Ben Hogan New Golf King 100.00 200.00
130 Braves Go to Milwaukee 20.00 40.00
154 26-Inning Tie 25.00 50.00
156 World's Largest Telescope 15.00 30.00

1976 Keller and Son Scottish Heritage
COMPLETE SET (25) 12.00 30.00
COMMON CARD (1-25) .75 2.00

1974 Brooke Bond The Sea
COMPLETE SET (50) 10.00 25.00
COMMON CARD (1-50) .40 1.00

1958 ABC Minors Sea Scenes
COMPLETE SET (10) 6.00 15.00
COMMON CARD (1-10) .50 1.25

VINTAGE

1976 Bassett Secret Island
COMPLETE SET (40) 4.00 10.00
COMMON CARD (1-40) .15 .40

1950 Quaker Sergeant Preston of the Yukon
COMPLETE SET (36) 75.00 150.00
COMMON CARD (1-36) 1.50 4.00

1978 Donruss Sgt. Pepper's Lonely Hearts Club Band
COMPLETE SET (66) 3.00 8.00
UNOPENED BOX (36 PACKS) 30.00 60.00
UNOPENED PACK (7 CARDS) 1.00 2.00
COMMON CARD (1-66) .06 .15

1964 Scanlens Shintaro Master Swordsman of the Samurai
COMPLETE SET (73) 350.00 700.00
COMMON CARD (1-73) 3.00 8.00
NNO Shintaro Master Swordsman of the Samurai Header 6.00 15.00

1956 Pecheur Lozenges Ships and Planes
COMPLETE SET (30) 90.00 175.00
COMMON CARD (1-30) 2.00 5.00

1961 Ching Ships and Their Workings
COMPLETE SET (25) 10.00 25.00
COMMON CARD (1-25) .30 .75

1971 Clover Dairies Ships and Their Workings
COMPLETE SET (25) 10.00 25.00
COMMON CARD (1-25) .50 1.25

1961 Ewbanks Ships Around Britain
COMPLETE SET (25) 12.00 30.00
COMMON CARD (1-25) .40 1.00

1962 Kellogg's Ships of the British Navy
COMPLETE SET (16) 5.00 12.00
COMMON CARD (1-16) .25 .60

1961 Ringtons Ships of the Royal Navy
COMPLETE SET (25) 12.00 30.00
COMMON CARD (1-25) .40 1.00

1964 Reddings Tea Ships of the World
COMPLETE SET (48) 12.00 30.00
COMMON CARD (1-48) .25 .60
NO. 13 NOT ISSUED

1957 Ewbanks Ships Through the Ages
COMPLETE SET (25) 6.00 15.00
COMMON CARD (1-25) .20 .50

1975 Topps Shock Theater
COMPLETE SET (51) 275.00 550.00
COMMON CARD (1-51) 3.00 8.00
NO. 17 HAS A VARIANT
CARD NO. 47 DOESN'T EXIST

1976 Topps UK Shock Theater
COMPLETE SET (53) 75.00 150.00
COMMON CARD (1-53) 1.50 4.00

1971 Donruss Silly Cycles
COMPLETE SET (66) 90.00 175.00
COMMON CARD (1-66) 1.00 2.50

1965 Topps Silly Stickers
COMPLETE SET (53) 150.00 300.00
COMMON CARD 2.00 5.00

1975 Donruss Six Million Dollar Man
COMPLETE SET (66) 30.00 80.00
UNOPENED BOX (24 PACKS) 300.00 500.00
UNOPENED PACK 12.00 20.00
COMMON STICKER (1-66) .50 1.25

1974 Topps Six Million Dollar Man
COMPLETE SET (55) 1000.00 2000.00
COMMON CARD (1-55) 20.00 50.00

1974 Topps Mexican Six Million Dollar Man
COMPLETE SET (55) 400.00 800.00
COMMON CARD (1-55) 10.00 25.00
1 Col. Steve Austin 20.00 50.00
55 Prime Mover 12.00 30.00

1976 Scanlens Skateboard Safety Tips
COMPLETE SET (24) 30.00 75.00
COMMON CARD (1-24) 1.50 4.00

1976 Donruss Skateboard Stickers
COMPLETE SET (44) 8.00 20.00
UNOPENED BOX (24 PACKS) 20.00 30.00
UNOPENED PACK (STICKERS) 1.50 2.00
COMMON STICKER (1-44) .40 1.00

1978 Wall's Ice Cream Skateboard Surfer
COMPLETE SET (20) 8.00 20.00
COMMON CARD (1-20) .60 1.50

1966 Topps Slob Stickers 1st Series
COMPLETE SET (44) 125.00 250.00
COMMON CARD (1-44) 2.00 5.00
*SERIES A: .5X TO 1.2X BASIC CARDS 2.50 6.00
*SERIES B: .6X TO 1.5X BASIC CARDS 3.00 8.00

1980 Dolly Madison Snoopy for President Stickers
COMPLETE SET (12) 6.00 15.00
COMMON STICKER 1.00 2.50

1970 Wonder Bread Snoopy World War I Airplanes
COMPLETE SET (8) 8.00 20.00
COMMON CARD 1.25 3.00

1965 Brooke Bond Songbirds of the United States
COMPLETE SET (50) 30.00 75.00
COMMON CARD (1-50) .60 1.50

1967 Topps Soupy Sales
COMPLETE SET (66) 125.00 250.00
UNOPENED BOX 350.00 400.00
UNOPENED PACK 25.00 30.00
COMMON CARD (1-66) 1.25 3.00

1976 Donruss Space 1999
COMPLETE SET (66) 6.00 15.00
UNOPENED BOX (24 PACKS) 25.00 40.00
UNOPENED PACK (5 CARDS) 2.00 2.50
COMMON CARD (1-66) .10 .25

1969 Brooke Bond Space Age
COMPLETE SET (48) 12.00 30.00
COMMON CARD (1-48) .25 .60

1969 Taylor-Reed Space Candy
COMPLETE SET (20) 50.00 100.00
COMMON CARD (1-20) 1.50 4.00

1957 Topps Space Cards
COMPLETE SET (88) 200.00 500.00
COMMON CARD (1-88) 2.50 6.00

1963 Topps Space Popsicle
COMPLETE SET (55) 400.00 800.00
COMMON CARD (1-55) 5.00 12.00

1952 Exhibit Space Ships
COMPLETE SET (4) 20.00 50.00
COMMON CARD (1-4) 4.00 10.00

1962 Space-Pak
COMPLETE SET (10) 25.00 60.00
COMMON CARD 2.00 5.00

1960 Fleer Spins and Needles
COMPLETE SET (80) 250.00 500.00
UNOPENED PACK 175.00 200.00
COMMON CARD (1-80) 2.00 5.00

1963 Leaf Spook Stories
COMPLETE SET (144) 200.00 400.00
COMPLETE SERIES 1 SET (72) 75.00 150.00
COMPLETE SERIES 2 SET (72) 120.00 250.00
COMMON CARD (1-72) .75 2.00
COMMON CARD (73-144) 1.25 3.00

1955 Mother's Cookies Sports Car
COMPLETE SET (42) 105.00 210.00
COMMON CARD (1-42) 1.50 4.00

1956 Mother's Cookies Sports Cars
COMPLETE SET (42) 100.00 200.00
COMMON CARD (1-42) 1.50 4.00

1961 Topps Sports Cars
COMPLETE SET (66) 200.00 300.00
COMMON CARD (1-66) 1.50 4.00
CL Checklist 3.00 8.00

1961 Topps Sports Cars License Plate Stickers
COMPLETE SET (20) 40.00 80.00
COMMON CARD (1-20) 2.00 5.00

1961 Sweetule Stamp Cards
COMPLETE SET (25) 8.00 20.00
COMMON CARD (1-25) .25 .60

1976 Fleer Stick It To 'Em
COMPLETE SET (66) 12.00 30.00
UNOPENED BOX (36 PACKS) 40.00 50.00
UNOPENED PACK (6 STICKERS) 2.00 2.50
COMMON CARD (1-66) .30 .75

1964 Kellogg's Story of the Bicycle
COMPLETE SET (12) 15.00 40.00
COMMON CARD (1-12) 1.00 2.50

1970 Clover Dairies Story of Milk
COMPLETE SET (25) 5.00 12.00
COMMON CARD (1-25) .40 1.00

1965 Home Counties Dairies The Story of Milk
COMPLETE SET (25) 12.00 30.00
COMMON CARD (1-25) .40 1.00

1966 United Dairies The Story of Milk
COMPLETE SET (25) 12.00 30.00
COMMON CARD (1-25) .40 1.00

1977 Sanitarium Story of New Zealand Aviation
COMPLETE SET (20) 4.00 10.00
COMMON CARD (1-20) .30 .75

1965 A&BC The Story of Sir Winston Churchill
COMPLETE SET (55) 100.00 200.00
COMMON CARD (1-55) 1.25 3.00

1949 Nabisco Straight Arrow Injun-Uities Book 1
COMPLETE SET (36) 50.00 100.00
COMMON CARD 1.00 2.50

1950 Nabisco Straight Arrow Injun-Uities Book 2
COMPLETE SET (36) 50.00 100.00
COMMON CARD (1-36) 1.00 2.50

1952 Nabisco Straight Arrow Injun-Uities Book 3
COMPLETE SET (36) 50.00 100.00
COMMON CARD (1-36) 1.00 2.50

1952 Nabisco Straight Arrow Injun-Uities Book 4
COMPLETE SET (36) 50.00 100.00
COMMON CARD (1-36) 1.00 2.50

1970 Cadbury's Strange but True
COMPLETE SET (24) 6.00 15.00
COMMON CARD (1-24) .50 1.25

1961 Cooper's Tea Strange but True Complete Series
COMPLETE SET (50) 12.00 30.00
COMMON CARD (1-50) .50 1.25

1961 Miranda Limited Strange Creatures
COMPLETE SET (50) 10.00 25.00
COMMON CARD (1-50) .30 .75

1952 Mars Candy Super Circus
COMMON CARD (1-21) 5.00 12.00

1950 Canada Dry Super Circus Action Toys
COMPLETE SET (10) 25.00 60.00
COMMON CARD 2.00 5.00

1956 Knockout Super Planes of Today
COMPLETE SET (20) 20.00 50.00
COMMON CARD (1-20) .75 2.00

1960 Ad-Trix Tales of the Vikings
COMPLETE SET (66) 75.00 150.00
COMMON CARD (1-66) .75 2.00

1958 Topps Target Moon
COMPLETE SET (88) 300.00 600.00
COMMON CARD (1-88) 2.00 5.00

1958 Topps Target Moon Salmon Backs
COMPLETE SET (44) 225.00 450.00
COMMON CARD 3.00 8.00
SKIP-NUMBERED SET
ALSO KNOWN AS PINK BACKS
ISSUED AS POPSICLE PROMOTION

1966 Philadelphia Gum Tarzan
COMPLETE SET (66) 120.00 250.00
UNOPENED PACK 40.00 50.00
COMMON CARD (1-66) 1.25 3.00

1967 Barratt Tarzan
COMPLETE SET (50) 25.00 60.00
COMMON CARD (1-50) .30 .75

1953 Topps Tarzan and the She Devil
COMPLETE SET (60) 300.00 600.00
COMMON CARD (1-60) 3.00 8.00

1967 Anglo Confectionery Tarzan
COMPLETE SET (66) 75.00 150.00
COMMON CARD (1-66) .75 2.00

1953 Topps Tarzan's Savage Fury
COMPLETE SET (60) 300.00 600.00
COMMON CARD (1-60) 2.50 6.00

1963 Rosan Terror Monsters
COMPLETE SET (130) 700.00 1200.00
COMMON CARD (1-130) 3.00 8.00
NNO Bonus Card 1 15.00 30.00
NNO Bonus Card 2 15.00 30.00

1967 Topps Terror Tales
COMPLETE SET (88) 700.00 1400.00
COMMON CARD (1-88) 5.00 12.00
1 Don't move, there's a bug on your coat 12.00 30.00
88 I hate doing dishes 8.00 20.00

1959 Parkhurst Texas John Slaughter
COMPLETE SET (50) 90.00 175.00
COMMON CARD (1-50) 1.25 3.00

1955 Bibby & Sons This Wonderful World
COMPLETE SET (25) 15.00 40.00
COMMON CARD (1-25) .50 1.25

1959 Fleer The Three Stooges
COMPLETE SET W/O CL SP (96) 600.00 1000.00
UNOPENED PACK 1000.00 1500.00
COMMON CARD (1-96) 5.00 12.00
1 Curly 125.00 250.00
2 Moe 60.00 120.00
3 Larry 50.00 100.00
16B You Can't Keep Your Money CL 450.00 700.00
63B Curly, the First Thing CL 600.00 1000.00
64B You Won't Fool Anybody CL 75.00 150.00

1966 Fleer The Three Stooges
COMPLETE SET (66) 350.00 700.00
UNOPENED BOX (24 PACKS) 650.00 800.00
UNOPENED PACK 30.00 40.00
COMMON CARD (1-66) 3.00 8.00

1978 Topps Three's Company
COMPLETE SET (44) 7.50 20.00
UNOPENED BOX (36 PACKS) 75.00 125.00
UNOPENED PACK (5 STICKERS) 2.00 4.00
COMMON STICKER (1-44) .30 .75

1968 Barratt Thunderbirds Second Series
COMPLETE SET (50) 20.00 50.00
COMMON CARD (1-50) .30 .75

1966 Somportex Thunderbirds Series 1
COMPLETE SET (72) 25.00 60.00
COMMON CARD (1-72) .30 .75

1966 Somportex Thunderbirds Series 2
COMPLETE SET (73) 25.00 60.00
COMMON CARD (1-73) .30 .75

1954 Tip Top Bread Tip Top Circus
COMPLETE SET (12) 45.00 90.00
COMMON CARD 2.50 6.00

1954 Tip Top Bread Tip Top Circus 3-Card Panels
COMPLETE SET (4) 50.00 100.00
COMMON PANEL 8.00 20.00

1954 Tip Top Space Cards
COMPLETE SET (24)
COMMON CARD

1954 Tip Top Sports Cars
COMPLETE SET (28) 200.00 400.00
COMMON CARD 4.00 10.00

1971 Barratt Tom and Jerry
COMPLETE SET (50) 15.00 40.00
COMMON CARD (1-50) .60 1.50

1979 Grandee Top Dogs Collection
COMPLETE SET (25) 3.00 8.00
COMMON CARD (1-25) .30 .75

1946 Nabisco Toytown Carnival
COMPLETE SET (36) 112.50 225.00
COMMON CARD (1-36) 2.00 5.00

1970 Barratt Trains
COMPLETE SET (50) 8.00 20.00
COMMON CARD (1-50) .25 .60

1971 Clover Dairies Transport Through the Ages
COMPLETE SET (25) 2.00 5.00
COMMON CARD (1-25) .12 .30

1957 Ewbanks Transport Through the Ages Black Backs
COMPLETE SET (25) 12.00 30.00
COMMON CARD (1-25) .40 1.00
*BLUE BACKS: .6X TO 1.5X BLACK BACKS

1957 Ewbanks Transport Through the Ages Blue Backs
COMPLETE SET (25) 20.00 50.00
COMMON CARD (1-25) .60 1.50
*BLUE BACKS: .6X TO 1.5X BLACK BACKS

1961 Cooper's Tea Transport Through the Ages Complete Series
COMPLETE SET (50) 15.00 40.00
COMMON CARD (1-50) .25 .60

1962 Typhoo Tea Travel Through the Ages
COMPLETE SET (24) 8.00 20.00
COMMON CARD (1-24) .30 .75

1956 Kellogg's Travel-Cals
COMPLETE SET (5) 75.00 150.00
COMMON DECAL 10.00 25.00

1960 Grant Products Treasure Island
COMPLETE SET (60) 20.00 50.00
COMMON CARD (1-60) .50 1.25
*CANADIAN: SAME VALUE

1966 Brooke Bond Trees in Britain
COMPLETE SET (50) 12.00 30.00
COMMON CARD (1-50) .20 .50

1975 Donruss Truckin'
COMPLETE SET (44) 4.00 10.00
UNOPENED BOX (24 PACKS) 100.00 125.00
UNOPENED PACK 5.00 6.00
COMMON CARD (1-44) .10 .25
UNC 44-Card Base Set Uncut Sheet

1977 Kellogg's The True West
COMPLETE SET (10) 6.00 15.00
COMMON CARD (1-10) .75 2.00

1952 Bowman TV and Radio Stars of NBC
COMPLETE SET (36) 150.00 250.00
COMMON CARD (1-36) 2.00 5.00

1953 Bowman TV and Radio Stars of NBC
COMPLETE SET (96) 200.00 400.00
COMMON CARD (1-96) 2.00 5.00
1 Jack Lescoulie SP 3.00 8.00
7 Carl Reiner SP 3.00 8.00
8 Groucho Marx SP 3.00 8.00
10 Dinah Shore SP 3.00 8.00
95 Bob Hope SP 3.00 8.00
96 Dan Gibson 3.00 8.00

1980 Fleer TV Smelly Awards
COMPLETE SET (64) 12.00 30.00
UNOPENED BOX (24 PACKS) 70.00 90.00
UNOPENED PACK 4.00 5.00
COMMON CARD (1-64) .20 .50

1964 Donruss Twelve O'Clock High
COMMON CARD 15.00 40.00

1971 Topps 21 Tattoos
COMPLETE SET (16) 75.00 150.00
COMMON TATTOO SHEET 5.00 12.00

1967 Topps Twiggy Test Series
COMMON CARD 50.00 100.00

1976 Sports Stars Publishing 200 Years of Freedom
COMPLETE SET (45) 8.00 20.00
COMMON CARD (1-45) .30 .75

1955 Ty-Phoo Tea Types of Ships
COMPLETE SET (20) 15.00 40.00
COMMON CARD (1-20) .60 1.50

1970 A&BC UFO
COMPLETE SET (64) 120.00 250.00
COMMON CARD (1-64) 2.50 6.00
64 S.H.A.D.O. Badge 4.00 10.00

1966 Topps Ugly Buttons
COMPLETE SET (24) 150.00 300.00
COMMON CARD (UNNUMBERED) 4.00 10.00

1965 Topps Ugly Stickers
COMPLETE SET (164) 500.00 1000.00
UNOPENED PACK 120.00 150.00
COMMON CARD (1-164) 2.00 5.00

1976 Topps Ugly Stickers
COMPLETE SET (110) 110.00 225.00
COMMON CARD .75 2.00

1942 Gum Inc. Uncle Sam
COMPLETE SET (48) 1800.00 3600.00
COMMON CARD (97-120) 6.00 15.00
COMMON CARD (121-144) 50.00 100.00

1966 Fleer Underdog Tattoos
COMMON CARD 1.00 2.50

1966 Anglo American Chewing Gum Underwater Adventure
COMPLETE SET (40) 25.00 60.00
COMMON CARD (1-40) .50 1.25

1962 Leaf The Untouchables

COMPLETE SET (16)	60.00	120.00
UNOPENED PACK	90.00	100.00
COMMON BOOKLET (1-16)	5.00	12.00

1962 Leaf The Untouchables Stickers

COMPLETE SET (16)	50.00	100.00
COMMON STICKER (1-16)	4.00	10.00

1961 Rosan US Army in Action

COMPLETE SET (64)	100.00	200.00
COMMON CARD (1-64)	1.00	2.50

1960 Post U.S. License Plates

COMPLETE SET (50)	90.00	175.00
COMMON CARD	1.25	3.00

1954 Bowman U.S. Navy Victories

COMPLETE SET (48)	275.00	550.00
COMMON CARD (1-48)	4.00	10.00

1952 Bowman U.S. Presidents

COMPLETE SET (36)	125.00	250.00
COMMON CARD (1-36)	2.00	5.00
1 Washington Takes Command	8.00	20.00
19 Abraham Lincoln	8.00	20.00
36 Dwight D.Eisenhower	5.00	12.00

1956 Topps U.S. Presidents

COMPLETE SET (36)	100.00	200.00
COMMON CARD (1-36)	1.25	3.00
1 Washington Takes Command	6.00	15.00
3 George Washington	5.00	12.00
19 Abraham Lincoln	5.00	12.00
36 Dwight D. Eisenhower	4.00	10.00

1972 Topps US Presidents

COMPLETE SET (43)	30.00	80.00
COMPLETE SET W/POSTERS (58)	60.00	120.00
UNOPENED PACK	8.00	12.00
COMMON CARD (1-36)	.40	1.00
COMMON CARD (37-43)	.60	1.50
1 George Washington DP	4.00	10.00
3 Thomas Jefferson	3.00	8.00
16 Abraham Lincoln	3.00	8.00
31 Franklin Roosevelt	3.00	8.00
34 John F. Kennedy	3.00	8.00

1972 Topps US Presidents Posters

COMPLETE SET (15)	20.00	50.00
COMMON CARD (1-15)	.75	2.00
STATED ODDS 1:1		
1 Abraham Lincoln	3.00	8.00
3 John F. Kennedy	3.00	8.00
10 George Washington	4.00	10.00
12 Thomas Jefferson	3.00	8.00

1957 Cracker Jack U.S. Presidents

COMPLETE SET (33)	200.00	400.00
COMMON CARD	4.00	10.00

1963 Topps Valentine Foldees

COMPLETE SET (55)	100.00	200.00
COMMON CARD (1-55)	1.50	4.00

1970 Topps Valentine Foldees

COMPLETE SET (55)	80.00	150.00
COMMON CARD (1-55)	2.00	5.00

1970 Topps Valentine Postcards

COMPLETE SET (33)	30.00	80.00
COMMON CARD (1-33)	1.50	4.00

1962 Topps Valentine Stickers

COMPLETE SET (44)	75.00	150.00
UNOPENED BOX (PACKS)		
UNOPENED PACK (CARDS)		
COMMON CARD	1.25	3.00

1960 Topps Valentine Wood Plaks

UNOPENED PACK (2 PLAKS)	65.00	80.00

1978 Brooke Bond Vanishing Wildlife

COMPLETE SET (40)	8.00	20.00
COMMON CARD (1-40)	.20	.50

1962 Kellogg's Veteran Motor Cars

COMPLETE SET (16)	15.00	40.00
COMMON CARD (1-16)	.75	2.00

1965 Autobrite Vintage Cars

COMPLETE SET (25)	15.00	40.00
COMMON CARD (1-25)	.50	1.25

1973 Sanitarium Vintage Cars

COMPLETE SET (20)	10.00	25.00
COMMON CARD (1-20)	.60	1.50

1966 Mobil Oil Vintage Cars The Great Days of Motoring

COMPLETE SET (24)	60.00	120.00
COMMON CARD (1-24)	1.50	4.00

1972 Donruss Vote Stickers

COMPLETE SET (33)	15.00	40.00
UNOPENED BOX (24 PACKS)	125.00	150.00
UNOPENED PACK	6.00	8.00
COMMON CARD (1-33)	1.00	2.50

1964 Donruss Voyage to the Bottom of the Sea

COMPLETE SET (66)	120.00	250.00
UNOPENED BOX (24 PACKS)		
UNOPENED PACK		
COMMON CARD (1-66)	1.25	3.00

1969 Topps Wacky Ads

COMPLETE SET W/#25 (36)	1000.00	2000.00
COMPLETE SET W/O #25 (35)	400.00	800.00
COMMON CARD (2-24; 26-36)	6.00	15.00
1 Melty Way	12.00	30.00
5 Vile Soap	8.00	20.00
6 Ajerx	8.00	20.00
7 Blunder Bread	12.00	30.00
10 Boo-Hoo	12.00	30.00
15 Blecch Shampoo	8.00	20.00
20 Dopey Whip/Minute Lice Hostage	15.00	40.00
25 Good And Empty SP	500.00	1000.00
29 Crust/Weakies Gadzooka/Kook Aid	8.00	20.00
32 Botch Tape	10.00	25.00
34 Pest Awful Bits	10.00	25.00
35 Fish-Bone	8.00	20.00
36 Mrs. Klean/6Up Breadcrust	12.00	30.00

1959 Topps Wacky Plaks

COMPLETE SET (88)	275.00	550.00
COMMON CARD (1-88)	2.00	5.00

1978 Hostess Wacky TV Shows Panels

COMPLETE SET (16)	50.00	100.00
COMMON PANEL	3.00	8.00
*SINGLES: .10X TO .25X BASIC PANELS		

1972 Spar Grocer Walt Disney on Parade

COMPLETE SET (19)	50.00	100.00
COMMON CARD	3.00	8.00

1973 Topps The Waltons

COMMON CARD (1-50)	50.00	100.00

1967 Topps Wanted Posters

COMPLETE SET (24)	75.00	150.00
UNOPENED BOX (24 PACKS)	400.00	600.00
COMMON POSTER	2.00	5.00

1975 Topps Wanted Stickers

COMPLETE SET (42)	20.00	50.00
COMMON CARD (1-42)	.60	1.50

1965 Philadelphia Gum War Bulletin

COMPLETE SET (88)	250.00	400.00
UNOPENED BOX	650.00	800.00
UNOPENED PACK	50.00	60.00
COMMON CARD (1-88)	1.50	4.00
CL Checklist 1-88	10.00	25.00

1962 Barratt Warriors Through the Ages

COMPLETE SET (25)	8.00	20.00
COMMON CARD (1-25)	.25	.60

1954 British Automatic Warships of the World

COMPLETE SET (24)	15.00	40.00
COMMON CARD (1-24)	.50	1.25

1957 Granose Foods Water Transport

COMPLETE SET (16)	8.00	20.00
COMMON CARD (1-16)	.40	1.00

1972 Nabisco Water World Heroes

COMPLETE SET (50)	12.00	30.00
COMMON CARD (1-50)	.40	1.00

1970 Topps Way Out Wheels

COMPLETE SET (36)	25.00	60.00
COMPLETE SET W/STICKERS (58)	50.00	100.00
COMMON CARD (1-36)	.75	2.00
*OPC: SAME VALUE		

1970 Topps Way Out Wheels Stickers

COMPLETE SET (22)	12.00	30.00
COMMON CARD (1-22)	.75	2.00
*OPC: SAME VALUE		

1959 Sweetule Weapons of Defence

COMPLETE SET (25)	12.00	30.00
COMMON CARD (1-25)	.40	1.00

1980 Topps Weird Wheels

COMPLETE SET (55)	6.00	15.00
UNOPENED BOX (36 PACKS)	50.00	70.00
UNOPENED PACK (6 STICKERS)	2.00	3.00
COMMON CARD (1-55)	.12	.30

1966 Fleer Weird-Ohs Baseball Cards

COMPLETE SET (66)	80.00	150.00
UNOPENED BOX	250.00	300.00
UNOPENED PACK	15.00	20.00
COMMON CARD (1-66)	.75	2.00

1968 Somportex Weirdies

COMPLETE SET (36)	100.00	200.00
COMMON CARD (1-36)	1.50	4.00

1976 Topps Welcome Back Kotter

COMPLETE SET (53)	10.00	25.00
UNOPENED BOX (36 PACKS)	150.00	300.00
UNOPENED PACK (7 CARDS)	5.00	8.00
COMMON CARD (1-53)	.20	.50
*OPC: SAME VALUE		

1959 Weetabix Western Story

COMPLETE SET (25)	25.00	60.00
COMMON CARD (1-25)	.75	2.00

1957 Lyons Tea What Do You Know?

COMPLETE SET (48)	20.00	50.00
COMMON CARD (1-48)	.30	.75

1964 Barratt What Do You Know?

COMPLETE SET (25)	8.00	20.00
COMMON CARD (1-25)	.25	.60

1965 Leaf What's My Job?

COMPLETE SET (72)	110.00	225.00
UNOPENED PACK	30.00	40.00
COMMON CARD (1-72)	1.00	2.50

1965 Leaf What's My Job? Stickers

COMPLETE SET (16)	25.00	60.00
COMMON CARD	1.25	3.00

1953 Topps Who-Z-At Star

COMPLETE SET (80)	400.00	750.00
COMMON CARD (1-80)	4.00	10.00

1958 A&BC Who-Z-At-Star?

COMPLETE SET (70)	350.00	700.00
COMMON CARD (1-70)	3.00	8.00

1965 Brooke Bond Wild Birds in Britain

COMPLETE SET (50)	15.00	40.00
COMMON CARD (1-50)	.25	.60

1950 Bowman Wild Man

COMPLETE SET (72)	800.00	1500.00
COMMON CARD (1-36)	5.00	12.00
COMMON CARD (37-72)	8.00	20.00

1949 Bowman Wild West

COMPLETE SET (180)	900.00	1600.00
COMMON SERIES 1 A (1-8), B-H (1-4)	3.00	8.00
COMMON SERIES 2 A (9-16), B-H (5-8)	3.00	8.00
COMMON SERIES 3 A (17-24), B-H (9-12)	3.00	8.00
COMMON SERIES 4 A (25-32), B-H (13-16)	3.00	8.00
COMMON SERIES 5 A (33-40), B-H (17-20)	7.50	20.00
A1 Capturing British Fort	6.00	15.00
C8 Daniel Boone	6.00	15.00
C9 Davy Crockett	6.00	15.00
C10 Annie Oakley	6.00	15.00
C15 Geronimo	6.00	15.00
C16 Sitting Bull	6.00	15.00
F7 Bill Hickok at Hays City	6.00	15.00
F17 Jesse James Holdup	15.00	40.00

1961 Barratt Wild West

COMPLETE SET (24)	15.00	40.00
COMMON CARD (1-24)	.50	1.25

1960 Sweetule Wild West Black Backs

COMPLETE SET (25)	10.00	25.00
COMMON CARD (1-25)	.30	.75

1960 Sweetule Wild West Blue Backs

COMPLETE SET (25)	10.00	25.00
COMMON CARD (1-25)	.30	.75

1960 Mills Tobacco Wild West

COMPLETE SET (25)	10.00	25.00
COMMON CARD (1-25)	.30	.75

1968 Barratt Wild Wild West

COMPLETE SET (50)	90.00	175.00
COMMON CARD (1-50)	1.25	3.00

1969 Nabisco Wildlife Baby Animals

COMPLETE SET (50)	15.00	40.00
COMMON CARD (1-50)	.75	2.00

1963 Brooke Bond Wildlife in Danger

COMPLETE SET (50)	10.00	25.00
COMMON CARD (1-50)	.20	.50

1952 Topps Wings

COMPLETE SET (200)	300.00	600.00
COMMON CARD (1-200)	1.00	2.50

1955 Doeskin Tissues Wings

COMPLETE SET (80)	150.00	300.00
COMMON CARD (1-80)	1.25	3.00

1942 Quaker Wings of Today

COMPLETE SET (12)	90.00	175.00
COMMON CARD (1-12)	5.00	12.00

1946 Quaker Wings of Victory

COMMON CARD (1-23)	6.00	15.00

1970 Barratt Wise Cracks Series 1

COMPLETE SET (50)	8.00	20.00
COMMON CARD (1-50)	.30	.75

1965 Topps Wise Guy Buttons

COMPLETE SET (23)	30.00	75.00
UNOPENED BOX (24 PACKS)	650.00	800.00
UNOPENED PACK		
COMMON BUTTON (UNNUMBERED)	2.50	6.00

1953-54 Albers Cereals Woody Woodpecker's Drawing Lessons

COMPLETE SET (36)	175.00	350.00
COMMON CARD (1-36)	3.00	8.00

1978 Sanitarium Wonderful Ways of Nature

COMPLETE SET (20)	8.00	20.00
COMMON CARD (1-20)	.60	1.50

1965 Browne's Tea Wonders of the Deep

COMPLETE SET (25)	10.00	25.00
COMMON CARD (1-25)	.30	.75

1965 H.E. Empson and Sons Wonders of the Deep

COMPLETE SET (25)	10.00	25.00
COMMON CARD (1-25)	.30	.75

1965 Northern Cooperative Society Wonders of the Deep

COMPLETE SET (25)	10.00	25.00
COMMON CARD (1-25)	.30	.75

1963 Tonibell Wonders of the Heavens

COMPLETE SET (25)	15.00	40.00
COMMON CARD (1-25)	.50	1.25

1960 Foto Gum Wonders of the Universe

COMPLETE SET (25)	6.00	15.00
COMMON CARD (1-25)	.50	1.25

1962 Barratt Wonders of the World

COMPLETE SET (50)	15.00	40.00
COMMON CARD (1-50)	.25	.60

1954-55 Topps World on Wheels

COMPLETE SET W/O SP (160)	500.00	1000.00
COMMON CARD (1-160)	2.00	5.00
COMMON BLUE BACK (171-180)		
COMMON RED BACK (161-180)		
CARDS 161-180 ARE EXTREMELY SCARCE		
1 Diamond T	3.00	8.00
7A Norton German Motorcycle ERR	4.00	10.00
7B Norton English Motorcycle COR	2.00	5.00
160 Haynes-Apperson	3.00	8.00
161 Chevrolet Corvette	10.00	25.00
162 Mercury Monterey	12.00	30.00
163 Packard Carribean	15.00	40.00
164 Cadillac Series	30.00	80.00
165 German Miniature Car	12.00	30.00
166 Hudson Italia		
167 Microbo Miniature Car	20.00	50.00
168 Bristol Convertible	15.00	40.00
169 Ford Thunderbird	15.00	40.00
170 Buick Skylark	25.00	60.00
171A Pontiac Strato-Star Blue Back	12.00	30.00
171B Pontiac Strato-Star Red Back		
172A Chevrolet Biscayne Blue Back	20.00	50.00
172B Chevrolet Biscayne Red Back	60.00	120.00
173A Buick Wildcat III Blue Back	10.00	25.00
173B Buick Wildcat III Red Back	50.00	100.00
174A Messerschmitt Blue Back	15.00	40.00
174B Messerschmitt Red Back	50.00	100.00
175A De Soto Fireflite Blue Back	12.00	40.00
175B De Soto Fireflite Red Back		
176A Chrysler 300 Blue Back	10.00	25.00
176B Chrysler 300 Red Back	20.00	50.00
177A Cadillac Eldorado Blue Back	12.00	30.00
177B Cadillac Eldorado Red Back		
178A Nash Rambler Blue Back	10.00	25.00
178B Nash Rambler Red Back	20.00	50.00
179A Dodge Royal Lancer Blue Back	12.00	30.00
179B Dodge Royal Lancer Red Back		
180A Ford Crown Victoria Blue Back	12.00	30.00
180B Ford Crown Victoria Red Back		

1963 Tonibell World's Passenger Liners

COMPLETE SET (25)	15.00	40.00
COMMON CARD (1-25)	.50	1.25

1949 Topps X-Ray Round Up

COMPLETE SET (200)	375.00	750.00
COMMON CARD (1-200)	1.25	3.00

1973 Topps You'll Die Laughing

COMPLETE SET (128)	80.00	150.00
COMPLETE SERIES 1 SET (62)	30.00	80.00
COMPLETE SERIES 2 SET (66)	50.00	100.00
UNOPENED BOX (36 PACKS)	150.00	300.00
UNOPENED PACK (2 CARDS)	3.00	8.00
SERIES 1 COMMON (1-62)	.60	1.25
SERIES 2 COMMON (63-128)	.60	1.50
*OPC: SAME VALUE AS TOPPS		

1980 Topps You'll Die Laughing Creature Feature

COMPLETE SET (88)	10.00	25.00
COMPLETE SET W/STICKERS (110)	12.00	30.00
UNOPENED BOX (36 PACKS)	80.00	150.00
UNOPENED PACK (12 CARDS+STICKER)	1.50	4.00
COMMON CARD (1-88)	.15	.40

1980 Topps You'll Die Laughing Creature Feature Stickers

COMPLETE SET (22)	3.00	8.00
COMMON CARD (1-22)	.20	.50
STATED ODDS 1:1		

1959 Topps You'll Die Laughing Funny Monsters

COMPLETE SET (66)	200.00	400.00
COMMON CARD (1-66)	2.00	5.00
1 I Just Came Back From the Beauty Parlor	4.00	10.00
66 This Photographer Does Beautiful Work.	3.00	8.00

1967 A&BC You'll Die Laughing

COMPLETE SET (48)	75.00	150.00
COMMON CARD (1-48)	1.00	2.50

1965 Barratt Young Adventurer

COMPLETE SET (25)	12.00	30.00
COMMON CARD (1-25)	.40	1.00

1963 Nabisco Young Heroes and Heroines

COMPLETE SET (30)	112.50	225.00
COMMON CARD (1-30)	2.50	6.00

1966 Fine Fare Tea Your Fortune in a Tea-Cup

COMPLETE SET (12)	8.00	20.00
COMMON CARD (1-12)	.50	1.25

1960 Fleer Yule Laff

COMPLETE SET (66)	50.00	100.00
COMMON CARD (1-66)	.75	2.00

1954 Zoo Animals

COMPLETE SET (50)	30.00	75.00
COMMON CARD (1-50)	.50	1.25

1975 Topps Zoo's Who Stick-Ons

COMPLETE SET (40)	10.00	25.00
COMMON CARD (1-40)	.30	.75

1975 Topps Zoo's Who Stick-Ons Puzzle A

COMPLETE SET (9)	5.00	12.00
COMMON CARD	.60	1.50

1975 Topps Zoo's Who Stick-Ons Puzzle B

COMPLETE SET (9)	5.00	12.00
COMMON CARD	.60	1.50

1958 Topps Zorro

COMPLETE SET (88)	250.00	450.00
COMMON CARD (1-88)	1.50	5.00
1 Zorro	4.00	10.00
88 Man of Mystery	4.00	10.00

1960 Parkhurst Zorro

COMPLETE SET (50)	100.00	200.00
COMMON CARD (1-50)	2.50	6.00

1983 Topps The A-Team
COMPLETE SET (66) 6.00 15.00
UNOPENED BOX (36 PACKS) 150.00 250.00
UNOPENED PACK (10 CARDS+1 STICKER) 4.00 6.00
COMMON CARD (1-66) .15 .40

1983 Topps The A-Team Stickers
COMPLETE SET (12) 3.00 8.00
STATED ODDS 1:1

1994 Hearst Entertainment A&E Biography Promos
COMPLETE SET (18) 10.00 25.00
COMMON CARD (1-18) .75 2.00

1996 DuoCards Abbott and Costello
COMPLETE SET (72) 6.00 15.00
UNOPENED BOX (30 PACKS) 20.00 30.00
UNOPENED PACK (7 CARDS) .75 1.00
COMMON CARD (1-72) .15 .40

1996 DuoCards Abbott and Costello Chromium
COMPLETE SET (6) 10.00 25.00
COMMON CARD (C1-C6) 2.50 6.00
STATED ODDS 1:15

1996 DuoCards Abbott and Costello Promos
COMMON CARD (P1-P2) .75 2.00
NNO Promo 3 (Who's on First?) 2.50 6.00
(25th Philly Non-Sports Show Exclusive)

2003 ABC Kids Promos
COMPLETE SET (5) 2.00 5.00
COMMON CARD (UNNUMBERED) .60 1.50

1993 AC Comics Promos
COMPLETE SET (9) 4.00 10.00
COMMON CARD .75 2.00

1993 Accolade Video Games Promos
COMPLETE SET (10) 2.00 5.00
COMMON CARD .30 .75

1995 Donruss Ace Ventura When Nature Calls
COMPLETE SET (90) 6.00 15.00
UNOPENED BOX (36 PACKS) 100.00 150.00
UNOPENED PACK (8 CARDS) 3.00 4.00
COMMON CARD (1-90) .12 .30
P1 When Nature Calls PROMO .75 2.00

1995 Donruss Ace Ventura When Nature Calls Foil
COMPLETE SET (9) 6.00 15.00
COMMON CARD (H1-H9) 1.25 3.00
STATED ODDS 1:4
HOBBY EXCLUSIVE

1995 Donruss Ace Ventura When Nature Calls Foil Embossed
COMPLETE SET (9) 4.00 10.00
COMMON CARD (F1-F9) .75 2.00
STATED ODDS 1:4
RETAIL EXCLUSIVE

1994 Kenner Action Masters Metal Figurine Promos
COMPLETE SET (20) 20.00 50.00
COMMON CARD 1.50 4.00

1991 Topps The Addams Family
COMPLETE SET (99) 4.00 10.00
COMPLETE SET W/STICKERS (110) 6.00 15.00
UNOPENED BOX (36 PACKS) 15.00 20.00
UNOPENED PACK (8 CARDS+1 STICKER) .50 .75
COMMON CARD (1-99) .08 .20

1991 Topps The Addams Family Stickers
COMPLETE SET (11) 2.00 5.00
COMMON CARD (1-11) .30 .75
STATED ODDS 1:1

2014 Adventure Time
COMPLETE SET (54) 5.00 12.00
UNOPENED BOX (24 PACKS) 300.00 400.00
UNOPENED PACK (5 CARDS) 12.00 15.00
COMMON CARD (1-54) .15 .40

2014 Adventure Time Autographs
COMMON AUTO (A1-A20) 6.00 15.00
STATED ODDS 1:24
SOME AUTOGRAPHS
CONTAIN RANDOM INSCRIPTIONS
A1 Justin Roiland 200.00 350.00
A2 Hynden Walch 15.00 40.00
A3 Maria Bamford 8.00 20.00
A4 Olivia Olson 20.00 50.00
A6 Miguel Ferrer 12.00 30.00
A11 Michael Dorn 12.00 30.00
A12 M. Emmet Walsh 10.00 25.00
A13 Steve Little 8.00 20.00
A14 Brian Baumgartner 8.00 20.00
A15 Erik Estrada 10.00 25.00
A17 Dee Bradley Baker 10.00 25.00
A19 Brian Posehn 10.00 25.00
A20 Neil Patrick Harris 20.00 50.00

2014 Adventure Time Katie Cook Puzzle
COMPLETE SET (9) 8.00 20.00
COMMON CARD (KC1-KC9) 1.25 3.00
STATED ODDS 1:12

2014 Adventure Time Steam Punk Foil
COMPLETE SET (9) 8.00 20.00
COMMON CARD (SP01-SP09) 1.25 3.00
STATED ODDS 1:12

2014 Adventure Time Totally Fabricated Wardrobes
COMPLETE SET (7) 25.00 60.00
COMMON MEM (TF1-TF7) 4.00 10.00
STATED ODDS 1:96
TF7 ISSUED AS ALBUM EXCLUSIVE
TF3 Princess Bubblegum 5.00 12.00
TF6 Marceline 5.00 12.00
TF7 Peppermint Butler ALB 6.00 15.00

2014 Adventure Time Promos
COMMON CARD .75 1.50
P2 Promo 2 NSU 1.25 3.00
HE1 Finn Jake and Friends HE 1.50 4.00

2013 Adventure Time Dog Tags Series 1
COMPLETE SET (20) 25.00 60.00
COMMON TAG (1-20) 2.00 5.00
NNO Checklist .10 .25

2014 Adventure Time Dog Tags Series 2
COMPLETE SET (20) 25.00 60.00
COMMON TAG (1-20) 2.00 5.00

2014 Adventure Time PlayPaks
COMPLETE SET (18) 4.00 10.00
COMMON CARD (1-18) .30 .75
STATED ODDS 2:1

2014 Adventure Time PlayPaks Princess Glitter
COMPLETE SET (9) 6.00 15.00
COMMON CARD (1-9) .75 2.00
STATED ODDS 1:1

2014 Adventure Time PlayPaks Scratch 'n Sniff
COMPLETE SET (3) 3.00 8.00
COMMON CARD (1-3) 1.50 4.00
STATED ODDS 1:3

2014 Adventure Time PlayPaks Standees
COMPLETE SET (3) 2.50 6.00
COMMON CARD (1-3) 1.25 3.00
STATED ODDS 1:3

2014 Adventure Time PlayPaks Stickers
COMPLETE SET (9) 3.00 8.00
COMMON CARD (1-9) .50 1.25
STATED ODDS 1:1

2014 Adventure Time PlayPaks Temporary Tattoos
COMPLETE SET (3) 2.50 6.00
COMMON CARD (UNNUMBERED) 1.25 3.00
STATED ODDS 1:3

2015 Adventure Time PlayPaks Series 2
COMPLETE SET (18) 4.00 10.00
COMMON CARD (1-18) .30 .75

2015 Adventure Time PlayPaks Series 2 Rainbow Foil
COMPLETE SET (9) 6.00 15.00
COMMON CARD (R1-R9) .75 2.00
STATED ODDS 1:1

2015 Adventure Time PlayPaks Series 2 Scratch 'n Sniff
COMPLETE SET (3) 3.00 8.00
COMMON CARD (N1-N3) 1.50 4.00
STATED ODDS 1:3

2015 Adventure Time PlayPaks Series 2 Standees
COMPLETE SET (3) 2.50 6.00
COMMON CARD (E1-E3) 1.25 3.00
STATED ODDS 1:3

2015 Adventure Time PlayPaks Series 2 Stickers
COMPLETE SET (9) 3.00 8.00
COMMON CARD (S1-S9) .50 1.25
STATED ODDS 1:1

2015 Adventure Time PlayPaks Series 2 Temporary Tattoos
COMPLETE SET (3) 2.50 6.00
COMMON CARD (UNNUMBERED) 1.25 3.00
STATED ODDS 1:3

2002 Adventures of Jimmy Neutron Boy Genius Ore Ida
COMPLETE SET (32) 6.00 15.00
COMMON CARD (1-32) .75 2.00

2002 Adventures of Jimmy Neutron Boy Genius Ore Ida Mail-In
COMPLETE SET (6) 4.00 10.00
COMMON CARD 1.00 2.50

1996 Inkworks Adventures of Pinocchio
COMPLETE SET (90) 5.00 12.00
UNOPENED BOX (36 PACKS) 15.00 20.00
UNOPENED PACK (8 CARDS) .40 .60
LW1 Lucky Game Winner (CD-ROM) .40 1.00

1996 Inkworks Adventures of Pinocchio Chase
COMPLETE SET (9) 10.00 25.00
COMMON CARD (P1-P9) 1.50 4.00
STATED ODDS 1:7

1996 Inkworks Adventures of Pinocchio FoilWorks
COMPLETE SET (3) 15.00 40.00
COMMON CARD (F1-F3) 6.00 15.00
STATED ODDS 1:35

1996 Inkworks Adventures of Pinocchio Lenticular
COMPLETE SET (2) 15.00 40.00
COMMON CARD (L1-L2) 10.00 25.00
STATED ODDS 1:72

1996 Inkworks Adventures of Pinocchio Promo
S1 Pinocchio S1 1.25 3.00

2013 Adventures of Sherlock Holmes
COMPLETE SET (27) 8.00 20.00
UNOPENED PREMIUM PACK 20.00 30.00
COMMON CARD (1-27) .40 1.00

2013 Adventures of Sherlock Holmes Bonus Promos
P1 Dracula 4.00 10.00
P1 The Memoirs of Sherlock Holmes 4.00 10.00
BP1 The Art of Burlesque
BP2 The Art of Burlesque
PDP2 Pulp Detectives

1990 Victoria Gallery Aeroplanes Civil Reprints
COMPLETE SET (50) 8.00 20.00
COMMON CARD (1-50) .30 .75

1996 Gothic Afraid of the Bear Promo

NNO John Malloy/100 3.00 8.00

2011 Age of Sorcery

COMPLETE SET (18) 12.00 30.00
UNOPENED PREMIUM BOX (24-29 CARDS) 20.00 50.00
COMMON CARD 1.00 2.50
B1 Bookmark Gold/Red/Gray
BC1 Midnite Diner Bonus
P1 Breathing Red Dragon PROMO/500 2.00 5.00

2011 Age of Sorcery Canvas

COMPLETE SET (4) 6.00 15.00
COMMON CARD (J1-J4) 2.00 5.00
JC1 Green Warrior
MD1 Lizard Man
NNO Cow
NNO Rare Cow

1993 Eclipse AIDS Awareness

COMPLETE SET (110) 6.00 15.00
UNOPENED BOX (36 PACKS) 20.00 30.00
UNOPENED PACK (12 + CONDOM) .75 1.00
COMMON CARD (1-110) .08 .20

1993 Eclipse AIDS Awareness Hotline Stickers

COMPLETE SET (6) 8.00 20.00
COMMON CARD (1-6) 2.00 5.00
STATED ODDS 1:12

1990 Imperial Publishing '38 Aircraft of the Royal Air Force Reprints

COMPLETE SET (50) 8.00 20.00
COMMON CARD (1-50) .30 .75

1994 Cornerstone Akira Previews

COMPLETE SET (10) 2.50 6.00
COMMON CARD (1-10) .50 1.25

1994 Cornerstone Akira

COMPLETE SET (100) 10.00 25.00
UNOPENED FACTORY SET 6.00 15.00
UNOPENED BOX (36 PACKS) 65.00 80.00
UNOPENED PACK (10 CARDS) 2.00 3.00
COMMON CARD (1-100) .12 .30
P Tetsuo and Kaori (prism) 60.00 120.00

1994 Cornerstone Akira Otomo Katsuhiro Chromium

COMPLETE SET (3) 6.00 15.00
COMMON CARD (1-3) 3.00 8.00
STATED ODDS 1:18

1994 Cornerstone Akira Promos

COMMON CARD .75 2.00
P1 Promo 1 1.25 3.00
P2 Promo 2 1.25 3.00
NNO Neo Tokyo is going to explode! (CCPG) 2.00 5.00

1993 Panini Aladdin

COMPLETE SET (100) 5.00 12.00
UNOPENED HOBBY BOX (36 PACKS) 20.00 30.00
UNOPENED PACK (10 CARDS) .75 1.00
UNOPENED JUMBO BOX (24 PACKS) 30.00 40.00
UNOPENED JUMBO PACK (15 CARDS) 1.25 1.75
COMMON CARD (1-100) .15 .40

1993 Panini Aladdin Stickers

COMPLETE SET (10) 2.00 5.00
COMMON CARD (1-10) .30 .75

1993 SkyBox Aladdin

COMPLETE SET (90) 6.00 15.00
UNOPENED BOX (36 PACKS) 20.00 30.00
UNOPENED PACK (8 CARDS) .75 1.00
COMMON CARD (1-90) .08 .25

1993 SkyBox Aladdin Spectra-Etch

COMPLETE SET (3) 10.00 25.00
COMMON CARD (S1-S3) 5.00 12.00
STATED ODDS 1:30

1987-88 Topps Alf

COMPLETE SET (91) 8.00 20.00
COMPLETE SERIES 1 SET (47) 5.00 12.00
COMPLETE SERIES 2 SET (44) 5.00 12.00
SER.1 BOX (48 PACKS) 50.00 75.00
SER.1 PACK (5 CARDS+1 STICKER) 1.50 2.00
SER.2 BOX (48 PACKS) 50.00 75.00
SER.2 PACK (5 CARDS+1 STICKER) 1.50 2.00
COMMON CARD (1-47) .20 .50
COMMON CARD (48-91) .20 .50
*OPC: SAME VALUE

1987-88 Topps Alf Bouillabaseball

COMPLETE SET (44) 5.00 12.00
COMPLETE SERIES 1 SET (22) 3.00 8.00
COMPLETE SERIES 2 SET (22) 3.00 8.00
COMMON CARD (1B-22B) .30 .75
COMMON CARD (23B-44B) .30 .75
*OPC: SAME VALUE
STATED ODDS 1:1

1987-88 Topps Alf Stickers

COMPLETE SET (33) 2.00 8.00
COMPLETE SERIES 1 SET (22) 2.00 5.00
COMPLETE SERIES 2 SET (11) 1.50 4.00
COMMON CARD (1-22) .15 .40
COMMON CARD (23-33) .15 .40
STATED ODDS 1:1

2002 Alias Season One

COMPLETE SET (81) 5.00 12.00
UNOPENED BOX (24 PACKS) 80.00 100.00
UNOPENED PACK (8 CARDS) 4.00 5.00
COMMON CARD (1-81) .15 .40
CIA47 STATED ODDS 1:90
CIA47 CIA.net: Bristow Sydney 6.00 15.00

2002 Alias Season One Autographs

COMMON AUTO (A1-A7) 6.00 15.00
STATED ODDS 1:39
A1 Jennifer Garner 300.00 600.00
A2 J.J. Abrams 100.00 200.00
A3 Victor Garber 25.00 50.00
A4 Bradley Cooper 150.00 300.00

2002 Alias Season One Box-Loaders

COMPLETE SET (4) 10.00 25.00
COMMON CARD 1.50 4.00
CL1 ISSUED AS CASE TOPPER
CL1 Sydney Bristow CT 12.00 30.00

2002 Alias Season One Double Agent Files

COMPLETE SET (6) 10.00 25.00
COMMON CARD (D1-D6) 2.00 5.00
STATED ODDS 1:17

2002 Alias Season One Pieceworks

COMPLETE SET (3) 125.00 250.00
COMMON MEM (1-3) 15.00 40.00
STATED ODDS 1:78
PW3 Jennifer Garner (bead hat) 125.00 200.00

2002 Alias Season One Secret Life

COMPLETE SET (9) 8.00 20.00
COMMON CARD (SL1-SL9) 1.25 3.00
STATED ODDS 1:11

2002 Alias Season One Promos

G1 Coming December 2002/1000* 2.50 6.00
(Non-Sport Update Gummie Award Exclusive)
P0 Sometimes the Truth Hurts 1.25 3.00
(SDCC Exclusive)

2002 Alias Season One CD Promos

COMPLETE SET (4) 4.00 10.00
COMMON CARD (IS1-IS4) 1.25 3.00

2003 Alias Season Two

COMPLETE SET (81) 5.00 12.00
UNOPENED BOX (24 PACKS) 100.00 200.00
UNOPENED PACK (8 CARDS) 5.00 8.00
COMMON CARD (1-81) .15 .40

2003 Alias Season Two Autographs

COMMON AUTO (A8-A19) 7.50 20.00
STATED ODDS 1:24
A8 Jennifer Garner 150.00 300.00
A10 Carl Lumbly 10.00 25.00
A12 Ron Rifkin 10.00 25.00
A14 Amy Irving 10.00 25.00
A16 Rutger Hauer 50.00 75.00
A17 Richard Lewis 10.00 25.00
A18 Terry O'Quinn 12.00 30.00

2003 Alias Season Two Box-Loaders

COMPLETE SET (4) 10.00 25.00
COMMON CARD 1.50 4.00
CL1 Sydney Bristow CT 12.00 30.00

2003 Alias Season Two Pieceworks

COMPLETE SET (10) 75.00 200.00
COMMON MEM (PW1-PW9) 6.00 15.00
STATED ODDS 1:24
PW1 Jennifer Garner (cowboy hat) 50.00 100.00
PW2 Jennifer Garner (cowboy shirt) 10.00 25.00
PW3 Jennifer Garner (cowboy pants) 10.00 25.00
PW4 Jennifer Garner (geisha kimono) 10.00 25.00

2003 Alias Season Two Seeking Sydney

COMPLETE SET (6) 7.50 20.00
COMMON CARD (1-6) 2.00 5.00
STATED ODDS 1:17

2003 Alias Season Two Undercover

COMPLETE SET (9) 6.00 15.00
COMMON CARD (1-9) 1.25 3.00
STATED ODDS 1:11

2003 Alias Season Two Promos

SD1 Sometimes The Truth Hurts .75 2.00
(SDCC Exclusive)
A2UK Coming December 2003 2.00 5.00
(UK Exclusive)
A2NSU Coming December 2003 1.50 4.00
(Non-Sport Update Exclusive)
INK2003 Inkworkscards.com

2004 Alias Season Three

COMPLETE SET (81) 6.00 15.00
UNOPENED BOX (24 PACKS) 70.00 80.00
UNOPENED PACK (8 CARDS) 3.00 3.50
COMMON CARD (1-81) .15 .40

2004 Alias Season Three Autographs

COMMON AUTO (A20-A31) 6.00 15.00
STATED ODDS 1:24
AR1 REDEMPTION 2.00 5.00
A20 Melissa George 15.00 40.00
A21 David Cronenberg 15.00 40.00
A22 Mia Maestro 10.00 25.00
A23 David Carradine 20.00 50.00
A24 Vivica A. Fox 15.00 40.00
A30 Peggy Lipton 12.00 30.00

2004 Alias Season Three Box-Loaders

COMPLETE SET (3) 2.50 6.00
COMMON CARD (BL1-BL3) 1.25 3.00
CL1 INCLUDED AS A CASE-TOPPER EXCLUSIVE
CL1 Julie Bell Artwork AU CI 20.00 50.00

2004 Alias Season Three Pieceworks

COMPLETE SET (10) 60.00 120.00
COMMON MEM (1-10) 6.00 15.00
STATED ODDS 1:24
PW1 Jennifer Garner Dress 15.00 30.00

2004 Alias Season Three Lost Years

COMPLETE SET (9) 8.00 20.00
COMMON CARD (1-9) 1.25 3.00
STATED ODDS 1:11

2004 Alias Season Three Wicked Games

COMPLETE SET (6) 8.00 20.00
COMMON CARD (1-6) 1.50 4.00
STATED ODDS 1:17

2004 Alias Season Three Tangled Previews

COMPLETE SET (7) 4.00 10.00
COMMON CARD (T1-T7) .75 2.00

2004 Alias Season Three Promos

A31 General Distribution .75 2.00
A32 Non-Sport Update .75 2.00
A3i Inkworks.com
(New Jersey Non-Sport Card Show Exclusive)
SD1 San Diego Comic Con 2.00 5.00
A3MS UK Memorabilia Show 1.50 4.00
A3UK Cards Inc. 1.50 4.00

2006 Alias Season Four

COMPLETE SET (81) 5.00 12.00
UNOPENED BOX (24 PACKS) 70.00 80.00
UNOPENED PACK (8 CARDS) 3.00 3.50
COMMON CARD (1-81) .15 .40

2006 Alias Season Four Autographs

COMPLETE SET (10)
COMMON AUTO (A32-A40) 4.00 10.00
STATED ODDS 1:24
A32 Joel Grey 8.00 20.00
A33 Gina Torres 6.00 15.00
A34 Sonia Braga 10.00 25.00
A35 Michael McKean 10.00 25.00
A37 Izabella Scorupco 6.00 15.00
A40 Angus Scrimm 30.00 75.00
ATS R.Rifkin/J.Grey 25.00 60.00

2006 Alias Season Four Box-Loaders

COMPLETE SET (4) 6.00 15.00
COMMON CARD (BL1-BL3) 1.50 4.00
STATED ODDS 1:BOX
CL1 Realities Collide /CASE INSERT 4.00 10.00

2006 Alias Season Four Pieceworks

COMPLETE SET (10) 60.00 120.00
COMMON MEM (1-10) 4.00 10.00
STATED ODDS 1:24
PW1 Jennifer Garner Dress 15.00 40.00
PW2 Jennifer Garner Top 15.00 40.00

2006 Alias Season Four Predictions

COMPLETE SET (9) 10.00 25.00
COMMON CARD (1-9) 2.00 5.00
STATED ODDS 1:11

2006 Alias Season Four Regrets

COMPLETE SET (6) 8.00 20.00
COMMON CARD (1-6) 1.50 4.00
STATED ODDS 1:17

2006 Alias Season Four Promos

P1 General Distribution 1.50 4.00
P2 Non-Sport Update 1.00 2.50
Pi Inkworks.com Exclusive 2.50 6.00
PSD San Diego Comic Con .75 2.00
PUK UK Exclusive 1.00 2.50

2017 Alien

COMPLETE SET (100) 10.00 25.00
UNOPENED BOX (18 PACKS) 120.00 130.00
UNOPENED PACK (5 CARDS) 6.00 8.00
COMMON CARD (1-100) .25 .60
*SILVER FOIL: 2X TO 5X BASIC CARDS 1.25 3.00
*BLUE FOIL/99: 4X TO 10X BASIC CARDS 2.50 6.00
*RED FOIL/25: 6X TO 15X BASIC CARDS 4.00 10.00
*CANVAS/15: 15X TO 40X BASIC CARDS 10.00 25.00
SHADOW BOX ALIEN EGG ODDS 1:270 HOBBY/ePACK
AES1 Shadow Box Alien Egg SP 20.00 50.00

2017 Alien Aperture Autographs

STATED PRINT RUN 50 SER.#'d SETS
AA1 Tom Skerritt 50.00 100.00
AA2 Ian Holm 25.00 60.00
AA3 Veronica Cartwright 25.00 60.00
AA4 Sigourney Weaver 400.00 600.00
AA5 Yaphet Kotto 30.00 75.00

AA6 Ron Shusett 60.00 120.00
AA7 Chris Foss 50.00 100.00

2017 Alien Deleted Scenes

COMPLETE SET (5) 8.00 20.00
COMMON CARD (DS1-DS5) 2.50 6.00
STATED ODDS 1:10 HOBBY/ePACK
DS1 Ripley and Parker 2.50 6.00
DS2 Ripley Soothes Lambert 2.50 6.00
DS3 Entering the Derelict 2.50 6.00
DS4 Airlock Sequence 2.50 6.00
DS5 Cocooned Dallas 2.50 6.00

2017 Alien Dual Stasis Signatures

COMMON CARD (SSD1-SSD5) 20.00 50.00
GROUP A ODDS 1:6,300
GROUP B ODDS 1:1,575
GROUP C ODDS 1:450
GROUP D ODDS 1:394
STATED ODDS 1:180 HOBBY/ePACK
SSD1 Weaver/Holm A 300.00 450.00
SSD3 Kotto/Shusett B 30.00 75.00
SSD4 Skeritt/Holm C 30.00 75.00
SSD5 Cartwright/Skeritt C 30.00 75.00

2017 Alien How It's Done

COMPLETE SET (5) 8.00 20.00
COMMON CARD (HID1-HID5) 2.50 6.00
STATED ODDS 1:10 HOBBY/ePACK

2017 Alien Inside the Nostromo

COMPLETE SET (6) 10.00 25.00
COMMON CARD (NOS1-NOS6) 2.00 5.00
STATED ODDS 1:10 HOBBY/ePACK

2017 Alien Nostromo Minerals Ore Relics

COMPLETE SET (3) 75.00 150.00
COMMON RELIC (MO1-MO3) 25.00 60.00
STATED ODDS 1:270 HOBBY/ePACK
MO1 Bismuth 30.00 75.00
MO3 Cobalt 30.00 75.00

2017 Alien Paranoid Android

COMPLETE SET (5) 8.00 20.00
COMMON CARD (PA1-PA5) 2.50 6.00
STATED ODDS 1:10 HOBBY/ePACK

2017 Alien Robot Parts Manufactured Relics

COMPLETE SET (3) 60.00 120.00
COMMON MEM (R1-R3) 15.00 40.00
STATED ODDS 1:270 HOBBY/ePACK
R1 Synthetic Core 30.00 75.00

2017 Alien Semiotic Manufactured Patches

COMPLETE SET W/O EPACK (29) 120.00 250.00
COMMON CARD 4.00 10.00
STATED ODDS 1:18 HOBBY/ePACK
SP0 Coffee/E-Pack 15.00 40.00

2017 Alien Special Order 937

COMPLETE SET (10) 10.00 25.00
COMMON CARD (SO1-SO10) 1.50 4.00
STATED ODDS 1:7 HOBBY/ePACK

2017 Alien Stasis Signatures

COMMON AUTO (SSS1-SSS7) 10.00 25.00
GROUP A ODDS 1:3,127
GROUP B ODDS 1:241
GROUP C ODDS 1:139
GROUP D ODDS 1:109
STATED ODDS 1:48 HOBBY/ePACK
SSS1 Sigourney Weaver A 300.00 500.00
SSS2 Ian Holm B 25.00 60.00
SSS3 Yaphet Kotto D 25.00 60.00
SSS4 Veronica Cartwright D 15.00 40.00
SSS5 Tom Skeritt B 25.00 60.00

2017 Alien Triple Stasis Signatures

COMMON CARD (SST1-SST5) 50.00 100.00
GROUP A ODDS 1:6,307
GROUP B ODDS 1:3,154
GROUP C ODDS 1:2,102
GROUP D ODDS 1:733
STATED ODDS 1:432 HOBBY/ePACK
SST1 Skeritt/Holm/Cartwright D 75.00 150.00
SST2 Foss/Kotto/Holm B 60.00 120.00
SST3 Cartwright/Shusett/Skeritt C 50.00 100.00
SST4 Kotto/Cartwright/Skeritt D 60.00 120.00
SST5 Weaver/Shusett/Kotto A 300.00 500.00

2017 Alien Weapons and Tools

COMPLETE SET (9) 8.00 20.00
COMMON CARD (WT1-WT9) 1.50 4.00
STATED ODDS 1:8 HOBBY/ePACK

2017 Alien Xeneology

COMPLETE SET (6) 8.00 20.00
COMMON CARD (X1-X6) 2.50 6.00
STATED ODDS 1:10 HOBBY/ePACK

1992 Star Pics Alien 3

COMPLETE SET (80) 5.00 12.00
UNOPENED BOX (36 PACKS) 10.00 20.00
UNOPENED PACK (10 CARDS) .50 .75
COMMON CARD (1-80) .12 .30

2021 Upper Deck Alien 3

COMPLETE SET (100) 10.00 25.00
UNOPENED BOX (15 PACKS) 100.00 150.00
UNOPENED PACK (8 CARDS) 6.00 10.00
COMMON CARD (1-100) .20 .50
*BARCODE: 1.2X TO 3X BASIC CARDS
*RUST: 4X TO 10X BASIC CARDS

2021 Upper Deck Alien 3 30th Anniversary Diamond Relic

30THCD Charles Dutton 60.00 150.00

2021 Upper Deck Alien 3 Behind-the-Scenes

COMPLETE SET (6) 4.00 10.00
COMMON CARD (BTS1-BTS6) 1.00 2.50
STATED ODDS 1:8

2021 Upper Deck Alien 3 Bishop Takes the Queen

COMPLETE SET (12) 6.00 15.00
COMMON CARD (BTQ1-BTQ12) 1.00 2.50
STATED ODDS 1:8

2021 Upper Deck Alien 3 Chest Burster

COMPLETE SET W/O SP (12) 100.00 200.00
COMMON CARD (CB1-CB12) 8.00 20.00
COMMON SP/50 (CB13-CB24) 30.00 75.00
STATED ODDS 1:16
CB12 Ripley 15.00 40.00
CB24 Ripley/50 50.00 100.00
CB25 Oxen/25 100.00 200.00
CB26 Oxen/25 100.00 200.00
CB27 Dog/15
CB28 Dog/15

2021 Upper Deck Alien 3 Choose Your Cut

COMPLETE SET (11) 5.00 12.00
COMMON CARD (CYC1-CYC11) .75 2.00
STATED ODDS 1:4

2021 Upper Deck Alien 3 Dillon's Dogma

COMPLETE SET (12) 6.00 15.00
COMMON CARD (DD1-DD12) 1.00 2.50
STATED ODDS 1:8

2021 Upper Deck Alien 3 The Dragon Inserts

COMPLETE SET (8) 4.00 10.00
COMMON CARD (TD1-TD8) .75 2.00
STATED ODDS 1:6

2021 Upper Deck Alien 3 Harmonious Brotherhood

COMPLETE SET (8) 4.00 10.00
COMMON CARD (HB1-HB8) .75 2.00
STATED ODDS 1:6

2021 Upper Deck Alien 3 The Lead Works

COMMON CARD (LW1-L15) 3.00 8.00
COMMON SP (LW16-LW25) 6.00 15.00
COMMON SP (LW26-LW32) 8.00 20.00
LW1-LW15 ODDS 1:24
LW16-LW25 ODDS 1:50
LW26-LW32 ODDS 1:200
LW29 It's Very Quick, Painless SP 15.00 40.00

2021 Upper Deck Alien 3 The Lead Works Autographs

STATED PRINT RUN 25 SER.#'d SETS
LWCD Charles S. Dutton 40.00 100.00
LWCF Christopher Fairbank 25.00 60.00
LWCJ Christopher John Fields 50.00 120.00
LWDW Danny Webb 40.00 100.00
LWLH Lance Henriksen
LWPG Peter Guinness 30.00 75.00
LWPM Paul McGann 50.00 120.00
LWRB Ralph Brown 30.00 75.00
LWVN Vincenzo Nicoli 25.00 60.00

2021 Upper Deck Alien 3 Chest Burster Minis

COMPLETE SET (20) 50.00 120.00
COMMON CARD (M1-M20) 3.00 8.00
INSIDE CHEST BURSTER CARDS
M11 Aaron 5.00 12.00
M12 Dillon 5.00 12.00
M13 Murphy 5.00 12.00
M14 Rains 5.00 12.00
M15 Jude 5.00 12.00
M16 Golic 5.00 12.00
M17 Gregor 5.00 12.00
M18 Dillon 5.00 12.00
M19 Clemens 5.00 12.00
M20 Ripley 8.00 20.00

2021 Upper Deck Alien 3 Mug Shots Autograph Inscriptions

COMMON AUTO 5.00 12.00
RANDOMLY INSERTED INTO PACKS
MSCD Charles S. Dutton 15.00 40.00
MSDU Charles S. Dutton 15.00 40.00
MSLH Lance Henriksen 15.00 40.00

2021 Upper Deck Alien 3 Mug Shots Autographs

COMMON AUTO 4.00 10.00
STATED ODDS 1:28
MSCD Charles S. Dutton 10.00 25.00
MSCF Christopher Fairbank 6.00 15.00
MSDU Charles S. Dutton 10.00 25.00
MSDW Danny Webb 5.00 12.00
MSLH Lance Henriksen 20.00 50.00
MSPG Peter Guinness 5.00 12.00
MSPM Paul McGann 5.00 12.00
MSVN Vincenzo Nicoli 6.00 15.00

2021 Upper Deck Alien 3 Mug Shots Autographs Green

*GREEN: X TO X BASIC CARDS
STATED ODDS 1:60
MSSW Sigourney Weaver
MSWE Sigourney Weaver

2021 Upper Deck Alien 3 Mug Shots Dual Autographs

COMMON AUTO
STATED ODDS 1:240
DACD D.Webb/C.Dutton 50.00 100.00
DADP D.Webb/P.McGann 50.00 100.00

2016 Alien Anthology

COMPLETE SET (100) 8.00 20.00
UNOPENED BOX (20 PACKS) 200.00 300.00
UNOPENED PACK (5 CARDS) 10.00 15.00
COMMON CARD (1-100) .20 .50
*SILVER: .60X TO 2X BASIC CARDS

2016 Alien Anthology Autographs

COMMON AUTO 6.00 15.00
STATED ODDS 1:20 W/OTHER AUTOS AND SKETCHES
SABP Bill Paxton 60.00 120.00
SACD Charles S. Dutton 15.00 40.00
SACH Carrie Henn 12.00 30.00
SADP Dominique Pinon 10.00 25.00
SAHS Harry Dean Stanton 50.00 100.00
SAIH Ian Holm EPACK 20.00 50.00
SALH Lance Henriksen 50.00 100.00
SAMR Mark Rolston 12.00 30.00
SAPR Paul Reiser 30.00 75.00
SARP Ron Perlman 15.00 40.00
SASW Sigourney Weaver 300.00 500.00
SATS Tom Skerritt 30.00 80.00
SAVC Veronica Cartwright 15.00 40.00

2016 Alien Anthology Character Bios

COMPLETE SET (12) 12.00 30.00
COMMON CARD 2.00 5.00
STATED ODDS 1:8

2016 Alien Anthology Dual Autographs

STATED ODDS 1:20 W/OTHER AUTOS AND SKETCHES
DACH Henriksen/Henn 100.00 200.00
DACS Stanton/Cartwright 60.00 120.00
DADD Dance/Dutton 25.00 60.00
DAHR Rolston/Henriksen 30.00 75.00
DAHS Skerritt/Holm 50.00 100.00
DAPH Paxton/Henriksen 100.00 200.00
DAPR Rolston/Paxton 90.00 175.00
DAPW Paxton/Weaver 200.00 400.00
DARH Henn/Reiser 30.00 75.00
DASC Skerritt/Cartwright 30.00 75.00
DASH Stanton/Holm 50.00 100.00
DASS Stanton/Skerritt 30.00 75.00
DAVH Cartwright/Holm 30.00 80.00
DAWH Weaver/Henn 150.00 300.00
DAWS Weaver/Skerritt 200.00 400.00

2016 Alien Anthology Legendary Encounters Art

COMPLETE SET (10) 12.00 30.00
COMMON CARD (LA1-LA10) 2.00 5.00
STATED ODDS 1:8

2016 Alien Anthology Legendary Game Art Autographs

COMMON CARD (LA1-LA10) 6.00 15.00
STATED ODDS 1:20 W/OTHER AUTOS AND SKETCHES

2016 Alien Anthology Space Marine Dog Tags

COMPLETE SET (15) 75.00 150.00
COMMON CARD 5.00 12.00
STATED ODDS 1:20

2016 Alien Anthology Weyland Yutani Propaganda Poster Autographs

COMPLETE SET (10) 50.00 100.00
COMMON CARD (WY1-WY10) 5.00 12.00
STATED PRINT RUN 70 SER.#'d SETS
ALL CARDS ARE SIGNED BY
PATTY MCPANCAKES EARP

2016 Alien Anthology Weyland Yutani Propaganda Posters

COMPLETE SET (10) 15.00 40.00
COMMON CARD (WY1-WY10) 2.50 6.00
STATED ODDS 1:8

1998 Inkworks Alien Legacy

COMPLETE SET (90) 5.00 12.00
UNOPENED BOX (36 PACKS) 60.00 100.00
UNOPENED PACK (8 CARDS) 2.00 3.00
COMMON CARD (1-90) .15 .40
RE1 STATED ODDS 1:108
RE1 Alien Acid Bath SP 6.00 15.00

1998 Inkworks Alien Legacy DVD Collection

COMPLETE SET (9) 5.00 12.00
COMMON CARD (AU1-AU9) .75 2.00
*K-MART VIDEO: SAME VALUE
ISSUED IN ALIEN DVD COLLECTION

MODERN

1998 Inkworks Alien Legacy Evolution of Ripley

COMPLETE SET (4) 6.00 15.00
COMMON CARD (C21-C24) 2.00 5.00
STATED ODDS 1:27

1998 Inkworks Alien Legacy Poster Gallery

COMPLETE SET (9) 6.00 15.00
COMMON CARD (CP1-CP9) 1.00 2.50
STATED ODDS 1:17

1990 FTCC Alien Nation

COMPLETE SET (60) 4.00 10.00
UNOPENED BOX (36 PACKS) 20.00 40.00
UNOPENED PACK (5 CARDS) 1.00 1.50
COMMON CARD (1-60) .10 .25

2004 Alien vs. Predator

COMPLETE SET (90) 4.00 10.00
UNOPENED BOX (36 PACKS) 70.00 80.00
UNOPENED PACK (7 CARDS) 2.50 3.00
COMMON CARD (1-90) .10 .30

2004 Alien vs. Predator Autographs

COMPLETE SET (8) 60.00 120.00
COMMON AUTO (A1-A7) 6.00 15.00
STATED ODDS 1:36
A1 Sanaa Lathan 20.00 50.00

2004 Alien vs. Predator Blood Hunters

COMPLETE SET (3) 5.00 12.00
COMMON CARD (BL1-BL3) 2.00 5.00
STATED ODDS 1:36

2004 Alien vs. Predator Pieceworks

COMPLETE SET (7) 25.00 60.00
COMMON MEM (PW1-PW7) 5.00 12.00
STATED ODDS 1:36

2004 Alien vs. Predator Survival of the Fiercest Puzzle

COMPLETE SET (9) 10.00 25.00
COMMON CARD (SF1-SF9) 1.50 4.00
STATED ODDS 1:11

2004 Alien vs. Predator Deadliest Game

COMPLETE SET (6) 6.00 15.00
COMMON CARD (DG1-DG6) 1.50 4.00
STATED ODDS 1:17

2004 Alien vs. Predator Promos

Pi Alien IW 2.50 6.00
PUK Predator UK 2.50 6.00
AVPSD2004 Predator SDCC 1.50 4.00

2007 Alien vs. Predator Requiem

COMPLETE SET (81) 4.00 10.00
UNOPENED BOX (24 PACKS) 40.00 60.00
UNOPENED PACK (8 CARDS) 2.00 2.50
COMMON CARD (1-81) .10 .30
CL1 STATED ODDS ONE PER CASE

2007 Alien vs. Predator Requiem Autographs

COMMON AUTO (A1-A10) 5.00 10.00
STATED ODDS 1:BOX
A1 Reiko Aylesworth 30.00 60.00
A2 John Ortiz 6.00 15.00
A4 Kristen Hager 15.00 30.00
A5 Ariel Gade 10.00 20.00
A7 Gina Holden 15.00 30.00
A9 Robert Joy 6.00 15.00
A10 Ian Whyte 6.00 15.00

2007 Alien vs. Predator Requiem Battlefield on Earth Puzzle

COMPLETE SET (9) 4.00 10.00
COMMON CARD (B1-B9) .75 2.00
STATED ODDS 1:11

2007 Alien vs. Predator Requiem Deadly

COMPLETE SET (3) 4.00 10.00
COMMON CARD (D1-D3) 2.00 5.00
STATED ODDS 1:24

2007 Alien vs. Predator Requiem Massacre on Main Street

COMPLETE SET (6) 4.00 10.00
COMMON CARD (M1-M6) 1.25 3.00
STATED ODDS 1:17

2007 Alien vs. Predator Requiem Pieceworks

COMMON MEM (PW1-PW12) 4.00 10.00
STATED ODDS 1:BOX
PW12A, PW12B ISSUED AS MULTI-CASE INCENTIVES
PW1 Kelly 8.00 20.00
PW3B Sheriff Morales Fur 8.00 20.00
PW6 Jesse 8.00 20.00
PW7 Molly 10.00 25.00
PW9 Ricky 8.00 20.00
PW10 Darcy 6.00 15.00
PW12A Dallas MCI 25.00 50.00
PW12B Kelly MCI 25.00 50.00
PWR1 Redemption card EXCH

2007 Alien vs. Predator Requiem Promos

COMMON CARD 2.00 5.00
APSD2007 SDCC Exclusive 4.00 10.00

1994 Comic Images Alien World of Wayne Barlowe

COMPLETE SET (90) 4.00 10.00
UNOPENED BOX (48 PACKS) 20.00 30.00
UNOPENED PACK (10 CARDS) .75 1.00
COMMON CARD (1-90) .10 .25
P1 The Alien World of Wayne Barlowe Promo .75 2.00
RC Jumbo Card (5-1/4 x 8, images of 90-card Corben base
MWB Wayne Barlowe Medallion 10.00 25.00
AUWB Wayne Barlowe AU/500* 20.00 50.00

1994 Comic Images Alien World of Wayne Barlowe Case Bonus

COMPLETE SET (4) 25.00 60.00
COMMON CARD 8.00 20.00
STATED ODDS 1:CASE

1994 Comic Images Alien World of Wayne Barlowe Prisms

COMPLETE SET (6) 5.00 12.00
COMMON CARD (1-6) 1.50 4.00
STATED ODDS 1:18

1994 Comic Images Alien World of Wayne Barlowe Space Traveler

COMPLETE SET (3) 10.00 25.00
COMMON CARD (1-3) 4.00 10.00
RANDOMLY INSERTED INTO PACKS

2018 Aliens

COMPLETE SET (100) 10.00 25.00
UNOPENED BOX (20 PACKS) 100.00 120.00
UNOPENED PACK (5 CARDS) 5.00 6.00
COMMON CARD (1-100) .20 .50
*ALIEN BLOOD: 3X TO 8X BASIC CARDS
*SYNTHETIC/99: 6X TO 15X BASIC CARDS
*ACID BLOOD/25: 10X TO 25X BASIC CARDS

2018 Aliens Actor Reactor Autograph Inscriptions

GROUP A ODDS 1:915
GROUP B ODDS 1:549
GROUP C ODDS 1:441
STATED ODDS 1:193
ARBI Lance Henriksen 60.00 120.00
Bishop B
ARBU Paul Reiser 75.00 150.00
I Made a Bad Call A
ARCB Paul Reiser 75.00 150.00
Carter Burke A
ARCD Cynthia Scott 20.00 50.00
Corporal Dietrich C
ARJJ Christopher Henn 30.00 75.00
Timmy Jorden C
ARJO Carrie Henn 50.00 100.00
Can I Dream? B
ARLB Lance Henriksen 100.00 200.00
Not Bad… A
ARLG William Hope 20.00 50.00
Lieutenant Gorman C
ARPF Ricco Ross 10.00 25.00
Private Frost C
ARPS Daniel Kash 10.00 25.00
Private Spunkmeyer C
ARRJ Carrie Henn 50.00 100.00
Newt B
ARCF1 Colette Hiller 60.00 120.00
Corporal Ferro B
ARCF2 Colette Hiller 60.00 120.00
We're in the Pipe… B
ARPD1 Mark Rolston 50.00 100.00
Private Drake A
ARPD2 Mark Rolston 50.00 100.00
They Ain't Payin… B

2018 Aliens Actor Reactor Autographs

COMMON AUTO 10.00 25.00
GROUP A ODDS 1:915
GROUP B ODDS 1:549
GROUP C ODDS 1:441
GROUP D ODDS 1:46
STATED ODDS 1:38
ARBI Lance Henriksen C 25.00 60.00
ARBU Paul Reiser B 30.00 75.00
ARCB Paul Reiser B 30.00 75.00
ARER Sigourney Weaver A 300.00 500.00
ARJJ Christopher Henn D 12.00 30.00
ARJO Carrie Henn C 20.00 50.00
ARLB Lance Henriksen C 25.00 60.00
ARLG William Hope D 12.00 30.00
ARRI Sigourney Weaver A 300.00 500.00
ARRJ Carrie Henn C 20.00 50.00

2018 Aliens Actor Reactor Dual Autographs

GROUP A ODDS 1:10,440
GROUP B ODDS 1:1,253
GROUP C ODDS 1:1,044
STATED OVERALL ODDS 1:540
DRBB L.Henriksen/P.Reiser B 100.00 200.00
DRBG P.Reiser/W.Hope B 60.00 120.00
DRCD C.Hiller/D.Kash C 20.00 50.00
DRDD M.Rolston/C.Scott C 30.00 60.00
DRFD R.Ross/M.Rolston B 60.00 120.00
DRFS R.Ross/D.Kash B 20.00 50.00
DRJG C.Henn/W.Hope B 60.00 120.00
DRJJ Carrie & Christopher Henn C 25.00 60.00
DRRB S.Weaver/L.Henriksen A 400.00 800.00
DRRN S.Weaver/C.Henn/E-Pack 400.00 800.00

2018 Aliens Alien Skin

COMPLETE SET W/SP (25) 100.00 200.00
COMPLETE SET W/O SP (15) 12.00 30.00
COMMON CARD (AS1-AS15) 1.50 4.00
COMMON SP (AS16-AS20) 6.00 15.00
COMMON SP (AS21-AS25) 10.00 25.00
STATED ODDS (AS1-AS15) 1:11
STATED ODDS (AS16-AS20) 1:81
STATED ODDS (AS21-AS25) 1:162

2018 Aliens Colonial Marines

COMPLETE SET (10) 6.00 15.00
COMMON CARD (CS01-CS010) 1.00 2.50
STATED ODDS 1:5

2018 Aliens Locked and Loaded

COMPLETE SET (10) 6.00 15.00
COMMON CARD (ABA1-ABA10) 1.00 2.50
STATED ODDS 1:5

2018 Aliens Look Into My Eye

COMPLETE SET (10) 6.00 15.00
COMMON CARD (EEH1-EEH10) 1.00 2.50
STATED ODDS 1:5

2018 Aliens Weyland-Yutani Plexi Business Card Autographs

COMMON AUTO 10.00 25.00
GROUP A ODDS 1:6,840
GROUP B ODDS 1:3,420
GROUP C ODDS 1:570
GROUP D ODDS 1:297
STATED OVERALL ODDS 1:180
WYBI Lance Henriksen C 30.00 75.00
WYCB Paul Reiser B 100.00 200.00
WYLG William Hope C 12.00 30.00
WYPD Mark Rolston C 20.00 50.00
WYPF Ricco Ross D 25.00 60.00
WYPS Daniel Kash D 20.00 50.00
WYRI Sigourney Weaver A 500.00 1000.00
WYRJ Carrie Henn C 30.00 75.00

2018 Aliens Weyland-Yutani Plexi Business Cards

COMPLETE SET (11) 50.00 100.00
COMMON CARD (WY1-WY11) 3.00 8.00
STATED ODDS 1:23
WY0 Alien Egg/E-Pack
WY00 Facehugger/E-Pack
WY000 Alien Queen/E-Pack
WY1 Ripley 6.00 15.00
WY3 Private Frost 4.00 10.00
WY6 Bishop 5.00 12.00
WY7 Carter Burke 8.00 20.00
WY8 Private Drake 4.00 10.00
WY10 Lt. Gorman 6.00 15.00
WY11 Timmy Jorden 4.00 10.00

1992 Fantasma Aliens Among Us Limited Edition

UNOPENED FACTORY SET (8 CARDS) 6.00 15.00
COMMON CARD (1-8) 1.25 3.00

1994 Topps Aliens Predator Universe

COMPLETE SET (87) 6.00 15.00
UNOPENED BOX (36 PACKS) 20.00 50.00
UNOPENED PACK (9 CARDS) 1.00 1.50
COMMON CARD (1-72) .15 .40
COMMON CARD (A1-A15) .40 1.00
OPERATION ALIENS STATED ODDS 1:1

1994 Topps Aliens Predator Universe Topps Finest Chromium

COMPLETE SET (6) 10.00 25.00
COMMON CARD (1-6) 3.00 8.00
STATED ODDS 1:17

1994 Topps Aliens Predator Universe Promos

COMPLETE SET (3) 2.00 5.00
COMMON CARD .75 2.00

2019 Alita Motorball Champions

COMPLETE SET (14) 75.00 150.00
COMMON CARD 5.00 12.00
NNO Ajakutty 6.00 15.00
NNO Alita 15.00 40.00
NNO Claymore 6.00 15.00
NNO Kumaza 10.00 25.00
NNO Mace 10.00 25.00
NNO Stinger 6.00 15.00
NNO Zariki 6.00 15.00

1991 Star Pics All My Children

COMPLETE SET (72) 6.00 15.00
COMPLETE BOX FACTORY SET (72) 8.00 20.00
UNOPENED BOX (36 PACKS) 10.00 20.00
UNOPENED PACK (10 CARDS) .50 .75

1991 Star Pics All My Children ABC Soaps

COMPLETE SET (6) .75 2.00
COMMON CARD (A-F) .40 1.00
RANDOM INSERT IN PACKS

1991 Star Pics All My Children Autographs

COMMON AUTO 6.00 15.00
KR Kelly Ripa 30.00 75.00
SL Susan Lucci 25.00 60.00

1996 Upper Deck All-Time Toons

COMPLETE SET (108) 6.00 15.00
COMPLETE BOX FACTORY SET (153) 50.00 100.00
UNOPENED BOX (36 PACKS) 15.00 25.00
UNOPENED PACK (5 CARDS) .50 .75
COMMON CARD (1-108) .10 .25
CI1 PROMO IS OVERSIZED 4 1/2 X 2 1/2
CI1A The Rabbit of Seville 2.00 5.00
CI1B Rabbit of Seville PROMO 2.50 6.00
(excludes 'The' from title)

1996 Upper Deck All-Time Toons Classic Ink

COMPLETE SET (15) 15.00 40.00
COMMON CARD (CI1-CI15) 2.00 5.00
STATED ODDS 1:12

1996 Upper Deck All-Time Toons Time Capsule

COMPLETE SET (15) 6.00 15.00
COMMON CARD (TC1-TC15) .75 2.00
STATED ODDS 1:3

2013 Alphas Season One

COMPLETE SET (60) 5.00 12.00
UNOPENED BOX (24 PACKS) 50.00 75.00
UNOPENED PACK (5 CARDS) 2.50 3.00
COMMON CARD (1-60) .15 .40

2013 Alphas Season One Autographs

COMMON AUTO (A1-A9) 8.00 20.00
STATED ODDS 1:24
A1 Ryan Cartwright 10.00 25.00
A2 Warren Christie 15.00 40.00
A3 Azita Ghanizada 20.00 50.00
A4 Laura Mennell 15.00 40.00
A6 Mahershala Ali 50.00 100.00
A9 Liane Balaban 10.00 25.00

2013 Alphas Season One Behind the Alphas

COMPLETE SET (9) 12.00 30.00
COMMON CARD (CH1-CH9) 2.00 5.00
STATED ODDS 2:24

2013 Alphas Season One Dual Wardrobes

COMMON WARDROBE 8.00 20.00
STATED ODDS 1:96

2013 Alphas Season One Alphas Team

COMPLETE SET (7) 10.00 25.00
COMMON CARD (CB1-CB7) 2.50 6.00
STATED ODDS 2:24

2013 Alphas Season One Wardrobes

COMMON WARDROBE (M1-M11) 5.00 12.00
STATED ODDS 1:24
M11 ISSUED AS ALBUM EXCLUSIVE
M1 Rachel Pirzad 8.00 20.00
M8 Gary Bell (jacket) 6.00 15.00
M9 Gary Bell (shirt) 6.00 15.00
M10 Nina Theroux 8.00 20.00
M11 Rachel Pirzad ALB

1985 Sanitarium Amazing Animals of the World

COMPLETE SET (12) 2.00 5.00
COMMON CARD (1-12) .25 .60

2009 America at War Band of Brothers Series 1

COMPLETE SET (192) 30.00 75.00
UNOPENED BOX (24 PACKS) 75.00 100.00
UNOPENED PACK (8 CARDS) 3.00 4.00
COMMON CARD (1-192) .25 .60

2009 America at War Band of Brothers Series 1 Veteran Autographs

COMMON AUTO 20.00 50.00
SP3 & SP9 ARE UNSIGNED

2009 America at War Band of Brothers Series 1 Promo Inserts

COMPLETE SET (4) 4.00 10.00
COMMON CARD (AD1-AD4) 1.25 3.00

2009 America at War Band of Brothers Series 1 Promos

COMMON PROMO .75 2.00
CH1 Coming September 2009 CECE/NSU 1.25 3.00
PH1 Coming September 2009 PHILLY/NSU 1.25 3.00

1992 America's Most Wanted Promos

COMPLETE SET (9) 10.00 25.00
COMMON CARD (UNNUMBERED) 1.50 4.00

1993 Collect-a-Card American Bandstand

COMPLETE SET (100) 6.00 15.00
UNOPENED BOX (36 PACKS) 10.00 25.00
UNOPENED PACK (8 CARDS) .30 .75
COMMON CARD (1-100) .12 .30
NNO Super Embossed Hologram 4.00 10.00
NNO Uncut Sheet

1993 Collect-a-Card American Bandstand Legends Signatures

COMPLETE SET (3) 25.00 60.00
COMMON CARD (1-3) 10.00 25.00
STATED PRINT RUN 100 SERIAL #'d SETS

1995 Kitchen Sink Press American Beauties and Cuties

COMPLETE BOXED SET (37) 6.00 15.00
COMMON CARD (1-36) .25 .60
COVER CARD IS UNNUMBERED

2004 American Chopper

COMPLETE SET (50) 5.00 12.00
UNOPENED HOBBY BOX (24 PACKS) 15.00 40.00
UNOPENED RETAIL BOX (8 PACKS) 10.00 15.00
UNOPENED PACK (5 CARDS + INSERT) 1.00 1.50
COMMON CARD (1-50) .15 .40

2004 American Chopper Autographs

COMPLETE SET (5) 150.00 250.00
COMMON CARD (UNNUMBERED) 20.00 50.00
NNO Mikey 50.00 100.00
NNO Paul Teutel Jr. 25.00 60.00
NNO Paul Teutel Sr. 50.00 100.00

2004 American Chopper Cool Threads

COMPLETE SET (6) 60.00 120.00
COMMON CARD (CT1-CT6) 8.00 20.00
STATED ODDS 1:120
CT1 Paul Sr 15.00 40.00
CT2 Paul Jr. 10.00 25.00
CT5 Paul Sr. 15.00 40.00
CT6 Paul Jr. 10.00 25.00

1991 Topps American Gladiators

COMPLETE SET (88) 3.00 8.00
COMPLETE SET W/STICKERS (99) 5.00 12.00
UNOPENED BOX (36 PACKS) 10.00 15.00
UNOPENED PACK (8 CARDS + STICKER) .40 .50
COMMON CARD (1-88) .05 .15

1991 Topps American Gladiators Stickers

COMPLETE SET (11) 4.00 10.00
COMMON CARD (1-11) .50 1.50
STATED ODDS 1:1

2013 American Horror Story Previews

COMPLETE SET (12) 15.00 30.00
COMMON CARD (AP1-AP12) 1.50 4.00

2013 American Horror Story Previews Autograph Costumes

COMMON AUTO (ACAP1-ACAP2) 25.00 60.00
STATED ODDS 1:
ACAP2 Evan Peters Shirt/100 30.00 75.00

2013 American Horror Story Previews Autographs

COMMON AUTO 20.00 50.00
EPP Evan Peters/150 50.00 100.00
ZQP Zachary Quinto/50 60.00 120.00

2013 American Horror Story Previews Costumes

COMMON CARD 10.00 25.00

2013 American Horror Story Previews Foil

COMPLETE SET (6) 10.00 25.00
COMMON CARD (APC1-APC6 2.00 5.00

2013 American Horror Story Previews Promos

COMPLETE SET (7) 8.00 20.00
COMMON CARD 2.00 5.00

2014 American Horror Story Album

COMPLETE SET (2) 6.00 15.00
COMMON CARD 4.00 10.00

2014 American Horror Story Autographs

COMMON AUTO 4.00 10.00
ZQR1 ISSUED AS 3-CASE INCENTIVE
AR1 Sarah Paulson 15.00 40.00
ABR1 Alexandra Breckenridge 20.00 50.00
ABR2 Alexandra Breckenridge 30.00 75.00
CBR1 Connie Britton 15.00 40.00
CER1 Christine Estabrook 6.00 15.00
DMR1 Dylan McDermott/100 15.00 40.00
DMR2 Dylan McDermott/100 15.00 40.00
DOR1 D.O'Hare Hat 6.00 15.00
DOR2 D.O'Hare No Hat 6.00 15.00
EPR1 Evan Peters Sweater/100 30.00 75.00
EPR2 Evan Peters Shirt/100 30.00 75.00
FCR1 Frances Conroy 10.00 25.00
JBR1 Jamie Brewer 8.00 20.00
LRR1 Lily Rabe 20.00 50.00
ROR1 Rosa Salazar 30.00 75.00
SPR1 Sarah Paulson 15.00 40.00
TFR1 Taissa Farmiga 25.00 60.00
ZQR1 Zachary Quinto/100 3CI 25.00 60.00
ZQR2 Zachary Quinto/100 20.00 50.00

2014 American Horror Story Creepiest Moments

COMPLETE SET (9) 4.00 10.00
COMMON CARD (1-9) .75 2.00
STATED ODDS 1:12

2014 American Horror Story Dual Autographs

COMMON AUTO 20.00 50.00
AR2 C.Britton/S.Paulson 30.00 75.00
AMR1 D.McDermott/C.Britton 30.00 75.00
AMR2 D.McDermott/D.O'Hare 25.00 60.00
AMR3 C.Britton/T.Farmiga 50.00 100.00
AMR6 A.Breckenridge/F.Conroy 50.00 100.00
AMR7 E.Peters/T.Farmiga 50.00 120.00
AMR8 S.Paulson/C.Britton 25.00 60.00

2014 American Horror Story Puzzle

COMPLETE SET (9) 5.00 12.00
COMMON CARD (ARP1-ARP9) .75 2.00
STATED ODDS 1:12

2014 American Horror Story Quotes

COMPLETE SET (9) 4.00 10.00
COMMON CARD (ARQ1-ARQ9) .75 2.00
STATED ODDS 1:12

2014 American Horror Story Wardrobes

COMMON WARDROBE (ARC1-ARC34) 8.00 20.00
STATED ODDS 3:BOX WITH AUTOS
ARC1 E.Peters/J.Lange/87 15.00 40.00
ARC2 E.Peters/J.Lange/105 12.00 30.00
ARC3 E.Peters/J.Lange/115 12.00 30.00
ARC4 Peters/McDermott/133 12.00 30.00
ARC5 Peters/McDermott/80 15.00 40.00
ARC6 E.Peters/J.Lange/90 15.00 40.00
ARC9 Peters/McDermott/99 15.00 40.00
ARC10 E.Peters/R.Schmidt/98 12.00 30.00
ARC11 Peters/McDermott/101 12.00 30.00
ARC14 Lange/McDermott/115 12.00 30.00
ARC16 Lange/McDermott/95 12.00 30.00
ARC18 Lange/McDermott/95 12.00 30.00
ARC20 J.Lange/E.Peters/118 12.00 30.00
ARC25 J.Lange/E.Peters/99 15.00 40.00
ARC28 Evan Peters/75 15.00 40.00
ARC31 Dylan McDermott/95 15.00 40.00
ARC32 Evan Peters 12.00 30.00
ARC33 Jessica Lange/102 12.00 30.00

2014 American Horror Story Promos

COMMON CARD 1.25 3.00
ARA Evan Peters 8.00 20.00
ARD T.Farmiga/Peters/99 15.00 40.00
APRR Burned man/99 20.00 50.00
ARRR Fist to forehead/99 12.00 30.00
ARUK T.Farmiga/.Peters 8.00 20.00
CHI1 Taissa Farmiga 8.00 20.00
CHI2 Evan Peters 8.00 20.00

2014 American Horror Story SDCC Mystery Packs Woodgrain Autographs

COMMON AUTO 4.00 10.00
ABC Alexandra Breckenridge 20.00 50.00
BSC Bodhi Schulz 12.00 30.00
CBC Connie Britton 20.00 50.00
CEC Christine Estabrook 5.00 12.00
DOC Denis O'Hare 5.00 12.00
FCC Frances Conroy 6.00 15.00
LRC Lily Rabe 20.00 50.00
MRC Matt Ross 5.00 12.00
RSC Riley Schmidt 5.00 12.00
SPC Sarah Paulson 20.00 50.00
TFC Taissa Farmiga 30.00 75.00

2016 American Horror Story Asylum

COMPLETE SET (72) 6.00 15.00
COMPLETE FACTORY SET (87) 80.00 120.00
COMMON CARD (1-72) .20 .50
*FOIL: 5X TO 12X BASIC CARDS
FACTORY SETS CONTAIN 1 BASE SET, 1 PARALLEL, 8 AUTO/RELICS, AND 6 CHASE INSERTS

2016 American Horror Story Asylum Autographed Wardrobe Materials

COMMON AUTO 15.00 40.00
SOME AUTOS CONTAIN INSCRIPTIONS
ACS Chloe Sevigny 30.00 80.00
AEP Evan Peters
AJC James Cromwell 12.00 30.00
ALR Lily Rabe 25.00 60.00
AZQ Zachary Quinto 25.00 60.00

2016 American Horror Story Asylum Autographs

COMMON AUTO 8.00 20.00
SOME AUTOS CONTAIN INSCRIPTIONS
ABO Britne Oldford 10.00 25.00
ACS Chloe Sevigny 25.00 60.00
ADM Dylan McDermott/50 12.00 30.00
AEP Evan Peters 30.00 80.00
AFC Frances Conroy 10.00 25.00
AJC James Cromwell/50 15.00 40.00
AJF Joseph Fiennes 12.00 30.00
ALR Lily Rabe/5 15.00 40.00
ANG Naomi Grossman 12.00 30.00
ASP Sarah Paulson 12.00 30.00
AZQ Zachary Quinto 50.00 100.00

2016 American Horror Story Asylum Costume Prop Relics

COMPLETE SET (6) 60.00 120.00
COMMON PROP 8.00 20.00

MODERN

RANDOMLY INSERTED INTO PACKS
CP1 Peters/Quinto/Cromwell/Lange 10.00 25.00
CP5 Sarah Paulson Book Cover 10.00 25.00
CP6 Jessica Lange Leg Restraints 10.00 25.00

2016 American Horror Story Asylum Costume Relics

COMPLETE SET (15) 150.00 300.00
COMMON RELIC 8.00 20.00
C4 Lily Rabe/65 20.00 50.00
C5 Evan Peters/65 10.00 25.00
C6 Jessica Lange/5 10.00 25.00
C9 Zachary Quinto/65 10.00 25.00
C10 Zachary Quinto/65 10.00 25.00
C11 Sarah Paulson/65 12.00 30.00
C12 Sarah Paulson/65 12.00 30.00
C13 Lily Rabe/65 20.00 50.00
C14 Lily Rabe/65 20.00 50.00

2016 American Horror Story Asylum Dual Costume Relics

COMPLETE SET (20) 200.00 400.00
COMMON RELIC 10.00 25.00
CD1 Sevigny/Cromwell 12.00 30.00
CD5 Paulson/Quinto 12.00 30.00
CD7 Cromwell/Lange 12.00 30.00
CD11 Lange/Peters 12.00 30.00
CD12 Lange/Sevigny 12.00 30.00
CD13 Lange/Peters 12.00 30.00
CD18 Quinto/Lange 12.00 30.00
CD20 Lange/Rabe 15.00 40.00

2016 American Horror Story Asylum Into the Mind of Madness

COMPLETE SET (9) 12.00 30.00
COMMON CARD (MM1-MM9) 2.00 5.00
RANDOMLY INSERTED IN FACTORY SETS

2016 American Horror Story Asylum Prop Relics

COMPLETE SET (8) 80.00 150.00
COMMON CARD 6.00 15.00
P2 Lily Rabe Clippings & Ribbons/107 8.00 20.00
P6 Sarah Paulson Vinyl Record/5 10.00 25.00
P7 Sarah Paulson Book Cover/67 15.00 40.00
P8 Jessica Lange Leg Restraints/69 15.00 40.00

2016 American Horror Story Asylum Quad Costume Relics

COMPLETE SET (3) 30.00 80.00
COMMON RELIC 12.00 30.00

2016 American Horror Story Asylum Quotes Puzzle

COMPLETE SET (9) 6.00 15.00
COMMON CARD (Q1-Q9) 1.25 3.00
RANDOMLY INSERTED IN FACTORY SET

2016 American Horror Story Asylum Same-Scene Dual Costume Relics

COMPLETE SET (13) 150.00 300.00
COMMON RELIC (CSD1-CSD13) 10.00 25.00
CSD8 Lily Rabe/67 15.00 40.00
CSD10 Lily Rabe, Jessica Lange/67 12.00 30.00
CSD13 Jessica Lange/71 12.00 30.00

2016 American Horror Story Asylum Welcome to Briarcliff

COMPLETE SET (9) 6.00 15.00
COMMON CARD (WB1-WB9) 1.25 3.00
RANDOM INSERTS IN FACTORY SET

2004 American Idol Season Three

COMPLETE SET (89) 6.00 15.00
UNOPENED BOX (36 PACKS) 25.00 60.00
UNOPENED PACK (5 CARDS) 1.00 1.75
COMMON CARD (1-89) .15 .40
*SILVER: 1X TO 2.5X BASIC CARDS
*GOLD: 6X TO 15X BASIC CARDS

2004 American Idol Season Three Behind-the-Scenes

COMPLETE SET (15) 5.00 12.00
COMMON CARD (BS1-BS15) .40 1.00
STATED ODDS 1:4

2004 American Idol Season Three Idol Chatter

COMPLETE SET (32) 6.00 15.00
COMMON CARD (IC1-IC32) .40 1.00
STATED ODDS 1:6

2004 American Idol Season Three Reality Bits

COMPLETE SET (12) 200.00 350.00
COMMON CARD 5.00 12.00
*SILVER/100: .5X TO 1.2X BASIC CARDS
*GOLD/25: .75X TO 2X BASIC CARDS
OVERALL AUTO/MEM ODDS 1:18
RBFB Fantasia Barrino 8.00 20.00
RBJH Jennifer Hudson 15.00 40.00
RBJT Jasmine Trias 5.00 30.00

2004 American Idol Season Three Signed Sealed Delivered Autographs

COMMON AUTO 3.00 8.00
OVERALL AUTO/MEM ODDS 1:18
SSDAA Amy Adams 4.00 10.00
SSDCV Camile Velasco 5.00 12.00
SSDDD Diana DeGarmo 5.00 12.00
SSDFB Fantasia Barrino 5.00 12.00
SSDJH Jennifer Hudson 12.00 30.00
SSDJT Jasmine Trias 10.00 25.00
SSDRJ Randy Jackson 15.00 40.00
SSDRS Ryan Seacrest 12.00 30.00
SSDLL2 Leah LaBelle 4.00 10.00

2005 American Idol Season Four

COMPLETE SET (80) 6.00 15.00
UNOPENED BOX (36 PACKS) 20.00 50.00
UNOPENED PACK (5 CARDS) 1.00 1.50
COMMON CARD (1-80) .15 .40
*GOLD: 1.2X TO 3X BASIC CARDS
*PLATINUM: 4X TO 10X BASIC CARDS

2005 American Idol Season Four Behind-the-Scenes

COMPLETE SET (15) 6.00 15.00
COMMON CARD (BS1-BS15) .50 1.25
STATED ODDS 1:4

2005 American Idol Season Four Idol Chatter

COMPLETE SET (24) 8.00 20.00
COMMON CARD (IC1-IC24) .40 1.00
STATED ODDS 1:6
IC2 Jessica Sierra .75 2.00
IC12 Carrie Underwood 1.50 4.00

2005 American Idol Season Four Reality Bits

COMMON CARD 5.00 12.00
*SILVER: .5X TO 1.2X BASIC CARDS
*GOLD: .8X TO 2X BASIC CARDS
OVERALL AUTO/MEM ODDS 1:18
RBCU Carrie Underwood 15.00 30.00

2005 American Idol Season Four Signed Sealed Delivered Autographs

COMMON AUTO 3.00 8.00
*SILVER/100: .6X TO 1.5X BASIC AUTOS
*GOLD/25: .75X TO 2X BASIC AUTOS
OVERALL AUTO/MEM ODDS 1:18
SSCJS Jessica Sierra 10.00 25.00
SSDBB Bo Bice 5.00 12.00
SSDCM Constantine Maroulis 6.00 15.00
SSDCU Carrie Underwood 200.00 400.00
SSDLC Lindsey Cardinale 6.00 15.00
SSDMG Mikalah Gordon 8.00 20.00
SSDNS Nikko Smith 5.00 12.00
SSDSS Scott Savol 4.00 10.00
SSDVS Vonzell Solomon 4.00 10.00

2007 American Idol Season Six

COMPLETE SET (72) 4.00 10.00
UNOPENED BOX (36 PACKS) 25.00 40.00
UNOPENED PACK (6 CARDS) 1.00 1.25
COMMON CARD (1-72) .10 .25

2007 American Idol Season Six Autographs

COMPLETE SET (12) 80.00 150.00
COMMON AUTO 3.00 8.00
STATED ODDS 1:15
NNO Gina Glocksen 4.00 10.00
NNO Jordin Sparks 30.00 80.00

2009 American Idol Season Eight

COMPLETE SET (97) 60.00 120.00
COMMON CARD (1-30) .15 .40
COMMON CARD (31-61) .20 .50
COMMON CARD (62-97) 1.50 4.00
31-61 ARE SWEEPSTAKES ENTRIES
62-97 ARE LENTICULAR
SWEEPSTAKES STATED ODDS 1:1
LENTICULAR STATED ODDS 1:8
SP: RANDOM INSERT IN PACKS
13 Carrie Underwood .40 1.00
18 Clay Aiken .30 .75
19 Kelly Clarkson .30 .75
27 Bikini Girl .30 .75
44 David Cook .30 .75
45 David Cook .30 .75
46 William Hung .30 .75
54 Carrie Underwood .50 1.25
59 Clay Aiken .40 1.00
60 Kelly Clarkson .40 1.00
63 Kris Allen 4.00 10.00
70 Megan Corkrey 3.00 8.00
72 Anoop Desai 2.50 6.00
75 Danny Gokey 6.00 15.00
76 Alexis Grace 3.00 8.00
82 Adam Lambert 20.00 40.00
90 Lil Rounds 3.00 8.00
NNO Beyonce
Madonna SP
NNO Bruce Springsteen
Diddy SP

2009 American Idol Season Eight Autographs

COMMON AUTO 3.00 8.00
STATED ODDS 1:12 HOBBY, 1:65 RETAIL
NNO Adam Lambert 125.00 250.00
NNO Alexis Grace 8.00 20.00
NNO Allison Iraheta 6.00 15.00
NNO Ann Marie Boskovich 4.00 10.00
NNO Anoop Desai 5.00 12.00
NNO Carly Smithson 10.00 25.00
NNO Casey Carlson 6.00 15.00
NNO Danny Gokey 8.00 20.00
NNO David Archuleta (gray background) 60.00 60.00
NNO David Archuleta (red background) 25.00 60.00
NNO Elliot Yamin 6.00 15.00
NNO Fantasia Barrino 10.00 25.00
NNO Felicia Barton 5.00 12.00
NNO Jasmine Murray 4.00 10.00
NNO Jesse Langseth 4.00 10.00
NNO Jordin Sparks 15.00 40.00
NNO Kris Allen 6.00 15.00
NNO Kristen McNamara 5.00 12.00
NNO Matt Giraud 5.00 12.00
NNO Megan Corkrey 30.00 60.00
NNO Michael Johns 10.00 25.00
NNO Mishavonna Henson 4.00 10.00
NNO Ricky Braddy 4.00 10.00
NNO Scott MacIntyre 5.00 12.00
NNO Stephen Fowler 4.00 10.00
NNO Stevie Wright 6.00 15.00
NNO Tatiana Del Toro 4.00 10.00

2011 American Pie

COMPLETE SET (200) 50.00 120.00
UNOPENED HOBBY BOX (24 PACKS) 300.00 500.00
UNOPENED HOBBY PACK (8 CARDS) 15.00 20.00
UNOPENED RETAIL BOX (24 PACKS)
UNOPENED RETAIL PACK (6 CARDS)
UNOPENED BONUS BOX (8 PACKS)
UNOPENED BONUS PACK (6 CARDS)
COMMON CARD (1-200) .20 .50
*FOIL: 1X TO 2.5X BASIC CARDS
*SPOTLIGHT FOIL/76: 5X TO 12X BASIC CARDS
100 Jimi Hendrix .40 1.00
104 John Wayne .25 .60
106 Johnny Cash .25 .60
108 John Lennon .25 .60
122 Apple Founded 4.00 10.00
162 Seinfeld Premieres 12.00 30.00
166 Freddie Mercury Tribute 2.00 5.00
170 Kurt Cobain Suicide 10.00 25.00
196 Kanye Interrupts Swift 75.00 200.00
199 Steve Jobs 1955-2011 8.00 20.00

2011 American Pie American Pieces Relics

COMPLETE SET (4) 60.00 120.00
COMMON RELIC 15.00 40.00
STATED ODDS 1:176
APCRGB Gettysburg 15.00 40.00
APCRGK Grassy Knoll 30.00 75.00
APCRSL Statue of Liberty 20.00 50.00

2011 American Pie Autograph Relics

COMPLETE SET (35) 500.00 900.00
COMMON AUTO 4.00 10.00
STATED ODDS 1:250
EXCHANGE DEADLINE 11/30/2014
APAR1 Mickey Rooney 100.00 200.00
APAR2 A.J. Hammer 6.00 15.00
APAR3 Maksim Chmerkovskiy 10.00 25.00
APAR4 Shanna Moakler EXCH 12.00 30.00
APAR5 Trista Sutter 10.00 25.00
APAR6 Kato Kaelin 10.00 25.00
APAR7 Joe Gannascoli 8.00 20.00
APAR9 Andrew Zimmern EXCH 10.00 25.00
APAR10 John O'Hurley EXCH 8.00 20.00
APAR11 Tia Carrere 15.00 40.00
APAR12 Tom Arnold EXCH 12.00 30.00
APAR13 Paul Teutul, Sr. 15.00 40.00
APAR14 Joey Fatone EXCH 10.00 25.00
APAR15 Gilbert Gottfried 20.00 50.00
APAR16 Dean Cain 15.00 40.00
APAR18 Sean Astin 8.00 20.00
APAR19 Buddy Valastro 12.00 30.00
APAR20 Carmen Electra 30.00 75.00
APAR21 Jack Hanna EXCH 12.00 30.00
APAR23 Naomi Judd 20.00 50.00
APAR24 Susan Lucci 25.00 60.00
APAR25 Butch Patrick 15.00 40.00
APAR26 John Ratzenberger 15.00 40.00
APAR28 Bret Michaels EXCH 25.00 60.00
APAR29 Don McLean 60.00 120.00
APAR30 Wilmer Valderrama 12.00 30.00
APAR31 Henry Winkler 50.00 100.00
APAR33 Vincent Pastore 12.00 30.00
APAR35 Carrot Top 8.00 20.00
APAR36 Enrique Iglesias EXCH 15.00 40.00
APAR37 Louie Anderson 8.00 20.00
APAR38 Jamie Foxx EXCH 75.00 150.00

2011 American Pie Autographs

COMMON AUTO 4.00 10.00
STATED ODDS 1:61
EXCHANGE DEADLINE 11/30/2014
APA1 Mickey Rooney 60.00 120.00
APA3 Maksim Chmerkovskiy 8.00 20.00
APA4 Shanna Moakler 6.00 15.00
APA6 Kato Kaelin 10.00 25.00
APA8 Jimmie Walker 8.00 20.00
APA9 Andrew Zimmern 12.00 30.00
APA10 John O'Hurley 6.00 15.00
APA11 Tia Carrere 30.00 75.00
APA12 Tom Arnold 10.00 25.00
APA13 Paul Teutul, Sr. 10.00 25.00
APA14 Joey Fatone 8.00 20.00
APA15 Gilbert Gottfried 10.00 25.00
APA16 Dean Cain 8.00 20.00
APA18 Sean Astin 15.00 40.00
APA19 Buddy Valastro 8.00 20.00
APA20 Carmen Electra 25.00 60.00

APA21 Jack Hanna 10.00 25.00
APA23 Naomi Judd 12.00 30.00
APA24 Susan Lucci 20.00 50.00
APA25 Butch Patrick 10.00 25.00
APA26 John Ratzenberger 12.00 30.00
APA28 Bret Michaels 15.00 40.00
APA29 Don McLean 30.00 75.00
APA30 Wilmer Valderrama 10.00 25.00
APA31 Henry Winkler 25.00 60.00
APA33 Vincent Pastore 10.00 25.00
APA35 Carrot Top 5.00 12.00
APA36 Enrique Iglesias EXCH 12.00 30.00
APA37 Louie Anderson 6.00 15.00
APA38 Bob Costas 15.00 40.00
APA39 Jamie Foxx 50.00 100.00
ACSH Charlie Sheen 125.00 250.00

2011 American Pie Coin Collection Dime

COMMON RELIC 12.00 30.00
STATED PRINT RUN 25 SER. #'d SETS
APCC2 John Wayne 25.00 60.00
APCC3 Marilyn Monroe 100.00 200.00
APCC4 Groucho Marx 15.00 40.00
APCC5 Humphrey Bogart 15.00 40.00
APCC7 Clark Gable 50.00 100.00
APCC8 Gary Cooper 20.00 50.00
APCC9 Christopher Reeve EXCH 20.00 50.00
APCC11 Jimi Hendrix 25.00 60.00
APCC15 Walt Disney 60.00 120.00

2011 American Pie Coin Collection Half-Dollar

COMMON RELIC 12.00 30.00
STATED PRINT RUN 25 SER. #'d SETS
APCC2 John Wayne 25.00 60.00
APCC3 Marilyn Monroe 200.00 350.00
APCC4 Groucho Marx 15.00 40.00
APCC5 Humphrey Bogart 15.00 40.00
APCC7 Clark Gable 25.00 60.00
APCC8 Gary Cooper 20.00 50.00
APCC9 Christopher Reeve EXCH 20.00 50.00
APCC11 Jimi Hendrix 25.00 60.00
APCC15 Walt Disney 25.00 60.00

2011 American Pie Coin Collection Penny

COMMON CARD (APCC1-APCC15) 12.00 30.00
*NICKEL/25: SAME VALUE
*DIME/25: SAME VALUE
*QUARTER/25: SAME VALUE
*HALF-DOLLAR/25: SAME VALUE
STATED PRINT RUN 25 SER. #'d SETS
APCC2 John Wayne 25.00 60.00
APCC3 Marilyn Monroe 60.00 120.00
APCC4 Groucho Marx 15.00 40.00
APCC5 Humphrey Bogart 15.00 40.00
APCC7 Clark Gable 25.00 60.00
APCC8 Gary Cooper 20.00 50.00
APCC9 Christopher Reeve EXCH 20.00 50.00
APCC11 Jimi Hendrix 25.00 60.00
APCC15 Walt Disney 25.00 60.00

2011 American Pie Fads and Fashions

COMPLETE SET (30) 12.00 30.00
COMMON CARD (FF1-FF30) .75 2.00
STATED ODDS 1:4

2011 American Pie Hirsute History

COMPLETE SET (20) 12.00 30.00
COMMON CARD (HH1-HH20) 1.00 2.50
STATED ODDS 1:6

2011 American Pie Hollywood Sign Letter Patches

COMPLETE SET (25) 120.00 250.00
COMMON PATCH (HSLP1-HSLP25) 5.00 12.00
STATED ODDS 1:93
STATED PRINT RUN 25 SER. #'d SETS
HSLP2 Bob Hope 6.00 15.00
HSLP3 Buster Keaton 6.00 15.00
HSLP4 Cary Grant 6.00 15.00
HSLP6 Charlie Chaplin 8.00 20.00
HSLP7 Clark Gable 8.00 20.00
HSLP9 Elizabeth Taylor 8.00 20.00
HSLP11 Frank Sinatra 8.00 20.00
HSLP15 Groucho Marx 8.00 20.00
HSLP16 Humphrey Bogart 6.00 15.00
HSLP19 John Wayne 10.00 25.00
HSLP20 Marilyn Monroe 15.00 40.00

2011 American Pie Hollywood Walk of Fame

COMPLETE SET (50) 15.00 40.00
COMMON CARD (HWF1-HWF50) .75 2.00
STATED ODDS 1:3
HWF18 Jimi Hendrix 1.25 3.00
HWF20 John Lennon 1.00 2.50
HWF21 John Wayne 1.00 2.50
HWF22 Johnny Cash 1.00 2.50
HWF25 Marilyn Monroe 1.50 4.00

2011 American Pie Hollywood Walk of Fame Patches

COMPLETE SET (50) 450.00 700.00
COMMON PATCH (HWF1-HWF50) 6.00 15.00
STATED PRINT RUN 50 SER. #'d SETS
HWF4 Cary Grant 8.00 20.00
HWF5 Christopher Reeve 8.00 20.00
HWF6 Chuck Berry 8.00 20.00
HWF7 Dean Martin 8.00 20.00
HWF9 Elizabeth Taylor 10.00 25.00
HWF10 Frank Sinatra 8.00 20.00
HWF13 Gene Roddenberry 8.00 20.00
HWF14 George Carlin 8.00 20.00
HWF18 Jimi Hendrix 10.00 25.00
HWF19 John Belushi 8.00 20.00
HWF20 John Lennon 8.00 20.00
HWF21 John Wayne 15.00 40.00
HWF22 Johnny Cash 8.00 20.00
HWF25 Marilyn Monroe 15.00 40.00
HWF28 Richard Pryor 8.00 20.00
HWF30 Walt Disney 8.00 20.00
HWF32 Groucho Marx 8.00 20.00
HWF44 Harry Houdini 8.00 20.00

2011 American Pie Relics

COMPLETE SET (36) 200.00 350.00
COMMON RELIC 2.50 6.00
STATED ODDS 1:13
EXCHANGE DEADLINE 11/30/2014
Apr-03 Maksim Chmerkovskiy 3.00 8.00
Apr-04 Shanna Moakler EXCH 4.00 10.00
Apr-09 Andrew Zimmern EXCH 3.00 8.00
Apr-11 Tia Carrere 4.00 10.00
Apr-13 Paul Teutul, Sr. 4.00 10.00
Apr-14 Joey Fatone 3.00 8.00
Apr-16 Dean Cain 3.00 8.00
Apr-20 Carmen Electra 5.00 12.00
Apr-21 Jack Hanna EXCH 6.00 15.00
Apr-23 Naomi Judd 4.00 10.00
Apr-24 Susan Lucci 5.00 12.00
Apr-28 Bret Michaels EXCH 8.00 20.00
Apr-31 Henry Winkler 3.00 8.00
Apr-34 Jimi Hendrix EXCH 125.00 200.00
Apr-36 Enrique Iglesias EXCH 8.00 20.00
Apr-38 Jamie Foxx EXCH 6.00 15.00

2011 American Pie Stamp Collection

STATED PRINT RUN 76 SER. #'d SETS
APSC1 Johnny Cash 25.00 50.00
APSC5 John Wayne 40.00 80.00
APSC6 James Stewart 20.00 40.00
APSC8 Frank Sinatra 20.00 40.00
APSC9 Mickey Rooney 20.00 40.00
APSC10 Marlon Brando 30.00 60.00
APSC11 Marilyn Monroe 40.00 80.00
APSC12 Grace Kelly 25.00 50.00
APSC13 Elizabeth Taylor 25.00 50.00
APSC15 Lucille Ball 20.00 40.00

2001 American Pride Commemorative Stickers

COMPLETE SET (45) 4.00 10.00
UNOPENED BOX (48 PACKS) 30.00 40.00
UNOPENED PACK (5 STICKERS) 1.00 1.25
COMMON CARD (1-45) .15 .40

1992-93 Champs American Vintage Cycles

COMPLETE SET (200) 6.00 15.00
COMP.SER. 1 SET (100) 4.00 10.00
COMP.SER. 2 SET (100) 4.00 10.00
UNOPENED SERIES 1 BOX (36 PACKS) 10.00 25.00
UNOPENED SERIES 1 PACK (12 CARDS) .30 .75
UNOPENED SERIES 2 BOX (36 PACKS) 12.00 30.00
UNOPENED SERIES 2 PACK (12 CARDS) .40 1.00
COMMON CARD (1-200) .12 .30

1992-93 Champs American Vintage Cycles Foil Sport Figures

COMPLETE SET (3) 2.50 6.00
COMMON CARD (FC1-FC3) 1.00 2.50
RANDOM INSERT IN SERIES 2 PACKS
FC1 Mitch Frerotte 1.00 2.50
FC2 Kenny Lofton 1.00 2.50
FC3 Jerry Glanville 1.00 2.50

1992 Starline Americana

COMPLETE SET (250) 8.00 20.00
UNOPENED BOX (36 PACKS) 15.00 25.00
UNOPENED PACK (12 CARDS) .75 1.00
COMMON CARD (1-250) .12 .30
2 Abraham Lincoln .30 .75
10 George Washington .20 .50
13 Wyatt Earp 1.25 3.00
17 Geronimo .60 1.50
26 Albert Einstein 1.25 3.00
28 George S. Patton 1.25 3.00
39 Thomas Jefferson .75 2.00
46 Thomas Edison .75 2.00
83 Ronald Reagan 1.25 3.00
90 Theodore Roosevelt .60 1.50
200 Martin Luther King Jr. .75 2.00
237 Jackie Robinson .40 1.00
245 Babe Ruth 1.50 4.00

1992 Starline Americana Promos

COMPLETE SET (7) 6.00 15.00
COMMON CARD (SKIP #'d) 1.50 4.00
2 Abraham Lincoln 2.00 5.00
10 George Washington 2.00 5.00

2011 Americana

COMPLETE SET (100) 12.00 25.00
UNOPENED HOBBY BOX (4 PACKS) 200.00 300.00
UNOPENED HOBBY PACK (5 CARDS) 50.00 75.00
COMMON CARD (1-100) .40 1.00
*RETAIL: .3X TO .75X HOBBY
*SILVER PROOF/100: 1.5X TO 4X BASIC CARDS
*GOLD PROOF/50: 2.5X TO 6X BASIC CARDS
1 Pamela Anderson 1.00 2.50
5 Justin Bieber .75 2.00
6 Ric Flair .75 2.00

2011 Americana Casting Call Quad Autographs

STATED PRINT RUN 10-25
4 Charl/Pearl/Deez/Donn /25 30.00 60.00

2011 Americana Casting Call Triple Autographs

STATED PRINT RUN 5-25
1 Nielsen/Borgnine/Stevens /17 100.00 150.00
3 Hegyes/Palillo/H-Jacobs /25 30.00 60.00

2011 Americana Celebrity Cut Autographs

COMMON AUTO 7.00 15.00
STATED PRINT RUN 5-99
1A Josie Davis /20 10.00 20.00
2A Peter Mayhew /20 20.00 40.00
2B Peter Mayhew /20 20.00 40.00
2C Peter Mayhew /20 20.00 40.00
3 Bonnie Piesse /50 12.00 25.00
4A Tony Todd /20 12.00 25.00
4B Tony Todd /20 12.00 25.00
4C Tony Todd /20 12.00 25.00
5 Daniel Logan /99 10.00 20.00
6 Linda Evans /20 15.00 30.00
7 Jane Russell /8
8 Christina Applegate /20 30.00 60.00
9 Joey Lawrence /20 10.00 20.00
10A Brigitte Nielsen /20 20.00 40.00
10B Brigitte Nielsen /20 20.00 40.00
10C Brigitte Nielsen /20 20.00 40.00
10D Brigitte Nielsen /40 20.00 40.00
11 Ron Howard 75.00 150.00
12A Dom DeLuise /15 20.00 40.00
12B Dom DeLuise /25 20.00 40.00
13 Doug Jones /20 10.00 20.00
14 Hugh O'Brian /40 20.00 40.00
15 Josh Duhamel /20 30.00 60.00
16A Larry Hagman /20 20.00 40.00
16B Larry Hagman /10 25.00 50.00
16C Larry Hagman /20 20.00 40.00
17 Margaret O'Brien /9
18A Michael Pare /50 20.00 40.00
18B Michael Pare /25 20.00 40.00
19 Richard Anderson /30 20.00 40.00
1B Josie Davis /10 10.00 20.00
20 Richard Kiel /50 20.00 40.00
21A Stella Stevens /30 12.00 25.00
21B Stella Stevens /30 12.00 25.00
21C Stella Stevens /30 12.00 25.00
22A Warwick Davis /20 20.00 40.00
22B Warwick Davis /20 20.00 40.00
22C Warwick Davis /20 20.00 40.00
25 Michael Madsen /10
26A Bo Hopkins /10
27 Corey Feldman /10 30.00 60.00
28 John Hurt /20 25.00 50.00
29A Pasha Lychnikoff /20 10.00 20.00
29B Pasha Lychnikoff /20 10.00 20.00
30A Alan Ruck /20 10.00 20.00
30B Alan Ruck /20 10.00 20.00
32A Jeffrey Tambor /20 12.00 25.00
32B Jeffrey Tambor /20 12.00 25.00
32C Jeffrey Tambor /10 15.00 30.00
33 D.Van Valkenburgh /15
34 Erin Moran /10
35A Clint Howard /10 20.00 40.00
35B Clint Howard /5 20.00 40.00
37 Willie Aames /5
38A Kenny Baker /30 20.00 40.00
38B Kenny Baker /30 20.00 40.00
39 Lawrence Hilton-Jacobs /40 10.00 20.00
40A Robert Hegyes /40 10.00 20.00
40B Robert Hegyes /10 10.00 20.00
42B Michael Beck /15 25.00 50.00
42C Michael Beck /40 12.00 25.00
43 George A. Romero /75 30.00 60.00
44 Tom Savini 12.00 30.00
45A Donna Pescow /40 10.00 20.00
45B Donna Pescow /40 10.00 20.00
46A Paul Le Mat /40 10.00 20.00
46B Paul Le Mat /35 10.00 20.00
48A Barry Pearl /20 10.00 20.00
48B Barry Pearl /40 10.00 20.00
48C Barry Pearl /15 10.00 20.00
49A Annette Charles /40 12.00 25.00
49B Annette Charles /35 12.00 25.00
50 Edd Byrnes /60 10.00 20.00
51 Eddie Deezen /60 12.00 25.00
52A Barry Bostwick /20 10.00 20.00
52B Barry Bostwick /20 10.00 20.00
52C Barry Bostwick /40 10.00 20.00
52D Barry Bostwick /10 12.00 25.00
53A Ele. Avellan/Eli. Avellan /20 20.00 40.00
53B Electra Avellan /30 15.00 30.00
53C Electra Avellan /15 15.00 30.00
54 Elise Avellan /30 15.00 30.00
55A Ed Asner /40 12.00 25.00
55B Ed Asner /40 12.00 25.00
57A Anson Williams /20 12.00 25.00
57B Anson Williams /25 12.00 25.00
58 Tab Hunter
59A Dina Meyer /20 20.00 40.00
59B Dina Meyer /50 20.00 40.00
59C Dina Meyer /40 15.00 30.00
62 Catherine Hicks /15

63A Shawnee Smith /20 20.00 40.00
63B Shawnee Smith /20 20.00 40.00
63C Shawnee Smith /20 20.00 40.00
63D Shawnee Smith /40 20.00 40.00
64A Lisa Marie /40 10.00 20.00
64B Lisa Marie /19 10.00 20.00
65A Martin Kove /20
65B Martin Kove /10
67A Daniel Baldwin /20 12.00 25.00
67B Daniel Baldwin /80 12.00 25.00
69A Bruce Davison /20 12.00 25.00
69B Bruce Davison /30 12.00 25.00
70A John Saxon /40 12.00 25.00
70B John Saxon /20 12.00 25.00

2011 Americana Co-Stars Materials

COMMON CARD 6.00 15.00
*SILVER SCREEN: .5X TO 1.25X BASIC CARDS
*GOLDEN ERA: .6X TO 1.5X BASIC CARDS
STATED PRINT RUN 25-249
1 J.Dean/N.Wood
2 J.Dean/R.Hudson
7 B.Davis/N.Wood/99 8.00 20.00
8 A.Gardner/L.Nielsen/89 8.00 20.00

2011 Americana Co-Stars Signatures

STATED PRINT RUN 5-49
NO PRICING ON CARDS #'d 20 OR LESS
2 Margot Kidder/Noel Neill /49 25.00 50.00
4 G.Kennedy/L.Nielsen /49 35.00 70.00
6 L.Hamilton/R.Carradine /49 30.00 60.00
10 Luke Goss/Val Kilmer /20 20.00 40.00
11 M.Dolenz/P.Tork /29 25.00 50.00
15 D.Hart/H.O'Brian /30 15.00 30.00
18 G.Kennedy/W.Forsythe /25 20.00 40.00
20 B.Nielsen/C.Haim /49 25.00 50.00

2011 Americana Combo Cuts Autographs

STATED PRINT RUN 10-25
NO PRICING ON CARDS #'d 15 OR LESS
1 Ventimiglia/Gray-Cabey /25 10.00 20.00
4 Josie Davis/Willie Aames /20 15.00 30.00
5 McDowell/Feldman /20 40.00 80.00
6 P.Mayhew/K.Baker /25 35.00 70.00
8 Hilton-Jacobs/Palillo /25 15.00 30.00
9 R.Hegyes/R.Palillo /25 15.00 30.00
10 Pare/Van Valkenburgh /25 10.00 20.00
13 Tony Todd/Tom Savini /20 25.00 50.00
14 Bo Hopkins/Paul Le Mat /25 20.00 40.00
15 R.Kleiser/J.Donnelly /25 10.00 20.00
16 A.Charles/B.Pearl /25 15.00 30.00
17 E.Byrnes/E.Deezen /25 10.00 20.00
18 A.Williams/E.Moran /25
19 Alan Ruck/Barry Bostwick /10
20 Ele. Avellan/Eli.Avellan /25 25.00 50.00
21 C.Feldman/C.Haim /22 75.00 125.00
27 Ed Asner/M.Boatman /20 15.00 30.00

2011 Americana Matinee Legends

COMPLETE SET (20) 10.00 20.00
COMMON CARD (1-20) .75 2.00
1 James Dean 1.50 3.00
2 Bettie Page 1.50 3.00

2011 Americana Matinee Legends Materials

COMMON CARD 5.00 12.00
*SILVER SCREEN/99: .5X TO 1.2X BASIC/499
*GOLDEN ERA/49: .6X TO 1.5X BASIC/499
*SUPER STARS/25: 1.5X TO 3X BASIC/499
STATED PRINT RUN 499 SER. #'d SETS
1 James Dean/5
2 Bettie Page 20.00 40.00
4 Ingrid Bergman 6.00 15.00
5 Bette Davis 6.00 15.00
6 Ava Gardner 6.00 15.00
10 Natalie Wood 8.00 20.00
12 Peter Sellers/99 6.00 15.00
13 Jayne Mansfield 8.00 20.00
16 Hedy Lamarr/49 6.00 15.00
17 Jean Harlow 6.00 15.00
19 Leslie Howard/59 6.00 15.00

2011 Americana Movie Posters Dual Materials

COMMON CARD 8.00 20.00
STATED PRINT RUN 499 SER. #'d SETS
2 Hayworth/Mature 10.00 25.00
4 Jean Harlow/Clark Gable 10.00 25.00
6 S.McQueen/R.Wagner 15.00 30.00
7 Jerry Lewis/Donna Reed 15.00 30.00
13 Cary Grant/Grace Kelly 15.00 30.00
14 Bogart/K.Hepburn 10.00 25.00
18 J.Russell/M.Monroe 20.00 40.00
19 Gary Cooper/Grace Kelly 10.00 25.00
31 Clark Gable/Vivien Leigh 15.00 30.00
32 Vivien Leigh/Clark Gable 15.00 30.00
33 Clark Gable/Vivien Leigh 15.00 30.00
34 Vivien Leigh/Clark Gable 15.00 30.00
35 C.Colbert/C.Gable 10.00 25.00
36 M.Monroe/J.Russell 20.00 40.00
38 Natalie Wood/Sal Mineo 10.00 25.00
40 K.Hepburn/Cary Grant 10.00 25.00
41 M.Monroe/C.Jones 20.00 40.00
42 C.Jones/M.Monroe 20.00 40.00
43 Deborah Kerr/Donna Reed 10.00 25.00
49 A.Hepburn/Bogart 15.00 30.00
50 G.Peck/A.Hepburn 15.00 30.00
51 M.Astor/H.Bogart 10.00 25.00

2011 Americana Movie Posters Materials

COMMON CARD 8.00 20.00
STATED PRINT RUN 499 SER. #'d SETS
2 Rita Hayworth 10.00 25.00
4 Jean Harlow 15.00 30.00
6 Steve McQueen 20.00 40.00
11 Mae West 15.00 30.00
12 Mae West 15.00 30.00
14 Humphrey Bogart/250 10.00 25.00
15 Shirley Temple 15.00 30.00
16 Liza Minelli 15.00 30.00
24 Leslie Howard/99 10.00 25.00
26 Elizabeth Taylor/250 10.00 25.00
31 Clark Gable/99 15.00 30.00
32 Vivien Leigh/250 10.00 25.00
33 Clark Gable/99 15.00 30.00
34 Vivien Leigh/250 10.00 25.00
36 Marilyn Monroe/350 20.00 40.00
37 Grace Kelly 10.00 25.00
38 Natalie Wood 10.00 25.00
40 Katharine Hepburn/300 10.00 25.00
41 Marilyn Monroe 15.00 30.00
42 Carolyn Jones 10.00 25.00
44 Liza Minelli 15.00 30.00
49 Audrey Hepburn 15.00 30.00
54 Bing Crosby/99 10.00 25.00

2011 Americana Movie Posters Quad Materials

6 McQ/Wagn/Vaug/Hold
53 Quin/Lamo/Cros/Hope 20.00 40.00

2011 Americana Movie Posters Triple Materials

COMMON CARD 10.00 25.00
STATED PRINT RUN 20-499
6 McQueen/Wagner/Vaughn /50 40.00 80.00
24 Howard/Davis/Bogart /20 75.00 125.00
26 Taylor/Clift/Winters /150 15.00 30.00
38 Wood/Mineo/Dean /50 75.00 125.00
49 Hepburn/Bogart/Holden /25 40.00 80.00

2011 Americana Prime Time Stars

COMPLETE SET (20) 6.00 15.00
COMMON CARD (1-20) .60 1.50
9 Pam Anderson 1.25 3.00
12 Selma Blair .75 2.00
19 Emmanuelle Chriqui .75 2.00

2011 Americana Prime Time Stars Director's Cut Signatures

COMMON CARD 10.00 20.00
STATED PRINT RUN 10-75
1A Linda Evans/20 15.00 30.00
1B Linda Evans/10
2 Erika Eleniak/40 12.00 25.00
3A Noel Neill/40 20.00 40.00
3B Noel Neill/60 20.00 40.00
4A Milo Ventimiglia/20
4B Milo Ventimiglia/15
5 Leslie Nielsen /40 30.00 60.00
6 Peter Tork/75 20.00 40.00
8A Erin Gray/40 15.00 30.00
8B Erin Gray/20 15.00 30.00
8C Erin Gray/40 15.00 30.00
9 Pam Anderson
10 Josie Davis
11 Linda Hamilton/20 40.00 80.00
12 Selma Blair/20 20.00 40.00
13 Piper Laurie/20
14 Luke Goss/20
15A Willie Aames/15
15B Willie Aames/20
16 Chris Noth
17 Lee Majors
18 Erin Moran/20
19A Emmanuelle Chriqui/20
19B Emmanuelle Chriqui/10
20 Michael Ontkean

2011 Americana Prime Time Stars Materials Big Screen

STATED PRINT RUN 10-49
5 Leslie Nielsen/29 12.00 25.00
6 Peter Tork/49 7.50 15.00
17 Lee Majors/49 12.00 25.00

2011 Americana Prime Time Stars Materials Small Screen

STATED PRINT RUN 125
5 Leslie Nielsen
9 Pam Anderson/125 20.00 40.00
13 Piper Laurie 5.00 12.00
17 Lee Majors/125 5.00 12.00

2011 Americana Prime Time Stars Signatures

COMMON CARD 8.00 15.00
STATED PRINT RUN 29-99
1 Linda Evans/29 15.00 30.00
2 Erika Eleniak/99 12.00 25.00
3 Noel Neill/29 15.00 30.00
5 Leslie Nielsen/49 20.00 40.00
6 Peter Tork/49 12.00 25.00
7 John Schneider/39 10.00 20.00
8 Erin Gray/99 10.00 20.00
9 Pam Anderson/29 50.00 100.00
10 Josie Davis
11 Linda Hamilton/99 20.00 40.00
12 Selma Blair/49 20.00 40.00
13 Piper Laurie
14 Luke Goss/49
16 Chris Noth
17 Lee Majors
18 Erin Moran/29 10.00 20.00
19 Emmanuelle Chriqui/95 40.00 80.00
20 Michael Ontkean

2011 Americana Prime Time Stars Signatures Materials

STATED PRINT RUN 29-49
4 Milo Ventimiglia/39 7.50 15.00
6 Peter Tork/49 10.00 20.00
7 John Schneider/29 10.00 20.00
9 Pam Anderson/29 50.00 100.00

2011 Americana Private Signings

COMMON CARD 4.00 10.00
STATED PRINT RUN 6-799
1 Pamela Anderson/29 50.00 100.00
2 Chris Noth/49 20.00 40.00
3 Burt Reynolds
4 Linda Hamilton/99 20.00 40.00
5 Justin Bieber/299 60.00 120.00
6 Ric Flair/99 50.00 100.00
8 Linda Evans/99 20.00 40.00
9 Selma Blair/99 25.00 50.00
10 John Schneider/99 10.00 20.00
12 Gloria Stuart
13 Josie Davis/49 10.00 20.00
14 Kenny Baker/49 15.00 30.00
15 Lawrence Hilton-Jacobs
17 Bo Hopkins/49
18 Michael Madsen/20 10.00 20.00
19 Daniel Logan/19
21 Charlene Tilton/25
22 Piper Laurie
25 Eric Roberts/49 6.00 15.00
26 Robert Vaughn/49 15.00 30.00
28 Sofia Milos/49 6.00 15.00
29 Tori Spelling/15
30 Willie Aames/49 6.00 15.00
31 David Carradine/49
32 Tony Todd/29 12.00 25.00
33 Christina Applegate
34 Tab Hunter
36 John Hurt/99 10.00 20.00
37 Scott Schwartz/199 6.00 15.00
38 Erin Moran/49 12.00 25.00
40 Alan Ruck/49 6.00 15.00
41 Barry Bostwick/49 10.00 20.00
42 Electra Avellan/99 10.00 25.00
43 Elise Avellan/99 10.00 20.00
44 Eileen Dietz/49 6.00 15.00
45 Erin Gray/49 10.00 20.00
46 Noel Neill/99 15.00 30.00
48 Patty Duke/49 15.00 30.00
49 Noureen DeWulf/99 10.00 20.00
50 Emmanuelle Chriqui/99 30.00 60.00
51 Barry Pearl/25 10.00 20.00
52 Corey Haim/149 30.00 60.00
53 Daniel Baldwin/29 10.00 20.00
56 Erika Eleniak/99 12.00 25.00
57 George A. Romero
58 James Duval/29 10.00 20.00
59 Jill-Michele Melean/19
60 Annette Charles/49 12.00 25.00
61 Meredith Salenger/39 10.00 20.00
62 Anson Williams/49 10.00 20.00
63 Micky Dolenz/19 15.00 30.00
64 Edd Byrnes/49 6.00 15.00
65 Mitzi Gaynor/29
67 George Kennedy/49 20.00 40.00
69 Joey Lawrence/49 6.00 15.00
70 Brigitte Nielsen/6
71 Peter Tork/39 15.00 30.00
72 Barry Williams/49 6.00 15.00
73 Ralph Macchio/49 15.00 30.00
75 Rhonda Fleming/29
76 Jeffrey Tambor
77 Katie Hoff/199 10.00 20.00
78 Lorna Luft/49 6.00 15.00
79 Barbara Morgan/49 20.00 40.00
82 Bill Pogue/25 30.00 60.00
83 Dean McDermott/15 20.00 40.00
84 Kathryn Thornton/59 20.00 40.00
85 Heidi Androl/59 15.00 30.00
87 Leslie Nielsen
88 Dick Gordon/15
90 D.Van Valkenburgh/199 10.00 20.00
91 Michelle Beadle/59 25.00 50.00
92 John Buccigross
93 Walt Cunningham/59 20.00 40.00
94 Fred Gregory/25 20.00 40.00
95 Ed Gibson/29 25.00 50.00
96 Tommy Chong/59 20.00 40.00
98 Willa Ford
99 John Kerr/49 12.00 25.00
100 Ami Dolenz/49 6.00 15.00

2011 Americana Private Stars Signature Materials

COMMON CARD 4.00 10.00
STATED PRINT RUN 10-249
NO PRICING ON CARDS #'d 20 OR LESS
1 Pamela Anderson/49 75.00 125.00
2 Chris Noth
3 Burt Reynolds
4 Linda Hamilton
5 Justin Bieber

6 Ric Flair/69 50.00 100.00
8 Linda Evans
9 Selma Blair
10 John Schneider/99 10.00 20.00
11 Marc McClure
12 Gloria Stuart/15
13 Josie Davis/49 12.00 25.00
14 Kenny Baker
15 Lawrence Hilton-Jacobs/25
16 Luke Goss
18 Michael Madsen
21 Charlene Tilton/25
22 Piper Laurie/18
24 Randal Kleiser
25 Eric Roberts/10
26 Robert Vaughn
27 Grayson Boucher
29 Tori Spelling/10
30 Willie Aames
31 David Carradine
32 Tony Todd/49 7.50 15.00
33 Christina Applegate/79 30.00 60.00
34 Tab Hunter/20 7.50 15.00
36 John Hurt/25 12.00 25.00
37 Scott Schwartz/249 7.50 15.00
38 Erin Moran
40 Alan Ruck
41 Barry Bostwick
42 Electra Avellan
43 Elise Avellan
44 Eileen Dietz
45 Erin Gray
46 Noel Neill
47 Jamie Donnelly
48 Patty Duke
49 Noureen DeWulf
50 Emmanuelle Chriqui
52 Corey Haim
56 Erika Eleniak
57 George A. Romero/99 20.00 40.00
60 Annette Charles
61 Meredith Salenger/99 10.00 20.00
62 Anson Williams/99 10.00 20.00
63 Micky Dolenz/24 12.00 25.00
64 Edd Byrnes
65 Mitzi Gaynor/99 7.50 15.00
67 George Kennedy
68 Pash Lychnikoff
70 Brigitte Nielsen
71 Peter Tork/149 12.00 25.00
73 Ralph Macchio
75 Rhonda Fleming/99 20.00 40.00
76 Jeffrey Tambor
77 Katie Hoff
78 Lorna Luft
79 Barbara Morgan/49
81 Peter Vanderkaay
82 Bill Pogue/99 15.00 30.00
83 Dean McDermott/10
84 Kathryn Thornton/189 12.00 25.00
85 Heidi Androl
86 Lenny Krayzelburg
87 Leslie Nielsen/119 30.00 60.00
88 Dick Gordon/99 25.00 50.00
90 Deborah Van Valkenburgh
91 Michelle Beadle
92 John Buccigross
93 Walt Cunningham/99 20.00 40.00
94 Fred Gregory/109 12.00 25.00
95 Ed Gibson/99 20.00 40.00
96 Tommy Chong
97 Robert Carradine
98 Willa Ford

2011 Americana ReCollection Buyback Signatures

1 Cindy Morgan 25.00 50.00
2 Karen Lynn Gorney/40 12.00 25.00
3 Micky Dolenz/33 25.00 50.00
4 Tatu/90 4.00 10.00
5 Peter Tork/38 20.00 40.00
6 John Schneider/55 20.00 40.00

2011 Americana Screen Gems

COMPLETE SET (20) 6.00 15.00
COMMON CARD (1-20) .60 1.50
2 Selma Blair .75 2.00
18 Justin Bieber 1.25 3.00

2011 Americana Screen Gems Director's Cut Autographs

COMMON CARD 7.50 15.00
PRINT RUN 4-99
1A Linda Hamilton /20 30.00 60.00
1B Linda Hamilton /20 30.00 60.00
1C Linda Hamilton /20 30.00 60.00
1D Linda Hamilton /20 30.00 60.00
2A Selma Blair /20 20.00 40.00
2B Selma Blair /20 20.00 40.00
2C Selma Blair /10 25.00 50.00
2D Selma Blair /4
3A Corey Haim /20 40.00 80.00
3B Corey Haim /41 30.00 60.00
4A Leslie Nielsen /60 30.00 60.00
4B Leslie Nielsen /20
4C Leslie Nielsen /40 30.00 60.00
4D Leslie Nielsen /20
5 George Kennedy /99 20.00 40.00
6 Robert Carradine
8A Gloria Stuart /40 20.00 40.00
8B Gloria Stuart /40 20.00 40.00
8C Gloria Stuart /20 20.00 40.00
9A Meredith Salenger /20 10.00 20.00
9B Meredith Salenger /20 10.00 20.00
9C Meredith Salenger /20 10.00 20.00
11 Willa Ford
12 Noureen DeWulf
14 Linda Evans /20 15.00 30.00
15 John Schneider /20 10.00 20.00
16A Erika Eleniak /19 12.00 25.00
16B Erika Eleniak /20 12.00 25.00
16C Erika Eleniak /20 12.00 25.00
17 Willie Aames /20 10.00 20.00
18 Justin Bieber
19A Josie Davis /10
19B Josie Davis /10
20A John Hurt /20 25.00 50.00
20B John Hurt /20 25.00 50.00

2011 Americana Screen Gems Material

COMMON CARD 3.00 8.00
*SILVER SCREEN/99: .5X TO 1.25X BASIC CARDS
*GOLDEN ERA/49: .6X TO 1.5X BASIC CARDS
PRINT RUN 99-249

2011 Americana Screen Gems Signature

COMMON CARD 10.00 20.00
PRINT RUN 29-99
1 Linda Hamilton
2 Selma Blair/99 25.00 50.00
3 Corey Haim/99 30.00 60.00
4 Leslie Nielsen
5 George Kennedy/79 15.00 30.00
6 Robert Carradine/49
7 Piper Laurie
8 Gloria Stuart
12 Noureen DeWulf
13 Milo Ventimiglia/29
14 Linda Evans
15 John Schneider/29 15.00 40.00
16 Erika Eleniak
17 Willie Aames
18 Justin Bieber/99 100.00 150.00

2011 Americana Screen Gems Signature Material

COMMON CARD 10.00 20.00
PRINT RUN 20-79
1 Linda Hamilton
2 Selma Blair
3 Corey Haim
4 Leslie Nielsen/39 30.00 60.00
5 George Kennedy
6 Robert Carradine
7 Piper Laurie/49
8 Gloria Stuart/35 20.00 40.00
10 Luke Goss
11 Willa Ford
12 Noureen DeWulf
14 Linda Evans
16 Erika Eleniak
17 Willie Aames
18 Justin Bieber
19 Josie Davis/69 12.00 25.00
20 John Hurt/20 25.00 50.00

2015 Americana

COMPLETE SET (73) 6.00 15.00
UNOPENED BOX (10 PACKS) 60.00 100.00
UNOPENED PACK (5 CARDS) 4.00 5.00
COMMON CARD (1-73) .20 .50
*BLUE: .75X TO 2X BASIC CARDS
*GREEN/25: 3X TO 8X BASIC CARDS

2015 Americana Big Screen Combo Signatures

1 Pacino
Bauer/25
3 Pacino
Mastrantonio/25
4 Mastrantonio 8.00 20.00
Bauer/25
5 Mastrantonio
Rourke/99
6 Rourke 150.00 300.00
Stallone/10
7 Hart
Jenkins/99
8 Knapp 15.00 40.00
Gonzalo/99
11 Gonzalo 10.00 25.00
Schirripa/99
12 Orlando 12.00 30.00
Vanilla Ice/99
13 Dushku
Vanilla Ice/25
14 Dushku 50.00 100.00
Elizabeth/25
15 McGinley
Stallone/10
16 McGinley
L.Dern/49
17 K.Hart 20.00 50.00
L.Dern/99
18 McDaniels 20.00 50.00
Rev Run/99
21 Jones
Short/10
23 D.B. Sweeney
Jones/49
24 Meade
Jones/49

2015 Americana Big Screen Signatures

1 Tony Orlando/99
2 John C. McGinley/99 12.00 30.00
3 Al Pacino/25 80.00 150.00
4 Steven Bauer/99 6.00 15.00
5 Laz Alonso/99
6 Terrence Jenkins/99
7 Alexa PenaVega/99 6.00 15.00
8 Corbin Bernsen/99 6.00 15.00
9 D.B. Sweeney/99 4.00 10.00
10 Hulk Hogan/99 20.00 50.00
11 Mary E. Mastrantonio/99 12.00 30.00
12 Mickey Rourke/99 6.00 15.00
13 Sylvester Stallone/49
14 Gabrielle Reece/99 8.00 20.00
15 Tony Sirico/99 6.00 15.00
16 Kevin Hart/99 25.00 60.00
17 Molly Ringwald/25 25.00 60.00
18 Bradley Cooper/99 50.00 100.00
19 Common/99 10.00 25.00
20 Gary Owen/99 4.00 10.00
21 Joe Manganiello/99 8.00 20.00
22 Martin Short/49 25.00 60.00
23 Roger Moore/99 20.00 50.00
24 Alexis Knapp/99 12.00 30.00
25 Jill Wagner/99
26 Jordana Brewster/99 50.00 100.00
27 Shannon Elizabeth/99 12.00 30.00
28 Rose McGowan/99 12.00 30.00
29 Eliza Dushku/99 30.00 80.00
30 Laura Dern/99 12.00 30.00
31 Ali Larter/99 15.00 40.00
32 James Earl Jones/75 20.00 50.00

2015 Americana Certified Albums

COMPLETE SET (6) 2.00 5.00
COMMON CARD (1-6) .50 1.25
*SILVER: .75X TO 2X BASIC CARDS
*GOLD/49: 2X TO 5X BASIC CARDS
*PLAT/25: 3X TO 8X BASIC CARDS

2015 Americana Certified Albums Signatures

COMMON CARD (1-6)
RANDOMLY INSERTED INTO PACKS
1 Paula Abdul 20.00 50.00
3 Coolio 40.00 100.00
5 Common 12.00 30.00
6 Vanilla Ice 12.00 30.00

2015 Americana Certified Singles

COMPLETE SET (7) 2.00 5.00
COMMON CARD (1-7) .50 1.25
*SILVER: .75X TO 2X BASIC CARDS
*GOLD/49: 2X TO 5X BASIC CARDS
*PLAT/25: 3X TO 8X BASIC CARDS

2015 Americana Certified Singles Signatures

COMMON CARD 6.00 15.00
1 Paula Abdul 20.00 50.00
3 Coolio 40.00 100.00
7 Vanilla Ice 12.00 30.00

2015 Americana Co-Stars Materials

COMMON CARD 8.00 20.00
6 Eliza Dushku 20.00 50.00
Laura Prepon/20
10 Eliza Dushku
Vanilla Ice/10
11 Eliza Dushku 25.00 60.00
Shannon Elizabeth/10

2015 Americana Double Materials

COMMON CARD 4.00 10.00
1 Alexis Knapp/99 5.00 12.00
2 Emily Meade/49
3 Eva Marie/99 8.00 20.00
4 Jill Wagner/99 15.00 40.00
5 Al Pacino/299 8.00 20.00
6 Hope Solo/99 10.00 25.00
7 Eliza Dushku/199 10.00 25.00
9 Padma Lakshmi/49 5.00 12.00
10 Jordana Brewster/49 15.00 40.00
11 Cody Simpson/299 5.00 12.00
13 La Toya Jackson/99 5.00 12.00
14 Ali Larter/49 5.00 12.00
15 Brooke Hogan/49
16 Coolio/49
17 Corbin Bernsen/49
19 Danica McKellar/49 12.00 30.00
20 Vanilla Ice/49
21 Shannon Elizabeth/99 10.00 25.00
22 Gretchen Rossi/49 6.00 15.00
23 Hulk Hogan/49 10.00 25.00
24 Joan Collins/49 8.00 20.00
27 Gabrielle Reece/199 5.00 12.00
28 Slade Smiley/49
29 Sylvester Stallone/299 8.00 20.00
30 Taryn Manning/10 6.00 15.00
32 Vince Neil/49 8.00 20.00
33 Kevin Hart/49 8.00 20.00
34 Chris Jericho/49 5.00 12.00
37 Roger Moore/49

2015 Americana Freeze Frame

COMMON CARD (1-55) 3.00 8.00
4 Al Pacino 5.00 12.00
6 Padma Lakshmi 4.00 10.00
7 Laz Alonso 4.00 10.00
9 Alexa PenaVega
10 Brooke Hogan 4.00 10.00
12 D.B. Sweeney 8.00 20.00
13 Danica McKellar 4.00 10.00
14 Daphne Oz 4.00 10.00
15 Hulk Hogan 4.00 10.00
16 Joan Collins 4.00 10.00
17 Kelly Rowland
19 Mickey Rourke 4.00 10.00
21 Paula Abdul 4.00 10.00
23 Sylvester Stallone 5.00 12.00
27 Vince Neil 4.00 10.00
28 Kevin Hart 4.00 10.00
29 Molly Ringwald 8.00 20.00
30 Bradley Cooper 6.00 15.00
31 Chris Jericho 4.00 10.00
32 Common 4.00 10.00
37 Roger Moore 4.00 10.00
38 Alexis Knapp 4.00 10.00
39 Emily Meade
40 Rutina Wesley 4.00 10.00
41 Ian Ziering 4.00 10.00
42 Jordana Brewster 6.00 15.00
43 Nick Cannon
45 Shannon Elizabeth 5.00 12.00
48 Laura Prepon 4.00 10.00
49 Eliza Dushku 6.00 15.00
50 Laura Dern 4.00 10.00
51 La Toya Jackson 4.00 10.00
53 James Earl Jones 4.00 10.00
54 Jill Wagner 4.00 10.00

2015 Americana Jumbo Materials

COMMON CARD 4.00 10.00
1 Alexis Knapp/10
3 Eva Marie/38
4 Jill Wagner/25
5 Al Pacino/499 12.00 30.00
6 Hope Solo/25 20.00 50.00
7 Eliza Dushku/72
9 Padma Lakshmi/99 6.00 15.00
10 Jordana Brewster/49 30.00 80.00
11 Cody Simpson/499 6.00 15.00
12 Laura Dern/25 8.00 20.00
13 La Toya Jackson/99 6.00 15.00
14 Ali Larter/125 12.00 30.00
15 Brooke Hogan/99
16 Coolio/125 6.00 15.00
17 Corbin Bernsen/149 5.00 12.00
18 D.B. Sweeney/199 5.00 12.00
19 Danica McKellar/149 12.00 30.00
20 Vanilla Ice/149 6.00 15.00
21 Shannon Elizabeth/10 6.00 15.00
22 Gretchen Rossi/299 5.00 12.00
23 Hulk Hogan/299 10.00 25.00
24 Joan Collins/49 12.00 30.00
26 Mickey Rourke/499 6.00 15.00
27 Gabrielle Reece/49 5.00 12.00
29 Sylvester Stallone/499 8.00 20.00
30 Taryn Manning/10
31 Teresa Giudice/199 6.00 15.00
32 Vince Neil/99 10.00 25.00
33 Kevin Hart/399 8.00 20.00
34 Chris Jericho/99 10.00 25.00
36 Rutina Wesley/31
37 Roger Moore/299 10.00 25.00

2015 Americana On the Tube Modern

COMPLETE SET (46) 30.00 80.00
COMMON CARD (1-46) 1.25 3.00
*GOLD: .75X TO 2X BASIC CARDS

2015 Americana On the Tube Modern Materials

COMMON CARD 5.00 12.00
1 Jill Wagner/199 10.00 25.00
2 Eliza Dushku/99 12.00 30.00
3 Laura Prepon/499 8.00 20.00
4 Emily Meade/299
9 Corbin Bernsen/299
11 Danica McKellar/299
13 Jordana Brewster/175
15 Hulk Hogan/272
17 Ali Larter/499 6.00 15.00
18 Patti Stanger/199
21 Joe Manganiello/150 6.00 15.00
26 Chris Jericho/49

2015 Americana On the Tube Modern Signatures

COMMON CARD 5.00 12.00
2 Katrina Bowden 12.00 30.00
3 John C. McGinley
4 Steven Bauer
8 Brooke Hogan 6.00 15.00
9 Corbin Bernsen 6.00 15.00
10 D.B. Sweeney 6.00 15.00
11 Danica McKellar 15.00 40.00
15 Hulk Hogan 15.00 40.00
17 Mary Elizabeth Mastrantonio 10.00 25.00
19 Paula Abdul 30.00 80.00
21 Steve Schirripa 6.00 15.00
22 Tony Sirico 6.00 15.00
23 Vince Neil 10.00 25.00
24 Molly Ringwald
25 Bradley Cooper 50.00 100.00
27 Common 6.00 15.00
28 Rutina Wesley
30 Joe Manganiello 6.00 15.00
31 Martin Short
33 Eva Marie 8.00 20.00
35 Jordana Brewster 50.00 100.00
36 Nick Cannon 8.00 20.00
37 Tiffani Thiessen 25.00 60.00
38 James Earl Jones
39 Rose McGowan 12.00 30.00
40 Julie Gonzalo 8.00 20.00
41 Laura Prepon 10.00 25.00
42 Eliza Dushku 50.00 100.00
43 La Toya Jackson 8.00 20.00
44 Ali Larter 15.00 40.00
45 Jill Wagner 8.00 20.00
46 Lea Michele

2015 Americana On the Tube Vintage

COMPLETE SET (10) 6.00 15.00
COMMON CARD (1-10) 1.25 3.00
*GOLD: .75X TO 2X BASIC CARDS

2015 Americana On the Tube Vintage Materials

COMMON CARD 5.00 12.00
1 Joan Collins/299 6.00 15.00
5 Jimmy Stewart/499 4.00 25.00
7 Lana Turner/499 6.00 15.00
9 Mickey Rooney/109 8.00 20.00
10 Robert Mitchum/63

2015 Americana On the Tube Vintage Signatures

1 Joan Collins 10.00 25.00

2015 Americana Screen Legends

COMPLETE SET (16) 10.00 25.00
COMMON CARD (1-16) 1.25 3.00
*SILVER: .75X TO 2X BASIC CARDS
*GOLD/49: 1.5X TO 4X BASIC CARDS
*PLAT: 2X TO 5X BASIC CARDS

2015 Americana Screen Legends Co-Stars

COMPLETE SET (17) 15.00 40.00
COMMON CARD (1-17) 2.00 5.00
*SILVER: .75X TO 2X BASIC CARDS
*GOLD/49: 1.2X TO 3X BASIC CARDS
*PLAT/25: 2X TO 5X BASIC CARDS

2015 Americana Signatures

COMMON CARD 4.00 10.00
*RED: .6X TO 1.5X BASIC CARDS
1 Tony Orlando 6.00 15.00
2 Audrina Patridge 5.00 12.00
4 John C. McGinley 10.00 25.00
5 Al Pacino 80.00 150.00
6 Hope Solo 15.00 40.00
7 Aly Raisman 8.00 20.00
8 Steven Bauer 5.00 12.00
9 Padma Lakshmi 5.00 12.00
11 Eliza Dushku 30.00 80.00
14 Biz Markie 5.00 12.00
15 Brooke Hogan 8.00 20.00
16 Coolio 30.00 75.00
17 Corbin Bernsen 5.00 12.00
18 D.B. Sweeney 6.00 15.00
19 Danica McKellar 15.00 40.00
20 Daphne Oz 6.00 15.00
21 DJ Jazzy Jeff 5.00 12.00
22 DJ Kool 5.00 12.00
23 Gretchen Rossi 5.00 12.00
24 Hulk Hogan 20.00 50.00
25 Joan Collins 10.00 25.00
27 Kelly Rowland 5.00 12.00
28 Mary Elizabeth Mastrantonio 8.00 20.00
29 MC Lyte 5.00 12.00
30 Mickey Rourke 15.00 40.00
31 Patti Stanger 5.00 12.00
32 Paula Abdul 50.00 100.00
34 Steve Schirripa 5.00 12.00
35 Sylvester Stallone 150.00 250.00
36 Taryn Manning 5.00 12.00
37 Gabrielle Reece 6.00 15.00
38 Teresa Giudice 5.00 12.00
39 Tony Sirico 6.00 15.00
40 Vince Neil 8.00 20.00
41 Kevin Hart 30.00 80.00
42 Molly Ringwald 25.00 60.00
43 Bradley Cooper 60.00 120.00
44 Chris Jericho 10.00 25.00
45 Common 6.00 15.00
48 Jaleel White 5.00 12.00
49 Joe Manganiello 8.00 20.00
50 Martin Short 25.00 60.00
51 Roger Moore 50.00 100.00
52 Alexis Knapp 10.00 25.00
53 Emily Meade 5.00 12.00
54 Eva Marie 12.00 30.00
55 Lea Michele 15.00 40.00
56 Ian Ziering 5.00 12.00
57 Jordana Brewster 30.00 80.00
58 Nick Cannon 8.00 20.00
59 Rev Run 6.00 15.00
60 Tiffani Thiessen 8.00 20.00
61 James Earl Jones 50.00 100.00
62 Vanilla Ice 5.00 12.00
63 Shannon Elizabeth 12.00 30.00
64 Rose McGowan 12.00 30.00
65 Julie Gonzalo 8.00 20.00
66 Laura Prepon 12.00 30.00
67 Cody Simpson 5.00 12.00
68 Laura Dern 8.00 20.00
69 La Toya Jackson 8.00 20.00
70 Ali Larter 12.00 30.00
71 Darryl McDaniels 10.00 25.00
72 Jill Wagner 10.00 25.00
73 Josie Davis 5.00 12.00

2015 Americana Silver Screen Co-Stars Materials

COMPLETE SET (17) 250.00 500.00
COMMON CARD 15.00 40.00

2015 Americana Silver Screen Double Materials

COMMON CARD 4.00 10.00
1 Alan Ladd/10
2 Ava Gardner/299 5.00 12.00
3 Bette Davis/299
5 Gene Tierney/299 8.00 20.00
6 Ginger Rogers/299 5.00 12.00
8 Ingrid Bergman/299 8.00 20.00
9 Jayne Mansfield/299 10.00 25.00
10 Jimmy Stewart/299 8.00 20.00
11 Jane Russell/70
12 Lana Turner/299
14 Mickey Rooney/49 8.00 20.00
15 Robert Mitchum/49
16 Bela Lugosi/299 6.00 15.00

2015 Americana Silver Screen Jumbo Materials

COMMON CARD 4.00 10.00
2 Ava Gardner/499 5.00 12.00
3 Bette Davis/499 5.00 12.00
5 Gene Tierney/499 5.00 12.00
6 Ginger Rogers/499 5.00 12.00
8 Ingrid Bergman/499 5.00 12.00
9 Jayne Mansfield/499 6.00 15.00
10 Jimmy Stewart/499 10.00 25.00
11 Jane Russell/499 5.00 12.00
13 Lillian Gish/499 5.00 12.00
14 Mickey Rooney/199 5.00 12.00
15 Robert Mitchum/180 5.00 12.00
16 Bela Lugosi/499 10.00 25.00

2015 Americana Silver Screen Triple Materials

COMMON CARD 6.00 15.00
1 Alan Ladd/5
2 Ava Gardner/299 10.00 25.00
4 Dorothy Lamour/299
5 Gene Tierney/299 8.00 20.00
6 Ginger Rogers/299 8.00 20.00
7 Hedy Lamarr/299 10.00 25.00
8 Ingrid Bergman/299 8.00 20.00
9 Jayne Mansfield/199 15.00 40.00
10 Jimmy Stewart/299
11 Jane Russell/17
14 Mickey Rooney/49
15 Robert Mitchum/49
16 Bela Lugosi/299 12.00 30.00

2015 Americana Star Materials

1 Alan Ladd
2 Ava Gardner 8.00 20.00
3 Bette Davis 5.00 12.00
4 Dorothy Lamour 5.00 12.00
5 Gene Tierney 5.00 12.00
7 Hedy Lamarr 5.00 12.00
8 Ingrid Bergman 5.00 12.00
9 Jayne Mansfield 8.00 20.00
10 Jimmy Stewart 10.00 25.00
11 Jane Russell
12 Lana Turner 5.00 12.00
15 Robert Mitchum
16 Bela Lugosi 10.00 25.00
17 Alexis Knapp 8.00 20.00
18 Emily Meade
19 Eva Marie
20 Gabrielle Reece 5.00 12.00
21 Al Pacino 5.00 12.00
22 Hope Solo
23 Eliza Dushku 8.00 20.00
24 Ian Ziering
26 Jordana Brewster
28 Laura Dern
29 La Toya Jackson 5.00 12.00
30 Ali Larter
31 Brooke Hogan 5.00 12.00
32 Coolio
33 Corbin Bernsen
34 D.B. Sweeney
35 Danica McKellar
36 Vanilla Ice
37 Shannon Elizabeth
38 Gretchen Rossi 6.00 15.00
39 Hulk Hogan 8.00 20.00
40 Joan Collins
42 Mickey Rourke
43 Patti Stanger 6.00 15.00
45 Sylvester Stallone 6.00 15.00
46 Taryn Manning
47 Teresa Giudice
48 Vince Neil 5.00 12.00
49 Kevin Hart 5.00 12.00
50 Chris Jericho 6.00 15.00
51 Common

MODERN

52 Rutina Wesley
53 Roger Moore 6.00 15.00
54 Jill Wagner 8.00 20.00

2015 Americana Triple Materials

COMMON CARD 5.00 12.00
1 Alexis Knapp/99 8.00 20.00
2 Emily Meade/49 6.00 15.00
3 Eva Marie/49
4 Jill Wagner/99 12.00 30.00
5 Al Pacino/299 8.00 20.00
7 Eliza Dushku/49 20.00 50.00
8 Ian Ziering/49 6.00 15.00
10 Jordana Brewster/49 15.00 40.00
11 Cody Simpson/299
12 Laura Dern/99 6.00 15.00
13 La Toya Jackson/99 6.00 15.00
14 Ali Larter/49
15 Brooke Hogan/49
17 Corbin Bernsen/49
19 Danica McKellar/27 15.00 40.00
20 Vanilla Ice/49
21 Shannon Elizabeth/99 6.00 15.00
23 Hulk Hogan/49
25 Joe Giudice/49
27 Gabrielle Reece/99 6.00 15.00
29 Sylvester Stallone/299 10.00 25.00
30 Taryn Manning/10
31 Teresa Giudice/49 6.00 15.00
32 Vince Neil/49 8.00 20.00
33 Kevin Hart/49
34 Chris Jericho/49 6.00 15.00
37 Roger Moore/49 8.00 20.00

2015 Americana Winner's Circle

COMPLETE SET (10) 15.00 40.00
COMMON CARD (1-10) 3.00 8.00

2015 Americana Winner's Circle Combo Materials

COMMON CARD 6.00 15.00

2015 Americana Winner's Circle Combo Signatures

COMMON CARD 12.00 30.00
1 Calvin Borel 15.00 40.00
Todd Pletcher
3 Bob Baffert 25.00 60.00
Gary Stevens
4 Bob Baffert 15.00 40.00
Chantal Sutherland-Kruse
5 D. Wayne Lukas 15.00 40.00
Pat Day
6 D. Wayne Lukas 15.00 40.00
Jerry Bailey
7 D. Wayne Lukas 15.00 40.00
Gary Stevens
8 Gary Stevens 15.00 40.00
Pat Day
10 Bob Baffert 30.00 80.00
D. Wayne Lukas

2015 Americana Winner's Circle Combos

COMPLETE SET (10) 8.00 20.00
COMMON CARD (1-10) 1.50 4.00

2015 Americana Winner's Circle Materials

COMMON CARD (1-10) 4.00 10.00
5 Calvin Borel/372 5.00 12.00
9 D. Wayne Lukas/151 6.00 15.00

2015 Americana Winner's Circle Signatures

COMMON CARD (10) 4.00 10.00
1 Chantal Sutherland-Kruse 5.00 12.00
2 Gary Stevens 8.00 20.00
3 Mike Smith 6.00 15.00
4 Pat Day 8.00 20.00
5 Calvin Borel 8.00 20.00
7 Todd Pletcher 6.00 15.00
8 Bob Baffert 15.00 40.00
9 D. Wayne Lukas 6.00 15.00

1991 Impel An American Tail

COMPLETE SET (150) 6.00 15.00
UNOPENED BOX (36 PACKS) 8.00 20.00
UNOPENED PACK (12 CARDS) .20 .50
COMMON CARD (1-150) .10 .25

1991 Impel An American Tail Holograms

COMPLETE SET (5) 3.00 8.00
COMMON CARD (H1-H5) 1.25 3.00
RANDOMLY INSERTED INTO PACKS

1991 Impel An American Tail Promos

COMMON CARD 1.25 3.00

1998 Upper Deck Anastasia

COMPLETE SET W/O SP (99) 8.00 20.00
COMPLETE SET W/SP (126) 20.00 50.00
UNOPENED BOX (36 PACKS) 15.00 25.00
UNOPENED PACK (5 CARDS) .50 .75
COMMON CARD (1-99) .15 .40
PORTRAITS (100-117); 1:8 .75 2.00
PUZZLE (118-123); 1:36 1.25 3.00
MOTION (124-126); 1:18 1.50 4.00

2011 Anchorman The Legend of Ron Burgundy

COMPLETE SET (12) 6.00 15.00
COMMON CARD (1-12) .75 2.00
BLU-RAY VIDEO EXCLUSIVE SET
1 Ron Burgundy 2.00 5.00
3 Brian Fantana 1.50 4.00
4 Brick Tamland 1.50 4.00
7 Wes Mantooth 2.00 5.00

2001 Inkworks Andromeda Season One

COMPLETE SET (90) 5.00 12.00
UNOPENED BOX (36 PACKS) 40.00 50.00
UNOPENED PACK (7 CARDS) 1.25 1.50
COMMON CARD (1-90) .15 .40
R1 The Three Faces Of Rommie 6.00 15.00

2001 Inkworks Andromeda Season One Autographs

COMMON AUTO (A1-A7) 5.00 12.00
STATED ODDS 1:45
A1 Kevin Sorbo 12.00 30.00
A2 Lisa Ryder 8.00 20.00
A3 Lexa Doig 30.00 75.00
A4 Laura Bertram 6.00 15.00
A7 Sam Sorbo 6.00 15.00

2001 Inkworks Andromeda Season One Diaries of the Mad Perseid

COMPLETE SET (6) 5.00 12.00
COMMON CARD (D1-D6) 1.25 3.00
STATED ODDS 1:17

2001 Inkworks Andromeda Season One Pieceworks

COMPLETE SET (4) 25.00 60.00
COMMON MEM (PW1-PW4) 8.00 20.00
STATED ODDS 1:65
PW2 Rommie's Vest 25.00 60.00

2001 Inkworks Andromeda Season One Crew of Andromeda

COMPLETE SET (9) 6.00 15.00
COMMON CARD (C1-C9) 1.00 2.50
STATED ODDS 1:11

2001 Inkworks Andromeda Season One Promos

COMMON CARD 1.25 3.00
DVD1 Explosive US 3.00 8.00

2004 Andromeda Reign of the Commonwealth

COMPLETE SET (90) 4.00 10.00
UNOPENED BOX (36 PACKS) 50.00 60.00
UNOPENED PACK (7 CARDS) 1.75 2.00
COMMON CARD (1-90) .10 .30

2004 Andromeda Reign of the Commonwealth Autographs

COMMON AUTO (A1-A6) 5.00 12.00
STATED ODDS 1:36
A1 Kevin Sorbo 12.00 30.00
A2 Lisa Ryder 8.00 20.00
A3 Lexa Doig 25.00 60.00

2004 Andromeda Reign of the Commonwealth Battle for the Commonwealth

COMPLETE SET (9) 10.00 25.00
COMMON CARD (BC1-BC9) 1.50 4.00
STATED ODDS 1:11

2004 Andromeda Reign of the Commonwealth Box-Loaders

COMPLETE SET (4) 8.00 20.00
COMMON CARD (BL1-BL3; CL1) 1.50 4.00
CL1 Andromeda Ascendant 6.00 15.00

2004 Andromeda Reign of the Commonwealth Fragile Allegiances

COMPLETE SET (6) 8.00 20.00
COMMON CARD (FA1-FA6) 1.50 4.00
STATED ODDS 1:17

2004 Andromeda Reign of the Commonwealth Pieceworks

COMPLETE SET (6) 80.00 150.00
COMMON MEM (PW1-PW6) 6.00 15.00
STATED ODDS 1:36
PW6 Beka's Top 20.00 40.00
PW9 Rommie's Vest 20.00 40.00
PW10 Beka's Top 20.00 40.00

2004 Andromeda Reign of the Commonwealth Promos

COMMON CARD 1.50 4.00

1990-91 Pacific Andy Griffith Show Complete Series

COMPLETE SET (330) 12.00 30.00
COMP.SER.1 SET (110) 5.00 12.00
COMP.SER.2 SET (110) 5.00 12.00
COMP.SER.3 SET (110) 5.00 12.00
UNOPENED SERIES 1 BOX (36 PACKS) 30.00 40.00
UNOPENED SERIES 1 PACK (10 CARDS) 1.00 1.25
UNOPENED SERIES 2 BOX (36 PACKS) 10.00 20.00
UNOPENED SERIES 2 PACK (10 CARDS) .50 .75
UNOPENED SERIES 3 BOX (36 PACKS) 10.00 20.00
UNOPENED SERIES 3 PACK (10 CARDS) .50 .75
COMMON CARD (1-110) .20 .50
COMMON CARD (111-220) .15 .40
COMMON CARD (221-330) .15 .40

1995 ACME Studios Andy Warhol

COMPLETE BOXED SET (36) 6.00 15.00
COMMON CARD (1-36) .30 .60
1 Andy Warhol .40 1.00

2012 Angry Birds

COMPLETE SET (180) 25.00 60.00
COMMON CARD (1-160) .10 .25
COMMON SILVER FOIL (161-176) 1.00 2.50
COMMON GOLD FOIL (177-180) 2.50 5.00

1993 Comic Images Ania

COMPLETE SET (7) 12.00 30.00
COMMON CARD 3.00 8.00
NNO Ebony Warrior - Coming in August (promo)1.25 3.00

1994 Mother Productions Animal Freaks

COMPLETE SET (40) 5.00 12.00
COMMON CARD .25 .60

2017 Animal Jam

COMPLETE SET (54) 6.00 15.00
UNOPENED BOX (24 PACKS)
UNOPENED PACK (14 CARDS/1 FIGURE)
COMMON CARD (1-54) .30 .75
ONLINE CODE CARDS 1:1
44b Spring Bunny GOLD SP

2017 Animal Jam 3-D Cards

COMPLETE SET (9) 5.00 12.00
COMMON CARD (1-9) 1.00 2.50
STATED ODDS 1:6

2017 Animal Jam Coloring Cards

COMPLETE SET (9) 3.00 8.00
COMMON CARD (1-9) .60 1.50
STATED ODDS 1:2

2017 Animal Jam Fuzzy Cards

COMPLETE SET (9) 10.00 25.00
COMMON CARD (1-9) 2.00 5.00
STATED ODDS 1:12

2017 Animal Jam Pop-Up Cards

COMPLETE SET (9) 3.00 8.00
COMMON CARD (1-9) .60 1.50
STATED ODDS 1:2

1996 Comic Images Animal Mystic

COMPLETE SET (90) 5.00 12.00
UNOPENED BOX (48 PACKS) 15.00 40.00
UNOPENED PACK (8 PACKS) .40 1.00
COMMON CARD (1-90) .12 .30
DARK ONE KEDA AU RANDOMLY INSERTED
NNO1 Keda AU/500 25.00 60.00

1996 Comic Images Animal Mystic Characters

COMPLETE SET (3) 10.00 25.00
COMMON CARD (1-3) 4.00 10.00
STATED ODDS 1:48

1996 Comic Images Animal Mystic Glow-in-the-Dark Ones

COMPLETE SET (6) 8.00 20.00
COMMON CARD (1-6) 2.50 6.00
STATED ODDS 1:16

1996 Comic Images Animal Mystic Promos

COMMON CARD .75 2.00

1998 Media One Animal Planet Promos

COMPLETE SET (10) 8.00 20.00
COMMON CARD (UNNUMBERED) 1.25 3.00

1990 Red Rose Tea Animals and Their Young

COMPLETE SET (48) 5.00 12.00
COMMON CARD (1-48) .20 .50

1995 Topps Animaniacs

COMPLETE SET (72) 6.00 15.00
UNOPENED BOX (36 PACKS) 50.00 75.00
UNOPENED PACK (9 CARDS) 2.00 3.00
COMMON CARD (1-72) .15 .40

1995 Topps Animaniacs Promos

COMMON CARD .60 1.50

1995 Topps Animaniacs Static Clings

COMPLETE SET (4) 15.00 40.00
COMMON CARD (SC1-SC4) 5.00 12.00
STATED ODDS 1:18

1995 Topps Animaniacs Stickers

COMPLETE SET (12) 1.50 4.00
COMMON CARD (1-12) .25 .60
INCLUDED IN THE BASE SET
STATED ODDS 1:1

1995 WildStorm Animated WildC.A.T.s

COMPLETE SET (135) 8.00 20.00
UNOPENED BOX (36 PACKS) 30.00 40.00
UNOPENED PACK (8 CARDS) 1.00 1.25
COMMON CARD (1-135) .12 .30

1995 WildStorm Animated WildC.A.T.s Animation Cels
COMPLETE SET (9) 15.00 40.00
COMMON CARD (CEL1-CEL9) 2.00 5.00
RANDOMLY INSERTED INTO PACKS

1995 WildStorm Animated WildC.A.T.s Box-Toppers
COMPLETE SET (5) 15.00 40.00
COMMON CARD (OS1-OS5) 4.00 10.00
STATED ODDS 1:BOX

1995 WildStorm Animated WildC.A.T.s Foil-Etched
COMPLETE SET (9) 15.00 40.00
COMMON CARD (FE1-FE9) 2.00 5.00
RANDOMLY INSERTED INTO PACKS

2017 Anovos Promos
COMPLETE SET (3) 5.00 12.00
COMMON CARD (UNNUMBERED) 2.50 6.00

1992 Panini Antique Cars
COMPLETE SET (100) 5.00 12.00
BOXED FACTORY SET (100) 6.00 15.00
UNOPENED BOX (36 PACKS) 25.00 30.00
UNOPENED PACK (8 CARDS) .75 1.00
COMMON CARD (1-100) .12 .30

2000 Aphrodite IX
BOXED FACTORY SET (5) 6.00 15.00
COMMON CARD 1.50 4.00

2005 The Apprentice
COMPLETE SET (72) 5.00 12.00
UNOPENED BOX (36 PACKS) 85.00 100.00
UNOPENED PACK (6 CARDS) 2.50 3.00
COMMON CARD (1-72) .12 .30
1 Donald J. Trump 2.00 5.00
NNO Donald Trump Multi Case Incentive AU 600.00 1000.00

2005 The Apprentice Autographs
COMMON AUTO 6.00 15.00
STATED ODDS 1:40
DT1 Donald Trump (red tie) SP 1000.00 2000.00
DT2 Donald Trump (pink tie) 1000.00 2000.00
GR George Ross 8.00 20.00

2005 The Apprentice Costumes
COMPLETE SET (2) 150.00 300.00
COMMON MEM 100.00 200.00
STATED ODDS 1:216

2005 The Apprentice Promos
COMMON CARD 1.50 4.00
P1 The Donald 10.00 25.00

1994 Arby's Hanna Barbera
COMPLETE SET (30) 30.00 75.00
UNOPENED PACK (6 CARDS) 4.00 10.00
COMMON CARD (1-30) 1.50 4.00

2014 Archer Seasons One Through Four
COMPLETE SET (73) 5.00 12.00
UNOPENED BOX (24 PACKS) 250.00 400.00
UNOPENED PACK (5 CARDS) 10.00 15.00
COMMON CARD (1-73) .15 .40
B1 Archer (standee) 6.00 15.00
P1 Get a Piece of the Action PROMO 1.25 3.00

2014 Archer Seasons One Through Four Autographs
COMMON AUTO (A1-A15) 8.00 20.00
STATED ODDS 1:24
A1 Jessica Walter 20.00 50.00
A2 Amber Nash 12.00 30.00
A3 Chris Parnell 12.00 30.00
A4 George Coe 15.00 40.00
A5 Lucky Yates 12.00 30.00
A7 Ona Grauer 10.00 25.00
A9 James Hong 10.00 25.00
A10 Judy Greer 30.00 75.00
A11 Adam Reed 10.00 25.00
A12 David Cross 10.00 25.00
A15 Burt Reynolds 75.00 150.00

2014 Archer Seasons One Through Four Inappropriate Workplace Moments
COMPLETE SET (9) 5.00 12.00
COMMON CARD (C1-C9) 1.25 3.00
STATED ODDS 1:12

2014 Archer Seasons One Through Four Sterling Archer's Spy (Just the) Tips
COMPLETE SET (9) 5.00 12.00
COMMON CARD (ISIS01-ISIS09) 1.25 3.00
STATED ODDS 1:12

2014 Archer Seasons One Through Four Totally Fabricated
COMPLETE SET (4) 60.00 120.00
COMMON MEM (TF1-TF4) 15.00 40.00
STATED ODDS 1:144

2014 Archer Seasons One Through Four Welcome to Whore Island
COMPLETE SET (9) 5.00 12.00
COMMON CARD (WHR01-WHR09) 1.25 3.00
STATED ODDS 1:12

1992 SkyBox Archie
COMPLETE SET (120) 6.00 15.00
UNOPENED BOX (36 PACKS) 12.00 30.00
UNOPENED PACK (10 CARDS) .30 .75
COMMON CARD (1-120) .10 .25

1992 SkyBox Archie Eternal Triangle Holograms
1 Eternal Triangle 2.00 5.00
2 Congratulations Redemption Card .40 1.00

1992 SkyBox Archie Holograms
COMPLETE SET (4) 5.00 12.00
COMMON CARD (H1-H4) 2.50 6.00
STATED ODDS 1:12

1992 SkyBox Archie Prototypes
COMPLETE SET (3) 4.00 10.00
COMMON CARD 2.00 5.00

1996 Krome Archie Chromium
COMPLETE SET (90) 10.00 25.00
UNOPENED BOX (36 PACKS) 25.00 40.00
UNOPENED PACK (7 CARDS) 1.25 1.50
COMMON CARD (1-90) .20 .50
P1 Promo 2.00 5.00
(General Distribution)

1996 Krome Archie Chromium Holochrome
COMPLETE SET (5) 8.00 20.00
COMMON CARD (C1-C5) 2.50 6.00

1998 Nestle Nuclear Chocolate Armageddon
COMPLETE SET (15) 12.00 30.00
COMMON CARD (1-15) 1.00 2.50

2001 Army National Guard
COMPLETE SET W/O SP (200) 50.00 100.00
COMPLETE SET W/SP (220) 120.00 250.00
UNOPENED BOX (28 PACKS) 85.00 100.00
UNOPENED PACK (11 CARDS) 3.00 4.00
COMMON CARD (1-20) 3.00 8.00
COMMON CARD (21-217; CL) .40 1.00

2005 Army of Darkness
COMPLETE SET (72) 6.00 15.00
UNOPENED BOX (36 PACKS) 25.00 60.00
UNOPENED PACK (7 CARDS) 1.00 1.75
COMMON CARD (1-72) .12 .30
BRUCE CAMPBELL PROMO 1:BOX
NNO1 Bruce Campbell Box-Topper Promo 1.25 3.00

2005 Army of Darkness Autographs
COMMON AUTO 8.00 20.00
STATED ODDS 1:18

2005 Army of Darkness Glow-in-the-Dark
COMPLETE SET (6) 3.00 8.00
COMMON CARD (1-6) .75 2.00
STATED ODDS 1:18

2015 Arrested Development Autographs
AW Allan Wasserman 12.00 30.00
DT Dave Thomas
JK Jamie Kennedy 20.00 50.00
JR Judge Reinhold

2015 Arrested Development Promo
P1 Coming Soon!
(Non-Sports Magazine Exclusive)

2010 The Art Hustle Series 1
COMPLETE SET (160) 15.00 40.00
COMPLETE SET W/EXTRAS (184) 20.00 50.00
UNOPENED BOX (36 PACKS) 120.00 130.00
UNOPENED PACK (7 CARDS) 4.00 5.00
COMMON CARD (1-184) .20 .50
NNO Metal as F*ck Silkscreen LE (factory set exclusive)
NNO Vectar Original Artwork
NNO Guess the Hand Contest Card

2010 The Art Hustle Series 1 Promos
COMMON CARD .75 2.00

2013 Art of Burlesque
COMPLETE SET (27) 3.00 8.00
PREMIUM PACK 20.00 25.00
COMMON CARD .25 .60
*LIPSTICK: 1X TO 2.5X BASIC CARDS

2013 Art of Burlesque Headline Honeys
COMPLETE SET (10) 8.00 20.00
COMMON CARD (CHASE1-CHASE10) 1.25 3.00

2013 Art of Burlesque Promos
F1 Huy Truong Feather Card (No Feather Attachment)
P1 Philly Non-Sports Card Show Mini Promo .75 2.00
BP1 Mamie Lamb (The High Rollers Extravaganza) .75 2.00
BP2 Lili St. Cyr (Phoenix) .75 2.00
LJP1 Liza Johnson
MCP1 Scott Houseman (Mega City 5; straighten stockings) 1.50 4.00
SFi-1 Terry Pavlet (SciFiCards; golden goddess) 4.00 10.00

1996 WildStorm Art of Chiodo
COMPLETE SET (90) 10.00 25.00
UNOPENED BOX (36 PACKS) 20.00 25.00
UNOPENED PACK (8 CARDS) .60 .75
COMMON CARD (1-90) .15 .40

1996 WildStorm Art of Chiodo Women in Swimsuits
COMPLETE SET (9) 20.00 50.00
COMMON CARD (L1-L9) 3.00 8.00
STATED ODDS 1:9

1999 Comic Images Art of Coca-Cola
COMPLETE SET (70) 4.00 10.00
UNOPENED BOX (36 PACKS) 30.00 40.00
UNOPENED PACK (7 CARDS) 1.00 1.25
COMMON CARD (1-70) .12 .30

1999 Comic Images Art of Coca-Cola Santa Omnichrome
COMPLETE SET (6) 12.00 30.00
COMMON CARD (C1-C6) 2.50 6.00
STATED ODDS 1:18

1999 Comic Images Art of Coca-Cola Promos
1 Lady Facing Right .75 2.00
2 Lady Facing Left .75 2.00

1994 Lime Rock Art of Curves
COMPLETE SET (100) 5.00 12.00
COMPLETE FACTORY SET/300 (100) 10.00 25.00
UNOPENED BOX
UNOPENED PACK
COMMON CARD (1-100) .08 .25

1994 Lime Rock Art of Curves Prisms
COMPLETE SET (4) 6.00 15.00
COMMON CARD (1-4) 2.00 5.00
STATED ODDS 1:36

1994 Lime Rock Art of Curves Promos
COMPLETE SET (6) 3.00 8.00
COMMON CARD (UNNUMBERED) .75 2.00

2018 The Art of Dan Allen
COMPLETE SET (6) 5.00 12.00
COMMON CARD (1-6) 1.50 4.00

2018 The Art of Dan Allen Foil
F1 Native American Skull 3.00 8.00

2018 The Art of Dan Allen Promos
P1 MHopOnHop Presents
P2 Tiger Skulls 2.50 6.00
(US & UK Set Exclusive)
P3 A 2018 Release! (black)/300 6.00 15.00
P3 A 2018 Release! (blue)/150*.
P3 A 2018 Release! (red)/50*

2008 Art of David Nestler
COMPLETE SET (45) 5.00 12.00
UNOPENED BOX (12 PACKS) 40.00 50.00
UNOPENED PACK (8 CARDS) 4.00 5.00
COMMON CARD (1-45) .20 .50
CT Art of Dave Nestler Case-Topper (unraveling)
SKDN Dave Nestler Sketch Card
OASKR Original Art Sketch Card Redemption
OASKDN Dave Nestler Original Art Sketch Card (8X10)/5 EXCH

2008 Art of David Nestler Attractive
COMPLETE SET (9) 8.00 20.00
COMMON CARD (1-9) 1.50 4.00
STATED ODDS 1:6

2008 Art of David Nestler Delicious
COMPLETE SET (9) 6.00 15.00
COMMON CARD (1-9) 1.25 3.00
STATED ODDS 1:4

2008 Art of David Nestler Erotica
COMPLETE SET (9) 6.00 15.00
COMMON CARD (1-9) 1.25 3.00
STATED ODDS 1:6

2008 Art of David Nestler Sexy
COMPLETE SET (5) 8.00 20.00
COMMON CARD (1-5) 2.50 6.00
STATED ODDS 1:12

2008 Art of David Nestler Vixens
COMPLETE SET (9) 15.00
COMMON CARD (1-9) 1.25 3.00
STATED ODDS 1:6

2008 Art of David Nestler Promos
COMMON CARD (DN1-DN4) 1.25 3.00

1993 Dynacomm Art of Frank Kelly Freas Freas Frames
COMPLETE SET (43)) 8.00 20.00
COMMON CARD (1-43) .30 .75
NNO1 About the Artist
NNO2 Frank Kelly Freas Collection Offer Card

1993 Dynacomm Art of Frank Kelly Freas Freas Frames 2

COMPLETE SET (43) 8.00 20.00
COMMON CARD (1-43) 30.00 .75
NNO1 About the Artist
NNO2 Frank Kelly Freas Collection Offer Card

1995 Comic Images The Art of Heavy Metal

COMPLETE SET (90) 5.00 12.00
UNOPENED BOX (48 PACKS) 30.00 40.00
UNOPENED PACK (10 CARDS) 1.00 1.25
COMMON CARD (1-90) 12.00 .30
MED Medallion Card/1,754* 10.00 25.00

1995 Comic Images The Art of Heavy Metal Black Magic

COMPLETE SET (3) 12.00 30.00
COMMON CARD (BM1-BM3) 6.00 15.00
STATED ODDS 1:48

1995 Comic Images The Art of Heavy Metal Chromium

COMPLETE SET (6) 15.00 40.00
COMMON CARD (C1-C6) 3.00 8.00
STATED ODDS 1:16

1995 Comic Images The Art of Heavy Metal Promos

NNO Case Bonus 6-up panel 2.50 6.00
NNO The Art of Heavy Metal (image from #31).75 2.00

1998 WildStorm Art of Jim Lee

BOXED FACTORY SET (50) 6.00 15.00
COMMON CARD (1-50) .25 .60

2014 Art of Kevin Seconds Promos

COMMON CARD 1.00 2.50
NSUB Foil 2.00 5.00

2019 Art of TMNT

COMPLETE SET (100) 15.00 40.00
UNOPENED BOX SET (106 CARDS) 100.00 150.00
COMMON CARD (1-100) .30 .75
*GREEN/99: 2X TO 5X BASIC CARDS
*PURPLE/50: 6X TO 15X BASIC CARDS
*ORANGE/25: 15X TO 40X BASIC CARDS

2019 Art of TMNT Autographs

COMMON AUTO 10.00 25.00
*PURPLE/50: .5X TO 1.2X BASIC AUTOS
*ORANGE/25: .6X TO 1.5X BASIC AUTOS
STATED ODDS 1:BOXED SET
STATED PRINT RUN 99 SER.#'d SETS
1 Kevin Eastman 20.00 50.00
23 Kevin Eastman 20.00 50.00
24 Kevin Eastman 20.00 50.00
25 Kevin Eastman 20.00 50.00
26 Kevin Eastman 20.00 50.00
27 Kevin Eastman 20.00 50.00
28 Kevin Eastman 20.00 50.00

1996 FPG Art of TSR

COMPLETE SET (50) 15.00 40.00
UNOPENED BOX (18 PACKS) 30.00 40.00
UNOPENED PACK (5 CARDS) 2.00 2.50
COMMON CARD (1-50) .60 1.50

1995 FPG Art Suydam

COMPLETE SET (90) 4.00 10.00
UNOPENED BOX (36 PACKS) 8.00 20.00
UNOPENED PACK (10 CARDS) .25 .60
COMMON CARD (1-90) .10 .25
NNO Art Suydam AU/1000* 20.00 50.00

1995 FPG Art Suydam Metallic

COMPLETE SET (5) 10.00 25.00
COMMON CARD (M1-M5) 3.00 8.00
STATED ODDS 1:12

1997 Keepsake Collection Art Treasures of the Vatican Library

COMPLETE SET (72) 6.00 15.00
UNOPENED BOX (48 PACKS) 12.00 30.00
UNOPENED PACK (8 CARDS) .25 .60
COMMON CARD (1-72) .15 .40

1997 Keepsake Collection Art Treasures of the Vatican Library Chromium

COMPLETE SET (6) 12.00 30.00
COMMON CARD (C1-C6) 3.00 8.00
STATED ODDS 1:18

1997 Keepsake Collection Art Treasures of the Vatican Library Promos

NNO Combine Some .75 2.00
NNO Finally a Trading Card .75 2.00

2003 Artwork of Boris and Julie Strokes of Genius

COMPLETE SET (72) 4.00 10.00
UNOPENED BOX (36 PACKS) 35.00 50.00
UNOPENED PACK (7 CARDS) 1.25 1.50
COMMON CARD (1-72) .10 .25
UNC2 6-Card Panel 2.00 5.00
(Album Exclusive)

2003 Artwork of Boris and Julie Strokes of Genius Autographs

COMMON CARD 25.00 60.00
STATED PRINT RUN 500 SETS

2003 Artwork of Boris and Julie Strokes of Genius Boris Lithographs

1 Limited Edition Lithograph
R1 Pumping Iron Redemption 25.00 60.00

2003 Artwork of Boris and Julie Strokes of Genius Silver Foil

COMPLETE SET (6) 10.00 25.00
COMMON CARD (F1-F6) 2.00 5.00
STATED ODDS 1:12

2003 Artwork of Boris and Julie Strokes of Genius Promos

COMMON CARD (P1-P2) 1.00 2.50

1997 Dynamic Forces Ash

COMPLETE SET (90) 8.00 20.00
UNOPENED BOX (24 PACKS) 10.00 25.00
UNOPENED PACK (8 CARDS) .50 1.25
COMMON CARD (1-90) .20 .50

1997 Dynamic Forces Ash Autographs

COMPLETE SET (9) 120.00 250.00
COMMON AUTO 12.00 30.00
STATED ODDS 1:36
C10 Joe Quesada/Jimmy Palmiotti AU/500

1997 Dynamic Forces Ash Chromium

COMPLETE SET (9) 15.00 40.00
COMMON CARD (C1-C10) 3.00 8.00
STATED ODDS 1:4
C10 AU/500 RANDOMLY INSERTED

1997 Dynamic Forces Ash Sketches

COMPLETE SET (5) 6.00 15.00
COMMON CARD (S1-S5) 2.00 5.00
STATED ODDS 1:7

1997 Dynamic Forces Ash Promos

COMPLETE SET (9) 5.00 12.00
COMMON CARD .75 2.00

1991 Mother Productions Assassins

COMPLETE BOXED SET (42) 6.00 15.00
COMMON CARD (1-42) .60

1994 21st Century Archives Astounding Science Fiction

COMPLETE SET (50) 3.00 8.00
UNOPENED BOX (36 PACKS) 40.00 50.00
UNOPENED PACK (8 CARDS) 1.25 1.50
COMMON CARD (1-50) .10 .30
NNO The Shadow Out of Time PROMO .75 2.00

1994 21st Century Archives Astounding Science Fiction Robert A. Heinlein

COMPLETE SET (5) 5.00 20.00
COMMON CARD (RH1-RH5) 2.00 5.00
RANDOMLY INSERTED INTO PACKS

1999 Panini Austin Powers Photocards

COMPLETE SET (72) 12.00 30.00
UNOPENED BOX (36 PACKS) 25.00 40.00
UNOPENED PACK (6 CARDS) 1.00 1.50
COMMON CARD (1-72) .40 1.00

1999 Cornerstone Austin Powers The Spy Who Shagged Me

COMPLETE SET (72) 5.00 12.00
UNOPENED BOX (36 PACKS) 30.00 50.00
UNOPENED PACK (8 CARDS) 1.50 2.50
COMMON CARD (1-72) .12 .30
UNNUMBERED LICENSE TO SHAG 1:72 PACKS
NNO License To Shag 3.00 8.00

1999 Cornerstone Austin Powers The Spy Who Shagged Me Help Austin Find His Mojo

COMPLETE SET (5) 10.00 25.00
COMMON CARD (M0-M4) 2.50 6.00
STATED ODDS 1:18

1999 Cornerstone Austin Powers The Spy Who Shagged Me Movie Posters

COMPLETE SET (3) 1.50 4.00
COMMON CARD (MP1-MP3) 1.00 2.50
STATED ODDS 1:12

1999 Cornerstone Austin Powers The Spy Who Shagged Me Promos

COMMON CARD 1.25 3.00
P5 The key to life is to rotate your vices 2.00 5.00
P8 Three blondes 6.00 15.00

1999 Cornerstone Austin Powers The Spy Who Shagged Me Blockbuster Promos

COMPLETE SET (5) 2.50 6.00
COMMON CARD (V1-V5) .75 2.00

1990 Weetabix Australian Natural Wonders

COMPLETE SET (10) 6.00 15.00
COMMON CARD (1-10) 1.00 2.50

2021 Topps On-Demand Avatar The Last Airbender Set

COMPLETE SET (20) 10.00 25.00
COMMON CARD (1-20) 1.25 3.00
*BLUE/149: 2X TO 5X BASIC CARDS
*GREEN/50: 4X TO 10X BASIC CARDS
*RED/25: 8X TO 20X BASIC CARDS
ANNCD PRINT RUN 4,750 SETS

1996 WildStorm Avengelyne

COMPLETE SET (189) 20.00 50.00
COMPLETE SERIES 1 SET (99) 12.00 30.00
COMPLETE SERIES 2 SET (99) 10.00 25.00
UNOPENED SERIES 1 BOX (24 PACKS) 25.00 60.00
UNOPENED SERIES 1 PACK (7 CARDS) 1.00 2.50
UNOPENED SERIES 2 BOX (24 PACKS) 25.00 60.00
UNOPENED SERIES 2 PACK (6 CARDS) 1.00 2.50
COMMON CARD SERIES 1 (1-99) .12 .30
COMMON CARD SERIES 2 (100-189) .12 .30
MOR1 RANDOMLY INSERTED IN SERIES 2 PACKS
MOR1 Sign of the Cross 10.00 25.00

1996 WildStorm Avengelyne Embossed

COMPLETE SET (9) 12.00 30.00
COMMON CARD (E1-E9) 2.50 6.00
STATED ODDS 1:6

1996 WildStorm Avengelyne Glow-in-the-Dark

COMPLETE SET (9) 20.00 50.00
COMMON CARD (G1-G9) 4.00 10.00
STATED ODDS 1:8 SERIES 1 PACKS

1996 WildStorm Avengelyne Motion

COMPLETE SET (9) 15.00 40.00
COMMON CARD (M1-M9) 3.00 8.00
RANDOMLY INSERTED INTO SERIES 2 PACKS

1992-95 Cornerstone The Avengers

COMPLETE SET (261) 15.00 40.00
COMPLETE FIRST SERIES SET (81) 8.00 20.00
COMPLETE IN COLOR SET (99) 6.00 15.00
COMPLETE RETURNS SET (81) 5.00 12.00
COMPLETE RETURNS FACTORY SET (87) 8.00 20.00
UNOPENED FIRST SERIES BOX (36 PACKS)65.00 80.00
UNOPENED FIRST SERIES PACK (10 CARDS)2.00 2.50
UNOPENED IN COLOR BOX (36 PACKS) 30.00 40.00
UNOPENED IN COLOR PACK (10 CARDS) 1.00 1.25
UNOPENED RETURNS BOX (36 PACKS) 30.00 40.00
UNOPENED RETURNS PACK (10 CARDS) 1.00 1.25
COMMON CARD (1-81) .12 .30
COMMON CARD IN COLOR (82-180) .12 .30
COMMON CARD RETURNS (181-261) .12 .30
AU1 Patrick MacNee AU/500* 150.00 300.00
(The Avengers Returns Exclusive)

1992-95 Cornerstone The Avengers Premiere

COMPLETE SET (9) 15.00 35.00
COMPLETE INSERT SET (6) 3.00 8.00
COMPLETE MAIL-IN SET (3) 12.00 30.00
COMMON CARD (P1-P6) .75 2.00
COMMON CARD (P7-P9) 5.00 12.00
P1-P6 RANDOMLY INSERTED INTO PACKS
P7-P9 MAIL-IN OFFER EXCLUSIVE
AVAILABLE EXCLUSIVELY IN RETURNS PACKS

1992-95 Cornerstone The Avengers Promos

A0-A1 FIRST SERIES EXCLUSIVE
B1-B9 IN COLOR EXCLUSIVE
C1-C3; IT7 RETURNS EXCLUSIVE
A0A We Did It/10* 150.00 300.00
A0B We Did It 5.00 12.00
(no serial number)
A7 Thanks for Your Support/100* 60.00 120.00
A8 It's Good to Hear From You 8.00 20.00
A9 Your Opinion Is Appreciated 8.00 20.00
B8 Talented Amateurs/100* 15.00 40.00
B9 We Did It Take 2/10* 25.00 60.00
IT7 Insider Trader Club Exclusive 8.00

2003 The Avengers Definitive Series One

COMPLETE SET (100) 6.00 15.00
UNOPENED BOX (36 PACKS) 50.00 60.00
UNOPENED PACK (8 CARDS) 1.75 2.00
COMMON CARD (1-100) .12 .30

2003 The Avengers Definitive Series One Autographs

COMMON AUTO (A1-A13) 6.00 15.00
STATED ODDS 1:12
A12 INSERTED INTO COLLECTOR ALBUM
A1 Honor Blackman 60.00 120.00
A2 Linda Thorson 20.00 50.00
A3 Elizabeth Shepherd 12.00 30.00
A8 Ray Brooks 8.00 20.00
A9 Barrie Ingham 10.00 25.00
A13 Patrick Macnee 150.00 300.00

2003 The Avengers Definitive Series One Bonus Gold Foil

COMPLETE SET (12) 5.00 12.00
COMMON CARD (F1-F12) .60 1.50
STATED ODDS 1:3

2003 The Avengers Definitive Series One Costumes

COMPLETE SET (2) 25.00 60.00
COMMON COSTUME (AVC1-AVC2) 10.00 25.00
STATED ODDS 2:CASE
AVC2 Emma Peel's Boots 15.00 40.00

2003 The Avengers Definitive Series One Promos
COMPLETE SET (3) 5.00 12.00
COMMON CARD 2.00 5.00

2014 Women of the Avengers
COMPLETE SET (54) 6.00 15.00
UNOPENED BOX (24 PACKS) 70.00 90.00
UNOPENED PACK (5 CARDS) 3.00 4.00
COMMON CARD (1-54) .20 .50

2014 Women of the Avengers Autographs
COMMON AUTO 6.00 15.00
STATED ODDS 1:10
A4 Diana Rigg/20
AVPM Patrick Macnee MCI 75.00 150.00
WAHB Honor Blackman 30.00 80.00
WAJP Jacqueline Pearce/199 ALB 12.00 30.00
WALT Linda Thorson 30.00 80.00

2014 Women of the Avengers Gold Foil
COMPLETE SET (9) 8.00 20.00
COMMON CARD (F1-F9) 1.25 3.00
STATED ODDS 1:4

2014 Women of the Avengers Promos
COMMON CARD 2.00 5.00
UCP1 Rigg seated holding pistol/200 6.00 15.00
(Unstoppable)
UCP1 Unstoppable Cards Proof/5

1988 Donruss Awesome All-Stars
COMPLETE SET (99) 6.00 15.00
COMPLETE SET W/VARIATIONS (127) 8.00 20.00
UNOPENED BOX (36 PACKS) 8.00 20.00
UNOPENED PACK (5 STICKERS) .20 .50
COMMON CARD (1-99) .12 .30
COMMON VARIATION .15 .40

1985 Topps Baby
COMPLETE SET (66) 3.00 8.00
COMPLETE SET W/STICKERS (77) 4.00 10.00
UNOPENED BOX (36 PACKS) 25.00 40.00
UNOPENED PACK (10 CARDS+1 STICKER) 1.00 1.20
COMMON CARD (1-66) .10 .25

1985 Topps Baby Stickers
COMPLETE SET (11) 1.25 3.00
COMMON CARD (1-11) .15 .40
STATED ODDS 1:1

1991 Topps Baby-Sitter's Club
COMPLETE SET (55) 6.00 15.00
UNOPENED BOX (48 PACKS) 30.00 50.00
UNOPENED PACK (5 CARDS)
COMMON CARD (1-55) .20 .50

Babylon 5

1996 SkyBox Babylon 5
COMPLETE SET (60) 6.00 15.00
UNOPENED BOX (48 PACKS) 40.00 60.00
UNOPENED PACK (8 CARDS) 1.50 2.00
COMMON CARD (1-60) .20 .50
JMS J Michael Straczynski AU 30.00 80.00
NNO1 Four Crew Members (dealer) 1.50 4.00

1996 SkyBox Babylon 5 Creator's Collection
COMPLETE SET (10) 8.00 20.00
COMMON CARD (CC1-CC10) 1.25 3.00
STATED ODDS 1:10

1996 SkyBox Babylon 5 Laser-Cuts
COMPLETE SET (2) 6.00 15.00
COMMON CARD (L1-L2) 4.00 10.00
STATED ODDS 1:48

1996 SkyBox Babylon 5 Nightwatch Posters
COMPLETE SET (10) 5.00 12.00
COMMON CARD (P1-P10) 1.00 2.50
STATED ODDS 1:5

1996 SkyBox Babylon 5 The Coming of Shadows
COMPLETE SET (9) 8.00 20.00
COMMON CARD (S1-S9) 2.00 5.00
STATED ODDS 1:10

1996 SkyBox Babylon 5 Trivia
COMPLETE SET (50) 8.00 20.00
COMMON CARD (T1-T50) .30 .75
STATED ODDS 1:2

1997 TBS Babylon 5 on TNT Promos
COMPLETE SET (5) 5.00 12.00
COMMON CARD .75 2.00
DRAGON CON EXCLUSIVE

1998 TBS Babylon 5 on TNT SDCC Promos
COMPLETE SET (12) 8.00 20.00
COMMON CARD .75 2.00

1999 SkyBox Babylon 5 Profiles
COMPLETE SET (100) 4.00 10.00
UNOPENED BOX (36 PACKS) 40.00 60.00
UNOPENED PACK (9 CARDS) 1.50 2.50
HE1 STATED PRINT RUN 1000
HE1 Harlon Ellison/1000 25.00 50.00
NNO Group of five PROMO 1.25 3.00

1999 SkyBox Babylon 5 Profiles Autographs
COMMON AUTO (A1-A8) 12.00 25.00
OVERALL AUTO ODDS 1:36
A1 Harlan Ellison 15.00 40.00
A2 Martin Sheen 25.00 60.00
A3 Peter Jurasik 15.00 40.00
A4 Bill Mumy 15.00 40.00
A6 Adrienne Barbeau 12.00 30.00

1999 SkyBox Babylon 5 Profiles Cage Props
COMPLETE SET (18) 8.00 20.00
COMMON CARD (PC1-PC18) 1.25 3.00
STATED ODDS 1:4

1999 SkyBox Babylon 5 Profiles Director's Chair
COMPLETE SET (5) 6.00 15.00
COMMON CARD (DC1-DC5) 2.00 5.00
STATED ODDS 1:16

1999 SkyBox Babylon 5 Profiles Optic Nerve
COMPLETE SET (9) 10.00 25.00
COMMON CARD (ON1-ON9) 2.00 5.00
STATED ODDS 1:12

1999 SkyBox Babylon 5 Profiles Sleeping in Light Autographs
COMMON AUTO 15.00 30.00
OVERALL AUTO ODDS 1:36
SA1 Bruce Boxleitner 20.00 50.00
SA2 Claudia Christian 20.00 50.00
SA4 Mira Furlan 25.00 60.00
SA7 Jeff Conaway 50.00 100.00

1999 SkyBox Babylon 5 Profiles Writer's Desk
COMPLETE SET (3) 4.00 10.00
COMMON CARD (WD1-WD3) 2.00 5.00
STATED ODDS 1:16

1998 Fleer SkyBox Babylon 5 Season Four
COMPLETE SET (81) 6.00 15.00
UNOPENED BOX (36 PACKS) 25.00 40.00
UNOPENED PACK (7 CARDS) 1.00 1.50
COMMON CARD (1-81) .15 .40
*LANGUAGE: .5X TO 1.2X BASIC CARDS
B1 BONUS ONE PER BOX .75 2.00
B1 Entertainment (box bonus) .75 2.00

1998 Fleer SkyBox Babylon 5 Season Four Autographs
COMMON AUTO (A1-A10) 12.00 30.00
STATED ODDS 1:90
A2 Jeff Conaway 50.00 100.00
A3 Stephen Furst 20.00 50.00
A4 Peter Jurasik 15.00 40.00
A5 Andreas Katsulas 50.00 100.00
A6 Bill Mumy 15.00 40.00
A7 Patricia Tallman 20.00 50.00
A8 Jeffrey Willerth 25.00 60.00
A9 Jerry Doyle 15.00 40.00
A10 Bruce Boxleitner 30.00 75.00

1998 Fleer SkyBox Babylon 5 Season Four Fleet of the First Ones
COMPLETE SET (6) 2.00 5.00
COMMON CARD (F1-F6) .60 1.50
STATED ODDS 1:6

1998 Fleer SkyBox Babylon 5 Season Four Promos
COMMON CARD 2.00 5.00
SDCC EXCLUSIVE
2 Non-Sport Update 1997 60.00 120.00
Gummies Awards Exclusive

1998 Fleer SkyBox Babylon 5 Season Four Season One Retrospective
COMPLETE SET (12) 3.00 8.00
COMMON CARD (S1-S12) .50 1.25
STATED ODDS 1:4

1998 Fleer SkyBox Babylon 5 Season Four SkyMotion Space Action
COMPLETE SET (4) 25.00 60.00
COMMON CARD (L1-L4) 8.00 20.00
STATED ODDS 1:90

1998 Fleer SkyBox Babylon 5 Season Four Starfury Nose Art
COMPLETE SET (9) 10.00 25.00
COMMON CARD (V1-V9) 1.50 4.00
STATED ODDS 1:8

1998 Fleer SkyBox Babylon 5 Season Four TNT in the Beginning
COMPLETE SET (2) 6.00 15.00
COMMON CARD (T1-T2) 4.00 10.00
STATED ODDS 1:36

1998 Fleer SkyBox Babylon 5 Season Five
COMPLETE SET (81) 5.00 12.00
UNOPENED BOX (36 PACKS) 25.00 40.00
UNOPENED PACK (9 CARDS) 1.00 1.50
COMMON CARD (1-81) .15 .40
*EMBOSSED: 1X TO 2.5 BASIC CARDS

1998 Fleer SkyBox Babylon 5 Season Five Autographs
COMPLETE SET (22) 400.00 700.00
COMMON AUTO (A1-A22) 7.50 20.00
STATED ODDS 1:36
A1 Bruce Boxleitner 25.00 60.00
A2 Tracy Scoggins 20.00 50.00
A3 Walter Koenig 25.00 50.00
A5 Marjorie Monaghan 12.00 30.00
A7 Denise Gentile 12.00 30.00
A10 P.Tallman 30.00 75.00
J. Willerth
A11 Marie Marshall 10.00 25.00
A16 Penn & Teller 50.00 100.00
A17 Ed Wasser 20.00 50.00
A18 Patricia Tallman 15.00 40.00
A19 Fabiano Udenio 15.00 40.00
A21 Robin A. Downes 10.00 25.00

1998 Fleer SkyBox Babylon 5 Season Five One Exit
COMPLETE SET (6) 5.00 12.00
COMMON CARD (E1-E6) 1.25 3.00
STATED ODDS 1:9

1998 Fleer SkyBox Babylon 5 Season Five River of Souls
COMPLETE SET (9) 6.00 15.00
COMMON CARD (R1-R9) .75 2.00
STATED ODDS 1:4

1998 Fleer SkyBox Babylon 5 Season Five Sleeping Light
COMPLETE SET (9) 10.00 25.00
COMMON CARD (S1-S9) 1.50 4.00
STATED ODDS 1:9

1998 Fleer SkyBox Babylon 5 Season Five Thirdspace
COMPLETE SET (9) 10.00 25.00
COMMON CARD (T1-T9) 1.50 4.00
STATED ODDS 1:6

1998 Fleer SkyBox Babylon 5 Season Five Promos
COMPLETE SET (2) 2.00 5.00
COMMON CARD (NNO) 1.25 3.00

1997 SkyBox Babylon 5 Special Edition
COMPLETE SET (72) 5.00 12.00
UNOPENED BOX (36 PACKS) 25.00 40.00
UNOPENED PACK (8 CARDS) 1.00 1.50
COMMON CARD (1-72) .12 .30
P1 Promo 1.25 3.00

1997 SkyBox Babylon 5 Special Edition Costumes
COMPLETE SET (18) 5.00 12.00
COMMON CARD (C1-C18) .40 1.00
STATED ODDS 1:2

1997 SkyBox Babylon 5 Special Edition Faces of Delenn
COMPLETE SET (4) 6.00 15.00
COMMON CARD (D1-D4) 2.00 5.00
STATED ODDS 1:12

1997 SkyBox Babylon 5 Special Edition Holograms
COMPLETE SET (2) 20.00 50.00
COMMON CARD (H1-H2) 12.00 30.00
STATED ODDS 1:72

1997 SkyBox Babylon 5 Special Edition Trivia
COMPLETE SET (36) 8.00 20.00
COMMON CARD (T51-T86) .20 .50
STATED ODDS 1:1

1997 SkyBox Babylon 5 Special Edition Worlds of Babylon 5
COMPLETE SET (9) 6.00 15.00
COMMON CARD (W1-W9) 1.25 3.00
STATED ODDS 1:6

1995 Fleer Ultra Babylon 5
COMPLETE SET (118) 50.00 100.00
UNOPENED BOX (36 PACKS) 200.00 300.00
UNOPENED PACK (8 CARDS) 6.00 8.00
COMMON CARD (1-118) .40 1.00
4-UP PANEL PROMO MEASURES 5X7 INCHES
P1 4-Up Panel Promo 4.00 10.00

1995 Fleer Ultra Babylon 5 Holograms
COMPLETE SET (8) 100.00 200.00
COMMON CARD (H1-H8) 12.00 30.00
STATED ODDS 1:12

1995 Fleer Ultra Babylon 5 Prismatic Foil
COMPLETE SET (8) 10.00 25.00
COMMON CARD (PF1-PF8) 2.50 6.00
STATED ODDS 1:4

1995 Fleer Ultra Babylon 5 Space Gallery
COMPLETE SET (8) 8.00 20.00

COMMON CARD (SG1-SG8) 2.00 5.00
STATED ODDS 1:4

2002 Complete Babylon 5
COMPLETE SET (120) 4.00 10.00
UNOPENED BOX (40 PACKS) 25.00 60.00
UNOPENED PACK (9 CARDS) 1.00 1.50
P1 Complete Babylon 5 Collage PROMO .40 1.00

2002 Complete Babylon 5 Autographs
COMMON AUTO (A1-A13; DA1) 6.00 15.00
STATED ODDS 1:20
A1b ISSUED AS CASE TOPPER
A1a Michael O'Hare 20.00 50.00
A1b J.M.Straczynski CT/500* 50.00 100.00
A4 Tamlyn Tomita 8.00 20.00
A6 Julia Nickson 8.00 20.00
A7 Tim Choate 8.00 20.00
A8 Mary Kay Adams 8.00 20.00
A10 Jason Carter 8.00 20.00
A12 Phil Morris 8.00 20.00
A13 Sarah Douglas 10.00 25.00
DA1 B.Boxleitner/M. Gilbert 75.00 150.00

2002 Complete Babylon 5 Classic Confrontations
COMPLETE SET (9) 2.00 5.00
COMMON CARD (CC1-CC9) .50 1.25
STATED ODDS 1:4

2002 Complete Babylon 5 Costumes
COMMON COSTUME (C1-C6) 8.00 20.00
STATED ODDS 1:40
C6 ISSUED AS ALBUM EXCLUSIVE
C3 Londo Molari/900* 35.00 70.00
C6 Susan Ivanova ALB/1500* 10.00 25.00

2002 Complete Babylon 5 Legend of the Rangers
COMPLETE SET (6) 8.00 20.00
COMMON CARD (L1-L6) 2.50 6.00
STATED ODDS 1:BOX

2002 Complete Babylon 5 The Movies
COMPLETE SET (12) 8.00 20.00
COMMON CARD (M1-M12) 1.25 3.00
STATED ODDS 1:8

2002 Complete Babylon 5 Women of Babylon 5 in Motion
COMPLETE SET (21) 25.00 50.00
COMMON CARD (W1-W21) 2.00 5.00
STATED ODDS 1:10

2001 Women of Babylon 5 Archive Collection
COMPLETE SET (5) 15.00 40.00
COMMON CARD (1-5) 5.00 12.00

1985 Kellogg's Back to the Future Canadian
COMPLETE SET (8) 12.00 30.00
COMMON CARD (1-8) 2.00 5.00
SCRATCH-OFF CARD NNO .40 1.00
STATED ODDS 1:CEREAL BOX

1989 Topps Back to the Future Part II
COMPLETE SET (88) 5.00 12.00
COMPLETE SET W/STICKERS (99) 6.00 15.00
UNOPENED BOX (36 PACKS) 50.00 75.00
UNOPENED PACK (9 CARDS+STICKER) 2.00 3.00
COMMON CARD (1-88) .12 .30

1989 Topps Back to the Future Part II Stickers
COMPLETE SET (11) 1.50 4.00
COMMON CARD (1-11) .20 .50
STATED ODDS 1:1

1996 Topps Barb Wire
COMPLETE SET (72) 8.00 20.00
UNOPENED BOX (36 PACKS) 50.00 75.00
UNOPENED PACK (8 CARDS) 2.00 3.00
COMMON CARD (1-72) .20 .50

1996 Topps Barb Wire Embossed
COMPLETE SET (12) 5.00 12.00
COMMON CARD (E1-E12) .75 2.00
STATED ODDS 1:1

1996 Topps Barb Wire Laser-Cuts
COMPLETE SET (4) 12.00 30.00
COMMON CARD (L1-L4) 4.00 10.00
STATED ODDS 1:18

1996 Topps Barb Wire Promos
COMMON CARD 1.25 3.00

1992 Panini Barbie and Friends
COMPLETE SET (198) 8.00 20.00
COMMON CARD (1-198) .08 .20

1992 Panini Barbie and Friends Stickers
COMPLETE SET (15) 2.00 5.00
COMMON CARD (1-15) .25 .60

1990 Mattel Barbie Series 1
COMPLETE SET (300) 15.00 40.00
UNOPENED BOX (24 PACKS) 30.00 80.00
UNOPENED PACK (10 CARDS) 1.25 3.00
COMMON CARD (1-300) .10 .25

1991 Mattel Barbie Series 2
COMPLETE SET (320) 15.00 40.00
UNOPENED BOX (24 PACKS) 10.00 25.00
UNOPENED PACK (10 CARDS) .40 1.00
COMMON CARD (1-320) .10 .25

1995 FPG Barclay Shaw
COMPLETE SET (90) 5.00 12.00
UNOPENED BOX (36 PACKS) 8.00 20.00
UNOPENED PACK (10 CARDS) .25 .60
COMMON CARD (1-90) .12 .30
NNO1 Barclay Shaw AU 25.00 60.00
NNO2 Barclay Shaw PROMO

1995 FPG Barclay Shaw Metallic Storm
COMPLETE SET (5) 12.00 30.00
COMMON CARD (MS1-MS5) 3.00 8.00
RANDOMLY INSERTED INTO PACKS

1992 Confex Baseball Enquirer
COMPLETE SET (64) 5.00 12.00
FACTORY SET/185000 (64) 6.00 15.00
COMMON CARD (1-64) .20 .50

1988 Donruss Baseball's Greatest Grossouts
COMPLETE SET (88) 5.00 12.00
COMPLETE SET W/VARIATIONS (124) 6.00 15.00
UNOPENED BOX (36 PACKS) 6.00 15.00
UNOPENED PACK (9 STICKERS) .15 .40
COMMON CARD (1-88) .12 .30

1992 Spoof Comics Batbabe
COMPLETE SET (37) 3.00 8.00
COMMON CARD (1-36; NNO) .12 .30

2015 Bates Motel Season One
COMPLETE SET (72) 6.00 15.00
COMPLETE FACTORY SET (81) 75.00 125.00
COMMON CARD (1-72) .12 .30
*BLUE LOGO: 2X TO 5X BASIC CARDS .60 1.50

2015 Bates Motel Season One Autographed Costumes
COMMON AUTO 10.00 25.00
BC1 Mike Vogel 12.00 30.00
BC4 Freddie Highmore 25.00 60.00
BC5 Freddie Highmore 25.00 60.00
BC6 Freddie Highmore 25.00 60.00
BC7 Olivia Cooke 30.00 75.00
BC8 Diana Bang 12.00 30.00
BC9 Diana Bang 12.00 30.00
BC10 Diana Bang 12.00 30.00

2015 Bates Motel Season One Autographs
COMMON AUTO 5.00 12.00
RANDOMLY INSERTED INTO PACKS
2 Mike Vogel 6.00 15.00
4 Brittney Wilson 6.00 15.00
5 Max Thieriot 8.00 20.00
6 David Cubitt 6.00 15.00
7 Diana Bang 15.00 40.00
9 Freddie Highmore 20.00 50.00
13 Keegan Connor Tracy 8.00 20.00
14 Nestor Carbonell 12.00 30.00
15 Vera Farmiga 60.00 120.00
17 Olivia Cooke 25.00 60.00

2015 Bates Motel Season One The Making of Norman Bates
COMPLETE SET (9) 10.00 25.00
COMMON CARD (M1-M9) 2.00 5.00
STATED ODDS 2:FACTORY SET

2015 Bates Motel Season One Postcards from White Pine Bay
COMPLETE SET (9) 25.00 60.00
COMMON CARD (BP1-BP9) 4.00 10.00
STATED ODDS 2:FACTORY SET

2015 Bates Motel Season One Props
COMPLETE SET (9) 30.00 80.00
COMMON (BP1-BP9) 5.00 12.00
BP3 Bates House Covers 8.00 20.00
BP4 Bates Motel Note Pad 6.00 15.00
BP7 Bedspread (Orange) 6.00 15.00
BP8 Wi-Fi Pamphlet 8.00 20.00

2015 Bates Motel Season One Victims
COMPLETE SET (9) 8.00 20.00
COMMON CARD (V1-V9) 1.50 4.00
STATED ODDS 2:FACTORY SET

2016 Bates Motel Season Two
COMPLETE SET (72) 6.00 15.00
COMMON CARD (1-72) .12 .30
*SILVER: 8X TO 20X BASIC CARDS 2.50 6.00

2016 Bates Motel Season Two Autographed Costumes
COMMON AUTO 8.00 20.00
CAKR Kathleen Robertson 12.00 30.00
CAPK Paloma Kwiatkowski 10.00 25.00

2016 Bates Motel Season Two Autographed Dual Costumes
COMMON AUTO 15.00 40.00
*BLUE INK: SAME VALUE
*GREEN INK: SAME VALUE
*PURPLE INK: SAME VALUE
*RED INK: SAME VALUE
DCFH Freddie Highmore 30.00 75.00
DCOC Olivia Cooke 25.00 60.00
DCVA Vera Farmiga 30.00 75.00
DCVF Vera Farmiga 30.00 75.00

2016 Bates Motel Season Two Autographs
COMMON AUTO 4.00 10.00
*BLUE INK: SAME VALUE
*GREEN INK: SAME VALUE
*RED INK: SAME VALUE
AFH1 Freddie Highmore 20.00 50.00
AKC2 Keegan Connor Tracy 5.00 12.00
AKR1 Kathleen Robertson 10.00 25.00
AMT1 Max Theriot 5.00 12.00
ANC1 Nestor Carbonell 10.00 25.00
AOC1 Olivia Cooke 20.00 50.00
APK1 Paloma Kwiatkowski 8.00 20.00
AVF1 Vera Farmiga 25.00 60.00
AVG1 Vincent Gale 5.00 12.00

2016 Bates Motel Season Two Bates Property
COMPLETE SET (9) 6.00 15.00
COMMON CARD (BP1-BP9) 1.00 2.50
STATED ODDS 2:SET

2016 Bates Motel Season Two Norma and Norman Love-Hate Relationship
COMPLETE SET (9) 8.00 20.00
COMMON CARD (LH1-LH9) 1.25 3.00
STATED ODDS 2:SET

2016 Bates Motel Season Two Props
COMMON PROP (BP1-BP4)
BP1 Door Hangers 8.00 20.00
BP2 Taxidermy Feathers 10.00 25.00
BP3 White Pine Bay's Newspaper 6.00 15.00
BP4 The Living Room

2016 Bates Motel Season Two Rest in Peace
COMPLETE SET (9) 6.00 15.00
COMMON CARD (RP1-RP9) 1.00 2.50
STATED ODDS 2:SET

1996 Topps Bathroom Buddies Test Issue
COMPLETE SET (44) 10.00 25.00
UNOPENED BOX (48 PACKS)
UNOPENED PACK (5 STICKERS)
COMMON CARD (1A-22A;1B-22B) .40 1.00

1996 Topps Bathroom Buddies
COMPLETE SET (66) 20.00 50.00
UNOPENED BOX (48 PACKS) 60.00 100.00
UNOPENED PACK (5 CARDS) 2.00 3.00
COMMON CARD (1A-33A;1B-33B) .40 1.00

2002 Battle of the Planets
COMPLETE SET (72) 4.00 10.00
UNOPENED BOX (40 PACKS) 75.00 125.00
UNOPENED PACK (7 CARDS) 2.00 3.00
COMMON CARD (1-72) .10 .25

2002 Battle of the Planets Animation Cels
COMPLETE SET (6) 5.00 12.00
COMMON CARD (AC1-AC6) 1.50 4.00
STATED ODDS 1:18

2002 Battle of the Planets Autographs
COMMON AUTO (A1-A15) 3.00 8.00
STATED ODDS 1:18
A2 AND A9 NOT ISSUED
A1 Angel Medina 4.00 10.00
A4 Dan Brereton 10.00 25.00
A5 Kevin McCarthy 12.00 30.00
A6 Jason Hofius 4.00 10.00
A8 J. Scott Campbell 6.00 15.00
A10 Alex Horley 4.00 10.00
A11 Brian Rood 4.00 10.00
A12 John Watson 4.00 10.00
A13 Dan Parsons/2000 4.00 10.00
A14 Kevin McCarthy 30.00
A15 Jae Lee 8.00 20.00
NNO Alex Ross ALB 15.00 40.00

2002 Battle of the Planets Premium Previews
COMPLETE BOXED SET (6) 4.00 10.00
COMMON CARD (1-6) 1.25 3.00
STATED PRINT RUN 1978 SER.#'d SETS

2002 Battle of the Planets Princess Exclusives
COMPLETE BOXED SET (6) 4.00 10.00
COMMON CARD (1-6) 1.25 3.00
STATED PRINT RUN 1000 SER.#'d SETS

1994 Merlin BattleCards
COMPLETE SET (140) 4.00 10.00
UNOPENED BOX (36 PACKS) 15.00 25.00
UNOPENED PACK (10 CARDS) .75 1.00
COMMON CARD (1-140) .05 .15
140 The Emperor of Vangoria SP

1994 Merlin BattleCards Treasure

COMPLETE SET (8) 6.00 15.00
COMMON CARD (T1-T8) 1.50 4.00
STATED ODDS 1:12

2000 Upper Deck Battlefield Earth

COMPLETE SET (90) 6.00 15.00
UNOPENED BOX (36 PACKS) 20.00 40.00
UNOPENED PACK (3 CARDS) 1.00 1.50
COMMON CARD (1-90) .12 .30

2000 Upper Deck Battlefield Earth Autographs

COMMON AUTO 20.00 50.00
STATED PRINT RUN 200 SER. #'d SETS
FW2 Forest Whitaker 50.00 100.00
JT1 John Travolta 150.00 300.00

2000 Upper Deck Battlefield Earth PowerDeck

COMPLETE SET (4) 12.00 30.00
COMMON CARD (PD1-PD4) 5.00 12.00
STATED ODDS 1:17 HOBBY
PD2 Terl SP 6.00 15.00

Battlestar Galactica

1978 Battlestar Galactica

COMPLETE SET (132) 12.00 30.00
COMPLETE SET W/STICKERS (154) 15.00 40.00
UNOPENED BOX (36 PACKS) 300.00 500.00
UNOPENED PACK (10 CARDS+1 STICKER) 10.00 15.00
COMMON CARD (1-132) .10 .25

1978 Topps Battlestar Galactica Stickers

COMPLETE SET (22) 3.00 8.00
COMMON CARD (1-22) .20 .50

1996 Dart FlipCards Battlestar Galactica

COMPLETE SET (72) 5.00 12.00
UNOPENED BOX (30 PACKS) 40.00 60.00
UNOPENED PACK (7 CARDS) 1.50 2.00
COMMON CARD (1-72) .12 .30

1996 Dart FlipCards Battlestar Galactica Big Boy

COMPLETE SET (4) 8.00 20.00
COMMON CARD (BB1-BB4) 2.50 6.00
STATED ODDS 1:30

1996 Dart FlipCards Battlestar Galactica Gold Foil

COMPLETE SET (6) 6.00 15.00
COMMON CARD (GF1-GF6) 1.50 4.00
STATED ODDS 1:15

1996 Dart FlipCards Battlestar Galactica Tall Boy Oversized

TB Mechanical Menace 2.50 6.00

1996 Dart FlipCards Battlestar Galactica Promos

P1a Deluxe Trading Cards 1.25 3.00
P1b Deluxe Trading Cards 1.25 3.00
(Collectors International Exclusive)
P2 Deluxe Trading Cards 1.25 3.00
NNO Revell-Monogram Model Ship 50.00 100.00
Limited Edition Collectible Offer
NNO VHS Insert

2006 Battlestar Galactica Colonial Warriors

COMPLETE SET (72) 4.00 10.00
UNOPENED BOX (40 PACKS) 30.00 80.00
UNOPENED PACK (5 CARDS) 1.00 2.00
COMMON CARD (1-72) .10 .30

2006 Battlestar Galactica Colonial Warriors 1978 Battlestar Galactica Expansion

COMPLETE SET (54) 20.00 50.00
COMMON CARD (133-186) .50 1.25
STATED ODDS 1:8

2006 Battlestar Galactica Colonial Warriors ArtiFEX

COMPLETE SET (9) 25.00 60.00
COMMON CARD (S1-S9) 3.00 8.00
STATED ODDS 1:40

2006 Battlestar Galactica Colonial Warriors Autograph Costumes

COMMON AUTO 30.00 75.00
DB Dirk Benedict 100.00 200.00
RH Richard Hatch 75.00 150.00

2006 Battlestar Galactica Colonial Warriors Autographs

COMMON AUTO 6.00 15.00
STATED ODDS 1:BOX
VL (VERY LIMITED): LESS THAN 300 CARDS
A8 ODDS 1: CASE
DA1 ODDS 1:6-CASE PURCHASE
A8 Alex Hyde-White 15.00 40.00
(Case-Topper)
A12 Jane Seymour VL 60.00 120.00
A17 Anne Lockhart VL 15.00 40.00
A18 Sarah Rush VL 12.00 30.00
A19 Glen A. Larson VL 30.00 75.00
A20 Ed Begley, Jr VL 15.00 40.00
A22 Arlene Martel VL 12.00 30.00
A23 Britt Ekland VL 30.00 75.00
A24 Richard Lynch VL 12.00 30.00
A25 Melody Anderson VL 10.00 25.00
A28 Randolph Mantooth VL 25.00 60.00
DA1 Richard Hatch 125.00 250.00
Dirk Benedict

2006 Battlestar Galactica Colonial Warriors Casting Call

COMPLETE SET (9) 30.00 60.00
COMMON CARD (W1-W9) 3.00 8.00
STATED ODDS 1:20

2006 Battlestar Galactica Colonial Warriors Costumes

COMMON COSTUME 8.00 20.00
STATED ODDS 1:BOX
CC12 ODDS 1:COLLECTORS ALBUM
DC1 ODDS 1:2-CASE PURCHASE
DC1 Comm. Adama/Capt. Apollo 50.00 100.00

2006 Battlestar Galactica Colonial Warriors Tribute

COMPLETE SET (2) 30.00 80.00
COMMON CARD (T1-T2) 20.00 50.00
STATED ODDS 1:480

2006 Battlestar Galactica Colonial Warriors Promos

COMMON CARD .75 2.00
P1 Lt. Starbuck 1.00 2.50
P2 Capt. Apollo NSU 1.25 3.00
P3 Ens. Greenbeam ALB .75 2.00
UK Lt. Boomer UK 1.25 3.00

2006 Battlestar Galactica DVD Series

COMPLETE SET (3) 5.00 12.00
COMMON CARD (DVD1-DVD3) 2.00 5.00

1978 General Mills Battlestar Galactica

COMPLETE SET (16) 60.00 120.00
COMMON CARD (1-16) 5.00 12.00

2005 Battlestar Galactica Premiere

COMPLETE SET (72) 4.00 10.00
UNOPENED BOX (40 PACKS) 30.00 80.00
UNOPENED PACK (5 CARDS) 1.00 2.00
COMMON CARD (1-72) .10 .30

2005 Battlestar Galactica Premiere Autographs

COMMON AUTO 6.00 15.00
STATED ODDS 1:40
L (LIMITED): 300-500 CARDS
VL (VERY LIMITED): 200-300 CARDS
AD Aaron Douglas L 15.00 40.00
CR Callum Keith Rennie 10.00 25.00
KS Katee Sackhoff VL 50.00 100.00
MB Matthew Bennett L 10.00 25.00
MH Michael Hogan L 8.00 20.00
TH Tricia Helfer VL 75.00 150.00
JBKS Jamie Bamber 100.00 200.00
Katee Sackhoff

2005 Battlestar Galactica Premiere Costumes

COMMON COSTUME 6.00 15.00
STATED ODDS 1:40
CC1 Number Six 10.00 25.00
CC2 Lt. Kara Starbuck Thrace 8.00 20.00
CC3 Lt. Sharon Boomer Valerii 8.00 20.00
CC4 Lt. Kara Starbuck Thrace 8.00 20.00

2005 Battlestar Galactica Premiere Cylon Threat

COMPLETE SET (9) 10.00 25.00
COMMON CARD (CT1-CT9) 1.25 3.00
STATED ODDS 1:20

2005 Battlestar Galactica Premiere Quotables

COMPLETE SET (9) 12.00 30.00
COMMON CARD (Q1-Q9) 2.00 5.00
STATED ODDS 1:40

2005 Battlestar Galactica Premiere Roll Call

COMPLETE SET (9) 8.00 20.00
COMMON CARD (R1-R9) 1.00 2.50
STATED ODDS 1:10

2005 Battlestar Galactica Premiere Promos

COMMON CARD .75 2.00
P3 Number 6/Baltar ALB 2.50 6.00
UK Cmdr. Adama/Laura Roslin UK 5.00 12.00

2006 Battlestar Galactica Season One

COMPLETE SET (81) 4.00 10.00
UNOPENED BOX (40 PACKS) 30.00 80.00
UNOPENED PACK (5 CARDS) 1.00 2.00
COMMON CARD (1-81) .10 .30
WBG ODDS 1:480
HEND SKETCH ODDS ONE PER 2-CASE PURCHASE
WBG Women of Battlestar Galactica 20.00 50.00
HEND Chris Henderson Sketch

2006 Battlestar Galactica Season One ArtiFEX

COMPLETE SET (9) 8.00 20.00
COMMON CARD (SPA1-SPA9) 1.00 2.50
STATED ODDS 1:20

2006 Battlestar Galactica Season One Autographs

COMMON AUTO 5.00 12.00
STATED ODDS 1:40
THJC ODDS ONE PER 6-CASE PURCHASE
L (LIMITED): 300-500 CARDS
VL (VERY LIMITED): LESS THAN 300 CARDS
GP Grace Park L 30.00 75.00
JB Jamie Bamber VL 50.00 100.00
KM Kandyse McClure L 8.00 20.00
MM Mary McDonnell VL 75.00 150.00
RH Richard Hatch VL 50.00 100.00
RW Robert Wisden L 6.00 15.00
SW Sam Witwer L 8.00 20.00
TP Tahmoh Penikett L 6.00 15.00
THJC Tricia Helfer 100.00 200.00
James Callis

2006 Battlestar Galactica Season One Costumes

COMMON COSTUME 10.00 25.00
STATED ODDS 1:40
CC9 ISSUED AS ALBUM EXCLUSIVE
LC ODDS ONE PER CASE
LC Leoben Conoy DUAL 15.00 40.00

2006 Battlestar Galactica Season One Crossroads

COMPLETE SET (9) 20.00 50.00
COMMON CARD (CR1-CR9) 2.50 6.00
STATED ODDS 1:10

2006 Battlestar Galactica Season One In Motion

COMPLETE SET (6) 40.00 100.00
COMMON CARD (M1-M6) 8.00 20.00
STATED ODDS 1:80

2006 Battlestar Galactica Season One Number Six

COMPLETE SET (6) 40.00 100.00
COMMON CARD (N1-N6) 8.00 20.00
STATED ODDS 1:80

2006 Battlestar Galactica Season One Promos

COMMON CARD .75 2.00
P3 Number 6/Apollo ALB 1.50 4.00
UK Apollo UK 8.00 20.00
CP1 Starbuck CON 1.50 4.00

2007 Battlestar Galactica Season Two

COMPLETE SET (72) 4.00 10.00
UNOPENED BOX (40 PACKS) 75.00 125.00
UNOPENED PACK (5 CARDS) 2.50 3.00
COMMON CARD (1-72) .12 .30
KYLE SKETCH ODDS 1:6-CASE PURCHASE
KYLE Jim Kyle Sketch 150.00 300.00

2007 Battlestar Galactica Season Two Alliances

COMPLETE SET (9) 6.00 15.00
COMMON CARD (A1-A9) 1.25 3.00
STATED ODDS 1:20

2007 Battlestar Galactica Season Two Autographs

COMMON AUTO 6.00 15.00
STATED ODDS 1:40
L (LIMITED): 300-500 CARDS
VL (VERY LIMITED): LESS THAN 300 CARDS
CF Colm Feore L 8.00 20.00
EC Erica Cerra L 10.00 25.00
JC James Callis VL 20.00 50.00
JH John Heard L 12.00 30.00
LC Leah Cairns L 8.00 20.00
LL Lucy Lawless VL 80.00 150.00
MT Michael Trucco L 8.00 20.00
TH Tricia Helfer VL 30.00 75.00

2007 Battlestar Galactica Season Two Costumes

COMMON COSTUME (CC21-CC31) 5.00 12.00
STATED ODDS 1:40
CC31 ISSUED AS ALBUM EXCLUSIVE
DC2 ISSUED AS CASE EXCLUSIVE
KS ISSUED AS 2-CASE INCENTIVE
CC21 Number Six 10.00 25.00
CC22 Galen Tyrol 6.00 15.00
CC24 Samuel Anders 6.00 15.00
CC27 Sharon Valerii 6.00 15.00
CC28 Saul Tigh 6.00 15.00
CC30 Kara Thrace 8.00 20.00
CC31 Number Six ALB
DC2 Priest Elosha CI 25.00 50.00
KS Katie Sackoff AU 2CI

MODERN

2007 Battlestar Galactica Season Two Crew

COMPLETE SET (9)	15.00	40.00
COMMON CARD (T1-T9)	3.00	8.00
STATED ODDS 1:40		

2007 Battlestar Galactica Season Two Rag Tag Fleet

COMPLETE SET (9)	4.00	10.00
COMMON CARD (R1-R9)	.75	2.00
STATED ODDS 1:13		

2007 Battlestar Galactica Season Two Shelter Posters

COMPLETE SET (4)	60.00	120.00
COMMON CARD (S1-S4)	15.00	40.00
STATED ODDS 1:240		
STATED PRINT RUN 250 SER. #'d SETS		

2007 Battlestar Galactica Season Two Women of Battlestar Galactica

COMPLETE SET (6)	12.00	30.00
COMMON CARD (W1-W6)	4.00	10.00
STATED ODDS 1:40		

2007 Battlestar Galactica Season Two Promos

COMMON CARD	.75	2.00
P2 Lee Adama NSU	1.25	3.00
P3 Lee Adama ALB	5.00	12.00

2008 Battlestar Galactica Season Three

COMPLETE SET (63)	4.00	10.00
UNOPENED BOX (24 PACKS)	125.00	200.00
UNOPENED PACK (5 CARDS)	5.00	8.00
UNOPENED ARCHIVE BOX	600.00	1000.00
COMMON CARD (1-63)	.12	.30

2008 Battlestar Galactica Season Three Autographs

COMMON AUTO	6.00	15.00
STATED ODDS 1:12		
EO ODDS ONE PER 6-CASE PURCHASE		
L (LIMITED): 300-500 CARDS		
BD2 Bill Duke L	10.00	25.00
EO Edward James Olmos 6CI	250.00	400.00
GP Grace Park	50.00	100.00
JB Jamie Bamber L	20.00	50.00
JC James Callis L	15.00	40.00
KS Katee Sackhoff	50.00	100.00
MF Michelle Forbes L	20.00	50.00
MM Mary McDonnell L	50.00	100.00
MS Mark Sheppard L	8.00	20.00
RM Ronald D. Moore	12.00	30.00
RW Rick Worthy	8.00	20.00
TP Tahmoh Penikett	8.00	20.00

2008 Battlestar Galactica Season Three Costumes

COMMON COSTUME	4.00	10.00
STATED ODDS 1:24		
TH ODDS ONE PER 2-CASE PURCHASE		
L (LIMITED): 300-500 CARDS		
CC32 William Adama	5.00	12.00
CC34 D'anna Biers	5.00	12.00
CC35 Number Six	6.00	15.00
CC36 Sharon Valerii	10.00	25.00
CC37 Sharon Valerii	10.00	25.00
CC39 Number Six	6.00	15.00
DC3 Gaius Baltar Number Six L	12.00	30.00
DC4 Gaius Baltar Sharon Valerii	12.00	30.00
DC5 Gaius Baltar Number Six L	12.00	30.00
TH Number 6 Tricia Helfer AU	50.00	100.00

2008 Battlestar Galactica Season Three Film Clip Gallery

COMPLETE SET (9)	25.00	60.00
COMMON CARD (F1-F9)	4.00	10.00
STATED ODDS 1:24		

2008 Battlestar Galactica Season Three Love in War

COMPLETE SET (9)	10.00	25.00
COMMON CARD (L1-L9)	1.50	4.00
STATED ODDS 1:12		

2008 Battlestar Galactica Season Three Shelter Posters

COMPLETE SET (3)	30.00	80.00
COMMON CARD (S5-S7)	12.00	30.00
STATED ODDS 1:144		

2008 Battlestar Galactica Season Three Significant Seven

COMPLETE SET (7)	6.00	15.00
COMMON CARD (SS1-SS7)	1.25	3.00
STATED ODDS 1:8		

2008 Battlestar Galactica Season Three Promos

COMMON CARD	.75	2.00
P3 Apollo/Number 6 ALB	4.00	10.00

2009 Battlestar Galactica Season Four

COMPLETE SET (63)	6.00	15.00
UNOPENED BOX (24 PACKS)	125.00	200.00
UNOPENED PACK (5 CARDS)	5.00	8.00
COMMON CARD (1-63)	.15	.40

2009 Battlestar Galactica Season Four Autographs

COMMON AUTO	4.00	10.00
STATED ODDS 1:12		
EICK STATED ODDS ONE PER CASE		
HOGAN/VERNON STATED ODDS ONE PER 2 CASE PURCHASE		
8 Edward James Olmos	250.00	500.00
9 James Callis	12.00	30.00
10 Jamie Bamber	15.00	40.00
11 Kate Vernon	6.00	15.00
12 Katee Sackhoff	30.00	75.00
13 Keegan Connor Tracy	6.00	15.00
14 Leah Cairns	12.00	30.00
15 Leela Savasta	8.00	20.00
16 Matthew Bennett	8.00	20.00
17 Michael Hogan	30.00	75.00
18 Nicki Clyne	10.00	25.00
19 Rekha Sharma	10.00	25.00
20 Rick Worthy	8.00	20.00
21 Stephanie Jacobsen	15.00	40.00
22 David Eick	8.00	20.00
23 M.Hogan/K.Vernon	60.00	120.00

2009 Battlestar Galactica Season Four Autograph Costumes

COMMON AUTO	20.00	50.00
CALLIS STATED ODDS ONE PER 4 CASE PURCHASE		
1 Jamie Bamber	30.00	75.00
4 Nicki Clyne	25.00	60.00
5 Rekha Sharma	30.00	75.00
7 James Callis SP	75.00	150.00

2009 Battlestar Galactica Season Four Costumes

COMMON COSTUME (C41-C51)	4.00	10.00
COSTUME/RELIC COMBINED ODDS 1:12		
C42 Lee Adama	5.00	12.00
C44 Elosha	5.00	12.00
C45 Tory Foster	5.00	12.00

2009 Battlestar Galactica Season Four Dual Costumes

COMMON COSTUME (DC6-DC20)	6.00	15.00
COSTUME/RELIC COMBINED ODDS 1:12		
DC7 Shevon	8.00	20.00
DC9 Lee Adama	10.00	25.00
DC10 Cally Tyrol	8.00	20.00
DC11 Racetrack	8.00	20.00
DC12 Laura Roslin	8.00	20.00

2009 Battlestar Galactica Season Four Final Five

COMPLETE SET (5)	4.00	10.00
COMMON CARD (FF1-FF5)	1.50	4.00
STATED ODDS 1:12		

2009 Battlestar Galactica Season Four Gallery

COMPLETE SET (9)	15.00	40.00
COMPLETE SET W/SP (10)	50.00	100.00
COMMON CARD (G1-G9)	3.00	8.00
STATED ODDS 1:24		
G10 AVAILABLE AS REDEMPTION ONLY		
G10 K.Thrace/L.Roslin SP	35.00	70.00

2009 Battlestar Galactica Season Four Razor

COMPLETE SET (9)	4.00	10.00
COMMON CARD (R1-R9)	1.00	2.50
STATED ODDS 1:8		

2009 Battlestar Galactica Season Four Relics

COMMON CARD (RC1-RC5)	25.00	50.00
PRINT RUN B/WN 200-350		
RC2 Cylon Integration Question	40.00	80.00
RC4 New Caprica Documents	40.00	80.00
RC5 Election Documents	50.00	100.00

2009 Battlestar Galactica Season Four Shelter Posters

COMPLETE SET (3)	30.00	80.00
COMMON CARD (S8-S10)	12.00	30.00
STATED ODDS 1:144		
PRINT RUN 375 SER. #'d SETS		

2009 Battlestar Galactica Season Four Promos

COMMON CARD (P1-P3, CP1)	.75	2.00
P2 Crew (Non-Sport Update Exclusive)	1.25	3.00
P3 Album Exclusive	3.00	8.00
CP1 William Adama/(Philly Spring)	4.00	10.00
P1b Crew (P2 front) (Non-Sport Update Exclusive)		

1978 Wonder Bread Battlestar Galactica

COMPLETE SET (36)	6.00	15.00
COMMON CARD (1-36)	.30	.75

2004 Complete Battlestar Galactica

COMPLETE SET (72)	4.00	10.00
UNOPENED BOX (40 PACKS)	125.00	200.00
UNOPENED PACK (8 CARDS)	3.00	5.00
COMMON CARD (1-72)	.10	.30
CC1 ISSUED AS ALBUM EXCLUSIVE		
CT1 ISSUED AS CASE TOPPER		
CC1 Commander Adama MEM ALB	12.00	30.00
CT1 Opening Monologue/600 CT	20.00	50.00

2004 Complete Battlestar Galactica Autographs

COMMON AUTO (A1-A14; CIA)	6.00	15.00
STATED ODDS TWO PER BOX		
CIA ISSUED AS 2-CASE INCENTIVE		
L (LIMITED): 300-500 COPIES		
VL (VERY LIMITED): 200-300 COPIES		
A1 Richard Hatch L	75.00	150.00
A2 Dirk Benedict VL	75.00	150.00
A4 Noah Hathaway	10.00	25.00
A5 Lloyd Bochner	8.00	20.00
A6 Lance LeGault	8.00	20.00
A7 Audrey Landers	20.00	50.00
A9 Herbert Jefferson Jr.	12.00	30.00
A10 Patrick Macnee L	50.00	100.00
A13 Felix Silla	10.00	25.00
A14 George Murdock	8.00	20.00
A15 Laurette Spang	25.00	60.00
A16 Terry Carter	10.00	25.00
CIA Kent McCord 2CI	25.00	60.00

2004 Complete Battlestar Galactica Colonial Warriors

COMPLETE SET (9)	10.00	25.00
COMMON CARD (CW1-CW9)	1.25	3.00
STATED ODDS 1:10		

2004 Complete Battlestar Galactica Galactica 1980

COMPLETE SET (20)	3.00	8.00
COMMON CARD (G1-G20)	.20	.50
STATED ODDS 1:3		

2004 Complete Battlestar Galactica Matt Busch ArtiFEX

COMPLETE SET (6)	10.00	25.00
COMMON CARD (N1-N6)	2.00	5.00
STATED ODDS 1:20		

2004 Complete Battlestar Galactica Promos

COMMON CARD	.75	2.00
P3 Album Exclusive	2.00	5.00
CON2003 Convention Exclusive	1.50	4.00
GUM2003 NSU Gummie Voting	15.00	40.00

1995 Sports Time Baywatch

COMPLETE SET (100)	6.00	15.00
UNOPENED BOX (36 PACKS)	25.00	60.00
UNOPENED PACK (9 CARDS)	1.50	2.00
COMMON CARD (1-100)	.12	.30

1995 Sports Time Baywatch Autographs

COMMON AUTO	12.00	30.00
STATED ODDS 1:432		
1 David Hasselhoff/200*	120.00	250.00
13 Yasmine Bleeth/1400*	25.00	60.00
44 Yasmine Bleeth	20.00	50.00
45 Yasmine Bleeth	20.00	50.00
72 Alexandra Paul/1300*	30.00	75.00
12A Yasmine Bleeth/1400*	25.00	60.00
12B Yasmine Bleeth	20.00	50.00
14A Yasmine Bleeth/1400*	25.00	60.00
14B Yasmine Bleeth	20.00	50.00

1995 Sports Time Baywatch Phone Cards

COMPLETE SET (11)	30.00	80.00
COMMON CARD (PC1-PC7)	6.00	15.00
COMMON MAIL-IN (PC8-PC10)	2.00	5.00
STATED ODDS 1:36		

1995 Sports Time Baywatch Platinum

COMPLETE SET (26)	20.00	50.00
COMMON CARD (P1-P26)	1.25	3.00

1995 Sports Time Baywatch Rainbow

COMPLETE SET (26)	12.00	30.00
COMMON CARD (R1-R26)	.75	2.00
STATED ODDS 1:6		

1995 Sports Time Baywatch Promos

P David Hasselhoff and Pamela Anderson	.75	2.00

2013 The Beach Boys

COMPLETE SET (120)	10.00	25.00
UNOPENED BOX (24 PACKS)	60.00	100.00
UNOPENED PACK (8 CARDS)	3.00	4.00
COMMON CARD (1-120)	.15	.40
*GOLD SURFER: .75X TO 2X BASIC CARDS		
*ARTIST'S PROOF/99: 8X TO 20X BASIC CARDS		

2013 The Beach Boys Autographs

COMMON MARKS	30.00	80.00
COMMON JARDINE	100.00	200.00
COMMON JOHNSTON	100.00	200.00
COMMON LOVE	100.00	200.00
COMMON WILSON	100.00	200.00
STATED PRINT RUN 65-70		

2013 The Beach Boys Commemorative Guitar Picks

COMPLETE SET (35)	100.00	200.00
COMMON CARD	4.00	10.00

2013 The Beach Boys Commemorative Guitar Picks Dual

COMMON CARD	12.00	30.00

MODERN

2013 The Beach Boys Concert Gear

COMPLETE SET (20)	60.00	120.00
COMMON CARD	5.00	12.00

2013 The Beach Boys Gold Albums

COMPLETE SET (23)	250.00	500.00
COMMON CARD (1-23)	12.00	30.00

2013 The Beach Boys Honors

COMPLETE SET (16)	10.00	25.00
COMMON CARD (1-16)	.75	2.00
*GOLD SURFER: 1X TO 2.5X BASIC CARDS		
*ARTIST PROOF/99: 1.5X TO 4X BASIC CARDS		

2013 The Beach Boys In Their Own Words

COMPLETE SET (14)	15.00	40.00
COMMON CARD (1-14)	1.25	3.00
*GOLD SURFER: 1X TO 2.5X BASIC CARDS		
*ARTIST PROOF/99: 1.5X TO 4X BASIC CARDS		

2013 The Beach Boys On the Record

COMPLETE SET (30)	60.00	120.00
COMMON CARD (1-30)	2.00	5.00
STATED ODDS 1:12		

2013 The Beach Boys Sounds of Summer

COMPLETE SET (12)	6.00	15.00
COMMON CARD (1-12)	.60	1.50
*GOLD SURFER: 1X TO 2.5X BASIC CARDS		
*ARTIST PROOF/99: 1.5X TO 4X BASIC CARDS		

2013 The Beach Boys Top 10 Hits

COMPLETE SET (18)	5.00	12.00
COMMON CARD (1-18)	.40	1.00
*GOLD SURFER: 1X TO 2.5X BASIC CARDS		
*ARTIST PROOF/99: 1.5X TO 4X BASIC CARDS		

1995 Kitchen Sink Press Beat Characters

COMPLETE BOXED SET (36)	5.00	12.00
COMMON CARD (1-36)	.25	.60

1996 Sports Time The Beatles

COMPLETE SET (100)	8.00	20.00
UNOPENED BOX (36 PACKS)	15.00	40.00
UNOPENED PACK (10 CARDS)	.75	1.25
COMMON CARD (1-100)	.15	.40

1996 Sports Time The Beatles Blockbuster Promos

COMPLETE SET (9)	6.00	15.00
COMMON CARD	1.25	3.00
BLOCKBUSTER VIDEO EXCLUSIVE		

1996 Sports Time The Beatles Gold Records

COMPLETE SET (12)	10.00	25.00
COMMON CARD (1-12)	1.50	4.00
STATED ODDS 1:7		

1996 Sports Time The Beatles Magical Mystery Tour

COMPLETE SET (5)	12.00	30.00
COMMON CARD (1-5)	4.00	10.00
STATED ODDS 1:36		

1996 Sports Time The Beatles Meet the Beatles

COMPLETE SET (10)	15.00	40.00
COMMON CARD (1-8)	2.00	5.00
STATED ODDS 1:14		

1996 Sports Time The Beatles Signature Series

COMPLETE SET (4)	120.00	250.00
COMMON CARD (1-4)	20.00	50.00
STATED ODDS 1:144		
24-KT GOLD CARDS		
1 John Lennon	50.00	100.00
2 Paul McCartney	50.00	100.00

1996 Sports Time The Beatles Promo

P1 Dealer Promo and Conventions	.75	2.00

1993 The River Group Beatles Collection

COMPLETE SET (200)	12.00	40.00
UNOPENED BOX (36 PACKS)	20.00	50.00
UNOPENED PACK (10 CARDS)	1.00	1.50
UNOPENED JUMBO PACK (21 CARDS)		
COMMON CARD (1-220)	.15	.40

1993 The River Group Beatles Collection Classic Hits

COMPLETE SET (8)	5.00	12.00
COMMON CARD (1-8)	.75	2.00
STATED ODDS 1:1		
JUMBO PACK EXCLUSIVE		

1993 The River Group Beatles Collection Number 1 Hits

COMPLETE SET (10)	25.00	60.00
COMMON CARD (1-10)	3.00	8.00
STATED ODDS 1:54		

1993 The River Group Beatles Collection US Concert

COMPLETE SET (2)	30.00	80.00
COMMON CARD (1-2)	20.00	50.00
STATED ODDS 1:288		

1993 The River Group Beatles Collection Promos

COMPLETE SET (10)	6.00	15.00
COMMON CARD (1-9, PROMO)	.75	2.00

1996 Tempo Beatrix Potter The Tale of Peter Rabbit

COMPLETE SET (110)	4.00	10.00
UNOPENED BOX (36 PACKS)	20.00	30.00
UNOPENED PACK (7 CARDS)	1.00	1.25
COMMON CARD (1-110)	.08	.20

1996 Tempo Beatrix Potter The Tale of Peter Rabbit Gold Foil Pets

COMPLETE SET (8)	5.00	12.00
COMMON CARD (PS1-PS8)	.75	2.00
STATED ODDS 1:18		

1996 Tempo Beatrix Potter The Tale of Peter Rabbit Pop-Ups

COMPLETE SET (4)	6.00	15.00
COMMON CARD (PU1-PU4)	2.00	5.00
STATED ODDS 1:25		

1987 Mother's Cookies Beauty and the Beast

COMPLETE SET (16)	10.00	25.00
COMMON CARD	1.25	3.00

1992 Upper Deck Beauty and the Beast

COMPLETE SET (198)	20.00	50.00
UNOPENED BOX (36 PACKS)	30.00	40.00
UNOPENED PACK (10 CARDS)	1.00	1.25
COMMON CARD (1-198)	.12	.30

1992 Upper Deck Beauty and the Beast Holograms

COMPLETE SET (9)	12.00	30.00
COMMON CARD (1-9)	2.00	5.00
RANDOMLY INSERTED INTO PACKS		

1994 Fleer Ultra Beavis and Butt-Head

COMPLETE SET (150)	10.00	25.00
UNOPENED BOX (36 PACKS)	100.00	150.00
UNOPENED PACK (5 CARDS)	3.00	4.00
COMMON CARD	.20	.50

1994 Fleer Ultra Beavis and Butt-Head Scratch 'n Sniff

COMPLETE SET (10)	12.00	30.00
COMMON CARD (SKIP-#'d)	1.50	4.00
RANDOMLY INSERTED INTO PACKS		

1993 Heritage Beer Cans Around the World

COMPLETE BOXED SET (100)	5.00	12.00
COMMON CARD (1-100)	.10	.25
STATED PRINT RUN 8,000 SETS		

1995 Authentix Beetle Bailey

COMPLETE SET (50)	5.00	12.00
UNOPENED BOX (36 PACKS)	15.00	25.00
UNOPENED PACK (6 CARDS)	.75	1.00
COMMON CARD (1-50)	.20	.50
P1 Beetle as baseball pitcher PROMO	.60	1.50
PC Production Certificate (factory set insert)/5000*		
NNO Mort Walker Jumbo	.75	2.00

1995 Authentix Beetle Bailey Silver

COMPLETE SET (5)	6.00	15.00
COMMON CARD (AX1-AX5)	1.50	4.00
STATED ODDS 1:6		

1990 Dart FlipCards Beetlejuice

COMPLETE SET (100)	4.00	10.00
COMPLETE SET W/STICKERS (120)	6.00	15.00
COMPLETE FACTORY SET/3000	8.00	20.00
UNOPENED BOX (36 PACKS)	15.00	20.00
UNOPENED PACK (10 CARDS)	.50	.75
COMMON CARD (1-100)	.06	.15

1990 Dart FlipCards Beetlejuice Glow-in-the-Dark Stickers

COMPLETE SET (20)	1.25	3.00
COMMON CARD (1-20)	.12	.30

2001 Beetlejuice

COMPLETE SET (24)	2.50	6.00
COMMON CARD (1-24)	.20	.50

1995 Performance Unlimited Beginner's Bible

COMPLETE SET (50)	2.00	5.00
UNOPENED BOX (24 PACKS)	6.00	10.00
UNOPENED PACK (6 CARDS)		
COMMON CARD (1-50)	.08	.20

1995 Performance Unlimited Beginner's Bible Pop-Ups

COMPLETE SET (10)	1.50	4.00
COMMON CARD (1-10)	.20	.50
STATED ODDS 1:1		

2020 Topps Benefit for Australia

COMPLETE SET (20)	10.00	25.00
COMMON CARD (1-20)	.75	2.00
STATED PRINT RUN SER.#'d SETS		

1992 Berenstain Bears

COMPLETE SET (72)	3.00	8.00
UNOPENED BOX (54 PACKS)	20.00	30.00
UNOPENED PACK (12 CARDS)	.50	.60
COMMON CARD (1-72)	.10	.25

1992 Berenstain Bears Promos

COMPLETE SET (4)		
17 Meanwhile, you cubs	2.00	5.00
93 The attic sure was cluttered	2.00	5.00
103 And other wedding pictures	2.00	5.00
139 Give back those books	2.00	5.00

1993 FPG Bernie Wrightson Master of the Macabre

COMPLETE SET (90)	5.00	12.00
UNOPENED BOX (36 PACKS)	30.00	40.00
UNOPENED PACK (10 CARDS)	.10	1.25
COMMON CARD (1-90)	.10	.30
AU1 Bernie Wrightson AU/1000		
NNO1 Snapper's Quest (album excl.)		

1993 FPG Bernie Wrightson Master of the Macabre Holograms

COMPLETE SET (3)	10.00	25.00
COMMON CARD (1-3)	4.00	10.00
RANDOMLY INSERTED INTO PACKS		

1993 FPG Bernie Wrightson Master of the Macabre Promos

NNO Frankenstein Hologram	2.00	5.00
NNO Advance Comics	.75	2.00
NNO monster chasing woman	1.25	3.00
NNO 6-card panel with cards from Achilleos 2, Joe Jusko ERB 1, Mike Ploog;		

1994 FPG Bernie Wrightson II More Macabre Promos

P3 Two Men Running	.75	2.00
P4 Tree Monsters	.75	2.00
NNO Swamp Thing (NSU)		
NNO Werewolf		
NNO Deluxe #17, oversized		
NNO 5-card panel (SDCC)		

2002 Best Defense Premiere Edition

COMPLETE SET (90)	8.00	20.00
UNOPENED BOX (PACKS)		
UNOPENED PACK (CARDS)		
COMMON CARD (1-90)	.20	.50
UNC 90-Card Uncut Sheet		

2002 Best Defense Premiere Edition Promos

COMPLETE SET (4)	3.00	8.00
COMMON CARD (1-4)	1.25	3.00

2016 Best Dumplings in New York

COMPLETE SET (51)	12.00	30.00
UNOPENED PACK (15 CARDS)	8.00	10.00
COMMON CARD (1-50; CL)	.30	.75

1995 Comic Images Best of Boris

COMPLETE SET (90)	12.00	30.00
UNOPENED BOX (36 PACKS)	75.00	90.00
UNOPENED PACK (7 CARDS)	2.50	3.00
COMMON CARD (1-90)	.20	.50
*REFRACTORS: 5X TO 12X BASIC CARDS	2.50	6.00
M1 Two-Headed Beast (Medallion Card)/3401*	10.00	25.00
AU1 The Magnificent AU/500	20.00	50.00
NNO Promo (unnumbered) (General Distribution)	.75	2.00
6PAN2 6-Card Panel (Album Exclusive)	3.00	8.00

1995 Comic Images Best of Boris OmniChrome

COMPLETE SET (6)	15.00	40.00
COMMON CARD (1-6)	3.00	8.00
STATED ODDS 1:16		

1995 Comic Images Best of Boris Triadmiration

COMPLETE SET (3)	15.00	40.00
COMMON CARD (1-3)	6.00	15.00
STATED ODDS 1:36		

1996 FPG Best of Dave Dorman

COMPLETE SET (90)	15.00	40.00
UNOPENED BOX (36 PACKS)	20.00	30.00
UNOPENED PACK (7 CARDS)	1.00	1.25
COMMON CARD (1-90)	.30	.75

1996 FPG Best of Dave Dorman Holochrome

COMPLETE SET (6)	15.00	40.00
COMMON CARD (1-6)	3.00	8.00
STATED ODDS 1:12		

1994 Comic Images Best of Frazetta

COMPLETE SET (90)	10.00	25.00
UNOPENED BOX (36 PACKS)	20.00	25.00
UNOPENED PACK (7 CARDS)	.75	1.00
COMMON CARD (1-90)	.20	.50
*REFRACTOR: 4X TO 10X BASIC CARDS		

1994 Comic Images Best of Frazetta Comic Covers

COMPLETE SET (3)	15.00	40.00
COMMON CARD (S1-S3)	6.00	15.00
STATED ODDS 1:108		

1994 Comic Images Best of Frazetta MagnaChrome

COMPLETE SET (6)	12.00	30.00
COMMON CARD (M1-M6)	3.00	8.00
STATED ODDS 1:16		
UNC 6-Up Panel (M1-M6)		

1996 FPG Best of Rowena

COMPLETE SET (90)	6.00	15.00
UNOPENED BOX (36 PACKS)	15.00	20.00
UNOPENED PACK (7 CARDS)	.40	.60
COMMON CARD (1-90)	.12	.30

1996 FPG Best of Rowena Holochrome

COMPLETE SET (6)	12.00	30.00
COMMON CARD (1-6)	3.00	8.00
STATED ODDS 1:16		

1995 Comic Images Best of Royo

COMPLETE SET (90)	10.00	25.00
UNOPENED BOX (36 PACKS)	50.00	60.00
UNOPENED PACK (7 CARDS)	2.00	2.25
COMMON CARD (1-90)	.30	.60
*HOLOCHROME: 4X TO 10X BASIC CARDS		
AU Nine Tongues and One Tear AU/500*	20.00	50.00
NNO The Best of Royo All-Chromium PROMO	1.25	3.00
NNO Look into the Sun (Medallion)	10.00	25.00

1995 Comic Images Best of Royo Creatures

COMPLETE SET (3)	15.00	40.00
COMMON CARD (1-3)	6.00	15.00
STATED ODDS 1:36		

1995 Comic Images Best of Royo Metallic

COMPLETE SET (6)	15.00	40.00
COMMON CARD (M1-M6)	3.00	8.00
STATED ODDS 1:16		

1996 Comic Images Best of the Hildebrandts

COMPLETE SET (90)	10.00	25.00
UNOPENED BOX (36 PACKS)	15.00	25.00
UNOPENED PACK (7 CARDS)	1.25	1.50
COMMON CARD (1-90)	.25	.60
*HOLOCHROME: 4X TO 10X BASIC CARDS	2.50	6.00
P1 Woman Riding Unicorn PROMO	.75	2.00
AU Greg Hildebrandt (gold ink) AU/500	20.00	50.00
AU Tim Hildebrandt (gold ink) AU/500	20.00	50.00
NNO Ekedadhim MagnaChrome Bonus	2.00	5.00
NNO Non-Chromium 6-Up Panel		

1996 Comic Images Best of the Hildebrandts MagnaChrome

COMPLETE SET (6)	15.00	40.00
COMMON CARD (M1-M6)	3.00	8.00
STATED ODDS 1:16		

1996 Comic Images Best of the Hildebrandts MagnaChrome Subset

COMPLETE SET (3)	15.00	40.00
COMMON CARD (1-3)	6.00	15.00
STATED ODDS 1:36		

2000 Best of The Wild Wild West Season One

COMPLETE SET (100)	5.00	12.00
UNOPENED BOX (36 PACKS)	200.00	300.00
UNOPENED PACK (9 CARDS)	6.00	8.00
COMMON CARD (1-100)	.15	.40
UNC 100-Card Base Set Uncut Sheet (Steve Charendoff Autograph)/100		

2000 Best of The Wild Wild West Season One Autographs

COMMON AUTO (A1-A14)	6.00	15.00
RANDOMLY INSERTED INTO PACKS		
A1 Robert Conrad	50.00	100.00
A2 Yvonne Craig	50.00	100.00
A3 Lloyd Bochner	10.00	25.00
A4 Jean Hale	12.00	30.00
A5 Richard Kiel	20.00	50.00
A6 Phoebe Dorin	12.00	30.00
A7 J.D. Cannon	8.00	20.00
A8 BarBara Luna	25.00	60.00
A10 Sigrid Valdis	25.00	60.00
A12 Sue Ane Langdon	15.00	40.00
A13 William Campbell	50.00	100.00
A14 Don Rickles	60.00	120.00

2000 Best of The Wild Wild West Season One Case-Toppers

COMPLETE SET (5)	10.00	25.00
STATED ODDS ONE PER CASE		

2000 Best of The Wild Wild West Season One Commemorative

COMPLETE SET (2)	6.00	15.00
COMMON CARD (C1-C2)	4.00	10.00
STATED ODDS 1:36		

2000 Best of The Wild Wild West Season One Master of Disguise

COMPLETE SET (9)	7.50	20.00
COMMON CARD (M1-M9)	1.00	2.50
STATED ODDS 1:6		

2000 Best of The Wild Wild West Season One Vintage West

COMPLETE SET (9)	5.00	12.00
COMMON CARD (W1-W9)	.75	2.00
STATED ODDS 1:4		

2000 Best of The Wild Wild West Season One Promos

COMPLETE SET (2)	2.00	5.00
COMMON CARD	1.25	3.00
P1 Wild Wild West GEN	1.25	3.00
P2 Wild Wild West ALB	1.25	3.00

2001 Best of The Wild Wild West Season Two Promo

P1 Promo	6.00	15.00

2016 Better Call Saul Dog Tags

COMPLETE SET (24)	30.00	80.00
UNOPENED BOX (24 PACKS)	85.00	100.00
UNOPENED PACK (1 TAG+1 STICKER)	4.00	5.00
COMMON TAG (1-24)	2.00	5.00
*FOIL: .75X TO 2X BASIC CARDS		

2016 Better Call Saul Dog Tags 3-D Tags

COMPLETE SET (4)	30.00	80.00
COMMON TAG (3D1-3D4)	10.00	25.00
STATED ODDS 1:24		

2016 Better Call Saul Dog Tags Stickers

COMPLETE SET (24)	6.00	15.00
COMMON STICKER (1-24)	.60	1.25
FOIL: .75X TO 2.5X BASIC STICKERS		
STATED ODDS 1:1		

2014 Bettie Page

COMPLETE SET (72)	6.00	15.00
UNOPENED BOX (24 PACKS)	150.00	200.00
UNOPENED PACK (6 CARDS)	6.00	8.00
COMMON CARD (1-72)	.20	.50

2014 Bettie Page Calendar Girl

COMPLETE SET (12)	12.00	30.00
COMMON CARD (1-12)	2.00	5.00

2014 Bettie Page Cut Signatures

COMMON AUTO (BPCS1-BPCS5)	120.00	200.00
*GOLD FOIL/10: .75X TO 1.2X BASIC AUTOS		

2014 Bettie Page Pajamas

COMPLETE SET (10)	225.00	450.00
COMMON MEM (BPPJ1-BPPJ10)	20.00	50.00
*GOLD FOIL/25: .75X TO 2X BASIC MEM	50.00	100.00

2014 Bettie Page Queen of the Pin-Ups

COMPLETE SET (16)	8.00	20.00
COMMON CARD (1-16)	1.25	3.00

1995 21st Century Archives Bettie Page In Black Lace

COMPLETE SET (50)	5.00	12.00
COMPLETE FACTORY SET (51)	6.00	15.00
UNOPENED BOX (36 PACKS)	30.00	40.00
UNOPENED PACK (8 CARDS)	1.00	1.25
COMMON CARD (1-50)	.20	.50

1995 21st Century Archives Bettie Page In Black Lace Bettie in Jungle Land

COMPLETE SET (5)	6.00	15.00
COMMON CARD (1B-5B)	1.50	4.00

1995 21st Century Archives Bettie Page In Black Lace SpectraTone

COMPLETE SET (5)	8.00	20.00
COMMON CARD (ST1-ST5)	2.00	5.00
RANDOMLY INSERTED INTO PACKS		

1995 Krome Betty Boop

COMPLETE SET (110)	8.00	20.00
UNOPENED BOX (36 PACKS)	50.00	75.00
UNOPENED PACK (5 CARDS)	2.00	2.50
COMMON CARD (1-110)	.15	.40
NNO Oversized Chromium AU		
NNO Uncut Sheet		

1995 Krome Betty Boop Chrome

COMPLETE SET (20)	6.00	15.00
COMMON CARD (C1-C20)	.40	1.00
*HOLOCHROME: 4X TO 10X BASIC CARDS	4.00	10.00
STATED ODDS 1:1		

2001 Betty Boop

COMPLETE SET (72)	5.00	12.00
UNOPENED BOX (36 PACKS)	30.00	40.00
UNOPENED PACK (6 CARDS)	1.00	1.25
COMMON CARD (1-72)	.12	.30
A1 Richard Fleischer AU	15.00	40.00
BT1 Box Topper Holographic Foil	1.25	3.00
CT1 Max Fleischer	10.00	25.00

2001 Betty Boop All About Betty Risky Foil

COMPLETE SET (6)	12.00	30.00
COMMON CARD (RF1-RF6)	2.50	6.00
STATED ODDS 1:11		

2001 Betty Boop Friends of Betty Boop

COMPLETE SET (4)	5.00	12.00
COMMON CARD (FB1-FB4)	1.50	4.00
STATED ODDS 1:16		

2001 Betty Boop Promos

CC San Diego Comic Con	1.50	4.00
P1 Non-chromium	.75	2.00
PF1 Chromium	2.00	5.00

1997 Krome Betty Boop Pin-Ups

COMPLETE SET (45)	5.00	12.00
UNOPENED BOX (36 PACKS)		
UNOPENED PACK		
COMMON CARD (1-45)	.10	.25

1997 Krome Betty Boop Pin-Ups Oversized Refractors

COMPLETE SET (6)		
COMMON CARD (OS1-OS6)	2.00	5.00
STATED ODDS 1:		

1997 Krome Betty Boop Pin-Ups Series 2

COMPLETE SET (45)	5.00	12.00
UNOPENED BOX (36 PACKS)		
UNOPENED PACK		
COMMON CARD (1-45)	.10	.25

1997 Krome Betty Boop Pin-Ups Series 2 NecroChrome

COMPLETE SET (6)	6.00	15.00
COMMON CARD (NC1-NC6)	1.50	4.00
RANDOMLY INSERTED INTO PACKS		

1997 Krome Betty Boop Pin-Ups Series 2 Oversized Refractors

COMPLETE SET (6)	8.00	20.00
COMMON CARD (OS1-OS6)	2.00	5.00
STATED ODDS 1:3 CASES		

1994 Topps Betty Page Illustrated Promo

NNO Betty Page (green background)	6.00	15.00

1993 Eclipse Beverly Hillbillies

COMPLETE SET (110)	5.00	12.00
UNOPENED BOX (36 PACKS)	30.00	50.00
UNOPENED PACK (12 CARDS)	1.00	1.50
PROMO PACK (5 CARDS)		
COMMON CARD (1-110)	.08	.20

1993 Eclipse Beverly Hillbillies Black Gold Foil

COMPLETE SET (9)	15.00	40.00
COMMON CARD (1-9)	2.50	6.00
STATED ODDS 1:12		

1991 Topps Beverly Hills 90210

COMPLETE SET (88)	5.00	12.00
COMPLETE SET W/STICKERS (99)	6.00	15.00
UNOPENED BOX (36 PACKS)	20.00	25.00
UNOPENED PACK (8 CARDS+1 STICKER)	.50	.75
COMMON CARD (1-88)	.08	.20

1991 Topps Beverly Hills 90210 Stickers

COMPLETE SET (11)	1.25	3.00
COMMON CARD (1-11)	.20	.50
STATED ODDS 1:1		

1991 General Mills Beverly Hills 90210 Black Backs

COMPLETE SET (12)	3.00	8.00
COMMON CARD	.50	1.25
*PURPLE BACKS: SAME VALUE		

2003 Beyblade

COMPLETE SET (72)	6.00	15.00
UNOPENED BOX (36 PACKS)	15.00	20.00
UNOPENED PACK (6 CARDS)	.50	.75
COMMON CARD (1-72)	.15	.40
*FOIL: .5X TO 1.2X BASIC CARDS	.20	.50

1993 Comic Images Beyond Bizarre Jim Warren's Surrealism

COMPLETE SET (90)	8.00	20.00
UNOPENED BOX (48 PACKS)	30.00	40.00
UNOPENED PACK (10 CARDS)	.75	1.00
COMMON CARD (1-90)	.15	.40

1993 Comic Images Beyond Bizarre Jim Warren's Surrealism OptiPrisms

COMPLETE SET (3)	3.00	8.00
COMMON CARD (1-3)	2.00	5.00
STATED ODDS 1:16		

1993 Comic Images Beyond Bizarre Jim Warren's Surrealism Spectrascope

COMPLETE SET (3)	3.00	8.00
COMMON CARD (S1-S3)	2.00	5.00
STATED ODDS 1:16		

1995 TCM Associates Bicycle Museum of America

COMPLETE SET (3)	2.00	5.00
COMMON CARD (1-3)	.75	2.00

2012 The Big Bang Theory Seasons One and Two

COMPLETE SET (72)	8.00	20.00
UNOPENED BOX (24 PACKS)	600.00	1200.00
UNOPENED PACK (5 CARDS)	25.00	50.00
COMMON CARD (1-72)	.25	.60
P1 Big Bang Theory PROMO	3.00	8.00

2012 The Big Bang Theory Seasons One and Two Wardrobes

COMMON MEM (M1-M18)	12.00	30.00
STATED ODDS 1:24		
M18 ISSUED AS BINDER EXCLUSIVE		
M1 Sheldon's Bathrobe	15.00	40.00
M2 Sheldon's Purple Undershirt	15.00	40.00
M3 Sheldon's Blue Undershirt	15.00	40.00
M4 Sheldon's Plaid Pants	15.00	40.00
M15 Penny's Hoodie	60.00	120.00
M16 Penny's Sweatpants	100.00	200.00
M17 Penny's Top	50.00	100.00
M18 Sheldon's Pajamas SP ALB	15.00	40.00
NNO Five-Piece	300.00	450.00

2012 The Big Bang Theory Seasons One and Two Autographs

COMMON AUTO (A1-A11)	8.00	20.00
STATED ODDS 1:24		
R=RARE, U=UNCOMMON		
A1 Johnny Galecki R	150.00	300.00
A2 Jim Parsons R	300.00	500.00
A3 Kaley Cuoco R	1500.00	3000.00
A4 Simon Helberg R	200.00	350.00
A5 Kunal Nayyar R	200.00	350.00
A6 Kevin Sussman U	25.00	60.00
A8 Laurie Metcalf U	15.00	40.00
A10 Alice Amter	10.00	25.00
A11 Courtney Henggeler	30.00	75.00

2012 The Big Bang Theory Seasons One and Two Behind-the-Scenes

COMPLETE SET (9)	25.00	50.00
COMMON CARD (C1-C9)	4.00	10.00
OVERALL CHASE ODDS 1:6		

2012 The Big Bang Theory Seasons One and Two Special Moments

COMPLETE SET (9)	10.00	25.00
COMMON CARD (F1-F9)	2.00	5.00
OVERALL CHASE ODDS 1:6		

2012 The Big Bang Theory Seasons Three and Four

COMPLETE SET (68)	6.00	15.00
UNOPENED BOX (24 PACKS)	150.00	250.00
UNOPENED PACK (5 CARDS)	6.00	10.00
COMMON CARD (1-67)	.20	.50

2012 The Big Bang Theory Seasons Three and Four Autograph Wardrobes

COMMON AUTO	150.00	300.00
OVERALL AUTO ODDS 1:24		
A1 Johnny Galecki	200.00	400.00
A2 Jim Parsons	300.00	450.00
A3 Kaley Cuoco	1000.00	1500.00
A6 Mayim Bialik	250.00	400.00
A7 Melissa Rauch	200.00	350.00

2012 The Big Bang Theory Seasons Three and Four Autographs

COMMON AUTO (A8-A20)	8.00	20.00
OVERALL AUTO ODDS 1:24		
A8 Aarti Mann	12.00	30.00
A11 Christine Baranski	12.00	30.00
A12 Laurie Metcalf	12.00	30.00
A15 Carol Ann Susi	50.00	100.00
A16 Danica McKellar	20.00	50.00
A17 Wil Wheaton	20.00	50.00
A18 Rick Fox	10.00	25.00
A19 Levar Burton	20.00	50.00

2012 The Big Bang Theory Seasons Three and Four Dual Wardrobes

COMMON MEM (DM1-DM7)	20.00	50.00
OVERALL WARDROBE ODDS 1:24		
DM1 Penny/Sheldon	50.00	100.00
DM2 Amy/Sheldon	20.00	50.00
DM3 Leonard/Sheldon	20.00	50.00
DM5 Penny/Leonard	30.00	75.00
DM6 Howard/Bernadette	20.00	50.00

2012 The Big Bang Theory Seasons Three and Four Duos

COMPLETE SET (9)	10.00	25.00
COMMON CARD (CPL1-CPL9)	2.00	5.00
STATED ODDS 1:12		

2012 The Big Bang Theory Seasons Three and Four The Elevator

COMPLETE SET (9)	10.00	25.00
COMMON CARD (E1-E9)	2.00	5.00
STATED ODDS 1:12		

2012 The Big Bang Theory Seasons Three and Four Wardrobes

COMMON MEM	10.00	25.00
OVERALL WARDROBE ODDS 1:24		
M29 ISSUED AS ALBUM EXCLUSIVE		
M1a Sheldon's Purple Shirt	20.00	50.00
M1b Shelbot's Purple Shirt	20.00	50.00
M2 Leonard's Boxers	20.00	50.00
M3 Penny's Blue Tank	20.00	50.00
M4 Raj's Cream Shirt	12.00	30.00
M7 Bernadette's Floral Shirt	20.00	50.00
M8 Sheldon's Green Shirt	12.00	30.00
M9 Leonard's Blue Shirt	12.00	30.00
M10 Penny's Yellow Tank	20.00	50.00
M13 Bernadette's Red Scarf	12.00	30.00
M14 Sheldon's Lt. Blue Shirt	15.00	40.00
M15 Leonard's Grey Sweatshirt	12.00	30.00
M16 Penny's Floral Dress	25.00	60.00
M19 Sheldon's Green Shirt	15.00	40.00
M20 Leonard's Blue Shirt	20.00	50.00
M21 Penny's Pink PJ Pants	50.00	100.00
M23 Sheldon's Purple Undershirt	12.00	30.00
M24 Leonard's Red Shirt	12.00	30.00
M26 Penny's Pink Tank	20.00	50.00
M27 Sheldon's Red Shirt	12.00	30.00
M29 Howard's Shirt ALB	25.00	50.00

2013 The Big Bang Theory Season Five

COMPLETE SET (68)	6.00	15.00
UNOPENED BOX (24 PACKS)	65.00	80.00
UNOPENED PACK (5 CARDS)	3.00	3.50
COMMON CARD (1-68)	.20	.50
P1 Full Cast PROMO NSU	1.50	4.00

2013 The Big Bang Theory Season Five Autographs

COMMON AUTO (A1-A21)	6.00	15.00
STATED ODDS 1:24		
A1 Johnny Galecki	150.00	300.00
A2 Jim Parsons	250.00	400.00
A4 Simon Helberg	125.00	250.00
A5 Kunal Nayyar	125.00	250.00
A6 Jim Parsons	150.00	300.00
A7 Simon Helberg	150.00	300.00
A8 Leonard Nimoy	250.00	400.00
A9 Becky O'Donohue	12.00	30.00
A10 Brent Spiner	20.00	50.00
A12 Joshua Malina	10.00	25.00
A14 Kevin Sussman	12.00	30.00
A15 John Ross Bowie	10.00	25.00
A18 Katie Leclerc	12.00	30.00
A19 Lance Barber	8.00	20.00
A20 Laurie Metcalf	10.00	25.00

2013 The Big Bang Theory Season Five Quotables

COMPLETE SET (9)	12.00	30.00
COMMON CARD (QTB01-QTB09)	2.50	6.00
STATED ODDS 1:12		

2013 The Big Bang Theory Season Five Standees

COMPLETE SET (7)	10.00	25.00
COMMON CARD (CS01-CS07)	2.50	6.00
STATED ODDS 2:24		

2013 The Big Bang Theory Season Five Wardrobes

COMMON MEM	8.00	20.00
STATED ODDS 1:18		
M39 ISSUED AS ALBUM EXCLUSIVE		
M1 Sheldon Cooper	12.00	30.00
M2 Leonard Hofstadter	15.00	40.00
M3 Penny	25.00	60.00
M6 Bernadette	15.00	40.00
M7 Amy Farrah Fowler	12.00	30.00
M8 Sheldon Cooper	10.00	25.00
M9 Leonard Hofstadter	10.00	25.00
M12 Penny	25.00	60.00
M13 Bernadette	15.00	40.00
M14 Sheldon Cooper	12.00	30.00
M15 Leonard Hofstadter	10.00	25.00
M16 Amy Farrah Fowler	12.00	30.00
M17 Rajesh Koothrappali	10.00	25.00
M19 Bernadette	12.00	30.00
M20 Amy Farrah Fowler	12.00	30.00
M21 Sheldon Cooper	20.00	50.00
M22 Leonard Hofstadter	12.00	30.00
M23 Penny	25.00	60.00
M24 Rajesh Koothrappali	10.00	25.00
M25 Howard Wolowitz	15.00	40.00
M26 Amy Farrah Fowler	10.00	25.00
M27 Leonard Hofstadter	10.00	25.00
M29 Penny	25.00	60.00
M30 Rajesh Koothrappali	10.00	25.00
M31 Bernadette	12.00	30.00
M32 Barry Kripke	10.00	25.00
M33 Penny	25.00	60.00
M34 Sheldon Cooper	10.00	25.00
M35 Leonard Hofstadter	12.00	30.00
M36 Amy Farrah Fowler	10.00	25.00
M37 Rajesh Koothrappali	12.00	30.00
M39 Penny ALB	30.00	60.00

2016 The Big Bang Theory Seasons 6 and 7

COMPLETE SET (72)	6.00	15.00
UNOPENED BOX (24 PACKS)	65.00	80.00
UNOPENED PACK (5 CARDS)	3.00	4.00
COMMON CARD (1-72)	.20	.50
*SILVER FOIL: 1.5X TO 4X BASIC CARDS		
P1 The Big Bang Theory Seasons 6 and 7 Promo GEN2.00 5.00		

2016 The Big Bang Theory Seasons 6 and 7 Algorithm Puzzle

COMPLETE SET (9)	6.00	15.00
COMMON CARD (Z1-Z9)	1.00	2.50
*SILVER FOIL: .75X TO 2X BASIC CARDS		
STATED ODDS 1:4		

2016 The Big Bang Theory Seasons 6 and 7 Artist Series

COMPLETE SET (7)	8.00	20.00
COMMON CARD (01-07)	2.00	5.00
*SILVER FOIL: .75X TO 2X BASIC CARDS		
*CRYPTOMIUM: 1X TO 2.5X BASIC CARDS		
STATED ODDS 1:4		

2016 The Big Bang Theory Seasons 6 and 7 Autographed Memorabilia

COMMON AUTO	125.00	250.00
MBM Mayim Bialik	150.00	300.00
MRM Melissa Rauch	150.00	300.00

2016 The Big Bang Theory Seasons 6 and 7 Autographs

COMMON AUTO	6.00	15.00
STATED ODDS 1:32		
BN1 Bob Newhart	60.00	120.00
BN2 Bob Newhart	30.00	75.00
BP1 Brian Posehn	12.00	30.00
BP2 Brian Posehn	8.00	20.00
CB1 Christine Baranski	8.00	20.00
CB2 Christine Baranski	8.00	20.00
KM1 Kate Micucci	20.00	50.00
KM2 Kate Micucci	20.00	50.00
LM1 Laurie Metcalf	8.00	20.00
LM2 Laurie Metcalk	8.00	20.00
LS1 Laura Spencer	8.00	20.00
LS2 Laura Spencer	8.00	20.00
MB1 Mayim Bialik	125.00	250.00
MB2 Mayim Bialik	125.00	250.00
MH1 Margo Harshman	12.00	30.00
MH2 Margo Harshman	8.00	20.00
MR1 Melissa Rauch	100.00	200.00
MR2 Melissa Rauch	100.00	200.00
SH1 Simon Helberg	125.00	250.00
SH2 Simon Helberg	100.00	200.00

2016 The Big Bang Theory Seasons 6 and 7 Dual Memorabilia

COMMON MEM (DM1-DM9)	12.00	30.00
STATED ODDS 1:96		
DM2 Kaley Cuoco/Johnny Galecki	15.00	40.00
DM7 Mayim Bialik/Kaley Cuoco	20.00	50.00
DM8 Melissa Rauch/Jim Parsons	20.00	50.00
DM9 Simon Helberg/Kunal Nayyar	25.00	60.00

2016 The Big Bang Theory Seasons 6 and 7 Memorabilia

COMMON MEM (M1-M37)	5.00	12.00
STATED ODDS 1:15		
M1 Kaley Cuoco	10.00	25.00
M2 Mayim Bialik	8.00	20.00
M3 Kunal Nayyar	6.00	15.00
M6 Rubber gloves	12.00	30.00
M8 Kunal Nayyar	8.00	20.00
M10 Jim Parsons	10.00	25.00
M11 Kaley Cuoco	10.00	25.00
M12 Jigsaw Puzzle	20.00	50.00
M14 Kaley Cuoco	12.00	30.00
M15 Melissa Rauch	12.00	30.00
M16 Kunal Nayyar	6.00	15.00
M17 Jim Parsons	10.00	25.00
M18 Simon Helberg	6.00	15.00
M19 Kaley Cuoco	10.00	25.00
M21 Mayim Bialik	20.00	50.00
M22 Model Train Set Felt	12.00	30.00
M24 Johnny Galecki	10.00	25.00
M25 Simon Helberg	8.00	20.00
M26 Kaley Cuoco	12.00	30.00
M29 Mayim Bialik	6.00	15.00
M30 Kaley Cuoco	25.00	60.00
M31 Jim Parsons	8.00	20.00
M34 Johnny Galecki	6.00	15.00
M35 Kaley Cuoco	12.00	30.00
M36 Mayim Bialik	8.00	20.00
M37 Jim Parsons ALB	30.00	75.00

2016 The Big Bang Theory Seasons 6 and 7 Portraits

COMPLETE SET (7)	6.00	15.00
COMMON CARD (CP1-CP7)	1.25	3.00
*SILVER FOIL: 1X TO 2.5X BASIC CARDS		
STATED ODDS 1:4		

1992 Tundra Big Budget Circus

COMPLETE SET (36)	5.00	12.00
COMMON CARD (1-36)	.25	.60

2014 Big Hero 6 Dog Tags

COMPLETE SET (24)	25.00	60.00
COMMON TAG (1-24)	1.50	4.00
*FOIL: .75X TO 2X BASIC TAGS		

2014 Big Hero 6 Dog Tags Stickers

COMPLETE SET (8)	3.00	8.00
COMMON STICKER	.50	1.25

1988 Leesley Bigfoot

COMPLETE SET (100)	5.00	12.00
COMMON CARD (1-100)	.10	.25

1992 Bikini Open

COMPLETE SET (45)	2.00	5.00

MODERN

COMPLETE BOXED SET (45) 2.00 5.00
UNOPENED BOX (36 PACKS) 8.00 10.00
UNOPENED PACK (8 CARDS) .40 .50
COMMON CARD (1-45) .10 .25

1992 Bikini Open Promos

COMPLETE SET (5) 3.00 8.00
COMMON CARD .75 2.00
1C Patricia Ford 1.25 3.00
(no name)

1991 Pro Set Bill and Ted's Atypical Movie

COMPLETE SET (100) 8.00 20.00
UNOPENED BOX (36 PACKS) 20.00 40.00
UNOPENED PACK (10 CARDS) 1.00 1.50
COMMON CARD (1-100) .15 .40
NNO Bill and Ted's PROMO .60 1.50

1995 SkyBox Bill Nye the Science Guy

COMPLETE SET (94) 5.00 12.00
UNOPENED BOX (36 PACKS) 30.00 40.00
UNOPENED PACK (8 CARDS+SWEEPSTAKES)1.00 1.25
COMMON CARD (1-94) .10 .25

1995 SkyBox Bill Nye the Science Guy Promos

COMPLETE SET (2) .75 2.00
COMMON CARD (1-2) .50 1.25
1 Will the Sun Ever Burn Out? .50 1.25
2 Crack-It-Open .50 1.25

1994 Comic Images Bill Ward 50 Fabulous Years of Torchy

COMPLETE SET (90) 4.00 10.00
UNOPENED BOX (48 PACKS) 20.00 30.00
UNOPENED PACK (10 CARDS) .75 1.00
COMMON CARD (1-90) .08 .20
NNO You say you'd like to dress me Mr. Gardner (medallion) 10.00 25.00
NNO Bill Ward AU/500 12.00 30.00
NNO 6UP Panel
NNO I Had No Idea Promo .60 1.50

1994 Comic Images Bill Ward 50 Fabulous Years of Torchy OmniChrome

COMPLETE SET (6) 15.00 40.00
COMMON CARD (1-6) 3.00 8.00
STATED ODDS 1:16

1994 Comic Images Bill Ward 50 Fabulous Years of Torchy Rare

COMPLETE SET (3) 15.00 40.00
COMMON CARD (1-3) 6.00 15.00
STATED ODDS 1:48

1991 Pacific Bingo

COMPLETE SET (110) 4.00 10.00
COMPLETE FACTORY SET 4.00 10.00
UNOPENED BOX (36 PACKS) 15.00 25.00
UNOPENED PACK (10 CARDS) .50 .75
COMMON CARD (1-110) .10 .25

1991 Acorn Biosphere Promos

COMMON CARD (SKIP #'d) 8.00 20.00
10 Blue-Spotted Salamander 50.00 100.00
25 Florida Bog Frog 50.00 100.00
125 George Bush on Turtle Protection 10.00 25.00
135 Bill Bradley on Turtle Protection 10.00 25.00
145 Mario Cuomo on Turtle Protection 10.00 25.00

1991 Bon Air Birds and Flowers

COMPLETE BOXED SET (50) 4.00 10.00
COMMON CARD (1-50) .15 .40

1992 Kitchen Sink Press Bizarre Detective

COMPLETE BOXED SET (36) 5.00 12.00
COMMON CARD (1-36) .25 .60

2008 Bizarro Series 1

COMPLETE SET (105) 10.00 25.00
UNOPENED BOX (48 PACKS) 45.00 60.00
UNOPENED PACK (7 CARDS) 1.25 1.50
COMMON CARD (1-105) .15 .40
NNO Dan Piraro Oversized Sketch

2008 Bizarro Series 1 Golden Secret Symbol Icons

COMPLETE SET (10) 10.00 25.00
COMMON CARD 2.00 5.00
STATED ODDS 1:48

2001 Black Scorpion Previews

COMPLETE SET (9) 6.00 15.00
COMMON CARD (P1-P9) 1.00 2.50

2001 Black Scorpion Costumes

COMPLETE SET (6) 60.00 120.00
COMMON MEM (BR1-BR6) 10.00 25.00

1994 SkyBox Blackball Comics

COMMON CARD .75 2.00
P1 Trade Show exclusive/2,500* 2.00 5.00
P2 Trade Show exclusive/2,500* 2.00 5.00

1999 Topps Blair Witch Project

COMPLETE SET (72) 4.00 10.00
UNOPENED HOBBY BOX (36 PACKS) 25.00 30.00
UNOPENED HOBBY PACK (8 CARDS) .75 1.00
UNOPENED RETAIL BOX (12 PACKS)
UNOPENED RETAIL PACK (8 CARDS)
COMMON CARD (1-72) .10 .25

1999 Topps Blair Witch Project Foil

COMPLETE SET (5) 8.00 20.00
COMMON CARD (1-5) 2.00 5.00
STATED ODDS 1:9

2013 Blakes 7

COMPLETE SET (54) 5.00 12.00
UNOPENED BOX (24 PACKS) 60.00 70.00
UNOPENED PACK (5 CARDS) 2.50 3.00
COMMON CARD (1-54) .20 .50

2013 Blakes 7 Autographs

COMMON AUTO 6.00 15.00
STATED ODDS 1:8
S1GB Glynis Barber 10.00 25.00
S1GT Gareth Thomas 15.00 40.00
S1JC Jan Chappell 20.00 50.00
S1JG Julian Glover 8.00 20.00
S1MK Michael Keating 15.00 40.00
S1PD Paul Darrow 15.00 40.00

2013 Blakes 7 Case-Toppers

SK Sean Pence
Sketch card
SM1 Servalan Made Costume Card EXCH 8.00 20.00
S1BB Brian Blessed AU EXCH 10.00 25.00
S1JP Jacqueline Pearce AU EXCH 10.00 25.00
S1PG Jacqueline Pearce 15.00 40.00
Stephen Greif AU EXCH

2013 Blakes 7 Dual Autograph

STATED ODDS 1: 2 CASES
S1TK Gareth Thomas 20.00 50.00
Sally Knyvette

2013 Blakes 7 Gold Foil

COMPLETE SET (9) 8.00 20.00
COMMON CARD (1-9) 1.50 4.00

2013 Blakes 7 Promos

COMMON CARD 1.25 3.00
CT1 Crew 6.00 15.00
The Card Trove
NS1 Avon 4.00 10.00
Blake#{Vila#{Non-Sports Trading Cards
PT1 Blake 4.00 10.00
Premier Trading Cards
TB1 Ship 2.50 6.00
Tom Breyer Unique
AP1A Big Finish 6.00 15.00
Servalan in hat
AP1B Blake 6.00 15.00
Applecards
AP1C Servalan 6.00 15.00
Rydeclive

2014 Blakes 7 Series Two

COMPLETE SET (54) 5.00 12.00
UNOPENED BOX (24 PACKS)
UNOPENED PACK (5 CARDS0
COMMON CARD (55-108) .20 .50

2014 Blakes 7 Series Two Autographs

COMMON AUTO 6.00 15.00
S1BB Brian Blessed
Series 1 design
S1MB Director Michael Briant 4.00 10.00
Series 1 design
S2BC Brian Croucher
S2DT Damien Thomas 6.00 15.00
S2GB Glynis Barber 25.00 60.00
S2GT Gareth Thomas
S2JC Jan Chappell 10.00 25.00
S2JP Jacqueline Pearce 6.00 15.00
S2JS Josette Simon 6.00 15.00
S2MK Michael Keating 15.00 40.00
S2MT Michael Troughton 6.00 15.00
S2PD Paul Darrow
S2RF Richard Franklin 6.00 15.00
S2SP Steven Pacey

2014 Blakes 7 Series Two Case-Topper Autograph

STATED ODDS
S2CH Carol Hawkins 10.00 25.00

2014 Blakes 7 Series Two Costumes

COMMON MEM 5.00 12.00
COS2B Jacqueline Pearce 10.00 25.00
Servalan RED

2014 Blakes 7 Series Two Dual Autographs

S2PD Steven Pacey 30.00 80.00
Paul Darrow#(50
S2PK Steven Pacey 20.00 50.00
Michael Keating
S2SB Josette Simon
Glynis Barber

2014 Blakes 7 Series Two Gold Foil

COMPLETE SET (9) 8.00 20.00
COMMON CARD (F1-F9) 1.50 4.00

2014 Blakes 7 Series Two Triple Autograph

STATED ODDS
S2KDP Michael Keating 80.00 150.00
Paul Darrow#{Steven Pacey

2014 Blakes 7 Series Two Promos

RPR1 Avon 4.00 10.00
Sooli/100#{Radickal Trading Cards
RPR2 Servalan 4.00 10.00
Radickal Trading Cards
RPR3 Tarrant 4.00 10.00
Radickal Trading Cards
SDPR1A Logo/100
Non Sport Trading Cards UK
SDPR1B Ship
Non Sport Trading Cards UK
SDPR1C 6 Cast
Non Sport Trading Cards UK

1995 Authentix Blondie

COMPLETE SET (50) 4.00 10.00
UNOPENED BOX (36 PACKS) 15.00 25.00
UNOPENED PACK (6 CARDS) .75 1.00
COMMON CARD (1-50) .15 .40
NNO Blondie PROMO 6X4 2.00 5.00
(Dealer and Mail-In Wrapper Exclusive)

1995 Authentix Blondie Silver

COMPLETE SET (5) 3.00 8.00
COMMON CARD (AX1-AX5) .75 2.00
*GOLD: 2X TO 5X BASIC CARDS
STATED ODDS 1:6
ANNCD PRINT RUN 7000 SETS
AX1 Alexander .75 2.00
AX2 Cookie .75 2.00
AX3 Blondie and Dagwood .75 2.00
AX4 Dagwood .75 2.00
AX5 Blondie .75 2.00

2013 Blood and Glory

COMPLETE SET (15) 5.00 12.00
COMMON CARD (1-15) .40 1.00
EB1 Kris Cagle, Tommy Shelton (Art Society excl.)

2013 Blood and Glory Promos

COMMON CARD 1.25 3.00
PACP2 Tim Shay NSU 2.00 5.00

1994 Sky Comics Blood and Roses

COMPLETE SET (29) 6.00 15.00
COMMON CARD (1-28; CL) .50 1.25

2017 Blood Drive Parody Collection

COMPLETE BOXED SET (64) 12.00 30.00
COMMON CARD (1-63, STICKER) .40 1.00
NNO Darth Batter Sticker .75 2.00

2017 Blood Drive Parody Collection Creature Collection

COMPLETE SET (6) 4.00 10.00
COMMON CARD (1-5) 1.25 3.00
NNO Mr Funnybones (printed suger-free gum stick)

2017 Blood Drive Parody Collection Promos

COMMON CARD 1.50 4.00
NNO Little Bat Big Imagination
(orange foil)

1996 Comic Images Blood Sucking Beasts from Hell

COMPLETE SET (3) 2.00 5.00
COMMON CARD (P1-P3) .75 2.00

1995 Krome Bloom County Outland

COMPLETE SET (100) 5.00 12.00
UNOPENED BOX (36 PACKS) 30.00 40.00
UNOPENED PACK (7 CARDS+1 STICKER) 1.00 1.50
COMMON CARD (1-100) .08 .20
*STICKERS: 1X TO 2.5X BASIC CARDS .20 .50
NNO 6-Card Panel Case Bonus

1995 Krome Bloom County Outland Holochrome

COMPLETE SET (5) 12.00 30.00
COMMON CARD (H1-H5) 3.00 8.00
STATED ODDS 1:18

1995 Krome Bloom County Outland Promos

COMPLETE SET (3) 2.00 5.00
COMMON CARD 1.00 2.50

1996 Keepsake Collection The Blue and the Gray

COMPLETE SET (72) 5.00 12.00
UNOPENED BOX (48 PACKS) 40.00 50.00
UNOPENED PACK (8 CARDS)
COMMON CARD (1-72) .12 .30
NNO Mort Kunstler AU/500* 20.00 50.00

1996 Keepsake Collection The Blue and the Gray Chromium

COMPLETE SET (6) 12.00 30.00
COMMON CARD (C1-C6) 3.00 8.00
STATED ODDS 1:16

1996 Keepsake Collection The Blue and the Gray Promos

COMPLETE SET (4) 2.00 5.00
COMMON CARD .75 2.00
NNO 6-Card Panel ALB

1991 Sterling Blue Angels

COMPLETE SET (21) 5.00 12.00
COMMON CARD (1-21) .40 1.00
*PROMO: 2X TO 5X BASIC CARDS

1995 FPG Bob Eggleton

COMPLETE SET (90) 4.00 10.00
UNOPENED BOX (36 PACKS) 10.00 20.00
UNOPENED PACK (10 CARDS) .50 .75
COMMON CARD (1-90) .10 .25
NNO B. Eggleton AU/1000 20.00 50.00
NNO Oversized PROMO 1.25 3.00

1995 FPG Bob Eggleton Metallic

COMPLETE SET (6) 12.00 30.00
COMMON CARD (M1-M5) 2.50 6.00
STATED ODDS 1:12

1996 Island Vibes Bob Marley Legend

COMPLETE SET (50) 8.00 20.00
UNOPENED BOX (36 PACKS) 30.00 50.00
UNOPENED PACK (9 CARDS) 1.50 2.00
COMMON CARD (1-50) .30 .75
*GOLDEN SIG.: .6X TO 1.5X BASIC CARDS .50 1.25
M1 Emancipate Yourself Medallion Coin
GE1 Bob Marley Legend Gold Embossed

1996 Island Vibes Bob Marley Legend Embossed

COMPLETE SET (3) 8.00 20.00
COMMON CARD (1-3) 3.00 8.00
STATED ODDS 1:17

1996 Island Vibes Bob Marley Legend Foil

COMPLETE SET (3) 8.00 20.00
COMMON CARD (1-3) 3.00 8.00
STATED ODDS 1:17

1996 Island Vibes Bob Marley Legend Oversized Ken Kelly

COMPLETE SET (3) 8.00 20.00
COMMON CARD (1-3) 3.00 8.00
STATED ODDS 1:17

1996 Island Vibes Bob Marley Legend Promos

COMPLETE SET (8) 5.00 12.00
COMMON CARD .75 2.00

2017 Bob's Burgers Music Album

COMPLETE SET (6) 15.00 40.00
COMMON CARD 4.00 10.00

1991 Boeing 75 Years 1916-1991

COMPLETE SET (10) 3.00 8.00
COMMON CARD (1-10) .50 1.25

2017 Bojack Horseman Horsin' Around

COMPLETE SET (20) 15.00 40.00
COMMON CARD (1-20) 1.25 30.00
STATED PRINT RUN 256 SETS

1997 Bolt Entertainment Promo

NNO Company Logo/Address 2.00 5.00

1996 Comic Images Bone Dragonslayer

COMPLETE SET (90) 4.00 10.00
UNOPENED BOX (36 PACKS) 30.00 40.00
UNOPENED PACK (8 CARDS) 1.25 1.50
COMMON CARD (1-90) .10 .25
B1 Box Bonus 2.00 5.00
P1 Beloved Bones are Back Promo .75 2.00
AU1 Jeff Smith AU/500* 20.00 50.00

1996 Comic Images Bone Dragonslayer Covers

COMPLETE SET (6) 15.00 40.00
COMMON CARD (C1-C6) 3.00 8.00
STATED ODDS 1:16

1996 Comic Images Bone Dragonslayer Villains

COMPLETE SET (3) 10.00 25.00
COMMON CARD (1-3) 4.00 10.00
STATED ODDS 1:48

1994 Comic Images Bone Series One

COMPLETE SET (90) 3.00 8.00
UNOPENED BOX (48 PACKS) 20.00 30.00
UNOPENED PACK (10 CARDS) .75 1.00
COMMON CARD (1-90) .08 .20
M1 Medallion 10.00 25.00
P1 Ron Miller's Firebrands Promo
AU1 Jeff Smith '94 AU/100 30.00 80.00

1994 Comic Images Bone Series One 6-Up Panels

COMPLETE SET (6) 25.00 60.00
COMMON CARD 6.00 15.00

1994 Comic Images Bone Series One Chromium Foil

COMPLETE SET (6) 15.00 40.00
COMMON CARD (C1-C6) 3.00 8.00
STATED ODDS 1:24

1994 Comic Images Bone Series One Cover Art

COMPLETE SET (3) 12.00 30.00
COMMON CARD (1-3) 5.00 12.00
RANDOMLY INSERTED INTO PACKS

1994 Comic Images Bone Series One Promos

1 Dealer Promo .75 2.00
2 Wizard Press
3 4-Up Panel Previews Magazine

1995 Comic Images Bone Series Two

COMPLETE SET (90) 8.00 20.00
UNOPENED BOX (36 PACKS) 40.00 50.00
UNOPENED PACK (7 CARDS) 1.50 1.75
COMMON CARD (1-90) .15 .40
*HOLOCHROME: 6X TO 15X BASIC CARDS 2.50 6.00
M1 Bone Series Two Medallion/1669* 10.00 25.00
AU1 Jeff Smith AU/500* 20.00 50.00
NNO Unnumbered Promo 1.25 3.00
4PAN2 4-Up Panel
6PAN2 6-Up Comic Panel Album Excl. 4.00 10.00

1995 Comic Images Bone Series Two MagnaChrome

COMPLETE SET (6) 15.00 40.00
COMMON CARD (M1-M6) 3.00 8.00
STATED ODDS 1:16

1995 Comic Images Bone Series Two MagnaChrome Thorne

COMPLETE SET (3) 10.00 25.00
COMMON CARD (T1-T3) 4.00 10.00
RANDOMLY INSERTED INTO PACKS

1998 Good Stuff Boris Karloff Beyond the Monster Series One

COMPLETE FACTORY SET (100) 6.00 15.00
COMMON CARD (1-100) .12 .30
STATED PRINT RUN 2,500 SETS

1998 Good Stuff Boris Karloff Beyond the Monster Series One Promos

COMPLETE SET (3) 2.00 5.00
COMMON CARD (P1-P3) .75 2.00

1998 Good Stuff Boris Karloff Beyond the Monster Series Two

COMPLETE FACTORY SET (106) 6.00 15.00
COMMON CARD (1-106) .12 .30
P4 Promo GEN 1.25 3.00

1992 Comic Images Boris Series Two

COMPLETE SET (90) 6.00 15.00
UNOPENED BOX (36 PACKS) 20.00 25.00
UNOPENED PACK (10 CARDS) .75 1.00
COMMON CARD (1-90) .12 .30
P1 Base #14 Workout Promo 1.50 4.00
UNC1 6-Card Prism Panel UNC

1992 Comic Images Boris Series Two Prisms

COMPLETE SET (6) 8.00 20.00
COMMON CARD (P1-P6) 1.50 4.00
STATED ODDS 1:16

1993 Comic Images Boris Series Three

COMPLETE SET (72) 8.00 20.00
UNOPENED BOX (36 PACKS) 25.00 40.00
UNOPENED PACK (7 CARDS) 1.00 1.25
COMMON CARD (1-72) .20 .50

1993 Comic Images Boris Series Three Chromium

COMPLETE SET (6) 5.00 12.00
COMMON CARD (1-6) 1.25 3.00

1994 Comic Images Boris Series Four

COMPLETE SET (90) 4.00 10.00
UNOPENED BOX (36 PACKS) 45.00 60.00
UNOPENED PACK (7 CARDS) 1.50 2.00
COMMON CARD (1-90) .10 .25
M1 Suzle 10.00 25.00
AU1 Boris Vallejo AU/500 30.00 75.00

1994 Comic Images Boris Series Four HoloChrome

COMPLETE SET (6) 12.00 30.00
COMMON CARD (H1-H6) 3.00 8.00
STATED ODDS 1:16

1994 Comic Images Boris Series Four Sci-Fi Sensations

COMPLETE SET (3) 12.00 30.00
COMMON CARD (1-3) 5.00 12.00
STATED ODDS 1:48

1991 Comic Images Boris Vallejo

COMPLETE SET (90) 8.00 20.00
UNOPENED BOX (36 PACKS) 50.00 60.00
UNOPENED PACK (10 CARDS) 1.75 2.00
COMMON CARD (1-90) .15 .40
NNO Boris Vallejo PROMO

1996 Comic Images Boris with Julie

COMPLETE SET (90) 10.00 25.00
UNOPENED BOX (36 PACKS) 35.00 50.00
UNOPENED PACK (7 CARDS) 1.25 1.50
COMMON CARD (1-90) .25 .60
*HOLOCHROME: 4X TO 10X BASIC CARDS 2.50 6.00
P1 Woman Fighting Monster Promo 1.00 2.50
AU1 Boris AU/250 20.00 50.00
AU2 Julie AU/250 20.00 50.00
BT1 Alabaster City BT 2.00 5.00
OV1 Future Trouble OV 7 X 7 1/2
UNC1 6-Up MagnaChrome Panel UNC 8.00 20.00

1996 Comic Images Boris with Julie MagnaChrome

COMPLETE SET (6) 15.00 40.00
COMMON CARD (M1-M6) 3.00 8.00
STATED ODDS 1:16

1996 Comic Images Boris with Julie Unicorns

COMPLETE SET (3) 12.00 30.00
COMMON CARD (1-3) 6.00 15.00
STATED ODDS 1:48

2017 Boss Baby Subway Kids Meal Tags

COMPLETE SET (6) 5.00 12.00
COMMON TAG (UNNUMBERED) 1.25 3.00

1994 Lime Rock Bozo

COMPLETE SET (54) 6.00 15.00
UNOPENED BOX (36 PACKS) 20.00 30.00
UNOPENED PACK (9 CARDS) 1.00 1.25
COMMON CARD (1-50, 54, P1-P3) .25 .60
NNO Bozo Birthday Card Offer 2.00 5.00

1994 Lime Rock Bozo Prisms

COMPLETE SET (3) 6.00 15.00
COMMON CARD 2.50 6.00
STATED ODDS 1:18

1994 Lime Rock Bozo Prototype Promos

COMMON CARD 1.25 3.00
P1b Football prism 2.50 6.00
P2b Golf prism 2.50 6.00
P3b Baseball prism 2.50 6.00
P4 Bozo with two women 2.00 5.00
P5 Bozo and bananas 2.00 5.00
P6 Water skiing 2.00 5.00

1992 Topps Bram Stoker's Dracula

COMPLETE SET (100) 12.00 30.00
UNOPENED BOX (36 PACKS) 60.00 100.00
UNOPENED PACK (10 CARDS) 2.00 3.00
COMMON CARD (1-100) .25 .60

1992 Topps Bram Stoker's Dracula Promos

COMPLETE SET (3) 2.50 6.00
COMMON CARD (1-3) 1.50 4.00

1992 Topps Bram Stoker's Dracula Comic Promos

COMPLETE SET (16) 10.00 25.00
COMMON CARD (1-16) 1.00 2.50
STATED ODDS 4:CELLO PACK OF COMICS
CARDS 1-4 INSERTED IN ISSUE #1
CARDS 5-8 INSERTED IN ISSUE #2
CARDS 9-12 INSERTED IN ISSUE #3
CARDS 13-16 INSERTED IN ISSUE #4

1997 Ground Zero Comics Brandi Five-One Promo

1 Art by Mike Wolfer 4.00 10.00
(Motor City Comic Con Exclusive)

1992 NAC Branson On Stage

COMPLETE SET (100) 6.00 15.00
UNOPENED BOX (36 PACKS) 10.00 20.00
UNOPENED PACK (10 CARDS) .50 .75
COMMON CARD (1-100) .10 .30

1996 Bravo Studios

COMPLETE SET (9) 5.00 12.00
COMMON CARD (P1-P9) .75 2.00

2014 Breaking Bad

COMPLETE SET (134) 12.00 30.00
UNOPENED BOX (24 PACKS) 250.00 400.00
UNOPENED PACK (5 CARDS) 10.00 15.00
COMMON CARD (1-134) .20 .50

2014 Breaking Bad Autographs

COMMON AUTO (A1-A21) 6.00 15.00
STATED ODDS 1:24
A1 Dean Norris 50.00 100.00
A2 Betsy Brandt 30.00 75.00
A3 RJ Mitte 30.00 75.00
A4 Giancarlo Esposito 150.00 300.00
A5 David Costabile 20.00 50.00

A6 Matt Jones 12.00 30.00
A7 Mark Margolis 20.00 50.00
A8 Michael Shamus Wiles 12.00 30.00
A9 Daniel Moncada 15.00 40.00
A10 Luis Moncada 15.00 40.00
A11 Jere Burns 8.00 20.00
A12 Nigel Gibbs 8.00 20.00
A13 Larry Hankin 12.00 30.00
A14 Michael Bowen 15.00 40.00
A15 Emily Rios 10.00 25.00
A21 Anna Gunn 25.00 60.00

2014 Breaking Bad Blue Sky

COMPLETE SET (8) 6.00 15.00
COMMON CARD (1-8) 1.25 3.00
STATED ODDS 1:24

2014 Breaking Bad Fan Art

COMPLETE SET (9) 8.00 20.00
COMMON CARD (BBFA01-BBFA09) 1.50 4.00
STATED ODDS 1:24

2014 Breaking Bad Los Pollos Hermanos

COMPLETE SET (9) 5.00 12.00
COMMON CARD (LPH1-LPH9) .75 2.00
STATED ODDS 1:12

2014 Breaking Bad Props

COMMON MEM (PC1-PC2) 30.00 80.00
STATED ODDS 1:576
PC1 Walter White 50.00 100.00

2014 Breaking Bad Wardrobes

COMMON CARD (1-22) 6.00 15.00
STATED ODDS 1:24
M22 ISSUED AS ALBUM EXCLUSIVE
M1 Walter White 15.00 40.00
M3 Jesse Pinkman 12.00 30.00
M4 Gustavo Gus Fring 10.00 25.00
M5 Skyler White 8.00 20.00
M6 Walter White 15.00 40.00
M9 Skyler White 8.00 20.00
M12 Walter White 15.00 40.00
M13 Gustavo Gus Fring 15.00 40.00
M14 Gustavo Gus Fring 8.00 20.00
M17 Jesse Pinkman 12.00 30.00
M18 Gustavo Gus Fring 8.00 20.00
M22 Walter White ALB 15.00 40.00

2014 Breaking Bad Promo

P1 Test Tubes NSU 2.00 5.00

1989 Tom Thumb Britain's Maritime History

COMPLETE SET (30) 5.00 12.00
COMMON CARD (1-30) .25 .60

2002 Britney Spears Pepsi Thai

COMPLETE SET (8) 30.00 75.00
COMMON CARD 6.00 15.00

1995 FPG Brom

COMPLETE SET (90) 4.00 10.00
UNOPENED BOX (36 PACKS) 15.00 25.00
UNOPENED PACK (10 CARDS) .50 1.00
COMMON CARD (1-90) .10 .25
AU1 Brom AU/1000* 20.00 50.00
DEL28 Brom/Tom Kidd Set Promo

1995 FPG Brom Metallic

COMPLETE SET (5) 12.00 30.00
COMMON CARD (M1-M5) 3.00 8.00
RANDOMLY INSERTED

1994 Comic Images Brothers Hildebrandt

COMPLETE SET (90) 3.00 8.00
UNOPENED BOX (48 PACKS) 15.00 25.00
UNOPENED PACK (10 CARDS) .50 .75
COMMON CARD (1-90) .08 .20
NNO1 Tim and Greg Hildebrandt AU/500 20.00 50.00
NNO2 Medallion Card/4256* 10.00 25.00

1994 Comic Images Brothers Hildebrandt Case-Toppers

COMPLETE SET (5) 50.00 100.00
COMMON CARD (1-5) 10.00 25.00
STATED ODDS 1:CASE

1994 Comic Images Brothers Hildebrandt Creatures of Tolkien

COMPLETE SET (3) 15.00 40.00
COMMON CARD (1-3) 6.00 15.00
STATED ODDS 1:48

1994 Comic Images Brothers Hildebrandt Foil

COMPLETE SET (6) 8.00 20.00
COMMON CARD (F1-F6) 2.50 6.00
STATED ODDS 1:16

1981 Amurol Bubble Funnies

COMPLETE SET (6) 12.00 30.00
COMMON MINI COMIC 2.00 5.00
MINI-COMICS SET
PRODUCED BY AMUROL
1 Amazing Spider-Man 4.00 10.00
2 Incredible Hulk 3.00 8.00
3 Captain America 3.00 8.00

2000 Bubblegum Promos

COMPLETE SET (5) 3.00 8.00
COMMON CARD (GUM1-GUM5) .75 2.00

Buffy the Vampire Slayer

1998 Inkworks Buffy the Vampire Slayer Season One

COMPLETE SET (72) 12.50 30.00
UNOPENED BOX (36 PACKS) 250.00 400.00
UNOPENED PACK (7 CARDS) 8.00 12.00
COMMON CARD (1-72) .20 .50
BL1 Season Two Promo 2.00 5.00
NNO How To Kill A Vampire 5.00 12.00

1998 Inkworks Buffy the Vampire Slayer Season One Autographs

COMMON AUTO (A1-A4) 50.00 100.00
RANDOM INSERTS IN PACKS
A1 Joss Whedon 120.00 250.00
A2 David Boreanaz 150.00 300.00
A3 Alyson Hannigan 250.00 400.00

1998 Inkworks Buffy the Vampire Slayer Season One Slayer Kit

COMPLETE SET (6) 40.00 100.00
COMMON CARD (S1-S6) 8.00 20.00
STATED ODDS 1:27

1998 Inkworks Buffy the Vampire Slayer Season One The Chosen One

COMPLETE SET (9) 30.00 75.00
COMMON CARD (C1-C9) 4.00 10.00
STATED ODDS 1:11

1998 Inkworks Buffy the Vampire Slayer Season One Promos

COMPLETE SET (3) 2.50 6.00
COMMON CARD .75 2.00
BP2 Buffy the Vampire Slayer SDCC 1.50 4.00
MS1 Buffy the Vampire Slayer VS .75 2.00

2001-02 Inkworks Buffy the Vampire Slayer Season One and Two DVD Promos

COMPLETE SET (12) 15.00 40.00
S1 PROMO PACK (5 CARDS) 8.00 20.00
S2 PROMO PACK (7 CARDS) 2.00 5.00
COMMON CARD (M1-M12) 2.00 5.00

1999 Inkworks Buffy the Vampire Slayer Season Two

COMPLETE SET (90) 5.00 12.00
UNOPENED BOX (36 PACKS) 250.00 400.00
UNOPENED PACK (7 CARDS) 8.00 12.00
COMMON CARD (1-90) .15 .40
NNO How To Lose Your Soul 4.00 10.00

1999 Inkworks Buffy the Vampire Slayer Season Two Autographs

COMMON AUTO (A5-A9) 30.00 75.00
RANDOM INSERTS IN PACKS
A5 Charisma Carpenter 250.00 400.00
A6 Anthony Stewart Head 120.00 200.00
A7 John Ritter 150.00 300.00
A8 Robia Lamorte 50.00 100.00

1999 Inkworks Buffy the Vampire Slayer Season Two Dark Destiny

COMPLETE SET (9) 15.00 40.00
COMMON CARD (D1-D9) 2.50 6.00
STATED ODDS 1:11

1999 Inkworks Buffy the Vampire Slayer Season Two Love Bites

COMPLETE SET (6) 12.50 30.00
COMMON CARD (B1-B6) 3.00 8.00
STATED ODDS 1:18

1999 Inkworks Buffy the Vampire Slayer Season Two Promos

COMPLETE SET (3) 5.00 12.00
COMMON CARD 2.00 5.00

1999 Inkworks Buffy the Vampire Slayer Season Three

COMPLETE SET (90) 5.00 12.00
UNOPENED BOX (36 PACKS) 125.00 200.00
UNOPENED PACK (7 CARDS) 4.00 6.00
COMMON CARD (1-90) .15 .40

1999 Inkworks Buffy the Vampire Slayer Season Three Autographs

COMMON AUTO (A10-A15) 25.00 60.00
RANDOM INSERTS IN PACKS
A10 Julie Benz 40.00 80.00
A11 Nicholas Brendon 30.00 80.00
A12 James Marsters 50.00 100.00
A13 Juliet Landau 30.00 75.00
A15 Eliza Dushku 120.00 200.00

1999 Inkworks Buffy the Vampire Slayer Season Three Graduation Day

COMPLETE SET (9) 12.50 30.00
COMMON CARD (G1-G9) 2.00 5.00
STATED ODDS 1:11

1999 Inkworks Buffy the Vampire Slayer Season Three The Future Is Ours

COMPLETE SET (6) 12.50 30.00
COMMON CARD (Y1-Y6) 3.00 8.00
STATED ODDS 1:18

1999 Inkworks Buffy the Vampire Slayer Season Three Promos

COMPLETE SET (9) 6.00 15.00
COMMON CARD .40 1.00
B31 Angel and Buffy 1.25 3.00
B33 Angel and Buffy 1.25 3.00
B35 Angel, Buffy, and Xander .75 2.00
B3SC Angel and Buffy 2.00 5.00
SFX1 Buffy cast .75 2.00
SD1999 Angel, Buffy, and Xander .75 2.00
WC1999 Angel, Buffy, and Xander 1.25 3.00

2000 Buffy the Vampire Slayer Season Four

COMPLETE SET (90) 5.00 12.00
UNOPENED BOX (36 PACKS) 90.00 100.00
UNOPENED PACK (7 CARDS) 4.00 5.00
COMMON CARD (1-90) .15 .40

2000 Buffy the Vampire Slayer Season Four Autographs

COMMON AUTO (A16-A21) 10.00 25.00
RANDOM INSERTS IN PACKS
A16 Emma Caulfield 50.00 100.00
A20 Mercedes Mcnab 30.00 75.00

2000 Buffy the Vampire Slayer Season Four New Beginnings

COMPLETE SET (9) 15.00 40.00
COMMON CARD (NB1-NB9) 2.50 6.00
STATED ODDS 1:11

2000 Buffy the Vampire Slayer Season Four Ritual of Enjoining

COMPLETE SET (6) 10.00 25.00
COMMON CARD (R1-R6) 2.00 5.00
STATED ODDS 1:17

2000 Buffy the Vampire Slayer Season Four Promos

COMPLETE SET (7) 6.00 15.00
COMMON CARD 1.25 3.00

2001 Buffy the Vampire Slayer Season Five

COMPLETE SET (90) 5.00 12.00
UNOPENED BOX (36 PACKS) 100.00 150.00
UNOPENED PACK (7 CARDS) 5.00 8.00
COMMON CARD (1-90) .15 .40
SLAYER'S GIFT STATED ODDS 1:100
SG1 Slayer's Gift FOIL 7.50 20.00

2001 Buffy the Vampire Slayer Season Five Autographs

COMPLETE SET (7) 250.00 500.00
COMMON AUTO (A22-A28) 15.00 40.00
RANDOM INSERTS IN PACKS
A22 Michelle Trachtenberg 80.00 150.00
A23 Amber Benson 50.00 100.00
A27 Bailey Chase 20.00 50.00
A28 Joel Grey 20.00 50.00
AR1 Autograph Redemption

2001 Buffy the Vampire Slayer Season Five Big Bad Crush

COMPLETE SET (6) 15.00 40.00
COMMON CARD (B1-B6) 3.00 8.00
STATED ODDS 1:17

2001 Buffy the Vampire Slayer Season Five Box-Loaders

COMPLETE SET (3) 5.00 12.00
COMMON CARD (BL1-BL3) 2.00 5.00

2001 Buffy the Vampire Slayer Season Five Protectors of the Key

COMPLETE SET (9) 12.50 30.00
COMMON CARD (K1-K9) 1.50 4.00
STATED ODDS 1:11

2001 Buffy the Vampire Slayer Season Five Promos

COMPLETE SET (6) 4.00 10.00
COMMON CARD .40 1.00
B5i Buffy 1.25 3.00
B52 Rupert and Buffy 4.00 8.00
B5SD2001 Buffy 1.25 3.00

2002 Buffy the Vampire Slayer Season Six

COMPLETE SET (90) 5.00 12.00
UNOPENED BOX (36 PACKS) 75.00 125.00
UNOPENED PACK (7 CARDS) 2.50 4.00
COMMON CARD (1-90) .15 .40

2002 Buffy the Vampire Slayer Season Six Autographs

COMMON AUTO (A29-A39) 10.00 25.00
STATED ODDS 1:35
A30 Dean Butler 12.00 30.00
A31 Elizabeth Anne Allen 12.00 30.00
A32 Adam Busch 15.00 40.00
A35 Ivana Milicevic 15.00 40.00
A36 Jeff Kober 12.00 30.00
A37 Andy Umberger 12.00 30.00
A38 Amelinda Embry 12.00 30.00

2002 Buffy the Vampire Slayer Season Six Box-Loaders

COMPLETE SET (3) 7.50 20.00

COMMON CARD (BL1-BL3)	.75	2.00
B6CL Where Does She Go From Here?	7.50	20.00

2002 Buffy the Vampire Slayer Season Six Love Bites Back

COMPLETE SET (6)	12.50	30.00
COMMON CARD (LBB1-LBB6)	2.50	6.00
STATED ODDS 1:17		

2002 Buffy the Vampire Slayer Season Six Once More with Feeling

COMPLETE SET (9)	12.50	30.00
COMMON CARD (H1-H9)	1.50	4.00
STATED ODDS 1:11		

2002 Buffy the Vampire Slayer Season Six Pieceworks

COMPLETE SET (5)	75.00	200.00
COMMON MEM (PW1-PW5)	20.00	50.00
STATED ODDS 1:64		

2002 Buffy the Vampire Slayer Season Six Promos

COMMON CARD	.75	2.00
NSUSD Buffy	.75	2.00

2003 Buffy the Vampire Slayer Season Seven

COMPLETE SET (90)	5.00	12.00
UNOPENED BOX (36 PACKS)	50.00	100.00
UNOPENED PACK (7 CARDS)	3.00	4.00
COMMON CARD (1-90)	.15	.40

2003 Buffy the Vampire Slayer Season Seven Autographs

COMPLETE SET (14)	150.00	300.00
COMMON AUTO (A40-A53)	10.00	25.00
STATED ODDS 1:36		
A42 Clare Kramer	20.00	50.00
A44 Iyari Limon	15.00	40.00
A45 Indigo	12.00	30.00
A46 Sarah Hagan	15.00	40.00
A47 Clara Bryant	12.00	30.00
A48 Felicia Day	30.00	80.00
A49 Kristy Wu	12.00	30.00
A50 Lalaine	12.00	30.00
A53 Nathan Fillion	50.00	100.00

2003 Buffy the Vampire Slayer Season Seven Box-Loaders

COMPLETE SET (3)	2.50	6.00
COMPLETE SET W/CL (4)	75.00	150.00
COMMON CARD (BL1-BL3)	1.00	2.50
CL1 Final Farewell - Joss Whedon AU	75.00	150.00

2003 Buffy the Vampire Slayer Season Seven Pieceworks

COMPLETE SET (8)	120.00	225.00
COMMON MEM (PW1-PW8)	8.00	20.00
STATED ODDS 1:36		
PW3 Kennedy T-Shirt	25.00	60.00
PW4 Kennedy Pants	10.00	25.00
PW7 Rachel Blouse	10.00	25.00
PW8 Rachel Pants	10.00	25.00

2003 Buffy the Vampire Slayer Season Seven Slayer's Legacy

COMPLETE SET (6)	10.00	25.00
COMMON CARD (SL1-SL6)	2.00	5.00
STATED ODDS 1:17		

2003 Buffy the Vampire Slayer Season Seven Final Battle

COMPLETE SET (9)	7.50	20.00
COMMON CARD (FB1-FB9)	1.25	3.00
*PARALLEL: 1X TO 2.5X BASIC CARDS		
STATED ODDS 1:11		

2003 Buffy the Vampire Slayer Season Seven Promos

COMMON CARD	.40	1.00
B7i Buffy the Vampire Slayer Inkworks	1.50	4.00
B71 Buffy the Vampire Slayer	.75	2.00
B72 Buffy the Vampire Slayer	1.50	4.00
B74 Buffy the Vampire Slayer LVCC	.75	2.00
B7UK Buffy the Vampire Slayer UK EMB	6.00	15.00
B7MEM Buffy the Vampire Slayer UK	2.00	5.00
NSUSD Buffy the Vampire Slayer NSU	6.00	15.00

Buffy the Vampire Slayer Universe

2007 Buffy the Vampire Slayer 10th Anniversary

COMPLETE SET (90)	5.00	12.00
UNOPENED BOX (24 PACKS)		
UNOPENED PACK (8 CARDS)		
COMMON CARD (1-90)	.15	.40
M1 STATED ODDS 1:145		
CL1 ISSUED AS CASE EXCLUSIVE		
M1 Welcome To Sunnydale Map	6.00	15.00
CL1 Buffy - Legendary CL	8.00	20.00

2007 Buffy the Vampire Slayer 10th Anniversary Forever

COMPLETE SET (9)	10.00	25.00
COMMON CARD (F1-F9)	2.00	5.00
STATED ODDS 1:11		

2007 Buffy the Vampire Slayer 10th Anniversary Friends Forever Pieceworks

COMPLETE SET (4)	120.00	250.00
COMMON MEM (FF1-FF4)	30.00	60.00
STATED ODDS 1:287		
FF1 Buffy's Coat	50.00	100.00
FF2 Willow's Jacket	40.00	80.00

2007 Buffy the Vampire Slayer 10th Anniversary Leader of Slayers

COMPLETE SET (3)	4.00	10.00
COMMON CARD (L1-L3)	2.50	6.00
STATED ODDS 1:23		

2007 Buffy the Vampire Slayer 10th Anniversary Pieceworks

STATED ODDS 1:24		
SE1 STATED ODDS 1:2304		
PW1 Buffy's Coat	12.00	30.00
PW2 Buffy's Pants	12.00	30.00
PW3a Buffy's Jacket	12.00	30.00
PW3b Buffy's Jacket w/trim		
PW4b Willow's Jacket w/trim		
PW10b Dawn's Pajama Pants w/lace	12.00	30.00
SE1 Slayer's Essential Stake Card	600.00	800.00
PR1 Pieceworks Redemption - PW3 Variant		
PR2 Pieceworks Redemption - PW4 Variant		

2007 Buffy the Vampire Slayer 10th Anniversary Recollections

COMPLETE SET (8)	10.00	25.00
COMMON CARD (R1-R8)	2.50	6.00
STATED ODDS 1:17		
R1 Buffy	3.00	8.00
R2 Willow	3.00	8.00

2007 Buffy the Vampire Slayer 10th Anniversary Promos

COMMON CARD	1.00	2.50
P1 Buffy (General Distribution)	1.25	3.00
Pi Buffy (Inkworks.com Exclusive)	1.50	4.00
PK Buffy (UK Exclusive)	1.25	3.00
NSU Buffy (Non-Sport Update Exclusive)	5.00	10.00

2004 Buffy the Vampire Slayer Big Bads

COMPLETE SET (72)	5.00	12.00
UNOPENED BOX (24 PACKS)	50.00	75.00
UNOPENED PACK (7 CARDS)	2.50	3.00
COMMON CARD (1-72)	.15	.40

2004 Buffy the Vampire Slayer Big Bads Box-Loaders

COMPLETE SET (3)	6.00	15.00
COMMON CARD (BL1-BL3)	1.25	3.00
CL1 Bad Boys	4.00	10.00

2004 Buffy the Vampire Slayer Big Bads Pieceworks

COMPLETE SET (7)	80.00	150.00
COMMON MEM (PW1-PW7)	8.00	20.00
STATED ODDS 1:24		
PW1 Spike (t-shirt)	15.00	40.00
PW2 Dru (top)	12.00	30.00
PW3 D'Hoffryn (robe)	10.00	25.00
PW4 Adam (pants)	12.00	30.00

2004 Buffy the Vampire Slayer Big Bads Seasons of Evil

COMPLETE SET (9)	10.00	25.00
COMMON CARD (SE1-SE9)	1.50	4.00
STATED ODDS 1:11		

2004 Buffy the Vampire Slayer Big Bads Other Side

COMPLETE SET (6)	8.00	20.00
COMMON CARD (OS1-OS6)	1.50	4.00
STATED ODDS 1:17		

2004 Buffy the Vampire Slayer Big Bads Promos

COMMON CARD	.40	1.00
P1 Buffy and The Master	1.00	2.50
PUK Buffy and Glory	1.00	2.50

2003 Buffy the Vampire Slayer Chaos Bleeds

COMPLETE SET (3)	6.00	15.00
COMMON CARD (VU1-VU3)	3.00	8.00

2003 Buffy the Vampire Slayer Connections

COMPLETE SET (72)	5.00	12.00
UNOPENED BOX (24 PACKS)	60.00	70.00
UNOPENED PACK (6 CARDS)	2.50	3.00
COMMON CARD (1-72)	.15	.40
*PARALLEL: 1X TO 2.5X BASIC CARDS		
STATED ODDS 1:1		

2003 Buffy the Vampire Slayer Connections Box-Loaders

COMPLETE SET (4)	20.00	50.00
COMMON CARD (BL1-BL3)	1.00	2.50
CL1 Coffin DIE CUT	20.00	50.00

2003 Buffy the Vampire Slayer Connections Heartbreaks

COMPLETE SET (6)	10.00	25.00
COMMON CARD (HB1-HB6)	2.00	5.00
STATED ODDS 1:14		

2003 Buffy the Vampire Slayer Connections Pieceworks

COMPLETE SET (3)	40.00	100.00
COMMON MEM (PWC1-PWC3)	15.00	40.00
STATED ODDS 1:24		
PWC1 Buffy and Spike	25.00	60.00

2003 Buffy the Vampire Slayer Connections Slayer's Circle

COMPLETE SET (9)	12.50	30.00
COMMON CARD (SC1-SC9)	1.50	4.00
STATED ODDS 1:11		

2003 Buffy the Vampire Slayer Connections Promos

COMPLETE SET (5)	3.00	8.00
COMMON CARD	.40	1.00
Pi Angel and Buffy	.75	2.00
PUK Rupert and Buffy	.75	2.00
PFOA Angel and Buffy (Friends of Allan Exclusive)	2.00	5.00
PUKP Rupert and Buffy	.75	2.00

2002 Buffy the Vampire Slayer Evolution

COMPLETE SET (50)	5.00	12.00
UNOPENED BOX (24 PACKS)	50.00	100.00
UNOPENED PACK (5 CARDS)	2.50	4.00
COMMON CARD (1-50)	.15	.40
*REF.: 1X TO 2.5X BASIC CARDS		

2002 Buffy the Vampire Slayer Evolution Box-Loaders

COMPLETE SET (3)	2.50	6.00
COMMON CARD (BL1-BL3)	.75	2.00

2002 Buffy the Vampire Slayer Evolution Portraits

COMPLETE SET (9)	30.00	80.00
COMMON CARD (PT1-PT9)	4.00	10.00
STATED ODDS 1:11		

2000 Buffy the Vampire Slayer Fan Club SDCC Promos

COMPLETE SET (4)	2.50	6.00
COMMON CARD	.75	2.00
*WW: .6X TO 1.5X BASIC CARDS		

2006 Buffy the Vampire Slayer Memories

COMPLETE SET (90)	5.00	12.00
UNOPENED BOX (36 PACKS)	125.00	200.00
UNOPENED PACK (11 CARDS)	4.00	6.00
COMMON CARD (1-90)	.15	.40

2006 Buffy the Vampire Slayer Memories Apocalypses

COMPLETE SET (6)	6.00	15.00
COMMON CARD (AP1-AP6)	1.25	3.00
STATED ODDS 1:17		

2006 Buffy the Vampire Slayer Memories Box-Loaders

COMPLETE SET (3)	10.00	25.00
COMMON CARD (BL1-BL3)	2.00	5.00
STATED ODDS ONE PER BOX		
CL1 Legacy	5.00	12.00

2006 Buffy the Vampire Slayer Memories Pieceworks

COMMON MEM (PW1-PW17)	4.00	10.00
STATED ODDS 1:18		
PW1 Buffy's Pants	10.00	25.00
PW2 Buffy's Sweater & Camisole	25.00	60.00
PW3 Buffy's Leather Jacket	15.00	40.00
PW7 Willow's Top	10.00	25.00
PW8 Tara's Sweater	8.00	20.00
PW15 Rona's Overalls	6.00	15.00
PW16a Andrew's Jacket	25.00	60.00
PW16b Andrew's Jacket w Stripe	25.00	60.00
PW17A Molly & Kennedy	80.00	150.00
PW17B Rona, Vi, & Amanda	80.00	150.00
PR1 Pieceworks Redemption		

2006 Buffy the Vampire Slayer Memories Reinforcements

COMPLETE SET (9)	6.00	15.00
COMMON CARD (R1-R9)	.75	2.00
STATED ODDS 1:11		

2006 Buffy the Vampire Slayer Memories Promos

COMMON CARD	.75	2.00
B2 Buffy	2.00	5.00
Bi Buffy	2.00	5.00
BUK Buffy	1.25	3.00
BSD2006 Buffy	2.00	5.00

2005 Buffy the Vampire Slayer Men of Sunnydale

COMPLETE SET (81)	4.00	10.00
UNOPENED BOX (36 PACKS)	60.00	100.00
UNOPENED PACK (7 CARDS)	2.00	3.00
COMMON CARD (1-81)	.10	.30

2005 Buffy the Vampire Slayer Men of Sunnydale Autographs

COMMON AUTO (A1-A11)	4.00	10.00
STATED ODDS 1:36		
A1 Nicholas Brendan	20.00	50.00

MODERN

A2 Marc Blucas 8.00 20.00
A3 Mark Metcalf 6.00 15.00
A6 Danny Strong 8.00 20.00
A7 Tom Lenk 8.00 20.00
A8 Adam Busch 8.00 20.00
A9 Charlie Weber 6.00 15.00
A11 D.Strong/T.Lenk/A.Busch 50.00 100.00

2005 Buffy the Vampire Slayer Men of Sunnydale Box-Loaders

COMPLETE SET (3) 5.00 12.00
COMMON CARD (BL1-BL3) 2.00 5.00
CL1 Angel, Riley, and Spike 6.00 15.00

2005 Buffy the Vampire Slayer Men of Sunnydale Dressed to Kill

COMPLETE SET (9) 6.00 15.00
COMMON CARD (DK1-DK9) .75 2.00
STATED ODDS 1:11

2005 Buffy the Vampire Slayer Men of Sunnydale Pieceworks

COMMON MEM (PW1-PW5) 4.00 10.00
STATED ODDS 1:36
PW2 Xander (trousers) 6.00 15.00
PW3 Giles (shirt) 6.00 15.00
PW5b Principal Wood's Tie 60.00 120.00

2005 Buffy the Vampire Slayer Men of Sunnydale Women Men Adore

COMPLETE SET (6) 6.00 15.00
COMMON CARD (WA1-WA6) 1.25 3.00
STATED ODDS 1:17

2005 Buffy the Vampire Slayer Men of Sunnydale Promos

COMPLETE SET (5) 5.00 12.00
COMMON CARD .40 1.00
P1 Angel, Xander, Giles, Spike 2.00 5.00
P2 Xander & Buffy 3.00 8.00
Pi Spike & Angel 2.00 5.00

1999 Inkworks Buffy the Vampire Slayer PhotoCards

COMPLETE SET (54) 6.00 15.00
UNOPENED BOX (36 PACKS) 40.00 50.00
UNOPENED PACK (6 CARDS) 1.75 2.00
COMMON CARD (1-54) .20 .50

1999 Buffy the Vampire Slayer PhotoCards Bonus Foil

COMPLETE SET (6) 20.00 50.00
COMMON CARD (B1-B6) 4.00 10.00
STATED ODDS 1:17

2000 Buffy the Vampire Slayer Reflections

COMPLETE SET (72) 6.00 15.00
UNOPENED BOX (24 PACKS) 100.00 150.00
UNOPENED PACK (5 CARDS) 4.00 6.00
COMMON CARD (1-72) .15 .40

2000 Buffy the Vampire Slayer Reflections Autographs

COMMON AUTO (A1-A6) 8.00 20.00
A1 Anthony Stewart Head 50.00 100.00
A2 Eliza Dushku 100.00 200.00
A3 Armin Shimmerman 15.00 40.00
A5 Serena Scott Thomas 12.00 30.00
A6 Juliet Landau 20.00 50.00

2000 Buffy the Vampire Slayer Reflections Portrait of a Slayer

COMPLETE SET (9) 15.00 40.00
COMMON CARD (S1-S9) 2.50 6.00
STATED ODDS 1:11

2000 Buffy the Vampire Slayer Reflections Slayer's Journal

COMPLETE SET (6) 10.00 25.00
COMMON CARD (J1-J6) 2.50 6.00
STATED ODDS 1:17

2000 Buffy the Vampire Slayer Reflections Promos

COMPLETE SET (3) 2.50 6.00
COMMON CARD (P1-P3) .75 2.00
P2 Buffy and Angel 1.50 4.00

2004 Buffy the Vampire Slayer Sky Promos

COMPLETE SET (7) 12.00 30.00
COMMON CARD (BTVS1-BTVS7) 2.50 6.00

2003 Buffy the Vampire Slayer The Story Continues

COMPLETE SET (81) 5.00 12.00
UNOPENED BOX (36 PACKS) 50.00 60.00
UNOPENED PACK (7 CARDS) 2.00 2.50
COMMON CARD (1-81) .12 .30
A1 The Story Continues 3.00 8.00

2003 Buffy the Vampire Slayer The Story Continues Box-Toppers

COMPLETE SET (2) 6.00 15.00
COMMON CARD (BC1-BC2) 4.00 10.00
STATED ODDS 1:BOX

2003 Buffy the Vampire Slayer The Story Continues Buffy and Spike

COMPLETE SET (4) 50.00 100.00
COMMON CARD (BS1-BS4) 12.00 30.00
STATED ODDS 1:72

2003 Buffy the Vampire Slayer The Story Continues Case-Toppers

COMPLETE SET (2) 80.00 150.00
COMMON CARD (CC1-CC2) 30.00 80.00
STATED ODDS 1:CASE

2003 Buffy the Vampire Slayer The Story Continues Shattered

COMPLETE SET (9) 6.00 15.00
COMMON CARD (S1-S9) 1.25 3.00
STATED ODDS 1:18

2003 Buffy the Vampire Slayer The Story Continues Sunnydale Evil

COMPLETE SET (9) 5.00 12.00
COMMON CARD (SE1-SE9) 1.00 2.50
STATED ODDS 1:6

2003 Buffy the Vampire Slayer The Story Continues The Gang

COMPLETE SET (6) 30.00 80.00
COMMON CARD (TG1-TG6) 6.00 15.00
STATED ODDS 1:36

2003 Buffy the Vampire Slayer The Story Continues Promos

COMMON CARD (P1-P4) 1.00 2.50
P3 Drusilla/Spike 4.00 10.00
P4 Buffy/Riley 4.00 10.00

2001 Buffy the Vampire Slayer The Story So Far

COMPLETE SET (81) 5.00 12.00
UNOPENED BOX (36 PACKS) 50.00 75.00
UNOPENED PACK (7 CARDS) 2.00 2.50
COMMON CARD (1-81) .12 .30
A1 Buffy 6.00 15.00
B1 Buffy EMBOSSED 8.00 20.00

2001 Buffy the Vampire Slayer The Story So Far Box-Toppers

COMPLETE SET (2) 12.00 30.00
COMMON CARD (BC1-BC2) 8.00 20.00
STATED ODDS 1:BOX

2001 Buffy the Vampire Slayer The Story So Far Case-Toppers

COMPLETE SET (2) 80.00 150.00
COMMON CARD (CC1-CC2) 30.00 80.00
STATED ODDS 1:CASE

2001 Buffy the Vampire Slayer The Story So Far Classic Quotes

COMPLETE SET (6) 20.00 50.00
COMMON CARD (CQ1-CQ6) 6.00 15.00
STATED ODDS 1:36

2001 Buffy the Vampire Slayer The Story So Far Couples

COMPLETE SET (9) 4.00 10.00
COMMON CARD (C1-C9) .75 2.00
STATED ODDS 1:6

2001 Buffy the Vampire Slayer The Story So Far Sunnydale Evil

COMPLETE SET (9) 10.00 25.00
COMMON CARD (SE1-SE9) 2.00 5.00
STATED ODDS 1:18

2001 Buffy the Vampire Slayer The Story So Far Promos

COMPLETE SET (4) 8.00 20.00
COMMON CARD (P1-P4) 1.50 4.00
P3 Buffy/Master 4.00 10.00
P4 Buffy Summers 4.00 10.00

2015 Buffy the Vampire Slayer Ultimate Collector's Set

COMPLETE SET w/o AU (11) 10.00 25.00
COMMON STICKER (9) 2.00 5.00
SMG1 Sarah Michelle Gellar AU/200 (bordered) 120.00 200.00
SMG2 Sarah Michelle Gellar AU/200 (full bleed) 120.00 200.00

2017 Buffy the Vampire Slayer Ultimate Collector's Set 2

COMPLETE BASE SET (7) 12.00 30.00
COMPLETE FACTORY SET 350.00 400.00
COMMON CARD (C1-C7) 2.50 6.00

2017 Buffy the Vampire Slayer Ultimate Collector's Set 2 Autographs

ONE AUTO PER SET
AH1 Alyson Hannigan Bordered 120.00 250.00
AH2 Alyson Hannigan Full Bleed 120.00 250.00
SMG Sarah Michelle Gellar COST 150.00 300.00

2017 Buffy the Vampire Slayer Ultimate Collector's Set 2 Metal

COMPLETE SET (5) 25.00 60.00
COMMON CARD (BM1-BM5) 6.00 15.00

2017 Buffy the Vampire Slayer Ultimate Collector's Set 3

COMPLETE SET (8) 25.00 60.00
UNOPENED FACTORY SET (5 CARDS) 450.00 500.00
COMMON CARD 4.00 10.00

2017 Buffy the Vampire Slayer Ultimate Collector's Set 3 Autographs

NNO Seth Green Bordered 50.00 100.00
NNO Seth Green Full Bleed 50.00 100.00

2017 Buffy the Vampire Slayer Ultimate Collector's Set 3 Dual Autograph

NNO Alyson Hannigan/Alexis Denisof (2-Set Incentive) 75.00 150.00

2017 Buffy the Vampire Slayer Ultimate Collector's Set 3 Gold Autographs

NNO Alyson Hannigan 75.00 150.00
NNO Sarah Michelle Gellar 120.00 200.00
NNO Seth Green 50.00 100.00

1997 The WB Buffy the Vampire Slayer WB29

COMPLETE SET (6) 30.00 75.00
COMMON CARD (UNNUMBERED) 8.00 20.00

2004 Buffy the Vampire Slayer Women of Sunnydale

COMPLETE SET (90) 5.00 12.00
UNOPENED BOX (36 PACKS) 100.00 150.00
UNOPENED PACK (7 CARDS) 3.00 5.00
TFR1 Tara Figure Redemption

2004 Buffy the Vampire Slayer Women of Sunnydale Autographs

COMMON AUTO (A1-A15) 8.00 20.00
STATED ODDS 1:36
A1 Emma Caulfield 30.00 60.00
A2 Amber Benson 30.00 60.00
A3 Juliet Landau 12.00 30.00
A5 Clare Kramer 12.00 30.00
A7 Bianca Lawson 12.00 30.00
A8 Julie Benz 20.00 50.00
A12 Elizabeth Anne Allen 20.00 40.00
A13 Robia La Morte 12.00 30.00
A15 Iyari Limon 12.00 30.00
AR1 Autograph Redemption

2004 Buffy the Vampire Slayer Women of Sunnydale Box-Loaders

COMPLETE SET (3) 5.00 12.00
COMMON CARD (BL1-BL3) 1.25 3.00
CL1 Working Girl 4.00 10.00

2004 Buffy the Vampire Slayer Women of Sunnydale Fashion Emergency

COMPLETE SET (9) 10.00 25.00
COMMON CARD (FE1-FE9) 1.50 4.00
STATED ODDS 1:11

2004 Buffy the Vampire Slayer Women of Sunnydale Ladies Choice

COMPLETE SET (6) 8.00 20.00
COMMON CARD (LC1-LC6) 1.50 4.00
STATED ODDS 1:17

2004 Buffy the Vampire Slayer Women of Sunnydale Pieceworks

COMPLETE SET (6) 40.00 100.00
COMMON MEM (PW1-PW6) 8.00 20.00
STATED ODDS 1:36

2004 Buffy the Vampire Slayer Women of Sunnydale Promos

COMMON CARD .40 1.00
D1 Tara Diamond Select Toys .75 2.00
P1 Buffy .75 2.00
Pi Dawn .75 2.00
WOSGG Cordelia Gum Guide 2.00 5.00
SD2004 Tara .75 2.00

2004 Ultimate Buffy the Vampire Slayer Collection

COMPLETE SET (612) 120.00 250.00
COMPLETE SET W/BONUS (619) 150.00 300.00
COMMON CARD .30 .75
UBC1 You're Invited PROMO 2.00 5.00

2004 Ultimate Buffy the Vampire Slayer Collection Bonus

COMPLETE SET (7) 15.00 40.00
COMMON CARD (BUCP1-BUCP7) 4.00 10.00

2000 Angel Season One

COMPLETE SET (90) 5.00 12.00
UNOPENED BOX (36 PACKS) 25.00 60.00
UNOPENED PACK (7 CARDS) 1.00 1.50
COMMON CARD (1-90) .15 .40

2000 Angel Season One Autographs

COMMON AUTO (A1-A6) 20.00 50.00
RANDOM INSERTS INTO PACKS
A1 David Boreanaz 125.00 250.00
A3 Glenn Quinn 30.00 75.00
A4 Elisabeth Rohm 30.00 75.00
A5 James Marsters 25.00 60.00

2000 Angel Season One Dark Avengers

COMPLETE SET (9)	15.00	40.00
COMMON CARD (DA1-DA9)	2.00	5.00

2000 Angel Season One I Love L.A.

COMPLETE SET (6)	15.00	40.00
COMMON CARD (LA1-LA6)	3.00	8.00

2000 Angel Season One Promos

COMMON CARD	1.25	3.00
AP2 Non-Sport Update	4.00	10.00
AP3 Cards Inc. UK	3.00	8.00
SD2000 San Diego Comic Con Exclusive	1.50	4.00
WW2000 Wizard World Exclusive	1.50	4.00

2001 Inkworks Angel Season Two

COMPLETE SET (90)	5.00	12.00
UNOPENED BOX (36 PACKS)	25.00	60.00
UNOPENED PACK (7 CARDS)	1.00	1.50
COMMON CARD (1-90)	.15	.40

2001 Inkworks Angel Season Two Autographs

COMPLETE SET (9)		
COMMON AUTO	15.00	40.00
RANDOM INSERTS IN PACKS		
A7 Charisma Carpenter	60.00	120.00
A9 Julie Benz	40.00	80.00
A10 Juliet Landau	60.00	120.00
A11 Stephanie Romanov	20.00	50.00
A13 Brigid Brannagh	20.00	50.00
A14 Julia Lee	20.00	50.00
DA1 Juliet Landau/Julie Benz	100.00	200.00

2001 Inkworks Angel Season Two City of Angel

COMPLETE SET (9)	10.00	25.00
COMMON CARD (CA1-CA9)	1.50	4.00
STATED ODDS 1:11		

2001 Inkworks Angel Season Two L.A. Women

COMPLETE SET (6)	7.50	20.00
COMMON CARD (LA1-LA6)	1.50	4.00
STATED ODDS 1:17		

2001 Inkworks Angel Season Two Promos

COMMON CARD	.75	2.00
A22 Coming August 2001! (Cards Inc.)	2.00	5.00
A2i Coming August 2001! (Internet offer)	2.00	5.00
AL1 (Box-loader promo from Season One)	2.00	5.00
A2SD2001 Coming August 2001! (San Diego Comic Con Exclusive)	2.00	5.00

2002 Angel Season Three

COMPLETE SET (90)	5.00	12.00
UNOPENED BOX (36 PACKS)	60.00	100.00
UNOPENED PACK (7 CARDS)	2.00	3.00
COMMON CARD (1-90)	.15	.40

2002 Angel Season Three Autographs

COMPLETE SET (9)	60.00	150.00
COMMON AUTO (A17-A23)	6.00	15.00
STATED ODDS 1:36		
A15 Amy Acker	40.00	80.00

2002 Angel Season Three Pieceworks

COMPLETE SET (2)	15.00	40.00
COMMON MEM (PW1-PW2)	10.00	25.00
STATED ODDS 1:54		

2002 Angel Season Three Prophesies Unfold

COMPLETE SET (9)	7.50	20.00
COMMON CARD (PR1-PR9)	1.25	3.00
STATED ODDS 1:11		

2002 Angel Season Three Triangulation

COMPLETE SET (6)	10.00	25.00
COMMON CARD (TR1-TR6)	2.00	5.00
STATED ODDS 1:17		

2002 Angel Season Three Promos

COMMON CARD	.75	2.00
A3i (Angel head shot; Inkworks.com web offer)	1.50	4.00
A3UK Angel Season Three (UK dealers)	1.50	4.00
A3WW2002 Coming August 2002 (Philly Con, Wizard World)	1.25	3.00

2003 Angel Season Four

COMPLETE SET (90)	5.00	12.00
UNOPENED BOX (36 PACKS)	25.00	60.00
UNOPENED PACK (7 CARDS)	1.00	1.50
COMMON CARD (1-90)	.15	.40

2003 Angel Season Four Autographs

COMPLETE SET (10)	100.00	200.00
COMMON AUTO (A24-A33)	6.00	15.00
STATED ODDS 1:36		
A24 Eliza Dushku	70.00	120.00
A29 Jack Kehler	8.00	20.00

2003 Angel Season Four Deceptions

COMPLETE SET (9)	10.00	25.00
COMMON CARD (D1-D9)	1.50	4.00
STATED ODDS 1:11		

2003 Angel Season Four Impossible Dreams

COMPLETE SET (3)	4.00	10.00
COMMON CARD (1-3)	1.50	4.00
STATED ODDS 1:BOX		

2003 Angel Season Four Pieceworks

COMPLETE SET (4)	20.00	50.00
COMMON MEM (PW1-PW4)	5.00	12.00
STATED ODDS 1:36		
PW1 David Boreanaz	6.00	15.00
PW2 Charisma Carpenter	8.00	20.00
PW4 Gina Torres	6.00	15.00

2003 Angel Season Four Redemptions

COMPLETE SET (6)	12.50	30.00
COMMON CARD (R1-R6)	2.50	6.00
STATED ODDS 1:17		

2003 Angel Season Four Promos

COMMON CARD	.75	2.00
A4i Coming August 2003 (three; inkworkscards.com exclusive)	2.00	5.00
A4UK Coming August 2003 (Connor and Angel)	2.00	5.00
A4UKE Coming August 2003 (Connor and Angel) (Embossed Variant Case-Incentive)/200	15.00	40.00
INK-2003 (10-card panel with 9 other series)		

2004 Angel Season Five

COMPLETE SET (90)	5.00	12.00
UNOPENED BOX (36 PACKS)	25.00	60.00
UNOPENED PACK (7 CARDS)	1.00	1.50
COMMON CARD (1-90)	.15	.40

2004 Angel Season Five Autographs

COMPLETE SET (12)	60.00	150.00
COMMON AUTO	6.00	15.00
STATED ODDS 1:36		
A34 Mercedes McNab	15.00	30.00
A35 David Fury	8.00	20.00
A36 Adam Baldwin	15.00	30.00
A40 Alec Newman	8.00	20.00

2004 Angel Season Five Breaking the Circle

COMPLETE SET (9)	10.00	25.00
COMMON CARD (BC1-BC9)	1.50	4.00
STATED ODDS 1:11		

2004 Angel Season Five Pieceworks

COMPLETE SET (7)	60.00	150.00
COMMON MEM (PW1-PW7)	10.00	25.00
STATED ODDS 1:36		
PW2 Amy Acker	20.00	50.00
PW3 David Boreanaz	12.00	30.00

2004 Angel Season Five Last Days

COMPLETE SET (6)	8.00	20.00
COMMON CARD (LD1-LD6)	1.50	4.00
STATED ODDS 1:17		

2004 Angel Season Five Promos

COMMON CARD	.75	2.00
A5i (3 cast; inkworks.com exclusive)	2.00	5.00
A5CE (7 cast; Collectors Expo)	2.00	5.00
A5UK (Angel; U.K. distribution)	2.00	5.00
A5WW (Angel; Wizard World Chicago)	1.25	3.00
INK-2004 (10-card panel with 9 other promos)		

2005 Spike The Complete Story

COMPLETE SET (72)	3.00	8.00
UNOPENED BOX (36 PACKS)	50.00	100.00
UNOPENED PACK (6 CARDS)	1.50	3.00
COMMON CARD (1-72)	.10	.25
BV1 PTR1 STATED ODDS 1:432		
BV1 Boris Vallejo AU	25.00	60.00
PTR1 Palz Figure Redemption	10.00	25.00

2005 Spike The Complete Story Autographs

COMPLETE SET (10)	150.00	300.00
COMMON AUTO (A1-A10)	10.00	25.00
STATED ODDS 1:36		
A1 James Marsters	50.00	100.00
A2 Juliet Landau	20.00	50.00
A3 Julie Benz	15.00	40.00
A4 Mercedes McNab	15.00	40.00
AR1 Autograph Redemption		

2005 Spike The Complete Story Box-Loaders

COMPLETE SET (3)	3.00	8.00
COMMON CARD (BL1-BL3)	1.25	3.00
STATED ODDS 1:BOX		
CL1 Bloodlines	15.00	40.00

2005 Spike The Complete Story Heart and Soul

COMPLETE SET (9)	8.00	20.00
COMMON CARD (HS1-HS9)	1.25	3.00
STATED ODDS 1:11		

2005 Spike The Complete Story Pieceworks

COMMON MEM	10.00	25.00
PW1A James Marsters Leather Coat AU	100.00	200.00
PW2A James Marsters Leather Coat AU	100.00	200.00
PR1 Redemption Card for PW1 PW2		
Apr-01 Redemption Card for PW1A PW2A		

2005 Spike The Complete Story Spike and Buffy

COMPLETE SET (6)	7.50	20.00
COMMON CARD (SB1-SB6)	2.00	5.00
STATED ODDS 1:17		

2005 Spike The Complete Story Promos

COMMON CARD	1.25	2.00
D1 Spike (Diamond Select action figures exclusive)	6.00	15.00
Pi Spike#(Inkworks Website Exclusive)	2.00	5.00
PUK Spike (UK Distribution)	1.50	4.00
PUKP Spike FOIL (UK Exclusive)	4.00	10.00

1994 21st Century Archives Bunny Yeager's Bettie Page

COMPLETE SET (50)	6.00	15.00
UNOPENED BOX (36 PACKS)	30.00	40.00
UNOPENED PACK (8 CARDS)	1.00	1.25
COMMON CARD (1-50)	.25	.60
P1 (Bettie, hanging from tree; dealer promo)	.75	2.00

1994 21st Century Archives Bunny Yeager's Bettie Page Beach Bettie in the Buff

COMPLETE SET (5)	5.00	12.00
COMMON CARD (N1-N5)	1.25	3.00
MAIL-IN EXCLUSIVE		

1994 21st Century Archives Bunny Yeager's Bettie Page Bunny Yeager's Girls of the Fifties

COMPLETE SET (5)	8.00	20.00
COMMON CARD (BY1-BY5)	2.50	6.00
STATED ODDS 1:18		

2002 Butt-Ugly Martians

COMPLETE SET (72)	8.00	20.00
UNOPENED BOX (36 PACKS)	30.00	40.00
UNOPENED PACK (7 CARDS)	1.25	1.50
UNOPENED JUMBO BOX (24 PACKS)		
UNOPENED JUMBO PACK (11 CARDS)		
COMMON CARD (1-72)	.25	.60

2002 Butt-Ugly Martians Foil

COMPLETE SET (6)	12.00	30.00
COMMON CARD (C1-C6)	2.50	6.00
RANDOMLY INSERTED INTO PACKS		

2002 Butt-Ugly Martians Pop-Ups

COMPLETE SET (3)	1.00	2.50
COMMON CARD (1-3)	.40	1.00
STATED ODDS 1:1 JUMBO PACKS		

2002 Butt-Ugly Martians Promos

COMPLETE SET (3)	2.00	5.00
COMMON CARD (P1-P3)	.75	2.00

1988 Hardee's California Raisins

COMPLETE SET (6)	3.00	8.00
COMMON CARD (UNNUMBERED)	.75	2.00

1988 Zoot California Raisins World Tour

COMPLETE SET (25)	2.50	6.00
COMMON CARD (1-25)	.12	.30

2008 Camp Rock

COMPLETE SET (71)	4.00	10.00
COMMON CARD (1-71)	.10	.30
P1 Reach for the Stars	1.00	2.50

2008 Camp Rock Stickers

COMPLETE SET (10)	2.00	5.00
COMMON CARD (1-10)	.25	.60
STATED ODDS 1:2		

2008 Camp Rock Foil Stickers

COMPLETE SET (10)	2.00	5.00
COMMON CARD	.25	.60
STATED ODDS 1:2		

1995 Collect-A-Card Campbell's Collection

COMPLETE SET (72)	4.00	10.00
UNOPENED BOX (36 PACKS)	20.00	25.00
UNOPENED PACK (8 CARDS)	.75	1.00
COMMON CARD (1-72)	.10	.25

1995 Collect-A-Card Campbell's Collection Phone Cards

COMPLETE SET (5)	25.00	60.00
COMMON CARD	6.00	15.00
STATED ODDS 1:60		
STATED PRINT RUN 10,500		
UNNUMBERED SET		

1995 Collect-A-Card Campbell's Collection Postcards

COMPLETE SET (4)	12.00	30.00
COMMON CARD (PC1-PC4)	4.00	10.00
STATED ODDS 1:25		

1995 Collect-A-Card Campbell's Collection Souper Cards

COMPLETE SET (12)	10.00	50.00
COMMON CARD (SC1-SC12)	3.00	8.00

1995 Collect-A-Card Campbell's Collection Static Cling

COMPLETE SET (6) 3.00 8.00
COMMON CARD .60 1.50
STATED ODDS 1:5

1995 Collect-A-Card Campbell's Collection Promos

COMPLETE SET (4) 2.00 5.00
COMMON CARD .60 1.50

2010 Canada at War

COMPLETE SET (112) 10.00 25.00
UNOPENED BOX (24 PACKS)
UNOPENED PACK (8 CARDS)
COMMON CARD (1-112) .20 .50

2001 Captain Scarlet

COMPLETE SET (72) 4.00 10.00
UNOPENED BOX (36 PACKS) 30.00 40.00
UNOPENED PACK (5 CARDS) 1.25 1.50
COMMON CARD (1-72) .12 .30
P1 This Is the Voice of the Mysterons PROMO.75 2.00

2001 Captain Scarlet Autographs

COMPLETE SET (2) 20.00 50.00
COMMON AUTO (CSA1-CSA2) 12.00 30.00
RANDOMLY INSERTED

2001 Captain Scarlet Box-Toppers

COMPLETE SET (3) 3.00 8.00
COMMON CARD (BT1-BT3) 1.25 3.00
STATED ODDS 1:BOX

2001 Captain Scarlet SIG Embossed

COMPLETE SET (6) 4.00 10.00
COMMON CARD (SIG1-SIG6) .75 2.00
STATED ODDS 1:9

MODERN

2018 Captain Scarlet and the Mysterons 50 Years

COMPLETE SET (36) 8.00 20.00
COMMON CARD (1-36) .30 .75

2018 Captain Scarlet and the Mysterons 50 Years Autographs

COMMON AUTO 8.00 20.00
STATED OVERALL ODDS 2 AUTO OR SKETCH:BOX
EM1 Elizabeth Morgan 25.00 60.00
EM2 Elizabeth Morgan 20.00 50.00
EM3 Elizabeth Morgan 30.00 75.00
EM4 Elizabeth Morgan/36
GF1 Gary Files 12.00 30.00
GF2 Gary Files 15.00 40.00
GF3 Gary Files 20.00 50.00
GF4 Gary Files 12.00 30.00
SR1 Shane Rimmer 15.00 40.00
SR2 Shane Rimmer 12.00 30.00
SR3 Shane Rimmer 20.00 50.00

2018 Captain Scarlet and the Mysterons 50 Years Promos

COMMON PROMO 3.00 8.00
NNO Dealer Promo
{(Roman Krause, wrongshoe)
NNO Dealer Promo
{(mitchy9210)
PH1 Coming Soon 20.00 50.00
{(Paul Hart; color; Gerry Anderson Show Sept 29 - Oct 1 2017)
PH1 Coming Soon
{(Paul Hart; black and white, Gerry Anderson Show Sept 29 - Oct 1 2017)/10
PR1 Coming Soon
(Year Set Exclusive)/20
CCP1 Dealer Promo 12.00 30.00
{(The Cyber Cellar, waltermabon1@cky.com)/20
DCP1 Dealer Promo
{(Derek's Trading Cards, derek_f)
EMP1 Dealer Promo 12.00 30.00
{(Acme 3000, elliotsmorris@aol.com)
GGP1 Dealer Promo 6.00 15.00
{(Gazza Games)
JWP1 Dealer Promo 5.00 12.00
{(completed image from JWP2+JWP3, Jason Wright, doctorjas73)
JWP2 Dealer Promo
{(puzzle left, Jason Wright, doctorjas73)
JWP3 Dealer Promo
{(puzzle right, Jason Wright, doctorjas73)
MBP1 Dealer Promo 15.00 40.00
{(marked MB-Trading-Cards, but from Try Trading Cards, taekwondo888)
OCP1 Dealer Promo 10.00 25.00
{(Of Course Collectables, of-course)
PCP1 Dealer Promo 20.00 50.00
{(Premier Cards, premier_cards@hotmail.co.uk)/20
PHP1 Dealer Promo 20.00 50.00
{(Paul Hart Trading cards, paul.hart@tinyworld.co.uk)/18
TCP1 Dealer Promo
{(Dean Rogers, Top Cards)
WEB1 Unstoppable Cards Web Exclusive

2004 Captain Spaulding's Museum of Monsters and Madmen

COMPLETE SET (6) 5.00 12.00
COMMON CARD (1-6) 1.25 3.00

2000 CardCaptors Series One

COMPLETE SET (90) 6.00 15.00
UNOPENED BOX (24 PACKS)
UNOPENED PACK (7 CARDS)
COMMON CARD (1-90) .10 .25
S1 Sakura Avalon PROMO .75 2.00

2000 CardCaptors Series One The Clow

COMPLETE SET (18) 25.00 60.00
COMMON CARD (C1-C18) 1.50 4.00
STATED ODDS 1:4

2004 Cardlings

COMPLETE FACTORY SET (30) 5.00 12.00
COMMON CARD .30 .75

2005-06 Strictly Ink Carnivale Promo

P Enter the fascinating mystical world of Carnivale 2.00 5.00

1993 CMK Cars of the World

COMPLETE SET (25) 5.00 12.00
COMMON CARD (1-25) .25 .60

1996 Fox Kids Network Casper Promo Panel

NNO 4-Card Panel 4.00 10.00

1995 Fleer Ultra Casper Movie

COMPLETE SET (119) 6.00 15.00
UNOPENED HOBBY BOX (36 PACKS) 25.00 60.00
UNOPENED HOBBY PACK (6 CARDS) 1.50 2.50
UNOPENED JUMBO BOX (24 PACKS)
UNOPENED JUMBO PACK (10 CARDS)
UNOPENED RETAIL BOX (18 PACKS) 15.00 20.00
UNOPENED RETAIL PACK (6 CARDS) .50 .75
COMMON CARD (1-119) .12 .30
*FLEER: .25X TO .6X BASIC CARDS .08 .20
NNO1 9-Card Panel Premier Edition May 1995 Promo 3.00 8.00

1995 Fleer Ultra Casper Movie Holograms

COMPLETE SET (4) 6.00 15.00
COMMON CARD (1-4) 2.00 5.00
STATED ODDS 1:12

1995 Fleer Ultra Casper Movie Prismatic Foil

COMPLETE SET (15) 5.00 12.00
COMMON CARD (1-15) .60 1.50
STATED ODDS 1:3

1995 Fleer Ultra Casper Movie Spectre-Blast

COMPLETE SET (15) 8.00 20.00
COMMON CARD (1-15) 1.00 2.50
STATED ODDS 1:4

1997 Krome Cast of Chaos

COMPLETE SET (90) 8.00 20.00
UNOPENED BOX (36 PACKS) 40.00 50.00
UNOPENED PACK (6 CARDS) 1.50 1.75
COMMON CARD (1-90) .15 .40
P1 Evil Ernie .75 2.00
NNO1 (Lady Death; unnumbered; a .75 2.00

1997 Krome Cast of Chaos ClearChrome

COMPLETE SET (5) 10.00 25.00
COMMON CARD (C1-C5) 2.50 6.00
RANDOMLY INSERTED INTO PACKS

2013 Castle Seasons One and Two

COMPLETE SET (72) 6.00 15.00
UNOPENED BOX (24 PACKS) 65.00 80.00
UNOPENED PACK (5 CARDS) 3.00 4.00
COMMON CARD (1-72) .20 .50

2013 Castle Seasons One and Two Autographs

COMMON AUTO (A1-A12; AE1) 6.00 15.00
STATED ODDS 1:24
A1 Nathan Fillion 25.00 50.00
A2 Jon Huertas 12.00 30.00
A4 Susan Sullivan 15.00 40.00
A5 Tamala Jones 8.00 20.00
A6 Ruben Santiago-Hudson 12.00 30.00
A7 Dana Delany 60.00 120.00
A8 Arye Gross 10.00 25.00
AE1 Nathan Fillion MEM 50.00 100.00

2013 Castle Seasons One and Two Behind-the-Scenes

COMPLETE SET (9) 20.00 40.00
COMMON CARD (BTS1-BTS9) 3.00 8.00
STATED ODDS 1:12

2013 Castle Seasons One and Two Characters

COMPLETE SET (9) 20.00 40.00
COMMON CARD (C1-C9) 3.00 8.00
STATED ODDS 1:12

2013 Castle Seasons One and Two Dual Wardrobes

COMMON MEM (DM1-DM11) 12.00 30.00
STATED ODDS 1:57
DM11 ISSUED AS ALBUM EXCLUSIVE
DM1 Richard/Kate 30.00 60.00
DM2 Richard/Alexis 20.00 40.00
DM3 Martha/Alexis 20.00 40.00
DM5 Roy/Kate 20.00 40.00
DM6 Richard/Martha 20.00 40.00
DM9 Kate/Lanie 20.00 40.00
DM11 Richard/Kate ALB 20.00 40.00

2013 Castle Seasons One and Two Scene of the Crime

COMPLETE SET (9) 15.00 30.00
COMMON CARD (CS1-CS9) 2.50 6.00
STATED ODDS 1:12

2013 Castle Seasons One and Two Wardrobes

COMMON MEM (M1-M31) 10.00 25.00
STATED ODDS 1:18
M3 Kate Beckett Green Jacket 15.00 40.00
M4 Richard Castle Suit 20.00 50.00
M7 Kate Beckett Dress 20.00 50.00
M8 Richard Castle Burgundy Shirt 15.00 40.00
M9 Martha Rodgers Dress 15.00 40.00
M10 Kate Beckett Black Jacket 25.00 60.00
M11 Alexis Castle Jacket 15.00 40.00
M12 Javier Esposito Jeans 10.00 30.00
M13 Kate Beckett Jeans 15.00 40.00
M15 Richard Castle Lavender Shirt 15.00 40.00
M17 Alexis Castle Shirt 10.00 50.00
M20 Kate Beckett Shirt 20.00 50.00
M21 Alexis Castle Pajamas 15.00 40.00
M22 Richard Castle Pants 15.00 40.00
M24 Kate Beckett Brown Jacket 15.00 40.00
M27 Richard Castle Pinstripe Shirt 15.00 40.00
M29 Richard Castle Navy Suit 15.00 40.00

2013 Castle Seasons One and Two Promos

COMMON CARD 2.00 5.00
P1 Beckett/Castle SDCC 6.00 15.00
P3 Cast Licensing Show 6.00 15.00

2014 Castle Seasons Three and Four

COMPLETE SET (72) 8.00 20.00
UNOPENED BOX (24 PACKS) 150.00 250.00
UNOPENED PACK (5 CARDS) 6.00 10.00
COMMON CARD (1-72) .25 .60
*FOIL: 8X TO 20X BASIC CARDS

2014 Castle Seasons Three and Four Autographs

COMMON AUTO (A1-A14) 5.00 12.00
STATED ODDS 1:24
A1 Nathan Fillion 50.00 100.00
A2 Molly C. Quinn 75.00 150.00
A3 Tamala Jones 8.00 20.00
A4 Seamus Dever 12.00 30.00
A5 Penny Johnson Jerald 8.00 20.00
A10 Derek Webster 6.00 15.00
A11 Richard Burgi 6.00 15.00
A12 Teri Polo 25.00 60.00

2014 Castle Seasons Three and Four Behind-the-Scenes

COMPLETE SET (9) 15.00 40.00
COMMON CARD (B1-B9) 3.00 8.00
STATED ODDS 1:12

2014 Castle Seasons Three and Four Caskett

COMPLETE SET (9) 10.00 25.00
COMMON CARD (C1-C9) 2.50 6.00
STATED ODDS 1:12

2014 Castle Seasons Three and Four Dual Wardrobes

COMMON MEM (DM1-DM4) 12.00 30.00
DM1 R.Hudson 25.00 60.00
S. Katic
DM3 M.Quinn 20.00 50.00
S.Sullivan
DM4 S.Katic 25.00 60.00
T.Jones

2014 Castle Seasons Three and Four Family Ties

COMPLETE SET (9) 10.00 25.00
COMMON CARD (FT1-FT9) 2.50 6.00
STATED ODDS 1:12

2014 Castle Seasons Three and Four Wardrobes

COMMON MEM (M1-M21) 10.00 25.00
STATED ODDS 1:24
M1 Nathan Fillion 12.00 30.00
M2 Stana Katic 30.00 80.00
M3 Susan Sullivan 12.00 30.00
M4 Ruben Santiago-Hudson 12.00 30.00
M5 Molly C. Quinn 15.00 40.00
M6 Susan Sullivan 15.00 40.00
M7 Jon Huertas 20.00 50.00
M8 Nathan Fillion 12.00 30.00
M11 Nathan Fillion 15.00 40.00
M15 Stana Katic 60.00 120.00
M16 Nathan Fillion 12.00 30.00
M17 Stana Katic 50.00 100.00
M21 Seamus Dever 12.00 30.00

1993 Purrfecto Cat Baseball Promos

COMPLETE SET (3) 2.50 6.00
COMMON CARD 1.25 3.00

2003 Cat in the Hat Movie

COMPLETE SET (72)	4.00	10.00
UNOPENED BOX (24 PACKS)	25.00	40.00
UNOPENED PACK (11 CARDS)	1.25	2.50
COMMON CARD (1-72)	.12	.30

2003 Cat in the Hat Movie Die-Cuts

COMPLETE SET (6)	10.00	25.00
COMMON CARD (DC1-DC6)	2.00	5.00
STATED ODDS 1:12		

2003 Cat in the Hat Movie Memorabilia

COMPLETE SET (6)	80.00	150.00
COMMON CARD (CW1-CW6)	12.00	30.00
STATED ODDS 1:24		

2003 Cat in the Hat Movie Promos

COMPLETE SET (3)	2.00	5.00
COMMON CARD (P1-P3)	.75	2.00

2011 CBLDF Liberty Trading Cards

COMPLETE SET (72)	6.00	15.00
UNOPENED BOX (24 PACKS)	65.00	80.00
UNOPENED PACK (5 CARDS)	3.00	3.50
COMMON CARD (1-72)	.15	.40

2011 CBLDF Liberty Trading Cards Autographs

COMMON CARD (UNNUMBERED)	5.00	12.00
RANDOMLY INSERTED INTO PACKS		
NNO Amanda Conner	6.00	15.00
NNO Bill Morrison	10.00	25.00
NNO Brad Meltzer	6.00	15.00
NNO Brian Azzarello	10.00	25.00
NNO Charlie Adlard	6.00	15.00
NNO Darwyn Cooke	12.00	30.00
NNO Denny O'Neil	12.00	30.00
NNO Eric Powell	6.00	15.00
NNO Erik Larsen	15.00	40.00
NNO Frank Quitely	6.00	15.00
NNO Gail Simone	8.00	20.00
NNO James Kochalka	8.00	20.00
NNO Jeff Smith	12.00	30.00
NNO Jim Valentino	6.00	15.00
NNO John Layman	8.00	20.00
NNO Kurt Busiek	10.00	25.00
NNO Mark Waid	6.00	15.00
NNO Marv Wolfman	6.00	15.00
NNO Mike Richardson	8.00	20.00
NNO Neil Gaiman	50.00	100.00
NNO Peter David	6.00	15.00
NNO Peter Kuper	8.00	20.00
NNO Phil Hester	6.00	15.00
NNO Rick Veitch	6.00	15.00
NNO Rob Liefeld	20.00	50.00
NNO Robert Kirkman	60.00	120.00
NNO Ryan Ottley	6.00	15.00
NNO Scott McCloud	6.00	15.00
NNO Steve Bissette	12.00	30.00

2011 CBLDF Liberty Trading Cards Puzzle Stickers

COMPLETE SET (9)	12.00	30.00
COMMON CARD	2.00	5.00
RANDOMLY INSERTED INTO PACKS		

2011 CBLDF Liberty Trading Cards Promos

COMPLETE SET (4)	6.00	15.00
COMMON CARD	2.00	5.00

2011 Cereal Killers Series One

COMPLETE SET (55)	8.00	20.00
UNOPENED BOX (24 PACKS)	100.00	150.00
UNOPENED PACK (8 CARDS)	4.00	6.00
COMMON CARD (1-55)	.30	.75
TAT Zomb'a Crunch Tattoo		

2011 Cereal Killers Series One Blacklight Stickers

COMPLETE SET (3)	10.00	25.00
COMMON CARD (1-3)	5.00	12.00

2011 Cereal Killers Series One Gold Bonus

GB1 Cereal Killers First Series	3.00	8.00

2011 Cereal Killers Series One Magnets

COMPLETE SET (3)	6.00	15.00
COMMON CARD (1-3)	3.00	8.00

2011 Cereal Killers Series One Silver Spoon Foil Fusion

COMPLETE SET (8)	8.00	20.00
COMMON CARD (1-8)	2.00	5.00

2012 Cereal Killers Series Two

COMPLETE SET (55)	8.00	20.00
UNOPENED BOX (24 PACKS)	75.00	125.00
UNOPENED PACK (8 CARDS)	3.00	5.00
COMMON CARD (1-55)	.30	.75

2012 Cereal Killers Series Two Glo Flo

COMPLETE SET (3)	5.00	12.00
COMMON CARD (1-3)	2.50	6.00

2012 Cereal Killers Series Two Silver Spoon Foil Fusion

COMPLETE SET (9)	8.00	20.00
COMMON CARD (1-9)	2.00	5.00

2012 Cereal Killers Series Two Sugar Glitter

COMPLETE SET (8)	12.00	30.00
COMMON CARD (1-8)	2.00	5.00

2012 Cereal Killers Series Two Promos

P1 Cereal Killers Glitter	2.00	5.00
P2 Cereal Killers Glitter	2.00	5.00
NNO Cinnamon Ghost Crunch NSU Glitter	2.00	5.00
4 Freakin' Berry NSU	2.00	5.00
5 Puffed Polterrice NSU	2.00	5.00

1995 FPG Charles Vess

COMPLETE SET (90)	5.00	12.00
UNOPENED BOX (36 PACKS)	30.00	40.00
UNOPENED PACK (10 CARDS)	1.25	1.50
COMMON CARD (1-90)	.12	.30
AU1 Charles Vess AU/1000*	20.00	50.00

1995 FPG Charles Vess Metal

COMPLETE SET (4)	10.00	25.00
COMMON CARD (M1-M4)	3.00	8.00
RANDOMLY INSERTED INTO PACKS		

2005 Charlie and the Chocolate Factory

COMPLETE SET (90)	5.00	12.00
UNOPENED BOX (36 PACKS)	500.00	800.00
UNOPENED PACK (8 CARDS)	15.00	25.00
COMMON CARD (1-90)	.15	.40
T1 STATED ODDS ONE PER TIN		
T1 Johnny Depp TIN	6.00	15.00

2005 Charlie and the Chocolate Factory Autographs

COMMON AUTO (UNNUMBERED)	12.00	30.00
STATED ODDS 1:72		
NNO Annasophia Robb	125.00	250.00
NNO Christopher Lee	150.00	300.00
NNO David Kelly	50.00	100.00
NNO Freddie Highmore	150.00	300.00
NNO Helena Bonham Carter	125.00	250.00
NNO Johnny Depp	4000.00	8000.00
NNO Julia Winter	30.00	60.00
NNO Missi Pyle	30.00	75.00

2005 Charlie and the Chocolate Factory Costumes

COMMON CARD	8.00	20.00
OVERALL COSTUME/PROP ODDS ONE PER HOBBY BOX		
15 ISSUED AS A CASE TOPPER		
16 ISSUED AS UK 2-CASE INCENTIVE		
17 ISSUED AS 10-CASE INCENTIVE		
18 ISSUED IN SDCC TINS		
4 Mike Teavee's skull shirt/305	10.00	25.00
6 Mr. Salt's tie/165	12.00	30.00
11 Oompa Loompa's red outfit/240	10.00	25.00
13 Violet Beauregarde's tracksuit top/330	15.00	40.00
16 Oompa Loompa's white outfit/210 2CI	10.00	25.00

2005 Charlie and the Chocolate Factory Foil Hobby

COMPLETE SET (9)	4.00	10.00
COMMON CARD (R1-R9)	.75	2.00
*RETAIL: SAME VALUE		
STATED ODDS 1:5 HOBBY		

2005 Charlie and the Chocolate Factory Props Hobby

COMMON CARD	6.00	15.00
OVERALL COSTUME/PROP ODDS ONE PER HOBBY BOX		
14 ISSUED AS CASE TOPPER		
15 ISSUED AS 25-CASE INCENTIVE		
16 ISSUED AS NEW YORK EXCLUSIVE		
3 Chocolate Bar/490	10.00	25.00
4 Contest Announcement/490	10.00	25.00
5 Golden Ticket/18	450.00	600.00
7 Red Ribbon/340	10.00	25.00
8 Smilex Toothpaste Box/340	15.00	30.00
10 Triple Dazzle Caramel Candy wrapper/290	15.00	30.00
12 Wonka Box of Chocolates/390	12.00	30.00
13 Wrapping Paper from Charlie's Birthday/72	150.00	250.00
14 Wonka Display Box/290 CT	15.00	30.00
15 Short Grass from factory/39 25CI	250.00	500.00
16 Long Grass from factory/95 NY	100.00	200.00

2005 Charlie and the Chocolate Factory Props Retail

COMPLETE SET (4)	12.00	30.00
COMMON CARD	4.00	10.00
STATED ODDS 1:RETAIL BOX		

2005 Charlie and the Chocolate Factory Scratch 'n Sniff Box-Toppers

COMPLETE SET (4)	5.00	12.00
COMMON CARD (BT1-BT4)	1.50	4.00
STATED ODDS ONE PER BOX		

Charmed

2004 Charmed Connections

COMPLETE SET (72)	4.00	10.00
UNOPENED BOX (24 PACKS)	50.00	60.00
UNOPENED PACK (6 CARDS)	2.00	2.50
COMMON CARD (1-72)	.10	.30
*FOIL: .8X TO 2X BASIC CARDS		
STATED ODDS ONE PER PACK		

2004 Charmed Connections Box-Loaders

COMPLETE SET (3)	3.00	8.00
COMMON CARD (BL1-BL3)	1.25	3.00
STATED ODDS 1:BOX		
CL1 STATED ODDS 1:CASE		
CL1 P3 CASE INSERT	6.00	15.00

2004 Charmed Connections Pieceworks

COMMON MEM (1-9)	8.00	20.00
STATED ODDS 1:24		
PWC1 Alyssa Milano Rose McGowan	15.00	40.00
PWC2 Holly Marie Combs Rose McGowan	15.00	40.00
PWC3 Alyssa Milano	15.00	40.00
PWC4 Brian Krause	10.00	25.00
PWC7 Alyssa Milano	10.00	25.00
PWC8 Holly Marie Combs	10.00	25.00
PWC9 Rose McGowan	20.00	40.00

2004 Charmed Connections Under Their Spell

COMPLETE SET (9)	10.00	25.00
COMMON CARD (1-9)	1.50	4.00
STATED ODDS 1:11		

2004 Charmed Connections Vanquishing Evil

COMPLETE SET (6)	8.00	20.00
COMMON CARD (1-6)	1.50	4.00
STATED ODDS 1:14		

2004 Charmed Connections Promos

COMMON CARD	1.50	4.00
CCi Phoebe Inkworks.com	2.00	5.00
CCP1 Charmed FOIL	4.00	10.00
CCP2 Paige NSU	2.00	5.00
CCP3 Charmed FOIL	3.00	8.00
CCUK Piper UK	2.00	5.00
CCFOA Phoebe Friends of Allan	3.00	8.00
CCPUK Piper FOIL	6.00	15.00

2005 Charmed Conversations

COMPLETE SET (72)	4.00	10.00
UNOPENED BOX (24 PACKS)	100.00	150.00
UNOPENED PACK (6 CARDS)	4.00	6.00
COMMON CARD (1-72)	.10	.30

2005 Charmed Conversations Autographs

COMMON AUTO (A1-A10)	5.00	12.00
STATED ODDS 1:36		
A1 Alyssa Milano	100.00	200.00
A2 Dorian Gregory	6.00	15.00
A5 Billy Drago	15.00	40.00
A6 Oded Fehr	6.00	15.00
A7 James Avery	20.00	50.00

2005 Charmed Conversations Box-Loaders

COMPLETE SET (3)	3.00	8.00
COMMON CARD (BL1-BL3)	1.25	3.00
STATED ODDS 1:BOX		
CL1 STATED ODDS 1:CASE		
CL1 Sisters (case insert)	6.00	15.00

2005 Charmed Conversations Charming Men

COMPLETE SET (6)	6.00	15.00
COMMON CARD (1-6)	1.25	3.00
STATED ODDS 1:14		

2005 Charmed Conversations Pieceworks

COMMON MEM (1-8)	8.00	20.00
STATED ODDS 1:36		
PWCC1 Alyssa Milano	12.00	30.00
PWCC2 Holly Marie Combs	10.00	25.00
PWCC3 Rose McGowan	10.00	25.00
PWCC7 Alyssa Milano	10.00	25.00
PWCC8 Holly Marie Combs	10.00	25.00

2005 Charmed Conversations Transformations

COMPLETE SET (9)	8.00	20.00
COMMON CARD (1-9)	1.00	2.50
STATED ODDS 1:11		

2005 Charmed Conversations Promos

COMPLETE SET (4)	4.00	10.00
COMMON CARD	.75	2.00
Pi Charmed Conversations (Inkworks)	2.50	6.00
PUK Charmed Conversations (UK)	2.50	6.00

2006 Charmed Destiny

COMPLETE SET (72)	4.00	10.00
UNOPENED BOX (24 PACKS)	60.00	70.00
UNOPENED PACK (6 CARDS)	3.00	3.50
COMMON CARD (1-72)	.10	.30

2006 Charmed Destiny Autographs

COMMON AUTO (A1-A11)	5.00	12.00
STATED ODDS 1:36		
A1 Holly Marie Combs	60.00	120.00

A2 Holly Marie Combs Brian Krause	75.00	150.00
A6 Eric Dane	6.00	15.00
A9 Billy Drago	15.00	40.00
A11 Marnette Patterson	6.00	15.00

2006 Charmed Destiny Bad Karma

COMPLETE SET (6)	5.00	12.00
COMMON CARD (1-6)	1.00	2.50
STATED ODDS 1:17		

2006 Charmed Destiny Box-Loaders

COMPLETE SET (3)	3.00	8.00
COMMON CARD (BL1-BL3)	1.25	3.00
STATED ODDS 1:BOX		
CL1 STATED ODDS 1:CASE		
CL1 Brad Kern AU		
CASE INSERT		

2006 Charmed Destiny Pieceworks

COMMON MEM (1-8)	4.00	10.00
STATED ODDS 1:36		
PW1a Rose McGowan	15.00	30.00
PW1b Rose McGowan Bead and Lace variant)	60.00	120.00
PW2 Alyssa Milano	20.00	40.00
PW3 Holly Marie Combs	15.00	30.00
PW5 Kaley Cuoco	20.00	50.00
PW8 Alyssa Milano	20.00	40.00
PW9 Holly Marie Combs Alyssa Milano	25.00	50.00
PWR1 Redemption Card		

2006 Charmed Destiny Unforgettable

COMPLETE SET (9)	8.00	20.00
COMMON CARD (1-9)	1.00	2.50
STATED ODDS 1:11		

2006 Charmed Destiny Promos

COMPLETE SET (5)	4.00	10.00
COMMON CARD	.75	2.00
Pi Piper, Phoebe, Paige, and Billie	1.25	3.00
PUK Phoebe, Piper, and Paige	1.25	3.00
PC2006 San Diego Comic Con Exclusive	1.25	3.00

2007 Charmed Forever

COMPLETE SET (72)	4.00	10.00
UNOPENED BOX (36 PACKS)		
UNOPENED PACK (6 CARDS)		
COMMON CARD (1-72)	.10	.30
CL1 The Power Of 4/CASE INSERT	8.00	20.00

2007 Charmed Forever And They Lived Happily Ever After

COMPLETE SET (3)	4.00	10.00
COMMON CARD (1-3)	2.00	5.00
STATED ODDS 1:35		

2007 Charmed Forever Family

COMPLETE SET (6)	4.00	10.00
COMMON CARD (1-6)	1.25	3.00
STATED ODDS 1:17		

2007 Charmed Forever Legacy

COMPLETE SET (9)	4.00	10.00
COMMON CARD (1-9)	.75	2.00
STATED ODDS 1:11		

2007 Charmed Forever Pieceworks

COMMON MEM (1-13)	8.00	20.00
STATED ODDS 1:18		
PW14 ISSUED AS MULTI-CASE INCENTIVE		
PW1 Alyssa Milano	10.00	25.00
PW4 Kaley Cuoco	6.00	50.00
PW6 Alyssa Milano	10.00	25.00
PW7b Holly Marie Combs	10.00	25.00
PW9 Alyssa Milano	10.00	25.00
PW11 Holly Marie Combs	15.00	30.00
PW14 Milano/Combs/McGowan MCI	30.00	60.00

2007 Charmed Forever Promos

COMPLETE SET (4)	3.00	8.00
COMMON CARD	.75	2.00
PSD Piper	1.50	4.00

2003 Charmed Power of Three

COMPLETE SET (72)	5.00	12.00
UNOPENED BOX (24 PACKS)	50.00	60.00
UNOPENED PACK (8 CARDS)	2.00	2.50
COMMON CARD (1-72)	.15	.40

2003 Charmed Power of Three Autographs

COMPLETE SET (14)		
COMMON AUTO	5.00	12.00
STATED ODDS 1:24		
A3 Alyssa Milano	125.00	250.00
A8 Rose McGowan	125.00	250.00
A9 Julian McMahon	25.00	60.00
A10 Robert Englund	50.00	100.00
A11 Billy Drago	15.00	40.00
A13 Adrian Paul	12.00	30.00
A14 Melinda Clarke	12.00	30.00

2003 Charmed Power of Three Box-Loaders

COMPLETE SET (3)	7.50	20.00
COMMON CARD (BL1-BL3)	2.50	6.00
STATED ODDS 1:BOX		
CL1 STATED ODDS 1:CASE		
CL1 Charmed CT	6.00	15.00

2003 Charmed Power of Three Pieceworks

COMPLETE SET (5)	60.00	120.00
COMMON MEM (1-5)	8.00	20.00
STATED ODDS 1:24		
PW4 Rose McGowan	20.00	50.00
PW5 Alyssa Milano	20.00	50.00

2003 Charmed Power of Three Puzzle

COMPLETE SET (9)	8.00	20.00
COMMON CARD (1-9)	1.25	3.00
STATED ODDS 1:11		

2003 Charmed Power of Three Spellbinders

COMPLETE SET (6)	4.00	10.00
COMMON CARD (1-6)	1.00	2.50
STATED ODDS 1:11		

2000 Charmed Season One

COMPLETE SET (72)	5.00	12.00
UNOPENED BOX (36 PACKS)	200.00	300.00
UNOPENED PACK (7 CARDS)	6.00	8.00
COMMON CARD (1-72)	.15	.40
S1 Spirit Board	10.00	25.00

2000 Charmed Season One Autographs

COMMON AUTO (A1-A7)	5.00	12.00
RANDOM INSERTS IN PACKS		
A1 Shannen Doherty	30.00	75.00
A2 Holly Marie Combs	100.00	200.00
A4 T.W. King	10.00	25.00
A5 Brian Krause	10.00	25.00
A7 David Carradine	15.00	40.00

2000 Charmed Season One Book of Shadows

COMPLETE SET (6)	15.00	40.00
COMMON CARD (1-6)	4.00	10.00
STATED ODDS 1:18		

2000 Charmed Season One Charmed Ones

COMPLETE SET (9)	20.00	50.00
COMMON CARD (P1-P9)	3.00	8.00
STATED ODDS 1:11		

2000 Charmed Season One Promos

COMPLETE SET (8)	8.00	20.00
COMMON CARD	.75	2.00
P1 Piper, Prue, and Phoebe	1.50	4.00
P2 Piper, Prue, and Phoebe	1.50	4.00
ML1 Phoebe, Prue, and Piper	1.50	4.00
P0b Phoebe, Prue, and Piper w/TM	2.00	5.00
PB1 Phoebe, Prue, and Piper	1.50	4.00
SF1 Piper, Prue, and Phoebe	1.50	4.00
NSU1 Piper, Prue, and Phoebe FOIL NSU	1.50	4.00

1992 Collect-a-Card Chevy

COMPLETE SET (100)	5.00	12.00
COMPLETE FACTORY SET (111)	25.00	60.00
UNOPENED BOX (36 PACKS)	30.00	40.00
UNOPENED PACK (10 CARDS)	1.25	1.50
COMMON CARD (1-100)	.10	.25

1992 Collect-a-Card Chevy Chrome

COMPLETE SET (8)	12.00	30.00
COMMON CARD (1-8	2.00	5.00
RANDOMLY INSERTED INTO PACKS		

1992 Collect-a-Card Chevy Promos

COMPLETE SET (4)	2.50	6.00
COMMON CARD	.75	2.00

2013 Chevy Series One

COMPLETE SET (8)	4.00	10.00
COMMON CARD (1-8)	1.00	2.50

2013 Chevy Series Two

COMPLETE SET (8)	4.00	10.00
COMMON CARD (1-8)	1.00	2.50

1993 Kitchen Sink Press Chicago Mob Wars

COMPLETE BOXED SET (36)	4.00	10.00
COMMON CARD (1-36)	.25	.60

2000 Chicken Run Platinum Collection

COMPLETE BOXED SET (19)	10.00	25.00
COMMON CARD (1-19)	.75	2.00

1991 Universal Child's Play 3 SDCC Promos

COMPLETE SET (5)	1.50	4.00
COMMON CARD (1-5)	.50	1.25

1997 Studio E Chopper Chicks of Mars

COMPLETE SET (60)	6.00	15.00
UNOPENED BOX (36 PACKS)	40.00	60.00
UNOPENED PACK (7 CARDS)	1.50	2.50
COMMON CARD (1-60)	.20	.50

1997 Studio E Chopper Chicks of Mars Alien Foil

COMPLETE SET (6)	8.00	20.00
COMMON CARD (A1-A6)	1.50	4.00
RANDOMLY INSERTED INTO PACKS		

1997 Studio E Chopper Chicks of Mars Character Foil

COMPLETE SET (3)	10.00	25.00
COMMON CARD (C1-C3)	4.00	10.00
RANDOMLY INSERTED INTO PACKS		

1997 Studio E Chopper Chicks of Mars Electronic

COMPLETE SET (2)	60.00	120.00
COMMON CARD (ETC1-ETC2)	30.00	75.00
RANDOMLY INSERTED INTO PACKS		

1997 Studio E Chopper Chicks of Mars Electronic Promos

ETC1 Sarah (marked "Prototype")	4.00	10.00
ETC2 Sandy (marked "Prototype")	4.00	10.00

1997 Studio E Chopper Chicks of Mars Embossed

COMPLETE SET (3)	6.00	15.00
COMMON CARD (S1-S3)	3.00	8.00
MAIL-IN EXCLUSIVE		

1997 Studio E Chopper Chicks of Mars Redemption

COMMON CARD	15.00	40.00

1997 Studio E Chopper Chicks of Mars Promos

COMPLETE SET (9)	5.00	12.00
COMMON CARD	.75	2.00

1992 FPG Chris Achilleos

COMPLETE SET (90)	5.00	12.00
UNOPENED BOX (36 PACKS)	20.00	30.00
UNOPENED PACK (10 CARDS)	1.00	1.25
COMMON CARD (1-90)	.10	.25
*SILVER: .75X TO 2X BASIC CARDS		
*GOLD: 1.5X TO 4X BASIC CARDS		
NNO Chris Achilleos PROMO	2.00	5.00
NNO Album Exclusive Insert		

1995 FPG Chris Achilleos Colossal

COMPLETE SET (50)	10.00	25.00
COMMON CARD (1-50)	.30	.75

1995 FPG Chris Foss

COMPLETE SET (90)	5.00	12.00
UNOPENED BOX (36 PACKS)	30.00	40.00
UNOPENED PACK (10 CARDS)	1.25	1.50
COMMON CARD (1-90)	.12	.30
NNO Chris Foss AU/1000*	20.00	50.00

1995 FPG Chris Foss Metallic

COMPLETE SET (5)	12.00	30.00
COMMON CARD (M1-M5)	3.00	8.00
STATED ODDS 1:12		

2000 Upper Deck Christina Aguilera

COMPLETE SET (45)	4.00	10.00
UNOPENED BOX (36 PACKS)	100.00	150.00
UNOPENED PACK (4 CARDS)	3.00	4.00
COMMON CARD (1-45)	.20	.50
AGUILERA AU SER.#'d 250		
NNO Christina Aguilera AU/250	300.00	600.00

1995 Fleer Christmas

COMPLETE SET (42)	3.00	8.00
UNOPENED BOX (36 PACKS)	15.00	25.00
UNOPENED PACK (7 CARDS)	.75	1.00
COMMON CARD	.12	.30
A CHRISTMAS CAROL (A1-A7)		
CHRISTMAS SONGS (B1-B7)		
THE NUTCRACKER (C1-C7)		
'TWAS THE NIGHT (D1-D7)		
TWELVE DAYS OF (E1-E7)		
VELVETEEN RABBIT (F1-F7)		

1995 Fleer Christmas Golden Memories

COMPLETE SET (6)	2.50	6.00
COMMON CARD	.75	1.50
STATED ODDS 1:6		

2004 Chronicles of Riddick

COMPLETE SET (72)	4.00	10.00
UNOPENED BOX (40 PACKS)	40.00	50.00
UNOPENED PACK (7 CARDS)	1.25	1.50
COMMON CARD (1-72)	.10	.30

2004 Chronicles of Riddick Autographs

COMMON AUTO (A1-A10)	10.00	25.00
STATED ODDS 1:20		
L (LIMITED): 300-500 COPIES		
VL (VERY LIMITED): 200-300 COPIES		
A1 Vin Diesel VL	300.00	450.00
A2 Judi Dench	30.00	75.00
A3 Karl Urban	25.00	60.00
A5 Alexa Davalos	40.00	100.00
A6 Thandie Newton	50.00	125.00
A10 Keith David L	15.00	40.00

2004 Chronicles of Riddick Casting Call

COMPLETE SET (9)	7.50	20.00
COMMON CARD (CC1-CC9)	1.25	3.00
STATED ODDS 1:10		

2004 Chronicles of Riddick Pitch Black

COMPLETE SET (18) 10.00 25.00
COMMON CARD (PB1-PB18) .75 2.00
STATED ODDS 1:3

2004 Chronicles of Riddick Pitch Black Autographs

COMMON AUTO (A7-A9) 10.00 25.00
A7 ISSUED AS CASE TOPPER
A8 ISSUED AS ALBUM EXCLUSIVE
A9 ISSUED AS MULTI-CASE INCENTIVE
A7 Keith David CT 20.00 50.00
A8 Radha Mitchell ALB 12.00 30.00
A9 Claudia Black MCI 125.00 300.00

2004 Chronicles of Riddick Promos

COMPLETE SET (3) 2.50 6.00
COMMON CARD (P1-P3) 1.00 2.50
P3 Riddick ALB 2.00 5.00

2014-16 RRParks Chronicles of the Three Stooges Complete Series

COMPLETE SET (258) 15.00 40.00
COMPLETE SERIES 1 SET 4.00 10.00
COMPLETE SERIES 2 SET 4.00 10.00
COMPLETE SERIES 3 SET 4.00 10.00
COMPLETE SERIES 4 SET 4.00 10.00
COMPLETE SERIES 5 SET 4.00 10.00
UNOPENED SERIES 1 BOX (36 PACKS) 60.00 120.00
UNOPENED SERIES 1 PACK (10 CARDS) 2.00 3.50
UNOPENED SERIES 2 BOX (36 PACKS) 50.00 90.00
UNOPENED SERIES 2 PACK (10 PACKS) 1.25 2.50
UNOPENED SERIES 3 BOX (36 PACKS) 60.00 120.00
UNOPENED SERIES 3 PACK (10 PACKS) 2.00 3.50
UNOPENED SERIES 4 BOX (36 PACKS) 50.00 90.00
UNOPENED SERIES 4 PACK (10 PACKS) 1.25 2.50
UNOPENED SERIES 5 FACTORY SET 30.00 50.00
COMMON CARD .08 .20

2014-16 RRParks Chronicles of the Three Stooges Complete Series Caricatures

COMPLETE SET (6) 5.00 12.00
COMMON CARD (1-6) 1.25 3.00

2014-16 RRParks Chronicles of the Three Stooges Complete Series Collector's Kit Promos

COMMON CARD 2.50 6.00

2014-16 RRParks Chronicles of the Three Stooges Complete Series Kickstarter Campaign Promos

COMMON CARD (1-4) 1.50 4.00

2014-16 RRParks Chronicles of the Three Stooges Complete Series NSU Promos

COMPLETE SET (4) 6.00 15.00
COMMON CARD (1-4) 2.00 5.00

2014-16 RRParks Chronicles of the Three Stooges Complete Series Pain-O-Rama Puzzle Series Three

COMPLETE SET (6) 8.00 20.00
COMMON CARD (PZ1-PZ6) 1.50 4.00

2014-16 RRParks Chronicles of the Three Stooges Complete Series Retro-Stalgic

COMPLETE SET (121) 10.00 80.00
COMMON CARD (97 - 217) .50 1.25
STATED ODDS 1:1
NNO1 Dewey, Cheatem And Howe (box-topper) 2.00 5.00

2014-16 RRParks Chronicles of the Three Stooges Complete Series Special Artist Portraits Series One

COMPLETE SET (9) 6.00 15.00
COMMON CARD (MC1-MC9) .75 2.00

2014-16 RRParks Chronicles of the Three Stooges Complete Series Special Artist Portraits Series Two

COMPLETE SET (9) 6.00 15.00
COMMON CARD (1-9) .75 2.00

2014-16 RRParks Chronicles of the Three Stooges Complete Series Special Stooge Gals

COMPLETE SET (5) 3.00 8.00
COMMON CARD (CM1-CM5) 1.00 2.50

2014-16 RRParks Chronicles of the Three Stooges Complete Series The Wrapper Promos

COMPLETE SET (4) 6.00 15.00
COMMON CARD (1-4) 2.00 5.00

2014-16 RRParks Chronicles of the Three Stooges Complete Series XMas Foil

COMPLETE SET (8) 6.00 15.00
COMMON CARD (1-8) 1.25 3.00

1989 South Wales Constabulary City of Cardiff

COMPLETE SET (36) 5.00 12.00
COMMON CARD (1-36) .25 .60

1996 Keepsake Collection Civil War The Art of Mort Kunstler

COMPLETE SET (90) 8.00 20.00
UNOPENED BOX (36 PACKS) 40.00 50.00
UNOPENED PACK (8 CARDS) 1.50 2.00
COMMON CARD (1-90) .15 .40
MKAU Until We Meet Again AU 20.00 50.00
X Confederate Sunset Bonus Insert

1996 Keepsake Collection Civil War The Art of Mort Kunstler Chromium Generals

COMPLETE SET (6) 15.00 40.00
COMMON CARD (C1-C6 3.00 8.00
STATED ODDS 1:12

1996 Keepsake Collection Civil War The Art of Mort Kunstler Promos

COMPLETE SET (3) 2.00 5.00
COMMON CARD (1-3) .75 2.00

1991 Bon Air Civil War Heritage

COMPLETE SET (20) 2.50 6.00

1992 Bon Air Civil War Heritage

COMPLETE SET (12) 3.00 8.00
COMMON CARD (1-12) .50 1.25

1986 De-Lish-Us Civil War Scenes

COMPLETE SET (36) 17.50 35.00
COMMON CARD (1-36) .75 2.00

1981 Post Clash of the Titans Canadian

COMPLETE SET (10) 20.00 50.00
COMMON CARD 2.50 6.00
INSERTED INTO POST CANADIAN CEREALS

1989 Universe Games Classic Aircraft

COMPLETE BOXED SET (50) 3.00 8.00
COMMON CARD (1-50) .10 .25

1993 M.C. Productions Classic American Guitars

COMPLETE SET (30) 3.00 8.00
COMMON CARD (1-30) .15 .40
NNO4 Uncut Sheet/1000*

1990 Classic Monster Trucks

COMPLETE SET (125) 15.00 40.00
UNOPENED BOX (36 PACKS) 50.00 75.00
UNOPENED PACK (12 CARDS) 1.50 2.00
COMMON CARD (1-125) .25 .60

2012 Classic Mythology I Previews

COMPLETE SET (5) 5.00 12.00
COMMON CARD (1-5) 1.50 4.00
STATED PRINT RUN 500 SER. #'d SETS

2012 Classic Mythology I

COMPLETE SET (30) 6.00 15.00
COMMON CARD (1-30) .30 .75

2012 Classic Mythology I Frosted Clear

COMPLETE SET (5) 6.00 15.00
COMMON CARD (1-5) 2.00 5.00
STATED ODDS ONE SET PER BASE SET

2012 Classic Mythology I Inserts

AC1 Artist Checklist – Perseus .40 1.00
SH1 Sticker header card – Sekhmet .40 1.00

2012 Classic Mythology I Promos

COMMON CARD (P1-P5) 5.00 12.00
P1 Horus (Philly) 6.00 15.00

2014 Classic Mythology II Previews

COMPLETE SET (5) 3.00 8.00
COMMON CARD (CM1-CM5) 1.25 3.00

2014 Classic Mythology II

COMPLETE SET (30) 10.00 25.00
COMMON CARD (1-30) .40 1.00
SH1 Hercules Sticker Header 1.25 3.00
L1 Medusa (lenticular)

2014 Classic Mythology II Frosted Clear

COMPLETE SET (6) 8.00 20.00
COMMON CARD (1-6) 2.50 6.00

2014 Classic Mythology II Metal Chase

HMC1 Hermes Metal Chase EXCH 12.00 30.00

2014 Classic Mythology II Promos

COMPLETE SET (5) 2.50 6.00
COMMON CARD (P1 - P5) .75 2.00

2018 Classic Mythology III Goddesses

COMPLETE SET (30) 6.00 15.00
COMMON CARD (1-30) .30 .75

2018 Classic Mythology III Goddesses Frosted Clear Chase

COMPLETE SET (5) 6.00 15.00
COMMON CARD (UNNUMBERED) 2.00 5.00

2018 Classic Mythology III Goddesses Lenticular Chase

L1 Amaterasu 15.00 40.00

1992 Sperry Mini Mags Classic Pulps

COMPLETE SET (100) 6.00 15.00
UNOPENED BOX (36 PACKS) 40.00 50.00
UNOPENED PACK (7 CARDS) 1.25 1.50
COMMON CARD (1-100) .10 .30
93B Forgotten World (upside down image) .40 1.00

1993 That's Entertainment Classic Toys

COMPLETE SET (66) 5.00 12.00
UNOPENED BOX (36 PACKS) 15.00 25.00
UNOPENED PACK (7 CARDS) .75 1.00
COMMON CARD (1-66) .15 .40

2017 SkyBox Clerks

COMPLETE SET (90) 8.00 20.00
UNOPENED BOX (20 PACKS) 80.00 100.00
UNOPENED PACK (5 CARDS) 4.00 5.00
COMMON CARD (1-90) .15 .40
*RAINBOW FOIL: .6X TO 1.5 BASIC CARDS .25 .60
*QUICK STOP FOIL: .75X TO 2X BASIC CARDS .40 1.00
*37 FOIL/37: 12X TO 30X BASIC CARDS 5.00 12.00

2017 SkyBox Clerks Autographs

COMMON AUTO 10.00 25.00
OVERALL AUTO ODDS 1:10
AMKS Kevin Smith 60.00 120.00
AMLS Lisa Spoonauer 10.00 25.00
AMMG Marilyn Ghigliotti 8.00 20.00
AMSM Scott Mosier 15.00 40.00
AMWF Walt Flanagan 15.00 40.00

2017 SkyBox Clerks Big Choice Autographs

COMMON AUTO 6.00 15.00
OVERALL AUTO ODDS 1:10
ABCAN Jeff Anderson 25.00 60.00
ABCBB Betsy Broussard 5.00 12.00
ABCBO Brian O'Halloran 50.00 100.00
ABCDK David Klein 8.00 20.00
ABCEO Ernest O'Donnell 10.00 25.00
ABCFL Walt Flanagan 15.00 40.00
ABCJA Jeff Anderson 25.00 60.00
ABCJM Jason Mewes 25.00 60.00
ABCKL Kimberly Loughran 8.00 20.00
ABCKS Kevin Smith 60.00 120.00
ABCLS Lisa Spoonauer 10.00 25.00
ABCME Jason Mewes 25.00 60.00
ABCMG Marilyn Ghigliotti 8.00 20.00
ABCMO Scott Mosier 15.00 40.00
ABCOH Brian O'Halloran 50.00 100.00
ABCSM Kevin Smith 60.00 120.00
ABCSP Lisa Spoonauer 10.00 25.00
ABCSS Scott Schiaffo 5.00 12.00
ABCWA Walt Flanagan 15.00 40.00
ABCWF Walt Flanagan 15.00 40.00

2017 SkyBox Clerks Big Words

COMPLETE SET (14) 8.00 20.00
COMMON CARD (BW1-BW14) 1.00 2.50
STATED ODDS 1:3

2017 SkyBox Clerks Dual Autographs

COMMON CARD 20.00 50.00
OVERALL AUTO ODDS 1:10
A2AG Anderson/Ghigliotti 20.00 50.00
A2AS Anderson/Spoonauer 30.00 75.00
A2GS Ghigliotti/Spoonauer 20.00 50.00
A2HA O'Halloran/Anderson 50.00 100.00
A2MS Mewes/Smith 120.00 250.00
A2MS Mewes/Smith 120.00 250.00
A2OA O'Halloran/Anderson 75.00 150.00
A2OG O'Halloran/Ghigliotti 30.00 75.00
A2OM O'Halloran/Mosier 30.00 75.00
A2OS O'Halloran/Spoonauer 60.00 120.00
A2SM Smith/Mosier 75.00 150.00

2017 SkyBox Clerks I Assure You It's Fake Patches

COMPLETE SET (13) 50.00 100.00
COMMON CARD (FAKE1-FAKE13) 4.00 10.00
STATED ODDS 1:20

2017 SkyBox Clerks Insight

COMPLETE SET (9) 12.00 30.00
COMMON CARD (IN1-IN9) 2.00 5.00
STATED ODDS 1:10

2017 SkyBox Clerks Quad Autographs

COMMON CARD 150.00 300.00
OVERALL AUTO ODDS 1:10
A4OAMS O'Halloran/Anderson Mewes/Smith 150.00 300.00

2017 SkyBox Clerks RST Video Autographs

COMMON AUTO 5.00 12.00
OVERALL AUTO ODDS 1:10
AAN Jeff Anderson 25.00 60.00
ABH Brian O'Halloran 50.00 100.00
ABO Brian O'Halloran 50.00 100.00
ADK David Klein 8.00 20.00

AEO Ernest O'Donnell 10.00 25.00
AFL Walt Flanagan 15.00 40.00
AGH Marilyn Ghigliotti 8.00 20.00
AJA Jeff Anderson 25.00 60.00
AJM Jason Mewes 25.00 60.00
AKE Kevin Smith 60.00 120.00
AKL Kimberly Loughran 8.00 20.00
AKS Kevin Smith 60.00 120.00
ALS Lisa Spoonauer 10.00 25.00
AME Jason Mewes 25.00 60.00
AMG Marilyn Ghigliotti 8.00 20.00
AMO Scott Mosier 15.00 40.00
ASC Scott Mosier 15.00 40.00
ASM Kevin Smith 60.00 120.00
ASP Lisa Spoonauer 10.00 25.00
AVS Virginia Smith 6.00 15.00
AWA Walt Flanagan 15.00 40.00
AWF Walt Flanagan 15.00 40.00

2017 SkyBox Clerks The List

COMPLETE SET (22) 10.00 25.00
COMMON CARD (TL1-TL22) .75 2.00
STATED ODDS 1:2

2017 SkyBox Clerks The List Steve Stark Autographs

COMMON AUTO (TL1-TL22) 12.00 30.00
STATED PRINT RUN 10 SER.#'d SETS

2017 SkyBox Clerks Triple Autographs

COMMON AUTO 30.00 75.00
OVERALL AUTO ODDS 1:10
A3HOA Loughran/O'Halloran/O'Donnell 50.00 100.00
A3MOA Schiaffo/O'Halloran/Flanagan 50.00 100.00
A3MSM Mewes/Mosier/Smith 75.00 150.00
A3OVA O'Halloran/Smith/Anderson 50.00 100.00
A3SKO Schiaffo/Klein/O'Halloran 100.00 200.00
A3SOA Anderson/Spoonauer/O'Halloran 60.00 120.00
A3SOS O'Halloran/Spoonauer/Smith 75.00 150.00
A3WAO Flanagan/Anderson/O'Halloran 75.00 150.00

2017 SkyBox Clerks Walt Art

COMPLETE SET (4) 12.00 30.00
COMMON CARD (WF1-WF4) 4.00 10.00
STATED ODDS 1:20

1993 Eclipse Clive Barker's Box of Blood

COMPLETE SET (32) 4.00 10.00
COMMON CARD (1-32) .25 .60

1992 Planet Mirth Productions Clown Collector Series Promos

COMMON CARD (SKIP #'d) 2.00 5.00

1995 FPG Clyde Caldwell

COMPLETE SET (90) 6.00 15.00
UNOPENED BOX (36 PACKS) 15.00 20.00
UNOPENED PACK (10 CARDS) .50 .75
COMMON CARD (1-90) .12 .30
NNO1 Clyde Caldwell AU/1000* 15.00 40.00
NNO2 Oversized PROMO 1.25 3.00

1995 FPG Clyde Caldwell Metallic

COMPLETE SET (5) 12.00 30.00
COMMON CARD (M1-M5) 3.00 8.00
RANDOMLY INSERTED INTO PACKS

2001 Coaster Cards

COMPLETE BOXED SET (82) 6.00 15.00
COMMON CARD (1-81) .10 .25
M1 Magnum XL-200 Motion Card 2.00 5.00

2001 Coaster Cards Promos

COMMON CARD 1.25 3.00
P1 The Mantis 2.00 5.00
P2 Twister, No UV Coating/200* 2.00 5.00
P3 Corkscrew, No UV Coating/200* 2.00 5.00
PM1 Magnum XL-200 Motion Card 4.00 10.00

1993 Coca-Cola

COMPLETE SET (100) 3.00 8.00
UNOPENED BOX (36 PACKS)
UNOPENED PACK (8 CARDS+1 CAP)
COMMON CARD (1-100) .05 .15
TC1 Ty Cobb RED FOIL 30.00 80.00

2001 Coca-Cola Christmas

COMPLETE SET (72) 4.00 10.00
UNOPENED BOX (36 PACKS) 40.00 50.00
UNOPENED PACK (7 CARDS) 1.25 1.50
COMMON CARD (1-72) .12 .30

2001 Coca-Cola Christmas Canvas

COMPLETE SET (6) 10.00 25.00
COMMON CARD (C1-C6) 2.00 5.00
RANDOMLY INSERTED INTO PACKS

1996 Collect-a-Card Coca-Cola Sign of Good Taste

COMPLETE SET (72) 5.00 12.00
UNOPENED BOX (36 PACKS) 40.00 50.00
UNOPENED PACK (8 CARDS) 1.25 1.50
COMMON CARD (1-72) .12 .30
NNO Sign of The Times 50.00 100.00
TL1 Dateline: 1907 Sold Everywhere 5c Drink Coca-Cola 15.00 40.00

1996 Collect-a-Card Coca-Cola Sign of Good Taste Polar Bears

COMPLETE SET (8) 20.00 50.00
COMMON CARD (PB1-PB8) 3.00 8.00
STATED ODDS 1:13

1996 Collect-a-Card Coca-Cola Sign of Good Taste Santa Jumbos

COMPLETE SET (6) 25.00 60.00
COMMON CARD (OS1-OS6) 5.00 12.00
STATED ODDS 1:BOX

1995 Collect-a-Card Coca-Cola Super Premium

COMPLETE SET (62) 4.00 10.00
UNOPENED BOX (24 PACKS) 40.00 50.00
UNOPENED PACK (10 CARDS) 2.00 2.25
COMMON CARD (1-60) .10 .25
NNO Girl in Blue Dress PROMO 1.25 3.00
NNO Uncut Sheet

1995 Collect-a-Card Coca-Cola Super Premium Embossed Santa

COMPLETE SET (6) 15.00 40.00
COMMON CARD (1-6) 3.00 8.00
STATED ODDS 1:11

1995 Collect-a-Card Coca-Cola Super Premium Mirage Holograms

COMPLETE SET (3) 20.00 50.00
COMMON CARD (1-3) 8.00 20.00
STATED ODDS 1:11

1995 Collect-a-Card Coca-Cola Super Premium Polar Bear

COMPLETE SET (8) 50.00 100.00
COMMON CARD (SPB1-SPB8) 6.00 15.00
STATED ODDS 1:7

1992-93 Mother Productions Cold Blooded Killers

COMPLETE BOXED SET (40) 4.00 10.00
COMMON CARD (1-40) .15 .40

1998 Gollner Cold War Cards

COMPLETE SET (20) 4.00 10.00
COMMON CARD .30 .75

1995 FPG Colossal Series 1

COMPLETE SET (50) 25.00 60.00
UNOPENED BOX (18 PACKS) 70.00 80.00
UNOPENED PACK (5 CARDS) 4.00 4.50
COMMON CARD (1-50) .75 2.00
PROMO Ken Kelly (#22 Card Front) 1.25 3.00

1995 FPG Colossal Series 2

COMPLETE SET (50) 20.00 50.00
UNOPENED BOX (18 PACKS) 40.00 50.00
UNOPENED PACK (5 CARDS) 2.50 3.00
COMMON CARD (1-50) .60 1.50
P27 Deluxe Promo 1.25 3.00

1995 FPG Colossal Series 2 Autographs

COMPLETE SET (10) 200.00 400.00
COMMON CARD 20.00 50.00
RANDOMLY INSERTED INTO PACKS

1991 Focus Columbus Quincentenary Jubilee

COMPLETE SET (100) 6.00 15.00
COMMON CARD (1-100) .12 .30

1994 21st Century Archives Comic Art Tribute to Joe Simon and Jack Kirby

COMPLETE SET (50) 3.00 8.00
UNOPENED BOX (36 PACKS) 15.00 20.00
UNOPENED PACK (8 CARDS) .40 .60
COMMON CARD (1-50) .10 .30
P1 Promo (unnumbered)

1994 21st Century Archives Comic Art Tribute to Joe Simon and Jack Kirby Jack Kirby's Great Machines

COMPLETE SET (5) 5.00 12.00
COMMON CARD (KM1-KM5) 1.25 3.00
AVAILABLE VIA MAIL-IN OFFER

1994 21st Century Archives Comic Art Tribute to Joe Simon and Jack Kirby Limited Edition DiamondChro

COMPLETE SET (5) 50.00 100.00
COMMON CARD (K1-K5) 10.00 25.00
STATED ODDS 1:12

1998 Comic Images Comic Greats '98

COMPLETE SET (72) 6.00 15.00
UNOPENED BOX (48 PACKS) 12.00 30.00
UNOPENED PACK (8 CARDS) .50 .75
COMMON CARD (1-72) .15 .40
NNO Comic Greats '98 PROMO 1.00 2.50
NNO Joe Quesada/Jimmy Palmiotti 20.00 50.00
NNO Uncut Sheet 25.00 60.00

1998 Comic Images Comic Greats '98 OmniChrome

COMPLETE SET (6) 10.00 25.00
COMMON CARD (1-6) 2.50 6.00
RANDOMLY INSERTED INTO PACKS

1993 Majestic Entertainment Comics FutureStars

COMPLETE SET (100) 5.00 12.00
UNOPENED BOX (36 PACKS) 25.00 40.00
UNOPENED PACK (9 CARDS) 1.00 1.25
COMMON CARD (1-100) .08 .20
MVP Snake
MVPAU Snake 6.00 15.00
Dan Lawlis AU
UNC 100-Card Base Set Uncut Sheet

1993 Majestic Entertainment Comics FutureStars Artist Photos Promos

COMMON SERIES 1 (1-3) .75 2.00
COMMON SERIES 2 (4-6) .75 2.00

1993 Majestic Entertainment Comics FutureStars Hot Pick

COMPLETE SET (8) 15.00 40.00
COMMON CARD (1-8) 2.50 6.00
STATED ODDS 1:18

1993 Majestic Entertainment Comics FutureStars Legacy #0 Ashcan

COMPLETE SET (9) 4.00 10.00
COMMON CARD (1-9) .60 1.50
STATED ODDS 1:18

1993 Majestic Entertainment Comics FutureStars Star Players

COMPLETE SET (5) 5.00 12.00
COMMON CARD (1-5) 1.25 3.00
STATED ODDS 1:7

1994 Topps Comics' Greatest World

COMPLETE SET (100) 6.00 15.00
UNOPENED BOX (36 PACKS) 40.00 50.00
UNOPENED PACK (8 CARDS) 1.25 1.50
COMMON CARD (1-100) .12 .30

1994 Topps Comics' Greatest World Topps Matrix

COMPLETE SET (6) 12.00 30.00
COMMON CARD (M1-M6) 2.50 6.00
*JUMBO: .6X TO 1.5X BASIC CARDS 4.00 10.00
STATED ODDS 1:18

1994 Topps Comics' Greatest World Promos

101 Vortex 1.25 3.00
102 X 1.25 3.00
103 Catalyst 1.25 3.00
104 Barb Wire 1.25 3.00
105 Motorhead 1.25 3.00
106 Titan 1.25 3.00
107 Will to Power 1.25 3.00
108 Division 13 1.25 3.00
109 Mecha 1.25 3.00
NNO X by Frank Miller .60 1.50
NNO Rebel by Jerry Ordway .60 1.50
NNO Barb Wire .60 1.50
NNO Machine .60 1.50
NNO Division 13 .60 1.50
NNO Catalyst
NNO The Machine
NNO Vortex B&W
NNO Vortex Color
NNO X B&W by Chris Warner
NNO Oversized Blue Background
NNO Oversized Red Background
NNO Oversized Silver Background
NNO Oversized Yellow Background
NNO Barb Wire/The Machine/Wolf Gang/Motorhead
NNO Division 13/Hero Zero/King Tiger/Vortex
NNO Comics Greatest Cards

2013 Complete Bionic Collection

CCMPLETE SET (163) 75.00 125.00
COMMON CARD (1-163) .60 1.50

2013 Complete Bionic Collection Anatomical Damage Box-Toppers

COMPLETE SET (3) 10.00 25.00
COMMON CARD (CT1-CT3) 5.00 12.00
STATED ODDS 1:BOX

2013 Complete Bionic Collection Bionic Woman Autographs

COMMON AUTO 6.00 15.00
STATED ODDS OVERALL 2:PACK
BROOKS AUTO ISSUED IN ARCHIVE BOX
NNO Gary Lockwood VL 8.00 20.00
NNO Janice Whitby VL 10.00 25.00
NNO John Saxon EL 25.00 60.00
NNO Kristy McNichol L 15.00 40.00
NNO Lee Majors EL 60.00 120.00
NNO L. Wagner (sweatshirt) EL 75.00 150.00
NNO L. Wagner (scarf) EL 75.00 150.00
NNO Martin E. Brooks AB 25.00 60.00
NNO Richard Anderson VL 20.00 50.00
NNO Roger Perry EL 10.00 25.00
NNO Stefanie Powers VL 30.00 75.00
NNO Terry Kiser VL 10.00 25.00

2013 Complete Bionic Collection Silver Ink Autographs

COMMON AUTO 25.00 60.00
MAJORS AUTO ISSUED AS 4-BOX INCENTIVE
WAGNER AUTO ISSUED IN ARCHIVE BOX
ANDERSON AUTO ISSUED AS 2-BOX INCENTIVE
NNO Lee Majors 4BI 100.00 200.00
NNO Lindsay Wagner AB 75.00 150.00

2013 The Complete Bionic Collection Six Million Dollar Man Autographs

COMMON AUTO 6.00 15.00
STATED ODDS OVERALL 2:PACK
SHATNER AUTO ISSUED IN ARCHIVE BOX
NNO Erik Estrada VL 15.00 40.00
NNO Joan Van Ark VL 15.00 40.00
NNO John Saxon EL 30.00 75.00
NNO Louis Gossett Jr. VL 25.00 60.00
NNO Martin E. Brooks EL 20.00 50.00
NNO Martine Beswick L 8.00 20.00
NNO Meg Foster EL 12.00 30.00
NNO Robert Walker Jr.EL 12.00 30.00
NNO Roger Perry EL 10.00 25.00
NNO Sandy Duncan VL 15.00 40.00
NNO Terry Kiser VL 10.00 25.00
NNO William Shatner AB 150.00 300.00
NNO Yvonne Craig VL 50.00 100.00

2013 Complete Bionic Collection Promos

COMMON CARD 1.25 3.00
P2 The Six Million Dollar Man ALB 4.00 10.00

2011 Complete Brady Bunch

COMPLETE SET (59) 20.00 50.00
COMPLETE SET W/AU 100.00 175.00
COMMON CARD (1-59) .75 2.00
STATED PRINT RUN 500 SETS

2011 Complete Brady Bunch Autographs

COMPLETE SET (6)
COMP.SET W/O DAVIS AUTO (5)
COMMON AUTO 10.00 25.00
5 AUTOS PER FACTORY SET
DAVIS AUTO ISSUED AS 2-SET INCENTIVE
NNO Ann B. Davis 2SI 50.00 100.00
NNO Barry Williams 12.00 30.00
NNO Christopher Knight 12.00 30.00
NNO Eve Plumb 25.00 60.00

2011 Complete Brady Bunch Promos

COMPLETE SET (2) 5.00 12.00
COMMON CARD 1.50 4.00
P2 Greg Brady NSU 4.00 10.00

2003 Complete Highlander The Series

COMPLETE SET (129) 4.00 10.00
UNOPENED BOX (40 PACKS) 50.00 75.00
UNOPENED PACK (9 CARDS) 2.00 3.00
COMMON CARD (1-126; C1-C3) .10 .25
CC1 ISSUED AS ALBUM EXCLUSIVE
CC1 Duncan MacLeod MEM ALB 8.00 20.00
DC1 McLeod's Arms/600 12.00 30.00

2003 Complete Highlander The Series Autographs

COMMON AUTO (A1-A20) 5.00 12.00
STATED ODDS THREE PER BOX
L (LIMITED): 300-500 COPIES
A1 Adrian Paul L 30.00 75.00
A2 Jim Byrnes 10.00 25.00
A3 Stan Kirsch L 15.00 40.00
A4 Elizabeth Gracen L 60.00 120.00
A5 Traci Lords L 20.00 50.00
A9 Marcia Strassman 10.00 25.00
A10 Sandra Bernhard 6.00 15.00
A11 Claudia Christian 8.00 20.00
A14 Amanda Wyss 6.00 15.00
A15 Anthony Head 8.00 20.00
A16 Tamlyn Tomita 8.00 20.00
A18 Ron Perlman 12.00 30.00
A19 Don S. Davis 6.00 15.00

2003 Complete Highlander The Series Lover

COMPLETE SET (9) 5.00 12.00
COMMON CARD (L1-L9) .60 1.50
STATED ODDS 1:8

2003 Complete Highlander The Series The Raven

COMPLETE SET (22) 6.00 15.00
COMMON CARD (R1-R22) .40 1.00
STATED ODDS 1:3

2003 Complete Highlander The Series Wanderer

COMPLETE SET (6) 12.00 30.00
COMMON CARD (W1-W6) 3.00 8.00
STATED ODDS 1:40

2003 Complete Highlander The Series Warrior

COMPLETE SET (9) 10.00 25.00
COMMON CARD (Q1-Q9) 1.50 4.00
STATED ODDS 1:20

2003 Complete Highlander The Series Promos

COMMON CARD (P1-P3) .75 2.00
P3 Album Exclusive 3.00 8.00
PCE2003 Encyclopedia Exclusive 2.00 5.00

2005 Complete Lost in Space

COMPLETE SET (90) 4.00 10.00
UNOPENED BOX (40 PACKS) 50.00 60.00
UNOPENED PACK (5 CARDS) 1.50 1.75
COMMON CARD (1-90) .10 .30
FS ISSUED AS ALBUM EXCLUSIVE
FS Fugitives in Space ALB MEM 15.00 40.00

2005 Complete Lost in Space 1966 Expansion

COMPLETE SET (55) 12.00 30.00
COMMON CARD (R56-R110) .30 .75
STATED ODDS 1:8

2005 Complete Lost in Space 1966 Reprints

COMPLETE SET (55) 12.00 30.00
COMMON CARD (R1-R55) .30 .75
STATED ODDS 1:8

2005 Complete Lost in Space Autographs

COMMON AUTO 10.00 25.00
STATED ODDS TWO PER BOX
HARRIS AU ISSUED AS 6-CASE INCENTIVE
AC Angela Cartwright 150.00 300.00
AJ Arte Johnson 30.00 75.00
BM Bill Mumy 100.00 200.00
DH Dee Hartford 30.00 75.00
DT Daniel J. Travanti 12.00 30.00
FY Francine York 15.00 40.00
JH Jonathan Harris CUT/50 6CI 400.00 650.00
JL June Lockhart 125.00 250.00
LS Leonard Stone 25.00 60.00
MG Mark Goddard 75.00 150.00
MK Marta Kristen 125.00 250.00
MT Malachi Throne 15.00 40.00
SJ Sherry Jackson 25.00 60.00
VM Vitina Marcus 30.00 75.00
DM1 Don Matheson (Idak) 60.00 120.00
DM2 Don Matheson (Rethso) 60.00 120.00
LKC June Lockhart/Marta Kristen
Angela Cartwright 250.00 400.00
SA1 Sheila Allen (Aunt Gamma) 30.00 75.00
SA2 Sheila Allen (Brynhilde) 30.00 75.00
SA3 Sheila Allen (Ruth Templeton) 30.00 75.00
BMAC Bill Mumy/Angela Cartwright 125.00 250.00
BMDT Bob May/Dick Tufeld 150.00 300.00
MGMK Mark Goddard/Marta Kristen 125.00 250.00

2005 Complete Lost in Space Characters

COMPLETE SET (7) 10.00 25.00
COMMON CARD (R1-R7) 1.50 4.00
STATED ODDS 1:20

2005 Complete Lost in Space Faces of Dr. Smith

COMPLETE SET (9) 10.00 25.00
COMMON CARD (F1-F9) 1.25 3.00
STATED ODDS 1:16

2005 Complete Lost in Space The Good, The Bad, and the Ugly

COMPLETE SET (9) 6.00 15.00
COMMON CARD (S1-S9) .75 2.00
STATED ODDS 1:8

2005 Complete Lost in Space Promos

COMMON CARD .75 2.00
P3 Album Exclusive 2.00 5.00
UK United Kingdom 1.50 4.00
SD2005 San Diego 2005 1.25 3.00

2004 Complete Six Million Dollar Man Seasons One and Two

COMPLETE SET (72) 3.00 8.00
UNOPENED BOX (40 PACKS) 65.00 75.00
UNOPENED PACK (7 CARDS) 1.75 2.00
COMMON CARD (1-72) .10 .25

2004 Complete Six Million Dollar Man Seasons One and Two Autographs

COMMON AUTO (A1-A13) 6.00 15.00
STATED ODDS TWO PER BOX
A11 ISSUED AS ALBUM EXCLUSIVE
A12 ISSUED AS CASE TOPPER
A13 ISSUED AS MULTI-CASE INCENTIVE
A1 Lee Majors VL 30.00 75.00
A2 Richard Anderson L 15.00 40.00
A3 Alan Oppenheimer VL 12.00 30.00
A5 John Saxon 12.00 30.00
A7 Arlene Martel 12.00 30.00
A8 Meg Foster 8.00 20.00
A11 Jennifer Darling ALB 10.00 25.00
A12 Gary Lockwood CT 8.00 20.00
A13 William Shatner MCI 150.00 300.00

2004 Complete Six Million Dollar Man Seasons One and Two Bionics

COMPLETE SET (3) 5.00 12.00
COMMON CARD (B1-B3) 2.00 5.00
STATED ODDS 1:40

2004 Complete Six Million Dollar Man Seasons One and Two Made for Each Other

COMPLETE SET (9) 6.00 15.00
COMMON CARD (SJ1-SJ9) .75 2.00
STATED ODDS 1:10

2004 Complete Six Million Dollar Man Seasons One and Two OSI Files

COMPLETE SET (9) 10.00 25.00
COMMON CARD (01-09) 1.25 3.00
STATED ODDS 1:20

2004 Complete Six Million Dollar Man Seasons One and Two The Movies

COMPLETE SET (9) 5.00 12.00
COMMON CARD (M1-M9) .75 2.00
STATED ODDS 1:6

2004 Complete Six Million Dollar Man Seasons One and Two Promos

COMPLETE SET (2)
COMMON CARD (P1-P2) .75 2.00
P2 Oscar Goldman ALB 3.00 8.00

1993 William Tell Publishing Composers

COMPLETE SET (72) 6.00 15.00
COMMON CARD (1-72) .15 .40

1993 Comic Images Conan

COMPLETE SET (90) 12.00 30.00
UNOPENED BOX (36 PACKS) 100.00 120.00
UNOPENED PACK (7 CARDS) 3.00 4.00
COMMON CARD (1-90) .25 .60
*HOLO: 4X TO 10X BASIC CARDS 2.50 6.00
COLOR VARIATIONS LISTED BELOW

1993 Comic Images Conan Prisms

COMPLETE SET (6) 10.00 25.00
COMMON CARD (1-6) 3.00 8.00

2004 Conan Art of the Hyborian Age

COMPLETE SET (72) 4.00 10.00
COMMON CARD (1-72) .10 .30
STAN LEE AU ISSUED AS CASE TOPPER
A1 Stan Lee AU CT 200.00 400.00

2004 Conan Art of the Hyborian Age Ode to the Cimmerian

COMPLETE SET (12) 3.00 8.00
COMMON CARD (C1-C12) .40 1.00
STATED ODDS 1:4

2004 Conan Art of the Hyborian Age Rise of the King

COMPLETE SET (6) 12.50 30.00
COMMON CARD (R1-R6) 2.50 6.00
STATED ODDS 1:40

2004 Conan Art of the Hyborian Age Savage Sisterhood

COMPLETE SET (9) 6.00 15.00
COMMON CARD (S1-S9) .75 2.00
STATED ODDS 1:8

2004 Conan Art of the Hyborian Age Promos

P1 Conan in snow 1.00 2.50
P2 Conan w/dead pterodactyl 1.50 4.00
SD2004 Conan under full moon 1.00 2.50

1994 Comic Images Conan Series Two

COMPLETE SET (90) 4.00 10.00
UNOPENED BOX (36 PACKS) 40.00 50.00
UNOPENED PACK (7 CARDS) 1.50 1.75
COMMON CARD (1-90) .08 .25
*HOLOCHROME: 8X TO 20X BASIC CARDS
NNO Gold Medallion 10.00 25.00

1994 Comic Images Conan Series Two Case-Toppers

COMPLETE SET (4) 25.00 60.00
COMMON CARD 8.00 20.00
STATED ODDS 1:CASE

1994 Comic Images Conan Series Two Elements

COMPLETE SET (3) 10.00 25.00
COMMON CARD (1-3) 4.00 10.00
STATED ODDS 1:36

1994 Comic Images Conan Series Two Prisms

COMPLETE SET (6) 15.00 40.00
COMMON CARD (P1-P6) 3.00 8.00
STATED ODDS 1:16
PAN Prisms P1-P6 Panel

1994 Comic Images Conan Series Two Promos

1 Earl Norem Art 1.25 3.00
2 2-Card Panel, D19 and D20 1.25 3.00
3 2-Card Panel, D19 and D20 Foil

1995 Comic Images Conan Series Three

COMPLETE SET (90) 10.00 25.00
UNOPENED BOX (48 PACKS) 35.00 50.00
UNOPENED PACK (7 CARDS) 1.00 1.50
COMMON CARD (1-90) .20 .50
CB Oversized Case Bonus Card
M1 Fighting Force Medallion Card 10.00 25.00
6PAN Shipboard Axe Fighting
(6-Panel Card Album Exclusive)
PROMO Joe Jusko Art PROMO 1.25 3.00

1995 Comic Images Conan Series Three Blas Gallego Art

COMPLETE SET (3) 8.00 20.00

COMMON CARD (1-3) 3.00 8.00
STATED ODDS 1:36

1995 Comic Images Conan Series Three MagnaChrome

COMPLETE SET (6) 20.00 50.00
COMMON CARD (M1-M6) 4.00 10.00
STATED ODDS 1:16

2009 Conan Movies Autographs Extension

ANNOUNCED PRINT RUN 333 SETS
SCHWARZNEGGER ISSUED AS 10-CASE INCENTIVE
AS Arnold Schwarzenegger 10SI 400.00 600.00
BD Ben Davidson AU
CG Cassandra Gava AU 10.00 25.00
JJ James Earl Jones AU 60.00 120.00
MA Mako AU 25.00 60.00
SD Sarah Douglas AU 10.00 25.00
CC1 Conan
CC2 Conan
CC3 Conan

1993 Topps Coneheads

COMPLETE SET (66) 5.00 12.00
UNOPENED BOX (48 PACKS) 20.00 30.00
UNOPENED PACK (5 CARDS) .50 .75
COMMON CARD (1-66) .15 .40

1993 Kitchen Sink Press Confidential

COMPLETE SET (36) 5.00 12.00
COMMON CARD (1-36) .25 .60

1995 Upper Deck Congo

COMPLETE SET (90) 8.00 20.00
UNOPENED BOX (36 PACKS) 30.00 40.00
UNOPENED PACK (8 CARDS) 1.00 1.25
COMMON CARD (1-90) .15 .40
PR1 Half Gorilla Face (dealer) 1.00 2.50
PR2 Half Gorilla Face (dealers/collector) 1.00 2.50

1995 Upper Deck Congo Action FX Foil

COMPLETE SET (6) 3.00 8.00
COMMON CARD (CF1-CF6) .75 2.00
STATED ODDS 1:12

1993 Eclipse Congressional Medal of Honor

COMPLETE BOXED SET (36) 4.00 10.00
COMMON CARD (1-36) .25 .60

2008 Conspiracy Files of Dean Haglund

COMPLETE SET (45) 5.00 12.00
UNOPENED BOX (12 PACKS) 40.00 50.00
UNOPENED PACK (8 CARDS) 3.00 4.00
COMMON CARD (1-45) .20 .50
NNO 45-Card Panel Sketch/200*
NNO 45-Card Panel Art Redemption/5*
NNO 45-Card Panel Uncut Sheet

2008 Conspiracy Files of Dean Haglund Alien DNA

COMPLETE SET (9) 6.00 15.00
COMMON CARD (DNA1-DNA9) 1.25 3.00
STATED ODDS 1:4

2008 Conspiracy Files of Dean Haglund Alien Tech Puzzle

COMPLETE SET (9) 6.00 15.00
COMMON CARD (AT1-AT9) 1.25 3.00
STATED ODDS 1:4

2008 Conspiracy Files of Dean Haglund Evidence

COMPLETE SET (2) 2.50 6.00
COMMON CARD (EC1-EC2) 1.50 4.00
STATED ODDS 1:12

2008 Conspiracy Files of Dean Haglund Fingerprints

COMPLETE SET (6) 6.00 15.00
COMMON CARD (FP1-FP6) 1.25 3.00
STATED ODDS 1:12

2008 Conspiracy Files of Dean Haglund Hair

COMPLETE SET (2) 8.00 20.00
COMMON CARD (HC1-HC2) 5.00 12.00
STATED ODDS 1:72

2008 Conspiracy Files of Dean Haglund Mystery Fingerprint

COMPLETE SET (2) 2.50 6.00
COMMON CARD (MFP1-MFP2) 1.50 4.00
STATED ODDS 1:12

2008 Conspiracy Files of Dean Haglund Top Secret Puzzle

COMPLETE SET (9) 8.00 20.00
COMMON CARD (TS1-TS9) 1.50 4.00
STATED ODDS 1:6

2008 Conspiracy Files of Dean Haglund Promos

COMPLETE SET (4) 3.00 8.00
COMMON CARD (P1-P4) 1.00 2.50

2012 Contemporary Pin-Ups Holiday Edition

COMPLETE SET (41) 6.00 15.00
COMMON CARD .25 .60

2014 Contemporary Pin-Ups Pin-Ups and Pitbulls

COMPLETE SET (38) 2.00 5.00
COMMON CARD .10 .25

2014 Contemporary Pin-Ups Pin-Ups and Pitbulls Meet the Artist Promos

COMPLETE SET (2)
COMMON CARD
1 Danny Silva [black lace] 4.00 10.00
(C2E2 Exclusive)
2 John Haun [feet] 4.00 10.00
(C2E2 Exclusive)

1993 Continuity Comics Promos

COMPLETE SET W/SP (29) 20.00 50.00
COMPLETE SET W/O SP (27) 6.00 15.00
COMMON CARD (1-29) .40 1.00
12 Valeria the She-Bat SP 8.00 20.00
13 Shaman SP 12.00 30.00

2014 Continuum Seasons One and Two

COMPLETE SET (69) 8.00 20.00
UNOPENED BOX (24 PACKS) 75.00 125.00
UNOPENED PACK (5 CARDS) 3.00 5.00
COMMON CARD (1-69) .20 .50
*GOLD: 5X TO 12X BASIC CARDS 2.50 6.00

2014 Continuum Seasons One and Two Autographs

COMMON AUTO 5.00 12.00
STATED ODDS 1:12
NNO Erik Knudsen EL 10.00 25.00
NNO Ian Tracey VL 6.00 15.00
NNO Lexa Doig EL 30.00 75.00
NNO Luvia Petersen EL 10.00 25.00
NNO Magda Apanowicz VL 12.00 30.00
NNO Rachel Nichols EL 75.00 150.00
NNO Richard Harmon EL 6.00 15.00
NNO Stephen Lobo EL 6.00 15.00
NNO Tony Amendola VL 6.00 15.00
NNO Victor Webster EL 15.00 40.00
NNO William B. Davis VL 6.00 15.00

2014 Continuum Seasons One and Two Case-Incentives

CAMERON ISSUED AS 2-CASE INCENTIVE
NICHOLS/KNUDSEN ISSUED AS 4-CASE INCENTIVE
1 R.Nichols 120.00 250.00
E.Knudsen AU
MC1 Kiera Cameron relic 2CI 40.00 80.00

2014 Continuum Seasons One and Two Characters

COMPLETE SET (18) 10.00 25.00
COMMON CARD (H1-H18) 1.25 3.00
STATED ODDS 1:12

2014 Continuum Seasons One and Two Future Self Case-Toppers

COMPLETE SET (2) 15.00 40.00
COMMON CARD (CT1-CT2) 10.00 25.00
STATED ODDS 1 PER CASE

2014 Continuum Seasons One and Two Future Tech

COMPLETE SET (6) 8.00 20.00
COMMON CARD (T1-T6) 2.00 5.00
STATED ODDS 1:24

2014 Continuum Seasons One and Two Relics

COMPLETE SET (16) 120.00 250.00
COMMON MEM (CC1-CC16) 4.00 10.00
STATED ODDS 1:24
CC1 Kiera Cameron 40.00 80.00
CC4 Jasmine Garza 10.00 25.00
CC8 Kiera Cameron 15.00 30.00
CC14 Curtis Chen 20.00 40.00

2014 Continuum Seasons One and Two Stars

COMPLETE SET (7) 8.00 20.00
COMMON CARD (C1-C7) 2.50 6.00
STATED ODDS 1:24

2014 Continuum Seasons One and Two Promos

P1 Promo 1 GEN 2.00 5.00
P2 Promo 2 Philly 3.00 8.00
P3 Promo 3 ALB 2.00 5.00
SD1 Promo 4 SDCC 3.00 8.00

2015 Continuum Season Three

COMPLETE SET (60) 6.00 15.00
UNOPENED BOX (24 PACKS) 75.00 125.00
UNOPENED PACK (5 CARDS 3.00 5.00
COMMON CARD .20 .50
*GOLD/100: 5X TO 12X BASIC CARDS

2015 Continuum Season Three Behind-the-Scenes

COMPLETE SET (9) 15.00 40.00
COMMON CARD (BS1-BS9) 3.00 8.00
STATED ODDS 1:24

2015 Continuum Season Three Bordered Autographs

COMMON AUTO 4.00 10.00
STATED ODDS 1:8
NNO Brian Markinson 5.00 12.00
NNO Erik Knudsen 8.00 20.00
NNO Ian Tracey 6.00 15.00
NNO Jennifer Spence 5.00 12.00
NNO Lexa Doig 25.00 60.00
NNO Luvia Peterson 6.00 15.00
NNO Magda Apanowicz 10.00 25.00
NNO Rachel Nichols 100.00 200.00
NNO Roger Cross 6.00 15.00
NNO Tanaya Beatty 5.00 12.00
NNO Victor Webster 8.00 20.00
NNO William B. Davis 6.00 15.00

2015 Continuum Season Three Case-Incentives

COMMON CARD
NNO Keira Black Nano Suit/100 50.00 100.00
NNO Rachel Nichols Archive Box AU 300.00 600.00
NNO Rachel Nichols Silver AU 100.00 200.00

2015 Continuum Season Three Cast

COMPLETE SET (8) 12.00 30.00
COMMON CARD (C1-C9) 2.50 6.00
STATED ODDS 1:24
C8 ISSUED AS CASE-TOPPER
C8 Erik Knudsen CT 6.00 15.00

2015 Continuum Season Three Full Bleed Autographs

COMMON AUTO 4.00 10.00
STATED ODDS 1:8
NNO Erik Knudsen 8.00 20.00
NNO Hugh Dillon 8.00 20.00
NNO Lexa Doig 30.00 75.00
NNO Nicholas Lea 6.00 15.00
NNO Richard Harmon 10.00 25.00
NNO Roger Cross 5.00 12.00
NNO Stephen Lobo 6.00 15.00
NNO Tanaya Beatty 6.00 15.00
NNO Victor Webster 10.00 25.00

2015 Continuum Season Three Quotables

COMPLETE SET (18) 12.00 30.00
COMMON CARD (Q1-Q018) 1.50 4.00
STATED ODDS 1:12

2015 Continuum Season Three Promos

COMPLETE SET (3) 4.00 10.00
COMMON CARD (P1-P3) 1.50 4.00
P2 Album Exclusive 2.50 6.00

1995 Subway Cool Coral Reefs Promos

COMPLETE SET (11) 6.00 15.00
COMMON CARD .75 2.00

1995 Coors

COMPLETE SET (100) 6.00 15.00
UNOPENED BOX (36 PACKS) 15.00 25.00
UNOPENED PACK (8 CARDS) .50 .75
COMMON CARD (1-100) .12 .30
CI Inaugural Season Coors Field 8.00 20.00
(case insert exclusive)

1995 Coors Bright Lights

COMPLETE SET (12) 25.00 60.00
COMMON CARD (1-12) 2.50 6.00
STATED ODDS 1:8

1995 Coors Golden Moments

COMPLETE SET (10) 25.00 60.00
COMMON CARD (1-10) 4.00 10.00
STATED ODDS 1:24

1995 Coors Promos

COMPLETE SET (2) 1.25 3.00
COMMON CARD (P1-P2) .75 2.00

1995 Coors Rocky Mountain Heritage

COMPLETE SET (6) 50.00 100.00
COMMON CARD (1-6) 8.00 20.00
STATED ODDS 1:108

1996 Collect-a-Card Corvette Heritage Collection 1953-1996

COMPLETE SET (90) 8.00 20.00
UNOPENED BOX (36 PACKS) 30.00 40.00
UNOPENED PACK (8 CARDS) 1.00 1.25
COMMON CARD (1-90) .15 .40
NNO Uncut Sheet
NNO 63 Corvette PROMO 1.25 3.00

1996 Collect-a-Card Corvette Heritage Collection 1953-1996 Dufex Corvette Cutaways

COMPLETE SET (3) 10.00 25.00
COMMON CARD (DK1-DK3) 4.00 10.00
STATED ODDS 1:36

1996 Collect-a-Card Corvette Heritage Collection 1953-1996 Fast Lane

COMPLETE SET (9) 25.00 60.00
COMMON CARD (FL1-FL9) 3.00 8.00
STATED ODDS 1:11

1996 Collect-a-Card Corvette Heritage Collection 1953-1996 Milestones

COMPLETE SET (10) 20.00 50.00
COMMON CARD (MS1-MS10) 2.50 6.00
STATED ODDS 1:9

1992 Collect-a-Card Country Classics

COMPLETE SET (100) 6.00 15.00
COMPLETE BOXED SET (102) 5.00 12.00
UNOPENED BOX (36 PACKS) 20.00 30.00
UNOPENED PACK (10 CARDS) 1.00 1.25
COMMON CARD (1-100) .12 .30
H1 Trophy HOLO .75 2.00
H2 Instruments HOLO .75 2.00

1992 Collect-a-Card Country Classics Autographs

COMPLETE SET (4) 25.00 60.00
COMMON CARD 8.00 20.00
RANDOMLY INSERTED INTO PACKS

1992 Collect-a-Card Country Classics Gold

COMPLETE SET (2) 6.00 15.00
COMMON CARD 4.00 10.00
RANDOMLY INSERTED INTO PACKS

1992 Sterling Country Gold

COMPLETE SET (100) 6.00 15.00
UNOPENED BOX (36 PACKS) 15.00 25.00
UNOPENED PACK (9 CARDS) .75 1.00
COMMON CARD (1-100) .12 .30

1993 Sterling Country Gold Series 2

COMPLETE SET (150) 12.00 30.00
UNOPENED BOX (36 PACKS) 20.00 30.00
UNOPENED PACK (9 CARDS) 1.00 1.25
COMMON CARD (1-150) .15 .40

1993 Sterling Country Gold Series 2 Singing Cowboys of the Silver Screen Gold

COMPLETE SET (9) 10.00 25.00
COMMON CARD (1-9) 1.50 4.00
*BLACK: SAME VALUE
*SILVER: SAME VALUE
STATED ODDS 1:8

1993 Sterling Country Gold Series 2 Promos

COMPLETE SET (12)
COMMON CARD (UNNUMBERED) .75 2.00
NNO Barbara Mandrell (auto prototype)
NNO Tracy Lawrence (auto prototype)
NNO Billy Ray Cyrus (auto prototype)

2015 Panini Country Music

COMPLETE SET (100) 12.00 30.00
UNOPENED HOBBY BOX (4 PACKS)
UNOPENED HOBBY PACK (8 CARDS)
UNOPENED BLASTER BOX (6 PACKS)
UNOPENED BLASTER PACK (8 CARDS)
UNOPENED RETAIL BOX (24 PACKS)
UNOPENED RETAIL PACK (8 CARDS)
COMMON CARD (1-100) .30 .75
*RETAIL: SAME VALUE
*GREEN: .6X TO 1.5X BASIC CARDS
*BLUE/199: .75X TO 2X BASIC CARDS
*PURPLE/99: 1.2X TO 3X BASIC CARDS
*RED/99: 1.2X TO 3X BASIC CARDS
*SILVER/49: 1.5X TO 4X BASIC CARDS
*GOLD/25: 2X TO 5X BASIC CARDS

2015 Panini Country Music Award Winners

COMPLETE SET (25) 25.00 60.00
COMMON CARD (1-25) 1.25 3.00
*RETAIL: SAME VALUE
*GREEN: .6X TO 1.5X BASIC CARDS
*BLUE/199: .75X TO 2X BASIC CARDS
*PURPLE/99: 1.2X TO 3X BASIC CARDS
*RED/99: 1.2X TO 3X BASIC CARDS
*SILVER/49: 1.5X TO 4X BASIC CARDS
*GOLD/25: 2X TO 5X BASIC CARDS

2015 Panini Country Music Backstage Pass

COMPLETE SET (20) 15.00 40.00
COMMON CARD (1-20) 1.25 3.00
*RETAIL: SAME VALUE
*GREEN: .6X TO 1.5X BASIC CARDS
*BLUE/199: .75X TO 2X BASIC CARDS
*PURPLE/99: 1.2X TO 3X BASIC CARDS
*RED/99: 1.2X TO 3X BASIC CARDS
*SILVER/49: 1.5X TO 4X BASIC CARDS
*GOLD/25: 2X TO 5X BASIC CARDS

2015 Panini Country Music Combo Signatures

*GREEN/25: 2X TO 5X BASIC CARDS
*SILVER/25: 2X TO 5X BASIC CARDS
2 Shawna Thompson 6.00 15.00
Keifer Thompson/49
3 Brian Kelley 6.00 15.00
Tyler Hubbard/49
4 Brantley Gilbert
Colt Ford/49
5 Josh Gracin
Lauren Alaina/49
6 John Rich 10.00 25.00
Big Kenny Alphin/199
7 Gretchen Wilson
Terri Clark/49
8 Troy Gentry 15.00 40.00
Eddie Montgomery/199
9 Joe Diffie
Tracy Lawrence/49
10 Heidi Newfield 8.00 20.00
Keith Burns/199
11 Brian King
Clay Sharpe/49
12 Pat Green
Chuck Wicks/49

2015 Panini Country Music Fresh Faces

COMPLETE SET (14) 12.00 30.00
COMMON CARD (1-14) 1.50 4.00
*RETAIL: SAME VALUE
*GREEN: .6X TO 1.5X BASIC CARDS
*BLUE/199: .75X TO 2X BASIC CARDS
*PURPLE/99: 1.2X TO 3X BASIC CARDS
*RED/99: 1.2X TO 3X BASIC CARDS
*SILVER/49: 1.5X TO 4X BASIC CARDS
*GOLD/25: 2X TO 5X BASIC CARDS

2015 Panini Country Music I Love Country Patches

COMMON MEM (1-25) 4.00 10.00
RANDOMLY INSERTED INTO PACKS
1 Brantley Gilbert 5.00 12.00
4 Darius Rucker 8.00 20.00
10 John Rich 5.00 12.00
11 Jaren Johnston 6.00 15.00
14 Neal McCoy 5.00 12.00
15 Pat Green 5.00 12.00
18 Ronnie Milsap 6.00 15.00

2015 Panini Country Music Instrumentals

COMPLETE SET (15) 12.00 30.00
COMMON CARD (1-15) 1.25 3.00
*RETAIL: SAME VALUE
*GREEN: .6X TO 1.5X BASIC CARDS
*BLUE/199: .75X TO 2X BASIC CARDS
*PURPLE/99: 1.2X TO 3X BASIC CARDS
*RED/99: 1.2X TO 3X BASIC CARDS
*SILVER/49: 1.5X TO 4X BASIC CARDS
*GOLD/25: 2X TO 5X BASIC CARDS
1 Brantley Gilbert 2.00 5.00
2 Darius Rucker 2.50 6.00
4 Gretchen Wilson 1.50 4.00
6 Pat Green 1.50 4.00
10 John Rich 1.50 4.00

2015 Panini Country Music Musician Combo Materials

SPR 99 SER.#'d SETS
1 Jana Kramer
Lindsay Ell/25
2 Shawna Thompson
Keifer Thompson
3 Brian Kelley
Tyler Hubbard
4 Brantley Gilbert
Colt Ford
5 Josh Gracin 20.00 50.00
Lauren Alaina
6 John Rich
Big Kenny Alphin
8 Troy Gentry 4.00 10.00
Eddie Montgomery
9 Joe Diffie
Tracy Lawrence
10 Heidi Newfield
Keith Burns/49
11 Brian King 4.00 10.00
Clay Sharpe
12 Pat Green 5.00 12.00
Chuck Wicks

2015 Panini Country Music Musician Materials

COMMON CARD (1-49) 5.00 12.00
*GREEN/499: .6X TO 1.5X BASIC CARDS
*SILVER/399: .75X TO 2X BASIC CARDS
*GOLD/199: 1.2X TO 3X BASIC CARDS
1 Barry Knox/399 6.00 15.00
2 Terri Clark/399 6.00 15.00
7 Darius Rucker/220 15.00 40.00
9 Sara Evans/399 20.00 50.00
11 Chris Young/399 6.00 15.00
13 Josh McSwain/399 6.00 15.00
14 Lauren Alaina/232 8.00 20.00
15 Lindsay Ell/299 8.00 20.00
17 Matt Thomas/399 6.00 15.00
18 Ronnie Milsap/399 12.00 30.00
21 Scotty McCreery/399 6.00 15.00
22 Wynonna/349 12.00 30.00
23 Scott Thomas/399 6.00 15.00
25 Joe Diffie/399 6.00 15.00
26 Kimberly Perry/199 12.00 30.00
27 Neil Perry/399 6.00 15.00
28 Reid Perry/399 6.00 15.00
29 Rachel Reinert/215 8.00 20.00
30 Pat Green/399 8.00 20.00
31 Chuck Wicks/399 6.00 15.00
33 Dustin Lynch/399 6.00 15.00
34 Mark Chesnutt/399 6.00 15.00
35 Joe Nichols/399 6.00 15.00
36 Maggie Rose/299 8.00 20.00
41 Jana Kramer/399 6.00 15.00
42 Jerrod Niemann/399 6.00 15.00
43 Colt Ford/399 6.00 15.00
44 Jamie Lynn Spears/175 15.00 40.00
45 Chase Rice/399 6.00 15.00
47 Jon Pardi/399 6.00 15.00
48 Ashley Monroe/299 8.00 20.00
49 Brantley Gilbert/140 15.00 40.00
50 Neal McCoy/249 8.00 20.00

2015 Panini Country Music Musician Quad Materials

COMMON CARD 20.00 50.00
*GREEN/49: 1.5X TO 4X BASIC CARDS
*SILVER/25: 2X TO 5X BASIC CARDS
SPR 99 SER.#'d SETS
2 Bob Carpenter 25.00 60.00
Jeff Hanna#{Jimmie Fadden#{John McEuen
3 Chris Thompson 25.00 60.00
James Young#{Jon Jones#{Mike Eli

2015 Panini Country Music Musician Triple Materials

COMMON CARD 15.00 40.00
STATED PRINT RUN 99 SER.#'d SETS
3 Reid Perry 25.00 60.00
Kimberly Perry#{Neil Perry

2015 Panini Country Music Pick Collection

COMPLETE SET (50) 200.00 400.00
COMMON CARD (1-50) 5.00 12.00

2015 Panini Country Music Quad Signatures

COMMON CARD 25.00 60.00
*GREEN/25: 1.2X TO 3X BASIC CARDS
*SILVER/25: 1.2X TO 3X BASIC CARDS
SPR 49 SER.#'d SETS
1 B.Knox 30.00 80.00
J.McSwain#{M.Thomas#{S.Thomas
2 B.Carpenter 50.00 100.00
J.McEuen#{J.Hanna#{J.Fadden

2015 Panini Country Music Signatures

COMMON CARD (1-62) 6.00 15.00
*BLUE/299: .5X TO 1.2X BASIC CARDS
*RED/199: .6X TO 1.5X BASIC CARDS
*GOLD/25: 1X TO 2.5X BASIC CARDS
*GREEN/25: 1X TO 2.5X BASIC CARDS
*SILVER/25: 1X TO 2.5X BASIC CARDS
2 Terri Clark/317 12.00 30.00
7 Darius Rucker/358 30.00 80.00
8 Josh Gracin/198 8.00 20.00
9 David Nail/344 10.00 25.00
11 Neil Mason/394 8.00 20.00
12 Tracy Lawrence/254 10.00 25.00
14 Lauren Alaina/265 10.00 25.00
15 Lindsay Ell/339 8.00 20.00
16 Gretchen Wilson/494 12.00 30.00
18 Ronnie Milsap/367 12.00 30.00
19 Kelsey Harmon/333 10.00 25.00
21 Josh Thompson/338 8.00 20.00
22 Wynonna/499 15.00 40.00
25 Joe Diffie/356 8.00 20.00
28 Scotty McCreery/399 10.00 25.00
29 LeAnn Rimes/453 25.00 60.00
30 Pat Green/279 10.00 25.00
32 Miranda Lambert/163 100.00 250.00
34 Brian King/394 8.00 20.00
35 Joe Nichols/335 8.00 20.00
36 Maggie Rose/368 10.00 25.00
40 Sara Evans/299 30.00 80.00
41 Clay Sharpe/394 10.00 25.00
42 Rodney Atkins/499 8.00 20.00
43 Colt Ford/285 12.00 30.00
44 Jamie Lynn Spears/376 15.00 40.00
46 Jana Kramer/344 12.00 30.00
48 Ashley Monroe/423 15.00 40.00
49 Brantley Gilbert/499 12.00 30.00
50 Neal McCoy/359 8.00 20.00
51 Rachel Reinert/335 8.00 20.00
52 Brian Kelley/399 6.00 15.00
53 Tyler Hubbard/399 10.00 25.00
58 Kimberly Perry/499 12.00 30.00
59 Neil Perry/499 8.00 20.00
60 Reid Perry/499 8.00 20.00
61 Jennifer Nettles/344 20.00 50.00
62 Shawna Thompson/285 10.00 25.00

2015 Panini Country Music Silhouette Signature Materials

*GREEN/25: 2X TO 5X BASIC CARDS
*PRIME/49: 1.5X TO 4X BASIC CARDS
*PR.GREEN/25: 2X TO 5X BASIC
*PR.SILVER/25: 2X TO 5X BASIC
*SILVER/25: 2X TO 5X BASIC CARDS
1 Big Kenny Alphin/126
2 Terri Clark/306 10.00 25.00
3 Brian Kelley/199
4 Josh Thompson/199 4.00 10.00
5 James Young/199
6 Kimberly Perry/99
7 Darius Rucker/199
8 Josh Gracin/399
9 Keifer Thompson/199 5.00 12.00

10 Eddie Montgomery/399 10.00 25.00
11 Rodney Atkins/199 10.00 25.00
12 Tracy Lawrence/348
13 Sara Evans/199
14 Lauren Alaina/349 15.00 40.00
15 Lindsay Ell/99
17 Scotty McCreery/199 8.00 20.00
18 Ronnie Milsap/344 25.00 60.00
19 Kelsey Harmon/399 5.00 12.00
20 Mike Eli/340
22 Heidi Newfield/84 15.00 40.00
23 Wynonna/199 15.00 40.00
24 Chris Young/199
25 Joe Diffie/246
26 David Nail/199
27 Shawna Thompson/199
28 John Rich/233
29 Rachel Reinert/149
30 Pat Green/199
31 Chuck Wicks/147 10.00 25.00
32 Miranda Lambert/175 60.00 120.00
33 Dustin Lynch/199
34 Randy Owen/199 12.00 30.00
35 Joe Nichols/199 12.00 30.00
36 Maggie Rose/49
37 Mark Chesnutt/330
38 Jerrod Niemann/231
39 Chase Rice/99
40 Jennifer Nettles/199 20.00 50.00
41 Teddy Gentry/338
42 Jana Kramer/199 25.00 60.00
43 Colt Ford/149
44 Jamie Lynn Spears/83
45 Troy Gentry/199
46 Tyler Hubbard/199 25.00 60.00
47 Jon Pardi/149
48 Ashley Monroe/99
49 Brantley Gilbert/99
50 Neal McCoy/333

2015 Panini Country Music Top of the Charts

COMPLETE SET (25) 20.00 50.00
COMMON CARD (1-25) 1.00 2.50
*RETAIL: SAME VALUE
*GREEN: .6X TO 1.5X BASIC CARDS
*BLUE/199: .75X TO 2X BASIC CARDS
*PURPLE/99: 1.2X TO 3X BASIC CARDS
*RED/99: 1.2X TO 3X BASIC CARDS
*SILVER/49: 1.5X TO 4X BASIC CARDS
*GOLD/25: 2X TO 5X BASIC CARDS
2 Florida Georgia Line 3.00 8.00
3 Alabama 1.50 4.00
9 Ronnie Milsap 3.00 8.00
16 Brantley Gilbert 2.50 6.00
19 Mark Chesnutt 2.00 5.00
21 LeAnn Rimes 3.00 8.00
23 Sara Evans 4.00 10.00
24 Wynonna 3.00 8.00

2015 Panini Country Music Triple Signatures

COMMON CARD (1-4) 20.00 50.00
*GREEN/25: 2X TO 5X BASIC CARDS
*SILVER/25: 2X TO 5X BASIC CARDS
4 R.Perry 60.00 120.00
K.Perry#(N.Perry

2015 Panini Country Music United States Flag Patches

COMMON CARD (1-25) 5.00 12.00
1 Brantley Gilbert 6.00 15.00
4 LeAnn Rimes 10.00 25.00
5 Darius Rucker 12.00 30.00
9 John Rich 8.00 20.00
11 Neal McCoy 6.00 15.00
12 Pat Green 6.00 15.00
14 Ronnie Milsap 8.00 20.00
21 Reid Perry 8.00 20.00

1991 Unbeatables Coup Cards

COMPLETE PACKAGED SET (10) 1.50 4.00
COMMON CARD (1-10) .30 .75

1990 Eclipse Coup D'Etat

COMPLETE SET (36) 4.00 10.00
COMMON CARD (1-36) .25 .60

1999 Comic Images CPM Manga The Art of Satoshi Urushihara

COMPLETE SET (72) 5.00 12.00
UNOPENED BOX (36 PACKS) 30.00 40.00
UNOPENED PACK (7 CARDS) 1.00 1.25
COMMON CARD (1-72) .12 .30

1999 Comic Images CPM Manga The Art of Satoshi Urushihara OmniChrome

COMPLETE SET (6) 10.00 25.00
COMMON CARD (1-6) 2.50 6.00
RANDOMLY INSERTED INTO PACKS

1999 Comic Images CPM Manga The Art of Satoshi Urushihara Promos

COMPLETE SET (3) 2.00 5.00
COMMON CARD (P1-P3) .75 2.00

1996 Cracker Jack Creatures of the Deep

COMPLETE SET (8) 4.00 10.00
COMMON CARD (1-8) .75 2.00
STATED ODDS 1:CRACKER JACK BOX

1992 Sears Craftsman Tools

COMPLETE SET (110) 15.00 40.00
UNOPENED BOX (PACKS)
UNOPENED PACK (CARDS)
COMMON CARD (1-110) .30 .75

1996 Cornerstone Crash and Burn Promos

COMPLETE SET (4) 2.50 6.00
COMMON CARD (A-D) .75 2.00

1995 SkyBox Creator's Edition

COMPLETE SET (90) 6.00 15.00
UNOPENED BOX (36 PACKS) 40.00 50.00
UNOPENED PACK (6 CARDS) 1.25 1.50
COMMON CARD (1-90) .12 .30

1995 SkyBox Creator's Edition Embossed Spectra

COMPLETE SET (5) 10.00 25.00
COMMON CARD (B1-B5) 3.00 8.00
STATED ODDS 1:12

1995 SkyBox Creator's Edition Promos

COMMON CARD () .75 2.00
P 1995 Biohazard 8.00 20.00
P01 1995 Kroma
P01 1994 Dr. Phobic
P03 1994 Shokk 1.25 3.00
P3 1995

1996 Dynamic Entertainment Creator's Alternate Universe

COMPLETE SET (90) 5.00 12.00
UNOPENED BOX (36 PACKS) 20.00 25.00
UNOPENED PACK (8 CARDS) .75 1.00
COMMON CARD (1-90) .12 .30
BLASTOFF PHONE CARD 1:36
PC Lance Blastoff Phone Card 8.00 20.00

1996 Dynamic Entertainment Creator's Alternate Universe Autographs

COMPLETE SET (87) 1100.00 2000.00
COMMON AUTO (1-87) 10.00 25.00
STATED ODDS 1:18
STATED PRINT RUN 100 SER.#'d SETS

1993 Dynamic Entertainment The Creators Universe

COMPLETE SET (100) 6.00 15.00
COMMON CARD (1-100) .12 .30
NNO Hellshock Hellshock Print Insert

1993 Dynamic Entertainment The Creators Universe 24 kt Autographs

COMPLETE SET (12) 250.00 500.00
COMMON AUTO 20.00 50.00
STATED ODDS 1:360

1993 Dynamic Entertainment The Creators Universe All American Family

COMPLETE SET (4) 5.00 12.00
COMMON CARD (1-4) 2.00 5.00
STATED ODDS 1:12

1993 Dynamic Entertainment The Creators Universe Checklist

COMPLETE SET (5) 10.00 25.00
COMMON CARD (1-5) 3.00 8.00
STATED ODDS 1:18

1993 Dynamic Entertainment The Creators Universe Family Fusion Titanium

COMPLETE SET (3) 8.00 20.00
COMMON CARD (1-3) 3.00 8.00
STATED ODDS 1:12

1993 Dynamic Entertainment The Creators Universe Jae Lee Serigraphs

NNO Hellshock Redemption Card
SG1 Hellshock 20.00 50.00
SG1 Hellshock Close-Up
SG1 Hellshock Full Body With Cross

1993 Dynamic Entertainment The Creators Universe Promos

COMPLETE SET (16) 5.00 12.00
COMMON CARD .40 1.00
NNO 4-Up Panel, Cards P1-P3 1.50 4.00

2019 Creatures of Myth and Legend

COMPLETE SET (20) 6.00 15.00
COMMON CARD (1-20) 40 1.00

2019 Creatures of Myth and Legend Canvas

COMPLETE SET (4) 5.00 12.00
COMMON CARD (CC1-CC4) 2.00 5.00
STATED ODDS 1:SET

2019 Creatures of Myth and Legend Lenticular Chase

LPL La Patasola 8.00 20.00

2019 Creatures of Myth and Legend Metal Chase

COMPLETE SET (2) 20.00 50.00
COMMON CARD (KMC & PMC) 12.00 30.00
YETI NOT INCLUDED IN SET PRICE
NNO Yeti/20 EXCH 60.00 120.00
PMC Piasa 15.00 40.00

2019 Creatures of Myth and Legend Promos

COMPLETE SET (3) 4.00 10.00
COMMON CARD (P1-P3) 1.50 4.00
P1 Chupacabra 2.50 6.00
(2018 Philly Non-Sports Card Show Exclusive)
P2 Mothman 1.50 4.00
P3 Lizard Man Chicago 1.50 4.00
(2019 Non-Sport Card Show Exclusive)

1996 Krome Creed

COMPLETE SET (50) 8.00 20.00
UNOPENED BOX (36 PACKS) 40.00 50.00
UNOPENED PACK (6 CARDS+1 STICKER) 1.25 1.50
COMMON CARD (1-50) .30 .75
HOLOCHROME: .5X TO 1.2X BASIC CARDS .40 1.00
NNO Trent Kaniuga AU/500* 20.00 50.00
NNO Oversized PROMO

1996 Krome Creed ClearChrome Mystery

COMPLETE SET (4) 10.00 25.00
COMMON CARD (1-4) 3.00 8.00
STATED ODDS 1:18

1996 Krome Creed NecroChrome

COMPLETE SET (5) 6.00 15.00
COMMON CARD (1-5) 1.50 4.00
STATED ODDS 1:6

2022 Fright-Rags Creepshow

COMPLETE SET (80) 30.00 75.00
UNOPENED BOX (24 PACKS) 200.00 250.00
UNOPENED PACK (9 CARDS+1 STICKER) 8.00 12.00
COMMON CARD (1-80, CL) .60 1.50
*BLUE: 1.5X TO 4X BASIC CARDS
STATED PRINT RUN 325 TOTAL BOXES

2022 Fright-Rags Creepshow Autographs

COMMON AUTO
STATED ODDS 1:24
NNO Adrienne Barbeau/53
NNO Darryl Ferrucci/55 75.00 200.00
NNO John Amplas/55 50.00 125.00
NNO Tom Atkins/52
NNO Tom Savini/55 125.00 300.00
NNO Warner Shook/55

2022 Fright-Rags Creepshow Stickers

COMPLETE SET (9) 12.00 30.00
COMMON CARD 2.00 5.00
STATED ODDS 1:1

1991 Kitchen Sink Press Crimes Against the Eye

COMPLETE SET (36) 10.00 25.00
COMMON CARD (1-36) .25 .60

1992 Eclipse Crime and Punishment

COMPLETE SET (110) 6.00 15.00
UNOPENED BOX (36 PACKS) 30.00 40.00
UNOPENED PACK (12 CARDS) 1.00 1.25
COMMON CARD (1-110) .10 .25
NNO Charles Manson PROMO .75 2.00

2001 Crimson Commemorative

COMPLETE SET (90) 5.00 12.00
UNOPENED BOX (36 PACKS) 30.00 40.00
UNOPENED PACK (6 CARDS) 1.00 1.25
COMMON CARD (1-90) .12 .30
NNO Humberto Ramos
Brian Augustyn AU

2001 Crimson Commemorative Autographs

COMMON CARD 4.00 10.00
STATED ODDS 1:18

2001 Crimson Commemorative Humberto Ramos Classic Images Holo Rainbow Chrome

COMPLETE SET (6) 6.00 15.00
COMMON CARD (C1-C6) 1.25 3.00
STATED ODDS 1:12

2001 Crimson Commemorative Key Character Glow

COMPLETE SET (6) 6.00 15.00
COMMON CARD (G1-G6) 1.25 3.00
STATED ODDS 1:12

2001 Crimson Commemorative Out There First Look

COMPLETE SET (6) 2.00 5.00
COMMON CARD (1-6) .40 1.00
STATED ODDS 1:12

2001 Crimson Commemorative Promos

COMMON CARD .75 2.00
H1 Bryan Augustyn AU
BC1 Joe Quesada Artwork 3.00 8.00

1998 Comic Images Crimson Embrace

COMPLETE SET (72)	8.00	20.00
UNOPENED BOX (48 PACKS)	50.00	65.00
UNOPENED PACK (7 CARDS)	1.25	1.50
COMMON CARD (1-72)	.25	.60
NNO Red-Headed Vampiress PROMO	1.00	2.50

1998 Comic Images Crimson Embrace OmniChrome

COMPLETE SET (9)	15.00	40.00
COMMON CARD (1-9)	2.50	6.00
RANDOMLY INSERTED INTO PACKS		

1998 Comic Images Crimson Embrace OmniChrome Autographs

COMMON CARD (1-9)	20.00	50.00
RANDOMLY INSERTED INTO PACKS		

2002 Crocodile Hunter

COMPLETE SET (72)	8.00	20.00
UNOPENED BOX (36 PACKS)		
UNOPENED PACK (6 CARDS)		
COMMON CARD (1-72)	.25	.60
B1 ISSUED ON BOX BOTTOM		
CT1 ISSUED AS CASE TOPPER		
B1 Steve Irwin BB	2.50	6.00
CT1 Have a Look CT	8.00	20.00

2002 Crocodile Hunter Authentic Danger-Ware

COMPLETE SET (2)	5.00	12.00
COMMON CARD (DW1-DW2)	3.00	8.00
OVERALL AUTO/MEM ODDS 1:36		

2002 Crocodile Hunter Autographs

COMMON AUTO (A1-A2)	25.00	60.00
OVERALL AUTO/MEM ODDS 1:36		
A1 Steve Irwin	600.00	1000.00

2002 Crocodile Hunter Most Dangerous Reptiles

COMPLETE SET (9)	6.00	15.00
COMMON CARD (DR1-DR9)	1.25	3.00
OVERALL INSERT ODDS 1:7		

2002 Crocodile Hunter Most Lethal Insects

COMPLETE SET (6)	4.00	10.00
COMMON CARD (LI1-LI6)	1.25	3.00
OVERALL INSERT ODDS 1:7		

2002 Crocodile Hunter Promos

P1 Steve Irwin	.75	2.00
NSU Steve Irwin NSU	.75	2.00
SDCC Steve Irwin SDCC	.75	2.00

2002 Brach's Crocodile Hunter

COMPLETE SET (5)	6.00	15.00
COMMON CARD	2.00	5.00

1994 Kitchen Sink Press The Crow

COMPLETE SET (100)	8.00	20.00
UNOPENED BOX (36 PACKS)	35.00	50.00
UNOPENED PACK (10 CARDS)	1.25	1.50
COMMON CARD (1-100)	.15	.40
STATED PRINT RUN 1800 SER.#'d SETS		
NNO Embossed Metal Poster/2000		

1994 Kitchen Sink Press The Crow Crow Vision

COMPLETE SET (10)	20.00	50.00
COMMON CARD (1-10)	3.00	8.00
STATED ODDS 1:18		

1994 Kitchen Sink Press The Crow Crow-mium

COMPLETE SET (6)	25.00	60.00
COMMON CARD (C1-C6)	5.00	12.00
STATED ODDS 1:36		

1994 Kitchen Sink Press The Crow Promos

P1 (standing, hands down)	1.50	4.00
P2 (2-card strip; Heroes magazine)	2.00	5.00
P3 (sitting, slight R profile)	1.50	4.00
P4 (squatting in window)	1.50	4.00
P5 (crow on shoulder)	1.50	4.00
1995V (1995; inserted in videos)	1.50	4.00

1997 Kitchen Sink Press The Crow City of Angels

COMPLETE SET (92)	6.00	15.00
UNOPENED BOX (36 PACKS)	30.00	50.00
UNOPENED PACK (8 CARDS)	1.50	2.50
COMMON CARD (1-92)	.12	.30
AU1 James O'Barr AU (factory set excl.)	15.00	40.00
RED1 Ultra Chase Art EXCH	10.00	25.00

1997 Kitchen Sink Press The Crow City of Angels Crowmium O'Barr

COMPLETE SET (6)	12.00	30.00
COMMON CARD (1-6)	4.00	10.00
STATED ODDS 1:18		

1997 Kitchen Sink Press The Crow City of Angels Embossed Legend of the Crow

COMPLETE SET (10)	6.00	15.00
COMMON CARD (1-10)	1.25	3.00
STATED ODDS 1:4		

1997 Kitchen Sink Press The Crow City of Angels Tattoos

COMPLETE SET (10)	2.50	6.00
COMMON CARD (1-10)	.40	1.00
STATED ODDS 1:1		

1997 Kitchen Sink Press The Crow City of Angels Promos

1 Wizard	1.00	2.50
2 NSU	1.00	2.50
3 Combo	1.00	2.50
4 Advance Comics	1.00	2.50
5 Promo 5	1.00	2.50

2002 The Crow Collector's Premium Previews

COMPLETE BOXED SET (6)	4.00	10.00
COMMON CARD (1-6)	1.00	2.50

2003 The Crow J. O'Barr Art

COMPLETE BOXED SET (10)	8.00	20.00
COMMON CARD (1-10)	1.25	3.00

2018 Cryptkins

P1 Chupacabra	1.25	3.00
P2 Nessie	1.25	3.00
P3 Yeti	1.25	3.00
P4 Bigfoot	1.25	3.00
P5 Phoenix	1.25	3.00
P6 Cthulhu	1.25	3.00
P7 Nightcrawler	3.00	10.00
P8 Twilight Mothman	3.00	8.00
P9 Nightcrawler	3.00	8.00
P10 Jersey Devil	3.00	8.00
P11 Nightcrawler	3.00	8.00
P12 Ogopogo	3.00	8.00
P13 Cosmic Cthulhu	3.00	8.00
P14 Midnight Chupacabra (Wondercon Cryptozoic Booth Redemption)	5.00	12.00
P15 Irradiated Cthulhu (SDCC Exclusive)	8.00	20.00
P16 Jersey Devil (SDCC Exclusive)		

2003 CSI Previews A

COMPLETE SET (10)	6.00	15.00
COMMON CARD (A1-A10)	1.00	2.50
STATED PRINT RUN 499 SER.#'d SETS		

2003 CSI Previews B

COMPLETE SET (10)	6.00	15.00
COMMON CARD (B1-B10)	1.00	2.50
STATED PRINT RUN 499 SER.#'d SETS		

2003 CSI Series One

COMPLETE SET (100)	6.00	15.00
UNOPENED BOX (36 PACKS)	50.00	60.00
UNOPENED PACK (7 CARDS)	1.75	2.00
COMMON CARD (1-100)	.10	.25
CC1 Casino Chip EXCH	150.00	300.00
DI1 100-Card UNC (dealer incentive)	15.00	40.00
SS1 Win Signed Script	.40	1.00

2003 CSI Series One Autographs

COMMON AUTO (CSIA1-CSIA21)	6.00	15.00
STATED ODDS 1:18		
CSIA1 William Petersen	20.00	50.00
CSIA2 Gary Dourden	10.00	25.00
CSIA3 Jorja Fox	20.00	50.00
CSIA4 Eric Szmanda	10.00	25.00
CSIA5 Robert David Hall	10.00	25.00
CSIA13 Eileen Cox Baker	8.00	20.00
CSIA20 Danny Cannon ALB	15.00	40.00

2003 CSI Series One Costumes

STATED ODDS 1:144		
CSIC1 William Petersen (lab coat)	20.00	50.00
CSIC4 Eric Szmanda (shirt)	15.00	40.00
CSIC5 Eric Szmanda (lab coat)	12.00	30.00

2003 CSI Series One DNA Fingerprint Gold Foil

COMPLETE SET (6)	4.00	10.00
COMMON CARD (DNA1-DNA6)	.75	2.00
STATED ODDS 1:3		

2003 CSI Series One Stars of CSI Gold Foil

COMPLETE SET (8)	5.00	12.00
COMMON CARD (F1-F8)	.75	2.00
STATED ODDS 1:3		

2003 CSI Series One Promos

COMPLETE SET (5)	2.50	6.00
COMMON CARD	.75	2.00

2004 CSI Series Two Previews

COMPLETE SET (10)	6.00	15.00
COMMON CARD (1-10)	1.00	2.50
STATED PRINT RUN 999 SER.#'d SETS		

2004 CSI Series Two

COMPLETE SET (100)	6.00	15.00
UNOPENED BOX (36 PACKS)	55.00	70.00
UNOPENED PACK (7 CARDS)	1.75	2.00
COMMON CARD (1-100)	.10	.25
AU1 M. Helgenberger W. Peterson AU/100	100.00	200.00
CC2 Casino Chip/50	30.00	80.00
DSB1 Gil Grissom Catherine Willows/250		

2004 CSI Series Two Autographs

COMMON AUTO	5.00	12.00
STATED ODDS 1:12		
CSIA22 Marg Helgenberger	30.00	75.00
CSIA23 George Eads	20.00	50.00
CSIA24 Paul Guilfoyle	20.00	50.00
CSIB1 William Petersen	30.00	80.00
CSIB2 Robert David Hall	15.00	40.00
CSIB17 Melinda Clarke/250 (Case-Topper)	15.00	40.00

2004 CSI Series Two Case-Toppers Cast

COMPLETE SET (8)	12.00	30.00
COMMON CARD	1.50	4.00
STATED ODDS 1 SET:CASE		
STATED PRINT RUN 250 SER.#'d SETS		

2004 CSI Series Two Costumes

COMPLETE SET (2)	25.00	60.00
COMMON CARD (CSIC2-CSIC3)	15.00	40.00
STATED ODDS 1:108		

2004 CSI Series Two Gold Foil Cast

COMPLETE SET (6)	4.00	10.00
COMMON CARD (CSI2F1-CSI2F6)	.75	2.00
STATED ODDS 1:3		

2004 CSI Series Two Gold Foil ID Badge

COMPLETE SET (6)	4.00	10.00
COMMON CARD (B1-B6	.75	2.00
STATED ODDS 1:3		

2004 CSI Series Two Promos

COMPLETE SET (4)	4.00	10.00
COMMON CARD	1.50	4.00

2006 CSI Series Three Previews

COMPLETE SET (9)	6.00	15.00
COMMON CARD (P1-P9)	1.00	2.50
STATED PRINT RUN 999 SER.#'d SETS		

2006 CSI Series Three

COMPLETE SET (72)	5.00	12.00
UNOPENED BOX (36 PACKS)		
UNOPENED PACK (5 CARDS)		
COMMON CARD (1-72)	.10	.25
B1 Gold Bonus ALB		
CH1 Casino Chip $25		
RED1 Congratulations EXCH		

2006 CSI Series Three Autographs

COMMON CARD (A1-A11)	6.00	15.00
STATED ODDS 1:18		
A1 William Petersen	30.00	80.00
A2 Marg Helgenberger	50.00	100.00
A3 Gary Dourdan	10.00	25.00
A4 George Eads	30.00	80.00
A5 Jorja Fox	15.00	40.00
A6 Eric Szmanda	15.00	40.00
A7 Louise Lombard	12.00	30.00
A11 Anthony E. Zuiker	8.00	20.00

2006 CSI Series Three Casino Chips

COMPLETE SET (5)	100.00	200.00
COMMON CARD (1-5)	20.00	50.00
STATED PRINT RUN 500 SER.#'d SETS		

2006 CSI Series Three Costumes

COMMON CARD (CSIS3C1-CSIS3C3)	6.00	15.00
CSIS3C2 Paul Guilfoyle (Armani tie)	20.00	50.00
CSIS3C3 George Eads (shirt)	8.00	20.00

2006 CSI Series Three Foil Bonus

COMPLETE SET (9)	6.00	15.00
COMMON CARD (F1-F9)	.75	2.00
STATED ODDS 1:6		

2006 CSI Series Three Promos

B1 8 Cast Gold Foil		
PR1 Willows and Grissom	1.25	3.00
PR2 Grissom	1.25	3.00

2004 CSI Miami Series One Previews

COMPLETE SET (11)	15.00	40.00
COMMON CARD (MIP1-MIP10; MIA0)	2.00	5.00
STATED PRINT RUN 999 SER.#'d SETS		
MIA0 Anthony E. Zuiker/AU	6.00	15.00

2004 CSI Miami Series One

COMPLETE SET (100)	6.00	15.00
UNOPENED BOX (36 PACKS)	40.00	50.00
UNOPENED PACK (7 CARDS)	1.25	1.50
COMMON CARD (1-100)	.10	.25

2004 CSI Miami Series One Autographs

COMMON AUTO (A1-A13)	6.00	15.00
STATED ODDS 1:12		
MIA1 David Caruso	50.00	100.00
MIA2 Emily Procter	10.00	25.00
MIA3 Khandi Alexander	15.00	40.00
MIA4 Rory Cochrane	20.00	50.00
MIA6 Ann Bliss	10.00	25.00
MIA7 Rex Linn	8.00	20.00
MIA8 Anthony E. Zuiker	8.00	20.00
MIA11 Cristian de la Fuente ALB	10.00	25.00
MIA12 Carol Mendelson	8.00	20.00

2004 CSI Miami Series One Case Bonus

Ultra1 David Caruso
Emily Procter AU/100
Ultra2 David Caruso 150.00 300.00
Emily Procter AU/100
Ultra3 David Caruso as Horatio Caine 8.00 20.00
Sofia Milos as Yelina Salas
Ultra4 William Peterson as Gil Grissom 8.00 20.00
Marg Helgenberger as Catherine Willows

2004 CSI Miami Series One Case-Toppers

COMPLETE SET (8) 15.00 40.00
COMMON CARD 2.50 6.00
STATED ODDS 1 SET:CASE
STATED PRINT RUN 250 SER.#'d SETS

2004 CSI Miami Series One Case-Toppers UK

COMPLETE SET (5) 12.00 30.00
COMMON CARD (DVD1-DVD5) 3.00 8.00
STATED ODDS 1:CASE

2004 CSI Miami Series One Costumes

COMMON CARD (CSIMC1-CSIMC2) 10.00 25.00
STATED ODDS 1:216

2004 CSI Miami Series One Forensics Gold Foil

COMPLETE SET (5) 3.00 8.00
COMMON CARD (MIAF1-MIAF5) .75 2.00
RANDOMLY INSERTED INTO PACKS

2004 CSI Miami Series One Starring Cast Profiles Gold Foil

COMPLETE SET (7) 4.00 10.00
COMMON CARD (F1-F2) .75 2.00
RANDOMLY INSERTED INTO PACKS

2004 CSI Miami Series One Promos

CSIM2 David Caruso 2.00 5.00
CSIM3 Emily Procter 2.00 5.00
CISM1b 5 Cast (error in card #) 4.00 10.00
CSIM1a 5 Cast 2.00 5.00
CSIWEB1 Duquesne And Caine
(Strictly Ink Excl.) 2.00 5.00
CSIM1CI1 Tim Speedle 5.00 12.00
CSIM1CI2 Eric Delko 2.00 5.00

2005 CSI Miami Series Two Previews

COMPLETE SET (9) 6.00 15.00
COMMON CARD (P1-P9) 1.00 2.50
STATED PRINT RUN 999 SER.#'d SETS

2005 CSI Miami Series Two

COMPLETE SET (72) 6.00 15.00
UNOPENED BOX (30 PACKS) 40.00 50.00
UNOPENED PACK (5 CARDS) 1.50 2.00
COMMON CARD (1-72) .12 .30

2005 CSI Miami Series Two Autographs

COMMON CARD (MIB1-MIB7) 6.00 15.00
STATED ODDS 1:30
MIB1 David Caruso 50.00 100.00
MIB2 Adam Rodriguez 15.00 40.00
MIB4 Emily Procter 20.00 50.00
MIB5 Khandi Alexander 15.00 40.00
MIB7 Boti Bliss 10.00 25.00

2005 CSI Miami Series Two ID Badges

COMPLETE SET (6) 6.00 15.00
COMMON CARD (MIID1-MIID6) 1.50 4.00
STATED ODDS 1:12

2005 CSI Miami Series Two Costumes

COMMON CARD 8.00 20.00
STATED ODDS 1:30 W/SKETCHES
CSIMS2C1 Tony Hawk (Quicksilver t-shirt) 15.00 40.00
CSIMS2C3 Emily Procter (bloody pants) 10.00 25.00
CSIMS3C1 David Caruso (shirt) 15.00 40.00

2005 CSI Miami Series Two Promos

PR1 Caine In Sunglasses 2.50 6.00
PR2 Yelina At The Beach 2.50 6.00
CSIM2WEB1 Horatio Caine (online offer) 4.00 10.00

2005 CSI New York Series One

COMPLETE SET (72) 6.00 15.00
UNOPENED BOX (30 PACKS) 50.00 60.00
UNOPENED PACK (5 CARDS) 2.00 2.50
COMMON CARD (1-72) .12 .30
BT1 CSI NY Series One Gold BT
RED1 Congrats Sketch EXCH

2005 CSI New York Series One Autographs

COMMON CARD (CSINYA1-CSINYA8) 6.00 15.00
CSINYA1 Gary Sinise
CSINYA3 Eddie Cahill
CSINYA4 Carmine Giovinazzo 15.00 40.00
CSINYA5 Hill Harper 12.00 30.00
CSINYA6 Anna Belknap 25.00 60.00
CSINYB1 Gary Sinise Gold (facsimile)
CSINYB2 Melina Kanakaredes Gold (facsimile)

2005 CSI New York Series One Costumes

CSINYS1 Mac Taylor (tie) 20.00 50.00
CSINYS2 Detective Flack (tie) 12.00 30.00
CSINYS3 Dr. Sheldon Hawkes (shirt) 8.00 20.00

2005 CSI New York Series One ID Badges

COMPLETE SET (5) 6.00 15.00
COMMON CARD (1-5) 1.50 4.00

2005 CSI New York Series One Promos

COMPLETE SET (2) 3.00 8.00
COMMON CARD (PR1-PR2) 2.50 6.00

1984 Sanitarium Curious Conveyances

COMPLETE SET (12) 4.00 10.00
COMMON CARD (1-12) .60 1.50

1981 Topps Cute 'N Cuddly Animal Posters

COMPLETE SET (12) 8.00 20.00
UNOPENED BOX (36 PACKS) 20.00 25.00
UNOPENED PACK (1 POSTER) 1.00 1.50
COMMON POSTER .75 2.00

1993-94 Vanguard Productions Cutting Edge Creator

COMPLETE SET (25) 6.00 15.00
COMMON CARD (1-25) .30 .75

1995 Topps Cyber-Force

COMPLETE SET (72) 6.00 15.00
UNOPENED BOX (24 PACKS) 35.00 45.00
UNOPENED PACK (5 CARDS) 1.75 2.00
COMMON CARD (1-72) .15 .40

1995 Topps Cyber-Force Clearzone Triptych

COMPLETE SET (3) 12.00 30.00
COMMON CARD (B1-B3) 5.00 12.00
STATED ODDS 1:24

1995 Topps Cyber-Force Hero Promos

COMPLETE SET 5.00 12.00
COMMON CARD .75 2.00

1996 Intrepid Cyber-Force Summer

COMPLETE SET (90) 10.00 25.00
UNOPENED BOX (36 PACKS) 40.00 50.00
UNOPENED PACK (7 CARDS) 1.25 1.50
COMMON CARD (1-90) .25 .60

1996 Intrepid Cyber-Force Summer Creators Series Puzzle

COMPLETE SET (9) 25.00 60.00
COMMON CARD (MS1-MS9) 3.00 8.00
STATED ODDS 1:8

1996 Intrepid Cyber-Force Summer Overheat Acetate

COMPLETE SET (3) 15.00 40.00
COMMON CARD (OH1-OH3) 6.00 15.00
STATED ODDS 1:36

1996 Intrepid Cyber-Force Summer Red Hot Foil

COMPLETE SET (6) 10.00 25.00
COMMON CARD (RH1-RH6) 2.50 6.00
STATED ODDS 1:6

1985 Topps Cyndi Lauper

COMPLETE SET (33) 4.00 10.00
COMPLETE SET W/STICKERS (66) 6.00 15.00
UNOPENED BOX (36 PACKS) 60.00 100.00
UNOPENED PACK (3 CARDS+3 STICKERS) 2.00 3.00
COMMON CARD (1-33) .20 .50

1985 Topps Cyndi Lauper Stickers

COMPLETE SET (33) 5.00 12.00
COMMON STICKERS (1-33) .30 .75
STATED ODDS 1:1

2005 D-Day Commemorative

COMPLETE FACTORY SET (82) 15.00 40.00
COMMON CARD (1-79, 2 CL) .30 .75

1992 Nonsports Illustrated Dactyls

COMPLETE FACTORY SET (22) 3.00 8.00
COMMON CARD (1-22) .30 .75

1992 Enor Dallas Cowboy Cheerleaders

COMPLETE BOXED SET (41) 5.00 12.00
COMMON CARD (1-41) .20 .50

1992 Enor Dallas Cowboy Cheerleaders Promos

COMPLETE SET (3) 2.00 5.00
COMMON CARD .75 2.00

1993 Score Dallas Cowboy Cheerleaders

COMPLETE FACTORY SET (45) 10.00 25.00
COMMON CARD (1-45) .30 .75
P1 1994 Calendar Promo

1993 Score Dallas Cowboy Cheerleaders 3-D

COMPLETE SET (4) 5.00 12.00
COMMON CARD (1-4) 1.50 4.00
STATED ODDS 1:BOXED SET

1993 Score Dallas Cowboy Cheerleaders Autographs

COMPLETE SET (34) 80.00 150.00
COMMON CARD 2.00 5.00
STATED ODDS 1:BOXED SET

1991 Potshot Productions Damn Saddam!

COMPLETE FACTORY SET (36) 5.00 12.00
COMMON CARD (1-36) .25 .60

1994 Topps Damn Yankees

COMPLETE SET (20) 6.00 15.00
COMMON CARD (1-20) .50 1.25
NNO Jerry Lewis as Applegate (1995) 4.00 10.00

2002 Dark Angel

COMPLETE SET (72) 5.00 12.00
UNOPENED HOBBY BOX (36 PACKS) 500.00 700.00
UNOPENED HOBBY PACK (7 CARDS) 15.00 20.00
UNOPENED RETAIL BOX (24 PACKS)
UNOPENED RETAIL PACK (7 CARDS)
COMMON CARD (1-72) .15 .40
P1 Built For Action PROMO 1.25 3.00

2002 Dark Angel Autographs

COMMON AUTO 6.00 15.00
STATED ODDS 1:33 HOBBY
BYRON MANN AUTO 1:78 RETAIL EXCLUSIVE
NNO Byron Mann RET 50.00 100.00
NNO James Cameron 3000.00 6000.00
NNO Jessica Alba 2500.00 5000.00

2002 Dark Angel Foil

COMPLETE SET (5) 4.00 10.00
COMMON CARD (1-5) 1.25 3.00
STATED ODDS 1:6

1982 Donruss The Dark Crystal

COMPLETE SET (78) 6.00 15.00
UNOPENED BOX (36 PACKS) 50.00 75.00
UNOPENED PACK (8 CARDS) 1.50 2.50
COMMON CARD (1-78) .15 .40

1993 The River Group Dark Dominion

COMPLETE SET (150) 6.00 15.00
UNOPENED BOX (36 PACKS) 15.00 25.00
UNOPENED PACK (9 CARDS) .50 .75
COMMON CARD (1-150) .08 .20

1993 The River Group Dark Dominion Level 1

COMPLETE SET (9) 12.00 30.00
COMMON CARD (1-9) 1.50 4.00
STATED ODDS 1:18

1993 The River Group Dark Dominion Level 2

COMPLETE SET (4) 60.00 120.00
COMMON CARD (1-4) 15.00 40.00
STATED ODDS 1:72

1993 The River Group Dark Dominion Promos

COMMON CARD .75 2.00

1997 Dark Horse Comics Convention Signing Promos

COMMON CARD (UNNUMBERED) .75 2.00
NNO Bettie Page 2.50 6.00
NNO Star Wars Tales of the Jedi: The Fall of the Sith Empire 2.00 5.00
NNO Star Wars: Dark Force Rising 2.00 5.00
NNO Star Wars: Protocol Offensive 5.00 12.00

1998 Dark Horse Comics Convention Signing Promos

COMMON CARD (UNNUMBERED) .75 2.00
NNO Buffy the Vampire Slayer 1.50 4.00
NNO Star Wars: Crimson Empire 2.00 5.00
NNO Star Wars: Last Command 2.00 5.00
NNO Star Wars: Mara Jade 2.00 5.00
NNO Star Wars Tales of the Jedi: Redemption2.00 5.00

1999 Dark Horse Comics Convention Signing Promos

COMMON CARD (UNNUMBERED) .75 2.00
NNO Buffy the Vampire Slayer 1.50 4.00
NNO Star Wars: Crimson Empire II 2.00 5.00
NNO Star Wars Tales 2.00 5.00
NNO Star Wars : Vader's Quest 2.00 5.00
NNO Star Wars Episode I: The Phantom Menace2.00 5.00
NNO Star Wars Manga 2.00 5.00
NNO Xena Warrior Princess 1.50 4.00

2000 Dark Horse Comics Convention Signing Promos

COMPLETE SET (15)
COMMON CARD .75 2.00
NNO Star Wars: Darth Maul 1.25 3.00
NNO Star Wars: Jedi Council 1.25 3.00
NNO Star Wars Tales 1.25 3.00
NNO Star Wars: Twilight 1.25 3.00

2001 Dark Horse Comics Convention Signing Promos

COMMON CARD .75 2.00
INFNH1 Star Wars: Infinities 1.25 3.00

SWJVS1 Star Wars: Jedi vs. Sith 1.25 3.00
TALES9 Star Wars Tales #9 1.25 3.00

1997 Comic Images Dark Horse Presents Ghost

COMPLETE SET (72) 5.00 12.00
UNOPENED BOX (36 PACKS) 35.00 50.00
UNOPENED PACK (8 CARDS) 1.00 1.50
COMMON CARD (1-72) .12 .30
NNO Congratulations Eric Luke AU/500* 25.00 60.00

1997 Comic Images Dark Horse Presents Ghost Chromium

COMPLETE SET (6) 10.00 25.00
COMMON CARD (C1-C6) 3.00 8.00
STATED ODDS 1:18

1997 Comic Images Dark Horse Presents Ghost Promos

P1 Ships May 1997 1.25 3.00
P2 Ships May 1997 1.25 3.00

1993 Imagine Dark Shadows

COMPLETE SET (62) 6.00 15.00
UNOPENED BOX (36 PACKS) 30.00 40.00
UNOPENED PACK (5 CARDS) 1.00 1.25
COMMON CARD (1-62) .20 .50

1993 Imagine Dark Shadows Promos

1 (wedding preparation) 1.00 2.50
2 (presenting cane) 1.00 2.50
3 (presenting ring) 1.00 2.50
NNO (unsigned autograph, same scene as Promo 3; art by John Graziano)
NNO (unnumbered, same image as above, blank back; oversized 5" x 7") 1.00 2.50

2000-01 Dynamic Forces DarkChylde 5th Anniversary

COMPLETE BOXED SET (6) 6.00 15.00
COMMON CARD 1.50 4.00

1997 Krome DarkChylde

COMPLETE SET (50) 12.00 30.00
UNOPENED BOX (32 PACKS) 20.00 30.00
UNOPENED PACK (5 CARDS) 1.00 1.25
COMMON CARD (1-50) .30 .75
*HOLOCHROME: .5X TO 1.2X BASIC CARDS .40 1.00
*CLEARCHROME: .75X TO 2X BASIC CARDS .60 1.50

1997 Top Cow The Darkness Witchblade Family Ties

COMPLETE SET (90) 6.00 15.00
UNOPENED BOX (48 PACKS) 25.00 40.00
UNOPENED PACK (6 CARDS) 1.00 1.25
COMMON CARD (1-90) .12 .30

1997 Top Cow The Darkness Witchblade Family Ties Puzzle Portrait Foil

COMPLETE SET (9) 12.00 30.00
COMMON CARD (1-9) 2.00 5.00
STATED ODDS 1:4

1997 Top Cow The Darkness Witchblade Family Ties Signatures

COMPLETE SET (3) 8.00 20.00
COMMON CARD 3.00 8.00
STATED ODDS 1:48

1997 Top Cow The Darkness Witchblade Family Ties The Darkness Motion

NNO Congratulations 15.00 40.00
NNO Congratulations (redemption)

1997 Top Cow The Darkness Witchblade Family Ties Promos

COMMON CARD (UNNUMBERED) .75 2.00
NNO Same Front Image as Above 2.00 5.00

1994 FPG Darrell K. Sweet

COMPLETE SET (90) 4.00 10.00
UNOPENED BOX (36 PACKS) 15.00 25.00
UNOPENED PACK (10 CARDS) .50 .75
COMMON CARD (1-90) .10 .25
NNO1 Darrell K. Sweet AU/1000* 50.00
NNO2 Darrell K. Sweet 10-Card Panel AU

1994 FPG Darrell K. Sweet Metallic Storm

COMPLETE SET (5) 12.00 30.00
COMMON CARD (MS1-MS5) 3.00 8.00
STATED ODDS 1:12

1994 FPG Darrell K. Sweet Promos

P1 Knight on Horse .60 1.50
P2 Slain Dragon .60 1.50
NNO Deluxe #19

1993 Jamison David and Goliath Story

COMPLETE BOXED SET (19) 3.00 8.00
COMMON CARD (1-18) .25 .60
NNO2 The Attack PROMO .75 2.00

1995 FPG David Cherry

COMPLETE SET (90) 5.00 12.00
UNOPENED BOX (36 PACKS) 30.00 40.00
UNOPENED PACK (10 CARDS) 1.00 1.25
COMMON CARD (1-90) .12 .30
NNO David A. Cherry AU/1000* 20.00 50.00
P27 Promo Sheet PROMO

1995 FPG David Cherry Metallic

COMPLETE SET (5) 10.00 25.00
COMMON CARD (M1-M5) 2.50 6.00
STATED ODDS 1:12

1995 FPG David Mattingly

COMPLETE SET (90) 5.00 12.00
UNOPENED BOX (36 PACKS) 30.00 40.00
UNOPENED PACK (10 CARDS) 1.00 1.25
COMMON CARD (1-90) .12 .30
NNO1 David B. Mattingly AU/1000* 20.00 50.00
NNO2 Oversized PROMO

1995 FPG David Mattingly Metallic

COMPLETE SET (5) 10.00 25.00
COMMON CARD (M1-M5) 2.50 6.00
STATED ODDS 1:12

1995 Comic Images Dawn and Beyond

COMPLETE SET (90) 6.00 15.00
UNOPENED BOX (48 PACKS) 100.00 120.00
UNOPENED PACK (10 CARDS) 2.50 3.00
COMMON CARD (1-90) .12 .30
SP Showcase Presentation Card
MED Medallion Card/4,735* 10.00 25.00
UNC (6-card panel) (Album Exclusive)
JMLAU Joseph Michael Linsner AU/500* 20.00 50.00
NNO Promo (Dealer Exclusive)

1995 Comic Images Dawn and Beyond Chromium

COMPLETE SET (6) 10.00 25.00
COMMON CARD (C1-C6) 2.50 6.00
STATED ODDS 1:16

1995 Comic Images Dawn and Beyond Dawn Subset

COMPLETE SET (3) 12.00 30.00
COMMON CARD (SS1-SS3) 6.00 15.00
STATED ODDS 1:48

1998 Sirius Dawn Another Set

COMPLETE SET (72) 4.00 10.00
UNOPENED BOX (36 PACKS) 30.00 40.00
UNOPENED PACK (7 CARDS) 1.25 1.50
COMMON CARD (1-72) .12 .30
OS Oversized Card ALB
JMLAU Joseph Michael Linsner AU/1000* 25.00 60.00

1998 Sirius Dawn Another Set Special Inserts

COMPLETE SET (5) 12.00 30.00
COMMON CARD (C1-C5) 3.00 8.00
RANDOMLY INSERTED INTO PACKS

2018 Fright-Rags Dawn of the Dead

COMPLETE SET W/SP (80) 20.00 50.00
COMPLETE SET W/O SP (73) 15.00 40.00
COMMON CARD (1-73) .40 1.00
COMMON SP (74-80) 1.25 3.00
*RED: .75X TO 2X BASIC CARDS .75 2.00
*RAINBOW FOIL: 1X TO 2.5X BASIC CARDS 1.00 2.50
CL Checklist .50 1.25

2018 Fright-Rags Dawn of the Dead Stickers

COMPLETE SET (9) 8.00 20.00
COMMON CARD (UNNUMBERED) 1.25 3.00
STATED ODDS 1:1

2021 Fright-Rags Day of the Dead

COMPLETE SET (83) 30.00 75.00
UNOPENED BOX (24 PACKS) 200.00 350.00
UNOPENED PACK (9 CARDS+1 STICKER) 8.00 15.00
COMMON CARD (1-83) .75 2.00
*PARALLEL: X TO X BASIC CARDS

2021 Fright-Rags Day of the Dead Autographs

COMMON AUTO
RANDOMLY INSERTED INTO PACKS
NNO Antone DiLeo 100.00 200.00
NNO Gary Klar
NNO Greg Nicotero 125.00 250.00
NNO Jarlath Conroy 75.00 150.00
NNO Lori Cardille 125.00 250.00
NNO Terry Alexander

2021 Fright-Rags Day of the Dead Stickers

COMPLETE SET (9) 12.00 30.00
COMMON STICKER 2.00 5.00
STATED ODDS 1:1

2002 Definitive Dawn

COMPLETE SET (72) 5.00 12.00
UNOPENED BOX (36 PACKS) 55.00 70.00
UNOPENED PACK (7 CARDS) 2.00 2.50
COMMON CARD (1-72) .12 .30
SK Linsner Sketch/650* 20.00 50.00
UNC 6-up Rainbow Chrome Panel Linsner AU/699*

2002 Definitive Dawn Autographs

COMMON CARD (A1-A10; B1) 8.00 20.00
STATED ODDS 1:18
STATED PRINT RUN 999 SER.#'d SETS
ALL CARDS SIGNED BY JOSEPH LINSNER
B1 IS AN ALBUM EXCLUSIVE

2002 Definitive Dawn Box-Toppers

COMPLETE SET (2) 2.00 5.00
COMMON CARD (T1-T2) 1.25 3.00
STATED ODDS 1:BOX

2002 Definitive Dawn Rainbow Chromium

COMPLETE SET (6) 10.00 25.00
COMMON CARD (C1-C6)) 2.50 6.00
STATED ODDS 1:12

2002 Definitive Dawn Promos

NNO1 The Definitive Dawn .75 2.00
NNO2 The Definitive Dawn AU/399 (Diamond Distribution Exclusive)

1993 Eagle Daytona Beach Bike Week Promos

1 Forever Panheads 2.00 5.00
2 HD Indian 2.00 5.00
3 One Wheel 2.00 5.00
4 Day at the Beach 2.00 5.00
NNO Vacation/1000*

2004 The Dead Zone Seasons One and Two

COMPLETE SET (100) 4.00 10.00
UNOPENED BOX (40 PACKS) 45.00 50.00
UNOPENED PACK (5 CARDS) 1.25 1.50
UNOPENED ARCHIVE BOX 150.00 250.00
COMMON CARD (1-100) .10 .30

2004 The Dead Zone Seasons One and Two Autographs

COMMON CARD 3.00 8.00
STATED ODDS TWO PER BOX
L (LIMITED): 300-500 COPIES
13 ISSUED ALBUM EXCLUSIVE
14 ISSUED AS MULTI-CASE INCENTIVE
3 Ally Sheedy L 30.00 75.00
5 Anthony Michael Hall L 50.00 100.00
9 John L. Adams L 12.00 30.00
10 Julie Patzwald 5.00 12.00
11 Kristen Dalton L 15.00 40.00
13 Rick Tae ALB 10.00 25.00
14 Robert Picardo CI 25.00 60.00
16 Sean Patrick Flanery L 20.00 50.00

2004 The Dead Zone Seasons One and Two Behind-the-Scenes

COMPLETE SET (13) 5.00 12.00
COMMON CARD (B1-B13) .50 1.25
STATED ODDS 1:5

2004 The Dead Zone Seasons One and Two Casting Call

COMPLETE SET (5) 25.00 60.00
COMMON CARD (DZ1-DZ5) 5.00 12.00
STATED ODDS 1:160
DZ5 ISSUED AS CASE TOPPER
DZ5 Cast CT 15.00 30.00

2004 The Dead Zone Seasons One and Two Stars of the Zone

COMPLETE SET (7) 5.00 12.00
COMMON CARD (S1-S7) .75 2.00
STATED ODDS 1:20

2004 The Dead Zone Seasons One and Two Promos

P1 Group of five .75 2.00
P2 Johnny Smith/Sarah Bannerman .75 2.00
P3 Group of seven 3.00 8.00

2006 The Dead Zone Autograph Expansion

COMMON CARD 5.00 12.00
DEBOER/BRUNO AUTO ISSUED AS 2-SET INCENTIVE
2 Anne Marie Loder 6.00 15.00
3 Anthony Michael Hall 20.00 50.00
6 Frank Whaley 6.00 15.00
7 Ione Skye 6.00 15.00
10 Nicole deBoer 15.00 40.00
11 Nicole deBoer/Chris Bruno 2SI 20.00 50.00

2012 Deadworld

COMPLETE SET (72) 5.00 12.00
UNOPENED PREMIUM PACK 60.00 70.00
COMMON CARD (1-72) .12 .30

2012 Deadworld 3-D Lenticular

COMPLETE SET (15) 20.00 50.00
COMMON CARD (DW3D1-DW3D15) 1.50 4.00
STATED ODDS 5:1

2012 Deadworld Girls of Deadworld Holographic

COMPLETE SET (12) 15.00 40.00
COMMON CARD (DWG1-DWG12) 2.50 6.00
STATED ODDS 4:1

1991 Escape Cards The Dean Gunnarson Collection

COMPLETE SET (40) 5.00 12.00
COMMON CARD (1-40) .25 .60

1991 Escape Cards The Dean Gunnarson Collection Promo

NNO Promo 1.25 3.00

1993 Upper Deck Deathmate

COMPLETE SET (110) 3.00 8.00
UNOPENED BOX (36 PACKS) 30.00 40.00
UNOPENED PACK (8 CARDS) 1.25 1.50
COMMON CARD (1-110) .06 .15

1993 Upper Deck Deathmate Lithograms

COMPLETE SET (2) 10.00 25.00
COMMON CARD (D1-D2) 6.00 15.00
STATED ODDS 1:90

1993 Upper Deck Deathmate Players of Deathmate

COMPLETE SET (6) 12.00 30.00
COMMON CARD (P1-P6) 2.50 6.00
STATED ODDS 1:18

1993 Upper Deck Deathmate Transitions

COMPLETE SET (8) 20.00 50.00
COMMON CARD (T1-T8) 3.00 8.00
STATED ODDS 1:12

1993 Classic Deathwatch 2000

COMPLETE SET (100) 6.00 15.00
UNOPENED BOX (36 PACKS) 20.00 30.00
UNOPENED PACK (8 CARDS) 1.00 1.25
UNOPENED JUMBO BOX (20 PACKS)
UNOPENED JUMBO PACK (16 CARDS)
COMMON CARD (1-100) .12 .30
NNO Neal Adams AUTO 20.00 50.00

1993 Classic Deathwatch 2000 Hybrid Cels

COMPLETE SET (7) 12.00 30.00
COMMON CARD (HC1-HC7) 2.50 6.00
RANDOMLY INSERTED INTO PACKS

1993 Classic Deathwatch 2000 Prisms

COMPLETE SET (20) 12.00 30.00
COMMON CARD (BC1-BC20) 1.50 3.00
STATED ODDS ONE PER JUMBO PACK

1993 Classic Deathwatch 2000 Sport Superheros

COMPLETE SET (3) 25.00 60.00
COMMON CARD (SS1-SS3) 8.00 20.00
RANDOMLY INSERTED INTO PACKS
SS1 Shaquille O'Neal 12.00 30.00
SS3 Ken Griffey, Jr. 10.00 25.00

1993 Classic Deathwatch 2000 Promos

PR1 Desperate Rescue .60 1.50
PR1 Desperate Rescue 2.00 5.00
May 2-5, 1993 Capitol
PR2 Escape From Death-Jaws .60 1.50
PR3 Inches From Death .60 1.50
PR4 Lith Kasti .60 1.50
PR5 Valeria the She-Bat .60 1.50

1992 Wild Card Decision '92

COMPLETE SET (100) 6.00 15.00
UNOPENED BOX (36 PACKS) 15.00 25.00
UNOPENED PACK (8 CARDS) .75 1.00
COMMON CARD (1-100) .12 .30
*5-STRIPE: 1.25X TO 3X BASIC CARDS .40 1.00
*10-STRIPE: 1.5X TO 4X BASIC CARDS .50 1.25
*20-STRIPE: 2X TO 5X BASIC CARDS .60 1.50
*50-STRIPE: 2.5X TO 6X BASIC CARDS .75 2.00
*100-STRIPE: 4X TO 10X BASIC CARDS 1.25 3.00
*1000-STRIPE: 20X TO 50X BASIC CARDS 6.00 15.00

1992 Wild Card Decision '92 Ross Perot

COMPLETE SET (5) 2.00 5.00
COMMON CARD (1-5) .60 1.50
RANDOMLY INSERTED INTO PACKS

1992 Wild Card Decision '92 Promos

COMPLETE SET (6) 5.00 12.00
COMMON CARD (P1-P6) 1.25 3.00

2016 Decision 2016

COMPLETE SET (340) 120.00 250.00
COMPLETE SET W/O SP (298) 75.00 150.00
COMPLETE SER.1 SET (135) 30.00 80.00
COMPLETE SER.1 SET W/O SP (110) 5.00 12.00
COMPLETE SER.2 SET (111) 60.00 120.00
COMPLETE UPDATE SET (94) 50.00 100.00
COMPLETE UPDATE SET W/O SP (77) 20.00 50.00
UNOPENED SER.1 BOX (24 PACKS) 30.00 50.00
UNOPENED SER.1 PACK (6 CARDS) 2.00 3.00
UNOPENED SER.2 BOX (30 CARDS) 100.00 120.00
UNOPENED UPDATE BOX (30 CARDS) 100.00 120.00
COMMON CARD (1-110) .25 .60
COMMON SP (111-135) 2.00 5.00
COMMON SER.2 CARD (136-246) .75 2.00
COMMON UPDATE CARD (247-323) .75 2.00
COMMON UPDATE SP (324-340) 2.00 5.00
*A.A.GOLD: .5X TO 1.2X BASIC CARDS .30 .75
*A.A.BLUE: .6X TO 1.5X BASIC CARDS .40 1.00
*A.A.RED: .75X TO 2X BASIC CARDS .50 1.25
SERIES 2 & UPDATE DO NOT CONTAIN PARALLELS
1 Ben Carson .75 2.00
2 Bernie Sanders 2.50 6.00
3 Bobby Jindal .40 1.00
4A Carly Fiorina ERR (reverse negative) 8.00 20.00
4B Carly Fiorina COR 1.50 4.00
5 Chris Christie .50 1.25
6 Donald Trump 2.50 6.00
8 Hillary Clinton 1.50 4.00
15A Lincoln Chaffee ERR 1.50 4.00
(last name misspelled)
15B Lincoln Chafee COR 1.25 3.00
16 Lindsey Graham .75 2.00
17 Marco Rubio .40 1.00
19 Mike Huckabee .30 .75
20 Rand Paul .40 1.00
21A Rick Perry ERR 2.00 5.00
(Rick Santorum Name on Front)
21B Rick Perry COR 6.00 15.00
22 Rick Santorum .40 1.00
24 Ted Cruz .60 1.50
25 Al Franken .60 1.50
26 Bill Clinton 1.25 3.00
31 Elizabeth Warren 1.25 3.00
33 Ivanka Trump 2.00 5.00
37 John McCain .40 1.00
40 Michelle Obama 2.00 5.00
41 Mitch McConnell .40 1.00
45 Paul Ryan .75 2.00
46 President Obama 2.00 5.00
47 Reince Priebus .40 1.00
48 Ronald Reagan 1.50 4.00
49 Sarah Palin 1.50 4.00
50A Tom Kaine ERR .60 1.50
(first name misspelled)
50B Tim Kaine COR 2.00 5.00
63 Melania Trump 2.00 5.00
64 Bill Clinton 1.25 3.00
77 Ben Carson .75 2.00
78 Bernie Sanders 1.50 4.00
81 Donald Trump 1.50 4.00
82 Hillary Clinton 1.25 3.00
88 Rand Paul COR 6.00 15.00
(case-incentive)
89 Rick Santorum .50 1.25
97 President Barack Obama 1.50 4.00
107 Mike Pence .75 2.00
108B Pat McCrory COR 1.25 3.00
112 Gary Johnson SP 4.00 10.00
115 George W. Bush SP 3.00 8.00
117 Tulsi Gabbard SP 3.00 8.00
123 Palin endorses Trump SP 3.00 8.00
131 Trump Huge SP 2.50 6.00
135 Trump Wins Nevada SP 2.50 6.00
137 Donald Trump 2.50 6.00
139 Gary Johnson 1.25 3.00
140 Hillary Clinton 1.50 4.00
142 Mike Pence 2.00 5.00
146 Bill Clinton 1.50 4.00
148 Melania Trump 2.50 6.00
151 Kamala Harris 2.00 5.00
155 Tulsi Gabbard 2.00 5.00
159 Elizabeth Warren 2.00 5.00
160 Jeff Sessions 2.50 6.00
170 Ben Carson 1.25 3.00
172 Bernie Sanders 1.50 4.00
177 Donald Trump Jr. .75 2.00
178 Eric Trump .75 2.00
180 Ivanka Trump 2.50 6.00
187 Justin Trudeau 2.50 6.00
192 Paul Ryan 1.00 2.50
198 Sheriff Joe Arpaio 2.00 5.00
207 Elizabeth Warren 2.50 6.00
213 Kellyanne Conway 3.00 8.00
215 Sarah Palin 2.00 5.00
243 Ross Perot 1.25 3.00
244 Ron Paul 1.50 4.00
245 Vladimir Putin 4.00 10.00
246 Julian Assange 1.50 4.00
250 First Lady Melania Trump 6.00 15.00
260 Kellyanne Conway 2.00 5.00
262 Sean Spicer 2.00 5.00
264 Ivanka Trump 3.00 8.00
280A James Mattis 1.50 4.00
280B James Mad Dog Mattis 2.50 6.00
285B Andrew Puzder 2.00 5.00
333B Sarah Huckabee SP 5.00 10.00
337 Robert Mueller SP 5.00 12.00

2016 Decision 2016 Battleground States

COMPLETE SET (10) 15.00 40.00
COMMON CARD (BGS1-BGS10) 2.00 5.00
STATED ODDS 1:BOX
SERIES 2 EXCLUSIVE

2016 Decision 2016 Candidate Portraits

COMPLETE SET W/O SP (44) 30.00 80.00
COMPLETE SET W/SP (58) 60.00 120.00
COMMON CARD (CP1-CP28) 1.50 4.00
COMMON SP (CP1-CP59) 2.50 6.00
COMMON SERIES 2 CARD (CP29-CP59) 2.00 5.00
COMMON SERIES 2 SP 2.50 6.00
COMMON UPDATE CARD (CP60-CP66) 2.50 6.00
*RETAIL: SAME VALUE AS HOBBY
STATED ODDS 1:6 HOBBY; 1:10 RETAIL
RETAIL VERSIONS ARE BLACK AND WHITE
SERIES 2 HAS NO RETAIL VERSION
CP1 Barack Obama 3.00 8.00
CP3 Bernie Sanders 2.00 5.00
CP4 Bill Clinton 2.50 6.00
CP5 Carly Fiorina 2.00 5.00
CP7A Donald Trump (smiling) 6.00 15.00
CP7B Donald Trump (not smiling) SP 8.00 20.00
CP8 George W. Bush 2.00 5.00
CP9 Hillary Clinton 3.00 8.00
CP17 Ronald Reagan 3.00 8.00
CP19 George H. W. Bush SP 6.00 15.00
CP20 Mitt Romney SP 5.00 12.00
CP21 Joe Biden SP CI 4.00 10.00
CP22 Sarah Palin SP 8.00 20.00
CP23 Lindsey Graham SP 3.00 8.00
CP25 John McCain SP 3.00 8.00
CP26 Rick Santorum SP 4.00 10.00
CP28 Gary Johnson SP CI 6.00 15.00
CP29 Al Gore 2.50 6.00
CP33 Donald Trump 5.00 12.00
CP34 Dwight D Eisenhower 2.50 6.00
CP35 George H.W. Bush 3.00 8.00
CP38 Gary Johnson 2.50 6.00
CP40 Hillary Clinton 3.00 8.00
CP45 John F. Kennedy 4.00 10.00
CP48 Mike Pence 4.00 10.00
CP49 Newt Gingrich 2.50 6.00
CP50 Richard Nixon 3.00 8.00
CP51 Robert Kennedy 3.00 8.00
CP54 William Weld 2.50 6.00
CP55 Walter Mondale SP 3.00 8.00
CP56 Michael Dukakis SP 4.00 10.00
CP58 Nelson Rockefeller SP 3.00 8.00
CP59 Victoria Woodhull SP 4.00 10.00
CP60 Donald J. Trump 3.00 8.00
CP62 George Washington 4.00 10.00
CP63 Ralph Nadar 4.00 10.00
CP64 Jerry Brown 3.00 8.00
CP65 Mike Pence 3.00 8.00
CP66 Thomas Jefferson 3.00 8.00

2016 Decision 2016 The Clinton Controversies

COMPLETE SET (42) 60.00 120.00
COMPLETE SERIES 2 SET (24) 30.00 80.00
COMPLETE UPDATE SET (18) 20.00 50.00
COMMON SERIES 2 CARD (CC1-CC24) 1.50 4.00
COMMON UPDATE CARD (CC25-CC42) 1.50 4.00
*GOLD: SAME VALUE 1.50 4.00
*PINK: .5X TO 1.2X BASIC CARDS 2.00 5.00
*GREEN: .6X TO 1.5X BASIC CARDS 2.50 6.00
*BLUE: .75X TO 2X BASIC CARDS 3.00 8.00
*RED: 1X TO 2.5X BASIC CARDS 4.00 10.00
*ICE BLUE: 1.2X TO 3X BASIC CARDS 5.00 12.00
STATED ODDS 3:BOX
ICE BLUE IS UPDATE EXCLUSIVE

2016 Decision 2016 Cut Signatures

COMMON CARD (CS1-CS22) 15.00 40.00
STATED ODDS 1 PER CASE
CS2 Donald Trump 600.00 1200.00
CS3 George W. Bush SP 100.00 200.00
CS4 Hillary Clinton 200.00 400.00
CS5 Jeb Bush 30.00 75.00
CS8 Rand Paul 25.00 60.00
CS11 John Kasich 30.00 75.00
CS12 Ted Cruz SP 30.00 75.00
CS13 Carly Fiorina SP 30.00 75.00
CS15 Mitt Romney SP 25.00 60.00
CS17 Martin O'Malley 30.00 75.00
CS18 Rick Perry 25.00 60.00
CS19 Paul Ryan 60.00 120.00
CS20 John McCain 30.00 75.00
CS21 Sarah Palin SP 150.00 300.00
CS22 Bernie Sanders SP 150.00 300.00

2016 Decision 2016 Cut Signatures Series 2

STATED ODDS 1:4 BOXES
NNO Barack Obama 300.00 600.00
NNO Barbara Boxer 30.00 80.00
NNO Ben Carson 20.00 50.00
NNO Bernie Sanders 250.00 500.00
NNO Bill Clinton 250.00 500.00
NNO Bobby Jindal 25.00 60.00
NNO Carly Fiorina 25.00 60.00
NNO Chris Christie 25.00 60.00
NNO Donald Trump 800.00 1200.00
NNO Donald Trump SP 1000.00 1600.00
NNO Elizabeth Warren 120.00 250.00
NNO George W. Bush 120.00 250.00
NNO Hillary Clinton 120.00 250.00
NNO Hillary Clinton SP 200.00 400.00
NNO Jeb Bush 25.00 60.00
NNO Jimmy Carter 80.00 150.00
NNO Joe Biden 500.00 1000.00
NNO John Kasich 30.00 80.00
NNO John McCain 50.00 100.00
NNO Lindsey Graham 50.00 100.00
NNO Marco Rubio 25.00 60.00
NNO Martin O'Malley 120.00 200.00
NNO Mike Pence
NNO Mitt Romney 50.00 100.00
NNO Newt Gingrich 50.00 100.00
NNO Paul Ryan 30.00 75.00
NNO Rand Paul 50.00 100.00
NNO Rick Perry 30.00 75.00
NNO Rick Santorum 20.00 50.00
NNO Rudy Giuliani
NNO Sarah Palin 100.00 200.00
NNO Scott Walker 20.00 50.00
NNO Ted Cruz 25.00 60.00
NNO Tim Kaine

2016 Decision 2016 Cut Signatures Series 2 Update

COMMON CARD	15.00	40.00
NNO Ben Sasse	15.00	40.00
NNO Donald J. Trump	1100.00	2000.00
NNO Donald Trump	500.00	800.00
NNO George W. Bush	150.00	300.00
NNO Hillary Clinton	75.00	150.00
NNO Hillary Rodham Clinton	120.00	200.00
NNO Ivanka	150.00	300.00
NNO Ivanka Trump	200.00	400.00
NNO KellyAnne Conway	250.00	400.00
NNO Nikki Haley	75.00	150.00
NNO W.	150.00	300.00

2016 Decision 2016 Elite Premium

COMPLETE SET (30)	500.00	1000.00
COMPLETE SERIES 1 SET (7)	120.00	250.00
COMPLETE SERIES 2 SET (13)	250.00	500.00
COMPLETE UPDATE SET (10)	150.00	300.00
COMMON CARD (E1-E7)	10.00	25.00
COMMON SER.2 CARD (E8-E20)	10.00	25.00
COMMON UPDATE (E21-E30; PBO)	10.00	25.00
*GREEN: SAME VALUE AS BASIC CARDS		
*BLUE: .5X TO 1.2X BASIC CARDS		
*RED: ..6X TO 1.5X BASIC CARDS		
*ICE BLUE: .6X TO 1.5X BASIC CARDS		
STATED ODDS 1 PER CASE		
ICE BLUE AND GREEN ARE UPDATE EXCLUSIVE		
E1 Justice Scalia SP	12.00	30.00
E2 Nancy Reagan SP	20.00	50.00
E3 Bush Dynasty	12.00	30.00
E5 Trump and Palin	12.00	30.00
E6 The White House	12.00	30.00
E7 George Washington	20.00	50.00
E8 Lincoln Memorial	15.00	40.00
E10 Statue of Liberty	15.00	40.00
E11 Bernie - FEEL THE BERN	12.00	30.00
E12 Five Presidents	30.00	75.00
E13 Five First Ladies	25.00	60.00
E14 Kennedy - Nixon first debate	15.00	40.00
E20 Mount Rushmore	25.00	60.00
E21 John Glenn	20.00	50.00
E24 Fidel Castro	12.00	30.00
E25 Andrew Jackson	15.00	40.00
E26 Abraham Lincoln	20.00	50.00
E27 Dr. Martin Luther King Jr.	12.00	30.00
E30 Donald J. Trump	20.00	50.00
PBO Obama Presidential Premium	12.00	30.00

2016 Decision 2016 First Lady Portraits

COMPLETE SET (15)	60.00	120.00
COMPLETE SERIES 1 SET (9)	30.00	80.00
COMPLETE SERIES 2 SET (4)	10.00	25.00
COMPLETE UPDATE SET (2)	8.00	20.00
COMMON CARD (FLP1-FLP9)	2.00	5.00
COMMON CARD (FLP10-FLP13)	2.50	6.00
COMMON CARD (FLP14-FLP15)	3.00	8.00
STATED ODDS 1:24 RETAIL ONLY		
FLP2 Michelle Obama	5.00	12.00
FLP3 Hillary Clinton	3.00	8.00
FLP5 Nancy Reagan	4.00	10.00
FLP6 Jacqueline Kennedy	5.00	12.00
FLP7 Rosalynn Carter	3.00	8.00
FLP8 Betty Ford	3.00	8.00
FLP9 Pat Nixon	4.00	10.00
FL10 Lady Bird Johnson SP	3.00	8.00
FLP14 Melania Trump	5.00	12.00

2016 Decision 2016 God Bless America Mini Flag Patches

COMMON SERIES 1 CARD (GBA1-GBA18)	6.00	15.00
COMMON SERIES 2 CARD (GBA19-GBA47)	6.00	15.00
*GREEN: .5X TO 1.2X BASIC CARDS		
*BLUE: .6X TO 1.5X BASIC CARDS		
*RED: .6X TO 1.5X BASIC CARDS		
STATED ODDS 4:CASE		
GBA1 Barack Obama	12.00	30.00
GBA3 Bernie Sanders	8.00	20.00
GBA4 Bill Clinton	10.00	25.00
GBA7 Donald Trump	15.00	40.00
GBA10 John Kasich	12.00	30.00
GBA14 Rand Paul	8.00	20.00
GBA15 Ronald Reagan	20.00	50.00
GBA16 Ted Cruz	8.00	20.00
GBA17 Hillary Clinton SP	15.00	40.00
GBA18 Donald Trump SP	15.00	40.00
GBA19 Bill Clinton	8.00	20.00
GBA22 Donald & Melania Trump	25.00	60.00
GBA23 Donald Trump	15.00	40.00
GBA27 George H.W. Bush	8.00	20.00
GBA28 Hillary Clinton	8.00	20.00
GBA29 James Comey	12.00	30.00
GBA30 Jill Stein	8.00	20.00
GBA31 John F. Kennedy	12.00	30.00
GBA33 Mike Pence	12.00	30.00
GBA36 Ronald Reagan	12.00	30.00
GBA42 Tulsi Gabbard	10.00	25.00
GBA44 Donald Trump SP	20.00	50.00
GBA45 Hillary Clinton SP	8.00	20.00
GBA47 Ted Cruz SP	12.00	30.00

2016 Decision 2016 Inauguration Premium

COMPLETE SET (9)	60.00	120.00
COMMON CARD (IP1-IP9)	6.00	15.00
*GREEN: SAME VALUE	6.00	15.00
*BLUE: .5X TO 1.2X BASIC CARDS	8.00	20.00
*RED: .6X TO 1.5X BASIC CARDS	10.00	25.00
*ICE BLUE: .6X TO 1.5X BASIC CARDS	10.00	25.00
RANDOMLY INSERTED INTO PACKS		
UPDATE EXCLUSIVE		

2016 Decision 2016 Jumbo Box-Toppers

COMPLETE SET (24)	60.00	120.00
COMMON CARD (J1-J24)	2.50	6.00
STATED ODDS 1:BOX		
J1 Barack Obama	4.00	10.00
J3 Bernie Sanders	3.00	8.00
J4 Bill Clinton	3.00	8.00
J5 Carly Fiorina SP	3.00	8.00
J7 Donald Trump	6.00	15.00
J8 Elizabeth Warren SP (very limited)	3.00	8.00
J9 George W. Bush SP	4.00	10.00
J10 Hillary Clinton	6.00	15.00
J12 Joe Biden SP	5.00	12.00
J14 Bernie and Hillary e-mails	5.00	12.00
J18 Michelle Obama SP	5.00	12.00
J20 Mitt Romney SP	3.00	8.00
J22 Ronald Reagan	4.00	10.00
J23 Sarah Palin SP (very limited)	3.00	8.00
J24 Ted Cruz	3.00	8.00

2016 Decision 2016 Money Relics

COMMON SERIES 1 (MO1-MO18)	15.00	40.00
COMMON SERIES 2 (MO19-MO38)	15.00	40.00
COMMON UPDATE (MO39-MO56)	15.00	40.00
*GREEN: SAME VALUE AS BASIC RELICS		
*BLUE: .5X TO 1.2X BASIC RELICS		
*RED: .5X TO 1.2X BASIC RELICS		
*ICE BLUE: .6X TO 1.5X BASIC RELICS		
STATED ODDS 1:2 CASES		
ICE BLUE IS UPDATE EXCLUSIVE		
MO1 Barack Obama	75.00	150.00
MO2 Ben Carson	25.00	60.00
MO3 Bernie Sanders	60.00	120.00
MO4 Bill Clinton	60.00	120.00
MO6 Chris Christie	20.00	50.00
MO7 Donald Trump	200.00	400.00
MO8 George W. Bush	75.00	150.00
MO9 Hillary Clinton	60.00	120.00
MO10 Jeb Bush	20.00	50.00
MO13 Michael Bloomberg	50.00	100.00
MO17 Ronald Reagan	50.00	100.00
MO18 Ted Cruz	25.00	60.00
MO19 Bernie Sanders	75.00	150.00
MO21 Dick Cheney	25.00	60.00
MO22 Donald Trump	200.00	400.00
MO23 Elizabeth Warren	20.00	50.00
MO24 Gary Johnson	25.00	60.00
MO25 Hillary Clinton	30.00	75.00
MO27 John F. Kennedy	75.00	150.00
MO28 Mike Pence	30.00	75.00
MO29 Newt Gingrich	25.00	60.00
MO31 Richard Nixon	50.00	100.00
MO34 Sarah Palin	30.00	75.00
MO35 Tim Geithner SP UER (Bernie Sanders back)	30.00	75.00
MO38 George Soros SP	50.00	100.00
MO39 Donald J. Trump	60.00	120.00
MO41 Barack Obama	25.00	60.00
MO42 Bernie Sanders	20.00	50.00
MO44 Ivanka Trump	50.00	100.00
MO51 Melania Trump	30.00	75.00

2016 Decision 2016 Party Pals Bookcards

COMMON CARD	6.00	15.00
*BLUE: .5X TO 1.2X BASIC CARDS	8.00	20.00
*RED: .6X TO 1.5X BASIC CARDS	10.00	25.00
RANDOMLY INSERTED INTO PACKS		
UPDATE EXCLUSIVE		
NNO Barack Obama/Hillary Clinton	10.00	25.00
NNO Barack Obama/Joe Biden	8.00	20.00
NNO Donald Trump/Chris Christie	8.00	20.00
NNO Donald Trump/Melania Trump	20.00	50.00
NNO Donald Trump/Mike Pence	12.00	30.00
NNO Donald Trump/Rudy Giuliani	10.00	25.00
NNO George H.W. Bush/George W. Bush	12.00	30.00
NNO Hillary Clinton/Elizabeth Warren	12.00	30.00
NNO Hillary Clinton/George Soros	8.00	20.00

2016 Decision 2016 Pieces of America

COMMON SERIES 1 CARD (PA1-PA21)	5.00	12.00
COMMON SERIES 2 CARD (PA22-PA53)	5.00	12.00
COMMON UPDATE CARD (PA54-PA71)	6.00	15.00
*GREEN: SAME VALUE AS BASIC CARDS		
*BLUE: ..5X TO 1.2X BASIC CARDS		
*RED: ..6X TO 1.5X BASIC CARDS		
STATED ODDS 1:CASE		
PA1A Hillary Clinton (IL)	15.00	40.00
PA1B Hillary Clinton (NY) SP	12.00	30.00
PA2A Donald Trump (NY)	20.00	50.00
PA2B Donald Trump (FL) SP	15.00	40.00
PA3A Bernie Sanders (VT)	12.00	30.00
PA3B Bernie Sanders (NY) SP	10.00	25.00
PA4 Marco Rubio (FL)	6.00	15.00
PA5 Ted Cruz (TX)	10.00	25.00
PA6 John Kasich (OH)	6.00	15.00
PA7 Ben Carson (MI)	10.00	25.00
PA8 Bill Clinton (AR)	6.00	15.00
PA9 George W. Bush (TX)	12.00	30.00
PA10 Barack Obama (HI)	15.00	40.00
PA11 Chris Christie (NJ)	6.00	15.00
PA12 Jeb Bush (FL)	10.00	25.00
PA13A Mitt Romney (UT)	6.00	15.00
PA13B Mitt Romney (MA) SP	8.00	20.00
PA14 Rand Paul (KY)	8.00	20.00
PA17 Mike Bloomberg (NY)	8.00	20.00
PA18 Ronald Reagan (CA)	10.00	25.00
PA19 Carly Fiorina (VA)	8.00	20.00
PA20 Sarah Palin (AK)	10.00	25.00
PA21 Joe Biden (PA)	8.00	20.00
PA22 Bill Clinton (AR)	10.00	25.00
PA23 Dick Cheney (NE)	10.00	25.00
PA24 Donald Trump (NY)	30.00	75.00
PA25 Elizabeth Warren (OK)	12.00	30.00
PA27A Gary Johnson (ND)	12.00	30.00
PA27B Gary Johnson (NM)	10.00	25.00
PA28 George H.W. Bush (MA)	12.00	30.00
PA29 Hillary Clinton (NY)	10.00	25.00
PA30 Jill Stein (MA)	10.00	25.00
PA31 Joe Biden (PA)	6.00	15.00
PA32 John F. Kennedy (MA)	30.00	75.00
PA33 John McCain (AZ)	10.00	25.00
PA34 Mike Pence (IN)	12.00	30.00
PA35 Newt Gingrich (PA)	12.00	30.00
PA36 Paul Ryan (WI)	10.00	25.00
PA37 Ronald Reagan (CA)	15.00	40.00
PA38 Rudy Giuliani (NY)	10.00	25.00
PA39 Sarah Palin (AK)	10.00	25.00
PA41A William Weld (MA)	40.00	80.00
PA41B William Weld (NY)	40.00	80.00
PA42 Jill Stein (IL)	6.00	15.00
PA44 Hillary Clinton (IL)	10.00	25.00
PA45 Ronald Reagan (IL)	20.00	50.00
PA46 Donald Trump (FL)	30.00	75.00
PA47 Colin Powell (NY)	12.00	30.00
PA48 Donald J. Trump (DC)	20.00	50.00
PA49 Al Franken (MN)	10.00	25.00
PA50 Arnold Schwarzenegger (CA)	15.00	40.00
PA51 Barack Obama (DC)	12.00	30.00
PA52 Bernie Sanders (NY)	10.00	25.00
PA53 Chuck Schumer (NY)	10.00	25.00
PA54 Ivanka Trump (NY)	12.00	30.00
PA55 James Mattis "Mad Dog" (WA)	12.00	30.00
PA58 Justin Trudeau (Canada)	12.00	30.00
PA59 Kellyanne Conway (DC)	8.00	20.00
PA60 Melania Trump (DC)	15.00	40.00
PA61 Mike Pence (DC)	15.00	40.00
PA64 Nikki Haley (SC)	10.00	25.00
PA65 Donald J. Trump (DC) SP	15.00	40.00

2016 Decision 2016 Political Gems

COMMON SERIES 1 CARD (PG1-PG24)	6.00	15.00
COMMON SERIES 2 CARD (PG25-PG44)	6.00	15.00
COMMON UPDATE CARD (PG45-PG62)	6.00	15.00
*GREEN: SAME VALUE AS BASIC CARDS		
*BLUE: .5X TO 1.2X BASIC CARDS		
*RED: .6X TO 1.5X BASIC CARDS		
*ICE BLUE: .75X TO 2X BASIC CARDS		
STATED ODDS 2:CASE		
ICE BLUE IS UPDATE EXCLUSIVE		
G1 Barack Obama	20.00	50.00
G2 Ben Carson	10.00	25.00
G3 Bernie Sanders	15.00	40.00
G4 Bill Clinton	10.00	25.00
G6 Chris Christie	8.00	20.00
G7 Donald Trump	20.00	50.00
G8 George W. Bush	15.00	40.00
G9 Hillary Clinton	15.00	40.00
G10 Jeb Bush	8.00	20.00
G11 John Kasich	8.00	20.00
G13 Michael Bloomberg SP	8.00	20.00
G15 Michelle Obama	12.00	30.00
G16 Rand Paul	8.00	20.00
G17 Ronald Reagan	20.00	50.00
G18 Ted Cruz	8.00	20.00
G19 Mitt Romney SP	12.00	30.00
G21 Melania Trump SP	20.00	50.00
G22 Joe Biden	10.00	25.00
G23 Sarah Palin	20.00	50.00
G24 Donald J. Trump SP	20.00	50.00
PG27 Barack Obama	12.00	30.00
PG29 Donald Trump	12.00	30.00
PG33 Hillary Clinton	8.00	20.00
PG34 Jill Stein	8.00	20.00
PG36 John F. Kennedy	12.00	30.00
PG38 Mike Pence	10.00	25.00
PG41 Ronald Reagan	12.00	30.00
PG42 Rudy Giuliani	8.00	20.00
PG43 Sarah Palin	8.00	20.00
PG45 Donald J. Trump	10.00	25.00
PG47 Arnold Schwarzenegger	8.00	20.00
PG48 Barack Obama	10.00	25.00
PG49 Benjamin Netanyahu	8.00	20.00
PG50 Bernie Sanders	12.00	30.00
PG52 Ivanka Trump	12.00	30.00
PG54 Jeff Sessions	10.00	25.00
PG57 Kellyanne Conway	8.00	20.00
PG58 Linda McMahon	10.00	25.00

2016 Decision 2016 Presidential Premiums Donald J. Trump

COMPLETE SET (10)	75.00	150.00
COMMON CARD (PPDT1-PPDT10)	8.00	20.00
*BLUE: .6X TO 1.5X BASIC CARDS	12.00	30.00
*RED: .75X TO 2X BASIC CARDS	15.00	40.00
STATED ODDS 1:2 BOXES		

2016 Decision 2016 Presidential Premiums Hillary Rodham Clinton

COMPLETE SET (10)	60.00	120.00
COMMON CARD (PPHC1-PPHC10)	6.00	15.00
*BLUE: .6X TO 1.5X BASIC CARDS	10.00	25.00
*RED: .75X TO 2X BASIC CARDS	12.00	30.00
STATED ODDS 1:2 BOXES		

2016 Decision 2016 Road to the White House Letters

COMPLETE SET (68)	400.00	800.00
COMMON CARSON	6.00	15.00
COMMON SANDERS	10.00	25.00
COMMON FIORINA	4.00	10.00
COMMON CHRISTIE	4.00	10.00
COMMON TRUMP	12.00	30.00
COMMON CLINTON	8.00	20.00
COMMON BUSH	6.00	15.00
COMMON KASICH	4.00	10.00
COMMON RUBIO	4.00	10.00
COMMON O'MALLEY	4.00	10.00
COMMON HUCKABEE	4.00	10.00
COMMON CRUZ	6.00	15.00
*BLUE FOIL: .5X TO 1.2X BASIC CARDS		
*RED FOIL: .6X TO 1.5X BASIC CARDS		
STATED ODDS 4:CASE		

2016 Decision 2016 Super Flags Commemorative Jumbo Patches

COMMON SERIES 1 PATCH (SF1-SF23)	6.00	15.00
COMMON SERIES 2 PATCH (SF24-SF49)	6.00	15.00
COMMON UPDATE PATCH (SF50-SF67)	6.00	15.00
*BLUE: .5X TO 1.2X BASIC PATCHES		
*RED: .6X TO 1.5X BASIC PATCHES		
SF1 Barack Obama	25.00	60.00
SF3 Bernie Sanders	10.00	25.00
SF4 Bill Clinton	12.00	30.00
SF5 Carly Fiorina	8.00	20.00
SF6 Chris Christie	8.00	20.00
SF7 Donald Trump	25.00	50.00
SF8 Hillary Clinton	12.00	30.00
SF9 Jeb Bush	10.00	25.00
SF15 Ronald Reagan	20.00	50.00
SF16 Ted Cruz	8.00	20.00
SF17 Hillary Clinton	10.00	25.00
SF18 Donald Trump	15.00	40.00
SF21 Sarah Palin	12.00	30.00
SF22 Michelle Obama	10.00	25.00
SF23 Joe Biden	10.00	25.00
SF24 Bill Clinton	10.00	25.00
SF25 Colin Powell	8.00	20.00
SF26 Dick Cheney	10.00	25.00
SF27 Donald Trump	20.00	50.00
SF28 Elizabeth Warren	12.00	30.00
SF29 Gabby Giffords	12.00	30.00
SF30 Gary Johnson	10.00	25.00
SF31 George H.W. Bush	8.00	20.00
SF32 Hillary Clinton	10.00	25.00
SF33 James Comey	12.00	30.00
SF35 John F. Kennedy	12.00	30.00
SF36 Melania Trump	15.00	40.00
SF37 Mike Pence	8.00	20.00
SF38 Paul Ryan	8.00	20.00
SF39 Ronald Reagan	15.00	40.00
SF41 Sarah Palin	10.00	25.00
SF44 William Weld	15.00	40.00
SF45 Donald Trump SP	15.00	40.00
SF46 Hillary Clinton SP	10.00	25.00
SF47 Ted Cruz SP	8.00	20.00
SF49 Michael T. Flynn SP	10.00	25.00
SF50 Donald J. Trump	15.00	40.00
SF51 Arnold Schwarzenegger	8.00	20.00
SF52 Barack Obama	12.00	30.00
SF53 Bernie Sanders	8.00	20.00
SF55 H.R. McMaster	10.00	25.00
SF56 Ivanka Trump	12.00	30.00
SF57 James Mattis "Mad Dog"	10.00	25.00
SF59 John F. Kelly	8.00	20.00
SF64 Nikki Haley	8.00	20.00
SF67 Steve Bannon	8.00	20.00

2016 Decision 2016 Thank You Tour

COMPLETE SET (8)	50.00	100.00
COMMON CARD (TT1-TT8)	3.00	8.00
*GREEN: SAME VALUE AS BASIC CARDS	3.00	8.00
*BLUE: .5X TO 1.2X BASIC CARDS	4.00	10.00
*RED: .5X TO 1.2X BASIC CARDS	4.00	10.00
*ICE BLUE: 1.2X TO 3BASIC CARDS	10.00	25.00
RANDOMLY INSERTED INTO PACKS		
UPDATE EXCLUSIVE		

2016 Decision 2016 Trump Under Fire

COMPLETE SET (82)	120.00	250.00
COMPLETE SERIES 1 SET (24)	30.00	80.00
COMPLETE SERIES 2 SET (36)	60.00	120.00
COMPLETE UPDATE SET (22)	25.00	60.00
COMMON SERIES 1 CARD (TUF1-TUF24)	1.50	4.00
COMMON SERIES 2 CARD (TUF25-TUF60)	1.50	4.00
COMMON UPDATE CARD (TUF61-82)		
*GOLD FOIL: .5X TO 1.2X BASIC CARDS	2.00	5.00
*GREEN FOIL: .5X TO 1.2X BASIC CARDS	2.00	5.00
*PINK FOIL: .6X TO 1.5X BASIC CARDS	2.50	6.00
*BLUE FOIL: .75X TO 2X BASIC CARDS	3.00	8.00
*RED FOIL: 1.2X TO 3X BASIC CARDS	5.00	12.00
*ICE BLUE: 1.5X TO 4X BASIC CARDS	6.00	15.00
STATED ODDS 1:6		

2016 Decision 2016 World Leader Flag Patches

COMMON PATCH (WL1-WL22)	6.00	15.00
*GREEN: SAME VALUE AS BASIC PATCHES		
*BLUE: .5X TO 1.2X BASIC PATCHES		
*RED: .6X TO 1.5X BASIC PATCHES		
*ICE BLUE: .75X TO 2X BASIC PATCHES		
RANDOMLY INSERTED INTO PACKS		
UPDATE EXCLUSIVE		
WL1 Donald J. Trump/United States of America	25.00	60.00
WL2 Barack Obama/United States of America	25.00	60.00
WL3 Justin Trudeau/Canada	15.00	40.00
WL4 Enrique Pena Nieto/Mexico	12.00	30.00
WL5 Benjamin Netanyahu/Israel	25.00	60.00
WL6 Malcolm Turnbull/Australia	12.00	30.00
WL7 Shinzo Abe/Japan	15.00	40.00
WL8 Xi Jinping/China	75.00	150.00
WL9 Vladimir Putin/Russia	50.00	100.00
WL10 Theresa May/United Kingdom	10.00	25.00
WL11 Angela Merkel/Germany	12.00	30.00
WL12 Rodrigo Duterte/Philippines	15.00	40.00
WL13 Tsai Ing-wen/Taiwan	12.00	30.00
WL14 Raul Castro/Cuba	15.00	40.00
WL15 Francois Hollande and Emmanuel Macron/France	10.00	25.00
WL17 Ayatollah Ali Khamenei/Iran	30.00	75.00
WL18 Kim Jong-un/North Korea	25.00	60.00
WL19 Stefan Loefven/Sweden	12.00	30.00
WL21 Marine Le Pen/France	12.00	30.00
WL22 Pope Francis/Vatican	20.00	50.00

2016 Decision 2016 Promos

*POLITICON: SAME VALUE AS BASIC PROMOS		
*POL.BLUE: .5X TO 1.2X BASIC PROMOS		
POL.RED/50: .6X TO 1.5X BASIC PROMOS		
P1 Donald Trump	6.00	15.00
P2 Hillary Clinton	4.00	10.00
P3 Bernie Sanders	4.00	10.00
P4 Chris Christie	2.50	6.00
P5 Ted Cruz	3.00	8.00
P6 Ben Carson	2.50	6.00
P7 Republicans Debate Moments	2.00	5.00
P8 Bernie Sanders, Hillary Clinton	2.50	6.00
P9 Melania Trump	6.00	15.00
P10 Bill Clinton	2.50	6.00
P11 Nikki Haley	5.00	12.00
P12 Marco Rubio	2.00	5.00
P13 John Kasich (No P prefix)	2.50	6.00
P14 Carly Fiorina	2.00	5.00
P15 Jeb Bush	2.00	5.00
P16 Bernie Sanders	5.00	12.00
P17 Hillary Clinton	4.00	10.00
P18 Donald Trump	6.00	15.00

2016 Decision 2016 Industry Summit Promos

COMPLETE SET (18)	60.00	120.00
COMMON CARD (P1-P18)	2.00	5.00
INDUSTRY SUMMIT EXCLUSIVE		
P1 Donald Trump	8.00	20.00
P2 Hillary Clinton	5.00	12.00
P3 Bernie Sanders	3.00	8.00
P7 Republicans Debate Moments	4.00	10.00
P8 Bernie Sanders, Hillary Clinton Campaign Moments	4.00	10.00
P9 Melania Trump	10.00	25.00
P10 Bill Clinton	5.00	12.00
P11 Nikki Haley	5.00	12.00
P13 John Kasich	3.00	8.00
P15 Jeb Bush	3.00	8.00
P16 Bernie Sanders	6.00	15.00
P17 Hillary Clinton	5.00	12.00
P18 Donald Trump	6.00	15.00

2016 Decision 2016 RNC Promos

COMPLETE SET (3)		
COMMON CARD (RNC1-RNC3)		
RNC1 Donald J. Trump (giving thumbs up)	4.00	10.00
RNC2 Donald J. Trump (blue tie)	4.00	10.00
RNC3 Donald J. Trump Candidate Portraits	4.00	10.00

2020 Decision 2020

UNOPENED BOX (30 CARDS)	75.00	125.00
UNOPENED SER.2 BOX (25 CARDS)	75.00	125.00
PREVIEW BOX	100.00	150.00
PREMIUM CUT SIGNATURE BOX	175.00	250.00
COMMON CARD (341-500)	.40	1.00
COMMON SP (501-507)	2.00	5.00
COMMON CARD (508-697)		
COMMON SP (698-707)		
*ELECTION DAY/45: 1.2X TO 3X BASIC CARDS		
*SILVER/25: 2X TO 5X BASIC CARDS		
341 Donald Trump	3.00	8.00
342 Kanye West	4.00	10.00
343 Kamala Harris	2.50	6.00
344 Elizabeth Warren	.75	2.00
345 Joe Biden	1.50	4.00
346 Tulsi Gabbard	2.00	5.00
347 Mike Bloomberg	.40	1.00
348 Bill Weld	.40	1.00
349 Kirsten Gillibrand	1.25	3.00
350 Amy Klobuchar	.40	1.00
351 Bernie Sanders	1.00	2.50
352 Pete Buttigieg	1.00	2.50
353 Marianne Williamson	.60	1.50
354 Andrew Yang	.40	1.00
355 John Hickenlooper	.75	2.00
356 Julian Castro	1.25	3.00
357 Steve Bullock	.40	1.00
358 Howard Schultz	.40	1.00
359 Jay Inslee	1.50	4.00
360 John Delaney	1.00	2.50
361 John Kasich	1.25	3.00
362 Larry Hogan	.40	1.00
363 Wayne Messam	.40	1.00
364 Tim Ryan	.60	1.50
365 Mike Gravel	.60	1.50
366 Bill De Blasio	.40	1.00
367 Michael Bennet	.60	1.50
368 Eric Swalwell	.40	1.00
369 Seth Moulton	.40	1.00
370 Tom Steyer	.40	1.00
371 Joe Sestak	.40	1.00
372 Mark Sanford	.40	1.00
373 Joe Walsh	.40	1.00
374 Beto O'Rourke	.40	1.00
375 Cory Booker	.40	1.00
376 Deval Patrick	.40	1.00
377 Roque De La Fuente	.75	2.00
378 Alexandria Ocasio-Cortez	4.00	10.00
379 Steve Scalise	.40	1.00
380 Mike Pence	2.50	6.00
380b Mike Pence (w/mask) SP		
381 Rashida Tlaib	1.00	2.50
382 Ayanna Pressley	.40	1.00
383 Ilhan Omar	1.25	3.00
384 First Lady Melania Trump	3.00	8.00
384b First Lady Melania Trump (w/mask) SP		
385 Lindsey Graham	.40	1.00
386 Dan Crenshaw	2.00	5.00
387 Nancy Pelosi	3.00	8.00
387b Nancy Pelosi (w/mask) SP		
388 Jim Jordan	.40	1.00
389 Bill Barr	2.50	6.00
389b William Barr SP		
390 Matt Whitaker	.60	1.50
391 Jerry Nadler	1.00	2.50
392 Robert Mueller	.40	1.00
393 John Huber	.40	1.00
394 Kyrsten Sinema	1.50	4.00
395 Michael Horowitz	.40	1.00
396 Matt Gaetz	.40	1.00
396b Matt Gaetz (w/gas mask) SP		
397 Doug Collins	.40	1.00
398 Andrew McCabe	.40	1.00
399 Susan Collins	.40	1.00
400 Adam Schiff	1.25	3.00
401 Val Demings	.40	1.00
402 Pramila Jayapal	.40	1.00
403 Paul Gosar	.40	1.00
404 Elise Stefanik	.40	1.00
405 Marie Yovanovitch	.40	1.00
406 Hakeem Jeffries	.40	1.00
407 Debbie Stabenow	.40	1.00
408 Gina Haspel	.40	1.00
409 Louie Gohmert	.40	1.00
410 Mike Lee	.40	1.00
411 Stacey Abrams	1.25	3.00
412 Conor Lamb	.40	1.00
413 Al Green	.40	1.00
414 Chuck Grassley	.40	1.00
415 Ron Johnson	.40	1.00
416 John Kennedy	.40	1.00
417 Martha McSally	.75	2.00
418 Debbie Lesko	1.25	3.00
419 Lisa Murkowski	.40	1.00
420 Cory Gardner	.40	1.00
421 Deb Fischer	.40	1.00
422 Mitt Romney	.40	1.00
423 Don McGahn	.40	1.00
424 Pat Cipollone	.40	1.00
425 Richard Briggs	.40	1.00
426 John Ratcliffe	.40	1.00
427 Debbie Dingell	.40	1.00
428 Ronna McDaniel	.40	1.00
429 Mitch McConnell	.40	1.00
430 Andy Biggs	.40	1.00
431 Ron DeSantis	.40	1.00
432 Peter Strzok	.40	1.00
433 Matt Mowers	.40	1.00
434 Wanda Vazquez Garced•	.40	1.00
435 Carmen Cruz	.40	1.00
436 Devin Nunes	2.50	6.00
437 Jackie Speier	.40	1.00
438 Kevin McCarthy	.40	1.00
439 Jim Clyburn	.40	1.00
440 Steny Hoyer	.40	1.00
441 Doug Jones	.40	1.00
442 Jay Sekulow	.40	1.00
443 Rick Scott	.40	1.00
444 Jacky Rosen	.40	1.00
445 Donna Shalala	.40	1.00
446 Christopher A. Wray	.40	1.00
447 Kayleigh McEnany	2.50	6.00
448 Tom Perez	.40	1.00
449 Mike Rogers	.40	1.00
450 Chris Coons	1.25	3.00
451 Fiona Hill	.60	1.50
452 Gordon Sondland	.40	1.00
453 Ivanka Trump	4.00	10.00
454 Kelly Loeffler	.40	1.00
455 Josh Hawley	.40	1.00
456 Mark Esper	.40	1.00
457 Marsha Blackburn	.40	1.00
458 Tim Scott	.40	1.00
459 Mario Diaz-Balart	.40	1.00
460 Anthony Fauci M.D.	4.00	10.00
460b Anthony Fauci M.D. (w/mask) SP		
461 Dr. Jerome Adams	.40	1.00
462 Deborah Birx	3.00	8.00
462b Deborah Birx (w/mask) SP		
463 Alex Azar	.40	1.00
464 Steven Mnuchin	1.50	4.00
465 Robert R. Redfield	.40	1.00
466 Larry Kudlow	.40	1.00
467 Robert O'Brien	.40	1.00
468 Seema Verma	.40	1.00
469 Stephen Hahn M.D.	.40	1.00
470 Ben Carson M.D.	.40	1.00
471 Mark Milley	.40	1.00

472 Pete Gaynor .40 1.00
473 Terrence J. O'Shaughnessy .40 1.00
474 Peter Navarro .40 1.00
475 Gretchen Whitmer .40 1.00
476 Jennifer Wexton .40 1.00
477 Jerome Powell .40 1.00
478 Brett Giroir .40 1.00
479 John P. Polowczyk .40 1.00
480 Brad Parscale .40 1.00
481 Andrew Cuomo 2.00 5.00
482 Joseph Maldonado-Passage .40 1.00
483 John James .40 1.00
484 Ralph Northam .40 1.00
485 Dan Scavino .40 1.00
486 Sheila Jackson-Lee .40 1.00
487 Mike Lindell .40 1.00
488 Jo Jorgensen .40 1.00
489 Katie Hill .40 1.00
490 Mark Meadows .40 1.00
491 Jeff Van Drew .40 1.00
492 Gavin Newsom .40 1.00
493 Eric Garcetti .40 1.00
494 Tedros Adhanom Ghebreyesus .40 1.00
495 Conan The Hero Dog 2.00 5.00
496 Maxine Waters .40 1.00
497 Keisha Lance Bottoms .40 1.00
498 Mike Pompeo 1.25 3.00
499 Roger Stone 1.25 3.00
500 John Durham .40 1.00
501 Anthony Scaramucci .40 1.00
502 Lt. Col. Alexander Vindman .40 1.00
503 Stormy Daniels 2.00 5.00
504 Michael Avenatti .40 1.00
505 Michael Cohen .40 1.00
506 Kim Klacik .40 1.00
507 John Brennan .40 1.00

2020 Decision 2020 America's Game Football Lace Relics

COMMON MEM 30.00 75.00
RANDOMLY INSERTED INTO PACKS
NNO Trump (hand on heart) 50.00 100.00

2020 Decision 2020 America's Game Football Relics

COMMON MEM 15.00 40.00
RANDOMLY INSERTED INTO PACKS
NNO Trump (w/mask)
NNO Trump Waving to the Crowd
NNO Trump with Sailors
NNO Trump and General 30.00 75.00
NNO Trump, Mattis and Leaders 25.00 60.00

2020 Decision 2020 Biden Gaffes

COMPLETE SET (27) 20.00 50.00
COMMON CARD (GAF1-GAF27) 1.25 3.00
RANDOMLY INSERTED INTO PACKS

2020 Decision 2020 Candidate Portraits

COMPLETE SET (30) 20.00 50.00
COMMON CARD (CP1-CP30) 1.00 2.50
RANDOMLY INSERTED INTO PACKS
CP1 Amy Klobuchar 1.25 3.00
CP2 Alexandria Ocasio-Cortez 5.00 12.00
CP3 Bernie Sanders 2.50 6.00
CP4 Andrew Yang 3.00 8.00
CP6 Beto O'Rourke 2.00 5.00
CP9 Donald J. Trump 2.50 6.00
CP11 Elizabeth Warren 2.00 5.00
CP12 Gretchen Whitmer 2.00 5.00
CP13 Joe Biden 3.00 8.00
CP15 Kamala Harris 3.00 8.00
CP21 Pete Buttigieg 3.00 8.00
CP22 Stacey Abrams 2.50 6.00
CP24 Tulsi Gabbard 4.00 8.00
CP25 Abraham Lincoln 3.00 8.00

2020 Decision 2020 Chicago

COMPLETE SET (47) 50.00 100.00
COMMON CARD (C1-C46: HEADER) 1.50 4.00
RANDOMLY INSERTED INTO PACKS
C9 Barack Obama 10.00 25.00
C10 Michelle Robinson Obama 6.00 15.00
C11 Hillary Rodham Clinton 2.00 5.00
C27 Dan Rostenkowski 5.00 12.00
C40 Ronald Reagan 8.00 20.00
C41 Abraham Lincoln 6.00 15.00
C44 Al Capone 6.00 15.00
C46 Saul Alinsky 2.50 6.00

2020 Decision 2020 Chicago SP

COMPLETE SET (2)
COMMON CARD (SP1-SP2)
RANDOMLY INSERTED INTO PACKS
SP1 Ronald Reagan and Harry Caray 4.00 10.00

2020 Decision 2020 COVID-19 White House Task Force

COMMON CARD (COV1-COV26: HEADER) 1.25 3.00
RANDOMLY INSERTED INTO PACKS
NNO Header Checklist 4.00 10.00
COV1 Donald Trump 3.00 8.00
COV2 Mike Pence 2.50 6.00
COV3 Anthony Fauci 4.00 10.00
COV4 Dr. Jerome Adams 1.50 4.00
COV5 Deborah Birx 3.00 8.00
COV6 Alex Azar 2.00 5.00
COV7 Steve Mnuchin 3.00 8.00
COV8 Robert R. Redfield 2.50 6.00
COV9 Larry Kudlow 2.00 5.00
COV10 Robert O'Brien 1.50 4.00
COV11 Seema Verma 1.50 4.00
COV12 Stephen Hahn 2.50 6.00
COV13 Dr. Ben Carson 2.00 5.00
COV18 Robert Wilkie 2.00 5.00
COV19 Robert Blair 2.00 5.00
COV20 Sonny Perdue 2.00 5.00
COV26 Hospital Ship Comfort 2.50 6.00
COV37 Donald J. Trump 3.00 8.00
COV38 Donald J. Trump 3.00 8.00
COV39 Donald J. Trump 3.00 8.00
COV40 Donald J. Trump 3.00 8.00
COV41 Donald J. Trump 3.00 8.00
COV42 Donald J. Trump 3.00 8.00
COV43 Donald J. Trump 3.00 8.00
COV46 Joe Biden 2.00 5.00

2020 Decision 2020 Cut Signatures

RANDOMLY INSERTED INTO PACKS
NNO Alan Dershowitz 40.00 100.00
NNO Amy Klobuchar 30.00 75.00
NNO Andrew Yang 30.00 75.00
NNO Barack Obama 400.00 1000.00
NNO Bernie Sanders 100.00 250.00
NNO Beto O'Rourke 30.00 75.00
NNO Bill Clinton
NNO Bill Weld 40.00 100.00
NNO Chelsea Clinton 60.00 150.00
NNO Chris Christie 25.00 60.00
NNO Cory Booker
NNO Deval Patrick 30.00 75.00
NNO Dick Cheney 40.00 100.00
NNO Dan Bongino 40.00 100.00
NNO Don Trump Jr. 1 60.00 150.00
NNO Don Trump Jr. 2 60.00 150.00
NNO Donald Rumsfeld 40.00 100.00
NNO Donald Trump 1 1200.00 3000.00
NNO Donald Trump 2 1200.00 3000.00
NNO Elizabeth Warren 50.00 125.00
NNO George W. Bush 150.00 400.00
NNO Herman Cain 50.00 125.00
NNO Hillary Clinton 60.00 150.00
NNO Ilhan Ohmar 50.00 125.00
NNO Ivanka Trump 200.00 500.00
NNO Jimmy Carter• 75.00 200.00
NNO Joe Biden 400.00 1000.00
NNO John Hickenlooper
NNO John McCain 60.00 150.00
NNO Kamala Harris 250.00 600.00
NNO Karl Rove 20.00 50.00
NNO Kayleigh McEnany 250.00 600.00
NNO Kirsten Gillibrand 25.00 60.00
NNO Liz Cheney 20.00 50.00
NNO Marco Rubio 25.00 60.00
NNO Mike Huckabee 30.00 75.00
NNO Mitt Romney
NNO Newt Gingrich 25.00 60.00
NNO Nikki Haley 60.00 150.00
NNO Paul Ryan 30.00 75.00
NNO Pete Buttigieg 30.00 75.00
NNO Rand Paul 40.00 100.00
NNO Scott Walker 20.00 50.00
NNO Ted Cruz 40.00 100.00
NNO Tulsi Gabbard 40.00 100.00

2020 Decision 2020 Cut Signatures Series 2

NNO Alan Dershowitz #2 20.00 50.00
NNO Alan Dershowitz #3 20.00 50.00
NNO Barack Obama 800.00 1200.00
NNO Ben Carson
NNO Bernie Sanders
NNO Chelsea Clinton 20.00 50.00
NNO David Bossie 15.00 40.00
NNO Dick Cheney
NNO Donald Trump
NNO Donald Trump Jr. #3 50.00 100.00
NNO Donald Trump Junior #4
NNO George W. Bush
NNO Hillary Clinton 50.00 100.00
NNO Ivanka Trump
NNO Jason Chaffetz 15.00 40.00
NNO Jeanine Pirro 25.00 60.00
NNO Jimmy Carter
NNO Joe Biden 300.00 600.00
NNO John Hickenlooper
NNO Kamala Harris
NNO Liz Cheney 15.00 40.00
NNO Marsha Blackburn #1 20.00 50.00
NNO Marsha Blackburn #2 20.00 50.00
NNO Matt Gaetz #1 20.00 50.00
NNO Matt Gaetz #2 20.00 50.00
NNO Michele Bachmann
NNO Mitt Romney 30.00 75.00
NNO Newt Gingrich 15.00 40.00
NNO Pete Buttigieg 30.00 75.00
NNO Richard Nixon 150.00 300.00
NNO Sarah Palin 60.00 120.00
NNO Ted Cruz #2 50.00 100.00
NNO Ted Cruz #3 50.00 100.00
NNO Tim Kaine

2020 Decision 2020 Dual Cut Signatures

RANDOMLY INSERTED INTO PACKS
NNO Dick and Liz Cheney
NNO Hillary & Chelsea Clinton 100.00 200.00

2020 Decision 2020 Elite Premium

COMMON CARD (E1-E27) 6.00 15.00
COMMON CARD (E28-E54) 6.00 15.00
RANDOMLY INSERTED INTO PACKS
E2 George HW Bush 12.00 30.00
E3 John Dingell 10.00 25.00
E4 Paul Laxault 8.00 20.00
E5 Elijah Cummings 8.00 20.00
E8 JFK 55th Anniversary 15.00 40.00
E9 RFK 50th Anniversary 10.00 25.00
E10 MLK 50th Anniversary 10.00 25.00
E11 JFK Jr. 20th Anniversary 15.00 40.00
E12 Moon Landing 50th Anniversary 8.00 20.00
E13 Air Force One 12.00 30.00
E14 The Beast 12.00 30.00
E15 Marine One 12.00 30.00
E16 Trumps Visit Taj Mahal 12.00 30.00
E17 White House Task Force 10.00 25.00
E18 National Champs Visit WH 12.00 30.00
E19 John Lewis 10.00 25.00
In Memorium
E20 Herman Cain 8.00 20.00
In Memorium
E40 Ruth Bader Ginsburg 10.00 25.00

2020 Decision 2020 First Lady Portraits

COMPLETE SET (6) 8.00 20.00
COMMON CARD (FL1-FL6) 2.00 5.00
RANDOMLY INSERTED INTO PACKS

2020 Decision 2020 God Bless America Flag Patches

COMMON MEM (GBA1-GBA62B) 4.00 10.00
COMMON MEM (GBA63-GBA89) 10.00
RANDOMLY INSERTED INTO PACKS
GBA1 Donald Trump 20.00 50.00
GBA1B President Trump SP 25.00 60.00
GBA2 Alexandria Ocasio-Cortez 15.00 40.00
GBA3 Amy Klobuchar 8.00 20.00
GBA4 Andrew Yang 5.00 12.00
GBA6 Dr. Anthony Fauci 12.00 30.00
GBA7 Barack Obama 10.00 25.00
GBA8 Bernie Sanders 10.00 25.00
GBA9 Beto O'Rourke 5.00 12.00
GBA10 Bill Barr 5.00 12.00
GBA11 Christopher Wray 10.00 25.00
GBA12 Chuck Grassley 8.00 20.00
GBA13 Conan The Hero Dog 12.00 30.00
GBA15 Cory Booker 5.00 12.00
GBA16 Devin Nunes 6.00 15.00
GBA17 Dianne Feinstein 6.00 15.00
GBA18 Donald Trump Jr. 8.00 20.00
GBA19 Doug Collins 5.00 12.00
GBA21 Elizabeth Warren 10.00 25.00
GBA23 Ivanka Trump 12.00 30.00
GBA24 James Mattis 5.00 12.00
GBA26 John F. Kennedy 12.00 30.00
GBA27 Jim Jordan 5.00 12.00
GBA28 Joe Biden 20.00 50.00
GBA31 Joseph Dunford 6.00 15.00
GBA33 Kamala Harris 15.00 40.00
GBA34 Kellyanne Conway 6.00 15.00
GBA35 Kevin McCarthy 6.00 15.00
GBA39 Mark Meadows 5.00 12.00
GBA41 Marsha Blackburn 5.00 12.00
GBA44 Matt Whitaker 5.00 12.00
GBA45 Melania Trump 12.00 30.00
GBA47 Michael Flynn 15.00 40.00
GBA48 Michael S. Rogers 6.00 15.00
GBA49 Michelle Obama 12.00 30.00
GBA50 Mike Pence 15.00 40.00
GBA51 Mike Pompeo 8.00 20.00
GBA52 Mitch McConnell 6.00 15.00
GBA53 Nancy Pelosi 8.00 20.00
GBA54 Pete Buttigieg 15.00
GBA56 Rudy Giuliani 8.00 20.00
GBA58 Tim Scott 5.00 12.00
GBA60 Trey Gowdy 5.00 12.00
GBA61 Tulsi Gabbard 8.00 20.00
GBA62 Donald J. Trump 15.00 40.00
GBA62B POTUS-45 SP 25.00 60.00
GBA63 Joe Biden 15.00 40.00
GBA64 Joe Biden 15.00 40.00
GBA65 Jill Biden 12.00 30.00
GBA66 Joe and Jill Biden 12.00 30.00
GBA67 Kamala Harris 5.00 12.00
GBA68 Ruth Bader Ginsburg 10.00 25.00
GBA69 Amy Coney Barrett 8.00 20.00
GBA70 Kayleigh McEnany 10.00 25.00
GBA71 Lauren Boebert 5.00 12.00
GBA72 Marjorie Taylor Greene 15.00 40.00
GBA80 Kanye West 25.00 60.00
GBA84 Nikki Haley 10.00 25.00
GBA87 Donald J. Trump 20.00 50.00
GBA88 Donald Trump 20.00 50.00

2020 Decision 2020 Governor State Flag Patches

COMMON MEM (GF1-GF51) 6.00 15.00
RANDOMLY INSERTED INTO PACKS
SERIES 2 ONLY
GF1 Kay Ivey 25.00 60.00
GF3 Doug Ducey 15.00 40.00
GF4 Asa Hutchinson 10.00 25.00
GF5 Gavin Newsom 12.00 30.00
GF6 Jared Polis 10.00 25.00
GF7 Ned Lamont 10.00 25.00
GF9 Ron DeSantis 75.00 200.00
GF11 David Ige 15.00 40.00
GF12 Brad Little 8.00 20.00
GF13 J.B. Pritzker 12.00 30.00
GF14 Eric Holcomb 12.00 30.00

MODERN

GF15 Kim Reynolds 15.00 40.00
GF16 Laura Kelly 8.00 20.00
GF18 John Bel Edwards 15.00 40.00
GF19 Janet Mills 12.00 30.00
GF20 Larry Hogan 15.00 40.00
GF22 Gretchen Whitmer 25.00 60.00
GF24 Tate Reeves 15.00 40.00
GF25 Mike Parson 12.00 30.00
GF26 Steve Bullock 8.00 20.00
GF28 Steve Sisolak 12.00 30.00
GF32 Andrew Cuomo 12.00 30.00
GF33 Roy Cooper 8.00 20.00
GF35 Mike Dewine 12.00 30.00
GF36 Kevin Stitt 8.00 20.00
GF38 Tom Wolf 10.00 25.00
GF39 Gina Raimondo 8.00 20.00
GF40 Henry McMaster 12.00 30.00
GF41 Kristi Noem 20.00 50.00
GF43 Greg Abbott 20.00 50.00
GF46 Ralph Northam 10.00 25.00
GF47 Jay Inslee 10.00 25.00
GF48 Jim Justice 12.00 30.00
GF50 Mark Gordon 12.00 30.00
GF51 Wanda Vazquez Garced 8.00 20.00

2020 Decision 2020 Inauguration Premium

COMPLETE SET (9) 25.00 60.00
COMMON CARD (IP1-IP9) 5.00 12.00
RANDOMLY INSERTED INTO PACKS

2020 Decision 2020 Keep America Great

COMPLETE SET (54) 75.00 150.00
COMP.SER.1 SET (27) 50.00 100.00
COMP.SER.2 SET (27) 50.00 100.00
COMMON CARD (KAG1-KAG27) 3.00 8.00
COMMON CARD (KAG28-KAG54) 3.00 8.00
RANDOMLY INSERTED INTO PACKS

2020 Decision 2020 Make America Great Again

COMPLETE SET (45) 150.00 300.00
COMP.SER.1 SET (27) 100.00 200.00
COMP.SER.2 SET (18) 75.00 150.00
COMMON CARD (M1-M27) 4.00 10.00
COMMON CARD (M28-M45) 4.00 10.00
RANDOMLY INSERTED INTO PACKS

2020 Decision 2020 Money Relics

COMMON MEM (MO1-MO45) 6.00 15.00
COMMON MEM (MO46-MO72) 6.00 15.00
RANDOMLY INSERTED INTO PACKS
MO1 Donald Trump 40.00 100.00
MO1B POTUS-45 30.00 75.00
MO2 Adam Schiff 10.00 25.00
MO3 Alexandria Ocasio-Cortez 15.00 40.00
MO5 Andrew Cuomo 8.00 20.00
MO6 Andrew Yang 10.00 25.00
MO7 Anthony Fauci 12.00 30.00
MO8 Barack Obama 20.00 50.00
MO9 Bernie Sanders 10.00 25.00
MO10 Beto O'Rourke 8.00 20.00
MO14 Donald Trump Jr. 15.00 40.00
MO15 Elizabeth Warren 10.00 25.00
MO16 Gretchen Whitmer 15.00 40.00
MO18 Ivanka Trump 20.00 50.00
MO23 Joe Biden 15.00 40.00
MO24 John F. Kennedy Jr. 15.00 40.00
MO25 Kamala Harris 25.00 60.00
MO26 Kevin McCarthy 8.00 20.00
MO30 Melania Trump 20.00 50.00
MO31 Mike Bloomberg 10.00 25.00
MO32 Mike Pence 8.00 20.00
MO33 Mike Pompeo 10.00 25.00
MO34 Nancy Pelosi 8.00 20.00
MO35 Pete Buttigieg 8.00 20.00
MO38 Rudy Giuliani 15.00 40.00
MO41 Tom Cotton 8.00 20.00
MO42 Tulsi Gabbard 10.00 25.00
MO43 William Barr 8.00 20.00
MO44 Donald J. Trump
MO48 Joe Biden 10.00 25.00
MO49 Joseph R. Biden 10.00 25.00
MO51 Donald Trump 40.00 100.00
MO52 Kamala Harris 8.00 20.00
MO53 Dr. Fauci 12.00 30.00
MO54 AOC 12.00 30.00
MO55 Marjorie Taylor Greene 15.00 40.00
MO57 Kanye West 15.00 40.00
MO58 Kayleigh McEnany 10.00 25.00
MO60 Ruth Bader Ginsburg 8.00 20.00
MO62 Nikki Haley 12.00 30.00
MO63 Kristi Noem 12.00 30.00
MO66 Ron Desantis 20.00 50.00
MO70 Lauren Boebert 10.00 25.00
MO74 Donald J. Trump 40.00 100.00

2020 Decision 2020 Nicknames

COMPLETE SET (54) 60.00 150.00
COMP.SER.1 SET (27) 40.00 100.00
COMP.SER.2 SET (27) 40.00 100.00
COMMON CARD (NN1-NN26: HEADER) 2.50 6.00
COMMON CARD (NN27-NN53) 2.50 6.00
RANDOMLY INSERTED INTO PACKS

2020 Decision 2020 Political Gems

COMMON MEM (G1-G64) 5.00 12.00
COMMON MEM (G65-G89) 5.00 12.00
RANDOMLY INSERTED INTO PACKS
G1 Donald Trump 20.00 50.00
G1A President Trump SP 30.00 75.00
G2 Alexandria Ocasio-Cortez 20.00 50.00
G3 Amy Klobuchar 8.00 20.00
G4 Andrew Yang 6.00 15.00
G6 Dr. Anthony Fauci 25.00
G7 Barack Obama 10.00 25.00
G8 Bernie Sanders 8.00 20.00
G9 Beto O'Rourke 6.00 15.00
G10 Bill Barr 8.00 20.00
G11 Christopher Wray 6.00 15.00
G13 Conan The Hero Dog 10.00 25.00
G17 Dianne Feinstein 8.00 20.00
G18 Donald Trump Jr. 12.00 30.00
G21 Elizabeth Warren 8.00 20.00
G23 Ivanka Trump 12.00 30.00
G24 James Mattis 6.00 15.00
G25 Jeff Sessions 6.00 15.00
G26 John F. Kennedy 15.00 40.00
G28 Joe Biden 15.00 40.00
G33 Kamala Harris 20.00 50.00
G34 Kellyanne Conway 8.00 20.00
G36 Lindsey Graham 6.00 15.00
G37 Louie Gohmert 10.00 25.00
G43 Matt Gaetz 8.00 20.00
G45 Melania Trump 15.00 40.00
G46 Mike Bloomberg 6.00 15.00
G49 Michelle Obama 10.00 25.00
G50 Mike Pence 8.00 20.00
G51 Mike Pompeo 8.00 20.00
G53 Nancy Pelosi 6.00 15.00
G54 Pete Buttigieg 8.00 20.00
G56 Rudy Giuliani 10.00 25.00
G60 Trey Gowdy 8.00 20.00
G61 Tulsi Gabbard 8.00 20.00
G62 Donald J. Trump 20.00 50.00
G62B POTUS-45 SP 30.00 75.00
PG63 Joe Biden 15.00 40.00
PG64 Joe Biden 15.00 40.00
PG65 Jill Biden 10.00 25.00
PG66 Joe & Jill Biden 12.00 30.00
PG67 Kamala Harris 6.00 15.00
PG68 Ruth Bader Ginsburg 10.00 25.00
PG69 Amy Coney Barrett 8.00 20.00
PG70 Kayleigh McEnany 10.00 25.00
PG71 Lauren Boebert 10.00 25.00
PG72 Marjorie Taylor Greene 12.00 30.00
PG80 Kanye West 15.00 40.00
PG82 Kristi Noem 6.00 15.00
PG84 Nikki Haley 10.00 25.00
PG87 Donald J. Trump 20.00 50.00
PG88 Donald Trump 20.00 50.00

2020 Decision 2020 Presidential Medal of Freedom

COMPLETE SET (36) 30.00 75.00
COMP.SER.1 SET (18) 20.00 50.00
COMP.SER.2 SET (18) 15.00 40.00
COMMON (PMOF1-PMOF15, BC1-2, NNO) 1.25 3.00
COMMON CARD (PMOF16-PMOF33) 1.25 3.00
RANDOMLY INSERTED INTO PACKS
NNO Header Card 2.50 6.00
PMOF1 Babe Ruth 3.00 8.00
PMOF4 Miriam Adelson 1.50 4.00
PMOF6 Elvis Presley 2.50 6.00
PMOF7 Anton Scalia 1.50 4.00
PMOF8 Mariano Rivera 2.00 5.00
PMOF9 Bob Cousy 1.50 4.00
PMOF10 Jerry West 3.00 8.00
PMOF13 Roger Penske 1.50 4.00
PMOF14 Rush Limbaugh 6.00 15.00
PMOF16 Lou Holtz 2.50 6.00
PMOF17 Dan Gable 2.00 5.00
PMOF22 Gary Player 1.50 4.00
PMOF23 Annika Sorenstam 3.00 8.00
PMOF30 Vin Scully 4.00 10.00
PMOFBC1 Edwin "Buzz" Aldrin 2.00 5.00
PMOFBC2 Dr. Anthony Fauci 8.00 20.00

2020 Decision 2020 Road to the White House Candidate Letters

COMMON BIDEN 6.00 15.00
COMMON HARRIS 10.00 25.00
COMMON PENCE 5.00 12.00
COMMON TRUMP 8.00 20.00
RANDOMLY INSERTED INTO PACKS

2020 Decision 2020 Russiagate

COMPLETE SET (82) 100.00 200.00
COMMON CARD (RG1-RG82) 1.50 4.00
RANDOMLY INSERTED INTO PACKS

2020 Decision 2020 Super Flags Commemorative Jumbo Patches

COMMON MEM 4.00 10.00
RANDOMLY INSERTED INTO PACKS
SF1 Donald Trump 25.00 60.00
SF1B POTUS-45 SP 50.00 100.00
SF2 Adam Schiff 6.00 15.00
SF3 Alexandria Ocasio-Cortez 10.00 25.00
SF5 Andrew Cuomo 10.00 25.00
SF6 Anthony Fauci 12.00 30.00
SF7 Bernie Sanders 10.00 25.00
SF8 Beto O'Rourke 8.00 20.00
SF10 Dan Crenshaw 8.00 20.00
SF11 Deborah Birx 5.00 12.00
SF12 Devin Nunes 6.00 15.00
SF13 Donald Trump Jr. 12.00 30.00
SF14 Doug Collins 5.00 12.00
SF16 Elizabeth Warren 6.00 15.00
SF17 Eric Prince 6.00 15.00
SF19 Ivanka Trump 20.00 50.00
SF20 Jack Keane 5.00 12.00
SF23 Joe Biden 15.00 40.00
SF24 John F. Kennedy Jr. 10.00 25.00
SF27 Kamala Harris 25.00 60.00
SF29 Lindsey Graham 6.00 15.00
SF30 Mark Esper 5.00 12.00
SF31 Mark Meadows 6.00 15.00
SF32 Mark Milley 5.00 12.00
SF34 Matt Gaetz 8.00 20.00
SF35 Melania Trump 15.00 40.00
SF37 Mike Bloomberg 5.00 12.00
SF38 Mike Pence 12.00 30.00
SF39 Nancy Pelosi 10.00 25.00
SF40 Pete Buttigieg 8.00 20.00
SF43 Tulsi Gabbard 8.00 20.00
SF44 Barack Obama 15.00 40.00
SF45 Donald J. Trump 30.00 75.00
SF46 Michelle Obama 12.00 30.00

2020 Decision 2020 Supreme Court Justice Portraits

COMPLETE SET (9) 10.00 25.00
COMMON CARD (SCOTUS1-SCOTUS9) 1.25 3.00
RANDOMLY INSERTED INTO PACKS
SCOTUS2 Clarence Thomas 2.00 5.00
SCOTUS3 Ruth Bader Ginsburg 5.00 12.00
SCOTUS5 Samuel A. Alito, Jr 2.50 6.00
SCOTUS8 Neil M. Gorsuch 2.00 5.00
SCOTUS9 Brett M. Kavanaugh 1.50 4.00

2020 Decision 2020 Trump Gold Plated Commemorative Coin Relics

COMMON CARD (TC1-TC11) 60.00 150.00
STATED PRINT RUN 45 SER.#'d SETS

2020 Decision 2020 World Leader Flag Patches

COMMON MEM (WL1-WL54) 8.00 20.00
COMMON MEM (WL55-WL104) 5.00 12.00
RANDOMLY INSERTED INTO PACKS
WL1 Sheikh Mohammed bin Zayed Al Nahyan 15.00 40.00
WL2 Alberto Fernandez 12.00 30.00
WL3 Jair Bolsonaro 30.00 75.00
WL4 Justin Trudeau 10.00 25.00
WL5 Li Keqiang 150.00 300.00
WL6 Xi Jinping 200.00 400.00
WL7 Ivan Duque 10.00 25.00
WL8 Carlos Alvarado Quesada 10.00 25.00
WL10 Mette Frederiksen 10.00 25.00
WL13 Emmanuel Macron 10.00 25.00
WL14 Angela Merkel 25.00 60.00
WL15 Frank-Walter Steinmeier 12.00 30.00
WL16 Kim Kielsen 15.00 40.00
WL17 Juan Orlando Hernandez 20.00 50.00
WL18 Guani Th. Johannesson 12.00 30.00
WL19 Ram Nath Kovind 12.00 30.00
WL20 Narendra Modi 15.00 40.00
WL21 Qassem Soleimani 20.00 50.00
WL22 Barham Salih 15.00 40.00
WL23 Sergio Mattarella 25.00 60.00
WL24 Naruhito 30.00 75.00
WL25 Shinzo Abe 30.00 75.00
WL26 George Weah 12.00 30.00
WL29 Jacinda Ardern 15.00 40.00
WL30 Kim Jong-un 60.00 120.00
WL33 Michael D. Higgins 10.00 25.00
WL34 Vladimir Putin 100.00 250.00
WL35 King Salman 50.00 100.00
WL37 Recep Tayyip Erdogan 10.00 25.00
WL38 Sheikh Khalifa bin Zayed Al Nahyan 15.00 40.00
WL39 Volodymyr Zelensky 100.00 250.00
WL40 Boris Johnson 20.00 50.00
WL41 Queen Elizabeth II 50.00 100.00
WL42A Donald Trump (hugging flag) 30.00 75.00
WL42B Donald Trump (smiling) 20.00 50.00
WL43 Juan Guaido 20.00 50.00
WL44 Nicolas Maduro 15.00 40.00
WL45 Nguyen Phu Trong 30.00 75.00
WL46 Benjamin Netanyahu 20.00 50.00
WL47 Mohammed bin Salman Al Saud 12.00 30.00
WL49 Uhuru Kenyatta 15.00 40.00
WL51 Alejandro Giammattei 10.00 25.00
WL53 Melania Trump 20.00 50.00
WL54 Donald Trump 15.00 40.00
WL59 Xi Jinping 100.00 250.00
WL62 Luis Abinader 10.00 25.00
WL65 Carrie Lam 10.00 25.00
WL73 Fayez al-Sarraj 12.00 30.00
WL74 Aung San Suu Kyi 15.00 40.00
WL75 Kim Jung Un 30.00 75.00
WL76 Jens Stoltenberg 12.00 30.00
WL77 Muhammadu Buhari 10.00 25.00
WL80 Mahmoud Abbas 6.00 15.00
WL86 Vlad Putin 100.00 250.00
WL87 Chung Sye-kyun 30.00 75.00
WL89 Halimah Yacob 25.00 60.00
WL94 Pedro Sanchez 12.00 30.00
WL97 Tsai Ing-wen 125.00 300.00
WL99 Joe Biden 15.00 40.00
WL100 Pope Francis 40.00 100.00
WL102 Armen Sarksyan 12.00 30.00
WL104 Wavel Ramkalawan 12.00 30.00

2020 Decision 2020 World Leader Flag Patches Preview Stamped

COMPLETE SET (53)
STATED PRINT RUN 5 SER.#'d SETS
UNPRICED DUE TO SCARCITY

2020 Decision 2020 Promos

COMPLETE SET (9)	15.00	40.00
COMMON CARD (PC1-PC9)	2.50	6.00
PC1 Donald Trump	6.00	15.00
PC2 Joe Biden	5.00	12.00
PC3 Dr. Anthony Fauci w/ mask	3.00	8.00
PC4 Kamala Harris	5.00	12.00
PC6 Kayleigh McEnany	4.00	10.00
PC7 Alexandria Ocasio-Cortez	3.00	8.00

2020 Decision Direct Holiday Edition

UNOPENED FACTORY SET (39)	50.00	75.00
COMMON CARD (1-36)	.75	2.00
1 Donald J. Trump	4.00	10.00
2 The White House	1.00	2.50
3 Joe Biden	2.00	5.00
4 Melania Trump	5.00	12.00
6 Mike Pence	1.25	3.00
7 Kamala Harris	2.50	6.00
8 Ivanka Trump	2.50	6.00
9 Dr. Anthony Fauci	1.25	3.00
10 Alexandria Ocasio-Cortez	3.00	8.00
11 Michelle Obama	1.00	2.50
12 Kayleigh McEnany	2.00	5.00
15 Mike Pompeo	1.00	2.50
15 Barack Obama UER	2.00	5.00
17 Bernie Sanders	1.25	3.00
18 Amy Coney Barrett	1.00	2.50
19 Conan	1.25	3.00
20 Donald Trump Jr.	1.00	2.50
27 Stacey Abrams	1.25	3.00

2022 Decision 2022

COMMON CARD (1-200)	.40	1.00
COMMON SP (201-227)	3.00	8.00
1 President Joe Biden	2.00	5.00
2 Kamala Harris	1.50	4.00
3 Donald J. Trump	5.00	12.00
4 Ron DeSantis	10.00	25.00
5 Alexandria Ocasio-Cortez	6.00	15.00
6 Jill Biden	2.50	6.00
7 Nancy Pelosi	1.25	3.00
8 Dr. Mehmet Oz	2.00	5.00
9 Kyrsten Sinema	1.50	4.00
10 Volodymyr Zelenskyy	4.00	10.00
24 Bernie Sanders	1.00	2.50
27 Brett Kavanaugh	1.25	3.00
33 Hunter Biden	1.50	4.00
34 Tulsi Gabbard	2.00	5.00
36 Kristi Noem	2.50	6.00
38 Liz Cheney	1.50	4.00
40 Marjorie Taylor Greene	3.00	8.00
41 Matthew McConaughey	3.00	8.00
43 Nikki Haley	2.00	5.00
45 Vladimir Putin	4.00	10.00
48 Barack Obama	2.50	6.00
50 Caitlyn Jenner	2.00	5.00
68 J.D. Vance	1.50	4.00
71 Joe Manchin	3.00	8.00
73 Kari Lake	6.00	15.00
75 Kellyanne Conway	2.00	5.00
76 Ketanji Brown Jackson	1.50	4.00
80 Lauren Boebert	2.00	5.00
94 Donald Trump Jr.	2.00	5.00
96 King Charles	4.00	10.00
100 Herschel Walker	2.00	5.00
101 Sarah Palin	1.50	4.00
118 Gavin Newsom	2.50	6.00
133 Sarah Huckabee Sanders	2.00	5.00
154 Katie Porter	2.00	5.00
164 Casey Desantis	2.50	6.00
167 Ye	6.00	15.00
175 The McCloskeys	4.00	10.00
200 Biden & Desantis	2.00	5.00
201 Kathy Salvi SP	8.00	20.00
204 Randi Weingarten SP	5.00	12.00
205 Patrisse Cullors SP	5.00	12.00
206 Tina Forte SP	6.00	15.00
208 Maura Healey SP	6.00	15.00
209 Greta Thunberg SP	25.00	60.00
212 Rishi Sunak SP	5.00	12.00
213 Sam Bankman-Fried SP	8.00	20.00
215 Klaus Schwab SP	5.00	12.00
216 Allan Fung SP	10.00	25.00
223 Jeff Landry SP	6.00	15.00
225 Derek Schmidt SP	6.00	15.00
226 Frank Biden SP	6.00	15.00
227 Elon Musk SP	50.00	125.00

2022 Decision 2022 Atlantic City NSCC Promos

COMMON CARD (AC1-AC18)	1.25	3.00
RANDOMLY INSERTED INTO PACKS		
AC1 Chris Christie	1.50	4.00
AC2 Phil Murphy	1.50	4.00
AC3 Christine Todd Whitman	1.50	4.00
AC4 Donald Trump	6.00	15.00
AC5 Grover Cleveland	1.50	4.00
AC7 Enoch "Nucky" Johnson	1.50	4.00
AC8 Brendan Byrne	2.00	5.00
AC9 Thomas Kean	2.50	6.00
AC10 Cory Booker	2.00	5.00
AC11 Bob Menendez	2.00	5.00
AC14 Jim McGreevey	1.50	4.00
AC15 Jon Corzine	1.50	4.00
AC16 Charles "Lucky" Luciano	2.50	6.00

2022 Decision 2022 Biden Gold-Plated Commemorative Coin Relics

COMMON MEM (BD1-BD3)	15.00	40.00
RANDOMLY INSERTED INTO PACKS		
STATED PRINT RUN 46 SER.#'d SETS		

2022 Decision 2022 Cut Signatures

COMMON AUTO	12.00	30.00
RANDOMLY INSERTED INTO PACKS		
NNO Al Sharpton	30.00	75.00
NNO Barack Obama	300.00	800.00
NNO Ben Carson	15.00	40.00
NNO Bill Barr	40.00	100.00
NNO Bill Clinton	150.00	400.00
NNO Donald J. Trump	600.00	1500.00
NNO Donald Trump Jr.	25.00	60.00
NNO Jared Kushner	30.00	75.00
NNO Jeanine Pirro	15.00	40.00
NNO Joe Biden	100.00	250.00
NNO Josh Hawley	15.00	40.00
NNO Kayleigh McEnany	30.00	75.00
NNO Kellyanne Conway	25.00	60.00
NNO Kristi Noem	30.00	75.00
NNO Newt Gingrich	15.00	40.00
NNO Paul Manafort	30.00	75.00
NNO Robert F. Kennedy Jr.	40.00	100.00
NNO Sarah Huckabee Sanders	15.00	40.00
NNO Sebastian Gorka	15.00	40.00
NNO Ted Cruz	15.00	40.00
NNO Tom Cotton	15.00	40.00

2022 Decision 2022 Elite In Memoriam

COMMON CARD (IM1-IM27)	3.00	8.00
RANDOMLY INSERTED INTO PACKS		
IM2 G. Gordon Liddy	5.00	12.00
IM3 Madeleine Albright	5.00	12.00
IM5 Robert "Bud" McFarlane	6.00	15.00
IM6 Harry Reid	6.00	15.00
IM7 Bob Dole	6.00	15.00
IM8 Walter F. Mondale	6.00	15.00
IM13 John Warner	6.00	15.00
IM16 Michael Collins	6.00	15.00
IM17 George Floyd	12.00	30.00
IM18 Ivana Trump	5.00	12.00
IM20 Vernon Jordan	6.00	15.00
IM23 Shinzo Abe	8.00	20.00
IM24 Queen Elizabeth II	6.00	15.00
IM25 Queen Elizabeth II	6.00	15.00
IM26 Queen Elizabeth II	6.00	15.00
IM27 Prince Philip	10.00	25.00

2022 Decision 2022 God Bless America Flag Patches

COMMON MEM (GBA1-GBA27)	3.00	8.00
RANDOMLY INSERTED INTO PACKS		
GBA2 Alexandria Ocasio-Cortez	12.00	30.00
GBA4 Caitlyn Jenner	6.00	15.00
GBA6 Donald Trump	10.00	25.00
GBA8 Dr. Mehmet Oz	10.00	25.00
GBA10 Glenn Youngkin	5.00	12.00
GBA12 Herschel Walker	10.00	25.00
GBA13 Hunter Biden	8.00	20.00
GBA15 Joe Biden	10.00	25.00
GBA17 Kari Lake	12.00	30.00
GBA18 Karine Jean-Pierre	10.00	25.00
GBA19 Kellyanne Conway	6.00	15.00
GBA23 Nancy Pelosi	8.00	20.00
GBA24 Ron DeSantis	25.00	60.00
GBA25 Sarah Huckabee Sanders	6.00	15.00
GBA26 Sarah Palin	8.00	20.00

2022 Decision 2022 Money Relics

COMMON MEM (MO01-MO27)	3.00	8.00
RANDOMLY INSERTED INTO PACKS		
MO01 Alan Greenspan	6.00	15.00
MO02 Alexander Hamilton	15.00	40.00
MO03 Alexandria Ocasio-Cortez	15.00	40.00
MO04 Allen Weisselberg	5.00	12.00
MO05 Antony Blinken	8.00	20.00
MO06 Caitlyn Jenner	5.00	12.00
MO07 Donald Trump	40.00	100.00
MO08 Dr. Mehmet Oz	8.00	20.00
MO09 Gavin Newsom	10.00	25.00
MO10 Glenn Youngkin	6.00	15.00
MO11 Herschel Walker	12.00	30.00
MO12 J.D. Vance	6.00	15.00
MO14 Joe Manchin	6.00	15.00
MO15 Kari Lake	20.00	50.00
MO17 Kyrsten Sinema	5.00	12.00
MO20 Joe Biden	10.00	25.00
MO21 Ron Desantis	25.00	60.00
MO22 Sarah Huckabee Sanders	5.00	12.00
MO23 Sarah Palin	15.00	40.00
MO24 Steve Bannon	15.00	40.00
MO26 Kanye West	40.00	100.00
MO27 John Durham	10.00	25.00

2022 Decision 2022 Nicknames

COMPLETE SET (18)	20.00	50.00
COMMON CARD (NN28-NN45)	2.50	6.00
RANDOMLY INSERTED INTO PACKS		
NN32 Christie Crème	4.00	10.00
NN39 Brandon	4.00	10.00
NN43 The Great MAGA King	10.00	25.00
NN44 The Governator	4.00	10.00

2022 Decision 2022 Pieces of America

COMMON MEM (POA1-POA27)	3.00	8.00
RANDOMLY INSERTED INTO PACKS		
POA2 Alexandria Ocasio-Cortez	20.00	50.00
POA3 Brett Kavanaugh	8.00	20.00
POA6 Donald Trump	15.00	40.00
POA7 Donald Trump Jr.	10.00	25.00
POA9 Eric Adams	6.00	15.00
POA10 Glenn Youngkin	6.00	15.00
POA11 Greg Abbott	5.00	12.00
POA12 Herschel Walker	8.00	20.00
POA13 Hunter Biden	5.00	12.00
POA14 J.D. Vance	8.00	20.00
POA15 Joe Biden	10.00	25.00
POA16 Joe Manchin	10.00	25.00
POA17 Kari Lake	12.00	30.00
POA19 Kellyanne Conway	12.00	30.00
POA20 Ketanji Brown Jackson	6.00	15.00
POA21 Kyrsten Sinema	5.00	12.00
POA22 Larry Elder	6.00	15.00
POA23 Nancy Pelosi	8.00	20.00
POA24 Ron DeSantis	30.00	75.00
POA25 Sarah Huckabee Sanders	6.00	15.00
POA26 Sarah Palin	8.00	20.00

2022 Decision 2022 Political Gems

COMMON MEM (PG1-PG27)	4.00	10.00
RANDOMLY INSERTED INTO PACKS		
PG1 Al Sharpton	12.00	30.00
PG2 Alexandria Ocasio-Cortez	15.00	40.00
PG4 Caitlyn Jenner	6.00	15.00
PG6 Donald Trump	25.00	60.00
PG7 Donald Trump Jr.	12.00	30.00
PG8 Dr. Mehmet Oz	5.00	12.00
PG9 Eric Adams	8.00	20.00
PG10 Glenn Youngkin	6.00	15.00
PG12 Herschel Walker	8.00	20.00
PG13 Hunter Biden	5.00	12.00
PG15 President Joe Biden	6.00	15.00
PG16 Joe Manchin	5.00	12.00
PG17 Kari Lake	10.00	25.00
PG20 Ketanji Brown Jackson	5.00	12.00
PG21 Kyrsten Sinema	8.00	20.00
PG23 Nancy Pelosi	10.00	25.00
PG24 Ron DeSantis	15.00	40.00
PG25 Sarah Huckabee Sanders	5.00	12.00
PG26 Sarah Palin	8.00	20.00
PG27 Volodymyr Zelenskyy	20.00	50.00

2022 Decision 2022 World Leader Flag Patches

COMMON MEM (WL5-WL72)	6.00	15.00
RANDOMLY INSERTED INTO PACKS		
WL55 Ali Asadov	15.00	40.00
WL56 Anas Haqqani	30.00	75.00
WL57 Dinesh Gunawardena	15.00	40.00
WL58 Gustavo Petro	8.00	20.00
WL59 Mohammad Hasan Akhund	30.00	75.00
WL61 Joe Biden	10.00	25.00
WL62 Justin Trudeau	12.00	30.00
WL63 Kim Jong-Un	20.00	50.00
WL64 Liz Truss	15.00	40.00
WL68 Vladimir Putin	60.00	150.00
WL69 Volodymyr Zelenskyy	30.00	75.00
WL70 Xi Jinping	125.00	300.00
WL72 Yoon Suk-Yeol	10.00	25.00

2013 The Deep

COMPLETE SET (9)	4.00	10.00
UNOPENED BOX	30.00	40.00
COMMON CARD (S1-S9)	.60	1.50

2013 The Deep Artist Chips Black

COMPLETE SET (10)	12.00	30.00
COMMON CARD (AC1-AC10)	2.00	5.00
*SILVER/25: .75X TO 2X BASIC CHIPS	4.00	10.00
STATED ODDS 1:		

1993 Active Marketing Defective Comics

COMPLETE SET (50)	2.50	6.00
UNOPENED BOX (36 PACKS)	35.00	45.00
UNOPENED PACK (8 CARDS+1 ENTRY FORM)	1.25	1.50
COMMON CARD (1-50)	.08	.25
*SILVER: .75X TO 2X BASIC CARDS	.20	.50
*GOLD: 15X TO 40X BASIC CARDS	4.00	10.00

1991 Historical Images Defenders of Freedom Crisis in the Gulf

COMPLETE SET (144)	8.00	20.00
COMPLETE SET W/ERRORS (161)	30.00	75.00
COMPLETE FACTORY SET (145)	10.00	25.00
UNOPENED BOX (36 PACKS)	25.00	40.00
UNOPENED PACK	1.00	1.25
COMMON CARD (1-144)	.12	.30
1B B-1 Bomber COR	2.00	5.00
3B F-15 Eagle Soars COR	2.00	5.00
7B B-52H Takes off COR (eight turbojets)	2.00	5.00
14B Loading M1A1 COR	2.00	5.00
16B Oil Fields Afire COR (text added)	2.00	5.00
17B Hussein's Legacy COR (text added)	2.00	5.00
63B Avenger COR (Consist of A)	2.00	5.00
66B Apache Tank Killer COR	2.00	5.00
74B M551 Sheridan COR	2.00	5.00
106B F-4 Phantom Lurks COR (Air Force Planes)	2.00	5.00
110B AWACs in Saudi COR	2.00	5.00
111B AWACs Protection COR	2.00	5.00
119B F-4 on Approach COR (corrected lines)	2.00	5.00

121B Chemical/ Biological Protect COR 2.00 5.00
134B Falcon on the Prowl COR 2.00 5.00
(U.S. Air Force)
138B T-30 Talon COR 2.00 5.00
(T-38 Talon)
144A Checklist ERR .12 .30
(Lists 74 and 120 error descriptions)
144B Checklist COR 2.00 5.00
(Lists 74 and 120 corrected descriptions)

1991 Historical Images Defenders of Freedom Crisis in the Gulf Promos

COMMON CARD (P1-P6) 3.00 8.00
NNO1 6UP (P1 to P6) 20.00 50.00

1993 SkyBox Demolition Man

COMPLETE SET (100) 4.00 10.00
UNOPENED BOX (36 PACKS) 15.00 25.00
UNOPENED PACK (8 CARDS) .75 1.00
COMMON CARD (1-100) .10 .25

1991 America's Major Players Desert Storm Card and Map

COMPLETE BOXED SET (110) 10.00 25.00
COMMON CARD (1-110) .15 .40
*VICTORY PRINT.: .30X TO .75X BASIC CARDS
NNO1 Iraq Map and poster
NNO2 110-Card Panel Uncut Sheet

1991 America's Major Players Desert Storm Card and Map Promos

COMPLETE SET (10)
COMMON CARD
NNO AH-64 Apache 60.00 120.00
NNO B-52G Stratofortress 60.00 120.00
NNO F/A-18 Hornet 60.00 120.00
NNO F-117 Night Hawk 60.00 120.00
NNO F-15C Eagle 60.00 120.00
NNO F-16C Fighting Falcon 60.00 120.00
NNO FMC M2/M3 Bradley 60.00 120.00
NNO M1A1 Abrams 60.00 120.00
NNO MIG-29 Fulcrum A 60.00 120.00
NNO MIL Mi24 Hind E 60.00 120.00

1991 Crown Desert Storm Card Collection

COMPLETE SET (21) 3.00 8.00
COMPLETE SERIES 1 SET (9) 2.00 5.00
COMPLETE SERIES 2 SET (10) 2.00 5.00
COMMON CARD (1-9) .30 .75
COMMON CARD (10-19) .30 .75
INCLUDES TWO UNNUMBERED CHECKLISTS

1991 Dart FlipCards Desert Storm Gulf War Facts

COMPLETE SET (100) 10.00 25.00
COMMON CARD (1-100) .15 .40

1991 Crown Desert Storm Landforce

COMPLETE SET (9) 6.00 15.00
COMMON CARD (1-9; CL) 1.00 2.50
*PROMOS: 1.2X TO 3X BASIC CARDS
NNO General Colin Powell 60.00 120.00

1991 AMA Desert Storm Operation Yellow Ribbon

COMPLETE SET (60) 3.00 8.00
COMMON CARD (1-60) .08 .25

1991 AMA Desert Storm Operation Yellow Ribbon Promos

COMPLETE SET (11)
COMMON CARD (P1-P11)
P1 Commander In Chief .60 1.50
P2 Stealth Fighter F-117A .60 1.50
P3 Gas Mask .60 1.50
P4 HAWK Missles .60 1.50
P5 M-1 Abrams Tank .60 1.50
P6 Troops at Ready .60 1.50
P7 U.S. Aircraft Carrier .60 1.50
P8 Harrier AV-8B .60 1.50
P9 Tomcats F-14 .60 1.50
P10 Patriot Missle Scud Buster .60 1.50
P11 General Norman H. Schwarzkopf 1.00 2.50

1991 Pro Set Desert Storm

COMPLETE SET (250) 10.00 25.00
COMPLETE FACTORY SET (250) 10.00 25.00
COMPLETE PX FACTORY SET (253) 12.00 30.00
COMPLETE DENNY FACTORY SET (254) 15.00 40.00
UNOPENED BOX (36 PACKS)
UNOPENED PACK (10 CARDS)
COMMON CARD (1-250) .06 .15
COMMON CARD (251-253) 1.25 3.00
250B Let us strive on... LUCITE
(Fact. excl.)
NNO1 Desert Storm Series Header/(Factory Set exclusive)
NNO2 Service in the Sand/(Factory Set exclusive)

1991 Pro Set Desert Storm Prototypes

COMPLETE SET (9) 4.00 10.00
COMMON CARD .75 2.00

1991 Crown Desert Storm Seaforce

COMPLETE SET (9) 8.00 20.00
COMMON CARD (1-8; CL) 1.25 3.00
*PROMO: 1X TO 2.5X BASIC CARDS
NNO1 President Bush PROMO 20.00 50.00

1991 Crown Desert Storm Skyforce

COMPLETE SET (10) 8.00 20.00
COMMON CARD (1-8 CL) 1.25 3.00
*PROMO: 1X TO 2.5X BASIC CARDS
NNO Norman Schwarzkopf

1991 Crown Desert Storm Skyforce Landforce Seaforce Promos

NNO Victory (Bush, Powell, Schwarzkopf) 6.00 12.00
(gold border)
NNO Victory (Bush, Powell, Schwarzkopf) 30.00 75.00
(black border)

1991 Topps UK Desert Storm

COMPLETE SET (88) 30.00 75.00
UNOPENED BOX (36 PACKS) 175.00 200.00
UNOPENED PACK
COMMON CARD (1-88) 2.00

1991 Topps UK Desert Storm Stickers

COMPLETE SET (22) 20.00 50.00
COMMON CARD (1-22) 1.25 3.00
STATED ODDS 1:1

2014 Despicable Me 2 Dog Tags

COMPLETE SET (24) 25.00 60.00
COMMON TAG (1-24) 2.00 5.00

2014 Despicable Me 2 Dog Tags Stickers

COMPLETE SET (24) 12.00 30.00
COMMON STICKER (1-24) 1.25 3.00
STATED ODDS 1:1

Dexter

2009 Dexter

COMPLETE SET (72) 6.00 15.00
UNOPENED BOX (24 PACKS) 60.00 70.00
UNOPENED PACK (6 CARDS) 2.50 3.00
COMMON CARD (1-72) .15 .40

2009 Dexter Autographs

COMMON CARD (DA1-DA11) 10.00 20.00
STATED ODDS 1:48
DA1 Michael C. Hall 50.00 100.00
DA2 Julie Benz 50.00 100.00
DA3 Jennifer Carpenter 30.00 75.00
DA4 Lauren Velez 8.00 20.00
DA5 David Zayas 20.00 50.00
DA6 James Remar 15.00 40.00
DA7 C.S. Lee 15.00 40.00
DA8 Erik King 12.00 30.00
DA9 Margo Martindale 8.00 20.00

2009 Dexter Behind-the-Scenes

COMPLETE SET (5) 4.00 10.00
COMMON CARD (DB1-DB5) 1.25 3.00
STATED ODDS 1:24

2009 Dexter Case-Incentives

DCI1 STATED ODDS ONE PER 3 CASE PURCHASE
DCI2 STATED ODDS ONE PER 10 CASE PURCHASE
DCI1 Dexter Morgan 30.00 75.00
DCI2 Blood Slide 250.00 350.00

2009 Dexter Costumes

COMMON CARD (DC1-DC21) 6.00 15.00
STATED ODDS 1:13
DC3 Angel Batista 8.00 20.00
DC4 Angel Batista 8.00 20.00
DC5 Cody 8.00 20.00
DC6 Cody 8.00 20.00
DC7 Debra Morgan 10.00 25.00
DC8a Debra Morgan Uniform Shirt 10.00 25.00
DC8b Debra Morgan Patch 250.00 500.00
DC9 Dexter Morgan 10.00 25.00
DC11 Frank Lundy 8.00 20.00
DC12 Frank Lundy 10.00 25.00
DC14 Lila 8.00 20.00
DC17 Lt. Maria LaGuerta 8.00 20.00
DC18 Rita Bennett 10.00 25.00
DC19 Rudy Cooper 8.00 20.00

2009 Dexter Dexter's Relationships

COMPLETE SET (4) 4.00 10.00
COMMON CARD (DR1-DR4) 1.50 4.00
STATED ODDS 1:24

2009 Dexter Dream Scenes

COMPLETE SET (2) 4.00 10.00
COMMON CARD (DS1-DS2) 2.50 6.00
STATED ODDS 1:24
DS1 Not a Drag to Dexter 2.50 6.00
DS2 Hey 2.50 6.00

2009 Dexter Group

COMPLETE SET (2) 2.50 6.00
COMMON CARD (DG1-DG2) 1.50 4.00
STATED ODDS 1:24

2009 Dexter Portraits

COMPLETE SET (4) 5.00 12.00
COMMON CARD (DT1-DT4) 1.50 4.00
STATED ODDS 1:24

2009 Dexter Props

COMMON CARD (DPC1-DPC5) 6.00 15.00
STATED ODDS 1:96
DPC1 Foot 50.00 100.00
DPC2 Hand 60.00 120.00

2009 Dexter Dark Defender

COMPLETE SET (4) 4.00 10.00
COMMON CARD (DD1-DD4) 1.50 4.00
STATED ODDS 1:24

2009 Dexter The Killer

COMPLETE SET (6) 6.00 15.00
COMMON CARD (DK1-DK6) 1.50 4.00
STATED ODDS 1:24

2010 Dexter Season Three

COMPLETE SET (72) 4.00 10.00
UNOPENED BOX (24 PACKS) 150.00 200.00
UNOPENED PACK (6 CARDS) 6.00 8.00
COMMON CARD (1-72) .12 .30

2010 Dexter Season Three Autograph Costumes

COMMON AUTO 20.00 40.00
OVERALL AUTO ODDS 1:48
JB Julie Benz 75.00 150.00
JC Jennifer Carpenter 25.00 60.00
MCH Michael C Hall 75.00 150.00

2010 Dexter Season Three Autographs

COMMON CARD 15.00 40.00
OVERALL AUTO ODDS 1:48
MCHS Michael C Hall 30.00 75.00
MCHJB M.Hall/J.Benz 60.00 120.00
MCHJS M.Hall/J.Smits 50.00 100.00

2010 Dexter Season Three Costumes

COMPLETE SET (29) 250.00 500.00
COMMON CARD (C1-C29) 6.00 15.00
OVERALL COSTUME/PROP CARD ODDS 1:10
CI ISSUED AS A CASE INCENTIVE
C1 Dexter Morgan 10.00 25.00
C2 Dexter Morgan 10.00 25.00
C3 Dexter Morgan 10.00 25.00
C4 Dexter Morgan 10.00 25.00
C5 Dexter Morgan 10.00 25.00
C6 Rita Bennett 10.00 25.00
C7 Rita Bennett 10.00 25.00
C8 Rita Bennett 10.00 25.00
C9 Rita Bennett 10.00 25.00
C24 D.Morgan/M.Prado 8.00 20.00
C25 R.Bennett/D.Morgan 15.00 40.00
C26 M.Laguerta/M.Prado 10.00 25.00
C27 D.Morgan/J.Quinn 8.00 20.00
C28 Dexter/Angel/Debra/Vince 15.00 40.00
C29 8 Swatch 15.00 40.00
CI 7 Swatch CI 15.00 40.00

2010 Dexter Season Three Dexter's Victims

COMPLETE SET (9) 10.00 25.00
COMMON CARD (V1-V9) 1.50 4.00
STATED ODDS 1:12

2010 Dexter Season Three Metallogloss Case-Toppers

COMPLETE SET (2) 10.00 25.00
COMMON CARD (1-2) 6.00 15.00
STATED ODDS 1:CASE

2010 Dexter Season Three Props

COMPLETE SET (11) 175.00 350.00
COMMON CARD 12.00 30.00
OVERALL COSTUME/PROP CARD ODDS 1:10
P1 Target Paper 15.00 40.00
P5 Wedding Invitation 15.00 40.00
P7 Milk Carton 60.00 120.00
P10 Forensics Quarterly 15.00 40.00
P11 Dry Cleaner Tag 30.00 60.00

2010 Dexter Season Three Puzzle

COMPLETE SET (9) 10.00 25.00
COMMON CARD (CP1-CP9) 1.50 4.00
STATED ODDS 1:12

2010 Dexter Season Three Quotes

COMPLETE SET (10) 10.00 25.00
COMMON CARD (Q1-Q10) 1.25 3.00
STATED ODDS 1:12

2010 Dexter Season Three Promos

COMMON CARD .75 2.00
P4 Dexter 2.00 5.00
P5 Dexter 2.00 5.00
AP1 Dexter ALB 2.00 5.00
AP2 Dexter ALB 2.00 5.00

2012 Dexter Season Four

COMPLETE SET (72) 8.00 20.00
UNOPENED BOX (24 PACKS) 60.00 100.00
UNOPENED PACK (5 CARDS) 4.00 5.00
COMMON CARD (1-72) .20 .50

2012 Dexter Season Four Autographs

COMMON AUTO 10.00 25.00
RANDOM INSERTS IN BOXES
AJL John Lithgow 30.00 75.00
AMCH Michael C. Hall 30.00 80.00

2012 Dexter Season Four Costumes

COMMON CARD 6.00 15.00
TWO COSTUME OR PROP CARDS PER BOX

CAMJ Arthur Mitchell jacket 8.00 20.00
CAMV Arthur Mitchell shirt 10.00 25.00
CCHP Christine Hill purple dress 8.00 20.00
CCHR Christine Hill red dress 8.00 20.00
CDMC Dexter Morgan sleeve covers 8.00 20.00

2012 Dexter Season Four Dexter's Justice

COMPLETE SET (9) 10.00 25.00
COMMON CARD (JM1-JM9) 2.50 6.00
THREE CARDS PER BOX

2012 Dexter Season Four Locations

COMPLETE SET (9) 10.00 25.00
COMMON CARD (L1-L9) 2.50 6.00
THREE CARDS PER BOX

2012 Dexter Season Four Props

COMMON CARD 6.00 15.00
TWO COSTUME OR PROP CARDS PER BOX
PAB Miami Metro Archive Box 8.00 20.00
PHR Hammer 20.00 40.00
PKP Kill Room Plastic 8.00 20.00
PPC Postcard 12.00 30.00
PWH 4 Walls 1 Heart Flyer 15.00 40.00

2012 Dexter Season Four SDCC Autographs

CARDS ISSUED IN 2012 SDCC MYSTERY PACKS
1 John Lithgow 30.00 75.00
who plays Arthur Mitchell
2 Michael C. Hall 50.00 100.00
who plays Dexter Morgan

2012 Dexter Season Four SDCC Costumes

CARDS ISSUED IN 2012 SDCC MYSTERY PACKS
CABB Sgt. Angel Batista shirt 6.00 15.00
CAMS Arthur Mitchell shirt 8.00 20.00
CCHT Christine Hill shirt 8.00 20.00
CDMA Dexter Morgan apron 10.00 25.00

2012 Dexter Season Four SDCC Props

CARDS ISSUED IN 2012 SDCC MYSTERY PACKS
PBL Blood/35
PSD Splatter Dummy/80 20.00 50.00
PSH Silicone Head/299 10.00 25.00
PSH Silicone Hand/200 10.00 25.00
PVL Q-Tip/Latex Glove/255 12.00 30.00

2012 Dexter Season Four Trinity's Kill

COMPLETE SET (9) 10.00 25.00
COMMON CARD (TM1-TM9) 2.50 6.00
THREE CARDS PER BOX

2012 Dexter Season Four Promos

COMPLETE SET 2.00 5.00
CH Dexter hunched over 10.00 25.00
(Chicago)
NY Dexter/Arthur 6.00 15.00
(NYC)
PH Dexter with tools 6.00 15.00
(Philly)
SD Dexter in a hoodie 3.00 8.00
(SDCC)
AP1 Dexter Morgan 5.00 12.00
(album excl.)
AP2 Dexter Morgan 5.00 12.00
(album excl.)

2015 Dexter Seasons Five and Six

COMPLETE SET (72) 8.00 20.00
COMPLETE FACTORY SET 20.00 50.00
COMMON CARD (1-72) .20 .50

2015 Dexter Seasons Five and Six Autographs

COMMON CARD 5.00 12.00
AAG1 Aimee Garcia 12.00 30.00
AAG2 Aimee Garcia 12.00 30.00
ACC1 Christian Camargo 10.00 25.00
ACC2 Christian Camargo 10.00 25.00
AJS1 Julia Stiles 30.00 75.00
AJS2 Julia Stiles 30.00 75.00
AMH1 Michael C. Hall 50.00 100.00

2015 Dexter Seasons Five and Six Beyond the Script

COMPLETE SET (9) 6.00 15.00
COMMON CARD (DB1-DB9) 1.25 3.00

2015 Dexter Seasons Five and Six Dual Autographs

COMMON CARD 50.00 100.00

2015 Dexter Seasons Five and Six Dual Costumes

COMPLETE SET (8) 80.00 150.00
COMMON CARD (DC1-DC8) 8.00 20.00
DC3 Lumen Ann Pierce 10.00 25.00
Dexter Morgan
DC4 Dexter Morgan 10.00 25.00
Lumen Ann Pierce
DC5 Lumen Ann Pierce 12.00 30.00
Dexter Morgan
DC7 Dexter Morgan 10.00 25.00

2015 Dexter Seasons Five and Six Props

COMPLETE SET (5) 60.00 120.00
COMMON CARD 8.00 20.00
DP1 Jordan Chase badge 10.00 25.00
DP3 Noah's Ark pageant script 10.00 25.00
DP4 Chain Link piece 15.00 40.00
DP5 Jordan Chase t-shirt 12.00 30.00

2015 Dexter Seasons Five and Six Quotes

COMPLETE SET (9) 10.00 25.00
COMMON CARD (DQ1-DQ9) 2.50 6.00

2015 Dexter Seasons Five and Six Triple Costumes

COMPLETE SET (2) 30.00 80.00
COMMON CARD 20.00 50.00

2015 Dexter Seasons Five and Six Red Robin Promos

COMPLETE SET (2) 8.00 20.00
COMMON CARD (1-2) 5.00 12.00

2016 Dexter Seasons Seven and Eight

COMPLETE SET (72) 8.00 20.00
COMMON CARD (1-72) .20 .50
*RED FOIL: 4X TO 10X BASIC CARDS

2016 Dexter Seasons Seven and Eight Autographed Costumes

COMMON CARD 10.00 25.00
CA2 Aimee Garcia as Jamie Batista 15.00 40.00

2016 Dexter Seasons Seven and Eight Autographs

COMMON CARD 6.00 15.00
ACR Charlotte Rampling 12.00 30.00
AYS Yvonne Strahovski 150.00 300.00
ACR2 Charlotte Rampling 12.00 30.00
AYS2 Yvonne Strahovski 150.00 300.00
DAMY Michael C. Hall/Yvonne Strahovski 200.00 400.00

2016 Dexter Seasons Seven and Eight Costumes

COMPLETE SET (32) 200.00 400.00
COMMON CARD 5.00 12.00
C1 David Zayas 10.00 25.00
(brown/white shirt)
C2 David Zayas 6.00 15.00
(jean shirt)
C3 C.S. Lee 6.00 15.00
(blue paisley shirt)
C5 Michael C. Hall 8.00 20.00
(gray shirt, standing)
C6 Michael C. Hall 8.00 20.00
(lavender shirt, hands in pockets)
C9 Desmond Harrington 6.00 15.00
(red shirt)
TC Lauren Velez TRIPLE 6.00 15.00
C10 Desmond Harrington 6.00 15.00
(blue/white/red shirt)
C11 Lauren Vélez 6.00 15.00
(flowered top, sitting)
C12 Jennifer Carpenter 8.00 20.00
(peach top)
C18 Michael C. Hall 8.00 20.00
(lt. blue shirt, badge)
C19 Sean Patrick Flanery 6.00 15.00
(blue shirt, striped tie)
C21 Desmond Harrington 6.00 15.00
(brown shirt)
C24 Lauren Vélez 6.00 15.00
(orange top)
C25 Jennifer Carpenter 8.00 20.00
(brown/white striped top)
C26 Jennifer Carpenter 6.00 15.00
(gray/white striped top)
DC1 David Zayas DUAL 8.00 20.00
DC2 C.S. Lee DUAL 8.00 20.00
DC3 Sean Patrick Flanery 6.00 15.00
(blue suit and tie) DUAL
DC4 Sean Patrick Flanery 6.00 15.00
(purple jacket) DUAL
DC5 Ray Stevenson DUAL 10.00 25.00

2016 Dexter Seasons Seven and Eight Dexter's Justice

COMPLETE SET (9) 8.00 20.00
COMMON CARD (DJ1-DJ9) 1.50 4.00
STATED ODDS 1:12

2016 Dexter Seasons Seven and Eight Friend or Foe

COMPLETE SET (9) 10.00 25.00
COMMON CARD (DF1-DF9) 1.50 4.00
STATED ODDS 1:12

2016 Dexter Seasons Seven and Eight Quotes

COMPLETE SET (9) 10.00 25.00
COMMON CARD (DQ1-DQ9) 2.50 6.00
STATED ODDS 1:12

2001 Dexter's Laboratory

COMPLETE SET (72) 4.00 10.00
UNOPENED BOX (24 PACKS) 30.00 40.00
UNOPENED PACK (6 CARDS+1 OFFER CARD) 1.50 2.00
COMMON CARD (1-72) .12 .30
NNO 9-Card Uncut Sheet 2.00 5.00

2001 Dexter's Laboratory Plasma Chase

COMPLETE SET (12) 15.00 40.00
COMMON CARD (P1-P12) 2.00 5.00
STATED ODDS 1:4

2001 Dexter's Laboratory Pre-Release

COMPLETE SET (12) 3.00 8.00
COMMON CARD (PR1-PR12) .40 1.00

2001 Dexter's Laboratory Promos

DL1a Are You (larger image) .75 2.00
DL1b Are You (smaller image)
DL2 At Last .75 2.00
DL3 Oooh, What's .75 2.00

1990 Topps Dick Tracy

COMPLETE SET (88) 8.00 20.00
COMPLETE SET W/STICKERS (99) 10.00 25.00
UNOPENED BOX (36 PACKS) 20.00 30.00
UNOPENED PACK (8 CARDS+1 STICKER) 1.00 1.25
UNOPENED JUMBO BOX (24 PACKS) 20.00 30.00
UNOPENED JUMBO PACK
(16 CARDS+1 STICKER) 1.00 1.25
COMMON CARD (1-88) .20 .50
*OPC: SAME VALUE

1990 Topps Dick Tracy Stickers

COMPLETE SET (11) 2.00 5.00
COMMON STICKERS (1-11) .40 1.00

1990 Dandy Gum Dick Tracy

COMPLETE SET (84) 5.00 12.00
UNOPENED BOX (PACKS)
UNOPENED PACK (CARDS)
COMMON CARD (1-84) .10 .25

2000 Digimon Animated Series Two

COMPLETE SET (32) 5.00 12.00
UNOPENED BOX (24 PACKS) 50.00 100.00
UNOPENED PACK (8 CARDS) 2.50 4.00
COMMON CARD (1-32) .30 .75
*SILVER: .5X TO 1.2X BASIC CARDS .40 1.00
*JAPANESE: 2.5X TO 6X BASIC CARDS 2.00 5.00
*GOLD/100: 5X TO 12X BASIC CARDS 4.00 10.00

2000 Digimon Animated Series Two Digimon Inserts

COMPLETE SET (10) 8.00 20.00
COMMON CARD (D1-D10) 1.25 3.00
STATED ODDS 1:6

1992 Star Pics Dinamation

COMPLETE SET (80) 4.00 10.00
UNOPENED BOX (36 PACKS) 15.00 25.00
UNOPENED PACK (10 CARDS) .75 1.00
COMMON CARD (1-80) .08 .25
NNO Dinamation PROMO 1.25 3.00

1993 Jiffy Pop Dinamation Babies

COMPLETE SET (5) 12.00 30.00
COMMON CARD (1-5) 4.00 10.00

1987 Willy Wonka Dina-Sour Eggs Dinosaurs

COMPLETE SET (12) 8.00 20.00
COMMON CARD 1.00 2.50

1992 DinoCardz

COMPLETE SET (80) 4.00 10.00
UNOPENED BOX (36 PACKS) 40.00 50.00
UNOPENED PACK (10 CARDS) 1.25 2.00
COMMON CARD (1-80) .10 .25
*FLAT FINISH: UNPRICED DUE TO SCARCITY

1992 DinoCardz Pepsi Promos

COMPLETE SET (20) 10.00 25.00
COMMON CARD (1-20) .75 2.00

1991 Kraft Dinomac

COMPLETE SET (3) 2.00 5.00
COMMON CARD .75 2.00

2015 Dinosaur Galaxy

COMPLETE SET (123) 15.00 40.00
COMMON CARD (1-123) .30 .75

2015 Dinosaur Galaxy Promos

COMPLETE SET (6) 10.00 25.00
COMMON CARD (P1-P6) 1.25 3.00
P6 Hal Robins 8.00 20.00

1993 Kitchen Sink Press Dinosaur Nation

COMPLETE BOXED SET (36) 5.00 12.00
COMMON CARD (1-36) .30 .75

1987 Dino-Card Co. Dinosaurs

COMPLETE SET (20) 4.00 10.00
COMMON CARD (1-20) .30 .75

2015 Dinosaurs

COMPLETE SET W/SP (150) 100.00 200.00
COMPLETE SET W/O SP (100) 20.00 50.00
COMMON CARD (1-100) .20 .50
COMMON SP (101-150) 1.25 3.00
*CANVAS MINI: 2.5X TO 6X BASIC CARDS 1.25 3.00
*CANVAS MINI SP: SAME VALUE 1.25 3.00

2015 Dinosaurs 3-D

COMPLETE SET (42) 100.00 200.00
COMMON HERBIVORES (1-24) 1.50 4.00
COMMON PREDATORS (25-33) 3.00 8.00

COMMON MARINE (34-39) 5.00 12.00
COMMON FLYING (40-42) 12.00 30.00
STATED ODDS 1:5 HOBBY; 1:2 LUNCHBOX
HERBIVORES 1:7.5 HOBBY; 1:3 LUNCHBOX
PREDATORS 1:25 HOBBY; 1:10 LUNCHBOX
MARINE 1:50 HOBBY; 1:20 LUNCHBOX
FLYING 1:150 HOBBY; 1:60 LUNCHBOX

2015 Dinosaurs Age of the Dinosaurs Patches

COMMON CARD GROUP A 50.00 100.00
COMMON CARD GROUP B 12.00 30.00
COMMON CARD GROUP C 6.00 15.00
COMMON CARD GROUP D 4.00 10.00
STATED ODDS 1:20 OVERALL
STATED ODDS GROUP A 1:578
STATED ODDS GROUP B 1:179
STATED ODDS GROUP C 1:84
STATED ODDS GROUP D 1:32
AOD9 Amargasaurus D 8.00 20.00
AOD13 Leptoceratops D 5.00 12.00
AOD14 Ankylosaurus D 5.00 12.00
AOD17 Pachyrhinosaurus D 5.00 12.00
AOD22 Maiasaura D 10.00 25.00
AOD32 Carnotaurus D 8.00 20.00
AOD35 Oviraptor D 8.00 20.00
AOD38 Tyrannosaurus Rex C 15.00 40.00
AOD39 Velociraptor B 15.00 40.00
AOD41 Utahraptor D 5.00 12.00
AOD43 Suchomimus B 15.00 40.00
AOD44 Albertosaurus B 20.00 50.00
AOD46 Kronosaurus D 5.00 12.00
AOD47 Elasmosaurus B 15.00 40.00
AOD48 Ichthyosaurus D 6.00 15.00
AOD49 Mosasaurus D 6.00 15.00
AOD50 Plesiosaurus B 15.00 40.00
AOD56 Woolly Mammoth A 250.00 400.00
AOD58 Smilodon A 100.00 200.00
AOD60 Neanderthal Man A 250.00 400.00

2015 Dinosaurs Apex Predators

COMPLETE SET (4) 50.00 100.00
COMMON CARD (AP1-AP4) 10.00 25.00
AP4 Man 15.00 40.00

2015 Dinosaurs Artist Autographs

COMMON AUTO 6.00 15.00
STATED ODDS 1:20
ALL SIGNED BY BENITO GALLEGO
STATED PRINT RUN 49 SER.#'d SETS

2015 Dinosaurs Predators of the Sea

COMPLETE SET (21) 150.00 300.00
COMMON CARD (POS1-POS21) 8.00 20.00
STATED ODDS 1:40
POS2 Megalodon 10.00 25.00

2015 Dinosaurs ROAR Audio Booklets

COMPLETE SET (6) 250.00 500.00
COMMON CARD (1-6) 50.00 100.00
STATED ODDS 1:500
1 Tyrannosaurus Rex 60.00 120.00
4 Triceratops 60.00 120.00

2015 Dinosaurs Stickers

COMPLETE SET (30) 8.00 20.00
COMMON CARD (S1-S30) .60 1.50
STATED ODDS 1:4 HOBBY; 1:LUNCHBOX

1986 Trend Dinosaurs and Prehistorics Fun-to-Know

COMPLETE SET (27) 5.00 12.00
COMMON CARD (1-27) .30 .75

1988 Topps Dinosaurs Attack

COMPLETE SET (55) 3.00 8.00
COMPLETE SET W/STICKERS (66) 4.00 10.00
UNOPENED BOX (48 PACKS) 40.00 60.00
UNOPENED PACK (5 CARDS+1 STICKER) 1.00 1.50
COMMON CARD (1-55) .10 .25

1988 Topps Dinosaurs Attack Stickers

COMPLETE SET (11) 1.25 3.00

COMMON CARD (1-11) .15 .40
STATED ODDS 1:1

1993 Redline Marketing Dinosaurs Mesozoic Era

COMPLETE SET (46) 6.00 15.00
COMMON CARD (1-46) .25 .60

1992 Pro Set Dinosaurs

COMPLETE SET (65) 4.00 10.00
UNOPENED BOX (36 PACKS) 15.00 20.00
UNOPENED PACK (10 CARDS) .75 1.00
COMMON CARD (1-50) .10 .30
COMMON PUZZLE (1P-10P) .10 .30
COMMON TRIVIA (1T-5T) .10 .30

1995 Collect-a-Card Dinotopia

COMPLETE SET (72) 4.00 10.00
UNOPENED BOX (36 PACKS) 20.00 30.00
UNOPENED PACK (8 CARDS) .75 1.00
COMMON CARD (1-72) .10 .25
CT Canyon City Jumbo Case-Topper (8 X 10) 15.00 40.00
NNO Dinotopia PROMO .75 2.00

1995 Collect-a-Card Dinotopia Dino-Fold

COMPLETE SET (10) 20.00 50.00
COMMON CARD (1-10) 2.50 6.00
STATED ODDS 1:12

1995 Collect-a-Card Dinotopia Dino-Vision

COMPLETE SET (8) 20.00 50.00
COMMON CARD (DV1-DV8) 3.00 8.00
STATED ODDS 1:18

1989 Brooke Bond Discovering Our Coast

COMPLETE SET (50) 5.00 12.00
COMMON CARD (1-50) .20 .50

1993 Dynamic Marketing Disney Adventures

COMPLETE SET (100) 8.00 20.00
COMMON CARD (1-100) .15 .40

1993 Dynamic Marketing Disney Adventures Chromium

COMPLETE SET (5) 8.00 20.00
COMMON CARD (1-5) 2.50 6.00

1992 Pro Set Disney Afternoon Promos

COMPLETE SET (10) 25.00 60.00
UNOPENED PACK 4.00 5.00
COMMON CARD (1-10) 3.00 8.00
NNO Darkwing Duck .40 1.00

2003 Disney Classic Movie FilmCardz

COMPLETE SET (72) 6.00 15.00
UNOPENED BOX (24 PACKS)
UNOPENED PACK (5 CARDS)
COMMON CARD (1-72) .15 .40

2003 Disney Classic Movie FilmCardz Rare Prisms

COMPLETE SET (6) 10.00 25.00
COMMON CARD (R1-R6) 2.50 6.00
STATED ODDS 1:8

2003 Disney Classic Movie FilmCardz Ultra Rare Prisms

COMPLETE SET (3) 8.00 20.00
COMMON CARD (UR1-UR3) 3.00 8.00
STATED ODDS 1:24

2003 Disney Classic Movie FilmCardz Promos

COMPLETE SET (3)
COMMON CARD (P1-P3)
P1 A Kiss for Dopey .75 2.00
P2 A Wish Come True .75 2.00
P3 The Sorcerer's Apprentice .75 2.00

2004 Disney Holiday Treasures

COMPLETE SET (50) 12.00 30.00
UNOPENED BOX (5 PACKS+2 FIGURINES) 35.00 40.00
UNOPENED PACK (5 CARDS) 1.25 1.50
COMMON CARD (HT1-HT50) .50 1.25

2014 Disney Infinity Power Play Battle Cards

COMPLETE SET (30) 6.00 15.00
COMMON CARD .40 1.00
COMMON PANEL 2.00 5.00

2016 Disney Movie Stars Woolworth's Australian

COMPLETE SET (42) 25.00 60.00
COMMON CARD (1-42) .75 2.00

2016 Disney Movie Stars Woolworth's Australian Stickers

COMPLETE SET (42) 12.00 30.00
COMMON CARD (1-42) .50 1.25
STATED ODDS 1:1

2004 Disney Pixar Treasures

COMPLETE SET W/SP (175) 25.00 60.00
COMPLETE SET (150) 12.00 30.00
UNOPENED BOX (24 PACKS) 30.00 40.00
UNOPENED PACK (5 CARDS) 1.50 1.75
COMMON CARD (DPT1-DPT150) .15 .40
COMMON CARD (DPT151-DPT160) .40 1.00
COMMON CARD (DPT161-DPT170) .75 2.00
COMMON CARD (DPT171-DPT175) 2.00 5.00
DPT1-DPT100 STATED ODDS THREE PER PACK
DPT101-DPT150 STATED ODDS ONE TO TWO PER PACK
DPT151-DPT160 STATED ODDS 1:3
DPT161-DPT170 STATED ODDS 1:6
DPT171-DPT175 STATED ODDS 1:24

1995 SkyBox Disney Premium

COMPLETE SET W/SP (91) 30.00 60.00
COMPLETE SET (91) 12.00 30.00
UNOPENED BOX (36 PACKS) 50.00 60.00
UNOPENED PACK (6 CARDS) 1.75 2.00
COMMON CARD (1-80) .30 .75
COMMON CARD (81-89) 1.50 4.00
COMMON CARD (90-91) 4.00 10.00

1995 SkyBox Disney Premium Promos

P1 Donald Duck - Good Scouts .60 1.50
P2 The Giant - Brave Little Tailor .60 1.50
SP1 Three Little Pigs 1933 12.00 30.00

2019 Disney Princess

COMPLETE SET (100) 12.00 30.00
UNOPENED BOX (20 PACKS)
UNOPENED PACK (5 CARDS)
COMMON CARD (1-100) .25 .60

2019 Disney Princess Relics

PD1 Tiana 40.00 100.00
PD2 Aurora
PD3 Merida 30.00 75.00
PD4 Pocahontas
PD5 Jasmine
PD6 Rapunzel 50.00 120.00
PD7 Belle 60.00 150.00
PD8 Snow White
PD9 Cinderella
PD10 Ariel 40.00 100.00
PD11 Mulan
PD12 Single Diamond EPACK
PD13 Triple Diamond EPACK
PD14 11 Diamonds EPACK

2019 Disney Princess Stickers

COMPLETE SET (25) 6.00 15.00
COMMON STICKER (S1-S25) .50 1.25

1991 Impel Disney Series One

COMPLETE SET (210) 10.00 25.00
UNOPENED BOX (36 PACKS) 20.00 30.00
UNOPENED PACK (12 CARDS) .75 1.00
COMMON CARD (1-210) .12 .30

1991 Impel Disney Series One Holograms

COMPLETE SET (2) 15.00 40.00
COMMON CARD (H1-H2) 10.00 25.00
RANDOMLY INSERTED INTO PACKS

1991 Impel Disney Series One Promos

COMPLETE SET (5) 4.00 10.00
COMMON CARD 1.25 3.00
6 Conquer the Giant 1.25 3.00
65 One for All 1.25 3.00
111 The Sorcerer's Apprentice 1940 1.25 3.00
190 Paris Originals 1.25 3.00
202 Miki Tiki 1.25 3.00

1992 SkyBox Disney Series Two

COMPLETE SET (200) 6.00 15.00
UNOPENED BOX (36 PACKS) 30.00 40.00
UNOPENED PACK (12 CARDS) 1.00 1.25
COMMON CARD (1-200) .10 .25

1992 SkyBox Disney Series Two Holograms

COMPLETE SET (3) 15.00 40.00
COMMON CARD (1-3) 6.00 15.00
RANDOMLY INSERTED INTO PACKS

1992 SkyBox Disney Series Two Promos

COMPLETE SET (3) 1.25 3.00
COMMON CARD .50 1.25
7 Following in His Footsteps .50 1.25
25 A Lucky Break .50 1.25
193 Air Art .50 1.25

2009 Disney Transportation

COMPLETE SET (25) 20.00
COMMON CARD .60 1.50

2003 Disney Treasures Aladdin Special Edition

COMPLETE SET (10) 1.00 2.50
COMMON CARD (AL1-AL10) .15 .40

2003 Disney Treasures Donald Duck Filmography

COMPLETE SET (45) 10.00 25.00
COMMON CARD (DD1-DD45) .40 1.00
STATED ODDS 1:1
DD1 The Wise Little Hen .40 1.00
DD2 The Band Concert .40 1.00
DD3 Mickey's Firebrigade .40 1.00
DD4 Mickey's Service Station .40 1.00
DD5 Mickey's Circus .40 1.00
DD6 Moving Day .40 1.00
DD7 Don Donald .40 1.00
DD8 Magician Mickey .40 1.00
DD9 Moose Hunters .40 1.00
DD10 Modern Inventions .40 1.00
DD11 Clock Cleaners .40 1.00
DD12 Lonesome Ghosts .40 1.00
DD13 Donald's Better Self .40 1.00
DD14 Donald's Nephews .40 1.00
DD15 The Autograph Hound .40 1.00
DD16 Donald's Dog Laundry .40 1.00
DD17 Mr. Duck Steps Out .40 1.00
DD18 The Nifty Nineties .40 1.00
DD19 Old MacDonald Duck .40 1.00
DD20 Orphan's Benefit .40 1.00
DD21 Mickey's Birthday Party .40 1.00
DD22 Symphony Hour .40 1.00
DD23 The Plastic's Inventor .40 1.00
DD24 The Clock Watcher .40 1.00
DD25 Donald's Crime .40 1.00
DD26 Donald's Double Trouble .40 1.00
DD27 Clown of the Jungle .40 1.00
DD28 Chip and Dale .40 1.00
DD29 Daddy Duck .40 1.00

DD30 Donald's Dream Voice	.40	1.00
DD31 Inferior Decorator	.40	1.00
DD32 Soup's On	.40	1.00
DD33 Tea for Two Hundred	.40	1.00
DD34 Donald's Happy Birthday	.40	1.00
DD35 Crazy Over Daisy	.40	1.00
DD36 Out of Scale	.40	1.00
DD37 Trick or Treat	.40	1.00
DD38 Rugged Bear	.40	1.00
DD39 Working for Peanuts	.40	1.00
DD40 Donald's Diary	.40	1.00
DD41 Grand Canyonscope	.40	1.00
DD42 Donald in Mathmagic Land	.40	1.00
DD43 Donald and the Wheel	.40	1.00
DD44 Mickey's Christmas Carol	.40	1.00
DD45 The Prince and The Pauper	.40	1.00

2003 Disney Treasures Mickey Mouse Filmography

COMPLETE SET (45)	12.00	30.00
COMMON CARD (MM1-MM45)	.50	1.25
STATED ODDS 1:1		

2003 Disney Treasures Pinocchio

COMPLETE SET (10)	12.00	30.00
COMMON CARD (P01-P010)	2.00	5.00
STATED ODDS 1:10		

2003 Disney Treasures Reel Piece of History Patches

COMMON CARD (PH31-PH40)	15.00	40.00
STATED ODDS 1:96		

2003 Disney Treasures Reel Piece of History Quads

COMMON CARD (PH21-PH30)	15.00	40.00
STATED ODDS 1:48		

2003 Disney Treasures Silly Symphonies

COMPLETE SET (9)	10.00	25.00
COMMON CARD (S1-S9)	1.50	4.00
STATED ODDS 1:10		

2003 Disney Treasures Snow White and the Seven Dwarfs

COMPLETE SET (10)	12.00	30.00
COMMON CARD (SW1-SW10)	2.50	6.00

2003 Disney Treasures The Lion King 10th Anniversary

COMPLETE SET (10)	1.00	2.50
COMMON CARD (LK1-LK10)	.15	.40

2003 Disney Treasures Walt Disney Retrospective

COMPLETE SET (10)	1.00	2.50
COMMON CARD (WD1-WD10)	.15	.40

2003 Disney Treasures Winnie the Pooh Filmography

COMPLETE SET (45)	15.00	40.00
COMMON CARD (WP1-WP45)	.60	1.50
STATED ODDS 1:1		

2003 Disney Treasures Promos

P1 Pinocchio		
P2 Mickey Mouse	1.25	3.00
P3 Captain Hook	5.00	12.00
P4 Scrooge McDuck	2.50	6.00

2001 Disney World Signature

COMPLETE SET (25)	8.00	20.00
UNOPENED PACK (5 CARDS)		
COMMON CARD (1-25)	.60	1.50
*GOLD SIG: .5X TO 1.2X BASIC CARDS	.75	2.00

2001 Disney World Signature Cast Member Exclusives

COMPLETE SET (5)	15.00	40.00
COMMON CARD (C1-C5)	4.00	10.00
*GOLD: 1X TO 2.5X BASIC CARDS	10.00	25.00

1997 SkyBox Disney's Hercules

COMPLETE SET (90)	6.00	15.00
UNOPENED BOX (18 PACKS)	15.00	25.00
UNOPENED PACK (8 CARDS)	1.00	1.50
COMMON CARD (1-90)	.12	.30
P1 PROMO (general distribution)	.75	2.00

1997 SkyBox Disney's Hercules Gold Medal

COMPLETE SET (4)	6.00	15.00
COMMON CARD (GM1-GM4)	2.50	6.00
STATED ODDS 1:9		

1997 SkyBox Disney's Hercules Holograms

COMPLETE SET (2)	4.00	10.00
COMMON CARD (H1-H2)	2.50	6.00
STATED ODDS 1:24		

1997 SkyBox Disney's Hercules Stickers

COMPLETE SET (6)	4.00	10.00
COMMON CARD (1-6)	.75	2.00
STATED ODDS 1:3		

2005 Disneyland 50th Anniversary

COMPLETE SET (65)	8.00	20.00
COMPLETE SET W/SP (125)	60.00	120.00
UNOPENED BOX (24 PACKS)	40.00	50.00
UNOPENED PACK (5 CARDS)	2.00	2.50
COMMON CARD (D1-DL125)	.25	.60
POSTERS SP (DL51-100)	.60	1.50
DIE-CUTS SP (DL116-DL125)	2.00	5.00

1991 Upper Deck Disneyland Previews

COMPLETE SET (5)	2.00	5.00
COMMON CARD (1-5)	.60	1.50

2014 Divergent

COMPLETE SET (72)	12.00	30.00
UNOPENED BOX (24 PACKS)	25.00	40.00
UNOPENED PACK (6 CARDS)	1.00	1.50
COMMON CARD (1-72)	.30	.75
A1 Tris PROMO	2.00	5.00
(Hot Topic exclusive)		

Doctor Who

2015 Doctor Who

COMPLETE SET w/o SP (200)	15.00	40.00
UNOPENED BOX (24 PACKS)	150.00	250.00
UNOPENED PACK (8 CARDS)	6.00	10.00
COMMON CARD (1-200)	.15	.40
COMMON SP	2.00	5.00
*BLUE/199: 4X TO 10X BASIC CARDS		
*PURPLE/99: 8X TO 20X BASIC CARDS		
*RED/50: 12X TO 30X BASIC CARDS		
9B The Ninth Doctor SP	6.00	15.00
10B The Tenth Doctor SP	5.00	12.00
11B The Eleventh Doctor SP	4.00	10.00
12B The Twelfth Doctor SP	6.00	15.00
25B Amy Pond SP	2.50	6.00
41B River Song SP	6.00	15.00
42B Rose Tyler SP	4.00	10.00
59B Dalek SP	15.00	40.00

2015 Doctor Who Autographs

COMMON AUTO	10.00	25.00
*BLUE/50: .5X TO 1.2X BASIC AUTOS		
STATED ODDS 1:123		
NNO Bernard Cribbins	15.00	40.00
NNO Bonnie Langford	12.00	30.00
NNO Catrin Stewart	20.00	50.00
NNO Deborah Watling	12.00	30.00
NNO Eric Roberts	60.00	120.00
NNO Eve Myles	30.00	80.00
NNO Frazer Hines	12.00	30.00
NNO Gareth David-Lloyd	20.00	50.00
NNO John Barrowman	50.00	100.00
NNO Mark Strickson	12.00	30.00
NNO Neve McIntosh	15.00	40.00
NNO Noel Clarke	15.00	40.00
NNO Sophie Aldred	12.00	30.00

2015 Doctor Who Christmas Time

COMPLETE SET (10)	8.00	20.00
COMMON CARD (CT1-CT10)	1.25	3.00
STATED ODDS 1:6		

2015 Doctor Who Companions

COMPLETE SET (10)	6.00	15.00
COMMON CARD (C1-C10)	1.00	2.50
STATED ODDS 1:4		

2015 Doctor Who Costumes

STATED ODDS 1:57		
1 Ood Costume	6.00	15.00
2 Rory William's Green Shirt	25.00	60.00
3 Sally Sparrow's Coat	10.00	25.00
4 Tenth Doctor's Striped Trousers	15.00	40.00

2015 Doctor Who Dual Autographs

STATED ODDS 1:14,501		
NNO Colin Baker/Bonnie Langford	250.00	400.00
NNO David Tennant/Freema Agyeman	250.00	400.00

2015 Doctor Who Gadgets

COMPLETE SET (7)	6.00	15.00
COMMON CARD (G1-G7)	1.25	3.00
STATED ODDS 1:12		

2015 Doctor Who Memorable Moments

COMPLETE SET (10)	5.00	12.00
COMMON CARD (MM1-MM10)	.75	2.00
STATED ODDS 1:2		

2015 Doctor Who Tardis Patches

COMMON CARD	5.00	12.00
*PURPLE/99: .5X TO 1.2X BASIC PATCHES		
*RED/25: .75X TO 2X BASIC PATCHES		
STATED ODDS 1:43		
P3 The Third Doctor	8.00	20.00
P4 The Fourth Doctor	6.00	15.00
P5 The Fifth Doctor	6.00	15.00
P7 The Seventh Doctor	8.00	20.00
P8 The Eighth Doctor	8.00	20.00
P9 The Ninth Doctor	8.00	20.00
P10 The Tenth Doctor	8.00	20.00
P11 The Eleventh Doctor	8.00	20.00
P12 The Twelfth Doctor	6.00	15.00
P14 Amy Pond	8.00	20.00
P16 Barbara Wright	6.00	15.00
P17 Christina de Souza	6.00	15.00
P18 Clara Oswald	6.00	15.00
P20 Leela	6.00	15.00
P21 Martha Jones	6.00	15.00
P22 Nyssa	6.00	15.00
P23 River Song	6.00	15.00
P24 Rose Tyler	8.00	20.00
P25 Sarah Jane Smith	6.00	15.00
P28 Tegan Jovanka	6.00	15.00
P30 Zoe	6.00	15.00

2015 Doctor Who Who Is the Doctor

COMPLETE SET (12)	10.00	25.00
COMMON CARD (D1-D12)	1.50	4.00
STATED ODDS 1:8		

2003 Doctor Who Big Screen Previews

COMPLETE SET (10)	6.00	15.00
COMMON CARD (P1-P10)	1.00	2.50

2003 Doctor Who Big Screen

COMPLETE SET (100)	5.00	10.00
UNOPENED BOX (36 PACKS)	50.00	60.00
UNOPENED PACK (8 CARDS)	1.75	2.00
COMMON CARD (1-100)	.08	.20
A0 Peter Cushing CT		

2003 Doctor Who Big Screen Autographs

COMMON CARD (A1-A13)	6.00	15.00
STATED ODDS 1:12		
A1 Roberta Tovey	20.00	50.00
A2 Jill Curzon	8.00	20.00
A3 Bernard Cribbins	15.00	40.00
A4 Ray Brooks	8.00	20.00
A5 Keith Marsh	8.00	20.00
A6 Philip Madoc	8.00	20.00
A8 Jennie Linden	12.00	30.00
A9 Barrie Ingram	8.00	20.00
A10 Michael Coles	8.00	20.00
A12 Sheila Steafel	8.00	20.00
A13 Geoffrey Toone	8.00	20.00
R1 Jill Curzon Redemption		

2003 Doctor Who Big Screen Foil Movie Posters

COMPLETE SET (12)	8.00	20.00
COMMON CARD (F1-F12)	.75	2.00
STATED ODDS 1:3		

2003 Doctor Who Big Screen Promos

COMPLETE SET (9)	12.00	30.00
COMMON PROMO	2.00	5.00

2008 Doctor Who Big Screen Additions

COMPLETE SET (72)	8.00	20.00
UNOPENED BOX (30 PACKS)	55.00	65.00
UNOPENED PACK (5 CARDS)	2.00	2.50
COMMON CARD ()	.15	.40
MC1 Movie Clip	8.00	20.00
NNO2 Dalek 2500/BT		

2008 Doctor Who Big Screen Additions Gold Ink Chase

COMPLETE SET (9)	5.00	12.00
COMMON CARD (F1-F9)	.75	2.00
STATED ODDS 1:6		

2008 Doctor Who Big Screen Additions Promos

COMPLETE SET (2)	3.00	8.00
COMMON CARD (PF1-PR2)	2.00	5.00

2000 Doctor Who Definitive Collection Series One Previews

COMPLETE SET (10)	6.00	15.00
COMMON CARD	1.00	2.50
STATED PRINT RUN 4,000 SER.#'d SETS		

2000 Doctor Who Definitive Collection Series One

COMPLETE SET (120)	6.00	15.00
UNOPENED BOX (36 PACKS)	40.00	50.00
UNOPENED PACK (8 CARDS)	1.25	1.50
COMMON CARD (1-120)	.10	.25

2000 Doctor Who Definitive Collection Series One Autographs

COMMON CARD (A1-A15)	6.00	15.00
STATED ODDS 1:18		
A1 Tom Baker	30.00	80.00
A2 Peter Davison	100.00	200.00
A3 Colin Baker	20.00	50.00
A4 Sylvester McCoy	10.00	25.00
A5 Paul McGann	15.00	40.00
A6 Anneke Wills	10.00	25.00
A8 Wendy Padbury	8.00	20.00
A9 John Levene	8.00	20.00
A10 Caroline John	8.00	20.00
A11 Katy Manning	12.00	30.00
A12 Elisabeth Sladen	10.00	25.00
A14 Nicola Bryant	15.00	40.00
A15 Sophie Aldred	8.00	20.00

2000 Doctor Who Definitive Collection Series One Doctors and Companions

COMPLETE SET (2)	50.00	100.00
COMMON CARD (A1-A2)	25.00	60.00
STATED ODDS 1 SET:CASE		
STATED PRINT RUN 300 SETS		

2000 Doctor Who Definitive Collection Series One Radio Times Covers

COMPLETE SET (17) 2.50 6.00
COMMON CARD (R1-R17) .20 .50
STATED ODDS 1:3

2000 Doctor Who Definitive Collection Series One Promos

COMMON CARD 1.50 4.00
B1 Two Doctors 2.00 5.00
(album exclusive)
NS1 The Fourth Doctor 4.00 10.00
SI1b Doctors, Daleks, Cybermen (No Copyright)
(NSU magazine)

2001 Doctor Who Definitive Collection Series Two Previews

COMPLETE SET (10) 6.00 15.00
COMMON CARD 1.00 2.50
STATED PRINT RUN 999 SETS

2001 Doctor Who Definitive Collection Series Two

COMPLETE SET (120) 6.00 15.00
UNOPENED BOX (36 PACKS) 40.00 50.00
UNOPENED PACK (8 CARDS) 1.25 1.50
COMMON CARD (1-120) .10 .25

2001 Doctor Who Definitive Collection Series Two Autographs

COMMON CARD 8.00 20.00
STATED ODDS 1:18
AU13 ISSUED AS CASE TOPPER
AU1 Lalla Ward 12.00 30.00
AU2 Tom Baker 30.00 80.00
AU8 Elisabeth Sladen 15.00 40.00
AU13 Anthony Ainley 30.00 80.00
(issued as case topper)

2001 Doctor Who Definitive Collection Series Two Case-Toppers

COMPLETE SET (5) 12.00 30.00
COMMON CARD (D1-D5) 3.00 8.00
STATED ODDS 1:CASE

2001 Doctor Who Definitive Collection Series Two Comics of Doctor Who

COMPLETE SET (13) 10.00 25.00
COMMON CARD (F1-F13) 1.00 2.50
STATED ODDS 1:3

2001 Doctor Who Definitive Collection Series Two Promos

COMPLETE SET (11) 12.00 30.00
COMMON CARD 1.50 4.00
WEB1 The Doctor and Romana 2.00 5.00

2002 Doctor Who Definitive Collection Series Three Previews

COMPLETE SET (10) 6.00 15.00
COMMON CARD 1.00 2.50
STATED PRINT RUN 999 SETS

2002 Doctor Who Definitive Collection Series Three

COMPLETE SET (120) 6.00 15.00
UNOPENED BOX (36 PACKS) 30.00 40.00
UNOPENED PACK (8 CARDS) 1.00 1.25
COMMON CARD (1-120) .10 .25

2002 Doctor Who Definitive Collection Series Three Autographs

COMMON CARD (AU1-AU21) 6.00 15.00
STATED ODDS 1:18
AU1 Colin Baker 15.00 40.00
AU2 Sylvester McCoy 20.00 50.00
AU5 Jean Marsh 12.00 30.00
AU9 Mark Eden 10.00 25.00
AU15 Kate O'Mara 10.00 25.00
AU17 Janet Fielding 12.00 30.00
AU20 Peter Davison CT 30.00 80.00
AU21 Jacqueline Pearce ALB 10.00 25.00

2002 Doctor Who Definitive Collection Series Three Case-Toppers

COMPLETE SET (9) 20.00 50.00
COMMON CARD (1-9) 3.00 8.00
STATED ODDS 1 SET:CASE

2002 Doctor Who Definitive Collection Series Three Memories of Doctor Who

COMPLETE SET (14) 4.00 10.00
COMMON CARD (F1-F14) .40 1.00
STATED ODDS 1:3

2002 Doctor Who Definitive Collection Series Three Promos

B2 Two Doctors ALB 2.00 5.00
AE2 Royal Connections 2.00 5.00
CI5 Hands Up 1.25 3.00
TP2 Disguise 2.00 5.00

2016 Doctor Who Extraterrestrial Encounters

COMPLETE SET (100) 6.00 15.00
UNOPENED BOX (24 PACKS) 80.00 100.00
UNOPENED PACK (8 CARDS) 3.00 4.00
COMMON CARD (1-100) .12 .30
*YELLOW: .75X TO 2X BASIC CARDS
*BLUE/99: 8X TO 20X BASIC CARDS
*PURPLE/50: 12X TO 30X BASIC CARDS
*RED/25: 15X TO 40X BASIC CARDS

2016 Doctor Who Extraterrestrial Encounters 50 Years of the Cybermen

COMPLETE SET (8) 6.00 15.00
COMMON CARD (1-8) 1.00 2.50
STATED ODDS 1:4

2016 Doctor Who Extraterrestrial Encounters Autographs

COMMON AUTO 8.00 20.00
STATED ODDS 1:52
NNO Adrian Scarborough 12.00 30.00
NNO Alex Kingston
NNO Angela Bruce 15.00 40.00
NNO Annette Badland 6.00 15.00
NNO Anthony Head
NNO Ariyon Bakare 12.00 30.00
NNO Arthur Darvill
NNO Barnaby Edwards 12.00 30.00
NNO Bernard Cribbins 15.00 40.00
NNO Billie Piper
NNO Catrin Stewart
NNO Chipo Chung 12.00 30.00
NNO Christina Cole 20.00 50.00
NNO Christine Adams 15.00 40.00
NNO Claire Rushbrook 20.00 50.00
NNO Clare Higgins 12.00 30.00
NNO Colin Baker
NNO Dan Starkey
NNO David Gooderson 20.00 50.00
NNO David Tennant
NNO Derek Jacobi
NNO Frances Barber 12.00 30.00
NNO Freema Agyeman
NNO Gabriel Woolf 8.00 20.00
NNO Geoffrey Palmer 20.00 50.00
NNO Georgia Moffett
NNO Ian McNiece 12.00 30.00
NNO Ingrid Oliver
NNO Jacqueline King 20.00 50.00
NNO James Corden
NNO Jami Reid-Quarrel
NNO Jenna Coleman
NNO John Barrowman
NNO John Hurt
NNO John Levene 20.00 50.00
NNO John Simm 25.00 60.00
NNO Keeley Hawes
NNO Kemi-Bo Jacobs 12.00 30.00
NNO Lalla Ward 25.00 60.00
NNO Mark Gatniss
NNO Martha Cope
NNO Michael Jayston 12.00 30.00
NNO Michelle Gomez
NNO Neve McIntosh
NNO Nicholas Briggs
NNO Nick Frost
NNO Nina Toussaint-White 15.00 40.00
NNO Noel Clarke
NNO Paul McGann
NNO Peter Davison
NNO Peter De Jersey
NNO Peter Purves 15.00 40.00
NNO Richard Hope 12.00 30.00
NNO Russell Tovey
NNO Samuel Anderson 15.00 40.00
NNO Sarah Louisse Madison
NNO Sean Gallagher
NNO Simon Fisher-Becker
NNO Simon Williams
NNO Stuart Milligan
NNO Sylvester McCoy
NNO Terry Molloy 15.00 40.00
NNO Tom Baker
NNO Tom Wilton 15.00 40.00
NNO Will Thorp

2016 Doctor Who Extraterrestrial Encounters Companions in Space

COMPLETE SET (12) 8.00 20.00
COMMON CARD (1-12) 1.25 3.00
STATED ODDS 1:12

2016 Doctor Who Extraterrestrial Encounters Costumes

COMMON CARD 5.00 12.00
STATED ODDS 1:37
1 The Tenth Doctor's Suit Trousers/199 12.00 30.00
2 Rose Tyler's Union Jack Shirt/199 6.00 15.00
3 River Song's Black Dress/499 6.00 15.00
5 Jenny's Green T-Shirt/199 8.00 20.00
7 Sally Sparrow's Coat/499 6.00 15.00
8 Ood's Costume/499 6.00 15.00
9 The Eleventh Doctor's Football Jersey/199 8.00 20.00

2016 Doctor Who Extraterrestrial Encounters Doctors Across Space

COMPLETE SET (13) 6.00 15.00
COMMON CARD (1-13) 1.00 2.50
STATED ODDS 1:2

2003 Doctor Who 40th Anniversary Previews

COMPLETE SET (10) 6.00 15.00
COMMON CARD (PR1-PR10) 1.00 2.50
STATED PRINT RUN 999 SETS

2003 Doctor Who 40th Anniversary

COMPLETE SET (100) 5.00 12.00
UNOPENED BOX (36 PACKS) 50.00 60.00
UNOPENED PACK (8 CARDS) 1.50 1.75
COMMON CARD (1-100) .10 .25

2003 Doctor Who 40th Anniversary Autographs

COMMON CARD 6.00 15.00
STATED ODDS 1:12
B1 Brian Blessed ALB 8.00 20.00
WA1 Eric Roberts 25.00 60.00
WA2 Daphne Ashbrook 15.00 40.00
WA3 Paul McGann 20.00 50.00
WA5 Sylvester McCoy 20.00 50.00
WA6 Sophie Aldred 20.00 50.00
WA7 Colin Baker 15.00 40.00
WA8 Peter Davison 15.00 40.00
WA9 Tom Baker 20.00 50.00
WA11 Peter Barkworth 10.00 25.00
WA12 Tony Selby 8.00 20.00
WA13 Martin Jarvis 10.00 25.00
WA14 Sheila Hancock 8.00 20.00
WA15 Elisabeth Sladen 20.00 50.00
WA16 Sarah Sutton 10.00 25.00
WA17 Richard Briers 10.00 25.00
WA18 Burt Kwouk CT 30.00 80.00

2003 Doctor Who 40th Anniversary Costumes

COMPLETE SET (3) 60.00 120.00
COMMON CARD 20.00 50.00
STATED ODDS 1:144

2003 Doctor Who 40th Anniversary Foil Merchandise

COMPLETE SET (14) 6.00 15.00
COMMON CARD (F1-F14) .60 1.50
STATED ODDS 1:3

2003 Doctor Who 40th Anniversary Promos

P1 Doctor Who 1963 - 2003 1.50 4.00
CI7 Peri (Cards, Inc.) 1.25 3.00

2014 Doctor Who + The Daleks Previews

COMPLETE SET (6) 8.00 20.00
P1 Dalek towering over TARDIS 2.00 5.00
P2 Companion cooling forehead 2.00 5.00
P3 smirking Doctor 2.00 5.00
P4 carrying the torch 2.00 5.00
P5 rocky fight at shoreline 2.00 5.00
P6 Dalek controllers 2.00 5.00

2015 Doctor Who + The Daleks

COMPLETE SET (54) 5.00 12.00
UNOPENED BOX (24 PACKS) 50.00 60.00
UNOPENED PACK (5 CARDS) 2.50 3.00
COMMON CARD (1-54) .15 .40

2015 Doctor Who + The Daleks Autographs

COMMON CARD
STATED ODDS 1:
DWBC Bernard Cribbins as Tom 6.00 15.00
DWJC Jill Curzon as Louise 8.00 20.00
(Album Exclusive)

2015 Doctor Who + The Daleks Film Cell

FC1 Congratulations 8.00 20.00

2015 Doctor Who + The Daleks Publicity Gold Foil

COMPLETE SET (9) 6.00 15.00
COMMON CARD (F1-F9) .75 2.00

2015 Doctor Who + The Daleks Promos

MP1 Dealer Promo 8.00 20.00
(@mitchy9210)/100
PR1 Coming Soon 1.50 4.00
(Dalek Tower)
CCP1 Dealer Promo 5.00 12.00
(The Cyber Cellar)/50
MHP1 Dealer Promo
(Matthew Hawkins)/40
NSP1 Dealer Promo
(nonsporttradingcardsuk)/100
RTP1 Dealer Promo 10.00 25.00
(Radickal Cards)
UCP1 Coming Soon 6.00 15.00
(Dalek Tower online excl.)/100
JDWP1 Dealer Promo 8.00 20.00
(JDW Cards)/50
rydeclive1 Dealer Promo
(Rydeclive)/100

2015 Doctor Who Re-Generation Who Promos

COMPLETE SET (2) 2.00 5.00
COMMON CARD 1.25 3.00

1994 Cornerstone Doctor Who Series One

COMPLETE SET (110) 10.00 25.00

UNOPENED BOX (36 PACKS)	50.00	75.00
UNOPENED PACK (10 CARDS)	2.00	2.50
COMMON CARD (1-110)	.15	.40
*GLOSSY: 1X TO 2.5X BASIC CARDS		

1994 Cornerstone Doctor Who Series One Autographs

STATED ODDS 1:432		
1 Anthony Ainley/81	20.00	50.00
2 Colin Baker/80	50.00	100.00
3 John Leeson/82	8.00	20.00
4 John Levene/82	30.00	75.00
5 Peter Davison/83	50.00	100.00
6 Sophie Aldred/84		
7 William Russell/57	20.00	50.00
8 John Levene (gold)/150		

1994 Cornerstone Doctor Who Series One Box Bottoms

COMPLETE SET (2)	2.00	5.00
COMMON CARD	1.25	3.00
STATED ODDS 1:BOX BOTTOM		

1994 Cornerstone Doctor Who Series One Prisms

COMPLETE SET (7)	12.00	30.00
COMMON CARD (P1-P7)	3.00	8.00
STATED ODDS 1:18		

1994 Cornerstone Doctor Who Series One Promos

COMPLETE SET (3)	2.00	5.00
COMMON CARD (A1-A3)	.75	2.00

1995 Cornerstone Doctor Who Series Two Autographs

1 John Levene		
2 Jon Pertwee	75.00	150.00
3 Nicholas Courtney	12.00	30.00
4 Sophie Aldred		

1995 Cornerstone Doctor Who Series Two Box-Bottoms

COMPLETE SET (2)	1.25	3.00
COMMON CARD (1-2)	.75	2.00
STATED ODDS 1:BOX BOTTOM		

1995 Cornerstone Doctor Who Series Two Foil Villains

COMPLETE SET (7)	15.00	40.00
COMMON CARD (F1-F7)	3.00	8.00
STATED ODDS 1:12		

1995 Cornerstone Doctor Who Series Two Premiere

COMPLETE SET (9)	2.50	6.00
COMMON CARD (1-9)	.40	1.00
STATED ODDS 1:2		

1995 Cornerstone Doctor Who Series Two Promos

B1a Doctor Who logo (orange back)	.75	2.00
B1b Doctor Who logo (red back)	.75	2.00
B2a 1st Doctor and friend (green back)	.75	2.00
B2b 1st Doctor and friend (purple back)	.75	2.00
B3a 4th Doctor/Leela/K9 (blue back)	.75	2.00
B3b 4th Doctor/Leela/K9 (yellow back)	.75	2.00
B4a 7th Doctor (blue back)	.75	2.00
B4b 7th Doctor (pink back)	.75	2.00

1995 Cornerstone Doctor Who Series Three

COMPLETE SET (110)	10.00	25.00
UNOPENED BOX (36 PACKS)	20.00	30.00
UNOPENED PACK (10 CARDS)	1.00	1.25
COMMON CARD (221-330)	.15	.40
*GLOSSY: 1X TO 2.5X BASIC CARDS		
NNO The Master FOIL	5.00	12.00

1995 Cornerstone Doctor Who Series Three Box Bottoms

COMPLETE SET (2)	1.25	3.00
COMMON CARD	.75	2.00
STATED ODDS 1:BOX BOTTOM		

1995 Cornerstone Doctor Who Series Three Companions Premiere

COMPLETE SET (6)	5.00	12.00
COMMON CARD (10-15)	1.25	3.00
STATED ODDS 1:6		

1995 Cornerstone Doctor Who Series Three Foil Doctors

COMPLETE SET (7)	12.00	30.00
COMMON CARD (F1-F7)	2.50	6.00
STATED ODDS 1:9		

1995 Cornerstone Doctor Who Series Three Inside Trader Exclusives

COMPLETE SET (2)	1.25	3.00
COMMON CARD	.75	2.00
STATED ODDS 1:BOX BOTTOM		
Pr15 3rd Doctor and Dalek	.75	2.00
Pr16 3rd Doctor and K9	.75	2.00

1995 Cornerstone Doctor Who Series Three Promos

COMPLETE SET (4)	8.00	20.00
COMMON CARD	.75	2.00
IT4 4th Doctor on bike (Inside Trader excl.)	8.00	20.00

1996 Cornerstone Doctor Who Series Four

COMPLETE SET (90)	6.00	15.00
UNOPENED BOX (36 PACKS)	15.00	20.00
UNOPENED PACK (10 CARDS)	.50	.75
COMMON CARD (1-90)	.12	.30
*GLOSSY: 1X TO 2.5X BASIC CARDS	.30	.75

1996 Cornerstone Doctor Who Series Four Autographs

COMPLETE SET (4)	90.00	175.00
COMMON CARD	20.00	50.00
STATED ODDS 1:432		
STATED PRINT RUN 90 SER.#'d SETS		

1996 Cornerstone Doctor Who Series Four Foil Doctors

COMPLETE SET (8)	15.00	40.00
COMMON CARD (i1-i8)	3.00	8.00
STATED ODDS 1:9		
i8 IS FACTORY SET EXCLUSIVE		
i8 The Eighth Doctor FACT	4.00	10.00

1996 Cornerstone Doctor Who Series Four Oversized Tribute

COMPLETE SET (2)	6.00	15.00
COMMON CARD (E1-E2)	4.00	10.00
STATED ODDS 1:BOX		

1996 Cornerstone Doctor Who Series Four Promos

COMPLETE SET (5)	4.00	10.00
COMMON CARD	.75	2.00
D3 Behind the Scenes	1.25	3.00
D4 Behind the Scenes	1.25	3.00
IT6 3rd Doctor and friend (Inside Trader exclusive)	2.00	5.00

2023 Rittenhouse Doctor Who Series 1-4

COMPLETE SET (156)	15.00	40.00
UNOPENED BOX (24 PACKS)	100.00	125.00
UNOPENED PACK (5 CARDS)	5.00	6.00
COMMON CARD (1-156)	.20	.50
*GOLD TARDIS/50: 10X TO 25X BASIC CARDS		
*RED TARDIS/25: 20X TO 50X BASIC CARDS		

2023 Rittenhouse Doctor Who Series 1-4 Adversaries

COMPLETE SET (31)	15.00	40.00
COMMON CARD (ADV01-ADV31)	.75	2.00
STATED ODDS 1:8		

2023 Rittenhouse Doctor Who Series 1-4 Allies

COMPLETE SET W/O RR (21)	12.00	30.00
COMMON CARD (AL01-AL22)	1.00	2.50
STATED ODDS 1:12		
AL05a Pete Tyler Alt Universe RR		

2023 Rittenhouse Doctor Who Series 1-4 Bordered Autographs

COMMON AUTO	6.00	15.00
STATED OVERALL ODDS 1:8		
L = 300-500 COPIES		
VL = 200-300 COPIES		
EL = 100-200 COPIES		
S = 100 OR FEWER COPIES		
NNO Anna Hope VL	8.00	20.00
NNO Annette Badland VL	8.00	20.00
NNO Billie Piper S	100.00	250.00
NNO Camille Coduri S AB	25.00	60.00
NNO Christina Cole VL	8.00	20.00
NNO Christopher Eccleston S	150.00	400.00
NNO Dan Starkey EL	12.00	30.00
NNO David Tennant (Tardis) S AB	200.00	500.00
NNO Ellen Thomas VL	8.00	20.00
NNO Freema Agyeman VL	20.00	50.00
NNO Sean Gilder VL	10.00	25.00
NNO Shaun Dingwall VL	10.00	25.00
NNO Tom Goodman-Hill VL	10.00	25.00

2023 Rittenhouse Doctor Who Series 1-4 Case-Toppers

COMPLETE SET (2)	15.00	40.00
COMMON CARD (CT1-CT2)	10.00	25.00
STATED ODDS 1:CASE		

2023 Rittenhouse Doctor Who Series 1-4 The Companions Donna Noble Puzzle

COMPLETE SET (9)	10.00	25.00
COMMON CARD (CD1-CD9)	1.50	4.00
STATED ODDS 1:24		

2023 Rittenhouse Doctor Who Series 1-4 The Companions Martha Jones Puzzle

COMPLETE SET (9)	10.00	25.00
COMMON CARD (CM1-CM9)	1.50	4.00
STATED ODDS 1:24		

2023 Rittenhouse Doctor Who Series 1-4 The Companions Rose Tyler Puzzle

COMPLETE SET (9)	12.00	30.00
COMMON CARD (CR1-CR9)	2.50	6.00
STATED ODDS 1:24		

2023 Rittenhouse Doctor Who Series 1-4 Dual Autographs

COMMON AUTO	100.00	250.00
RANDOMLY INSERTED INTO PACKS		
EL = 100-200		
S = 100 OR FEWER		
NNO B.Piper/C.Coduri EL	150.00	400.00
NNO C.Eccleston/B.Piper 6CI	250.00	600.00
NNO D.Tennant/B.Piper 6CI	250.00	600.00

2023 Rittenhouse Doctor Who Series 1-4 Full Bleed Autographs

COMMON AUTO	6.00	15.00
STATED OVERALL ODDS 1:8		
L = 300-500 COPIES		
VL = 200-300 COPIES		
EL = 100-200 COPIES		
S = 100 OR FEWER COPIES		
NNO Andrew Garfield S	500.00	1200.00
NNO Billie Piper S	100.00	250.00
NNO Billie Piper S AB	125.00	300.00
NNO Camille Coduri EL	25.00	60.00
NNO Chipo Chung L	8.00	20.00
NNO Christina Cole L	12.00	30.00
NNO Christopher Eccleston S	150.00	400.00
NNO Christopher Eccleston S AB	200.00	500.00
NNO Dan Starkey VL	8.00	20.00
NNO David Tennant EL	200.00	500.00
NNO Freema Agyeman EL	30.00	75.00
NNO Gabriel Woolf L	10.00	25.00
NNO Ruari Mears VL	10.00	25.00
NNO Ruari Mears VL	10.00	25.00
NNO Sarah Parish L	8.00	20.00
NNO Sean Gilder L	8.00	20.00
NNO Simon Callow	12.00	30.00
NNO Will Thorp L	10.00	25.00
NNO Yasmin Bannerman as Jabe	8.00	20.00

2023 Rittenhouse Doctor Who Series 1-4 Holiday Specials

COMPLETE SET (48)	20.00	50.00
COMMON CARD	1.00	2.50
STATED ODDS 1:8		

2023 Rittenhouse Doctor Who Series 1-4 Inscriptions

COMMON ADAMS	12.00	30.00
COMMON AGYEMAN	25.00	60.00
COMMON BADLAND	15.00	40.00
COMMON BANNERMAN	20.00	50.00
COMMON BENTON	10.00	25.00
COMMON BURING	25.00	60.00
COMMON CARNES	12.00	30.00
COMMON CHUNG	25.00	60.00
COMMON CLARKE	15.00	40.00
COMMON CODURI	30.00	75.00
COMMON COLE	15.00	40.00
COMMON COLLINS	12.00	30.00
COMMON DINGWALL	12.00	30.00
COMMON ECCLESTON	250.00	600.00
COMMON GILDER	12.00	30.00
COMMON GOODMAN-HILL	12.00	30.00
COMMON HART	15.00	40.00
COMMON HAYDEN-SMITH	12.00	30.00
COMMON HAYES	10.00	25.00
COMMON HOPE	10.00	25.00
COMMON JAMES	12.00	30.00
COMMON JOHNSON	10.00	25.00
COMMON JOYNER	15.00	40.00
COMMON KASEY	30.00	75.00
COMMON KING	10.00	25.00
COMMON KNIGHT	8.00	20.00
COMMON LLOYD	15.00	40.00
COMMON LOREN	12.00	30.00
COMMON MARC	8.00	20.00
COMMON MEARS	10.00	25.00
COMMON NEWTON	15.00	40.00
COMMON PARISH	12.00	30.00
COMMON PIPER	100.00	250.00
COMMON PLOWMAN	15.00	40.00
COMMON RIDDELL	8.00	20.00
COMMON RUSCOE	10.00	25.00
COMMON RYAN	10.00	25.00
COMMON STARKEY	12.00	30.00
COMMON STINTON	10.00	25.00
COMMON THORP	10.00	25.00
COMMON TSHABALALA	20.00	50.00
COMMON WOOLF	15.00	40.00
STATED OVERALL ODDS 1:24		

2023 Rittenhouse Doctor Who Series 1-4 The 9th Doctor Puzzle

COMPLETE SET (9)	12.00	30.00
COMMON CARD (DE1-DE9)	2.50	6.00
STATED ODDS 1:48		

2023 Rittenhouse Doctor Who Series 1-4 The 10th Doctor Puzzle

COMPLETE SET (9)	12.00	30.00
COMMON CARD (DT1-DT9)	2.50	6.00
STATED ODDS 1:48		

2023 Rittenhouse Doctor Who Series 1-4 Promos

P1 General Distribution	2.00	5.00
P2 Album Exclusive	10.00	25.00

2022 Rittenhouse Doctor Who Series 11 and 12

COMPLETE SET (60)	10.00	25.00
UNOPENED BOX (24 PACKS)	60.00	100.00
UNOPENED PACK (5 CARDS)	3.00	5.00
COMMON CARD (1-60)	.40	1.00
*PARALLEL: .75X TO 2X BASIC CARDS		
*UK PARALLEL: .75X TO 2X BASIC CARDS		

*GOLD/99: 3X TO 8X BASIC CARDS
*TEAL/99: 3X TO 8X BASIC CARDS
*ORANGE/50: 6X TO 15X BASIC CARDS
*RED/50: 6X TO 15X BASIC CARDS

2022 Rittenhouse Doctor Who Series 11 and 12 Red TARDIS

COMPLETE SET (60)
*RED: 6X TO 15X BASIC CARDS
STATED PRINT RUN 50 SER.#'d SETS

2022 Rittenhouse Doctor Who Series 11 and 12 3-D Case-Toppers

COMPLETE SET (2) 15.00 40.00
COMMON CARD (CT1-CT2) 10.00 25.00
STATED ODDS 1:CASE

2022 Rittenhouse Doctor Who Series 11 and 12 Allies and Adversaries

COMPLETE SET (18) 20.00 50.00
COMMON CARD (HA01-HA18) 2.50 6.00
STATED ODDS 1:12

2022 Rittenhouse Doctor Who Series 11 and 12 Allies and Adversaries UK

COMPLETE SET (18) 15.00 40.00
COMMON CARD (UA1-UA18) 2.00 5.00
STATED ODDS 1:12
UK EXCLUSIVE

2022 Rittenhouse Doctor Who Series 11 and 12 Asia Paintbrush Posters

COMPLETE SET (7) 25.00 60.00
COMMON CARD (AP1-AP7) 5.00 12.00
STATED ODDS 1:48
UK EXCLUSIVE

2022 Rittenhouse Doctor Who Series 11 and 12 Asia Posters

COMPLETE SET (7) 30.00 75.00
COMMON CARD (APP1-APP7) 6.00 15.00
STATED ODDS 1:48

2022 Rittenhouse Doctor Who Series 11 and 12 Bordered Autographs

L = 300-500 COPIES
VL = 200-300 COPIES
EL = 100-200 COPIES
S = 100 OR FEWER
STATED OVERALL ODDS 1:8
NNO Alan Cumming as King James EL UK 20.00 50.00
NNO Bhavnisha Parmar VL 12.00 30.00
NNO Charlotte Ritchie as Lin EL UK 12.00 30.00
NNO Ian Gelder as Zellin VL UK 6.00 15.00
NNO Jo Martin EL 25.00 60.00
NNO Jodie Whittaker as The Doctor EL UK 200.00 500.00
NNO Kevin Eldon VL 8.00 20.00
NNO Mandip Gill as Yasmin Khan EL UK 60.00 150.00
NNO Mark Addy as Paltraki VL UK 10.00 25.00
NNO Patrick O'Kane VL 6.00 15.00
NNO Paul Kasey VL 8.00 20.00
NNO Ritu Arya as Gat VL UK 6.00 15.00
NNO Samuel Oatley as Tzim-Sha VL UK 6.00 15.00
NNO Sharon D. Clarke VL 6.00 15.00
NNO Tosin Cole EL 30.00 75.00

2022 Rittenhouse Doctor Who Series 11 and 12 Character Mirror

COMPLETE SET (5) 10.00 25.00
COMMON CARD (B1-B5) 2.50 6.00
STATED ODDS 1:48
M1 The Thirteenth Doctor 6.00 15.00

2022 Rittenhouse Doctor Who Series 11 and 12 Dual Autographs

COMMON AUTO 20.00 50.00
RANDOMLY INSERTED INTO PACKS
NNO I.Gelder/CH Ashitey VL 25.00 60.00
NNO J.Whittaker/J.Martin 8CI UK 300.00 600.00
NNO J.Whittaker/S.Dhawan 8CI 200.00 400.00
NNO S.Dhawan/P.O'Kane 4CI 60.00 150.00

2022 Rittenhouse Doctor Who Series 11 and 12 Full Bleed Autographs

COMMON AUTO 5.00 12.00
L = 300-500 COPIES
EL = 100-200 COPIES
S = 100 OR FEWER
STATED OVERALL ODDS 1:8
NNO Alan Cumming EL 25.00 60.00
NNO Amy Booth-Steel 10.00 25.00
NNO Barbara Fadden L 6.00 15.00
NNO Bhavnisha Parmar L UK 12.00 30.00
NNO Brett Goldstein EL UK 60.00 150.00
NNO Charlotte Ritchie VL 10.00 25.00
NNO Christian Rubeck L 6.00 15.00
NNO Clare-Hope Ashitey VL 8.00 20.00
NNO Gia Re 8.00 20.00
NNO Haley McGee L 6.00 15.00
NNO Jo Martin VL UK 25.00 60.00
NNO Joana Borja L 10.00 25.00
NNO Jodie Whittaker EL 200.00 500.00
NNO Julie Hesmondhalgh 6.00 15.00
NNO Kirsty Besterman 10.00 25.00
NNO Laura Fraser L 10.00 25.00
NNO Mandip Gill EL 50.00 125.00
NNO Mark Addy VL 10.00 25.00
NNO Molly Harris 8.00 20.00
NNO Nadia Parkes L 8.00 20.00
NNO Nicholas Briggs/Voice of Cybermen VL 12.00 30.00
NNO Nicholas Briggs/Voice of Daleks VL 12.00 30.00
NNO Patrick O'Kane VL UK 10.00 25.00
NNO Paul Kasey VL UK 8.00 20.00
NNO Samuel Oatley VL 8.00 20.00
NNO Sharon D. Clarke L UK 6.00 15.00
NNO Tosin Cole EL UK 40.00 100.00

2022 Rittenhouse Doctor Who Series 11 and 12 Graffiti Art Character

COMPLETE SET (4) 40.00 100.00
COMMON CARD (CA1-CA4) 12.00 30.00
STATED ODDS 1:144
UK EXCLUSIVE
CA1 The Doctor 25.00 60.00

2022 Rittenhouse Doctor Who Series 11 and 12 Inscriptions

COMMON ADDY 10.00 25.00
COMMON ARYA 25.00 60.00
COMMON ASHITEY 10.00 25.00
COMMON BALDRY 8.00 20.00
COMMON BAXTER 10.00 25.00
COMMON BESTERMAN 15.00 40.00
COMMON BOOTH-STEEL 8.00 20.00
COMMON BORJA 12.00 30.00
COMMON BOWMAN 10.00 25.00
COMMON BRIGGS 8.00 20.00
COMMON CHIMIMBA 8.00 20.00
COMMON CLARKE 8.00 20.00
COMMON COLE 12.00 30.00
COMMON COLLINS-LEVY 8.00 20.00
COMMON CUMMING 40.00 100.00
COMMON CUZNER
COMMON DHAWAN 50.00 125.00
COMMON DOOLEY 8.00 20.00
COMMON ELDON 10.00 25.00
COMMON FADDEN 8.00 20.00
COMMON FINNERAN 10.00 25.00
COMMON FLANAGAN 8.00 20.00
COMMON FOSTER 10.00 25.00
COMMON FRASER 8.00 20.00
COMMON GALIEVA 12.00 30.00
COMMON GELDER 10.00 25.00
COMMON GILL 30.00 75.00
COMMON GLENISTER 12.00 30.00
COMMON GOLDSTEIN 75.00 200.00
COMMON GRAHAM 10.00 25.00
COMMON HARRIS 10.00 25.00
COMMON HESMONDHALGH 10.00 25.00
COMMON HUSSAIN 8.00 20.00
COMMON KASEY 10.00 25.00
COMMON LLOYD 10.00 25.00
COMMON MARTIN 30.00 75.00
COMMON MCELHINNEY 8.00 20.00
COMMON MCGEE 8.00 20.00
COMMON MILLER 10.00 25.00
COMMON MOHINDRA 8.00 20.00
COMMON OATLEY 8.00 20.00
COMMON O'KANE 15.00 40.00
COMMON PACKER 10.00 25.00
COMMON PARKES 10.00 25.00
COMMON PARMAR 8.00 20.00
COMMON PATEL 8.00 20.00
COMMON RAINER
COMMON RE 25.00 60.00
COMMON RITCHIE 20.00 50.00
COMMON ROBINSON 12.00 30.00
COMMON RUBECK 10.00 25.00
COMMON SHALLOO 12.00 30.00
COMMON SHIELDS 8.00 20.00
COMMON STEELE 8.00 20.00
COMMON STOKKE 10.00 25.00
COMMON TIHNGANG 10.00 25.00
COMMON WHITTAKER 200.00 500.00
COMMON ZAZA 8.00 20.00
STATED ODDS 1:24

2022 Rittenhouse Doctor Who Series 11 and 12 New Year Specials

COMPLETE SET (16) 30.00 75.00
COMMON CARD 2.50 6.00
STATED ODDS 1:24
ROTD1 The Doctor 8.00 20.00

2022 Rittenhouse Doctor Who Series 11 and 12 New Year Specials Posters

COMPLETE SET (2) 30.00 75.00
COMMON CARD 20.00 50.00
STATED ODDS 1:288

2022 Rittenhouse Doctor Who Series 11 and 12 Space for All Metal Portraits

COMPLETE SET W/RR (5) 60.00 150.00
COMPLETE SET W/O RR (4) 50.00 125.00
COMMON CARD (M1-M5) 15.00 40.00
STATED ODDS 1:288
B5 The Doctor RR 25.00 60.00

2022 Rittenhouse Doctor Who Series 11 and 12 TARDIS

COMPLETE SET (9) 10.00 25.00
COMMON CARD (T1-T9) 1.50 4.00
STATED ODDS 1:48

2022 Rittenhouse Doctor Who Series 11 and 12 The Universe Is Calling

COMPLETE SET (4) 30.00 75.00
COMMON CARD (U1-U4) 8.00 20.00
STATED ODDS 1:144
U1 The Doctor 12.00 30.00

2022 Rittenhouse Doctor Who Series 11 and 12 Promos

COMPLETE SET (5)
COMMON CARD
P2 Philly Non-Sports Show
P3 Album Exclusive
HP1 General Distribution
PT1 General Distribution
UKP1 General Distribution

2017 Doctor Who Signature Series

COMPLETE SET (100) 20.00 50.00
UNOPENED BOX (4 PACKS) 100.00 120.00
UNOPENED PACK (5 CARDS) 25.00 30.00
COMMON CARD (1-100) .20 .50
*GREEN/50: 3X TO 8X BASIC CARDS
*YELLOW/25: 6X TO 15X BASIC CARDS
*PURPLE/10: 12X TO 30X BASIC CARDS

2017 Doctor Who Signature Series Autographs

COMMON AUTO (SKIP #'d) 6.00 15.00
*GREEN/50: .5X TO 1.2X BASIC AUTOS
STATED ODDS 1:1
16 Arthur Darvill 15.00 40.00
17 Alex Kingston 20.00 50.00
26 Carol Anne Ford 15.00 40.00
27 Richard Hope 6.00 15.00
28 Ralph Watson 8.00 20.00
30 Christine Adams 8.00 20.00
33 Annette Badland 8.00 20.00
34 Peter De Jersey 6.00 15.00
35 David Gooderson 6.00 15.00
36 Georgia Moffett 15.00 40.00
37 Matthew Waterhouse 6.00 15.00
39 Geoffrey Beevers 10.00 25.00
40 Velile Tshabalala 8.00 20.00
42 Adjoa Andoh 5.00 12.00
44 Ross Mullan 6.00 15.00
45 Eric Loren 6.00 15.00
46 Ben Righton 6.00 15.00
47 Sarah Sutton 15.00 40.00
49 Deborah Watling 6.00 15.00
50 Mark Strickson 8.00 20.00
53 Keeley Hawes 15.00 40.00
61 Lalla Ward 12.00 30.00
62 Chris Bowen 6.00 15.00
64 Adrian Scarborough 4.00 10.00
65 Peter Purves 8.00 20.00
67 Ellie Haddington 6.00 15.00
69 Russell Tovey 8.00 20.00
73 Louise Jameson 12.00 30.00
74 Michael Goldsmith 6.00 15.00
76 Christina Cole 6.00 15.00
77 Angela Bruce 6.00 15.00
78 Nicholas Briggs 10.00 25.00
80 Jemma Redgrave 15.00 40.00
81 Trevord Laird 6.00 15.00
82 Michael Jayston 12.00 30.00
84 Simon Williams 6.00 15.00
88 David Garfield 6.00 15.00
89 Tom Goodman-Hill 8.00 20.00
90 Joe Dempsie 6.00 15.00
91 Frazer Hines 10.00 25.00
92 Sophie Aldred 15.00 40.00
95 Bonnie Langford 8.00 20.00
96 Shaun Dingwall
97 Stewart Bevan 6.00 15.00
99 Derek Jacobi 15.00 40.00

2018 Doctor Who Signature Series Autographs

COMMON AUTO 6.00 15.00
*GREEN/50: .5X TO 1.2X BASIC AUTOS
*BLUE/25: .6X TO 1.5X BASIC AUTOS
DWAAD Arthur Darvill 15.00 40.00
Rory Last Centurion
DWACB Colin Baker 30.00 75.00
DWACR Claire Rushbrook 8.00 20.00
DWACS Catrin Stewart 15.00 40.00
DWADS Dan Starkey 12.00 30.00
DWAFA Freema Agyeman 20.00 50.00
DWAFB Frances Barber 15.00 40.00
DWAGM Georgia Moffett 15.00 40.00
DWAIO Ingrid Oliver 25.00 60.00
DWAJB John Barrowman 20.00 50.00
DWAJC James Corden 30.00 75.00
DWAJH John Hurt 60.00 120.00
DWAJL John Levene 8.00 20.00
DWAKH Keeley Hawes 10.00 25.00
DWAKM Katy Manning 20.00 50.00
DWANB Nicholas Briggs 12.00 30.00
DWANF Nick Frost 30.00 75.00
DWAPD Peter Davison 20.00 50.00
DWART Russell Tovey 8.00 20.00
DWASH Sonita Henry 8.00 20.00
DWASP Sarah Parish 15.00 40.00
DWASR Struan Rodger 10.00 25.00
DWATK Tommy Knight 8.00 20.00
DWATM Terry Molloy 10.00 25.00
DWAADR Arthur Darvill 15.00 40.00
Rory Williams
DWAAKR Alex Kingston 25.00 60.00
DWAAKS Alex Kingston 25.00 60.00
DWAASH Anthony Head 12.00 30.00
DWABPM Billie Piper 60.00 120.00
The Moment

DWABPR Billie Piper 75.00 150.00
Rose Tyler
DWACAF Carol Anne Ford 8.00 20.00
DWADJM Derek Jacobi 15.00 40.00
The Master
DWADJY Derek Jacobi 12.00 30.00
Professor Yana
DWAGDL Gareth David-Lloyd 8.00 20.00
DWAJCO James Corden 30.00 75.00
DWAJRQ Jami Reid-Quarrell 10.00 25.00
DWAKMJ Kemi-Bo Jacobs 8.00 20.00
DWAMGG Mark Gatiss 8.00 20.00
Gantok
DWAMGM Michelle Gomez 12.00 30.00
DWANTW Nina Toussaint-White 10.00 25.00
DWAPMG Paul McGann 25.00 60.00
DWASMC Sylvester McCoy 30.00 75.00
DWASMS Sylvester McCoy 30.00 75.00
DWACLKH Chris Lew Kum Hoi 8.00 20.00

2018 Doctor Who Signature Series Autographs Green

*GREEN: .5X TO 1.2X BASIC AUTO
STATED PRINT RUN 50 SER.#'d SETS
DWAJCC Jenna Coleman 200.00 350.00

2016 Doctor Who Tenth Doctor Adventures Widevision

COMPLETE SET (88) 10.00 25.00
FACTORY SEALED SET
COMMON CARD (1-88) .25 .60

2016 Doctor Who Tenth Doctor Adventures Widevision Autographs

COMMON CARD 10.00 25.00
STATED ODDS OVERALL 2:BOX
WAAA Adjoa Andoh 15.00 40.00
WAAH Anthony Head 15.00 40.00
WAAK Alex Kingston 30.00 80.00
WABC Bernard Cribbins 15.00 40.00
WABE Barnaby Edwards 20.00 50.00
WABP Billie Piper 100.00 200.00
WABR Ben Righton 12.00 30.00
WACC Camille Coduri 12.00 30.00
WACH Clare Higgins 20.00 50.00
WACR Claire Rushbrook 12.00 30.00
WADC Debbie Chazen 15.00 40.00
WADJ Derek Jacobi 60.00 120.00
WADT David Tennant 150.00 300.00
WAFA Freema Agyeman 30.00 80.00
WAGM Georgia Moffett 30.00 80.00
WAGP Geoffrey Palmer 12.00 30.00
WAJB John Barrowman 50.00 100.00
WAJK Jacqueline King 25.00 60.00
WAJS John Simm 60.00 120.00
WANB Nicholas Briggs 15.00 40.00
WANC Noel Clarke 15.00 40.00
WAPd Peter de Jersey 12.00 30.00
WASD Shaun Dingwall 15.00 40.00
WASP Sarah Parish 15.00 40.00
WATB Thomas Brodie-Sangster 15.00 40.00
WAWT Will Tharp 15.00 40.00
WAABA Annette Badland 20.00 50.00
WAJRE Jemma Redgrave 30.00 75.00

2016 Doctor Who Timeless

COMPLETE SET (100) 8.00 20.00
UNOPENED BOX (24 PACKS) 60.00 70.00
UNOPENED PACK (8 CARDS) 2.50 3.00
COMMON CARD (1-100) .15 .40
*GREEN: 2X TO 5X BASIC CARDS
*BLUE/99: 8X TO 20X BASIC CARDS
*PURPLE/50: 12X TO 30X BASIC CARDS
*RED/25: 15X TO 40X BASIC CARDS

2016 Doctor Who Timeless Autographs

COMMON CARD 10.00 25.00
STATED ODDS 1:24
NNO Alan Ruscoe
NNO Alex Kingston 25.00 60.00
NNO Ariyon Bakare 12.00 30.00
NNO Arthur Darvill
NNO Billie Piper 60.00 120.00
NNO Bonnie Langford
NNO Camille Coduri 15.00 40.00
NNO Carole Ann Ford
NNO Catrin Stewart
NNO Chipo Chung 15.00 40.00
NNO Clare Higgins 15.00 40.00
NNO Colin Baker
NNO Dan Starkey
NNO Daphne Ashbrook 15.00 40.00
NNO David Tennant
NNO Debbie Chazen 12.00 30.00
NNO Deborah Watling
NNO Derek Jacobi
NNO Elizabeth Fost 15.00 40.00
NNO Eric Loren
NNO Eric Roberts 15.00 40.00
NNO Eve Myles
NNO Frances Barber
NNO Frazer Hines
NNO Freema Agyeman
NNO Gabriel Woolf
NNO Gareth David-Lloyd
NNO Geoffrey Palmer 12.00 30.00
NNO Georgia Moffett
NNO Ian McNiece
NNO Ingrid Oliver
NNO Jami Reid-Quarrell 15.00 40.00
NNO Jenna Coleman
NNO Jimmy Vee
NNO John Barrowman
NNO John Hurt
NNO John Simm 60.00 120.00
NNO Katy Manning 15.00 40.00
NNO Kemi-Bo Jacobs 15.00 40.00
NNO Mark Strickson 12.00 30.00
NNO Marnix van den Broeke 12.00 30.00
NNO Matthew Waterhouse 12.00 30.00
NNO Michelle Gomez 50.00 100.00
NNO Neve McIntosh 15.00 40.00
NNO Nicholas Briggs 15.00 40.00
NNO Nick Frost
NNO Nina Toussaint-White 20.00 50.00
NNO Noel Clarke 15.00 40.00
NNO Paul McGann 75.00 150.00
NNO Peter Davison 100.00 200.00
NNO Peter De Jersey 12.00 30.00
NNO Russell Tovey 12.00 30.00
NNO Samuel Anderson
NNO Sarah Parish 15.00 40.00
NNO Silas Carson
NNO Sophie Aldred 12.00 30.00
NNO Sylvester McCoy 60.00 120.00
NNO Terry Molloy 12.00 30.00
NNO Thomas Brodie-Sangster 15.00 40.00
NNO Tom Baker
NNO Will Thorp 15.00 40.00

2016 Doctor Who Timeless Companions Across Time

COMPLETE SET (10) 6.00 15.00
COMMON CARD (1-10) 1.00 2.50
STATED ODDS 1:

2016 Doctor Who Timeless Costume Relics Blue

COMPLETE SET (9) 100.00 200.00
COMMON CARD 6.00 15.00
*PURPLE/50: .6X TO 1.5X BASIC CARDS

2016 Doctor Who Timeless Daleks Across Time

COMPLETE SET (10) 6.00 15.00
COMMON CARD (1-10) 1.00 2.50

2016 Doctor Who Timeless Dual Autographs

BPNC B.Piper
N.Clarke
CBSM C.Baker
S.McCoy
DTBP D.Tennant 300.00 500.00
B.Piper
JBEM J.Barrowman
E.Myles
PDCB P.Davison
C.Baker
PMER P.McGann
E.Roberts
SMPM S.McCoy
P.McGann
TBPD T.Baker 200.00 350.00
P.Davison

2016 Doctor Who Timeless Historical Figures

COMPLETE SET (12) 10.00 25.00
COMMON CARD (1-12) 1.50 4.00
RANDOMLY INSERTED INTO PACKS

2016 Doctor Who Timeless Signed TARDIS Medallions

STATED PRINT RUN 10 SER.#'d SETS
ALKI Alex Kingston
ARDA Arthur Darvill 80.00 150.00
BECR Bernard Cribbins
BIPI Billie Piper
BOLA Bonnie Langford
CAAF Carole Ann Ford
COBA Colin Baker 100.00 200.00
DATE David Tennant
DEWA Deborah Watling
FRAG Freema Agyeman 80.00 150.00
FRHI Frazer Hines 80.00 150.00
JOBA John Barrowman 60.00 120.00
LOBA Louise Jameson
MAST Mark Strickson
NOCL Noel Clarke 60.00 120.00
PAMC Paul McGann
PEDA Peter Davison
SOAL Sophie Aldred
SYMC Sylvester McCoy 100.00 200.00
TOBA Tom Baker

2016 Doctor Who Timeless TARDIS Medallions

COMPLETE SET (36) 300.00 600.00
COMMON CARD (1-36) 8.00 20.00
*SILVER/25: .6X TO 1.5X BASIC CARDS
STATED PRINT RUN 150 SER.#'d SETS

2016 Doctor Who Timeless The Doctors Across Time

COMPLETE SET (13) 6.00 15.00
COMMON CARD (1-13) .75 2.00
RANDOMLY INSERTED INTO PACKS

2016 Doctor Who Timeless Time Travelers

COMPLETE SET (10) 8.00 20.00
COMMON CARD (1-10) 1.25 3.00
RANDOMLY INSERTED INTO PACKS

2016 Doctor Who Timeless Triple Autographs

BDB Baker
Davison#(Baker
FWH Ford 150.00 300.00
Watling#(Hines
MRA McGann 200.00 400.00
Roberts#(Ashbrook
TPA Tennant 500.00 800.00
Piper#(Agyeman

2006 Doctor Who Trilogy

COMPLETE SET (200) 8.00 20.00
UNOPENED BOX (36 PACKS)
UNOPENED PACK (10 CARDS)
COMMON CARD (1-200) .10 .25

2006 Doctor Who Trilogy Costumes

COMMON COSTUME (WHOTC1-WHOTC4)
STATED ODDS 1:
WHOTC1 Frazer Hines Coat 15.00 40.00
WHOTC2 Sergeant Benton Uniform
WHOTC3 Uniform Worn in "The Caves of Androzani" 40.00 80.00
WHOTC4 Vogan Outfit 12.00 30.00

2006 Doctor Who Trilogy Gold Foil Annuals

COMPLETE SET (18) 12.00 30.00
COMMON CARD (F1-F18) 1.00 2.50
STATED ODDS 1:6

2006 Doctor Who Trilogy Promos

COMPLETE SET (5)
COMMON CARD
B1 Companions Doctors Villains 2.00 5.00
WEB1 Companions Doctors Villains
WHOTAE1 6th Doctor 1.25 3.00
WHOTPR1 7th Doctor 1.25 3.00
WHOTPR2 Companions Villains The Doctors 1.25 3.00

1993 Victoria Doctor Who

COMPLETE SET (20) 8.00 20.00
COMMON CARD (1-20) .75 2.00

2017 Topps Now Doctor Who

1 BBC Announces the Thirteenth Doctor Jodie Whittaker/1400* 6.00 15.00

1994 FPG Don Maitz

COMPLETE SET (90) 4.00 10.00
UNOPENED BOX (36 PACKS) 30.00 40.00
UNOPENED PACK (10 CARDS) 1.00 1.25
COMMON CARD (1-90) .10 .25
NNO1 Don Maitz AU 20.00 50.00
NNO2 10-Up Panel Uncut Sheet AU
Deluxe14 4-Up Panel Plus Logo PROMO

1994 FPG Don Maitz Metallic Storm

COMPLETE SET (5) 12.00 30.00
COMMON CARD (MS1-MS5) 3.00 8.00
STATED ODDS 1:12

1996 FPG Don Maitz

COMPLETE SET (90) 4.00 10.00
UNOPENED BOX (36 PACKS) 25.00 30.00
UNOPENED PACK (10 CARDS) .75 1.00
COMMON CARD (1-90) .10 .25
NNO1 Don Maitz AU 20.00 50.00

1996 FPG Don Maitz Metallic Storm

COMPLETE SET (5) 12.00 30.00
COMMON CARD (M1-M5) 3.00 8.00
STATED ODDS 1:12

1997 The Illustration Studio Don Paresi's Fatal Beauty

COMPLETE SET (90) 4.00 10.00
UNOPENED BOX (36 PACKS) 35.00 50.00
UNOPENED PACK (8 CARDS) 1.50 1.75
COMMON CARD (1-90) .10 .25

1992-98 Don Rosa Uncle Scrooge Adventures Promos

COMPLETE SET (4) 6.00 15.00
COMMON CARD 2.00 5.00

2003 Don't Let It Happen Here

COMPLETE SET (50) 6.00 15.00
UNOPENED BOX (36 PACKS)/450*
UNOPENED PACK (6 CARDS)
COMMON CARD (1-50) .25 .60
RGAU Ricardo Garijo Autograph

1984 WTW Productions '38 Don't Let It Happen Over Here Reprints

COMPLETE SET (24) 5.00 12.00
COMMON CARD (1-24) .40 1.00

1991 Card Collectors Co. Don't Let It Happen Over Here Reprints

COMPLETE SET (24) 3.00 8.00
COMMON CARD (1-24) .20 .50

2016 Doom GameStop Pre-Order Promos

COMPLETE SET (4) 8.00 20.00
COMMON CARD (UNNUMBERED) 2.50 6.00

2005 Doom Movie

COMPLETE SET (72) 4.00 10.00
UNOPENED BOX (24 PACKS) 50.00 60.00
UNOPENED PACK (8 CARDS) 2.25 2.50
COMMON CARD (1-72) .10 .30

2005 Doom Movie Autographs

COMMON CARD 6.00 15.00
STATED ODDS 1:24
BRST Brian Steele 12.00 30.00
(Multi-Case Incentive)
DOJO Doug Jones 15.00 40.00
DWJO Dwayne Johnson 300.00 500.00
KAUR Karl Urban 15.00 40.00
ROPI Rosamund Pike 60.00 120.00

2005 Doom Movie Villains

COMPLETE SET (9) 6.00 15.00
COMMON CARD (R1-R9) .75 2.00
STATED ODDS 5:24

2005 Doom Movie Promos

COMPLETE SET (2) 2.50 6.00
COMMON CARD 1.50 4.00

1997 Comic Images Doug Beekman

COMPLETE SET (6) 25.00 60.00
COMMON CARD (1-6) 5.00 12.00
NNO Doug Beekman AU

1997 Comic Images Doug Beekman Promos

COMPLETE SET (2) 1.25 3.00
COMMON CARD .75 2.00

2014 Downton Abbey Seasons One and Two

COMPLETE SET (126) 10.00 25.00
UNOPENED BOX (24 PACKS) 60.00 100.00
UNOPENED PACK (5 CARDS) 3.00 4.00
COMMON CARD (1-126) .15 .40
*MINI: 2X TO 5X BASIC CARDS

2014 Downton Abbey Seasons One and Two At War

COMPLETE SET (9) 4.00 10.00
COMMON CARD (WWI1-WWI9) .75 2.00
STATED ODDS 1:12

2014 Downton Abbey Seasons One and Two Autographs

COMMON AUTO (A1-A14) 10.00 25.00
STATED ODDS 1:24
A1 Jim Carter 50.00 100.00
A2 Laura Carmichael 25.00 60.00
A3 Phyllis Logan 30.00 75.00
A4 Siobhan Finneran 15.00 40.00
A6 Thomas Howes 20.00 50.00
A7 Michelle Dockery 25.00 60.00
A8 Jessica Brown Findlay 30.00 75.00
A9 Joanne Froggatt 20.00 50.00
A10 Rob James-Collier 20.00 50.00
A11 Lesley Nicol 25.00 60.00
A13 Iain Glen 12.00 30.00
A14 Allen Leech 20.00 50.00

2014 Downton Abbey Seasons One and Two Downstairs

COMPLETE SET (12) 5.00 12.00
COMMON CARD (DWN1-DWN12) .75 2.00
STATED ODDS 1:12

2014 Downton Abbey Seasons One and Two Upstairs

COMPLETE SET (12) 5.00 12.00
COMMON CARD (UP1-UP12) .75 2.00
STATED ODDS 1:12

2014 Downton Abbey Seasons One and Two Dual Wardrobes

COMMON CARD (DW1-DW5) 6.00 15.00
STATED ODDS 1:24
DW1 E.Crawley/M.Crawley 8.00 20.00
DW2 C. Crawley/M. Crawley 12.00 30.00
DW3 C. Crawley/E. Crawley 8.00 20.00

2014 Downton Abbey Seasons One and Two Wardrobes

STATED ODDS 1:24
W1 E.Crawley Dress 8.00 20.00
W4 Mary Crawley's Dress 12.00 30.00
W5 Cora Crawley's Dress 8.00 20.00
W6 Mary Crawley's Dress 12.00 30.00
W7 E.Crawley Exclusive 12.00 30.00

2014 Downton Abbey Seasons One and Two Promos

PRINT RUNS B/WN 100-300 COPIES PER
P1 NSU Special Issue/300 3.00 8.00
P2 UK Mem Show Metal/100 6.00 15.00

1995 Artbox Dragon Ball

COMPLETE SET (100) 8.00 20.00
UNOPENED BOX (24 PACKS) 30.00 40.00
UNOPENED PACK (6 CARDS) 1.50 1.75
COMMON CARD (1-100) .15 .40

1995 Artbox Dragon Ball Chromium

COMPLETE SET (12) 4.00 10.00
COMMON CARD (C1-C12) .40 1.00
RANDOMLY INSERTED INTO PACKS

2003 Dragon Ball GT

COMPLETE SET (72) 8.00 20.00
UNOPENED BOX (24 PACKS)
UNOPENED PACK (5 CARDS)
COMMON CARD (1-72) .15 .40

2002 Dragon Ball Z FilmCardz

COMPLETE SET (72) 5.00 12.00
UNOPENED BOX (24 PACKS) 40.00 50.00
UNOPENED PACK (5 CARDS) 2.00 2.25
COMMON CARD (1-72) .12 .30

2002 Dragon Ball Z FilmCardz Mass Market

COMPLETE SET (9) 8.00 20.00
COMMON CARD (Pm1-Pm9) 1.25 3.00
RANDOMLY INSERTED INTO RETAIL PACKS

2002 Dragon Ball Z FilmCardz Rare

COMPLETE SET (6) 6.00 15.00
COMMON CARD (R1-R6) 1.25 3.00
RANDOMLY INSERTED INTO PACKS

2002 Dragon Ball Z FilmCardz Ultra-Rare

COMPLETE SET (3) 5.00 12.00
COMMON CARD (UR1-UR3) 2.50 6.00
RANDOMLY INSERTED INTO PACKS

2002 Dragon Ball Z FilmCardz Promos

P1 Piccolo .75 2.00
P2 Doore, Salza and Neiz .75 2.00
P3 Super Saiyan Goku .75 2.00
P4 Cooler .75 2.00

1984 Fleer Dragon's Lair Rub-Off Game

COMPLETE SET (27) 3.00 8.00
COMMON CARD .20 .50

1996 Topps Dragonheart

COMPLETE SET (72) 6.00 15.00
UNOPENED BOX (36 PACKS) 20.00 30.00
UNOPENED PACK (6 CARDS) .75 1.00
COMMON CARD (1-72) .15 .40

1996 Topps Dragonheart Dracofoil

COMPLETE SET (6) 8.00 20.00
COMMON CARD (C1-C6) 2.50 6.00
STATED ODDS 1:9

1992 Panini Dream Cars

COMPLETE SET (100) 6.00 15.00
COMMON CARD (1-100) .12 .30
NNO 4-Card Panel 4.00 10.00
(44, 93, 43, 71)

1991 Panini Dream Cars 100

COMPLETE SET (100) 8.00 20.00
COMMON CARD (1-100) .15 .40

1991-92 Lime Rock Dream Machines

COMPLETE SET (165) 8.00 20.00
COMP.SER. 1 SET (110) 6.00 15.00
COMP.SER. 2 SET (55) 4.00 10.00
UNOPENED SERIES I BOX (36 PACKS) 10.00 20.00
UNOPENED SERIES I PACK (12 CARDS) .50 .75
UNOPENED SERIES II BOX (36 PACKS) 15.00 25.00
UNOPENED SERIES II PACK (12 CARDS) .75 1.00
COMMON CARD (1-110) .12 .30
COMMON CARD (111-165) .15 .40

1991-92 Lime Rock Dream Machines Promos

COMPLETE SET (12) 10.00 25.00
COMMON SERIES I (1-6) .50 1.25
COMMON SERIES II (P1-P6) .75 2.00
*FOIL: .5X TO 1.2X BASIC PROMOS

2010 Dreamers of Darkness

COMPLETE SET (51) 5.00 12.00
COMMON CARD (1-50; C) .15 .40
C Dreamers of Darkness .75 2.00
(cover card)

2014 Dreamworks Heroes

COMPLETE SET (42) 8.00 20.00
COMMON CARD (1-42) .40 1.00

1991 Eclipse Drug Wars

COMPLETE BOXED SET (36) 4.00 10.00
COMMON CARD (1-36) .25 .60

1983 Donruss Dukes of Hazzard

COMPLETE SET (44) 12.00 30.00
UNOPENED BOX (36 PACKS)
UNOPENED PACK (5 CARDS+1 STICKER)
COMMON CARD (1-44) .25 .60

1984 Fleer Dune

COMPLETE SET (132) 15.00 40.00
COMPLETE SET W/STICKERS (176) 25.00 60.00
UNOPENED BOX (36 PACKS) 125.00 200.00
UNOPENED PACK (10 CARDS+1 STICKER) 4.00 6.00
COMMON CARD (1-132) .25 .60

1984 Fleer Dune Stickers

COMPLETE SET (44) 12.00 30.00
COMMON STICKER (1-44) .60 1.50

1985 Topps Duran Duran

COMPLETE SET (33) 5.00 12.00
COMPLETE SET W/STICKERS (66) 6.00 15.00
UNOPENED BOX (36 PACKS) 50.00 75.00
UNOPENED PACK (3 CARDS+3 STICKERS) 1.50 2.50
COMMON CARD (1-33) .20 .50

1985 Topps Duran Duran Stickers

COMPLETE SET (33) 1.50 4.00
COMMON CARD (1-33) .10 .25
STATED ODDS 1:1

1996 WildStorm DV8

COMPLETE SET (90) 10.00 25.00
UNOPENED BOX (36 PACKS) 40.00 50.00
UNOPENED PACK (8 CARDS) 1.25 1.50
COMMON CARD (1-90) .25 .60
NNO Team Picture PROMO/2500* 10.00

1996 WildStorm DV8 MiniCelz

COMPLETE SET (9) 15.00 40.00
COMMON CARD (MC1-MC9) 2.50 6.00
RANDOMLY INSERTED INTO PACKS

1998 Good Stuff Dwight Frye True Character

COMPLETE FACTORY SET (72) 10.00 25.00
COMMON CARD (1-72) .20 .50
STATED PRINT RUN 1000 SETS

2011 Dynamo 5

COMPLETE SET (10) 8.00 20.00
COMMON CARD (1-10) 1.25 3.00
P1 Adam Cleveland Promo 3.00 8.00

1982 Topps E.T.

COMPLETE SET (87) 6.00 15.00
COMPLETE SET W/STICKERS (99) 8.00 20.00
UNOPENED BOX (36 PACKS) 75.00 125.00
UNOPENED PACK (10 CARDS) 2.00 3.00
COMMON CARD (1-87) .10 .25
*OPC: SAME VALUE

1982 Topps E.T. Stickers

COMPLETE SET (12) 2.00 5.00
COMMON CARD (1-12) .20 .50
STATED ODDS 1:1
10 E.T. image, bigger .40 1.00
with just blue background
11 E.T., with just yellow background .40 1.00
12 E.T. image, bigger .40 1.00
with just red background

1996 Topps Widevision E.T. The Extra-Terrestrial Promo

NNO E.T. The Extra-Terrestrial 2.00 5.00

1982 Monty Gum E.T.

COMPLETE SET (100) 12.00 30.00
COMMON CARD (1-100) .15 .40

1983 Nabisco E.T.

COMPLETE SET (12) 6.00 15.00
COMMON CARD (1-12) 1.00 2.50

1983-84 Hershey Reese's Pieces E.T. Magic Motion Stickers

COMPLETE SET (8) 6.00 15.00
COMMON CARD 1.00 2.50

1982 Hershey Reese's Pieces E.T. Rainbow Reflection Stickers

COMPLETE SET (8) 8.00 20.00
COMMON STICKER 1.50 4.00

1992 Kitchen Sink Press Early Jazz Greats

COMPLETE SET (36) 4.00 10.00
COMMON CARD (1-36) .25 .60
P3 Heroes of the Blues PROMO .40 1.00
P4 Pioneers of Country Music PROMO .40 1.00
NNO Early Jazz Greats Poster PROMO .40 1.00

1995 Fleer Easter

COMPLETE SET (42) 3.00 8.00
UNOPENED HOBBY BOX (36 PACKS)
UNOPENED HOBBY PACK (7 CARDS+3 STICKERS)
UNOPENED RETAIL BOX (36 PACKS)
UNOPENED RETAIL PACK (7 CARDS)
COMMON CARD .15 .40
*STICKER: .5X TO 1.2X BASIC CARDS .20 .50

1995 Fleer Easter Golden Memories

COMPLETE SET (6) 6.00 15.00
COMMON CARD 1.25 3.00
STATED ODDS 1:6
MG1 Humpty Dumpty 1.25 3.00
PCS1 It was the first day of spring, 1.25 3.00
TUD1 It was a lovely summer in the c 1.25 3.00
IALT1 I'm a little teapot, short and 1.25 3.00
LCET1 It was Easter morning and Littl 1.25 3.00
TSOTEB1 Little Bunny, come close, Mam 1.25 3.00

1992 Shel-Tone Electrified! Bass Legends

COMPLETE SET (37) 5.00 12.00
COMMON CARD (1-36; CL) .25 .60

1997 Comic Images Elvgren and Friends

COMPLETE SET (36) 4.00 10.00
UNOPENED BOX (30 PACKS) 20.00 30.00
UNOPENED PACK (4 CARDS) 1.00 1.25
COMMON CARD (1-36) .20 .50
NNO Cleopatra Scene/Art by Gil Elvgren (Dealer Promo) 1.25 3.00

1997 Comic Images Elvgren and Friends ClearChrome

COMPLETE SET (6) 15.00 40.00
COMMON CARD 3.00 8.00
STATED ODDS 1:15

1995 21st Century Archives Elvgren Pin-Ups

COMPLETE SET (50) 5.00 12.00
COMPLETE BOXED SET (50) 6.00 15.00
UNOPENED BOX (36 PACKS) 20.00 30.00
UNOPENED PACK (8 CARDS) 1.00 1.25
COMMON CARD (1-50) .15 .40
NNO Fire Bell Promo .75 2.00

1995 21st Century Archives Elvgren Pin-Ups Bathing Beauties

COMPLETE SET (5) 8.00 20.00
COMMON CARD (B1-B5) 2.00 5.00
RANDOMLY INSERTED INTO PACKS

1995 21st Century Archives Elvgren Pin-Ups Beach Girls

COMPLETE SET (5) 4.00 10.00
COMMON CARD (EB1-EB5) 1.25 3.00
MAIL-IN WRAPPER OFFER EXCLUSIVE

1995 21st Century Archives Elvgren Pin-Ups Innocent Nudes

COMPLETE SET (5) 4.00 10.00
COMMON CARD (EN1-EN5) 1.25 3.00
MAIL-IN WRAPPER OFFER EXCLUSIVE

1997 Comic Images Elvira Mistress of Omnichrome

COMPLETE SET (72) 8.00 20.00
UNOPENED BOX (36 PACKS) 25.00 35.00
UNOPENED PACK (8 CARDS) .75 1.00
COMMON CARD (1-72) .25 .60
NNO1 Elvira AU 20.00 50.00
NNO2 6-Card Panel Uncut Sheet

1997 Comic Images Elvira Mistress of Omnichrome Clearchrome

COMPLETE SET (6) 15.00 40.00
COMMON CARD (1-6) 3.00 8.00
STATED ODDS 1:15

1997 Comic Images Elvira Mistress of Omnichrome Promos

1 Elvira Crouching With Skulls .75 2.00
2 Elvira With Redhead Dog .75 2.00

1996 Comic Images Elvira Mistress of the Dark

COMPLETE SET (72) 4.00 10.00
UNOPENED BOX (48 PACKS) 30.00 40.00
UNOPENED PACK (8 CARDS) .75 1.00
COMMON CARD (1-72) .12 .30
AU1 Elvira AU/500 20.00 50.00
NNO1 Posing on Pumpkin PROMO .75 2.00

1996 Comic Images Elvira Mistress of the Dark Spook Show

COMPLETE SET (6) 10.00 25.00
COMMON CARD (C1-C6) 2.50 6.00
RANDOMLY INSERTED INTO PACKS

2008 Elvis By the Numbers

COMPLETE SET (80) 5.00 12.00
UNOPENED BOX (28 PACKS) 65.00 75.00
UNOPENED PACK (6 CARDS) 2.50 3.00
COMMON CARD (1-80) .15 .40
*CANVAS: 1X TO 2.5X BASIC CARDS
ST1 '56 Concert Ticket/56 120.00 200.00

2008 Elvis By the Numbers Celebrity Signatures Bronze

COMMON AUTO 15.00 40.00
CSNS Nancy Sinatra 80.00 150.00
CSYC Yvonne Craig 20.00 50.00

2007 Elvis Is

COMPLETE SET (100) 4.00 10.00
UNOPENED BOX (24 PACKS) 40.00 60.00
UNOPENED PACK (5 CARDS) 2.00 3.00
UNOPENED BLASTER BOX (10 PACKS) 25.00 40.00
UNOPEND BLASTER PACK (5 CARDS) 2.50 4.00
COMMON CARD (1-100) .10 .30
CONTEST ENTRY CARD STATED ODDS 1:20
NNO Contest Entry Card

2007 Elvis Is Al Wertheimer Artist's Proofs Autographs

OVERALL AUTO ODDS 1:96
AW3 The Kiss/100 100.00 200.00
AW4 Fan Mail/400 50.00 100.00

2007 Elvis Is Autographs

COMMON CARD 15.00 40.00
STATED ODDS 1:96
1 Barbara Eden 25.00 60.00
4 Nancy Sinatra 80.00 150.00
NNO Elvis Presley/4
NNO Elvis Presley Auto Redemption

2007 Elvis Is Elvis Worn Memorabilia

COMMON CARD 20.00 50.00
MEMORABILIA COMBINED ODDS 1:84

2007 Elvis Is Foil Inserts

COMPLETE SET (6) 4.00 10.00
COMMON CARD (EI1-E6) .75 2.00
STATED ODDS 1:12

2007 Elvis Is On the Record

COMPLETE SET (9) 4.00 10.00
COMMON CARD (OR1-OR9) .60 1.50
STATED ODDS 1:8

2007 Elvis Is Timelines

COMPLETE SET (4) 3.00 8.00
COMMON CARD (1-4) 1.00 2.50
STATED ODDS ONE PER BLASTER BOX

1992 River Group The Elvis Collection

COMPLETE SET (660) 50.00 100.00
COMPLETE SERIES 1 SET (220) 12.00 30.00
COMPLETE SERIES 2 SET (220) 12.00 30.00
COMPLETE SERIES 3 SET (220) 20.00 50.00
UNOPENED SERIES 1 BOX (36 PACKS) 30.00 40.00
UNOPENED SERIES 1 PACK (12 CARDS) 1.00 1.25
UNOPENED SERIES 2 BOX (36 PACKS) 30.00 40.00
UNOPENED SERIES 2 PACK (12 CARDS) 1.00 1.25
UNOPENED SERIES 3 BOX (36 PACKS) 85.00 100.00
UNOPENED SERIES 3 PACK (12 CARDS) 2.50 3.00
SERIES 1 (1-220) .12 .30
SERIES 2 (221-440) .12 .30
SERIES 3 (441-660) .20 .50
NNO 48-card panel Uncut Dufex Sheet

1992 River Group The Elvis Collection Elvis The King

COMPLETE SET (5) 10.00 25.00
COMMON CARD (1-5) 2.50 6.00

1992 River Group The Elvis Collection Gold and Platinum Records

COMPLETE SET (50) 25.00 60.00
COMMON CARD (1-50) .60 1.50
STATED ODDS ONE PER JUMBO

1992 River Group The Elvis Collection Promos

COMMON CARD 1.25 3.00

1992 River Group The Elvis Collection Top Ten Hits

COMPLETE SET (40) 200.00 450.00
COMPLETE SERIES 1 SET (12) 80.00 150.00
COMPLETE SERIES 2 SET (16) 100.00 200.00
COMPLETE SERIES 3 SET (12) 80.00 150.00
COMMON CARD (1-40) 6.00 15.00
STATED ODDS SERIES 1 - 1:36
STATED ODDS SERIES 2 AND 3 - 1:18

2006 Elvis Lives

COMPLETE SET (90) 4.00 10.00
UNOPENED BOX (24 PACKS) 30.00 50.00
UNOPENED PACK (5 CARDS) 1.50 2.50
UNOPENED BLASTER BOX (8 PACKS+1 DIE CAST)
COMMON CARD (1-90) .10 .30

2006 Elvis Lives Autographs

COMMON CARD 30.00 80.00
STATED ODDS 1:144
CARDS LISTED ALPHABETICALLY

2006 Elvis Lives Elvis Worn Memorabilia

COMPLETE SET (3) 50.00 100.00
COMMON CARD 15.00 40.00
*GOLD/299: .6X TO 1.5X BASIC CARDS
*PLATINUM/99: 2X TO 5X BASIC CARDS
MEMORABILIA COMBINED ODDS 1:240
EWS1 Blue Shirt with White Polka Dots 15.00 40.00
EWS2 Red Shirt 15.00 40.00
EWS3 Blue Scarf 15.00 40.00

2006 Elvis Lives Fashions

COMPLETE SET (12) 12.00 30.00
COMMON CARD (1-12) 1.50 4.00
STATED ODDS 1:6

2010 Elvis Milestones

COMPLETE SET (75) 4.00 10.00
UNOPENED BOX (24 PACKS)
UNOPENED PACK (5 CARDS)
COMMON CARD (1-75) .10 .30
*75TH ANNIV: 1.5X TO 4X BASIC CARDS
*DIAMOND: 15X TO 40X BASIC CARDS

2010 Elvis Milestones Celebrity Signatures Blue

COMMON CARD 15.00 30.00
*RED/50: .8X TO 2X BASIC CARDS
*GREEN/25: 1.2X TO 3X BASIC CARDS
OVERALL AUTO/MEM ODDS ONE PER BOX
CSDJ DJ Fontana 20.00 40.00
CSNS Nancy Sinatra 50.00 100.00
CSPP Pat Priest 20.00 40.00
CSYC Yvonne Craig 20.00 40.00

2010 Elvis Milestones King Size Swatches

COMPLETE SET (3) 250.00 500.00
COMMON CARD (KS1-KS3) 100.00 200.00
OVERALL AUTO/MEM ODDS ONE PER BOX
STATED PRINT RUN 25 SER. #'d SETS

2010 Elvis Milestones The King of Hollywood Pop-Ups

COMPLETE SET (6) 5.00 12.00
COMMON CARD (PU1-PU6) 1.50 4.00
STATED ODDS 1:8

2010 Elvis Milestones The King's Things Memorabilia

COMPLETE SET (6) 80.00 150.00
COMMON CARD (KT1-KT6) 12.00 30.00
*HOLOFOIL/99: .6X TO 1.2X BASIC CARDS
*RED/25: .75X TO 1.5X BASIC CARDS
OVERALL AUTO/MEM ODDS ONE PER BOX

2010 Elvis Milestones Under the Lights

COMPLETE SET (12) 10.00 25.00
COMMON CARD (UTL1-UTL12) 1.00 2.50
STATED ODDS 1:6

2007 Elvis The Music

COMPLETE SET (81) 4.00 10.00
UNOPENED BOX (28 PACKS) 40.00 60.00
UNOPENED PACK (6 CARDS) 2.00 3.00
UNOPENED VALUE BOX (12 PACKS)
UNOPENED VALUE PACK (6 CARDS)
COMMON CARD (1-81) .12 .30
*TCB: 1.2X TO 3X BASIC CARDS

2007 Elvis The Music Celebrity Signatures

*SILVER: .6X TO 1.2X BASIC CARDS
*BLUE/30: .6X TO 1.5X BASIC CARDS
*RED/25-30: .6X TO 1.5X BASIC CARDS
ONE RELIC OR AUTO PER BOX
CSCN Chris Noel 20.00 40.00
CSCP Cynthia Pepper 25.00 50.00
CSDF DJ Fontana 25.00 50.00
CSGS Gordon Stoker 15.00 30.00
CSJB James Burton 15.00 30.00
CSMM Mary Ann Mobley 20.00 40.00
CSNS Nancy Sinatra 75.00 150.00
CSRW Ray Walker 30.00 60.00
CSSM Scotty Moore 30.00 60.00
CSYC Yvonne Craig 20.00 40.00
NNO Elvis Presley

2007 Elvis The Music Rock 'n Roll Relics

COMPLETE SET (5) 60.00 120.00
COMMON CARD 15.00 30.00
*GOLD/299: .6X TO 1.2X BASIC CARDS
*PLATINUM/99: .75X TO 1.5X BASIC CARDS
ONE RELIC OR AUTO PER BOX

2007 Elvis The Music Wertheimer Negatives

COMPLETE SET (7) 5.00 12.00
COMMON CARD (WN1-WN7) 1.25 3.00
STATED ODDS 1:14
WN4b Listening To His Music AU/199 20.00 50.00
WN4c Listening To His Music AU/56

1999 Inkworks Elvis Platinum Collection

COMPLETE SET (90) 5.00 12.00
UNOPENED BOX (36 PACKS) 40.00 50.00
UNOPENED PACK (6 CARDS) 1.25 1.50
COMMON CARD (1-90) .15 .40
SP1 STATED ODDS 1:108
G1 STATED ODDS 1:1411
G1 Elvis Presley 12.00 30.00
SP1 Elvis Presley 8.00 20.00

1999 Inkworks Elvis Platinum Collection Gold Records

COMPLETE SET (9) 10.00 25.00
COMMON CARD (R1-R9) 1.50 4.00
STATED ODDS 1:11

1999 Inkworks Elvis Platinum Collection Return To Sender Postcards

COMPLETE SET (6) 8.00 20.00
COMMON CARD (PC1-PC6) 1.50 4.00
STATED ODDS 1:17

2022 Topps Elvis Presley The King of Rock and Roll

COMPLETE SET (150) 200.00 500.00
COMMON CARD (1-150) 2.50 6.00
*PINK/45: 2.5X TO 6X BASIC CARDS

2022 Topps Elvis Presley The King of Rock and Roll Album Covers

COMPLETE SET (10) 25.00 60.00
COMMON CARD (C1-C10) 4.00 10.00
*FOIL/45: 1.2X TO 3X BASIC CARDS

MODERN

2022 Topps Heritage Elvis Presley

COMPLETE SET (40) 75.00 200.00
UNOPENED BOX (8 CARDS)
COMMON CARD (1-40) 3.00 8.00
*FAC.SIG./199: 1X TO 2.5X BASIC CARDS

2022 Topps Heritage Elvis Presley Movies

COMPLETE SET (10) 60.00 150.00
COMMON CARD (M1-M10) 12.00 30.00
STATED OVERALL ODDS 1:1

2022 Topps Heritage Elvis Presley Relic

R1 Elvis 100.00 250.00
Shirt

2005 Elvis TV Guide Covers

COMPLETE FACTORY SET (16) 6.00 15.00
COMMON CARD (TV1-TV16) .60 1.50

2016 Emoji Tags

COMPLETE SET (24) 30.00 80.00
UNOPENED BOX (24 PACKS) 85.00 100.00
UNOPENED PACK (1 TAG+1 STICKER)
COMMON TAG (1-24) 2.00 5.00

2016 Emoji Tags Stickers

COMPLETE SET (8) 2.50 6.00
COMMON STICKER (1-8) .40 1.00
STATED ODDS 1:1

1990 CaliCo Graphics Endangered Species

COMPLETE SET (36) 3.00 8.00
COMMON CARD (1-36) .15 .40
NNO Spider Monkey OS

1991 Victoria Gallery Endangered Wild Animals

COMPLETE SET (20) 4.00 12.00
COMMON CARD (1-20) .30 .75

2014 Ender's Game

COMPLETE SET (69) 8.00 20.00
UNOPENED BOX (24 PACKS) 100.00 150.00
UNOPENED PACK (5 CARDS) 4.00 6.00
COMMON CARD (1-69) .20 .50
P1 NON-SPORT UPDATE PROMO 2.00 5.00
P1 Non-Sport Update PROMO 2.00 5.00

2014 Ender's Game Autographs

COMMON AUTO (A1-A15) 8.00 15.00
STATED ODDS 1:24
A1 Harrison Ford 600.00 1200.00
A2 Asa Butterfield 30.00 75.00
A3 Hailee Steinfeld 300.00 500.00
A4 Aramis Knight 10.00 20.00
A11 Khylin Rhambo 10.00 20.00

2014 Ender's Game Dual Wardrobes

STATED ODDS 1:144
DM1 Ender and Petra 20.00 50.00
DM4 Ender's Suit and Pads 15.00 40.00
DM5 Ender's Suit and Pads 15.00 40.00

2014 Ender's Game Formic Foil

COMPLETE SET (8) 8.00 20.00
COMMON CARD (SB01-SB08) 2.00 5.00
STATED ODDS 1:12

2014 Ender's Game International Fleet

COMPLETE SET (13) 10.00 25.00
COMMON CARD (RF1-RF13) 1.25 3.00
STATED ODDS 1:12

2014 Ender's Game Replica Patches

COMPLETE SET (2) 25.00 60.00
COMMON CARD (PC01-PC02) 15.00 40.00
STATED ODDS 1:144

2014 Ender's Game Wardrobes

COMPLETE SET (12) 120.00 225.00
COMPLETE SET W/SP (13) 150.00 300.00
COMMON CARD (M1-M13) 8.00 20.00
STATED ODDS 1:24
M13 ALBUM EXCLUSIVE
M1 Ender Wiggin 12.00 30.00
M3 Petra 15.00 40.00
M5 Petra Arkanian 15.00 40.00
M9 Ender Wiggin 12.00 30.00
M12 Valentine Wiggin 12.00 30.00
M13 Yellow Launchie Suit ALB 20.00 50.00

1993 Portfolio Endless Summer

COMPLETE SET (50) 4.00 10.00
UNOPENED BOX (36 PACKS) 20.00 30.00
UNOPENED PACK (9 CARDS) .75 1.00
COMMON CARD (1-50) .15 .40
*ENDLESS WAVE: 1X TO 2.5X BASIC CARDS .40 1.00
P1 Maci Wilkins PROMO .75 2.00

1993 Portfolio Endless Summer Covers

COMPLETE SET (5) 1.25 3.00
COMMON CARD (1-5) .30 .75
INCLUDED WITH THE BASE SET

1993 Portfolio Endless Summer Hot!

COMPLETE SET (6) 5.00 12.00
COMMON CARD (1-6) 1.00 2.50
RANDOMLY INSERTED INTO PACKS

1993 Portfolio Endless Summer Medal

COMPLETE SET (6) 5.00 12.00
COMMON CARD (1-6) 1.00 2.50

2001 Enduring Freedom

COMPLETE SET (90) 8.00 20.00
COMPLETE SET W/STICKERS (90) 10.00 25.00
UNOPENED BOX (24 PACKS) 40.00 60.00
UNOPENED PACK (7 CARDS+1 STICKER) 2.00 2.50
COMMON CARD (1-90) .15 .40

2001 Enduring Freedom Stickers

COMPLETE SET (9) 2.50 6.00
COMMON CARD (1-9) .40 1.00
STATED ODDS 1:1

1993 Mundus Amicus Environmental Action Endangered Animals

COMPLETE SET (50) 3.00 8.00
UNOPENED BOX (36 PACKS)
UNOPENED PACK (9 CARDS)
COMMON CARD (1-50) .12 .30

1993 Dynamic Marketing Escape of the Dinosaurs

COMPLETE SET (60) 5.00 12.00
COMMON CARD (1-60) .15 .40

1993 Dynamic Marketing Escape of the Dinosaurs Chromium

COMPLETE SET (5) 5.00 12.00
COMMON CARD (1-5) 1.25 3.00

2012 Essential Elvis

COMPLETE SET (35) 60.00 120.00
COMMON CARD (1-35) 2.50 6.00
*HOLOFOIL: .6X TO 1.5X BASIC CARDS

2012 Essential Elvis Autographs Silver

COMMON CARD 12.00 30.00
*GOLD/100: .5X TO 1.25X SILVER
*SILVER/50: .6X TO 1.5X SILVER
OVERALL AUTO ODDS AT LEAST ONE PER BOX
RED INK VARIATIONS EXIST
APAW Alfred Wertheimer 15.00 40.00
APGK George Kalinsky 15.00 40.00
ESBE Barbara Eden 20.00 50.00
ESNS Nancy Sinatra 15.00 40.00
ESYC Yvonne Craig 15.00 40.00
ESMAM Mary Ann Mobley 15.00 40.00
ESMTM Mary Tyler Moore 50.00 100.00

2012 Essential Elvis Essential Materials Gold

STATED PRINT RUN 35-299
*BLUE: .6X TO 1.5X GOLD
EM4 Swim Trunks/149 15.00 40.00
EM6 Kimono/199 15.00 40.00
EMD1 Plaid PJs/Green suit/149 20.00 50.00
EMD2 Tweed/Green/199 20.00 50.00
EMD3 Red/Tweed/299 20.00 50.00
EMQ1 Red/Plaid/Tweed/Grn/35 60.00 120.00
EMT1 Red/Tweed/Green/99 30.00 60.00
EMT2 Red/Plaid/Tweed/149 30.00 60.00

2012 Essential Elvis Essential Materials King Size Gold

COMMON CARD (KS1-KS3) 20.00 40.00
STATED PRINT RUN 99-299
*BLUE: 2X TO 5X GOLD
KS1 Sun Records jacket/99 35.00 70.00
KS2 Bathrobe/299 20.00 40.00
KS3 Black shirt/White dickey/99 35.00 70.00

2012 Essential Elvis Essential Materials Silver

COMMON CARD (EM1-EM4) 10.00 25.00
*BLUE: .6X TO 1.5X SILVER
EM1 Sun Records jacket 12.00 30.00

2007 eTopps Allen and Ginter Presidents

COMPLETE SET (6) 25.00 60.00
COMMON CARD (1-6) 2.00 5.00
STATED PRINT RUN 999 SER. #'d SETS
2 John F. Kennedy 8.00 20.00
4 Ronald Reagan 10.00 25.00
5 Bill Clinton 5.00 12.00
6 George W. Bush 3.00 8.00

2009 eTopps Allen and Ginter Moments

STATED PRINT RUN 999 SER. #'d SETS
EMK Ted Kennedy 2.00 5.00

2009 eTopps Allen and Ginter Presidents

COMPLETE SET (5) 8.00 20.00
COMMON CARD (7-11) 2.00 5.00
STATED PRINT RUN 999 SER. #'d SETS

1993 Press Pass Eudaemon Promos

LT Card Collector's Price Guide Magazine .60 1.50
RT Comic Book Collector Magazine .60 1.50
NNO 2-Card Panel 1.25 3.00
NNO 3-Card Panel 1.25 3.00

2011 Eureka Seasons One and Two

COMPLETE SET (25) 20.00 50.00
COMMON CARD (1-25) 1.00 2.50
STATED PRINT RUN 250 SER. #'d SETS

2011 Eureka Seasons One and Two Artifacts

COMPLETE SET (9) 80.00 150.00
COMMON CARD (AF1-AF9) 8.00 20.00
STATED ODDS ONE PER PACK
STATED PRINT RUN 350 SER. #'d SETS

2011 Eureka Seasons One and Two Autographs

COMMON AUTO 4.00 12.00
STATED ODDS TWO PER PACK
2 Chris Gauthier 12.00 30.00
3 Christopher Jacot 5.00 12.00
4 Colin Ferguson 30.00 75.00
6 Erica Cerra 15.00 40.00
7 Joe Morton 10.00 25.00
8 Matt Frewer 15.00 40.00
10 Neil Grayston 8.00 20.00
11 Niall Matter 6.00 15.00
13 Shayn Solberg 5.00 12.00
14 Tamlyn Tomita 8.00 20.00

2011 Eureka Seasons One and Two Casting Call

COMPLETE SET (11) 20.00 50.00
COMPLETE SET W/SP (12) 30.00 80.00
COMMON CARD (C1-C11) 2.50 6.00
STATED ODDS 1:1
STATED PRINT RUN 350 SER. #'d SETS
C12 ISSUED AS RITTENHOUSE REWARD
C12 Sheriff Jack Carter/350 RR 10.00 25.00

2011 Eureka Seasons One and Two Promos

COMPLETE SET (3) 2.50 6.00
P1 Sheriff Carter and company .75 2.00
P2 Allison Blake/Jack Carter 1.50 4.00
P3 Jo Lupo/Jack Carter 1.50 4.00

2012 Eureka Autograph Expansion

COMMON AUTO 6.00 15.00
ANNOUNCED PRINT RUN 250 SETS
2 Colin Ferguson 5SI/50* 200.00 300.00
3 Ed Quinn 25.00 60.00
4 Erica Cerra 15.00 40.00
6 Matt Frewer 8.00 20.00
7 Neil Grayston 3SI/100* 30.00 75.00

1995 FPG Everway

COMPLETE SET (90) 5.00 12.00
UNOPENED BOX (36 PACKS)
UNOPENED PACK (10 CARDS)
COMMON CARD (1-90) .12 .30

1995 FPG Everway Metallic Muse

COMPLETE SET (6) 10.00 25.00
COMMON CARD (M1-M6) 2.00 5.00
STATED ODDS 1:12

1995 FPG Everway Promos

COMMON CARD 1.25 3.00

2019 Fright-Rags The Evil Dead

COMPLETE SET W/SP (76) 25.00 60.00
UNOPENED BOX (24 PACKS)
UNOPENED PACK (9 CARDS+1 STICKER)
COMMON CARD (1-68, CL) .75 1.50
COMMON SP (69-75)
69 Ash SP 2.00 5.00

1993 Krome Evil Ernie

COMPLETE SET (100) 8.00 20.00
UNOPENED BOX (36 PACKS) 20.00 30.00
UNOPENED PACK (8 CARDS) .75 1.00
COMMON CARD (1-100) .15 .40
C2 Necrochrome (commemorative boxed set)
SN1 Krome Signed and Numbered

1993 Krome Evil Ernie Krome

COMPLETE SET (5) 15.00 40.00
COMMON CARD (1-5) 4.00 10.00
STATED ODDS 1:18 packs

1993 Krome Evil Ernie Promos

4 Evil Ernie 10.00 25.00
Lady Death (Brian Pulido AU)

1995 Krome Evil Ernie Glow-in-the-Dark

COMPLETE SET (100) 10.00 25.00
UNOPENED BOX (36 PACKS) 40.00 50.00
UNOPENED PACK (8 CARDS) 1.25 1.50
COMMON CARD (1-100) .20 .50
*HOLOCHROME: 1.2X TO 3X BASIC CARDS .40 1.00
A2 Necro Chase Card
(Album Exclusive)
B3 Bonus Card (commemorative set)

1995 Krome Evil Ernie Glow-in-the-Dark Clear

COMPLETE SET (5) 15.00 40.00
COMMON CARD (C1-C5) 4.00 10.00
RANDOMLY INSERTED INTO PACKS

1997 Krome Evil Ernie Master of Annihilation

COMPLETE SET (90) 8.00 20.00
UNOPENED BOX (36 PACKS) 40.00 50.00
UNOPENED PACK (6 CARDS) 1.25 1.50
COMMON CARD (1-90) .15 .40
*FRACTAL: .5X TO 1.2X BASIC CARDS .20 .50
P1 Artwork by Justiniano PROMO
PA1 Psycho Apocalypse 8.00 20.00

1997 Krome Evil Ernie Master of Annihilation Box-Toppers

COMPLETE SET (5) 8.00 20.00
COMMON CARD (N1-N5) 2.50 6.00
STATED ODDS 1:BOX

1997 Krome Evil Ernie Master of Annihilation Fractal Autographs

COMMON CARD 20.00 50.00
STATED PRINT RUN 500 SER.#'d SETS

1997 Krome Evil Ernie Master of Annihilation Fractal Chromium

COMPLETE SET (5) 6.00 15.00
COMMON CARD (S1-S5) 1.50 4.00
STATED ODDS 1:12

1997 Krome Evil Ernie Master of Annihilation NecroChrome Stickers

COMPLETE SET (72) 10.00 25.00
COMMON CARD (1-72) .20 .50
STATED ODDS 1:1

1997 Krome Evil Ernie Master of Annihilation Super Real-O-Rama

COMPLETE SET (3) 5.00 12.00
COMMON CARD (SRORS1-SRORS3) 2.00 5.00
STATED ODDS 1:36

1998 Crown Sports Executive Privilege

COMPLETE SET (9) 2.50 6.00
COMMON CARD .50 1.25
*PROTOTYPE: SAME VALUE

1992 All Sports Marketing Exotic Dreams

COMPLETE SET (100) 8.00 20.00
UNOPENED BOX (36 PACKS) 15.00 20.00
UNOPENED PACK (9 CARDS) .50 .75
COMMON CARD (1-100) .15 .40

1992 All Sports Marketing Exotic Dreams Prototype Panels

COMPLETE SET (8) 15.00 40.00
COMMON CARD 2.50 6.00

1992 All Sports Marketing Exotic Dreams Prototypes

COMPLETE SET (8) 6.00 15.00
COMMON CARD (SKIP #'d) 1.25 3.00

1982 Sanitarium Exploring Our Solar System

COMPLETE SET (20) 6.00 15.00
COMMON CARD (1-20) .40 1.00

1994 The Ikon Face the Fire

COMPLETE BOXED SET (50) 4.00 10.00
COMMON CARD (1-50) .15 .40

1994 The Ikon Face the Fire Promos

COMMON CARD 1.25 3.00

1994 Mother Productions Faces of Death

COMPLETE BOXED SET (42) 5.00 12.00
COMMON CARD .25 .60

2012 Falling Skies Season One

COMPLETE SET (30) 20.00 50.00
COMMON CARD (1-30) 1.00 2.50

2012 Falling Skies Season One 2nd Mass

COMPLETE SET W/SP (10) 30.00 80.00
COMPLETE SET (9) 25.00 50.00
COMMON CARD (SM1-SM9) 3.00 8.00
STATED ODDS ONE PER PACK
SM10 ISSUED AS A RITTENHOUSE REWARD
STATED PRINT RUN 325 SER. #'d SETS
SM10 Anthony RR 12.00 30.00

2012 Falling Skies Season One Autographs

COMMON AUTO 4.00 10.00
STATED ODDS 1:1
2 Colin Cunningham 15.00 40.00
3 Connor Jessup 15.00 40.00
5 Drew Roy 6.00 15.00
7 Jessy Schram 15.00 40.00
8 Maxim Knight 6.00 15.00
10 Moon Bloodgood 50.00 100.00
12 Noah Wyle 30.00 75.00
14 Sarah Carter 15.00 40.00
15 Seychelle Gabriel 12.00 30.00
16 Will Patton 10.00 25.00

2012 Falling Skies Season One Costumes

COMMON CARD 6.00 15.00
STATED ODDS TWO PER PACK
STATED PRINT RUN 350 SER. #'d SETS
DC1/225 ISSUED AS CASE TOPPER
CC3 Sarah Carter 10.00 25.00
CC4 Anne Glass 8.00 20.00
CC5 Moon Bloodgood 8.00 20.00
CC13 Seychelle Gabriel 8.00 20.00
CC14 Seychelle Gabriel 8.00 20.00
CC17 Moon Bloodgood/200 25.00 50.00
DC1 Drew Roy/Noah Wyle 225 CT 20.00 40.00

2012 Falling Skies Season One Costumes Autographs

JESSUP ISSUED AS A 2-BOX INCENTIVE
BLOODGOOD ISSUED AS A 4-BOX INCENTIVE
1 Connor Jessup 2BI 50.00 100.00
2 Moon Bloodgood 4BI 125.00 200.00

2012 Falling Skies Season One Promos

P1 Group of 6 GEN 1.50 4.00
P2 Tom Mason 1.00 2.50
(SDCC)

2013 Falling Skies Season Two

COMPLETE SET (30) 20.00 50.00
COMMON CARD (1-30) 1.50 4.00
BT1 ISSUED AS BOX TOPPER
BT1 Get Off My Planet BT 5.00 12.00

2013 Falling Skies Season Two Autograph Costumes

WYLE ISSUED AS 4-BOX INCENTIVE
PATTON ISSUED AS 2-BOX INCENTIVE
NW Noah Wyle 4BI 50.00 100.00
WP Will Patton 2BI 25.00 60.00

2013 Falling Skies Season Two Autographs

COMMON AUTO 4.00 10.00
STATED ODDS 1:1
EL (EXTREMELY LIMITED): LESS THAN 200 COPIES
2 Brad Kelly EL 6.00 15.00
3 Colin Cunningham EL 10.00 25.00
4 Connor Jessup EL 10.00 25.00
6 Drew Roy EL 6.00 15.00
8 Jessy Schram EL 10.00 25.00
9 Luciana Carro EL 8.00 20.00
11 Melissa Kramer EL 5.00 12.00
12 Moon Bloodgood EL 30.00 75.00
13 Mpho Koaho EL 5.00 12.00
14 Noah Wyle EL 30.00 75.00
16 Sarah Carter EL 15.00 40.00
17 Seychelle Gabriel EL 15.00 40.00
18 Terry O'Quinn EL 12.00 30.00
19 Will Patton EL 15.00 40.00

2013 Falling Skies Season Two Costumes

COMPLETE SET (19) 80.00 150.00
COMMON CARD 4.00 10.00
TWO COSTUME CARDS PER PACK
STATED PRINT RUN 375 SER. #'d SETS
CC18 Tom Mason shirt 5.00 12.00
CC19 Anne Glass jacket 5.00 12.00
CC20 Anne Glass shirt 5.00 12.00
CC24 Ben Mason shirt 5.00 12.00
CC25 Ben Mason shirt 5.00 12.00
CC26 Maggie hoodie 6.00 15.00
CC27 Maggie pants 6.00 15.00
CC31 Karen shirt 6.00 15.00

2013 Falling Skies Season Two International Pin-Ups

COMPLETE SET (9) 25.00 60.00
COMMON CARD (1-9) 3.00 8.00
STATED ODDS 1:2

2013 Falling Skies Season Two Quotables

COMPLETE SET (9) 25.00 60.00
COMMON CARD (Q1-Q9) 3.00 8.00
STATED ODDS 1:2
Q10 ISSUED AS RITTENHOUSE REWARD
Q10 Captain Weaver RR 15.00 40.00

2013 Falling Skies Season Two Promos

P1 Cast GEN 1.25 3.00
P2 Tom Mason ALB 4.00 10.00
P3 Four dudes SDCC 1.50 4.00

2015 Falling Skies Autographs Expansion

COMMON AUTO 5.00 12.00
TERRY O'QUINN CASE-INCENTIVE 25.00 60.00
10 Terry O'Quinn 3SI 20.00 50.00

2018 Fallout Series 1

COMPLETE SET (144) 12.00 30.00
UNOPENED BOX (24 PACKS)
UNOPENED PACK (10 CARDS)
COMMON CARD (1-144) .15 .40

2018 Fallout Series 1 Die-Cuts

COMPLETE SET (10) 75.00 150.00
COMMON CARD (1-10) 8.00 20.00
RANDOMLY INSERTED INTO PACKS

2018 Fallout Series 1 Vault Boy Ultra-Rare Inserts

COMPLETE SET (5)
COMMON CARD (1-5)
STATED PRINT RUN 120 SER.#'d SETS
1 Vault Boy
2 Vault Boy
3 Vault Boy
4 Vault Boy
5 Vault Boy

2005 Family Guy Season One

COMPLETE SET (72) 4.00 10.00
UNOPENED BOX (24 PACKS) 100.00 150.00
UNOPENED PACK (7 CARDS) 4.00 6.00
COMMON CARD (1-72) .10 .30

2005 Family Guy Season One Autographs

COMMON AUTO (1-6) 4.00 10.00
RANDOMLY INSERTED INTO PACKS
A1 Seth MacFarlane 350.00 600.00
A2 Alex Borstein 15.00 40.00
A3 Erik Estrada 8.00 20.00
A4 Mike Henry 15.00 40.00

2005 Family Guy Season One Bad Dog

COMPLETE SET (6) 5.00 12.00
COMMON CARD (BD1-BD6) 1.00 2.50
STATED ODDS 1:17

2005 Family Guy Season One Box-Loaders

COMPLETE SET (3) 4.00 10.00
COMPLETE SET W/TOPPER (4) 8.00 20.00
COMMON CARD (BL1-BL3) 1.50 4.00
STATED ODDS 1:BOX
CL1 The Peter Principle 5.00 12.00
(Case-Topper)

2005 Family Guy Season One Griffin Family Photos

COMPLETE SET (9) 6.00 15.00
COMMON CARD (FP1-FP9) .75 2.00
STATED ODDS 1:11

2005 Family Guy Season One Promos

COMPLETE SET (6) 5.00 12.00
COMMON CARD .75 2.00
Pi Excuse Me Do I Know You? 1.25 3.00
PUK That Is Freakin' Sweet 2.00 5.00

2006 Family Guy Season Two

COMPLETE SET (72) 4.00 10.00
UNOPENED BOX (24 PACKS) 55.00 70.00
UNOPENED PACK (7 CARDS) 2.50 3.00
COMMON CARD (1-72) .10 .30

2006 Family Guy Season Two Autographs

COMMON CARD (1-6) 6.00 15.00
STATED ODDS 1:24
A7 Alex Borstein 10.00 25.00
A8 Adam Carolla 10.00 25.00
A11 Jennifer Tilly 10.00 20.00

2006 Family Guy Season Two Box-Loaders

COMPLETE SET (4) 8.00 20.00
COMMON CARD (BL1-BL3) 1.50 4.00
STATED ODDS 1:BOX
CL1 STATED ODDS 1:CASE
CL1 The Real World 5.00 12.00
CASE INSERT

2006 Family Guy Season Two Griffin Family Tree

COMPLETE SET (9) 6.00 15.00
COMMON CARD (1-9) .75 2.00
STATED ODDS 1:11

2006 Family Guy Season Two Life of Brian

COMPLETE SET (6) 5.00 12.00
COMMON CARD (1-6) 1.00 2.50
STATED ODDS 1:17

2006 Family Guy Season Two Promos

COMPLETE SET (5) 4.00 10.00
COMMON CARD .75 2.00
Pi Free Card Offer – Inkworks.Com 1.25 3.00
PUK Poppycock 2.00 5.00

2011 Family Guy Seasons Three Through Five

COMPLETE SET (50) 8.00 20.00
COMMON CARD (1-50) .30 .75

2011 Family Guy Seasons Three Through Five Autographs

COMMON CARD 8.00 20.00
STATED ODDS 1:24
CF1 Carrie Fisher 125.00 250.00
EA1 Ed Asner 10.00 25.00
GG1 Gina Gershon 12.00 30.00
JG1 Jennie Garth 12.00 30.00
LB1 Levar Burton 10.00 25.00
LG1 Leif Garrett 15.00 40.00
MH1 Mark Hamill 350.00 600.00
PD1 Patrick Duffy 10.00 25.00
PS1 Patrick Stewart 100.00 200.00
PW1 Patrick Warburton 20.00 50.00
TS1 Tori Spelling 15.00 40.00
LGJ1 Lou Gossett Jr. 12.00 30.00

MODERN

2011 Family Guy Seasons Three Through Five Meet the Characters

COMPLETE SET (10) 10.00 25.00
COMMON CARD (1-10) 2.00 5.00

2011 Family Guy Seasons Three Through Five Quotables

COMPLETE SET (24) 20.00 40.00
COMMON CARD (Q1-Q24) 1.25 3.00
*REFRACTOR/70: .75X TO 2X BASIC CARDS
*BLACK REF./25: 1.25X TO 3X BASIC CARDS

1991 Tuff Stuff Famous Battles of the Civil War

COMPLETE SET (100) 6.00 15.00
COMMON CARD (1-100) .12 .30

1992 Eclipse Famous Comic Book Creators

COMPLETE SET (110) 8.00 20.00
UNOPENED BOX (36 PACKS) 15.00 20.00
UNOPENED PACK (12 CARDS) .50 .75
COMMON CARD (1-110) .10 .30

1993 Eclipse Famous Comic Book Creators Update

COMPLETE BOXED SET (36) 4.00 10.00
COMMON CARD (1-36) .20 .50

1993 Zone Productions Famous Dope Fiends

COMPLETE BOXED SET (36) 4.00 10.00
COMMON CARD (1-36) .20 .50

1992 Cecil Court Collection Famous Film Directors

COMPLETE SET (20) 4.00 10.00
COMMON CARD (1-20) .40 1.00
NNO Promo Card 1.50 4.00
(General Distribution)

1994 Race Promotions Famous Hot Rod

COMPLETE SET (123) 10.00 25.00
UNOPENED BOX (PACKS)
UNOPENED PACK (10 CARDS)
COMMON CARD (1-120+3 CL) .20 .50

1981 Grandee Famous MG Marques

COMPLETE SET (28) 2.50 6.00
COMMON CARD (1-28) .12 .30

1992 Contact Press Famous UFO Sightings

COMPLETE SET (20) 4.00 10.00
COMMON CARD (1-20) .40 1.00

1992 Comic Images Fangoria

COMPLETE SET (90) 4.00 10.00
UNOPENED BOX (48 PACKS) 125.00 200.00
UNOPENED PACK (10 CARDS) 3.00 4.00
COMMON CARD (1-90) .08 .20
P1 6-Card Panel Uncut Sheet Chromium 4.00 10.00
NNO Bride of Re-Animator PROMO 2.00 5.00

1992 Comic Images Fangoria Chromium

COMPLETE SET (6) 6.00 15.00
COMMON CARD (1C-6C) 1.50 4.00
2C Predator 2.00 5.00
3C The Terminator 2.00 5.00
6C Jason 2.00 5.00

1993 Imagine Fantasy Girls I

COMPLETE BOXED SET (60) 4.00 10.00
COMPLETE AU BOXED SET (63) 8.00 20.00
COMMON CARD (1-60) .15 .30
61 Constance AU 2.00 5.00
62 Victoria AU 2.00 5.00
63 Ronda AU 2.00 5.00

1994 Imagine Fantasy Girls II

COMPLETE SET (65) 2.00 10.00
COMMON CARD (1-65) .12 .30
AU1 Mandy Leigh AU
AU9 Julianna Masterson AU
AU19 Michelle Clark AU

2003 Fantasy Worlds of Irwin Allen

COMPLETE SET (100) 8.00 20.00
UNOPENED BOX (40 PACKS) 65.00 80.00
UNOPENED PACK (7 CARDS) 1.75 2.00
COMMON CARD (1-100) .20 .50
C1 ISSUED AS ALBUM EXCLUSIVE
C1 Captain Crane MEM 6.00 15.00

2003 Fantasy Worlds of Irwin Allen Autographs

COMMON CARD 6.00 15.00
THREE AUTOS PER BOX
A5 ISSUED AS CASE TOPPER
A1 Bill Mumy L 12.00 60.00
A3 Lee Meriwether 15.00 25.00
A4 David Hedison 12.00 25.00
A5 Bob May CT 25.00 50.00
A6 Don Marshall 12.00 50.00
A7 Marta Kristen L 15.00 50.00
A9 Deanna Lund L 15.00 50.00
A10 Angela Cartwright 25.00 30.00
A17 June Lockhart 25.00 30.00

2003 Fantasy Worlds of Irwin Allen Behind-the-Scenes

COMPLETE SET (9) 12.00 30.00
COMMON CARD (B1-B9) 2.00 5.00
STATED ODDS 1:40

2003 Fantasy Worlds of Irwin Allen Gallery

COMPLETE SET (4) 30.00 80.00
COMMON CARD (G1-G4) 10.00 25.00
STATED ODDS 1:120

2003 Fantasy Worlds of Irwin Allen Sci-Fi Legends

COMPLETE SET W/MCI (22) 50.00 100.00
COMPLETE SET (21) 6.00 15.00
COMMON CARD (R1-R21) .40 1.00
STATED ODDS 1:6
R22 ISSUED AS MULTICASE INCENTIVE
R22 Robot B9/250 MCI 30.00 80.00

2003 Fantasy Worlds of Irwin Allen The Openings

COMPLETE SET (12) 8.00 20.00
COMMON CARD (L1-L12) .40 1.00
STATED ODDS 1:8

2003 Fantasy Worlds of Irwin Allen Promos

P1 Holiday 2003 GEN .75 2.00
P2 Holiday 2003 NSU 2.00 5.00
P3 ALB 4.00 10.00

1992 Calfun Fantazy Cards

COMPLETE SET (99) 4.00 10.00
COMMON CARD (1-97, CL1 & CL2) .10 .25
BONUS CARD IS UNNUMBERED

1981 Sanitarium Farewell to Steam

COMPLETE SET (20) 5.00 12.00
COMMON CARD (1-20) .50 1.25

Farscape

2000 Farscape In Motion Lenticular Previews

COMPLETE SET (9) 7.50 20.00
COMMON CARD (M1-M9) 1.25 3.00

2001 Farscape In Motion

COMPLETE SET (60) 5.00 12.00
UNOPENED BOX (24 PACKS) 125.00 200.00
UNOPENED PACK (4 CARDS) 6.00 8.00
COMMON CARD (1-60) .15 .40
P1 John Crichton PROMO .75 2.00

2001 Farscape In Motion Archive Collection

COMPLETE SET (12) 80.00 150.00
COMMON CARD (AC1-AC12) 6.00 15.00
OVERALL ARCHIVE COLLECTION ODDS THREE PER BOX
STATED PRINT RUN 999 SER. #'d SETS

2001 Farscape In Motion Archive Collection Gold

COMPLETE SET (3) 50.00 100.00
COMMON CARD (WC1-WC3) 15.00 40.00
OVERALL ARCHIVE COLLECTION ODDS THREE PER BOX
STATED PRINT RUN 500 SER. #'d SETS

2001 Farscape In Motion Close Encounters

COMPLETE SET (9) 10.00 25.00
COMMON CARD (C1-C9) 1.50 4.00
STATED ODDS 1:6

2001 Farscape In Motion From the Archives Costumes

COMPLETE SET (4) 80.00 150.00
COMMON CARD (C8-C12) 15.00 40.00
STATED ODDS 1:24
C11 WAS DOES NOT EXIST

2001 Farscape In Motion Portraits in Motion

COMPLETE SET (9) 15.00 40.00
COMMON CARD (P1-P9) 2.00 5.00
STATED ODDS 1:8

2001 Farscape In Motion Ships of Farscape

COMPLETE SET (9) 6.00 15.00
COMMON CARD (S1-S9) .75 2.00
STATED ODDS 1:3

2001 Farscape In Motion Sound in Motion

COMPLETE SET (6) 30.00 80.00
COMMON CARD (S1-S6) 8.00 20.00
STATED ODDS ONE PER BOX

2001 Farscape In Motion The Good the Bad and the Ugly

COMPLETE SET (18) 5.00 12.00
COMMON CARD (U1-U18) .40 1.00
STATED ODDS 1:2

2001 Farscape John Crichton Promos

COMPLETE SET (6) 6.00 15.00
COMMON CARD (D1-D6) 1.25 3.00
STATED PRINT RUN 999 SETS

1999 Rittenhouse Farscape Previews

COMPLETE SET (6) 12.00 30.00
COMMON CARD (1-6) 3.00 8.00
STATED PRINT RUN 1,999 SER. #'d SETS

2000 Farscape Season One

COMPLETE SET (72) 5.00 12.00
UNOPENED BOX (36 PACKS) 60.00 90.00
UNOPENED PACK (9 CARDS) 2.00 3.00
COMMON CARD (1-72) .15 .40
PM1 STATED ODDS 1:36
PM1 Farscape In Motion PROMO 2.00 5.00

2000 Farscape Season One Autographs

COMPLETE SET W/A6 (6)
COMPLETE SET (5)
COMMON CARD (A1-A5) 12.00 30.00
STATED ODDS 1:72
A5 ISSUED AS ALBUM EXCLUSIVE
A1 Ben Browder 60.00 120.00
A2 Anthony Simcoe 20.00 50.00
A3 Gigi Edgley 30.00 80.00
A6 Claudia Black CT 50.00 100.00

2000 Farscape Season One Behind-the-Scenes

COMPLETE SET (9) 10.00 25.00
COMMON CARD (BTS1-BTS9) 1.50 4.00
STATED ODDS 1:6

2000 Farscape Season One Farscape Stars

COMPLETE SET (9) 6.00 15.00
COMMON CARD (FS1-FS9) 1.00 2.50
STATED ODDS 1:4

2000 Farscape Season One From the Archives Costumes

COMPLETE SET (7) 150.00 300.00
COMMON CARD (C1-C7) 12.00 30.00
STATED ODDS ONE PER BOX
C7 ISSUED AS CASE TOPPER
C1 Ben Browder 30.00 80.00
C2 Claudia Black 30.00 80.00
C6 Lani Tupu 30.00 80.00
C7 Chiana CT 30.00 80.00

2000 Farscape Season One Promos

COMPLETE SET (4) 4.00 10.00
P1 Zhaan .75 2.50
P2 Aeryn Sun 2.00 5.00
TV1 Zhaan 2.00 5.00
DVD1 Group of seven 2.00 5.00

2000 Farscape Season Two Previews

COMPLETE SET (9) 15.00 40.00
COMMON CARD (P1-P9) 2.00 5.00
STATED ODDS 1:8

2001 Farscape Season Two

COMPLETE SET (72) 5.00 12.00
UNOPENED BOX (40 PACKS) 55.00 70.00
UNOPENED PACK (9 CARDS) 1.50 1.75
COMMON CARD (73-144) .15 .40
*PP BLACK/50: 3X TO 8X BASIC CARDS 1.25 3.00
*PP CYAN/50: 3X TO 8X BASIC CARDS 1.25 3.00
*PP MAGENTA/50: 3X TO 8X BASIC CARDS 1.25 3.00
*PP YELLOW/50: 3X TO 8X BASIC CARDS 1.25 3.00

2001 Farscape Season Two Alien Life

COMPLETE SET (12) 6.00 15.00
COMMON CARD (A1-A12) .75 2.00
STATED ODDS 1:10

2001 Farscape Season Two Autographs

COMMON AUTO 6.00 15.00
STATED ODDS 1:100
A11 ISSUED IN COLLECTORS ALBUM
A12 ISSUED AS CASE TOPPER
A7 Virginia Hey 20.00 50.00
A8 Lani Tupu 10.00 25.00
A9 Wayne Pygram 12.00 30.00

2001 Farscape Season Two Behind-the-Scenes

COMPLETE SET (22) 8.00 20.00
COMMON CARD (BK1-BK22) .60 1.50
STATED ODDS 1:5

2001 Farscape Season Two Costume Contest

COMPLETE SET W/O SP (10) 6.00 15.00
COMPLETE SET W/SP (11)
COMMON CARD .75 2.00
STATED ODDS 1:1
F F SP

2001 Farscape Season Two From the Archives Costumes

COMPLETE SET (13) 200.00 400.00
COMMON CARD (C1-C13) 6.00 15.00
STATED ODDS TWO PER BOX

CC3 John Crichton	25.00	60.00
CC4 Stark	10.00	25.00
CC5 Rygel XVI	8.00	20.00
CC8 Captain Crais	60.00	120.00
CC10 Chiana	60.00	120.00

2001 Farscape Season Two Quotables

COMPLETE SET (22)	10.00	25.00
COMMON CARD (Q1-Q22)	.75	2.00
STATED ODDS 1:5		

2001 Farscape Season Two Promos

BP1 Chiana ALB	1.50	4.00
NNO Scorpius	1.00	2.50

2002 Farscape Season Three

COMPLETE SET (72)	5.00	12.00
UNOPENED BOX (40 PACKS)	55.00	70.00
UNOPENED PACK (9 CARDS)	1.50	1.75
COMMON CARD (145-216)	.15	.40
*PP BLACK/50: 3X TO 8X BASIC CARDS	1.25	3.00
*PP CYAN/50: 3X TO 8X BASIC CARDS	1.25	3.00
*PP MAGENTA/50: 3X TO 8X BASIC CARDS	1.25	3.00
*PP YELLOW/50: 3X TO 8X BASIC CARDS	1.25	3.00

2002 Farscape Season Three Autographs

COMMON AUTO	4.00	10.00
STATED ODDS 1:1		
A15 ISSUED AS ALBUM EXCLUSIVE		
ZA1 ISSUED AS CASE TOPPER		
A13 Paul Goddard	8.00	20.00
A14 Tammy MacIntosh	12.00	30.00
A15 Jonathan Hardy ALBUM	10.00	25.00
A16 Matt Newton	6.00	15.00
A17 Linda Cropper	6.00	15.00
A20 Francesca Buller	6.00	15.00
A21 Andrew Prowse	6.00	15.00
ZA1 Virginia Hey CT	10.00	25.00

2002 Farscape Season Three Behind-the-Scenes

COMPLETE SET (22)	3.00	8.00
COMMON CARD (BTS23-BTS44)	.20	.50
STATED ODDS 1:5		

2002 Farscape Season Three Family Ties

COMPLETE SET (6)	4.00	10.00
COMMON CARD (F1-F6)	.75	2.00
STATED ODDS 1:20		

2002 Farscape Season Three From the Archives Costumes

COMPLETE SET (2)	30.00	80.00
COMMON CARD (CC14-CC15)	12.00	30.00
STATED ODDS 1:240		
CC14 Scorpius	25.00	60.00
Harvey		

2002 Farscape Season Three Revenging Angel Animation Cels

COMPLETE SET (18)	30.00	60.00
COMMON CARD (R1-R18)	2.00	5.00
STATED ODDS 1:20		

2002 Farscape Season Three Quotables

COMPLETE SET (22)	3.00	8.00
COMMON CARD (Q23-Q44)	.20	.50
STATED ODDS 1:5		

2002 Farscape Season Three Promos

COMPLETE SET (2)	2.00	5.00
COMMON CARD (P1-P2)	1.00	2.50
P2 Group of seven ALB	2.00	5.00

2003 Farscape Season Four

COMPLETE SET (72)	5.00	12.00
UNOPENED BOX (40 PACKS)	50.00	60.00
UNOPENED PACK (9 CARDS)	1.25	1.50
COMMON CARD (217-288)	.15	.40
JC ISSUED AS CASE TOPPER		
JC John Czop (Sikozu) SKETCH	20.00	50.00

2003 Farscape Season Four Behind-the-Scenes

COMPLETE SET (22)	3.00	8.00
COMMON CARD (BTS45-BTS66)	.40	1.00
STATED ODDS 1:5		

2003 Farscape Season Four Farscape ArtiFEX

COMPLETE SET (9)	8.00	20.00
COMPLETE SET W/SP (10)	25.00	60.00
COMMON CARD (X1-X9)	1.25	3.00
STATED ODDS 1:10		
HEY AUTO STATED ODDS 1:480		
XH6 Virginia Hey AU (Zhaan)	25.00	50.00

2003 Farscape Season Four Farscape Autographs

COMMON CARD (A22-A34)	6.00	15.00
STATED ODDS 2:BOX		
A22 Raelee Hill	12.00	30.00
A23 Melissa Jaffer	6.00	15.00
A24 Rebecca Riggs	8.00	20.00
A25 David Franklin	6.00	15.00
A26 Lani Tupu	10.00	25.00
A29 Murray Bartlett	6.00	15.00
A32 Wayne Pygram	10.00	25.00
A33 Gigi Edgley	15.00	40.00
A34 Kent McCord	50.00	100.00

2003 Farscape Season Four Farscape Gallery

COMPLETE SET (8)	40.00	80.00
COMMON CARD (G1-G8)	5.00	12.00
STATED ODDS 1:40		

2003 Farscape Season Four From the Archives Costumes

COMMON CARD (C16-C21)	8.00	20.00
STATED ODDS 1:BOX		
C21 ISSUED AS ALBUM EXCLUSIVE		
C16 Jool	12.00	30.00
C17 Jothee	12.00	30.00
C21 Moya ALBUM	12.00	30.00

2003 Farscape Season Four Quotables

COMPLETE SET (22)	5.00	12.00
COMMON CARD (Q45-Q66)	.40	1.00
STATED ODDS 1:5		

2003 Farscape Season Four Promos

COMPLETE SET (3)	2.50	6.00
COMMON CARD (P1-P3)	.75	2.00
P3 Aeryn/John	3.00	8.00

2004 Farscape Through the Wormhole

COMPLETE SET (72)	4.00	10.00
UNOPENED BOX (40 PACKS)	65.00	80.00
UNOPENED PACK (5 CARDS)	1.75	2.00
COMMON CARD (1-72)	.10	.30

2004 Farscape Through the Wormhole Autographs

COMMON CARD (A35-A70)	6.00	15.00
OVERALL AUTO ODDS TWO PER BOX		
A39 ISSUED AS ALBUM EXCLUSIVE		
ALL AUTOS LIMITED (300-500 COPIES) UNLESS NOTED		
VL (VERY LIMITED): 200-300 COPIES		
A37 Alyssa-Jane Cook	8.00	20.00
A38 Claudia Black VL	100.00	200.00
A39 Bianca Chiminello ALB	8.00	20.00
A43 Marta Dusseldorp	6.00	15.00
A45 Tina Bursil	6.00	15.00
A49 Imogen Annesley	6.00	15.00
A54 Angie Milliken	6.00	15.00
A55 Jamie Croft	6.00	15.00
A56 Darlene Vogel	6.00	15.00
A60 Felicity Price	6.00	15.00
A66 Gigi Edgley	30.00	75.00
A67 Anthony Simcoe	20.00	50.00
A68 Wayne Pygram VL	50.00	100.00
A69 Raelee Hill	12.00	30.00
A70 Paul Goddard	6.00	15.00

2004 Farscape Through the Wormhole Crichton's Women

COMPLETE SET (9)	25.00	60.00
COMMON CARD (W1-W9)	3.00	8.00
STATED ODDS 1:40		

2004 Farscape Through the Wormhole Dual Autographs

OVERALL AUTO ODDS TWO PER BOX		
DA2 ISSUED AS MULTI-CASE INCENTIVE		
VL (VERY LIMITED): 200-300 COPIES		
DA1 B.Browder/C.Black VL	200.00	350.00
DA2 B.Browder/W.Pygram CI	75.00	150.00
DA3 V.Hey/P.Goddard	20.00	50.00

2004 Farscape Through the Wormhole Peacekeeper Wars

COMPLETE SET (18)	8.00	20.00
COMMON CARD (PW1-PW18)	.60	1.50
STATED ODDS 1:5		

2004 Farscape Through the Wormhole Sean Pence ArtiFEX

COMPLETE SET (9)	5.00	12.00
COMMON CARD (SPA1-SPA9)	.75	2.00
STATED ODDS 1:13		

2004 Farscape Through the Wormhole Season One Quotables

COMPLETE SET (22)	6.00	15.00
COMMON CARD (Q1-Q22)	.40	1.00
STATED ODDS 1:5		

2004 Farscape Through the Wormhole Promos

COMPLETE SET (4)	5.00	12.00
COMMON CARD	.75	2.00
P2 Aeryn Sun	1.50	4.00
P3 Chiana	3.00	8.00

1999 Comic Images Fastner and Larson Flesh and Blood

COMPLETE SET (9)	4.00	10.00
COMMON CARD (1-9)	.75	2.00

2001 Fathom

COMPLETE SET (90)	5.00	12.00
UNOPENED BOX (36 PACKS)		
UNOPENED PACK (6 CARDS)		
COMMON CARD (1-90)	.12	.30
NNO 90-Card Panel Full-Set Uncut Sheet		

2001 Fathom Glow-in-the-Dark

COMPLETE SET (6)	6.00	15.00
COMMON CARD (G1-G6)	1.25	3.00
STATED ODDS 1:12		

2001 Fathom Holograph Autographs

COMMON CARD	5.00	12.00
STATED ODDS 1:18		
STATED PRINT RUN 600 SETS		

2001 Fathom Premium Previews

COMPLETE BOXED SET (6)	4.00	10.00
COMMON CARD	1.25	3.00

2001 Fathom Rainbow Chrome

COMPLETE SET (6)	6.00	15.00
COMMON CARD (C1-C6)	1.25	3.00
STATED ODDS 1:12		

2001 Fathom Jumbo Promos

COMPLETE SET (6)	15.00	40.00
COMMON CARD (1-6)	3.00	8.00
STATED ODDS 1:BOX		

2001 Fathom Promos

COMMON CARD	.75	2.00
P1 Previews	1.25	3.00
P2 Previews	1.25	3.00
P3 Previews	1.25	3.00
P4 Previews	1.25	3.00
W1 Wizard World	1.25	3.00
W2 Wizard World	1.25	3.00
W3 Wizard World	1.25	3.00
W4 Wizard World	1.25	3.00
NNO 4-Up Panel AU		
PC1 4-Card Panel of the Above		
NSU1 Busty	1.25	3.00

1981 K.F. Byrnes FD

COMPLETE SET (22)	4.00	10.00
COMMON CARD (1-22)	.30	.75

1982 KF Byrnes FD

COMPLETE SET (22)	8.00	20.00
COMMON CARD (1-22)	.50	1.25

1983 K.F. Byrnes FD

COMPLETE SET (22)	12.00	30.00
COMMON CARD (1-22)	.75	2.00

1986 K.F. Byrnes FD

COMPLETE SET (22)	12.00	30.00
COMMON CARD (1-22)	.75	2.00

2011 FemForce

COMPLETE SET (51)	4.00	10.00
UNOPENED SKETCH PACK (52 CARDS)	30.00	40.00
COMMON CARD (1-51)	.15	.40

2011 FemForce Promos

COMPLETE SET (3)	2.50	6.00
COMMON CARD		2.50
CCCE3 Stardust	1.50	4.00
PCCEP3 Alizarin Crimson	1.50	4.00

1996 FPG Femme Fatales

COMPLETE SET (90)	12.00	30.00
UNOPENED BOX (36 PACKS)	15.00	20.00
UNOPENED PACK (6 CARDS)	.50	.75
COMMON CARD (1-90)	.30	.75

1996 FPG Femme Fatales Gold Metallic

COMPLETE SET (5)	12.00	30.00
COMMON CARD (1G-5G)	3.00	8.00
STATED ODDS 1:12		

1992 Dart Flipcards FernGully

COMPLETE SET (100)	5.00	12.00
COMPLETE FACTORY SET (100)/3000	8.00	20.00
UNOPENED BOX (48 PACKS)	15.00	20.00
UNOPENED PACK (8 CARDS)	.50	.75
COMMON CARD (1-100)	.10	.25

1992 Mother Productions 50's Pin-Up Girls Series 1

COMPLETE SET (40)	3.00	8.00
COMMON CARD (1-40)	.12	.30

1992 Mother Productions 50's Pin-Up Girls Series 2

COMPLETE SET (40)	3.00	8.00
COMMON CARD (1-40)	.12	.30

2001 Final Fantasy Spirits Within

COMPLETE SET (72)	6.00	15.00
UNOPENED BOX (24 PACKS)	40.00	50.00
UNOPENED PACK (7 CARDS)	2.00	2.25
COMMON CARD (1-72)	.15	.40
NNO Uncut Sheet		

2001 Final Fantasy Spirits Within Holochrome

COMPLETE SET (7)	12.00	30.00
COMMON CARD (C1-C7)	2.50	6.00
RANDOMLY INSERTED INTO PACKS		

2001 Final Fantasy Spirits Within Promos

P1 Perchance to Dream	.75	2.00
P2 Two soldiers in full helmets	.75	2.00

2017 Find Your Hero Promos

COMPLETE SET (7) 8.00 20.00
COMMON CARD (UNNUMBERED) 2.00 5.00

2016 Finding Dory

COMPLETE SET (40) 6.00 15.00
UNOPENED BOX (24 PACKS) 40.00 50.00
UNOPENED PACK (5 CARDS) 2.00 2.50
COMMON CARD (P1-P40) .15 .40

2016 Finding Dory Dog Tags Bulls-i-Toy

COMPLETE SET (24) 25.00 60.00
UNOPENED BOX (24 PACKS) 80.00 100.00
UNOPENED PACK (1 DOG TAG+1 STICKER) 4.50 5.00
COMMON TAG 1.50 4.00
*FOIL: .6X TO 1.5X BASIC TAGS 2.50 6.00

2016 Finding Dory Dog Tags Bulls-i-Toy Stickers

COMPLETE SET (8) 2.00 5.00
COMMON CARD .40 1.00
STATED ODDS 1:1

2016 Finding Dory Dog Tags Upper Deck

COMPLETE SET (12) 25.00 60.00
UNOPENED BOX (24 PACKS)
UNOPENED PACK (5 CARDS)
COMMON CARD (1-12) 3.00 8.00

2003 Finding Nemo FilmCardz

COMPLETE SET (72) 6.00 15.00
UNOPENED BOX (24 PACKS) 50.00 60.00
UNOPENED PACK (5 CARDS) 2.00 2.50
COMMON CARD (1-72) .15 .40

2003 Finding Nemo FilmCardz Rare Prism

COMPLETE SET (6) 10.00 25.00
COMMON CARD (R1-R6) 2.50 6.00
STATED ODDS 1:8

2003 Finding Nemo FilmCardz Ultra Rare

COMPLETE SET (3) 8.00 20.00
COMMON CARD (UR1-UR3) 3.00 8.00
STATED ODDS 1:24

2003 Finding Nemo FilmCardz Promos

COMPLETE SET (2) 1.25 3.00
COMMON CARD (P1-P2) .75 2.00

1995 MT Productions Fine Custom Rides Promos

NNO Ford Sedan 1.25 3.00
NNO Chevrolet Truck 1.25 3.00

2017 Fingerlakes Comic Con Zombie Promos

COMPLETE SET (3) 3.00 8.00
COMMON CARD (1-3) 1.50 4.00

1993-98 Bon Air Fire Engines Complete Series

COMPLETE SET (500) 20.00 50.00
COMPLETE SERIES 1 SET (100) 6.00 15.00
COMPLETE SERIES 2 SET (100) 5.00 12.00
COMPLETE SERIES 3 SET (100) 5.00 12.00
COMPLETE SERIES 4 SET (100) 5.00 12.00
COMPLETE SERIES 5 SET (100) 5.00 12.00
UNOPENED SERIES 1 BOX (36 PACKS) 30.00 40.00
UNOPENED SERIES 1 PACK (10 CARDS) 1.00 1.25
UNOPENED SERIES 2 BOX (36 PACKS) 25.00 35.00
UNOPENED SERIES 2 PACK (10 CARDS) 1.00 1.25
UNOPENED SERIES 3 BOX (36 PACKS) 25.00 35.00
UNOPENED SERIES 3 PACK (10 CARDS) 1.00 1.25
UNOPENED SERIES 4 BOX (36 PACKS) 25.00 35.00
UNOPENED SERIES 4 PACK (10 CARDS) 1.00 1.25
COMMON SERIES 1 CARD (1-100) .12 .30
COMMON SERIES 2 CARD (101-200) .10 .25
COMMON SERIES 3 CARD (201-300) .10 .25
COMMON SERIES 4 CARD (301-400) .10 .25
COMMON SERIES 5 CARD (401-500) .10 .25

1993-98 Bon Air Fire Engines Complete Series 24-Kt Gold Cards

1 Series 1 24-Kt Gold Card/1000 100.00 200.00
2 Series 2 24-Kt Gold Card/1000 200.00 400.00
3 Series 3 24-Kt Gold Card/1000 200.00 400.00
4 Series 4 24-Kt Gold Card/1000 200.00 400.00

1993-98 Bon Air Fire Engines Complete Series Fire-O-Graphics Series 4 Set

COMPLETE SET (6) 10.00 25.00
COMMON CARD (1-6) 2.00 5.00
STATED ODDS 1:12

1993-98 Bon Air Fire Engines Complete Series Prisms

COMPLETE SET (18) 25.00 60.00
COMPLETE SERIES 1 SET (6) 8.00 20.00
COMPLETE SERIES 2 SET (6) 10.00 25.00
COMPLETE SERIES 3 SET (6) 12.00 30.00
COMMON CARD (1-6) 1.50 4.00
COMMON CARD (7-12) 2.00 5.00
COMMON CARD (13-18) 2.50 6.00
STATED ODDS 1:12

1993-98 Bon Air Fire Engines Complete Series Promos

COMPLETE SET (9) 5.00 12.00
COMMON CARD (P1-P9) .75 2.00

2006 Firefly The Complete Collection

COMPLETE SET (72) 5.00 12.00
UNOPENED BOX (36 PACKS) 55.00 70.00
UNOPENED PACK (6 CARDS) 1.50 2.00
COMMON CARD (1-72) .15 .40

2006 Firefly The Complete Collection Autographs

COMMON AUTO (A1-A11) 8.00 20.00
STATED ODDS 1:36
A1 Nathan Fillion 50.00 100.00
A2 Gina Torres 15.00 40.00
A3 Morena Baccarin 60.00 120.00
A4 Adam Baldwin 25.00 60.00
A5 Jewel Staite 30.00 75.00
A6 Sean Maher 25.00 50.00
A7 Ron Glass 25.00 60.00
A8 Michael Fairman 10.00 25.00
A10 Christina Hendricks 75.00 150.00

2006 Firefly The Complete Collection Box-Loaders

COMPLETE SET (3) 4.00 10.00
COMMON CARD (BL1-BL3) 1.50 4.00
STATED ODDS 1:36
CL1 Outlaws 4.00 10.00
CASE INSERT

2006 Firefly The Complete Collection Firefly Forever

COMPLETE SET (9) 10.00 25.00
COMMON CARD (F1-F9) 1.25 3.00
STATED ODDS 1:11
PAN 9-Card Panel (F1-F9)/199

2006 Firefly The Complete Collection Battle of Serenity

COMPLETE SET (6) 6.00 15.00
COMMON CARD (B1-B6) 1.25 3.00
STATED ODDS 1:17

2006 Firefly The Complete Collection Promos

COMPLETE SET (4) 3.00 8.00
COMMON CARD .75 2.00
Pi Firefly 1.25 3.00
PUK Firefly 2.00 5.00

2015 Firefly The Verse

COMPLETE SET (171) 8.00 20.00
UNOPENED BOX (20 PACKS) 75.00 85.00
UNOPENED PACK (7 CARDS) 4.00 5.00
COMMON CARD (1-171) .10 .25
*EMERALD FOIL: 3X TO 8X BASIC CARDS .75 2.00
*LEATHER/99: 8X TO 20X BASIC CARDS 2.00 5.00

2015 Firefly The Verse Artist Autographs

COMMON CLARK (1-9) 5.00 12.00
COMMON BRINKERHOFF (10-18) 5.00 12.00
COMMON GLEBE (19-27) 8.00 20.00
COMMON HALLION (28-36) 4.00 10.00
COMMON PARNELL (37-45) 4.00 10.00
COMMON EDGE (46-54) 4.00 10.00
COMMON GILES (55-63) 5.00 12.00
COMMON BRAZIER (64-72) 6.00 15.00
COMMON PETRECCA (73-81) 5.00 12.00
COMMON SHARPE (82-90) 6.00 15.00
COMMON PULKOVSKI (91-99) 4.00 10.00
COMMON GRIMOEUVRE (100-108) 5.00 12.00
COMMON REDFERN (109-117) 4.00 10.00
COMMON SANTIAGO (118-126) 5.00 12.00
COMMON HINDELANG (127-135) 6.00 15.00
COMMON SHAY (136-144) 6.00 15.00
COMMON GOMEZ (145-154) 5.00 12.00
COMMON JIMENEZ (155-162) 5.00 12.00
COMMON MEEKS (163-171) 4.00 10.00
STATED ODDS 1:20

2015 Firefly The Verse Autographs

COMMON AUTO 5.00 12.00
STATED ODDS 1:20
AB Adam Baldwin 25.00 60.00
AN Andrew Bryniarski 6.00 15.00
BU Richard Burgi 6.00 15.00
DS Doug Savant 6.00 15.00
GI Gregory Itzin 6.00 15.00
JR Jeff Ricketts 6.00 15.00
JS Jewel Staite 100.00 200.00
KG Kevin Gage 6.00 15.00
LD Larry Drake 10.00 25.00
MB Morena Baccarin 60.00 120.00
MC Melinda Clarke 15.00 40.00
MF Michael Fairman 6.00 15.00
MS Mark Sheppard 6.00 15.00
NF Nathan Fillion 75.00 150.00
RB Richard Brooks 10.00 25.00
RG Ron Glass 30.00 75.00
SM Sean Maher 25.00 60.00
WO Jonathan Woodward 6.00 15.00

2015 Firefly The Verse Dual Autographs

COMMON AUTO 12.00 30.00
BA Atterton/Baccarin 60.00 120.00
BG Baldwin/Gage 20.00 50.00
FB Bryniarski/Fairman 15.00 40.00
FM Fillion/Baccarin 200.00 400.00
FT Fillion/Maher 75.00 150.00
GM Maher/Baldwin 50.00 100.00
GS Baldwin/Glass 50.00 100.00
HB Glass/Baccarin 100.00 200.00
HF Baldwin/Fillion 100.00 200.00
SD Sheppard/Drake 20.00 50.00

2015 Firefly The Verse Original Art Autographs

COMMON CARD 25.00 60.00
OADB Ron Glass 30.00 75.00
OAIS Morena Baccarin 50.00 100.00
OAKF Jewel Staite 30.00 75.00
OAMR Nathan Fillion 75.00 150.00

2015 Firefly The Verse Triple Autographs

COMMON AUTO 25.00 60.00
FBT Maher/Fillion/Baldwin 100.00 200.00
FSF Fillion/Fairman/Sheppard 75.00 150.00
GBM Maher/Glass/Baldwin 125.00 250.00
HFB Glass/Fillion/Baccarin 200.00 350.00
SFD Fillion/Sheppard/Drake 60.00 120.00

2001 First Wave Previews

COMPLETE SET (6) 5.00 12.00
COMMON CARD (FW1-FW6) 1.25 3.00
STATED PRINT RUN 2001 SETS

2002 First Wave

COMPLETE SET (16) 6.00 15.00
COMPLETE FACTORY SET 75.00 100.00
COMMON CARD (1-16) .50 1.25

2002 First Wave Autographs

COMPLETE SET (4) 30.00 80.00
COMMON CARD (A1-A4) 6.00 15.00
STATED PRINT RUN 999 SETS
A2 Traci Elizabeth Lords 20.00 50.00

2002 First Wave Costumes

COMPLETE SET (8) 60.00 120.00
COMMON CARD 8.00 20.00
STATED PRINT RUN 750 SETS

1988 Comic Images Flaming Carrot Comics

COMPLETE SET (40) 12.00 30.00
UNOPENED BOX (50 PACKS)
UNOPENED PACK (5 CARDS)
COMMON CARD (1-40) .50 1.50

1993 Arena Magazine Flare Promo

NNO Art by Daerick Gross 1.25 3.00

1982 Cadbury Flight The World's Most Spectacular Birds

COMPLETE SET (12) 6.00 15.00
COMMON CARD (1-12) 1.00 2.50

1993 Cardz The Flintstones

COMPLETE SET (100) 6.00 15.00
UNOPENED BOX (36 PACKS) 25.00 30.00
UNOPENED PACK (8 CARDS) .75 1.00
COMMON CARD (1-100) .12 .30
T1 Flintstones Theme (tekchrome) 8.00 20.00

1993 Cardz The Flintstones Whatzit Coloring Cards

COMPLETE SET (10) 1.50 4.00
COMMON CARD (1-10) .40 1.00

1993 Cardz The Flintstones Promos

1 The Flintstone Flyer - Dealer Prototype .75 2.00
2 Dating - Dealer Prototype .75 2.00

1993 Topps The Flintstones Movie

COMPLETE SET (88) 5.00 12.00
COMPLETE SET W/STICKERS (99) 6.00 15.00
UNOPENED BOX (36 PACKS) 20.00 25.00
UNOPENED PACK (8 CARDS) .50 .75
COMMON CARD (1-88) .12 .30

1993 Topps The Flintstones Movie Stickers

COMPLETE SET (11) 1.50 4.00
COMMON STICKERS (1-11) .30 .75

1993 Topps The Flintstones Movie Promos

1 Unnumbered .75 2.00
2 4-Up Panel
3 9-Up Panel 3.00 8.00

1996 Donruss Flipper

COMPLETE SET (90) 10.00 25.00
UNOPENED BOX (36 PACKS) 20.00 30.00
UNOPENED PACK (8 CARDS) .75 1.00
COMMON CARD (1-90) .25 .60
NNO Flipper Trading Cards PROMO .75 2.00

2008 The Forbidden Kingdom Theater Promos

COMPLETE SET (6) 6.00 15.00
COMMON CARD 1.25 4.00

MODERN

Card	Low	High
NNO The Drunken Immortal	1.50	4.00
NNO The Jade Warlord	1.50	4.00
NNO The Orphan Warrior	1.50	4.00
NNO The Silent Monk	1.50	4.00
NNO The Traveler	1.50	4.00
NNO The White Haired Assassin	1.50	4.00

1995 Hershey's Forrest Gump Canada

Card	Low	High
COMPLETE SET (6)	3.00	8.00
COMMON CARD	.75	2.00

2019 Panini Fortnite Series 1

Card	Low	High
COMPLETE SET W/O SP (100)	30.00	75.00
UNOPENED BOX (24 PACKS)	125.00	200.00
UNOPENED PACK (6 CARDS)	6.00	8.00
UNLISTED COMMON (1-100)	.50	1.25
UNLISTED UNCOMMON (101-150)	.75	2.00
UNLISTED RARE (151-200)	1.25	3.00
UNLISTED EPIC (201-250)	2.00	5.00
UNLISTED LEGENDARY (251-300)	2.50	6.00
COMMON (1-100) HAVE NO PARALLELS		
128 Highrise Assault Trooper U	3.00	8.00
145 Angular Axe U	2.00	5.00
150 Yuletide Ranger U	2.00	5.00
155 Backbone R	2.00	5.00
162 Chromium R	2.00	5.00
163 Cipher R	10.00	25.00
166 Dark Bomber R	3.00	8.00
172 Fortune R	2.00	5.00
186 Firewalker R	2.50	6.00
187 Fishstick R	2.50	6.00
189 Red-Nosed Raider R	1.50	4.00
192 Riot R	1.50	4.00
200 Triple Threat R	1.50	4.00
202 Archetype E	5.00	12.00
211 Far Out Man E	4.00	10.00
214 Ghoul Trooper E	5.00	12.00
216 Ginger Gunner E	2.50	6.00
229 Rosa E	3.00	8.00
232 Ember E	2.50	6.00
233 Peely E	10.00	25.00
235 Skull Trooper E	12.00	30.00
237 Spooky Team Leader E	3.00	8.00
238 Stage Slayer E	2.50	6.00
241 Sun Strider E	2.50	6.00
246 The Ace E	2.50	6.00
247 Tomatohead E	3.00	8.00
252 Black Knight L	150.00	400.00
253 Calamity L	5.00	12.00
254 Carbide L	4.00	10.00
256 Crackshot L	5.00	12.00
258 Cuddle Team Leader L	4.00	10.00
261 Deadfire L	5.00	12.00
262 Dire L	6.00	15.00
263 Drift L	6.00	15.00
264 Enforcer L	4.00	10.00
266 Fate L	4.00	10.00
268 Frostbite L	5.00	12.00
270 Hime L	5.00	12.00
271 Leviathan L	6.00	15.00
277 Omega L	6.00	15.00
278 Omen L	5.00	12.00
279 P.A.N.D.A. Team Leader L	3.00	8.00
280 Power Chord L	3.00	8.00
281 Ragnarok L	5.00	12.00
282 Raptor L	5.00	12.00
284 Raven L	8.00	20.00
285 Red Knight L	10.00	25.00
286 Rex L	4.00	10.00
290 Spider Knight L	8.00	20.00
293 Tricera Ops L	5.00	12.00
294 Valkyrie L	4.00	10.00
296 Vertex L	4.00	10.00
299 Wukong L	3.00	8.00
300 Luxe L	25.00	60.00

2019 Panini Fortnite Series 1 Crystal Shard

Card	Low	High
UNLISTED UNCOMMON (101-150)	6.00	15.00
UNLISTED RARE (151-200)	8.00	20.00
UNLISTED EPIC (201-250)	10.00	25.00
UNLISTED LEGENDARY (251-300)	12.00	30.00
RANDOMLY INSERTED INTO PACKS		
102 Assault Rifle U	8.00	20.00
105 Pistol U	10.00	25.00
106 Pump Shotgun U	25.00	60.00
107 Tactical Shotgun U	60.00	150.00
110 Clinger U	15.00	40.00
111 Axcordion U	8.00	20.00
114 Jackspammer U	30.00	75.00
116 Lead Swinger U	50.00	120.00
117 Armadillo U	12.00	30.00
118 Hayseed U	30.00	75.00
119 Brainiac U	15.00	40.00
120 Bullseye U	15.00	40.00
121 Bunnymoon U	12.00	30.00
122 Prickly Patroller U	10.00	25.00
123 Crimson Scout U	25.00	60.00
124 Red-Nosed Ranger U	15.00	40.00
125 Dominator U	10.00	25.00
126 Garrison U	12.00	30.00
127 Grill Sergeant U	10.00	25.00
129 Sunflower U	12.00	30.00
130 Liteshow U	50.00	120.00
131 Nitelite U	15.00	40.00
132 Nog Ops U	20.00	50.00
133 Patch Patroller U	30.00	75.00
134 Tinseltoes U	40.00	100.00
135 Dark Glyph U	50.00	120.00
137 Scarlet Defender U	12.00	30.00
138 Scorpion U	10.00	25.00
140 Sgt. Green Clover U	12.00	30.00
141 Star-Spangled Ranger U	30.00	75.00
142 Star-Spangled Trooper U	50.00	120.00
143 Striped Soldier U	15.00	40.00
144 Med Kit U	12.00	30.00
145 Angular Axe U	60.00	150.00
149 Whistle Warrior U	12.00	30.00
151 Absolute Zero R	30.00	75.00
152 Bandolette R	15.00	40.00
154 Arctic Assassin R	25.00	60.00
155 Backbone R	10.00	25.00
156 Blue Squire R	30.00	75.00
159 Brilliant Striker R	30.00	75.00
160 Brite Bomber R	400.00	1000.00
161 Chopper R	12.00	30.00
162 Chromium R	12.00	30.00
163 Cipher R	10.00	25.00
164 Circuit Breaker R	20.00	50.00
165 Codename E.L.F. R	12.00	30.00
166 Dark Bomber R	100.00	250.00
167 Dazzle R	15.00	40.00
168 Buccaneer R	15.00	40.00
169 Diecast R	15.00	40.00
170 Dynamo R	30.00	75.00
173 Hyperion R	15.00	40.00
174 Infiltrator R	15.00	40.00
175 Insight R	15.00	40.00
176 Jumpshot R	12.00	30.00
177 Longshot R	15.00	40.00
178 Maki Master R	20.00	50.00
180 Maximilian R	30.00	75.00
181 Mayhem R	15.00	40.00
182 Midnight Ops R	12.00	30.00
184 Munitions Major R	30.00	75.00
186 Firewalker R	40.00	100.00
187 Fishstick R	125.00	300.00
188 Heartbreaker R	15.00	40.00
189 Red-Nosed Raider R	12.00	30.00
190 Reflex R	50.00	120.00
191 Mezmer R	30.00	75.00
193 Royale Knight R	300.00	800.00
194 Ruckus R	30.00	75.00
195 Sash Sergeant R	15.00	40.00
196 Skull Ranger R	125.00	300.00
197 Snorkel Ops R	15.00	40.00
198 Sunbird R	12.00	30.00
199 Sushi Master R	30.00	75.00
200 Triple Threat R	10.00	25.00
202 Archetype E	25.00	60.00
203 Beef Boss E	30.00	75.00
204 Brite Gunner E	40.00	100.00
205 Bunny Brawler E	20.00	50.00
206 Castor E	12.00	30.00
207 DJ Yonder E	50.00	120.00
208 Dusk E	25.00	60.00
210 Fable E	30.00	75.00
211 Far Out Man E	30.00	75.00
214 Ghoul Trooper E	100.00	250.00
215 Giddy-Up E	12.00	30.00
216 Ginger Gunner E	25.00	60.00
217 Growler E	40.00	100.00
220 Heidi E	15.00	40.00
221 Hollowhead E	30.00	75.00
222 Mission Specialist E	12.00	30.00
224 Mothmando E	15.00	40.00
226 Plague E	40.00	100.00
227 Redline E	15.00	40.00
229 Rosa E	30.00	75.00
230 Rust Lord E	20.00	50.00
232 Ember E	20.00	50.00
233 Peely E	300.00	800.00
234 Shadow Ops E	15.00	40.00
235 Skull Trooper E	40.00	100.00
236 Sparkle Specialist E	250.00	600.00
237 Spooky Team Leader E	15.00	40.00
241 Sun Strider E	15.00	40.00
243 Synth Star E	15.00	40.00
244 Taro E	30.00	75.00
245 Tender Defender E	125.00	300.00
247 Tomatohead E	30.00	75.00
248 Funk Ops E	15.00	40.00
249 Zoey E	100.00	250.00
250 Aerobic Assassin E	30.00	75.00
252 Black Knight L	2000.00	4000.00
253 Calamity L	75.00	200.00
254 Carbide L	30.00	75.00
255 Chomp Sr. L	15.00	40.00
256 Crackshot L	15.00	40.00
257 Hybrid L	20.00	50.00
258 Cuddle Team Leader L	15.00	40.00
259 Dark Vanguard L	60.00	150.00
260 Dark Voyager L	15.00	40.00
261 Deadfire L	15.00	40.00
262 Dire L	50.00	120.00
263 Drift L	60.00	150.00
264 Enforcer L	50.00	120.00
265 Blackheart L	15.00	40.00
266 Fate L	20.00	50.00
267 Flytrap L	20.00	50.00
268 Frostbite L	15.00	40.00
269 Havoc L	40.00	100.00
271 Leviathan L	15.00	40.00
272 Love Ranger L	30.00	75.00
273 Magnus L	60.00	150.00
274 Moisty Merman L	100.00	250.00
275 Musha L	30.00	75.00
276 Oblivion L	75.00	200.00
277 Omega L	50.00	120.00
278 Omen L	25.00	60.00
279 P.A.N.D.A. Team Leader L	15.00	40.00
280 Power Chord L	30.00	75.00
281 Ragnarok L	60.00	150.00
283 Ravage L	100.00	250.00
284 Raven L	100.00	250.00
285 Red Knight L	150.00	400.00
286 Rex L	50.00	120.00
290 Spider Knight L	125.00	300.00
291 A.I.M. L	25.00	60.00
293 Tricera Ops L	20.00	50.00
295 Valor L	100.00	250.00
296 Vertex L	15.00	40.00
297 Arachne L	30.00	75.00
298 Wild Card L	75.00	200.00
299 Wukong L	200.00	500.00
300 Luxe L	150.00	400.00

2019 Panini Fortnite Series 1 Holofoil

Card	Low	High
UNLISTED UNCOMMON (101-150)	3.00	8.00
UNLISTED RARE (151-200)	4.00	10.00
UNLISTED EPIC (201-250)	5.00	12.00
UNLISTED LEGENDARY (251-300)	6.00	15.00
RANDOMLY INSERTED INTO PACKS		
101 Burst Assault Rifle U	4.00	10.00
103 Hunting Rifle U	12.00	30.00
104 Submachine Gun U	12.00	30.00
105 Pistol U	6.00	15.00
106 Pump Shotgun U	25.00	60.00
107 Tactical Shotgun U	8.00	20.00
108 Semi-Auto Sniper Rifle U	5.00	12.00
109 Six Shooter U	6.00	15.00
110 Clinger U	5.00	12.00
112 Drumbeat U	6.00	15.00
113 Gatekeeper U	6.00	15.00
117 Armadillo U	8.00	20.00
123 Crimson Scout U	12.00	30.00
126 Garrison U	10.00	25.00
127 Grill Sergeant U	6.00	15.00
128 Highrise Assault Trooper U	8.00	20.00
129 Sunflower U	6.00	15.00
130 Liteshow U	8.00	20.00
132 Nog Ops U	10.00	25.00
134 Tinseltoes U	10.00	25.00
135 Dark Glyph U	6.00	15.00
138 Scorpion U	6.00	15.00
139 Drum Gun U	6.00	15.00
140 Sgt. Green Clover U	5.00	12.00
141 Star-Spangled Ranger U	6.00	15.00
144 Med Kit U	10.00	25.00
150 Yuletide Ranger U	8.00	20.00
152 Bandolette R	10.00	25.00
153 Airheart R	12.00	30.00
154 Arctic Assassin R	6.00	15.00
155 Backbone R	8.00	20.00
156 Blue Squire R	12.00	30.00
157 Abominable Axe R	4.00	10.00
158 Guiding Glow R	15.00	40.00
159 Brilliant Striker R	6.00	15.00
160 Brite Bomber R	25.00	60.00
165 Codename E.L.F. R	10.00	25.00
166 Dark Bomber R	30.00	75.00
169 Diecast R	10.00	25.00
170 Dynamo R	15.00	40.00
171 First Strike Specialist R	6.00	15.00
178 Maki Master R	10.00	25.00
182 Midnight Ops R	10.00	25.00
185 Radiant Striker R	6.00	15.00
187 Fishstick R	30.00	75.00
188 Heartbreaker R	8.00	20.00
192 Riot R	8.00	20.00
193 Royale Knight R	30.00	75.00
196 Skull Ranger R	25.00	60.00
197 Snorkel Ops R	6.00	15.00
200 Triple Threat R	8.00	20.00
201 Abstrakt E	8.00	20.00
202 Archetype E	6.00	15.00
203 Beef Boss E	8.00	20.00
204 Brite Gunner E	8.00	20.00
206 Castor E	8.00	20.00
207 DJ Yonder E	12.00	30.00
208 Dusk E	8.00	20.00
209 Elmira E	12.00	30.00
210 Fable E	12.00	30.00
212 Fireworks Team Leader E	15.00	40.00
213 Flapjackie E	8.00	20.00
214 Ghoul Trooper E	30.00	75.00
215 Giddy-Up E	8.00	20.00
216 Ginger Gunner E	12.00	30.00
218 Hay Man E	10.00	25.00
219 Master Key E	8.00	20.00
221 Hollowhead E	10.00	25.00
222 Mission Specialist E	6.00	15.00
223 Moonwalker E	8.00	20.00
231 Sanctum E	10.00	25.00
232 Ember E	8.00	20.00
233 Peely E	60.00	150.00
235 Skull Trooper E	75.00	200.00
236 Sparkle Specialist E	10.00	25.00
237 Spooky Team Leader E	6.00	15.00
238 Stage Slayer E	12.00	30.00
240 Straw Ops E	10.00	25.00
245 Tender Defender E	10.00	25.00
246 The Ace E	10.00	25.00
247 Tomatohead E	15.00	40.00
249 Zoey E	10.00	25.00
252 Black Knight L	600.00	1500.00

253 Calamity L	10.00	25.00
254 Carbide L	10.00	25.00
255 Chomp Sr. L	20.00	50.00
256 Crackshot L	10.00	25.00
257 Hybrid L	12.00	30.00
258 Cuddle Team Leader L	15.00	40.00
259 Dark Vanguard L	10.00	25.00
260 Dark Voyager L	15.00	40.00
261 Deadfire L	10.00	25.00
262 Dire L	15.00	40.00
263 Drift L	30.00	75.00
264 Enforcer L	10.00	25.00
266 Fate L	15.00	40.00
267 Flytrap L	10.00	25.00
268 Frostbite L	15.00	40.00
269 Havoc L	12.00	30.00
270 Hime L	25.00	60.00
271 Leviathan L	20.00	50.00
272 Love Ranger L	15.00	40.00
273 Magnus L	12.00	30.00
274 Moisty Merman L	12.00	30.00
275 Musha L	12.00	30.00
276 Oblivion L	15.00	40.00
277 Omega L	25.00	60.00
279 P.A.N.D.A. Team Leader L	10.00	25.00
280 Power Chord L	30.00	75.00
281 Ragnarok L	15.00	40.00
282 Raptor L	15.00	40.00
283 Ravage L	12.00	30.00
284 Raven L	15.00	40.00
285 Red Knight L	50.00	120.00
286 Rex L	25.00	60.00
287 Rose Team Leader L	12.00	30.00
288 Shogun L	20.00	50.00
289 Sky Stalker L	15.00	40.00
290 Spider Knight L	25.00	60.00
291 A.I.M. L	12.00	30.00
292 The Visitor L	12.00	30.00
293 Tricera Ops L	15.00	40.00
294 Valkyrie L	20.00	50.00
295 Valor L	12.00	30.00
296 Vertex L	15.00	40.00
297 Arachne L	12.00	30.00
298 Wild Card L	15.00	40.00
299 Wukong L	25.00	60.00
300 Luxe L	100.00	250.00

2019 Panini Fortnite Series 1 Holofoil Crystal Shard Exclusives

COMPLETE SET W/P10 (10)	600.00	1500.00
COMPLETE SET W/O P10 (9)	400.00	1000.00
COMMON CARD (P1-P9)	60.00	150.00
EBAY EXCLUSIVE		
P1 Trailblazer	100.00	250.00
P2 Cloaked Star	100.00	250.00
P3 Galaxy	250.00	600.00
P5 Merry Marauder	150.00	400.00
P7 Rabbit Raider	125.00	300.00
P8 Rogue Agent	125.00	300.00
P9 Teknique	75.00	200.00

2020 Panini Fortnite Series 2

COMPLETE SET W/O SP (50)	10.00	25.00
UNOPENED HOBBY BOX (24 PACKS)	75.00	120.00
UNOPENED MEGA BOX (12 PACKS)	125.00	200.00
UNOPENED BLASTER BOX (6 PACKS)	20.00	30.00
UNOPENED PACK (6 CARDS)	2.00	3.00
COMMON U (1-50)	.75	2.00
COMMON R (51-110)	1.50	4.00
COMMON E (111-170)	2.50	6.00
COMMON L (171-200)	3.00	8.00
2 Aura U	1.25	3.00
8 Bracer U	4.00	10.00
15 Devastator U	2.50	6.00
26 Plastic Patroller U	1.50	4.00
44 Clash U	2.50	6.00
65 Shot Caller R	8.00	20.00
72 Bull Shark R	5.00	12.00
86 Journey R	6.00	15.00
106 Wolf R	5.00	12.00
125 Vega E	6.00	15.00
130 Guan Yu E	8.00	20.00
131 Fyra E	12.00	30.00
136 Kitbash E	8.00	20.00
139 Powder E	6.00	15.00
140 Shaman E	4.00	10.00
175 Krampus L	6.00	15.00
176 Lynx L	5.00	12.00
177 Malice L	6.00	15.00
183 The Ice King L	15.00	40.00
184 The Ice Queen L	12.00	30.00
185 The Prisoner L	6.00	15.00
186 Ultima Knight L	15.00	40.00
195 Ruin L	5.00	12.00

2020 Panini Fortnite Series 2 Cracked Ice

COMMON U (1-50)	8.00	20.00
COMMON R (51-110)	8.00	20.00
COMMON E (111-170)	10.00	25.00
COMMON L (171-200)	12.00	30.00
1 Anarchy Agent U	15.00	40.00
2 Aura U	60.00	150.00
3 B.R.U.T.E. Gunner U	25.00	60.00
4 B.R.U.T.E. Navigator U	15.00	40.00
5 Banner Trooper U	15.00	40.00
6 Birdie U	12.00	30.00
7 Bolt U	12.00	30.00
8 Bracer U	12.00	30.00
9 Branded Brawler U	10.00	25.00
10 Cabbie U	10.00	25.00
11 Cole U	10.00	25.00
12 Crystal U	40.00	100.00
15 Devastator U	12.00	30.00
16 Gage U	15.00	40.00
17 Grit U	12.00	30.00
18 Guild U	12.00	30.00
19 Hard Charger U	10.00	25.00
20 Jungle Scout U	10.00	25.00
22 Manic U	20.00	50.00
23 Marked Marauder U	12.00	30.00
24 Match Point U	15.00	40.00
25 Pastel U	25.00	60.00
26 Plastic Patroller U	12.00	30.00
27 Recon Ranger U	15.00	40.00
28 Red Jade U	25.00	60.00
29 Relay U	10.00	25.00
31 Sizzle Sgt. U	10.00	25.00
34 Swamp Stalker U	10.00	25.00
35 Symbol Stalwart U	10.00	25.00
37 Toy Trooper U	20.00	50.00
39 Vice U	12.00	30.00
40 World Warrior U	25.00	60.00
41 Arctic Intel U	12.00	30.00
42 Jolly Jammer U	12.00	30.00
44 Clash U	20.00	50.00
45 Cozy Commander U	10.00	25.00
46 Crusher U	15.00	40.00
47 EX U	12.00	30.00
48 Chill Count U	10.00	25.00
49 Holly Jammer U	10.00	25.00
52 Bravo Leader R	15.00	40.00
53 Bubble Bomber R	25.00	60.00
56 Fennix R	25.00	60.00
58 Guaco R	60.00	150.00
59 Limelight R	30.00	75.00
60 Moxie R	15.00	40.00
63 Rio Grande R	15.00	40.00
64 Ruby R	60.00	150.00
65 Shot Caller R	15.00	40.00
67 Starlie R	100.00	250.00
68 Street Striker R	12.00	30.00
69 The Paradigm R	40.00	100.00
70 Toxic Tagger R	15.00	40.00
72 Bull Shark R	12.00	30.00
73 Bundles R	12.00	30.00
74 Burial Threat R	25.00	60.00
76 Cutiepie R	12.00	30.00
77 Dolph R	12.00	30.00
78 Flatfoot R	12.00	30.00
80 Hazard R	12.00	30.00
81 Haze R	25.00	60.00
84 Echo R	12.00	30.00
85 Hugo R	12.00	30.00
86 Journey R	12.00	30.00
87 Metal Mouth R	25.00	60.00
88 Monks R	20.00	50.00
90 Remedy R	12.00	30.00
93 Riptide R	20.00	50.00
96 Sludge R	50.00	120.00
97 Snuggs R	25.00	60.00
98 Stingray R	40.00	100.00
99 Surf Rider R	20.00	50.00
100 Swift R	12.00	30.00
101 The Autumn Queen R	15.00	40.00
102 The Brat R	25.00	60.00
109 Wrath R	30.00	75.00
110 Zadie R	50.00	120.00
111 Astro Assassin E	15.00	40.00
112 Bunker Jonesy E	75.00	200.00
113 Demi E	20.00	50.00
114 Doggo E	30.00	75.00
115 Eternal Voyager E	75.00	200.00
116 Freestyle E	20.00	50.00
122 Starfish E	15.00	40.00
123 Stoneheart E	100.00	250.00
124 Stratus E	30.00	75.00
125 Vega E	20.00	50.00
126 Versa E	12.00	30.00
127 Vulture E	12.00	30.00
129 Yonder E	50.00	120.00
130 Guan Yu E	15.00	40.00
131 Fyra E	15.00	40.00
132 Terns E	20.00	50.00
135 Kenji E	12.00	30.00
136 Kitbash E	30.00	75.00
137 Lace E	12.00	30.00
138 Noir E	40.00	100.00
139 Powder E	30.00	75.00
140 Shaman E	25.00	60.00
141 Trog E	15.00	40.00
143 Wilde E	15.00	40.00
144 Willow E	15.00	40.00
145 Wonder E	12.00	30.00
146 Whiteout E	25.00	60.00
147 8-Ball E	60.00	150.00
148 Astra E	20.00	50.00
150 Bash E	40.00	100.00
151 Big Chuggus E	25.00	60.00
152 Big Mouth E	20.00	50.00
154 Chaos Agent E	30.00	75.00
155 Chic E	15.00	40.00
156 Delirium E	15.00	40.00
157 Dominion E	12.00	30.00
158 Globe Shaker E	20.00	50.00
159 Grim Fable E	60.00	150.00
160 Hemlock E	15.00	40.00
161 Kane E	30.00	75.00
162 Peely Bone E	125.00	300.00
163 Polar Patroller E	30.00	75.00
165 Scratch E	40.00	100.00
166 Shiver E	30.00	75.00
167 Sklaxis E	15.00	40.00
168 Smoke Dragon E	25.00	60.00
169 Teef E	30.00	75.00
170 Yule Trooper E	75.00	200.00
171 Ark L	15.00	40.00
172 Catalyst L	25.00	60.00
173 DJ Bop L	15.00	40.00
174 Glimmer L	20.00	50.00
175 Krampus L	30.00	75.00
176 Lynx L	30.00	75.00
177 Malice L	20.00	50.00
178 Oppressor L	25.00	60.00
179 Rox L	25.00	60.00
180 Sentinel L	20.00	50.00
181 Supersonic L	12.00	30.00
182 Tempest L	20.00	50.00
183 The Ice King L	300.00	800.00
184 The Ice Queen L	125.00	300.00
185 The Prisoner L	20.00	50.00
186 Ultima Knight L	200.00	500.00
187 Velocity L	15.00	40.00
189 Warpaint L	15.00	40.00
190 Zenith L	30.00	75.00
191 Criterion L	30.00	75.00
192 Dark Vertex L	30.00	75.00
193 Eon L	20.00	50.00
194 Glow L	25.00	60.00
195 Ruin L	75.00	200.00
196 Singularity L	15.00	40.00
197 Oro L	30.00	75.00
198 Deadeye L	40.00	100.00
199 Fusion L	40.00	100.00
200 Zero L	75.00	200.00

2020 Panini Fortnite Series 2 Holofoil

COMPLETE SET (200)		
COMMON U (1-50)	3.00	6.00
COMMON R (51-110)	3.00	8.00
COMMON E (111-170)		10.00
COMMON L (171-200)		
2 Aura U	12.00	30.00
3 B.R.U.T.E. Gunner U	5.00	12.00
4 B.R.U.T.E. Navigator U	5.00	12.00
5 Banner Trooper U	6.00	15.00
13 Deadfall U	4.00	10.00
14 Desert Dominator U	4.00	10.00
17 Grit U	6.00	15.00
18 Guild U	6.00	15.00
20 Jungle Scout U	5.00	12.00
21 King Flamingo U	8.00	20.00
22 Manic U	8.00	20.00
29 Relay U	6.00	15.00
37 Toy Trooper U	6.00	15.00
39 Vice U	5.00	12.00
40 World Warrior U	8.00	20.00
43 Caution U	6.00	15.00
44 Clash U	5.00	12.00
45 Cozy Commander U	8.00	20.00
46 Crusher U	5.00	12.00
47 EX U	4.00	10.00
48 Chill Count U	4.00	10.00
49 Holly Jammer U	4.00	10.00
50 Tower Recon Specialist U	4.00	10.00
51 Aeronaut R	5.00	12.00
58 Guaco R	6.00	15.00
62 PJ Pepperoni R	10.00	25.00
63 Rio Grande R	6.00	15.00
64 Ruby R	4.00	10.00
65 Shot Caller R	4.00	10.00
66 Sledge R	4.00	10.00
67 Starlie R	8.00	20.00
68 Street Striker R	4.00	10.00
69 The Paradigm R	6.00	15.00
73 Bundles R	4.00	10.00
75 Bushranger R	5.00	12.00
76 Cutiepie R	5.00	12.00
77 Dolph R	5.00	12.00
79 Gan R	5.00	12.00
80 Hazard R	4.00	10.00
81 Haze R	4.00	10.00
82 Hush R	5.00	12.00
84 Echo R	6.00	15.00
85 Hugo R	5.00	12.00
87 Metal Mouth R	5.00	12.00
90 Remedy R	6.00	15.00
92 Rippley R	4.00	10.00
93 Riptide R	6.00	15.00
96 Sludge R	10.00	25.00
101 The Autumn Queen R	15.00	40.00
102 The Brat R	10.00	25.00
109 Wrath R	8.00	20.00
110 Zadie R	6.00	15.00
111 Astro Assassin E	8.00	20.00
112 Bunker Jonesy E	6.00	15.00
114 Doggo E	5.00	12.00
118 Infinity E	10.00	25.00
119 Mecha Team Leader E	6.00	15.00
123 Stoneheart E	6.00	15.00
124 Stratus E	6.00	15.00
125 Vega E	8.00	20.00
129 Yonder E	25.00	60.00
130 Guan Yu E	6.00	15.00
134 Jack Gourdon E	15.00	40.00
136 Kitbash E	5.00	12.00
137 Lace E	5.00	12.00

138 Noir E 5.00 12.00
139 Powder E 5.00 12.00
140 Shaman E 6.00 15.00
142 Ventura E 8.00 20.00
145 Wonder E 8.00 20.00
146 Whiteout E 6.00 15.00
147 8-Ball E 15.00 40.00
150 Bash E 6.00 15.00
155 Chic E 5.00 12.00
157 Dominion E 6.00 15.00
158 Globe Shaker E 10.00 25.00
159 Grim Fable E 12.00 30.00
160 Hemlock E 8.00 20.00
162 Peely Bone E 15.00 40.00
163 Polar Patroller E 6.00 15.00
166 Shiver E 6.00 15.00
167 Sklaxis E 5.00 12.00
168 Smoke Dragon E 5.00 12.00
170 Yule Trooper E 20.00 50.00
172 Catalyst L 10.00 25.00
175 Krampus L 12.00 30.00
176 Lynx L 12.00 30.00
177 Malice L 10.00 25.00
178 Oppressor L 15.00 40.00
180 Sentinel L 10.00 25.00
182 Tempest L 12.00 30.00
183 The Ice King L 40.00 100.00
184 The Ice Queen L 30.00 75.00
186 Ultima Knight L 30.00 75.00
189 Warpaint L 12.00 30.00
191 Criterion L 10.00 25.00
192 Dark Vertex L 10.00 25.00
193 Eon L 12.00 30.00
195 Ruin L 10.00 25.00
196 Singularity L 30.00 75.00
198 Deadeye L 12.00 30.00
200 Zero L 30.00 75.00

2020 Panini Fortnite Series 2 Cracked Ice Bonus Set

COMPLETE SET (10) 30.00 75.00
COMMON CARD (P1-P10) 4.00 10.00
P1 Bone Wasp 12.00 30.00
P3 Ether 6.00 15.00
P4 Flare 6.00 15.00
P5 Gutbomb 10.00 25.00
P6 Hothouse 8.00 20.00
P7 Luminos 8.00 20.00
P10 Takara 10.00 25.00

2020 Panini Fortnite Series 2 Epic Harvesting Tools

COMPLETE SET (37) 12.00 30.00
COMMON CARD (H1-H37) .75 2.00
RANDOMLY INSERTED INTO PACKS

2020 Panini Fortnite Series 2 Maps

COMPLETE SET (13) 5.00 12.00
COMMON CARD (M1-M13) .60 1.50
RANDOMLY INSERTED INTO PACKS

2020 Panini Fortnite Series 2 Optichrome Holo

COMMON U (1-50) 3.00 8.00
COMMON R (51-110) 4.00 10.00
COMMON E (111-170) 5.00 12.00
COMMON L (171-200) 10.00 25.00
2 Aura U 8.00 20.00
3 B.R.U.T.E. Gunner U 8.00 20.00
4 B.R.U.T.E. Navigator U 5.00 12.00
5 Banner Trooper U 6.00 15.00
7 Bolt U 10.00 25.00
12 Crystal U 10.00 25.00
18 Guild U 12.00 30.00
20 Jungle Scout U 6.00 15.00
21 King Flamingo U 6.00 15.00
22 Manic U 8.00 20.00
28 Red Jade U 6.00 15.00
31 Sizzle Sgt. U 6.00 15.00
32 Slingshot U 6.00 15.00
35 Symbol Stalwart U 5.00 12.00
36 Tactics Officer U 6.00 15.00
37 Toy Trooper U 6.00 15.00
38 Verge U 5.00 12.00
42 Jolly Jammer U 8.00 20.00
47 EX U 8.00 20.00
48 Chill Count U 6.00 15.00
50 Tower Recon Specialist U 5.00 12.00
53 Bubble Bomber R 12.00 30.00
54 Catastrophe R 6.00 15.00
55 Facet R 8.00 20.00
56 Fennix R 6.00 15.00
57 Frontier R 5.00 12.00
58 Guaco R 5.00 12.00
59 Limelight R 6.00 15.00
60 Moxie R 6.00 15.00
61 Payback R 6.00 15.00
62 PJ Pepperoni R 10.00 25.00
64 Ruby R 10.00 25.00
67 Starlie R 6.00 15.00
69 The Paradigm R 5.00 12.00
72 Bull Shark R 6.00 15.00
80 Hazard R 6.00 15.00
82 Hush R 8.00 20.00
87 Metal Mouth R 6.00 15.00
90 Remedy R 8.00 20.00
92 Rippley R 8.00 20.00
94 Rustler R 5.00 12.00
96 Sludge R 12.00 30.00
97 Snuggs R 6.00 15.00
98 Stingray R 10.00 25.00
101 The Autumn Queen R 20.00 50.00
102 The Brat R 12.00 30.00
110 Zadie R 10.00 25.00
111 Astro Assassin E 6.00 15.00
113 Demi E 8.00 20.00
117 Hotwire E 6.00 15.00
118 Infinity E 6.00 15.00
119 Mecha Team Leader E 10.00 25.00
120 Slumber E 10.00 25.00
121 Sparkle Supreme E 6.00 15.00
127 Vulture E 6.00 15.00
129 Yonder E 25.00 60.00
131 Fyra E 6.00 15.00
132 Terns E 6.00 15.00
133 Hacivat E 8.00 20.00
134 Jack Gourdon E 6.00 15.00
135 Kenji E 6.00 15.00
136 Kitbash E 8.00 20.00
137 Lace E 6.00 15.00
138 Noir E 6.00 15.00
141 Trog E 10.00 25.00
143 Wilde E 6.00 15.00
144 Willow E 8.00 20.00
145 Wonder E 6.00 15.00
146 Whiteout E 8.00 20.00
147 8-Ball E 30.00 75.00
150 Bash E 10.00 25.00
151 Big Chuggus E 8.00 20.00
152 Big Mouth E 6.00 15.00
154 Chaos Agent E 8.00 20.00
159 Grim Fable E 10.00 25.00
162 Peely Bone E 20.00 50.00
165 Scratch E 6.00 15.00
166 Shiver E 10.00 25.00
170 Yule Trooper E 30.00 75.00
172 Catalyst L 10.00 25.00
173 DJ Bop L 15.00 40.00
175 Krampus L 12.00 30.00
176 Lynx L 25.00 60.00
177 Malice L 12.00 30.00
180 Sentinel L 12.00 30.00
181 Supersonic L 30.00 75.00
182 Tempest L 30.00 75.00
183 The Ice King L 100.00 250.00
184 The Ice Queen L 60.00 150.00
185 The Prisoner L 12.00 30.00
186 Ultima Knight L 125.00 300.00
187 Velocity L 15.00 40.00
188 Vendetta L 12.00 30.00
189 Warpaint L 30.00 75.00
190 Zenith L 20.00 50.00
192 Dark Vertex L 12.00 30.00
194 Glow L 12.00 30.00
195 Ruin L 12.00 30.00
196 Singularity L 12.00 30.00
197 Oro L 25.00 60.00
198 Deadeye L 12.00 30.00
199 Fusion L 20.00 50.00
200 Zero L 30.00 75.00

2021 Panini Fortnite Series 3

COMPLETE SET W/O SP (100) 20.00 50.00
UNOPENED BOX (24 PACKS)
UNOPENED PACK (6 CARDS)
COMMON U (1-25) .40 1.00
COMMON R (26-100) .60 1.50
COMMON E (101-200) .75 2.00
COMMON L (201-223) 2.00 5.00
COMMON F (224-232) 3.00 8.00

2021 Panini Fortnite Series 3 Cracked Ice

COMMON U (1-25) 3.00 8.00
COMMON R (26-100) 4.00 10.00
COMMON E (101-200) 5.00 12.00
COMMON L (201-223) 6.00 15.00
COMMON F (224-232) 20.00 50.00
RANDOMLY INSERTED INTO PACKS
27 Athleisure Assassin R 8.00 20.00
31 Bigfoot R 15.00 40.00
36 Bronto R 10.00 25.00
39 Chance R 25.00 60.00
48 Doublecross R 10.00 25.00
52 Focus R 50.00 120.00
55 Guff R 10.00 25.00
56 Hopper R 6.00 15.00
59 Iris R 12.00 30.00
62 Maven R 10.00 25.00
64 Mystify R 6.00 15.00
66 Pinkie R 6.00 15.00
67 Fanatic R 8.00 20.00
71 Relaxed Fit Jonesy R 15.00 40.00
72 Karve R 6.00 15.00
77 Siren R 25.00 60.00
86 Tek R 6.00 15.00
89 Tsuki R 12.00 30.00
90 Twistie R 8.00 20.00
95 Waypoint R 8.00 20.00
97 Wiretap R 6.00 15.00
99 Yellowjacket R 6.00 15.00
101 Agent Peely E 150.00 400.00
105 Bash (Dark) E 10.00 25.00
106 Battlehawk E 40.00 100.00
108 Britestorm Bomber E 10.00 25.00
111 Bun Bun E 12.00 30.00
113 Bunnywolf E 8.00 20.00
116 Cloaked Shadow E 15.00 40.00
117 Cobalt E 8.00 20.00
123 Double Agent Hush E 30.00 75.00
124 Double Agent Wildcard E 40.00 100.00
126 Dread Fate E 8.00 20.00
127 Dread Omen E 6.00 15.00
129 Elite Agent E 30.00 75.00
132 Ghoul Trooper (Zombie) E 20.00 50.00
134 Hit Man E 8.00 20.00
135 Cluck E 15.00 40.00
136 Jaeger E 10.00 25.00
137 Jules E 40.00 100.00
138 Kit E 50.00 120.00
139 Kuno E 12.00 30.00
140 Kurohomura E 12.00 30.00
143 Lucky Rider E 8.00 20.00
145 Malcore E 6.00 15.00
149 Morro E 8.00 20.00
151 Nightlife E 15.00 40.00
152 Nightshade E 8.00 20.00
153 Nightwitch E 12.00 30.00
154 Nite Nite (Nite Fright) E 6.00 15.00
155 Nitehare E 6.00 15.00
174 Skull Trooper (Inverted) E 60.00 150.00
176 Mancake E 30.00 75.00
177 Mave E 8.00 20.00
178 Pulse E 8.00 20.00
187 Snowmando E 12.00 30.00
190 Summer Fable E 12.00 30.00
192 Synth E 8.00 20.00
195 Triage Trooper E 12.00 30.00
196 Tropical Punch Zoey E 15.00 40.00
197 Unpeely E 25.00 60.00
201 Backlash L 8.00 20.00
203 Crackshot (Pink) L 10.00 25.00
204 Cyclo L 15.00 40.00
205 Dynamo Dancer L 8.00 20.00
206 Eternal Knight L 75.00 200.00
208 Firebrand L 15.00 40.00
210 Vi L 75.00 200.00
213 Maya L 10.00 25.00
215 Hypersonic L 12.00 30.00
216 Inferno L 40.00 100.00
221 Galaxia L 40.00 100.00
222 Raz L 25.00 60.00
223 The Mighty Volt L 20.00 50.00
224 Frozen Love Ranger F 25.00 60.00
225 Frozen Raven F 125.00 300.00
226 Frozen Red Knight F 100.00 250.00
228 Frozen Fishstick F 125.00 300.00
230 Snow Drift F 40.00 100.00
232 The Devourer F 60.00 150.00

2021 Panini Fortnite Series 3 Holofoil

COMPLETE SET (232)
COMMON U (1-25) 1.50 4.00
COMMON R (26-100) 2.50 6.00
COMMON E (101-200)
COMMON L (201-223)
COMMON F (224-232)
1 Aura (Winter Hunter) U 8.00 20.00
30 Beach Bomber R 6.00 15.00
41 Contract Giller R 15.00 40.00
55 Guff R 12.00 30.00
65 Pillar R 10.00 25.00
68 Psion R 4.00 10.00
88 Showdown R 5.00 12.00
101 Agent Peely E 25.00 60.00
124 Double Agent Wildcard E 8.00 20.00
132 Ghoul Trooper (Zombie) E 5.00 12.00
137 Jules E 12.00 30.00
146 Mariana E 5.00 12.00
157 Onesie (Winter) E 8.00 20.00
174 Skull Trooper (Inverted) E 10.00 25.00
197 Unpeely E 15.00 40.00
209 The Scientist L 6.00 15.00
212 Menace L 12.00 30.00
218 Midas L 60.00 150.00
220 Raptor (Glow) L 6.00 15.00
228 Frozen Fishstick F 8.00 20.00
229 Frozen Nog Ops F 10.00 25.00

2021 Panini Fortnite Series 3 Laser

COMMON U (1-25) 2.00 5.00
COMMON R (26-100) 2.50 6.00
COMMON E (101-200) 3.00 8.00
COMMON L (201-223) 5.00 12.00
COMMON F (224-232) 6.00 15.00
31 Bigfoot R 6.00 15.00
36 Bronto R 3.00 8.00
50 Fastball R 4.00 10.00
52 Focus R 5.00 12.00
56 Hopper R 6.00 15.00
67 Fanatic R 5.00 12.00
70 Redux R 3.00 8.00
77 Siren R 15.00 40.00
81 SparkPlug R 5.00 12.00
87 Terra R 6.00 15.00
101 Agent Peely E 30.00 75.00
117 Cobalt E 6.00 15.00
123 Double Agent Hush E 20.00 50.00
124 Double Agent Wildcard E 8.00 20.00
126 Dread Fate E 4.00 10.00
129 Elite Agent E 8.00 20.00
130 Envision E 6.00 15.00
157 Onesie (Winter) E 12.00 30.00
163 Kondor (Unshackled Wrath) E 5.00 12.00
167 Revolt E 5.00 12.00
174 Skull Trooper (Inverted) E 20.00 50.00
176 Mancake E 15.00 40.00
190 Summer Fable E 6.00 15.00

197 Unpeely E 20.00 50.00
204 Cyclo L 6.00 15.00
206 Eternal Knight L 30.00 75.00
209 The Scientist L 8.00 20.00
211 Blastoff L 6.00 15.00
218 Midas L 60.00 120.00
221 Galaxia L 8.00 20.00
224 Frozen Love Ranger F 10.00 25.00
225 Frozen Raven F 20.00 50.00
227 Frost Broker F 15.00 40.00
228 Frozen Fishstick F 25.00 60.00
231 Snowheart F 10.00 25.00
232 The Devourer F 15.00 40.00

2021 Panini Fortnite Series 3 Optichrome Holo

COMMON U (1-25) 2.00 5.00
COMMON R (26-100)
COMMON E (101-200)
COMMON L (201-223)
COMMON F (224-232)
7 Clover Team Leader U 6.00 15.00
39 Chance R 6.00 15.00
41 Contract Giller R 10.00 25.00
55 Guff R 10.00 25.00
62 Maven R 6.00 15.00
101 Agent Peely E 40.00 100.00
112 Bunny Brawler (Dark) E 6.00 15.00
133 Hazard Agent E 5.00 12.00
137 Jules E 30.00 75.00
174 Skull Trooper (Inverted) E 25.00 60.00
175 Sleuth E 20.00 50.00
197 Unpeely E 15.00 40.00
209 The Scientist L 12.00 30.00
210 Vi L 25.00 60.00
218 Midas L 200.00 350.00
220 Raptor (Glow) L 6.00 15.00
226 Frozen Red Knight F 12.00 30.00
227 Frost Broker F 12.00 30.00
228 Frozen Fishstick F 25.00 60.00
230 Snow Drift F 20.00 50.00
231 Snowheart F 12.00 30.00
232 The Devourer F 15.00 40.00

2021 Panini Fortnite Series 3 Cracked Ice Bonus Set

COMPLETE SET (10) 75.00 200.00
COMMON CARD (P1-P10) 12.00 30.00
P1 Chaos Double Agent 30.00 75.00
P3 Party MVP 25.00 60.00
P5 Rabbit Raider (Dark) 15.00 40.00
P9 TNTina (Ghost) 20.00 50.00

2021 Panini Fortnite Series 3 Harvesting Tools

COMPLETE SET (65) 25.00 60.00
COMMON U (H1-H12) .40 1.00
COMMON R (H13-H57) .75 2.00
COMMON E (H58-H65) 1.25 3.00
RANDOMLY INSERTED INTO PACKS

2021 Panini Fortnite Series 3 Wraps

COMPLETE SET (35) 25.00 60.00
COMMON U (W1-W12) 1.25 3.00
COMMON R (W13-W35) 1.50 4.00
RANDOMLY INSERTED INTO PACKS

1990 Mother Productions 40 Famous Murderers

COMPLETE SET (40) 4.00 10.00
COMMON CARD (1-40) .15 .40

2006 The 4400 Season One

COMPLETE SET (72) 4.00 10.00
UNOPENED BOX (36 PACKS) 50.00 75.00
UNOPENED PACK (6 CARDS) 2.50 3.00
COMMON CARD (1-72) .10 .30
CL1 STATED ODDS ONE:CASE
CL1 Emerging Power 3.00 8.00

2006 The 4400 Season One Autographs

COMMON AUTO (A1-A9) 4.00 10.00
STATED ODDS 1:BOX
A1 Jacqueline McKenzie 5.00 12.00
A2 Peter Coyote 6.00 15.00
A3 Billy Campbell 6.00 15.00
A5 Laura Allen 5.00 12.00
A7 Brooke Nevin 6.00 15.00
AR1 Redemption card

2006 The 4400 Season One Changed Puzzle

COMPLETE SET (9) 10.00 25.00
COMMON CARD (C1-C9) 1.25 3.00
STATED ODDS 1:11
PAN 9-Card Puzzle Panel/99

2006 The 4400 Season One Ripples

COMPLETE SET (6) 6.00 15.00
COMMON CARD (R1-R6) 1.25 3.00
STATED ODDS 1:17

2006 The 4400 Season One Turf Wars

COMPLETE SET (3) 4.00 10.00
COMMON CARD (BL1-BL3) 1.50 4.00
STATED ODDS 1:BOX

2006 The 4400 Season One Promos

COMMON CARD 1.00 2.50

2006 The 4400 Season One SDCC Promo Pack

COMPLETE SET (4) 3.00 8.00
COMMON CARD 1.00 2.50

2007 The 4400 Season Two

COMPLETE SET (81) 4.00 10.00
UNOPENED BOX (36 PACKS) 50.00 75.00
UNOPENED PACK (7 CARDS) 2.00 3.00
COMMON CARD (1-81) .10 .30
CL1 STATED ODDS ONE PER CASE

2007 The 4400 Season Two 4400 and Counting Puzzle

COMPLETE SET (9) 12.00 30.00
COMMON CARD (AC1-AC9) 2.50 6.00
STATED ODDS 1:11
NNO 9-Card Panel Mini Press Sheet/99

2007 The 4400 Season Two Autographs

COMMON AUTO (A10-A18) 5.00 12.00
STATED ODDS 1:36
A12 Joel Gretsch 6.00 15.00
A13 Mahershalalhashbaz Ali 50.00 100.00
A14 Samantha Ferris 6.00 15.00
A15 Natasha Gregson Wagner 8.00 20.00
A16 Robert Picardo 8.00 20.00
A17 Jeffrey Combs 8.00 20.00
A18 Kavan Smith 6.00 15.00
AR1 Redemption card

2007 The 4400 Season Two Life Interrupted

COMPLETE SET (6) 10.00 25.00
COMMON CARD (L1-L6) 2.00 5.00
STATED ODDS 1:17

2007 The 4400 Season Two Pieceworks

COMMON MEM (PW1-PW10) 6.00 15.00
STATED ODDS 1:BOX
PW10 ISSUED AS MULTI-CASE INCENTIVE
PW8 Owen DUAL 12.00 30.00
PW10 J.Collier/R.Tyler DUAL CI 12.00 30.00

2007 The 4400 Season Two States of Being

COMPLETE SET (3) 5.00 12.00
COMMON CARD (BL1-BL3) 2.50 6.00
STATED ODDS 1:BOX
CL1 Unlock Your Mind 4.00 10.00

2007 The 4400 Season Two Promos

COMMON CARD 1.25 3.00
Pi Free Card Offer 3.00 8.00
PSD San Diego Comic Con 1.50 4.00

2018 Four Feather Falls

COMPLETE SET (18) 4.00 10.00
COMMON CARD (1-18) .30 .75

2018 Four Feather Falls Autographs

COMMON AUTO 8.00 20.00
DB1 Denise Bryer 10.00 25.00
DB2 Denise Bryer 20.00 50.00
DB3 Denise Bryer 20.00 50.00
DG1 David Graham 15.00 40.00
DG2 David Graham 20.00 50.00
DG3 David Graham 15.00 40.00
NP1 Nicholas Parsons 30.00 75.00
NP2 Nicholas Parsons 30.00 75.00

2018 Four Feather Falls Promos

COMMON PROMO 6.00 15.00
CCP1 Dealer Promo (The Cyber Cellar, waltermabon1@cky.com)) 10.00 25.00
DCP1 Dealer Promo (Derek's Trading Cards, derek_f)
EMP1 Dealer Promo (Acme 30000, elliotsmorris@aol.com)/24 12.00 30.00
GGP1 Dealer Promo (Gazza Games) 12.00 30.00
JWP1 Dealer Promo (Jason Wrightm, doctorjas73)/18 10.00 25.00
MBP1 Dealer Promo (marked MB-Trading-Cards, but from Try Trading Cards, taekwondo888)
MPP1 Dealer Promo (mitchy9210) 8.00 20.00
PCP1 Dealer Promo (Premier Cards)/20 15.00 40.00
PHP1 Dealer Promo (Paul Hart Trading Cards)/18 15.00 40.00
RKP1 Dealer Promo (Roman Krause, wrongshoe) 15.00 40.00
TCP1 Dealer Promo (Dean Rogers, Top Cards)
TMP1 Dealer Promo (telly-mania)/23
UTP1 Dealer Promo (Umbrella Trading Cards)12.00 30.00

1995 Fleer Fox Kids Network

COMPLETE SET (150) 6.00 15.00
UNOPENED HOBBY BOX (36 PACKS) 35.00 45.00
UNOPENED HOBBY PACK (8 CARDS+1 POP-UP) 1.25 1.50
UNOPENED RETAIL BOX (18 PACKS)
UNOPENED RETAIL PACK (6 CARDS)
COMMON CARD (1-150) .08 .20

1991 Comic Images Frank Frazetta

COMPLETE SET (90) 3.00 8.00
UNOPENED BOX (36 PACKS) 20.00 25.00
UNOPENED PACK (10 CARDS) .50 .75
COMMON CARD (1-90) .05 .15

1999 Comic Images Frank Miller's Sin City

COMPLETE SET (72) 6.00 15.00
UNOPENED BOX (36 PACKS) 30.00 40.00
UNOPENED PACK (7 CARDS) 1.00 1.25
COMMON CARD (1-72) .15 .40

1999 Comic Images Frank Miller's Sin City LustreChrome

COMPLETE SET (6) 15.00 40.00
COMMON CARD (L1-L6) 3.00 8.00
STATED ODDS 1:18

2006 Frankenstein

COMPLETE SET (72) 4.00 10.00
UNOPENED BOX (24 PACKS) 50.00 60.00
UNOPENED PACK (8 CARDS) 2.00 2.50
COMMON CARD (1-72) .10 .25
P1 Electrical Wiring 200.00 350.00
NNO Boris Karloff Cut Signature

2006 Frankenstein Bonus Glow-in-the-Dark

COMPLETE SET (3) 2.50 6.00
COMMON CARD 1.25 3.00
STATED ODDS 1:BOX

2006 Frankenstein Cinema Film

COMPLETE SET (9) 120.00 250.00
COMMON CARD (CFC1-CFC9) 12.00 30.00
STATED ODDS 1:80

2006 Frankenstein Promos

COMPLETE SET (6) 5.00 12.00
COMMON CARD .75 2.00
Promo3 Escaping This Summer 2006 3.00 8.00
SDPromo1 Unleashed This Fall 2005 1.25 3.00
SDPromo2 Light on Forehead 1.25 3.00

1993 Comic Images Frazetta The Legend Continues

COMPLETE SET (90) 3.00 8.00
UNOPENED BOX (48 PACKS) 20.00 25.00
UNOPENED PACK (10 CARDS) .50 .75
COMMON CARD (1-90) .10 .25

1993 Comic Images Frazetta The Legend Continues Chromium

COMPLETE SET (3) 8.00 20.00
COMMON CARD (1-3) 3.00 8.00
UNC 3-Up Panel (C1-C3)

1993 Comic Images Frazetta The Legend Continues Spectrascope

COMPLETE SET (3) 8.00 20.00
COMMON CARD (1-3) 3.00 8.00

1993 Comic Images Frazetta The Legend Continues Promos

1 Wolf-Man Attacks .75 2.00
2 Mini-Press Sheet .75 2.00

1993 21st Century Archives Frazetta Limited Edition Holograms Series I

COMPLETE SET (3) 20.00 50.00
COMMON CARD 8.00 20.00
*GOLD: .75X TO 2X BASIC CARDS

1988 Shel-Tone Freakards I

COMPLETE SET (48) 5.00 12.00
COMMON CARD (1-48) .20 .50

1991 Shel-Tone Freakards II

COMPLETE SET (47) 4.00 10.00
COMMON CARD (1-46, CL) .15 .40

1997 Freakies

COMPLETE SET (3) 2.50 6.00
COMMON CARD (UNNUMBERED) 1.25 3.00

1997 Inkworks Freaks Promos

COMMON CARD .75 1.50
P1 Twank! 2.00 5.00
P2 Rasty!#{P3 Ligme!#{P4 Caplan!

1995 SkyBox Free Willy 2

COMPLETE SET (90) 4.00 10.00
UNOPENED HOBBY BOX (36 PACKS) 20.00 30.00
UNOPENED HOBBY PACK (8 CARDS) 1.00 1.25
UNOPENED RETAIL BOX (36 PACKS)
UNOPENED RETAIL PACK (5 CARDS)
COMMON CARD (1-90) .10 .25
NNO Free Willy 2 PROMO 3.00 8.00

1995 SkyBox Free Willy 2 Coloring Cards

COMPLETE SET (9) 2.00 5.00
COMMON CARD (CC1-CC9) .30 .75
STATED ODDS 1:1 RETAIL

1995 SkyBox Free Willy 2 Lenticular

COMPLETE SET (2) 10.00 25.00
COMMON CARD (L1-L2) 6.00 15.00
STATED ODDS 1:36

1995 SkyBox Free Willy 2 Pop-Ups

COMPLETE SET (9) 2.00 5.00
COMMON CARD (P1-P9) .30 .75
STATED ODDS 1:1 HOBBY

1995 SkyBox Free Willy 2 Spectra-Etch Puzzle

COMPLETE SET (9) 10.00 25.00

COMMON CARD (SP1-SP9) 1.50 4.00
STATED ODDS 1:5

1989 Eclipse Friendly Dictators

COMPLETE SET (36) 4.00 10.00
COMMON CARD (1-36) .25 .60

1988 Topps Fright Flicks

COMPLETE SET (90) 8.00 20.00
COMPLETE SET W/STICKERS (101) 10.00 25.00
UNOPENED BOX (36 PACKS) 150.00 250.00
UNOPENED PACK (9 CARDS) 4.00 8.00
COMMON CARD (1-90) .15 .40
*OPC: SAME VALUE

1988 Topps Fright Flicks Stickers

COMPLETE SET (11) 1.50 4.00
COMMON CARD (1-11) .25 .60
STATED ODDS 1:1

1996 Dart FlipCards The Frighteners

COMPLETE SET (72) 8.00 20.00
UNOPENED BOX (30 PACKS) 25.00 40.00
UNOPENED PACK (7 CARDS) 1.00 1.50
COMMON CARD (1-72) .30 .60
TB AVAILABLE VIA MAIL-IN OFFER
TB Unearthly Struggle Tall Boy 5.00 12.00

1996 Dart FlipCards The Frighteners Big Boy

COMPLETE SET (4) 8.00 20.00
COMMON CARD (BB1-BB8) 3.00 8.00
STATED ODDS 1:BOX

1996 Dart FlipCards The Frighteners Gold Foil

COMPLETE SET (6) 12.00 30.00
COMMON CARD (1-6) 3.00 8.00
STATED ODDS 1:15

1996 Dart FlipCards The Frighteners Promos

COMPLETE SET (3) 2.50 6.00
COMMON CARD (P1-P3) .75 2.00
P3 Collector's International Trade Show Exclusive 2.00 5.00

2012 Fringe Seasons One and Two

COMPLETE SET (72) 5.00 12.00
UNOPENED BOX (24 PACKS) 500.00 750.00
UNOPENED PACK (5 CARDS) 20.00 30.00
COMMON CARD (1-71) .15 .40
P1 Olivia/Peter/Walter PROMO 2.50 6.00

2012 Fringe Seasons One and Two Wardrobes

COMMON CARD 6.00 15.00
STATED ODDS ONE PER BOX
M1 Astrid's blouse 8.00 20.00
M3 Broyles' tie SP 30.00 60.00
M8 Olivia's shirt 12.00 30.00
M9 Olivia's suit 10.00 25.00
M10 Peter's shirt 10.00 25.00
M11 Peter's shirt 10.00 25.00
M13 Rachel's pants 8.00 20.00
M14 Walter's shirt 8.00 20.00
M15 Walter's shirt 8.00 20.00
M16 Walter's coat 8.00 20.00
M17 Officer's jacket 10.00 25.00

2012 Fringe Seasons One and Two Autographs

COMMON AUTO 6.00 15.00
C = COMMON
U = UNCOMMON
R = RARE
STATED ODDS ONE PER BOX
A1 Anna Torv R 200.00 400.00
A2 Joshua Jackson R 200.00 400.00
A3 Lance Reddick R 75.00 150.00
A4 Blair Brown R 150.00 300.00
A5 Jasika Nicole R 60.00 120.00
A6 John Noble R 200.00 400.00
A7 Seth Gabel R 100.00 200.00
A8 Sebastian Roche U 8.00 20.00
A9 Michael Cerveris U 15.00 40.00
A10 Kevin Corrigan U 10.00 25.00
A11 Ari Graynor C 10.00 25.00
A12 Kirk Acevedo C 10.00 25.00
A14b Jeff Pinkner R 60.00 120.00
A15 J.H. Wyman R 60.00 120.00
A16 Meghan Markle U 500.00 1000.00

2012 Fringe Seasons One and Two Our Universe

COMPLETE SET (9) 15.00 40.00
COMMON CARD (F1-F9) 3.00 8.00
RANDOMLY INSERTED INTO PACKS
F1 Olivia Dunham 4.00 10.00

2012 Fringe Seasons One and Two Universe B

COMPLETE SET (9) 15.00 40.00
COMMON CARD (D1-D9) 3.00 8.00
RANDOMLY INSERTED INTO PACKS
D1 Olivia Dunham 4.00 10.00

2013 Fringe Seasons Three and Four

COMPLETE SET (73) 6.00 15.00
COMMON CARD (1-73) .20 .50
NSP2 GTS Come and Play PROMO 10.00 25.00

2013 Fringe Seasons Three and Four Autographs

COMMON AUTO 6.00 15.00
STATED ODDS 1:24
A1 Anna Torv 200.00 350.00
A3 John Noble 100.00 200.00
A4 Lance Reddick 30.00 75.00
A5 Blair Brown 100.00 200.00
A6 Jasika Nicole 60.00 120.00
A7 Seth Gabel 60.00 120.00
A8 Kirk Acevedo 10.00 25.00
A9 Leonard Nimoy 300.00 500.00
A14 Michelle Krusiec 15.00 40.00
A16 Paula Giroday 8.00 20.00
A19 Lily Pilblad 25.00 60.00

2013 Fringe Seasons Three and Four Behind-the-Scenes

COMPLETE SET (9) 6.00 15.00
COMMON CARD (D1-D9) 1.25 3.00
OVERALL CHASE ODDS 1:6

2013 Fringe Seasons Three and Four The Other Side

COMPLETE SET (9) 8.00 20.00
COMMON CARD (ALT1-ALT9) 1.50 4.00
OVERALL CHASE ODDS 4:24

2013 Fringe Seasons Three and Four Wardrobes

COMMON CARD 6.00 15.00
COMMON OLIVIA/BOLIVIA 10.00 25.00
COMMON WALTER BISHOP 8.00 20.00
STATED ODDS 1:24

2016 Fringe Season 5

COMPLETE FACTORY SET (22) 200.00 400.00
A1 Anna Torv/AU 100.00 200.00
A3 John Noble/AU 30.00 75.00
A4 Jasika Nicole/AU 20.00 50.00
A12 Michael Cerveris/AU 10.00 25.00
CT O.Dunham CT/37 15.00 40.00
DM1 A.Farnsworth MEM2/200 12.00 30.00
DM2 O.Dunham MEM2/100 15.00 40.00
DM3 P.Bishop MEM2/50 25.00 60.00
G1 Butterfly/200 12.00 30.00
G2 Hand/100 12.00 30.00
G3 Frog/50 10.00 25.00
G3 Seahorse/25 10.00 25.00
M1 O.Dunham MEM/200 12.00 30.00
M2 P.Bishop MEM/200 10.00 25.00
M3 W.Bishop MEM/200 8.00 20.00
M4 P.Broyles MEM/100 8.00 20.00
M5 A.Farnsworth MEM/100 12.00 30.00
M6 O.Dunham MEM/50 20.00 50.00
M7 P.Bishop MEM/50 15.00 40.00
M8 O.Dunham MEM/25 100.00 200.00
M9 P.Bishop MEM/25 8.00 20.00
TM1 Dunham/Bishop/Bishop
TRIPLE MEM/25 150.00 300.00

2014 Frozen Dog Tags

COMPLETE SET (24) 25.00 60.00
COMMON TAG (1-24) 2.00 5.00
*FOIL: .75X TO 2X BASIC CARDS

2014 Frozen Dog Tags Stickers

COMPLETE SET (8) 2.00 5.00
COMMON STICKER .50 1.25
STATED ODDS 1:1
UNNUMBERED SET

2004 Fullmetal Alchemist

COMPLETE SET (45) 5.00 12.00
UNOPENED BOX (24 PACKS) 30.00 40.00
UNOPENED PACK (5 CARDS) 1.50 1.75
COMMON CARD (1-45) .20 .50

2004 Fullmetal Alchemist Prisms

COMPLETE SET (30) 8.00 20.00
COMPLETE RARE SET (18) 2.50 6.00
COMPLETE ULTRA RARE SET (12) 6.00 15.00
COMMON RARE (SP1-SP18) .25 .60
COMMON ULTRA RARE (SP19-SP30) .75 2.00
STATED ODDS RARE 2:3
STATED ODDS ULTRA RARE 1:3

2017 Funko Disney Treasures Patches

COMMON CARD (UNNUMBERED) 1.25 3.00
NNO Dot 2.50 6.00
NNO Magic Mirror 2.00 5.00
NNO Piglet 2.00 5.00
NNO Scrooge McDuck 2.50 6.00

2015 Furious 7 Vudu Pizza Promos

COMPLETE SET (4) 10.00 25.00
COMMON CARD (UNNUMBERED) 3.00 8.00

2018 Galaxy Goo Planetary Fact Cards

COMPLETE SET (9) 5.00 12.00
COMMON CARD (1-9) .75 2.00

1999 DreamWorks Galaxy Quest Promos

COMPLETE SET (9) 6.00 15.00
COMMON CARD 1.00 2.50

Game of Thrones

2012 Rittenhouse Game of Thrones Season One

COMPLETE SET (72) 5.00 12.00
UNOPENED BOX (24 PACKS) 1200.00 2000.00
UNOPENED PACK (5 CARDS) 50.00 85.00
UNOPENED ARCHIVE BOX 2000.00 4000.00
COMMON CARD (1-72) .15 .40
*FOIL: 2X TO 5X BASIC CARDS
T1/900 ISSUED AS CASE TOPPER
T1 Title Sequence/900 10.00 25.00
(Case-Topper)

2012 Rittenhouse Game of Thrones Season One Autographs

COMMON AUTO 10.00 25.00
L (LE) - LIMITED LOWER END: 300-400 COPIES
L (UE) - LIMITED UPPER END: 400-500 COPIES
OVERALL AUTO ODDS TWO PER BOX
BEAN AUTO ISSUED AS 3-CASE INCENTIVE
DINKLAGE AUTO ISSUED AS 6-CASE INCENTIVE
NNO Aidan Gillen L (UE) 25.00 60.00
NNO Alfie Allen L (UE) 30.00 75.00
NNO Art Parkinson L (LE) 30.00 75.00
NNO Charles Dance L (LE) 60.00 120.00
NNO Conleth Hill L (UE) 20.00 50.00
NNO Elyes Gabel L (UE) 20.00 50.00
NNO Emilia Clarke L (LE) 1000.00 2000.00
NNO Esme Bianco L (UE) 20.00 50.00
NNO Harry Lloyd L (UE) 15.00 40.00
NNO Ian McElhinney L (UE) 15.00 40.00
NNO I.Hempstead-Wright L (UE) 50.00 100.00
NNO Jack Gleeson L (UE) 30.00 75.00
NNO Jamie Sives L (UE) 12.00 30.00
NNO Jason Momoa L (LE) 200.00 400.00
NNO Jerome Flynn L (UE) 25.00 60.00
NNO John Bradley L (UE) 15.00 40.00
NNO Kit Harington L (LE) 300.00 600.00
NNO Kristian Nairn L (UE) 15.00 40.00
NNO Lena Headey L (LE) 75.00 150.00
NNO Maisie Williams L (UE) 250.00 500.00
NNO Mark Addy L (LE) 50.00 100.00
NNO Michelle Fairley L (LE) 60.00 120.00
NNO N.Coster-Waldau L (LE) 75.00 150.00
NNO Owen Teale L (UE) 15.00 40.00
NNO Peter Dinklage 6CI 200.00 400.00
NNO Richard Madden L (LE) 125.00 250.00
NNO Rory McCann L (UE) 30.00 75.00
NNO Sean Bean 3CI 100.00 200.00

2012 Rittenhouse Game of Thrones Season One Full Bleed Autographs

COMMON AUTO 10.00 25.00
L (LE) - LIMITED LOWER END: 300-400 COPIES
L (UE) - LIMITED UPPER END: 400-500 COPIES
OVERALL AUTO ODDS TWO PER BOX
NNO Aidan Gillen L (UE) 30.00 75.00
NNO Alfie Allen L (UE) 25.00 60.00
NNO Art Parkinson L (LE) 50.00 100.00
NNO Conleth Hill L (UE) 20.00 50.00
NNO Esme Bianco L (UE) 25.00 60.00
NNO Harry Lloyd L (UE) 25.00 60.00
NNO Ian McElhinney L (UE) 15.00 40.00
NNO I. Hempstead-Wright L (UE) 60.00 120.00
NNO Jack Gleeson L (UE) 25.00 60.00
NNO Jamie Sives L (UE) 15.00 40.00
NNO Jason Momoa L (LE) 200.00 400.00
NNO Jerome Flynn L (UE) 60.00 120.00
NNO John Bradley L (UE) 15.00 40.00
NNO Julian Glover L (UE) 15.00 40.00
NNO Kristian Nairn L (UE) 25.00 60.00
NNO Maisie Williams L (UE) 150.00 300.00
NNO Mark Addy L (LE) 50.00 100.00
NNO Miltos Yerolemou L (UE) 25.00 60.00
NNO Rory McCann L (UE) 30.00 75.00

2012 Rittenhouse Game of Thrones Season One Quotables

COMPLETE SET (9) 8.00 20.00
COMMON CARD (Q1-Q9) 1.50 4.00
STATED ODDS 1:12
Q10 ISSUED AS RITTENHOUSE REWARD
Q10 What Do We Say SP RR 25.00 50.00

2012 Rittenhouse Game of Thrones Season One Shadowbox

COMPLETE SET (6) 35.00 70.00
COMMON CARD 8.00 20.00
STATED ODDS 1:48
2 Daenerys Targaryen 10.00 25.00

2012 Rittenhouse Game of Thrones Season One The Houses

COMPLETE SET (9) 8.00 20.00
COMMON CARD (H1-H9) 1.50 4.00
STATED ODDS 1:12

2012 Rittenhouse Game of Thrones Season One You Win or You Die

COMPLETE SET (5) 10.00 25.00
COMMON CARD (SP1-SP5) 3.00 8.00
STATED ODDS 1:24
SP4 I Do Not Have A Gentle Heart 4.00 10.00

2012 Rittenhouse Game of Thrones Season One Promos

P1 Daenerys Targaryen GEN 4.00 10.00

MODERN

P2 Ned Stark NSU 5.00 12.00
P3 Ned Stark ALB 8.00 20.00

2013 Rittenhouse Game of Thrones Season Two

COMPLETE SET (88) 6.00 15.00
UNOPENED BOX (24 PACKS) 400.00 600.00
UNOPENED PACK (5 CARDS) 15.00 25.00
COMMON CARD (1-88) .15 .40
*FOIL: 1.5X TO 4X BASIC CARDS .60 1.50

2013 Rittenhouse Game of Thrones Season Two Autographs

COMMON AUTO 6.00 15.00
TWO AUTOGRAPHS PER BOX
L (LIMITED): 300-500 COPIES
VL (VERY LIMITED): 200-300
WEISS OR BENIOFF ISSUED AS 3-CASE INCENTIVE
MARTIN ISSUED AS 6-CASE INCENTIVE
NNO Aidan Gillen L 20.00 50.00
NNO Aimee Richardson 10.00 25.00
NNO Amrita Acharia 10.00 25.00
NNO Conan Stevens L 10.00 25.00
NNO Conleth Hill L 15.00 40.00
NNO D.B. Weiss 3CI 15.00 40.00
NNO David Benioff 3CI 25.00 60.00
NNO Donald Sumpter L 10.00 25.00
NNO Finn Jones 12.00 30.00
NNO Francis Magee 12.00 30.00
NNO Gemma Whelan 15.00 40.00
NNO George R.R. Martin 6CI 125.00 250.00
NNO Gethin Anthony 10.00 25.00
NNO Jack Gleeson VL 30.00 75.00
NNO John Bradley 12.00 30.00
NNO Kate Dickie 10.00 25.00
NNO Kerr Logan L 12.00 30.00
NNO Laura Pradelska L 12.00 30.00
NNO Maisie Williams L 100.00 200.00
NNO Natalie Dormer 30.00 75.00
NNO Natalia Tena 15.00 40.00
NNO Nicholas Blane 10.00 25.00
NNO Roger Allam 8.00 20.00
NNO Rory McCann L 30.00 75.00
NNO Roxanne McKee 12.00 30.00
NNO Sibel Kekilli L 15.00 40.00
NNO Simon Armstrong 10.00 25.00
NNO Stephen Dillane VL 20.00 50.00

2013 Rittenhouse Game of Thrones Season Two Battle of Blackwater Case-Toppers

COMPLETE SET (2) 20.00 40.00
COMMON CARD (CT1-CT2) 10.00 25.00
STATED ODDS 1:CASE

2013 Rittenhouse Game of Thrones Season Two Family Sigil

COMPLETE SET (6) 10.00 25.00
COMMON CARD (S1-S6) 3.00 8.00
STATED ODDS 1:24

2013 Rittenhouse Game of Thrones Season Two Full Bleed Autographs

COMMON AUTO 8.00 20.00
TWO AUTOGRAPHS PER BOX
L (LIMITED): 300-500 COPIES
VL (VERY LIMITED): 200-300 COPIES
NNO Charles Dance VL 75.00 150.00
NNO Emilia Clarke VL 2000.00 4000.00
NNO Gwendoline Christie 50.00 100.00
NNO Iain Glen L 20.00 50.00
NNO Kit Harington VL 200.00 400.00
NNO Lena Headey VL 75.00 150.00
NNO Michelle Fairley VL 75.00 150.00
NNO Nikolaj Coster-Waldau VL 75.00 150.00
NNO Peter Dinklage VL 125.00 250.00
NNO Richard Madden VL 150.00 300.00
NNO Rose Leslie 60.00 120.00
NNO Sophie Turner 75.00 150.00
NNO Tom Wlaschiha 15.00 40.00

2013 Rittenhouse Game of Thrones Season Two Gallery

COMPLETE SET (6) 20.00 50.00
COMMON CARD (PL1-PL6) 6.00 15.00
STATED ODDS 1:48

2013 Rittenhouse Game of Thrones Season Two Quotables

COMPLETE SET (9) 8.00 20.00
COMPLETE SET W/SP (10) 25.00 60.00
COMMON CARD (Q11-Q19) 1.50 4.00
STATED ODDS 1:12
Q20 ISSUED AS RITTENHOUSE REWARD

2013 Rittenhouse Game of Thrones Season Two Relics

COMMON CAPE 8.00 20.00
COMMON BANNER 10.00 25.00
STATED ODDS 1:48
PRINT RUN 300-625
RL2 Tyrion Lannister/325 12.00 30.00
RL3 Cersei Lannister/325 30.00 75.00
RL4 Jaime Lannister/325 25.00 60.00
RS1 Eddard Stark/375 12.00 30.00
RS3 Robb Stark/375 15.00 40.00
RS4 Sansa Stark/375 25.00 60.00
RS5 Arya Stark/375 12.00 30.00
RNW1 Watch Cloak/625 20.00 50.00

2013 Rittenhouse Game of Thrones Season Two Storyboard Art

COMPLETE SET (20) 12.00 30.00
COMMON CARD (SB1-SB20) 1.50 4.00
STATED ODDS 1:12

2013 Rittenhouse Game of Thrones Season Two Promos

P1 Daenerys Targaryen GEN .75 2.00
P2 King Joffrey Baratheon NSU 2.50 6.00
P3 Tyrion Lannister ALB 10.00 25.00
P4 Robb Stark (Chicago) 6.00 15.00
P5 Daenerys Targaryen (Philly) 4.00 10.00

2014 Rittenhouse Game of Thrones Season Three

COMPLETE SET (98) 10.00 25.00
UNOPENED BOX (24 PACKS) 150.00 250.00
UNOPENED PACK (5 CARDS) 6.00 10.00
COMMON CARD (1-98) .20 .50
*GOLD/150: 6X TO 15X BASIC CARDS 65.00 80.00
*HOLO: 1.5X TO 4X BASIC CARDS 3.00 3.50

2014 Rittenhouse Game of Thrones Season Three Blue Autographs

COMMON AUTO 6.00 15.00
STATED ODDS 1:12
NNO Anton Lesser 8.00 20.00
NNO Carice van Houten L 25.00 60.00
NNO David Bradley 10.00 25.00
NNO Ellie Kendrick L 8.00 20.00
NNO Hannah Murray L 10.00 25.00
NNO Iwan Rheon L 12.00 30.00
NNO Kristofer Hivju L 30.00 75.00
NNO Nikolaj Coster-Waldau EL 60.00 120.00
NNO Peter Dinklage EL 75.00 150.00
NNO Thomas Brodie Sangster L 15.00 40.00

2014 Rittenhouse Game of Thrones Season Three Bordered Autographs

STATED ODDS 1:12
NNO Daniel Portman L 8.00 20.00
NNO Gwendoline Christie 30.00 75.00
NNO Iain Glen L 15.00 40.00
NNO Lena Headey EL 75.00 150.00
NNO Michael McElhatton L 6.00 15.00
NNO Rose Leslie 30.00 75.00
NNO Sophie Turner 75.00 150.00

2014 Rittenhouse Game of Thrones Season Three Case-Incentive Autographs

COMMON AUTO 75.00 150.00
HEADEY ISSUED AS 3-CASE INCENTIVE
COSTER-WALDAU ISSUED AS 3-CASE INCENTIVE
DINKLAGE ISSUED AS 3-CASE INCENTIVE
NNO Peter Dinklage 6CI 100.00 200.00

2014 Rittenhouse Game of Thrones Season Three Case-Topper

STATED ODDS 1 PER CASE
1 House Martell Sigil Die-Cut Card 8.00 20.00

2014 Rittenhouse Game of Thrones Season Three Full Bleed Autographs

COMMON AUTO 5.00 12.00
STATED ODDS 1:12
NNO Aidan Gillen L 20.00 50.00
NNO Conan Stevens L 10.00 25.00
NNO Conleth Hill L 12.00 30.00
NNO Gemma Whelan 10.00 25.00
NNO Gethin Anthony 6.00 15.00
NNO Ian Whyte L 8.00 20.00
NNO Jack Gleeson VL 30.00 75.00
NNO John Bradley 12.00 30.00
NNO Maisie Williams L 125.00 250.00
NNO Natalia Tena 10.00 25.00
NNO Natalie Dormer 50.00 100.00
NNO Oona Chaplin EL 100.00 200.00
NNO Rory McCann L 60.00 120.00
NNO Roxanne McKee 6.00 15.00
NNO Sibel Kekilli L 12.00 30.00
NNO Stephen Dillane 12.00 30.00
NNO Tobias Menzies 10.00 25.00

2014 Rittenhouse Game of Thrones Season Three Gallery

COMPLETE SET (12) 12.00 30.00
COMMON CARD (G01-G12) 2.00 5.00
STATED ODDS 1:12

2014 Rittenhouse Game of Thrones Season Three Map Marker Sigil

COMPLETE SET (6) 80.00 200.00
COMMON CARD (MM1-MM6) 15.00 40.00
STATED ODDS 1:144

2014 Rittenhouse Game of Thrones Season Three Quotables

COMPLETE SET (9) 8.00 20.00
COMMON CARD (Q21-Q29) 1.50 4.00
STATED ODDS 1:12
Q30 Dead Rats Don't Squeak RR 15.00 40.00

2014 Rittenhouse Game of Thrones Season Three Relationships

COMPLETE SET (20) 12.00 30.00
COMMON CARD (DL1-DL20) 1.25 3.00
*GOLD: 1.2X TO 3X BASIC CARDS
STATED ODDS 1:12

2014 Rittenhouse Game of Thrones Season Three Relics

COMPLETE SET (2) 60.00 120.00
COMMON CARD (R1-R2) 30.00 75.00
STATED ODDS 1:2 CASES
STATED PRINT RUN 325 SER.#'d SETS

2014 Rittenhouse Game of Thrones Season Three Promos

P1 Daenerys and Troops GEN 2.00 5.00
P2 Desert Dragons NSU 2.50 6.00
P3 Flying Dragon ALB 4.00 10.00
P4 Daenerys and Dragons (Philly) 4.00 10.00

2015 Rittenhouse Game of Thrones Season Four

COMPLETE SET (100) 10.00 25.00
UNOPENED BOX (24 PACKS) 150.00 250.00
UNOPENED PACK (5 CARDS) 6.00 10.00
COMMON CARD (1-100) .20 .50
*HOLO: 1.5X TO 4X BASIC CARDS
*GOLD: 6X TO 15X BASIC CARDS

2015 Rittenhouse Game of Thrones Season Four Beautiful Death

COMPLETE SET (20) 15.00 40.00
COMMON CARD (BD1-BD20) 1.50 4.00
*GOLD: 1X TO 2.5X BASIC CARDS
STATED ODDS 1:24

2015 Rittenhouse Game of Thrones Season Four Blue Autographs

COMMON AUTO 10.00 25.00
OVERALL AUTO STATED ODDS 1:12
REGULAR = >500
L = 300-500
VL = 200-300
EL = <200
NNO Nathalie Emmanuel L 25.00 60.00

2015 Rittenhouse Game of Thrones Season Four Bordered Autographs

COMMON AUTO 5.00 12.00
OVERALL AUTO STATED ODDS 1:12
REGULAR = >500
L = 300-500
VL = 200-300
EL = <200
NNO Ben Hawkey L 6.00 15.00
NNO Burn Gorman L 6.00 15.00
NNO Indira Varma L 12.00 30.00
NNO Kerry Ingram L 10.00 25.00
NNO Oona Chaplin EL 75.00 150.00
NNO Will Tudor L 6.00 15.00
NNO Yuri Kolokolnikov L 6.00 15.00

2015 Rittenhouse Game of Thrones Season Four Case-Incentive Autographs

NNO Jack Gleeson Gold AU 6CI 50.00 100.00
NNO Kit Harington Gold AU 9CI 200.00 400.00

2015 Rittenhouse Game of Thrones Season Four Case-Topper

NNO1 Embossed Raven 5.00 12.00

2015 Rittenhouse Game of Thrones Season Four Full Bleed Autographs

COMMON AUTO 5.00 12.00
OVERALL AUTO STATED ODDS 1:12
REGULAR = >500
L = 300-500
VL = 200-300
EL = <200
NNO Aimee Richardson 10.00 25.00
NNO Alexandra Dowling 10.00 25.00
NNO Anton Lesser 6.00 15.00
NNO Carice van Houten L 25.00 60.00
NNO Daniel Portman L 6.00 15.00
NNO David Bradley 10.00 25.00
NNO Donald Sumpter L 6.00 15.00
NNO Ellie Kendrick L 8.00 20.00
NNO Finn Jones 10.00 25.00
NNO Fintan McKeown L 8.00 20.00
NNO Hafthor Julius Bjornsson VL 50.00 100.00
NNO Hannah Murray L 6.00 15.00
NNO Jacob Anderson VL 50.00 100.00
NNO Kate Dickie 6.00 15.00
NNO Kit Harington EL 300.00 600.00
NNO Kristofer Hivju L 8.00 20.00
NNO Laura Pradelska L 8.00 20.00
NNO Lena Headey EL 75.00 150.00
NNO Nikolaj Coster-Waldau EL 75.00 150.00
NNO Peter Dinklage EL 125.00 250.00
NNO Sean Bean L 75.00 150.00
NNO Thomas Brodie Sangster L 15.00 40.00
NNO Tony Way L 6.00 15.00

2015 Rittenhouse Game of Thrones Season Four Quotables

COMPLETE SET (9) 8.00 20.00
COMMON CARD (Q31-Q39) 1.50 4.00
STATED ODDS 1:12
Q40 Nothing Isn't Better or Worse...RR 15.00 40.00

2015 Rittenhouse Game of Thrones Season Four Shields

COMMON CARD (H1-H4) 15.00 40.00
STATED ODDS 1:144 W/SKETCHES
H1 House Stark 30.00 75.00

H3 House Baratheon (Stannis)	20.00	50.00
H4 House Greyjoy	20.00	50.00

2015 Rittenhouse Game of Thrones Season Four Valar Morghulis

COMPLETE SET (20)	25.00	60.00
COMMON CARD (G1-G20)	2.50	6.00
STATED ODDS 1:24		

2015 Rittenhouse Game of Thrones Season Four Promos

COMMON CARD (P1-P3)	2.50	6.00
P3 Margaery and Joffrey ALB	10.00	25.00

2016 Rittenhouse Game of Thrones Season Five

COMPLETE SET (100)	10.00	25.00
UNOPENED BOX (24 PACKS)	50.00	80.00
UNOPENED PACK (5 CARDS)	2.25	3.50
COMMON CARD (1-100)	.20	.50
*FOIL: 1.5X TO 4X BASIC CARDS		
*GOLD: 6X TO 15X BASIC CARDS		

2016 Rittenhouse Game of Thrones Season Five Beautiful Death

COMPLETE SET (20)	20.00	50.00
COMMON CARD (BD21-BD40)	1.50	4.00
*GOLD: 1X TO 2.5X BASIC CARDS		
STATED ODDS 1:24		

2016 Rittenhouse Game of Thrones Season Five Blue Autographs

COMMON AUTO	6.00	15.00
L = 300-500 COPIES		
VL = 200-300 COPIES		
EL = 100-200 COPIES		
ALL AUTOGRAPHS STATED ODDS 1:12		
NNO Aidan Gillen EL	25.00	60.00
NNO Birgitte Hjort Sorensen L	8.00	20.00
NNO Hafpor Julius Bjornsson L	15.00	40.00
NNO Jacob Anderson L	15.00	40.00
NNO Kit Harington VL	200.00	350.00
NNO Sophie Turner EL	75.00	150.00

2016 Rittenhouse Game of Thrones Season Five Bordered Autographs

COMMON AUTO	5.00	12.00
L = 300-500 COPIES		
VL = 200-300 COPIES		
EL = 100-200 COPIES		
ALL AUTOGRAPHS STATED ODDS 1:12		
NNO Paul Bentley L	6.00	15.00
NNO Alexander Siddig EL	30.00	75.00
NNO Carice van Houten L	20.00	50.00
NNO Charlotte Hope L	15.00	40.00
NNO Dean-Charles Chapman L	10.00	25.00
NNO Enzo Cilenti L	6.00	15.00
NNO Hannah Murray L	8.00	20.00
NNO Ian Whyte L	6.00	15.00
NNO Jessica Henwick L	12.00	30.00
NNO Keisha Castle-Hughes L	10.00	25.00
NNO Lino Facioli L	6.00	15.00
NNO Nathalie Emmanuel L	20.00	50.00
NNO Reece Noi as Mossador L	10.00	25.00
NNO Rosabell Laurenti Sellers L	15.00	40.00
NNO Toby Sebastian L	6.00	15.00
NNO Tom Wlaschiha L	8.00	20.00

2016 Rittenhouse Game of Thrones Season Five Case-Incentive Autographs

COMMON AUTO	100.00	200.00
NNO Sophie Turner/Aidan Gillen AU	150.00	300.00
NNO Peter Dinklage Bordered AU	150.00	300.00

2016 Rittenhouse Game of Thrones Season Five Case-Toppers

COMPLETE SET (2)	8.00	20.00
COMMON CARD (H11-H12)	5.00	12.00
STATED ODDS 1:CASE		

2016 Rittenhouse Game of Thrones Season Five Dragonglass Relic

STATED ODDS 1:1440		
DG1 Dragonglass	150.00	300.00

2016 Rittenhouse Game of Thrones Season Five Full Bleed Autographs

COMMON AUTO	5.00	12.00
L = 300-500 COPIES		
VL = 200-300 COPIES		
EL = 100-200 COPIES		
STATED ODDS 1:12 OVERALL		
NNO Daniel Portman L	8.00	20.00
NNO Elizabeth Webster	6.00	15.00
NNO Hannah Waddingham	6.00	15.00
NNO Indira Varma L	12.00	30.00
NNO Iwan Rheon L	10.00	25.00
NNO Jonathan Pryce VL	25.00	60.00
NNO Kerry Ingram L	6.00	15.00
NNO Lena Headey VL	75.00	150.00
NNO Maisie Williams VL	125.00	250.00
NNO Michael McElhatton L	8.00	20.00
NNO Natalie Dormer L	30.00	75.00
NNO Paul Bentley L	6.00	15.00
NNO Peter Dinklage VL	125.00	250.00
NNO Ross O'Hennessy	6.00	15.00

2016 Rittenhouse Game of Thrones Season Five Night Watch Relics

COMMON CARD (CC1-CC5)	12.00	30.00
STATED ODDS 1:288		
CC1 Jon Snow	20.00	50.00
CC2 Samwell Tarly	15.00	40.00
CC4 Eddison Tollett	15.00	40.00

2016 Rittenhouse Game of Thrones Season Five Quotables

COMPLETE SET W/O SP(9)	10.00	25.00
COMMON CARD (Q41-Q50)	1.50	4.00
STATED ODDS 1:12		
Q50 SP OFFERED AS RITTENHOUSE REWARD		
Q50 Lannister/Targaryen/Baratheon Stark/Tyrell RR	25.00	60.00

2016 Rittenhouse Game of Thrones Season Five Reflections

COMPLETE SET (16)	80.00	150.00
COMMON CARD (RM1-RM16)	4.00	10.00
STATED ODDS 1:48		
RM02 T.Lannister and Varys	6.00	15.00
RM03 A.Stark and J.H'ghar	6.00	15.00
RM04 Daenerys and Khal	8.00	20.00
RM06 Jon Snow and Ygritte	6.00	15.00
RM10 C.Lannister and J.Lannister	6.00	15.00
RM12 Samwell Tarly and Gilly	6.00	15.00
RM14 M.Tyrell and Lady Olenna	6.00	15.00
RM16 R.Snow and T.Greyjoy	6.00	15.00

2016 Rittenhouse Game of Thrones Season Five Relationships

COMPLETE SET (10)	8.00	20.00
COMMON CARD (DL21-DL30)	1.25	3.00
*GOLD: 1X TO 2.5X BASIC CARDS		
STATED ODDS 1:24		

2016 Rittenhouse Game of Thrones Season Five Promos

COMMON CARD (P1-P3)	1.50	4.00
P1 Daenerys Targaryen GEN	2.00	5.00
P3 Night's King ALB	10.00	25.00

2017 Rittenhouse Game of Thrones Season Six

COMPLETE SET (100)	6.00	15.00
UNOPENED BOX (24 PACKS)	50.00	75.00
UNOPENED PACK (5 CARDS)	2.50	3.50
COMMON CARD (1-100)	.15	.40
*FOIL: 3X TO 8X BASIC CARDS	1.25	3.00
*GOLD: 8X TO 20X BASIC CARDS	3.00	8.00
CT1 Valyrian Steel Metal Card CT	6.00	15.00

2017 Rittenhouse Game of Thrones Season Six Beautiful Death Posters

COMPLETE SET (20)	30.00	80.00
COMMON CARD (BD41-BD60)	2.50	6.00
*FOIL: 1X TO 2.5X BASIC CARDS	6.00	15.00
STATED ODDS 1:24		

2017 Rittenhouse Game of Thrones Season Six Blue Autographs

COMMON AUTO	10.00	25.00
STATED ODDS OVERALL 1:12		
REGULAR AUTO <500		
L (LIMITED) = 300-500		
VL (VERY LIMITED) = 200-300		
EL (EXTREMELY LIMITED) = 100-200		
NNO John Bradley VL	12.00	30.00
NNO Jonathan Pryce VL	15.00	40.00
NNO Lena Headey VL	60.00	120.00
NNO Maisie Williams VL	75.00	150.00
NNO Tom Wlaschiha VL	15.00	40.00

2017 Rittenhouse Game of Thrones Season Six Bordered Autographs

COMMON AUTO	5.00	12.00
STATED ODDS OVERALL 1:12		
REGULAR AUTO <500		
L (LIMITED) = 300-500		
VL (VERY LIMITED) = 200-300		
EL (EXTREMELY LIMITED) = 100-200		
NNO Clive Russell VL	12.00	30.00
NNO Eline Powell L	12.00	30.00
NNO Elizabeth Cadwallader L	6.00	15.00
NNO Elizabeth Webster L	8.00	20.00
NNO Eros Vlahos VL	12.00	30.00
NNO Eugene Simon L	6.00	15.00
NNO Faye Marsay VL	15.00	40.00
NNO Hafpor Julius Bjornsson L	30.00	75.00
NNO Jacob Anderson L	15.00	40.00
NNO Julian Glover	8.00	20.00
NNO Natalie Dormer VL	20.00	50.00
NNO Richard E. Grant VL	20.00	50.00
NNO Robert Aramayo L	8.00	20.00

2017 Rittenhouse Game of Thrones Season Six Case-Incentive Autographs

COMMON AUTO	50.00	100.00
NNO Michiel Huisman Gold AU	50.00	100.00
NNO Williams/Wlaschiha DUAL AU	125.00	250.00

2017 Rittenhouse Game of Thrones Season Six Full Bleed Autographs

COMMON AUTO	5.00	12.00
STATED ODDS OVERALL 1:12		
REGULAR AUTO <500		
L (LIMITED) = 300-500		
VL (VERY LIMITED) = 200-300		
EL (EXTREMELY LIMITED) = 100-200		
NNO Alexander Siddig EL	30.00	75.00
NNO Ben Crompton L	8.00	20.00
NNO Ben Hawkey L	6.00	15.00
NNO Birgitte Hjort L	12.00	30.00
NNO Brenock O'Connor L	8.00	20.00
NNO Charlotte Hope L	15.00	40.00
NNO Conleth Hill EL	25.00	60.00
NNO Dean-Charles Chapman L	10.00	25.00
NNO Enzo Cilenti L	6.00	15.00
NNO Essie Davis L	8.00	20.00
NNO Gwyneth Keyworth L	10.00	25.00
NNO Hannah John-Kamen L	20.00	50.00
NNO Hannah Murray VL	20.00	50.00
NNO Ian Whyte L	10.00	25.00
NNO Isaac Hempstead-Wright VL	30.00	75.00
NNO James Faulkner L	6.00	15.00
NNO Jessica Hunwick L	12.00	30.00
NNO Kae Alexander L	10.00	25.00
NNO Keisha Castle-Hughes L	12.00	30.00
NNO Luke Barnes L	6.00	15.00
NNO Nathalie Emmanuel L	60.00	120.00
NNO Paola Dionisotti VL	12.00	30.00
NNO Richard Brake L	25.00	60.00
NNO Rosabell Laurenti Sellers L	20.00	50.00
NNO Sophie Turner EL	100.00	200.00
NNO Struan Rodger	6.00	15.00
NNO Tim Plester VL	12.00	30.00
NNO Toby Sebastian L	6.00	15.00
NNO Vladimir Furdik L	25.00	60.00

2017 Rittenhouse Game of Thrones Season Six Hall of Faces

COMPLETE SET (16)	100.00	200.00
COMMON CARD (HF1-HF16)	6.00	15.00
STATED ODDS 1:96		
HF1 Arya Stark	8.00	20.00
HF5 Daenerys Targaryen	10.00	25.00

2017 Rittenhouse Game of Thrones Season Six Quotables

COMPLETE SET (10)	10.00	25.00
COMMON CARD (Q51-Q59)	1.50	4.00
STATED ODDS 1:12		
Q60 IS RITTENHOUSE REWARD EXCLUSIVE		
Q60 Sometimes Before We Can...RR	20.00	50.00

2017 Rittenhouse Game of Thrones Season Six Relationships

COMPLETE SET (10)	12.00	30.00
COMMON CARD (DL31-DL40)	2.50	6.00
*GOLD: 1X TO 2.5X BASIC CARDS	6.00	15.00
STATED ODDS 1:24		

2017 Rittenhouse Game of Thrones Season Six Relics

COMMON CARD (S6R1-S6R2)	20.00	50.00
S6R1 Daenerys Targaryen	100.00	200.00

2017 Rittenhouse Game of Thrones Season Six Promos

COMMON CARD (P1-P3)	2.00	5.00
P2 Jon Snow Going into Battle NSU	2.50	6.00
P3 Daenerys and Dragon ALB	6.00	15.00

2018 Rittenhouse Game of Thrones Season Seven

COMPLETE SET (81)	8.00	20.00
UNOPENED BOX (24 PACKS)	100.00	150.00
UNOPENED PACK (5 CARDS)	4.00	6.00
UNOPENED ARCHIVE BOX	1000.00	1500.00
COMMON CARD (1-81)	.20	.50
*FOIL: 1.5X TO 4X BASIC CARDS	.75	2.00
*GOLD: 8X TO 20X BASIC CARDS	4.00	10.00

2018 Rittenhouse Game of Thrones Season Seven Beautiful Death Poster Art

COMPLETE SET (7)	10.00	25.00
COMMON CARD (BD61-BD67)	2.50	6.00
*FOIL: 1.2X TO 3X BASIC CARDS	8.00	20.00
STATED ODDS 1:42		

2018 Rittenhouse Game of Thrones Season Seven Blue Autographs

COMMON AUTO	10.00	25.00
STATED OVERALL ODDS 1:12		
REGULAR AUTO <500		
L (LIMITED) = 300-500		
VL (VERY LIMITED) = 200-300		
EL (EXTREMELY LIMITED) = 100-200		
NNO Gemma Whalen VL	12.00	30.00

2018 Rittenhouse Game of Thrones Season Seven Bordered Autographs

COMMON AUTO	5.00	12.00
STATED OVERALL ODDS 1:12		
NNO Ania Bukstein L	8.00	20.00
NNO Bella Ramsey VL	50.00	125.00
NNO Ben Crompton L	6.00	15.00
NNO Birgitte Hjort Sorensen L	8.00	20.00
NNO Brenock O'Connor L	6.00	15.00
NNO Danny Kirrane VL	8.00	20.00
NNO Essie Davis L	8.00	20.00
NNO Ian Gelder L	6.00	15.00
NNO Jonathan Pryce VL	15.00	40.00
NNO Joseph Mawle VL	15.00	40.00
NNO Joseph Quinn VL	30.00	75.00
NNO Kae Alexander L	8.00	20.00
NNO Lucy Hayes L	12.00	30.00
NNO Maisie Williams VL	50.00	100.00
NNO Paola Dionisotti VL	12.00	30.00
NNO Rob Callender L	10.00	25.00
NNO Sara Dylan L	10.00	25.00

NNO Sebastien Croft L 8.00 20.00
NNO Sophie Turner EL 60.00 120.00
NNO Tim Plester VL 12.00 30.00

2018 Rittenhouse Game of Thrones Season Seven Full Bleed Autographs

COMMON AUTO 6.00 15.00
STATED OVERALL ODDS 1:12
REGULAR AUTO <500
L (LIMITED) = 300-500
VL (VERY LIMITED) = 200-300
EL (EXTREMELY LIMITED) = 100-200
NNO Aidan Gillen EL 15.00 40.00
NNO Aisling Franciosi L 12.00 30.00
NNO Bella Ramsey VL 60.00 150.00
NNO Clive Russell VL 15.00 40.00
NNO Eline Powell L 12.00 30.00
NNO Eros Vlahos VL 8.00 20.00
NNO Faye Marsay VL 10.00 25.00
NNO Ian McElhinney VL 10.00 25.00
NNO Indira Varma VL 10.00 25.00
NNO Jim Broadbent EL 75.00 150.00
NNO Joe Dempsie EL 100.00 200.00
NNO Joseph Mawle VL 15.00 40.00
NNO Michael Feast L 8.00 20.00
NNO Michiel Huisman VL 15.00 40.00
NNO Nell Tiger Free VL 30.00 75.00
NNO Nikolaj Coster-Waldau EL 75.00 150.00
NNO Paul Kaye VL 20.00 50.00
NNO Pilou Asbaek VL 25.00 60.00
NNO Richard E. Grant VL 20.00 50.00
NNO Robert Aramayo L 8.00 20.00
NNO Roger Allam 6.00 15.00
NNO Tom Hopper VL 15.00 40.00
NNO Wilf Scolding L 8.00 20.00
NNO Yuri Kolokolnikov L 6.00 15.00

2018 Rittenhouse Game of Thrones Season Seven Multi-Case Incentive Autographs

NNO Michelle Fairley GOLD 6CI 50.00 100.00
NNO Dinklage/Hill DUAL 9CI 75.00 150.00

2018 Rittenhouse Game of Thrones Season Seven Quotables

COMPLETE SET W/RR (10) 25.00 60.00
COMPLETE SET W/O RR (9) 12.00 30.00
COMMON CARD (Q61-Q69) 2.50 6.00
STATED ODDS 1:12
Q70 Quotables RR 15.00 40.00

2018 Rittenhouse Game of Thrones Season Seven Relationships

COMPLETE SET (10) 12.00 30.00
COMMON CARD (DL41-DL50) 2.50 6.00
*GOLD: .6X TO 1.5X BASIC CARDS 4.00 10.00
STATED ODDS 1:24

2018 Rittenhouse Game of Thrones Season Seven Relics

VR6 Daenerys Targaryen Dual Relic 300.00 500.00

2018 Rittenhouse Game of Thrones Season Seven Valyrian Steel Alternate Case-Toppers

COMPLETE SET (3) 30.00 75.00
COMMON CARD (UNNUMBERED) 12.00 30.00
*GOLD: 1X TO 2.5X BASIC CARDS
STATED ODDS 1:CASE
NNO Cersei 15.00 40.00

2018 Rittenhouse Game of Thrones Season Seven Valyrian Steel Autographs

COMMON AUTO 6.00 15.00
STATED OVERALL ODDS 1:12
REGULAR AUTO <500
L (LIMITED) = 300-500
VL (VERY LIMITED) = 200-300
EL (EXTREMELY LIMITED) = 100-200
NNO Elle Kendrick VL 8.00 20.00
NNO Harry Lloyd VL 12.00 30.00
NNO Jessice Henwick L 10.00 25.00
NNO Rory McCann L 25.00 60.00
NNO Thomas Brodie Sangster L 10.00 25.00

2018 Rittenhouse Game of Thrones Season Seven Winter Is Here

COMPLETE SET (12) 75.00 150.00
COMMON CARD (W1-W12) 6.00 15.00
STATED ODDS 1:144
W5 Daenerys Targaryen 20.00 50.00
W9 Sansa Stark 8.00 20.00
W11 Tormund Giantsbane 10.00 25.00
W12 Tyrion Lannister 10.00 25.00

2018 Rittenhouse Game of Thrones Season Seven Promos

COMMON CARD (P1-P4) 3.00 8.00
P2 Non-Sport Update 5.00 12.00
P3 Album Exclusive 6.00 15.00
P4 Spring 2018 Philly NonSport Show 5.00 12.00

2020 Rittenhouse Game of Thrones Season Eight

COMPLETE SET (60) 8.00 20.00
UNOPENED BOX (24 PACKS) 100.00 150.00
UNOPENED PACK (5 CARDS) 4.00 6.00
COMMON CARD (1-60) .20 .50
*FOIL: .75X TO 2X BASIC CARDS
*GOLD: 3X TO 8X BASIC CARDS

2020 Rittenhouse Game of Thrones Season Eight Acetate

COMPLETE SET (20) 100.00 200.00
COMMON CARD (T01-T20) 6.00 15.00
STATED ODDS 1:96
T05 Daenerys Targaryen 10.00 25.00

2020 Rittenhouse Game of Thrones Season Eight Autographed Relic

NNO Sophie Turner S 100.00 200.00

2020 Rittenhouse Game of Thrones Season Eight Beautiful Death Poster Art

COMPLETE SET (6) 12.00 30.00
COMMON CARD (BD68-BD73) 3.00 8.00
*GOLD: 1.2X TO 3X BASIC CARDS
STATED ODDS 1:72

2020 Rittenhouse Game of Thrones Season Eight Blue Autographs

COMMON AUTO 15.00 40.00
STATED OVERALL ODDS 1:24
L = 300-500 COPIES
VL = 200-300 COPIES
EL = 100-200 COPIES
S = 100 OR FEWER COPIES
FAIRLEY IS ARCHIVE BOX EXCLUSIVE
NNO Michelle Fairley S AB 60.00 120.00

2020 Rittenhouse Game of Thrones Season Eight Bordered Autographs

COMMON AUTO 6.00 15.00
STATED OVERALL ODDS 1:24
L = 300-500 COPIES
VL = 200-300 COPIES
EL = 100-200 COPIES
S = 100 OR FEWER COPIES
NNO Joe Dempsie S 75.00 150.00
NNO Lena Headey S 75.00 150.00

2020 Rittenhouse Game of Thrones Season Eight Case-Toppers

COMPLETE SET (4) 12.00 30.00
COMMON CARD (CT1-CT4) 4.00 10.00
STATED ODDS 1:CASE
CT2 The Lannisters Send Their Regards 8.00 20.00

2020 Rittenhouse Game of Thrones Season Eight Dragonstone Markers

COMPLETE SET (8) 25.00 60.00
COMMON CARD (DM1-DM8) 5.00 12.00
STATED ODDS 1:288
DM3 Targaryen 6.00 15.00

2020 Rittenhouse Game of Thrones Season Eight Dual Autographs

COMMON AUTO 12.00 30.00
STATED OVERALL ODDS 1:24
L = 300-500 COPIES
VL = 200-300 COPIES
EL = 100-200 COPIES
S = 100 OR FEWER COPIES
NNO Faye Marsay/Tom Wlaschiha L 15.00 40.00
NNO Iain Glen/Bella Ramsey VL 75.00 200.00
NNO Lena Headey/Dean-Charles Chapman EL75.00150.00
NNO Maisie Williams/David Bradley S 125.00 250.00
NNO Rory McCann/Hafpor Julius Bjornsson EL 60.00 120.00
NNO Rory McCann/Maisie Williams S 250.00 500.00
NNO Sean Bean/Michelle Fairley EL 100.00 200.00
NNO Maisie Williams/Joe Dempsie 9CI 125.00 250.00
NNO Lena Headey/Pilou Asbaek S AB 75.00 150.00

2020 Rittenhouse Game of Thrones Season Eight Dual Booklet Autograph

NNO Peter Dinklage/Sophie Turner S 200.00 400.00

2020 Rittenhouse Game of Thrones Season Eight Dual Relic

COMPLETE SET (1)
6-CASE INCENTIVE EXCLUSIVE
NNO Daenerys Targaryen 6CI 75.00 150.00

2020 Rittenhouse Game of Thrones Season Eight For the Throne

COMPLETE SET (11) 100.00 200.00
COMMON CARD (F01-F11) 8.00 20.00
STATED ODDS 1:144
F02 Daenerys Targaryen 20.00 50.00

2020 Rittenhouse Game of Thrones Season Eight Full Bleed Autographs

COMMON AUTO 6.00 15.00
STATED OVERALL ODDS 1:24
L = 300-500 COPIES
VL = 200-300 COPIES
EL = 100-200 COPIES
S = 100 OR FEWER COPIES
NNO Richard Dormer L 12.00 30.00
NNO Dan Hildebrand VL 8.00 20.00
NNO Marc Rissmann VL 8.00 20.00
NNO Andy Kellegher VL 8.00 20.00
NNO Nell Williams VL 10.00 25.00

2020 Rittenhouse Game of Thrones Season Eight Gold Autographs

COMMON AUTO 6.00 15.00
STATED ODDS 1:24
L = 300-500 COPIES
VL = 200-300 COPIES
EL = 100-200 COPIES
S = 100 OR FEWER COPIES
NNO David Bradley EL 10.00 25.00
NNO Hafpor Julius Bjornsson EL 25.00 60.00
NNO Miltos Yerolemou VL 8.00 20.00
NNO Nell Williams VL 8.00 20.00
NNO Pilou Asbaek VL 8.00 20.00
NNO Rose Leslie EL 30.00 75.00
NNO Tom Wlaschiha EL 15.00 40.00

2020 Rittenhouse Game of Thrones Season Eight Inscriptions

COMMON ASBAEK 15.00 40.00
COMMON BEAN
COMMON BEATTIE 12.00 30.00
COMMON BLANE 10.00 25.00
COMMON BRAKE 15.00 40.00
COMMON BROWN 10.00 25.00
COMMON CARTER 8.00 20.00
COMMON CHAPMAN 12.00 30.00
COMMON COSTER-WALDAU 125.00 250.00
COMMON DIONISOTTI 6.00 15.00
COMMON EMMANUEL 30.00 75.00
COMMON FACIOLI 15.00 40.00
COMMON FAIRLEY 60.00 120.00
COMMON FLYNN 50.00 100.00
COMMON GORMAN 8.00 20.00
COMMON HANMORE 8.00 20.00
COMMON HAYES 8.00 20.00
COMMON JONES 10.00 25.00
COMMON KEKILLI 12.00 30.00
COMMON LESLIE 100.00 200.00
COMMON MAGEE 10.00 25.00
COMMON MARSAY 15.00 40.00
COMMON MCCANN 50.00 100.00
COMMON MCELHINNEY 12.00 30.00
COMMON MCKEE 10.00 25.00
COMMON NAIR 6.00 15.00
COMMON NAIRN 25.00 60.00
COMMON PLESTER 6.00 15.00
COMMON RAMSEY 125.00 300.00
COMMON RHEON 20.00 50.00
COMMON RUSSELL 10.00 25.00
COMMON SCOLDING 10.00 25.00
COMMON SIMON 6.00 15.00
COMMON STANLEY 10.00 25.00
COMMON SUMPTER 10.00 25.00
COMMON TENA 15.00 40.00
COMMON TUDOR 6.00 15.00
COMMON VANSITTART 12.00 30.00
COMMON VLAHOS 8.00 20.00
COMMON WADDINGHAM 10.00 25.00
COMMON WEBSTER 10.00 25.00
COMMON WHYTE 10.00 25.00
COMMON WILLIAMS 75.00 150.00
COMMON WLASCHIHA 30.00 75.00
COMMON YEROLEMOU 20.00 50.00
STATED ODDS 1:24

2020 Rittenhouse Game of Thrones Season Eight Map Markers

COMPLETE SET (3) 12.00 30.00
COMMON CARD (MM7-MM9) 6.00 15.00
STATED ODDS 1:288
MM7 The Sellswords 6.00 15.00
MM8 House Bolton 6.00 15.00
MM9 Stannis Baratheon 6.00 15.00

2020 Rittenhouse Game of Thrones Season Eight Quotables

COMPLETE SET W/RR (10) 25.00 60.00
COMPLETE SET W/O RR (9) 6.00 15.00
COMMON CARD (Q71-Q80) 1.25 3.00
STATED ODDS 1:12
Q80 IS RITTENHOUSE REWARD
Q80 Quotable RR 20.00 50.00

2020 Rittenhouse Game of Thrones Season Eight Relationships

COMPLETE SET (18) 12.00 30.00
COMMON CARD (DL51-DL68) 1.00 2.50
*GOLD: 2X TO 5X BASIC CARDS
STATED ODDS 1:24

2020 Rittenhouse Game of Thrones Season Eight Relics

COMMON MEM 15.00 40.00
STATED ODDS 1:192
VR13 Tyrion Lannister 20.00 50.00
VR14 Sansa Stark 25.00 60.00
VR15 Daenerys Targaryen 30.00 75.00

2020 Rittenhouse Game of Thrones Season Eight Valyrian Steel Autographs

COMMON AUTO 6.00 15.00
STATED OVERALL ODDS 1:24
L = 300-500 COPIES
VL = 200-300 COPIES
EL = 100-200 COPIES
S = 100 OR FEWER COPIES
NNO Dean-Charles Chapman EL 8.00 20.00
NNO Hannah Waddingham L 10.00 25.00
NNO Kate Dickie EL 8.00 20.00
NNO Natalia Tena EL 12.00 30.00

2020 Rittenhouse Game of Thrones Season Eight Promos

COMPLETE SET (2)
COMMON CARD (P1-P2)

P1 General Distribution 2.50 6.00
P2 Album Exclusive

2020 Rittenhouse Game of Thrones The Complete Series

COMPLETE SET (73) 8.00 20.00
UNOPENED BOX (24 PACKS) 75.00 125.00
UNOPENED PACK (5 CARDS) 3.00 5.00
UNOPENED ARCHIVE BOX 600.00 1000.00
COMMON CARD (1-73) .25 .60
*GOLD/175: 5X TO 12X BASIC CARDS

2020 Rittenhouse Game of Thrones The Complete Series Archive Cut Autograph Relic

NNO Emilia Clarke 3500.00 7000.00

2020 Rittenhouse Game of Thrones The Complete Series Blue Autographs

COMMON AUTO 6.00 15.00
STATED OVERALL ODDS 1:24
NNO Finn Jones VL 8.00 20.00
NNO Roxanne McKee VL 10.00 25.00
NNO Sibel Kekilli L 12.00 30.00

2020 Rittenhouse Game of Thrones The Complete Series Bordered Autographs

COMMON AUTO 8.00 20.00
STATED OVERALL ODDS 1:24
NNO Anton Lesser EL 12.00 30.00
NNO Mark Gatiss EL 12.00 30.00

2020 Rittenhouse Game of Thrones The Complete Series The Cast

COMPLETE SET (100) 150.00 300.00
COMMON CARD (C001-C100) 2.00 5.00
*GOLD/75: .75X TO 2X BASIC CARDS
RANDOMLY INSERTED INTO PACKS

2020 Rittenhouse Game of Thrones The Complete Series Dual Autographs

COMMON AUTO 15.00 40.00
STATED OVERALL ODDS 1:24
NNO A.Gillen/K.Dickie EL 30.00 75.00
NNO A.Gillen/R.Vansittart S 50.00 100.00
NNO A.Gillen/S.Bean EL 100.00 200.00
NNO A.Lesser/H.Bjornsson EL 25.00 60.00
NNO A.Lesser/L.Headey EL 60.00 120.00
NNO A.Lesser/N.Coster-Waldau EL 60.00 120.00
NNO A.Lesser/P.Asbaek EL 20.00 50.00
NNO C.Hope/I.Rheon EL 30.00 75.00
NNO I.Glen/I.McElhinney VL 20.00 50.00
NNO J.Anderson/N.Emmanuel VL 50.00 100.00
NNO J.Flynn/D.Portman VL 20.00 50.00
NNO K.Nairn/S.Coleman VL 20.00 50.00
NNO L.Headey/H.Bjornsson EL 75.00 150.00
NNO L.Headey/H.Waddingham EL 60.00 120.00
NNO M.Williams/F.Marsay S 150.00 300.00
NNO M.Stanley/J.Bradley EL 25.00 60.00
NNO M.Fairley/K.Dickie EL 50.00 100.00
NNO M.Fairley/R.Donachie VL 20.00 50.00
NNO N.Emmanuel/I.McElhinney VL 25.00 60.00
NNO R.McCann/E.Simon EL 30.00 75.00

2020 Rittenhouse Game of Thrones The Complete Series Dual Relics

RANDOMLY INSERTED INTO PACKS
SD1 Daenerys-Tyrion 100.00 200.00
(9-Case Incentive)
SD2 Tyrion-Daenerys 75.00 150.00

2020 Rittenhouse Game of Thrones The Complete Series Full Bleed Autographs

COMMON AUTO 6.00 15.00
STATED OVERALL ODDS 1:24
NNO Bella Ramsey VL 60.00 150.00
NNO Daniel Portman S 30.00 75.00
NNO Donald Sumpter VL 8.00 20.00
NNO Faye Marsay VL 10.00 25.00
NNO Hafpor Julius Bjornsson EL 25.00 60.00
NNO Ian Davies VL 8.00 20.00
NNO Maisie Williams S 150.00 300.00
NNO Nathalie Emmanuel S 60.00 120.00
NNO Nicolaj Coster-Waldau S 125.00 250.00
NNO Pilou Asbaek S 20.00 50.00
NNO Samantha Spiro VL 12.00 30.00
NNO Tara Fitzgerald VL 12.00 30.00

2020 Rittenhouse Game of Thrones The Complete Series Gold Autographs

COMMON AUTO 6.00 15.00
STATED OVERALL ODDS 1:24
NNO Burn Gorman EL 10.00 25.00
NNO Cedric Henderson EL 12.00 30.00
NNO Dominic Carter EL 8.00 20.00
NNO Ian Whyte VL 12.00 30.00
NNO Kate Dickie EL 10.00 25.00
NNO Rupert Vansittart EL 8.00 20.00
NNO Tim Plester EL 10.00 25.00

2020 Rittenhouse Game of Thrones The Complete Series Inscription Autographs

COMMON D. BRADLEY 50.00 100.00
COMMON J. BRADLEY 50.00 100.00
COMMON COLEMAN 30.00 75.00
COMMON DAVIES 15.00 40.00
COMMON DICKIE 50.00 100.00
COMMON GATISS 60.00 120.00
COMMON GILLEN 250.00 500.00
COMMON GLEN 60.00 120.00
COMMON HEADEY 200.00 350.00
COMMON HOPE 30.00 75.00
COMMON LESSER 50.00 100.00
COMMON PARKINSON 30.00 75.00
COMMON PORTMAN 30.00 75.00
COMMON SPIRO 30.00 75.00
COMMON WADDINGHAM
STATED OVERALL ODDS 1:24

2020 Rittenhouse Game of Thrones The Complete Series Maps of the Realm

COMPLETE SET (18) 12.00 30.00
COMMON CARD (M01-M18) 1.25 3.00
STATED ODDS 1:24

2020 Rittenhouse Game of Thrones The Complete Series Pairs

COMPLETE SET W/RR (19) 50.00 100.00
COMPLETE SET W/O RR (18) 15.00 40.00
COMMON CARD (R01-R18) 1.25 3.00
STATED ODDS 1:24
R19 IS RITTENHOUSE REWARD EXCLUSIVE
R19 Daenerys Targaryen/Ser
Jorah Mormont RR 30.00 75.00

2020 Rittenhouse Game of Thrones The Complete Series Progressions Then and Now Metal

COMMON CARD (T01-T14) 10.00 25.00
STATED ODDS 1:144
T01 Daenerys Targaryen 25.00 60.00
T07 Sansa Stark 15.00 40.00

2020 Rittenhouse Game of Thrones The Complete Series Relics

COMPLETE SET (5)
COMMON MEM 30.00 75.00
RANDOMLY INSERTED INTO PACKS
DC1 Jon Snow/Robb Stark Cloaks 50.00 100.00
DC2 The Hound/Jaqen H'ghar Capes 50.00 100.00
DC4 Cersei's Dresses 50.00 100.00
VR18 Daenerys Targaryen Gloves 75.00 150.00
(6-Case Incentive)

2020 Rittenhouse Game of Thrones The Complete Series Sigil Case-Toppers

COMPLETE SET (2) 8.00 20.00
COMMON CARD 6.00 15.00
STATED ODDS 1:CASE

2020 Rittenhouse Game of Thrones The Complete Series Valyrian Steel Autographs

COMMON AUTO 6.00 15.00
STATED OVERALL ODDS 1:24
NNO David Bradley VL 8.00 20.00
NNO Ian Hanmore EL 8.00 20.00
NNO Lino Facioli EL 8.00 20.00

2022 Rittenhouse Game of Thrones The Complete Series Volume 2

COMPLETE SET (72) 10.00 25.00
UNOPENED BOX (3 PACKS) 125.00 200.00
UNOPENED PACK (10 CARDS) 50.00 75.00
COMMON CARD (1-72) .25 .60
*GOLD/50: 6X TO 12X BASIC CARDS
*RED/25: 6X TO 15X BASIC CARDS

2022 Rittenhouse Game of Thrones The Complete Series Volume 2 '21 Iron Anniversary Expansion

COMPLETE SET (99) 20.00 50.00
COMMON CARD (199-297) .40 1.00
*COPPER/99: 3X TO 8X BASIC CARDS
*GOLD/50: 3X TO 8X BASIC CARDS
*RED/25: 6X TO 15X BASIC CARDS
STATED ODDS 1:1

2022 Rittenhouse Game of Thrones The Complete Series Volume 2 '21 Iron Anniversary Metal Expressions

COMPLETE SET (18) 30.00 75.00
COMMON CARD (H37-H54) 3.00 8.00
STATED ODDS 1:3

2022 Rittenhouse Game of Thrones The Complete Series Volume 2 Artifex Metal

COMMON CARD (AF28-AF39) 125.00 300.00
STATED PRINT RUN 25 SER.#'d SETS
AF28 Daenerys Targaryen by Chris Meeks 300.00 800.00
AF30 Jaime Lannister by Chris Meeks 150.00 400.00
AF31 Jon Snow 250.00 600.00
AF32 Robb Stark by Carlos Cabaleiro 400.00 1000.00
AF36 Missandei by Carlos Cabaleiro 200.00 500.00
AF39 Ramsay Bolton by Louise Draper 200.00 500.00

2022 Rittenhouse Game of Thrones The Complete Series Volume 2 Autographed Costume

NNO Kit Harington

2022 Rittenhouse Game of Thrones The Complete Series Volume 2 Blue Autographs

COMMON AUTO 8.00 20.00
STATED OVERALL ODDS 2:BOX
L = 300-500 COPIES
VL = 200-300 COPIES
EL = 100-200 COPIES
S = 100 OR FEWER COPIES
NNO Gethin Anthony L 10.00 25.00
NNO Iain Glen VL 30.00 75.00
NNO Jessica Henwick L 20.00 50.00
NNO Keisha Castle-Hughes L 12.00 30.00
NNO Kerry Ingram L
NNO Kerry Ingram VL
NNO Natalia Tena L 12.00 30.00
NNO Ron Donachie VL 15.00 40.00
NNO Yuri Kolokolnikov L 10.00 25.00

2022 Rittenhouse Game of Thrones The Complete Series Volume 2 Bordered Autographs

COMMON AUTO 8.00 20.00
STATED OVERALL ODDS 2:BOX
L = 300-500 COPIES
VL = 200-300 COPIES
EL = 100-200 COPIES
S = 100 OR FEWER COPIES
NNO Dar Salim VL 10.00 25.00
NNO Harry Grasby VL 12.00 30.00
NNO Joseph Naufahu VL 15.00 40.00
NNO Robert Pugh VL 30.00 75.00
NNO Ross Mullan L 12.00 30.00
NNO Steven Cole VL 20.00 50.00

2022 Rittenhouse Game of Thrones The Complete Series Volume 2 Cut Signature

NNO Diana Rigg 1000.00 2000.00

2022 Rittenhouse Game of Thrones The Complete Series Volume 2 Dragonstone

COMPLETE SET (9) 10.00 25.00
COMMON CARD (D1-D9) 1.50 4.00
STATED ODDS 1:3

2022 Rittenhouse Game of Thrones The Complete Series Volume 2 Dual Autographs

COMMON AUTO 50.00 125.00
STATED OVERALL ODDS 2:BOX
L = 300-500 COPIES
VL = 200-300 COPIES
EL = 100-200 COPIES
S = 100 OR FEWER COPIES
NNO Emilia Clarke/Kit Harington S 3000.00 7500.00
NNO Jacob Anderson/Nikolaj
Coster-Waldau VL 100.00 250.00

2022 Rittenhouse Game of Thrones The Complete Series Volume 2 Full Bleed Autographs

COMMON AUTO 6.00 15.00
STATED OVERALL ODDS 2:BOX
L = 300-500 COPIES
VL = 200-300 COPIES
EL = 100-200 COPIES
S = 100 OR FEWER COPIES
NNO Art Parkinson L 8.00 20.00
NNO Brian Fortune 8.00 20.00
NNO Dean S. Jagger L 8.00 20.00
NNO Eddie Jackson 8.00 20.00
NNO Edward Dogliani L 10.00 25.00
NNO Emilia Clarke S 3000.00 8000.00
NNO Finn Jones L 12.00 30.00
NNO Gemma Whelan L 12.00 30.00
NNO Gerard Jordan L 8.00 20.00
NNO Gwendoline Christie S
NNO Jack Gleeson L 30.00 75.00
NNO Jacob Anderson VL 50.00 125.00
NNO Jazzy de Lisser 10.00 25.00
NNO Joseph Naufahu VL 15.00 40.00
NNO Ross Mullan L 25.00 60.00
NNO Sophie Turner VL 125.00 300.00
NNO Trevor Allan Davies L 10.00 25.00
NNO Wilko Johnson L 15.00 40.00

2022 Rittenhouse Game of Thrones The Complete Series Volume 2 Gold Autographs

COMMON AUTO 10.00 25.00
STATED OVERALL ODDS 2:BOX
L = 300-500 COPIES
VL = 200-300 COPIES
EL = 100-200 COPIES
S = 100 OR FEWER COPIES
NNO Andy Kellegher VL 15.00 40.00
NNO Dean S. Jagger VL 20.00 50.00
NNO Eline Powell VL 25.00 60.00
NNO Kae Alexander VL 25.00 60.00
NNO Kerry Ingram VL 40.00 100.00
NNO Mark Stanley VL 15.00 40.00
NNO Steven Cole VL 12.00 30.00

2022 Rittenhouse Game of Thrones The Complete Series Volume 2 Head of the House

COMPLETE SET (11) 10.00 25.00
COMMON CARD (HH01-HH11) 1.50 4.00
STATED ODDS 1:3

2022 Rittenhouse Game of Thrones The Complete Series Volume 2 In Memoriam

COMPLETE SET (36) 60.00 150.00
COMMON CARD (M01-M36) 3.00 8.00
STATED ODDS 1:3

2022 Rittenhouse Game of Thrones The Complete Series Volume 2 Inscriptions

COMMON ANDERSON 75.00 200.00
COMMON BLOWERS 15.00 40.00
COMMON DAVIS 15.00 40.00
COMMON DE LISSER 20.00 50.00
COMMON DINKLAGE
COMMON DOGLIANI
COMMON FARESS 30.00 75.00
COMMON FITZGERALD 10.00 25.00
COMMON FORTUNE 10.00 25.00
COMMON HARINGTON 2500.00 6000.00
COMMON JACKSON 8.00 20.00
COMMON JAGGER 12.00 30.00
COMMON JOHNSON 30.00 75.00
COMMON JONES 15.00 40.00
COMMON JORDAN 12.00 30.00
COMMON KOLOKOLNIKOV 12.00 30.00
COMMON MCGINLEY 8.00 20.00
COMMON MCKEOWN 10.00 25.00
COMMON NAUFAHU 30.00 75.00
COMMON OPAREI 8.00 20.00
COMMON PRADELSKA 12.00 30.00
COMMON QUINN 40.00 100.00
COMMON RATTRAY 10.00 25.00
COMMON RODGER 8.00 20.00
COMMON TEALE 10.00 25.00
COMMON VAN HOUTEN 30.00 75.00
COMMON WAY 8.00 20.00
STATED ODDS 1:BOX

2022 Rittenhouse Game of Thrones The Complete Series Volume 2 Quotables

COMPLETE SET W/RR (13)
COMPLETE SET W/O RR (12) 12.00 30.00
COMMON CARD (Q81-Q93) 2.00 5.00
STATED ODDS 1:3
Q93 Quotable Game of Thrones
(Rittenhouse Reward)

2022 Rittenhouse Game of Thrones The Complete Series Volume 2 Red Sigil Autographs

COMMON AUTO 8.00 20.00
STATED OVERALL ODDS 2:BOX
L = 300-500 COPIES
VL = 200-300 COPIES
EL = 100-200 COPIES
S = 100 OR FEWER COPIES
NNO Daniel Portman L 10.00 25.00
NNO Gemma Whelan L 12.00 30.00
NNO Gethin Anthony L 10.00 25.00
NNO Iain Glen VL 40.00 100.00
NNO Jack Gleeson L 20.00 50.00
NNO Jack Gleeson L/(blue ink)
NNO Jessica Henwick L 15.00 40.00
NNO Kae Alexander VL 15.00 40.00
NNO Keisha Castle-Hughes L 15.00 40.00
NNO Kerry Ingram VL 12.00 30.00
NNO Natalia Tena L 12.00 30.00
NNO Sophie Turner VL 100.00 250.00

2022 Rittenhouse Game of Thrones The Complete Series Volume 2 Valyrian Steel Autographs

COMMON AUTO 6.00 15.00
STATED OVERALL ODDS 2:BOX
L = 300-500 COPIES
VL = 200-300 COPIES
EL = 100-200 COPIES
S = 100 OR FEWER COPIES
NNO Kerr Logan L 8.00 20.00
NNO Wilf Scolding 8.00 20.00

2022 Rittenhouse Game of Thrones The Complete Series Volume 2 Vistas

COMPLETE SET (21) 30.00 75.00
COMMON CARD (V01-V21) 2.50 6.00
STATED ODDS 1:3

2022 Rittenhouse Game of Thrones The Complete Series Volume 2 Promos

P1 Album Exclusive 8.00 20.00

2019 Rittenhouse Game of Thrones Inflexions

COMPLETE SET (150) 60.00 120.00
UNOPENED BOX (3 PACKS) 125.00 200.00
UNOPENED PACK (15 CARDS) 45.00 70.00
COMMON CARD (1-150) .60 1.50
*SILVER/75: 1.2X TO 3X BASIC CARDS
*WHITE/50: 1.5X TO 4X BASIC CARDS
*GOLD PLATINUM/40: 3X TO 8X BASIC CARDS
*RED/25: 4X TO 10X BASIC CARDS

2019 Rittenhouse Game of Thrones Inflexions Archive Cut Autograph Relics

COMMON AUTO 75.00 150.00
STATED OVERALL ODDS 2:BOX
EL = 100-200 COPIES
S = 100 OR FEWER COPIES
NNO Emilia Clarke S 2500.00 4000.00
NNO Jason Momoa S 125.00 250.00
NNO Kit Harington S 500.00 1000.00
NNO Kristian Nairn S 300.00 600.00
NNO Peter Dinklage EL 100.00 200.00

2019 Rittenhouse Game of Thrones Inflexions Artifex Metal Expansion

COMMON HOBBY (AF7-AF13) 125.00 250.00
COMMON INTERNATIONAL (AF14-AF17)
RANDOMLY INSERTED INTO PACKS
AF7 Daenerys Targaryen 500.00 1000.00
AF8 Jon Snow 200.00 400.00
AF11 Arya Stark 400.00 700.00
AF13 Night King 150.00 300.00
AF14 Daenerys Targaryen 800.00 1200.00
AF15 Jon Snow 350.00 700.00
AF16 Arya Stark 500.00 1000.00
AF17 Night King

2019 Rittenhouse Game of Thrones Inflexions Blue Autograph

NNO Tara Fitzgerald EL IE 60.00 120.00

2019 Rittenhouse Game of Thrones Inflexions Bordered Autographs

COMMON AUTO 6.00 15.00
STATED OVERALL ODDS 2:BOX
L = 300-500 COPIES
VL = 200-300 COPIES
EL = 100-200 COPIES
S = 100 OR FEWER COPIES
1 Carice Van Houten EL 30.00 75.00
2 John Bradley L 10.00 25.00
4 Michiel Huisman VL 12.00 30.00
6 Tara Fitzgerald EL 15.00 40.00
(Hobby Exclusive)

2019 Rittenhouse Game of Thrones Inflexions Dual Autographs

COMMON AUTO 15.00 40.00
STATED OVERALL ODDS 2:BOX
L = 300-500 COPIES
VL = 200-300 COPIES
EL = 100-200 COPIES
S = 100 OR FEWER COPIES
NNO C.Van Houten/S.Dillane EL 125.00 250.00
NNO E.Kendrick/I.Hempstead-Wright VL 25.00 60.00
NNO E.Kendrick/T.Brodie Sangster VL 25.00 60.00
NNO G.Whelan/M.Feast VL 20.00 50.00
NNO I.Hempstead-Wright/J.Mawle VL 20.00 50.00
NNO J.Gleeson/L.Headey EL 75.00 150.00
NNO J.Broadbent/J.Bradley EL 75.00 150.00
NNO J.Dempsie/C.Van Houten EL 75.00 150.00
NNO J.Quinn/D.Kirrane L 20.00 75.00
NNO K.Castle-Hughes/J.Henwick VL 30.00 75.00
NNO K.Hivju/R.Leslie VL 50.00 100.00
NNO N.Tiger Free/T.Sebastianl VL 25.00 60.00
NNO P.Dinklage/S.Kekilli EL 100.00 200.00
NNO S.Turner/J.Gleeson EL 100.00 200.00
NNO T.Fitzgerald/S.Dillane VL 20.00 50.00
NNO W.Scolding/A.Franciosi VL 20.00 50.00

2019 Rittenhouse Game of Thrones Inflexions Full-Bleed Autographs

COMMON AUTO 6.00 15.00
STATED OVERALL ODDS 2:BOX
L = 300-500 COPIES
VL = 200-300 COPIES
EL = 100-200 COPIES
S = 100 OR FEWER COPIES
NNO Isaac Hempstead-Wright VL 30.00 75.00
NNO Joseph Quinn VL 40.00 100.00
NNO Lena Headey EL 125.00 250.00
NNO Megan Parkinson L 8.00 20.00
NNO Sophie Turner EL 75.00 150.00

2019 Rittenhouse Game of Thrones Inflexions Gold Autographs

COMMON AUTO 6.00 15.00
STATED OVERALL ODDS 2:BOX
L = 300-500 COPIES
VL = 200-300 COPIES
EL = 100-200 COPIES
S = 100 OR FEWER COPIES
NNO Aisling Franciosi VL 10.00 25.00
NNO Bella Ramsey VL 100.00 250.00
NNO Donald Sumpter VL 8.00 20.00
NNO Ellie Kendrick VL 10.00 25.00
NNO Esme Bianco L 8.00 20.00
NNO Gemma Whelan VL 12.00 30.00
NNO Harry Lloyd VL 12.00 30.00
NNO Jack Gleeson S 100.00 200.00
NNO James Faulkner VL 8.00 20.00
NNO Jessica Henwick VL 15.00 40.00
NNO Jim Broadbent EL 50.00 100.00
NNO Joe Dempsie EL 60.00 120.00
NNO Joseph Mawle VL 15.00 40.00
NNO Keisha Castle-Hughes VL 12.00 30.00
NNO Kristofer Hivju VL 25.00 60.00
NNO Michael Feast VL 8.00 20.00
NNO Nathalie Emmanuel VL 20.00 50.00
NNO Nell Tiger Free VL 20.00 50.00
NNO Owen Teale L 8.00 20.00
NNO Paul Kaye VL 10.00 25.00
NNO Richard Dormer VL IE 60.00 120.00
NNO Roger Allam VL 10.00 25.00
NNO Rory McCann L 20.00 50.00
NNO Rosabell Laurenti Sellers EL 50.00 100.00
NNO Stephen Dillane EL 15.00 40.00
NNO Tara Fitzgerald VL 15.00 40.00
NNO Thomas Brodie Sangster L 8.00 20.00
NNO Toby Sebastian VL 8.00 20.00
NNO Tom Hopper VL 12.00 30.00
NNO Wilf Scolding VL 8.00 20.00

2019 Rittenhouse Game of Thrones Inflexions Laser Cuts

COMPLETE SET (18) 10.00 25.00
COMMON CARD (L19-L36) 1.25 3.00
STATED ODDS 1:1 HOBBY BOX

2019 Rittenhouse Game of Thrones Inflexions Lenticular

COMPLETE SET (20) 15.00 40.00
COMMON CARD (L1-L20) 2.00 5.00
STATED ODDS 1:1

2019 Rittenhouse Game of Thrones Inflexions Mirror Relationships

COMPLETE SET (12) 30.00 75.00
COMMON CARD (RM17-RM28) 3.00 8.00
STATED ODDS 1:1 INTERNATIONAL BOX
RM17 Daenerys Targaryen and Jon Snow 12.00 30.00
RM22 Bran Stark and Hodor 6.00 15.00
RM23 Night King and Benjen Stark 5.00 12.00
RM24 Davos Seaworth and Gendry 4.00 10.00
RM25 Arya Stark and The Hound 4.00 10.00
RM26 Tyrion Lannister and Shae 8.00 20.00

2019 Rittenhouse Game of Thrones Inflexions Relics

COMPLETE SET (5) 100.00 200.00
COMMON CARD (VR7-VR11) 15.00 40.00
RANDOMLY INSERTED INTO PACKS
VR7 Daenerys Targaryen 50.00 100.00
VR9 Daenerys Targaryen 60.00 120.00
VR11 Daenerys Targaryen 30.00 75.00

2019 Rittenhouse Game of Thrones Inflexions Stamps

COMPLETE SET (15) 200.00 400.00
COMMON CARD (S1-S15) 12.00 30.00
RANDOMLY INSERTED INTO PACKS
S1 Iron Throne 20.00 50.00
S2 Sansa Stark 20.00 50.00
S3 Tyrion Lannister 20.00 50.00
S7 Arya Stark 15.00 40.00
S11 Daenerys Targaryen 25.00 60.00

2019 Rittenhouse Game of Thrones Inflexions Valyrian Autographs

COMMON AUTO 6.00 15.00
STATED OVERALL ODDS 2:BOX
L = 300-500 COPIES
VL = 200-300 COPIES
EL = 100-200 COPIES
S = 100 OR FEWER COPIES
NNO Aidan Gillen VL 15.00 40.00
NNO Bella Ramsey VL 50.00 125.00
NNO Carice Van Houten EL 20.00 50.00
NNO Esme Bianco L 10.00 25.00
NNO Gemma Whelan VL 12.00 30.00
NNO Jack Gleeson VL 15.00 40.00
NNO Joseph Mawle VL 10.00 25.00
NNO Kristofer Hivju VL 25.00 60.00
NNO Michelle Fairley VL 25.00 60.00
NNO Nathalie Emmanuel L 20.00 50.00
NNO Nell Tiger Free VL 15.00 40.00
NNO Paul Kaye L 8.00 20.00
NNO Pilou Asbaek L 8.00 20.00
NNO Richard Dormer VL HE 12.00 30.00
NNO Roger Allam VL 8.00 20.00
NNO Ron Donachie L 8.00 20.00
NNO Rosabell Laurenti Sellers VL 20.00 50.00
NNO Roxanne McKee L 8.00 20.00
NNO Stephen Dillane L 10.00 25.00
NNO Tom Hopper VL 8.00 20.00

2019 Rittenhouse Game of Thrones Inflexions Promo

P1 GOT Inflexions ALB 10.00 25.00

2021 Rittenhouse Game of Thrones Iron Anniversary

COMPLETE SET (99) 10.00 25.00
UNOPENED BOX (8 PACKS) 125.00 200.00
UNOPENED PACK (48 CARDS) 15.00 25.00
COMMON CARD (1-99) .30 .75
*COPPER/199: 4X TO 10X BASIC CARDS
*IRON/99: 6X TO 15X BASIC CARDS
*GOLD/99: 6X TO 15X BASIC CARDS
*RED/50: 8X TO 20X BASIC CARDS

2021 Rittenhouse Game of Thrones Iron Anniversary 3-D Dectation

COMMON CARD (T1-T2) 25.00 60.00
RANDOMLY INSERTED INTO PACKS
T2 Raven 30.00 75.00

2021 Rittenhouse Game of Thrones Iron Anniversary Artifex Metal

COMMON CARD () 250.00 500.00
STATED PRINT RUN 25 SER.#'d SETS
AF19 Jon Snow 400.00 800.00
AF25 Davos Seaworth 300.00 600.00
AF27 Daenerys Targaryen 600.00 1000.00

2021 Rittenhouse Game of Thrones Iron Anniversary Autographed Quotes

COMMON AUTO 300.00 600.00
STATED OVERALL ODDS 1:24

2021 Rittenhouse Game of Thrones Iron Anniversary Autographed Relic
NNO Lena Headey/Cersei Lannister EL 200.00

2021 Rittenhouse Game of Thrones Iron Anniversary Battles
COMPLETE SET (11) 10.00 25.00
COMMON CARD 2.00 5.00
STATED ODDS 1:9

2021 Rittenhouse Game of Thrones Iron Anniversary Blue Autographs
STATED OVERALL ODDS 1:24
L = 300-500 COPIES
VL = 200-300 COPIES
EL = 100-200 COPIES
S = 100 OR FEWER COPIES
NNO Bella Ramsey VL 60.00 150.00
NNO Ian Beattie EL 12.00 30.00
NNO Jerome Flynn VL 25.00 60.00

2021 Rittenhouse Game of Thrones Iron Anniversary Case-Toppers
COMMON CARD 8.00 20.00
STATED ODDS 1:CASE

2021 Rittenhouse Game of Thrones Iron Anniversary Dual Autographs
COMMON AUTO 15.00 40.00
STATED OVERALL ODDS 1:24
L = 300-500 COPIES
VL = 200-300 COPIES
EL = 100-200 COPIES
S = 100 OR FEWER COPIES
NNO Alfie Allen/Iwan Rheon EL 50.00 100.00
NNO Amrita Acharia/Roxanne McKee VL 30.00 75.00
NNO Ben Crompton/Mark Stanley EL 30.00 75.00
NNO Conleth Hill/Nathalie Emmanuel S 75.00 150.00
NNO Conleth Hill/Sean Bean EL 150.00 300.00
NNO Dean-Charles Chapman/Julian Glover VL20.00 50.00
NNO Isaac Hempstead-Wright/Burn Gorman VL20.0050.00
NNO Iwan Rheon/Natalia Tena EL 25.00 60.00
NNO Lena Headey/Ian Beattie S 75.00 150.00
NNO Lena Headey/Mark Gatiss EL 75.00 150.00
NNO Maisie Williams/Miltos Yerolemou S 200.00 400.00

2021 Rittenhouse Game of Thrones Iron Anniversary Expressions
COMPLETE SET (18) 20.00 50.00
COMMON CARD 2.50 6.00
STATED ODDS 1:9

2021 Rittenhouse Game of Thrones Iron Anniversary Full Bleed Autographs
STATED OVERALL ODDS 1:24
L = 300-500 COPIES
VL = 200-300 COPIES
EL = 100-200 COPIES
S = 100 OR FEWER COPIES
NNO Carice Van Houten EL 60.00 120.00
NNO James Cosmo VL 50.00 100.00
NNO John Bradley VL 25.00 60.00
NNO Nicolaj Coster-Waldau EL 100.00 200.00
NNO Rory McCann EL 50.00 100.00

2021 Rittenhouse Game of Thrones Iron Anniversary Gold Autographs
COMMON AUTO 6.00 15.00
STATED OVERALL ODDS 1:12
L = 300-500 COPIES
VL = 200-300 COPIES
EL = 100-200 COPIES
S = 100 OR FEWER COPIES
NNO Birgitte Hjort Sorensen EL 30.00 75.00
NNO Jamie Sives EL 12.00 30.00
NNO Noah Taylor EL 8.00 20.00
NNO Ralph Ineson EL 15.00 40.00
NNO Reece Noi EL 10.00 25.00
NNO Richard Brake 15.00 40.00

2021 Rittenhouse Game of Thrones Iron Anniversary Gold Icons
COMPLETE SET (5) 100.00 200.00
COMMON CARD 20.00 50.00
RANDOMLY INSERTED INTO PACKS

2021 Rittenhouse Game of Thrones Iron Anniversary Inscriptions
COMMON ACHARIA 10.00 25.00
COMMON ADDY 50.00 100.00
COMMON ALEXANDER 8.00 20.00
COMMON ALLEN 30.00 75.00
COMMON ALTIN 8.00 20.00
COMMON ANTHONY 10.00 25.00
COMMON ARMSTRONG 10.00 25.00
COMMON ASHTON-GRIFFITHS 6.00 15.00
COMMON BARNES 10.00 25.00
COMMON BENTLEY 6.00 15.00
COMMON BIANCO 15.00 40.00
COMMON BUKSTEIN 20.00 50.00
COMMON CADWALLADER 6.00 15.00
COMMON CASTLE-HUGHES 15.00 40.00
COMMON CILENTI 6.00 15.00
COMMON CLARKE 3000.00 6000.00
COMMON COLE 8.00 20.00
COMMON COSMO 20.00 50.00
COMMON CROMPTON 10.00 25.00
COMMON DAVIES 8.00 20.00
COMMON DYLAN 10.00 25.00
COMMON ELLIOTT 6.00 15.00
COMMON FAULKNER 10.00 25.00
COMMON FRY 8.00 20.00
COMMON FURDIK 60.00 120.00
COMMON GLEESON 60.00 120.00
COMMON GLOVER 10.00 25.00
COMMON HENWICK 30.00 75.00
COMMON HILL 50.00 100.00
COMMON HOPPER 12.00 30.00
COMMON HUISMAN 15.00 40.00
COMMON INESON 15.00 40.00
COMMON INGRAM 20.00 50.00
COMMON JOHANNESSON 6.00 15.00
COMMON KENDRICK 6.00 15.00
COMMON LEATHAM 8.00 20.00
COMMON LLOYD 12.00 30.00
COMMON LOGAN
COMMON NOI 6.00 15.00
COMMON O'CONNOR 8.00 20.00
COMMON O'HENNESSEY 8.00 20.00
COMMON RICHARDSON 15.00 40.00
COMMON RISSMAN 8.00 20.00
COMMON SEBASTIAN 15.00 40.00
COMMON SELLERS 25.00 60.00
COMMON SIVES 10.00 25.00
COMMON SORENSEN 15.00 40.00
COMMON STEVENS 12.00 30.00
COMMON TAYLOR 10.00 25.00
COMMON TURNER 125.00 250.00
COMMON VARMA 15.00 40.00
COMMON WOODRUFF 6.00 15.00
STATED ODDS 1:24

2021 Rittenhouse Game of Thrones Iron Anniversary Laser Cuts
COMPLETE SET (27) 30.00 75.00
COMMON CARD 2.50 6.00
STATED ODDS 1:9

2021 Rittenhouse Game of Thrones Iron Anniversary Relic Quotes
COMMON DAENERYS 60.00 120.00
COMMON JON SNOW 50.00 100.00
COMMON TYRION 50.00 100.00
S = 100 OR FEWER COPIES

2021 Rittenhouse Game of Thrones Iron Anniversary Valyrian Steel Autographs
COMMON AUTO 6.00 15.00
STATED OVERALL ODDS 1:24
L = 300-500 COPIES
VL = 200-300 COPIES
EL = 100-200 COPIES
S = 100 OR FEWER COPIES
NNO Hafpor Julius Bjornsson EL 30.00 75.00
NNO Ian Whyte VL 12.00 30.00
NNO Josef Altin L 10.00 25.00

2021 Rittenhouse Game of Thrones Iron Anniversary Promos
P1 Daenerys & Jon Snow GEN 2.50 6.00
P2 Arya Stark ALB 10.00 25.00

2021 Rittenhouse Game of Thrones Iron Anniversary Series Two
COMPLETE SET (99) 10.00 25.00
UNOPENED BOX (8 PACKS) 100.00 150.00
UNOPENED PACK (6 CARDS) 12.00 20.00
COMMON CARD .25 .60
*COPPER/199: 2X TO 5X BASIC CARDS
*GOLD/99: 12X TO 30X BASIC CARDS
*IRON/99: 15X TO 40X BASIC CARDS
*RED/50: 20X TO 50X BASIC CARDS

2021 Rittenhouse Game of Thrones Iron Anniversary Series Two 3-D Dectation
COMPLETE SET (3) 60.00 120.00
COMMON CARD 20.00 50.00
RANDOMLY INSERTED INTO PACKS

2021 Rittenhouse Game of Thrones Iron Anniversary Series Two Artifex Metal
COMMON CARD 150.00 300.00
STATED PRINT RUN 25 SER.#'d SETS
AF18 Arya Stark 200.00 400.00
AF24 Brienne of Tarth 200.00 400.00
AF26 Daenerys Targaryen 1500.00 3000.00

2021 Rittenhouse Game of Thrones Iron Anniversary Series Two Autographed Relic Quote
NNO Sophie Turner

2021 Rittenhouse Game of Thrones Iron Anniversary Series Two Battles
COMPLETE SET (11) 8.00 20.00
COMMON CARD 1.00 2.50
STATED ODDS 1:9

2021 Rittenhouse Game of Thrones Iron Anniversary Series Two Blue Autographs
COMMON AUTO 60.00 120.00
STATED OVERALL ODDS 1:24
L = 300-500 COPIES
VL = 200-300 COPIES
EL = 100-200 COPIES
S = 100 OR FEWER COPIES
NNO Sean Bean EL 75.00 150.00

2021 Rittenhouse Game of Thrones Iron Anniversary Series Two Bordered Autographs
STATED OVERALL ODDS 1:24
L = 300-500 COPIES
VL = 200-300 COPIES
EL = 100-200 COPIES
S = 100 OR FEWER COPIES
NNO Emilia Clarke S
NNO Noah Taylor EL 25.00 60.00
NNO Patrick Malahide EL 15.00 40.00

2021 Rittenhouse Game of Thrones Iron Anniversary Series Two Case-Toppers
COMPLETE SET (2) 8.00 20.00
COMMON CARD 6.00 15.00
STATED ODDS 1:CASE

2021 Rittenhouse Game of Thrones Iron Anniversary Series Two Dual Autographs
COMMON AUTO 20.00 50.00
STATED OVERALL ODDS 1:24
L = 300-500 COPIES
VL = 200-300 COPIES
EL = 100-200 COPIES
S = 100 OR FEWER COPIES
NNO S.Turner/F.Jones EL 75.00 150.00
NNO A.Gillen/C.Hill EL 75.00 150.00
NNO A.Allen/G.Whelan VL 25.00 60.00
NNO C.Hill/S.Kekilli S 100.00 200.00
NNO L.Headey/N.Williams EL 50.00 100.00
NNO L.Headey/N.Coster-Waldau S 250.00 400.00

2021 Rittenhouse Game of Thrones Iron Anniversary Series Two Expressions
COMPLETE SET (18) 30.00 75.00
COMMON CARD 2.50 6.00
STATED ODDS 1:9

2021 Rittenhouse Game of Thrones Iron Anniversary Series Two Full Bleed Autographs
COMMON AUTO 6.00 15.00
STATED OVERALL ODDS 1:24
L = 300-500 COPIES
VL = 200-300 COPIES
EL = 100-200 COPIES
S = 100 OR FEWER COPIES
NNO Clifford Barry VL 10.00 25.00
NNO Dar Salim L 8.00 20.00
NNO Ellie Kendrick VL 10.00 25.00
NNO Emilia Clarke S 4000.00 6000.00
NNO Gemma Whelan L 8.00 20.00
NNO Gerald Lepkowski VL 8.00 20.00
NNO Harry Grasby VL 12.00 30.00
NNO Mia Soteriou VL 12.00 30.00
NNO Michael McElhatton VL 10.00 25.00
NNO Patrick Malahide EL 20.00 50.00
NNO Sean Blowers VL 10.00 25.00

2021 Rittenhouse Game of Thrones Iron Anniversary Series Two Gold Autographs
STATED OVERALL ODDS 1:24
L = 300-500 COPIES
VL = 200-300 COPIES
EL = 100-200 COPIES
S = 100 OR FEWER COPIES
NNO Brenock O'Connor EL 15.00 40.00
NNO Emilia Clarke S
NNO Gwendoline Christie S 125.00 250.00
NNO Yuri Kolokolnikov VL 10.00 25.00

2021 Rittenhouse Game of Thrones Iron Anniversary Series Two Gold Icons
COMPLETE SET (5) 50.00 100.00
COMMON CARD 12.00 30.00
STATED ODDS 1:80
G02 Dragonstone 15.00 40.00
G06 House Baratheon 15.00 40.00
G08 House Stark 20.00 50.00

2021 Rittenhouse Game of Thrones Iron Anniversary Series Two Inscriptions
COMMON ALLAM 6.00 15.00
COMMON BARRY 8.00 20.00
COMMON BECKWITH 8.00 20.00
COMMON BRODIE-SANGSTER 10.00 25.00
COMMON CALLENDER 5.00 12.00
COMMON CALLENDER/1: UNPRICED DUE TO SCARCITY
COMMON CHRISTIE 100.00 200.00
COMMON CROFT 6.00 15.00
COMMON DEMPSIE 15.00 40.00
COMMON DILLANE 10.00 25.00
COMMON DONACHIE 5.00 12.00
COMMON DOWLING 6.00 15.00
COMMON FEAST 6.00 15.00
COMMON GELDER 10.00 25.00
COMMON GRASBY 5.00 12.00
COMMON HEMPSTEAD-WRIGHT 20.00 50.00
COMMON HILLENBRAND
COMMON HIVJU 60.00 120.00
COMMON INGRAM 8.00 20.00
COMMON KAYE 6.00 15.00
COMMON KILLEEN 12.00 30.00
COMMON KIRRANE 8.00 20.00

MODERN

COMMON LEPKOWSKI 6.00 15.00
COMMON MALAHIDE 20.00 50.00
COMMON MCELHATTON 6.00 15.00
COMMON MCINNERNY 6.00 15.00
COMMON MENZIES 10.00 25.00
COMMON MSAMATI 8.00 20.00
COMMON MURRAY 12.00 30.00
COMMON PARKINSON 6.00 15.00
COMMON POWELL 6.00 15.00
COMMON PRYCE 15.00 40.00
COMMON PUGH 10.00 25.00
COMMON RYCROFT 6.00 15.00
COMMON SALIM 15.00 40.00
COMMON VERREY 8.00 20.00
STATED OVERALL ODDS 1:24
L = 300-500 COPIES
VL = 200-300 COPIES
EL = 100-200 COPIES
S = 100 OR FEWER COPIES

2021 Rittenhouse Game of Thrones Iron Anniversary Series Two Laser Cuts

COMPLETE SET (27) 30.00 75.00
COMMON CARD 2.00 5.00
STATED ODDS 1:9

2021 Rittenhouse Game of Thrones Iron Anniversary Series Two Promos

P1 General Distribution 3.00 8.00
P2 Convention 5.00 12.00

2021 Rittenhouse Game of Thrones Iron Anniversary Series Two Relic Quotes

COMMON CERSEI 25.00 60.00
COMMON ROBB 20.00 50.00
COMMON SANSA 20.00 50.00
STATED PRINT RUN 100 COPIES OR FEWER

2021 Rittenhouse Game of Thrones Iron Anniversary Series Two Valyrian Steel Autographs

COMMON AUTO 10.00 25.00
STATED OVERALL ODDS 1:24
L = 300-500 COPIES
VL = 200-300 COPIES
EL = 100-200 COPIES
S = 100 OR FEWER COPIES
NNO Birgitte Hjort Sorensen EL 15.00 40.00
NNO Emilia Clarke S
NNO Gwendoline Christie S 75.00 150.00
NNO Jamie Sives EL 12.00 30.00
NNO Noah Taylor S 15.00 40.00
NNO Reece Noi EL 12.00 30.00
NNO Steven Cole VL 20.00 50.00

2017 Rittenhouse Game of Thrones Valyrian Steel

COMPLETE SET (100) 120.00 250.00
UNOPENED BOX (3 PACKS) 110.00 150.00
UNOPENED PACK (4 CARDS) 40.00 50.00
COMMON CARD (1-100) 2.50 6.00
*GOLD/100: .75X TO 2X BASIC CARDS 5.00 12.00
*PLATINUM/35: 1.5X TO 4X BASIC CARDS 10.00 25.00
1A IS AN ALBUM EXCLUSIVE
4A IS A RITTENHOUSE REWARD
PLATINUM IS 10-CASE INCENTIVE
CARDS 101-109 INSERTED IN SEASON SEVEN PACKS
1 Tyrion Lannister 3.00 8.00
1A Tyrion Lannister ALB 10.00 25.00
2 Cersei Lannister 4.00 10.00
3 Ser Jaime Lannister 4.00 10.00
4 Daenerys Targaryen 8.00 20.00
4A Daenerys Targaryen RR 120.00 250.00
5 Jon Snow 8.00 20.00
6 Sansa Stark 5.00 12.00
7 Arya Stark 5.00 12.00
9 Theon Greyjoy 3.00 8.00
15 Bronn 3.00 8.00
17 Ser Davos Seaworth 3.00 8.00
18 Sandor Clegane 4.00 10.00
24 Margaery Tyrell 5.00 12.00
27 Tormund Giantsbane 4.00 10.00
34 Robb Stark 4.00 10.00
41 Jaqen H'ghar 3.00 8.00
43 Ygritte 4.00 10.00
49 Lancel Lannister 3.00 8.00
54 Rickon Stark 3.00 8.00
58 Dragons 4.00 10.00
60 Yara Greyjoy 3.00 8.00
70 Lord Eddard Stark 4.00 10.00
84 Tyene Sand 4.00 10.00
85 Nymeria Sand 3.00 8.00
97 Doran Martell 3.00 8.00

2017 Rittenhouse Game of Thrones Valyrian Steel 3-D Lenticular

COMPLETE SET (18) 75.00 150.00
COMMON CARD (L1-L18) 3.00 8.00
L1 Daenerys' Gift 6.00 15.00
L5 Tywin arrives at Harrenhal 4.00 10.00
L11 A Test of Loyalty 5.00 12.00
L12 A Grim Wedding 4.00 10.00
L13 Drogon's Warning 6.00 15.00
L17 Failed Power Play 5.00 12.00

2017 Rittenhouse Game of Thrones Valyrian Steel ArtiFex Metal

COMPLETE SET (6) 600.00 1200.00
COMMON CARD (AF1-AF6) 120.00 250.00
STATED PRINT RUN 25 SER.#'d SETS
AF1 Tyrion Lannister 150.00 300.00
AF2 Arya Stark 150.00 300.00

2017 Rittenhouse Game of Thrones Valyrian Steel Dual Autographs

COMMON AUTO 25.00 60.00
NNO Bradley/Murray VL 30.00 75.00
NNO Harington/Leslie VL 200.00 400.00
NNO Nairn/Hempstead-Wright EL 75.00 150.00
NNO Addy/Bean EL 100.00 200.00
NNO Coster-Waldau/Flynn VL 75.00 150.00
NNO Dinklage/Portman EL 125.00 250.00
NNO Dinklage/Coster-Waldua EL 125.00 250.00

2017 Rittenhouse Game of Thrones Valyrian Steel Gold Autographs

COMMON AUTO 8.00 20.00
RANDOMLY INSERTED INTO PACKS
NNO Aidan Gillen L 15.00 40.00
NNO Alfie Allen VL 12.00 30.00
NNO Art Parkinson VL 10.00 25.00
NNO Carice van Houten VL 20.00 50.00
NNO Charles Dance VL 25.00 60.00
NNO Clive Russell VL 12.00 30.00
NNO Conleth Hill EL 20.00 50.00
NNO Faye Marsay VL 10.00 25.00
NNO Iain Glen VL 20.00 50.00
NNO Ian McElhinney VL 12.00 30.00
NNO Indira Varma L 15.00 40.00
NNO Isaac Hempstead-Wright VL 25.00 60.00
NNO Iwan Rheon VL 12.00 30.00
NNO Jacob Anderson L 12.00 30.00
NNO Jerome Flynn VL 25.00 60.00
NNO John Bradley VL 15.00 40.00
NNO Maisie Williams VL 125.00 250.00
NNO Mark Addy EL 60.00 120.00
NNO Michael McElhatton EL 25.00 60.00
NNO Natalie Dormer VL 25.00 60.00
NNO Roger Ashton-Griffiths VL 10.00 25.00
NNO Sean Bean EL 75.00 150.00
NNO Sibel Kekilli L 10.00 25.00
NNO Sophie Turner EL 75.00 150.00

2017 Rittenhouse Game of Thrones Valyrian Steel Laser Cuts

COMMON CARD (LC1-LC18) 3.00 8.00
LC1 Tyrion Lannister 4.00 10.00
LC2 Daenerys Targaryen 10.00 25.00
LC4 Jon Snow 3.00 12.00
LC5 Sansa Stark 4.00 10.00
LC10 Brienne of Tarth 4.00 10.00
LC17 Ygritte 8.00 20.00

2017 Rittenhouse Game of Thrones Valyrian Steel Pin and Coin Cards

COMPLETE SET (3) 60.00 120.00
COMMON CARD 20.00 50.00
H8 Hand of the Queen Pin 25.00 60.00

2017 Rittenhouse Game of Thrones Valyrian Steel Relics

COMMON MEM 12.00 30.00
RANDOMLY INSERTED INTO PACKS
TR1 Triple Banner Relic Card (Stark, Baratheon, Lannister) 30.00 75.00
VR1 Daenerys Targaryen Pants 300.00 450.00
VR2 Daenerys Targaryen Die-Cut Blue Dress 300.00 450.00
VR3 Daenerys Targaryen Cape 60.00 120.00
VR4 Daenerys Targaryen White Dress 60.00 120.00
VR5 Tywin Lannister Jacket 150.00 300.00
NNO Jason Momoa Autograph Dothraki Leather 100.00 200.00

2017 Rittenhouse Game of Thrones Valyrian Steel Valyrian Autographs

COMMON AUTO 6.00 15.00
RANDOMLY INSERTED INTO PACKS
NNO Alfie Allen VL 15.00 40.00
NNO Anton Lesser VL 8.00 20.00
NNO Charles Dance L 20.00 50.00
NNO Clive Russell VL 10.00 25.00
NNO Conleth Hill EL 15.00 40.00
NNO Daniel Portman L 8.00 20.00
NNO Faye Marsay VL 10.00 25.00
NNO Finn Jones VL 8.00 20.00
NNO Iain Glen L 15.00 40.00
NNO Ian McElhinney VL 10.00 25.00
NNO Indira Varma L 10.00 25.00
NNO Isaac Hempstead-Wright VL 15.00 40.00
NNO Iwan Rheon L 10.00 25.00
NNO Jacob Anderson L 8.00 20.00
NNO Jerome Flynn VL 20.00 50.00
NNO John Bradley VL 8.00 20.00
NNO Julian Glover L 8.00 20.00
NNO Kristian Nairn VL 20.00 50.00
NNO Lena Headey VL 60.00 120.00
NNO Maisie Williams VL 75.00 150.00
NNO Mark Addy EL 50.00 100.00
NNO Michael McElhatton EL 15.00 40.00
NNO Michiel Huisman VL 12.00 30.00
NNO Nikolaj Coster-Waldau EL 75.00 150.00
NNO Owen Teale L 8.00 20.00
NNO Peter Dinklage EL 75.00 150.00
NNO Richard Brake L 15.00 40.00
NNO Roger Ashton-Griffiths VL 8.00 20.00
NNO Rose Leslie VL 30.00 75.00
NNO Sean Bean EL 75.00 150.00
NNO Tom Wlaschiha VL 12.00 30.00

1992 SkyBox Garfield

COMPLETE SET (100) 5.00 12.00
COMPLETE SET W/TATTOOS (109) 6.00 15.00
UNOPENED BOX (36 PACKS) 25.00 40.00
UNOPENED PACK (8 CARDS) .75 1.00
COMMON CARD (1-100) .12 .30

1992 SkyBox Garfield Holograms

COMPLETE SET (5) 10.00 25.00
COMMON CARD (H1-H5) 3.00 8.00
RANDOMLY INSERTED INTO PACKS

1992 SkyBox Garfield Tattoos

COMPLETE SET (9) 1.50 4.00
COMMON CARD (1-9) .20 .50
STATED ODDS 1:1
CONSIDERED A PART OF THE BASE SET

1992 SkyBox Garfield Promos

COMMON CARD .75 1.50
1 Garfield 1.50 4.00
2 Odie#{(2-Card Panel)

1995 Krome Garfield

COMPLETE SET (90) 10.00 25.00
UNOPENED BOX (24 PACKS) 15.00 25.00
UNOPENED PACK (5 CARDS) .60 1.00
COMMON CARD (1-90) .25 .60
*HOLOCHROME: 1.2X TO 3X BASIC CARDS

1995 Krome Garfield Holochrome Chromium

COMPLETE SET (9) 8.00 20.00
COMMON CARD (GC1-GC9) 1.25 3.00
STATED ODDS 1:12

1995 Krome Garfield Holochrome Promos

COMPLETE SET (3) 2.00 5.00
COMMON CARD .75 2.00

1997 Krome Garfield

COMPLETE SET (45) 8.00 20.00
UNOPENED BOX (24 PACKS) 25.00 30.00
UNOPENED PACK (5 CARDS) 1.00 1.25
COMMON CARD (1-45) .25 .60
*SPARKLE: .75X TO 2X BASIC CARDS
*SPARKLE STICKERS: 1X TO 2.5 BASIC CARDS

1997 Krome Garfield Holochrome

COMPLETE SET (5) 15.00 40.00
COMMON CARD (GC1-GC5) 4.00 10.00

2004 Garfield Collection

COMPLETE SET (72) 3.00 8.00
COMMON CARD .10 .25
*PAW PRINT: 2.5X TO 6X BASIC CARDS
JIM DAVIS AUTO ANNOUNCED PRINT RUN 500
AU Jim Davis AUTO 25.00 60.00

2004 Garfield Collection Garfield the Movie

COMPLETE SET (28) 1.00 2.50
COMMON CARD (1-28) .10 .25
*PAW PRINT: 2.5X TO 6X BASIC CARDS
STATED ODDS 1:1

2004 Garfield Collection Vinyl Cling Stickers

COMPLETE SET (42) 3.00 8.00
COMMON CARD (1-42) .15 .40
STATED ODDS 1:1

1995 SkyBox Gargoyles Series One

COMPLETE SET (90) 6.00 15.00
UNOPENED BOX (36 PACKS) 30.00 40.00
UNOPENED PACK (7 CARDS) 1.00 1.25
COMMON CARD (1-90) .12 .30
S1 Goliath Prototype .75 2.00

1995 SkyBox Gargoyles Series One Double-Sided Spectra

COMPLETE SET (4) 10.00 25.00
COMMON CARD (DS1-DS4) 3.00 8.00
STATED ODDS 1:24

1995 SkyBox Gargoyles Series One Foil

COMPLETE SET (9) 10.00 25.00
COMMON CARD (F1-F9) 1.25 3.00
STATED ODDS 1:1 JUMBO PACKS

1995 SkyBox Gargoyles Series One Pop-Ups

COMPLETE SET (10) 1.50 4.00
COMMON CARD (P1-P10) .20 .50
STATED ODDS 1:1 HOBBY PACKS

1995 SkyBox Gargoyles Series One SkyMotion

1 Redemption
2 SkyMotion 15.00 40.00

1995 SkyBox Gargoyles Series One Video

1 Gargoyles Video
2 Redemption 8.00 20.00

1995 SkyBox Gargoyles Series Two

COMPLETE SET (75) 6.00 15.00
UNOPENED BOX (48 PACKS) 30.00 40.00
UNOPENED PACK (5 CARDS) .75 1.00
COMMON CARD (1-75) .12 .30

1995 SkyBox Gargoyles Series Two Static Glow Decals

COMPLETE SET (9) 15.00 40.00
COMMON CARD (1-9) 2.00 5.00
RANDOMLY INSERTED INTO PACKS

1995 SkyBox Gargoyles Series Two Promos

COMPLETE SET (2) 1.25 3.00
COMMON CARD .75 2.00

1995 WildStorm Gen13

COMPLETE SET (107) 12.00 30.00
UNOPENED BOX (36 PACKS) 15.00 25.00
UNOPENED PACK (7 CARDS) .40 .75
COMMON CARD (1-107) .25 .60
*REFRACTORS: .6X TO 1.5X BASIC CARDS .40 1.00

1995 WildStorm Gen13 Gen Active Motion

COMPLETE SET (9) 20.00 50.00
COMMON CARD (GA1-GA9) 4.00 10.00
STATED ODDS 1:6

1995 WildStorm Gen13 Glow-in-the-Dark Chromium

COMPLETE SET (9) 15.00 40.00
COMMON CARD (GL1-GL9) 3.00 8.00
STATED ODDS 1:8

1996 WildStorm Gen13 Series 2

COMPLETE SET (90) 6.00 15.00
UNOPENED BOX (36 PACKS) 15.00 20.00
UNOPENED PACK (8 CARDS) .40 .40
COMMON CARD (1-90) .12 .30

1996 WildStorm Gen13 Series 2 Gen-Alloy

COMPLETE SET (9) 15.00 40.00
COMMON CARD (GA1-GA9) 3.00 8.00
STATED ODDS 1:9

1996 WildStorm Gen13 Series 2 Oversized Storyboard

COMPLETE SET (5) 12.00 30.00
COMMON CARD (OS1-OS5) 4.00 10.00
STATED ODDS 1:BOX

1998 WildStorm Gen13 Power Pack

COMPLETE BOXED SET (50) 12.00 30.00
COMMON CARD (1-50) .30 .75

1997 Upper Deck George of the Jungle

COMPLETE SET (45) 6.00 15.00
UNOPENED BOX (24 PACKS) 25.00 40.00
UNOPENED PACK (7 CARDS) 1.50 1.75
COMMON CARD (1-45) .30 .75

1997 Upper Deck George of the Jungle Pop-Ups

COMPLETE SET (10) 1.25 3.00
COMMON CARD (B1-B10) .20 .50
STATED ODDS 2:1

1997 Upper Deck George of the Jungle Posters and Game Boards

COMPLETE SET (10) 1.25 3.00
COMMON CARD (A1-A10) .20 .50
STATED ODDS 1:1

2017 Gerry Anderson Collection Case-Topper Autographs

JWCO Jeremy Wilkin 25.00 60.00
JWCB Jeremy Wilkin 15.00 40.00

2017 Gerry Anderson Collection Fireball XL5

COMPLETE SET (54) 5.00 12.00
COMMON CARD (1-54) .20 .50
PS1 Fly Around the Universe 12.00 30.00
(Postage Stamp Insert)

2017 Gerry Anderson Collection Fireball XL5 Autographs

COMMON CARD 6.00 15.00
DG1 David Graham 10.00 25.00
DG2 David Graham 10.00 25.00
DG3 David Graham 12.00 30.00

2017 Gerry Anderson Collection Fireball XL5 Foil

COMPLETE SET (6) 6.00 15.00
COMMON CARD (F1-F6) 1.25 3.00
STATED ODDS 1:SET PER BOX

2017 Gerry Anderson Collection Fireball XL5 Promos

B2 Fireball XL5 8.00 20.00
(Album Exclusive)
GP1 Dealer Promo (Gazza Games) 8.00 20.00
PR2 Coming in 2016 (The Lost Worlds of Gerry Anderson Incentive)/100
RP1 Dealer Promo (Rydeclive)
YS1 Coming in 2016
(Unstoppable Yearbox)/125 6.00 15.00
CCP1 Dealer Promo (The Cyber Cellar) 10.00 25.00
DTP1 Dealer Promo (Derek's Trading Cards)
EMP1 Dealer Promo (Acme 3000)
PCP1 Dealer Promo (Premier Cards)/30 12.00 30.00
PHP1 Dealer Promo (Paul Hart Trading Cards)/50
RAP1 Dealer Promo (Radickal Trading Cards)
TCP1 Dealer Promo (Dean Rogers Top Cards)
WEB1 The Gerry Anderson Collection (Website Exclusive)
HCPR1 Coming Soon (British Horror
Collection Case Incentive)/100 10.00 25.00

2017 Gerry Anderson Collection Joe 90

COMPLETE SET (54) 5.00 12.00
COMMON CARD (1-54) .20 .50
PS1 Most Special Agent 12.00 30.00
(Postage Stamp Insert)

2017 Gerry Anderson Collection Joe 90 Autographs

COMMON CARD 6.00 15.00
EM1 Elizabeth Morgan 12.00 30.00
GF1 Gary Files 10.00 25.00
GF2 Gary Files 10.00 25.00
GF3 Gary Files 12.00 30.00
GF4 Gary Files 10.00 25.00
JW1 Jeremy Wilkin 15.00 40.00
JW2 Jeremy Wilkin 12.00 30.00
JW3 Jeremy Wilkin 8.00 20.00
SR1 Shane Rimmer 10.00 25.00
SR2 Shane Rimmer 8.00 20.00

2017 Gerry Anderson Collection Joe 90 Foil

COMPLETE SET (6) 6.00 15.00
COMMON CARD (F1-F6) 1.25 3.00
STATED ODDS 1:SET PER BOX

2017 Gerry Anderson Collection Joe 90 Promos

B4 Joe 30 8.00 20.00
(Album Exclusive)
GP1 Dealer Promo (Gazza Games) 10.00 25.00
PR4 Coming in 2016 (The Lost Worlds of Gerry Anderson Incentive)/100
RP1 Dealer Promo (Rydeclive)
YS1 Coming in 2016
(Unstoppable Yearbox)/125 5.00 12.00
ASP1 Dealer Promo (AMS-78)
CCP1 Dealer Promo (The Cyber Cellar) 8.00 20.00
DTP1 Dealer Promo (Derek's Trading Cards)
EMP1 Dealer Promo (Acme 3000) 12.00 30.00
MBP1 Dealer Promo (Trytradingcards) 10.00 25.00
PCP1 Dealer Promo (Premier Cards)/30
RAP1 Dealer Promo (Radickal Trading Cards)
RKP1 Dealer Promo (Roman Krause)
TCP1 Dealer Promo (Dean Rogers Top Cards)
WEB1 The Gerry Anderson Collection (Website Exclusive)
HCPR1 Coming Soon (British Horror Collection Case Incentive)/100 10.00 25.00

2017 Gerry Anderson Collection Stingray

COMPLETE SET (54) 5.00 12.00
COMMON CARD (1-54) .20 .50
PS1 Stingray 15.00 40.00
(Postage Stamp Insert)
PS2 We Are About to Launch Stingray 15.00 40.00
(Postage Stamp Insert)

2017 Gerry Anderson Collection Stingray Autographs

COMMON CARD 6.00 15.00
DG1 David Graham 8.00 20.00
DG2 David Graham 8.00 20.00

2017 Gerry Anderson Collection Stingray Foil

COMPLETE SET (6) 6.00 15.00
COMMON CARD (F1-F6) 1.25 3.00
STATED ODDS 1:SET PER BOX

2017 Gerry Anderson Collection Stingray Promos

B3 Stingray 4.00 10.00
(Album Exclusive)
GP1 Dealer Promo (Gazza Games) 6.00 15.00
MP1 Dealer Promo (Mitchy9210) 6.00 15.00
PR3 Coming in 2016 (The Lost Worlds of Gerry Anderson Incentive)/100 4.00 10.00
RP1 Dealer Promo (Rydeclive) 4.00 10.00
YS1 Coming in 2016
(Unstoppable Yearbox)/125 5.00 12.00
ASP1 Dealer Promo (AMS-78)
CCP1 Dealer Promo (The Cyber Cellar) 3.00 8.00
DTP1 Dealer Promo (Derek's Trading Cards)
EMP1 Dealer Promo (Acme 3000) 10.00 25.00
PCP1 Dealer Promo (Premier Cards)/30 15.00 40.00
PHP1 Dealer Promo (Paul Hart
Trading Cards)/50 10.00 25.00
RAP1 Dealer Promo (Radickal Trading Cards)8.00 20.00
RKP1 Dealer Promo (Roman Krause)
UMP1 Dealer Promo (Umbrella Trading Cards)12.00 30.00
WEB1 The Gerry Anderson Collection
(Website Exclusive) 2.50 6.00
HCPR1 Coming Soon (British Horror Collection Case Incentive)/100

2017 Gerry Anderson Collection Supercar

COMPLETE SET (54) 5.00 12.00
COMMON CARD (1-54) .20 .50
PS1 It's the Marvel of the Age! 10.00 25.00
(Postage Stamp Insert)

2017 Gerry Anderson Collection Supercar Autographs

COMMON CARD 6.00 15.00
DG1 David Graham 10.00 25.00
DG2 David Graham 12.00 30.00
DG3 David Graham 8.00 20.00

2017 Gerry Anderson Collection Supercar Foil

COMPLETE SET (6) 6.00 15.00
COMMON CARD (F1-F2) 1.25 3.00
STATED ODDS 1:SET PER BOX

2017 Gerry Anderson Collection Supercar Promos

B1 Supercar 8.00 20.00
(Album Exclusive)
GP1 Dealer Promo (Gazza Games) 10.00 25.00
PR1 Coming in 2016 (The Lost Worlds fo Gerry Anderson Incentive)/100 6.00 15.00
RP1 Dealer Promo (Rydeclive) 3.00 8.00
YS1 Coming in 2016
(Unstoppable Yearbox)/125 6.00 15.00
CCP1 Dealer Promo (The Cyber Cellar) 3.00 8.00
DTP1 Dealer Promo (Derek's Trading Cards)
EMP1 Dealer Promo (Acme 3000) 6.00 15.00
PCP1 Dealer Promo (Premier Cards)/30 12.00 30.00
RAP1 Dealer Promo (Radickal Trading Cards)2.50 6.00
TCP1 Dealer Promo (Dean Rogers Top Cards)
WEB1 The Gerry Anderson Collection
(Website Exclusive) 8.00 20.00
HCPR1 Coming Soon (British Horror Collection Case Incentive)/100

1997 JPP Armada Ghost in the Shell

COMPLETE SET (54) 4.00 10.00
UNOPENED BOX (24 PACKS) 40.00 55.00
UNOPENED PACK (7 CARDS) 2.00 2.50
COMMON CARD (1-54) .15 .40
NNO Unnumbered, Holochrome PROMO .75 2.00
SP1 Special Reflector 5.00 12.00

1997 JPP Armada Ghost in the Shell Acetate

COMPLETE SET (9) 15.00 40.00
COMMON CARD (C1-C9) 2.50 6.00
STATED ODDS 1:12

1997 JPP Armada Ghost in the Shell Reflectors

COMPLETE SET (15) 4.00 10.00
COMMON CARD (S1-S15) .40 1.00
STATED ODDS 1:1

2009 Ghost Whisperer Seasons One and Two

COMPLETE SET (72) 6.00 15.00
COMMON CARD (1-72) .15 .40
SN1 STATED ODDS 1:CASE
SN1 Same As It Never Was 12.50 30.00

2009 Ghost Whisperer Seasons One and Two Autograph Costumes

COMMON AUTO 10.00 25.00
GA1 Jennifer Love Hewitt 100.00 200.00
GAC2 David Conrad 15.00 40.00

2009 Ghost Whisperer Seasons One and Two Autographs

COMMON AUTO (GA1-GA9; GCI1-GCI2) 5.00 12.00
STATED ODDS 1:48
GCI1 ISSUED AS 6-CASE INCENTIVE
GCI2 ISSUED AS 10-CASE INCENTIVE
GA1 Jennifer Love Hewitt 75.00 150.00
GA2 David Conrad 10.00 25.00
GA3 Camryn Manheim 8.00 20.00
GA4 Christoph Sanders 8.00 20.00
GA5 Jamie Kennedy 10.00 25.00
GA6 J.Kennedy/C.Sanders 15.00 40.00
GCI1 J.L.Hewitt/D.Conrad 6CI 100.00 200.00
GCI2 Hewitt/Conrad/Manheim 10CI 125.00 250.00

2009 Ghost Whisperer Seasons One and Two Costumes

COMMON CARD (GC1-GC20; GCI3) 6.00 15.00
STATED ODDS 1:12
GCI3 STATED ISSUED AS 3-CASE INCENTIVE
GC1 Melinda Gordon Jacket 10.00 25.00
GC2 Melinda Gordon Dress 8.00 20.00
GC3 Melinda Gordon Teddy 8.00 20.00
GC4 Melinda Gordon Nightgown 20.00 50.00
GC5 Melinda Gordon Robe 8.00 20.00
GC6 Melinda Gordon Dress 10.00 25.00
GC7 Melinda Gordon Sweater 8.00 20.00
GC8 Melinda Gordon Shirt 15.00 40.00
GC9 Melinda Gordon Dress 8.00 20.00
GC10 Melinda Gordon Nightgown 8.00 20.00
GC11 Melinda Gordon Dress 8.00 20.00
GC12 Melinda Gordon Dress 8.00 20.00
GC13 Melinda Gordon Dress 8.00 20.00
GC14 Melinda Gordon Jacket 10.00 25.00
Scarf
GC15 Melinda Gordon Robe 10.00 25.00
Robe

GC16 Melinda Gordon PJs PJs 10.00 25.00
GC20 Sarah Applewhite Nightgown 8.00 20.00
GCI3 Melinda Gordon Dress/Dress 3CI 30.00 60.00

2009 Ghost Whisperer Seasons One and Two Crossing Over

COMPLETE SET (3) 4.00 10.00
COMMON CARD (C1-C3) 1.50 4.00
RANDOM INSERTS IN PACKS

2009 Ghost Whisperer Seasons One and Two Kindred Spirits

COMPLETE SET (9) 6.00 15.00
COMMON CARD (K1-K9) 1.00 2.50
RANDOM INSERTS IN PACKS

2009 Ghost Whisperer Seasons One and Two SDCC-Exclusive Autographs

STATED ODDS 2 PER SDCC BOX
NNO Camryn Manheim 10.00 25.00
NNO Jamie Kennedy 10.00 25.00
NNO Jennifer Love Hewitt

2009 Ghost Whisperer Seasons One and Two Signs

COMPLETE SET (6) 6.00 15.00
COMMON CARD (S1-S6) 1.50 4.00
RANDOM INSERTS IN PACKS

2009 Ghost Whisperer Seasons One and Two Trivia

COMPLETE SET (9) 6.00 15.00
COMMON CARD (T1-T9) 1.00 2.50
RANDOM INSERTS IN PACKS

2010 Ghost Whisperer Seasons Three and Four

COMPLETE SET (72) 6.00 15.00
COMMON CARD (1-72) .15 .40

2010 Ghost Whisperer Seasons Three and Four Autographs

COMMON AUTO 8.00 20.00
STATED ODDS 1:48
ACS Christoph Sanders 10.00 25.00
AHD Hillary Duff 25.00 60.00
AJLH Jennifer Love Hewitt 60.00 120.00
AJLHCM J.L.Hewitt/C.Manheim DUAL 30.00 75.00
AJLHJK J.L.Hewitt/J.Kennedy DUAL 30.00 75.00

2010 Ghost Whisperer Seasons Three and Four Costumes

COMMON CARD (C1-C29; CI1) 12.00 30.00
OVERALL COSTUME/PROP ODDS 1:10
CI1 SHOE ISSUED AS CASE INCENTIVE
C1 M.Gordon pants/shirt DUAL 15.00 40.00
C2 Melinda Gordon shirt shirt DUAL 15.00 40.00
C3 Melinda Gordon dress dress DUAL 15.00 40.00
C4 Melinda Gordon dress dress DUAL 15.00 40.00
C5 Melinda Gordon jacket jacket DUAL 15.00 40.00
C6 Melinda Gordon jacket jacket DUAL 15.00 40.00
C7 Melinda Gordon dress dress DUAL 15.00 40.00
C8 Melinda Gordon pjs pjs DUAL 15.00 40.00
C9 Melinda Gordon shirt shirt DUAL 15.00 40.00
C10 Melinda Gordon dress sweater DUAL 15.00 40.00
C12B Jim Clancy patch SP 30.00 60.00
C20 Ned Banks tie 15.00 40.00
C28 9 Swatch 20.00 50.00
C29 6 Swatch 20.00 50.00
CI1 Melinda Gordon shoe/ (issued as case incentive) 100.00 200.00

2010 Ghost Whisperer Seasons Three and Four Props

COMMON CARD 15.00 40.00
OVERALL COSTUME/PROP ODDS 1:10
TOOTH ISSUED AS CASE TOPPER

2010 Ghost Whisperer Seasons Three and Four Puzzle

COMPLETE SET (9) 6.00 15.00
COMMON CARD (CP1-CP9) 1.00 2.50
STATED ODDS 1:12

2010 Ghost Whisperer Seasons Three and Four Quotes

COMPLETE SET (9) 6.00 15.00
STATED ODDS 1:12

2010 Ghost Whisperer Seasons Three and Four Trivia

COMPLETE SET (9) 6.00 15.00
COMMON CARD (T1-T9) 1.00 2.50
STATED ODDS 1:12

2016 Ghostbusters

COMPLETE SET (54) 8.00 20.00
UNOPENED BOX (24 PACKS) 65.00 80.00
UNOPENED PACK (5 CARDS) 3.00 4.00
COMMON CARD (1-54) .30 .75
*SILVER FOIL: 1.5X TO 4X BASIC CARDS

2016 Ghostbusters Autographs

COMMON AUTO 10.00 25.00
STATED ODDS 1:30
SOME AUTOS CONTAIN INSCRIPTIONS
GROUP A: 175-225 COPIES
GROUP B: 350-375 COPIES
AH Arsenio Hall B 25.00 60.00
AP Annie Potts B 30.00 75.00
BB Bobby Brown B 15.00 40.00
BS Ben Stein A 25.00 60.00
DA Dan Aykroyd B 125.00 250.00
EH Ernie Hudson B 20.00 50.00
HY Harris Yulin A 15.00 40.00
IR Ivan Reitman B 30.00 75.00
JR Jason Reitman A 30.00 75.00
LK Larry King B 50.00 100.00
LS Laura Summer A 15.00 40.00
ME Michael Ensign A 20.00 50.00
ML Maurice LaMarche A 20.00 50.00
JRU Jennifer Runyon A 20.00 50.00

2016 Ghostbusters Behind-the-Scenes

COMPLETE SET (9) 5.00 12.00
COMMON CARD (B1-B9) 1.00 2.50
*SILVER FOIL: .75X TO 2X BASIC CARDS
STATED ODDS 1:3

2016 Ghostbusters Character Bios

COMPLETE SET (7) 6.00 15.00
COMMON CARD (C1-C7) 1.50 4.00
*SILVER FOIL: .75X TO 2X BASIC CARDS
STATED ODDS 1:3
C1 Dr. Peter Venkman 2.00 5.00

2016 Ghostbusters Quotes

COMPLETE SET (9) 5.00 12.00
COMMON CARD (Q1-Q9) 1.00 2.50
*SILVER FOIL: .75X TO 2X BASIC CARDS
STATED ODDS 1:3

2016 Ghostbusters Replica Patches

COMMON CARD (H1-H9) 4.00 10.00
STATED ODDS 1:72
H1 Venkman 8.00 20.00
H2 Stantz 6.00 15.00
H3 Spengler 5.00 12.00
H4 Zeddemore 5.00 12.00
H9 Rookie (Binder Exclusive) 8.00 20.00

2016 Ghostbusters Sing for Your Specter

COMPLETE SET (9) 6.00 15.00
COMMON CARD (E1-E9) 1.25 3.00
*SILVER FOIL: .75X TO 2X BASIC CARDS
STATED ODDS 1:3

2016 Ghostbusters Totally Fabricated Slime Relics

COMPLETE SET (6) 50.00 100.00
COMMON CARD (S1-S6) 10.00 25.00
STATED ODDS 1:200
S2 Standard Ectoplasmic Residue, Weakened 12.00 30.00
S3 Psychomagnotheric Ectoplasm 15.00 40.00
S4 Necrotic Ectoplasm 12.00 30.00

2016 Ghostbusters Tricks and Traps

COMPLETE SET (9) 5.00 12.00
COMMON CARD (D1-D9) 1.00 2.50
*CRYPTONIUM: 2X TO 5X BASIC CARDS
STATED ODDS 1:3

1989 Topps Ghostbusters II

COMPLETE SET (88) 5.00 12.00
COMPLETE SET W/STICKERS (99) 6.00 15.00
UNOPENED BOX (48 PACKS) 50.00 75.00
UNOPENED PACK (8 CARDS) 2.00 3.00
COMMON CARD (1-88) .12 .30

1989 Topps Ghostbusters II Stickers

COMPLETE SET (11) 1.50 4.00
COMMON STICKER (1-11) .25 .60
STATED ODDS 1:1

1991 Impel G.I. Joe

COMPLETE SET (200) 15.00 40.00
COMPLETE FOOTLOCKER BOXED SET (200) 30.00 50.00
UNOPENED BOX (36 PACKS) 40.00 60.00
UNOPENED PACK (12 CARDS) 1.50 2.50
COMMON CARD (1-200) .10 .25
1 Cesspool .75 2.00
6 Septic Tank .60 1.50
15 Rattler .75 2.00
22 Duke 1.50 4.00
25 Shipwreck .75 2.00
28 Storm Shadow 2.50 6.00
31 Gung-Ho .40 1.00
32 Cobra Commander 1.25 3.00
41 Snake-Eyes 8.00 20.00
133 Cobra Commander 1.25 3.00
135 Snake-Eyes 5.00 12.00

1994 Comic Images G.I. Joe 30th Salute

COMPLETE SET (90) 5.00 12.00
UNOPENED BOX (48 PACKS) 25.00 35.00
UNOPENED PACK (10 CARDS) .50 .75
COMMON CARD (1-90) .12 .30
M1 Nurse with Crutch Medallion/2372* 25.00
AU1 Joe Kubert AU/500 20.00 50.00

1994 Comic Images G.I. Joe 30th Salute Chromium

COMPLETE SET (6) 6.00 15.00
COMMON CARD (1-6) 2.00 5.00
STATED ODDS 1:6

1994 Comic Images G.I. Joe 30th Salute Comic Anthology

COMPLETE SET (3) 10.00 25.00
COMMON CARD (1-3) 5.00 12.00
RANDOMLY INSERTED INTO PACKS

1994 Comic Images G.I. Joe 30th Salute Uncut Sheets

1 6-Card Panel (1 per case) 8.00 20.00

1994 Comic Images G.I. Joe 30th Salute Promos

1 30th Salute (dealer) 1.50 4.00

1986 Hasbro G.I. Joe Action

COMPLETE SET (192) 75.00 150.00
COMMON CARD (1-192) .75 2.00

1986 Hasbro G.I. Joe Action Stickers

COMPLETE SET (12) 8.00 20.00
COMMON CARD .75 2.00

1987 Comic Images G.I. Joe Files

COMPLETE SET (55) 6.00 15.00
COMMON CARD (1-55) .20 .50

1991 Impel G.I. Joe Hall of Fame

COMPLETE SET (20) 150.00 300.00
COMMON CARD (1-20) 8.00 20.00
1 Duke 20.00 50.00
7 Snake Eyes 50.00 100.00
10 Falcon 10.00 25.00
17 Major Bludd 15.00 40.00
18 Cobra Commander 20.00 50.00
19 Baroness 15.00 40.00

1993 Hasbro G.I. Joe Mission Search and Destroy

COMPLETE SET (20) 20.00 50.00
COMMON CARD (1-20) 1.25 3.00

1993 Hasbro G.I. Joe Mission Search and Destroy Comic Book

COMPLETE SET (4) 3.00 8.00
M1 Code Name Duke 1.50 4.00
M2 Trouble for Scarlett 1.50 4.00
M3 Cobra Cyber-Viper 1.50 4.00
M4 Cobra's Ultimate Weapon 1.50 4.00

2013 GI Joe Retaliation

COMPLETE SET (48) 8.00 20.00
COMPLETE SET W/TATS (54) 10.00 25.00
UNOPENED BOX (48 PACKS) 40.00 50.00
UNOPENED PACK (3 CARDS+1 TATTOO) 1.00 1.25
COMMON CARD (1-48) .30 .75

2013 GI Joe Retaliation Tattoos

COMPLETE SET (6) 2.00 5.00
COMMON CARD (T1-T6) .40 1.00
STATED ODDS 1:1

1981 Topps Giant Movie Pin-Ups

COMPLETE SET (12) 15.00 40.00
UNOPENED BOX (36 PACKS) 35.00 50.00
UNOPENED PACK (1 PIN-UP)
COMMON CARD (UNNUMBERED) 2.00 5.00
5 Star Wars 4.00 10.00
8 The Empire Strikes Back 4.00 10.00

1993 Comic Images Comic Images Gil Elvgren's Calendar Pin-Ups 1

COMPLETE SET (90) 4.00 10.00
UNOPENED BOX (48 PACKS) 20.00 30.00
UNOPENED PACK (10 CARDS) .75 1.00
COMMON CARD (1-90) .10 .25
NNO1 Promo 1 .75 2.00

1993 Comic Images Gil Elvgren's Calendar Pin-Ups 1 OptiPrisms

COMPLETE SET (3) 6.00 15.00
COMMON CARD (1-3) 2.50 6.00
RANDOMLY INSERTED INTO PACKS

1993 Comic Images Gil Elvgren's Calendar Pin-Ups 1 SpectraScope

COMPLETE SET (3) 6.00 15.00
COMMON CARD (1-3) 2.50 6.00
RANDOMLY INSERTED INTO PACKS

1994 Comic Images Gil Elvgren's Calendar Pin-Ups 2

COMPLETE SET (90) 4.00 10.00
UNOPENED BOX (48 PACKS) 30.00 40.00
UNOPENED PACK (10 CARDS) .75 1.00
COMMON CARD (1-90) .10 .25
M1 Medallion Card/2495* 10.00 25.00
6UP 6UP Panel (case insert) 8.00 20.00
NNO1 Promo (dealers) .75 2.00

MODERN

1994 Comic Images Gil Elvgren's Calendar Pin-Ups 2 OmniChrome

COMPLETE SET (6)	10.00	25.00
COMMON CARD (1-6)	2.50	6.00
STATED ODDS 1:16		

1994 Comic Images Gil Elvgren's Calendar Pin-Ups 2 Soft and Cuddly

COMPLETE SET (3)	10.00	25.00
COMMON CARD (1-3)	5.00	12.00
STATED ODDS 1:48		

1998 Dart FlipCards Gilligan's Island

COMPLETE SET (72)	5.00	12.00
UNOPENED BOX (36 PACKS)	60.00	100.00
UNOPENED PACK (6 CARDS)	2.00	3.00
COMMON CARD (1-72)	.12	.30

1998 Dart FlipCards Gilligan's Island Lenticular

COMPLETE SET (6)	12.00	30.00
COMMON CARD (L1-L6)	3.00	8.00
STATED ODDS 1:18		

1998 Dart FlipCards Gilligan's Island Lenticular Send-Away

COMPLETE SET (6)	6.00	15.00
COMMON CARD (S1-S6)	1.50	4.00
WRAPPER OFFER EXCLUSIVE		

1998 Dart FlipCards Gilligan's Island Promos

COMMON CARD	.75	2.00
2A Philly	1.50	4.00
3A Toronto Sportscard Expo 1 (same image as P1)	1.50	4.00
3B Toronto Sportscard Expo 2 (same image as P2)	1.50	4.00
NNO Non-Sport Update	2.00	5.00

2013 Girls of Snake and Mongoose Promos

COMPLETE SET (6)	10.00	25.00
COMMON CARD (UNNUMBERED)	2.00	5.00
SDCC EXCLUSIVE PROMO SET		

1996 Tempo Gladiators

COMPLETE SET (99)	5.00	12.00
UNOPENED BOX (30 PACKS)		
UNOPENED PACK (7 CARDS)		
COMMON CARD (1-99)	.10	.25

1996 JPP Amada Godzilla

COMPLETE SET (54)	8.00	20.00
UNOPENED BOX (24 PACKS)	150.00	250.00
UNOPENED PACK (5 CARDS)	6.00	10.00
COMMON CARD (1-54)	.30	.75
*HOLO STICKERS: 1.5X TO 4X BASIC CARDS	1.25	3.00

1996 JPP Amada Godzilla Holochrome Stickers

COMPLETE SET (54)
*HOLO STICKERS: 1.2X TO 3X BASIC CARDS
STATED ODDS 1:1

2006 Godzilla King of the Monsters

COMPLETE SET (72)	6.00	15.00
UNOPENED BOX (36 PACKS)	150.00	250.00
UNOPENED PACK (6 CARDS)	4.00	8.00
COMMON CARD (1-72)	.15	.40

2006 Godzilla King of the Monsters Artist Sketches

COMMON CARD	10.00	25.00
STATED ODDS 1:36		

2006 Godzilla King of the Monsters Foil Posters

COMPLETE SET (6)	10.00	25.00
COMMON CARD	2.50	6.00
STATED ODDS 1:12		

2006 Godzilla King of the Monsters Promos

COMPLETE SET (4)	3.00	8.00
COMMON CARD (P1-P4)	.75	2.00
P4 G-Fan Magazine Exclusive	1.50	4.00

1998 Maggi Noodles Godzilla Australian

COMPLETE SET (10)	4.00	10.00
COMMON CARD (1-10)	.60	1.50

1998 Inkworks Godzilla The Movie Supervue

COMPLETE SET (72)	5.00	12.00
UNOPENED BOX (36 PACKS)	35.00	50.00
UNOPENED PACK (5 CARDS)	1.00	1.50
COMMON CARD (1-72)	.15	.40
GS1 Mother of all Monsters	12.00	30.00

1998 Inkworks Godzilla The Movie Supervue Silverzilla

COMPLETE SET (3)	6.00	15.00
COMMON CARD (S1-S3)	3.00	8.00
STATED ODDS 1:27		

1998 Inkworks Godzilla The Movie Supervue Promos

0 Starlog Magazine Exclusive		
MP1 Suncoast and Media Play 3-Card Panel Exclusive	2.00	5.00
P1A General Distribution		
P1B General Distribution SP/25*	150.00	300.00
GP00 UK Distributor Exclusive	4.00	10.00

1995 Comic Images Golden Age of Comics

COMPLETE SET (90)	10.00	25.00
UNOPENED BOX (36 PACKS)	50.00	75.00
UNOPENED PACK (7 CARDS)	1.50	2.50
COMMON CARD (1-90)	.25	.60
*HOLOCHROME: 4X TO 10X BASIC CARDS		
NNO1 Case Topper Panel	2.00	5.00
NNO2 Gill Fox AU/500*		
NNO3 Master Comics #27 Medallion/1048*	10.00	25.00

1995 Comic Images Golden Age of Comics Prisms

COMPLETE SET (6)	10.00	25.00
COMMON CARD (1-6)	3.00	8.00
STATED ODDS 1:16		

1995 Comic Images Golden Age of Comics Schomburg MagnaChrome

COMPLETE SET (3)	12.00	30.00
COMMON CARD (1-3)	6.00	15.00
RANDOMLY INSERTED INTO PACKS		

1995 Comic Images Golden Age of Comics Promos

F1 Startling Comics #53	.75	2.00
F2 Exciting Comics	.75	2.00
F3 Claw	.75	2.00
NNO Wonder Comics #1 (General Distribution)	.40	1.00

2010 Golden Age of Comics Heroes and Villians

COMPLETE SET (40)	20.00	50.00
UNOPENED BOX (100 PACKS)		
UNOPENED PACK (2 CARDS)		
COMMON CARD (1-40)	.75	2.00
NNO S.Miller 3-Card Panel	12.00	30.00

2010 Golden Age of Comics Heroes and Villians Promos

COMP. SET w/o SP (7)	4.00	10.00
COMPLETE SET (8)	8.00	20.00
COMMON CARD (1-7)	.75	2.00
STATED ODDS ONE PER PACK		
SP ONLY AVAILABLE FROM 2010 PHILLY NONSPORT EXPO		
NNO Green Lama SP	4.00	10.00

2007 The Golden Compass

COMPLETE SET (72)	4.00	10.00
UNOPENED BOX (24 PACKS)	40.00	60.00
UNOPENED PACK (9 CARDS)	2.00	3.00
COMMON CARD (1-72)	.10	.30
CL1 Other Worlds (Case-Loader)	3.00	8.00

2007 The Golden Compass Daemon Forms

COMPLETE SET (3)	6.00	15.00
COMMON CARD (DF1-DF3)	3.00	8.00
STATED ODDS 1:23		
DF2 Lord Asriel and Stelmaria	3.00	8.00
DF3 Mrs. Coulter and The Golden Monkey	3.00	8.00

2007 The Golden Compass Fight to the Death

COMPLETE SET (6)	5.00	12.00
COMMON CARD (FD1-FD6)	1.25	3.00
STATED ODDS 1:7		

2007 The Golden Compass Lyra's World

COMPLETE SET (6)	8.00	20.00
COMMON CARD (LW1-LW6)	2.00	5.00
STATED ODDS 1:9		

2007 The Golden Compass Pieceworks

COMPLETE SET (11)	80.00	150.00
COMMON CARD (PW1-PW11)	8.00	20.00
STATED ODDS 1:24		
PWR1 Pieceworks Redemption Card		

2007 The Golden Compass Truth Teller

COMPLETE SET (6)	8.00	20.00
COMMON CARD (TT1-TT6)	2.00	5.00
STATED ODDS 1:9		

2007 The Golden Compass Promos

COMMON CARD	.75	2.00
GCBF Golden Compass/London Book Fair	20.00	50.00
GCLS Iorek & Lyra/New York Licensing Show	1.25	3.00
GCPi Mrs. Coulter/Inkworks.com	2.50	6.00
GCCFF Golden Compass/Cannes	25.00	60.00
GCUKP Lyra & Iorek	6.00	15.00
GCSD2007 Iorek & Lyra SDCC	2.00	5.00

1996 Sellar Publishing Golden Horseshu Series 1

COMPLETE SET (52)	12.00	30.00
COMPLETE FACTORY SET (52)	15.00	40.00
COMMON CARD (1-52)	.40	1.00

1996 Sellar Publishing Golden Horseshu Series 1 Cameo

COMPLETE SET (15)	5.00	12.00
COMMON CARD (C1-C15)	.50	1.25
STATED ODDS 1:1		

2000 Golden Horseshu Series 2

COMPLETE SET (52)	12.00	30.00
COMPLETE FACTORY SET (52)	20.00	50.00
COMMON CARD (52)	.40	1.00

2000 Golden Horseshu Series 2 Cameo

COMPLETE SET (15)	5.00	12.00
COMMON CARD (C1-C15)	.50	1.25
STATED ODDS 1:1		

2000 Golden Horseshu Series 2 Fame

COMPLETE SET (2)	3.00	8.00
COMMON CARD (F1-F2)	2.00	5.00
STATED ODDS 1:24		

1996 DuoCards Gone with the Wind

COMPLETE SET (90)	5.00	12.00
UNOPENED BOX (36 PACKS)	20.00	30.00
UNOPENED PACK (8 CARDS)	.60	1.00
COMMON CARD (1-90)	.15	.40

1996 DuoCards Gone with the Wind Chrome

COMPLETE SET (6)	4.00	10.00
COMMON CARD (1-6)	1.00	2.50

1996 DuoCards Gone with the Wind Promos

COMMON CARD	.60	1.50
1 Limited Release	2.00	5.00
2 Non-Sport Update Exclusive	.75	2.00
3 Limited Release	2.00	5.00

2018 Fright-Rags Good Guys Official Chucky Photo Cards

COMPLETE SET (78)	15.00	40.00
UNOPENED BOX (24 PACKS)	150.00	250.00
UNOPENED PACK (9 CARDS+1 STICKER)	6.00	10.00
COMMON CARD (1-77, NNO)	.30	.75
*BLACK: X TO X BASIC CARDS		
*RAINBOW: X TO X BASIC CARDS		

2018 Fright-Rags Good Guys Official Chucky Photo Cards Stickers

COMPLETE SET (9)	3.00	8.00
COMMON STICKER	.60	1.50
STATED ODDS 1:1		

1994 Pacific Goofy Monsters Promos

COMPLETE SET (6)	5.00	12.00
COMMON CARD (S1-S2)	1.25	3.00

1992 Kitchen Sink Press Goon Squad

COMPLETE SET (36)	5.00	12.00
COMMON CARD (1-36)	.25	.60

1992 Kitchen Sink Press Goon Squad Promos

COMPLETE SET (4)	4.00	10.00
COMMON CARD (1-4)	1.25	3.00

1985 Topps The Goonies

COMPLETE SET (86)	5.00	12.00
COMPLETE SET W/STICKERS (101)	6.00	15.00
COMPLETE SET W/VAR.STICKERS (108)	8.00	20.00
UNOPENED BOX (36 PACKS)	400.00	800.00
UNOPENED PACK (10 CARDS+1 STICKER)	12.00	20.00
COMMON CARD (1-86)	.10	.25

1985 Topps The Goonies Stickers

COMPLETE SET (15)	1.50	4.00
COMPLETE SET W/VARIATIONS (22)	2.50	6.00
COMMON CARD (1-15)	.20	.50
STATED ODDS 1:1		

1985 General Mills Goonies Canadian

COMPLETE SET (10)	50.00	100.00
COMMON CARD (1-10)	6.00	15.00

1985 Ziploc The Goonies Stickers

COMPLETE SET (4)	12.00	30.00
COMMON STICKER	5.00	12.00

1996 Topps Goosebumps

COMPLETE SET (54)	4.00	10.00
UNOPENED BOX (36 PACKS)	30.00	40.00
UNOPENED PACK (8 CARDS)	1.00	1.25
COMMON CARD (1-54)	.15	.40
P1 General Distribution	.75	2.00
NNOS2 Series Two Promo Worms	.75	2.00

1996 Topps Goosebumps Foil Stickers

COMPLETE SET (6)	10.00	25.00
COMMON CARD (1-6)	2.00	5.00
STATED ODDS 1:12		

1996 Topps Goosebumps Glow-in-the-Dark

COMPLETE SET (6)	8.00	20.00
COMMON CARD (G1-G6)	1.50	4.00
STATED ODDS 1:12		

1996 Topps Goosebumps Monster Magic

COMPLETE SET (6)	10.00	25.00
COMMON CARD (M1-M6)	2.00	5.00
STATED ODDS 1:12		

1992 Creative Card Congress Grateful Dead Promos

COMPLETE SET (3)	2.50	6.00
COMMON CARD	1.25	3.00

1993 Performance Years Great Guns

COMPLETE SET (100)	8.00	20.00
COMPLETE FACTORY SET (101)	10.00	25.00
UNOPENED BOX (36 PACKS)	20.00	30.00
UNOPENED PACK (10 CARDS)	.60	1.00
COMMON CARD (1-100)	.15	.40
*GOLD: 1X TO 2.5X BASIC CARDS	.40	1.00
NNO Colt Army .45 Hologram	1.50	4.00

1993 Performance Years Great Guns Promos

1 Colt M-16	1.25	3.00
2 1855 Volcanic	1.25	3.00
3 1860 Henry Rifle	1.25	3.00
4 Colt Single Action Army	2.00	5.00

1992 Oo-La-La Great Ventriloquists 1

COMPLETE SET (12)	4.00	10.00
COMMON CARD (1-12)	.50	1.25

1993 Mun-War Enterprises Greatest Cards Unearthed!

COMPLETE SET (144)	8.00	20.00
COMMON CARD (1-144)	.10	.25

2010 Green Hornet Movie Series One

COMPLETE SET (17)	75.00	125.00
COMMON CARD (C1-C14)	.40	1.00
STATED PRINT RUN 500 SER. #'d SETS		
GH Green Hornet coat MEM	6.00	15.00
KATO Kato jacket MEM	60.00	120.00
JC Jay Chou AU	1250.00	2500.00
CP1 Green Hornet	1.50	4.00
Kato PROMO		

2010 Green Hornet Movie Series Two

COMPLETE SET (5)	30.00	60.00
COMPLETE SET W/ROGEN AU (6)	125.00	200.00
COMMON CARD (1-5)	8.00	20.00
ROGEN AUTO ISSUED AS 3-SET INCENTIVE		
SR Seth Rogen AU 3CI	200.00	400.00

2010 Greetings from the Onion Postcards

COMPLETE SET (100)	20.00	50.00
COMMON CARD (1-100)	.40	1.00

1995 Comic Images Greg and Tim Hildebrandt Separate and Together

COMPLETE SET (90)	10.00	25.00
UNOPENED BOX (36 PACKS)	40.00	50.00
UNOPENED PACK (7 CARDS)	1.50	1.75
COMMON CARD (1-90)	.25	.60
*REFRACTOR: 4X TO 10X BASIC CARDS	2.50	6.00
NNO Reg and Tim Hildebrandt AU	20.00	50.00
NNO Medallion Card/2103*	10.00	25.00
NNO People at the Door PROMO	1.25	3.00

1995 Comic Images Greg and Tim Hildebrandt Separate and Together Magnachrome

COMPLETE SET (6)	12.00	30.00
COMMON CARD (1-6)	2.50	6.00
RANDOMLY INSERTED INTO PACKS		

1995 Comic Images Greg and Tim Hildebrandt Separate and Together Robin Hood

COMPLETE SET (3)	10.00	25.00
COMMON CARD (1-3)	4.00	10.00
RANDOMLY INSERTED INTO PACKS		

2002 Greg and Tim Hildebrandt Their Tolkien Art Previews

COMPLETE BOXED SET (6)	8.00	20.00
COMMON CARD (1-6)	1.25	4.00

1984 Topps Gremlins

COMPLETE SET (82)	5.00	12.00
COMPLETE SET W/STICKERS (93)	6.00	15.00
UNOPENED BOX (36 PACKS)	100.00	150.00
UNOPENED PACK (10 CARDS+1 STICKER)	3.00	4.00
UNOPENED RACK PACK (45 CARDS)		
COMMON CARD (1-82)	.15	.40
*OPC: SAME VALUE AS TOPPS		

1984 Topps Gremlins Stickers

COMPLETE SET (11)	1.25	3.00
COMMON CARD	.20	.50

1984 Topps Gremlins Stickers Blank Backs

COMPLETE SET (11)	15.00	40.00
COMMON CARD (11)	2.50	6.00

1990 Topps Gremlins 2

COMPLETE SET (88)	4.00	10.00
COMPLETE SET W/STICKERS (99)	5.00	12.00
COMPLETE SET W/ALL STICKERS (110)	8.00	20.00
COLLECTOR'S EDITION SET (110)	8.00	20.00
UNOPENED BOX (36 PACKS)	60.00	100.00
UNOPENED PACK (9 CARDS+1 STICKER)	2.00	3.00
COMMON CARD (1-88)	.10	.25

1990 Topps Gremlins 2 Green Border Stickers

COMPLETE SET (11)	2.50	6.00
COMMON CARD (1-11)	.50	1.00
STATED ODDS 1:1		

1990 Topps Gremlins 2 Red Border Stickers

COMPLETE SET (11)	1.50	4.00
COMMON CARD (1-11)	.20	.50
STATED ODDS 1:1		

2013 Grimm

COMPLETE SET (72)	5.00	12.00
UNOPENED BOX (24 PACKS)	40.00	50.00
UNOPENED PACK (6 CARDS)	2.00	2.25
COMMON CARD (1-72)	.15	.40
*BLACK: 1.5X TO 4X BASIC CARDS	.60	1.50
*CYAN: 1.5X TO 4X BASIC CARDS	.60	1.50
*MAGENTA: 1.5X TO 4X BASIC CARDS	.60	1.50
*YELLOW: 1.5X TO 4X BASIC CARDS	.60	1.50

2013 Grimm Aunt Marie's Trailer Puzzle

COMPLETE SET (9)	5.00	12.00
COMMON CARD (AMT1-AMT9)	1.25	3.00
STATED ODDS 1:12		

2013 Grimm Autographs

COMMON CARD	6.00	15.00
3 AUTO/MEM/PROP CARDS PER BOX		
BTAC1 Bitsie Tulloch	15.00	40.00
BTAC2 Bitsie Tulloch	15.00	40.00
CCAC1 Claire Coffee	15.00	40.00
CCAC2 Claire Coffee	15.00	40.00
DBAC1 Daniel Baldwin	8.00	20.00
DBAC2 Daniel Baldwin	8.00	20.00
DGAC1 David Giuntoli	20.00	50.00
DGAC2 David Giuntoli	20.00	50.00
DPAC1 Danielle Panabaker	15.00	40.00
DPAC2 Danielle Panabaker	15.00	40.00
FKAC1 Frederick Koehler	8.00	20.00
FKAC2 Frederick Koehler	8.00	20.00
MMAC1 Mary Elizabeth Mastrantonio	20.00	50.00
RLAC1 Reggie Lee	10.00	25.00
RLAC2 Reggie Lee	10.00	25.00
SRAC1 Sasha Roiz	8.00	20.00
SRAC2 Sasha Roiz	8.00	20.00
SWAC1 Silas Weir Mitchell	8.00	20.00
SWAC2 Silas Weir Mitchell	8.00	20.00
TWAC1 Titus Welliver	12.00	30.00
TWAC2 Titus Welliver	12.00	30.00
BRTAC1 Bree Turner	15.00	40.00
BRTAC2 Bree Turner	15.00	40.00
DBRAC1 Danny Bruno	10.00	25.00
DBRAC2 Danny Bruno	10.00	25.00

2013 Grimm Costumes

COMPLETE SET (21)	120.00	250.00
COMMON CARD	3.00	8.00
3 AUTO/MEM/PROP CARDS PER BOX		
GC1 Nick Burkhardt coat	6.00	15.00
GC2 Nick Burkhardt jacket	6.00	15.00
GC3 Hank Griffin shirt	3.00	8.00
GC4 Hank Griffin coat	3.00	8.00
GC5 Captain Renard jacket	3.00	8.00
GC6 Captain Renard shirt	3.00	8.00
GC7 Juliette Silverton shirt	5.00	12.00
GC8 Juliette Silverton jeans	5.00	12.00
GC9 Monroe shirt	3.00	8.00
GC10 Monroe shirt	3.00	8.00
GC11 Rosalee Calvert shirt	6.00	15.00
GC12 Rosalee Calvert shirt	6.00	15.00
GC13 Sergeant Wu shirt	3.00	8.00
GC14 Sergeant Wu scarf	3.00	8.00
GC15 Burnhardt/Griffin	12.00	30.00
GC16 Burnhard/Monroe	8.00	20.00
GC17 Wu/Renard	5.00	12.00
GC18 Wu/Griffin	4.00	10.00
GC19 Calvert/Monroe	6.00	15.00
GC20 Calvert/Monroe	6.00	15.00
GC21 7 cast members	20.00	50.00

2013 Grimm Props

COMPLETE SET (17)	450.00	800.00
COMMON CARD (GPR1-GPR7)	8.00	20.00
COMMON PAGE CARD (GPR8-GPR17)	30.00	80.00
3 AUTO/MEM/PROP CARDS PER BOX		
GPR2 Scythe Blade	15.00	40.00
GPR6 Medieval Hammer Pick	10.00	25.00
GPR9 Schakal Page	50.00	100.00

2013 Grimm Secrets

COMPLETE SET (3)	4.00	10.00
COMMON CARD (GS1-GS3)	2.50	6.00
STATED ODDS 1:24		

2013 Grimm Wesen Lenticular

COMPLETE SET (15)	15.00	40.00
COMMON CARD (GL1-GL15)	2.00	5.00
STATED ODDS 1:12		

2013 Grimm Album Promos

ISSUED AS ALBUM EXCLUSIVE		
AP1 Nick Burkhardt/Juliette Silverton	5.00	12.00
AP2 Nick Burkhardt and 6 others	5.00	12.00

2013 Grimm Foil Promos

PROMO1 Nick Burkhardt/Hank Griffin/Philly Fan Expo	2.50	6.00
PROMO2 Weapons/Philly Fan Expo	2.50	6.00
PROMO3 Body on table/Philly Fan Expo	2.50	6.00

2013 Grimm Promos

AC Nick Burkhardt/Monroe/AppleCards	15.00	40.00
GTS Nick Burkhardt/Hank Griffin/GTS	4.00	10.00
NYCC Scary lady NYCC	.75	2.00
SDCC Monster SDCC	.75	2.00
PNSCS Bearded guy/Philly	2.00	5.00
PROMO1 Nick Burkhardt/Hank Griffin	1.50	4.00
PROMO2 Weapons	1.50	4.00
PROMO3 Body on table	1.50	4.00
PROMO4 Nick w/Axe SDCC	1.50	4.00

2011 Grimm Fairy Tales Promos

COMPLETE SET (5)		
COMMON CARD		
P1 J. Scott Campbell/2500		
P2 J. Scott Campbell (Philly)		
PDI1 Dealer Incentive 1		
PDI2 Dealer Incentive 2		
PDI3 Dealer Incentive 3		

2015 Grimm Season Two

COMPLETE SET (72)	6.00	15.00
COMPLETE BOXED SET	30.00	80.00
COMMON CARD (1-72)	.15	.40

2015 Grimm Season Two Autographs

COMMON CARD	6.00	15.00
SMA Silas Weir Mitchell as Monroe, a Blutbad (blue)	10.00	25.00
SMA Silas Weir Mitchell as Monroe, a Blutbad (red)	10.00	25.00

2015 Grimm Season Two Costume Autographs

2 AUTOS OR COSTUMES PER BOX		
BTAC Bitsie Tulloch as Juliette Silverton (black)	8.00	20.00
BTAC Bitsie Tulloch as Juliette Silverton (blue)	8.00	20.00
BTAC Bitsie Tulloch as Juliette Silverton (red)	8.00	20.00
DGAC David Giuntoli as Detective Nick Burkhardt (blue)	12.00	30.00

2015 Grimm Season Two Duo Autographs

COMMON CARD	20.00	50.00
2 AUTOS OR COSTUMES PER BOX		
DBC1 B.Tulloch/C.Coffee (black/black)	25.00	60.00
DDB1 D.Giuntoli/B.Tulloch black/black)	30.00	80.00
DDR1 R.Hornsby/D.Giuntoli black/black)	25.00	60.00
DDS1 D.Giuntoli/S.Mitchell black/black)	30.00	80.00
DJC1 J.Tuck/C.Coffee black/black)	25.00	60.00
DSC1 S.Rois/C.Coffee black/black)	25.00	60.00
DSC1 Sasha Roiz as Captain Sean Renard Claire Coffee as Adalind Schade (green/black)	25.00	60.00

2015 Grimm Season Two Exotic Spice and Tea Shop Puzzle

COMPLETE SET (9)	12.00	30.00
COMMON CARD (GPC1-GPC9)	1.50	4.00
STATED ODDS 2:BOX		

2015 Grimm Season Two Illustrated Wesen

COMPLETE SET (15)	15.00	40.00
COMMON CARD (GW1-GW15)	1.25	3.00
STATED ODDS 3:BOX		

2015 Grimm Season Two Monroe's Halloween

COMPLETE SET (3)	6.00	15.00
COMMON CARD (GH1-GH3)	2.50	6.00
STATED ODDS 1:BOX		

2015 Grimm Season Two Promos

DP growling gal		
P2 picnic		
SP sitting chair & pillows, through window grate		
AP1 Soul Dreams album excl.	2.00	5.00
AP2 A Grimm World album excl.	2.00	5.00
APP dressed in sheet in kitchen Applecards	15.00	40.00
CC2 skeletal grimace SDCC	3.00	8.00
CC3 lying on ground, bloody neck SDCC	3.00	8.00
P1A scarface		
P1B scarface, holographic foil; Philly 60th Anniversary D		
RR1 meeting small witch/100	6.00	15.00

RR2 screaming removing shirt/100	6.00	15.00
BIGT domehead in woods	4.00	10.00
Big T		
NSU1 pointy ears snarling		
NSU2 red hair pointy ear		
NSU		
PUS1A woodchuck man	1.50	4.00
PUS1B woodchuck man; holofoil	1.50	4.00
PCAN1A wolfman	1.50	4.00
PCAN1B wolfman, holofoil	1.50	4.00
PCHI1A crouching stripehead	8.00	20.00
Chicago Non-Sport Card Show		
PCHI1B crouching stripehead, holofoil	8.00	20.00
Chicago Non-Sport Card Show		
PHILLY National Gold Medal		

1996 WildStorm Groo

COMPLETE SET (153)	100.00	200.00
UNOPENED BOX (36 PACKS)	300.00	400.00
UNOPENED PACK (8 CARDS)	8.00	12.00
COMMON CARD (1-153)	.75	2.00
AU1 Sergio Argones AU/500	25.00	60.00
SK1 Sergio Argones SKETCH/50	200.00	400.00

1996 WildStorm Groo Images of Groo Chromium

COMPLETE SET (9)	80.00	150.00
COMMON CARD (IG1-IG9)	8.00	20.00
RANDOMLY INSERTED INTO PACKS		

1985 Topps Gross Bears Buttons

COMPLETE SET (29)	120.00	250.00
UNOPENED BOX (36 PACKS)	80.00	120.00
UNOPENED PACK (1 BIG BAD BUTTON)	2.50	4.00
COMMON BUTTON	4.00	10.00

2006 Gross Out US Edition

COMPLETE SET (80)	6.00	15.00
UNOPENED BOX (36 PACKS)	25.00	40.00
UNOPENED PACK (7 CARDS)	1.00	1.25
COMMON CARD (1-60)	.12	.30
COMMON CARD (61-80)	.20	.50

2017 Grossery Gang

COMPLETE SET (118)	15.00	40.00
COMPLETE SET W/O SP (52)	5.00	12.00
COMMON CARD (1-52)	.20	.50
STICKERS (53-69)	.60	1.50
FRIDGE PUZZLE (70-78)	.60	1.50
MOST WANTED PUZZLE (79-87)	.60	1.50
TOUCH 'N FEEL (88-98)	.75	2.00
HEAT 'N REVEAL (99-112)	.75	2.00
SILVER HOLOGRAPHIC (113-118)	2.50	6.00

1986 Fleer Grossville High

COMPLETE SET (66)	8.00	20.00
UNOPENED BOX (48 PACKS)	35.00	50.00
UNOPENED PACK (5 STICKERS)	1.25	1.50
COMMON CARD (1-66)	.20	.50

1988 Topps Growing Pains

COMPLETE SET (66)	4.00	10.00
COMPLETE SET W/STICKERS (77)	6.00	15.00
UNOPENED BOX (36 PACKS)	50.00	75.00
UNOPENED PACK (9 CARDS+STICKER)	1.50	2.50
COMMON CARD (1-66)	.12	.30

1988 Topps Growing Pains Stickers

COMPLETE SET (11)	2.00	5.00
COMMON STICKER (1-11)	.30	.75
STATED ODDS 1:1		

1992 Topps Gruesome Greeting Cards

COMPLETE SET (44)	3.00	8.00
UNOPENED BOX (36 PACKS)	20.00	30.00
UNOPENED PACK (3 CARDS)	1.00	1.25
COMMON CARD (1-44)	.15	.40

2012 The Guild Seasons One Through Three

COMPLETE SET (63)	6.00	15.00
UNOPENED BOX (24 PACKS)	30.00	50.00
UNOPENED PACK (5 CARDS)	1.75	2.50
COMMON CARD (1-63)	.15	.40
P1 The Guild PROMO	6.00	15.00

2012 The Guild Seasons One Through Three Autographs

COMMON AUTO (A1-A25)	5.00	12.00
STATED ODDS 1:24		
A23 DOES NOT EXIST		
A1 Sandeep Parikh SP	15.00	40.00
A2 Felicia Day SP	100.00	200.00
A3 Jeff Lewis SP	15.00	40.00
A4 Amy Okuda SP	50.00	100.00
A5 Robin Thorsen SP	12.00	30.00
A6 Vincent Caso SP	50.00	100.00
A7 Sandeep Parikh	10.00	25.00
A8 Felicia Day	30.00	75.00
A9 Jeff Lewis	8.00	20.00
A10 Amy Okuda	20.00	50.00
A11 Robin Thorsen	6.00	15.00
A12 Vincent Caso	10.00	25.00
A13 Wil Wheaton	30.00	75.00
A18 Michele Boyd	12.00	30.00
A22 Tara Caso	6.00	15.00
A24 Kim Evey	8.00	20.00
A25 Sean Becker	10.00	25.00

2012 The Guild Seasons One Through Three Characters

COMPLETE SET (6)	5.00	12.00
COMMON CARD (TG1-TG6)	1.50	4.00
OVERALL CHASE ODDS 1:6		

2012 The Guild Seasons One Through Three Costumes

COMPLETE SET (7)	80.00	150.00
COMMON CARD	8.00	20.00
STATED ODDS 1:24		
M1 Felicia Day	25.00	60.00
M4 Amy Okuda	10.00	25.00
M5 Robin Thorsen	10.00	25.00

2012 The Guild Seasons One Through Three Vlog

COMPLETE SET (9)	5.00	12.00
COMMON CARD (1-9)	1.25	3.00
OVERALL CHASE ODDS 1:6		

1992 Pro Set Guinness Book of Records

COMPLETE SET (100)	6.00	15.00
UNOPENED BOX (36 PACKS)	10.00	15.00
UNOPENED PACK (10 CARDS)	.30	.40
COMMON CARD (1-100)	.12	.30

1992 Pro Set Guinness Book of Records Promos

COMMON CARD	1.25	3.00
6 Head and Shoulders Above (variant back)	1.50	4.00
(Pro Set Gazette Magazine Exclusive)		

2001 Gumby Previews

COMPLETE PREVIEW SET (7)	6.00	15.00
COMMON CARD	1.25	3.00
ANNCD PRINT RUN 2500 SER.#'d SETS		
P1 Gumby 6-Card Preview PROMO	.75	2.00

2000 Gundam Wing

COMPLETE SET (90)	5.00	12.00
UNOPENED BOX (24 PACKS)	30.00	40.00
UNOPENED PACK (7 CARDS)	1.25	1.75
COMMON CARD (1-90)	.10	.25
*SILVER: .75X TO 2X BASIC CARDS		
*GOLD/100: 5X TO 12X BASIC CARDS		
GWC1 Checklist	1.25	3.00

2000 Gundam Wing Gundam Clear

COMPLETE SET (15)	20.00	50.00
COMMON CARD (GC1-GC15)	2.00	5.00
STATED ODDS 1:4		

2001 Gundam Wing Endless Waltz

COMPLETE SET (90)	4.00	10.00
UNOPENED BOX (24 PACKS)	15.00	25.00
UNOPENED PACK (7 CARDS)	.75	1.25
COMMON CARD (1-90)	.06	.15
*GOLD: 12X TO 30X BASIC CARDS		

2001 Gundam Wing Endless Waltz GW Gallery

COMPLETE SET (13)	6.00	15.00
COMMON CARD (G1-G13)	.75	2.00
*GOLD/100: 1X TO 2.5X BASIC CARDS		
RANDOMLY INSERTED INTO PACKS		

2001 Gundam Wing Endless Waltz GW MS Collection

COMPLETE SET (17)	4.00	10.00
COMMON CARD (MS1-MS17)	.40	1.00
*GOLD/100: 2X TO 5X BASIC CARDS		
RANDOMLY INSERTED INTO PACKS		

1993 Pacific Gunsmoke

COMPLETE SET (110)	5.00	12.00
COMPLETE FACTORY SET (110)	5.00	12.00
UNOPENED BOX (36 PACKS)	20.00	30.00
UNOPENED PACK (CARDS)	.60	1.00
COMMON CARD (1-110)	.08	.20

1995 Hagar the Horrible

COMPLETE SET (50)	5.00	12.00
UNOPENED BOX (36 PACKS)	20.00	30.00
UNOPENED PACK (6 CARDS)	.75	1.00
COMMON CARD (1-50)	.20	.50
P1 Hagar Running PROMO	.75	2.00
UNC 50-Card Uncut Sheet/100*		
NNO1 Jumbo Card/500*	.75	2.00

2014 Hallowe'en All Hallows' Eve

COMPLETE SET (20)	5.00	12.00
COMMON CARD	.50	1.25

2014 Hallowe'en All Hallows' Eve Frosted Clear

COMPLETE SET (4)	8.00	20.00
COMMON CARD	3.00	8.00
*METAL: .75X TO 2X BASIC CARDS		

2014 Hallowe'en All Hallows' Eve Promos

COMPLETE SET (3)	5.00	12.00
*METAL: .75X TO 2X BASIC PROMOS		
P1 Witch (Facebook)	1.50	4.00
P2 Zombies (Philly)	1.50	4.00
P3 The Monster (Philly)	1.50	4.00
P4 Graveyard (SDCC 2014)	2.00	5.00
P5 She-Devil (Fan Expo Canada)	2.00	5.00

2014 Hallowe'en All Hallows' Eve Promos Metal

*METAL: .75X TO 2X BASIC CARDS		
P1 Witch (Facebook)	3.00	8.00
P2 Zombies (Philly)	3.00	8.00
P3 The Monster (Philly)	3.00	8.00
P4 Graveyard (SDCC 2014)	3.00	8.00
P5 She-Devil (Fan Expo Canada)	3.00	8.00

2015 Hallowe'en 2 Trick or Treat

COMPLETE SET (20)
COMMON CARD (1-20)
STATED ODDS 1:
1 Black Cat
2 Bogeyman
3 Cemetery
4 Creepy Clown
5 Devil
6 Gargoyle
7 Grave Robber
8 Hell Hound
9 Jack-O-Lanterns
10 Mad Scientist's Monster
11 Monster!
12 Mummies
13 Samhain
14 Scarecrow
15 Swamp Monster
16 Trick or Treat!
17 Vampire
18 Werewolf
19 Witch
20 Zombies
H2L The Grim Reaper (lenticular)

2015 Hallowe'en 2 Trick or Treat Double-Thick Metal

COMPLETE SET (2)
COMMON CARD (SP3-SP4)
STATED ODDS 1:
SP3 Day of the Dead (orange female)
SP4 Day of the Dead (green male)

2015 Hallowe'en 2 Trick or Treat Frosted Clear

COMPLETE SET (4)
COMMON CARD
STATED ODDS 1:
1 Mummy
2 Swamp Monster
3 The Bat
4 The Vampyre's Bride

2015 Hallowe'en 2 Trick or Treat Promos

COMPLETE SET (5)
COMMON CARD (P1-P5)
*METAL: X TO X BASIC CARDS
P1 Ghost
P2 Headless Horseman
P3 Haunted House
P4 Demon's Ball
P5 Goblin

2018 Hallowe'en 3 The Witching Hour

COMPLETE SET (21)	.60	15.00
COMMON CARD (1-20, HH)	.60	1.50

2018 Hallowe'en 3 The Witching Hour Frosted Clear

COMPLETE SET (3)	8.00	20.00
COMMON CARD	4.00	10.00
STATED ODDS 1:SET		

2018 Hallowe'en 3 The Witching Hour Lenticular Insert

H3L Restless Spirit	20.00	50.00

2018 Hallowe'en 3 The Witching Hour Limited Edition Metal

COMPLETE SET (2)		
COMMON CARD	25.00	60.00
JC1 Day of the Dead	30.00	75.00

2018 Hallowe'en 3 The Witching Hour Metal Chase

NNO Grim Reaper	60.00	120.00

2018 Hallowe'en 3 The Witching Hour Promos

COMPLETE SET (3)	5.00	12.00
COMMON CARD (P1-P3	2.50	6.00

2007 Halo

COMPLETE SET (90)	6.00	15.00
UNOPENED BOX (24 PACKS)	300.00	450.00
UNOPENED PACK (7 CARDS)	15.00	20.00
COMMON CARD (1-90)	.12	.30

2007 Halo Embossed Foil

COMPLETE SET (10)	12.00	30.00
COMMON CARD (1-10)	1.50	4.00
STATED ODDS 1:6		

2007 Halo Flix-Pix Lenticular

COMPLETE SET (5)	20.00	50.00
COMMON CARD (1-5)	5.00	12.00
STATED ODDS 1:12		
RETAIL EXCLUSIVE		

MODERN

2007 Halo Foil

COMPLETE SET (10) 5.00 12.00
COMMON CARD (1-10) .60 1.50
STATED ODDS 1:6

2007 Halo Promos

COMPLETE SET (2) 2.00 5.00
COMMON CARD (P1-P2) 1.25 3.00

1997 CMA Hammer Horror 40th Anniversary

COMPLETE FACTORY SET (9) 15.00 40.00
COMMON CARD (T1-T9) 3.00 8.00

1995-96 Cornerstone Hammer Horror

COMPLETE SET (162) 12.00 30.00
COMPLETE SERIES ONE SET (81) 6.00 15.00
COMPLETE SERIES TWO SET (82) 5.00 12.00
UNOPENED SERIES ONE BOX (36 PACKS) 25.00 40.00
UNOPENED SERIES ONE PACK (10 CARDS) .75 1.25
UNOPENED SERIES TWO BOX (36 PACKS) 25.00 40.00
UNOPENED SERIES TWO PACK (10 CARDS) .75 1.25
COMMON CARD (1-81) .15 .40
COMMON CARD (81-162; CL) .12 .30
IT1 Frankenstein (inside traders) (Series 1 Exclusive) 5.00 12.00
IT5 Blood from the Mummy's Tomb (Series 2 Exclusive) 1.25 3.00
UNC1 81-Card Series 1 Base Set Uncut Sheet
UNC2 80-Card Series 2 Base Set Uncut Sheet

1995-96 Cornerstone Hammer Horror Autographs

COMMON CARD 30.00 80.00
STATED ODDS 1:216 IN SERIES TWO BOXES

1995-96 Cornerstone Hammer Horror Crip-tych

COMPLETE SET (6) 6.00 15.00
COMMON CARD (A1-A6) 1.50 4.00
RANDOMLY INSERTED INTO SERIES ONE PACKS
PAN1 3-Card Panel (A1-A3)
PAN2 3-Card Panel (A4-A6)

1995-96 Cornerstone Hammer Horror The Hammer That Never Was Foil

COMPLETE SET (6) 12.00 30.00
COMMON CARD (F1-F6) 3.00 8.00
STATED ODDS 1:9 SERIES TWO PACKS

1995-96 Cornerstone Hammer Horror MonsterMotion Lenticular

COMPLETE SET (2) 6.00 15.00
COMMON CARD 4.00 10.00
MM MonsterMotion Order Card 4.00 10.00
MR MonsterMotion Redemption 4.00 10.00

1995-96 Cornerstone Hammer Horror Promos

COMMON CARD .75 2.00
M1 The Curse of Frankenstein (Model Mart Kits) 1.25 3.00
M2 The Curse of the Werewolf (Model Mart Kits) 1.25 3.00
M3 The Reptile (Model Mart Kits) 1.25 3.00
P1A Promo 1 1.25 3.00
P1B Stake Pounding 1.25 3.00
P2C Werewolf artwork (George Bush not issued)/12* 120.00 200.00
P4A Combo 1.25 3.00

2000 Hammer Horror III Entombed

COMPLETE FACTORY SET (74) 5.00 12.00
COMMON CARD (1-72; TC AND CL) .12 .30

2000 Hammer Horror III Entombed Discount Cards

COMPLETE SET (3) 2.00 5.00
COMMON CARD .75 2.00
STATED ODDS 1:SET

2000 Hammer Horror III Entombed Promos

P1 Sarcophagus 1.50 4.00
P2 Holding Lanter 1.50 4.00
NNO Pop-Up/50* 125.00 200.00
NNO Don't Scream! (dealer postcard)

2004 Hammer Horror IV Behind the Screams

COMPLETE FACTORY SET (72) 4.00 10.00
COMMON CARD (1-72) .12 .30

2004 Hammer Horror IV Behind the Screams Magazine Tribute Ultra Rare

COMPLETE SET (3) 20.00 50.00
COMMON CARD (T1-T3 8.00 20.00

2004 Hammer Horror IV Behind the Screams Rare Prize

COMPLETE SET (3) 5.00 12.00
COMMON CARD (R1-R3 2.00 5.00

2004 Hammer Horror IV Behind the Screams Transition Rare

COMPLETE SET (15) 12.00 30.00
COMMON CARD 1.00 2.50
RANDOMLY INSERTED

2004 Hammer Horror IV Behind the Screams Promos

COMPLETE SET (2) 3.00 8.00
COMMON CARD (P1-P2) 2.00 5.00

2007-08 Strictly Ink Hammer Horror Series One Promos

P1 Coming 2007 GEN
PR3 Peter Cushing Christopher Lee 1.00 2.50

1994 Madison Square Productions Hammer Horror Tribute Promos

COMPLETE SET (3) 10.00 25.00
COMMON CARD (P1-P3) 4.00 10.00

2002-03 Artbox Hamtaro

COMPLETE SET (60) 5.00 12.00
COMPLETE SERIES 1 SET (30) 3.00 8.00
COMPLETE SERIES 2 SET (30) 3.00 8.00
UNOPENED SERIES 1 BOX (12 PACKS) 20.00 25.00
UNOPENED SERIES 1 PACK (5 CARDS) 2.00 2.25
UNOPENED SERIES 2 BOX (12 PACKS) 20.00 25.00
UNOPENED SERIES 2 PACK (5 CARDS) 2.00 2.25
COMMON CARD (1-30) .15 .40
COMMON CARD (31-60) .15 .40
*STICKERS: 1X TO 2.5X BASIC CARDS
NNO How to play with the face/map side (S1)
NNO Hamtaro Trading Card Collectibles Order Form (S1)
NNO Hamtaro Trading Cards (S2)
NNO Checklist Sheet / Merchandise Form / Game Instructions (S2)

2002-03 Artbox Hamtaro Promos

COMPLETE SET (2) 2.00 5.00
COMMON CARD (HP1-HP2) 1.25 3.00

1994 Cardz Hanna-Barbera Classics

COMPLETE SET (60) 5.00 12.00
UNOPENED BOX (36 PACKS) 25.00 30.00
UNOPENED PACK (8 CARDS+1 BANDAGE) .75 1.00
COMMON CARD (1-60) .12 .30
PROMOS P1, P2, P3 ARE GENERAL DISTRIBUTION
P1 Yogi Bear - Ice Box Raider PROMO .75 2.00
P2 Jetsons .75 2.00
P3 Scooby Doo .75 2.00

1994 Cardz Hanna-Barbera Classics Tekchromes

COMPLETE SET (3) 6.00 15.00
COMMON CARD (T1-T3) 2.50 6.00
STATED ODDS 1:36

2008 Hannah Montana

COMPLETE SET (90) 4.00 10.00
UNOPENED BOX (24 PACKS) 40.00 50.00
UNOPENED PACK (7 CARDS) 2.00 2.50
COMMON CARD (1-90) .10 .30

2008 Hannah Montana Foil Stickers

COMPLETE SET (10) 2.00 5.00
COMMON CARD (F1-F10) .40 1.00
STATED ODDS 1:3

2008 Hannah Montana Glitter Stickers

COMPLETE SET (10) 3.00 8.00
COMMON CARD (G1-G10) .60 1.50
STATED ODDS 1:6

2008 Hannah Montana Mega Stickers

COMPLETE SET (10) 3.00 8.00
COMMON CARD (1-10) .40 1.00
STATED ODDS 1:2

2008 Hannah Montana Pop Star Quiz

COMPLETE SET (120) 5.00 12.00
UNOPENED BOX (24 PACKS) 30.00 40.00
UNOPENED PACK (7 CARDS) 1.50 1.75
COMMON CARD (1-120) .12 .30
P1 Part-Time Pop Star PROMO (SDCC Exclusive) 1.50 4.00

2008 Hannah Montana Pop Star Quiz Glitter Stickers

COMPLETE SET (5) 2.00 5.00
COMMON STICKER (1-5) .60 1.50
STATED ODDS 1:6

2008 Hannah Montana Pop Star Quiz Jewel Foil

COMPLETE SET (12) 3.00 8.00
COMMON CARD (1-12) .40 1.00
STATED ODDS 1:2

2008 Hannah Montana Pop Star Quiz Stick-Ons

COMPLETE SET (10) 2.50 6.00
COMMON STICK-ON (1-10) .30 .75
STATED ODDS 1:3

1998 DuoCards Happy Days

COMPLETE SET (72) 4.00 10.00
UNOPENED BOX (30 PACKS) 75.00 125.00
UNOPENED PACK (7 CARDS) 3.00 4.00
COMMON CARD (1-72) .12 .30

1998 DuoCards Happy Days Autographs

STATED PRINT RUN 150 SER.#'d SETS
1 Henry Winkler/150 50.00 100.00
2 Marion Ross/150 30.00 80.00

1998 DuoCards Happy Days The Fonz OmniChrome

COMPLETE SET (6) 10.00 25.00
COMMON CARD (1-6) 2.00 5.00
STATED ODDS 1:15

1998 DuoCards Happy Days Promos

COMPLETE SET (2) 1.25 3.00
COMMON CARD (P1-P2) .75 2.00

1994 Disney Hardball

COMPLETE SET (8) 5.00 12.00
COMMON CARD .75 2.00

1987 Topps Harry and the Hendersons

COMPLETE SET (77) 3.00 8.00
COMPLETE SET W/STICKERS (99) 5.00 12.00
UNOPENED BOX (36 PACKS) 35.00 50.00
UNOPENED PACK (9 CARDS+STICKER) 1.25 2.50
COMMON CARD (1-77) .10 .25

1987 Topps Harry and the Hendersons Stickers

COMPLETE SET (22) 2.00 5.00
COMMON CARD (1-22) .10 .30

Harry Potter Movies

2001 Harry Potter and the Sorcerer's Stone

COMPLETE SET (81) 12.00 30.00
COMPLETE HOLOFOIL SET (40) 25.00 60.00
UNOPENED BOX (36 PACKS) 30.00 40.00
UNOPENED PACK (7 CARDS) 1.00 1.25
COMMON CARD (1-81+CHECKLIST) .30 .75
*HOLOFOIL: 1.5X TO 4X BASIC CARDS
HOLOFOIL PARALLEL ONLY CONTAINS
THE FIRST 40 CARDS FROM THE BASE SET

2005 Harry Potter and the Sorcerer's Stone

COMPLETE SET (90) 3.00 8.00
UNOPENED BOX (24 PACKS) 600.00 1200.00
UNOPENED PACK (8 CARDS) 25.00 50.00
COMMON CARD (1-90) .10 .25

2005 Harry Potter and the Sorcerer's Stone Autographs

COMMON AUTO 15.00 40.00
STATED ODDS 1:48
NNO Devon Murray 20.00 50.00
NNO Geraldine Somerville 40.00 100.00
NNO Ian Hart 25.00 60.00
NNO John Cleese 150.00 400.00
NNO John Hurt 200.00 350.00
NNO Joshua Herdman 40.00 100.00
NNO Leslie Phillips 75.00 200.00
NNO Matthew Lewis 75.00 200.00
NNO Ray Fearon 30.00 75.00
NNO Warwick Davis/Bank Teller 40.00 100.00
NNO Warwick Davis/Prof. Flitwick 30.00 75.00

2005 Harry Potter and the Sorcerer's Stone Box-Loaders

COMPLETE SET (4) 4.00 10.00
COMMON CARD (BT1-BT4) 1.25 3.00
STATED ODDS ONE PER BOX

2005 Harry Potter and the Sorcerer's Stone Case-Loaders

COMPLETE SET (3) 50.00 100.00
COMMON CARD (1-3) 15.00 40.00
STATED ODDS ONE PER CASE

2005 Harry Potter and the Sorcerer's Stone Chase

COMPLETE SET (9) 6.00 15.00
COMMON CARD (R1-R9) .75 2.00
STATED ODDS 1:5

2005 Harry Potter and the Sorcerer's Stone Costumes

COMPLETE SET (12) 175.00 350.00
COMMON CARD (C1-C12) 10.00 25.00
STATED ODDS 1:48
C2 Griffindor Tie/360 25.00 60.00
C3 David Bradley Pants/360 20.00 50.00
C4 Robbie Coltrane Shirt/710 20.00 50.00
C5 Daniel Radcliffe Quiddich Sweater/410 30.00 75.00
C6 Daniel Radcliffe Quiddich Sweater/335 50.00 100.00
C7 Oliver Wood Sweater/300 60.00 120.00
C11 Hogwarts Skirts/510 25.00 60.00
C12 Tom Felton Scarf/485 75.00 150.00

2005 Harry Potter and the Sorcerer's Stone Dealer-Incentive Props

COMMON PROP 125.00 250.00
1 Platform 9 3/4 Ticket/40 800.00 1500.00
3 Wizard Coin Bronze/40 400.00 800.00
4 Wizard Coin Gold/40 400.00 800.00
5 Wizard Coin Silver/40 400.00 800.00

2005 Harry Potter and the Sorcerer's Stone Film Cels

COMPLETE SET (9) 120.00 250.00

COMMON CARD (CFC1-CFC9) 12.00 30.00
STATED ODDS 1:80

2005 Harry Potter and the Sorcerer's Stone Props

COMMON PROP 12.00 30.00
P1-P13 STATED ODDS 1:48
NNO NY TOY FAIR EXCLUSIVE
P1 Wand Box/842 20.00 50.00
P2 The Sorcerer's Stone/265 75.00 150.00
P3 4 Pivet Drive/130 150.00 300.00
P5 Practice Broom/450 30.00 75.00
P6 Fluffy's Fur/700 25.00 60.00
P7 Chocolate Frog/127 300.00 600.00
P8 The Daily Prophet/733 20.00 50.00
P9 Gringotts Top Secret Letter/140 250.00 500.00
P10 Shopping List/130 200.00 350.00
P12 Wizard Candy/538 150.00 300.00
P13 Devil's Snare/100 200.00 400.00
NNO Slytherin Sweater/165 125.00 250.00

2005 Harry Potter and the Sorcerer's Stone Promos Gold Foil

COMPLETE SET (4) 5.00 12.00
COMMON CARD (1-4) .75 2.00
*RED: .6X TO 1.5X BASIC PROMOS
*SILVER: .75X TO 2X BASIC PROMOS
*BLUE: 1.5X TO 4X BASIC PROMOS
*GREEN: 3X TO 8X BASIC PROMOS
3 Hermione, Harry, and Ron 3.00 8.00

2006 Harry Potter and the Chamber of Secrets

COMPLETE SET (90) 5.00 12.00
UNOPENED BOX (24 PACKS) 800.00 1200.00
UNOPENED PACK (8 CARDS) 35.00 50.00
COMMON CARD (1-90) .15 .40

2006 Harry Potter and the Chamber of Secrets Autographs

COMMON AUTO 25.00 60.00
STATED ODDS 1:48
NNO Bonnie Wright 125.00 300.00
NNO Chris Rankin 50.00 120.00
NNO Fiona Shaw 50.00 120.00
NNO Harry Melling 40.00 100.00
NNO Julian Glover 50.00 120.00
NNO Kenneth Branagh 75.00 150.00
NNO Miriam Margolyes 50.00 120.00
NNO Richard Griffiths 75.00 200.00
NNO Shirley Henderson 75.00 150.00

2006 Harry Potter and the Chamber of Secrets Box-Loaders

COMPLETE SET (4) 5.00 12.00
COMMON CARD (BT1-BT4) 1.50 4.00
STATED ODDS ONE PER BOX

2006 Harry Potter and the Chamber of Secrets Case-Loaders

COMPLETE SET (2) 10.00 25.00
COMMON CARD (1-2) 6.00 15.00
STATED ODDS ONE PER CASE

2006 Harry Potter and the Chamber of Secrets Costumes

COMMON CARD (C1-C17) 8.00 20.00
STATED ODDS 1:24
C1 Daniel Radcliffe Shirt/190 150.00 300.00
C2 Rupert Grint Sweater/290 150.00 300.00
C4 Daniel Radcliffe Shirt/540 25.00 60.00
C5 Rupert Grint Shirt/490 20.00 50.00
C6 Christian Coulson Sweater/240 30.00 75.00
C8 Jason Isaacs Cloak/640 15.00 40.00
C9 Bonnie Wright Sweater/190 100.00 200.00
C10 Emma Watson Sweater/165 100.00 200.00
C11 Daniel Radcliffe Blue Sweater/440 20.00 50.00
C12 Daniel Radcliffe Red Sweater/540 20.00 50.00
C13 Tom Felton Robe/165 125.00 250.00
C14 Robbie Coltrane Shirt/515 20.00 50.00
C15 Devon Murray Jacket/240 25.00 60.00
C16 Bonnie Wright Pajamas/340 25.00 60.00
C17 Richard Griffiths Suit/390 12.00 30.00

2006 Harry Potter and the Chamber of Secrets Dealer-Incentives

Ci1 Daniel Radcliffe Pajamas/340 20.00 50.00
Ci2 Hermione's Cauldron/160 40.00 80.00
Ci3 Basilisk Fang/100 120.00 250.00
Ci4 Hogwarts Letter/64 200.00 400.00

2006 Harry Potter and the Chamber of Secrets Film Cels

COMPLETE SET (9) 100.00 200.00
COMMON CARD (CFC1-CFC9) 10.00 25.00
STATED ODDS 1:80

2006 Harry Potter and the Chamber of Secrets Foil Chase

COMPLETE SET (9) 8.00 20.00
COMMON CARD (R1-R9) 1.00 2.50
STATED ODDS 1:5

2006 Harry Potter and the Chamber of Secrets Props

COMMON CARD (P1-P10) 25.00 50.00
STATED ODDS 1:80
P2 Howler/190 125.00 250.00
P3 Dumbledore's Books/290 30.00 60.00
P4 Fawkes' Feathers/140 125.00 250.00
P5 Mandrake/360 50.00 100.00
P6 Dueling Club Cloth/80 250.00 400.00
P8 Aragog's Legs/215 100.00 200.00
P9 Potions Book/115 150.00 300.00

2002 Harry Potter and the Chamber of Secrets Promos K-Mart

COMPLETE SET (4) 6.00 15.00
COMMON CARD 2.00 5.00

2004 Harry Potter and the Prisoner of Azkaban

COMPLETE SET (90) 5.00 12.00
UNOPENED BOX (24 PACKS) 1000.00 1500.00
UNOPENED PACK (6 CARDS) 45.00 65.00
COMMON CARD (1-90) .15 .40
HOLOFOIL IS SDCC EXCLUSIVE

2004 Harry Potter and the Prisoner of Azkaban Autographs

COMMON AUTO 25.00 60.00
STATED ODDS 1:48
NNO Bonnie Wright 75.00 200.00
NNO David Thewlis 60.00 150.00
NNO Emma Watson 1500.00 2500.00
NNO Gary Oldman 1200.00 2000.00
NNO James Phelps 75.00 200.00
NNO Julie Christie 50.00 120.00
NNO Matthew Lewis 60.00 150.00
NNO Michael Gambon 200.00 500.00
NNO Oliver Phelps 75.00 200.00

2004 Harry Potter and the Prisoner of Azkaban Box-Loaders

COMPLETE SET (4) 5.00 12.00
COMMON CARD (BT1-BT4) 1.25 3.00
STATED ODDS ONE PER BOX

2004 Harry Potter and the Prisoner of Azkaban Case-Loaders

COMPLETE SET (3) 60.00 120.00
COMMON CARD (1-3) 20.00 50.00
STATED ODDS ONE PER CASE

2004 Harry Potter and the Prisoner of Azkaban Chase Hobby

COMPLETE SET (9) 6.00 15.00
COMMON CARD (R1-R9) .75 2.00
*RETAIL: SAME VALUE AS HOBBY
STATED ODDS 1:5 HOBBY

2004 Harry Potter and the Prisoner of Azkaban Costumes

COMMON MEM (C1-C7) 15.00 40.00
STATED ODDS 1:24
C1 Daniel Radcliffe Robe/100 (UK Exclusive) 150.00 300.00
C2 Rupert Grint Robe/100 100.00 200.00
C3 Daniel Radcliffe Robe/750 20.00 50.00
C4 Emma Watson Robe/900 100.00 200.00
C5 Daniel Radcliffe Shirt/600 25.00 60.00
C6 Emma Watson Pink Sweater/450 100.00 200.00

2004 Harry Potter and the Prisoner of Azkaban Dealer Incentive Props

HONEYDUKES/75: 5-CASE INCENTIVE
PEAR TREE LEAVES/30: 25-CASE INCENTIVE
1 Honeydukes Candy/75 200.00 400.00
2 Pear Tree Leaves/30 1500.00 3000.00

2004 Harry Potter and the Prisoner of Azkaban Props

COMMON MEM (P1-P9) 15.00 40.00
STATED ODDS 1:24
P1 Chocolate Frog/86 200.00 400.00
P3 Spindle's Lick 'O' Rish Spiders/70 200.00 400.00
P4 Honeydukes Bag/434 30.00 75.00
P6 Black Pepper Imps/90 150.00 300.00
P7 Exploding Bon Bons/96 150.00 300.00
P8 The Daily Prophet/200 60.00 120.00
P9 Permission Form/100 200.00 400.00

2004 Harry Potter and the Prisoner of Azkaban UK Retail

COMPLETE SET (72) 5.00 12.00
UNOPENED BOX (24 PACKS) 15.00 20.00
UNOPENED PACK (6 CARDS) .75 1.00
COMMON CARD (1-72) .12 .30

2004 Harry Potter and the Prisoner of Azkaban UK Retail Foil

COMPLETE SET (17) 2.50 6.00
COMMON CARD (F1-F17) .20 .50
STATED ODDS 1:1 CARDS INC. PACKS

2004 Harry Potter and the Prisoner of Azkaban Promos Silver Foil

COMPLETE SET (5) 5.00 12.00
COMMON CARD (1-5) .75 2.00
*GOLD: .5X TO 1.2X BASIC PROMOS
*RED: .6X TO 1.5X BASIC PROMOS
*GREEN: 2.5X TO 6X BASIC PROMOS
*BLUE: 4X TO 10X BASIC PROMOS
5 Prisoner of Azkaban 3.00 8.00

2004 Harry Potter and the Prisoner of Azkaban Promos Holofoil

COMPLETE SET (5) 5.00 12.00
COMMON CARD (1-5) 1.25 3.00
SDCC EXCLUSIVE

2004 Harry Potter and the Prisoner of Azkaban Update

COMPLETE SET (90) 5.00 12.00
UNOPENED BOX (24 PACKS) 1500.00 2000.00
UNOPENED PACK (8 CARDS) 65.00 90.00
COMMON CARD (1-90) .15 .40

2004 Harry Potter and the Prisoner of Azkaban Update Autographs

COMMON AUTO 15.00 40.00
STATED ODDS 1:110 HOBBY
CARD 14 UK TIN SET ONLY
CARD 18 DEALER INCENTIVE ONLY
NNO Daniel Radcliffe 600.00 1200.00
NNO D.Radcliffe/E.Watson/R.Grint 2000.00 3000.00
NNO Dawn French 50.00 100.00
NNO Emma Watson 1500.00 2500.00
NNO Genevieve Gaunt 20.00 50.00
NNO Harry Melling 30.00 75.00
NNO J.Phelps/O.Phelps 150.00 400.00
NNO Jimmy Gardner 20.00 50.00
NNO Richard Griffiths 40.00 100.00
NNO Rupert Grint 300.00 600.00
NNO Warwick Davis 20.00 50.00
NNO Warwick Davis UK TIN 20.00 50.00

2004 Harry Potter and the Prisoner of Azkaban Update Box-Loaders

COMPLETE SET (4) 4.00 10.00
COMMON CARD (BT1-BT4) 1.25 3.00
STATED ODDS ONE PER HOBBY BOX

2004 Harry Potter and the Prisoner of Azkaban Update Case-Loaders

COMPLETE SET (3) 50.00 100.00
COMMON CARD (1-3) 15.00 40.00
STATED ODDS ONE PER CASE

2004 Harry Potter and the Prisoner of Azkaban Update Chase Hobby

COMPLETE SET (9) 6.00 15.00
COMMON CARD (R1-R9) .75 2.00
STATED ODDS 1:5 HOBBY

2004 Harry Potter and the Prisoner of Azkaban Update Chase Retail

COMPLETE SET (9) 6.00 15.00
COMMON CARD (M1-M9) .75 2.00
STATED ODDS 1:5 RETAIL

2004 Harry Potter and the Prisoner of Azkaban Update Costumes

COMMON CARD (C1-C21) 15.00 40.00
STATED ODDS C1-C19 1:36 HOBBY
STATED ODDS C20-C21 1:24 RETAIL
C2 Emma Watson Sweater/730 100.00 200.00
C3 Pam Ferris Jacket/430 20.00 50.00
C4 D.Radcliffe Quidditch w/Stripe/1,143 30.00 75.00
C5 D.Radcliffe Quidditch w/o Stripe/2,173 25.00 60.00
C6 Robert Hardy Coat/830 30.00 75.00
C7 Emma Thompson Dress/330 30.00 75.00
C8 Tom Felton Robe/628 60.00 120.00
C10 Emma Watson Pants/730 100.00 200.00
C11 David Thewlis Shirt/834 25.00 60.00
C12 Harry Cedric Quidditch Robes/628 25.00 60.00
C13 Cedric Diggory Quidditch Robe/2,173 25.00 60.00
C14 Griffindor House Members Tie/330 50.00 100.00
C15 Julie Christie Jacket/250 40.00 80.00
C17 Slytherin House Members Tie/380 60.00 120.00
C18 Daniel Radcliffe Robe/2,173 25.00 60.00
C19 Emma Watson Sweater/628 200.00 500.00
C20 Daniel Radcliffe Cloak/2,575 20.00 50.00
C21 Oliver Phelps Quidditch Robe/2,803 20.00 50.00

2004 Harry Potter and the Prisoner of Azkaban Update Dealer-Incentive Memorabilia

COMMON MEM 25.00 60.00
1 Monster Book of Monsters/310 150.00 300.00
2 Whomping Willow Tree/172 200.00 400.00
4 Daniel Radcliffe Shirt/475 75.00 150.00

2004 Harry Potter and the Prisoner of Azkaban Update Film Cels

COMPLETE SET (9) 60.00 120.00
COMMON CARD (CFC1-CFC9) 6.00 15.00
STATED ODDS 1:80 HOBBY
STATED PRINT RUN 900 SER. #'d SETS

2004 Harry Potter and the Prisoner of Azkaban Update Props

COMMON CARD (P1-P10) 12.00 30.00
STATED ODDS 1:80 HOBBY
P1 Buckbeak Feather/390 75.00 150.00
P3 The Marauder's Map/500 60.00 120.00
P4 Wanted Poster/335 30.00 75.00
P5 Daily Prophet Newspaper/480 50.00 100.00
P6 Fizzing Whizzbees/430 30.00 60.00
P7 Unfogging the Future (Cover & Pages)/93020.00 50.00
P9 Devination Class Purple/930 25.00 60.00
P10 Grim Fur/880 30.00 75.00

2004 Harry Potter and the Prisoner of Azkaban Update Promos Silver Foil

COMPLETE SET (4) 5.00 12.00
COMMON CARD (1-4) 1.00 2.50
*GOLD: SAME VALUE AS SILVER

MODERN

*BLUE: 1.2X TO 3X BASIC PROMOS		
*GREEN: 1.2X TO 3X BASIC PROMOS		
*RED: 1.5X TO 4X BASIC PROMOS		
*HOLOFOIL: 1.5X TO 4X BASIC PROMOS		
3 Harry	1.50	4.00
4 Hermione, Buckbeak, and Harry	1.50	4.00

2004 Harry Potter and the Prisoner of Azkaban FilmCardz

COMPLETE SET (72)	6.00	15.00
UNOPENED BOX (24 PACKS)	50.00	60.00
UNOPENED PACK (5 CARDS)	2.50	3.00
COMMON CARD (1-72)	.20	.50

2004 Harry Potter and the Prisoner of Azkaban FilmCardz Rare Chase

COMPLETE SET (9)	12.00	30.00
COMMON CARD (R1-R9)	1.50	4.00
STATED ODDS 1:5		

2004 Harry Potter and the Prisoner of Azkaban FilmCardz Ultra Rare Chase

COMPLETE SET (9)	15.00	40.00
COMMON CARD (UR1-UR9)	2.50	6.00
STATED ODDS 1:8		

2004 Harry Potter and the Prisoner of Azkaban FilmCardz Promos

COMPLETE SET (2)	2.50	6.00
COMMON CARD	1.50	4.00

2005 Harry Potter and the Goblet of Fire

COMPLETE SET (90)	5.00	12.00
UNOPENED BOX (24 PACKS)	800.00	1250.00
UNOPENED PACK (8 CARDS)	35.00	50.00
COMMON CARD (1-90)	.15	.40

2005 Harry Potter and the Goblet of Fire Autographs

COMMON AUTO	15.00	40.00
STATED ODDS 1:48 HOBBY		
NNO Angelica Mandy	60.00	120.00
NNO Brendan Gleeson	250.00	400.00
NNO Gary Oldman	400.00	600.00
NNO Henry Lloyd-Hughes	25.00	60.00
NNO James & Oliver Phelps	400.00	800.00
NNO Miranda Richardson	75.00	150.00
NNO Robert Pattinson	4000.00	8000.00
NNO Rupert Grint	300.00	600.00
NNO Shirley Henderson	150.00	400.00
NNO Stanislav Ianevski	50.00	100.00
NNO Tiana Benjamin	60.00	150.00
NNO Warwick Davis	30.00	75.00

2005 Harry Potter and the Goblet of Fire Box-Loaders

COMPLETE SET (4)	6.00	15.00
COMMON CARD (BT1-BT4)	1.50	4.00
STATED ODDS ONE PER HOBBY BOX		

2005 Harry Potter and the Goblet of Fire Case-Loaders

COMPLETE SET (3)	20.00	50.00
COMMON CARD (1-3)	8.00	20.00
STATED ODDS ONE PER HOBBY CASE		

2005 Harry Potter and the Goblet of Fire Costumes

COMMON MEM (C1-C14)	12.00	30.00
STATED ODDS 1:24 HOBBY		
C1 Daniel Radcliffe Outfit/400	30.00	75.00
C2 Robert Pattinson Shirt/500	25.00	60.00
C3 Clemence Poesy Outfit/250	30.00	75.00
C4 Stanislav Ianevski Outfit/700	15.00	40.00
C5 Stanislav Ianevski Shirt/400	50.00	100.00
C6 Durmstrang Student Outfit/725	15.00	40.00
C7 Beauxbatons Student Outfit/800	15.00	40.00
C8 Emma Watson Pants/300	100.00	200.00
C10 Clemence Poesy Sweater/275	100.00	200.00
C11 David Tennant Shirt/800	15.00	40.00
C12 Miranda Richardson Dress/300	60.00	120.00
C13 Death Eater Robe/250	15.00	40.00

2005 Harry Potter and the Goblet of Fire Dealer-Incentive Memorabilia

COMMON MEM	20.00	50.00
TF1 Michael Gambon Outfit/175	30.00	75.00
C13a Death Eater Robe/188	25.00	60.00
PI0a Trial Chamber Paper/317	30.00	75.00
PI3a Monolith Trophy/105	125.00	250.00
PI4a Death Eater Wand/64	300.00	500.00

2005 Harry Potter and the Goblet of Fire Film Cels

COMPLETE SET (9)	80.00	150.00
COMMON CARD (CFC1-CFC9)	8.00	20.00
STATED ODDS 1:80 HOBBY		
STATED PRINT RUN 300 SER.#'d SETS		

2005 Harry Potter and the Goblet of Fire Foil Chase

COMPLETE SET (9)	6.00	15.00
COMMON CARD (R1-R9)	.75	2.00
STATED ODDS 1:5 HOBBY		

2005 Harry Potter and the Goblet of Fire Props

COMMON MEM (P1-P12)	20.00	50.00
STATED ODDS 1:80 HOBBY		
P2 Yule Ball Program/125	75.00	150.00
P3 Yule Ball Poster/105	25.00	60.00
P5 Quidditch Burnt Tent/290	25.00	60.00
P6 Quidditch Program/205	30.00	80.00
P7 First Task Tent/250	75.00	150.00
P8 The Dark Forces Book/75	150.00	300.00
P9 First Task Sack/125	125.00	250.00
P10 Trial Chamber Paper/95	150.00	300.00
P12 Gryffindor Banner/265	30.00	75.00

2005 Harry Potter and the Goblet of Fire Tin Bonus

COMPLETE SET (2)	2.00	5.00
COMMON CARD (T1-T2)	1.25	3.00
STATED ODDS ONE PER RETAIL TIN		

2006 Harry Potter and the Goblet of Fire Update

COMPLETE SET (90)	5.00	12.00
UNOPENED BOX (24 PACKS)	65.00	80.00
UNOPENED PACK (8 CARDS)	3.00	4.00
COMMON CARD (1-90)	.15	.40

2006 Harry Potter and the Goblet of Fire Update Autographs

COMMON AUTO	12.00	30.00
STATED ODDS 1:48 HOBBY		
NNO Bonnie Wright	150.00	400.00
NNO Clemence Poesy	75.00	150.00
NNO Daniel Radcliffe	2000.00	4000.00
NNO Radcliffe/Janevski Posey/Pattinson	6000.00	10000.00
NNO David Tennant	75.00	150.00
NNO Frances de la Tour	30.00	75.00
NNO Katie Leung	50.00	100.00
NNO Michael Gambon	100.00	200.00
DE1 Ashley Artus MEM	15.00	40.00
DE2 Alex Palmer MEM	15.00	40.00

2006 Harry Potter and the Goblet of Fire Update Box-Loaders

COMPLETE SET (4)	5.00	12.00
COMMON CARD (BT1-BT4)	1.50	4.00
STATED ODDS ONE PER BOX		

2006 Harry Potter and the Goblet of Fire Update Case-Loaders

COMPLETE SET (3)	25.00	60.00
COMMON CARD (1-3)	10.00	25.00
STATED ODDS ONE PER CASE		

2006 Harry Potter and the Goblet of Fire Update Costumes

COMMON MEM (C1-C15)	6.00	15.00
STATED ODDS 1:24 HOBBY		
C1 Jason Isaacs Robe/475	20.00	50.00
C2 Katie Leung Dress/700	15.00	40.00
C3 Maggie Smith Dress/350	20.00	50.00
C5 Daniel Radcliffe Outfit/275	30.00	75.00
C7 Emma Watson Dress/600	75.00	150.00
C8 Robert Pattinson Robe/700	25.00	60.00
C10 Clemence Poesy Outfit/1025	15.00	40.00
C11 Daniel Radcliffe Outfit/250	60.00	120.00
C12 Robert Pattinson Shirt/300	15.00	40.00
C13 Clemence Poesy Shirt/900	20.00	50.00
C14 Daniel Radcliffe Outfit/300	15.00	40.00
C15 Gryffindor Tie/400	25.00	60.00

2006 Harry Potter and the Goblet of Fire Update Dealer-Incentives Memorabilia

COMMON MEM	15.00	40.00
BCI Slytherin Tie/114	25.00	60.00
Ci1 Clemence Poesy Dress/230	20.00	50.00
Ci2 Ralph Fiennes Cloak/155	125.00	250.00
Ci4a Daniel Radcliffe Wand/28	1000.00	2000.00
Ci4b Robert Pattinson Wand/28	2500.00	5000.00
Ci4c Clemence Poesy Wand/28	500.00	750.00
Ci4d Stanislav Ianevski Wand/28	500.00	1000.00

2006 Harry Potter and the Goblet of Fire Update Film Cels

COMPLETE SET (9)	60.00	120.00
COMMON CARD (CFC1-CFC9)	6.00	15.00
STATED ODDS 1:80 HOBBY		

2006 Harry Potter and the Goblet of Fire Update Foil Chase

COMPLETE SET (9)	8.00	20.00
COMMON CARD (R1-R9)	1.25	3.00
STATED ODDS 1:5		

2006 Harry Potter and the Goblet of Fire Update Jumbo Props

ONE PER SDCC ALBUM		
1 First Task Tent/200	60.00	120.00
2 Quidditch Burnt Tent/200	50.00	100.00

2006 Harry Potter and the Goblet of Fire Update Props

COMMON CARD (P1-P11)	15.00	40.00
STATED ODDS 1:80 HOBBY		
P2 Memorial Banner/355	20.00	50.00
P3 Books/350	25.00	60.00
P4 Weasley Tent/520	20.00	50.00
P5 Riddle House/305	25.00	60.00
P6 Chudley Cannons Poster/120	75.00	150.00
P8 Ron's Yule Ball Dress Robe Package Wrapping/240	20.00	50.00
P9 Rita Skeeter's Notepad/120	125.00	250.00
P10 Hermione's Book/130	150.00	300.00
P11 Harry's Letter to Sirius Black/90	200.00	400.00

2006 Harry Potter and the Goblet of Fire Update Promos Silver Foil

COMPLETE SET (4)	3.00	8.00
COMMON CARD (1-4)	.75	2.00
*GREEN: .6X TO 1.5X BASIC CARDS		
*BLUE: 1.2X TO 3X BASIC CARDS		
*RED: 1.5X TO 4X BASIC CARDS		
1 Dumbledore and Harry	.75	2.00
2 Teachers	.75	2.00
3 Harry	1.25	3.00
4 Ron, Hermione, and Harry	1.25	3.00

2007 Harry Potter and the Order of the Phoenix

COMPLETE SET (90)	5.00	12.00
UNOPENED BOX (24 PACKS)		
UNOPENED PACK (8 CARDS)		
COMMON CARD (1-90)	.15	.40
*RETAIL: SAME VALUE		
RETAIL VERSION HAS NO FOIL		

2007 Harry Potter and the Order of the Phoenix Autographs

COMMON AUTO	40.00	100.00
STATED ODDS 1:48		
NNO Bonnie Wright	150.00	400.00
NNO Daniel Radcliffe	500.00	1000.00
NNO Emma Watson	3000.00	7000.00
NNO Evanna Lynch	125.00	250.00
NNO Jason Isaacs	75.00	150.00
NNO Katie Leung	125.00	300.00
NNO Matthew Lewis	60.00	150.00
NNO Michael Gambon	125.00	300.00
NNO Rupert Grint	500.00	1200.00
NNO Tony Maudsley	60.00	150.00

2007 Harry Potter and the Order of the Phoenix Box-Loaders

COMPLETE SET (4)	5.00	12.00
COMMON CARD (BT1-BT4)	1.50	4.00
STATED ODDS ONE PER BOX		

2007 Harry Potter and the Order of the Phoenix Case-Loaders

COMPLETE SET (2)	15.00	30.00
COMMON CARD (CT1-CT2)	10.00	20.00
STATED ODDS ONE PER CASE		

2007 Harry Potter and the Order of the Phoenix Costumes

COMMON MEM (C1-C18)	12.00	30.00
STATED ODDS 1:24		
C1 Daniel Radcliffe Shirt/235	30.00	75.00
C2 Rupert Grint Shirt/560	15.00	40.00
C3 Emma Watson Sweater/250	125.00	250.00
C4 Oliver Phelps Shirt/260	30.00	75.00
C5 Bonnie Wright Sweater/660	15.00	40.00
C7 Katie Leung Tie/160	60.00	120.00
C8 Evanna Lynch Shirt/320	60.00	120.00
C9 Daniel Radcliffe Sweater/550	20.00	50.00
C10 Imelda Staunton Outfit/660	15.00	40.00
C12 Michael Gambon Outfit/560	25.00	60.00

2007 Harry Potter and the Order of the Phoenix Dealer-Incentives

COMMON MEM (Ci1-Ci4)	50.00	100.00
Ci1 Emma Watson Sweater/410	125.00	250.00
Ci2 Ralph Fiennes Outfit/200	50.00	100.00
Ci4 Hog's Head Hair/88	125.00	250.00

2007 Harry Potter and the Order of the Phoenix Death Eater Puzzle

COMPLETE SET (9)	4.00	10.00
COMMON CARD (R1-R9)	.75	2.00
STATED ODDS 1:5 RETAIL		

2007 Harry Potter and the Order of the Phoenix Film Cels

COMPLETE SET (9)	100.00	175.00
COMMON CARD (CFC1-CFC9)	12.00	30.00
STATED ODDS 1:80		

2007 Harry Potter and the Order of the Phoenix Foil Chase

COMPLETE SET (9)	5.00	12.00
COMMON CARD (R1-R9)	.75	2.00
STATED ODDS 1:5 HOBBY		

2007 Harry Potter and the Order of the Phoenix Props

COMMON MEM (P1-P12)	15.00	40.00
STATED ODDS 1:80		
P1 Dumbledore's Army Parchment/185	125.00	250.00
P2 Death Eater Mask/100	75.00	150.00
P3 Daily Prophet/310	20.00	50.00
P4 O.W.L./235	25.00	60.00
P5 Dolores Umbridge Doily/160	30.00	75.00
P6 Dolores Umbridge Progress Report/335	20.00	50.00
P7 Death Eater Mask/100	125.00	250.00
P12 Death Eater Mask/100	75.00	150.00

2007 Harry Potter and the Order of the Phoenix Promos

COMPLETE SET (6)	5.00	12.00
COMMON CARD	.75	2.00
3 James,Harry, and Lily	2.00	5.00
4 Harry	2.00	5.00
SD Harry	1.50	4.00
NSU Dolores Umbridge	.75	2.50

2007 Harry Potter and the Order of the Phoenix Update

COMPLETE SET (90)	5.00	12.00

UNOPENED BOX (24 PACKS)	1000.00	1500.00
UNOPENED PACK (8 CARDS)	40.00	65.00
COMMON CARD (91-180)	.15	.40

2007 Harry Potter and the Order of the Phoenix Update Autographs

COMMON AUTO	30.00	75.00
STATED ODDS 1:48		
NNO Radcliffe/Leung	1200.00	3000.00
NNO Tav MacDougall	75.00	150.00
NNO Richard Cubison	60.00	120.00
NNO Richard Trinder	60.00	120.00
NNO Tom Felton	1000.00	2500.00
NNO Helena Bonham Carter	600.00	1500.00
NNO Sian Thomas	40.00	100.00
NNO Jason Piper	40.00	100.00
NNO David Thewlis	40.00	100.00
NNO Natalia Tena	75.00	200.00
NNO Michael Gambon	500.00	1200.00

2007 Harry Potter and the Order of the Phoenix Update Box-Toppers

COMPLETE SET (4)	5.00	12.00
COMMON CARD (BT1-BT4)	1.50	4.00
STATED ODDS ONE PER BOX		

2007 Harry Potter and the Order of the Phoenix Update Case-Toppers

COMPLETE SET (6)	50.00	100.00
COMMON CARD	10.00	25.00
BLUE/YELLOW VARIATIONS		
STATED ODDS ONE PER CASE		

2007 Harry Potter and the Order of the Phoenix Update Costumes

COMMON MEM (C1-C15)	12.00	30.00
STATED ODDS 1:24		
C1 Daniel Radcliffe Shirt/375	20.00	50.00
C2 Emma Watson Sweater/400	75.00	150.00
C3 Evanna Lynch Sweater/475	25.00	60.00
C4 Katie Leung Sweater/680	20.00	50.00
C5 Daniel Radcliffe Sweater/275	20.00	50.00
C6 Rupert Grint Tie/120	50.00	100.00
C7 Bonnie Wright Jacket/625	15.00	40.00
C8 Evanna Lynch Pants/570	25.00	60.00
C13 James Phelps Oliver Phelps Shirt/475	25.00	60.00
C14 Ralph Fiennes Michael Gambon Outfit/185	75.00	150.00

2007 Harry Potter and the Order of the Phoenix Update Dealer-Incentives

COMMON MEM (Ci1-Ci4)	20.00	50.00
Ci2 Defense Against the Dark Arts Book/180	200.00	350.00
Ci3 Death Eater Costume/120	50.00	100.00
Ci4 Dumbledore/Umbridge Outfits/84	75.00	150.00

2007 Harry Potter and the Order of the Phoenix Update Film Cels

COMPLETE SET (9)	100.00	175.00
COMMON CARD (CFC1-CFC9)	12.00	30.00
STATED ODDS 1:80		

2007 Harry Potter and the Order of the Phoenix Update Foil Chase

COMPLETE SET (9)	4.00	10.00
COMMON CARD (R1-R9)	.75	2.00
STATED ODDS 1:5		

2007 Harry Potter and the Order of the Phoenix Update Props

COMMON MEM (P1-P12)	15.00	40.00
STATED ODDS 1:80		
P1 Cauldron/150	75.00	150.00
P2 Flying Memos/435	20.00	50.00
P3 The Daily Prophet/505	20.00	50.00
P4 Defense Against the Dark Arts Book/100	60.00	120.00
P7 Ravenclaw Outfit O.W.L. Exam Papers/100	75.00	150.00
P8 Death Eater Mask/Robe/100	60.00	120.00
P9 Death Eater Mask/Robe/95	75.00	150.00
P10 Death Eater Mask/Robe/90	60.00	120.00
P11 Dolores Umbridge Doily Curtains/115	60.00	120.00
P12 Severus Snape Test Tube Stand/100	50.00	100.00

2009 Harry Potter and the Half-Blood Prince

COMPLETE SET (90)	6.00	15.00
UNOPENED BOX (24 PACKS)	800.00	1200.00
UNOPENED PACK (8 CARDS)	35.00	50.00
COMMON CARD (1-90)	.15	.40

2009 Harry Potter and the Half-Blood Prince Autographs

COMMON AUTO	20.00	50.00
STATED ODDS 1:120		
NNO D.Radcliffe/T.Felton	2000.00	4000.00
NNO David Thewlis	75.00	200.00
NNO Emma Watson	1500.00	2500.00
NNO Evanna Lynch	200.00	500.00
NNO Helena Bonham Carter	400.00	1000.00
NNO Jessie Cave	50.00	125.00
NNO Maggie Smith	400.00	1000.00
NNO Michael Gambon	150.00	400.00
NNO Natalia Tena	50.00	125.00
NNO Rupert Grint	250.00	500.00

2009 Harry Potter and the Half-Blood Prince Case-Incentives

COMMON MEM (Ci1-Ci4)	10.00	25.00
Ci1 STATED ODDS ONE PER 2-CASE INCENTIVE		
Ci2 STATED ODDS ONE PER 5-CASE INCENTIVE		
Ci3 STATED ODDS ONE PER 10-CASE INCENTIVE		
Ci4 STATED ODDS ONE PER 25-CASE INCENTIVE		
Ci2 Boxing Telescope Boxes/220 5CI	60.00	120.00
Ci3 Beater's Bats/130 10CI	75.00	150.00
Ci4 Chicken Foot Goblets/108 25CI	100.00	200.00

2009 Harry Potter and the Half-Blood Prince Costumes

COMMON MEM (C1-C14)	10.00	25.00
STATED ODDS 1:30		
C1 Bellatrix Lestrange/390	25.00	60.00
C2 Horace Slughorn/240	15.00	40.00
C3 Ron Weasley/380	20.00	50.00
C4 Rubeus Hagrid/480	30.00	75.00
C7 Albus Dumbledore/500	25.00	60.00
C9 Professor McGonagall/490	30.00	75.00
C11 Ravenclaw Students/170	20.00	50.00
C14 Nymphadora Tonks/400	25.00	60.00

2009 Harry Potter and the Half-Blood Prince Crystal Case-Toppers

COMPLETE SET (6)	250.00	500.00
COMMON CARD	50.00	100.00
STATED ODDS ONE PER CASE		

2009 Harry Potter and the Half-Blood Prince FilmCards

COMPLETE SET (9)	100.00	150.00
COMMON CARD (CFC1-CFC9)	10.00	25.00
STATED ODDS 1:80		

2009 Harry Potter and the Half-Blood Prince Metal Box-Toppers

COMPLETE SET (4)	10.00	25.00
COMMON CARD (BT1-BT4)	3.00	8.00
STATED ODDS ONE PER CASE		

2009 Harry Potter and the Half-Blood Prince Props

COMMON MEM (P1-P12)	15.00	40.00
STATED ODDS 1:60		
P1 Slughorn's Christmas Party Lanterns/380	15.00	40.00
P2 Advanced Potion-Making Book Pages/380	30.00	75.00
P3 Cushions from The Burrow/480	20.00	50.00
P4 Quidditch Quaffle Ball/130	50.00	100.00
P5 Slughorn's Office Wall Covering/330	12.00	30.00
P7 Just Like That Hat Boxes/395	15.00	40.00
P8 Records from Slughorn's House/230	25.00	60.00
P10 Skiving Snackbox Boxes/280	25.00	60.00
P11 Advanced Potion-Making Book Covers/240	30.00	75.00
P12 Nose Biting Tea Cup Boxes/295	20.00	50.00

2009 Harry Potter and the Half-Blood Prince Puzzle

COMPLETE SET (9)	6.00	15.00
COMMON CARD (R1-R9)	1.00	2.50
STATED ODDS 5:24		

2009 Harry Potter and the Half-Blood Prince Promos

COMPLETE SET (5)	5.00	12.00
COMMON CARD (P1-P5)	.75	2.00
P4 Ron Weasley Cormac McLaggan	1.50	4.00
P5 Draco Malfoy	1.50	4.00

2009 Harry Potter and the Half-Blood Prince Update

COMPLETE SET (90)	6.00	15.00
UNOPENED BOX (24 PACKS)	600.00	1000.00
UNOPENED PACK (8 CARDS)	25.00	40.00
COMMON CARD (91-180)	.15	.40

2009 Harry Potter and the Half-Blood Prince Update Autographs

COMMON AUTO	30.00	75.00
STATED ODDS 1:48		
GALLACHER AUTO ONE PER 3 CASE PURCHASE		
NNO A.Evans/R.Evans SP	60.00	150.00
NNO Amelda Brown SP	40.00	100.00
NNO Anna Shaffer	40.00	100.00
NNO Dave Legeno	40.00	100.00
NNO Frank Dillane SP	100.00	200.00
NNO Helen McCrory SP	150.00	300.00
NNO Julie Walters SP	400.00	750.00
NNO R.Grint/J.Cave SP	300.00	600.00

2009 Harry Potter and the Half-Blood Prince Update Case-Incentives

COMMON MEM (Ci1-Ci4)	60.00	120.00
Ci1 STATED ODDS ONE PER 2-CASE INCENTIVE		
Ci2 STATED ODDS ONE PER 5-CASE INCENTIVE		
Ci3 STATED ODDS ONE PER 10-CASE INCENTIVE		
Ci4 STATED ODDS ONE PER 25-CASE INCENTIVE		
Ci1 Hermione Granger Shirt/330 2CI	125.00	250.00
Ci3 Luna Lovegood's Glasses/110 10CI	75.00	150.00
Ci4 Memory Vial/80 25CI	150.00	300.00

2009 Harry Potter and the Half-Blood Prince Update Case-Toppers

COMPLETE SET (3)	20.00	50.00
COMMON CARD (CT1-CT3)	10.00	25.00
STATED ODDS ONE PER CASE		

2009 Harry Potter and the Half-Blood Prince Update Costumes

COMMON MEM (C1-C14)	8.00	20.00
STATED ODDS 1:24		
C1 Harry Potter/280	25.00	60.00
C2 Ron Weasley/360	15.00	40.00
C3 Hermione Granger/280	100.00	200.00
C4 Draco Malfoy/460	25.00	60.00
C5 Ginny Weasley/460	20.00	50.00
C6 Harry Potter/280	25.00	60.00
C7 Luna Lovegood/490	50.00	100.00
C8 The Waitress/380	60.00	120.00
C9 Harry Potter/330	25.00	60.00
C10 Hermione Granger/360	100.00	200.00
C13 Luna Lovegood/450	25.00	60.00

2009 Harry Potter and the Half-Blood Prince Update FilmCards

COMPLETE SET (9)	80.00	150.00
COMMON CARD (CFC1-CFC9)	8.00	20.00
STATED ODDS 1:80		
CFC7 Hermione,Ron, and Harry	10.00	25.00

2009 Harry Potter and the Half-Blood Prince Update Props

COMMON MEM (P1-P12)	12.00	30.00
STATED ODDS 1:80		
P2 Slughorn Christmas Party Bottles/130	25.00	60.00
P3 Ron Weasley Hospital Bed Sheets/190	30.00	75.00
P4 Slughorn Classroom Bottles/120	30.00	75.00
P5 Quidditch Flags and Poles/280	25.00	60.00
P7 Slughorn House Pictures/130	75.00	150.00
P8 Seamus Finnegan Cauldron/180	30.00	75.00
P9 Potion Mixing Sticks/130	30.00	75.00
P10 Bellatrix Lestrange Wanted Poster/230	30.00	75.00
P11 Amycus Carrow Wanted Poster/240	15.00	40.00
P12 Alecto Carrow Wanted Poster/240	15.00	40.00

2009 Harry Potter and the Half-Blood Prince Update Puzzle

COMPLETE SET (9)	6.00	15.00
COMMON CARD (R1-R9)	1.50	4.00
STATED ODDS 5:24		

2009 Harry Potter and the Half-Blood Prince Update Wood Box-Toppers

COMPLETE SET (4)	8.00	20.00
COMMON CARD (BT1-BT4)	3.00	8.00
STATED ODDS ONE PER BOX		

2010 Harry Potter and the Deathly Hallows Part One

COMPLETE SET (90)	6.00	15.00
UNOPENED BOX (24 PACKS)	400.00	600.00
UNOPENED PACK (8 CARDS)	15.00	25.00
COMMON CARD (1-90)	.12	.30

2010 Harry Potter and the Deathly Hallows Part One Autographs

COMMON AUTO	15.00	40.00
STATED ODDS 1:48		
R = RARE		
UR = ULTRA RARE		
EXCH EXPIRATION: 12/01/2011		
NNO Andy Linden R	40.00	100.00
NNO Bonnie Wright	150.00	400.00
NNO Clemence Poesy UR	60.00	150.00
NNO David O'Hara	40.00	100.00
NNO David Thewlis R	100.00	250.00
NNO Evanna Lynch UR	100.00	250.00
NNO Guy Henry	50.00	120.00
NNO Helen McCrory R	125.00	250.00
NNO Natalia Tena	50.00	125.00
NNO Nick Moran UR	50.00	125.00
NNO Rade Serbedzija R	60.00	150.00
NNO Rhys Ifans R	125.00	300.00
NNO Rupert Grint UR	500.00	1000.00

2010 Harry Potter and the Deathly Hallows Part One Case-Incentives

COMMON MEM (Ci1-Ci4)	25.00	60.00
Ci1 ISSUED AS 2-CASE INCENTIVE		
Ci2 ISSUED AS 5-CASE INCENTIVE		
Ci3 ISSUED AS 10-CASE INCENTIVE		
Ci4 ISSUED AS 25-CASE INCENTIVE		
GOLD,SILVER, AND BRONZE VAR. EXIST FOR Ci4		
Ci2 Arthur Weasley/180 5CI	60.00	120.00
Ci3 Harry Potter/130 10CI	125.00	250.00
Ci4A Gringotts Copper Coin/88 25CI	200.00	400.00
Ci4B Gringotts Silver Coin/88 25CI	200.00	400.00
Ci4C Gringotts Gold Coin/88 25CI	500.00	1000.00

2010 Harry Potter and the Deathly Hallows Part One Clear Box-Toppers

COMPLETE SET (4)	5.00	12.00
COMMON CARD (BT1-BT4)	2.00	5.00
STATED ODDS ONE PER BOX		

2010 Harry Potter and the Deathly Hallows Part One Costumes

COMMON MEM (C1-C15)	12.00	30.00
STATED ODDS 1:24		
PRINT RUN 240-580		
C1 Hermione Granger shirt/310	100.00	200.00
C2 Bill Weasley vest/530	20.00	50.00
C3 Draco Malfoy shirt/460	30.00	75.00
C4 Hermione Granger shirt/280	150.00	300.00
C5 Lucius Malfoy coat/500	15.00	40.00
C6 Ron Weasley shirt/450	15.00	40.00
C7 Harry Potter shirt/310	30.00	75.00
C9 Wormtail shirt/380	15.00	40.00
C10 Luna Lovegood dress/240	20.00	50.00

MODERN

C11 Severus Snape robe/280 125.00 250.00
C14 Bellatrix Lestrange dress/510 30.00 75.00

2010 Harry Potter and the Deathly Hallows Part One Crystal Case-Toppers

COMPLETE SET (3) 20.00 50.00
COMMON CARD (CT1-CT3) 8.00 20.00
STATED ODDS ONE PER CASE

2010 Harry Potter and the Deathly Hallows Part One FilmCards

COMPLETE SET (9) 60.00 120.00
COMMON CARD (CFC1-CFC9) 6.00 15.00
STATED PRINT RUN 247 SER. #'d SETS

2010 Harry Potter and the Deathly Hallows Part One Foil

COMPLETE SET (9) 8.00 20.00
COMMON CARD (R1-R9) 1.00 2.50
STATED ODDS 1:4

2010 Harry Potter and the Deathly Hallows Part One Props

COMMON MEM (P1-P12) 12.00 30.00
STATED ODDS 1:80
PRINT RUN 110-330
P1 The Daily Prophet/260 60.00 120.00
P2 Tent Blanket/330 50.00 100.00
P3 Saucers and Candles/110 50.00 100.00
P6 Magic Wand/140 60.00 120.00
P7 Lovegood Drawings/200 60.00 120.00
P8 Ron's Rucksack/160 75.00 150.00
P9 The Daily Prophet/260 75.00 150.00
P10 Courtroom Paperwork/290 15.00 40.00
P11 Dumbledore Book/180 150.00 300.00
P12 Tent Clothes Peg/110 60.00 120.00

2010 Harry Potter and the Deathly Hallows Part One Promos

COMPLETE SET (5) 8.00 20.00
COMMON CARD 2.00 5.00

2011 Harry Potter and the Deathly Hallows Part Two

COMPLETE SET (54) 6.00 15.00
UNOPENED BOX (24 PACKS) 800.00 1200.00
UNOPENED PACK (8 CARDS) 35.00 50.00
COMMON CARD (1-54) .15 .40

2011 Harry Potter and the Deathly Hallows Part Two Autographs

COMMON AUTO 30.00 75.00
OVERALL AUTO ODDS ONE PER BOX
LEGENO ISSUED AS 2-CASE INCENTIVE
DUFF ISSUED AS 5-CASE INCENTIVE
PHELPS ISSUED AS 10-CASE INCENTIVE
HINDS ISSUED AS 25-CASE INCENTIVE
NNO Bonnie Wright 150.00 400.00
NNO Chris Rankin 40.00 100.00
NNO Ciaran Hinds 25CI 250.00 400.00
NNO Emma Watson 4000.00 8000.00
NNO John Hurt 150.00 400.00
NNO Maggie Smith 250.00 400.00
NNO Michael Gambon 150.00 400.00
NNO Warwick Davis 50.00 125.00

2011 Harry Potter and the Deathly Hallows Part Two Box-Toppers

COMPLETE SET (4) 12.00 30.00
COMMON CARD (BT1-BT4) 4.00 10.00
STATED ODDS ONE PER BOX

2011 Harry Potter and the Deathly Hallows Part Two Clear

COMPLETE SET (9) 6.00 15.00
COMMON CARD (BC1-BC9) 1.00 2.50

2011 Harry Potter and the Deathly Hallows Part Two Crystal Case-Toppers

COMPLETE SET (3) 50.00 100.00
COMMON CARD (CT1-CT3) 15.00 40.00
STATED ODDS ONE PER CASE

2011 Harry Potter and the Deathly Hallows Part Two FilmCards

COMPLETE SET (18) 200.00 400.00
COMMON CARD (CFC1-CFC18) 15.00 30.00
STATED PRINT RUN 213-214

2011 Harry Potter and the Deathly Hallows Part Two Foil

COMPLETE SET (9) 4.00 10.00
COMMON CARD (R1-R9) .50 1.25

2011 Harry Potter and the Deathly Hallows Part Two Puzzle

COMPLETE SET (9) 6.00 15.00
COMMON CARD (BP1-BP9) .75 2.00

2011 Harry Potter and the Deathly Hallows Part Two Puzzle Autographs

COMMON AUTO (PA1-PA9) 10.00 25.00
OVERALL AUTO ODDS ONE PER BOX
PA1 Jon Key 12.00 30.00
PA3 Jamie Campbell 15.00 40.00
PA7 Pauline Stone 12.00 30.00

Harry Potter Universe

2003 Harry Potter Chocolate Frog Series 1 US

COMPLETE SET (24) 50.00 100.00
COMMON CARD 2.00 5.00
14 Helga Hufflepuff 3.00 8.00
20 Newt Scamander 5.00 12.00
22 Rowena Ravenclaw 4.00 10.00

2004 Harry Potter Chocolate Frog Series 2 US

COMPLETE SET (12) 30.00 80.00
COMMON CARD (1-12) 2.00 5.00
1 Albus Dumbledore 10.00 25.00
3 Minerva McGonagall 4.00 10.00
5 Severus Snape 6.00 15.00
6 Rubeus Hagrid 3.00 8.00
10 Voldemort 4.00 10.00
NNO The Potter Family 3.00 8.00

2021 Panini Harry Potter Evolution

COMPLETE SET (300) 40.00 100.00
UNOPENED BOX (18 PACKS)
UNOPENED PACK (8 CARDS)
COMMON CARD (1-300) .40 1.00
*RAINBOW FOIL: 1.5X TO 4X BASIC CARDS
*GOLD: 3X TO 8X BASIC CARDS
*FRAG.REAL: 5X TO 12X BASIC CARDS

2010 Harry Potter Heroes and Villains

COMPLETE SET (72) 6.00 15.00
UNOPENED BOX (24 PACKS) 800.00 1200.00
UNOPENED PACK (8 CARDS) 30.00 50.00
COMMON CARD (1-54) .12 .30
COMMON CARD (55-72) .25 .60
55-72 STATED ODDS 1:2

2010 Harry Potter Heroes and Villains Autographs

COMMON AUTO 15.00 40.00
STATED ODDS 1:240
NNO Bonnie Wright 75.00 150.00
NNO David Thewlis 75.00 150.00
NNO Emma Watson 4000.00 8000.00
NNO Evanna Lynch 100.00 200.00
NNO Matthew Lewis 20.00 50.00
NNO N.Tena/G.Harris 50.00 100.00
NNO Rupert Grint 150.00 300.00
NNO Toby Jones 125.00 250.00

2010 Harry Potter Heroes and Villains Box-Toppers

COMPLETE SET (4) 8.00 20.00
COMMON CARD (BT1-BT4) 3.00 8.00
STATED ODDS ONE PER BOX
BT1 Harry Potter 4.00 10.00

2010 Harry Potter Heroes and Villains Case-Incentives

COMMON MEM (CI1-CI4) 75.00 150.00
CI1 ISSUED AS 2-CASE INCENTIVE
CI2 ISSUED AS 5-CASE INCENTIVE
CI3 ISSUED AS 10-CASE INCENTIVE
CI4 ISSUED AS 25-CASE INCENTIVE
STATED PRINT RUN 92-230
Ci1 Hermione Granger/230 2CI 100.00 200.00
Ci2 H.Potter/G.Weasley/140 5CI 125.00 250.00
Ci4 Slughorn Goblet/92 25CI 150.00 300.00

2010 Harry Potter Heroes and Villains Costumes

COMMON MEM (C1-C11) 8.00 20.00
OVERALL SINGLE/DUAL COSTUME ODDS 1:24
STATED PRINT RUN 130-480
C1 Fred Weasley/380 15.00 40.00
C2 Hermione Granger/130 75.00 150.00
C3 Kingsley Shacklebolt/460 12.00 30.00
C4 Narcissa Malfoy/430 20.00 50.00
C5 Tom Riddle/230 60.00 120.00
C7 Hermione Granger/160 60.00 120.00
C8 Dumbledore/280 30.00 75.00
C9 Slytherin Quidditch/480 15.00 40.00
C10 Bellatrix Lestrange/230 50.00 100.00
C11 Cedric Diggory/380 12.00 30.00

2010 Harry Potter Heroes and Villains Dual Costumes

COMMON MEM (DC1-DC3) 30.00 75.00
OVERALL SINGLE/DUAL COSTUME ODDS 1:24
STATED PRINT RUN 140-180
DC1 S.Black/H.Potter /140 60.00 120.00

2010 Harry Potter Heroes and Villains Dual Props

COMMON MEM 60.00 120.00
OVERALL SINGLE/DUAL PROP ODDS 1:60
DP1 Quaffle/Bristles/190 75.00 150.00

2010 Harry Potter Heroes and Villains Foil

COMPLETE SET (9) 6.00 15.00
COMMON CARD (R1-R9) 1.00 2.50
STATED ODDS 1:6

2010 Harry Potter Heroes and Villains Metal Case-Toppers

COMPLETE SET (3) 25.00 60.00
COMMON CARD (CT1-CT3) 10.00 25.00
STATED ODDS ONE PER CASE

2010 Harry Potter Heroes and Villains Props

COMMON PROP (P1-P11) 25.00 60.00
OVERALL SINGLE/DUAL PROP ODDS 1:60
STATED PRINT RUN 120-250
P1 Harry's Test Tube/140 60.00 120.00
P2 Hagrid's Candle/230 30.00 75.00
P3 Defence Test/200 30.00 75.00
P5 Burrow Picture/120 75.00 150.00
P6 Mortar and Pestle/150 30.00 75.00
P7 Hedwig's Cage/130 30.00 75.00
P8 Pixie Cage Base/180 50.00 100.00
P10 Ministry Coffee Cups/160 50.00 100.00
P11 Hagrid's Slughorn Cup/170 30.00 75.00

2010 Harry Potter Heroes and Villains Promos

COMPLETE SET (3) 3.00 8.00
COMMON CARD (P1-P3) 1.50 4.00

2005 Harry Potter Literary Series

COMPLETE FACTORY SET (45) 8.00 20.00
COMMON CARD (1-45) .25 .60

2006 Harry Potter Memorable Moments

COMPLETE SET (72) 5.00 12.00
UNOPENED BOX (24 PACKS) 250.00 400.00
UNOPENED PACK (8 CARDS) 12.00 20.00
COMMON CARD (1-72) .15 .40

2006 Harry Potter Memorable Moments Autographs

COMMON AUTO 15.00 40.00
OVERALL AUTO ODDS 1:48
NNO David Bradley 15.00 40.00
NNO Emma Watson 750.00 1500.00
NNO Jason Isaacs 60.00 120.00
NNO Maggie Smith 300.00 600.00

2006 Harry Potter Memorable Moments Coin Cards Silver

COMPLETE SET (2) 10.00 25.00
COMMON COIN 6.00 15.00
STATED ODDS ONE SET PER BOX

2006 Harry Potter Memorable Moments Costume Autographs

COMMON AUTO (DE3-DE6) 20.00 50.00
OVERALL AUTO ODDS 1:48
DE4 Paschal Friel 40.00 100.00
DE5 Olivia Higginbottom 40.00 100.00

2006 Harry Potter Memorable Moments Costumes

COMMON MEM (C1-C5) 8.00 20.00
STATED PRINT RUN 170-660
C2 Tom Felton/170 75.00 150.00
C5 Maggie Smith/360 20.00 50.00

2006 Harry Potter Memorable Moments Dealer-Incentives Memorabilia

COMMON MEM (Ci1-Ci3) 75.00 150.00
Ci2 Defense Against the Dark Arts Book/190100.00 200.00
Ci3 Letter from Sirius/50 500.00 1000.00

2006 Harry Potter Memorable Moments Dual Costumes

COMMON MEM (DC1-DC7) 20.00 50.00
STATED PRINT RUN 210-460
DC1 Rupert Grint/310 25.00 60.00
DC2 J.Phelps/O.Phelps/235 75.00 150.00
DC3 Daniel Radcliffe/360 75.00 150.00
DC5 S.Ianevski/R.Pattinson/275 75.00 150.00
DC7 C.Poesy/R.Pattinson/210 60.00 120.00

2006 Harry Potter Memorable Moments Foil Chase

COMPLETE SET (9) 8.00 20.00
COMMON CARD (R1-R9) 1.00 2.50
STATED ODDS 1:5

2006 Harry Potter Memorable Moments Props

COMMON MEM 25.00 60.00
STATED ODDS 1:80
P2 Norbert's Egg/140 50.00 100.00
P3 Basilisk Skin/160 50.00 100.00
P6 Christmas Card/180 30.00 80.00
P7 Moon and Star Christmas Ornaments/15050.00 100.00
P8 Student Wands and Quills/115 75.00 150.00
PC1 Buckbeak's Feather 200.00 375.00
Tom Felton Robe/50
PC2 Marauder's Map 30.00 80.00
David Thewlis Shirt/110
PC3 Daniel Radcliffe Shirt 50.00 100.00
Grim Fur/105
PC4 Daniel Radcliffe Pajamas/90 75.00 150.00

2009 Harry Potter Memorable Moments 2

COMPLETE SET (72) 5.00 12.00
UNOPENED BOX (24 PACKS) 300.00 500.00
UNOPENED PACK (8 CARDS) 12.00 20.00
COMMON CARD (1-72) .15 .40

2009 Harry Potter Memorable Moments 2 3-D Case-Toppers

COMPLETE SET (3) 30.00 60.00
COMMON CARD (CT1-CT3) 15.00 30.00
STATED ODDS ONE PER CASE

2009 Harry Potter Memorable Moments 2 Autographs

COMMON AUTO	10.00	20.00
OVERALL AUTO ODDS 1:48		
NNO Verne Troyer R	20.00	50.00

2009 Harry Potter Memorable Moments 2 Dual Autographs

COMPLETE SET (4)		
COMMON AUTO	30.00	75.00
OVERALL AUTO ODDS 1:48		
NNO D.Radcliffe/G.Oldman UR	600.00	1200.00
NNO J.Isaacs/T.Felton UR	125.00	250.00
NNO P.Bjelac/S.Ianevski R	75.00	200.00

2009 Harry Potter Memorable Moments 2 Case-Incentives

COMMON CARD (Ci1-Ci4)	15.00	40.00
Ci1 ISSUED AS 2-CASE INCENTIVE		
Ci2 ISSUED AS 5-CASE INCENTIVE		
Ci3 ISSUED AS 10-CASE INCENTIVE		
Ci4 ISSUED AS 25-CASE INCENTIVE		
Ci2 Harry Potter/Lord Voldemort/200 5CI	20.00	50.00
Ci3 Ron Weasley/Neville Longbottom/140 10CI	20.00	50.00
Ci4 Hermione Granger Professor Remus/104 25CI	100.00	200.00

2009 Harry Potter Memorable Moments 2 Costumes

COMMON MEM (C1-C12)	10.00	25.00
STATED ODDS 1:30		
C1 Ginny Weasley/670	20.00	50.00
C6 Dudley Dursley/590	12.00	30.00
C7 Harry Potter Oliver Wood/430	25.00	60.00
C8 Hermione Granger Harry Potter/350	75.00	150.00
C9 Hermione Granger Cho Chang/290	75.00	150.00
C10 Fleur Delacour/470	12.00	30.00
C11 Ron Weasley Ginny Weasley/300	20.00	40.00
C12 Hermione Granger Ginny Weasley/250	75.00	150.00

2009 Harry Potter Memorable Moments 2 Dumbledore's Army Box-Toppers

COMPLETE SET (5)	10.00	25.00
COMMON CARD (BT1-BT5)	3.00	8.00
STATED ODDS ONE PER BOX		

2009 Harry Potter Memorable Moments 2 Etched Binder Case-Incentives

COMPLETE SET (2)	12.00	30.00
COMMON CARD (BC1-BC2)	8.00	20.00

2009 Harry Potter Memorable Moments 2 Foil Puzzle

COMPLETE SET (9)	6.00	15.00
COMMON CARD (PZ1-PZ9)	1.25	3.00
STATED ODDS 5:24		

2009 Harry Potter Memorable Moments 2 Props

COMMON MEM (P1-P12)	10.00	25.00
STATED ODDS 1:80		
P1 Hedwig's Perch/100	50.00	100.00
P2 Ron's Compass/90	100.00	200.00
P3 Devil's Snare and Fluffy's Fur/260	50.00	100.00
P4 Mandrake and Fawkes's Feather/260	75.00	150.00
P5 Buckbeak's Feathers and Chain/150	50.00	100.00
P6 Honeydukes Candy Wrappers and Bags/100	30.00	75.00
P8 Yule Ball Drapes and Programs/400	25.00	60.00
P9 Defense Against the Dark Arts Books/190	75.00	150.00
P12 First Task Tent and Canopy Material/410	15.00	40.00

2009 Harry Potter Memorable Moments 2 Promos

COMPLETE SET (5)	4.00	10.00
COMMON CARD (P1-P5)	1.00	2.50
P4 Riddle Graveyard ALB	1.50	4.00
P5 Walkway ALB	1.50	4.00

2007 World of Harry Potter 3-D

COMPLETE SET (72)	5.00	12.00
UNOPENED BOX (24 PACKS)	800.00	1500.00
UNOPENED PACK (7 CARDS)	35.00	65.00
COMMON CARD (1-72)	.15	.40

2007 World of Harry Potter 3-D Autographs

COMMON AUTO	30.00	75.00
1-12 STATED ODDS 1:48		
CARDS 13 AND 14 SDCC EXCLUSIVE		
NNO Bonnie Wright/100 SDCC	75.00	150.00
NNO Daniel Radcliffe	3000.00	4500.00
NNO David Tennant/250 SDCC	125.00	250.00
NNO David Thewlis	100.00	200.00
NNO Harry Taylor	60.00	150.00
NNO James Phelps	50.00	100.00
NNO J.Herdman/J.Waylett	50.00	100.00
NNO Oliver Phelps	50.00	100.00
NNO Richard Bremmer	150.00	300.00
NNO R.Griffith/H.Melling	100.00	250.00
NNO R.Pattinson/S.Ianevski	2000.00	4000.00
NNO Warwick Davis	40.00	100.00

2007 World of Harry Potter 3-D Box-Loaders

COMPLETE SET (4)	8.00	20.00
COMMON CARD (BT1-BT4)	2.50	6.00
STATED ODDS ONE PER BOX		

2007 World of Harry Potter 3-D Case-Loaders

COMPLETE SET (2)	10.00	25.00
COMMON CARD (1-2)	6.00	15.00
STATED ODDS ONE PER CASE		

2007 World of Harry Potter 3-D Costumes

COMMON MEM (C1-C13)	8.00	20.00
STATED ODDS 1:24		
C3 Kenneth Branagh Jacket/600	12.00	30.00
C6 Slytherin Quidditch Robe/175	15.00	40.00
C8 Emma Watson Pants/400	30.00	75.00
C9 Daniel Radcliffe Quidditch Robe/250	20.00	50.00
C10 Gryffindor Cloak/175	20.00	50.00
C11 Daniel Radcliffe Stanislav Ianevski Outfits/125	15.00	40.00

2007 World of Harry Potter 3-D Dealer-Incentives

COMMON MEM (Ci1-Ci4)	50.00	100.00
Ci1 Gary Oldman Prison Outfit/240	75.00	150.00
Ci2 Dragon Selection Sack/120	75.00	150.00
Ci4 The Daily Prophet/56	250.00	500.00

2007 World of Harry Potter 3-D Props

STATED ODDS 1:80		
P1 Wand Box/200	20.00	50.00
P2 Broom/175	15.00	40.00
P3 Ashes/125	15.00	40.00
P4 Potions Book/100	100.00	200.00
P5 Magical Me Book/200	20.00	50.00
P6 Gilderoy Lockhart Photo/225	20.00	50.00
P7 Divination Book/150	15.00	40.00
P8 Marauder's Map/125	30.00	75.00
P9 Trial Chamber Papers/175	15.00	40.00
P10 Water Plants Book/125	60.00	120.00

2007 World of Harry Potter 3-D Puzzle

COMPLETE SET (9)	12.00	30.00
COMMON CARD (PZ1-PZ9)	1.50	4.00
STATED ODDS 1:5		

2007 World of Harry Potter 3-D Rare Chase

COMPLETE SET (6)	8.00	20.00
COMMON CARD (R1-R6)	1.50	4.00
STATED ODDS 1:8		

2007 World of Harry Potter 3-D Ultra Rare Chase

COMPLETE SET (3)	5.00	12.00
COMMON CARD (UR1-UR3)	2.00	5.00
STATED ODDS 1:12		

2008 World of Harry Potter 3-D Series Two

COMPLETE SET (72)	5.00	12.00
UNOPENED BOX (24 PACKS)	1000.00	1500.00
UNOPENED PACK (7 CARDS)	40.00	65.00
COMMON CARD (1-72)	.20	.50

2008 World of Harry Potter 3-D Series Two Autographs

COMMON AUTO	12.00	30.00
STATED ODDS 1:48		
R = RARE		
UR = ULTRA RARE		
NNO Alfred Enoch	30.00	75.00
NNO Charles Hughes R	20.00	50.00
NNO Christian Coulson R	200.00	500.00
NNO Daniel Radcliffe UR	2000.00	4000.00
NNO Emma Watson UR	800.00	1200.00
NNO Rupert Grint UR	400.00	1000.00

2008 World of Harry Potter 3-D Series Two Case-Loaders

COMPLETE SET (3)	20.00	50.00
COMMON CARD (CT1-CT3)	8.00	20.00
STATED ODDS ONE PER CASE		

2008 World of Harry Potter 3-D Series Two Costumes

COMMON MEM (C1-C6)	8.00	20.00
STATED ODDS 1:80		
C1 Harry Potter Quidditch sweater/360	20.00	50.00
C3 Hermione Granger pants/260	20.00	50.00
C4 Slytherin students/260 DUAL	10.00	25.00
C5 Gryffindor students/210 DUAL	10.00	25.00

2008 World of Harry Potter 3-D Series Two Dealer-Incentives

COMMON CARD (Ci1-Ci4)	25.00	60.00
Ci1 ISSUED AS 2-CASE INCENTIVE		
Ci2 ISSUED AS 5-CASE INCENTIVE		
Ci3 ISSUED AS 10-CASE INCENTIVE		
Ci4 ISSUED AS 25-CASE INCENTIVE		
Ci1 Pixie Cage/310 2CI	25.00	60.00
Ci2 Proclamations/160 5CI	25.00	60.00
Ci3 Umbridge's Special Quill/110 10CI	125.00	250.00
Ci4 Lupin's Wand/80 25CI	125.00	250.00

2008 World of Harry Potter 3-D Series Two Metal Box-Loaders

COMPLETE SET (4)	6.00	15.00
COMMON CARD (BT1-BT4)	2.00	5.00
STATED ODDS ONE PER BOX		

2008 World of Harry Potter 3-D Series Two Props

COMMON MEM (P1-P13)	8.00	20.00
STATED ODDS 1:40		
P1 Lantern/240	50.00	100.00
P2 Cage/260	30.00	75.00
P3 Quidditch Bat/180	50.00	100.00
P4 Quidditch Quaffle and Bludgers/270	30.00	75.00
P5 McGonagall's Class Books/310	20.00	50.00
P6 Bone/120	75.00	150.00
P7 Lockhart's Class Books/360	25.00	60.00
P8 Chain/310	30.00	75.00
P11 Durmstrang Staff/360	20.00	50.00
P12 Dagger/100	75.00	150.00
P13 Quidditch Programs and Flags/320	20.00	50.00

2008 World of Harry Potter 3-D Series Two Puzzle

COMPLETE SET (9)	6.00	15.00
COMMON CARD (PZ1-PZ9)	.75	2.00
STATED ODDS 5:24		

2008 World of Harry Potter 3-D Series Two SDCC-Exclusive Memorabilia

STATED PRINT RUN 550 SER. #'d SETS		
SD08C1 Harry Potter red sweater/550	25.00	60.00
SD08C2 Ron Weasley sweater/550		
SD08C3 Harry Potter blue jumper/550		
SD08C4 Harry Potter jeans/550	30.00	75.00

2008 World of Harry Potter 3-D Series Two Promos

COMMON CARD (P1-P5)	.75	2.00
P4 The Dark Arts	8.00	20.00
P5 Dumbledore's Army	10.00	25.00

1994 ERTL Harvest Heritage Inaugural Series

COMPLETE SET (150)	6.00	15.00
UNOPENED BOX (36 PACKS)	30.00	40.00
UNOPENED PACK (12 CARDS)		
COMMON CARD (1-150)	.08	.20

2018 Hatchimals

COMPLETE SET (100)	8.00	20.00
UNOPENED BOX (24 PACKS)		
UNOPENED PACK (5 CARDS+1 STICKER)		
COMMON CARD (1-100)	.15	.40
*STICKER: .75X TO 2X BASIC CARDS		
*GLITTER: 1.2X TO 3X BASIC CARDS		
*RAINBOW: 2.5X TO 6X BASIC CARDS		

2018 Hatchimals Coloring Cards

COMPLETE SET (10)	4.00	10.00
COMMON CARD (1-10)	.60	1.50
STATED OVERALL ODDS 1:1		

2018 Hatchimals Necklaces

COMPLETE SET (10)	6.00	15.00
COMMON CARD (1-10)	1.25	3.00
STATED ODDS 1:VALUE BOX		

2018 Hatchimals Temporary Tattoos

COMPLETE SET (10)	2.50	6.00
COMMON CARD (1-10)	.50	1.25
STATED ODDS 1:6		

2018 Hatchimals Thermo Egg Reveal

COMPLETE SET (10)	5.00	12.00
COMMON CARD (1-10)	1.00	2.50
STATED ODDS 1:3		

1991 Comic Images Heavy Metal

COMPLETE SET (90)	6.00	15.00
UNOPENED BOX (48 PACKS)	30.00	40.00
UNOPENED PACK (10 CARDS)		
COMMON CARD (1-90)	.12	.30

1996 Comic Images Heavy Metal The Movie and More

COMPLETE SET (90)	5.00	12.00
UNOPENED BOX (36 PACKS)	15.00	25.00
UNOPENED PACK (10 CARDS)		
COMMON CARD (1-90)	.10	.25
0 Art by Luis Royo Box-Topper	2.00	5.00
NNO Heavy Metal The Movie and More PROMO	.60	1.50

1996 Comic Images Heavy Metal The Movie and More Calendar

COMPLETE SET (3)	15.00	40.00
COMMON CARD (S1-S3)	6.00	15.00
STATED ODDS 1:36		

1996 Comic Images Heavy Metal The Movie and More Chromium

COMPLETE SET (6)	12.00	30.00
COMMON CARD (C1-C6)	2.50	6.00
STATED ODDS 1:12		

1998 Comic Images Heavy Metal Rough Cut F.A.K.K. 2

COMPLETE SET (72)	6.00	15.00
UNOPENED BOX (48 PACKS)	40.00	50.00
UNOPENED PACK (8 CARDS)	1.00	1.25
COMMON CARD (1-72)	.15	.40

1998 Comic Images Heavy Metal Rough Cut F.A.K.K. 2 Autographs

COMMON CARD (A1-A6)	20.00	50.00
RANDOMLY INSERTED INTO PACKS		

1998 Comic Images Heavy Metal Rough Cut F.A.K.K. 2 Omnichrome

COMPLETE SET (6) 12.00 30.00
COMMON CARD (OC1-OC6) 3.00 8.00
STATED ODDS 1:18

1998 Comic Images Heavy Metal Rough Cut F.A.K.K. 2 Promos

P1 As Heavy Metal's New Movie .75 2.00
P2 As Heavy Metal's New Movie .75 2.00

2004 Hellboy

COMPLETE SET (72) 3.00 8.00
UNOPENED BOX (36 PACKS) 60.00 100.00
UNOPENED PACK (6 CARDS) 2.00 3.00
COMMON CARD (1-72) .10 .25
PAN1 To Hell and Back 9-Up Panel/199 30.00 75.00

2004 Hellboy Autographs

COMPLETE SET (7)
COMMON AUTO (A1-A7) 6.00 15.00
STATED ODDS 1:36
A1 Ron Perlman 30.00 75.00
A2 Doug Jones 12.00 30.00
A3 Karel Roden 10.00 25.00
A5 Mike Mignola 10.00 25.00
A6 Guillermo Del Toro 200.00 400.00

2004 Hellboy Box-Loaders

COMPLETE SET (3) 3.00 8.00
COMMON CARD (BL1-BL3) 1.25 3.00
CL1 The Meaning Of Pain 8.00 20.00

2004 Hellboy BPRD

COMPLETE SET (6) 10.00 25.00
COMMON CARD (B1-B6) 2.00 5.00
STATED ODDS 1:17

2004 Hellboy Pieceworks

COMPLETE SET (12) 100.00 200.00
COMMON CARD (PW1-PW12) 8.00 20.00
STATED ODDS 1:36
PW1 Ron Perlman 10.00 25.00
PW2 Ron Perlman 10.00 25.00
PR1 Pieceworks Redemption Card

2004 Hellboy To Hell and Back

COMPLETE SET (9) 7.50 20.00
COMMON CARD (P1-P9) 1.25 3.00
STATED ODDS 1:11

2004 Hellboy Promos

COMPLETE SET (4) 4.00 10.00
COMMON CARD .75 2.00
Pi Hellboy 2.00 5.00
PUK Hellboy 2.00 5.00

2004 Hellboy SDCC Promos

COMPLETE SET (5) 2.50 6.00
COMMON CARD (1-5) .75 2.00

2007 Hellboy Animated The Sword of Storms

COMPLETE SET (72) 5.00 12.00
UNOPENED BOX (36 PACKS) 60.00 70.00
UNOPENED PACK (6 CARDS) 1.75 2.25
COMMON CARD (1-72) .15 .40
CL1 To Serve and Protect Case-Topper 8.00 20.00
NNO Uncut Sheet/99 30.00 80.00

2007 Hellboy Animated The Sword of Storms Box-Toppers

COMPLETE SET (3) 4.00 10.00
COMMON CARD (BL1-BL3) 1.50 4.00
STATED ODDS 1:BOX

2007 Hellboy Animated The Sword of Storms Demons Unleashed Puzzle

COMPLETE SET (9) 8.00 20.00
COMMON CARD (D1-D9) 1.25 3.00
STATED ODDS 1:11

2007 Hellboy Animated The Sword of Storms Hero's Journey Die-Cuts

COMPLETE SET (6) 12.00 30.00
COMMON CARD (H1-H6) 2.50 6.00
STATED ODDS 1:17

2007 Hellboy Animated The Sword of Storms Promos

COMPLETE SET (7)
COMMON CARD
HA1A Coming Fall 2006 .75 2.00
HA1B Coming January 2007 .75 2.00
HA2 Coming January 2007 .75 2.00
HAi Liz 2.50 6.00
HAT Army Attacks 1.25 3.00
HAUK Coming January 2007 1.25 3.00
HASD2006 Coming Fall 2006 .75 2.00

1992 Eclipse Hellraiser

COMPLETE SET (110) 6.00 15.00
UNOPENED BOX (36 PACKS) 30.00 40.00
UNOPENED PACK (12 CARDS) 1.00 1.25
COMMON CARD (1-110) .10 .30
NNO Clive Barker AU 80.00 150.00

1992 Eclipse Hellraiser Silver Holograms

COMPLETE SET (2) 20.00 50.00
COMMON CARD (1-2) 12.00 30.00
*GOLD: .5X TO 1.2X BASIC CARDS
RANDOMLY INSERTED INTO PACKS

2001 Henchmen of Horror

COMPLETE SET (50) 5.00 12.00
COMMON CARD (1-50) .20 .50
NNO Renfield PROMO .75 2.00

2001 Hercules The Complete Journeys Previews

COMPLETE SET (9) 6.00 15.00
COMMON CARD (H1-H9) 1.00 2.50
ANNOUNCED PRINT RUN 2,500 SETS

2001 Hercules The Complete Journeys

COMPLETE SET (120) 5.00 12.00
UNOPENED BOX (40 PACKS) 50.00 75.00
UNOPENED PACK (9 CARDS) 2.00 2.50
COMMON CARD (1-120) .08 .25
HC1 ISSUED AS CASE TOPPER
HC1 Hercules MEM CT 15.00 40.00

2001 Hercules The Complete Journeys Autographs

COMMON AUTO 4.00 10.00
STATED ODDS THREE PER BOX
A15 ISSUED AS ALBUM EXCLUSIVE
A1 Kevin Sorbo 20.00 50.00
A2 Sam Sorbo 12.00 30.00
A3 Martin Kove 8.00 20.00
A4 Cory Everson 15.00 40.00
A5 Kevin Smith 12.00 30.00
A6 Tawny Kitaen 30.00 75.00
A8 Robert Trebor 6.00 15.00
A9 Liddy Holloway 6.00 15.00
A11 Lisa Chappell 10.00 25.00
A12 Josephine Davison 8.00 20.00
A13 Joel Tobeck 5.00 12.00
A14 Michael Hurst 6.00 15.00
A15 Meighan Desmond ALB 6.00 15.00
A16 Gina Torres 10.00 25.00
A17 Alexandra Tydings 10.00 25.00

2001 Hercules The Complete Journeys Heavenly Bodies

COMPLETE SET (9) 6.00 15.00
COMMON CARD (HB1-HB9) .75 2.00
STATED ODDS 1:8
PAN 9-Card Panel (HB1-HB9)
(Steve Charendoff AU/50

2001 Hercules The Complete Journeys Hercules HoloFEX

COMPLETE SET (6) 12.00 30.00
COMMON CARD (H1-H6) 2.50 6.00
STATED ODDS 1:40

2001 Hercules The Complete Journeys Mythical Beasts

COMPLETE SET (9) 3.00 8.00
COMMON CARD (M1-M9) .40 1.00
STATED ODDS 1:4
PAN 9-Card Panel (M1-M9)
Steve Charendoff AU/50

2001 Hercules The Complete Journeys Xena Trilogy

COMPLETE SET (3) 6.00 15.00
STATED ODDS ONE PER BOX
XT1 Warrior Princess 3.00 8.00
XT2 The Gauntlet 3.00 8.00
XT3 The Unchained Heart 3.00 8.00

2001 Hercules The Complete Journeys Promos

BP1 Hercules ALB 3.00 8.00

1996 Topps Hercules The Legendary Journeys

COMPLETE SET (90) 12.00 30.00
UNOPENED BOX (36 PACKS) 70.00 80.00
UNOPENED PACK (9 CARDS) 2.50 3.00
COMMON CARD (1-90) .30 .75
P1 Hercules with Xena 4.00 10.00

1996 Topps Hercules The Legendary Journeys Embossed

COMPLETE SET (9) 20.00 50.00
COMMON CARD (E1-E9) 3.00 8.00
STATED ODDS 1:18

1996 Topps Hercules The Legendary Journeys Holograms

COMPLETE SET (2) 5.00 12.00
COMMON CARD (H1-H2) 3.00 8.00
STATED ODDS 1:18
H1 Hercules 3.00 8.00
H2 Xena 3.00 8.00

2003 Hercules The Movies Expansion

COMMON CARD () 1.50 4.00
HC2 Hercules MEM 8.00 20.00
HC3 Ioalus MEM 8.00 20.00
HXA Kevin Sorbo AU 20.00 50.00

2010 Heroes Archives

COMPLETE SET (72) 5.00 12.00
UNOPENED BOX (24 PACKS) 150.00 250.00
UNOPENED PACKS (5 CARDS) 6.00 10.00
COMMON CARD (1-72) .15 .40

2010 Heroes Archives Autographs

COMMON AUTO 4.00 10.00
STATED ODDS SIX PER BOX
OLIVERI AUTO ISSUED AS CASE TOPPER
TAKEI AUTO ISSUED AS 3-CASE INCENTIVE
ROBERTS UP AUTO IS 6-CASE INCENTIVE
CARDS 1A,19A,21A,24A, AND 37A ONLY IN ARCHIVE BOX
L (LIMITED): 300-500
VL (VERY LIMITED): 200-300
1A Adrian Pasdar/suit AB 15.00 40.00
1B Adrian Pasdar/t-shirt VL 15.00 40.00
4A Ashley Crow w/dog L 5.00 12.00
4B Ashley Crow no dog L 5.00 12.00
6 Bruce Boxleitner 8.00 20.00
7 Cristine Rose L 6.00 15.00
9A David Anders/Adam Monroe L 8.00 15.00
9B David Anders/Takezo Kensei L 8.00 15.00
11A Dawn Olivieri/hair clip CT 8.00 20.00
11B Dawn Olivieri/no hair clip 8.00 20.00
12 Deanne Bray 6.00 15.00
13A Eric Roberts/facing forward 6CI 30.00 75.00
13B E.Roberts/looking up RR 15.00 40.00
14 Ernie Hudson 12.00 30.00
17 George Takei 3CI 50.00 100.00
18 Greg Grunberg L 8.00 20.00
19A H.Panettiere/cheerleader outfit AB 150.00 300.00
19B H.Panettiere/shirt VL 125.00 250.00
20 Jack Coleman L 12.00 30.00
21A James Kyson Lee/white shirt AB 15.00 40.00
21B James Kyson Lee/red shirt VL 10.00 25.00
22 Jamie Hector 5.00 12.00
23 Jessalyn Gilsig 5.00 12.00
24A Jimmy Jean-Louis/striped shirt AB 6.00 15.00
24B Jimmy Jean-Louis/white shirt VL 6.00 15.00
25 Katherine Boecher 8.00 20.00
28 Kristen Bell VL 75.00 150.00
30 Madeline Zima 10.00 25.00
31 Malcolm McDowell VL 20.00 50.00
33 Nicholas D'Agosto 5.00 12.00
34 Richard Roundtree 8.00 20.00
35 Rick Worthy 5.00 12.00
37A S.Ramamurthy/facing forward AB 15.00 40.00
37B S.Ramamurthy/facing left VL 8.00 20.00
38 Shalim Ortiz 5.00 12.00
39 Swoosie Kurtz VL 8.00 20.00
40 Tamlyn Tomita 6.00 15.00
41 Tessa Thompson 30.00 75.00
42A Todd Stashwick/green light L 5.00 12.00
42B Todd Stashwick/no light L 5.00 12.00

2010 Heroes Archives Generations

COMPLETE SET (8) 6.00 15.00
COMMON CARD (G1-G8) 1.50 4.00
STATED ODDS 1:12

2010 Heroes Archives Quotable Heroes

COMPLETE SET (9) 6.00 15.00
COMMON CARD (Q1-Q9) 1.50 4.00
STATED ODDS 1:8
Q10 ISSUED AS RITTENHOUSE REWARD
Q10 Are you going to eat it SP 12.00 30.00

2010 Heroes Archives Relics

COMMON CARD 6.00 15.00
STATED ODDS ONE PER BOX
3 Claire Bennet 20.00 50.00
6 Missing Poster/165 50.00 100.00
7 Lydia 12.00 30.00
10 Campaign Poster/375 30.00 60.00
12 Peter Petrelli 8.00 20.00
13 Samuel Sullivan 8.00 20.00
15 Wanted Posters/250 25.00 60.00

2010 Heroes Archives Promos

P1 Sylar
P2 Hiro Nakamura 4.00 10.00
CP1 Claire Bennet 3.00 8.00

2010 Heroes of the Blues Reprints

COMPLETE SET (36) 5.00 12.00
COMMON CARD (1-36) .15 .40
P1 Early Jazz Greats PROMO 1.25 3.00
P2 Pioneers of Country Music PROMO 1.25 3.00
NNO Heroes of the Blues Poster PROMO 1.25 3.00

1991 Lime Rock Heroes of the Persian Gulf

COMPLETE SET (110) 8.00 20.00
COMMON CARD (1-110) .12 .30

1991 Lime Rock Heroes of the Persian Gulf Promos

COMPLETE SET (2) 15.00 40.00
COMMON CARD 10.00 25.00

2008 Heroes Series One

COMPLETE SET (90) 5.00 12.00
UNOPENED BOX (24 PACKS)
UNOPENED PACK (7 CARDS)
COMMON CARD (1-90) .15 .40

2008 Heroes Series One Authentic Worn Costumes

COMMON CARD 6.00 15.00
STATED ODDS 1:44 HOBBY
1 Claire Bennet Cheerleading Uniform (facing left) 25.00 50.00
2 Claire Bennet Cheerleading Patch (facing right) 125.00 200.00

3 Hiro Nakamura Jacket Shirt 8.00 20.00

2008 Heroes Series One Autographs

COMMON AUTO 8.00 20.00
STATED ODDS 1:135 HOBBY
1 Adrian Pasdar 10.00 25.00
2 Greg Grunberg 10.00 25.00
3 Hayden Panettiere 100.00 200.00
5 Jason Kyson Lee 15.00 30.00
6 Masi Oka 75.00 150.00
7 Milo Ventimiglia 25.00 50.00
10 Zachary Quinto 50.00 100.00

2008 Heroes Series One Foil

COMPLETE SET (10) 4.00 10.00
COMMON CARD (1-10) 1.00 2.50
STATED ODDS 1:3

2008 Heroes Series Two

COMPLETE SET (90) 5.00 12.00
UNOPENED BOX (24 PACKS)
UNOPENED PACK (7 CARDS)
COMMON CARD (1-90) .15 .40

2008 Heroes Series Two Autograph Costumes

COMMON AUTO 75.00 150.00
STATED ODDS 1:3,760
1 Adrian Pasdar 250.00 500.00
2 Dana Davis 150.00 300.00
3 Milo Ventimiglia 125.00 250.00

2008 Heroes Series Two Autographs

COMMON AUTO 4.00 10.00
STATED ODDS 1:72
1 Adair Tishler 12.00 30.00
2 Adrian Pasdar 10.00 25.00
4 Ali Larter 75.00 150.00
8 David Anders 8.00 20.00
11 Milo Ventimiglia 15.00 40.00
13 Sendhil Ramamurthy 8.00 20.00
14 Stephen Tobolowsky 5.00 12.00

2008 Heroes Series Two Costumes

COMMON CARD 3.00 8.00
STATED ODDS 1:72
1 Claire Bennet Uniform 15.00 40.00
2 Elle Bishop Shirt 10.00 25.00
4 Maya Herrera Shirt 4.00 10.00
5 Monica Dawson Uniform 8.00 20.00
6 Nathan Petrelli Shirt 5.00 12.00
7 Noah Bennet Shirt 5.00 12.00
8 Peter Petrelli Shirt 5.00 12.00
9 Sylar Jacket 10.00 25.00

2008 Heroes Series Two Dual Autographs

COMMON AUTO 200.00 400.00
STATED ODDS 1:9,610
1 C.Rose/A.Pasdar 300.00 600.00
2 C.Rose/M.Ventimiglia 250.00 500.00
4 M.Ventimiglia/D.Anders 300.00 600.00

2008 Heroes Series Two Dual Costumes

COMMON CARD 100.00 200.00
STATED ODDS 1:1,880
1 C.Bennet Uni/N.Bennet Shirt 120.00 250.00
2 C.Bennet Uni/W.Rosen Sweater 120.00 250.00

2008 Heroes Series Two Foil

COMPLETE SET (10) 4.00 10.00
COMMON CARD (1-10) 1.00 2.50
STATED ODDS 1:3

2008 Heroes Series Two Promos

COMPLETE SET (2) 1.50 4.00
COMMON CARD (P1-P2) 1.00 2.50

1988 Comic Images Heroic Origins

COMPLETE SET (90) 6.00 15.00
UNOPENED BOX (50 PACKS)
UNOPENED PACK (5 CARDS)
COMMON CARD (1-90) .12 .30

1995 Dart FlipCards Hershey's

COMPLETE SET (100) 4.00 10.00
UNOPENED BOX (36 PACKS) 20.00 30.00
UNOPENED PACK (8 CARDS) 1.00 1.25
COMMON CARD (1-100) .08 .20
UNC 100-Card Uncut Sheet/1000

1995 Dart FlipCards Hershey's Chromium

COMPLETE SET (6) 12.00 30.00
COMMON CARD (C1-C6) 2.50 6.00
STATED ODDS 1:18

1995 Dart FlipCards Hershey's Tall Boy

S1 Gone Fishing/3000* (mail-in) 4.00 10.00
S1 Gone Fishing Zina Saunders AU/500* 25.00 60.00
FC2 (Zina Saunders art)

1995 Dart FlipCards Hershey's Wood

COMPLETE SET (3) 10.00 25.00
STATED ODDS 1:36
W1 Sitting on Top of the World, ca 1935 4.00 10.00
W2 Stepping Stones to Health, ca 1935 4.00 10.00
W3 Topped with Hershey's Syrup, ca 1930-19354.0010.00

1995 Dart FlipCards Hershey's Promos

COMMON CARD .60 1.50

1993 Freedom Press High School Heroes

COMPLETE SET (30) 2.50 6.00
COMMON CARD (1-30) .15 .40

1993 Freedom Press High School Heroes II

COMPLETE SET (30) 6.00
COMMON CARD (1-30) .15 .40

2007 High School Musical

COMPLETE SET (50) 5.00 12.00
UNOPENED BOX (24 PACKS) 30.00 40.00
UNOPENED PACK (7 CARDS) 1.50 2.00
COMMON CARD (1-50) .20 .50

2007 High School Musical Costumes

COMPLETE SET (2) 12.00 30.00
COMMON CARD (1-2) 6.00 15.00
STATED ODDS 1:163

2007 High School Musical Felt Stickers

COMPLETE SET (5) 2.00 5.00
COMMON CARD (F1-F5) .60 1.50
STATED ODDS 1:6

2007 High School Musical Glitter Stickers

COMPLETE SET (10) 4.00 10.00
COMMON CARD (1-10) .60 1.50
STATED ODDS 1:6

2007 High School Musical Puzzle Stickers

COMPLETE SET (20) 2.50 6.00
COMMON CARD (1-20) .20 .50
STATED ODDS 2:3

2007 High School Musical Stickers

COMPLETE SET (30) 4.00 10.00
COMMON CARD (1-30) .30 .75
STATED ODDS 2:1

2008 High School Musical 3

COMPLETE SET (50) 5.00 12.00
UNOPENED BOX (24 PACKS) 40.00 50.00
UNOPENED PACKS (7 CARDS) 2.00 2.50
COMMON CARD (1-50) .15 .40
P1 Ready for the Future PROMO 1.25 3.00

2008 High School Musical 3 Foil Stickers

COMPLETE SET (10) 6.00 15.00
COMMON CARD (F1-F10) .75 2.00
STATED ODDS 1:6

2008 High School Musical 3 Glitter Stickers

COMPLETE SET (10) 5.00 12.00
COMMON CARD (G1-G10) .75 2.00
STATED ODDS 1:6

2008 High School Musical 3 Mega Stickers

COMPLETE SET (20) 6.00 15.00
COMMON CARD (1-20) .40 1.00
STATED ODDS 2:3

2008 High School Musical 3 Stickers

COMPLETE SET (30) 6.00 15.00
COMMON CARD (1-30) .20 .50
STATED ODDS 2:1

2008 High School Musical Expanded Edition

COMPLETE SET (50) 5.00 12.00
UNOPENED BOX (24 PACKS) 30.00 40.00
UNOPENED PACK (7 CARDS) 1.50 2.00
COMMON CARD (1-50) .20 .50

2008 High School Musical Expanded Edition Felt Stickers

COMPLETE SET (5) 3.00 8.00
COMMON CARD (F1-F5) 1.25 3.00
STATED ODDS 1:6

2008 High School Musical Expanded Edition Glitter Stickers

COMPLETE SET (10) 6.00 15.00
COMMON CARD (1-10) 1.25 3.00
STATED ODDS 1:6

2008 High School Musical Expanded Edition Puzzle Stickers

COMPLETE SET (20) 3.00 8.00
COMMON CARD (1-20) .25 .60
RANDOMLY INSERTED IN PACKS

2008 High School Musical Expanded Edition Stickers

COMPLETE SET (30) 2.00 5.00
COMMON CARD (1-30) .12 .30
STATED ODDS 2:1

2002 Highlander The Series Previews

COMPLETE SET (9) 6.00 15.00
COMMON CARD (1-9) 1.25 3.00

2007 Highlander Autograph Expansion

COMMON AUTO (IA2-IA5) 10.00 25.00
ANNOUNCED PRINT RUN 333 SETS
IA2 Adrian Paul 12.00 30.00
IA4 Elizabeth Gracen 15.00 40.00

1992 Comic Images Hildebrandt

COMPLETE SET (90) 6.00 15.00
UNOPENED BOX (48 PACKS) 40.00 50.00
UNOPENED PACK (10 CARDS) 1.75 2.00
COMMON CARD (1-90) .12 .30
NNO Woman and Unicorn Promo .75 2.00

1992 Comic Images Hildebrandt Prisms

COMPLETE SET (6) 12.00 30.00
COMMON CARD (1-6) 2.50 6.00
STATED ODDS 1:16
PAN 6-Card Panel (P1-P6)

1993 Comic Images Hildebrandt

COMPLETE SET (90) 4.00 10.00
UNOPENED BOX (48 PACKS) 10.00 20.00
UNOPENED PACK (10 CARDS)
COMMON CARD (1-90) .10 .25
HILDEBRANDT AU SER.#'d TO 250
NNO Two Men Riding Unicorns PROMO .75 2.00
NNO Greg Hildebrandt AU/250 20.00 50.00
NNO 6-Card Panel

1993 Comic Images Hildebrandt Chromium

COMPLETE SET (6) 15.00 40.00
COMMON CARD (C1-C6) 3.00 8.00
STATED ODDS 1:16

2015 Historic Autographs Civil War Appomattox

COMPLETE SET w/o SP (40) 25.00 60.00
COMPLETE SET w/SP (60) 60.00 120.00
COMMON CARD (1-40) .75 2.00
COMMON SP (41-60) 2.00 5.00
COMMON STATED PRINT RUN 1400 SER.#'d SETS
SP STATED PRINT RUN 700 SER.#'d SETS

2016 Historic Autographs The Mob

COMPLETE SET W/SP (60) 20.00 50.00
COMPLETE SET W/O SP (40) 5.00 12.00
COMMON CARD/3500 (1-40) .25 .60
COMMON SP/1750 (41-60) 1.25 3.00

2018 Historic Autographs P.O.T.U.S.

COMPLETE SET W/PREM (63) 12.00 30.00
COMPLETE SET W/O PREM (55) 5.00 12.00
UNOPENED BOX (10 PACKS)
UNOPENED PACK (12 CARDS)
COMMON CARD (1-55) .20 .50
COMMON PREM (PREM1-PREM8) 1.00 2.50

2018 Historic Autographs P.O.T.U.S. Coins

COMMON COIN 8.00 20.00
RANDOMLY INSERTED INTO PACKS
CNGW George Washington/5
CNJA John Adams/11
CNTJ Thomas Jefferson/11 100.00 200.00
CNJME James Madison/11 50.00 100.00
CNJME James Monroe/12 50.00 100.00
CNJQA John Quincy Adams/12 60.00 120.00
CNAJN Andrew Jackson/11
CNMVB Martin Van Buren/10
CNWH William Henry Harrison/10 60.00 120.00
CNJT John Tyler/11 25.00 60.00
CNJP James Polk/11 60.00 120.00
CNZT Zachary Taylor/10
CNMF Millard Fillmore/10 50.00 100.00
CNFP Franklin Pierce/18
CNJB James Buchanan/13 50.00 100.00
CNAL Abraham Lincoln/12 60.00 120.00
CNAJ Andrew Johnson/10 30.00 75.00
CNUG Ulysses Grant/15 30.00 75.00
CNRH Rutherford B. Hayes/16 15.00 40.00
CNJG James Garfield/5
CNCAA Chester A. Arthur/5
CNGC1 Grover Cleveland/11 15.00 40.00
CNBH Benjamin Harrison/16 20.00 50.00
CNGC2 Grover Cleveland/32 15.00 40.00
CNWM William McKinley/36 12.00 30.00
CNTR Theodore Roosevelt/50 15.00 40.00
CNWT William Howard Taft/41 25.00 60.00
CNWW Woodrow Wilson/41 12.00 30.00
CNWH Warren G. Harding/10 60.00 120.00
CNCC Calvin Coolidge/41 15.00 40.00
CNHH Herbert Hoover/35 12.00 30.00
CNFDR Franklin D. Roosevelt/44 15.00 40.00
CNHT Harry S. Truman/41 15.00 40.00
CNJFK John F. Kennedy/49 20.00 50.00
CNRN Richard Nixon/40 10.00 25.00
CNRR Ronald Reagan/41 12.00 30.00
CNGHWB George H.W. Bush/35 10.00 25.00
CNBC William J. Clinton/37 10.00 25.00
CNGWB George W. Bush/33 15.00 40.00
CNBO Barack Obama/37 10.00 25.00
CNDT Donald Trump/39 15.00 40.00

MODERN

2018 Historic Autographs P.O.T.U.S. Stamps

COMMON STAMP	4.00	10.00
RANDOMLY INSERTED INTO PACKS		
STGW George Washington/90	5.00	12.00
STJA John Adams/90	4.00	10.00
STTJ Thomas Jefferson/49	5.00	12.00
STJME James Madison/90	5.00	12.00
STJME James Monroe/49	5.00	12.00
STJQA John Quincy Adams/90	4.00	10.00
STAJN Andrew Jackson/24	6.00	15.00
STMVB Martin Van Buren/90	4.00	10.00
STWH William Henry Harrison/19	6.00	15.00
STJT John Tyler/17	10.00	25.00
STJP James Polk/19		
STZT Zachary Taylor/90	4.00	10.00
STMF Millard Fillmore/19		
STFP Franklin Pierce/19		
STJB James Buchanan/19	20.00	50.00
STAL Abraham Lincoln/49	10.00	25.00
STAJ Andrew Johnson/90	4.00	10.00
STUG Ulysses Grant/15		
STRH Rutherford B. Hayes/75	4.00	10.00
STJG James Garfield/75	4.00	10.00
STCAA Chester Arthur/75	4.00	10.00
STGC1 Grover Cleveland/90	4.00	10.00
STBH Benjamin Harrison/75	5.00	12.00
STGC2 Grover Cleveland/19	8.00	20.00
STWM William McKinley/90	4.00	10.00
STTR Theodore Roosevelt/90	5.00	12.00
STWT William Howard Taft/75	4.00	10.00
STWW Woodrow Wilson/75	4.00	10.00
STWH Warren G. Harding/19	20.00	50.00
STCC Calvin Coolidge/15	30.00	75.00
STHH Herbert Hoover/49	4.00	10.00
STFDR Franklin D. Roosevelt/90	6.00	15.00
STHT Harry S. Truman/49	5.00	12.00
STDE Dwight D. Eisenhower/48	4.00	10.00
STJFK John F. Kennedy/15		
STLBJ Lyndon B. Johnson/49		
STRN Richard Nixon/49	8.00	20.00
STGF Gerald Ford/17		
STRR Ronald Reagan/59	8.00	20.00

1984 Sanitarium Historic Buildings

COMPLETE SET (12)	2.50	6.00
COMMON CARD (1-12)	.40	1.00

1984 Chef & Brewer Historic Pub Signs

COMPLETE SET (20)	6.00	15.00
COMMON CARD	.50	1.25

1995 21st Century Archives History of Comic Strips Promo

NNO Milton Caniff artwork PROMO	.75	2.00

2004 History of the United States

COMPLETE SET (300)	20.00	40.00
COMMON CARD	.10	.25

2004 History of the United States Documents Monuments and Places

COMPLETE SET (15)	5.00	12.00
COMMON CARD (DMP1-DMP15)	.60	1.50
STATED ODDS 1:3		

2004 History of the United States Famous Americans

COMPLETE SET (10)	5.00	12.00
COMMON CARD (FA1-FA10)	1.00	2.50
STATED ODDS 1:5		

2004 History of the United States State Quarters

COMPLETE SET (22)	200.00	400.00
COMMON CARD (SQ1-SQ22)	8.00	20.00
STATED ODDS ONE PER BOX		

2004 History of the United States Greatest Moments in American History

COMPLETE SET (25)	10.00	25.00
COMMON CARD (GM1-GM25)	.75	2.00
STATED ODDS 1:4		

2004 History of the United States Making of America

COMPLETE SET (15)	6.00	15.00
COMMON CARD (MA1-MA15)	1.00	2.50
STATED ODDS 1:6		

1994 Cardz Hitchhiker's Guide to the Galaxy

COMPLETE SET (100)	6.00	15.00
UNOPENED BOX (24 PACKS)	15.00	20.00
UNOPENED PACK (8 CARDS)	.75	1.00
COMMON CARD (1-100)	.12	.30

1994 Cardz Hitchhiker's Guide to the Galaxy Holograms

COMPLETE SET (2)	3.00	8.00
COMMON CARD (H1-H2)	2.00	5.00
RANDOMLY INSERTED INTO PACKS		

1994 Cardz Hitchhiker's Guide to the Galaxy Tekchromes

COMPLETE SET (4)	6.00	15.00
COMMON CARD (T1-T4)	2.00	5.00
STATED ODDS 1:12		

1994 Cardz Hitchhiker's Guide to the Galaxy Promos

COMPLETE SET (3)	2.00	5.00
COMMON CARD	.75	2.00

1993 Personality Comics Hobo Patricide

COMPLETE BOXED SET (38)	6.00	15.00
COMMON CARD	.30	.75

1992 Panini Action Hockey Freaks

COMPLETE SET (100)	5.00	12.00
COMPLETE SET W/STICKERS (110)	6.00	15.00
UNOPENED BOX (36 PACKS)	15.00	20.00
UNOPENED PACK (7 CARDS)	.50	.75
COMMON CARD (1-100)	.10	.25

1992 Panini Action Hockey Freaks Stickers

COMPLETE SET (10)	1.00	2.50
COMMON STICKERS (1-10)	.20	.50
STATED ODDS 1:1		

2002 Hoffman Architect of Fantasy Series One

COMPLETE SET (50)	4.00	10.00
COMMON CARD (1-50)	.15	.40
BM (Signed Blue Metallic Nude Card)	.75	2.00

2002 Hoffman Architect of Fantasy Series Two

COMPLETE SET (50)	4.00	10.00
COMMON CARD (1-50)	.15	.40
BM Blue Metallic Nude Card (Card Set II)	.75	2.00

1993 Mother Productions Hollywood Dead

COMPLETE SET (40)	5.00	12.00
COMMON CARD (1-40)	.25	.60

1993 Victoria Gallery Hollywood Moviemen

COMPLETE BOXED SET (25)	3.00	8.00
COMMON CARD (1-25)	.25	.60

1993 Victoria Gallery Hollywood Moviemen Promos

COMPLETE SET (2)	3.00	8.00
COMMON CARD	2.00	5.00

1994 21st Century Archives Hollywood Pinups

COMPLETE SET (50)	6.00	15.00
UNOPENED BOX (36 PACKS)	20.00	30.00
UNOPENED PACK (8 CARDS)		
COMMON CARD (1-50)	.25	.60
NNO Non-Sport Update PROMO	.75	2.00

1994 21st Century Archives Hollywood Pinups Blonde Bombshells

COMPLETE SET (5)	2.50	6.00
COMMON CARD (BB1-BB5)	1.00	2.50
AVAILABLE THROUGH MAIL-IN OFFER		

1994 21st Century Archives Hollywood Pinups George Petty Old Gold

COMPLETE SET (5)	3.00	8.00
COMMON CARD (LE1-LE5)	.75	2.00

1994 21st Century Archives Hollywood Pinups Marilyn Monroe-Norma Jean

COMPLETE SET (5)	8.00	20.00
COMMON CARD (M1-M5)	2.00	5.00
STATED ODDS 1:18		

1975 Fleer Hollywood Slap Stickers

COMPLETE SET (66)	15.00	40.00
UNOPENED BOX (36 PACKS)	200.00	250.00
UNOPENED PACK	6.00	8.00
COMMON CARD	.30	.75
UNNUMBERED SET		

1991 Starline Hollywood Walk of Fame

COMPLETE SET (250)	10.00	25.00
UNOPENED BOX (36 PACKS)	25.00	40.00
UNOPENED PACK (12 CARDS)	.75	1.25
COMMON CARD (1-250)	.08	.20
27A Dorothy Lamour COR	.40	1.00
27B Dorothy Lamour ERR/Dorthy	.08	.20
48A Bobby Vinton COR	.40	1.00
48B Bobby Vinton ERR/Bobbie	.08	.20
49A Andy Williams COR	.40	1.00
49B Andy Williams ERR/Willams	.08	.20
4A Charlton Heston COR	.40	1.00
4B Charlton Heston ERR/Charleton	.08	.20
72A Zsa Zsa Gabor COR	.40	1.00
72B Zsa Zsa Gabor ERR/Car 72	.08	.20
106A Janet Leigh COR	.40	1.00
106B Janet Leigh ERR/Card 108	.08	.20
142A Vera Miles COR	.08	1.00
142B Vera Miles ERR/Mills	.08	.20

1991 Starline Hollywood Walk of Fame Gold Promos

COMPLETE SET (4)	12.00	30.00
COMMON CARD	4.00	10.00

1991 Starline Hollywood Walk of Fame Prototype Promos

COMMON CARD (SKIP #'d)	3.00	8.00
77 Ann-Margret SP	8.00	20.00

2007 Hollywood Zombies

COMPLETE SET (72)	8.00	20.00
UNOPENED BOX (24 PACKS)	100.00	150.00
UNOPENED PACK (7 CARDS)	4.00	6.00
COMMON CARD (1-72)	.20	.50
*FOIL: 2X TO 5X BASIC CARDS	1.00	2.50

2007 Hollywood Zombies Bonus

COMPLETE SET (2)	4.00	8.00
STATED ODDS 1:BLISTER PACK		
B1 Britney Speared (totally bald Britney)	2.00	5.00
B2 Britney Speared (bald with a few stringers)	2.00	5.00

2007 Hollywood Zombies Morbid Mugshots Gore-Glow

COMPLETE SET (10)	15.00	40.00
COMMON CARD (1-10)	2.00	5.00
STATED ODDS 1:4		

2007 Hollywood Zombies Promos

P1 Elijah Deadwood	.75	2.00
P2 Paris Hellton (NSU)	2.00	5.00
P3 Paris Hellton	.75	2.00
WJ Wacko Jacko Static Cling	2.00	5.00

2007 Hollywood Zombies Masks SDCC

COMPLETE SET (4)	8.00	20.00
COMMON CARD (1-4)	2.00	5.00
SDCC EXCLUSIVE		
3 Donald Stump	4.00	10.00

1994 Aziriah Holy Traders Series 1

COMPLETE SET (30)	3.00	8.00
COMMON CARD	.15	.40

1995 Aziriah Holy Traders Series 2

COMPLETE SET (24)	3.00	8.00
COMMON CARD (1-24)	.15	.40

2001 Holy Traders Series 3

COMPLETE SET (24)	3.00	8.00
COMMON CARD	.15	.40

2004 Holy Traders Series 4

COMPLETE SET (24)	3.00	8.00
COMMON CARD	.15	.40

2007 Holy Traders Series 5

COMPLETE SET (26)	3.00	8.00
COMMON CARD (1-26)	.15	.40

2008 Holy Traders Series 6

COMPLETE SET (26)	3.00	8.00
COMMON CARD (1-26)	.15	.40

1992 Topps Home Alone 2

COMPLETE SET (66)	4.00	10.00
COMPLETE SET W/STICKERS (77)	5.00	12.00
UNOPENED BOX (36 PACKS)	15.00	20.00
UNOPENED PACK (12 CARDS)	.75	1.00
COMMON CARD (1-66)	.10	.30

1992 Topps Home Alone 2 Stickers

COMPLETE SET (11)	1.00	2.50
COMMON STICKERS (1-11)	.15	.40

1987 Topps Home and Away

COMPLETE SET (33)	15.00	40.00
COMMON CARD (1-33)	.75	2.00

1994 SkyBox Home Improvement

COMPLETE SET (90)	6.00	15.00
UNOPENED BOX (24 PACKS)	20.00	30.00
UNOPENED PACK (7 CARDS)	1.00	1.25
S1 Tim Taylor and Al Borland	.40	1.00

1994 SkyBox Home Improvement Foil

COMPLETE SET (2)	5.00	12.00
COMMON CARD (F1-F2)	3.00	8.00
STATED ODDS 1:24		

2004 Homies Swap

COMPLETE SET (72)	6.00	15.00
UNOPENED BOX (36 PACKS)	35.00	50.00
UNOPENED PACK (7 CARDS)	1.25	1.50
COMMON CARD (1-72)	.12	.30

1988 Comic Images The Honeymooners

COMPLETE SET (50)	30.00	80.00
UNOPENED BOX (50 PACKS)	100.00	150.00
UNOPENED PACK (5 CARDS)	3.00	4.00
COMMON CARD (1-50)	.75	2.00

1992 Topps Hook

COMPLETE SET (99)	3.00	8.00
COMPLETE SET W/STICKERS (110)	5.00	12.00
UNOPENED BOX (36 PACKS)	8.00	10.00
UNOPENED PACK (8 CARDS+STICKER)	.40	.50
COMMON CARD (1-99)	.04	.10

1992 Topps Hook Stickers

COMPLETE SET (11)	1.50	4.00
COMMON STICKERS (1-11)	.25	.60

2017 Hoopla Wondercon Promos

COMMON CARD	2.50	6.00

1994 Star International Hooters

COMPLETE SET (100)	4.00	10.00
UNOPENED BOX (36 PACKS)	30.00	60.00
UNOPENED PACK (9 CARDS)	2.00	2.50
COMMON CARD (1-100)	.08	.20
NNO1 Uncut Sheet		
NNO2 Checklist Sheet PROMO		

1994 Star International Hooters Autographs

AVAILABLE VIA REDEMPTION		
1 Heidi Mark	2.00	5.00
2 Redemption Card		

1993 Star International Hooters Calendar Girls

COMPLETE SET (100)	10.00	25.00
UNOPENED BOX (36 PACKS)	8.00	12.00
UNOPENED PACK (9 CARDS)	.25	.30

1993 Star International Hooters Calendar Girls Promos

COMPLETE SET (2)	2.50	6.00
COMMON CARD	1.50	4.00
1 Heidi Tenety	1.50	4.00
2 Heidi Tenety	1.50	4.00

1993 Star International Hooters Calendar Girls Show Promos

COMPLETE SET (14)	12.00	30.00
COMMON CARD (SKIP #'d)	1.50	4.00

2018 Horroible Kids

COMPLETE SET (90)	15.00	40.00
UNOPENED BOX (24 PACKS)		
UNOPENED PACK (5 CARDS)		
COMMON CARD (1a-45b)	.40	1.00

1993 21st Century Archives Horror Stories and Terror Tales

COMPLETE SET (55)	4.00	10.00
COMPLETE FACTORY SET (56)	6.00	15.00
UNOPENED BOX (36 PACKS)	15.00	25.00
UNOPENED PACK (8 CARDS)	.75	1.00
COMMON CARD (1-55)	.15	.40

1993 21st Century Archives Horror Stories and Terror Tales SculptorCast

COMPLETE SET (5)	12.00	30.00
COMMON CARD (SC1-SC5)	3.00	8.00
RANDOMLY INSERTED INTO PACKS		

1993 21st Century Archives Horror Stories and Terror Tales Promos

NNO August Prototype (dealer promo)	.75	2.00
NNO October Prototype (dealer promo)	.75	2.00

2011 Horrors of War

COMPLETE SET (48)	400.00	800.00
COMMON CARD (1-48)	10.00	25.00
ANNOUNCED PRINT RUN 40		

2013 Horrors of War II

COMPLETE SET (40)	300.00	600.00
COMMON CARD (49-88)	10.00	25.00
ANNOUNCED PRINT RUN 40		

1991 Horrors of War Reprints

COMPLETE SET (288)	15.00	40.00
COMMON CARD (1-288)	.10	.25

1984 WTW Productions '38 Horrors of War Reprints

COMPLETE SET (48)	5.00	12.00
COMMON CARD (241-288)	.25	.60

1997 Hot Aire

COMPLETE SET (102)	10.00	25.00
COMMON CARD	.15	.40

1988 Topps Hot Hunks Test Series

COMPLETE SET (7)	30.00	75.00
COMMON CARD	6.00	15.00

1991 Dreamtrip Enterprises Hot Schlock Women in Crime Collection

COMPLETE SET (40)	8.00	20.00
COMMON CARD (1-40)	.40	1.00

1999 Comic Images Hot Wheels

COMPLETE SET (72)	6.00	15.00
UNOPENED BOX (36 PACKS)	40.00	50.00
UNOPENED PACK (6 CARDS)	1.25	1.50
COMMON CARD (1-72)	.15	.40

1999 Comic Images Hot Wheels Kyle Petty Gold Etched

COMPLETE SET (6)	5.00	12.00
COMMON CARD (C1-C6)	1.50	4.00
STATED ODDS 1:18		

1999 Comic Images Hot Wheels Promos

COMPLETE SET (2)	2.00	5.00
COMMON CARD (PR1-PR2)	1.25	3.00

2010 Hot Wheels

COMPLETE SET (88)	12.00	30.00
UNOPENED BOX (24 PACKS)		
UNOPENED PACK (7 CARDS)		
COMMON CARD (1-88)	.20	.50

2010 Hot Wheels Tattoos and Decals

COMPLETE SET (10)	5.00	12.00
COMMON CARD (1-10)	.75	2.00
STATED ODDS 1:2		

2018 Fright-Rags House of 1,000 Corpses

COMPLETE SET (88)	12.00	30.00
UNOPENED BOX (24 PACKS)	100.00	120.00
COMMON CARD (1-87, CL)	.30	.75

2018 Fright-Rags House of 1,000 Corpses Stickers

COMPLETE SET (9)	4.00	10.00
COMMON CARD (UNNUMBERED)	.75	2.00

2014 How to Train Your Dragon 2

COMPLETE SET (100)	8.00	20.00
UNOPENED BOX (24 PACKS)		
UNOPENED PACK (6 CARDS)		
COMMON CARD	.15	.40
CHARACTER (R1-R12)		
DRAGON (D1-D27)		
STORY (S1-S61)		

2014 How to Train Your Dragon 2 Bonus Cards

COMPLETE SET (4)	3.00	8.00
COMMON CARD	1.25	3.00
STATED ODDS 1 PER JUMBO PACK		

2014 How to Train Your Dragon 2 Dragon Footprint Autographs

COMPLETE SET (5)	25.00	60.00
COMMON CARD (1-5)	6.00	15.00
STATED ODDS 1:24		
1 Toothless	12.00	30.00
2 Stormfly	8.00	20.00

2014 How to Train Your Dragon 2 Foil Characters

COMPLETE SET (10)	2.50	6.00
COMMON CARD (1-10)	.40	1.00
STATED ODDS 1:2		

2014 How to Train Your Dragon 2 Pencil Toppers

COMPLETE SET (5)	15.00	40.00
COMMON CARD (1-5)	5.00	12.00
STATED ODDS 1:12		
1 Toothless	8.00	20.00

2014 How to Train Your Dragon 2 Rider's Licenses

COMPLETE SET (10)	12.00	30.00
COMMON CARD (1-10)	2.50	6.00
STATED ODDS 1:3		

2014 How to Train Your Dragon 2 Stickers

COMPLETE SET (20)	6.00	15.00
COMMON CARD (1-20)	.60	1.50
STATED ODDS 1:2		

2014 How to Train Your Dragon 2 Tattoos

COMPLETE SET (10)	5.00	12.00
COMMON CARD (1-10)	.75	2.00
STATED ODDS 1:4		

1986 Topps Howard the Duck

COMPLETE SET (77)	5.00	12.00
COMPLETE SET W/STICKERS (99)	6.00	15.00
UNOPENED BOX (36 PACKS)	75.00	125.00
UNOPENED PACK (9 CARDS+1 STICKER)	2.00	4.00
COMMON CARD (1-77)	.12	.30

1986 Topps Howard the Duck Stickers

COMPLETE SET (22)	2.00	5.00
COMMON CARD (1-22)	.15	.40
STATED ODDS 1:1		

1996 Fleer SkyBox Hunchback of Notre Dame

COMPLETE SET (101)	5.00	12.00
UNOPENED HOBBY BOX (48 PACKS)	20.00	30.00
UNOPENED HOBBY PACK (11 CARDS)		
UNOPENED WALMART BOX (20 PACKS)	5.00	10.00
UNOPENED WALMART PACK (11 CARDS)		
COMMON CARD (1-101)	.10	.25
NNO World of Card Collecting		
P1 Dance, Esmeralda, Dance 3-D Motion Insert		

1996 Fleer SkyBox Hunchback of Notre Dame 3-D Motions

COMPLETE SET (2)	8.00	20.00
COMMON CARD (1-2)	5.00	12.00
STATED ODDS 1:24 HOBBY		

1996 Fleer SkyBox Hunchback of Notre Dame Color-In

COMPLETE SET (10)	3.00	8.00
COMMON CARD (1-10)	.75	2.00
STATED ODDS 2:1 WALMART		

1996 Fleer SkyBox Hunchback of Notre Dame Iron-Ons

COMPLETE SET (6)	4.00	10.00
COMMON CARD (1-6)	.75	2.00
STATED ODDS 1:6 HOBBY		

1996 Fleer SkyBox Hunchback of Notre Dame Jester's Challenge

COMPLETE SET (35)	6.00	15.00
COMMON CARD (1-35)	.30	.75
STATED ODDS 1:1		

1996 Fleer SkyBox Hunchback of Notre Dame Mall Tour

COMPLETE SET (8)	2.00	5.00
COMMON CARD (1-8)	.40	1.00

1996 Fleer SkyBox Hunchback of Notre Dame Promos

1 6-Up Panel	2.00	5.00
2 Target	.75	2.00

2012 The Hunger Games

COMPLETE SET (72)	6.00	15.00
COMPLETE SET W/SP (105)		
UNOPENED BOX (24 PACKS)	20.00	30.00
UNOPENED PACK (6 CARDS)	1.00	1.50
COMMON CARD (1-72)	.15	.40
CD BONUS (73-81)		
WALMART EXCLUSIVES (82-105)		

2012 The Hunger Games Autographs

STATED ODDS 1:50		
WALMART EXCLUSIVE		
A1 Jennifer Lawrence	1000.00	2000.00
A2 Josh Hutcherson	50.00	100.00
A3 Liam Hemsworth	100.00	200.00
A5 Dayo Okenyl	25.00	60.00
A7 Isabelle Fuhrman	30.00	80.00
A9 Jack Quaid	25.00	60.00

2013 The Hunger Games Auction Promos

COMPLETE SET (6)	8.00	20.00
COMMON CARD (UNNUMBERED)	1.25	3.00

2013 The Hunger Games Catching Fire

COMPLETE SET (40)	10.00	25.00
COMMON CARD (1-40)	.40	1.00

1991 Pacific I Love Lucy

COMPLETE SET (110)	5.00	12.00
COMPLETE BOXED SET (110)	5.00	12.00
UNOPENED BOX (36 PACKS)	15.00	25.00
UNOPENED PACK (10 CARDS)	.75	1.00
COMMON CARD (1-110)	.07	.25
*PINK BORDER: SAME VALUE	.10	.25

2001 Dart FlipCards I Love Lucy 50th Anniversary

COMPLETE SET (72)	4.00	10.00
UNOPENED BOX (36 PACKS)	30.00	40.00
UNOPENED PACK (6 CARDS)	1.00	1.25
NNO God Bless America Stars and Stripes Sticker		

2001 Dart FlipCards I Love Lucy 50th Anniversary Bonus Cards

B1 Box Bottom	.75	2.00
BT1 Box Topper	1.50	4.00
CT1 Lucy and Ricky Case Loader	8.00	20.00

2001 Dart FlipCards I Love Lucy 50th Anniversary Character Holographic

COMPLETE SET (4)	5.00	12.00
COMMON CARD (C1-C4)	1.50	4.00
STATED ODDS 1:16		

2001 Dart FlipCards I Love Lucy 50th Anniversary Classic Moments

COMPLETE SET (6)	8.00	20.00
COMMON CARD (CM1-CM6)	1.50	4.00
STATED ODDS 1:11		

2001 Dart FlipCards I Love Lucy 50th Anniversary Promos

CC 50th Anniversary Trading Cards San Diego Comic Con	1.50	4.00
P1 50th Anniversary Trading Cards	.75	2.00

2002 Ice Age

COMPLETE SET (72)	4.00	10.00
UNOPENED BOX (24 PACKS)	25.00	40.00
UNOPENED PACK (6 CARDS)	1.25	1.75
COMMON CARD (1-72)	.10	.25
P1 Ice Age Trading Cards Are Coming PROMO	1.25	3.00

2002 Ice Age Ice

COMPLETE SET (12)	10.00	25.00
COMMON CARD (IC1-IC12)	1.25	3.00
STATED ODDS 1:4		

1992 MotorArt Iditarod
COMPLETE SET (110) 5.00 12.00
UNOPENED BOX (36 PACKS) 15.00 25.00
UNOPENED PACK (9 CARDS) .75 1.00
COMMON CARD (1-110) .10 .25

1992 MotorArt Iditarod Prototype Promos
COMPLETE SET (3) 4.00 10.00
COMMON CARD 1.50 4.00

2008 Igor
COMPLETE SET (70) 8.00 20.00
UNOPENED BOX (24 PACKS)
UNOPENED PACK (5 CARDS)
COMMON CARD (1-70) .25 .60

2008 Igor Autographs
COMMON AUTO 30.00 75.00
RANDOMLY INSERTED INTO PACKS
A1 John Cusack 100.00 200.00

2008 Igor Character Inserts
COMPLETE SET (11) 6.00 15.00
COMMON CARD (C1-C11) .75 2.00
STATED ODDS 1:1

2008 Igor Storyboard Concept Art
COMPLETE SET (9) 8.00 20.00
COMMON CARD (S1-S9) 1.50 4.00
RANDOMLY INSERTED INTO PACKS

1995 Topps Image Universe
COMPLETE SET (90) 12.00 30.00
UNOPENED BOX (24 PACKS) 50.00 75.00
UNOPENED PACK (6 CARDS) 2.00 3.00
COMMON CARD (1-90) .25 .60
0 Image Universe PROMO .75 2.00

1995 Topps Image Universe ClearZone
COMPLETE SET (6) 15.00 40.00
COMMON CARD (C1-C6) 3.00 8.00
STATED ODDS 1:11

1995 Topps Image Universe First Issue Covers
COMPLETE SET (6) 15.00 40.00
COMMON CARD (D1-D6) 3.00 8.00
STATED ODDS 1:7

1995 Topps Image Universe Interview Refractors
COMPLETE SET (6) 15.00 40.00
COMMON CARD (I1-I6) 3.00 8.00
STATED ODDS 1:7

1993 Jamison Images of Jesus
COMPLETE BOXED SET (19) 2.00 5.00
COMMON CARD (1-18; NNO1) .25 .60
NNO2 Calming the Sea PROMO 4.00 10.00

1994 Image Comics Images of ShadowHawk
COMPLETE SET (100) 6.00 15.00
UNOPENED BOX (36 PACKS) 30.00 40.00
UNOPENED PACK (8 CARDS) 1.00 1.25
COMMON CARD (1-100) .12 .30

1994 Image Comics Images of ShadowHawk Holofoil
COMPLETE SET (7) 12.00 30.00
COMMON CARD (SP1-SP7) 2.50 6.00
STATED ODDS 1:9

1992 Topps In Living Color
COMPLETE SET (88) 5.00 12.00
COMPLETE SET W/STICKERS (99) 6.00 15.00
UNOPENED BOX (36 PACKS) 125.00 200.00
UNOPENED PACK (8 CARDS) 4.00 5.00
COMMON CARD (1-88) .12 .30

1994 Interlink In Pursuit of Justice The Simpson Case
COMPLETE SET (50) 2.50 6.00
COMMON CARD (1-50) .08 .25

1994 Interlink In Pursuit of Justice The Simpson Case Promos
COMPLETE SET (10) 2.50 6.00
COMMON CARD (P1-P10) .50 1.25

1985 Brooke Bond Incredible Creatures
COMPLETE SET (40) 5.00 12.00
COMMON CARD (1-40) .25 .60

1996 Topps Independence Day
COMPLETE SET (72) 5.00 12.00
UNOPENED BOX (36 PACKS) 25.00 40.00
UNOPENED PACK (6 CARDS) 1.00 1.50
COMMON CARD (1-72) .15 .40

1996 Topps Independence Day Holofoil
COMPLETE SET (6) 8.00 20.00
COMMON CARD (ID1-ID6) 2.50 6.00
STATED ODDS 1:9

1996 Topps Independence Day Promos
COMPLETE SET (3) 2.00 5.00
COMMON CARD .75 2.00

1993 Indian Motorcycles II
COMPLETE SET (25) 5.00 12.00
UNOPENED BOX (24 PACKS) 15.00 25.00
UNOPENED PACK (8 CARDS) .75 1.00
COMMON CARD (1-25) .30 .75

1984 Topps Indiana Jones and the Temple of Doom
COMPLETE SET (88) 5.00 12.00
COMPLETE SET W/STICKERS (99) 6.00 15.00
UNOPENED BOX (36 PACKS) 75.00 125.00
UNOPENED PACK (10 CARDS+1 STICKER) 2.00 3.00
COMMON CARD (1-88) .15 .40

1984 Topps Indiana Jones and the Temple of Doom Stickers
COMPLETE SET (11) 1.25 3.00
COMMON CARD (1-11) .20 .50
STATED ODDS 1:1

2008 Indiana Jones and the Kingdom of the Crystal Skull
COMPLETE SET (90) 5.00 12.00
UNOPENED BOX (24 PACKS) 60.00 100.00
UNOPENED PACK (7 CARDS) 3.00 4.00
COMMON CARD (1-90) .15 .40
*HOLOFOIL: 3X TO 8X BASIC CARDS 1.25 3.00

2008 Indiana Jones and the Kingdom of the Crystal Skull Autographs
COMMON CARD 4.00 10.00
HOBBY STATED ODDS 1:78
RETAIL STATED ODDS 1:100
AUTOS ARE UNNUMBERED
NNO Alan Dale 5.00 12.00
NNO Andrew Divoff 6.00 15.00
NNO George Lucas 400.00 800.00
NNO Harrison Ford 2000.00 4000.00
NNO Ford/Lucas/Spielberg
NNO Jim Broadbent 20.00 50.00
NNO John Hurt 30.00 75.00
NNO Karen Allen H 15.00 40.00
NNO Karen Allen R 10.00 25.00
NNO Pasha Lychnikoff 4.00 15.00
NNO Ray Winstone 20.00 50.00
NNO Shia LaBeouf 100.00 200.00
NNO S.LaBeouf/K.Allen
NNO Steven Spielberg 700.00 1200.00

2008 Indiana Jones and the Kingdom of the Crystal Skull Foil
COMPLETE SET (10) 5.00 12.00
COMMON CARD .60 1.50
STATED ODDS 1:6

2008 Indiana Jones Heritage
COMPLETE SET (90) 5.00 12.00
UNOPENED BOX (24 PACKS) 200.00 350.00
UNOPENED PACK (5 CARDS) 8.00 15.00
COMMON CARD (1-90) .15 .40
*GOLD: 2.5X TO 6X BASIC CARDS

2008 Indiana Jones Heritage Autographs
COMMON CARD 4.00 10.00
STATED ODDS 1:42
NNO Karen Allen 50.00 100.00
NNO Michael Byrne 15.00 40.00
NNO Kate Capshaw 300.00 500.00
NNO Harrison Ford 1500.00 3000.00
NNO Paul Freeman 150.00 300.00
NNO Julian Glover 10.00 25.00
NNO George Harris 20.00 50.00
NNO Anthony Higgins 8.00 20.00
NNO Wolf Kahler 6.00 15.00
NNO Lawrence Kasdan 200.00 350.00
NNO Kathleen Kennedy 400.00 800.00
NNO George Lucas 800.00 1500.00
NNO Kevork Malikyan 60.00 120.00
NNO Frank Marshall 200.00 350.00
NNO Alfred Molina 200.00 350.00
NNO Ke Huy Quan 125.00 300.00
NNO John Rhys-Davies 250.00 500.00
NNO Roshan Seth 6.00 15.00
NNO Steven Spielberg 2000.00 4000.00
NNO Vic Tablian 6.00 15.00
NNO David Yip 8.00 20.00
NNO Denholm Elliot CUT/1
NNO Pat Roach CUT/1

2008 Indiana Jones Heritage Box-Loader Promos
COMPLETE SET (3) 4.00 10.00
COMMON CARD 1.50 4.00
STATED ODDS ONE PER BOX

2008 Indiana Jones Heritage Magnets
COMPLETE SET (9) 120.00 250.00
COMMON CARD 12.00 30.00
STATED ODDS 1:8

2008 Indiana Jones Masterpieces
COMPLETE SET (90) 6.00 15.00
UNOPENED BOX (24 PACKS) 300.00 500.00
UNOPENED PACK (7 CARDS) 12.00 20.00
COMMON CARD (1-90) .15 .40

2008 Indiana Jones Masterpieces Etched Foil
COMPLETE SET (6) 8.00 20.00
COMMON CARD (1-6) 2.00 5.00
STATED ODDS 1:6
HOBBY EXCLUSIVE
2 Indiana Jones 3.00 8.00

2008 Indiana Jones Masterpieces Foil Silver
COMPLETE SET (9) 5.00 12.00
COMMON CARD (1-9) 1.25 3.00
*BRONZE: .75X TO 2X BASIC CARDS 2.50 6.00
*GOLD/99: 2.5X TO 6X BASIC CARDS 8.00 20.00
STATED ODDS 1:4

1992 Pro Set The Young Indiana Jones Chronicles
COMPLETE SET (95) 4.00 10.00
COMMON CARD (1-95) .12 .30

1992 Pro Set The Young Indiana Jones Chronicles 3-D
COMPLETE SET (10) 2.00 5.00
COMMON CARD (3D1-3D10) .30 .75
STATED ODDS ONE PER PACK

1992 Pro Set The Young Indiana Jones Chronicles Hidden Treasures
COMPLETE SET (8) 2.00 5.00
COMMON CARD .30 .75
STATED ODDS 1:1

1993 Kitchen Sink Press Infant Earth
COMPLETE SET (36) 6.00 15.00
COMMON CARD (1-36) .30 .75
NNO Uncut Sheet Signed

1999 General Mills Inspector Gadget
COMPLETE SET (15) 5.00 12.00
COMMON CARD (1-15) .60 1.50

1999 McDonald's Inspector Gadget
COMPLETE SET (6) 2.50 6.00
COMMON CARD .60 1.50

1994 Cardz Interplanetary Lizards of the Texas Plains Promos
1 Interplanetary Lizards of the Texas Plains .60 1.50
2 Interplanetary Lizards of the Texas Plains .60 1.50
3 Interplanetary Lizards of the Texas Plains .60 1.50

1988 Eclipse Iran-Contra Scandal
COMPLETE BOXED SET (36) 4.00 10.00
COMMON CARD (1-36) .25 .60

1996 Inkworks Island of Dr. Moreau Promos
COMPLETE SET (8) 6.00 15.00
COMMON CARD 1.00 2.50

1996 DuoCards It's a Wonderful Life
COMPLETE SET (72) 6.00 15.00
UNOPENED BOX (30 PACKS) 30.00 50.00
UNOPENED PACK (7 CARDS) 1.50 2.00
COMMON CARD (1-72) .20 .50

1996 DuoCards It's a Wonderful Life Chromium
COMPLETE SET (6) 12.00 30.00
COMMON CARD (C1-C6) 3.00 8.00
STATED ODDS 1:15

1996 DuoCards It's a Wonderful Life Mail-In
COMPLETE SET (6) 8.00 20.00
COMMON CARD (R1-R6) 2.00 5.00
AVAILABLE VIA MAIL-IN OFFER

1996 DuoCards It's a Wonderful Life Talking Card
1 Every Time A Bell Rings 15.00 40.00
2 Redemption Card

1996 DuoCards It's a Wonderful Life Promos
COMPLETE SET (2) 1.25 3.00
COMMON CARD (1-2) .75 2.00

1994 Comic Images Jack Kirby The Unpublished Archives
COMPLETE SET (90) 5.00 12.00
UNOPENED BOX (48 PACKS) 15.00 20.00
UNOPENED PACK (10 CARDS) .30 .40
COMMON CARD (1-90) .10 .25
M1 Medallion 6.00 15.00
JK1 Jack Kirby 24K Gold Signature/500* 20.00 50.00
UNC1 6-Up Panel UNC 8.00 20.00

1994 Comic Images Jack Kirby The Unpublished Archives Chromium
COMPLETE SET (6) 8.00 20.00
COMMON CARD (C1-C6) 2.00 5.00
STATED ODDS 1:16

1994 Comic Images Jack Kirby The Unpublished Archives The Villains
COMPLETE SET (3) 12.00 30.00
COMMON CARD (1-3) 6.00 15.00
STATED ODDS 1:48

1994 Comic Images Jack Kirby The Unpublished Archives Promo

1 Dealer Promo 1.50 4.00

1993 Topps Jack Kirby's Teen Agents Promos

COMPLETE SET (9) 5.00 12.00
COMMON CARD (1-9) .75 2.00

2022 Zerocool Jackass

COMPLETE SET (38) 10.00 25.00
UNOPENED BOX (10 PACKS) 100.00 150.00
UNOPENED PACK (5 CARDS) 10.00 15.00
COMMON CAST (1-14) .60 1.50
COMMON "ROOKIES" (15-24) .60 1.50
COMMON LEGENDS (25-31) .60 1.50
COMMON CAMEOS (32-45) .60 1.50
COMMON GROUP SHOTS (46-50) .60 1.50
SILVER/250: 1.2X TO 3X BASIC CARDS
*SILVER SP: 2.5X TO 6X BASIC CARDS
*HOLO/100: 4X TO 10X BASIC CARDS
*BLUE/50: 8X TO 20X BASIC CARDS
*RED/25: 15X TO 40X BASIC CARDS
STATED CAST ODDS 1:5
STATED "ROOKIES" ODDS 1:7
STATED LEGENDS ODDS 1:5
STATED GROUP SHOTS ODDS 1:7
STATED CAMEOS ODDS 1:2
STATED PRINT RUN 2,880 SETS

2022 Zerocool Jackass Behind-the-Lens

COMPLETE SET (30) 25.00 60.00
COMMON CARD (btl1-btl30) 1.50 4.00
SILVER/250: SAME VALUE AS BASIC
*HOLO/100: .5X TO 1.2X BASIC CARDS
*BLUE/50: 1X TO 2.5X BASIC CARDS
STATED ODDS 1:1

2022 Zerocool Jackass Boxes

NNO Black/50*
NNO Cracked Ice/1*
NNO Gold/10*
NNO Green/1,490*
NNO Purple/890*
NNO Rainbow/50*
NNO Red/2,480*
NNO Regular
NNO Silver/4,979*

2022 Zerocool Jackass Movie Posters

COMPLETE SET (10) 30.00 75.00
COMMON CARD (mp1-mp10) 5.00 12.00
SILVER/250: SAME VALUE AS BASIC
*HOLO/100: .5X TO 1.2X BASIC CARDS
*BLUE/50: 1X TO 2.5X BASIC CARDS
STATED ODDS 1:3

2022 Zerocool Jackass Signatures

COMMON AUTO 15.00 40.00
*BLUE/50: .6X TO 1.5X BASIC AUTOS
STATED PRINT RUN 100 SER.#'d SETS
jsp Sean "Poopies" McInerney 25.00 60.00
jsbb Butterbean (Eric Esch) 30.00 75.00
jscp Chris Pontius 20.00 50.00
jsdj DJ Paul (Paul Beauregard) 40.00 100.00
jsdm Dimitry Elyashkevich
jsds Dark Shark (Compston Wilson)
jsea Eric Andre 60.00 150.00
jsem Eric Manaka 30.00 75.00
jsfn Francis Ngannou 40.00 100.00
jsjk Johnny Knoxville 100.00 250.00
jsjt Jeff Tremaine 40.00 100.00
jslf Loomis Fall 30.00 75.00
jspl Preston Lacy 25.00 60.00
jsps PK Subban 40.00 100.00
jsrd Rob Dyrdek 40.00 100.00
jsrk Rick Kosick 20.00 50.00
jsrw Rachel Wolfson 25.00 60.00
jssj Spike Jonze 60.00 150.00
jsso Steve-O 125.00 300.00
jstb Tory Belleci 20.00 50.00
jsth Tony Hawk 100.00 250.00
jswm Weeman (Jason Acuna) 40.00 100.00
jszh Zach Holmes 20.00 50.00

2022 Zerocool Jackass Stunts

COMPLETE SET (70) 60.00 150.00
COMMON CARD (s1-s70) 1.50 4.00
SILVER/250: SAME VALUE AS BASIC
*HOLO/100: .5X TO 1.2X BASIC CARDS
*BLUE/50: 1X TO 2.5X BASIC CARDS
STATED ODDS 1:1

2004 JAG Limited Edition Previews

COMPLETE SET (7) 6.00 15.00
COMMON CARD (J1-J6) 1.50 4.00
JFF1 EXCLUSIVE TO JAG FEST
JFF1 Promo 15.00 40.00
(JAG Fest Exclusive)

2006 JAG Premiere Edition

COMPLETE SET (60) 8.00 12.00
UNOPENED BOX (24 PACKS) 80.00 100.00
UNOPENED PACK (6 CARDS) 3.50 4.50
COMMON CARD .15 .40
P1 JAG Premiere Edition PROMO

2006 JAG Premiere Edition Autographs

COMMON AUTO (A1-A29) 4.00 10.00
STATED ODDS OVERALL 5:BOX
A1 David James Elliott 30.00 75.00
A2 Catherine Bell 75.00 150.00
A4 Nanci Chambers 6.00 15.00
A6 Meta Golding 8.00 20.00
A8 Tamlyn Tomita 6.00 15.00
A10 Karri Turner 12.00 30.00
A11 Patrick Labyorteaux 8.00 20.00
A12 Tracey Needham 8.00 20.00
A13 Isabella Hoffman 10.00 25.00
A16 Troian Bellisario 8.00 20.00
A17 Andrea Thompson 6.00 15.00
A18 Corbin Bernsen 10.00 25.00
A21 Zoe McLellan 8.00 20.00
A22 Susan Haskell 8.00 20.00
A24 David Andrews 6.00 15.00
A25 Mae Whitman 5.00 12.00
A26 Dee Wallace-Stone 12.00 30.00
A28 Andrew Divoff 6.00 15.00
A29 Vaughn Armstrong 6.00 15.00

2006 JAG Premiere Edition Black-Back Autographs

COMMON AUTO (D1-D3) 75.00 150.00
STATED ODDS 1:700
D1 David James Elliott/50 75.00 150.00
D2 Catherine Bell/50 100.00 200.00
D3 C.Bell 120.00 250.00
D.Elliott/40

2006 JAG Premiere Edition Heart-to-Heart

COMPLETE SET (5) 5.00 12.00
COMMON CARD (HH1-HH5) 1.25 3.00
STATED PRINT RUN 1,600 SER.#'d SETS

2006 JAG Premiere Edition JAG Clips Gallery

COMPLETE SET (4) 8.00 20.00
COMMON CARD (G1-G4) 3.00 8.00
STATED ODDS 1:24

2006 JAG Premiere Edition JAG Debut Autographs

COMMON AUTO (D1-D29) 4.00 10.00
STATED ODDS OVERALL 5:BOX
D1 David James Elliott 25.00 60.00
D2 Catherine Bell 60.00 120.00
D3 Randy Vasquez 5.00 12.00
D4 Nanci Chambers 10.00 25.00
D5 Rif Hutton 6.00 15.00
D6 Meta Golding 8.00 20.00
D8 Tamlyn Tomita 6.00 15.00
D10 Karri Turner 10.00 25.00
D11 Patrick Labyorteaux 12.00 30.00
D12 Tracey Needham 12.00 30.00
D13 Isabella Hoffman 10.00 25.00
D14 Julie Caitlin Brown 6.00 15.00
D16 Troian Bellisario 10.00 25.00
D17 Andrea Thompson 6.00 15.00
D18 Corbin Bernsen 10.00 25.00
D23 Anne-Marie Johnson 10.00 25.00
D25 Mae Whitman 5.00 12.00
D26 Dee Wallace-Stone 12.00 30.00
D28 Andrew Divoff 6.00 15.00

2006 JAG Premiere Edition JAG Ensemble Autographs

COMMON AUTO (JC1-JC5) 10.00 25.00
STATED ODDS 1:84
STATED ODDS OVERALL 5:BOX
JC1 N.Chambers 60.00 120.00
D.Elliott/100
JC3 C.Bell 75.00 150.00
D.Elliott/100
JC4 C.Carrington 15.00 40.00
R.Hutton#(R.Vasquez/200
JC5 T.Tomita 20.00 50.00
A.Thompson#(T.Needham/250

2006 JAG Premiere Edition JAG Spotlight

COMPLETE SET (10) 25.00 60.00
COMMON CARD (CB1-CB5; DE1-DE5) 3.00 8.00
STATED ODDS 1:24

2006 JAG Premiere Edition Trevor Goddard Tributes

COMPLETE SET (6) 8.00 20.00
COMMON CARD (TG1-TG6) 2.00 5.00
STATED ODDS 1:12

1990 Rosenbloom Jake's Jokes

COMPLETE SET (121) 6.00 15.00
UNOPENED CELLO PACK (18 CARDS) 3.00 4.00
COMMON CARD (1-121) .12 .30

James Bond

2007 Complete James Bond

COMPLETE SET (189) 8.00 20.00
UNOPENED BOX (40 PACKS) 60.00 100.00
UNOPENED PACK (5 CARDS) 3.00 4.00
COMMON CARD (1-189) .15 .40

2007 Complete James Bond Autographs

COMMON AUTO 6.00 15.00
STATED ODDS 1:40
A90 STATED ODDS ONE PER COLLECTOR'S ALBUM
LAZENBY AU STATED ODDS ONE PER 2 CASE PURCHASE
RICHARDS AU STATED ODDS ONE PER 6 CASE PURCHASE
L (LIMITED): 300-500 COPIES
VL (VERY LIMITED): 200-300 COPIES
A32 Ursula Andress VL 300.00 750.00
A51 Yaphet Kotto VL 125.00 300.00
A52 Lynn-Holly Johnson VL 30.00 75.00
A53 Kristina Wayborn VL 25.00 60.00
A54 Maud Adams VL 60.00 120.00
A55 Maud Adams VL 75.00 150.00
A56 Famke Janssen VL 200.00 500.00
A57 Tania Mallet L 15.00 40.00
A63 Lana Wood VL 15.00 40.00
A65 Timothy Moxon L 12.00 30.00
A66 Britt Ekland L 30.00 75.00
A68 Alan Cumming VL 50.00 100.00
A70 Caroline Bliss VL 15.00 40.00
A71 Izabella Scorupco VL 30.00 75.00
A72 Honor Blackman VL 100.00 250.00
A73 Marguerite Lewars VL 50.00 100.00
A75 Judi Dench VL 40.00 100.00
A77 Mads Mikkelsen VL 60.00 120.00
A78 Caterina Murino L 20.00 50.00
A79 Giancarlo Giannini L 20.00 50.00
A80 John Rhys-Davies VL 50.00 125.00
A81 Sebastien Foucan L 8.00 20.00
A90 Jeremy Bulloch ALB 30.00 75.00
NNO George Lazenby FB 2CI 60.00 150.00
NNO Denise Richards FB 6CI 250.00 500.00

2007 Complete James Bond Casino Royale Dangerous Liaisons

COMPLETE SET (9) 15.00 40.00
COMMON CARD (DL1-DL9) 2.50 6.00
STATED ODDS 1:14

2007 Complete James Bond Casino Royale Expansion

COMPLETE SET (10) 20.00 50.00
COMMON CARD 3.00 8.00
STATED ODDS 1:20

2007 Complete James Bond Relics

COMMON MEM (RC1-RC18) 10.00 25.00
STATED ODDS 1:40
DC1 STATED ODDS ONE PER CASE
L (LIMITED): 300-500 COPIES
VL (VERY LIMITED): 200-300 COPIES
RC2 James Bond Medical Report VL 15.00 40.00
RC3 Fontainebleau Letterhead VL 50.00 100.00
RC4 San Monique Flag 15.00 40.00
RC5 Circus Program 50.00 100.00
RC6 Casino Chip VL 100.00 200.00
RC7 Sir Robert King Bank Statement VL 75.00 150.00
RC8 Parahawk Parachute VL 300.00 600.00
RC9 Zorin Industries Patch 12.00 30.00
RC10 Fontainebleau Score Sheet VL 75.00 150.00
RC12 Tarot Card L 200.00 400.00
RC13 Casino Chip VL 300.00 600.00
RC14 Casino L'or Noir Check VL 75.00 150.00
RC16 Osato Stationary 20.00 50.00
RC17 Playing Card 30.00 75.00
RC18 Casino Chip VL 125.00 250.00
DC1 James Bond Dual Shirt CT 50.00 100.00

2007 Complete James Bond Casino Royale Quotables

COMPLETE SET (6) 8.00 20.00
COMMON CARD (Q1-Q6) 1.50 4.00
STATED ODDS 1:20

2007 Complete James Bond Promos

COMPLETE SET (3) 4.00 10.00
COMMON CARD (P1-P3) .75 2.00
P3 6 Bond Villains ALB 3.00 8.00

1965 Somportex Exciting World of James Bond

COMPLETE SET (49) 75.00 150.00
COMMON CARD (1-49) 1.00 2.50

1965 Philadelphia Gum James Bond

COMPLETE SET (66) 125.00 225.00
UNOPENED PACK (YELLOW) 100.00 120.00
COMMON CARD (1-66) 1.00 2.50
1 Debonair But Deadly 1.00 2.50
66 The Final Encounter 2.00 5.00

1993 Eclipse James Bond 007 Series One

COMPLETE SET (110) 12.00 30.00
UNOPENED BOX (36 PACKS) 85.00 100.00
UNOPENED PACK (12 CARDS) 2.50 3.00
COMMON CARD (1-110) .20 .50

1993 Eclipse James Bond 007 Series One Holograms

COMPLETE SET (2) 10.00 25.00
COMMON CARD (H1-H2) 6.00 15.00
RANDOMLY INSERTED INTO PACKS
H2A Oddjob ERR (overexposed image) 8.00 20.00

1993 Eclipse James Bond 007 Series Two

COMPLETE SET (110) 6.00 15.00
UNOPENED BOX (36 PACKS) 40.00 50.00

MODERN

UNOPENED PACK (12 CARDS)	1.25	1.50
COMMON CARD (1-110)	.12	.30

1993 Eclipse James Bond 007 Series Two Bond Girls

COMPLETE SET (6)	8.00	20.00
COMMON CARD (BG1-BG6)	2.00	5.00
RANDOMLY INSERTED INTO PACKS		

2002 James Bond 40th Anniversary

COMPLETE SET (60)	5.00	12.00
UNOPENED BOX (20 PACKS)	65.00	80.00
UNOPENED PACK (6 CARDS)	3.50	4.00
COMMON CARD (1-60)	.15	.40

2002 James Bond 40th Anniversary Autographs

COMMON AUTO (A1-A24)	8.00	20.00
STATED ODDS 1:10		
A4 CHAIM TOPOL NOT ISSUED		
A1 Jonathan Pryce	15.00	40.00
A2 Joe Don Baker	40.00	100.00
A3 Shirley Eaton	15.00	40.00
A6 George Lazenby	50.00	125.00
A8 Clifton James	60.00	120.00
A9 Christopher Lee	125.00	300.00
A10 Richard Kiel	50.00	125.00
A11 Lois Chiles	15.00	40.00
A12 Julian Glover	12.00	30.00
A14 Tanya Roberts	20.00	50.00
A16 David Hedison	10.00	25.00
A17 Steven Berkoff	10.00	25.00
A18 Robert Brown	15.00	40.00
A19 Samantha Bond	12.00	30.00
A20 Angela Scouler	10.00	25.00
A21 Bernard Horsfall	10.00	25.00
A22 Caroline Munro	15.00	40.00
A23 Vincent Schiavelli	25.00	60.00
A24 Patrick Macnee	40.00	100.00

2002 James Bond 40th Anniversary Bond Extras

COMPLETE SET (19)	6.00	15.00
COMMON CARD (BE1-BE19)	.40	1.00
STATED ODDS 1:1		

2002 James Bond 40th Anniversary Bond Villians

COMPLETE SET (19)	6.00	15.00
COMMON CARD (BV1-BV19)	.40	1.00
STATED ODDS 1:2		

2002 James Bond 40th Anniversary Bond Women

COMPLETE SET (19)	12.50	30.00
COMMON CARD (BW1-BW19)	.75	2.00
STATED ODDS 1:4		

2002 James Bond 40th Anniversary Costumes

COMPLETE SET (3)	50.00	100.00
COMMON COSTUME (CC1-CC3)	10.00	25.00
STATED ODDS 1:120		
CC1 James Bond	100.00	200.00

2002 James Bond 40th Anniversary Expansion

COMPLETE SET (11)	30.00	80.00
COMMON CARD	.75	2.00
A25 Geoffrey Keen AU	6.00	15.00
A26 Sean Bean AU	15.00	40.00
A27 Robert Davi AU	10.00	25.00

2002 James Bond 40th Anniversary Game

COMP.SET w/o SP (8)	5.00	12.00
COMMON CARD (A-S)	.75	2.00
STATED ODDS 1:1		
SP ANNOUNCED PRINT RUN 40 SETS		
D James Bond SP	250.00	500.00

2002 James Bond 40th Anniversary Promos

P1 Sean Connery	.75	2.00
P2 Roger Moore	.75	2.00
P3 Pierce Brosnan SDCC	1.25	3.00

2012 James Bond 50th Anniversary

COMPLETE SET (198)	12.00	30.00
COMP.SER. 1 SET (99)	6.00	15.00
COMP.SER. 2 SET (99)	8.00	20.00
UNOPENED SER.1 BOX (24 PACKS)	75.00	125.00
UNOPENED SER.1 PACK (5 CARDS)	4.00	6.00
UNOPENED SER.2 BOX (24 PACKS)	75.00	125.00
UNOPENED SER.2 PACK (5 CARDS)	4.00	6.00
COMMON CARD (1-198)	.15	.40
ODD #'d CARDS ISSUED IN SERIES 1		
EVEN #'d CARDS ISSUED IN SERIES 2		
*PARALLEL: 1.5X TO 4X BASIC CARDS		
SKYFALL CARD ISSUED AS SER. 1 CT		
CT1 ISSUED AS SER. 2 CASE TOPPER		
JBR27 ISSUED AS SER. 1 3-CASE INCENTIVE		
JBR28 ISSUED AS SER. 2 3-CASE INCENTIVE		
CT1 James Bond (007 logo in background) (Ser. 2 CT)	10.00	25.00
NNO SkyFall Movie Poster/700 (Ser. 1 CT)	10.00	25.00
JBR27 Gustav Graves' Ice Palace Interior MEM/375 (Ser. 1 3CI)	40.00	80.00
JBR28 Franz Sanchez's Airplane MEM/333 (3CI)	20.00	50.00

2012 James Bond 50th Anniversary Autographs

COMMON AUTO	5.00	12.00
OVERALL AUTO ODDS 3 PER BOX		
L (LIMITED): 300-500 COPIES		
VL (VERY LIMITED): 200-300 COPIES		
EL (EXTREMELY LTD): UNDER 200 COPIES		
A110 Daniel Craig EL	250.00	600.00
A138 Gemma Arterton EL	125.00	250.00
A145 Jill St. John L	20.00	50.00
A151 Eunice Gayson VL	15.00	40.00
A162 Anthony Zerbe L	20.00	50.00
A166 Luciana Paluzzi L	12.00	30.00
A170 Nina Muschallik	6.00	15.00
A171 Francisca Tu	6.00	15.00
A173 Michael Madsen L	12.00	30.00
A176 Lesley Langley L	8.00	20.00
A180 Toby Stephens L	10.00	25.00
A181 Simon Andreu L	6.00	15.00
A183 Cristina Contes L	8.00	20.00
A186 Veruschka L	6.00	15.00
A189 Pierce Brosnan EL	150.00	400.00
A194 Joie Vejjajiva L	6.00	15.00
A196 Mary Stavin VL	15.00	40.00
A198 Martine Beswicke EL	25.00	60.00
A199 Edward de Souza L	6.00	15.00
A200 Clifton James EL	60.00	120.00
A201 Christopher Muncke L	8.00	20.00
A202 Jeroen Krabbe L	6.00	15.00
A203 Sneh Gupta L	6.00	15.00
A204 Peter Fontaine L	6.00	15.00
A205 Al Matthews L	6.00	15.00
A207 Halle Berry EL	125.00	300.00
A208 Gotz Otto L	8.00	20.00
A209 Nadja Regin L	60.00	120.00
A210 Nadja Regin EL	60.00	120.00
A212 Irka Bochenko L	10.00	25.00
A213 Alizia Gur VL	20.00	50.00
A216 Frank McRae L	6.00	15.00
A217 Beatrice Libert L	6.00	15.00
A220 Gloria Hendry L	8.00	20.00
A221 Neville Jason L	6.00	15.00

2012 James Bond 50th Anniversary Bond James Bond

COMPLETE SET (11)	8.00	20.00
COMMON CARD (B12-B22)	2.00	5.00
STATED ODDS 1:12		
B23 ISSUED IN 2013 JAMES BOND A&R		
B23 Daniel Craig	8.00	20.00

2012 James Bond 50th Anniversary Dr. No Commemorative

COMPLETE SET (108)	12.00	30.00
COMMON CARD (1-108)	.30	.75
STATED ODDS ONE PER SER. 1 PACK		

2012 James Bond 50th Anniversary From Russia with Love Commemorative

COMPLETE SET (108)	15.00	40.00
COMMON CARD (1-108)	.30	.75
STATED ODDS ONE PER SER. 2 PACK		

2012 James Bond 50th Anniversary Full Bleed Autographs

COMMON AUTO	5.00	12.00
OVERALL AUTO ODDS 3 PER BOX		
L (LIMITED): 300-500 COPIES		
VL (VERY LIMITED): 200-300 COPIES		
EL (EXTREMELY LIMITED): LESS THAN 200 COPIES		
NNO Al Matthews L	6.00	15.00
NNO Aleta Morrison L	8.00	20.00
NNO Andreas Wisniewski L	6.00	15.00
NNO Burt Kwouk VL	10.00	25.00
NNO Carey Lowell EL	125.00	250.00
NNO Catherina von Schell VL	15.00	40.00
NNO Clifton James EL	50.00	100.00
NNO Corinne Clery VL	20.00	50.00
NNO Cristina Contes L	12.00	30.00
NNO Daniel Benzali VL	8.00	20.00
NNO Fiona Fullerton VL	20.00	50.00
NNO Frank McRae L	6.00	15.00
NNO George Leech L	6.00	15.00
NNO Honor Blackman 6CI	125.00	300.00
NNO Jan Williams L	10.00	25.00
NNO Lois Chiles L	20.00	50.00
NNO Mollie Peters L	15.00	40.00
NNO Nancy Sinatra L	25.00	60.00
NNO Sneh Gupta L	10.00	25.00
NNO Vernon Dobtcheff	6.00	15.00
NNO Veruschka L	8.00	20.00
NNO Anne Lonnberg L	10.00	25.00
NNO Catherine Rabett L	8.00	20.00
NNO Colin Salmon L	6.00	15.00
NNO Edward de Souza L	6.00	15.00
NNO Gotz Otto L	6.00	15.00
NNO Honor Blackman EL	75.00	200.00
NNO Jeroen Krabbe L	6.00	15.00
NNO John Rhys-Davies VL	50.00	125.00
NNO John Wyman L	6.00	15.00
NNO Joie Vejjajiva L	6.00	15.00
NNO Lois Chiles L	12.00	30.00
NNO Marilyn Galsworthy L	6.00	15.00
NNO Michelle Yeoh L	125.00	300.00
NNO Richard Kiel L	30.00	75.00
NNO Roger Moore EL	125.00	250.00
NNO Sean Bean L	30.00	75.00
NNO Serena Gordon L	6.00	15.00
NNO Steven Berkoff (hat) L	10.00	25.00
NNO Tania Mallett L	12.00	30.00
NNO Ulrich Thomsen L	6.00	15.00
NNO R.Moore/R.Kiel 6CI	125.00	300.00

2012 James Bond 50th Anniversary Gold Gallery

COMP.SET w/o SPs (36)	40.00	80.00
COMP.SER. 1 SET (18)	20.00	40.00
COMP.SER. 2 SET (18)	25.00	50.00
COMMON CARD (GG1-GG38)	2.00	5.00
STATED ODDS 1:12		
GG19, GG38 ISSUED AS RITTENHOUSE REWARD		
GG19 Honey Ryder RR SP	25.00	50.00
GG38 Vesper Lynd RR SP	30.00	60.00

2012 James Bond 50th Anniversary Gold Plaques

COMPLETE SET (22)	15.00	40.00
COMP.SER. 1 SET (11)	10.00	25.00
COMP.SER. 2 SET (11)	10.00	25.00
COMMON CARD (P1-P22)	2.00	5.00
STATED ODDS 1:12		

2012 James Bond 50th Anniversary Shadowbox

COMP.SER. 1 SET (3)	25.00	50.00
COMPLETE SET (6)	40.00	80.00
COMP.SER. 2 SET (3)	25.00	50.00
COMMON CARD (S1-S6)	10.00	25.00
STATED ODDS 1:96		

2012 James Bond 50th Anniversary SkyFall Posters

COMPLETE SET (4)	15.00	40.00
COMMON CARD (SF1-SF4)	5.00	12.00
STATED ODDS 1:48		

2012 James Bond 50th Anniversary Promos

P1 James Bond Connery GEN		
P1 Honey Ryder GEN	1.25	3.00
P2 Tatiana Romanova NSU	10.00	20.00
P2 James Bond Dalton NSU	2.00	5.00
P3 Jinx ALB	10.00	20.00
P3 James Bond Craig ALB	6.00	15.00
P4 James Bond Brosnan (Philly)	2.50	6.00
P4 JW Pepper (Philly)	2.50	6.00
UKP1 James Bond Connery (UK excl.)	6.00	15.00

2009 James Bond Archives

COMPLETE SET (66)	8.00	20.00
UNOPENED BOX (24 PACKS)	75.00	125.00
UNOPENED PACK (5 CARDS)	3.00	5.00
UNOPENED ARCHIVE BOX	2000.00	3000.00
COMMON CARD (1-66)	.15	.40

2009 James Bond Archives Autographs

STATED ODDS 1:12		
DENCH AUTO STATED ODDS ONE PER 3 CASE PURCHASE		
JANSSEN WOJB AUTO STATED ODDS ONE PER 6 CASE PURCHASE		
RHYS-DAVIES AUTO STATED ODDS ONE PER 15 CASE PURCHASE		
A128 Tobias Menzies L	15.00	40.00
A129 Christina Cole L	10.00	25.00
NNO Carmen du Sautoy VL	15.00	40.00
NNO Caroline Bliss VL	15.00	40.00
NNO Caterina Murino VL	30.00	75.00
NNO Cecilie Thomsen VL	15.00	40.00
NNO Chaim Topol VL	25.00	60.00
NNO Christina Cole L	12.00	30.00
NNO Eunice Gayson L	15.00	40.00
NNO Famke Janssen VL	250.00	600.00
NNO Geoffrey Holder VL	60.00	120.00
NNO George Lazenby VL	60.00	150.00
NNO Honor Blackman VL	150.00	400.00
NNO Izabella Scorupco VL	75.00	150.00
NNO Joe Don Baker VL	40.00	100.00
NNO John Cleese VL	100.00	250.00
NNO John Terry VL	15.00	40.00
NNO Mads Mikkelsen L	60.00	120.00
NNO Margaret Nolan	25.00	60.00
NNO Marguerite Lewars VL	60.00	120.00
NNO Olga Kurylenko VL	100.00	200.00
NNO Paul Ritter L	12.00	30.00
NNO Priscilla Barnes L	15.00	40.00
NNO Robert Carlyle VL	25.00	60.00
NNO Roger Moore VL	125.00	300.00
NNO Samantha Bond L	8.00	20.00
NNO Tobias Menzies L	15.00	40.00
NNO Wayne Newton VL	40.00	100.00
NNO Judi Dench (Full Bleed) 3CI	50.00	125.00
WA27 Famke Janssen (Women of James Bond) 6CI	150.00	400.00
NNO John Rhys-Davies 15CI	250.00	500.00

2009 James Bond Archives Quantum of Solace Dangerous Liaisons

COMPLETE SET (9)	8.00	20.00

COMMON CARD (DL10-DL18) 2.00 5.00
STATED ODDS 1:12

2009 James Bond Archives Quantum of Solace Expansion

COMPLETE SET (9) 8.00 20.00
COMMON CARD 2.00 5.00
STATED ODDS 1:12

2009 James Bond Archives Relics

COMMON MEM (QC1-QC27) 6.00 15.00
STATED ODDS 1:12
AMR1 STATED ODDS ONE PER CASE
QC1 Camille Camisole 20.00 50.00
Skirt
QC2 James Bond & Camille Jacket 12.00 30.00
Dress
QC3 James Bond Jacket 50.00 100.00
Tie
QC4 Camille Dress 8.00 20.00
QC5 Camille Tank Top 25.00 60.00
Blouse#{Pants
QC9 Mathis Shirt 8.00 20.00
Jacket#{Pants
QC12 James Bond Shirt 12.00 30.00
Jacket#{Pants
QC14 Mitchell Shirt 10.00 25.00
Tie
QC18 James Bond Shirt 8.00 20.00
Jacket
QC19 James Bond Pants 8.00 20.00
QC20 James Bond Jacket 8.00 20.00
QC22 James Bond Shirt 8.00 20.00
Pants
QC23 James Bond Jacket 10.00 25.00
QC24 James Bond Shirt 12.00 30.00
QC25 James Bond Tie 25.00 60.00
QC26 Greene's Driver Jacket 6.00 15.00
QC27 James Bond & Camille Jkt 50.00 100.00
Pnts#{Cmsl#{Skrt
AMR1 Aston Martin Windshield 25.00 60.00

2009 James Bond Archives The Complete James Bond 007 Expansion

COMPLETE SET (9) 8.00 20.00
COMMON CARD (190-198) 2.00 5.00
STATED ODDS 1:12

2009 James Bond Archives Quantum of Solace Quotables

COMPLETE SET (8) 8.00 20.00
COMMON CARD (Q7-Q14) 2.00 5.00
STATED ODDS 1:14

2009 James Bond Archives Promos

P2 Camille (Non-Sport Update Magazine) .75 2.00
P3 Strawberry Fields (Album Exclusive) 3.00 8.00

2014 James Bond Archives

COMPLETE SET (99) 10.00 25.00
UNOPENED BOX (24 PACKS) 150.00 200.00
UNOPENED PACKS (6 CARDS) 6.00 8.00
COMMON CARD (1-99) .25 .60
*GOLD: 5X TO 12X BASIC CARDS

2014 James Bond Archives 40th Anniversary Autographs

COMMON AUTO 5.00 12.00
REGULAR = >500
L = 300-500
VL = 200-300
EL = <200
STATED ODDS 1:12
A238 Ola Rapace L 10.00 25.00
A246 Oona Chaplin L 15.00 40.00
A248 Yvonne Shima EL 50.00 100.00
A249 Lizzie Warville VL 12.00 30.00
A251 Jeremy Bulloch VL 30.00 75.00
A253 Karin Dor VL 12.00 30.00
A255 Elize du Toit L 6.00 15.00

2014 James Bond Archives Case-Incentives

RMG Roger Moore Gold AU 6CI 50.00 120.00
BG74 Bond Girls Are Forever 5.00 12.00
Miss Moneypenny CT
DGJD Daniel Craig 125.00 250.00
Dame Judi Dench Dual AU 9CI

2014 James Bond Archives Full Bleed Autographs

COMMON AUTO 5.00 12.00
STATED ODDS 1:12
REGULAR = >500
L = 300-500
VL = 200-300
EL = <200
NNO Chichinou Kaeppler L 6.00 15.00
NNO Catherine Serre L 6.00 15.00
NNO Daniel Craig EL 250.00 600.00
NNO Eunice Gayson EL 25.00 60.00
NNO Jane Seymour EL 125.00 300.00
NNO Martine Beswicke EL 25.00 60.00
NNO Monty Norman L (Composer) 8.00 20.00
NNO Pierce Brosnan EL 150.00 400.00
NNO Roger Moore EL 75.00 200.00
NNO Elize du Toit L 8.00 20.00

2014 James Bond Archives Live and Let Die Throwbacks

COMPLETE SET (120) 50.00 100.00
COMMON CARD (1-120) .40 1.00

2014 James Bond Archives Relics

COMMON MEM 8.00 20.00
STATED ODDS 1:60
JBR11 Aston Marton VB Windshield/190 50.00 100.00
JBR13 Aston Martin Rear Side Panel/140 75.00 150.00
JBR29 Parahawk Canopy/300 10.00 25.00
JBR30 Franz Sanchez's Airplane Window/40010.00 25.00
JBR31 Elliot Carver's Stealth Boat/175 25.00 60.00
JBR32 Chemical Canister/375 12.00 30.00
JBR35 Lotus Esprit S1 Carpeting/490 10.00 25.00
JBR38 Alfa Romeo Interior/275 15.00 40.00
JBR39 Aston Martin DBS Interior/275 20.00 50.00
JBR40 Goldfinger Suit/275 60.00 120.00
JBR42 Kristatos Jacket/375 10.00 25.00
JBR43 Helicopter Panel/200 50.00 100.00
JBR44 Lotus Esprit S1 Window Pane/175 50.00 100.00
JBR45 Zukovsky's Cane/110 150.00 300.00

2014 James Bond Archives Thunderball Throwbacks

COMPLETE SET (99) 30.00 80.00
COMMON CARD (1-99) .50 1.25
STATED ODDS 1:6

2014 James Bond Archives Tomorrow Never Dies

COMPLETE SET (93) 30.00 80.00
COMMON CARD (1-93) .40 1.00
*GOLD: 3X TO 8X BASIC CARDS 3.00 8.00
STATED ODDS 1:6

2014 James Bond Archives Women of Bond Autographs

COMMON AUTO 5.00 12.00
STATED ODDS 1:12
REGULAR = >500
L = 300-500
VL = 200-300
EL = <200
WA37 Samantha Bond L 6.00 15.00
WA41 Catherina von Schell VL 10.00 25.00
WA42 Shirley Eaton L 15.00 40.00
WA43 Fiona Fullerton VL 12.00 30.00
WA44 Mary Stavin VL 10.00 25.00
WA45 Tania Mallett L 12.00 30.00
WA46 Jan Williams L 8.00 20.00
WA49 Halle Berry EL 125.00 300.00
WA50 Nadja Regin EL 50.00 100.00
WA51 Serena Gordon L 10.00 25.00
WA52 Teri Hatcher EL 100.00 250.00
WA53 Berenice Marlohe L 15.00 40.00
WA55 Oona Chaplin L 20.00 50.00
WA57 Lizzie Warville VL 10.00 25.00
WA58 Sheena Easton EL 60.00 150.00

2014 James Bond Archives Promos

P1 James Bond Archives GEN 1.50 4.00
P2 James Bond Archives CON 2.00 5.00
P3 James Bond Archives ALB 12.00 30.00

2015 James Bond Archives

COMPLETE SET (90) 10.00 25.00
UNOPENED BOX (24 PACKS) 75.00 125.00
UNOPENED PACK (6 CARDS) 3.00 5.00
COMMON CARD (1-90) .25 .60
*GOLD: 5X TO 12X BASIC CARDS

2015 James Bond Archives Autographs

COMMON AUTO 5.00 12.00
STATED ODDS 1:12
A222 Roger Moore EL 75.00 200.00
A252 Sheena Easton VL 60.00 150.00
A263 Caroline Bliss L 15.00 40.00
A271 Dolph Lundgren VL 50.00 125.00
A273 Mathieu Amalric VL 20.00 50.00
A279 Shane Rimmer L 12.00 30.00
A282 David Harbour L 30.00 75.00

2015 James Bond Archives Full Bleed Autographs

COMMON AUTO 5.00 12.00
STATED ODDS 1:12
NNO Blanche Ravalec L 8.00 20.00
NNO Caroline Munro L 15.00 40.00
NNO Christopher Lee EL 125.00 300.00
NNO David Hedison L 8.00 20.00
NNO George Lazenby EL 60.00 120.00
NNO Halle Berry VL 250.00 600.00
NNO Jeremy Bulloch VL 30.00 75.00
NNO Joe Don Baker VL 25.00 60.00
NNO Karin Dor VL 15.00 40.00
NNO Lizzie Warville VL 10.00 25.00
NNO Madeline Smith L 12.00 30.00
NNO Maryam d'Abo L 12.00 30.00
NNO Maud Adams VL 50.00 100.00
NNO Nadja Regin EL 50.00 100.00
NNO Rachel Grant L 8.00 20.00
NNO Samantha Bond L 10.00 25.00
NNO Tanya Roberts L 40.00 100.00
NNO Teri Hatcher VL 75.00 200.00
NNO Yvonne Shima EL 50.00 100.00

2015 James Bond Archives Case-Incentives

NNO Britt Ekland Silver AU 6CI 60.00 120.00
NNO Daniel Craig AU MEM 9CI 125.00 250.00

2015 James Bond Archives Case-Topper

SP Spectre Preview 6.00 15.00

2015 James Bond Archives GoldenEye

COMPLETE SET (102) 50.00 100.00
UNOPENED BOX (36 PACKS) 20.00 30.00
UNOPENED PACK (8 CARDS) .75 1.00
COMMON CARD (1-102) .75 2.00
*GOLD/125: 2.5X TO 6X BASIC CARDS
STATED ODDS 1:6

2015 James Bond Archives Skyfall Expansion

COMPLETE SET (14) 25.00 60.00
COMMON CARD 3.00 8.00
STATED ODDS 1:24

2015 James Bond Archives The Spy Who Loved Me Throwbacks

COMPLETE SET (93) 30.00 80.00
COMMON CARD (1-93) .40 1.00
STATED ODDS 1:6

2015 James Bond Archives Promos

P1 General Distribution 1.50 4.00
P2 Album Exclusive 8.00 20.00
P3 Philly Non-Sport Show 2.50 6.00

2017 James Bond Archives Final Edition

COMPLETE SET (83) 6.00 15.00
UNOPENED BOX (24 PACKS) 55.00 70.00
UNOPENED PACK (5 CARDS) 2.50 3.00
COMMON CARD (1-83) .15 .40
*GOLD: 4X TO 10X BASIC CARDS 1.50 4.00

2017 James Bond Archives Final Edition Autographed Costumes

COMMON AUTO 12.00 30.00
STATED OVERALL ODDS 1:12
NNO Berenice Marlohe/250 30.00 75.00

2017 James Bond Archives Final Edition Autographs

COMMON AUTO 5.00 12.00
STATED OVERALL ODDS 1:12
REGULAR AUTO <500
L (LIMITED) = 300-500
VL (VERY LIMITED) = 200-300
EL (EXTREMELY LIMITED) = 100-200
NNO Tanya Roberts L 30.00 75.00
A155 Daniel Craig EL 200.00 500.00
A223 Roger Moore VL 100.00 250.00
A224 Roger Moore VL 75.00 200.00
A225 Roger Moore VL 75.00 200.00
A283 Ben Whishaw L 30.00 75.00
A297 George Roubicek VL 15.00 40.00
WA54 Naomie Harris VL 50.00 100.00

2017 James Bond Archives Final Edition Case-Incentive Autographs

COMMON AUTO 50.00 100.00
NNO Sean Connery CUT 18CI 1250.00 2500.00
NNO Christopher Lee AU 9CI 200.00 500.00

2017 James Bond Archives Final Edition Double-Sided Mirror

COMPLETE SET (8) 80.00 150.00
COMMON CARD (SKIP #'d) 10.00 25.00
STATED ODDS 1:72

2017 James Bond Archives Final Edition For Your Eyes Only Throwback

COMPLETE SET (36) 12.00 30.00
COMMON CARD (1-36) 1.00 2.50
STATED ODDS 1:9

2017 James Bond Archives Final Edition Full-Bleed Autographs

COMMON AUTO 5.00 12.00
STATED OVERALL ODDS 1:12
REGULAR AUTO <500
L (LIMITED) = 300-500
VL (VERY LIMITED) = 200-300
EL (EXTREMELY LIMITED) = 100-200
NNO Berenice Marlohe L 10.00 25.00
NNO Britt Ekland VL 20.00 50.00
NNO Caroline Bliss L 15.00 40.00
NNO Christina Hui L 6.00 15.00
NNO Christopher Neame 6.00 15.00
NNO Daisy Beaumont L 6.00 15.00
NNO Daniela Bianchi VL 75.00 150.00
NNO Dave Bautista VL 30.00 75.00
NNO Deborah Moore 6.00 15.00
NNO Denise Perrier VL 12.00 30.00
NNO Diana Lee-Hsu L 6.00 15.00
NNO George Lazenby EL 60.00 120.00
NNO George Roubicek VL 10.00 25.00
NNO Halle Berry VL 150.00 400.00
NNO Helena Ronee L 10.00 25.00
NNO Jane Seymour VL 60.00 150.00
NNO Jeanne Roland L 6.00 15.00
NNO Jeffrey Wright VL 25.00 60.00
NNO Judi Dench VL 50.00 125.00
NNO Lea Seydoux L 50.00 100.00
NNO Mark Dymond L 6.00 15.00
NNO Mathieu Amalric L 6.00 15.00
NNO Michelle Yeoh L 150.00 400.00
NNO Nicaise Jean-Louis L 6.00 15.00
NNO Pavel Douglas L 6.00 15.00

NNO Rachel Grant L 6.00 15.00
NNO Richard Kiel L 40.00 100.00
NNO Roger Moore L 100.00 250.00
NNO Rory Kinnear L 6.00 15.00
NNO Shane Rimmer L 12.00 30.00
NNO Tom Chadbon 6.00 15.00
NNO Tula L 10.00 25.00

2017 James Bond Archives Final Edition Metal

COMPLETE SET (12) 200.00 400.00
COMMON CARD (M13-M24) 15.00 40.00
STATED ODDS 1:72
M20A OFFERED AS CASE-TOPPER

2017 James Bond Archives Final Edition Octopussy Throwback

COMPLETE SET (32) 15.00 40.00
COMMON CARD (1-32) .75 2.00
STATED ODDS 1:9

2017 James Bond Archives Final Edition Relics

COMMON MEM 10.00 25.00
STATED ODDS 1:144
STATED PRINT RUN 91-200
MR7 Palio de Siena Scarf/200 20.00 50.00
MR8 Opera Invitation/160 20.00 50.00
MR9 La Clinica Alvarez Admissions Documents/185 25.00 60.00
MR10 Rubeyon Royale Hotel Card/91 150.00 300.00
MR11 Opera Program/155 60.00 120.00
PR21 James Bond's Jacket/200 12.00 30.00
PR22 James Bond's Shirt/200 15.00 40.00
PR26 James Bond's Shirt/200 15.00 40.00
PR28 Moneypenny's Jacket/200 12.00 30.00

2017 James Bond Archives Final Edition Spectre-Skyfall Expansion

COMPLETE SET (24) 20.00 50.00
COMMON CARD (SKIP #'d) 2.00 5.00
STATED ODDS 1:24

2017 James Bond Archives Final Edition A View to a Kill Throwback

COMPLETE SET (30) 12.00 30.00
COMMON CARD (1-30) 1.00 2.50
STATED ODDS 1:9

2017 James Bond Archives Final Edition Promos

COMMON CARD 2.00 5.00
P3 Album Exclusive 4.00 10.00

2016 James Bond Archives Spectre Edition

COMPLETE SET (76) 6.00 15.00
UNOPENED BOX (24 PACKS) 55.00 70.00
UNOPENED PACK (5 CARDS) 2.50 3.00
COMMON CARD (1-76) .15 .40
*GOLD/100: 8X TO 20X BASIC CARDS 3.00 8.00
CT1 INSERTED AS CASE-TOPPER
CT1 Spectre Movie Poster Case-Topper 6.00 15.00

2016 James Bond Archives Spectre Edition Metal

COMPLETE SET (12) 150.00 300.00
COMMON CARD (M1-M12) 12.00 30.00
STATED ODDS 1:144

2016 James Bond Archives Spectre Edition Full Bleed Autographs

COMMON AUTO 5.00 12.00
VERY LIMITED (VL) = 200-300
LIMITED (L) = 300-500
STATED ODDS 1:12
NNO Berenice Marlohe L 15.00 40.00
NNO Britt Ekland L 20.00 50.00
NNO Caroline Munro L 12.00 30.00
NNO Dave Bautista VL 100.00 250.00
NNO Dolph Lundgren VL 75.00 200.00
NNO George Roubicek VL 8.00 20.00
NNO Jane Seymour VL 100.00 250.00
NNO Joe Don Baker VL 25.00 60.00
NNO Karin Dor VL 25.00 40.00
NNO Lea Seydoux L 60.00 120.00
NNO Maryam d'Abo L 12.00 30.00
NNO Roger Moore VL 100.00 250.00
NNO Sheena Easton VL 30.00 75.00
NNO Teri Hatcher VL 100.00 250.00

2016 James Bond Archives Spectre Edition Case-Incentives

6CI Aliza Gur/Martine Beswick Dual AU 60.00 120.00
9CI Johnathan Pryce AU Relic 60.00 120.00

2016 James Bond Archives Spectre Edition Diamonds Are Forever Throwbacks

COMPLETE SET (48) 15.00 40.00
COMMON CARD (1-48) .75 2.00
STATED ODDS 1:6

2016 James Bond Archives Spectre Edition Double-Sided Mirror

COMPLETE SET (8) 80.00 150.00
COMMON CARD 10.00 25.00
STATED ODDS 1:144

2016 James Bond Archives Spectre Edition Autographs

COMMON AUTO 5.00 12.00
VERY LIMITED (VL) = 200-300
LIMITED (L) = 300-500
STATED ODDS 1:12
A269 Jeffrey Wright VL 25.00 60.00
A284 Daniela Bianchi VL 125.00 300.00
A293 Denise Perrier VL 12.00 30.00
A298 George Roubicek VL 10.00 25.00
NNO Clifton James AB 150.00 300.00

2016 James Bond Archives Spectre Edition The Living Daylights

COMPLETE SET (55) 25.00 60.00
COMMON CARD (1-55) .75 2.00
*GOLD/125: 1.2X TO 3X BASIC CARDS 2.50 6.00
STATED ODDS 1:6

2016 James Bond Archives Spectre Edition Moonraker Throwbacks

COMPLETE SET (61) 15.00 40.00
COMMON CARD (1-61) .60 1.50
STATED ODDS 1:6

2016 James Bond Archives Spectre Edition Relics

COMMON MEM 10.00 25.00
STATED ODDS 1:96
MR1 La Clinica Alvarez Admissions Doc 25.00 60.00
MR2 Classified Documents 30.00 75.00
MR3 Draco's Calendar 20.00 50.00
MR4 Moneypenny's Files 25.00 60.00
MR5 Police Badge 60.00 120.00
MR6 Russian Atomic Energy ID Badge 60.00 120.00
PR16 Camille's Body Suit 15.00 40.00
PR19 Severine's Dress 12.00 30.00

2013 James Bond Autographs and Relics

COMPLETE SET (110) 8.00 20.00
COMMON CARD (1-110) .25 .60
*SILVER: 1X TO 2.5X BASIC CARDS
*GOLD/100: 10X TO 25X BASIC CARDS

2013 James Bond Autographs and Relics Autographs

COMMON AUTO 6.00 15.00
TWO AUTOS PER BOX
L (LIMITED): 300-500 COPIES
EL (EXTREMELY LIMITED): LESS THAN 200 COPIES
A99 Joe Don Baker EL 30.00 75.00
A111 Teri Hatcher EL 60.00 150.00
A227 Berenice Marlohe L 30.00 75.00
A228 Daniel Craig EL 200.00 500.00
A229 Judi Dench EL 50.00 125.00
A230 Jane Seymour EL 60.00 150.00
A231 Bruce Glover EL 30.00 75.00
A233 Catherine Serre L 8.00 20.00
A243 Naomie Harris EL 100.00 175.00

2013 James Bond Autographs and Relics Full Bleed Autographs

COMMON AUTO 5.00 12.00
TWO AUTOS PER BOX
L (LIMITED): 300-500 COPIES
VL (VERY LIMITED): 200-300 COPIES
EL (EXTREMELY LIMITED): LESS THAN 200 COPIES
RAPACE AUTO ISSUED AS 3-CASE INCENTIVE
NNO Alizia Gur VL 15.00 40.00
NNO Burt Kwouk VL 8.00 20.00
NNO Clifton James EL 100.00 200.00
NNO Geoffrey Palmer L 8.00 20.00
NNO Gloria Hendry L 6.00 15.00
NNO Irka Bochenko L 6.00 15.00
NNO John Rhys-Davies EL 30.00 75.00
NNO Kenneth Tsang L 6.00 15.00
NNO Lana Wood L 15.00 40.00
NNO Lulu 12.00 30.00
NNO Martine Beswicke EL 25.00 60.00
NNO Mary Stavin VL 15.00 40.00
NNO Mollie Peters L 10.00 25.00
NNO Ola Rapace 3CI 15.00 40.00
NNO Roger Moore EL 75.00 200.00
NNO Sophie Marceau EL 125.00 300.00
NNO Steven Berkoff L 6.00 15.00
NNO Valerie Leon L 10.00 25.00

2013 James Bond Autographs and Relics Gold Gallery

COMPLETE SET (9) 4.00 10.00
COMMON CARD (GG39-GG47) 1.25 3.00
STATED ODDS 1:24

2013 James Bond Autographs and Relics Goldfinger Commemorative

COMPLETE SET (110) 15.00 40.00
COMMON CARD (1-110) .40 1.00
STATED ODDS 1:1

2013 James Bond Autographs and Relics Single Relics

COMMON MEM (SSC1-SSC42) 6.00 15.00
STATED PRINT RUN 200 SER. #'d SETS
SSC1 James Bond Suit Jacket 15.00 40.00
SSC2 James Bond Suit Pants 10.00 25.00
SSC3 James Bond Tie 15.00 40.00
SSC4 James Bond Shirt 15.00 40.00
SSC5 Patrice Suit Jacket 12.00 30.00
SSC6 Patrice Shirt 10.00 25.00
SSC9 Moneypenny Tank Top 8.00 20.00
SSC10 James Bond Shirt 10.00 25.00
SSC11 James Bond Chinos 12.00 30.00
SSC12 Mallory Suit Jacket 10.00 25.00
SSC13 Q Trousers 10.00 25.00
SSC14 James Bond Shirt 8.00 20.00
SSC15 James Bond Trousers 10.00 25.00
SSC16 James Bond Chauffeur Jacket 12.00 30.00
SSC17 James Bond Sweater 10.00 25.00
SSC18 Patrice Dress Shirt 8.00 20.00
SSC19 Moneypenny Shirt 20.00 50.00
SSC20 James Bond Dinner Suit 20.00 50.00
SSC22 Severine Dress 20.00 50.00
SSC23 James Bond Jacket 12.00 30.00
SSC24 James Bond Shirt 12.00 30.00
SSC25 James Bond Pants 12.00 30.00
SSC26 James Bond Tie 15.00 40.00
SSC27 Silva Police Hat 8.00 20.00
SSC28 Silva Bullet Proof Vest 8.00 20.00
SSC32 James Bond Pants 10.00 25.00
SSC33 James Bond Jacket 10.00 25.00
SSC34 James Bond Shirt 12.00 30.00
SSC36 M Scarf 12.00 30.00
SSC37 M Coat 10.00 25.00
SSC39 Kincade Cap 10.00 25.00
SSC41 Silva Sweater 8.00 20.00
DCRA Daniel Craig AU/155 6CI 150.00 300.00

2013 James Bond Autographs and Relics Dual Relics

COMMON MEM (SDC1-SDC4) 10.00 25.00
STATED PRINT RUN 200 SER. #'d SETS
SDC1 Moneypenny 15.00 40.00
SDC2 James Bond 15.00 40.00
SDC3 Q 15.00 40.00

2013 James Bond Autographs and Relics Dual Character Relics

COMMON MEM (SCDC1-SCDC8) 12.00 30.00
STATED PRINT RUN 200 SER. #'d SETS
SCDC1 Bond/Ronson 15.00 40.00
SCDC2 Bond/Patrice 15.00 40.00
SCDC3 Bond/Bodyguard 15.00 40.00
SCDC4 Bond/Severine 20.00 50.00
SCDC5 Bond/M 15.00 40.00
SCDC8 Bond/M 15.00 40.00

2013 James Bond Autographs and Relics Quad Relics

COMMON MEM 25.00 60.00
STATED PRINT RUN 200 SER. #'d SETS
SQC1 James Bond 30.00 75.00

2013 James Bond Autographs and Relics Triple Relics

COMMON MEM 10.00 25.00
STATED PRINT RUN 200 SER. #'d SETS
STC1 Patrice 12.00 30.00
STC4 James Bond 15.00 40.00
STC5 Silva 15.00 40.00
STC6 James Bond 20.00 50.00

2013 James Bond Autographs and Relics Quotables

COMPLETE SET (21) 15.00 40.00
COMMON CARD (QS01-QS21) 1.50 4.00
STATED ODDS 1:12
QS22 ISSUED AS RITTENHOUSE REWARD
QS22 So, 007, Lots to Be Done RR SP 12.00 30.00

2013 James Bond Autographs and Relics Promos

P1 James Bond GEN 1.25 3.00
P2 James Bond (Philly) 3.00 8.00
P3 James Bond ALB 12.00 30.00
P4 James Bond CON 15.00 40.00
P5 James Bond (UK excl.) 4.00 10.00

2016 James Bond Classics

COMPLETE SET (72) 8.00 20.00
UNOPENED BOX (24 PACKS) 50.00 60.00
UNOPENED PACK (5 CARDS) 2.00 2.50
COMMON CARD (1-72) .20 .50
*GOLD: 6X TO 15X BASIC CARDS
CT1 INSERTED 1 PER CASE

2016 James Bond Classics 007 Mirror

COMPLETE SET (8) 100.00 200.00
STATED ODDS 1:144
M13 James Bond 15.00 40.00
Kamal Khan

2016 James Bond Classics Full Bleed Autographs

COMMON AUTO 5.00 12.00
STATED ODDS 1:12
NORMAL = < 500
L = 300-500
VL = 200-300
EL = 100-200
NNO Ben Whishaw VL 30.00 75.00
NNO Bruce Glover EL 20.00 50.00
NNO Cary-Hiroyuki Tagawa L 6.00 15.00
NNO Daniela Bianchi EL 150.00 400.00
NNO David Harbour EL 40.00 100.00
NNO David Hedison L 6.00 15.00
NNO Jeffrey Wright EL 25.00 60.00
NNO Jesper Christensen L 8.00 20.00
NNO Madeline Smith L 8.00 20.00
NNO Mathieu Amalric EL 15.00 40.00
NNO Maud Adams EL 50.00 100.00
NNO Nadja Regin EL 30.00 75.00
NNO Naomie Harris EL 50.00 100.00
NNO Oona Chaplin VL 20.00 50.00
NNO Pierce Brosnan EL 250.00 600.00
NNO Rachel McDowall L 6.00 15.00

NNO Samantha Bond L 6.00 15.00
NNO Sophie Marceau EL 100.00 250.00

2016 James Bond Classics Autographs

COMMON AUTO 5.00 12.00
STATED ODDS 1:12
NORMAL = < 500
L = 300-500
VL = 200-300
EL = 100-200
A226 Roger Moore EL 125.00 300.00
A265 Andy Bradford L 6.00 15.00
A270 Jeffrey Wright EL 25.00 60.00
A285 Diana Lee-Hsu L 6.00 15.00
A286 Daisy Beaumont L 6.00 15.00
A288 Claude-Oliver Rudolph L 6.00 15.00

2016 James Bond Classics Case Incentives Autographs

COMMON AUTO 60.00 120.00
NNO Honor Blackman AU Archive Box 100.00 250.00
NNO Judi Dench Silver AU 6CI 40.00 100.00
NNO Daniel Craig Gold AU 9CI 125.00 300.00

2016 James Bond Classics License to Kill

COMPLETE SET (65) 15.00 40.00
COMMON CARD (1-65) .50 1.25
*GOLD: 2X TO 5X BASIC CARDS
STATED ODDS 1:6

2016 James Bond Classics Man with the Golden Gun Throwbacks

COMPLETE SET (50) 30.00 80.00
COMMON CARD (1-50) 1.25 3.00
STATED ODDS 1:6

2016 James Bond Classics On Her Majesty's Secret Service Throwbacks

COMPLETE SET (60) 20.00 50.00
COMMON CARD (1-60) .60 1.50
STATED ODDS 1:6

2016 James Bond Classics Relics

COMMON MEM 8.00 20.00
STATED ODDS 1:96
STATED PRINT RUN 200 SER.#'d SETS
PR1 James Bond 12.00 30.00
PR2 Vesper Lynd 30.00 75.00
PR3 Le Chiffre 15.00 40.00
PR4 James Bond 12.00 30.00
PR6 Camille 12.00 30.00
PR8 James Bond 15.00 40.00
PR11 James Bond 10.00 25.00
PR12 James Bond 12.00 30.00
PR13 Vesper Lynd 25.00 60.00

2016 James Bond Classics Spectre Metal Gallery

COMPLETE SET (10) 150.00 300.00
COMMON CARD (G1-G10) 10.00 25.00
STATED PRINT RUN 150 SER.#'d SETS
G1 James Bond 15.00 40.00
G2 Oberhauser 12.00 30.00
G5 Moneypenny 12.00 30.00
G6 Lucia Sciarra 12.00 40.00
G8 Dr. Madeleine Swann 15.00 40.00
G9 C 15.00 40.00

2016 James Bond Classics Promos

P1 James Bond and Q 2.00 5.00
(General Distribution)
P2 Vesper 2.50 6.00
(Non-Sport Update Magazine Exclusive)
P3 On Her Majesty's Secret Service 15.00 40.00
(Album Exclusive)

2019 James Bond Collection

COMPLETE SET W/SP (200) 100.00 200.00
COMPLETE SET W/O SP (100) 10.00 25.00
UNOPENED BOX (18 PACKS)
UNOPENED PACK (6 CARDS)
COMMON CARD (1-100) .20 .50
COMMON SP (101-150) 1.00 2.50
COMMON SP (151-200) 1.50 4.00
*SILVER (1-100): 3X TO 8X BASIC CARDS
*RAINBOW (101-150): 4X TO 10X BASIC CARDS
*GOLD (151-200): X TO X BASIC CARDS
SP (101-150) ODDS 1:1
SP (151-200) ODDS 1:3

2019 James Bond Collection Autographs

COMMON AUTO 5.00 12.00
GROUP A ODDS 1:1,020
GROUP B ODDS 1:575
GROUP C ODDS 1:245
GROUP D ODDS 1:139
GROUP E ODDS 1:10
STATED OVERALL ODDS 1:9
ABO Maryam d'Abo E 12.00 30.00
ABW Ben Whishaw A 50.00 120.00
ABY Carole Ashby E 8.00 20.00
ACA Caterina Murino D 15.00 40.00
ACB Caroline Bliss E 15.00 40.00
ACC Corinne Clery E 10.00 25.00
ACT Chaim Topol C 25.00 60.00
AEA Shirley Eaton E 12.00 30.00
AEK Britt Ekland E 20.00 50.00
AEN Michael Madsen D 15.00 40.00
AFJ Famke Janssen B 125.00 300.00
AGL George Lazenby B 75.00 200.00
AIZ Izabella Scorupco C 30.00 75.00
AJD Judi Dench B 50.00 125.00
AJR John Rhys-Davies C 30.00 75.00
AJW Jeffrey Wright A 30.00 75.00
AKT Kenneth Tsang E 6.00 15.00
ALC Lois Chiles E 6.00 15.00
ALJ Lynn-Holly Johnson E 12.00 30.00
ANR Nadja Regin E 6.00 15.00
ARC Robert Carlyle D 12.00 30.00
ARI Denise Richards B 125.00 300.00
ASB Sean Bean A 75.00 150.00
ASR Shane Rimmer E 12.00 30.00
ATM Tania Mallet E 6.00 15.00
AVI Mary Stavin E 8.00 20.00
AWA Christoph Waltz C 125.00 300.00
AWN Wayne Newton C 50.00 125.00

2019 James Bond Collection Bond Legacy

COMPLETE SET W/SP (40)
COMPLETE SET W/O SP (25)
COMMON CARD (BL1-BL25) 4.00 10.00
COMMON TIER 2 (BL26-BL33)
COMMON TIER 3 (BL34-BL40)
STATED OVERALL ODDS 1:18
STATED TIER 1 ODDS 1:20
STATED TIER 2 ODDS 1:216
STATED TIER 3 ODDS 1:648

2019 James Bond Collection Bond Legacy Autographs

BLA1 Ben Whishaw 50.00 120.00
BLA2 Jeffrey Wright 40.00 100.00
BLA4 John Rhys-Davies 30.00 75.00
BLA5 Sean Bean 40.00 100.00
BLA6 Denise Richards 125.00 300.00
BLA7 Famke Janssen 125.00 300.00
BLA8 George Lazenby 75.00 200.00
BLA9 Judi Dench 125.00 300.00

2019 James Bond Collection Bond vs. Villains

COMPLETE SET (20) 10.00 25.00
COMMON CARD (BV1-BV20) 1.25 3.00
STATED ODDS 1:6

2019 James Bond Collection Inscription Autographs

COMMON AUTO 10.00 25.00
GROUP A ODDS 1:771
GROUP B ODDS 1:54
GROUP C ODDS 1:71
STATED OVERALL ODDS 1:30
AAC Alan Cumming B 25.00 60.00
AAS Anthony Starke B 12.00 30.00
ABO Maryam d'Abo B 15.00 40.00
ACA Caterina Murino B 20.00 50.00
ACB Caroline Bliss B 15.00 40.00
ACC Corinne Clery B 30.00 75.00
AEA Shirley Eaton B 15.00 40.00
AEK Britt Ekland B 20.00 50.00
AFJ Famke Janssen A 150.00 400.00
AGL George Lazenby A 150.00 400.00
AJC John Cleese B 50.00 100.00
AJD Judi Dench A 75.00 200.00
AJG Julian Glover B 15.00 40.00
AJW Jeffrey Wright A 75.00 200.00
ALC Lois Chiles B 15.00 40.00
ALJ Lynn-Holly Johnson B 30.00 75.00
AMB Martine Beswick C 12.00 30.00
ANR Nadja Regin B 25.00 60.00
AON Colin Salmon B 15.00 40.00
ARI Denise Richards A 125.00 300.00
ASB Sean Bean A 40.00 100.00
ASC Andrew Scott B 30.00 75.00
ASE Jane Seymour B 50.00 120.00
ASJ Jill St. John B 30.00 75.00
ASR Shane Rimmer B 12.00 30.00
ATM Tania Mallet B 15.00 40.00
AWN Wayne Newton A 125.00 300.00

2019 James Bond Collection Q Branch

COMPLETE SET (15) 12.00 30.00
COMMON CARD (QB1-QB15) 1.50 4.00
STATED ODDS 1:12

2019 James Bond Collection See the World

COMPLETE SET (10) 20.00 50.00
COMMON CARD (STW1-STW10) 4.00 10.00
STATED ODDS 1:36

2019 James Bond Collection Short-Printed Autographs

COMMON AUTO 60.00 120.00
STATED OVERALL ODDS 1:9
SPADR Denise Richards/99 125.00 250.00
SPAFJ Famke Janssen/99 150.00 400.00
SPAGL George Lazenby/99 150.00 300.00
SPAJD Judi Dench/99 60.00 150.00
SPAJW Jeffrey Wright/99 50.00 120.00
SPASB Sean Bean/99 50.00 125.00
SPAWA Christoph Waltz/99 150.00 400.00
SSPAGL George Lazenby/25 300.00 800.00
SSPAWA Christoph Waltz/25 400.00 1000.00

1996-97 Inkworks James Bond Connoisseur's Collection Complete Series

COMPLETE SET (270) 20.00 50.00
COMPLETE VOLUME ONE SET (90) 8.00 20.00
COMPLETE VOLUME TWO SET (90) 8.00 20.00
COMPLETE VOLUME THREE SET (90) 8.00 20.00
UNOPENED VOL. ONE BOX (36 PACKS) 45.00 60.00
UNOPENED VOL. ONE PACK (7 CARDS) 1.25 1.75
UNOPENED VOL. TWO BOX (36 PACKS) 35.00 50.00
UNOPENED VOL. TWO PACK (7 CARDS) 1.00 1.50
UNOPENED VOL. THREE BOX (36 PACKS) 35.00 50.00
UNOPENED VOL. THREE PACK (7 CARDS) 1.00 1.50
COMMON CARD VOL. ONE (1-90) .15 .40
COMMON CARD VOL. TWO (91-180) .15 .40
COMMON CARD VOL. THREE (181-270) .15 .40

1996-97 Inkworks James Bond Connoisseur's Collection Complete Series Metalworks Posters

COMPLETE SET (17) 30.00 80.00
COMPLETE VOLUME ONE SET (6) 10.00 25.00
COMPLETE VOLUME TWO SET (5) 15.00 40.00
COMPLETE VOLUME THREE SET (6) 10.00 25.00
COMMON CARD VOL. ONE (P1-P6) 3.00 8.00
COMMON CARD VOL. TWO (P7-P11) 6.00 15.00
COMMON CARD VOL. THREE (P12-P17) 3.00 8.00
STATED ODDS 1:24 FOR ALL THREE VOLUMES

1996-97 Inkworks James Bond Connoisseur's Collection Complete Series The Golden Touch

COMPLETE GOLD SET (3) 30.00 80.00
COMPLETE PLATINUM SET (3) 300.00 600.00
COMMON CARD (G1a-G3a) 15.00 40.00
COMMON CARD (G1b-G3b) 150.00 300.00
GOLD STATED ODDS 1:108
PLATINUM STATED ODDS 1:1080
G1a Sean Connery GOLD 20.00 50.00
G1b Sean Connery PLATINUM 150.00 300.00
G2a Roger Moore GOLD 15.00 40.00
G2b Roger Moore PLATINUM 200.00 400.00
G3a Pierce Brosnan GOLD 15.00 40.00
G3b Pierce Brosnan PLATINUM 150.00 300.00

1996-97 Inkworks James Bond Connoisseur's Collection Complete Series Women of Bond

COMPLETE SET (27) 50.00 100.00
COMPLETE VOLUME ONE SET (9) 15.00 40.00
COMPLETE VOLUME TWO SET (9) 15.00 40.00
COMPLETE VOLUME THREE SET (9) 15.00 40.00
COMMON CARD VOL. ONE (W1-W9) 3.00 8.00
COMMON CARD VOL. TWO (W10-W18) 3.00 8.00
COMMON CARD VOL. THREE (W19-W27) 3.00 8.00
STATED ODDS 1:11 FOR ALL THREE VOLUMES

1996-97 Inkworks James Bond Connoisseur's Collection Complete Series Promos

COMMON CARD .75 2.00
NNO Casino Chip
SD1 George Lazenby SDCC 4.00 10.00
SD2 Sean Connery SDCC 4.00 10.00
SD3 Timothy Dalton SDCC 4.00 10.00
SD4 Roger Moore SDCC 4.00 10.00

2006 James Bond Dangerous Liaisons

COMPLETE SET (110) 5.00 12.00
UNOPENED BOX (40 PACKS) 250.00 400.00
UNOPENED PACK (5 CARDS) 8.00 10.00
COMMON CARD (1-110) .15 .40

2006 James Bond Dangerous Liaisons Autographs

COMMON AUTO 8.00 20.00
STATED ODDS 1:20
MOORE AUTO STATED ODDS ONE PER 6 CASE PURCHASE
L (LIMITED): 300-500 COPIES
VL (VERY LIMITED): 200-300 COPIES
A62 Cary-Hiroyuki Tagawa 10.00 25.00
A66 Britt Ekland L 50.00 100.00
A67 George Baker ALB 20.00 50.00
WA19 Ursula Andress VL 250.00 600.00
WA26 Maud Adams VL 75.00 150.00
WA28 Lana Wood L 60.00 120.00
WA29 Tanya Roberts 30.00 75.00
WA30 Denise Richards L 75.00 200.00
NNO Alan Cumming VL 75.00 150.00
NNO Famke Janssen VL 100.00 250.00
NNO John Bowe 10.00 25.00
NNO Kristina Wayborn VL 150.00 300.00
NNO Lana Wood SP 50.00 100.00
NNO Lynn-Holly Johnson VL 50.00 100.00
NNO Madeline Smith L 15.00 40.00
NNO Maud Adams 100.00 200.00
Octopussy VL
NNO Maud Adams 75.00 150.00
The Man With The Golden Gun VL
NNO Robert Davi 10.00 25.00
NNO Tania Mallet 12.00 30.00
NNO Tanya Roberts 40.00 100.00
NNO Yaphet Kotto VL 125.00 300.00
NNO Roger Moore 6CI 150.00 400.00

2006 James Bond Dangerous Liaisons Bond Allies

COMPLETE SET (18) 12.00 30.00
COMMON CARD (BA1-BA18) .75 2.00
STATED ODDS 1:10

MODERN

MODERN

2006 James Bond Dangerous Liaisons Bond Girls Are Forever

COMPLETE SET (17) 10.00 25.00
COMMON CARD (BG30-BG45) 1.25 3.00
STATED ODDS 1:20
BG46 IS RITTENHOUSE REWARD EXCLUSIVE

2006 James Bond Dangerous Liaisons Bond Villains

COMPLETE SET (20) 40.00 80.00
COMMON CARD (F21-F40) 2.00 5.00
STATED ODDS 1:12

2006 James Bond Dangerous Liaisons Costumes

CC4 STATED ODDS ONE PER CASE
CC6 STATED ODDS ONE PER 2 CASE PURCHASE
CC4 James Bond Jacket 15.00 40.00
CC6 Jinx Dress 60.00 120.00
(2-Case Incentive)

2006 James Bond Dangerous Liaisons Art and Images of 007

COMPLETE SET (20) 250.00 500.00
COMMON CARD (AR1-AR20) 12.00 30.00
STATED ODDS 1:40
PRINT RUN 375 SER. #'d SETS

2006 James Bond Dangerous Liaisons Promos

COMMON CARD .75 2.00
P3 Bond Being Strangled ALB 3.00 8.00
UK Bond With Brandy UK 8.00 20.00

2002 James Bond Die Another Day

COMPLETE SET (90) 5.00 12.00
UNOPENED BOX (40 PACKS) 60.00 100.00
UNOPENED PACK (9 CARDS) 1.50 2.50
COMMON CARD (1-90) .15 .40

2002 James Bond Die Another Day Autographs

COMMON AUTO (A1-A8) 10.00 25.00
STATED ODDS 1:40
A1 John Cleese SP 60.00 120.00
A2 Judi Dench 60.00 150.00
A3 Michael Madsen 12.00 30.00
A4 Samantha Bond 12.00 30.00
A5 Rosamund Pike 150.00 300.00

2002 James Bond Die Another Day Case-Loaders

COMMON CARD 10.00 25.00
STATED ODDS ONE PER CASE
AC1 From the Archives Costume 10.00 25.00
MP1 Die Another Day Movie Poster 10.00 25.00

2002 James Bond Die Another Day Casting Call

COMPLETE SET (12) 4.00 10.00
COMMON CARD (C1-C12) .40 1.00
STATED ODDS 1:4

2002 James Bond Die Another Day Montage

COMPLETE SET (9) 4.00 10.00
COMMON CARD (M1-M9) .60 1.50
STATED ODDS 1:4

2002 James Bond Die Another Day Star Cards

COMPLETE SET (6) 7.50 20.00
COMMON CARD (S1-S6) 1.50 4.00
STATED ODDS 1:20

2002 James Bond Die Another Day Women of Bond

COMPLETE SET (9) 10.00 25.00
COMMON CARD (W1-W9) 1.25 3.00
STATED ODDS 1:10

2002 James Bond Die Another Day Promos

COMPLETE SET (2) 1.25 3.00
COMMON CARD (P1-P2) .75 2.00

2003 James Bond Die Another Day Expansion

COMPLETE SET (19) 20.00 50.00
COMMON CARD (1-18) .75 2.00
ANNOUNCED PRINT RUN 999 SETS
AC2 Wetsuit 15.00 40.00

2002 James Bond Dr. No Commemorative

COMP.FACT. SET (18) 10.00 25.00
COMMON CARD (1-18) .75 2.00

2003 James Bond From Russia with Love-Goldfinger

COMPLETE SET (18) 10.00 25.00
COMMON CARD .75 2.00

1995 Graffiti James Bond GoldenEye

COMPLETE SET (90) 5.00 12.00
UNOPENED BOX (36 PACKS) 30.00 50.00
UNOPENED PACK (8 CARDS) 1.00 1.50
COMMON CARD (1-90) .10 .25

1995 Graffiti James Bond GoldenEye 007 Puzzle

COMPLETE SET (3) 12.00 30.00
COMMON CARD (JB1-JB3) 5.00 12.00
STATED ODDS 1:35

1995 Graffiti James Bond GoldenEye Bond James Bond Puzzle

COMPLETE SET (9) 10.00 25.00
COMMON CARD (B1-B9) 2.00 5.00
STATED ODDS 1:11

1995 Graffiti James Bond GoldenEye Gadgets of Q

COMPLETE SET (6) 10.00 25.00
COMMON CARD (Q1-Q6) 2.50 6.00
STATED ODDS 1:17

1995 Graffiti James Bond GoldenEye Promos

COMMON CARD .60 1.50
2 Grafitti/Inkworks 10.00 25.00
(Hawaii Convention Exclusive)/500

2010 James Bond Heroes and Villains

COMPLETE SET (81) 6.00 15.00
UNOPENED BOX (24 PACKS) 100.00 200.00
UNOPENED PACK (5 CARDS) 4.00 8.00
COMMON CARD (1-81) .15 .40

2010 James Bond Heroes and Villains Autographs

COMMON AUTO 5.00 12.00
STATED ODDS 3 PER BOX
L (LIMITED): 300-500 CARDS
VL (VERY LIMITED): LESS THAN 300 CARDS
RMGL ODDS ONE PER 6-CASE PURCHASE
A119 Cecilie Thomsen VL 15.00 40.00
A123 Belle Avery VL 12.00 30.00
A124 Geoffrey Holder VL 60.00 120.00
A125 John Cleese VL 75.00 150.00
A131 Chaim Topol VL 25.00 60.00
A134 Simon Kassianides L 6.00 15.00
A136 Olga Kurylenko L 75.00 150.00
A137 Paul Ritter L 8.00 20.00
A140 Gottfried John L 10.00 25.00
A141 Kabir Bedi L 6.00 15.00
A142 Will Yun Lee VL 12.00 30.00
A143 Joanna Lumley L 15.00 40.00
A150 Olga Bisera L 8.00 20.00
A152 Carole Ashby L 8.00 20.00
A153 Corinne Clery L 15.00 40.00
A156 Bettine LeBeau L 6.00 15.00
A161 Gabriele Ferzetti L 10.00 25.00
NNO Daniel Craig VL 150.00 400.00
NNO Gemma Arterton VL 150.00 300.00
NNO Jonathan Pryce L 15.00 40.00
NNO Sean Bean L 25.00 60.00
NNO Gottfried John L 12.00 30.00
NNO Patrick Macnee VL 40.00 100.00
NNO Caroline Munro VL 30.00 75.00
NNO Gloria Hendry 8.00 20.00
NNO Kabir Bedi L 12.00 30.00
NNO Will Yun Lee VL 12.00 30.00
NNO Jill St. John L 25.00 60.00
NNO Blanche Ravalec L 10.00 25.00
NNO Trina Parks 8.00 20.00
NNO Serena Scott Thomas L 12.00 30.00
NNO Joaquin Cosio L 6.00 15.00
NNO Bettine LeBeau L 8.00 20.00
NNO David Meyer 12.00 30.00
Tony Meyer L
NNO Eunice Gayson 20.00 50.00
Kate Gayson L
NNO R.Moore/G.Lazenby 6CI 150.00 400.00
WA32 Caroline Munro VL 25.00 60.00
WA33 Izabella Scorupco L 25.00 60.00
WA34 Corinne Clery VL 25.00 60.00
WA35 Tsai Chin 6.00 15.00

2010 James Bond Heroes and Villains James Bond Expansion

COMMON CARD 2.50 6.00
STATED ODDS 1:24
AI21 James Bond AI /375 20.00 50.00
AI22 James Bond AI /375 20.00 50.00

2010 James Bond Heroes and Villains Lenticular Expansion

COMPLETE SET (9) 8.00 20.00
COMMON CARD 1.50 4.00
STATED ODDS 1:18

2010 James Bond Heroes and Villains Men of James Bond

COMPLETE SET (6) 4.00 10.00
COMMON CARD (B1-B6) 1.25 3.00
STATED ODDS 1:18

2010 James Bond Heroes and Villains Relics

COMMON MEM 10.00 25.00
STATED ODDS 1:120
JBR8 ODDS ONE PER CASE
JBR12 ODDS ONE PER 3-CASE PURCHASE
JBR1 King Canister/400 12.00 30.00
JBR2 King Dossier/175 100.00 200.00
JBR3 IDA Emblem /150 100.00 200.00
JBR5 XKR Interior/333 15.00 40.00
JBR7 Chase Leather/444 15.00 40.00
JBR8 Speed Leather/777 12.00 30.00
JBR10 Taxi Interior/200 60.00 120.00
JBR12 Windshield/333 50.00 100.00

2010 James Bond Heroes and Villains Promos

COMPLETE SET (4) 5.00 12.00
COMMON CARD .75 2.00
P3 Roger Moore ALB 3.00 8.00
CP1 Daniel Craig CON 2.50 6.00

2008 James Bond In Motion

COMPLETE SET (63) 5.00 12.00
UNOPENED BOX (24 PACKS) 75.00 125.00
UNOPENED PACK (4 CARDS) 3.00 5.00
COMMON CARD (1-63) .15 .40

2008 James Bond In Motion Autographs

COMMON AUTO 6.00 15.00
OVERALL AUTO ODDS 1:12
A113 ISSUED AS ALBUM EXCLUSIVE
HAMILTON AU ISSUED AS 3-CASE INCENTIVE
MOORE AU ISSUED AS 6-CASE INCENTIVE
L (LIMITED): 300-500 COPIES
VL (VERY LIMITED): 200-300 COPIES
A69 Denise Richards VL 150.00 400.00
A83 Thomas Wheatley VL 20.00 50.00
A87 Kate Gayson L 12.00 30.00
A89 Ivana Milicevic 12.00 30.00
A92 Isaach de Bankole L 8.00 20.00
A94 Sid Haig L 20.00 50.00
A95 Priscilla Barnes L 15.00 40.00
A98 Joe Don Baker VL 50.00 125.00
A101 Daud Shah L 8.00 20.00
A104 Joseph Millson L 10.00 25.00
A108 Margaret Nolan L 15.00 40.00
A113 Anthony Starke ALB 15.00 40.00
A115 Wayne Newton VL 75.00 200.00
A116 John Terry VL 30.00 75.00
A118 Robert Carlyle VL 20.00 50.00
A120 Carmen du Sautoy L 10.00 25.00
WA31 Honor Blackman VL 125.00 300.00
NNO Guy Hamilton 3CI 30.00 75.00
NNO Roger Moore 6CI 125.00 300.00

2008 James Bond In Motion Bond Allies

COMPLETE SET (17) 20.00 40.00
COMMON CARD (BA20-BA36) 1.50 4.00
STATED ODDS 1:12

2008 James Bond In Motion Bond Girls Are Forever

COMPLETE SET (24) 20.00 40.00
COMMON CARD (BG-49-BG72) 1.25 3.00
STATED ODDS 1:8

2008 James Bond In Motion Bond Villains

COMPLETE SET (22) 10.00 25.00
COMMON CARD (F42-F63) 1.00 2.50
STATED ODDS 1:9

2008 James Bond In Motion Costumes

COMMON CARD (SC1-SC5) 6.00 15.00
OVERALL COSTUME/RELIC ODDS 1:12
L (LIMITED): 300-500 COPIES
SC1 James Bond Shirt 12.00 30.00
SC2 M Shirt L 15.00 40.00
SC3 James Bond Pants 6.00 15.00

2008 James Bond In Motion Dual Costumes

COMMON CARD (DC2-DC7) 4.00 10.00
OVERALL COSTUME/RELIC ODDS 1:12
DC2 ISSUED AS CASE TOPPER
VL (VERY LIMITED): 200-300 COPIES
DC2 Vesper Lynd Dress/Cardigan CT 50.00 100.00
DC3 James Bond Shirt 10.00 25.00
Pants
DC6 Solange Bathing Suit 125.00 250.00
Sarong VL

2008 James Bond In Motion Full Bleed Autographs

COMMON AUTO 6.00 15.00
OVERALL AUTO ODDS 1:12
L (LIMITED): 300-500 COPIES
VL (VERY LIMITED): 200-300 COPIES
NNO Ivana Milicevic L 12.00 30.00
NNO Thomas Wheatley VL 30.00 75.00
NNO Giancarlo Giannini 15.00 40.00
NNO Joseph Millson L 10.00 25.00
NNO Virginia Hey 8.00 20.00
NNO Anthony Starke 8.00 20.00

2008 James Bond In Motion James Bond Lenticular

COMPLETE SET (6) 3.00 6.00
COMMON CARD (JB1-JB6) .60 1.50
STATED ODDS 1:4

2008 James Bond In Motion Relics

COMMON MEM (RC19-RC23) 8.00 20.00
OVERALL ODDS 1:12
L (LIMITED): 300-500 COPIES
VL (VERY LIMITED): 200-300 COPIES
RC19 Casino Table Felt L 30.00 75.00
RC20 Diamond Bed Sheet L 20.00 50.00

RC21 Vesper Lynd's Business Card VL 125.00 250.00
RC23 Miranda Frost Bed Cover L 15.00 40.00

2008 James Bond In Motion Triple Costumes

COMMON CARD (TC1-TC8) 5.00 12.00
OVERALL COSTUME/RELIC ODDS 1:12
VL (VERY LIMITED): 200-300 COPIES
TC1 James Bond Shirt Jacket#{Pants 10.00 25.00
TC3 James Bond Shirt Shirt#{Pants 10.00 25.00
TC5 James Bond Shirt Shirt#{Pants 12.00 30.00
TC6 James Bond Shirt Jacket#{Pants 10.00 25.00
TC7 James Bond Shirt Jacket#{Pants 15.00 40.00
TC8 James Bond Shirt Jacket#{Pants 12.00 30.00
QC1 Le Chiffre Shirt Vest#{Jacket#{Pants VL 60.00 120.00

2008 James Bond In Motion Promos

P2 Shadow ALB 3.00 8.00
NNO Smoking Gun GEN .75 2.00

2002 James Bond Limited Edition Previews

COMPLETE SET (6) 15.00 40.00
PRINT RUN 2002 SER. #'d SETS
1 40th Anniversary Logo 4.00 10.00
2 Sean Connery 4.00 10.00
3 George Lazenby 4.00 10.00
4 Roger Moore 4.00 10.00
5 Timothy Dalton 4.00 10.00
6 Pierce Brosnan 4.00 10.00

2011 James Bond Mission Logs

COMPLETE SET (66) 5.00 12.00
UNOPENED BOX (24 PACKS) 75.00 125.00
UNOPENED PACK (5 CARDS) 3.00 5.00
COMMON CARD (1-66) .15 .40
VB6 ISSUED AS CASE TOPPER
VB6 Daniel Craig VB/700 CT 10.00 25.00

2011 James Bond Mission Logs Autographs

COMMON AUTO 5.00 12.00
OVERALL AUTO ODDS TWO PER BOX
L (LIMITED): 300-500 COPIES
VL (VERY LIMITED): 200-300 COPIES
A157 Geoffrey Palmer L 10.00 25.00
A158 Ulrich Thomsen VL 10.00 25.00
A160 Eunice Gayson VL 15.00 40.00
A163 Marilyn Galsworthy L 6.00 15.00
A165 Anne Lonnberg L 10.00 25.00
A175 Aleta Morrison L 8.00 20.00
A178 Fernando Guillen Cuervo L 6.00 15.00
A179 Catherina von Schell VL 15.00 40.00
A182 Kenneth Tsang L 6.00 15.00
A185 Fiona Fullerton VL 8.00 20.00
A187 Ricky Jay L 12.00 30.00
A190 Daniel Benzali VL 10.00 25.00
A191 Valerie Leon L 12.00 30.00
A193 Andreas Wisniewski L 6.00 15.00
A197 Burt Kwouk VL 12.00 30.00

2011 James Bond Mission Logs Bond Allies

COMPLETE SET (11) 8.00 20.00
COMMON CARD (BA35-BA45) 1.50 4.00
STATED ODDS 1:12

2011 James Bond Mission Logs Bond Villains

COMPLETE SET (11) 8.00 20.00
COMMON CARD (F71-F81) 1.50 4.00
STATED ODDS 1:12

2011 James Bond Mission Logs Bond James Bond

COMPLETE SET (11) 8.00 20.00
COMMON CARD (B1-B11) 1.50 4.00
STATED ODDS 1:12

2011 James Bond Mission Logs Femme Fatales

COMPLETE SET (9) 15.00 30.00
COMMON CARD (F10-F18) 2.00 5.00
STATED ODDS 1:12

2011 James Bond Mission Logs Full Bleed Autographs

COMMON AUTO 5.00 12.00
OVERALL AUTO ODDS TWO PER BOX
L (LIMITED): 300-500 COPIES
VL (VERY LIMITED): 200-300 COPIES
EL (EXTREMELY LIMITED): 200 OR FEWER COPIES
MADSEN BLUE INK ISSUED AS RITT. REWARD
NNO Anthony Zerbe VL 20.00 50.00
NNO Daniel Craig EL 250.00 600.00
NNO Gabriele Ferzetti L 10.00 25.00
NNO Joanna Lumley L 15.00 40.00
NNO Lana Wood L 20.00 50.00
NNO Lesley Langley L 8.00 20.00
NNO Luciana Paluzzi L 15.00 40.00
NNO M. Madsen (red ink) VL 15.00 40.00
NNO M. Madsen (blue ink) RR 50.00 100.00
NNO Pierce Brosnan EL 200.00 500.00
NNO Shane Rimmer 12.00 30.00
NNO Toby Stephens L 12.00 30.00
NNO B.Ravalec/R.Kiel L 60.00 120.00

2011 James Bond Mission Logs Relics

COMMON MEM 6.00 15.00
STATED ODDS ONE PER BOX
JBR6 ISSUED AS 3-CASE INCENTIVE
CRAIG AUTO ISSUED AS 9-CASE INCENTIVE
JBR6 Boat Carpeting/199 3CI 75.00 150.00
JBR14 Seat Leather/400 15.00 40.00
JBR15 Opera Program/350 30.00 75.00
JBR17 Tosca Gift Bag/250 25.00 60.00
JBR20 Drax Jumpsuit/900 8.00 20.00
JBR21 Motorcycle Gloves/200 100.00 200.00
JBR22 Bond Vest/600 8.00 20.00
JBR26 Russian Bnkr Suit/875 8.00 20.00
NNO Daniel Craig Shirt AU/150 9CI 200.00 400.00

2011 James Bond Mission Logs Women of James Bond Autographs

COMMON AUTO 12.00 30.00
OVERALL AUTO ODDS TWO PER BOX
L (LIMITED): 300-500 COPIES
VL (VERY LIMITED): 200-300 COPIES
WA47 Martine Beswicke VL 25.00 60.00

2011 James Bond Mission Logs Promos

COMPLETE SET (5) 1.50 4.00
P3 Roger Moore ALB 6.00 15.00
P4 Sean Connery (Philly) 2.00 5.00
ISP1 Pierce Brosnan (Ind. Summit) 10.00 20.00

2010 James Bond Solitaire's Tarot Deck

COMPLETE SET (25) 20.00 50.00
COMMON CARD 1.50 4.00

1966 Philadelphia Gum James Bond Thunderball

COMPLETE SET (67) 125.00 250.00
UNOPENED PACK 400.00 600.00
COMMON CARD (1-67) 1.25 3.00
NNO Secret Code Capsule Decoder 8.00 20.00

1979 Topps James Bond Moonraker

COMPLETE SET (99) 4.00 10.00
COMPLETE SET W/STICKERS (121) 6.00 15.00
UNOPENED BOX (36 PACKS) 100.00 150.00
UNOPENED PACK (10 CARDS+1 STICKER) 3.00 5.00
COMMON CARD (1-99) .08 .20

1979 Topps James Bond Moonraker Stickers

COMPLETE SET (22) 2.50 6.00
COMMON CARD (1-22) .20 .50
STATED ODDS 1:1

1979 O-Pee-Chee James Bond Moonraker

COMPLETE SET (99) 4.00 10.00
COMMON CARD (1-99) .08 .20

1979 O-Pee-Chee James Bond Moonraker Stickers

COMPLETE SET (22) 2.50 6.00
COMMON CARD (1-22) .20 .50
STATED ODDS 1:1

2004 Quotable James Bond

COMPLETE SET (100) 4.00 10.00
UNOPENED BOX (40 PACKS) 75.00 125.00
UNOPENED PACK (5 CARDS) 2.00 3.00
COMMON CARD (1-100) .10 .30
CC5 STATED ODDS ONE PER COLLECTOR'S ALBUM
CC5 Aristotle Kristatos Clothing 12.00 30.00

2004 Quotable James Bond Autographs

COMMON AUTO 6.00 15.00
STATED ODDS 1:20
d'ABO AUTO ISSUED AS U.S. CASE TOPPER
KIEL AUTO ISSUED AS MULTI-CASE INCENTIVE
EATON AUTO ISSUED AS U.K. CASE TOPPER
L (LIMITED): 300-500 COPIES
VL (VERY LIMITED): 200-300 COPIES
A4 Serena Scott-Thomas L 15.00 40.00
A28 Sophie Marceau L 125.00 300.00
A29 Roger Moore VL 100.00 250.00
A30 Michelle Yeoh L 100.00 250.00
A31 Martine Beswick L 25.00 60.00
A33 Mollie Peters L 20.00 50.00
A34 Blanche Ravalec 8.00 20.00
A36 Will Yun Lee L 12.00 30.00
A37 Goldie 8.00 20.00
A43 Michael Billington 12.00 30.00
A44 Shane Rimmer 12.00 30.00
A45 Carey Lowell VL 75.00 200.00
A46 Maria Grazia Cucinotta L 25.00 60.00
A47 Burt Kwouk 10.00 25.00
A48 Rachel Grant L 20.00 50.00
A49 Madeline Smith VL 30.00 75.00
WA16 Sophie Marceau L 100.00 250.00
WA17 Michelle Yeoh L 100.00 250.00
WA18 Serena Scott-Thomas L 15.00 40.00
WA20 Mollie Peters L 15.00 40.00
WA21 Carey Lowell VL 125.00 250.00
WA22 Maria Grazia Cucinotta L 20.00 50.00
WA23 Martine Beswick L 15.00 40.00
WA24 Rachel Grant L 15.00 40.00
WA25 Madeline Smith VL 50.00 100.00
NNO Maryam d'Abo US CT 40.00 100.00
NNO Richard Kiel CI 50.00 125.00
NNO Shirley Eaton UK CT 50.00 100.00

2004 Quotable James Bond Bond Girls Are Forever

COMPLETE SET (9) 40.00 80.00
COMMON CARD (BG21-BG29) 6.00 15.00
STATED ODDS 1:40 U.S. PACKS

2004 Quotable James Bond Bond Villains

COMPLETE SET (20) 40.00 80.00
COMMON CARD (F1-F20)
STATED ODDS 1:14

2004 Quotable James Bond Theme Songs

COMPLETE SET (10) 8.00 20.00
COMMON CARD (T1-T10) 1.00 2.50
STATED ODDS 1:10

2004 Quotable James Bond Villains and Vixens

COMPLETE SET (9) 30.00 80.00
COMMON CARD (UK1-UK9) 5.00 12.00
STATED ODDS 1:40 U.K. PACKS

2004 Quotable James Bond Vintage Bond

COMPLETE SET (5) 60.00 120.00
COMMON CARD (VB1-VB5) 10.00 25.00
STATED ODDS 1:120
STATED PRINT RUN 700 SER. #'d SETS

2004 Quotable James Bond Promos

COMPLETE SET (4) 5.00 12.00
COMMON CARD .75 2.00
P3 Dr. No ALB 3.00 8.00
NSU1 Goldfinger NSU#(show excl.) 2.00 5.00

1997 Inkworks James Bond Tomorrow Never Dies

COMPLETE SET (90) 6.00 15.00
UNOPENED BOX (36 PACKS) 50.00 75.00
UNOPENED PACK (8 CARDS) 1.75 2.50
COMMON CARD (1-90) .12 .30
B1 STATED ODDS 1:108
B1 Bond Dressed to Kill 12.00 30.00

1997 Inkworks James Bond Tomorrow Never Dies Teri Hatcher Puzzle

COMPLETE SET (9) 20.00 50.00
COMMON CARD (T1-T9) 3.00 8.00
STATED ODDS 1:11

1997 Inkworks James Bond Tomorrow Never Dies Women of Bond

COMPLETE SET (4) 12.00 30.00
COMMON CARD (W1-W4) 4.00 10.00
STATED ODDS 1:24

1997 Inkworks James Bond Tomorrow Never Dies Promos

COMMON CARD 2.00 5.00
0 James Bond running 2.50 6.00

2021 Upper Deck James Bond Villains and Henchmen

COMPLETE SET (100) 10.00 25.00
UNOPENED BOX (18 PACKS) 150.00 250.00
UNOPENED PACK (5 CARDS) 8.00 15.00
COMMON CARD (1-100) .20 .50
*OBSIDIAN: 20X TO 50X BASIC CARDS
*ACETATE: X TO X BASIC CARDS
*ACETATE SP: X TO X BASIC CARDS
*ACETATE SSP: X TO X BASIC CARDS

2021 Upper Deck James Bond Villains and Henchmen Allies and Colleagues

COMPLETE SET (25) 30.00 75.00
COMMON CARD (AC1-AC25) 2.00 5.00
STATED ODDS 1:2 HOBBY/EPACK

2021 Upper Deck James Bond Villains and Henchmen As Quoted

COMPLETE SET (25) 60.00 120.00
COMMON CARD (AQ1-AQ25) 3.00 8.00
STATED ODDS 1:4 HOBBY/EPACK

2021 Upper Deck James Bond Villains and Henchmen Autographs

GROUP A ODDS 1:1,039
GROUP B ODDS 1:501
GROUP C ODDS 1:186
STATED ODDS 1:120 HOBBY/EPACK
AC Alan Cumming B 50.00 100.00
AS Andrew Scott B
BE Britt Ekland C 20.00 50.00
BW Ben Whishaw A
CA Carole Ashby C 20.00 50.00
CC Corinne Clery C 20.00 50.00
CZ Christoph Waltz A 200.00 500.00
DC Daniel Craig A 2000.00 4000.00
DR Denise Richards B 60.00 150.00

FJ Famke Janssen A 125.00 300.00
GL George Lazenby B 60.00 150.00
JC John Cleese A 50.00 125.00
JD Judi Dench A 60.00 150.00
JS Jane Seymour A 125.00 300.00
JW Jeffrey Wright A 30.00 75.00
MD Maryam d'Abo C 50.00 100.00
RY Rick Yune B
SB Sean Bean A 30.00 75.00
SE Shirley Eaton C 25.00 60.00
WN Wayne Newton B 30.00 75.00
JRD John Rhys-Davies B 30.00 75.00
LHJ Lynn-Holly Johnson C 30.00 75.00

2021 Upper Deck James Bond Villains and Henchmen Bond Premium Silver Redemption

COMPLETE SET (6)
STATED PRINT RUN SER.#'d SETS
UNPRICED DUE TO SCARCITY
S7 Harold Sakata as Oddjob
S8 Timothy Dalton as James Bond
S9 Pierce Brosnan as James Bond
S10 Sean Bean as Alec Trevelyan
S11 Lotte Lenya Rosa Klebb
S12 Famke Jansen as Xenia Onatopp

2021 Upper Deck James Bond Villains and Henchmen Bonded Materials

COMPLETE SET (20)
COMMON MEM (BM1-BM20) 10.00 25.00
GROUP A 1:706
GROUP B 1:38
STATED ODDS 1:36 HOBBY/EPACK
BM1 Daniel Craig/Coat A 20.00 50.00
BM4 Daniel Craig/Pants A 20.00 50.00
BM6 Ralph Fiennes/Jeans B 15.00 40.00
BM7 Ben Whishaw/Shirt B 12.00 30.00
BM9 Ben Whishaw/Beanie B
BM10 Ben Whishaw/Sweater B EXCH
BM13 Ralph Fiennes/Shirt B 12.00 30.00
BM15 Lea Seydoux/Blouse B 20.00 50.00
BM16 Lea Seydoux/Jacket B 25.00 60.00
BM17 Lea Seydoux/Dress B 30.00 75.00
BM18 Lea Seydoux/Dress B 20.00 50.00
BM19 Naomie Harris/Blouse B 12.00 30.00
BM20 Naomie Harris/Trousers B 20.00 50.00

2021 Upper Deck James Bond Villains and Henchmen Crystal Clear

COMMON CARD (CC21-CC50) 12.00 30.00
COMMON SP (CC6-CC20) 20.00 50.00
COMMON SSP (CC1-CC5) 50.00 100.00
STATED ODDS 1:18 HOBBY/EPACK
STATED SP ODDS 1:90 HOBBY/EPACK
STATED SSP ODDS 1:720 HOBBY/EPACK

2021 Upper Deck James Bond Villains and Henchmen Dual Bonded Materials

COMMON MEM (BM21-BM40) 10.00 25.00
GROUP A 1:2,155
GROUP B 1:74
STATED ODDS 1:72 HOBBY/EPACK
BM21 Dave Bautista/Suit B 12.00 30.00
BM23 Daniel Craig/Coat A 50.00 100.00
BM24 Daniel Craig/Pants A 30.00 75.00
BM25 Christoph Waltz/Jacket B 25.00 60.00
BM27 Ben Whishaw/Shirt B 15.00 40.00
BM28 Allesandro Cremona/Shirt B 20.00 50.00
BM29 Ben Whishaw Beanie B 15.00 40.00
BM30 Ben Whishaw/Sweater B
BM31 Ben Whishaw/Shirt B 15.00 40.00
BM32 Ben Whishaw/Pants B 20.00 50.00
BM35 Lea Seydoux Blouse B 30.00 75.00
BM36 Lea Seydoux/Jacket B 25.00 60.00
BM37 Lea Seydoux/Dress B 30.00 75.00
BM38 Lea Seydoux/Dress B 25.00 60.00
BM39 Naomie Harris Blouse B 12.00 30.00
BM40 Naomie Harris/Pants B 20.00 50.00

2021 Upper Deck James Bond Villains and Henchmen Dual Bonded Materials Combos

GROUP A 1:4,032
GROUP B 1:149
STATED ODDS 1:144 HOBBY/EPACK
BM41 A.Cremona/L.Seydoux/Tie-Blouse A
BM42 D.Craig/L.Seydoux/Coat-Blouse B 75.00 150.00
BM43 D.Bautista/B.Whishaw/Suit-Shirt B 15.00 40.00
BM44 B.Whishaw/R.Fiennes/Shirt-Jeans B 20.00 50.00
BM45 B.Whishaw/A.Scott/Shirt-Suit B 12.00 30.00
BM46 N.Harris/B.Whishaw/Blouse-Shirt B 20.00 50.00
BM47 D.Craig/D.Bautista/Coat-Suit B 25.00 60.00
BM48 L.Seydoux/B.Whishaw/Blouse-Shirt B25.00 60.00
BM49 L.Seydoux/C.Waltz/Blouse-Jacket B
BM50 D.Craig/C.Waltz/Coat-Jacket B
BM51 R.Fiennes/A.Cremona/Jeans-Coat B
BM52 N.Harris/B.Whishaw/Blouse-Shirt B

2021 Upper Deck James Bond Villains and Henchmen Master Plan

COMPLETE SET (15) 12.00 30.00
COMMON CARD (MP1-MP15) 1.25 3.00
STATED ODDS 1:7

2021 Upper Deck James Bond Villains and Henchmen Movie Posters Acetate

COMPLETE SET W/O SP & SSP (20) 200.00 400.00
COMMON CARD (MP16-MP35) 12.00 30.00
COMMON SP (MP6-MP15) 25.00 60.00
COMMON SSP (MP1-MP5) 50.00 100.00
STATED ODDS 1:45 HOBBY/EPACK
STATED SP ODDS 1:200 HOBBY/EPACK
STATED SSP ODDS 1:800 HOBBY/EPACK

2021 Upper Deck James Bond Villains and Henchmen Quad Bonded Materials Combos

COMPLETE SET (10)
COMMON MEM (BM63-BM72)
GROUP A 1:7,097
GROUP B 1:460
STATED OVERALL ODDS 1:432 HOBBY/EPACK
BM63 D.Craig/C.Waltz/Pants 2-Jacket 2 A
BM64 D.Craig/L.Seydoux/Pants 2-Dress 2 B
BM65 D.Bautista/B.Whishaw/Suit 2-Shirt 2 B
BM66 B.Whishaw/R.Fiennes/Shirt 2-Jeans 2 B
BM67 B.Whishaw/A.Scott/Shirt 2-Suit 2 B
BM68 N.Harris/B.Whishaw/Pants 2-Shirt 2 B
BM69 D.Craig/D.Bautista/Pants 2-Suit 2 B
BM70 L.Seydoux/B.Whishaw/Dress 2-Shirt 2 B
BM71 L.Seydoux/A.Cremona/Dress 2-Shirt 2 B30.0075.00
BM72 A.Cremona/L.Seydoux/Shirt 2-Dress 2 B

2021 Upper Deck James Bond Villains and Henchmen Star Signings

COMMON AUTO 8.00 20.00
GROUP A ODDS 1:7,635
GROUP B ODDS 1:109
GROUP C ODDS 1:31
GROUP D ODDS 1:73
STATED OVERALL ODDS 1:18
SSAC Alan Cumming B
SSAS Andrew Scott B 25.00 60.00
SSBE Britt Ekland C 25.00 50.00
SSBW Ben Whishaw C 30.00 75.00
SSCA Caroline Munro C 20.00 50.00
SSCB Caroline Bliss D 15.00 40.00
SSCC Corinne Clery C 20.00 50.00
SSCM Caterina Murino C 25.00 60.00
SSCZ Christoph Waltz B 150.00 300.00
SSDR Denise Richards B 150.00 300.00
SSFJ Famke Janssen B 125.00 250.00
SSGF Glenn Foster D 12.00 30.00
SSGH Gloria Hendry C 10.00 25.00
SSGL George Lazenby B 125.00 250.00
SSIS Izabella Scorupco B 20.00 50.00
SSJC Joaquin Cosio D 10.00 25.00
SSJD Judi Dench B 60.00 120.00
SSJG Julian Glover D 12.00 30.00
SSJK Jeroen Krabbe C 10.00 25.00
SSJL John Cleese C 75.00 150.00
SSJS Jane Seymour B 100.00 200.00
SSJW Jeffrey Wright B 30.00 75.00
SSKT Kenneth Tsang C 10.00 25.00
SSMM Michael Madsen C 12.00 30.00
SSMN Margaret Nolan C 15.00 40.00
SSMS Mary Stavin C 12.00 30.00
SSSA Samantha Bond C 12.00 30.00
SSSB Sean Bean B 60.00 120.00
SSSK Simon Kassianides C 15.00 40.00
SSTR Tanya Roberts C 50.00 100.00
SSWN Wayne Newton C 30.00 75.00
SSDC2 Daniel Craig A 300.00 600.00
SSJLS Jill St. John C 50.00 100.00
SSJRD John Rhys-Davies B 75.00 150.00
SSLHJ Lynn-Holly Johnson C 25.00 60.00

2021 Upper Deck James Bond Villains and Henchmen Triple Bonded Materials Trios

STATED ODDS 1:216 HOBBY/EPACK
BM53 Craig/Seydoux/Waltz
Coat-Jacket-Jacket B 100.00 200.00
BM54 Whishaw/Fiennes/Harris/Sweater-Shirt-Pants B EXCH
BM55 Craig/Waltz/Bautista
Coat-Jacket-Suit A 75.00 150.00
BM56 Seydoux/Whishaw/Fiennes/Jacket-Sweater-Shirt B EXCH
BM57 Seydoux/Whishaw/Harris/Jacket-Sweater-Pants B EXCH
BM58 Whishaw/Cremona/Scott/Sweater-Shirt-Suit B
BM59 Craig/Whishaw/Fiennes/Coat-Sweater-Shirt B EXCH
BM60 Waltz/Bautista/Scott/Jacket-Suit-Suit B50.00 100.00
BM61 Fiennes/Whishaw/Harris/Shirt-Sweater-Pants B
BM62 Fiennes/Cremona/Seydoux
Shirt-Shirt-Jacket B 50.00 100.00

2021 Upper Deck James Bond Villains and Henchmen The Upper Hand

COMPLETE SET (10) 15.00 40.00
COMMON CARD (UH1-UH10) 2.50 6.00
STATED ODDS 1:10 HOBBY/EPACK

1998 Inkworks The Women of James Bond

COMPLETE SET (72) 6.00 15.00
UNOPENED BOX (36 PACKS) 60.00 100.00
UNOPENED PACK (5 CARDS) 1.50 2.00
COMMON CARD (1-72) .15 .40
M1 STATED ODDS 1:108
M1 Minnie Driver 10.00 25.00
((Mystery Girl Insert)
PAN 9-Card Panel

1998 Inkworks The Women of James Bond Autographs

COMMON AUTO (A1-A5) 15.00 40.00
A1 Caroline Munro 20.00 50.00
A2 Lois Maxwell 50.00 100.00
A4 Shirley Eaton 20.00 50.00
A5 Lana Wood 20.00 50.00

1998 Inkworks The Women of James Bond Bond's Best

COMPLETE SET (3) 10.00 25.00
COMMON CARD (B1-B3) 4.00 10.00
STATED ODDS 1:35

1998 Inkworks The Women of James Bond Early Encounters

COMPLETE SET (6) 8.00 20.00
COMMON CARD (E1-E6) 2.50 6.00
STATED ODDS 1:17

1998 Inkworks The Women of James Bond Promos

P1 Pussy and the Flying Circus 1.25 3.00
P2 Paris Carver/James Bond 2.00 5.00

2003 Women of James Bond In Motion

COMPLETE SET (63) 5.00 12.00
UNOPENED BOX (20 PACKS) 60.00 100.00
UNOPENED PACK (6 CARDS) 3.00 8.00
COMMON CARD (1-63) .15 .40
C1 In Motion Checklist Card

2003 Women of James Bond In Motion Autographs

COMMON AUTO (WA1-WA15) 12.00 30.00
STATED ODDS 1:10
WA1 Jill St. John 30.00 75.00
WA2 Maryam d'Abo 15.00 40.00
WA3 Barbara Bach 250.00 500.00
WA7 Kristina Wayborn 20.00 50.00
WA8 Eunice Gayson 15.00 40.00
WA9 Lynn-Holly Johnson 20.00 50.00
WA10 Maud Adams 20.00 50.00
WA11 Britt Ekland 20.00 50.00
WA12 Luciana Paluzzi 15.00 40.00
WA13 Mie Hama 150.00 400.00
WA14 Jane Seymour 50.00 120.00
WA15 Lois Chiles 100.00 200.00

2003 Women of James Bond In Motion Bond Girls Are Forever

COMPLETE SET (20) 125.00 250.00
COMMON CARD (BG1-BG20) 6.00 15.00
STATED ODDS 1:5

2003 Women of James Bond In Motion Case-Toppers

COMPLETE SET (3) 12.50 30.00
COMMON CARD (CT1-CT3) 5.00 12.00
STATED ODDS ONE PER CASE

2003 Women of James Bond In Motion Femmes Fatales

COMPLETE SET (9) 8.00 20.00
COMMON CARD (F1-F9) 1.25 3.00
STATED ODDS 1:4

2003 Women of James Bond In Motion Jinx

COMPLETE SET (9) 4.00 10.00
COMMON CARD (J1-J9) .60 1.50
STATED ODDS 1:7

2003 Women of James Bond In Motion Women of MI6

COMPLETE SET (6) 3.00 8.00
COMMON CARD (M1-M6) .75 2.00
STATED ODDS 1:3.3

2003 Women of James Bond In Motion Promos

COMPLETE SET (3) 4.00 10.00
COMMON CARD (P1-P3) .75 2.00
P1 Honey Ryder 2.50 6.00
P3 Women of James Bond In Motion 2.50 6.00

1999 Inkworks James Bond The World Is Not Enough

COMPLETE SET (90) 5.00 12.00
COMMON CARD (1-90) .15 .40
S1 STATED ODDS 1:108
S1 Shaken Not Stirred SP 6.00 15.00

1999 Inkworks James Bond The World Is Not Enough Autographs

COMMON AUTO 8.00 20.00
A1 Denise Richards 60.00 125.00
A2 Judi Dench 40.00 100.00
A3 Desmond Llewelyn 60.00 120.00
A4 Serena Scott-Thomas 15.00 40.00
R1 Redemption Card

1999 Inkworks James Bond The World Is Not Enough Bond Is Back

COMPLETE SET (9) 4.00 10.00
COMMON CARD (B1-B9) .75 2.00
STATED ODDS 1:11

1999 Inkworks James Bond The World Is Not Enough Poker Chips

COMPLETE SET (3) 25.00 50.00
COMMON CARD (C1-C3) 8.00 20.00
STATED ODDS ONE PER BOX

1999 Inkworks James Bond The World Is Not Enough Promos

P1 Fire Girl	.75	2.00
DW1 James Bond (w/gun) UK	2.00	5.00
ML1 Elektra King/James Bond/Christmas Jones	1.25	3.00

1999 Inkworks James Bond The World Is Not Enough Q Branch

COMPLETE SET (6)	3.00	8.00
COMMON CARD (Q1-Q6)	1.00	2.50
STATED ODDS 1:17		

1992 Active Marketing James Dean Collection

COMPLETE BOXED SET (50)	4.00	10.00
COMMON CARD (1-50)	.15	.40
*PROMOS: 3X TO 8X BASIC CARDS	1.25	3.00

1995 FPG James Warhola

COMPLETE SET (90)	5.00	12.00
UNOPENED BOX (36 PACKS)	15.00	20.00
UNOPENED PACK (10 CARDS)	.50	.75
COMMON CARD (1-90)	.12	.30

1995 FPG James Warhola Metallic

COMPLETE SET (5)	12.00	30.00
COMMON CARD (M1-M5)	3.00	8.00
RANDOMLY INSERTED INTO PACKS		

1998 Comic Images Janesko Premiere Pin-Ups

COMPLETE SET (72)	8.00	20.00
UNOPENED BOX (36 PACKS)	40.00	50.00
UNOPENED PACK (8 CARDS)	1.75	2.00
COMMON CARD (1-72)	.20	.50

1998 Comic Images Janesko Premiere Pin-Ups Autographs

COMMON CARD (1-6)	20.00	50.00
STATED ODDS 1:360		
STATED PRINT RUN 500 SER.#'d SETS		

1998 Comic Images Janesko Premiere Pin-Ups LustreChrome

COMPLETE SET (6)	12.00	40.00
COMMON CARD (1-6)	3.00	8.00
RANDOMLY INSERTED INTO PACKS		

1998 Comic Images Janesko Premiere Pin-Ups Promos

COMPLETE SET (2)	1.25	3.00
COMMON CARD (1-2)	.75	2.00

1999 Comic Images Janesko Limited Edition

COMPLETE SET (9)	8.00	20.00
COMMON CARD (1-9)	.40	1.00
1 Avalanche AU/1000	6.00	15.00

2002 Janesko Select

COMPLETE SET (72)	4.00	10.00
UNOPENED BOX (36 PACKS)	40.00	50.00
UNOPENED PACK (7 CARDS)	1.75	2.00
COMMON CARD (1-72)	.12	.30
BT Flamenco Box-Topper	1.25	3.00
UNC (Exclusive 6-card uncut sheet) (Album Exclusive)		

2002 Janesko Select Autographs

COMMON CARD	10.00	25.00
RANDOMLY INSERTED INTO PACKS		
A1 Cherry Blossom	10.00	25.00
A2 Fade to Blue	10.00	25.00
A3 Flamenco	10.00	25.00
P2 Fade to Blue (both numbers distributed in packs)	10.00	25.00
P3 Flamenco (both numbers distributed in packs)	10.00	25.00

2002 Janesko Select Holofoil

COMPLETE SET (6)	10.00	25.00
COMMON CARD (C1-C6)	2.00	5.00
STATED ODDS 1:12		

2002 Janesko Select Promos

COMPLETE SET (3)	2.00	5.00
COMMON CARD (P1-P3)	.75	2.00

1996 FPG Janny Wurts

COMPLETE SET (60)	4.00	10.00
UNOPENED BOX (36 PACKS)	20.00	25.00
UNOPENED PACK (10 CARDS)	.75	1.00
COMMON CARD (1-60)	.12	.30
NNO Janny Wurts AU/1000*	20.00	50.00
NNO Double-Sided PROMO bookmark	4.00	10.00

1996 FPG Janny Wurts Metallic

COMPLETE SET (5)	12.00	30.00
COMMON CARD (M1-M5)	3.00	8.00
RANDOMLY INSERTED INTO PACKS		

1993 Eclipse Jason Goes to Hell

COMPLETE SET (110)	10.00	25.00
UNOPENED BOX (36 PACKS)	30.00	40.00
UNOPENED PACK (12 CARDS)	1.00	1.25
COMMON CARD (1-110)	.15	.40
J1 RANDOM INSERT IN PACKS		
J1 The Final Friday	2.00	5.00

1993 Topps Comics Jason Goes to Hell Promos

COMPLETE SET (9)	10.00	25.00
COMMON CARD (1-9)	2.00	5.00

1983 Topps Jaws 3-D

COMPLETE SET (44)	5.00	12.00
UNOPENED BOX (36 PACKS)	75.00	125.00
UNOPENED PACK (6 CARDS+VIEWER)	2.00	3.00
COMMON CARD (1-44)	.20	.50

1995 21st Century Archives J.C. Leyendecker

COMPLETE SET (50)	5.00	12.00
COMPLETE BOXED SET (50)	6.00	15.00
UNOPENED BOX (36 PACKS)	20.00	25.00
UNOPENED PACK (8 CARDS)	.75	1.00
COMMON CARD (1-50)	.20	.50

1995 21st Century Archives J.C. Leyendecker New Year's Babies

COMPLETE SET (5)	6.00	15.00
COMMON CARD (NY1-NY5)	2.00	5.00
STATED ODDS 1:8		

1995 FPG Jeff Easley

COMPLETE SET (90)	4.00	10.00
UNOPENED BOX (36 PACKS)	30.00	40.00
UNOPENED PACK (10 CARDS)	1.00	1.25
COMMON CARD (1-90)	.10	.25
NNO1 J Easley AU/1000*	20.00	50.00
NNO2 Jeff Easley 10-Card Panel AU		
NNO3 Oversized PROMO	2.00	5.00

1995 FPG Jeff Easley Metallic Storm

COMPLETE SET (6)	10.00	25.00
COMMON CARD (MS1-MS6)	2.50	6.00
RANDOMLY INSERTED INTO PACKS		

1993 FPG Jeffrey Jones

COMPLETE SET (90)	5.00	12.00
UNOPENED BOX (36 PACKS)	15.00	20.00
UNOPENED PACK (10 CARDS)	.50	.75
COMMON CARD (1-90)	.12	.30
NNO Jeffrey Jones AU/1000*	20.00	50.00

1993 FPG Jeffrey Jones Gold Holograms

COMPLETE SET (3)	25.00	60.00
COMMON CARD (GH1-GH3)	10.00	25.00
STATED ODDS 1:CASE		

1993 FPG Jeffrey Jones Holograms

COMPLETE SET (3)	6.00	15.00
COMMON CARD (H1-H3)	3.00	8.00
STATED ODDS 1:18		

1995 FPG Jeffrey Jones

COMPLETE SET (90)	5.00	12.00
UNOPENED BOX (36 PACKS)	25.00	40.00
UNOPENED PACK (10 CARDS)	1.00	1.25
COMMON CARD (1-90)	.10	.25
NNO1 Jeffrey Jones AU/1000*	20.00	50.00
NNO2 5-Card Panel PROMO		

1995 FPG Jeffrey Jones Canvas

COMPLETE SET (5)	12.00	30.00
COMMON CARD (C1-C5)	3.00	8.00
STATED ODDS 1:12		

2007 Jericho Season One

COMPLETE SET (72)	4.00	10.00
UNOPENED BOX (36 PACKS)	50.00	75.00
UNOPENED PACK (6 CARDS)	2.00	3.00
COMMON CARD (1-72)	.12	.30

2007 Jericho Season One Autographs

COMPLETE SET (8)		
COMMON AUTO (A1-A8)	4.00	10.00
STATED ODDS 1:36		
A1 Skeet Ulrich	20.00	50.00
A2 Ashley Scott	10.00	25.00
A3 Sprague Grayden	6.00	15.00
AR1 Redemption Card	1.50	4.00

2007 Jericho Season One Box-Loaders

COMPLETE SET (3)	5.00	12.00
COMMON CARD (CH1-CH3)	2.00	5.00
CH1-CH3 ISSUED ONE PER BOX		
CL1 ISSUED ONE PER CASE		
CL1 Welcome To Jericho	4.00	10.00

2007 Jericho Season One Fallout

COMPLETE SET (9)	3.00	8.00
COMMON CARD (F1-F9)	.75	2.00
STATED ODDS 1:11		

2007 Jericho Season One Pieceworks

COMPLETE SET (17)	150.00	300.00
COMMON CARD (PW1-PW13)	6.00	15.00
STATED ODDS 1:36		
PW2 Skeet Ulrich	8.00	20.00
PW4 Lennie James	8.00	20.00
PW5 Lennie James	8.00	20.00
PW6 Kenneth Mitchell	8.00	20.00
PW8 Ashley Scott	8.00	20.00
PW9 Ashley Scott	8.00	20.00
PW12 Alicia Coppola	8.00	20.00
PW13 Alicia Coppola	8.00	20.00
PWA1 Skeet Ulrich AU	15.00	40.00
PWA2 Ashley Scott AU	15.00	40.00
PWA3 Kenneth Mitchell AU	8.00	20.00
APWR1 Redemption Card		

2007 Jericho Season One Survivors

COMPLETE SET (6)	3.00	8.00
COMMON CARD (S1-S6)	1.00	2.50
STATED ODDS 1:17		

2007 Jericho Season One Promos

COMPLETE SET	.75	2.00
J1PK Jericho	2.50	6.00
JER2007 Jericho Flag	2.50	6.00
J1SD2007 Jericho - 11 cast members	2.00	5.00

1998 Comic Images Jerry Springer OmniChrome

COMPLETE SET (8)	12.00	30.00
COMMON CARD	2.50	6.00
AUC1 Steve Wilkos AU	12.00	30.00
AUC2 Todd Schultz AU	10.00	25.00

1998 Comic Images Jerry Springer Promos

COMPLETE SET (2)	1.25	3.00
COMMON CARD (P1-P2)	.75	2.00

1991 Freedom Press JFK Assassination

COMPLETE FACTORY SET (40)	6.00	15.00
COMMON CARD (1-40)	.30	.75

1995 FPG Jim Steranko

COMPLETE SET (78)	6.00	15.00
UNOPENED BOX (36 PACKS)	30.00	40.00
UNOPENED PACK (8 CARDS)	1.00	1.25
COMMON CARD (1-78)	.15	.40
NNO Jim Steranko AU/1000*	20.00	50.00

1995 FPG Jim Steranko Metallic

COMPLETE SET (12)	12.00	30.00
COMMON CARD (M1-M12)	1.50	4.00
RANDOMLY INSERTED INTO PACKS		

1995 FPG J.K. Potter

COMPLETE SET (90)	5.00	12.00
UNOPENED BOX (36 PACKS)	15.00	20.00
UNOPENED PACK (8 CARDS)	.50	.75
COMMON CARD (1-90)	.10	.25
NNO J. K. Potter AU/1000*	20.00	50.00

1995 FPG J.K. Potter Metallic

COMPLETE SET (5)	8.00	20.00
COMMON CARD (M1-M5)	2.50	6.00
STATED ODDS 1:12		

2002 Joe 90 Limited Edition Previews

COMPLETE SET (6)	8.00	20.00
COMMON CARD (J1-J6)	2.00	5.00

2002 Joe 90 Memorabilia Previews

COMPLETE SET (6)	8.00	20.00
COMMON CARD (JMP1-JMP6)	2.00	5.00

1995 FPG Joe DeVito

COMPLETE SET (90)	4.00	10.00
UNOPENED BOX (36 PACKS)	15.00	20.00
UNOPENED PACK (8 CARDS)	.50	.75
COMMON CARD (1-90)	.08	.20
NNO Joe DeVito AU/1000*	20.00	50.00

1995 FPG Joe DeVito Metallic

COMPLETE SET (6)	15.00	40.00
COMMON CARD (M1-M6)	3.00	8.00
STATED ODDS 1:12		

1996 Joe Jusko's Colossal Cards

COMPLETE SET (100)	30.00	75.00
COMPLETE SERIES 1 SET (50)	20.00	50.00
COMPLETE SERIES 2 SET (50)	20.00	50.00
UNOPENED BOX (18 PACKS)	80.00	100.00
UNOPENED PACK (5 CARDS)	4.50	6.00
UNOPENED BOX (18 PACKS)	80.00	100.00
UNOPENED PACK (5 CARDS)	4.50	6.00
COMMON CARD (1-50)	.75	2.00
COMMON CARD (51-100)	.75	2.00

1994 FPG Joe Jusko's Edgar Rice Burroughs Collection

COMPLETE SET (60)	4.00	10.00
COMMON CARD (1-60)	.12	.30
NNO1 Joe Jusko AU		
NNO2 Joe Jusko Case Premium Insert AU		
NNO3 Uncut Sheet		

1994 FPG Joe Jusko's Edgar Rice Burroughs Collection Metallic Storm

COMPLETE SET (6)	15.00	40.00
COMMON CARD (MS1-MS6)	3.00	8.00
STATED ODDS 1:18		

1996 Donruss Joe's Apartment

COMPLETE SET (90)	5.00	12.00
UNOPENED BOX (36 PACKS)	30.00	40.00
UNOPENED PACK (7 CARDS+1 TATTOO)	1.00	1.25
COMMON CARD (1-90)	.10	.25
NNO Joe's Apartment 4UP Panel	1.25	3.00

1996 Donruss Joe's Apartment Temporary Tattoos

COMPLETE SET (9)	1.50	4.00
COMMON CARD (TAT1-TAT9)	.25	.60
STATED ODDS 1:1		

MODERN

1996 FPG John Berkey Series 2

COMPLETE SET (90)	5.00	12.00
UNOPENED BOX (36 PACKS)	30.00	40.00
UNOPENED PACK (10 CARDS)	1.00	1.25
COMMON CARD (1-90)	.12	.30
NNO1 John Berkey AU	20.00	50.00

1996 FPG John Berkey Series 2 Metallic

COMPLETE SET (5)	12.00	30.00
COMMON CARD (M1-M5)	3.00	8.00
STATED ODDS 1:12		

1994 FPG John Berkey Science Fiction Ultraworks

COMPLETE SET (90)	10.00	25.00
UNOPENED BOX (36 PACKS)	30.00	40.00
UNOPENED PACK (10 CARDS)	1.00	1.25
COMMON CARD (1-90)	.20	.50
NNO1 John Berkey AU/1000*	20.00	50.00
NNO2 Flying Legs Redemption Card		

1994 FPG John Berkey Science Fiction Ultraworks Metallic Storm

COMPLETE SET (5)	15.00	40.00
COMMON CARD (MS1-MS5)	4.00	10.00
*GOLD: .75X TO 2X BASIC CARDS	8.00	20.00
STATED ODDS 1:12		

1994 FPG John Berkey Science Fiction Ultraworks Promos

1 3-Up Panel		
2 Amphibian (card #3)	.75	2.00
3 Painted Space (card #10)	.75	2.00
4 Title Card	4.00	10.00

2019 Fright-Rags John Carpenter's Halloween

COMPLETE SET (78)	40.00	100.00
UNOPENED BOX (24 PACKS)	600.00	800.00
UNOPENED PACK (9 CARDS+1 STICKER)	30.00	40.00
COMMON CARD (1-78; CL)	.75	2.00
*PUMPKIN: 2X TO 5X BASIC CARDS		
PARALLEL #'s ARE 4, 14, 23, 31, 49, 52		

2019 Fright-Rags John Carpenter's Halloween Autographs

COMMON AUTO	75.00	150.00
STATED ODDS 1:120		
NNO Nick Castle	200.00	400.00
NNO PJ Soles	250.00	500.00

2019 Fright-Rags John Carpenter's Halloween Stickers

COMPLETE SET (9)	25.00	60.00
COMMON STICKER	5.00	12.00
STATED ODDS 1:1		

1994 TCM Associates John Deere

COMPLETE SET (100)	8.00	20.00
UNOPENED BOX (36 PACKS)	40.00	50.00
UNOPENED PACK (10 CARDS)	1.25	1.50
COMMON CARD (1-100)	.15	.40

2005 John Wayne

COMPLETE SET (72)	6.00	15.00
UNOPENED BOX (40 PACKS)	40.00	60.00
UNOPENED PACK (6 CARDS)	2.00	3.00
COMMON CARD (1-72)	.15	.40

2005 John Wayne Costumes

COMPLETE SET (6)	80.00	150.00
COMMON CARD (C1-C6)	12.00	30.00
STATED ODDS 1:80		

2005 John Wayne Favorite Hobbies

COMPLETE SET (4)	20.00	50.00
COMMON CARD (FH1-FH4)	6.00	15.00
STATED ODDS 1:160		

2005 John Wayne Hero's Hats Die-Cuts

COMPLETE SET (9)	15.00	40.00
COMMON CARD (HH1-HH9)	3.00	8.00
STATED ODDS 1:40		

2005 John Wayne Leading Roles Holofoil

COMPLETE SET (12)	15.00	40.00
COMMON CARD (LR1-LR12)	2.50	6.00
STATED ODDS 1:40		

2005 John Wayne Limited Edition Wood Collector's Box Distribution

COMPLETE SET (3)	8.00	20.00
COMMON CARD (JWT1-JWT3)	3.00	8.00
WOOD DISTRIBUTION SET EXCLUSIVE		

2005 John Wayne Promos

COMPLETE SET (5)		
COMMON CARD	.60	1.50

1992 Tuff Stuff Johnny Clem

COMPLETE SET (10)	5.00	12.00
COMMON CARD (1-10)	.60	1.50

2009 Jonas

COMPLETE SET (50)	6.00	15.00
UNOPENED BOX (24 PACKS)	25.00	40.00
UNOPENED PACK (5 CARDS+2 STICKERS)	1.50	2.00
COMMON CARD (1-50)	.25	.60

2009 Jonas Foil Puzzle Stickers

COMPLETE SET (10)	2.50	6.00
COMMON CARD (1-10)	.40	1.00
STATED ODDS 2:1		

1996 Upper Deck Jonny Quest

COMPLETE SET (60)	6.00	15.00
UNOPENED HOBBY BOX (36 PACKS)	40.00	60.00
UNOPENED HOBBY PACK (6 CARDS)	1.50	2.00
UNOPENED RETAIL BOX (48 PACKS)	15.00	30.00
UNOPENED RETAIL PACK (5 CARDS)	.50	.75
COMMON CARD (1-60)	.20	.50
P1 Coming in Fall '96 PROMO		

1996 Upper Deck Jonny Quest Action Quest Pop-Ups

COMPLETE SET (4)	4.00	10.00
COMMON CARD (AQ1-AQ4)	1.25	3.00
STATED ODDS 1:18		

1996 Upper Deck Jonny Quest Hadji's Clues Hobby

COMPLETE SET (10)	6.00	15.00
COMMON CARD (HC1-HC10)	.75	2.00
STATED ODDS 1:3		

1996 Upper Deck Jonny Quest Hadji's Clues Retail

COMPLETE SET (7)	4.00	10.00
COMMON CARD (HC1-HC7)	.75	2.00
STATED ODDS 1:5		

1996 Upper Deck Jonny Quest Quest Challenge

COMPLETE SET (10)	1.25	3.00
COMMON CARD (QC1-QC10)	.20	.50
STATED ODDS 1:2		

2008 Journey to the Center of the Earth 3-D

COMPLETE SET (50)	4.00	10.00
COMMON CARD (1-50)	.15	.40
CL1 ISSUED AS CASE EXCLUSIVE		
CL1 Underworld Adventure CL	3.00	8.00

2008 Journey to the Center of the Earth 3-D Challenging the Unknown

COMPLETE SET (6)	5.00	12.00
COMMON CARD (CU1-CU6)	1.50	4.00
STATED ODDS 1:17		

2008 Journey to the Center of the Earth 3-D Forgotten World Puzzle

COMPLETE SET (9)	4.00	10.00
COMMON CARD (FW1-FW9)	1.00	2.50
STATED ODDS 1:11		

2008 Journey to the Center of the Earth 3-D Pieceworks

COMMON CARD	6.00	15.00
STATED ODDS 1:24		
PW12A, B, AND C ISSUED AS DEALER INCENTIVE		
PW12A Sean T-Shirt MCI	8.00	20.00
PW12B Trevor Shirt MCI	8.00	20.00
PW12C Hannah T-Shirt MCI	8.00	20.00

2008 Journey to the Center of the Earth 3-D Prehistoric Peril

COMPLETE SET (3)	4.00	10.00
COMMON CARD (PR1-PR3)	2.50	6.00
STATED ODDS 1:24		

2008 Journey to the Center of the Earth 3-D Promos

P1 Trevor/Sean/Hannah GEN	.60	1.50
Pi Trevor/Sean/Hannah (inkworks.com excl.)	.75	2.00

1992 Eclipse JRR Tolkien The Hobbit

COMPLETE BOXED SET (36)	5.00	12.00

1995 Edge Judge Dredd Movie

COMPLETE SET (82)	5.00	12.00
UNOPENED BOX (36 PACKS)	15.00	20.00
UNOPENED PACK (8 CARDS)	.50	.75
COMMON CARD (1-82)	.12	.30

1995 Edge Judge Dredd Movie Boing Acetate

COMPLETE SET (4)	80.00	150.00
COMMON CARD (1-4)	15.00	40.00
RANDOMLY INSERTED INTO PACKS		

1995 Edge Judge Dredd Movie Brit-Cit Babes Silver

COMPLETE SET (9)	25.00	60.00
COMMON CARD (1-9)	3.00	8.00
*PRISMS: .5X TO 1.2X BASIC CARDS	4.00	10.00
RANDOMLY INSERTED INTO PACKS		

1995 Edge Judge Dredd Movie Promos

1 Judge Dredd	1.25	3.00
2 ABC War Robot	1.25	3.00
3 Mean Machine	1.25	3.00

1995 Edge Judge Dredd Movie Sleep of the Just

COMPLETE SET (9)	6.00	15.00
COMMON CARD (10-11)	.75	2.00
RANDOMLY INSERTED INTO PACKS		

1995 Edge Judge Dredd Movie Video Game Tips

COMPLETE SET (9)	10.00	25.00
COMMON CARD (1-9)	1.25	3.00
RANDOMLY INSERTED INTO PACKS		

1995 Edge Judge Dredd The Epics

COMPLETE SET (90)	5.00	12.00
UNOPENED BOX (36 PACKS)	30.00	40.00
UNOPENED PACK (8 CARDS)	1.00	1.25
COMMON CARD (1-90)	.10	.25
4PAN 4-Card Panel		

1995 Edge Judge Dredd The Epics Death Dimensions Black

COMPLETE SET (4)	12.00	30.00
COMMON CARD (1-4)	4.00	10.00
*PRISMS: 2X TO 5X BASIC CARDS	20.00	50.00
STATED ODDS 1:19		

1995 Edge Judge Dredd The Epics Legends Artwork

COMPLETE SET (13)	10.00	25.00
COMMON CARD (1-13)	1.25	3.00
STATED ODDS 1:10		

1995 Edge Judge Dredd The Epics Movie Previews

COMPLETE SET (3)	5.00	12.00
COMMON CARD (MP1-MP3)	2.00	5.00
STATED ODDS 1:15		

1995 Edge Judge Dredd The Epics Sleep of the Just

COMPLETE SET (9)	6.00	15.00
COMMON CARD (1-9)	.75	2.00
STATED ODDS 1:4		

1997 Comic Images Judgment Day

COMPLETE SET (72)	5.00	12.00
UNOPENED BOX (48 PACKS)	15.00	20.00
UNOPENED PACK (8 CARDS)	.50	.60
COMMON CARD (1-72)	.12	.30

1997 Comic Images Judgment Day Autographs

COMMON AUTO	20.00	50.00

1997 Comic Images Judgment Day Promos

COMPLETE SET (2)	1.25	3.00
COMMON CARD	.75	2.00

1994 Cardz Julie Bell

COMPLETE SET (46)	5.00	12.00
UNOPENED BOX (36 PACKS)	15.00	25.00
UNOPENED PACK (8 CARDS)	.75	1.00
COMMON CARD (1-45, C1)	.20	.50
P2AU Julie Bell AU	20.00	50.00

1994 Cardz Julie Bell Promos

P1 Demon in the Palace	.60	1.50
P2 Beauty and the Steel Beast	1.00	2.50

1994 Cardz Julie Bell Tekchrome

COMPLETE SET (10)	6.00	15.00
COMMON CARD (T1-T10)	.75	2.00
STATED ODDS 1:1		

1998 Comic Images Julie Strain Bettie 2000 Autographs

COMMON CARD	10.00	25.00
STATED PRINT RUN 500 SETS		

1998 Comic Images Julie Strain Bettie 2000 ClearChrome

COMPLETE SET (6)	12.00	30.00
COMMON CARD (1-6)	3.00	8.00
STATED ODDS 1:18		

1998 Comic Images Julie Strain Bettie 2000 Promos

COMPLETE SET (2)	1.50	4.00
COMMON CARD	1.00	2.50

1995 SkyBox Jumanji

COMPLETE SET (90)	5.00	12.00
UNOPENED BOX (36 PACKS)	25.00	40.00
UNOPENED PACK (8 CARDS)	1.25	1.50
COMMON CARD (1-90)	.10	.25

1995 SkyBox Jumanji Disappearing Ink

COMPLETE SET (6)	15.00	40.00
COMMON CARD (J1-J6)	3.00	8.00
STATED ODDS 1:18		

1995 SkyBox Jumanji Holograms

COMPLETE SET (4)	10.00	25.00
COMMON CARD (H1-H4)	3.00	8.00
STATED ODDS 1:12		

1995 SkyBox Jumanji Promos

S1 Alan on alligator	.75	2.00
T1 Sarah scared of spiders (Target Exclusive)	1.25	3.00

1992 Bassett Jurassic Park

COMPLETE SET (20)	2.00	5.00
COMMON CARD (1-20)	.20	.50

1993 Topps Jurassic Park

COMPLETE SET (154)	15.00	40.00
COMPLETE SET W/STICKERS (176)	20.00	50.00
COMPLETE SER.1 SET (88)	5.00	12.00
COMPLETE SER.2 SET (66)	10.00	25.00
COMP.SER.1 SET W/STICKERS (99)	6.00	15.00
COMP.SER.2 SET W/STICKERS (77)	12.00	30.00
UNOPENED SER.1 BOX (36 PACKS)	75.00	125.00
UNOPENED SER.1 PACK (8 CARDS+1 STICKER)	3.00	4.00
UNOPENED SER.2 BOX (36 PACKS)	75.00	125.00
UNOPENED SER.2 PACK (8 CARDS+1 STICKER)	3.00	4.00
COMMON CARD (1-88)	.10	.25
COMMON CARD (89-154)	.20	.50
*GERMAN: SAME VALUE		
NNO Silver Holograms Uncut Sheet		

1993 Topps Jurassic Park Action Holograms

COMPLETE SET (4)	8.00	20.00
COMMON CARD (1-4)	3.00	8.00
STATED ODDS 1:18		

1993 Topps Jurassic Park Puzzle Stickers

COMPLETE SET (11)	2.00	5.00
COMMON STICKERS (1-11)	.40	1.00
*GERMAN: SAME VALUE		
STATED ODDS 1:1		

1993 Topps Jurassic Park Stickers

COMPLETE SET (11)	1.50	4.00
COMMON STICKERS (1-11)	.20	.50
STATED ODDS 1:1		

1993 Topps Jurassic Park Gold

COMPLETE SET (88)	4.00	15.00
COMPLETE SET W/ART AND STICKERS (109)	10.00	25.00
UNOPENED BOX (36 PACKS)	65.00	80.00
UNOPENED PACK (9 CARDS)	2.25	2.50
COMMON CARD (1-88)	.10	.25

1993 Topps Jurassic Park Gold Action Holograms

COMPLETE SET (4)	2.00	5.00
COMMON CARD (1-4)	1.00	2.50
STATED ODDS 1:18		

1993 Topps Jurassic Park Gold Arts

COMPLETE SET (10)	2.00	5.00
COMMON CARD (1-10)	.40	1.00

1993 Topps Jurassic Park Gold Promos

COMPLETE SET (2)	2.00	5.00
COMMON CARD (1-2)	1.25	3.00

1993-94 Kenner Jurassic Park

COMMON CARD	4.00	10.00
INSERTED INTO KENNER ACTION FIGURES		

1997 Topps Jurassic Park The Lost World

COMPLETE SET (72)	5.00	12.00
COMPLETE SET W/STICKERS (83)	6.00	15.00
UNOPENED BOX (36 PACKS)	150.00	250.00
UNOPENED PACK (6 CARDS+1 STICKER)	4.00	6.00
COMMON CARD (1-72)	.12	.30
NNO Tyrannosaurus Rex PROMO	1.50	4.00

1997 Topps Jurassic Park The Lost World Stickers

COMPLETE SET (11)	1.50	4.00
COMMON CARD (1-11)	.20	.50
STATED ODDS 1:1		

1993 Topps Jurassic Park Raptor

COMPLETE SET (6)	8.00	20.00
COMMON CARD (1-6)	1.50	4.00

2001 Jurassic Park III 3-D

COMPLETE SET (72)	5.00	12.00
UNOPENED BOX (36 PACKS)	100.00	150.00
UNOPENED PACK (7 CARDS)	3.00	4.00
COMMON CARD (1-72)	.15	.40
M1 STATED ODDS 1:107		
CL1 ISSUED AS CASE TOPPER		
DFX1 STATED ODDS 1:8		
DFX2 STATED ODDS ONE PER HOBBY BOX		
M1 Mega Mayhem FOIL	6.00	15.00
CL1 Reptile Rumble CT	8.00	20.00
DFX1 3-D Viewer	.40	1.00
DFX2 3-D Glasses	.40	1.00

2001 Jurassic Park III 3-D Extreme

COMPLETE SET (9)	12.50	30.00
COMMON CARD (JE1-JE9)	1.50	4.00
STATED ODDS 1:11		

2001 Jurassic Park III 3-D Ragin' Refractors Blue

COMPLETE SET (6)	12.50	30.00
COMMON CARD (RR1-RR6)	2.50	6.00
OVERALL REFRACTOR ODDS 1:17		

2001 Jurassic Park III 3-D Promos

COMMON CARD	.75	2.00
JP34 Uk Distribution	1.50	4.00
JP3A Ames Distribution	1.25	3.00
JP3i Inkworkscards.com	1.25	3.00
JP3SD2001 SDCC 2001	2.00	5.00

2015 Jurassic World Best Buy Promos

COMPLETE SET (8)	6.00	15.00
COMMON CARD	1.50	4.00
ISLA NUBLAR BROCHURE/MAP	2.00	5.00

2015 Jurassic World Dog Tags

COMPLETE SET (24)	30.00	80.00
COMMON CARD (1-24)	2.00	5.00
*FOIL: .75X TO 2X BASIC TAGS		

2015 Jurassic World Dog Tags Costumes

COMMON CARD (C1-C10)	6.00	15.00
C2 Morton	10.00	25.00
C4 Lowery	12.00	30.00
C6 Owen	15.00	40.00
C7 Gray	25.00	60.00
C8 Claire	15.00	40.00
C10 Prop (ticket)	30.00	80.00

2015 Jurassic World Dog Tags Stickers

COMPLETE SET (24)	5.00	12.00
BASE STICKER (1-12)	.40	1.00
3-D STICKER (13-24)	.60	1.50
STATED ODDS 1:1		
2A Triceratops ERR "Sticke"	2.00	5.00

2015 Jurassic World Vudu Pizza Promos

COMPLETE SET (8)	15.00	40.00
COMMON CARD	2.00	5.00
2 Indominus Rex	5.00	12.00
5 Tyrannosaurus Rex 1	3.00	8.00
6 Tyrannosaurus Rex 2 (roar)	3.00	8.00
7 Velociraptor 1	3.00	8.00
8 Velociraptor 2	3.00	8.00

2018 Jurassic World Fallen Kingdom

COMPLETE SET (39)	8.00	20.00
UNOPENED BOX (24 PACKS)		
UNOPENED PACK (7 CARDS)		
COMMON CARD (1-39)	.40	1.00

2018 Jurassic World Fallen Kingdom 3-D Action

COMPLETE SET (9)	6.00	15.00
COMMON CARD (1-9)	1.25	3.00
RANDOMLY INSERTED INTO PACKS		

2018 Jurassic World Fallen Kingdom Costumes

COMMON MEM	3.00	8.00
STATED ODDS 1:24		
C1 Chris Pratt	10.00	25.00
C2 Bryce Dallas Howard	15.00	40.00
C4 Daniella Pineda	20.00	50.00
C6 Chris Pratt	12.00	30.00

2018 Jurassic World Fallen Kingdom Dinos

COMPLETE SET (15)	5.00	12.00
COMMON CARD (1-15)	.50	1.25
RANDOMLY INSERTED INTO PACKS		

2018 Jurassic World Fallen Kingdom Glow-in-the-Dark

COMPLETE SET (9)	4.00	10.00
COMMON CARD (1-9)	.75	2.00
RANDOMLY INSERTED INTO PACKS		

2018 Jurassic World Fallen Kingdom Heat 'N Reveal

COMPLETE SET (9)	4.00	10.00
COMMON CARD (1-9)	.75	2.00
RANDOMLY INSERTED INTO PACKS		

2018 Jurassic World Fallen Kingdom Dog Tags

COMPLETE SET W/SP (48)	75.00	150.00
COMPLETE SET W/O SP (24)	20.00	50.00
COMMON CARD (1-24)	1.50	4.00
COMMON FOIL SP (25-48)	3.00	8.00

2018 Jurassic World Fallen Kingdom Dog Tags 3-D Stickers

COMPLETE SET (12)	6.00	15.00
COMMON CARD (1-12)	.75	2.00
STATED ODDS 1:1		

2018 Jurassic World Fallen Kingdom Dog Tags Costume Tags

COMMON TAG	8.00	20.00
STATED ODDS 1:24		
C1 Chris Pratt/Shirt	12.00	30.00
C2 Bryce Dallas Howard/Pants	15.00	40.00
C3 Daniella Pineda/Shirt	25.00	60.00
C5 Rafe Spall/Shirt	10.00	25.00
C7 Bryce Dallas Howard/Shirt	15.00	40.00

2001 Just a Pilgrim Previews

COMPLETE BOXED SET (7)	8.00	20.00
COMMON CARD (1-7)	1.50	4.00

2011 Justin Bieber 2.0

COMPLETE SET (131)	25.00	50.00
COMP.SET w/o SP's (100)	15.00	30.00
COMMON CARD (10-109)	.20	.50
COMMON SP (1-9,110-131)	.75	2.00
*HOLOKOTE: 1.5X TO 4X BASIC CARDS		
AU1 Justin Bieber AU	250.00	400.00

2011 Justin Bieber 2.0 Relics

COMPLETE SET (3)	50.00	100.00
COMMON CARD (I1-I3)	15.00	40.00

2011 Justin Bieber 2.0 Stickers

COMPLETE SET (30)	7.50	15.00
COMMON CARD (1-30)	.40	1.00

2011 Justin Bieber 2.0 Wide Scream

COMPLETE SET (16)	12.00	25.00
COMMON CARD	1.25	3.00

1996 Donruss Kazaam

COMPLETE SET (90)	5.00	12.00
UNOPENED BOX (48 PACKS)	150.00	250.00
UNOPENED PACK (10 CARDS)	6.00	10.00
COMMON CARD (1-90)	.12	.30

1996 Donruss Kazaam Foil Embossed

COMPLETE SET (9)	12.00	30.00
COMMON CARD (F1-F9)	1.50	4.00
STATED ODDS 1:9		

1994 FPG Keith Parkinson

COMPLETE SET (90)	5.00	12.00
UNOPENED BOX (36 PACKS)	30.00	40.00
UNOPENED PACK (10 CARDS)	1.00	1.25
COMMON CARD (1-90)	.12	.30
BC Life on the Edge Binder Card (Album Exclusive)	3.00	8.00
NNO1 Keith Parkinson AU/1000*	15.00	40.00
NNO2 Keith Parkinson Panel AU	25.00	60.00

1994 FPG Keith Parkinson Metallic Storm

COMPLETE SET (5)	12.00	30.00
COMMON CARD (MS1-MS5)	4.00	10.00

1994 FPG Keith Parkinson Promos

COMPLETE SET (4)	4.00	10.00
COMMON CARD	1.25	3.00
4 4-Up Panel	2.00	5.00

1996 FPG Keith Parkinson Colossal

COMPLETE SET (50)	20.00	50.00
UNOPENED BOX (18 PACKS)	15.00	25.00
UNOPENED PACK (5 CARDS)	1.00	1.50
COMMON CARD (1-50)	.75	2.00

1996 FPG Keith Parkinson Colossal Autographs

COMPLETE SET (50)	1000.00	1800.00
COMMON CARD (1-50)	15.00	40.00
STATED ODDS 1:18		

1994 Comic Images Ken Barr The Beast Within

COMPLETE SET (90)	4.00	10.00
UNOPENED BOX (48 PACKS)	20.00	30.00
UNOPENED PACK (10 CARDS)	.50	.75
COMMON CARD (1-90)	.08	.20
NNO1 Ken Barr AU/500		40.00
NNO2 Medallion Card/1104	8.00	20.00

1994 Comic Images Ken Barr The Beast Within Foils

COMPLETE SET (6)	12.00	25.00
COMMON CARD (F1-F6)	2.50	6.00
STATED ODDS 1:16		

1994 Comic Images Ken Barr The Beast Within Promos

COMPLETE SET (2)	2.00	5.00
COMMON CARD	1.25	3.00

1994 Comic Images Ken Barr The Beast Within Vampires Subset

COMPLETE SET (3)	8.00	20.00
COMMON CARD (1-3)	3.00	8.00
STATED ODDS 1:192		

1993 FPG Ken Kelly

COMPLETE SET (90)	5.00	12.00
UNOPENED BOX (36 PACKS)	15.00	25.00
UNOPENED PACK (10 CARDS)	.50	.75
COMMON CARD (1-90)	.12	.30
B1 Album excl. Card	2.00	5.00
AUKK Ken Kelly AU/1000	15.00	40.00

1993 FPG Ken Kelly Holograms

COMPLETE SET (3)	6.00	15.00
COMMON CARD (1-3)	2.50	6.00
RANDOM INSERTS IN PACKS		

1994 FPG Ken Kelly 2

COMPLETE SET (90)	6.00	15.00
UNOPENED BOX (36 PACKS)	30.00	40.00
UNOPENED PACK (10 CARDS)	1.00	1.25
COMMON CARD (1-90)	.10	.25
AUKK Ken Kelly AU/1000*	12.50	35.00
NNO1 The Enraged King (1985 - album excl.)	4.00	10.00

1994 FPG Ken Kelly 2 Metallic Storm

COMPLETE SET (5)	8.00	20.00
COMMON CARD (MS1-MS5)	2.00	5.00
STATED ODDS 1:12		

1994 FPG Ken Kelly 2 Promos

COMMON CARD 1.25 3.00
NNO Warrior Above a Pile of Skulls 2 1/2x7 3.00 8.00
(Rhode Island Collector's Expo Exclusive)
NNO Barbarian Choking Monster 6.00 15.00
(Capital City Exclusive)

1995 FPG Ken Kelly Colossal

COMPLETE SET (50) 20.00 50.00
UNOPENED BOX (18 PACKS) 65.00 80.00
UNOPENED PACK (5 CARDS) 3.00 4.00
COMMON CARD (1-50) .75 2.00

1995 FPG Ken Kelly Colossal Autographs

COMPLETE SET (50) 1000.00 1800.00
COMMON CARD (1-50) 15.00 40.00
STATED ODDS 1:18

1996 FPG Ken Kelly Stickers

COMPLETE SET (50) 6.00 15.00
COMMON CARD (1-50) .25 .60
NNO Ken Kelly Sticker AU/500* 20.00 50.00

1996 FPG Ken Kelly Stickers Promos

COMPLETE SET (20) 25.00 60.00
COMMON CARD 1.50 4.00

2016 Killer Babes

COMPLETE SET (25) 6.00 15.00
COMMON CARD .30 .75

1988 Killer Cards 1st Series

COMPLETE FACTORY SET (46) 6.00 15.00
COMMON CARD (1-46) .25 .60

1989 Killer Cards 2nd Series

COMPLETE SET (45) 5.00 12.00
COMMON CARD (1-45) .20 .50

2016 Killer Dudes

COMPLETE SET (25) 6.00 15.00
COMMON CARD .30 .75

1994 Cardz Killzone Promos

P1 Galaxinovels will change the way you look at superheros 1.50 4.00
P2 What would you say if you could get full-page illustrations... 1.50 4.00

1993 Eclipse King Kong

COMPLETE SET (110) 5.00 12.00
UNOPENED BOX (36 PACKS) 20.00 30.00
UNOPENED PACK (12 CARDS) 1.00 1.25
COMMON CARD (1-110) .10 .25
E1 King Kong Embossed Insert 5.00 12.00
NNO Uncut Sheet 20.00 50.00
Proto1 Birth of a Legend PROMO 4.00 10.00

2005 King Kong Movie

COMPLETE SET (80) 5.00 12.00
UNOPENED BOX (24 PACKS) 35.00 50.00
UNOPENED PACK (7 CARDS) 1.50 2.50
COMMON CARD (1-80) .15 .40

2005 King Kong Movie Autographs

COMMON CARD 4.00 10.00
STATED ODDS 1:24 HOBBY
1 Colin Hanks 12.00 30.00
3 Jamie Bell 15.00 40.00
4 Kyle Chandler 12.00 30.00

2005 King Kong Movie Blister Bonus

COMPLETE SET (3) 1.25 3.00
COMMON CARD (B1-B3) .75 2.00
STATED ODDS 1:1 BLISTER PACK EXCLUSIVE

2005 King Kong Movie Embossed Foil

COMPLETE SET (10) 6.00 15.00
COMMON CARD (1-10) 1.00 2.50
STATED ODDS 1:6 RETAIL PACKS

2005 King Kong Movie Flocked

COMPLETE SET (5) 5.00 12.00
COMMON CARD (1-5) 1.25 3.00
STATED ODDS 1:8

2005 King Kong Movie Memorabilia

COMPLETE SET (7) 100.00 200.00
COMMON CARD 15.00 30.00
STATED ODDS 1:24 HOBBY
1 Ann Darrow's Dressing Gown 25.00 50.00
2 Ann Darrow's Dressing Room Dress 20.00 40.00
3 Ann Darrow's Film Dress 20.00 40.00

2005 King Kong Movie Stickers

COMPLETE SET (10) 4.00 12.00
COMMON CARD (1-10) .75 2.00
STATED ODDS 1:4 RETAIL PACKS EXCLUSIVE

2005 King Kong Movie Tin Bonus

COMPLETE SET (12) 50.00 100.00
COMMON CARD (1-6) 5.00 12.00
COMMON CARD (A-F) 5.00 12.00
STATED ODDS 2:TIN

2005 King Kong Movie Video Game Creatures

COMPLETE SET (5) 8.00 20.00
COMMON CARD (C1-C5) 2.00 5.00
STATED ODDS 1:4 HOBBY PACKS EXCLUSIVE

2005 King Kong Movie Promos

P1 Kong GEN 1.00 2.50
P2 Kong NSU 1.50 4.00

1996 SkyBox Kingdom Come Xtra

COMPLETE SET (50) 8.00 20.00
UNOPENED BOX (36 PACKS) 50.00 60.00
UNOPENED PACK (6 CARDS) 1.50 1.75
COMMON CARD (1-50) .30 .75
NNO1 Alex Ross/Mark Wade Dual AU
NNO2 Superman Flying PROMO .60 1.50

1996 SkyBox Kingdom Come Xtra Alex Ross Autographs

COMPLETE SET (50) 3000.00 5000.00
COMMON CARD (1-50) 60.00 120.00
STATED ODDS 1:180

1996 SkyBox Kingdom Come Xtra Creator Collection

COMPLETE SET (6) 8.00 20.00
COMMON CARD (1-6) 1.50 4.00
STATED ODDS 1:9

1996 SkyBox Kingdom Come Xtra Kingdom Classics

COMPLETE SET (3) 8.00 20.00
COMMON CARD (KC1-KC3) 3.00 8.00
STATED ODDS 1:9

1996 SkyBox Kingdom Come Xtra Mark Wade Autographs

COMPLETE SET (50) 3000.00 5000.00
COMMON CARD (1-50) 60.00 120.00
STATED ODDS 1:180

1996 SkyBox Kingdom Come Xtra Sketchboards

COMPLETE SET (16) 2.50 6.00
COMMON CARD (1-15, S16) .20 .50
STATED ODDS 1:1

1997-98 Cornerstone KISS

COMPLETE SET (180) 15.00 40.00
UNOPENED SER.1 BOX (36 PACKS)
UNOPENED SER.1 PACK (9 CARDS)
UNOPENED SER.2 BOX (36 PACKS)
UNOPENED SER.2 PACK (9 CARDS)
COMMON CARD (1-180) .15 .40
*GOLD SEAL: X TO X BASIC CARDS
*GS BLUE: X TO X BASIC CARDS
*GS RED: 1X TO 2.5X BASIC CARDS .40 1.00

1997-98 Cornerstone KISS Foil Gold

COMPLETE SET (8)
*GOLD: X TO X BASIC CARDS
STATED ODDS 1:

1997-98 Cornerstone KISS Promos

COMPLETE SET (11)
COMMON CARD
P1 Promo 1 .60 1.50
P2 Promo 2 .60 1.50
P3 Promo 3 .60 1.50
P4 Promo 4 .60 1.50
P5 The KISS Years 2.00 5.00
(insert with photo book)
P6 (Dealer promo) .60 1.50
P7 NSU 1.25 3.00
P8 (Collect!)
P9 (Combo) .75 2.00
P10 Musicland/Sam Goody/Media Play
UNC1 Uncut Promo Sheet/10

1997-98 Cornerstone KISS Promos II

COMPLETE SET (3) 3.00 8.00
COMMON CARD (P1-P3) .75 2.00
P2 shout it out loud!! 1.50 4.00
P3 The KISS Years book (reprint) 2.50 6.00

2009 KISS 360

COMPLETE SET (90) 12.00 30.00
UNOPENED BOX (24 PACKS) 45.00 60.00
UNOPENED PACK (5 CARDS) 2.00 3.00
COMMON CARD (1-90) .15 .40
*BLUE KISS: .3X TO .8X BASIC CARDS
*BLOOD-SPITTING: 8X TO 20X BASIC CARDS
*DR. LOVE/50: 20X TO 50X BASIC CARDS
*$/50: 30X TO 80X BASIC CARDS
*KISSED/25: 50X TO 120X BASIC CARDS

2009 KISS 360 KISSignatures

STATED PRINT RUN 99 SER. #'d SETS
QUAD AUTO STATED PRINT RUN 5 SER. #'d SETS
QUAD AUTO UNPRICED DUE TO SCARCITY
AF Ace Frehley 150.00 250.00
GS Gene Simmons 200.00 300.00
PC Peter Criss 150.00 250.00
PS Paul Stanley 175.00 300.00
KISS Paul/Gene/Ace/Peter/5

2009 KISS 360 Rock Star Relics

COMPLETE SET (6) 200.00 400.00
COMMON CARD 25.00 60.00
*SILVER FOIL/99: .5X TO 1.2X BASIC RELICS
*RED FOIL/25: 1.2X TO 3X BASIC RELICS
STATED ODDS 1:90
EC Eric Carr Drumheads 60.00 120.00
GSPS G.Simmons Pants/P.Stanley Jmpst 60.00 120.00

2009 KISS 360 Snapshots

COMPLETE SET (12) 12.00 30.00
COMMON CARD (SS1-SS12) 1.25 3.00
STATED ODDS 1:6

2009 KISS 360 Transformations

COMPLETE SET (6) 12.00 30.00
COMMON CARD (TF1-TF6) 2.50 6.00
STATED ODDS 1:12

2001 KISS Alive

COMPLETE SET (72) 5.00 12.00
UNOPENED BOX (36 PACKS) 20.00 40.00
UNOPENED PACK (7 CARDS) 1.00 1.50
COMMON CARD (1-72) .12 .30
NNO KISS Alive Box Topper Card 1.50 4.00

2001 KISS Alive Gold Records

COMPLETE SET (25) 50.00 100.00
COMMON CARD (A1-A25) 2.00 5.00
STATED ODDS 1:12

2009 KISS Ikons

COMPLETE SET (90) 8.00 20.00
COMMON CARD (1-90) .15 .40
*BLUE KISS: .3X TO .8X BASIC CARDS
*BLOOD-SPITTING: 8X TO 20X BASIC CARDS
*FIRE-BREATHING: 40X TO 100X BASIC CARDS
*KISSED: 40X TO 100X BASIC CARDS
INSTANT WIN CARDS TOTAL PRINT RUN OF 100
NNO Instant Win. Autograph Gene EXCH 150.00 250.00
NNO Instant Win. Autograph Paul EXCH 150.00 250.00

2009 KISS Ikons Klothes

COMPLETE SET (2) 25.00 60.00
COMMON CARD (KK1-KK2) 15.00 40.00
STATED ODDS 1:96

2009 KISS Ikons Klothes Die-Cuts

COMMON CARD 30.00 80.00
K STATED PRINT RUN 249 SER. #'d SETS
I STATED PRINT RUN 149 SER. #'d SETS
S STATED PRINT RUN 99 SER. #'d SETS
KK1i Gene Simmons Pants - I 50.00 100.00
KK1s Gene Simmons Pants - S 75.00 150.00
KK2i Gene Simmons Jumpsuit - I 50.00 100.00
KK2s Gene Simmons Jumpsuit - S 75.00 150.00

2009 KISS Ikons Stickers

COMPLETE SET (12) 3.00 8.00
COMMON CARD (1-12) .40 1.00
STATED ODDS 1:2

2009 KISS Ikons Tattoos

COMPLETE SET (18) 5.00 12.00
COMMON CARD (1-18) .40 1.00
STATED ODDS 1:4 H, 1:2 R

2010 Legend of KISS

COMPLETE SET (100) 8.00 20.00
COMMON CARD (1-100) .15 .40
*BLACK: 4X TO 10X BASIC CARDS
*FIRST EDITION/33: 15X TO 40X BASIC CARDS
*BLUE/25: 20X TO 50X BASIC CARDS

2010 Legend of KISS KISSignatures

KSAF Ace Frehley/30 200.00 300.00
KSGS Gene Simmons/30 250.00 350.00
KSPC Peter Criss/35 200.00 300.00
KSPS Paul Stanley/30 200.00 300.00

2010 Legend of KISS Pop-Ups

COMPLETE SET (6) 5.00 12.00
COMMON CARD (PU1-PU6) 1.00 2.50
STATED ODDS 1:6
PU1 Gene Simmons 2.00 5.00
PU2 Paul Stanley 1.50 4.00
PU3 Peter Criss 1.50 4.00
PU4 Ace Frehley 1.50 4.00

2010 Legend of KISS Rockstar Relics

COMMON CARD 25.00 50.00
*HOLOFOIL/99: .5X TO 1.2X BASIC CARDS
*GOLD/25: .8X TO 2X BASIC CARDS (360-425)
*GOLD/25: .6X TO 1.5X BASIC CARDS (122-160)
OVERALL RELICS ODDS 1:90
PRINT RUN B/WN 122-425
RREC E.Carr Drum/122 30.00 60.00
RRGS Simmons Costume/160 30.00 60.00

2010 KISS Rock Tags

COMPLETE SET (24) 30.00 80.00
COMMON CARD (1-24) 1.50 4.00
*RAINBOW: .75X TO 2X BASIC TAGS

2010 KISS Rock Tags Stickers

COMPLETE SET (24) 8.00 20.00
COMMON CARD (1-24) .60 1.50
STATED ODDS 1:1

1999 Cornerstone KISS Series 3 Promos

COMMON CARD (P1-P2) 5.00 12.00
P2 Arriving Summer 1999 10.00 25.00

2019 KISS Ultra Premium

COMPLETE SET (18) 20.00 50.00
UNOPENED BOX (12 PACKS)
UNOPENED PACK (7 CARDS)
COMMON CARD (1-18) 1.50 4.00

2019 KISS Ultra Premium Autographs

COMMON AUTO (1-14)
STATED ODDS 1:1

1 Gene Simmons	125.00	250.00
2 Gene Simmons		
3 Paul Stanley	100.00	200.00
4 Paul Stanley	100.00	200.00
6 Anthony Marques	15.00	40.00
9 Kyle Strahm	15.00	40.00
10 Rodney Buchemi	15.00	40.00
11 Michael Adams	12.00	30.00
12 Kewber Baal	15.00	40.00

2019 KISS Ultra Premium Box-Toppers

COMPLETE SET (2)	50.00	100.00
COMMON CARD (1-2)	25.00	60.00
STATED ODDS 1:1		

2019 KISS Ultra Premium Pencil Art Concepts

COMPLETE SET (12)	8.00	20.00
COMMON CARD (1-12)	1.25	3.00
STATED ODDS 1:1		

2019 KISS Ultra Premium Puzzle

COMPLETE SET (9)	12.00	30.00
COMMON CARD (1-9)	2.00	5.00
STATED ODDS 1:1		

1983 Donruss Knight Rider

COMPLETE SET (55)	10.00	20.00
COMMON CARD (1-55)	.30	.75

1991 KSAS Nightmare

COMPLETE SET (25)	5.00	12.00
COMMON CARD (1-25)	.40	1.00

2008 Kung Fu Panda

COMPLETE SET (50)	5.00	12.00
COMMON CARD (1-50)	.15	.40

2008 Kung Fu Panda Masters of Kung Fu

COMPLETE SET (8)	8.00	20.00
COMMON CARD (M1-M8)	1.50	4.00
STATED ODDS 1:9		

2008 Kung Fu Panda Sparkly Stickers

COMPLETE SET (9)	2.00	5.00
COMMON CARD (S1-S9)	.30	.75
STATED ODDS 1:1		

2008 Kung Fu Panda True Warriors Die-Cuts

COMPLETE SET (6)	6.00	15.00
COMMON CARD (T1-T6)	1.25	3.00
STATED ODDS 1:5		

2008 Kung Fu Panda Promos

COMPLETE SET (4)	5.00	12.00
COMMON CARD	1.25	3.00
Pi Palms Together	2.00	5.00
H2007 Holiday Wishes Die-Cut	2.00	5.00

2011 Kung Fu Panda 2

COMPLETE SET (90)	8.00	20.00
COMMON CARD (1-90)	.15	.40

2011 Kung Fu Panda 2 Pop-Ups

COMPLETE SET (9)	4.00	10.00
COMMON CARD (1-9)	.60	1.50
STATED ODDS 1:2		

2011 Kung Fu Panda 2 Puzzle Foil

COMPLETE SET (9)	4.00	10.00
COMMON CARD (PZ1-PZ9)	.75	2.00
STATED ODDS 1:2		

2011 Kung Fu Panda 2 Tattoos

COMPLETE SET (10)	3.00	8.00
COMMON CARD	.50	1.25
STATED ODDS 1:1		

1994 Krome Lady Death

COMPLETE SET (100)	12.00	30.00
UNOPENED BOX (36 PACKS)	85.00	100.00
UNOPENED PACK (6 CARDS)	2.50	3.00
COMMON CARD (1-100)	.25	.60
1MC Mystery Card ClearChrome	6.00	15.00
C4 Bonus Mystery Card	.25	.60
NNO Brian Pulido and Steven Hughes AU/1500*	10.00	25.00
PROMO1 Update PROMO	.75	2.00

1994 Krome Lady Death Clearchrome Bonus

COMPLETE SET (5)	12.00	30.00
COMMON CARD (1-5)	4.00	10.00
*NECROCHROME: .5X TO 1.2X BASIC CARDS		
STATED ODDS 1:12		

1995 Krome Lady Death

COMPLETE SET (100)	10.00	25.00
UNOPENED BOX (36 PACKS)	70.00	80.00
UNOPENED PACK (8 CARDS)	2.25	2.50
COMMON CARD (1-100)	.20	.50
M1 Lady Death II Mystery Chase Card	5.00	12.00
NNO Pullido and Hughes AU	20.00	50.00

1995 Krome Lady Death Clearchrome

COMPLETE SET (5)	12.00	30.00
COMMON CARD (C1-C5)	3.00	8.00
RANDOMLY INSERTED INTO PACKS		

1995 Krome Lady Death Tryptic Chase

COMPLETE SET (3)	8.00	20.00
COMMON CARD (T1-T3)	3.00	8.00
RANDOMLY INSERTED INTO PACKS		
T1 Lady Death II Tryptic Chase Card 1	3.00	8.00
T2 Lady Death II Tryptic Chase Card 2	3.00	8.00
T3 Lady Death II Tryptic Chase Card 3	3.00	8.00

1995 Krome Lady Death Promos

COMMON CARD	1.25	3.00
NNO Sword in Left Hand	5.00	12.00
SPC1 Sword in Left Hand	4.00	10.00
SPC2 Hands on Knees	6.00	15.00
ESPC1 Head Shot, Fire in Back	10.00	25.00
ESPC1 On Horse, Capital	8.00	20.00
ESPC2 On Horse, Capital	4.00	10.00
ESPC2 Black and White, Standing in Water	6.00	15.00

1996 Krome Lady Death

COMPLETE SET (90)	10.00	25.00
UNOPENED BOX (36 PACKS)	70.00	80.00
UNOPENED PACK (6 CARDS)	2.25	2.50
COMMON CARD (1-90)	.20	.50
*BLACK MASK: .75X TO 2X BASIC CARDS	.40	1.00
*BL.MASK HOLO: 3X TO 8X BASIC CARDS	1.50	4.00
*BL.MASK FRAC: 3X TO 8X BASIC CARDS	1.50	4.00
*CLEARCHROME: 5X TO 12X BASIC CARDS	2.50	6.00
*FRACTAL: 5X TO 12X BASIC CARDS	2.50	6.00
*HOLOCHROME: 5X TO 12X BASIC CARDS	2.50	6.00

1996 Krome Lady Death Fractal Chromium

COMPLETE SET (6)	25.00	60.00
COMMON CARD (C1-C6)	5.00	12.00
STATED ODDS 1:12		

1996 Krome Lady Death Oversized

COMPLETE SET (5)	15.00	40.00
COMMON CARD (O1-O5)	4.00	10.00
STATED ODDS 1:BOX		

1997 Krome Lady Death Previews

COMPLETE SET (7)	8.00	20.00
COMMON CARD	1.50	4.00

2001 Lady Death and the Women of Chaos Love Bites

COMPLETE SET (72)	8.00	20.00
UNOPENED BOX (36 PACKS)	40.00	50.00
UNOPENED PACK (7 CARDS)	1.25	1.50
COMMON CARD (1-72)	.25	.60
NNO Brian Pulido AU/500*	8.00	20.00

2001 Lady Death and the Women of Chaos Love Bites Luscious Ladies of Chaos

COMPLETE SET (6)	6.00	15.00
COMMON CARD (C1-C6)	1.25	3.00
STATED ODDS 1:12		

1998 JPP Amada Lady Death Covenant Holofoil

COMPLETE SET (90)	12.00	30.00
UNOPENED BOX (24 PACKS)	30.00	40.00
UNOPENED PACK (6 CARDS)	1.50	1.75
COMMON CARD (1-90)	.30	.75
NNO LD in Black Leather PROMO	1.25	3.00

1998 JPP Amada Lady Death Covenant Holofoil Chaos Comics

COMPLETE SET (9)	15.00	40.00
COMMON CARD (C1-C9)	3.00	8.00
STATED ODDS 1:6		

1998 JPP Amada Lady Death Covenant Holofoil Evil Ernie

COMPLETE SET (9)	12.00	30.00
COMMON CARD (E1-E9)	2.50	6.00
RANDOMLY INSERTED INTO PACKS		

2002 Lady Death Dark Alliance

COMPLETE SET (72)	4.00	10.00
UNOPENED BOX (36 PACKS)	30.00	40.00
UNOPENED PACK (7 CARDS)	1.00	1.25
COMMON CARD (1-72)	.12	.30

2002 Lady Death Dark Alliance Autographs

1 Brian Pulido	4.00	10.00
2 David Michael Beck	8.00	20.00
3 Romano Molenaar	6.00	15.00

1999 Comic Images Lady Death Night Gallery Gold MetalTex

COMPLETE SET (6)	20.00	50.00
COMMON CARD (C1-C6)	5.00	12.00
RANDOMLY INSERTED INTO PACKS		

1999 Comic Images Lady Death Night Gallery Promos

NNO Graveyard in background	1.50	4.00
NNO Lady Death on red bed	1.50	4.00

1993 Chaos Comics Lady Death The Reckoning

NNO Comic Promo/15000*	2.00	5.00

1997 Krome Lady Death Wicked Ways

COMPLETE SET (90)	10.00	25.00
UNOPENED BOX (36 PACKS)	40.00	50.00
UNOPENED PACK (6 CARDS)	1.25	1.50
COMMON CARD (1-90)	.20	.50
*REFRACTOR: 1X TO 2.5X BASIC CARDS	.50	1.25

1997 Krome Lady Death Wicked Ways Fractal Chromium

COMPLETE SET (6)	15.00	40.00
COMMON CARD (1-6	4.00	10.00
STATED ODDS 1:12		

1997 Krome Lady Death Wicked Ways Promos

PROMO1 With Skeleton	1.25	3.00
PROMO2 With Skeleton (Refractor)	4.00	10.00

1991 Impel Laffs

COMPLETE SET (80)	3.00	8.00
UNOPENED BOX (36 PACKS)	8.00	10.00
UNOPENED PACK (8 CARDS)		
COMMON CARD (1-80)	.08	.20

1991 Impel Laffs Promos

COMPLETE SET (5)	1.50	4.00
COMMON CARD	.40	1.00

1994 FPG Larry Elmore

COMPLETE SET (90)	6.00	15.00
UNOPENED BOX (36 PACKS)	70.00	80.00
UNOPENED PACK (10 CARDS)	2.25	2.50
COMMON CARD (1-90)	.12	.30

1994 FPG Larry Elmore Autographs

10UP 10UP Panel (CI)		
AULE Larry Elmore AU/1000	15.00	40.00
UNC1 Full Uncut Sheet/500		

1994 FPG Larry Elmore Metallic Storm

COMPLETE SET (5)	12.00	30.00
COMMON CARD (MS1-MS5)	4.00	10.00
RANDOMLY INSERTED INTO PACKS		

1995 FPG Larry Elmore Colossal

COMPLETE SET (50)	20.00	50.00
UNOPENED BOX (18 PACKS)	40.00	50.00
UNOPENED PACK (5 CARDS)	2.50	2.75
COMMON CARD (1-50)	.75	2.00

1995 FPG Larry Elmore Colossal Autographs

COMPLETE SET (50)	200.00	400.00
COMMON CARD (1-50)	4.00	10.00
RANDOMLY INSERTED INTO PACKS		

1993 Topps Last Action Hero

COMPLETE SET (88)	3.00	8.00
COMPLETE SET W/STICKERS (99)	4.00	10.00
UNOPENED BOX (36 PACKS)	15.00	20.00
UNOPENED PACK (8 CARDS+1 STICKER)	.50	.75
COMMON CARD (1-88)	.08	.20

1993 Topps Last Action Hero Holofoils

COMPLETE SET (4)	8.00	20.00
COMMON CARD (1-4)	2.50	6.00
STATED ODDS 1:12		

1993 Topps Last Action Hero Stickers

COMPLETE SET (11)	.75	2.00
COMMON CARD (1-11)	.15	.40
STATED ODDS 1:1		

1993 Topps Last Action Hero Promos

1 Jack and Danny	.75	2.00
2 Last Action Hero movie ticket	.75	2.00

2001 Laurel and Hardy Millennium 2000

COMPLETE SET (72)	10.00	25.00
COMMON CARD (1-72)	.30	.75
STATED ODDS 1:		
B2 (No Info)	3.00	8.00
P1 The Boys in Bathing Suits PROMO	2.50	6.00
NNO Lenticular Card		

2001 Laurel and Hardy Millennium 2000 Dame's Gallery

COMPLETE SET (3)	5.00	12.00
COMMON CARD (DG1)	2.00	5.00
STATED ODDS 1:		

2001 Laurel and Hardy Millennium 2000 Villains Gallery

COMPLETE SET (3)	5.00	12.00
COMMON CARD (VG1-VG3)	2.00	5.00
STATED ODDS 1:		

2001 Laurel and Hardy Millennium 2000 Redemption

COMPLETE SET (6)	10.00	25.00
COMMON CARD	2.50	6.00
STATED ODDS 1:		

1997 RiverWye Productions Laurel and Hardy Premier Collection

COMPLETE SET (90)	8.00	20.00
COMMON CARD (1-90)	.20	.50
B1 70th Anniversary	2.50	6.00
NNO StanleyMotion Insert	10.00	25.00

1997 RiverWye Productions Laurel and Hardy Premier Collection Gold Foil-Stamped Signatures

COMPLETE SET (3)	6.00	15.00

COMMON CARD (S1-S3) 2.50 6.00
RANDOMLY INSERTED INTO PACKS

1997 RiverWye Productions Laurel and Hardy Premier Collection Mini-Posters

COMPLETE SET (4) 4.00 10.00
COMMON CARD (MP1-MP4) 1.50 4.00
STATED ODDS 1:

1997 RiverWye Productions Laurel and Hardy Premier Collection Redemptions

COMPLETE SET (3) 5.00 12.00
COMMON CARD (R1-R3) 2.00 5.00
STATED ODDS 1:

1997 RiverWye Productions Laurel and Hardy Premier Collection Promos

COMMON CARD 1.25 3.00
NNO Stan and Ollie Pop-Up Card 4.00 10.00

2016 Leaf Live

COMPLETE SET (10)
COMMON CARD (1-10)
1 In Memory of Gene Wilder/233* 6.00 15.00
6 Hillary Clinton vs. Donald Trump/181* 5.00 12.00
8 Harambe/243* 6.00 15.00
9 John Cusack 3.00 8.00

2020 Leaf Metal American Politics

COMPLETE SET (10) 75.00 150.00
UNOPENED BOX SET (10 CARDS) 150.00 200.00
COMMON CARD (PE01-PE10) 8.00 20.00
*CRYSTAL SILVER/35: .5X TO 1.2X BASIC CARDS
*RAINBOW BLUE/25: .75X TO 2X BASIC CARDS
STATED PRINT RUN 50 SER.#'d SETS
PE01 Alexandria Ocasio-Cortez 10.00 25.00
PE02 Barack Obama 12.00 30.00
PE03 Donald J. Trump 12.00 30.00
PE05 Ivanka Trump 10.00 25.00
PE08 Kayleigh McEnany 10.00 25.00

1989 CaliCo Graphics League of Nations

COMPLETE SET (18) 2.00 5.00
COMMON CARD (1-18) .25 .60

1990 CaliCo Graphics League of Nations

COMPLETE SET (54) 4.00 10.00
COMMON CARD (1-54) .15 .40

1983 Pacific Leave It to Beaver

COMPLETE SET (60) 15.00 40.00
UNOPENED BOX (36 PACKS) 250.00 300.00
UNOPENED PACK (10 CARDS) 8.00 10.00
COMMON CARD (1-60) .50 1.25

1994 Cardz Lee MacLeod

COMPLETE SET (50) 5.00 12.00
UNOPENED BOX (24 PACKS) 15.00 25.00
UNOPENED PACK (8 CARDS) 1.00 1.25
COMMON CARD (1-50) .20 .50

1994 Cardz Lee MacLeod Autographs

COMMON CARD 8.00 20.00
STATED ODDS 1:576

1994 Cardz Lee MacLeod Promos

COMPLETE SET (2) 1.00 2.50
COMMON CARD .60 1.50

1994 Cardz Lee MacLeod TekChromes

COMPLETE SET (10) 6.00 12.50
COMMON CARD (T1-T10) 1.00 2.50
STATED ODDS 1:1

1993 Majestic Entertainment Legacy

COMPLETE SET (150) 6.00 15.00
UNOPENED BOX (36 PACKS) 15.00 25.00
UNOPENED PACK (9 CARDS) .50 .75
COMMON CARD (1-150) .08 .20
NNO1 The Protector knew he was dying (album excl)

1993 Majestic Entertainment Legacy Dyna-tech

COMPLETE SET (9) 15.00 40.00
COMMON CARD (1-9) 2.00 5.00
STATED ODDS 1:18

1993 Majestic Entertainment Legacy STAT Ashcan Promos

COMPLETE SET (9) 3.00 8.00
COMMON CARD (1-9) .40 1.00
STATED ODDS 1:5

2016 The Legend of Zelda

COMPLETE SET (108) 30.00 80.00
COMPLETE SET W/O FOIL (90) 8.00 20.00
UNOPENED BOX (24 PACKS) 50.00 60.00
UNOPENED PACK (CARDS) 2.50 3.00
COMMON CARD (1-90) .15 .40
COMMON FOIL (91-108) 2.00 5.00

2016 The Legend of Zelda Decals

COMPLETE SET (12) 8.00 20.00
COMMON CARD (D1-D12) 1.00 2.50

2016 The Legend of Zelda Gold Foil

COMPLETE SET (9) 100.00 200.00
COMMON CARD (G1-G9) 4.00 10.00
STATED ODDS 1:
G1 Link 6.00 15.00
G3 The Skull Kid 8.00 20.00
G4 Yuga 6.00 15.00
G5 Ganondorf 15.00 40.00
(box-topper)
G6 Majora's Mask 20.00 50.00
(box-topper)
G7 Zant 30.00 80.00
(box-topper)
G8 Ghirahim 12.00 30.00
(box-topper)

2016 The Legend of Zelda Tattoos

COMPLETE SET (9) 5.00 12.00
COMMON CARD (1-9) 1.00 2.50
STATED ODDS 1:1

2007 Legend of Zelda Twilight Princess

COMPLETE SET (50) 10.00 25.00
UNOPENED BOX (24 PACKS) 250.00 400.00
UNOPENED PACK (7 CARDS) 10.00 15.00
COMMON CARD (1-50) .30 .75

2007 Legend of Zelda Twilight Princess Gold Foil

COMPLETE SET (9) 250.00 500.00
COMMON CARD (G1-G9) 12.00 30.00
STATED ODDS 1:24
G1 Dark Lord: Ganondorf 60.00 120.00
G3 Ganon's Puppet: Zelda 30.00 80.00
G4 Queen Rutela 30.00 80.00
G7 Great Fairy 50.00 100.00
G9 Great Spirit 50.00 100.00

2007 Legend of Zelda Twilight Princess Silver Foil

COMPLETE SET (27) 10.00 25.00
COMMON CARD (S1-S27) .75 2.00
STATED ODDS 1:1

2007 Legend of Zelda Twilight Princess Tattoos

COMPLETE SET (4) 3.00 8.00
COMMON CARD (1-4) 1.00 2.50
STATED ODDS 1:1

2005 Legend of Zorro Promos

COMPLETE SET (5) 3.00 8.00
COMMON CARD 1.00 2.50

2014 Legendary Lovecraft

COMPLETE SET (66) 6.00 15.00
COMMON CARD (1-66) .15 .40

2014 Legendary Lovecraft Mythical Monsters Foil

COMPLETE SET (6) 8.00 20.00
COMMON CARD (MM1-MM6) 2.50 5.00
STATED ODDS 1:4

2014 Legendary Lovecraft Sacred Souvenier Relics

COMPLETE SET (3) 8.00 20.00
COMMON CARD (1-3) 3.00 8.00
STATED ODDS 1:8

1991 Victoria Gallery Legends of Hollywood

COMPLETE SET (20) 5.00 12.00
COMMON CARD (1-20) .50 1.25
P1 John Wayne (promo) 1.25 3.00

2017 LEGO Create the World

COMPLETE SET (140) 10.00 25.00
COMMON CARD (1-140) .15 .40

2019 LEGO Movie 2

COMPLETE SET (36) 15.00 40.00
UNOPENED BOX
UNOPENED PACK (4 CARDS) 3.50 5.00
COMMON CARD (1-36) .75 2.00
1 Batman RED FOIL 1.25 3.00
2 Emmet FOIL 1.25 3.00
10 Lucy FOIL 1.25 3.00
15 Benny FOIL 1.25 3.00
16 Rex FOIL 1.25 3.00
19 Sweet Mayhem FOIL 1.25 3.00
22 Unikitty FOIL 1.25 3.00
28 Queen Watevra Wa-Nabi FOIL 1.25 3.00

2015-21 Headmistress Press Lesbian Poets

COMPLETE SET 25.00 60.00
SERIES 1 SET (12) 6.00 15.00
SERIES 2 SET (12) 6.00 15.00
SERIES 3 SET (12) 6.00 15.00
SERIES 4 SET (12) 6.00 15.00
SERIES 5 SET (12)
SERIES 6 SET (12)
SERIES 7 SET (12)
SERIES 1 (1-12) 1.00 2.50
SERIES 2 (13-24) 1.00 2.50
SERIES 3 (25-36) 1.00 2.50
SERIES 4 (37-48) 1.00 2.50
SERIES 5 (49-60)
SERIES 6 (61-72)
SERIES 7 (73-84)

2002 Lethal Ladies Lady Death Medieval Witchblade

COMPLETE SET (72) 4.00 10.00
UNOPENED BOX (36 PACKS) 40.00 50.00
UNOPENED PACK (7 CARDS) 1.25 1.50
COMMON CARD (1-72) .12 .30

2002 Lethal Ladies Lady Death Medieval Witchblade Artist's Proofs Autographs

COMMON AUTO (A1-A2) 8.00 20.00

2002 Lethal Ladies Lady Death Medieval Witchblade Autographs

COMMON CARD (A1-A8) 4.00 10.00
STATED ODDS 1:18
A1 Romano Molenaar/500* 6.00 15.00
A2 Roy Young/500* 6.00 15.00
A3 Brian Pulido/500* 6.00 15.00
A4 Curtis Arnold/500* 8.00 20.00

2002 Lethal Ladies Lady Death Medieval Witchblade Reflectors

COMPLETE SET (6) 10.00 25.00
COMMON CARD (C1-C6) 2.00 5.00
STATED ODDS 1:12

1997 Krome Lethal Strike

COMPLETE SET (35) 6.00 15.00
UNOPENED CARD BOX (20 PACKS)
UNOPENED CARD PACK (4 CARDS+1 STICKER)
UNOPENED STICKER BOX (20 PACKS)
UNOPENED STICKER PACK (4 STICKERS+1 CARD)
COMMON CARD (1-35) .25 .60
*CHROMIUM: .6X TO 1.5X BASIC CARDS .40 1.00
*HOLOCHROME: .6X TO 1.5X BASIC CARDS .40 1.00
*STICKERS: .6X TO 1.5X BASIC CARDS .40 1.00
1 Twisted Sisters .25 .60
2 Death Kiss .25 .60
3 Stryke of Lightning .25 .60
4 Cool Kill .25 .60
5 Attack .25 .60
6 Assassins Kiss .25 .60
7 Dive into Danger .25 .60
8 Cloud of Death .25 .60
9 Steady and Swift .25 .60
10 Vanity of Vengeance .25 .60
11 Bullseye .25 .60
12 One Woman Weapon .25 .60
13 Warrior of the Game .25 .60
14 Ace up the Sleeve .25 .60
15 Loner .25 .60
16 Vondrake .25 .60
17 Dead On .25 .60
18 In the Line of Fire .25 .60
19 All in the Family .25 .60
20 High Velocity .25 .60
21 Slumber Party .25 .60
22 Eternal Love .25 .60
23 Loaded and Lace .25 .60
24 Sexy Sleuth .25 .60
25 Dragons Kiss .25 .60
26 Naked Danger .25 .60
27 Blasting Bitch .25 .60
28 Look That Kills .25 .60
29 Greco .25 .60
30 Holding Steady .25 .60
31 Slice by Slice .25 .60
32 Come and Get It. .25 .60
33 Bang. Youre Dead .25 .60
34 Night Moves .25 .60
35 Lethal Strike Check List .25 .60

2021 Levi's 501 Originals

COMMON CARD (1-7, NNO)
*RED/50: .6X TO 1.2X BASIC CARDS
1 Barbie Ferreira 15.00 40.00
2 Emma Chamberlain 150.00 300.00
3 Hailey Bieber 150.00 300.00
4 Jaden Smith 15.00 40.00
NNO Checklist
(Ferreira/Chamberlain/Bieber/Smith/Rashford/Osaka/Gilgeous-Alexander)

2021 Levi's 501 Originals Autographed Relics

STATED PRINT RUN 15 SER.#'d SETS
2 Emma Chamberlain
3 Hailey Bieber

2021 Levi's 501 Originals Autographs

STATED PRINT RUN 50 SETS
2 Emma Chamberlain
3 Hailey Bieber 300.00 600.00

2021 Levi's 501 Originals Relics

1 Barbie Ferreira 125.00 250.00

2002 Lexx

COMPLETE SET (72) 5.00 12.00
UNOPENED BOX (40 PACKS)
UNOPENED PACK (6 CARDS)
COMMON CARD (1-72) .12 .30
NNO Uncut Sheet/400*

2002 Lexx Box-Toppers

COMPLETE SET (6) 6.00 15.00
COMMON CARD (1-6) 1.25 3.00
STATED ODDS 1:BOX

2002 Lexx Costumes
1 Xenia Seeberg as Xev Hands on Hips/19980.00 150.00
2 Xenia Seeberg as Xev Kicking
3 Xenia Seeberg as Xev Standing

2002 Lexx Rainbow Chrome
COMPLETE SET (6) 6.00 15.00
COMMON CARD (C1-C2) 1.25 3.00
STATED ODDS 1:12

2002 Lexx Promos
COMPLETE SET (4) 2.00 5.00
COMMON CARD .75 2.00

1994 Lift Off Promo
NNO America's Spirit of Adventure 4.00 10.00

1994 Photographic Concepts Lighthouses of Yesteryear
COMPLETE SET (50) 3.00 8.00
COMMON CARD (1-50) .10 .25

2021 Topps Lil Wayne Tha Carter IV 10th Anniversary Set
COMPLETE SET (20) 10.00 25.00
UNOPENED BOX (8 CARDS)
COMMON CARD (1-20) 1.25 3.00
*RAINBOW FOIL/10: 20X TO 50X BASIC CARDS

1992 Freedom Press Lincoln Assassination
COMPLETE BOXED SET (40) 6.00 15.00
COMMON CARD (1-40) .30 .75

1994 SkyBox The Lion King
COMPLETE SET (170) 8.00 20.00
COMPLETE SER.1 SET (90) 5.00 12.00
COMPLETE SER.2 SET (81) 4.00 10.00
UNOPENED SER.1 BOX (36 PACKS) 10.00 20.00
UNOPENED SER.1 PACK (8 CARDS) .50 .75
UNOPENED SER.1 JUMBO BOX (24 PACKS)50.00 60.00
UNOPENED SER.1 JUMBO PACK (16 CARDS)2.00 2.50
UNOPENED SER.2 BOX (36 PACKS) 10.00 20.00
UNOPENED SER.2 PACK (8 CARDS) .50 .75
UNOPENED SER.2 JUMBO BOX (24 PACKS)30.00 40.00
UNOPENED SER.2 JUMBO PACK (16 CARDS)1.00 1.25
COMMON CARD (1-90) .10 .25
COMMON CARD (91-170) .08 .20

1994 SkyBox The Lion King Activity
COMPLETE SET (5) 2.50 6.00
STATED ODDS 1 PER WALMART PACK
A1 Crossword Puzzle .75 2.00
A2 Connect the Dots .75 2.00
A3 Word Scramble .75 2.00
A4 Help Pumbaa Find His Favorite Food .75 2.00
A5 Find the Hidden Names .75 2.00

1994 SkyBox The Lion King Color-Ins
COMPLETE SET (5) 2.50 6.00
COMMON CARD (C1-C5) .75 2.00

1994 SkyBox The Lion King Embossed Foil
COMPLETE SET (9) 12.00 30.00
COMMON CARD (F1-F9) 3.00 8.00
STATED ODDS 1:12

1994 SkyBox The Lion King Foil Border
COMPLETE SET (2) 10.00 25.00
COMMON CARD (FB1-FB2) 6.00 15.00
STATED ODDS 1:90 HOBBY; 1:200 WALMART

1994 SkyBox The Lion King Lenticular Holograms
COMPLETE SET (2) 12.00 30.00
COMMON CARD (L1-L2) 8.00 20.00
STATED ODDS 1:180
L1 I Never Get To Go Anywhere 8.00 20.00
L2 Future King of the Jungle 8.00 20.00

1994 SkyBox The Lion King Pop-Ups
COMPLETE SET (10) 12.00 30.00
COMMON CARD SER.1 AND 2 (P1-P10) 2.50 6.00
STATED ODDS 1:24 HOBBY; 1:50 WALMART

1994 SkyBox The Lion King Thermographic
COMPLETE SET (9) 12.00 30.00
COMMON CARD (T1-T9) 2.00 5.00
STATED ODDS 1:9 HOBBY; 1:20 WALMART

1994 SkyBox The Lion King Promos
COMMON CARD .75 2.00
SB1 1994 Super Bowl Exclusive 250.00 400.00

1994 AMC Coca-Cola The Lion King Promos
COMPLETE SET (16) 6.00 15.00
COMMON CARD (1-16) .75 2.00
AMC THEATER EXCLUSIVES

1994 SkyBox The Lion King Australian Promos
COMMON CARD 8.00 20.00

1998 DuoCards Lionel Greatest Trains
COMPLETE SET (72) 6.00 15.00
UNOPENED BOX (36 PACKS) 20.00 30.00
UNOPENED PACK (7 CARDS) 1.00 1.25
COMMON CARD (1-72) .15 .40

1998 DuoCards Lionel Greatest Trains OmniChrome
COMPLETE SET (6) 10.00 25.00
COMMON CARD (1-6) 2.00 5.00
STATED ODDS 1:15

1998 DuoCards Lionel Greatest Trains Promos
COMPLETE SET (2) 1.25 3.00
COMMON CARD .75 2.00

1997 DuoCards Lionel Legendary Trains
COMPLETE SET (72) 5.00 12.00
UNOPENED BOX (30 PACKS) 30.00 40.00
UNOPENED PACK (7 CARDS) 1.00 1.25
COMMON CARD (1-72) .12 .30

1997 DuoCards Lionel Legendary Trains Chromium
COMPLETE SET (6) 12.00 30.00
COMMON CARD (C1-C6) 2.50 6.00
STATED ODDS 1:15

1997 DuoCards Lionel Legendary Trains Promos
COMPLETE SET (2) 1.50 4.00
COMMON CARD 1.00 2.50

1999 DuoCards Lionel Legendary Trains Centennial
COMPLETE SET (72) 8.00 20.00
UNOPENED BOX (30 PACKS) 40.00 50.00
UNOPENED PACK (7 CARDS) 1.25 1.50
COMMON CARD (1-72) .25 .60

1999 DuoCards Lionel Legendary Trains Centennial Gold MetalTex
COMPLETE SET (6) 15.00 40.00
COMMON CARD (C1-C6) 3.00 8.00
STATED ODDS 1:12

1999 DuoCards Lionel Legendary Trains Centennial Promos
COMPLETE SET (2) 1.25 3.00
COMMON CARD (PR1-PR2) .75 2.00

1991 Pro Set The Little Mermaid
COMPLETE SET (90) 2.00 5.00
FACTORY SET 10.00 25.00
UNOPENED BOX (36 PACKS) 15.00 25.00
UNOPENED PACK (8 CARDS) 1.00 1.50
COMMON CARD (1-90) .07 .20

1991 Pro Set The Little Mermaid Color-In Cards
COMPLETE SET (15) 2.00 5.00
COMMON CARD (1-15) .25 .60
RANDOMLY INSERTED INTO PACKS

1991 Pro Set The Little Mermaid Sponge
COMPLETE SET (6) 1.25 3.00
COMMON CARD (1-6) 4.00 1.00

1991 Pro Set The Little Mermaid Stand-Up
COMPLETE SET (15) 4.00 10.00
COMMON CARD (1-15) .50 1.25

1991 Pro Set The Little Mermaid Stick 'Ems
COMPLETE SET (7) 2.00 5.00
COMMON CARD (1-7) .50 1.25
STATED ODDS 1:5

1991 Pro Set The Little Mermaid Promos
NNO Little Mermaid Pop-Up Promo 30.00 75.00
NNO Little Mermaid Cello Pack Promo

1997 Upper Deck The Little Mermaid
COMPLETE SET (90) 6.00 15.00
UNOPENED BOX (24 PACKS) 20.00 30.00
UNOPENED PACK (7 CARDS) 1.25 1.50
COMMON CARD (1-90) .20 .50
*GOLD: 2X TO 5X BASIC CARDS 1.00 2.50

1997 Upper Deck Little Mermaid Lenticular
COMPLETE SET (5) 25.00 60.00
COMMON CARD (L1-L5) 6.00 15.00
STATED ODDS 1:23

1997 Upper Deck Little Mermaid Stick-Ums
COMPLETE SET (21) 12.00 30.00
COMMON CARD .75 2.00

1986 Topps Little Shop of Horrors
COMPLETE SET (44) 5.00 12.00
UNOPENED BOX (36 PACKS) 35.00 50.00
UNOPENED PACK (5 STICKERS) 1.00 2.00
COMMON STICKER (1-44) .20 .50

2009 Littlest Pet Shop
COMPLETE SET W/O INSERTS (54) 4.00 10.00
COMPLETE SET W/INSERTS (117) 12.00 30.00
UNOPENED BOX (24 PACKS) 40.00 50.00
UNOPENED PACK (4 CARDS) 2.00 2.25
COMMON CARD (1-54) .10 .25

2018 LOL Surprise!
COMPLETE SET (63) 10.00 25.00
UNOPENED BOX (24 PACKS)
UNOPENED PACK (14 CARDS)
COMMON CARD (1-63) .25 .60

2018 LOL Surprise! Foil
COMPLETE SET (9) 5.00 12.00
COMMON CARD (1-9) 1.00 2.50
RANDOMLY INSERTED IN SPECIAL PACK

2018 LOL Surprise! Glitter
COMPLETE SET (9) 6.00 15.00
COMMON CARD (1-9) 1.25 3.00
RANDOMLY INSERTED IN SPECIAL PACK

2018 LOL Surprise! Gold Inserts
COMPLETE SET (9) 6.00 15.00
COMMON CARD (1-9) 1.25 3.00
RANDOMLY INSERTED IN SPECIAL PACK

2018 LOL Surprise! Pop-Up Cards
COMPLETE SET (9) 5.00 12.00
COMMON CARD (1-9) .75 2.00
RANDOMLY INSERTED IN SPECIAL PACK

2010 Lombardi The Broadway Play
COMPLETE SET (7) 4.00 10.00
COMMON CARD (L1-L7) .75 2.00

1997 Dart FlipCards The Lone Ranger
COMPLETE SET (72) 6.00 15.00
UNOPENED BOX (30 PACKS) 30.00 40.00
UNOPENED PACK (7 CARDS) 1.25 1.50
COMMON CARD (1-72) .15 .40

1997 Dart FlipCards The Lone Ranger Die-Cuts
COMPLETE SET (6) 15.00 40.00
COMMON CARD (DC1-DC6) 3.00 8.00
STATED ODDS 1:15

1997 Dart FlipCards The Lone Ranger The Twelve Unpublish
COMPLETE SET (13) 15.00 40.00
COMMON CARD (49-60, NNO) 2.00 5.00
STATED ODDS 1:CASE

1997 Dart FlipCards The Lone Ranger Promos
COMMON CARD .75 2.00
2 Collectors International, Montreal 2.00 5.00
NNO Philadelphia NS Cards Show 2.00 5.00
Proto Non-Sport Update 1996 Gummies Awards2.00 5.00

1984 WTW Productions '40 Lone Ranger Reprints
COMPLETE SET (48) 8.00 20.00
COMMON CARD (1-48) .30 .75

2003 Looney Tunes Back in Action
COMPLETE SET (72) 5.00 12.00
UNOPENED BOX (36 PACKS) 50.00 60.00
UNOPENED PACK (6 CARDS) 1.75 2.00
COMMON CARD (1-72) .15 .40

2003 Looney Tunes Back in Action Acme Cards
COMPLETE SET (6) 6.00 15.00
COMMON CARD (A1-A6) 1.25 3.00
STATED ODDS 1:17

2003 Looney Tunes Back in Action Autographs
COMPLETE SET (8)
COMMON AUTO (A1-A8) 6.00 15.00
STATED ODDS 1:36
A1 Brendan Fraser 150.00 400.00
A2 Jenna Elfman 20.00 50.00
A3 Steve Martin 125.00 250.00
A4 Heather Locklear 60.00 120.00
A5 Bill Goldberg 50.00 100.00

2003 Looney Tunes Back in Action Box-Loaders
COMPLETE SET (3) 2.50 6.00
COMMON CARD (BL1-BL3) 1.00 2.50
STATED ODDS ONE PER BOX
CL1 STATED ODDS ONE PER CASE
CL1 To the Duck Cave 6.00 15.00

2003 Looney Tunes Back in Action Official Looney Tunes Tours
COMPLETE SET (9) 6.00 15.00
COMMON CARD (LTT1-LTT9) .75 2.00
STATED ODDS 1:11

2003 Looney Tunes Back in Action Wooden Nickel Casino Chips
COMPLETE SET (4) 60.00 120.00
COMMON CARD 25.00 50.00
STATED ODDS ONE CHIP AND HOLDER PER CASE

2003 Looney Tunes Back in Action Promos
COMPLETE SET (4) 3.00 8.00
COMMON CARD 1.00 2.50

1996 Upper Deck Looney Tunes OlympiCards

COMPLETE SET (45) 6.00 15.00
UNOPENED BOX (PACKS)
UNOPENED PACK (CARDS)
COMMON CARD (1-45) .20 .50

1996 Upper Deck Looney Tunes OlympiCards Go for the Gold Scratchers

COMPLETE SET (5) 4.00 10.00
COMMON CARD (GG1-GG5) 1.25 3.00
STATED ODDS 1:7

Lord of the Rings Universe

2001 Topps Lord of the Rings Fellowship of the Ring

COMPLETE SET (90) 5.00 12.00
UNOPENED HOBBY BOX (36 PACKS) 1000.00 1500.00
UNOPENED HOBBY PACK (8 CARDS) 30.00 40.00
UNOPENED RETAIL BOX (24 PACKS) 125.00 150.00
UNOPENED RETAIL PACK (8 CARDS) 7.00 8.00
COMMON CARD (1-90) .15 .40

2001 Topps Lord of the Rings Fellowship of the Ring Autographs

COMMON AUTO 50.00 100.00
HOBBY STATED ODDS 1:24
RETAIL STATED ODDS 1:72
SEAN BEAN AUTO UK HOBBY ONLY
NNO Cate Blanchett H 250.00 600.00
NNO Christopher Lee R 300.00 750.00
NNO Dominic Monaghan R 600.00 1500.00
NNO Elijah Wood H 150.00 400.00
NNO Hugo Weaving R 250.00 600.00
NNO John Rhys-Davies H 150.00 400.00
NNO Liv Tyler H 200.00 500.00
NNO Orlando Bloom R 400.00 1000.00
NNO Sean Bean UK 100.00 250.00
NNO Sir Ian McKellen H 1000.00 2500.00
NNO Viggo Mortensen H 125.00 250.00

2001 Topps Lord of the Rings Fellowship of the Ring Box-Loaders

COMPLETE SET (2) 8.00 20.00
COMMON CARD 5.00 12.00
STATED ODDS ONE PER BOX

2001 Topps Lord of the Rings Fellowship of the Ring Prismatic

COMPLETE SET (10) 7.50 20.00
COMMON CARD 1.00 2.50
STATED ODDS 1:6

2001 Topps Lord of the Rings Fellowship of the Ring Stickers

COMPLETE SET (10) 7.50 20.00
COMMON STICKER 1.00 2.50
RANDOM INSERTS IN RETAIL PACKS

2002 Lord of the Rings Fellowship of the Ring Update

COMPLETE SET (72) 5.00 12.00
UNOPENED BOX (36 PACKS) 40.00 50.00
UNOPENED PACK (7 CARDS) 1.25 1.50
COMMON CARD (91-162) .15 .40

2002 Lord of the Rings Fellowship of the Ring Update Memorabilia

COMPLETE SET (8) 500.00 750.00
COMMON MEM 50.00 100.00
GROUP A STATED ODDS 1:45
GROUP B STATED ODDS 1:180
NNO Arwen's Riding Outfit B 75.00 150.00
NNO Bilbo's Rivendell Waistcoat B 60.00 120.00
NNO Frodo's Elven Nightshirt B 60.00 120.00

2002 Lord of the Rings Two Towers

COMPLETE SET (90) 6.00 15.00
UNOPENED HOBBY BOX (36 PACKS) 200.00 300.00
UNOPENED HOBBY PACK (7 CARDS) 6.00 8.00
UNOPENED RETAIL BOX (24 PACKS) 40.00 50.00
UNOPENED RETAIL PACK (7 CARDS) 1.25 1.50
COMMON CARD (1-90) .15 .40

2002 Lord of the Rings Two Towers Autographs

COMMON AUTO 40.00 100.00
GROUP A STATED ODDS 1:45 H, 1:158 R
GROUP B STATED ODDS 1:232 H, 1:804 R
GROUP C STATED ODDS 1:518 H, 1:1796 R
GROUP D STATED ODDS ONE PER CASE
2 Billy Boyd A 50.00 120.00
3 Cate Blanchett A 150.00 400.00
4 Christopher Lee A 200.00 500.00
7 Dominic Monaghan B 125.00 250.00
8 Elijah Wood A 150.00 400.00
9 Karl Urban A 60.00 150.00
10 Liv Tyler A 150.00 400.00
11 Miranda Otto C 100.00 200.00
12 Orlando Bloom B 300.00 750.00
13 Peter Jackson A 300.00 750.00
14 Sean Astin A 50.00 120.00

2002 Lord of the Rings Two Towers Prismatic

COMPLETE SET (10) 8.00 20.00
COMMON CARD 1.25 3.00
STATED ODDS 1:6

2003 Lord of the Rings Two Towers Update

COMPLETE SET (72) 5.00 12.00
UNOPENED BOX (36 PACKS) 200.00 300.00
UNOPENED PACK (7 CARDS) 6.00 8.00
COMMON CARD (1-72) .15 .40

2003 Lord of the Rings Two Towers Update Autographs

COMMON AUTO 60.00 150.00
STATED ODDS 1:113
NNO Sean Bean 100.00 200.00
NNO Viggo Mortensen 125.00 300.00

2003 Lord of the Rings Two Towers Update Memorabilia

COMPLETE SET (9) 150.00 300.00
COMMON MEM 12.00 30.00
STATED ODDS 1:33
NNO Arwen's Requiem Cloak 30.00 80.00
NNO Eowyn's Underfrock 15.00 40.00

2003 Lord of the Rings Return of the King

COMPLETE SET (90) 5.00 12.00
UNOPENED HOBBY BOX (36 PACKS) 250.00 400.00
UNOPENED HOBBY PACK (7 CARDS) 8.00 12.00
UNOPENED RETAIL BOX (24 PACKS) 50.00 60.00
UNOPENED RETAIL PACK (7 CARDS) 2.00 2.50
COMMON CARD (1-90) .15 .40

2003 Lord of the Rings Return of the King Autographs

COMMON AUTO 20.00 50.00
STATED ODDS 1:36 H, 1:122 R
NNO Andy Serkis 60.00 150.00
NNO Bernard Hill 40.00 100.00
NNO Billy Boyd 50.00 100.00
NNO Bret McKenzie 30.00 75.00
NNO Christopher Lee SP 300.00 750.00
NNO David Wenham 30.00 75.00
NNO Ian Holm 50.00 120.00
NNO John Noble 25.00 60.00
NNO Karl Urban 50.00 120.00
NNO Lawrence Makoare 30.00 75.00
NNO Liv Tyler 150.00 400.00
NNO Sean Astin 60.00 150.00
NNO Viggo Mortensen 150.00 400.00

2003 Lord of the Rings Return of the King Box-Loaders

COMPLETE SET (2) 1.50 4.00
COMMON CARD 1.00 2.50
STATED ODDS ONE PER BOX

2003 Lord of the Rings Return of the King Prismatic

COMPLETE SET (10) 8.00 20.00
COMMON CARD (1-10) 1.25 3.00
STATED ODDS 1:6

2004 Lord of the Rings Return of the King Update

COMPLETE SET (72) 5.00 12.00
UNOPENED BOX (36 PACKS) 200.00 350.00
UNOPENED PACK (7 CARDS) 6.00 10.00
COMMON CARD (91-162) .15 .40

2004 Lord of the Rings Return of the King Update Autographs

COMMON AUTO 15.00 40.00
AUTO/MEM COMBINED ODDS 1:36
NNO Peter Jackson 1000.00 2500.00

2004 Lord of the Rings Return of the King Update Memorabilia

COMMON MEM 6.00 15.00
AUTO/MEM COMBINED ODDS 1:36
NNO Aragorn's Coronation Shirt 25.00 60.00
NNO Arwen's Coronation Dress 12.00 30.00
NNO Elrond's Bronze Silk Robe 12.00 30.00
NNO Eowyn's Coronation Dress 8.00 20.00
NNO Eowyn's Golden Hall Party Dress 10.00 25.00
NNO Frodo's Grey Havens Vest 50.00 100.00
NNO The Witch-King's Cloak 8.00 20.00

2002 Lord of the Rings Action Flipz Rare

COMPLETE SET (6) 8.00 20.00
COMMON CARD (R1-R6) 2.00 5.00
STATED ODDS 1:6

2002 Lord of the Rings Action Flipz Chromium Stickers

COMPLETE SET (24) 6.00 15.00
COMMON CARD (1-24) .40 1.00
STATED ODDS 1:2

2002 Lord of the Rings Action Flipz Ultra-Rare

COMPLETE SET (3) 8.00 20.00
COMMON CARD (UR1-UR3) 3.00 8.00
STATED ODDS 1:24

2002 Lord of the Rings Action Flipz Promos

COMPLETE SET (8) 10.00 25.00
COMMON CARD 1.50 4.00
ci1 The Fellowship BT 2.00 5.00
ci2 Ringwraiths BT 2.00 5.00

2006 Lord of the Rings Evolution

COMPLETE SET (72) 5.00 12.00
UNOPENED HOBBY BOX (24 PACKS) 400.00 600.00
UNOPENED HOBBY PACK (6 CARDS) 12.00 25.00
UNOPENED RETAIL BOX (24 PACKS) 30.00 40.00
UNOPENED RETAIL PACK (6 CARDS) 1.75 2.00
COMMON CARD (1-72) .15 .40

2006 Lord of the Rings Evolution A Uncommon

COMPLETE SET (20) 8.00 20.00
COMMON CARD (1A-20A) .75 2.00
STATED ODDS 1:4

2006 Lord of the Rings Evolution B Rare

COMPLETE SET (12) 20.00 40.00
COMMON CARD (1B-12B) 2.50 6.00
STATED ODDS 1:12

2006 Lord of the Rings Evolution Memorabilia

COMMON MEM 8.00 20.00
STATED ODDS 1:24 RETAIL
1 Arwen's Nightgown 25.00 50.00
2 Frodo's Travel Cloak 10.00 25.00
3 Galadriel's Grey Havens Cloak 10.00 25.00
4 Gandalf the White's Cloak 20.00 40.00
5 Gandalf the White's Shirt 12.00 30.00

2006 Lord of the Rings Evolution Stained Glass

COMPLETE SET (10) 8.00 20.00
COMMON CARD (S1-S10) 1.25 3.00
STATED ODDS 1:6

2006 Lord of the Rings Masterpieces

COMPLETE SET (90) 5.00 12.00
UNOPENED BOX (36 PACKS) 300.00 500.00
UNOPENED PACK (7 CARDS) 10.00 15.00
COMMON CARD (1-90) .15 .40

2006 Lord of the Rings Masterpieces Etched Foil

COMPLETE SET (6) 6.00 15.00
COMMON CARD (1-6) 1.25 3.00
STATED ODDS 1:6

2006 Lord of the Rings Masterpieces Foil

COMPLETE SET (9) 8.00 20.00
COMMON CARD (1-9) 1.25 3.00
*BRONZE: 2X TO 5X BASIC CARDS
*GOLD: 4X TO 10X BASIC CARDS
STATED ODDS 1:4

2008 Lord of the Rings Masterpieces II

COMPLETE SET (72) 5.00 12.00
UNOPENED BOX (36 PACKS) 250.00 500.00
UNOPENED PACK (7 CARDS) 8.00 15.00
COMMON CARD (1-72) .15 .40

2008 Lord of the Rings Masterpieces II Etched Foil

COMPLETE SET (6) 3.00 6.00
COMMON CARD (1-6) .60 1.50
STATED ODDS 1:6

2008 Lord of the Rings Masterpieces II Foil

COMPLETE SET (9) 3.00 6.00
COMMON CARD (1-9) .40 1.00
*BRONZE: 2X TO 5X SILVER
*GOLD: 10X TO 25X SILVER
STATED ODDS 1:4

2004 Lord of the Rings Trilogy Chrome

COMPLETE SET (100) 8.00 20.00
UNOPENED HOBBY BOX (36 PACKS) 200.00 350.00
UNOPENED HOBBY PACK (5 CARDS) 6.00 10.00
UNOPENED RETAIL BOX (24 PACKS) 70.00 80.00
UNOPENED RETAIL PACK (5 CARDS) 2.75 3.00
COMMON CARD (1-100) .20 .50

2004 Lord of the Rings Trilogy Chrome Autographs

COMMON AUTO 12.00 30.00
STATED ODDS 1:18 H, 1:83 R
NNO Bernard Hill 30.00 75.00
NNO Billy Boyd 30.00 75.00
NNO David Wenham SP 20.00 50.00
NNO Ian Holm 30.00 75.00
NNO Karl Urban 20.00 50.00
NNO Liv Tyler 100.00 250.00
NNO Sala Baker 20.00 50.00
NNO Viggo Mortensen 100.00 250.00
Aragorn
NNO Viggo Mortensen 75.00 200.00
King Elessar

2004 Lord of the Rings Trilogy Chrome Memorabilia

COMMON MEM 12.00 30.00
STATED ODDS 1:36 H, 1:55 R
NNO Bilbo's Waistcoat 20.00 50.00
NNO Eowyn's Golden Hall Dress 20.00 50.00

MODERN

NNO Pippin's Tunic 25.00 60.00
NNO Sam's Tunic 40.00 80.00

2014 The Hobbit An Unexpected Journey

COMPLETE SET (101) 6.00 15.00
UNOPENED BOX (24 PACKS) 200.00 300.00
UNOPENED PACK (5 CARDS) 8.00 12.00
COMMON CARD (1-101) .20 .50

2014 The Hobbit An Unexpected Journey 3-D Lenticular Posters

COMPLETE SET (4) 25.00 60.00
COMMON CARD (KA1-KA4) 10.00 25.00
STATED ODDS 1:144

2014 The Hobbit An Unexpected Journey Autographs

COMMON AUTO (A1-A21, CA2) 10.00 25.00
STATED ODDS 1:24
A1 Richard Armitage 75.00 150.00
A2 Ken Stott 15.00 40.00
A3 Graham McTavish 15.00 40.00
A6 Stephen Hunter 10.00 25.00
A7 Dean O'Gorman 100.00 200.00
A8 Aidan Turner 25.00 60.00
A9 John Callen 10.00 25.00
A12 Mark Hadlow 10.00 25.00
A14 Ian Holm 50.00 100.00
A15 Barry Humphries 12.00 30.00
A16 Manu Bennett 12.00 30.00
A17 Martin Freeman 75.00 150.00
A18 Andy Serkis 50.00 100.00
A19 Lee Pace 30.00 75.00
A20 Sylvester McCoy 20.00 50.00
CA2 Writer Phillipa Boyens 75.00 150.00

2014 The Hobbit An Unexpected Journey Character Biographies

COMPLETE SET (19) 15.00 40.00
COMMON CARD (CB01-CB19) 1.50 4.00
STATED ODDS 1:12

2014 The Hobbit An Unexpected Journey Lonely Mountain Flashback

COMPLETE SET (18) 6.00 15.00
COMMON CARD (P01-P18) .75 2.00
STATED ODDS 1:4

2014 The Hobbit An Unexpected Journey Promos

COMMON CARD (P1-P2) 1.25 3.00
P2 Bilbo and 13 Dwarves 3.00 8.00
(Chicago Non-Sport Card Show)

2012 The Hobbit An Unexpected Journey Denny's

COMPLETE SET (12) 5.00 12.00
COMMON CARD (1-10) .20 .50
BBS Bilbo Baggins/Sting LE 2.00 5.00
GGG Gandalf the Grey/Glamdring LE 2.00 5.00

2012 The Hobbit An Unexpected Journey Dog Tags

COMPLETE SET (48) 60.00 120.00
UNOPENED BOX (PACKS)
UNOPENED PACK (CARDS)
COMMON TAGS (1-48) 1.50 4.00
NNO Checklist 1.50 4.00

2012 The Hobbit An Unexpected Journey Dog Tags Tattoos

COMPLETE SET (12) 3.00 8.00
COMMON STICKER .40 1.00
STATED ODDS 1:1

2015 The Hobbit Desolation of Smaug

COMPLETE SET (72) 6.00 15.00
UNOPENED BOX (24 PACKS) 150.00 250.00
UNOPENED PACK (5 CARDS) 6.00 10.00
COMMON CARD (1-72) .20 .50
*SILVER: 5X TO 12X BASIC CARDS 2.50 6.00

2015 The Hobbit Desolation of Smaug 3-D Lenticular Posters

COMPLETE SET (4) 20.00 50.00
COMMON CARD (KA5-KA8) 8.00 20.00
STATED ODDS 1:444

2015 The Hobbit Desolation of Smaug Autographs

COMMON AUTO 6.00 15.00
STATED ODDS 1:24
AT Aidan Turner 30.00 75.00
GM Graham McTavish 15.00 40.00
JC John Callen 10.00 25.00
JN James Nesbitt 8.00 20.00
KS Ken Stott 15.00 40.00
LP Lee Pace 50.00 100.00
MB Manu Bennett 12.00 30.00
MF Martin Freeman 50.00 100.00
MN Mary Nesbitt 8.00 20.00
MP Mikael Persbrandt 10.00 25.00
PN Peggy Nesbitt 10.00 25.00
RA Richard Armitage 50.00 100.00
SF Stephen Fry 15.00 40.00
SH Stephen Hunter 10.00 25.00
SM Sylvester McCoy 25.00 60.00
WK William Kircher 10.00 25.00
CA3 Fran Walsh 50.00 100.00
CA4 Andy Serkis 20.00 50.00

2015 The Hobbit Desolation of Smaug Character Biographies

COMPLETE SET (9) 8.00 20.00
COMMON CARD (CB20-CB28) 1.50 4.00
STATED ODDS 1:12

2015 The Hobbit Desolation of Smaug Collage

COMPLETE SET (3) 5.00 12.00
COMMON CARD (CP1-CP3) 1.50 4.00
STATED ODDS 1:96
CP2 King Thranduil 2.00 5.00
CP3 Thorin Oakenshield 5.00 12.00

2015 The Hobbit Desolation of Smaug Dwarves

COMPLETE SET (13) 10.00 25.00
COMMON CARD (D1-D13) 1.50 4.00
STATED ODDS 1:24

2015 The Hobbit Desolation of Smaug Illustration Autographs

COMMON AUTO 100.00 200.00
LPI Lee Pace 100.00 200.00
MFI Martin Freeman 250.00 400.00
RAI Richard Armitage 150.00 300.00
SMI Sylvester McCoy 100.00 200.00

2015 The Hobbit Desolation of Smaug Lake-town

COMPLETE SET (6) 8.00 20.00
COMMON CARD (LT1-LT6) 2.50 6.00
STATED ODDS 1:24

2015 The Hobbit Desolation of Smaug Poster Autographs

COMMON AUTO 25.00 60.00
STATED ODDS 1:232
ATP Aidan Turner 60.00 120.00
GMP Graham McTavish 60.00 120.00
JNP James Nesbitt 30.00 75.00
JCP John Cullen 30.00 75.00
LPP Lee Pace 60.00 120.00
MFP Martin Freeman 75.00 150.00
PHP Peter Hambleton 30.00 75.00
RAP Richard Armitage 60.00 120.00

2015 The Hobbit Desolation of Smaug Smaug Inserts

COMPLETE SET (6) 30.00 80.00
COMMON CARD (S1-S6) 6.00 15.00
STATED ODDS 1:96

2015 The Hobbit Desolation of Smaug Promos

COMMON CARD (P1-P3) 1.50 4.00
P2 Dragon Chrome 2.50 6.00
Philly Fall Show 2014
P3 Bilbo and the hoard 2.50 6.00
Philly Fall Show 2014

2016 The Hobbit Battle of the Five Armies

COMPLETE SET (90) 6.00 15.00
UNOPENED BOX (24 PACKS) 60.00 80.00
UNOPENED PACK (5 CARDS) 3.00 4.00
COMMON CARD (1-90) .20 .50
*SILVER: 5X TO 12X BASIC CARDS 2.50 6.00
*CANVAS/75: 6X TO 15X BASIC CARDS 3.00 8.00

2016 The Hobbit Battle of the Five Armies 3-D Lenticular Posters

COMPLETE SET (5) 50.00 100.00
COMMON CARD (KA9-KA13) 12.00 30.00
STATED ODDS 1:144

2016 The Hobbit Battle of the Five Armies Autographs

COMMON AUTO 8.00 20.00
STATED ODDS 1:24 W/OTHER AUTOS
AB Adam Brown 8.00 20.00
AT Aidan Turner 25.00 60.00
EL Evangeline Lilly 125.00 250.00
GM Graham McTavish 15.00 40.00
IH Sir Ian Holm 250.00 400.00
JC John Callen 10.00 25.00
JT John Tui 8.00 20.00
KS Ken Stott 10.00 25.00
LE Luke Evans 50.00 100.00
LP Lee Pace 60.00 120.00
MB Manu Bennett 10.00 25.00
MF Martin Freeman 50.00 100.00
PH Peter Hambleton 8.00 20.00
RA Richard Armitage 50.00 100.00
SH Stephen Hunter 8.00 20.00
WK William Kircher 10.00 25.00
CA1 Peter Jackson 75.00 150.00
CA5 Howard Shore 20.00 50.00

2016 The Hobbit Battle of the Five Armies Character Biographies

COMPLETE SET (6) 5.00 12.00
COMMON CARD (CB29-CB34) 1.50 4.00
STATED ODDS 1:12

2016 The Hobbit Battle of the Five Armies Cryptomium Smaug Puzzle

COMPLETE SET (9) 15.00 40.00
COMMON CARD (S1-S9) 3.00 8.00
STATED ODDS 1:24

2016 The Hobbit Battle of the Five Armies Illustration Autographs

COMMON AUTO 80.00 150.00
STATED ODDS 1:24 W/OTHER AUTOS
ATI Aidan Turner 120.00 250.00
GMI Graham McTavish 150.00 300.00
LPI Lee Pace 150.00 300.00
MFI Martin Freeman 100.00 200.00
RAI Richard Armitage 100.00 200.00

2016 The Hobbit Battle of the Five Armies Portraits

COMPLETE SET (6) 30.00 80.00
COMMON CARD (BP1-BP6) 8.00 20.00
STATED ODDS 1:48

2016 The Hobbit Battle of the Five Armies Poster Autographs

COMMON AUTO 15.00 40.00
STATED ODDS 1:24 W/OTHER AUTOS
ATP Aidan Turner 50.00 100.00
LPP Lee Pace 50.00 100.00
MFP Martin Freeman 80.00 150.00
RAP Richard Armitage 50.00 100.00

2016 The Hobbit Battle of the Five Armies Weapons

COMPLETE SET (9) 5.00 12.00
COMMON CARD (W1-W9) 1.00 2.50
*SILVER: .6X TO 1.5X BASIC CARDS
*CANVAS/75: 1.5X TO 4X BASIC CARDS
STATED ODDS 1:4

2016 The Hobbit Battle of the Five Armies Promos

COMMON CARD (P1-P12) 1.25 3.00
P1 NSCC July 2015 1.50 4.00
P2 GTS July-Nov 2015 10.00 25.00
P3 GTS July-Nov 2015 10.00 25.00
P4 GTS July-Nov 2015 10.00 25.00
P7 NSU Dec-Jan 2016 6.00 15.00
P8 NSU Dec-Jan 2016 6.00 15.00
P9 NSU Dec-Jan 2016 6.00 15.00
P10 NSU Dec-Jan 2016 Variant 6.00 15.00
P11 NSU Dec-Jan 2016 Variant 6.00 15.00
P12 NSU Dec-Jan 2016 Variant 6.00 15.00

2022 CZX Middle-Earth

COMPLETE SET (50) 25.00 60.00
UNOPENED BOX (6 PACKS)
UNOPENED PACK (5 CARDS)
COMMON CARD (1-50) .75 2.00
*RED/125: 1.5X TO 4X BASIC CARDS
*GREEN/45: 6X TO 15X BASIC CARDS
*SILVER/25: 12X TO 30X BASIC CARDS

2022 CZX Middle-Earth Autographs

COMMON AUTO 25.00 60.00
STATED OVERALL AUTO ODDS 1:BOX
FW Fran Walsh/200 40.00 100.00
PB Philippa Boyens/200 50.00 125.00
PJ Peter Jackson/200 150.00 400.00
BHG Bruce Hopkins/200 75.00 200.00
CPH Craig Parker/175 50.00 125.00
ELT Evangeline Lilly/100 200.00 500.00
JBN Jed Brophy/180 30.00 75.00
JBS Jed Brophy/200 30.00 75.00
JDG John Rhys-Davies/75 200.00 500.00
JDT John Rhys-Davies/100 150.00 400.00
LMG Lawrence Makoare/155 30.00 75.00
LML Lawrence Makoare/180 40.00 100.00
LMW Lawrence Makoare/100 50.00 125.00
LTA Liv Tyler/105 200.00 500.00
MOE Miranda Otto/110 250.00 600.00
SCR Sylvester McCoy/200 30.00 75.00
SHB Stephen Hunter/200 30.00 75.00
SLR Sarah McLeod/200 60.00 150.00
TBA Orlando Bloom EXCH 250.00 600.00
VMA Viggo Mortensen/80 250.00 600.00
VMS Viggo Mortensen/70 250.00 600.00
WKT William Kircher/200 30.00 75.00
BBP1 Billy Boyd/110 40.00 100.00
BBP2 Billy Boyd/110 40.00 100.00
DMM1 Dominic Monaghan/120 40.00 100.00
DMM2 Dominic Monaghan/150 40.00 100.00
IMGG Ian McKellen/75 400.00 1000.00
IMGW Ian McKellen/75 400.00 1000.00
LTA2 Liv Tyler/105 150.00 400.00
VMKE Viggo Mortensen/65 500.00 1200.00
IMGG2 Ian McKellen/65 500.00 1200.00
IMGG3 Ian McKellen/60 500.00 1200.00
IMGW2 Ian McKellen/65 500.00 1200.00
IMGW3 Ian McKellen/60 500.00 1200.00

2022 CZX Middle-Earth Dual Autographs

COMMON AUTO 300.00 750.00
STATED OVERALL AUTO ODDS 1:BOX
IMSM I.McKellen/S.McCoy/35 1200.00 3000.00
MOBH M.Otto/B.Hill/55 600.00 1500.00
VMIM V.Mortensen/I.McKellen/30 2000.00 4000.00
VMLT V.Mortensen/L.Tyler/30 1000.00 2500.00
VMMO V.Mortensen/M.Otto/50 600.00 1500.00

2022 CZX Middle-Earth Film Cels

COMPLETE SET W/O B1 (19) 125.00 300.00
COMMON MEM 10.00 25.00

STATED ODDS 1:6
STATED PRINT RUN 375 SER.#'d SETS

2022 CZX Middle-Earth STR PWR

COMPLETE SET (25) 100.00 250.00
COMMON CARD (S01-S25) 6.00 15.00
*GREEN/85: .75X TO 2X BASIC CARDS
*SILVER/45: 2X TO 5X BASIC CARDS
STATED ODDS 1:6

1993 Skyline Cards Los Angeles Scenes Promos

COMPLETE SET (3) 2.50 6.00
COMMON CARD (P1-P3) 1.25 3.00

2004 Lost Previews

COMPLETE SET (15) 6.00 15.00
COMMON CARD (LP1-LP15) .60 1.50

2005 Lost Season One

COMPLETE SET (90) 5.00 12.00
UNOPENED BOX (36 PACKS) 50.00 60.00
UNOPENED PACK (7 CARDS) 1.75 2.00
COMMON CARD (1-90) .15 .40

2005 Lost Season One Autographs

COMMON AUTO (A1-A12) 6.00 15.00
STATED ODDS 1:36
A1 Evangeline Lilly 75.00 200.00
A2 Josh Holloway 50.00 100.00
A3 Maggie Grace 60.00 120.00
A5 Mira Furlan 10.00 25.00
A12 Swoosie Kurtz 8.00 20.00

2005 Lost Season One Box-Loaders

COMPLETE SET (3) 5.00 12.00
COMMON CARD (BL1-BL3) 2.00 5.00
BL STATED ODDS ONE PER BOX
CL STATED ODDS ONE PER CASE
CL1 The Hatch 5.00 12.00

2005 Lost Season One Missing Oceanic 815

COMPLETE SET (9) 8.00 20.00
COMMON CARD (M1-M9) 1.00 2.50
STATED ODDS 1:11

2005 Lost Season One Numbers

COMPLETE SET (6) 6.00 15.00
COMMON CARD (SKIP #'c) 1.25 3.00
STATED ODDS 1:17

2005 Lost Season One Pieceworks

COMMON CARD 8.00 20.00
STATED ODDS 1:36
PW1 Evangeline Lilly 15.00 40.00
PW3 Maggie Grace 15.00 40.00
PW4 Matthew Fox 10.00 25.00
PW6 Terry O'Quinn 10.00 25.00
PW10 Yunjin Kim 10.00 25.00
PW11 Emilie De Ravin 10.00 25.00
PW12 Harold Perrineau 12.00 30.00
Malcolm David Kelley
PWA1 Evangeline Lilly AU 150.00 300.00
PWA2 Josh Holloway AU 75.00 150.00
PWA3 Maggie Grace AU 100.00 200.00
Apr-01 Redemption Card

2005 Lost Season One Promos

COMMON CARD .75 2.00
L1i Jack, Kate, & Sawyer 2.00 5.00
L1DS Jack, Kate, & Sawyer 1.25 3.00
L1MS Cast 2.00 5.00
L1PN Jack, Kate, & Sawyer 1.25 3.00
L1UK Cast 1.25 3.00
L1NSV Cast 2.00 5.00

2006 Lost Season Two

COMPLETE SET (90) 5.00 12.00
UNOPENED BOX (36 PACKS) 60.00 70.00
UNOPENED PACK (7 CARDS) 2.00 2.50
COMMON CARD (1-90) .15 .40

2006 Lost Season Two Autographs

COMMON AUTO (A13-A24) 5.00 12.00
STATED ODDS 1:36
A13 Emilie De Ravin 25.00 60.00
A14 Yunjin Kim 20.00 50.00
A15 L. Scott Caldwell 6.00 15.00
A16 Sam Anderson 6.00 15.00
A17 Michael Emerson 20.00 50.00
A19 Tania Raymonde 10.00 25.00
A24 Sonya Walger 10.00 25.00
AR1 Autograph Redemption Card

2006 Lost Season Two Betrayal

COMPLETE SET (6) 6.00 15.00
COMMON CARD (B1-B6) 1.25 3.00
STATED ODDS 1:17

2006 Lost Season Two Box-Loaders

COMPLETE SET (3) 5.00 12.00
COMMON CARD (BL1-BL3) 2.00 5.00
BL1-BL3 STATED ODDS ONE PER BOX
CL1 STATED ODDS ONE PER CASE
CL1 Fail Safe 5.00 12.00

2006 Lost Season Two Pieceworks

COMMON CARD (PW1-PW12; PR1) 5.00 12.00
STATED ODDS 1:36
PW1 Terry O'Quinn 8.00 20.00
PW3 Yunjin Kim 10.00 25.00
PW4 Josh Holloway 8.00 20.00
PW6 Evangeline Lilly 25.00 50.00
PW9 Dominic Monaghan Sand 20.00 40.00
PW10 Jorge Garcia Sand 15.00 30.00
PW11 Josh Holloway Shirt/Sand 20.00 40.00
PW12A Harold Perrineau 15.00 30.00
PW12B Jack Shepard 15.00 30.00
PR1 Pieceworks Redemption Card

2006 Lost Season Two Question Mark

COMPLETE SET (9) 8.00 20.00
COMMON CARD (1-9) 1.00 2.50
STATED ODDS 1:11

2006 Lost Season Two Promos

COMPLETE SET (5) 5.00 12.00
COMMON CARD .75 2.00
L2i Lost 2.50 6.00
L2UK Lost 1.50 4.00

2007 Lost Season Three

COMPLETE SET (90) 5.00 12.00
UNOPENED BOX (36 PACKS) 60.00 100.00
UNOPENED PACK (7 CARDS) 2.00 3.00
COMMON CARD (1-90) .15 .40
CL1 STATED ODDS ONE PER CASE
CL1 Rescue Or Ruin 10.00 25.00

2007 Lost Season Three Autographs

COMMON AUTO (A25-A34) 5.00 12.00
STATED ODDS 1:36
A25 Michael Emerson 20.00 50.00
A26 Elizabeth Mitchell 20.00 50.00
A30 Nestor Carbonell 10.00 25.00
A33 Ian Somerhalder 15.00 40.00

2007 Lost Season Three Fighting Back

COMPLETE SET (9) 4.00 10.00
COMMON CARD (FB1-FB9) .75 2.00
STATED ODDS 1:11

2007 Lost Season Three Pieceworks

COMMON CARD (PW1-PW12) 5.00 12.00
PW1-PW11 STATED ODDS 1:36
PW12A AND PW12B DEALER EXCLUSIVE
PWA1 AND PWA2 RANDOM INSERTS IN PACKS
PW1 Evangeline Lilly 12.00 30.00
PW2 Marsha Thomason 6.00 15.00
PW3 Yunjin Kim 8.00 20.00
PW4 Elizabeth Mitchell 12.00 30.00
PW5 Matthew Fox 6.00 15.00
PW11 Matthew Fox 12.00 30.00
Elizabeth Mitchell
PW12A Rodgrigo Santoro 10.00 25.00
PW12B Kiele Sanchez 10.00 25.00
PWA1 Andrew Divoff AU 15.00 40.00
PWA2 Marsha Thomason AU 20.00 50.00

2007 Lost Season Three Propworks

PPW1 Exploding airplane 30.00 80.00
PPWA1 Greg Grunberg 30.00 80.00

2007 Lost Season Three Through the Looking Glass

COMPLETE SET (3) 4.00 10.00
COMMON CARD (LG1-LG3) 2.00 5.00
STATED ODDS 1:36

2007 Lost Season Three Ties to the Island

COMPLETE SET (6) 4.00 10.00
COMMON CARD (TI1-TI6) 1.00 2.50
STATED ODDS 1:17

2007 Lost Season Three Promos

COMMON CARD .75 2.00
L3i Lost 2.00 5.00
(Inkworks.com Exclusive)
L3P Lost 1.50 4.00

2010 Lost Seasons One Through Five

COMPLETE SET (108) 7.50 15.00
UNOPENED BOX (24 PACKS) 60.00 100.00
UNOPENED PACK (5 CARDS) 3.00 4.00
COMMON CARD (1-108) .15 .40
E. LILLY COST. ISSUED AS 6-CASE INCENTIVE
EL Evangeline Lilly MEM/175 6CI 150.00 250.00

2010 Lost Seasons One Through Five ArtiFEX

COMPLETE SET (25) 15.00 30.00
COMMON CARD (ART1-ART25) .75 2.00
STATED ODDS 1:6
A26 ISSUED AS RITTENHOUSE REWARD
A26 Richard Alpert RR SP 10.00 25.00

2010 Lost Seasons One Through Five Autographs

COMMON AUTO 5.00 12.00
STATED ODDS 1:8
LC STATED ODDS ONE PER CASE
HP STATED ODDS ONE PER 3-CASE PURCHASE
SB IS D23 EXPO EXCLUSIVE
L (LIMITED): 300-500 COPIES
VL (VERY LIMITED): 200-300 COPIES
NNO Alan Dale 10.00 25.00
NNO Andrea Roth 6.00 15.00
NNO Doug Hutchison 6.00 15.00
NNO Eric Lange 6.00 15.00
NNO Francois Chau L 6.00 15.00
NNO Henry Ian Cusick L 25.00 60.00
NNO Harold Perrineau 3CI 25.00 60.00
NNO Ian Somerhalder L 15.00 40.00
NNO Jon Gries L 6.00 15.00
NNO John Terry L 6.00 15.00
NNO Ken Leung VL 15.00 40.00
NNO Kiele Sanchez L 20.00 50.00
NNO L. Scott Caldwell CT 12.00 30.00
NNO Michael Emerson VL 25.00 60.00
NNO Mira Furlan L 12.00 30.00
NNO Malcolm David Kelley L 8.00 20.00
NNO Mark Pellegrino 15.00 40.00
NNO Michelle Rodriguez VL 100.00 200.00
NNO Nestor Carbonell L 12.00 30.00
NNO Sterling Beaumon D23 150.00 300.00
NNO Sonya Walger 12.00 30.00
NNO Terry O'Quinn 60.00 120.00
NNO Tania Raymonde 10.00 25.00
NNO Titus Welliver 10.00 25.00
NNO William Sanderson 6.00 15.00
NNO Yunjin Kim VL 50.00 100.00

2010 Lost Seasons One Through Five Flash Forward

COMPLETE SET (4) 4.00 10.00
COMMON CARD (FF1-FF4) 1.25 3.00
STATED ODDS 1:6

2010 Lost Seasons One Through Five In Motion

COMPLETE SET (9) 12.50 25.00
COMMON CARD (L1-L9) 1.50 4.00
STATED ODDS 1:12

2010 Lost Seasons One Through Five Oceanic Six

COMPLETE SET (6) 12.50 25.00
COMMON CARD (S1-S6) 2.50 6.00
STATED ODDS 1:24

2010 Lost Seasons One Through Five Promos

COMPLETE SET (10) 8.00 20.00
COMMON CARD (P1-P10) .75 2.00
P8 Sun-Hwa Kwon 4.00 10.00
(Album Exclusive)
P10 Desmond Hume 1.25 3.00

2010 Lost Archives

COMPLETE SET (72) 5.00 12.00
UNOPENED BOX (24 PACKS) 150.00 250.00
UNOPENED PACK (5 CARDS) 8.00 10.00
COMMON CARD (1-72) .15 .40
BT ISSUED AS 3-CASE INCENTIVE
BT Banyan Tree/250 3CI 30.00 60.00

2010 Lost Archives ArtiFEX Expansion

COMPLETE SET (9) 12.00 30.00
COMMON CARD (A27-A35) 2.50 6.00
STATED ODDS 1:12
A36 ISSUED AS RITTENHOUSE REWARD
A36 The Man in Black SP 10.00 25.00

2010 Lost Archives Autographs

COMMON AUTO 6.00 15.00
STATED ODDS FOUR PER BOX
MARIN AUTO ISSUED AS 6-CASE INCENTIVE
L (LIMITED): 300-500 COPIES
VL (VERY LIMITED): 200-300 COPIES
NNO L. Scott Caldwell L 8.00 20.00
NNO Nestor Carbonell VL 10.00 25.00
NNO Henry Ian Cusick VL 15.00 40.00
NNO Kim Dickens 12.00 30.00
NNO Michael Emerson VL 30.00 75.00
NNO Malcolm David Kelley VL 10.00 25.00
NNO Daniel Dae Kim L 20.00 50.00
NNO Yunjin Kim VL 30.00 75.00
NNO Swoosie Kurtz VL 12.00 30.00
NNO Ken Leung L 12.00 30.00
NNO Bai Ling VL 25.00 60.00
NNO Harold Perrineau VL 20.00 50.00
NNO Tania Raymonde L 12.00 30.00
NNO Zuleikha Robinson 10.00 25.00
NNO Ian Somerhalder L 15.00 40.00
NNO John Terry VL 12.00 30.00
NNO Sonya Walger L 10.00 25.00
NNO Cynthia Watros 12.00 30.00
NNO Cheech Marin 6CI 75.00 150.00

2010 Lost Archives Costumes

COMMON CARD 12.00 30.00
STATED ODDS 1:96
JARRAH COSTUME ISSUED AS CASE TOPPER
STATED PRINT RUN 375 SER. #'d SETS
1 Ben Linus 25.00 50.00
2 Hugo Hurley Reyes 25.00 50.00
3 Jack Shephard 30.00 60.00
4 James Sawyer Ford 25.00 50.00
5 John Locke 25.00 50.00
6 Kate Austin 30.00 60.00

2010 Lost Archives Dharma Patches

COMPLETE SET (9) 300.00 600.00
COMMON CARD (DP1-DP9) 30.00 80.00
STATED ODDS 1:144
STATED PRINT RUN 250 SER. #'d SETS

2010 Lost Archives Season Six

COMPLETE SET (18) 12.00 30.00
COMMON CARD (109-126) 1.50 4.00
STATED ODDS 1:6

2010 Lost Archives Promos

COMMON CARD	1.50	4.00
CP1 Lost ALB	6.00	15.00

2006 Lost Dharma Initiative 3 The Swan

COMPLETE SET (6)	2.00	5.00
COMMON CARD (1-6)	.50	1.25

2011 Lost Relics

COMMON CARD	6.00	15.00
STATED PRINT RUN 350 SER. #'d SETS		
RC2 ISSUED AS BOX TOPPER		
CC1 Jack Shephard	10.00	25.00
CC2 Juliet Burke	10.00	25.00
CC3 Charlie Pace	10.00	25.00
CC4 Claire Littleton	8.00	20.00
CC6 Ana Lucia Cortez	15.00	40.00
CC9 Sun Kwon	12.00	30.00
CC10 Sayid Jarrah	8.00	20.00
CC11 Shannon Rutherford	10.00	25.00
CC12 John Locke	8.00	20.00
CC13 Ben Linus	8.00	20.00
CC15 Penny Widmore	10.00	25.00
CC21 James Sawyer Ford	10.00	25.00
CC22 Goodwin Stanhope	8.00	20.00
CC23 Miles Straume	8.00	20.00
CC24 Ilana Verdansky	8.00	20.00
CC27 Naomi Dorrit	8.00	20.00
CC31 Sun Kwon	12.00	30.00
CC33 Shannon Rutherford	10.00	25.00
CC34 Charlie Pace	12.00	30.00
RC1 Chicken Shack Sign	25.00	50.00
RC2 Airplane/300 BT	50.00	100.00
P1 Group of Twelve PROMO	.75	2.00

2011 Lost Relics Autographs

COMMON AUTO	5.00	12.00
STATED ODDS ONE PER PACK		
NNO Bai Ling	15.00	40.00
NNO Carlton Cuse - Producer	30.00	75.00
NNO Damon Lindelof - Producer	30.00	75.00
NNO Kenton Duty	6.00	15.00
NNO Naveen Andrews w/hat	12.00	30.00
NNO Naveen Andrews w/o hat	25.00	60.00

2006 Lost Revelations

COMPLETE SET (81)	5.00	12.00
UNOPENED BOX (36 PACKS)	50.00	60.00
UNOPENED PACK (6 CARDS)	1.75	2.00
COMMON CARD (1-81)	.15	.40

2006 Lost Revelations Autographs

COMMON AUTO	6.00	15.00
STATED ODDS 1:36		
A1 Yunjin Kim	30.00	75.00
A3 Julie Bowen	30.00	75.00
A6 Tamara Taylor	10.00	25.00
A7 Katey Sagal	25.00	60.00
A10 Dustin Watchman	12.00	30.00

2006 Lost Revelations Black and White

COMPLETE SET (6)	6.00	15.00
COMMON CARD	1.25	3.00
STATED ODDS 1:17		

2006 Lost Revelations Box-Loaders

COMPLETE SET (3)	3.00	8.00
COMMON CARD (BL1-BL3)	1.25	3.00
BL1-BL3 STATED ODDS ONE PER BOX		
CL1 STATED ODDS ONE PER CASE		
CL1 Case Loader – Countdown	6.00	15.00

2006 Lost Revelations Inside the Island

COMPLETE SET (9)	8.00	20.00
COMMON CARD (I1-I9)	1.00	2.50
STATED ODDS 1:11		

2006 Lost Revelations Pieceworks

COMMON CARD	8.00	20.00
STATED ODDS 1:36		
PW2 Evangeline Lilly	12.00	30.00
PW6 Emilie De Ravin	10.00	25.00
PW8 Matthew Fox	125.00	200.00
Evangeline Lilly		
PW9 Josh Holloway	50.00	100.00
Evangeline Lilly		

2006 Lost Revelations Promos

COMPLETE SET (7)	6.00	15.00
COMMON CARD	.75	2.00
LR3 Hurley & Libby	1.25	3.00
LR4 Sun & Jin	1.25	3.00
LRi Mr.Eko, Claire, & Charlie	1.25	3.00
LRUK Jin, Michael, Sawyer	2.00	5.00
LRNSV Lost	2.00	5.00

1998 Kellogg's Lost in Space 3-D

COMPLETE SET (8)	8.00	20.00
COMMON CARD (1-8)	1.25	3.00

2018 Lost in Space Archives Series One

COMPLETE SET (43)	12.00	30.00
COMMON CARD (SKIP NUMBERED)	.60	1.50

2018 Lost in Space Archives Series One Character Art Autographs

COMMON AUTO	25.00	60.00
STATED ODDS 1:SET		
NNO Angela Cartwright	30.00	75.00

2018 Lost in Space Archives Series One Inscription Autographs

COMMON AUTO	15.00	40.00
STATED ODDS 2:SET		

2018 Lost in Space Archives Series One Metal

COMPLETE SET (8)	50.00	100.00
COMMON CARD (M1-M8)	8.00	20.00
STATED ODDS 4:SET		

2018 Lost in Space Archives Series One Triple Autograph

2-SET INCENTIVE		
NNO Bill Mumy	75.00	150.00
Marta Kristen#(Angela Cartwright#(2-Set Incentive)		

2018 Lost in Space Archives Series Two

COMPLETE FACTORY SET		
COMPLETE SET (42)	12.00	30.00
COMMON CARD (SKIP #'d)	.60	1.50

2018 Lost in Space Archives Series Two Autographed Relic

NNO Mark Goddard	75.00	150.00

2018 Lost in Space Archives Series Two Character Art Autographs

COMMON AUTO	30.00	75.00
STATED ODDS 1:FACTORY SET		
AO2 Marta Kristen	50.00	100.00

2018 Lost in Space Archives Series Two Inscription Autographs

COMMON AUTO	20.00	50.00
STATED ODDS 2:FACTORY SET		

2018 Lost in Space Archives Series Two Juan Ortiz Character Art

COMPLETE SET (7)	12.00	30.00
COMMON CARD (OC1-OC7)	3.00	8.00
RANDOMLY INSERTED INTO FACTORY SETS		

2018 Lost in Space Archives Series Two Ron Gross Painted Art

COMPLETE SET (9)	8.00	20.00
COMMON CARD (LP1-LP9)	1.50	4.00
RANDOMLY INSERTED INTO FACTORY SETS		

1998 Inkworks Lost in Space Classic Episodes Promos

COMPLETE SET (2)	1.25	3.00
COMMON CARD (P1-P2)	.75	2.00

1997 Inkworks Lost in Space The Classic Series

COMPLETE SET (81)	10.00	25.00
UNOPENED BOX (36 PACKS)	150.00	250.00
UNOPENED PACK (7 CARDS)	4.00	6.00
COMMON CARD (1-72; M1-M9)	.30	.75
R1 Danger, Will Robinson RoboMetallic Insert	15.00	40.00
NNO Uncut Press Sheet		
RP1 Part of the Display Box		

1997 Inkworks Lost in Space The Classic Series Autographs

P2 Mark Goddard	75.00	150.00
P3 Jonathan Harris	200.00	400.00

1997 Inkworks Lost in Space The Classic Series Promos

COMMON CARD	.75	2.00
P3 Signed by Jonathan Harris	20.00	50.00

1997 Inkworks Lost in Space The Classic Series Robinson Family

COMPLETE SET (9)	25.00	60.00
COMMON CARD (1-9)	3.00	8.00
STATED ODDS 1:11		

1997 Inkworks Lost in Space The Classic Series Weird Aliens

COMPLETE SET (6)	15.00	40.00
COMMON CARD (A1-A6)	3.00	8.00
STATED ODDS 1:17		

2022 Rittenhouse Lost in Space Collector's Set

COMPLETE SET (12)	12.00	30.00
COMMON CARD (1-12)	2.00	5.00

2022 Rittenhouse Lost in Space Collector's Set Autographs

COMMON AUTO	6.00	15.00
NNO Ignacio Serricchio	8.00	20.00
NNO Maxwell Jenkins	20.00	50.00
NNO Mina Sundwall	40.00	100.00
NNO Molly Parker	25.00	60.00
NNO Parker Posey	25.00	60.00
NNO Taylor Russell	20.00	50.00
NNO Toby Stephens	15.00	40.00

2022 Rittenhouse Lost in Space Collector's Set Characters

COMPLETE SET (8)	20.00	50.00
COMMON CARD (C1-C8)	5.00	12.00

2022 Rittenhouse Lost in Space Collector's Set Dual Autographs

COMMON AUTO	30.00	75.00
NNO M.Jenkins/M.Sundwall	50.00	125.00
NNO M.Jenkins/M.Parker	40.00	100.00

1998 General Mills Lost in Space

COMPLETE SET (4)	8.00	20.00
COMMON CARD (GM1-GM4)	2.50	6.00

1998 Inkworks Lost in Space The Movie

COMPLETE SET (90)	5.00	12.00
UNOPENED BOX (36 PACKS)	30.00	50.00
UNOPENED PACK (8 CARDS)	1.50	2.00
COMMON CARD (1-90)	.15	.40
J1 STATED ODDS 1:108		
J1 Jupiter 2	4.00	10.00

1998 Inkworks Lost in Space The Movie Autographs

COMPLETE SET (3)		
COMMON AUTO	6.00	15.00
RANDOMLY INSERTED INTO PACKS		
A1 Mimi Rogers	20.00	50.00
A2 Lacey Chabert	200.00	400.00
NNO Autograph Redemption Card		

1998 Inkworks Lost in Space The Movie Double Feature

COMPLETE SET (9)	5.00	12.00
COMMON CARD (DF1-DF9)	1.00	2.50
STATED ODDS 1:11		

1998 Inkworks Lost in Space The Movie War of the Robots

COMPLETE SET (4)	8.00	20.00
COMMON CARD (R1-R4)	3.00	8.00
STATED ODDS 1:24		

2019 Lost in Space Season One

COMPLETE SET (72)	6.00	15.00
UNOPENED BOX (24 PACKS)	60.00	100.00
UNOPENED PACK (5 CARDS)	2.50	4.00
COMMON CARD (1-72)	.15	.40

2019 Lost in Space Season One Bordered Autographs

COMMON AUTO	4.00	10.00
L = 300-500 COPIES		
VL = 200-300 COPIES		
EL = 100-200 COPIES		
S = 100< COPIES		
STATED OVERALL ODDS 1:12		
NNO Billy Mumy S AB	50.00	100.00
NNO Cary-Hiroyuki Tagawa S AB	15.00	40.00
NNO Kiki Sukezane EL	10.00	25.00

2019 Lost in Space Season One Case-Topper

CT For a Brighter Future Poster	4.00	10.00

2019 Lost in Space Season One Characters

COMPLETE SET (8)	8.00	20.00
COMMON CARD (CC1-CC8)	1.50	4.00
*METAL: 1.2X TO 3X BASIC CARDS		
STATED ODDS 1:48		

2019 Lost in Space Season One Chariot

COMPLETE SET (6)	6.00	15.00
COMMON CARD (C1-C6)	1.50	4.00
STATED ODDS 1:48		

2019 Lost in Space Season One Dual Autographs

COMMON AUTO	12.00	30.00
EL = 100-200 COPIES		
S = 100< COPIES		
STATED OVERALL ODDS 1:12		
STEPHEN/PARKER IS 9-CASE INCENTIVE		
NNO A.Friese/M.Sundwall S	50.00	100.00
NNO C.Tagawa/K.Sukezane S	20.00	50.00
NNO I.Serricchio/T.Russell EL	20.00	50.00
NNO P.Posey/B.Mumy EL	20.00	50.00
NNO P.Posey/M.Jenkins EL	30.00	75.00
NNO T.Stephens/M.Jenkins EL	15.00	40.00
NNO T.Stephens/M.Parker 9CI	50.00	100.00

2019 Lost in Space Season One Full Bleed Autographs

COMMON AUTO	4.00	10.00
L = 300-500 COPIES		
VL = 200-300 COPIES		
EL = 100-200 COPIES		
S = 100< COPIES		
STATED OVERALL ODDS 1:12		
NNO Billy Mumy EL	12.00	30.00
NNO Cary-Hiroyuki Tagawa S	12.00	30.00
NNO Ignacio Serricchio EL	12.00	30.00
NNO Kiki Sukezane EL	6.00	15.00
NNO Maxwell Jenkins EL	20.00	50.00
NNO Mina Sundwall EL	60.00	120.00
NNO Molly Parker EL	30.00	75.00
NNO Parker Posey EL	12.00	30.00
NNO Taylor Russell S	30.00	75.00
NNO Toby Stephens EL	15.00	40.00

2019 Lost in Space Season One Juan Ortiz Characters

COMPLETE SET (8)	5.00	12.00
COMMON CARD (OC1-OC8)	1.00	2.50
STATED ODDS 1:48		

2019 Lost in Space Season One Juan Ortiz Episode Title

COMPLETE SET (10) 8.00 20.00
COMMON CARD (OE1-OE10) 1.25 3.00
STATED ODDS 1:24

2019 Lost in Space Season One Jupiter 2

COMPLETE SET (6) 6.00 15.00
COMMON CARD (J1-J6) 1.50 4.00
STATED ODDS 1:48

2019 Lost in Space Season One Mirror Puzzle

COMPLETE SET (2) 5.00 12.00
COMMON CARD (MP1-MP2) 3.00 8.00
STATED ODDS 1:144

2019 Lost in Space Season One Quotables

COMPLETE SET (11) 8.00 20.00
COMMON CARD (Q1-Q11) 1.25 3.00
STATED ODDS 1:24

2019 Lost in Space Season One Relics

COMMON MEM 4.00 10.00
RANDOMLY INSERTED INTO PACKS
RC1 Will Robinson 5.00 12.00
RC5 Judy Robinson 15.00 40.00
RC7 Penny Robinson 8.00 20.00
RC8 John Robinson 6.00 15.00

2019 Lost in Space Season One Promos

P1 General Distribution 2.50 6.00
P2 Album Exclusive
PT1 General Distribution

1993 Comic Images Lost Worlds by William Stout

COMPLETE SET (90) 4.00 10.00
UNOPENED BOX (48 PACKS) 15.00 20.00
UNOPENED PACK (10 CARDS) .50 .75
COMMON CARD (1-90) .08 .25
P1 T-Rex .75 2.00
(Dealer Exclusive)
UNC1 6-Up Panel C1-C6 UNC
UNC2 William Stout 6-Up Panel AU UNC

1993 Comic Images Lost Worlds by William Stout Chromium

COMPLETE SET (6) 5.00 12.00
COMMON CARD (1-6) 1.50 4.00
STATED ODDS 1:16

1992 Fantagraphic Books Love and Rockets

COMPLETE BOXED SET (36) 6.00 15.00
COMMON CARD (1-36) .20 .50

1995 KRC International Lucy Moments and Memories

COMPLETE SET (80) 6.00 15.00
UNOPENED BOX (36 PACKS) 20.00 30.00
UNOPENED PACK (9 CARDS) .75 1.00
COMMON CARD (1-80) .15 .40

1995 KRC International Lucy Moments and Memories Golden Strips

COMPLETE SET (20) 15.00 40.00
COMMON CARD (S1-S20) 1.00 2.50
RANDOMLY INSERTED INTO PACKS

1995 KRC International Lucy Moments and Memories Moments and Memories Confirmation Checklist

COMPLETE SET (10) 8.00 20.00
COMMON CARD (CC1-CC10) 1.00 2.50
WRAPPER REDEMPTION EXCLUSIVE

1995 KRC International Lucy Moments and Memories Promos

P Lucy General Distribution .75 2.00
P Lucy Gold Foil

1994 Comic Images Luis Royo 2 Forbidden Universe

COMPLETE SET (90) 5.00 12.00
UNOPENED BOX (48 PACKS) 20.00 30.00
UNOPENED PACK (10 CARDS) .75 1.00
COMMON CARD (1-90) .10 .25
M1 Royo Medallion Card/1250* 10.00 25.00
AULR Bisectrix Luis Royo AU/500* 20.00 50.00

1994 Comic Images Luis Royo 2 Forbidden Universe Prism

COMPLETE SET (6) 10.00 25.00
COMMON CARD (P1-P6) 3.00 8.00
STATED ODDS 1:16

1994 Comic Images Luis Royo 2 Forbidden Universe Warrior Women

COMPLETE SET (3) 15.00 40.00
COMMON CARD (S1-S2) 6.00 15.00
STATED ODDS 1:48

2000 Luis Royo Prohibited

COMPLETE SET (72) 5.00 12.00
UNOPENED BOX (36 PACKS) 30.00 40.00
UNOPENED PACK (10 CARDS) 1.25 1.50
COMMON CARD (1-72) .15 .40

2000 Luis Royo Prohibited Metal Tex

COMPLETE SET (6) 10.00 25.00
COMMON CARD (CHASE1-CHASE6) 2.50 6.00
RANDOMLY INSERTED INTO PACKS

1994 Brainstorm Comics Luxura

COMPLETE SET (18) 5.00 12.00
COMMON CARD .30 .75

2013 Machete

COMPLETE SET (66) 12.00 30.00
COMMON CARD (1-66) 1.00 2.50
STATED PRINT RUN 300 SETS
LL1 Lindsay Lohan/Booth AU 100.00 200.00
LL2 Lindsay Lohan/The Sister AU 75.00 150.00

2013 Machete Promos

COMMON PROMO 2.00 5.00
P1a April Booth/Philly 50.00 100.00
P1b Machete/Philly 8.00 20.00
P2a Machete Wearing Vest/NYC 8.00 20.00
P2b Machete w/Two Ladies/NYC 50.00 100.00
P3a Machete/Chicago 6.00 15.00
P3b She/Chicago 30.00 75.00

1993 Lime Rock Mad Final Edition

COMPLETE SET (55) 12.00 30.00
FACTORY SET W/PRISMS & COA 12.00 30.00

1993 Lime Rock Mad Final Edition Prism Rookies

COMPLETE SET (3) 4.00 10.00
R1 The Gray Lady Spy Dossier 2.50 6.00
R2 The Black Spy Dossier 2.50 6.00
R3 The White Spy Dossier 2.50 6.00

1993 Lime Rock Mad Final Edition Promos

COMPLETE SET (3) 10.00 25.00
COMMON CARD (R1-R3) 4.00 10.00
R1 The Gray Lady Spy Dossier PROTO 4.00 10.00
R2 The Black Spy Dossier PROTO 4.00 10.00
R3 The White Spy Dossier PROTO 4.00 10.00

1985 Regina Mad Hot Rods

COMPLETE SET (45) 60.00 150.00
COMMON CARD (1-45) 2.00 5.00

1992 Lime Rock MAD Magazine

COMPLETE SET (110) 6.00 15.00
FACTORY SET 15.00 40.00
COMPLETE SER.1 SET (55) 4.00 10.00
COMPLETE SER.2 SET (55) 4.00 10.00
UNOPENED SER.1 BOX (36 PACKS) 30.00 50.00
UNOPENED SER.1 PACK (11 CARDS) 1.50 2.00
UNOPENED SER.2 BOX (36 PACKS) 30.00 50.00
UNOPENED SER.2 PACK (11 CARDS) 1.50 2.00
COMMON CARD (1-55) .12 .30
COMMON CARD (56-110) .12 .30
NNO Uncut Sheet

1992 Lime Rock MAD Magazine Dealer Promos

COMPLETE SET (10) 8.00 20.00
COMMON CARD (1-10) 1.25 3.00
RANDOMLY INSERTED INTO PACKS

1992 Lime Rock MAD Magazine Holograms

1 Alfred E. Neuman 10.00 25.00
2A Vote Mad Clinton/Bush Silver 6.00 15.00
2B Vote Mad Clinton/Bush Gold 12.00 30.00
(Mail-In)

1992 Lime Rock MAD Magazine Inside Trader Member Promos

COMPLETE SET (10) 12.00 30.00
COMMON CARD (1-10) 2.00 5.00

1992 Lime Rock MAD Magazine Inside Trader Promos

COMPLETE SET (10) 10.00 25.00
COMMON CARD (1-10) 1.50 4.00

1992 Lime Rock MAD Magazine Spy vs. Spy Promos

COMPLETE SET (4) 2.00 5.00
COMMON CARD (1-4) .75 2.00

2005 Madagascar

COMPLETE SET (72) 4.00 10.00
UNOPENED BOX (48 PACKS) 25.00 40.00
UNOPENED PACK (5 CARDS) 1.00 1.50
COMMON CARD (1-72) .12 .30

1994 Dark Horse Comics Madman X 50 Bubblegum

COMPLETE FACTORY SET (50) 5.00 12.00
COMMON CARD (1-50) .20 .50

1991 Mother Productions Mafia Family

COMPLETE BOXED SET (40) 6.00 15.00
COMMON CARD (1-40) .20 .50
NNO Willie Moretti Murdered .75 2.00

1983 Donruss Magnum P.I.

COMPLETE SET (66) 8.00 20.00
UNOPENED BOX (36 PACKS) 75.00 125.00
UNOPENED PACK (8 CARDS) 2.00 3.00
UNOPENED RACK BOX
UNOPENED RACK PACK (36 CARDS)
COMMON CARD (1-66) .25 .60

2017 Make Believe Promos

COMPLETE SET (2) 2.00 5.00
COMMON CARD (P1-P2) 1.50 4.00

1995 Bacon & Eggs Mallrats

COMPLETE SET (90) 6.00 15.00
UNOPENED BOX (36 PACKS) 15.00 20.00
UNOPENED PACK (6 CARDS) .50 .75
COMMON CARD (1-90) .12 .30

1995 Bacon & Eggs Mallrats Promos

COMPLETE SET (10) 6.00 15.00
COMMON CARD (1-10) 1.00 2.50
NNO Stan Lee, Comic Book God 6.00 15.00

1993 Kitchen Sink Press Mamie Van Doren

COMPLETE BOXED SET (36) 5.00 12.00
COMMON CARD (1-36) .25 .60
AUNC1 Mamie Van Doren 36-Card Panel AU

1985 Sanitarium Mammals of the Seas

COMPLETE SET (20) 3.00 8.00
COMMON CARD (1-20) .25 .60

1992 Kitchen Sink Press Man Bait

COMPLETE BOXED SET (36) 6.00 15.00
COMMON CARD (1-36) .30 .75

2015 Man Who Fell to Earth

COMPLETE SET (54) 4.00 10.00
UNOPENED BOX (24 PACKS) 150.00 200.00
UNOPENED PACK (5 CARDS) 8.00 10.00
COMMON CARD (1-54) .25 .60

2015 Man Who Fell to Earth Autographs

STATED ODDS 1:24
B1 BOWIE INSERTED 1 PER CASE
BERNIE CASEY HAS MULTIPLE INSCRIPTIONS
A1 David Bowie/50 (no hat) 750.00 1500.00
B1 David Bowie/50 (with hat) 1500.00 2500.00
MWFRT Rip Torn 30.00 75.00

2015 Man Who Fell to Earth Gold Foil

COMPLETE SET (9) 6.00 15.00
COMMON CARD (F1-F9) 1.00 2.50
STATED ODDS 1:7

2015 Man Who Fell to Earth Promos

MP1 Outdoors/mitchy9210/100
PR1 Mountains Artwork/Strictly Ink 1.50 4.00
PR1 Right Profile 1.50 4.00
PR2 Coming Soon/Mountains Artwork 1.25 3.00
NSP1 Coming Soon Signal Pole/Non Sport Trading Cards/100 6.00 15.00
RCP1 Signal Pole/Rydeclive
RTP1 Coming Soon Face/Radickal 6.00 15.00

1995 Comic Images Mandrake the Magician Promo

NNO Mandrake the Magician 2.00 5.00

1983 Sanitarium Many-Stranded Web of Nature

COMPLETE SET (20) 8.00 20.00
COMMON CARD (1-20) .60 1.50

1993 Sports Time Marilyn Monroe

COMPLETE SET (100) 8.00 20.00
UNOPENED BOX (36 PACKS) 30.00 40.00
UNOPENED PACK (7 CARDS) 1.00 1.25
COMMON CARD (1-100) .15 .40
RED1 Diamond Redemption Card EXCH 80.00 150.00
UNC1 Chromium Sheets UNC

1993 Sports Time Marilyn Monroe Checklists

COMPLETE SET (5) 3.00 8.00
COMMON CARD (1-5) .75 2.00
RANDOMLY INSERTED INTO PACKS

1993 Sports Time Marilyn Monroe Cover Girl Chromium

COMPLETE SET (10) 10.00 25.00
COMMON CARD (1-10) 2.00 5.00
*COL.CLUB: 4X TO 10X BASIC CARDS 20.00 50.00
RANDOMLY INSERTED INTO PACKS

1993 Sports Time Marilyn Monroe Promos

1 Card Sheet WCN 3.00 8.00
2 Card Sheet NSCC 3.00 8.00
P1 Silver Signature 1.25 3.00
P2 Gold Signature 1.25 3.00

1995 Sports Time Marilyn Monroe II

COMPLETE SET (100) 6.00 15.00
UNOPENED BOX (36 PACKS) 30.00 40.00
UNOPENED PACK (9 CARDS) 1.25 1.50
COMMON CARD (1-100) .12 .30
MI4 Club exclusive, Mail-In Offer Gold Signature

1995 Sports Time Marilyn Monroe II 24-kt Gold Signatures

COMPLETE SET (6) 8.00 20.00
COMMON CARD (1-3; 1R-3R) 2.00 5.00
STATED ODDS 1:144 (REDEMPTION ONLY)

1995 Sports Time Marilyn Monroe II Holochrome

COMPLETE SET (12) 25.00 60.00
COMMON CARD (1-12) 2.50 6.00
STATED ODDS 1:12

1995 Sports Time Marilyn Monroe II Ruby Ring

1 Contains Real Ruby in Ring 60.00 120.00
2 Ruby Ring Redemption Card 50.00 100.00

1993 The Private Collection Marilyn Monroe

COMPLETE SET (103) 12.00 30.00
UNOPENED BOX (36 PACKS) 40.00 50.00
UNOPENED PACK (10 CARDS) 1.50 1.75
COMMON CARD (1-103; CL1, CL2, CL3) .25 .60

1993 The Private Collection Marilyn Monroe Group 1 Promos

COMPLETE SET (5) 6.00 15.00
COMMON CARD (MMP1-MMP5) 2.00 5.00

1993 The Private Collection Marilyn Monroe Group 2 Promos Pink Foil

COMPLETE SET W/O SP (4) 8.00 20.00
COMMON CARD 3.00 8.00
1 Zuma Beach, California 1946 SP 30.00 75.00

1993 The Private Collection Marilyn Monroe Group 3 Promos Brown Border

COMPLETE SET (5) 50.00 100.00
COMMON CARD (1-5) 10.00 25.00

1993 The Private Collection Marilyn Monroe Group 4 Promos Green Stripe

COMPLETE SET (5) 15.00 40.00
COMMON CARD (100P-104P) 6.00 15.00

1993 The Private Collection Marilyn Monroe Group 5 Promos No Green Stripe

COMPLETE SET (5) 15.00 40.00
COMMON CARD (100P-104P) 6.00 15.00

1993 The Private Collection Marilyn Monroe Group 6 Promos

COMPLETE SET (3) 12.00 30.00
COMMON CARD 6.00 15.00

1993 The Private Collection Marilyn Monroe Group 7 Promos

COMMON CARD 2.50 6.00
NNO Cast of Drunkard 5.00 12.00
NNO Marilyn Drinking Coffee 5.00 12.00
NNO Blue Book Models 5.00 12.00
NNO Sitting on Beach/Drawing a Heart in the Sand 5.00 12.00

1993 The Private Collection Marilyn Monroe Limited Edition

COMPLETE SET (5) 25.00 60.00
COMMON CARD (1-5) 5.00 12.00
RANDOMLY INSERTED INTO PACKS
4 Limited Edition 4 12.00 30.00

1993 The Private Collection Marilyn Monroe Story Cards

COMPLETE SET (15) 10.00 25.00
COMMON CARD (SC1-SC15) .75 2.00
RANDOMLY INSERTED INTO PACKS

2007 Marilyn Monroe Shaw Family Archive

COMPLETE SET (72) 6.00 15.00
UNOPENED BOX (24 PACKS) 60.00 80.00
UNOPENED PACK (6 CARDS) 2.50 3.00
COMMON CARD (1-72) .15 .40
KMA Kevin McCarthy AU 15.00 40.00
NNO 72-Card Panel Uncut Sheets

2007 Marilyn Monroe Shaw Family Archive Marilyn Behind-the-Scenes

COMPLETE SET (9) 12.00 30.00
COMMON CARD (MB1-MB9) 2.50 6.00
STATED ODDS 1:8

2007 Marilyn Monroe Shaw Family Archive Marilyn Costumes

COMPLETE SET (5) 60.00 120.00
COMMON CARD (MP1-MP5) 12.00 30.00
STATED ODDS 1:48

2007 Marilyn Monroe Shaw Family Archive Marilyn Swim Suit Fun

COMPLETE SET (6) 10.00 25.00
COMMON CARD (MS1-MS6) 2.50 6.00
STATED ODDS 1:12

2007 Marilyn Monroe Shaw Family Archive Shot Seen 'Round the World

COMPLETE SET (9) 12.00 30.00
COMMON CARD (MD1-MD9) 1.50 4.00
STATED ODDS 1:8

2009 Mario Kart Wii Foil

COMPLETE SET W/O SP (24) 6.00 15.00
COMPLETE SET W/SP (25) 12.00 30.00
COMMON CARD (F1-F25) .50 1.25
STATED ODDS 2:3
F25 INSERTED AS TIN EXCLUSIVE

2009 Mario Kart Wii Tattoos

COMPLETE SET (14) 4.00 10.00
COMMON CARD (T1-T14) .40 1.00
STATED ODDS 1:1

2009 Mario Kart Wii Stickers

COMPLETE SET (12) 6.00 15.00
COMMON CARD (S1-S12) .75 2.00
STATED ODDS 1:3

Mars Attacks

1962 Topps Mars Attacks

COMPLETE SET (55) 3000.00 4200.00
UNOPENED BOX (36 PACKS)
UNOPENED PACK (8 CARDS)
WAX PACK WRAPPER 1500.00 2500.00
COMMON CARD (1-55) 30.00 75.00
1 The Invasion Begins 150.00 400.00
2 Martians Approaching 40.00 100.00
21 Prize Captive 125.00 300.00
55 Checklist 250.00 600.00

1964 A&BC Mars Attacks

COMPLETE SET (55) 750.00 1500.00
COMMON CARD (1-55) 8.00 20.00
1 The Invasion Begins 20.00 50.00
55 Checklist 50.00 100.00

1994 Topps Mars Attacks Archives

COMPLETE SET (99) 15.00 40.00
UNOPENED BOX (36 PACKS) 125.00 200.00
UNOPENED PACK (8 CARDS) 4.00 6.00
COMMON CARD (1-99) .20 .50
*1ST DAY ISSUE: 4X to 10X BASIC CARDS 2.00 5.00
*1ST DAY ISSUE SP: 6X to 15X BASIC CARDS3.00 8.00
STATED ODDS 1:9
NNO Zina Saunders AU/2000* 30.00 80.00

1994 Topps Mars Attacks Archives NSU Homage Series Promos

NNO (1994 Chicago Comiccon)/1000 6.00 15.00
NNO (Capital City Distribution, Inc.; 1994 Annual Trade Show)/1500 6.00 15.00
NNO (Diamond Comics Distributors, 1994 Annual Trade Show)/1500 8.00 20.00
NNO (Heroes World Distribution company; 1994 Annual Trade Show)/500 8.00 20.00
NNO (Heroes World; 1994 Heroes Convention in Charlotte)/1000 6.00 15.00
NNO (Homage Card)
NNO (Homage Card: 1994 Non-Sport Update Subscribers) 6.00 15.00
NNO (Special Autographed Homage card, unsigned; gold foil on front)/1500
NNO Jay Lynch (Special Autographed Homage card; gold foil on front)/1500 15.00 40.00

1996 Barclay's Mars Attacks UK

COMPLETE SET (8) 15.00 40.00
COMMON CARD (1-8) 2.50 6.00

2012 Mars Attacks Heritage

COMPLETE SET (55) 6.00 15.00
UNOPENED BOX (24 PACKS) 75.00 125.00
UNOPENED PACK (6 CARDS) 5.00 6.00
COMMON CARD (1-55) .20 .50
*GOLD: 50X TO 100X BASIC CARDS
*GREEN: 1.5X TO 4X BASIC CARDS
*SILVER: 10X TO 25X BASIC CARDS
1 The Invasion Begins .40 1.00
55 Checklist .30 .75

2012 Mars Attacks Heritage 3-D

COMPLETE SET (5) 8.00 20.00
COMMON CARD (1-5) 3.00 8.00
STATED ODDS 1:8

2012 Mars Attacks Heritage Deleted Scenes

COMPLETE SET (10) 5.00 12.00
COMMON CARD (1-10) .75 2.00
STATED ODDS 1:1

2012 Mars Attacks Heritage Len Brown Autographs

COMPLETE SET (55) 4000.00 7500.00
COMMON CARD 75.00 150.00
STATED ODDS 1:504 HOBBY

2012 Mars Attacks Heritage New Universe

COMPLETE SET (15) 5.00 12.00
COMMON CARD (1-15) .60 1.50
STATED ODDS 1:1

2013 Mars Attacks Invasion

COMPLETE SET (95) 12.00 30.00
UNOPENED BOX (24 PACKS) 125.00 200.00
UNOPENED PACK (5 CARDS) 5.00 8.00
COMMON CARD (1-95) .30 .75
*HERITAGE: 2X TO 5X BASIC CARDS
*GOLD: 4X TO 10X BASIC CARDS
NNO Asplode Their Heads 5.00 12.00

2013 Mars Attacks Invasion Anatomy of a Martian

COMPLETE SET (6) 10.00 25.00
COMMON CARD (1-6) 3.00 8.00
STATED ODDS 1:12

2013 Mars Attacks Invasion Artist Autographs

COMMON GALLUR 10.00 25.00
COMMON HORLEY 15.00 40.00
COMMON HORSLEY 15.00 40.00
COMMON JUSKO 15.00 40.00
COMMON KIDD 12.00 30.00
COMMON NELSON 15.00 40.00
COMMON ORBIK 15.00 40.00
COMMON PALUMBO 12.00 30.00
COMMON PETERSON 12.00 30.00
COMMON REPKA 15.00 40.00
COMMON SPEARS 15.00 40.00
COMMON WILKERSON 15.00 40.00
STATED ODDS 1:111
GREG STAPLES (16-18) NOT ISSUED IN SET

2013 Mars Attacks Invasion Classic Creator Autographs

COMMON CARD 40.00 80.00
STATED ODDS 1:417
1 Charles Adlard 60.00 120.00
3 Len Brown 100.00 175.00
4 Simon Bisley 50.00 100.00

2013 Mars Attacks Invasion Comic Creator Autographs

STATED ODDS 1:1,670
1 John Layman 40.00 80.00
2 John McCrea 50.00 100.00

2013 Mars Attacks Invasion Pencil Concepts

COMPLETE SET (58) 500.00 800.00
*CONCEPT: 8X TO 20X BASIC CARDS
STATED ODDS 1:48

2013 Mars Attacks Invasion Early Missions

COMPLETE SET (6) 5.00 12.00
COMMON CARD (1-6) 1.50 4.00
STATED ODDS 1:12

2013 Mars Attacks Invasion Extra Gore

COMPLETE SET (10) 80.00 150.00
*GOLD: 1.5X TO 4X BASIC CARDS 8.00 20.00
STATED ODDS 1:72

2013 Mars Attacks Invasion Join the Fight

COMPLETE SET (4) 6.00 15.00
COMMON CARD (1-4) 2.00 5.00
*GRAFFITI: 2.5X TO 6X BASIC CARDS
STATED ODDS 1:6

2013 Mars Attacks Invasion Masterpieces

COMPLETE SET (5) 5.00 12.00
COMMON CARD (1-5) 2.00 5.00
STATED ODDS 1:6

2013 Mars Attacks Invasion Medallions

COMMON CARD (MM1-MM16) 20.00 50.00
STATED ODDS 1:108
MM2 Beauty and the Beast SP 125.00 200.00
MM4 Giant Robot 40.00 80.00
MM6 Creeping Menace SP 125.00 200.00
MM7 Terror in the Railroad 35.00 70.00
MM11 Crushed to Death 30.00 60.00
MM14 Trapped SP 75.00 150.00
MM16 Destroying a Dog SP 125.00 200.00

2013 Mars Attacks Invasion Movie Autographs

STATED ODDS 1:167
1 Brian Haley 8.00 20.00
2 Frank Welker 20.00 50.00
3 O-Lan Jones 8.00 20.00
4 Pam Grier 15.00 40.00
5 Willie Garson 8.00 20.00

2013 Mars Attacks Invasion Patches

COMMON CARD (MP1-MP16) 20.00 50.00
STATED ODDS 1:109
MP2 Surviving Martians SP 75.00 150.00
MP4 Losing Ground SP 75.00 150.00
MP6 Twisted Experiments SP 75.00 150.00
MP7 Bred for Destruction SP 75.00 150.00
MP11 Retaking Red Square SP 75.00 150.00
MP14 Operation Earth SP 75.00 150.00

2013 Mars Attacks Invasion Promos

COMPLETE SET (4)
COMMON CARD
0 Invasion Begins 2.50 6.00
1 Stan Strikes 8.00 20.00
P1 Grinning Martian 2.50 6.00
NNO Mars Attacks Minis 2.00 5.00

2021 Topps Mars Attacks Invasion 2026

COMPLETE SET (10) 75.00 150.00

MODERN

COMMON CARD (1-10) 10.00 25.00
STATED PRINT RUN 1044 ANNCD SETS

1994 Topps Mars Attacks Model Kit

COMPLETE SET (9) 75.00 150.00
COMMON CARD 8.00 20.00
NNO Air Assault Martian 8.00 20.00
NNO Attacking Martian 8.00 20.00
NNO Contemplating Conquest 8.00 20.00
NNO Mars Attacks Modeling 8.00 20.00
NNO No Place to Hide 8.00 20.00
NNO Slaughter in the Streets 8.00 20.00
NNO Target Earth 8.00 20.00
NNO Terror in the Sky 8.00 20.00
NNO The Invasion Begins Bonus Chase/5000*
NNO Official Mars Attacks Conquest Oversized
NNO Official Mars Attacks Conquest AU
NNO Uncut Sheet/50*
NNO Slaughter in the Streets (Promotional Use Only)

1995 Del Rey Books Mars Attacks Novel Cards

COMPLETE SET (4) 2.50 6.00
COMMON CARD .75 2.00

2016 Mars Attacks Occupation

COMPLETE SET (81) 30.00 80.00
UNOPENED BOX (24 PACKS)
UNOPENED PACK (5 CARDS)
COMMON CARD (1-81) .60 1.50
*HERITAGE: .6X TO 1.5X BASIC CARDS
*CONCEPT ART: 1X TO 2.5X BASIC CARDS
*FOIL: 2.5X TO 6X BASIC CARDS

2016 Mars Attacks Occupation All-Star Sketch Artists

COMPLETE SET (9) 25.00 60.00
COMMON CARD (AS1-AS9) 4.00 10.00
STATED ODDS 1:7

2016 Mars Attacks Occupation Creator Autographs

COMMON CARD (A1-A11) 10.00 25.00
A1 Alex Horley 30.00 75.00
A2 Adam Levine
A3 Ralph Horsley 10.00 25.00
A4 Lars Grant-West
A5 Kieran Yanner
A6 Greg Staples 10.00 25.00
A7 Eric Wilkerson 10.00 25.00
A8 Ed Repka 12.00 30.00
A9 Bob Larkin 30.00 80.00
A10 Dan Brereton 10.00 25.00
A11 Jason Crosby 25.00 60.00

2016 Mars Attacks Occupation Dinosaurs Attack vs. Mars Attacks

COMPLETE SET (9) 30.00 80.00
COMMON CARD (DAMA1-DAMA9) 5.00 12.00
STATED ODDS 1:12

2016 Mars Attacks Occupation Judge Dredd Autographs

COMPLETE SET (4) 25.00 60.00
COMMON CARD 8.00 20.00
STATED ODDS 1:1 JUDGE DREDD PACKS

2016 Mars Attacks Occupation Judge Dredd Inserts

COMPLETE SET (18) 25.00 60.00
UNOPENED JUDGE DREDD PACK 80.00 150.00
COMMON CARD (1-18) 1.50 4.00
ONE SET PER JUDGE DREDD PACK

2016 Mars Attacks Occupation Mars Attacks Superstars

COMPLETE SET (9) 25.00 60.00
COMMON CARD (1-9) 3.00 8.00
STATED ODDS 1:2

2016 Mars Attacks Occupation Mars Attacky Packages

COMPLETE SET (13) 50.00 100.00
COMMON CARD 4.00 10.00
STATED ODDS 1:7

2016 Mars Attacks Occupation Original 1962 Series Metal

COMPLETE SET (55) 1500.00 3000.00
COMMON CARD (1-55) 25.00 60.00

2016 Mars Attacks Occupation Then and Now

COMPLETE SET (9) 15.00 40.00
COMMON CARD (TN1-TN9) 2.50 6.00
STATED ODDS 1:7

2016 Mars Attacks Occupation Promos

P1A Mars Rules (green)
P1B Mars Rules (gold)
P1C Mars Rules (red) 1.50 4.00
P3 Behold the Martian (art by Jeff Zapata)
GPK Slime Captive (Garbage Pail Kids) 5.00 12.00
IDW Mars-Attacks Occupation No. 1 Mar. (IDW) 30.00 80.00
IDW Submit (IDW)
KS1 Kickstarter (Non-Sport Update) 2.50 6.00
NNO Area 51 (Mars Attacks: The Dice Game! 4-3/8" x 3-3/8") 2.00 5.00
LB1962B The Armageddon Detective (Topps Books) 15.00 40.00

2017 Mars Attacks The Revenge

COMPLETE SET (55) 8.00 20.00
UNOPENED BOX (149 CARDS) 60.00 80.00
COMMON CARD (1-55) .30 .75
*EMERALD: .6X TO 1.5X BASIC CARDS .50 1.25
*PEN. EMERALD: .6X TO 1.5X BASIC CARDS .50 1.25
*YELLOW/199: 1.25X TO 3X BASIC CARDS 1.25 3.00
*PEN. YELLOW/199: 1.25X TO 3X BASIC CARDS 1.25 3.00
*RED/99: 5X TO 12X BASIC CARDS 4.00 10.00
*PEN. RED/99: 5X TO 12X BASIC CARDS 4.00 10.00
*BLACK/55: 6X TO 15X BASIC CARDS 5.00 12.00
*PEN. BLACK/55: 6X TO 15X BASIC CARDS 5.00 12.00
*BRONZE/25: 10X TO 25X BASIC CARDS 8.00 20.00
*PEN. BRONZE/25: 10X TO 25X BASIC CARDS 8.00 20.00
*SILVER/10: 15X TO 40X BASIC CARDS 12.00 30.00
*PEN. SILVER/10: 15X TO 40X BASIC CARDS 12.00 30.00

2017 Mars Attacks The Revenge Artist Autographs

COMMON HARPER 10.00 25.00
COMMON DEJARNETTE 8.00 20.00
*PENCILED/10: SAME VALUE
55 Brent Engstrom 100.00 175.00

2017 Mars Attacks The Revenge Commemorative Medallion Relics

COMPLETE SET (20) 200.00 400.00
COMMON RELIC 10.00 25.00
*SILVER/15: .5X TO 1.2X BASIC RELICS 12.00 30.00
STATED PRINT RUN 55 SER.#'d SETS

2017 Mars Attacks The Revenge Len Brown Co-Creator Autographs

COMMON AUTO (1-55) 10.00 25.00
*PENCILED/10: SAME VALUE

2014 Mars Attacks SDCC Scavenger Hunt

COMPLETE SET (9) 12.00 30.00

2019 Mars Attacks Uprising Promos

P1 Coming Soon to Kickstarter
P2 Coming Soon to Kickstarter
P3 Coming Soon to Kickstarter

2018 Mars Attacks Wacky Packages

COMPLETE SET (10) 25.00 60.00
COMMON CARD (1-10) 4.00 10.00
STATED PRINT RUN 348 SER.#'d SETS

2020 Topps Mars Attacks Wacky Packages Series 3

COMPLETE SET (15) 10.00 25.00
UNOPENED PACK (6 CARDS)
COMMON CARD (1-15) 1.25 3.00
*RED CRUDLOW: 1.5X TO 4X BASIC CARDS
STATED PRINT RUN 635 SETS

2020 Topps Mars Attacks Wacky Packages Series 4

COMPLETE SET (21) 12.00 30.00
UNOPENED PACK (28 CARDS)
COMMON CARD (1-20; HEADER) 1.00 2.50
*COUPON: 1.2X TO 3X BASIC CARDS
*RED LUDLOW: 2X TO 5X BASIC CARDS
STATED PRINT RUN 1,006 SETS

2020 Topps Mars Attacks Wacky Packages Series 4 Glow-in-the-Dark

COMPLETE SET (4) 15.00 40.00
COMMON CARD (G1-G4) 8.00 20.00
STATED ODDS 1:1

2022 Topps Mars Attacks Wacky Packages Series 6

COMPLETE SET (10)
COMMON CARD (1-9; CL)
*COUPON: 1.5X TO 4X BASIC CARDS
*RAINBOW: 3X TO 8X BASIC CARDS
STATED PRINT RUN 1,159 ANNCD SETS

2022 Topps Mars Attacks Wacky Packages Series 6 Sci-Fi Cereal Box

COMPLETE SET (3) 8.00 20.00
COMMON CARD (1-3) 4.00 10.00
STATED ODDS 1:1

1996 Topps Widevision Mars Attacks

COMPLETE SET (72) 8.00 20.00
UNOPENED BOX (36 PACKS) 50.00 75.00
UNOPENED PACK (9 CARDS) 2.00 3.00
COMMON CARD (1-72) .20 .50

1996 Topps Widevision Mars Attacks Destruct-O-Rama Foil

COMPLETE SET (6) 12.00 30.00
COMMON CARD (MA1-MA6) 4.00 10.00
STATED ODDS 1:9

1996 Topps Widevision Mars Attacks Promos

NNO Promo 1 (Martian - green logo) .75 2.00
NNO Promo 2 (Martian - red logo) .75 2.00
NNO Promo 3 (Martian reading magazine) .75 2.00
NNO Savage Dragon Mars Attacks .75 2.00

1992 Unbeatables Martin Luther King Jr.

COMPLETE BOXED SET (16) 3.00 8.00
COMMON CARD (1-16) .30 .75

1994 Topps Mary Shelley's Frankenstein The Movie

COMPLETE SET (12) 5.00 12.00
COMMON CARD (1-12) .50 1.25

1982 Donruss M.A.S.H.

COMPLETE SET (66) 7.50 20.00
UNOPENED BOX (36 PACKS) 75.00 150.00
UNOPENED PACK (6 CARDS) 2.00 4.00
COMMON CARD (1-66) .15 .40

1994 Cardz The Mask

COMPLETE SET (100) 8.00 20.00
UNOPENED BOX (24 PACKS) 15.00 20.00
UNOPENED PACK (8 CARDS) .75 1.00
COMMON CARD (1-100) .15 .40

1994 Cardz The Mask TekChromes

COMPLETE SET (10) 30.00 80.00
COMMON CARD (T1-T10) 4.00 10.00
STATED ODDS 1:12

1994 Cardz The Mask Promos

1 Promo Postcard (logo)
2 Promo Postcard (no logo)
P1 The Mask Returns .75 2.00
P2 Eyeballs and Tongue .75 2.00

1996 Inkworks The Mask Animated Series Inkworks Promos

COMPLETE SET (2) 1.25 3.00
COMMON CARD .75 2.00

1996 Maxx The Mask Animated Series Maxx Promos

COMPLETE SET (3) 2.00 5.00
COMMON CARD .75 2.00

1994 Edwards Cinemas The Mask Promos

COMPLETE SET (12) 8.00 20.00
COMMON CARD (1-12) 1.00 2.50

1998 DuoCards The Mask of Zorro

COMPLETE SET (72) 5.00 12.00
UNOPENED BOX (30 PACKS) 36.00 40.00
UNOPENED PACK (7 PACKS) 1.25 1.50
COMMON CARD (1-72) .12 .40

1998 DuoCards The Mask of Zorro Antonio Banderas OmniChrome

COMPLETE SET (3) 12.00 30.00
COMMON CARD (1-3) 5.00 12.00
WRAPPER REDEMPTION

1998 DuoCards The Mask of Zorro Catherine Zeta-Jones OmniChrome

COMPLETE SET (6) 12.00 30.00
COMMON CARD (1-6) 3.00 8.00
STATED ODDS 1:12

1998 DuoCards The Mask of Zorro Promos

COMPLETE SET (3) 3.00 8.00
COMMON CARD 1.50 4.00

2005 Mask of Zorro Promos

COMPLETE SET (2) 2.00 5.00
COMMON CARD 1.25 3.00

1996 Donruss Masked Rider Promo

NNO Masked Rider .60 1.50

1993 Comic Images Masterpiece Collection

COMPLETE SET (90) 5.00 12.00
UNOPENED BOX (48 PACKS) 40.00 50.00
UNOPENED PACK (10 CARDS) 1.00 1.25
COMMON CARD (1-90) .08 .25

1993 Comic Images Masterpiece Collection Chromium

COMPLETE SET (6) 2.50 6.00
COMMON CARD (1-6) .75 2.00
STATED ODDS 1:16

1993 Comic Images Masterpiece Collection Promos

COMPLETE SET (2) 1.25 3.00
COMMON CARD .75 2.00

1996 FPG Masters of Fantasy Metallic

COMPLETE SET (90) 12.00 30.00

UNOPENED BOX (36 PACKS) 30.00 40.00
UNOPENED PACK (6 CARDS) 1.00 1.25
COMMON CARD (1-90) .30 .75

1996 FPG Masters of Fantasy Metallic Gold

COMPLETE SET (6) 15.00 40.00
COMMON CARD (1-6) 3.00 8.00
STATED ODDS 1:12

1993 Imagine Masters of Horror Promos

COMPLETE SET (3) 2.00 5.00
COMMON CARD (1-3) .75 2.00

1996 Comic Images Masters of Japanimation

COMPLETE SET (90) 5.00 12.00
UNOPENED BOX (48 PACKS) 20.00 30.00
UNOPENED PACK (10 CARDS) .50 .75
COMMON CARD (1-90) .12 .30
NNO1 Gall Force Eternal Story Insert 2.00 5.00
NNO2 Koichi Ohata AU/500 20.00 50.00
NNO3 90 Cards Uncut Sheet

1996 Comic Images Masters of Japanimation Mighty Warriors of US Manga Corps

COMPLETE SET (3) 15.00 40.00
COMMON CARD (S1-S3) 6.00 15.00
RANDOMLY INSERTED INTO PACKS

1996 Comic Images Masters of Japanimation Overfiend Chromium

COMPLETE SET (6) 10.00 25.00
COMMON CARD (C1-C6) 2.50 6.00
STATED ODDS 1:16

1996 Comic Images Masters of Japanimation Promos

COMPLETE SET (2) 1.25 3.00
COMMON CARD .75 2.00

1984 Topps Masters of the Universe

COMPLETE SET (88) 8.00 20.00
UNOPENED BOX (36 PACKS) 300.00 500.00
UNOPENED PACK (10 CARDS+1 STICKER) 8.00 15.00
COMMON CARD (1-88) .20 .50

1984 Topps Masters of the Universe Stickers

COMPLETE SET (22) 2.00 5.00
COMMON CARD .15 .40
STATED ODDS 1:1

1986 Wonder Bread Masters of the Universe

COMPLETE SET (15) 25.00 60.00
COMMON CARD 2.50 6.00
NNO He-Man 4.00 10.00
NNO Skeletor 4.00 10.00

1995 Cardz Maverick The Movie

COMPLETE SET (60) 5.00 12.00
UNOPENED BOX (36 PACKS) 20.00 30.00
UNOPENED PACK (8 CARDS) .75 1.00
COMMON CARD (1-60) .15 .40

1995 Cardz Maverick The Movie TekChrome

COMPLETE SET (3) 8.00 20.00
COMMON CARD (T1-T3) 3.00 8.00
STATED ODDS 1:24

1995 Cardz Maverick The Movie Promos

COMPLETE SET (3) 1.25 3.00
COMMON CARD (P1-P3) .60 1.50

1986 Topps Max Headroom

COMPLETE SET (33) 6.00 15.00
COMMON CARD (1-33) .15 .40

1994 Comic Images Maxfield Parrish Portrait of America

COMPLETE SET (90) 4.00 10.00
UNOPENED BOX (48 PACKS) 20.00 30.00
UNOPENED PACK (10 CARDS) .50 .75
COMMON CARD (1-90) .10 .25
NNO Jason and His Teacher Medallion Card/1437* 10.00 25.00
NNO Le Parfum Irresistible PROMO .75 2.00

1994 Comic Images Maxfield Parrish Portrait of America Foil

COMPLETE SET (6) 8.00 20.00
COMMON CARD (F1-F6) 1.50 4.00
STATED ODDS 1:16

1994 Comic Images Maxfield Parrish Portrait of America Subset

COMPLETE SET (3) 10.00 25.00
COMMON CARD (1-3) 4.00 10.00
STATED ODDS 1:48

1993 SkyBox Maximum Force

P0 Preying Mantis
P00 Trencher Mobile
NNO Blitz .75 2.00

1993 Topps The Maxx

COMPLETE SET (90) 5.00 12.00
COMMON CARD (1-90) .12 .30

1993 Topps The Maxx Autographs

1 Redemption EXCH
2 Sam Keith 20.00 50.00

1993 Topps The Maxx Etched Foil

COMPLETE SET (4) 10.00 25.00
COMMON CARD (1-4) 3.00 8.00
STATED ODDS 1:18

1993 Topps The Maxx Winners

1 Redemption Card
5 Etched Foil Card 15.00 40.00

1996 WildStorm The Maxx

COMPLETE SET (99) 8.00 20.00
UNOPENED BOX (36 PACKS) 20.00 25.00
UNOPENED PACK (8 CARDS) .50 .75
COMMON CARD (1-99) .15 .40

1996 WildStorm The Maxx Gallery

COMPLETE SET (9) 12.00 30.00
COMMON CARD (P1-P9) 2.50 6.00
STATED ODDS 1:12

1996 WildStorm The Maxx Sam Kieth's Private Collection

COMPLETE SET (9) 12.00 30.00
COMMON CARD (E1-E9) 2.50 6.00
STATED ODDS 1:9

1995 Tempo May Gibbs

COMPLETE SET (110) 6.00 15.00
UNOPENED BOX (30 PACKS)
UNOPENED PACK (7 CARDS)
COMMON CARD (1-110) .12 .30

1995 Tempo May Gibbs Creature

COMPLETE SET (8) 6.00 15.00
COMMON CARD (C1-C8) 1.25 3.00
STATED ODDS 1:8

1995 Tempo May Gibbs Rare Issue

COMPLETE SET (3) 5.00 12.00
COMMON CARD (RI1-RI3) 2.00 5.00
STATED ODDS 1:25

1995 Tempo May Gibbs Promos

COMMON CARD 4.00 10.00

1996 Classic McDonald's Premiere Edition

COMPLETE SET (50) 4.00 10.00
UNOPENED BOX (24 PACKS) 35.00 60.00
UNOPENED PACK (5 CARDS) 2.00 3.00
COMMON CARD (1-50) .15 .40
*$2 PHONE CARD: 2X TO 5X BASIC CARDS .75 2.00
*GOLD FOIL: 5X TO 12X BASIC CARDS 2.00 5.00

1996 Classic McDonald's Premiere Edition $5 Phone Cards I

COMPLETE SET (10) 12.00 30.00
COMMON CARD (1-10) 2.00 5.00
STATED ODDS 1:24

1996 Classic McDonald's Premiere Edition $5 Phone Cards II

COMPLETE SET (10) 12.00 30.00
COMMON CARD 2.00 5.00
STATED ODDS 1:24

1996 Classic McDonald's Premiere Edition McDonald's Cels

COMPLETE SET (20) 15.00 40.00
COMMON CARD (MC1-MC20) 1.25 3.00

1996 Classic McDonald's Premiere Edition Promos

S2 Phone Card (test issue)
NNO1 1000 Phone Card 2.00 5.00

1998 Comic Images Meanie Babies

COMPLETE SET (61) 3.00 8.00
UNOPENED BOX (48 PACKS) 25.00 40.00
UNOPENED PACK (6 CARDS+1 STICKER) 1.00 1.50
COMMON CARD (1-61) .12 .30
*STICKER: .75X TO 2X BASIC CARDS .25 .60

1998 Comic Images Meanie Babies John Pound Autographs

COMPLETE SET (3) 30.00 80.00
COMMON CARD (1S-3S) 12.00 30.00
RANDOMLY INSERTED INTO PACKS

1998 Comic Images Meanie Babies Omnichrome

COMPLETE SET (6) 10.00 25.00
COMMON CARD (Omni1-Omni6) 2.00 5.00
STATED ODDS 1:16

1998 Comic Images Meanie Babies Sketches

COMPLETE SET (3) 12.00 30.00
COMMON CARD (1S-3S) 5.00 12.00
RANDOMLY INSERTED INTO PACKS

1998 Comic Images Meanie Babies Promos

COMPLETE SET (4) 2.00 5.00
COMMON CARD .75 2.00

1991 Impel Megametal

COMPLETE SET (150) 12.00 30.00
COMMON CARD (1-150) .20 .50

1991 Impel Megametal Holograms

COMPLETE SET (8) 2.50 6.00
COMMON CARD .50 1.25
STATED ODDS 1:5

1991 Impel Megametal Promos

COMPLETE SET (3) 4.00 10.00
COMMON CARD 2.00 5.00

1996 Sports Time Melrose Place Promos

1 Andrew Shue/60
2 Courtney Thorne Smith/8
3 Doug Savant/35
4 Grant Show/8
5 Jack Wagner/35
6 Josie Bisset/36
7 Thomas Calabro/8
P Promo (w/blue background) -1996 .75 2.00
P Promo (w/brown background) -1997 .75 2.00

1993 Comic Images Melting Pot

COMPLETE SET (90) 8.00 20.00
UNOPENED BOX (36 PACKS) 30.00 40.00
UNOPENED PACK (7 CARDS) 1.00 1.25
COMMON CARD (1-90) .20 .50
*REFRACTOR: 8X TO 20X BASIC CARDS 4.00 10.00

1993 Comic Images Melting Pot Prisms

COMPLETE SET (6) 15.00 40.00
COMMON CARD (P1-P6) 4.00 10.00
STATED ODDS 1:12

2014 Melty Misfits Series One

COMPLETE SET (60) 50.00 100.00
UNOPENED BOX (24 PACKS)
UNOPENED PACK (7 CARDS)
COMMON CARD (1a-30b) .75 2.00

1997 Inkworks Men in Black

COMPLETE SET (90) 4.00 10.00
UNOPENED BOX (36 PACKS) 50.00 75.00
UNOPENED PACK (8 CARDS) 1.50 2.50
COMMON CARD (1-90) .15 .40
CUNNINGHAM AUTO RANDOM INSERT IN PACKS
S1 Suncoast Video PROMO 2.00 5.00
LCAU Lowell Cunningham AU 6.00 15.00
NNO The Secret is Out! PROMO 2.00

1997 Inkworks Men in Black Alien Profiles

COMPLETE SET (5) 8.00 20.00
COMMON CARD (P1-P5) 2.00 5.00
STATED ODDS 1:11

1997 Inkworks Men in Black Cards in Black

COMPLETE SET (2) 12.00 30.00
COMMON CARD (B1-B2) 8.00 20.00
STATED ODDS 1:54

1997 Inkworks Men in Black Foilworks

COMPLETE SET (5) 10.00 25.00
COMMON CARD (S1-S5) 3.00 8.00
STATED ODDS 1:24

2002 Men in Black II

COMPLETE SET (81) 4.00 10.00
UNOPENED BOX (36 PACKS) 50.00 90.00
UNOPENED PACK (7 CARDS) 1.50 2.50
COMMON CARD (1-81) .10 .25

2002 Men in Black II Autographs

COMMON CARD (A1-A7) 6.00 15.00
STATED ODDS 1:50
A1 Tommy Lee Jones 450.00 900.00
A2 Barry Sonnenfeld 50.00 100.00
A3 Lara Flynn Boyle 50.00 100.00
A4 Tony Shalhoub 25.00 60.00

2002 Men in Black II Box-Loaders

COMPLETE SET (4) 7.50 20.00
COMMON CARD 1.25 3.00
STATED ODDS 1:36
BL1 They're Back in Business 1.25 3.00
BL2 They're Back in Action 1.25 3.00
BL3 They're Back in Black 1.25 3.00
CL1 Same Planet. New Scum. 6.00 15.00
CASE INSERT

2002 Men in Black II Neuralyzer

COMPLETE SET (2) 6.00 15.00
COMMON CARD (N1-N2) 4.00 10.00
STATED ODDS 1:35 HOBBY ONLY

2002 Men in Black II Pieceworks

COMPLETE SET (3) 30.00 60.00
COMMON CARD (PW1-PW3) 6.00 15.00
STATED ODDS 1:35
PW2 Tommy Lee Jones 15.00 30.00
PW3 Tommy Lee Jones 15.00 30.00

2002 Men in Black II Special

COMPLETE SET (3)	4.00	10.00
COMMON CARD (R1-R3)	1.50	4.00
STATED ODDS 1:11 RETAIL ONLY		

2002 Men in Black II Weapons Overview

COMPLETE SET (6)	7.50	20.00
COMMON CARD (W1-W6)	1.50	4.00
STATED ODDS 1:17		

2002 Men in Black II Promos

COMPLETE SET (6)	3.00	8.00
COMMON CARD	.75	2.00
Pi Lara Flynn Boyle	1.25	3.00

2002 Men in Black II Suncoast Video

NNO (Title Card)
NNO C'mon, J. She ain't even...
NNO Once you've had worm...
NNO Silly little planet...
NNO ...would someone please...
NNO You didn't neuralize...
NNO Thank you for participating...
NNO I'm not going to take advice...
NNO The Crelons are the...
NNO Why don't you go...
NNO (Coupon Card)

2021 Topps MetaZoo Cryptid Nation Series 0

COMPLETE SET (73)	150.00	400.00
UNOPENED BOX (30 TOTAL CARDS)	30.00	50.00
COMMON B (1-73)	1.25	3.00
COMMON S (1-73)	1.50	4.00
COMMON G (1-73)	2.50	6.00
*BLACK STAR: 3X TO 8X BASIC CARDS		
2 Alien Astronaut B	12.00	30.00
3 Babe the Blue Ox G	12.00	30.00
5 Beast of Busco G	15.00	40.00
6 Bigfoot G	10.00	25.00
7 Black Cat S	8.00	20.00
10 Chessie G	12.00	30.00
11 Chibi Mothman B	10.00	25.00
12 Chibi Quetza S	4.00	10.00
13 Chupacabra G	4.00	10.00
14 Dingbelle B	5.00	12.00
18 Frozen People B	5.00	12.00
19 Funeral Mountain Terrashot S	10.00	25.00
21 Ghost Deer B	4.00	10.00
22 Ghost Train G	15.00	40.00
23 Giant Salamander B	8.00	20.00
24 Gumberoo B	10.00	25.00
25 Hide Behind S	4.00	10.00
26 Hodag G	3.00	8.00
27 Hoop Snake S	8.00	20.00
28 Hopkinsville Goblin S	5.00	12.00
29 Huggin' Molly S	2.50	6.00
30 Jersey Devil G	5.00	12.00
31 Joint Snake B	2.00	5.00
33 Killer Clown B	10.00	25.00
34 Kushtaka S	10.00	25.00
35 Lake Worth Monster B	12.00	30.00
37 Lizard Man of Scape Ore Swamp G	6.00	15.00
38 Loveland Frogman G	6.00	15.00
39 Mantis Man B	8.00	20.00
42 Metal Man of Alabama G	6.00	15.00
43 Minnesota Iceman S	6.00	15.00
45 Mothman G	60.00	150.00
46 Old Green Eyes B	2.50	6.00
47 Piasa Bird G	10.00	25.00
48 Pukwudgie B	2.00	5.00
49 Quetzalcoatlus G	30.00	75.00
53 Salem's Witches S	3.00	8.00
54 Sam Sinclair G	6.00	15.00
55 Sewer Alligator B	6.00	15.00
57 Sinkhole Sam G	15.00	40.00
58 Slide-Rock Bolter G	3.00	8.00
60 Snallygaster G	3.00	8.00
61 Snow Snake B	6.00	15.00
64 Squonk S	6.00	15.00
66 The Char Man B	6.00	15.00
67 The Spookster S	8.00	20.00
70 Uncle Sam G	20.00	50.00
71 Walking Sam G	8.00	20.00
72 Wapaloosie B	10.00	25.00

2021 Topps MetaZoo Cryptid Nation Series 0 Black Star

*BLACK STAR: 3X TO 8X BASIC CARDS
STATED ODDS 1:1

2021 Topps MetaZoo Cryptid Nation Series 0 Creator Card Caster Gold

STATED ODDS 1:83 BOXES		
STATED PRINT RUN 299 SER.#'d SETS		
C1 Michael Waddell	200.00	400.00
C2 Steve Aoki	125.00	300.00

2021 Topps MetaZoo Cryptid Nation Series 0 First Sighting Gold

COMMON CARD	125.00	300.00
STATED ODDS 1:22 BOXES		
STATED PRINT RUN 99 SER.#'d SETS		
3G Babe the Blue Ox	250.00	600.00
5G Beast of Busco	150.00	400.00
6G Bigfoot	600.00	1500.00
10G Chessie	600.00	1500.00
13G Chupacabra	300.00	800.00
22G Ghost Train	400.00	1000.00
26G Hodag	250.00	600.00
30G Jersey Devil	300.00	800.00
38G Loveland Frogman	1200.00	3000.00
42G Metal Man of Alabama	250.00	600.00
45G Mothman	2000.00	5000.00
47G Piasa Bird	300.00	800.00
49G Quetzacoatlus	300.00	800.00
60G Snallygaster	200.00	500.00
68G Tizheruk	150.00	400.00

2021 Topps MetaZoo Cryptid Nation Series 0 Lore

COMPLETE SET (10)	15.00	40.00
COMMON CARD (L1-L10)	2.50	6.00
STATED ODDS 4:BOX		

2021 Topps MetaZoo Cryptid Nation Series 0 Promo Gold

STATED ODDS 1:50 BOXES		
STATED PRINT RUN 999 SER.#'d SETS		
P1 Topps x Cryptid Nation Collab	60.00	150.00

2022 Topps Chrome MetaZoo Cryptid Nation Series 0

COMPLETE SET (150)	30.00	75.00
UNOPENED BOX (20 PACKS)	100.00	125.00
UNOPENED PACK (4 CARDS)	6.00	8.00
BLASTER BOX (4 PACKS)	25.00	40.00
BLASTER PACK (4 CARDS)	6.00	10.00
COMMON CARD (1-150)	.40	1.00
*REFRACTOR: 1.5X TO 4X BASIC CARDS		
*XFRAC: 2X TO 5X BASIC CARDS		
*GREEN/99: 15X TO 40X BASIC CARDS		
*GOLD/50: 20X TO 50X BASIC CARDS		

2022 Topps Chrome MetaZoo Cryptid Nation Series 0 Battle

COMPLETE SET (6)	10.00	25.00
COMMON CARD (B1-B6)	2.50	6.00
*GREEN/99: 2X TO 5X BASIC CARDS		
*GOLD/50: 4X TO 10X BASIC CARDS		
STATED ODDS 1:10		
B6 Loveland Frogman vs. Flatwoods Monster	4.00	10.00

2022 Topps Chrome MetaZoo Cryptid Nation Series 0 Creator Cards

COMPLETE SET (2)	50.00	125.00
COMMON CARD (C1-C2)	25.00	60.00
STATED ODDS 1:160		
C2 Steve Aoki	40.00	100.00

2022 Topps Chrome MetaZoo Cryptid Nation Series 0 Cryptid Camera

COMPLETE SET (150)		
COMMON CARD (1F-150F)		
STATED ODDS 1:20		
3F Babe The Blue Ox	15.00	40.00
5F Beast of Busco	10.00	25.00
6F Bigfoot	10.00	25.00
10F Chessie	10.00	25.00
13F Chupacabra	10.00	25.00
17F Fresno Nightcrawlers	8.00	20.00
22F Ghost Train	10.00	25.00
26F Hodag	12.00	30.00
30F Jersey Devil	10.00	25.00
42F Metal Man of Alabama	8.00	20.00
45F Mothman	30.00	75.00
47F Piasa Bird	8.00	20.00
49F Quetzalcoatlus	6.00	15.00
54F Sam Sinclair	15.00	40.00
57F Sinkhole Sam	6.00	15.00
68F Tizheruk	10.00	25.00
70F Uncle Sam	10.00	25.00
71F Walking Sam	6.00	15.00
74F Adam Ackler	10.00	25.00
79F Ben B	6.00	15.00
118F Piasa Bird	12.00	30.00
121F Rainbow Wizard	6.00	15.00
144F Chaos Crystal	20.00	50.00
145F Death Beam	6.00	15.00
146F Eternal Snowflake	10.00	25.00
148F Medium's Third Eye	12.00	30.00

2022 Topps Chrome MetaZoo Cryptid Nation Series 0 Cryptid Camera Gold Refractors

STATED ODDS 1:1,195		
STATED PRINT RUN 50 SER.#'d SETS		
42F Metal Man of Alabama	25.00	60.00
47F Piasa Bird	50.00	125.00
57F Sinkhole Sam	50.00	125.00
58F Slide-Rock Bolter	30.00	75.00
79F Ben B	12.00	30.00
102F Indrid Cold	30.00	75.00
121F Rainbow Wizard	30.00	75.00
144F Chaos Crystal	75.00	200.00

2022 Topps Chrome MetaZoo Cryptid Nation Series 0 Cryptid Camera Green Refractors

STATED ODDS 1:604		
STATED PRINT RUN 99 SER.#'d SETS		
3F Babe The Blue Ox	60.00	150.00
22F Ghost Train	25.00	60.00
38F Loveland Frogman	50.00	125.00
41F Menehune	50.00	125.00
42F Metal Man of Alabama	25.00	60.00
45F Mothman	100.00	250.00
54F Sam Sinclair	20.00	50.00
57F Sinkhole Sam	20.00	50.00
60F Snallygaster	30.00	75.00
62F Snow Wasset	30.00	75.00
68F Tizheruk	25.00	60.00
74F Adam Ackler	20.00	50.00
77F Babe The Blue Ox	30.00	75.00
121F Rainbow Wizard	25.00	60.00
128F Sinkhole Sam	15.00	40.00
137F Tizheruk	15.00	40.00
143F Blood Ruby	15.00	40.00
144F Chaos Crystal	60.00	150.00

2022 Topps Chrome MetaZoo Cryptid Nation Series 0 Lore

COMPLETE SET (10)	6.00	15.00
COMMON CARD (L1-L10)	1.00	2.50
*GREEN/99: 8X TO 20X BASIC CARDS		
*GOLD/50: 12X TO 30X BASIC CARDS		
STATED ODDS 1:7		

1992 Shel-Tone Michael H. Price's Hollywood Horrors

COMPLETE BOXED.SET (37)	5.00	12.00
COMMON CARD (1-37)	.25	.60
NNO Hollywood Horrors PROMO	1.25	3.00

1984 Topps Michael Jackson

COMPLETE SET (66)	12.00	30.00
COMP.SER.1 SET (33)	8.00	20.00
COMP.SER.2 SET (33)	8.00	20.00
COMP.SER. 1 FACT.SET (33)	10.00	25.00
UNOPENED SER.1 BOX (36 PACKS)	75.00	125.00
UNOPENED SER.1 PACK (3 CARDS+3 STICKERS)	2.00	3.00
UNOPENED SER.2 BOX (36 PACKS)	75.00	125.00
UNOPENED SER.2 PACK (3 CARDS+3 STICKERS)	2.00	3.00
COMMON CARD (1-33)	.40	1.00
COMMON CARD (34-66)	.40	1.00

1984 Topps Michael Jackson Stickers

COMPLETE SET (66)	15.00	40.00
COMP.SER.1 SET (33)	10.00	25.00
COMP.SER.2 SET (33)	10.00	25.00
COMMON SER.1 STICKER (1-33)	.40	1.00
COMMON SER.2 STICKER (34-66)	.40	1.00
STATED ODDS 3:1		

2011 Michael Jackson

COMPLETE SET (190)	12.00	30.00
UNOPENED BOX (24 PACKS)	150.00	250.00
UNOPENED PACK (5 CARDS)	6.00	10.00
COMMON CARD (1-177)	.15	.40
COMMON CARD (178-190)	.30	.75
*GOLD/500: 6X TO 15X BASIC CARDS		
*PLATINUM/100: 12X TO 30X BASIC CARDS		
*DIAMOND/10: 40X TO 100X BASIC CARDS		

2011 Michael Jackson Charted Albums Gold

COMPLETE SET (10)	200.00	350.00
COMMON CARD (CA1-CA10)	15.00	40.00
*PLATINUM: .6X TO 1.5X BASIC CARDS	25.00	60.00
*DIAMOND: 1.2X TO 3X BASIC CARDS	60.00	120.00

2011 Michael Jackson Eclectic Threads

COMMON CARD (ET1-ET3)	100.00	175.00
ET3 Michael Jackson DUAL	125.00	225.00

2011 Michael Jackson Jackson Live

COMMON CARD (JL1-JL3)	100.00	175.00
JL3 Michael Jackson DUAL	125.00	225.00

2011 Michael Jackson Sequins

COMMON CARD (1-4)	10.00	25.00
ANNCD PRINT RUN 50 SETS		

2011 Michael Jackson Televised Fashions

COMMON CARD (TV1-TV5)	30.00	80.00
1 Michael Jackson 5 MEM	400.00	800.00

1984 Topps Michael Jackson Super Stickers

COMPLETE SET (13)	6.00	15.00
COMMON STICKER (1-13)	.75	2.00

1994 FPG Michael Kaluta

COMPLETE SET (90)	4.00	10.00
UNOPENED BOX (36 PACKS)	15.00	20.00
UNOPENED PACK (10 CARDS)	.50	.75
COMMON CARD (1-90)	.10	.25
AU1a MW Kaluta AU/1000*	20.00	50.00
AU1b Michael Kaluta AU UNC		

1994 FPG Michael Kaluta Metallic Storm

COMPLETE SET (5)	12.00	30.00
COMMON CARD (MS1-MS5)	3.00	8.00
STATED ODDS 1:12		

1994 FPG Michael Kaluta Promos

COMMON CARD	.75	2.00
3 5-Card Panel (SDCC)		

1995 FPG Michael Kaluta Series Two

COMPLETE SET (90)	4.00	10.00
UNOPENED BOX (36 PACKS)	15.00	20.00
UNOPENED PACK (10 CARDS)	.50	.75
COMMON CARD (1-90)	.10	.25
AU1 Michael Kaluta AU/1000*	20.00	50.00

1995 FPG Michael Kaluta Series Two Metallic

COMPLETE SET (5) 12.00 30.00
COMMON CARD (M1-M5) 3.00 8.00
STATED ODDS 1:12

2020 Upper Deck Mickey Mouse

COMPLETE SET W/SP (180) 100.00 200.00
COMPLETE SET W/O SP (90) 15.00 40.00
UNOPENED BOX (PACKS)
UNOPENED PACK (CARDS)
COMMON CARD (1-90) .40 1.00
COMMON SP/999 (91-140) .75 2.00
COMMON SP/699 (141-170) 1.25 3.00
COMMON SP/299 (171-180) 2.00 5.00
*ACETATE: 2.5X TO 6X BASIC CARDS
*ACETATE/999: 1.2X TO 3X BASIC CARDS
*ACETATE/699: .75X TO 2X BASIC CARDS
*ACETATE/299: .5X TO 1.2X BASIC CARDS

2020 Upper Deck Mickey Mouse Comic Cut Panels

COMMON MEM 8.00 20.00
RANDOMLY INSERTED INTO PACKS

2020 Upper Deck Mickey Mouse Film Cels

COMPLETE SET (47) 125.00 250.00
COMMON MEM (F1-F47) 3.00 8.00
RANDOMLY INSERTED INTO PACKS

2020 Upper Deck Mickey Mouse Medallions

COMPLETE SET (50) 100.00 200.00
COMMON CARD (M1-M50) 2.50 6.00
RANDOMLY INSERTED INTO PACKS

2020 Upper Deck Mickey Mouse Mickey Through the Ages 3-D Lenticular

COMPLETE SET (42) 60.00 120.00
COMMON CARD (MTA1-MTA42) 1.50 4.00
RANDOMLY INSERTED INTO PACKS

2003 Micronauts Previews

COMPLETE SET (10) 10.00 25.00
COMMON CARD (P1-P9) 1.50 4.00
NNO Space Glider Action Figure 2.00 5.00

2003 Micronauts

COMPLETE FACTORY SET (36) 3.00 8.00
COMMON CARD (1-36) .20 .50

1999 Mike Hoffman Worlds of Wonder

COMPLETE SET (9) 8.00 20.00
COMMON CARD (1-9) 1.25 3.00
STATED PRINT RUN 1000 SER.#'d SETS

1994 FPG Mike Ploog

COMPLETE SET (90) 6.00 15.00
UNOPENED BOX (36 PACKS) 10.00 20.00
UNOPENED PACK (10 CARDS) .50 .75
COMMON CARD (1-90) .12 .30
NNO1 Ploog AU/1000* 20.00 50.00
NNO2 Marvel Art Redemption Card/50*
NNO3 Mike Ploog 10-Card Panel AU

1994 FPG Mike Ploog Metallic Storm

COMPLETE SET (5) 12.00 30.00
COMMON CARD (MS1-MS5) 3.00 8.00
STATED ODDS 1:12

1994 FPG Mike Ploog Promos

12 Deluxe, Four-Up Panel
NNO Ork Games NSU 1.25 3.00
NNO The Impasse .75 2.00
NNO The Impasse Text Variant 2.50 6.00
NNO 6-Card Panel

1989 Comic Images Mike Zeck

COMPLETE SET (45) 10.00 25.00
UNOPENED BOX (50 PACKS) 80.00 90.00
UNOPENED PACK (5 CARDS) 1.75 2.00
COMMON CARD (1-45) .75 2.00

2012 Military Propaganda and Posters Previews

COMPLETE SET (6) 4.00 10.00
COMMON CARD (1-6) .75 2.00
STATED PRINT RUN 500 SER.#'d SETS

2012 Military Propaganda and Posters

COMPLETE SET (36) 10.00 25.00
COMMON CARD (1-36) .60 1.50
*CANVAS: 2X TO 5X BASIC CARDS
37 On to Victory - Case Card
MW1 Mirror-Wise - A Precarious Story

2012 Military Propaganda and Posters Memorabilia

COMMON CARD 10.00 25.00

2012 Military Propaganda and Posters Mini Propaganda Leaflet US Version

COMPLETE SET (4) 8.00 20.00
COMMON CARD (A1-A4) 3.00 8.00
STATED ODDS 2:SET

2012 Military Propaganda and Posters Promos

COMPLETE SET (9) 6.00 15.00
COMMON CARD 1.25 3.00

1995 21st Century Archives Milk and Cheese

COMPLETE SET (50) 4.00 10.00
COMPLETE FACTORY SET (51) 6.00 15.00
UNOPENED BOX (36 PACKS) 30.00 40.00
UNOPENED PACK (8 CARDS) 1.00 1.25
COMMON CARD (1-50) .15 .40
NNO1 Santa Claus Promo .75 2.00
(2-Card Panel 6X4)

1995 21st Century Archives Milk and Cheese Foil Embossed

COMPLETE SET (5) 8.00 20.00
COMMON CARD 2.00 5.00
RANDOMLY INSERTED INTO PACKS

1995 Sports Time Miller Genuine

COMPLETE SET (100) 6.00 15.00
UNOPENED BOX (36 PACKS) 20.00 25.00
UNOPENED PACK (9 CARDS) .50 .75
COMMON CARD (1-100) .12 .30
CT Die Cut CT

1995 Sports Time Miller Genuine Miller Crystal Gallery Acetate

COMPLETE SET (10) 25.00 60.00
COMMON CARD (C1-C10) 3.00 8.00
STATED ODDS 1:12

1995 Sports Time Miller Genuine Miller Moments

P New From Sports Time Promo .75 2.00
1J Miller Pays Tribute Jumbo Promo .75 2.00

1995 Sports Time Miller Genuine Miller Moments Embossed

COMPLETE SET (5) 30.00 80.00
COMMON CARD (M1-M5) 8.00 20.00
STATED ODDS 1:36

1995 Sports Time Miller Genuine Millery Holiday Chaser Foil

COMPLETE SET (15) 20.00 50.00
COMMON CARD (H1-H15) 1.50 4.00
STATED ODDS 1:6

1996 Upper Deck The Mini Collection

COMPLETE SET (45) 6.00 15.00
UNOPENED BOX (PACKS)
UNOPENED PACK (CARDS)
COMMON CARD (1-45) .20 .50
NNO1 Sir Alec Issignonis 4X6
NNO2 1959 Colours 4X6

2015 Minions Dog Tags

COMPLETE SET (24) 30.00 80.00
UNOPENED BOX (24 PACKS)
UNOPENED PACK (1 TAG+1 STICKER)
COMMON TAG (1-24) 2.00 5.00
*FOIL: ..5X TO 1.2X BASIC TAGS 2.50 6.00

2015 Minions Dog Tags Stickers

COMPLETE SET (24) 6.00 15.00
COMMON CARD .40 1.00
*FOIL: .75X TO 2X BASIC STICKERS .75 2.00
STATED ODDS 1:1

2015 Minions Movie

COMPLETE SET (54) 6.00 15.00
COMMON CARD (1-54) .20 .50
*GOLD: 1.5X TO 4X BASIC CARDS

2015 Minions Movie Foil

COMPLETE SET (18) 12.00 30.00
COMMON CARD (1-18) 1.25 3.00
STATED ODDS 1:4

2015 Minions Movie Jumbo Exclusives

COMPLETE SET (9) 10.00 25.00
COMMON CARD (9) 2.00 5.00
STATED ODDS 1:1 JUMBO PACK

2015 Minions Vudu Pizza Promos

COMPLETE SET (8) 10.00 25.00
COMMON CARD 2.00 5.00
WALMART VUDU PIZZA EXCLUSIVES
UNNUMBERED SET

1991 Impel Minnie 'n Me

COMPLETE SET (160) 6.00 15.00
UNOPENED BOX (36 PACKS) 15.00 20.00
UNOPENED PACK (12 CARDS) .50 .75
COMMON CARD (1-160) .07 .20

1992 SkyBox Minnie 'n Me Series Two

COMPLETE SET (150) 6.00 15.00
UNOPENED BOX (36 PACKS) 30.00 40.00
UNOPENED PACK (12 CARDS) 1.00 1.25
COMMON CARD (1-150) .08 .20

1992 SkyBox Minnie 'n Me Series Two Pink Holograms

COMPLETE SET (2) 10.00 25.00
COMMON CARD (1-2) 6.00 15.00
RANDOMLY INSERTED INTO PACKS

1992 SkyBox Minnie 'n Me Series Two Promos

COMPLETE SET (3) 1.00 2.50
COMMON CARD (1-3) .40 1.00

2005 MirrorMask Previews

COMPLETE SET (9) 8.00 20.00
COMMON CARD (1-9) 1.50 4.00

1991 Franks Miss Black America

COMPLETE BOXED SET (132) 15.00 40.00
COMMON CARD .25 .60

1993 Star International Miss USA

COMPLETE SET (100) 3.00 8.00
UNOPENED BOX (36 PACKS) 20.00 25.00
UNOPENED PACK (9 CARDS) .50 .75
COMMON CARD (2-101) .12 .30

2016 Moana

COMPLETE SET (20) 3.00 8.00
UNOPENED BOX (24 PACKS)
UNOPENED PACK (4 CARDS)
COMMON CARD (P1-P20) .20 .50

2016 Moana Tattoos

COMPLETE SET (12) 2.50 6.00
COMMON CARD (T1-T12) .30 .75
STATED ODDS 1:

1992 Modern Props

COMPLETE BOXED SET (30) 6.00 15.00
COMMON CARD (1-30) .40 1.00

1993 Comic Images Moebius

COMPLETE SET (90) 8.00 20.00
UNOPENED BOX (48 PACKS) 20.00 30.00
UNOPENED PACK (10 CARDS) .50 .75
COMMON CARD (1-90) .10 .25
NNO Moebius PROMO .75 2.00

1993 Comic Images Moebius Chromium

COMPLETE SET (6) 6.00 15.00
COMMON CARD (2-6) 2.00 5.00
STATED ODDS 1:16

1995 Cornerstone The Monkees

COMPLETE SET (90) 5.00 12.00
UNOPENED BOX (36 PACKS) 150.00 250.00
UNOPENED PACK (10 CARDS) 6.00 8.00
COMMON CARD (1-90) .12 .30

1995 Cornerstone The Monkees Autographs

COMPLETE SET (4) 300.00 500.00
COMMON AUTO 75.00 150.00
STATED ODDS 1:216
STATED PRINT RUN 250 AUTOS EACH
1 Davey Jones/250* 100.00 200.00
4 Peter Tork/250* 100.00 200.00

1995 Cornerstone The Monkees Foil-Stamped

COMPLETE SET (4) 5.00 12.00
COMMON CARD (F1-F4) 1.50 4.00
RANDOMLY INSERTED INTO PACKS

1995 Cornerstone The Monkees Promos

COMPLETE SET (4) 6.00 15.00
COMMON CARD 1.25 3.00
0 Album Exclusive 2.50 6.00
IT3 Inside Trading Club Exclusive 2.50 6.00

2011 Monster Art of Mike Sosnowski

COMPLETE SET (36) 5.00 12.00
COMPLETE BOXED SET (37) 8.00 20.00
COMMON CARD (1-36) .25 .60
NNO1 Mike Sosnowski Sketch Insert
NNO2 Mike Sosnowski AU

1997 Reed Monster Movie Classics 1

COMPLETE SET (50) 8.00 20.00
UNOPENED BOX (36 PACKS)
UNOPENED PACK (6 CARDS)
COMMON CARD (1-50) .30 .75
COA Certification Card

1997 Reed Monster Movie Classics 1 Promos

COMPLETE SET (6) 2.50 5.00
COMMON CARD (P1-P6) .40 1.00

1997 Reed Monster Movie Classics 2

COMPLETE SET (50) 6.00 15.00
UNOPENED BOX (36 PACKS)
UNOPENED PACK (6 CARDS)
COMMON CARD (1-50) .25 .60

1997 Reed Monster Movie Classics 2 Promos

COMPLETE SET (3) 2.50 5.00
COMMON CARD (P1-P3) .75 2.00

2007 Monsterfaces

COMPLETE SET (72) 5.00 12.00
UNOPENED BOX (36 PACKS) 50.00 60.00
UNOPENED PACK (7 CARDS)
COMMON CARD (1-72) .12 .30
NNO1 Frank Russo Color Auto Sketch Insert
NNO2 One of a Kind Monsterwax Metal Insert
NNO3 Actual Artist DNA Insert
NNO4 Queef Box-Bottom Insert

2007 Monsterfaces Promos

COMPLETE SET (2) 1.25 3.00
COMMON CARD (P1-P2) .75 2.00

1993 Contact Press Monsters and Mysteries of the Planet Earth

COMPLETE BOXED SET (30) 6.00 15.00
COMMON CARD (1-30) .40 1.00

2001 Monsters Inc

COMPLETE SET (50) 3.00 8.00
UNOPENED BOX (24 PACKS) 60.00 100.00
UNOPENED PACK (8 CARDS) 2.50 4.00
COMMON CARD (1-50) .12 .30

2001 Monsters Inc Badge Stickers

COMPLETE SET (6) 1.25 3.00
COMMON CARD (1-6) .25 .60
STATED ODDS 1:2

2001 Monsters Inc Glow-in-the-Dark

COMPLETE SET (6) 1.25 3.00
COMMON CARD (1-6) .25 .60
STATED ODDS 1:2

2001 Monsters Inc Jigsaw Puzzle

COMPLETE SET (6) 1.25 3.00
COMMON CARD (1-6) .25 .60
STATED ODDS 1:2

2001 Monsters Inc Mystery Monster

COMPLETE SET (6) 1.50 4.00
COMMON CARD (MM1-MM6) .40 1.00
STATED ODDS 1:4

2001 Monsters Inc Pop-Ups

COMPLETE SET (6) 1.25 3.00
COMMON CARD (P1-P6) .25 .60
STATED ODDS 1:2

2001 Monsters Inc Promos

COMPLETE SET (2) 1.25 3.00
COMMON CARD (P1-P2) .75 2.00

1996 Cornerstone Monty Python and the Holy Grail

COMPLETE SET (72) 6.00 15.00
UNOPENED BOX (24 PACKS) 20.00 25.00
UNOPENED PACK (9 CARDS) 1.00 1.25
COMMON CARD (1-72) .30 .75
NNO1 CD-ROM Merchandise Card .40 1.00
NNO2 The Holy Grail Card 6.00 15.00

1996 Cornerstone Monty Python and the Holy Grail Knights

COMPLETE SET (6) 12.00 30.00
COMMON CARD (K1-K6) 2.50 6.00
RANDOMLY INSERTED INTO PACKS

1996 Cornerstone Monty Python and the Holy Grail Promos

A Tim the Enchanter and 7 others .75 2.00
B King Arthur and 3 others .75 2.00
IT2 Sir Not-Appearing... 5.00 12.00
(Inside Trader)
P1a Coming in 1995 from - Knights
P1b Coming later this year from - Knights
P2a Coming in 1995 from - Turbans
P2b Coming later this year from - Turbans

1995 Cornerstone Monty Python's Flying Circus Promos

COMMON CARD 1.25 3.00
NNO Monty Python T-Shirt 2.50 6.00

1999 NostalgiaCards Morbid Monsters

COMPLETE SET (45) 3.00 8.00
UNOPENED BOX (36 PACKS) 30.00 40.00
UNOPENED PACK (8 CARDS) 1.00 1.25
COMMON CARD (1-45) .15 .40
TRWBAU Todd M. Riley, William D. Bristow AU

1994 Comic Images More Beyond Bizarre Jim Warren

COMPLETE SET (90) 4.00 10.00
UNOPENED BOX (48 PACKS) 20.00 30.00
UNOPENED PACK (10 CARDS) .75 1.00
COMMON CARD (1-90)
NNO Jim Warren AU 20.00 50.00
NNO Medallion Card/1317* 10.00 25.00
NNO Jim Warren 2 More Beyond Bizarre PROMO .75 2.00

1992 Kitchen Sink Press More Hollywood Characters

COMPLETE BOXED SET (36) 4.00 10.00
COMMON CARD (1-36) .25 .60
NNO Uncut sheet

1995 Comic Images More than Battlefield Earth

COMPLETE SET (90) 4.00 10.00
UNOPENED BOX (48 PACKS) 12.00 30.00
UNOPENED PACK (10 CARDS) .25 .60
COMMON CARD (1-90) .08 .20
M1 Medallion/1015* 10.00 25.00
UNC1 6-Up Panel UNC

1995 Comic Images More than Battlefield Earth Chromium

COMPLETE SET (6) 12.00 30.00
COMMON CARD (C1-C6) 3.00 8.00
STATED ODDS 1:16

1995 Comic Images More than Battlefield Earth Subset

COMPLETE SET (3) 10.00 25.00
COMMON CARD (1-3) 6.00 15.00
STATED ODDS 1:48
1 Windsplitter 6.00 15.00
2 Chrissie Dreams Of Rescue 6.00 15.00
3 Windsplitter II 6.00 15.00

1995 Comic Images More than Battlefield Earth Promos

1 Dawn Attack (Card #27) .75 2.00
2 More Than Battlefield Earth 10.00 25.00
NSU Gummie

2013 Mortal Instruments City of Bones

COMPLETE SET (100) 8.00 20.00
UNOPENED HOBBY BOX (24 PACKS)
UNOPENED HOBBY PACK (6 CARDS)
UNOPENED RETAIL BOX (24 PACKS)
UNOPENED RETAIL PACK (7 CARDS)
COMMON CARD .15 .40

2013 Mortal Instruments City of Bones Premiere Date Foil

COMPLETE SET (100)
*PREMIERE DATE: X TO X BASIC CARDS
STATED ODDS 1:

2013 Mortal Instruments City of Bones Autograph Memorabilia

COMMON CARD 10.00 25.00
AWJCB Jamie Campbell Bower 75.00 200.00
AWJRM Jonathan Rhys-Meyers 30.00 80.00
AWJW1 Jemima West 20.00 50.00
AWKZ1 Kevin Zegers 20.00 50.00
AWLC1 Lily Collins 60.00 120.00
AWLH1 Lena Headey EXCH
AWRS1 Robert Sheehan 12.00 30.00

2013 Mortal Instruments City of Bones Autographs

COMMON CARD 3.00 8.00
STATED ODDS 1:12
ACC1 Cassandra Clare EXCH
ACCH CCH Pounder
AGG1 Godfey Gao
AHZ2 Harald Zwart
AJCB Jamie Campbell Bower 50.00 125.00
AJRM Jonathan Rhys-Meyers
AJW1 Jemima West 12.00 30.00
AKD1 Kevin Durand
AKZ1 Kevin Zegers 8.00 20.00
ALC1 Lily Collins 25.00 60.00
ALH1 Lena Headey EXCH 15.00 40.00

2013 Mortal Instruments City of Bones Runes

COMPLETE SET (22) 12.00 30.00
COMMON CARD 1.25 3.00
TWO RUNES OR TAROT CARDS PER RETAIL PACK

2013 Mortal Instruments City of Bones Tarot

COMPLETE SET (13) 8.00 20.00
COMMON CARD 1.25 3.00
TWO RUNES OR TAROT CARDS PER RETAIL PACK

2013 Mortal Instruments City of Bones Wardrobes

COMMON CARD 6.00 15.00
WAT1 Aidan Turner 15.00 40.00
WJCB Jamie Campbell Bower 10.00 25.00
WJH1 Jared Harris 8.00 20.00
WJRM Jonathan Rhys-Meyers
WJW1 Jemima West
WKD1 Kevin Durand 15.00 40.00
WKZ1 Kevin Zegers 10.00 25.00
WLH1 Lean Headey 12.00 30.00
WRM1 Robert Maillet
WRS1 Robert Sheehan 10.00 25.00

1994 Classic Mortal Kombat Series I

COMPLETE SET (100) 6.00 15.00
UNOPENED BOX (36 PACKS) 100.00 150.00
UNOPENED PACK (10 CARDS) 3.00 4.00
COMMON CARD (1-100) .10 .25

1994 Classic Mortal Kombat Series I Arcade Previews

COMPLETE SET (5) 3.00 8.00
COMMON CARD (P1-P5) .75 2.00
STATED ODDS 1:6

1994 Classic Mortal Kombat Series I Collector's Edition

COMPLETE SET (10) 4.00 10.00
COMMON CARD (CE1-CE10) .60 1.50

1994 Classic Mortal Kombat Series I Limited Edition

COMPLETE SET (10) 6.00 15.00
COMMON CARD (LE1-LE10) .75 2.00
STATED ODDS 1:6

1994 Classic Mortal Kombat Series I Promos

D1 Sonya Blade Classic Games 1.25 3.00
D1 Sonya Blade Diamond Seminar 4.00 10.00
D1 Sonya Blade Capital Retailers 4.00 10.00

1994 Classic Mortal Kombat Series II

COMPLETE SET (80) 10.00 25.00
UNOPENED BOX (PACKS)
UNOPENED PACK (CARDS)
COMMON CARD (1-80) .20 .50

1994 Classic Mortal Kombat Series II Babality Moves

COMPLETE SET (12) 20.00 50.00
COMMON CARD (BAB1-BAB12) 2.50 6.00
STATED ODDS 1:12

1994 Classic Mortal Kombat Series II Finishing Moves

COMMON CARD (FM1-FM25) 6.00 15.00
STATED ODDS 1:48

1994 Classic Mortal Kombat Series II Friendship Moves

COMPLETE SET (12) 20.00 50.00
COMMON CARD (FD1-FD12) 2.50 6.00
STATED ODDS 1:24

1994 Classic Mortal Kombat Series II Spikes

COMPLETE SET (8) 50.00 100.00
COMMON CARD (SPK1-SPK8) 6.00 15.00
STATED ODDS 1:48

1994 Classic Mortal Kombat Series II Spikes and Pit II

COMPLETE SET (12) 40.00 100.00
COMMON CARD (SP1-12) 4.00 10.00
STATED ODDS 1:24

1995 SkyBox Mortal Kombat Movie

COMPLETE SET (90) 4.00 10.00
UNOPENED BOX (36 PACKS)
UNOPENED PACK (8 CARDS)
COMMON CARD (1-90) .10 .25

1995 SkyBox Mortal Kombat Movie Gold Foil Warrior Champions

COMPLETE SET (3) 8.00 20.00
COMMON CARD (W1-W3) 3.00 8.00
*PROMOS: .10X TO .25X BASIC CARDS
STATED ODDS 1:18

1995 SkyBox Mortal Kombat Movie Red Foil Kombat

COMPLETE SET (4) 15.00 40.00
COMMON CARD (F1-F4) 5.00 12.00
*PROMOS: .10X TO .25X BASIC CARDS 1.25 3.00
STATED ODDS 1:19

1995 SkyBox Mortal Kombat Movie Promo

S1 Nothing in This... 1.50 4.00

1991 WTE Movie Posters Promo Cards

COMPLETE SET (20) 12.00 30.00
COMMON CARD (1-20) .60 3.00
Proto1 Gone With the Wind
(Vivien Leigh, Clark Gable)

1998 Dart FlipCards Mr. Bean

COMPLETE SET (72) 5.00 12.00
UNOPENED BOX (36 PACKS) 50.00 75.00
UNOPENED PACK (6 CARDS) 3.00 4.00
COMMON CARD (1-72) .12 .30

1998 Dart FlipCards Mr. Bean Lenticular

COMPLETE SET (6) 10.00 25.00
COMMON CARD (L1-L6) 2.50 6.00
STATED ODDS 1:18

1998 Dart FlipCards Mr. Bean Prismatic

COMPLETE SET (6) 10.00 25.00
COMMON CARD (S1-S6) 2.50 6.00
MAIL-IN EXCLUSIVE SET

1998 Dart FlipCards Mr. Bean Promos

COMPLETE SET (3) 2.00 5.00
COMMON CARD .75 2.00
1 Prism (Toronto Spring Expo) 1.25 3.00

1981 Fleer Ms. Pac-Man Stickers

COMPLETE SET (54) 50.00 100.00
UNOPENED BOX (36 PACKS) 200.00 300.00
UNOPENED PACK (3 CARDS+3 STICKERS) 6.00 8.00
COMMON CARD-STICKER 1.25 3.00

1995 Fleer Ultra MTV Animation

COMPLETE SET (146)	8.00	20.00
UNOPENED BOX (36 PACKS)	35.00	45.00
UNOPENED PACK (10 CARDS)	1.00	1.25
COMMON CARD (1-146)	.12	.30

1995 Fleer Ultra MTV Animation Aeon Flux Chromium

COMPLETE SET (15)	12.00	30.00
COMMON CARD (C1-C15)	1.25	3.00
STATED ODDS 1:4		

1995 Fleer Ultra MTV Animation Holograms

COMPLETE SET (4)	6.00	15.00
COMMON CARD (1-4)	2.50	6.00
STATED ODDS 1:12		

1995 Fleer Ultra MTV Animation Prismatic Foil Puzzle

COMPLETE SET (18)	12.00	30.00
COMMON CARD (1-18)	.75	2.00
STATED ODDS 1:2		

1999 Inkworks The Mummy Promo

P1 The Mummy	3.00	8.00

2001 Inkworks The Mummy Returns

COMPLETE SET (81)	5.00	12.00
UNOPENED BOX (36 PACKS)	50.00	60.00
UNOPENED PACK (7 CARDS)	1.50	2.00
COMMON CARD (1-81)	.15	.40
MBL1 Scorpion King	4.00	10.00

2001 Inkworks The Mummy Returns Autographs

COMPLETE SET W/O A7 (7)	100.00	200.00
COMMON AUTO (A1-A7)	10.00	25.00
REDEMPTION CARDS ONLY		
RANDOMLY INSERTED INTO PACKS		
A1 Brendan Fraser	150.00	400.00
A2 Arnold Vosloo	15.00	40.00
A4 John Hannah	15.00	40.00
A6 Patricia Velasquez	15.00	40.00
A7 The Rock	2000.00	4000.00

2001 Inkworks The Mummy Returns Pieceworks

COMPLETE SET (3)	100.00	200.00
COMMON CARD (P1-P3)	25.00	60.00
RANDOM INSERTS IN PACKS		
P1 Rachel Weisz	30.00	80.00
P2 Rachel Weisz	30.00	80.00

2001 Inkworks The Mummy Returns Sands of Time

COMPLETE SET (6)	10.00	25.00
COMMON CARD (ST1-ST6)	2.00	5.00
STATED ODDS 1:17		

2001 Inkworks The Mummy Returns Scorpion King

COMPLETE SET (9)	15.00	40.00
COMMON CARD (SK1-SK9)	2.00	5.00
STATED ODDS 1:11		

2001 Inkworks The Mummy Returns Promos

COMPLETE SET (5)	5.00	12.00
MR1 The Mummy Returns	.75	2.00
MR2 The Mummy Returns	1.50	4.00
MR3 The Mummy Returns	2.50	6.00
MR4 The Mummy Returns	3.00	8.00
MRi The Mummy Returns	1.50	4.00

2005 The Munsters

COMPLETE SET (5)	30.00	75.00
COMMON CARD (F1-F5)	8.00	20.00

2005 The Munsters Autographs

COMMON AUTO (A1-A3)	20.00	50.00
A3 Yvonne DeCarlo/499	75.00	150.00

2005 The Munsters Promos

COMMON CARD (P1-P3)	.75	2.00
P3 Herman, Marilyn, Herman and Grandpa, Lilly	8.00	20.00

1996 Dart FlipCards The Munsters Deluxe

COMPLETE SET (90)	8.00	20.00
UNOPENED BOX (30 PACKS)	60.00	100.00
UNOPENED PACK (7 CARDS)	2.50	3.00
COMMON CARD (1-90)	.20	.50
P1 Same Card Front as Card 8 PROMO	.75	2.00
TB1 Munster Trivia Insert	4.00	10.00

1996 Dart FlipCards The Munsters Deluxe Die-Cuts

COMPLETE SET (3)	10.00	25.00
COMMON CARD (DC1-DC3)		10.00
STATED ODDS 1:30		

1996 Dart FlipCards The Munsters Deluxe Gold Foil

COMPLETE SET (4)	8.00	20.00
COMMON CARD (GF1-GF4)	3.00	8.00
STATED ODDS 1:10		

1997 Dart FlipCards The Munsters Deluxe

COMPLETE SET (72)	5.00	12.00
UNOPENED BOX (36 PACKS)	75.00	125.00
UNOPENED PACK (6 CARDS)	2.50	4.00
COMMON CARD (1-72)	.12	.30

1997 Dart FlipCards The Munsters Deluxe Autographs

COMMON CARD (A1-A4)	15.00	40.00
STATED ODDS 1:300		
A2 Al Lewis	60.00	150.00
A4 Yvonne DeCarlo	60.00	150.00

1997 Dart FlipCards The Munsters Deluxe Lenticular

COMPLETE SET (6)	10.00	25.00
COMMON CARD (L1-L6)	2.50	6.00
STATED ODDS 1:18		

1997 Dart FlipCards The Munsters Deluxe Prismatic

COMPLETE SET (6)	5.00	12.00
COMMON CARD (S1-S6)	1.00	2.50
AVAILABLE VIA MAIL-IN REDEMPTION		

1997 Dart FlipCards The Munsters Deluxe Promos

1 Same Image as P1, Prismatic Foil	1.25	3.00
Philly Non-Sport Show		
2 Same Image as P2, Prismatic Foil	1.25	3.00
Toronto Sportcard Expo		
ES Grandpa Al Lewis for Governor		
P1 Cast	.75	2.00
P2 Herman and Lily	.75	2.00
SP The Munster Family Show Synopsis at Back		
SP The Munster Family		

1993 Cardz Jim Henson's Muppet Trading Cards

COMPLETE SET (60)	3.00	8.00
UNOPENED BOX (36 PACKS)	15.00	25.00
UNOPENED PACK (8 CARDS)	.50	.75
COMMON CARD (1-60)	.10	.25

1993 Cardz Jim Henson's Muppet Trading Cards TekChrome

COMPLETE SET (3)	5.00	12.00
COMMON CARD (1-3)	2.50	6.00

1993 Cardz Jim Henson's Muppet Trading Cards Promos

COMPLETE SET (3)	1.00	2.50
COMMON CARD (1-3)	.50	1.25

1994 Cardz Muppets Take the Ice

COMPLETE SET (80)	4.00	10.00
UNOPENED BOX (36 PACKS)	15.00	25.00
UNOPENED PACK (8 CARDS)	.75	1.00
COMMON CARD (1-80)	.10	.25
P1 Goalie	.60	1.50
P2 Hooking	.60	1.50
P3 Schedule	.60	1.50

1994 Cardz Muppets Take the Ice TekChrome

COMPLETE SET (3)	4.00	10.00
COMMON CARD (1-3)	1.50	4.00
STATED ODDS 1:9		

1992 Collect-A-Card Musclecars

COMPLETE SET (100)	6.00	15.00
UNOPENED BOX (36 PACKS)	10.00	15.00
UNOPENED PACK (9 CARDS)	.40	.50
COMMON CARD (1-100)	.10	.30

1992 Collect-a-Card Musclecars Promos

COMPLETE SET (2)	2.50	6.00
COMMON CARD	1.50	4.00

1993 RPM Mustang 30th Anniversary Collection

COMPLETE SET (4)	2.50	6.00
COMMON CARD (MC1-MC4)	.75	2.00

2023 Fright-Rags My Bloody Valentine

COMPLETE SET (81)	20.00	50.00
UNOPENED BOX (24 PACKS)	150.00	250.00
UNOPENED PACK (9 CARDS+1 STICKER)	8.00	12.00
COMMON CARD (1-80+CL)	.60	1.50
*RED: 2X TO 5X BASIC CARDS		

2023 Fright-Rags My Bloody Valentine Autographs

COMMON AUTO	50.00	125.00
STATED ODDS 1:24		
NNO Helene Udy	75.00	200.00
NNO Jim Murchison	60.00	150.00
NNO Lori Hallier	60.00	150.00
NNO Peter Cowper	125.00	300.00
NNO Rob Stein	75.00	200.00
NNO Tom Kovacs	60.00	150.00

2023 Fright-Rags My Bloody Valentine Stickers

COMPLETE SET (9)	5.00	12.00
COMMON CARD	.75	2.00
STATED ODDS 1:1		

2014 My Favorite Martian Previews

COMPLETE SET (6)	6.00	15.00
COMMON CARD (PR1-PR6)	1.50	4.00

2018 Mysticons

COMPLETE SET (100)	6.00	15.00
UNOPENED BOX (5 PACKS)		
UNOPENED PACK (6 CARDS)		
COMMON CARD (1-100)	.12	.30

2018 Mysticons Characters

COMPLETE SET (20)	10.00	25.00
COMMON CARD (CO1-CO20)	.75	2.00

2018 Mysticons Coloring Cards

COMPLETE SET (10)	5.00	12.00
COMMON CARD (CC1-CC10)	.60	1.50

2018 Mysticons Stickers

COMPLETE SET (10)	4.00	10.00
COMMON CARD (ST1-ST10)	.50	1.25

2018 Mysticons Temporary Tattoos

COMPLETE SET (10)	4.00	10.00
COMMON CARD (1-10)	.50	1.25

1994 American Realist Myth or Real

COMPLETE SET (80)	10.00	25.00
COMMON CARD (1-80)	.20	.50

2005 Napoleon Dynamite

COMPLETE SET (50)	6.00	15.00
UNOPENED BOX (36 PACKS)	25.00	40.00
UNOPENED PACK (6 CARDS)	1.50	2.00
COMMON CARD (1-50)	.20	.50

1993 21st Century Archives National Lampoon

COMPLETE SET (100)	4.00	10.00
UNOPENED BOX (36 PACKS)	15.00	20.00
UNOPENED PACK (8 CARDS)	.75	1.00
COMMON CARD (1-100)	.07	.20

1993 21st Century Archives National Lampoon Promos

COMPLETE SET (10)	5.00	12.00
COMMON CARD (1-10)	.75	2.00

1993 21st Century Archives National Lampoon Sculptor-Cast

COMPLETE SET (10)	20.00	50.00
COMMON CARD (1-10)	2.50	6.00
STATED ODDS 1:12		

1993 Eclipse National Lampoon's Loaded Weapon I

COMPLETE SET (110)	6.00	15.00
UNOPENED BOX (36 PACKS)	15.00	20.00
UNOPENED PACK (12 CARDS)	.50	.75
COMMON CARD (1-110)	.12	.30
109P Loaded Weapon I PROMO	.75	2.00

1995-96 National Parks Collection

COMPLETE SET (200)	15.00	40.00
COMPLETE SERIES 1 SET (100)	10.00	25.00
COMPLETE SERIES 2 SET (100)	10.00	25.00
UNOPENED SERIES 1 BOX	65.00	80.00
UNOPENED SERIES 1 PACK		
UNOPENED SERIES 2 BOX	65.00	80.00
UNOPENED SERIES 2 PACK		
COMMON CARD (1-200)	.20	.50

1995 TCM Associates National Wildlife Federation Promos

COMPLETE SET (2)	2.00	5.00
COMMON CARD	1.25	3.00

1995 Bon Air Native Americans An Epic Struggle of Blood and Courage

COMPLETE SET (90)	4.00	10.00
UNOPENED BOX (36 PACKS)	15.00	20.00
UNOPENED PACK (8 CARDS)	.75	1.00
COMMON CARD (1-90)	.10	.25
*RETAIL: SAME VALUE AS HOBBY	.10	.25

1995 Bon Air Native Americans An Epic Struggle of Blood and Courage Prismatic

COMPLETE SET (6)	12.00	30.00
COMMON CARD (S1-S6)	2.50	6.00
STATED ODDS 1:12		

1995 Bon Air Native Americans An Epic Struggle of Blood and Courage Sculptured 24k Gold

NNO Gold Card	1.25	3.00
NNO Redemption Card		

1995 Bon Air Native Americans An Epic Struggle of Blood and Courage Promos

COMPLETE SET (4)	4.00	10.00
COMMON CARD	1.50	4.00

1994 Coors Nature Series Promos

COMPLETE SET (6)	8.00	20.00
COMMON CARD (1-6)	2.00	5.00

2012 NCIS

COMPLETE SET (36)	15.00	40.00
UNOPENED BOX (15 PACKS)		
UNOPENED PACK (7 CARDS)		
COMMON CARD (1-36)	.75	2.00

2012 NCIS Autographed Relics

CARROLL ISSUED AS 2-BOX INCENTIVE		
PERRETTE ISSUED AS 4-BOX INCENTIVE		
NNO Pauley Perrette 4BI	125.00	250.00
NNO Rocky Carroll 2BI	30.00	75.00

2012 NCIS Autographs

COMMON AUTO	6.00	15.00
STATED ODDS 1:1		
NNO Alicia Coppola	10.00	25.00
NNO Bob Newhart	30.00	75.00
NNO Brian Dietzen	8.00	20.00
NNO Charles Durning	15.00	40.00
NNO Cheryl Ladd	50.00	100.00
NNO Diane Neal	15.00	40.00
NNO Jessica Steen	10.00	25.00
NNO Lauren Holly	30.00	75.00
NNO Michael Nouri	10.00	25.00
NNO Pauley Perrette	75.00	150.00
NNO Rena Sofer	12.00	30.00

2012 NCIS Character Quote Box-Toppers

COMPLETE SET (2)	30.00	60.00
COMMON CARD (CT1-CT2)	20.00	40.00
STATED ODDS 1:BOX		
STATED PRINT RUN 225 SER. #'d SETS		

2012 NCIS Characters

COMPLETE SET (9)	20.00	40.00
COMMON CARD (C1-C9)	3.00	8.00
STATED ODDS 1:1		
STATED PRINT RUN 600 SER.#'d SETS		

2012 NCIS Relics

COMMON CARD (CC1-CC22)	6.00	15.00
STATED ODDS 2:1		
STATED PRINT RUN 500 SER. #'d SETS		
CC7 ISSUED AS A RITTENHOUSE REWARD		
CC1 Abby Sciuto	8.00	20.00
CC3 Ziva David	10.00	25.00
CC6 Abby Sciuto	8.00	20.00
CC7 Anthony Dinozzo/150 RR	125.00	250.00
CC10 Anthony Dinozzo	8.00	20.00
CC11 Leroy Jethro Gibbs	12.00	30.00
CC12 Ziva David	10.00	25.00
CC14 Abby Sciuto	8.00	20.00
CC16 Ziva David	10.00	25.00
CC17 Leroy Jethro Gibbs	12.00	30.00
CC20 Ziva David	10.00	25.00
CC21 Anthony Dinozzo	8.00	20.00
CC22 Abby Sciuto	12.00	30.00

2012 NCIS Promos

P1 6 cast shot GEN	1.25	3.00
P2 7 cast shot NSU	2.50	6.00
P3 5 cast shot ALB	12.00	30.00
P4 5 cast shot (Philly)	2.00	5.00

2009 Ndbag the Boogeyman SDCC Promos

COMPLETE SET (4)	6.00	15.00
COMMON CARD	2.00	5.00

2011 Ndbag the Boogeyman SDCC Promos

COMPLETE SET (4)	6.00	15.00
COMMON CARD	2.00	5.00

2012 Ndbag the Boogeyman SDCC Promos

COMPLETE SET (4)	6.00	15.00
COMMON CARD	2.00	5.00

2013 Ndbag the Boogeyman SDCC Promos

COMPLETE SET (4)	6.00	15.00
COMMON CARD	2.00	5.00

2014 Ndbag the Boogeyman SDCC Promos

COMPLETE SET (4)	6.00	15.00
COMMON CARD	2.00	5.00

2015 Ndbag the Boogeyman SDCC Promos

COMPLETE SET (4)	6.00	15.00
COMMON CARD	2.00	5.00

2016 Ndbag the Boogeyman SDCC Promos

COMPLETE SET (4)	6.00	15.00
COMMON CARD	2.00	5.00

1990 Starhead Neat Stuff

COMPLETE SET (10)	2.00	5.00
COMMON CARD (1-9 + HEADER)	.30	.75

1988 Topps Neighbours

COMPLETE SET (66)	2.50	6.00
COMMON CARD (1-66)	.10	.30

1997 Comic Images The New American Pin-Up ClearChrome

COMPLETE SET (5)	12.00	30.00
COMMON CARD (C1-C5)	3.00	8.00
RANDOMLY INSERTED INTO PACKS		

1997 Comic Images The New American Pin-Up ClearChrome Autographs

COMMON CARD (C1-C5)	20.00	50.00
RANDOMLY INSERTED INTO PACKS		

1997 Comic Images The New American Pin-Up Promos

COMPLETE SET (5)	2.50	6.00
COMMON CARD	.75	2.00

1997 Comic Images The New American Pin-Up

COMPLETE SET (72)	5.00	12.00
UNOPENED BOX (36 PACKS)	20.00	30.00
UNOPENED PACK (8 CARDS)	1.00	1.25
COMMON CARD (1-72)	.12	.30

1984 Sanitarium New Zealand Reef Fish

COMPLETE SET (20)	2.50	6.00
COMMON CARD (1-20)	.25	.60

1991 Capri Sun Nicktoons

COMPLETE SET (22)	12.00	30.00
COMMON CARD (1-22)	.75	2.00

2004 Nicktoons

COMPLETE SET (130)	10.00	25.00
UNOPENED BOX (24 PACKS)	30.00	40.00
UNOPENED PACK (5 CARDS)	1.25	1.75
COMMON CARD (NT1-NT100)	.08	.20
COMMON CARD (NT101-NT130)	.40	1.00

1992 Capri Sun Nicktoons Decals

COMPLETE SET (22)	10.00	25.00
COMMON CARD (1-22	.75	2.00
NNO SNICKS Promo	2.00	5.00

2009 Night at the Museum McDonald's

COMPLETE SET (8)	3.00	8.00
COMMON CARD (1-8)	.75	2.00

1987 Rosem Night of the Living Dead

COMPLETE SET (50)	10.00	25.00
COMMON CARD (1-50)	.30	.75

2012 Night of the Living Dead

COMPLETE SET (36)	10.00	25.00
COMMON CARD (1-36)	.50	1.25

2012 Night of the Living Dead Autographs

COMMON AUTO (A1-A9)	10.00	25.00
ORIGINAL CAST AU 100-250 COPIES		
DUAL CAST AU 100 COPIES		
A1 Russ Streiner	20.00	50.00
A2 Judith O'Dea	30.00	75.00
A5 Judith Ridley	12.00	30.00
A6 Kyra Schon	15.00	40.00
A7 Judith O'Dea Russ Streiner/100	75.00	150.00
A8 Judith O'Dea Judith Ridley/100	30.00	75.00
A9 Judith Ridley Kyra Schon/100	25.00	60.00

2012 Night of the Living Dead Gold Foil Poster Gallery

COMPLETE SET (9)	12.00	30.00
COMMON CARD (F1-F9)	2.50	6.00
STATED ODDS TWO PER MEGA PACK		

2012 Night of the Living Dead Promos

1 Green	1.25	3.00
2 Cast	1.50	4.00
3 Andy Fry Art		
4 Andy Fry Art Sketchlife	5.00	12.00
5 Avengers 50/NOTLD (web excl.)		
6 Avengers 50/NOTLD (NSU)		

2020 Fright-Rags Night of the Living Dead

COMPLETE SET (81)	20.00	50.00
UNOPENED BOX (24 PACKS)	150.00	200.00
UNOPENED PACK (9 CARDS+1 STICKER)	6.00	8.00
COMMON CARD (1-80+CL)	.50	1.25
*PARALLEL: 2X TO 5X BASIC CARDS		

2020 Fright-Rags Night of the Living Dead Autographs

COMMON AUTO	30.00	75.00
STATED PRINT RUN 50 SETS		
NNO Judith O'Dea	50.00	100.00
NNO Kyra Schon	50.00	100.00
NNO Marilyn Eastman	75.00	150.00
NNO Russ Streiner	60.00	120.00

2020 Fright-Rags Night of the Living Dead Portrait

NNO George Romero	250.00	400.00

2020 Fright-Rags Night of the Living Dead Stickers

COMPLETE SET (9)	8.00	20.00
COMMON STICKER	1.25	3.00
STATED ODDS 1:1		

1993 Imagine Night of the Living Dead Promos

COMPLETE SET (8)	10.00	25.00
COMMON CARD (1-8)	2.00	5.00

2004 Night Slasher

COMPLETE SET (36)	5.00	12.00
UNOPENED BOX (36 PACKS)		
UNOPENED PACK (6 CARDS)		
COMMON CARD (1-36)	.25	.60

1993 SkyBox The Nightmare Before Christmas

COMPLETE SET (90)	12.00	30.00
UNOPENED BOX (36 PACKS)	50.00	75.00
UNOPENED PACK (8 CARDS)	2.00	3.00
COMMON CARD (1-90)	.25	.60
S1 Skybox International Promo	1.50	4.00

1993 SkyBox The Nightmare Before Christmas Spectra

COMPLETE SET (4)	15.00	40.00
COMMON CARD (1-4)	6.00	15.00
STATED ODDS 1:18		

2001 Nightmare Before Christmas

COMPLETE SET (72)	6.00	15.00
UNOPENED BOX (36 PACKS)	30.00	50.00
UNOPENED PACK (7 CARDS)	1.00	1.50
COMMON CARD (1-72)	.15	.40
FILM FLIP CARD STATED ODDS 1:4		
FC Film Flip Card	6.00	15.00

2001 Nightmare Before Christmas Autographs

RANDOM INSERTS IN PACKS		
A1 Tim Burton	250.00	500.00
A2 Danny Elfman	100.00	200.00
A3 Chris Sarandon	15.00	40.00
A4 Glenn Shadix	12.00	30.00

2014 Nightmare Before Christmas Dog Tags

COMPLETE SET (24)	50.00	100.00
UNOPENED BOX (PACKS)		
UNOPENED PACK (TAG+1 STICKER)		
COMMON TAG (1-24)	2.50	6.00
*FOIL: .5X TO 1.2X BASIC TAG	3.00	8.00

2014 Nightmare Before Christmas Dog Tags Stickers

COMPLETE SET (8)	2.00	5.00
COMMON STICKER	.40	1.00
STATED ODDS 1:1		

1991 Impel Nightmare on Elm Street

COMPLETE SET (120)	12.00	30.00
COMPLETE COFFIN SET (132)	15.00	40.00
COMPIETE BOILER ROOM SET (132)	20.00	50.00
COMMON CARD (1-120)	.25	.60

1991 Impel Nightmare on Elm Street Boiler Room

COMPLETE SET (10)	2.50	6.00
COMMON CARD	.50	1.25
BOILER ROOM SET EXCLUSIVE		

1991 Impel Nightmare on Elm Street Coffin

COMPLETE SET (10)	2.50	6.00
COMMON CARD (S1-S10)	.50	1.25
COFFIN FACTORY SET EXCLUSIVE		

1991 Impel Nightmare on Elm Street FreddyVision Holograms

COMPLETE SET (2)	3.00	8.00
COMMON CARD	2.00	5.00
COFFIN FACTORY SET EXCLUSIVE		

1991 Impel Nightmare on Elm Street Holograms

COMPLETE SET (2)	3.00	8.00
COMMON CARD	2.00	5.00
BOILER ROOM SET EXCLUSIVE		

1991 Impel Nightmare on Elm Street Promos

COMPLETE SET (6)	15.00	40.00
COMMON CARD (SKIP #'d)	4.00	10.00

2003 Nightmare on Elm Street Previews

COMPLETE SET (6)	8.00	20.00
COMMON CARD (NMP1-NMP6)	2.00	5.00
STATED PRINT RUN 1000 SER.#'d SETS		

1993 Valiant Comics Ninjak Promos

1 Breaking Through Glass (chromium)/10,000*	2.00	5.00
2 Breaking Through Glass (chromium refractor)/1,000*	10.00	25.00
3 Breaking Through Glass (6 X 10 1/2) (oversized blank back)	4.00	10.00

MODERN

1993 Collect-a-Card Norfin Trolls

COMPLETE SET (50)	4.00	10.00
COMPLETE SET W/STICKERS (60)	5.00	12.00
UNOPENED BOX (48 PACKS)	15.00	20.00
UNOPENED PACK (7 CARDS+1 STICKER)	.50	.75
COMMON CARD (1-50)	.12	.30

1993 Collect-a-Card Norfin Trolls Stickers

COMPLETE SET (10)	1.00	2.50
COMMON CARD (1-10)	.15	.40
STATED ODDS 1:1		

1993 Collect-a-Card Norfin Trolls Promos

COMPLETE SET (4)	2.00	5.00
COMMON CARD	.75	2.00

1993 Sports Time Norma Jeane Collection Lost Portfolio of Marilyn Monroe

COMPLETE SET (75)	6.00	15.00
COMMON CARD (1-75)	.15	.40

1993 Comic Images Norman Rockwell Saturday Evening Post

COMPLETE SET (90)	5.00	12.00
UNOPENED BOX (48 PACKS)	35.00	45.00
UNOPENED PACK (10 CARDS)	1.00	1.25
COMMON CARD (1-90)	.10	.30
NNO Uncut Sheet		
NNO Available June 1993 PROMO	.75	2.00

1993 Comic Images Norman Rockwell Saturday Evening Post Wood

COMPLETE SET (6)	15.00	40.00
COMMON CARD (1-6)	3.00	8.00
STATED ODDS 1:18		

1995 Comic Images Norman Rockwell Two The Saturday Evening Post

COMPLETE SET (90)	4.00	10.00
UNOPENED BOX (48 PACKS)	30.00	40.00
UNOPENED PACK (10 CARDS)	.75	1.00
COMMON CARD (1-90)	.10	.25
NNO Medallion Card/1399*	10.00	25.00
NNO Norman Rockwell 2 PROMO	.60	1.50
NNO Uncut Sheet		

1995 Comic Images Norman Rockwell Two The Saturday Evening Post 24-Karat Signature

NNO Norman Rockwell/500*	3.00	8.00
NNO Redemption Card		

1995 Comic Images Norman Rockwell Two The Saturday Evening Post Chromium

COMPLETE SET (6)	10.00	25.00
COMMON CARD (C1-C6)	2.50	6.00
STATED ODDS 1:16		

1995 Comic Images Norman Rockwell Two The Saturday Evening Post Nostalgic Notes

COMPLETE SET (3)	12.00	30.00
COMMON CARD (1-3)	6.00	15.00
STATED ODDS 1:48		

1992 Ultimate Northern Exposure Promo

NNO Northern Exposure	1.50	4.00

2000 Nostalgicards Christmas Promo

P1 Santa Claus/Merry Christmas	4.00	10.00

1993 Kitchen Sink Press Not a Lie from My Mouth

COMPLETE SET (36)	4.00	10.00
COMMON CARD (1-36)	.25	.60

2000 NSYNC Rainbow Prism

COMPLETE SET (10)	1.25	3.00
COMMON CARD (1-10)	.20	.50
STATED ODDS 1:1		

2000 NSYNC Stickers

COMPLETE SET (10)	1.25	3.00
COMMON CARD (1-10)	.20	.50
STATED ODDS 1:1		

1993 Kitchen Sink Press Oddball Comics

COMPLETE BOXED SET (36)	5.00	12.00
COMMON CARD (1-36)	.25	.60

1994 Freedom Press Official Currier and Ives Civil War

COMPLETE SET (16)	5.00	12.00
COMMON CARD (1-16)	.60	1.50

1994 Freedom Press Official Currier and Ives Rails and Sails

COMPLETE SET (16)	6.00	15.00
COMMON CARD (1-16)	.50	1.25

1993 Kitchen Sink Press Omaha The Cat Dancer

COMPLETE SET (36)	6.00	15.00
COMMON CARD (1-36)	.30	.75
Promo1 Cherry Joins Kitchen Sink	.75	2.00
Promo2 Cherry's Jubilee -- Check Out the Talent	.75	2.00
Promo3 Melody -- The True Story	.75	2.00

1992 Bon Air On Guard Heritage Collection

COMPLETE SET (63)	6.00	15.00
COMMON CARD (1-63)	.20	.50

1992 Bon Air On Guard Heritage Collection Promos

COMPLETE SET (10)	8.00	20.00
COMMON CARD (1-10)	1.25	.30
NNO 10-Card Uncut Sheet	30.00	80.00

2014 Once Upon a Time Season 1

COMPLETE SET (45)	5.00	12.00
COMMON CARD (1-45)	.20	.50
P1 NON-SPORT UPDATE EXCLUSIVE		
P1 Snow White (NSU)	1.25	3.00

2014 Once Upon a Time Season 1 Autographs

COMMON AUTO (A1-A11)	6.00	15.00
STATED ODDS 2:FACTORY SET (w/MEM)		
A1 Lana Parrilla	60.00	120.00
A2 Robert Carlyle	75.00	150.00
A3 Jared S. Gilmore	8.00	20.00
A5 Eion Bailey	8.00	20.00
A6 Giancarlo Esposito	20.00	50.00
A8 Kristin Bauer	10.00	25.00
A9 Jessy Schram	15.00	40.00
A11 Jamie Dornan	20.00	50.00

2014 Once Upon a Time Season 1 Price of Magic

COMPLETE SET (9)	10.00	25.00
COMMON CARD (C1-C9)	2.00	5.00
STATED ODDS 2:FACTORY SET		

2014 Once Upon a Time Season 1 Wardrobes

COMMON MEM (M1-M14)	6.00	15.00
STATED ODDS 2:FACTORY SET (w/AU)		
M1 Snow White	8.00	20.00
M3 Rumplestiltskin	15.00	40.00
M4 The Evil Queen SP	50.00	100.00
M5 The Siren	10.00	25.00
M7 The Evil Queen	8.00	20.00
M9 Prince Charming	8.00	20.00
M10 The Evil Queen	10.00	25.00
M13 The Evil Queen	8.00	20.00
M14 Snow White ALB	20.00	50.00
NNO Snow White/Evil Queen		
Snow White/Prince Charming Oversized		

2013 One Direction

COMPLETE SET (100)	10.00	25.00
UNOPENED BOX (24 PACKS)	20.00	30.00
UNOPENED PACK (9 CARDS+1 STICKER)	1.25	1.50
COMMON CARD (1-100)	.15	.40

2013 One Direction Heart Throb

COMPLETE SET (20)	10.00	25.00
COMMON CARD (1-20)	.75	2.00

2013 One Direction On the Road

COMPLETE SET (17)	6.00	15.00
COMMON CARD (1-17)	.60	1.50

2013 One Direction Spellbound

COMPLETE SET (35)	12.00	30.00
COMMON CARD (1-35)	.60	1.50

2013 One Direction Stickers

COMPLETE SET (15)	4.00	10.00
COMMON CARD (1-15)	.30	.75
STATED ODDS 1:1		

2013 One Direction Take Me Home

COMPLETE SET (13)	4.00	10.00
COMMON CARD (1-13)	.40	1.00

2013 One Direction Up All Night

COMPLETE SET (15)	4.00	10.00
COMMON CARD (1-15)	.30	.75

1989 Euroflash 100 Great Cars of the World Stickers

COMPLETE SET (100)	5.00	12.00
COMMON CARD (1-100)	.10	.25

1996 SkyBox 101 Dalmatians

COMPLETE SET (101)	6.00	15.00
UNOPENED BOX (36 PACKS)	20.00	30.00
UNOPENED PACK (11 CARDS)	.75	1.00
COMMON CARD (1-101)	.12	.30

1996 SkyBox 101 Dalmatians Foil 'n Fur

COMPLETE SET (2)	6.00	15.00
COMMON CARD (1-2)	3.00	8.00
STATED ODDS 1:24		

1996 SkyBox 101 Dalmatians Magnetic Frame

COMPLETE SET (4)	3.00	8.00
COMMON CARD (1-4)	1.25	3.00
STATED ODDS 1:9		

1996 SkyBox 101 Dalmatians Mini-Mags

COMPLETE SET (4)	1.50	4.00
COMMON CARD (1-4)	.50	1.25

1996 SkyBox 101 Dalmatians Promos

P1 Foil 'N Fur	1.25	3.00
NNO 4-up Dealer Panel	2.00	5.00
SW1 Special Limited Edition Trading Card (Petsmart Exclusive)		

1996 Ralston Cookie Crisp 101 Dalmatians

COMPLETE SET (5)	6.00	15.00
COMMON CARD	2.00	5.00

1991 Pacific Operation Desert Shield

COMPLETE SET (110)	5.00	12.00
COMPLETE FACTORY SET (110)	8.00	20.00
UNOPENED BOX (36 PACKS)	15.00	25.00
UNOPENED PACK (12 CARDS)	.75	1.00
COMMON CARD (1-110)	.10	.25

1991 Pacific Operation Desert Shield Schwarzkopf

NNO Schwarzkopf Gold/500	4.00	10.00
NNO Schwarzkopf Silver/10		
NNO Schwarzkopf Prism/3		
NNO Schwarzkopf (factory set exclusive)	2.00	5.00

2016 Orphan Black Season 1

COMPLETE SET (72)	8.00	20.00
UNOPENED BOX (24 PACKS)	70.00	80.00
UNOPENED PACK (5 CARDS)	3.00	4.00
COMMON CARD (1-72)	.20	.50
*SILVER FOIL: 1.2X TO 3X BASIC CARDS		

2016 Orphan Black Season 1 Autographs

COMMON AUTO	6.00	15.00
STATED ODDS 1:24		
EB Evelyne Brochu	15.00	40.00
IC Inga Cadranel	10.00	25.00
JG Jordan Gavaris	8.00	20.00
KH Kevin Hanchard	8.00	20.00
SW Skyler Wexler	10.00	25.00
TMA Maslany/Alison Hendrix	75.00	150.00
TMB Maslany/Beth Childs	60.00	120.00
TMC Maslany/Cosima Niehaus		
TMD Maslany/Danielle Fournier	60.00	120.00
TMG Maslany/Aryanna Giordano	75.00	150.00
TMH Maslany/Helena	50.00	100.00
TMJ Maslany/Janika Zingler	75.00	150.00
TMK Maslany/Katja Obinger	60.00	120.00
TMR Maslany/Rachel Duncan	75.00	150.00
TMS Maslany/Sarah Manning	75.00	150.00

2016 Orphan Black Season 1 Character Bios

COMPLETE SET (9)	6.00	15.00
COMMON CARD (C1-C9)	1.25	3.00
*SILVER FOIL: .6X TO 1.5X BASIC CARDS		
STATED ODDS 1:3		

2016 Orphan Black Season 1 Dual Wardrobes

COMMON WARDROBE (DM1-DM3)	15.00	40.00
STATED ODDS 1:144		
DM1 Maslany/Gavaris	20.00	50.00
DM3 Maslany/Maslany	25.00	60.00

2016 Orphan Black Season 1 Felix's Loft

COMPLETE SET (9)	6.00	15.00
COMMON CARD (F1-F9)	1.25	3.00
*SILVER FOIL: .6X TO 1.5X BASIC CARDS		
STATED ODDS 1:3		

2016 Orphan Black Season 1 IDW Comic Covers

COMPLETE SET (6)	10.00	25.00
COMMON CARD (V1-V6)	3.00	8.00
STATED ODDS 1:36		

2016 Orphan Black Season 1 Quotes

COMPLETE SET (9)	5.00	12.00
COMMON CARD (Q1-Q9)	1.25	3.00
*SILVER FOIL: .6X TO 1.5X BASIC CARDS		
STATED ODDS 1:3		

2016 Orphan Black Season 1 Wardrobes

COMMON WARDROBE (M1-M13)	6.00	15.00
STATED ODDS 1:24		
M1 Maslany/Sarah Manning	15.00	40.00
M3 Maslany/Alison Hendrix	15.00	40.00
M4 Maslany/Helena	10.00	25.00
M5 Maslany/Sarah Manning	12.00	30.00
M7 Maslany/Alison Hendrix	12.00	30.00
M8 Maslany/Sarah Manning	12.00	30.00
M10 Maslany/Alison Hendrix	15.00	40.00
M13 Maslany/Sarah Manning	12.00	30.00

2016 Orphan Black Season 1 Promos

COMMON CARD (P1-P5)	2.00	5.00
P1 One of a Kind NSCC	5.00	12.00

2017 Orphan Black Season 2

COMPLETE SET (4)	30.00	80.00
COMMON CARD (S1-S4)	10.00	25.00

2017 Orphan Black Season 2 Autographed Wardrobes
COMMON AUTO 25.00 60.00
STATED ODDS 3:CASE
TMHW Tatiana Maslany 75.00 150.00

2017 Orphan Black Season 2 Autographs
COMMON AUTO 5.00 12.00
STATED ODDS 3:PREMIUM PACK
EB Evelyne Brochu 15.00 40.00
JG Jordan Gavaris 10.00 25.00
KB Kristian Bruun 8.00 20.00
SW Skyler Wexler 6.00 15.00
AML Ari Millen/Miller 6.00 15.00
AMM Ari Millen/Mark 6.00 15.00
AMR Ari Millen/Rudy 6.00 15.00
TMA Tatiana Maslany/Alison 60.00 120.00
TMC Tatiana Maslany/Cosima 60.00 120.00
TMH Tatiana Maslany/Helena 60.00 120.00
TMJ Tatiana Maslany/Jennifer 60.00 120.00
TMR Tatiana Maslany/Rachel 60.00 120.00
TMS Tatiana Maslany/Sarah 75.00 150.00
TMT Tatiana Maslany/Tony 60.00 120.00
ZDGM Zoe De Grand Maison 8.00 20.00

2017 Orphan Black Season 2 Promos
COMMON CARD 4.00 10.00

2017 Orphan Black Season 3
COMPLETE SET (4) 30.00 80.00
COMMON CARD (C1-C4) 10.00 25.00

2017 Orphan Black Season 3 Autographed Wardrobes
COMMON AUTO 10.00 25.00
STATED ODDS 3:CASE
TM1W Tatiana Maslany/Alison 75.00 150.00
TM2W Tatiana Maslany/Cosima 75.00 150.00
TM3W Tatiana Maslany/Helena 60.00 120.00
TM4W Tatiana Maslany/Rachel 50.00 100.00

2017 Orphan Black Season 3 Autographs
COMMON AUTO 5.00 12.00
STATED ODDS 3:1 PREMIUM PACK
EB Evelyne Brochu 12.00 30.00
JG Jordan Gavaris 10.00 25.00
JV Josh Vokey 6.00 15.00
KB Kristian Bruun 6.00 15.00
KB Kristin Booth 6.00 15.00
KS Ksenia Solo 15.00 40.00
SW Skyler Wexler 8.00 20.00
AM1 Ari Millen/Mark 6.00 15.00
AM2 Ari Millen/Miller 6.00 15.00
AM3 Ari Millen/Parsons 6.00 15.00
AM4 Ari Millen/Rudy 6.00 15.00
AM5 Ari Millen/Seth 6.00 15.00
TM1 Tatiana Maslany/Alison 50.00 100.00
TM2 Tatiana Maslany/Cosima 50.00 100.00
TM3 Tatiana Maslany/Helena 50.00 100.00
TM4 Tatiana Maslany/Rachel 50.00 100.00
TM5 Tatiana Maslany/Sarah 60.00 120.00
TM6 Tatiana Maslany/Krystal 60.00 120.00
ZDGM Zoe De Grand Maison 6.00 15.00

2020 Rittenhouse The Orville Archives Bordered Autographs
UNOPENED BOX (15 CARDS)
COMMON AUTO 5.00 12.00
NNO Adrianne Palicki 30.00 75.00
NNO J. Lee 12.00 30.00
NNO Jason Alexander 30.00 75.00
NNO Mark Jackson 8.00 20.00
NNO Molly Hagan 6.00 15.00
NNO Penny Johnson Jerald 10.00 25.00
NNO Peter Macon 12.00 30.00
NNO Scott Grimes 12.00 30.00
NNO Tim Russ 12.00 30.00

2020 Rittenhouse The Orville Archives Dual Autograph
NNO BJ Tanner/K.Wener 15.00 40.00

2020 Rittenhouse The Orville Archives Full Bleed Autographs
COMMON AUTO 5.00 12.00
RANDOMLY INSERTED INTO PACKS
A9 J. Lee 15.00 40.00
A11 Kelly Hu 12.00 30.00
A14 Michaela McManus 5.00 12.00
A17 Robert Picardo 12.00 30.00
A25 Jason Alexander 75.00 150.00

2020 Rittenhouse The Orville Archives Silver Autographs
COMMON AUTO 10.00 25.00
RANDOMLY INSERTED INTO PACKS
AS2 Adrianne Palicki 50.00 100.00
AS6 Peter Macon 12.00 30.00
AS8 J. Lee 15.00 40.00

2019 The Orville Season One
COMPLETE SET (72) 8.00 20.00
UNOPENED BOX (24 PACKS) 60.00 100.00
UNOPENED PACK (5 CARDS) 2.50 4.00
COMMON CARD (1-72) .25 .60

2019 The Orville Season One Bordered Autographs
COMMON AUTO 4.00 10.00
STATED OVERALL ODDS 1:12
L = 300-500 COPIES
VL = 200-300 COPIES
NNO Brett Rickaby L 5.00 12.00
NNO Catherine Shu L 5.00 12.00
NNO Dylan Kenin L 6.00 15.00
NNO Erica Tazel L 6.00 15.00
NNO Gavin Lee L 5.00 12.00
NNO Giorgia Whigham L 10.00 25.00
NNO J. Paul Boehmer L 6.00 15.00
NNO James Morrison L 5.00 12.00
NNO JD Cullum L 5.00 12.00
NNO Kelly Hu VL 12.00 30.00
NNO Larry Joe Campbell L 6.00 15.00
NNO Lenny Von Dohlen L 5.00 12.00
NNO Michaela McManus L 12.00 30.00
NNO Philip Anthony-Rodriguez L 6.00 15.00
NNO Ralph Garman L 5.00 12.00
NNO Rena Owen L 6.00 15.00
NNO Rob Lowe AB 75.00 150.00
NNO Robert Knepper VL 8.00 20.00
NNO Robert Picardo L 10.00 25.00

2019 The Orville Season One Bridge Crew
COMPLETE SET (8) 10.00 25.00
COMMON CARD (CC1-CC8) 2.50 6.00
*MIRROR: 2.5X TO 6X BASIC CARDS
STATED ODDS 1:24

2019 The Orville Season One Case-Topper
STATED ODDS 1:CASE
CT1 The Anhkana 8.00 20.00

2019 The Orville Season One Dual Autographs
COMMON AUTO 10.00 25.00
STATED OVERALL ODDS 1:12
NNO Adrianne Palicki/Rob Lowe 100.00 200.00
NNO Philip Anthony-Rodriguez/Eric Tazel 10.00 25.00
NNO Robert Picardo/Molly Hagen 25.00 60.00

2019 The Orville Season One Full-Bleed Autographs
COMMON AUTO 12.00 30.00
STATED OVERALL ODDS 1:12
EL = 100-200 COPIES
VL = 200-300 COPIES
S = 100 OR FEWER COPIES
A1 Seth MacFarlane S 200.00 400.00
A2 Adrianne Palicki VL 50.00 100.00
A6 Peter Macon EL 15.00 40.00
A9 Rob Lowe S 75.00 150.00

2019 The Orville Season One Off-Duty
COMPLETE SET (7) 8.00 20.00
COMMON CARD (D1-D7) 2.00 5.00
STATED ODDS 1:24

2019 The Orville Season One The Orville Ship
COMPLETE SET (9) 12.00 30.00
COMMON CARD (O1-O9) 2.50 6.00
STATED ODDS 1:24

2019 The Orville Season One Quotables
COMPLETE SET (14) 15.00 40.00
COMMON CARD (Q1-Q14) 2.50 6.00
STATED ODDS 1:24

2019 The Orville Season One Relics
COMMON MEM 8.00 20.00
RANDOMLY INSERTED INTO PACKS
RC1 Capt. Ed Mercer 20.00 50.00
RC2 Cmdr. Kelly Grayson 15.00 40.00
RC4 Lt. Gordon Malloy 10.00 25.00
RC5 Lt. Cmdr. Bortus 12.00 30.00
RC6 Lt. Alara Kitan 15.00 40.00
RC7 Lt. John Lamarr 12.00 30.00
RC8 Lt. Cmdr. Steve Newton 10.00 25.00
RC9 Teleya 10.00 25.00

2019 The Orville Season One Tour the Orville
COMPLETE SET W/RR (10)
COMPLETE SET W/O RR (9) 10.00 25.00
COMMON CARD (T1-T9) 1.50 4.00
STATED ODDS 1:24
T10 IS RITTENHOUSE REWARD

2019 The Orville Season One Promos
COMPLETE SET (4)
COMMON CARD (P1-P4)
P1 General Distribution 2.50 6.00
P2 Non-Sport Update Magazine 2.00 5.00
P3 Album Exclusive 8.00 20.00
P4 Facebook Fan Exclusive 25.00 60.00

2002 The Osbournes Season One
COMPLETE SET (72) 5.00 12.00
UNOPENED BOX (36 PACKS) 60.00 100.00
UNOPENED PACK (6 CARDS) 2.00 3.00
COMMON CARD (1-72) .15 .40

2002 The Osbournes Season One Autographs
COMMON AUTO (A1-A4) 6.00 15.00
STATED ODDS 1:137
A1 Ozzy 300.00 600.00
A2 Sharon 30.00 75.00
A3 Kelly 10.00 25.00

2002 The Osbournes Season One Box-Loaders
COMPLETE SET (5) 7.50 20.00
COMMON CARD 1.00 2.50
STATED ODDS ONE PER BOX
B6CL ISSUED AS CASE INSERT
B6CL Lola (CI) 6.00 15.00

2002 The Osbournes Season One Family Portrait
COMPLETE SET (9) 7.50 20.00
COMMON CARD (FP1-FP9) 1.25 3.00
STATED ODDS 1:11
PAN 9-Card Panel (FP1-FP9)

2002 The Osbournes Season One Head Bangers
COMPLETE SET (5) 3.00 8.00
COMMON CARD (H1-H5) .75 2.00
STATED ODDS 1:17

2002 The Osbournes Season One Pieceworks
COMPLETE SET (4) 20.00 40.00
COMMON CARD (PW1-PW4) 4.00 10.00
STATED ODDS 1:36
PW1 Ozzy 8.00 20.00

2002 The Osbournes Season One Promos
P0 The Osbournes .75 2.00
P1 The Osbournes .75 2.00
Pi Lola .75 2.00
PUK The Osbournes .75 2.00

1995 Comic Images Other Worlds Michael Whelan II
COMPLETE SET (90) 4.00 10.00
UNOPENED BOX (48 PACKS) 20.00 30.00
UNOPENED PACK (10 CARDS) .50 .75
COMMON CARD (1-90) .10 .25
6PAN 6-Card Panel
NNO Michael Whelan AU/1000* 10.00 25.00
NNO Medallion Card/1729* 10.00 25.00
PROMO Promo Card

1995 Comic Images Other Worlds Michael Whelan II Chromium
COMPLETE SET (6) 15.00 40.00
COMMON CARD (C1-C6) 3.00 8.00
RANDOMLY INSERTED INTO PACKS

1995 Comic Images Other Worlds Michael Whelan II Gunslinger
COMPLETE SET (3) 12.00 30.00
COMMON CARD (Sp1-Sp3) 5.00 12.00
RANDOMLY INSERTED INTO PACKS

1994 Comic Images Our Daughters
COMPLETE SET (3) 3.00 8.00
COMMON CARD (PC1-PC3) 1.25 3.00

1981 Sanitarium Our Golden Fleece
COMPLETE SET (20) 4.00 12.00
COMMON CARD (1-20) .50 1.25

2016 Outcast
COMPLETE SET (81) 20.00 50.00
UNOPENED BOX (24 PACKS) 80.00 100.00
UNOPENED PACK (8 CARDS) 5.00 6.00
COMMON CARD (1-76) .40 1.00
CHARACTER CARDS PART OF BASE SET

1997 DuoCards The Outer Limits
COMPLETE SET (81) 4.00 10.00
UNOPENED BOX (30 PACKS) 30.00 50.00
UNOPENED PACK (7 CARDS) 1.50 2.50
COMMON CARD (1-81) .10 .25

1997 DuoCards The Outer Limits Case Inserts
COMPLETE SET (6) 10.00 25.00
COMMON CARD (D1-D6) 3.00 8.00
STATED ODDS 1:CASE

1997 DuoCards The Outer Limits Gold Monster
COMPLETE SET (2) 15.00 40.00
COMMON CARD 10.00 25.00
STATED ODDS 2:CASE IN PACKS

1997 DuoCards The Outer Limits OmniChrome
COMPLETE SET (6) 5.00 12.00
COMMON CARD (1-6) 1.50 4.00
WRAPPER OFFER EXCLUSIVE SET

1997 DuoCards The Outer Limits Rare Art Chromium
COMPLETE SET (6) 6.00 15.00
COMMON CARD (1-6) 1.50 4.00
STATED ODDS 1:15

1997 DuoCards The Outer Limits Promos
COMPLETE SET (2) 1.25 3.00
COMMON CARD .75 2.00

2002 The Outer Limits Premiere

COMPLETE SET (72) 4.00 10.00
UNOPENED BOX (40 PACKS) 40.00 60.00
UNOPENED PACK (9 CARDS) 1.00 1.50
N1 ISSUED AS ALBUM EXCLUSIVE
C1 Checklist 1.00 2.50
N1 Opening and Closing Narrations ALB 6.00 15.00

2002 The Outer Limits Premiere Autographs

COMMON AUTO 6.00 15.00
STATED ODDS THREE PER BOX
A19 ISSUED AS CASE TOPPER
A20 ISSUED AS ALBUM EXCLUSIVE
A1 Adam West 100.00 200.00
A2 Robert Culp 30.00 75.00
A3 Leonard Nimoy 125.00 250.00
A4 William Shatner 125.00 250.00
A7 Michael Constantine 8.00 20.00
A8 Ed Asner 15.00 40.00
A11 Cliff Robertson 50.00 100.00
A12 Jacqueline Scott 10.00 25.00
A14 David McCallum 20.00 50.00
A16 Peter Mark Richman 8.00 20.00
A18 Harlan Ellison 15.00 40.00
A19 BarBara Luna CT 30.00 75.00
A20 Arlene Martel ALBUM 15.00 40.00

2002 The Outer Limits Premiere Beyond the Outer Limits

COMPLETE SET (9) 12.50 30.00
COMMON CARD (B1-B9) 2.00 5.00
STATED ODDS 1:20

2002 The Outer Limits Premiere Stars of the Outer Limits

COMPLETE SET (9) 5.00 12.00
COMMON CARD (S1-S9) .75 2.00
STATED ODDS 1:4

2002 The Outer Limits Premiere Strange but True

COMPLETE SET (9) 3.00 8.00
COMMON CARD (T1-T9) .50 1.25
STATED ODDS 1:8

2002 The Outer Limits Premiere Promos

BP1 Brig. Gen. Jefferson Barton ALB 2.00 5.00
NNO Major Charles Merritt GEN 2.00 5.00
NNO Mjr Charles Merritt (Adam West) Coming Soon 2001 SP

2003 The Outer Limits Sex Cyborgs and Science Fiction

COMPLETE SET (81) 4.00 10.00
UNOPENED BOX (40 PACKS) 60.00 100.00
UNOPENED PACK (9 CARDS) 2.50 3.00
COMMON CARD (1-81) .10 .30

2003 The Outer Limits Sex Cyborgs and Science Fiction Autographs

COMMON AUTO 6.00 15.00
STATED ODDS THREE PER BOX
L (LIMITED): 300-500 COPIES
A15 AND A18 WERE NOT ISSUED
A1 Natasha Henstridge 15.00 40.00
A2 Brent Spiner L 25.00 60.00
A3 Margot Kidder 12.00 30.00
A4 Michael Ironside 12.00 30.00
A5 Nana Visitor L 12.00 30.00
A6 Hal Holbrook L 20.00 50.00
A7 Alan Thicke 8.00 20.00
A8 Robert Picardo L 12.00 30.00
A9 Burt Young 8.00 20.00
A10 Beau Bridges 8.00 20.00
A12 Rebecca DeMornay 20.00 50.00
A13 Sofia Shinas 8.00 20.00
A14 William Sadler 8.00 20.00
A16 William B. Davis 8.00 20.00

2003 The Outer Limits Sex Cyborgs and Science Fiction From the Archives Costumes

COMMON CARD (CC1-CC12) 6.00 15.00
STATED ODDS 1:20
CC11 ISSUED AS CASE TOPPER
CC12 ISSUED AS ALBUM EXCLUSIVE
L (LIMITED): 300-500 COPIES
CC1 Gary Busey L 8.00 20.00
CC4 Sean Patrick Flanery L 8.00 20.00
CC9 Jeremy Sisto L 8.00 20.00
CC11 Brent Spiner CT 15.00 30.00
CC12 Robert Picardo ALB 10.00 20.00

2003 The Outer Limits Sex Cyborgs and Science Fiction Opening Monologue

COMPLETE SET (9) 2.00 5.00
COMMON CARD (M1-M9) .40 1.00
STATED ODDS 1:3

2003 The Outer Limits Sex Cyborgs and Science Fiction Stars of the Outer Limits

COMPLETE SET (18) 12.50 30.00
COMMON CARD (S1-S18) .75 2.00
STATED ODDS 1:6

2003 The Outer Limits Sex Cyborgs and Science Fiction Promos

P1 Woman 1.50 4.00
P2 Earth 2.50 6.00
P3 Picture 4.00 10.00
RAUKTOL Eye 8.00 20.00

2004 The Outer Limits Expansion

COMMON CARD 8.00 20.00
NIMOY AUTO ISSUED AS 5-SET INCENTIVE
MCCAMMON MEM ISSUED AS 5-SET INCENTIVE
A20 Leonard Nimoy AU 5SI 150.00 250.00
A21 Gary Busey AU 20.00 40.00
A22 Sheena Easton AU 40.00 80.00
CC13 Melissa McCammon MEM 5SI 20.00 50.00

2016 Outlander Season 1

COMPLETE SET (72) 15.00 40.00
UNOPENED BOX (24 PACKS) 250.00 500.00
UNOPENED PACK (5 CARDS) 10.00 20.00
COMMON CARD (1-72) .40 1.00
*FRASER: 8X TO 20X BASIC CARDS 4.00 10.00
*THISTLE/50: 10X TO 25X BASIC CARDS 10.00 25.00

2016 Outlander Season 1 Autographs

COMMON AUTO 8.00 20.00
STATED ODDS 1:24
AB Annette Badland 30.00 75.00
DL Duncan Lacroix 60.00 120.00
GL Gary Lewis 50.00 100.00
GM Graham McTavish 50.00 100.00
GO Grant O'Rourke 30.00 75.00
JF James Fleet 12.00 30.00
LD Laura Donnelly 75.00 150.00
LV Lotte Verbeek 20.00 50.00
NH Neil Hudson 100.00 200.00
SC Simon Callow 30.00 75.00
SH Sam Heughan 75.00 150.00
FDH Finn Den 50.00 100.00
SCR Steven Cree 25.00 60.00
TM1 Tobias Menzies 60.00 120.00
TM2 Tobias Menzies 60.00 120.00

2016 Outlander Season 1 Character Bios

COMPLETE SET (9) 8.00 20.00
COMMON CARD (C1-C9) 1.25 3.00
*FRASER: 1X TO 2.5X BASIC CARDS 3.00 8.00
*THISTLE/50: 3X TO 8X BASIC CARDS 10.00 25.00
STATED ODDS 1:3

2016 Outlander Season 1 Dual Wardrobes

COMMON CARD (DM1-DM9) 75.00 150.00
STATED ODDS 1:96
DM1 C.Balfe/T.Menzies 120.00 250.00
DM2 T.Menzies/C.Balfe 200.00 350.00
DM3 S.Heughan/C.Balfe 200.00 400.00
DM4 Lotte Verbeek 150.00 300.00
DM6 C.Balfe/S.Heughan 250.00 500.00
DM7 Caitriona Balfe 150.00 300.00
DM9 Caitriona Balfe 300.00 500.00

2016 Outlander Season 1 Quotes

COMPLETE SET (9) 6.00 15.00
COMMON CARD (Q1-Q9) 1.25 3.00
*FRASER: .5X TO 1.2X BASIC CARDS 1.50 4.00
*THISTLE/50: 3X TO 8X BASIC CARDS 10.00 25.00
STATED ODDS 1:3

2016 Outlander Season 1 Speak Outlander

COMPLETE SET (9) 5.00 12.00
COMMON CARD (S1-S9) 1.00 2.50
*FRASER: 1.2X TO 3X BASIC CARDS 3.00 8.00
*THISTLE/50: 3X TO 8X BASIC CARDS 8.00 20.00
STATED ODDS 1:3

2016 Outlander Season 1 Wardrobes

COMMON WARDROBE (M1-M37) 50.00 100.00
STATED ODDS 1:24
M1 Caitriona Balfe 100.00 200.00
M2 Sam Heughan 125.00 250.00
M3 Tobias Menzies 75.00 150.00
M6 Laura Donnelly 75.00 150.00
M7 Caitriona Balfe 75.00 150.00
M8 Sam Heughan 150.00 300.00
M9 Nell Hudson 75.00 150.00
M10 Caitriona Balfe 100.00 200.00
M11 Duncan Lacroix 100.00 200.00
M12 Graham McTavish 75.00 150.00
M13 Caitriona Balfe 300.00 600.00
M14 Sam Heughan 100.00 200.00
M16 Caitriona Balfe 125.00 250.00
M18 Sam Heughan 75.00 150.00
M20 Caitriona Balfe 250.00 500.00
M21 Tobias Menzies 100.00 200.00
M22 Sam Heughan 125.00 250.00
M23 Graham McTavish 60.00 120.00
M24 Caitriona Balfe 200.00 400.00
M25 Lotte Verbeek 200.00 400.00
M28 Duncan Lacroix 100.00 200.00
M29 Caitriona Balfe 200.00 350.00
M30 Tobias Menzies 100.00 200.00
M31 Laura Donnelly 75.00 150.00
M32 Gary Lewis 100.00 200.00
M33 Graham McTavish 75.00 150.00
M34 Caitriona Balfe 250.00 500.00
M35 Lotte Verbeek 125.00 250.00
M36 Sam Heughan 75.00 150.00
M37 Caitriona Balfe ALB 150.00 300.00

2016 Outlander Season 1 Promos

1 Non-Sport Update Aug/Sept 2015 8.00 20.00
2 National Sports Collectors Convention 201512.00 30.00
3 Non-Sport Update April/May 2016 12.00 30.00
4 Non-Sport Update April/May 2016 10.00 25.00
5 Philly Non-Sports Card Show 2016 20.00 50.00

2017 Outlander Season 2

COMPLETE SET (72) 8.00 20.00
UNOPENED BOX (24 PACKS) 60.00 90.00
UNOPENED PACK (5 CARDS) 3.00 4.00
COMMON CARD (1-72) .20 .50
*RAINBOW FOIL: 3X TO 8X BASIC CARDS 1.50 4.00
*GOLD JACOBITE: 6X TO 15X BASIC CARDS3.00 8.00
*RED JACOBITE/50: 20X TO 50X BASIC CARDS 10.00 25.00

2017 Outlander Season 2 Autographs

COMMON AUTO 8.00 20.00
STATED ODDS 1:24
CS Claire Sermonne 10.00 25.00
DL Duncan Lacroix 25.00 60.00
DP Dominique Pinon 10.00 25.00
GL Gary Lewis 30.00 75.00
GM Graham McTavish 25.00 60.00
GO Grant O'Rourke 15.00 40.00
LD Laura Donnelly 25.00 60.00
LL Lionel Lingelser 15.00 40.00
MD Mark Duret 10.00 25.00
NH Hell Hudson 25.00 60.00
RB Romann Berrux 20.00 50.00
RD Rosie Day 12.00 30.00
RR Richard Rankin 20.00 50.00
SH Sam Heughan 60.00 120.00
SK Scott Kyle 12.00 30.00
SS Sophie Skelton 50.00 100.00
SW Stephen Walters 20.00 50.00
AMZ Adrienne-Marie Zitt 12.00 30.00
LDZ Laurence Dobiesz 10.00 25.00
SCR Steven Cree 12.00 30.00
TM1 Tobias Menzies 30.00 75.00
TM2 Tobias Menzies 30.00 75.00

2017 Outlander Season 2 Character Bios

COMPLETE SET (9) 5.00 12.00
COMMON CARD (C1-C9) 1.00 2.50
*RAINBOW FOIL: .5X TO 1.2X BASIC CARDS1.25 3.00
*GOLD JACOBITE: 1X TO 2.5X BASIC CARDS2.50 6.00
*RED JACOBITE/50: 4X TO 10X BASIC CARDS
STATED ODDS 1:3

2017 Outlander Season 2 Dual Autographs

STATED OVERALL AUTO ODDS 1:24
RDLD Day/Dobiesz 300.00 600.00
RRSS Rankin/Skelton 200.00 400.00
SWDP Weber/Pinon 120.00 250.00

2017 Outlander Season 2 Dual Wardrobes

COMMON WARDROBE (DM1-DM6) 10.00 25.00
STATED ODDS 1:100
DM2 Weber/Heughan 75.00 150.00
DM4 Heughan/Lacroix 60.00 120.00
DM5 Heughan/Balfe 50.00 100.00
DM6 Walters/O'Rourke 50.00 100.00

2017 Outlander Season 2 Garden of Versailles

COMPLETE SET (9) 6.00 15.00
COMMON CARD (V1-V9) 1.25 3.00
*RAINBOW FOIL: .5X TO 1.2X BASIC CARDS1.50 4.00
*GOLD JACOBITE: 1X TO 2.5X BASIC CARDS3.00 8.00
*RED JACOBITE/50: 3X TO 8X BASIC CARDS10.00 25.00
STATED ODDS 1:3

2017 Outlander Season 2 Quotes

COMPLETE SET (9) 5.00 12.00
COMMON CARD (Q1-Q9) 1.00 2.50
*RAINBOW FOIL: .5X TO 1.2X BASIC CARDS1.25 3.00
*GOLD JACOBITE: 1X TO 2.5X BASIC CARDS3.00 8.00
*RED JACOBITE/50: 3X TO 8X BASIC CARDS8.00 20.00
STATED ODDS 1:3

2017 Outlander Season 2 STR PWR

COMPLETE SET (10) 120.00 250.00
COMMON CARD (S1-S10) 8.00 20.00
*RED: SAME VALUE AS BASIC 12.00 30.00
*SILVER: .6X TO 1.5X BASIC CARDS 15.00 40.00
*GOLD/25: .75X TO 2X BASIC CARDS
STATED ODDS 1:24

2017 Outlander Season 2 Vive Les Frasers

COMPLETE SET (9) 15.00 40.00
COMMON CARD (Z1-Z9) 3.00 8.00
STATED ODDS 1:24

2017 Outlander Season 2 Wardrobes

COMMON CARD (M1-M25) 10.00 25.00
STATED ODDS 1:24
B1 IS AN ALBUM EXCLUSIVE
B1 Sam Heughan ALB 30.00 75.00
M1 Caitriona Balfe 30.00 75.00
M2 Sam Heughan/99 50.00 100.00
M3 Stanley Weber 12.00 30.00
M5 Claire Sermonne 15.00 40.00

M6 Caitriona Balfe/49 300.00 600.00
M9 Caitriona Balfe 30.00 75.00
M10 Sam Heughan 75.00 150.00
M11 Tobias Menzies 20.00 50.00
M12 Stanley Weber 15.00 40.00
M13 Caitriona Balfe 125.00 250.00
M14 Sam Heughan/99 120.00 200.00
M15 Caitriona Balfe/99 75.00 150.00
M16 Caitriona Balfe 30.00 75.00
M18 Caitriona Balfe 30.00 75.00
M19 Sam Heughan/99 100.00 200.00
M20 Caitriona Balfe 20.00 50.00
M21 Stephen Walters/99 50.00 100.00
M22 Duncan Lacroix 15.00 40.00
M23 Sam Heughan 50.00 100.00
M25 Duncan Lacroix 15.00 40.00

2017 Outlander Season 2 Promos

COMMON CARD
P1 Emerald City Comic Con 50.00 100.00
P1 The Gathering Cologne Germany 10.00 25.00
P2 NY Tartan Day Parade
P2 WonderCon Anaheim/Fan Expo Dallas 8.00 20.00
P3 Industry Summit 8.00 20.00
P4 NSU Magazine 10.00 25.00
P5 NSU Magazine 6.00 15.00
P6 NSU Magazine 10.00 25.00
P7 Outlandish Gathering Boston 15.00 40.00
P8 Outlander in the City New York 60.00 120.00
P9 San Diego Comic Con 12.00 30.00

2019 Outlander Season 3

COMPLETE SET (72) 8.00 20.00
UNOPENED BOX (24 PACKS) 150.00 200.00
UNOPENED PACK (5 CARDS) 6.00 8.00
COMMON CARD (1-72) .25 .60
*CANVAS: 2X TO 5X BASIC CARDS
*FC GOLD: 6X TO 15X BASIC CARDS
*FC RED/50: 12X TO 30X BASIC CARDS

2019 Outlander Season 3 Autographs

COMMON AUTO 6.00 15.00
STATED ODDS 1:24
AM Albie Marber 8.00 20.00
CD Cesar Domboy 30.00 75.00
DB David Berry 20.00 50.00
HJ Hannah James 8.00 20.00
JB John Bell 20.00 50.00
LD Laura Donnelly 30.00 75.00
LL Lauren Lyle 25.00 60.00
NH Nell Hudson 12.00 30.00
RR Richard Rankin 30.00 75.00
SC Steven Cree 12.00 30.00
SS Sophe Skelton 50.00 100.00
CB1 Caitriona Balfe 450.00 600.00
CLB Clark Butler 12.00 30.00
TM1 Tobias Menzies 50.00 100.00
TM2 Tobias Menzies 50.00 100.00

2019 Outlander Season 3 Character Bios

COMPLETE SET (9) 6.00 15.00
COMMON CARD (C1-C9) 1.25 3.00
*CANVAS: .6X TO 1.5X BASIC CARDS
*FC GOLD: 1X TO 2.5X BASIC CARDS
*FC RED/50: X TO X BASIC CARDS
STATED ODDS 1:3

2019 Outlander Season 3 Convention Exclusive Wardrobes

COMMON MEM (CE1-CE6) 20.00 50.00
STATED PRINT RUN 299 SER.#'d SETS
CE1 Sam Heughan 50.00 100.00
CE2 Sam Heughan 30.00 75.00
CE4 Caitriona Balfe 30.00 75.00
CE5 Sam Heughan 75.00 150.00

2019 Outlander Season 3 Dual Autographs

RANDOMLY INSERTED INTO PACKS
APMH A.Pargeter/M.Hadfield 100.00 200.00
JBCD J.Bell/C.Domboy 125.00 250.00

2019 Outlander Season 3 Dual Wardrobes

COMMON MEM (DM1-DM8) 75.00 150.00
STATED OVERALL ODDS 1:275
DM1 Tobias Menzies/Sam Heughan/49 100.00 200.00
DM2 Sam Heughan/49 100.00 200.00
DM5 Sam Heughan/49 100.00 200.00
DM6 Lauren Lyle/49 125.00 250.00

2019 Outlander Season 3 Folding Card Insert

STATED ODDS 1:96
F1 A. Malcolm 8.00 20.00

2019 Outlander Season 3 Key Art Puzzle

COMPLETE SET (9) 6.00 15.00
COMMON CARD (Z1-Z9) 1.25 3.00
STATED ODDS 1:6

2019 Outlander Season 3 On Set

COMPLETE SET (9) 6.00 15.00
COMMON CARD (S1-S9) 1.00 2.50
*CANVAS: .6X TO 1.5X BASIC CARDS
*FC GOLD: 1.2X TO 3X BASIC CARDS
*FC RED/50: 2X TO 5X BASIC CARDS
STATED ODDS 1:3

2019 Outlander Season 3 The Skye Boat Song

COMPLETE SET (6) 6.00 15.00
COMMON CARD (Q1-Q6) 1.50 4.00
*CANVAS: .75X TO 2X BASIC CARDS
*FC GOLD: 1.2X TO 3X BASIC CARDS
*FC RED/50: 1.5X TO 4X BASIC CARDS
STATED ODDS 1:3

2019 Outlander Season 3 Triple Wardrobes

COMMON MEM (TM1-TM2) 150.00 300.00
STATED OVERALL ODDS 1:275
TM1 Sam Heughan/David Berry 200.00 400.00

2019 Outlander Season 3 Wardrobes

COMMON MEM (M1-M27, B1) 12.00 30.00
STATED ODDS 1:24
M1 Sam Heughan/99 75.00 150.00
M2 Caitriona Balfe 30.00 75.00
M3 Duncan Lacroix/99 30.00 75.00
M4 Tobias Menzies/99 30.00 75.00
M6 Romann Berrux/99 25.00 60.00
M10 Caitriona Balfe/99 75.00 150.00
M11 Ian Conningham/99 20.00 50.00
M12 John Bell/99 15.00 40.00
M13 Sam Heughan 20.00 50.00
M14 Caitriona Balfe/99 75.00 150.00
M15 Bill Paterson/99 20.00 50.00
M16 Sam Heughan 15.00 40.00
M17 Caitriona Balfe/99 50.00 100.00
M20 Laura Donnelly/99 50.00 100.00
M24 Sam Heughan/99 60.00 120.00
M25 Caitriona Balfe/99 60.00 120.00
B1 David Berry 15.00 40.00

2019 Outlander Season 3 Promos

COMMON CARD (P1-P8) 2.50 6.00
P1 WonderCon/Philly Non-Sports Card Show3.00 8.00
P2 Philly Non-Sports Card Show /National Sports Collectors Convention 5.00 12.00
P3 Non-Sport Update Magazine June/July 3.00 8.00
P7 Creation Entertainment's
Official Outlander Convention 6.00 15.00

2020 Cryptozoic Outlander Season 4

COMPLETE SET (72) 6.00 15.00
UNOPENED BOX (24 PACKS) 125.00 250.00
UNOPENED PACK (5 CARDS) 6.00 10.00
COMMON CARD (1-72) .20 .50
*CANVAS: 6X TO 15X BASIC CARDS
*GOLD FOIL: 10X TO 25X BASIC CARDS
*RED FOIL/50: 20X TO 50X BASIC CARDS

2020 Cryptozoic Outlander Season 4 Autographs

COMMON AUTO 10.00 25.00
OVERALL AUTO ODDS 1:24
BC Braeden Clarke 12.00 30.00
CM Colin McFarlane 25.00 60.00
CO Caitlin O'Ryan 20.00 50.00
MG Melanie Gray 12.00 30.00
NS Natalie Simpson 12.00 30.00
SH Simon Harrison 15.00 40.00
SM Sera-Lys McArthur 30.00 75.00
TC Tantoo Cardinal 20.00 50.00

2020 Cryptozoic Outlander Season 4 Characters

COMPLETE SET (9) 6.00 15.00
COMMON CARD (C1-C9) 1.00 2.50
*CANVAS: 1.2X TO 3X BASIC CARDS
*GOLD FOIL: 2X TO 5X BASIC CARDS
*RED FOIL/50: 4X TO 10X BASIC CARDS
STATED ODDS 1:3

2020 Cryptozoic Outlander Season 4 Convention Exclusive Oversized Wardrobe

OS01 Caitriona Balfe/200 75.00 150.00

2020 Cryptozoic Outlander Season 4 Convention Exclusive Wardrobes

COMMON MEM (CE1-CE5) 30.00 75.00
CE1 S.Heughan/C.Balfe/200 60.00 120.00
CE2 S.Heughan/C.Balfe/200 50.00 100.00
CE5 Sophie Skelton/99 125.00 250.00

2020 Cryptozoic Outlander Season 4 Dual Wardrobes

COMMON MEM (DM01-DM13) 25.00 60.00
OVERALL DUAL/TRIPLE ODDS 1:48
DM02 Caitriona Balfe/150 30.00 75.00
DM03 Sophie Skelton/99 50.00 100.00
DM04 Caitriona Balfe/99 50.00 100.00
DM05 L.Lyle/C.Domboy/99 50.00 100.00
DM06 C.Balfe/S.Skelton/150 60.00 120.00
DM07 S.Heughan/S.Skelton/200 60.00 120.00
DM09 C.Balfe/S.Heughan/150 75.00 150.00
DM11 S.Skelton/N.Simpson/200 50.00 100.00

2020 Cryptozoic Outlander Season 4 Father and Daughter

COMPLETE SET (9) 8.00 20.00
COMMON CARD (F1-F9) 1.25 3.00
*CANVAS: .75X TO 2X BASIC CARDS
*GOLD FOIL: 1.2X TO 3X BASIC CARDS
*RED FOIL/50: X TO X BASIC CARDS
STATED ODDS 1:3

2020 Cryptozoic Outlander Season 4 Fraser's Ridge

COMPLETE SET (9)
COMMON CARD (R1-R9)
*GOLD FOIL: 1X TO 2.5X BASIC CARDS
*CANVAS: 1.2X TO 3X BASIC CARDS
*RED FOIL/50: 2.5X TO 6X BASIC CARDS
STATED ODDS 1:3

2020 Cryptozoic Outlander Season 4 Oversized Wardrobes

COMPLETE SET (10)
COMMON MEM
OS02 Sam Heughan/99 300.00 450.00
OS03 Caitriona Balfe/99 200.00 400.00
OS04 S.Heughan/C.Balfe/99 350.00 600.00
OS05 Fraser Family/200 200.00 350.00
OSM03 Caitriona Balfe/25
OSM09 Caitriona Balfe/150 125.00 250.00
OSM10 Maria Doyle Kennedy/150 30.00 75.00
OSM15 Maria Doyle Kennedy/150 20.00 50.00
OSM25 Maria Doyle Kennedy/200 25.00 60.00
OSM26 Sophie Skelton/99 125.00 250.00

2020 Cryptozoic Outlander Season 4 Playing Cards

COMPLETE SET (54) 25.00 60.00
COMMON CARD 1.00 2.50
*GOLD: 2X TO 5X BASIC CARDS
STATED ODDS 1:2

2020 Cryptozoic Outlander Season 4 Puzzle

COMPLETE SET (9) 12.00 30.00
COMMON CARD (Z1-Z9) 2.50 6.00
STATED ODDS 1:6

2020 Cryptozoic Outlander Season 4 Quad Wardrobes

QM01 Balfe/Bell/Heughan/25 1200.00 2000.00

2020 Cryptozoic Outlander Season 4 Star Struck Autographs

COMMON AUTO 50.00 100.00
OVERALL AUTO ODDS 1:24
STCB Caitriona Balfe 300.00 500.00
STSH Sam Heughan 300.00 450.00

2020 Cryptozoic Outlander Season 4 Star Struck Dual Autographs

STSC S.Heughan/C.Balfe

2020 Cryptozoic Outlander Season 4 Triple Wardrobes

COMMON MEM (TM01-TM03) 50.00 100.00
OVERALL DUAL/TRIPLE ODDS 1:48
TM01 Caitriona Balfe/50 300.00 450.00
TM02 Balfe/Kennedy/McFarlane/150 75.00 150.00

2020 Cryptozoic Outlander Season 4 Wardrobes

COMMON MEM (M01-M30) 10.00 25.00
STATED ODDS 1:24
M03 Caitriona Balfe/99 75.00 150.00
M04 Sam Heughan/150 30.00 75.00
M06 Caitriona Balfe/150 30.00 75.00
M07 Cesar Domboy 12.00 30.00
M08 John Bell/99 50.00 100.00
M09 Caitriona Balfe/99 100.00 200.00
M10 Maria Doyle Kennedy/99 20.00 50.00
M11 John Bell/150 25.00 60.00
M12 Natalie Simpson/99 30.00 75.00
M13 Richard Rankin 15.00 40.00
M14 Lauren Lyle 12.00 30.00
M15 Maria Doyle Kennedy/150 25.00 60.00
M16 Sophie Skelton/99 30.00 75.00
M17 Tantoo Cardinal 15.00 40.00
M18 Ajuawak Kapashesit 12.00 30.00
M19 David Berry/99 60.00 120.00
M20 Richard Rankin/150 15.00 40.00
M21 Sophie Skelton/150 20.00 50.00
M22 Sophie Skelton/200 15.00 40.00
M23 Braeden Clarke/99 15.00 40.00
M24 Sophie Skelton/200 20.00 50.00
M25 Maria Doyle Kennedy/99 25.00 60.00
M26 Sophie Skelton/99 50.00 100.00
M27 Grant Stott 12.00 30.00
M28 John Bell/200 15.00 40.00
M29 Cesar Domboy/200 20.00 50.00
M30 Caitriona Balfe/99 60.00 120.00

2020 Cryptozoic Outlander Season 4 Promos

P1 Wizard World New Orleans 12.00 30.00
P2 Non-Sport Update FEB/MARCH 2.50 6.00
P3 Outlander Season 5 Premiere Event 25.00 60.00
P4 Emerald City Comic Con/Cryptozoic eStore8.00 20.00
P5 Cryptozoic Con
P6 Cryptozoic Con
P7 Cryptozoic Con II
P8 Cryptozoic Con II
P9 Cryptozoic Con II

2019 Outlander CZX

COMPLETE SET (54) 12.00 30.00
UNOPENED BOX (6 PACKS) 150.00 250.00
UNOPENED PACK (4 CARDS) 25.00 40.00
COMMON CARD (1-54) .50 1.25
*DF RED/50: 1.5X TO 4X BASIC CARDS
*DF GREEN/25: 2X TO 5X BASIC CARDS
*DF SILVER/15: 8X TO 20X BASIC CARDS

2019 Outlander CZX Autographed Wardrobes

COMMON AUTO 15.00 40.00
RANDOMLY INSERTED INTO PACKS
CFW UNPRICED DUE TO SCARCITY
ABW Annette Badland/90 20.00 50.00
AGW Andrew Gower/80 30.00 75.00
CBW Caitriona Balfe/50 250.00 500.00
CDW Cesar Domboy/80 20.00 50.00
CFW Caitriona Balfe/25
DBW David Berry/105 20.00 50.00
FRW Tobias Menzies/60 50.00 100.00
GLW Gary Lewis/90 20.00 50.00
GMW Graham McTavish/99 20.00 50.00
IMW Steven Cree/105 20.00 50.00
JBW John Bell/90 30.00 75.00
JFW Sam Heughan/60 250.00 500.00
LLW Lauren Lyle/90 25.00 60.00
LVW Lotte Verbeek/80 25.00 60.00
NHW Nell Hudson/80 30.00 75.00
SHW Sam Heughan/60 250.00 400.00
SWW Stephen Walters/25 125.00 250.00
TMW Tobias Menzies/60 60.00 120.00

2019 Outlander CZX Autographs

COMMON AUTO 15.00 40.00
RANDOMLY INSERTED INTO PACKS
CD Cesar Domboy/125 20.00 50.00
DG Diana Gabaldon, Author/120 75.00 150.00
ES Ed Speleers/105 20.00 50.00
GL Gary Lewis/110 25.00 60.00
GM Graham McTavish/60 100.00 200.00
GO Grant O'Rourke/105 20.00 50.00
LD Laura Donnelly/125 25.00 60.00
LV Lotte Verbeek/105 20.00 50.00
RR Richard Rankin/200 30.00 75.00
SM Simon Meacock/110 20.00 50.00
SS Sophie Skelton/80 50.00 100.00
MDK Maria Doyle Kennedy/110 25.00 60.00

2019 Outlander CZX Dual Autographed Wardrobes

RANDOMLY INSERTED INTO PACKS
CTW Caitriona Balfe/Tobias Menzies/50 500.00 800.00
DJW David Berry/Sam Heughan/60 300.00 500.00

2019 Outlander CZX Dual Autographs

COMMON AUTO 50.00 100.00
RANDOMLY INSERTED INTO PACKS
CBTM C.Balfe/T.Menzies/25 300.00 500.00
CDJB C.Domboy/J.Bell/60 60.00 120.00
CDLL C.Domboy/L.Lyle/35 75.00 150.00
CDSH C.Domboy/S.Heughan/50 200.00 350.00
DBSH D.Berry/S.Heughan/35 150.00 300.00
NHLL N.Hudson/L.Lyle/40 60.00 120.00
RRSS R.Rankin/S.Skelton/60 100.00 200.00
SCSH S.Cree/S.Heughan/30 125.00 250.00
SSSH S.Skelton/S.Heughan/30 200.00 350.00
TMSH T.Menzies/S.Heughan/35 500.00 1000.00
TMSS T.Menzies/S.Skelton/60 100.00 200.00

2019 Outlander CZX Dual Wardrobes

COMMON MEM (DW1-DW23, B1) 15.00 40.00
RANDOMLY INSERTED INTO PACKS
B1 IS AN ALBUM EXCLUSIVE
B1 S.Heughan/C.Balfe 25.00 60.00
DW1 S.Heughan/L.Donnelly/175 20.00 50.00
DW2 C.Balfe/L.Verbeek/150 20.00 50.00
DW3 C.Balfe/S.Heughan/75 75.00 150.00
DW4 Nell Hudson/99 25.00 60.00
DW6 C.Balfe/S.Heughan/150 60.00 120.00
DW8 S.Weber/C.Balfe/150 20.00 50.00
DW9 R.Berrux/L.Donnelly/110 20.00 50.00
DW12 D.Pinon/C.Balfe/99 30.00 75.00
DW14 L.Donnelly/D.Lacroix/99 30.00 75.00
DW15 B.Paterson/C.Balfe/99 25.00 60.00
DW16 M.Chatelier/T.Menzies/99 30.00 75.00
DW17 Caitriona Balfe/199 20.00 50.00
DW18 C.Balfe/S.Heughan/59 125.00 250.00
DW19 G.McTavish/S.Heughan/99 30.00 75.00
DW20 Caitriona Balfe/150 25.00 60.00
DW21 Caitriona Balfe/130 50.00 100.00
DW22 C.Balfe/A.Badland/150 20.00 50.00
DW23 C.Balfe/L.Donnelly/150 20.00 50.00

2019 Outlander CZX Lenticular

COMPLETE SET (20) 75.00 150.00
COMMON CARD (L1-L20) 4.00 10.00
STATED ODDS 1:6

2019 Outlander CZX STR PWR

COMPLETE SET (25) 100.00 200.00
COMMON CARD (S1-S25) 6.00 15.00
*GREEN/55: .6X TO 1.5X BASIC CARDS
*SILVER/30: 1.2X TO 3X BASIC CARDS
STATED ODDS 1:6

2019 Outlander CZX Triple Autographs

COMMON AUTO 200.00 400.00
RANDOMLY INSERTED INTO PACKS
CRS Balfe/Rankin/Skelton/50 300.00 500.00
CSJ Balfe/Heughan/Bell/25 500.00 750.00
CST Balfe/Heughan/Menzies/25 750.00 1000.00
CTS Balfe/Menzies/Skelton/50 300.00 500.00
DCS Berry/Balfe/Heughan/25 500.00 800.00
LCJ Verbeek/Balfe/Bell/25 400.00 700.00

2019 Outlander CZX Triple Wardrobes

COMMON MEM (TW1-TW12) 15.00 40.00
RANDOMLY INSERTED INTO PACKS
TW1 L.Lyle/C.Domboy/150 20.00 50.00
TW2 Heughan/O'Rourke/McTavish/80 60.00 120.00
TW4 L.Verbeek/C.Balfe/99 30.00 75.00
TW5 T.Menzies/C.Balfe/49 75.00 150.00
TW6 Weber/Pinon/Balfe/99 25.00 60.00
TW7 Heughan/Balfe/Menzies/199 25.00 60.00
TW8 Caitriona Balfe/150 30.00 75.00
TW10 S.Heughan/J.Bell/49 75.00 150.00
TW11 Lotte Verbeek/99 20.00 50.00
TW12 C.Balfe/S.Heughan/75 100.00 200.00

2019 Outlander CZX Wardrobes

COMMON MEM (W1-W15) 15.00 40.00
RANDOMLY INSERTED INTO PACKS
W1 Caitriona Balfe/40 100.00 200.00
W2 Sam Heughan/199 20.00 50.00
W4 Caitriona Balfel/99 25.00 60.00
W7 Grant O'Rourke/99 25.00 60.00
W8 Caitriona Balfe/99 30.00 75.00
W12 Sam Heughan/209 20.00 50.00
W14 Sam Heughan/250 20.00 50.00
W15 Sam Heughan/200 20.00 50.00

2019 Outlander CZX Promos

COMPLETE SET (9) 50.00 100.00
COMMON CARD (P1-P9) 4.00 10.00
P1 WonderCon 6.00 15.00
P2 Non-Sport Update Magazine 6.00 15.00
P3 Non-Sport Update Magazine 5.00 12.00
P4 Non-Sport Update Magazine 5.00 12.00
P5 Philly Non-Sports Card 10.00 25.00
P7 National Sports Collectors Convention 10.00 25.00
P8 San Diego Comic Con 6.00 15.00
P9 New York Comic Con 10.00 25.00

2001 Ozzy Osbourne

COMPLETE SET (68) 5.00 12.00
UNOPENED BOX (36 PACKS)
UNOPENED PACK (7 CARDS)
COMMON CARD (1-68) .15 .40

2001 Ozzy Osbourne Box-Toppers

COMPLETE SET (3) 8.00 20.00
COMMON CARD (A1-A3) 3.00 8.00
STATED ODDS 1:BOX

2001 Ozzy Osbourne Master of Metal Poster

COMPLETE SET (5) 5.00 12.00
COMMON CARD (P1-P5) .15 4.00
STATED ODDS 1:7

2000 Ozzy Osbourne and Black Sabbath Comic Images Promos

COMMON CARD .75 2.00

1999 Cornerstone Ozzy Osbourne and Black Sabbath Promos

COMPLETE SET (2) 1.25 3.00
COMMON CARD (P1-P2) .75 2.00

1994 SkyBox The Pagemaster

COMPLETE SET (90) 8.00 20.00
UNOPENED BOX (36 PACKS) 30.00 50.00
UNOPENED PACK (8 CARDS) 1.50 2.50
COMMON CARD (1-90) .15 .40

1994 SkyBox The Pagemaster Foil Embossed

COMPLETE SET (9) 10.00 25.00
COMMON CARD (F1-F9) 2.00 5.00
RANDOMLY INSERTED INTO PACKS

1997 Top Cow Painted Cow

PAN 6-Card Panel (66/49/31/24/3/56)
AUMS Marc Silvestri AU 20.00 50.00

1997 Top Cow Painted Cow Chromium

COMPLETE SET (6) 15.00 40.00
COMMON CARD 3.00 8.00
RANDOMLY INSERTED INTO PACKS

1997 Top Cow Painted Cow Promos

COMPLETE SET (3) 2.00 5.00
COMMON CARD .75 2.00

1993 Kitchen Sink Press Painted Ladies

COMPLETE SET (36) 5.00 12.00
COMMON CARD (1-36) .25 .60

2010 Paranormal Activity

COMPLETE SET (50) 10.00 25.00
UNOPENED PACK (8 CARDS)
COMMON CARD (1-50) .20 .50

2010 Paranormal Activity Autographs

COMPLETE SET (4) 50.00 100.00
COMMON CARD 8.00 20.00
OVERALL AUTO/MEM/FILM ODDS TWO PER PACK
2 Katie Featherston 20.00 40.00
4 Katie Featherston 25.00 50.00
Micah Sloat

2010 Paranormal Activity Costumes

COMPLETE SET (4) 25.00 60.00
COMMON CARD (C1-C4) 8.00 20.00
OVERALL AUTO/MEM/FILM ODDS TWO PER BOX
C2 Katie Featherston 10.00 25.00
C4 Katie Featherston 10.00 25.00

2010 Paranormal Activity Autograph Costumes

CI1 Katie Featherston 25.00 60.00

2010 Paranormal Activity Film Frames

COMPLETE SET (3) 25.00 50.00
COMMON CARD 8.00 20.00
OVERALL AUTO/MEM/FILM ODDS TWO PER BOX

2010 Paranormal Activity Portents of Evil

COMPLETE SET (9) 4.00 10.00
COMMON CARD (PE1-PE9) 1.00 2.50
STATED ODDS 1:1

2010 Paranormal Activity Puzzle

COMPLETE SET (9) 4.00 10.00
COMMON CARD (PU1-PU9) 1.00 2.50
STATED ODDS 1:1

2010 Paranormal Activity Promos

COMPLETE SET (4) 4.00 10.00
COMMON CARD .75 2.00
ALBUM1 Katie lights off ALB 2.00 5.00
ALBUM2 Katie lights on ALB 2.00 5.00

2013 Parks and Recreation

COMPLETE SET (90) 5.00 12.00
UNOPENED BOX (24 PACKS) 250.00 500.00
UNOPENED PACK (5 CARDS) 10.00 20.00
COMMON CARD (1-90) .15 .40
*FOIL: .6X TO 1.5X BASIC CARDS

2013 Parks and Recreation Autographs

COMMON AUTO 5.00 12.00
*GOLD/43-99: SAME AS BASIC AUTO
STATED ODDS 1:12
AP2 ISSUED AS 4-CASE INCENTIVE
AP Aubrey Plaza 150.00 400.00
AP1 Amy Poehler gray jkt 150.00 300.00
AP2 Amy Poehler black jkt 4CI 300.00 600.00
FA Fred Armisen 20.00 50.00
JO Jim O'Heir 20.00 50.00
MM Megan Mullally 30.00 75.00
NO Nick Offerman 125.00 250.00
PP Parker Posey 15.00 40.00
PR Paul Rudd 150.00 400.00
R Retta 8.00 20.00
RL Rob Lowe 75.00 200.00

2013 Parks and Recreation Autographs Gold Foil Red Ink

PRINT RUN 6-99
AA Aziz Ansari/99 15.00 40.00
MC Mo Collins/47* 8.00 20.00

2013 Parks and Recreation Autographs Red Ink

COMMON CARD 5.00 12.00
PRINT RUN 26-173
AA Azzi Ansari/173* 15.00 40.00
AP Aubrey Plaza/50* 25.00 60.00
MM Megan Mullally/38* 8.00 20.00
NO Nick Offerman/55* 15.00 40.00
PR Paul Rudd/50* 50.00 100.00

2013 Parks and Recreation Relics

COMMON MEM 6.00 15.00
*GOLD/99: SAME PRICE AS BASIC CARDS
STATED ODDS 1:24
RAA Aziz Ansari suit jacket 8.00 20.00
R1AP Amy Poehler dress 10.00 25.00
R2AP Amy Poehler suit jacket 10.00 25.00
RAP2 Aubrey Plaza hoodie 12.00 30.00

2013 Parks and Recreation Relics Dual Gold Foil

COMMON CARD 8.00 20.00
PRINT RUN 50-99
RDAP Amy Poehler/99 12.00 30.00
RDAP2 Aubrey Plaza/99 15.00 40.00

2013 Parks and Recreation Relics Triple Gold Foil

PRINT RUN 50-99
RTAP Amy Poehler/99 12.00 30.00
RTRL Rob Lowe/50 15.00 40.00

1992 Victoria Gallery Partners

COMPLETE SET (20) 4.00 10.00
COMMON CARD (1-20) .40 1.00

1995 FPG Paul Chadwick

COMPLETE SET (90) 4.00 10.00
UNOPENED BOX (36 PACKS) 12.00 20.00
UNOPENED PACK (8 CARDS) .50 .75
COMMON CARD (1-90) .10 .25
AU1 Paul Chadwick AU/1000* 20.00 50.00

1995 FPG Paul Chadwick Metallic

COMPLETE SET (5) 10.00 25.00
COMMON CARD (M1-M5) 3.00 8.00
STATED ODDS 1:12

1995 FPG Paul Chadwick Promos

COMPLETE SET (2) 1.25 3.00
COMMON CARD .75 2.00

1992 ProSport Specialities Peanuts Classics

COMPLETE SET (400) 12.00 30.00
COMPLETE SERIES 1 SET (1-200) 8.00 20.00
COMPLETE SERIES 2 SET (201-400) 6.00 15.00
UNOPENED SERIES 1 BOX (36 PACKS) 25.00 40.00
UNOPENED SERIES 1 PACK (10 CARDS) .75 1.00
UNOPENED SERIES 2 BOX (36 PACKS) 15.00 25.00
UNOPENED SERIES 2 PACK (10 CARDS) .40 .75
COMMON CARD (1-400) .08 .20
NNO Uncut Sheet 10.00 25.00

1992 ProSport Specialities Peanuts Classics Holograms

COMPLETE SET (2) 5.00 12.00
COMMON CARD (1-2) 3.00 8.00
RANDOMLY INSERTED INTO PACKS
1 Snoopy for President 4.00 10.00

1991 Tuff Stuff Peanuts Previews American

COMPLETE BOXED SET (33) 4.00 10.00
COMMON CARD (1-33) .15 .40
*CANADIAN: SAME VALUE
SCHULZ AUTOS RANDOMLY INSERTED
IN BOXED SETS
NNO1 Charles Schulz AU/33
NNO2 Uncut Sheet

1991 Tuff Stuff Peanuts Previews American Promos

1 The Peanuts Gang 2.00 5.00
2 Snoopy Playing Hockey 4.00 10.00

2015 Penny Dreadful Season 1

COMPLETE SET (72) 6.00 15.00
UNOPENED BOX (24 PACKS) 50.00 75.00
UNOPENED PACK (5 CARDS) 3.00 4.00
COMMON CARD (1-72) .15 .40
*SILVER FOIL: 2X TO 5X BASIC CARDS

2015 Penny Dreadful Season 1 Autographs

COMMON AUTO 5.00 12.00
STATED ODDS 1:24
AP Alex Price 6.00 15.00
HG Henry Goodman 5.00 12.00
HT Harry Treadaway 12.00 30.00
RC Reeve Carney 10.00 25.00
RK Rory Kinnear 10.00 25.00
RN Robert Nairne 6.00 15.00
HTO Hannah Tointon 6.00 15.00

2015 Penny Dreadful Season 1 Characters

COMPLETE SET (9) 6.00 15.00
COMMON CARD (C1-C9) 1.25 3.00
*SILVER FOIL: 1X TO 2.5X BASIC CARDS
STATED ODDS 1:4

2015 Penny Dreadful Season 1 Etchings

COMPLETE SET (8) 8.00 20.00
COMMON CARD (E1-E8) 1.50 4.00
*SILVER FOIL: .75X TO 2X BASIC CARDS
STATED ODDS 1:4

2015 Penny Dreadful Season 1 Props

COMMON CARD (M1-M15) 6.00 15.00
STATED ODDS 1:48
M15 Dr. Victor Frankenstein's Anatomy ALB10.00 25.00

2015 Penny Dreadful Season 1 Quotables

COMPLETE SET (9) 6.00 15.00
COMMON CARD (Q1-Q9) 1.25 3.00
*SILVER FOIL: 1X TO 2.5X BASIC CARDS
STATED ODDS 1:4

2015 Penny Dreadful Season 1 Tarot

COMPLETE SET (9) 25.00 60.00
COMMON CARD 5.00 12.00
STATED ODDS 1:32

2015 Penny Dreadful Season 1 Wardrobes

COMMON CARD (W1-W19) 6.00 15.00
STATED ODDS 1:24
W01 Eva Green 12.00 30.00
W02 Josh Hartnett 10.00 25.00
W03 Timothy Dalton 10.00 25.00
W04 Harry Treadaway 8.00 20.00
W06 Eva Green 12.00 30.00
W07 Reeve Carney 8.00 20.00
W08 Josh Hartnett 10.00 25.00
W09 Danny Sapani 10.00 25.00
W11 Eva Green 10.00 25.00
W12 Josh Hartnett 10.00 25.00
W13 Olivia Llewellyn 12.00 30.00
W14 Alun Armstrong 8.00 20.00
W15 Eva Green 10.00 25.00
W16 Reeve Carney 8.00 20.00
W17 Harry Treadaway 8.00 20.00
W18 Timothy Dalton 20.00 50.00
W19 Eva Green 12.00 30.00

2015 Penny Dreadful Season 1 Promos

COMMON CARD 6.00 15.00

2000 Pepsi Around the Globe

COMPLETE SET (72) 6.00 15.00
UNOPENED BOX (36 PACKS) 15.00 25.00
UNOPENED PACK (8 CARDS) .50 .75
COMMON CARD (1-72) .12 .30

2000 Pepsi Around the Globe Foil

COMPLETE SET (6) 8.00 20.00
COMMON CARD (F1-F6) 2.50 6.00
STATED ODDS 1:18

2000 Pepsi Around the Globe Promos

COMPLETE SET (3) 2.50 6.00
COMMON CARD (P1-P3) 1.25 3.00

1996 Dart FlipCards Pepsi Cola Premium

COMPLETE SET (90) 8.00 20.00
UNOPENED BOX (30 PACKS) 30.00 50.00
UNOPENED PACK (7 CARDS) 1.50 2.00
COMMON CARD (1-90) .15 .40
P1 Dealer Promo/400 2.00 5.00

1996 Dart FlipCards Pepsi Cola Premium Die-Cuts

COMPLETE SET (3) 8.00 20.00
COMMON CARD (DC1-DC3) 4.00 10.00
STATED ODDS 1:10

1996 Dart FlipCards Pepsi Cola Premium Gold Foil

COMPLETE SET (4) 10.00 25.00
COMMON CARD (GF1-GF4) 3.00 8.00
STATED ODDS 1:10

1994 Pepsi Cola Series One

COMPLETE SET (100) 5.00 12.00
UNOPENED BOX (36 PACKS) 30.00 40.00
UNOPENED PACK (8 CARDS) 1.00 1.25
COMMON CARD (1-100) .10 .25

1994 Pepsi Cola Series One Chromium

COMPLETE SET (10) 20.00 50.00
COMMON CARD (C1-C10) 3.00 8.00
STATED ODDS 1:12

1994 Pepsi Cola Series One Promos

COMPLETE SET (2) 2.00 5.00
COMMON CARD (P1-P2) 1.25 3.00

1995 Pepsi Cola Series Two

COMPLETE SET (100) 5.00 12.00
UNOPENED BOX (36 PACKS) 20.00 30.00
UNOPENED PACK (8 CARDS) .75 1.00
COMMON CARD (101-200) .10 .25

1995 Pepsi Cola Series Two Glamour Girls Foil

COMPLETE SET (3) 10.00 25.00
COMMON CARD (GG1-GG3) 4.00 10.00
STATED ODDS 1:36

1995 Pepsi Cola Series Two Pepsi and Pete Chromium

COMPLETE SET (6) 15.00 40.00
COMMON CARD (C11-C16) 3.00 8.00
STATED ODDS 1:18

1995 Pepsi Cola Series Two Tall Boys

1 2-Up Tall Boy Panel - Mail In
TB1 Zina Saunders (chromium) 20.00 50.00

1995 Pepsi Cola Series Two Promos

COMPLETE SET (3) 5.00
COMMON CARD (P3-P5) .75 2.00

1983 Topps Perlorian Cats

COMPLETE SET (55) 6.00 15.00
UNOPENED BOX (36 CARDS) 30.00 45.00
UNOPENED PACK (6 STICKERS) 1.25 1.50
COMMON CARD (1-55) .15 .40

2018 The Persuaders

COMPLETE SET (36) 6.00 15.00
COMMON CARD (1-36) .30 .75

2018 The Persuaders Autographs

COMMON AUTO 6.00 15.00
AA1 Annette Andre CI 12.00 30.00
AA2 Annette Andre ALB
AA3 Annette Andre ALB
CC1 Carol Cleveland 12.00 30.00
CC2 Carol Cleveland 12.00 30.00
CR1 Christian Roberts CI 10.00 25.00
CS1 Catherine Schell 10.00 25.00
DB1 Derren Nesbitt 8.00 20.00
GR1 Gary Raymond 10.00 25.00
GR2 Gary Raymond 10.00 25.00
MN1 Margaret Nolan 10.00 25.00
MN2 Margaret Nolan 10.00 25.00
MS1 Madeline Smith 8.00 20.00
MS2 Madeline Smith 8.00 20.00
RM1 Roger Moore 100.00 200.00
RM2 Roger Moore 100.00 200.00
SL1 Suzanna Leigh 12.00 30.00
VL1 Valerie Leon 15.00 40.00
VL2 Valerie Leon 15.00 40.00

2018 The Persuaders Promos

P1 Coming Soon (Curtis and Moore)
AS1 Dealer Promo (ams-78) 20.00 50.00
CC1 Dealer Promo (The Cyber Cellar) 12.00 30.00
DP1 Dealer Promo (humdrum1) 8.00 20.00
DP2 Dealer Promo
DT1 Dealer Promo (Derek's Trading Cards) 10.00 25.00
EM1 Dealer Promo (ACME 3000)
GP1 Dealer Promo (gazzagames) 12.00 30.00
HP1 Dealer Promo (twilightzone111)
JW1 Dealer Promo (doctorjas73)
JW2 Dealer Promo (doctorjas73)
MB1 Dealer Promo (MB-Trading-Cards, taekwondo888)
PC1 Dealer Promo (Premier Cards) 12.00 30.00
PR1 Coming Soon (British Horror Collection)/100
RK1 Dealer Promo (Roman Krause)
RK2 Dealer Promo (Roman Krause)
SF1 Dealer Promo (Scifi Cards) 8.00 20.00
EM2 Dealer Promo (ACME 3000)
TM1 Dealer Promo (telly-mania) 15.00 40.00
TZ1 Dealer Promo (twilightzone111) 10.00 25.00
UT1 Dealer Promo (Umbrella Trading Cards)12.00 30.00
UT2 Dealer Promo (Umbrella Trading Cards)12.00 30.00
BJB1 Dealer Promo (Brianjblues)
WEB1 Web Exclusive Promo Card/100

1993 Mother Productions Perverted Priests

COMPLETE BOXED SET (40) 6.00 15.00
COMMON CARD .30 .75

1994 Peter Max

COMPLETE SET (6) 3.00 8.00
COMMON CARD (1-6) .75 2.00

1995 Comic Images The Phantom

COMPLETE SET (90) 5.00 12.00
UNOPENED BOX (48 PACKS) 25.00 40.00
UNOPENED PACK (10 CARDS) .60 1.00
COMMON CARD (1-90) .10 .25
AU Lee Falk AUTO 20.00 50.00
M1 Medallion/1314* 10.00 25.00
6PAN 6-Card Panel
PROMO The Phantom PROMO .75 2.00

1995 Comic Images The Phantom Animals

COMPLETE SET (3) 12.00 30.00
COMMON CARD (1-3) 6.00 15.00
STATED ODDS 1:48

1995 Comic Images The Phantom Chromium

COMPLETE SET (6) 8.00 20.00
COMMON CARD (1-6) 2.50 6.00
STATED ODDS 1:16

1996 Intrepid Phantom Gallery

COMPLETE SET (100) 10.00 25.00
UNOPENED BOX (36 PACKS) 30.00 40.00
UNOPENED PACK (7 CARDS) .75 1.00
COMMON CARD (1-100) .20 .50

1996 Intrepid Phantom Gallery Legends

COMPLETE SET (9) 5.00 12.00
COMMON CARD (L1-L9) .75 2.00
STATED ODDS 1:4 PACKS

1996 Intrepid Phantom Gallery Past Present Future Phantom

COMPLETE SET (3) 12.00 30.00
COMMON CARD (P1-P3) 6.00 15.00
RANDOMLY INSERTED INTO PACKS

1996 Intrepid Phantom Gallery Phantom Year One

COMPLETE SET (6) 10.00 25.00
COMMON CARD (Y1-Y6) 3.00 8.00
RANDOMLY INSERTED INTO PACKS

1996 Inkworks The Phantom Movie

COMPLETE SET (90) 6.00 15.00
UNOPENED BOX (36 PACKS) 15.00 30.00
UNOPENED PACK (8 CARDS) .50 1.00
COMMON CARD (1-90) .12 .30
L1 The last hope of justice for 400 years 10.00 25.00
S1 The Phantom PROMO .75 2.00
(Non-Sport Update Magazine Exclusive)
NNO1 Uncut Sheet/2500
NNO2 Uncut Sheet Joe Jusko AU/400

1996 Inkworks The Phantom Movie Foilworks Skulls

COMPLETE SET (3) 10.00 25.00
COMMON CARD (F1-F3) 5.00 12.00
STATED ODDS 1:35

1996 Inkworks The Phantom Movie Joe Jusko Puzzle

COMPLETE SET (9) 10.00 25.00
COMMON CARD (P1-P9) 1.50 4.00
STATED ODDS 1:10

1994 Dynamic Marketing The Phantom Series One

COMPLETE SET (110) 5.00 12.00
UNOPENED BOX (36 PACKS)
UNOPENED PACK (7 CARDS)
COMMON CARD (1-110) .10 .25

1994 Dynamic Marketing The Phantom Series One Gallery

COMPLETE SET (6) 10.00 25.00
COMMON CARD (G1-G6) 2.50 6.00

1994 Dynamic Marketing The Phantom Series Two

COMPLETE SET (110) 4.00 10.00
UNOPENED BOX (36 PACKS)
UNOPENED PACK (7 CARDS)
COMMON CARD (1-110) .08 .20

1994 Dynamic Marketing The Phantom Series Two Gallery

COMPLETE SET (6) 10.00 25.00
COMMON CARD (G1-G6) 2.50 6.00
RANDOMLY INSERTED INTO PACKS

1995 Comic Images Phil Rizzuto's Baseball The National Pastime

COMPLETE SET (90) 8.00 20.00
UNOPENED BOX (36 PACKS) 35.00 50.00
UNOPENED PACK (10 CARDS) 1.00 1.50
COMMON CARD (1-90) .15 .40
*HOLOCHROME: 2X TO 5X BASIC CARDS
M1 Phil Rizzuto's Baseball Medallion Card 8.00 20.00
AUPR Philip Francis Rizzuto AU/1000 20.00 50.00
NNO1 Phil Rizzuto's Baseball Promo (dealers)1.25 3.00

1995 Comic Images Phil Rizzuto's Baseball The National Pastime Diamond Covers

COMPLETE SET (3) 8.00 20.00
COMMON CARD (1-3) 4.00 10.00
STATED ODDS 1:36

1995 Comic Images Phil Rizzuto's Baseball The National Pastime MagnaChrome

COMPLETE SET (6) 10.00 25.00
COMMON CARD (1-6) 3.00 8.00
STATED ODDS 1:16

1994-19 Philly Non-Sports Show Promos

COMMON CARD .75 2.00
1 Frank & Phyllis Reighter 2.00 5.00
2 Honoring Emergency Service Personnel 2.00 5.00
4 Zina Saunders 2.00 5.00
5 Marlin, Harris and Roxanne Toser 2.00 5.00
Non-Sport Update
5 Sally Star 2.00 5.00
61 Geary Kauffman/In Memoriam 2.00 5.00
62 Mike Ruggeri/In Memoriam 2.00 5.00
65 Fran Ross/In Memoriam 2.00 5.00
73 Phyllis Reighter/In Memoriam 2.00 5.00
90 Cliff H. Tooker, Jr./In Memoriam 2.00 5.00
93 Bill DeFranzo/In Memoriam 2.00 5.00
96 Jay Lynch 2.00 5.00
In Memoriam
103 Al Wexler 2.00 5.00
In Memoriam

1995 21st Century Archives Pin-Ups Uncovered

COMPLETE SET (50) 5.00 12.00
COMPLETE FACTORY SET (51) 6.00 15.00
UNOPENED BOX (36 PACKS) 30.00 40.00
UNOPENED PACK (8 CARDS) 1.50 1.75
COMMON CARD (1-50) .20 .50

1995 21st Century Archives Pin-Ups Uncovered Boudoir Beauties

COMPLETE SET (5) 8.00 20.00
COMMON CARD (1-5) 2.00 5.00
RANDOMLY INSERTED INTO PACKS

1995 21st Century Archives Pin-Ups Uncovered Promos

COMMON CARD .75 2.00

1992 Eclipse Pioneers of Country Music

COMPLETE BOXED SET (40) 5.00 12.00
COMMON CARD (1-40) .50

1995 Intrepid Pitt

COMPLETE SET (100) 10.00 25.00
UNOPENED BOX (48 PACKS) 25.00 40.00
UNOPENED PACK (7 CARDS) .60 1.00
COMMON CARD (1-100) .20 .50
NNO Pitt Promo .60 1.50
(general distribution)

1995 Intrepid Pitt Ashcan Characters

COMPLETE SET (9) 4.00 10.00
COMMON CARD (C1-C9) .75 2.00
STATED ODDS 1:3
CONTINUES NUMERICALLY INTO ASHCAN COVERS

1995 Intrepid Pitt Ashcan Covers

COMPLETE SET (9) 4.00 10.00
COMMON CARD (C10-C18) .75 2.00
STATED ODDS 1:3
CONTINUATION OF ASHCAN CHARACTERS

1995 Intrepid Pitt Holoforge

COMPLETE SET (6) 12.00 30.00
COMMON CARD (H1-H6) 3.00 8.00
RANDOMLY INSERTED INTO PACKS

1995 Intrepid Pitt Megamotion

1 EXCH 30.00 80.00
M1 Pitt 20.00 50.00

1995 Intrepid Pitt Siliconite

COMPLETE SET (3) 12.00 30.00
COMMON CARD (S1-S3) 6.00 15.00
STATED ODDS 1:48

2000 Pizza Monsters

COMPLETE SET (5) 5.00 12.00
COMMON CARD

1999 Inkworks Planet of the Apes Archives

COMPLETE SET (90) 5.00 12.00
UNOPENED BOX (36 PACKS)
UNOPENED PACK (8 CARDS)
COMMON CARD (1-90) .15 .40
L1 STATED ODDS 1:108
L1 Future of Liberty 8.00 20.00

1999 Inkworks Planet of the Apes Archives Autographs

COMMON AUTO (A1-A5) 12.00 30.00
RANDOMLY INSERTED INTO PACKS
A1 Linda Harrison 60.00 120.00
A3 Jeff Corey 20.00 50.00

1999 Inkworks Planet of the Apes Archives Posters

COMPLETE SET (9) 15.00 40.00
COMMON CARD (P1-P9) 2.50 6.00

1999 Inkworks Planet of the Apes Archives Roddy Revealed

COMPLETE SET (4) 5.00 12.00
COMMON CARD (R1-R4) 2.00 5.00

1999 Inkworks Planet of the Apes Archives Promos

COMPLETE SET (3) 3.00 8.00
COMMON CARD .75 2.00
SFX1 UK Distribution 2.50 6.00

2004 Planet of the Apes Charlton Heston Collection

COMPLETE SET (9) 8.00 20.00
COMMON CARD (1-9) 1.25 3.00
STATED PRINT RUN 999 SER.#'d SETS

2001 Coca-Cola Planet of the Apes

COMPLETE SET (4) 12.00 30.00
COMMON CARD (1-4) 4.00 10.00

2001 Topps Planet of the Apes Movie

COMPLETE SET (90) 6.00 15.00
UNOPENED HOBBY BOX (36 PACKS) 50.00 90.00
UNOPENED HOBBY PACK (8 CARDS) 2.00 3.00
COMMON CARD (1-90) .15 .40

2001 Topps Planet of the Apes Movie Authentic Movie Memorabilia

COMPLETE SET (7) 100.00 200.00
COMMON CARD 8.00 20.00
STATED ODDS 1:36
5 Karubi's Costume 10.00 25.00
6 Major Leo Davidson's 10.00 25.00
Astronaut Shirt
7 Thade's Father's Costume SP 50.00 100.00

2001 Topps Planet of the Apes Movie Autographs

COMMON AUTO 8.00 20.00
STATED ODDS 1:36
UNNUMBERED SET
NNO Charlton Heston 125.00 250.00
NNO Estella Warren SP 150.00 300.00
NNO Helena Bonham Carter 25.00 60.00
NNO Kris Kristofferson 75.00 150.00
NNO Linda Harrison 30.00 75.00
NNO Tim Roth 25.00 60.00

2001 Topps Planet of the Apes Movie Box-Topper Bonus Foil

COMPLETE SET (6) 6.00 15.00
COMMON CARD 1.50 4.00
STATED ODDS 1:BOX

2001 Topps Planet of the Apes Movie Embossed

COMPLETE SET (10) 8.00 20.00
COMMON CARD (F1-F10) 1.00 2.50
STATED ODDS 1:6 HOBBY

2001 Topps Planet of the Apes Movie Simian Suede

COMPLETE SET (6) 15.00 40.00
COMMON CARD (S1-S6) 3.00 8.00
RANDOMLY INSERTED INTO PACKS

2001 Topps Planet of the Apes Movie Stickers

COMPLETE SET (10) 60.00 120.00
COMMON CARD (1-10) 6.00 15.00
STATED ODDS 1:12

2001 Topps Planet of the Apes Movie Promos

1 Dark Horse Comics .75 2.00
2 Chimpanzee Warrior CON .75 2.00
3 Krull (May 2001) .75 2.00
4 Thade (Wizard #117) 1.25 3.00
5 Sales Tri-Fold (11 X 24)
6 Merchandising Opportunity
7 Rule The Planet Foil (5 X 9) 1.50 4.00
8 In Semos We Trust
A1 7-27-01 - 4-Up Panel 4.00 10.00

2001 Planet of the Apes Movie CD Cardz

COMPLETE SET (7) 12.00 30.00
COMMON CARD (1-7) 2.50 6.00

1995 SkyBox Pocahontas

COMPLETE SET (90) 5.00 12.00
UNOPENED BOX (36 PACKS) 15.00 25.00
UNOPENED PACK (9 CARDS) .40 .60
COMMON CARD (1-90) .12 .30

1995 SkyBox Pocahontas 3-D Panorama

COMPLETE SET (5) 6.00 15.00
COMMON CARD (1-5) 2.00 5.00
STATED ODDS 1:9

1995 SkyBox Pocahontas Animation

COMPLETE SET (2) 25.00 60.00
COMMON CARD (1-2) 15.00 40.00
STATED ODDS 1:90

1995 SkyBox Pocahontas Dufex

COMPLETE SET (5) 15.00 40.00
COMMON CARD (1-5) 5.00 12.00
STATED ODDS 1:36

1995 SkyBox Pocahontas Pop-Outs

COMPLETE SET (12) 2.00 5.00
COMMON CARD (1-12) .20 .50
STATED ODDS 1:1
INCLUDED AS PART OF THE BASE SET

1995 SkyBox Pocahontas Animation Discovery Adventure Promos

COMPLETE SET (10) 10.00 25.00
COMMON CARD 1.50 4.00

1995 SkyBox Pocahontas Blue Back Promos

COMPLETE SET (4) 4.00 10.00
COMMON CARD (1-4) 1.50 4.00

1995 SkyBox Pocahontas Premier in the Park Promos

COMPLETE SET (10) 12.00 30.00
COMMON CARD 2.00 5.00

1995 SkyBox Pocahontas Summer Spectacular Promos

COMPLETE SET (10) 10.00 25.00
COMMON CARD 1.50 4.00

1993 Kitchen Sink Press Pocket Pin-Ups

COMPLETE BOXED SET (36) 5.00 12.00
COMMON CARD (1-36) .25 .60

1993 Kitchen Sink Press Pocket Pin-Ups Promos

COMPLETE SET (3) 1.50 4.00
COMMON CARD (1-3) .60 1.50

1996 Comic Images Poison Elves

COMPLETE SET (75) 5.00 12.00
UNOPENED BOX (48 PACKS) 12.00 20.00
UNOPENED PACK (8 CARDS) .45 .60
COMMON CARD (1-75) .15 .40

1996 Comic Images Poison Elves Chromium

COMPLETE SET (6) 10.00 25.00
COMMON CARD (C1-C6) 2.50 6.00
RANDOMLY INSERTED INTO PACKS

1996 Comic Images Poison Elves Subset

COMPLETE SET (3) 8.00 20.00
COMMON CARD (S1-S3) 4.00 10.00
RANDOMLY INSERTED INTO PACKS

2000 Pokemon Action Flipz Premier

COMPLETE SET (40) 9.00 18.00
UNOPENED BOX (24 PACKS) 10.00 15.00
UNOPENED PACK (4 CARDS/1 STICKER) 1.00 2.00
STICKER SET (SP1-SP10) 4.00 8.00
COMMON STICKER .50 1.00
S CARDS (S1-S4) 2.00 4.00
SG CARDS (SG1-SG4) 3.00 6.00
SR CARDS (SR1-SR10) 1.00 3.00

2003 Pokemon Advanced

COMPLETE SET (90) 5.00 12.00
UNOPENED BOX (24 PACKS) 125.00 150.00
UNOPENED PACK (7 CARDS) 6.00 8.00
COMMON CARD (1-90) .10 .25
*FOIL: 1.5X TO 4X BASIC CARDS

2003 Pokemon Advanced Embossed Evolution

COMPLETE SET (18) 4.00 10.00

COMMON CARD (1-18) .50 1.25
STATED ODDS 1:4

2003 Pokemon Advanced Pop-Ups

COMPLETE SET (10) 3.00 8.00
COMMON CARD (1-10) .60 1.50
STATED ODDS 1:6

2004 Pokemon Advanced Challenge

COMPLETE SET (90) 4.00 10.00
UNOPENED BOX (24 PACKS) 15.00 30.00
UNOPENED PACK (7 CARDS) .60 1.25
COMMON CARD (1-90) .08 .20
*FOIL: 2X TO 5X BASIC CARDS

2004 Pokemon Advanced Challenge Evolution Die-Cuts

COMPLETE SET (18) 10.00 25.00
COMMON CARD (1-18) 1.25 3.00
STATED ODDS 1:4
18 Charizard 2.00 5.00

2004 Pokemon Advanced Challenge Pop-Ups

COMPLETE SET (10) 5.00 12.00
COMMON CARD (1-10) 1.00 2.50
STATED ODDS 1:6
1 Absol 1.50 4.00
8 Charizard 1.50 4.00

2000 Pokemon Chrome

COMPLETE SET (78) 10.00 25.00
COMPLETE SERIES 1 SET (78) 6.00 15.00
COMPLETE SERIES 2 SET (73) 6.00 15.00
UNOPENED SERIES 1 BOX (30 PACKS)
UNOPENED SERIES 2 PACK (5 CARDS)
UNOPENED SERIES 2 BOX (30 PACKS)
UNOPENED SERIES 2 PACK (5 CARDS)
COMMON CARD (1-78) .25 .60
COMMON CARD (79-151) .25 .60
*SPECTRA: .6X TO 1.5X BASIC CARDS
*SPARKLE: 1.2X TO 3X BASIC CARDS
*TECHNO: 3X TO 8X BASIC CARDS

1999 Kellogg's Pokemon Game Tips

COMPLETE SET (20)
COMMON CARD (SKIP #'d) 6.00 15.00

2000 Pokemon Movie

COMPLETE SET (72) 5.00 12.00
UNOPENED BOX (36 PACKS) 2000.00 3000.00
UNOPENED PACK (6 CARDS) 55.00 80.00
COMMON CARD (1-71; CL) .20 .50

2000 Pokemon Movie Animation Stick-Ons

COMPLETE SET (10) 8.00 20.00
COMMON CARD (1-10) 1.25 3.00
STATED ODDS 1:6

2000 Pokemon Movie First Appearance Holograms

COMPLETE SET (6)
COMMON CARD (1-6) 75.00 150.00
STATED ODDS 1:36

1999 Topps Pokemon Movie Animation Edition Blue Evolution Die-Cuts

COMPLETE SET (12) 10.00 25.00
COMMON CARD (E1-E12) 1.25 3.00
STATED ODDS 1:12

2009 Politicians

COMPLETE SET W/O SP (290) 50.00 100.00
COMMON CARD .20 .50
AZ2S John McCain 3.00 8.00
CA8R Nancy Pelosi 2.00 5.00
CT1S Joe Lieberman .40 1.00
MA1S Edward M. Kennedy 3.00 8.00
NY9R Anthony Weiner .50 1.25
TX14R Ron Paul 2.00 5.00
VT1S Bernard Sanders 2.50 6.00
WI1R Paul Ryan 2.00 5.00
EX1 Barack Hussein Obama 10.00 25.00
EX3 Hillary Rodham Clinton 6.00 15.00
EXG Barack Obama Gold SP 150.00 300.00
JU1 John Roberts 2.00 5.00
WH1 Michelle Obama 1.00 2.50
WH2 Bo .40 1.00
WH3 Air Force One .40 1.00
WH4 Marine One .40 1.00
NNO Barack Obama Sweepstakes

Pop Century

2010 Leaf Pop Century

COMMON CARD 6.00 15.00
AB1 Amber Benson AU 8.00 20.00
AC1 Adrianne Curry AU 8.00 20.00
AD1 Annie Duke AU 8.00 20.00
AJ1 Ashley Judd AU 40.00 80.00
AO1 Aubrey O'Day AU 10.00 25.00
AP1 Adrian Pasdar AU 8.00 20.00
AP2 Audrina Patridge AU 8.00 20.00
AT1 Andrea Thompson AU 8.00 20.00
AW1 Amy Weber AU 8.00 20.00
BB1 Beau Bridges AU 8.00 20.00
BC1 Bruce Campbell AU 12.00 30.00
BF1 Bethenny Frankel AU 10.00 25.00
BJ1 Bruce Jenner AU 8.00 20.00
BP1 Butch Patrick AU 10.00 25.00
CB1 Corbin Bernsen AU 10.00 25.00
CC1 Charisma Carpenter AU 20.00 50.00
CJ1 Christopher Judge AU 12.00 30.00
CK1 Christopher Knight AU 10.00 25.00
CL1 Christopher Lloyd AU 35.00 70.00
DB1 Debby Boone AU 8.00 20.00
DD1 Donna D'Errico AU 10.00 25.00
DD2 Donna Douglas AU 10.00 25.00
DJ1 Davy Jones AU 50.00 100.00
DW1 Dawn Wells AU 20.00 50.00
E1 Elvira AU 60.00 120.00
EB1 Ernest Borgnine AU 20.00 50.00
EE1 Erika Eleniak AU 10.00 25.00
EG1 Erin Gray AU 12.00 30.00
GG1 Gil Gerard AU 10.00 25.00
HF1 Harrison Ford AU 400.00 600.00
HP1 Hayden Panettiere AU 75.00 150.00
HS1 Helen Slater AU 12.00 30.00
HW1 Henry Winkler AU 35.00 70.00
IT1 Ice-T AU 10.00 25.00
JC2 Jennifer Coolidge AU 10.00 25.00
JD1 Joyce DeWitt AU 15.00 40.00
JG2 Jennie Garth AU 15.00 40.00
JK1 Jennifer Korbin AU 10.00 25.00
JM1 Jason Momoa AU 8.00 20.00
JRD John Rhys-Davies AU 8.00 20.00
JS1 Jewel Staite AU 15.00 40.00
JS2 John Schneider AU 10.00 25.00
JT1 Jeffrey Tambor AU 8.00 20.00
JW1 Jimmie Walker AU 10.00 25.00
KK1 Khloe Kardashian AU 15.00 40.00
KK2 Kim Kardashian AU 75.00 150.00
KK3 Kourtney Kardashian AU 20.00 50.00
KL1 Kristanna Loken AU 15.00 40.00
KP1 Kirsten Prout AU 15.00 40.00
KW1 Kendra Wilkinson AU 15.00 40.00
LB1 Levar Burton AU 10.00 25.00
LB2 Linda Blair AU 15.00 40.00
LH1 Lauren Holly AU 35.00 70.00
LH2 Larry Hagman AU 20.00 60.00
LH3 Linda Hamilton AU 10.00 25.00
LT1 Lea Thompson AU 15.00 40.00
MF1 Mira Furlan AU 8.00 20.00
MH1 Mark Hamill AU 75.00 150.00
MK1 Margot Kidder AU 8.00 20.00
MR1 Mickey Rooney AU 20.00 50.00
NE1 Nicole Eggert AU 25.00 60.00
NN1 Nichelle Nichols AU 12.00 30.00
PA1 Pamela Anderson AU 75.00 150.00
PF1 Peter Fonda AU 30.00 80.00
RC1 Richard Chamberlain AU 20.00 50.00
RD1 Richard Dreyfuss AU 15.00 40.00
RH1 Ron Howard AU 40.00 80.00
RK1 Richard Kiel AU 10.00 25.00
RM1 Rita Moreno AU 12.00 30.00
SA1 Sean Astin AU 8.00 20.00
SD1 Sarah Douglas AU 8.00 20.00
SF1 Steve-O AU 10.00 25.00
SL1 Shayne Lamas AU 8.00 20.00
SL2 Stan Lee AU 400.00 1000.00
SO1 Stephen Furst AU 8.00 20.00
SP1 Stephanie Pratt AU 10.00 25.00
T1 Tiffany AU 15.00 40.00
TC1 Tia Carrere AU 15.00 40.00
TD1 Taylor Dayne AU 10.00 25.00
TD2 Thomas Dekker AU 8.00 20.00
TM1 Taryn Manning AU 8.00 20.00
TR1 Tanya Roberts AU 10.00 25.00
TS1 Tori Spelling AU 8.00 20.00
TUC The Unknown Comic AU 10.00 25.00
VT1 Verne Troyer AU 12.00 30.00
WAY Weird Al Yankovic AU 20.00 50.00
WJ1 Wynonna Judd AU 20.00 50.00
WS1 William Shatner AU 50.00 100.00

2010 Leaf Pop Century Authentic Costumes Blue

COMMON CARD (SW1-SW50) 5.00 12.00
OVERALL COSTUME ODDS 3:1
SW3 Ali Larter 6.00 15.00
SW5 Anne Hathaway 6.00 15.00
SW7 Arnold Schwarzenegger 8.00 20.00
SW8 Ashley Judd 8.00 20.00
SW10 Jon Bon Jovi 10.00 25.00
SW11 Brad Pitt 6.00 15.00
SW12 Brenda Song 6.00 15.00
SW13 Britney Spears 15.00 40.00
SW14 Brittany Murphy 8.00 20.00
SW15 Cameron Diaz 10.00 25.00
SW16 Charlie Sheen 6.00 15.00
SW18 Corey Haim 8.00 20.00
SW21 Drew Barrymore 6.00 15.00
SW22 Dustin Hoffman 8.00 20.00
SW24 Elisha Cuthbert 6.00 15.00
SW25 Eliza Dushku 8.00 20.00
SW27 Gwyneth Paltrow 6.00 15.00
SW28 Harrison Ford 6.00 15.00
SW29 Hilary Duff 8.00 20.00
SW31 Jack Nicholson 6.00 15.00
SW32 Jaime Pressly 6.00 15.00
SW34 John Wayne 12.00 30.00
SW36 Cate Blanchett 6.00 15.00
SW37 Katherine Heigl 6.00 15.00
SW40 Madonna 25.00 50.00
SW47 Teri Hatcher 6.00 15.00
SW49 Uma Thurman 6.00 15.00

2010 Leaf Pop Century Award Winners Autographs Blue

COMMON CARD 8.00 20.00
STATED PRINT RUN 10-100
AWAD1 Annie Duke/50 10.00 25.00
AWCL1 Christopher Lloyd50 35.00 70.00
AWEB1 Ernest Borgnine/20 20.00 50.00
AWEF1 Edward Furlong/50 12.00 30.00
AWHP1 Hayden Panettiere/20 75.00 150.00
AWHW1 Henry Winkler/50 25.00 50.00
AWLB1 Linda Blair/50 15.00 40.00
AWLH1 Lauren Holly/50 35.00 70.00
AWLH3 Linda Hamilton/50 25.00 50.00
AWLT1 Lea Thompson/50 15.00 40.00
AWLW1 Lindsay Wagner/50 25.00 50.00
AWMR1 Mickey Rooney/50 30.00 60.00
AWPF1 Peter Fonda/10
AWRC1 R.Chamberlain/50 15.00 40.00
AWRD1 Richard Dreyfuss/20 15.00 40.00
AWRH1 Ron Howard/10
AWRM1 Rita Moreno/50 15.00 40.00
AWVT1 Verne Troyer/100 10.00 25.00
AWWAY Weird Al Yankovic/100 20.00 50.00
AWWJ1 Wynonna Judd/50 20.00 50.00
AWWS1 William Shatner/20 50.00 100.00

2010 Leaf Pop Century Co-Stars Autographs Silver

STATED PRINT RUN 25 SER. #'d SETS
CSACCK Adrianne Curry 15.00 40.00
Christopher Knight
CSAJWJ Ashley Judd 50.00 100.00
Wynonna Judd
CSAPSP Audrina Patridge 20.00 50.00
Stephanie Pratt
CSBBCJ Beau Bridges 20.00 50.00
Christopher Judge
CSBWCK Barry Williams 15.00 40.00
Christopher Knight
CSBWT Barry Williams 12.00 30.00
Tiffany
CSEEDE Erika Eleniak 15.00 40.00
Donna D'Errico
CSGGEG Gil Gerard 30.00 80.00
Erin Gray
CSJSCJ Jewel Staite 15.00 40.00
Christopher Judge
CSJTCB Jeffrey Tambor 15.00 40.00
Corbin Bernsen
CSJTCL Jeffrey Tambor 25.00 60.00
Christopher Lloyd
CSKLIT Kristanna Loken 15.00 40.00
Ice-T
CSLHEF Linda Hamilton 50.00 100.00
Edward Furlong
CSLWEB Lindsay Wagner 25.00 50.00
Ernest Borgnine
CSMBLH Michael Biehn 50.00 100.00
Linda Hamilton
CSNEEG Nicole Eggert 30.00 80.00
Erin Gray
CSPAEE Pamela Anderson 200.00 400.00
Erika Eleniak
CSPAJM Pamela Anderson 150.00 300.00
Jason Momoa
CSTRJC Tanya Roberts 15.00 40.00
Jeff Conaway
CSTSJG Tori Spelling 25.00 60.00
Jennie Garth
CSJRDJT John Rhys-Davies 20.00 50.00
Jeffrey Tambor
CSSAJRD Sean Astin 20.00 50.00
John Rhys-Davies

2010 Leaf Pop Century Signatures Previews

1 Christopher Kid Reid 5.00 10.00
2 Audrina Patridge 10.00 20.00
3 Annie Duke 12.00 25.00

2011 Leaf Pop Century

COMMON CARD 4.00 10.00
*SILVER/25: .5X TO 1.2X BASIC CARDS
BAAB1 Amber Benson 6.00 15.00
BAAJ1 Ashley Judd 40.00 80.00
BAAP2 Audrina Patridge 8.00 20.00
BAAW1 Amy Weber 6.00 15.00
BABE1 Barbara Eden SP 25.00 50.00
BABJ1 Bruce Jenner SP 20.00 50.00
BABL1 Bai Ling 10.00 25.00
BABM1 Bill Mumy 8.00 20.00
BABS2 Britney Spears SP 250.00 500.00
BACA2 Christina Applegate SP 30.00 60.00
BACE1 Carmen Electra 25.00 50.00
BACL1 Christopher Lloyd SP
BACN1 Cam Newton 50.00 100.00
BACS1A Charlie Sheen (suit) SP 75.00 150.00
BACS1B Charlie Sheen (Tiger Blood) SP 75.00 150.00
BACS1C Charlie Sheen (Winning) SP 75.00 150.00
BACT1 Cheryl Tiegs SP
BADB1 Debby Boone 8.00 20.00
BADD2 Donna Douglas 10.00 25.00
BADR1 Della Reese 6.00 15.00
BADR2 Dennis Rodman 20.00 40.00
BADW1 Dawn Wells 10.00 25.00
BAEC1 Emma Caulfield 8.00 20.00
BAECP Elvira 30.00 60.00
BAEM1 Erin Moran 8.00 20.00

Card	Low	High
BAER1 Elisabeth Rohm	8.00	20.00
BAER2 Eric Roberts	6.00	15.00
BAFW1 Fred Williamson	6.00	15.00
BAGG1 Gil Gerard	8.00	20.00
BAGH1 George Hamilton	8.00	20.00
BAGLN Gena Lee Nolin	10.00	25.00
BAHA1 Harry Anderson	8.00	20.00
BAHF1 Harrison Ford SP	400.00	600.00
BAHP1 Hayden Panettiere	40.00	80.00
BAJA1 Jason Alexander SP	30.00	60.00
BAJC1 Jeff Conaway	20.00	40.00
BAJC3 Jose Canseco	20.00	40.00
BAJD1 Joyce Dewitt SP	8.00	20.00
BAJK1 Jennifer Korbin	6.00	15.00
BAJM2 Jason Momoa	10.00	25.00
BAJS1 Jewel Staite	10.00	25.00
BAJS2 John Schneider	8.00	20.00
BAJT1 Jeffrey Tambor SP	6.00	15.00
BAJW1 Jimmy Walker	6.00	15.00
BAKB1 Kate Beckinsale SP	150.00	250.00
BAKD1 Kara DioGuardi	6.00	15.00
BAKK1 Khloe Kardashian	8.00	20.00
BAKK2 Kim Kardashian SP	40.00	80.00
BAKK3 Kourtney Kardashian	15.00	30.00
BAKL1 Kelly LeBrock	15.00	30.00
BAKP1 Kirsten Prout	6.00	15.00
BAKW1 Kendra Wilkinson	15.00	30.00
BALA1 Loni Anderson	20.00	40.00
BALF1 Lita Ford	10.00	25.00
BALH1 Larry Hagman	20.00	40.00
BALH2 Lauren Holly	15.00	30.00
BALL1 Lindsay Lohan SP	150.00	250.00
BAMC1 Mike Connors	8.00	20.00
BAMD1 Mickey Dolenz	10.00	25.00
BAMI1 Michael Imperioli	10.00	25.00
BAMI2 Mark Ingram	20.00	40.00
BAMK1 Margot Kidder	8.00	20.00
BAMR2 Mickey Rourke SP	20.00	40.00
BAMVD Mamie Van Doren	10.00	25.00
BAMW1 Mary Wilson SP	15.00	30.00
BANE1 Nicole Eggert SP	20.00	40.00
BANR1 Nolan Ryan SP	40.00	80.00
BAODA Olivia D'Abo	10.00	25.00
BAPA1 Pamela Anderson SP	75.00	150.00
BAPF1 Peter Fonda SP	20.00	40.00
BAPG1 Pam Grier	15.00	30.00
BAPP1 Pat Priest	8.00	20.00
BAPT1 Peter Tork	15.00	30.00
BARD1 Richard Dreyfuss SP	30.00	60.00
BARK1 Richard Kiel	6.00	15.00
BARM1 Ralph Macchio	10.00	25.00
BARM2 Rose Marie	6.00	15.00
BARON Ryan O'Neal	10.00	25.00
BARR1 Richard Roundtree	6.00	15.00
BASA1 Sean Astin	6.00	15.00
BASA2 Steven Adler	10.00	25.00
BASD1 Sarah Douglas	6.00	15.00
BASE1 Shannon Elizabeth	6.00	15.00
BASF1 Sherilyn Fenn	15.00	30.00
BASL2 Stan Lee	250.00	600.00
BASO2 Susan Olsen	8.00	20.00
BASY1 Sean Young	15.00	30.00
BATC1 Tia Carrere	15.00	30.00
BATL1 Traci Lords	40.00	80.00
BATR1 Tanya Roberts	10.00	25.00
BATW1 Tahnee Welch	6.00	15.00
BAVAF Vivica A. Fox	8.00	20.00
BAVN1 Vince Neil	10.00	25.00
BAWK1 Walter Koenig	10.00	25.00
BAWS1 William Shatner SP	60.00	120.00

2011 Leaf Pop Century Award Winners Autographs

Card	Low	High
COMMON CARD	4.00	10.00
RANDOM INSERT IN PACKS		
AWBS2 Britney Spears SP	120.00	250.00
AWCA2 Christina Applegate SP	25.00	50.00
AWCE1 Carmen Electra	25.00	50.00
AWCN1 Cam Newton	50.00	100.00
AWDB1 Debby Boone	8.00	20.00
AWDD2 Donna Douglas	10.00	25.00
AWDR1 Della Reese	6.00	15.00
AWDR2 Dennis Rodman	20.00	40.00
AWDW1 Dawn Wells	10.00	25.00
AWEM1 Erin Moran	8.00	20.00
AWGH1 George Hamilton	8.00	20.00
AWJA1 Jason Alexander SP	30.00	60.00
AWJRD John Rhys-Davies	10.00	25.00
AWJS2 John Schneider SP	8.00	20.00
AWKK1 Khloe Kardashian	8.00	20.00
AWKK2 Kim Kardashian SP	40.00	80.00
AWKK3 Kourtney Kardashian	15.00	30.00
AWLL1 Lindsay Lohan SP	150.00	250.00
AWMB1 Michael Biehn	20.00	40.00
AWMC1 Mike Connors	8.00	20.00
AWMI1 Michael Imperioli	10.00	25.00
AWMI2 Mark Ingram	20.00	40.00
AWMK1 Margot Kidder	8.00	20.00
AWMR2 Mickey Rourke SP	20.00	40.00
AWMSJ Mia St. John	6.00	15.00
AWNR1 Nolan Ryan SP	40.00	80.00
AWRR1 Richard Roundtree	6.00	15.00
AWSL2 Stan Lee SP	300.00	800.00
AWSO2 Susan Olsen	8.00	20.00
AWTL1 Traci Lords	40.00	80.00
AWVAF Vivica A. Fox	8.00	20.00
AWVN1 Vince Neil SP	10.00	25.00

2011 Leaf Pop Century Bettie Page Cut Signatures

Card	Low	High
COMMON CARD (BP1-BP4)	250.00	350.00
STATED PRINT RUN 10 SER. #'d SETS		

2011 Leaf Pop Century Dressing Room Autograph Memorabilia

Card	Low	High
COMMON CARD	20.00	40.00
STATED PRINT RUN 3-73 SER.#'d SETS		
DRBS2 Britney Spears		
DRKK2 Kim Kardashian/24	100.00	200.00
DRKK3 Kourtney Kardashian/51	25.00	50.00
DRNE1 Nicole Eggert/25	25.00	50.00
DRPA1 Pamela Anderson/19	100.00	200.00
DRRD1 Richard Dreyfuss/3		
DRWS1 William Shatner/29	75.00	150.00

2011 Leaf Pop Century Keeping It Real Autographs

Card	Low	High
COMMON CARD	4.00	10.00
RANDOM INSERT IN PACKS		
KRAP2 Audrina Patridge	8.00	20.00
KRBL1 Bai Ling	10.00	25.00
KRJC1 Jeff Conaway	20.00	40.00
KRJC3 Jose Canseco	20.00	40.00
KRKD1 Kara DioGuardi	6.00	15.00
KRKK2 Kim Kardashian SP	40.00	80.00
KRKK3 Kourtney Kardashian	15.00	30.00
KRKW1 Kendra Wilkinson	15.00	30.00
KRPA1 Pamela Anderson SP	75.00	150.00
KRSO1 Steve-O	10.00	25.00
KRSP1 Stephanie Pratt	6.00	15.00
KRSY1 Sean Young	15.00	30.00
KRTC1 Tia Carrere	15.00	30.00
KRVN1 Vince Neil SP	10.00	25.00

2011 Leaf Pop Century Sci-Fi Autographs

Card	Low	High
COMMON CARD	4.00	10.00
RANDOM INSERT IN PACKS		
SFAB1 Amber Benson	6.00	15.00
SFBB1 Beau Bridges	6.00	15.00
SFBC1 Bruce Campbell	15.00	30.00
SFBM1 Bill Mumy	8.00	20.00
SFCC1 Charisma Carpenter	15.00	30.00
SFCJ1 Christopher Judge SP		
SFEC1 Emma Caulfield	8.00	20.00
SFEF1 Edward Furlong	8.00	20.00
SFEG1 Erin Gray	15.00	30.00
SFER2 Eric Roberts	6.00	15.00
SFGG1 Gil Gerard	8.00	20.00
SFHP1 Hayden Panettiere	40.00	80.00
SFJM2 Jason Momoa	10.00	25.00
SFJS1 Jewel Staite	10.00	25.00
SFKL2 Kristanna Loken	20.00	40.00
SFLH3 Linda Hamilton SP	25.00	50.00
SFLT2 Lea Thompson	10.00	25.00
SFLW1 Lindsay Wagner	15.00	30.00
SFMB1 Michael Biehn	20.00	40.00
SFNN1 Nichelle Nichols	20.00	40.00
SFPM1 Peter Mayhew	6.00	15.00
SFRD1 Richard Dreyfuss SP	30.00	60.00
SFVAF Vivica A. Fox	8.00	20.00
SFWK1 Walter Koenig	10.00	25.00
SFWS1 William Shatner SP	60.00	120.00

2011 Leaf Pop Century Smash Hit Autographs

Card	Low	High
COMMON CARD	8.00	20.00
PRINT RUN 3-78		
SHBS2 Britney Spears/3		
SHDJ1 Davy Jones/28	40.00	80.00
SHIT1 Ice-T/20		
SHLF1 Lita Ford/60	10.00	25.00
SHMD1 Mickey Dolenz/56	20.00	40.00
SHMW1 Mary Wilson/26	15.00	30.00
SHPT1 Peter Tork/56	20.00	40.00
SHSA2 Steven Adler/40	10.00	25.00
SHTIF Tiffany/48	10.00	25.00
SHVN1 Vince Neil/19		
SHWJ1 Wynonna Judd/78	15.00	30.00

2011 Leaf Pop Century Stunning Starlets Autographs

Card	Low	High
COMMON CARD	6.00	15.00
RANDOM INSERT IN PACKS		
SSAJ1 Ashley Judd	50.00	100.00
SSAP2 Audrina Patridge	8.00	20.00
SSBD1 Bo Derek	30.00	60.00
SSBL1 Bai Ling	10.00	25.00
SSBS2 Britney Spears SP	150.00	250.00
SSCA2 Christina Applegate SP	25.00	50.00
SSCC1 Charisma Carpenter	15.00	30.00
SSCE1 Carmen Electra	25.00	50.00
SSCT1 Cheryl Tiegs SP		
SSDD1 Donna D'Errico SP	8.00	20.00
SSGLN Gena Lee Nolin	10.00	25.00
SSHP1 Hayden Panettiere	40.00	80.00
SSJG1 Jennie Garth SP		
SSKB1 Kate Beckinsale SP	150.00	250.00
SSKK1 Khloe Kardashian	8.00	20.00
SSKK2 Kim Kardashian SP	40.00	80.00
SSKK3 Kourtney Kardashian	15.00	30.00
SSKL1 Kelly LeBrock	15.00	30.00
SSKL2 Kristanna Loken	20.00	40.00
SSKW1 Kendra Wilkinson	15.00	30.00
SSLA1 Loni Anderson	20.00	40.00
SSLL1 Lindsay Lohan SP	150.00	250.00
SSMVD Mamie Van Doren	10.00	25.00
SSNE1 Nicole Eggert	20.00	40.00
SSPA1 Pamela Anderson SP	75.00	150.00
SSSE1 Shannon Elizabeth		
SSSF1 Sherilyn Fenn	15.00	30.00
SSTC1 Tia Carrere	15.00	30.00
SSTR1 Tanya Roberts	10.00	25.00
SSVAF Vivica A. Fox	8.00	20.00

2011 Leaf Pop Century Walk of Fame Autographs

Card	Low	High
COMMON CARD	8.00	20.00
RANDOM INSERT IN PACKS		
WFBE1 Barbara Eden SP	25.00	50.00
WFBS2 Britney Spears SP	250.00	400.00
WFDJ1 Davy Jones	40.00	80.00
WFHW1 Henry Winkler	20.00	40.00
WFLH1 Larry Hagman SP	20.00	40.00
WFLW1 Lindsay Wagner	15.00	30.00
WFMD1 Mickey Dolenz	10.00	25.00
WFMR1 Mickey Rooney	20.00	40.00
WFMVD Mamie Van Doren	10.00	25.00
WFMW1 Mary Wilson	15.00	30.00
WFNN1 Nichelle Nichols	20.00	40.00
WFPF1 Peter Fonda	20.00	40.00
WFPT1 Peter Tork	15.00	30.00
WFRC1 Richard Chamberlain	15.00	30.00
WFRD1 Richard Dreyfuss SP	30.00	60.00
WFRH1 Ron Howard	30.00	60.00
WFSL2 Stan Lee SP	200.00	500.00
WFVN1 Vince Neil SP	10.00	25.00
WFWS1 William Shatner SP	60.00	120.00

2012 Leaf Pop Century

Card	Low	High
COMMON CARD	5.00	12.00
*SILVER/25: .5X TO 1.2X BASIC CARD		
BAAB2 Amanda Beard	12.00	30.00
BAAC1 Arianny Celeste	20.00	40.00
BAAD1 Angie Dickinson	12.00	30.00
BAAE1 Angie Everhart	8.00	20.00
BAAF1 Amy Fisher	10.00	25.00
BAAQ1 Aileen Quinn	8.00	20.00
BAAR1 Austin Chumlee Russell	20.00	40.00
BAAW1 Adam West	25.00	50.00
BABDW Billy Dee Williams	25.00	50.00
BABE1 Barbara Eden	25.00	50.00
BABH1 Brooke Hogan	20.00	40.00
BABJ1 Bruce Jenner	8.00	20.00
BABP1 Bristol Palin	12.00	30.00
BABR1 Brande Roderick	8.00	20.00
BABR2 Burt Reynolds	25.00	50.00
BABS1 Britney Spears	200.00	300.00
BABW1 Burt Ward	20.00	40.00
BABZ1 Billy Zane	8.00	20.00
BACA1 Christina Applegate	30.00	60.00
BACE1 Carmen Electra	15.00	40.00
BACH1 Big Hoss Harrison	12.00	30.00
BACL1 Carla Laemmle	10.00	25.00
BACM1 Cindy Margolis	10.00	25.00
BACP1 Cassandra Peterson	30.00	60.00
BACS1 Charlie Sheen	40.00	80.00
BACS2 Claire Sinclair	8.00	20.00
BACT1 Cheryl Tiegs	30.00	60.00
BADL1 David Lander	10.00	25.00
BADMX DMX	12.00	30.00
BADR1 Dennis Rodman	20.00	40.00
BADS1 Dominique Swain	8.00	20.00
BADT1 Donald J. Trump	1200.00	1750.00
BADTJ Donald Trump Jr.	25.00	60.00
BAEB1 Ernest Borgnine	20.00	40.00
BAEE1 Erik Estrada	8.00	20.00
BAEL1 Emmanuel Lewis	8.00	20.00
BAEM1 Erin Moran	8.00	20.00
BAEP1 Emily Procter	8.00	20.00
BAFW1 Fred Williamson	8.00	20.00
BAGC1 Gina Carano	20.00	40.00
BAGG2 Gina Gershon	25.00	50.00
BAGLN Gena Lee Nolin	10.00	25.00
BAHA1 Harry Anderson	8.00	20.00
BAHF1 Harrison Ford		
BAHF2 Heidi Fleiss	12.00	30.00
BAHH1 Henry Hill	12.00	30.00
BAHP1 Hayden Panettiere	60.00	120.00
BAI1 Ichiro		
BAIS1 Ian Somerhalder	10.00	25.00
BAJA1 Jason Alexander	25.00	50.00
BAJA2 Julie Adams	12.00	30.00
BAJC1 Joanna Cassidy	8.00	20.00
BAJH1 Jessica Hall	8.00	20.00
BAJJ1 Jenna Jameson	20.00	40.00
BAJLO Jennifer Lopez	100.00	200.00
BAJN1 Jay North	12.00	30.00
BAJP1 Jason Priestley	10.00	25.00
BAJP2 Jeremy Piven	8.00	20.00
BAJS1 Jordin Sparks	10.00	25.00
BAKB1 Kate Beckinsale	175.00	300.00
BAKC1 Ken Climo	10.00	25.00
BAKC2 Kristin Cavallari	10.00	25.00
BAKS1 Kristy Swanson	12.00	30.00
BALAW Lesley Ann Warren	10.00	25.00
BALF1 Lou Ferrigno	20.00	40.00
BALH1 Larry Hagman	25.00	50.00
BALL1 Lindsay Lohan	100.00	200.00
BAMCD Michael C. Cuncan	25.00	50.00
BAMF1 Morgan Fairchild	20.00	40.00
BAML1 Martin Landau	20.00	40.00
BAMR1 Mickey Rourke	12.00	30.00
BANH1 Natasha Henstridge	20.00	40.00
BAPJS P.J. Soles	8.00	20.00
BAPL1 Piper Laurie	8.00	20.00
BAPP1 Pat Priest	10.00	25.00
BAPP2 Priscilla Presley	30.00	60.00
BAPS1 Patrick Stewart	30.00	60.00
BAPW1 Patrick Warburton	12.00	30.00

MODERN

BARD1 Richard Dreyfuss 30.00 60.00
BARG1 Rupert Grint 30.00 60.00
BARH1 Old Man Harrison 12.00 30.00
BARH2 Rick Harrison 20.00 40.00
BARK1 Rodney King 30.00 60.00
BASE1 Shannon Elizabeth 25.00 50.00
BASP1 Sarah Palin 50.00 100.00
BASU1 Sara Underwood 25.00 50.00
BATB1 Toni Basil 10.00 25.00
BATF1 Tom Felton 30.00 60.00
BATG2 Tracey Gold 8.00 20.00
BATL1 Tommy Lee 20.00 40.00
BATL2 Traci Lords 20.00 50.00
BATP1 The Professor
BATW1 Torrie Wilson 12.00 30.00
BAVN1 Vince Neil 10.00 25.00
BAVT1 Verne Troyer 8.00 20.00
BAVW1 Van Williams 12.00 30.00

2012 Leaf Pop Century Award Winners Autographs

COMMON CARD 6.00 15.00
AWAB2 Amanda Beard 20.00 40.00
AWAD1 Angie Dickinson 20.00 40.00
AWAQ1 Aileen Quinn 8.00 20.00
AWBR1 Brande Roderick 8.00 20.00
AWBR2 Burt Reynolds 20.00 50.00
AWCS1 Charlie Sheen 50.00 100.00
AWCS2 Claire Sinclair 8.00 20.00
AWEB1 Ernest Borgnine 20.00 40.00
AWIS1 Ian Somerhalder 10.00 25.00
AWJJ1 Jenna Jameson 25.00 50.00
AWJLO Jennifer Lopez 150.00 250.00
AWJS1 Jordin Sparks 8.00 20.00
AWKC1 Ken Climo 10.00 25.00
AWLAW Lesley Ann Warren 8.00 20.00
AWLF1 Lou Ferrigno 12.00 30.00
AWMCD Michael Clarke Duncan 20.00 40.00
AWML1 Martin Landau 12.00 30.00
AWNH1 Natasha Henstridge 20.00 40.00
AWPL1 Piper Laurie 8.00 20.00
AWRG1 Rupert Grint 30.00 60.00
AWTF1 Tom Felton 30.00 60.00
AWTL1 Tommy Lee 20.00 40.00
AWYB1 Yancy Butler 8.00 20.00

2012 Leaf Pop Century Co-Stars Autographs

COMMON CARD 8.00 20.00
AP2LB1 A.Patridge/L.Bosworth 10.00 25.00
AR1CH1 C.Russell/C.Harrison 25.00 50.00
AS1CA1 A.Sabato/C.Applegate 20.00 40.00
AW1BW1 A.West/B.Ward 60.00 120.00
BD1EB1 B.Dern/E.Borgnine 20.00 40.00
BD1MR1 B.Dern/M.Rourke 12.00 30.00
BZ1NK1 B.Zane/N.Kinski 12.00 30.00
CE1CS1 C.Electra/C.Sheen 50.00 100.00
EL1VT1 E.Lewis/V.Troyer 15.00 40.00
JA1GG1 J.Alexander/G.Gottfried 15.00 40.00
JC1PJS J.Cassidy/PJ Soles 10.00 25.00
JN1EL1 J.North/E.Lewis 10.00 25.00
JN1JP3 J.North/J.Provost 15.00 40.00
JP1IZ1 J.Priestley/I.Ziering 12.00 30.00
JS2NK1 J.Sands/N.Kinski 20.00 40.00
PA1CE1 P.Anderson/C.Electra 200.00 400.00
RH1RH2 R.Harrison/R.Harrison 30.00 60.00
SK1FW1 Kellerman/Williamson 10.00 25.00
SK1VW1 Kellerman/Williams 15.00 40.00
SP1BP1 S.Palin/B.Palin 150.00 300.00
VN1TL1 V.Neil/T.Lee 40.00 80.00
PSC Pawn Stars cast 100.00 200.00
SofM Sound of Music cast 300.00 450.00

2012 Leaf Pop Century Dressing Room Autograph Memorabilia

COMMON CARD 25.00 50.00
RANDOM INSERT IN PACKS
DRBS1 Britney Spears
DRCS1 Charlie Sheen 75.00 150.00
DRPA1 Pamela Anderson

2012 Leaf Pop Century Inscriptions Autographs Priscilla Presley

IPP2a Priscilla Presley 75.00 150.00
IPP2b Priscilla Presley (silver)/25 100.00 175.00
IPP2c Priscilla Presley (blue)/5
IPP2d Priscilla Presley (gold)/1

2012 Leaf Pop Century Keeping It Real Autographs

COMMON CARD 5.00 12.00
KRAE1 Angie Everhart 10.00 25.00
KRAF1 Amy Fisher 10.00 25.00
KRAR1 Austin Chumlee Russell 20.00 40.00
KRBE1 Barbara Eden 25.00 50.00
KRBH1 Brooke Hogan 20.00 40.00
KRBP1 Bristol Palin 20.00 40.00
KRBR1 Brande Roderick 8.00 20.00
KRCE1 Carmen Electra 20.00 40.00
KRCH1 Big Hoss Harrison 12.00 30.00
KRCM1 Cindy Margolis 8.00 20.00
KRCP1 Cassandra Peterson 30.00 60.00
KRDMX DMX 10.00 25.00
KRDTJ Donald Trump Jr. 25.00 60.00
KREE1 Erik Estrada 8.00 20.00
KREL1 Emmanuel Lewis 8.00 20.00
KREM1 Erin Moran
KRGR1 Gretchen Rossi 6.00 15.00
KRHF2 Heidi Fleiss 10.00 25.00
KRJH1 Jessica Hall 6.00 15.00
KRJLO Jennifer Lopez
KRJS1 Jordin Sparks 10.00 25.00
KRKC2 Kristin Cavallari 10.00 25.00
KRKS1 Kristy Swanson 10.00 25.00
KRLF1 Lou Ferrigno 12.00 30.00
KRMF1 Morgan Fairchild 12.00 30.00
KRRH1 Old Man Harrison 12.00 30.00
KRRH2 Rick Harrison 15.00 40.00
KRRK1 Rodney King 25.00 50.00
KRSE1 Shannon Elizabeth 25.00 50.00
KRTG1 Teresa Giudice 6.00 15.00
KRTG2 Tracey Gold 8.00 20.00
KRTW1 Torrie Wilson 12.00 30.00

2012 Leaf Pop Century Stunning Starlets Autographs

COMMON CARD 8.00 20.00
RANDOM INSERT IN PACKS
SSAB2 Amanda Beard 15.00 40.00
SSAC1 Arianny Celeste 20.00 40.00
SSAD1 Angie Dickinson 20.00 40.00
SSAE1 Angie Everhart 12.00 30.00
SSBH1 Brooke Hogan 25.00 50.00
SSBR1 Brande Roderick 10.00 25.00
SSCM1 Cindy Margolis 10.00 25.00
SSCS2 Claire Sinclair 10.00 25.00
SSDS1 Dominique Swain 12.00 30.00
SSEP1 Emily Procter 10.00 25.00
SSGG2 Gina Gershon 25.00 50.00
SSJJ1 Jenna Jameson 30.00 60.00
SSJLO Jennifer Lopez 175.00 300.00
SSKS1 Kristy Swanson 12.00 30.00
SSMF1 Morgan Fairchild 15.00 40.00
SSNH1 Natasha Henstridge 20.00 40.00
SSNK1 Nastassja Kinski 30.00 60.00
SSPL1 Piper Laurie 10.00 25.00
SSPP2 Priscilla Presley 40.00 80.00
SSSE1 Shannon Elizabeth 25.00 50.00
SSSU1 Sara Underwood 25.00 50.00
SSTL2 Traci Lords 30.00 60.00
SSTW1 Torrie Wilson 12.00 30.00

2013 Leaf Pop Century

COMMON CARD 3.00 8.00
*SILVER/25: .5X TO 1.2X BASIC CARDS
BAAD1 Andy Dick 3.00 8.00
BAAD2 Angie Dickinson 12.00 30.00
BAAGB Ashley Gold Broad 6.00 15.00
BAAL1 Ali Landry 10.00 25.00
BAAM1 Ali MacGraw 10.00 25.00
BAAP1 Al Pacino
BAAP3 Artimus Pyle 8.00 20.00
BAAS1 Ashley Scott 6.00 15.00
BABB1 Brooke Burns 8.00 20.00
BABB2 Barry Bostwick 6.00 15.00
BABG1 Bob Gibson 12.00 30.00
BABH1 Bo Hopkins 3.00 8.00
BABI1 Billy Idol 20.00 50.00
BABJ1 Bruce Jenner 5.00 12.00
BABM1 Bam Margera 6.00 15.00
BABT1 Becca Tobin 5.00 12.00
BABY1 Burt Young 8.00 20.00
BAC1 Coolio 30.00 75.00
BACB1 Candace Bailey 6.00 15.00
BACF1 Carrie Fisher 50.00 100.00
BACL1 Carl Lewis 10.00 25.00
BACL2 Carla Laemmle 10.00 25.00
BACP1 Carly Patterson 8.00 20.00
BACP2 Chris Pontius 6.00 15.00
BACRJ Cal Ripken Jr. 40.00 80.00
BACS1 Connie Stevens 6.00 15.00
BACW1 Cindy Williams 8.00 20.00
BADB1 Drake Bell 4.00 10.00
BADC1 Dean Cain 3.00 8.00
BADD1 Donna Douglas 12.00 30.00
BADG1 Debbie Gibson 15.00 40.00
BADH1 Dave Hester 5.00 12.00
BADR1 Debbie Reynolds 12.00 30.00
BADR2 Dennis Rodman 8.00 20.00
BADS1 Dee Snider 6.00 15.00
BADS2 Dwight Schultz 10.00 25.00
BAEA1 Ed Asner 6.00 15.00
BAEA2 Erin Andrews 30.00 60.00
BAEE1 Erika Eleniak 12.00 30.00
BAEM1 Erin Murphy 6.00 15.00
BAGC1 Gabrielle Carteris 4.00 10.00
BAGL1 George Lazenby 15.00 40.00
BAGM1 Garry Marshall 8.00 20.00
BAHH1 Hulk Hogan 35.00 70.00
BAHMC Holly Marie Combs 20.00 50.00
BAHR1 Helen Reddy 6.00 15.00
BAHS1 Hope Solo 20.00 50.00
BAJC1 Joan Collins 12.00 30.00
BAJE1 Jason Earles 3.00 8.00
BAJG1 James Gandolfini 60.00 120.00
BAJL1 Jennifer Lopez 60.00 120.00
BAJL2 Jerry Lewis 30.00 60.00
BAJL3 Jerry Lawler 10.00 25.00
BAJL4 Judy Landers 8.00 20.00
BAJM1 Jenny McCarthy 30.00 60.00
BAJM2 Jeremy Miller 3.00 8.00
BAKB1 Kate Beckinsale 150.00 250.00
BAKS1 Katey Sagal 20.00 50.00
BAKS2 Kevin Sorbo 6.00 15.00
BAKV1 Kate Vernon 4.00 10.00
BALA1 Loni Anderson 10.00 25.00
BALB1 Linda Blair 10.00 25.00
BALG1 Les Gold
BALL1 Lindsay Lohan 75.00 150.00
BALLJ Lolo Jones 15.00 40.00
BALP1 Lori Petty 8.00 20.00
BAMB1 Max Baer Jr. 10.00 25.00
BAMBJ Mark Boone Jr. 8.00 20.00
BAMDL Vini Mad Dog Lopez 8.00 20.00
BAMF1 Morgan Fairchild 6.00 15.00
BAML1 Mario Lopez 4.00 10.00
BAMS1 Mark Spitz 6.00 15.00
BANC1 Naked Cowboy 3.00 8.00
BANK1 Nancy Kerrigan 8.00 20.00
BANK2 Nastassja Kinski 12.00 30.00
BAPD1 Patty Duke 8.00 20.00
BAPG1 Pam Grier 6.00 15.00
BAPR1 Pete Rose 8.00 20.00
BAPT1 Peter Tork 10.00 25.00
BAPW1 Patrick Warburton 8.00 20.00
BARF1 Ric Flair 15.00 40.00
BARH1 Richard Hatch 8.00 20.00
BARL1 Robert Loggia 10.00 25.00
BASF1 Samantha Fox 10.00 25.00
BASG1 Seth Gold
BASK1 Stacy Keach 8.00 20.00
BASM1 Shannon Miller 8.00 20.00
BASM2 Sofia Milos 6.00 15.00
BASP1 Sarah Palin 40.00 80.00
BASS1 Serinda Swan 8.00 20.00
BAST1 Sam Trammell 6.00 15.00
BATH1 Tippi Hedren 20.00 50.00
BATH2 Tonya Harding 12.00 30.00
BATN1 Ted Nugent 15.00 40.00
BATO1 Tony Orlando 10.00 25.00
BATW1 Tom Wopat 10.00 25.00
BAVG1 Vida Guerra 12.00 30.00
BAVM1 Virginia Madsen 12.00 30.00
BAVP1 Vincent Pastore 5.00 12.00
BAWM1 Wink Martindale 5.00 12.00
BAYAT Y.A. Tittle 8.00 20.00

2013 Leaf Pop Century And the Nomination Is Autographs

COMMON CARD 6.00 15.00
*SILVER/25: .5X TO 1.2X BASIC CARDS
ANAM1 Ali MacGraw 10.00 25.00
ANAP1 Al Pacino 150.00 250.00
ANBI1 Billy Idol 15.00 40.00
ANDR1 Debbie Reynolds 12.00 30.00
ANJC1 Joan Collins 12.00 30.00
ANJG1 James Gandolfini 60.00 120.00
ANJL1 Jennifer Lopez 60.00 120.00
ANKS1 Katey Sagal 15.00 40.00
ANLB1 Linda Blair 10.00 25.00
ANSK1 Stacy Keach 8.00 20.00
ANSP1 Sarah Palin 40.00 80.00

2013 Leaf Pop Century Co-Stars Autographs

COMMON CARD 6.00 15.00
*SILVER/25: .5X TO 1.2X BASIC CARDS
CS01 A.Broad/L.Gold
CS02 A.Broad/S.Gold
CS03 S.Gold/L.Gold 12.00 30.00
CS04 B.Douglas/M.Tyson
CS06 C.Stevens/E.Asner 10.00 25.00
CS07 C.Williams/P.Marshall 20.00 50.00
CS09 D.Lander/P.Marshall 12.00 30.00
CS10 D.Bell/J.Lewis 15.00 40.00
CS13 D.Douglas/M.Baer Jr. 15.00 40.00
CS15 D.Snider/D.Rodman 12.00 30.00
CS16 P.Marshall/G.Marshall 15.00 40.00
CS17 H.Combs/A.Dickinson 15.00 40.00
CS18 K.Sagal/M.Junior 12.00 30.00
CS19 M.Oher/Q.Aaron 12.00 30.00
CS20 T.Dow/K.Osmond 15.00 40.00
CS21 C.Bach/T.Wopat 15.00 40.00
CS22 J.Gandolfini/V.Pastore 60.00 120.00
CS23 D.Moceanu/S.Miller 15.00 40.00
CS25 R.Flair/Animal 15.00 40.00
CS26 N.Kerrigan/T.Harding 15.00 40.00
CS27 D.Harris/G.Wilbur 12.00 30.00
CS007 007 Girls 50.00 100.00
CSHPC L.Gold/S.Gold/A.Broad 15.00 40.00
CSWKRP Ander/Hess/Reid/60 20.00 50.00

2013 Leaf Pop Century Dressing Room Autograph Memorabilia

COMMON CARD 75.00 150.00
RANDOMLY INSERTED INTO PACKS
DRJL1 Jennifer Lopez 100.00 175.00

2013 Leaf Pop Century Keeping It Real Autographs

COMMON CARD 3.00 8.00
*SILVER/25: .5X TO 1.2X BASIC CARDS
KRBM1 Bam Margera 6.00 15.00
KRC1 Coolio 25.00 60.00
KRDR2 Dennis Rodman 6.00 15.00
KRGC1 Gabrielle Carteris 4.00 10.00
KRML1 Mario Lopez 4.00 10.00
KRPR1 Pete Rose 8.00 20.00
KRTN1 Ted Nugent 15.00 40.00
KRVP1 Vincent Pastore 4.00 10.00

2013 Leaf Pop Century Perfectly Cast Autographs

COMMON CARD 6.00 15.00
*SILVER/25: .5X TO 1.2X BASIC CARDS
PCAP1 Al Pacino 150.00 250.00
PCAP2 Al Pacino 150.00 250.00
PCBE1 Barbara Eden 20.00 50.00

Card	Low	High
PCDC1 Dean Cain	8.00	20.00
PCGL1 George Lazenby	12.00	30.00
PCJL1 Jennifer Lopez	60.00	120.00
PCJL2 Jerry Lewis	35.00	70.00
PCLH1 Larry Hagman	20.00	50.00
PCPM1 Penny Marshall	12.00	30.00

2013 Leaf Pop Century Stunning Starlets Autographs

Card	Low	High
COMMON CARD	8.00	20.00
*SILVER/25: .5X TO 1.2X BASIC CARDS		
SSAL1 Ali Landry	12.00	30.00
SSBE1 Barbara Eden	15.00	40.00
SSJM1 Jenny McCarthy	15.00	40.00
SSLB1 Linda Blair	12.00	30.00

2014 Leaf Pop Century

Card	Low	High
UNOPENED BOX (4 CARDS)		
COMMON AUTO	4.00	10.00
BAT$ Too $hort	6.00	15.00
BAAB1 Adam Baldwin	8.00	20.00
BAAC1 Adrianne Curry	15.00	40.00
BAAD1 Ami Dolenz	6.00	15.00
BAAL1 Ali Landry	12.00	30.00
BAAM1 Andrew McCarthy	10.00	25.00
BAAP1 Al Pacino	100.00	250.00
BAAP2 Artimus Pyle	15.00	40.00
BAAY1 Al Yankovic	20.00	50.00
BABB1 Brooke Burns	10.00	25.00
BABR1 Brande Roderick	12.00	30.00
BABR2 Burt Reynolds	30.00	80.00
BABS1 Bruno Sammartino	20.00	50.00
BABT1 Bella Thorne	20.00	50.00
BACA1 Christina Applegate	30.00	80.00
BACF1 Carrie Fisher	120.00	200.00
BACH1 Chelsie Hightower	12.00	30.00
BACL1 Carla Laemmle	6.00	15.00
BACRJ Cal Ripken Jr.	30.00	80.00
BACTH C. Thomas Howell	5.00	12.00
BADD1 Donna D'Errico	10.00	25.00
BADDM Drea de Matteo	12.00	30.00
BADF1 Diane Franklin	8.00	20.00
BADG1 Danny Glover	20.00	50.00
BADG2 Debbie Gibson	12.00	30.00
BADH2 David Hasselhoff	20.00	50.00
BADH3 Daryl Hannah	15.00	40.00
BADR1 Debbie Reynolds	8.00	20.00
BADR2 Dennis Rodman	8.00	20.00
BADVD Dick Van Dyke	30.00	80.00
BAEA1 Erin Andrews	15.00	40.00
BAEE1 Erika Eleniak	10.00	25.00
BAEON Ed O'Neill	30.00	80.00
BAGLN Gena Lee Nolin	5.00	12.00
BAGM1 Gavin MacLeod	5.00	12.00
BAGS1 George Steele	8.00	20.00
BAHMC Holly Marie Combs	10.00	25.00
BAJB1 John Barrowman	12.00	30.00
BAJC1 Jose Canseco	20.00	50.00
BAJF1 Jennie Finch	10.00	25.00
BAJG1 James Gandolfini	50.00	120.00
BAJJ1 Jenna Jameson	20.00	50.00
BAJL1 Jerry Lewis	40.00	100.00
BAJL2 Jennifer Lopez	10.00	25.00
BAJLA Joey Lauren Adams	6.00	15.00
BAJLS Jamie Lynn Sigler	8.00	20.00
BAJM1 Johnny Manziel	40.00	100.00
BAJM2 Jenny McCarthy	30.00	80.00
BAJR1 John Ratzenberger	10.00	25.00
BAKC1 Kim Coates	6.00	15.00
BAKMN Kristy McNichol	10.00	25.00
BAKR1 Kristen Renton	10.00	25.00
BAKS1 Kevin Sorbo	8.00	20.00
BAKS2 Katey Sagal	50.00	120.00
BALA1 Loni Anderson	15.00	40.00
BALB1 Linda Blair	15.00	40.00
BALF1 Lita Ford	10.00	25.00
BALLJ Lolo Jones	8.00	20.00
BALM1 Lea Michele	25.00	60.00
BAMH1 Mariel Hemingway	12.00	30.00
BAMJ1 Magic Johnson	25.00	60.00
BAML1 Martin Landau	20.00	50.00
BAML2 Mario Lopez	5.00	12.00
BAMP1 Mackenzie Phillips	8.00	20.00
BAMR1 Melissa Rycroft	5.00	12.00
BAMR2 Molly Ringwald	20.00	50.00
BAMS1 Mark Spitz	8.00	20.00
BANE1 Nicole Eggert	15.00	40.00
BANN1 Nichelle Nichols	15.00	40.00
BANR1 Norman Reedus	25.00	60.00
BAODA Olivia d'Abo	5.00	12.00
BAPB1 Pat Boone	8.00	20.00
BAPD1 Patty Duke	12.00	30.00
BAPP1 Priscilla Presley	25.00	60.00
BAPR1 Pete Rose	15.00	40.00
BAPT1 Peter Tork	8.00	20.00
BARC1 Richard Chamberlain	10.00	25.00
BARF1 Ric Flair	25.00	60.00
BARH1 Robert Hays	10.00	25.00
BARL1 Robert Loggia	6.00	15.00
BARM1 Rose Marie	12.00	30.00
BARM2 Roger Moore	30.00	80.00
BASA1 Sean Astin	12.00	30.00
BASD1 Skylar Diggins	15.00	40.00
BASP1 Sarah Palin	50.00	120.00
BASRL Sugar Ray Leonard	30.00	80.00
BASS1 Serinda Swan	10.00	25.00
BATC1 Tim Curry	25.00	60.00
BATM1 Taryn Manning	6.00	12.00
BATN1 Ted Nugent	25.00	60.00
BATO1 Tony Orlando	10.00	25.00
BATR1 Tara Reid	30.00	80.00
BAVT1 Verne Troyer	6.00	15.00

2014 Leaf Pop Century Award Winners Autographs

Card	Low	High
COMMON AUTO	12.00	30.00
AWAP1 Al Pacino	100.00	200.00
AWAY1 Al Yankovic	30.00	80.00
AWBI1 Billy Idol	20.00	50.00
AWCRJ Cal Ripken Jr.	30.00	80.00
AWJF1 Jennie Finch	15.00	40.00
AWMJ1 Magic Johnson	25.00	60.00
AWML1 Martin Landau	20.00	50.00
AWPR1 Pete Rose	15.00	40.00
AWSRL Sugar Ray Leonard	30.00	80.00

2014 Leaf Pop Century Co-Stars Autographs

Card	Low	High
COMPLETE SET (10)		
COMMON AUTO	8.00	20.00
CS2 Ed Asner Gavin MacLeod	15.00	40.00
CS5 Lea Michele Kevin McHale	12.00	30.00
CS6 Donna D'Errico Erika Eleniak		
CS7 George Steele Bruno Sammartino	15.00	40.00
CS8 Tony Dow Ken Osmond	15.00	40.00
CS9 Cal Ripken Jr. Pete Rose	30.00	80.00
CSSOA Sons of Anarchy Cast	50.00	120.00

2014 Leaf Pop Century Inscriptions

Card	Low	High
COMPLETE SET (3)		
COMMON CARD	12.00	30.00
STATED PRINT RUN 60 SER.#'d SETS		
ILA1 Loni Anderson	15.00	40.00

2014 Leaf Pop Century Keeping It Real Autographs

Card	Low	High
COMMON CARD	4.00	10.00
KRJC1 Jose Canseco	12.00	30.00
KRMR1 Melissa Rycroft	6.00	15.00
KRVT1 Verne Troyer	6.00	15.00

2014 Leaf Pop Century Live Autographs

Card	Low	High
COMMON CARD	15.00	40.00
LAP1 Pele	150.00	300.00
LAAP1 Al Pacino SP	100.00	200.00
LALM1 Lea Michele	30.00	80.00
LAMT1 Mike Tyson	80.00	200.00
LANR1 Norman Reedus	40.00	100.00
LASL1 Stan Lee	150.00	400.00

2014 Leaf Pop Century Perfectly Cast Autographs

Card	Low	High
COMPLETE SET (17)		
COMMON CARD	5.00	12.00
PCBR Burt Reynolds	60.00	120.00
PCAB1 Adam Baldwin	8.00	20.00
PCCF1 Carrie Fisher	120.00	200.00
PCDH2 David Hasselhoff	20.00	50.00
PCDVD Dick Van Dyke	50.00	120.00
PCGM1 Gavin MacLeod	8.00	20.00
PCJB1 John Barrowman	6.00	15.00
PCJLS Jamie Lynn Sigler	8.00	20.00
PCJR1 John Ratzenberger	10.00	25.00
PCNN1 Nichelle Nichols	15.00	40.00
PCNR1 Norman Reedus	30.00	80.00
PCRH1 Robert Hays	8.00	20.00
PCRM2 Roger Moore	40.00	100.00
PCTC1 Tim Curry	30.00	80.00
PCVT1 Verne Troyer	8.00	20.00

2014 Leaf Pop Century Stunning Starlets Autographs

Card	Low	High
COMMON CARD	8.00	20.00
SSAD1 Ami Dolenz	10.00	25.00
SSBT1 Bella Thorne	20.00	50.00
SSDDM Drea de Matteo	12.00	30.00
SSDH3 Daryl Hannah	15.00	40.00
SSJLS Jamie Lynn Sigler	10.00	25.00
SSMH1 Mariel Hemingway	12.00	30.00

2014 Leaf Pop Century Walk of Fame Autographs

Card	Low	High
COMMON CARD	8.00	20.00
WFDVD Dick Van Dyke	30.00	80.00
WFGM2 Garry Marshall	10.00	25.00
WFJC2 Joan Collins	30.00	80.00
WFJL1 Jerry Lewis	40.00	100.00
WFML1 Martin Landau	12.00	30.00
WFNN1 Nichelle Nichols	10.00	25.00
WFPB1 Pat Boone	10.00	25.00
WFRC1 Richard Chamberlain	10.00	25.00
WFTO1 Tony Orlando	12.00	30.00

2015 Leaf Pop Century

Card	Low	High
COMMON AUTO	5.00	12.00
BAAB1 Angelica Bridges	10.00	25.00
BAAK1 Anna Kournikova	15.00	40.00
BAAM1 Andrew McCarthy	6.00	15.00
BAAP1 Al Pacino	80.00	150.00
BAAQ1 Aileen Quinn	8.00	20.00
BAAS1 Annabella Sciorra	12.00	30.00
BAAW1 Adam West	15.00	40.00
BABR1 Burt Reynolds	20.00	50.00
BABW1 Burt Ward	12.00	30.00
BACJ1 Chris Jericho	8.00	20.00
BACRJ Cal Ripken Jr.	12.00	30.00
BACW1 Cindy Williams	6.00	15.00
BADB1 Dale Bozzio	6.00	15.00
BADR1 Dennis Rodman	6.00	15.00
BAEE2 Erika Eleniak	6.00	15.00
BAEW1 Estella Warren	25.00	60.00
BAGC1 George Clinton	6.00	15.00
BAGW1 Gene Wilder	60.00	120.00
BAHH1 Hulk Hogan	20.00	50.00
BAHW1 Henry Winkler	10.00	25.00
BAJP1 Joe Pantoliano	6.00	15.00
BAKB1 Kristen Bell	30.00	80.00
BAKLB Kelly LeBrock	12.00	30.00
BALH1 Linda Hamilton	12.00	30.00
BAMF1 Megan Fox	100.00	200.00
BAMMK Michael McKean	10.00	25.00
BAMS1 Martin Short	12.00	30.00
BAMT1 Mike Tyson	30.00	80.00
BANN1 Nichelle Nichols	10.00	25.00
BANR1 Norman Reedus	15.00	40.00
BAPR1 Pete Rose	8.00	20.00
BARD1 Roger Daltrey	30.00	80.00
BARF1 Ric Flair	10.00	25.00
BARH1 Ryan Hurst	6.00	15.00
BARP1 Ron Perlman	15.00	40.00
BASS1 Sharon Stone	60.00	120.00
BATO1 Tony Orlando	6.00	15.00
BATON Tatum O'Neal	8.00	20.00
BATP1 Tera Patrick	12.00	30.00
BATT1 Tiffani Thiessen	15.00	40.00
BAVM1 Vanessa Marcil	10.00	25.00

2015 Leaf Pop Century Co-Stars

Card	Low	High
COMMON AUTO	15.00	40.00
CO01 Hulk Hogan / Ric Flair	50.00	100.00
CO03 Adam West / Burt Ward	100.00	200.00

2015 Leaf Pop Century Hitmakers

Card	Low	High
COMMON AUTO	5.00	12.00
HMGC1 George Clinton	8.00	20.00
HMRD1 Roger Daltrey	30.00	80.00

2015 Leaf Pop Century Inscription Autographs

Card	Low	High
IHW1 Henry Winkler	12.00	30.00

2015 Leaf Pop Century Live and Clear Autographs

Card	Low	High
COMMON AUTO	8.00	20.00
LCAS1 Annabella Sciorra	12.00	30.00
LCEJO Edward James Olmos	15.00	40.00
LCHW1 Henry Winkler	10.00	25.00
LCLH1 Linda Hamilton	15.00	40.00
LCTON Tatum O'Neal	10.00	25.00
LCWK1 Walter Koenig	10.00	25.00

2015 Leaf Pop Century Perfectly Cast

Card	Low	High
COMMON AUTO	5.00	12.00
PCAP1 Al Pacino	50.00	100.00
PCBDW Billy Dee Williams	15.00	40.00
PCGW1 Gene Wilder	60.00	120.00
PCHW1 Henry Winkler	8.00	20.00
PCNN1 Nichelle Nichols	8.00	20.00
PCRP1 Ron Perlman	10.00	25.00
PCSS1 Sharon Stone	30.00	80.00
PCTT1 Tiffani Thiessen		

2015 Leaf Pop Century Star Power Metal

Card	Low	High
COMMON AUTO	5.00	12.00
SPAK1 Anna Kournikova	12.00	30.00
SPBE1 Barbara Eden	20.00	50.00
SPCF1 Carrie Fisher	20.00	50.00
SPDB1 Dale Bozzio	8.00	20.00
SPDVD Dick Van Dyke		
SPEW1 Estella Warren	25.00	60.00
SPJG1 Josh Gad		
SPJLS Jamie-Lynn Sigler	6.00	15.00
SPKA1 Krista Allen	10.00	25.00
SPKLB Kelly LeBrock	12.00	30.00
SPLH1 Linda Hamilton	10.00	25.00
SPNN1 Nichelle Nichols		
SPRD1 Roger Daltrey	30.00	80.00
SPRF1 Ric Flair	12.00	30.00
SPTG1 Teri Garr		
SPTON Tatum O'Neal	6.00	15.00
SPTT1 Tiffani Thiessen		
SPVM1 Vanessa Marcil	8.00	20.00

2015 Leaf Pop Century Stunning Starlets

Card	Low	High
COMMON AUTO	6.00	15.00
SSAK1 Anna Kournikova	12.00	30.00
SSEW1 Estella Warren	15.00	40.00
SSKA1 Krista Allen	8.00	20.00
SSKB1 Kristen Bell	25.00	60.00
SSMF1 Megan Fox	100.00	200.00
SSSS1 Sharon Stone	60.00	120.00
SSTON Tatum O'Neal	8.00	20.00
SSTP1 Tera Patrick	10.00	25.00
SSTT1 Tiffani Thiessen	25.00	60.00

2016 Leaf Pop Century

Card	Low	High
COMMON CARD	4.00	10.00
BAAC1 Alice Cooper	20.00	50.00
BAAP1 Al Pacino	50.00	100.00
BAAR1 Alfonso Ribeiro	6.00	15.00
BABD1 Buster Douglas	5.00	12.00
BABE1 Barbara Eden	15.00	40.00

BABG1 Boy George	15.00	40.00
BACA1 Christina Applegate	25.00	60.00
BACC1 Chevy Chase	100.00	200.00
BACL1 Carl Lewis	8.00	20.00
BACN1 Chuck Negron	5.00	12.00
BACS1 Connie Stevens	8.00	20.00
BADC1 Dyan Cannon	6.00	15.00
BADC2 Dean Cain	12.00	30.00
BADR1 Daisy Ridley	250.00	400.00
BADR2 Dennis Rodman	5.00	12.00
BADVD Dick Van Dyke	15.00	40.00
BAEA1 Ed Asner	5.00	12.00
BAEON Ed O'Neill	15.00	40.00
BAER1 Eric Roberts		20.00
BAFT1 Frank Thomas	10.00	25.00
BAGA1 Gillian Anderson	30.00	80.00
BAGE1 Giancarlo Esposito	6.00	15.00
BAGL1 George Lazenby	12.00	30.00
BAGL2 Gina Lollobrigida	12.00	30.00
BAGW1 Gene Wilder	25.00	60.00
BAGW2 George Wendt	8.00	20.00
BAHMC Holly Marie Combs	15.00	40.00
BAIM1 Idina Menzel	12.00	30.00
BAJL1 Jerry Lewis	20.00	50.00
BAJQ1 Jonathan Ke Huy Quan	60.00	150.00
BAJR1 Jeri Ryan	25.00	60.00
BAKC1 Kevin Costner	50.00	100.00
BAKM1 Katie Morgan	12.00	30.00
BAKR1 Kim Richards	6.00	15.00
BAMB1 Max Baer Jr	6.00	15.00
BAMF1 Megan Fox	50.00	100.00
BAMF2 Mick Foley	8.00	20.00
BAML1 Martin Landau	10.00	25.00
BAMM1 Malcolm McDowell	12.00	30.00
BAMS1 Mena Suvari	15.00	40.00
BAMS2 Marina Sirtis	12.00	30.00
BANC1 Neve Campbell	15.00	40.00
BANR1 Norman Reedus	20.00	50.00
BAPMB Paul McBeth	12.00	30.00
BARC1 Richard Chamberlain	5.00	12.00
BARH1 Robert Hays	6.00	15.00
BARL1 Robert Loggia	8.00	20.00
BARM1 Ralph Macchio	10.00	25.00
BARM2 Roger Moore	25.00	60.00
BART1 Richard Thomas	6.00	15.00
BASD1 Shannen Doherty	15.00	40.00
BASF1 Samantha Fox	10.00	25.00
BASJ1 Shirley Jones	10.00	25.00
BASPF Sean Patrick Flanery	8.00	20.00
BATA1 Tatyana Ali	6.00	15.00
BATC1 Tim Curry	10.00	25.00
BATF1 Tom Felton	8.00	20.00
BATH1 Tippi Hedren	10.00	25.00
BATR1 Tara Reid	12.00	30.00
BAVH1 Valerie Harper	10.00	25.00
BAVP1 Vincent Pastore	12.00	30.00
BAVT1 Verne Troyer	6.00	15.00
BAWN1 Wayne Newton	6.00	15.00
BAWS1 William Shatner	30.00	80.00

2016 Leaf Pop Century Co-Stars

CS01 Kelly LeBrock / Ilan Mitchell-Smith	12.00	30.00
CS02 Idina Menzel / Kristen Bell		
CS03 Sean Patrick Flanery / Norman Reedus	15.00	40.00
CS04 Tatyana Ali / Alfonso Ribeiro Karyn Parsons	12.00	30.00

2016 Leaf Pop Century Dressing Room

DR-KB1 Kristen Bell Gold	25.00	60.00
DR-KB1 Kristen Bell Red/25	30.00	80.00
DR-KB1 Kristen Bell Blue Spectrum/10	50.00	100.00
DR-KB1 Kristen Bell Silver Spectrum/5		
DR-KB1 Kristen Bell Gold Spectrum/1		

2016 Leaf Pop Century Hit Makers

COMMON CARD	4.00	10.00
HMAC1 Alice Cooper	15.00	40.00
HMBG1 Boy George	8.00	20.00
HMSF1 Samantha Fox	8.00	20.00
HMWN1 Wayne Newton	6.00	15.00

2016 Leaf Pop Century Marquee Materials

COMMON CARD	4.00	10.00
MM01 Ashley Judd	5.00	12.00
MM02 Brad Pitt	5.00	12.00
MM04 Burt Reynolds	5.00	12.00
MM05 Charlize Theron	8.00	20.00
MM08 Dean Martin	5.00	12.00
MM09 Elvis Presley	20.00	50.00
MM10 Frank Sinatra	10.00	25.00
MM11 Halle Berry	5.00	12.00
MM12 Hayden Panettiere		
MM13 Jack Ruby	8.00	20.00
MM15 James Stewart	6.00	15.00
MM16 Jane Fonda		
MM17 Jennifer Aniston	5.00	12.00
MM18 Jennifer Lopez	5.00	12.00
MM19 Jennifer Love Hewitt	10.00	25.00
MM20 Julia Roberts	5.00	12.00
MM21 Mila Kunis	6.00	15.00
MM22 Molly Ringwald	6.00	15.00
MM24 Sarah Michelle Gellar	6.00	15.00
MM26 William Shatner	5.00	12.00

2016 Leaf Pop Century PC Live and Clear Autographs

LC-AK1 Anna Kournikova Gold	8.00	20.00
LC-AK1 Anna Kournikova Silver/20	12.00	30.00
LC-AK1 Anna Kournikova Blue/10		
LC-AK1 Anna Kournikova Purple/1		

2016 Leaf Pop Century Perfectly Cast

COMMON CARD	4.00	10.00
PCGE1 Giancarlo Esposito	5.00	12.00
PCGL1 George Lazenby	10.00	25.00
PCGW2 George Wendt	6.00	15.00
PCIM1 Idina Menzel	30.00	80.00
PCJOH John O'Hurley	5.00	12.00
PCKC1 Kevin Costner		
PCMM1 Malcolm McDowell	8.00	20.00
PCRT1 Richard Thomas	5.00	12.00

2016 Leaf Pop Century Sci-Fi Signatures

COMMON CARD	8.00	20.00
SFDR1 Daisy Ridley	200.00	300.00
SFGA1 Gillian Anderson	50.00	100.00
SFJR1 Jeri Ryan	15.00	40.00
SFMF1 Megan Fox	50.00	100.00
SFNN1 Nichelle Nichols	10.00	25.00
SFWS1 William Shatner	30.00	80.00

2016 Leaf Pop Century Stunning Starlets

COMMON CARD	8.00	20.00
SSDC1 Dyan Cannon	10.00	25.00
SSDR1 Daisy Ridley	250.00	400.00
SSGA1 Gillian Anderson	50.00	100.00
SSJR1 Jeri Ryan	20.00	50.00
SSMS1 Mena Suvari	12.00	30.00
SSNC1 Neve Campbell	20.00	50.00
SSSD1 Shannen Doherty	12.00	30.00
SSTR1 Tara Reid	10.00	25.00

2017 Leaf Pop Century

UNOPENED BOX (1 PACK/4 CARDS)	75.00	120.00
COMMON AUTO	4.00	10.00
BAAB1 Andrea Bocelli	20.00	50.00
BAAD1 Angie Dickinson	10.00	25.00
BAAM1 Aly Michalka	6.00	15.00
BAAMH Anthony Michael Hall	10.00	25.00
BAAP1 Adrian Paul	5.00	12.00
BAAT1 Alan Thicke SP	10.00	25.00
BABM1 Bam Margera	5.00	12.00
BABR1 Burt Reynolds	20.00	50.00
BABW1 Barry Williams	6.00	15.00
BABY1 Burt Young	6.00	15.00
BACB1 Catherine Bach	12.00	30.00
BACF1 Carrie Fisher SP	75.00	150.00
BACL1 Christopher Lloyd SP	30.00	75.00
BACMG Conor McGregor SP	60.00	120.00
BACS1 Christian Slater	8.00	20.00
BADR1 Daisy Ridley	120.00	250.00
BADS1 Dee Snider	6.00	15.00
BADVD Dick Van Dyke SP	20.00	50.00
BADW1 Dawn Wells	8.00	20.00
BAEC1 Emmanuelle Chriqui	8.00	20.00
BAEH1 Elizabeth Henstridge	12.00	30.00
BAEK1 Emily Kinney	6.00	15.00
BAFB1 Fairuza Balk	8.00	20.00
BAGW1 Gene Wilder SP	40.00	100.00
BAGW2 George Wendt	12.00	30.00
BAIA1 Iggy Azalea	10.00	25.00
BAJC1 Joan Cusack	5.00	12.00
BAJC2 John Cusack	15.00	40.00
BAJL1 Jonathan Lipnicki	5.00	12.00
BAJM1 Joe Manganiello	6.00	15.00
BAJN1 Jay North	5.00	12.00
BAJR1 Judge Reinhold	8.00	20.00
BAKMN Kristy McNichol	10.00	25.00
BAKR1 Kristen Renton	6.00	15.00
BAKS1 Kevin Sorbo	5.00	12.00
BALA1 Lisa Ann	10.00	25.00
BALA2 Loni Anderson	8.00	20.00
BALAW Lesley Ann Warren	5.00	12.00
BALH1 Lucy Hale	5.00	12.00
BAMF1 Megan Fox	30.00	75.00
BAMF2 Mick Foley SP	10.00	25.00
BAMS1 Mena Suvari	8.00	20.00
BAMT1 Mike Tyson	30.00	80.00
BANF1 Nathan Fillion	12.00	30.00
BANN1 Nichelle Nichols	15.00	40.00
BANR1 Norman Reedus	15.00	40.00
BANT1 Nicholas Turturro	5.00	12.00
BAPA1 Pamela Anderson	25.00	60.00
BAPC1 Peter Capaldi	15.00	40.00
BAPS1 Paul Sorvino	6.00	15.00
BARD1 Richard Dreyfuss	15.00	40.00
BARG1 Richard Grieco	5.00	12.00
BARL1 Robin Leach	5.00	12.00
BARM1 Ralph Macchio	8.00	20.00
BARM2 Roger Moore	25.00	60.00
BASB1 Selma Blair	12.00	30.00
BASE1 Shannon Elizabeth	8.00	20.00
BASF1 Sherilyn Fenn	8.00	20.00
BASI1 Scott Ian	10.00	25.00
BASU1 Sara Underwood SP	10.00	25.00
BATB1 Tom Berenger	12.00	30.00
BATG1 Teri Garr	10.00	25.00
BAVG1 Vida Guerra	6.00	15.00
BAVM1 Vanessa Marcil SP	12.00	30.00

2017 Leaf Pop Century Accolades Autographs

COMMON AUTO	6.00	15.00
AAP1 Al Pacino SP	50.00	100.00
ACL1 Christopher Lloyd SP	15.00	40.00
ACMG Conor McGregor SP	75.00	150.00
ACRJ Cal Ripken Jr.	10.00	25.00
ACS1 Christian Slater	10.00	25.00
ADVD Dick Van Dyke SP	25.00	60.00
AEA1 Ed Asner	8.00	20.00
AIM1 Idina Menzel SP	15.00	40.00
AMF1 Megan Fox	25.00	60.00
AMS1 Matt Stonie SP	8.00	20.00
ANF1 Nathan Fillion	10.00	25.00
APC1 Peter Capaldi	20.00	50.00
ARD1 Richard Dreyfuss	10.00	25.00
ASI1 Scott Ian	8.00	20.00

2017 Leaf Pop Century Clear Autographs

COMMON AUTO	5.00	12.00
CAD1 Angie Dickinson	8.00	20.00
CAT1 Alan Thicke SP	8.00	20.00
CCL1 Christopher Lloyd	25.00	60.00
CCS1 Christian Slater	8.00	20.00
CEK1 Emily Kinney	10.00	25.00
CLA1 Loni Anderson	12.00	30.00
CMB1 Max Baer Jr	10.00	25.00
CNN1 Nichelle Nichols	12.00	30.00
CNR1 Norman Reedus	20.00	50.00

2017 Leaf Pop Century Dressing Room Relics

DREC1 Emmanuelle Chriqui	12.00	30.00
DREC1 Emmanuelle Chriqui Silver/10		
DREC1 Emmanuelle Chriqui Gold/5		
DREC1 Emmanuelle Chriqui Purple/1		

2017 Leaf Pop Century Dual Autographs

COMMON AUTO	10.00	25.00
KJ Kylie & Kendall Jenner CUT	25.00	60.00
DA1 McDonald/Margera SP	15.00	40.00
DA4 Reid/Martin	12.00	30.00
DA5 John & Joan Cusack SP	25.00	60.00
DA6 Patrick/Ann	20.00	50.00
DA7 Fisher/Ridley SP	250.00	400.00
DA9 Berenger/Bernsen SP	15.00	40.00

2017 Leaf Pop Century In Memoriam Autographs

COMMON AUTO	8.00	20.00
IMCF1 Carrie Fisher SP	60.00	120.00
IMGW1 Gene Wilder SP	30.00	75.00
IMRM1 Roger Moore	25.00	60.00

2017 Leaf Pop Century Musically Yours Autographs

COMMON AUTO	5.00	12.00
*SILVER/10-25: X TO X BASIC AUTOS		
MYAP1 Artimus Pyle	6.00	15.00
MYDS1 Dee Snider	5.00	12.00
MYIA1 Iggy Azalea	8.00	20.00
MYIM1 Idina Menzel SP	15.00	40.00
MYJL1 Jerry Lewis	20.00	50.00
MYLH1 Lucy Hale	8.00	20.00
MYSI1 Scott Ian	5.00	12.00
MYTC1 Tim Curry	25.00	60.00

2017 Leaf Pop Century Prop Century Relics

COMMON RELIC	3.00	8.00
*PLAT.SPEC./20: .6X TO 1.5X BASIC RELICS		
PC1 Adam Sandler	5.00	12.00
PC2 Barbra Streisand	4.00	10.00
PC3 Benicio Del Toro	4.00	10.00
PC4 Beyonce	6.00	15.00
PC5 Billy Bob Thornton	4.00	10.00
PC7 Brad Pitt	5.00	12.00
PC11 Danny Kaye	5.00	12.00
PC13 Dwayne Johnson	4.00	10.00
PC16 Forest Whitaker	4.00	10.00
PC17 Helen Hunt	5.00	12.00
PC19 Jennifer Lawrence	10.00	25.00
PC20 Jennifer Lopez	6.00	15.00
PC21 Jesse Eisenberg	4.00	10.00
PC22 Jessica Simpson	5.00	12.00
PC26 Katherine Heigl	5.00	12.00
PC28 Matthew McConaughey	4.00	10.00
PC29 Mike Myers	5.00	12.00
PC30 Mila Kunis	6.00	15.00
PC33 Richard Pryor	4.00	10.00
PC34 Robert Duvall	4.00	10.00
PC35 Robin Williams	6.00	15.00
PC36 Russell Crowe	5.00	12.00
PC37 Sandra Bullock	6.00	15.00
PC38 Sarah Hyland	5.00	12.00
PC41 Will Ferrell	6.00	15.00

2017 Leaf Pop Century Stunning Starlets Autographs

COMMON AUTO	6.00	15.00
SSAM1 Aly Michalka	8.00	20.00
SSCB1 Catherine Bach	12.00	30.00
SSDW1 Dawn Wells	8.00	20.00
SSEH1 Elizabeth Henstridge	12.00	30.00
SSEK1 Emily Kinney	10.00	25.00
SSIA1 Iggy Azalea	10.00	25.00
SSKLB Kelly LeBrock	10.00	25.00
SSPA1 Pamela Anderson	25.00	60.00
SSSE1 Shannon Elizabeth	8.00	20.00
SSSF1 Sherilyn Fenn	8.00	20.00

2017 Leaf Pop Century Walk of Fame Autographs

COMMON AUTO	4.00	10.00
WFBE1 Barbara Eden	12.00	30.00
WFBR1 Burt Reynolds	20.00	50.00

WFCC1 Chevy Chase 30.00 75.00
WFJC1 Joan Collins 6.00 15.00
WFJC2 John Cusack 10.00 25.00
WFPA1 Pamela Anderson 20.00 50.00

2018 Leaf Pop Century Metal

UNOPENED BOX (4 CARDS) 110.00 150.00
COMMON AUTO 5.00 12.00
*BLUE: .5X TO 1.2X BASIC AUTOS
BAAD1 Adam Driver 60.00 120.00
BAAS1 Ally Sheedy 10.00 25.00
BAAW1 Anson Williams 8.00 20.00
BABA1 Ben Affleck 75.00 150.00
BABP2 Brook Power 6.00 15.00
BABW1 Burt Ward 15.00 40.00
BACB1 Corbin Bernsen
BACM1 Caleb McLaughlin 10.00 25.00
BACS1 Charlie Sheen 20.00 50.00
BADB1 Danny Bonaduce 6.00 15.00
BADC1 Diahann Carroll 6.00 15.00
BADDM Drea de Matteo 6.00 15.00
BADM1 Don Most 8.00 20.00
BADR1 Denise Richards 15.00 40.00
BAEC1 Emmanuelle Chriqui 6.00 15.00
BAEM1 Esai Morales 6.00 15.00
BAEON Ed O'Neill 20.00 50.00
BAGM1 Gaten Matarazzo 15.00 40.00
BAGS1 Gary Sinise 12.00 30.00
BAGW1 George Wendt 12.00 30.00
BAHL1 Hal Linden 6.00 15.00
BAHW1 Henry Winkler 20.00 50.00
BAJC1 James Caan 15.00 40.00
BAJC2 Jennifer Carpenter 6.00 15.00
BAJC3 John Cusack 8.00 20.00
BAJH1 Jon Heder 8.00 20.00
BAJM1 Jerry Mathers 12.00 30.00
BAJW1 Jimmie Walker 6.00 15.00
BAKT1 Kathleen Turner 12.00 30.00
BALD1 Laura Dern 10.00 25.00
BALDP Lou Diamond Phillips 10.00 25.00
BALF1 Lou Ferrigno 10.00 25.00
BALM1 Lee Majors 12.00 30.00
BALV1 Lark Voorhies 6.00 15.00
BAMBB Millie Bobby Brown 50.00 100.00
BAMF1 Morgan Fairchild 12.00 30.00
BAMJW Malcolm Jamal Warner 6.00 15.00
BAML1 Meat Loaf 12.00 30.00
BAMN1 Michael Nesmith 20.00 50.00
BAPA1 Pamela Anderson 25.00 60.00
BARL1 Robin Leach 6.00 15.00
BARM1 Rose McIver 10.00 25.00
BARQ1 Randy Quaid 10.00 25.00
BASA1 Steve Austin 30.00 75.00
BASB1 Scott Baio 8.00 20.00
BASC1 Sonny Chiba 12.00 30.00
BASD1 Shelley Duvall 12.00 30.00
BASP1 Stefanie Powers 15.00 40.00
BASS1 Sadie Sink 15.00 40.00
BATD1 Tony Dow 10.00 25.00
BAVH1 Valerie Harper 8.00 20.00
BAVK1 Val Kilmer 15.00 40.00
BAVT1 Verne Troyer 8.00 20.00
BAWK1 William Katt 15.00 40.00
BAWS1 William Shatner 50.00 100.00
BAWS2 Wallace Shawn 8.00 20.00

2018 Leaf Pop Century Metal Accolades Autographs

COMMON AUTO 6.00 15.00
*BLUE/50: .5X TO 1.2X BASIC AUTOS
ACS1 Charlie Sheen 20.00 50.00
AEON Ed O'Neill 25.00 60.00
AKT1 Kathleen Turner 8.00 20.00
ARQ1 Randy Quaid 10.00 25.00

2018 Leaf Pop Century Metal American Royalty Memorabilia

AR1 Jacqueline Kennedy Onassis 15.00 40.00

2018 Leaf Pop Century Metal Cut Signatures

RANDOMLY INSERTED INTO PACKS
PCCAG1 Al Gore 30.00 75.00
PCCAG2 Ava Gardner 30.00 75.00
PCCAK1 Anna Kendrick 60.00 120.00
PCCBB1 Barbara Bush 50.00 100.00
PCCBG1 Brian Gray
PCCGS1 Gene Simmons 50.00 100.00
PCCIT1 Ivanka Trump 75.00 150.00
PCCJB1 Joe Biden 50.00 100.00
PCCVP1 Vincent Price 50.00 100.00

2018 Leaf Pop Century Metal Dual Autographs

COMMON AUTO
*BLUE: .5X TO 1.2X BASIC AUTOS
DA1 A.Sheedy/E.Estevez
DA2 A.Williams/D.Most 15.00 40.00
DA3 B.Dern/L.Dern 20.00 50.00
DA4 E.Morales/L.Diamond Phillips
DA5 H.Winkler/S.Baio 25.00 60.00
DA6 R.Jackson/J.Heder 20.00 50.00
DA7 J.Mathers/T.Dow
DA8 K.Parsons/T.Ali 10.00 25.00
DA9 L.Majors/L.Wagner
DA10 C.Sheen/D.Richards
DA11 B.Affleck/V.Kilmer
DA12 G.Matarazzo/C.McLaughlin 20.00 50.00

2018 Leaf Pop Century Metal Heart Breaker Signatures

COMMON AUTO 5.00 12.00
*BLUE: .5X TO 1.2X BASIC AUTOS
HBBE1 Barbara Eden 25.00 60.00
HBBP1 Brook Power 6.00 15.00
HBDR1 Denise Richards 20.00 50.00
HBEC1 Emmanuelle Chriqui 10.00 25.00
HBKB1 Kristin Bauer 6.00 15.00
HBLD1 Laura Dern 8.00 20.00
HBMF1 Morgan Fairchild 8.00 20.00
HBPA1 Pamela Anderson 25.00 60.00
HBRM1 Rose McIver 10.00 25.00
HBSP1 Stefanie Powers 15.00 40.00
HBTK1 Tawny Kitaen 6.00 15.00

2018 Leaf Pop Century Metal Prop Century 4 Memorabilia

COMMON MEM 8.00 20.00
PC41 Farrell/Burghoff/Morgan/Swit 10.00 25.00
PC43 Latifah/Beyonce/Lopez/Spears 10.00 25.00
PC45 Presley/Crosby/Holly/Martin 30.00 75.00
PC48 Williams/Pryor/Martin/Murphy 15.00 40.00

2018 Leaf Pop Century Metal Prop Century 6 Memorabilia

COMMON MEM 10.00 25.00
PC61 Carrey/Williams/Martin Murphy/Pryor/Rock 15.00 40.00
PC62 Chase/Murray/Sandler Rock/Murphy/Ferrell 12.00 30.00
PC64 Heston/Cagney/Stewart Sinatra/Holden/Kaye 12.00 30.00
PC65 Pacino/Duvall/Hopkins Cagney/Crowe/Sinatra 30.00 75.00

2018 Leaf Pop Century Metal Prop Century 8 Memorabilia

COMMON MEM 8.00 20.00
PC81 Adams/Paltrow/Garner/Winslet Lane/Berry/Bullock/Theron 10.00 25.00
PC82 Berry/Lane/Gyllenhaal/Garner Hudson/Hunt/Judd/Ringwald 15.00 40.00
PC83 Douglas/Pacino/Pitt/Costner Washington/Reynolds/Wahlberg/Cooper 10.00 25.00
PC84 Gyllenhaal/Berry/Bates/Bullock Winslet/Roberts/Tomei/Theron 12.00 30.00

2018 Leaf Pop Century Metal Prop Century Duos Memorabilia

PC21 50 Cent/Ice Cube 3.00 8.00
PC22 A.Pacino/R.Duvall 6.00 15.00
PC23 B.Streisand/W.Houston 3.00 8.00
PC24 C.Chase/B.Murray 8.00 20.00
PC25 C.Walken/W.Ferrell 5.00 12.00
PC26 D.Kaye/B.Crosby 6.00 15.00
PC27 D.Martin/B.Crosby 6.00 15.00
PC28 D.Martin/J.Lewis 10.00 25.00
PC29 E.Murphy/M.Myers 6.00 15.00
PC210 E.Presley/B.Holly 25.00 60.00
PC211 F.Sinatra/B.Crosby 5.00 12.00
PC212 F.Sinatra/D.Martin 12.00 30.00
PC213 R.Pryor/E.Murphy 6.00 15.00
PC214 S.Rogan/J.Hill 3.00 8.00
PC215 Z.Galifianakis/B.Cooper 5.00 12.00

2018 Leaf Pop Century Metal Quad Autographs

QA1 Ridley/Driver/Dern/Fisher
QA2 Brown/Matarazzo/McLaughlin/Sink 120.00 250.00
QA3 Leopardi/York/Obedzinski/Di Mattia 75.00 150.00

2018 Leaf Pop Century Metal Vinyl Signs Autographs

VSDC1 Diahann Carroll 8.00 20.00
VSIA1 Iggy Azalea 12.00 30.00
VSML1 Meat Loaf 12.00 30.00
VSMN1 Michael Nesmith 20.00 50.00

2018 Leaf Pop Century Metal Walk of Fame Autographs

WFBD1 Bruce Dern 6.00 15.00
WFCS1 Charlie Sheen
WFDC1 Diahann Carroll 6.00 15.00
WFGS1 Gary Sinise 10.00 25.00
WFJC1 James Caan 12.00 30.00
WFLM1 Lee Majors 12.00 30.00
WFRQ1 Randy Quaid 10.00 25.00
WFWS1 William Shatner 25.00 60.00

2019 Leaf Pop Century Metal

UNOPENED BOX (1 PACK/4 CARDS) 200.00 400.00
COMMON AUTO 5.00 12.00
BAE1 Edge 6.00 15.00
BAAP1 Al Pacino 60.00 120.00
BABA1 Ben Affleck 50.00 100.00
BABR1 Brande Roderick 10.00 25.00
BABR2 Brandon Routh 12.00 30.00
BABT1 Bella Thorne 10.00 25.00
BACS1 Charlie Sheen 20.00 50.00
BACT1 Carrot Top 6.00 15.00
BADN1 Daniel Negreanu 6.00 15.00
BADR1 Daisy Ridley 100.00 200.00
BADR2 Denise Richards 15.00 40.00
BAEE1 Emilio Estevez 20.00 50.00
BAFD1 Felicia Day 12.00 30.00
BAGD1 Geena Davis 30.00 75.00
BAGLN Gena Lee Nolin 6.00 15.00
BAHF1 Harrison Ford
BAIZ1 Ian Ziering 6.00 15.00
BAJC1 James Caan 10.00 25.00
BAJF1 Jamie Foxx 20.00 50.00
BAJJL Jennifer Jason Leigh 15.00 40.00
BAJLH Jennifer Love Hewitt 60.00 120.00
BAJOH John O'Hurley 6.00 15.00
BAJR1 Jeremy Renner 20.00 50.00
BAJW1 Jaleel White 6.00 15.00
BALB1 Linda Blair 10.00 25.00
BALD1 Laura Dern 12.00 30.00
BALF1 Louise Fletcher 6.00 15.00
BALL1 Lorenzo Lamas 6.00 15.00
BALM1 Lee Majors 15.00 40.00
BALW1 Lindsay Wagner 12.00 30.00
BAMB1 Matthew Broderick 25.00 60.00
BAMB2 Michael Beck 10.00 25.00
BAMBB Millie Bobby Brown 60.00 120.00
BAMK1 Martin Klebba 6.00 15.00
BAML1 Mike Lookinland 6.00 15.00
BAMN1 Michael Nesmith 50.00 100.00
BAMP1 Michael Pare 6.00 15.00
BAMW1 Mary Wilson 8.00 20.00
BAPA1 Pamela Anderson 20.00 50.00
BAPB1 Pat Boone 6.00 15.00
BARD1 Richard Dreyfuss 10.00 25.00
BARH1 Ryan Hurst 12.00 30.00
BASG1 Steve Guttenberg 8.00 20.00
BASS1 Steven Seagal 25.00 60.00
BATB1 Tom Berenger 10.00 25.00
BATG1 Tracey Gold 8.00 20.00
BATH1 Tonya Harding 15.00 40.00
BAVK1 Val Kilmer 12.00 30.00
BAWB1 Wilford Brimley 8.00 20.00
BASMG1 Sarah Michelle Gellar
BASMG2 Sarah Michelle Gellar

2019 Leaf Pop Century Metal Classic Roles

CRBE1 Barbara Eden 25.00 60.00
CRBR1 Burt Reynolds 30.00 75.00
CRCL1 Christopher Lloyd 20.00 50.00
CRDW1 Dawn Wells 15.00 40.00
CRGL1 George Lazenby 15.00 40.00
CRGW1 George Wendt 10.00 25.00
CRJH1 Jon Heder 10.00 25.00
CRJR1 John Ratzenberger 8.00 20.00
CRJW1 Jaleel White 10.00 25.00
CRKS1 Kristy Swanson 12.00 30.00
CRLF1 Louise Fletcher 8.00 20.00
CRLM1 Lee Majors 15.00 40.00
CRLW1 Lindsay Wagner 15.00 40.00
CRRH1 Ryan Hurst 8.00 20.00
CRSJ1 Shirley Jones 10.00 25.00

2019 Leaf Pop Century Metal Dual Autographs

DA01 Vincent Pastore/Federico Castelluccio 8.00 20.00
DA02 Mickey Dolenz/Michael Nesmith
DA03 Michael Imperioli/Federico Castelluccio 8.00 20.00
DA04 Erik Estrada/Larry Wilcox 15.00 40.00
DA05 John Ratzenberger/George Wendt 30.00 75.00
DA06 Jeremy Miller/Tracey Gold
DA07 Harrison Ford/Adam Driver
DA08 Christopher Lloyd/Lea Thompson 50.00 100.00
DA09 Dennis Haysbert/Charlie Sheen
DA10 Brandon Routh/Dean Cain
DA11 Al Pacino/Jamie Foxx

2019 Leaf Pop Century Metal Heartbreakers

HBE1 Britt Ekland 10.00 25.00
HBR1 Brande Roderick 6.00 15.00
HBT1 Bella Thorne 5.00 12.00
HGLN Gena Lee Nolin 6.00 15.00
HJLH Jennifer Love Hewitt
HKS1 Kristy Swanson 6.00 15.00
HLT1 Lea Thompson 20.00 50.00
HLV1 Laura Vandervoort 20.00 50.00
HNE1 Nicole Eggert
HTH1 Tricia Helfer 8.00 20.00
HTL1 Traci Lords 15.00 40.00
HTON Tatum O'Neal 6.00 15.00

2019 Leaf Pop Century Metal Inscription Autograph

ICH1 Chris Hansen 15.00 40.00

2019 Leaf Pop Century Metal Prop Century Co-Stars Memorabilia

PC201 Jack Nicholson/Dennis Hopper 6.00 15.00
PC202 Matthew McConaughey/Kate Hudson 5.00 12.00
PC203 Jennifer Lopez/Alex Rodriguez 6.00 15.00
PC204 Russell Crowe/Paul Giamatti 4.00 10.00
PC205 Robert Redford/Dustin Hoffman 5.00 12.00
PC206 Christopher Walken/Bruce Willis 4.00 10.00
PC207 Bill Murray/Chevy Chase 6.00 15.00
PC208 Jack Black/Ben Stiller 5.00 12.00
PC209 Ewan McGregor/Samuel L. Jackson 6.00 15.00
PC210 Sacha Baron Cohen/Will Ferrell
PC211 Kim Kardashian/Kourtney Kardashian 8.00 20.00

2019 Leaf Pop Century Metal Sci-Fi Signatures

SFSCM1 Caleb McLaughlin
SFSFD1 Felicia Day 10.00 25.00
SFSGM1 Gaten Matarazzo 8.00 20.00
SFSLV1 Laura Vandervoort 10.00 25.00
SFSSS1 Sadie Sink
SFSTH1 Tricia Helfer 6.00 15.00
SFSWS1 William Shatner 50.00 100.00

2019 Leaf Pop Century Metal Stars of Sandlot

SA601 Sandlot Cast 25.00 60.00

2019 Leaf Pop Century Metal Stars of Sopranos

SS601 Sopranos Cast 25.00 60.00

2019 Leaf Pop Century Metal Vinyl Signs

VSAP1 Artimus Pyle 8.00 20.00
VSBT1 Bella Thorne 8.00 20.00
VSMD1 Mickey Dolenz 15.00 40.00
VSMW1 Mary Wilson 6.00 15.00
VSPB1 Pat Boone 5.00 12.00

2020 Leaf Pop Century Metal

BAC1 Coolio/27 25.00 60.00
BAAD1 Adam Driver/10 100.00 200.00
BAAD2 Angie Dickinson/25 15.00 40.00
BAAG1 Annabeth Gish/20 8.00 20.00
BAAP1 Al Pacino/5
BAAQ1 Aileen Quinn/50 10.00 25.00
BAAR1 Anthony Rapp/15 8.00 20.00
BAAS1 Alicia Silverstone/5
BABT1 Bella Thorne/50 10.00 25.00
BACB1 Clive Barker/50 20.00 50.00
BACE1 Carmen Electra/15 30.00 75.00
BACK1 Camille Kostek/15 8.00 20.00
BACM1 Cheech Marin/50 20.00 50.00
BACR1 Christina Ricci/24 60.00 120.00
BACS1 Charlie Sheen/15
BACT1 Charlene Tilton/15 10.00 25.00
BADB1 Delta Burke/15 8.00 20.00
BADDM Drea de Matteo/15 12.00 30.00
BADR1 Daisy Ridley/14 125.00 250.00
BADR2 Denise Richards/30 25.00 60.00
BADR3 Dennis Rodman/50 15.00 40.00
BADVD Dick Van Dyke/15 50.00 100.00
BAEA1 Ed Asner/15 10.00 25.00
BAEB1 Elizabeth Berkley/15 30.00 75.00
BAEE1 Emilio Estevez/41 25.00 60.00
BAER1 Eric Roberts/15 8.00 20.00
BAEW1 Elijah Wood/16 15.00 40.00
BAFJ1 Fat Joe/33 10.00 25.00
BAGL1 George Lopez/50 12.00 30.00
BAHF1 Harrison Ford/3
BAHT1 Heather Thomas/20 20.00 50.00
BAJJ1 Jesse Jane/15 20.00 50.00
BAJL1 Joey Lawrence/15 8.00 20.00
BAJM1 Joe Montana/50 75.00 150.00
BAJR1 Jeremy Renner/50 20.00 50.00
BAJT1 John Travolta/50 50.00 100.00
BAKJ1 Kate Jackson/30 30.00 75.00
BALB1 Linda Blair/8 15.00 40.00
BALP1 Lori Petty/35 12.00 30.00
BALR1 Lisa Rinna/24 15.00 40.00
BAMBB Millie Bobby Brown/45 60.00 120.00
BAMC1 Mark Cuban/50 30.00 75.00
BAMI1 Michael Imperioli/23 8.00 20.00
BAMJ1 Michelle Johnson/15 12.00 30.00
BAML1 Mike Love/25 20.00 50.00
BAMM1 Michael Madsen/50 10.00 25.00
BAMR1 Marion Ross/20 15.00 40.00
BAMR2 Meg Ryan/24 75.00 150.00
BAND1 Nina Dobrev/25 25.00 60.00
BANK1 Nancy Kovack/50 8.00 20.00
BANS1 Nicole Sullivan/22 10.00 25.00
BARO1 Robert O'Neill/50 10.00 25.00
BARW1 Robert Wagner/15 12.00 30.00
BASA1 Sean Astin/25 15.00 40.00
BASP1 Stefanie Powers/15 15.00 40.00
BASS1 Steven Seagal/5
BATB1 Toni Basil/15 8.00 20.00
BAVP1 Vincent Pastore/50 10.00 25.00
BAWM1 Wink Martindale/15 8.00 20.00
BAWS1 William Shatner/50 50.00 100.00

2020 Leaf Pop Century Metal And the Winner Is

COMMON AUTO (ATW01-ATW22) 4.00 10.00
ATW01 Catherine Zeta-Jones/50 10.00 25.00
ATW02 Charlton Heston/50 5.00 12.00
ATW03 Christopher Walken/50 6.00 15.00
ATW04 Dustin Hoffman/50 5.00 12.00
ATW06 Frank Sinatra/40 12.00 30.00
ATW07 Ginger Rogers/30 8.00 20.00
ATW09 Jack Nicholson/50 6.00 15.00
ATW10 James Cagney/40 5.00 12.00
ATW11 James Stewart/30 5.00 12.00
ATW12 Jennifer Lawrence/50 8.00 20.00
ATW13 Julia Roberts/50 6.00 15.00
ATW16 Marisa Tomei/50 6.00 15.00
ATW17 Matthew McConaughey/50 5.00 12.00
ATW18 Morgan Freeman/50 6.00 15.00
ATW20 Robin Williams/50 8.00 20.00
ATW22 William Holden/50 5.00 12.00

2020 Leaf Pop Century Metal Classic Roles

CRAR1 Anthony Rapp/15 8.00 20.00
CRAW1 Anson Williams/15 12.00 30.00
CRBT1 Bella Thorne/38 12.00 30.00
CRCB1 Creed Bratton/15 15.00 40.00
CRCS1 Charlie Sheen/15 25.00 60.00
CRDB1 Delta Burke/15
CRDDM Drea de Matteo/15 12.00 30.00
CRDM1 Don Most/15 10.00 25.00
CRDVD Dick Van Dyke/31 50.00 100.00
CREA1 Ed Asner/15 8.00 20.00
CREW1 Elijah Wood/16 25.00 60.00
CRFC1 Federico Castelluccio/50 8.00 20.00
CRHF1 Harrison Ford/3
CRJM1 Jerry Mathers/15 12.00 30.00
CRJT1 John Travolta/50 50.00 100.00
CRJW1 Jimmie Walker/50 8.00 20.00
CRKF1 Kate Flannery/15 10.00 25.00
CRLD1 Laura Dern/18 15.00 40.00
CRMBB Millie Bobby Brown/45 75.00 150.00
CRMI1 Michael Imperioli/22 10.00 25.00
CRML1 Mario Lopez/35 12.00 30.00
CRMM1 Michael Madsen/50 8.00 20.00
CRMPG Mark-Paul Gosselaar/35 20.00 50.00
CRND1 Nina Dobrev/25 30.00 75.00
CRON1 Oscar Nunez/15 10.00 25.00
CRPB1 Peter Billingsley/15 30.00 75.00
CRRT1 Richard Thomas/50 25.00 50.00
CRSA1 Sean Astin/24 15.00 40.00
CRSS1 Shawnee Smith/29 15.00 40.00
CRVP1 Vincent Pastore/50 8.00 20.00
CRWK1 William Katt/15 25.00 60.00

2020 Leaf Pop Century Metal Co-Stars Autographs

CS01 Aileen Quinn/Tim Curry/15
CS02 Charlie Sheen/John Cusack/15 30.00 75.00
CS03 Charlie Sheen/Shawnee Smith/15
CS04 Cheech Marin/Tommy Chong/50 75.00 150.00
CS05 Daisy Ridley/Laura Dern/6
CS06 Don Most/Anson Williams/50 15.00 40.00
CS07 Elijah Wood/Sean Astin/6
CS08 Elizabeth Berkley/Mario Lopez/6
CS09 Elizabeth Berkley/Mark-Paul Gosselaar/6
CS10 Eric Roberts/William Katt/15 15.00 40.00
CS11 Harrison Ford/Daisy Ridley/2
CS12 Henry Winkler/Anson Williams/26
CS13 Henry Winkler/Don Most/26 20.00 50.00
CS14 Jamie Foxx/George Lopez/15 20.00 50.00
CS15 Jeremy Renner/Michael Madsen/15
CS16 Jeremy Renner/Tommy Chong/15
CS17 Jerry Mathers/Tony Dow/15 30.00 75.00
CS18 Lori Petty/Megan Cavanagh/26
CS19 Mario Lopez/Mark-Paul Gosselaar/6
CS20 Nicole Sullivan/John O'Hurley/4
CS21 Scott Baio/Anson Williams/5
CS22 Scott Baio/Don Most/5
CS23 Scott Baio/Marion Ross/5
CS24 Tim Curry/Richard Thomas/15
CS25 Tom Arnold/Laura Dern/9
CS26 Kate Flannery/Creed Bratton Oscar Nunez/15 50.00 100.00
CS27 Marion Ross/Don Most Anson Williams/26 30.00 75.00
CS28 Sopranos Cast/42 50.00 100.00
CS29 Doyle Brunson/Daniel Negreanu/13
CS30 Robert Wagner/Stefanie Powers/15 30.00 75.00

2020 Leaf Pop Century Metal Famous Fabrics 4

STATED PRINT RUN 25 SER.#'d SETS
FFF01 Elvis Presley/Buddy Holly/Frank Sinatra/Bing Crosby
FFF02 Brad Pitt/Matthew McConaughey/Bradley Cooper/Mark Wahlberg
FFF03 Steve Carell/Seth Rogen Jonah Hill/Will Ferrell 15.00 40.00
FFF04 David Spade/Chris Rock/Mike Myers/Will Ferrell
FFF05 Charles Bronson/Dwayne Johnson/Russell Crowe/Burt Reynolds
FFF06 Michelle Pfeiffer/Maggie Gyllenhaal/Charlize Theron/Jennifer Lawrence 12.00 30.00
FFF07 Adam Sandler/Chris Rock/David Spade/Shaquille O'Neal
FFF08 Bradley Cooper/Jennifer Lawrence/Matthew McConaughey/Kate Hudson
FFF09 Benicio Del Toro/Brad Pitt/Bradley Cooper/Matthew McConaughey
FFF10 Jack Black/Ben Stiller Seth Rogen/Jonah Hill 20.00 50.00

2020 Leaf Pop Century Metal Heartbreakers

HAD1 Angie Dickinson/25 15.00 40.00
HAS1 Alicia Silverstone/5
HCE1 Carmen Electra/10
HCK1 Camille Kostek/15
HCR1 Christina Ricci/24 75.00 150.00
HEB1 Elizabeth Berkley/15
HHT1 Heather Thomas/15
HJJ1 Jesse Jane/15 20.00 50.00
HKJ1 Kate Jackson/30 30.00 75.00
HLR1 Lisa Rinna/24
HMJ1 Michelle Johnson/15 12.00 30.00
HMR1 Meg Ryan/24 60.00 120.00
HND1 Nina Dobrev/25 30.00 75.00

2020 Leaf Pop Century Metal Hooray for Hollywood

STATED PRINT RUN 20 SER.#'d SETS
HFH01 Frank Sinatra/Dean Martin/Bing Crosby25.0060.00
HFH02 James Cagney/Charlton Heston/Danny Kaye 15.00 40.00
HFH03 Debbie Reynolds/Ginger Rogers/Yvonne De Carlo 5.00 12.00
HFH04 Jerry Lewis/Dean Martin/Frank Sinatra
HFH05 James Stewart/James Cagney/Charlton Heston 5.00 12.00
HFH06 Lon Chaney/Yvonne De Carlo/Cloris Leachman 30.00 75.00
HFH07 Robert Redford/Dennis Hopper/Dustin Hoffman

2020 Leaf Pop Century Metal Keeping It Real

COMMON AUTO 8.00 20.00
KIRDR1 Denise Richards/30 25.00 60.00
KIRLR1 Lisa Rinna/24 10.00 25.00
KIRMC1 Mark Cuban/50 50.00 100.00
KIRTC1 Tommy Chong/50 20.00 50.00

2020 Leaf Pop Century Metal Vinyl Signs

COMMON AUTO 8.00 20.00
VSDB1 Dale Bozzio/15 15.00 40.00
VSFJ1 Fat Joe/33 12.00 30.00
VSML1 Mike Love/24 20.00 50.00
VSSS1 Shawnee Smith/29 12.00 30.00

2008 Popcardz

COMPLETE SET (40) 5.00 12.00
UNOPENED BOX (24 PACKS) 50.00 75.00
UNOPENED PACK (5 CARDS) 2.00 3.00
COMMON CARD (1-40) .20 .50
*GOLD: 2.5X TO 6X BASIC CARDS
1 Jessica Biel .75 2.00
4 Scarlett Johansson 1.25 3.00
11 Chris Evans .75 2.00
15 Dwayne Johnson .75 2.00
16 Anton Yelchin 1.00 2.50
17 Jessica Alba 1.25 3.00
24 Megan Fox 1.25 3.00
33 Hayden Panettiere .75 2.00
38 Amanda Seyfried .75 2.00
39 Kristen Stewart 1.25 3.00

2008 Popcardz Memorabilia

COMPLETE SET (8) 60.00 120.00
COMMON CARD 5.00 12.00
SKIP-NUMBERED SET
STATED ODDS 1:5
1 Jessica Biel 10.00 25.00
17 Jessica Alba 15.00 40.00
18 Mandy Moore 8.00 20.00

1994 Card Creations Popeye

COMPLETE SET (100) 5.00 12.00
UNOPENED BOX (36 PACKS) 15.00 20.00
UNOPENED PACK (6 CARDS) .50 .75
COMMON CARD (1-100) .10 .25
CI1 RELEASED AS CASE-TOPPER
MI1 RELEASED AS WRAPPER REDEMPTION
CI1 Bruiserboy University/1929 (issued as case-topper) 8.00 20.00
MI1 The Champ MIO 6.00 15.00

1994 Card Creations Popeye Evolution Chrome

COMPLETE SET (8) 10.00 25.00
COMMON CARD (EC1-EC8) 2.00 5.00
STATED ODDS 1:36

1994 Card Creations Popeye Power Cels

COMPLETE SET (3) 50.00 100.00
COMMON CARD (1-3) 15.00 40.00
STATED ODDS 1:360

1994 Card Creations Popeye Promos

COMPLETE SET (4) 2.50 6.00
COMMON CARD 1.00 2.50

1996 Card Creations Popeye Premium

COMPLETE SET (99) 6.00 15.00
UNOPENED BOX (16 PACKS) 30.00 50.00
UNOPENED PACK (8 CARDS) 2.00 3.00
COMMON CARD (1-99) .12 .30

1996 Card Creations Popeye Premium Sericels

COMPLETE SET (8) 20.00 50.00
COMMON CARD (1-8) 4.00 10.00
STATED ODDS 1:16

1992-93 Portfolio

COMPLETE SET (108) 12.00 30.00
COMPLETE '92 INT SET (50) 8.00 20.00
COMPLETE '93 SERIES ONE SET (58) 6.00 15.00
UNOPENED '92 INT BOX (36 PACKS) 15.00 20.00
UNOPENED '92 INT PACK (8 CARDS) .50 .75
UNOPENED '93 SERIES ONE BOX (36 PACKS)12.00 15.00
UNOPENED '93 SERIES ONE PACK (8 CARDS).40 .50
COMMON CARD '92 INT (1-50) .30 .75
COMMON CARD '93 SERIES ONE (51-108) .25 .60

1992-93 Portfolio Autographs

KE Kelly Emberg AU/1000 6.00 15.00
SG Steffi Graf AU/100 15.00 40.00

1992-93 Portfolio Promos

COMMON CARD (1-5) .75 2.00
5 Guest Celebrity Steffi Graf 2.00 5.00
NNO 2-Card Panel (9 X 4) (1992)

2013 Portraits of Poe

COMPLETE SET (9) 2.50 6.00
COMMON CARD (1-9) .40 1.00

2013 Portraits of Poe Promo

1 Coming Fall of 2013 2.00 5.00

2019 Posty Fest

COMPLETE FACTORY SET (12) 20.00 50.00
COMPLETE BASE SET (10) 12.00 30.00
COMMON CARD (1-10) 2.00 5.00
TOPPS ONLINE EXCLUSIVE

2019 Posty Fest Collectibles

NNO Posty Patch	4.00	10.00
NNO Posty Pin	4.00	10.00

1995 Fleer Ultra Power Rangers The Movie

COMPLETE SET (150)	6.00	15.00
COMPLETE SET W/POP-UPS (174)	8.00	20.00
UNOPENED BOX (36 PACKS)	50.00	75.00
UNOPENED PACK (8 CARDS)	1.50	2.50
COMMON CARD (1-150)	.10	.25
*RETAIL: SAME VALUE	.10	.25

1995 Fleer Ultra Power Rangers The Movie Holograms

COMPLETE SET (12)	12.00	30.00
COMMON CARD (1-12)	1.50	4.00

1995 Fleer Ultra Power Rangers The Movie Power Pop-Ups

COMPLETE SET (24)	2.00	5.00
COMMON CARD (1-24)	.10	.25
INCLUDED WITH BASE SET		

1995 Fleer Ultra Power Rangers The Movie Zord Holofoil

COMPLETE SET (8)	25.00	60.00
COMMON CARD (1-8)	4.00	10.00

1994 Collect-a-Card Power Rangers The New Season

COMPLETE SET (72)	5.00	12.00
UNOPENED BOX (36 PACKS)	20.00	30.00
UNOPENED PACK (7 CARDS)	.75	1.00
COMMON CARD (1-72)	.12	.30
*FOIL: 1X TO 2.5X BASIC CARDS	.40	1.00
*RETAIL: SAME VALUE AS BASIC CARDS	.12	.30
*RET.FOIL: SAME VALUE AS FOIL CARDS	.40	1.00
*WALMART: ..30X TO .75X BASIC CARDS	.10	.25
D2 Tommy, the White Ranger	2.00	5.00

1994 Collect-a-Card Power Rangers The New Season Acetate Characters

COMPLETE SET (8)	15.00	40.00
COMMON CARD (CS1-CS8)	2.50	6.00
STATED ODDS 1:18		

1994 Collect-a-Card Power Rangers The New Season Bonus

COMPLETE SET (3)	1.25	3.00
COMMON CARD (1-3)	.50	1.25

1994 Collect-a-Card Power Rangers The New Season Foil Characters

COMPLETE SET (8)	3.00	8.00
COMMON CARD (AN1-AN8)	.50	1.25

1994 Collect-a-Card Power Rangers The New Season White Ranger

COMPLETE SET (8)	15.00	40.00
COMMON CARD (WR1-WR8)	3.00	8.00

1994 Power Rangers Series One

COMPLETE SET (72)	5.00	12.00
UNOPENED BOX (36 PACKS)	15.00	25.00
UNOPENED PACK (7 CARDS)	.75	1.00
COMMON CARD (1-72)	.12	.30
*WALMART: .2X TO .5X BASIC CARDS	.06	.15
*POWERFOIL: 3X TO 8X BASIC CARDS	1.00	2.50

1994 Power Rangers Series One Promos

COMPLETE SET (3)	2.00	5.00
COMMON CARD 1-3)	.75	2.00

1994 Power Rangers Series One Wal-Mart Power Foil

COMPLETE SET (12)	6.00	15.00
COMMON CARD (1-12)	.75	2.00

1994 Power Rangers Series Two

COMPLETE SET (73)	5.00	12.00
UNOPENED BOX (36 PACKS)	20.00	30.00
UNOPENED PACK (8 CARDS)	1.00	1.25
COMMON CARD (73-144)	.10	.25
*FOIL: .75X TO 2X BASIC CARDS	.20	.50
*RETAIL: SAME VALUE AS BASIC CARDS	.10	.25
*RAINBOW: .75X TO 2X BASIC CARDS	.20	.50
*WALMART: .30X TO .75X BASIC CARDS	.08	.20
*JUMBO: SAME VALUE AS BASIC CARDS	.10	.25
D1 Mighty Morphin Power Rangers CT	3.00	8.00

1994 Power Rangers Series Two Jumbo Power Foil

COMPLETE SET (12)	4.00	10.00
COMMON CARD (1-12)	.50	1.25
STATED ODDS 1:1 JUMBO		

1994 Power Rangers Series Two Magic Morphers

COMPLETE SET (12)	15.00	40.00
COMMON CARD (1-12)	2.00	5.00
STATED ODDS 1:18		

1994 Power Rangers Series Two Promos

COMPLETE SET (2)	1.50	4.00
COMMON CARD	1.00	2.50

2000 Powerpuff Girls

COMPLETE SET (72)	8.00	20.00
UNOPENED BOX (24 PACKS)	100.00	200.00
UNOPENED PACK (6 CARDS)	4.00	8.00
COMMON CARD (1-72)	.25	.60

2000 Powerpuff Girls Mojo Jojo Villain

COMPLETE SET (12)	1.50	4.00
COMMON CARD (P1-P12)	.20	.50
STATED ODDS 1:1		

2000 Powerpuff Girls Silver Foil

COMPLETE SET (12)	10.00	25.00
COMMON CARD (Pr1-Pr12)	1.25	3.00
*PINK: SAME VALUE		
STATED ODDS 1:4		

2001 Powerpuff Girls

COMPLETE SET (72)	8.00	20.00
UNOPENED BOX (24 PACKS)	15.00	25.00
UNOPENED PACK (6 CARDS)	1.00	1.25
COMMON CARD (1-72)	.25	.60
NNO Uncut Sheet		

2001 Powerpuff Girls Foil-Enhanced Villains

COMPLETE SET (12)	5.00	12.00
COMMON CARD (V1-V12)	.60	1.50
STATED ODDS 1:3		

2001 Powerpuff Girls Motion

COMPLETE SET (12)	3.00	8.00
COMMON CARD (M1-M12)	.40	1.00
STATED ODDS 1:1		

2001 Powerpuff Girls Promos

PPGS21 Promo Lenticular	.75	2.00
PPGS22 Promo	.75	2.00
PPGS23 Promo	.75	2.00
PPGS24 Promo	.75	2.00

2002 Powerpuff Girls Sneak Previews

COMPLETE SET (6)	4.00	10.00
COMMON CARD (SP1-SP6)	1.00	2.50
RANDOMLY INSERTED INTO PACKS		

2002 Powerpuff Girls

COMPLETE SET (72)	5.00	12.00
UNOPENED BOX (24 PACKS)	30.00	40.00
UNOPENED PACK (6 CARDS)	1.50	2.00
COMMON CARD (1-72)	.15	.40
NNO The Powerpuff Girls Ad Insert		

2002 Powerpuff Girls Prisms

COMPLETE SET (12)	10.00	25.00
COMMON CARD (PR1-PR12)	1.25	3.00
STATED ODDS 1:3		

2002 Powerpuff Girls Movie FilmCardz

COMPLETE SET (84)	4.00	10.00
UNOPENED BOX (24 PACKS)	15.00	25.00
UNOPENED PACK (6 CARDS)	1.25	1.50
COMMON CARD (1-84)	.10	.25

2002 Powerpuff Girls Movie FilmCardz Foil

COMPLETE SET (9)	8.00	20.00
COMMON CARD (Pr1-Pr9)	1.25	3.00
STATED ODDS 1:3		

2002 Powerpuff Girls Movie FilmCardz Rare

COMPLETE SET (6)	10.00	25.00
COMMON CARD (R1-R6)	2.00	5.00
STATED ODDS 1:18		

2002 Powerpuff Girls Movie FilmCardz Ultra-Rare

COMPLETE SET (3)	6.00	15.00
COMMON CARD (UR1-UR3)	2.50	6.00
STATED ODDS 1:24		

2002 Powerpuff Girls Movie FilmCardz Promos

P1 Thanks for the snack Professor	1.25	3.00
P2 What are you lookin' at	1.25	3.00
P3 Hobo Jojo	1.25	3.00

2016 Preacher

COMPLETE SET (50)	100.00	200.00
COMPLETE EP.1 SET (5)	8.00	20.00
COMPLETE EP.2 SET (5)	6.00	15.00
COMPLETE EP.3 SET (5)	6.00	15.00
COMPLETE EP.4 SET (5)	12.00	30.00
COMPLETE EP.5 SET (5)	12.00	30.00
COMPLETE EP.6 SET (5)	10.00	25.00
COMPLETE EP.7 SET (5)	8.00	20.00
COMPLETE EP.8 SET (5)	8.00	20.00
COMPLETE EP.9 SET (5)	12.00	30.00
COMPLETE EP.10 SET (5)	10.00	25.00
EP.1 (1-5) - MAY 23, 2016/362*	2.00	5.00
EP.2 (6-10) - JUNE 5, 2016/232*	1.50	4.00
EP.3 (11-15) - JUNE 12, 2016/184*	1.50	4.00
EP.4 (16-20) - JUNE 19, 2016/149*	3.00	8.00
EP.5 (21-25) - JUNE 26, 2016/162*	3.00	8.00
EP.6 (26-30) - JULY 3, 2016/166*	2.50	6.00
EP.7 (31-35) - JULY 10, 2016/170*	2.00	5.00
EP.8 (36-40) - JULY 17, 2016/167*	2.00	5.00
EP.9 (41-45) - JULY 24, 2016/151*	3.00	8.00
EP.10 (46-50) - JULY 31, 2016/181*	2.50	6.00
TOPPS.COM 24-HOUR EXCLUSIVE		
COINCIDED WITH SEASON 1 EPISODES		
OF THE AMC TV SERIES PREACHER		

2017 Preacher Season 2

COMPLETE SET (65)	225.00	450.00
COMPLETE EP.1 SET (5)	15.00	40.00
COMPLETE EP.2 SET (5)	15.00	40.00
COMPLETE EP.3 SET (5)	15.00	40.00
COMPLETE EP.4 SET (5)	15.00	40.00
COMPLETE EP.5 SET (5)	15.00	40.00
COMPLETE EP.6 SET (5)	15.00	40.00
COMPLETE EP.7 SET (5)	15.00	40.00
COMPLETE EP.8 SET (5)	15.00	40.00
COMPLETE EP.9 SET (5)	15.00	40.00
COMPLETE EP.10 SET (5)	15.00	40.00
COMPLETE EP.11 SET (5)	15.00	40.00
COMPLETE EP.12 SET (5)	15.00	40.00
COMPLETE EP.13 SET (6)	15.00	40.00
EP.1 (1-5) - JUNE 25, 2017/80*	5.00	12.00
EP.2 (6-10) - JUNE 26, 2017/71*	5.00	12.00
EP.3 (11-15) - JULY 3, 2017/82*	5.00	12.00
EP.4 (16-20) - JULY 10, 2017/75*	5.00	12.00
EP.5 (21-25) - JULY 18, 2017/72*	5.00	12.00
EP.6 (26-30) - JULY 24, 2017/79*	5.00	12.00
EP.7 (31-35) - JULY 31, 2017/65*	5.00	12.00
EP.8 (36-40) - AUGUST 7, 2017/70*	5.00	12.00
EP.9 (41-45) - AUGUST 14, 2017/72*	5.00	12.00
EP.10 (46-50) - AUGUST 21, 2017/63*	5.00	12.00
EP.11 (51-55) - AUGUST 28, 2017/54*	5.00	12.00
EP.12 (56-60) - SEPTEMBER 4, 2017/58*	5.00	12.00
EP.13 (61-66) - SEPTEMBER 11, 2017/66*	5.00	12.00

2017 Preacher Season 2 Relics

4A Jesse Custer's Black Trousers	30.00	75.00

2016 Preacher SDCC Promos

COMPLETE SET (3)	3.00	8.00
COMMON CARD (1-3)	1.50	4.00

1992 Enesco Precious Moments

COMPLETE SET (16)	3.00	8.00
COMMON CARD (1-16)	.40	1.00

1985 Kellogg's Prehistoric Animals and the Present 3-D

COMPLETE SET (8)	8.00	20.00
COMMON CARD (1-8)	1.50	4.00

1993 Ross Prehistoric Artifacts

COMPLETE SET (25)	8.00	20.00
COMMON CARD (1-25)	.50	1.25

2009 President Barack Obama The First 100 Days in Office

COMPLETE SET (50)	4.00	10.00
COMPLETE BOXED SET (51)	6.00	15.00
COMMON CARD (1-50)	.15	.40
NNO JUMBO DIE-CUT INSERTED AS BOX-TOPPER		
NNO Barack Obama Jumbo Die-Cut (Box-Topper)	1.00	2.50

2009 President Obama Inaugural

COMPLETE SET (90)	20.00	50.00
COMPLETE SET W/SP (93)	60.00	120.00
UNOPENED BOX (24 PACKS)	50.00	100.00
UNOPENED PACK (7 CARDS)	2.50	4.00
COMMON (1-93)	.15	.40
*SILVER: 2X TO 5X BASIC CARDS		
*GOLD: 4X TO 10X BASIC CARDS		
BK ALL STAR #44B ODDS 1:192 PACKS		
PRESIDENTIAL PUP ODDS 1:384 PACKS		
ONE POSTER PER BOX		
PUP EXCHANGE DEADLINE 1/20/2011		
44b Barack Obama All Star SP	20.00	40.00
NNO Barack Obama Poster	4.00	10.00
NNO Presidential Pup	20.00	40.00

2009 President Obama Inaugural Stickers

COMPLETE SET (18)	6.00	15.00
COMMON STICKER (1-18)	.60	1.50
*FOIL: .6X TO 1.5X BASIC STICKER		
STATED ODDS 1:1		

1994 Comic Images Previews Promos

COMPLETE SET (20)	6.00	15.00
COMMON CARD (D1-D20)	.60	1.50
NNO Frankenstein Hologram		

1995 Comic Images Prince Valiant

COMPLETE SET (90)	3.00	8.00
UNOPENED BOX (48 PACKS)	15.00	25.00
UNOPENED PACK (10 CARDS)	.75	1.00
COMMON CARD (1-90)	.08	.20
M1 Medallion Card/991*	10.00	25.00
PROMO Prince Valiant PROMO GEN	.75	2.00
6PAN 6-Card Panel Case Insert		

1995 Comic Images Prince Valiant 24k Gold Signatures

1 Hal Foster	20.00	50.00
2 Redemption Card		

1995 Comic Images Prince Valiant Chromium

COMPLETE SET (6)	12.00	30.00
COMMON CARD (C1-C6)	3.00	8.00
STATED ODDS 1:16		

1995 Comic Images Prince Valiant Hal Foster

COMPLETE SET (3)	12.00	30.00
COMMON CARD (1-3)	6.00	15.00
STATED ODDS 1:48		

1997 TCI Princess Diana Queen of Hearts

COMPLETE BOXED SET (50)	8.00	20.00
COMMON CARD (1-50)	.30	.75

1996 Upper Deck Princess Gwenevere and the Jewel Riders

COMPLETE SET (55)	4.00	10.00
UNOPENED BOX (36 PACKS)	25.00	40.00
UNOPENED PACK (8 CARDS)	1.25	1.50
COMMON CARD (1-55)	.15	.40

1996 Upper Deck Princess Gwenevere and the Jewel Riders Jewel Readers

COMPLETE SET (3)	1.00	2.50
COMMON CARD (JR1-JR3)	.40	1.00
STATED ODDS 1:3		

1996 Upper Deck Princess Gwenevere and the Jewel Riders Secrets

COMPLETE SET (15)	3.00	8.00
COMMON CARD (PS1-PS15)	.30	.75
STATED ODDS 1:1		

2018 The Prisoner 50th Anniversary

COMPLETE SET (36)	6.00	15.00
COMMON CARD (1-36)	.30	.75

2018 The Prisoner 50th Anniversary Autographs

COMMON AUTO	5.00	12.00
AA1 Annette Andre	15.00	40.00
CB1 Christopher Benjamin	6.00	15.00
CB2 Christopher Benjamin	6.00	15.00
CB3 Christopher Benjamin	8.00	20.00
DB1 Denise Buckley	10.00	25.00
DB2 Denise Buckley	10.00	25.00
DN1 Derren Nesbitt	10.00	25.00
DN2 Derren Nesbitt	15.00	40.00
FF1 Fenella Fielding	8.00	20.00
JL1 Justine Lord	10.00	25.00
JL2 Justine Lord CTE	12.00	30.00
JM1 Jane Merrow	25.00	60.00
JM2 Jane Merrow	30.00	75.00
JM3 Jane Merrow 3BOPI	25.00	60.00
NW1 Norma West	10.00	25.00
NW2 Norma West	12.00	30.00
NW3 Norma West	10.00	25.00
PW1 Peter Wyngarde CE	25.00	60.00
PW1 Tony Sloman	8.00	20.00
PW2 Peter Wyngarde CE	25.00	60.00
PW3 Peter Wyngarde CE	25.00	60.00

2002 The Prisoner Autograph Series Volume 1

COMPLETE SET (72)	6.00	15.00
UNOPENED BOX (36 PACKS)	45.00	60.00
UNOPENED PACK (6 CARDS)	2.00	2.50
COMMON CARD (1-72)	.15	.40
P1 Autograph Series Volume One PROMO	1.25	3.00

2002 The Prisoner Autograph Series Volume 1 Autographs

COMMON CARD (PA1-PA16)	6.00	15.00
STATED ODDS 1:24		
PA1 Patrick McGoohan as No 6 (scarce, redemption card)	175.00	250.00
PA2 Annette Andre is Monique	10.00	25.00
PA4 Peter Bowles is A	10.00	25.00
PA6 Mark Eden is No 100	10.00	25.00
PA11 Jane Merrow is No 24	10.00	25.00
PA15 Norma West is No 240	10.00	25.00

2002 The Prisoner Autograph Series Volume 1 Classic Dialogue Holofoil

COMPLETE SET (6)	12.00	30.00
COMMON CARD (PHF1-PHF6)	3.00	8.00
STATED ODDS 1:12		

2002 The Prisoner Autograph Series Volume 1 Costumes

PC2 Patrick McGoohan (dark red cape)		
PC3 Patrick McGoohan (red)		
PC1A Patrick McGoohan (orange cape)		
PC1B Patrick McGoohan (blue cape)/150*		
SDC1 Patrick McGoohan (blue cape - 2002 SDCC exclusive)	10.00	25.00

2002 The Prisoner Autograph Series Volume 1 Guardians of the Village Foil

COMPLETE SET (6)	10.00	25.00
COMMON CARD (PF1-PF6)	2.50	6.00
STATED ODDS 1:12		

2002 The Prisoner Autograph Series Volume 1 Silva Screen Promos

SSP1 (Leo McKern; bicycle in blue)	4.00	10.00
SSP2 (No 6 in jacket; bicycle in magenta)	4.00	10.00
SSP3 (Rover in your face; bicycle in grey)	4.00	10.00

2010 The Prisoner Collector Series Volume 2

COMPLETE SET (50)	5.00	12.00
UNOPENED BOX (24 PACKS)	60.00	75.00
UNOPENED PACK (6 CARDS)	2.00	3.00
COMMON CARD (1-50)	.20	.50
NNO1 Clayton McCormack Case-Topper Insert		

2010 The Prisoner Collector Series Volume 2 Autographs

COMMON CARD (PA1-PA6)	10.00	25.00
STATED ODDS 1:24		
PA1 Patrick McGoohan/75*	250.00	400.00

2010 The Prisoner Collector Series Volume 2 Promos

COMMON CARD (P1-P7)	1.25	3.00
P7 Village Bus	10.00	25.00

1989 Six of One The Prisoner Fan Club

COMPLETE SET (64)	20.00	50.00
COMMON CARD (1-64)	.50	1.25

1996 Cornerstone The Prisoner Promos

IT8 Inside Trader Club Exclusive	6.00	15.00
Promoa1 Gray-Blue Back (512 Area Code) ERR		
Promoa2 Gray-Blue Back (520 Area Code) COR		
Promoa3 Blue Back	.75	2.00
Promob1 512 Area Code ERR		
Promob2 520 Area Code COR		

1991 Lime Rock Pro Cheerleaders NBA

COMPLETE SET (44)	3.00	8.00
UNOPENED BOX (36 PACKS)	10.00	15.00
UNOPENED PACK (12 CARDS)	.50	.75
COMMON CARD (1-44)	.15	.40

1991 Lime Rock Pro Cheerleaders NBA Promos

COMPLETE SET (10)		
COMMON CARD		
13A Lisa Marie Byram (SCA logo)	1.00	2.50
13B Lisa Marie Byram (no SCA logo)	.75	2.00
13C Terri Derryberry (error name, with SCA logo)		
16 Felicia "Crickett" Harris		
17A Terri Derryberry (with SCA logo)	1.00	2.50
17B Terri Derryberry (no SCA logo)	.75	2.00
19A Cheryl M Washington (with SCA logo)	1.00	2.50
19B Cheryl M Washington (no SCA logo)	.75	2.00
22 Maryann Wenger (no SCA logo)	.75	2.00
26A Julie Carmichael (with SCA logo)	1.00	2.50
26B Julie Carmichael (no SCA logo)	.75	2.00

1992 Lime Rock Pro Football Cheerleaders

COMPLETE SET (160)	5.00	12.00
UNOPENED BOX (36 PACKS)	10.00	15.00
UNOPENED PACK (11 CARDS)	.75	1.00
COMMON CARD (42-197, CL's)	.06	.15

1992 Lime Rock Pro Football Cheerleaders Promos

COMMON NO LOGO	.75	2.00
COMMON LOGO	1.50	4.00

2011 Project Superpowers

COMPLETE SET (72)	6.00	15.00
COMPLETE FACTORY SET (81)	25.00	60.00
COMMON CARD (1-72)	.15	.40

2011 Project Superpowers Alex Ross Autographs

COMPLETE SET (2)	15.00	30.00
COMMON CARD	10.00	20.00
PSAAR1 Masquerade	8.00	20.00
PSAAR2 The Team Forms	8.00	20.00

2011 Project Superpowers Artist Puzzle

COMPLETE SET (9)	10.00	25.00
COMMON CARD (1-9)	1.50	4.00
INSERTED IN SDCC MYSTERY PACKS		

2011 Project Superpowers Chrome Inserts

COMPLETE SET (9)	5.00	12.00
COMMON CARD (1-9)	1.00	2.50
STATED ODDS 2:BOX		

2011 Project Superpowers Chrome Puzzle

COMPLETE SET (9)	4.00	10.00
COMMON CARD (1-9)	.75	2.00
STATED ODDS 2:BOX		

2011 Project Superpowers Fighting Yank's War Journal

COMPLETE SET (18)	8.00	20.00
COMMON CARD (1-18)	1.00	2.50
STATED ODDS 5:BOX		

2011 Project Superpowers Promos

P1 Devil	.75	2.00
AP1 Album Promo 1	3.00	8.00
AP2 Album Promo 2	3.00	8.00
NNO The Black Terror (Philly Non-Sports Show Exclusive)	.75	2.00
NNO Devil (SDCC Exclusive)	.75	2.00
NNO Miss Masque (foil) (SDCC Exclusive)	.75	2.00
NNO Black Terror/Masquerade (Non-Sport Update Exclusive)	1.25	3.00
NNO Foil (Sketchlife Exclusive)	1.25	3.00

1996 SkyBox Prophet Collection

COMPLETE SET (90)	4.00	10.00
UNOPENED BOX (24 PACKS)	30.00	40.00
UNOPENED PACK (6 CARDS)	1.25	1.75
COMMON CARD (1-90)	.10	.25

1996 SkyBox Prophet Collection Promos

COMMON CARD	.75	2.00

2013 Psych Seasons One Through Four

COMPLETE SET (68)	5.00	12.00
COMMON CARD (1-68)	.15	.40

2013 Psych Seasons One Through Four Autographs

COMPLETE SET (11)		
COMMON AUTO (A1-A12)	10.00	25.00
STATED ODDS 1:24		
A10 DOES NOT EXIST		
A1 James Roday	60.00	120.00
A2 Dule Hill	75.00	150.00
A3 Kirsten Nelson	15.00	40.00
A4 Corbin Bernsen	15.00	40.00
A5 Rachael Leigh Cook	50.00	100.00
A7 Ally Sheedy	20.00	50.00
A8 Robert Patrick	30.00	75.00
A9 George Takei	30.00	75.00
A11 Timothy Omundson	25.00	60.00
A12 Jaleel White	12.00	30.00

2013 Psych Seasons One Through Four Henry's Wisdom

COMPLETE SET (9)	6.00	15.00
COMMON CARD (HL1-HL9)	1.25	3.00
STATED ODDS 1:12		

2013 Psych Seasons One Through Four Psychic Moments

COMPLETE SET (9)	6.00	15.00
COMMON CARD (PM01-PM09)	1.25	3.00
STATED ODDS 1:12		

2013 Psych Seasons One through Four Undercover

COMPLETE SET (9)	6.00	15.00
COMMON CARD (UC1-UC9)	1.25	3.00
STATED ODDS 1:12		

2013 Psych Seasons One Through Four Wardrobes

COMPLETE SET (22)	200.00	400.00
COMMON CARD (M1-M22)	8.00	20.00
OVERALL MEMORABILIA ODDS 1:24		
M22 ISSUED AS ALBUM EXCLUSIVE		
M1 Shawn Spencer shirt	10.00	25.00
M3 Juliet O'Hara blouse	10.00	25.00
M7 Shawn Spencer blue plaid shirt	10.00	25.00
M9 Det. Juliet O'Hara blue blouse	10.00	25.00
M12 Det. Juliet O'Hara green sweater	10.00	25.00
M13 Shawn Spencer plaid blue shirt	10.00	25.00
M16 Det. Juliet O'Hara pink blouse	10.00	25.00
M20 Shawn Spencer grey shirt	10.00	25.00
M22 Juliet O'Hara blouse BE	10.00	25.00

2013 Psych Seasons One Through Four Dual Wardrobes

COMPLETE SET (5)	60.00	120.00
COMMON CARD (DM1-DM5)	10.00	25.00
OVERALL MEMORABILIA ODDS 1:24		
DM1 S. Spencer/J. O'Hara	12.00	30.00
DM2 S. Spencer/B. Guster	12.00	30.00

2015 Psych Seasons Five Through Eight

COMPLETE SET (90)	8.00	20.00
COMMON CARD (1-90)	.15	.40

2015 Psych Seasons Five Through Eight Autographs

COMPLETE SET (26)	400.00	800.00
COMMON AUTO	6.00	15.00
STATED ODDS 1:8		
AA Anthony Anderson	10.00	25.00
BZ Billy Zane	10.00	25.00
CB Corbin Bernsen	15.00	40.00
CS Curt Smith	25.00	60.00
DB Diedrich Bader	12.00	30.00
DH Dule Hill	30.00	75.00
FS French Stewart	8.00	20.00
JP Jason Priestley	15.00	40.00
JR James Roday	30.00	75.00
JS Jimmi Simpson	20.00	50.00
KF Kurt Fuller	15.00	40.00
KN Kirsten Nelson	10.00	25.00
LW Lesley Ann Warren	12.00	30.00
MM Malcolm McDowell	15.00	40.00
MP Mekhi Phifer	8.00	20.00
RM Ralph Macchio	20.00	50.00
SB Sage Brocklebank	10.00	25.00

VK Val Kilmer	30.00	75.00
VL Vanessa Lachey	30.00	75.00
DA1 James Roday	200.00	350.00
Dule Hill		
JSM Jean Smart	12.00	30.00

2015 Psych Seasons Five Through Eight Character Bios

COMPLETE SET (6)	12.00	30.00
COMMON CARD (C1-C6)	4.00	10.00
STATED ODDS 1:12		

2015 Psych Seasons Five Through Eight Psych The Musical

COMPLETE SET (6)	15.00	40.00
COMMON CARD (PM1-PM6)	5.00	12.00
STATED ODDS 1:24		

2015 Psych Seasons Five Through Eight Undercover

COMPLETE SET (9)	6.00	15.00
COMMON CARD (UC1-UC9)	1.25	3.00
STATED ODDS 1:24		

2003 Psychedelic Republicans

COMPLETE SET (24)	5.00	12.00
UNOPENED BOX (36 PACKS)	60.00	75.00
UNOPENED PACK (8 CARDS)	2.00	2.50
COMMON CARD (1-24)	.30	.75

1994 Vintage Animation Psycho Cards

COMPLETE SET (4)	2.50	6.00
COMMON CARD (1-4)	.75	2.00

1994 Cottage Cards Pterosaurs

COMPLETE SET (18)	4.00	10.00
COMMON CARD (1-18)	.30	.75

2000 Pukey-Mon

COMPLETE SET (69)	2.50	6.00
COMPLETE SET W/SP (116)	6.00	15.00
UNOPENED BOX (36 PACKS)	20.00	40.00
UNOPENED PACK (5 CARDS)	1.00	1.50
COMMON CARD (1-69)	.06	.15
COMMON "U" CARD (70-96)	.10	.25
U STATED ODDS 1:2		
COMMON "R" CARD (97-116)	.20	.50
R STATED ODDS 1:4		

2000 Pukey-Mon Gold Foil

COMPLETE SET (20)	12.00	30.00
COMMON CARD (W97-W116)	.75	2.00
STATED ODDS 1:18		

2000 Pukey-Mon Greek

COMPLETE SET (4)	1.25	3.00
COMMON CARD	.40	1.00
STATED ODDS 1:9		

2000 Pukey-Mon Holographic Foil

COMPLETE SET (20)	15.00	40.00
COMMON CARD (W97-W116)	1.25	3.00
STATED ODDS 1:37		

2000 Pukey-Mon Scratch 'n Sniff

COMPLETE SET (10)	3.00	8.00
COMMON CARD (SKIP #'d)	.40	1.00
STATED ODDS 1:9		

1996 Tempo Pumped Up Down Under

COMPLETE SET (100)	12.00	30.00
UNOPENED BOX (30 PACKS)		
UNOPENED PACK (CARDS)		
COMMON CARD (1-100)	.25	.60

2004 Quacky Cardz

COMPLETE SET (66)	4.00	10.00
UNOPENED BOX (24 PACKS)	20.00	30.00
UNOPENED PACK (5 CARDS)	1.00	1.25
COMMON CARD	.12	.30
NNO Be the Next Quacky Card		
NNO On Sale Here		
NNO Ben Dumped PROMO	1.25	3.00

1989 Kitchen Sink Press R. Crumb

COMPLETE SET (36)	5.00	12.00
COMMON CARD (1-36)	.25	.60
*2nd PRINTING: SAME VALUE		

1981 Topps Raiders of the Lost Ark

COMPLETE SET (88)	5.00	12.00
UNOPENED BOX (36 PACKS)	200.00	300.00
UNOPENED PACK (10 CARDS)	6.00	8.00
COMMON CARD (1-88)	.15	.40
*OPC: SAME VALUE		

1985 Topps Rambo II First Blood

COMPLETE SET (66)	5.00	12.00
COMPLETE SET W/STICKERS (88)	6.00	15.00
UNOPENED BOX (36 PACKS)	150.00	250.00
UNOPENED PACK (8 CARDS)	5.00	8.00
COMMON CARD (1-66)	.15	.40

1985 Topps Rambo II First Blood Stickers

COMPLETE SET (22)	2.50	6.00
COMMON CARD (1-22)	.20	.50
STATED ODDS 1:1		

2010 Rantz Angels

COMPLETE SET (51)	4.00	10.00
COMPLETE FACTORY SET (52)	12.00	30.00
COMMON CARD (1-50, COVER CARD)	.15	.40
NNO Nadia PROMO	1.25	3.00

1992 GNM Rapid Transit System

COMPLETE FACTORY SET (101)	6.00	15.00
COMMON CARD (1-100, CL)	.15	.40

1992 GNM Rapid Transit System Promos

COMPLETE SET (2)		
RTSP1 1969 Dodge Charger R/T/2500*	3.00	8.00
RTSP2 1970 Plymouth Superbird/2500*	3.00	8.00

1991 Collectible Imagery Rare and Endangered Species

COMPLETE SET (21)	5.00	12.00
COMMON CARD (1-21, CL)	.30	.75
P1 Giant Panda	6.00	15.00
P2 Woodland Caribou	6.00	15.00

1991 Collectible Imagery Rare and Endangered Species Promos

COMPLETE SET (4)	12.00	30.00
COMMON CARD	4.00	10.00

1993 Topps Ray Bradbury Comics

COMPLETE SET (15)	20.00	50.00
COMMON CARD	2.00	5.00

1995 Krome Razor Chromium

COMPLETE SET (90)	5.00	12.00
UNOPENED BOX (36 PACKS)	30.00	40.00
UNOPENED PACK (7 CARDS)	1.00	1.25
COMMON CARD (1-90)	.12	.30
NNO1 Razor, Everett Hartsoe AU/500*	20.00	50.00

1995 Krome Razor Chromium Character Subset Holochrome

COMPLETE SET (5)	15.00	40.00
COMMON CARD (C1-C5)	4.00	10.00
RANDOMLY INSERTED INTO PACKS		

1997 Krome Razor Mega Chromium

COMPLETE SET (36)	10.00	25.00
UNOPENED BOX (36 PACKS)	30.00	40.00
UNOPENED PACK (3 CARDS)	1.25	1.50
COMMON CARD (1-36)	.30	.75
*FRACTAL: .5X TO 1.2X BASIC CARDS		
NNO Jackhammer AU/1000*	25.00	60.00

1997 Krome Razor Mega Chromium Fractal

COMPLETE SET (36)		
*FRACTAL: .5X TO 1.2X BASIC CARDS		
STATED ODDS 1:6		

1997 Krome Razor Mega Chromium Previews

COMPLETE SET (7)	5.00	12.00
COMMON CARD	1.50	4.00

1996 Krome Razor Metal and Flesh

COMPLETE SET (90)	8.00	20.00
UNOPENED BOX (36 PACKS)	15.00	20.00
UNOPENED PACK (6 CARDS)	.75	1.00
COMMON CARD (1-90)	.15	.40

1996 Krome Razor Metal and Flesh Autographs

COMMON CARD	20.00	50.00
RANDOMLY INSERTED INTO PACKS		

1996 Krome Razor Metal and Flesh HoloChrome

COMPLETE SET (5)	10.00	25.00
COMMON CARD (1-5)	2.50	6.00
RANDOMLY INSERTED INTO PACKS		

1996 Krome Razor Metal and Flesh PhotoChrome

COMPLETE SET (2)	10.00	25.00
COMMON CARD (PC1-PC2)	6.00	15.00
RANDOMLY INSERTED INTO PACKS		

1996 Krome Razor Metal and Flesh Promos

Promo1 Tommi Gunn (fire background)	1.25	3.00
Promo2 Razor (purple background)	1.25	3.00
Promo3 Razor (moon background)	1.25	3.00
Promo4 Razor (wall background)		
Promo5 HoloChrome		
NNO1 Chromium 2UP Panel Preview		
NNO2 James O'Barr Runaway Promo (OS)		

2006 Razor Poker

COMPLETE SET (76)	10.00	25.00
COMMON CARD (1-76)	.25	.60

2006 Razor Poker Poker Paraphernalia Autographs

STATED ODDS 1:288		
CARD PP1 WAS NOT ISSUED		
PP2 Phil Hellmuth	30.00	80.00
PP3 Ted Forrest		
PP4 Phil Laak	20.00	50.00
PP5 Antonio Esfandiari		

2006 Razor Poker Showdown Signatures

COMMON CARD (A1-A38)	4.00	10.00
STATED ODDS 1:12		
A38 AVAILABLE THROUGH CASE PURCHASE ONLY		
A1 Daniel Negreanu	6.00	15.00
A8 Erick Lindgren SP	12.00	30.00
A11 Phil Hellmuth	8.00	20.00
A12 John Juanda SP	6.00	15.00
A14 Phil Laak	6.00	15.00
A17 Ted Forrest SP	6.00	15.00
A21 Michael Mizrachi SP	6.00	15.00
A25 Jerry Buss	25.00	60.00
A27 Jennifer Tilly	12.00	30.00
A28 Greg Raymer SP	6.00	15.00
A30 Joe Hachem SP	6.00	200.00
A36 Sammy Farha SP	10.00	25.00
A38 Cindy Margolis	15.00	40.00

2010 Razor Poker

COMMON CARD (1-43)	6.00	15.00
*GOLD/25: .5X TO 1.2X BASIC CARDS		
5 Cindy Margolis	10.00	25.00
6 Cyndy Violette	8.00	20.00
7 Daniel Negreanu	12.00	30.00
9 David Pham		
11 Erica Schoenberg	8.00	20.00
13 Evelyn Ng	8.00	20.00
17 Isabelle Mercier	8.00	20.00
21 Jennifer Harman	8.00	20.00
22 Jerry Buss	8.00	20.00
26 Lacey Jones UER	8.00	20.00
31 Mike Matusow	8.00	20.00
36 Phil Hellmuth	35.00	70.00
37 Scott Fischman		
42 Tom Dwan	10.00	25.00
43 Vanessa Rousso	12.00	30.00
SU1 Stu Ungar MEM	25.00	60.00

2010 Razor Poker Bracelet Winner Signatures

COMMON CARD (BH1-BH27)	6.00	15.00
UNPRICED PARALLEL PRINT RUN 1-10		
BH1 Doyle Brunson		
BH2 Greg Raymer		
BH3 Howard Lederer		
BH4 Johnny Chan		
BH5 Daniel Negreanu	12.00	30.00
BH8 Phil Hellmuth	12.00	30.00
BH12 Cyndy Violette	8.00	20.00
BH14 David Pham		
BH18 Jennifer Harman	8.00	20.00
BH23 Mike Matusow	8.00	20.00

2010 Razor Poker Dual Autographs

COMMON CARD	20.00	50.00
STATED PRINT RUN 50 SER. #'d SETS		
DS3 P.Hellmuth/D. Negreanu	30.00	80.00
DS6 E.Schoenberg/E.Ng	25.00	60.00
DS7 L.Jones/C.Margolis	25.00	60.00
DS8 C.Violette/I.Mercier	25.00	60.00
DS11 M.Matusow/P.Hellmuth		
DS15 J.Gold/C.Moneymaker	25.00	60.00
ELAE E.Lindgren/A.Esfandiari		
JADW J.Arieh/D.Williams		
MMTD M.Mizrachi/T.Dwan		
PATD P.Antonius/T.Dwan		

2010 Razor Poker Favorite Hands Autographs

COMMON CARD (FHS1-FHS49)	10.00	25.00
STATED PRINT RUN 10-50		
FHS5 Cindy Margolis	15.00	40.00
FHS6 Cyndy Violette	12.00	30.00
FHS7 Daniel Negreanu		
FHS9 David Pham		
FHS11 Doyle Brunson		
FHS12 Erica Schoenberg	12.00	30.00
FHS14 Evelyn Ng	12.00	30.00
FHS16 Greg Raymer		
FHS17 Howard Lederer		
FHS19 Humberto Brenes	12.00	30.00
FHS20 Isabelle Mercier	12.00	30.00
FHS24 Jennifer Harman	12.00	30.00
FHS25 Jerry Buss	12.00	30.00
FHS27 Johnny Chan		
FHS30 Lacey Jones	15.00	40.00
FHS37 Orel Hershiser		
FHS40 Phil Gordon	12.00	30.00
FHS41 Phil Hellmuth	50.00	100.00
FHS45 Shannon Elizabeth		
FHS48 Tom Dwan	25.00	60.00
FHS49 Vanessa Rousso	20.00	50.00

2010 Razor Poker Final Table Signatures

COMMON CARD (FTS1-FTS10)	20.00	40.00
STATED PRINT RUN 25 SER. #'d SETS		
FTS1 Chris Moneymaker		
FTS2 Daniel Negreanu	50.00	100.00
FTS7 Mike Matusow		
FTS8 Phil Hellmuth	60.00	120.00

2010 Razor Poker Las Vegas Summit Signatures Promos

COMMON CARD	5.00	12.00
SE Shannon Elizabeth	40.00	80.00

2010 Razor Poker Tournament Fabrics and Signatures

COMMON CARD 12.00 30.00
STATED PRINT RUN 99 SER. #'d SETS
CM Cindy Margolis 15.00 40.00
PH Phil Hellmuth 25.00 60.00

1995 Fleer Real Monsters

COMPLETE SET (90) 4.00 10.00
COMPLETE SET W/COLORING (100) 5.00 12.00
UNOPENED BOX (48 PACKS) 30.00 40.00
UNOPENED PACK (6 CARDS) 1.00 1.25
COMMON CARD (1-90) .08 .20
COMMON COLORING CARD (1-10) .10 .25

1995 Fleer Ultra Real Monsters

COMPLETE SET (90) 5.00 12.00
COMPLETE SET W/POP-UPS (114) 6.00 15.00
UNOPENED BOX (36 PACKS) 30.00 40.00
UNOPENED PACK (8 CARDS) 1.00 1.25
COMMON CARD (1-90) .10 .25
COMMON POP-UP CARD (PU1-PU24) .12 .30

1995 Fleer Ultra Real Monsters Holograms

COMPLETE SET (4) 6.00 15.00
COMMON CARD (1-4) 2.00 5.00
STATED ODDS 1:12 HOBBY PACKS

1995 Fleer Real Monsters Promo Panels

COMPLETE SET (3) 2.50 6.00
COMMON PANEL (UNNUMBERED) 1.25 3.00

1995 Fleer Ultra Reboot

COMPLETE SET (150) 6.00 15.00
UNOPENED HOBBY BOX (36 PACKS) 15.00 20.00
UNOPENED RETAIL BOX (100 PACKS) 10.00 15.00
UNOPENED RETAIL PACK (6 CARDS)
UNOPENED HOBBY PACK (8 CARDS)
COMMON CARD (1-150) .08 .20
*NON-ENHANCED BASE: .12X TO .30X BASIC CARDS

1995 Fleer Ultra Reboot Game Players Chromium

COMPLETE SET (10) 10.00 25.00
COMMON CARD (1-10) 1.25 3.00
STATED ODDS 1:6

1995 Fleer Ultra Reboot HoloBlast

COMPLETE SET (5) 8.00 20.00
COMMON CARD (1-5) 2.00 5.00
STATED ODDS 1:9

1995 Fleer Ultra Reboot Suspended Animation

COMPLETE SET (10) 6.00 15.00
COMMON CARD (1-10) .75 2.00
STATED ODDS 1:6

1995 Fleer Ultra Reboot UltraPrints

COMPLETE SET (5) 8.00 20.00
COMMON CARD 2.50 6.00
STATED ODDS 1:CASE
UNNUMBERED SET LISTED ALPHABETICALLY
OVERSIZED MEASURING 6 1/2 X 10 INCHES

1995 Fleer Ultra Reboot Promos

NNO Dot Patrol (Wizard) .75 2.00
NNO 9UP perforated (Preview) 1.50 4.00
NNO 9UP non-perforated (NSU) 1.50 4.00

2002 Red Dwarf Previews

COMPLETE SET (6) 5.00 12.00
COMMON CARD (PC1-PC6) 1.50 4.00

2002 Red Dwarf

COMPLETE SET (64) 5.00 12.00
UNOPENED BOX (24 PACKS) 65.00 80.00
UNOPENED PACK (6 CARDS) 3.00 4.00
COMMON CARD .15 .40
CC1 STATED ODDS ONE PER CASE
DC1 STATED PRINT RUN 50 SER. #'d SETS
GR1 STATED ODDS 1:1080
20 CREDIT BANKNOTE SER. #'D TO 250
CC1 Case Topper 12.00 30.00
DC1 Dealer Card
GR1 Gold Redemption Card
NNO XL 20 Credit Banknote

2002 Red Dwarf Autographs

COMMON AUTO 25.00 60.00
OVERALL AUTO/MEM ODDS 1:24
STATED PRINT RUN 250 SER.#'d SETS
3 Chloe Annett 30.00 75.00
4 Robert Llewellyn 30.00 75.00
AC1 Doug Naylor MEM ALB 30.00 80.00

2002 Red Dwarf Chloe Annett Photoshoot

COMPLETE SET (6) 5.00 12.00
COMMON CARD (CA1-CA6) 1.25 3.00
STATED ODDS 1:8

2002 Red Dwarf Chrome

COMPLETE SET (32) 10.00 25.00
COMMON CARD (C1-C32) .40 1.00
STATED ODDS 1:2

2002 Red Dwarf Memorabilia

COMPLETE SET (11) 200.00 400.00
COMPLETE SET W/VARIANTS (16) 300.00 600.00
COMMON CARD (MEM1-MEM11) 8.00 20.00
OVERALL AUTO/MEM ODDS 1:24
MEM4 Kryten Head and Ear/300 10.00 25.00
MEM5A Monster Lucky (Emohawk Feather)/100 10.00 25.00
MEM5B Monster Lucky (Gelf Mask)/100 10.00 25.00
MEM5C Monster Lucky (Psiren Skin)/100 10.00 25.00
MEM6 JMC 5 Credit Note/500 15.00 40.00
MEM7 Lister Cigarette Pack/135 15.00 40.00
MEM8 JMC 10 Credit Note/450 15.00 40.00
MEM9 Morris Dancer Monthly/135 25.00 60.00
MEM10A RD Lucky Dip (Red Dwarf Ship)/325 25.00 60.00
MEM10B RD Lucky Dip (Landing Bay Logo Panel)/325 25.00 60.00
MEM10C RD Lucky Dip (Set Plans Episode VI)/325 25.00 60.00
MEM10D RD Lucky Dip (Mr. Fibble)/325 25.00 60.00
MEM11 Gold Uniform/225 25.00 60.00

2002 Red Dwarf Smeg

COMPLETE SET (6) 4.00 10.00
COMMON CARD 1.00 2.50
STATED ODDS 1:8

2002 Red Dwarf Sylvain Despretz

COMPLETE SET (6) 5.00 12.00
COMMON CARD 1.25 3.00
STATED ODDS 1:8

2005 Red Sonja

COMPLETE SET (72) 6.00 15.00
UNOPENED BOX (36 PACKS) 60.00 75.00
UNOPENED PACK (7 CARDS) 2.00 2.50
COMMON CARD (1-72) .15 .40

2005 Red Sonja Autographs

COMMON CARD 6.00 15.00
STATED ODDS 1:18

2005 Red Sonja Fiery Glow-in-the-Dark

COMPLETE SET (6) 6.00 15.00
COMMON CARD (1-6) 1.25 3.00
STATED ODDS 1:18

2011 Red Sonja

COMPLETE SET (72) 4.00 10.00
UNOPENED BOX (36 PACKS) 65.00 80.00
UNOPENED PACK (7 CARDS)
COMMON CARD (1-72) .10 .25

2011 Red Sonja 3-D Lenticular

COMPLETE SET (15) 12.00 30.00
COMMON CARD (RS1-RS15) 1.50 4.00
STATED ODDS 4:BOX

2011 Red Sonja Autographs

COMMON CARD 5.00 12.00
STATED ODDS 1:2 BOXES

2011 Red Sonja Red Sonja vs. Thulsa Doom

COMPLETE SET (3) 4.00 10.00
COMMON CARD (RST1-RST3) 2.00 5.00
STATED ODDS 1:BOX

2011 Red Sonja Robert E. Howard Puzzle

COMPLETE SET (9) 8.00 20.00
COMMON CARD (RSP1-RSP9) 1.25 3.00
STATED ODDS 4:BOX

2011 Red Sonja Promos

COMMON CARD 1.50 4.00
NNO1 NSU 2.50 6.00
NNO2 Philly NS Card Show 2.50 6.00
Album1 Lounging 6.00 15.00
Album2 Battlefield w/axe 6.00 15.00
Rare Promo Sitting at table/100 15.00 40.00
Special Three views 2.50 6.00
PromoPFT Standing over coffin/50 30.00 80.00
PromoUK1 Sitting on wooden throne 5.00 12.00
PromoUK2 Wearing hood in snow 5.00 12.00
PuzzleA1 MegaCon 8.00 20.00
PuzzleA2 MegaCon 8.00 20.00
PuzzleB1 Pop Art Con 6.00 15.00
PuzzleB2 Pop Art Con 6.00 15.00

2009 Red Sonja 35th Anniversary Back to Basics

COMPLETE SET (72) 4.00 10.00
UNOPENED BOX (36 PACKS) 60.00 75.00
UNOPENED PACK (7 CARDS) 2.00 2.50
COMMON CARD (1-72) .12 .30
NNO1 Greg Hildebrandt Hand-Painted Dream insert
NNO2 Roy Thomas 2-Case Incentive AU

2009 Red Sonja 35th Anniversary Back to Basics Foil Puzzle

COMPLETE SET (9) 10.00 25.00
COMMON CARD (UNNUMBERED SET) 2.00 5.00
STATED ODDS 1:7

2009 Red Sonja 35th Anniversary Back to Basics Holographic Foil

COMPLETE SET (9) 10.00 25.00
COMMON CARD (1-9) 2.00 5.00
STATED ODDS 1:7

1991 Tuff Stuff Remember Pearl Harbor

COMPLETE SET (50) 3.00 8.00
COMMON CARD (1-50) .10 .30
NNO Uncut Sheet PROMO

1995 Dynamic Marketing The Ren and Stimpy Show

COMPLETE SET (110) 8.00 20.00
UNOPENED BOX (48 PACKS) 40.00 50.00
UNOPENED PACK (7 CARDS) 1.00 1.25
COMMON CARD (1-110) .15 .40
NNO Ren and Stimpy 6-card promo sheet (general distribution) 2.00 5.00

1995 Dynamic Marketing The Ren and Stimpy Show International Eediots Chrome Foild Postcards

COMPLETE SET (18) 10.00 25.00
COMMON CARD (E1-E18) .75 2.00
RANDOMLY INSERTED INTO PACKS

1995 Dynamic Marketing The Ren and Stimpy Show Kitty Glitter

COMPLETE SET (5) 12.00 30.00
COMMON CARD (K1-K5) 3.00 8.00
RANDOMLY INSERTED INTO PACKS

1992 Kitchen Sink Press Republicans Attack

COMPLETE BOXED SET (36) 5.00 12.00
COMMON CARD (1-36) .25 .60

1998 JPP Amada Resident Evil

COMPLETE SET (90) 8.00 20.00
UNOPENED BOX (24 PACKS) 40.00 50.00
UNOPENED PACK (6 CARDS) 2.00 2.25
COMMON CARD .20 .50
SP1 Jim Lee AU

1998 JPP Amada Resident Evil Holochrome Refractors

COMPLETE SET (9) 6.00 15.00
COMMON CARD (S1-S9) 1.00 2.50
STATED ODDS 1:3

1998 JPP Amada Resident Evil Motions

COMPLETE SET (3) 12.00 30.00
COMMON CARD (M1-M3) 6.00 15.00
RANDOMLY INSERTED INTO PACKS

1998 JPP Amada Resident Evil Promos

COMMON CARD .75 2.00
P2 Promo

1994 Cardz Return of the Flintstones

COMPLETE SET (60) 5.00 12.00
UNOPENED BOX (36 PACKS) 15.00 25.00
UNOPENED PACK (8 CARDS) .50 .75
COMMON CARD (1-50) .12 .30
COMMON POP-UP (51-60) .20 .50

1994 Cardz Return of the Flintstones TekChromes

COMPLETE SET (3) 8.00 20.00
COMMON CARD (T1-T3) 3.00 8.00
STATED ODDS 1:18

1994 Cardz Return of the Flintstones Promos

1 3-Up Panel - TekChrome 8.00 20.00
P1 Promo 1 .75 2.00
P2 Promo 2 .75 2.00

1985 Topps Return to Oz

COMPLETE SET (44) 6.00 15.00
UNOPENED BOX (36 PACKS) 75.00 125.00
UNOPENED PACK (6 CARDS) 2.50 4.00
COMMON CARD (1-44) .25 .60

2013 Revenge Season One

COMPLETE SET (108) 6.00 15.00
UNOPENED BOX (24 PACKS) 55.00 70.00
UNOPENED PACK (5 CARDS) 2.50 3.00
COMMON CARD (1-108) .20 .50

2013 Revenge Season One Autographs

COMPLETE SET (14) 200.00 400.00
COMMON CARD (A1-A14) 6.00 15.00
OVERALL AUTO/MEM ODDS ONE PER BOX
A1 Nick Wechsler 20.00 50.00
A2 Ashley Madekwe 30.00 60.00
A3 Christa Allen 30.00 60.00
A7 James Morrison 10.00 25.00
A9 Margarita Levieva 20.00 50.00
A10 Amber Valletta 15.00 40.00
A12 Merrin Dungey 8.00 20.00
A13 Veronica Cartwright 8.00 20.00

2013 Revenge Season One Behind-the-Scenes

COMPLETE SET (9) 6.00 15.00
COMMON CARD (BS1-BS9) 1.25 3.00
OVERALL CHASE ODDS 1:12

2013 Revenge Season One Flashback

COMPLETE SET (9) 6.00 15.00
COMMON CARD (FB1-FB9) 1.25 3.00
OVERALL CHASE ODDS 2:24

2013 Revenge Season One Wardrobes

COMPLETE SET (13) 120.00 250.00
COMMON CARD (M1-M13) 5.00 12.00
OVERALL AUTO/MEM ODDS ONE PER BOX
M2 Emily Thorne 12.00 30.00
M4 Ashley Davenport 8.00 20.00
M5 Nolan Ross 6.00 15.00
M6 Charlotte Grayson 10.00 25.00
M7 Amanda Clarke 10.00 25.00
M9 Victoria Grayson 12.00 30.00
M12 Emily Thorne 15.00 40.00
M13 Victoria Grayson 10.00 25.00

2017 Fright-Rags Re-Animator

COMPLETE SET (60) 15.00 40.00
UNOPENED BOX/75
UNOPENED FACTORY BOX/200
UNOPENED PACK/600
COMMON CARD (1-60) .30 .75
*PARALLEL: 2.5X TO 6X BASIC CARDS 2.00 5.00
BARBARA CRAMPTON AUTOS
LIMITED TO 200
NNO Barbara Crampton/200* 25.00 60.00

2017 Fright-Rags Re-Animator Behind-the-Scenes

COMPLETE SET (9) 6.00 15.00
COMMON CARD (UNNUMBERED) 1.00 2.50

2017 Fright-Rags Re-Animator Characters

COMPLETE SET (8) 8.00 20.00
COMMON CARD (UNNUMBERED) 1.25 3.00

2017 Fright-Rags Re-Animator Stickers

COMPLETE SET (9) 10.00 25.00
COMMON CARD (UNNUMBERED) 1.50 4.00

1993 Imagine Rhonda Keeps You Up All Nite

COMPLETE FACTORY SET (60) 4.00 10.00
COMMON CARD (1-60) .12 .30

1993 Imagine Rhonda Keeps You Up All Nite Promos

COMPLETE SET (4) 2.50 6.00
COMMON CARD .75 2.00

1993 Comic Images Richard Corben

COMPLETE SET (90) 8.00 10.00
UNOPENED BOX (48 PACKS) 20.00 30.00
UNOPENED PACK (10 CARDS) .75 1.00
COMMON CARD (1-90) .10 .25
NNO Richard Corben PROMO .75 2.00

1993 Comic Images Richard Corben Prisms

COMPLETE SET (6) 6.00 15.00
COMMON CARD (1-6) 2.00 5.00
STATED ODDS 1:16

1994 FPG Richard Hescox

COMPLETE SET (90) 6.00 15.00
UNOPENED BOX (36 PACKS) 30.00 45.00
UNOPENED PACK (10 CARDS) 1.00 1.25
COMMON CARD (1-90) .12 .30

1994 FPG Richard Hescox Metallic Storm

COMPLETE SET (5) 10.00 25.00
COMMON CARD (MS1-MS5) 3.00 8.00
RANDOMLY INSERTED INTO PACKS

1994 FPG Richard Hescox Promos

COMMON CARD .75 2.00
NNO (title card) 4.00 10.00
(Never-released Dealer Incentive)

2018 Rick and Morty Season 1

COMPLETE SET (45) 8.00 20.00
UNOPENED BOX (24 PACKS) 120.00 200.00
UNOPENED PACK (5 CARDS) 5.00 8.00
COMMON CARD (1-45) .30 .75
*SILVER FOIL: .75X TO 2X BASIC CARDS .60 1.50
*LASER GUN DECO: 2.5X TO 6X BASIC CARDS1.50 4.00

2018 Rick and Morty Season 1 Album Exclusive Stickers

COMPLETE SET (3)
COMMON CARD (BK1-BK3)
ALBUM EXCLUSIVE
BK1 Spaceship
BK2 Meeseeks Box
BK3 Mr. Meeseeks

2018 Rick and Morty Season 1 Anatomy Park

COMPLETE SET (18) 10.00 25.00
COMMON CARD (AP1-AP18) 1.25 3.00
STATED ODDS 1:3

2018 Rick and Morty Season 1 Autographs

COMMON AUTO 12.00 30.00
STATED ODDS 1:48
JHD Jess Harnell/100 15.00 40.00
JHR Jess Harnell/100 15.00 40.00
JRK Justin Roiland/50 250.00 400.00
JRM Justin Roiland/50 300.00 500.00
JRR Justin Roiland/50 250.00 400.00
JRX Justin Roiland/10
KWC Kari Wahlgren/50 15.00 40.00
KWJ Kari Wahlgren/50 30.00 75.00
KWP Kari Wahlgren/50 15.00 40.00
KWS Kari Wahlgren/50 15.00 40.00
MLA Maurice LaMarche/100 CON 25.00 60.00
MLB Maurice LaMarche/50 25.00 60.00
MLC Maurice LaMarche/50 25.00 60.00
PHM Phil Hendrie/100 15.00 40.00
RPC Rob Paulsen/100 20.00 50.00
RPG Rob Paulsen/100 15.00 40.00
RPR Rob Paulsen/100 15.00 40.00
RPS Rob Paulsen/100 20.00 50.00
RRB Ryan Ridley/50 15.00 40.00
RRT Ryan Ridley/50 50.00 100.00
TKC Tom Kenny/50 50.00 100.00
TKF Tom Kenny/50 120.00 200.00
TKM Tom Kenny/50 120.00 200.00
TKP Tom Kenny/50 15.00 40.00
TKS Tom Kenny/50 150.00 300.00
TKZ Tom Kenny/50 SDCC 30.00 75.00
CPAC Chris Parnell/100 100.00 200.00
CPJS Chris Parnell/100 60.00 120.00
JHRR Jess Harnell/100 15.00 40.00
JHRR Jess Harnell/100 CON
KWGJ Kari Wahlgren/50 25.00 60.00
KWHW Kari Wahlgren/50 50.00 100.00
KWTD Kari Wahlgren/50 30.00 75.00
RRFP Ryan Ridley/50 20.00 50.00
RRGL Ryan Ridley/50 30.00 75.00
RRTM Ryan Ridley/50 CON 15.00 40.00

2018 Rick and Morty Season 1 Characters

COMPLETE SET W/CE (10) 12.00 30.00
COMPLETE SET W/O CE (9) 8.00 20.00
COMMON CARD (CB1-CB10) 1.50 4.00
STATED ODDS 1:6
CB10 IS A CONVENTION EXCLUSIVE
CB10 Snuffles CON 5.00 12.00

2018 Rick and Morty Season 1 Rixty Minutes

COMPLETE SET W/CE (10) 15.00 40.00
COMPLETE SET W/O CE (9) 10.00 25.00
COMMON CARD (RM1-RM10) 2.00 5.00
STATED ODDS 1:6
RM10 IS A CONVENTION EXCLUSIVE
RM10 Corns of Action CON 5.00 12.00

2018 Rick and Morty Season 1 Scratch and Sniff

COMPLETE SET W/EXCL. (10) 25.00 60.00
COMPLETE SET W/O EXCL. (7) 8.00 20.00
COMMON CARD (SS1-SS10) 2.00 5.00
STATED ODDS 1:12
SS8-SS9 ARE RETAIL EXCLUSIVES
SS10 IS A CONVENTION EXCLUSIVE
SS8 Eat Your Big Meat RET 10.00 25.00
SS9 Ass World RET 6.00 15.00
SS10 Hot Dog CON 5.00 12.00

2018 Rick and Morty Season 1 Standees

COMPLETE SET W/ SE (12) 30.00 75.00
COMPLETE SET W/O SE (6) 15.00 40.00
COMMON STANDEE (E1-E9) 4.00 10.00
COMMON STANDEE (E10-E12)
STATED ODDS 1:12
E7-E9 ARE RETAIL EXCLUSIVES
E10-E12 ARE CONVENTION EXCLUSIVES
E10 Rick CON 5.00 12.00
E11 Morty CON 5.00 12.00
E12 Summer CON 5.00 12.00

2018 Rick and Morty Season 1 Stickers

COMPLETE SET W/RE (6) 12.00 30.00
COMPLETE SET W/O RE (3) 5.00 12.00
COMMON STICKER (K1-K6) 2.50 6.00
STATED ODDS 1:12
K4-K6 ARE RETAIL EXCLUSIVES
K4 Anatomy Park RET 3.00 8.00
K5 Rick's Gym RET 3.00 8.00
K6 Gwendolyn RET 3.00 8.00

2018 Rick and Morty Season 1 Temporary Tattoos

COMPLETE SET W/TE (12) 30.00 75.00
COMPLETE SET W/O TE (7) 12.00 30.00
COMMON TATTOO (T1-T9) 3.00 8.00
COMMON TATTOO (T10-T12) 5.00 12.00
STATED ODDS 1:12
T8-T9 ARE RETAIL EXCLUSIVES
T10-T12 ARE CONVENTION EXCLUSIVES
T8 Rick and Morty Spaceship RET 3.00 8.00
T9 Rick and Morty Rorschach Test RET 4.00 10.00
T10 Scary Terry CON 5.00 12.00
T11 Skull with Rick and Morty Eyeballs CON 5.00 12.00
T12 Rick and Morty in Black Rectangle CON 5.00 12.00

2018 Rick and Morty Season 1 Promos

COMPLETE SET (8) 10.00 75.00
COMMON CARD (P1-P8) 4.00 10.00
P1 Philly Non-Sports Card Show 10.00 25.00
P2 Non-Sport Update Magazine 6.00 15.00
P4 Non-Sport Update Magazine 8.00 20.00
P5 Non-Sport Update Magazine 6.00 15.00
P6 Non-Sport Update Magazine 8.00 20.00
P7 Philly Non-Sports Card Show 6.00 15.00
P8 San Diego Comic Con 10.00 25.00

2019 Rick and Morty Season 2

COMPLETE SET (45) 6.00 15.00
UNOPENED BOX (24 PACKS) 200.00 300.00
UNOPENED PACK (5 CARDS) 8.00 12.00
COMMON CARD (1-45) .25 .60
*SILVER FOIL: 1X TO 2.5X BASIC CARDS
*PLUMBUS DECO FOIL: 2X TO 5X BASIC CARDS

2019 Rick and Morty Season 2 Autographs

COMMON AUTO 8.00 20.00
STATED ODDS 1:24
ATC Alan Tudyk/300 20.00 50.00
JHS Jess Harnell/50 15.00 40.00
JRC Justin Roiland/25 300.00 600.00
MLA Maurice LaMarche/25 20.00 50.00
MLR Maurice LaMarche/25 50.00 100.00
SCG Scott Chernoff 10.00 25.00
SCX Sarah Chalke/100 50.00 100.00
TKH Tom Kenny/50 30.00 75.00
TKP Tom Kenny/50 30.00 75.00
TKT Tom Kenny/50 30.00 75.00
TSD Tara Strong/150 15.00 40.00
TST Tara Strong/200 15.00 40.00
CPAJ Chris Parnell/25 75.00 150.00
CPGJ Chris Parnell/25 75.00 150.00
CPHJ Chris Parnell/25 75.00 150.00
CPOJ Chris Parnell/25 75.00 150.00
CPSH Chris Parnell/25 75.00 150.00
CPTT Chris Parnell/25 75.00 150.00
CPWJ Chris Parnell/25 75.00 150.00
CSTG Cassie Steele 20.00 50.00
GCAD Gary Cole 12.00 30.00
JREM Justin Roiland/25 300.00 600.00
JRMR Justin Roiland/25 300.00 600.00
KDRG Keith David 12.00 30.00
KDTP Keith David 12.00 30.00
KMRF Kevin Michael Richardson/200 12.00 30.00
KMRH Kevin Michael Richardson/100 12.00 30.00
KWJ2 Kari Wahlgren/50 25.00 60.00
KWRW Kari Wahlgren/50 30.00 75.00
MLMG Maurice LaMarche/25 30.00 75.00
MLMP Maurice LaMarche/50 15.00 40.00
MLND Maurice LaMarche/25 30.00 75.00
RRCN Ryan Ridley/50 30.00 75.00
RRHV Ryan Ridley/25 30.00 75.00
RRLK Ryan Ridley/50 25.00 60.00
RRRD Ryan Ridley/25 30.00 75.00
RRTA Ryan Ridley/50 25.00 60.00
SCBS Sarah Chalke/100 50.00 100.00
SCGB Sarah Chalke/50 50.00 100.00
SCPB Sarah Chalke/100 50.00 100.00
SGSS Spencer Grammer/300 30.00 75.00
TKAI Tom Kenny/50 30.00 75.00
TKGN Tom Kenny/50 30.00 75.00
TKNL Tom Kenny/50 30.00 75.00
TKPO Tom Kenny/50 30.00 75.00
TKWB Tom Kenny/50 30.00 75.00
TMRM Tress MacNeille 10.00 25.00
CPJS2 Chris Parnell/25 75.00 150.00
GAWBA Gary Anthony Williams/250 12.00 30.00
KMRMR Kevin Michael Richardson/200 10.00 25.00

2019 Rick and Morty Season 2 Beth Knows Best

COMPLETE SET (9) 5.00 12.00
COMMON CARD (BKB1-BKB9) 1.00 2.50
STATED ODDS 1:6

2019 Rick and Morty Season 2 Characters

COMPLETE SET (12) 6.00 15.00
COMMON CARD (C1-C12) 1.00 2.50
STATED ODDS 1:3

2019 Rick and Morty Season 2 Crimes of Rick Sanchez

COMPLETE SET (12) 8.00 20.00
COMMON CARD (CRS1-CRS12) 1.25 3.00
STATED ODDS 1:6

2019 Rick and Morty Season 2 Face the Music

COMPLETE SET (9) 6.00 15.00
COMMON CARD (M1-M9) 1.25 3.00
STATED ODDS 1:3

2019 Rick and Morty Season 2 Interdimensional Cable II

COMPLETE SET (12) 6.00 15.00
COMMON CARD (IDC1-IDC12) 1.00 2.50
STATED ODDS 1:3

2019 Rick and Morty Season 2 Metallic

COMPLETE SET (9) 75.00 150.00
COMMON CARD (M1-M9) 10.00 25.00
CONVENTION EXCLUSIVE

2019 Rick and Morty Season 2 Stickers

COMPLETE SET (15) 6.00 15.00
COMMON STICKER (S1-S15) .75 2.00
STATED ODDS 1:3

MODERN

2019 Rick and Morty Season 2 STR PWR

COMPLETE SET (9) 75.00 150.00
COMMON CARD (SP1-SP9) 10.00 25.00
*BLUE: .5X TO 1.2X BASIC CARDS
*GOLD/25: 1.5X TO 4X BASIC CARDS
STATED ODDS 1:144

2019 Rick and Morty Season 2 Totally Fabricated Fake Memorabilia

COMMON MEM 5.00 12.00
STATED ODDS 1:60
B1 Toy Antennae ALB 8.00 20.00
CE1 Rick's Bloody Lab Coat/100 LACC 30.00 75.00
TF1 Squanchy's Fur 12.00 30.00
TF2 Dinglebop 8.00 20.00
TF6 Plushy Beth 8.00 20.00
TF7 Yummy Yums Wrapper 6.00 15.00
TF8 Morty's Tribal Mask 15.00 40.00
TF9 Rick's Sombrero 10.00 25.00
TF12 Fart's Golden Poop 6.00 15.00
TF14 Roy's Carpet 6.00 15.00
TF15 Tammy's Wedding Ring 6.00 15.00
TF16 Zeep's Alien Costume 10.00 25.00
TF17 Eyeholes 10.00 25.00

2019 Rick and Morty Season 2 Promos

COMPLETE SET (8)
COMMON CARD (P1-P8)
P1 New York Comic-Con 2018 2.00 5.00
P2 Philly Non-Sports Card Show 2.50 6.00
P3 Box Break Promotion at Philly Show 3.00 8.00
P4 Non-Sport Update Magazine OCT/NOV 185.00 12.00
P5 Non-Sport Update Magazine OCT/NOV 185.00 10.00
P6 Non-Sport Update Magazine OCT/NOV 185.00 10.00
P7 GTS National Hobby Shop Day 2.00 5.00
P8 Emerald City Comic Con 2019 6.00 15.00

2019 Rick and Morty Season 3 Autographs

UNOPENED PACK (4 CARDS)
COMMON AUTO 8.00 20.00
STATED ODDS 1:1
EACH UNOPENED PACK CONTAINS
1 AUTO & 3 SKETCH CARDS
MBJ Melique Berger/105 15.00 40.00
MLC Maurice LaMarche/50 15.00 40.00
MLW Maurice LaMarche/50 15.00 40.00
RRA Ryan Ridley/50 15.00 40.00
TKC Tom Kenny/50 15.00 40.00
TSS Tara Strong/160 12.00 30.00
CPCJ Chris Parnell/25 60.00 120.00
JRPR Justin Roiland/25 600.00 1200.00
KWDS Kari Wahlgren/50 15.00 40.00
KWJ3 Kari Wahlgren/50 15.00 40.00
MBFK Melique Berger/55 15.00 40.00
MLFP Maurice LaMarche/40 15.00 40.00
MLGL Maurice LaMarche/50 15.00 40.00
RRAW Ryan Ridley/50 15.00 40.00
RRCA Ryan Ridley/50 15.00 40.00
RRSO Ryan Ridley/50 15.00 40.00
SCCB Sarah Chalke/50 30.00 75.00
SCYB Sarah Chalke/50 30.00 75.00
SGCS Spencer Grammer/105 20.00 50.00
TKGN Tom Kenny/25 25.00 60.00
TKMA Tom Kenny/50 15.00 40.00
TKS1 Tom Kenny/25 25.00 60.00
TKSA Tom Kenny/25 25.00 60.00
TKSB Tom Kenny/50 15.00 40.00
CPJS3 Chris Parnell/25 60.00 120.00
MBMRS Melique Berger/105 12.00 30.00
SCBS2 Sarah Chalke/50 30.00 75.00
SGSS2 Spencer Grammer/105 20.00 50.00
TKTG3 Tom Kenny/25 25.00 60.00
TSPMG Tara Strong/120 15.00 40.00

2019 Rick and Morty Season 3 Promos

COMMON CARD (P1-P9) 2.50 6.00
P1 Morty Fighting 4.00 10.00
(SDCC Exclusive)
P2 Pickle Rick 4.00 10.00
(Non-Sport Update Exclusive)
P3 Jerry Meditating 5.00 12.00
(Non-Sport Update Exclusive)
P7 Rick with Agent 4.00 10.00
(LA Comic Con Exclusive)
P8 Rick with Vindicators 3.00 8.00
(Philly Non-Sports Card Show Exclusive)
P9 Rick with Guitar 3.00 8.00
(National Hobby Shop Day Exclusive)

1999 Upper Deck Ricky Martin

COMPLETE SET (90) 8.00 20.00
UNOPENED BOX (24 PACKS) 25.00 40.00
UNOPENED PACK (6 CARDS) 1.25 2.00
COMMON CARD (1-90) .20 .50
*GOLD SCRIPT/500: 4X TO 10X BASIC CARDS2.00 5.00
*PLATINUM/100: 6X TO 15X BASIC CARDS 3.00 8.00
NNO Ricky Super Script Card

1993 Rocky Mountain Knife Works Riders of the Silver Screen

COMPLETE SET (300) 15.00 40.00
COMMON CARD (1-300) .12 .30

1993 Rocky Mountain Knife Works Riders of the Silver Screen Promos

COMPLETE SET (4) 3.00 8.00
COMMON CARD 1.25 3.00

1994 Kitchen Sink Press R.I.P. Real Monsters Demons and Ghosts

COMPLETE BOXED SET (42) 6.00 15.00
COMMON CARD (1-42) .30 .75

1992 Eclipse Rise and Fall of the Soviet Union

COMPLETE BOXED SET (36) 4.00 10.00
COMMON CARD (1-36) .15 .40

2012 RMS Titanic 1912-2012 Commemorative

COMPLETE SET (27) 5.00 12.00
COMMON CARD (1-27) .30 .75
*RETAIL: SAME VALUE
NNO1 Hobby Canvas Case-Topper Insert
NNO2 Retail Canvas Case-Topper Insert
NNO3 Largest Steamer in the World

2012 RMS Titanic 1912-2012 Commemorative 3-Card Chase

COMPLETE SET (3) 4.00 10.00
COMMON CARD (TP1-TP3) 2.00 5.00

2012 RMS Titanic 1912-2012 Commemorative Canvas Retail

COMPLETE SET (9) 15.00 40.00
COMMON CARD 2.50 6.00

2012 RMS Titanic 1912-2012 Commemorative Promos

COMMON CARD 1.25 3.00
Test This Mock Up Sample Card

1992 GNM Road Warriors Past and Present

COMPLETE FACTORY SET (50) 8.00 20.00
COMMON CARD (1-50) .30 .75

1992 GNM Road Warriors Past and Present Promos

S1 Chevrolet Impala 2.00 5.00
S3 Dodge Viper 2.00 5.00

1996 FPG Robh Ruppel

COMPLETE SET (90) 4.00 10.00
UNOPENED BOX (36 PACKS) 15.00 20.00
UNOPENED PACK (10 CARDS) .50 .75
COMMON CARD (1-90) .10 .25
NNO1 Robh Ruppel AU/1000* 20.00 50.00
NNO2 Medallion Card

1996 FPG Robh Ruppel Metallic

COMPLETE SET (5) 12.00 30.00
COMMON CARD (M1-M5) 3.00 8.00
STATED ODDS 1:12

1991 Topps Robin Hood Prince of Thieves Test Series

COMPLETE SET (88) 5.00 12.00
COMPLETE SET W/STICKERS (97) 6.00 15.00
UNOPENED BOX (36 PACKS)
UNOPENED PACK (8 CARDS+1 STICKER)
COMMON CARD (1-88) .20 .50

1991 Topps Robin Hood Prince of Thieves Test Series Stickers

COMPLETE SET (9) 1.50 4.00
COMMON CARD (1-9) .20 .50
STATED ODDS 1:1

1990 Topps Robocop 2

COMPLETE SET (88) 4.00 10.00
COMPLETE SET W/STICKERS (99) 5.00 12.00
COLLECTOR'S EDITION SET (121) 8.00 20.00
UNOPENED BOX (36 PACKS) 30.00 60.00
UNOPENED PACK (9 CARDS+1 STICKER) 1.25 2.00
COMMON CARD (1-88) .08 .25

1990 Topps Robocop 2 Behind-the-Scenes

COMPLETE SET (22) 3.00 8.00
COMMON CARD (A-V) .20 .50
INCLUDED IN THE COLLECTOR'S SET

1990 Topps Robocop 2 Puzzle Stickers

COMPLETE SET (11) 1.25 3.00
COMMON CARD (1-11) .20 .50
STATED ODDS 1:1

1994 Cornerstone Robot Carnival Masters of Japanese Animation

COMPLETE SET (81) 6.00 15.00
UNOPENED BOX (36 PACKS) 15.00 25.00
UNOPENED PACK (10 CARDS) .75 1.00
COMMON CARD (1-81) .15 .40

1994 Cornerstone Robot Carnival Masters of Japanese Animation Foil

COMPLETE SET (6) 15.00 40.00
COMMON CARD (F1-F6) 3.00 8.00
STATED ODDS 1:12

1994 Cornerstone Robot Carnival Masters of Japanese Animation Promos

COMMON CARD .60 1.50
NNO Uncut Sheet

1985 Fleer Robot Wars

COMPLETE SET (41) 10.00 25.00
UNOPENED BOX (36 PACKS) 50.00 80.00
UNOPENED PACK (3 CARDS&2 STICKERS) 2.00 3.00
COMMON CARD (1-41) .40 1.00

2002 Robotech

COMPLETE SET (50) 4.00 10.00
UNOPENED BOX (24 PACKS) 40.00 50.00
UNOPENED PACK (6 CARDS) 2.00 2.25
COMMON CARD (1-50) .15 .40

2002 Robotech Autographs

COMMON CARD (A1-A5) 12.00 30.00
STATED ODDS 1:24

2002 Robotech Codename Robotech Holofoil

COMPLETE SET (9) 6.00 15.00
COMMON CARD (D1-D9) .75 2.00
STATED ODDS 1:4

2002 Robotech Masterpiece Holofoil

COMPLETE SET (9) 6.00 15.00
COMMON CARD (C1-C9) .75 2.00
STATED ODDS 1:4

2002 Robotech Promos

COMPLETE SET (2) 1.25 3.00
COMMON CARD (P1-P2) .75 2.00

1986 FTCC Robotech The Macross Saga

COMPLETE SET (60) 4.00 10.00
COMMON CARD (1-60) .12 .30
NNO Uncut Sheet

2005 Robots

COMPLETE SET (90) 4.00 10.00
UNOPENED BOX (36 PACKS) 35.00 50.00
UNOPENED PACK (7 CARDS) 1.25 2.00
COMMON CARD (1-90) .10 .30

2005 Robots Box-Loaders

COMPLETE SET (3) 2.50 6.00
COMMON CARD (BL1-BL3) 1.50 3.00
STATED ODDS ONE PER HOBBY BOX
CL1 ISSUED AS HOBBY CASE TOPPER
CL1 Bigweld CT 4.00 10.00

2005 Robots Fender Bender

COMPLETE SET (6) 6.00 15.00
COMMON CARD (FB1-FB6) 2.00 5.00
STATED ODDS 1:11 HOBBY

2005 Robots Postcards From the Big City Film

COMPLETE SET (6) 8.00 20.00
COMMON CARD (PC1-PC6) 2.50 6.00
STATED ODDS 1:17 HOBBY

2005 Robots Retail Foil

COMPLETE SET (4) 8.00 20.00
COMMON CARD (RE1-RE4) 2.50 6.00
STATED ODDS 1:11 RETAIL

2005 Robots Rusties to the Rescue

COMPLETE SET (9) 8.00 20.00
COMMON CARD (RR1-RR9) 1.50 4.00
STATED ODDS 1:11

2005 Robots Promos

COMPLETE SET (7) 6.00 15.00
COMMON CARD .75 2.00
P3 Miscellaneous 1.25 3.00
P4 Promo Card Encyclopedia 2.50 6.00
PI Free Card Offer 2.00 5.00
PUK Cards Inc. UK Distribution 2.00 5.00

1986 Dandy Rock 'n Bubble

COMPLETE SET (56) 15.00 40.00
COMMON CARD .40 1.00

1990 Eclipse Rock Bottom Awards

COMPLETE BOXED SET (36) 3.00 8.00
COMMON CARD (1-36) .15 .40

1991 Brockum Rock Cards

COMPLETE SET (288) 15.00 40.00
COMPLETE SET W/16 STICKERS 12.00 30.00
COMPLETE SET W/18 STICKERS 15.00 40.00
UNOPENED BOX (36 PACKS) 15.00 25.00
UNOPENED PACK (12 CARDS+STICKER) .40 .75
COMMON CARD (1-288) .20 .50

1991 Brockum Rock Cards Art Stickers

COMPLETE SET W/SP (18) 8.00 20.00
COMPLETE SET W/O SP (16) 6.00 15.00
COMMON CARD (1-16) .40 1.00
COMMON SP (17-18) 2.50 6.00
STATED ODDS 1:1
17 Ball and Chain SP 2.50 6.00
18 Souls of Black (Testament) SP 2.50 6.00

1991 Brockum Rock Cards Grateful Dead Legacy

COMPLETE SET (10) 8.00 20.00
COMMON CARD (1-10) 1.00 2.50
STATED ODDS 1:6
1 Jerry Garcia 3.00 8.00

2 Bob Weir 1.25 3.00
7 Grateful Dead 1.50 4.00
10 Grateful Dead 1.50 4.00

1991 Brockum Rock Cards Holograms
COMPLETE SET (9) 12.00 30.00
COMMON CARD (1-9) 2.00 5.00
STATED ODDS 1:18

1991 Brockum Rock Cards Promos
COMPLETE SET (20) 25.00 60.00
COMMON CARD 1.50 4.00

1985 Amurol Rock Star Concert
COMPLETE SET (108) 20.00 50.00
COMMON CARD (1-108) .40 1.00

1991 Topps The Rocketeer
COMPLETE SET (99) 4.00 10.00
COMPLETE SET W/STICKERS (110) 5.00 12.00
COMPLETE BOXED SET (132) 8.00 20.00
UNOPENED BOX (36 PACKS) 10.00 15.00
UNOPENED PACK (8 CARDS+1 STICKER) .30 .40
COMMON CARD (1-99) .02 .10

1991 Topps The Rocketeer Stickers
COMPLETE SET (11) 1.50 4.00
COMMON STICKER (1-11) .15 .40
STATED ODDS 1:1

2016 Rocky 40th Anniversary Factory Set
COMPLETE FACTORY SET (330) 30.00 80.00
COMMON CARD (1-330) .15 .40
ROCKY (1-31)
ROCKY II (32-108)
ROCKY III (109-158)
ROCKY IV (159-214)
ROCKY V (215-245)
ROCKY BALBOA (246-330)
STALLONE AU's UNPRICED DUE TO SCARCITY

1985 Topps Rocky IV
COMPLETE SET (66) 5.00 12.00
COMPLETE SET W/STICKERS (77) 6.00 15.00
UNOPENED BOX (36 PACKS) 150.00 250.00
UNOPENED PACK (9 CARDS+1 STICKER) 6.00 8.00
COMMON CARD (1-66) .10 .25

1985 Topps Rocky IV Stickers
COMPLETE SET (11) 1.25 3.00
COMMON CARD (1-11) .15 .40
STATED ODDS 1:1

1993 FPG Roger Dean
COMPLETE SET (90) 5.00 12.00
UNOPENED BOX (36 PACKS) 15.00 20.00
UNOPENED PACK (10 CARDS) .40 .60
COMMON CARD (1-90) .10 .25
NNO1 Roger Dean AU/1000* 20.00 50.00
NNO2 Redemption Card

1993 FPG Roger Dean Metallic Storm
COMPLETE SET (5) 12.00 30.00
COMMON CARD (1-5) 3.00 8.00
*GOLD: .75X TO 2X BASIC CARDS
RANDOMLY INSERTED INTO PACKS

1993 FPG Roger Dean Promos
COMMON CARD (1-3) .75 2.00
1 4-Card Panel

2007-08 Whosontour Entertainment The Rolling Stones
COMPLETE SET (150) 20.00 50.00
UNOPENED BOX (24 PACKS) 80.00 100.00
UNOPENED PACK (6 CARDS+1 TATTOO) 4.00 5.00
COMMON CARD (1-150) .30 .75

2007-08 Whosontour Entertainment The Rolling Stones Guitar Picks
COMPLETE SET (3) 8.00 20.00
COMMON CARD 4.00 10.00
STATED ODDS 1:6

2007-08 Whosontour Entertainment The Rolling Stones Holographic Tongues
COMPLETE SET (6) 12.00 30.00
COMMON CARD (SKIP #'d) 3.00 8.00
STATED ODDS 1:12

2007-08 Whosontour Entertainment The Rolling Stones Satin Stickers
COMPLETE SET (15) 12.00 30.00
COMMON CARD (UNNUMBERED SET) 1.50 4.00
STATED ODDS 1:8

2007-08 Whosontour Entertainment The Rolling Stones Temporary Tattoos
COMPLETE SET (12) 5.00 12.00
COMMON CARD .50 1.25
STATED ODDS 1:1

1994 Comic Images Ron Miller's Firebrands
COMPLETE SET (90) 5.00 12.00
UNOPENED BOX (48 PACKS) 20.00 30.00
UNOPENED PACK (10 CARDS) .40 .60
COMMON CARD (1-90) .10 .25
M1 World of US Manga Corps Medallion Promo/628* 10.00 25.00
AURM Ron Miller AU/500 20.00 50.00
NNO 6UP Panel 8.00 20.00
NNO Ron Miller's Firebrands Promo (dealers) .75 2.00

1994 Comic Images Ron Miller's Firebrands Galaxy Prisms
COMPLETE SET (6) 12.00 30.00
COMMON CARD (P1-P6) 3.00 8.00
STATED ODDS 1:16

1994 Comic Images Ron Miller's Firebrands Winged Women
COMPLETE SET (3) 10.00 25.00
COMMON CARD (WW1-WW3) 5.00 12.00
STATED ODDS 1:48

2000 Roswell Season One
COMPLETE SET (90) 5.00 12.00
UNOPENED BOX (36 PACKS) 50.00 75.00
UNOPENED PACK (7 CARDS) 1.50 2.50
COMMON CARD (1-90) .15 .40
RL1 STATED ODDS ONE PER BOX
RL1 Season Two Promo 1.25 3.00

2000 Roswell Season One Alien Orbs
COMPLETE SET (2) 8.00 20.00
COMMON CARD (01-02) 5.00 12.00
STATED ODDS 1:72

2000 Roswell Season One Aliens Among Us
COMPLETE SET (9) 7.50 20.00
COMMON CARD (A1-A9) 1.50 4.00
STATED ODDS 1:11

2000 Roswell Season One Autographs
COMMON AUTO (A1-A6) 8.00 20.00
STATED ODDS 1:108
A1 Jonathan Frakes 15.00 40.00
A2 Shiri Appleby 15.00 40.00
A3 Colin Hanks 10.00 25.00
A6 Julie Benz 10.00 25.00
R1 Redemption AU EXCH

2000 Roswell Season One Not of This Earth
COMPLETE SET (6) 6.00 15.00
COMMON CARD (N1-N6) 2.00 5.00
STATED ODDS 1:17

2000 Roswell Season One Promos
PR1B Roswell cast 1.25 3.00
(copyright information on back in green ink)
PR2 Roswell cast .75 2.00
PR3 Roswell cast 2.00 5.00
PRi Roswell cast 1.25 3.00

1989 Eclipse Rotten to the Core
COMPLETE BOXED SET (36) 200.00 400.00
COMMON CARD (1-36) .20 .50
26 Donald Trump 200.00 400.00

1993 FPG Rowena
COMPLETE SET (90) 5.00 12.00
UNOPENED BOX (36 PACKS) 15.00 20.00
UNOPENED PACK (10 CARDS) .40 .60
COMMON CARD (1-90) .10 .25
NNO Rowena AU/1000 20.00 50.00

1993 FPG Rowena Holograms
COMPLETE SET (3) 8.00 20.00
COMMON CARD (H1-H3) 3.00 8.00
*GOLD: 2X TO 5X BASIC CARDS
RANDOMLY INSERTED INTO PACKS
H1 Golden Devil 3.00 8.00
H2 The Magic Carpet 3.00 8.00
H3 The Wrong Place to Sit 3.00 8.00

1992 Arrowcatch Productions Roy Rogers King of the Cowboys
COMPLETE BOXED SET (72) 8.00 20.00
COMMON CARD (1-72) .20 .50
UNC1 Uncut Sheet

1992 Arrowcatch Productions Roy Rogers King of the Cowboys Red Border Promos
COMPLETE SET (5) 4.00 10.00
COMMON CARD (TC1-TC5) 1.25 3.00
*BLUE: SAME VALUE AS RED

1993 Press Pass The Royal Family
COMPLETE SET (110) 2.50 6.00
UNOPENED BOX (48 PACKS) 15.00 20.00
UNOPENED PACK (9 CARDS) .30 .40
UNOPENED JUMBO BOX 20.00 25.00
UNOPENED JUMBO PACK
COMMON CARD (1-110) .12 .30

1993 Press Pass The Royal Family Promos
COMPLETE SET (3) 3.00 8.00
COMMON CARD 1.50 4.00

2018 The Royal Wedding On-Demand
COMPLETE SET (20) 25.00 60.00
COMMON CARD (1-20) 2.00 5.00
STATED PRINT RUN 1134 SETS

1997 Comic Images Royo Secret Desires
COMPLETE SET (72) 5.00 12.00
UNOPENED BOX (48 PACKS) 30.00 40.00
UNOPENED PACK (8 CARDS) 1.25 1.50
COMMON CARD (1-72) .12 .30
NNO Royo/Congratulations AU 20.00 50.00
NNO Coming February 1997 PROMO .75 2.00

1997 Comic Images Royo Secret Desires Omnichrome
COMPLETE SET (6) 15.00 40.00
COMMON CARD (Omni1-Omni6) 3.00 8.00
STATED ODDS 1:16

1998 Comic Images Royo Millennium
COMPLETE SET (72) 8.00 20.00
UNOPENED BOX (36 PACKS) 40.00 50.00
UNOPENED PACK (8 CARDS) 1.75 2.00
COMMON CARD (1-72) .20 .50
NNO Luis Royo AU 10.00 25.00

1998 Comic Images Royo Millennium Oil on Canvas
COMPLETE SET (6) 20.00 50.00
COMMON CARD (1-6) 4.00 10.00
STATED ODDS 1:18

1998 Comic Images Royo Millennium Promos
COMPLETE SET (3) 2.00 5.00
COMMON CARD .75 2.00

2001 Rudolph the Red-Nosed Reindeer and the Island of the Misfit Toys
COMPLETE SET (9) 6.00 15.00
COMMON CARD (M1-M9) 1.25 3.00

2001 Rudolph the Red-Nosed Reindeer and the Island of the Misfit Toys Holofoil Original Cartoons
COMPLETE SET (6) 5.00 12.00
COMMON CARD (C1-C6) 1.25 3.00

2001 Rudolph the Red-Nosed Reindeer and the Island of the Misfit Toys Promos
2 Coming October 2001 2.00 5.00
CC Coming October 2001 1.25 3.00
P1 Coming October 2001 .75 2.00

1997 Tempo Rugrats
COMPLETE SET (100) 5.00 12.00
UNOPENED BOX (36 PACKS) 75.00 125.00
UNOPENED PACK (7 CARDS) 2.50 4.00
COMMON CARD (1-100) .10 .25

1997 Tempo Rugrats Rugrats at Play
COMPLETE SET (3) 3.00 8.00
COMMON CARD (RP1-RP3) 1.50 4.00
STATED ODDS 1:28
ANNCD PRINT RUN OF 2500

1997 Tempo Rugrats Tommy's Favorite Things
COMPLETE SET (7) 2.50 6.00
COMMON CARD (TFT1-TFT7) .60 1.50
STATED ODDS 1:5
ANNCD PRINT RUN OF 6000

1997 Tempo Rugrats Ultimate Chase
COMPLETE SET (2) 15.00 40.00
COMMON CARD 10.00 25.00
STATED ODDS 1:2100
STATED PRINT RUN 50 SER.#'d SETS

1987 Mother's Cookies Rumpelstiltskin
COMPLETE SET (16) 6.00 15.00
COMMON CARD (1-16) .50 1.25

1992 Topps Russ Trolls
COMPLETE SET (66) 4.00 10.00
COMPLETE SET W/STICKERS (77) 5.00 12.00
UNOPENED BOX (36 PACKS) 15.00 20.00
UNOPENED PACK (8 CARDS+1 STICKER) .75 1.00
COMMON CARD (1-66) .12 .30

1992 Topps Russ Trolls Stickers
COMPLETE SET (11) 1.50 3.00
COMMON STICKERS (1-11) .20 .50

2001 Sabrina The Animated Series Promos
COMPLETE SET (2) 2.50 6.00
COMMON CARD 1.50 4.00

1999 Dart FlipCards Sabrina the Teenage Witch
COMPLETE SET (72) 6.00 15.00
UNOPENED BOX (36 PACKS) 40.00 60.00
UNOPENED PACK (6 CARDS) 1.50 2.50
COMMON CARD (1-72) .15 .40

1999 Sabrina the Teenage Witch Autographs
COMPLETE SET (6) 100.00 200.00
COMMON CARD (A1-A6) 10.00 25.00
STATED ODDS 1:360
A2 Martin Mull 12.00 30.00
A5 Melissa Joan Hart 30.00 80.00

MODERN

1999 Dart FlipCards Sabrina the Teenage Witch Collectible Bears

COMPLETE SET (2) 15.00 40.00
COMMON BEAR 10.00 25.00
STATED ODDS 1:BOX

1999 Dart FlipCards Sabrina the Teenage Witch Prisms

COMPLETE SET (6) 8.00 20.00
COMMON CARD (S1-S6) 1.50 4.00
STATED ODDS 1:18

1999 Dart FlipCards Sabrina the Teenage Witch Promos

1 Playing Bass (Philly) 2.00 5.00
2 No One Said Being 2.00 5.00
A Teen Was Easy NSCC
3 No One Said Being 2.00 5.00
A Teen Was Easy (Toronto)
4 Hobby Version Excl.
P1 Holding Cat .75 2.00
P2 Playing Bass .75 2.00

1992 Comic Images Sachs and Violens

COMPLETE SET (90) 5.00 12.00
UNOPENED BOX (48 PACKS) 15.00 25.00
UNOPENED PACK (10 CARDS) .75 1.00
COMMON CARD (1-90) .10 .25

1992 Comic Images Sachs and Violens Prism

COMPLETE SET (6) 12.00 30.00
COMMON CARD (1-6) 2.50 6.00
STATED ODDS 1:16

1992 Comic Images Sachs and Violens Promos

COMPLETE SET (3) 2.00 5.00
COMMON CARD .75 2.00

2000 Sailor Moon Archival

COMPLETE SET (72) 6.00 15.00
UNOPENED BOX (30 PACKS) 100.00 150.00
UNOPENED PACK (7 CARDS) 3.00 5.00
6 CARDS+1 CCG PROMO PER PACK
COMMON CARD (1-72) .15 .40
NNO Collectible Card Game Promo .40 1.00

2000 Sailor Moon Archival Holofoil Game

COMPLETE SET (9) 50.00 100.00
COMMON CARD (1-9) 1.25 3.00
STATED ODDS (1-3) - 1:10
STATED ODDS (4-6) - 1:15
STATED ODDS (7-8) - 1:45
STATED ODDS (9) - 1:360
4 Doom and Gloom Girls 2.00 5.00
5 Sammy Tsukino 2.00 5.00
6 Luna Pen 2.00 5.00
7 Insectia 6.00 15.00
8 Confusion 6.00 15.00
9 Wicked Lady 25.00 60.00

1997 Dart FlipCards Sailor Moon Awesome

COMPLETE SET (72) 8.00 20.00
UNOPENED BOX (30 PACKS) 65.00 80.00
UNOPENED PACK (7 CARDS) 2.50 3.00
COMMON CARD (1-72) .25 .60

1997 Dart FlipCards Sailor Moon Awesome Die-Cuts

COMPLETE SET (6) 15.00 40.00
COMMON CARD (DC1-DC6) 3.00 8.00
RANDOMLY INSERTED INTO PACKS

1997 Dart FlipCards Sailor Moon Awesome Stand-Ups

COMPLETE SET (6) 5.00 12.00
COMMON CARD (S1-S6) 1.25 3.00
MAIL-IN EXCLUSIVE

2000 Sailor Moon FilmCardz

COMPLETE SET (45) 6.00 15.00
UNOPENED BOX (24 PACKS)
UNOPENED PACK (5 CARDS)
COMMON CARD (1-45) .25 .60

2000 Sailor Moon FilmCardz Prism

COMPLETE SET (10) 10.00 25.00
COMMON CARD (H1-H10) 1.25 3.00
RANDOMLY INSERTED INTO PACKS

1997 Dart FlipCards Sailor Moon Prismatic

COMPLETE SET (72) 10.00 25.00
UNOPENED BOX (36 PACKS) 65.00 80.00
UNOPENED PACK (5 CARDS) 2.25 2.50
COMMON CARD (1-72) .25 .60

1997 Dart FlipCards Sailor Moon Prismatic Jumbos

COMPLETE SET (6) 10.00 25.00
COMMON CARD (S1-S6) 3.00 8.00
AVAILABLE THROUGH MAIL-IN OFFER

1997 Dart FlipCards Sailor Moon Prismatic Lenticular

COMPLETE SET (6) 6.00 15.00
COMMON CARD (L1-L6) 1.25 3.00
STATED ODDS 1:18

1997 Dart FlipCards Sailor Moon Prismatic Promos

COMMON CARD 1.25 3.00
NNO1 2UP Panel

2017 The Saint Series One

COMPLETE SET (36) 5.00 12.00
COMMON CARD (1-36) .30 .75

2017 The Saint Series One Autographs

COMMON AUTO 8.00 20.00
AA1 Annette Andre 10.00 25.00
AA2 Annette Andre 10.00 25.00
AA3 Annette Andre 10.00 25.00
AA4 Annette Andre 20.00 50.00
AA5 Annette Andre 10.00 25.00
AW1 Anneke Wills 12.00 30.00
AW2 Anneke Wills 12.00 30.00
AW3 Anneke Wills 12.00 30.00
CC1 Carol Cleveland 12.00 30.00
CC1 Isla Blair 15.00 40.00
CC2 Isla Blair 15.00 40.00
CC2 Carol Cleveland 12.00 30.00
CC3 Carol Cleveland 12.00 30.00
CC3 Isla Blair 15.00 40.00
DG1 David Graham 10.00 25.00
DG2 David Graham 10.00 25.00
DP1 David Prowse 15.00 40.00
DP2 David Prowse 15.00 40.00
JG1 Julian Glover 15.00 40.00
JG2 Julian Glover 15.00 40.00
JL1 Jennie Linden 10.00 25.00
JL2 Jennie Linden 10.00 25.00
JL3 Jennie Linden 10.00 25.00
PD1 Paul Darrow 10.00 25.00
PD2 Paul Darrow 10.00 25.00
PD3 Paul Darrow 10.00 25.00
RM1 Roger Moore 50.00 100.00
RM2 Roger Moore 50.00 100.00
SE1 Shirley Eaton
SE2 Shirley Eaton
SL1 Suzanna Leigh 25.00 60.00
SR1 Shane Rimmer
WG1 William Gaunt 10.00 25.00
WG2 William Gaunt 10.00 25.00
WG3 William Gaunt 10.00 25.00

2017 The Saint Series One Promos

AS1 Dealer Promo
(ams-78)/5
CC1 The Cyber Cellar waltermadbon1@sky.com8.0020.00
DR1 Dean Rogers Top Cards
DR2 Dean Rogers Top Cards
DR3 Dean Rogers Top Cards
DT1 Derek's Trading Cards, derek_f
DT2 Derek's Trading Cards, derek_f
EM1 Acme 3000 elliotsmorris@aol.com
EM2 Acme 3000 elliotsmorris@aol.com
GP1 Gazza Games 6.00 15.00
JW1 Jason Wright doctorjas73/50
JW2 Jason Wright doctorjas73/50
JW3 Jason Wright doctorjas73/50
MB1 MB-TRADING-CARDS/5
MB1 MB-TRADING-CARDS/5
MB2 MB-TRADING-CARDS/5
MB2 MB-TRADING-CARDS/5
MP1 mitchy9210
MP2 mitchy9210
PC1 Premier Trading Cards
PC2 Premier Trading Cards
PC3 Premier Trading Cards 10.00 25.00
PR1 Coming Soon
(British Horror Collection Case-Incentive)/100
PR3 Gerry Anderson Collection case-topper
RK1 Roman Krause, wrongshoe
RK2 Roman Krause, wrongshoe
SF1 Sci-Fi Trading Cards, scifi_cards 8.00 20.00
TM1 telly-mania/30
UT1 Umbrella Trading Cards 10.00 25.00
UT2 Umbrella Trading Cards 12.00 30.00
WEB1 Web Exclusive Promo Card 2.50 6.00

2018 The Saint Series Two

COMPLETE SET (36) 5.00 12.00
COMMON CARD (1-36) .30 .75

2018 The Saint Series Two Autographs

COMMON AUTO 6.00 15.00
STATED ODDS 1:
AD1 Angela Douglas 10.00 25.00
AD1 Alexandra Dane 12.00 30.00
AD2 Alexandra Dane 12.00 30.00
AD2 Angela Douglas 10.00 25.00
AD3 Angela Douglas 10.00 25.00
AD3 Alexandra Dane 12.00 30.00
AM1 Aimi MacDonald 10.00 25.00
AM2 Aimi MacDonald 8.00 20.00
AM3 Aimi MacDonald 8.00 20.00
CB1 Caroline Blakiston 10.00 25.00
CB2 Caroline Blakiston 10.00 25.00
CB3 Caroline Blakiston 10.00 25.00
CG1 Caron Gardner 10.00 25.00
CG2 Caron Gardner 10.00 25.00
CG3 Caron Gardner 10.00 25.00
DN1 Derren Nesbitt 10.00 25.00
JC1 Jill Curzon 10.00 25.00
JC3 Jill Curzon 8.00 20.00
JL2 Justine Lord 25.00 60.00
JL3 Justine Lord 25.00 60.00
JL5 Justine Lord 25.00 60.00
JL6 Justine Lord 25.00 60.00
JM1 Jane Merrow 12.00 30.00
JM2 Jane Merrow 10.00 25.00
JM3 Jane Merrow 10.00 25.00
NW1 Norma West 20.00 50.00
PW1 Peter Wyngarde 20.00 50.00
PW2 Peter Wyngarde 20.00 50.00
PW3 Peter Wyngarde 20.00 50.00
RM1 Roger Moore 75.00 150.00
SS1 Sylvia Sims CI 20.00 50.00
SS2 Sylvia Sims CI 20.00 50.00
SS3 Sylvia Sims CI 20.00 50.00
VD3 Vera Day 15.00 40.00
VL1 Valerie Leon 12.00 30.00
VL3 Valerie Leon 12.00 30.00

2018 The Saint Series Two Promos

AS1 Dealer Promo (ams-78) 20.00 50.00
CC1 Dealer Promo (The Cyber Cellar) 12.00 30.00
DP1 Dealer Promo (humdrum1) 5.00 12.00
DP2 Dealer Promo
DT1 Dealer Promo (Derek's Trading Cards) 10.00 25.00
GP1 Dealer Promo (gazzagames) 12.00 30.00
HP1 Dealer Promo (twilightzone111)
JW1 Dealer Promo (doctorjas73)
JW2 Dealer Promo (doctorjas73)
MB1 Dealer Promo (MB-Trading-Cards, taekwondo888)
PC1 Dealer Promo (Premier Cards) 12.00 30.00
RK1 Dealer Promo (Roman Krause, romankrause@yahoo.co.uk)
RK2 Dealer Promo (Roman Krause)
SF1 Dealer Promo (Scifi Cards)
TM1 Dealer Promo (telly-mania) 10.00 25.00
TZ1 Dealer Promo (twilightzone111)
UT1 Dealer Promo (Umbrella Trading Cards)12.00 30.00
UT2 Dealer Promo (Umbrella Trading Cards)12.00 30.00

1995 Comic Images Salvador Dali

COMPLETE SET (90) 15.00 40.00
UNOPENED BOX (36 PACKS) 45.00 60.00
UNOPENED PACK (7 CARDS) 1.25 1.75
COMMON CARD (1-90) .30 .75
*HOLOCHROME: .75X TO 2X BASIC CARDS .60 1.50
M1 Medallion/869 10.00 25.00
CT1 6-Up Panels CT 8.00 20.00
24K1 Salvador Dali/500 (gold signature) 20.00 50.00
NNO Promo NNO 1.25 3.00

1995 Comic Images Salvador Dali MagnaChrome

COMPLETE SET (6) 15.00 40.00
COMMON CARD (1-6) 3.00 8.00
STATED ODDS 1:16

1995 Comic Images Salvador Dali Precious Time Prisms

COMPLETE SET (3) 10.00 25.00
COMMON CARD (1-3) 4.00 10.00
STATED ODDS 1:36

2002 Samurai Jack

COMPLETE SET (72) 5.00 12.00
UNOPENED BOX (24 PACKS) 40.00 50.00
UNOPENED PACK (6 CARDS) 2.00 2.25
COMMON CARD (1-72) .15 .40
NNO Genndy Tartakovsky AU 15.00 40.00

2002 Samurai Jack Die-Cuts

COMPLETE SET (6) 8.00 20.00
COMMON CARD (DC1-DC6) 1.50 4.00
RANDOMLY INSERTED INTO PACKS

2002 Samurai Jack Japanese Chrome

COMPLETE SET (6) 10.00 25.00
COMMON CARD (JP1-JP6) 2.00 5.00
RANDOMLY INSERTED INTO PACKS

2002 Samurai Jack Promos

COMPLETE SET (2) 1.25 3.00
COMMON CARD (SJ1-SJ2) .75 2.00

1993 EicherWick Productions San Francisco Scenes

COMPLETE SET (28) 5.00 12.00
COMMON CARD (1-28) .30 .75

1994 FPG SanJulian Collection

COMPLETE SET (90) 5.00 12.00
UNOPENED BOX (36 PACKS) 15.00 20.00
UNOPENED PACK (10 CARDS) .75 1.00
COMMON CARD (1-90) .12 .30
NNO1 Sanjulian AU/1000* 20.00 50.00
NNO2 Uncut Sheet 4-Up Panel

1994 FPG SanJulian Collection Metallic Storm

COMPLETE SET (5) 12.00 30.00
COMMON CARD (MS1-MS5) 3.00 8.00
*GOLD: .75X TO 2X BASIC CARDS 6.00 15.00
RANDOMLY INSERTED INTO PACKS

1994 FPG SanJulian Collection Promos

COMPLETE SET (4) 4.00 10.00

COMMON CARD	.60	1.50
2 Title Card	3.00	8.00

1995 TCM Associates Santa and Snowflakes

COMPLETE SET (72)	4.00	10.00
UNOPENED BOX (36 PACKS)	30.00	40.00
UNOPENED PACK (8 CARDS)	1.25	1.50
COMMON CARD (1-72)	.12	.30
NNO1 The Complete Santa Around the World		

1995 TCM Associates Santa and Snowflakes Distinctly Textured

COMPLETE SET (12)	12.00	30.00
COMMON CARD (SF1-SF12)	1.25	3.00
STATED ODDS 1:6		

1995 TCM Associates Santa and Snowflakes Gold Cards

1 Roof Top Santa	175.00	300.00
2 Work Shop Santa	120.00	200.00
3 Redemption Card		

1995 TCM Associates Santa and Snowflakes Santa's Children

COMPLETE SET (4)	10.00	25.00
COMMON CARD (SC1-SC4)	3.00	8.00
*GOLD: .50X TO 1.2X BASIC CARDS		
STATED ODDS 1:36		

1994 TCM Associates Santa Around the World Premier Edition

COMPLETE SET (72)	4.00	10.00
UNOPENED BOX (36 PACKS)	20.00	30.00
UNOPENED PACK (8 CARDS)	1.00	1.25
COMMON CARD (1-72)	.12	.30
G1 22k Gold Santa/1000*	80.00	150.00
G2 Redemption EXCH/1000*		
Ph1 Kris Kringle Mail In Phone Card	2.00	5.00

1994 TCM Associates Santa Around the World Premier Edition Foil

COMPLETE SET (12)	12.00	30.00
COMMON CARD (F1-F12)	1.25	3.00
STATED ODDS 1:6		

1994 21st Century Archives Santa Claus Nostalgic Art Collection

COMPLETE SET (50)	4.00	10.00
UNOPENED BOX (36 PACKS)	30.00	40.00
UNOPENED PACK (8 CARDS)	1.25	1.50
COMMON CARD (1-50)	.12	.30

1994 21st Century Archives Santa Claus Nostalgic Art Collection Foil

COMPLETE SET (5)	5.00	12.00
COMMON CARD (S1-S5)	1.25	3.00
RANDOMLY INSERTED INTO PACKS		

1992 Star Pics Saturday Night Live

COMPLETE SET (150)	10.00	25.00
UNOPENED BOX (36 PACKS)	60.00	100.00
UNOPENED PACK (10 CARDS)	3.00	4.00
COMMON CARD (1-150)	.12	.30

1992 Star Pics Saturday Night Live Autographs

COMMON AUTO (SKIP #'d)	8.00	20.00
9 Al Franken	20.00	50.00
18 Julia Sweeney	20.00	50.00
19 Rob Schneider	15.00	40.00
27 Mike Myers	250.00	500.00
33 Chris Rock	40.00	100.00
47 Chris Farley	800.00	2000.00
53 Adam Sandler	60.00	150.00
83 Phil Hartman	300.00	800.00

1988 Epic Cards Saturday Serials

COMPLETE SET (40)	4.00	10.00
COMMON CARD (1-40)	.20	.50
NNO Lone Ranger on Trigger		

1991 Epic Cards Saturday Serials

COMPLETE SET (40)	4.00	10.00
COMMON CARD (41-80)	.20	.50

1992 Kitchen Sink Press Saucer People

COMPLETE BOXED SET (36)	5.00	12.00
COMMON CARD (1-36)	.25	.60
NNO Saucer People PROMO (general distribution)	2.00	5.00

1992 Comic Images Savage Dragon

COMPLETE SET (90)	3.00	8.00
UNOPENED BOX (48 PACKS)	15.00	25.00
UNOPENED PACK (10 CARDS)		
COMMON CARD (1-90)	.08	.20

1992 Comic Images Savage Dragon Prisms

COMPLETE SET (6)	15.00	40.00
COMMON CARD (1-6)	3.00	8.00
STATED ODDS 1:16		

1997 WildStorm Savage Dragon

COMPLETE SET (90)	5.00	12.00
UNOPENED BOX (36 PACKS)	15.00	20.00
UNOPENED PACK (8 CARDS)	.75	1.00
COMMON CARD (1-90)	.10	.25

1997 WildStorm Savage Dragon Eric Larsen Gallery

COMPLETE SET (9)	10.00	25.00
COMMON CARD (EL1-EL9)	1.25	3.00
STATED ODDS 1:9		

1997 WildStorm Savage Dragon Stickers

COMPLETE SET (9)	1.50	4.00
COMMON CARD (ST1-ST9)	.20	.50
STATED ODDS 1:9		

1988 Comic Images Savage Sword of Conan the Barbarian

COMPLETE SET (50)	60.00	120.00
UNOPENED BOX (50 PACKS)	175.00	200.00
UNOPENED PACK (5 CARDS)	4.00	5.00
COMMON CARD (1-50)	1.25	3.00

1992 Pacific Saved By the Bell

COMPLETE SET (110)	6.00	15.00
UNOPENED BOX (100 PACKS)	60.00	100.00
UNOPENED PACK (5 CARDS)	1.00	1.25
COMMON CARD (1-110)	.12	.30

1994 Pacific Saved by the Bell The College Years

COMPLETE SET (110)	5.00	12.00
UNOPENED BOX (36 PACKS)	20.00	30.00
UNOPENED PACK (10 CARDS)	.75	1.00
COMMON CARD (1-110)	.08	.20

1994 Pacific Saved by the Bell The College Years Prisms

COMPLETE SET (10)	10.00	25.00
COMMON CARD (1-10)	1.25	3.00
STATED ODDS 1:18		

1994 Pacific Saved by the Bell The College Years Promos

COMPLETE SET (5)	4.00	10.00
COMMON CARD (P1-P5)	1.25	3.00

1993 Kellogg's Saved by the Bell New Class

COMPLETE SET (10)	5.00	12.00
COMMON CARD	.75	2.00

1991 Eclipse Savings and Loan Scandal

COMPLETE BOXED SET (36)	4.00	10.00
COMMON CARD (1-36)	.25	.60

2002 Scooby Doo The Movie

COMPLETE SET (72)	5.00	12.00
UNOPENED BOX (36 PACKS)	40.00	50.00
UNOPENED PACK (6 CARDS+1 STICKER)	1.50	1.75
COMMON CARD (1-72)	.15	.40
*STICKER: .8X TO 2X BASIC CARDS		

2002 Scooby Doo The Movie Box-Loaders

COMPLETE SET (4)	2.50	6.00
COMMON CARD (BL1-BL4)	.75	2.00
STATED ODDS ONE PER BOX		
CL1 STATED ODDS ONE PER CASE		
CL1 Another Mystery Solved	4.00	10.00

2002 Scooby Doo The Movie Lenticular

COMPLETE SET (6)	7.50	20.00
COMMON CARD (L1-L6)	1.50	4.00
STATED ODDS 1:11		

2002 Scooby Doo The Movie Sparkly

COMPLETE SET (6)	10.00	25.00
COMMON CARD (SP1-SP6)	2.00	5.00
STATED ODDS 1:11		

2002 Scooby Doo The Movie Promos

SD1 Scooby and the Gang GEN	.75	2.00
SD2 Scooby and the Gang NSU	1.25	3.00
SD3 Scooby and the Gang (UK excl.)	2.00	5.00
SDI Scooby and the Gang (free card offer)	1.25	3.00
SDWW Scooby and the Gang (Wizard Wizard)	2.50	6.00

2004 Scooby Doo 2 Monsters Unleashed

COMPLETE SET (72)	3.00	8.00
UNOPENED BOX (36 PACKS)	50.00	60.00
UNOPENED PACK (7 CARDS)	1.50	1.75
COMMON CARD (1-72)	.08	.25

2004 Scooby Doo 2 Monsters Unleashed Autographs

COMMON CARD (A1-A8)	4.00	10.00
STATED ODDS 1:36		
CARD A3 WAS NOT ISSUED		
A1 Matthew Lillard	25.00	60.00
A2 Linda Cardellini	75.00	150.00
A4 Alicia Silverstone	50.00	100.00
A5 Pat O'Brien	15.00	40.00
A7 C. Ernst Harth	5.00	12.00
A8 Kevin Durand	6.00	15.00

2004 Scooby Doo 2 Monsters Unleashed Box-Loaders

COMPLETE SET (3)	6.00	10.00
COMMON CARD (BL1-BL3)	1.50	4.00
STATED ODDS ONE PER BOX		
CL1 STATED ODDS ONE PER CASE		
CL1 Yo Bro	4.00	10.00

2004 Scooby Doo 2 Monsters Unleashed Mystery, Inc.

COMPLETE SET (6)	12.00	30.00
COMMON CARD (MI1-MI6)	3.00	8.00
STATED ODDS 1:17		

2004 Scooby Doo 2 Monsters Unleashed Pieceworks

COMPLETE SET (12)	80.00	150.00
COMMON CARD	5.00	12.00
STATED ODDS 1:36		
PW9 Daphne's Jacket	7.50	20.00
PW10 Daphne's Pants	7.50	20.00
PW11 Daphne's Top	7.50	20.00

2004 Scooby Doo 2 Monsters Unleashed Puzzle

COMPLETE SET (9)	2.50	6.00
COMMON CARD (MU1-MU9)	.40	1.00
STATED ODDS 1:11		

2004 Scooby Doo 2 Monsters Unleashed Promos

COMPLETE SET (4)	3.00	8.00
COMMON CARD	1.00	2.50

2003 Scooby Doo Mysteries and Monsters

COMPLETE SET (72)	5.00	12.00
UNOPENED BOX (24 PACKS)	40.00	50.00
UNOPENED PACK (7 CARDS+1 STICKER)	1.75	2.25
COMMON CARD (1-72)	.15	.40

2003 Scooby Doo Mysteries and Monsters Autographs

COMPLETE SET (6)	100.00	200.00
COMMON CARD	7.50	20.00
STATED ODDS 1:62 HOBBY		
A1 Casey Kasem	200.00	400.00
A2 Tim Conway	50.00	100.00
A4 Frank Welker	100.00	200.00
A5 Nicole (Jaffe) David	75.00	150.00
A6 Heather (Kenney) North	125.00	250.00

2003 Scooby Doo Mysteries and Monsters Box-Loaders

COMPLETE SET (4)	7.50	20.00
COMMON CARD (BL1-BL4)	1.00	2.50
STATED ODDS 1:BOX		
CL1 STATED ODDS 1:CASE		
CL1 We'd Have Put a Great Illustration	6.00	15.00

2003 Scooby Doo Mysteries and Monsters Sparkly

COMPLETE SET (6)	10.00	25.00
COMMON CARD (SP1-SP6)	2.00	5.00
STATED ODDS 1:7 HOBBY		

2003 Scooby Doo Mysteries and Monsters Stickers

COMPLETE SET (9)	1.50	4.00
COMMON CARD (S1-S9)	.20	.50
STATED ODDS ONE PER PACK		

2003 Scooby Doo Mysteries and Monsters Promos

COMPLETE SET (3)	2.00	5.00
COMMON CARD	1.00	2.50

2002 The Scorpion King Previews

COMPLETE SET (7)	6.00	15.00
COMMON CARD (PC1-PC7)	1.25	3.00
PC2 Mathayus	2.00	5.00

2002 The Scorpion King

COMPLETE SET (72)	3.00	8.00
UNOPENED BOX (36 PACKS)	40.00	50.00
UNOPENED PACK (6 CARDS)	1.25	1.50
COMMON CARD (1-72)	.10	.25
CL1 STATED ODDS ONE PER CASE		
CL1 Cassandra Mathayus	4.00	10.00

2002 The Scorpion King Autographs

COMMON AUTO (A1-A5)	4.00	10.00
STATED ODDS 1:51		
A1 The Rock	2000.00	4000.00

2002 The Scorpion King Pieceworks

COMPLETE SET (4)	20.00	50.00
COMMON CARD	6.00	15.00
STATED ODDS 1:36		

2002 The Scorpion King The Future King Puzzle

COMPLETE SET (9)	8.00	20.00
COMMON CARD (P1-P9)	1.25	3.00
STATED ODDS 1:11		

2002 The Scorpion King The Rock

COMPLETE SET (3) 4.00 10.00
COMMON CARD (BL1-BL3) 1.50 4.00
STATED ODDS ONE PER BOX
BL1 Cassandra 1.50 4.00
BL2 Isis 1.50 4.00
BL3 Balthazar 1.50 4.00

2002 The Scorpion King Visions of the Sorceress

COMPLETE SET (6) 10.00 25.00
COMMON CARD (S1-S6) 2.00 5.00
STATED ODDS 1:17

2002 The Scorpion King Promos

BB1 Best Buy Exclusive
SKP1 Mathayus GEN .75 2.00
SKP2 Mathayus 1.25 3.00
Balthazar NSU
SKPi Mathayus (free card offer) 1.25 3.00
UMJ1 Soundtrack
(Japanese Exclusive)
SKPUK Mathayus 1.50 4.00
(UK excl.)

1996 Scott Barnett's Brushstrokes

COMPLETE SET (9) 4.00 10.00
COMMON CARD (1-9) .75 2.00

1993 SkyBox SeaQuest DSV

COMPLETE SET (100) 6.00 15.00
UNOPENED BOX (36 PACKS) 30.00 40.00
UNOPENED PACK (8 CARDS) 1.00 1.25
COMMON CARD (1-100) .12 .30

1993 SkyBox SeaQuest DSV Foil

COMPLETE SET (4) 12.00 30.00
COMMON CARD (1-4) 4.00 10.00
STATED ODDS 1:20

1993 SkyBox SeaQuest DSV Promos

COMPLETE SET (2) 1.25 3.00
COMMON CARD (S1-S2) .75 2.00

2018 The Secret Service

COMPLETE SET (18) 4.00 10.00
COMMON CARD (1-18) .30 .75

2018 The Secret Service Autographs

COMMON AUTO 8.00 20.00
DG1 David Graham 12.00 30.00
DG2 David Graham 12.00 30.00
GF1 Gary Files 15.00 40.00
GF2 Gary Files 15.00 40.00
JW1 Jeremy Wilkin
SR1 Shane Rimmer 12.00 30.00

2018 The Secret Service Promos

CCP1 The Cyber Cellar 10.00 25.00
DCP1 Derek's Trading Cards, derek_f
EMP1 Acme 30000/elliotsmorris@aol.com 12.00 30.00
GGP1 Gazza Games 12.00 30.00
JWP1 Jason Wright, doctorjas73 10.00 25.00
MBP1 marked MB-Trading-Cards 12.00 30.00
but from Try Trading Cards#(taekwondo888
MPP1 mitchy9210
PCP1 Premier Cards 15.00 40.00
PHP1 Paul Hart Trading Cards 15.00 40.00
RKP1 Roman Krause/wrongshoe
TCP1 Dean Rogers/Top Cards
TMP1 telly-mania 20.00 50.00
UTP1 Umbrella Trading Cards 12.00 30.00
WEB1 Web Exclusive

2007 Seeker The Dark is Rising

COMPLETE SET (72) 4.00 10.00
COMMON CARD (1-72) .10 .30
CL1 ISSUED AS CASE TOPPER
CL1 Unlikely Warrior CT 3.00 8.00

2007 Seeker The Dark is Rising Autographs

COMMON CARD 4.00 10.00
STATED ODDS ONE PER BOX
AEE Edmund Entin 8.00 20.00
AFC Frances Conroy 10.00 25.00
AGS Gregory Smith 12.00 30.00
AIM Ian McShane 10.00 25.00
AJH John Benjamin Hickey 10.00 25.00

2007 Seeker The Dark is Rising Eternal Enemies

COMPLETE SET (6) 10.00 25.00
COMMON CARD (E1-E6) 2.00 5.00
STATED ODDS 1:17

2007 Seeker The Dark is Rising Hidden

COMPLETE SET (3) 8.00 20.00
COMMON CARD (H1-H3) 3.00 8.00
STATED ODDS 1:23

2007 Seeker The Dark is Rising Pieceworks

COMPLETE SET (6) 50.00 100.00
COMMON CARD (PW1-PW6) 5.00 12.00
STATED ODDS ONE PER BOX
PW1 Will Stanton Sweater 8.00 20.00
PW2 The Rider Cloak 8.00 20.00
PW3 Max Stanton Jacket 10.00 25.00
PW5 Miss Greythorne Jacket 10.00 25.00

2007 Seeker The Dark is Rising Signs of Light Puzzle

COMPLETE SET (9) 12.00 30.00
COMMON CARD (S1-S9) 1.50 4.00
STATED ODDS 1:11

2007 Seeker The Dark is Rising Promos

COMPLETE SET (6) 6.00 15.00
COMMON CARD 1.25 3.00
Pi inkworks.com exclusive 1.50 4.00
PK U.K. distribution 2.50 6.00
PFW Dee's Show NJ-NY 2007 2.50 6.00
PSD2007 SDCC 2007 2.00 5.00

1995 SEGA Team Blockbuster

COMPLETE SET (50) 80.00 150.00
COMMON CARD (1-50) 1.50 4.00

2019 Seinfeld Night New York Mets Set

COMPLETE SET (4) 30.00 75.00
COMMON CARD 12.00 30.00
NNO Cosmo Kramer 12.00 30.00
NNO Elaine Benes 12.00 30.00
NNO George Costanza 12.00 30.00
NNO Jerry Seinfeld 12.00 30.00

2005 Serenity

COMPLETE SET (72) 4.00 10.00
UNOPENED BOX (36 PACKS) 50.00 80.00
UNOPENED PACK (6 CARDS) 1.50 2.25
COMMON CARD (1-72) .10 .25
CL1 STATED ODDS 1:CASE
CL1 Browncoats Unite 12.00 30.00

2005 Serenity Action Figure Inserts

COMPLETE SET (5) 10.00 25.00
COMMON CARD (DSS1-DSS5) 2.50 6.00

2005 Serenity Autographs

COMMON AUTO (A1-A10) 15.00 40.00
STATED ODDS 1:BOX
A1 Nathan Fillion 75.00 150.00
A3 Adam Baldwin 25.00 60.00
A4 Alan Tudyk 75.00 150.00
A5 Jewel Staite 30.00 75.00
A6 Morena Baccarin 75.00 200.00
A7 Summer Glau 200.00 400.00
A9 Ron Glass 30.00 75.00
A10 Chiwetel Ejiofor 50.00 125.00

2005 Serenity Pieceworks

COMPLETE SET (8) 80.00 150.00
COMMON CARD (PW1-PW8) 8.00 20.00
STATED ODDS ONE PER BOX
PW1 Mal 12.00 30.00
PW2 Zoe 10.00 25.00
PW3 Jayne 10.00 25.00
PW4 Wash 10.00 25.00
PW5 Kaylee 12.00 30.00

2005 Serenity Renegades Puzzle

COMPLETE SET (9) 10.00 25.00
COMMON CARD (R1-R9) 1.50 4.00
STATED ODDS 1:11

2005 Serenity Truth Within

COMPLETE SET (3) 3.00 8.00
COMMON CARD (BL1-BL3) 1.25 3.00
STATED ODDS 1:BOX

2005 Serenity Women of Serenity

COMPLETE SET (5) 6.00 15.00
COMMON CARD (WS1-WS5) 1.50 4.00
STATED ODDS 1:17

2005 Serenity Promos

Spi Jayne 2.00 5.00
DST1 Mal/Jayne 1.25 3.00
SPUK Group of six 2.00 5.00
(UK excl.)
SPWW Mal/Jayne 2.00 5.00
(Wizard World)
SPCEE Wash/Mal/Zoe 2.00 5.00
(Chicagoland)
SPNSUSD Group of seven NSU 2.00 5.00

1992 CTW Sesame Street

COMPLETE SET (100) 6.00 15.00
UNOPENED BOX (36 PACKS) 15.00 25.00
UNOPENED PACK (10 CARDS) .75 1.00
COMMON CARD (1-100) .10 .25
NNO1 Checklist 1 .20 .50
NNO2 Checklist 2 .20 .50
NNO3 How well do you know
Sesame Street? Insert .20 .50

2010 Seven Revelations

COMPLETE SET (18) 12.00 30.00
UNOPENED PREMIUM PACK 30.00 80.00
COMMON CARD (1-18) 1.00 2.50
NNO1 Paul Allen Ballard Hand-Finish Insert
NNO2 Jennifer Mercer Multiple-Pack-Purchase Insert

2010 Seven Revelations Puzzle

COMPLETE SET (9) 20.00 50.00
COMMON CARD (N1-N9) 3.00 8.00
STATED ODDS 1:1

2013 Sgt Fury and His Howling Commandos

COMPLETE SET (30) 20.00 50.00
COMMON CARD (1-30) 1.50 4.00

2013 Sgt Fury and His Howling Commandos Characters

COMPLETE SET (9) 10.00 25.00
COMMON CARD (C1-C9) 2.00 5.00
ONE CHARACTER CARD PER PACK

1994 Topps The Shadow

COMPLETE SET (100) 12.00 30.00
UNOPENED BOX (36 PACKS) 30.00 40.00
UNOPENED PACK (7 CARDS) 1.25 1.50
COMMON CARD (1-90; L1-L10) .20 .50
NNO The Shadow PROMO .75 2.00

1994 Topps The Shadow Finest

COMPLETE SET (4) 12.00 30.00
COMMON CARD (S1-S4) 4.00 10.00
STATED ODDS 1:45

1992 Comic Images Shadowhawk

COMPLETE SET (90) 4.00 10.00
UNOPENED BOX (48 PACKS) 20.00 30.00
UNOPENED PACK (10 CARDS) .75 1.00
COMMON CARD (1-90) .10 .25
NNO Shadowhawk PROMO .75 2.00

1992 Comic Images Shadowhawk Prisms

COMPLETE SET (6) 15.00 40.00
COMMON CARD (1-6) 3.00 8.00
STATED ODDS 1:16

2003 Shark Tale Promos

COMPLETE SET (12) 6.00 15.00
COMMON CARD (UNNUMBERED) .75 2.00

2018 Sharknado Series One

COMPLETE SET (90) 10.00 25.00
UNOPENED BOX (36 PACKS)
UNOPENED PACK (10 CARDS)
COMMON CARD (1-90) .20 .60

2018 Sharknado Series One Sharknado 2 The Second One

COMPLETE SET (90) 10.00 25.00
COMMON CARD (1-90) .25 .60
SECONDARY BASE SET

2018 Sharknado Series One Actor Subset

COMPLETE SET (36) 15.00 40.00
COMMON CARD (1-36) .75 2.00
STATED ODDS 1:1

2018 Sharknado Series One Bloody Subset

COMPLETE SET (27) 10.00 25.00
COMMON CARD (1-27) .75 2.00
STATED ODDS 1:1

2018 Sharknado Series One Costume Relics

COMMON MEM 10.00 25.00
STATED ODDS 1:36
R1 Tara Reid 15.00 40.00
R3 Tara Reid 15.00 40.00
R4 Cassie Scerbo 12.00 30.00

2018 Sharknado Series One Faux Film Cells

COMMON MEM 8.00 20.00
RANDOMLY INSERTED INTO PACKS
FC1 Tara Reid 12.00 30.00
FC3 Cassie Scerbo 10.00 25.00

2018 Sharknado Series One Full Metal Box-Toppers

COMPLETE SET (9) 25.00 60.00
COMMON CARD (BT1-BT9) 5.00 12.00
STATED ODDS 1:BOX

2018 Sharknado Series One Header

H1 Build Your Complete Collection 2.00 5.00

2018 Sharknado Series One Limited Edition Portrait Cards

COMPLETE SET (9) 12.00 30.00
COMMON CARD (PC1-PC9) 2.50 6.00
STATED ODDS 1:12

2018 Sharknado Series One Sharknado 6 Puzzle Backs

COMPLETE SET ()
COMMON CARD ()
STATED ODDS 1:
E1 They're Re-Making History
E2 He Came. He Sawed. He Conquered.
E3 She Slays in Every Time Period
E4 When It Pours, She Reigns

2018 Sharknado Series One Sharknado in 3-D

COMPLETE SET (18) 12.00 30.00
COMMON CARD (1-18) 1.00 2.50
STATED ODDS 1:2

2018 Sharknado Series One Promos

COMPLETE SET (3) 5.00 12.00
COMMON CARD (P1-P3) 2.00 5.00

2002 Sherlock Holmes Premiere Collection Previews

COMPLETE SET (9)	6.00	15.00
COMMON CARD (B1-B9)	1.00	2.50

2002 Sherlock Holmes Premiere Collection

COMPLETE FACTORY SET (72)	6.00	15.00
COMMON CARD (1-72)	.15	.40
BM Premiere Collection		
Foil-Blocked Bookmark		
M Moriarty Mystery Card		

2002 Sherlock Holmes Premiere Collection Clues

COMPLETE SET (3)	12.00	30.00
COMMON CARD	5.00	12.00
STATED ODDS 1:3 SETS		

2002 Sherlock Holmes Premiere Collection Disguise

COMPLETE SET (6)	10.00	25.00
COMMON CARD (D1-D6)	2.00	5.00
STATED ODDS 1:3 SETS		

2002 Sherlock Holmes Premiere Collection Promos

COMMON CARD	1.25	3.00

1995 Comic Images Shi

COMPLETE SET (90)	8.00	20.00
UNOPENED BOX (36 PACKS)	50.00	60.00
UNOPENED PACK (7 CARDS)	2.00	2.25
COMMON CARD (1-90)	.15	.40
ALB Album Promo Sheet		
AU William Tucci AU/500*	20.00	50.00
M1 Medallion Card/7681*	10.00	25.00
CB Jumbo Card Case Bonus	6.00	15.00
UNCAU 90-Card Uncut Sheet AU		
PROMO Shi All-Chromium PROMO	1.25	3.00

1995 Comic Images Shi MagnaChrome

COMPLETE SET (6)	15.00	40.00
COMMON CARD (M1-M6)	3.00	8.00
STATED ODDS 1:16		

1995 Comic Images Shi New Crusade

COMPLETE SET (3)	15.00	40.00
COMMON CARD (1-3)	6.00	15.00
STATED ODDS 1:36		

1998 Krome Shi Mega Chromium

COMPLETE SET (30)	6.00	15.00
UNOPENED BOX (PACKS)		
UNOPENED PACK (CARDS)		
COMMON CARD (1-30)	.30	.75

1998 Krome Shi Mega Chromium Chase

COMPLETE SET (4)	10.00	25.00
COMMON CARD (CHASE1-CHASE4)	3.00	8.00
RANDOMLY INSERTED INTO PACKS		

1996 Comic Images Shi Visions of the Golden Empire

COMPLETE SET (90)	8.00	20.00
UNOPENED BOX (36 PACKS)	40.00	50.00
UNOPENED PACK (7 CARDS)	1.50	1.75
COMMON CARD (1-90)	.20	.50
*HOLOCHROME: 4X TO 10X BASIC CARDS	2.00	5.00
NNO Atomik Angels Bonus Insert	2.00	5.00
NNO William Tucci AU/500*	20.00	50.00
NNO 90-Card Holochrome Panel		

1996 Comic Images Shi Visions of the Golden Empire Embossed 23kt Gold

1 Copyright 1996/1000	8.00	20.00
2 Exchange Card/1000		

2000 Ships of Farscape

COMPLETE SET (9)	8.00	12.00
COMMON CARD (FS1-FS9)	1.00	2.50
ANNOUNCED PRINT RUN 2,500 SETS		

2015 Shopkins Dog Tags

COMPLETE SET (18)	25.00	60.00
UNOPENED BOX (24 PACKS)	60.00	120.00
UNOPENED PACK (1 DOG TAG+STICKER)	2.00	5.00
COMMON DOG TAG (1-18)	2.50	6.00

2015 Shopkins Dog Tags Foil

COMPLETE SET (6)	12.00	30.00
COMMON CARD (S1-S6)	3.00	8.00
RANDOMLY INSERTED INTO PACKS		

2015 Shopkins Dog Tags Stickers

COMPLETE SET (20)	5.00	12.00
COMMON CARD	.40	1.00
STATED ODDS 1:1		

2016 Shopkins Magnets

COMPLETE SET (16)	10.00	25.00
COMPLETE SET W/DC (24)	15.00	40.00
UNOPENED BOX (24 PACKS)	80.00	100.00
UNOPENED PACK (2 MAGNETS+POSTER)	1.50	4.00
COMMON MAGNET	.75	2.00
5 Kooky Cookie	1.50	4.00
Poppy Corn#{Soda Pops		
7 Dum Mee Mee	1.25	3.00
8 I Heart SPK	1.25	3.00
Poppy Corn#{Apple Blossum#{Cupcake Chic		
12 Sneaky Sally	1.25	3.00
14 Suzie Sundae	1.25	3.00

2016 Shopkins Magnets Posters

COMPLETE SET (4)	2.50	6.00
COMMON POSTER	.75	2.00
STATED ODDS 1:1		

2015 Shopkins Seasons 1 and 2

COMPLETE SET W/O SP (90)	12.00	30.00
COMPLETE SET W/SP (130)	50.00	100.00
UNOPENED BOX (24 PACKS)	50.00	90.00
UNOPENED PACK (6 CARDS+STICKER)	1.50	4.00
COMMON CARD (1-90)	.20	.50
COMMON SP (91-130)	1.25	3.00

2001 Shrek

COMPLETE SET (72)	5.00	12.00
UNOPENED BOX (30 PACKS)	50.00	75.00
UNOPENED PACK (6 CARDS)	2.00	2.50
COMMON CARD (1-72)	.12	.30
B1 Shrek And Princess Fiona Box Bonus		

2001 Shrek Animation Cels

COMPLETE SET (6)	10.00	25.00
COMMON CARD (AC1-AC6)	2.00	5.00
STATED ODDS 1:15		

2001 Shrek Stand-Up Characters

COMPLETE SET (6)	8.00	20.00
COMMON CARD (S1-S6)	1.50	4.00
STATED ODDS 1:10		

2001 Shrek Promos

COMMON CARD	.75	2.00
1 Toronto Spring Expo	2.00	5.00
2 SDCC	1.25	3.00
3 Shrek Trading Cards	1.25	3.00

2004 Comic Images Shrek 2

COMPLETE SET (72)	5.00	12.00
UNOPENED BOX (36 PACKS)	30.00	40.00
UNOPENED PACK (6 CARDS)	1.25	1.50
COMMON CARD (1-72)	.12	.30
*UK: SAME VALUE AS BASIC CARDS	.12	.30
*UK FOIL: 1.5X TO 4X BASIC CARDS	.50	1.25

2004 Comic Images Shrek 2 Autographs

COMMON CARD (A1-A2)	15.00	40.00
AVAILABLE THROUGH REDEMPTION ONLY		

2004 Comic Images Shrek 2 Foil Characters

COMPLETE SET (6)	8.00	20.00
COMMON CARD (C1-C6)	1.50	4.00
RANDOMLY INSERTED INTO PACKS		

2004 Shrek 2 Promos

COMPLETE SET (5)		
COMMON CARD ()		
P1 Shrek and Fiona	.75	2.00
P2 Shrek hugging Donkey	.75	2.00
P3 Shrek running	1.25	3.00
NNO Coming Spring 2004	.75	2.00
Donkey and Shrek		
NNO Shrek 2 Oversized	.75	2.00

2004 Cards Inc. Shrek 2 Promos

COMMON CARD (P1-P4)	.75	2.00
P3 Shrek Running	1.25	3.00
P4 Puss in Boots	2.00	5.00

2007 Shrek the Third

COMPLETE SET (72)	4.00	10.00
COMMON CARD (1-72)	.10	.30
CL1 STATED ODDS ONE PER HOBBY CASE		
CL1 Ogre Love	3.00	8.00

2007 Shrek the Third Fiona's Fairytale Five

COMPLETE SET (5)	8.00	20.00
COMMON CARD (F1-F5)	2.00	5.00
STATED ODDS 1:17		

2007 Shrek the Third Raul's Make-Up Tips

COMPLETE SET (3)	3.00	8.00
COMMON CARD (BL1-BL3)	1.25	3.00
STATED ODDS ONE PER HOBBY BOX		

2007 Shrek the Third Scratch 'n Stink Gold

COMPLETE SET (6)	5.00	12.00
COMMON CARD (SH1-SH6)	1.00	2.50
STATED ODDS 1:5 HOBBY		

2007 Shrek the Third Scratch 'n Stink Green

COMPLETE SET (6)	1.50	4.00
COMMON CARD (S1-S6)	.30	.75
STATED ODDS 1:1 RETAIL		

2007 Shrek the Third Tattoos

COMPLETE SET (6)	2.00	5.00
COMMON CARD (T1-T6)	.40	1.00
STATED ODDS 1:2 RETAIL		

2007 Shrek the Third Promos

COMMON CARD	.75	2.00
S3i Shrek/Puss/Donkey	1.25	3.00
S3T Donkey/Shrek/Puss	1.25	3.00
S3NY Shrek/Puss/Donkey NYCC	1.25	3.00

2019 Fright-Rags Silent Night Deadly Night

COMPLETE SET (80)	25.00	60.00
UNOPENED BOX (24 PACKS)		
UNOPENED PACK (9 CARDS+1 STICKER)		
COMMON CARD (1-80)	.50	1.25
*PARALLEL: 1.5X TO 4X BASIC CARDS		

2019 Fright-Rags Silent Night Deadly Night Autograph

NNO Linnea Quigley	25.00	60.00

2019 Fright-Rags Silent Night Deadly Night Stickers

COMPLETE SET (6)	3.00	8.00
COMMON STICKER	.75	2.00
STATED ODDS 1:1		

2001 Silly CDs

COMPLETE SET (33)	8.00	20.00
PUZZLE CARDS SETS 1-4 AND 6	12.00	30.00
PUZZLE CARDS SET 5	8.00	20.00
COMPLETE SET W/PUZZLES (69)	25.00	60.00
UNOPENED BOX (36 PACKS)	50.00	60.00
UNOPENED PACK (5 CARDS)	1.50	1.75
COMMON CARD (1-33)	.40	1.00
COMMON PUZZLE 1-4 AND 6	.75	2.00
COMMON PUZZLE 5	2.00	5.00
12 Pariah SP	1.50	4.00

2001 Silly CDs Promos

COMMON CARD	1.25	3.00
1 4-Up Panel		

2001 Silly CDs Stickers

COMPLETE SET W/SP (11)	10.00	25.00
COMPLETE SET W/O SP (9)	1.25	3.00
COMMON CARD (1-11)	.20	.50
STICKERS #4 and #6 ARE SP		
4 Sickie Fartin' Rare SP	6.00	15.00
6 Moronna Rare SP	6.00	15.00

2003 Silly CDs Series 2

COMPLETE SET (34)	10.00	25.00
COMMON CARD (1-36)	.50	1.25

2008 Silly Supermarket All-New Series

COMPLETE SET (30)	8.00	20.00
UNOPENED BOX (24 PACKS)	20.00	25.00
UNOPENED PACK (6 CARDS)	1.00	1.25
COMMON CARD	.40	1.00

2003 Silly Supermarket Stickers Series One

COMPLETE SET (24)	6.00	15.00
COMMON CARD	.50	1.25

2003 Silly Supermarket Stickers Series Two

COMPLETE SET (24)	6.00	15.00
COMMON CARD	.50	1.25

2005-06 Top Shelf Enterprises Silly Supermarket Stickers Series Three

COMPLETE SET (30)	5.00	12.00
COMMON CARD	.25	.60
P1 Krusty Kreme Doughnuts Promo		
P2 Liquid Mold Promo (excl.)		
AU1 Jay Lynch AU/50		
NNO1 Got Wheels? (blank back)		
NNO2 Land O' Snakes Venom (blank back)		
NNO3 Waggy Packages (blank back)		

1990 Topps The Simpsons

COMPLETE SET (88)	6.00	12.00
COMPLETE SET W/STICKERS (110)	6.00	15.00
UNOPENED BOX (36 PACKS)	75.00	125.00
UNOPENED PACK (8 CARDS+1 STICKER)	2.50	4.00
COMMON CARD (1-88)	.20	.50

1990 Topps The Simpsons Stickers

COMPLETE SET (22)	2.50	6.00
COMMON CARD (1-22)	.20	.50
STATED ODDS 1:1		

2000 The Simpsons Anniversary Celebration

COMPLETE SET (81)	5.00	12.00
UNOPENED BOX (24 PACKS)	40.00	50.00
UNOPENED PACK (7 CARDS)	2.00	2.25
COMMON CARD (1-81)	.15	.40
T1 STATED ODDS 1:1		
SC1 STATED ODDS 1:CASE		
T1 Decoder Thingy	.40	1.00
SC1 Greetings From Springfield	10.00	25.00

2000 The Simpsons Anniversary Celebration Autographs

COMPLETE SET (5)	100.00	200.00
COMMON CARD (A1-A5)	20.00	50.00
RANDOM INSERT IN PACKS		

2000 The Simpsons Anniversary Celebration Cut-Ups

COMPLETE SET (8) 15.00 40.00
COMMON CARD (C1-C8) 2.50 6.00
STATED ODDS 1:11

2000 The Simpsons Anniversary Celebration Diorama-Rama

COMPLETE SET (4) 12.00 30.00
COMMON CARD (D1-D4) 4.00 10.00
STATED ODDS 1:27

2000 The Simpsons Anniversary Celebration Nuclear Neon

COMPLETE SET (6) 10.00 25.00
COMMON CARD (N1-N6) 2.00 5.00
STATED ODDS 1:17

2000 The Simpsons Anniversary Celebration Promos

COMPLETE SET (3) 2.00 5.00
COMMON CARD (P1-P3) 1.25 3.00

1996 Tempo The Simpsons Down Under

COMPLETE SET (100) 12.00 30.00
UNOPENED BOX (30 PACKS) 45.00 60.00
UNOPENED PACK (7 CARDS) 1.50 2.00
COMMON CARD (1-100) .25 .60
SDBC1 Binder Card 20.00 50.00

1996 Tempo The Simpsons Down Under Bartarang

1 Bartarang
BART1 Bartarang EXCH 200.00 400.00

1996 Tempo The Simpsons Down Under Homer as Famous Australians

COMPLETE SET (7) 15.00 40.00
COMMON CARD (HA1-HA7) 3.00 8.00
STATED ODDS 1:7

1996 Tempo The Simpsons Down Under Springfield's Finest

COMPLETE SET (4) 20.00 50.00
COMMON CARD (SF1-SF4) 6.00 15.00
STATED ODDS 1:60

1996 Tempo The Simpsons Down Under The Seven Duffs Beer Die-Cuts

COMPLETE SET (7) 60.00 120.00
COMMON CARD (D1-D7) 8.00 20.00
STATED ODDS 1:30

1996 Tempo The Simpsons Down Under Promos

COMPLETE SET (4) 6.00 15.00
COMMON CARD 2.00 5.00

2000 The Simpsons FilmCardz

COMPLETE SET (45) 8.00 20.00
UNOPENED UK BOX (24 PACKS)
UNOPENED HOBBY BOX (24 PACKS) 30.00 40.00
UNOPENED HOBBY PACK (5 CARDS) 1.75 2.00
UNOPENED UK PACK (2 CARDS)
COMMON CARD (1-45) .30 .75

2000 The Simpsons FilmCardz Foil Cels

COMPLETE SET (10) 12.00 30.00
COMMON CARD (S1-S10) 2.00 5.00
RANDOMLY INSERTED IN PACKS

2000 The Simpsons FilmCardz Promos

COMPLETE SET (3) 2.50 6.00
COMMON CARD (P1-P3) 1.25 3.00

2003 The Simpsons FilmCardz Series Two

COMPLETE SET (45) 6.00 15.00
UNOPENED BOX (24 PACKS) 30.00 40.00
UNOPENED PACK (5 CARDS) 1.25 1.75
COMMON CARD (1-45) .25 .60

2003 The Simpsons FilmCardz Series Two Follow Suit Foil Rare

COMPLETE SET (6) 10.00 25.00
COMMON CARD 2.00 5.00
STATED ODDS 1:8

2003 The Simpsons FilmCardz Series Two Follow Suit Foil Ultra Rare

COMPLETE SET (3) 8.00 20.00
COMMON CARD (UR1-UR3) 3.00 8.00
STATED ODDS 1:24

2003 The Simpsons FilmCardz Series Two Promos

COMPLETE SET (2) 1.25 3.00
COMMON CARD (P1-P2) .75 2.00

2001 Simpsons Mania

COMPLETE SET (72) 4.00 10.00
UNOPENED BOX (36 PACKS) 50.00 60.00
UNOPENED PACK (7 CARDS) 1.50 1.75
COMMON CARD (1-72) .12 .30
NNO Homer PROMO 1.25 3.00

2001 Simpsons Mania Autographs

COMPLETE SET (7) 150.00 300.00
COMMON CARD (A1-A7) 25.00 50.00
STATED ODDS 1:72
A1 Nancy Cartwright 30.00 80.00
A3 Hank Azaria 25.00 60.00

2001 Simpsons Mania SimpsaDelic

COMPLETE SET (9) 10.00 25.00
COMMON CARD (S1-S9) 1.25 3.00
STATED ODDS 1:11

1993 SkyBox The Simpsons Series One

COMPLETE SET (80) 4.00 10.00
UNOPENED BOX (36 PACKS) 500.00 750.00
UNOPENED PACK (8 CARDS) 15.00 20.00
COMMON CARD .15 .40

1993 SkyBox The Simpsons Series One Cel Cards

COMPLETE SET (6) 15.00 40.00
COMMON CARD (1-6) 3.00 8.00
STATED ODDS 1:18

1993 SkyBox The Simpsons Series One Glow-in-the-Dark

COMPLETE SET (4) 12.00 30.00
COMMON CARD (1-4) 4.00 10.00
STATED ODDS 1:36

1993 SkyBox The Simpsons Series One Tattoos

COMPLETE SET (10) .75 2.00
COMMON CARD (1-10) .10 .25
RANDOMLY INSERTED INTO PACKS

1993 SkyBox The Simpsons Series One Wiggle

COMPLETE SET (9) 6.00 15.00
COMMON CARD (1-9) .75 2.00
STATED ODDS 1:4

1994 SkyBox The Simpsons Series Two

COMPLETE SET (81) 4.00 10.00
UNOPENED BOX (36 PACKS) 250.00 400.00
UNOPENED PACK (8 CARDS) 8.00 12.00
COMMON CARD .12 .30
NNO Bartscreen Decoder .75 2.00

1994 SkyBox The Simpsons Series Two Arty Art

COMPLETE SET (4) 80.00 150.00
COMMON CARD (A1-A4) 15.00 40.00
STATED ODDS 1:180

1994 SkyBox The Simpsons Series Two Disappearing Ink

COMPLETE SET (4) 20.00 50.00
COMMON CARD (D1-D4) 6.00 15.00
STATED ODDS 1:36

1994 SkyBox The Simpsons Series Two Smell-O-Rama

COMPLETE SET (10) 4.00 10.00
COMMON CARD (1-10 .50 1.25
STATED ODDS 1:3

1994 SkyBox The Simpsons Series Two Wiggle

COMPLETE SET (9) 10.00 25.00
COMMON CARD (W1-W9) 2.00 5.00
STATED ODDS 1:6

1994 SkyBox The Simpsons Series Two Promos

COMMON CARD .75 2.00
B1 Willy the Dupe Dupkin 1.25 3.00
Bongo Comics
B2 Radioactive Man Bongo Comics 1.25 3.00
B3 Bongo Comics 1.25 3.00
B4 Bongo Comics 1.25 3.00
B5 Bartman/Radioactive Man 1.25 3.00
B6 Bongo Comics 1.25 3.00
P4 Willy the Dupe Dupkin 6.00 15.00
Diamond Distribution
NNO Upcoming Series II
How to Use Spinner Card

1998 Comic Images Sirius Gallery

COMPLETE SET (72) 6.00 15.00
UNOPENED BOX (48 PACKS) 20.00 30.00
UNOPENED PACK (8 CARDS) .75 1.00
COMMON CARD (1-72) .15 .40

1998 Comic Images Sirius Gallery Autographs

COMPLETE SET (3)
COMMON CARD 15.00 40.00
RANDOMLY INSERTED INTO PACKS

1998 Comic Images Sirius Gallery Omnichrome

COMPLETE SET (6) 12.00 30.00
COMMON CARD (Omni1-Omni6) 2.50 6.00
STATED ODDS 1:18

1998 Comic Images Sirius Gallery Promos

1 6-Up Panel
2 Unnumbered, Dawn .75 2.00

2004 Six Feet Under Seasons One and Two

COMPLETE SET (81) 4.00 10.00
UNOPENED BOX (40 PACKS) 45.00 60.00
UNOPENED PACK (5 CARDS) 1.25 1.50
COMMON CARD (1-81) .10 .30

2004 Six Feet Under Seasons One and Two Autographs

COMPLETE SET (17) 200.00 400.00
COMMON CARD 6.00 15.00
STATED ODDS THREE PER BOX
BALL AUTO ISSUED AS CASE TOPPER
BLACK AUTO ISSUED AS ALBUM EXCLUSIVE
DOUGLAS AUTO ISSUED AS MULTI-CASE INCENTIVE
L (LIMITED): 300-500 COPIES
1 Alan Ball CT 20.00 40.00
4 Joanna Cassidy L 20.00 40.00
5 Illeana Douglas Cl 15.00 30.00
6 Michael C. Hall L 20.00 50.00
8 Peter Krause L 15.00 40.00

2004 Six Feet Under Seasons One and Two Opening Montage

COMPLETE SET (9) 6.00 15.00
COMMON CARD (M1-M9) .75 2.00
STATED ODDS 1:14

2004 Six Feet Under Seasons One and Two Players

COMPLETE SET (9) 8.00 20.00
COMMON CARD (PL1-PL9) 1.25 3.00
STATED ODDS 1:14

2004 Six Feet Under Seasons One and Two Relationships

COMPLETE SET (27) 4.00 10.00
COMMON CARD (R1-R27) .20 .50
STATED ODDS 1:5

2004 Six Feet Under Seasons One and Two Promos

COMPLETE SET (3) 2.00 5.00
COMMON CARD .75 2.00
P3 Brotherhood 2.50 6.00

2007 Six Million Dollar Man Color Autograph Expansion

MAJORS/WAGNER AUTO ISSUED AS 2-SET INCENTIVE
A14 Lee Majors 20.00 50.00
A15 Richard Anderson 10.00 25.00
A16 Lindsay Wagner 50.00 100.00
A21 Alan Oppenheimer 8.00 20.00
DA1 Lee Majors/Richard Anderson 125.00 250.00
DA2 Lee Majors/Lindsay Wagner 2SI 125.00 250.00

1994 FunFax 60's Sci-Fi and Terror TV

COMPLETE SET (100) 12.00 30.00
COMPLETE SERIES 1 SET (50) 8.00 20.00
COMPLETE SERIES 2 SET (50) 6.00 15.00
UNOPENED S1 BOX (36 PACKS)
UNOPENED S1 PACK (6 CARDS)
UNOPENED S2 BOX (36 PACKS)
UNOPENED S2 PACK (6 CARDS)
COMMON CARD (1-100) .25 .60

1994 FunFax 60's Sci-Fi and Terror TV Promos

COMPLETE SET (6) 8.00 20.00
COMMON CARD (P1-P6) 2.00 5.00

1995 Fleer Ultra Skeleton Warriors

COMPLETE SET (100) 8.00 20.00
UNOPENED HOBBY BOX (36 PACKS) 35.00 45.00
UNOPENED HOBBY PACK (6 CARDS) 1.25 1.50
UNOPENED RETAIL BOX (36 PACKS) 15.00 20.00
UNOPENED RETAIL PACK (6 CARDS) .75 1.00
COMMON CARD (1-100) .15 .40
*FLEER: SAME VALUE AS BASIC CARDS .15 .40

1995 Fleer Ultra Skeleton Warriors Comics Promos

COMMON CARD .75 2.00

1995 Fleer Ultra Skeleton Warriors Luma Bone

COMPLETE SET (5) 2.50 6.00
COMMON CARD (1-5) .60 1.50
STATED ODDS 1:4 HOBBY; 1:7 RETAIL

1995 Fleer Ultra Skeleton Warriors PowerBlast

COMPLETE SET (9) 12.00 30.00
COMMON CARD (1-9) 1.50 4.00
STATED ODDS 1:6 HOBBY; 1:11 RETAIL

1995 Fleer Ultra Skeleton Warriors Suspended Animation

COMPLETE SET (10) 5.00 12.00
COMMON CARD (1-10) .60 1.50
STATED ODDS 1:4 HOBBY; 1:6 RETAIL

2004 Sky Captain and the World of Tomorrow Promos

COMPLETE SET (8) 5.00 12.00
COMMON CARD (1-8) 1.00 2.50

2001 The Slayers

COMPLETE SET (72) 5.00 12.00
UNOPENED BOX (36 PACKS) 30.00 40.00
UNOPENED PACK (7 CARDS) 1.25 1.50
COMMON CARD (1-72) .12 .30

2001 The Slayers Foil

COMPLETE SET (6)	12.00	30.00
COMMON CARD (C1-C6)	2.50	6.00
RANDOMLY INSERTED INTO PACKS		

2001 The Slayers Promos

P1 Shipping May 2001 Group of 5	.75	2.00
P2 Shipping May 2001 Lina and Zelgadis	.75	2.00

1999 Inkworks Sleepy Hollow

COMPLETE SET (90)	5.00	12.00
UNOPENED BOX (36 PACKS)	40.00	50.00
UNOPENED PACK (8 CARDS)	1.25	1.50
COMMON CARD (1-90)	.10	.25
T1 STATED ODDS 1:108		
T1 Colonial Post newspaper	6.00	15.00

1999 Inkworks Sleepy Hollow Autographs

COMMON AUTO (A2-A5)	10.00	25.00
RANDOM INSERTS IN PACKS		
A4 Casper van Dien	20.00	50.00
A5 Danny Elfman	75.00	150.00
R1 Redemption EXCH		

1999 Inkworks Sleepy Hollow Foil Lobby Cards

COMPLETE SET (6)	8.00	20.00
COMMON CARD (LC1-LC6)	2.50	6.00
STATED ODDS 1:17		

1999 Inkworks Sleepy Hollow Heads Will Roll

COMPLETE SET (9)	5.00	12.00
COMMON CARD (CC1-CC9)	1.25	3.00
STATED ODDS 1:11		

1999 Inkworks Sleepy Hollow Promos

COMMON PROMO	1.25	3.00
P2 The Headless Horseman	1.50	4.00
P3 Christina Ricci	2.00	5.00

2015 Sleepy Hollow Season One

COMPLETE SET (63)	6.00	15.00
UNOPENED BOX (24 PACKS)	30.00	50.00
UNOPENED PACK (5 CARDS)	1.50	2.50
COMMON CARD (1-63)	.15	.40
*FOIL: 1X TO 2.5X BASIC CARDS	.40	1.00

2015 Sleepy Hollow Season One Autographs

COMMON AUTO	5.00	12.00
STATED ODDS 1:24		
AS Amandla Stenberg	12.00	30.00
EC Erin Cahill	8.00	20.00
KY Kathleen York	8.00	20.00
NG Nicholas Gonzalez	6.00	15.00
PG Patrick Gorman	8.00	20.00
TM Tom Mison	30.00	75.00
DJM D.J. Mifflin	10.00	25.00

2015 Sleepy Hollow Season One Behind-the-Scenes

COMPLETE SET (9)	6.00	15.00
COMMON CARD (BTS1-BTS9)	1.25	3.00
STATED ODDS 1:12		

2015 Sleepy Hollow Season One Character Bios

COMPLETE SET (6)	8.00	20.00
COMMON CARD (C1-C6)	2.00	5.00
STATED ODDS 1:12		

2015 Sleepy Hollow Season One Monsters

COMPLETE SET (9)	8.00	20.00
COMMON CARD (MN1-MN9)	1.50	4.00
STATED ODDS 1:12		
MN8 The Headless Horseman	2.50	6.00

2015 Sleepy Hollow Season One Posters

COMPLETE SET (3)	30.00	80.00
COMMON CARD (PS1 - PS3)	12.00	30.00
STATED ODDS 1:288		

2015 Sleepy Hollow Season One Wardrobes

COMPLETE SET (14)	75.00	150.00
COMMON CARD (M1-M14)	4.00	10.00
STATED ODDS 1:24		
M1 Nicole Beharie	5.00	12.00
M2 Tom Mison	5.00	12.00
M5 Nicole Beharie	6.00	15.00
M6 Orlando Jones	5.00	12.00
M7 Nicholas Gonzalez	6.00	15.00
M8 Nicole Beharie	5.00	12.00
M9 Tom Mison	6.00	15.00
M12 Katia Winter	6.00	15.00
M13 Richard Cetrone	6.00	15.00
M14 Nicole Beharie	8.00	20.00

2015 Sleepy Hollow Season One Promos

COMPLETE SET (2)	1.25	3.00
COMMON CARD (P1-P2)	.75	2.00
*CRYPTO.: .75X TO 2X BASIC CARDS		

1997 Inkworks Sliders

COMPLETE SET (72)	5.00	12.00
UNOPENED BOX (36 PACKS)	25.00	40.00
UNOPENED PACK (8 CARDS)	1.00	1.50
COMMON CARD (1-72)	.15	.40
NNO Dealer Issue Promo Card	2.00	5.00

1997 Inkworks Sliders Embossed

COMPLETE SET (9)	7.50	20.00
COMMON CARD (1-9)	1.25	3.00
STATED ODDS 1:12		

1997 Inkworks Sliders Foilworks

COMPLETE SET (6)	7.50	20.00
COMMON CARD (1-6)	1.50	4.00
STATED ODDS 1:18		

1998 Inkworks Small Soldiers

COMPLETE SET (99)	4.00	10.00
UNOPENED BOX (36 PACKS)	50.00	75.00
UNOPENED PACK (8 CARDS+1 TATTOO)	2.00	3.00
COMMON CARD (1-90; T1-T9)	.08	.25
S1 STATED ODDS 1:108		
S1 The Gorgonites	12.00	30.00
The Commando Elite		

1998 Small Soldiers Autographs

COMPLETE SET (4)	120.00	250.00
COMMON CARD (A1-A4)	20.00	50.00
RANDOMLY INSERTED INTO PACKS		
A2 Kristen Dunst	70.00	120.00
A4 Stan Winston	25.00	60.00

1998 Inkworks Small Soldiers Battle

COMPLETE SET (6)	6.00	15.00
COMMON CARD (B1-B6)	1.25	3.00
STATED ODDS 1:27		

1998 Inkworks Small Soldiers Promos

COMPLETE SET (3)	2.00	5.00
COMMON CARD (P1-P3)	.75	2.00
NNO Phil Hartman Tribute 1948-1998 (Dealer Exclusive)	30.00	75.00

1981 Brooke Bond Small Wonders

COMPLETE SET (40)	8.00	20.00
COMMON CARD (1-40)	.30	.75

1996 Dart FlipCards Smokey Bear Collector's Series

COMPLETE SET (50)	4.00	10.00
UNOPENED BOX (36 PACKS)	25.00	35.00
UNOPENED PACK (7 CARDS)	1.00	1.25
COMMON CARD (1-50)	.12	.30
P1 Smokey With Binoculars PROMO	.75	2.00
S1 Smokey With Binoculars Die-Cuts	6.00	15.00
S2 Thanks for Listening Gold Foil-Stamp	6.00	15.00
TB Tall Boy Card	4.00	10.00

1982 Topps Smurf SuperCards

COMPLETE SET (56)	10.00	25.00
UNOPENED BOX (24 PACKS)		
UNOPENED PACK (7 CARDS)		
UNOPENED RACK PACK		
COMMON CARD (1-56)	.30	.75

1986 Topps Snotty Signs Stickers

COMPLETE SET (44)	4.00	10.00
COMMON CARD (1-44)	.20	.50

1993 SkyBox Snow White and the Seven Dwarfs Series One

COMPLETE SET (90)	6.00	15.00
UNOPENED BOX (36 PACKS)	30.00	40.00
UNOPENED PACK (8 CARDS)	1.25	1.50
COMMON CARD (1-90)	.12	.30

1993 SkyBox Snow White and the Seven Dwarfs Series One Spectra

COMPLETE SET (4)	8.00	20.00
COMMON CARD (1-4)	2.50	6.00
STATED ODDS 1:18		

1994 SkyBox Snow White and the Seven Dwarfs Series Two

COMPLETE SET (90)	5.00	12.00
UNOPENED HOBBY BOX (36 PACKS)	20.00	30.00
UNOPENED HOBBY PACK (8 CARDS)	1.00	1.25
UNOPENED JUMBO BOX (24 PACKS)	10.00	15.00
UNOPENED JUMBO PACK (16 CARDS)	.50	.75
UNOPENED RETAIL BOX (12 PACKS)	10.00	15.00
UNOPENED RETAIL PACK (8 CARDS)	.50	.75
COMMON CARD (1-90)	.10	.25
S1 Snow White and Dopey Promo	.75	2.00

1994 SkyBox Snow White and the Seven Dwarfs Series Two Foil

COMPLETE SET (9)	15.00	40.00
COMMON CARD (F1-F9)	2.50	6.00
STATED ODDS 1:18 HOBBY AND RETAIL; 1:9 JUMBO		

1989 Red Star Soap Stars

COMPLETE BOXED SET (15)	5.00	12.00
COMMON CARD	.60	1.50

2015 Sonic Boom Dog Tags

COMPLETE SET (24)	30.00	80.00
COMMON CARD (1-24)	2.00	5.00

2015 Sonic Boom Dog Tags Stickers

COMPLETE SET (24)	5.00	12.00
COMMON CARD (1-24)	.40	1.00
STATED ODDS 1:1		

1993 Topps Sonic the Hedgehog

COMPLETE SET (33)	8.00	8.00
COMPLETE SET W/STICKERS (66)	5.00	12.00
UNOPENED BOX (36 PACKS)	15.00	25.00
UNOPENED PACK (8 CARDS)	.75	1.00
COMMON CARD (1-33)	.12	.30

1993 Topps Sonic the Hedgehog Stickers

COMPLETE SET (33)	2.50	6.00
COMMON CARD (1-33)	.12	.30

2014 Sons of Anarchy Seasons 1-3

COMPLETE SET (100)	5.00	12.00
UNOPENED BOX (24 PACKS)	100.00	200.00
UNOPENED PACK (5 CARDS)	4.00	8.00
COMMON CARD (1-100)	.20	.50

2014 Sons of Anarchy Seasons 1-3 Autographs

COMMON AUTO (A1-A26)	8.00	20.00
STATED ODDS 1:24		
A1 Charlie Hunnam	60.00	120.00
A2 Katey Sagal	25.00	60.00
A3 Ron Perlman	20.00	50.00
A4 Kim Coates	15.00	40.00
A5 Dayton Callie	10.00	25.00
A6 Ryan Hurst	25.00	60.00
A7 William Lucking	15.00	40.00
A8 Theo Rossi	15.00	40.00
A9 Emilio Rivera	12.00	30.00
A11 Taylor Sheridan	10.00	25.00
A12 Jeff Kober	15.00	40.00
A14 Patrick St. Esprit	10.00	25.00
A17 Mitch Pileggi	12.00	30.00
A19 Dendrie Taylor	10.00	25.00
A20 Sprague Grayden	15.00	40.00
A21 Henry Rollins	15.00	40.00
A23 Kristen Renton	12.00	30.00
A25 Tommy Flanagan	25.00	50.00
A26 David Labrava	12.00	30.00

2014 Sons of Anarchy Seasons 1-3 Character Bios

COMPLETE SET (11)	8.00	20.00
COMMON CARD (C01-C11)	1.25	3.00
STATED ODDS 1:12		

2014 Sons of Anarchy Seasons 1-3 Dual Wardrobes

COMPLETE SET (4)	60.00	120.00
COMMON MEM (DM01-DM04)	12.00	30.00
STATED ODDS 1:24		
DM01 Jax and Opie	15.00	40.00
DM03 Jax and Juice	15.00	40.00

2014 Sons of Anarchy Seasons 1-3 Patches

COMPLETE SET (3)	25.00	60.00
COMMON MEM (RP01-RP03)	10.00	25.00
STATED ODDS 1:96		
RP01 Men of Mayhem	12.00	30.00

2014 Sons of Anarchy Seasons 1-3 Prop Relics

COMMON MEM (P1-P3)	10.00	25.00
RANDOMLY INSERTED INTO PACKS		
P1 Movie Money	12.00	30.00
P3 Piney's Oxygen Tank	200.00	350.00

2014 Sons of Anarchy Seasons 1-3 Temporary Tattoos

COMPLETE SET (9)	8.00	20.00
COMMON CARD (TT01-TT09)	2.00	5.00
STATED ODDS 1:24		

2014 Sons of Anarchy Seasons 1-3 Triple Wardrobe

STATED PRINT RUN 25 SER. #'d CARDS		
TW1 Gemma/Jax/Tara	125.00	250.00

2014 Sons of Anarchy Seasons 1-3 Wardrobes

COMMON CARD (M1-M12)	6.00	15.00
STATED ODDS 1:24		
M1 Jax	10.00	25.00
M2 Gemma	8.00	20.00
M4 Gemma	10.00	25.00
M5 Jax	10.00	25.00
M6 Opie	10.00	25.00
M7 Bobby	8.00	20.00
M9 Gemma	10.00	25.00
M10 Tig	8.00	20.00
M11 Clay	12.00	30.00
M12 Opie	12.00	30.00

2014 Sons of Anarchy Seasons 1-3 Promos

P1a Promo (Philly)	3.00	8.00
P1b Promo 1 Metal (Philly)	25.00	60.00

2015 Sons of Anarchy Seasons 4-5

COMPLETE SET (72)	5.00	12.00
UNOPENED BOX (24 PACKS)	100.00	150.00
UNOPENED PACK (5 CARDS)	4.00	6.00
COMMON CARD (1-72)	.20	.50
*RAINBOW/25: 8X TO 20X BASIC CARDS	4.00	10.00
*RED/10: 15X TO 40X BASIC CARDS	8.00	20.00

2015 Sons of Anarchy Seasons 4-5 Autographs

COMMON AUTO	10.00	25.00
STATED ODDS 1:24		
AT Ashley Tisdale	50.00	100.00
CH Charlie Hunnam	75.00	150.00
DC Dayton Callie	25.00	60.00
DD Drea de Matteo	30.00	75.00
KS Katey Sagal	20.00	50.00
MO Michael Marisi Ornstein	15.00	40.00
RH Ryan Hurst	30.00	75.00
RM Rachel Miner	12.00	30.00
RP Ron Perlman	20.00	50.00
RW Robin Weigert	12.00	30.00
TA Tom Arnold	15.00	40.00
WL William Lucking	20.00	50.00
WZ Winter Ave Zoli	25.00	60.00
DL1 David Labrava 1	15.00	40.00

2015 Sons of Anarchy Seasons 4-5 Character Bios

COMPLETE SET (9)	3.00	8.00
COMMON CARD (C12-C20)	.60	1.50
*RAINBOW/25: 4X TO 10X BASIC CARDS	6.00	15.00
STATED ODDS 1:4		

2015 Sons of Anarchy Seasons 4-5 Dual Wardrobes

COMMON CARD (DW1-DW9)	6.00	15.00
STATED ODDS 1:144		
DW1 W.Unser C.Marstein	10.00	25.00
DW2 P.Winston O.Winston	8.00	20.00
DW4 T.Knowles-Teller W.Case	12.00	30.00
DW5 J.Teller O.Winston	30.00	75.00
DW6 L.Winston O.Winston	12.00	30.00
DW9 G.Teller P.Winston	12.00	30.00

2015 Sons of Anarchy Seasons 4-5 Gallery

COMPLETE SET (9)	4.00	10.00
COMMON CARD (G1-G9)	.75	2.00
*RAINBOW/25: 6X TO 15X BASIC CARDS		
STATED ODDS 1:4		

2015 Sons of Anarchy Seasons 4-5 Patches

COMPLETE SET (3)	25.00	60.00
COMMON MEM (RP4-RP6)	8.00	20.00
STATED ODDS 1:192		
RP5 Charming, CA	12.00	30.00

2015 Sons of Anarchy Seasons 4-5 Temporary Tattoos

COMPLETE SET (9)	10.00	25.00
COMMON CARD (TT10-TT18)	2.00	5.00
STATED ODDS 1:24		

2015 Sons of Anarchy Seasons 4-5 Triple Wardrobes

COMMON MEM (TW1-TW3)	15.00	40.00
STATED ODDS 1:576		
TW2 Jax Piney#{Opie	25.00	60.00

2015 Sons of Anarchy Seasons 4-5 Wardrobes

COMMON MEM	5.00	12.00
STATED ODDS 1:24		
W03 Gemma Teller Morrow	8.00	20.00
W04 Bobby Munson	6.00	15.00
W05 Tara Knowles-Teller	6.00	15.00
W06 Harry Opie Winston	8.00	20.00
W09 Jackson Jax Teller	10.00	25.00
W11 Tara Knowles-Teller	8.00	20.00
W13 Wayne Unser	6.00	15.00
W14 Wendy Case	8.00	20.00
W15 Happy Lowman	8.00	20.00
W17 Tara Knowles-Teller	8.00	20.00
W18 Piermont Piney WInston	8.00	20.00

2015 Sons of Anarchy Seasons 4-5 Promo

P1 NSU APR/MAY 2015	2.00	5.00

2015 Sons of Anarchy Seasons 6-7

COMPLETE SET (63)	6.00	15.00
UNOPENED BOX (24 PACKS)	100.00	150.00
UNOPENED PACK (6 CARDS)	4.00	6.00
COMMON CARD (1-63)	.20	.50
*SILVER FOIL/100: 4X TO 10X BASIC CARDS		

2015 Sons of Anarchy Seasons 6-7 Autographs

COMMON AUTO	10.00	25.00
STATED ODDS 1:24		
CH Charlie Hunnam	75.00	150.00
KD Kim Dickens	20.00	50.00
KS Katey Sagal	20.00	50.00
MM Marilyn Manson	250.00	500.00
RW Robin Weigert	25.00	60.00
TR Theo Rossi	12.00	30.00
WG Walton Goggins	20.00	50.00
DDM Drea de Matteo	50.00	100.00
MMO Michael Marisi Ornstein	12.00	30.00
WAZ Winter Ave Zoli	15.00	40.00

2015 Sons of Anarchy Seasons 6-7 Brawl

COMPLETE SET (9)	5.00	12.00
COMMON CARD (Z1-Z9)	1.00	2.50
*SILVER FOIL/100: 1.5X TO 4X BASIC CARDS		
STATED ODDS 1:4		

2015 Sons of Anarchy Seasons 6-7 Dual Wardrobes

COMMON MEM (DM1-DM9)	10.00	25.00
STATED ODDS 1:120		
DM2 Case Padilla	12.00	30.00
DM3 Unser Roosevelt	15.00	40.00
DM8 Knowles-Teller Teller	25.00	60.00

2015 Sons of Anarchy Seasons 6-7 Gallery

COMPLETE SET (9)	4.00	10.00
COMMON CARD (G1-G9)	.75	2.00
*SILVER FOIL/100: 2X TO 5X BASIC CARDS		
STATED ODDS 1:4		

2015 Sons of Anarchy Seasons 6-7 Mug Shots

COMPLETE SET (9)	5.00	12.00
COMMON CARD (MG1-MG9)	1.00	2.50
*SILVER FOIL/100: 1.5X TO 4X BASIC CARDS		
STATED ODDS 1:4		

2015 Sons of Anarchy Seasons 6-7 Patches

COMPLETE SET (3)	20.00	50.00
COMMON MEM (RP5-RP7)	8.00	20.00
STATED ODDS 1:192		
RP8 Sons of Anarchy	10.00	25.00

2015 Sons of Anarchy Seasons 6-7 Prop Relics

STATED ODDS 1:481		
M1 Pipe	50.00	100.00

2015 Sons of Anarchy Seasons 6-7 Temporary Tattoos

COMPLETE SET (9)	10.00	25.00
COMMON CARD (TT1-TT9)	2.00	5.00
STATED ODDS 1:16		

2015 Sons of Anarchy Seasons 6-7 Triple Wardrobes

COMPLETE SET (6)	125.00	250.00
COMMON MEM (TM1-TM6)	10.00	25.00
STATED ODDS 1:192		
TM3 Case Teller#{Knowles-Teller	20.00	50.00
TM4 Unser Knowles-Teller#{Roosevelt	25.00	60.00
TM5 Telford Munson#{Trager	25.00	60.00
TM6 Case Teller#{Padilla	20.00	50.00

2015 Sons of Anarchy Seasons 6-7 Wardrobes

COMMON MEM (M1-M23)	4.00	10.00
STATED ODDS 1:24		
M1 Filip Chibs Telford	6.00	15.00
M2 Eli Roosevelt	5.00	12.00
M4 Tara Knowles-Teller	12.00	30.00
M5 Jackson Jax Teller	10.00	25.00
M7 Ratboy Skogstrom	5.00	12.00
M8 Wayne Unser	8.00	20.00
M9 Lyla Winston	5.00	12.00
M12 Alex Tig Trager	8.00	20.00
M13 Nero Padilla	8.00	20.00
M14 Juan Carlos Juice Ortiz	6.00	15.00
M15 Wayne Unser	5.00	12.00
M16 Nero Padilla	8.00	20.00
M17 Lyla Winston	6.00	15.00
M18 Wendy Case	6.00	15.00
M19 Tara Knowles-Teller	6.00	15.00
M20 Wayne Unser	5.00	12.00
M21 Happy Lowman	6.00	15.00
M22 Filip Chibs Telford	15.00	40.00
M23 Wendy Case	6.00	15.00
M24 Gemma Teller Morrow ALB	12.00	30.00

2005 The Sopranos Season One

COMPLETE SET (72)	5.00	12.00
UNOPENED BOX (36 PACKS)	200.00	300.00
UNOPENED PACK (8 CARDS)	6.00	8.00
COMMON CARD (1-72)	.15	.40

2005 The Sopranos Season One Autographs

COMPLETE SET (9)		
COMMON AUTO	8.00	20.00
AAT Aida Turturro SP	12.00	30.00
ADC Dominic Chianese CI	30.00	75.00
AJA Jerry Adler	10.00	25.00
AJD Jamie Lynn DiScala SP	30.00	75.00

2005 The Sopranos Season One Box-Toppers

COMPLETE SET (3)	3.00	8.00
COMMON CARD (BL1-BL3)	1.25	3.00

2005 The Sopranos Season One Family Matters

COMPLETE SET (9)	10.00	25.00
COMMON CARD (FM1-FM9)	1.25	3.00

2005 The Sopranos Season One La Belle Donne

COMPLETE SET (6)	8.00	20.00
COMMON CARD (BD1-BD6)	1.50	4.00

1999 Comic Images South Park

COMPLETE SET (70)	5.00	12.00
UNOPENED BOX (30 PACKS)	125.00	200.00
UNOPENED PACK (10 CARDS)	5.00	8.00
COMMON CARD (1-70)	.15	.40

1999 Comic Images South Park Many Deaths of Kenny OmniChrome

COMPLETE SET (6)	6.00	15.00
COMMON CARD (1-6)	2.00	5.00
STATED ODDS 1:20		

1999 Comic Images South Park Promos

P1 Eric/Kyle/Stan/Kenny	.75	2.00
P2 South Park	.75	2.00

1996 Collect-a-Card South Pole Vacation feat. the Coca-Cola Polar Bears

COMPLETE SET (50)	2.00	5.00
UNOPENED BOX (36 PACKS)	10.00	15.00
UNOPENED PACK (8 CARDS)	.50	.75
COMMON CARD (1-50)	.08	.20
PBL1 Fish Tales Case Bonus	15.00	40.00

1996 Collect-a-Card South Pole Vacation feat. the Coca-Cola Polar Bears T-Ball Practice

COMPLETE SET (6)	5.00	12.00
COMMON CARD (SP1-SP6)	1.00	2.50
STATED ODDS 1:4		

2016 Space 1999 Series 1

COMPLETE SET (54)	6.00	15.00
COMMON CARD (1-54)	.20	.50

2016 Space 1999 Series 1 Autographs

COMMON CARD	8.00	20.00
BB1 Barbara Bain	100.00	200.00
BB1 Brian Blessed	75.00	150.00
BB2 Barbara Bain	100.00	200.00
BC2 Bernard Cribbins	15.00	40.00
CS1 Catherine Schell	20.00	50.00
CS2 Catherine Schell	15.00	40.00
JC1 Jess Conrad	12.00	30.00
JC2 Jess Conrad	15.00	40.00
NT1 Nick Tate	20.00	50.00
NT2 Nick Tate	20.00	50.00
SH1 Suzanne Heimer	12.00	30.00
SH2 Suzanne Heimer	12.00	30.00
SH3 Suzanne Heimer	20.00	50.00
SJ1 Susan Jameson	12.00	30.00
SJ2 Susan Jameson	15.00	40.00
SR1 Shane Rimmer	30.00	75.00
SR2 Shane Rimmer	12.00	30.00
VL1 Valerie Leon	15.00	40.00
ZM3 Zienia Merton	15.00	40.00

2016 Space 1999 Series 1 Cut Signatures

COMMON CARD		
STATED PRINT RUN 10 SER.#'d SETS		
BM Barry Morse		
GA Gerry Anderson/Co-Creator		
ML Martin Landau	100.00	200.00

2016 Space 1999 Series 1 Mirror Foil

COMPLETE SET (9)	6.00	15.00
COMMON CARD (F1-F9)	1.00	2.50

2016 Space 1999 Series 1 Promos

COMMON CARD	4.00	10.00
CP1 Coming in 2016 (landing; Captain Scarlet incentive pack)	8.00	20.00
MP1 Professor; Mitchy 9210 (Dealers Exclusive)	10.00	25.00
NNO Space: 1999 - Winter 2015/Early 2016 (printing plate of UP1)		
RP1 Koenig at console; Radickal Trading Cards (Dealers Exclusive)	10.00	25.00
YS1 Coming in 2016/125	10.00	25.00
ASP1 Moonbase Alpha; ams-78 (Dealers Exclusive)	15.00	40.00
BJB1 Maya and Tony; brianjblues (Dealers Exclusive)	8.00	20.00
CCP2 Maya; The Cyber Cellar (Dealers Exclusive)	8.00	20.00
GGP1 Koenig on surface; Gazzagames Trading Cards (Dealers Exclusive)	8.00	20.00
MBP1 Russell and Koenig (Dealer's Exclusive)		
PHP2 Russell hands on Koenig forehead; Paul Hart Trading Cards (Dealer's Exclusive)	12.00	30.00
WEBE1 Eagle landing (internet exclusive)	8.00	20.00

2018 Space 1999 Series 2

COMPLETE FACTORY SET (39)	75.00	100.00
COMPLETE SET (36)	6.00	15.00
COMMON CARD (1-36)	.30	.75

2018 Space 1999 Series 2 Autographs

COMMON CARD	5.00	12.00
STATED OVERALL ODDS 3:FACTORY SET		
AP1 Anton Phillips	6.00	15.00
BB3 Barbara Bain/50 3CPI	75.00	150.00
BJ1 Brian Johnson	8.00	20.00
CP1 Christopher Penfold	6.00	15.00
CS1 Catherine Schell	20.00	50.00
CS2 Catherine Schell	15.00	40.00
CS3 Catherine Schell	15.00	40.00
DP1 David Prowse	60.00	120.00
DP2 David Prowse	60.00	120.00
DR1 David Robb	6.00	15.00
IS1 Isla Blair/75 3BPI	10.00	25.00
IS2 Isla Blair	10.00	25.00
JG1 Julian Glover/75 3BPI	12.00	30.00
JG2 Julian Glover		
LH1 Laraine Humphrys	6.00	15.00
MC1 Michael Culver	50.00	100.00
MC2 Michael Culver	50.00	100.00
MC3 Michael Culver	50.00	100.00
NW1 Norma West	30.00	75.00
PH1 Prentis Hancock		
PH2 Prentis Hancock		
RB1 Roy Boyd	8.00	20.00
RB2 Roy Boyd	6.00	15.00
SJ1 Susan Jameson/150 CPI	20.00	50.00
SJ2 Susan Jameson	12.00	30.00
SR2 Shane Rimmer	6.00	15.00
VL1 Valerie Leon	20.00	50.00

2018 Space 1999 Series 2 Promos

PH1 Coming Soon (Paul Hart Trading Cards 2017, FAnderson Convention, paul.hart@tinworld.co.uk)		
PR1 Coming Soon/50		
PR2 Coming Soon/50		
TZ1 Dealer Promo (twilightzone111)		
ASP1 Dealer Promo (ams-78)		
ASP2 Dealer Promo (ams-78)		
CCP1 Dealer Promo (The Cyber Cellar/waltermabon1@sky.com)		
CCP2 Dealer Promo (The Cyber Cellar/waltermabon1@sky.com)		
DTP1 Dealer Promo (Derek's Trading Cards)/30		
DTP2 Dealer Promo (Derek's Trading Cards)/30		
GGP1 Dealer Promo (Gazza Games)	12.00	30.00
GGP2 Dealer Promo (Gazza Games)	12.00	30.00
JWP1 Dealer Promo (Jason Wright, doctorjas73)		
JWP2 Dealer Promo (Jason Wright, doctorjas73)		
JWP2 Dealer Promo (completed JWP1+JWP2; Jason Wright, doctorjas73)/20		
MBP1 Dealer Promo (MB-Trading-Cards [Try-Trading-Cards], taekwondo888)/8		
MBP2 Dealer Promo (MB-Trading-Cards [Try-Trading-Cards], taekwondo888)/8		
PCP1 Dealer Promo (Premier Cards, premier_cards@hotmail.co.uk)/20		
PCP2 Dealer Promo (Premier Cards, premier_cards@hotmail.co.uk)/20		
PCP3 Dealer Promo (completed PCP1+PCP2, Premier Cards, premier_cards@hotmail.co.uk)/20		
PCP3 Dealer Promo (color error)		
PHP1 Dealer Promo (Paul Hart Trading Cards)		
PHP1 Space 1999 (Gerry Anderson Show Sept 29 - Oct 1 2017)		
PZP1 Special Promo (Patrick Zimmerman)		
PZP2 Special Promo (Patrick Zimmerman)		
TCP1 Dealer Promo (Deal Rogers Top Cards, www.topcards.uk)		
TCP2 Dealer Promo (Deal Rogers Top Cards, www.topcards.uk)		
TCP3 Dealer Promo (completed TCP1+TCP2; Deal Rogers Top Cards, www.topcards.uk)		
TMP1 Dealer Promo (telly-mania)/30	10.00	25.00
UTP1 Dealer Promo (Umbrella Trading Cards)/20	12.00	30.00
UTP2 Dealer Promo (Umbrella Trading Cards)/20	12.00	30.00
WEB1 Web Exclusive Promo Card/100	10.00	25.00
WEB1 Web Promo/100	8.00	20.00

2019 Space 1999 Series 3

COMPLETE SET (54)	10.00	25.00
COMMON CARD (1-54)	.40	1.00

2019 Space 1999 Series 3 Autographs

COMMON AUTO	5.00	12.00
GH1 Gay Hamilton	8.00	20.00
GH2 Gay Hamilton	8.00	20.00
JH1 John Hug	12.00	30.00
JH2 John Hug	12.00	30.00
SB1 Sarah Bullen	15.00	40.00
SB2 Sarah Bullen	15.00	40.00
SD1 Sam Dastor	10.00	25.00
SD2 Sam Dastor	10.00	25.00
ERS1 Eva Reuber-Staier	20.00	50.00
S3BB1 Barbara Bain	30.00	75.00
S3BB2 Barbara Bain	30.00	75.00
S3BB3 Barbara Bain	30.00	75.00
S3CP1 Christopher Penfold	6.00	15.00
S3CP2 Christopher Penfold	6.00	15.00
S3CS1 Catherine Schell	15.00	40.00
S3CS2 Catherine Schell	15.00	40.00
S3DR1 David Robb	6.00	15.00
S3DR2 David Robb	6.00	15.00
S3PH1 Prentis Hancock	8.00	20.00
S3PH2 Prentis Hancock	8.00	20.00
S3RB1 Roy Boyd	6.00	15.00
S3RB2 Roy Boyd	6.00	15.00
S3SJ1 Susan Jameson	8.00	20.00
S3SJ2 Susan Jameson	8.00	20.00
S3TO1 Tony Osaba	6.00	15.00
S3TO2 Tony Osaba	6.00	15.00
S3VL1 Valerie Leon	10.00	25.00
S3VM1 Vicki Michelle	10.00	25.00
S3VM2 Vicki Michelle	10.00	25.00

1993 World Class Marketing Space Art Fantastic

COMPLETE SET (55)	4.00	10.00
UNOPENED BOX (36 PACKS)	15.00	20.00
UNOPENED PACK (9 CARDS)	.75	1.00
COMMON CARD (1-55)	.20	.50
H1 Bob McCall Hologram Insert	3.00	8.00

2021 Upper Deck Space Jam A New Legacy

COMPLETE SET (100)	15.00	40.00
UNOPENED BOX (PACKS)		
UNOPENED PACK (CARDS)		
COMMON CARD (1-100)	.40	1.00
*NEON ORANGE: .5X TO 1.2X BASIC CARDS		
*NEON PINK: .5X TO 1.2X BASIC CARDS		
*NEON TURQ.: X TO X BASIC CARDS		

2021 Upper Deck Space Jam A New Legacy Retail

COMPLETE SET (50)	15.00	40.00
COMMON CARD (1-50)	.75	1.00
*BLUE: .75X TO 2X BASIC CARDS		
1 LeBron James Cartoon	1.25	3.00
34 LeBron James Portrait	1.25	3.00
46 LeBron and Bugs "Space Jam 6"	1.25	3.00
47 Bugs, Lola and Cartoon LeBron	1.25	3.00
48 Bugs, Lola and LeBron	1.25	3.00
49 LeBron James Profile	1.25	3.00
50 Bugs, LeBron and Tweety	1.25	3.00

2021 Upper Deck Space Jam A New Legacy Autographed Film Cels

COMMON AUTO	15.00	40.00
GROUP A ODDS 1:234,496		
GROUP B ODDS 1:11,274		
GROUP C ODDS 1:6,777		
GROUP D ODDS 1:1,242		
GROUP E ODDS 1:481		
OVERALL ODDS 1:320 HOBBY/EPACK		
FCAAD Anthony Davis B	50.00	125.00
FCABA Eric Bauza E	20.00	50.00
FCABE Jeff Bergman E	20.00	50.00
FCACJ Cedric Joe C	30.00	75.00
FCADC Don Cheadle C	60.00	150.00
FCAEB Eric Bauza E	20.00	50.00
FCAER Eric Bauza E	20.00	50.00
FCAGI Gabriel "Fluffy" Iglesias E	40.00	100.00
FCAJB Jeff Bergman E	30.00	75.00
FCALJ LeBron James A		
FCAEB2 Eric Bauza E	20.00	50.00
FCAJE2 Jeff Bergman E	30.00	75.00

2021 Upper Deck Space Jam A New Legacy Breaking the Game 3-D Lenticular

COMMON CARD (3D1-3D24)	2.00	5.00
COMMON SP (3D25-3D30)	8.00	20.00
STATED ODDS 1:17 HOBBY/EPACK		
STATED ODDS 1:16 BLASTER/MEGA		
STATED SP ODDS 1:400 HOBBY/EPACK		
STATED SP ODDS 1:240 BLASTER/MEGA		
3D1 LeBron James Cartoon	12.00	30.00
3D18 Arachnneka	2.50	6.00
3D21 White Mamba	3.00	8.00
3D27 Granny SP	10.00	25.00
3D28 Lola Bunny SP	10.00	25.00
3D29 The Brow SP	10.00	25.00
3D30 LeBron James SP	40.00	100.00

2021 Upper Deck Space Jam A New Legacy Dual Autographed Film Cels

STATED PRINT RUN 49 SER.#'d SETS		
FCDABI J.Bergman/G.Iglesia		
FCDABM B.Bergen/C.Milo		
FCDAJK C.Joe/S.Martin-Green	25.00	60.00
FCDABB1 J.Bergman/E.Bauza	60.00	150.00
FCDABB2 B.Bergen/J.Bergman	75.00	200.00

2021 Upper Deck Space Jam A New Legacy Film Cels

COMMON T1 MEM	4.00	10.00
COMMON T2 MEM	5.00	12.00
COMMON T3 MEM	5.00	12.00
COMMON T4 MEM	6.00	15.00
STATED ODDS T1 1:36		
STATED ODDS T2 1:48		
STATED ODDS T3 1:96		
STATED ODDS T4 1:290		
OVERALL ODDS 1:36		
FC2 Wile E. Coyote T1	5.00	12.00
FC3 LeBron James Cartoon T1	12.00	30.00
FC4 Sylvester T1	5.00	12.00
FC12 Lola Bunny T2	6.00	15.00
FC13 Bugs Bunny T2	6.00	15.00
FC17 Marvin the Martian T2	6.00	15.00
FC18 LeBron James Cartoon T2	15.00	40.00
FC20 The Brow T3	6.00	15.00
FC21 Chronos T3	6.00	15.00
FC23 White Mamba T3	6.00	15.00
FC27 LeBron James T4	25.00	60.00
FC30 LeBron James T4	12.00	30.00
FC32 Don Cheadle as Al G. Rhythm T4	12.00	30.00

2021 Upper Deck Space Jam A New Legacy Horizontal Autographs

COMMON AUTO	10.00	25.00
GROUP A ODDS 1:24,340		
GROUP B ODDS 1:4,951		
GROUP C ODDS 1:2,655		
GROUP D ODDS 1:532		
STATED ODDS 1:400 HOBBY/EPACK		
HSAD Anthony Davis A	60.00	150.00
HSBA Eric Bauza D	12.00	30.00
HSBE Jeff Bergman D	15.00	40.00
HSCM Candi Milo D	15.00	40.00
HSDC Don Cheadle B	60.00	150.00
HSEB Eric Bauza D	12.00	30.00
HSEF Eric Bauza D	12.00	30.00
HSGI Gabriel "Fluffy" Iglesias D	20.00	50.00
HSJB Jeff Bergman D	20.00	50.00
HSJE Jeff Bergman D	15.00	40.00
HSNO Nneka Ogwumike C	15.00	40.00
HSSM Sonequa Martin-Green C	12.00	30.00
HSER2 Eric Bauza D	12.00	30.00
HSJE2 Jeff Bergman B	20.00	50.00
HSMI2 Candi Milo B	15.00	40.00

2021 Upper Deck Space Jam A New Legacy Letterman Manufactured Patches

COMMON T1 MEM	2.50	6.00
COMMON T2 MEM	2.50	6.00
COMMON T3 MEM		
STATED ODDS T1 1:87		
STATED ODDS T2 1:556		
STATED ODDS T3 1:1,607		
OVERALL ODDS 1:72 HOBBY/EPACK		
LPAR Arachnneka T1	4.00	10.00
LPBB Bugs Bunny T3	10.00	25.00
LPCH Chronos T1	4.00	10.00
LPLB Lola Bunny T2	6.00	15.00
LPLJ LeBron James T3	60.00	150.00
LPTH The Brow T2	3.00	8.00
LPWH White Mamba T1	3.00	8.00

2021 Upper Deck Space Jam A New Legacy Looney Tunes Character Manufactured Patches

COMMON MEM	2.00	5.00
STATED ODDS 1:120 HOBBY/EPACK		
LTCPBB Bugs Bunny	5.00	12.00
LTCPBU Bugs Bunny	5.00	12.00
LTCPDD Daffy Duck	3.00	8.00
LTCPJA LeBron James	20.00	50.00
LTCPLB Lola Bunny	4.00	10.00
LTCPLJ LeBron James Cartoon	15.00	40.00
LTCPLO Lola Bunny	4.00	10.00
LTCPTA Taz	3.00	8.00

2021 Upper Deck Space Jam A New Legacy Looney Tunes in Action

COMPLETE SET (18)	10.00	25.00
COMMON CARD (IA1-IA18)	.75	2.00
*GREEN/599: 1.5X TO 4X BASIC CARDS		
*GOLD: 4X TO 10X BASIC CARDS		
RANDOMLY INSERTED INTO PACKS		
IA1 LeBron James	2.00	5.00
IA10 Lola Bunny	1.25	3.00
IA15 LeBron James Cartoon	2.00	5.00
IA18 Bugs Bunny	1.25	3.00

2021 Upper Deck Space Jam A New Legacy Pink Autographs

COMMON AUTO	10.00	25.00
GROUP A ODDS 1:234,160		
GROUP B ODDS 1:2,060		
GROUP C ODDS 1:468		
GROUP D ODDS 1:362		
GROUP E ODDS 1:340		
STATED ODDS 1:120 HOBBY/EPACK		
STATED ODDS 1:1,200 BLASTER/MEGA		
PSAD Anthony Davis B	150.00	400.00
PSBE Jeff Bergman D	15.00	40.00
PSCM Candi Milo B	12.00	30.00
PSDA Khris Davis D	12.00	30.00
PSDC Don Cheadle B	50.00	125.00
PSGI Gabriel "Fluffy" Iglesias E	20.00	50.00
PSJB Jeff Bergman C	25.00	60.00
PSJE Jeff Bergman D	15.00	40.00

PSLJ LeBron James A
PSMA Sonequa Martin-Green E 15.00 40.00
PSNO Nneka Ogwumike E 12.00 30.00
PSAN2 Anthony Davis C 150.00 400.00
PSBN3 Jeff Bergman C 25.00 60.00
PSCH2 Don Cheadle B 50.00 125.00
PSEF3 Jeff Bergman D 15.00 40.00
PSER2 Jeff Bergman C 25.00 60.00
PSIG2 Gabriel "Fluffy" Iglesias E 20.00 50.00
PSJG3 Jeff Bergman C 15.00 40.00
PSKD2 Khris Davis D 12.00 30.00
PSMI2 Candi Milo D 12.00 30.00
PSOG2 Nneka Ogwumike E 12.00 30.00
PSSM2 Sonequa Martin-Green E 15.00 40.00
PSSY2 Jeff Bergman C 15.00 40.00
PSYS2 Jeff Bergman D 15.00 40.00

2021 Upper Deck Space Jam A New Legacy Power Moves

COMPLETE SET (15)
COMMON CARD (PM1-PM15)
*GOLD: X TO X BASIC CARDS
*GREEN/499: 2X TO 5X BASIC CARDS
RANDOMLY INSERTED INTO PACKS
PM1 LeBron James 2.50 6.00
PM10 Lola Bunny 1.25 3.00
PM15 Bugs Bunny 1.50 4.00

2021 Upper Deck Space Jam A New Legacy Ready to Jam

COMPLETE SET (10) 10.00 25.00
COMMON CARD (RJ1-RJ10) 1.25 3.00
*RED/999: .75X TO 2X BASIC CARDS
*BLUE/799: 1.2X TO 3X BASIC CARDS
*ORANGE/449: 1.2X TO 3X BASIC CARDS
*YELLOW/599: 3X TO 8X BASIC CARDS
*TURQ./349: 3X TO 8X BASIC CARDS
STATED ODDS 1:6 BLASTER/MEGA
RJ1 LeBron James 3.00 8.00
RJ5 Bugs Bunny 2.00 5.00

2021 Upper Deck Space Jam A New Legacy Teal Autographs

COMMON AUTO 10.00 25.00
GROUP A ODDS 1:229,640
GROUP B ODDS 1:2,088
GROUP C ODDS 1:395
GROUP D ODDS 1:383
GROUP E ODDS 1:370
STATED ODDS 1:120 HOBBY/EPACK
STATED ODDS 1:1,200 BLASTER/MEGA
SAD Anthony Davis B 60.00 150.00
SBA Eric Bauza C 15.00 40.00
SBB Bob Bergen E 15.00 40.00
SBE Jeff Bergman D 12.00 30.00
SBU Eric Bauza D 15.00 40.00
SCM Candi Milo B 20.00 50.00
SDC Don Cheadle B 60.00 150.00
SEB Eric Bauza C 15.00 40.00
SGI Gabriel "Fluffy" Iglesias E 30.00 75.00
SJB Jeff Bergman D 20.00 50.00
SJE Jeff Bergman C 12.00 30.00
SLJ LeBron James A
SMA Sonequa Martin-Green E 15.00 40.00
SNO Nneka Ogwumike E 12.00 30.00
SAA2 Eric Bauza C 15.00 40.00
SAN2 Anthony Davis B 60.00 150.00
SBN3 Jeff Bergman D 20.00 50.00
SBO2 Bob Bergen E 15.00 40.00
SCH2 Don Cheadle B 60.00 150.00
SEB2 Eric Bauza C 15.00 40.00
SEF3 Jeff Bergman C 12.00 30.00
SEI3 Eric Bauza C 15.00 40.00
SER2 Jeff Bergman C 20.00 50.00
SEU3 Eric Bauza C 15.00 40.00
SIG2 Gabriel "Fluffy" Iglesias E 30.00 75.00
SJG3 Jeff Bergman C 12.00 30.00
SMI2 Candi Milo B 20.00 50.00
SOG2 Nneka Ogwumike E 12.00 30.00
SPP2 Eric Bauza C 15.00 40.00
SSM2 Sonequa Martin-Green E 15.00 40.00
SSY2 Jeff Bergman D 12.00 30.00
SYS2 Jeff Bergman C 12.00 30.00
SZA3 Eric Bauza D 15.00 40.00

2021 Upper Deck Space Jam A New Legacy Tune and Goon Squad Autographed Jersey Patches Manufactured R

COMMON AUTO 15.00 40.00
STATED PRINT RUN 10-99
TSJAAD Anthony Davis/10
TSJABB Bob Bergen/99 30.00 75.00
TSJACM Candi Milo/99 30.00 75.00
TSJADC Don Cheadle/10
TSJAGI Gabriel Iglesias/99 40.00 100.00
TSJAJB Jeff Bergman/99 25.00 60.00
TSJALJ LeBron James/10

2021 Upper Deck Space Jam A New Legacy Tune and Goon Squad Manufactured Jersey Patches

COMMON MEM 2.50 6.00
STATED ODDS 1:320 HOBBY/EPACK
TSJP1 White Mamba 5.00 12.00
TSJP2 Arachnneka 3.00 8.00
TSJP4 The Brow 3.00 8.00
TSJP6 Bugs Bunny 6.00 15.00
TSJP7 Lola Bunny 8.00 20.00
TSJP8 LeBron James 40.00 100.00
TSJP9 Porky Pig 4.00 10.00

2021 Upper Deck Space Jam A New Legacy Tune and Goon Squad Rookies

COMPLETE SET (6)
COMMON CARD (RC1-RC6)
*GREEN/99: .75X TO 2X BASIC CARDS
*GOLD: 1.2X TO 3X BASIC CARDS
RANDOMLY INSERTED INTO PACKS
RC6 LeBron James 5.00 12.00

2021 Upper Deck Space Jam A New Legacy Tune Squad All-Stars

COMPLETE SET (10) 6.00 15.00
COMMON CARD (AS1-AS10) .75 2.00
*GOLD: .75X TO 2X BASIC CARDS
*GREEN/199: 1X TO 2.5X BASIC CARDS
RANDOMLY INSERTED INTO PACKS

1990 Space Ventures Space Shots

COMPLETE SET (110) 6.00 15.00
COMPLETE FACTORY SET 20.00 50.00
UNOPENED BOX (36 PACKS) 15.00 25.00
UNOPENED PACK (12 CARDS) .75 1.00
COMMON CARD (1-110) .10 .30

1990 Space Ventures Space Shots Promos

COMPLETE SET (9) 8.00 20.00
COMMON CARD (1-9) 1.25 3.00

1991 Space Shots

COMPLETE SET (110) 5.00 15.00
COMPLETE FACTORY SET (111) 15.00 40.00
UNOPENED BOX (36 PACKS) 15.00 20.00
UNOPENED PACK (12 CARDS) .75 1.00
COMMON CARD (111-220) .12 .30

1991 Space Shots Moon Mars

COMPLETE SET (36) 2.00 5.00
COMMON CARD (1-36) .30 .75

1992 Space Ventures Space Shots

COMPLETE SET (110) 6.00 15.00
COMPLETE FACTORY SET (111) 8.00 20.00
UNOPENED BOX (36 PACKS) 15.00 20.00
UNOPENED PACK (8 CARDS) .75 1.00
COMMON CARD (221-330) .12 .30
NNO1 First Earthrise Hologram
NNO2 Jim Lovell AU

2011 Spartacus Blood and Sand

COMPLETE SET (26) 50.00 100.00
COMMON CARD (1-26) 3.00 8.00
STATED PRINT RUN 250 SER. #'d SETS
1B AVAILABLE VIA REDMPTION

2011 Spartacus Blood and Sand Autographs

COMMON AUTO 12.00 30.00
OVERALL AUTO ODDS 2:1
2 Viva Bianca 15.00 40.00
3 Lesley-Ann Brandt 25.00 60.00
4 Jai Courtney 20.00 50.00
5 Erin Cummings 15.00 40.00
6 John Hannah 25.00 60.00
7 Katrina Law 15.00 40.00
8 Lucy Lawless 75.00 150.00
11 Andy Whitfield 400.00 800.00

2011 Spartacus Blood and Sand Gods of the Arena Autographs

COMMON AUTO 8.00 20.00
OVERALL AUTO ODDS TWO PER PACK
2 Lesley-Ann Brandt 12.00 30.00

2011 Spartacus Blood and Sand Savage

COMPLETE SET (9) 20.00 40.00
COMMON CARD (SA1-SA9) 2.50 6.00
STATED ODDS ONE PER PACK
STATED PRINT RUN 350 SER. #'d SETS

2011 Spartacus Blood and Sand Seductive

COMPLETE SET (9) 25.00 50.00
COMMON CARD (SE1-SE9) 3.00 8.00
STATED ODDS ONE PER PACK
STATED PRINT RUN 350 SER. #'d SETS

2009 Spartacus Blood and Sand Promos

COMPLETE SET (12) 12.00 30.00
COMMON CARD (1-12) 1.50 4.00

2013 Spartacus Expansion

COMPLETE SET (22) 75.00 150.00
COMMON CARD 2.00 5.00
LM Liam McIntyre AU 60.00 120.00
CAR C. Addai-Robinson AU 20.00 50.00

2012 Spartacus Gods of the Arena

COMPLETE SET (18) 20.00 50.00
COMMON CARD (G1-G18) 2.00 5.00
CC1 ISSUED AS 2-BOX INCENTIVE
SHADOWBOX ISSUED AS BOX TOPPER
CC1 Spartacus MEM 2BI 50.00 100.00
NNO Whitfield Mem.Shadowbox BT 25.00 50.00

2012 Spartacus Gods of the Arena Autographs

COMMON AUTO 5.00 12.00
STATED ODDS 2:1
MENSAH AUTO ISSUED AS 4-BOX INCENTIVE
L (LIMITED): 300-500 COPIES
VL (VERY LIMITED): 200-300 COPIES
EL (EXTREMELY LIMITED): 200 OR LESS
1 Craig Walsh Wrighton VL 8.00 20.00
3 Dustin Clare VL 50.00 100.00
5 Jaime Murray EL 60.00 120.00
8 Jessica Grace Smith L 10.00 25.00
10 John Hannah EL 60.00 120.00
11 Lliam Powell L 6.00 15.00
12 Lucy Lawless EL 50.00 100.00
13 Manu Bennett VL 20.00 50.00
14 Nick Tarabay VL 10.00 25.00
16 Peter Mensah 4BI 50.00 100.00
17 Reuben de Jong L 10.00 25.00
20 Temuera Morrison L 12.00 30.00

2012 Spartacus Gods of the Arena Battle for Freedom

COMPLETE SET (9) 15.00 30.00
COMMON CARD (B1-B9) 2.50 6.00
STATED ODDS 1:1

2012 Spartacus Gods of the Arena Die-Cut Gold Plaques

COMPLETE SET (12) 30.00 60.00
COMMON CARD 3.00 8.00
STATED ODDS 1:1
GG7 Barca GOTA SP RR 20.00 50.00

2012 Spartacus Gods of the Arena Gladiators In Action

COMPLETE SET (9) 15.00 30.00
COMMON CARD (G1-G9) 2.50 6.00
STATED ODDS 1:1

2012 Spartacus Gods of the Arena Vengeance

COMPLETE SET (9) 15.00 30.00
COMMON CARD (V1-V9) 2.50 6.00
STATED ODDS 1:1

2012 Spartacus Gods of the Arena Women of Spartacus

COMPLETE SET (9) 20.00 40.00
COMPLETE SET 3.00 8.00
STATED ODDS 1:1

2012 Spartacus Gods of the Arena Promos

COMPLETE SET (2) 8.00 20.00
COMMON CARD 2.00 5.00
P2 Spartacus ALB 10.00 25.00

2013 Spartacus Vengeance

COMPLETE SET (30) 30.00 60.00
CT1 Spartacus Poster BT 8.00 20.00

2013 Spartacus Vengeance Autographs

COMMON AUTO 8.00 20.00
TWO AUTOS PER PACK
DEKNIGHT AUTO ISSUED AS 4 BOX INCENTIVE
L (LIMITED): 300-500 COPIES
VL (VERY LIMITED): 200-300 COPIES
EL (EXTREM. LTD): LESS THAN 200 COPIES
1 Brooke Williams L 10.00 25.00
2 Conan Stevens EL 25.00 60.00
3 Cynthia Addai-Robinson EL 25.00 60.00
4 Katrina Law L 15.00 40.00
5 Katrina Law L 15.00 40.00
7 Liam McIntyre EL 60.00 120.00
10 Viva Bianca VL 25.00 50.00
11 Viva Bianca VL 25.00 50.00
12 Steven S. DeKnight 4BI 30.00 75.00

2013 Spartacus Vengeance Blood and Sand Autographs

COMMON AUTO 8.00 20.00
TWO AUTOS PER PACK
L (LIMITED): 300-500 COPIES
VL (VERY LIMITED): 200-300 COPIES
EL (EXTREM. LTD): LESS THAN 200 COPIES
2 Craig Parker 12.00 30.00
7 Peter Mensah EL 50.00 100.00

2013 Spartacus Vengeance Die-Cut Gold Plaques

COMPLETE SET (8) 12.00 30.00
COMMON CARD (GV1-GV8) 2.50 6.00
ONE PER PACK

2013 Spartacus Vengeance Relics

COMMON CARD 10.00 25.00
STATED ODDS 1:1
SPARTACUS MAP ISSUED AS 2 BOX INCENTIVE
3 Ilithyia 15.00 40.00
4 Lucretia 15.00 40.00
5 Seppia 12.00 30.00
7 Ilithyia's Dress HOR 15.00 40.00
8 Lucretia's Dress HOR 15.00 40.00
9 Seppia's Dress HOR 12.00 30.00
11 Mira's Map 12.00 30.00
13 Spartacus' Map 2BI 40.00 80.00

2013 Spartacus Vengeance Promos

P1 Spartacus GEN 1.25 3.00
P2 Spartacus ALB 5.00 12.00

1996 WildStorm Spawn
COMPLETE SET (99) 10.00 25.00
UNOPENED BOX (24 PACKS) 20.00 25.00
UNOPENED PACK (6 CARDS) 1.00 1.25
COMMON CARD (1-99) .20 .50
M1 Spawn Morph Lenticular 6.00 15.00

1996 WildStorm Spawn Spawn Motion
COMPLETE SET (9) 20.00 50.00
COMMON CARD (SM1-SM9) 3.00 8.00
STATED ODDS 1:6

1997 WildStorm Spawn Archives Chromium
COMPLETE FACTORY SET (50) 6.00 15.00
COMMON CARD (1-50) .25 .60

1997 Inkworks Spawn Movie
COMPLETE SET (81) 4.00 10.00
UNOPENED BOX (36 PACKS) 60.00 100.00
UNOPENED PACK (8 CARDS) 2.00 3.00
COMMON CARD (1-81) .10 .25
K1 The Devil's Own (Kay Bee Toys) 6.00 15.00
HOLO1 Spawn - The Devil's Own Holofoil 10.00 25.00

1997 Inkworks Spawn Movie Autographs
1 Todd McFarlane AU/700* 50.00 100.00
2 Todd McFarlane Gold AU
3 Todd McFarlane Silver AU
4 Todd McFarlane Black AU

1997 Inkworks Spawn Movie From Comics to Film
COMPLETE SET (9) 15.00 40.00
COMMON CARD (1-9) 2.50 6.00
STATED ODDS 1:11

1997 Inkworks Spawn Movie Promos
COMPLETE SET (5) 3.00 8.00
COMMON CARD .75 2.00
P0 Starlong Mail In 2.00 5.00
P3 NSU Subscribers at SDCC 3.00 8.00

1997 Inkworks Spawn Movie Spawn Revealed
COMPLETE SET (4) 12.00 30.00
COMMON CARD (1-4) 4.00 10.00

1998 Inkworks Spawn Toy Files
COMPLETE SET (90) 8.00 20.00
UNOPENED BOX (36 PACKS) 40.00 50.00
UNOPENED PACK (8 CARDS) 1.25 1.50
COMMON CARD (1-90) .15 .40
SR1 Blue Spawn 10.00 25.00
TMAU Todd McFarlane AU 25.00 60.00

1998 Inkworks Spawn Toy Files Design Sketch Foil
COMPLETE SET (9) 15.00 40.00
COMMON CARD (D1-D9) 2.50 6.00
STATED ODDS 1:11

1998 Inkworks Spawn Toy Files Promos
P1 Spawn 1.25 3.00
Hotter Than Hell! C
MS1 Spawn 8.00 20.00
Hotter Than Hell! R
ST1 Spawn 20.00 50.00
Hotter Than Hell! VR
ST2 Spawn 20.00 50.00
Hotter Than Hell! VR

1995 WildStorm Spawn Widevision
COMPLETE SET (152) 4.00 10.00
UNOPENED BOX (36 PACKS) 15.00 20.00
UNOPENED PACK (8 CARDS) .40 .60
COMMON CARD (1-152) .10 .25
AU1 Autographs Widevision AU
TC1 ToddChrome New Costume 20.00 50.00
TTA1 Todd Toys Ad Insert

1995 WildStorm Spawn Widevision Painted
COMPLETE SET (12) 10.00 25.00
COMMON CARD (P1-P12) 1.25 3.00
STATED ODDS 1:9

1995 WildStorm Spawn Widevision Todd McFarlane Gallery
COMPLETE SET (4) 10.00 25.00
COMMON CARD (TG1-TG4) 4.00 10.00
STATED ODDS 1:36

1995 WildStorm Spawn Widevision Todd Toys
COMPLETE SET (6) 12.00 30.00
COMMON CARD (TT1-TT6) 2.50 6.00
STATED ODDS 1:18

1995 WildStorm Spawn Widevision Promos
COMPLETE SET (8)
COMMON CARD .75 2.00
P1 The Comic Of The Decade - OV 1.25 3.00
P2 Scott Clark Art 1.25 3.00
PROTO1 Same Art as P1 - (chain border) 1.25 3.00
PROTO2 Brett Booth Art - (chain border) 1.25 3.00
PROTO3 Same Front as P2 - (chain border) 1.25 3.00
PROTO4 Alex Garner Art - (chain border) 1.25 3.00
NNO 4-Up Sheet (Prototypes 1-4) 2.00 5.00

1995 Comic Images Species
COMPLETE SET (90) 5.00 12.00
UNOPENED BOX (36 PACKS) 20.00 30.00
UNOPENED PACK (10 CARDS) 1.00 1.25
COMMON CARD (1-90) .10 .25
6PAN 6-Card Panel PROMO
9PAN 9-Card Panel
(Card Album Exclusive)
M1 Boy Sil Medallion/694* 10.00 25.00
PROMO Species PROMO .75 2.00

1995 Comic Images Species Sil
COMPLETE SET (3) 15.00 40.00
COMMON CARD (1-3) 6.00 15.00
RANDOMLY INSERTED INTO PACKS

1995 Comic Images Species Superstars
COMPLETE SET (6) 12.00 30.00
COMMON CARD (C1-C6) 2.50 6.00
STATED ODDS 1:16

1993 Prime Time Speed Racer
COMPLETE SET (55) 4.00 10.00
UNOPENED BOX (36 PACKS) 20.00 30.00
UNOPENED PACK (8 CARDS) 1.00 1.25
COMMON CARD (1-55) .15 .40
*GOLD: .6X TO 1.5X BASIC CARDS

1993 Prime Time Speed Racer Chromium
COMPLETE SET (6) 15.00 40.00
COMMON CARD (C1-C6) 3.00 8.00

1993 Prime Time Speed Racer Promos
COMMON CARD (P1-P3) 1.50 4.00
P3 Mail-in Promo 12.00 30.00

2008 Speed Racer General Mills
COMPLETE SET (4) 6.00 15.00
COMMON CARD 2.50 6.00

2013 Spellcasters Previews
COMPLETE SET (5) 4.00 10.00
COMMON CARD (S1-S5) 1.00 2.50

2013 Spellcasters
COMPLETE SET (20) 5.00 12.00
COMMON CARD (1-20) .50 1.25
L1 Chaos Magic Lenticular

2013 Spellcasters Frosted Clear
COMPLETE SET (6) 8.00 20.00
COMMON CARD (1-6) 1.50 4.00
STATED ODDS 1:1
6 Fantasy Magic (rare Craig Yeung)

2013 Spellcasters Promos
COMMON CARD (P1-P5) 1.50 4.00
P5 Black Magic (foil) 6.00 15.00
TY Fantasy Magic (Thank You mail-in)

1997 Magic Box International Spice Girls Photos
COMPLETE SET (220) 6.00 15.00
COMPLETE SERIES 1 SET (120) 4.00 10.00
COMPLETE SERIES 2 SET (100) 4.00 10.00
UNOPENED SERIES 1 BOX (25 PACKS)
UNOPENED SERIES 1 PACK (8 CARDS)
UNOPENED SERIES 2 BOX (25 PACKS)
UNOPENED SERIES 2 PACK (8 CARDS)
COMMON SERIES 1 CARD (1-120) .20 .50
COMMON SERIES 2 CARD (121-220) .20 .50

1993 Kitchen Sink Press Spicy Pulp Covers Series 2
COMPLETE SET (39) 5.00 12.00
COMMON CARD (1-39) .25 .60
NNO Uncut Sheet (22" x 18-1/4")/500

1995 Kitchen Sink Press The Spirit
COMPLETE BOXED SET (36) 6.00 15.00
COMMON CARD (1-36) .30 .75
UNC1 Will Eisner 36-Card Panel UNC AU

2008 The Spirit
COMPLETE SET (72) 4.00 10.00
UNOPENED BOX (24 PACKS)
UNOPENED PACK (7 CARDS)
COMMON CARD (1-72) .10 .30
CL1 STATED ODDS ONE PER CASE
CL1 The Key To The City

2008 The Spirit Autographs
COMMON CARD 6.00 15.00
STATED ODDS 1:48
A1 Gabriel Macht 8.00 20.00
A2 Jaime King 8.00 20.00
A4 Paz Vega 10.00 25.00
A5 Stana Katic 12.00 30.00
A7 Samuel L. Jackson 250.00 500.00
AR1 Redemption card
AR1B Redemption card for Samuel L. Jackson

2008 The Spirit Good Guys Bad Guys
COMPLETE SET (6) 6.00 15.00
COMMON CARD (GB1-GB6) 1.25 3.00
STATED ODDS 1:17

2008 The Spirit My City Screams
COMPLETE SET (3) 5.00 12.00
COMMON CARD (MC1-MC3) 2.00 5.00
STATED ODDS 1:24

2008 The Spirit Pieceworks
COMPLETE SET (13) 120.00 250.00
COMMON CARD 5.00 12.00
STATED ODDS 1:36
PW12A, PW12B ISSUED AS MULTI-CASE INCENTIVES
PW2 Plaster of Paris 10.00 25.00
PW4 Sand Saref 20.00 40.00
PW9 Silken Floss 20.00 40.00
PW10 Silken Floss 20.00 40.00
PW11 The Octopus/Silken Floss DUAL 10.00 25.00
PW12A The Spirit CI 8.00 20.00
PW12B The Spirit CI 8.00 20.00

2008 The Spirit Spirit of the City Puzzle
COMPLETE SET (9) 8.00 20.00
COMMON CARD (SC1-SC9) 1.00 2.50
STATED ODDS 1:11

2008 The Spirit Promos
COMMON CARD .60 1.50
Pi Silken Floss 2.00 5.00
PMS I'm Gonna Kill You 1.50 4.00
All Kinds of Dead
PPS Sand Seref (Philly) 1.50 4.00
PUK Lorelei 2.00 5.00
(UK excl.)
H2008 The Spirit
(Holiday excl.)

1990 Topps Ireland Spitting Image
COMPLETE SET (66) 30.00 75.00
UNOPENED BOX (36 PACKS)
UNOPENED PACK
COMMON CARD (1-66) 1.00 2.50
31 Mike Tyson 25.00 60.00

2016 Splashlings Wave 1
COMPLETE SET (104) 12.00 30.00
UNOPENED BOX (24 PACKS) 70.00 80.00
UNOPENED PACK (5 CARDS+1 FIGURE) 3.00 3.50
COMMON CARD (1-104) .25 .60

1993 The River Group Splatter Bowl
COMPLETE BOXED TIN SET (31) 4.00 10.00
COMMON CARD (1-31) .25 .60
NNO Grimmax; Eyepike 2UP Panel 5X7 Promo1.25 3.00

2009 SpongeBob Squarepants Series 1
COMPLETE SET (90) 15.00 40.00
UNOPENED BOX (PACKS)
UNOPENED PACK (CARDS)
COMMON CARD (1-90) .40 1.00

2009 SpongeBob Squarepants Series 1 Alphabet Stickers
COMPLETE SET (15) 12.00 30.00
COMMON STICKER (1-15) 1.25 3.00
STATED ODDS 1:1

2009 SpongeBob Squarepants Series 1 Create-a-Scene Stickers
COMPLETE SET (10) 5.00 12.00
COMMON CARD (1-10) .75 2.00
STATED ODDS 1:3

2009 SpongeBob Squarepants Series 1 Real Sponge Cards
COMMON CARD 15.00 40.00
STATED ODDS 1:12

2009 SpongeBob Squarepants Series 2
COMPLETE SET (90) 15.00 40.00
UNOPENED BOX (24 PACKS)
UNOPENED PACK (9 CARDS)
COMMON CARD (1-90) .40 1.00

2009 SpongeBob Squarepants Series 2 Magnets
COMPLETE SET (9) 6.00 15.00
COMMON CARD (1-9) 1.00 2.50
STATED ODDS 1:12

2009 SpongeBob Squarepants Series 2 Make-Your-Own Clings
COMPLETE SET (10) 5.00 12.00
COMMON CARD (1-10) .75 2.00
STATED ODDS 1:12

2009 SpongeBob Squarepants Series 2 Pop-Ups
COMPLETE SET (10) 6.00 15.00
COMMON CARD (1-10) 1.25 3.00
STATED ODDS 1:4

2009 SpongeBob Squarepants Series 2 Stickers
COMPLETE SET (10) 10.00 25.00
COMMON STICKER 2.00 5.00
STATED ODDS 1:2

MODERN

2009 SpongeBob Squarepants Series 2 Temporary Tattoos

COMPLETE SET (9) 10.00 25.00
COMMON CARD (1-9) 2.00 5.00
STATED ODDS 1:6

1993 Butthedz Spoofy Tunes

COMPLETE SET (55) 5.00 12.00
UNOPENED BOX (36 PACKS) 15.00 20.00
UNOPENED PACK (8 CARDS) .75 1.00
COMMON CARD (1-55) .05 .40
NNO1 Miss Manners Biography 2.00 5.00
NNO2 Miss Manners AU 8.00 20.00

1993 Butthedz Spoofy Tunes Promos

P1 The Next Degeneration .75 2.00
P2 Night Rhyme .75 2.00
P3 The Lonely Ranger .75 2.00

2011 Spook Show

COMPLETE SET (66) 6.00 15.00
UNOPENED BOX (24 PACKS) 50.00 60.00
UNOPENED PACK (8 CARDS) 2.00 3.00
COMMON CARD (1-66) .20 .50
CLA Checklist A
CLB Checklist B
NNO Credits Card

2011 Spook Show Autographs

COMMON CARD 8.00 20.00
STATED ODDS 1:24

2011 Spook Show Emerge-O-Vision

COMPLETE SET (2) 3.00 8.00
COMMON CARD (E1-E2) 2.00 5.00
STATED ODDS 1:12

2011 Spook Show Frightening Foil

COMPLETE SET (6) 5.00 12.00
COMMON CARD (F1-F6) 1.00 2.50
STATED ODDS 1:4

2011 Spook Show Gruesome Gimmicks

COMPLETE SET (3) 4.00 10.00
COMMON CARD (G1-G3) 2.00 5.00
STATED ODDS 1:8

2011 Spook Show Promos

COMPLETE SET (6) 5.00 12.00
COMMON CARD (P1-P6) .75 2.00
P4 Kara-Kum 1.50 4.00
Philly Non-Sport Show 2011
P5 Midnight Zombie's Jamboree 1.50 4.00
Chicagoland 2011
P6 Horror Strikes At Midnight 1.50 4.00
The Wrapper

2003 Sports Illustrated Swimsuit

COMPLETE SET (100) 10.00 25.00
COMMON CARD (1-100) .20 .50

2003 Sports Illustrated Swimsuit Autographs

COMMON AUTO 10.00 25.00
RANDOMLY INSERTED INTO PACKS
3 Elsa Benitez 50.00 100.00
4 Melissa Keller 12.00 30.00
5 Molly Sims 100.00 200.00
6 Noemie Lenoir 25.00 60.00
7 Petra Nemcova 50.00 100.00
8 Rachel Hunter 20.00 50.00
10 Yamila Diaz-Rahi 60.00 120.00
CB Christie Brinkley 150.00 300.00
CT Cheryl Tiegs 200.00 400.00

2003 Sports Illustrated Swimsuit Body Sand

COMPLETE SET (10) 100.00 175.00
COMMON CARD (S1-S10) 3.00 8.00
STATED ODDS 1:24
S2 Daniela Pestova 20.00 50.00
S3 Daniela Pestova 20.00 50.00
S5 Molly Sims 15.00 40.00
S8 Petra Nemcova 6.00 15.00
S9 Petra Nemcova 6.00 15.00

2003 Sports Illustrated Swimsuit Classic

COMPLETE SET (10) 6.00 15.00
COMMON CARD (1-10) 1.25 3.00
STATED ODDS 1:4

2003 Sports Illustrated Swimsuit Covers

COMPLETE SET (5) 5.00 12.00
COMMON CARD (CC1-CC5) 1.50 4.00
STATED ODDS 1:12

2003 Sports Illustrated Swimsuit Memorabilia

COMPLETE SET (6) 30.00 80.00
COMMON CARD 6.00 15.00
STATED ODDS 1:24

2004 Sports Illustrated Swimsuit

COMPLETE SET (100) 10.00 25.00
COMMON CARD (1-100) .20 .50

2004 Sports Illustrated Swimsuit Autographs

COMMON AUTO 8.00 20.00
1 Carolyn Murphy BT 10.00 25.00
3 Jessica Van Der Steen 10.00 25.00
4 Marisa Miller (back view) 120.00 250.00
5 Marisa Miller (front view) 120.00 250.00
6 May Anderson
7 Melissa Keller 10.00 25.00
9 Noemie Lenoir 12.00 30.00

2004 Sports Illustrated Swimsuit Body Paint

COMPLETE SET (10) 80.00 150.00
COMMON CARD (BP1-BP10) 6.00 15.00
STATED ODDS 1:24
BP2 Bridget Hall 8.00 20.00
BP3 Bridget Hall 8.00 20.00
BP4 Marisa Miller 8.00 20.00
BP5 Marisa Miller 8.00 20.00
BP7 Noemie Lenoir 10.00 25.00
BP8 Noemie Lenoir 10.00 25.00

2004 Sports Illustrated Swimsuit Fresh Face Michelle Lombardo

COMPLETE SET (10) 10.00 25.00
COMMON CARD (FF1-FF10) 1.50 4.00
STATED ODDS 1:4

2004 Sports Illustrated Swimsuit Hall of Fame

COMPLETE SET (10) 8.00 20.00
COMMON CARD (HF1-HF10) 1.25 3.00
STATED ODDS 1:4

2004 Sports Illustrated Swimsuit Memorabilia

COMPLETE SET (8) 100.00 175.00
COMMON CARD (SM1-SM8) 8.00 20.00
STATED ODDS 1:24
SM1 Fernanda Motta 12.00 30.00
SM2 Fernanda Motta 12.00 30.00
SM5 Michelle Lombardo 10.00 25.00
SM6 Michelle Lombardo 10.00 25.00
SM7 Marisa Miller 12.00 30.00
SM8 Michelle Lombardo 10.00 25.00

2005 Sports Illustrated Swimsuit

COMPLETE SET (100) 10.00 25.00
COMMON CARD (1-100) .20 .50

2005 Sports Illustrated Swimsuit Autographs

COMMON CARD 10.00 25.00
STATED ODDS 1:24
1 Ana Beatriz Barros 15.00 40.00
2 Alicia Hall 12.00 30.00
3 Anne V 12.00 30.00
4 Daniella Sarahyba 12.00 30.00
8 Yamila Diaz-Rahi 30.00 75.00

2005 Sports Illustrated Swimsuit Fresh Face Alicia Hall

COMPLETE SET (8) 10.00 25.00
COMMON CARD (FF1-FF8) 1.50 4.00
STATED ODDS 1:6

2005 Sports Illustrated Swimsuit Memorabilia

COMPLETE SET (7) 60.00 120.00
COMMON CARD 6.00 15.00
STATED ODDS 1:24
BHM Bridget Hall 10.00 25.00
DSM Daniella Sarahyba 8.00 20.00
MMM Marisa Miller 15.00 40.00
AH1M Alicia Hall 8.00 20.00
AH2M Alicia Hall 8.00 20.00

2005 Sports Illustrated Swimsuit Olympians

COMPLETE SET (8) 8.00 20.00
COMMON CARD (OL1-OL8) 1.25 3.00
STATED ODDS 1:6

2005 Sports Illustrated Swimsuit Underwater Beauties

COMPLETE SET (12) 12.00 30.00
COMMON CARD (UB1-UB12) 1.50 4.00
STATED ODDS 1:4

2006 Sports Illustrated Swimsuit

COMPLETE SET (100) 10.00 25.00
COMMON CARD (1-100) .20 .50

2006 Sports Illustrated Swimsuit Autographs

STATED ODDS 1:24
1 Aline Nakashima 12.00 30.00
2 Brooklyn Decker 75.00 150.00
3 Daniela Pestova 10.00 25.00
4 Daniella Sarahyba 10.00 25.00
5 Elisa Benitez SP 30.00 75.00
6 Fernanda Motta 10.00 25.00
7 Maria Sharapova SP 600.00 1200.00
8 Oluchi Onweagba 10.00 25.00
9 Veronica Varekova 12.00 30.00
10 Yamila Diaz-Rahi 20.00 50.00
11 Yesica Toscanini 12.00 30.00

2006 Sports Illustrated Swimsuit Bombshell Beach

COMPLETE SET (10) 10.00 25.00
COMMON CARD (1-10) 1.50 4.00
STATED ODDS 1:4

2006 Sports Illustrated Swimsuit Memorabilia

COMPLETE SET (9) 200.00 400.00
COMMON CARD 10.00 25.00
STATED ODDS 1:24
BDM Brooklyn Decker 50.00 100.00
MSM Maria Sharapova 100.00 200.00
RRM Rebecca Romjin-Stamos 20.00 50.00
VVM Veronica Varekova

2006 Sports Illustrated Swimsuit Net Gains Maria Sharapova

COMPLETE SET (10) 25.00 60.00
COMMON CARD (NG1-NG10) 5.00 12.00
STATED ODDS 1:4

2007 Sports Illustrated Swimsuit

COMPLETE SET (100) 15.00 40.00
UNOPENED BOX (PACKS)
UNOPENED PACK (CARDS)
COMMON CARD (1-100) .15 .40
21 Bar Refaeli .40 1.00
22 Bar Refaeli .40 1.00
23 Bar Refaeli .40 1.00
24 Bar Refaeli .40 1.00
25 Bar Refaeli .40 1.00
26 Bar Refaeli .40 1.00
27 Bar Refaeli .40 1.00
28 Bar Refaeli .40 1.00
29 Bar Refaeli .40 1.00
30 Bar Refaeli .40 1.00
31 Brooklyn Decker .60 1.50
32 Brooklyn Decker .60 1.50
33 Brooklyn Decker .60 1.50
34 Brooklyn Decker .60 1.50
35 Brooklyn Decker .60 1.50
54 Marisa Miller .60 1.50
55 Marisa Miller .60 1.50
56 Marisa Miller .60 1.50
57 Marisa Miller .60 1.50
58 Marisa Miller .60 1.50
59 Marisa Miller .60 1.50
60 Marisa Miller .60 1.50
61 Marisa Miller .60 1.50
62 Marisa Miller .60 1.50
63 Marisa Miller .60 1.50
64 Marisa Miller .60 1.50
99 Checklist 12.00 30.00
100 Checklist 12.00 30.00

2007 Sports Illustrated Swimsuit Autographs

COMMON AUTO 15.00 30.00
STATED ODDS 1:18
3 Bar Refaeli 120.00 250.00
4 Brooklyn Decker 100.00 200.00
7 Irina Shayk 60.00 120.00
9 Tori Praver 20.00 40.00
10 Yamila Diaz-Rahi 20.00 50.00

2007 Sports Illustrated Swimsuit Beyonce

COMPLETE SET (10) 125.00 300.00
COMMON CARD (1-10) 20.00 50.00
STATED ODDS 1:4

2007 Sports Illustrated Swimsuit Rookies

COMPLETE SET (10) 8.00 20.00
STATED ODDS 1:4
2 Bar Refaeli 2.00 5.00
8 Heidi Klum 2.00 5.00
9 Kathy Ireland 2.00 5.00

2008 Sports Illustrated Swimsuit

COMPLETE SET (75) 6.00 15.00
UNOPENED BOX (PACKS)
UNOPENED PACK (CARDS)
COMMON CARD (1-75) .15 .40
13 Bar Refaeli .40 1.00
14 Bar Refaeli .40 1.00
15 Bar Refaeli .40 1.00
16 Bar Refaeli .40 1.00
17 Bar Refaeli .40 1.00
18 Bar Refaeli .40 1.00
19 Brooklyn Decker .60 1.50
20 Brooklyn Decker .60 1.50
21 Brooklyn Decker .60 1.50
22 Brooklyn Decker .60 1.50
23 Brooklyn Decker .60 1.50
24 Brooklyn Decker .60 1.50
49 Marisa Miller .60 1.50
50 Marisa Miller .60 1.50
51 Marisa Miller .60 1.50
52 Marisa Miller .60 1.50
53 Marisa Miller .60 1.50
54 Marisa Miller .60 1.50

2008 Sports Illustrated Swimsuit Autographs

COMMON CARD 10.00 25.00
STATED ODDS 1:16
JC1 Jeisa Chiminazzo - ruffled top 20.00 40.00
JC2 Jeisa Chiminazzo - striped top 20.00 40.00
JG1 Jessica Gomes - blue and white bikini 30.00 75.00

JG2 Jessica Gomes - brown and red bikini 30.00 75.00
JH1 Julie Henderson - gold one-piece 12.00 30.00
JH2 Julie Henderson - yellow bikini 12.00 30.00
JM1 Jarah Mariano 50.00 100.00
JM2 Jarah Mariano 50.00 100.00

2008 Sports Illustrated Swimsuit Danica Patrick

COMPLETE SET (10) 75.00 150.00
COMMON CARD (DP1-DP10) 8.00 20.00
STATED ODDS 1:4

2008 Sports Illustrated Swimsuit Editor's Choice

EC1 Ana Beatriz Barros 15.00 30.00
EC2 Brooklyn Decker 20.00 40.00
EC3 Daniella Sarahyba
EC4 Marisa Miller 30.00 60.00
EC5 Danica Patrick

2008 Sports Illustrated Swimsuit Material

COMMON CARD 15.00 30.00
STATED ODDS 1:16
PRAVER JEWEL ODDS 1:6 CASES
BDM Brooklyn Decker 20.00 40.00
BRM Bar Refaeli 20.00 40.00
DPM Danica Patrick 75.00 125.00
MMM Marisa Miller 30.00 60.00
TPMJ Tori Praver JEWEL/20*

2008 Sports Illustrated Swimsuit Rookies

COMPLETE SET (10) 8.00 20.00
COMMON CARD (R1-R10) 1.25 3.00
STATED ODDS 1:4
R2 Jessica Gomes 1.50 4.00
R7 Jarah Mariano 1.50 4.00
R8 Christie Brinkley 2.00 5.00
R9 Elle Macpherson 2.50 6.00

2009 Sports Illustrated Swimsuit

COMPLETE SET (80) 6.00 15.00
UNOPENED BOX (PACKS)
UNOPENED PACK (CARDS)
COMMON CARD (1-80) .15 .40
9 Bar Refaeli .40 1.00
10 Bar Refaeli .40 1.00
11 Bar Refaeli .40 1.00
12 Bar Refaeli .40 1.00
13 Bar Refaeli .40 1.00
14 Brooklyn Decker .60 1.50
15 Brooklyn Decker .60 1.50
16 Brooklyn Decker .60 1.50
17 Brooklyn Decker .60 1.50
18 Brooklyn Decker .60 1.50
19 Cintia Dicker .30 .75
20 Cintia Dicker .30 .75
21 Cintia Dicker .30 .75
33 Hillary Rhoda .30 .75
34 Hillary Rhoda .30 .75
35 Hillary Rhoda .30 .75
41 Jarah Mariano .30 .75
42 Jarah Mariano .30 .75
43 Jarah Mariano .30 .75
44 Jarah Mariano .30 .75
45 Jarah Mariano .30 .75
46 Jessica Gomes .30 .75
47 Jessica Gomes .30 .75
48 Jessica Gomes .30 .75
49 Jessica Gomes .30 .75
50 Jessica Gomes .30 .75

2009 Sports Illustrated Swimsuit Body Paint

COMPLETE SET (10) 8.00 20.00
COMMON CARD (B1-B10) 1.25 3.00
STATED ODDS 1:4
B1 Brooklyn Decker 2.50 6.00
B2 Brooklyn Decker 2.50 6.00
B3 Heidi Klum 2.00 5.00
B4 Heidi Klum 2.00 5.00

2009 Sports Illustrated Swimsuit Danica Patrick

COMPLETE SET (10) 50.00 100.00
COMMON CARD (D1-D10) 6.00 15.00
STATED ODDS 1:4

2009 Sports Illustrated Swimsuit Materials

STATED ODDS 1:8
BRM Bar Refaeli 25.00 50.00
CDM Cintia Dicker 8.00 20.00
EMM Elle Macpherson CT 20.00 40.00
HKM Heidi Klum 20.00 40.00
HRM Hillary Rhoda 8.00 20.00
JGM Jessica Gomes 8.00 20.00
MKM Maria Kirilenko 20.00 40.00
MMM Marisa Miller 25.00 50.00
MSM Maria Sharapova 40.00 80.00
PRM Pania Rose 8.00 20.00
DP1M Danica Patrick 75.00 150.00
DP2M Danica Patrick 75.00 150.00

2012 Sports Illustrated Swimsuit Decade of Supermodels

COMPLETE SET (70) 10.00 25.00
UNOPENED BOX (96 CARDS)
COMMON CARD (1-70) .40 1.00
12 Beyonce 1.00 2.50
13 Brooklyn Decker .75 2.00
18 Danica Patrick 6.00 15.00
24 Elle Macpherson .60 1.50
29 Heidi Klum .60 1.50
47 Maria Sharapova 2.00 5.00
48 Marisa Miller .60 1.50

2012 Sports Illustrated Swimsuit Decade of Supermodels Celebrities

COMPLETE SET (10) 12.00 30.00
COMMON CARD (C1-C10) 2.00 5.00
STATED ODDS 4:1
C2 Beyonce 3.00 8.00
C3 Brooklyn Decker 2.50 6.00
C4 Danica Patrick 6.00 15.00
C8 Maria Sharapova 4.00 10.00

2012 Sports Illustrated Swimsuit Decade of Supermodels Danica Patrick Memorabilia

COMMON CARD (DP1-DP10) 25.00 60.00
STATED ODDS 1:1

2012 Sports Illustrated Swimsuit Decade of Supermodels Decade's Best

COMPLETE SET (10) 8.00 20.00
COMMON CARD (DB1-DB10) 2.00 5.00
STATED ODDS 4:1
DB1 Bar Refaeli 2.50 6.00
DB2 Brooklyn Decker 2.50 6.00
DB7 Marisa Miller 2.50 6.00

2012 Sports Illustrated Swimsuit Decade of Supermodels Memorabilia

COMMON CARD 10.00 25.00
STATED ODDS 2:1
AV Anne V 12.00 30.00
BD Brooklyn Decker 25.00 50.00
BR Bar Refaeli 15.00 40.00
BR2 Bar Refaeli 15.00 40.00
DP Daniela Pestova 12.00 30.00
EM Elle Macpherson 15.00 40.00
HK Heidi Klum 15.00 40.00
JM Jarah Mariano 12.00 30.00
KC Kim Cloutier 12.00 30.00
MK Maria Kirilenko 15.00 40.00
MM2 Marisa Miller 20.00 50.00
MS Maria Sharapova 25.00 60.00
PN Petra Nemcova 12.00 30.00
TP Tori Praver 12.00 30.00

2012 Sports Illustrated Swimsuit Decade of Supermodels Natural Colors

COMPLETE SET (10) 10.00 25.00
COMMON CARD (NC1-NC10) 2.00 5.00
STATED ODDS FOUR PER BOX
NC2 Brooklyn Decker 2.50 6.00
NC8 Marisa Miller 2.50 6.00

1994 Imagine Spring Break

COMPLETE SET (60) 6.00 15.00
COMMON CARD (1-60) .20 .50

1993 Lime Rock Spy vs. Spy

COMPLETE SET (55) 4.00 10.00
COMPLETE SET W/VARIATIONS (110) 8.00 20.00
UNOPENED BOX (36 PACKS) 30.00 40.00
UNOPENED PACK (9 CARDS) 1.25 1.50
COMMON CARD (1a-55b) .15 .40

1993 Lime Rock Spy vs. Spy Silver Holograms

COMPLETE SET (3) 4.00 10.00
COMMON CARD (H1-H3) 1.50 4.00
*GOLD: 1.2X TO 3X BASIC CARDS 5.00 12.00
RANDOMLY INSERTED INTO PACKS

2021 Parkside Squishmallows Series 1

COMPLETE SET (100) 20.00 50.00
UNOPENED BOX (24 PACKS) 300.00 600.00
UNOPENED PACK (8 CARDS*) 12.00 25.00
UNOPENED RACK BOX (8 CARDS*)
COMMON CARD (1-100) .50 1.25
*MINI: 1.5X TO 4X BASIC CARDS
*BLACK LIGHT: 8X TO 20X BASIC CARDS
*FOIL: X TO X BASIC CARDS
*HOLOGRAPH: X TO X BASIC CARDS

2021 Parkside Squishmallows Series 1 Founder's Redemption

1 Jonathan Kelly/250 EXCH

2021 Parkside Squishmallows Series 1 Lenticular Flip-a-Mallows

COMMON CARD (L1-L10) 40.00 100.00
RANDOMLY INSERTED INTO PACKS

2021 Parkside Squishmallows Series 1 Puzzle Inserts

COMPLETE SET (20) 15.00 40.00
COMMON CARD 1.50 4.00
RANDOMLY INSERTED INTO PACKS

2021 Parkside Squishmallows Series 1 Relics

COMMON MEM (R1-R10) 125.00 300.00
RANDOMLY INSERTED INTO PACKS

2021 Parkside Squishmallows Series 1 Squish in the Wild

COMPLETE SET (20) 60.00 150.00
COMMON CARD (SW1-SW20) 5.00 12.00
RANDOMLY INSERTED INTO PACKS

2021 Parkside Squishmallows Series 1 Storybook Series

COMMON CARD (SB1-SB10) 30.00 75.00
RANDOMLY INSERTED INTO PACKS

2021 Parkside Squishmallows Series 1 Street Art

COMMON CARD (ST1-ST20) 8.00 20.00
RANDOMLY INSERTED INTO PACKS

1993 Star International Star '93 Show Promos

COMPLETE SET (33) 60.00 120.00
COMMON CARD (1-33) 2.00 5.00

Stargate

1994 Collect-a-Card Stargate

COMPLETE SET (100) 6.00 15.00
UNOPENED BOX (36 PACKS) 15.00 20.00
UNOPENED PACK (8 CARDS) .75 1.00
COMMON CARD (1-100) .12 .30

1994 Collect-a-Card Stargate Adventure

COMPLETE SET (12) 10.00 25.00
COMMON CARD (AS1-AS12) 1.25 3.00
STATED ODDS 1:6

1994 Collect-a-Card Stargate Characters

COMPLETE SET (8) 15.00 40.00
COMMON CARD (CS1-CS8) 3.00 8.00
STATED ODDS 1:24

1994 Collect-a-Card Stargate Game Tips

COMPLETE SET (8) 5.00 12.00
COMMON CARD (TS1-TS8) .75 2.00
STATED ODDS 1:4

1994 Collect-a-Card Stargate Stargate Mail-In Redemption

COMPLETE SET (3) 20.00 50.00
COMMON CARD (G1-G3) 8.00 20.00
MAIL-IN REDEMPTION SET EXCLUSIVE

1994 Collect-a-Card Stargate Unlock the Stargate Game

COMPLETE SET (12) 2.00 5.00
COMMON CARD 1-12 .20 .50
STATED ODDS 1:1

1994 Collect-a-Card Stargate Promos

COMPLETE SET (4) 2.00 5.00
COMMON CARD .75 2.00

2000 Stargate SG-1 Previews

COMPLETE SET (6) 8.00 20.00
COMMON CARD (P1-P6) 1.50 4.00

2001 Stargate SG-1

COMPLETE SET (72) 8.00 20.00
UNOPENED BOX (40 PACKS) 15.00 20.00
UNOPENED PACK (9 CARDS) .75 1.00
COMMON CARD (1-72) .25 .60
*P.P.BLACK/25: 1.2X TO 3X BASIC CARDS 1.25 3.00
*P.P.CYAN/25: 1.2X TO 3X BASIC CARDS 1.25 3.00
*P.P.MAGENTA/25: 1.2X TO 3X BASIC CARDS1.25 3.00
*P.P.YELLOW/25: 1.2X TO 3X BASIC CARDS1.25 3.00
UNC 72-Card Base Set Uncut Sheet/100*

2001 Stargate SG-1 Autographs

COMMON CARD (A1-A9) 10.00 25.00
STATED ODDS 1:40
A1 Richard Dean Anderson 80.00 150.00
A2 Don Davis 25.00 60.00
A3 Teryl Rothery 12.00 30.00
A7 Vince Crestejo 12.00 30.00
A8 Jay Acovone 12.00 30.00

2001 Stargate SG-1 From the Archives Costumes

COMPLETE SET (4) 100.00 250.00
COMMON CARD (C1-C4) 15.00 30.00
STATED ODDS 1:80
C4 ISSUED AS CASE TOPPER
C3 Major Samantha Carter 80.00 150.00
C4 Teal'c CT 30.00 80.00

2001 Stargate SG-1 Stargate Aliens

COMPLETE SET (9) 1.50 4.00
COMMON CARD (X1-X9) .20 .50
STATED ODDS 1:3

2001 Stargate SG-1 Stargate in Motion

COMPLETE SET (6) 15.00 40.00
COMMON CARD (M1-M6) 3.00 8.00
STATED ODDS 1:27
UNC 18-Card Uncut Sheet (3 Base Sets)/20*

2001 Stargate SG-1 Stargate Stars

COMPLETE SET (5) 3.00 8.00
COMMON CARD (S1-S5) .75 2.00
STATED ODDS 1:7

2001 Stargate SG-1 Promos

COMPLETE SET (2) 2.00 5.00
P1 Group shot GEN .75 2.00
P2 Colonel Jack O'Neill ALB 1.50 4.00

2002 Stargate SG-1 Season Four

COMPLETE SET (72) 3.00 8.00
UNOPENED BOX (40 PACKS) 65.00 80.00
UNOPENED PACK (9 CARDS) 1.75 2.00
COMMON CARD (1-72) .10 .25

2002 Stargate SG-1 Season Four Autographs

COMMON CARD (A10-A19) 6.00 15.00
STATED ODDS ONE PER BOX
A19 ISSUED AS ALBUM EXCLUSIVE
A10 Suanne Braun 8.00 20.00
A11 Amanda Tapping 25.00 60.00
A12 Carmen Angenziano 8.00 20.00
A13 Michael Shanks 25.00 60.00
A14 Peter Wingfield 8.00 20.00
A16 Vanessa Angel 8.00 20.00
A18 J.R. Bourne 8.00 20.00
A19 Erick Avari ALB 12.00 30.00

2002 Stargate SG-1 Season Four Dial Us Home

COMPLETE SET (6) 2.00 5.00
COMMON CARD (D1-D6) .40 1.00
STATED ODDS 1:6

2002 Stargate SG-1 Season Four From the Archives Costumes

COMMON CARD (C5-C12) 6.00 15.00
STATED ODDS 1:40
C12 ISSUED AS CASE TOPPER
ANNOUNCED PRINT RUN 625-1450
C6 General Hammond/1350* 8.00 20.00
C8 Colonel Maybourne/1300* 8.00 20.00
C9 Anise 30.00 60.00
Freya/625*
C11 Major Samantha Carter/625* 30.00 80.00
C12 Major Samantha Carter DUAL CT/667* 40.00 80.00

2002 Stargate SG-1 Season Four Goa'uld Technology

COMPLETE SET (9) 4.00 10.00
COMMON CARD (G1-G9) .60 1.50
STATED ODDS 1:8

2002 Stargate SG-1 Season Four Heroes in Action

COMPLETE SET (4) 10.00 25.00
COMMON CARD (H1-H4) 3.00 8.00
STATED ODDS 1:40

2002 Stargate SG-1 Season Four SketchaFEX

COMMON CARD 40.00 80.00
STATED ODDS 1:480

2002 Stargate SG-1 Season Four Promos

P1 Group of five GEN 1.00 2.50
BP1 Group of four ALB 1.50 4.00

2003 Stargate SG-1 Season Five

COMPLETE SET (72) 4.00 10.00
UNOPENED BOX (40 PACKS) 45.00 60.00
UNOPENED PACK (9 CARDS) 1.25 1.50
COMMON CARD (1-72) .10 .30
UNC 72-Card Base Set Uncut Sheet

2003 Stargate SG-1 Season Five Autographs

COMMON CARD (A20-A25) 6.00 15.00
OVERALL AUTO ODDS 1:20
A25 ISSUED AS CASE TOPPER
A21 Christopher Judge 12.00 30.00
A25 John de Lancie CT 20.00 50.00

2003 Stargate SG-1 Season Five Dr. Daniel Jackson Tribute

COMPLETE SET (9) 2.00 5.00
COMMON CARD (D1-D9) .30 .75
STATED ODDS 1:4
PAN 9-Card Panel (D1-D9)

2003 Stargate SG-1 Season Five False Gods

COMPLETE SET (12) 8.00 20.00
COMMON CARD (F1-F12) .75 2.00
STATED ODDS 1:12
PAN 12-Card Panel (F1-F12)

2003 Stargate SG-1 Season Five From the Archives Costumes

COMMON CARD (C13-C16) 12.00 30.00
STATED ODDS 1:160
C16 ISSUED AS ALBUM EXCLUSIVE
C14 Bra'tac 25.00 60.00

2003 Stargate SG-1 Season Five Wormhole X-Treme

COMPLETE SET (9) 6.00 15.00
COMMON CARD (W1-W9) .75 2.00
STATED ODDS 1:8
PAN 9-Card Panel (W1-W9)

2003 Stargate SG-1 Season Five Wormhole X-Treme Autographs

COMMON CARD (WXA1-WXA6) 6.00 15.00
OVERALL AUTO ODDS 1:20

2003 Stargate SG-1 Season Five Promos

COMPLETE SET (3) 2.50 6.00
COMMON CARD (P1-P3) 1.00 2.50
P3 Dr. Daniel Jackson ALB 1.50 4.00

2004 Stargate SG-1 Season Six

COMPLETE SET (72) 4.00 10.00
UNOPENED BOX (40 PACKS) 45.00 60.00
UNOPENED PACK (7 CARDS) 1.25 1.50
UNOPENED ARCHIVE BOX 800.00 1200.00
COMMON CARD (1-72) .10 .30
UNC 72-Card Uncut Sheet/25*

2004 Stargate SG-1 Season Six Autographs

COMMON CARD 6.00 15.00
STATED ODDS TWO PER BOX
A33 ISSUED AS CASE TOPPER
DA1 ISSUED AS MULTI-CASE INCENTIVE
L (LIMITED): 300-500 COPIES
A26 Corin Nemec 12.00 30.00
A33 Musetta Vander CT 20.00 50.00
A37 Amanda Tapping L 25.00 60.00
A38 Michael Shanks L 50.00 100.00
A40 Brad Wright L 20.00 50.00
DA1 Michael Shanks/Amanda Tapping MCI 100.00 200.00

2004 Stargate SG-1 Season Six Behind-the-Scenes

COMPLETE SET (9) 8.00 20.00
COMMON CARD (B1-B9) 1.25 3.00
STATED ODDS 1:5

2004 Stargate SG-1 Season Six Costumes

COMMON CARD (C17-C21) 12.00 30.00
STATED ODDS 1:120
C21 ISSUED AS ALBUM EXCLUSIVE
C17 Major Samantha Carter 20.00 50.00
C21 Colonel O'Neill ALBUM 15.00 40.00

2004 Stargate SG-1 Season Six In the Line of Duty Colonel O'Neill

COMPLETE SET (9) 15.00 40.00
COMMON CARD (CO1-CO9) 2.50 6.00
STATED ODDS 1:10 US PACKS

2004 Stargate SG-1 Season Six In the Line of Duty Major Carter

COMPLETE SET (9) 12.00 30.00
COMMON CARD (MC1-MC9) 2.00 5.00
STATED ODDS 1:10 UK PACKS

2004 Stargate SG-1 Season Six Stargate Gallery

COMPLETE SET (6) 15.00 40.00
COMMON CARD (G1-G6) 3.00 8.00
STATED ODDS 1:40

2004 Stargate SG-1 Season Six Promos

COMPLETE SET (5) 5.00 12.00
COMMON CARD .75 2.00
P3 Group of five ALB 2.00 5.00
GG2004 Group of four 2.00 5.00
(Gum Guide)
PCE2004 Promo Card Encyclopedia 2004 Edition 2.00 5.00

2005 Stargate SG-1 Season Seven

COMPLETE SET (72) 4.00 10.00
UNOPENED BOX (40 PACKS) 50.00 60.00
UNOPENED PACK (5 CARDS) 1.25 1.50
COMMON CARD (1-72) .10 .30
UNC 72-Card Uncut Sheet/25*

2005 Stargate SG-1 Season Seven Autographs

COMMON AUTO (A42-A61) 6.00 15.00
STATED ODDS ONE PER BOX
A42 ISSUED AS 6-CASE INCENTIVE
A46 ISSUED AS 2-CASE INCENTIVE
L (LIMITED): 300-500 COPIES
VL (VERY LIMITED): 200-300 COPIES
A42 Michael Shanks 6CI 200.00 400.00
A43 Robert Picardo VL 30.00 80.00
A44 Don Davis L 12.00 30.00
A45 Teryl Rothery L 15.00 40.00
A46 Jolene Blalock 2CI 60.00 120.00
A47 Anna-Louise Plowman L 15.00 40.00
A48 Jessica Steen L 15.00 40.00
A49 Saul Rubinek L 10.00 25.00
A50 Kristen Dalton L 10.00 25.00
A51 David Palffy L 12.00 30.00
A53 Christopher Cousins L 12.00 30.00
A57 Katie Smart L 10.00 25.00
A59 Dom DeLuise L 15.00 40.00
A60 Tony Amendola L 12.00 30.00
A61 Christopher Judge VL 30.00 80.00

2005 Stargate SG-1 Season Seven Behind-the-Scenes

COMPLETE SET (9) 3.00 8.00
COMMON CARD (B10-B18) .40 1.00
STATED ODDS 1:10

2005 Stargate SG-1 Season Seven Costumes

COMPLETE SET (6) 60.00 120.00
COMMON CARD (C22-C27) 10.00 25.00
OVERALL COSTUME/RELIC ODDS ONE PER BOX
C26 ISSUED IN COLLECTORS ALBUM

2005 Stargate SG-1 Season Seven Dr. Frasier Tribute

COMPLETE SET (2) 50.00 100.00
COMMON CARD (F1-F2) 25.00 60.00
STATED ODDS 1:480

2005 Stargate SG-1 Season Seven In the Line of Duty Dr. Jackson

COMPLETE SET (9) 12.00 30.00
COMMON CARD (DJ1-DJ9) 2.00 5.00
STATED ODDS 1:20 UK PACKS

2005 Stargate SG-1 Season Seven In the Line of Duty Teal'C

COMPLETE SET (9) 8.00 20.00
COMMON CARD (T1-T9) 1.25 3.00
STATED ODDS 1:20 N.AMERICAN PACKS

2005 Stargate SG-1 Season Seven Relics

COMPLETE SET (9) 100.00 200.00
COMMON CARD (R1-R9) 10.00 25.00
OVERALL COSTUME/RELIC ODDS ONE PER BOX
R8 ISSUED AS N.AMERICAN CASE TOPPER
R9 ISSUED AS UK CASE TOPPER
STATED PRINT RUN 240-481

2005 Stargate SG-1 Season Seven SG-1 Team

COMPLETE SET (4) 50.00 100.00
COMMON CARD (S1-S4) 12.00 30.00
STATED ODDS 1:200
STATED PRINT RUN 600 SER. #'d SETS

2005 Stargate SG-1 Season Seven Stargate Casting Call

COMPLETE SET (4) 8.00 20.00
COMMON CARD (CC1-CC4) 2.50 6.00
STATED ODDS 1:40

2005 Stargate SG-1 Season Seven Promos

COMPLETE SET (4) 6.00 15.00
COMMON CARD .75 2.00
P3 Major Samantha Carter ALB 4.00 10.00
UK Colonel Jack O'Neill 3.00 8.00
(UK excl.)

2006 Stargate SG-1 Season Eight

COMPLETE SET (72) 4.00 10.00
UNOPENED BOX (40 PACKS) 65.00 80.00
UNOPENED PACK (5 CARDS) 1.75 2.00
COMMON CARD (1-72) .10 .30

2006 Stargate SG-1 Season Eight Autographs

COMMON CARD (A62-A78) 6.00 15.00
OVERALL AUTO ODDS ONE PER BOX
A68 ISSUED AS ALBUM EXCLUSIVE
L (LIMITED): 300-500 COPIES
VL (VERY LIMITED): 200-300 COPIES
A63 Cary-Hiroyuki Tagawa L 8.00 20.00
A64 Kevin McNulty 8.00 20.00
A67 Claudia Black VL 120.00 200.00
A68 Erica Durance ALB 15.00 40.00
A72 Mel Harris 8.00 20.00
A73 Isaac Hayes VL 60.00 120.00
A76 Dan Castelleneta VL 40.00 80.00
A78 George Dzundza 8.00 20.00

2006 Stargate SG-1 Season Eight Costumes

COMP.SET w/o C35 30.00 80.00
COMMON CARD (C28-C35) 6.00 15.00
OVERALL COSTUME/RELIC ODDS ONE PER BOX
C35 ISSUED AS CASE TOPPER
C28 Jonas Quinn 8.00 20.00
C29 Dr. Daniel Jackson 8.00 20.00
C30 Colonel Jack O'Neill 8.00 20.00
C31 Teal'c 8.00 20.00
C32 Major Kawalsky 12.00 30.00
C35 Apophis DUAL CT 15.00 40.00

2006 Stargate SG-1 Season Eight Dual Autographs

OVERALL AUTO ODDS 1:BOX
DA2 ISSUED AS 2-CASE INCENTIVE
DA3 ISSUED AS 6-CASE INCENTIVE
DA2 Christoper Judge/Tony Amendola 2CI 50.00 100.00
DA3 Claudia Black/Michael Shanks 6CI 200.00 350.00

2006 Stargate SG-1 Season Eight Kneel Before Your God

COMPLETE SET (2) 30.00 80.00
COMMON CARD (G1-G2) 20.00 50.00
STATED ODDS 1:480
STATED PRINT RUN 375 SER. #'d SETS

2006 Stargate SG-1 Season Eight Personnel Files

COMPLETE SET (9) 6.00 15.00
COMMON CARD (PF1-PF9) 1.00 2.50
STATED ODDS 1:20

2006 Stargate SG-1 Season Eight Relics

COMPLETE SET (5) 50.00 100.00
COMMON CARD (R10-R14) 8.00 20.00
OVERALL COSTUME/RELIC ODDS ONE PER BOX
STATED PRINT RUN 403-434
R10 Kelownan Files/434 12.00 30.00
R12 Alien Newspaper/407 10.00 25.00
R13 Mission Report/403 12.00 30.00

2006 Stargate SG-1 Season Eight Twisted

COMPLETE SET (9) 6.00 15.00
COMMON CARD (TW1-TW9) .60 1.50
STATED ODDS 1:10

2006 Stargate SG-1 Season Eight Promos

P1 Vala/Dr. Jackson GEN .75 2.00
P2 Major Samantha Carter NSU 1.50 4.00
P3 Teal'c ALB 6.00 15.00
UK Dr. Daniel Jackson (UK) 2.00 5.00

2007 Stargate SG-1 Season Nine

COMPLETE SET (72) 4.00 10.00
COMMON CARD (1-72) .10 .30

2007 Stargate SG-1 Season Nine Autographs

COMMON CARD 4.00 10.00
STATED ODDS TWO PER BOX
DA4 ISSUED AS MULTI-CASE INCENTIVE
VL (VERY LIMITED): 200-300 COPIES
A74 William B. Davis 6.00 15.00
A82 Amy Sloan 6.00 15.00
A83 Alessandro Juliani 5.00 12.00
A84 Michael Ironside 8.00 20.00
A85 Ben Browder VL 80.00 150.00
A87 Lexa Doig 25.00 60.00
A88 Ernie Hudson 8.00 20.00
A90 Tony Todd 10.00 25.00
A91 Matthew Walker 6.00 15.00
A92 Cameron Bright 10.00 25.00
A93 Peter Flemming 6.00 15.00
A94 Kendall Cross 8.00 20.00
DA4 Michael Shanks/Ben Browder CI 50.00 100.00

2007 Stargate SG-1 Season Nine Cast Posters

COMPLETE SET (7) 25.00 60.00
COMMON CARD (CP1-CP7) 5.00 12.00
STATED ODDS 1:40

2007 Stargate SG-1 Season Nine Costumes

COMPLETE SET (9) 80.00 150.00
COMMON CARD (C35-C43) 5.00 12.00
OVERALL COSTUME/RELIC ODDS ONE PER BOX
C35 Daniel Jackson 10.00 25.00
C36 Daniel Jackson 10.00 25.00
C37 Daniel Jackson 10.00 25.00
C40 General Jack O'Neill 12.00 30.00
C43 Rya'c 8.00 20.00

2007 Stargate SG-1 Season Nine Dual Costumes

C13 ISSUED AS ALBUM EXCLUSIVE
C14 ISSUED AS CASE TOPPER
C13 Cronus ALB 15.00 40.00
C14 Kali CT 20.00 50.00

2007 Stargate SG-1 Season Nine Production Sketches

COMPLETE SET (18) 15.00 40.00
COMMON CARD (S1-S18) 1.50 4.00
STATED ODDS 1:10

2007 Stargate SG-1 Season Nine Relics

COMMON CARD 8.00 20.00
OVERALL COSTUME/RELIC ODDS ONE PER BOX
R75 ISSUED AS MULTI-CASE INCENTIVE
R15 Alien Newspaper/500 8.00 20.00
R16 Roses/378 8.00 20.00
R17 Alien Documents/454 8.00 20.00
R75 R75 Bug/120 CI 50.00 100.00

2007 Stargate SG-1 Season Nine The Book of Origin

COMPLETE SET (9) 12.00 30.00
COMMON CARD (B1-B9) 2.50 6.00
STATED ODDS 1:20

2007 Stargate SG-1 Season Nine Promos

P1 Lt. Col. Mitchell GEN 1.25 3.00
P2 Dr.Jackson/Lt.Col.Mitchell NSU 1.25 3.00
P3 Teal'c ALB 6.00 15.00
UK Vala 2.00 5.00
(UK excl.)
DVD Collect all 9 seasons
(Promotional DVD Exclusive)
DST6 Series Three Action Figures Are Available Now!
SD07 Dr. Jackson SDCC 2.00 5.00

2008 Stargate SG-1 Season Ten

COMPLETE SET (72) 4.00 10.00
UNOPENED BOX (40 PACKS)
UNOPENED PACK (5 CARDS)
COMMON CARD (1-72) .10 .30

2008 Stargate SG-1 Season Ten Ark of Truth

COMPLETE SET (18) 15.00 40.00
COMMON CARD (S1-S18) 1.50 4.00
STATED ODDS 1:8

2008 Stargate SG-1 Season Ten Autographs

COMMON CARD 6.00 15.00
STATED ODDS TWO PER BOX
L (LIMITED): 300-500 COPIES
VL (VERY LIMITED): 200-300 COPIES
SOME AUTOS NOT PRICED DUE TO
LACK OF MARKET ACTIVITY
A95 Armin Shimerman VL 15.00 40.00
A96 Rene Auberjonois VL 15.00 40.00
A97 Morena Baccarin 30.00 80.00
A101 Fred Willard 10.00 25.00
A107 April Telek 10.00 25.00
A108 Claudia Black L 30.00 75.00
AT Amanda Tapping VL 50.00 100.00
CJ Christopher Judge VL 30.00 80.00

2008 Stargate SG-1 Season Ten Costumes

COMMON CARD 10.00 25.00
STATED ODDS TWO PER BOX
AC1 ISSUED AS 3-CASE INCENTIVE
LANDRY DUAL ISSUED AS CASE TOPPER
VL (VERY LIMITED): 200-300 COPIES
AC1 Michael Shanks AU 3CI 30.00 80.00
CT President Landry DUAL CT 12.00 30.00

2008 Stargate SG-1 Season Ten Film Clip Gallery

COMMON CARD (F1-F9) 5.00 12.00
STATED ODDS 1:24
F10 ISSUED AS RITTENHOUSE REWARD
F10 Cameron Mitchell SP RR

2008 Stargate SG-1 Season Ten Stargate Patches

STATED ODDS 1:48
PC1 Colonel Jack O'Neill
PC2 Dr. Daniel Jackson 5.00 12.00
PC3 Lt. Col. Cameron Mitchell 4.00 10.00
PC4 Lt. Col. Samantha Carter
PC5 Teal'c 8.00 20.00
PC6 Vala Mal Doran

2008 Stargate SG-1 Season Ten Women of Stargate

COMPLETE SET (17) 25.00 60.00
COMMON CARD (W1-W17) 2.00 5.00
STATED ODDS 1:8

2008 Stargate SG-1 Season Ten Promos

COMMON CARD .75 2.00
P3 Dr. Jackson (album excl.) 4.00 10.00
CP1 Group of six (con. excl.) 2.00 5.00

2012 Stargate SG-1 Expansion Autographs

ISSUED VIA RITTENHOUSE WEBSITE
A70 Richard Dean Anderson/160* AU 150.00 200.00
AC4 Christopher Judge/500* AU MEM 40.00 75.00
AC5 Richard Dean Anderson/100* AU MEM 200.00 250.00

2004 Stargate Atlantis Previews

COMPLETE SET (6) 8.00 20.00
COMMON CARD 2.00 5.00
STATED PRINT RUN 999 SER.#'d SETS

2005 Stargate Atlantis Season One

COMPLETE SET (63) 4.00 10.00
UNOPENED BOX (40 PACKS) 75.00 125.00
UNOPENED PACK (5 CARDS) 2.00 3.00
COMMON CARD (1-63) .10 .25

2005 Stargate Atlantis Season One Ancient Technology

COMPLETE SET (9) 25.00 60.00
COMMON CARD (AT1-AT9) 3.00 8.00
STATED ODDS 1:20

2005 Stargate Atlantis Season One Atlantis Crew

COMPLETE SET (9) 15.00 40.00
COMMON CARD (C1-C9) 2.50 6.00
STATED ODDS 1:40

2005 Stargate Atlantis Season One Autographs

COMMON AUTO 6.00 15.00
STATED ODDS 1:40
CHAMBERS AUTO ISSUED AS CASE TOPPER
DAVI AUTO ISSUED AS 2-CASE INCENTIVE
SCARFE AU ISSUED AS ALBUM EXCLUSIVE
L (LIMITED: 300-500 COPIES
VL (VERY LIMITED): 200-300 COPIES
1 Alan Scarfe ALB 10.00 25.00
3 Boyan Vukelic 8.00 20.00
5 Colm Meaney L 15.00 40.00
7 David Nykl 8.00 20.00
8 Erin Chambers CT 10.00 25.00
10 Jana Mitsoula 6.00 15.00
11 Joe Flanigan VL 20.00 50.00
12 Laura Mennell 8.00 20.00
13 Melia McClure 8.00 20.00
14 Paul McGillion VL 15.00 40.00
15 Robert Davi 2CI 50.00 100.00

2005 Stargate Atlantis Season One Costumes

COMMON CARD 8.00 20.00
STATED ODDS ONE PER BOX
AC1 ISSUED AS 6-CASE INCENTIVE
AC1 Rachel Luttrell AU 6CI 150.00 300.00

2005 Stargate Atlantis Season One Fallen Hero

COMPLETE SET (2) 30.00 80.00
COMMON CARD (H1-H2) 20.00 50.00
STATED ODDS 1:480

2005 Stargate Atlantis Season One Quotables

COMPLETE SET (20) 6.00 15.00
COMMON CARD (Q1-Q20) .40 1.00
STATED ODDS 1:6

2005 Stargate Atlantis Season One Promos

COMPLETE SET (5) 3.00 8.00
COMMON CARD .75 2.00
P3 Maj. Sheppard/Lt. Ford 1.25 3.00
UK Dr. McKay/Dr. Weir 1.25 3.00
SD2005 Ford/Sheppard/Weir/McKay 1.25 3.00

2006 Stargate Atlantis Season Two

COMPLETE SET (72) 4.00 10.00
UNOPENED BOX (40 PACKS) 45.00 60.00
UNOPENED PACK (5 CARDS) 1.25 1.50
COMMON CARD (1-72) .10 .30

2006 Stargate Atlantis Season Two Atlantis Team

COMPLETE SET (7) 15.00 40.00
COMMON CARD (P1-P7) 3.00 8.00
STATED ODDS 1:40

2006 Stargate Atlantis Season Two Autographs

COMMON CARD 6.00 15.00
STATED ODDS 1:20
SANFORD AU ISSUED AS ALBUM EXCLUSIVE
TAPPING AU ISSUED AS 2-CASE INCENTIVE
2 Brandy Ledford 12.00 30.00
7 Connor Trinneer 12.00 30.00
9 James Lafazanos 8.00 20.00
10 Kavan Smith 12.00 30.00
11 Pascale Hutton 8.00 20.00
12 Peter Woodward 8.00 20.00
13 Rachel Luttrell 50.00 100.00
14 Ryan Robbins 12.00 30.00
15 Torri Higginson 30.00 80.00
16 Garwin Sanford ALBUM 10.00 25.00
17 Amanda Tapping 2CI 25.00 60.00

2006 Stargate Atlantis Season Two Costumes

COMPLETE SET (4) 50.00 100.00
COMMON CARD 12.00 30.00
STATED ODDS 1:120

2006 Stargate Atlantis Season Two In Motion

COMPLETE SET (3) 50.00 100.00
COMMON CARD (M1-M3) 15.00 40.00
STATED ODDS 1:240

2006 Stargate Atlantis Season Two Quotables

COMPLETE SET (20) 6.00 15.00
COMMON CARD (Q21-Q40) .40 1.00
STATED ODDS 1:8

2006 Stargate Atlantis Season Two Warriors in Action

COMPLETE SET (9) 8.00 20.00
COMMON CARD (W1-W9) 1.25 3.00
STATED ODDS 1:20

2006 Stargate Atlantis Season Two Promos

COMMON CARD .75 2.00
P3 Group of Five ALB 3.00 8.00
UK Weir/McKay UK 1.50 4.00
CP1 Teyla Emmagan 4.00 10.00
(Summer Cons)

2008 Stargate Atlantis Seasons Three and Four

COMPLETE SET (81) 4.00 10.00
UNOPENED BOX (24 PACKS)
UNOPENED PACK (5 CARDS)
COMMON CARD (1-81) .10 .30

2008 Stargate Atlantis Seasons Three and Four Atlantis Team

COMPLETE SET (9) 15.00 40.00
COMMON CARD (T1-T9) 2.50 6.00
STATED ODDS 1:24

2008 Stargate Atlantis Seasons Three and Four Autographs

COMMON CARD 6.00 15.00
STATED ODDS TWO PER BOX
L (LIMITED): 300-500 COPIES
VL (VERY LIMITED): 200-300 COPIES
4 Joe Flanigan VL 15.00 40.00
6 Torri Higginson L 12.00 30.00

8 Richard Kind L 10.00 25.00
9 Rachel Luttrell VL 60.00 120.00
10 Jason Momoa VL 25.00 60.00
13 Robert Picardo VL 20.00 50.00
14 Mitch Pileggi L 8.00 20.00
15 Jewel Staite L 20.00 50.00
16 Danny Trejo L 20.00 50.00

2008 Stargate Atlantis Seasons Three and Four Costumes

COMMON CARD 4.00 10.00
STATED ODDS TWO PER BOX
JF ODDS ONE PER 3-CASE PURCHASE
SBTMW ODDS ONE PER CASE
1 Torri Higginson 8.00 20.00
2 Jewel Staite 8.00 20.00
9 Jason Momoa 5.00 12.00
10 Torri Higginson 8.00 20.00
11 Jason Momoa 5.00 12.00
12 Joe Flanigan 5.00 12.00
13 Joe Flanigan 5.00 12.00
14 Rachel Luttrell 6.00 15.00
15 Rachel Luttrell 6.00 15.00
16 Rachel Luttrell 6.00 15.00
17 Rachel Luttrell 6.00 15.00
JF Joe Flanigan AU 3CI 25.00 60.00
SBTMW Sheppard/Beckett
Teyla/McKay/Weir CT 30.00 80.00

2008 Stargate Atlantis Seasons Three and Four Pegasus Galaxy Starships

COMPLETE SET (9) 15.00 40.00
COMMON CARD (PG1-PG9) 2.00 5.00
STATED ODDS 1:12

2008 Stargate Atlantis Seasons Three and Four Quotables

COMPLETE SET (18) 6.00 15.00
COMMON CARD (Q41-Q58) .40 1.00
STATED ODDS 1:6

2008 Stargate Atlantis Seasons Three and Four Promos

COMPLETE SET (3) 2.50 6.00
COMMON CARD (P1-P3) 1.25 3.00

2009 Stargate Heroes Stargate Universe Previews

COMPLETE SET (9) 8.00 20.00
COMMON CARD (SU1-SU9) 2.00 5.00
STATED ODDS 1:24
SU10 ISSUED AS RITTENHOUSE REWARD
SU10 5 Cast Members RR SP 10.00 25.00

2009 Stargate Heroes

COMPLETE SET (90) 4.00 10.00
UNOPENED BOX (24 PACKS) 40.00 60.00
UNOPENED PACK (5 CARDS) 2.00 2.50
UNOPENED ARCHIVE BOX 800.00 1500.00
COMMON CARD (1-90) .10 .30
CARD 91 ISSUED AS RITTENHOUSE REWARD
91 Hammond SP RR 10.00 25.00

2009 Stargate Heroes Continuum

COMPLETE SET (18) 15.00 40.00
COMMON CARD (SC1-SC18) 1.25 3.00
STATED ODDS 1:8

2009 Stargate Heroes In Motion

COMPLETE SET (9) 10.00 25.00
COMMON CARD (M1-M9) 1.50 4.00
STATED ODDS 1:12

2009 Stargate Heroes Stargate Atlantis Autographs

COMMON CARD 4.00 10.00
OVERALL AUTOGRAPH ODDS 1:8
VL (VERY LIMITED): 200-300 COPIES
AT Amanda Tapping VL 60.00 120.00
BN Bill Nye 6.00 15.00
DH1 David Hewlett VL 30.00 60.00
DH2 David Hewlett VL 30.00 60.00
JM Jason Momoa VL 60.00 120.00
JN Jaime Ray Newman 10.00 20.00
MM Michelle Morgan 6.00 15.00
PS Patrick Sabongui 6.00 15.00
RF1 Rainbow Francks VL 30.00 60.00
RF2 Rainbow Francks VL 30.00 60.00
RP Robert Picardo VL 60.00 120.00

2009 Stargate Heroes Stargate Atlantis Relics

COMMON CARD 6.00 15.00
OVERALL RELIC ODDS 1:12
TE1 Teyla 8.00 20.00
TE2 Teyla 8.00 20.00
TE3 Teyla DUAL 10.00 25.00

2009 Stargate Heroes Stargate Atlantis Season Five

COMPLETE SET (20) 4.00 10.00
COMMON CARD (1-20) .30 .75
STATED ODDS 1:4

2009 Stargate Heroes Stargate SG-1 Autograph Relics

COMMON CARD 20.00 50.00
OVERALL AUTOGRAPH ODDS 1:8
VL (VERY LIMITED): 200-300 COPIES

2009 Stargate Heroes Stargate SG-1 Autographs

COMMON CARD 6.00 15.00
OVERALL AUTOGRAPH ODDS 1:8
SHANKS AUTO STATED ODDS ONE PER 3-CASE PURCHASE
L (LIMITED): 300-500 COPIES
A86 Beau Bridges 40.00 80.00
MS Michael Shanks 3CI 30.00 60.00

2009 Stargate Heroes Stargate SG-1 Dual Relics

COMMON CARD 8.00 20.00
OVERALL RELIC ODDS 1:12

2009 Stargate Heroes Stargate SG-1 Relics

COMMON CARD (C59-C72) 4.00 10.00
OVERALL RELIC ODDS 1:12
C59 Samantha Carter 8.00 20.00
C60 Samantha Carter 8.00 20.00
C61 Samantha Carter 8.00 20.00
C62 Samantha Carter 8.00 20.00
C63 Vala Mal Doran 6.00 15.00
C64 Vala Mal Doran 6.00 15.00
C65 Vala Mal Doran 6.00 15.00
C66 Cameron Mitchell 6.00 15.00

2009 Stargate Heroes Promos

COMMON CARD (P1-P4) .75 2.00
P3 Sheppard ALB 8.00 20.00
P4 Teyla SDCC 2.00 5.00

2010 Stargate Universe Season One

COMPLETE SET (72) 5.00 12.00
UNOPENED BOX (24 PACKS)
UNOPENED PACK (5 CARDS)
COMMON CARD (1-72) .15 .40

2010 Stargate Universe Season One Autographs

COMMON CARD 5.00 12.00
STATED ODDS THREE PER BOX
PHILLIPS AU ISSUED AS 3-CASE INCENTIVE
VL (VERY LIMITED): 200-300 COPIES
1 Alaina Huffman VL 45.00 90.00
2 Brian J. Smith VL 25.00 50.00
4 Christopher McDonald 8.00 20.00
5 David Blue VL 40.00 80.00
6 Elyse Levesque VL 50.00 100.00
8 Jamil Walker Smith VL 30.00 60.00
9 Jennifer Spence 8.00 20.00
11 Julia Benson 8.00 20.00
12 Louis Ferreira VL 40.00 80.00
14 Ona Grauer 8.00 20.00
15 Patrick Gilmore VL 8.00 20.00
17 Reiko Aylesworth 8.00 20.00
19 Lou Diamond Phillips 3CI 75.00 150.00

2010 Stargate Universe Season One Costumes

COMMON CARD (R1-R9) 5.00 12.00
STATED ODDS TWO PER BOX
DUAL COSTUME CARD ISSUED AS CASE TOPPER
R5 Tamara Johansen pants 6.00 15.00
R7 Chloe Armstrong dress 8.00 20.00
NNO Chloe/Alan/333 CT 30.00 60.00

2010 Stargate Universe Season One Crew

COMPLETE SET (9) 20.00 50.00
COMMON CARD (PL1-PL9) 4.00 10.00
STATED ODDS 1:24

2010 Stargate Universe Season One In Motion

COMPLETE SET (9) 15.00 40.00
COMMON CARD (L1-L9) 3.00 8.00
STATED ODDS 1:12

2010 Stargate Universe Season One Quotable Eli

COMPLETE SET (9) 8.00 20.00
COMMON CARD (Q1-Q9) 1.50 4.00
STATED ODDS 1:8

2010 Stargate Universe Season One Sketches

STATED ODDS ONE PER 6-CASE PURCHASE
1 David Desbois 250.00 400.00
2 Sean Pence 250.00 400.00

2010 Stargate Universe Season One Promos

CE Eli Wallace (Cleveland)
P1 Young/Rush/Wray GEN .75 2.00
P2 E.Wallace/Dr. Rush NSU 1.25 3.00
P3 Stargate Universe ALB
CP1 Group of five SDCC .75 2.00
CP2 Wray/Wallace/Telford (Philly)

2011 Stargate Universe Season Two

COMPLETE SET (20) 30.00 60.00
COMMON CARD (1-20) 2.00 5.00
STATED PRINT RUN 400 SER. #'d SETS

2011 Stargate Universe Season Two Autographs

COMMON CARD 6.00 15.00
STATED ODDS TWO PER PACK
L (LIMITED): 300-500 COPIES
VL (VERY LIMITED): 200-300 COPIES
EL (EXTREMELY LIMITED): LESS THAN 200 COPIES
1 Alaina Huffman VL 25.00 50.00
2 Brian J. Smith VL 15.00 30.00
3 David Blue VL 15.00 40.00
4 Elyse Levesque VL 30.00 60.00
6 Jamil Walker Smith VL 10.00 25.00
7 Julie McNiven L 10.00 25.00
8 Lou Diamond Phillips VL 25.00 50.00
9 Louis Ferreira VL 15.00 40.00
11A Ming-Na (full bleed) VL 30.00 60.00
11B Ming-Na (bordered) VL 20.00 40.00
12A R.D. Anderson SG1 EL 150.00 250.00
12B R.D. Anderson SGU EL 200.00 300.00

2011 Stargate Universe Season Two Destiny

COMPLETE SET (9) 15.00 30.00
COMMON CARD (D1-D9) 2.50 6.00
STATED ODDS ONE PER PACK
STATED PRINT RUN 444 SER. #'d SETS

2011 Stargate Universe Season Two Secrets

COMPLETE SET (9) 15.00 30.00
COMMON CARD (S1-S9) 2.50 6.00
STATED ODDS ONE PER PACK
STATED PRINT RUN 444 SER. #'d SETS

2011 Stargate Universe Season Two Promos

P1 Johansen/Wray/Armstrong 1.25 3.00
P2 Greer/Telford/Young 2.00 5.00

1993 World Class Marketing Starlog Science Fiction Universe

COMPLETE SET (106) 8.00 20.00
UNOPENED BOX (36 PACKS) 20.00 30.00
UNOPENED PACK (9 CARDS) 1.25 1.50
COMMON CARD (1-100; CK1-CK6) .15 .40
HC1 Kirk/Spock Silver Hologram 4.00 10.00
HC1 Kirk/Spock Gold Hologram 4.00 10.00
NNO Kirk/Spock 4-Card Panel PROMO

1993 World Class Marketing Starlog Science Fiction Universe Star Trek Covers

COMPLETE SET (5) 5.00 12.00
COMMON CARD (1-5) 1.25 3.00
MAIL-IN EXCLUSIVE SET

1997 Inkworks Starship Troopers

COMPLETE SET (81) 6.00 15.00
UNOPENED BOX (36 PACKS) 20.00 40.00
UNOPENED PACK (9 CARDS) 1.00 1.50
COMMON CARD (1-81) .15 .40

1997 Inkworks Starship Troopers Art

COMPLETE SET (4) 12.00 30.00
COMMON CARD (1-4) 4.00 10.00
STATED ODDS 1:17

1997 Inkworks Starship Troopers Bug War

COMPLETE SET (9) 15.00 40.00
COMMON CARD (BW1-BW9) 2.50 6.00
STATED ODDS 1:11

1997 Inkworks Starship Troopers Gold

COMPLETE SET (2) 15.00 40.00
COMMON CARD (1-2) 10.00 25.00
STATED ODDS 1:54

1997 Inkworks Starship Troopers Promos

COMPLETE SET (5) 4.00 10.00
COMMON CARD .75 2.00
0 Starlog Mail-Away Offer Promo 1.25 3.00
NNO 3-Up Panel Oversized 2.00 5.00

1995 FPG Stephen Hickman

NNO Collector's Edition Promo .60 1.50

1995 Lime Rock Steve Rude Nexus

COMPLETE SET (3) 1.25 3.00
COMMON CARD (P1-P3) .60 1.50

2019 Steven Universe

COMPLETE SET (72) 8.00 20.00
UNOPENED BOX (24 PACKS) 75.00 125.00
UNOPENED PACK (5 CARDS) 3.00 5.00
COMMON CARD (1-72) .25 .60
*PINK: 2X TO 5X BASIC CARDS

2019 Steven Universe Autographs

COMMON AUTO 15.00 40.00
STATED ODDS 1:24
EG Estelle/200 20.00 50.00
ES Estelle/150 20.00 50.00
RS Rebecca Sugar/225 200.00 350.00
AMO Aimee Mann/150 20.00 50.00
CYA Charlyne Yi/75 50.00 100.00
CYD Charlyne Yi/50 75.00 150.00
CYE Charlyne Yi/75 30.00 75.00
CYL Charlyne Yi/50 60.00 120.00
CYN Charlyne Yi/75 20.00 50.00
CYR Charlyne Yi/75 25.00 60.00
DMP Deedee Magno Hall/175 25.00 60.00

ELP Erica Luttrell/55 60.00 120.00
ELS Erica Luttrell/125 30.00 75.00
MDA Michaela Dietz/225 20.00 50.00
SRP Shelby Rabara/125 75.00 150.00
ZCO Zach Callison/55 60.00 120.00
ZCP Zach Callison/55 60.00 120.00
CEWD Christine Ebersole/150 30.00 75.00
CEWP Christine Ebersole/80 50.00 100.00
DBBC Dee Bradley Baker/55 30.00 75.00
DBBF Dee Bradley Baker/55 25.00 60.00
DBBL Dee Bradley Baker/100 25.00 60.00
DMBP Deedee Magno Hall/80 25.00 60.00
DMYP Deedee Magno Hall80 30.00 75.00
GRCC Grace Rolek/55 30.00 75.00
GRCM Grace Rolek/125 25.00 60.00
JPLL Jennifer Paz/225 30.00 75.00
KMSK Kate Micucci/55 25.00 60.00
MDPP Michaela Dietz/125 20.00 50.00
MMLB Matthew Moy/175 25.00 60.00
ZCSU Zach Callison/125 60.00 120.00
ZCTM Zach Callison/50 75.00 150.00
ZCWS Zach Callison/55 50.00 100.00

2019 Steven Universe Crystal Gem Friends

COMPLETE SET (9) 5.00 12.00
COMMON CARD (C1-C9) .75 2.00
*PINK: .75X TO 2X BASIC CARDS
STATED OVERALL ODDS 1:3

2019 Steven Universe Fusions

COMPLETE SET (10) 5.00 12.00
COMMON CARD (F1-F10) .75 2.00
*PINK: .75X TO 2X BASIC CARDS
STATED ODDS 1:3
F1 Alexandrite .75 2.00
F2 Opal .75 2.00
F3 Sugilite .75 2.00
F4 Rainbow Quartz .75 2.00
F5 Sardonyx .75 2.00
F6 Smoky Quartz .75 2.00
F7 Malachite .75 2.00
F8 Stevonnie .75 2.00
F9 Sunstone .75 2.00
F10 Obsidian .75 2.00

2019 Steven Universe Greatest Hits

COMPLETE SET (9) 8.00 20.00
COMMON CARD (GH1-GH8) 1.25 3.00
STATED ODDS 1:3

2019 Steven Universe Totally Fabricated Bubble Gems

COMMON MEM (TF1-TF9; B1) 8.00 20.00
STATED ODDS 1:72
TF3 Centipeetle Mother 10.00 25.00
TF4 Flower Monster 12.00 30.00
TF5 Ice Monster 10.00 25.00
TF7 Giant Bird 10.00 25.00
B1 Peridot ALB

2019 Steven Universe Promos

COMMON CARD (P1-P6) 1.50 4.00
CE1 EXCLUSIVE TO NYCC
P1 Non-Sport Update Magazine 2.00 5.00
P2 Non-Sport Update Magazine 2.00 5.00
P3 Non-Sport Update Magazine 2.50 6.00
P6 Philly Non-Sports Card Show 2.00 5.00
CE1 NYCC Exclusive 8.00 20.00

1992 Pacific The Story of World War II 50th Anniversary

COMPLETE SET (110) 5.00 12.00
UNOPENED BOX (36 PACKS) 20.00 30.00
UNOPENED PACK (10 CARDS)
COMMON CARD (1-110) .10 .25

Stranger Things

2020 Topps Stranger Things Autograph Collection

*ORANGE/50: .5X TO 1.2X BASIC AUTOS
*RED/25: .6X TO 1.5X BASIC AUTOS
CA Chelsea Talmadge 12.00 30.00
EA Millie Bobby Brown 200.00 500.00
KA Linnea Berthelsen 20.00 50.00
MA Brett Gelman 50.00 100.00
PA Rob Morgan 15.00 40.00
11A Millie Bobby Brown 200.00 500.00
BNA Sean Astin 20.00 50.00
CFA Catherine Dyer 8.00 20.00
CHA Catherine Curtin 30.00 75.00
DRA Matthew Modine 30.00 75.00
ESA Priah Ferguson 25.00 60.00
FWA Finn Wolfhard 60.00 150.00
GBA Finn Wolfhard 60.00 150.00
JHA David Harbour 75.00 150.00
KWA Cara Buono 20.00 50.00
MBA Matthew Modine 30.00 75.00
MHA Cynthia Barrett 8.00 20.00
MSA Karen Ceesay 12.00 30.00
MWA Finn Wolfhard 60.00 150.00
SBA Joe Keery 75.00 200.00
SHA Joe Keery 75.00 200.00
TWA Joe Chrest

2020 Topps Stranger Things Autograph Collection Orange

STATED PRINT RUN 50 SER.#'d SETS
DB Gaten Matarazzo 75.00 200.00
DHB Gaten Matarazzo 75.00 200.00
MMB Sadie Sink 150.00 400.00

2020 Topps Stranger Things Autograph Collection Red

STATED PRINT RUN 25 SER.#'d SETS
WBC Noah Schnapp 125.00 300.00
WLC Noah Schnapp 125.00 300.00

2022 Zerocool Stranger Things Billy Butcher Artist Series

COMPLETE SET (14) 10.00 25.00
UNOPENED BOX (4 PACKS) 40.00 60.00
UNOPENED PACK (8 CARDS) 10.00 15.00
COMMON CARD (1-14) 1.25 3.00
*RED METAL/250: 1.2X TO 3X BASIC CARDS
*ORANGE METAL/199: 2.5X TO 6X BASIC CARDS
*YELLOW METAL/99: 3X TO 8X BASIC CARDS
*PRE.ART VARIANT/86: 8X TO 20X BASIC CARDS
*GREEN RAINBOW/50: 12X TO 30X BASIC CARDS

2022 Zerocool Stranger Things Billy Butcher Artist Series Characters

COMPLETE SET (18) 12.00 30.00
COMMON CARD (1-18) 1.25 3.00
*RED METAL/250: 1.2X TO 3X BASIC CARDS
*ORANGE METAL/199: 2.5X TO 6X BASIC CARDS
*YELLOW METAL/99: 3X TO 8X BASIC CARDS
*GREEN RAINBOW/50: 12X TO 30X BASIC CARDS
RANDOMLY INSERTED INTO PACKS

2022 Zerocool Stranger Things Billy Butcher Artist Series The Party Lenticular

COMPLETE SET (9) 12.00 30.00
COMMON CARD (1-9) 2.00 5.00
RANDOMLY INSERTED INTO PACKS

2018 Stranger Things Season 1

COMPLETE SET (100) 10.00 25.00
UNOPENED BOX (24 PACKS)
UNOPENED PACK (7 CARDS)
COMMON CARD (1-100) .20 .50
*UPSIDE DOWN/99: 8X TO 20X BASIC CARDS
*WAFFLE/11: 30X TO 80X BASIC CARDS

2018 Stranger Things Season 1 Autographed Commemorative Patches

COMPLETE SET (9)
COMMON AUTO 30.00 75.00
STATED ODDS 1:2,605
STATED PRINT RUN 10 SER.#'d SETS
AP11 Millie Bobby Brown 200.00 500.00
APDH Gaten Matarazoo 150.00 300.00
APEV Millie Bobby Brown 200.00 500.00
APJH David Harbour 250.00 400.00
APJM David Harbour 250.00 400.00
APSH Joe Keery 150.00 300.00
APWB Noah Schnapp 125.00 300.00

2018 Stranger Things Season 1 Autographed Costume Relic

STATED ODDS 1:8,110
ARJH David Harbour 200.00 500.00

2018 Stranger Things Season 1 Autographs

COMMON AUTO 8.00 20.00
*ORANGE/99: .6X TO 1.5X BASIC AUTOS
*GREEN/50: ..75X TO 2X BASIC AUTOS
*PURPLE/25: 1.2X TO 3X BASIC AUTOS
STATED ODDS 1:79
AKW Cara Buono 12.00 30.00
AJH David Harbour 125.00 300.00
ADH Gaten Matarazzo 125.00 300.00

2018 Stranger Things Season 1 Autographs Green

STATED ODDS 1:365
STATED PRINT RUN 50 SER.#'d SETS
A11 Millie Bobby Brown 300.00 800.00
AMD Matt Duffer 75.00 200.00
ARD Ross Duffer 100.00 250.00
ASH Joe Keery 150.00 400.00
AWB Noah Schnapp 200.00 500.00

2018 Stranger Things Season 1 Character Stickers

COMPLETE SET (20) 8.00 20.00
COMMON CARD (1-20) .75 2.00
STATED ODDS 1:2

2018 Stranger Things Season 1 Characters

COMPLETE SET (20) 12.00 30.00
COMMON CARD (1-20) 1.25 3.00
STATED ODDS 1:4

2018 Stranger Things Season 1 Commemorative Patches

COMMON PATCH 3.00 8.00
*ORANGE/99: SAME VALUE AS BASIC
*GREEN/50: .5X TO 1.2X BASIC PATCHES
*PURPLE/25: .6X TO 1.5X BASIC PATCHES
STATED ODDS 1:49
P11 Eleven 8.00 20.00
PBH Barb 4.00 10.00
PCF Connie 5.00 12.00
PEV Eleven 8.00 20.00
PJH Hopper 6.00 15.00
PJM Hopper 6.00 15.00
PLS Lucas 6.00 15.00
PMB Martin 4.00 10.00
PMW Mike 4.00 10.00
PNW Nancy 6.00 15.00
PSC Scott 4.00 10.00
PSH Steve 5.00 12.00
PSP Shepard 5.00 12.00
PTH Tommy 5.00 12.00
PWB Will 6.00 15.00

2018 Stranger Things Season 1 Costume Relics

COMMON MEM 8.00 20.00
*ORANGE/99: .5X TO 1.2X BASIC MEM
*GREEN/50: .6X TO 1.5X BASIC MEM
*PURPLE/25: .75X TO 2X BASIC MEM
STATED ODDS 1:249
NNO Jim Hopper 12.00 30.00
NNO Mike Wheeler 10.00 25.00
NNO Mike Wheeler 10.00 25.00
NNO Nancy Wheeler 15.00 40.00

2018 Stranger Things Season 1 Dual Autographs

STATED ODDS 1:11,520
STATED PRINT RUN 10 SER.#'d SETS
DADB Matt & Ross Duffer 250.00 500.00

2018 Stranger Things Season 1 Scene Stickers

COMPLETE SET (10) 6.00 15.00
COMMON CARD (1-10) 1.00 2.50
STATED ODDS 1:6

2018 Stranger Things Season 1 Promo

NYCC4 Stronger Together NYCC

2019 Stranger Things Season 2

COMPLETE SET (100) 10.00 25.00
UNOPENED BOX (24 PACKS) 200.00 300.00
UNOPENED PACK (7 CARDS) 8.00 12.00
COMMON CARD (1-100) .20 .50
*UPSIDE DOWN/99: 6X TO 15X BASIC CARDS
*WAFFLE/11: 20X TO 50X BASIC CARDS

2019 Stranger Things Season 2 Autographed Commemorative Medallions

COMMON AUTO 40.00 100.00
STATED PRINT RUN 10 SER.#'d SETS
ACMHT David Harbour 150.00 400.00
ACMGB Gaten Matarazzo 100.00 250.00
ACMGT Gaten Matarazzo 100.00 250.00
ACMET Millie Bobby Brown 400.00 1000.00
ACMWB Noah Schnapp 100.00 250.00
ACMWW Noah Schnapp 100.00 250.00

2019 Stranger Things Season 2 Autographed Commemorative Patches

COMMON AUTO 30.00 75.00
STATED PRINT RUN 10 SER.#'d SETS
ACPJM David Harbour 150.00 400.00
ARGM Gaten Matarazzo 100.00 250.00
ACPSP Joe Keery 100.00 250.00
ACPES Millie Bobby Brown 250.00 600.00
ACPWAV Noah Schnapp 125.00 300.00
ACPWA Noah Schnapp 125.00 300.00
ACPMMA Sadie Sink 200.00 500.00
ACPMMS Sadie Sink 200.00 500.00

2019 Stranger Things Season 2 Autographed Relics

COMMON AUTO 100.00 250.00
STATED PRINT RUN 10 SER.#'d SETS
CRHH David Harbour 250.00 500.00
CRHU David Harbour 250.00 500.00
CREO Millie Bobby Brown 750.00 1500.00

2019 Stranger Things Season 2 Autographs

COMMON AUTO 8.00 20.00
*ORANGE/99: .5X TO 1.2X BASIC AUTOS
*GREEN/50: .6X TO 1.5X BASIC AUTOS
*PURPLE/25: .75X TO 2X BASIC AUTOS
RANDOMLY INSERTED INTO PACKS
ABA Brian Gelman 15.00 40.00
ACA Chelsea Talmadge 10.00 25.00
ADB Linnea Berthelsen 25.00 60.00
AES Priah Ferguson 20.00 50.00
AMM Sadie Sink 100.00 250.00
AMS Karen Ceesay 10.00 25.00
AOP Rob Morgan 10.00 25.00

2019 Stranger Things Season 2 Autographs Green

STATED PRINT RUN 50 SER.#'d SETS
ADH Gaten Matarazzo
AJH David Harbour 125.00 300.00
AMD Matt Duffer 60.00 150.00
ARD Ross Duffer 60.00 150.00
ASH Joe Keery 150.00 400.00
AWB Noah Schnapp 100.00 250.00

2019 Stranger Things Season 2 Autographs Orange

STATED PRINT RUN 99 SER.#'d SETS
AKW Cara Buono 20.00 50.00
ATW Joe Chrest 8.00 20.00

2019 Stranger Things Season 2 Autographs Purple

STATED PRINT RUN 25 SER.#'d SETS
A11 Millie Bobby Brown 250.00 600.00

2019 Stranger Things Season 2 Character Stickers

COMPLETE SET (20) 6.00 15.00
COMMON STICKER (CS1-CS20) .75 2.00
RANDOMLY INSERTED INTO PACKS

2019 Stranger Things Season 2 Characters

COMPLETE SET (20) 10.00 25.00
COMMON CARD (C1-C20) 1.25 3.00
RANDOMLY INSERTED INTO PACKS

2019 Stranger Things Season 2 Commemorative Medallions

COMMON MEM
*ORANGE/99: .5X TO 1.2X BASIC MEM
*GREEN/50: .6X TO 1.5X BASIC MEM
*PURPLE/25: .75X TO 2X BASIC MEM
RANDOMLY INSERTED INTO PACKS
CMBC Billy 6.00 15.00
CMBW Bob
CMCC Jonathan 5.00 12.00
CMDB Dustin 6.00 15.00
CMDD Dustin 6.00 15.00
CMDW Dustin 6.00 15.00
CMET Eleven 8.00 20.00
CMHT Hopper 10.00 25.00
CMJC Joyce 6.00 15.00
CMJT Joyce 6.00 15.00
CMLB Lucas 5.00 12.00
CMLD Lucas 5.00 12.00
CMLW Lucas 5.00 12.00
CMMB Mike 6.00 15.00
CMMD Mike 6.00 15.00
CMMT Murray 6.00 15.00
CMMW Mike 6.00 15.00
CMWB Will 8.00 20.00
CMWC Will 5.00 12.00
CMWD Will 5.00 12.00
CMWW Will 5.00 12.00

2019 Stranger Things Season 2 Commemorative Patches

COMMON MEM 3.00 8.00
*ORANGE/99: .5X TO 1.2X BASIC MEM
*GREEN/50: .6X TO 1.5X BASIC MEM
*PURPLE/25: .75X TO 2X BASIC MEM
RANDOMLY INSERTED INTO PACKS
CPCP Carol 5.00 12.00
CPJM Hopper 6.00 15.00
CPKA Keith 4.00 10.00
CPMM Merrill 5.00 12.00
CP11S Eleven 10.00 25.00
CPBHP Billy
CPMAV Mike 4.00 10.00
CPMWA Mike 5.00 12.00
CPMWS Mike 6.00 15.00
CPSAV Will 4.00 10.00
CPSOM Sam 4.00 10.00
CPWBA Will 6.00 15.00

2019 Stranger Things Season 2 Costume Relics

COMMON MEM 4.00 10.00
*ORANGE/99: .5X TO 1.2X BASIC MEM
*GREEN/50: .6X TO 1.5X BASIC MEM
*PURPLE/25: .75X TO 2X BASIC MEM
RANDOMLY INSERTED INTO PACKS
CREO Eleven 10.00 25.00
CRHH Jim Hopper 1 6.00 15.00
CRHU Jim Hopper 2 6.00 15.00
CRMJ Max Mayfield 8.00 20.00
CRSW Steve Harrington 6.00 15.00

2019 Stranger Things Season 2 Dual Autographs

COMMON AUTO 100.00 250.00
STATED PRINT RUN 10 SER.#'d SETS
DADB The Duffer Brothers 200.00 500.00
DAHB D.Harbour/M.Bobby Brown 600.00 1500.00
DAHG D.Harbour/B.Gelman 200.00 500.00
DAKM J.Keery/G.Matarazzo 500.00 1200.00

2019 Stranger Things Season 2 Dual Costume Relics

*PURPLE/25: SAME VALUE AS BASIC
RANDOMLY INSERTED INTO PACKS
DRDL Dustin/Lucas 20.00 50.00
DRDM Dustin/Max 15.00 40.00
DREJ Eleven/Hopper 20.00 50.00
DRJE Eleven/Hopper 30.00 75.00
DRJW Hopper/Will
DRLM Lucas/Max 15.00 40.00
DRMX Eleven/Max 25.00 60.00
DRSD Steve/Dustin 15.00 40.00
DRWS Will/Sam

2019 Stranger Things Season 2 Scene Stickers

COMPLETE SET (20) 12.00 30.00
COMMON STICKER (S1-S20) 1.00 2.50
RANDOMLY INSERTED INTO PACKS

2019 Stranger Things Season 2 Triple Autographs

COMPLETE SET (2)
COMMON AUTO 150.00 400.00
STATED PRINT RUN 10 SER.#'d SETS
TAKID Brown/Schnapp/Matarazzo 600.00 1500.00

2019 Stranger Things Welcome to the Upside Down

COMPLETE SET (80) 8.00 20.00
UNOPENED BOX (24 PACKS) 200.00 300.00
UNOPENED PACK (7 CARDS) 8.00 12.00
COMMON CARD (1-80) .15 .40
*ORANGE/99: 3X TO 8X BASIC CARDS
*RED/50: 5X TO 12X BASIC CARDS
*PURPLE/25: 8X TO 20X BASIC CARDS

2019 Stranger Things Welcome to the Upside Down Autographs

COMMON AUTO 6.00 15.00
*ORANGE/99: .5X TO 1.2X BASIC AUTOS
*RED/50: .6X TO 1.5X BASIC AUTOS
*PURPLE/25: .75X TO 2X BASIC AUTOS
RANDOMLY INSERTED INTO PACKS
ACB Cara Buono 12.00 30.00
ACC Catherine Curtin 8.00 20.00
AJC Joe Chrest 8.00 20.00
ALB Linnea Berthelsen 12.00 30.00
APF Priah Ferguson 20.00 50.00
ASA Sean Astin 30.00 75.00
ANS2 Noah Schnapp 75.00 200.00

2019 Stranger Things Welcome to the Upside Down Autographs Mindflayer Orange

COMPLETE SET (19)
*ORANGE: X TO X BASIC CARDS
STATED PRINT RUN 99 SER.#'d SETS
ABG Brett Gelman EXCH 25.00 60.00
AMM Matthew Modine
AMX Sadie Sink 150.00 400.00

2019 Stranger Things Welcome to the Upside Down Characters

COMPLETE SET (20) 10.00 25.00
COMMON CARD (1-20) .75 2.00
RANDOMLY INSERTED INTO PACKS
1 Eleven 1.50 4.00

2019 Stranger Things Welcome to the Upside Down Commemorative Button Pin Relics

COMMON MEM 2.50 5.00
*ORANGE/99: .5X TO 1.2X BASIC MEM
*RED/50: .6X TO 1.5X BASIC MEM
*PURPLE/25: .75X TO 2X BASIC MEM
RANDOMLY INSERTED INTO PACKS
HPBN Bob 2.50 6.00
HPCJ Joyce 2.50 6.00
HPDC Dustin 4.00 10.00
HPEC Eleven 6.00 15.00
HPLC Lucas 2.50 6.00
HPMC Mike 3.00 8.00
HPSS Steve 2.50 6.00
VP8D Dustin 5.00 12.00
VP8M Max 2.50 6.00
VPBS Steve 2.50 6.00
VPHB Billy 3.00 8.00
VPHJ Steve 2.50 6.00
VPMW Mike 3.00 8.00
VPNW Nancy 2.50 6.00

2019 Stranger Things Welcome to the Upside Down Evolution of Demogorgon

COMPLETE SET (6) 3.00 8.00
COMMON CARD (EV1-EV6) .75 2.00
*ORANGE/99: .75X TO 2X BASIC CARDS
*RED/50: 1.2X TO 3X BASIC CARDS
*PURPLE/25: 1.5X TO 4X BASIC CARDS
RANDOMLY INSERTED INTO PACKS

2019 Stranger Things Welcome to the Upside Down Relics

*RED/50: X TO X BASIC MEM
*PURPLE/25: X TO X BASIC MEM
STATED PRINT RUN 99 SER.#'d SETS
RC11 Eleven 10.00 25.00
RCDH Dustin Henderson
RCJB Jonathan Byers
RCJH Jim Hopper 8.00 20.00
RCLS Lucas Sinclair
RCMM Max Mayfield 10.00 25.00
RCNW Nancy Wheeler
RCSH Steve Harrington
RCSO Sam Owens
RCWB Will Byers 8.00 20.00

2019 Stranger Things Welcome to the Upside Down Tribute to Barb

COMPLETE SET (9) 6.00 15.00
COMMON CARD (B1-B9) 1.25 3.00
*ORANGE/99: .6X TO 1.5X BASIC CARDS
*RED/50: .75X TO 2X BASIC CARDS
*PURPLE/25: 1X TO 2.5X BASIC CARDS
RANDOMLY INSERTED INTO PACKS

2019 Stranger Things Welcome to the Upside Down Triple Autographs

COMPLETE SET (4)
STATED PRINT RUN 10 SER.#'d SETS
UNPRICED DUE TO SCARCITY
TABBV Brown/Berthelsen/Vince
TABWS Brown/Wolfhard/Sink
TAHBW Harbour/Brown/Wolfhard
TAWBC Wolfhard/Buono/Chrest

2019 Stranger Things Welcome to the Upside Down Welcome to Hawkins

COMPLETE SET (15) 6.00 15.00
COMMON CARD (HWK1-HWK15) .75 2.00
*ORANGE/99: .6X TO 1.5X BASIC CARDS
*RED/50: 1.2X TO 3X BASIC CARDS
*PURPLE/25: 1.5X TO 4X BASIC CARDS
RANDOMLY INSERTED INTO PACKS

2019 Stranger Things Welcome to the Upside Down Promo

NNO Dr. Martin Brenner NYCC 6.00 15.00

1996 Comic Images Strangers in Paradise

COMPLETE SET (90) 4.00 10.00
UNOPENED BOX (36 PACKS) 30.00 40.00
UNOPENED PACK (10 CARDS) 1.25 1.50
COMMON CARD (1-90) .10 .25
BC0 Bonus Card 2.00 5.00
AUTM Terry Moore AU/500 20.00 50.00
NNO1 Promo 1 GEN .60 1.50

1996 Comic Images Strangers in Paradise Covers Chromium

COMPLETE SET (6) 15.00 40.00
COMMON CARD (C1-C6) 3.00 8.00
STATED ODDS 1:16

1996 Comic Images Strangers in Paradise Miniseries Covers

COMPLETE SET (3) 12.00 30.00
COMMON CARD (1-3) 5.00 12.00
STATED ODDS 1:36

1993 Topps Street Fighter II

COMPLETE SET (88) 5.00 12.00
COMPLETE SET W/STICKERS (99) 6.00 15.00
UNOPENED BOX (36 PACKS) 300.00 500.00
UNOPENED PACK (8 CARDS+1 STICKER) 10.00 15.00
COMMON CARD (1-88) .10 .30

1993 Topps Street Fighter II Foil

COMPLETE SET (4) 8.00 20.00
COMMON CARD (1-4) 2.50 6.00
RANDOMLY INSERTED INTO PACKS

1993 Topps Street Fighter II Stickers

COMPLETE SET (11) 1.25 3.00
COMMON CARD (1-11) .20 .50

1995 Upper Deck Street Fighter Movie

COMPLETE SET (90) 6.00 15.00
UNOPENED BOX (36 PACKS) 25.00 30.00
UNOPENED PACK (8 CARDS) .75 1.00
COMMON CARD (1-90) .15 .40
AN1 Guile vs. M. Bison Animation
LE1 Jean-Claude Van Damme Litho 30.00 80.00

1995 Upper Deck Street Fighter Movie Special F/X

COMPLETE SET (10) 20.00 50.00
COMMON CARD (SF1-SF10) 2.50 6.00
STATED ODDS 1:8

1995 Upper Deck Street Fighter Movie Promos

COMPLETE SET (3) 2.00 5.00
COMMON CARD .75 2.00

1995 Edge Street Sharks

COMPLETE SET (100) 4.00 10.00
UNOPENED BOX (24 PACKS) 20.00 30.00
UNOPENED PACK (8 CARDS) 1.25 1.50
COMMON CARD (1-100) .08 .20
*HOLOFOIL: 1X TO 2.5X BASIC CARDS

1995 Edge Street Sharks 9-Card Puzzle

COMPLETE SET (9) 3.00 8.00
COMMON CARD .40 1.00
STATED ODDS 1:1 RETAIL

1995 Edge Street Sharks Jawsome Animators Lenticular

COMPLETE SET (5) 6.00 15.00
COMMON CARD (1-5) 1.50 4.00
STATED ODDS 1:48

1995 Edge Street Sharks Sharkbites Die-Cuts

COMPLETE SET (9) 12.00 30.00
COMMON CARD (SB1-SB9) 2.00 5.00
STATED ODDS 1:72

1995 Edge Street Sharks Sharkglow

COMPLETE SET (9) 6.00 15.00
COMMON CARD .75 2.00
STATED ODDS 1:24

1995 Edge Street Sharks Sharkskins Static Decals

COMPLETE SET (9) 2.00 5.00
COMMON CARD .30 .75
STATED ODDS 1:4

1995 Edge Street Sharks Promos

COMPLETE SET (4)	4.00	10.00
COMMON CARD	1.50	4.00

2014 Stupid Heroes

COMPLETE SET (110)	6.00	15.00
UNOPENED BOX (24 PACKS)	50.00	100.00
UNOPENED PACK (8 CARDS)	2.50	4.00
COMMON CARD (1a-55b)	.30	.75
P1 Stupid Heroes Promo (Stuporman)	2.50	6.00

1989 Topps Stupid Smiles

COMPLETE SET (44)	5.00	12.00
UNOPENED BOX (48 PACKS)	25.00	40.00
UNOPENED PACK	.75	1.00
COMMON CARD (1-44)	.20	.50
*OPC: SAME VALUE AS TOPPS		

1992 Super Country Music

COMPLETE SET (100)	6.00	15.00
UNOPENED BOX (36 PACKS)	15.00	25.00
UNOPENED PACK (10 CARDS)	.75	1.00
COMMON CARD (1-100)	.10	.30

1992 Tenny Super Country Music Promos

COMPLETE SET (4)	3.00	8.00
COMMON CARD	1.25	3.00

1993 SkyBox Super Mario Brothers

COMPLETE SET (100)	4.00	10.00
UNOPENED BOX (36 PACKS)	50.00	75.00
UNOPENED PACK (8 CARDS)	2.00	3.00
COMMON CARD (1-100)	.08	.20
NNO Super Mario Brothers PROMO	.75	2.00

1993 SkyBox Super Mario Brothers Flip Holograms

COMPLETE SET (3)	8.00	20.00
COMMON CARD (1-3)	3.00	8.00
STATED ODDS 1:18		

1983 Fleer Super Pac-Man Stickers

COMPLETE SET (54)	6.00	15.00
UNOPENED BOX (36 PACKS)	200.00	300.00
UNOPENED PACK (3 CARDS+3 STICKERS)	6.00	8.00
COMMON CARD-STICKER	.30	.75

Supernatural

2006 Supernatural Season One

COMPLETE SET (90)	4.00	10.00
UNOPENED BOX (36 PACKS)	65.00	80.00
UNOPENED PACK (6 CARDS)	2.25	2.50
COMMON CARD (1-90)	.10	.30

2006 Supernatural Season One Autographs

COMMON AUTO (A1-A8)	5.00	12.00
STATED ODDS 1:36		
A1 Jared Padalecki	60.00	120.00
A2 Jensen Ackles	75.00	150.00
A3 Amy Acker	25.00	60.00
A4 Julie Benz	12.00	30.00
A6 Marnette Patterson	10.00	25.00

2006 Supernatural Season One Box-Loaders

COMPLETE SET (3)	4.00	10.00
COMMON CARD (BL1-BL3)	1.25	4.00
STATED ODDS ONE PER BOX		
CL1 STATE ODDS ONE PER CASE		
CL1 Crash	5.00	12.00
CASE INSERT		

2006 Supernatural Season One Dead End

COMPLETE SET (6)	6.00	15.00
COMMON CARD (D1-D6)	1.25	3.00
STATED ODDS 1:17		

2006 Supernatural Season One Pieceworks

COMMON CARD	12.00	30.00
STATED ODDS 1:36		
PW1 Jared Padalecki	50.00	100.00
PW2 Jensen Ackles	50.00	100.00
PW3 Jared Padalecki	30.00	75.00
PW4 Jensen Ackles	50.00	100.00
PW5 Jeffrey Dean Morgan	25.00	50.00
PW6 Jeffrey Dean Morgan	25.00	50.00
PW7 Jeffrey Dean Morgan	25.00	50.00
PW9 Julie Benz	25.00	50.00
PW11 Amy Acker	15.00	40.00
PW13A Jensen Ackles CI	75.00	150.00
PW13B Jared Padalecki CI	75.00	150.00
PWA1 Julie Benz AU	25.00	50.00
PWA2 Amy Acker AU	25.00	50.00

2006 Supernatural Season One Searching

COMPLETE SET (9)	8.00	20.00
COMMON CARD (S1-S9)	1.00	2.50
STATED ODDS 1:11		

2006 Supernatural Season One Promos

COMPLETE SET (5)	4.00	10.00
COMMON CARD	.75	2.00
SNi Sam and Dean	1.25	3.00
SNT Dean and Sam	1.25	3.00
SNUK Dean and Sam	1.50	4.00

2007 Supernatural Season Two

COMPLETE SET (90)	4.00	10.00
UNOPENED BOX (36 PACKS)	65.00	80.00
UNOPENED PACK (6 CARDS)	2.00	2.50
COMMON CARD (1-90)	.10	.30

2007 Supernatural Season Two Autographs

COMMON AUTO (A9-A17)	5.00	12.00
STATED ODDS 1:36		
A9 Jared Padalecki	125.00	250.00
A10 Jensen Ackles	150.00	300.00
A11 Samantha Ferris	12.00	30.00
A12 Alona Tal	15.00	40.00
A13 Chad Lindberg	6.00	15.00
A14 Amber Benson	12.00	30.00
A16 Samantha Smith	8.00	20.00

2007 Supernatural Season Two Box-Loaders

COMPLETE SET (3)	5.00	12.00
COMMON CARD (FM1-FM3)	2.00	5.00
STATED ODDS ONE PER BOX		
CL1 Intervention	10.00	25.00
CASE INSERT		

2007 Supernatural Season Two Hunters

COMPLETE SET (6)	8.00	20.00
COMMON CARD (H1-H6)	1.50	4.00
STATED ODDS 1:17		

2007 Supernatural Season Two Pieceworks

COMMON CARD	8.00	20.00
STATED ODDS 1:36		
PW1A Jared Padalecki	15.00	40.00
PW1B Jensen Ackles	15.00	40.00
PW2 Jensen Ackles	20.00	50.00
PW3 Jared Padalecki	15.00	40.00
PW4 Jeffrey Dean Morgan	15.00	40.00
PW5 Alona Tal	20.00	50.00
Jensen Ackles		
PW8 Amber Benson	12.00	30.00
PW10 Tricia Helfer	12.00	30.00
PW11 Tricia Helfer	12.00	30.00
PW13 Fredric Lehne	12.00	30.00
PW14 Linda Blair	12.00	30.00
PW15 Linda Blair	15.00	40.00
Jared Padalecki		
PW17A Jensen Ackles	50.00	100.00
PW17B Jared Padalecki	60.00	120.00
PWYA Jensen Ackles	60.00	120.00
PWYB Jared Padalecki	60.00	120.00

2007 Supernatural Season Two The Devil's Due

COMPLETE SET (9)	8.00	20.00
COMMON CARD (DD1-DD9)	1.25	3.00
STATED ODDS 1:11		

2007 Supernatural Season Two Promos

COMPLETE SET (6)	5.00	12.00
COMMON CARD	.75	2.00
Pi Sam & Dean	2.50	6.00
PDS Dean & Sam	1.25	3.00
PFE Dean & Sam	2.50	3.00
PUK Dean & Sam	1.50	4.00

2008 Supernatural Season Three

COMPLETE SET (81)	4.00	10.00
UNOPENED BOX (24 PACKS)	250.00	400.00
UNOPENED PACK (8 CARDS)	10.00	15.00
COMMON CARD (1-81)	.10	.30
CL1 STATED ODDS ONE PER CASE		
CL1 Hellfire	12.00	30.00

2008 Supernatural Season Three Autographs

COMMON AUTO	5.00	12.00
STATED ODDS ONE PER BOX		
SD1 ISSUED AS 10-CASE INCENTIVE		
A18 Jared Padalecki	30.00	75.00
A19 Lauren Cohan	15.00	40.00
A20 Jim Beaver	8.00	20.00
A21 Sterling K. Brown	6.00	15.00
A25 Billy Drago	12.00	30.00
A28 Peter Macon	6.00	15.00
SD1 J.Padalecki/J.Ackles 10CI	300.00	600.00

2008 Supernatural Season Three Betrayed

COMPLETE SET (6)	10.00	25.00
COMMON CARD (BT1-BT6)	2.00	5.00
STATED ODDS 1:17		

2008 Supernatural Season Three Hell on Earth Puzzle

COMPLETE SET (9)	8.00	20.00
COMMON CARD (HE1-HE9)	1.25	3.00
STATED ODDS 1:11		

2008 Supernatural Season Three Out of Time

COMPLETE SET (3)	6.00	15.00
COMMON CARD (OT1-OT3)	2.50	6.00
STATED ODDS 1:24		

2008 Supernatural Season Three Pieceworks

COMMON CARD (PW1-PW13)	5.00	12.00
STATED ODDS ONE PER BOX		
PW13A, PW13B ISSUED AS MULTI-CASE INCENTIVES		
PW1 Dean Winchester	15.00	40.00
PW2 Sam Winchester	15.00	40.00
PW4A Sam Winchester	25.00	50.00
PW4B Dean Winchester	25.00	50.00
PW7 Isaac	8.00	20.00
Tamara DUAL		
PW11 Casey	12.00	30.00
PW13A Sam Winchester CI	60.00	120.00
PW13B Dean Winchester CI	50.00	100.00

2008 Supernatural Season Three Promos

COMPLETE SET (4)	4.00	10.00
COMMON CARD	.75	2.00
Pi Sam/Dean	2.00	5.00
PPS Sam/Dean	1.25	3.00
PUK Sam/Dean (UK)	2.00	5.00

2014 Supernatural Seasons 1-3

COMPLETE SET (72)	5.00	12.00
UNOPENED BOX (24 PACKS)	125.00	250.00
UNOPENED PACK (5 CARDS)	6.00	10.00
COMMON CARD (1-72)	.20	.50
*MEGA MOON: 4X TO 10X BASIC CARDS	2.00	5.00
*SILVER/25: 8X TO 20X BASIC CARDS	4.00	10.00
*GOLD/10: 12X TO 30X BASIC CARDS	6.00	15.00

2014 Supernatural Seasons 1-3 Autographs

COMMON AUTO (A1-A20)	6.00	15.00
STATED ODDS 1:24		
A1 Jim Beaver	30.00	75.00
A2 Jeffrey Dean Morgan	125.00	250.00
A3 Samantha Smith	10.00	25.00
A4 Alona Tal	15.00	40.00
A5B Katie Cassidy/Authentic	60.00	120.00
A6 Lauren Cohan	25.00	60.00
A7 Nicki Aycox	15.00	40.00
A8 Richard Speight, Jr.	15.00	40.00
A11 A.J. Buckley	8.00	20.00
A13 Travis Wester	8.00	20.00
A14 Amber Benson	8.00	20.00
A15 Billy Drago	12.00	30.00
A16 Linda Blair	15.00	40.00
A18 Emmanuelle Vaugier	12.00	30.00
A20 Eric Kripke, Creator	15.00	40.00

2014 Supernatural Seasons 1-3 Shadowbox

COMPLETE SET (9)	15.00	40.00
COMMON CARD (CP1-CP9)	3.00	8.00

2014 Supernatural Seasons 1-3 Dual Wardrobes

COMPLETE SET (6)		
COMMON CARD (DM1-DM5, HT6)		
STATED ODDS 1:		
DM1 J.Padalecki	15.00	40.00
J.Ackles		
DM2 J.Ackles	15.00	40.00
J.Padalecki		
DM3 J.Padalecki	12.00	30.00
J.D.Morgan		
DM4 J.Ackles	20.00	50.00
J.Padalecki		
DM5 J.Padalecki	10.00	25.00
M.Whitfield		
HT6 J.Ackles	30.00	80.00
J.Padalecki		

2014 Supernatural Seasons 1-3 Locations

COMPLETE SET (9)	8.00	20.00
COMMON CARD (L01-L09)	1.25	3.00
STATED ODDS 1:12		
*MEGA MOON: .8X TO 2X BASIC CARDS	2.50	6.00
*SILVER/25: 2X TO 4X BASIC CARDS	5.00	12.00
*GOLD/10: 2.5X TO 6X BASIC CARDS	10.00	25.00

2014 Supernatural Seasons 1-3 Wardrobes

COMMON CARD (M01-M21)	6.00	15.00
STATED ODDS 1:24		
M1 Sam Winchester	15.00	40.00
M2 Sam Winchester	15.00	40.00
M3 Sam Winchester	15.00	40.00
M4 Dean Winchester	12.00	30.00
M5 Sam Winchester	10.00	25.00
M6 Meg Masters	12.00	30.00
M7 Dean Winchester	20.00	50.00
M8 Sam Winchester	15.00	40.00
M10 John Winchester	15.00	40.00
M11 Sam Winchester	12.00	30.00
M12 Dean Winchester	15.00	40.00
M13 Sam Winchester	12.00	30.00
M14 Sam Winchester	12.00	30.00
M15 Sam Winchester	15.00	40.00
M16 Dean Winchester	15.00	40.00
M17 Sam Winchester	10.00	25.00
M19 Sam Winchester	15.00	40.00
M21 Dean Winchester ALB	20.00	50.00

2014 Supernatural Seasons 1-3 Winchester Brothers

COMPLETE SET (9) 8.00 20.00
COMMON CARD (J1-J9) 1.25 3.00
*MEGA MOON: .75X TO 2X BASIC CARDS 2.50 6.00
*SILVER/25: 1.5X TO 4X BASIC CARDS 5.00 12.00
*GOLD/10: 2.5X TO 6X BASIC CARDS 10.00 25.00
STATED ODDS 1:12

2016 Supernatural Seasons 4-6

COMPLETE SET (72) 5.00 12.00
UNOPENED BOX (24 PACKS)
UNOPENED PACK (5 CARDS)
COMMON CARD (1-72) .25 .60
*RAINBOW: 2X TO 5X BASIC CARDS
*GOLD/50: 6X TO 15X BASIC CARDS

2016 Supernatural Seasons 4-6 Autographs

COMMON AUTO 8.00 20.00
STATED ODDS 1:14
AG Amy Gumenick 20.00 50.00
CH Christopher Heyerdahl 10.00 25.00
EP Emily Perkins 15.00 40.00
GC Genevieve Cortese Padalecki 60.00 120.00
JB Jim Beaver 50.00 100.00
JH Jessica Heafey 12.00 30.00
JM Julia Maxwell 15.00 40.00
JR Julian Richings 20.00 50.00
KB Katherine Boecher 25.00 60.00
KR Kim Rhodes 12.00 30.00
LM Lindsey McKeon 20.00 50.00
LW Lanette Ware 10.00 25.00
MP Mitch Pileggi 15.00 40.00
MS Mark Sheppard 75.00 150.00
RB Rob Benedict 15.00 40.00
RM Rachel Miner 25.00 50.00
RS Richard Speight, Jr. 12.00 30.00
SR Sebastian Roche 10.00 25.00
CAF Carrie Anne Fleming 10.00 25.00
JAB Jake Abel 15.00 40.00
JMC Julie McNiven 20.00 50.00

2016 Supernatural Seasons 4-6 Character Bios

COMPLETE SET (6) 5.00 12.00
COMMON CARD (C1-C6) 1.25 3.00
*RAINBOW: 1X TO 2.5X BASIC CARDS
*GOLD/50: 2X TO 5X BASIC CARDS
STATED ODDS 1:4

2016 Supernatural Seasons 4-6 Disguises

COMPLETE SET (9) 10.00 25.00
COMMON CARD (D1-D9) 1.50 4.00
*RAINBOW: .6X TO 1.5X BASIC CARDS
*GOLD/50: 1.2X TO 3X BASIC CARDS
STATED ODDS 1:4

2016 Supernatural Seasons 4-6 Dual Wardrobes

COMMON CARD 15.00 40.00
HT5 Castiel and Sam 25.00 60.00
(Hot Topic Exclusive)

2016 Supernatural Seasons 4-6 Locations

COMPLETE SET (9) 6.00 15.00
COMMON CARD (L10-L18) 1.25 3.00
*RAINBOW: .75X TO 2X BASIC CARDS
*GOLD/50: 1.5X TO 4X BASIC CARDS
STATED ODDS 1:4

2016 Supernatural Seasons 4-6 Wardrobes

COMMON CARD (M1-M15) 6.00 15.00
STATED ODDS 1:24 W/DUAL WARDROBES
M1 Jared Padalecki 10.00 25.00
M2 Misha Collins 12.00 30.00
M3 Jensen Ackles 15.00 40.00
M8 Emily Perkins 10.00 25.00
M9 Rick Worthy 8.00 20.00
M10 Genevieve Cortese Padalecki 12.00 30.00
M11 Rob Benedict 10.00 25.00
M12 Jared Padalecki 12.00 30.00
M13 Julia Maxwell 12.00 30.00
M14 Demore Barnes 8.00 20.00
M15 Julie McNiven 10.00 25.00

2008 Supernatural Connections

COMPLETE SET (72) 4.00 10.00
UNOPENED BOX (24 PACKS) 50.00 75.00
UNOPENED PACK (6 CARDS) 2.00 3.00
COMMON CARD (1-72) .10 .30
CL1 STATED ODDS ONE PER CASE
CL1 The Devil In Me 10.00 25.00

2008 Supernatural Connections Autographs

COMMON AUTO (A1-A11) 5.00 12.00
STATED ODDS ONE PER BOX
A1 Jensen Ackles 100.00 200.00
A2 Linda Blair 15.00 40.00
A6 Jim Beaver 10.00 25.00
A7 Alona Tal 8.00 20.00
A8 Fredric Lane 12.00 30.00
A10 Sterling K. Brown 6.00 15.00
A11 Jensen Ackles/Fredric Lane 75.00 150.00

2008 Supernatural Connections Becoming

COMPLETE SET (3) 4.00 10.00
COMMON CARD (B1-B3) 1.50 4.00
STATED ODDS 1:24

2008 Supernatural Connections Fear No Evil Puzzle

COMPLETE SET (9) 8.00 20.00
COMMON CARD (F1-F9) 1.25 3.00
STATED ODDS 1:11

2008 Supernatural Connections Pieceworks

COMMON CARD 6.00 15.00
STATED ODDS ONE PER BOX
PW14A AND PW14B ISSUED AS MULTI-CASE INCENTIVES
PW1 Dean Winchester shirt NO BLOOD 15.00 40.00
PW2A Dean Winchester T-Shirt w/o blood stain 25.00 50.00
PW3 John Winchester Shirt 10.00 25.00
PW4 Andrea Barr Shirt 12.00 30.00
PW5 Meg Top 12.00 30.00
PW6 Sam Winchester T-Shirt 10.00 25.00
PW7 Dean Winchester T-Shirt 10.00 25.00
PW12 Lenore Top 10.00 25.00
PW14A Sam Winchester Jacket CI 80.00 150.00
PW14B Dean Winchester Jacket CI 80.00 150.00

2008 Supernatural Connections Road to Ruin

COMPLETE SET (6) 6.00 15.00
COMMON CARD (R1-R6) 1.25 3.00
STATED ODDS 1:17

2008 Supernatural Connections Promos

PI Sam and Dean/(Inkworks.com) 2.00 5.00
PUK Sam and Dean 3.00 8.00
(UK excl.)
SCFOA Friend Of Allan 10.00 25.00

2008 Very Supernatural Christmas

COMPLETE FACTORY SET (7+1 PW) 12.00 30.00
COMMON CARD (XM1-XM7) .75 2.00
COMMON PIECEWORKS 8.00 20.00
STATED PRINT RUN 2,500

1993 Jamison Supernatural Images

COMPLETE BOXED SET (18) 3.00 8.00
COMMON CARD .30 .75

1996 Comic Images Supreme

COMPLETE SET (90) 8.00 20.00
UNOPENED BOX (36 PACKS) 15.00 25.00
UNOPENED PACK (7 CARDS)
COMMON CARD .15 .40
NNO Silver Foil, Dealers PROMO .75 2.00

1996 Comic Images Supreme Autographs

COMPLETE SET (9) 200.00 400.00
COMMON CARD 20.00 50.00
RANDOMLY INSERTED INTO PACKS
STATED PRINT RUN 500 SETS

1996 Comic Images Supreme Chase

COMPLETE SET (9) 25.00 60.00
COMMON CARD 3.00 8.00
STATED ODDS 1:12

1995 Illustration Studio Swimsuits and Mermaids

COMPLETE SET (50) 3.00 8.00
COMPLETE FACTORY SET (50) 4.00 10.00
UNOPENED BOX (36 PACKS) 20.00 25.00
UNOPENED PACK (8 CARDS) .75 1.00
COMMON CARD (1-50) .12 .30

1993 Cardz Tales from the Crypt

COMPLETE SET (110) 6.00 15.00
UNOPENED BOX (36 PACKS) 75.00 125.00
UNOPENED PACK (8 CARDS) 3.00 4.00
COMMON CARD (1-110) .10 .25
T1 The Cryptkeeper TekChrome 8.00 20.00

1993 Cardz Tales from the Crypt Holograms

COMPLETE SET (3) 6.00 15.00
COMMON CARD (1-3) 2.50 6.00
STATED ODDS 1:18

1993 Cardz Tales from the Crypt Promos

COMPLETE SET (5) 3.00 8.00
COMMON CARD 1.00 2.50

2008 Tales of Despereaux

COMPLETE SET (50) 6.00 15.00
UNOPENED BOX (24 PACKS) 25.00 40.00
UNOPENED PACK (5 CARDS) 1.25 2.00
COMMON CARD (1-50) .25 .60

2008 Tales of Despereaux Autographs

COMMON AUTO 8.00 20.00
RANDOMLY INSERTED INTO PACKS
74 Matthew Broderick SP 75.00 150.00
75 Frances Conroy 10.00 25.00

1992 Design Dimensions Tall Stacks

COMPLETE SET (24) 4.00 10.00
COMMON CARD (1-24) .30 .75

1995 Comic Images Tank Girl

COMPLETE SET (90) 5.00 12.00
UNOPENED BOX (48 PACKS) 30.00 40.00
UNOPENED PACK (10 CARDS) 1.00 1.25
COMMON CARD (1-90) .12 .30
M1 Medallion Insert/461* 10.00 25.00
AU1 Lori Petty AU/500* 20.00 50.00
CT1 6-Card Panel UNC CT 4.00 10.00
PROMO She's definitely the girl PROMO

1995 Comic Images Tank Girl MagnaChrome

COMPLETE SET (6) 15.00 40.00
COMMON CARD (1-6) 3.00 8.00
STATED ODDS 1:16

1995 Comic Images Tank Girl The Rippers

COMPLETE SET (3) 15.00 40.00
COMMON CARD (1-3) 6.00 15.00
STATED ODDS 1:48

2012 Tarzan 100th Anniversary

COMPLETE SET (55) 6.00 15.00
UNOPENED BOX (24 PACKS) 65.00 80.00
UNOPENED PACK (7 CARDS) 3.00 4.00
COMMON CARD (1-55) .15 .40
*FOIL: 4X TO 10X BASIC CARDS 1.50 4.00

2012 Tarzan 100th Anniversary Book Covers

COMPLETE SET (9) 15.00 40.00
COMMON CARD (B01-B09) 2.50 6.00
OVERALL CHASE ODDS 1:4

2012 Tarzan 100th Anniversary Characters

COMPLETE SET (9) 15.00 40.00
COMMON CARD (FP01-FP09) 2.50 6.00
OVERALL CHASE ODDS 1:4

2012 Tarzan 100th Anniversary Movie Posters

COMPLETE SET (9) 15.00 40.00
COMMON CARD (MOV01-MOV09) 2.50 6.00
OVERALL CHASE ODDS 6:24

2012 Tarzan 100th Anniversary Promos

P1 Tarzan 1.50 4.00
(Non-Sport Update)
P2 Tarzan 3.00 8.00
(ERB Chain of Friendship)
P3 Tim Shay art 2.00 5.00
(Pop-Art Con)
P4 Gary Kezele art 2.00 5.00
(Pop-Art Con)
P5 Tarzan 5.00 12.00
(Pre-Order)
P6 Tarzan 5.00 12.00
(Licensing Show)

1996 FPG Tarzan Epic Adventures Promos

COMPLETE SET (10) 12.00 30.00
COMMON CARD (1-10) 1.50 4.00

2014 Taylor Swift 1989 Album Polaroids

COMPLETE SET (65) 50.00 100.00
COMPLETE SET #1 (1-13) 10.00 25.00
COMPLETE SET #2 (14-26) 10.00 25.00
COMPLETE SET #3 (27-39) 10.00 25.00
COMPLETE SET #4 (40-52) 10.00 25.00
COMPLETE SET #5 (53-65) 10.00 25.00
COMMON CARD (1-65) 1.25 3.00

1990 The Unusually Funny Factory Team-Spirits

COMPLETE SET (40) 4.00 10.00
UNOPENED BOX (PACKS)
UNOPENED PACK (CARDS)
COMMON CARD (1-40) .20 .50

1990 Brooke Bond Teenage Mutant Hero Turtles Dimension X Escapade

COMPLETE SET (12) 3.00 8.00
COMMON CARD (1-12) .50 1.25

1989 Topps Teenage Mutant Ninja Turtles

COMPLETE SET (176) 10.00 25.00
COMPLETE SER.1 SET (88) 6.00 15.00
COMPLETE SER.2 SET (88) 6.00 15.00
COMMON CARD (1-88) .15 .40
*OPC: SAME VALUE AS TOPPS
*REGINA: SAME VALUE AS TOPPS

1989 Topps Teenage Mutant Ninja Turtles Collector's Edition Bonus

COMPLETE SET (22) 4.00 10.00
COMMON CARD (A-V) .30 .75
COLLECTOR'S EDITION EXCLUSIVE

1989 Topps Teenage Mutant Ninja Turtles Series 1 Stickers

COMPLETE SET (11)	2.50	6.00
COMMON CARD (1-11)	.40	1.00
STATED ODDS 1:1		

1989 Topps Teenage Mutant Ninja Turtles Series 2 Stickers

COMPLETE SET (11)	2.50	6.00
COMMON CARD (1-11)	.40	1.00
STATED ODDS 1:1		

1991 Hostess Pudding Pie Teenage Mutant Ninja Turtles Stickers

COMPLETE SET (5)	5.00	12.00
COMMON STICKERS	1.25	3.00

1990 Topps Teenage Mutant Ninja Turtles Movie

COMPLETE SET (132)	8.00	20.00
UNOPENED BOX (36 PACKS)	10.00	15.00
UNOPENED PACK (9 CARDS)	.50	.75
COMMON CARD (1-132)	.20	.50

1990 Topps Teenage Mutant Ninja Turtles Movie Stickers

COMPLETE SET (11)	3.00	8.00
COMMON CARD (1-11)	.60	1.50

1991 Topps Teenage Mutant Ninja Turtles II Secret of the Ooze

COMPLETE SET (99)	6.00	15.00
UNOPENED BOX (36 PACKS)	8.00	15.00
UNOPENED PACK (8 CARDS)	.25	.50
COMMON CARD (1-99)	.10	.25

1991 Topps Teenage Mutant Ninja Turtles II Secret of the Ooze Stickers

COMPLETE SET (11)	2.00	5.00
COMMON STICKERS (1-11)	.20	.50

1991 Hostess Pudding Pie Teenage Mutant Ninja Turtles II Secret of the Ooze Stickers

COMPLETE SET (5)	5.00	12.00
COMMON STICKER	1.25	3.00

1992 Topps Teenage Mutant Ninja Turtles III

COMPLETE SET W/STICKERS (99)	5.00	12.00
UNOPENED BOX (36 PACKS)	75.00	125.00
UNOPENED PACK (8 CARDS)	2.50	4.00
COMMON CARD (1-88)	.10	.30

1992 Topps Teenage Mutant Ninja Turtles III Stickers

COMPLETE VARIANT SET (22)	1.50	4.00
COMPLETE A SET (11)	1.00	2.50
COMPLETE B SET (11)	1.00	2.50
COMMON CARD (1A-11B)	.12	.30
STATED ODDS 1:1		

2014 Teenage Mutant Ninja Turtles Movie Dog Tags

COMPLETE SET (24)	50.00	100.00
COMMON CARD (1-24)	2.00	5.00
*RAINBOW FOIL: .8X TO 2X BASIC CARDS		

2014 Teenage Mutant Ninja Turtles Movie Dog Tags Stickers

COMPLETE SET (8)	6.00	15.00
COMMON CARD (1-8)	1.25	3.00
STATED ODDS 1:1		

2009 Teenage Mutant Ninja Turtles Red Baron Pizza

COMPLETE SET (4)	12.00	30.00
COMMON CARD	4.00	10.00
STATED ODDS 1:RED BARON BOX		

2003 Teenage Mutant Ninja Turtles Series One Previews

COMPLETE SET (20)	6.00	15.00
COMMON CARD (1-20)	.40	1.00
STATED ODDS 1:4		

2003 Teenage Mutant Ninja Turtles Series One

COMPLETE SET (125)	5.00	12.00
UNOPENED BOX (36 PACKS)	30.00	40.00
UNOPENED PACK (5 CARDS)	1.00	1.25
COMMON CARD (1-125)	.10	.25
*GOLD: .75X TO 2X BASIC CARDS		
CARDS 85 TO 125 NOT INCLUDED AS PARALLELS		

2003 Teenage Mutant Ninja Turtles Series One Mutant Ooze

COMPLETE SET (8)	12.00	30.00
COMMON CARD (1-8)	2.00	5.00
STATED ODDS 1:72		

2003 Teenage Mutant Ninja Turtles Series One Sewer Covers

COMPLETE SET (10)	10.00	25.00
COMMON CARD (1-10)	1.25	3.00
STATED ODDS 1:36		

2003 Teenage Mutant Ninja Turtles Series Two

COMPLETE SET (136)	6.00	15.00
UNOPENED BOX (36 PACKS)	30.00	40.00
UNOPENED PACK (5 CARDS)	1.00	1.25
COMMON CARD (1-136)	.10	.25
*GOLD: .75X TO 2X BASIC CARDS		
CARDS 101 TO 136 NOT INCLUDED AS PARALLELS		

2003 Teenage Mutant Ninja Turtles Series Two Ninja Mask

COMPLETE SET (4)	10.00	25.00
COMMON CARD (1-4)	3.00	8.00
STATED ODDS 1:36		

2003 Teenage Mutant Ninja Turtles Series Two Raising Shell

COMPLETE SET (10)	8.00	20.00
COMMON CARD (1RS-10RS)	1.25	3.00
STATED ODDS 1:9		

2003 Teenage Mutant Ninja Turtles Series Two Standups

COMPLETE SET (15)	10.00	25.00
COMMON CARD (1-15)	1.00	2.50
STATED ODDS 1:9		

2014 Teenage Mutant Ninja Turtles Vudu Pizza Promos

COMPLETE SET (4)	15.00	40.00
COMMON CARD	5.00	12.00
STATED ODDS 1:MARKETSIDE PIZZA BOX		

2000 Tenchi Muyo

COMPLETE SET (72)	5.00	12.00
UNOPENED BOX (36 PACKS)	40.00	50.00
UNOPENED PACK (7 CARDS)	1.50	2.00
COMMON CARD (1-72)	.12	.30
PAN Tenchi Muyo 9-Card Panel (Album Exclusive)		

2000 Tenchi Muyo Metal Tex

COMPLETE SET (6)	12.00	30.00
COMMON CARD (C1-C6)	2.50	6.00
STATED ODDS 1:18		

1997 Krome Tenth Chromium Previews

COMPLETE SET (7)	4.00	10.00
COMMON CARD	1.00	2.50

2000-01 Dynamic Forces 10th Muse Collector's Previews

COMPLETE SET (6)	12.00	30.00
COMMON CARD (1-6)	2.00	5.00
COA INCLUDED		

1991 Impel Terminator II

COMPLETE SET (140)	5.00	12.00
COMP.FACTORY SET (142)	15.00	40.00
UNOPENED BOX (36 PACKS)	12.00	15.00
UNOPENED PACK (12 CARDS)	.50	.75
COMMON CARD (1-140)	.15	.40
HOLOGRAM FOUND IN FACTORY SETS		
NNO Arnold Schwarzenegger HOLO	8.00	20.00
NNO Stan Winston, SFX Artist	5.00	12.00

1991 Topps Terminator II Judgment Day Stickers

COMPLETE SET (44)	3.00	8.00
COMMON STICKER (1-44)	.12	.30

2003 Terminator 2 Judgment Day FilmCardz Previews

COMPLETE SET (5)	4.00	10.00
COMMON CARD (PS1-PS5)	1.00	2.50
STATED PRINT RUN 1008 SER. #'d SETS		

2003 Terminator 2 Judgment Day FilmCardz

COMPLETE SET (72)	5.00	12.00
UNOPENED BOX (24 PACKS)	50.00	60.00
UNOPENED PACK (5 CARDS)	2.00	3.00
COMMON CARD (1-72)	.15	.40
T2 STATED ODDS ONE PER COLLECTOR'S TIN		
FX1 ANNOUNCED PRINT RUN 30		
T2 On the Inside (collector's tin exclusive)	1.50	4.00
FX1 Liquid Metal from T1000 MEM	150.00	300.00

2003 Terminator 2 Judgment Day FilmCardz Autographs

COMMON AUTO	15.00	40.00
STATED ODDS 1:24		
CARD 8 ISSUED AS CASE TOPPER		
4 Edward Fulong	75.00	150.00
6 Linda Hamilton/275*	250.00	400.00
7 Robert Patrick/275*	125.00	250.00
8 D.Stanton/D.Stanton DUAL CT	30.00	75.00

2003 Terminator 2 Judgment Day FilmCardz CyberEtch

COMPLETE SET (24)	5.00	12.00
COMMON CARD (CE1-CE24)	.40	1.00
STATED ODDS 1:1		

2003 Terminator 2 Judgment Day FilmCardz FilmWear

COMPLETE SET (5)	30.00	80.00
COMMON CARD	5.00	10.00
STATED ODDS 1:24		
FW1 T800 Pants	12.00	25.00
FW4 Sarah Connor Shirt	6.00	15.00
FW5 T800 Leather Jacket	15.00	30.00
CT1 T800 Shirt CT	20.00	40.00

2003 Terminator 2 Judgment Day FilmCardz Rare Metal

COMPLETE SET (6)	6.00	15.00
COMMON CARD (R1-R6)	1.25	3.00
STATED ODDS 1:8		

2003 Terminator 2 Judgment Day FilmCardz Ultra Rare Metal

COMPLETE SET (3)	8.00	20.00
COMMON CARD (UR1-UR3)	3.00	8.00
STATED ODDS 1:12		

2003 Terminator 2 Judgment Day FilmCardz Ultra Rare Metal Box-Toppers

COMPLETE SET (3)	5.00	12.00
COMMON CARD (BT1-BT3)	2.00	5.00
STATED ODDS 1:BOX		

2003 Terminator 2 Judgment Day FilmCardz Promos

COMPLETE SET (2)	2.00	5.00
COMMON CARD	1.25	3.00

2003 Terminator 3 FilmCardz Previews

COMPLETE SET (5)	5.00	12.00
COMMON CARD (PS1-PS5)	1.50	4.00

2003 Terminator 3 FilmCardz

COMPLETE SET (54)	6.00	15.00
UNOPENED BOX (24 PACKS)	40.00	50.00
UNOPENED PACK (5 CARDS)	2.00	2.50
COMMON CARD (1-54)	.25	.60

2003 Terminator 3 FilmCardz Box-Toppers

COMPLETE SET (2)	10.00	25.00
COMMON CARD (BT1-BT2)	6.00	15.00
STATED ODDS 1:BOX		

2003 Terminator 3 FilmCardz CyberEtch

COMPLETE SET (6)	15.00	40.00
COMMON CARD (CE1-CE6)	3.00	8.00
STATED ODDS 1 SET:BOXED SET		

2003 Terminator 3 FilmCardz Rare T-X

COMPLETE SET (5)	10.00	25.00
COMMON CARD (TX1-TX5)	2.50	6.00
STATED ODDS 1:3		

2003 Terminator 3 FilmCardz Ultra-Rare Metal

COMPLETE SET (3)	8.00	20.00
COMMON CARD (UR1-UR3)	3.00	8.00
STATED ODDS 1:6		

2003 Terminator 3 FilmCardz Promos

COMPLETE SET (2)	3.00	8.00
COMMON CARD (P1-P2)	2.00	5.00

2003 Terminator 3 Rise of the Machines

COMPLETE SET (72)	5.00	12.00
UNOPENED BOX (36 PACKS)	75.00	125.00
UNOPENED PACK (7 CARDS)	3.00	4.00
COMMON CARD (1-72)	.12	.30

2003 Terminator 3 Rise of the Machines Autographs

COMMON AUTO	10.00	25.00
STATED ODDS 1:96 HOBBY, 1:144 RETAIL		
A1 AND A2 ONLY IN HOBBY PACKS		
A5 ISSUED AS CASE INCENTIVE		
A1 Arnold Schwarzenegger/300*	400.00	600.00
A2 Kristanna Loken/300*	30.00	75.00
A5 Nick Stahl CI	20.00	50.00

2003 Terminator 3 Rise of the Machines T-Worn Costumes

COMPLETE SET (3)	25.00	60.00
COMMON CARD (T1-T3)	10.00	25.00
STATED ODDS 1:58		
T1 T-800 (shirt)/600*	12.00	30.00
R1 T1 Redemption		
R2 T2 Redemption		
R3 T3 Redemption		

2003 Terminator 3 Rise of the Machines Skynet War Machines

COMPLETE SET (6)	8.00	20.00
COMMON CARD (C1-C6)	1.50	4.00
STATED ODDS 1:12		

2009 Terminator Salvation

COMPLETE SET (90)	4.00	10.00
UNOPENED BOX (24 PACKS)	30.00	50.00
UNOPENED PACK (7 CARDS)	2.00	2.50
COMMON CARD (1-90)	.10	.25
P1 A nuclear bomb can ruin your day PROMO	1.25	3.00

2009 Terminator Salvation Autographs

COMMON AUTO	4.00	10.00
STATED ODDS 1:24 HOBBY		
UNNUMBERED CARDS LISTED ALPHABETICALLY		

1 Chris Ashworth	6.00	15.00
2 Dylan Kenin	5.00	12.00
5 Michael Ironside	10.00	25.00

2009 Terminator Salvation Battle Pop-Ups

COMPLETE SET (9)	2.00	5.00
COMMON CARD (1-9)	.30	.75
STATED ODDS 1:4 RETAIL		

2009 Terminator Salvation Embossed Foil

COMPLETE SET (9)	2.50	6.00
COMMON CARD (1-9)	.40	1.00
STATED ODDS 1:6		

2009 Terminator Salvation Memorabilia

COMMON CARD	6.00	15.00
STATED ODDS 1:48 HOBBY		
UNNUMBERED CARDS LISTED ALPHABETICALLY		
1 John Connor Fatigues	12.00	30.00
2 John Connor Jacket	12.00	30.00

2004 Terror Cards

COMPLETE SET (52)	4.00	10.00
UNOPENED BOX (12 PACKS)	10.00	15.00
UNOPENED PACK (10 CARDS)	.50	.75
COMMON CARD (1-50; CL; HEADER)	.15	.40

2004 Terror Cards Autographics

COMPLETE SET (4)	60.00	120.00
COMMON CARD	15.00	40.00
STATED ODDS 1:62		

2004 Terror Cards Scream Queens

COMPLETE SET (3)	8.00	20.00
COMMON CARD	3.00	8.00
STATED ODDS 1:42		

2005-06 Necroscope Terror Cards XL

COMPLETE SET (23)	80.00	150.00
COMMON CARD (1-25)	2.00	5.00
CARDS 21 AND 23 DO NOT EXIST		
3 Gunnar Hansen	8.00	20.00
7 Linnea Quigley	5.00	12.00
9 Ben Chapman	3.00	8.00
14 Reggie Bannister	3.00	8.00
15 Irwin Keyes	3.00	8.00
16 Joe Bob Briggs	3.00	8.00
17 Allan Trautman	3.00	8.00
21 Kane Hodder	4.00	10.00
P1 Scream Queens SDCC Promo	.75	2.00

2005-06 Necroscope Terror Cards XL Death by Engagement

COMPLETE SET (2)	12.00	30.00
COMMON CARD	6.00	15.00
UNNUMBERED SET LISTED ALPHABETICALLY		
1 PJ Soles	10.00	25.00
Christa Campbell#{Juliane Berlin#{Edie Dearing AU/15		

2005-06 Necroscope Terror Cards XL Scream Queen Autographs

COMPLETE SET (8)	20.00	50.00
COMMON CARD	2.50	6.00
UNNUMBERED SET LISTED ALPHABETICALLY		
1 Christa Campbell	4.00	10.00
2 Edie Dearing	3.00	8.00
5 P. J. Soles	6.00	15.00
7 Tiffany Shepis (reclining)	3.00	8.00
8 Tiffany Shepis (standing)	3.00	8.00

1987 Piedmont Candy Terrorist Attack

COMPLETE SET (35)	10.00	25.00
UNOPENED BOX (36 PACKS)	30.00	40.00
UNOPENED PACK (8 CARDS)	1.00	1.50
COMMON CARD (1-35)	.40	1.00

1996 Tempo 36 Years of Barbie

COMPLETE SET (110)	6.00	15.00
UNOPENED BOX (30 PACKS)	30.00	40.00
UNOPENED PACK (7 CARDS)	1.00	1.50
COMMON CARD (1-110)	.10	.25

1996 Tempo 36 Years of Barbie Barbie Goes Wild

BGW1 Barbie Goes Wild!/36*	100.00	200.00

1996 Tempo 36 Years of Barbie The Beginning 1959

COMPLETE SET (5)	4.00	10.00
COMMON CARD (TB1-TB5)	1.25	3.00
STATED PRINT RUN 7500 SETS		

1996 Tempo 36 Years of Barbie Bride Barbie Pop-Ups

COMPLETE SET (6)	10.00	25.00
COMMON CARD (BR1-BR6)	2.50	6.00
STATED PRINT RUN 2000 SETS		

1996 Tempo 36 Years of Barbie Happy Birthday

COMPLETE SET (3)	4.00	10.00
COMMON CARD (HB1-HB3)	1.50	4.00
STATED PRINT RUN 5000 SETS		

1996 Tempo 36 Years of Barbie Ken and Barbie

COMPLETE SET (3)	3.00	8.00
COMMON CARD (KB1-KB3)	1.50	4.00
STATED PRINT RUN 5000 SETS		

1996 Tempo 36 Years of Barbie Promos

COMPLETE SET (4)	2.50	6.00
COMMON CARD (B1-B4)	.75	2.00
B1 Uptown Chic	8.00	20.00
B2 Swim & Dive Barbie 1995#{B3 Happy Birthday Barbie#{The Beginning 1959#{4-Card Panel		

2000 This Is Spinal Tap

COMPLETE FACTORY SET (36)	6.00	15.00
COMMON CARD (1-36)	.25	.60

1996 FPG Thomas Canty

COMPLETE SET (90)	4.00	10.00
UNOPENED BOX (36 PACKS)	25.00	30.00
UNOPENED PACK (10 CARDS)	1.00	1.25
COMMON CARD (1-90)	.10	.25
AUTC Thomas Canty AU	20.00	50.00

1996 FPG Thomas Canty Metallic

COMPLETE SET (5)	12.00	30.00
COMMON CARD (M1-M5)	3.00	8.00
STATED ODDS 1:12		

1993 Spectrum Thomas the Tank Engine & Friends Promos

COMPLETE SET (4)	6.00	15.00
COMMON CARD	2.00	5.00

1994 The River Group Three by Shooter

COMPLETE BOXED SET (30)	2.00	5.00
COMMON CARD (1-30)	.12	.30

1993 SkyBox The Three Musketeers

COMPLETE SET (90)	6.00	15.00
UNOPENED BOX (36 PACKS)	20.00	30.00
UNOPENED PACK (8 CARDS)	1.00	1.25
COMMON CARD (1-90)	.10	.30
S1 The Three Musketeers PROMO	.75	2.00

1993 SkyBox The Three Musketeers Foil

COMPLETE SET (4)	15.00	40.00
COMMON CARD (1-4)	5.00	12.00
STATED ODDS 1:36		

1993 SkyBox The Three Musketeers Spectra Embossed

COMPLETE SET (3)	4.00	10.00
COMMON CARD (1-3)	2.00	5.00
STATED ODDS 1:8		

1985 FTCC The Three Stooges

COMPLETE SET (60)	20.00	50.00
UNOPENED BOX (36 PACKS)	85.00	100.00
UNOPENED PACK (7 CARDS)	2.50	3.00
COMMON CARD (1-60)	.40	1.00

1989 FTCC The Three Stooges

COMPLETE SET (60)	10.00	25.00
UNOPENED BOX (36 PACKS)	30.00	40.00
UNOPENED PACK (7 CARDS)	1.25	1.50
COMMON CARD (1-60)	.20	.50

1997 DuoCards The Three Stooges

COMPLETE SET (72)	6.00	15.00
UNOPENED BOX (36 PACKS)	100.00	150.00
UNOPENED PACK (8 CARDS)	3.00	4.00
COMMON CARD (1-72)	.12	.30
P1 Pokes in the Eyes! Promo	.75	2.00

1997 DuoCards The Three Stooges Chromium Antics

COMPLETE SET (3)	6.00	15.00
COMMON CARD (C1-C3)	3.00	8.00
STATED ODDS 1:15		

1997 DuoCards The Three Stooges Die-Cuts

COMPLETE SET (3)	8.00	20.00
COMMON CARD (1-3)	3.00	8.00
STATED ODDS 1:15		

1997 Market Square Productions The Three Stooges Promos

COMPLETE SET (2)	1.25	3.00
COMMON CARD	.75	2.00

2005 The Three Stooges

COMPLETE SET (72)	6.00	15.00
UNOPENED BOX (40 PACKS)	65.00	80.00
UNOPENED PACK (6 CARDS)	2.00	2.25
COMMON CARD (1-72)	.20	.50
BC Larry Moe and Curly (Box Cutout Exclusive)		
P4 Spook Louder (Album Exclusive)		
UNC 72-Card Base Set Uncut Sheet		

2005 The Three Stooges Costume Memorabilia

COMPLETE SET (6)	30.00	80.00
COMMON CARD (C1-C6)	6.00	15.00
OVERALL COSTUME/PROP ODDS 1:80		

2005 The Three Stooges Curly Years

COMPLETE SET (9)	25.00	60.00
COMMON CARD (CY1-CY9)	3.00	8.00
STATED ODDS 1:40		

2005 The Three Stooges Film Cel Case-Toppers

COMPLETE SET (2)	15.00	40.00
COMMON CARD (F1-F2)	10.00	25.00
STATED ODDS 1:CASE		

2005 The Three Stooges Prop Memorabilia

OVERALL COSTUME/PROP ODDS 1:80		
DP ISSUED AS 6-CASE INCENTIVE		
DP Curly Joe Desk 6CI		
RC Larry Fine Residual Check	12.00	40.00
S1 Curly Joe Stationery/24	20.00	50.00
SGJ Moe Howard Necklace/57	100.00	200.00

2005 The Three Stooges Shemp the Original Third Stooge

COMPLETE SET (12)	15.00	40.00
COMMON CARD (SS1-SS12)	2.00	5.00
STATED ODDS 1:40		

2005 The Three Stooges Stooge Milestones

COMPLETE SET (4)	20.00	50.00
COMMON CARD (SM1-SM4)	6.00	15.00
STATED ODDS 1:160		

2005 The Three Stooges Promos

COMPLETE SET (6)	4.00	10.00
COMMON CARD	.75	2.00
NNO Seltzer (Philly)	2.00	5.00

2007 The Three Stooges Update

COMPLETE SET (16)	5.00	12.00
COMMON CARD (1-16)	.60	1.50

2007 The Three Stooges Update Larry Fine Tie Materials

COMPLETE SET (8)	125.00	250.00
COMMON CARD	15.00	40.00
STATED ODDS 1:SET		

2007 300 Circuit City DVD Promos

COMPLETE SET (4)	6.00	15.00
COMMON CARD (UNNUMBERED)	2.00	5.00

1991-97 J&W Productions Thunder on the Water Complete Series

COMPLETE SET (175)	20.00	50.00
UNOPENED BOX (PACKS)		
UNOPENED PACK (CARDS)		
COMMON CARD (1-175)	.25	.60

1991-97 J&W Productions Thunder on the Water Hydro Legends

COMPLETE SET (16)	8.00	20.00
COMMON CARD (HL1-HL16)	1.00	2.50

2015 Thunderbirds 50th Anniversary Autographs

COMMON CARD	10.00	25.00
MZ Matt Zimmerman	15.00	40.00
DG1 David Graham	12.00	30.00
DG2 David Graham	12.00	30.00
DG4 David Graham ALB	12.00	30.00
G3D David Graham	12.00	30.00
MZ2 Matt Zimmerman	15.00	40.00
MZ3 Matt Zimmerman	15.00	40.00
SA1 Sylvia Anderson	20.00	50.00
SA2 Sylvia Anderson	20.00	50.00
MZ1V Matt Zimmerman	15.00	40.00
MZ2V Matt Zimmerman	15.00	40.00
MZ3V Matt Zimmerman	15.00	40.00
NNO1 Matt Zimmerman	15.00	40.00
DA1 S.Anderson/D.Graham DUAL AU	75.00	150.00

2015 Thunderbirds 50th Anniversary Case-Toppers

COMPLETE SET (6)	8.00	20.00
COMMON CARD (CT1-CT6)	2.00	5.00

2015 Thunderbirds 50th Anniversary Mirror Foil

COMPLETE SET (10)	8.00	20.00
COMMON CARD (F1-F10)	1.00	2.50

2004 Thunderbirds Are Go Movie Previews

COMPLETE SET (6)	6.00	15.00
COMMON CARD (TMP1-TMP6)	1.50	4.00

2004 Thunderbirds Are Go Movie

COMPLETE SET (72)	6.00	15.00
UNOPENED BOX (36 PACKS)		
UNOPENED PACK (6 CARDS)		
COMMON CARD (1-72)	.15	.40

2004 Thunderbirds Are Go Movie Autographs

COMMON CARD		
STATED ODDS 1:		
AC4 Ron Cook	5.00	12.00
AC5 Philip Winchester	8.00	20.00

AC6 Dominic Colenso 6.00 15.00
AC7 Lex Shrapnel 5.00 12.00
AC8 Brady Corbet
AC9 Rose Keegan (album excl.)
AC1A Jonathan Frakes
AC1B Jonathan Frakes Redemption
AC2A Sir Ben Kingsley 15.00 40.00
AC2B Sir Ben Kingsley Redemption
AC3A Sophia Myles
AC3B Sophia Myles Redemption
AC10A Mike Trim
AC10B Mike Trim Redemption

2004 Thunderbirds Are Go Movie Promos

COMMON CARD 1.50 4.00
CZP2 Thunderbird 1 3.00 8.00
GGTB FAB 1 (Gum Guide 2) 2.00 5.00
NNO1 (9-card puzzle promo; The Sun/Woolworths) 6.00 15.00
CIWTB The Mighty Mole (NSU) 2.00 5.00
NECP5 Thunderbird 4 2.00 5.00

1992 Club Pro Set Thunderbirds Are Go! UK

COMPLETE SET (100) 8.00 20.00
UNOPENED BOX (66 PACKS) 20.00 30.00
UNOPENED PACK (6 CARDS) .75 1.00
COMMON CARD (1-100) .15 .40

2001 Thunderbirds Premium Previews

COMPLETE SET (10) 6.00 15.00
COMMON CARD (TBP1-TBP10) 1.25 3.00

2001 Thunderbirds Premium

COMPLETE SET (72) 4.00 10.00
UNOPENED BOX (36 PACKS)
UNOPENED PACK (5 CARDS)
COMMON CARD (1-72) .12 .30

2019 Thunderbirds Series 2

COMPLETE SET (36) 6.00 15.00
COMMON CARD (1-36) .30 .75
*PRINT PROOF/20: 3X TO 8X BASIC CARDS

2019 Thunderbirds Series 2 Autographs

COMMON AUTO 5.00 12.00
*B&W: X TO X BASIC AUTOS
BJ1 Brian Johnson 5.00 12.00
DE1 David Elliott 5.00 12.00
DG1 David Graham 12.00 30.00
DG2 David Graham 12.00 30.00
DG3 David Graham 12.00 30.00
DG4 David Graham 15.00 40.00
DG5 David Graham 12.00 30.00
DG6 David Graham 15.00 40.00
JC1 Joy Cuff 6.00 15.00
JC2 Joy Cuff 6.00 15.00
JW1 Jeremy Wilkin 60.00 120.00
MT1 Mary Turner 5.00 12.00
MT1 Mike Trim 8.00 20.00
MT2 Mike Trim 8.00 20.00
MZ1 Matt Zimmerman 15.00 40.00
MZ2 Matt Zimmerman 12.00 30.00
MZ3 Matt Zimmerman 12.00 30.00
MZ4 Matt Zimmerman 12.00 30.00
MZ5 Matt Zimmerman 10.00 25.00
MZ6 Matt Zimmerman 12.00 30.00

2019 Thunderbirds Series 2 Dual Autographs

GZ1 D.Graham/M.Zimmerman 25.00 60.00

2019 Thunderbirds Series 2 Postage Stamps

COMMON STAMP 6.00 15.00
MS1 Genuine Thunderbirds British Stamp Miniature Sheet

1997 Comic Images The Tick

COMPLETE SET (72) 4.00 10.00
UNOPENED BOX (48 PACKS) 20.00 30.00
UNOPENED PACK (8 CARDS) 1.00 1.25
COMMON CARD (1-72) .12 .30
NNO Citizens of The Fan-Land - Dealers 2.00 5.00
AU1 Ben Edlund AU/500* 20.00 50.00

1997 Comic Images The Tick Chromium Covers

COMPLETE SET (6) 15.00 40.00
COMMON CARD (C1-C6) 3.00 8.00
STATED ODDS 1:18

1994 Comic Images Tim Hildebrandt's Flights of Fantasy

COMPLETE SET (90) 4.00 10.00
UNOPENED BOX (48 PACKS) 20.00 30.00
UNOPENED PACK (10 CARDS) .50 .75
COMMON CARD (1-90) .08 .20
GM Gold Medallion 25.00
AUTH Tim Hildebrandt AU/500 100.00 150.00

1994 Comic Images Tim Hildebrandt's Flights of Fantasy Flying Dragons

COMPLETE SET (3) 12.00 30.00
COMMON CARD (D1-D3) 5.00 12.00
STATED ODDS 1:48

1994 Comic Images Tim Hildebrandt's Flights of Fantasy HoloChrome

COMPLETE SET (6) 15.00 40.00
COMMON CARD (H1-H6) 3.00 8.00
STATED ODDS 1:16
H6UP (6-up panel of holochrome cards, H1-H6)

1994 FPG Tim White

COMPLETE SET (90) 5.00 12.00
UNOPENED BOX (36 PACKS) 30.00 40.00
UNOPENED PACK (10 CARDS) 1.25 1.50
COMMON CARD (1-90) .12 .30
AUTW Tim White AU/1000* 20.00 50.00
NNO1 Promo Card (Deluxe #15, oversized)
AU10UP Tim White 10UP AU (CT)

1994 FPG Tim White Metallic Storm

COMPLETE SET (5) 15.00 40.00
COMMON CARD (MS1-MS5) 4.00 10.00
STATED ODDS 1:12

2003 Timeline Commemorative

COMPLETE SET (18) 5.00 12.00
COMMON CARD (1-18) .60 1.50

2003 Timeline Commemorative Costumes

COMMON COSTUME 8.00 20.00
C1 Paul Walker 10.00 25.00

1991 Topps Tiny Toon Adventures

COMPLETE SET (77) 6.00 15.00
UNOPENED BOX (60 PACKS) 30.00 50.00
UNOPENED PACK (5 CARDS+1 STICKER) 1.00 1.25
COMMON CARD (1-77) .15 .40

1991 Topps Tiny Toon Adventures Stickers Variations

COMPLETE SET (11)
*VARIATIONS: X TO X BASIC STICKERS
STATED ODDS 1:

2000 Titan AE

COMPLETE SET (90) 4.00 10.00
UNOPENED BOX (36 PACKS) 40.00 50.00
UNOPENED PACK (8 CARDS) 1.50 1.75
COMMON CARD (1-90) .10 .25
T1 Etched Foil Card 12.00 30.00

2000 Titan AE Die-Cuts

COMPLETE SET (6) 10.00 25.00
COMMON CARD (CC1-CC6) 2.00 5.00
STATED ODDS 1:17

2000 Titan AE Future of Earth Foil

COMPLETE SET (9) 10.00 25.00
COMMON CARD (C1-C9) 1.25 3.00
STATED ODDS 1:11
PAN Future of Earth Foil 9-Card Panel

2000 Titan AE Promos

COMMON CARD .75 2.00
P4 Promo 4 UK 3.00 8.00
9UP Future of Earth PAN

1998 Dart FlipCards Titanic

COMPLETE SET (72) 6.00 15.00
UNOPENED BOX (36 PACKS) 30.00 40.00
UNOPENED PACK (6 CARDS) 1.25 1.50
COMMON CARD (1-72) .15 .40
NNO1 Titanic Jumbo Lenticular Card

1998 Dart FlipCards Titanic Autographs

MD Millvina Dean 20.00 50.00
RW Ralph White 8.00 20.00

1998 Dart FlipCards Titanic White Star Gold Foil Die-Cuts

COMPLETE SET (6) 12.00 30.00
COMMON CARD (DC1-DC6) 2.50 6.00
STATED ODDS 1:8

1998 Inkworks Titanic Movie

COMPLETE FACTORY SET (25) 30.00 80.00
COMMON CARD (1-25) 1.25 3.00

1993 Cardz Tom and Jerry

COMPLETE SET (60) 5.00 12.00
UNOPENED BOX (36 PACKS) 12.00 15.00
UNOPENED PACK (8 CARDS) .50 .75
COMMON CARD (1-60) .15 .40

1993 Cardz Tom and Jerry Promos

COMPLETE SET (3) 5.00
COMMON CARD (p1-p3) .75 2.00

1993 Cardz Tom and Jerry TekChrome

COMPLETE SET (3) 6.00 15.00
COMMON CARD (T1-T3) 2.50 6.00
STATED ODDS 1:18

1995 FPG Tom Kidd

COMPLETE SET (90) 6.00 15.00
UNOPENED BOX (36 PACKS) 30.00 40.00
UNOPENED PACK (10 CARDS) 1.00 1.25
COMMON CARD (1-90) .12 .30
AUTK Tom Kidd AU/1000* 20.00 50.00

1995 FPG Tom Kidd Metallic

COMPLETE SET (5) 12.00 30.00
COMMON CARD (M1-M5) 3.00 8.00
STATED ODDS 1:12

1988 Grande Illusions Tom Savini's Gotcha

COMPLETE SET (60) 5.00 12.00
COMMON CARD (1-60) .15 .40
61 Tom Savini AU 8.00 20.00
62 Demon 3 PROMO 4.00 10.00

1997 Comic Images Tomb Raider 2 Video Game

COMPLETE SET (7) 5.00 12.00
COMMON CARD 1.00 2.50

2001 Tomb Raider

COMPLETE SET (90) 5.00 12.00
UNOPENED BOX (36 PACKS) 40.00 50.00
UNOPENED PACK (8 CARDS) 1.25 1.50
COMMON CARD (1-90) .15 .40
BL1 STATED ODDS ONE PER BOX
BL1 Lara Croft Tomb Raider 4.00 10.00
PAN Tomb Raider 9-Card Foil Panel/500

2001 Tomb Raider Autographs

COMMON AUTO (A1-A4) 8.00 20.00
RANDOMLY INSERTED INTO PACKS
A1 Angelina Jolie 500.00 1000.00
A2 Leslie Phillips 20.00 50.00

2001 Tomb Raider Pieceworks

RANDOM INSERTS IN PACKS
P1 Angelina Jolie EXCH 20.00 50.00
PT1 Pieceworks Redemption Card

2001 Tomb Raider Puzzle

COMPLETE SET (9) 12.50 30.00
COMMON CARD 2.00 5.00
STATED ODDS 1:11

2001 Tomb Raider Promos

COMPLETE SET (5) 6.00 15.00
COMMON CARD .75 2.00
TR4 Lara Croft Tomb Raider 3.00 8.00

2001 Tomb Raider The Quest

COMPLETE SET (6) 10.00 25.00
COMMON CARD 2.50 6.00
STATED ODDS 1:17

2003 Tomb Raider Cradle of Life

COMPLETE SET (81) 5.00 12.00
UNOPENED BOX (36 PACKS) 500.00 800.00
UNOPENED PACK (8 CARDS) 15.00 25.00
COMMON CARD (1-81) .15 .40

2003 Tomb Raider Cradle of Life Autographs

COMMON AUTO (A1-A6) 4.00 10.00
STATED ODDS 1:36
A1 Angelina Jolie 1250.00 2500.00
A2 Chris Barrie 6.00 15.00
A4 Til Schweiger 10.00 25.00
A5 Simon Yam 20.00 50.00

2003 Tomb Raider Cradle of Life Box-Loaders

COMPLETE SET (3) 2.50 6.00
COMMON CARD (BL1-BL3) 1.00 2.50
BL1-BL3 STATED ODDS ONE PER BOX
CL1 STATED ODDS ONE:CASE
BL1 Brave and Beautiful 1.00 2.50
BL2 Easy Rider Deadly Mission 1.00 2.50
BL3 Statuesque 1.00 2.50
CL1 Lara Croft Tomb Raider (Case-Loader) 10.00 25.00

2003 Tomb Raider Cradle of Life Pieceworks

COMMON MEM 12.00 30.00
STATED ODDS 1:36
PW1b Angelina Jolie (red jacket lining) 25.00 60.00
PW1c Angelina Jolie (jacket patch) 30.00 75.00

2003 Tomb Raider Cradle of Life Puzzle Cards

COMPLETE SET (9) 7.50 20.00
COMMON CARD (COL1-COL9) 1.25 3.00
STATED ODDS 1:11

2003 Tomb Raider Cradle of Life Secret of the Orb

COMPLETE SET (6) 7.50 20.00
COMMON CARD (SO1-SO6) 1.50 4.00
STATED ODDS 1:17

2003 Tomb Raider Cradle of Life Promos

COMPLETE SET (4) 3.00 8.00
COMMON CARD .75 2.00
TR2UK Lara Croft Tomb Raider 2.00 5.00

1997 Krome Tony Daniel's The Tenth

COMPLETE SET (50) 8.00 20.00
UNOPENED BOX (32 PACKS) 30.00 40.00
UNOPENED PACK (5 CARDS) 1.25 1.50
COMMON CARD (1-50) .30 .75
*NECROCHROME: .5X TO 1.2X BASIC CARDS.40 1.00
*FRACTAL CHROMIUM: .75X TO 2X BASIC CARDS .60 1.50

MODERN

1997 Krome Tony Daniel's The Tenth ClearChrome

COMPLETE SET (6) 15.00 40.00
COMMON CARD (1-6) 3.00 8.00
STATED ODDS 1:

1996 Top Cow Classics Promos

Promo1 Cyblade/Shi 5.00 12.00
Promo2 Ripclaw 5.00 12.00

2002 Top Cow Universe

COMPLETE SET (72) 4.00 10.00
UNOPENED BOX (36 PACKS) 40.00 50.00
UNOPENED PACK (7 CARDS) 1.25 1.50
COMMON CARD (1-72) .12 .30
MSAU Mark Silvestri/500 (album excl.) 8.00 20.00
NNO1 6-up Chromium panel
P1 Promo 1 (Coming Winter 2001) .75 2.00

2018 Topps 80th Anniversary Wrapper Art

COMPLETE SET (115) 700.00 1200.00
COMMON CARD (1-45) 5.00 12.00
1 1966 Batman/707* 25.00 60.00
2 1956 U.S. Presidents/596* 8.00 20.00
3 1972 Baseball/605* 12.00 30.00
4 1964 The Beatles/515* 20.00 50.00
6 1968 Hot Rods/413* 6.00 15.00
7 1977 Charlie's Angels/224* 6.00 15.00
8 1989 Back to the Future II/213* 8.00 20.00
11 1978 Three's Company/220* 8.00 20.00
12 1965 Ugly Stickers/207* 6.00 15.00
13 1965 King Kong/152* 25.00 60.00
14 1985 Cyndi Lauper/146* 25.00 60.00
16 1966 Superman/343* 10.00 25.00
19 1984 Michael Jackson 1st Series/234* 6.00 15.00
20 1982 Donkey Kong/256* 6.00 15.00
22 1973 Kung Fu/190* 6.00 15.00
23 1985 Garbage Pail Kids/969* 6.00 15.00
24 1988 Dinosaurs Attack!/199* 6.00 15.00
29 1966 Lost in Space/247* 8.00 20.00
34 1965 Gilligan's Island/304* 6.00 15.00
41 1975 Bay City Rollers/238* 6.00 15.00
43 1978 Grease/271* 6.00 15.00
49 1956 Elvis Presley/356* 8.00 20.00
52 1985 The Goonies/244* 6.00 15.00
60 1966 Get Smart/278* 6.00 15.00
69 1984 Supergirl/249* 6.00 15.00
71 1969 Mod Squad/214* 6.00 15.00
74 1971 Partridge Family/215* 6.00 15.00
77 1986 Duran Duran/178* 6.00 15.00
79 1971 Brady Bunch/294* 6.00 15.00
82 1976 Welcome Back Kotter/220* 8.00 20.00
83 1978 Battlestar Galactica/237* 6.00 15.00
86 1965 The Man from U.N.C.L.E./220* 6.00 15.00
91 1984 Masters of the Universe/224* 6.00 15.00
95 1979 James Bond Moonraker/199* 6.00 15.00
97 1962 Mars Attacks/405* 8.00 20.00
103 1964 Addams Family/227* 20.00 50.00
106 1965 Monster Greeting Cards/207* 6.00 15.00
109 1957 Space Cards/191* 10.00 25.00
112 1973 Wacky Packages/498* 6.00 15.00

2022 Topps Entertainment Blend

COMPLETE SET W/SP (28) 100.00 250.00
COMPLETE SET W/O SP (20) 40.00 100.00
UNOPENED BOX (6 CARDS) 25.00 40.00
COMMON CARD (1-20) 4.00 10.00
COMMON SP 10.00 25.00
*A.P.SILVER/49: 6X TO 15X BASIC CARDS
*BLUE/25: 4X TO 10X BASIC CARDS
1b Blasted Billy SP 20.00 50.00
2b Jay Decay SP 15.00 40.00
3b Evil Eddie SP 20.00 50.00
4b Thin Lynn SP 12.00 30.00
7b Beth Death SP 15.00 40.00
8b Foul Bill SP 12.00 30.00

2022 Topps Entertainment Blend Chopped

COMPLETE SET (5) 15.00 40.00
COMMON CARD (C1-C5) 5.00 12.00
RANDOMLY INSERTED INTO BOXES
C1 Mars Attacks 5.00 12.00
C2 Bruce 5.00 12.00
C3 Blasted Billy 5.00 12.00
C4 Wrapper Art #1 5.00 12.00
C5 Wrapper Art #2 5.00 12.00

2022 Topps Entertainment Blend Chopped Ermsy Autographs

COMMON AUTO (C1-C5) 300.00 800.00
STATED PRINT RUN 20 SER.#'d SETS

2019 Topps Now Entertainment

ENT1 Lil Nas X 8.00 20.00

2019 Topps Now Entertainment Autographs

COMMON AUTO
*BLACK/75: .5X TO 1.2X BASIC AUTOS
*BLUE/49: .75X TO 2X BASIC AUTOS
STATED PRINT RUN 99 SER.#'d SETS
ENT1A Lil Nas X 125.00 250.00

2016 Topps Now Election

1 Donald Trump/Hillary Clinton/277* 75.00 150.00
2 Hillary Clinton/328* 50.00 100.00
3 Donald Trump/334* 75.00 150.00
4 Mike Pence and Tim Kaine/71* 200.00 400.00
5 Tim Kaine/65* 75.00 150.00
6 Mike Pence/65* 75.00 150.00
7 Donald Trump/Hillary Clinton/143* 10.00 25.00
8 Hillary Clinton/165* 125.00 250.00
9 Donald Trump/145* 8.00 20.00
10 Donald Trump/158* 15.00 40.00
11 Hillary Clinton/157* 8.00 20.00
12 Donald Trump/Hillary Clinton/144* 50.00 100.00
13 Donald Trump Wins Election/2011* 125.00 250.00
14 Donlad Trump Sworn In/847* 75.00 150.00
15 President Trump Inaugural Address/474* 150.00 300.00
16 Obamas Leave White House/675* 200.00 400.00
17 Donald and Melania White House/551* 100.00 200.00
18 Mike Pence Sworn In/456* 60.00 120.00

2020-21 Topps Now Election

COMMON CARD 3.00 8.00
*BLUE/46: 4X TO 10X BASIC CARDS
1 Donald Trump/Joe Biden/4365* 6.00 15.00
2 Joe Biden/3946* 4.00 10.00
3 Donald Trump/6634* 10.00 25.00
4 Kamala Harris/Mike Pence/2138* 4.00 10.00
5 Kamala Harris/3216* 5.00 12.00
7 Donald Trump/Joe Biden/1830* 5.00 12.00
8 Joe Biden/1821* 5.00 12.00
9 Donald Trump/2413* 5.00 12.00
11 Kamala Harris/5045* 6.00 15.00
12 Kamala Harris/Joe Biden/4746* 5.00 12.00
13 Kamala Harris/17016* 4.00 10.00
14 Joe Biden/8925* 6.00 15.00
17 Lady Gaga/8271* 6.00 15.00
18 Jennifer Lopez/6659* 4.00 10.00
20 Amanda Gorman/14716* 4.00 10.00
21 Bernie Sanders/91169* 8.00 20.00

2021 Topps Now NASA Perseverance Mars Rover Landing

COMPLETE SET (2) 6.00 15.00
COMMON CARD (1-2) 4.00 10.00

2016 Topps Santa Claus

COMPLETE SET (8) 6.00 15.00
COMMON CARD (1-8) 1.25 3.00

2016 Topps Santa Claus Autographs

COMMON AUTO 10.00 25.00

2013 Topps 75th Anniversary

COMPLETE SET (100) 6.00 15.00
UNOPENED BOX (24 PACKS) 55.00 70.00
UNOPENED PACK (8 CARDS) 2.50 3.00
COMMON CARD (1-100) .12 .30
*RAINBOW: 1.2X TO 3X BASIC CARDS .75 1.00
*DIAMOND: 10X TO 25X BASIC CARDS 3.00 8.00
*GLOSS/10: 50X TO 100X BASIC CARDS 12.00 30.00

2013 Topps 75th Anniversary Autographs

COMMON CARD 4.00 10.00
*RAINBOW FOIL/150: SAME AS BASIC AUTO
*DIAMOND/75: .5X TO 1.2X BASIC AUTO
STATED ODDS 1:8
NNO Anson Williams 12.00 30.00
NNO Barbara Feldon 20.00 50.00
NNO Bill Mumy 10.00 25.00
NNO Burt Young 10.00 25.00
NNO Corey Feldman 15.00 40.00
NNO Dawn Wells 12.00 30.00
NNO Ed Gale 10.00 25.00
NNO Ernie Hudson 15.00 40.00
NNO Jeff Cohen 50.00 100.00
NNO Joshua Rudoy 6.00 15.00
NNO Joyce DeWitt 10.00 25.00
NNO Julia Nickson 8.00 20.00
NNO Karen Allen 12.00 30.00
NNO Mark Goddard 6.00 15.00
NNO Marta Kristen 10.00 25.00
NNO Richard Kiel 10.00 25.00
NNO Roger Moore 50.00 100.00
NNO Russell Johnson 12.00 30.00
NNO Van Williams 20.00 50.00

2013 Topps 75th Anniversary Minis

COMPLETE SET (8) 5.00 12.00
COMMON CARD (1-8) 1.25 3.00
STATED ODDS 1:6

2013 Topps 75th Anniversary Test Issue

COMPLETE SET (8) 20.00 50.00
COMMON CARD (1-8) 5.00 12.00
STATED ODDS 1:24

1990 Pacific Total Recall

COMPLETE BOXED SET (110) 8.00 20.00
COMMON CARD (1-110) .15 .40

1992 Kitchen Sink Press Total Trash Paperback Cover Art of the 40's and 50's

COMPLETE BOXED SET (36) 5.00 12.00
COMMON CARD (1-36) .25 .60

1991 Topps Toxic Crusaders

COMPLETE SET (88) 5.00 12.00
COMPLETE SET W/STICKERS (96) 6.00 15.00
UNOPENED BOX (36 PACKS) 15.00 20.00
UNOPENED PACK (8 CARDS+1 STICKER) .75 1.00
COMMON CARD (1-88) .12 .30

1991 Topps Toxic Crusaders Hologram Stickers

COMPLETE SET (8) 1.50 3.00
COMMON STICKER (1-8) .30 .75
STATED ODDS 1:1

1992 Topps Toxic High

COMPLETE SET (88) 5.00 12.00
UNOPENED BOX (48 PACKS) 10.00 15.00
UNOPENED PACK (5 STICKER-CARDS) .50 .75
COMMON CARD (1-88) .12 .30

1991 Mother Productions Toxic Waste Zombies

COMPLETE BOXED SET (40) 5.00 12.00
COMMON CARD (1-40) .25 .60

1995 SkyBox Toy Story

COMPLETE SET (90) 6.00 15.00
UNOPENED BOX (36 PACKS) 75.00 125.00
UNOPENED PACK (16 CARDS) 2.50 4.00
COMMON CARD (1-90) .12 .30

1995 SkyBox Toy Story 3-D Motion

COMPLETE SET (2) 12.00 30.00
COMMON CARD (1-2) 8.00 20.00
STATED ODDS 1:48

1995 SkyBox Toy Story Badge Stickers

COMPLETE SET (8) 1.50 4.00
COMMON CARD (1-8) .20 .50
STATED ODDS 1:1

1995 SkyBox Toy Story Foil Embossed

COMPLETE SET (9) 25.00 60.00
COMMON CARD (F1-F9) 3.00 8.00
STATED ODDS 1:18

1995 SkyBox Toy Story Promos

1A Totally Toy Story .75 2.00
1B Tri-Fold Video Promo (Target) 1.25 3.00
2 It's Out of This World - Skybox CD-ROM
S1 Toy Story .75 2.00
NNO Buzz Lightyear - 4-Card Panel 6.00 15.00

1996 SkyBox Toy Story Series Two

COMPLETE SET (74) 5.00 12.00
UNOPENED BOX (48 PACKS) 15.00 20.00
UNOPENED PACK (12 CARDS) .50 .75
COMMON CARD (1-74) .12 .30

1996 SkyBox Toy Story Series Two 3-D Motion

COMPLETE SET (2) 10.00 25.00
COMMON CARD (1-2) 6.00 15.00
STATED ODDS 1:24

1996 SkyBox Toy Story Series Two Color Me Iron-Ons

COMPLETE SET (6) 4.00 10.00
COMMON CARD (1-6) .75 2.00
STATED ODDS 1:6

1991 Impel Trading Card Treats

COMPLETE SET (36) 5.00 12.00
ARCHIE SET (1-6) 1.00 2.50
INSPECTOR GADGET SET (7-12) 1.00 2.50
MARVEL SET (13-18) 1.25 3.00
NINTENDO SET (19-24) 1.00 2.50
UNIVERSAL MONSTERS SET (25-30) 1.00 2.50
WIDGET SET (31-36) 1.00 2.50
COMMON CARD (1-36) .20 .50
13 Spider-Man / Traffic Safety .40 1.00

1985 Hasbro Transformers Action Cards

COMPLETE SET W/O VARIANTS (192) 100.00 200.00
COMPLETE SET W/VARIANTS (246) 300.00 600.00
COMMON CARD (1-192) 1.25 3.00
COMMON VARIANT 4.00 10.00
BASE CARDS ARE ORANGE/YELLOW
VARIANTS ARE BLUE/PURPLE
103C IS CONSIDERED A VARIANT
1 Optimus Prime 5.00 12.00
4A Ratchet (yellow) 6.00 15.00
5 Tracks 3.00 8.00
10A Sunstreaker (orange) 8.00 20.00
15A Ironhide (yellow) 6.00 15.00
16 Prowl 2.00 5.00
34A Grimlock (yellow) 8.00 20.00
38A Jetfire (yellow) 5.00 12.00
96 Checklist 2.00 5.00
97A Megatron (yellow) 5.00 12.00
98A Starscream (yellow) 2.00 5.00
104A Soundwave (orange) 2.00 5.00
14B Wheeljack (yellow trans.) 5.00 12.00

1985 Hasbro Transformers Action Cards Motto Stickers

COMPLETE SET (24) 40.00 100.00
COMMON CARD (1-24) 1.50 4.00
SKYWARP EXTREMELY SHORT PRINTED
3 Grimlock 2.50 6.00
8 Megatron 4.00 10.00
9 Optimus Prime 4.00 10.00
15 Skywarp SP 20.00 50.00
18 Soundwave 2.50 6.00
19 Starscream 2.50 6.00
24 Wheeljack 2.50 6.00

2003 Transformers Armada
COMPLETE SET (122) 6.00 15.00
UNOPENED BOX (36 PACKS) 50.00 60.00
UNOPENED PACK (5 CARDS) 1.75 2.00
COMMON CARD (1-122) .10 .25
*GOLD: .75X TO 2X BASIC CARDS
AUPL Pat Lee AU/700
SKDP Dreamwave Productions Sketchagraph/50
AURed Autograph Redemption EXCH/700
SKRed Sketchagraph Redemption EXCH/50

2003 Transformers Armada Autobots Deceptions Die-Cuts
COMPLETE SET (9) 10.00 25.00
COMMON CARD (1AD-9AD) 1.25 3.00
STATED ODDS 1:6

2003 Transformers Armada Comic Art
COMPLETE SET (12) 12.00 30.00
COMMON CARD (1ACA-12ACA) 1.25 3.00
STATED ODDS 1:9

2003 Transformers Armada Flappers
COMPLETE SET (8) 12.00 30.00
COMMON CARD (1TF-8TF) 2.00 5.00
STATED ODDS 1:18

2003 Transformers Armada Posters
COMPLETE SET (10) 10.00 25.00
COMMON CARD (1AP-10AP) 1.25 3.00
STATED ODDS 1:9

2003 Transformers Armada Promos
COMPLETE SET (4) 2.50 6.00
COMMON CARD (1-4) .75 2.00

2002 Transformers Generation One Previews
COMPLETE SET (6) 6.00 15.00
COMMON CARD (TMP1-TMP6) 1.50 4.00

2017 Transformers The Last Knight Sonic Drive-In Wacky Pack Stickers
COMPLETE SET (27) 8.00 20.00
COMMON CARD (UNNUMBERED) .60 1.50
*FOIL: .75X TO 2X BASIC STICKERS
FOIL IS NOT A FULL PARALLEL SET

2013 Transformers Optimum Collection
COMPLETE SET (72) 10.00 25.00
UNOPENED BOX (24 PACKS) 50.00 60.00
UNOPENED PACK (6 CARDS) 2.25 2.50
COMMON CARD (1-72) .15 .40

2013 Transformers Optimum Collection Autographs
COMMON AUTO 6.00 15.00
STATED ODDS 1:29
JBTA Jess Harnell Barricade 10.00 25.00
JITA Jess Harnell Ironhide 8.00 20.00
LNTA Leonard Nimoy/90 200.00 400.00
RFTA Robert Foxworth 10.00 25.00
RTTA Rachael Taylor SP 50.00 100.00

2013 Transformers Optimum Collection Case-Incentives
TTIP ISSUED AS 3-CASE INCENTIVE
TTIP Tire Prop Card (3CI) 30.00 80.00

2013 Transformers Optimum Collection Film Relics
COMMON CARD 5.00 12.00
STATED ODDS 1:36

2013 Transformers Optimum Collection G1 Foil
COMPLETE SET (18) 12.00 30.00
COMMON CARD (TF1-TF18) 1.25 3.00
STATED ODDS 1:4
TF1 Optimus Prime 2.00 5.00
TF2 Bumblebee 1.50 4.00
TF3 Megatron 2.00 5.00
TF12 Starscream 1.50 4.00
TF15 Soundwave 1.50 4.00

2013 Transformers Optimum Collection Holographic Foil Puzzle
COMPLETE SET (9) 6.00 15.00
COMMON CARD (PF1-PF9) 1.00 2.50
STATED ODDS 1:8

2013 Transformers Optimum Collection SDCC Promos Autographs
COMMON AUTO 6.00 15.00
2012 SDCC EXCLUSIVE
DMTA Darius McCrary 8.00 20.00
RTTA Rachael Taylor SP 30.00 75.00
LNCCTA Leonard Nimoy/45 300.00 600.00

2013 Transformers Optimum Collection Promos
AC Jolt (Applecards) 2.50 6.00
P1 Things Just Got a Lot Worse SDCC 1.50 4.00
P2 Day of the Decepticons SDCC 1.50 4.00
P3 Dylan Gould (Philly) 2.50 6.00
P4 Alice ALB 3.00 8.00
PH Demolishor (Philly) 2.50 6.00
RR Rampage (Red Robin) 2.50 6.00
NSU Bruce Brazos NSU 1.50 4.00
TKP Decepticon No More (Tilted Kilt)

2007 Transformers
COMPLETE SET (90) 6.00 15.00
UNOPENED BOX (24 PACKS) 75.00 125.00
UNOPENED PACK (7 CARDS) 3.00 5.00
COMMON CARD (1-90) .15 .40
FOX AUTO STATED ODDS 1:396 HOBBY
NNO Megan Fox AU 350.00 500.00

2007 Transformers Authentic Movie Memorabilia
COMMON CARD 6.00 15.00
STATED ODDS 1:39 HOBBY

2007 Transformers Embossed Foil
COMPLETE SET (10) 5.00 12.00
COMMON CARD (1-10) .75 2.00
STATED ODDS 1:6

2007 Transformers Flix-Pix
COMPLETE SET (5) 4.00 10.00
COMMON CARD (1-5) 1.25 3.00
STATED ODDS 1:12 RETAIL

2007 Transformers Foil
COMPLETE SET (10) 5.00 12.00
COMMON CARD (1-10) .75 2.00
STATED ODDS 1:6

2009 Transformers Revenge of the Fallen Previews
COMPLETE SET (3) .40 1.00
COMMON CARD (1-3) .25 .60
COMIC ART/MOVIE RECAP/PREVIEW COMBINED ODDS 2:1

2009 Transformers Revenge of the Fallen
COMPLETE SET (45) 3.00 8.00
UNOPENED BOX (24 PACKS) 50.00 75.00
UNOPENED PACK (6 CARDS) 2.00 3.00
COMMON CARD (1-45) .15 .40

2009 Transformers Revenge of the Fallen Autographs
COMMON AUTO 10.00 25.00
STATED ODDS 1:91
UNNUMBERED CARDS LISTED ALPHABETICALLY
NNO Shia LaBeouf 100.00 200.00
NNO Peter Cullen 60.00 120.00
NNO Robert Foxworth 15.00 40.00
NNO Jess Harnell 15.00 40.00
NNO Mark Ryan 12.00 30.00

2009 Transformers Revenge of the Fallen Comic Art
COMPLETE SET (12) 2.00 5.00
COMMON CARD (1-12) .25 .60
COMIC ART/MOVIE RECAP/PREVIEW COMBINED ODDS 2:1

2009 Transformers Revenge of the Fallen Movie Recap
COMPLETE SET (9) 1.25 3.00
COMMON CARD (1-9) .25 .60
COMIC ART/MOVIE RECAP/PREVIEW COMBINED ODDS 2:1

2009 Transformers Revenge of the Fallen Pop-Ups
COMPLETE SET (9) 2.00 5.00
COMMON CARD (1-9) .40 1.00
STATED ODDS 1:2

2009 Transformers Revenge of the Fallen Tattoos
COMPLETE SET (10) 2.00 5.00
COMMON CARD (1-10) .30 .75
STATED ODDS 1:2

2011 Transformers Rescue Bots Promos
COMPLETE SET (4) 2.00 5.00
ISSUED AS PERFORATED SHEET AT SDCC
1 Blades .75 2.00
2 Boulder .75 2.00
3 Chase .75 2.00
4 Heatwave .75 2.00

1992 Topps Trash Can Trolls
COMPLETE SET (88) 6.00 15.00
UNOPENED BOX (36 PACKS) 10.00 15.00
UNOPENED PACK (6 STICKER-CARDS) .50 .75
COMMON CARD (1-88) .12 .30

2002 Treasure Planet FilmCardz
COMPLETE SET (72) 6.00 15.00
UNOPENED BOX (24 PACKS) 35.00 40.00
UNOPENED PACK (5 CARDS) 1.50 1.75
COMMON CARD (1-72) .15 .40
P1 Promo 1 (SDCC)

2002 Treasure Planet FilmCardz Rare
COMPLETE SET (6) 12.00 30.00
COMMON CARD (R1-R6) 2.50 6.00
STATED ODDS 1:8

2002 Treasure Planet FilmCardz Ultra Rare
COMPLETE SET (3) 8.00 20.00
COMMON CARD (UR1-UR3) 3.00 8.00
STATED ODDS 1:24

1993 Press Pass Tribe The Intro
COMPLETE SET (90) 5.00 12.00
UNOPENED BOX (36 PACKS) 15.00 20.00
UNOPENED PACK (8 CARDS) .75 1.00
COMMON CARD (1-90) .10 .25

1993 Press Pass Tribe The Intro Prism
COMPLETE SET (5) 8.00 20.00
COMMON CARD (P1-P5) 2.00 5.00
STATED ODDS 1:12

1993 Press Pass Tribe The Intro Promos
COMPLETE SET (4) 2.50 6.00
COMMON CARD (1-4) .75 2.00

1993 Press Pass Tribe The Intro Thermofoil
COMPLETE SET (5) 8.00 20.00
COMMON CARD (T1-T5) 2.00 5.00
STATED ODDS 1:36

1991 Manning Triumphs and Horrors of the Gulf War
COMPLETE SET (50) 6.00 15.00
COMMON CARD (1-50) .15 .40
*PROMO: 2X TO 5X BASIC CARDS
*TEST: 4X TO 10X BASIC CARDS
UNC 50-Card Base Set Uncut Sheet

1984 Topps Trivia Battle
COMPLETE SET (132) 5.00 12.00
COMMON CARD (ODD SKIP #'d) .08 .20
SCRATCH OFF GAME RULES CARD HAS #NNO

1984 Topps Trivia Battle Stickers
COMPLETE SET (12) 1.25 3.00
COMMON STICKERS .15 .40

1992 Star Pics Troll Force
COMPLETE SET (50) 3.00 8.00
UNOPENED BOX (48 PACKS) 20.00 25.00
UNOPENED PACK (7 CARDS+1 STICKER) 1.00 1.25
COMMON CARD (1-50) .12 .30

1992 Star Pics Troll Force Promos
COMPLETE SET (3) 1.00 2.50
COMMON CARD (S1-S3) .40 1.00

1992 Star Pics Troll Force Stickers
COMPLETE SET (6) .75 2.00
COMMON CARD .25 .60
STATED ODDS 1:1

1982 Donruss Tron
COMPLETE SET (66) 4.00 10.00
COMPLETE SET W/STICKERS (74) 5.00 12.00
UNOPENED BOX (36 PACKS) 200.00 300.00
UNOPENED PACK (8 CARDS+1 STICKER) 6.00 8.00
COMMON CARD (1-66) .08 .20
CARD #9 NOT ISSUED
TWO VARIANTS OF CARD #6 EXIST

1982 Donruss Tron Stickers
COMPLETE SET (8) 1.25 3.00
COMMON CARD (1-8) .20 .50

1982 York Peanut Butter Tron Discs
COMPLETE SET (6) 12.00 30.00
COMMON CARD (1-6) 3.00 8.00

1992 Classic Trouble Trolls
COMPLETE SET (60) 2.50 5.00
UNOPENED BOX (48 PACKS) 8.00 12.00
UNOPENED PACK (6 CARDS) .40 .50
COMMON CARD (1-60) .10 .30

1992 Classic Trouble Trolls Promos
NNO Chunky Troll .40 1.00
NNO Snotty Troll .40 1.00
NNO Zit Troll .40 1.00

2013 True Blood Archives
COMPLETE SET (72) 5.00 12.00
UNOPENED BOX (24 PACKS) 75.00 125.00
UNOPENED PACK (5 CARDS) 4.00 6.00
COMMON CARD (1-48, 99-122) .15 .40
*FOIL: 1.25X TO 3X BASIC CARDS
CT1 ISSUED AS CASE TOPPER
CT1 Season Six Preview CT 8.00 20.00

2013 True Blood Archives Autographs
COMMON AUTO (UNNUMBERED) 5.00 12.00
STATED ODDS 1:12
L (LIMITED): 300-500 COPIES
VL (VERY LIMITED): 200-300 COPIES
EL (EXTREMELY LIMITED): LESS THAN 200 COPIES
WOLL AUTO ISSUED AS 3-CASE INCENTIVE
MOYER AUTO ISSUED AS 6-CASE INCENTIVE
NNO Alexander Skarsgard EL 60.00 120.00
NNO Allan Hyde L 6.00 15.00
NNO Anna Camp EL 15.00 40.00
NNO Anna Paquin EL 75.00 150.00
NNO Carrie Preston L 6.00 15.00
NNO Chris Bauer EL 8.00 20.00

MODERN

NNO Deborah Ann Woll 3CI	30.00	75.00
NNO Denis O'Hare VL	6.00	15.00
NNO James Frain EL	6.00	15.00
NNO Janina Gavankar EL	15.00	40.00
NNO Jessica Tuck L	6.00	15.00
NNO Kelly Overton EL	10.00	25.00
NNO Kristin Bauer L	10.00	25.00
NNO Lauren Bowles L	6.00	15.00
NNO Mehcad Brooks VL	10.00	25.00
NNO Michelle Forbes EL	15.00	40.00
NNO Nelsan Ellis L	15.00	40.00
NNO Rutina Wesley EL	10.00	25.00
NNO Ryan Kwanten EL	12.00	30.00
NNO Stephen Moyer 6CI	60.00	120.00
NNO Todd Lowe VL	6.00	15.00
NNO Valentina Cervi EL	8.00	20.00
NNO William Sanderson EL	6.00	15.00

2013 True Blood Archives Costumes

COMPLETE SET (15)	150.00	300.00
COMMON CARD (C1-C15)	8.00	20.00
COSTUME/PROP ODDS 1:24		
C1 Sookie Stackhouse shirt	10.00	25.00
C2 Jason Stackhouse shirt	10.00	25.00
C3 Jessica Hamby shirt	12.00	30.00
C4 Pam De Beaufort dress	10.00	25.00
C5 Sookie Stackhouse dress	10.00	25.00
C8 Sam Merlotte shirt	10.00	25.00
C9 Russell Edgington jacket	10.00	25.00
C10 Sookie Stackhouse shirt	15.00	40.00
C12 Sookie Stackhouse dress	10.00	25.00
C14 Sookie Stackhouse dress	10.00	25.00
C15 Eric Northman shirt	10.00	25.00

2013 True Blood Archives Gallery Characters

COMPLETE SET (11)	15.00	40.00
COMMON CARD (PL01-PL11)	3.00	8.00
STATED ODDS 1:24		

2013 True Blood Archives Props

COMPLETE SET (4)	25.00	60.00
COMMON PROP (R1-R4)	8.00	20.00
COSTUME/PROP ODDS 1:24		

2013 True Blood Archives Quotables

COMPLETE SET (12)	8.00	20.00
COMPLETE SET W/SP (13)	20.00	50.00
COMMON CARD (Q11-Q22)	1.25	3.00
STATED ODDS 1:12		
Q23 ISSUED AS RITTENHOUSE REWARD		
Q23 I Made Her Vampire RR	15.00	40.00

2013 True Blood Archives Relationships

COMPLETE SET (18)	10.00	25.00
COMMON CARD (R1-R18)	1.00	2.50
STATED ODDS 1:8		

2013 True Blood Archives Promos

P1 Jessica Hamby GEN	1.50	4.00
P2 Sookie Stackhouse NSU	2.50	6.00
P3 Bill Compton ALB	5.00	12.00
P4 Tara Thornton (Philly)	2.00	5.00
P5 Pam De Beaufort SDCC	2.00	5.00

2011 Legends of True Blood Hoyt Fortenberry

COMPLETE SET (9)	8.00	20.00
COMMON CARD (C1-C9)	1.50	4.00
STATED PRINT RUN 500 SER.#'d SETS		

2011 Legends of True Blood Sam Merlotte

COMPLETE SET (9)	8.00	20.00
STATED PRINT RUN 500 SER.#'d SETS		

2011 Legends of True Blood Sookie Stackhouse

COMPLETE SET (9)	8.00	20.00
STATED PRINT RUN 500 SER.#'d SETS		

2013 Legends of True Blood Andy Bellefleur

COMPLETE SET (9)	8.00	20.00
COMMON CARD (C1-C9)	1.50	4.00
STATED PRINT RUN 500 SER.#'d SETS		

2013 Legends of True Blood Bill Compton

COMPLETE SET (9)	8.00	20.00
COMMON CARD (C1-C9)	1.50	4.00
STATED PRINT RUN 500 SER.#'d SETS		

2013 Legends of True Blood Jessica Hamby

COMPLETE SET (9)	8.00	20.00
COMMON CARD (C1-C9)	1.50	4.00
STATED PRINT RUN 500 SER.#'d SETS		

2012 True Blood Premiere

COMPLETE SET (98)	6.00	15.00
UNOPENED BOX (24 PACKS)	60.00	100.00
UNOPENED PACK (8 CARDS)	2.50	4.00
COMMON CARD (1-98)	.20	.50
*PARALLEL: 1.5X TO 4X BASIC		
DIECUT BOTTLE ISSUED AS CASE TOPPER		
CT Tru Blood Bottle DIECUT CT	10.00	25.00

2012 True Blood Premiere Autographs

COMMON AUTO (UNNUMBERED)	5.00	12.00
OVERALL AUTO ODDS 2 PER BOX		
L (LIMITED): 300-500 COPIES		
VL (VERY LIMITED): 200-300 COPIES		
EL (EXTREMELY LIMITED): LESS THAN 200 COPIES		
BAUER AUTO ISSUED AS 3-CASE INCENTIVE		
SKARSGARD AUTO ISSUED AS 6-CASE INCENTIVE		
NNO Alexander Skarsgard 6CI	75.00	150.00
NNO Allan Hyde VL	15.00	40.00
NNO Anna Camp L	15.00	40.00
NNO Anna Paquin EL	75.00	150.00
NNO Brit Morgan VL	8.00	20.00
NNO Carrie Preston L	6.00	15.00
NNO Courtney Ford L	10.00	25.00
NNO Deborah Ann Woll L	50.00	100.00
NNO Kevin Alejandro L	6.00	15.00
NNO Kristin Bauer 3CI	20.00	50.00
NNO Lauren Bowles L	6.00	15.00
NNO Lindsay Pulsipher L	6.00	15.00
NNO Lizzy Caplan VL	20.00	50.00
NNO Mariana Klaveno L	8.00	20.00
NNO Melissa Rauch	30.00	75.00
NNO Michael Raymond James L	6.00	15.00
NNO Michelle Forbes EL	15.00	40.00
NNO Nelsan Ellis L	6.00	15.00
NNO Raoul Trujillo L	6.00	15.00
NNO Stephen Moyer EL	75.00	150.00
NNO Todd Lowe VL	8.00	20.00

2012 True Blood Premiere Black and White

COMPLETE SET (6)	10.00	25.00
COMMON CARD (BW1-BW6)	3.00	8.00
STATED ODDS 1:18		
BW1 Sookie Stackhouse	4.00	10.00
BW2 Bill Compton	4.00	10.00

2012 True Blood Premiere Characters

COMPLETE SET (9)	10.00	25.00
COMMON CARD (D1-D9)	2.00	5.00
STATED ODDS 1:12		

2012 True Blood Premiere Full Bleed Autographs

COMMON AUTO (UNNUMBERED)	5.00	12.00
OVERALL AUTO ODDS 2 PER BOX		
L (LIMITED): 300-500 COPIES		
VL (VERY LIMITED): 200-300 COPIES		
NNO Brit Morgan L	6.00	15.00
NNO Courtney Ford L	8.00	20.00
NNO Lizzy Caplan VL	20.00	40.00

2012 True Blood Premiere Quotables

COMPLETE SET (9)	8.00	20.00
COMPLETE SET W/SP (10)	20.00	50.00
COMMON CARD (Q1-Q9)	2.00	5.00
STATED ODDS 1:12		
Q10 ISSUED AS A RITTENHOUSE REWARD		
Q10 I'm Sorry You Fell In Love RR	10.00	25.00

2012 True Blood Premiere Shadowbox

COMPLETE SET (4)	25.00	50.00
COMMON CARD (UNNUMBERED)	6.00	15.00
STATED ODDS 1:72		

2012 True Blood Premiere Promos

COMPLETE SET (5)	6.00	15.00
COMMON PROMO	1.25	3.00
P3 Sookie/Bill ALB	6.00	15.00

2014 True Blood Season Six Collector's Set

COMP. SET w/o AU's (20)	8.00	20.00
COMP. FACT. SET (30)	80.00	120.00
COMMON CARD (123-142)	.60	1.25
ANNOUNCED PRINT RUN 500 SETS		

2014 True Blood Season Six Collector's Set Autographs

COMMON AUTO	6.00	15.00
AUTOGRAPH SET INCLUDED IN FACT. SET		
NNO Janina Gavankar	12.00	30.00
NNO Kelly Overton	10.00	25.00
NNO Rutina Wesley	12.00	30.00
NNO Ryan Kwanten	15.00	40.00
NNO Valentina Cervi	15.00	40.00

2014 True Blood Season Six Collector's Set Incentives

MOYER AU ISSUED AS 3-SET INCENTIVE		
SKARSGARD AU ISSUED AS 6-SET INCENTIVE		
1 Alex Skarsgard silver 6SI	60.00	120.00
2 Stephen Moyer 3SI	50.00	100.00

2015 True Blood Season Seven Collector's Set

COMPLETE SET w/o AU's (10)	6.00	15.00
COMPLETE FACTORY SET (15)	30.00	80.00
COMMON CARD (1-10)	1.25	3.00

2015 True Blood Season Seven Collector's Set Autographs

COMMON AUTO	6.00	15.00
NNO Chris Heyerdahl B	8.00	20.00
NNO Chris Heyerdahl FB	8.00	20.00
NNO Rutina Wesley	12.00	30.00
NNO Ryan Kwanten	15.00	40.00

1992 Eclipse True Crime

COMPLETE SET (220)	12.00	30.00
COMPLETE SER.1 SET (110)	8.00	20.00
COMPLETE SER.2 SET (110)	8.00	20.00
UNOPENED SER.1 BOX (36 PACKS)	30.00	40.00
UNOPENED SER.1 PACK (12 CARDS)	1.00	1.50
UNOPENED SER.2 BOX (36 PACKS)	20.00	30.00
UNOPENED SER.2 PACK (12 CARDS)	1.00	1.25
COMMON SER.1 CARD (1-110)	.12	.30
COMMON SER.2 CARD (111-220)	.12	.30
H1 Electric Chair Hologram/1000*	50.00	100.00
P179 Prototype Card	.75	2.00

1992 Eclipse True Crime Rodney King

COMPLETE SET (4)	6.00	15.00
COMMON CARD (A-D)	2.00	5.00
RANDOMLY INSERTED INTO PACKS		

1984 WTW Productions True Spy Stories Reprints

COMPLETE SET (24)	6.00	15.00
COMMON CARD (1-24)	.40	1.00

2011 The Tudors Seasons One Two and Three

COMPLETE SET (72)	6.00	15.00
COMMON CARD (1-72)	.15	.40

2011 The Tudors Seasons One Two and Three Autographs

COMMON AUTO	5.00	12.00
OVERALL AUTO ODDS 1:1		
TAGA Gabrielle Anwar	15.00	40.00
TAJF James Frain	6.00	15.00
TAJM Jonathan Rhys Meyers	15.00	40.00
TAMK Maria Doyle Kennedy	12.00	30.00
TAND Natalie Dormer	25.00	60.00
TASB Sarah Bolger	10.00	25.00
TATM Tamzin Merchant	10.00	25.00

2011 The Tudors Seasons One Two and Three Costumes

COMMON CARD	12.00	30.00
OVERALL COSTUME/PROP ODDS 1:1		
STATED PRINT RUN 200 SER. #'d SETS		
ABBD Anne Boleyn	15.00	40.00
ABGD Anne Boleyn	15.00	40.00
ABWG Anne Boleyn	15.00	40.00
JSGD Jane Seymour	15.00	40.00
JSPD Jane Seymour	15.00	40.00
KHBC King Henry VIII	15.00	40.00
KHCS King Henry VIII	15.00	40.00
KHGL King Henry VIII	15.00	40.00
KHNC King Henry VIII	15.00	40.00
KHST King Henry VIII	15.00	40.00
HJD J.Seymour/Henry VIII	15.00	40.00

2011 The Tudors Seasons One Two and Three Heads Will Roll

COMPLETE SET (9)	15.00	30.00
COMMON CARD (HWR1-HWR9)	2.50	6.00
OVERALL INSERT ODDS 9 PER BOX		

2011 The Tudors Seasons One Two and Three Henry's Legacy

COMPLETE SET (3)	5.00	12.00
COMMON CARD (HL1-HL3)	2.50	6.00
OVERALL INSERT ODDS 9 PER BOX		

2011 The Tudors Seasons One Two and Three Location

COMPLETE SET (9)	10.00	20.00
OVERALL INSERT ODDS 9 PER BOX		

2011 The Tudors Seasons One Two and Three Props

COMMON CARD	15.00	30.00
OVERALL COSTUME/PROP ODDS ONE PER BOX		
STATED PRINT RUN 200 SER. #'d SETS		
TQ Quills	20.00	40.00
TKM The King's Mirror/100	20.00	40.00
TMP Lady Ursula's Painting	20.00	40.00
TWP Five Wounds Poster	20.00	40.00

2011 The Tudors Seasons One Two and Three The Leisurely King

COMPLETE SET (6)	5.00	12.00
COMMON CARD (LK1-LK6)	2.00	5.00
OVERALL INSERT ODDS 9 PER BOX		

2013 The Tudors The Final Season

CL The Tudors CL	1.50	4.00

2013 The Tudors The Final Season Autographs

COMMON AUTO	8.00	20.00
JM Jonathan Rhys Meyers	30.00	75.00

2013 The Tudors The Final Season Costumes

COMMON CARD (C1-C11)	10.00	25.00
C2 Henry Cavill/155	15.00	40.00
C6 Henry Cavill/155	15.00	40.00
C11 Jonahan Rhys Meyers/65	30.00	75.00

2013 The Tudors The Final Season Props

COMMON CARD (P1-P8)	12.00	30.00
P2 Queen Catherine's Quill/30	60.00	120.00

1992 Mystery Playhouse Tune in for Terror

COMPLETE SET (33)	5.00	12.00
UNOPENED BOX (PACKS)		
UNOPENED PACK (CARDS)		
COMMON CARD	.20	.50
B1 Prototype Strip Case-Topper	2.00	5.00
B2 Bonus Coupon!	2.00	5.00

1992 Mystery Playhouse Tune in for Terror Promos

COMMON CARD	2.00	5.00
43 Hairy Monster	4.00	10.00
44 Jar of Acid	4.00	10.00
45 The Old Hermit	4.00	10.00
46 Shrunken Head	4.00	10.00
47 Terror Out of Space	4.00	10.00
48 Mask of Medusa	4.00	10.00

1992 Mystery Playhouse Tune in for Terror Stickers

COMPLETE SET (9)	1.25	3.00
COMMON CARD	.20	.50
STATED ODDS 1:SET PER FACTORY SET		

1994 TV Week Series 1

COMPLETE SET (24)	30.00	75.00
COMMON CARD (1-24)	2.00	5.00
*GOLD: .75X TO 2X BASIC CARDS	4.00	10.00

1993 Imagine TV's Greatest Hits Promos

1 The Dick Van Dyke Show	.75	2.00
2 The Invaders	.75	2.00

1995 Comic Images 20 Years of The Rocky Horror Picture Show

COMPLETE SET (90)	5.00	12.00
UNOPENED BOX (36 PACKS)	25.00	40.00
UNOPENED PACK (7 CARDS)	.75	1.00
COMMON CARD (1-90)	.10	.25
MEDALLION 1:108		
NNO Medallion/837*	8.00	20.00
NNO This ain't no time warp PROMO	1.50	4.00
NNO Uncut Sheet	4.00	10.00

1995 Comic Images 20 Years of The Rocky Horror Picture Show Janet and Brad

COMPLETE SET (3)	5.00	12.00
COMMON CARD (1-3)	2.50	6.00
RANDOMLY INSERTED INTO PACKS		

1995 Comic Images 20 Years of The Rocky Horror Picture Show Sweet Transvestite

COMPLETE SET (2)	5.00	12.00
COMMON CARD (1-2)	3.00	8.00
RANDOMLY INSERTED INTO PACKS		

1987 Topps 21 Jump Street

COMPLETE SET (44)	4.00	10.00
UNOPENED BOX (48 PACKS)	40.00	60.00
UNOPENED PACK (5 STICKER-CARDS)	1.50	3.00
COMMON STICKER-CARD (1-44)	.15	.40

2003 24 Seasons One and Two

COMPLETE SET (90)	8.00	20.00
UNOPENED BOX (36 PACKS)	50.00	60.00
UNOPENED PACK (7 CARDS)	2.00	2.25
COMMON CARD (1-90)	.15	.40
NNO 6-Card Panel		

2003 24 Seasons One and Two Autographs

COMMON AUTO (A1-A7)	5.00	12.00
STATED ODDS 1:36		
A2 Penny Johnson Jerald	10.00	25.00
A3 Carlos Bernard	10.00	25.00

2003 24 Seasons One and Two Costumes

COMMON COSTUME (M1-M6)	8.00	20.00
STATED ODDS 1:36		
M2 Kim Bauer - shirt CT	15.00	40.00
M3 Senator Palmer	60.00	120.00
Tie		

2003 24 Seasons One and Two Moment of Truth

COMPLETE SET (6)	8.00	20.00
COMMON CARD (C1-C6)	2.00	5.00
STATED ODDS 1:12		

2003 24 Seasons One and Two Promos

COMMON CARD	2.00	5.00
P1 Jack Bauer	4.00	10.00
P2 President Palmer	3.00	8.00
P3 Group of five	3.00	8.00
NNO Card Album 6-Card Panel		

2005 24 Season Three

COMPLETE SET (72)	6.00	15.00
UNOPENED BOX (36 PACKS)	50.00	60.00
UNOPENED PACK (6 CARDS)	1.75	2.00
COMMON CARD (1-72)	.15	.40
NNO Card Album 6-Card Panel		

2005 24 Season Three Autographs

COMMON AUTO (A1-A6)	5.00	12.00
STATED ODDS 1:36		
A3 WAS NOT ISSUED		
A1 Kim Raver	12.00	30.00
A6 Mary Lynn Rajskub	10.00	25.00

2005 24 Season Three Costumes

COMMON COSTUME (M1-M6)	6.00	15.00
STATED ODDS 1:36		
M3 ISSUED AS CASE TOPPER		
M3 Jack Bauer - jacket CT	10.00	20.00

2006 24 Season Four Previews

COMPLETE SET (9)	8.00	20.00
COMMON CARD (PS1-PS9)	1.25	3.00

2006 24 Season Four

COMPLETE SET (90)	6.00	15.00
UNOPENED BOX (36 PACKS)	55.00	70.00
UNOPENED PACK (7 CARDS)	2.00	2.50
COMMON CARD (1-90)	.15	.40

2006 24 Season Four Autographs

COMMON AUTO	6.00	15.00
STATED ODDS 1:36		
NNO Aisha Tyler	25.00	60.00
NNO Carlos Bernard	12.00	30.00
NNO Gregory Itzin	12.00	30.00
NNO Lana Parrilla	30.00	75.00
NNO Louis Lombardi	8.00	20.00
NNO Mary Lynn Rajskub	10.00	25.00
NNO Shohreh Aghdashloo	12.00	30.00

2006 24 Season Four Case-Incentive Costumes

COMMON COSTUME (Ci1-Ci3)	12.00	30.00
Ci1 ISSUED AS 2-CASE INCENTIVE		
Ci2 ISSUED AS 5-CASE INCENTIVE		
Ci3 ISSUED AS 10-CASE INCENTIVE		
Ci2 President Keeler 5CI	50.00	100.00
Ci3 James Heller 10CI	80.00	150.00

2006 24 Season Four Case-Topper Costumes

COMMON COSTUME (CT1-CT2)	15.00	40.00
STATED ODDS ONE PER CASE		
CT2 Jack Bauer	15.00	40.00

2006 24 Season Four Character Box-Toppers

COMPLETE SET (3)	8.00	20.00
COMMON CARD (BT1-BT3)	3.00	8.00
STATED ODDS 1:BOX		

2006 24 Season Four Costumes

COMMON COSTUME (C1-C12)	6.00	15.00
STATED ODDS 1:36		
C1 Jack Bauer/125	20.00	50.00
C2 Chloe O'Brian/500	15.00	40.00
C3 Tony Almeida/150	15.00	40.00
C4 Habib Marwan/290	8.00	20.00
C6 Curtis Manning/125	12.00	30.00
C7 Navi Araz/325	8.00	20.00
C8 Thomas Sherek/200	8.00	20.00
C9 Edgar Stiles/195	8.00	20.00
C10 Richard Hell/200	8.00	20.00

2006 24 Season Four Props

COMMON PROP (P1-P7)	10.00	25.00
STATED ODDS 1:120		
P2 CTU Folder/150	15.00	40.00
P3 James Heller Gag/90	60.00	120.00
P4 Jack Bauer Tie and CTU Badge/60	120.00	250.00
P5 Embassy Folder cover/190	15.00	40.00
P6 Playbook/125	50.00	100.00

2006 24 Season Four Puzzle

COMPLETE SET (9)	4.00	10.00
COMMON CARD (PZ1-PZ9)	.75	2.00
STATED ODDS 5:36		

2006 24 Season Four Rare Foil

COMPLETE SET (6)	5.00	12.00
COMMON CARD (R1-R6)	1.25	3.00
STATED ODDS 1:12		

2006 24 Season Four Ultra Rare Foil

COMPLETE SET (3)	5.00	12.00
COMMON CARD (UR1-UR3)	2.50	6.00
STATED ODDS 1:36		

2006 24 Season Four Promos

COMPLETE SET (4)	6.00	15.00
COMMON CARD	2.00	5.00

2007 24 Season Four Expansion

COMPLETE SET (90)	6.00	15.00
UNOPENED BOX (36 PACKS)	55.00	70.00
UNOPENED PACK (7 CARDS)	2.00	2.50
COMMON CARD (1-90)	.15	.40

2007 24 Season Four Expansion Autograph Costumes

COMMON AUTO	12.00	30.00
OVERALL AUTO ODDS 1:36		
NNO Gregory Itzin	15.00	40.00
NNO Mary Lynn Rajskub	25.00	60.00
NNO Roger Cross SDCC	15.00	40.00

2007 24 Season Four Expansion Autographs

COMMON AUTO	6.00	15.00
OVERALL AUTO ODDS 1:36		
NNO Dennis Haysbert	50.00	100.00
NNO Geoff Pierson	8.00	20.00
NNO Glenn Morshower	12.00	30.00
NNO James Morrison	10.00	25.00
NNO John Allen Nelson	8.00	20.00
NNO Tomas Arana	8.00	20.00
NNO Tzi Ma	10.00	25.00
NNO Gregory Itzin/Dennis Haysbert	150.00	300.00

2007 24 Season Four Expansion Box-Toppers

COMPLETE SET (3)	5.00	12.00
COMMON CARD (BT1-BT3)	2.50	6.00
STATED ODDS 1:BOX		

2007 24 Season Four Expansion Case-Incentive Props

Ci1 Marwans Hideout/115 2CI	12.00	30.00
Ci2 Presidential Case/70 5CI	50.00	100.00
Ci3 Detonator Computer Chip/55 10CI	80.00	150.00

2007 24 Season Four Expansion Case-Topper Costumes

COMMON COSTUME (CT1-CT2)	20.00	50.00
STATED ODDS 1:CASE		

2007 24 Season Four Expansion Costumes

COMMON COSTUME (C1-C12)	6.00	15.00
STATED ODDS 1:36		
STATED PRINT RUN 90-350		
C1 Jack Bauer/90	120.00	250.00
C4 Tony Almeida/90	30.00	80.00
C11 Chloe O'Brian/105	20.00	50.00

2007 24 Season Four Expansion Props

COMMON PROP (P1-P9)	12.00	30.00
STATED ODDS 1:90		
STATED PRINT RUN 60-140		
P1 CTU Patch/60	100.00	200.00
P4 Train Schedule/90	100.00	200.00
P8 Playbook Pages/100	25.00	60.00
P9 Plant Diagram/70	80.00	150.00

2007 24 Season Four Expansion Puzzle

COMPLETE SET (9)	5.00	12.00
COMMON CARD (PZ1-PZ9)	1.00	2.50
STATED ODDS 1:12		

2007 24 Season Four Expansion Rare Foil

COMPLETE SET (6)	6.00	15.00
COMMON CARD (R1-R6)	1.50	4.00
STATED ODDS 1:18		

2007 24 Season Four Expansion Ultra Rare Foil

COMPLETE SET (3)	6.00	15.00
COMMON CARD (UR1-UR3)	2.50	6.00
STATED ODDS 1:36		

2007 24 Season Four Expansion Promos

COMMON CARD (P1-P3)	2.00	5.00
P3 Coming February 2007 ALB	8.00	20.00

2008 24 Season Five

COMPLETE SET (90)	6.00	15.00
UNOPENED BOX (36 PACKS)	50.00	60.00
UNOPENED PACK (7 CARDS)	2.00	2.50
COMMON CARD (1-90)	.15	.40

2008 24 Season Five Autographs

COMMON AUTO	8.00	20.00
STATED ODDS 1:36		
NNO Carlo Rota	10.00	25.00
NNO Connie Britton	15.00	40.00
NNO James Morrison	10.00	25.00
NNO Jayne Atkinson	15.00	40.00
NNO Jean Smart	10.00	25.00
NNO Mark Sheppard	12.00	30.00
NNO Mary Lynn Rajskub	15.00	40.00
NNO Ray Wise	12.00	30.00
NNO Sean Astin	20.00	50.00

2008 24 Season Five Box-Toppers

COMPLETE SET (3)	6.00	15.00
COMMON CARD (BT1-BT3)	2.50	6.00
STATED ODDS 1:BOX		

2008 24 Season Five Case-Incentive Costumes

COMMON COSTUME	20.00	50.00
CI2 Chloe O'Brian - shirt/85 5CI	40.00	80.00
CI3 Kim Bauer - blouse/63 10CI	60.00	120.00

2008 24 Season Five Case-Topper Costumes

COMPLETE SET (2)	20.00	50.00
COMMON CARD	12.00	30.00
STATED ODDS ONE PER CASE		

2008 24 Season Five Costumes

COMMON COSTUME (C1-C15)	5.00	12.00
STATED ODDS 1:36		
PRINT RUN 90-265		
C1 Jack Bauer (jacket)/115	30.00	60.00
C2 President Palmer (shirt)/105	8.00	20.00
C3 Haas (jacket)200	6.00	15.00

C4 Tony Almeida (pants)/200 6.00 15.00
C5 Michelle Dessler (pants)/175 15.00 40.00
C6 Chloe O'Brian (sweater)/115 15.00 40.00
C7 Bill Buchanan (tie)/115 20.00 40.00
C8 Walt Cummings (tie)/90 40.00 80.00
C10 Curtis Manning (shirt)/115 8.00 20.00
C14 Wayne Palmer (sweater)/165 6.00 15.00
C15 Anton Beresch (mask)/115 8.00 20.00

2008 24 Season Five Props

COMMON PROP (P1-P6; S6P1-S6P3) 6.00 15.00
STATED PRINT RUN 60-190
P2 CTU Folder/165 10.00 25.00
P4 Bloody Bandages/115 30.00 60.00
P5 CTU ID Card/60 100.00 200.00
P6 Timing Mechanism/90 50.00 100.00
P7 Mall Bag/150 35.00 70.00
P8 Terrorist's Bomb Vest/110 35.00 70.00
S6P1 Explosion Debris (stool)/100 40.00 80.00
S6P2 Explosion Debris (lectern)/90 40.00 80.00
S6P3 Explosion Debris (body)/80 40.00 80.00

2008 24 Season Five Puzzle

COMPLETE SET (9) 4.00 10.00
COMMON CARD (PZ1-PZ9) .75 2.00
STATED ODDS 1:9

2008 24 Season Five Rare Foil

COMPLETE SET (6) 4.00 10.00
COMMON CARD (R1-R6) 1.00 2.50
STATED ODDS 1:12

2008 24 Season Five Ultra Rare Foil

COMPLETE SET (3) 5.00 12.00
COMMON CARD (UR1-UR3) 2.50 6.00
STATED ODDS 1:36

2008 24 Season Five Promos

COMMON CARD 1.00 2.50
P3 Jack Bauer ALB 2.00 5.00

Twilight

2008 Twilight

COMPLETE SET (72) 8.00 20.00
COMMON CARD (1-72) .25 .60
CL1 ISSUED AS CASE TOPPER
HT1 ISSUED AS HOT TOPIC EXCLUSIVE
CL1 Protector CT 25.00 50.00
HT1 Who Is Bella HOT TOPIC 3.00 8.00

2008 Twilight Always Puzzle

COMPLETE SET (9) 25.00 60.00
COMMON CARD (AL1-AL9) 4.00 10.00
STATED ODDS 1:11
PAN 9-Card Panel Always Set/199

2008 Twilight Different

COMPLETE SET (6) 8.00 20.00
COMMON CARD (D1-D6) 1.50 4.00
STATED ODDS 1:17

2008 Twilight In Pursuit

COMPLETE SET (3) 12.00 30.00
COMMON CARD (IP1-IP3) 5.00 12.00
STATED ODDS 1:23

2008 Twilight Pieceworks

COMMON CARD (PW1-PW12) 15.00 40.00
STATED ODDS 1:24
PW1 Bella Swan - Jacket 150.00 250.00
PW2 Edward Cullen - Shirt 250.00 400.00
PW3 Alice Cullen - Jacket 60.00 120.00
PW4 Jasper Cullen - Jacket 75.00 150.00
PW6 Rosalie Hale - Vest 30.00 80.00
PW7 Jacob Black - Jeans 50.00 100.00
PW9 Carlisle Cullen - Shirt 60.00 120.00
PW10 Victoria - Shirt 50.00 100.00
PW12 James - Jeans 50.00 100.00

2008 Twilight Promos

P1 Bella/Edward GEN 1.50 4.00
Pi Bella/Billy/Charlie/Inkworks.com 40.00 80.00
PMS Bella/Edward CON 4.00 10.00
PPS Belle/Edward/Philly 4.00 10.00
PUK Bella UK 4.00 10.00

2009-12 Summit Entertainment Twilight All About Edward NAT Complete Series

COMPLETE SET (48) 30.00 80.00
SERIES 1 (AAE1-AAE12) 1.25 3.00
SERIES 2 (AAE21-AAE29) 1.25 3.00
SERIES 3 (AAE31-AAE39) 1.25 3.00
SERIES 4 (AAE41-AAE49) 1.25 3.00
SERIES 5 (AAE51-AAE59) 1.25 3.00

2009 Twilight New Moon

COMPLETE SET (84) 10.00 25.00
COMMON CARD (1-84) .25 .60
CL1 STATED ODDS 1:104
HT1 STATED ODDS 1:24 HOT TOPIC PACKS
T1 STATED ODDS 1:15 TARGET PACKS
CL1 Reckless 6.00 15.00
HT1 Temptations 25.00 50.00
T1 Goodbye 4.00 10.00

2009 Twilight New Moon Autographs

STATED ODDS 1:24 UPDATE PACKS
NNO Ashley Green 10.00 25.00
NNO Peter Facinelli 4.00 10.00

2009 Twilight New Moon Puzzle

COMPLETE SET (9) 10.00 25.00
COMMON CARD (T1-T9) 2.00 5.00
STATED ODDS 1:7

2009 Twilight New Moon Seeing Alice

COMPLETE SET (3) 8.00 20.00
STATED ODDS 1:23

2009 Twilight New Moon The Wolfpack Puzzle

COMPLETE SET (6) 8.00 20.00
STATED ODDS 1:11

2009 Twilight New Moon Volturi Coven

COMPLETE SET (6) 8.00 20.00
COMMON CARD (VO1-VO6) 2.50 6.00
STATED ODDS 1:11

2009 Twilight New Moon SDCC Characters

COMPLETE SET (4) 2.50 6.00
1 Bella Swan, Edward, and Jacob Black 1.25 3.00
2 Bella 1.25 3.00
3 Edward 1.25 3.00
4 Jacob 1.25 3.00

2010 Twilight Eclipse

COMPLETE SET (160) 25.00 50.00
COMP.SER. 1 SET (80) 15.00 30.00
COMP.SER. 2 SET (80) 15.00 30.00
B1 STATED ODDS 1:104 SER. 1 PACKS
H1 STATED ODDS 1:104 SER. 2 PACKS
B1 Marry Me 5.00 12.00
H1 Welcome to the Army 30.00 60.00

2010 Twilight Eclipse Protagonists

COMPLETE SET (3) 5.00 12.00
COMMON CAPD (F1-F3) 3.00 8.00
STATED ODDS 1:23 SERIES 1 PACKS

2010 Twilight Eclipse Puzzle

COMPLETE SET (9) 8.00 20.00
COMMON CARD (A1-A9) 1.50 4.00
STATED ODDS 1:7

2010 Twilight Eclipse Riley

COMPLETE SET (3) 10.00 25.00
COMMON CARD (G1-G3) 5.00 12.00
STATED ODDS 1:23

2010 Twilight Eclipse The Cullens Puzzle

COMPLETE SET (6) 6.00 15.00
COMMON CARD (D1-D6) 2.00 5.00
STATED ODDS 1:11

2010 Twilight Eclipse The Wolfpack Puzzle

COMPLETE SET (6) 6.00 15.00
COMMON CARD (WP1-WP6) 1.50 4.00
STATED ODDS 1:11

2010 Twilight Eclipse Trio and Villains Puzzle

COMPLETE SET (9) 15.00 30.00
COMMON CARD (C1-C9) 2.50 6.00
STATED ODDS 1:7 SERIES 2 PACKS

2010 Twilight Eclipse Volturi Coven

COMPLETE SET (12) 10.00 25.00
COMP.SER. 1 SET (6) 5.00 12.00
COMP.SER. 2 SET (6) 5.00 12.00
COMMON CARD (VO1-VO12) 1.50 4.00
VO1-VO6 STATED ODDS 1:11 SER. 1 PACKS
VO7-VO12 STATED ODDS 1:11 SER. 2 PACKS

2010 Twilight Eclipse All About Jacob

COMPLETE SET (9) 6.00 15.00
COMMON CARD (AAJ1 - AAJ9) 1.25 3.00

2010 Twilight Eclipse Faces of Battle The Battle of Forks

COMPLETE SET (8) 15.00 40.00
COMMON CARD 2.50 6.00

2010 Twilight Eclipse Fan Club Promos

COMPLETE SET (20) 30.00 80.00
COMMON CARD 2.00 5.00

2010 Twilight Eclipse Fold-Out Booklet Promos

COMPLETE SET (5) 8.00 20.00
COMMON CARD 2.00 5.00

2010 Twilight Eclipse Master Portrait Promos

COMPLETE SET (26) 50.00 100.00
COMMON CARD 2.00 5.00

2010 Twilight Eclipse On the Set Promos

COMPLETE SET (15) 12.00 30.00
COMMON CARD (P1-P15) 1.50 4.00

2010 Twilight Eclipse Portrait Promos

COMPLETE SET (7) 8.00 20.00
COMMON CARD (1-7) 2.50 6.00

2010 Twilight Eclipse Red Border Promos

COMPLETE SET (10) 10.00 25.00
COMMON CARD 2.00 5.00

2010 Twilight Eclipse Red Ribbon Border Promos

COMPLETE SET (10) 8.00 20.00
COMMON CARD 1.50 4.00

2010 Twilight Eclipse Signature

COMPLETE SET (21) 20.00 50.00
COMMON CARD (SS1-SS21) 1.50 4.00
SS1 Robert Pattinson 3.00 8.00

2010 Twilight Eclipse Twilightgraphs Complete Series

COMPLETE SET (20) 25.00 60.00
COMMON CARD (1-20) 2.00 5.00

2011 Twilight Breaking Dawn Limited Editions Promos

COMPLETE SET (36) 100.00 175.00
COMMON CARD (P1-P36) 2.50 6.00
SP1 9 Cast Montage

2011 Twilight Breaking Dawn Part 1 Limited Edition Promos

COMPLETE SET (11) 15.00 40.00
COMMON CARD 2.50 6.00

2011 Twilight Breaking Dawn Part 1 NAT Complete Promo Series

COMPLETE SET (33) 30.00 80.00
COMMON CARD (1-33) 2.00 5.00

2011 Twilight Breaking Dawn Part 1 SDCC Bella Promos

COMPLETE SET (5) 6.00 15.00
COMMON CARD 1.50 4.00

2011 Twilight Breaking Dawn Part 1 SDCC Edward Promos

COMPLETE SET (5) 8.00 20.00
COMMON CARD 2.00 5.00

2011 Twilight Breaking Dawn Part 1 Wedding Album Promos

COMPLETE SET (3) 5.00 12.00
COMMON CARD 2.50 6.00

2011 Twilight Breaking Dawn Part 1 Wedding Album Set

COMPLETE SET (12) 15.00 40.00
COMMON CARD 2.50 6.00

2012 Twilight Breaking Dawn Part 2

COMPLETE SET (72) 8.00 20.00
COMMON CARD (1-19) .40 1.00
COMMON CARD (20-72) .25 .60

2012 Twilight Breaking Dawn Part 2 Twilightgraphs

COMPLETE SET (11) 10.00 25.00
COMMON CARD 2.00 5.00
*PARALLEL: 1.5X TO 4X BASIC CARDS

1999 Rittenhouse Twilight Zone

COMPLETE SET (72) 5.00 12.00
UNOPENED BOX (36 PACKS) 200.00 300.00
UNOPENED PACK (9 CARDS) 5.00 8.00
COMMON CARD (1-72) .15 .40
*BLACK PP/99: 2X TO 5X BASIC CARDS
*CYAN PP/99: 2X TO 5X BASIC CARDS
*MAGENTA PP/99: 2X TO 5X BASIC CARDS
*YELLOW PP/99: 2X TO 5X BASIC CARDS
Z1 Checklist
UNC 72-Card Base Set Uncut Sheet/250

1999 Rittenhouse Twilight Zone Autograph Challenge

COMP.SET w/o SP (9) 10.00 25.00
COMMON CARD 2.00 5.00
STATED ODDS ONE PER PACK
Z Rod Serling SP 60.00 120.00

1999 Rittenhouse Twilight Zone Autographs

COMPLETE SET (18)
COMMON AUTO (A1-A19) 15.00 40.00
STATED ODDS TWO PER BOX
A19 ISSUED AS ALBUM EXCLUSIVE
A1 William Shatner 500.00 750.00
A2 Donna Douglas 30.00 75.00
A3 Richard Kiel 75.00 150.00
A5 Ann Blyth 20.00 50.00
A6 Kevin McCarthy 30.00 75.00
A7 Martin Milner 20.00 50.00
A8 Vera Miles 25.00 60.00
A9 Rod Taylor 30.00 75.00
A10 William Windom 20.00 50.00
A12 Fritz Weaver 25.00 60.00
A14 Anne Francis 60.00 120.00
A17 Cloris Leachman 50.00 100.00

A18 Bill Mumy 30.00 75.00
A19 Ruta Lee ALB 20.00 50.00

1999 Rittenhouse Twilight Zone Commemorative

COMPLETE SET (2) 2.50 6.00
COMMON CARD (C1-C2) 1.50 4.00
STATED ODDS 1:36

1999 Rittenhouse Twilight Zone Stars

COMPLETE SET (9) 6.00 15.00
COMMON CARD (S1-S9) .75 2.00
RANDOMLY INSERTED INTO PACKS

2020 Rittenhouse Twilight Zone Archives

COMPLETE SET (64) 6.00 15.00
UNOPENED BOX (24 PACKS) 75.00 125.00
UNOPENED PACK (5 CARDS) 3.00 5.00
UNOPENED ARCHIVE BOX 1000.00 1500.00
COMMON CARD (J93-J156) .25 .60
*FOIL/150: 3X TO 8X BASIC CARDS

2020 Rittenhouse Twilight Zone Archives Acetate

COMPLETE SET (9) 60.00 120.00
COMMON CARD (PC1-PC9) 10.00 25.00
STATED ODDS 1:144

2020 Rittenhouse Twilight Zone Archives Autographs

COMMON AUTO (A172-A177) 5.00 12.00
OVERALL AUTO ODDS 1:12
L = 300-500
A173 Derrik Lewis L 6.00 15.00
A174a Pamela Austin L 20.00 50.00
A174b Pamela Austin AB 200.00 350.00

2020 Rittenhouse Twilight Zone Archives Case-Topper

CT1 60th Anniversary Montage 8.00 20.00

2020 Rittenhouse Twilight Zone Archives Dual Autographed Booklets

NNO Rod Serling/Billy Mumy 550.00 1000.00
NNO Rod Serling/William Shatner 800.00 1400.00

2020 Rittenhouse Twilight Zone Archives Dual Autographs

COMMON AUTO 12.00 30.00
OVERALL AUTO ODDS 1:12
L = 300-500
NNO Tim Stafford/Jeffrey Byron L 10.00 25.00

2020 Rittenhouse Twilight Zone Archives Inscription Autographs

COMMON ALEXANDER 8.00 20.00
COMMON ASTIN 20.00 50.00
COMMON BADHAM 10.00 25.00
COMMON BARRIE 15.00 40.00
COMMON BEAN 12.00 30.00
COMMON BEECHER 15.00 40.00
COMMON BOWER 15.00 40.00
COMMON BYRON 12.00 30.00
COMMON CALL 10.00 25.00
COMMON DILLAWAY 15.00 40.00
COMMON GING 12.00 30.00
COMMON IRVIN 12.00 30.00
COMMON JACKSON 20.00 50.00
COMMON JILLIAN 30.00 75.00
COMMON MASAK 8.00 20.00
COMMON MORGAN 12.00 30.00
COMMON MUMY 75.00 150.00
COMMON RICHMAN 12.00 30.00
COMMON SCOTT 15.00 40.00
COMMON SHATNER 150.00 300.00
COMMON STAFFORD 15.00 40.00
COMMON TAKEI 30.00 75.00
COMMON TITUS 12.00 30.00
COMMON VAN PATTEN 25.00 60.00
COMMON WYNANT 8.00 20.00
OVERALL AUTO ODDS 1:12

2020 Rittenhouse Twilight Zone Archives Portfolio Print Autographs

PPA1 Billy Mumy (It's A Good Life) 30.00 75.00
(6-Case Incentive)
PPA2 William Shatner in
Nightmare At 20,000 Feet 125.00 250.00
(9-Case Incentive)

2020 Rittenhouse Twilight Zone Archives Portfolio Prints

COMPLETE SET (5) 8.00 20.00
COMMON CARD (C11-C15) 2.50 6.00
STATED ODDS 1:96

2020 Rittenhouse Twilight Zone Archives Portraits

COMPLETE SET (9) 6.00 15.00
COMMON CARD (POR10-POR18) 1.25 3.00
STATED ODDS 1:24

2020 Rittenhouse Twilight Zone Archives Stars of the Twilight Zone

COMPLETE SET (18) 10.00 25.00
COMMON CARD (S55-S72) 1.00 2.50
STATED ODDS 1:12

2020 Rittenhouse Twilight Zone Archives Twilight Zone Hall of Fame

COMPLETE SET (9) 100.00 200.00
COMMON CARD (H13-H21) 12.00 30.00
STATED ODDS 1:144

2020 Rittenhouse Twilight Zone Archives Promos

COMMON CARD (P1-P3) 1.50 4.00
P1 Collage 2.50 6.00
(General Distribution)
P3 Jack Klugman 30.00 75.00
(Album Exclusive)

2009 Complete Twilight Zone

COMPLETE SET (79) 5.00 12.00
UNOPENED BOX (24 PACKS) 65.00 75.00
UNOPENED PACK (5 CARDS) 2.75 3.00
COMMON CARD (1-79) .15 .40

2009 Complete Twilight Zone Autographs

COMMON AUTO 10.00 20.00
STATED ODDS 1:6
A126 ISSUED AS CASE INCENTIVE
A136 ISSUED AS 3-CASE INCENTIVE
A149 ISSUED AS 6-CASE INCENTIVE
ALL AUTOS LIMITED (300-500 COPIES) UNLESS NOTED
VL (VERY LIMITED): 200-300 COPIES
A098 Morgan Brittany 60.00 120.00
Susanne Cupito VL
A099 Mariette Hartley 25.00 60.00
A100 Tom Reese 10.00 25.00
A103 Brooke Hayward 30.00 75.00
A105 June Foray 100.00 200.00
A106 Dee Hartford 20.00 50.00
A107 Patrick Macnee 50.00 100.00
A111 Cliff Osmond VL 50.00 100.00
A112 Larrian Gillespie 20.00 50.00
A113 Sarah Marshall 15.00 40.00
A116 Mary Badham 20.00 50.00
A117 Jean Marsh 25.00 60.00
A118 Doris Singleton 15.00 40.00
A119 Arlene Martel (Arline Sax) 15.00 40.00
A120 Earl Holliman 10.00 25.00
A123 Linden Chiles 10.00 25.00
A124 Susan Harrison 20.00 50.00
A125 Paul Comi 15.00 40.00
A126 Dana Dillaway CT 30.00 75.00
A127 Tom Lowell 12.00 30.00
A128 Tim Stafford (Jeffrey Byron) VL 30.00 75.00
A129 Tim O'Connor 15.00 40.00
A134 Randy Boone 12.00 30.00
A135 Cliff Robertson 100.00 200.00
The Dummy VL
A136 Cliff Robertson/A Hundred Yards 3CI150.00 300.00
A141 John Astin 50.00 100.00
A143 Margarita Cordova 15.00 40.00
A148 Joyce Van Patten 20.00 50.00
A149 George Clayton Johnson (Writer) 6CI200.00 350.00

2009 Complete Twilight Zone In Motion

COMPLETE SET (18) 20.00 40.00
COMMON CARD (L1-L18) 1.50 4.00
STATED ODDS 1:12

2009 Complete Twilight Zone Life of It's Own

COMPLETE SET (9) 10.00 25.00
COMMON CARD (Z1-Z9) 1.50 4.00
STATED ODDS 1:12

2009 Complete Twilight Zone Portraits

COMPLETE SET (9) 10.00 25.00
COMMON CARD (POR1-POR9) 1.50 4.00
STATED ODDS 1:12

2009 Complete Twilight Zone Promos

COMMON CARD (P1-P3) .75 2.00
P3 Album Exclusive 3.00 8.00

2000 Twilight Zone The Next Dimension

COMPLETE SET (73) 5.00 12.00
UNOPENED BOX (40 PACKS) 200.00 300.00
UNOPENED PACK (9 CARDS) 5.00 8.00
COMMON CARD (73-144) .15 .40
*PP BLACK/50: 2.5X TO 6X BASIC CARDS
*PP CYAN/50: 2.5X TO 6X BASIC CARDS
*PP MAGENTA/50: 2.5X TO 6X BASIC CARDS
*PP YELLOW/50: 2.5X TO 6X BASIC CARDS
H1 SERIAL #'d TO 777
Z2 Checklist .15 .40
H1 Serling w/Charendoff AU
UNC 72-Card Base Set Uncut Sheet/99

2000 Twilight Zone The Next Dimension Autograph Challenge

COMP.SET w/o SP (8) 6.00 15.00
COMMON CARD 1.25 3.00
STATED ODDS ONE PER PACK
S S SP 225.00 450.00

2000 Twilight Zone The Next Dimension Autographs

COMMON AUTO (A20-A38) 10.00 25.00
STATED ODDS TWO PER BOX
A15 AUTOGRAPH CHALLENGE WINNER
A37 ISSUED AS ALBUM EXCLUSIVE
A38 ISSUED AS CASE TOPPER
A15 Elizabeth Allen WINNER 250.00 500.00
A20 William Shatner 300.00 600.00
A21 Beverly Garland 15.00 40.00
A22 Burt Reynolds 60.00 120.00
A25 Don Rickles 50.00 100.00
A27 Jean Carson 15.00 40.00
A29 Jack Klugman 30.00 75.00
A31 Peter Mark Richman 12.00 30.00
A32 James Best 30.00 75.00
A33 Sherry Jackson 20.00 50.00
A34 Buddy Ebsen 50.00 100.00
A36 Dennis Weaver 25.00 60.00

2000 Twilight Zone The Next Dimension Promos

COMMON CARD (P1-P3) .75 2.00
P3 William Shatner ALB 15.00 40.00

2000 Twilight Zone The Next Dimension Rod Serling

COMPLETE SET (3) 5.00 12.00
COMMON CARD (RS1-RS3) 2.00 5.00
STATED ODDS 1:40

2000 Twilight Zone The Next Dimension Twilight Zone Stars

COMPLETE SET (9) 6.00 15.00
COMMON CARD (S10-S18) .75 2.00
STATED ODDS 1:6

2019 Twilight Zone Rod Serling Edition

COMPLETE SET (156) 10.00 25.00
UNOPENED BOX (24 PACKS) 100.00 150.00
UNOPENED PACK (8 CARDS) 4.00 6.00
COMMON CARD (1-156) .15 .40

2019 Twilight Zone Rod Serling Edition Autographs

COMMON AUTO 5.00 12.00
STATED OVERALL ODDS 1:3
NNO Ann Jillian L 12.00 30.00
NNO Barbara Barrie L 6.00 15.00
NNO Billy Mumy EL 60.00 120.00
NNO Carol Byron L 6.00 15.00
NNO Denise Lynn L 6.00 15.00
NNO Jim Houghton L 6.00 15.00
NNO John Clarke S AB 550.00 1000.00
NNO John Considine L 6.00 15.00
NNO Martin Landau/Dan Hotaling VL 50.00 100.00
NNO Martin Landau/Mjr. Ivan Kuchenko VL 50.00 100.00
NNO Morgan Brittany/Nightmare as a Child L15.00 40.00
NNO Morgan Brittany/Valley of the Shadow L15.00 40.00
NNO Nehemiah Persoff L 15.00 40.00
NNO Shelley Fabares L 25.00 60.00

2019 Twilight Zone Rod Serling Edition Characters

COMPLETE SET (9) 30.00 75.00
COMMON CARD (M1-M9) 5.00 12.00
STATED ODDS 1:60

2019 Twilight Zone Rod Serling Edition Cut Signature

NNO Rod Serling/50 S 1000.00 2000.00

2019 Twilight Zone Rod Serling Edition Dual Autographs

DA2 D.Dillaway/V.Cartwright VL 20.00 50.00
NNO C.Leachman/Bill Mumy CI 75.00 150.00

2019 Twilight Zone Rod Serling Edition Inscription Autographs

COMMON BRITTANY 25.00 60.00
COMMON BRITTANY/CUPITO 25.00 60.00
COMMON CARTWRIGHT 25.00 60.00
COMMON FABARES 30.00 75.00
COMMON FOREST 75.00 150.00
COMMON HOLLIMAN 60.00 120.00
COMMON HOWARD 250.00 500.00
COMMON LEACHMAN 50.00 100.00
COMMON LEE 30.00 75.00
COMMON MUMY 125.00 250.00
COMMON SHATNER 200.00 350.00
STATED OVERALL ODDS 1:12
AI01 William Shatner
Gremlins S

2019 Twilight Zone Rod Serling Edition Opening Monologue Case-Toppers

COMPLETE SET (3) 10.00 25.00
COMMON CARD (M1-M3) 5.00 12.00
STATED ODDS 1:CASE

2019 Twilight Zone Rod Serling Edition Stars of the Twilight Zone

COMPLETE SET (18) 15.00 40.00
COMMON CARD (S37-S54) 1.25 3.00
STATED ODDS 1:12

2019 Twilight Zone Rod Serling Edition Twilight Zone Portfolio Prints Character Art

COMPLETE SET W/RR (10)
COMPLETE SET W/O RR (9) 10.00 25.00
COMMON CARD (C1-C9) 2.00 5.00
STATED ODDS 1:24
C10 IS RITTENHOUSE REWARD
C10 Barney Phillips as Haley/John Hoyt as Ross RR

2019 Twilight Zone Rod Serling Edition Twilight Zone Portfolio Prints The Serling Episodes

COMPLETE SET (92) 50.00 100.00

COMMON CARD (J1-J92) .75 2.00
STATED ODDS 1:3

2019 Twilight Zone Rod Serling Edition Promos

COMPLETE SET (3)
COMMON CARD (P1-P3) 1.50 4.00
P1 Rod Serling 2.50 6.00
P3 Bill Mumy 4.00 10.00
(Album Exclusive)

2005 Twilight Zone Science and Superstition

COMPLETE SET (73) 4.00 10.00
UNOPENED BOX (40 PACKS) 50.00 65.00
UNOPENED PACK (5 CARDS) 1.25 1.75
COMMON CARD (217-288) .10 .30
UNPRICED SERLING AUTO PRINT RUN 5
STATED ODDS OF STERLING AUTO 1:100,000
NNO Rod Serling HOF AU/5*

2005 Twilight Zone Science and Superstition Autographs

COMMON CARD (A66-A97) 6.00 15.00
STATED ODDS FOUR PER BOX
A97 ISSUED AS ALBUM EXCLUSIVE
L (LIMITED): 300-500 COPIES
VL (VERY LIMITED): 200-300 COPIES
A66 Barry Morse 12.00 30.00
A67 Ron Howard VL 400.00 800.00
A68 Joanne Linville 12.00 30.00
A72 Mickey Rooney L 60.00 120.00
A73 Sydney Pollack 15.00 40.00
A74 Alan Sues 8.00 20.00
A75 Lois Nettleton 15.00 40.00
A76A Jason Wingreen/Mr.Schuster L 25.00 60.00
A76B Jason Wingreen/The Bard L 25.00 60.00
A77 Veronica Cartwright 15.00 40.00
A80 Russell Johnson L 30.00 75.00
A82 Orson Bean L 25.00 60.00
A83 William Schallert 10.00 25.00
A85 Patricia Barry 8.00 20.00
A86 Susan Gordon 10.00 25.00
A87 Natalie Trundy 12.00 30.00
A90 Arte Johnson L 25.00 50.00
A92 Jeanne Cooper 10.00 25.00
A94 Kevin Hagen 10.00 25.00
A95 James Doohan L 300.00 500.00
A96 Anne Francis L 50.00 100.00
A97 Edson Stroll ALB 8.00 20.00

2005 Twilight Zone Science and Superstition The Quotable Twilight Zone

COMPLETE SET (18) 20.00 50.00
COMMON CARD (Q1-Q18) 1.25 3.00
STATED ODDS 1:7

2005 Twilight Zone Science and Superstition Twilight Zone Hall of Fame

COMPLETE SET (8) 250.00 500.00
COMMON CARD (H5-H12) 40.00 80.00
STATED ODDS 1:100
STATED PRINT RUN 333 SER. #'d SETS

2005 Twilight Zone Science and Superstition Twilight Zone Stars

COMPLETE SET (9) 8.00 20.00
COMMON CARD (S28-S36) 1.00 2.50
STATED ODDS 1:14

2005 Twilight Zone Science and Superstition Promos

COMPLETE SET (4) 5.00 12.00
COMMON CARD .75 2.00
P3 Rod Serling ALB 2.00 5.00
CP1 Group of Six CON 3.00 8.00

2002 Twilight Zone Shadows and Substance

COMPLETE SET (72) 5.00 12.00
UNOPENED BOX (40 PACKS) 75.00 125.00
UNOPENED PACK (9 CARDS) 2.00 3.00
COMMON CARD (145-216) .15 .40
Z3 Checklist
P1 Group Shot PROMO .75 2.00

2002 Twilight Zone Shadows and Substance Autographs

COMMON AUTO (A39-A65) 6.00 15.00
STATED ODDS FOUR PER BOX
A51A ISSUED AS CASE TOPPER
A65 ISSUED IN COLLECTORS ALBUM
CARDS A53, A54, A59, AND A60 WERE NOT ISSUED
A39 Dean Stockwell 30.00 75.00
A40 Patricia Breslin 20.00 50.00
A41 Hazel Court 20.00 50.00
A42 Jonathan Winters 50.00 100.00
A43 Jack Klugman 50.00 100.00
A44 Leonard Nimoy 250.00 500.00
A45 Russell Johnson 25.00 60.00
A46 Nan Martin 12.00 30.00
A48 Michael Constantine 10.00 25.00
A49 Bill Mumy 30.00 75.00
A50 Julie Newmar 100.00 200.00
A51A George Takei CT 30.00 75.00
A52A George Murdock 12.00 30.00
A52B H.M. Wynant 12.00 30.00
A55B Steve Forrest 10.00 25.00
A56A Jonathan Harris 60.00 120.00
A57 Arlene Martel 20.00 50.00
A61 Jacqueline Scott 12.00 30.00
A62 Gloria Pall 15.00 40.00
A63 Asa Maynor 12.00 30.00
A65 George Lindsey ALB 20.00 50.00

2002 Twilight Zone Shadows and Substance Twilight Zone Hall of Fame

COMPLETE SET (4) 100.00 200.00
COMMON CARD (H1-H4) 30.00 60.00
STATED ODDS 1:100

2002 Twilight Zone Shadows and Substance Twilight Zone Stars

COMPLETE SET (9) 6.00 15.00
COMMON CARD (S19-S27) 1.00 2.50
STATED ODDS 1:5

1991 Star Pics Twin Peaks

COMPLETE BOXED SET (76) 8.00 20.00
COMMON CARD (1-76) .20 .50
*LTD ED: SAME VALUE

1991 Star Pics Twin Peaks Autographs

COMMON AUTO 10.00 25.00
RANDOMLY INSERTED INTO BOXED SETS
4 Kyle McLachlan R 125.00 250.00
9 Michael Ontkean 125.00 250.00
10 Harry Goaz 50.00 100.00
11 Kimmy Robertson 30.00 75.00
12 Michael Horse 50.00 100.00
14 Sheryl Lee as Laura Palmer R 125.00 250.00
17 Russ Tamblyn 20.00 50.00
20 Lara Flynn Boyle 75.00 150.00
21 Austin Lynch 15.00 40.00
22 Sheryl Lee as Madeleine Ferguson 60.00 120.00
23 Jack Nance 25.00 60.00
28 Joan Chen R 50.00 100.00
34 Madchen Amick 100.00 200.00
37 Everett McGill 50.00 100.00
46 Richard Beymer 80.00 150.00
47 Sherilyn Fenn 120.00 250.00
59 Ray Wise 75.00 150.00
64 Don Davis 100.00 200.00

2018 Twin Peaks

COMPLETE SET (90) 8.00 20.00
UNOPENED BOX (24 PACKS) 75.00 90.00
UNOPENED PACK (5 CARDS) 3.00 4.00
COMMON CARD (1-90) .20 .50
*RETRO: 6X TO 15X BASIC CARDS

2018 Twin Peaks Autographed Costume

NNO Kyle MacLachlan 6CI 100.00 200.00

2018 Twin Peaks Case-Topper Insert

STATED ODDS 1:CASE
CT1 Laura Palmer Memorial 15.00 40.00

2018 Twin Peaks Characters

COMPLETE SET (42) 75.00 150.00
COMMON CARD (CC1-CC42) 2.00 5.00
STATED ODDS 1:12
CC1 Kyle MacLachlan as Dale Cooper 2.00 5.00
CC2 Michael Ontkean as Harry S. Truman 2.00 5.00
CC3 Sheryl Lee as Laura Palmer 2.00 5.00

2018 Twin Peaks Classic Autographs

COMMON AUTO 6.00 15.00
STATED OVERALL ODDS 1:12
REGULAR AUTO <500
L (LIMITED) = 300-500
VL (VERY LIMITED) = 200-300
EL (EXTREMELY LIMITED) = 100-200
S (SCARCE) = 100 OR FEWER
NNO Carel Struycken EL 12.00 30.00
NNO Charlotte Stewart VL 8.00 20.00
NNO Dana Ashbrook VL 10.00 25.00
NNO David Duchovny S 200.00 400.00
NNO Everett McGill EL 15.00 40.00
NNO Harry Goaz VL 15.00 40.00
NNO James Marshall VL 12.00 30.00
NNO Kimmy Robertson VL 8.00 20.00
NNO Kyle MacLachlan EL 125.00 250.00
NNO Lenny Von Dohlen VL 10.00 25.00
NNO Madchen Amick EL 50.00 100.00
NNO Michael Horse VL 10.00 25.00
NNO Michael Ontkean S 250.00 500.00
NNO Peggy Lipton EL 50.00 100.00
NNO Piper Laurie EL 25.00 60.00
NNO Ray Wise VL 12.00 30.00
NNO Sherilynn Fenn VL 50.00 100.00
NNO Sheryl Lee EL 75.00 150.00
NNO Wendy Robie EL 10.00 25.00

2018 Twin Peaks Dual Autographs

COMMON AUTO 50.00 100.00
RANDOMLY INSERTED INTO PACKS
NNO D.Lynch/K.MacLachlan 1250.00 2500.00
NNO K.MacLachlan/M.Ontkean 9CI 200.00 400.00
NNO P.Lipton/C.Mulkey 60.00 120.00
NNO S.Fenn/K.MacLachlan 125.00 250.00
NNO S.Lee/J.Marshall 125.00 250.00
NNO S.Lee/K.MacLachlan 150.00 300.00
NNO W.Robie/E.McGill 60.00 120.00

2018 Twin Peaks It Is Happening Again

COMPLETE SET (2) 50.00 100.00
COMMON CARD (HA1-HA2) 20.00 50.00
STATED ODDS 1:288
HA1 Dale Cooper 25.00 60.00

2018 Twin Peaks A Limited Event Series

COMPLETE SET (54) 100.00 200.00
COMMON CARD (1-54) 2.50 6.00
STATED ODDS 1:8

2018 Twin Peaks Limited Event Series Autographs

COMMON AUTO 6.00 15.00
STATED OVERALL ODDS 1:12
REGULAR AUTO <500
L (LIMITED) = 300-500
VL (VERY LIMITED) = 200-300
EL (EXTREMELY LIMITED) = 100-200
S (SCARCE) = 100 OR FEWER
NNO Carel Struycken EL 20.00 50.00
NNO Chrysta Bell L 8.00 20.00
NNO Dana Ashbrook EL 12.00 30.00
NNO David Lynch S 400.00 800.00
NNO Everett McGill EL 15.00 40.00
NNO Harry Goaz EL 12.00 30.00
NNO James Marshall EL 12.00 30.00
NNO Jim Belushi VL 25.00 60.00
NNO Kimmy Robertson VL 8.00 20.00
NNO Madchen Amick EL 30.00 75.00
NNO Michael Horse VL 10.00 25.00
NNO Peggy Lipton S 30.00 75.00
NNO Ray Wise VL 15.00 40.00
NNO Sherilyn Fenn EL 25.00 60.00
NNO Sheryl Lee S 75.00 150.00
NNO Wendy Robie EL 8.00 20.00

2018 Twin Peaks Quotables

COMPLETE SET W/O EXCLUSIVE (14) 12.00 30.00
COMMON CARD (Q1-Q14) 2.00 5.00
STATED ODDS 1:24
Q15 IS RITTENHOUSE REWARD EXCLUSIVE
Q15 Quotable Twin Peaks RR

2018 Twin Peaks Promos

COMMON CARD (P1-P4) 2.50 6.00
P2 Non-Sport Update Magazine 3.00 8.00
P3 Binder Exclusive
P4 Philly Non-Sport Show Spring 2018 8.00 20.00

2019 Twin Peaks Archives

COMPLETE SET (72) 8.00 20.00
UNOPENED BOX (24 PACKS) 75.00 125.00
UNOPENED PACK (5 CARDS) 3.00 5.00
ARCHIVE BOX (222 CARDS) 1300.00 2000.00
COMMON CARD (1-72) .25 .60

2019 Twin Peaks Archives Case-Topper

CT1 Two Coopers 8.00 20.00

2019 Twin Peaks Archives Classic Autographs

COMMON AUTO 6.00 15.00
STATED OVERALL ODDS 1:12
REGULAR AUTO <500
L (LIMITED) = 300-500
VL (VERY LIMITED) = 200-300
EL (EXTREMELY LIMITED) = 100-200
S (SCARCE) = 100 OR FEWER
NNO Richard Beymer EL 25.00 60.00
NNO Ian Buchanan EL 8.00 20.00
NNO Ian Buchanan S AB 15.00 40.00
NNO Victoria Catlin EL AB 12.00 30.00
NNO Eric Da Re EL 10.00 25.00
NNO Eric Da Re S AB 15.00 40.00
NNO David Patrick Kelly EL 12.00 30.00
NNO Robyn Lively S AB 15.00 40.00
NNO Brenda Strong VL 8.00 20.00
NNO David Warner EL 12.00 30.00
NNO Clay Wilcox VL 8.00 20.00
NNO Kathleen Wilhoite L 8.00 20.00
NNO Billy Zane EL 15.00 40.00
NNO Billy Zane S AB 20.00 50.00

2019 Twin Peaks Archives Classic Inscription Autographs

COMMON ASHBROOK 25.00 60.00
COMMON GOAZ 15.00 40.00
COMMON HERSHBERGER 12.00 30.00
COMMON LAURIE 30.00 75.00
COMMON LEE 60.00 120.00
COMMON ONTKEAN 75.00 150.00
STATED OVERALL ODDS 1:12
VL (VERY LIMITED) = 200-300
EL (EXTREMELY LIMITED) = 100-200

2019 Twin Peaks Archives Dual Autographs

COMMON AUTO 15.00 40.00
STATED OVERALL ODDS 1:12
EL (EXTREMELY LIMITED) = 100-200
S (SCARCE) = 100 OR FEWER
LIPTON/AMICK IS ARCHIVE BOX EXCLUSIVE
NNO R.Beymer/D. Kelly S 60.00 120.00
NNO S.Fenn/B.Zane EL 50.00 100.00
NNO P.Lipton/M.Amick 9CI 75.00 150.00

2019 Twin Peaks Archives Modern Autographs

COMMON AUTO 6.00 15.00
STATED OVERALL ODDS 1:12
L (LIMITED) = 300-500
VL (VERY LIMITED) = 200-300
EL (EXTREMELY LIMITED) = 100-200

S (SCARCE) = 100 OR FEWER
NNO Richard Beymer S AB 30.00 75.00
NNO Robert Forster L 15.00 40.00
NNO Robert Forster S AB 30.00 75.00
NNO David Patrick Kelly EL 12.00 30.00
NNO Kyle MacLachlan EL 60.00 120.00
NNO Walter Olkewicz VL 10.00 25.00
NNO John Pirruccello S AB 15.00 40.00
NNO Amy Shiels VL 10.00 25.00
NNO Tom Sizemore VL 10.00 25.00
NNO Nae Yuuki S AB 12.00 30.00
NNO Christophe Zajac-Denek S AB

2019 Twin Peaks Archives Original Stars of Twin Peaks

COMPLETE SET (27) 12.00 30.00
COMMON CARD (S1-S27) .75 2.00
STATED ODDS 1:12

2019 Twin Peaks Archives Poker Chip Relics

COMMON MEM (PC1-PC2)
RANDOMLY INSERTED INTO PACKS
PC2 ARCHIVE BOX EXCLUSIVE
PC1 Poker Chip 75.00 150.00
PC2 Poker Chip Broken AB 100.00 200.00

2019 Twin Peaks Archives Quotables

COMPLETE SET (13) 15.00 40.00
COMMON CARD (Q16-Q28) 2.00 5.00
STATED ODDS 1:24

2019 Twin Peaks Archives Relationships

COMPLETE SET (42) 12.00 30.00
COMMON CARD (LR1-LR42) .75 2.00
STATED ODDS 1:8

2019 Twin Peaks Archives Scratch-n-Sniff

COMPLETE SET W/O RR (9) 15.00 40.00
COMMON CARD (SS1-SS9) 3.00 8.00
STATED ODDS 1:12
SS10 IS A RITTENHOUSE REWARD
SS10 Multi-Pies RR 25.00 60.00

2019 Twin Peaks Archives Sheriff's Department Patches

COMMON CARD (SP1-SP7) 8.00 20.00
STATED ODDS 1:288
SP1 Harry S. Truman 12.00 30.00
SP3 Andy Brennan 10.00 25.00
SP4 Frank Truman 10.00 25.00
SP5 Bobby Briggs 12.00 30.00

2019 Twin Peaks Archives Promos

COMMON CARD (P1-P2)
P1 Welcome to Twin Peaks 2.50 6.00
P2 Dougie Jones and Janey-E Jones 8.00 20.00

2019 Twin Peaks Archives Welcome to Twin Peaks

COMPLETE SET (18) 12.00 30.00
COMMON CARD (W1-W18) 1.00 2.50
STATED ODDS 1:24

1996 Donruss Twister

COMPLETE SET (90) 6.00 15.00
UNOPENED BOX (36 PACKS) 15.00 20.00
UNOPENED PACK (8 CARDS) .75 1.00
COMMON CARD (1-90) .12 .30
CARDS 89 AND 90 DO NOT EXIST
NNO1 NSU Promo .75 2.00

1996 Donruss Twister Foil

COMPLETE SET (9) 12.00 30.00
COMMON CARD (F1-F9) 2.00 5.00
STATED ODDS 1:4

2017 Twitster

COMPLETE SET (5) 30.00 75.00
COMMON CARD (1-5) 6.00 15.00
3 Trump/Putin/201* 8.00 20.00
4 Donald Trump/191* 8.00 20.00
6 Donald Trump Covfefe/188* 10.00 25.00

1998 Inkworks TV's Coolest Classics

COMPLETE SET (90) 5.00 12.00
UNOPENED BOX (36 PACKS) 25.00 30.00
UNOPENED PACK (8 CARDS) .75 1.00
COMMON CARD (1-90) .15 .40
BH1 ISSUED IN COLLECTORS ALBUM
BH1 Beverly Hillbillies ALB 1.50 4.00

1998 Inkworks TV's Coolest Classics Autographs

COMPLETE SET (7)
COMMON CARD (A1-A7) 8.00 20.00
STATED ODDS 1:180
A1 Barbara Feldon 20.00 50.00
A2 Donna Douglas 30.00 75.00
A3 Susan Olsen 15.00 40.00
A6 Barry Williams 20.00 50.00

1998 Inkworks TV's Coolest Classics Dream Girls

COMPLETE SET (6) 12.50 30.00
COMMON CARD (D1-D6) 2.50 6.00
STATED ODDS 1:20

1998 Inkworks TV's Coolest Classics Memorable Moments

COMPLETE SET (9) 7.50 20.00
COMMON CARD (M1-M9) 1.25 3.00
STATED ODDS 1:11

1998 Inkworks TV's Coolest Classics Promos

P1 Greg Brady 1.00 2.50
P2 Maxwell Smart 1.00 2.50
P3 Sgt. Schultz 1.00 2.50

1998 Inkworks TV's Coolest Classics Smell-o-Rama

COMPLETE SET (3) 10.00 25.00
COMMON CARD (S1-S3) 4.00 10.00
STATED ODDS 1:30

2004 UFO

COMPLETE SET (100) 5.00 12.00
UNOPENED BOX (24 PACKS) 50.00 60.00
UNOPENED PACK (6 CARDS) 2.50 3.00
COMMON CARD .10 .25
*FOIL: .75X TO 2X BASIC CARDS .20 .50

2004 UFO Autographs

COMMON CARD 15.00 40.00
RANDOMLY INSERTED INTO PACKS
NNO Ed Bishop 30.00 80.00
NNO Gerry Anderson 30.00 80.00
NNO Stuart Myres 20.00 50.00
NNO Wanda Ventham 20.00 50.00

2004 UFO Costumes

COMMON CARD 25.00 60.00
RANDOMLY INSERTED INTO PACKS

2004 UFO Future Fashions

COMPLETE SET (9) 15.00 40.00
COMMON CARD (FF001-FF009) 2.50 6.00
RANDOMLY INSERTED INTO PACKS

2004 UFO Promos

COMPLETE SET (4) 3.00 8.00
COMMON CARD (P1-P4) 1.25 3.00

2016 UFO

COMPLETE SET (54) 12.00 30.00
UNOPENED BOX (24 PACKS)
UNOPENED PACK (5 CARDS)
COMMON CARD (1-54)

2016 UFO Autographs

COMMON AUTO 8.00 20.00
STATED ODDS 2:BOX
AB1 Ayshea Brough 12.00 30.00
AB2 Ayshea Brough 12.00 30.00
AB3 Ayshea Brough 12.00 30.00
DN1 Derren Nesbitt 10.00 25.00
DN2 Derren Nesbitt 10.00 25.00
DN3 Derren Nesbitt 10.00 25.00
GD1 Gabrielle Drake 15.00 40.00
GD2 Gabrielle Drake 15.00 40.00
GM1 Georgina Moon 12.00 30.00
GM2 Georgina Moon 12.00 30.00
GM3 Georgina Moon 12.00 30.00
JL1 John Levene 12.00 30.00
JL2 John Levene 15.00 40.00
JM1 Jane Merror 10.00 25.00
JM2 Jane Merror 10.00 25.00
JW1 Jeremy Wilkin 15.00 40.00
JW2 Jeremy Wilkin 15.00 40.00
JW3 Jeremy Wilkin 20.00 50.00
MJ1 Michael Jayston 10.00 25.00
MJ2 Michael Jayston 10.00 25.00
SJ1 Susan Jameson 15.00 40.00
SJ2 Susan Jameson 15.00 40.00
SJ3 Susan Jameson 20.00 50.00
WV1 Wanda Ventham 25.00 60.00
WV2 Wanda Ventham 25.00 60.00

2016 UFO Mirror Foil

COMPLETE SET (9) 10.00 25.00
COMMON CARD (F1-F9) 1.50 4.00
RANDOMLY INSERTED INTO PACKS

2019 UFO Series 2

COMPLETE SET (36) 6.00 15.00
COMMON CARD (1-36) .30 .75
*PRINT PROOF/20: 3X TO 8X BASIC CARDS

2019 UFO Series 2 Autographs

COMMON AUTO 6.00 15.00
*B&W: X TO X BASIC AUTOS
AB1 Ayshea Brough 10.00 25.00
AB2 Ayshea Brough 12.00 30.00
AB3 Ayshea Brough 10.00 25.00
AB4 Ayshea Brough/50 WEB 25.00 60.00
CR1 Christian Roberts 10.00 25.00
DN3 Derren Nesbitt/7 CI
GB3 Gabrielle Drake Holiday Special 25.00 60.00
GM1 Georgina Moon 10.00 25.00
GM2 Georgina Moon 10.00 25.00
GM3 Georgina Moon 10.00 25.00
GR1 Gary Raymond 10.00 25.00
GR2 Gary Raymond 10.00 25.00
GR3 Gary Raymond 10.00 25.00
JM1 Jane Merrow 12.00 30.00
JM2 Jane Merrow 12.00 30.00
JM3 Jane Merrow 12.00 30.00
JW1 Jeremy Wilkin/10 CI 150.00 300.00
PS1 Penny Spencer 15.00 40.00
PS2 Penny Spencer CT 20.00 50.00
SJ1 Susan Jameson 12.00 30.00
SJ2 Susan Jameson 12.00 30.00
TW2 Tessa Wyatt 10.00 25.00
TW3 Tessa Wyatt 12.00 30.00
WV1 Wanda Ventham 25.00 60.00
WV2 Wanda Ventham 30.00 75.00
WV3 Wanda Ventham 30.00 75.00
WV4 Wanda Ventham 25.00 60.00

2019 UFO Series 2 Previews

COMPLETE SET (6)
COMMON CARD (PV1-PV6
STATED ODDS 1:
PV1 (purple back)
PV2 (purple back)
PV3 (purple back)
PV4 (purple back)
PV5 (purple back)
PV6 (purple back)

1998 Dark Horse Comics UFO Trading Cards

COMPLETE BOXED SET (50) 6.00 15.00
COMMON CARD (1-50) .25 .60

2020 Topps On-Demand Ugly Stickers

COMPLETE SET (20)
COMMON CARD (1-20)
*TAN BACKS: 3X TO 8X BASIC CARDS
STATED PRINT RUN 500 SETS

2020 Topps On-Demand Ugly Stickers 5x7 Posters

COMPLETE SET (10) 20.00 50.00
COMMON CARD 3.00 8.00
STATED ODDS 1:1

1993 Comic Images Ujena's Swimwear Illustrated

COMPLETE SET (90) 4.00 10.00
COMPLETE FACTORY SET (91) 6.00 15.00
UNOPENED BOX (48 PACKS) 20.00 25.00
UNOPENED PACK (10 CARDS) .50 .75
COMMON CARD (1-90) .02 .10

1993 Comic Images Ujena's Swimwear Illustrated Promos

NNO1 Available May 1993 (gen dist) .75 2.00
NNO2 (4-up panel, above card)

1993 Comic Images Ujena's Swimwear Illustrated Spectrascope

COMPLETE SET (6) 20.00 50.00
COMMON CARD (S1-S6) 4.00 10.00
STATED ODDS 1:16

1994 Comic Images Ujena's Swimwear Illustrated

COMPLETE SET (90) 6.00 15.00
UNOPENED BOX (48 PACKS) 20.00 25.00
UNOPENED PACK (10 CARDS) .50 .75
COMMON CARD (1-90) .10 .25
NNO1 Dealer Promo .75 2.00
NNO2 Medallion Card/847 10.00 25.00

1994 Comic Images Ujena's Swimwear Illustrated Cool Covers

COMPLETE SET (3) 12.00 30.00
COMMON CARD (1-3) 6.00 15.00
STATED ODDS 1:48

1994 Comic Images Ujena's Swimwear Illustrated Foil

COMPLETE SET (6) 15.00 40.00
COMMON CARD (F1-F6) 3.00 8.00
STATED ODDS 1:16

2002 Ultimate Anime

COMPLETE SET (72) 4.00 10.00
UNOPENED BOX (36 PACKS) 25.00 40.00
UNOPENED PACK (7 CARDS) 1.25 1.50
COMMON CARD (1-72) .12 .30

2002 Ultimate Anime OmniChrome

COMPLETE SET (8) 12.00 30.00
COMMON CARD (C1-C8) 2.00 5.00
RANDOMLY INSERTED INTO PACKS

1986 Hostess Ultimate Backstage Pass Stickers

COMPLETE SET (30) 20.00 50.00
COMMON CARD (1-30) 1.00 2.50

1993 SkyBox Ultraverse

COMPLETE SET (100) 6.00 15.00
UNOPENED BOX (36 PACKS) 30.00 50.00
UNOPENED PACK (8 CARDS) 1.00 1.50
COMMON CARD (1-100) .12 .30

1993 SkyBox Ultraverse Promos

COMPLETE SET (13) 15.00 40.00
COMMON CARD .75 2.00
C1 Prime (Issued with Prime #2) 1.50 4.00
C2 Hardcase 1.50 4.00
C3 Strangers (issued with Hardcase #2) 1.50 4.00
C4 Freex (Issued with Freex #1) 1.50 4.00
C5 Mantra/Prototype 1.50 4.00
(Issued with Mantra #1
P0a Warstrike (yellow U on back) 1.25 3.00
P0b Warstrike (Capital City logo on back) 3.00 8.00
P0c Warstrike (Heros World logo on back) 4.00 10.00

1993 SkyBox Ultraverse Rookies

COMPLETE SET (9) 6.00 15.00
COMMON CARD (R1-R9) 1.00 2.50
STATED ODDS 1:5

MODERN

1993 SkyBox Ultraverse Star Rookies

COMPLETE SET (4) 4.00 10.00
COMMON CARD (S1-S4) 1.25 3.00
STATED ODDS 1:18

1993 SkyBox Ultraverse Ultra Tech

COMPLETE SET (2) 4.00 10.00
COMMON CARD (U1-U2) 2.50 6.00
STATED ODDS 1:36

1994 SkyBox Ultraverse II

COMPLETE SET (90) 6.00 15.00
COMPLETE FACTORY SET (101) 25.00 60.00
UNOPENED BOX (36 PACKS) 40.00 75.00
UNOPENED PACK (8 CARDS) 2.00 3.00
COMMON CARD (1-90) .12 .30
SB1 Topaz 6.00 15.00
SB2 Contrary 6.00 15.00
NNO Original Artwork

1994 SkyBox Ultraverse II Autographs

COMPLETE SET (7) 250.00 500.00
COMMON CARD (SKIP #'d) 30.00 80.00
RANDOMLY INSERTED INTO PACKS

1994 SkyBox Ultraverse II Painted Bonus

COMPLETE SET (7) 12.00 30.00
COMMON CARD (B1-B7) 2.00 5.00
STATED ODDS 1:10

1994 SkyBox Ultraverse II Ultra Etched Foil

COMPLETE SET (2) 6.00 15.00
COMMON CARD (UB1-UB2) 4.00 10.00
STATED ODDS 1:36

1994 SkyBox Ultraverse II Promos

COMPLETE SET (6) 4.00 10.00
COMMON CARD .75 1.50
NNO The Solution, Mantra,
Darkwave/Prime, Strangers 1.50 4.00
NNO The Solution, Mantra,
Darkwave/Prime, Strangers Previews 1.50 4.00

1994 SkyBox Ultraverse Master Series

COMPLETE SET (90) 6.00 15.00
UNOPENED BOX (36 PACKS) 30.00 40.00
UNOPENED PACK (6 CARDS) 1.25 1.50
COMMON CARD (1-90) .12 .30
AU1 Dave Dorman AU 30.00 80.00
ART1 Original Art

1994 SkyBox Ultraverse Master Series Hololithograms

COMPLETE SET (2) 10.00 25.00
COMMON CARD (H1-H2) 6.00 15.00
STATED ODDS 1:36

1994 SkyBox Ultraverse Master Series Promos

COMMON CARD .75 2.00
NNO Heater/Solitaire/Mantra/Sludge 12.00 30.00

1994 SkyBox Ultraverse Master Series UltraFlash Foil

COMPLETE SET (5) 15.00 40.00
COMMON CARD (U1-U5) 4.00 10.00
STATED ODDS 1:12

2020 Rittenhouse The Umbrella Academy Season One

COMPLETE SET (63) 8.00 20.00
UNOPENED BOX (24 PACKS) 75.00 125.00
UNOPENED PACK (5 CARDS) 3.00 5.00
COMMON CARD (1-63) .25 .60

2020 Rittenhouse The Umbrella Academy Season One Autographed Relic

NNO Aidan Gallagher 6CI 100.00 200.00

2020 Rittenhouse The Umbrella Academy Season One Autographs

COMMON AUTO 6.00 15.00
STATED ODDS 1:24
NNO Aidan Gallagher EL 75.00 150.00
NNO Alyssa Gervasi VL 8.00 20.00
NNO Blake Talabis VL 8.00 20.00
NNO Cameron Britton EL 25.00 60.00
NNO Cameron Brodeur EL 8.00 20.00
NNO Colm Feore EL 25.00 60.00
NNO Dante Albidone EL 10.00 25.00
NNO Eden Cupid EL 25.00 60.00
NNO Ellen Page EL 125.00 250.00
NNO Ellen Piggford VL 8.00 20.00
NNO Emmy River-Lampman EL 60.00 120.00
NNO Ethan Hwang EL 8.00 20.00
NNO Jordan Claire Robbins EL 25.00 60.00
NNO Justin Min EL 30.00 75.00
NNO Robert Sheehan S 100.00 200.00
NNO Sean Sullivan VL 8.00 20.00
NNO Sheila McCarthy VL 20.00 50.00
NNO T.J. McGibbon VL 10.00 25.00
NNO Zachary Bennett VL 8.00 20.00

2020 Rittenhouse The Umbrella Academy Season One Case-Topper

NNO Space Boy Poster 6.00 15.00

2020 Rittenhouse The Umbrella Academy Season One Collector's Set

COMPLETE SET (9) 20.00 50.00
COMMON CARD (E1-E9) 4.00 10.00
STATED PRINT RUN 500 SER.#'d SETS
EBAY EXCLUSIVE

2020 Rittenhouse The Umbrella Academy Season One Dual Autographs

COMMON AUTO 30.00 75.00
NNO E.Page/E.Raver-Lampman 9CI 150.00 300.00
NNO Robert Sheehan/Cody Ray Thompson EL60.00120.00

2020 Rittenhouse The Umbrella Academy Season One Heist at the Museum

COMPLETE SET (7) 10.00 25.00
COMMON CARD (M1-M7) 2.00 5.00
STATED ODDS 1:24

2020 Rittenhouse The Umbrella Academy Season One Quotables

COMPLETE SET W/RR (13) 10.00 25.00
COMPLETE SET W/O RR (12)
COMMON CARD (Q1-Q12) 2.00 5.00
STATED ODDS 1:24
Q4A Klaus Hargreeves
(Rittenhouse Reward)

2020 Rittenhouse The Umbrella Academy Season One Relics

COMMON MEM (RC01-RC14) 8.00 20.00
STATED ODDS 1:24
RC01 Luther Hargreeves 12.00 30.00
RC04 Klaus Hargreeves 20.00 50.00
RC05 Number Five 30.00 75.00
RC06 Ben Hargreeves 10.00 25.00
RC07 Vanya Hargreeves 15.00 40.00
RC08 Vanya's Sheet Music 25.00 60.00
RC09 Allison's Pink Boa 10.00 25.00
RC10 Hazel and Cha-Cha Termination letters125.00250.00
RC11 Number Five's Time
Travel Calculation Notes 125.00 250.00
RC12 Extra Ordinary book cover 12.00 30.00
RC13 Vanya's Orchestra Program 15.00 40.00
RC14 Luther's Space Boy Poster 15.00 40.00

2020 Rittenhouse The Umbrella Academy Season One Starring Characters Acetate

COMPLETE SET (9) 30.00 75.00
COMMON CARD (PC1-PC9) 6.00 15.00
STATED ODDS 1:48

2020 Rittenhouse The Umbrella Academy Season One Then and Now

COMPLETE SET (7) 12.00 30.00
COMMON CARD (TN1-TN7) 2.50 6.00
STATED ODDS 1:24

2020 Rittenhouse The Umbrella Academy Season One Promos

COMPLETE SET (3)
COMMON CARD (P1-P3)
P1 General Distribution 1.50 4.00
P2 Social Media
P3 Binder Exclusive 2.50 6.00

1984 WTW Productions Uncle Sam Reprints

COMPLETE SET (48) 6.00 15.00
RELEASED BY WTW

2014 Under the Dome Season One

COMPLETE SET (81) 8.00 20.00
UNOPENED BOX (24 PACKS) 60.00 100.00
UNOPENED PACK (5 CARDS) 3.00 4.00
COMMON CARD (1-81) .20 .50
*GOLD: 8X TO 20X BASIC CARD
CT1 ISSUED AS CASE TOPPER
CT1 Don't Halve a Cow! CT 6.00 15.00

2014 Under the Dome Season One Autographs

COMMON AUTO 4.00 10.00
STATED ODDS 1:12
ROBERTSON ISSUED AS 3-CASE INCENTIVE
VOGEL ISSUED AS 6-CASE INCENTIVE
NNO Aisha Hinds 5.00 12.00
NNO Beth Broderick 5.00 12.00
NNO Britt Robertson 25.00 60.00
NNO Britt Robertson Silver 3CI 50.00 100.00
NNO Colin Ford 5.00 12.00
NNO Jeff Fahey 8.00 20.00
NNO John Elvis 10.00 25.00
NNO Leon Rippy 5.00 12.00
NNO Mackenzie Lintz 6.00 15.00
NNO Mike Vogel 6.00 15.00
NNO Mike Vogel Silver 6CI 12.00 30.00
NNO Natalie Martinez 12.00 30.00
NNO Rachelle Lefevre 25.00 60.00
NNO Samantha Mathis 10.00 25.00

2014 Under the Dome Season One Characters

COMPLETE SET (18) 15.00 40.00
COMMON CARD (C01-C18) 1.50 4.00
STATED ODDS 1:12

2014 Under the Dome Season One Quotables

COMPLETE SET (12) 12.00 30.00
COMMON CARD (Q01-Q12) 2.00 5.00
STATED ODDS 1:12

2014 Under the Dome Season One Relics

COMPLETE SET (15) 120.00 250.00
COMMON CARD (R1-R15) 5.00 12.00
STATED ODDS 1:24
R1 Dale "Barbie" Barbara 15.00 40.00
R2 Angie McAlister 25.00 60.00
R3 James "Big Jim" Rennie 12.00 30.00
R4 Dodee Weaver 12.00 30.00
R5 Joe McAlister 8.00 20.00
R6 Julia Shumway 15.00 40.00
R8 Dale "Barbie" Barbara 10.00 25.00
R9 James "Junior" Rennie 8.00 20.00
R11 Norrie Calvert-Hill 8.00 20.00
R12 Julia Shumway 15.00 40.00
R14 Joe McAlister 12.00 30.00

2014 Under the Dome Season One Promos

COMPLETE SET (4) 5.00 12.00
COMMON CARD (P1-P4) .75 2.00
P3 Promo 3 ALB 4.00 10.00
P4 Promo 4 SDCC 2.00 5.00

2015 Under the Dome Season Two

COMPLETE FACTORY SET (31) 120.00 200.00
COMMON CARD .40 1.00
COMMON AUTO 5.00 12.00
ALEXANDER KOCH ISSUED AS 3-CASE INCENTIVE
AK Alexander Koch 3SI 50.00 100.00
BR Britt Robertson 15.00 40.00
CF Colin Ford 8.00 20.00
GV Grace Victoria Cox 15.00 40.00
JE John Elvis 6.00 15.00
ML Mackenzie Lintz 12.00 30.00
MV Mike Vogel 15.00 40.00
NM Natalie Martinez 10.00 25.00
SM Samantha Mathis 12.00 30.00

1987 Brooke Bond Unexplained Mysteries of the World

COMPLETE SET (40) 2.00 5.00
COMMON CARD (1-40) .08 .20

2020 Fascinating Cards United States Congress

UNOPENED BOX (24 PACKS)
UNOPENED PACK (10 CARDS)
COMMON CARD (1-535) 1.50 4.00
STATED PRINT RUN 100 ANNCD SETS
6 Kyrsten Sinema 25.00 60.00
8 Tom Cotton 15.00 40.00
9 Dianne Feinstein 12.00 30.00
10 Kamala Harris 30.00 75.00
11 Michael Bennet 12.00 30.00
12 Cory Gardner 10.00 25.00
13 Richard Blumenthal 12.00 30.00
14 Chris Murphy 12.00 30.00
15 Tom Carper 12.00 30.00
16 Chris Coons 12.00 30.00
17 Marco Rubio 10.00 25.00
18 Rick Scott 12.00 30.00
19 Kelly Loeffler 12.00 30.00
20 David Perdue 8.00 20.00
21 Mazie Hirono 10.00 25.00
30 Chuck Grassley 12.00 30.00
33 Mitch McConnell 15.00 40.00
34 Rand Paul 10.00 25.00
36 John Kennedy 12.00 30.00
38 Angus King 10.00 25.00
42 Elizabeth Warren 12.00 30.00
43 Gary Peters 10.00 25.00
46 Tina Smith 10.00 25.00
50 Josh Hawley 10.00 25.00
59 Cory Booker 12.00 30.00
64 Chuck Schumer 15.00 40.00
82 John Thune 10.00 25.00
86 Ted Cruz 20.00 50.00
90 Bernie Sanders 12.00 30.00
94 Patty Murray 10.00 25.00
95 Shelley Capito 12.00 30.00
96 Joe Manchin 12.00 30.00
98 Ron Johnson 10.00 25.00
113 Andy Biggs 10.00 25.00
133 Nancy Pelosi 25.00 60.00
136 Eric Swalwell 10.00 25.00
143 Devin Nunes 10.00 25.00
166 Katie Porter 10.00 25.00
173 Scott Peters 10.00 25.00
188 Matt Gaetz 20.00 50.00
219 John Lewis 15.00 40.00
271 Thomas Massie 8.00 20.00
393 Dan Bishop 10.00 3.00
463 Dan Crenshaw 60.00 120.00
465 John Ratcliffe 12.00 30.00

1992 Comic Images Unity

COMPLETE SET (90) 4.00 10.00
UNOPENED BOX (48 PACKS) 15.00 20.00
UNOPENED PACK (10 CARDS) .75 1.00
COMMON CARD (1-90) .12 .30

1992 Comic Images Unity Chromium

COMPLETE SET (6) 3.00 8.00
COMMON CARD (1-6) 1.00 2.50
STATED ODDS 1:6

1994 Topps Universal Monsters Illustrated

COMPLETE SET (100) 10.00 25.00
UNOPENED BOX (36 PACKS) 125.00 250.00
UNOPENED PACK (8 CARDS) 4.00 8.00
COMMON CARD (1-100) .20 .50

1994 Topps Universal Monsters Illustrated Horror Glow

COMPLETE SET (4) 8.00 20.00
COMMON CARD (H1-H4) 3.00 8.00
STATED ODDS 1:18

1994 Topps Universal Monsters Illustrated MonsterChrome

COMPLETE SET (10) 15.00 40.00
COMMON CARD (M1-M10) 2.50 6.00
STATED ODDS 1:9

1994 Topps Universal Monsters Illustrated Promos

NNO The Mummy (Horror Glow) 1.25 3.00
NNO Bride of Frankenstein .40 1.00
NNO This Island Earth NSU .40 1.00
NNO Classic Creatures of Horror Oversized (Previews) 1.25 3.00

1996 Kitchen Sink Press Universal Monsters of the Silver Screen

COMPLETE SET (90) 5.00 12.00
COMPLETE SET W/STICKERS (100) 6.00 15.00
UNOPENED BOX (36 PACKS) 15.00 20.00
UNOPENED PACK (8 CARDS+1 STICKER) .50 .60
COMMON CARD (1-90) .10 .25
U1 Bride of Frankenstein EXCH (uncut sheet red) 15.00 40.00

1996 Kitchen Sink Press Universal Monsters of the Silver Screen Bio-Chrome

COMPLETE SET (12) 25.00 60.00
COMMON CARD 3.00 8.00
STATED ODDS 1:9

1996 Kitchen Sink Press Universal Monsters of the Silver Screen Lobby Card and Poster Stickers

COMPLETE SET (10) 1.50 4.00
COMMON CARD (S1-S10) .20 .50

1992 Pizza Hut Universal Monsters Holograms

COMPLETE SET (3) 4.00 10.00
COMMON CARD (1-3) 2.50 6.00

1992 Pepsi Universal Party Monsters

COMPLETE SET (6) 1.50 4.00
COMMON CARD (1-6) .50 1.25

1986 Ting Uranus Strikes!

COMPLETE SEALED SET (36) 15.00 40.00
COMMON CARD (1-36) .75 2.00

2009 Urban Legends

COMPLETE SET (51) 10.00 25.00
COMMON CARD (1-50, C1) .40 1.00

2009 Urban Legends Promos

COMMON CARD .75 2.00
P1 The Mexican Pet UL 5.00 12.00
P2 The Rent-Free Roommate UL 4.00 10.00
P2 Living Hell SS 1.25 3.00
P3 Date With A Doctor UL 2.00 5.00
P4 The Brain Suckers Of Saturn SS

1992 Mother's Cookies U.S. Presidents

COMPLETE SET (42) 3.00 8.00
COMMON CARD (1-42) .15 .40
1 George Washington .40 1.00
3 Thomas Jefferson .20 .50
16 Abraham Lincoln .75 2.00
35 John F. Kennedy .60 1.50
37 Richard M. Nixon .30 .75
40 Ronald Reagan .40 1.00
41 George Bush .20 .50

2017 U.S.S. Arizona The Greatest Escape

COMPLETE SET (18) 15.00 40.00
COMMON CARD (GE1-GE18) 1.25 3.00
STATED PRINT RUN 1512 SETS

1984 Fleer V

COMPLETE SET (66) 25.00 60.00
UNOPENED BOX (36 PACKS) 125.00 200.00
UNOPENED PACK (10 CARDS+1 STICKER) 3.00 5.00
COMMON CARD (1-66) .40 1.00

Fleer V Stickers

COMPLETE SET (22) 8.00 20.00
COMMON CARD (1-22) .40 1.00
STATED ODDS 1:1

1993 Upper Deck Valiant Era

COMPLETE SET (120) 6.00 15.00
UNOPENED BOX (36 PACKS) 15.00 20.00
UNOPENED PACK (8 CARDS) .75 1.00
COMMON CARD (1-120) .10 .25
HOLO The Valiant Era Hologram 1.25 3.00
SP1 The Art of Joe Quesada 8.00 20.00

1993 Upper Deck Valiant Era First Appearance

COMPLETE SET (9) 25.00 60.00
COMMON CARD (FA1-FA9) 3.00 8.00

1993 Upper Deck Valiant Era Foil Art

COMPLETE SET (9) 12.00 30.00
COMMON CARD (1-9) 2.00 5.00
STATED ODDS 1:12

1994 Upper Deck Valiant Era

COMPLETE SET (140) 4.00 10.00
UNOPENED BOX (36 PACKS) 15.00 25.00
UNOPENED PACK (8 CARDS) .75 1.00
COMMON CARD (121-260) .08 .20
NNO L-E Manowar Holoview 6.00 15.00

1994 Upper Deck Valiant Era Electric Box-Toppers

COMPLETE SET (9) 25.00 60.00
COMMON CARD (OS1-OS9) 3.00 8.00
STATED ODDS 1:BOX

1994 Upper Deck Valiant Era First Appearance

COMPLETE SET (9) 6.00 15.00
COMMON CARD (FA10-FA18) .75 2.00
STATED ODDS 1:12

1994 Upper Deck Valiant Era Promo Art

COMPLETE SET (9) 6.00 15.00
COMMON CARD (PA1-PA9) .75 2.00
STATED ODDS 1:12

1994 Upper Deck Valiant Era Valiant Comics Promos

COMPLETE SET (14) 5.00 12.00
COMMON CARD (VP1-VP14) .60 1.50

1994 Upper Deck Valiant Era Valiant Comics Promos Chromium

COMPLETE SET (7) 8.00 20.00
COMMON CARD (CH1-CH7) 2.00 5.00

1994 Upper Deck Valiant Files Promos

COMPLETE SET (5) 3.00 8.00
COMMON CARD .75 2.00
NNO Promo Oversize (Previews) 1.25 3.00
SLE1 Promo Card Oversize 1.25 3.00
SLE2 Promo Oversize 1.25 3.00

2018 Valiant Harbinger Wars 2

COMPLETE SET (6) 6.00 15.00
COMMON CARD (1-6) 1.50 4.00
STATED PRINT RUN 1000 SETS

2014 Vampire Academy Blood Sisters

COMPLETE SET (100) 6.00 15.00
UNOPENED BOX (24 PACKS) 25.00 40.00
UNOPENED PACK (6 CARDS) 1.50 2.00
COMMON CARD (1-100) .15 .40
*GOLD: 5X TO 12X BASIC CARDS 2.00 5.00

2014 Vampire Academy Blood Sisters Autographs

COMMON AUTO 4.00 10.00
*RED: SAME AS BASIC AUTOS
STATED ODDS 1:12
ACF1 Claire Foy 15.00 40.00
ADS1 Dominic Sherwood 6.00 15.00
AJR1 Joely Richardson 6.00 15.00
ALF1 Lucy Fry 12.00 30.00
AOK1 Olga Kurylenko 12.00 30.00
ASG1 Sami Gayle 5.00 12.00
ASH1 Sarah Hyland 20.00 50.00
ASH2 Sarah Hyland 30.00 75.00
ASH3 Sarah Hyland 20.00 50.00
AZD2 Zoey Deutch 50.00 100.00

2014 Vampire Academy Blood Sisters Character Crests

COMPLETE SET (6) 6.00 15.00
COMMON CARD (CC1-CC6) 2.00 5.00
STATED ODDS 1:24

2014 Vampire Academy Blood Sisters Crests

COMPLETE SET (12) 6.00 15.00
COMMON CARD (C1-C12) 1.00 2.50
STATED ODDS 1:12

2011 The Vampire Diaries Season One

COMPLETE SET (63) 5.00 12.00
UNOPENED BOX (24 PACKS) 125.00 200.00
UNOPENED PACK (5 CARDS) 5.00 8.00
COMMON CARD (1-63) .15 .40

2011 The Vampire Diaries Season One Autographs

COMMON CARD (A1-A20) 6.00 15.00
OVERALL AUTO/MEM ODDS 1:BOX
A1 Nina Dobrev 100.00 200.00
A2 Paul Wesley 50.00 100.00
A3 Ian Somerhalder 50.00 100.00
A4 Steven R. McQueen 12.00 30.00
A5 Katerina Graham 20.00 50.00
A6 Candice Accola 20.00 50.00
A7 Zach Roerig 10.00 25.00
A9 Sara Canning 12.00 30.00
A10 Matt Davis 10.00 25.00
A12 Kevin Williamson 12.00 30.00
A14 Arielle Kebbel 12.00 30.00
A15 Kelly Hu 15.00 40.00
A16 Kayla Ewell 8.00 20.00
A19 Malese Jow 20.00 50.00

2011 The Vampire Diaries Season One Die-Cuts

COMPLETE SET (9) 15.00 40.00
COMMON CARD (D1-D9) 3.00 8.00
STATED ODDS 1:4

2011 The Vampire Diaries Season One Foil

COMPLETE SET (9) 10.00 25.00
COMMON CARD (F1-F9) 2.00 5.00
STATED ODDS 1:4

2011 The Vampire Diaries Season One Wardrobes

COMMON CARD (M1-M21) 10.00 25.00
OVERALL AUTO/MEM ODDS 1:BOX
M21 ISSUED AS BINDER EXCLUSIVE
M1 Stefan Salvatore 12.00 30.00
M2 Stefan Salvatore 12.00 30.00
M3 Elena Gilbert 30.00 80.00
M4 Elena Gilbert 30.00 80.00
M5 Elena Gilbert 30.00 80.00
M6 Bonnie Bennet 12.00 30.00
M7 Bonnie Bennet 20.00 50.00
M9 Caroline Forbes 15.00 40.00
M10 Caroline Forbes 15.00 40.00
M11 Caroline Forbes 15.00 40.00
M12 Damon Salvatore 15.00 40.00
M13 Damon Salvatore 15.00 40.00
M14 Damon Salvatore 20.00 50.00
M17 Vicki Donovan 15.00 40.00
M20 Katherine Pierce 50.00 100.00
M21 Elena Gilbert ALB 20.00 50.00

2011 The Vampire Diaries Season One Promos

P2 Stefan Salvatore GEN 2.00 5.00
P3 Damon Salvatore SDCC 3.00 8.00
P5 Damon/Elena/Stefan PALEYFEST 20.00 50.00

2013 The Vampire Diaries Season Two

COMPLETE SET (69) 8.00 20.00
UNOPENED BOX (24 PACKS) 60.00 70.00
UNOPENED PACK (5 CARDS) 2.50 3.00
COMMON CARD (1-69) .25 .60

2013 The Vampire Diaries Season Two Autographed Wardrobes

COMMON AUTO (A1-A3) 75.00 150.00
OVERALL AUTO ODDS 1:BOX
A1 Nina Dobrev 150.00 300.00
A2 Paul Wesley 100.00 200.00

2013 The Vampire Diaries Season Two Autographs

COMMON AUTO (A4-A21) 6.00 15.00
OVERALL AUTO ODDS 1:BOX
A4 Steven R. McQueen 10.00 25.00
A5 Kat Graham 25.00 60.00
A6 Candice Accola 30.00 75.00
A7 Zach Roerig 10.00 25.00
A8 Michael Trevino 12.00 30.00
A9 Matt Davis 8.00 20.00
A10 Joseph Morgan 50.00 100.00
A11 Sara Canning 8.00 20.00
A12 Daniel Gillies 12.00 30.00
A13 Michaela McManus 10.00 25.00
A14 Taylor Kinney 8.00 20.00
A15 Lauren Cohan 25.00 60.00
A21 Marguerite MacIntyre 10.00 25.00

2013 The Vampire Diaries Season Two Behind-the-Scenes

COMPLETE SET (9) 10.00 25.00
COMMON CARD (BTS1-BTS9) 2.00 5.00
STATED ODDS 2:24

2013 The Vampire Diaries Season Two Dual Wardrobes

COMMON CARD 10.00 25.00
OVERALL WARDROBE ODDS ONE PER BOX
DM2 Damon/Stefan 25.00 50.00
DM3A Elena/Stefan 25.00 50.00
DM3B Elena/Stefan/175
DM4 Matt/Caroline 20.00 40.00
DM5 Elena/Damon 30.00 60.00
DM6 Jeremy/Bonnie 20.00 40.00

2013 The Vampire Diaries Season Two Katerina Petrova
COMPLETE SET (7) 8.00 20.00
COMMON CARD (KP1-KP7) 2.00 5.00
STATED ODDS 2:24

2013 The Vampire Diaries Season Two Wardrobes
COMMON CARD (M1-M29) 6.00 15.00
OVERALL WARDROBE ODDS ONE PER BOX
M1 Tyler Lockwood 8.00 20.00
M2 Caroline Forbes 15.00 40.00
M3 Caroline Forbes 15.00 40.00
M6 Stefan Salvatore 12.00 30.00
M7 Damon Salvatore 15.00 40.00
M8 Stefan Salvatore 12.00 30.00
M9 Elena Gilbert 25.00 50.00
M10 Damon Salvatore 15.00 40.00
M11 Katherine Pierce 25.00 50.00
M12 Rose 12.00 30.00
M13 Jules 10.00 25.00
M14 Jenna Sommers 12.00 30.00
M15 Jeremy Gilbert 10.00 25.00
M16 Rose 12.00 30.00
M17 Katherine Pierce 25.00 50.00
M19 Tyler Lockwood 8.00 20.00
M20 Elena Gilbert 25.00 50.00
M21 Caroline Forbes 15.00 40.00
M22 Jules 10.00 25.00
M23 Bonnie Bennett 15.00 40.00
M25 Elena Gilbert 25.00 50.00
M27 Matt Donovan 8.00 20.00
M29 Elena Gilbert 25.00 50.00

2013 The Vampire Diaries Season Two Promos
P1 Stefan/Elena/Damon NSU 2.00 5.00
P2 Damon/Elena/Stefan 3.00 8.00
(Chicago)

2014 The Vampire Diaries Season Three
COMPLETE SET (72) 10.00 25.00
UNOPENED BOX (24 PACKS) 50.00 60.00
UNOPENED PACK (5 CARDS) 2.00 2.50
COMMON CARD (1-72) .25 .60

2014 The Vampire Diaries Season Three Autograph Wardrobes
STATED ODDS 1:288
AM1 Nina Dobrev 100.00 200.00
AM2 Paul Wesley 50.00 100.00
AM3 Ian Somerhalder 75.00 150.00

2014 The Vampire Diaries Season Three Autographs
COMMON CARD (A5-A21) 8.00 20.00
STATED ODDS 1:24
A5 Steven R. McQueen 15.00 40.00
A6 Kat Graham 15.00 40.00
A7 Candice Accola 25.00 60.00
A8 Zach Roerig 12.00 30.00
A9 Michael Trevino 12.00 30.00
A11 Claire Holt 15.00 40.00
A18 Torrey DeVitto 10.00 25.00

2014 The Vampire Diaries Season Three Mystic Falls
COMPLETE SET (5) 4.00 10.00
COMMON CARD (NV1-NV5) 1.25 3.00
STATED ODDS 1:12

2014 The Vampire Diaries Season Three Original Vampires
COMPLETE SET (7) 3.00 8.00
COMMON CARD (RF1-RF7) .75 2.00
STATED ODDS 1:12

2014 The Vampire Diaries Season Three Wardrobes
COMMON MEM (M1-M29) 6.00 15.00
STATED ODDS 1:24
M29 ISSUED AS ALBUM EXCLUSIVE
M1 Elena Gilbert 15.00 40.00
M2 Stefan Salvatore 8.00 20.00
M3 Damon Salvatore 12.00 30.00
M4 Caroline Forbes 8.00 20.00
M5 Rebekah 8.00 20.00
M6 Katherine Pierce 15.00 40.00
M10 Stefan Salvatore 8.00 20.00
M11 Rebekah 8.00 20.00
M13 Caroline Forbes 8.00 20.00
M15 Elena Gilbert 15.00 40.00
M17 Damon Salvatore 12.00 30.00
M18 Bonnie Bennett 12.00 30.00
M21 Caroline Forbes 8.00 20.00
M22 Elena Gilbert 15.00 40.00
M24 Bonnie Bennett 12.00 30.00
M26 Rebekah 8.00 20.00
M28 Caroline Forbes 8.00 20.00
M29 Damon Salvatore ALB 8.00 20.00

2014 The Vampire Diaries Season Three Dual Wardrobes
COMMON CARD (DM1-DM6) 15.00 40.00
STATED ODDS 1:96
DM1 Elena/Rebekah 25.00 60.00
DM2 Caroline/Klaus 20.00 50.00
DM3 Damon/Alaric 20.00 50.00
DM4 Elena/Damon 25.00 60.00

2016 The Vampire Diaries Season Four
COMPLETE SET (72) 10.00 25.00
UNOPENED BOX (24 PACKS) 65.00 80.00
UNOPENED PACK (5 CARDS) 3.00 4.00
COMMON CARD (1-72) .25 .60
*FOIL: 2X TO 5X BASIC CARDS

2016 The Vampire Diaries Season Four Autographed Wardrobes
COMMON AUTO 75.00 150.00
STATED ODDS 1:24 W/BASIC AUTOS
ISM Ian Somerhalder 125.00 250.00

2016 The Vampire Diaries Season Four Autographs
COMMON AUTO 5.00 12.00
STATED ODDS 1:24
AD Alyssa Diaz 15.00 40.00
AK Arielle Kebbel 10.00 25.00
CA Candice Accola 25.00 60.00
CG Camille Guaty 8.00 20.00
CH Claire Holt 12.00 30.00
DG Daniel Gillies 20.00 50.00
GP Grace Phipps 8.00 20.00
IS Ian Somerhalder 60.00 120.00
PT Phoebe Tonkin 75.00 150.00
PW Paul Wesley 50.00 100.00
RW Rick Worthy 6.00 15.00
SM Steven R. McQueen 8.00 20.00
TD Torrey DeVitto 6.00 15.00
ZR Zach Roerig 15.00 40.00
CMD Charles Michael Davis 30.00 75.00
PTE Paul Telfer 8.00 20.00

2016 The Vampire Diaries Season Four Dual Wardrobes
COMMON CARD (DM1-DM6) 12.00 30.00
STATED ODDS 1:96
DM1 Elena Gilbert/Stefan Salvatore 25.00 60.00
DM2 Damon Salvatore/Elena Gilbert 20.00 50.00
DM3 Rebekah/Klaus 20.00 50.00
DM4 Caroline Forbes/Klaus 25.00 60.00
DM6 Caroline Forbes/Tyler Lockwood 15.00 40.00

2016 The Vampire Diaries Season Four Portraits
COMPLETE SET (9) 6.00 15.00
COMMON CARD (T1-T9) 1.00 2.50
*FOIL: .6X TO 1.5X BASIC CARDS
STATED ODDS 1:3

2016 The Vampire Diaries Season Four Studio
COMPLETE SET (9) 6.00 15.00
COMMON CARD (S1-S9) 1.00 2.50
*FOIL: .6X TO 1.5X BASIC CARDS
STATED ODDS 1:3

2016 The Vampire Diaries Season Four Trios
COMPLETE SET (9) 6.00 15.00
COMMON CARD (H1-H9) 1.00 2.50
*FOIL: .6X TO 1.5X BASIC CARDS
STATED ODDS 1:3

2016 The Vampire Diaries Season Four Wardrobes
COMMON CARD (M1-M24) 8.00 20.00
STATED ODDS 1:18
M1 Elena Gilbert 12.00 30.00
M2 Stefan Salvatore 10.00 25.00
M4 Tyler Lockwood 10.00 25.00
M5 Matt Donovan 10.00 25.00
M6 Klaus Mikaelson 10.00 25.00
M7 Rebekah Mikaelson 25.00 60.00
M8 Bonnie Bennett 10.00 25.00
M10 Elena Gilbert 15.00 40.00
M12 Rebekah Mikaelson 10.00 25.00
M13 Klaus Mikaelson 15.00 40.00
M14 Damon Salvatore 12.00 30.00
M16 Caroline Forbes 10.00 25.00
M19 Stefan Salvatore 10.00 25.00
M20 Elena Gilbert 15.00 40.00
M21 Rebekah Mikaelson 12.00 30.00
M22 Klaus Mikaelson 12.00 30.00
M23 Damon Salvatore 12.00 30.00
M24 Graduation Robe
(Album Exclusive)

1997 Comic Images Vampirella Bloodlust
COMPLETE SET (72) 6.00 15.00
UNOPENED BOX (48 PACKS) 40.00 50.00
UNOPENED PACK (8 CARDS) 1.25 1.50
COMMON CARD (1-72) .15 .40
NNO1 Chromium Panel ALB 2.00 5.00

1997 Comic Images Vampirella Bloodlust Chromium
COMPLETE SET (6) 8.00 20.00
COMMON CARD (1-6) 1.50 4.00
STATED ODDS 1:18

1997 Comic Images Vampirella Bloodlust Promos
COMPLETE SET (2) 1.25 3.00
COMMON CARD .75 2.00

1995 Topps Vampirella Gallery
COMPLETE SET (72) 8.00 20.00
UNOPENED BOX (36 PACKS) 30.00 40.00
UNOPENED PACK (7 CARDS) 1.00 1.25
COMMON CARD (1-72) .20 .50
*GOLD: .75X TO 2X BASIC CARDS
NNO1 Art by Jose Gonzalez Hologram 20.00 50.00

1995 Topps Vampirella Gallery Fellow Femme Fatales
COMPLETE SET (6) 12.00 30.00
COMMON CARD (C1-C6) 2.50 6.00
STATED ODDS 1:18

1995 Topps Vampirella Gallery Promos
COMPLETE SET (7) 6.00 15.00
COMMON CARD 1.25 3.00

1996 Topps Vampirella Mastervisions
COMPLETE SET (36) 12.00 30.00
COMMON CARD (1-36) .40 1.00
P1 Art by Ray Lago 2.00 5.00

1996 Krome Vampress Luxura
COMPLETE SET (90) 12.00 30.00
UNOPENED BOX (24 PACKS) 40.00 50.00
UNOPENED PACK (6 CARDS) 2.00 2.25
COMMON CARD (1-90) .25 .60
*HOLOCHROME: 1.2X TO 3X BASIC CARDS .75 2.00
P1 Promo 1 (gen dist) 1.25 3.00
AU0 Kirk Lindo AU/500 15.00 40.00

1996 Krome Vampress Luxura Legends of Luxura Triptych
COMPLETE SET (9) 15.00 40.00
COMMON CARD (C1-C9) 2.00 5.00
STATED ODDS 1:4

2004 Van Helsing
COMPLETE SET (72) 6.00 15.00
UNOPENED BOX (36 PACKS) 40.00 50.00
UNOPENED PACK (7 CARDS) 1.25 1.50
COMMON CARD (1-72) .15 .40

2004 Van Helsing Autographs
COMMON AUTO 10.00 25.00
AVAILABLE VIA REDEMPTION CARDS
HJ Hugh Jackman L 250.00 500.00
RR Richard Roxburgh 15.00 40.00
SH Shuler Hensley 15.00 40.00
SS Stephen Sommers 12.00 30.00

2004 Van Helsing Monster Piece Costumes
COMMON CARD 12.00 30.00
REDEMPTION EXCLUSIVE
RM Redemption Card EXCH
MP1 Hugh Jackman (brown jacket) 20.00 50.00
MP2 Kate Beckinsale (red gown) 15.00 40.00
MP4 Hugh Jackman (ball costume) 20.00 50.00
MPUK Dracula's Brides UK CI 50.00 100.00

2004 Van Helsing Silver Foil
COMPLETE SET (6) 10.00 25.00
COMMON CARD (C1-C6) 2.00 5.00
STATED ODDS 1:15

2004 Van Helsing Promos
COMPLETE SET (3) 4.00 10.00
COMMON CARD (P1-P3) 2.00 5.00

1992-93 21st Century Archives Vargas Girls Pin-Ups
COMPLETE SET (100) 8.00 20.00
COMPLETE SER.1 SET (50) 5.00 12.00
COMPLETE SER.1 FACT. SET (51) 6.00 15.00
COMPLETE SER.2 SET (50) 5.00 12.00
COMPLETE SER.2 FACT. SET (51) 6.00 15.00
UNOPENED SER.1 BOX (36 PACKS) 30.00 40.00
UNOPENED SER.1 PACK (8 CARDS) 1.25 1.50
UNOPENED SER.2 BOX (36 PACKS) 30.00 40.00
UNOPENED SER.2 PACK (8 CARDS) 1.25 1.50
COMMON CARD SERIES 1 (1-50) .15 .40
COMMON CARD SERIES 2 (51-100) .15 .40

1992-93 21st Century Archives Vargas Girls Pin-Ups Series 1 Promos
COMMON CARD (UNNUMBERED) .75 2.00
NNO 2-Card Panel (8 7/8 X 4 Inches) 1.25 3.00
(Previews Magazine Exclusive)
NNO 3-card panel (8 7/8 X 4 3/8 Inches) 4.00 10.00
(SDCC Exclusive)

1992-93 21st Century Archives Vargas Girls Pin-Ups Series 2 Promos
NNO Dec. 1945 Prototype .60 1.50
(general distribution)
NNO Dec. 1945 Prototype (prism) 4.00 10.00
(general distribution)

1995 21st Century Archives Vargas Girls Pin-Ups
COMPLETE SET (50) 4.00 10.00
COMPLETE FACTORY SET (51) 6.00 15.00
UNOPENED BOX (36 PACKS) 30.00 40.00
UNOPENED PACK (8 CARDS) 1.25 1.50
COMMON CARD (1-50) .15 .40
*PRISM: 2X TO 5X BASIC CARDS
NNO Varga Prototype Jan. 1941 (same as cover of factory set; similar to card #1) .60 1.50

1995 21st Century Archives Vargas Girls Pin-Ups Innocent Prism

COMPLETE SET (5) 8.00 20.00
COMMON CARD (N1-N5) 2.00 5.00
*METALLIC: .5X TO 1.2X BASIC CARDS
RANDOMLY INSERTED INTO PACKS

1995 21st Century Archives Vargas Girls Pin-Ups Military Edition

COMPLETE SET (9) 5.00 12.00
COMMON CARD (1-9) 1.00 2.50
MAIL-IN EXCLUSIVE SET

2022 Zerocool Veefriends Series 1

UNOPENED BOX (10 CARDS) 3000.00 5000.00
STATED PRINT RUN 22 SER.#'d SETS
1 Content Condor 150.00 400.00
2 Diamond Hands Hen 300.00 800.00
4 Hot Sh*t Hornet 75.00 200.00
5 Rare Robot 125.00 300.00
6 Turnt Tick 300.00 750.00
8 You're Gonna Die Fly 250.00 600.00
9 5555 Fan 500.00 1200.00
10 Accountable Ant 150.00 400.00
11 Accountable Anteater 400.00 1000.00
12 Adaptable Alien 150.00 400.00
13 Adventurous Astronaut 500.00 1200.00
14 Alert Ape 150.00 400.00
15 Ambitious Angel 600.00 1500.00
16 Amiable Anchovy 150.00 400.00
17 Amped Aye Aye 200.00 500.00
18 Arbitraging Admiral 500.00 1200.00
19 Articulate Armadillo 200.00 500.00
20 Aspiring Alpaca 400.00 1000.00
21 Authentic Anaconda 125.00 300.00
22 Awesome African Civet 150.00 400.00
23 Bad Intentions 125.00 300.00
24 Bad Ass Bulldog 125.00 300.00
25 Balanced Beetle 250.00 600.00
26 Bashful Blobfish 150.00 400.00
28 Be the Bigger Person 75.00 200.00
29 Befuddled Burglar 600.00 1500.00
30 Benevolent Barn Owl 75.00 200.00
31 Big Game Bandicoot 150.00 400.00
32 Boisterous Beaver 75.00 200.00
33 Bold as F*ck Bat 200.00 500.00
34 Bombastic Baboon
35 Boss Bobcat 200.00 500.00
37 Brave Bison
39 Brilliant Barb 250.00 600.00
40 Brilliant Barracuda 150.00 400.00
43 Bubbly Buzzard
44 Bullish Bull 1500.00 4000.00
45 Calm Clam
46 Candid Clownfish 1200.00 3000.00
47 Capable Caterpillar 300.00 750.00
48 Caring Camel 200.00 500.00
49 Charismatic Chameleon 75.00 200.00
50 Charming Cheetah 250.00 600.00
52 Cheerful Chipmunk 150.00 400.00
53 Chill Chinchilla 250.00 600.00
54 Clever Crocodile 200.00 500.00
55 Common Sense Cow 500.00 1200.00
56 Compassionate Catfish 150.00 400.00
57 Confident Cobra 150.00 400.00
58 Considerate Cowboy 300.00 800.00
59 Consistent Cougar 150.00 400.00
60 Conviction Cockroach 125.00 300.00
61 Courageous Cockatoo 125.00 300.00
62 Courteous Coyote 500.00 1200.00
64 Creative Crab 200.00 500.00
65 Curious Crane
66 Cynical Cat 125.00 300.00
67 Dapper Dachshund 150.00 400.00
68 Daring Dragonfly 150.00 400.00
69 Decisive Duck 125.00 300.00
70 Dedicated Dragonfly 200.00 500.00
71 Detail-Oriented Dumbo Octopus 150.00 400.00
72 Determined Dolphin 150.00 400.00
73 Dialed-In Dog 200.00 500.00
75 Dope Dodo 150.00 400.00
76 Driven Dragon 150.00 400.00
77 Dynamic Dinosaur
78 Eager Eagle 150.00 400.00
79 Earnest Ermine 75.00 200.00
80 Empathy Elephant 1200.00 3000.00
81 Enamoured Emu 150.00 400.00
82 Energetic Electric Eel
83 Entrepreneur Elf 300.00 750.00
89 Faithful Pheasant 150.00 400.00
90 Flex'n Fox 200.00 500.00
91 Fly Firefly
92 Focused Falcon 200.00 500.00
93 Forever Phoenix 600.00 1500.00
94 Forgiving Horned Frog
95 Forthright Flamingo 200.00 500.00
96 F*ck You Monday Mole 125.00 300.00
98 Gary Bee 500.00 1200.00
99 Generous Gerbil 100.00 250.00
100 Gentle Giant 125.00 300.00
101 Genuine Giraffe 500.00 1200.00
103 Gifted Gopher 150.00 400.00
104 Gleeful Sugar Glider 125.00 300.00
105 Glowing Glow Worm 400.00 1000.00
106 Graceful Goldfish 200.00 500.00
107 Gracious Goose 250.00 600.00
108 Gracious Grasshopper 300.00 800.00
109 Gracious Grizzly Bear 250.00 600.00
110 Grateful Gar 150.00 400.00
111 Gratitude Gorilla 2500.00 6000.00
112 Gutsy Gecko
114 Happy Hermit Crab
115 Hard-Working Wombat 100.00 250.00
116 Headstrong Honey Badger 250.00 600.00
117 Heart-Trooper
118 Helpful Hippo 250.00 600.00
119 Hodl Hyena 200.00 500.00
120 Honest Honey Bee
121 Honorable Olm
122 Humble Hedgehog
123 Humble Hummingbird
124 Hungry Hammerhead 150.00 400.00
125 Hustling Hamster
126 Hype Horse
127 Impeccable Inostranet 300.00 800.00
128 Independent Inch Worm 250.00 600.00
129 Innovative Impala 300.00 750.00
130 Insightful Irish Terrier 200.00 500.00
131 Intuitive Iguana 125.00 300.00
133 Jolly Jack-O 200.00 500.00
134 Joyous Jellyfish 125.00 300.00
135 Juicy Jaguar 125.00 300.00
136 Just Jackal
137 Karma Kiwi 150.00 400.00
138 Keen Kingfisher
140 Kind Kudu
141 Kind-Warrior 250.00 600.00
142 Kindred Kangaroo
143 Knowing Gnome 400.00 1000.00
144 Last Glass Standing 250.00 600.00
145 Legendary Lemur 150.00 400.00
146 Legit Llama 100.00 250.00
147 Level Headed Lizard 125.00 300.00
148 Likable Leopard
149 Like a Sponge
150 Lit Lamb 300.00 800.00
151 Logical Lion 150.00 400.00
152 Loyal Lobster 125.00 300.00
154 Macho Manta Ray 250.00 600.00
155 Macro Micro 200.00 500.00
156 Magnanimous Maltese 300.00 800.00
157 Major Moth 150.00 400.00
158 Mature Mule 125.00 300.00
160 Methodical Mammoth 500.00 1200.00
161 Meticulous Magpie 300.00 750.00
162 Mint Mink 200.00 500.00
163 Modest Moose 200.00 500.00
164 Mojo Mouse 125.00 300.00
165 Moral Monkey 100.00 250.00
166 Motivated Monster 300.00 800.00
167 Nifty Narwhal
168 Noble Numbat 150.00 400.00
169 O.G. Ox
170 Observant Oyster 125.00 300.00
171 Offense Oriented Orangutan
172 Optimistic Otter 250.00 600.00
173 Organized Ostrich
175 Passionate Parrot 200.00 500.00
176 Patient Panda
177 Patient Pig
178 Pea Salad 150.00 400.00
179 Peaceful Pelican 250.00 600.00
180 Perceptive Puma 125.00 300.00
181 Perfect Persian Cat
182 Perspective Pigeon 250.00 600.00
183 Persuasive Pigeon 100.00 250.00
185 Pleasant Platypus 200.00 500.00
187 Poised Pug 300.00 750.00
189 Polished Poodle 300.00 750.00
190 Ponder It from All Angles 150.00 400.00
191 Positive Porcupine 150.00 400.00
192 Practical Peacock
193 Proactive Piranha 200.00 500.00
194 Productive Puffin 150.00 400.00
195 Profound Possum 250.00 600.00
196 Prudent Polar Bear
197 Quick Quail 150.00 400.00
198 Radical Rabbit 600.00 1500.00
199 Rational Rattlesnake 400.00 1000.00
200 Reflective Rhinoceros 125.00 300.00
201 Reliable Rat 300.00 750.00
202 Resourceful Robin
203 Respectful Racoon 150.00 400.00
204 Responsive Ram 150.00 400.00
205 Secure Sparrow 200.00 500.00
206 Self-Aware Hare 300.00 750.00
207 Selfless Sloth 250.00 600.00
208 Sensible Sommelier 250.00 600.00
209 Sensitive Centipede 150.00 400.00
210 Sentimental Salamander 400.00 1000.00
211 Serious Sperm Whale 150.00 400.00
213 Sharing Squirrel
214 Shrewd Shark
215 Shrewd Sheep 125.00 300.00
216 Sincere Skunk 125.00 300.00
217 Skilled Skeleton
218 Slay'n Slug 200.00 500.00
219 Sophisticated Stingray 300.00 800.00
221 Spiffy Salmon
222 Spontaneous Seahorse
223 Steadfast Snake 250.00 600.00
224 Stoic Slime
225 Stunned Sun 300.00 750.00
226 Sufficient Shrimp 125.00 300.00
227 Suffocate Hate 250.00 600.00
229 Swaggy Sea Lion
230 Sweet Swan 250.00 600.00
231 Sympathetic Squid 125.00 300.00
232 Tasteful Malayan Tapir
233 Tenacious Termite 200.00 500.00
234 Tenacious Turkey 400.00 1000.00
236 The Oak Monster
237 The World Has Plenty of Love Start Listening to It 125.00 300.00
238 Thoughtful Three Horned Harpik
239 Tidy Troll
240 To the Moon Meerkat 300.00 750.00
241 Tolerant Tortoise 200.00 500.00
242 Tolerant Tuna 300.00 800.00
243 Toronto St. Louis 200.00 500.00
244 Tough to Beat a Worm from the Dirt! 150.00 400.00
245 Tremendous Tiger 150.00 400.00
246 Truculent T-Rex
247 Trusting Tarantula
249 Unwavering Urchin
250 Very, Very, Very, Very Lucky Black Cat
251 Vibe'n Vampire 400.00 1000.00
253 Warm Wolverine 500.00 1200.00
254 Well-Connected Werewolf 400.00 1000.00
255 Well-Rounded Warthog 400.00 1000.00
256 When You Live for their Validation You Aren't Living 250.00 600.00
257 Who Was Born in 1997? 100.00 250.00
258 Wild Wallaby 100.00 250.00
259 Willful Wizard 125.00 300.00
260 Wily Wild Boar
261 Wise Wasp
262 Witty Weasel
263 Woke Walrus
265 Yolo Yak 250.00 600.00
266 Your Poor Relationship with Time Is Your Biggest Vulnerability 300.00 800.00
267 Zealous-Zombie
268 Zestful Zebra

1996 Kitchen Sink Press Veil of Delirium

COMPLETE BOXED SET (36) 6.00 15.00
COMMON CARD (1-36) .30 .75
AU Todd Schorr AU Uncut Sheet
P1 Oversized Promo 1.25 3.00

2006 Veronica Mars Season One

COMPLETE SET (72) 3.00 8.00
UNOPENED BOX (24 PACKS) 60.00 100.00
UNOPENED PACK (7 CARDS) 3.00 5.00
COMMON CARD (1-72) .08 .25

2006 Veronica Mars Season One Autographs

COMMON AUTO (A1-A11) 5.00 12.00
STATED ODDS 1:24
A1 Kristen Bell 150.00 300.00
A6 Amanda Seyfried 60.00 120.00
A7 Tina Majorino 10.00 25.00
A8 Anthony Anderson 10.00 25.00
A9 Max Greenfield 6.00 15.00
A10 Paula Marshall 6.00 15.00
AR1 Autograph Redemption Card

2006 Veronica Mars Season One Box-Loaders

COMPLETE SET (3) 3.00 8.00
COMMON CARD (BL1-BL3) 1.25 3.00
STATED ODDS 1:BOX
CL1 Veronica & Lilly 10.00 25.00

2006 Veronica Mars Season One Pieceworks

COMMON CARD (1-12) 4.00 10.00
STATED ODDS 1:24
PW1 Kristen Bell 60.00 120.00
PW2 Jason Dohring 10.00 25.00
PW3 Percy Daggs III 8.00 20.00
PW4 Teddy Dunn 8.00 20.00
PW6 Amanda Seyfried 12.00 30.00
PW8 Lisa Rinna 12.00 30.00
PW9 Alona Tal 10.00 25.00
PW10 Ryan Hansen 10.00 25.00
PW11 Kyle Secor 10.00 25.00
PW12 Paris Hilton 25.00 60.00

2006 Veronica Mars Season One Revolving around Mars

COMPLETE SET (6) 6.00 15.00
COMMON CARD (1-6) 1.25 3.00
STATED ODDS 1:17

2006 Veronica Mars Season One Who Killed Lilly Kane

COMPLETE SET (9) 8.00 20.00
COMMON CARD (1-9) 1.00 2.50
STATED ODDS 1:11

2006 Veronica Mars Season One Promos

COMPLETE SET (4) 4.00 10.00
COMMON CARD .75 2.00
P2 Veronica Mars NSU 2.00 5.00
P3 Cast CON 1.25 3.00
Pi Veronica Mars (Inkworks) 1.50 4.00

2007 Veronica Mars Season Two

COMPLETE SET (81) 3.00 8.00
UNOPENED BOX (24 PACKS) 50.00 75.00
UNOPENED PACK (8 CARDS) 2.50 3.00
COMMON CARD (1-81) .10 .25

MODERN

2007 Veronica Mars Season Two Autographed Pieceworks

COMMON AUTO (APW1-APW4)	10.00	25.00
APW1 Enrico Colantoni	15.00	40.00
APW3 Kyle Gallner	15.00	40.00
APW4 Charisma Carpenter	30.00	75.00

2007 Veronica Mars Season Two Autographs

COMMON AUTO (A12-A21)	5.00	12.00
STATED ODDS 1:24		
A12 Kristen Bell	75.00	150.00
A13 Enrico Colantoni	12.00	30.00
A14 Percy Daggs III	5.00	20.00
A15 Kyle Gallner	10.00	25.00
A16 Kristin Cavallari	10.00	25.00
A17 Krysten Ritter	60.00	120.00
A18 Alona Tal	10.00	25.00
A19 Charisma Carpenter	25.00	60.00

2007 Veronica Mars Season Two Box-Loaders

COMPLETE SET (3)	3.00	8.00
COMMON CARD (BL1-BL3)	1.25	3.00
STATED ODDS 1:BOX		
CL1 Transition	10.00	25.00
CASE INSERT		

2007 Veronica Mars Season Two Cliffhanger

COMPLETE SET (9)	6.00	15.00
COMMON CARD (1-9)	1.00	2.50
STATED ODDS 1:11		

2007 Veronica Mars Season Two Justice

COMPLETE SET (6)	4.00	10.00
COMMON CARD (1-6)	1.00	2.50
STATED ODDS 1:17		

2007 Veronica Mars Season Two Pieceworks

COMMON CARD (PW1-PW13; PWR)	5.00	12.00
STATED ODDS 1:24		
PW13 DEALER INCENTIVE		
PW1 Kristen Bell	20.00	50.00
PW2 Enrico Colantoni	6.00	15.00
PW3 Jason Dohring	6.00	15.00
PW6A Tessa Thompson	8.00	20.00
PW6B Tessa Thompson	8.00	20.00
PW7 Kyle Gallner	10.00	25.00
PW9 Alyson Hannigan	20.00	50.00
PW10 Charisma Carpenter	20.00	50.00
PW13 K.Bell/J.Dohring/T.Dunn (Dealer Incentive Exclusive)	100.00	200.00
PR1 Pieceworks Redemption Card		

2007 Veronica Mars Season Two Promos

COMPLETE SET (4)	3.00	8.00
COMMON CARD	.75	2.00
VM2Pi Duncan, Veronica, & Logan (Inkworks)	2.00	5.00

2003 The Very Best of the Saint

COMPLETE SET (100)	4.00	10.00
UNOPENED BOX (36 PACKS)	30.00	40.00
UNOPENED PACK (6 CARDS)	1.25	1.50
COMMON CARD (1-100)	.10	.25
SKGB Graham Bleathman (CT sketch)		

2003 The Very Best of the Saint Autographs

COMMON CARD (SA1-SA20)	10.00	25.00
STATED ODDS 1:36		
SA9, SA11, SA16 DO NOT EXIST		
SA1 Roger Moore	120.00	200.00
SA6 Stephanie Beacham	25.00	60.00
SA10 Johnny Briggs	20.00	50.00
SA14 Julian Glover	15.00	40.00
SA18 Francis Matthews	15.00	40.00
SA19 John Savident	20.00	50.00
SA20 Edward Woodward/200 (sold seperately)	25.00	60.00

2003 The Very Best of the Saint Costumes

COMMON CARD	12.00	30.00
STATED ODDS 1:360		
SC1 Simon Templar's Suit Jacket	15.00	40.00
SC3 Simon Templar's Suit Waist Jacket (CT excl.)	15.00	40.00
SDC1 Roger Moore Simon Templar's Jacket (SDCC 2002)		

2003 The Very Best of the Saint Infamous Simon Templar Foil Puzzle

COMPLETE SET (9)	10.00	25.00
COMMON CARD (1-9)	1.25	3.00
STATED ODDS 1:8		

2003 The Very Best of the Saint Saintly Merchandise Foil

COMPLETE SET (6)	10.00	25.00
COMMON CARD (SM1-SM6)	2.00	5.00
STATED ODDS 1:12		

2003 The Very Best of the Saint Promos

COMPLETE SET (2)	1.50	4.00
COMMON CARD (P1-P2)	1.00	2.50

1991 Collect-a-Card Vette Set

COMPLETE SET (100)	8.00	20.00
COMPLETE BOXED SET (110)	6.00	15.00
UNOPENED BOX (36 PACKS)	10.00	15.00
UNOPENED PACK (10 CARDS)	.40	.50
COMMON CARD (1-100)	.15	.40
NNO1 1988 Corvette Callaway Sledgehammer Hologram	.75	2.00
NNO3 Uncut Sheet		

1991 Collect-a-Card Vette Set Mario Andretti

COMPLETE SET (10)	5.00	12.00
COMMON CARD (1-10)	.60	1.50
MAILAWAY AND BOXED SET EXCLUSIVE		

1991 Collect-a-Card Vette Set Promos

COMPLETE SET (2)	2.00	5.00
COMMON CARD	1.25	3.00

1994 Star International VI Talent Search Venus Swimwear

COMPLETE SET (100)	6.00	15.00
UNOPENED BOX (36 PACKS)		
UNOPENED PACK (9 CARDS)		
COMMON CARD (1-100)	.12	.30

1983 Topps Video City

COMPLETE SET (32)	12.00	30.00
UNOPENED BOX (36 PACKS)	125.00	200.00
UNOPENED PACK (3 CARDS & 3 STICKERS)	3.50	5.00
COMMON CARD	.50	1.25

1988 Dart FlipCards Vietnam Facts Series I

COMPLETE SET (66)	8.00	20.00
COMPLETE BOXED SET (66)	8.00	20.00
UNOPENED BOX (48 PACKS)	15.00	25.00
UNOPENED PACK (6 CARDS)	.50	.75
COMMON CARD (1-66)	.25	.60

1991 Dart FlipCards Vietnam Facts Series II

COMPLETE BOXED SET (100)	8.00	20.00
COMMON CARD (1-100)	.15	.40

1991 Dart FlipCards Vietnam Facts Series II 4UP Panels

COMMON CARD	2.00	5.00

1994 Comic Images Vincent Di Fate's Blueprints of the Future

COMPLETE SET (90)	4.00	10.00
UNOPENED BOX (48 PACKS)	20.00	30.00
UNOPENED PACK (10 CARDS)	.75	1.00
COMMON CARD (1-90)	.10	.25
M1 Medallion Card	10.00	25.00
AUVDF Vincent Di Fate/500*	20.00	50.00

1994 Comic Images Vincent Di Fate's Blueprints of the Future Larger Than Life

COMPLETE SET (3)	12.00	30.00
COMMON CARD (1-3)	5.00	12.00
STATED ODDS 1:48		

1994 Comic Images Vincent Di Fate's Blueprints of the Future OmniChrome

COMPLETE SET (6)	15.00	40.00
COMMON CARD (OC1-OC6)	3.00	8.00
STATED ODDS 1:16		

1994 Comic Images Vincent Di Fate's Blueprints of the Future Promos

6UP (6-up panel of OC1-OC6)	8.00	20.00
NNO1 Jim Warren 2 Insert Promo	.75	2.00

1992 Mother Productions Vintage Aircraft Nose Art

COMPLETE SET (42)	5.00	12.00
COMMON CARD (1-42)	.25	.60

1993 Mother Productions Vintage Art Nose Art Series II

COMPLETE SET (42)	5.00	12.00
COMMON CARD (1-42)	.25	.60

1997 Ultimate Art Visions of Freedom

COMPLETE BOXED SET (39)	4.00	10.00
COMMON CARD (1-39)	.20	.50

1995 Topps Visions of Vampirella

COMPLETE SET (90)	8.00	20.00
UNOPENED BOX (24 PACKS)	40.00	50.00
UNOPENED PACK (11 CARDS)	2.00	2.50
COMMON CARD (1-90)	.20	.50
91 (Art by Caesar album excl)	1.50	4.00

1995 Topps Visions of Vampirella HorrorGlow

COMPLETE SET (6)	15.00	40.00
COMMON CARD (1-6)	3.00	8.00
STATED ODDS 1:8		

1995 Topps Visions of Vampirella Pin-Up Gallery Box-Toppers

COMPLETE SET (6)	15.00	40.00
COMMON CARD (1-6)	3.00	8.00
STATED ODDS 1:BOX		

1995 Topps Visions of Vampirella Promos

COMMON CARD	1.25	3.00
91 Vampirella		
P3 Art by Joseph Linsner; cello-packed with	2.00	5.00
NNO1 unnumbered panel; inset is P2, external	2.50	6.00

1984 Topps Voltron Tattoos

COMPLETE SET (12)	5.00	12.00
UNOPENED BOX (36 PACKS)	45.00	60.00
UNOPENED PACK (1 SHEET OF 24)	1.50	2.00
COMMON SHEET	.60	1.50

1995 Saban VR Troopers

COMPLETE SET (20)	5.00	12.00
J.B. REESE SET (5)	1.25	3.00
JEB SET (5)	1.25	3.00
KAITLIN HALL SET (5)	1.25	3.00
RYAN STEEL SET (5)	1.25	3.00
COMMON CARD	.50	1.25

1987 Zoot Wacko-Saurs

COMPLETE SET (48)	3.00	8.00
UNOPENED BOX (50 PACKS)	10.00	15.00
UNOPENED PACK (5 CARDS)	.30	.40
COMMON CARD	.12	.30

1985 Glenn Confections Wacky Wax Dinosaurs

COMPLETE SET (36)	15.00	40.00
COMMON CARD (1-36)	1.10	2.25

The Walking Dead

2011 The Walking Dead

COMPLETE SET (81)	8.00	20.00
UNOPENED BOX (24 PACKS)	350.00	600.00
UNOPENED PACK (5 CARDS)	15.00	25.00
COMMON CARD (1-81)	.15	.40
BT New Season Oct.16 BT PROMO		

2011 The Walking Dead Autographs

COMMON AUTO (A1-A18)	10.00	25.00
STATED ODDS 1:24		
A3 AND A4 ISSUED WITH SEASON TWO		
A1 Jon Bernthal	50.00	100.00
A2 Jon Bernthal	30.00	75.00
A3 Laurie Holden	60.00	120.00
A4 Laurie Holden	50.00	100.00
A5 Steven Yeun	30.00	75.00
A6 Steven Yeun	30.00	75.00
A7 Chandler Riggs	50.00	100.00
A8 Chandler Riggs	50.00	100.00
A9 Emma Bell	20.00	50.00
A10 Emma Bell	20.00	50.00
A11 Lennie James	60.00	120.00
A12 Lennie James	50.00	100.00
A13 Michael Rooker	100.00	200.00
A14 Michael Rooker	100.00	200.00
A17 Norman Reedus	50.00	100.00
A18 Norman Reedus	60.00	120.00

2011 The Walking Dead Behind-the-Scenes

COMPLETE SET (9)	20.00	40.00
COMMON CARD (C1-C9)	3.00	8.00
STATED ODDS 1:12		

2011 The Walking Dead Foil Walkers

COMPLETE SET (9)	12.00	30.00
COMMON CARD (W1-W9)	2.50	6.00
STATED ODDS 1:6		

2011 The Walking Dead Wardrobes

COMMON MEM (M1-M18)	6.00	15.00
STATED ODDS 1:12		
M18 ANNOUNCED PRINT RUN 500		
M1 Rick Grimes	50.00	100.00
M2 Lori Grimes	50.00	100.00
M3 Lori Grimes	15.00	40.00
M4 Carl Grimes	30.00	60.00
M5 Shane Walsh	12.00	30.00
M6 Shane Walsh	12.00	30.00
M7 Glenn	25.00	60.00
M8 Andrea	20.00	40.00
M9 Amy	20.00	50.00
M10 Dale	12.00	30.00
M11 Daryl	50.00	100.00
M13 Deer Eating Zombie	8.00	20.00
M18 Rick's First Kill/500* ALB	15.00	40.00

2011 The Walking Dead Promos

COMMON CARD	2.00	5.00
P3 Rick Grimes and friend GEN	3.00	8.00
P4 Rick and mini walker S1 DVD	6.00	15.00
NNO Rick Grimes SDCC	4.00	10.00

2012 The Walking Dead Season Two

COMPLETE SET (80)	8.00	20.00
UNOPENED BOX (24 PACKS)	200.00	300.00
UNOPENED PACK (5 CARDS)	8.00	12.00
COMMON CARD (1-80)	.20	.50

2012 The Walking Dead Season Two Autographs

COMMON CARD (A1-A14)	8.00	20.00
STATED ODDS 1:24 H, 1:2,000 R		
A1 Andrew Lincoln	60.00	120.00

A2 Jon Bernthal 60.00 120.00
A3 Jeffrey DeMunn 30.00 75.00
A4 Steven Yeun 20.00 50.00
A5 Norman Reedus 50.00 100.00
A6 Melissa Suzanne McBride 25.00 50.00
A7 Madison Lintz 15.00 40.00
A8 Madison Lintz 25.00 60.00
A9 Lauren Cohan 30.00 75.00
A10 Scott Wilson 20.00 50.00
A13 Laurie Holden 20.00 50.00
A14 Sarah Wayne Callies 20.00 50.00

2012 The Walking Dead Season Two Character Bios

COMPLETE SET (9) 12.00 30.00
COMMON CARD (CB1-CB9) 2.50 6.00
STATED ODDS 1:12

2012 The Walking Dead Season Two Dual Wardrobes

COMMON MEM (DM1-DM3) 30.00 75.00
SINGLE/DUAL MEM ODDS 1:12 H, 1:2,000 R
DM1 Rick Grimes/Sophia 50.00 100.00

2012 The Walking Dead Season Two Puzzle

COMPLETE SET (9) 10.00 25.00
COMMON CARD (1-9) 1.25 3.00
STATED ODDS 1:12

2012 The Walking Dead Season Two Shadowbox

COMPLETE SET (9) 40.00 80.00
COMMON CARD (SB1-SB9) 6.00 15.00
STATED ODDS 1:24

2012 The Walking Dead Season Two Wardrobes

COMMON MEM (M1-M33) 6.00 15.00
SINGLE/DUAL MEM ODDS 1:12 H, 1:2,000 R
M33 ISSUED AS BINDER EXCLUSIVE
M1 Rick Grimes white t-shirt 25.00 60.00
M2 T-Dog 12.00 30.00
M3 Shane Walsh 20.00 50.00
M4 Carl Grimes 15.00 40.00
M5 Andrea 25.00 50.00
M6 Glenn blue shirt 10.00 25.00
M7 Lori Grimes 15.00 40.00
M8 Dale Horvath 15.00 40.00
M9 Sophia (human) 25.00 50.00
M10 Maggie Greene 15.00 40.00
M11 Shane Walsh 12.00 30.00
M12 Andrea 15.00 40.00
M13 Carol Peletier 25.00 60.00
M14 Hershel Greene 12.00 30.00
M15 Glenn 12.00 30.00
M16 Rick Grimes 25.00 60.00
M17 Lori Grimes 30.00 60.00
M18 Carl Grimes 15.00 40.00
M19 Andrea 10.00 25.00
M20 Sophia (walker) 20.00 50.00
M21 Carol Peletier 15.00 40.00
M22 Hershel Greene 15.00 40.00
M23 Maggie Greene 15.00 40.00
M24 Dale Horvath 15.00 40.00
M25 T-Dog 10.00 25.00
M26 Andrea 15.00 40.00
M27 Daryl Dixon 30.00 75.00
M33 Bus Walker ALB 8.00 20.00

2012 The Walking Dead Season Two Promos

P1 Rick Grimes NSU 2.50 6.00
RC1 Michonne RCBD
SDCC1 Michonne SDCC 3.00 8.00

2013 The Walking Dead Season 2 Dog Tags

COMPLETE SET (24) 30.00 80.00
UNOPENED BOX (24 PACKS) 85.00 100.00
UNOPENED PACK (1 TAG+1 STICKER) 4.00 5.00
COMMON CARD (1-24) 2.00 5.00
*FOIL: .8X TO 2X BASIC TAGS
1 Rick Grimes 4.00 10.00
7 Daryl Dixon 5.00 12.00
16 Merle and Daryl 5.00 12.00
22 Shane Walker 3.00 8.00

2013 The Walking Dead Season 2 Dog Tags Costumes

COMPLETE SET (10) 120.00 250.00
COMMON TAG (C1-C10) 8.00 20.00
STATED ODDS 1:24
HOBBY EXCLUSIVE
C1 IronE Singleton L 20.00 50.00
C2 Laurie Holden 12.00 30.00
C3 Scott Wilson 20.00 50.00
C4 Steven Yeun 20.00 50.00
C7 Jon Bernthal 15.00 40.00
C10 Sarah Wayne Calles 25.00 60.00

2013 The Walking Dead Season 2 Dog Tags Costumes Target

COMPLETE SET (10) 120.00 250.00
COMMON TAG (CT1-CT10) 8.00 20.00
STATED ODDS 1:24
TARGET EXCLUSIVE
CT1 Andrew Lincoln 12.00 30.00
CT2 Jon Bernthal 10.00 25.00
CT3 Lauren Cohan 12.00 30.00
CT5 IronE Singleton 10.00 25.00
CT6 Madison Lintz R 30.00 80.00
CT7 School Bus Walker L 10.00 25.00
CT9 Lauren Cohan L 15.00 40.00
CT10 Laurie Holden 12.00 30.00

2013 The Walking Dead Season 2 Dog Tags Costumes Wal-Mart

COMPLETE SET (10) 100.00 200.00
COMMON TAG (CW1-CW10) 8.00 20.00
STATED ODDS 1:24
WALMART EXCLUSIVE
CW1 Andrew Lincoln 15.00 40.00
CW3 Lauren Cohan L 12.00 30.00
CW4 IronE Singleton 12.00 30.00
CW6 Steven Yeun L 12.00 30.00
CW8 Laurie Holden 12.00 30.00
CW9 IronE Singleton (AMC) R 12.00 30.00
CW10 Lauren Cohan L 10.00 25.00

2013 The Walking Dead Season 2 Dog Tags Stickers

COMPLETE SET (24) 5.00 12.00
COMMON STICKER (S1-S24) .40 1.00
*FOIL: .8X TO 2X BASIC STICKERS
STATED ODDS 1:1

2013 The Walking Dead Season 2 Dog Tags Update

COMPLETE SET (24) 30.00 80.00
COMMON TAG (1-24) 2.00 5.00
*FOIL: .5X TO 1.2X BASIC TAGS
STATED ODDS 1:1
PR1 RANDOMLY INSERTED
4 Daryl Dixon 3.00 8.00
5 Daryl Dixon 3.00 8.00
6 Daryl Dixon 3.00 8.00
12 Rick Grimes 3.00 8.00
13 Rick Grimes 3.00 8.00
17 Michonne 2.50 6.00
PR1 Farmhouse Bedroom Prop Relic 30.00 80.00

2013 The Walking Dead Season 2 Dog Tags Update Costumes

COMPLETE SET (10) 100.00 200.00
COMMON TAG (C1-C10) 8.00 20.00
*FOIL: .8X TO 2X BASIC TAGS
STATED ODDS 1:24
HOBBY EXCLUSIVE
C1 Andrew Lincoln 20.00 50.00
C3 Jeffrey DeMunn 15.00 40.00
C4 Laurie Holden 15.00 40.00
C6 Chandler Riggs 10.00 25.00
C9 Lauren Cohan 15.00 40.00
C10 Steven Yeun 12.00 30.00

2013 The Walking Dead Season 2 Dog Tags Update Costumes Retail

COMPLETE SET (11) 120.00 250.00
COMMON TAG (CR1-CR11) 8.00 20.00
*FOIL: .8X TO 2X BASIC TAGS
STATED ODDS 1:24
RETAIL EXCLUSIVE
CR1 Andrew Lincoln 15.00 40.00
CR2 Jon Bernthal 10.00 25.00
CR3 Chandler Riggs 10.00 25.00
CR4 Pruitt Taylor Vince 10.00 25.00
CR6A Chandler Riggs/Red 10.00 25.00
CR6B Chandler Riggs/Gray 10.00 25.00
CR6C Chandler Riggs/Navy 10.00 25.00
CR8 Sarah Wayne Callies 12.00 30.00
CR9 Jeffrey DeMunn 12.00 30.00
CR11 Chandler Riggs 10.00 25.00

2013 The Walking Dead Season 2 Dog Tags Update Stickers

COMPLETE SET (24) 5.00 12.00
COMMON STICKER (S1-S24) .40 1.00
*FOIL: .8X TO 2X BASIC STICKERS
STATED ODDS 1:1

2014 The Walking Dead Season Three Part 1

COMPLETE SET (72) 8.00 20.00
UNOPENED BOX (24 PACKS) 100.00 150.00
UNOPENED PACK (5 CARDS) 4.00 6.00
COMMON CARD (1-72) .20 .50

2014 The Walking Dead Season Three Part 1 Autographed Wardrobes

COMMON AUTO (AM1-AM7) 20.00 50.00
STATED ODDS 1:144
AM1 Steven Yeun 30.00 60.00
AM2 Lauren Cohan 75.00 150.00
AM3 Melissa McBride 30.00 60.00

2014 The Walking Dead Season Three Part 1 Autographs

COMMON AUTO (A1-A12) 5.00 12.00
STATED ODDS 1:24
A1 Andrew Lincoln 60.00 120.00
A2 Norman Reedus 50.00 100.00
A3 Lauren Cohan 50.00 100.00
A4 Steven Yeun 15.00 40.00
A5 IronE Singleton 10.00 25.00
A6 Melissa McBride 15.00 40.00
A7 Emily Kinney 15.00 40.00
A8 Danai Gurira 25.00 60.00
A11 Scott Wilson 10.00 25.00
A12 Sarah Wayne Callies 25.00 60.00

2014 The Walking Dead Season Three Part 1 Grimes Family Shadowbox

COMPLETE SET (9) 6.00 15.00
COMMON CARD (GF1-GF9) 1.25 3.00
STATED ODDS 1:12

2014 The Walking Dead Season Three Part 1 Props

STATED ODDS 1:769
SC01 Shell Casings 80.00 150.00

2014 The Walking Dead Season Three Part 1 Season Two Wardrobes

COMMON MEM (M34-M37) 10.00 25.00
STATED ODDS 1:24
M35 Maggie 15.00 40.00
M36 Glenn 15.00 30.00

2014 The Walking Dead Season Three Part 1 The Prison

COMPLETE SET (9) 8.00 20.00
COMMON CARD (TP1-TP9) 1.50 4.00
STATED ODDS 1:12

2014 The Walking Dead Season Three Part 1 Wardrobes

COMMON MEM (M1-M30) 6.00 15.00
STATED ODDS 1:24
M29 WALGREEN'S EXCLUSIVE
M30 HOT TOPIC EXCLUSIVE
M1 Daryl 25.00 60.00
M2 Lori 10.00 25.00
M3 Maggie 10.00 25.00
M4 Carol 8.00 20.00
M5 Beth 25.00 50.00
M6 Rick 40.00 80.00
M9 Glenn 15.00 30.00
M10 Carl 10.00 20.00
M11 Maggie 15.00 40.00
M12 Carol 8.00 20.00
M15 Lori 8.00 20.00
M17 Carl 10.00 25.00
M18 Carol 8.00 20.00
M19 Glenn 8.00 20.00
M20 Maggie 10.00 25.00
M21 Carl 8.00 20.00
M22 Lori 15.00 30.00
M23 Carol 12.00 25.00
M24 Beth SP 100.00 200.00
M25 T-Dog 15.00 30.00
M26 Lori 10.00 25.00
M27 Maggie SP 30.00 75.00
M29 Walker Wardrobe WG 75.00 150.00
M30 Walker Wardrobe HT 50.00 100.00

2014 The Walking Dead Season Three Part 2

COMPLETE SET (72) 8.00 20.00
UNOPENED BOX (24 PACKS) 100.00 150.00
UNOPENED PACK (5 CARDS) 4.00 6.00
COMMON CARD (1-72) .20 .50

2014 The Walking Dead Season Three Part 2 Autographed Wardrobes

COMMON AUTO (AM8-AM10) 50.00 100.00
STATED ODDS 1:144
AM8 Danai Gurira 60.00 120.00
AM9 Andrew Lincoln 60.00 120.00

2014 The Walking Dead Season Three Part 2 Autographs

COMMON AUTO (A13-A23) 6.00 15.00
STATED ODDS 1:24
A13 Greg Nicotero 10.00 25.00
A14 Laurie Holden 15.00 40.00
A15 Dallas Roberts/Human 8.00 20.00
A18 Chad L. Coleman 12.00 30.00
A19 Sonequa Martin-Green 15.00 40.00
A22 Lennie James 20.00 50.00
A23 David Morrissey 25.00 60.00

2014 The Walking Dead Season Three Part 2 Dual Wardrobes

COMMON MEM (DM01-DM05) 15.00 40.00
STATED ODDS 1:24 w/SINGLE WARDROBE
DM1 Andrea/The Governor 30.00 75.00
DM2 Andrea/Merle 20.00 50.00
DM4 Merle/The Governor 30.00 75.00
DM5 Bowman/Merle 25.00 60.00

2014 The Walking Dead Season Three Part 2 Props

RANDOMLY INSERTED INTO PACKS
SC02A Shell Casting 80.00 120.00
SC02B Shell Casting (cap variant) 200.00 350.00

2014 The Walking Dead Season Three Part 2 The Governor

COMPLETE SET (9) 10.00 25.00
COMMON CARD (TG01-TG09) 2.00 5.00
STATED ODDS 1:12

2014 The Walking Dead Season Three Part 2 Wardrobes

COMMON MEM#((M29-M52; W01-14) 6.00 15.00
STATED ODDS 1:24
M52 ALBUM EXCLUSIVE
W13 WALGREEN'S EXCLUSIVE
W14 HOT TOPIC EXCLUSIVE
M29 Andrea 12.00 30.00
M30 Michonne 50.00 100.00
M31 The Governor 20.00 50.00
M32 Tyreese 10.00 25.00

MODERN

M33 Merle 15.00 40.00
M34 Andrea 10.00 25.00
M35 Milton 8.00 20.00
M36 Morgan 10.00 25.00
M37 The Governor 15.00 40.00
M38 Rick 30.00 80.00
M39 Michonne 60.00 120.00
M40 Tyreese 10.00 25.00
M41 Andrea 15.00 40.00
M42 Caesar 10.00 25.00
M43 Bowman 8.00 20.00
M44 Sasha 10.00 25.00
M45 Morgan 12.00 30.00
M47 Michonne 80.00 150.00
M49 Rick 25.00 60.00
M51 Merle 30.00 80.00
M52 Andrea ALB 20.00 50.00
W13WG Walker WG 120.00 250.00
W14HT Walker HT 50.00 100.00

2014 The Walking Dead Season Three Part 2 Woodbury

COMPLETE SET (9) 8.00 20.00
COMMON CARD (WB1-WB9) 1.50 4.00
STATED ODDS 1:12

2014 The Walking Dead Season Three Part 2 Promos

COMPLETE SET (2) 6.00 15.00
COMMON CARD (NSU1-NSU2) 4.00 10.00

2014 The Walking Dead Season 3 Dog Tags

COMPLETE SET (36) 60.00 120.00
UNOPENED BOX (24 PACKS) 120.00 150.00
UNOPENED PACK (1 TAG+1 STICKER) 5.00 6.50
COMMON CARD (1-36) 2.00 5.00
*FOIL: .5X TO 1.2X BASIC TAGS
3 Beth Greene 3.00 8.00
6 Daryl Dixon 3.00 8.00
7 Daryl Dixon (w/Harley) 6.00 15.00
11 The Governor 3.00 8.00
16 Michonne 3.00 8.00
17 Michonne (aiming katana) 4.00 10.00
21 Rick Grimes (aiming gun) 5.00 12.00
22 Rick Grimes 4.00 10.00
27 Merle Walker (Walker #3) 3.00 8.00

2014 The Walking Dead Season 3 Dog Tags Stickers

COMPLETE SET (24) 6.00 15.00
COMMON CARD (S1-S24) .40 1.00
*3-D: .6X TO 1.5X BASIC STICKERS
STATED ODDS 1:1

2014 The Walking Dead Season 3 Dog Tags Dual Costumes Hobby

COMMON CARD (DC1-DC2)
RANDOMLY INSERTED INTO PACKS
DC1 Carl/Michonne 30.00 80.00
DC2 Glenn/Maggie 30.00 80.00

2014 The Walking Dead Season 3 Dog Tags Dual Costumes Retail

COMMON CARD (DCR1-DCR2)
RANDOMLY INSERTED INTO PACKS
DCR1 Axel/Carol 25.00 60.00
DCR2 Andrea/Milton 25.00 60.00

2014 The Walking Dead Season 3 Dog Tags Costumes Hobby

COMMON CARD (C1-C12) 6.00 15.00
C1A Andrea 8.00 20.00
C1B Andrea ERR/Beth's Pic 50.00 100.00
C2 Beth 20.00 50.00
C3 Carl 8.00 20.00
C4 Carol 15.00 40.00
C5 Glenn 10.00 25.00
C6 Maggie 12.00 30.00
C7 Merle 15.00 40.00
C8 Michonne 20.00 50.00
C9 Milton 8.00 20.00
C11 Michonne 25.00 60.00

2014 The Walking Dead Season 3 Dog Tags Costumes Retail

COMMON TAG (CR1-CR14; HTC1) 6.00 15.00
STATED ODDS 1:24
HTC1 IS HOT TOPIC EXCLUSIVE
CR1 Carl 8.00 20.00
CR2 Glenn 10.00 25.00
CR3 Maggie 10.00 25.00
CR4 Beth 15.00 40.00
CR5 Carol 12.00 30.00
CR6 Andrea 8.00 20.00
CR7 Lori 8.00 20.00
CR8 Merle 20.00 50.00
CR9 Axel 8.00 20.00
HTC1 The Governor HT 12.00 30.00

2014 The Walking Dead Season 3 Dog Tags Season 4 Teaser Tags

COMPLETE SET (12) 25.00 60.00
COMMON CARD (1-12) 3.00 8.00
RANDOMLY INSERTED INTO PACKS
4 Daryl Dixon 5.00 12.00
7 Michonne 5.00 12.00
8 Rick Grimes 5.00 12.00

2016 The Walking Dead Season Four Part 1

COMPLETE SET (72) 8.00 20.00
UNOPENED BOX (24 PACKS) 70.00 80.00
UNOPENED PACK (5 CARDS) 4.00 5.00
COMMON CARD (1-72) .20 .50
*BLACK: 2X TO 5X BASIC CARDS 1.00 2.50
*SILVER/99: 4X TO 10X BASIC CARDS 2.00 5.00
*GOLD/25: 8X TO 20X BASIC CARDS 4.00 10.00

2016 The Walking Dead Season Four Part 1 Autographs

COMMON AUTO 6.00 15.00
*BLACK/125: SAME VALUE AS BASIC AUTOS
*SILVER/75: .5X TO 1.2X BASIC AUTOS
*GOLD/25: .6X TO 1.5X BASIC AUTOS
STATED ODDS 1:24
AL1 Andrew Lincoln 50.00 100.00
AL2 Andrew Lincoln 50.00 100.00
BS1 Brighton Sharbino 30.00 75.00
BS2 Brighton Sharbino 30.00 75.00
DM1 David Morrisey 20.00 50.00
DM2 David Morrisey 20.00 50.00
EK1 Emily Kinney 12.00 30.00
EK2 Emily Kinney 12.00 30.00
KK1 Kyla Kenedy 10.00 25.00
KK2 Kyla Kenedy 10.00 25.00
NR1 Norman Reedus 50.00 100.00
NR2 Norman Reedus 50.00 100.00
SW1 Scott Wilson 15.00 40.00
SW2 Scott Wilson 15.00 40.00
CLC1 Chad L. Coleman 10.00 25.00
CLC2 Chad L. Coleman 10.00 25.00
MMB1 Melissa McBride 15.00 40.00
MMB2 Melissa McBride 15.00 40.00

2016 The Walking Dead Season Four Part 1 Character Bios

COMPLETE SET (9) 8.00 20.00
COMMON CARD (C1-C9) 1.50 4.00
*SILVER/99: .5X TO 1.2X BASIC CARDS
*GOLD/25: 1.2X TO 3X BASIC CARDS
STATED ODDS 1:3

2016 The Walking Dead Season Four Part 1 Dual Memorabilia

COMMON CARD (DM1-DM5) 50.00 100.00
STATED ODDS 1:1,555
DM1 Daryl/Beth 60.00 120.00
DM4 Rick/Carl 60.00 120.00

2016 The Walking Dead Season Four Part 1 Memorabilia

COMMON CARD (M1-M28) 5.00 12.00
STATED ODDS 1:24
M1 Carl Grimes 8.00 20.00
M3 Wine Bottle 12.00 30.00
M4 The Governor 10.00 25.00
M7 Tyreese 6.00 15.00
M9 Michonne 12.00 30.00
M11 Barbed Wire 25.00 60.00
M13 Daryl Dixon 25.00 60.00
M15 Carol Peletier 12.00 30.00
M16 Ammo Box 15.00 40.00
M17 Carl Grimes 10.00 25.00
M19 Tyreese 6.00 15.00
M21 Wine Bottle 12.00 30.00
M22 Beth Greene 20.00 50.00
M24 Ammo Box 60.00 120.00
M25 Rick Grimes 12.00 30.00
M26 Carl Grimes 8.00 20.00
M27 Ammo Box 15.00 40.00
M28 Ammo Box HT

2016 The Walking Dead Season Four Part 1 Posters

COMPLETE SET (4) 6.00 15.00
COMMON CARD (D1-D4) 2.00 5.00
*SILVER/99: .5X TO 1.2X BASIC CARDS
*GOLD/25: 1.2X TO 3X BASIC CARDS
STATED ODDS 1:6
D3 Norman Reedus 3.00 8.00
D4 Emily Kinney 2.50 6.00

2016 The Walking Dead Season Four Part 1 Terminus

COMPLETE SET (9) 5.00 12.00
COMMON CARD (Z1-Z9) 1.00 2.50
*CRYPTOMIUM: 1.5X TO 3X BASIC CARDS
*SILVER/99: 2X TO 5X BASIC CARDS
*GOLD/25: 3X TO 8X BASIC CARDS
STATED ODDS 1:3

2016 The Walking Dead Season Four Part 1 Promos

P1 Survive Rick NYCC/PHILLY 1.25 3.00
P2 Rick NSU 4.00 10.00
P3 Terminus Map NSU 3.00 8.00
P4 Daryl 4.00 10.00

2016 The Walking Dead Season Four Part 2

COMPLETE SET (72) 8.00 20.00
UNOPENED BOX (24 PACKS) 60.00 80.00
UNOPENED PACK (5 CARDS) 3.00 4.00
COMMON CARD (1-72) .20 .50
*BLACK: 4X TO 10X BASIC CARDS 2.00 5.00
*SILVER/99: 8X TO 20X BASIC CARDS 4.00 10.00
*GOLD/25: 12X TO 30X BASIC CARDS 6.00 15.00

2016 The Walking Dead Season Four Part 2 Autographs

COMMON AUTO 6.00 15.00
*BLACK/125: SAME VALUE AS BASIC AUTOS
*SILVER/75: .5X TO 1.2X BASIC AUTOS
*GOLD/25: .6X TO 1.5X BASIC AUTOS
STATED ODDS 1:24
AL3 Andrew Lincoln 50.00 100.00
AL4 Andrew Lincoln 50.00 100.00
AM1 Alanna Masterson 12.00 30.00
AM2 Alanna Masterson 12.00 30.00
CS1 Christian Serratos 25.00 60.00
CS2 Christian Serratos 25.00 60.00
DG1 Danai Gurira 20.00 50.00
DG2 Danai Gurira 20.00 50.00
DG3 Danai Gurira 20.00 50.00
DG4 Danai Gurira 20.00 50.00
MC1 Michael Cudlitz 15.00 40.00
MC2 Michael Cudlitz 15.00 40.00
NR3 Norman Reedus 30.00 75.00
NR4 Norman Reedus 30.00 75.00
SY1 Steven Yeun 15.00 40.00
SY2 Steven Yeun 15.00 40.00
JMD1 Josh McDermitt 15.00 40.00
JMD2 Josh McDermitt 15.00 40.00
SMG1 Sonequa Martin-Green 15.00 40.00
SMG2 Sonequa Martin-Green 15.00 40.00

2016 The Walking Dead Season Four Part 2 Character Bios

COMPLETE SET (9) 8.00 20.00
COMMON CARD (C10-C18) 1.50 4.00
*SILVER/99: 1.25X TO 3X BASIC INSERTS 5.00 12.00
*GOLD/25: 2.5X TO 6X BASIC INSERTS 10.00 25.00
STATED ODDS 1:3

2016 The Walking Dead Season Four Part 2 Dual Memorabilia

COMMON CARD (DM6-DM9) 20.00 50.00
STATED ODDS 1:481
DM6 Abraham and Eugene 20.00 50.00
DM7 Sasha and Maggie 20.00 50.00
DM8 Rosita and Abraham 25.00 60.00
DM9 Maggie and Glenn 30.00 80.00

2016 The Walking Dead Season Four Part 2 Memorabilia

COMMON CARD (M29-M61) 6.00 15.00
STATED ODDS 1:24
M29 Sasha 10.00 25.00
M31 Rick Grimes 10.00 25.00
M33 Glenn Rhee 8.00 20.00
M35 Wine Bottle 12.00 30.00
M36 Abraham Ford 8.00 20.00
M40 Maggie Greene 8.00 20.00
M41 Rosita Espinosa 12.00 30.00
M44 Glenn Rhee 10.00 25.00
M46 Wine Bottle 15.00 40.00
M47 Rosita Espinosa 12.00 30.00
M48 Ammo Box 8.00 20.00
M50 Wine Bottle 12.00 30.00
M51 Eugene Porter 12.00 30.00
M52 Ammo Box 20.00 50.00
M53 Maggie Greene 8.00 20.00
M54 Glenn Rhee 10.00 25.00
M55 Rosita Espinosa 12.00 30.00

2016 The Walking Dead Season Four Part 2 Posters

COMPLETE SET (4) 6.00 15.00
COMMON CARD (D5-D8) 2.00 5.00
*SILVER/99: 1.25X TO 3X BASIC INSERTS 6.00 15.00
*GOLD/25: 2.5X TO 6X BASIC INSERTS 12.00 30.00
STATED ODDS 1:6

2016 The Walking Dead Season Four Part 2 Reunion

COMPLETE SET (9) 5.00 12.00
COMMON CARD (Z1-Z9) 1.00 2.50
*SILVER/99: 2X TO 5X BASIC INSERTS 5.00 12.00
*GOLD/25: 3X TO 8X BASIC INSERTS 8.00 20.00
STATED ODDS 1:3

2015 The Walking Dead Season 4 Dog Tags

COMPLETE SET (36) 60.00 120.00
UNOPENED BOX (24 PACKS) 80.00 100.00
UNOPENED PACK (1 TAG+1 STICKER) 4.00 5.00
COMMON TAG (1-36) 2.00 5.00
*FOIL: .5X TO 1.2X BASIC TAGS 2.50 6.00
1 Rick Grimes 5.00 12.00
2 Daryl Dixon 4.00 10.00
8 Tyreese Williams 4.00 10.00
9 Michonne 4.00 10.00
10 Rick Grimes 3.00 8.00
11 Daryl Dixon 4.00 10.00
12 Beth Greene 3.00 8.00
21 Beth Greene 3.00 8.00
24 Michonne 3.00 8.00

2015 The Walking Dead Season 4 Dog Tags Costumes

COMPLETE SET (17) 150.00 300.00
COMMON CARD (C1-C17) 5.00 12.00
RANDOMLY INSERTED INTO PACKS
C1 Rick 10.00 25.00
C2 Daryl 30.00 75.00
C3 Michonne 8.00 20.00
C4 Carl 6.00 15.00
C5 Maggie 15.00 40.00
C6 Glenn 8.00 20.00
C7 Tyreese 8.00 20.00
C8 Sasha 8.00 20.00
C9 Abraham 8.00 20.00

C10 Rosita	10.00	25.00
C11 Rick	12.00	30.00
C12 Beth	15.00	40.00

2015 The Walking Dead Season 4 Dog Tags Stickers

COMPLETE SET (24)	6.00	15.00
COMMON CARD (1-24)	.40	1.00
*3-D: 1.5X TO 4X BASIC STICKERS		

2016 The Walking Dead Season 5

COMPLETE SET (100)	10.00	25.00
UNOPENED BOX (24 PACKS)	50.00	60.00
UNOPENED PACK (5 CARDS)	3.00	4.00
COMMON CARD (1-100)	.20	.50
*RUST/99: 4X TO 10X BASIC CARDS	2.00	5.00
*MUD/50: 8X TO 20X BASIC CARDS	4.00	10.00
*MOLD/25: 12X TO 30X BASIC CARDS	6.00	15.00
*SEPIA/10: 15X TO 40X BASIC CARDS	8.00	20.00

2016 The Walking Dead Season 5 Autographs

COMMON AUTO	6.00	15.00
*RUST/99: SAME VALUE AS BASIC AUTOS		
*MUD/50: .5X TO 1.2X BASIC AUTOS		
*MOLD/25: .6X TO 1.5X BASIC AUTOS		
*SEPIA/10: .75X TO 2X BASIC AUTOS		
STATED ODDS 1:61		
NNO Alanna Masterson	12.00	30.00
NNO Chad L. Coleman	10.00	25.00
NNO Chandler Riggs	15.00	40.00
NNO Danai Gurira	20.00	50.00
NNO David Morrissey	15.00	40.00
NNO Emily Kinney	15.00	40.00
NNO Katelyn Nacon	15.00	40.00
NNO Melissa McBride	12.00	30.00
NNO Michael Cudlitz	15.00	40.00
NNO Norman Reedus	25.00	60.00
NNO Seth Gilliam	8.00	20.00
NNO Sonequa Martin-Green	12.00	30.00
NNO Steven Yeun	25.00	60.00
NNO Tyler James Williams	10.00	25.00

2016 The Walking Dead Season 5 Characters

COMPLETE SET (18)	12.00	30.00
COMMON CARD (C1-C18)	1.25	3.00
STATED ODDS 1:2		
C1 Rick Grimes	2.00	5.00
C3 Michonne	2.00	5.00
C4 Daryl Dixon	2.50	6.00
C5 Glenn Rhee	1.50	4.00

2016 The Walking Dead Season 5 Dual Autographs

COMMON CARD	20.00	50.00
STATED ODDS 1:2,566		
2 K.Nacon/J.Douglas	25.00	60.00
3 M.McBride/B.Samuel	20.00	50.00
4 M.McBride/C.L.Coleman	25.00	60.00
5 M.McBride/S.Gilliam	30.00	80.00

2016 The Walking Dead Season 5 Locations

COMPLETE SET (7)	6.00	15.00
COMMON CARD (L1-L7)	1.25	3.00
STATED ODDS 1:4		

2016 The Walking Dead Season 5 Relics

COMPLETE SET (18)	120.00	250.00
COMMON RELIC	3.00	8.00
*RUST/99: .5X TO 1.2X BASIC RELICS		
*MUD/50: .6X TO 1.5X BASIC RELICS		
*MOLD/25: .75X TO 2X BASIC RELICS		
*SEPIA/10: 1X TO 2.5X BASIC RELICS		
STATED ODDS 1:29		
NNO Abraham Ford	8.00	20.00
NNO Beth Greene	8.00	20.00
NNO Carl Grimes	6.00	15.00
NNO Daryl Dixon	12.00	30.00
NNO Enid	10.00	25.00
NNO Glenn Rhee	6.00	15.00
NNO Maggie Greene	10.00	25.00
NNO Rick Grimes	8.00	20.00
NNO Sasha Williams	12.00	30.00
NNO Tara Chambler	6.00	15.00
NNO Tyreese Williams/Pants	6.00	15.00
NNO Tyreese Williams/Shirt	5.00	12.00

2016 The Walking Dead Season 5 Triple Autograph

STATED ODDS 1:11,290		
1 McBride/Coleman/Gilliam	150.00	300.00

2016 The Walking Dead Season 5 Walkers

COMPLETE SET (10)	6.00	15.00
COMMON CARD (W1-W10)	1.00	2.50

2016 The Walking Dead Season 5 Dog Tags

COMPLETE SET (36)	80.00	150.00
UNOPENED BOX (24 PACKS)	80.00	100.00
UNOPENED PACK (1 TAG+1 STICKER)	4.00	5.00
COMMON TAG (1-36)	2.00	5.00
*FOIL: .5X TO 1.2X BASIC TAGS		
1 Rick Grimes	3.00	8.00
2 Daryl Dixon	5.00	12.00
3 Michonne	2.50	6.00
10 Glenn Rhee	2.50	6.00
21 Daryl Dixon	5.00	12.00
23 Michonne	2.50	6.00
24 Rick Grimes	3.00	8.00

2016 The Walking Dead Season 5 Dog Tags Stickers

COMPLETE SET (24)	6.00	15.00
COMMON CARD (1-24)	.40	1.00
*3-D: 1.2X TO 3X BASIC STICKERS		
STATED ODDS 1:1		

2016 The Walking Dead Season 5 Dog Tags Costumes

COMPLETE SET (18)	150.00	300.00
COMMON TAG (C1-C18)	6.00	15.00
RANDOMLY INSERTED INTO PACKS		
C1 Daryl	25.00	60.00
C2 Rick	15.00	40.00
C3 Glenn	15.00	40.00
C4 Maggie	15.00	40.00
C5 Abraham	15.00	40.00
C6 Beth	12.00	30.00
C8 Eugene	12.00	30.00
C9 Sasha	15.00	40.00
C10 Rick	20.00	50.00
C11 Rosita	25.00	60.00
C12 Noah	12.00	30.00

2016 The Walking Dead Season 5 Dog Tags Season 6 Teaser Tags

COMPLETE SET (12)	30.00	80.00
COMMON TAG (S1-S12)	2.50	6.00
RANDOMLY INSERTED INTO PACKS		
S1 Daryl Dixon	6.00	15.00
S3 Rick Grimes	3.00	8.00
S4 Rick Grimes	3.00	8.00
S6 Michonne	3.00	8.00
S8 Carol Peletier	5.00	12.00
S9 Glenn Rhee	3.00	8.00
S12 Daryl Dixon	4.00	10.00

2017 The Walking Dead Season 6

COMPLETE SET (100)	6.00	15.00
UNOPENED BOX (24 PACKS)	60.00	100.00
UNOPENED PACK (6 CARDS)	3.00	4.00
COMMON CARD (1-100)	.12	.30
*RUST: 1.2X TO 3X BASIC CARDS	2.00	5.00
*MUD/50: 8X TO 20X BASIC CARDS	2.50	6.00
*MOLD/25: 10X TO 25X BASIC CARDS	3.00	8.00
*SEPIA/10: 20X TO 50X BASIC CARDS	6.00	15.00

2017 The Walking Dead Season 6 Autographed Relics

STATED PRINT RUN 10 SER.#'d SETS	30.00	80.00
NNO Chandler Riggs	50.00	100.00
NNO Christian Serratos	60.00	120.00
NNO Danai Gurira	60.00	120.00
NNO Josh McDermitt	30.00	80.00
NNO Melissa McBride	30.00	80.00

2017 The Walking Dead Season 6 Autographs

COMMON AUTO	10.00	25.00
*RUST/99: SAME VALUE AS BASIC AUTOS		
*MUD/50: .5X TO 1.2X BASIC AUTOS		
*MOLD/25: .6X TO 1.5X BASIC AUTOS		
*SEPIA/10: .75X TO 2X BASIC AUTOS		
STATED ODDS 1:24		
NNO Alanna Masterson	12.00	30.00
NNO Alexandra Breckenridge	15.00	40.00
NNO Chandler Riggs	15.00	40.00
NNO Christian Serratos	12.00	30.00
NNO Danai Gurira	20.00	50.00
NNO Josh McDermitt	12.00	30.00
NNO Melissa McBride	15.00	40.00
NNO Michael Cudlitz	12.00	30.00
NNO Norman Reedus	30.00	75.00
NNO Sonequa Martin-Green	15.00	40.00
NNO Steven Yeun	15.00	40.00
NNO Tom Payne	25.00	60.00
NNO Tovah Feldshuh	15.00	40.00

2017 The Walking Dead Season 6 Characters

COMPLETE SET (20)	8.00	20.00
COMMON CARD (C1-C20)	1.25	3.00
*RUST/99: .6X TO 1.5X BASIC CARDS	2.00	5.00
*MUD/50: .75X TO 2X BASIC CARDS	2.50	6.00
*MOLD/25: 1X TO 2.5X BASIC CARDS	3.00	8.00
*SEPIA/10: 2X TO 5X BASIC CARDS	6.00	15.00

2017 The Walking Dead Season 6 Chop

COMPLETE SET (10)	6.00	15.00
COMMON CARD (1-10)	1.00	2.50
*RUST: .6X TO 1.5X BASIC CARDS	1.50	4.00
*MUD/50: .75X TO 2X BASIC CARDS	2.00	5.00
*MOLD/25: 1X TO 2.5X BASIC CARDS	2.50	6.00
*SEPIA/10: 2X TO 5X BASIC CARDS	5.00	12.00

2017 The Walking Dead Season 6 In Memoriam

COMPLETE SET (9)	8.00	20.00
COMMON CARD (M1-M9)	1.50	4.00
*RUST/99: .75X TO 2X BASIC CARDS		
*MUD/50: 1X TO 2.5X BASIC CARDS		
*MOLD/25: 1.2X TO 3X BASIC CARDS		
*SEPIA/10: 1.5X TO 4X BASIC CARDS		
TARGET EXCLUSIVE		

2017 The Walking Dead Season 6 Locations

COMPLETE SET (8)	6.00	15.00
COMMON CARD (L1-L8)	1.00	2.50
*MUD/50: X TO X BASIC CARDS		
*MOLD/25: X TO X BASIC CARDS		

2017 The Walking Dead Season 6 Negan Dual Relics

*MOLD/25: .6X TO 1.5X BASIC RELICS		
WALMART EXCLUSIVE		
NNO Negan/Carl	20.00	50.00
NNO Negan/Carol	20.00	50.00
NNO Negan/Eugene	20.00	50.00
NNO Negan/Maggie	20.00	50.00
NNO Negan/Michonne	20.00	50.00
NNO Negan/Walker	20.00	50.00

2017 The Walking Dead Season 6 Relics

COMMON RELIC (UNNUMBERED)	6.00	15.00
*RUST/99: SAME VALUE AS BASIC RELICS		
*MUD/50: .5X TO 1.2X BASIC RELICS		
*MOLD/25: .6X TO 1.5X BASIC RELICS		
NNO Carl Grimes	8.00	20.00
NNO Carol Peletier	6.00	15.00
NNO Maggie Greene	12.00	30.00
NNO Michonne	12.00	30.00
NNO Morgan Jones	4.00	10.00
NNO Negan WM	15.00	40.00

2017 The Walking Dead Season 6 Relics Mud

*MUD: .5X TO 1.2X BASIC RELICS		
STATED PRINT RUN 50 SER.#'d SETS		
NNO Rosita Espinosa	20.00	50.00

2017 The Walking Dead Season 6 Ties That Bind

COMPLETE SET (9)	8.00	20.00
COMMON CARD (M1-M9)	2.00	5.00
*RUST/99: .75X TO 2X BASIC CARDS		
*MUD/50: 1.2X TO 3X BASIC CARDS		
*MOLD/25: 1.5X TO 4X BASIC CARDS		
*SEPIA/10: 2X TO 5X BASIC CARDS		
WALMART EXCLUSIVE		

2017 The Walking Dead Season 6 Walker Relics

COMPLETE SET (5)	20.00	50.00
COMMON RELIC (UNNUMBERED)	4.00	10.00
*RUST/99: .5X TO 1.2X BASIC RELICS	5.00	12.00
*MUD/50: .6X TO 1.5X BASIC RELICS	6.00	15.00
*MOLD/25: .75X TO 2X BASIC RELICS	8.00	20.00
*SEPIA/10: 1X TO 2.5X BASIC RELICS	10.00	25.00
WALMART EXCLUSIVE		

2017 The Walking Dead Season 6 Dog Tags

COMPLETE SET (36)	60.00	120.00
UNOPENED BOX (24 PACKS)		
UNOPENED PACK (1 TAG)		
COMMON TAG (1-36)	2.00	5.00
*FOIL: .5X TO 1.2X BASIC TAGS		
1 Rick Grimes	5.00	12.00
3 Daryl Dixon	3.00	8.00
4 Glenn Rhee	2.50	6.00
5 Maggie Greene	2.50	6.00
6 Michonne	2.50	6.00
12 Rick Grimes	5.00	12.00
14 Daryl Dixon	3.00	8.00
15 Carl Grimes	4.00	10.00
16 Glenn Rhee	2.50	6.00
20 Michonne	2.50	6.00
21 Maggie Greene	2.50	6.00
23 Daryl Dixon	3.00	8.00
24 Rick Grimes	5.00	12.00

2017 The Walking Dead Season 6 Dog Tags Costumes

COMPLETE SET (17)	100.00	200.00
COMMON TAG	3.00	8.00
STATED ODDS 1:24		
C1 Negan	30.00	75.00
C2 Morgan	10.00	25.00
C3 Carl	8.00	20.00
C4 Eugene	6.00	15.00
C5 Maggie	8.00	20.00
C6 Carol	8.00	20.00
C7 Morgan	10.00	25.00
C8 Carl	8.00	20.00
C9 King Ezekiel	10.00	25.00
C10 Daryl	10.00	25.00
C11 Tara	6.00	15.00
C12 Dwight	6.00	15.00
C13 Carol	8.00	20.00

2017 The Walking Dead Season 6 Dog Tags Season 7 Teaser Tags

COMPLETE SET (12)	20.00	50.00
COMMON TAG (1-12)	2.00	5.00
1 Rick Grimes	2.50	6.00
2 Negan	4.00	10.00
3 Daryl Dixon	2.50	6.00
4 Carol Peletier	2.50	6.00
7 Michonne	3.00	8.00
9 Carl Grimes	3.00	8.00

2017 The Walking Dead Season 7

COMPLETE SET (100)	6.00	15.00

UNOPENED BOX (24 PACKS) 65.00 75.00
UNOPENED PACK (8 CARDS) 3.00 3.50
COMMON CARD (1-100) .12 .30
*RUST: 1.2X TO 3X BASIC CARDS .40 1.00
*MUD/50: 8X TO 20X BASIC CARDS 2.50 6.00
*MOLD/25: 10X TO 25X BASIC CARDS 3.00 8.00
*SEPIA/10: 20X TO 50X BASIC CARDS 6.00 15.00

2017 The Walking Dead Season 7 Allegiances

COMPLETE SET (7) 6.00 15.00
COMMON CARD (A1-A7) 1.50 4.00
*RUST/99: .6X TO 1.5X BASIC CARDS 2.50 6.00
*MUD/50: .75X TO 2X BASIC CARDS 3.00 8.00
*MOLD/25: 1.2X TO 3X BASIC CARDS 5.00 12.00
STATED ODDS 1:2 WALMART EXCLUSIVE

2017 The Walking Dead Season 7 Autographed Relics

STATED PRINT RUN 10 SER.#'d SETS
RMI Danai Gurira 60.00 120.00
RNE Jeffrey Dean Morgan
RCP Melissa McBride 50.00 100.00
RDDI Norman Reedus 100.00 200.00
RSW Sonequa Martin-Green 75.00 150.00

2017 The Walking Dead Season 7 Autographs

COMMON AUTO 6.00 15.00
*RUST: .6X TO 1.5X BASIC AUTOS
*MUD/50: .75X TO 2X BASIC AUTOS
*MOLD/25: 1.2X TO 3X BASIC AUTOS
AAN Austin Nichols 8.00 20.00
ABV Briana Venskus 8.00 20.00
ACE Christine Evangelista 12.00 30.00
AJH Joshua Hoover 8.00 20.00
AJM Josh McDermitt 12.00 30.00
AJW Jordan Woods-Robinson 10.00 25.00
AKC Kerry Cahill 8.00 20.00
AKM Karl Makinen 8.00 20.00
ALM Logan Miller 10.00 25.00
ANB Nicole Barre 8.00 20.00
ARM Ross Marquand 10.00 25.00
ATP Tom Payne 15.00 40.00
AXB Xander Berkeley 10.00 25.00
AAMA Ann Mahoney 8.00 20.00

MODERN

2017 The Walking Dead Season 7 Autographs Rust

AJDM Jeffrey Dean Morgan 120.00 250.00

2017 The Walking Dead Season 7 Characters

COMPLETE SET (19) 8.00 20.00
COMMON CARD (C1-C19) 1.25 3.00
*RUST: .75X TO 2X BASIC CARDS 2.50 6.00
*MUD/50: 1.2X TO 3X BASIC CARDS 4.00 10.00
*MOLD/25: 1.5X TO 4X BASIC CARDS 5.00 12.00

2017 The Walking Dead Season 7 Chop

COMPLETE SET (9) 10.00 25.00
COMMON CARD (1-9) 2.00 5.00
*RUST: .6X TO 1.5X BASIC CARDS 3.00 8.00
*MUD/50: .75X TO 2X BASIC CARDS 4.00 10.00
*MOLD/25: 1X TO 2.5X BASIC CARDS 5.00 12.00

2017 The Walking Dead Season 7 Dual Autographs

STATED PRINT RUN 10 SER.#'d SETS
DAGM D.Gurira/M.McBride
DAMC J.D.Morgan/M.Cudlitz 150.00 300.00
DACY M.Cudlitz/S.Yeun
DARM N.Reedus/R.Marquand 120.00 200.00
DAYM S.Yeun/M.McBride

2017 The Walking Dead Season 7 Dual Relics

COMMON CARD 10.00 25.00
STATED PRINT RUN 25 SER.#'d SETS
DRCW Carol/Walker 15.00 40.00
DRDC Daryl/Carol 20.00 50.00
DRDS Daryl/Sasha 20.00 50.00
DRDT Daryl/Tara 15.00 40.00
DRDW Dwight/Walker 12.00 30.00
DREW Ezekiel/Walker 12.00 30.00
DRSC Sasha/Carol 15.00 40.00
DRTC Tara/Carol 12.00 30.00

2017 The Walking Dead Season 7 In Memoriam

COMPLETE SET (9) 10.00 25.00
COMMON CARD (M1-M9) 1.50 4.00
*RUST/99: .6X TO 1.5X BASIC CARDS 2.50 6.00
*MUD/50: .75X TO 2X BASIC CARDS 3.00 8.00
*MOLD/25: 1.2X TO 3X BASIC CARDS 5.00 12.00
STATED ODDS 1:2 TARGET EXCLUSIVE

2017 The Walking Dead Season 7 Negan Dual Relics

COMMON RELIC 12.00 30.00
DRNC Negan/Carol 15.00 40.00
DRNDD Negan/Daryl 30.00 75.00
DRND Negan/Dwight 15.00 40.00
DRNE Negan/Ezekiel 15.00 40.00
DRNW Negan/Walker 15.00 40.00

2017 The Walking Dead Season 7 Relics

COMMON RELIC 6.00 15.00
*RUST: .5X TO 1.2X BASIC RELICS
*MUD/50: .6X TO 1.5X BASIC RELICS
*MOLD/25: .75X TO 2X BASIC RELICS
RDD Daryl Dixon's Shirt 8.00 20.00
RDW Dwight's Pants 8.00 20.00
REZ Ezekiel's Shirt 10.00 25.00
RDDI Daryl Dixon's Jacket 12.00 30.00

2017 The Walking Dead Season 7 Relics Mud

*MUD/50: .6X TO 1.5X BASIC RELICS
RNE Negan's Pants 12.00 30.00

2017 The Walking Dead Season 7 Rivalries

COMPLETE SET (4) 2.50 6.00
COMMON CARD (R1-R4) 1.00 2.50
*RUST: .5X TO 1.2X BASIC CARDS 1.25 3.00
*MUD/50: .6X TO 1.5X BASIC CARDS 1.50 4.00
*MOLD/25: .75X TO 2X BASIC CARDS 2.50 5.00

2017 The Walking Dead Season 7 Shell Casing Relics

COMMON RELIC 25.00 60.00
*MOLD/18-20: .5X TO 1.2X BASIC RELICS
BRAA Aaron/50 30.00 75.00
BRAF Abraham Ford/50 30.00 75.00
BRCP Carol Peletier/35 25.00 60.00
BRDD Daryl Dixon/75 50.00 125.00
BREP Eugene Porter/35 30.00 75.00
BREZ Ezekiel/60 30.00 75.00
BRRE Rosita Espinosa/97 25.00 60.00
BRTC Tara Chambler/35 25.00 60.00

2017 The Walking Dead Season 7 Walker Relics

COMMON RELIC 4.00 10.00
*RUST/99: .5X TO 1.2X BASIC RELICS 5.00 12.00
*MUD/50: .6X TO 1.5X BASIC RELICS 6.00 15.00
*MOLD/25: .75X TO 2X BASIC RELICS 8.00 20.00

2017 The Walking Dead Season 7 Walkers

COMPLETE SET (10) 6.00 15.00
COMMON CARD (W1-W10) 1.25 3.00
*RUST: .6X TO 1.5X BASIC CARDS 2.00 5.00
*MUD/50: .75X TO 2X BASIC CARDS 2.50 6.00
*MOLD/25: 1.2X TO 3X BASIC CARDS 4.00 10.00
STATED ODDS 1:4 TARGET BLASTER BOX
STATED ODDS 1:4 WALMART BLASTER BOX

2016 The Walking Dead Season 7 In Memoriam

COMPLETE SET (2) 12.00 30.00
COMMON CARD (1-2) 8.00 20.00
2 Glenn Rhee/200* 10.00 25.00

2018 The Walking Dead Season 8 Part 1

COMPLETE SET (90) 8.00 20.00
UNOPENED BOX (24 PACKS) 75.00 90.00
UNOPENED PACK (8 CARDS) 3.50 4.00
COMMON CARD (1-90) .15 .40
*RUST/99: 2.5X TO 6X BASIC CARDS
*MUD/50: 5X TO 12X BASIC CARDS
*MOLD/25: 10X TO 25X BASIC CARDS
*SEPIA/10: 20X TO 50X BASIC CARDS

2018 The Walking Dead Season 8 Part 1 Allegiances

COMPLETE SET (9) 10.00 25.00
COMMON CARD (A1-A9) 1.50 4.00

2018 The Walking Dead Season 8 Part 1 Autographed Costumes

COMMON AUTO
STATED ODDS 1:
ARCE Josh McDermitt 20.00 50.00
ARCN Jeffrey Dean Morgan
ARCDD Norman Reedus
ARCRE Christian Serratos
ARCPJR Tom Payne 30.00 75.00

2018 The Walking Dead Season 8 Part 1 Autographed Manufactured Bat Medallion Relics

CCMPLETE SET (2)
STATED PRINT RUN SER.#'d SETS
UNPRICED DUE TO SCARCITY
ABRD Austin Amelio
ABRN Jeffrey Dean Morgan

2018 The Walking Dead Season 8 Part 1 Autographs

COMMON AUTO 5.00 12.00
*RUST/99: .5X TO 1.2X BASIC AUTOS
*MUD/50: .6X TO 1.5X BASIC AUTOS
*MOLD/25: .75X TO 2X BASIC AUTOS
RANDOMLY INSERTED INTO PACKS
ADN Daniel Newman 8.00 20.00
AJMD Josh McDermitt 15.00 40.00
AKN Katelyn Nacon 12.00 30.00
ASGT Sabrina Gennarino 10.00 25.00

2018 The Walking Dead Season 8 Part 1 Autographs Mud

COMPLETE SET (11)
*MUD: .6X TO 1.5X BASIC AUTOS
STATED PRINT RUN 50 SER.#'d SETS
AMM Melissa McBride 20.00 50.00
ASO Steven Ogg 20.00 50.00

2018 The Walking Dead Season 8 Part 1 Characters

COMPLETE SET (25) 15.00 40.00
COMMON CARD (C1-C25) 1.25 3.00
*RUST/99: .5X TO 1.2X BASIC CARDS
*MUD/50: .6X TO 1.5X BASIC CARDS
*MOLD/25: .75X TO 2X BASIC CARDS

2018 The Walking Dead Season 8 Part 1 Costumes

COMMON COSTUME 3.00 8.00
*RUST/99: .5X TO 1.2X BASIC COSTUMES
*MUD/50: .6X TO 1.5X BASIC COSTUMES
*MOLD/25: .75X TO 2X BASIC COSTUMES
RANDOMLY INSERTED INTO PACKS
RCDD Daryl Dixon 5.00 12.00
RCMJ Morgan Jones 4.00 10.00
RCN Negan 6.00 15.00
RCPJR Jesus 4.00 10.00
RCRG Rick Grimes 5.00 12.00

2018 The Walking Dead Season 8 Part 1 Dual Costumes

COMMON COSTUME 10.00 25.00
RANDOMLY INSERTED INTO PACKS
DCMR Negan & Daryl 20.00 50.00
DCLR Rick & Daryl 15.00 40.00
DCLS Rick & Rosita 12.00 30.00

2018 The Walking Dead Season 8 Part 1 Dual Walker Relics

COMMON RELIC
*RUST/99:
*MUD/50: X TO X BASIC RELICS
*MOLD/25: X TO X BASIC RELICS
RANDOMLY INSERTED INTO PACKS
WDR1 Negan & Walker
WDR2 Rick Grimes & Walker
WDR3 Daryl Dixon & Walker
WDR4 Rosita Espinosa & Walker
WDR5 Morgan & Walker

2018 The Walking Dead Season 8 Part 1 In Memoriam

COMPLETE SET (5) 3.00 8.00
COMMON CARD (IM1-IM5) 1.00 2.50
TARGET EXCLUSIVE

2018 The Walking Dead Season 8 Part 1 Manufactured Bat Medallion Relics

COMMON RELIC 6.00 15.00
*RUST/99: .5X TO 1.2X BASIC RELICS
*MUD/50: .6X TO 1.5X BASIC RELICS
*MOLD/25: .75X TO 2X BASIC RELICS
WALMART EXCLUSIVE
BRMR Maggie Rhee 12.00 30.00
BRN Negan 15.00 40.00
BRRG Rick Grimes 12.00 30.00

2018 The Walking Dead Season 8 Part 1 Manufactured Faction Patches

COMMON PATCH 4.00 10.00
*RUST/99: SAME VALUE
*MUD/50: .5X TO 1.2X BASIC PATCHES
*MOLD/25: .6X TO 1.5X BASIC PATCHES
RANDOMLY INSERTED INTO PACKS
PRHA Andy 4.00 10.00
PRHE Enid 4.00 10.00
PRHG Gregory 5.00 12.00
PRSA Aaron 6.00 15.00
PRSD Dwight 5.00 12.00
PRSE Eric Raleigh 4.00 10.00
PRSG Gavin 5.00 12.00
PRSM Mara 4.00 10.00
PRSN Negan 6.00 15.00
PRSR Regina 4.00 10.00
PRSS Simon 5.00 12.00
PRST Tobin 4.00 10.00
PRHMR Maggie Rhee 6.00 15.00
PRHPJ Jesus 5.00 12.00
PRKMJ Morgan 6.00 15.00
PRSCG Carl Grimes 10.00 25.00
PRSDD Daryl Dixon 8.00 20.00
PRSEG Eugene Porter 5.00 12.00
PRSGS Gabriel Stokes 4.00 10.00
PRSMC Michonne 6.00 15.00
PRSRG Rick Grimes 10.00 25.00
PRSRO Rosita Espinosa 6.00 15.00
PRSTC Tara Chambler 4.00 10.00

2018 The Walking Dead Season 8 Part 1 Manufactured Faction Patches Target Exclusives

COMMON PATCH 4.00 10.00
*RUST/99: SAME VALUE
*MUD/50: .5X TO 1.2X BASIC PATCHES
*MOLD/25: .6X TO 1.5X BASIC PATCHES
RANDOMLY INSERTED INTO PACKS
PRKCP Carol Peletier 6.00 15.00
PRKDI Dianne 6.00 15.00
PRKJ Jerry 5.00 12.00
PRKKE King Ezekiel 6.00 15.00

2018 The Walking Dead Season 8 Part 1 Many Sides of War

COMPLETE SET (7) 6.00 15.00
COMMON CARD (MSW1-MSW7) 1.25 3.00
RANDOMLY INSERTED INTO PACKS

2018 The Walking Dead Season 8 Part 1 Rivalries

COMPLETE SET (7) 5.00 12.00
COMMON CARD (R1-R7) 1.00 2.50
RANDOMLY INSERTED INTO PACKS

2018 The Walking Dead Season 8 Part 1 Walker Relics

COMMON RELIC 3.00 8.00
*RUST/99: SAME VALUE
*MUD/50: .5X TO 1.2X BASIC RELICS
*MOLD/25: .6X TO 1.5X BASIC RELICS
RANDOMLY INSERTED INTO PACKS

2018 The Walking Dead Season 8 Part 1 Walkers

COMPLETE SET (10) 4.00 10.00
COMMON CARD (W1-W10) .75 2.00
RANDOMLY INSERTED INTO PACKS

The Walking Dead Universe

2017 Fear the Walking Dead Seasons 1 and 2 Dog Tags

COMPLETE SET (48) 60.00 150.00
COMPLETE SET W/O FOIL (24) 25.00 60.00
UNOPENED BOX (24 PACKS)
UNOPENED PACK (1 TAG+1 STICKER)
COMMON TAG (1-24) 2.00 5.00
COMMON FOIL TAG (25-48) 2.50 6.00
1 Madison Clark 2.50 6.00
4 Alicia Clark 4.00 10.00
19 Madison Clark 2.50 6.00
22 Alicia Clark 4.00 10.00
25 Madison Clark FOIL 3.00 8.00
28 Alicia Clark FOIL 5.00 12.00
43 Madison Clark FOIL 3.00 8.00
46 Alicia Clark FOIL 5.00 12.00

2017 Fear the Walking Dead Seasons 1 and 2 Dog Tags Vinyl Stickers

COMPLETE SET (12) 5.00 12.00
COMMON STICKER (1-12) .60 1.50
*3-D: .75X TO 2X BASIC STICKERS 1.25 3.00
STATED ODDS 1:1

2017 Fear the Walking Dead Seasons 1 and 2 Dog Tags Costume Tags

COMPLETE SET (12) 50.00 100.00
COMMON TAG (C1-C12) 2.50 6.00
STATED ODDS 1:24
C1 Cliff Curtis 3.00 8.00
C2 Frank Dillane 5.00 12.00
C3 Ruben Blades 3.00 8.00
C4 Frank Dillane 4.00 10.00
C5 Lorenzo James Henrie 3.00 8.00
C6 Jesse McCartney 3.00 8.00
C7 Frank Dillane 5.00 12.00
C8 Daniel Zovatto 3.00 8.00
C10 Jesse McCartney 6.00 15.00
C12 Frank Dillane 5.00 12.00

2017 Fear the Walking Dead Seasons 1 and 2 Widevision

COMPLETE SET (80) 12.00 30.00
UNOPENED FACTORY SET (82 CARDS) 90.00 120.00
COMMON CARD (1-82) .20 .50
*MUD/25: 5X TO 12X BASIC CARDS 2.50 6.00
*MOLD/10: 10X TO 25X BASIC CARDS 5.00 12.00

2017 Fear the Walking Dead Seasons 1 and 2 Widevision Autographs

COMMON AUTO 8.00 20.00
*MUD/25: .5X TO 1.2X BASIC AUTOS
STATED ODDS OVERALL 2 AUTOS:BOX
CD1 Colman Domingo 15.00 40.00
CD2 Colman Domingo 15.00 40.00
KD1 Kim Dickens 25.00 60.00
KD2 Kim Dickens 25.00 60.00
MM1 Mercedes Mason 12.00 30.00
MM2 Mercedes Mason 12.00 30.00
ADC1 Alycia Debnam-Carey 100.00 250.00
ADC2 Alycia Debnam-Carey 100.00 250.00

2017 The Walking Dead 100th Episode and Season 8 Premiere

COMPLETE SET (25) 20.00 50.00
COMMON CARD (1-25) 1.50 4.00
*MUD/50: .75X TO 2X BASIC CARDS 3.00 8.00
*MOLD/25: 1.5X TO 4X BASIC CARDS 6.00 15.00
*SEPIA/10: 3X TO 8X BASIC CARDS 12.00 30.00
STATED PRINT RUN 282 SETS
RELEASED 10/23/2017

2017 The Walking Dead 100th Episode and Season 8 Premiere Autographs

COMMON AUTO
*MUD/50: X TO X BASIC AUTOS
*MOLD/25: X TO X BASIC AUTOS
STATED ODDS 1:SET
NNO Norman Reedus
NNO Jeffrey Dean Morgan
NNO Sarah Wayne Callies
NNO Chandler Riggs
NNO David Morrissey
NNO Danai Gurira
NNO Melissa McBride
NNO Steven Yeun
NNO Michael Cudlitz
NNO Josh McDermitt
NNO Christian Serratos
NNO Seth Gilliam
NNO Ross Marquand
NNO Scott Wilson
NNO Katelyn Nacon
NNO Tom Payne
NNO Chad L. Coleman
NNO Tovah Feldshuh

2018 The Walking Dead Autograph Collection

COMMON AUTO 6.00 15.00
*RUST/50: .5X TO 1.2X BASIC AUTOS
*MUD/25: .6X TO 1.5X BASIC AUTOS
STATED PRINT RUN 99 OR FEWER
ABA Brighton Sharbino/91 12.00 30.00
ABB Brighton Sharbino/91 12.00 30.00
ABC Brighton Sharbino/91 12.00 30.00
AEK Emily Kinney/54 20.00 50.00
AKN Katelyn Nacon/53 15.00 40.00
AMC Michael Cudlitz/81 15.00 40.00
AMD Major Dodson/77 8.00 20.00
AML Madison Lintz/79 10.00 25.00
AMM Melissa McBride/65 30.00 75.00
ANR Norman Reedus/90 50.00 100.00
ASG Sabrina Gennarino/68 8.00 20.00
AAMA Ann Mahoney/99 8.00 20.00
AAMB Ann Mahoney/54 8.00 20.00
ABSA Benedict Samuel/79 8.00 20.00
ABSB Benedict Samuel/79 8.00 20.00
ABSC Benedict Samuel/78 8.00 20.00
ACCA Chad Coleman/74 12.00 30.00
ACCB Chad Coleman/70 12.00 30.00
ACCC Chad Coleman/70 12.00 30.00
ACEA Christine Evangelista/83 20.00 50.00
ACRA Chandler Riggs/69 20.00 50.00
ACRB Chandler Riggs/69 20.00 50.00
AEBA Emma Bell/77 12.00 30.00
AJBA Jon Bernthal/80 25.00 60.00
AJBB Jon Bernthal/79 25.00 60.00
AJDA Jeffrey Dean Morgan/79 75.00 150.00
AJDB Jeffrey Dean Morgan/79 75.00 150.00
AJMA Josh McDermitt/82 12.00 30.00
AJMB Josh McDermitt/99 12.00 30.00
AKKA Kyla Kenedy/66 10.00 25.00
ATFA Tovah Feldshuh/99 8.00 20.00
ASWCA Sarah Wayne Callies/99 30.00 75.00

2012 The Walking Dead Comic Book

COMPLETE SET (91) 8.00 20.00
UNOPENED BOX (24 PACKS) 75.00 125.00
UNOPENED PACK (5 CARDS) 4.00 6.00
COMMON CARD (1-91) .20 .50
*FOIL: 1.2X TO 3X BASIC CARDS

2012 The Walking Dead Comic Book Autographs

COMMON AUTO (A1-A4) 20.00 50.00
RANDOMLY INSERTED INTO PACKS
A1 Robert Kirkman 100.00 200.00
A2 Charlie Adlard 80.00 150.00
A4 Sina Grace 25.00 60.00

2012 The Walking Dead Comic Book Killed In Action

COMPLETE SET (9) 12.00 30.00
COMMON CARD (KIA1-KIA9) 2.00 5.00
STATED ODDS 1:12

2012 The Walking Dead Comic Book Mini-Books

COMPLETE SET (9) 12.00 30.00
COMMON CARD (CB1-CB9) 2.00 5.00
STATED ODDS 1:12

2012 The Walking Dead Comic Book Promos

P1 TWD Comic Book CHI 4.00 10.00
P2 TWD Comic Book NSU 1.25 3.00
P3 TWD Comic Book SDCC 12.00 30.00

2013 The Walking Dead Comic Book 2

COMPLETE SET (72) 8.00 20.00
UNOPENED BOX (24 PACKS) 60.00 100.00
UNOPENED PACK (5 CARDS) 3.00 4.00
COMMON CARD (1-72) .20 .50
*FOIL: 1.2X TO 3X BASIC CARDS
B1 ISSUED AS ALBUM EXCLUSIVE
B1 Rick STANDEE ALB 15.00 40.00
P1 TWD Comic Book 2 PROMO NSU 2.00 5.00

2013 The Walking Dead Comic Book 2 Autographs

COMMON AUTO 15.00 40.00
STATED ODDS 1:576
A1 Robert Kirkman 80.00 150.00
A2 Charlie Adlard 30.00 80.00
A4 Sean Mackiewicz 20.00 50.00

2013 The Walking Dead Comic Book 2 Quotables

COMPLETE SET (9) 12.00 30.00
COMMON CARD (QTB1-QTB9) 2.00 5.00
STATED ODDS 1:12

2013 The Walking Dead Comic Book 2 Something to Fear

COMPLETE SET (9) 12.00 30.00
COMMON CARD (STF1-STF9) 2.00 5.00
STATED ODDS 1:12

2017 The Walking Dead Evolution

COMPLETE SET (100) 6.00 15.00
UNOPENED BOX (24 PACKS) 60.00 90.00
UNOPENED PACK (8 CARDS) 3.00 4.00
COMMON CARD (1-100) .15 .40
*BROWN: 1X TO 2.5X BASIC CARDS .40 1.00
*BLACK/50: 8X TO 20X BASIC CARDS 3.00 8.00
*GREEN/25: 12X TO 30X BASIC CARDS 5.00 12.00
*B&W/10: 15X TO 40X BASIC CARDS 6.00 15.00

2017 The Walking Dead Evolution Adversaries

COMPLETE SET (12) 6.00 15.00
COMMON CARD (AD1-AD12) .75 2.00
*BROWN/99: 1X TO 2.5X BASIC CARDS 2.00 5.00
*BLACK/50: 1.5X TO 4X BASIC CARDS 3.00 8.00
*GREEN/25: 2X TO 5X BASIC CARDS 4.00 10.00

2017 The Walking Dead Evolution Allegiances

COMPLETE SET (10) 6.00 15.00
COMMON CARD (AL1-AL10) .75 2.00
*BROWN/99: 1X TO 2.5X BASIC CARDS 2.00 5.00
*BLACK/50: 1.5X TO 4X BASIC CARDS 3.00 8.00
*GREEN/25: 2X TO 5X BASIC CARDS 4.00 10.00
WALMART EXCLUSIVE

2017 The Walking Dead Evolution Autographed Relics

COMMON AU MEM 20.00 50.00
STATED PRINT RUN 10 SER.#'d SETS
RDAAB Alexandra Breckenridge 50.00 100.00
RDACR Chandler Riggs 75.00 150.00
RDAJM Josh McDermitt 30.00 75.00
RDAKN Katelyn Nacon 30.00 75.00
RDALG Lawrence Gilliard Jr. 25.00 60.00
RDAMC Michael Cudlitz 60.00 120.00
RDASM Sonequa Martin-Green 75.00 150.00
RDASY Steven Yeun 60.00 120.00

2017 The Walking Dead Evolution Autographs

COMMON AUTO 6.00 15.00
*BROWN/99: SAME VALUE
*BLACK/50: .5X TO 1.2X BASIC AUTOS
*GREEN/25: .6X TO 1.5X BASIC AUTOS
STATED ODDS 1:24
ABS Brighton Sharbino 12.00 30.00
AEB Emma Bell 12.00 30.00
AJP Jeremy Palko 10.00 25.00
AJW Jordan Woods 8.00 20.00
ALT Lew Temple 8.00 20.00
AML Madison Lintz 12.00 30.00
ASG Seth Gilliam 8.00 20.00
ATF Tovah Feldshuh 10.00 25.00
ATP Tom Payne 12.00 30.00
AXB Xander Berkeley 8.00 20.00
ASGI Seth Gilliam 8.00 20.00
ASWC Sarah Wayne 20.00 50.00
ATPA Tom Payne 12.00 30.00

2017 The Walking Dead Evolution Autographs Black

*BLACK: .5X TO 1.2X BASIC AUTOS
STATED PRINT RUN 50 SER.#'d SETS
AMC Michael Cudlitz 15.00 40.00
AMCU Michael Cudlitz 15.00 40.00
AMEM Melissa McBride 15.00 40.00
AMMC Melissa McBride 15.00 40.00
AMEMC Melissa McBride 15.00 40.00
AMMCB Melissa McBride 15.00 40.00

2017 The Walking Dead Evolution Autographs Brown

*BROWN: SAME VALUE
STATED PRINT RUN 99 SER.#'d SETS
AAA Austin Amelio 12.00 30.00
AAN Austin Nichols 10.00 25.00
AJB Jon Bernthal 20.00 50.00
ARM Ross Marquand 10.00 25.00
ASC Sarah Wayne 20.00 50.00
ATF Tovah Feldshuh 10.00 25.00
ATP Tom Payne 12.00 30.00
AAAM Austin Amelio 12.00 30.00
AANI Austin Nichols 8.00 20.00
AJBE Jon Bernthal 20.00 50.00
AJDM Jeffrey Dean Morgan 75.00 150.00
AJMC Josh McDermitt 10.00 25.00
AJOM Josh McDermitt 10.00 25.00
ARMA Ross Marquand 10.00 25.00
ASWC Sarah Wayne 20.00 50.00
ATPA Tom Payne 12.00 30.00

2017 The Walking Dead Evolution Autographs Green

*GREEN: .6X TO 1.5X BASIC AUTOS
STATED PRINT RUN 25 SER.#'d SETS
ACR Chandler Riggs 30.00 75.00
ANR Norman Reedus 50.00 100.00
ACHR Chandler Riggs 30.00 75.00
ANOR Norman Reedus 50.00 100.00
ANRD Norman Reedus 50.00 100.00
ANRE Norman Reedus 50.00 100.00
ACHAR Chandler Riggs 30.00 75.00
ACRIG Chandler Riggs 30.00 75.00

2017 The Walking Dead Evolution Bat Relics

COMMON RELIC 10.00 25.00
*BROWN/99: SAME VALUE AS BASIC RELICS
*BLACK/50: .6X TO 1.5X BASIC RELICS
BRAF Abraham Ford 15.00 40.00
BRGR Glenn Rhee 15.00 40.00
BRN1 Negan 20.00 50.00

BRN2 Negan 20.00 50.00
BRN3 Negan 20.00 50.00
BRN4 Negan 20.00 50.00

2017 The Walking Dead Evolution Costume Relics

*BROWN/99: SAME VALUE AS BASIC RELICS
*BLACK/50: .5X TO 1.2X BASIC RELICS
*GREEN/25: .6X TO 1.5X BASIC RELICS
RANDOMLY INSERTED INTO PACKS
RCG Carl Grimes 6.00 15.00
RDD Daryl Dixon 8.00 20.00
RDL Dawn Lerner 5.00 12.00
RDW Dwight 5.00 12.00
RGR Glenn Rhee 8.00 20.00
RJA Jessie Anderson 5.00 12.00
RMG Maggie Greene 6.00 15.00
RRE Rosita Espinosa 6.00 15.00
RRG Rick Grimes 20.00 50.00
RSW Sasha Williams 5.00 12.00
RTC Tara Chambler 5.00 12.00

2017 The Walking Dead Evolution In Memoriam

COMPLETE SET (9) 8.00 20.00
*BROWN/99: .5X TO 1.2X BASIC CARDS 1.50 4.00
*BLACK/50: 1X TO 2.5X BASIC CARDS 3.00 8.00
*GREEN/25: 1.5X TO 4X BASIC CARDS 5.00 12.00
TARGET EXCLUSIVE

2017 The Walking Dead Evolution No Safe Haven

COMPLETE SET (9) 4.00 10.00
COMMON CARD (NSF1-NSF9) .60 1.50
*BROWN/99: .75X TO 2X BASIC CARDS 1.25 3.00
*BLACK/50: 1.5X TO 4X BASIC CARDS 2.50 6.00
*GREEN/25: 2.5X TO 6X BASIC CARDS 4.00 10.00

2017 The Walking Dead Evolution Rick Grimes Dual Relics

COMMON CARD (DWRRG1-DWRRG5)
DWRRG1 Rick Grimes and Walker
DWRRG2 Rick Grimes and Walker
DWRRG3 Rick Grimes and Walker
DWRRG4 Rick Grimes and Walker
DWRRG5 Rick Grimes and Walker

2017 The Walking Dead Evolution Terminus Butcher Relics

COMPLETE SET (3) 15.00 40.00
COMMON CARD (TBRTB1-TBRTB3) 6.00 15.00
*BROWN/99: .5X TO 1.2X BASIC RELICS 8.00 20.00
*BLACK/50: .6X TO 1.5X BASIC RELICS 10.00 25.00

2017 The Walking Dead Evolution Triple Relics

TRAER Abraham/Eugene/Rosita 30.00 75.00
TRRCD Rick/Carl/Daryl 50.00 100.00

2017 The Walking Dead Evolution Walker Costume Relics

COMMON CARD (RW1-RW5) 4.00 10.00
*BROWN/99: SAME VALUE AS BASIC RELICS4.00 10.00
*BLACK/50: .5X TO 1.2X BASIC RELICS 4.00 12.00
*GREEN/25: .6X TO 1.5X BASIC RELICS 6.00 15.00

2017 The Walking Dead Evolution Walkers

COMPLETE SET (10) 5.00 12.00
COMMON CARD (WA1-WA10) .60 1.50
*BROWN/99: .75X TO 2X BASIC CARDS 1.25 3.00
*BLACK/50: 1.5X TO 4X BASIC CARDS 2.50 6.00
*GREEN/25: 2.5X TO 6X BASIC CARDS 4.00 10.00

2017 The Walking Dead Evolution Weapons

COMPLETE SET (12) 6.00 15.00
COMMON CARD (W1-W12) .75 2.00
*BROWN/99: .75X TO 2X BASIC CARDS 1.25 3.00
*BLACK/50: 1.5X TO 4X BASIC CARDS 2.50 6.00
*GREEN/25: 2.5X TO 6X BASIC CARDS 4.00 10.00

2018 The Walking Dead Hunters and the Hunted

COMPLETE SET W/SP (120)
COMPLETE SET W/O SP (100) 8.00 20.00
UNOPENED BOX (24 PACKS) 50.00 75.00
UNOPENED PACK (8 CARDS) 2.50 3.00
COMMON CARD (1-100) .20 .50
COMMON SP 4.00 10.00
*ORANGE/99: 2X TO 5X BASIC CARDS
*BLUE/50: 4X TO 10X BASIC CARDS
*GREEN/25: 6X TO 15X BASIC CARDS
*PURPLE/10: 10X TO 25X BASIC CARDS
1 Rick Grimes SP 8.00 20.00
2 Negan SP 8.00 20.00
3 Daryl Dixon SP 8.00 20.00
5 Carl Grimes SP 12.00 30.00
6 Carol Peletier SP 6.00 15.00
8 Glenn Rhee SP 5.00 12.00
10 Sasha Williams SP 10.00 25.00
15 Abraham Ford SP 6.00 15.00
33 Dale Horvath SP 8.00 20.00
35 Merle Dixon SP 8.00 20.00

2018 The Walking Dead Hunters and the Hunted Autographs

COMMON AUTO
*ORANGE/99: .5X TO 1.2X BASIC AUTOS
*BLUE/50: .6X TO 1.5X BASIC AUTOS
*GREEN/25: .75X TO 2X BASIC AUTOS
RANDOMLY INSERTED INTO PACKS
HAAA Austin Amelio 12.00 30.00
HADB Daniel Bonjour 6.00 15.00
HAEE Ethan Embry 10.00 25.00
HAKN Katelyn Nacon 8.00 20.00
HAPZ Peter Zimmerman 6.00 15.00
HASG Seth Gilliam 12.00 30.00
HASO Steven Ogg 12.00 30.00
HAPTV Pruitt Taylor Vince 6.00 15.00
HASWC Sarah Wayne Callies 20.00 50.00

2018 The Walking Dead Hunters and the Hunted Bat Relics

COMMON MEM 5.00 12.00
*ORANGE/99: .5X TO 1.2X BASIC MEM
*BLUE/50: .6X TO 1.5X BASIC MEM
*GREEN/25: .75X TO 2X BASIC MEM
WALMART EXCLUSIVE
MBAL Rick Grimes 15.00 40.00
MBJM Negan 12.00 30.00
MBMC Abraham Ford 8.00 20.00
MBSY Glenn Rhee 12.00 30.00

2018 The Walking Dead Hunters and the Hunted Commemorative Weapon Medallions

COMMON MEM 6.00 15.00
*ORANGE/99: .5X TO 1.2X BASIC MEM
*BLUE/50: .6X TO 1.5X BASIC MEM
*GREEN/25: .75X TO 2X BASIC MEM
WMBA Amy 10.00 25.00
WMBN Nicholas 12.00 30.00
WMHN Negan 12.00 30.00
WMKG The Governor 10.00 25.00
WMKM Michonne 15.00 40.00
WMBDM Deanna Monroe 8.00 20.00
WMBJA Jessie Anderson 8.00 20.00
WMBOT Otis 8.00 20.00
WMBSW Shane Walsh 8.00 20.00
WMBTW Tyreese Williams 12.00 30.00
WMCDD Daryl Dixon 20.00 50.00
WMHRG Rick Grimes 12.00 30.00
WMKMD Merle Dixon 10.00 25.00
WMMCP Carol Peletier 10.00 25.00
WMMGR Glenn Rhee 10.00 25.00
WMMRG Rick Grimes 12.00 30.00
WMMSW Shane Walsh 8.00 20.00
WMRCP Carol Peletier 10.00 25.00
WMRGR Glenn Rhee 10.00 25.00
WMRRG Rick Grimes 15.00 40.00
WMRSW Shane Walsh 10.00 25.00

2018 The Walking Dead Hunters and the Hunted Costume Relics

COMMON MEM
*ORANGE/99: .5X TO 1.2X BASIC MEM
*BLUE/50: .6X TO 1.5X BASIC MEM
*GREEN/25: .75X TO 2X BASIC MEM
RE Enid 5.00 12.00
RAL Rick Grimes A 12.00 30.00
RCG Carl Grimes 8.00 20.00
RDD Daryl Dixon 6.00 15.00
RKE King Ezekiel 6.00 15.00
RMR Maggie Rhee 10.00 25.00
RALS Rick Grimes B 10.00 25.00
RCPJ Carol Peletier A 8.00 20.00
RCPS Carol Peletier B 6.00 15.00
RSWJ Sasha Williams B 5.00 12.00
RSWP Sasha Williams A 5.00 12.00

2018 The Walking Dead Hunters and the Hunted Dual Costume Relics

STATED PRINT RUN 25 SER.#'d SETS
DRCE Carl/Enid 20.00 50.00
DRDM Daryl/Morgan 20.00 50.00
DRGM Glenn/Maggie 25.00 60.00
DRRC Rick/Carl 30.00 75.00
DRRD Rick/Daryl 25.00 60.00
DRRN Rick/Negan 20.00 50.00
DRSE Sasha/Eugene 25.00 60.00

2018 The Walking Dead Hunters and the Hunted Epic Battles

COMPLETE SET (11) 6.00 15.00
COMMON CARD (EB1-EB11) 1.25 3.00
RANDOMLY INSERTED INTO PACKS

2018 The Walking Dead Hunters and the Hunted How to Take Down a Walker

COMPLETE SET (7) 4.00 10.00
COMMON CARD (HT1-HT7) 1.25 3.00
RANDOMLY INSERTED INTO PACKS

2018 The Walking Dead Hunters and the Hunted Leaders

COMPLETE SET (9) 5.00 12.00
COMMON CARD (L1-L9) 1.00 2.50
RANDOMLY INSERTED INTO PACKS

2018 The Walking Dead Hunters and the Hunted Partners

COMPLETE SET (13) 20.00 50.00
COMMON CARD (P1-P13) 3.00 8.00
WALMART EXCLUSIVE

2018 The Walking Dead Hunters and the Hunted Sacrifices

COMPLETE SET (7) 8.00 20.00
COMMON CARD (S1-S7) 2.50 6.00
TARGET EXCLUSIVE

2018 The Walking Dead Hunters and the Hunted Walker Dual Relics

COMMON MEM
WALMART EXCLUSIVE
STATED PRINT RUN 25 SER.#'d SETS
NNO Daryl Dixon/Walker 15.00 50.00
NNO Michonne/Walker 15.00 40.00
NNO Negan/Walker 20.00 50.00

2018 The Walking Dead Hunters and the Hunted Walker Relics

COMMON MEM 3.00 8.00
*ORANGE/99: .5X TO 1.2X BASIC MEM
*BLUE/50: .6X TO 1.5X BASIC MEM
*GREEN/25: .75X TO 2X BASIC MEM
WALMART EXCLUSIVE

2017 The Walking Dead Rise Up Magnets

COMPLETE SET (24) 50.00 100.00
UNOPENED BOX (24 PACKS)
UNOPENED PACK (1 METAL SIGN)
COMMON MAGNET (1-24) 2.00 5.00
1 Negan 3.00 8.00
2 Daryl 3.00 8.00
3 Carol 3.00 8.00
7 Michonne 5.00 12.00
8 King Ezekiel 2.50 6.00
9 Negan 3.00 8.00
10 Maggie 2.50 6.00
11 Rise Up (Rick) 2.50 6.00
12 Michonne & Rick 3.00 8.00
13 Daryl 3.00 8.00
15 Rick 3.00 8.00
16 King Ezekiel (w/Shiva) 2.50 6.00
19 Carol 2.50 6.00
20 Daryl 3.00 8.00
22 Maggie 2.50 6.00
23 Michonne 5.00 12.00
24 Rick 3.00 8.00

2017 The Walking Dead Rise Up Magnetic Metal Signs Special Silver

COMPLETE SET (9) 60.00 120.00
COMMON MAGNET (S1-S9) 6.00 15.00
STATED ODDS 1:24
S1 Negan 12.00 30.00
S2 Rick 10.00 25.00
S3 Michonne 10.00 25.00
S5 Maggie 8.00 20.00
S6 Daryl 12.00 30.00
S8 Carl 20.00 50.00

2018 The Walking Dead Road to Alexandria

COMPLETE SET (100) 8.00 20.00
UNOPENED BOX (24 PACKS) 60.00 90.00
UNOPENED PACK (8 CARDS) 3.00 4.00
COMMON CARD (1-100) .15 .40
*RUST: .6X TO 1.5X BASIC CARDS
*BLUE/50: 2.5X TO 6X BASIC CARDS
*MOLD/25: 8X TO 20X BASIC CARDS
*SEPIA/10: 12X TO 30X BASIC CARDS

2018 The Walking Dead Road to Alexandria Autographs

COMMON AUTO 5.00 12.00
*RUST/99: .5X TO 1.2X BASIC AUTOS
*BLUE/50: .6X TO 1.5X BASIC AUTOS
*MOLD/25: .75X TO 2X BASIC AUTOS
RANDOMLY INSERTED INTO PACKS
NNO Carlos Navarro 6.00 15.00
NNO Jeremy Palko 6.00 15.00
NNO Josh McDermitt 10.00 25.00
NNO Karen Ceesay 6.00 15.00
NNO Kenric Green 8.00 20.00
NNO Michael Cudlitz 10.00 25.00
NNO Steve Coulter 6.00 15.00
NNO Steven Ogg 25.00 60.00

2018 The Walking Dead Road to Alexandria Bat Relics

COMMON MEM 4.00 10.00
*RUST/99: SAME VALUE AS BASIC 4.00 10.00
*BLUE/50: .5X TO 1.2X BASIC MEM 5.00 12.00
*MOLD/25: .6X TO 1.5X BASIC MEM 6.00 15.00
WALMART EXCLUSIVE
NNO Abraham Ford 5.00 12.00
NNO Arat 5.00 12.00
NNO Daryl Dixon 6.00 15.00
NNO Glenn Rhee 8.00 20.00
NNO Maggie Greene 10.00 25.00
NNO Negan 6.00 15.00
NNO Rick Grimes 8.00 20.00

2018 The Walking Dead Road to Alexandria Better Days

COMPLETE SET (10) 5.00 12.00
COMMON CARD (BD1-BD10) .75 2.00
RANDOMLY INSERTED INTO PACKS

2018 The Walking Dead Road to Alexandria Captured

COMPLETE SET (10) 6.00 15.00
COMMON CARD (CA1-CA10) 1.00 2.50
TARGET EXCLUSIVE

2018 The Walking Dead Road to Alexandria Characters

COMPLETE SET (20) 6.00 15.00
COMMON CARD (C1-C20) .60 1.50
STATED OVERALL ODDS 1:1

C1 Rick Grimes 1.50 4.00
C5 Daryl Dixon 1.50 4.00
C6 Carol Peletier 1.25 3.00
C10 Michonne 1.25 3.00
C20 Negan 1.25 3.00

2018 The Walking Dead Road to Alexandria Costume Relics

COMMON MEM 4.00 10.00
*RUST/99: SAME VALUE AS BASIC
*BLUE/50: .5X TO 1.2X BASIC MEM
*MOLD/25: .6X TO 1.5X BASIC MEM
RANDOMLY INSERTED INTO PACKS
NNO Abraham Ford 5.00 12.00
NNO Beth 6.00 15.00
NNO Carl Grimes 6.00 15.00
NNO Carol Peletier 8.00 20.00
NNO Daryl Dixon 12.00 30.00
NNO Dawn Lerner 5.00 12.00
NNO Dwight 5.00 12.00
NNO Ezekiel 5.00 12.00
NNO Jessie Anderson 5.00 12.00
NNO Maggie Greene 6.00 15.00
NNO Negan 12.00 30.00
NNO Rick Grimes 12.00 30.00
NNO Rosita Espinosa 8.00 20.00

2018 The Walking Dead Road to Alexandria Daryl Dixon Walker Costume Relics

COMMON MEM 12.00 30.00
*RUST/99: .5X TO 1.2X BASIC MEM
*BLUE/50: .6X TO 1.5X BASIC MEM
*MOLD/25: .75X TO 2X BASIC MEM
WALMART EXCLUSIVE

2018 The Walking Dead Road to Alexandria Dual Autographed Costume Relics

COMPLETE SET (3)
STATED PRINT RUN 10 SER.#'d SETS
UNPRICED DUE TO SCARCITY
NNO C.Riggs/E.Kinney
NNO E.Kinney/T.J.Williams
NNO M.McBride/S.Martin-Green

2018 The Walking Dead Road to Alexandria Dual Costume Relics

COMMON MEM
*RUST/99: X TO X BASIC MEM
*BLUE/50: X TO X BASIC MEM
*MOLD/25: X TO X BASIC MEM
RANDOMLY INSERTED INTO PACKS
DRLK Rick/Beth
DRLR Rick/Carl
DRRK Carl/Beth
DRLMB Rick/Carol
DRMBK Carol/Beth
DRMBM Carol/Tara
DRMBR Carl/Carol

2018 The Walking Dead Road to Alexandria Factions

COMPLETE SET (10) 4.00 10.00
COMMON CARD (F1-F10) .60 1.50
RANDOMLY INSERTED INTO PACKS

2018 The Walking Dead Road to Alexandria Manufactured Location Patches

COMMON PATCH 4.00 10.00
*RUST/99: .5X TO 1.2X BASIC PATCHES
*BLUE/50: .6X TO 1.5X BASIC PATCHES
*MOLD/25: .75X TO 2X BASIC PATCHES
RANDOMLY INSERTED INTO PACKS
PAL Rick Grimes 8.00 20.00
PCR Carl Grimes 6.00 15.00
PCS Rosita Espinosa 6.00 15.00
PDM The Governor 5.00 12.00
PJB Shane Walsh 5.00 12.00
PKN Enid 5.00 12.00
PLC Maggie Greene 5.00 12.00
PLH Andrea 5.00 12.00
PMC Abraham Ford 6.00 15.00
PMM Carol Peletier 6.00 15.00
PNR Daryl Dixon 6.00 15.00
PRM Aaron 5.00 12.00
PSY Glenn Rhee 5.00 12.00
PTP Jesus 5.00 12.00
PBSL Lizzie Samuels 6.00 15.00
PJDD Dale Horvath 5.00 12.00
PJDM Negan 8.00 20.00

2018 The Walking Dead Road to Alexandria Rise Up

COMPLETE SET (10) 8.00 20.00
COMMON CARD (RU1-RU10) 1.25 3.00
WALMART EXCLUSIVE

2018 The Walking Dead Road to Alexandria Walker Costume Relics

COMMON MEM 4.00 10.00
*RUST/99: SAME VALUE AS BASIC
*BLUE/50: .5X TO 1.2X BASIC MEM
*MOLD/25: .6X TO 1.5X BASIC MEM
RANDOMLY INSERTED INTO PACKS

2018 The Walking Dead Road to Alexandria Walker Hall of Fame

COMPLETE SET (9) 6.00 15.00
COMMON CARD (W1-W2) 1.00 2.50
RANDOMLY INSERTED INTO PACKS

2016 The Walking Dead Survival Box

COMPLETE SET W/O SP (50) 30.00 80.00
COMPLETE SET W/SP (75) 80.00 150.00
UNOPENED BOX (4 PACKS) 100.00 120.00
UNOPENED PACK (5 CARDS) 30.00 40.00
COMMON CARD (1-50) 1.00 2.50
COMMON SP (1B-25B) 3.00 8.00
*INFECTED/99: .6X TO 1.5X BASIC CARDS
*INFECTED SP/99: .20X TO .5X BASIC CARDS
*ROTTEN/25: 1X TO 2.5X BASIC CARDS
*ROTTEN SP/25: .30X TO .75X BASIC CARDS
*MAGGOTS/10: 1.5X TO 3X BASIC CARDS
*MAGGOTS SP/10: SAME VALUE AS BASIC CARDS

2016 The Walking Dead Survival Box Autographs

COMMON CARD 8.00 20.00
*INFECTED/99: .5X TO 1.2X BASIC CARDS
*ROTTEN/25: .75X TO 2X BASIC CARDS
*MAGGOTS/10: 1X TO 2.5 BASIC CARDS
RANDOMLY INSERTED INTO PACKS
NNO Alexandra Breckenridge 25.00 60.00
NNO Brighton Sharbino 25.00 60.00
NNO Chad L. Coleman 10.00 25.00
NNO Christian Serratos 15.00 40.00
NNO Jeffrey Dean Morgan
NNO Jose Pablo Cantillo 6.00 15.00
NNO Josh McDermitt
NNO Major Dodson 10.00 25.00
NNO Norman Reedus 60.00 120.00
NNO Pruitt Taylor Vince 10.00 25.00
NNO Ross Marquand 15.00 40.00
NNO Scott Wilson 15.00 40.00

2016 The Walking Dead Survival Box Dual Autographs

COMMON CARD 15.00 40.00
NNO B.Sharbino/K.Kenedy/99 60.00 120.00
NNO C.L.Coleman/S.Martin-Green/99 30.00 80.00
NNO C.Brill/M.Dodson/99 20.00 50.00
NNO M.McBride/J.Douglas/99 25.00 60.00
NNO M.McBride/B.Samuel/99 25.00 60.00
NNO M.McBride/S.Gilliam/97 30.00 80.00
NNO S.Yeun/K.Nacon/99 50.00 100.00

2016 The Walking Dead Survival Box Dual Relic Books

COMMON CARD 25.00 60.00
STATED PRINT RUN 10 SER.#'d SETS
NNO Daryl/Beth 60.00 150.00
NNO Glenn/Maggie 75.00 200.00
NNO Rick/Carl 30.00 80.00

2016 The Walking Dead Survival Box Kill or Be Killed

COMPLETE SET (10) 12.00 30.00
COMMON CARD (1-10) 2.50 6.00
*INFECTED/99: .6X TO 1.5X BASIC CARDS
*ROTTEN/25: .75X TO 2X BASIC CARDS
*MAGGOTS/10: 1X TO 2.5X BASIC CARDS
RANDOMLY INSERTED INTO PACKS

2016 The Walking Dead Survival Box Relics

COMMON CARD 5.00 12.00
*INFECTED/99: .5X TO 1.2X BASIC CARDS
*ROTTEN/25: .6X TO 1.5X BASIC CARDS
*MAGGOTS/10: .75X TO 2X BASIC CARDS
RANDOMLY INSERTED INTO PACKS
NNO Abraham/Pants 6.00 15.00
NNO Beth/Pants 10.00 25.00
NNO Carl/Shirt 10.00 25.00
NNO Daryl/Shirt 15.00 40.00
NNO Dawn/Shirt 6.00 15.00
NNO Enid/Jacket 12.00 30.00
NNO Glenn/Black Shirt 10.00 25.00
NNO Glenn/Maroon Shirt 10.00 25.00
NNO Jessie/Shirt 15.00 40.00
NNO Noah/Black Shirt 8.00 20.00
NNO Rick/Shirt 10.00 25.00
NNO Rosita/Shirt 12.00 30.00
NNO Sasha/Shirt 10.00 25.00
NNO Tara/Shirt 8.00 20.00

2016 The Walking Dead Survival Box Survival Guide

COMPLETE SET (8) 10.00 25.00
COMMON CARD 2.50 6.00
*INFECTED/99: .60X TO 1.5X BASIC CARDS
*ROTTEN/25: .75X TO 2X BASIC CARDS
*MAGGOTS/10: 1X TO 2.5X BASIC CARDS
RANDOMLY INSERTED INTO PACKS

2016 The Walking Dead Survival Box Walker Bite

COMPLETE SET (5) 10.00 25.00
COMMON CARD (1-5) 3.00 8.00
*INFECTED/99: .6X TO 1.5X BASIC CARDS
*ROTTEN/25: .75X TO 2X BASIC CARDS
*MAGGOTS/10: 1X TO 2.5X BASIC CARDS
RANDOMLY INSERTED INTO PACKS

2014 The Walking Dead Tokenz

COMPLETE SET (42) 10.00 25.00
UNOPENED BOX (24 PACKS) 65.00 80.00
UNOPENED PACK (4 TOKENZ) 3.00 4.00
COMMON CARD (1-42) .50 1.25
*FOIL: .75X TO 2X BASIC TOKENZ 1.00 2.50

2014 The Walking Dead Tokenz Virtual Reality Walkers

COMPLETE SET (6) 4.00 10.00
COMMON CARD (VR1-VR6) 1.25 3.00
STATED ODDS 1:1

1993 Federal Card Company Wanted by FBI

COMPLETE SET W/SP1 (100) 4.00 10.00
UNOPENED BOX (40 PACKS) 15.00 25.00
UNOPENED PACK (8 CARDS) .50 .75
COMMON CARD (1-100) .08 .20
SP2 J. Edgar Hoover FOIL 3.00 8.00

1993 Federal Card Company Wanted by FBI Promos

COMPLETE SET (8) 6.00 15.00
COMMON CARD 1.25 3.00
PAN1 24-card sheet (18X24) 250.00 500.00

1980 Topps Wanted Posters

COMPLETE SET (24) 20.00 50.00
UNOPENED BOX (36 PACKS) 45.00 60.00
UNOPENED PACK (1 POSTER) 2.00 5.00
COMMON POSTER (1-24) 1.50 4.00

1992 Kitchen Sink Press War Cry Propaganda Poster Art of WWII

COMPLETE BOXED SET (36) 5.00 12.00
COMMON CARD (1-36) .25 .60

2014 War Illustrated 1914

COMPLETE SET (18) 5.00 12.00
COMMON CARD (1-18) .30 .75

2014 War Illustrated 1914 Artefacts

COMMON CARD 4.00 10.00

2014 War Illustrated 1914 Promos

COMPLETE SET (5)
COMMON CARD
P1 1914 Preview Set 1.50 4.00
(foundering ship)
MC5 Cult-Stuff website
PTC1 Double sided magno/15
NSTC1 magno nonsportstradingcards/25 15.00 40.00
NSUP1 Your Country Needs You NSU 4.00 10.00

2010 Warehouse 13 Season One

COMPLETE SET (72) 5.00 12.00
UNOPENED BOX (24 PACKS) 75.00 125.00
UNOPENED PACK (5 CARDS) 3.00 5.00
UNOPENED ARCHIVE BOX 350.00 500.00
COMMON CARD (1-72) .15 .40

2010 Warehouse 13 Season One Autographs

COMMON AUTO 5.00 12.00
STATED ODDS TWO PER BOX
L (LIMITED): 300-500 COPIES
VL (VERY LIMITED): 200-300 COPIES
NNO Eddie McClintock VL 25.00 60.00
NNO Erica Cerra L 10.00 25.00
NNO Genelle Williams VL 15.00 40.00
NNO Joanne Kelly VL 20.00 50.00
NNO Joe Morton L 6.00 15.00
NNO Saul Rubinek VL 15.00 40.00
NNO Tricia Helfer L 12.00 30.00

2010 Warehouse 13 Season One Gallery

COMPLETE SET (6) 15.00 40.00
COMMON CARD (G1-G6) 4.00 10.00
STATED ODDS 1:24

2010 Warehouse 13 Season One Relics

COMMON CARD (R1-R8) 6.00 15.00
STATED ODDS 1:12
VOLTA RELIC ISSUED AS CASE TOPPER
MCLINTOCK AUTO ISSUED AS 3-CASE INCENTIVE
R1 Peter Lattimer 8.00 20.00
R3 Myka Bering 8.00 20.00
R4 Myka Bering 8.00 20.00
R6 Claudia Donovan 8.00 20.00
NNO Volta CT/333 15.00 30.00
NNO Lattimer/McClint AU 3CI 75.00 125.00

2010 Warehouse 13 Season One Snag It Bag It Tag It

COMPLETE SET (18) 20.00 50.00
COMMON CARD (A1-A18) 2.00 5.00
STATED ODDS 1:8
A19 ISSUED AS RITTENHOUSE REWARD
A19 Moon Rock SP 10.00 25.00

2010 Warehouse 13 Season One Promos

P1 Pete Lattimer/Myka Bering GEN 1.50 4.00
P2 Pete Lattimer/Myka Bering NSU 2.00 5.00
P3 Artie Nielsen/Claudia Donovan ALB 6.00 15.00
CP1 Myka Bering/Pete Lattimer SDCC 2.00 5.00

2011 Warehouse 13 Season Two

COMPLETE SET (26) 30.00 60.00
UNOPENED BOX (15 PACKS) 60.00 100.00

UNOPENED PACK (6 CARDS)	4.00	6.00
COMMON CARD (1-26)	2.00	5.00
STATED PRINT RUN 250 SER. #'d SETS		

2011 Warehouse 13 Season Two Artifacts

COMPLETE SET (9)	20.00	40.00
COMMON CARD (A20-A28)	3.00	8.00
STATED PRINT RUN 350 SER. #'d SETS		

2011 Warehouse 13 Season Two Autographs

COMMON AUTO	5.00	12.00
STATED ODDS TWO PER PACK		
NNO Allison Scagliotti	25.00	60.00
NNO Armin Shimerman	8.00	20.00
NNO CCH Pounder	10.00	25.00
NNO Eddie McClintock	15.00	40.00
NNO Genelle Williams	6.00	15.00
NNO Jaime Murray	25.00	60.00
NNO Joanne Kelly	20.00	50.00
NNO Neil Grayston	10.00	25.00
NNO Roberta Maxwell	6.00	15.00
NNO Saul Rubinek	15.00	40.00
NNO Tia Carrere	15.00	40.00

2011 Warehouse 13 Season Two Relics

COMMON CARD	8.00	20.00
STATED PRINT RUN 350 SER. #'d SETS		
7 Myka Bering dress	10.00	25.00

2011 Warehouse 13 Season Two Promos

P1 Pete Lattimer/Myka Bering GEN	.75	2.00
P2 Pete Lattimer/Myka Bering NSU	1.50	4.00
P3 Artie Nielsen/Claudia Donovan SDCC	2.00	5.00

2012 Warehouse 13 Season Three

COMPLETE SET (26)	25.00	50.00
UNOPENED BOX (15 PACKS)		
UNOPENED PACK (6 CARDS)		
COMMON CARD (1-26)	2.00	5.00

2012 Warehouse 13 Season Three Artifacts

COMP.SET w/o A38 (9)	15.00	40.00
COMPLETE SET (10)	20.00	50.00
COMMON CARD (A29-A37)	3.00	8.00
STATED PRINT RUN 350 SER. #'d SETS		
A38 ISSUED AS RITTENHOUSE REWARD		
A38 Upholstery Brush RR	15.00	30.00

2012 Warehouse 13 Season Three Autograph Relics

COMMON AUTO	50.00	100.00
RUBINEK ISSUED AS 2-BOX INCENTIVE		
McCLINTOCK ISSUED AS 4-BOX INCENTIVE		

2012 Warehouse 13 Season Three Autographs

COMMON AUTO	5.00	12.00
L (LIMITED): 300-500 COPIES		
VL (VERY LIMITED): 200-300 COPIES		
EL (EXTREMELY LIMITED): LESS THAN 200 COPIES		
NNO Aaron Ashmore VL	10.00	25.00
NNO Allison Scagliotti VL	20.00	50.00
NNO CCH Pounder VL	12.00	30.00
NNO Eddie McClintock VL	20.00	50.00
NNO Jeri Ryan EL	50.00	100.00
NNO Kate Mulgrew EL	30.00	75.00
NNO Lindsay Wagner EL	30.00	75.00
NNO Rene Auberjonois VL	12.00	30.00
NNO Saul Rubinek VL	15.00	40.00

2012 Warehouse 13 Season Three Relics

COMMON CARD	6.00	15.00
STATED ODDS TWO RELICS PER PACK		
1 Amanda Lattimer	12.00	30.00
4 Claudia Donovan	15.00	40.00
5 Claudia Donovan	15.00	40.00
6 H.G. Wells jacket	10.00	25.00
7 H.G. Wells vest	10.00	25.00
8 H.G. Wells shirt	10.00	25.00
9 H.G. Wells sweater	10.00	25.00
10 Jane Lattimer	10.00	25.00
13 Mrs. Irene Frederic	12.00	30.00
14 Myk Bering	10.00	25.00
15 Myka Bering dress	10.00	25.00
16 Myka Bering shirt	10.00	25.00
17 Myka Bering	10.00	25.00
18 Pete Lattimer hoodie	8.00	20.00
19 Pete Lattimer t-shirt	8.00	20.00
20 Pete Lattimer jacket	8.00	20.00
21 Pete Lattimer shirt	8.00	20.00

2012 Warehouse 13 Season Three Promos

P1 Artie/Myka/Pete GEN	1.00	2.50
P2 Four Ladies BT	6.00	15.00

2013 Warehouse 13 Season Four

COMPLETE SET (20)	20.00	50.00
UNOPENED BOX (15 PACKS)		
UNOPENED PACK (6 CARDS)		
COMMON CARD (1-20)	2.00	5.00
BT1 ISSUED AS BOX TOPPER		
BT1 Claudia/Pete/Myka/Artie BT	8.00	20.00

2013 Warehouse 13 Season Four Autograph Relics

COMMON AUTO	15.00	40.00
ONE AUTO OR AUTO RELIC PER PACK		
NNO Allison Scagliotti/160	50.00	100.00
NNO Brent Spiner jacket/160	20.00	50.00
NNO Jamie Murray/150	25.00	60.00
NNO Joanne Kelly jacket/160	25.00	60.00
NNO Jeri Ryan dress/107 2BI	60.00	120.00

2013 Warehouse 13 Season Four Autographs

COMMON AUTO	5.00	12.00
ONE AUTO OR AUTO RELIC PER PACK		
NNO Allison Scagliotti	15.00	40.00
NNO Brent Spiner	20.00	50.00
NNO CCH Pounder	6.00	15.00
NNO Jamie Murray	20.00	50.00
NNO Jeri Ryan	25.00	60.00
NNO Joanne Kelly	15.00	40.00

2013 Warehouse 13 Season Four Grand Designs

COMPLETE SET (10)	20.00	50.00
COMMON CARD (GD1-GD10)	3.00	8.00
OVERALL CHASE ODDS ONE PER PACK		

2013 Warehouse 13 Season Four Of Monsters and Men

COMPLETE SET (10)	15.00	40.00
COMMON CARD (MM1-MM10)	2.50	6.00
OVERALL CHASE ODDS ONE PER PACK		

2013 Warehouse 13 Season Four Relics

COMMON CARD	5.00	12.00
TWO RELICS PER PACK		
3 Brother Adrian jacket/150	15.00	40.00
4 Claudia Donovan kimono/350	10.00	25.00
5 Claudia Donovan sweater/350	10.00	25.00
6 Dr. Vanessa Calder blouse/150	15.00	40.00
7 H.G. Wells shirt/150	30.00	60.00
8 Hugo Miller/350 DUAL	8.00	20.00
9 Kate Logan blouse/350	6.00	15.00
10 Kate Logan jacket/450	6.00	15.00
11 Leena blouse/450	6.00	15.00
13 Myka Bering jacket/350	8.00	20.00
14 Myka Bering shirt/450	8.00	20.00
20 Pete Lattimer tie/150 2BI	25.00	50.00

2013 Warehouse 13 Season Four Promos

P1 Pete/Claudia/Steve GEN	.75	2.00
P2 Artie/Claudia (Philly)	.60	1.50

1997 Bolt Entertainment Warrior Nun Areala

COMPLETE SET (91)	5.00	12.00
UNOPENED BOX (32 PACKS)	40.00	50.00
UNOPENED PACK (8 CARDS)	1.50	1.75
COMMON CARD (1-90, WIDOW)	.10	.25

1997 Bolt Entertainment Warrior Nun Areala Autographs

COMMON CARD	8.00	20.00
RANDOMLY INSERTED INTO PACKS		

1997 Bolt Entertainment Warrior Nun Areala Foil

COMPLETE SET (5)	10.00	25.00
COMMON CARD (C1-C5)	2.50	6.00
STATED ODDS 1:10		

1997 Bolt Entertainment Warrior Nun Areala Leather

COMPLETE SET (9)	25.00	60.00
COMMON CARD (L1-L9)	3.00	8.00
RANDOMLY INSERTED INTO PACKS		

1997 Bolt Entertainment Warrior Nun Areala Promos

COMPLETE SET (6)	5.00	12.00
COMMON CARD (P1-P6)	1.25	3.00

2014 The Warriors 5X7

COMPLETE SET (17)	25.00	60.00
COMMON CARD (WI1-WI16; COVER CARD)	2.50	6.00

1995 Fleer Ultra Waterworld

COMPLETE SET (150)	6.00	15.00
UNOPENED BOX (36 PACKS)	30.00	40.00
UNOPENED PACK (8 CARDS)	1.00	1.25
COMMON CARD (1-150)	.08	.20
4UP Waterworld Fleer Ultra (4UP panel)		3.00

1995 Fleer Ultra Waterworld Double Foil

COMPLETE SET (6)	5.00	12.00
COMMON CARD (F1-F6)	1.00	2.50
STATED ODDS 1:4		

1995 Fleer Ultra Waterworld Holograms

COMPLETE SET (6)	4.00	10.00
COMMON CARD (H1-H6)	.75	2.00
STATED ODDS 1:4		

1995 Fleer Ultra Waterworld Prismatic Foil

COMPLETE SET (6)	5.00	12.00
COMMON CARD (P1-P6)	1.00	2.50
STATED ODDS 1:6		

2007 Webkinz Series 1

COMPLETE SET (80)	15.00	30.00
UNOPENED BOX (36 PACKS)	20.00	30.00
UNOPENED PACK (6 CARDS)	1.00	1.25
COMMON CARD (1-80)	.12	.30
CODE CARDS	.50	1.00
VIRTUAL PET CODE (UNUSED)	6.00	12.00
1 Arte Fact	.30	.75
3 Dr. Quack	.30	.75
4 Ms. Birdy	.20	.50
5 Plumpy	.40	1.00
8 Black Lab	.75	2.00
9 Cocker Spaniel	.30	.75
10 Golden Retriever	.30	.75
11 St. Bernard	.75	2.00
12 Elephant	.30	.75
13 Hippo	.40	1.00
14 Lion	.30	.75
15 Monkey	.30	.75
16 Alley Cat	.30	.75
17 Black and White Cat	.30	.75
18 Gold and White Cat	.30	.75
19 Persian Cat	.30	.75
20 Cow	.30	.75
21 Frog	.30	.75
22 Pig	.30	.75
23 Rabbit	.75	2.00
27 Poncho	.20	.50
28 Wacky Zingoz	.20	.50
29 Zacky Zingoz	.20	.50
30 Zangos	.20	.50
35 Hungry Hog	.20	.50
37 Wacky Zingoz	.20	.50
47 Wacky Zingoz 600 Trophy	.40	1.00
48 Zacky's Quest Trophy	.20	.50
49 Zingos Bounce Trophy	.20	.50
50 Zingoz Pop Gold Trophy	.20	.50
58 Ultimate Experiment Table	.30	.75
71 Always Be Prepared	.20	.50
72 Call A Friend	.20	.50
73 DiceKinz Blowback	.20	.50
74 New Job in the Employment Office	.20	.50
75 Something Shiny	.40	1.00
76 Sometimes Good Things Just Happen	.20	.50
77 Spin the Wheel of WOW	.20	.50
78 Spin the Wishing Well	.20	.50
79 Tradesies, No Return	.20	.50
CC Code Card	.40	1.00
OPC Online Pet Card	5.00	12.00

2007 Webkinz Series 1 Challenge Cards

COMPLETE SET (15)	3.00	8.00
COMMON CARD (C11-C115)	.40	1.00
STATED ODDS 1:2		

2007 Webkinz Series 1 Curio Shop Curiosities

COMPLETE SET (8)	6.00	15.00
COMMON CARD (A11-A18)	1.00	2.50
STATED ODDS 1:9		

2007 Webkinz Series 1 Doodlez

COMPLETE SET (8)	10.00	25.00
COMMON CARD (D11-D18)	2.00	5.00
STATED ODDS 1:18		

2008 Webkinz Series 2

COMPLETE SET (85)	6.00	15.00
UNOPENED BOX (36 PACKS)	60.00	75.00
UNOPENED PACK (6 CARDS)	2.75	3.50
COMMON CARD (1-85)		

2008 Webkinz Series 2 At Paw Level

COMPLETE SET (8)	10.00	25.00
COMMON CARD (P11-P18)	2.00	5.00
STATED ODDS 1:18		

2008 Webkinz Series 2 Challenge Cards

COMPLETE SET (15)	3.00	8.00
COMMON CARD (C21-C215)	.40	1.00
STATED ODDS 1:2		

2008 Webkinz Series 2 W-Tales Snapshots

COMPLETE SET (8)	6.00	15.00
COMMON CARD (W11-W18)	1.00	2.50
STATED ODDS 1:9		

2009 Webkinz Series 4

COMPLETE SET (90)	6.00	15.00
UNOPENED BOX (36 PACKS)		
UNOPENED PACK (6 CARDS)		
COMMON CARD (1-90)	.08	.20

1986 Appel Enterprises Weird Ball

COMPLETE SET (42)	6.00	15.00
UNOPENED BOX (36 PACKS)	50.00	75.00
UNOPENED PACK (5 CARDS)	1.50	2.50
UNOPENED RACK PACK (24 CARDS)	4.00	5.00
COMMON CARD (1-42)	.30	.75

1993 21st Century Archives Weird Tales Women in Peril

COMPLETE SET (55)	4.00	10.00
UNOPENED BOX (36 PACKS)	15.00	25.00
UNOPENED PACK (8 CARDS)	.75	1.00
COMMON CARD (1-55)	.15	.40

1993 21st Century Archives Weird Tales Women in Peril Promos

COMPLETE SET (7)	3.00	8.00
COMMON CARD	.75	2.00

MODERN

1993 21st Century Archives Weird Tales Women in Peril Sculptor-Cast

COMPLETE SET (5)	12.00	30.00
COMMON CARD (1-5)	3.00	8.00
RANDOMLY INSERTED INTO PACKS		

2017 Welcome to the Show Series 1

COMPLETE SET (20)	6.00	15.00
COMMON CARD	.50	1.25
*RED: 1.2X TO 3X BASIC CARDS	1.50	4.00
UNC Complete Set Uncut Sheet		

2017 Welcome to the Show Series 1 Autographs

COMMON CARD	6.00	15.00
*RED: .6X TO 1.5X BASIC CARDS		
STATED ODDS 1:SET		

1995 WildStorm WetWorks

COMPLETE SET (107)	8.00	20.00
UNOPENED BOX (24 PACKS)	10.00	15.00
UNOPENED PACK (7 CARDS)	.50	.75
COMMON CARD (1-107)	.15	.40

1995 WildStorm WetWorks Die-Cuts

COMPLETE SET (9)	25.00	60.00
COMMON CARD (C1-C9)	3.00	8.00
STATED ODDS 1:5		

1995 WildStorm WetWorks Gold Chromium

COMPLETE SET (9)	25.00	60.00
COMMON CARD (G1-G9)	3.00	8.00
STATED ODDS 1:8		

1991 Pacific Where Are They?

COMPLETE SET (110)	6.00	15.00
UNOPENED BOX (36 PACKS)	15.00	25.00
UNOPENED PACK (10 CARDS)	.75	1.00
COMMON CARD (1-110)	.12	.30
AU1 Tony Tallarico AU/2500*	2.00	5.00

1991 Mattel Where's Waldo?

COMPLETE SET (128)	6.00	15.00
UNOPENED BOX (24 PACKS)	10.00	20.00
UNOPENED PACK (8 CARDS)	.75	1.00
COMMON CARD (1-128)	.10	.25

1991 Mattel Life Cereal Where's Waldo?

COMPLETE SET (12)	6.00	15.00
COMMON CARD (1-12)	.75	2.00
PRODUCED BY MATTEL		
INSERTED IN BOXES OF LIFE CEREAL		

1988 Topps Who Framed Roger Rabbit?

COMPLETE SET (132)	5.00	12.00
COMPLETE SET W/STICKERS (154)	6.00	15.00
UNOPENED BOX (36 PACKS)	30.00	60.00
UNOPENED PACK (9 CARDS+1 STICKER)	1.25	2.00
COMMON CARD (1-132)	.06	.15

1988 Topps Who Framed Roger Rabbit? Puzzle Stickers

COMPLETE SET (22)	2.00	5.00
COMMON CARD (1-22)	.15	.40
STATED ODDS 1:1		

2014 The Wicker Man Previews

COMPLETE SET (6)	6.00	12.00
COMMON CARD (P1-P6)	1.25	3.00

2014 The Wicker Man

COMPLETE SET (54)	6.00	15.00
UNOPENED BOX (24 PACKS)	40.00	60.00
UNOPENED PACK (5 CARDS)	2.00	3.00
COMMON CARD (1-54)	.20	.50

2014 The Wicker Man Autographs

COMMON CARD	10.00	25.00
STATED ODDS 1:24		
WMBE Britt Ekland	20.00	50.00
WMCL Christopher Lee	120.00	200.00

2014 The Wicker Man Film Cell

FC1 Hailing Wicker Man	5.00	12.00

2014 The Wicker Man Gold Foil Chase

COMPLETE SET (9)	6.00	15.00
COMMON CARD (F1-F9)	1.25	3.00
STATED ODDS 1:6		

2014 The Wicker Man Promos

COMMON CARD	1.00	2.50
NSP1 Howie/100 (Nonsporttradingcardsuk)	4.00	10.00
RTP1 Summerisle/100 (Radickal)	3.00	8.00
UCP1 Hailing Wicker/100 ALB	4.00	10.00

1996 Amurol Wild Pitch

COMPLETE SET (12)	8.00	20.00
COMMON CARD (1-12)	1.25	3.00
NNO Lightning Rod/20,000		

1986 Sanitarium Wild South

COMPLETE SET (20)	10.00	25.00
COMMON CARD (1-20)	.75	2.00

1999 SkyBox Wild Wild West

COMPLETE SET (81)	5.00	12.00
UNOPENED BOX (36 PACKS)		
UNOPENED PACK (9 CARDS)		
COMMON CARD (1-81)	.15	.40
NNO Wild Wild West PROMO	1.25	3.00

1999 SkyBox Wild Wild West Autographs

COMMON CARD (A1-A15)	5.00	10.00
STATED ODDS 1:36		
A1 Kevin Kline	125.00	250.00
A2 Barry Sonnenfeld	5.00	12.00
A3 Kenneth Branagh	60.00	120.00
A5 Musetta Vander	6.00	15.00
A6 Frederique Van Der Wal	20.00	50.00
A8 M. Emmet Walsh	30.00	75.00
A9 Ted Levine	8.00	20.00
A12 Ian Abercrombie	6.00	15.00
A14 Jon Peters	5.00	12.00
A15 Salma Hayek	500.00	1000.00

1999 SkyBox Wild Wild West Concept Sketches

COMPLETE SET (9)	5.00	12.00
COMMON CARD (S1-S9)	.75	2.00
STATED ODDS 1:4		

1999 SkyBox Wild Wild West Gordon's Gadgets

COMPLETE SET (9)	10.00	25.00
COMMON CARD (G1-G9)	1.50	4.00
STATED ODDS 1:12		

1999 SkyBox Wild Wild West Platinum Portraits

COMPLETE SET (3)	50.00	120.00
COMMON CARD (P1-P3)	20.00	50.00
STATED PRINT RUN 750 SER.#'d SETS		

2003 The Wild Wild West The Dr. Loveless Episodes

COMPLETE SET (13)	25.00	60.00
COMMON CARD	.40	1.00
STATED PRINT RUN 999 SETS		
A1 Robert Conrad AU	20.00	50.00
CC1 James T. West's Outfit	4.00	10.00
P1 Wild Wild West	.75	2.00

1993 Topps WildCATs Prism

COMPLETE SET (100)	4.00	10.00
UNOPENED BOX (36 PACKS)	20.00	30.00
UNOPENED PACK (8 CARDS)	.75	1.00
COMMON CARD (1-100)	.07	.25
32AU Jim Lee AUTO		
COMPLETE SET (6)	10.00	25.00
COMMON CARD (1-6)	2.00	5.00
STATED ODDS 1:18		

1994 Topps WildC.A.T.s

COMPLETE SET (96)	8.00	20.00
UNOPENED BOX (36 PACKS)	20.00	30.00
UNOPENED PACK (6 CARDS)	1.00	1.25
COMMON CARD (1-96)	.15	.40

1994 Topps WildC.A.T.s Double-Sided

COMPLETE SET (6)	15.00	40.00
COMMON CARD (D1-D6)	3.00	8.00
STATED ODDS 1:12		

1994 Topps WildC.A.T.s Painted

COMPLETE SET (12)	25.00	60.00
COMMON CARD (P1-P12)	2.50	6.00
STATED ODDS 1:8		

1994 Topps WildC.A.T.s Promos

COMMON CARD	1.25	3.00
P1B Direct Market	2.00	5.00

1994 Topps WildC.A.T.s WildDISCs

COMPLETE SET (5)	12.00	30.00
COMMON CARD (C1-C5)	3.00	8.00
STATED ODDS 1:BOX		

1991 Bon Air Wildlife America

COMPLETE BOXED SET (50)	3.00	8.00
COMMON CARD (1-50)	.12	.30

1992 Panini Wildlife in Danger

COMPLETE SET (100)	6.00	15.00
UNOPENED BOX (36 PACKS)	8.00	10.00
UNOPENED PACK (8 CARDS)	.50	.60
COMMON CARD (1-100)	.02	.30

1994 WildStorm Set I

COMPLETE SET (100)	20.00	50.00
UNOPENED BOX (36 PACKS)	40.00	50.00
UNOPENED PACK (6 CARDS)	1.25	1.50
COMMON CARD (1-100)	.40	1.00

1994 WildStorm Set I Autographs

COMMON CARD (A1-A15; VARIANTS)	6.00	15.00
STATED ODDS 1:		
A11A Mr. Majestic Jim Lee/500	10.00	25.00
A15A Helspont Mark Silvestri/500	30.00	80.00

1994 WildStorm Set I HoloChrome

COMPLETE SET (9)	30.00	80.00
COMMON CARD (C1-C9)	4.00	10.00
RANDOMLY INSERTED INTO PACKS		

1994 WildStorm Set I Promos

COMMON CARD	.75	2.00

1996 WildStorm Set II

COMPLETE SET (90)	10.00	25.00
UNOPENED BOX (36 PACKS)	30.00	40.00
UNOPENED PACK (6 CARDS)		
COMMON CARD (1-90)	.20	.50

1996 WildStorm Set II Battle Motion

COMPLETE SET (9)	30.00	80.00
COMMON CARD (BM1-BM9)	4.00	10.00
STATED ODDS 1:8		

1996 WildStorm Archives

COMPLETE SET (198)	20.00	50.00
COMPLETE SER.1 SET (99)	12.00	30.00
COMPLETE SER.2 SET (99)	10.00	25.00
UNOPENED SER.1 BOX (24 PACKS)	30.00	50.00
UNOPENED SER.1 PACK (6 CARDS)	1.50	2.00
UNOPENED SER.2 BOX (24 PACKS)	30.00	50.00
UNOPENED SER.2 PACK (6 CARDS)	1.50	2.00
COMMON CARD (1-99)	.25	.60
COMMON CARD (100-198)	.20	.50
P1A Series I Promo	1.50	4.00
P1B Series II Promo NSU		

1996 WildStorm Archives Holo-Foil

COMPLETE SET (11)	20.00	50.00
COMMON CARD (G1-G11)	2.50	6.00
STATED ODDS 1:6		

1996 WildStorm Archives HoloChrome

COMPLETE SET (9)	25.00	60.00
COMMON CARD (WP1-WP9)	3.00	8.00
RANDOMLY INSERTED INTO PACKS		

1996 WildStorm Archives Jim Lee Lithograph

JLL Lithograph	15.00	40.00
JLLR Redemption Card		

1995 WildStorm Gallery

COMPLETE SET (127)	10.00	25.00
UNOPENED BOX (36 PACKS)	30.00	40.00
UNOPENED PACK (8 CARDS)	1.00	1.25
COMMON CARD (1-126, 138)	.15	.40
WILDSTORM RISING (127-137)		
WILDSTORM RISING ARE COMIC EXCLUSIVE		

1995 WildStorm Gallery Battle

COMPLETE SET (12)	12.00	30.00
COMMON CARD (B1-B12)	1.25	3.00
STATED ODDS 1:9		

1995 WildStorm Gallery Promos

COMPLETE SET (3)	2.50	6.00
COMMON CARD	1.25	3.00

1995 WildStorm Gallery Reader's Choice

COMPLETE SET (6)	15.00	40.00
COMMON CARD (RC1-RC6)	3.00	8.00
STATED ODDS 1:18		

1997 WildStorm Photoblast

COMPLETE SET (50)	8.00	20.00
COMMON CARD (1-50)	.30	.75

1997 WildStorm Stickers

COMPLETE SET (90)	10.00	25.00
UNOPENED BOX (36 PACKS)		
UNOPENED PACK (8 CARDS)		
COMMON CARD (1-90)	.25	.60

1996 WildStorm Swimsuit

COMPLETE SET (99)	8.00	20.00
UNOPENED BOX (36 PACKS)	40.00	50.00
UNOPENED PACK (8 CARDS)	1.25	1.50
COMMON CARD (1-99)	.15	.40

1996 WildStorm Swimsuit Miss WildStorm Pageant Stickers

COMPLETE SET (9)	15.00	40.00
COMMON CARD (S1-S9)	2.50	6.00
STATED ODDS 1:9		

1994 Cardz William Shatner's Tek World

COMPLETE SET (100)	4.00	10.00
UNOPENED BOX (36 PACKS)	15.00	20.00
UNOPENED PACK (8 CARDS)	.75	1.00
COMMON CARD (1-100)	.08	.20

1994 Cardz William Shatner's Tek World Autographs

1 William Shatner	100.00	150.00
2 Lee Sullivan	30.00	80.00

1994 Cardz William Shatner's Tek World Promos

COMMON CARD	.75	2.00
NNO 4-Up Panel (Comicfest '93)	2.00	5.00
NNO 4-Up Panel (SDCC)	2.00	5.00

1994 Cardz William Shatner's Tek World TekChrome

COMPLETE SET (4)	10.00	25.00
COMMON CARD (T1-T4)	3.00	8.00
RANDOMLY INSERTED INTO PACKS		

1994 Comic Images William Stout

COMPLETE SET (90)	4.00	10.00
UNOPENED BOX (48 PACKS)	20.00	30.00
UNOPENED PACK (10 CARDS)	.75	1.00

COMMON CARD (1-90) .10 .25
M1 Medallion/1844* 10.00 25.00
P1 William Stout PROMO .75 2.00
AU1 William Stout AU/500* 20.00 50.00

1994 Comic Images William Stout Antarctica

COMPLETE SET (3) 15.00 40.00
COMMON CARD (1-3) 6.00 15.00
RANDOMLY INSERTED INTO PACKS

1994 Comic Images William Stout Holochrome

COMPLETE SET (6) 15.00 40.00
COMMON CARD (H1-H6) 3.00 8.00
RANDOMLY INSERTED INTO PACKS

1996 Comic Images William Stout 3 Saurians and Sorcerers

COMPLETE SET (90) 4.00 10.00
UNOPENED BOX (36 PACKS) 20.00 30.00
UNOPENED PACK (10 CARDS) .75 1.00
COMMON CARD (1-90) .10 .25
BT The Ghoulish Trio
(Box Topper Exclusive)
6UP 6UP Panel
AUWS William Stout AU/500* 20.00 50.00
NNO1 Promo 1 (gen. dist.) .60 1.50

1996 Comic Images William Stout 3 Saurians and Sorcerers Ghoulish Trio

COMPLETE SET (3) 15.00 40.00
COMMON CARD (1-3) 6.00 15.00
STATED ODDS 1:36

1996 Comic Images William Stout 3 Saurians and Sorcerers Masters of the Universe MagnaChrome

COMPLETE SET (6) 12.00 30.00
COMMON CARD (M1-M6) 2.50 6.00
STATED ODDS 1:16
GHOULISH TRIO ODDS 1:BOX

1993 Kitchen Sink Press Window on the Unspeakable

COMPLETE BOXED SET (36) 4.00 10.00
COMMON CARD (1-36) .20 .50

1999 X-Toys Wing Commander Action Figure Cards

COMPLETE SET (8) 12.00 30.00
COMMON CARD 2.00 5.00
STATED ODDS 1:1 ACTION FIGURE

1992 Panini Wings of Fire

COMPLETE SET (100) 6.00 15.00
COMPLETE BOXED SET (100) 6.00 15.00
UNOPENED BOX (36 PACKS) 15.00 20.00
UNOPENED PACK (8 CARDS) .20 .50
COMMON CARD (1-100) .12 .30

1991 Eagle Wings of Gold Series 1

COMPLETE SET (19) 3.00 8.00
COMMON CARD (1-18, CL) .30 .75

1991 Eagle Wings of Gold Series 1 Promos

COMMON CARD 4.00 10.00

1994 TCM Associates Winnebago

COMPLETE SET (100) 4.00 10.00
UNOPENED BOX (36 PACKS) 10.00 12.00
UNOPENED PACK (10 CARDS) .50 .60
COMMON CARD (1-100) .08 .20

1994 TCM Associates Winnebago Holograms

COMPLETE SET (2) 3.00 8.00
COMMON CARD (1-2) 2.00 5.00
RANDOMLY INSERTED INTO PACKS

1994 TCM Associates Winnebago Prototypes

COMPLETE SET (2) 1.25 3.00
COMMON CARD .75 2.00

1996 Top Cow Witchblade

COMPLETE SET (90) 10.00 25.00
UNOPENED BOX (36 PACKS) 40.00 50.00
UNOPENED PACK (8 CARDS) 1.25 1.50
COMMON CARD (1-90) .15 .40
*GOLD: .1X TO 2.5X BASIC CARDS
NNO1 The Witchblade 15.00 40.00
NNO2 90-Card Panel Uncut Sheets
NNO3 24-Card Panel Uncut Sheets

1996 Top Cow Witchblade Etched Foil Puzzle

COMPLETE SET (9) 10.00 25.00
COMMON CARD (P1-P9) 1.50 4.00
STATED ODDS 1:4

1996 Top Cow Witchblade Promos

1 FAN and Wizard Magazines .75 2.00
2 Orange Border

1996 Top Cow Witchblade Signatures

COMPLETE SET (3) 20.00 50.00
COMMON CARD (S1-S3) 8.00 20.00
RANDOMLY INSERTED INTO PACKS

2014 Witchblade

COMPLETE SET (72) 8.00 20.00
UNOPENED BOX (24 PACKS) 45.00 60.00
UNOPENED PACK (6 CARDS) 2.00 2.50
COMMON CARD (1-72) .15 .40
*GREEN: 2X TO 5X BASIC CARDS
*PURPLE: 5X TO 12X BASIC CARDS
*SILVER: 5X TO 12X BASIC CARDS
*GOLD/50: 6X TO 15X BASIC CARDS

2014 Witchblade #170 Cover Puzzle Chase

COMPLETE SET (9) 6.00 15.00
COMMON CARD (W1-W9) 1.25 3.00
STATED ODDS 1:12

2014 Witchblade Artifacts Map Puzzle Chase

COMPLETE SET (9) 6.00 15.00
COMMON CARD (A1-A9) 1.25 3.00
STATED ODDS 1:12

2014 Witchblade Card Album

COMPLETE SET (2) 6.00 15.00
COMMON CARD (AP1-AP2) 4.00 10.00

2014 Witchblade Gauntlet Puzzle Chase

COMPLETE SET (9) 6.00 15.00
COMMON CARD (G1-G9) 1.25 3.00
STATED ODDS 1:12

2014 Witchblade Optispex

COMPLETE SET (2) 20.00 50.00
COMMON CARD (1-2) 12.00 30.00

2014 Witchblade Optispex Oversized

1 Blue Throne 15.00 40.00

2014 Witchblade Promos

1 Ian in leather; AppleCards 15.00 40.00
2 Pedestal, flames, gargoyle
3 Gray skull behind UV
4 Gray skull behind no UV
5 Right arm swiping; Fan Expo Canada 2.00 5.00
6 Ian in gauntlet UV
7 Ian in gauntlet no UV
8 Orange flame throne UV
9 Orange flame throne no UV
10 Silver gauntlet splatters face
11 Red orb Red Robin/100 12.00 30.00
12 Flying in blue hair
PCAN1 Cop Sara with gun UV 2.00 5.00
PCAN2 Cop Sara with gun no UV 2.00 5.00
PUSA1 gauntlet hand behind UV 2.00 5.00
PUSA2 gauntlet hand behind no UV 2.00 5.00

2002 Witchblade Disciples of the Blade

COMPLETE SET (72) 4.00 10.00
UNOPENED BOX (36 PACKS) 25.00 35.00
UNOPENED PACK (7 CARDS) 1.00 1.25
COMMON CARD (1-72) .10 .25

2002 Witchblade Disciples of the Blade Autographs

COMPLETE SET (10) 30.00 80.00
COMMON CARD (A1-10) 4.00 10.00
STATED ODDS 1:18
A10 IS ALBUM EXCLUSIVE

2002 Witchblade Disciples of the Blade Rainbow Chrome

COMPLETE SET (6) 5.00 12.00
COMMON CARD (C1-C6) 1.25 3.00
STATED ODDS 1:12

2002 Witchblade Disciples of the Blade Promos

BT1 Inkworks TV Season 1 (BT) 2.00 5.00
NNO Belly-dancer .75 2.00
NSU1 NSU 1.25 3.00

2000 Witchblade Millennium

COMPLETE SET (72) 6.00 15.00
UNOPENED BOX (36 PACKS) 50.00 60.00
UNOPENED PACK (6 CARDS) 1.50 1.75
COMMON CARD (1-72) .12 .30
AUKC Keu Cha AU/1500* (album excl.) 5.00 12.00

2000 Witchblade Millennium Autographs Black Ink

COMMON CARD 4.00 10.00
*BLUE INK/200: .6X TO 1.5X BASIC AUTOS
*RED INK/100: .75X TO 2X BASIC AUTOS
STATED ODDS 1:18
1 Christina Z 6.00 15.00
3 Dorian 6.00 15.00
5 JD Smith 6.00 15.00
6 Joe Jusko 8.00 20.00
11 Michael Turner
12 Paul Jenkins 10.00 25.00
13 Randy Green 6.00 15.00

2000 Witchblade Millennium Chrome

COMPLETE SET (6) 8.00 20.00
COMMON CARD (C1-C6) 1.50 4.00
STATED ODDS 1:12

2000 Witchblade Millennium Glow-in-the-Dark

COMPLETE SET (6) 8.00 20.00
COMMON CARD (G1-G6) 1.50 4.00
STATED ODDS 1:12

2000 Witchblade Millennium Promos

COMMON CARD 1.25 3.00
NNO 4-Up Panel D1-D4 4.00 10.00
(Previews Magazine Exclusive)
NNO Summer 2000 2.00 5.00
(Coni Convention Exclusive)

2002 Witchblade Season One

COMPLETE SET (81) 4.00 10.00
UNOPENED BOX (24 PACKS) 20.00 30.00
UNOPENED PACK (9 CARDS) 1.00 1.25
COMMON CARD (1-81) .10 .30
MPS Quest for Justice/177*
(9-Card Panel Mini-Press Sheet)

2002 Witchblade Season One Autographs

COMPLETE SET (6) 100.00 175.00
COMMON CARD (A1-A6) 10.00 25.00
STATED ODDS 1:27
A1 Yancy Butler 50.00 100.00
A4 Anthony Cistaro 12.00 30.00
A5 Eric Etebari 12.00 30.00

2002 Witchblade Season One Box-Loaders

COMPLETE SET (4) 2.50 6.00
COMMON CARD (1-4) .75 2.00
CL1 Witchblade 6.00 15.00

2002 Witchblade Season One Legacy of the Witchblade

COMPLETE SET (6) 5.00 12.00
COMMON CARD (L1-L6) 1.25 3.00
STATED ODDS 1:17

2002 Witchblade Season One Pieceworks

COMPLETE SET (2) 20.00 50.00
COMMON CARD (PW1-PW2) 12.00 30.00
STATED ODDS 1:27

2002 Witchblade Season One Quest For Justice

COMPLETE SET (9) 8.00 20.00
COMMON CARD (Q1-Q9) 1.25 3.00
STATED ODDS 1;11

2002 Witchblade Season One Promos

COMPLETE SET (4) 10.00 25.00
COMMON CARD .75 2.00
UKP Witchblade 4.00 10.00
DFP1 Witchblade 5.00 12.00

2000 Witchblade TV Series

COMPLETE SET (18) 12.00 30.00
COMMON CARD 1.00 2.50

1990 Pacific Wizard of Oz

COMPLETE SET (110) 6.00 15.00
COMPLETE BOXED SET (110) 5.00 12.00
UNOPENED BOX (36 PACKS) 30.00 40.00
UNOPENED PACK (10 CARDS) 1.00 1.25
COMMON CARD (1-110) .12 .30

1996 DuoCards The Wizard of Oz

COMPLETE SET (72) 6.00 15.00
UNOPENED BOX (36 PACKS) 25.00 40.00
UNOPENED PACK (7 CARDS) .75 1.25
COMMON CARD (1-72) .15 .40

1996 DuoCards The Wizard of Oz Chromium

COMPLETE SET (6) 15.00 40.00
COMMON CARD (C1-C6) 3.00 8.00
RANDOMLY INSERTED INTO PACKS

1996 DuoCards The Wizard of Oz Promos

COMPLETE SET (2) 1.25 3.00
COMMON CARD .75 2.00

2006 The Wizard of Oz

COMPLETE SET (72) 4.00 10.00
UNOPENED BOX (40 PACKS) 55.00 70.00
UNOPENED PACK (6 CARDS) 1.50 2.00
COMMON CARD (1-72) .12 .30
NNO2 Dorothy Box Bottom Insert

2006 The Wizard of Oz Before and After

COMPLETE SET (2) 10.00 25.00
COMMON CARD (BA1-BA2) 6.00 15.00
STATED ODDS 1:240

2006 The Wizard of Oz Binder Inserts

COMPLETE SET (2) 2.00 5.00
COMMON CARD (A-B) 1.25 3.00

2006 The Wizard of Oz Cut Signatures

COMMON CARD
CSD1 Judy Garland/10 1600.00 2000.00
CSD2 Judy Garland/10 1600.00 2000.00
CSJH Tin Man - Jack Haley/130 200.00 300.00

2006 The Wizard of Oz Props

COMMON CARD 20.00 50.00
STATED ODDS 1:160
HCLS Hair from Cowardly Lion 80.00 150.00
SCSS Straw from Scarecrow 100.00 175.00

MODERN

2006 The Wizard of Oz Signatures

COMPLETE SET (4) 30.00 80.00
COMMON CARD 10.00 25.00
STATED ODDS 1:240

2006 The Wizard of Oz Toto

COMPLETE SET (6) 6.00 15.00
COMMON CARD (TD1-TD6) 1.25 3.00
STATED ODDS 1:20

2006 The Wizard of Oz Wicked Words

COMPLETE SET (6) 6.00 15.00
COMMON CARD (WW1-WW6) 1.25 3.00
STATED ODDS 1:20

2006 The Wizard of Oz Wiz Quiz Puzzle

COMPLETE SET (9) 6.00 15.00
COMMON CARD (1-9) .75 2.00
STATED ODDS 1:13

1994 Women of the World

COMPLETE SET (100) 4.00 10.00
UNOPENED BOX (36 PACKS) 10.00 15.00
UNOPENED PACK (10 CARDS) .50 .75
COMMON CARD (1-100) .08 .20

1994 Women of the World Gatefolds

COMPLETE SET (12) 25.00 60.00
COMMON CARD (1-12) 3.00 8.00

1994 Women of the World Mystery Box-Toppers

COMPLETE SET (5) 15.00 40.00
COMMON CARD 5.00 12.00

1994 Women of the World Signed Mystery Box-Toppers

COMMON CARD 8.00 20.00
STATED ODDS 1:CASE

1993 Weetabix Wonderful World of Disney

COMPLETE SET (20) 10.00 25.00
COMMON CARD (1-20) 1.00 2.50

1994 Saldino Woodstock

COMPLETE FACTORY SET (9) 3.00 8.00
COMMON CARD (1-9) .90 1.75

1993 Cardz World Famous San Diego Zoo

COMPLETE SET (110) 4.00 10.00
UNOPENED BOX (36 PACKS) 15.00 20.00
UNOPENED PACK (8 CARDS) .75 1.00
COMMON CARD (1-110) .10 .25
T1 Sumatran Tiger TekChrome 5.00 12.00

1993 Cardz World Famous San Diego Zoo Holograms

COMPLETE SET (3) 8.00 20.00
COMMON CARD (1-3) 3.00 8.00
STATED ODDS 1:36

1997 Tempo World of Barbie

COMPLETE SET (100) 6.00 15.00
UNOPENED BOX (30 PACKS)
UNOPENED PACK (7 CARDS)
COMMON CARD (1-100) .12 .30
NNO Dolls of the World Case-Topper

1997 Tempo World of Barbie Barbie Years

COMPLETE SET (4) 4.00 10.00
COMMON CARD (BY1-BY4) 1.25 3.00
STATED ODDS 1:5

1997 Tempo World of Barbie Bob Mackie Collection

COMPLETE SET (9) 12.00 30.00
COMMON CARD (BMC1-BCM9) 2.00 5.00
STATED ODDS 1:12

1997 Tempo World of Barbie Prima Ballerina Barbie

COMPLETE SET (2) 6.00 15.00
COMMON CARD (PBB1-PBB2) 4.00 10.00
STATED ODDS 1:60

1997 Tempo World of Barbie Promos

COMPLETE SET (4) 3.00 8.00
COMMON CARD (P1-P4) 1.25 3.00

1997 Tempo World of Barbie Summit Redemption Series

COMMON CARD 6.00 15.00

1994 Comic Images World of US Manga Corps

COMPLETE SET (90) 4.00 10.00
UNOPENED BOX (48 PACKS) 15.00 20.00
UNOPENED PACK (10 CARDS) .50 .75
COMMON CARD (1-90) .10 .25
NNO Koichi Ohata AU/500* 20.00 50.00
NNO Promo 1 (gen. dist.) .75 2.00
NNO 6UP Panel of Chromium
NNO Animation Cel/5*
NNO Medallion Card/1876* 10.00 25.00

1994 Comic Images World of US Manga Corps Chromium

COMPLETE SET (6) 15.00 40.00
COMMON CARD (C1-C6) 3.00 8.00
STATED ODDS 1:16

1994 Comic Images World of US Manga Corps Women of US Manga Corps

COMPLETE SET (3) 15.00 40.00
COMMON CARD (1-3) 6.00 15.00
STATED ODDS 1:48

1994 Cardz World War II A Grateful Nation Remembers

COMPLETE SET (100) 4.00 10.00
UNOPENED BOX (24 PACKS) 15.00 20.00
UNOPENED PACK (8 CARDS) .75 1.00
COMMON CARD (1-100) .08 .20

1994 Cardz World War II A Grateful Nation Remembers Promos

COMPLETE SET (3) 1.25 3.00
COMMON CARD (P1-P3) .60 1.50

1994 Cardz World War II A Grateful Nation Remembers TekChrome

COMPLETE SET (10) 6.00 15.00
COMMON CARD (T1-T10) .75 2.00
STATED ODDS 1:1

1991 Tuff Stuff World War II Propaganda

COMPLETE SET (15) 3.00 8.00
COMMON CARD (1-15) .40 1.00

1993 The Richards Group World War II War Machines

COMPLETE BOXED SET (100) 8.00 20.00
COMMON CARD (1-100)
*PROMO: 1X TO 2.5X BASIC CARDS .60 1.50
NNO1 Factory Set Uncut Sheet/250

X-Files

1995 Topps The X-Files

COMPLETE SET (72) 5.00 12.00
COMMON CARD (1-72) .15 .40
*FOIL: 1.5X TO 4X BASIC CARDS
0 Mulder and Scully
(Album Exclusive)

1995 Topps The X-Files Chromium Finest

COMPLETE SET (4) 12.50 30.00
COMMON CARD (X1-X4) 4.00 10.00

1995 Topps The X-Files Etched Foil

COMPLETE SET (6) 15.00 40.00
COMMON CARD (I1-I6) 4.00 10.00
PAN 6-Card Panel of Etched Foil Set

1995 Topps The X-Files MasterVisions

COMPLETE BOXED SET (30) 15.00 40.00
COMMON CARD (1-30) 1.25 3.00

1996 Topps The X-Files Season Two

COMPLETE SET (72) 6.00 15.00
UNOPENED BOX (36 PACKS) 40.00 60.00
UNOPENED PACK (9 CARDS) 1.50 2.50
COMMON CARD (1-72) .15 .40
*FOIL: 1X TO 2.5X BASIC CARDS

1996 Topps The X-Files Season Two Holograms

COMPLETE SET (4) 12.00 30.00
COMMON CARD (X1-X4) 4.00 10.00
STATED ODDS 1:18

1996 Topps The X-Files Season Two Etched Foil

COMPLETE SET (6) 15.00 40.00
COMMON CARD (i1-i6) 3.00 8.00
STATED ODDS 1:12
PAN 6UP Panel of Etched Foils

1996 Topps The X-Files Season Two Promos

COMMON CARD 1.50 4.00
P0 X-Files Magazine 2.00 5.00
P1 Levitating person OS 6.00
P2 Mulder and Scully 8.00 20.00
P5 Old Mulder GEN 8.00 20.00

1996 Topps The X-Files Season Three

COMPLETE SET (72) 5.00 12.00
UNOPENED BOX (36 PACKS) 40.00 60.00
UNOPENED PACK (9 CARDS) 1.50 2.50
COMMON CARD (1-72) .15 .40
*FOIL: .8X TO 2X BASIC CARDS

1996 Topps The X-Files Season Three Etched Foil

COMPLETE SET (6) 10.00 20.00
COMMON CARD (i1-i6) 2.00 5.00
STATED ODDS 1:12

1996 Topps The X-Files Season Three Holograms

COMPLETE SET (2) 3.00 8.00
COMMON CARD (X1-X2) 2.00 5.00
STATED ODDS 1:18

1996 Topps The X-Files Season Three Paranormal's Finest

COMPLETE SET (2) 3.00 8.00
COMMON CARD (X3PF1-X3PF2) 2.00 5.00
STATED ODDS 1:18

1996 Topps The X-Files Season Three Promos

COMMON CARD .75 2.00
P3 Dead Alien 1.50 4.00
P4 Two Guys Fighting 1.25 3.00
P5 Scully/Mulder 8.00 20.00

2001 Inkworks The X-Files Seasons 4 and 5

COMPLETE SET (90) 5.00 12.00
UNOPENED BOX (24 PACKS) 60.00 100.00
UNOPENED PACK (9 CARDS) 2.50 4.00
COMMON CARD (1-90) .15 .40

2001 Inkworks The X-Files Seasons 4 and 5 Autographs

COMMON AUTO (A1-A5) 8.00 20.00
STATED ODDS 1:72
A1 Chris Carter 100.00 200.00
A4 Laurie Holden 15.00 40.00

2001 Inkworks The X-Files Seasons 4 and 5 Black Oil

COMPLETE SET (6) 20.00 50.00
COMMON CARD (B1-B6) 4.00 10.00
STATED ODDS 1:17

2001 Inkworks The X-Files Seasons 4 and 5 Box-Loaders

COMPLETE SET (2) 2.00 5.00
COMMON CARD 1.25 3.00

2001 Inkworks The X-Files Seasons 4 and 5 Death

COMPLETE SET (3) 25.00 60.00
COMMON CARD (D1-D3) 10.00 25.00
STATED ODDS 1:48

2001 Inkworks The X-Files Seasons 4 and 5 I Want to Believe

COMPLETE SET (3) 4.00 10.00
COMMON CARD (P1-P3) 1.50 4.00
STATED ODDS 1:11

2001 Inkworks The X-Files Seasons 4 and 5 Pieceworks

STATED ODDS 1:115
PW1 Mulder's Sweatshirt 20.00 50.00

2001 Inkworks The X-Files Seasons 4 and 5 Promos

COMPLETE SET (4) 4.00 10.00
COMMON CARD 1.25 3.00

2001 Inkworks The X-Files Seasons 6 and 7

COMPLETE SET (90) 5.00 12.00
UNOPENED BOX (24 PACKS) 100.00 150.00
UNOPENED PACK (9 CARDS) 4.00 6.00
COMMON CARD (1-90) .15 .40

2001 Inkworks The X-Files Seasons 6 and 7 Autographs

COMMON AUTO (A6-A11) 10.00 25.00
RANDOM INSERTS IN PACKS
A7 Don S. Williams 12.00 30.00
A9 Gillian Anderson 200.00 400.00
A11 Michael McKean 25.00 60.00

2001 Inkworks The X-Files Seasons 6 and 7 Box-Loaders

COMPLETE SET (3) 4.00 10.00
COMMON CARD (BL1-BL3) 1.50 4.00

2001 Inkworks The X-Files Seasons 6 and 7 Inside the Syndicate

COMPLETE SET (6) 6.00 15.00
COMMON CARD (I1-I6) 1.25 3.00
STATED ODDS 1:17

2001 Inkworks The X-Files Seasons 6 and 7 Pieceworks

COMPLETE SET (2) 40.00 80.00
COMMON CARD 20.00 50.00
EXCH RANDOM INSERTS IN PACKS

2001 Inkworks The X-Files Seasons 6 and 7 The Truth Is Revealed

COMPLETE SET (3) 4.00 10.00
COMMON CARD (P4-P6) 2.00 5.00
STATED ODDS 1:11

2001 Inkworks The X-Files Seasons 6 and 7 Promos

COMPLETE SET (4) 4.00 10.00
COMMON CARD 1.25 3.00

2002 X-Files Season 8

COMPLETE SET (90) 5.00 12.00
COMMON CARD (1-90) .15 .40

2002 X-Files Season 8 Autographs

COMMON AUTO (A12-A15) 10.00 25.00
STATED ODDS 1:48
A12 Annabeth Gish 50.00 100.00
A14 Adam Baldwin 12.00 30.00

2002 X-Files Season 8 Believe to Understand

COMPLETE SET (3) 4.00 10.00

COMMON CARD (P7-P9) 1.50 4.00
STATED ODDS 1:11
PAN Believe to Understand 3-Card Panel (P7-P9)

2002 X-Files Season 8 Box-Loaders

COMPLETE SET (4) 7.50 20.00
COMMON CARD 1.25 3.00
X8CL1 X-Files 7.50 20.00

2002 X-Files Season 8 Pieceworks

COMPLETE SET (2) 20.00 50.00
COMMON MEM 12.00 30.00
STATED ODDS 1:115

2002 X-Files Season 8 The Search for Mulder

COMPLETE SET (6) 15.00 40.00
COMMON CARD (B1-B6) 3.00 8.00
STATED ODDS 1:17

2002 X-Files Season 8 Promos

COMPLETE SET (4) 3.00 8.00
COMMON CARD 1.00 2.50

2003 X-Files Season 9

COMPLETE SET (90) 5.00 12.00
UNOPENED BOX (24 PACKS) 200.00 300.00
UNOPENED PACK (9 CARDS) 8.00 12.00
COMMON CARD (1-90) .15 .40

2003 X-Files Season 9 Autographs

COMMON AUTO (A16-A20) 8.00 20.00
STATED ODDS 1:41
AF Gillian Anderson 250.00 400.00
A16 Mitch Pileggi 30.00 75.00
A16 Robert Patrick 100.00 200.00
A17 William B. Davis 15.00 40.00
A19 Steven Williams 15.00 40.00
A20 Burt Reynolds 60.00 120.00

2003 X-Files Season 9 Box-Loaders

COMPLETE SET (4) 7.50 20.00
COMMON CARD 1.50 4.00
CL1 Smoking Man 6.00 15.00

2003 X-Files Season 9 Pieceworks

COMPLETE SET (5) 75.00 150.00
COMMON MEM (PW1-PW5) 6.00 15.00
STATED ODDS 1:24
PW1 Mr. Burt (shirt) 8.00 20.00
PW4 Skinner (tie) 60.00 120.00

2003 X-Files Season 9 Reunion

COMPLETE SET (6) 7.50 20.00
COMMON CARD (R1-R6) 1.50 4.00
STATED ODDS 1:17

2003 X-Files Season 9 The Truth on Trial

COMPLETE SET (9) 12.50 30.00
COMMON CARD (T1-T9) 1.50 4.00
STATED ODDS 1:11
PAN The Truth on Trial 9-Card Panel (T1-T9)/299

2003 X-Files Season 9 Promos

COMPLETE SET (3) 3.00 8.00
COMMON CARD 1.00 2.50
PUK Scully and Skinner 2.00 5.00

2018 X-Files Seasons 10 and 11

COMPLETE SET (96) 8.00 20.00
UNOPENED BOX (24 PACKS)
UNOPENED PACK (5 CARDS)
ARCHIVE BOX
COMMON CARD (1-96) .20 .50
*BLUE/99: 6X TO 15X BASIC CARDS

2018 X-Files Seasons 10 and 11 Autographs

COMMON AUTO 4.00 10.00
STATED ODDS 1:8
NNO Alex Diakun/Motel Manager L 5.00 12.00
NNO Alex Diakun/Devil AB 15.00 40.00
NNO Annet Mahendru 8.00 20.00
NNO Barbara Hershey L 12.00 30.00
NNO David Duchovny S 150.00 300.00
NNO Dean Haglund VL 8.00 20.00
NNO Dean Haglund Variant AB 15.00 40.00
NNO Gillian Anderson S 150.00 300.00
NNO Haley Joel Osment/Davey James VL 12.00 30.00
NNO Haley Joel Osment Kitten James Variant AB 20.00 50.00
NNO Jere Burns L 5.00 12.00
NNO Jeremy Schuetze L 5.00 12.00
NNO Karin Konoval/Chucky Variant AB 15.00 40.00
NNO Karin Konoval/Judy L 5.00 12.00
NNO Keith Arbuthnot/Alien Variant AB 30.00 75.00
NNO Keith Arbuthnot/Ghouli VL 5.00 12.00
NNO Keith Arbuthnot/Mr. Chuckleteeth VL 8.00 20.00
NNO Lauren Ambrose VL 20.00 50.00
NNO Rhys Darby/Guy Mann Human L 8.00 20.00
NNO Rhys Darby/Guy Mann Variant AB 15.00 40.00
NNO Roger Cross 5.00 12.00
NNO Stuart Margolin VL 8.00 20.00
NNO William B. Davis EL 20.00 50.00

2018 X-Files Seasons 10 and 11 Bronze Metal

COMMON CARD (B1-B3) 20.00 50.00
ARCHIVE BOX EXCLUSIVE
B2 Scully 50.00 100.00
B3 Skinner 50.00 100.00

2018 X-Files Seasons 10 and 11 Case-Toppers

COMPLETE SET (2) 12.00 30.00
COMMON CARD (CT1-CT2) 8.00 20.00
STATED ODDS 1:CASE

2018 X-Files Seasons 10 and 11 Dual Autographs

COMMON AUTO 50.00 100.00
DAVIS/SCHUETZE 6-CASE INCENTIVE
DUCHOVNY/ANDERSON 9-CASE INCENTIVE
NNO David Duchovny/Gillian Anderson 9CI 400.00 750.00

2018 X-Files Seasons 10 and 11 Monsters Aliens and More

COMPLETE SET (6) 15.00 40.00
COMMON CARD (M1-M6) 5.00 12.00
STATED ODDS 1:48

2018 X-Files Seasons 10 and 11 Mulder Conspiracy Monologues

COMMON CARD (CM1-CM2) 12.00 30.00
STATED ODDS 1:288

2018 X-Files Seasons 10 and 11 My Struggle Monologues

COMPLETE SET (8) 12.00 30.00
COMMON CARD (MS1-MS8) 3.00 8.00
STATED ODDS 1:24

2018 X-Files Seasons 10 and 11 Quotable X-Files

COMPLETE SET W/RR (28)
COMPLETE SET W/O RR (27) 12.00 30.00
COMMON CARD (Q1-Q28) 1.00 2.50
STATED ODDS 1:8
Q28 The Quotable X-Files (Rittenhouse Rewards)

2018 X-Files Seasons 10 and 11 Relationships

COMPLETE SET (12) 15.00 40.00
COMMON CARD (R1-R12) 2.50 6.00
STATED ODDS 1:24

2018 X-Files Seasons 10 and 11 Stars of the X-Files

COMPLETE SET (10) 15.00 40.00
COMMON CARD (S1-S10) 3.00 8.00
STATED ODDS 1:24

2018 X-Files Seasons 10 and 11 Promos

COMPLETE SET (2)
COMMON CARD (P1-P2)
P1 Fall 2018 4.00 10.00
P2 Fall 2018 8.00 20.00
(Chicago Exclusive)
P3 Fall 2018

1998 Topps The X-Files Fight the Future

COMPLETE SET (72) 5.00 12.00
UNOPENED BOX (36 PACKS) 30.00 50.00
UNOPENED PACK (8 CARDS) 1.50 2.50
COMMON CARD (1-72) .15 .40

1998 Topps The X-Files Fight the Future Autographs

COMMON AUTO 12.00 30.00
STATED ODDS 1:72
NNO John Neville 15.00 40.00
NNO Mitch Pileggi 30.00 75.00
NNO Tom Braidwood 25.00 60.00
NNO William B. Davis 15.00 40.00

1998 Topps The X-Files Fight the Future Foil Mystery

COMPLETE SET (6) 10.00 25.00
COMMON CARD (M1-M6) 2.50 6.00
STATED ODDS 1:12

1998 Topps The X-Files Fight the Future Promos

P0 The X-Files Fight the Future 5.00 12.00
(Cards Inc UK Exclusive/Oversized 3.1 x 4.4)/3000
P1A The X-Files Fight the Future 1.25 3.00
P1B The X-Files Fight the Future 4.00 10.00
(Cards Inc UK Exclusive)

2008 X-Files I Want to Believe

COMPLETE SET (72) 5.00 12.00
UNOPENED BOX (24 PACKS) 100.00 150.00
UNOPENED PACK (7 CARDS) 4.00 6.00
COMMON CARD (1-72) .15 .40
CL1 STATED ODDS 1:CASE
CL1 Out of Darkness 10.00 25.00

2008 X-Files I Want to Believe Autographs

COMMON AUTO 5.00 12.00
STATED ODDS ONE PER BOX
AD1 ISSUED AS 10-CASE INCENTIVE
A1 David Duchovny 150.00 300.00
A2 Gillian Anderson 125.00 250.00
A3 Chris Carter 50.00 100.00
A4 Frank Spotnitz 8.00 20.00
A5 Xzibit 10.00 25.00
A9 Nestor Serrano 6.00 15.00
AD1 D.Duchovny/G.Anderson 10CI 400.00 600.00

2008 X-Files I Want to Believe Back to Basics

COMPLETE SET (3) 4.00 10.00
COMMON CARD (BB1-BB3) 2.50 6.00
STATED ODDS 1:24

2008 X-Files I Want to Believe In Search of Puzzle

COMPLETE SET (9) 5.00 12.00
COMMON CARD (S1-S9) 1.25 3.00
STATED ODDS 1:11
PAN In Search of 9-Card Panel (S1-S9)/99

2008 X-Files I Want to Believe Pieceworks

COMMON MEM (PW1-PW14; PWR) 4.00 10.00
STATED ODDS 1:24
PW14A, PW14B ISSUED AS 3-CASE INCENTIVES
PW1A Mulder Jacket 15.00 30.00
PW1B Mulder Fur 40.00 80.00
PW2 Scully 20.00 50.00
PW3 Scully 10.00 25.00
PW8 Scully DUAL 15.00 40.00
PW9 Scully 15.00 30.00
PW10 Mulder DUAL 12.00 30.00
PW14A David Duchovny 3CI 30.00 80.00
PW14B Gillian Anderson 3CI 30.00 80.00
PWR1 Redemption card

2008 X-Files I Want to Believe Wanting to Believe

COMPLETE SET (6) 5.00 12.00
COMMON CARD (WB1-WB6) 1.50 4.00
STATED ODDS 1:17

2008 X-Files I Want to Believe Promos

COMPLETE SET (4) 5.00 12.00
COMMON CARD 1.25 3.00
Xi Mulder/Scully 2.00 5.00
(Free Card Offer)
XF1 Mulder GEN 1.50 4.00
XFP Scully 1.50 4.00

2019 X-Files Archives Metal

COMPLETE SET (9) 100.00 200.00
COMMON CARD (XC1-XC9) 10.00 25.00
STATED PRINT RUN 50 SER.#'d SETS
STATED ODDS 3:SET
XC1 Fox Mulder 12.00 30.00
XC2 Fox Mulder 12.00 30.00
XC3 Fox Mulder 12.00 30.00
XC4 Dana Scully 15.00 40.00
XC5 Dana Scully 15.00 40.00
XC6 Dana Scully 15.00 40.00
XC7 Walter Skinner 10.00 25.00
XC8 Walter Skinner 10.00 25.00
XC9 Walter Skinner 10.00 25.00

2019 X-Files Archives Autographs

COMMON AUTO 20.00 50.00
STATED ODDS 2:SET
NNO David Duchovny/50 150.00 300.00
NNO Gillian Anderson/100 150.00 300.00

2005 X-Files Connections

COMPLETE SET (72) 5.00 12.00
COMMON CARD (1-72) .15 .40
*PARALLEL: 1X TO 2.5X BASIC CARDS

2005 X-Files Connections Autographs

COMMON AUTO (A1-A11) 6.00 15.00
STATED ODDS 1:24
A1 Gillian Anderson 125.00 250.00
A2 Annabeth Gish 75.00 150.00
A3 Mimi Rogers 15.00 40.00
A4 William B. Davis 20.00 50.00
A6 Nicholas Lea 12.00 30.00
A7 Tom Braidwood 10.00 25.00
A8 Bruce Harwood 6.00 15.00
A9 Dean Haglund 8.00 20.00
A11 Veronica Cartwright 10.00 25.00

2005 X-Files Connections Box-Loaders

COMPLETE SET (4) 8.00 20.00
COMMON CARD 1.50 4.00
STATED ODDS ONE PER BOX
CL1 The Truth Is Out There 5.00 12.00

2005 X-Files Connections Haunting Cases

COMPLETE SET (6) 6.00 15.00
COMMON CARD (HC1-HC6) 1.25 3.00
STATED ODDS 1:14

2005 X-Files Connections Mulder's Secret Files

COMPLETE SET (9) 8.00 20.00
COMMON CARD (M1-M9) 1.00 2.50
STATED ODDS 1:11
PAN Mulder's Secret Files 9-Card Panel (M1-M9)/199

2005 X-Files Connections Pieceworks

COMMON CARD
STATED ODDS 1:
PW1 Scully's Shirt 25.00 50.00
PW1A Scully's Shirt 150.00 250.00
Gillian Anderson AU
PW2 Mulder's Shirt 8.00 20.00
PR1 Pieceworks Redemption

2005 X-Files Connections Promos

COMMON CARD 2.00 5.00
Pi Scully 3.00 8.00
PP1 Mulder & Scully 4.00 10.00
PFOA Scully 10.00 25.00
PPUK Reyes & Doggett 6.00 15.00

1997 Intrepid The X-Files Contact

COMPLETE SET (90) 8.00 20.00
UNOPENED BOX (36 PACKS) 25.00 40.00
UNOPENED PACK (7 CARDS) 1.00 1.50
COMMON CARD (1-90) .15 .40
NNO1 Box-Topper (bonus)
NNO2 Teen Taken from Tent by Aliens CT 10.00 25.00
NNO3 Promo GEN 1.25 3.00

1997 Intrepid The X-Files Contact Alien Visitations Foil

COMPLETE SET (9) 12.00 30.00
COMMON CARD (A1-A9) 2.00 5.00
*NO SHINE: .6X TO 1.5X BASIC CARDS
RANDOMLY INSERTED INTO PACKS

1997 Intrepid The X-Files Contact Colony Cels Acetate

COMPLETE SET (3) 10.00 25.00
COMMON CARD (C1-C3 4.00 10.00
RANDOMLY INSERTED INTO PACKS

1997 Topps The X-Files Showcase

COMPLETE SET (72) 6.00 15.00
UNOPENED BOX (36 PACKS) 25.00 40.00
UNOPENED PACK (9 CARDS) 1.00 1.50
COMMON CARD .20 .50

1997 Topps The X-Files Showcase Laser

COMPLETE SET (6) 6.00 15.00
COMMON CARD (L1-L6) 2.00 5.00

1997 Topps X-Files Showcase Promo

P1 Pilot Episode 1X79P1 .60 1.50

1997 Topps The X-Files Showcase X-Effect

COMPLETE SET (6) 5.00 12.00
COMMON CARD (E1-E6) 1.50 4.00

2019 X-Files UFOs and Aliens

COMPLETE SET W/SP (300) 150.00 300.00
COMPLETE SET W/O SP (100) 10.00 25.00
UNOPENED BOX (20 PACKS) 75.00 125.00
UNOPENED PACK (6 CARDS) 4.00 6.00
COMMON CARD (1-100) .20 .50
COMMON SP (101-200) .75 2.00
COMMON SP (201-300) 2.50 6.00
SP ODDS (101-200) 1:1
SP ODDS (201-300) 1:2

2019 X-Files UFOs and Aliens Behind-the-Scenes

COMPLETE SET (10) 5.00 12.00
COMMON CARD (BTS1-BTS10) 1.00 2.50
STATED ODDS 1:7

2019 X-Files UFOs and Aliens Characters

COMPLETE SET (30) 12.00 30.00
COMMON CARD (C1-C30) .75 2.00
STATED ODDS 1:3

2019 X-Files UFOs and Aliens Paranormal Script Autographs

COMMON AUTO 5.00 12.00
GROUP A ODDS 1:694
GROUP B ODDS 1:211
GROUP C ODDS 1:102
GROUP D ODDS 1:61
GROUP E ODDS 1:47
GROUP F ODDS 1:33
STATED OVERALL ODDS 1:12
AAB Adam Baldwin D 15.00 40.00
AAD Doug Abrahams C 6.00 15.00
AAG Annabeth Gish C 25.00 60.00
AAN Gillian Anderson C 100.00 200.00
ACC Chris Carter A 60.00 120.00
ACE Cary Elwes A 50.00 100.00
ACO Chris Owens C 8.00 20.00
ACS Carrie Cain-Sparks D 6.00 15.00
ACU Colin Cunningham C 6.00 15.00
ADD David Duchovny B 125.00 250.00
ADH Dean Haglund E 8.00 20.00
ADM Dwight McFee F 6.00 15.00
ADU David Duchovny B 125.00 250.00
AEL Cary Elwes A 50.00 100.00
AGA Gillian Anderson C 100.00 200.00
AJH Jerry Hardin B 12.00 30.00
AJP James Pickens Jr. C 6.00 15.00
AKT Ken Camroux-Taylor E 6.00 15.00
ALH Laurie Holden F 12.00 30.00
ALR Leon Russom C 8.00 20.00
AML Megan Leitch D 12.00 30.00
AMP Mitch Pileggi B 25.00 60.00
ANL Nicholas Lea D 12.00 30.00
APA Robert Patrick B 60.00 120.00
APS Pat Skipper D 6.00 15.00
ARO Mimi Rogers D 10.00 25.00
ARP Robert Patrick B 60.00 120.00
ART Rebecca Toolan D 8.00 20.00
ASB Scott Bellis D 8.00 20.00
ASW Steven Williiams D 10.00 25.00
ATB Tom Braidwood E 8.00 20.00
AVC Veronica Cartwright E 8.00 20.00
AVG Vince Gilligan C 30.00 75.00
AWD William B. Davis B 15.00 40.00

2019 X-Files UFOs and Aliens Paranormal Script Dual Autographs

COMMON AUTO 100.00 200.00
STATED ODDS 1:1,706
ADCG C.Carter/V.Gilligan 200.00 400.00
ADDA G.Anderson/D.Duchovny 400.00 800.00
ADMW M.Pileggi/W.Davis 125.00 250.00

2019 X-Files UFOs and Aliens Paranormal Script Dual Inscriptions

ADDA Anderson "What's Going On?" Duchovny "Something Cosmic"

2019 X-Files UFOs and Aliens Paranormal Script Inscriptions

COMMON AUTO 12.00 30.00
GROUP A ODDS 1:2,842
GROUP B ODDS 1:189
STATED OVERALL ODDS 1:177
AAB Adam Baldwin 75.00 150.00
Knowle Rohrer B
AAD Doug Abrahams 20.00 50.00
Patrolman #1 B
AAG Annabeth Gish 75.00 150.00
Monica Reyes B
AAN Gillian Anderson 500.00 1000.00
The Truth Is Out There A
ABD Bill Dow 15.00 40.00
Dr. Charles Burks B
ABH Bruce Harwood 15.00 40.00
John Fitzgerald Byers B
ACC Chris Carter 150.00 300.00
The Truth Is Out There B
ACE Cary Elwes 175.00 350.00
Agent Brad Follmer B
ACO Chris Owens 25.00 60.00
Jeffrey Spendor B
ACS Carrie Cain-Sparks 30.00 75.00
Train Station Clerk B
ACU Colin Cunningham 15.00 40.00
Lt. Terry Wilmer B
ADD David Duchovny 500.00 1000.00
The Truth Is Out There A
ADH Dean Haglund 25.00 60.00
Richard Ringo Langly B
ADU David Duchovny 500.00 1000.00
Fox Mulder A
AEB Eric Breker 15.00 40.00
Ambulance Driver B
AGA Gillian Anderson 500.00 1000.00
Dana Scully A
AJF John Finn 20.00 50.00
Michael Kritschgau B
AJG Jeff Gulka
Gibson Praise B
AJH Jerry Hardin 60.00 120.00
Deep Throat B
AJP James Pickens Jr. 20.00 50.00
Director Alvin Kersh B
AJS Jerry Schram
Larold Rebhun B
AKT Ken Camroux-Taylor 30.00 75.00
2nd Senior Agent B
AMP Mitch Pileggi 100.00 200.00
Director Walter Skinner B
ANL Nicholas Lea 50.00 100.00
Alex Krycek B
ARD Rick Dobran
Sergeant Armando Gonzales A
ARO Mimi Rogers 30.00 75.00
Diana Fowley B
ART Rebecca Toolan 25.00 60.00
Teena Mulder B
ASK Sarah Koskoff 25.00 60.00
Theresa Newman House B
ASL Sheila Larken 15.00 40.00
Margaret Scully B
ASP Joe Spano 20.00 50.00
Mike Millar B
ASR Steve Railsback 15.00 40.00
Duane Berry B
ATB Tom Braidwood 20.00 50.00
Melvin Frohike B
ATO Tom O'Brien
Sgt. Louis Frisch B
AVC Veronica Cartwright 20.00 50.00
Cassandra Spender B
AWD William B. Davis 300.00 600.00
Cigarette Smoking Man B

2019 X-Files UFOs and Aliens Redacted Files

COMMON LEVEL 1 (FBI1-FBI20) 8.00 20.00
COMMON LEVEL 2 (FBI21-FBI25) 75.00 150.00
STATED L1 ODDS 1:66
STATED L2 ODDS 1:660

2019 X-Files UFOs and Aliens Stickers

COMPLETE SET (100) 125.00 250.00
COMMON STICKER (S1-S100) 1.50 4.00
STATED ODDS 1:5

2019 X-Files UFOs and Aliens Unexplained Phenomena

COMPLETE SET (10) 10.00 25.00
COMMON CARD (UP1-UP10) 2.00 5.00
STATED ODDS 1:7

1996-99 Fox Entertainment The X-Files Video Cards

COMPLETE SET (42) 100.00 200.00
COMMON CARD (V1-V42) 2.50 6.00

Xena

2003 The Quotable Xena Warrior Princess

COMPLETE SET (138) 5.00 12.00
COMMON CARD .08 .25
*FOIL: .6X TO 1.5X BASIC CARDS
C14 ISSUED AS ALBUM EXCLUSIVE
C14 Xena MEM ALB 25.00 50.00

2003 The Quotable Xena Warrior Princess Autograph Costumes

COMMON CARD (AC4-AC10) 20.00 50.00
STATED ODDS 1:200
AC10 ISSUED AS MULTI-CASE INCENTIVE
AC4 Lucy Lawless 30.00 75.00
AC6 Bruce Campbell 25.00 60.00
AC10 Renee O'Connor CI 50.00 100.00

2003 The Quotable Xena Warrior Princess Autographs

COMMON CARD (A35-A51) 4.00 10.00
OVERALL AUTO ODDS TWO PER BOX
L (LIMITED): 300-500 COPIES
A35 Tsianina Joelson 6.00 15.00
A36 Alex Mendoza 6.00 15.00
A37 Jacqueline Kim 6.00 15.00
A38 Bruce Campbell 15.00 40.00
A40 Tony Todd 12.00 30.00
A42 Colin Moy 6.00 15.00
A44 Jay Laga'aia 6.00 15.00
A45 Dean O'Gorman 5.00 12.00
A46 Jeffrey Thomas 6.00 15.00
A47 Charles Mesure 6.00 15.00
A48 Daniel Sing L 6.00 15.00
A49 George Kee Cheung 5.00 12.00
A50 William Gregory Lee 8.00 20.00
A51 Gina Torres 6.00 15.00

2003 The Quotable Xena Warrior Princess Dual Autographs

COMMON CARD (DA3-DA8) 20.00 40.00
OVERALL AUTO ODDS TWO PER BOX
L (LIMITED): 300-500 COPIES
DA8 T.Raimi/L.Lawless L 30.00 60.00

2003 The Quotable Xena Warrior Princess Eternal Friends

COMPLETE SET (9) 6.00 15.00
COMMON CARD (E1-E9) .75 2.00
STATED ODDS 1:10

2003 The Quotable Xena Warrior Princess Forged in the Heat of Battle

COMPLETE SET (6) 12.50 30.00
COMMON CARD (F1-F6) 2.50 6.00
STATED ODDS 1:40

2003 The Quotable Xena Warrior Princess Words from the Bard

COMPLETE SET (9) 2.50 6.00
COMMON CARD (B1-B9) .40 1.00
STATED ODDS 1:4

2003 The Quotable Xena Warrior Princess Xena in Motion

COMPLETE SET (6) 10.00 25.00
COMMON CARD 6.00 15.00
STATED ODDS 1:40
CT1 ISSUED AS CASE TOPPER
CT1 Xena In Motion CT 15.00 40.00

2003 The Quotable Xena Warrior Princess Promos

COMPLETE SET (4) 3.00 8.00
COMMON CARD 1.00 2.50
P3 Gabrielle/Xena/Argo ALB 1.50 4.00
C2003 Xena CON 1.50 4.00

2001 Xena A Taste of Honey Case Bonus

COMPLETE SET (3) 2.50 6.00
COMMON CARD (XC1-XC3) 1.25 3.00

2005 Xena and Hercules Animated Series

COMPLETE SET (72) 4.00 10.00
UNOPENED BOX (40 PACKS) 250.00 400.00
UNOPENED PACK (5 CARDS) 6.00 10.00
COMMON CARD (1-72) .10 .30

2005 Xena and Hercules Animated Series Animated Casting Call

COMPLETE SET (14) 6.00 15.00
COMMON CARD (C1-C14) .60 1.50
STATED ODDS 1:14

MODERN

MODERN

2005 Xena and Hercules Animated Series Animated Extras
COMPLETE SET (18) 12.50 30.00
COMMON CARD (X1-X18) 1.25 3.00
STATED ODDS 1:20

2005 Xena and Hercules Animated Series Animated Mythical Beasts
COMPLETE SET (6) 15.00 40.00
COMMON CARD (B1-B6) 3.00 8.00
STATED ODDS 1:60

2005 Xena and Hercules Animated Series Autographs
COMMON AUTO 6.00 15.00
STATED ODDS TWO PER BOX
TREBOR AUTO ISSUED IN COLLECTORS ALBUM
L (LIMITED): 300-500 COPIES
VL (VERY LIMITED): 200-300 COPIES
1 Bruce Campbell L 20.00 50.00
11 Lucy Lawless VL 25.00 60.00
12 Hudson Leick VL 10.00 25.00
18 Ted Raimi Joxer VL 12.00 30.00
19 Peter Rowley L 6.00 15.00
20 Karen Sheperd L 6.00 15.00
21 Kevin Sorbo VL 20.00 50.00
22 Claire Stansfield L 8.00 20.00

2005 Xena and Hercules Animated Series Dual Autographs
LAWLESS/O'CONNOR AUTO ISSUED AS 2-CASE INCENTIVE
SORBO/LAWLESS AUTO ISSUED AS 6-CASE INCENTIVE
1 L.Lawless/R.O'Connor 2CI 50.00 100.00
2 K.Sorbo/L.Lawless 6CI 120.00 250.00

2005 Xena and Hercules Animated Series Limited Edition
COMPLETE SET (3) 50.00 100.00
COMMON CARD 15.00 40.00
STATED ODDS 1:240 UK PACKS

2005 Xena and Hercules Animated Series The Musical Xena and Hercules
COMPLETE SET (9) 8.00 20.00
COMMON CARD (M1-M9) 1.25 3.00
STATED ODDS 1:14

2005 Xena and Hercules Animated Series Xena and Hercules in Action
COMPLETE SET (9) 8.00 20.00
COMMON CARD (HX1-HX9) 1.25 3.00
STATED ODDS 1:14

2005 Xena and Hercules Animated Series Xena Hercules ArtiFEX
COMPLETE SET (6) 15.00 40.00
COMMON CARD (CZ1-CZ6) 3.00 8.00
STATED ODDS 1:40 US PACKS

2005 Xena and Hercules Animated Series Promos
COMPLETE SET (4) 4.00 10.00
COMMON CARD .75 2.00
P3 Iolaus/Hercules/Xena/Gabrielle ALB 3.00 8.00
UK Iolaus/Hercules (UK excl.) 1.25 3.00

2002 Xena Beauty and Brawn
COMPLETE SET (72) 4.00 10.00
COMMON CARD (1-73) .10 .30

2002 Xena Beauty and Brawn Amazon Warriors
COMPLETE SET (9) 6.00 15.00
COMMON CARD (AW1-AW9) .75 2.00
STATED ODDS 1:10

2002 Xena Beauty and Brawn Autographs
COMMON AUTO 5.00 12.00
OVERALL AUTO ODDS ONE PER BOX
A30 ISSUED AS CASE TOPPER
A33 ISSUED AS ALBUM EXCLUSIVE
A23 Melinda Clarke 8.00 20.00
A24 Alison Bruce 6.00 15.00
A26 Josephine Davison 6.00 15.00
A28 Kate Elliott 6.00 15.00
A29 Erik Thomson 6.00 15.00
A30 Meg Foster CT 10.00 25.00
A31 Tim Thomerson 6.00 15.00
A32A Marie Matiko as K'ao Hsin 6.00 15.00
A32B Marie Matiko as Pao S'su 6.00 15.00
A34 Sheeri Rappaport 6.00 15.00

2002 Xena Beauty and Brawn Beauty and Brawn
COMPLETE SET (2) 12.00 30.00
COMMON CARD (BB1-BB2) 10.00 20.00
STATED ODDS 1:480

2002 Xena Beauty and Brawn Dual Autographs
OVERALL AUTO ODDS ONE PER BOX
DA1 L.Lawless/R.O'Connor 100.00 200.00
DA2 H.Leick/R.O'Connor 60.00 120.00

2002 Xena Beauty and Brawn Footsteps of a Warrior
COMPLETE SET (9) 2.50 6.00
COMMON CARD (FW1-FW9) .40 1.00
STATED ODDS 1:4

2002 Xena Beauty and Brawn From the Archives Autograph Costumes
COMMON CARD (AC1-AC3) 25.00 50.00
OVERALL COSTUME ODDS TWO PER BOX
AC2 Hudson Leick 25.00 50.00
AC3 Meighan Desmond 25.00 50.00

2002 Xena Beauty and Brawn From the Archives Costumes
COMMON CARD (C1-C13) 6.00 15.00
OVERALL COSTUME ODDS TWO PER BOX
C3 Autolycus 8.00 20.00
C4 Tyrella 8.00 20.00
C6 Xena 8.00 20.00
C7 Xena 8.00 20.00
C9 Xena 8.00 20.00

2002 Xena Beauty and Brawn From the Archives Dual Costumes
COMMON MEM (DC1-DC8) 8.00 20.00
OVERALL COSTUME ODDS TWO PER BOX
DC1 Autolycus 10.00 25.00
DC3 Gabrielle 50.00 100.00
DC4 Xena Gabrielle 15.00 40.00
DC6 Gabrielle Aphrodite 15.00 30.00
DC7 Gabrielle 20.00 50.00
DC8 Xena 10.00 25.00

2002 Xena Beauty and Brawn Kevin Smith Tribute
COMPLETE SET (9) 8.00 20.00
COMMON CARD (KS1-KS9) 1.25 3.00
STATED ODDS 1:20

2002 Xena Beauty and Brawn Xena Scrolls
COMPLETE SET (6) 15.00 40.00
COMMON CARD (XS1-XS6) 3.00 8.00
STATED ODDS 1:40

2002 Xena Beauty and Brawn Promos
COMPLETE SET (3) 2.50 6.00
COMMON CARD 1.00 2.50
P3 Ares ALB 1.50 4.00

2007 Xena Dangerous Liaisons
COMPLETE SET (72) 4.00 10.00
UNOPENED BOX (40 PACKS)
UNOPENED PACK (5 CARDS)
COMMON CARD (1-72) .10 .30

2007 Xena Dangerous Liaisons Autograph Costumes
COMMON AU MEM 8.00 20.00
OVERALL COSTUME ODDS TWO PER BOX
AC11 Bruce Campbell 12.00 30.00

2007 Xena Dangerous Liaisons Autographs
COMPLETE SET (2)
A52 Musetta Vander CT 30.00 80.00
DA9 L.Lawless/K.Sorbo DUAL 3CI 80.00 150.00

2007 Xena Dangerous Liaisons Costumes
COMMON MEM (C1-C11) 6.00 15.00
OVERALL COSTUME ODDS TWO PER BOX
C1 Pao Ssu 8.00 20.00
C2 Xena 10.00 25.00
C3 Gabrielle 8.00 20.00
C6 Xena 8.00 20.00
C7 Xena 8.00 20.00
C8 Xena 10.00 25.00
C9 Xena 10.00 25.00
C10 Gabrielle 8.00 20.00

2007 Xena Dangerous Liaisons Dual Costumes
COMMON MEM (DC1-DC12) 6.00 15.00
OVERALL COSTUME ODDS TWO PER BOX
DC12 ISSUED AS ALBUM EXCLUSIVE
QC1 ISSUED AS 2-CASE INCENTIVE
VL (VERY LIMITED): 200-300 COPIES
DC1 Xena/Borias VL 15.00 40.00
DC3 Xena/Callisto 15.00 40.00
DC4 Xena/Cyane 10.00 25.00
DC5 Xena/Gabrielle 20.00 50.00
DC6 Discord/Autolycus VL 20.00 50.00
DC7 Xena/Hercules 15.00 40.00
DC8 Xena/Autolycus 8.00 20.00
DC9 Alti/Gabrielle 8.00 20.00
DC10 Xena/Gabrielle VL 50.00 100.00
DC11 Gabrielle/Aphrodite 10.00 25.00
QC1 Xena/Gabrielle/Hercules/Iolaus QUAD 2CI25.0060.00

2007 Xena Dangerous Liaisons Rise and Fall of the Warrior Queen
COMPLETE SET (9) 25.00 60.00
COMMON CARD (WQ1-WQ9) 5.00 12.00
STATED ODDS 1:40

2007 Xena Dangerous Liaisons Women and Weapons
COMPLETE SET (18) 20.00 50.00
COMMON CARD (WW1-WW18) 2.50 6.00
STATED ODDS 1:20

2007 Xena Dangerous Liaisons Xena Comics
COMPLETE SET (9) 8.00 20.00
COMMON CARD (XC1-XC9) 1.50 4.00
STATED ODDS 1:10

2007 Xena Dangerous Liaisons Promos
COMMON CARD .75 2.00
P3 Autolycus/Xena ALB 4.00 10.00
INT Ares/Xena 1.25 3.00

1998 MotionVision Xena Warrior Princess
COMPLETE SET (5) 12.00 30.00
COMMON CARD 3.00 8.00

1997 Topps Xena Warrior Princess
COMPLETE SET (72) 8.00 20.00
UNOPENED BOX (36 PACKS) 85.00 100.00
UNOPENED PACK (8 CARDS) 2.50 3.00
COMMON CARD (1-72) .20 .50
B1 Xena 20.00 50.00
P1 The Gods Have Spoken PROMO 1.00 2.50

1997 Topps Xena Warrior Princess Finest Chromium
COMPLETE SET (2) 15.00 40.00
COMMON CARD (C1-C2) 10.00 25.00
*REFRACTOR: SAME VALUE
STATED ODDS 1:36

1997 Topps Xena Warrior Princess Foil
COMPLETE SET (6) 15.00 40.00
COMMON CARD (X1-X6) 3.00 8.00
STATED ODDS 1:12

1998 Topps Xena Warrior Princess Series Two
COMPLETE SET (72) 8.00 20.00
UNOPENED BOX (36 PACKS) 60.00 100.00
UNOPENED PACK (8 CARDS) 2.00 3.00
COMMON CARD (1-72) .20 .50
P2 Xena: Warrior Princess Series Two Promo1.50 4.00

1998 Topps Xena Warrior Princess Series Two Autographs
COMMON AUTO (A1-A12) 15.00 40.00
STATED ODDS 1:36
A1 Ted Raimi 15.00 40.00
A2 Kevin Smith 30.00 75.00
A3 Bruce Campbell 30.00 75.00
A4 Hudson Leick 25.00 60.00
A5 Melinda Clarke 30.00 75.00
A6 Michael Hurst 15.00 40.00
A7 Alexandra Tydings 12.00 30.00
A11 Karl Urban 15.00 40.00

1998 Topps Xena Warrior Princess Series Two Finest Chromium
COMPLETE SET (6) 8.00 20.00
COMMON CARD (XC1-XC6) 2.50 6.00
RANDOMLY INSERTED IN PACKS

1999 Topps Xena Warrior Princess Series 3
COMPLETE SET (72) 8.00 20.00
UNOPENED BOX (36 PACKS) 65.00 80.00
UNOPENED PACK (8 CARDS) 2.00 2.50
P1 Xena Warrior Princess PROMO 1.25 3.00

1999 Topps Xena Warrior Princess Series 3 Destiny Bound
COMPLETE SET (2) 6.00 15.00
COMMON CARD (1-2) 4.00 10.00
STATED ODDS 1:18

1999 Topps Xena Warrior Princess Series 3 Incarnations
COMPLETE SET (9) 20.00 50.00
COMMON CARD (1-9) 3.00 8.00
STATED ODDS 1:9

2001 Xena Warrior Princess Previews
COMPLETE SET (9) 6.00 15.00
COMMON CARD (P1-P9) .75 2.00
ANNOUNCED PRINT RUN 2,500 SETS

2001 Xena Warrior Princess Previews UK
COMPLETE SET (6) 10.00 25.00
COMMON CARD (X1-X6) 2.50 6.00

2001 Xena Warrior Princess Seasons Four and Five
COMPLETE SET (72) 5.00 12.00
UNOPENED BOX (40 PACKS)
UNOPENED PACK (9 CARDS)
COMMON CARD (1-72) .15 .40
R1 ISSUED AS CASE TOPPER
X1 STATED ODDS 1:480
X1 STATED PRINT RUN 999 SER. #'d SETS
R1 Lucy Lawless MEM CT 30.00 60.00
X1 Xena Argo/999 7.50 20.00

2001 Xena Warrior Princess Seasons Four and Five Autographs

COMMON CARD (A1-A6) 8.00 20.00
STATED ODDS 1:80
A6 ISSUED AS ALBUM EXCLUSIVE
A6 ANNOUNCED PRINT RUN 2000
A1 Lucy Lawless 30.00 75.00
A5 Claire Stansfield 12.00 30.00

2001 Xena Warrior Princess Seasons Four and Five Face of a Warrior

COMPLETE SET (9) 15.00 40.00
COMMON CARD (W1-W9) 3.00 8.00
STATED ODDS 1:40

2001 Xena Warrior Princess Seasons Four and Five Gabrielle the Battling Bard

COMPLETE SET (9) 12.50 30.00
COMMON CARD (G1-G9) 2.00 5.00
STATED ODDS 1:10

2001 Xena Warrior Princess Seasons Four and Five Xena Allies

COMPLETE SET (9) 4.00 10.00
COMMON CARD (F1-F9) .60 1.50
STATED ODDS 1:4

2001 Xena Warrior Princess Seasons Four and Five Xena Enemies

COMPLETE SET (6) 7.50 20.00
COMMON CARD (E1-E6) 1.50 4.00
STATED ODDS 1:9

2001 Xena Warrior Princess Seasons Four and Five Xena Undressed

COMPLETE SET (6) 50.00 100.00
COMMON CARD (U1-U6) 8.00 20.00
STATED ODDS 1:80

2001 Xena Warrior Princess Seasons Four and Five Promos

COMPLETE SET (5) 6.00 15.00
COMMON CARD .75 2.00
P2 Gabrielle 1.50 4.00
P3 Xena 2.50 6.00
Gabrielle
P4 Xena NSU 1.50 4.00
BP1 Xena 3.00 8.00
Gabrielle ALB

2001 Xena Warrior Princess Season Six

COMPLETE SET (72) 5.00 12.00
UNOPENED BOX (40 PACKS) 100.00 150.00
UNOPENED PACK (9 CARDS) 2.50 4.00
COMMON CARD (1-72) .15 .40
*PP BLACK/25: 3X TO 8X BASIC CARDS 1.25 3.00
*PP CYAN/25: 3X TO 8X BASIC CARDS 1.25 3.00
*PP MAGENTA/25: 3X TO 8X BASIC CARDS 1.25 3.00
*PP YELLOW/25: 3X TO 8X BASIC CARDS 1.25 3.00

2001 Xena Warrior Princess Season Six Autographs

COMMON AUTO (A7-A21) 6.00 15.00
STATED ODDS ONE PER BOX
A7 Hudson Leick 20.00 40.00
A11 Alexandra Tydings 20.00 40.00
A12 Renee O'Connor 25.00 60.00
A14 Lucy Lawless 40.00 80.00
A15 Ebonie Smith 8.00 20.00

2001 Xena Warrior Princess Season Six Busting Loose

COMPLETE SET (9) 5.00 12.00
COMMON CARD (BL1-BL9) .75 2.00
STATED ODDS 1:8

2001 Xena Warrior Princess Season Six Forever Gabrielle

COMPLETE SET (2) 25.00 50.00
COMMON CARD (G1-G2) 12.50 30.00
STATED ODDS 1:480
STATED PRINT RUN 750 SER. #'d SETS

2001 Xena Warrior Princess Season Six From the Archives Costumes

COMMON MEM (R3-R11) 6.00 15.00
STATED ODDS ONE PER BOX
R6 ISSUED AS ALBUM EXCLUSIVE
ANNOUNCED PRINT RUN 275-1575
R4 Xena/275* 50.00 100.00
R5 Xena/1210* 15.00 30.00
R6 Xena/1500* ALB 8.00 20.00
R7 Alti/1125* 10.00 25.00

2001 Xena Warrior Princess Season Six God of War

COMPLETE SET (9) 4.00 10.00
COMMON CARD (GW1-GW9) .60 1.50
STATED ODDS 1:4

2001 Xena Warrior Princess Season Six Wet Wicked and Wild

COMPLETE SET (9) 15.00 40.00
COMMON CARD (WWW1-WWW9) 2.50 6.00
STATED ODDS 1:20

2001 Xena Warrior Princess Season Six Promos

COMMON CARD 1.00 2.50
P1B Xena (headshot) SP 100.00 150.00
BP1 Xena ALB 4.00 10.00
GUMMIE2001 Xena/1000* (NSU GUMMIE) 12.00 30.00

2001 Xena Warrior Princess Archive Collection

COMPLETE SET (5) 20.00 35.00
COMMON CARD (X1-X5) 5.00 12.00
STATED PRINT RUN 999 SER. #'d SETS

2004 Xena Warrior Princess Art and Images

COMPLETE SET (63) 4.00 10.00
UNOPENED BOX (20 PACKS) 55.00 65.00
UNOPENED PACK (6 CARDS) 2.75 3.25
COMMON CARD (1-63) .10 .30

2004 Xena Warrior Princess Art and Images Autographs

COMMON CARD 6.00 15.00
STATED ODDS 1:CASE
A54 ISSUED IN COLLECTORS ALBUM
DA7 ISSUED AS MULTI-CASE INCENTIVE
XA1 ISSUED AS N.AMER. CASE TOPPER
XA2 ISSUED AS INT'L CASE TOPPER
DA7 T.Raimi/R.O'Connor CI 50.00 100.00
XA1 Lucy Lawless CT (US) 40.00 80.00
XA2 Renee O'Connor CT (Int'l) 30.00 60.00

2004 Xena Warrior Princess Art and Images Douglas Shuler ArtiFEX

COMPLETE SET (9) 6.00 15.00
COMMON CARD (IA1-IA9) 1.25 3.00
STATED ODDS 1:10 INT'L PACKS

2004 Xena Warrior Princess Art and Images Portraits of a Warrior

COMPLETE SET (18) 15.00 40.00
COMMON CARD (PP1-PP18) 1.00 2.50
STATED ODDS 1:4

2004 Xena Warrior Princess Art and Images Rebekah Lynn ArtiFEX

COMPLETE SET (9) 40.00 80.00
COMMON CARD (NA1-NA9) 4.00 10.00
STATED ODDS 1:10 N.AMER. PACKS

2004 Xena Warrior Princess Art and Images Renee O'Connor ArtiFEX

COMPLETE SET (9) 40.00 80.00
COMMON CARD (R1-R9) 6.00 15.00
STATED ODDS 1:20

2004 Xena Warrior Princess Art and Images Women and Warriors

COMPLETE SET (5) 100.00 175.00
COMMON CARD (WW1-WW5) 15.00 40.00
STATED ODDS 1:90
STATED PRINT RUN 500 SER. #'d SETS

2004 Xena Warrior Princess Art and Images Women of Xena

COMPLETE SET (9) 25.00 50.00
COMMON CARD (WX1-WX9) 2.50 6.00
STATED ODDS 1:20

2004 Xena Warrior Princess Art and Images Xena Gallery

COMPLETE SET (6) 20.00 40.00
COMMON CARD (GX1-GX6) 3.00 8.00
STATED ODDS 1:30

2004 Xena Warrior Princess Art and Images Promos

COMPLETE SET (4) 4.00 10.00
COMMON CARD .75 2.00
P3 Xena/Gabrielle ALB 3.00 8.00
C2004 Xena CON 1.25 3.00

1995 Kitchen Sink Press The Yellow Kid

COMPLETE BOXED SET (36) 5.00 12.00
COMMON CARD .15 .40

1999 Comic Images DuoCards Yellow Submarine

COMPLETE SET (72) 6.00 15.00
UNOPENED BOX (36 PACKS) 30.00 40.00
UNOPENED PACK (7 CARDS) 1.00 1.25
COMMON CARD (1-72) .15 .40

1999 Comic Images DuoCards Yellow Submarine Chromium

COMPLETE SET (6) 8.00 20.00
COMMON CARD (1-6) 2.50 6.00
STATED ODDS 1:24

1999 Comic Images DuoCards Yellow Submarine Promos

NNO1 Promo 1 (card #66) .75 2.00
NNO2 Promo 2 .75 2.00

2012 Yo Gabba Gabba

COMPLETE SET (90) 6.00 15.00
COMMON CARD (1-90) .15 .40
*STKR: 1X TO 2.5X BASIC CARDS
NNO Yo Gabba Gabba PROMO 1.00 2.50

2012 Yo Gabba Gabba DJ Lance in Motion

COMPLETE SET (6) 10.00 25.00
COMMON CARD (DL1-DL6) 3.00 8.00
STATED ODDS 1:24

2012 Yo Gabba Gabba Mark's Magic Pictures

COMPLETE SET (6) 4.00 10.00
STATED ODDS 1:12

2012 Yo Gabba Gabba Pop-Ups

COMPLETE SET (6) 3.00 8.00
COMMON CARD (PU1-PU6) 1.00 2.50
STATED ODDS 1:8

1991 Pro Set YO! MTV Raps Complete Series

COMPLETE SET (150) 5.00 12.00
COMPLETE SERIES 1 SET (100) 4.00 10.00
COMPLETE SERIES 2 SET (50) 2.00 5.00
UNOPENED SERIES 1 BOX (36 PACKS) 10.00 15.00
UNOPENED SERIES 1 PACK (10 CARDS) .75 1.00
UNOPENED SERIES 2 BOX (36 PACKS) 10.00 15.00
UNOPENED SERIES 3 PACK (10 CARDS) .75 1.00
COMMON CARD (1-100) .15 .40
COMMON CARD (101-150) .12 .30
NNO Instant Winner Series 1 (pack insert) .15 .40
NNO All New Prizes! Series 2 (pack insert) .15 .40
NNO Yo! MTV Raps Series 1 (checklist send-in)
NNO Yo! MTV Raps Series 2 (checklist send-in)
NNO YO! MTV Raps Hologram 50.00 100.00

1986 Scanlens Young Talent Time

COMPLETE SET (33) 30.00 75.00
COMMON CARD (1-33) 1.25 3.00

1992 Comic Images Youngblood

COMPLETE SET (90) 4.00 10.00
UNOPENED BOX (48 PACKS) 25.00 40.00
UNOPENED PACK (10 CARDS) 1.00 1.50
COMMON CARD (1-90) .12 .30

1992 Comic Images Youngblood Prisms

COMPLETE SET (6) 3.00 8.00
COMMON CARD (P1-P6) 1.00 2.50
STATED ODDS 1:16
UNC 6-Card Prism Uncut Sheet

1992 Comic Images Youngblood Promos

1 Capitol City/Wizard Press 6.00 15.00
2 Bedrock, Shaft, Cougar, Riptide 2.50 6.00
3 General Distribution 2.00

1995 SkyBox Youngblood

COMPLETE SET (90) 10.00 25.00
UNOPENED BOX (24 PACKS) 40.00 50.00
UNOPENED PACK (8 CARDS) 2.00 2.25
COMMON CARD (1-90) .20 .50
ESD1 Badrock (SkyDisk) 30.00 80.00

1995 SkyBox Youngblood Promos

C1 Combo Magazine Exclusive .75 2.00
N1 Promo 5 .75 2.00
P0 Promo 1 .75 2.00
P1 Team Youngblood Comic #16 Insert .75 2.00
S1 Promo 4 .75 2.00
NNO1 Badrock
NNO2 Badrock (SkyDisk, in case)

1995 SkyBox Youngblood Stickers

COMPLETE SET (9) 6.00 15.00
COMMON CARD (S1-S9) .75 2.00
STATED ODDS 1:1

1995 SkyBox Youngblood Wiggle

COMPLETE SET (5) 15.00 40.00
COMMON CARD (W1-W5) 4.00 10.00
STATED ODDS 1:8

1992 Cardz Zap Pax

COMPLETE SET (110) 8.00 20.00
UNOPENED BOX (36 PACKS) 10.00 15.00
UNOPENED PACK (8 CARDS) .50 .75
COMMON CARD (1-110) .10 .25
NNO Skull Hologram 2.00 5.00

1992 Cardz Zap Pax Promos

COMPLETE SET (4) 2.00 5.00
COMMON CARD .75 2.00

1983 Donruss Zero Heroes

COMPLETE SET (66) 6.00 15.00
UNOPENED BOX (36 PACKS) 35.00 50.00
UNOPENED PACK (6 CARDS) 1.25 1.50
COMMON CARD (1-66) .12 .30

1992 FantaCo Zombie War

COMPLETE BOXED SET (45) 10.00 25.00
COMPLETE DELUXE BOXED SET (46) 15.00 40.00
COMPLETE COMIC SUBSET (5) 5.00 12.00
COMMON CARD (1-45) .30 .75
COMMON CARD (46-50) 1.25 3.00
51 Dead on Target AU 8.00 20.00
Kevin Eastman/Charles Lang/Tom Skulan/Jim Whiting
P50 The Emperor Zombie 1.25 3.00
NNO Earth Must Die #1 1.25 3.00
(Comic Exclusive Bonus)

DC/Marvel

DC

1991 DC Comics Armageddon 2001 Checklist Promo

NNO Guy Running in Space 1.00 2.50

2015 Arrow Season One

COMPLETE SET (95) 10.00 25.00
UNOPENED BOX (24 PACKS) 75.00 125.00
UNOPENED PACK (5 CARDS) 3.00 5.00
COMMON CARD (1-95) .30 .75
*BRONZE: 1.2X TO 3X BASIC CARDS .75 2.00
*GOLD/40: 6X TO 15X BASIC CARDS 1.50 4.00

2015 Arrow Season One Autographs

COMMON CARD (A2-A23) 5.00 12.00
STATED ODDS 1:24
A1 AND A12 DO NOT EXIST
A2 Katie Cassidy SP 100.00 200.00
A3 David Ramsey SP 60.00 120.00
A4 Willa Holland SP 300.00 500.00
A5 Susanna Thompson SP 30.00 75.00
A6 Paul Blackthorne SP 30.00 75.00
A7 Emily Bett Rickards SP 150.00 300.00
A8 Colin Donnell 8.00 20.00
A9 Manu Bennett 10.00 25.00
A10 Celina Jade 50.00 100.00
A11A John Barrowman 20.00 50.00
A11B John Barrowman 15.00 40.00
A13 Byron Mann 6.00 15.00
A15 Kelly Hu 25.00 60.00
A16 Christie Laing 6.00 15.00
A18A Jessica De Gouw 12.00 30.00
A18B Jessica De Gouw 12.00 30.00
A19 Alex Kingston 20.00 50.00

2015 Arrow Season One Character Bios

COMPLETE SET (18) 20.00 50.00
COMMON CARD (CB1-CB18) 2.50 6.00
*BRONZE: .50X TO 1.2X BASIC CARDS 3.00 8.00
*GOLD/40: 2X TO 5X BASIC CARDS 12.00 30.00
STATED ODDS 1:12

2015 Arrow Season One Comic Covers

COMPLETE SET (6) 6.00 15.00
COMMON CARD (CC1-CC6) 2.00 5.00
*ACETATE: .75X TO 2X BASIC CARDS
STATED ODDS 1:12

2015 Arrow Season One Dual Wardrobes

COMMON CARD (DM1-DM3) 12.00 30.00
DM1 S.Amell
E.B.Rickards 20.00 50.00
DM2 C.Haynes
W.Holland 20.00 50.00

2015 Arrow Season One Training

COMPLETE SET (9) 8.00 20.00
COMMON CARD (TR1-TR9) 1.50 4.00
*BRONZE: .75X TO 2X BASIC CARDS 3.00 8.00
*GOLD/40: 2X TO 5X BASIC CARDS 8.00 20.00
STATED ODDS 1:12

2015 Arrow Season One Wardrobes

COMMON CARD (M1-M25) 6.00 15.00
STATED ODDS 1:24
M1 Stephen Amell 12.00 30.00
M2 Katie Cassidy 15.00 40.00
M4 Willa Holland 10.00 25.00
M5 Susanna Thompson 8.00 20.00
M6 Stephen Amell 15.00 40.00
M7 Jessica De Gouw 8.00 20.00
M9 Emily Bett Rickards 25.00 60.00
M10 Colton Haynes 10.00 25.00
M11 John Barrowman 15.00 40.00
M13 Colin Donnell 8.00 20.00
M14 Susanna Thompson 8.00 20.00
M15 Stephen Amell 30.00 75.00
M16 Colin Donnell 10.00 25.00
M17 Katie Cassidy 15.00 40.00
M18 Colton Haynes 10.00 25.00
M19 Michael Rowe 12.00 30.00
M20 Byron Mann 10.00 25.00
M21 Willa Holland 12.00 30.00
M22 John Barrowman 8.00 20.00
M24 Roger Cross 10.00 25.00
M25 Stephen Amell (album excl.) 25.00 60.00

2015 Arrow Season One Promos

P1 Philly Spring 2014 2.50 6.00
P2 NSU Dec/Jan 2015 UK Issue 10.00 25.00
CP1 NSU Feb/Mar 2015 Variant Issue 2.50 6.00

2015 Arrow Season Two

COMPLETE SET (72) 8.00 20.00
UNOPENED BOX (24 PACKS) 100.00 150.00
UNOPENED PACK (5 CARDS) 4.00 6.00
COMMON CARD (1-72) .25 .60
*GREEN: .6X TO 1.5X BASIC CARDS .40 1.00
*RED: 2X TO 5X BASIC CARDS 1.25 3.00
*SILVER/40: 8X TO 20X BASIC CARDS 5.00 12.00

2015 Arrow Season Two Archers

COMPLETE SET (3) 4.00 10.00
COMMON CARD (A1-A3) 1.50 4.00
*GREEN: .6X TO 1.5X BASIC CARDS
*RED: .75X TO 2X BASIC CARDS
*SILVER: 2.5X TO 6X BASIC CARDS
STATED ODDS 1:8

2015 Arrow Season Two Autographs

COMMON AUTO 5.00 12.00
STATED ODDS 1:24
CJ Celina Jade 30.00 75.00
CL1 Caity Lotz 50.00 100.00
CL2 Caity Lotz 60.00 120.00
CR Cynthia Addai-Robinson 10.00 25.00
DNY David Nykl 15.00 40.00
JB John Barrowman 20.00 50.00
JDG1 Jessica de Gouw 12.00 30.00
JDG2 Jessica de Gouw 12.00 30.00
KA1 Kevin Alejandro 8.00 20.00
KA2 Kevin Alejandro 12.00 30.00
KC Katie Cassidy 100.00 200.00
KH Kelly Hu 20.00 50.00
KL Katrina Law 25.00 60.00
MR Michael Rowe 6.00 15.00
SG1 Summer Glau 60.00 120.00
SG2 Summer Glau 50.00 100.00

2015 Arrow Season Two Characters

COMPLETE SET (9) 5.00 12.00
COMMON CARD (CB1-CB9) 1.00 2.50
*GREEN: .6X TO 1.5X BASIC CARDS
*RED: .75X TO 2X BASIC CARDS
*SILVER: 2.5X TO 6X BASIC CARDS
STATED ODDS 1:4

2015 Arrow Season Two Dual Wardrobes

COMMON CARD 12.00 30.00
DM1 Willa Holland/John Barrowman 20.00 50.00
DM2 Katrina Law/Summer Glau 25.00 60.00
DM4 Katrina Law/Caity Lotz 25.00 60.00
DM5 Caity Lotz/Stephen Amell 15.00 40.00
DM6 Emily Bett Rickards 20.00 50.00

2015 Arrow Season Two Mirakuru

COMPLETE SET (6) 4.00 10.00
COMMON CARD (U1-U6) 1.25 3.00
*GREEN: .6X TO 1.5X BASIC CARDS
*RED: .75X TO 2X BASIC CARDS
*SILVER: 2.5X TO 6X BASIC CARDS
STATED ODDS 1:4

2015 Arrow Season Two Stickers

COMPLETE SET (9) 10.00 25.00
COMMON CARD (S1-S9) 2.50 6.00
STATED ODDS 1:24

2015 Arrow Season Two Suicide Squad

COMPLETE SET (9) 5.00 12.00
COMMON CARD (Z1-Z9) 1.00 2.50
*GREEN: .6X TO 1.5X BASIC CARDS
*RED: .75X TO 2X BASIC CARDS
*SILVER: 2.5X TO 6X BASIC CARDS
STATED ODDS 1:4

2015 Arrow Season Two Wardrobes

COMMON CARD 5.00 12.00
M1 Stephen Amell 10.00 25.00
M3 Willa Holland 10.00 25.00
M4 Manu Bennett 15.00 40.00
M5 John Barrowman 6.00 15.00
M6 Caity Lotz 6.00 15.00
M8 Paul Blackthorne 6.00 15.00
M9 Colton Haynes 6.00 15.00
M10 Caity Lotz 8.00 20.00
M11 Michael Rowe 6.00 15.00
M12 Stephen Amell 20.00 50.00
M13 Emily Bett Rickards 12.00 30.00
M14 Katrina Law 30.00 80.00
M15 Manu Bennett 6.00 15.00
M16 Colton Haynes 8.00 20.00
M17 Willa Holland 10.00 25.00
M18 John Barrowman 12.00 30.00
M19 Kevin Alejandro 6.00 15.00
M20 Manu Bennett 6.00 15.00
M21 David Ramsey 10.00 25.00
M22 Caity Lotz 12.00 30.00
M23 Michael Jai White 6.00 15.00
M25 Willa Holland ALB 15.00 40.00

2015 Arrow Season Two Promos

P1 Convention Exclusive 1.25 3.00

2017 Arrow Season Three

COMPLETE SET (81) 6.00 15.00
UNOPENED BOX (24 PACKS) 60.00 80.00
UNOPENED PACK (5 CARDS) 3.00 4.00
COMMON CARD (1-81) .20 .50
*SILVER FOIL: .6X TO 1.5X BASIC CARDS .30 .75
P1 Arrow Season Three Promo NSU 2.50 6.00

2017 Arrow Season Three Autographs

COMMON AUTO 5.00 12.00
STATED ODDS 1:24
SOME AUTOS CONTAIN INSCRIPTIONS
AG Amy Gumenick 15.00 40.00
CC Christina Cox 8.00 20.00
CR Charlotte Ross 10.00 25.00
DJ Doug Jones 8.00 20.00
FY Francoise Yip 6.00 15.00
KY Karl Yune 8.00 20.00
MS Marc Singer 12.00 30.00
RF Rila Fukushima 25.00 60.00
AMA Audrey Marie Anderson 10.00 25.00
BTK Bex Taylor-Klaus 10.00 25.00
CL1 Caity Lotz 30.00 75.00
CL2 Caity Lotz 50.00 100.00
EBR Emily Bett Rickards 125.00 250.00
JRR J.R. Ramirez 6.00 15.00
KC1 Katie Cassidy 60.00 120.00
KC2 Katie Cassidy 150.00 300.00
KL1 Katrina Law 20.00 50.00
KL2 Katrina Law 25.00 60.00

2017 Arrow Season Three Character Bios

COMPLETE SET (6) 5.00 12.00
COMMON CARD (C1-C6) 1.25 3.00
*SILVER FOIL: .75X TO 2X BASIC CARDS
STATED ODDS 1:4

2017 Arrow Season Three Dual Wardrobes

COMMON MEM (DM1-DM5) 6.00 15.00
STATED ODDS 1:209
DM1 Stephen Amell/Matt Nable 20.00 50.00
DM3 Colton Haynes/Stephen Amell/19 250.00 500.00
DM4 Rila Fukushima/Karl Yune/99 12.00 30.00
DM5 Charlotte Ross/Emily Bett Rickards/19200.00 350.00

2017 Arrow Season Three Props

COMMON CARD (PR1-PR4) 12.00 30.00
STATED ODDS 1:24
PR2 Roy's note to Thea/19 200.00 400.00
PR3 Wildcat Gym boxing glove/49 80.00 150.00

2017 Arrow Season Three Team Arrow

COMPLETE SET (6) 5.00 12.00
COMMON CARD (Z1-Z6) 1.25 3.00
*SILVER FOIL: .75X TO 2X BASIC CARDS
STATED ODDS 1:4

2017 Arrow Season Three Wardrobes

COMMON MEM (M1-M24) 5.00 12.00
STATED ODDS 1:24
M1 Stephen Amell/99 60.00 120.00
M3 Emily Bett Rickards 10.00 25.00
M4 Rila Fukushima 6.00 15.00
M5 Karl Yune/99 20.00 50.00

M7 Katie Cassidy 8.00 20.00
M8 John Barrowman/99 15.00 40.00
M10 Willa Holland 6.00 15.00
M11 Marc Singer/99 10.00 25.00
M12 Katrina Law 6.00 15.00
M13 Matt Nable/49 60.00 120.00
M18 Stephen Amell/49 125.00 250.00
M19 Colton Haynes/99 20.00 50.00
M20 Emily Bett Rickards 12.00 30.00
M21 Brandon Routh/99 25.00 60.00
M23 Brandon Routh/99 60.00 120.00
M24 John Barrowman ALB 12.00 30.00

2017 Arrow Season Three Wedding

COMPLETE SET (6) 5.00 12.00
COMMON CARD (B1-B6) 1.25 3.00
*SILVER FOIL: .75X TO 2X BASIC CARDS
STATED ODDS 1:4

2017 Arrow Season Four

COMPLETE SET (72) 6.00 15.00
UNOPENED BOX (24 PACKS) 65.00 85.00
UNOPENED PACK (5 CARDS) 3.00 4.00
COMMON CARD (1-72) .15 .40
*SILVER FOIL: .6X TO 1.5X BASIC CARDS .25 .60

2017 Arrow Season Four Autographs

COMMON AUTO 5.00 12.00
STATED ODDS 1:24
AG Amy Gumenick 25.00 60.00
AH Anna Hopkins 10.00 25.00
CC Casper Crump 12.00 30.00
JR Jeri Ryan 30.00 75.00
KL Katrina Law 30.00 75.00
MR Matt Ryan 50.00 100.00
NM Neal McDonough 12.00 30.00
TS Tiera Skovbye 6.00 15.00
AC2 Alexander Calvert 6.00 15.00
AMA Audrey Marie Anderson 12.00 30.00
CHR Charlotte Ross 12.00 30.00
CL1 Caity Lotz 50.00 100.00
CL2 Caity Lotz 60.00 120.00
CR1 Ciara Renee 15.00 40.00
CR2 Ciara Renee 20.00 50.00
EBR Emily Bett Rickards 100.00 200.00
EMK Emily Kinney 12.00 30.00
FH1 Falk Hentschel 8.00 20.00
FH2 Falk Hentschel 20.00 50.00
JRB JR Bourne 6.00 15.00
KC1 Katie Cassidy 75.00 150.00
RF1 Rila Fukushima 20.00 50.00
RF2 Rila Fukushima 25.00 60.00
SA1 Stephen Amell 750.00 1500.00
SA2 Stephen Amell 600.00 1000.00

2017 Arrow Season Four Character Bios

COMPLETE SET (9) 6.00 15.00
COMMON CARD (CB1-CB9) 1.25 3.00
*SILVER FOIL: .75X TO 2X BASIC CARDS 2.50 6.00
STATED ODDS 1:3

2017 Arrow Season Four Dual Autograph

CRFH C.Renee/F.Hentschel 60.00 120.00

2017 Arrow Season Four Dual Wardrobes

COMMON CARD (DM1-DM7) 6.00 15.00
STATED ODDS 1:146
DM3 Cupid 20.00 50.00
DM4 The Atom 60.00 120.00
DM5 The Canary and Black Canary 100.00 200.00
DM6 Green Arrow and Speedy 150.00 300.00
DM7 Nyssa al Ghul and Ra's al Ghul 50.00 100.00

2017 Arrow Season Four Locations

COMPLETE SET (9) 6.00 15.00
COMMON CARD (L1-L9) 1.00 2.50
*SILVER FOIL: .6X TO 1.5X BASIC CARDS 1.50 4.00
STATED ODDS 1:3

2017 Arrow Season Four Olicity

COMPLETE SET (9) 5.00 12.00
COMMON CARD (OF1-OF9) .75 2.00
*SILVER: .75X TO 2X BASIC CARDS 1.50 4.00
STATED ODDS 1:3

2017 Arrow Season Four Props

COMMON MEM (PR1-PR7) 6.00 15.00
STATED ODDS OVERALL 1:24 W/WARDROBES
PR1 Mayoral Campaign Flyer/99 8.00 20.00
PR2 Double Down's Playing Card/99 8.00 20.00
PR3 Oliver's Note/49 50.00 100.00
PR4 Constantine's Scroll/49 30.00 75.00

2017 Arrow Season Four Stickers

COMPLETE SET (9) 12.00 30.00
COMMON CARD (S1-S9) 1.50 4.00
STATED ODDS 1:24
S8 Green Arrow and Felicity 2.50 6.00

2017 Arrow Season Four STR PWR

COMPLETE SET (10) 60.00 120.00
COMMON CARD (S1-S10) 6.00 15.00
*RED: .5X TO 1.2X BASIC CARDS 8.00 20.00
*GOLD/25: .75X TO 2X BASIC CARDS 12.00 30.00

2017 Arrow Season Four Triple Wardrobe

TM1 Arsenal/Spartan/Black Canary 200.00 350.00

2017 Arrow Season Four Wardrobes

COMMON CARD (M1-M23, B1) 5.00 12.00
STATED ODDS OVERALL 1:24 W/PROPS
B1 IS AN ALBUM EXCLUSIVE
M1 Stephen Amell 6.00 15.00
M2 Katie Cassidy 10.00 25.00
M4 Willa Holland 10.00 25.00
M6 Stephen Amell/99 20.00 50.00
M7 JR Bourne/99 10.00 25.00
M8 John Barrowman/99 12.00 30.00
M11 Stephen Amell 12.00 30.00
M12 Willa Holland/99 20.00 50.00
M13 Caity Lotz/99 30.00 75.00
M14 John Barrowman/49 25.00 60.00
M15 Katrina Law/49 60.00 120.00
M17 Katie Cassidy/49 50.00 100.00
M18 Stephen Amell/25 120.00
M19 Colton Haynes/49 60.00 120.00
M22 Neal McDonough/99 12.00 30.00
M23 Amy Gumenick/99 12.00 30.00
B1 Stephen Amell 10.00 25.00

2017 Arrow Season Four Promo

P1 Oct/Nov NSU 2.00

Batman

1995 SkyBox Adventures of Batman and Robin

COMPLETE SET (90) 8.00 20.00
UNOPENED HOBBY BOX (36 PACKS) 60.00 100.00
UNOPENED HOBBY PACK (8 CARDS) 2.00 3.00
UNOPENED WAL-MART BOX (18 PACKS)30.00 50.00
UNOPENED WAL-MART PACK (5 CARDS) 2.00 3.00
COMMON CARD (1-90) .15 .40

1995 SkyBox Adventures of Batman and Robin Color-In

COMPLETE SET (9) 5.00 12.00
COMMON CARD (C1-C9) 1.00 2.50
STATED ODDS 1:1
WAL-MART EXCLUSIVE

1995 SkyBox Adventures of Batman and Robin Dark Knight Thermal

COMPLETE SET (3) 8.00 20.00
COMMON CARD (T1-T3) 5.00 12.00
STATED ODDS 1:36
HOBBY EXCLUSIVE

1995 SkyBox Adventures of Batman and Robin Pop-Ups

COMPLETE SET (12) 5.00 12.00
COMMON CARD (P1-P12) .75 2.00
STATED ODDS 1:1
HOBBY EXCLUSIVE

1995 SkyBox Adventures of Batman and Robin RAS Foil

COMPLETE SET (9) 10.00 25.00
COMMON CARD (R1-R9) 2.00 5.00
STATED ODDS 1:11
HOBBY EXCLUSIVE

1966 Topps Batman A Series Red Bat

COMPLETE SET (44) 125.00 300.00
COMMON CARD (1-44) 5.00 12.00
1A The Ghostly Foe 15.00 40.00
2A Grappling a Gator 8.00 20.00
44A Batman on Broadway 6.00 15.00

1997 SkyBox Batman and Robin

COMPLETE SET (70) 5.00 12.00
UNOPENED BOX (36 PACKS) 200.00 400.00
UNOPENED PACK (8 CARDS) 6.00 12.00
COMMON CARD (1-70) .15 .40

1997 SkyBox Batman and Robin Autographs

COMMON AUTO 75.00 150.00
STATED ODDS 1:720
NNO Alicia Silverstone 100.00 250.00
NNO Arnold Schwarzenegger 500.00 1200.00
NNO George Clooney 600.00 1500.00
NNO Dir. Joel Schumacher 100.00 250.00
NNO Uma Thurman 250.00 600.00

1997 SkyBox Batman and Robin Celluloid Action

COMPLETE SET (6) 10.00 25.00
COMMON CARD (1-6) 3.00 8.00
STATED ODDS 1:24

1997 SkyBox Batman and Robin Mini-Posters

COMPLETE SET (5) 2.50 6.00
COMMON CARD 1.00 2.50
STATED ODDS 1:6
UNNUMBERED SET

1997 SkyBox Batman and Robin Profiles

COMPLETE SET (12) 4.00 10.00
COMMON CARD (P1-P12) .75 2.00
STATED ODDS 1:3

1997 SkyBox Batman and Robin Storyboard

COMPLETE SET (24) 6.00 15.00
COMMON CARD (S1-S24) .50 1.25
STATED ODDS 1:1

1997 SkyBox Batman and Robin Promos

1 Batman and Robin OV (dealers) .75 2.00
2 Batman/Mr. Freeze 2-Card Panel 1.25 3.00

1997 Kellogg's Batman and Robin Bat Discs

COMPLETE SET (16) 8.00 20.00
COMMON DISC (1-16) 1.00 2.50

1997 Kenner Batman and Robin

COMPLETE SET (4) 3.00 8.00
COMMON CARD (K1-K4) 1.25 3.00
RANDOM INSERTS

2005 Batman Animated Season One

COMPLETE SET (90) 6.00 15.00
UNOPENED BOX (24 PACKS) 15.00 40.00
UNOPENED PACK (7 CARDS) 1.00 1.50
COMMON CARD (1-90) .15 .40

2005 Batman Animated Season One Flix-Pix Motion

COMPLETE SET (5) 3.00 8.00
COMMON CARD (1-5) .75 2.00
STATED ODDS 1:3

2005 Batman Animated Season One Magnets

COMPLETE SET (9) 5.00 12.00
COMMON CARD (1-9) .75 2.00
STATED ODDS 1:6

2005 Batman Animated Season One Tin Bonus

COMPLETE SET (6) 6.00 15.00
COMMON CARD (TB1-TB6) 1.50 4.00
STATED ODDS 1:TIN

2005 Batman Animated Season One Tin Matching Bonus

COMPLETE SET (6) 8.00 20.00
COMMON CARD (T1-T6) 1.50 4.00
STATED ODDS 1:1

2005 Batman Animated Season One Tins

COMPLETE SET (6) 20.00 50.00
COMMON UNOPENED TIN 5.00 12.00

2005 Batman Animated Season One Promos

D1 Intense Cool Collectible
(Dealer Exclusive)
P1 To Catch a Thief .75 2.00
P2 Hunger for Vengeance .75 2.00

1993 Topps Batman Animated Series One

COMPLETE SET (100) 6.00 15.00
UNOPENED BOX (36 PACKS) 125.00 200.00
UNOPENED PACK (10 CARDS) 4.00 6.00
COMMON CARD (1-100) .12 .30

1993 Topps Batman Animated Series One Vinyl Mini Cells

COMPLETE SET (6) 6.00 15.00
COMMON CARD (1-6) 2.00 5.00
*BLANK BACKS: SAME VALUE
STATED ODDS 1:12

1993 Topps Batman Animated Series One Promos

COMPLETE SET (5)
1 Fiery Background (NSU) .75 2.00
2 Batman Fighting Man (comic excl.) 1.25 3.00
3 Batman Holding Man (OS) .75 2.00
4 Batman Sitting (OS) .75 2.00
5 2-Up Panel (con. excl.) 2.00 5.00

1993 Topps Batman Animated Series Two

COMPLETE SET (90) 6.00 15.00
UNOPENED BOX (36 PACKS) 125.00 200.00
UNOPENED PACK (10 CARDS) 4.00 6.00
COMMON CARD (101-190) .12 .30
DEVITO AU ISSUED AS STADIUM CLUB EXCLUSIVE
DDAU Danny DeVito AU/2000 (SC excl.) 50.00 100.00

1993 Topps Batman Animated Series Two Vinyl Mini Cells

COMPLETE SET (4) 4.00 10.00
STATED ODDS 1:12
1 Batman 2.00 5.00
2 Batman Battles the Joker 2.00 5.00
3 Batman Faces the Phantasm 2.00 5.00
4 The Dark Knight of Gotham City 2.00 5.00

1993 Topps Batman Animated Series Two Promos

PROMOS ARE UNNUMBERED
1 Catwoman/Batman (dealer excl.) 1.25 3.00
2 Batman Walking (OS) 10.00 25.00

2008 Batman Archives

COMPLETE SET (63)	6.00	15.00
UNOPENED BOX (24 PACKS)	100.00	150.00
UNOPENED PACK (5 CARDS)	3.00	5.00
COMMON CARD (1-63)	.15	.40
ROBINSON AU STATED ODDS ONE PER CASE		
NNO Jerry Robinson AU		

2008 Batman Archives 1940 Batman Gum

COMPLETE SET (9)	6.00	15.00
COMMON CARD (1-9)	1.25	3.00
STATED ODDS 1:8		

2008 Batman Archives Dark Victory

COMPLETE SET (9)	10.00	25.00
COMMON CARD (DV1-DV9)	2.00	5.00
STATED ODDS 1:12		

2008 Batman Archives Lenticular

COMPLETE SET (9)	15.00	40.00
COMMON CARD (L1-L9)	3.00	8.00
STATED ODDS 1:24		

2008 Batman Archives Promos

P1 Batman standing on rooftop GEN	1.50	4.00
P2 Batman and Robin NSU	2.00	5.00
P3 Batgirl ALB	5.00	12.00
CP1 Batman behind castle CON	8.00	20.00
SD08 Batman throwing batarangs SDCC	2.50	6.00

1966 Topps Batman B Series Blue Bat

COMPLETE SET (44)	150.00	400.00
COMMON CARD (1-44)	6.00	15.00
1B The Joker's Icy Jest	20.00	50.00
35B Holy Rodents	8.00	20.00
44B Riddler Robs a Rainbow!	15.00	40.00

2005 Batman Begins Movie

COMPLETE SET (90)	5.00	12.00
UNOPENED HOBBY BOX (24 PACKS)	200.00	300.00
UNOPENED HOBBY PACK (7 CARDS)	8.00	12.00
COMMON CARD (1-90)	.15	.40

2005 Batman Begins Movie Autographs

COMMON AUTO	60.00	120.00
STATED ODDS 1:120 HOBBY		
NNO Gary Oldman	600.00	1500.00
NNO Katie Holmes	150.00	400.00
NNO Liam Neeson	1200.00	3000.00
NNO Michael Caine	300.00	750.00

2005 Batman Begins Movie Blister Bonus

COMPLETE SET (3)	1.25	3.00
COMMON CARD (B1-B3)	.75	2.00
STATED ODDS 1:1		
BLISTER PACK EXCLUSIVE		

2005 Batman Begins Movie Embossed Foil

COMPLETE SET (5)	3.00	6.00
COMMON CARD (1-5)	1.00	2.50
STATED ODDS 1:8		

2005 Batman Begins Movie Holograms

COMPLETE SET (5)	4.00	8.00
COMMON CARD (1-5)	1.25	3.00
STATED ODDS 1:12		

2005 Batman Begins Movie Memorabilia

COMMON CARD	10.00	25.00
STATED ODDS 1:24 HOBBY		
1 Batman's Cape	15.00	40.00
2 Batman's Costume	100.00	200.00

2005 Batman Begins Movie Stickers

COMPLETE SET (10)	1.50	4.00
COMMON CARD (1-10)	.40	1.00
STATED ODDS 1:2 RETAIL		

2005 Batman Begins Movie Tattoos

COMPLETE SET (10)	2.00	5.00
COMMON CARD (1-10)	.60	1.50
STATED ODDS 1:4 RETAIL		

1966 Topps Batman Black Bat

COMPLETE SET (55)	300.00	750.00
1 The Batman	75.00	200.00
55 Hidden Loot	20.00	50.00

1966 Topps Batman Color

COMPLETE SET (55)	150.00	400.00
COMMON CARD (1-55)	4.00	10.00
1 Bruce Wayne	20.00	50.00
2 Robin	10.00	25.00
4 Batman and Robin	12.00	30.00

1988 DC Comics Batman The Cult Promo

NNO Art by Bernie Wrightson	2.50	6.00

1999 DC Comics Batman Dark Victory Promos

COMPLETE SET (12)	5.00	12.00
COMMON CARD (1-12)	.60	1.50

1995 Dynamic Marketing Batman Forever

COMPLETE SET (110)	10.00	25.00
COMMON CARD (1-110)	.20	.50

1995 Dynamic Marketing Batman Forever Promos

COMPLETE SET (3)	2.50	6.00
COMMON CARD (P1-P3)	1.25	3.00
P1 Batman	1.25	3.00
P2 Riddler	1.25	3.00
P3 Two-Face	1.25	3.00

1995 Fleer Batman Forever

COMPLETE SET (120)	5.00	12.00
UNOPENED RETAIL BOX (18 PACKS)	30.00	40.00
UNOPENED RETAIL PACK (6 CARDS)	2.00	2.50
COMMON CARD (1-120)	.12	.30

1995 Fleer Metal Batman Forever

COMPLETE SET (100)	8.00	20.00
UNOPENED HOBBY BOX (36 PACKS)	125.00	250.00
UNOPENED HOBBY PACK (8 CARDS)	4.00	8.00
UNOPENED RETAIL BOX (20 PACKS)		
UNOPENED RETAIL PACK (6 CARDS)		
UNOPENED JUMBO BOX (24 PACKS)	125.00	200.00
UNOPENED JUMBO PACK (10 CARDS)	6.00	8.00
COMMON CARD (1-100)	.20	.50
*SILVER: .8X TO 2X BASIC CARDS 1:1		
A1 STATED ODDS 1:18		

1995 Fleer Metal Batman Forever Gold Blaster

COMPLETE SET (10)	5.00	12.00
COMMON CARD (1-10)	1.00	2.50
STATED ODDS 1:3		

1995 Fleer Metal Batman Forever Holograms

COMPLETE SET (4)	12.00	30.00
COMMON CARD (H1-H4)	4.00	10.00
STATED ODDS 1:18		

1995 Fleer Metal Batman Forever Movie Previews

COMPLETE SET (8)	5.00	12.00
COMMON CARD (1-8)	1.25	3.00
STATED ODDS 1:6		

1995 Fleer Metal Batman Forever Promos

1 Batman, Unnumbered 5X7, Perforated	.75	2.00
2 Batman, Unnumbered 5X7, Unperforated	.75	2.00

1995 McDonald's Batman Forever Pop-Ups

COMPLETE SET (16)	10.00	25.00
COMMON CARD (1-16)	1.25	3.00
NNO Instruction card		

1995 Topps Batman Forever Stickers

COMPLETE SET (88)	8.00	20.00
UNOPENED BOX (36 PACKS)		
UNOPENED PACK (5 CARDS)		
COMMON CARD (1-88)	.20	.50

1995 Topps Batman Forever Stickers Chromium

COMPLETE SET (4)	4.00	10.00
COMMON CARD (B1-B4)	1.50	4.00
STATED ODDS 1:18		
B1 Batman	2.00	5.00

1995 Fleer Ultra Batman Forever

COMPLETE SET (120)	6.00	15.00
UNOPENED HOBBY BOX (36 PACKS)	50.00	75.00
UNOPENED HOBBY PACK (8 CARDS)	2.00	2.50
UNOPENED RETAIL BOX (18 PACKS)		
UNOPENED RETAIL PACK (6 CARDS)		
UNOPENED JUMBO BOX (24 PACKS)		
UNOPENED JUMBO PACK (17 CARDS)		
COMMON CARD (1-120)	.12	.30
A1 Batman PROMO	.75	2.00

1995 Fleer Ultra Batman Forever Acclaim Video Game Tips

COMPLETE SET (2)	1.00	2.50
COMMON CARD (G1-G2)	.75	2.00
STATED ODDS 1:18		

1995 Fleer Ultra Batman Forever Animaction

COMPLETE SET (10)	5.00	12.00
COMMON CARD (1-10)	1.00	2.50
STATED ODDS 1:4		

1995 Fleer Ultra Batman Forever Holograms

COMPLETE SET (36)	5.00	12.00
COMMON CARD (1-36)	.30	.75
STATED ODDS 1:1		

1995 Unocal Batman Forever

COMPLETE SET (5)	6.00	15.00
COMMON CARD	1.50	4.00

1996 SkyBox Batman Holo Series

COMPLETE SET (50)	8.00	20.00
UNOPENED BOX (24 PACKS)	150.00	250.00
UNOPENED PACK (4 CARDS)	6.00	10.00
COMMON CARD (1-50)	.20	.50
*GOLD: .75X TO 2X BASIC CARDS		
*BLUE: 4X TO 10X BASIC CARDS		
H1 The Dark Knight	6.00	15.00
NNO Batman PROMO	1.25	3.00

1996 SkyBox Batman Holo Series HoloAction

COMPLETE SET (4)	3.00	8.00
*GOLD: .60X TO 1.5X BASIC CARDS		
*BLUE: 4X TO 10X BASIC CARDS		
STATED ODDS 1:4		
H1 The Joker	1.25	3.00
H2 The Riddler	1.25	3.00
H3 Batman	1.25	3.00
H4 Two-Face	1.25	3.00

1995 SkyBox Batman Master Series

COMPLETE SET (90)	8.00	20.00
UNOPENED BOX (36 PACKS)	150.00	250.00
UNOPENED PACK (10 CARDS)	4.00	8.00
COMMON CARD (1-90)	.20	.50
*AP: .8X TO 2X BASIC CARDS		

1995 SkyBox Batman Master Series Chromium

COMPLETE SET (2)	6.00	15.00
COMMON CARD (1-2)	4.00	10.00
STATED ODDS 1:24		

1995 SkyBox Batman Master Series Clearchrome

COMPLETE SET (2)	20.00	40.00
COMMON CARD (1-2)	10.00	25.00
STATED ODDS 1:120		

1995 SkyBox Batman Master Series Master Villains

COMPLETE SET (10)	10.00	25.00
COMMON CARD (1-10)	2.00	5.00
STATED ODDS 1:10		

1995 SkyBox Batman Master Series Spectra Etch

COMPLETE SET (6)	5.00	12.00
COMMON CARD (1-6)	1.25	3.00
STATED ODDS 1:6		

1989 Topps Batman Movie

COMPLETE SET (264)	10.00	25.00
COMPLETE SET W/STICKERS (308)	12.00	30.00
SERIES ONE SET (132)	5.00	12.00
SERIES ONE SET W/STICKERS (144)	6.00	15.00
SERIES TWO SET (132)	5.00	12.00
SERIES TWO SET W/STICKERS (144)	6.00	15.00
UNOPENED SERIES ONE BOX (36 PACKS)	60.00	100.00
UNOPENED SERIES ONE PACK (9 CARDS+STICKER)	2.00	3.00
UNOPENED SERIES TWO BOX (36 PACKS)	50.00	75.00
UNOPENED SERIES TWO PACK (9 CARDS+STICKER)	2.00	2.50
COMMON CARD (1-264)	.12	.30
*OPC: SAME VALUE		
*REGINA: SAME VALUE		

1989 Topps Batman Movie Stickers

COMPLETE SET (44)	4.00	10.00
SERIES ONE SET (22)	2.50	6.00
SERIES TWO SET (22)	2.50	6.00
COMMON STICKER (1-44)	.20	.50
STATED ODDS 1:1		

1989 Topps Batman Movie Collector's Edition

COMPLETE SET (264)	10.00	25.00
COMP. SER. ONE (132)	6.00	15.00
COMP. SER. ONE FACT. SET (165)	8.00	20.00
COMP. SER. TWO (132)	6.00	15.00
COMP. SER. TWO FACT. SET (165)	8.00	20.00
COMMON CARD (1-264)	.10	.25

1989 Topps Batman Movie Collector's Edition Bonus

COMPLETE SET (22)	3.00	8.00
COMP. SER. ONE SET (11)	2.00	5.00
COMP. SER. TWO SET (11)	2.00	5.00
COMMON CARD (A-V)	.30	.75

1989 DC Comics Batman Movie Special Promo

NNO Batman 1989	2.50	6.00

1992 Topps Batman Returns

COMPLETE SET (88)	6.00	15.00
COMPLETE SET W/STADIUM CL. INSERTS (99)	8.00	20.00
UNOPENED BOX (36 PACKS)	25.00	40.00
UNOPENED PACK (9 CARDS)	1.00	1.50
COMMON CARD (1-88)	.12	.30
*OPC: SAME VALUE		

1992 Stadium Club Batman Returns

COMPLETE SET (100)	5.00	12.00
UNOPENED BOX (36 PACKS)	30.00	50.00
UNOPENED PACK (10 CARDS)	1.50	2.00
COMMON CARD (1-100)	.15	.40

1992 Stadium Club Batman Returns Inserts

COMPLETE SET (10)	2.00	5.00
COMMON CARD (A-J)	.40	1.00
*OPC: SAME VALUE		
STATED ODDS 1:1		

1992 Dynamic Marketing Batman Returns

COMPLETE SET (150)	15.00	40.00
COMMON CARD (1-150)	.20	.50

1992 Dynamic Marketing Batman Returns Holograms

COMPLETE SET (9)	6.00	15.00
COMMON CARD (1-9)	1.00	2.50

1992 Dynamic Marketing Batman Returns Limited Edition Gold

COMPLETE SET (10)	10.00	25.00
COMMON CARD (1-10)	2.00	5.00

1992 Dynamic Marketing Batman Returns Stickers

COMPLETE SET (20)	5.00	12.00
COMMON CARD (1-20)	.40	1.00

1992 O-Pee-Chee Batman Returns Stadium Club Inserts

COMPLETE SET (10)	2.50	6.00
COMMON CARD (1-10)	.40	1.00
*TOPPS: SAME VALUE		
STATED ODDS 1:1		

1992 Zellers Batman Returns

COMPLETE SET (24)	4.00	10.00
COMMON CARD (1-24)	.30	.75

1966 Topps Batman Riddler Backs

COMPLETE SET (38)	150.00	400.00
UNOPENED BOX (24 PACKS)		
UNOPENED PACK (4 CARDS)		
COMMON CARD (1-38)	8.00	20.00
6 Bookworm Batman	12.00	30.00
35 A Dastardly Duo	8.00	20.00
SD Secret Decoder	10.00	25.00

1994 SkyBox Batman Saga of the Dark Knight

COMPLETE SET (100)	6.00	15.00
UNOPENED BOX (36 PACKS)	75.00	125.00
UNOPENED PACK (8 CARDS)	2.50	4.00
COMMON CARD (1-100)	.15	.40
SD1 STATED ODDS 1:240		

1994 SkyBox Batman Saga of the Dark Knight Spectra Etch Portraits

COMPLETE SET (5)	6.00	15.00
COMMON CARD (B1-B5)	2.50	6.00
STATED ODDS 1:18		

1989 Dandy Batman Stickers Australian

COMPLETE SET (42)	8.00	20.00
COMMON CARD (1-42)	.40	1.00

1966 Weeties and Rice Krinkles Batman

COMPLETE SET (36)	200.00	400.00
COMMON CARD	6.00	15.00

2012 DC Comics Batman The Legend

COMPLETE SET (63)	6.00	15.00
UNOPENED BOX (24 PACKS)	125.00	200.00
UNOPENED PACK (5 CARDS)	5.00	8.00
COMMON CARD (1-63)	.20	.50
*FOIL: 2X TO 5X BASIC CARDS		

2012 DC Comics Batman The Legend Batcave Puzzle

COMPLETE SET (9)	10.00	25.00
COMMON CARD (TBC1-TBC9)	2.00	5.00
STATED ODDS		

2012 DC Comics Batman The Legend Batmobile

COMPLETE SET (9)	12.00	30.00
COMMON CARD (BM1-BM9)	2.00	5.00

2012 DC Comics Batman The Legend Circus of Villains

COMPLETE SET (8)	12.00	30.00
COMMON CARD (CP1-CP8)	2.50	6.00
STATED ODDS		
CP1 The Joker	4.00	10.00

2012 DC Comics Batman The Legend Promos

P1 Batman/Joker NSU	.75	2.00
BP1 Gothem City ALB		

1995 SkyBox Kenner Legends of Batman Promos

COMPLETE SET (27)	30.00	80.00
COMMON CARD (K1-K27)	2.00	5.00

2004 Catwoman

COMPLETE SET (72)	4.00	10.00
UNOPENED BOX (36 PACKS)	50.00	60.00
UNOPENED PACK (6 CARDS)	2.00	2.50
COMMON CARD (1-72)	.10	.30

2004 Catwoman Autographs

COMMON CARD (A1-A7)	6.00	15.00
STATED ODDS 1:36		
A4 Kim Smith	20.00	50.00

2004 Catwoman Box-Loaders

COMMON CARD	1.25	3.00
STATED ODDS 1:BOX		
CL1 I Rule The Night	4.00	10.00
CASE INSERT		

2004 Catwoman Cat Vision

COMPLETE SET (6)	8.00	20.00
COMMON CARD (CV1-CV6)	1.50	4.00
STATED ODDS 1:17		

2004 Catwoman Fearless

COMPLETE SET (9)	10.00	25.00
COMMON CARD (F1-F9)	1.50	4.00
STATED ODDS 1:11		

2004 Catwoman Pieceworks

COMMON CARD (PW1-PW14)	8.00	20.00
STATED ODDS 1:36		
PW1 Halle Berry	15.00	40.00
PW2 Halle Berry	15.00	40.00
PW4 Halle Berry	15.00	40.00

2004 Catwoman Promos

COMPLETE SET (5)	4.00	10.00
COMMON CARD	1.00	2.50
PUK Catwoman	1.50	4.00
FCBD1 Catwoman FOIL	1.50	4.00
SDCC2004 Catwoman		

1966 Topps Comic Book Foldees

COMPLETE SET (44)	200.00	350.00
UNOPENED BOX	400.00	650.00
UNOPENED PACK	15.00	40.00
COMMON CARD (1-44)	2.00	5.00

1966 Topps Comic Book Foldees Oversized

COMPLETE SET (43)	300.00	600.00
COMMON CARD (1-43)	5.00	12.00

1970 Topps Comic Cover Stickers

COMPLETE SET (44)	80.00	150.00
UNOPENED PACK	20.00	50.00
COMMON CARD (1-44)	1.25	3.00

1995 DC Comics Contagion Promo

NNO Batman Story Promo	.75	2.00

2022 CZX Crisis on Infinite Earths

COMPLETE SET (50)	15.00	40.00
UNOPENED BOX (6 CARDS)	250.00	400.00
COMMON CARD (1-50)	.75	2.00
*RED/125: 1.5X TO 4X BASIC CARDS		
*GREEN/45: 2X TO 5X BASIC CARDS		
*SILVER/25: 3X TO 8X BASIC CARDS		

2022 CZX Crisis on Infinite Earths Autographs

COMMON AUTO	12.00	30.00
STATED ODDS 1:24		
MW Marv Wolfman/175	15.00	40.00
BRS Brandon Routh/75	300.00	800.00
GGF Grant Gustin/100	300.00	800.00
MBS Melissa Benoist/100	400.00	1000.00
NMD Nicole Maines/120	60.00	150.00
TCP Tom Cavanagh/100	60.00	150.00
BRRP Brandon Routh/115	75.00	200.00
BRTA Brandon Routh/100	125.00	300.00
CLBC Caity Lotz/85	100.00	250.00
CLSL Caity Lotz/115	75.00	200.00
CLWC Caity Lotz/100	75.00	200.00
DPKF Danielle Panabaker/150	100.00	250.00
EDLL Erica Durance/150	50.00	125.00
GGBA Grant Gustin/115	250.00	600.00
JMAS Jes Macallan/125	40.00	100.00
JRB5 Jesse Rath/125	20.00	50.00
JRQD Jesse Rath/150	20.00	50.00
KCBC Katie Cassidy/125	100.00	250.00
KCLL Katie Cassidy/150	50.00	125.00
KMMS Katherine McNamara/160	125.00	300.00
MBKD Melissa Benoist/115	300.00	750.00
NMNN Nicole Maines/130	100.00	200.00
RWAK Robert Wuhl/200	15.00	40.00
SAGA Stephen Amell/100	400.00	1000.00
SAOQ Stephen Amell/115	400.00	1000.00
TCHW Tom Cavanagh/115	125.00	300.00
TCRF Tom Cavanagh/85	100.00	250.00
TWCK Tom Welling/125	300.00	750.00
DPDCS Danielle Panabaker/175	75.00	200.00
EDAZE Erica Durance/125	60.00	150.00

2022 CZX Crisis on Infinite Earths Dual Autographs

COMMON AUTO	300.00	800.00
BRGG B.Routh/G.Gustin/40	400.00	1000.00
CLBR C.Lotz/B.Routh/40	300.00	800.00
CLMB C.Lotz/M.Benoist/40	300.00	800.00
EDTW E.Durance/T.Welling/40	400.00	1000.00
GGMB G.Gustin/M.Benoist/40	1500.00	3000.00
GGSA G.Gustin/S.Amell/20	400.00	1000.00
MBBR M.Benoist/B.Routh/40	1500.00	3000.00
MBSA M.Benoist/S.Amell/20	500.00	1200.00
SABR S.Amell/B.Routh/20	300.00	800.00
SACL S.Amell/C.Lotz/20		
SAKM S.Amell/K.McNamara/40	400.00	1000.00
TWBR T.Welling/B.Routh/40	300.00	800.00

2022 CZX Crisis on Infinite Earths Dual Relics

COMMON MEM	10.00	25.00
B1 M.Benoist/G.Gustin		
DM01 S.Amell/C.Lotz/150	60.00	120.00
DM03 C.Patton/G.Gustin/150	30.00	75.00
DM04 S.Amell/D.Ramsey/250	15.00	40.00
DM05 G.Gustin/M.Benoist/175	50.00	100.00
DM06 Carlos Valdes/75	25.00	60.00
DM07 M.Benoist/C.Leigh/250	60.00	120.00
DM08 G.Gustin/T.Cavanagh/150	30.00	75.00
DM09 M.Benoist/K.McGrath/199	150.00	300.00
DM10 G.Gustin/J.W.Shipp/99	50.00	100.00
DM11 C.Lotz/K.Cassidy/199	30.00	75.00
DM12 G.Gustin/C.Patton/85	20.00	50.00
DM13 B.Routh/C.Lotz/25	175.00	350.00
DM14 T.Hoechlin/M.Benoist/50	200.00	400.00
DM15 M.Benoist/C.Leigh/50	200.00	400.00
DM16 D.Panabaker/C.Valdes/225	20.00	50.00
DM17 M.Benoist/T.Hoechlin/199	60.00	120.00
DM18 Stephen Amell/75	50.00	100.00
DM20 Katie Cassidy/75		

2022 CZX Crisis on Infinite Earths Relics

COMMON MEM (M01-M20)	12.00	30.00
M01 Melissa Benoist/250	60.00	120.00
M02 Grant Gustin/250	15.00	40.00
M04 Grant Gustin/250	15.00	40.00
M05 Katie McGrath/250	75.00	150.00
M06 Stephen Amell/150	20.00	50.00
M08 Chyler Leigh/250	30.00	75.00
M09 Candice Patton/199	20.00	50.00
M10 Caity Lotz/99	50.00	100.00
M11 Melissa Benoist/99	75.00	150.00
M13 Danielle Panabaker/299	15.00	40.00
M14 Chyler Leigh/199	30.00	75.00
M15 Stephen Amell/150	20.00	50.00
M16 Katie McGrath/250	125.00	250.00
M17 Candice Patton/199	15.00	40.00
M18 Tom Cavanagh/299	15.00	40.00
M19 John Wesley Shipp/99	25.00	60.00
M20 Brandon Routh/299	15.00	40.00

2022 CZX Crisis on Infinite Earths STR PWR

COMMON CARD (S01-S20)	3.00	8.00
*SILVER/105: .5X TO 1.2X BASIC CARDS		
*GOLD/55: .6X TO 1.5X BASIC CARDS		
S01 Stephen Amell as Green Arrow	6.00	15.00
S02 Melissa Benoist as Supergirl	12.00	30.00
S03 Grant Gustin as The Flash	6.00	15.00
S05 Brandon Routh as The Atom	4.00	10.00
S06 Ruby Rose as Batwoman	6.00	15.00
S08 Tyler Hoechlin as Superman	8.00	20.00
S10 Katherine McNamara as Mia Smoak	6.00	15.00
S11 Tom Welling as Clark Kent	8.00	20.00
S12 Jon Cryer as Lex Luthor	5.00	12.00
S13 Brandon Routh as Superman	6.00	15.00
S15 Osric Chau as Ryan Choi	4.00	10.00
S16 Chyler Leigh as Alex Danvers	10.00	25.00
S19 John Wesley Shipp as The Flash	5.00	12.00

2022 CZX Crisis on Infinite Earths Triple Relics

COMMON MEM	50.00	100.00
TM01 Amell/Gustin/Benoist/75	400.00	800.00
TM02 Amell/Gustin/Benoist/75	150.00	300.00
TM05 Amell/Ramsey/Cassidy/125	75.00	150.00
TM06 Benoist/Brooks/Leigh/125	60.00	120.00

2022 CZX Crisis on Infinite Earths Promos

PBR Superman NSU	4.00	10.00
PMB Supergirl NSU	3.00	8.00
PGSR Three Flashes NSU	4.00	10.00

2019 CZX Super Heroes and Super-Villains

COMPLETE SET (54)	10.00	25.00
UNOPENED BOX (6 PACKS)	600.00	1000.00
UNOPENED PACK (5 CARDS)	100.00	175.00
COMMON CARD (1-54)	.25	.60
*RED/80: 1X TO 2.5X BASIC CARDS		
*GREEN/30: 6 TO 15X BASIC CARDS		
*SILVER/20: 20X TO 50X BASIC CARDS		

2019 CZX Super Heroes and Super-Villains Autographs

COMMON AUTO 5.00 12.00
STATED OVERALL ODDS 1:6
BAB3 NOT PRICED DUE TO SCARCITY
ATF Antje Traue/210 30.00 75.00
DKV Doutzen Kroes/300 25.00 60.00
AZLL Ayelet Zurer/205 20.00 50.00
BAB1 Ben Affleck/10 1500.00 3000.00
BAB2 Ben Affleck/10 2000.00 4000.00
BAB3 Ben Affleck/10
EMBA Ezra Miller/30 300.00 500.00
EMF1 Ezra Miller/50 300.00 500.00
EMF2 Ezra Miller/30 400.00 600.00
GMKA Graham McTavish/310 12.00 30.00
HCCK Henry Cavill/20 500.00 1000.00
HCS1 Henry Cavill/50 400.00 800.00
HCS2 Henry Cavill/25 600.00 1000.00
HCS3 Henry Cavill/25 600.00 1000.00
JMA1 Jason Momoa/105 200.00 400.00
JMA2 Jason Momoa/55 150.00 300.00
JMAC Jason Momoa/55 150.00 300.00
TMAC Temuera Morrison/210 15.00 40.00
TMAS Temuera Morrison/210 15.00 40.00
TOMG Tao Okamoto/205 8.00 20.00
GGWW1 Gal Gadot/99 1000.00 2000.00
GGWW2 Gal Gadot/25 1500.00 3000.00
GGWW3 Gal Gadot/25 1500.00 3000.00
JDGFF Jack Dylan Grazer/300 8.00 20.00
TOMG2 Tao Okamoto/205 12.00 30.00

2019 CZX Super Heroes and Super-Villains Film Cels

COMMON MEM 2.50 6.00
STATED ODDS 1:6
FC27 IS AN ALBUM EXCLUSIVE
FC7 Wonder Woman 8.00 20.00
FC10 Suicide Squad 20.00 50.00
FC12 Suicide Squad 6.00 15.00
FC15 Batman v Superman: Dawn of Justice4.00 10.00
FC18 Man of Steel 5.00 12.00
FC21 The Dark Knight Rises 5.00 12.00
FC22 The Dark Knight 12.00 30.00
FC25 Batman Begins 8.00 20.00
FC27 Batman Begins ALB 8.00

2019 CZX Super Heroes and Super-Villains STR PWR

COMPLETE SET (24) 75.00 150.00
COMMON CARD (S1-S24) 3.00 8.00
*SILVER/60: .6X TO 1.5X BASIC CARDS
*GOLD/30: 1.2X TO 3X BASIC CARDS
STATED ODDS 1:6
S03 Gal Gadot as Wonder Woman 8.00 20.00
S09 Margot Robbie as Harley Quinn 6.00 15.00
S21 Heath Ledger as The Joker 8.00 20.00

2019 CZX Super Heroes and Super-Villains Promos

COMMON CARD (P1-P6) 1.50 4.00
P1 Wonder Woman WON 12.00 30.00
P2 Superman NSU 2.00 5.00
P3 Batman NSU 3.00 8.00
P5 The Flash SDCC 2.00 5.00

1993 SkyBox DC Bloodlines

COMPLETE SET (81) 5.00 12.00
UNOPENED BOX (36 PACKS) 25.00 40.00
UNOPENED PACK (8 CARDS) 1.00 1.50
COMMON CARD (1-81) .12 .30

1993 SkyBox DC Bloodlines Embossed Foil

COMPLETE SET (5) 12.00 30.00
COMPLETE SET w/o SP (4) 8.00 20.00
COMMON CARD (S1-S5) 3.00 8.00
STATED ODDS 1:18
SP EXCH STATED ODDS 1:72
S5 Superman Redemption SP EXCH 8.00 20.00
NNO The One True Superman 15.00 40.00

1993 SkyBox DC Bloodlines Logo Promos

COMPLETE SET (4) 4.00 10.00
COMMON CARD 1.50 4.00
NNO The Man of Steel! 1.50 4.00
NNO The Man of Tomorrow! 1.50 4.00
NNO The Last Son of Krypton! 1.50 4.00
NNO The Metropolis Kid! 1.50 4.00

1993 SkyBox DC Bloodlines No Logo Promos

COMPLETE SET (4) 4.00 10.00
COMMON CARD 1.50 4.00
NNO The Man of Steel! 1.50 4.00
NNO The Man of Tomorrow! 1.50 4.00
NNO The Last Son of Krypton! 1.50 4.00
NNO The Metropolis Kid! 1.50 4.00

1993 SkyBox DC Bloodlines Promos

COMMON CARD .75 2.00
NNO (Unnumbered, embossed foil 1994)
NNO Which, if any, is the real Man of Steel?

2017 DC Comics Bombshells

COMPLETE SET (64) 8.00 20.00
UNOPENED BOX (24 PACKS+1 FIGURINE)85.00 105.00
UNOPENED PACK (5 CARDS) 4.00 5.00
COMMON CARD .30 .75
*COPPER DECO: .75X TO 2X BASIC CARDS.60 1.50
*RAINBOW FOIL: 2.5X TO 6X BASIC CARDS2.00 5.00

2017 DC Comics Bombshells Characters

COMPLETE SET (9) 6.00 15.00
COMMON CARD (C1-C9) 1.25 3.00
*COPPER DECO: .6X TO 1.5X BASIC CARDS2.00 5.00
*RAINBOW FOIL: .75X TO 2X BASIC CARDS2.50 6.00
STATED ODDS 1:2

2017 DC Comics Bombshells Lil Bombshells

COMPLETE SET (18) 5.00 12.00
COMMON CARD (L1-L18) .60 1.50
*COPPER DECO: .75X TO 2X BASIC CARDS1.25 3.00
*RAINBOW FOIL: 1.5X TO 4X BASIC CARDS2.50 6.00
STATED ODDS 1:2

2017 DC Comics Bombshells Men

COMPLETE SET (3) 4.00 10.00
COMMON CARD (N1-N3) 2.00 5.00
*COPPER DECO: .5X TO 1.2X BASIC CARDS2.50 6.00
*RAINBOW FOIL: .6X TO 1.5X BASIC CARDS3.00 8.00
STATED ODDS 1:8

2017 DC Comics Bombshells Pennant Stickers

COMPLETE SET (4) 12.00 30.00
COMMON CARD (K1-K4) 4.00 10.00
STATED ODDS 1:24

2017 DC Comics Bombshells Sketch Inserts

COMPLETE SET (6) 5.00 12.00
COMMON CARD (V1-V6) 1.00 2.50
*COPPER DECO: .6X TO 1.5X BASIC CARDS1.50 4.00
*RAINBOW FOIL: .75X TO 2X BASIC CARDS2.00 5.00
STATED ODDS 1:3

2017 DC Comics Bombshells STR PWR

COMPLETE SET (12) 100.00 200.00
COMMON CARD (S1-S12) 8.00 20.00
*SILVER: .75X TO 2X BASIC CARDS 15.00 40.00
*GOLD/25: 1.2X TO 3X BASIC CARDS 25.00 60.00
STATED ODDS 1:

2017 DC Comics Bombshells Promos

COMMON CARD
B1 She's Poison! ALB 8.00 20.00
P1 Supergirl Wondercon 4.00 10.00
P2 Mera Industry Summit 6.00 15.00
P3 Stargirl Philly Non-Sports Card Show 5.00 12.00
P4 Catwoman Magazine NSU 2.00 5.00
P5 The Canary Sings All the Hits! SDCC 1.50 4.00
P6 Katana SDCC 5.00 12.00
P7 Magic Conjuring Set/Zantana SDCC 12.00 30.00
P8 Stargirl SDCC 4.00 10.00
P9 Harley Quinn SDCC 5.00 12.00
P10 The Iceberg Lounge/Harley Quinn NSCC10.00 25.00

2018 DC Comics Bombshells II

COMPLETE SET (64) 10.00 25.00
UNOPENED BOX (24 PACKS) 80.00 95.00
UNOPENED PACK (5 CARDS) 3.50 4.00
COMMON CARD (1-64) .30 .75
*GOLD: 1.2X TO 3X BASIC CARDS
*RAINBOW: 2.5X TO 6X BASIC CARDS

2018 DC Comics Bombshells II Batgirls

COMPLETE SET (9) 6.00 15.00
COMMON CARD (G1-G9) 1.25 3.00
*GOLD: .75X TO 2X BASIC CARDS
*RAINBOW: 1X TO 2.5X BASIC CARDS
STATED ODDS 1:3

2018 DC Comics Bombshells II Lil Bombshells Production Sketch Inserts

COMPLETE SET (9) 8.00 20.00
COMMON CARD (A1-A9) 1.50 4.00
*GOLD: .75X TO 2X BASIC CARDS
*RAINBOW: 1X TO 2.5X BASIC CARDS
STATED ODDS 1:3

2018 DC Comics Bombshells II New Bombshells Covers

COMPLETE SET (9) 6.00 15.00
COMMON CARD (C1-C9) 1.25 3.00
*GOLD: .75X TO 2X BASIC CARDS
*RAINBOW: 1X TO 2.5X BASIC CARDS
STATED ODDS 1:3

2018 DC Comics Bombshells II Official Membership Cards

COMPLETE SET (9) 30.00 75.00
COMMON CARD (V1-V9) 6.00 15.00
STATED ODDS 1:28

2018 DC Comics Bombshells II STR PWR

COMPLETE SET (10)
COMMON CARD (ST1-ST10) 6.00 15.00
*SILVER: .5X TO 1.2X BASIC CARDS
*GOLD/25: .6X TO 1.5X BASIC CARDS
STATED ODDS 1:144
ST1 Wonder Woman 12.00 30.00
ST2 Harley Quinn 12.00 30.00
ST3 Batwoman 15.00 40.00
ST5 Batman 10.00 25.00
ST6 The Joker 8.00 20.00
ST8 Batgirl 10.00 25.00
ST9 Eloisa Lane 10.00 25.00
ST10 Catwoman 10.00 25.00

2018 DC Comics Bombshells II Terrific Twosomes

COMPLETE SET (9) 6.00 15.00
COMMON CARD (T1-T9) 1.25 3.00
*GOLD: .75X TO 2X BASIC CARDS
*RAINBOW: 1X TO 2.5X BASIC CARDS
STATED ODDS 1:3

2018 DC Comics Bombshells II Totally Fabricated

COMPLETE SET (3) 30.00 75.00
COMMON MEM 12.00 30.00
STATED PRINT RUN 100 SER.#'d SETS
CONVENTION EXCLUSIVE

2018 DC Comics Bombshells II Promos

COMPLETE SET (4) 10.00 25.00
COMMON CARD (P1-P3) 3.00 8.00
P3 2018 SDCC 5.00 12.00
P4 2018 GTS National Hobby Shop Day 6.00 15.00

2019 DC Comics Bombshells III

COMPLETE SET (64) 8.00 20.00
UNOPENED BOX (24 PACKS) 100.00 150.00
UNOPENED PACK (5 CARDS) 4.00 6.00
COMMON CARD (1-64) .30 .75
*GOLD: .75X TO 2X BASIC CARDS
*RAINBOW: 1.5X TO 4X BASIC CARDS

2019 DC Comics Bombshells III Gotham's Greatest

COMPLETE SET (9) 6.00 15.00
COMMON CARD (GG1-GG9) 1.00 2.50
*GOLD: .6X TO 1.5X BASIC CARDS
*RAINBOW: 1X TO 2.5X BASIC CARDS
STATED ODDS 1:3

2019 DC Comics Bombshells III On the Front Line

COMPLETE SET (9) 6.00 15.00
COMMON CARD (SH1-SH9) 1.00 2.50
*GOLD: .5X TO 1.2X BASIC CARDS
*RAINBOW: .75X TO 2X BASIC CARDS

2019 DC Comics Bombshells III Showstoppers

COMPLETE SET (9) 5.00 12.00
COMMON CARD (SH1-SH9) .75 2.00
*GOLD: .6X TO 1.5X BASIC CARDS
*RAINBOW: 1X TO 2.5X BASIC CARDS
STATED ODDS 1:3

2019 DC Comics Bombshells III STR PWR

COMPLETE SET (10) 50.00 100.00
COMMON CARD (S01-S10) 6.00 15.00
*SILVER: .6X TO 1.5X BASIC CARDS
*GOLD/25: 1.5X TO 4X BASIC CARDS
STATED ODDS 1:144

2019 DC Comics Bombshells III Vintage Photographs

COMPLETE SET (10)
COMMON CARD (V1-V10) 2.50 6.00
*GOLD: X TO X BASIC CARDS
*RAINBOW: X TO X BASIC CARDS
STATED ODDS 1:12

2019 DC Comics Bombshells III Wonder Girls

COMPLETE SET (9) 6.00 15.00
COMMON CARD (WG1-WG9) 1.00 2.50
*GOLD: .5X TO 1.2X BASIC CARDS
*RAINBOW: .75X TO 2X BASIC CARDS
STATED ODDS 1:3

2019 DC Comics Bombshells III Promos

COMPLETE SET (6) 8.00 20.00
COMMON CARD (P1-P6) 1.25 3.00
P1 Batwoman SDCC 2.00 5.00
P2 Batgirl NSCC 5.00 12.00
P3 Poison Ivy NSU 2.00 5.00
P4 Mera NSU 1.50 4.00
P5 Katana NSU 2.00 5.00
P6 Stargirl NYCC 1.25 3.00

2019 DC Comics Bombshells Funko Target Deluxe Collector Box

COMPLETE SET (5) 4.00 10.00
COMMON CARD (UNNUMBERED) 1.25 3.00
*SILVER FOIL: 1.5X TO 4X BASIC CARDS
NNO Batgirl 1.25 3.00
NNO Batwoman 1.25 3.00
NNO Harley Quinn 1.25 3.00
NNO Poison Ivy 1.25 3.00
NNO Wonder Woman 1.25 3.00

2017 Raw Thrills DC Comics Injustice Gods Among Us

COMPLETE SET (100)	120.00	250.00
COMMON CARD (1-100)	.75	2.00
*HOLOFOIL: .6X TO 1.5X BASIC CARDS		
23 Insurgency Harley Quinn	1.50	4.00
29 The Joker	1.25	3.00
30 Wonder Woman	1.50	4.00
32 Batman	1.25	3.00
33 Arkham Origins Batman	2.50	6.00
40 Animated Harley Quinn	1.25	3.00
44 Shazam	5.00	12.00
52 Ares	2.00	5.00
53 Arkham Origins Bane	1.50	4.00
54 Luchador Bane	1.50	4.00
55 Batgirl	2.00	5.00
56 Cassandra Cain Batgirl	8.00	20.00
57 Arkham Knight Batman	8.00	20.00
59 Animated Batman Beyond	1.50	4.00
60 Blackest Night Batman	1.50	4.00
61 Red Son Batman	1.50	4.00
62 Darkseid	2.50	6.00
63 Arkham Origins Deathstroke	1.50	4.00
64 Red Son Deathstroke	1.50	4.00
65 Containment Doomsday	1.50	4.00
68 Red Son Green Lantern	2.50	6.00
69 Red Lantern Hal Jordan	3.00	8.00
70 Arkham Harley Quinn	2.50	6.00
71 Arkham Knight Harley Quinn	1.50	4.00
73 Regime Hawkgirl	1.50	4.00
74 Killer Frost	8.00	20.00
75 Regime Killer Frost	1.25	3.00
77 Martian Manhunter	1.50	4.00
78 Blackest Night Martian Manhunter	8.00	20.00
79 Raven	6.00	15.00
80 Regime Raven	1.25	3.00
81 Reverse Flash	10.00	25.00
83 Mortal Kombat X Scorpion	1.50	4.00
84 Boss Solomon Grundy	2.50	6.00
85 Red Son Solomon Grundy	2.50	6.00
86 Static	1.50	4.00
87 Goodfall Superman	8.00	20.00
89 Prison Superman	2.50	6.00
90 Red Son Superman	1.50	4.00
91 Arkham Knight The Arkham Knight	3.00	8.00
92 Elseworld The Flash	2.50	6.00
93 Metahuman The Flash	4.00	10.00
94 Arkham Origins The Joker	1.50	4.00
95 The Killing Joke The Joker	8.00	20.00
96 600 Wonder Woman	6.00	15.00
97 Justice League Wonder Woman	1.50	4.00
98 Red Son Wonder Woman	1.50	4.00

2019 Raw Thrills DC Comics Injustice Gods Among Us Series 2

COMPLETE SET (110)	30.00	75.00
COMMON CARD (1-110)	.60	1.50
*HOLOFOIL: .75X TO 2X BASIC CARDS		

2021 Raw Thrills DC Comics Injustice Gods Among Us Series 3

COMPLETE SET (120)	75.00	200.00
COMMON CARD (1-120)	1.25	3.00
*HOLOFOIL: .75X TO 2X BASIC CARDS		

2016 DC Comics Justice League

COMPLETE SET (63)	6.00	15.00
UNOPENED BOX (24 PACKS)	60.00	80.00
UNOPENED PACK (5 CARDS)	3.00	4.00
COMMON CARD (1-63)	.20	.50
*SILVER: 2X TO 5X BASIC CARDS		

2016 DC Comics Justice League All-Star Comics

COMPLETE SET (9)	10.00	25.00
COMMON CARD (C1-C9)	1.50	4.00
*SILVER: .75X TO 2X BASIC CARDS		
STATED ODDS 1:3		

2016 DC Comics Justice League Batman Classic TV Series Cryptomium Reissue

COMPLETE SET (9)	60.00	120.00
COMMON CARD (DC71-DC79)	6.00	15.00
STATED ODDS 1:24		

2016 DC Comics Justice League Blank Cover Box-Toppers

COMPLETE SET (9)	25.00	60.00
COMMON CARD (BT1-BT9)	4.00	10.00
STATED ODDS 1:BOX		
BT1 Superman	6.00	15.00
BT2 Batman	6.00	15.00
BT3 Wonder Woman	5.00	12.00
BT4 Green Lantern	5.00	12.00
BT6 The Flash	5.00	12.00

2016 DC Comics Justice League Madame Xanadu Tarot Cards

COMPLETE SET (9)	8.00	20.00
COMMON CARD (X1-X9)	1.25	3.00
*SILVER: 1X TO 2.5X BASIC CARDS		
STATED ODDS 1:3		

2016 DC Comics Justice League Model Sheets

COMPLETE SET (9)	8.00	20.00
COMMON CARD (MS1-MS9)	1.00	2.50
*SILVER: .75X TO 2X BASIC CARDS		
STATED ODDS 1:3		
MS1 Superman	2.00	5.00
MS2 Batman	2.00	5.00
MS3 Wonder Woman	1.50	4.00
MS4 Green Lantern	1.50	4.00
MS5 Aquaman	1.25	3.00
MS6 The Flash	1.50	4.00
MS7 Green Arrow	1.25	3.00

2016 DC Comics Justice League Replica Patches

COMPLETE SET (6)	100.00	200.00
COMMON CARD (E7-E12)	12.00	30.00
STATED ODDS 1:96		
E10 Green Lantern	15.00	40.00
E11 Superman	25.00	60.00
E12 Wonder Woman	20.00	50.00

2016 DC Comics Justice League Retro

COMPLETE SET (6)	10.00	25.00
COMMON CARD (G1-G6)	1.50	4.00
*SILVER: .75X TO 2X BASIC CARDS		
STATED ODDS 1:4		
G1 Superman	2.50	6.00
G2 Batman	2.50	6.00
G3 Wonder Woman	2.00	5.00
G4 Green Lantern	2.00	5.00

2016 DC Comics Justice League Totally Fabricated

COMMON CARD (TF12-TF15)	15.00	40.00
TF15 Green Arrow ALB	25.00	60.00

2016 DC Comics Justice League Promos

P1 Philly Non-Sports Show May 2016	1.50	4.00
DC7P1 NSU Magazine June/July 2016	2.00	5.00
DC7P2 NSU Magazine June/July 2016	2.00	5.00
DC7P3 NSU Magazine June/July 2016	2.00	5.00
DC7P4 NSU Magazine June/July 2016	2.00	5.00
DC7P5 NSU Magazine June/July 2016	2.00	5.00
DC7P6 NSU Magazine June/July 2016	2.00	5.00

2012 DC Comics New 52

COMPLETE SET (61)	6.00	15.00
UNOPENED BOX (24 PACKS)	200.00	300.00
UNOPENED PACK (5 CARDS)	8.00	12.00
COMMON CARD (1-61)	.20	.50
*FOIL: 2.5X TO 6X BASIC CARDS		

2012 DC Comics New 52 Binder Inserts

COMPLETE SET (9)	15.00	30.00
COMMON CARD (B1-B9)	2.50	6.00
ONE SET PER BINDER		

2012 DC Comics New 52 Lanterns

COMPLETE SET (9)	15.00	30.00
COMMON CARD (1-9)	3.00	8.00
STATED ODDS 2:24		

2012 DC Comics New 52 Work in Progress

COMPLETE SET (9)	15.00	30.00
COMMON CARD (WIP1-WIP9)	3.00	8.00
STATED ODDS 2:24		

1982 Nature Made DC Comics Super Heroes

COMPLETE SET (12)	15.00	40.00
COMMON CARD (1-12)	2.00	5.00
1 Superman	4.00	10.00
3 Batman	4.00	10.00
7 Wonder Woman	3.00	8.00
11 The Joker	2.50	6.00

2015 DC Comics Super Villains

COMPLETE SET (63)	8.00	20.00
UNOPENED BOX (24 PACKS)	60.00	100.00
UNOPENED PACK (5 CARDS)	2.50	4.00
COMMON CARD (1-63)	.30	.75
*SILVER: .75X TO 2X BASIC CARDS		
*GOLD/25: 3X TO 8X BASIC CARDS		

2015 DC Comics Super Villains Batman Classic TV Series

COMPLETE SET (9)	12.00	30.00
COMMON CARD (DC61-DC69)	2.50	6.00
STATED ODDS 1:24		

2015 DC Comics Super Villains Crime Syndicate of America

COMPLETE SET (6)	5.00	12.00
COMMON CARD (CS1-CS6)	1.50	4.00
*SILVER: .6X TO 1.5X BASIC CARDS		
*GOLD/25: 1.2X TO 3X BASIC CARDS		
STATED ODDS 1:4		

2015 DC Comics Super Villains Forever Evil

COMPLETE SET (9)	6.00	15.00
COMMON CARD (FE1-FE9)	1.25	3.00
*SILVER: .75X TO 2X BASIC CARDS		
*GOLD/25: 1.5X TO 4X BASIC CARDS		
STATED ODDS 1:4		

2015 DC Comics Super Villains Forever Evil Box-Toppers

COMPLETE SET (9)	20.00	50.00
COMMON CARD (BT1-BT9)	3.00	8.00
STATED ODDS 1:BOX		
BT1 Black Adam #1	6.00	15.00
BT3 Brainiac #1	6.00	15.00
BT4 Deadshot #1	8.00	20.00
BT5 Doomsday #1	5.00	12.00
BT8 Sinestro #1	6.00	15.00

2015 DC Comics Super Villains NOIR

COMPLETE SET (9)	10.00	25.00
COMMON CARD (N1-N9)	2.00	5.00
*SILVER: .6X TO 1.5X BASIC CARDS		
*GOLD/25: 1.2X TO 3X BASIC CARDS		
STATED ODDS 1:4		

2015 DC Comics Super Villains Replica Patches

COMPLETE SET (6)	30.00	80.00
COMMON CARD (E1-E6)	10.00	25.00
STATED ODDS 1:96		
E3 Owlman	12.00	30.00
E4 Power Ring	12.00	30.00

2015 DC Comics Super Villains Sirens

COMPLETE SET (3)	3.00	8.00
COMMON CARD (S1-S3)	2.00	5.00
*SILVER: .6X TO 1.5X BASIC CARDS		
*GOLD/25: 1.5X TO 4X BASIC CARDS		
STATED ODDS 1:8		
S1 Harley Quinn	2.50	6.00

2015 DC Comics Super Villains Totally Fabricated

STATED ODDS 1:192		
TF8 Bane	20.00	50.00
TF9 Lex Luthor	15.00	40.00
TF10 Deathstroke	25.00	60.00
TF11 The Joker ALB		

2013 DC Comics Women of Legend

COMPLETE SET (63)	8.00	20.00
UNOPENED BOX (24 PACKS)	125.00	200.00
UNOPENED PACK (5 CARDS)	6.00	8.00
COMMON CARD (1-63)	.25	.60
*FOIL: 1.2X TO 3X BASIC CARDS		
P1 The Women of Legend PROMO	2.50	6.00

2013 DC Comics Women of Legend Gail's Picks

COMPLETE SET (9)	15.00	30.00
COMMON CARD (GP01-GP09)	2.50	6.00
STATED ODDS 2:24		

2013 DC Comics Women of Legend Katie Cook Stickers

COMPLETE SET (9)	15.00	30.00
COMMON CARD (KC1-KC9)	2.50	6.00
STATED ODDS 1:12		

2013 DC Comics Women of Legend Totally Fabricated

COMMON CARD	20.00	40.00
STATED ODDS 1:175		

1975 Wonder Bread DC Comics

COMPLETE SET (20)	8.00	25.00
COMMON CARD (1-20)	.60	1.50

1992 Impel DC Comics Cosmic

COMPLETE SET (180)	4.00	10.00
COMPLETE FACTORY SET (190)	12.00	30.00
UNOPENED BOX (36 PACKS)	15.00	20.00
UNOPENED PACK (10 CARDS)	.50	.75
COMMON CARD (1-180)	.12	.30

1992 Impel DC Comics Cosmic Holograms

COMPLETE SET (10)	15.00	40.00
COMMON CARD (DCH1-DCH10)	1.50	4.00
STATED ODDS 1:10		
DCH1 Clark Kent and Lois Lane	2.00	5.00
DCH2 Darkseid	3.00	8.00
DCH4 Flash	2.50	6.00
DCH5 Green Lantern	2.50	6.00
DCH7 Lobo	2.50	6.00
DCH8 Superman	5.00	12.00
DCH9 Wonder Woman	4.00	10.00

1993 SkyBox DC Cosmic Teams

COMPLETE SET (150)	8.00	20.00
UNOPENED BOX (36 PACKS)	40.00	60.00
UNOPENED PACK (8 CARDS)	1.50	2.00
COMMON CARD (1-150)	.10	.25

1993 SkyBox DC Cosmic Teams Holograms

COMPLETE SET (6)	10.00	25.00
COMMON CARD (DCH11-DCH16)	2.00	5.00
STATED ODDS 1:12		

1993 SkyBox DC Cosmic Teams Promos

COMMON CARD .75 2.00
0 Deathstroke NYCC 12.00 30.00
NNO Superman MOS Wizard Silver
NNO Superman MOS Wizard Gold

2014 DC Epic Battles

COMPLETE SET (63) 8.00 20.00
UNOPENED BOX (20 PACKS) 200.00 300.00
UNOPENED PACK (5 CARDS) 8.00 12.00
COMMON CARD (1-63) .30 .75
*COPPER: 1.5X TO 4X BASIC CARDS
*GOLD: 2.5X TO 6X BASIC CARDS
*METAL: 4X TO 10X BASIC CARDS

2014 DC Epic Battles Totally Fabricated

COMMON CARD (TF5-TF7) 12.00 30.00
STATED ODDS 1:160
TF7 Harley Quinn 20.00 50.00

2014 DC Epic Battles Bombshells

COMPLETE SET (8) 12.00 30.00
COMMON CARD (B1-B8) 2.50 6.00
STATED ODDS 1:10
B1 Supergirl 3.00 8.00
B2 Wonder Woman 3.00 8.00
B3 Harley Quinn 4.00 10.00
B4 Poison Ivy 3.00 8.00

2014 DC Epic Battles Make Believe

COMPLETE SET (9) 12.00 30.00
COMMON CARD (PB1-PB9) 2.50 6.00
*COPPER: .50X TO 1.2X BASIC CARDS
*GOLD: .75X TO 2X BASIC CARDS
*METAL: 1X to 2.5X BASIC CARDS
STATED ODDS 1:10

2014 DC Epic Battles Promos

COMPLETE SET (2) 3.00 8.00
COMMON CARD (P1-P2) 1.50 4.00
P2 Cryptomium PHILLY 2.50 6.00

1974 Wonder Bread DC Heroes

COMMON DC CHARACTER 10.00 25.00
COMMON WB CHARACTER 3.00 8.00
INSERTED INTO PACKS OF WONDER BREAD
NNO Batman 75.00 150.00
NNO Bugs Bunny 10.00 25.00
NNO Catwoman 25.00 60.00
NNO Clark Kent 12.00 30.00
NNO Cool Cat 6.00 15.00
NNO Daffy Duck 4.00 10.00
NNO Henery Hawk 6.00 15.00
NNO Joker 60.00 120.00
NNO Lois Lane 12.00 30.00
NNO Pepe Le Pew 15.00 40.00
NNO Petunia Pig 4.00 10.00
NNO Riddler 30.00 75.00
NNO Robin 15.00 40.00
NNO Speedy Gonzales 4.00 10.00
NNO Superman 30.00 75.00
NNO Tasmanian Devil
NNO Tweety 5.00 12.00
NNO Wile E. Coyote 4.00 10.00
NNO Wonder Woman 30.00 75.00
NNO Yosemite Sam 6.00 15.00

2007 DC Legacy

COMPLETE SET (50) 4.00 10.00
UNOPENED BOX (24 PACKS) 50.00 75.00
UNOPENED PACK (4 CARDS) 2.50 3.00
COMMON CARD (1-50) .10 .30
*GOLD: 2X TO 5X BASIC CARDS .60 1.50

2007 DC Legacy Autographs

O'NEIL ISSUED AS CASE EXCLUSIVE
KUBERT ISSUED AS ALBUM EXCLUSIVE
PROMOS ARE UNNUMBERED
1 Denny O'Neil CT 10.00 20.00
2 Joe Kubert ALB 15.00 30.00

2007 DC Legacy DC Gallery

COMPLETE SET (9) 10.00 25.00
COMMON CARD (AR1-AR9) 2.00 5.00
STATED ODDS 1:24

2007 DC Legacy First Title Covers

COMPLETE SET (9) 4.00 10.00
COMMON CARD (FC1-FC9) .75 2.00
STATED ODDS 1:12

2007 DC Legacy Legendary Heroes

COMPLETE SET (6) 20.00 50.00
COMMON CARD (L1-L6) 6.00 15.00
STATED ODDS 1:48

2007 DC Legacy Promos

COMPLETE SET (5) 5.00 12.00
COMMON CARD .75 2.00
P3 Wonder Woman ALB 3.00 8.00
CP1 Flash 1.50 4.00

1995 SkyBox DC Legends Power Chrome

COMPLETE SET (150) 15.00 40.00
UNOPENED BOX (36 PACKS) 175.00 300.00
UNOPENED PACK (9 CARDS) 5.00 8.00
COMMON CARD (1-150) .20 .50

1995 SkyBox DC Legends Power Chrome Battlezone

COMPLETE SET (6) 20.00 50.00
COMMON CARD (B1-B6) 4.00 10.00
STATED ODDS 1:12

1995 SkyBox DC Legends Power Chrome Hard Hitters

COMPLETE SET (18) 15.00 40.00
COMMON CARD (H1-H18) 1.00 2.50
STATED ODDS 1:2
H1 Superman 2.00 5.00
H2 Batman 2.00 5.00
H3 Wonder Woman 2.00 5.00
H4 Green Lantern 2.00 5.00
H5 Flash 2.00 5.00
H10 Superman 2.00 5.00
H11 Batman 2.00 5.00
H12 Wonder Woman 2.00 5.00
H13 Green Lantern 2.00 5.00
H14 Flash 2.00 5.00

1995 SkyBox DC Legends Power Chrome Legacy

COMPLETE SET (3) 12.00 30.00
COMMON CARD (L1-L3) 6.00 15.00
STATED ODDS 1:36

1995 SkyBox DC Legends Power Chrome Promos

COMPLETE SET (2) 1.25 3.00
COMMON CARD .75 2.00

1994 SkyBox DC Master Series

COMPLETE SET (90) 6.00 15.00
UNOPENED BOX (36 PACKS) 125.00 200.00
UNOPENED PACK (6 CARDS) 4.00 6.00
COMMON CARD (1-90) .15 .40
SD2 STATED ODDS 1:240
SD2 Superman Skydisc Redemption EXCH 20.00 50.00

1994 SkyBox DC Master Series Double-Sided Spectra

COMPLETE SET (5) 25.00 60.00
COMMON CARD (DS1-DS5) 6.00 15.00
STATED ODDS 1:36

1994 SkyBox DC Master Series Foil

COMPLETE SET (4) 10.00 25.00
COMMON CARD (F1-F4) 3.00 8.00
STATED ODDS 1:18

1993 SkyBox DC Milestone The Dakota Universe

COMPLETE SET (100) 6.00 15.00
UNOPENED BOX (36 PACKS) 25.00 40.00
UNOPENED PACK (8 CARDS) 1.00 1.50
COMMON CARD (1-100) .12 .30

1993 SkyBox DC Milestone The Dakota Universe Embossed

COMPLETE SET (2) 6.00 15.00
COMMON CARD (M1-M2) 3.00 8.00
STATED ODDS 1:36

1996 SkyBox DC Outburst Firepower

COMPLETE SET (80) 5.00 12.00
COMMON CARD (1-80) .15 .40

1996 SkyBox DC Outburst Firepower Holoburst

COMPLETE SET (2) 6.00 15.00
COMMON CARD (1-2) 4.00 10.00
STATED ODDS 1:36

1996 SkyBox DC Outburst Firepower Maximum Firepower

COMPLETE SET (20) 6.00 15.00
COMMON CARD (1-20) .60 1.50
STATED ODDS 2:3

1994 SkyBox DC Stars

COMPLETE SET (45) 6.00 15.00
UNOPENED BOX (36 PACKS) 50.00 75.00
UNOPENED PACK (6 CARDS) 2.00 3.00
COMMON CARD (1-45) .25 .60

1994 SkyBox DC Stars Foil

COMPLETE SET (4) 8.00 20.00
COMMON CARD (F1-F2) 2.00 5.00
STATED ODDS 1:18
F1 Superman 4.00 10.00
F2 Batman 4.00 10.00
F3 Wonder Woman 3.00 8.00

1994 SkyBox DC Stars Puzzle

COMPLETE SET (9) 4.00 10.00
COMMON CARD (P1-P9) 1.00 2.50
STATED ODDS 1:1
P1 Batman 2.00 5.00
P5 Superman 2.00 5.00
P6 Wonder Woman 1.25 3.00

1978 DC Super Heroes Stickers

COMPLETE SET (30) 15.00 40.00
COMMON STICKER (1-30) .40 1.00
*TAYSTEE: SAME VALUE
*SUNBEAM: SAME VALUE
*LANG: .6X TO 1.5X BASIC STICKER
BASE SET HAS NO SPECIFIC LOGO
1 Superman 2.00 5.00
2 The Man of Steel 2.00 5.00
9 Superman and Lois Lane 1.50 4.00
10 Superman and Supergirl 2.00 5.00
11 Wonder Woman 1.50 4.00
12 Batman and Robin 2.00 5.00
13 Batgirl 1.25 3.00
14 The Riddler 1.25 3.00
15 The Joker 1.50 4.00
16 Batman 2.50 6.00
18 The Penquin .75 2.00
22 Aquaman 1.00 2.50
24 Flash 1.25 3.00
25 Green Arrow 1.25 3.00
26 Hawkman .75 2.00
30 Green Lantern 1.25 3.00

1995 Fleer SkyBox DC Versus Marvel

COMPLETE SET (100) 30.00 75.00
UNOPENED BOX (36 PACKS) 300.00 500.00
UNOPENED PACK (8 CARDS) 8.00 15.00
COMMON CARD (1-100) .60 1.50
1 Superman vs. Hulk 5.00 12.00
2 Captain America .75 2.00
11 Spider-Man 2.00 5.00
13 Thor 1.25 3.00
14 Wolverine 2.00 5.00
17 Batman 2.50 6.00
19 Captain Marvel vs. Thor .75 2.00
20 Catwoman .75 2.00
21 Flash 1.00 2.50
22 Green Lantern 1.25 3.00
24 Robin .75 2.00
26 Superman 1.50 4.00
27 Wonder Woman 1.25 3.00
37 Wonder Woman vs. Storm 1.50 4.00
39 Thanos 1.25 3.00
45 The Joker 2.00 5.00
55 Wolverine vs. Lobo 1.50 4.00
58 Deathstroke vs. Punisher .60 1.50
59 Ghost Rider vs. Demon .50 1.25
62 Steel vs. Iron Man 1.00 2.50
65 Venom vs. Lobo 1.50 4.00
67 Thor vs. Wonder Woman 1.25 3.00
69 Captain America vs. Bane 1.25 3.00
70 Batman vs. Bullseye 1.50 4.00
73 Spider-Man vs. Superboy 1.25 3.00
74 Green Lantern vs. Green Goblin 1.25 3.00
77 Doctor Doom vs. Capt. Marvel 1.50 4.00
78 The Joker vs. Spider-Man 3.00 8.00
80 Superman vs. Juggernaut 1.50 4.00
82 Catwoman vs. Elektra 1.25 3.00
91 Captain America vs. Batman 2.00 5.00
92 Darkseid vs. Thanos 1.50 4.00
95 Green Goblin vs. The Joker 1.25 3.00

1995 Fleer SkyBox DC Versus Marvel Holo F/X

COMPLETE SET (12) 60.00 150.00
COMMON CARD (1-12) 3.00 8.00
STATED ODDS 1:8
3 Captain America vs. Batman 25.00 60.00
4 Catwoman vs. Elektra 12.00 30.00
5 Quicksilver vs. Flash 12.00 30.00
6 Superman vs. Hulk 15.00 40.00
8 Robin vs. Jubilee 6.00 15.00
9 Wolverine vs. Lobo 25.00 60.00
10 Captain Marvel vs. Thor 6.00 15.00
11 Spider-Man vs. Superboy 8.00 20.00
12 Wonder Woman vs. Storm 5.00 12.00

1995 Fleer SkyBox DC Versus Marvel Impact

COMPLETE SET (18) 15.00 40.00
COMMON CARD (1-18) 1.25 3.00
STATED ODDS 1:2
1 Thor 2.50 6.00
2 Metamorpho 1.50 4.00
3 Iron Man 2.00 5.00
5 Wonder Woman vs. Black Widow 2.00 5.00
6 Hawkman 1.50 4.00
10 Gambit 3.00 8.00
11 Supergirl 2.00 5.00
12 Beast 3.00 8.00
13 Split 1.50 4.00
17 Impulse 1.50 4.00
18 Wolverine 6.00 15.00

1995 Fleer SkyBox DC Versus Marvel Mirage

COMPLETE SET (2) 200.00 500.00
COMMON CARD (1-2) 125.00 300.00
STATED ODDS 1:360
2 Wolverine 150.00 400.00
Batman#{Dark Claw

1995 Fleer SkyBox DC Versus Marvel Case-Topper Promos

NNO Justice League vs. The Avengers 30.00 75.00

1995 Fleer SkyBox DC Versus Marvel Ballot Promo

NNO The Battles of the Century (unglued)
NNO The Battles of the Century (glued)
(Wizard #53, FAN #7)

1994 SkyBox DC Vertigo

COMPLETE SET (90)	6.00	15.00
UNOPENED BOX (36 PACKS)	40.00	60.00
UNOPENED PACK (6 CARDS)	2.00	2.50
COMMON CARD (1-90)	.12	.30
SD4 Death (SkyDisc)	30.00	80.00

1994 SkyBox DC Vertigo Gold Foil

COMPLETE SET (6)	25.00	60.00
COMMON CARD	5.00	12.00
*SILVER: 1.2X TO 3X BASIC INSERTS		
STATED ODDS 1:18		

1994 SkyBox DC Vertigo Promos

COMPLETE SET (4)	3.00	8.00
COMMON CARD	1.25	3.00

1994 SkyBox DC Vertigo The Sandman

COMPLETE SET (90)	8.00	20.00
UNOPENED BOX (36 PACKS)	40.00	60.00
UNOPENED PACK (6 CARDS)	2.00	2.50
COMMON CARD (1-90)	.15	.40
S1 The Doll's House PROMO	.60	1.50
NNO Morpheus 3-D Stereo Hologram	30.00	75.00

1994 SkyBox DC Vertigo The Sandman Cards Illustrated Promos

COMPLETE SET (9)	6.00	15.00
COMMON CARD (CI1-CI9)	.75	2.00
CARDS ILLUSTRATED MAGAZINE EXCLUSIVE		

1994 SkyBox DC Vertigo The Sandman Endless Galaxy

COMPLETE SET (7)	60.00	120.00
COMMON CARD (1-7)	8.00	20.00
*SILVER: 1X TO 2.5 BASIC CARDS		
STATED ODDS 1:18		

1994 SkyBox DC Vertigo The Sandman Panels

COMMON PANEL	8.00	20.00
13 4-Card Panel		
2-52-10-60		

1995 SkyBox DC Villains Dark Judgment

COMPLETE SET (90)	6.00	15.00
COMMON CARD (1-90)	.15	.40
SM1 STATED ODDS 1:180		
SM1 Two-Face Redemption EXCH	8.00	20.00

1995 SkyBox DC Villains Dark Judgment Gathering of Evil

COMPLETE SET (9)	6.00	15.00
COMMON CARD (GE1-GE9)	1.25	3.00
STATED ODDS 1:7		

1995 SkyBox DC Villains Dark Judgment Villains Attack

COMPLETE SET (3)	8.00	20.00
COMMON CARD (CC1-CC3)	4.00	10.00
STATED ODDS 1:30		

2018 DC's Legends of Tomorrow Seasons 1 and 2

COMPLETE SET (72)	8.00	20.00
UNOPENED BOX (24 PACKS)	75.00	125.00
UNOPENED PACK (5 CARDS)	3.00	6.00
COMMON CARD (1-72)	.25	.60
*SILVER FOIL: 1.5X TO 4X BASIC CARDS	.75	2.00
*RIP HUNTER DECO: 3X TO 8X BASIC CARDS	2.00	5.00

2018 DC's Legends of Tomorrow Seasons 1 and 2 Autographs

COMMON AUTO	6.00	15.00
STATED ODDS 1:24		
AD Arthur Darvill	30.00	75.00
DP Dan Payne	8.00	20.00
EL Elyse Levesque	12.00	30.00
FK Faye Kingslee	6.00	15.00
LM Laura Mennell	8.00	20.00
NM Neal McDonough	12.00	30.00
SC Stephanie Corneliussen	12.00	30.00
SG Sarah Grey	15.00	40.00
AP1 Amy Pemberton	20.00	50.00
AP2 Amy Pemberton	20.00	50.00
BR1 Brandon Routh	50.00	100.00
BR2 Brandon Routh	50.00	100.00
CL1 Caity Lotz	50.00	100.00
CL2 Caity Lotz	50.00	100.00
FD1 Franz Drameh	12.00	30.00
FD2 Franz Drameh	12.00	30.00
ML1 Matt Letscher	15.00	40.00
ML2 Matt Letscher	15.00	40.00
NZ1 Nick Zano	12.00	30.00
NZ2 Nick Zano	12.00	30.00
MRS1 Maisie Richardson-Sellers	50.00	100.00
MRS2 Maisie Richardson-Sellers	50.00	100.00

2018 DC's Legends of Tomorrow Seasons 1 and 2 Characters

COMPLETE SET (9)	6.00	15.00
COMMON CARD (C1-C9)	1.00	2.50
*SILVER FOIL: .5X TO 1.2X BASIC CARDS	1.25	3.00
*RIP HUNTER DECO: .6X TO 1.5X BASIC CARDS	1.50	4.00
STATED ODDS 1:3		

2018 DC's Legends of Tomorrow Seasons 1 and 2 Dual Wardrobe

DM1 W.Miller D.Purcell	30.00	75.00

2018 DC's Legends of Tomorrow Seasons 1 and 2 Icons

COMPLETE SET (9)	6.00	15.00
COMMON CARD (I1-I9)	1.00	2.50
*SILVER FOIL: .5X TO 1.2X BASIC CARDS	1.25	3.00
*RIP HUNTER DECO: .6X TO 1.5X BASIC CARDS	1.50	4.00
STATED ODDS 1:3		

2018 DC's Legends of Tomorrow Seasons 1 and 2 Legendary Objects

COMPLETE SET (9)	8.00	20.00
COMMON CARD (L1-L9)	1.25	3.00
*SILVER FOIL: .5X TO 1.2X BASIC CARDS	1.50	4.00
*RIP HUNTER DECO: .6X TO 1.5X BASIC CARDS	2.00	5.00
STATED ODDS 1:3		

2018 DC's Legends of Tomorrow Seasons 1 and 2 Puzzle

COMPLETE SET (9)	10.00	25.00
COMMON CARD (Z1-Z9)	1.50	4.00
*SILVER FOIL: .5X TO 1.2X BASIC CARDS	2.00	5.00
*RIP HUNTER DECO: .6X TO 1.5X BASIC CARDS	2.50	6.00
STATED ODDS 1:12		

2018 DC's Legends of Tomorrow Seasons 1 and 2 STR PWR

COMPLETE SET (10)	50.00	100.00
COMMON CARD (S1-S10)	6.00	15.00
*RED: .5X TO 1.2X BASIC CARDS	8.00	20.00
*SILVER: .6X TO 1.5X BASIC CARDS	10.00	25.00

2018 DC's Legends of Tomorrow Seasons 1 and 2 Wardrobes

COMMON MEM (M1-M27; B1)	5.00	12.00
STATED ODDS 1:24		
B1 IS AN ALBUM EXCLUSIVE		
M1 Arthur Darvill	6.00	15.00
M2 Caity Lotz	12.00	30.00
M3 Dominic Purcell	8.00	20.00
M4 Wentworth Miller	10.00	25.00
M5 Franz Drameh	6.00	15.00
M7 Maisie Richardson-Sellers	10.00	25.00
M9 Neal McDonough	6.00	15.00
M10 Casper Crump	6.00	15.00
M12 Matt Letscher	6.00	15.00
M13 Falk Hentschel	6.00	15.00
M14 Maisie Richardson-Sellers/99	25.00	60.00
M16 Neal McDonough	6.00	15.00
M17 Brandon Routh/49	30.00	75.00
M18 Franz Drameh/25	125.00	250.00
M19 Caity Lotz/25	150.00	300.00
M20 Matt Letscher/25	100.00	200.00
M21 Ciara Renee/49	60.00	120.00
M22 Victor Garber/25	60.00	120.00
M23 Arthur Darvill/49	100.00	200.00
M24 Casper Crump/49	50.00	100.00
M25 Dan Payne/25	60.00	120.00
M26 Maisie Richardson-Sellers/25	125.00	250.00
M27 Falk Hentschel/49	75.00	150.00
B1 Caity Lotz ALB	25.00	60.00

2018 DC's Legends of Tomorrow Seasons 1 and 2 Promos

COMMON CARD (P1-P3)	3.00	8.00
P2 Coming Soon ACE	15.00	40.00

2016 The Flash Season 1

COMPLETE SET (72)	8.00	20.00
UNOPENED BOX (24 PACKS)	60.00	75.00
UNOPENED PACK (5 CARDS)	3.50	4.00
COMMON CARD (1-72)	.20	.50
*FOIL: 1.2X TO 3X BASIC CARDS	.60	1.50
*GOLD LOGO: 5X TO 12X BASIC CARDS	2.50	6.00

2016 The Flash Season 1 Autographs

COMMON AUTO	6.00	15.00
STATED ODDS 1:24		
AP Amanda Pays	12.00	30.00
AM1 Andy Mientus	10.00	25.00
AM2 Andy Mientus	10.00	25.00
AC1 Anthony Carrigan	10.00	25.00
AC2 Anthony Carrigan	10.00	25.00
CR1 Chad Rook	12.00	30.00
CR2 Chad Rook	12.00	30.00
DP Danielle Panabaker	75.00	150.00
DG1 Devon Graye	12.00	30.00
DG2 Devon Graye	12.00	30.00
DJ1 Doug Jones	8.00	20.00
DJ2 Doug Jones	12.00	30.00
EK Emily Kinney	12.00	30.00
JLM Jesse L. Martin	25.00	60.00
KF1 Kelly Frye	12.00	30.00
KF2 Kelly Frye	12.00	30.00
LM Liam McIntyre	10.00	25.00
LW Logan Williams	10.00	25.00
MJ Malese Jow	20.00	50.00
PL1 Peyton List	75.00	150.00
PL2 Peyton List	75.00	150.00
RK Robert Knepper	25.00	60.00
TC2 Tom Cavanagh	75.00	150.00
VG Victor Garber	12.00	30.00
WM1 Wentworth Miller	30.00	75.00
WM2 Wentworth Miller	30.00	75.00

2016 The Flash Season 1 Character Bios

COMPLETE SET (7)	6.00	15.00
COMMON CARD (CB1-CB7)	1.25	3.00
*FOIL: .6X TO 1.5X BASIC CARDS	2.00	5.00
*GOLD LOGO: .75X TO 2X BASIC CARDS	2.50	6.00
STATED ODDS 1:4		

2016 The Flash Season 1 Dual Wardrobes

COMMON CARD (DM1-DM7)	10.00	25.00
STATED ODDS 1:96		
DM2 G.Gustin/J.W.Shipp	15.00	40.00
DM3 D.Panabaker#/C.Valdes	15.00	40.00
DM6 G.Gustin/T.Cavanagh	125.00	250.00
DM7 Victor Garber	12.00	30.00

2016 The Flash Season 1 Locations

COMPLETE SET (9)	6.00	15.00
COMMON CARD (L1-L9)	1.00	2.50
*FOIL: .6X TO 1.5X BASIC CARDS	2.00	5.00
*GOLD LOGO: .75X TO 2X BASIC CARDS	2.50	6.00
STATED ODDS 1:3		

2016 The Flash Season 1 Memorabilia

COMMON CARD (M1-M30)	5.00	12.00
STATED ODDS 1:24		
M1 Grant Gustin	8.00	20.00
M2 Candice Patton	6.00	15.00
M3 Danielle Panabaker	10.00	25.00
M6 Rick Cosnett	6.00	15.00
M7 Tom Cavanagh	8.00	20.00
M8 Victor Garber	6.00	15.00
M9 Patrick Sabongui	6.00	15.00
M11 Grant Gustin	8.00	20.00
M12 Danielle Panabaker	10.00	25.00
M17 Tom Cavanagh	8.00	20.00
M18 Grant Gustin	8.00	20.00
M20 Candice Patton	6.00	15.00
M22 Patrick Sabongui	6.00	15.00
M23 Grant Gustin	20.00	50.00
M24 Rick Cosnett	12.00	30.00
M25 CC Jitters Coffee Cup	15.00	40.00
M26 Fire and Ice Painting	12.00	30.00
M27 Missing Dr. Martin Stein Flyer	10.00	25.00
M28 Picture News	10.00	25.00
M30 Address Label ALB	10.00	25.00

2016 The Flash Season 1 Rogues

COMPLETE SET (9)	8.00	20.00
COMMON CARD (G1-G9)	1.25	3.00
*FOIL: .6X TO 1.5X BASIC CARDS	2.00	5.00
*GOLD LOGO: .75X TO 2X BASIC CARDS	2.50	6.00
STATED ODDS 1:3		

2017 The Flash Season 2

COMPLETE SET (72)	6.00	15.00
UNOPENED BOX (24 PACKS)	80.00	100.00
UNOPENED PACK (5 CARDS)	3.50	4.50
COMMON CARD (1-72)	.20	.50
*RAINBOW FOIL: 1.2X TO 3X BASIC CARDS	.60	1.50
*SCARLET SPEEDSTER: 5X TO 12X BASIC CARDS	2.50	6.00

2017 The Flash Season 2 Autographs

COMMON AUTO	6.00	15.00
STATED ODDS 1:24		
GUSTIN AUTOS UNPRICED DUE TO SCARCITY		
CC Casper Crump	12.00	30.00
KC Katie Cassidy	75.00	150.00
LW Logan Williams	15.00	40.00
NM Neal McDonough	15.00	40.00
SV Shantel VanSanten	50.00	100.00
VB Violett Beane	15.00	40.00
VG Victor Garber	10.00	25.00
AC1 Adam Copeland	15.00	40.00
AC2 Adam Copeland	20.00	50.00
AP1 Allison Paige	20.00	50.00
AP2 Allison Paige	30.00	75.00
APY Amanda Pays	10.00	25.00
EBR Emily Bett Rickards	125.00	250.00
LM1 Liam McIntyre	10.00	25.00
LM2 Liam McIntyre	10.00	25.00
MJ1 Malese Jow	12.00	30.00
MJ2 Malese Jow	12.00	30.00
PL1 Peyton List	75.00	150.00
PL2 Peyton List	75.00	150.00
TS1 Teddy Sears	30.00	75.00
TS2 Teddy Sears	30.00	75.00
TS3 Teddy Sears	60.00	120.00
TS4 Teddy Sears	25.00	60.00
WM1 Wentworth Miller	30.00	75.00
WM2 Wentworth Miller	30.00	75.00
JWS1 John Wesley Shipp	25.00	60.00
JWS2 John Wesley Shipp	15.00	40.00

2017 The Flash Season 2 Dual Wardrobes

COMMON CARD (DM1-DM6) 10.00 25.00
STATED OVERALL ODDS 1:24
DM1 Malese Jow/Candice Patton 12.00 30.00
DM3 Tom Cavanagh/Grant Gustin 12.00 30.00
DM5 Grant Gustin/Shantel VanSanten 12.00 30.00
DM6 John Wesley Shipp/25

2017 The Flash Season 2 Locations

COMPLETE SET (9) 8.00 20.00
COMMON CARD (L1-L9) 1.25 3.00
*RAINBOW FOIL: .6X TO 1.5X BASIC CARDS2.00 5.00
*SCARLET SPEEDSTER: .75X TO
2X BASIC CARDS 2.50 6.00
STATED ODDS 1:3

2017 The Flash Season 2 Metas

COMPLETE SET (9) 6.00 15.00
COMMON CARD (MT1-MT9) 1.00 2.50
*RAINBOW FOIL: .6X TO 1.5X BASIC CARDS1.50 4.00
*SCARLET SPEEDSTER: .75X TO
2X BASIC CARDS 2.00 5.00
STATED ODDS 1:3

2017 The Flash Season 2 Quotable Cisco

COMPLETE SET (9) 6.00 15.00
COMMON CARD (Q1-Q9) 1.00 2.50
*RAINBOW FOIL: .6X TO 1.5X BASIC CARDS1.50 4.00
*SCARLET SPEEDSTER: .75X TO
2X BASIC CARDS 2.00 5.00
STATED ODDS 1:3

2017 The Flash Season 2 STR PWR Character Bios

COMPLETE SET (13) 80.00 150.00
COMMON CARD (CB1-CB13) 6.00 15.00
*RAINBOW FOIL: .5X TO 1.2X BASIC CARDS8.00 20.00
*RED: .6X TO 1.5X BASIC CARDS 10.00 25.00
*SILVER: .75X TO 2X BASIC CARDS 12.00 30.00
*GOLD/25: 1X TO 2.5X BASIC CARDS 15.00 40.00
BLACK/1: UNPRICED DUE TO SCARCITY
RANDOMLY INSERTED INTO PACKS

2017 The Flash Season 2 Triple Wardrobe

STATED PRINT RUN 25 SER.#'d SETS
TM1 Grant Gustin/Jay Garrick 120.00 250.00

2017 The Flash Season 2 Wardrobes

COMMON CARD (M1-M33; B1) 6.00 15.00
STATED ODDS 1:24
B1 IS AN ALBUM EXCLUSIVE
M1 Grant Gustin 8.00 20.00
M2 Carlos Valdes 8.00 20.00
M3 Danielle Panabaker 10.00 25.00
M6 Violett Beane 10.00 25.00
M8 Teddy Sears 8.00 20.00
M10 Malese Jow/99 15.00 40.00
M11 Candice Patton/99 15.00 40.00
M12 Grant Gustin/99 25.00 60.00
M14 Greg Finley 8.00 20.00
M15 Shantel VanSanten 12.00 30.00
M18 Keiynan Lonsdale/99 15.00 40.00
M19 Tom Cavanagh/25 100.00 200.00
M20 Katie Cassidy/25 120.00 250.00
M22 Violett Beane 10.00 25.00
M23 Candice Patton/99 20.00 50.00
M24 Carlos Valdes 8.00 20.00
M25 Picture News 10.00 25.00
M26 Drawing of Vandal Savage/25 100.00 200.00
M27 Flash Day Flyer/65 30.00 80.00
M28 Bart Allen Mail/25 75.00 150.00
M29 Mr. Jiggle Wiggle/99 25.00 60.00
M30 Picture News 10.00 25.00
M31 Picture News 10.00 25.00
M32 Trickster's Drawing/75 20.00 50.00
M33 Picture News 8.00 20.00
B1 Wentworth Miller ALB 10.00 25.00

2017 The Flash Season 2 Promos

COMMON CARD
P1 NSU Magazine 3.00 8.00
P2 WonderCon/Fan Expo 5.00 12.00
P3 Industry Summit 10.00 25.00
P4 Philly Non-Sport Card Show 8.00 20.00

2016-17 Funko DC Legion of Collectors Patches

COMMON PATCH 2.00 5.00
DC LEGION OF COLLECTORS EXCLUSIVE
NNO Green Arrow 2.50 6.00
NNO Joker 3.00 8.00
NNO Superman 2.50 6.00
NNO Wonder Woman 3.00 8.00
NNO Wonder Woman (logo) 3.00 8.00

2016 Gotham Season One

COMPLETE SET (72) 6.00 15.00
UNOPENED BOX (24 PACKS) 80.00 100.00
UNOPENED PACK (5 CARDS) 4.00 5.00
COMMON CARD (1-72) .15 .40
*SILVER: 1.2X TO 3X BASIC CARDS .50 1.25

2016 Gotham Season One Autographs

COMMON AUTO 6.00 15.00
STATED ODDS 1:24
AC Anthony Carrigan 12.00 30.00
CB Camren Bicondova GE 125.00 250.00
CF Clare Foley 12.00 30.00
CK Carol Kane 15.00 40.00
DM David Mazouz 75.00 150.00
ER Erin Richards 50.00 100.00
MV Milo Ventimiglia 15.00 40.00
ND Nicholas D'Agosto 15.00 40.00
NT Nicholle Tom 12.00 30.00
SP Sean Pertwee 20.00 50.00
CMO Cameron Monaghan 50.00 100.00
CMS Cory Michael Smith 25.00 60.00
LAB Lesley-Ann Brandt 12.00 30.00
RLT Robin Lord Taylor 75.00 150.00
TS2 Todd Stashwick 10.00 25.00

2016 Gotham Season One Character Bios

COMPLETE SET (15) 6.00 15.00
COMMON CARD (C1-C15) .75 2.00
*SILVER: .75X TO 2X BASIC CARDS 1.50 4.00
STATED ODDS 1:2

2016 Gotham Season One Dual Wardrobes

COMMON CARD (DM1-DM9) 8.00 20.00
STATED ODDS 1:96
DM2 David Zayas 15.00 40.00
DM3 Zabryna Guevara 20.00 50.00
DM4 John Doman 15.00 40.00
DM7 Mazouz/Bicondova 15.00 40.00
DM8 McKenzie/Baccarin 25.00 60.00
DM9 Robin Lord Taylor 15.00 40.00

2016 Gotham Season One Quotes

COMPLETE SET (9) 6.00 15.00
COMMON CARD (Q1-Q9) 1.00 2.50
*SILVER: .6X TO 1.5X BASIC CARDS 1.50 4.00
STATED ODDS 1:3

2016 Gotham Season One Triple Wardrobes

COMMON CARD (TM1-TM3) 12.00 30.00
STATED ODDS 1:192
TM1 Bicondova/Doman/McKenzie 20.00 50.00
TM2 Camren Bicondova 20.00 50.00

2016 Gotham Season One Villains

COMPLETE SET (4) 3.00 8.00
COMMON CARD (V1-V4) 1.00 2.50
*SILVER: .6X TO 1.5X BASIC CARDS 1.50 4.00
STATED ODDS 1:6

2016 Gotham Season One Wardrobes

COMMON CARD (M1-M30) 8.00 20.00
STATED ODDS 1:24
M1 Ben McKenzie 30.00 80.00
M4 Erin Richards 12.00 30.00
M5 David Zayas 25.00 60.00
M6 Ben McKenzie 25.00 60.00
M9 Camren Bicondova 30.00 80.00
M12 Ben McKenzie 15.00 40.00
M13 Cory Michael Smith 10.00 25.00
M15 Camren Bicondova 12.00 30.00
M16 David Mazouz 15.00 40.00
M17 Robin Lord Taylor 10.00 25.00
M20 Morena Baccarin 15.00 40.00
M23 Jada Pinkett Smith 10.00 25.00
M24 Camren Bicondova 15.00 40.00
M25 Ben McKenzie 15.00 40.00
M27 Erin Richards 12.00 30.00
M30 Jada Pinkett Smith ALB 10.00 25.00

2016 Gotham Season One Promos Metal

*METAL: X TO X BASIC CARDS
P1 Philly NonÂSports Card Show, MAY 201615.00 40.00
P2 NSU Magazine, AUG/SEP 2016 12.00 30.00
P3 San Diego Comic Con, JUL 2016 30.00 75.00

2017 Gotham Season Two

COMPLETE SET (72) 6.00 15.00
UNOPENED BOX (24 PACKS) 65.00 80.00
UNOPENED PACK (5 CARDS) 3.00 4.00
COMMON CARD (1-72) .20 .50
*SILVER: 1X TO 2.5X BASIC CARDS .50 1.25
*PENGUIN DECO: 2X TO 5X BASIC CARDS1.00 2.50

2017 Gotham Season Two Autographs

COMMON AUTO 6.00 15.00
STATED ODDS 1:24
AC Anthony Carrigan 25.00 60.00
CB Camren Bicondova 100.00 200.00
CF Clare Foley 15.00 40.00
CK Carol Kane 12.00 30.00
DM David Mazouz 60.00 120.00
ER Erin Richards 50.00 100.00
JL Jessica Lucas 125.00 250.00
SP Sean Pertwee 15.00 40.00
TS Todd Stashwick 8.00 20.00
CMO Cameron Monaghan 30.00 75.00
CMS Cory Michael Smith 30.00 75.00
JF1 James Frain 20.00 50.00
JF2 James Frain 20.00 50.00
MV1 Michelle Veintimilla 12.00 30.00
MV2 Michelle Veintimilla 12.00 30.00
NAL Natalie Alyn Lind 60.00 120.00
ND1 Nathan Darrow 10.00 25.00
ND2 Nathan Darrow 10.00 25.00
RLT Robin Lord Taylor 50.00 100.00
BDW1 B.D. Wong 15.00 40.00
BDW2 B.D. Wong 15.00 40.00

2017 Gotham Season Two Bad and Beautiful

COMPLETE SET (6) 6.00 15.00
COMMON CARD (MX1-MX6) 1.50 4.00
*SILVER: .6X TO 1.5X BASIC CARDS
*PENGUIN DECO: .75X TO 2X BASIC CARDS
STATED ODDS 1:4

2017 Gotham Season Two Dual Autographs

COMMON CARD 60.00 120.00
STATED PRINT RUN 10 SER.#'d SETS
LF1 J.Frain/J.Lucas 125.00 250.00
LF2 J.Frain/J.Lucas 125.00 250.00
JFNL J.Frain/N.Lind 200.00 400.00
NDMV N.Darrow/M.Veintimilla 150.00 300.00
NLJL N.Lind/J.Lucas 200.00 400.00

2017 Gotham Season Two Dual Wardrobes

COMMON CARD (DM1-DM8) 8.00 20.00
STATED ODDS 1:96
DM1 Ben McKenzie 30.00 75.00
DM4 C.Bicondova/M.Veintimilla 12.00 30.00
DM6 C.Bicondova/D.Mazouz 15.00 40.00
DM7 Camren Bicondova 30.00 75.00

2017 Gotham Season Two New Day Dark Knights

COMPLETE SET (7) 6.00 15.00
COMMON CARD (ND1-ND7) 1.50 4.00
*SILVER: .6X TO 1.5X BASIC CARDS
*PENGUIN DECO: .75X TO 2X BASIC CARDS
STATED ODDS 1:4

2017 Gotham Season Two Rising Villains

COMPLETE SET (9) 8.00 20.00
COMMON CARD (V1-V9) 1.25 3.00
*SILVER: .6X TO 1.5X BASIC CARDS
*PENGUIN DECO: .75X TO 2X BASIC CARDS
STATED ODDS 1:3

2017 Gotham Season Two STR PWR Character Bios

COMPLETE SET (15) 100.00 200.00
COMMON CARD (CB1-CB15) 6.00 15.00
*SILVER: .5X TO 1.2X BASIC CARDS
*GOLD/25: .75X TO 2X BASIC CARDS
STATED ODDS 1:144

2017 Gotham Season Two The Maniax

COMPLETE SET (6) 6.00 15.00
COMMON CARD (MX1-MX6) 1.50 4.00
*SILVER: .6X TO 1.5X BASIC CARDS
*PENGUIN DECO: .75X TO 2X BASIC CARDS
STATED ODDS 1:4

2017 Gotham Season Two Triple Autographs

STATED PRINT RUN 3 SER.#'d SETS
UNPRICED DUE TO SCARCITY
FYB Fisher/Ybarra/Brill
LFL Lucas/Frain/Lind

2017 Gotham Season Two Triple Wardrobes

STATED ODDS 1:288
TM1 Smith/McKenzie/Baccarin 25.00 60.00
TM2 Bicondova/Mazouz 20.00 50.00

2017 Gotham Season Two Promos

P1 Non-Sport Update (April/May, 2017) 6.00 15.00
P2 Non-Sport Update (April/May, 2017) 6.00 15.00
P3 Non-Sport Update (April/May, 2017) 4.00 10.00
P4 Non-Sport Update (April/May, 2017) 8.00 20.00

2017 Gotham Season Two Wardrobes

COMMON CARD (M1-M26; B1) 4.00 10.00
STATED ODDS 1:24
B1 ALBUM EXCLUSIVE
M1 Ben McKenzie 20.00 50.00
M2 David Mazouz 8.00 15.00
M3 Donal Logue 20.00 50.00
M4 Cory Michael Smith 6.00 15.00
M5 Morena Baccarin 30.00 75.00
M6 Robin Lord Taylor 8.00 20.00
M7 Camren Bicondova 20.00 50.00
M8 Natalie Alyn Lind 75.00 150.00
M9 Erin Richards 15.00 40.00
M11 Robin Lord Taylor 5.00 12.00
M12 Cory Michael Smith 5.00 12.00
M13 Ben McKenzie 10.00 25.00
M15 Robin Lord Taylor 12.00 30.00
M16 Cory Michael Smith 6.00 15.00
M17 Camren Bicondova 12.00 30.00
M18 Erin Richards 25.00 60.00
M19 David Mazouz 6.00 15.00
M20 Cory Michael Smith 15.00 40.00
M22 Ben McKenzie 5.00 12.00
M23 Robin Lord Taylor 6.00 15.00
M26 Erin Richards 8.00 20.00
B1 Ben McKenzie 10.00 25.00

2022 Hro DC Unlock the Multiverse Chapter 1

COMMON CARD 4.00 10.00
NNO Amanda Waller as seen in Justice League vs. Suicide Squad #2 (2016) S 8.00 20.00
NNO Aquaman L 50.00 125.00
NNO Aquaman S 8.00 20.00
NNO Aquaman U 5.00 12.00
NNO Aquaman vs. Black Manta E 6.00 15.00
NNO Bane Breaks Batman : Batman #497 (1993) U 5.00 12.00
NNO Barry Allen / The Flash S 8.00 20.00
NNO Batman & Catwoman E 6.00 15.00
NNO Batman & Catwoman S 8.00 20.00
NNO Batman & Robin E 6.00 15.00
NNO Batman (Inks) S 8.00 20.00
NNO Batman (Pencils) S 8.00 20.00
NNO Batman L 60.00 150.00
NNO Batman M 2500.00 6000.00
NNO Batman of Earth-32 E 6.00 15.00
NNO Batman U 5.00 12.00
NNO Batman vs. The Joker E 6.00 15.00
NNO Batmobile U 5.00 12.00
NNO Bruce Wayne / Batman S 8.00 20.00
NNO Clark Kent / Superman S 8.00 20.00
NNO Crime Syndicate of America E 6.00 15.00
NNO Cyborg U 5.00 12.00
NNO Cyborg Upgrades : Justice League #33 (2017) U 5.00 12.00
NNO Darkseid Defeats Zeus : Wonder Woman #37 (2017) U 5.00 12.00
NNO Darkseid L 30.00 75.00
NNO Darkseid S 8.00 20.00
NNO David Singh as seen in The Flash #33 (2014) S 8.00 20.00
NNO Death of Superman : Superman #75 (1992) U 5.00 12.00
NNO Detective Comics #1000 (2019) Variant Cover S 8.00 20.00
NNO Earth's Mightiest Mortal - Shazam! U 5.00 12.00
NNO Green Lantern & Black Lanterns S 8.00 20.00
NNO Green Lantern Corps E 6.00 15.00
NNO Hal Jordan / Green Lantern S 8.00 20.00
NNO Half Man Half Machine - Cyborg U 5.00 12.00
NNO Harley Quinn L 25.00 60.00
NNO Helmet of Fate as seen in Justice Society of America #30 (2009) U 5.00 12.00
NNO In brightest day, in blackest night, no evil shall escape my sight - Green Lantern Corps U 5.00 12.00
NNO Iris West as seen in The Flash #8 (2012) S 8.00 20.00
NNO John Constantine S 8.00 20.00
NNO John Stewart Kills Mogo : Green Lantern Corps #60 (2011) U 5.00 12.00
NNO Justice League E 6.00 15.00
NNO Justice League of America U 5.00 12.00
NNO King of the Seven Seas - Aquaman U 5.00 12.00
NNO Lasso of Truth U 5.00 12.00
NNO Lex Luthor L 25.00 60.00
NNO Mera & Aquaman Embrace : Aquaman #48 (2016) U 5.00 12.00
NNO Mongul Is Briefed By His Ring : Green Lantern Corps #20 (2008) U 5.00 12.00
NNO Mother Box as seen in Justice League #41 (2015) U 5.00 12.00
NNO Owlman E 6.00 15.00
NNO Page 2 of Batman #1 (1940) - Panel 1 E 6.00 15.00
NNO Page 2 of Batman #1 (1940) - Panel 2 E 6.00 15.00
NNO Page 2 of Batman #1 (1940) - Panel 3 E 6.00 15.00
NNO Page 2 of Batman #1 (1940) - Panel 4 E 6.00 15.00
NNO Page 2 of Batman #1 (1940) - Panel 5 E 6.00 15.00
NNO Page 2 of Batman #1 (1940) - Panel 6 E 6.00 15.00
NNO Page 2 of Batman #1 (1940) - Panel 7 E 6.00 15.00
NNO Page 2 of Batman #1 (1940) - Panel 8 E 6.00 15.00
NNO Page 2 of Batman #1 (1940) - Panel 9 E 6.00 15.00
NNO Power Ring U 5.00 12.00
NNO Reverse-Flash vs. The Flash E 6.00 15.00
NNO Shazam U 5.00 12.00
NNO Sinestro Corps Attacks Earth : Green Lantern #24 (2007) U 5.00 12.00
NNO Sinestro vs. Green Lantern E 6.00 15.00
NNO Stephen Shin as seen in Aquaman #15 (2012) S 8.00 20.00
NNO Superman (Inks) S 8.00 20.00
NNO Superman (Pencils) S 8.00 20.00
NNO Superman L 30.00 75.00
NNO Superman of Earth-3 E 6.00 15.00
NNO Superman U 5.00 12.00
NNO Superman vs. Lex Luthor E 6.00 15.00
NNO Teen Titans E 6.00 15.00
NNO The Cheetah vs. Wonder Woman E 6.00 15.00
NNO The Flash (Inks) S 8.00 20.00
NNO The Flash (Pencils) S 8.00 20.00
NNO The Flash U 5.00 12.00
NNO The Green Lantern U 5.00 12.00
NNO The Joker L 40.00 100.00
NNO The Joker M 1200.00 3000.00
NNO The Joker S 8.00 20.00
NNO The Last Son of Krypton - Superman U 5.00 12.00
NNO White Lantern Transformation : Blackest Night #8 (2010) U 5.00 12.00
NNO Wonder Woman (Flashpoint) E 6.00 15.00
NNO Wonder Woman (Inks) S 8.00 20.00
NNO Wonder Woman (Pencils) S 8.00 20.00
NNO Wonder Woman L 40.00 100.00
NNO Wonder Woman M 1500.00 4000.00
NNO Wonder Woman U 5.00 12.00

2022 Hro DC Unlock the Multiverse Chapter 1 The Batman A Cruel Riddle

COMMON CARD 10.00 25.00
STATED PRINT RUN 16,668 SER.#'d SETS
LOW PRINT RUNS MAY SELL AT A PREMIUM

2022 Hro DC Unlock the Multiverse Chapter 1 The Batman Case Files

COMMON CARD 10.00 25.00
STATED PRINT RUN 72,351 SER.#'d SETS
LOW PRINT RUNS MAY SELL AT A PREMIUM
NNO Cowl U 12.00 30.00
NNO Hero U 12.00 30.00
NNO Shadows U 12.00 30.00
NNO Vengeance U 12.00 30.00
NNO Vigilante U 12.00 30.00

2022 Hro DC Unlock the Multiverse Chapter 1 The Batman Fear Is a Tool

COMMON CARD 6.00 15.00
STATED PRINT RUN 23,720 SER.#'d SETS
LOW PRINT RUNS MAY SELL AT A PREMIUM
NNO Batman strikes again! HOLO E 25.00 60.00
NNO The Caped Crusader HOLO E 15.00 40.00
NNO I'm here HOLO E 12.00 30.00

2022 Hro DC Unlock the Multiverse Chapter 1 The Batman From Gotham City

COMMON CARD
STATED PRINT RUN 56,273 SER.#'d SETS
LOW PRINT RUNS MAY SELL AT A PREMIUM

2022 Hro DC Unlock the Multiverse Chapter 1 The Batman Movie Posters

COMMON CARD 10.00 25.00
STATED PRINT RUN 102,398 SER.#'d SETS
LOW PRINT RUNS MAY SELL AT A PREMIUM

2022 Hro DC Unlock the Multiverse Chapter 1 The Batman Stills

COMMON CARD 5.00 12.00
STATED PRINT RUN 105,512 SER.#'d SETS
LOW PRINT RUNS MAY SELL AT A PREMIUM

2003 Justice League

COMPLETE SET (81) 6.00 15.00
UNOPENED BOX (36 PACKS) 50.00 60.00
UNOPENED PACK (7 CARDS) 1.75 2.00
COMMON CARD (1-81) .15 .40
NNO World's Greatest Heroes Uncut Sheet 30.00 80.00
AWCL The Justice League Case-Loader 12.00 30.00

2003 Justice League ActionWorks Lenticular

COMPLETE SET (7) 12.00 30.00
COMMON CARD (AW1-AW7) 2.00 5.00
STATED ODDS 1:17
AW1 Superman 3.00 8.00
AW2 Batman 3.00 8.00
AW3 Wonder Woman 2.50 6.00

2003 Justice League Autographs

A1 Bruce Timm, Producer and Designer 12.00 30.00
AR1 Redemption Card

2003 Justice League Friends and Foes Foil

COMPLETE SET (18) 3.00 8.00
COMMON CARD (FF1-FF18) .20 .50
STATED ODDS 1:1

2003 Justice League World's Greatest Heroes

COMPLETE SET (9) 6.00 15.00
COMMON CARD (WGS1-WGS9) .75 2.00
STATED ODDS 1:11

2009 Justice League of America Archives

COMPLETE SET (72) 5.00 12.00
UNOPENED BOX (24 PACKS) 60.00 100.00
UNOPENED PACK (5 CARDS) 2.50 4.00
COMMON CARD (1-72) .15 .40
ANDERSON AUTO INSERTED ONE PER CASE
MA Murphy Anderson AU 15.00 30.00
P1 Justice League PROMO .75 2.00

2009 Justice League of America Archives Founding Members

COMPLETE SET (7) 15.00 40.00
COMMON CARD (FM1-FM7) 3.00 8.00
STATED ODDS 1:24

2009 Justice League of America Archives Other Earths

COMPLETE SET (6) 4.00 10.00
COMMON CARD (OE1-OE6) 1.25 3.00
STATED ODDS 1:12

2009 Justice League of America Archives Super Friends

COMPLETE SET (18) 12.50 30.00
COMMON CARD (SF1-SF18) 1.00 2.50
STATED ODDS 1:8

2004 Justice League of America Post Cereal

COMPLETE SET (7) 8.00 20.00
COMMON CARD (1-7) .75 2.00
1 Batman 4.00 10.00
2 The Flash 1.50 4.00
3 Green Lantern 1.50 4.00
6 Superman 4.00 10.00
7 Wonder Woman 2.50 6.00

1969 Fleer Justice League of America Tattoos

COMMON CARD (1-28) 4.00 10.00
3 Batman Full Body 6.00 15.00
4 Batman Torso-Up Punching 6.00 15.00
5 Batman Chest-Up Punching 6.00 15.00
6 Batman Chest-Up Punching THUP 6.00 15.00
7 Batman Chest-Up Punching to Side 6.00 15.00
8 Batman Near-Full Body 6.00 15.00

1997 DC Comics New Year's Evil Promos

COMPLETE SET (8) 3.00 8.00
COMMON CARD (1-8) .60 1.50

1991 DC Comics Robin II The Joker's Wild Hologram Promos

COMPLETE SET (4) 10.00 25.00
COMMON CARD 3.00 8.00
2 Batman 5.00 12.00
3 Joker 5.00 12.00

1984 Topps Supergirl

COMPLETE SET (44) 4.00 10.00
UNOPENED BOX (36 PACKS) 40.00 75.00
UNOPENED PACK (6 CARDS) 2.00 3.00
COMMON STICKER (1-44) .15 .40

1984 Nabisco Supergirl DC Super Heroes Cookies Singles

COMPLETE SET (15) 15.00 40.00
COMMON CARD (1-15) 2.00 5.00

2018 Supergirl Season 1

COMPLETE SET (72) 10.00 25.00
UNOPENED BOX (24 PACKS) 100.00 125.00
UNOPENED PACK (5 CARDS) 5.00 6.00
COMMON CARD (1-72) .30 .75
*RAINBOW: 1.5X TO 4X BASIC CARDS 1.25 3.00
*RED FOIL: 3X TO 8X BASIC CARDS 2.50 6.00

2018 Supergirl Season 1 Artifacts

COMPLETE SET (9) 5.00 12.00
COMMON CARD (A1-A9) .75 2.00
*RAINBOW: 1X TO 2.5X BASIC CARDS 2.00 5.00
*RED FOIL: 1.2X TO 3X BASIC CARDS 2.50 6.00
STATED ODDS 1:3

2018 Supergirl Season 1 Autographs

COMMON AUTO 6.00 15.00
STATED ODDS 1:24
BV Briana Venskus 8.00 20.00
CL Chyler Leigh 60.00 120.00
DC Dean Cain 10.00 25.00
EC Emma Caulfield 10.00 25.00
ET Eve Torres 8.00 20.00
HS Helen Slater 12.00 30.00
JJ Jeremy Jordan 12.00 30.00
MB Mehcad Brooks 8.00 20.00
MW Malina Weissman 12.00 30.00
BM1 Brit Morgan 15.00 40.00
BM2 Brit Morgan 20.00 50.00
CB1 Chris Browning 8.00 20.00
CB2 Chris Browning 12.00 30.00
DH1 David Harewood 25.00 60.00
DH2 David Harewood 30.00 75.00
HL1 Hope Lauren 10.00 25.00
HL2 Hope Lauren 15.00 40.00
IG1 Iddo Goldberg 8.00 20.00
IG2 Iddo Goldberg 10.00 25.00
IR1 Italia Ricci 20.00 50.00
IR2 Italia Ricci 30.00 75.00
JB1 Jeff Branson 10.00 25.00
JB2 Jeff Branson 10.00 25.00
MB1 Melissa Benoist 300.00 500.00
MB2 Melissa Benoist 400.00 650.00
MB3 Melissa Benoist 350.00 600.00

2018 Supergirl Season 1 Cat Quotes

COMPLETE SET (18) 60.00 120.00
COMMON CARD (CQ1-CQ9) 3.00 8.00
COMMON CARD (CQ10-CQ18) 4.00 10.00
CQ1-CQ9 STATED ODDS 1:18
CQ10-CQ18 STATED ODDS

2018 Supergirl Season 1 Character Bios

COMPLETE SET (9) 6.00 15.00
COMMON CARD (L1-L9) 1.00 2.50
*RAINBOW: .75X TO 2X BASIC CARDS 2.00 5.00
*RED FOIL: 1.25X TO 3X BASIC CARDS 3.00 8.00
STATED ODDS 1:3

2018 Supergirl Season 1 Dual Wardrobes

COMMON MEM 10.00 25.00

STATED ODDS 1:120

DM1 Melissa Benoist	20.00	50.00
DM2 Melissa Benoist	20.00	50.00
DM4 Melissa Benoist/99	75.00	150.00
DM5 Henry Czerny/99	30.00	75.00
DM7 Jenna Dewan Tatum/99	25.00	60.00
DM8 Melissa Benoist/25	500.00	800.00

2018 Supergirl Season 1 Locations

COMPLETE SET (9)	6.00	15.00
COMMON CARD (L1-L9)	1.00	2.50
*RAINBOW: .6X TO 1.5X BASIC CARDS	1.50	4.00
*RED FOIL: 1X TO 2.5X BASIC CARDS	2.50	6.00
STATED ODDS 1:3		

2018 Supergirl Season 1 Props

COMMON PROP	20.00	50.00
STATED OVERALL ODDS 1:24		
PR2 National City Tribune Newspaper/99	60.00	120.00
PR3 TOYCON Vinyl Banner/49	75.00	150.00
PR4 Noonan's Coffee/99	75.00	150.00
PR5 Lord Technologies VIP Super Rail Pass	120.00	250.00

2018 Supergirl Season 1 STR PWR

COMPLETE SET (10)	75.00	150.00
COMMON CARD (S1-S10)	6.00	15.00
*SILVER: .6X TO 1.5X BASIC CARDS		
STATED ODDS 1:144		
S1 Supergirl	10.00	25.00
S2 Kara Danvers	10.00	25.00
S3 Kara Zor-El	10.00	25.00
S5 Alex Danvers	8.00	20.00
S6 Winn Schott	8.00	20.00
S8 Cat Grant	12.00	30.00
S9 Astra	10.00	25.00
S10 Maxwell Lord	8.00	20.00

2018 Supergirl Season 1 Supergirl Key Art

COMPLETE SET (9)	15.00	40.00
COMMON CARD (Z1-Z9)	3.00	8.00
STATED ODDS 1:18		

2018 Supergirl Season 1 Wardrobes

COMMON MEM	6.00	15.00
STATED OVERALL ODDS 1:24		
M1 Melissa Benoist	30.00	75.00
M3 Chyler Leigh	12.00	30.00
M4 Jeremy Jordan	10.00	25.00
M5 David Harewood/49	75.00	150.00
M6 Calista Flockhart	10.00	25.00
M7 Melissa Benoist	20.00	50.00
M8 Helen Slater	10.00	25.00
M9 Italia Ricci	8.00	20.00
M10 Levi Miller/99	10.00	25.00
M11 Melissa Benoist	20.00	50.00
M12 Jenna Dewan Tatum	15.00	40.00
M13 Calista Flockhart	10.00	25.00
M14 Iddo Goldberg/49	60.00	120.00
M15 Melissa Benoist	20.00	50.00
M17 Laura Vandervoort/49	100.00	200.00
M19 Calista Flockhart	8.00	20.00
M20 Jeff Branson/25	120.00	250.00
M22 Chyler Leigh	12.00	30.00
M24 Melissa Benoist	50.00	100.00
M25 Italia Ricci	10.00	25.00
M26 Melissa Benoist/99	50.00	100.00
M27 Calista Flockhart	8.00	20.00
M28 Laura Benanti/99	25.00	60.00
M30 Helen Slater	12.00	30.00
M31 Melissa Benoist	20.00	50.00
M32 Calista Flockhart	8.00	20.00
M33 Chyler Leigh	15.00	40.00
M34 Italia Ricci/49	120.00	250.00
M35 Jenna Dewan Tatum	8.00	20.00
M36 Jeremy Jordan	8.00	20.00
B1 Melissa Benoist ALB	20.00	50.00

2018 Supergirl Season 1 Promos

COMPLETE SET (3)	8.00	20.00
COMMON CARD (P1-P3)	2.50	6.00
P1 2017 Philly Non-Sports Show	3.00	8.00
P2 2017 Philly Non-Sports Show	3.00	8.00
P3 2017 Philly Non-Sports Show	4.00	10.00

Superman

2013 DC Comics Superman The Legend

COMPLETE SET (62)	6.00	15.00
UNOPENED BOX (24 PACKS)	75.00	125.00
UNOPENED PACK (5 CARDS)	4.00	6.00
COMMON CARD (1-62)	.15	.40

2013 DC Comics Superman The Legend Alternate Worlds

COMPLETE SET (9)	8.00	20.00
COMMON CARD (ARS1-ARS9)	1.50	4.00
OVERALL CHASE ODDS 4:24		

2013 DC Comics Superman The Legend Secret Origin

COMPLETE SET (6)	6.00	15.00
COMMON CARD (SO1-SO6)	1.50	4.00
OVERALL CHASE ODDS 4:24		

2013 DC Comics Superman The Legend Women of Superman

COMPLETE SET (9)	8.00	20.00
COMMON CARD (WOS1-WOS9)	1.50	4.00
OVERALL CHASE ODDS 4:24		

2013 DC Comics Superman The Legend X-Ray Vision

COMPLETE SET (9)	8.00	20.00
COMMON CARD (XR1-XR9)	1.50	4.00
OVERALL CHASE ODDS 4:24		

1992 SkyBox Doomsday The Death of Superman

COMPLETE SET (100)	8.00	20.00
UNOPENED BOX (36 PACKS)	60.00	100.00
UNOPENED PACK (8 CARDS)	2.00	3.00
COMMON CARD (1-100)	.25	.60

1992 SkyBox Doomsday The Death of Superman A Memorial Tribute

COMPLETE SET (4)	25.00	60.00
COMMON CARD (1-4)	8.00	20.00

1992 SkyBox Doomsday The Death of Superman Bloody S Puzzle

COMPLETE SET (2)	15.00	40.00
COMMON CARD (F1-F2)	10.00	25.00
STATED ODDS 1:36		

1992 SkyBox Doomsday The Death of Superman Promos

COMPLETE SET (3)	3.00	8.00
COMMON CARD	.75	2.00
00 Here Lies Earth's Greatest Hero	3.00	8.00

1995 SkyBox Lois and Clark

COMPLETE SET (90)	5.00	12.00
UNOPENED BOX (36 PACKS)	20.00	30.00
UNOPENED PACK (8 CARDS+1 TATTOO)	.75	1.00
COMMON CARD (1-90)	.10	.25
NNO Lapel Pin Box Topper		

1995 SkyBox Lois and Clark Diffuser Chip Foil

COMPLETE SET (9)	25.00	60.00
COMMON CARD (LC1-LC9)	3.00	8.00
STATED ODDS 1:7		

1995 SkyBox Lois and Clark Holochip Painted Foil

COMPLETE SET (6)	10.00	25.00
COMMON CARD (BJ1-BJ6)	2.50	6.00
STATED ODDS 1:15		

1995 SkyBox Lois and Clark Tattoos

COMPLETE SET (6)	1.50	4.00
COMMON CARD	.30	.75
INCLUDED WITH BASE SET		

1995 SkyBox Lois and Clark Promos

COMPLETE SET (3)	2.50	6.00
COMMON CARD (LC1-LC2; NSU1)	1.25	3.00

1993 SkyBox Return of Superman

COMPLETE SET (100)	10.00	25.00
UNOPENED BOX (36 PACKS)	15.00	20.00
UNOPENED PACK (8 CARDS)	.75	1.00
COMMON CARD (1-100)	.20	.50
P0 Coming August 25 PROMO	.75	2.00
S5 Foil Redemption Card	2.00	5.00
NNO The One True Superman	2.00	5.00

1993 SkyBox Return of Superman Foil SP

COMPLETE SET (4)	20.00	50.00
COMMON CARD (SP1-SP4)	6.00	15.00
STATED ODDS 1:36		

2002 Smallville Season One Previews

COMPLETE SET (9)	7.50	20.00
COMMON CARD (PR1-PR9)	1.25	3.00
*SDCC: .60X TO 1.5X BASIC CARDS		
STATED PRINT RUN 2500 SETS		

2002 Smallville Season One

COMPLETE SET (90)	5.00	12.00
UNOPENED BOX (36 PACKS)	150.00	250.00
UNOPENED PACK (7 CARDS)	5.00	8.00
COMMON CARD (1-90)	.10	.25

2002 Smallville Season One Autographs

COMMON AUTO (A1-A6)	6.00	15.00
STATED ODDS 1:59		
A1 John Schneider	30.00	75.00
A2 Allison Mack	75.00	150.00
A3 Eric Johnson	10.00	25.00
A4 Kelly Brook	15.00	40.00
A6 Joe Morton	10.00	25.00

2002 Smallville Season One Box-Loaders

COMPLETE SET (3)	7.50	20.00
COMMON CARD (BL1-BL3)	1.25	3.00
B6CL Reign of Blood	6.00	15.00
CASE INSERT		

2002 Smallville Season One Pieceworks

COMPLETE SET (4)	50.00	100.00
COMMON CARD (PW1-PW4)	10.00	25.00
STATED ODDS 1:59		
PW1 Tom Welling	15.00	40.00
PW2 Kristin Kreuk	15.00	40.00

2002 Smallville Season One Smallville High

COMPLETE SET (9)	12.50	30.00
COMMON CARD (SH1-SH9)	1.50	4.00
STATED ODDS 1:11		

2002 Smallville Season One Spring Formal

COMPLETE SET (6)	7.50	20.00
COMMON CARD (LBB1-LBB6)	1.50	4.00
STATED ODDS 1:17		

2002 Smallville Season One Promos

COMPLETE SET (6)	6.00	15.00
COMMON CARD	1.25	3.00

2003 Smallville Season Two

COMPLETE SET (90)	5.00	12.00
UNOPENED BOX (36 PACKS)	75.00	125.00
UNOPENED PACK (7 CARDS)	3.00	4.00
COMMON CARD (1-90)	.10	.25

2003 Smallville Season Two Autographs

COMMON AUTO (A7-A16)	8.00	20.00
STATED ODDS 1:36		
A7 Annette O'Toole	15.00	40.00
A8 Sam Jones III	10.00	25.00
A11 John Glover	12.00	30.00
A12 Emmanuelle Vaugier	10.00	25.00

2003 Smallville Season Two Box-Loaders

COMPLETE SET (3)	7.50	20.00
COMMON CARD (BL1-BL3)	1.00	2.50
CL1 ISSUED AS CASE TOPPER		
CL1 The Mark Of Jor-El CT	6.00	15.00

2003 Smallville Season Two Pieceworks

COMPLETE SET (8)	60.00	120.00
COMMON CARD (PW1-PW8)	8.00	20.00
STATED ODDS 1:36		
PW1 Tom Welling	12.00	30.00
PW2 Kristin Kreuk	12.00	30.00
PW3 Allison Mack	12.00	30.00
PW6 John Schneider	10.00	25.00
PW8 Michael Rosenbaum	10.00	25.00

2003 Smallville Season Two The Day Is Coming

COMPLETE SET (9)	12.50	30.00
COMMON CARD (1-9)	1.50	4.00
STATED ODDS 1:11		

2003 Smallville Season Two Till Death Do Us Part

COMPLETE SET (6)	7.50	20.00
COMMON CARD (DP1-DP6)	1.50	4.00
STATED ODDS 1:17		

2003 Smallville Season Two Promos

COMPLETE SET (5)	3.00	8.00
COMMON CARD	.75	2.00

2004 Smallville Season Three

COMPLETE SET (90)	5.00	12.00
UNOPENED BOX (36 PACKS)	50.00	75.00
UNOPENED PACK (7 CARDS)	2.00	3.00
COMMON CARD (1-90)	.10	.25

2004 Smallville Season Three Autographs

COMMON AUTO (A17-A25)	6.00	15.00
STATED ODDS 1:36		
A18 Michael McKean	12.00	30.00
A23 Neil Flynn	6.00	15.00
A24 Adrianne Palicki	30.00	75.00

2004 Smallville Season Three Box-Loaders

COMPLETE SET (3)	5.00	12.00
COMMON CARD (BL1-BL3)	2.00	5.00
STATED ODDS 1:BOX		
CL1 The Last Son of Krypton	4.00	10.00
CASE INSERT		

2004 Smallville Season Three Departures

COMPLETE SET (6)	8.00	20.00
COMMON CARD (1-6)	1.50	4.00
STATED ODDS 1:17		

2004 Smallville Season Three Generations

COMPLETE SET (9)	10.00	25.00
COMMON CARD (1-9)	1.25	3.00
STATED ODDS 1:11		

2004 Smallville Season Three Pieceworks

COMMON CARD (PW1-PW7)	8.00	20.00
STATED ODDS 1:36		
PW1 Tom Welling Shirt	12.00	30.00
PW2 Kristin Kreuk Sweater	12.00	30.00
PW3 Allison Mack Dress	12.00	30.00
PWR1 Redemption Card		

2004 Smallville Season Three Promos

COMPLETE SET (5)	4.00	10.00
COMMON CARD	1.00	2.50
SM3i Clark Kent	2.00	5.00

2005 Smallville Season Four

COMPLETE SET (90)	4.00	10.00
UNOPENED BOX (36 PACKS)	75.00	125.00
UNOPENED PACK (7 CARDS)	2.50	4.00
COMMON CARD (1-90)	.10	.25

2005 Smallville Season Four Autographs

COMMON AUTO (A26-A34)	6.00	15.00
STATED ODDS 1:36		
A26 Michael Rosenbaum	25.00	60.00
A27 Erica Durance	30.00	75.00
A28 Margot Kidder	20.00	50.00
A29 Sarah Carter	10.00	25.00
A30 Peyton List	15.00	40.00

2005 Smallville Season Four Box-Loaders

COMPLETE SET (3)	5.00	12.00
COMMON CARD (BL1-BL3)	2.00	5.00
BL STATED ODDS 1:BOX		
CL STATED ODDS 1:CASE		
CL1 Nemesis	4.00	10.00
CASE INSERT		

2005 Smallville Season Four Lois and Clark

COMPLETE SET (9)	8.00	20.00
COMMON CARD (1-9)	1.25	3.00
STATED ODDS 1:11		

2005 Smallville Season Four Pieceworks

COMMON CARD (PW1-PW7)	8.00	20.00
STATED ODDS 1:36		
PW1A Michael Rosenbaum AU	75.00	150.00
PW2 Tom Welling	12.00	30.00
PW3 Kristin Kreuk	12.00	30.00
PW4 Erica Durance	12.00	30.00
PW5 Jensen Ackles	10.00	25.00

2005 Smallville Season Four Switchcraft

COMPLETE SET (6)	10.00	25.00
COMMON CARD (1-6)	2.00	5.00
STATED ODDS 1:17		

2005 Smallville Season Four Promos

COMPLETE SET (3)	3.00	8.00
COMMON CARD	1.25	3.00
SM4i Clark & Lois	2.00	5.00

2006 Smallville Season Five

COMPLETE SET (90)	5.00	12.00
UNOPENED BOX (36 PACKS)	60.00	100.00
UNOPENED PACK (7 CARDS)	2.00	2.25
COMMON CARD (1-90)	.10	.25

2006 Smallville Season Five Autographs

COMMON AUTO (A35-A45)	6.00	15.00
STATED ODDS 1:36		
A35 James Marsters	20.00	50.00
A36 Tom Wopat	20.00	50.00
A38 Lee Thompson Young	10.00	25.00

2006 Smallville Season Five Box-Loaders

COMPLETE SET (3)	8.00	20.00
COMMON CARD (BL1-BL3)	2.00	5.00
STATED ODDS 1:BOX		
CL1 ISSUED AS CASE TOPPER		
CL1 Banished CT	4.00	10.00

2006 Smallville Season Five Pieceworks

COMMON CARD (PW1-PW10)	10.00	25.00
STATED ODDS 1:36		
PW11A/B ISSUED AS MULTI-CASE INCENTIVE		
PW1 Tom Welling	12.00	30.00
PW3 Kristin Kreuk	12.00	30.00
PW4 Allison Mack	12.00	30.00
PW5 Erica Durance	12.00	30.00
PW11A Tom Wopat MCI	30.00	60.00
PW11B John Schneider MCI	30.00	60.00

2006 Smallville Season Five Price of Life

COMPLETE SET (6)	8.00	20.00
COMMON CARD (1-6)	1.50	4.00
STATED ODDS 1:17		

2006 Smallville Season Five Triangles

COMPLETE SET (9)	8.00	20.00
COMMON CARD (1-9)	1.25	3.00
STATED ODDS 1:11		

2006 Smallville Season Five Promos

COMPLETE SET (4)	3.00	8.00
COMMON CARD	1.25	3.00

2007 Smallville Season Six

COMPLETE SET (90)	5.00	12.00
UNOPENED BOX (36 PACKS)		
UNOPENED PACK (7 CARDS)		
COMMON CARD (1-90)	.10	.25
CL1 ISSUED AS CASE TOPPER		
CL1 Wrath of Zod CT	8.00	20.00

2007 Smallville Season Six Archer's Quest

COMPLETE SET (3)	10.00	25.00
COMMON CARD (AQ1-AQ3)	4.00	10.00
STATED ODDS 1:35		

2007 Smallville Season Six Autographs

COMMON AUTO (A46-A54)	6.00	15.00
STATED ODDS 1:36		
A46 Justin Hartley	15.00	40.00
A47 Aaron Ashmore	10.00	25.00
A49 Tori Spelling	12.00	30.00
AJA Justin Hartley	50.00	100.00
Kyle Gallner		
AJB Alan Ritchson	50.00	100.00
Lee Thompson Young		

2007 Smallville Season Six Justice

COMPLETE SET (9)	5.00	12.00
COMMON CARD (J1-J9)	1.50	4.00
STATED ODDS 1:11		

2007 Smallville Season Six Pieceworks

COMMON CARD (PW1-PW11)	8.00	20.00
STATED ODDS 1:36		
PW1 Tom Welling	12.00	30.00
PW2 Kristin Kreuk	12.00	30.00
PW3 Michael Rosenbaum	10.00	25.00
PW4 Allison Mack	12.00	30.00
PW5 Erica Durance	20.00	40.00
PW6 Justin Hartley	12.00	30.00
PW9 Lynda Carter	12.00	30.00

2007 Smallville Season Six The Powers That Be

COMPLETE SET (6)	10.00	25.00
COMMON CARD (PB1-PB6)	2.50	6.00
STATED ODDS 1:17		

2007 Smallville Season Six Promos

COMPLETE SET (3)	2.50	6.00
COMMON CARD	1.25	3.00
SM6P Clark, Lois, & Oliver	1.50	4.00

2012 Smallville Seasons Seven Through Ten

COMPLETE SET (85)	5.00	12.00
UNOPENED BOX (24 PACKS)	60.00	100.00
UNOPENED PACK (5 CARDS)	2.50	4.00
COMMON CARD (1-85)	.12	.30

2012 Smallville Seasons Seven Through Ten Wardrobes

COMMON CARD (M1-M30)	8.00	20.00
STATED ODDS 1:8		
M1 Clark's jacket	12.00	30.00
M2 Clark's t-shirt	12.00	30.00
M3 Clark's t-shirt	12.00	30.00
M4 Clark's jacket	12.00	30.00
M5 Clark's jacket	15.00	40.00
M6 Clark's t-shirt	10.00	25.00
M7 Clark's shirt	10.00	25.00
M11 Jimmy's shirt	10.00	25.00
M12 Lois' top	15.00	40.00
M13 Lois' top	15.00	40.00
M14 Chloe's dress	15.00	40.00
M15 Chloe's shirt	20.00	50.00
M16 Kara's hoodie	30.00	60.00
M20 Tess' tank	25.00	50.00
M21 Tess' tank	25.00	50.00
M22 Tess' pants	15.00	40.00
M23 Tess' blouse	15.00	40.00
M26 Linda's dress	12.00	30.00
M27 Curtis' apron	10.00	25.00
M30 Clark's t-shirt	10.00	25.00

2012 Smallville Seasons Seven Through Ten Autographs

COMMON AUTO (A1-A14)	12.00	30.00
STATED ODDS 1:24		
A1 Cassidy Freeman	30.00	60.00
A2 Justin Hartley	15.00	40.00
A4 John Glover	20.00	50.00
A6 Aaron Ashmore	15.00	40.00
A7 Eric Johnson	15.00	40.00
A8 Laura Vandervoort	250.00	500.00
A9 Margot Kidder	25.00	60.00
A12 John Schneider	30.00	75.00
A13 James Marsters	20.00	50.00
A14 Terence Stamp	25.00	60.00

2012 Smallville Seasons Seven Through Ten Behind-the-Scenes

COMPLETE SET (9)	8.00	20.00
COMMON CARD (BTS1-BTS9)	1.50	4.00
RANDOMLY INSERTED INTO PACKS		

2012 Smallville Seasons Seven Through Ten Clark and Lois

COMPLETE SET (9)	12.00	30.00
COMMON CARD (LC1-LC9)	2.00	5.00
RANDOMLY INSERTED INTO PACKS		

2012 Smallville Seasons Seven Through Ten Promos

P1 Clark Kent black jacket NSU	.75	2.00
P2 Clark Kent red jacket C2E2	3.00	8.00
P3 Lois Lane/Clark Kent PHILLY	3.00	8.00

1940 Gum Inc. Superman

COMPLETE SET (72)	2500.00	6000.00
COMMON CARD (2-48)	15.00	40.00
COMMON CARD (49-71)	40.00	100.00
1 Superman	300.00	800.00
72 Superman vs. Torpedo	75.00	150.00

1966 Topps Superman

COMPLETE SET (66)	125.00	250.00
UNOPENED BOX (24 PACKS)		
UNOPENED PACK		
COMMON CARD (1-66)	1.25	3.00

1966 Topps Superman Test Series

COMPLETE SET (44)	2050.00	4100.00
COMMON CARD (1-44)	30.00	75.00

1996 Fleer SkyBox Superman Action Packs

COMPLETE SET (46)	6.00	15.00
UNOPENED BOX (48 PACKS)	30.00	50.00
UNOPENED PACK (7 CARDS)	1.00	1.50
COMMON CARD	.25	.60
STATED ODDS 2:1		

1978 Drake's Cakes Superman The Movie

COMPLETE SET (24)	50.00	100.00
COMMON CARD (1-24)	2.50	6.00
STATED ODDS 1:1 PACKAGE		

1996 Fleer SkyBox Superman Holo Series Promos

NNO 6-Card Panel (11, 35, 7, 38, 4, 29)
NNO 6-Card Panel (37, 47, 43, 10, 41, 44)
NNO Silver Hologram
(Superman busting through brick wall)
NNO Silver Hologram
(Superman busting through brick wall)/Checklist Back

1966 Topps Superman in the Jungle

COMPLETE SET (66)	4100.00	8200.00
COMMON CARD (1-66)	50.00	100.00

1968 A&BC Superman in the Jungle

COMPLETE SET (66)	150.00	300.00
COMMON CARD (1-66)	1.50	4.00

1994 SkyBox Superman Man of Steel Platinum Series Collector's Edition

COMPLETE SET (90)	5.00	12.00
UNOPENED BOX (36 PACKS)	40.00	75.00
UNOPENED PACK (6 CARDS)	2.00	3.00
COMMON CARD (1-90)	.10	.25
SC1 Superman Fighting Robot PROMO	.75	2.00

1994 SkyBox Superman Man of Steel Platinum Series Collector's Edition Spectra-Etch

COMPLETE SET (6)	15.00	40.00
COMMON CARD (S1-S6)	3.00	8.00
STATED ODDS 1:7		

1994 SkyBox Superman Man of Steel Platinum Series Premium Edition

COMPLETE SET (90)	15.00	40.00
UNOPENED BOX (36 PACKS)		
UNOPENED PACK (6 CARDS)		
COMMON CARD (1-90)	.30	.75
SD3 STATED ODDS 1:240		
SD3 The Man of Steel SkyDisc	50.00	100.00

1994 SkyBox Superman Man of Steel Platinum Series Premium Edition Forged-in-Gold

COMPLETE SET (4)	80.00	150.00
COMMON CARD (FG1-FG4)	20.00	50.00
RANDOMLY INSERTED INTO PACKS		
HOBBY EXCLUSIVE		

1994 SkyBox Superman Man of Steel Platinum Series Premium Edition Forged-in-Steel

COMPLETE SET (4)	30.00	80.00
COMMON CARD (FS1-FS4)	10.00	25.00
STATED ODDS 1:18		
WAL-MART/SAM'S CLUB EXCLUSIVE		

1994 SkyBox Superman Man of Steel Platinum Series Premium Edition Promos

FS1 Brought to His Knees	12.00	30.00
FS2 Three Men of Steel	12.00	30.00
FS3 Showdown with Doomsday	12.00	30.00
FS4 The Man of Tomorrow	12.00	30.00
SP1 Metallic	1.25	3.00
SW1 Wal-Mart excl.	20.00	50.00
NNO1 2-UP Panel	1.25	3.00
Superman Planting Flag#(NSU		

NNO2 2-UP Panel 1.25 3.00
Superman on Moon
NNO3 2-UP Panel 1.25 3.00
Doomsday/Darkseid

1978 Topps Superman The Movie

COMPLETE SET (165) 12.00 30.00
UNOPENED BOX (36 PACKS) 150.00 250.00
UNOPENED PACK (10 CARDS+1 STICKER) 4.00 6.00
COMMON CARD (1-165) .15 .40

1978 Topps Superman The Movie Blue-Border Stickers

COMPLETE SET (12) 1.50 4.00
COMMON CARD .20 .50

1978 Topps Superman The Movie Foil Stickers

COMPLETE SET (16) 3.00 8.00
COMMON STICKER .30 .75

1978 O-Pee-Chee Superman The Movie

COMPLETE SET (77) 8.00 20.00
UNOPENED BOX (36 PACKS)
UNOPENED PACK (10 CARDS+1 STICKER)
COMMON CARD (1-77) .15 .40

1978 O-Pee-Chee Superman The Movie Blue-Border Stickers

COMPLETE SET (6) .80 2.00
COMMON CARD (1-6) .25 .60
STATED ODDS 1:1

1978 O-Pee-Chee Superman The Movie Foil Stickers

COMPLETE SET (6) .80 2.00
COMMON CARD (1-6) .25 .60
STATED ODDS 1:1

1978 Weston Bakeries Superman The Movie

COMPLETE SET (9) 12.00 30.00
COMMON CARD (1-9) 2.00 5.00

1940 Leader Novelty Superman R146

COMPLETE SET (36) 1200.00 2500.00
COMMON CARD (1-24) 20.00 50.00
COMMON CARD (25-36) 30.00 80.00
*COMPLETE BOXES: 1.5X TO 4X BASIC CARDS

1984 WTW Productions Superman Reprints Thick Stock

COMPLETE SET (72) 8.00 20.00
COMMON CARD (1-72) .25 .60

1984 WTW Productions Superman Reprints Thin Stock

COMPLETE SET (72) 6.00 15.00
COMMON CARD .20 .50

2006 Superman Returns

COMPLETE SET (90) 5.00 12.00
UNOPENED HOBBY BOX (24 PACKS)
UNOPENED HOBBY PACK (7 CARDS)
UNOPENED RETAIL BONUS BOX (6 PACKS)
UNOPENED RETAIL BONUS PACK (7 CARDS)
UNOPENED RETAIL BLISTER BOX (26 PACKS)
UNOPENED RETAIL BLISTER PACK (7 CARDS)
UNOPENED RETAIL TIN (37 CARDS)
COMMON CARD (1-90) .15 .40

2006 Superman Returns Autographs

COMMON AUTO 8.00 20.00
STATED ODDS 1:58 HOBBY
NNO Brandon Routh 400.00 800.00
NNO James Marsden 12.00 30.00
NNO Kate Bosworth 50.00 100.00
NNO Kevin Spacey 750.00 1500.00
NNO Parker Posey 10.00 25.00

2006 Superman Returns Blister Bonus

COMPLETE SET (3) 6.00 15.00
COMMON CARD (B1-B3) 2.50 6.00
STATED ODDS 1:BLISTER PACK

2006 Superman Returns Embossed

COMPLETE SET (5) 5.00 12.00
COMMON CARD (1-5) 1.25 3.00
STATED ODDS 1:12

2006 Superman Returns Magnets

COMPLETE SET (9) 12.00 30.00
COMMON CARD (1-9) 2.00 5.00
STATED ODDS 1:12 RETAIL

2006 Superman Returns Promos

COMPLETE SET (3) 2.00 5.00
COMMON CARD (P1-P3) 1.50 2.00
P3 Return of a Hero 1.50 4.00

2006 Superman Returns Saved by Superman Memorabilia

COMMON CARD 8.00 20.00
STATED ODDS 1:12 HOBBY
2 Clark Kent's Suit 15.00 40.00
5 Lex Luthor's Coat 12.00 30.00
6 Lex Luthor's Suit 12.00 30.00
11 Superman's Briefs 30.00 80.00
12 Superman's Cape 12.00 30.00
13 Superman's Suit 15.00 40.00

2006 Superman Returns Stickers

COMPLETE SET (10) 12.00 30.00
COMMON CARD (1-10) 1.50 4.00
STATED ODDS 1:6 RETAIL

2006 Superman Returns Tin Lid

COMPLETE SET (6) 6.00 15.00
COMMON CARD (A-F) 1.25 3.00
STATED ODDS ONE PER TIN

2006 Superman Returns Tin Story

COMPLETE SET (6) 6.00 15.00
COMMON CARD (1-6) 1.25 3.00
STATED ODDS 1:TIN

2006 Superman Returns Tattoos

COMPLETE SET (50) 12.00 30.00
COMMON CARD .40 1.00

1981 Topps Superman II

COMPLETE SET (88) 6.00 15.00
COMPLETE SET W/STICKERS (110) 8.00 20.00
UNOPENED BOX (36 PACKS) 100.00 150.00
UNOPENED PACK (11 CARDS+1 STICKER) 3.00 4.00
UNOPENED RACK BOX (PACKS)
UNOPENED RACK PACK (48 CARDS)
COMMON CARD (1-88) .12 .30

1981 Topps Superman II Stickers

COMPLETE SET (22) 2.00 5.00
COMMON CARD (1-22) .20 .50
STATED ODDS 1:1

1983 Topps Superman III

COMPLETE SET (99) 6.00 15.00
COMPLETE SET W/STICKERS (121) 8.00 20.00
UNOPENED BOX (36 PACKS) 75.00 125.00
UNOPENED PACK (10 CARDS+1 STICKER) 3.00 4.00
COMMON CARD (1-99) .15 .40

1983 Topps Superman III Stickers

COMPLETE SET (22) 3.00 8.00
COMMON CARD (1-22) .40 1.00
STATED ODDS 1:1

1978 Weetabix Superman

COMPLETE SET (18) 12.00 30.00
COMMON CARD (1-18) 1.00 2.50

Marvel

1994 Fleer SkyBox Amalgam Previews

COMPLETE SET (4) 1.50 4.00
COMMON CARD (1-4) .40 1.00
INSERTED IN DC VERSUS MARVEL WAL-MART PACKS
1 Dark Claw .75 2.00
3 Dark Claw .75 2.00

1996 Fleer SkyBox Amalgam

COMPLETE SET (90) 15.00 40.00
UNOPENED BOX (24 PACKS) 150.00 200.00
UNOPENED PACK (7 CARDS) 6.00 8.00
COMMON CARD (1-90) .30 .75
1 Super-Soldier 1.50 4.00
3 Dark Claw 3.00 8.00
65 Super-Soldier vs. Ultra-Metallo .30 .75
66 Ultra-Metallo vs. Super-Soldier .30 .75
77 Dark Claw vs. Hyena .30 .75
78 Hyena vs. Dark Claw .30 .75

1996 Fleer SkyBox Amalgam Classics PowerBlast

COMPLETE SET (9) 15.00 40.00
COMMON CARD (1-9) 2.50 6.00
STATED ODDS 1:5
1 Super-Soldier Action #1 5.00 12.00
2 Judgment League Avengers #4 3.00 8.00
9 Secret Crisis of the Infinity Hour #7 3.00 8.00

1996 Fleer SkyBox Amalgam Holopix

COMPLETE SET (6) 75.00 150.00
COMMON CARD (1-6) 12.00 30.00
STATED ODDS 1:12
1 Dark Claw 30.00 75.00

1996 Fleer SkyBox Amalgam Secret Crisis of the Infinity Hour Canvas

COMPLETE SET (9) 15.00 40.00
COMMON CARD (1-9) 2.00 5.00
STATED ODDS 1:5
3 Dark Claw 4.00 10.00
8 Wonder Woman 3.00 8.00
9 Super-Soldier 3.00 8.00

1996 Fleer SkyBox Amalgam Promos

COMPLETE SET (3) 6.00 15.00
COMMON CARD 3.00 8.00
1 Batman, Dark Claw, Wolverine 4.00 10.00

1989 Comic Images Arthur Adams

COMPLETE SET (45) 10.00 25.00
UNOPENED BOX (50 PACKS)
UNOPENED PACK (5 CARDS+HEADER)
COMMON CARD (1-45) .40 1.00

1995 Marvel Comics Atlantis Rising Checklist Promo

NNO Atlantis Rising .75 2.00

2011 Avengers Kree Skrull War

COMPLETE SET (90) 6.00 15.00
UNOPENED BOX (24 PACKS) 60.00 100.00
UNOPENED PACK (9 CARDS) 3.00 5.00
COMMON CARD .15 .40
NNO Cover Card Checklist 4.00 10.00

2011 Avengers Kree Skrull War Characters

COMPLETE SET (9) 1.50 4.00
COMMON CARD (1-9) .30 .75
OVERALL CHARACTER ODDS 2.33:1

2011 Avengers Kree Skrull War Covers

COMPLETE SET (9) 1.50 4.00
COMMON CARD (C1-C9) .30 .75
OVERALL COVER ODDS 1:1

2011 Avengers Kree Skrull War Covers Black and White

COMPLETE SET (9) 8.00 20.00
COMMON CARD (B1-B9) 1.50 4.00
OVERALL COVER ODDS 1:1

2011 Avengers Kree Skrull War Covers Variant Art

COMPLETE SET (9) 3.00 8.00
COMMON CARD (V1-V9) .60 1.50
OVERALL COVER ODDS 1:1

2011 Avengers Kree Skrull War Power

COMPLETE SET (18) 3.00 8.00
COMMON CARD .40 1.00
OVERALL MINI STORY ODDS 1.67:1

2011 Avengers Kree Skrull War Retro Characters

COMPLETE SET (27) 4.00 10.00
COMMON CARD (R1-R27) .30 .75
COMMON SP .40 1.00
OVERALL CHARACTER ODDS 2.33:1

2011 Avengers Kree Skrull War Soldiers' Honor

COMPLETE SET (18) 3.00 8.00
COMMON CARD .40 1.00
OVERALL MINI STORY ODDS 1.67:1

2011 Avengers Kree Skrull War The Debt

COMPLETE SET (36) 5.00 12.00
COMMON CARD .40 1.00
OVERALL MINI STORY ODDS 1.67:1

2011 Avengers Kree Skrull War The Fall

COMPLETE SET (27) 4.00 10.00
COMMON CARD .40 1.00
OVERALL MINI STORY ODDS 1.67:1

2015 Avengers Lowe's Build and Grow Patches

COMPLETE SET (6) 8.00 20.00
COMMON PATCH 1.50 4.00
1 Black Widow 2.50 6.00
2 Captain America 4.00 10.00
5 Iron Man 4.00 10.00

2016 Avengers Lowe's Build and Grow Patches

COMPLETE SET (6) 25.00 60.00
COMMON CARD (1-6) 5.00 12.00
1 Black Widow 6.00 15.00
2 Captain America 10.00 25.00
5 Iron Man 6.00 15.00

2015 Avengers Silver Age

COMPLETE SET (100) 8.00 20.00
UNOPENED BOX (24 PACKS) 150.00 250.00
UNOPENED CARDS (5 CARDS) 6.00 10.00
COMMON CARD (1-100) .25 .60
*SILVER/100: 4X TO 10X BASIC CARDS
*GOLD/10: 15X TO 40X BASIC CARDS

2015 Avengers Silver Age Avengers Assemble

COMPLETE SET (17) 8.00 20.00
COMMON CARD (AA1-AA17) .75 2.00
STATED ODDS 1:24
AA1 Iron Man 2.50 6.00
AA2 Thor 1.25 3.00
AA3 Ant-Man 1.50 4.00
AA5 Hulk 1.25 3.00
AA7 Captain America 1.25 3.00
AA8 Hawkeye 1.00 2.50
AA14 Black Panther 1.00 2.50
AA15 Vision 1.00 2.50

2015 Avengers Silver Age Case-Toppers

COMMON CARD (CT1-CT3)	15.00	15.00
STATED ODDS 1:CASE		
CT3 Neal Adams	10.00	25.00

2015 Avengers Silver Age Classic Villains

COMPLETE SET (12)	12.00	30.00
COMMON CARD (V1-V12)	2.00	5.00
STATED ODDS 1:24		

2015 Avengers Silver Age Cut Archives Tales of Suspense

COMPLETE SET (41)	500.00	1000.00
COMMON CARD	20.00	50.00
STATED ODDS 1:144		

2015 Avengers Silver Age Cut Archives The Avengers

COMPLETE SET (104)	400.00	800.00
COMMON CARD	6.00	15.00
STATED ODDS 1:12		

2015 Avengers Silver Age Tales of Suspense

COMPLETE SET (41)	20.00	50.00
COMMON CARD (TSC1-TSC41)	1.00	2.50
STATED ODDS 1:12		

2015 Avengers Silver Age Promos

COMMON CARD (P1-P3)	1.50	4.00
P2 Album Exclusive	10.00	25.00

2006 Blade TV Series Wizard World LA

COMPLETE SET (4)	6.00	15.00
COMMON CARD	2.00	5.00

2006 Blade TV Series Wizard World Philly

COMPLETE SET (3)	10.00	25.00
COMMON CARD	5.00	10.00

1993 Marvel Bloodties Checklist Promo

NNO Bunch of X-Men	.60	1.50

1990 Comic Images Captain America

COMPLETE SET (45)	20.00	50.00
UNOPENED BOX (50 PACKS)	100.00	120.00
UNOPENED PACK (5 CARDS)	2.00	2.50
COMMON CARD (1-45)	.75	2.00

2021 Upper Deck Cloak and Dagger Season 1 Autographs

COMMON AUTO	5.00	12.00
CAJ Aubrey Joseph	10.00	25.00
CDH Dalon J. Holland	6.00	15.00
CEL Emma Lahana	6.00	15.00
CJZ Jaime Zevallos	6.00	15.00
CLM Lane Miller	6.00	15.00
CMC Marqus Clae	6.00	15.00
CMM Miles Mussenden	6.00	15.00
COH Olivia Holt	6.00	15.00
DAJ Aubrey Joseph	10.00	25.00
DAM Ally Maki	8.00	20.00
DAR Andrea Roth	6.00	15.00
DDH Dalon J. Holland	6.00	15.00
DEL Emma Lahana	6.00	15.00
DJZ Jaime Zevallos	6.00	15.00
DLM Lane Miller	6.00	15.00
DOH Olivia Holt	6.00	15.00

2021 Upper Deck Cloak and Dagger Season 1 Inscription Autographs

COMMON AUTO	15.00	40.00
CAJ Aubrey Joseph/"Ty Ty"	100.00	200.00
CAJ Aubrey Joseph/"Master of Space"	100.00	200.00
DAJ Aubrey Joseph/"Cloak"	100.00	200.00
DOH Olivia Holt/"Harbinger of Hope"	75.00	150.00
DOH Olivia Holt/"Manipulator of Light"	75.00	150.00

2021 Upper Deck Cloak and Dagger Season 1 Photo Variant Autographs

COMMON AUTO	12.00	30.00
STATED PRINT RUN 50 SER.#'d SETS		
CD1AJ Aubrey Joseph	20.00	50.00
CD1AN Angela M. Davis	15.00	40.00

1981 Leaf Comic Book Candy Secret Origins Stories

COMPLETE SET (8)	12.00	30.00
COMMON CARD	1.50	4.00
2 Batman	2.00	5.00
6 Superman	2.00	5.00
8 Wonder Woman	2.00	5.00

1975 Topps Comic Book Heroes Stickers White Backs

COMPLETE SET W/CL (49)	100.00	200.00
COMPLETE SET (40)	75.00	150.00
UNOPENED BOX (36 PACKS)	1000.00	2000.00
UNOPENED PACK	30.00	55.00
COMMON STICKER	1.00	2.50
COMMON CHECKLIST	2.50	6.00
1 Black Widow	3.00	8.00
2 Captain America 1	10.00	25.00
3 Captain America 2	10.00	25.00
4a Captain Marvel (Which Way to the John?)	4.00	10.00
4b Captain Marvel (Friendly Skies of United)	4.00	10.00
5 Checklist	1.00	2.50
6 Conan	5.00	12.00
7 Daredevil	5.00	12.00
16 Hulk 1	1.25	3.00
17 Hulk 2	1.25	3.00
21 Iron Man	2.00	5.00
30 Spider-Man 1	12.00	30.00
31a Spider-Man 2 (Bug Off!)	12.00	30.00
31b Spider-Man 2 (You Drive Me Up a Wall!)	12.00	30.00
39 Thor 1	1.50	4.00
40 Thor 2	3.00	8.00

2006 Complete Avengers

COMPLETE SET (81)	4.00	10.00
COMMON CARD (1-81)	.10	.30
ARCHIVE CUT ISSUED AS 2-CASE INCENTIVE		
NNO Archive Cut 2CI	25.00	60.00

2006 Complete Avengers Autographs

COLAN STATED ODDS 1:CASE		
THOMAS STATED ODDS 1:ALBUM		
1 Gene Colan	10.00	25.00
2 Roy Thomas	10.00	25.00

2006 Complete Avengers Earth's Mightiest Heroes

COMPLETE SET (18)	15.00	40.00
COMMON CARD (MH1-MH18)	1.50	4.00
STATED ODDS 1:20		

2006 Complete Avengers Greatest Enemies

COMPLETE SET (9)	4.00	10.00
COMMON CARD (GE1-GE9)	1.00	2.50
STATED ODDS 1:10		

2006 Complete Avengers Legendary Heroes

COMMON CARD (LH1-LH9)	2.50	6.00
STATED ODDS 1:40		
LH1 Captain America	4.00	10.00
LH2 Thor	3.00	8.00
LH3 Iron Man	4.00	10.00
LH6 Hulk	3.00	8.00

2006 Complete Avengers Promos

P3 Thor ALB	4.00	10.00
CP1 Avengers	2.00	5.00

1996 Comic Images Conan The Marvel Years

COMPLETE SET (90)	10.00	25.00
UNOPENED BOX (36 PACKS)	75.00	125.00
UNOPENED PACK (7 CARDS)	3.00	4.00
COMMON CARD (1-90)	.20	.50
*REFRACTOR: 4X TO 10 X BASIC CARDS		
NNO Simon Bisley AUTO/500	20.00	50.00
NNO Conan PROMO	.75	2.00
0 Conan#[(issued as box topper)	2.00	5.00

1996 Comic Images Conan The Marvel Years Conan the Savage

COMPLETE SET (3)	10.00	25.00
COMMON CARD (S1-S3)	4.00	10.00
STATED ODDS 1:18		

1996 Comic Images Conan The Marvel Years MagnaChrome

COMPLETE SET (6)	15.00	40.00
COMMON CARD (M1-M6)	3.00	8.00
STATED ODDS 1:12		

2011 Dangerous Divas

COMPLETE SET (72)	8.00	20.00
UNOPENED BOX (24 PACKS)	150.00	250.00
UNOPENED PACK (5 CARDS)	6.00	10.00
COMMON CARD (1-72)	.20	.50
*FOIL: 2X TO 5X BASIC CARDS		
1 Black Panther	1.25	3.00
2 Black Panther	1.25	3.00
3 Black Panther	1.25	3.00
7 Ms. Marvel	.40	1.00
8 Ms. Marvel	.40	1.00
9 Ms. Marvel	.40	1.00
13 Black Widow	1.25	3.00
14 Black Widow	1.25	3.00
15 Black Widow	1.25	3.00
22 Spider-Woman	.40	1.00
23 Spider-Woman	.40	1.00
24 Spider-Woman	.40	1.00
25 Rogue	.50	1.25
26 Rogue	.50	1.25
27 Rogue	.50	1.25
31 Elektra	.40	1.00
32 Elektra	.40	1.00
33 Elektra	.40	1.00
34 Storm	.75	2.00
35 Storm	.75	2.00
36 Storm	.75	2.00
37 Black Cat	.30	.75
38 Black Cat	.30	.75
39 Black Cat	.30	.75
49 Mystique	.50	1.25
50 Mystique	.50	1.25
51 Mystique	.50	1.25
64 Scarlet Witch	1.25	3.00
65 Scarlet Witch	1.25	3.00
66 Scarlet Witch	1.25	3.00

2011 Dangerous Divas Case-Toppers

COMPLETE SET (3)	60.00	120.00
COMMON CARD (CT1-CT3)	20.00	50.00
STATED ODDS ONE PER CASE		
STATED PRINT RUN 350 SER. #'d SETS		

2011 Dangerous Divas Embrace

COMPLETE SET W/RR (10)	30.00	75.00
COMPLETE SET W/O RR (9)	15.00	40.00
COMMON CARD (E10-E18)	2.50	6.00
STATED ODDS 1:24		
E19 ISSUED AS RITTENHOUSE REWARD		
E11 Medusa/Black Bolt	4.00	10.00
E12 Spider-Woman/IronMan	3.00	8.00
E13 Mary Jane/Spider-Man	4.00	10.00
E14 Emma Frost/Namor	3.00	8.00
E15 Ms. Marvel/Wolverine	5.00	12.00
E16 Domino/Wolverine	4.00	10.00
E19 She-Hulk/Starfox SP RR	25.00	60.00

2011 Dangerous Divas Sultry Seductresses

COMPLETE SET (9)	15.00	40.00
COMMON CARD (S1-S9)	2.50	6.00
STATED ODDS 1:12		
S1 Black Cat	4.00	10.00
S7 Mary Jane Watson	6.00	15.00
S8 Psylocke	4.00	10.00

2011 Dangerous Divas Women of Marvel

COMPLETE SET (12)	12.00	30.00
COMMON CARD (W1-W12)	1.25	3.00
STATED ODDS 1:8		
W1 Mary Jane/Black Cat	2.50	6.00
W3 Scarlet Witch	5.00	12.00
W4 Natasha Romanoff	2.00	5.00
W5 Storm	2.00	5.00
W11 Anya Corazon	1.50	4.00

2011 Dangerous Divas Promos

COMMON CARD	1.00	2.50
P1 Group of Four GEN	1.25	3.00
P3 Group of Four HV	3.00	8.00
P4 Group of Four ALB	10.00	25.00
ISP1 Group of Four IS	6.00	15.00

2014 Dangerous Divas 2

COMPLETE SET (90)	12.00	30.00
UNOPENED BOX (24 PACKS)	400.00	600.00
UNOPENED PACK (5 CARDS)	15.00	25.00
COMMON CARD (1-90)	.30	.75
*EMERALD: 5X TO 12X BASIC CARDS		
*RUBY/50: 10X TO 25X BASIC CARDS		
*DIAMOND/10: 80X TO 150X BASIC CARDS		

2014 Dangerous Divas 2 Art of Milo Manara

COMPLETE SET (9)	12.00	30.00
COMMON CARD (MM1-MM9)	2.00	5.00
STATED ODDS 1:24		
MM1 Storm	3.00	8.00
MM4 Angela	3.00	8.00
MM7 Captain Marvel	3.00	8.00
MM9 Scarlet Witch	4.00	10.00

2014 Dangerous Divas 2 Case-Toppers

COMPLETE SET (5)	30.00	80.00
COMMON CARD (E38-E42)	8.00	20.00
STATED ODDS 1:CASE		
E40 Lady Sinister and Daken	10.00	25.00
E41 Mystique and Wolverine	8.00	30.00
E42 Spider-Man and Sarah Stacy	8.00	25.00

2014 Dangerous Divas 2 Cut Archives

COMMON CARD	6.00	15.00
STATED ODDS 1:96		
BW2 ISSUED AS ARCHIVE BOX EXCLUSIVE		
BW1 Black Widow #/72	12.00	30.00
BW2 Black Widow #/74 (Archive Box excl.)	20.00	50.00
SW1 Scarlet Witch #/50	10.00	25.00
SW2 Scarlet Witch #/23	10.00	25.00
SW3 Scarlet Witch #/37	10.00	25.00
SW4 Scarlet Witch #/21	10.00	25.00
SW5 Scarlet Witch #/35	10.00	25.00
SW6 Scarlet Witch #/24	10.00	25.00

2014 Dangerous Divas 2 Marvel 75th Anniversary

COMMON CARD	12.00	30.00
STATED ODDS 1:144		
STATED PRINT RUN 75 SER. #'d SETS		
SKIP-NUMBERED SET		
3 Angela	15.00	40.00
18 X-23	15.00	40.00
21 Jubilee	15.00	40.00
27 Black Widow	15.00	40.00
33 Captain Marvel	15.00	40.00
36 Storm	15.00	40.00
42 Mystique	20.00	50.00

45 Jean Grey	15.00	40.00
54 Scarlet Witch	20.00	50.00
57 Red She-Hulk	15.00	40.00
60 Hela	15.00	40.00
66 Sif	15.00	40.00
69 Wasp	15.00	40.00
75 Emma Frost	20.00	50.00

2014 Dangerous Divas 2 Sultry Seductresses

COMPLETE SET (9)	12.00	30.00
COMMON CARD (S10-S18)	2.00	5.00
STATED ODDS 1:24		
S10 Black Cat	2.50	6.00
S11 Psylocke	2.50	6.00
S13 Mystique	3.00	8.00
S16 Rogue	4.00	10.00
S17 Black Widow	3.00	8.00

2014 Dangerous Divas 2 Promos

COMPLETE SET (4)	5.00	12.00
COMMON CARD (P1-P4)	1.50	4.00
P4 Fall 2014 Philly Non-Sport Show	2.50	6.00

2003 Daredevil Movie

COMPLETE SET (72)	6.00	15.00
UNOPENED HOBBY BOX (36 PACKS)	70.00	80.00
UNOPENED HOBBY PACK (7 CARDS)	2.50	3.00
UNOPENED RETAIL BOX (24 PACKS)		
UNOPENED RETAIL PACK (7 CARDS)		
COMMON CARD (1-72)	.15	.40
DD COSTUME STATED ODDS 1:72		
NNO Daredevil Costume MEM	10.00	25.00

2003 Daredevil Movie Autographs

COMMON CARD	5.00	12.00
STATED ODDS 1:72		
GARNER AUTO ISSUED AS DEALER CONTEST EXCLUSIVE		
1 Ben Affleck	350.00	600.00
2 Coolio	60.00	150.00
3 Joe Pantoliano	120.00	200.00
6 Jennifer Garner/50*	300.00	600.00

2003 Daredevil Movie Promos

COMPLETE SET (3)	2.50	6.00
COMMON CARD	1.25	3.00

1993 Triton Magazine Daredevil

COMPLETE SET (3)	3.00	8.00
COMMON CARD (1-3)	2.00	5.00

2019 Deadpool

COMPLETE SET W/SP (130)	125.00	250.00
COMPLETE SET W/O SP (100)	12.00	30.00
UNOPENED BOX (18 PACKS)	150.00	250.00
UNOPENED PACK (5 CARDS)	8.00	12.00
COMMON CARD (1-100)	.25	.60
COMMON SP (101-130)	5.00	12.00
*SILVER: X TO X BASIC CARDS		
*BLACK: 1X TO 2.5X BASIC CARDS		
*PINK: 3X TO 8X BASIC CARDS		

2019 Deadpool 3-D Lenticular

COMPLETE SET W/SP (42)	125.00	250.00
COMPLETE SET W/O SP (30)	60.00	120.00
COMMON CARD (3D1-3D30)	3.00	8.00
COMMON SP (3D31-3D42)	8.00	20.00
STATED ODDS TIER 1 1:27		
STATED ODDS TIER 2 1:180		
3D32 Sharp Edges SP	15.00	40.00
3D33 Under Control SP	15.00	40.00
3D35 Pizza Time SP	15.00	40.00

2019 Deadpool Chimichangas with Deadpool

COMPLETE SET (8)	8.00	20.00
COMMON CARD (CWD1-CWD8)	1.50	4.00
STATED ODDS 1:13		

2019 Deadpool Deadglass

COMPLETE SET (20)	100.00	200.00
COMMON CARD (DG1-DG20)	5.00	12.00
STATED ODDS 1:72		
DG2 Venompool	8.00	20.00
DG6 Green Deadpool	8.00	20.00
DG9 Ultimate Deadpool	10.00	25.00
DG11 New Costume	15.00	40.00
DG13 Widdle Wade	8.00	20.00
DG16 Thunderbolts Deadpool	12.00	30.00
DG18 Wolverinepool	12.00	30.00
DG19 Hulkpool	12.00	30.00

2019 Deadpool Deadpatches

COMPLETE SET W/O SP (24)		
COMMON MEM (DP1-DP24)	3.00	8.00
COMMON MEM (DP25-DP33)	8.00	20.00
COMMON MEM (DP34-DP39)	10.00	25.00
COMMON MEM (DP40-DP42)	75.00	150.00
STATED ODDS TIER 1 1:32		
STATED ODDS TIER 2 1:144		
STATED ODDS TIER 3 1:360		
STATED ODDS TIER 4 1:1,800		

2019 Deadpool Deadpool Bombing

COMPLETE SET (12)	8.00	20.00
COMMON CARD (DB1-DB12)	1.50	4.00
STATED ODDS 1:8		

2019 Deadpool Meet the Pools!

COMPLETE SET (18)	10.00	25.00
COMMON CARD (MTP1-MTP18)	1.25	3.00
STATED ODDS 1:6		

2019 Deadpool New Mutants #98 Comic Cuts Covers

STATED PRINT RUN 10 SER.#'d SETS		
NMC1-NMC9 UNPRICED DUE TO SCARCITY		
CARD #NM98 1:432		
NM98 New Mutants #98	15.00	40.00

2019 Deadpool Pooling Around

E-PACK ACHIEVEMENT EXCLUSIVE		
PA1 Deadpool & Juggernaut	10.00	25.00
PA2 Deadpool & Rogue	6.00	15.00
PA3 Deadpool & Wolverine	30.00	75.00
PA4 Deadpool & Sentinel		
PA5 Deadpool & Honey Badger		
PA6 Deadpool & Beast		

2019 Deadpool Sport Ball!

COMPLETE SET (12)	15.00	40.00
COMMON CARD (SB1-SB12)	2.00	5.00
STATED ODDS 1:8		
SB1 89 UD BB Nolan Ryan	3.00	8.00
SB4 89 FL BB Billy Ripken ERR	4.00	10.00
SB5 87 FL BB Barry Bonds	2.50	6.00
SB9 94 CC BB Jose Canseco	3.00	8.00
SB12 84 FL BB Jay Johnstone	2.50	6.00

2016 Deadpool Collectible Postcards

COMPLETE SET (8)	4.00	10.00
COMMON CARD	.75	2.00
UNNUMBERED SET LISTED ALPHABETICALLY		
TARGET DVD EXCLUSIVE		

1988 Marvel Comics Evolutionary War Promo

NNO Comic Story Promo	1.25	3.00

1989 Comic Images Excalibur

COMPLETE SET (46)	8.00	20.00
UNOPENED BOX (50 PACKS)	30.00	45.00
UNOPENED PACK (5 CARDS)	1.00	1.25
COMMON CARD (1-45)	.30	.75

2008 Fantastic Four Archives

COMPLETE SET (72)	6.00	15.00
UNOPENED BOX (24 PACKS)	125.00	200.00
UNOPENED PACK (5 CARDS)	5.00	8.00
COMMON CARD (1-72)	.15	.40

2008 Fantastic Four Archives Legendary Heroes

COMPLETE SET (9)	25.00	50.00
COMMON CARD (LH1-LH9)	3.00	8.00
STATED ODDS 1:24		

2008 Fantastic Four Archives Nemesis

COMPLETE SET (9)	5.00	10.00
COMMON CARD (N1-N9)	1.00	2.50
STATED ODDS 1:8		

2008 Fantastic Four Archives Ready for Action

COMPLETE SET (18)	12.00	30.00
COMMON CARD (A1-A18)	1.25	3.00
STATED ODDS 1:12		

2005 Fantastic Four Movie

COMPLETE SET (100)	8.00	20.00
UNOPENED BOX (36 PACKS)	50.00	75.00
UNOPENED PACK (5 CARDS)	2.00	2.50
COMMON CARD (1-100)	.15	.40

2005 Fantastic Four Movie Costumes

COMMON CARD	4.00	10.00
STATED ODDS 1:20		
DD4 Dr. Doom Cloak BLUE/499	8.00	20.00
FF1 Human Torch - Suit ORANGE/969	12.00	30.00
FF2 Human Torch - Suit BLUE/499	20.00	50.00
FF3 Mr. Fantastic - Suit ORANGE/969	12.00	30.00
FF4 Mr. Fantastic - Suit BLUE/499	20.00	50.00
FF5 Invisible Woman - Suit ORANGE/349	40.00	80.00
FF6 Invisible Woman - Suit BLUE/299	60.00	120.00
FF7 The Thing - Suit ORANGE/399	20.00	50.00
FF8 The Thing - Suit BLUE/299	20.00	50.00
FF9 Sue Storm Suit BLUE/699	30.00	60.00

2011 50 Years of the Fantastic Four

COMPLETE SET (9)	20.00	50.00
COMMON CARD (FA1-FA9)	3.00	8.00

2019 Flair Marvel

COMPLETE SET W/O SP (90)	25.00	60.00
UNOPENED BOX (9 PACKS)	400.00	800.00
UNOPENED PACK (6 CARDS)	45.00	90.00
COMMON CARD (1-90)	.50	1.25
FLARIUM TIER 1 (91-100)	.75	2.00
FLARIUM TIER 2 (101-110)	1.00	2.50
FLARIUM TIER 3 (111-120)	1.00	2.50
FLARIUM TIER 4 (121-130)	1.25	3.00
FLARIUM TIER 5 (131-140)	2.50	6.00
FLARIUM TIER 6 (141-150)	8.00	20.00
E-PACK ACHIEVEMENT (151-156)	3.00	8.00
FLARIUM TIER 1 ODDS 1:3		
FLARIUM TIER 2 ODDS 1:4		
FLARIUM TIER 3 ODDS 1:6		
FLARIUM TIER 4 ODDS 1:9		
FLARIUM TIER 5 ODDS 1:18		
FLARIUM TIER 6 ODDS 1:80		
91 Wolverine SP	2.00	5.00
92 Spider-Man SP	2.00	5.00
96 Moonstar SP	1.00	2.50
98 Nick Fury SP	1.00	2.50
100 Red Goblin SP	1.25	3.00
101 Storm SP	1.25	3.00
102 Captain America SP	2.00	5.00
103 Angel SP	1.50	4.00
105 Black Cat SP	1.50	4.00
107 Ant-Man SP	1.25	3.00
108 Squirrel Girl SP	2.00	5.00
111 Iron Man SP	2.50	6.00
112 Captain Marvel SP	2.00	5.00
113 Loki SP	1.50	4.00
116 Groot SP	1.25	3.00
118 Vision SP	1.25	3.00
120 Magik SP	1.50	4.00
121 Dr. Stephen Strange SP	3.00	8.00
122 Scarlet Witch SP	2.00	5.00
125 Psylocke SP	2.50	6.00
126 Gamora SP	1.50	4.00
128 Xorn SP	2.00	5.00
129 Doctor Octopus SP	1.50	4.00
131 Daredevil SP	4.00	10.00
132 Beast SP	6.00	15.00
133 Mystique SP	8.00	20.00
134 Spider-Gwen SP	10.00	25.00
136 Lady Deathstrike SP	3.00	8.00
140 Cyclops SP	4.00	10.00
141 Green Goblin SP	12.00	30.00
142 Iceman SP	12.00	30.00
143 Beta Ray Bill SP	10.00	25.00
144 Rogue SP	15.00	40.00
146 Ultron SP	15.00	40.00
148 Rocket Raccoon SP	15.00	40.00
149 Moon Knight SP	20.00	50.00
150 Thanos SP	20.00	50.00
152 Doctor Voodoo SP EPACK	5.00	12.00
153 Electro SP EPACK	8.00	20.00
154 Spider-Man 2099 SP EPACK	6.00	15.00
155 Iron Patriot SP EPACK	10.00	25.00
156 Magneto SP EPACK	60.00	120.00

2019 Flair Marvel Anti-Matter

COMPLETE SET W/SP (35)		
COMPLETE SET W/O SP (5)	8.00	20.00
COMMON CARD (AM1-AM5)	2.00	5.00
COMMON SP (AM6-AM15)	2.00	5.00
COMMON SP (AM16-AM35)	2.50	6.00
STATED ODDS 1:30		
STATED SP (AM6-AM15) ODDS 1:50		
STATED SP (AM16-AM35) ODDS 1:80		
AM0 Diamond Head EPACK	6.00	15.00
AM00 Fitzroy SP EPACK	30.00	75.00
AM000 Dark Phoenix SP EPACK		
AM2 Superior Spider-Man	2.50	6.00
AM3 Thanos	4.00	10.00
AM6 Ultron SP	2.50	6.00
AM11 Taskmaster SP	2.50	6.00
AM15 Stryfe SP	2.50	6.00
AM16 Magneto SP	6.00	15.00
AM17 Loki SP	3.00	8.00
AM18 Red Skull SP	6.00	15.00
AM19 Green Goblin SP	12.00	30.00
AM20 Kingpin SP	8.00	20.00
AM21 Carnage SP	6.00	15.00
AM22 Sabretooth SP	4.00	10.00
AM23 Shadow King SP	8.00	20.00
AM25 Dormammu SP	4.00	10.00
AM26 Jigsaw SP	10.00	25.00
AM27 Leader SP	8.00	20.00
AM28 Mandarin SP	10.00	25.00
AM32 Ares SP	4.00	10.00
AM34 Steel Serpent SP	4.00	10.00
AM35 Magus SP	4.00	10.00

2019 Flair Marvel Artist Autographs

COMPLETE SET (141)		
COMMON CACAU	8.00	20.00
COMMON DEVRIES	12.00	30.00
COMMON DORMAN	15.00	40.00
COMMON EASLEY	15.00	40.00
COMMON EGGLETON	15.00	40.00
COMMON EVANS	6.00	15.00
COMMON FAE	10.00	25.00
COMMON FLEMING	20.00	50.00
COMMON GALLOWAY	10.00	25.00
COMMON GIST	15.00	40.00
COMMON GREGORY	10.00	25.00
COMMON HAMMERMEISTER	15.00	40.00
COMMON HETRICK	30.00	75.00
COMMON HORNE	6.00	15.00
COMMON LAGO	8.00	20.00
COMMON MACNEIL	6.00	15.00
COMMON MANGUM	25.00	60.00
COMMON MARTIMIANO	8.00	20.00
COMMON MILLET	8.00	20.00
COMMON MOMOKO	50.00	100.00
COMMON OLIVETTI	8.00	20.00
COMMON PAVELEC	15.00	40.00
COMMON PONCE	15.00	40.00

COMMON POZAS 20.00 50.00
COMMON SASS 25.00 60.00
COMMON SIENKIEWICZ 12.00 30.00
COMMON STANKO 12.00 30.00
COMMON STEELE 10.00 25.00
COMMON TARGETE 10.00 25.00
COMMON WAYSHAK 400.00 1000.00
STATED PRINT RUN 30 SER.#'d SETS

2019 Flair Marvel Lucky 8's

COMPLETE SET (30) 125.00 250.00
COMMON CARD (LJ1-LJ30) 3.00 8.00
STATED PRINT RUN 88 SER.#'d SETS
LJ0 E-PACK ACHIEVEMENT
LJ0 Binary EPACK
LJ1 Emma Frost 10.00 25.00
LJ2 Psylocke 10.00 25.00
LJ3 Fantomex 5.00 12.00
LJ4 Wonder Man 8.00 20.00
LJ5 Mister Sinister 5.00 12.00
LJ9 Ultimate Spider-Man 6.00 15.00
LJ10 Moonstone 5.00 12.00
LJ11 Ghost Rider 8.00 20.00
LJ13 Mockingbird 10.00 25.00
LJ14 Juggernaut 6.00 15.00
LJ15 Daken 8.00 20.00
LJ16 Gwen Stacy 8.00 20.00
LJ19 Iron Fist 5.00 12.00
LJ20 Moon Knight 6.00 15.00
LJ21 Jessica Jones 4.00 10.00
LJ22 Agent Venom 6.00 15.00
LJ23 Vision 4.00 10.00
LJ24 Colossus 5.00 12.00
LJ25 Mystique 6.00 15.00
LJ26 Honey Badger 10.00 25.00
LJ27 Dark Beast 5.00 12.00
LJ29 Moon Boy 4.00 10.00

2019 Flair Marvel Matter

COMPLETE SET W/SP (35) 75.00 150.00
COMPLETE SET W/O SP (20) 30.00 75.00
COMMON CARD (M1-M20) 2.50 6.00
COMMON SP (M21-M30) 2.50 6.00
COMMON SP (M31-M35) 3.00 8.00
STATED ODDS 1:30
STATED SP (M21-M30) ODDS 1:50
STATED SP (M31-M35) ODDS 1:80
M0, M00, M000 E-PACK ACHIEVEMENT
M0 Nova EPACK 12.00 30.00
M00 Bishop SP EPACK 12.00 30.00
M000 Jean Grey SP EPACK 60.00 120.00
M2 Thor 3.00 8.00
M3 Captain America 3.00 8.00
M4 Spider-Man 4.00 10.00
M6 Venom 3.00 8.00
M7 Wolverine 5.00 12.00
M10 Doctor Strange 5.00 12.00
M11 Punisher 5.00 12.00
M13 Iron Man 3.00 8.00
M21 Hank Pym SP 3.00 8.00
M22 X-Men SP 3.00 8.00
M26 Deadpool SP 12.00 30.00
M28 Ghost Rider SP 6.00 15.00
M29 Howard The Duck SP 5.00 12.00
M31 Black Bolt SP 5.00 12.00
M32 Peter Parker SP 5.00 12.00
M34 Moon Knight SP 6.00 15.00
M35 Colossus SP 5.00 12.00

2019 Flair Marvel Pieces of Flair Comic Corner Patches

COMPLETE SET W/SP (37) 100.00 200.00
COMPLETE SET W/O SP (19) 25.00 60.00
COMMON PATCH (POF1-POF19) 2.00 5.00
COMMON SP (POF20-POF29) 2.50 6.00
COMMON SP (POF30-POF37) 5.00 12.00
STATED ODDS 1:12
STATED SP (POF20-POF29) ODDS 1:45
STATED SP (POF30-POF37) ODDS 1:120
POF3 Tales to Astonish #56 2.50 6.00
POF4 Spectacular Spider-Man #90 6.00 15.00
POF5 Daredevil #257 2.50 6.00
POF7 Ghost Rider #18 3.00 8.00
POF8 Marvel Premiere #48 3.00 8.00
POF9 Marvel Spotlight #32 2.50 6.00
POF10 The Amazing Spider-Man #2 2.50 6.00
POF12 The Incredible Hulk #377 3.00 8.00
POF17 The Punisher #53 3.00 8.00
POF18 Venom #1 3.00 8.00
POF20 Captain Britain #27 SP 5.00 12.00
POF21 Marvel Comics Presents #113 SP 3.00 8.00
POF25 Spectacular Spider-Man #107 SP 6.00 15.00
POF27 The Incredible Hulk #296 SP 4.00 10.00
POF29 The Punisher #53 SP 3.00 8.00
POF30 Amazing Spider-Man
Annual Vol 1 #21 SP 15.00 40.00
POF31 The Amazing Spider-Man #252 SP15.00 40.00
POF32 The Amazing Spider-Man #250 SP 6.00 15.00
POF33 Captain America #341 SP 12.00 30.00
POF35 The Incredible Hulk #299 SP 15.00 40.00
POF36 The Incredible Hulk #300 SP 8.00 20.00
POF37 The New Mutants #21 SP 8.00 20.00
POF38 Spider-Man #1 EPACK
POF39 Ghost Rider #39 SP EPACK
POF40 Marvel Premiere #51 SP EPACK

2019 Flair Marvel Power Blast

STATED ODDS 1:18
STATED SP ODDS 1:90
PB1 Killmonger 20.00 50.00
PB3 Humbug 60.00 150.00
PB4 Ultron 50.00 125.00
PB6 Jack of Hearts 2.50 6.00
PB7 Boom Boom 1.50 4.00
PB8 Weapon H 2.50 6.00
PB9 Mar-Vell 3.00 8.00
PB10 Ahab 3.00 8.00
PB11 Dagger 4.00 10.00
PB12 Captain Marvel 2.00 5.00
PB13 Wolverine 4.00 10.00
PB14 Hawkeye 5.00 12.00
PB16 X-23 6.00 15.00
PB17 Maria Hill 2.50 6.00
PB18 Rictor 3.00 8.00
PB19 Mr. Negative 2.00 5.00
PB20 Warpath 1.50 4.00
PB23 Venom 4.00 10.00
PB25 Sleepwalker 1.50 4.00
PB27 Northstar 5.00 12.00
PB28 Okoye 2.00 5.00
PB31 Jean Grey 2.00 5.00
PB32 Prowler 2.00 5.00
PB33 Odin 6.00 15.00
PB35 War Machine 2.50 6.00
PB37 Hellcat 2.50 6.00
PB38 Hammerhead 3.00 8.00
PB40 Tiger Shark 1.50 4.00
PB41 Bushmaster SP 8.00 20.00
PB42 Silver Sable SP 6.00 15.00
PB43 SP//dr SP 10.00 25.00
PB46 Ghost Rider SP 10.00 25.00
PB47 Shatterstar SP 5.00 12.00
PB49 Speedball SP 5.00 12.00

2019 Flair Marvel Power Blast Exclusives

PBE0 Voyager EPACK

2019 Flair Marvel Singularity

COMPLETE SET W/SP (29) 50.00 100.00
COMPLETE SET W/O SP (14) 12.00 30.00
COMMON CARD (S1-S14) 1.25 3.00
COMMON SP (S15-S24) 2.00 5.00
COMMON SP (S25-S29) 5.00 12.00
STATED ODDS 1:16
STATED SP (S15-S24) ODDS 1:30
STATED SP (S25-S29) ODDS 1:70
S0 Green Goblin EPACK
S00 Star-Lord SP EPACK
S000 Havok SP EPACK
S1 Spider-Man 1.50 4.00
S3 Wolverine 4.00 10.00
S4 Rogue 1.50 4.00
S5 Thor 2.50 6.00
S6 Jean Grey 2.00 5.00
S7 Captain America 2.50 6.00
S12 Daredevil 2.50 6.00
S13 Captain Marvel 2.00 5.00
S14 Hulk 1.50 4.00
S15 Iron Man SP 6.00 15.00
S16 Scarlet Witch SP 2.50 6.00
S19 She-Hulk SP 3.00 8.00
S22 Doctor Strange SP 2.50 6.00
S23 Cable SP 3.00 8.00
S24 Punisher SP 6.00 15.00
S25 Deadpool SP 6.00 15.00
S29 Thanos SP 12.00 30.00

2019 Flair Marvel Stained Glass

COMPLETE SET W/SP (20) 75.00 150.00
COMPLETE SET W/O SP (10) 15.00 40.00
COMMON CARD (SG1-SG10) 2.50 6.00
COMMON SP (SG11-SG20) 5.00 12.00
STATED ODDS 1:15
STATED SP ODDS 1:40
SG0 Dormammu EPACK
SG00 Martinex SP EPACK
SG1 Iron Man 5.00 12.00
SG2 Magneto 3.00 8.00
SG3 Wolverine 6.00 15.00
SG6 Captain America 3.00 8.00
SG7 Thanos 8.00 20.00
SG10 Black Panther 3.00 8.00
SG11 Daredevil SP 8.00 20.00
SG12 Elektra SP 5.00 12.00
SG13 Thor SP 6.00 15.00
SG14 Ultron SP 3.00 8.00
SG15 Storm SP 8.00 20.00
SG17 Captain Marvel SP 15.00 40.00
SG18 Spider-Man SP 15.00 40.00
SG19 Doctor Stephen Strange SP 8.00 20.00

2019 Flair Marvel Through the Ages Bronze Age

TTAB0 Moon Knight EPACK

2019 Flair Marvel Through the Ages Copper Age

COMPLETE SET (25) 20.00 50.00
COMMON CARD (TTAC1-TTAC25) 1.25 3.00
*BRONZE: .6X TO 1.5X BASIC CARDS
*SILVER: 1.2X TO 3X BASIC CARDS
*GOLDEN: 2X TO 5X BASIC CARDS
STATED ODDS 1:12
TTAC0 Elektra EPACK
TTAC1 Namor The Sub-Mariner 1.50 4.00
TTAC2 Captain America 2.00 5.00
TTAC3 Bucky Barnes 1.50 4.00
TTAC6 Spider-Man 2.50 6.00
TTAC7 X-Men 2.00 5.00
TTAC8 Iron Man 2.50 6.00
TTAC9 The Hulk 1.50 4.00
TTAC10 Thor 2.00 5.00
TTAC11 Wolverine 3.00 8.00
TTAC12 Ghost Rider 1.50 4.00
TTAC14 The Punisher 2.00 5.00
TTAC15 Thanos 2.50 6.00
TTAC16 Venom 1.50 4.00
TTAC17 Deadpool 2.00 5.00
TTAC19 Cable 1.50 4.00
TTAC22 Rocket Raccoon 1.50 4.00
TTAC23 Rogue 1.50 4.00

2019 Flair Marvel Through the Ages Golden Age

TTAG0 The Angel EPACK
TTAG00 Ka-Zar EPACK

2019 Flair Marvel Through the Ages Silver Age

TTAS0 Ant-Man EPACK

2019 Flair Marvel Totemic Teams

COMPLETE SET W/SP (49) 60.00 120.00
COMPLETE SET W/O SP (28) 15.00 40.00
COMMON CARD (TT1-TT28) 1.00 2.50
COMMON SP (TT29-TT42) 1.50 4.00
COMMON SP (TT43-TT49) 2.00 5.00
STATED ODDS 1:6
STATED SP (TT29-TT42) ODDS 1:30
STATED SP (TT43-TT49) ODDS 1:70
CARDS TT50-TT56 E-PACK EXCLUSIVE
TT1 Hulk 1.50 4.00
TT2 Black Widow 1.25 3.00
TT5 Kitty Pryde 1.50 4.00
TT7 Beast 1.25 3.00
TT8 Jean Grey 2.00 5.00
TT9 Drax 1.25 3.00
TT10 Gamora 1.50 4.00
TT11 Groot 1.50 4.00
TT12 Rocket Raccoon 1.50 4.00
TT17 Namor 1.25 3.00
TT18 Black Panther 1.50 4.00
TT19 Doctor Strange 2.50 6.00
TT24 Shaman 1.25 3.00
TT27 Squirrel Girl 2.00 5.00
TT29 Hank Pym SP 2.50 6.00
TT32 Iceman SP 4.00 10.00
TT33 Mantis SP 5.00 12.00
TT35 Crystal SP 3.00 8.00
TT38 Professor X SP 2.50 6.00
TT41 Grasshopper SP 3.00 8.00
TT43 Captain America SP 10.00 25.00
TT45 Star-Lord SP 3.00 8.00
TT47 Iron Man SP 8.00 20.00
TT48 Guardian SP 3.00 8.00
TT49 Mr. Immortal SP 2.00 5.00
TT50 Blink EPACK 12.00 30.00
TT51 Morph EPACK 8.00 20.00
TT52 Thunderbird EPACK 10.00 25.00
TT53 Mimic EPACK 10.00 25.00
TT54 Sunfire EPACK 10.00 25.00
TT55 Magnus EPACK 10.00 25.00
TT56 Magik EPACK 15.00 40.00

2013 Fleer Retro Marvel

COMPLETE SET (60) 100.00 250.00
UNOPENED BOX (20 PACKS)
UNOPENED PACK (6 CARDS)
COMMON CARD (1-60) 1.25 3.00
1 Black Bolt 6.00 15.00
2 Black Panther 3.00 8.00
3 Black Widow 2.00 5.00
4 Cable 8.00 20.00
5 Captain America 2.50 6.00
6 Captain Marvel 1.50 4.00
10 Deadpool 8.00 20.00
11 Doctor Strange 6.00 15.00
12 Elektra 1.50 4.00
14 Ghost Rider 3.00 8.00
16 Hawkeye 1.50 4.00
17 Hulk 2.50 6.00
22 Iron Man 6.00 15.00
24 Moon Knight 10.00 25.00
25 Mr. Fantastic 5.00 12.00
26 Namor 2.00 5.00
30 Professor X 3.00 8.00
31 Psylocke 1.50 4.00
32 Punisher 3.00 8.00
33 Red Hulk 3.00 8.00
34 Red She-Hulk 2.50 6.00
36 Rogue 1.50 4.00
37 Scarlet Witch 5.00 12.00
38 She-Hulk 2.50 6.00
39 Silver Surfer 3.00 8.00
40 Spider-Man 12.00 30.00
41 Spider-Woman 1.50 4.00
42 Star-Lord 1.50 4.00
43 Storm 2.00 5.00
45 Thor 5.00 12.00
46 Ultimate Spider-Man 15.00 40.00
47 Venom 6.00 15.00
48 Wasp 1.50 4.00
49 Wolverine 5.00 12.00
50 X-23 6.00 15.00

52 Doctor Doom 2.00 5.00
53 Galactus 1.50 4.00
55 Loki 3.00 8.00
56 Magneto 3.00 8.00
58 Mystique 3.00 8.00
59 Norman Osborn 1.50 4.00
60 Thanos 4.00 10.00

2013 Fleer Retro Marvel Autographs

COMMON AUTO 5.00 12.00
STATED ODDS 1:10
1 Brandon Peterson 6.00 15.00
2 Adi Granov 50.00 120.00
4 Dave Wilkins 6.00 15.00
5 Steve Epting 15.00 40.00
6 Terry Dodson 6.00 15.00
8 Jim Cheung 10.00 25.00
9 Chris Samnee 12.00 30.00
10 Paco Medina 50.00 120.00
14 Matthew Clark 10.00 25.00
16 Mike Deodato Jr. 8.00 20.00
17 Olivier Coipel 6.00 15.00
21 Mike Deodato Jr. 8.00 20.00
22 Salvador Larroca Martinez 12.00 30.00
23 Mike Deodato Jr. 6.00 15.00
24 Alex Maleev 20.00 50.00
25 Steve Epting 10.00 25.00
29 Andy Lanning 15.00 40.00
31 Jorge Molina 20.00 50.00
34 Carlo Pagulayan 8.00 20.00
35 Salvador Larroca Martinez 6.00 15.00
38 Ryan Stegman 8.00 20.00
39 Lee Weeks 10.00 25.00
42 Mark Bagley 12.00 30.00
43 David Lopez 8.00 20.00
44 Ryan Stegman 8.00 20.00
46 Jim Cheung 75.00 200.00
47 Patrick Zircher 6.00 15.00
48 Olivier Coipel 6.00 15.00
49 Clay Mann 40.00 100.00
50 Stefano Caselli 25.00 60.00
53 Barry Kitson 6.00 15.00
54 Chris Bachalo 6.00 15.00
55 Mike Mayhew 8.00 20.00
56 Ale Garza 6.00 15.00
57 Adam Kubert 6.00 15.00
58 Adam Kubert 6.00 15.00
59 Mike Deodato Jr. 6.00 15.00
60 Mark Bagley 20.00 50.00

2013 Fleer Retro Marvel 1990 Impel Marvel Universe

COMMON CARD (1-25) 10.00 25.00
STATED ODDS 1:6
1 Cable 25.00 60.00
2 Captain America 30.00 75.00
3 Captain Marvel 20.00 50.00
4 Colossus 15.00 40.00
5 Cyclops 15.00 40.00
6 Daredevil 40.00 100.00
7 Deadpool 60.00 150.00
8 Hawkeye 15.00 40.00
9 Hulk 20.00 50.00
10 Human Torch 12.00 30.00
14 Iron Man 30.00 75.00
17 Wolverine 75.00 200.00
19 Nova 30.00 75.00
20 Spider-Man 100.00 250.00
21 Storm 15.00 40.00
22 Thing 40.00 100.00
23 Thor 40.00 100.00
24 Magneto 20.00 50.00
25 Red Skull 15.00 40.00

2013 Fleer Retro Marvel 1990 Impel Marvel Universe Autographs

STATED ODDS 1:576
1 Adi Granov 20.00 50.00
2 Steve Epting
3 Ed McGuinness
5 Adi Granov 60.00 150.00
6 Mike Deodato Jr.
7 Carlo Barberi 200.00 500.00
8 Paul Renaud 60.00 150.00
9 Steve McNiven 250.00 600.00
11 Pablo Raimondi 100.00 250.00
12 Phil Noto 75.00 200.00
13 Mike Deodato Jr.
14 Salvador Larroca Martinez 150.00 400.00
16 Mike Deodato Jr.
17 Jim Cheung 300.00 750.00
19 Clayton Henry
20 Stefano Caselli 600.00 1500.00

2013 Fleer Retro Marvel 1991 Impel Marvel Universe

COMMON CARD (1-20) 12.00 30.00
STATED ODDS 1:7.5
1 Captain America 25.00 60.00
2 Captain Marvel 20.00 50.00
4 Cyclops 20.00 50.00
5 Daredevil 15.00 40.00
6 Deadpool 25.00 60.00
7 Hulk 25.00 60.00
10 Invisible Woman 15.00 40.00
11 Iron Man 20.00 50.00
12 Loki 30.00 75.00
13 Wolverine 30.00 75.00
14 Mr. Fantastic 20.00 50.00
15 Spider-Man 100.00 250.00
16 Storm 20.00 50.00
17 Thing 20.00 50.00
18 Thor 25.00 60.00
19 Magneto 30.00 75.00
20 Thanos 25.00 60.00

2013 Fleer Retro Marvel 1991 Impel Marvel Universe Autographs

STATED ODDS 1:720
2 Dexter Soy 125.00 300.00
3 Adi Granov 125.00 300.00
4 Brandon Peterson 150.00 400.00
5 Paolo Rivera 100.00 250.00
6 Jason Pearson
7 Carlo Pagulayan 125.00 300.00
10 Randy Green
11 Scot Eaton 150.00 400.00
12 Stephanie Hans 250.00 600.00
14 Joe Jusko 300.00 750.00
15 Brad Walker
16 Brandon Peterson 150.00 400.00
17 Joe Jusko 200.00 500.00
19 Paco Medina
20 Mark Bagley 150.00 400.00

2013 Fleer Retro Marvel 1992 Impel Marvel Universe

COMMON CARD (1-15) 10.00 25.00
STATED ODDS 1:10
1 Captain America 15.00 40.00
2 Cyclops 12.00 30.00
3 Daredevil 15.00 40.00
4 Deadpool 30.00 75.00
5 Hulk 15.00 40.00
7 Iron Man 20.00 50.00
8 Loki 15.00 40.00
10 Spider-Man 60.00 150.00
11 Storm 15.00 40.00
12 Thor 15.00 40.00
13 Wolverine 50.00 120.00
14 Magneto 15.00 40.00
15 Thanos 20.00 50.00

2013 Fleer Retro Marvel 1992 Impel Marvel Universe Autographs

COMMON AUTO 10.00 25.00
STATED ODDS 1:960
2 Giuseppe Camuncoli 250.00 600.00
4 Patrick Zircher
5 Michael Golden 60.00 150.00
6 Ryan Stegman 100.00 250.00
8 Stephanie Hans
9 Stefano Caselli 60.00 150.00
10 Brad Walker 600.00 1500.00
11 Arthur Adams 30.00 75.00
13 Arthur Adams 250.00 600.00
14 Mike Perkins 150.00 400.00
15 Mark Bagley

2013 Fleer Retro Marvel Hardware

COMMON CARD (1-10) 12.00 30.00
STATED ODDS 1:60
1 Punisher 40.00 100.00
2 Deadpool 125.00 300.00
3 Iron Man 60.00 150.00
5 Thor 60.00 150.00
8 Black Widow 40.00 100.00
9 Mandarin 15.00 40.00

2013 Fleer Retro Marvel Holograms

COMMON CARD (H1-H3) 75.00 200.00
STATED ODDS 1:80
H1 Fantastic Four vs Dr. Doom 125.00 300.00
H2 New Avengers vs Dark Avengers 250.00 600.00

2013 Fleer Retro Marvel Intimidation Nation

COMMON CARD (1-20) 20.00 50.00
STATED ODDS 1:30
1 Wolverine 60.00 150.00
3 Hulk 75.00 200.00
4 Ghost Rider 75.00 200.00
5 Punisher 40.00 100.00
6 Silver Surfer 60.00 150.00
7 Black Panther 40.00 100.00
8 Red Hulk 30.00 75.00
10 Deadpool 100.00 250.00
11 Galactus 60.00 150.00
12 Magneto 75.00 200.00
16 Thanos 40.00 100.00
17 Venom 75.00 200.00
18 Carnage 60.00 150.00
19 Doctor Doom 60.00 150.00
20 Juggernaut 30.00 75.00

2013 Fleer Retro Marvel Jambalaya

COMMON CARD (1-21) 200.00 500.00
STATED ODDS 1:200
2 Invisible Woman 1000.00 2500.00
4 Human Torch 600.00 1500.00
5 Spider-Man 2000.00 5000.00
6 Iron Man 1200.00 3000.00
8 Thor 2000.00 4000.00
10 Wolverine 2000.00 5000.00
11 Cyclops 300.00 800.00
12 Iceman 300.00 800.00
14 Silver Surfer 500.00 1000.00
15 Daredevil 1200.00 3000.00
16 Deadpool 2000.00 4000.00
18 Doctor Doom 400.00 800.00
19 Venom 500.00 1000.00

2013 Fleer Retro Marvel Metal

COMMON CARD (1-42) 10.00 25.00
STATED ODDS 7:20
2 Invisible Woman 15.00 40.00
3 Thing 25.00 60.00
4 Human Torch 12.00 30.00
5 Spider-Man 200.00 500.00
8 Iron Man 100.00 250.00
9 Captain America 75.00 200.00
10 Thor 40.00 100.00
11 Hulk 30.00 75.00
13 Doctor Strange 30.00 75.00
14 Ms. Marvel 30.00 75.00
15 Scarlet Witch 30.00 75.00
16 Wolverine 200.00 500.00
17 Emma Frost 25.00 60.00
18 Cyclops 15.00 40.00
19 Jean Grey 12.00 30.00
22 Storm 20.00 50.00
23 Psylocke 60.00 150.00
24 Nova 15.00 40.00
25 Silver Surfer 60.00 150.00
26 Daredevil 30.00 75.00
27 Deadpool 100.00 250.00
29 Punisher 30.00 75.00
30 Ghost Rider 30.00 75.00
31 Venom 60.00 150.00
32 Phoenix 30.00 75.00
33 Green Goblin 20.00 50.00
35 Loki 30.00 75.00
36 Magneto 50.00 120.00
37 Doctor Doom 40.00 100.00
39 Thanos 60.00 150.00
40 Mystique 20.00 50.00
41 Apocalypse 20.00 50.00
42 Galactus 25.00 60.00

2013 Fleer Retro Marvel Metal Precious Metal Gems Blue

COMMON CARD (1-42) 400.00 1000.00
STATED PRINT RUN 50 SER.#'d SETS
1 Mr. Fantastic 2500.00 6000.00
2 Invisible Woman 1500.00 4000.00
3 Thing 1500.00 4000.00
4 Human Torch 1200.00 3000.00
5 Spider-Man 20000.00 40000.00
6 Luke Cage 1250.00 2500.00
7 Domino 1000.00 2000.00
8 Iron Man 15000.00 30000.00
9 Captain America 10000.00 25000.00
10 Thor 3000.00 7500.00
11 Hulk 7500.00 15000.00
13 Doctor Strange 1000.00 2000.00
14 Ms. Marvel 1500.00 3000.00
15 Scarlet Witch 1000.00 2000.00
16 Wolverine 15000.00 30000.00
17 Emma Frost 1000.00 2500.00
18 Cyclops 1200.00 3000.00
20 Rogue 500.00 1200.00
22 Storm 2500.00 5000.00
23 Psylocke 1200.00 3000.00
24 Nova 1500.00 4000.00
25 Silver Surfer 3000.00 7500.00
26 Daredevil 3000.00 7500.00
27 Deadpool 4000.00 10000.00
29 Punisher 2000.00 4000.00
31 Venom 2000.00 4000.00
32 Phoenix 5000.00 10000.00
33 Green Goblin 600.00 1200.00
34 Red Skull 1600.00 3200.00
35 Loki 2500.00 5000.00
36 Magneto 2500.00 5000.00
38 Sabretooth 1250.00 2500.00
39 Thanos 1250.00 2500.00
40 Mystique 1500.00 3000.00
41 Apocalypse 1250.00 2500.00
42 Galactus 1500.00 3000.00

2013 Fleer Retro Marvel Metal Precious Metal Gems Green

STATED PRINT RUN 10 SER.#'d SETS
1 Mr. Fantastic 2000.00 4000.00
2 Invisible Woman 2000.00 4000.00
3 Thing 6000.00 15000.00
4 Human Torch 2500.00 5000.00
13 Doctor Strange 5000.00 10000.00
14 Ms. Marvel 2000.00 4000.00
15 Scarlet Witch 5000.00 10000.00
22 Storm 10000.00 20000.00
37 Doctor Doom 4000.00 8000.00
40 Mystique 15000.00 30000.00

2013 Fleer Retro Marvel Metal Precious Metal Gems Red

COMMON CARD (1-42) 150.00 400.00
STATED PRINT RUN 100 SER.#'d SETS
1 Mr. Fantastic 600.00 1500.00
3 Thing 250.00 600.00
4 Human Torch 300.00 800.00
5 Spider-Man 10000.00 20000.00
7 Domino 500.00 1200.00
8 Iron Man 2000.00 5000.00
9 Captain America 1200.00 3000.00

10 Thor 1200.00 3000.00
11 Hulk 1200.00 3000.00
12 Iron Fist 250.00 600.00
13 Doctor Strange 1000.00 2500.00
14 Ms. Marvel 500.00 1200.00
15 Scarlet Witch 1000.00 2500.00
16 Wolverine 4000.00 10000.00
17 Emma Frost 400.00 1000.00
18 Cyclops 600.00 1500.00
20 Rogue 400.00 1000.00
22 Storm 1000.00 2000.00
23 Psylocke 1000.00 2500.00
24 Nova 800.00 2000.00
25 Silver Surfer 2000.00 4000.00
26 Daredevil 1000.00 2500.00
27 Deadpool 2500.00 6000.00
28 She-Hulk 400.00 1000.00
29 Punisher 600.00 1500.00
30 Ghost Rider 1000.00 2000.00
31 Venom 1200.00 3000.00
32 Phoenix 300.00 600.00
33 Green Goblin 400.00 1000.00
35 Loki 1000.00 2000.00
36 Magneto 600.00 1500.00
37 Doctor Doom 2000.00 5000.00
39 Thanos 1000.00 2500.00
40 Mystique 1200.00 3000.00
41 Apocalypse 600.00 1500.00
42 Galactus 1000.00 2000.00

2013 Fleer Retro Marvel Power Blast

COMMON CARD (1-21) 40.00 100.00
STATED ODDS 1:33
1 Black Panther 75.00 200.00
2 Black Widow 150.00 400.00
4 Captain America 125.00 300.00
5 Colossus 60.00 150.00
6 Cyclops 50.00 120.00
8 Deadpool 250.00 600.00
10 Hulk 60.00 150.00
11 Human Torch 50.00 120.00
12 Iron Man 75.00 200.00
13 Moon Knight 200.00 500.00
16 Punisher 60.00 150.00
18 Spider-Man 300.00 750.00
19 Thing 60.00 150.00
21 Wolverine 200.00 500.00

2013 Fleer Retro Marvel Quick Strike

COMMON CARD (1-21) 25.00 60.00
STATED ODDS 1:40
1 Iron Fist 40.00 100.00
2 Spider-Man 300.00 800.00
3 Spider-Woman 60.00 150.00
4 Daredevil 75.00 200.00
6 Silver Surfer 200.00 500.00
7 Nightcrawler 75.00 200.00
9 Black Panther 60.00 150.00
10 Beast 75.00 200.00
11 Captain America 400.00 1000.00
12 Moon Knight 250.00 600.00
15 Gamora 30.00 75.00
16 Ka-Zar 60.00 150.00
17 Tigra 75.00 200.00
18 Psylocke 50.00 120.00
20 Iron Man 300.00 800.00

2013 Fleer Retro Marvel Stickers

COMPLETE SET (25) 75.00 200.00
COMMON CARD (1-25) 2.50 6.00
STATED ODDS 1:5
2 Invisible Woman 3.00 8.00
5 Spider-Man 12.00 30.00
6 Captain America 4.00 10.00
7 Hulk 2.50 8.00
8 Iron Man 8.00 20.00
9 Thor 4.00 10.00
12 Silver Surfer 5.00 12.00
13 Black Panther 15.00
15 Daredevil 3.00 8.00
16 Doctor Strange 3.00 8.00

19 Wolverine 10.00 25.00
20 Black Widow 4.00 10.00
22 Magneto 8.00 20.00
23 Doctor Doom 6.00 15.00
24 Kang The Conquerer 3.00 8.00
25 Galactus 5.00 12.00

2013 Fleer Retro Marvel Ti-22

COMMON CARD (1-21) 60.00 150.00
STATED ODDS 1:40
1 Captain America 500.00 1200.00
2 Cyclops 75.00 200.00
3 Deadpool 250.00 600.00
4 Hulk 125.00 300.00
5 Human Torch 75.00 200.00
7 Invisible Woman 100.00 250.00
9 Iron Man 400.00 1000.00
11 Ms. Marvel 100.00 250.00
12 Punisher 150.00 400.00
13 Silver Surfer 150.00 400.00
14 Spider-Man 600.00 1500.00
17 Thor 200.00 500.00
19 Wolverine 600.00 1500.00
20 Doctor Doom 125.00 300.00
21 Magneto 75.00 200.00

2013 Fleer Retro Marvel Ultra Stars

COMPLETE SET (15) 200.00 500.00
COMMON CARD (1-15) 15.00 40.00
STATED ODDS 1:40
1 Beta Ray Bill 20.00 50.00
2 Adam Warlock 20.00 50.00
4 Thanos 50.00 120.00
5 Thor 40.00 100.00
6 Mr. Fantastic 20.00 50.00
7 Thing 20.00 50.00
8 Invisible Woman 25.00 60.00
9 Human Torch 20.00 50.00
10 Nova 30.00 75.00
11 Star-Lord 25.00 60.00
12 Galactus 30.00 75.00
15 Darkhawk 20.00 50.00

2013 Fleer Retro Marvel Ultra X-Men

COMPLETE SET (30) 125.00 300.00
COMMON CARD (1-30) 5.00 12.00
STATED ODDS 1:4
1 Angel 8.00 20.00
4 Beast 6.00 15.00
5 Bishop 6.00 15.00
6 Cable 6.00 15.00
8 Colossus 8.00 20.00
9 Cyclops 10.00 25.00
11 Emma Frost 8.00 20.00
12 Gambit 20.00 50.00
13 Havok 6.00 15.00
14 Hope 6.00 15.00
16 Jean Grey 6.00 15.00
18 Kitty Pryde 10.00 25.00
22 Namor 8.00 20.00
23 Nightcrawler 6.00 15.00
24 Professor X 8.00 20.00
25 Psylocke 10.00 25.00
26 Rogue 6.00 15.00
27 Storm 12.00 30.00
29 Wolverine 30.00 75.00
30 X-23 10.00 25.00

2015 Fleer Retro Marvel

COMPLETE SET (60) 12.00 30.00
UNOPENED BOX (20 PACKS) 120.00 150.00
COMMON CARD (1-60) .40 1.00
1 Ant-Man 1.50 4.00
5 Black Widow .75 2.00
8 Captain America 1.25 3.00
13 Daredevil 1.25 3.00
14 Deadpool 1.25 3.00
23 Hawkeye .75 2.00
25 Hulk .75 2.00
29 Iron Man 1.50 4.00
40 Punisher 1.25 3.00
47 Spider-Man 1.50 4.00
50 Star-Lord .75 2.00
59 Wolverine 1.50 4.00

2015 Fleer Retro Marvel 1960 Fleer

COMPLETE SET (21) 150.00 400.00
COMMON CARD (1-21) 10.00 25.00
RANDOM INSERTS IN PACKS
1 Captain America 25.00 60.00
2 Thor 15.00 40.00
4 Spider-Man 30.00 75.00
6 Doctor Strange 40.00 100.00
7 Daredevil 15.00 40.00
8 Black Widow 12.00 30.00
9 Black Panther 15.00 40.00
11 Hulk 12.00 30.00
15 Scarlet Witch 12.00 30.00
16 Iron Man 30.00 75.00
17 Iron Fist 12.00 30.00

2015 Fleer Retro Marvel 1982 Fleer

COMPLETE SET (21) 300.00 800.00
COMMON CARD (1-21) 10.00 25.00
RANDOM INSERTS IN PACKS
1 Captain America 30.00 75.00
2 Nick Fury 15.00 40.00
3 Red Skull 12.00 30.00
4 Wolverine 100.00 250.00
5 Storm 12.00 30.00
6 Magneto 12.00 30.00
7 Hulk 12.00 30.00
10 Spider-Man 125.00 300.00
11 Daredevil 20.00 50.00
12 Venom 100.00 250.00
13 Iron Man 20.00 50.00
14 Black Widow 30.00 75.00
15 Blade 12.00 30.00
17 Rogue 25.00 60.00
18 Cyclops 30.00 75.00
19 Spider-Woman 20.00 50.00
20 Black Cat 15.00 40.00
21 Mysterio 15.00 40.00

2015 Fleer Retro Marvel 1990 Marvel Universe Impel

COMPLETE SET (18) 300.00 750.00
COMMON CARD (1-18) 12.00 30.00
STATED ODDS 1:9
1 Black Panther 40.00 100.00
2 Black Widow 25.00 60.00
4 Captain America 30.00 75.00
5 Captain Marvel 15.00 40.00
6 Magneto 15.00 40.00
8 Doctor Strange 30.00 75.00
9 Red Skull 15.00 40.00
10 Hulk 25.00 60.00
11 Iron Man 30.00 75.00
12 Thanos 50.00 120.00
13 Spider-Man 60.00 150.00
15 Ultron 15.00 40.00
16 Thor 20.00 50.00
17 Wolverine 60.00 150.00
18 Venom 60.00 150.00

2015 Fleer Retro Marvel 1990 Marvel Universe Impel Autographs

COMPLETE SET (13)
COMMON CARD (1-13) 4.00 10.00
STATED ODDS 1:5 FOR ALL AUTOS
1 Dave Wilkins 6.00 15.00
3 Jenny Frison 6.00 15.00
5 Dexter Soy 5.00 12.00
7 Chris Samnee 5.00 12.00
13 Patrick Scherberger 5.00 12.00
14 Aleksi Briclot 6.00 15.00
15 George Perez 12.00 30.00
16 Esad Ribic 6.00 15.00

2015 Fleer Retro Marvel 1992 X-Men Impel

COMPLETE SET (15) 100.00 250.00
COMMON CARD (1-15) 6.00 15.00
STATED ODDS 1:11
3 Captain America 10.00 25.00
5 Emma Frost 8.00 20.00
6 Gambit 20.00 50.00
7 Iron Man 15.00 40.00
8 Magneto 10.00 25.00
13 Scarlet Witch 20.00 50.00
14 Storm 15.00 40.00
15 Wolverine 30.00 75.00

2015 Fleer Retro Marvel 1992 X-Men Impel Autographs

COMMON CARD (1-12) 4.00 10.00
STATED ODDS 1:5 FOR ALL AUTOS
2 Adam Kubert
5 Olivier Coipel 10.00 25.00
8 Olivier Coipel 6.00 15.00
9 Jim Cheung 10.00 25.00
10 Olivier Coipel 5.00 12.00
13 Olivier Coipel 12.00 30.00
15 Stuart Immonen 6.00 15.00

2015 Fleer Retro Marvel 1993 Marvel Skybox Universe

COMPLETE SET (27) 50.00 125.00
COMMON CARD (1-27) 1.50 4.00
STATED ODDS 1:6
1 Captain America 2.00 5.00
3 Doctor Octopus 2.00 5.00
5 Spider-Man 15.00 40.00
8 Wolverine 12.00 30.00
10 Captain America 4.00 10.00
12 Daredevil 2.50 6.00
13 Iron Man 10.00 25.00
17 Spider-Man 20.00 50.00
18 Ant-Man 3.00 8.00
20 Captain America 1.50 4.00
21 Iron Patriot 3.00 8.00
22 Iron Man 2.00 5.00

2015 Fleer Retro Marvel 1994 Flair Prints

COMMON CARD (1-9) 12.00 30.00
RANDOMLY INSERTED INTO PACKS
1 Cyclops 15.00 40.00
2 Hulk 15.00 40.00
3 Spider-Man 25.00 60.00
6 Thor 20.00 50.00
7 Ultron 15.00 40.00
8 Venom 20.00 50.00
9 Wolverine 25.00 60.00

2015 Fleer Retro Marvel 1994 Fleer Suspended Animation

COMPLETE SET W/VAR (42) 250.00 600.00
COMPLETE SET W/O VAR (30) 150.00 400.00
COMMON CARD (1-42) 2.50 6.00
RANDOMLY INSERTED INTO PACKS
1A Captain America/Shield Right Hand 25.00 60.00
1B Captain America/Shield Left Hand 40.00 100.00
3A Black Widow/Left Fist Front 6.00 15.00
3B Black Widow/Left Fist Back 8.00 20.00
4 Falcon 6.00 15.00
5 Hawkeye 2.00 5.00
6 Hulk 6.00 15.00
7A Iron Man/Facing Front 20.00 50.00
7B Iron Man/Facing Left 30.00 75.00
8B M.O.D.O.K./Facing Left 2.00 5.00
9 Nick Fury 5.00 12.00
11 Thor 10.00 25.00
12B Hulk/Left Forearm Up 8.00 20.00
14 Devil Dinosaur 2.00 5.00
15 Hulk Jump Jet 3.00 8.00
16A Leader/Touching Head 2.00 5.00
17B Red Hulk/Drawing Gun 8.00 20.00
18B She-Hulk/Posing 6.00 15.00
19 Skaar 2.00 5.00
20A Spider-Man/Leaping 30.00 75.00
20B Spider-Man/Swinging 400.00 100.00
22A Iron Fist/Fist on Fire 2.50 6.00
23 Nick Fury 2.50 6.00
26 Sandman 3.00 8.00
27 Scorpion 2.50 6.00

28 Spider-Man 60.00 150.00
29A Venom/Hands Down 25.00 60.00
29B Venom/Hands Up 40.00 100.00
30 White Tiger 3.00 8.00

2015 Fleer Retro Marvel 1994 Marvel Flair

COMPLETE SET (30) 125.00 300.00
COMMON CARD (1-30) 2.50 6.00
STATED ODDS 1:4
1 Black Widow 4.00 10.00
3 Enchantress 3.00 8.00
4 Captain America 10.00 25.00
5 Captain Marvel 4.00 10.00
6 Green Goblin 3.00 8.00
7 Cyclops 5.00 12.00
8 Doctor Strange 10.00 25.00
9 Loki 4.00 10.00
10 Gambit 8.00 20.00
12 Magneto 3.00 8.00
15 Mystique 3.00 8.00
16 Iron Man 12.00 30.00
17 Jean Grey 3.00 8.00
20 Scarlet Witch 8.00 20.00
21 Sabretooth 3.00 8.00
22 Spider-Man 40.00 100.00
24 Thanos 12.00 30.00
25 Star-Lord 4.00 10.00
26 Storm 8.00 20.00
28 Thor 6.00 15.00
29 Wolverine 40.00 100.00
30 Venom 15.00 40.00

2015 Fleer Retro Marvel 1994 Marvel Flair Power Blast

COMPLETE SET (18) 300.00 800.00
COMMON CARD (1-18) 6.00 15.00
STATED ODDS 1:33
1 Blade 20.00 50.00
3 Cyclops 10.00 25.00
4 Black Cat 20.00 50.00
5 Deadpool 75.00 200.00
6 Ghost Rider 25.00 60.00
7 Hulk 25.00 60.00
8 Black Widow 20.00 50.00
9 Iron Man 75.00 200.00
10 Moon Knight 60.00 150.00
11 Namor 25.00 60.00
12 Elektra 30.00 75.00
13 Punisher 15.00 40.00
15 Rocket Raccoon 12.00 30.00
17 Winter Soldier 12.00 30.00
18 Wolverine 125.00 300.00

2015 Fleer Retro Marvel 1995 Flair Holoblast

COMMON CARD (1-3) 75.00 200.00
STATED ODDS 1:240
1 The Avengers/Ultron 150.00 400.00
2 Spider-Man/Venom 300.00 800.00

2015 Fleer Retro Marvel 1995 Marvel Metal Blaster

COMPLETE SET (42) 250.00 600.00
COMMON CARD (1-42) 6.00 15.00
STATED ODDS 1:2
2 Black Panther 20.00 50.00
3 Apocalypse 8.00 20.00
4 Black Widow 20.00 50.00
5 Captain America 30.00 75.00
7 Captain Marvel 10.00 25.00
8 Cyclops 15.00 40.00
9 Dark Phoenix 30.00 75.00
10 Daredevil 10.00 25.00
11 Deadpool 40.00 100.00
12 Doctor Octopus 10.00 25.00
13 Doctor Strange 30.00 75.00
16 Falcon 8.00 20.00
17 Gambit 20.00 50.00
18 Juggernaut 8.00 20.00
19 Ghost Rider 15.00 40.00
20 Hulk 15.00 40.00
21 Loki 12.00 30.00
23 Iron Man 30.00 75.00
24 Magneto 25.00 60.00
26 Namor 10.00 25.00
27 Mystique 12.00 30.00
28 Nova 12.00 30.00
29 Punisher 10.00 25.00
30 Red Skull 8.00 20.00
31 Scarlet Witch 15.00 40.00
32 She-Hulk 15.00 40.00
34 Spider-Man 125.00 300.00
36 Thanos 30.00 75.00
37 Storm 15.00 40.00
38 Thor 12.00 30.00
39 Ultron 8.00 20.00
41 Wolverine 40.00 100.00
42 Venom 40.00 100.00

2015 Fleer Retro Marvel 1995 Marvel Metal Blaster Precious Metal Gems PMG Blue

COMMON CARD (1-42) 150.00 300.00
STATED PRINT RUN 50 SER.#'d SETS
2 Black Panther 750.00 1500.00
3 Apocalypse 300.00 600.00
4 Black Widow 500.00 1000.00
5 Captain America 2500.00 6000.00
6 Bullseye 500.00 1200.00
7 Captain Marvel 600.00 1500.00
8 Cyclops 250.00 500.00
9 Dark Phoenix 1000.00 2000.00
10 Daredevil 350.00 700.00
11 Deadpool 2000.00 4000.00
12 Doctor Octopus 600.00 1500.00
13 Doctor Strange 1000.00 2500.00
14 Elektra 300.00 800.00
15 Green Goblin 600.00 1500.00
16 Falcon 200.00 400.00
17 Gambit 250.00 500.00
18 Juggernaut 200.00 400.00
20 Hulk 1200.00 3000.00
21 Loki 500.00 1000.00
22 Iceman 600.00 1500.00
23 Iron Man 3000.00 7500.00
24 Magneto 2000.00 4000.00
26 Namor 200.00 400.00
27 Mystique 300.00 600.00
28 Nova 200.00 400.00
29 Punisher 250.00 500.00
30 Red Skull 300.00 800.00
31 Scarlet Witch 600.00 1200.00
32 She-Hulk 250.00 500.00
33 Sabretooth 250.00 600.00
34 Spider-Man 8000.00 15000.00
35 Star-Lord 250.00 500.00
36 Thanos 750.00 1500.00
37 Storm 400.00 1000.00
38 Thor 400.00 800.00
39 Ultron 400.00 800.00
40 Vision 750.00 1500.00
41 Wolverine 10000.00 20000.00
42 Venom 2500.00 5000.00

2015 Fleer Retro Marvel 1995 Marvel Metal Blaster Precious Metal Gems PMG Green

STATED PRINT RUN 10 SER.#'d SETS
1 Ant-Man 2000.00 4000.00
2 Black Panther 2500.00 5000.00
3 Apocalypse 1500.00 3000.00
5 Captain America 3000.00 6000.00
6 Bullseye 300.00 600.00
7 Captain Marvel 1500.00 3000.00
13 Doctor Strange 2500.00 5000.00
14 Elektra 300.00 600.00
17 Gambit 1500.00 3000.00
20 Hulk 2500.00 5000.00
23 Iron Man 3000.00 6000.00
24 Magneto 1500.00 3000.00
31 Scarlet Witch 1250.00 2500.00
33 Sabretooth 600.00 1200.00
35 Star-Lord 1500.00 3000.00
36 Thanos 1500.00 3000.00
39 Ultron 1250.00 2500.00
40 Vision 1250.00 2500.00

2015 Fleer Retro Marvel 1995 Marvel Metal Blaster Precious Metal Gems PMG Red

COMMON CARD (1-42) 75.00 150.00
STATED PRINT RUN 100 SER.#'d SETS
1 Ant-Man 100.00 200.00
2 Black Panther 500.00 1000.00
3 Apocalypse 100.00 200.00
4 Black Widow 200.00 400.00
5 Captain America 600.00 1200.00
6 Bullseye 150.00 300.00
7 Captain Marvel 200.00 400.00
8 Cyclops 200.00 400.00
9 Dark Phoenix 150.00 300.00
10 Daredevil 200.00 400.00
11 Deadpool 600.00 1200.00
12 Doctor Octopus 150.00 300.00
13 Doctor Strange 300.00 600.00
14 Elektra 125.00 250.00
15 Green Goblin 150.00 300.00
17 Gambit 200.00 400.00
19 Ghost Rider 400.00 800.00
20 Hulk 150.00 300.00
21 Loki 200.00 400.00
23 Iron Man 500.00 1000.00
24 Magneto 300.00 600.00
26 Namor 100.00 200.00
27 Mystique 125.00 250.00
29 Punisher 150.00 300.00
30 Red Skull 125.00 250.00
31 Scarlet Witch 200.00 400.00
32 She-Hulk 200.00 400.00
33 Sabretooth 100.00 200.00
34 Spider-Man 1000.00 2000.00
36 Thanos 250.00 500.00
37 Storm 200.00 400.00
38 Thor 350.00 700.00
39 Ultron 100.00 200.00
40 Vision 150.00 300.00
41 Wolverine 1250.00 2500.00
42 Venom 400.00 800.00

2015 Fleer Retro Marvel 1997-98 Fleer Ultra Star Power Supreme

COMPLETE SET (12) 30.00 80.00
COMMON CARD (1-12) 3.00 8.00
RANDOM INSERTS IN PACKS
1 Ant-Man 12.00 30.00
3 Leader 12.00 30.00
4 Black Panther 40.00 100.00
5 Doctor Strange 60.00 150.00
6 Loki 15.00 40.00
7 Emma Frost 30.00 75.00
8 Iron Man 60.00 150.00
9 Magneto 40.00 100.00
10 Jean Grey 20.00 50.00
12 Mister Sinister 15.00 40.00

2015 Fleer Retro Marvel 1999 Skybox E-X Century

COMPLETE SET (18) 75.00 200.00
COMMON CARD (1-18) 3.00 8.00
RANDOM INSERTS IN PACKS
1 Namor 10.00 25.00
2 Ka-Zar 6.00 15.00
3 Angel 5.00 12.00
4 Captain America 60.00 150.00
6 Red Skull 12.00 30.00
7 Destroyer 5.00 12.00
8 Miss America 6.00 15.00
9 Dracula 5.00 12.00
10 Droom 5.00 12.00
11 The Rawhide Kid 5.00 12.00
13 Goom 5.00 12.00
14 Grogg 5.00 12.00
15 Doctor Druid 6.00 15.00
16 Fin Fang Foom 5.00 12.00
17 Nick Fury 5.00 12.00

2015 Fleer Retro Marvel 2000 Fleer Focus Star Studded

COMPLETE SET (12) 75.00 200.00
COMMON CARD (1-12) 6.00 15.00
RANDOM INSERTS IN PACKS
3 Abomination 10.00 25.00
4 Hercules 10.00 25.00
5 Hulk 15.00 40.00
8 She-Hulk 20.00 50.00
9 Red Hulk 8.00 20.00
10 Thor 20.00 50.00
11 Wonder Man 8.00 20.00
12 Thanos 20.00 50.00

2015 Fleer Retro Marvel Autographs

COMMON CARD 3.00 8.00
STATED ODDS 1:5 FOR ALL AUTOS
1 Terry Dodson 5.00 12.00
2 Simone Bianchi 4.00 10.00
3 Julian Totino Tedesco 4.00 10.00
4 Simone Bianchi 4.00 10.00
5 Phil Noto 4.00 10.00
9 Paolo Rivera 6.00 15.00
12 Walt Simonson 10.00 25.00
16 Terry Dodson 8.00 20.00
23 Mike Deodato Jr. 4.00 10.00
35 Terry Dodson 4.00 10.00
40 Kenneth Rocafort 5.00 12.00
44 Jim Cheung 4.00 10.00
45 Chris Bachalo 6.00 15.00
47 Ramon Perez 4.00 10.00
50 Mark Bagley 6.00 15.00
55 Brandon Peterson 5.00 12.00
56 Adi Granov 5.00 12.00

2015 Fleer Retro Marvel Jambalaya

COMMON CARD (1-21) 75.00 200.00
STATED ODDS 1:200
1 Captain America 250.00 500.00
2 Cyclops 150.00 400.00
5 Deadpool 300.00 600.00
6 Loki 300.00 750.00
7 Doctor Strange 1200.00 3000.00
8 Elektra 500.00 1200.00
10 Hulk 300.00 600.00
13 Iron Man 2000.00 5000.00
14 Scarlet Witch 1500.00 4000.00
15 Thanos 125.00 250.00
16 Spider-Man 750.00 1500.00
17 Storm 400.00 1000.00
18 Ultron 300.00 750.00
19 Thor 150.00 300.00
20 Wolverine 1500.00 4000.00
21 Venom 250.00 500.00

2015 Fleer Retro Marvel Skybox Universe Autographs

COMMON AUTO 5.00 12.00
STATED ODDS 1:5 FOR ALL AUTOS
1 Michael Zeck 30.00 75.00
2 Michael Zeck 10.00 25.00
4 Michael Zeck 25.00 60.00
5 Michael Zeck 150.00 400.00
8 Michael Zeck 60.00 150.00
9 Michael Zeck 10.00 25.00
10 Mike Perkins 30.00 75.00
14 Ariel Olivetti 10.00 25.00
18 Phil Hester 25.00 60.00
20 Olivier Coipel 20.00 50.00
21 Stuart Immonen 8.00 20.00
22 Olivier Coipel 20.00 50.00
25 Olivier Coipel 6.00 15.00

2022 Fleer Ultra Avengers

COMPLETE SET W/SP (105)
COMPLETE SET W/O SP (90) 125.00 300.00
UNOPENED BOX (12 PACKS) 250.00 300.00
UNOPENED PACK (6 CARDS) 20.00 25.00

COMMON CARD (1-90) 2.50 6.00
COMMON SP (91-105) 5.00 12.00
*GREEN: .5X TO 1.2X BASIC CARDS
*ORANGE/549: .6X TO 1.5X BASIC CARDS
*BLUE/360: .75X TO 2X BASIC CARDS
*BURGUNDY/141: 1.5X TO 4X BASIC CARDS

2022 Fleer Ultra Avengers 1st Appearances

COMPLETE SET (15) 15.00 40.00
COMMON CARD (FA1-FA15) 2.00 5.00
*GREEN: .5X TO 1.2X BASIC CARDS
*ORANGE/549: .6X TO 1.5X BASIC CARDS
*BLUE/360: .75X TO 2X BASIC CARDS
*BURGUNDY/141: 1.2X TO 3X BASIC CARDS
*RED/63: 1.5X TO 4X BASIC CARDS
STATED ODDS 1:6.7 HOBBY/EPACK/BLASTER

2022 Fleer Ultra Avengers 3 X 3

COMPLETE SET (9) 60.00 150.00
COMMON CARD (1-9) 8.00 20.00
STATED ODDS 1:24 HOBBY/EPACK/BLASTER
1 Spider-Man 15.00 40.00
2 Hulk 10.00 25.00
3 Thor 10.00 25.00
4 Iron Man 12.00 30.00
7 Captain Marvel 12.00 30.00
8 Scarlet Witch & Quicksilver 10.00 25.00
9 Vision & Captain America 12.00 30.00

2022 Fleer Ultra Avengers Artist Spotlight

COMPLETE SET (10) 10.00 25.00
COMMON CARD (AS1-AS10) 1.50 4.00
*GREEN: SAME VALUE AS BASIC
*ORANGE/549: .5X TO 1.2X BASIC CARDS
*BLUE/360: .6X TO 1.5X BASIC CARDS
*BURGUNDY/141: .75X TO 2X BASIC CARDS
*RED/63: 1.2X TO 3X BASIC CARDS
STATED ODDS 1:5 HOBBY/EPACK/BLASTER

2022 Fleer Ultra Avengers Checkmates

COMPLETE SET W/O SP (16) 50.00 125.00
COMMON CARD 5.00 12.00
COMMON SP 10.00 25.00
COMMON SSP 40.00 100.00
WHITE PAWNS (CP1-CP8)
WHITE ROOKS (CP9-CP10)
WHITE KNIGHTS (CP11-CP12)
WHITE BISHOPS (CP13-CP14)
WHITE QUEEN (CP15)
BLACK QUEEN (CP16)
BLACK PAWNS (CP17-CP24)
BLACK ROOKS (CP25-CP28)
BLACK KNIGHTS (CP27-CP28)
BLACK BISHOPS (CP29-CP30)
BLACK KING (CP31)
WHITE KING (CP32)
OVERALL PAWN ODDS 1:18
OVERALL ROOK ODDS 1:144
OVERALL KNIGHT ODDS 1:108
OVERALL BISHOP ODDS 1:120
OVERALL QUEEN ODDS 1:540
OVERALL KING ODDS 1:720
INSERTED IN HOBBY/EPACK/BLASTER
CP1 Namor 6.00 15.00
CP4 Vision 6.00 15.00
CP5 Scarlet Witch 8.00 20.00
CP7 Ant-Man 6.00 15.00
CP9 Spider-Man SP 25.00 60.00
CP10 Black Widow SP 15.00 40.00
CP13 Iron Man SP 15.00 40.00
CP14 Thor SP 12.00 30.00
CP15 Captain Marvel SSP 50.00 125.00
CP17 Magneto 8.00 20.00
CP20 Korvac 6.00 15.00
CP29 Ultron SP 12.00 30.00
CP30 Loki SP 12.00 30.00
CP31 Thanos SSP 75.00 200.00
CP32 Captain America SSP 125.00 300.00

2022 Fleer Ultra Avengers Checkmates Black Gilbert Martimiano Autographs

STATED PRINT RUN 25 SER.#'d SETS
CP1 Namor
CP2 Hercules 75.00 200.00
CP3 Hawkeye
CP4 Vision
CP5 Scarlet Witch
CP6 Quicksilver
CP7 Ant-Man
CP8 Wasp
CP9 Spider-Man
CP10 Black Widow
CP11 Black Panther
CP12 Hulk
CP13 Iron Man
CP14 Thor
CP15 Captain Marvel
CP16 Enchantress
CP17 Magneto 125.00 300.00
CP18 Ronan the Accuser 75.00 200.00
CP19 Winter Soldier 125.00 300.00
CP20 Korvac 60.00 150.00
CP21 Red Hulk
CP22 Iron Patriot
CP23 Sentry 75.00 200.00
CP24 High Evolutionary
CP25 Red Skull
CP26 Baron Zemo
CP27 M.O.D.O.K. 75.00 200.00
CP28 Taskmaster
CP29 Ultron
CP30 Loki
CP31 Thanos
CP32 Captain America

2022 Fleer Ultra Avengers Checkmates White Jason Juta Autographs

STATED PRINT RUN 25 SER.#'d SETS
CP1 Namor 75.00 200.00
CP2 Hercules 100.00 250.00
CP3 Hawkeye 30.00 75.00
CP4 Vision 75.00 200.00
CP5 Scarlet Witch 50.00 125.00
CP6 Quicksilver 60.00 150.00
CP7 Ant-Man 30.00 75.00
CP8 Wasp 75.00 200.00
CP9 Spider-Man 400.00 1000.00
CP10 Black Widow
CP11 Black Panther
CP12 Hulk
CP13 Iron Man 125.00 300.00
CP14 Thor
CP15 Captain Marvel 60.00 150.00
CP16 Enchantress
CP17 Magneto
CP18 Ronan the Accuser
CP19 Winter Soldier
CP20 Korvac
CP21 Red Hulk
CP22 Iron Patriot
CP23 Sentry
CP24 High Evolutionary
CP25 Red Skull
CP26 Baron Zemo
CP27 M.O.D.O.K.
CP28 Taskmaster
CP29 Ultron
CP30 Loki
CP31 Thanos
CP32 Captain America

2022 Fleer Ultra Avengers Comic Clippings

COMMON MEM/30-55 40.00 100.00

2022 Fleer Ultra Avengers Comic Clippings Coinage

COMMON MEM/20-40 60.00 150.00
RANDOMLY INSERTED INTO PACKS
CARDS SER.#'d 12-15
UNPRICED DUE TO SCARCITY
CCCAVG151 Avengers (1963) #151/30 75.00 200.00
CCCAVG183 Avengers (1963) #183/40 75.00 200.00
CCCAVG185 Avengers (1963) #185/40 75.00 200.00
CCCAVG195 Avengers (1963) #195/40 75.00 200.00
CCCAVG196 Avengers (1963) #196/40 75.00 200.00

2022 Fleer Ultra Avengers Comic Covers

COMMON MEM/26-49 50.00 125.00
COMMON MEM/50-108 40.00 100.00
RANDOMLY INSERTED INTO PACKS

2022 Fleer Ultra Avengers Earth's Mightiest Spin-Offs

COMPLETE SET (10) 10.00 25.00
COMMON CARD (SO1-SO10) 1.50 4.00
*GREEN: .5X TO 1.2X BASIC CARDS
*ORANGE/549: .6X TO 1.5X BASIC CARDS
*BLUE/360: .75X TO 2X BASIC CARDS
*BURGUNDY/141: 1.2X TO 3X BASIC CARDS
*RED/63: 1.5X TO 4X BASIC CARDS
STATED ODDS 1:5 HOBBY/EPACK/BLASTER

2022 Fleer Ultra Avengers Greatest Battles

COMPLETE SET (13) 12.00 30.00
COMMON CARD (EB1-EB13) 1.50 4.00
*GREEN: .5X TO 1.2X BASIC CARDS
*ORANGE/549: .6X TO 1.5X BASIC CARDS
*BLUE/360: .75X TO 2X BASIC CARDS
*BURGUNDY/141: 1.2X TO 3X BASIC CARDS
*RED/63: 1.5X TO 4X BASIC CARDS
STATED ODDS 1:6.7 HOBBY/EPACK/BLASTER

2022 Fleer Ultra Avengers Jambalaya

COMMON CARD (1-30) 60.00 150.00
STATED ODDS 1:144 HOBBY/EPACK
STATED ODDS 1:288 BLASTER
1 Ant-Man 125.00 300.00
2 Black Panther 200.00 500.00
3 Captain America 250.00 600.00
4 Falcon 75.00 200.00
5 Hawkeye 100.00 250.00
6 Hercules 75.00 200.00
7 Hulk 125.00 300.00
8 Iron Man 500.00 1200.00
9 Ares 60.00 150.00
10 Valkyrie 75.00 200.00
11 Daredevil 150.00 400.00
12 Thor 200.00 500.00
13 Vision 100.00 250.00
14 Wasp 75.00 200.00
15 Baron Zemo 75.00 200.00
16 Crossbones 60.00 150.00
17 Dormammu 75.00 200.00
18 Loki 150.00 400.00
19 Red Skull 100.00 250.00
20 Taskmaster 75.00 200.00
21 War Machine 125.00 300.00
22 Winter Soldier 75.00 200.00
23 Ultron 100.00 250.00
24 Korvac 125.00 300.00
25 Thanos 250.00 600.00
26 Wonder Man 75.00 200.00
27 Maria Hill 60.00 150.00
28 Ronan the Accuser 60.00 150.00
29 Ego The Living Planet 60.00 150.00
30 Captain Marvel 150.00 400.00

2022 Fleer Ultra Avengers Marvel Value Stamp Relics

COMMON MEM 15.00 40.00
STATED PRINT RUN 99 SER.#'d SETS
VS1 Ant-Man 40.00 100.00
VS2 Ares 30.00 75.00
VS3 Black Bolt 25.00 60.00
VS4 Black Panther 75.00 200.00
VS5 Black Widow 40.00 100.00
VS6 Captain America 75.00 200.00
VS7 Captain Marvel 60.00 150.00
VS8 Collector 25.00 60.00
VS9 Crystal 50.00 125.00
VS10 Daredevil 40.00 100.00
VS12 Dormammu 20.00 50.00
VS15 Hawkeye 25.00 60.00
VS16 Hela 20.00 50.00
VS17 Hellcat 30.00 75.00
VS18 Hercules 20.00 50.00
VS19 Hulk 75.00 200.00
VS20 Iron Man 75.00 200.00
VS26 Mantis 20.00 50.00
VS28 Moon Knight 75.00 200.00
VS33 Red Skull 30.00 75.00
VS34 Ronan The Accuser 20.00 50.00
VS35 Valkyrie 25.00 60.00
VS36 Patriot 30.00 75.00
VS37 Stature 25.00 60.00
VS40 Stingray 25.00 60.00
VS41 Thanos 125.00 300.00
VS42 Thor 60.00 150.00
VS44 Ultron 40.00 100.00
VS45 Vision 30.00 75.00
VS46 War Machine 50.00 125.00
VS47 Wasp 25.00 60.00
VS48 Winter Soldier 20.00 50.00

2022 Fleer Ultra Avengers Medallions

COMPLETE SET (50) 125.00 300.00
COMMON CARD (M1-M50) 4.00 10.00
*AMETHYST: .6X TO 1.5X BASIC CARDS
*GOLD/200: .75X TO 2X BASIC CARDS
*PLATINUM/100: 1X TO 2.5X BASIC CARDS
*RUBY RED/65: 2X TO 5X BASIC CARDS
STATED ODDS 1:2 HOBBY/EPACK
STATED ODDS 1:3 BLASTER
M1 Ant-Man 2.00 5.00
M2 Ares 1.50 4.00
M3 Black Bolt 2.50 6.00
M4 Black Panther 3.00 8.00
M5 Black Widow 3.00 8.00
M6 Captain America 4.00 10.00
M7 Captain Marvel 2.50 6.00
M8 Collector 1.50 4.00
M9 Crystal 1.50 4.00
M10 Daredevil 4.00 10.00
M11 Doctor Druid 1.50 4.00
M12 Dormammu 1.50 4.00
M13 Falcon 2.50 6.00
M14 Firebird 1.50 4.00
M15 Hawkeye 2.50 6.00
M16 Hela 2.00 5.00
M17 Hellcat 1.50 4.00
M18 Hercules 2.00 5.00
M19 Hulk 3.00 8.00
M20 Iron Man 4.00 10.00
M21 Korvac 1.50 4.00
M22 Living Lightning 1.50 4.00
M23 Lockjaw 1.50 4.00
M24 Rick Jones 1.50 4.00
M25 Malekith 1.50 4.00
M26 Mantis 2.00 5.00
M27 Mockingbird 2.00 5.00
M28 Moon Knight 3.00 8.00
M29 Nick Fury 2.00 5.00
M30 Photon 1.50 4.00
M31 Quasar 1.50 4.00
M32 Ego The Living Planet 1.50 4.00
M33 Red Skull 2.50 6.00
M34 Ronan the Accuser 1.50 4.00
M35 Maria Hill 1.50 4.00
M36 Patriot 1.50 4.00
M37 She-Hulk 2.00 5.00
M38 M.O.D.O.K. 1.50 4.00
M39 Beyonder 1.50 4.00
M40 Valkyrie 2.00 5.00
M41 Stingray 1.50 4.00
M42 U.S. Agent 1.50 4.00
M43 Thanos 4.00 10.00
M44 Thor 3.00 8.00

M45 Tigra	1.50	4.00
M46 Ultron	2.00	5.00
M47 Vision	2.00	5.00
M48 War Machine	2.00	5.00
M49 Wasp	2.00	5.00
M50 Winter Soldier	1.50	4.00

2022 Fleer Ultra Avengers Ultra Power

COMPLETE SET (30)	150.00	400.00
COMMON CARD (UP1-UP30)	5.00	12.00
*VARIATION/50: .75X TO 2X BASIC CARDS		
STATED ODDS 1:36 HOBBY/EPACK/BLASTER		
UP1 Captain America	20.00	50.00
UP2 Thanos	30.00	75.00
UP3 Captain Marvel	15.00	40.00
UP6 Daredevil	20.00	50.00
UP7 Ant-Man	6.00	15.00
UP11 Ultron		25.00
UP15 Loki	12.00	30.00
UP16 Thor	12.00	30.00
UP17 Doctor Strange	15.00	40.00
UP18 Dormammu	6.00	15.00
UP20 Black Bolt	6.00	15.00
UP22 Iron Man	30.00	75.00
UP23 Black Widow	12.00	30.00
UP26 Black Panther	10.00	25.00
UP27 Hawkeye	6.00	15.00
UP29 Hulk	15.00	40.00
UP30 Bruce Banner	10.00	25.00

2022 Fleer Ultra Avengers Ultra Stars

COMPLETE SET (50)	150.00	400.00
COMMON CARD (US1-US50)	2.50	6.00
*GOLD: 2X TO 5X BASIC CARDS		
STATED ODDS 1:3 BLASTER EXCLUSIVE		
US1 Ant-Man	4.00	10.00
US2 Ares	5.00	12.00
US4 Baron Zemo	4.00	10.00
US5 Black Knight	3.00	8.00
US6 Black Panther	8.00	20.00
US7 Black Widow	8.00	20.00
US8 Captain America	10.00	25.00
US9 Captain Britain	6.00	15.00
US10 Captain Marvel	8.00	20.00
US11 Daredevil	8.00	20.00
US12 Deadpool	12.00	30.00
US13 Doctor Strange	6.00	15.00
US14 Falcon	3.00	8.00
US15 Gamora	5.00	12.00
US17 Hawkeye	3.00	8.00
US18 Hellcat	4.00	10.00
US19 Hercules	4.00	10.00
US20 Hulk	10.00	25.00
US21 Hulkling	4.00	10.00
US22 Iron Fist	3.00	8.00
US23 Iron Lad	6.00	15.00
US24 Iron Man	12.00	30.00
US25 Jessica Jones	6.00	15.00
US26 Loki	8.00	20.00
US27 Luke Cage	4.00	10.00
US31 Nick Fury	3.00	8.00
US32 Patriot	4.00	10.00
US33 Red Skull	5.00	12.00
US34 Ronan the Accuser	3.00	8.00
US35 Ego The Living Planet	4.00	10.00
US36 Sentry	4.00	10.00
US37 She-Hulk	6.00	15.00
US39 Speed	3.00	8.00
US41 Swordsman	4.00	10.00
US42 Thanos	10.00	25.00
US43 Thor	8.00	20.00
US44 Jane Foster	5.00	12.00
US45 Ultron	6.00	15.00
US46 Vision	4.00	10.00
US47 War Machine	3.00	8.00
US48 Wasp	6.00	15.00
US49 Winter Soldier	3.00	8.00

2022 Fleer Ultra Avengers Universe Power Supreme

COMMON CARD (UPS1-UPS42)	5.00	12.00
*BLACK DIE-CUT: 2X TO 5X BASIC CARDS		
STATED ODDS 1:36 HOBBY/EPACK/BLASTER		
UPS1 Ant-Man	10.00	25.00
UPS2 Baron Zemo	6.00	15.00
UPS3 Black Bolt	6.00	15.00
UPS4 Black Panther	12.00	30.00
UPS5 Black Widow	15.00	40.00
UPS6 Captain America	15.00	40.00
UPS7 Collector	6.00	15.00
UPS9 Daredevil	12.00	30.00
UPS10 Doctor Strange	12.00	30.00
UPS12 Falcon	6.00	15.00
UPS14 Hawkeye	6.00	15.00
UPS15 Hela	8.00	20.00
UPS17 Hulk	10.00	25.00
UPS18 Iron Man	20.00	50.00
UPS19 Jessica Jones	8.00	20.00
UPS20 Loki	8.00	20.00
UPS21 Luke Cage	6.00	15.00
UPS23 Ego The Living Planet	8.00	20.00
UPS27 Nick Fury	6.00	15.00
UPS28 Red Hulk	12.00	30.00
UPS29 Red Skull	8.00	20.00
UPS30 Captain Marvel	20.00	50.00
UPS31 Beyonder	8.00	20.00
UPS32 Taskmaster	6.00	15.00
UPS33 Thanos	15.00	40.00
UPS35 Thor	10.00	25.00
UPS36 Tigra	6.00	15.00
UPS37 Ultron	6.00	15.00
UPS38 Vision	6.00	15.00
UPS39 Wasp	6.00	15.00
UPS40 Winter Soldier	8.00	20.00

2015-17 Funko Marvel Collector's Corp Patches

COMPLETE SET (15)		
COMMON PATCH	2.00	5.00
MARVEL COLLECTOR'S CORP EXCLUSIVE		
NNO Ant-Man	2.00	5.00
NNO Captain America	4.00	10.00
NNO Crossbones	2.00	5.00
NNO Deadpool	3.00	8.00
NNO Doctor Strange	2.00	5.00
NNO Falcon	2.00	5.00
NNO Iron Man & Ultron	2.00	5.00
NNO Ms. Marvel	2.00	5.00
NNO Red Skull	2.00	5.00
NNO Rocket Raccoon	2.00	5.00
NNO Spider-Man	3.00	8.00
NNO Star-Lord	2.00	5.00
NNO Storm	2.00	5.00
NNO Ultron	2.00	5.00
NNO Vulture	2.00	5.00

1990 Comic Images Ghost Rider I

COMPLETE SET (46)	4.00	10.00
UNOPENED BOX (50 PACKS)	20.00	30.00
UNOPENED PACK (5 CARDS+HEADER)	.40	.60
COMMON CARD (0-45)	.15	.40

1992 Comic Images Ghost Rider II

COMPLETE SET (80)	8.00	20.00
UNOPENED BOX (48 PACKS)	30.00	50.00
UNOPENED PACK (10 CARDS)	1.00	1.50
COMMON CARD (1-80)	.20	.50
NNO PROMO	.75	2.00

1992 Comic Images Ghost Rider II Glow-in-the-Dark

COMPLETE SET (10)	5.00	12.00
COMMON CARD (G1-G10)	.60	1.50
G1 Illuminating	1.00	2.50
G2 Vigilantes	1.25	3.00
G5 Wolverine	1.50	4.00
G7 Punisher	1.25	3.00
G9 Cable	.75	2.00

2015 Guardians of the Galaxy Animated Series Promos

COMPLETE SET (6)	5.00	12.00
COMMON CARD	1.25	3.00
3 Groot	1.50	4.00
5 Rocket Raccoon	1.50	4.00
6 Star-Lord	2.00	5.00

2013 Guardians of the Galaxy Marvel Now SDCC Promos

COMPLETE SET (6)	12.00	30.00
COMMON CARD	.60	1.50
4 Iron Man SP	10.00	25.00

2003 Hulk Film and Comic Series

COMPLETE SET (81)	5.00	12.00
UNOPENED BOX (24 PACKS)	60.00	100.00
UNOPENED PACK (5 CARDS)	3.00	5.00
COMMON CARD (1-81)	.12	.30

2003 Hulk Film and Comic Series Famous Hulk Covers

COMPLETE SET (45)	25.00	60.00
COMMON CARD (1-45)	1.00	2.50
STATED ODDS 1:1		

2003 Hulk Film and Comic Series Illustrated Film Scenes

COMPLETE SET (10)	8.00	20.00
COMMON CARD (IF01-IF02)	1.25	3.00
STATED ODDS 1:6		

2003 Hulk Film and Comic Series Promos

COMPLETE SET (2)	3.00	8.00
COMMON CARD (PC1-PC2)	2.00	5.00

2003 Hulk Fla-Vor-Ice

COMPLETE SET (5)	8.00	20.00
COMMON CARD (1-5)	2.50	6.00

1979 Topps Incredible Hulk

COMPLETE SET (88)	10.00	25.00
COMPLETE SET W/STICKERS (110)	12.00	30.00
UNOPENED BOX (36 PACKS)	250.00	500.00
UNOPENED PACK (7 CARDS+STICKER)	8.00	15.00
COMMON CARD (1-88)	.12	.30

1979 Topps Incredible Hulk Stickers

COMPLETE SET (22)	3.00	8.00
COMMON CARD (1-22)	.20	.50
STATED ODDS 1:1		

1991 Incredible Hulk

COMPLETE SET (90)	15.00	40.00
UNOPENED BOX (48 PACKS)	150.00	250.00
UNOPENED PACK (10 CARDS)	3.00	6.00
COMMON CARD (1-90)	.50	1.25

2003 Incredible Hulk

COMPLETE SET (72)	5.00	12.00
UNOPENED BOX (24 PACKS)	75.00	125.00
UNOPENED PACK (7 CARDS)	4.00	6.00
COMMON CARD (1-72)	.12	.30

2003 Incredible Hulk Crystal Clear

COMPLETE SET (5)	8.00	20.00
COMMON CARD (1-5)	2.00	5.00
STATED ODDS 1:12		

2003 Incredible Hulk Gamma Ray Foil

COMPLETE SET (10)	15.00	40.00
COMMON CARD (1-10)	2.00	5.00
STATED ODDS 1:6		

1978 Drake's Cakes Incredible Hulk

COMPLETE SET (24)	20.00	50.00
COMMON CARD (1-8)	3.00	8.00
COMMON CARD (9-24)	1.50	4.00

1979 Wall's Ice Cream Incredible Hulk

COMPLETE SET (20)	30.00	80.00
COMMON CARD (1-20)	2.00	5.00

1990 Comic Images Jim Lee I

COMPLETE SET (45)	10.00	25.00
UNOPENED BOX (50 PACKS)	20.00	25.00
UNOPENED PACK (5 CARDS+HEADER)	.50	.75
COMMON CARD (1-45)	.40	1.00

1991 Comic Images Jim Lee II

COMPLETE SET (45)	12.00	30.00
UNOPENED BOX (50 PACKS)	20.00	25.00
UNOPENED PACK (5 CARDS+HEADER)	.50	.75
COMMON CARD (1-45)	.50	1.25

1989 Comic Images John Byrne

COMPLETE SET (45)	5.00	12.00
UNOPENED BOX (50 PACKS)	30.00	40.00
UNOPENED PACK (5 CARDS)	.75	1.00
COMMON CARD (1-45)	.20	.50

2010 Legends of Marvel Black Widow

COMPLETE SET (9)	6.00	15.00
COMMON CARD (L1-L9)	1.25	3.00
STATED PRINT RUN 1939 SER.#'d SETS		

2010 Legends of Marvel Captain America

COMPLETE SET (9)	8.00	20.00
COMMON CARD (L1-L9)	1.50	4.00
STATED PRINT RUN 1939 SER.#'d SETS		

2010 Legends of Marvel Iron Man

COMPLETE SET (9)	8.00	20.00
COMMON CARD (L1-L9)	1.50	4.00
STATED PRINT RUN 1939 SER.#'d SETS		

2011 Legends of Marvel Elektra

COMPLETE SET (9)	5.00	12.00
COMMON CARD (L1-L9)	.75	2.00
STATED PRINT RUN 1939 SER.#'d SETS		

2011 Legends of Marvel Thor

COMPLETE SET (9)	6.00	15.00
COMMON CARD (L1-L9)	1.25	3.00
STATED PRINT RUN 1939 SER.#'d SETS		

2012 Legends of Marvel Ghost Rider

COMPLETE SET (9)	6.00	15.00
COMMON CARD (L1-L9)	1.25	3.00
STATED PRINT RUN 1939 SER.#'d SETS		

2012 Legends of Marvel Hulk

COMPLETE SET (9)	8.00	20.00
COMMON CARD (L1-L9)	1.50	4.00
STATED PRINT RUN 1939 SER.#'d SETS		

2012 Legends of Marvel Ms. Marvel

COMPLETE SET (9)	6.00	15.00
COMMON CARD (L1-L9)	1.25	3.00
STATED PRINT RUN 1939 SER.#'d SETS		

2012 Legends of Marvel Moon Knight

COMPLETE SET (9)	4.00	10.00
COMMON CARD (L1-L9)	.75	2.00
STATED PRINT RUN 1939 SER.#'d SETS		

2012 Legends of Marvel Thing

COMPLETE SET (9)	6.00	15.00
COMMON CARD (L1-L9)	1.25	3.00
STATED PRINT RUN 1939 SER.#'d SETS		

2013 Legends of Marvel Daredevil

COMPLETE SET (9)	8.00	20.00
COMMON CARD (L1-L9)	1.50	4.00
STATED PRINT RUN 1939 SER.#'d SETS		

2013 Legends of Marvel Marvel Girl

COMPLETE SET (9)	5.00	12.00
COMMON CARD (L1-L9)	1.00	2.50
STATED PRINT RUN 1939 SER.#'d SETS		

2013 Legends of Marvel Nova

COMPLETE SET (9)	5.00	12.00
COMMON CARD (L1-L9)	1.00	2.50
STATED PRINT RUN 1939 SER.#'d SETS		

2014 Legends of Marvel She-Hulk

COMPLETE SET (9)	4.00	10.00
COMMON CARD (L1-L9)	.75	2.00
STATED PRINT RUN 1939 SER.#'d SETS		

2014 Legends of Marvel War Machine

COMPLETE SET (9)	4.00	10.00
COMMON CARD (L1-L9)	.75	2.00
STATED PRINT RUN 1939 SER.#'d SETS		

1991 Comic Images Marvel 1st Covers II

COMPLETE SET (100)	15.00	40.00
UNOPENED BOX (48 PACKS)	100.00	150.00
UNOPENED PACK (10 CARDS)	2.50	4.00
COMMON CARD (1-100)	.20	.50
(LS) - LIMITED SERIES		
2 Giant-Size Chillers Curse of Dracula	.40	1.00
3 The Spectacular Spider-Man	1.25	3.00
5 The Marvel No-Prize Book	.40	1.00
8 Wolverine (LS)	.40	1.00
10 Uncanny X-Men at the Texas State Fair	1.25	3.00
14 Hawkeye (LS)	.75	1.50
16 The Spectacular Spider-Ham	1.50	4.00
18 Magik (LS)	.40	1.00
19 The Jack of Hearts (LS)	2.50	6.00
20 The X-Men and the Micronauts	.50	1.25
26 Moon Knight	1.50	4.00
32 Vision and Scarlet Witch (LS)	.50	1.25
33 Nightcrawler (LS)	.75	2.00
34 Official History of the Marvel Universe	1.25	3.00
36 The Punisher (LS)	.75	2.00
43 Strange Tales	.75	2.00
45 Silver Surfer	1.00	2.50
46 The Punisher	1.25	3.00
47 Hawkeye and Mockingbird	.75	2.00
48 Marvel Comics Presents Wolverine	1.25	3.00
50 Nick Fury vs. S.H.I.E.L.D.	1.25	3.00
58 Wolverine	.40	1.00
59 Semper Fi'	.50	1.25
61 What If ...	.50	1.25
63 Damage Control (LS)	.75	2.00
65 Marc Spector - Moon Knight	1.25	3.00
69 The Wolverine Saga	1.50	4.00
76 The Thanos Quest	1.25	3.00
78 Namor, The Sub-Mariner	.50	1.25
83 Guardians of the Galaxy	.60	1.50
87 Spider-Man	2.00	5.00
90 Black Panther: Panther's Prey (LS)	.60	1.50
95 The Deadly Foes of Spider-Man (LS)	.75	2.00
100 Checklist	1.00	2.50

2021 Upper Deck Marvel Ages

COMPLETE SET W/SP (300)	150.00	300.00
COMPLETE SET W/O SP (100)	10.00	25.00
UNOPENED BOX (16 PACKS)	150.00	250.00
UNOPENED PACK (12 CARDS)	10.00	15.00
COMMON LOW SERIES (1-100)	.20	.50
COMMON MID SERIES (101-200)	1.25	3.00
COMMON HIGH SERIES (201-300)	1.25	3.00
*STICKERS: 4X TO 10X BASIC CARDS		
*PHOTO VAR.: 4X TO 10X BASIC CARDS		
*FOILBOARD: 6X TO 15X BASIC CARDS		
STICKERS PARALLEL LOW SERIES ONLY		
PHOTO VARIANTS PARALLEL MID SERIES ONLY		
FOILBOARD PARALLEL HIGH SERIES ONLY		

2021 Upper Deck Marvel Ages 3-D Lenticular Puzzles

COMMON 3D1-3D4	15.00	40.00
COMMON 3D5-3D8	15.00	40.00
COMMON 3D9-3D12	15.00	40.00
COMMON 3D13-3D16	20.00	50.00
COMMON 3D17-3D20	10.00	25.00
STATED ODDS 1:136 HOBBY/EPACK		

2021 Upper Deck Marvel Ages Artist Spotlight Featuring Steve Ditko

COMPLETE SET (10)	20.00	50.00
COMMON CARD (ASF1-ASF10)	3.00	8.00
STATED ODDS 1:5 HOBBY/EPACK		

2021 Upper Deck Marvel Ages Bronze Metal Relics

COMPLETE SET (20)	200.00	500.00
COMMON MEM (BMR1-BMR20)	15.00	40.00
STATED PRINT RUN 65 SER.#'d SETS		

2021 Upper Deck Marvel Ages Comic Clippings

COMMON MEM	20.00	50.00
STATED PRINT RUN VARIES 10-75 CARDS		
CM26 Captain Marvel #26/25		
MP15 Marvel Premiere #15/10		
MSM1 Ms. Marvel #1/20		
MSP32 Marvel Spotlight #32/10		
ST167 Strange Tales #167/25		
TH169 Thor #169/25		

2021 Upper Deck Marvel Ages Copper Metal Relics

COMMON MEM (CMR1-CMR5)	25.00	60.00
STATED PRINT RUN 99 SER.#'d SETS		
CMR1 New Mutants #98	50.00	120.00
CMR4 Infinity Gauntlet #4	50.00	100.00
CMR5 Spider-Man #1	75.00	150.00

2021 Upper Deck Marvel Ages Decades 1960s

COMPLETE SET (10)	300.00	600.00
COMMON CARD	20.00	50.00
STATED ODDS 1:160		
D61 Captain America	50.00	100.00
D63 Thor	50.00	100.00
D64 Hulk	30.00	75.00
D65 Iron Man	75.00	150.00
D66 Doctor Strange	30.00	75.00
D67 Black Panther	75.00	150.00
D68 Spider-Man	150.00	300.00

2021 Upper Deck Marvel Ages Decades 1970s

COMPLETE SET (10)	125.00	250.00
COMMON CARD	10.00	25.00
STATED ODDS 1:80		
D71 Ghost Rider	25.00	60.00
D72 Blade	12.00	30.00
D73 Howard The Duck	15.00	40.00
D74 Valkyrie	15.00	40.00
D75 Wolverine	30.00	75.00
D76 Nova	15.00	40.00
D77 Captain Britain	12.00	30.00
D79 Morbius	15.00	40.00

2021 Upper Deck Marvel Ages Decades 1980s

COMPLETE SET (10)	60.00	120.00
COMMON CARD	6.00	15.00
STATED ODDS 1:53		
D82 Venom	20.00	50.00
D83 Cloak	8.00	20.00
D85 Magik	10.00	25.00
D86 Silver Sable	8.00	20.00
D87 Psylocke	10.00	25.00
D88 War Machine	12.00	30.00
D810 She-Hulk	8.00	20.00

2021 Upper Deck Marvel Ages Decades 1990s

COMPLETE SET (10)	60.00	120.00
COMMON CARD	6.00	15.00
STATED ODDS 1:40		
D91 Wolverine	15.00	40.00
D94 Jean Grey	10.00	25.00
D95 Deadpool	12.00	30.00
D96 Cable	12.00	30.00
D98 Magneto	8.00	20.00
D910 Spider-Man	15.00	40.00

2021 Upper Deck Marvel Ages Decades 2000s

COMPLETE SET (10)	30.00	75.00
COMMON CARD	5.00	12.00
STATED ODDS 1:32		
D104 Kate Bishop	8.00	20.00
D106 Wolverine	10.00	25.00
D107 Spider-Man	10.00	25.00
D109 Thor	6.00	15.00
D1010 Thanos	6.00	15.00

2021 Upper Deck Marvel Ages Decades 2010s

COMPLETE SET (10)	50.00	100.00
COMMON CARD	5.00	12.00
STATED ODDS 1:32		
D111 America Chavez	6.00	15.00
D112 Kamala Khan	6.00	15.00
D115 Wolverine	8.00	20.00
D116 Captain America	6.00	15.00
D117 Spider-Man	8.00	20.00
D118 Doctor Strange	10.00	25.00
D119 Loki	10.00	25.00
D1110 Mighty Thor	8.00	20.00

2021 Upper Deck Marvel Ages Flavorful

COMMON CARD (F1-F45)	6.00	15.00
COMMON SP	10.00	25.00
STATED ODDS 1:53		
1/6/7/8/11/12/15/16/18/24/29/30/33/39/43 ODDS 1:96		
3/4/5/13/17 ODDS 1:480		
F1 Cyclops SP	15.00	40.00
F2 Carnage	12.00	30.00
F3 Spider-Man SP	100.00	200.00
F4 Captain America SP	75.00	150.00
F5 Wolverine SP	50.00	100.00
F6 Hulk SP	20.00	50.00
F7 Magneto SP	15.00	40.00
F8 Thanos SP	12.00	30.00
F11 Daredevil SP	12.00	30.00
F12 Black Panther SP	15.00	40.00
F13 Thor SP	75.00	150.00
F14 Moon Knight	10.00	25.00
F15 Iron Man SP	20.00	50.00
F17 Taskmaster SP	15.00	40.00
F18 Venom SP	50.00	100.00
F21 Ebony Maw	8.00	20.00
F22 Black Widow	10.00	25.00
F24 Captain Marvel SP	20.00	50.00
F25 Doctor Strange	12.00	30.00
F26 Black Bolt	10.00	25.00
F28 Miles Morales	12.00	30.00
F29 Cable SP	20.00	50.00
F30 Deadpool SP	75.00	150.00
F33 Punisher SP	15.00	40.00
F34 Mystique	8.00	20.00
F36 Nick Fury	8.00	20.00
F39 Dark Phoenix SP	15.00	40.00
F40 Ultron	8.00	20.00
F41 Bullseye	8.00	20.00
F42 Jubilee	12.00	30.00
F44 Mysterio	8.00	20.00

2021 Upper Deck Marvel Ages Fresnel

COMMON CARD (F1-F25)	8.00	20.00
COMMON SP (F26-F40)	20.00	50.00
COMMON SP (F41-F45)	75.00	150.00
STATED ODDS 1:75		
SP (F26-F40) ODDS 1:300		
SP (F41-F45) ODDS 1: 1,720		
F2 Nick Fury	10.00	25.00
F3 Elektra	15.00	40.00
F4 Black Cat	25.00	60.00
F5 Falcon	10.00	25.00
F6 Spider-Woman	12.00	30.00
F7 Isaiah Bradley	20.00	50.00
F9 Dr. Stephen Strange	30.00	75.00
F10 Carnage	20.00	50.00
F11 Dagger	12.00	30.00
F12 Cloak	12.00	30.00
F13 Punisher	30.00	75.00
F14 Daredevil	25.00	60.00
F15 Sentry	12.00	30.00
F16 Wasp	12.00	30.00
F17 Jessica Jones	12.00	30.00
F18 Iron Fist	15.00	40.00
F19 Luke Cage	12.00	30.00
F21 Eternity	10.00	25.00
F22 Ant-Man	15.00	40.00
F23 She-Hulk	15.00	40.00
F24 Moon Knight	12.00	30.00
F25 Gamora	10.00	25.00
F26 Rocket Raccoon SP	60.00	120.00
F27 Groot SP	50.00	100.00
F31 Blade SP	75.00	150.00
F32 Professor X SP	30.00	75.00
F33 Storm SP	60.00	120.00
F34 Magneto SP	50.00	100.00
F35 Black Widow SP	50.00	100.00
F36 Thanos SP	60.00	150.00
F37 Star-Lord SP	30.00	75.00
F38 Hulk SP	50.00	125.00
F39 Captain Marvel SP	30.00	75.00
F40 Iron Man SP	75.00	150.00
F42 Spider-Man SP	400.00	800.00
F43 Wolverine SP	200.00	400.00
F44 Thor SP	150.00	300.00
F45 Black Panther SP	150.00	300.00

2021 Upper Deck Marvel Ages Gamerverse

COMPLETE SET (10)	15.00	40.00
COMMON CARD (G1-G10)	2.00	5.00
STATED ODDS 1:5 HOBBY/EPACK		
G1 Spider-Man	4.00	10.00
G2 Kingpin	2.50	6.00
G9 Black Cat	3.00	8.00

2021 Upper Deck Marvel Ages Golden Metal Relics

COMPLETE SET (5)
STATED PRINT RUN 10 SER.#'d SETS
UNPRICED DUE TO SCARCITY
GMR1 Captain America Comics #9
GMR2 Motion Picture Funnies Weekly #1
GMR3 Marvel Mystery Comics #2
GMR4 Marvel Mystery Comics #3
GMR5 Captain America Comics #10

2021 Upper Deck Marvel Ages Saturday Morning Cartoons

COMPLETE SET (9)	5.00	12.00
COMMON CARD (SMC1-SMC9)	1.00	2.50
STATED ODDS 1:2 HOBBY/EPACK		

2021 Upper Deck Marvel Ages Totally Toys

COMPLETE SET (15)	10.00	25.00
COMMON CARD (TT1-TT15)	1.00	2.50
STATED ODDS 1:1		

TT1 Beast 1.00 2.50
TT2 Ghost Rider 1.00 2.50
TT3 Nick Fury 1.00 2.50
TT4 Black Widow 1.25 3.00
TT5 Captain America 1.50 4.00
TT6 Rogue 1.00 2.50
TT7 Miles Morales 1.25 3.00
TT8 Colossus 1.00 2.50
TT9 Falcon 1.00 2.50
TT10 Green Goblin 1.00 2.50
TT11 Shuri 1.00 2.50
TT12 Thanos 1.00 2.50
TT13 Gambit 1.25 3.00
TT14 M.O.D.O.K. 1.00 2.50
TT15 Wolverine 2.00 5.00

2021 Upper Deck Marvel Ages Word Cloud

COMMON CARD (WC1-WC55) 8.00 20.00
COMMON SP 15.00 40.00
STATED ODDS 1:46
8/9/16/18/35/36/37/38/44/45/46/47/48/50/55 ODDS 1:160
1/2/3/5/12/15/20/27/39/54 ODDS 1:320
WC1 Spider-Man SP 75.00 200.00
WC2 Captain America SP 30.00 75.00
WC3 Wolverine SP 40.00 100.00
WC4 Jean Grey 15.00 40.00
WC5 Cyclops SP 75.00 150.00
WC6 Beast 12.00 30.00
WC7 Thor 12.00 30.00
WC8 Beta Ray Bill SP 20.00 50.00
WC9 Valkyrie SP 25.00 60.00
WC10 Odin 12.00 30.00
WC11 Quicksilver 10.00 25.00
WC12 Black Panther SP 75.00 150.00
WC13 Doctor Voodoo 10.00 25.00
WC15 Daredevil SP 60.00 120.00
WC16 Storm SP 25.00 60.00
WC17 Red Hulk 12.00 30.00
WC20 Captain Marvel SP 40.00 100.00
WC22 Nova 10.00 25.00
WC24 Baron Zemo 10.00 25.00
WC26 Quasar 12.00 30.00
WC27 Taskmaster SP 20.00 50.00
WC30 America Chavez 10.00 25.00
WC31 Nebula 12.00 30.00
WC32 Punisher 20.00 50.00
WC33 US Agent 10.00 25.00
WC34 Misty Knight 10.00 25.00
WC36 She-Hulk SP 30.00 75.00
WC37 Moon Knight SP 20.00 50.00
WC38 Mandarin SP 15.00 40.00
WC39 Deadpool SP 25.00 60.00
WC41 Wasp 10.00 25.00
WC44 Hawkeye SP 20.00 50.00
WC45 Groot SP 20.00 50.00
WC48 Venom SP 125.00 250.00
WC49 Hercules 10.00 25.00
WC50 Miles Morales SP 25.00 60.00
WC52 Falcon 12.00 30.00
WC53 Ms. Marvel 10.00 25.00
WC54 Doctor Strange SP 75.00 150.00
WC55 Scarlet Witch SP 50.00 100.00

2020 Upper Deck Marvel Anime

COMPLETE SET (90) 20.00 50.00
UNOPENED BOX (16 PACKS) 250.00 400.00
UNOPENED PACK (5 CARDS) 15.00 25.00
COMMON CARD (1-90) .50 1.25
*MEGA MOON: 2.5X TO 6X BASIC CARDS
*HYPER MOSAIC: 3X TO 8X BASIC CARDS

2020 Upper Deck Marvel Anime Capsule Characters

COMPLETE SET (5) 12.00 30.00
COMMON CARD (G1-G5) 4.00 10.00
*GREEN/99: 1.2X TO 3X BASIC CARDS
*RED/49: 2X TO 5X BASIC CARDS
STATED ODDS 1:12
G1 Avengers 10.00 25.00
G2 X-Men 6.00 15.00

2020 Upper Deck Marvel Anime Capsule Characters Minis

COMPLETE SET (50) 125.00 300.00
COMMON CARD (CCM1-CCM50) 2.50 6.00
STATED ODDS 1:12
1 PER CAPSULE CHARACTER CARD
CCM1 Captain America 10.00 25.00
CCM2 Thor 8.00 20.00
CCM3 Black Widow 8.00 20.00
CCM4 Hulk 5.00 12.00
CCM5 Scarlet Witch 6.00 15.00
CCM8 Doctor Strange 6.00 15.00
CCM9 Captain Marvel 6.00 15.00
CCM11 Luke Cage 5.00 12.00
CCM12 Iron Fist 3.00 8.00
CCM13 Daredevil 3.00 8.00
CCM14 Jessica Jones 4.00 10.00
CCM15 Hulk 6.00 15.00
CCM16 Doctor Strange 3.00 8.00
CCM17 She-Hulk 3.00 8.00
CCM18 Hellcat 4.00 10.00
CCM19 Nighthawk 2.50 6.00
CCM21 Adam Warlock 5.00 12.00
CCM23 Gamora 2.50 6.00
CCM24 Groot 8.00 20.00
CCM26 Mantis 3.00 8.00
CCM27 Quasar 6.00 15.00
CCM28 Rocket Raccoon 2.00 5.00
CCM29 Star-Lord 3.00 8.00
CCM30 Yondu 3.00 8.00
CCM32 Captain America 8.00 20.00
CCM40 Captain America 8.00 20.00
CCM41 Wolverine 12.00 30.00
CCM43 Professor X 8.00 20.00
CCM44 Beast 5.00 12.00
CCM46 Beast 5.00 12.00
CCM47 Rogue 8.00 20.00
CCM48 Jean Grey 6.00 15.00

2020 Upper Deck Marvel Anime Chibis

COMPLETE SET W/O SP (30) 150.00 400.00
COMMON TIER 1 (1-30) 4.00 10.00
TIER 1 ODDS 1:80
TIER 2 ODDS 1:240
TIER 3 ODDS 1:800
TIER 4 ODDS 1:2,300
1 Ant-Man 10.00 25.00
2 Black Widow 20.00 50.00
3 Captain Marvel 6.00 15.00
4 Carnage 20.00 50.00
5 Daredevil 10.00 25.00
6 Captain America 25.00 60.00
7 Drax 15.00 40.00
13 Iron Man 25.00 60.00
15 Miles Morales 15.00 40.00
16 Groot 20.00 50.00
17 Nick Fury 6.00 15.00
18 Nebula 10.00 25.00
19 Rocket Raccoon 10.00 25.00
20 Ronan 8.00 20.00
21 She-Hulk 12.00 30.00
22 Spider-Man 30.00 75.00
24 Star-Lord 8.00 20.00
25 Thor 12.00 30.00
26 Ultron 6.00 15.00
27 Venom 25.00 60.00
28 Vision 5.00 12.00
31 Captain America SP 40.00 100.00
32 Captain Marvel SP 25.00 60.00
33 Carnage SP 40.00 100.00
34 Daredevil SP 12.00 30.00
35 Thor SP 10.00 25.00
36 Star-Lord SP 12.00 30.00
37 Spider-Man SP 60.00 150.00
38 Miles Morales SP 25.00 60.00
39 Ghost-Spider SP 25.00 60.00
40 Drax SP 8.00 20.00
41 Hulk SP 10.00 25.00
42 Iron Man SP
43 Falcon SP 8.00 20.00
44 Groot SP 20.00 50.00
45 Luke Cage SP 25.00 60.00
46 Daredevil SP 15.00 40.00
47 Wasp SP 30.00 75.00
48 Doctor Strange SP
49 Rocket Raccoon SP 25.00 60.00
50 Gamora SP 30.00 75.00
51 Yondu SP 20.00 50.00
52 Nebula SP 30.00 75.00
53 Guardians of the Galaxy SP
54 Ronan SP 40.00 100.00
55 Drax SP 50.00 125.00
56 Black Panther SP
57 Miles Morales SP 40.00 100.00
58 Medusa SP
59 Ultron SP 30.00 75.00
60 Iron Fist SP 25.00 60.00
61 Spider-Man SP 250.00 600.00
62 Spider-Woman SP
63 Captain Marvel SP 75.00 200.00
64 Venom SP
65 Ghost-Spider SP 150.00 400.00

2020 Upper Deck Marvel Anime Hanafuda

COMMON CARD (P1-P12; P25-P36) 8.00 20.00
COMMON SP (P13-P20; P37-P44) 12.00 30.00
COMMON SP (P21-P24; P45-P48) 25.00 60.00
P1-P12; P25-P36 ODDS 1:90
P13-P20; P37-P44 ODDS 1:180
P21-P24; P45-P48 ODDS 1:600
P1 Cloak 15.00 40.00
P2 Dagger 12.00 30.00
P3 Falcon 10.00 25.00
P6 She-Hulk 15.00 40.00
P7 Jubilee 15.00 40.00
P8 Iron Man 25.00 60.00
P9 Vision 10.00 25.00
P10 Jessica Jones 20.00 50.00
P13 Red Skull SP 25.00 60.00
P14 Thor SP 15.00 40.00
P15 Black Panther SP 50.00 100.00
P18 Ghost Rider SP 50.00 100.00
P19 Namor SP 30.00 75.00
P20 Magneto SP 30.00 75.00
P21 Wolverine SP 60.00 120.00
P22 Spider-Man SP 250.00 500.00
P23 Professor X SP 60.00 125.00
P24 Captain Marvel SP 60.00 150.00
P25 Dark Phoenix 12.00 30.00
P27 Beta Ray Bill 12.00 30.00
P29 Kitty Pryde 15.00 40.00
P30 Gamora 10.00 25.00
P31 Scarlet Witch 15.00 40.00
P32 X-23 20.00 50.00
P34 Nick Fury 10.00 25.00
P35 Punisher 15.00 40.00
P37 Daredevil SP 75.00 150.00
P39 Cable SP 20.00 50.00
P40 Rogue SP 75.00 150.00
P42 Black Widow SP 30.00 75.00
P44 Cyclops SP 20.00 50.00
P46 Hulk SP 50.00 100.00
P47 Domino SP 60.00 120.00
P48 Thanos SP 50.00 100.00

2020 Upper Deck Marvel Anime Idols

COMPLETE SET (7) 10.00 25.00
COMMON CARD (I1-I7) 2.00 5.00
STATED ODDS 1:13

2020 Upper Deck Marvel Anime Kaiju

COMPLETE SET (8) 8.00 20.00
COMMON CARD (K1-K8) 1.50 4.00
STATED ODDS 1:13

2020 Upper Deck Marvel Anime Kaiju Artist Autographs

COMMON AUTO 50.00 125.00
STATED PRINT RUN 60 SER.#'d SETS

2020 Upper Deck Marvel Anime Mechanized

COMPLETE SET (10) 15.00 40.00
COMMON CARD (M1-M10) 3.00 8.00
STATED ODDS 1:10
M1 Wolverine 6.00 15.00
M2 Spider-Man 5.00 12.00
M3 Black Widow 4.00 10.00
M4 Captain America 4.00 10.00
M9 Deadpool 5.00 12.00

2020 Upper Deck Marvel Anime Mechanized Artist Autographs

COMMON AUTO 60.00 120.00
STATED PRINT RUN 60 SER.#'d SETS

2020 Upper Deck Marvel Anime Red Foil Artist Autographs

COMMON AUTO 20.00 50.00
STATED PRINT RUN 120 SER.#'d SETS

2020 Upper Deck Marvel Anime Stax Middle Layer

COMMON MIDDLE (SS1A-SS10A) 1.50 4.00
COMMON MIDDLE SP (SS11A-SS15A) 8.00 20.00
*TOP: SAME VALUE
*TOP SP: SAME VALUE
*BOTTOM: SAME VALUE
*BOTTOM SP: SAME VALUE
STATED ODDS 1:16
STATED SP ODDS 1:180
SS2A Cable 2.00 5.00
SS6A Hulk 1.50 5.00
SS7A Spider-Woman 2.50 6.00
SS8A Sentry 1.50 4.00
SS10A Moon Knight 2.00 5.00
SS11A Captain America SP 12.00 30.00
SS12A Wolverine SP 15.00 40.00
SS13A Iron Man SP 12.00 30.00
SS14A Spider-Man SP 15.00 40.00

2020 Upper Deck Marvel Anime Stax Top Layer

COMPLETE SET ()
*: X TO X BASIC CARDS
STATED ODDS 1:

1994 Flair Marvel Annual

COMPLETE SET (150) 50.00 100.00
UNOPENED BOX (24 PACKS) 250.00 400.00
UNOPENED PACK (10 CARDS) 10.00 15.00
COMMON CARD (1-150) .40 1.00
11 Avengers 1.50 4.00
16 Captain America 3.00 8.00
34 Wolverine vs Hulk 2.50 6.00
35 The Scarlet Witch 1.25 3.00
48 The Black Costume .75 2.00
65 Cap vs Cap 1.25 3.00
67 Cosmic Spider-Man .75 2.00
69 Thanos 1.50 4.00
75 Gambit 1.25 3.00
78 Deadpool 2.00 5.00
86 Omega Red vs Wolverine 1.00 2.50
94 Spider-Man 2099 1.50 4.00
104 Maximum Carnage 2.00 5.00
116 Daredevil 1.25 3.00
135 Carnage 1.25 3.00
136 Venom 2.50 6.00
137 Spider-Demon 1.00 2.50
139 Spider-Man 2.50 6.00

1994 Flair Marvel Annual FlairPrint

COMPLETE SET (10) 15.00 40.00
COMMON CARD (1-10) 2.00 5.00
STATED ODDS 1:CASE
1 Cable 3.00 8.00
2 Cyclops 5.00 12.00
4 Iron Man 2.50 6.00
6 Phoenix 2.50 6.00
10 Wolverine 6.00 15.00

1994 Flair Marvel Annual PowerBlast

COMPLETE SET (18)	25.00	60.00
COMMON CARD (1-18)	2.00	5.00
STATED ODDS 1:2		
3 Iron Man	3.00	8.00
4 Magneto	4.00	10.00
5 Phoenix	3.00	8.00
6 Storm	3.00	8.00
7 Venom	5.00	12.00
8 Wolverine	8.00	20.00
9 Ghost Rider	2.50	6.00
10 Punisher	2.50	6.00
11 Captain America	2.50	6.00
12 Gambit	3.00	8.00
13 Thor	3.00	8.00
15 Spider-Man	6.00	15.00
16 Deadpool	5.00	12.00
17 Invisible Woman	2.50	6.00
18 Dr. Doom	2.50	6.00

1995 Flair Marvel Annual

COMPLETE SET (150)	20.00	50.00
UNOPENED BOX (24 PACKS)	500.00	800.00
UNOPENED PACK (10 CARDS)	20.00	35.00
COMMON CARD (1-150)	.20	.50

1995 Flair Marvel Annual Chromium

COMPLETE SET (12)	6.00	15.00
COMMON CARD (1-12)	.75	2.00
STATED ODDS 1:2		

1995 Flair Marvel Annual DuoBlast

COMPLETE SET (3)	5.00	12.00
COMMON CARD (1-3)	2.00	5.00
STATED ODDS 1:6		

1995 Flair Marvel Annual FlairPrint

COMPLETE SET (10)	10.00	25.00
COMMON CARD (1-10)	2.00	5.00
STATED ODDS 1:CASE		

1995 Flair Marvel Annual HoloBlast

COMPLETE SET (12)	12.00	30.00
COMMON CARD (1-12)	1.50	4.00
STATED ODDS 1:3		

1995 Flair Marvel Annual PowerBlast

COMPLETE SET (24)	10.00	25.00
COMMON CARD (1-24)	.60	1.50
STATED ODDS 1:1		

1995 Flair Marvel Annual Promo Panels

NNO Title Card/Spider-Man/Storm/Sabretooth	2.00	5.00
Salome/Info Card/Hobgoblin/Namor		

2017 Marvel Annual 2016

COMPLETE SET W/O SP (100)	12.00	30.00
COMPLETE SET W/SP (150)	100.00	200.00
UNOPENED BOX (20 PACKS)		
UNOPENED PACK (5 CARDS)		
COMMON CARD (1-100)	.30	.75
COMMON SP (101-150)	2.50	6.00
*GOLD: 2X TO 5X BASIC CARDS		
*GOLD SP: .25X TO .60X BASIC CARDS		
*RED: 12X TO 30X BASIC CARDS		
*RED SP: 2X TO 5X BASIC CARDS		

2017 Marvel Annual 2016 Base Variants

COMPLETE SET (12)	50.00	100.00
COMMON CARD (BV1-BV12)	3.00	8.00
STATED ODDS 1:80		
BV1 Star-Lord	5.00	12.00
BV2 Silk	5.00	12.00
BV3 Captain Marvel	10.00	25.00
BV4 Captain America	8.00	20.00
BV5 Beast	5.00	12.00
BV7 Valkyrie	6.00	15.00
BV8 Punisher	12.00	30.00
BV9 Hawkeye	5.00	12.00
BV11 Agent Venom	6.00	15.00
BV12 Black Panther	12.00	30.00

2017 Marvel Annual 2016 Civil War II

COMPLETE SET (40)	100.00	200.00
COMMON CARD (CW1-CW40)	2.50	6.00
STATED ODDS 1:3		

2017 Marvel Annual 2016 Comic Variants

COMPLETE SET (6)	60.00	120.00
COMMON CARD (TIV1-TIV6)	10.00	25.00
STATED ODDS 1:240		

2017 Marvel Annual 2016 Dual Patches

COMPLETE SET W/O SP (10)	60.00	120.00
COMPLETE SET W/SP (15)	120.00	250.00
COMMON PATCH (DCP1-DCP15)	5.00	12.00
STATED ODDS 1:285		
STATED ODDS SP 1:480		
DCP1 Captain Marvel/She-Hulk	6.00	15.00
DCP4 Medusa/Spider-Man	6.00	15.00
DCP6 Black Panther/Luke Cage	8.00	20.00
DCP9 Iron Man/Black Widow	10.00	25.00
DCP10 Deadpool/Daredevil	10.00	25.00
DCP11 Captain Marvel/Iron Man SP	6.00	15.00
DCP12 Hawkeye/Black Widow SP	15.00	40.00
DCP13 Deadpool/Spider-Man SP	15.00	40.00
DCP14 Vision/Daredevil SP	6.00	15.00
DCP15 Captain America/Captain America SP	20.00	50.00

2017 Marvel Annual 2016 Happy Birthday

COMPLETE SET (5)	8.00	20.00
COMMON CARD (HB1-HB5)	2.00	5.00
STATED ODDS 1:36		

2017 Marvel Annual 2016 In Memoriam

COMPLETE SET (5)	10.00	25.00
COMMON CARD (IM1-IM5)	2.50	6.00
STATED ODDS 1:36		

2017 Marvel Annual 2016 New Alliances

COMPLETE SET (5)	8.00	20.00
COMMON CARD (NA1-NA5)	2.00	5.00
STATED ODDS 1:36		

2017 Marvel Annual 2016 Patches

COMPLETE SET W/O SP (10)	50.00	100.00
COMPLETE SET W/SP (15)	100.00	200.00
COMMON PATCH (CP1-CP15)	4.00	10.00
STATED ODDS 1:240		
STATED ODDS SP 1:285		
CP1 Captain America	5.00	12.00
CP2 Iron Man	6.00	15.00
CP3 Black Panther	6.00	15.00
CP4 Black Widow	6.00	15.00
CP7 Rocket Raccoon	6.00	15.00
CP8 Spider-Gwen	5.00	12.00
CP10 Doctor Strange	6.00	15.00
CP11 Kitty Pryde SP	10.00	25.00
CP12 Scarlet Witch SP	15.00	40.00
CP13 Deadpool SP	15.00	40.00
CP14 Captain Marvel SP	10.00	25.00
CP15 Spider-Man SP	15.00	40.00

2017 Marvel Annual 2016 Plexi Die-Cuts

COMPLETE SET (10)	200.00	400.00
COMMON CARD (PD1-PD10)	8.00	20.00
STATED ODDS 1:300		
PD2 Doctor Strange	30.00	80.00
PD5 Deadpool	25.00	60.00
PD6 Wolverine	30.00	80.00
PD7 Iron Man	25.00	60.00
PD8 Rocket Raccoon	25.00	60.00
PD9 Spider-Gwen	20.00	50.00
PD10 Spider-Man	30.00	80.00

2017 Marvel Annual 2016 Plot Twists

COMPLETE SET (10)	15.00	40.00
COMMON CARD (PT1-PT10)	2.00	5.00
STATED ODDS 1:18		

2017 Marvel Annual 2016 Rookie Heroes

COMPLETE SET (5)	15.00	40.00
COMMON CARD (RH1-RH5)	3.00	8.00
*FOIL: X TO X BASIC CARDS		
STATED ODDS 1:37		
RH1 Deadpool 2099	6.00	15.00
RH5 Wolverine	8.00	20.00

2017 Marvel Annual 2016 Team Logo Patches

COMPLETE SET (5)	30.00	80.00
COMMON PATCH (TLP1-TLP5)	8.00	20.00
STATED ODDS 1:480		

2017 Marvel Annual 2016 Team Name Patches

COMPLETE SET (5)	25.00	60.00
COMMON PATCH (TNP1-TNP5)	6.00	15.00
STATED ODDS 1:480		

2017 Marvel Annual 2016 Top 10 Fights

COMPLETE SET (10)	20.00	50.00
COMMON CARD (TF1-TF10)	3.00	8.00
STATED ODDS 1:20		

2017 Marvel Annual 2016 Top 10 Heroes

COMPLETE SET (10)	20.00	50.00
COMMON CARD (TH1-TH10)	3.00	8.00
STATED ODDS 1:20		

2017 Marvel Annual 2016 Top 10 Issues

COMPLETE SET (10)	20.00	50.00
COMMON CARD (TI1-TI10)	3.00	8.00
STATED ODDS 1:20		

2017 Marvel Annual 2016 Top 10 Story Arcs

COMPLETE SET (10)	20.00	50.00
COMMON CARD (TS1-TS10)	3.00	8.00
STATED ODDS 1:20		

2017 Marvel Annual 2016 Top 10 Villains

COMPLETE SET (10)	20.00	50.00
COMMON CARD (TV1-TV10)	3.00	8.00
STATED ODDS 1:20		

2018 Marvel Annual 2017

COMPLETE SET (150)	100.00	200.00
COMPLETE SET W/O SP (100)	15.00	40.00
UNOPENED BOX (20 PACKS)	55.00	75.00
UNOPENED PACK (5 CARDS)	3.00	4.00
COMMON CARD (1-100)	.30	.75
COMMON SP (101-150)	1.00	2.50
*BLUE: 2X TO 5X BASIC CARDS	1.50	4.00
*PURPLE: 5X TO 12X BASIC CARDS	4.00	10.00
SP CARDS HAVE NO PARALLELS		
101 Thor SP	2.00	5.00
103 Spider-Man 2099 SP	1.25	3.00
105 Iron Man SP	2.50	6.00
106 Groot SP	2.00	5.00
108 Spider-Woman SP	1.50	4.00
109 Rogue SP	1.25	3.00
112 Magneto SP	1.50	4.00
114 Silk SP	2.00	5.00
115 Captain Marvel SP	3.00	8.00
116 Iceman SP	1.25	3.00
117 Spectrum SP	1.50	4.00
125 Black Panther SP	2.50	6.00
126 Venom SP	2.00	5.00
127 Thanos SP	2.50	6.00
129 Deadpool SP	3.00	8.00
141 Shuri SP	1.50	4.00
144 Mystique SP	1.25	3.00
150 Captain America SP	2.50	6.00

2018 Marvel Annual 2017 Patches

COMMON PATCH (CP1-CP14)	3.00	8.00
COMMON SP PATCH (CP15-CP23)	6.00	15.00
STATED ODDS CP1-CP14 - 1:60		
STATED ODDS CP15-CP23 - 1:240		
CP0 Red Skull/E-Pack		
CP00 Captain America/E-Pack		
CP1 Captain Marvel	8.00	20.00
CP2 Doctor Strange	6.00	15.00
CP4 Hulk	6.00	15.00
CP5 Nova	5.00	12.00
CP8 Wasp	4.00	10.00
CP9 Storm	5.00	12.00
CP11 Karnak	6.00	15.00
CP12 Magneto	5.00	12.00
CP13 Daredevil	6.00	15.00
CP14 Spider-Woman	6.00	15.00
CP15 Ultron SP	10.00	25.00
CP16 Old Man Logan SP	20.00	50.00
CP17 Medusa SP	15.00	40.00
CP18 Captain America SP	20.00	50.00
CP19 Rogue SP	15.00	40.00
CP21 Superior Octopus SP	12.00	30.00
CP22 Jean Grey SP	12.00	30.00

2018 Marvel Annual 2017 Dual Patches

COMMON PATCH (DCP1-DCP14)	3.00	8.00
COMMON SP PATCH (DCP15-DCP23)	8.00	20.00
STATED ODDS DCP1-DCP14 - 1:60		
STATED ODDS DCP15-DCP23 - 1:240		
DCP0 Kobik & Winter Soldier/E-Pack		
DCP00 Squirrel Girl & Red Hulk/E-Pack		
DCP2 Hive and Doctor Faustus	5.00	12.00
DCP3 Spectrum and Blue Marvel	5.00	12.00
DCP5 Captain America and Madame Hydra	6.00	15.00
DCP6 Magik and Colossus	8.00	20.00
DCP7 Spider-Man and Jackal	6.00	15.00
DCP8 Luke Cage and Iron Fist	5.00	12.00
DCP9 Hercules and Mockingbird	8.00	20.00
DCP10 Silk and Black Cat	6.00	15.00
DCP11 Vision and Scarlet Witch	10.00	25.00
DCP12 Cloak and Dagger	10.00	25.00
DCP14 Groot and Rocket	5.00	12.00
DCP15 Ultimate Spider-Man and Black Widow SP	30.00	75.00
DCP17 Blackout and Baron Zemo SP	15.00	40.00
DCP18 Devil Dinosaur and Moon Girl SP	10.00	25.00
DCP21 Captain Marvel and Ms. Marvel SP	30.00	75.00
DCP22 Wolverine and Wolverine SP	20.00	50.00
DCP23 Ironheart and Tony Stark A.I. SP	15.00	40.00

2018 Marvel Annual 2017 In Memoriam

COMPLETE SET (5)	10.00	25.00
COMMON CARD (IM1-IM5)	3.00	8.00
STATED ODDS 1:16		

2018 Marvel Annual 2017 Rookie Heroes

COMPLETE SET (5)	15.00	40.00
COMMON CARD (RH1-RH5)	5.00	12.00
STATED ODDS 1:16		

2018 Marvel Annual 2017 Secret Empire Comic Covers

COMPLETE SET (40)	50.00	100.00
COMMON CARD (SE1-SE40)	1.50	4.00
STATED ODDS 1:2		

2018 Marvel Annual 2017 Top 10 Fights

COMPLETE SET (10)	8.00	20.00
COMMON CARD (TF1-TF10)	1.25	3.00
STATED ODDS 1:10		

2018 Marvel Annual 2017 Top 10 Heroes

COMPLETE SET (10)	8.00	20.00

COMMON CARD (TH1-TH10) 1.25 3.00
STATED ODDS 1:10

2018 Marvel Annual 2017 Top 10 Issues

COMPLETE SET (10) 8.00 20.00
COMMON CARD (TI1-TI10) 1.25 3.00
STATED ODDS 1:10

2018 Marvel Annual 2017 Top 10 Story Arcs

COMPLETE SET (10) 8.00 20.00
COMMON CARD (TS1-TS10) 1.25 3.00
STATED ODDS 1:10

2018 Marvel Annual 2017 Top 10 Villains

COMPLETE SET (10) 8.00 20.00
COMMON CARD (TV1-TV10) 1.25 3.00
STATED ODDS 1:10

2018-19 Upper Deck Marvel Annual

COMPLETE SET W/SP (150) 125.00 250.00
COMPLETE SET W/O SP (100) 15.00 40.00
UNOPENED BOX (20 PACKS) 125.00 250.00
UNOPENED PACK (5 CARDS) 6.00 12.00
COMMON CARD (1-100) .40 1.00
COMMON SP (101-150) 2.50 6.00

2018-19 Upper Deck Marvel Annual Dual Patches

COMMON PATCH (PD1-PD14) 8.00 20.00
COMMON SP (PD15-PD23) 12.00 30.00
STATED ODDS 1:60
STATED ODDS SP 1:240
PD1 Red Wolf/Living Lightning 10.00 25.00
PD3 Peggy Carter/Ms. Marvel 10.00 25.00
PD4 Valkyrie/Wolverine 12.00 30.00
PD8 Doctor Strange/Black Panther 10.00 25.00
PD9 Savage Hulk/Ghost Rider 10.00 25.00
PD10 Captain Marvel/Dark Celestial 12.00 30.00
PD11 Challenger/Grandmaster 10.00 25.00
PD16 Rocket Raccoon/Groot SP 15.00 40.00
PD17 Magus/Ego SP 15.00 40.00
PD20 Iron Heart/Iron Man SP 20.00 50.00
PD21 Anti-Venom/Spider-Man SP 15.00 40.00
PD22 Miles Morales/Silk SP 15.00 40.00
PD23 Spider-Gwen/Kingpin SP 30.00 75.00
PD24 Wasp/Beast EPACK 30.00 75.00
PD25 Jarvis/Voyager SP EPACK 60.00 120.00

2018-19 Upper Deck Marvel Annual Happy Birthday

COMPLETE SET (9) 8.00 20.00
COMMON CARD (HB1-HB9) 1.25 3.00
E-PACK ACHIEVEMENT EXCLUSIVE
HB1 Blade 1.50 4.00
HB3 Mantis 1.50 4.00
HB5 Phyla-Vell 1.50 4.00
HB7 Beta Ray Bill 2.00 5.00
HB8 Shang-Chi 1.50 4.00

2018-19 Upper Deck Marvel Annual In Memoriam

COMPLETE SET (5) 8.00 20.00
COMMON CARD (IM1-IM5) 2.50 6.00
STATED ODDS 1:16
IM2 The Mighty Thor 3.00 8.00
IM4 Thanos 4.00 10.00

2018-19 Upper Deck Marvel Annual Infinity Wars Comic Covers

COMMON CARD (CC1-CC40) 1.25 3.00
STATED ODDS 1:2

2018-19 Upper Deck Marvel Annual Patches

COMMON PATCH (P1-P14) 5.00 12.00
COMMON SP (P15-P23) 12.00 30.00
STATED ODDS 1:60
STATED ODDS SP 1:240
P1 Ghost Rider 8.00 20.00
P2 Iron Man 6.00 15.00
P4 Captain America 6.00 15.00
P5 Black Panther 6.00 15.00
P6 Captain Marvel 8.00 20.00
P7 Thor Odinson 6.00 15.00
P10 Spider-Man 10.00 25.00
P12 Venom 6.00 15.00
P13 Doctor Strange 6.00 15.00
P14 Iron Lad 8.00 20.00
P16 Ms. Marvel SP 20.00 50.00
P18 Wolvie SP 20.00 50.00
P19 Voyager SP 20.00 50.00
P20 Vision SP 15.00 40.00
P22 Jean Grey SP 15.00 40.00
P24 Nova/E-Pack 30.00 75.00
P25 Adam Warlock SP/E-Pack 60.00 120.00

2018-19 Upper Deck Marvel Annual Rookie Heroes

COMPLETE SET (5) 10.00 25.00
COMMON CARD (RH1-RH5) 3.00 8.00
STATED ODDS 1:16
RH3 Iron Hulk 4.00 10.00
RH4 Cosmic Ghost Rider 4.00 10.00

2018-19 Upper Deck Marvel Annual Top 10 Fights

COMPLETE SET (10) 10.00 25.00
COMMON CARD (TF1-TF10) 1.50 4.00
STATED ODDS 1:10

2018-19 Upper Deck Marvel Annual Top 10 Heroes

COMPLETE SET (10) 12.00 30.00
COMMON CARD (TH1-TH10) 2.00 5.00
STATED ODDS 1:10

2018-19 Upper Deck Marvel Annual Top 10 Issues

COMPLETE SET (10) 10.00 25.00
COMMON CARD (TI1-TI10) 1.50 4.00
STATED ODDS 1:10

2018-19 Upper Deck Marvel Annual Top 10 Story Arcs

COMPLETE SET (10) 10.00 25.00
COMMON CARD (TS1-TS10) 1.50 4.00
STATED ODDS 1:10

2018-19 Upper Deck Marvel Annual Top 10 Villains

COMPLETE SET (10) 12.00 30.00
COMMON CARD (TV1-TV10) 2.00 5.00
STATED ODDS 1:10

2019-20 Upper Deck Marvel Annual

COMPLETE SET (100) 25.00 60.00
UNOPENED BOX (16 PACKS) 125.00 200.00
UNOPENED PACK (5 CARDS) 8.00 12.00
COMMON CARD (1-100) .60 1.50
*VARIANTS: .75X TO 2X BASIC CARDS

2019-20 Upper Deck Marvel Annual Creators Corner Autographs

COMMON AUTO 10.00 25.00
STATED ODDS 1:64
CCBG Butch Guice 12.00 30.00
CCCS Charles Soule 12.00 30.00
CCEN Eric Nguyen 25.00 60.00
CCES Ethan Sacks 12.00 30.00
CCKT Kelly Thompson 25.00 60.00
CCADC Donny Cates
(E-Pack Achievement)

2019-20 Upper Deck Marvel Annual Future Watch Heroes

COMPLETE SET (5) 12.00 30.00
COMMON CARD (FWH1-FWH5) 4.00 10.00
STATED ODDS 1:10

2019-20 Upper Deck Marvel Annual Humble Beginnings

COMPLETE SET (10) 20.00 50.00
COMMON CARD (HB1-HB10) 3.00 8.00
STATED ODDS 1:5

2019-20 Upper Deck Marvel Annual Marvel Com-Mix

COMPLETE SET (10) 30.00 75.00
COMMON CARD (MC1-MC10) 5.00 12.00
STATED ODDS 1:5

2019-20 Upper Deck Marvel Annual Number 1 Spot

COMPLETE SET (25) 20.00 50.00
COMMON CARD (N1S1-N1S25) 1.50 4.00
STATED ODDS 1:2

2019-20 Upper Deck Marvel Annual Splash-ticular 3-D

COMMON CARD (S1-S10) 4.00 10.00
COMMON SP (S11-S20) 8.00 20.00
STATED ODDS 1:23
STATED SP ODDS 1:64

2020-21 Upper Deck Marvel Annual

COMPLETE SET (100) 30.00 75.00
UNOPENED BOX (16 PACKS) 125.00 200.00
UNOPENED PACK (5 CARDS) 8.00 12.00
COMMON CARD (1-100) .75 2.00
3 Gwen Stacy 1.25 3.00
5 America Chavez 1.50 4.00
18 X-23 2.00 5.00
25 Spider-Man 2.50 6.00
27 Black Panther 1.25 3.00
28 Ironheart 1.00 2.50
33 Doctor Strange 1.25 3.00
34 Iron Man 1.50 4.00
37 Deadpool 2.00 5.00
38 Moon Knight 1.50 4.00
50 Wolverine 2.00 5.00
53 Ghost-Spider 1.25 3.00
71 Miles Morales 2.00 5.00

2020-21 Upper Deck Marvel Annual Annual Impact

COMPLETE SET (10) 12.00 30.00
COMMON CARD (AI1-AI10) 1.25 3.00
STATED ODDS 1:5 HOBBY/EPACK
STATED ODDS 1:25 PACK WARS
AI1 Thor 1.50 4.00
AI5 Wolverine 3.00 8.00
AI7 Captain America 2.00 5.00
AI8 Black Panther 2.50 6.00
AI10 Knull 3.00 8.00

2020-21 Upper Deck Marvel Annual Base Cover Variants

COMMON TIER 1 1.25 3.00
COMMON TIER 2 1.50 4.00
COMMON TIER 3 2.00 5.00
COMMON TIER 4 15.00 40.00
TIER 1 STATED ODDS 1:2 H/E; 1:6 PW
TIER 2 STATED ODDS 1:4 H/E; 1:20 PW
TIER 3 STATED ODDS 1:8 H/E; 1:40 PW
TIER 4 STATED ODDS 1:64 H/E; 1:320 PW
5 America Chavez T2 2.00 5.00
6 Venom T3 3.00 8.00
17 Storm T3 2.50 6.00
18 X-23 T2 2.50 6.00
25 Spider-Man T4 20.00 50.00
34 Iron Man T4 20.00 50.00
37 Deadpool T4 25.00 60.00
38 Moon Knight T3 2.50 6.00
42 Star-Lord T4 20.00 50.00
47 Blade T2 3.00 8.00
50 Wolverine T4 25.00 60.00
52 Cosmic Ghost Rider T1 2.00 5.00
71 Miles Morales T3 3.00 8.00

2020-21 Upper Deck Marvel Annual Creators Corner Autographs

COMMON AUTO 10.00 25.00
GROUP A ODDS 1:5,684
GROUP B ODDS 1:364
GROUP C ODDS 1:301
STATED ODDS 1:160 HOBBY/EPACK
CCBP Benjamin Percy C 15.00 40.00
CCCZ Chip Zdarsky C 12.00 30.00
CCDC Donny Cates B 25.00 60.00
CCKT Kelly Thompson A 15.00 40.00
CCSM Steve McNiven C 15.00 40.00
CCTH Tini Howard B 25.00 60.00
CCVS Valerio Schiti B 20.00 50.00
CCLFY Leinil Francis Yu B 15.00 40.00

2020-21 Upper Deck Marvel Annual Humble Beginnings

COMPLETE SET (10) 10.00 25.00
COMMON CARD (HB1-HB10) 1.25 3.00
STATED ODDS 1:5 HOBBY/EPACK
STATED ODDS 1:25 PACK WARS
HB1 Captain America 2.00 5.00
HB3 Wolverine 2.50 6.00
HB4 Black Panther 2.00 5.00
HB7 Scarlet Witch 2.50 6.00
HB10 Spider-Man 4.00 10.00

2020-21 Upper Deck Marvel Annual Number 1 Spot

COMPLETE SET (25) 15.00 40.00
COMMON CARD (N1S1-N1S25) 1.25 3.00
STATED ODDS 1:2 HOBBY/EPACK
STATED ODDS 1:10 PACK WARS

2020-21 Upper Deck Marvel Annual Splash-ticular 3-D

COMMON CARD (S1-S20) 5.00 12.00
COMMON SP 6.00 15.00
COMMON SSP 10.00 25.00
STATED ODDS 1:23
STATED SP ODDS 1:64
STATED SSP ODDS 1:256
S3 Empyre: X-Men (2020) #2 SP 15.00 40.00
S4 Captain Marvel (2019) #19 SP 10.00 25.00
S5 Empyre (2020) #0: Avengers SP 12.00 30.00
S6 Empyre (2020) #1 SSP 20.00 50.00
S9 Empyre (2020) #4 SSP 15.00 40.00
S10 Daredevil (2019) #19 6.00 15.00
S11 Falcon & Winter Soldier (2020) #1 8.00 20.00
S12 Immortal Hulk (2018) #34 6.00 15.00
S13 Avengers (2018) #29 8.00 20.00
S14 Thor (2020) #1 8.00 20.00
S15 Venom (2018) #25 15.00 40.00
S16 The Amazing Spider-Man (2018) #45 8.00 20.00
S17 The Amazing Spider-Man (2018) #4512.00 30.00
S18 Wolverine (2020) #1 10.00 25.00
S19 Wolverine (2020) #1 20.00 50.00
S20 Venom (2018) #25 12.00 30.00

2020-21 Upper Deck Marvel Annual Star Rookies

COMPLETE SET (5) 6.00 15.00
COMMON CARD (SR1-SR5) 1.50 4.00
STATED ODDS 1:10 HOBBY/EPACK
STATED ODDS 1:50 PACK WARS
SR1 Knull 4.00 10.00

2021-22 Upper Deck Marvel Annual

COMPLETE SET (100) 40.00 100.00
UNOPENED BOX (16 PACKS) 75.00 100.00
UNOPENED PACK (5 CARDS) 5.00 7.50
COMMON CARD (1-100) .75 2.00
*CANVAS: .6X TO 1.5X BASIC CARDS
*SILVER SPARKLE: 1X TO 2.5X BASIC CARDS
*BLUE: 1.2X TO 3X BASIC CARDS
*GOLD LIN./88: 3X TO 8X BASIC CARDS

2021-22 Upper Deck Marvel Annual Gold Linearity

Card	Low	High
*GOLD LIN.: 3X TO 8X BASIC CARDS		
STATED PRINT RUN 88 SER.#'d SETS		
10 Blade	30.00	75.00
18 Doctor Doom	60.00	150.00
34 Human Torch	40.00	100.00
37 Iron Man	60.00	150.00
51 Marvel Girl	40.00	100.00
54 Moon Knight	125.00	300.00
74 Scream	75.00	200.00
76 Shang-Chi	40.00	100.00
78 Silk	40.00	100.00
79 Spider-Man	75.00	200.00
89 Thor	125.00	300.00
97 Wolverine	150.00	400.00

2021-22 Upper Deck Marvel Annual Annual Impact

Card	Low	High
COMPLETE SET (10)	10.00	25.00
COMMON CARD (AI1-AI10)	1.25	3.00
STATED ODDS 1:5 HOBBY/EPACK		
STATED ODDS 1:10 BLASTER		
STATED ODDS 1:50 PACK WARS		
AI1 Captain Marvel	1.50	4.00
AI2 Dr. Strange	1.50	4.00
AI8 Steve Rogers	2.00	5.00

2021-22 Upper Deck Marvel Annual Backscatters

Card	Low	High
COMPLETE SET (15)	50.00	125.00
COMMON CARD (B1-B15)	3.00	8.00
STATED ODDS 1:16 HOBBY/EPACK		
STATED ODDS 1:24 BLASTER		
B1 Captain America	8.00	20.00
B2 Doctor Doom	6.00	15.00
B3 Doctor Stephen Strange	5.00	12.00
B4 Galactus	6.00	15.00
B6 Hulk	4.00	10.00
B9 Iron Man	8.00	20.00
B10 Magneto	4.00	10.00
B12 Silver Surfer	6.00	15.00
B13 Spider-Man	10.00	25.00
B15 Wolverine	8.00	20.00

2021-22 Upper Deck Marvel Annual Creators Corner Autographs

Card	Low	High
COMMON AUTO	8.00	20.00
GROUP A ODDS 1:10,430		
GROUP B ODDS 1:130		
STATED ODDS 1:128 HOBBY/EPACK		
STATED ODDS 1:600 BLASTER		
CCBP Benjamin Percy B	10.00	25.00
CCDC Donny Cates B	12.00	30.00
CCEM Ed McGuinness B	10.00	25.00
CCJA Jason Aaron B	12.00	30.00
CCOC Olivier Coipel A	10.00	25.00

2021-22 Upper Deck Marvel Annual Creators Corner Dual Autographs

Card	Low	High
STATED ODDS 1:2,176 HOBBY/EPACK		
DCCAF J.Aaron/L.F.Yu	15.00	40.00
DCCAM J.Aaron/E.McGuinness	20.00	50.00
DCCBB B.M.Bendis/M.Bagley		
DCCBM B.M.Bendis/E.McGuinness		
DCCCC D.Cates/O.Coipel	30.00	75.00
DCCDO D.Cates/O.Coipel	30.00	75.00

2021-22 Upper Deck Marvel Annual Humble Beginnings

Card	Low	High
COMPLETE SET (10)	8.00	20.00
COMMON CARD (HB1-HB10)	1.50	4.00
STATED ODDS 1:5 HOBBY/EPACK		
STATED ODDS 1:10 BLASTER		
STATED ODDS 1:50 PACK WARS		
HB7 Spider-Man	2.50	6.00
HB10 Wolverine	2.00	5.00

2021-22 Upper Deck Marvel Annual Number 1 Spot

Card	Low	High
COMPLETE SET (25)	12.00	30.00
COMMON CARD (N1S1-N1S25)	1.00	2.50
STATED ODDS 1:2 HOBBY/EPACK		
STATED ODDS 1:4 BLASTER		
STATED ODDS 1:20 PACK WARS		

2021-22 Upper Deck Marvel Annual Splash-ticular

Card	Low	High
COMPLETE SET W/SP (20)	60.00	150.00
COMPLETE SET W/O SP (10)	20.00	50.00
COMMON CARD (N1S1-N1S10)	3.00	8.00
COMMON SP (N1S11-N1S17)	5.00	12.00
COMMON SSP (N1S18-N1S20)	8.00	20.00
STATED ODDS 1:23 HOBBY/EPACK		
STATED ODDS 1:35 BLASTER		
STATED SP ODDS 1:64 HOBBY/EPACK		
STATED SP ODDS 1:96 BLASTER		
STATED SSP ODDS 1:256 HOBBY/EPACK		
STATED SSP ODDS 1:384 BLASTER		

2021-22 Upper Deck Marvel Annual Star Rookies

Card	Low	High
COMPLETE SET (5)	12.00	30.00
COMMON CARD (SR1-SR5)	3.00	8.00
STATED ODDS 1:10 HOBBY/EPACK		
STATED ODDS 1:20 BLASTER		
STATED ODDS 1:100 PACK WARS		

2021-22 Upper Deck Marvel Annual Suspended Animation

Card	Low	High
COMPLETE SET W/O SP (20)	125.00	300.00
COMMON CARD/699 (1-20)	6.00	15.00
COMMON CARD/399 (21-35)	8.00	20.00
COMMON CARD/199 (36-45)	15.00	40.00
COMMON CARD/99 (46-50)	75.00	200.00
1 Kang/699	10.00	25.00
3 Valkyrie/699	8.00	20.00
4 Beta Ray Bill/699	10.00	25.00
5 Franklin Richards/699	8.00	20.00
8 Black Winter/699	20.00	50.00
9 Knull/699	15.00	40.00
12 Kraven/699	10.00	25.00
13 Aaron Fischer/699	10.00	25.00
14 Storm/699	15.00	40.00
15 Thena/699	8.00	20.00
17 X-23/699	20.00	50.00
18 Magik/699	20.00	50.00
20 Sersi/699	8.00	20.00
21 Magneto/399	30.00	75.00
22 Spider-Woman/399	20.00	50.00
23 Miles Morales/399	40.00	100.00
24 Immortal Hulk/399	20.00	50.00
25 Jessica Jones/399	15.00	40.00
27 Cable/399		
28 Namor/399	20.00	50.00
30 Venom/399	50.00	125.00
31 Daredevil/399	40.00	100.00
32 Moon Knight/399	40.00	100.00
33 Ikaris/399	20.00	50.00
34 Shang-Chi/399	15.00	40.00
35 Cyclops/399	20.00	50.00
36 Iron Man/199	25.00	60.00
37 Loki/199	50.00	125.00
38 Mr. Fantastic/199	40.00	100.00
40 Thing/199	30.00	75.00
41 Thor/199	40.00	100.00
42 Black Panther/199	30.00	75.00
43 Black Widow/199	40.00	100.00
44 Captain Marvel/199	30.00	75.00
45 Thanos/199	20.00	50.00
46 Captain America/99	125.00	300.00
47 Galactus/99	100.00	250.00
49 Spider-Man/99	150.00	400.00
50 Wolverine/99	125.00	300.00

2011 Marvel Beginnings

Card	Low	High
COMPLETE SET (180)	20.00	50.00
UNOPENED BOX (24 PACKS)	500.00	900.00
UNOPENED PACK (7 CARDS)	20.00	40.00
COMMON CARD (1-180)	.25	.60

2011 Marvel Beginnings Breakthrough Issues

Card	Low	High
COMPLETE SET (45)	15.00	40.00
COMMON CARD (B1-B45)	.50	1.25
STATED ODDS 1:1		
B1 Amazing Fantasy #15	1.25	3.00
B2 Giant-Size X-Men #1	.75	2.00
B3 Avengers #4	.75	2.00
B4 Wolverine #75	1.25	3.00
B5 Incredible Hulk #1	1.00	2.50
B7 Amazing Spider-Man #122	1.25	3.00
B9 Uncanny X-Men #141	1.25	3.00
B13 Wolverine Mini-Series #4	1.00	2.50
B14 Wolverine #145	1.00	2.50
B15 Amazing Spider-Man #6	1.25	3.00
B18 Amazing Spider-Man #2	1.25	3.00
B19 Iron Man #225	.75	2.00
B23 Amazing Spider-Man #13	1.25	3.00
B28 Amazing Spider-Man #90	1.25	3.00
B29 Amazing Spider-Man #238	1.25	3.00
B37 Captain America #1	1.25	3.00
B39 Amazing Spider-Man #583	1.25	3.00

2011 Marvel Beginnings Breakthrough Issues Autographs

Card	Low	High
COMMON CARD (B1-B45)	6.00	15.00
OVERALL AUTO ODDS 1:72		
B1 Stan Lee	500.00	1200.00
B2 Len Wein	60.00	150.00
B3 Stan Lee	500.00	1200.00
B4A Adam Kubert	8.00	20.00
B4C Larry Hama	8.00	20.00
B5 Stan Lee	500.00	1200.00
B6B Matthew Ryan	10.00	25.00
B7 Gerry Conway	8.00	20.00
B9 Terry Austin	10.00	25.00
B10A Joe Sinnott	15.00	40.00
B10B Stan Lee	500.00	1200.00
B11A Joe Sinnott	15.00	40.00
B11B Larry Lieber	12.00	30.00
B11C Stan Lee	500.00	1200.00
B12A Joe Sinnott	15.00	40.00
B12B Stan Lee	500.00	1200.00
B13 Tom Orzechowski	60.00	150.00
B15 Stan Lee	500.00	1200.00
B16A George Perez	12.00	30.00
B16B Kurt Busiek	12.00	30.00
B16C Tom Smith	10.00	25.00
B17A Bob Wiacek	10.00	25.00
B17B Ron Zalme	8.00	20.00
B18 Stan Lee	500.00	1200.00
B19A David Michelinie	10.00	25.00
B19B Mark D. Bright	12.00	30.00
B20A Joe Sinnott	15.00	40.00
B20B Stan Lee	500.00	1200.00
B22 Tom Orzechowski	60.00	150.00
B23 Stan Lee	500.00	1200.00
B24 Stan Lee	500.00	1200.00
B25 Joe Sinnott	15.00	40.00
B27 Stan Lee	500.00	1200.00
B28 Stan Lee	500.00	1200.00
B29 Roger Stern	10.00	25.00
B31 Terry Austin	10.00	25.00
B32 Stan Lee	500.00	1200.00
B33A Joe Quesada	12.00	30.00
B33B Peter David	10.00	25.00
B35 Mark Waid	15.00	40.00
B36 Bryan Hitch	12.00	30.00
B39 Mark Waid	15.00	40.00
B41 Stan Lee	500.00	1200.00
B42A Alex Irvine	12.00	30.00
B42B Tomm Coker	12.00	30.00
B43B Fred Van Lente	8.00	20.00
B44 Salvador Larroca	10.00	25.00
B45B Brian Michael Bendis	8.00	20.00

2011 Marvel Beginnings Breakthrough Issues Dual Autographs

Card	Low	High
COMMON AUTO	20.00	50.00
OVERALL AUTO ODDS 1:72		
B4 Larry Hama/Adam Kubert	25.00	60.00
B9 Terry Austin/Tom Orzechowski	30.00	75.00
B10 Joe Sinnott/Stan Lee	600.00	1500.00
B11 Stan Lee/Larry Lieber	250.00	500.00
B12 Joe Sinnott/Stan Lee	600.00	1500.00
B16 George Perez/Tom Smith	25.00	60.00
B17B Tom Orzehowski/Bob Wiacek	25.00	60.00
B20 Joe Sinnott/Stan Lee	600.00	1500.00
B45 Brian Michael Bendis/Alex Maleev	25.00	60.00

2011 Marvel Beginnings Breakthrough Issues Triple Autographs

Card	Low	High
OVERALL AUTO ODDS 1:72		
B4 Kubert/Green/Hama	50.00	100.00
B11 Sinnott/Lieber/Lee	350.00	700.00
B16 Perez/Busiek/Smith	60.00	120.00
B17 Wiacek/Zalme/Orzechowski		

2011 Marvel Beginnings Comic Book Panels

Card	Low	High
COMMON MEM (UM1-UM13)	50.00	100.00
STATED ODDS 1:288		
UM5 The Amazing Spider-Man #14 /66	60.00	120.00
UM8 The Amazing Spider-Man #50 /39	60.00	120.00
UM12 The Avengers #57 /50	60.00	120.00

2011 Marvel Beginnings Marvel Prime

Card	Low	High
COMPLETE SET (60)	150.00	400.00
COMMON CARD (M1-M60)	2.00	5.00
STATED ODDS 1:2		

2011 Marvel Beginnings Villain Holograms

Card	Low	High
COMMON CARD (H1-H42)	15.00	40.00
STATED ODDS 1:72		
H3 Bullseye	20.00	50.00
H4 Carnage	40.00	100.00
H5 Dark Phoenix	20.00	50.00
H6 Deadpool	30.00	75.00
H8 Doctor Octopus	30.00	75.00
H9 Dormammu	25.00	60.00
H10 Dracula	20.00	50.00
H11 Electro	25.00	60.00
H13 Enchantress	25.00	60.00
H14 Fin Fang Foom	25.00	60.00
H15 Galactus	20.00	50.00
H16 Green Goblin	30.00	75.00
H20 Kang the Conquerer	25.00	60.00
H21 Kingpin	30.00	75.00
H22 Kraven	60.00	150.00
H24 Lizard	20.00	50.00
H25 Loki	40.00	100.00
H26 Magneto	40.00	100.00
H31 Mystique	30.00	75.00
H32 Red Skull	20.00	50.00
H33 Sabretooth	25.00	60.00
H34 Sandman	25.00	60.00
H38 Stryfe	30.00	75.00
H39 Super Skrull	40.00	100.00
H40 Thanos	40.00	100.00
H42 Venom	40.00	100.00

2011 Marvel Beginnings X-Men Die-Cuts

Card	Low	High
COMPLETE SET (45)	30.00	75.00
COMMON CARD (X1-X45)	.75	1.50
STATED ODDS 1:2		
X1 Angel	2.00	5.00
X3 Banshee	.75	2.00
X4 Beast	1.25	3.00
X5 Bishop	1.50	4.00
X7 Cable	2.50	6.00
X9 Chamber	.75	2.00
X10 Cloak	.75	2.00
X11 Colossus	1.25	3.00
X12 Cyclops	3.00	8.00
X14 Darwin	.75	2.00
X15 Dazzler	1.25	3.00
X16 Domino	.75	2.00
X17 Emma Frost	1.50	4.00
X19 Gambit	10.00	25.00
X20 Havok	.75	2.00
X23 Iceman	1.25	3.00

X24 Jean Grey	5.00	12.00
X25 Jubilee	3.00	8.00
X27 Kitty Pryde	.75	2.00
X30 Marvel Girl	.75	2.00
X31 Namor	1.25	3.00
X32 Nightcrawler	1.25	3.00
X35 Polaris	1.00	2.50
X36 Professor X	1.50	4.00
X37 Psylocke	6.00	15.00
X38 Rogue	2.50	6.00
X39 Storm	1.25	3.00
X42 Warpath	1.00	2.50
X43 Wolverine	6.00	15.00
X44 X-23	6.00	15.00

2012 Marvel Beginnings 2

COMPLETE SET (180)	15.00	40.00
UNOPENED BOX (24 PACKS)	300.00	500.00
UNOPENED PACK (7 CARDS)	12.00	20.00
COMMON CARD (181-360)	.15	.40

2012 Marvel Beginnings 2 Avengers Die-Cuts

COMPLETE SET (45)	12.00	30.00
COMMON CARD (A1-A45)	.40	1.00
STATED ODDS 1:2		
A2 Ant-Man	.50	1.25
A4 Black Panther	.60	1.50
A5 Black Widow	.75	2.00
A6 Captain America	1.25	3.00
A7 Captain America	1.25	3.00
A10 Doctor Strange	.50	1.25
A18 Hulk	1.00	2.50
A20 Iron Man	1.50	4.00
A26 Moon Knight	.50	1.25
A32 Scarlet Witch	.50	1.25
A35 Spider-Man	1.50	4.00
A38 Thor	1.25	3.00
A42 War Machine	.50	1.25
A44 Wolverine	2.00	5.00

2012 Marvel Beginnings 2 Breakthrough Issues

COMPLETE SET (45)	10.00	25.00
COMMON CARD (B46-B90)	.40	1.00
STATED ODDS 1:1		

2012 Marvel Beginnings 2 Breakthrough Issues Autographs

COMMON CARD	15.00	30.00
OVERALL AUTO ODDS 1:48		
B46 Roy Thomas	20.00	50.00
B47 Stan Lee	300.00	750.00
B48A Brian Michael Bendis	15.00	40.00
B48B Bill Jemas	15.00	40.00
B50 Stan Lee	300.00	750.00
B51 Stan Lee	300.00	750.00
B52 Stan Lee	300.00	750.00
B53 Stan Lee	300.00	750.00
B54 Stan Lee	300.00	750.00
B55 Stan Lee	300.00	750.00
B56 Stan Lee	300.00	750.00
B57A John Beatty	15.00	40.00
B57B Mike Zeck	15.00	40.00
B58 Tom DeFalco	50.00	125.00
B59 Stan Lee	300.00	750.00
B60 Stan Lee	300.00	750.00
B61A Chris Claremont	15.00	40.00
B61B Len Wein	15.00	40.00
B62 Fabian Nicieza	15.00	40.00
B63 Gary Friedrich	40.00	100.00
B64A David Michelinie	15.00	40.00
B64B Jim Salicrup	15.00	40.00
B64C Janet Jay Jay Jackson	15.00	40.00
B65 Tom DeFalco	50.00	125.00
B66A Chris Claremont	15.00	40.00
B66B Dan Green	15.00	40.00
B66C Jim Shooter	30.00	60.00
B67A Jim Shooter	30.00	60.00
B67B Jackson Guice	15.00	40.00
B68B Chris Claremont	15.00	40.00
B69A Len Wein	15.00	40.00
B69B Roy Thomas	15.00	40.00
B70 Tom DeFalco	50.00	125.00
B71 Stan Lee	300.00	750.00
B72 Joe Sinnott	15.00	40.00
B73 Marv Wolfman	15.00	40.00
B74B Tom DeFalco	50.00	125.00
B75 Whilce Portacio	15.00	40.00
B77A Jim Salicrup	15.00	40.00
B77B David Michelinie	15.00	40.00
B79A Laura Martin	15.00	40.00
B80A Frank D'Armata	15.00	40.00
B80B Steve Epting	15.00	40.00
B81A Steve Epting	15.00	40.00
B81B Frank D'Armata	15.00	40.00
B82A Laura Martin	15.00	40.00
B82C Mark Morales	15.00	40.00
B84 Tim Bradstreet	15.00	40.00
B90 Marv Wolfman	15.00	40.00

2012 Marvel Beginnings 2 Breakthrough Issues Dual Autographs

COMMON CARD	30.00	60.00
OVERALL AUTO ODDS 1:48		
B57 T.DeFalco/J.Beatty	30.00	80.00
B64A T.DeFalco/J.Salicrup	30.00	80.00
B66 C.Claremont/J.Shooter	30.00	80.00
B68 J.Shooter/C.Claremont	30.00	70.00
B75 T.DeFalco/W.Portacio	30.00	70.00
B79 C.Eliopoulos/L.Martin		
B80 F.D'Armata/S.Epting		
B81 S.Epting/F.D'Armata		

2012 Marvel Beginnings 2 Comic Book Panels

COMMON CARD	30.00	80.00
STATED ODDS 1:288		

2012 Marvel Beginnings 2 Marvel Prime

COMPLETE SET (60)	50.00	125.00
COMMON CARD (M1-M60)	.75	2.00
STATED ODDS 1:2		
M1 Anti-Venom	3.00	8.00
M3 Beta Ray Bill	2.00	5.00
M4 Black Cat	2.00	5.00
M5 Black Panther	2.50	6.00
M8 Captain America	3.00	8.00
M9 Captain Marvel	1.50	4.00
M10 Carnage	3.00	8.00
M11 Cyclops	1.50	4.00
M12 Daredevil	1.25	3.00
M13 Deadpool	25.00	60.00
M15 Doctor Doom	1.50	4.00
M18 Gambit	2.50	6.00
M19 Ghost Rider	1.50	4.00
M20 Havok	1.25	3.00
M21 Hawkeye	2.50	6.00
M22 Howard The Duck	1.50	4.00
M23 Hulk	1.25	3.00
M26 Iron Fist	1.50	4.00
M27 Iron Man	6.00	15.00
M28 Loki	3.00	8.00
M30 Magneto	1.50	4.00
M31 Man-Thing	1.00	2.50
M33 Moon Knight	6.00	15.00
M34 Multiple Man	1.25	3.00
M35 Namor	1.25	3.00
M37 Nova	1.25	3.00
M39 Psylocke	12.00	30.00
M40 Punisher	2.00	5.00
M41 Red Hulk	1.00	2.50
M42 Red She-Hulk	2.00	5.00
M44 Rescue	1.50	4.00
M45 Rogue	2.00	5.00
M47 She-Hulk	3.00	8.00
M48 Silver Surfer	2.50	6.00
M50 Spider-Man	8.00	20.00
M52 Super Skrull	1.00	2.50
M54 Thing	2.50	6.00
M55 Thor	3.00	8.00
M57 Venom	5.00	12.00
M59 Wolverine	12.00	30.00
M60 X-23	3.00	8.00

2012 Marvel Beginnings 2 X-Men Holograms

COMMON CARD (H43-H84)	20.00	50.00
STATED ODDS 1:72		
H77 Psylocke	25.00	60.00
H78 Rogue	30.00	80.00
H83 Wolverine	50.00	100.00

2012 Marvel Beginnings 3

COMPLETE SET (180)	15.00	30.00
UNOPENED BOX (24 PACKS)	300.00	500.00
UNOPENED PACK (5 CARDS)	12.00	20.00
COMMON CARD (361-540)	.15	.40

2012 Marvel Beginnings 3 Avengers Holograms

COMPLETE SET (42)	500.00	800.00
COMMON CARD (HA1-HA42)	12.00	30.00
STATED ODDS 1:72		
HA1 Ant-Man	40.00	100.00
HA21 Moon Knight	250.00	600.00
HA30 Spider-Man	600.00	1200.00
HA33 Storm	150.00	400.00
HA34 Thing	40.00	100.00
HA37 US Agent	60.00	120.00
HA41 Wolverine	40.00	80.00

2012 Marvel Beginnings 3 Breakthrough Issues

COMPLETE SET (45)	10.00	25.00
COMMON CARD (B91-B135)	.40	1.00
STATED ODDS 1:1		

2012 Marvel Beginnings 3 Breakthrough Issues Autographs

COMMON CARD	6.00	15.00
OVERALL AUTO ODDS 1:48		
B91 Stan Lee	300.00	750.00
B92 Glynis Oliver Marsh	15.00	40.00
B95 Jim Salicrup	60.00	150.00
B97 Steve Epting	10.00	25.00
B98 Stan Lee	300.00	750.00
B100 Stan Lee	300.00	750.00
B101 Matt Hollingsworth	10.00	25.00
B102 Stan Lee	300.00	750.00
B103 Stan Lee	300.00	750.00
B104 Stan Lee	300.00	750.00
B105 Stan Lee	300.00	750.00
B108 Stan Lee	300.00	750.00
B109 Stan Lee	300.00	750.00
B110 Dan Green	10.00	25.00
B111A Chris Claremont	20.00	50.00
B113 Fabian Nicieza	12.00	30.00
B115 Jackson Guice	10.00	25.00
B117 Stan Lee	300.00	750.00
B118 Stan Lee	300.00	750.00
B120B Mike Zeck	60.00	150.00
B122 Sean Chen	15.00	40.00
B123 Jim Salicrup	60.00	150.00
B124 Laura Martin	10.00	25.00
B125B Jim Cheung	12.00	30.00
B126C Mark Bagley	10.00	25.00
B127A John Ney Rieber	10.00	25.00
B129 Stan Lee	300.00	750.00
B130 Louise Simonson	10.00	25.00
B131B Dexter Vines	12.00	30.00
B132 Tim Bradstreet	12.00	30.00

2012 Marvel Beginnings 3 Breakthrough Issues Dual Autographs

COMPLETE SET (15)		
COMMON CARD	10.00	25.00
OVERALL AUTO ODDS 1:48		
B92 C.Claremont/J.Salicrup	30.00	80.00
B93 T.DeFalco/C.Claremont	100.00	250.00
B95 J.Salicrup/T.DeFalco	30.00	80.00
B96 R.Thomas/L.Wein	30.00	80.00
B107 L.Wein/R.Thomas	30.00	80.00
B111 C.Claremont/G.Marsh	25.00	60.00
B127 R.Starkings/J.Rieber	25.00	60.00

2012 Marvel Beginnings 3 Breakthrough Issues Triple Autographs

OVERALL ODDS 1:48		
B126 Ponsor/Bagley/Lanning	25.00	60.00

2012 Marvel Beginnings 3 Comic Book Panels

COMMON CARD	40.00	80.00
STATED ODDS 1:288		

2012 Marvel Beginnings 3 Marvel Prime

COMPLETE SET (60)	40.00	100.00
COMMON CARD (M1-M60)	.75	2.00
STATED ODDS 1:2		
M37 Psylocke	5.00	12.00
M45 Spider-Man	10.00	25.00
M50 Toxin	2.50	6.00
M52 Ultimate Spider-Man	20.00	50.00

2012 Marvel Beginnings 3 Villains Die-Cuts

COMPLETE SET (45)	12.00	30.00
COMMON CARD (V1-V45)	.75	2.00
STATED ODDS 1:2		
V3 Baron Zemo	1.25	3.00
V4 Black Cat	1.25	3.00
V6 Carnage	1.50	4.00
V9 Doctor Octopus	1.50	4.00
V13 Green Goblin	1.25	3.00
V23 Loki	1.00	2.50
V24 Magneto	1.50	4.00
V31 Mystique	1.50	4.00
V42 Thanos	1.50	4.00
V44 Ultron	1.25	3.00
V45 Venom	2.00	5.00

2021 Black Diamond Marvel

UNOPENED BOX (6 CARDS))	1250.00	2500.00
COMMON CARD (1-99)	8.00	20.00
STATED PRINT RUN 149 SER.#'d SETS		
1 Robert Downey Jr.	60.00	120.00
2 Gwyneth Paltrow	12.00	30.00
4 Don Cheadle	15.00	40.00
7 Natalie Portman	15.00	40.00
8 Tom Hiddleston	20.00	50.00
9 Clark Gregg	10.00	25.00
12 Kat Dennings	15.00	40.00
13 Chris Evans	30.00	75.00
14 Hayley Atwell	25.00	60.00
15 Sebastian Stan	20.00	50.00
16 Mark Ruffalo	10.00	25.00
17 Chris Hemsworth	20.00	50.00
18 Scarlett Johansson	50.00	100.00
19 Jeremy Renner	12.00	30.00
20 Samuel L. Jackson	12.00	30.00
22 Tom Hiddleston	40.00	100.00
23 Zachary Levi	10.00	25.00
24 Chris Evans	30.00	75.00
25 Sebastian Stan	15.00	40.00
28 Georges St-Pierre	10.00	25.00
29 Chris Pratt	12.00	30.00
30 Zoe Saldana	15.00	40.00
32 Vin Diesel	15.00	40.00
33 Bradley Cooper	15.00	40.00
34 Lee Pace	10.00	25.00
35 Michael Rooker	12.00	30.00
36 Karen Gillan	15.00	40.00
37 Scarlett Johansson	30.00	75.00
39 Elizabeth Olsen	25.00	60.00
41 James Spader	20.00	50.00
42 Paul Rudd	10.00	25.00
44 Chris Evans	40.00	100.00
45 Robert Downey Jr.	25.00	60.00
46 Emily VanCamp	15.00	40.00
47 Tom Holland	25.00	60.00
48 Daniel Bruhl	12.00	30.00

49 Benedict Cumberbatch 20.00 50.00
54 Chris Pratt 12.00 30.00
55 Zoe Saldana 12.00 30.00
56 Vin Diesel 15.00 40.00
57 Bradley Cooper 12.00 30.00
58 Elizabeth Debicki 10.00 25.00
59 Pom Klementieff 12.00 30.00
61 Chris Hemsworth 30.00 75.00
62 Cate Blanchett 12.00 30.00
63 Idris Elba 10.00 25.00
65 Tessa Thompson 12.00 30.00
66 Mark Ruffalo 12.00 30.00
68 Chadwick Boseman 30.00 75.00
69 Michael B. Jordan 15.00 40.00
74 Letitia Wright 10.00 25.00
76 Angela Bassett 12.00 30.00
78 Benedict Cumberbatch 30.00 75.00
79 Chadwick Boseman 30.00 75.00
80 Elizabeth Olsen 20.00 50.00
81 Paul Bettany 12.00 30.00
82 Paul Bettany 12.00 30.00
83 Josh Brolin 15.00 40.00
86 Brie Larson 30.00 75.00
87 Samuel L. Jackson 12.00 30.00
90 Goose 15.00 40.00
91 Jude Law 15.00 40.00
92 John Slattery 12.00 30.00
93 Robert Downey Jr. 75.00 200.00
95 Scarlett Johansson 30.00 75.00
96 Brie Larson 50.00 120.00
97 Tom Holland 50.00 100.00
98 Karen Gillan 15.00 40.00
100 Josh Brolin 30.00 75.00

2021 Black Diamond Marvel Diamond Cutters

COMMON CARD (DC2-DC12) 10.00 25.00
STATED PRINT RUN 199 SER.#'d SETS
CARD NUMBER DC1 NOT ISSUED
DC2 Benedict Cumberbatch 25.00 60.00
DC3 Bradley Cooper 15.00 40.00
DC4 Brie Larson 20.00 50.00
DC5 Chris Evans 20.00 50.00
DC6 Chris Hemsworth 20.00 50.00
DC11 Robert Downey Jr. 30.00 75.00
DC12 Tom Holland 30.00 75.00

2021 Black Diamond Marvel Diamond Facet

COMMON CARD (DF1-DF24) 8.00 20.00
STATED PRINT RUN 299 SER.#'d SETS
DF2 Brie Larson 15.00 40.00
DF3 Cate Blanchett 12.00 30.00
DF4 Chadwick Boseman 15.00 40.00
DF5 Chris Evans 12.00 30.00
DF6 Chris Pratt 10.00 25.00
DF9 Elizabeth Olsen 20.00 50.00
DF10 Goose 12.00 30.00
DF12 Josh Brolin 15.00 40.00
DF13 Karen Gillan 12.00 30.00
DF14 Mark Ruffalo 10.00 25.00
DF16 Paul Bettany 10.00 25.00
DF19 Samuel L. Jackson 12.00 30.00
DF20 Scarlett Johansson 25.00 60.00
DF21 Sebastian Stan 15.00 40.00
DF22 Tilda Swinton 10.00 25.00
DF23 Tom Holland 20.00 50.00
DF24 Vin Diesel 10.00 25.00

2021 Black Diamond Marvel Diamond Facet Autographs

DFAEO Elizabeth Olsen/25 400.00 800.00
DFAJR Jeremy Renner/49 125.00 250.00
DFAKG Karen Gillan/49 125.00 250.00
DFAPB Paul Bettany/10
DFAPK Pom Klementieff/49 75.00 150.00
DFASS Sebastian Stan/49 400.00 600.00
DFATH Tom Holland/10 2000.00 3000.00
DFATS Tilda Swinton/49 75.00 150.00

2021 Black Diamond Marvel Diamond Plate Autographs

GROUP A ODDS 1:1,239
GROUP B ODDS 1:326
GROUP C ODDS 1:86
GROUP D ODDS 1:45
GROUP E ODDS 1:44
GROUP F ODDS 1:35
GROUP G ODDS 1:19
STATED OVERALL ODDS 1:7 HOBBY/EPACK
DPAM Anthony Mackie D 250.00 500.00
DPBW Benedict Wong E 25.00 60.00
DPCE Chris Evans B 1250.00 2500.00
DPCH Chris Hemsworth A
DPCO Chris Evans B 1250.00 2500.00
DPCS Cobie Smulders E 125.00 250.00
DPED Elizabeth Debicki D 100.00 200.00
DPEO Elizabeth Olsen E 450.00 900.00
DPFG Frank Grillo F 30.00 75.00
DPHA Hayley Atwell C 100.00 200.00
DPJR Jeremy Renner D 150.00 300.00
DPJS John Slattery D 30.00 75.00
DPKG Karen Gillan D 75.00 150.00
DPMG Monique Ganderton G 30.00 75.00
DPPB Paul Bettany E 300.00 600.00
DPPK Pom Klementieff D 60.00 120.00
DPRS Ray Stevenson G 30.00 75.00
DPSS Sebastian Stan C 200.00 400.00
DPTS Tilda Swinton C 50.00 100.00
DPWD Winston Duke F 60.00 120.00
DPEVC Emily VanCamp C 100.00 200.00
DPGSP Georges St-Pierre F 60.00 120.00
DPTBN Tim Blake Nelson G 30.00 75.00

2021 Black Diamond Marvel Diamond Shard Dual Relics

COMMON MEM 20.00 50.00
STATED ODDS 1:8 HOBBY/EPACK
DS2BP Chadwick Boseman/Michael B. Jordan50.00100.00
DS2AMW P.Rudd/E.Lilly 25.00 60.00
DS2CW1 R.Downey Jr./C.Evans 75.00 150.00
DS2CW2 C.Evans/S.Stan 50.00 100.00
DS2DRS B.Cumberbatch/T.Swinton 30.00 75.00
DS2RAG1 C.Hemsworth/T.Hiddleston 30.00 75.00
DS2RAG2 Chris Hemsworth/Cate Blanchett25.00 60.00

2021 Black Diamond Marvel Diamond Shard Relics

COMMON MEM 20.00 50.00
STATED ODDS 1:4 HOBBY/EPACK
DSCE Chris Evans/Shirt 60.00 120.00
DSCH Chris Hemsworth/Cape 30.00 75.00
DSCO Chadwick Boseman/Tunic 75.00 150.00
DSNP Natalie Portman/Shirt 50.00 100.00
DSSJ Scarlett Johansson/Jacket 75.00 150.00
DSTT Tessa Thompson/Suit 25.00 60.00
DSRDJ Robert Downey Jr./Shirt 60.00 120.00

2021 Black Diamond Marvel Diamond Shard Triple Relics

COMMON MEM 60.00 120.00
STATED ODDS 1:20 HOBBY/EPACK
DS3CW Chris Evans/Anthony
Mackie/Scarlett Johansson 75.00 200.00
DS3IM3 Downey Jr./Paltrow/Favreau 60.00 150.00
DS3RAG Thompson/Hemsworth/Hiddleston60.00 150.00

2021 Black Diamond Marvel Diamond Shards Autographs

STATED PRINT RUN 25-99 SER.#'d SETS
DSAAM Anthony Mackie/49 500.00 1000.00
DSACE Chris Evans/25 1000.00 2000.00
DSACH Chris Hemsworth/25 1200.00 2000.00
DSAED Elizabeth Debicki/99 125.00 250.00
DSAEO Elizabeth Olsen/49 600.00 1200.00
DSAKG Karen Gillan/99 100.00 200.00
DSASS Sebastian Stan/25
DSATS Tilda Swinton/99 75.00 150.00
DSAEVC Emily VanCamp/25 150.00 300.00

2021 Black Diamond Marvel Exquisite Collection

COMMON CARD (2-50) 8.00 20.00
STATED PRINT RUN 125 SER.#'d SETS
2 Anthony Mackie 15.00 40.00
3 Benedict Cumberbatch 20.00 50.00
5 Bradley Cooper 10.00 25.00
6 Brie Larson 50.00 100.00
7 Cate Blanchett 15.00 40.00
8 Chadwick Boseman 20.00 50.00
9 Chris Evans 20.00 50.00
10 Chris Hemsworth 25.00 60.00
11 Chris Pratt 12.00 30.00
13 Cobie Smulders 10.00 25.00
15 Danai Gurira 12.00 30.00
16 Dave Bautista 10.00 25.00
17 Don Cheadle 10.00 25.00
19 Elizabeth Olsen 30.00 75.00
20 Emily VanCamp 20.00 50.00
21 Evangeline Lilly 12.00 30.00
22 Goose 12.00 30.00
23 Gwyneth Paltrow 12.00 30.00
24 Hayley Atwell 12.00 30.00
26 Idris Elba 12.00 30.00
27 Jaimie Alexander 15.00 40.00
28 James Spader 15.00 40.00
29 Jeff Goldblum 12.00 30.00
30 Jeremy Renner 12.00 30.00
31 Josh Brolin 20.00 50.00
32 Karen Gillan 10.00 25.00
34 Mark Ruffalo 20.00 50.00
35 Michael B. Jordan 10.00 25.00
36 Natalie Portman 20.00 50.00
37 Paul Bettany 12.00 30.00
38 Paul Rudd 15.00 40.00
39 Pom Klementieff 15.00 40.00
40 Robert Downey Jr. 50.00 100.00
41 Samuel L. Jackson 12.00 30.00
42 Scarlett Johansson 60.00 120.00
43 Sebastian Stan 15.00 40.00
44 Tessa Thompson 20.00 50.00
45 Tilda Swinton 12.00 30.00
46 Tom Hiddleston 25.00 60.00
47 Tom Holland 250.00 600.00
49 Winston Duke 12.00 30.00
50 Zoe Saldana 10.00 25.00

2021 Black Diamond Marvel Exquisite Collection Autographs

STATED PRINT RUN 15-99 SER.#'d SETS
AAM Anthony Mackie/35 500.00 1000.00
ABW Benedict Wong/99 50.00 100.00
ACE Chris Evans/35 800.00 1200.00
ACH Chris Hemsworth/65 1500.00 3000.00
ACS Cobie Smulders/65 150.00 300.00
AED Elizabeth Debicki/99 40.00 100.00
AEO Elizabeth Olsen/35
AFG Frank Grillo/99 40.00 100.00
AHA Hayley Atwell/35 200.00 400.00
AJR Jeremy Renner/35 250.00 500.00
AJS John Slattery/35 60.00 120.00
AKG Karen Gillan/35 125.00 250.00
APB Paul Bettany/15
APK Pom Klementieff/65 75.00 150.00
ASS Sebastian Stan/35 125.00 300.00
ATH Tom Holland/15 2000.00 3000.00
ATS Tilda Swinton/35 75.00 150.00
AWD Winston Duke/99 40.00 120.00
AEVC Emily VanCamp/65 125.00 250.00

2021 Black Diamond Marvel Gemography Diamond Autographs

COMMON AUTO 75.00 200.00
STATED PRINT RUN 25 SER.#'d SETS
GAM Anthony Mackie 300.00 800.00
GBW Benedict Wong 125.00 300.00
GCE Chris Evans 1500.00 4000.00
GCH Chris Hemsworth 600.00 1500.00
GCS Cobie Smulders 100.00 250.00
GED Elizabeth Debicki 125.00 300.00
GEO Elizabeth Olsen 1000.00 2500.00
GEV Emily VanCamp 125.00 300.00
GHA Hayley Atwell 150.00 400.00
GJR Jeremy Renner 150.00 400.00
GKG Karen Gillan 250.00 600.00
GPB Paul Bettany 500.00 1200.00
GPK Pom Klementieff 125.00 300.00
GSS Sebastian Stan 200.00 500.00
GTH Tom Holland 1200.00 3000.00

2021 Black Diamond Marvel Gold Autographs

COMMON AUTO 60.00 150.00
RANDOMLY INSERTED INTO PACKS
6 Chris Hemsworth/10 1000.00 2500.00
13 Chris Evans/49 500.00 1200.00
14 Hayley Atwell/49 125.00 300.00
15 Sebastian Stan/49 150.00 400.00
17 Chris Hemsworth/10 1000.00 2500.00
24 Chris Evans/25 750.00 2000.00
26 Anthony Mackie/35 300.00 800.00
36 Karen Gillan/49 75.00 200.00
39 Elizabeth Olsen/25 500.00 1200.00
40 Cobie Smulders/49 75.00 200.00
44 Chris Evans/25 750.00 2000.00
46 Emily VanCamp/49 100.00 250.00
47 Tom Holland/10
61 Chris Hemsworth/10 600.00 1500.00
75 Winston Duke/49 75.00 200.00
80 Elizabeth Olsen/25 500.00 1200.00
81 Paul Bettany/25 400.00 1000.00
82 Paul Bettany/10
98 Karen Gillan/25 75.00 200.00

2021 Black Diamond Marvel Infinity Stone Diamond Relics

COMMON MEM 100.00 250.00
STATED PRINT RUN 23 SER.#'d SETS
1 Robert Downey Jr. 1500.00 4000.00
3 Jon Favreau 150.00 400.00
4 Don Cheadle 200.00 500.00
6 Chris Hemsworth 500.00 1200.00
7 Natalie Portman 400.00 1000.00
8 Tom Hiddleston 400.00 1000.00
13 Chris Evans 600.00 1500.00
14 Hayley Atwell 200.00 500.00
16 Mark Ruffalo 300.00 800.00
17 Chris Hemsworth 500.00 1200.00
18 Scarlett Johansson 1200.00 3000.00
19 Jeremy Renner 200.00 500.00
20 Samuel L. Jackson 150.00 400.00
22 Tom Hiddleston 400.00 1000.00
24 Chris Evans 600.00 1500.00
25 Sebastian Stan 300.00 800.00
26 Anthony Mackie 200.00 500.00
27 Frank Grillo 200.00 500.00
29 Chris Pratt 300.00 750.00
30 Zoe Saldana 150.00 400.00
32 Vin Diesel 300.00 800.00
33 Bradley Cooper 250.00 600.00
36 Karen Gillan 300.00 800.00
37 Scarlett Johansson 1200.00 3000.00
39 Elizabeth Olsen 600.00 1500.00
40 Cobie Smulders 150.00 400.00
42 Paul Rudd 200.00 500.00
43 Evangeline Lilly 250.00 600.00
44 Chris Evans 600.00 1500.00
45 Robert Downey Jr. 1500.00 4000.00
47 Tom Holland
49 Benedict Cumberbatch 500.00 1200.00
53 Tilda Swinton 150.00 400.00
54 Chris Pratt 300.00 750.00
55 Zoe Saldana 125.00 300.00
56 Vin Diesel 300.00 800.00
57 Bradley Cooper 125.00 300.00
61 Chris Hemsworth 500.00 1200.00
63 Idris Elba 150.00 400.00
66 Mark Ruffalo 300.00 800.00
67 Taika Waititi 200.00 500.00
68 Chadwick Boseman 1500.00 4000.00
71 Danai Gurira 150.00 400.00
74 Letitia Wright 150.00 400.00

78 Benedict Cumberbatch 300.00 750.00
79 Chadwick Boseman 1500.00 4000.00
80 Elizabeth Olsen 600.00 1500.00
81 Paul Bettany 125.00 300.00
82 Paul Bettany 125.00 300.00
83 Josh Brolin 750.00 2000.00
84 Paul Rudd 200.00 500.00
85 Evangeline Lilly 200.00 500.00
86 Brie Larson 400.00 1000.00
87 Samuel L. Jackson 200.00 500.00
92 John Slattery 125.00 300.00
93 Robert Downey Jr. 1000.00 2500.00
94 Jeremy Renner 150.00 400.00
95 Scarlett Johansson 1200.00 3000.00
96 Brie Larson 400.00 1000.00
97 Tom Holland
98 Karen Gillan 300.00 800.00
99 Tom Vaughan-Lawlor 150.00 400.00
100 Josh Brolin 1000.00 2500.00

2021 Black Diamond Marvel Polished Patches Autographed Manufactured Relics

COMMON AUTO 60.00 150.00
STATED PRINT RUN 5-99 SER.#'d SETS
PPAAM Anthony Mackie/25 250.00 600.00
PPACE Chris Evans/25 600.00 1500.00
PPACS Cobie Smulders/49 75.00 200.00
PPAED Elizabeth Debicki/99 125.00 300.00
PPAEO Elizabeth Olsen/25 400.00 1000.00
PPAHA Hayley Atwell/25 100.00 250.00
PPAJR Jeremy Renner/25 100.00 250.00
PPAJS John Slattery/25 75.00 200.00
PPAKG Karen Gillan/25 100.00 250.00
PPAPB Paul Bettany/5
PPASS Sebastian Stan/25 125.00 300.00
PPATH Tom Holland/5
PPATS Tilda Swinton/25 75.00 200.00
PPATBN Tim Blake Nelson/25 50.00 125.00

2021 Black Diamond Marvel Polished Patches Manufactured Relics

COMMON MEM 10.00 25.00
STATED PRINT RUN 49 SER.#'d SETS
PPAV1 Chris Evans 100.00 200.00
PPAV2 Chris Hemsworth 25.00 60.00
PPAV3 Robert Downey Jr. 75.00 150.00
PPAV4 Scarlett Johansson 125.00 250.00
PPAV5 Mark Ruffalo 15.00 40.00
PPAV6 Jeremy Renner 15.00 40.00
PPBP1 Chadwick Boseman 30.00 75.00
PPBP2 Lupita Nyong'o 12.00 30.00
PPBP3 Michael B. Jordan 12.00 30.00
PPCA1 Chris Evans 20.00 50.00
PPCA2 Sebastian Stan 20.00 50.00
PPCA3 Hayley Atwell 12.00 30.00
PPCA4 Hugo Weaving 20.00 50.00
PPCA6 Tommy Lee Jones 12.00 30.00
PPCM1 Goose 15.00 40.00
PPCM2 Brie Larson 30.00 75.00
PPCM5 Lashana Lynch 15.00 40.00
PPCM6 Samuel L. Jackson 12.00 30.00
PPGG1 Chris Pratt 20.00 50.00
PPGG2 Zoe Saldana 12.00 30.00
PPGG3 Vin Diesel 12.00 30.00
PPGG4 Bradley Cooper 12.00 30.00
PPGG6 Karen Gillan 15.00 40.00
PPIM1 Robert Downey Jr. 75.00 150.00
PPIM3 Gwyneth Paltrow 12.00 30.00
PPTH1 Chris Hemsworth 25.00 60.00
PPTH2 Natalie Portman 50.00 100.00
PPTH3 Tom Hiddleston 25.00 60.00
PPTH4 Idris Elba 12.00 30.00
PPTH6 Kat Dennings 12.00 30.00

2021 Black Diamond Marvel Polished Patches Puzzles Manufactured Relics

COMMON MEM 6.00 15.00
STATED ODDS 1:8 HOBBY/EPACK
PPAV1 Chris Evans 12.00 30.00
PPAV2 Chris Hemsworth 12.00 30.00
PPAV3 Robert Downey Jr. 20.00 50.00
PPAV4 Scarlett Johansson 15.00 40.00
PPBP1 Chadwick Boseman 15.00 40.00
PPBP3 Michael B. Jordan 8.00 20.00
PPCA1 Chris Evans 15.00 40.00
PPCA2 Sebastian Stan 8.00 20.00
PPCA3 Hayley Atwell 8.00 20.00
PPCA6 Tommy Lee Jones 8.00 20.00
PPCM1 Goose 8.00 20.00
PPCM2 Brie Larson 12.00 30.00
PPGG1 Chris Pratt 10.00 25.00
PPGG2 Zoe Saldana 8.00 20.00
PPIM1 Robert Downey Jr. 20.00 50.00
PPTH1 Chris Hemsworth 15.00 40.00
PPTH2 Natalie Portman 10.00 25.00
PPTH3 Tom Hiddleston 12.00 30.00
PPTH5 Ray Stevenson 10.00 25.00

2021 Black Diamond Marvel Triskelion Autographs

COMMON AUTO
RANDOMLY INSERTED INTO PACKS
TAM Anthony Mackie/35 1000.00 1500.00
TBW Benedict Wong/99 60.00 120.00
TCS Cobie Smulders/65 100.00 250.00
THA Hayley Atwell/65 60.00 150.00
TJR Jeremy Renner/99 125.00 250.00
TKG Karen Gillan/35 125.00 250.00
TMG Monique Ganderton/125 50.00 100.00
TPB Paul Bettany/15 1000.00 1500.00
TRS Ray Stevenson/125 30.00 75.00
TSS Sebastian Stan/35 125.00 250.00
TTH Tom Holland/15 2000.00 3000.00
TTS Tilda Swinton/65 75.00 150.00
TEVC Emily VanCamp/35 50.00 125.00
TTBN Tim Blake Nelson/99 50.00 100.00

2012 Marvel Bronze Age

COMPLETE SET (81) 6.00 15.00
UNOPENED BOX (24 PACKS) 300.00 500.00
UNOPENED PACK (5 CARDS) 12.00 20.00
COMMON CARD (1-81) .15 .40
*PARALLEL: 1.2X TO 3X BASIC CARDS

2012 Marvel Bronze Age Case-Toppers

COMPLETE SET (2) 20.00 40.00
COMMON CARD (CT1-CT2) 10.00 25.00
STATED ODDS 1:CASE

2012 Marvel Bronze Age Classic Heroes

COMPLETE SET (9) 8.00 20.00
COMPLETE SET W/SP (10) 15.00 40.00
COMMON CARD (CH1-CH10) 1.50 4.00
STATED ODDS 1:12
CH10 ISSUED AS RITTENHOUSE REWARD
CH10 Silver Surfer RR SP 12.00 30.00

2012 Marvel Bronze Age Dual-Sided Posters

COMPLETE SET (18) 15.00 30.00
COMMON CARD (PP1-PP18) 1.25 3.00
STATED ODDS 1:8

2012 Marvel Bronze Age Embossed

COMPLETE SET (12) 15.00 40.00
COMMON CARD (E1-E12) 2.50 6.00
STATED ODDS 1:24
E9 Wolverine 4.00 10.00
E10 Punisher 3.00 8.00

2012 Marvel Bronze Age Promos

P1 Wolverine/Hulk 1974 GEN .75 2.00
P2 Spider-Man 1984 NSU .75 2.00
P3 Promo 3 ALB 3.00 8.00
P4 X-Men 1976 SDCC 1.25 3.00

1979 General Mills Marvel Cereal Stickers

COMPLETE SET (8) 8.00 20.00
COMPLETE VARIANT 1 SET (4) 5.00 12.00
COMPLETE VARIANT 2 SET (4) 5.00 12.00
COMMON CARD (1-4) 1.25 3.00
ALL CARDS HAVE 2 VARIANTS
1A Captain America (variant 1) 1.50 4.00
1B Captain America (variant 2) 1.50 4.00
3A Spider-Man (swinging on web) 2.00 5.00
3B Spider-Man (jumping or leaping) 2.00 5.00

Marvel Cinematic Universe

2015 Agent Coulson's Vintage Captain America

COMPLETE SET (21) 10.00 25.00
COMMON CARD .50 1.25

2019 Agents of S.H.I.E.L.D. Compendium

COMPLETE SET W/SP (210) 200.00 350.00
COMPLETE SET W/O SP (50) 5.00 12.00
UNOPENED BOX (16 PACKS) 100.00 200.00
UNOPENED PACK (6 CARDS) 6.00 12.00
SEASON 1 COMMON (1-50) .20 .50
SEASON 2 COMMON (51-90) 1.00 2.50
SEASON 3 COMMON (91-130) 1.00 2.50
SEASON 4 COMMON (131-170) 2.00 5.00
SEASON 5 COMMON (171-210) 2.00 5.00
SEASON 2 ODDS 1:3
SEASON 3 ODDS 1:3
SEASON 4 ODDS 1:7
SEASON 5 ODDS 1:7

2019 Agents of S.H.I.E.L.D. Compendium Autographs

COMMON AUTO 5.00 12.00
GROUP A ODDS 1:89
GROUP B ODDS 1:66
GROUP C ODDS 1:39
GROUP D ODDS 1:16
STATED OVERALL ODDS 1:9
AAAK Adam Kulbersh D 6.00 15.00
AAAP Adrian Pasdar A 15.00 40.00
AABB B.J. Britt A 12.00 30.00
AABC Chloe Bennet C 150.00 300.00
AABD Brett Dalton A 10.00 25.00
AABJ B.J. Britt B 8.00 20.00
AABV Briana Venskus C 10.00 25.00
AACB Chloe Bennet A 200.00 350.00
AACN Natalia Cordova-Buckley A 25.00 60.00
AADB Brett Dalton C 10.00 25.00
AADL Dichen Lachman A 12.00 30.00
AADO David O'Hara C 6.00 15.00
AAEH Elizabeth Henstridge B 50.00 100.00
AAHE Elizabeth Henstridge C 30.00 75.00
AAHS Henry Simmons C 8.00 20.00
AAJM Mallory Jansen B 30.00 75.00
AAKS Kerr Smith D 6.00 15.00
AALD Dichen Lachman A 12.00 30.00
AALM Luke Mitchell B 10.00 25.00
AAMJ Mallory Jansen C 25.00 60.00
AAML Luke Mitchell B 12.00 30.00
AAMN Ming-Na Wen A 40.00 100.00
AAMW Matthew Willig D 6.00 15.00
AANC Natalia Cordova-Buckley D 15.00 40.00
AAPA Adrian Pasdar B 12.00 30.00
AASH Henry Simmons B 10.00 25.00
AASK Simon Kassianides B 6.00 15.00
AASS Simon Kassianides A 10.00 25.00
AATW Titus Welliver D 8.00 20.00
AAWM Ming-Na Wen C 25.00 60.00

2019 Agents of S.H.I.E.L.D. Compendium Character Profiles

COMPLETE SET (20) 10.00 25.00
COMMON CARD (CB1-CB20) 1.25 3.00
STATED ODDS 1:5

2019 Agents of S.H.I.E.L.D. Compendium Character Profiles Autographs

GROUP A ODDS 1:978
GROUP B ODDS 1:254
GROUP C ODDS 1:150
STATED OVERALL ODDS 1:90
CBAK Adam Kulbersh B 15.00 40.00
CBBB B.J. Britt C 6.00 15.00
CBBD Brett Dalton A 10.00 25.00
CBBV Briana Venskus C 15.00 40.00
CBCA Christine Adams B 5.00 12.00
CBCB Chloe Bennet A 250.00 400.00
CBDL Dichen Lachman C 12.00 30.00
CBEH Elizabeth Henstridge A 100.00 200.00
CBHS Henry Simmons B 8.00 20.00
CBJH Jamie Harris B 10.00 25.00
CBJR J. August Richards B 4.00 10.00
CBJS Joel Stoffer C 10.00 25.00
CBLM Luke Mitchell B 10.00 25.00
CBMJ Mallory Jansen C 60.00 120.00
CBMN Ming-Na Wen A 30.00 75.00
CBMO Maximilian Osinski C 5.00 12.00
CBMW Matthew Willig C 6.00 15.00
CBNC Natalia Cordova-Buckley B 5.00 12.00
CBSK Simon Kassianides C 10.00 25.00
CBTW Titus Welliver C 5.00 12.00

2019 Agents of S.H.I.E.L.D. Compendium Character Profiles Variant Autographs

CPAO1 Chloe Bennett 200.00 350.00
CPAO2 Ming-Na Wen
CPAO3 Elizabeth Henstridge

2019 Agents of S.H.I.E.L.D. Compendium The Plot Thickens

COMPLETE SET (10) 10.00 25.00
COMMON CARD (PT1-PT10) 1.50 4.00
STATED ODDS 1:13

2015 Agents of SHIELD Season 1

COMPLETE SET (72) 8.00 20.00
UNOPENED BOX (24 PACKS) 125.00 200.00
UNOPENED PACK (5 CARDS) 5.00 8.00
COMMON CARD (1-72) .20 .50
*GOLD/100: 5X TO 12X BASIC CARDS 2.50 6.00

2015 Agents of SHIELD Season 1 Advanced Technology

COMPLETE SET (9) 5.00 12.00
COMMON CARD (AT1-AT9) 1.00 2.50
STATED ODDS 1:24

2015 Agents of SHIELD Season 1 Allegiance

COMPLETE SET (18) 25.00 60.00
COMMON CARD (FF1-FF18)) 3.00 8.00
STATED ODDS 1:24

2015 Agents of SHIELD Season 1 Art of 7

COMPLETE SET (6) 6.00 15.00
COMMON CARD (CB1-CB6) 2.00 5.00
STATED ODDS 1:24

2015 Agents of SHIELD Season 1 Bordered Autographs

COMMON CARD 5.00 12.00
STATED ODDS 1:18
NNO Elena Satine VL 10.00 25.00
NNO Glenn Morshower VL 6.00 15.00
NNO J. August Richards VL 8.00 20.00
NNO Saffron Burrows VL 8.00 20.00
NNO Titus Welliver VL 10.00 25.00

2015 Agents of SHIELD Season 1 Case-Incentives

NNO Bill Paxton BOR AU/AB 75.00 150.00
NNO Cobie Smulders AU/9CI 120.00 200.00
NNO Stan Lee AU/6CI 200.00 500.00

2015 Agents of SHIELD Season 1 Case-Toppers

COMMON CARD (CT1-CT2) 8.00 20.00
STATED ODDS 1:CASE

2015 Agents of SHIELD Season 1 Costumes

COMMON CARD (CC1-CC19)	4.00	10.00
STATED ODDS 1:24		
CC1 Agent Phil Coulson	5.00	12.00
CC2 Agent Phil Coulson	5.00	12.00
CC3 Agent Melinda May	15.00	40.00
CC6 Agent Jemma Simmons	6.00	15.00
CC7 Agent Leo Fitz	5.00	12.00
CC8 Agent Skye	30.00	75.00
CC9 Agent Maria Hill	10.00	25.00
CC11 Ian Quinn	5.00	12.00
CC12 Agent John Garrett	6.00	15.00
CC15 Agent Jasper Sitwell	6.00	15.00
CC16 Raina	5.00	12.00
CC17 Agent Felix Blake	5.00	12.00
CC18 Debonair Gentleman	12.00	30.00
CC19 Mike Peterson	5.00	12.00

2015 Agents of SHIELD Season 1 Full Bleed Autographs

COMMON CARD	5.00	12.00
STATED ODDS 1:18		
NNO Adrian Pasdar VL	8.00	20.00
NNO Bill Paxton EL	100.00	200.00
NNO Brad Dourif L	8.00	20.00
NNO Brett Dalton EL	20.00	50.00
NNO Christine Adams L	6.00	15.00
NNO Clark Gregg EL	20.00	50.00
NNO Elena Satine VL	10.00	25.00
NNO Elizabeth Henstridge EL	25.00	60.00
NNO J. August Richards EL	10.00	25.00
NNO Leonor Varela L	6.00	15.00
NNO Louis Changchien L	6.00	15.00
NNO Ming-Na Wen EL	30.00	75.00
NNO Patton Oswalt EL	20.00	50.00
NNO Ruth Negga EL	25.00	60.00
NNO Saffron Burrows VL	10.00	25.00
NNO Titus Welliver EL	12.00	30.00

2015 Agents of SHIELD Season 1 ID Cards

COMPLETE SET (6)	10.00	25.00
COMMON CARD (ID1-ID6)	3.00	8.00
STATED ODDS 1:24		

2015 Agents of SHIELD Season 1 Silver Signature Autograph

CS1 Cobie Smulders EL	300.00	500.00

2015 Agents of SHIELD Season 1 Promos

COMMON CARD (P1-P2)	2.00	5.00
P2 Album Exclusive	15.00	40.00

2015 Agents of SHIELD Season 2

COMPLETE SET (72)	8.00	20.00
UNOPENED BOX (24 PACKS)	200.00	400.00
UNOPENED PACK (5 CARDS)	8.00	15.00
UNOPENED ARCHIVE BOX	1000.00	1500.00
COMMON CARD (1-72)	.20	.50
*GOLD/100: 5X TO 12X BASIC CARDS		

2015 Agents of SHIELD Season 2 Agents of Shield

COMPLETE SET (10)	10.00	25.00
COMMON CARD (AS1-AS10)	1.50	4.00
*METAL/75: 2.5X TO 6X BASIC CARDS		
STATED ODDS 1:24		

2015 Agents of SHIELD Season 2 Archive Box Exclusive Autographs

COMMON CARD	12.00	30.00
2 Chloe Bennet (Silver)	100.00	200.00
3 Clark Gregg (Silver)	25.00	60.00
4 Elizabeth Henstridge (Silver)	30.00	75.00
5 Hayley Atwell (Silver)	75.00	150.00
7 Kyle MacLachlan (Full Bleed)	25.00	60.00
8 Ming-Na (Silver)	30.00	75.00
9 Ruth Negga (Silver)	15.00	40.00

2015 Agents of SHIELD Season 2 Art of Evolution

COMPLETE SET (12)	15.00	40.00
COMMON CARD (CB1-CB24)	2.50	6.00
STATED ODDS 1:24		

2015 Agents of SHIELD Season 2 Bordered Autographs

COMMON CARD	5.00	12.00
STATED ODDS 1:24 WITH FULL BLEED		
NNO B.J. Britt VL	6.00	15.00
NNO Brett Dalton EL	12.00	30.00
NNO Chloe Bennet EL	75.00	150.00
NNO Clark Gregg EL	20.00	50.00
NNO Dichen Lachman EL	10.00	25.00
NNO Elizabeth Henstridge EL	25.00	60.00
NNO Henry Simmons EL	10.00	25.00
NNO Iain De Caestecker EL	15.00	40.00
NNO Jaimie Alexander as Lady Sif S	80.00	150.00
NNO Kyle MacLachlan EL	25.00	60.00
NNO Luke Mitchell EL	10.00	25.00
NNO Maya Stojan EL	12.00	30.00
NNO Ming-Na EL	30.00	75.00
NNO Nick Blood EL	8.00	20.00
NNO Ruth Negga EL	12.00	30.00

2015 Agents of SHIELD Season 2 Full Bleed Autographs

COMMON AUTO	6.00	15.00
STATED ODDS 1:24 WITH BORDERED		
L = 300-500		
VL = 200-300		
EL = <200		
NNO Chloe Bennet EL	75.00	150.00
NNO Dichen Lachman EL	10.00	25.00
NNO Fred Dryer EL	10.00	25.00
NNO Hayley Atwell EL	60.00	120.00
NNO Henry Simmons EL	10.00	25.00
NNO Iain De Caestecker EL	15.00	40.00
NNO Luke Mitchell EL	12.00	30.00
NNO Maya Stojan EL	10.00	25.00
NNO Nick Blood EL	8.00	20.00
NNO Patton Oswalt EL	12.00	40.00
NNO Ruth Negga EL	12.00	30.00

2015 Agents of SHIELD Season 2 Case-Incentives

NNO Kyle MacLachlan Silver Sig	50.00	100.00
9CI Jaimie Alexander Silver Sig	75.00	150.00

2015 Agents of SHIELD Season 2 Case-Topper

STATED ODDS 1:CASE		
CT1 Real SHIELD Embossed Logo	6.00	15.00

2015 Agents of SHIELD Season 2 Costumes

COMMON CARD (CC1-CC17)	5.00	12.00
STATED ODDS 1:24		
CC1 Director Phil Coulson	8.00	20.00
CC2 Agent Skye	15.00	40.00
CC5 Agent Jemma Simmons	10.00	25.00
CC9 Agent Bobbi Morse	10.00	25.00
CC13 Agent 33/Kara Lynn Palamas	8.00	20.00
CC15 Lady Sif	6.00	15.00

2015 Agents of SHIELD Season 2 Gifted Index

COMPLETE SET (18)	15.00	40.00
COMMON CARD (G1-G18)	2.00	5.00
STATED ODDS 1:24		

2015 Agents of SHIELD Season 2 Promos

COMMON CARD (P1-P4)	1.50	4.00
P3 ALB	10.00	25.00

2015 Ant-Man

COMPLETE SET (90)	6.00	15.00
UNOPENED BOX (20 PACKS)	100.00	150.00
UNOPENED PACK (5 CARDS)	5.00	8.00
COMMON CARD (1-90)	.15	.40
*BRONZE: 2.5X TO 6X BASIC CARDS	1.00	2.50

2015 Ant-Man Ant Construction

COMPLETE SET (7)	5.00	12.00
COMMON CARD (AC1-AC7)	1.25	3.00
STATED ODDS 1:8		

2015 Ant-Man Ant Heritage

COMPLETE SET (10)	10.00	25.00
COMMON CARD (AH1-AH10)	1.50	4.00
STATED ODDS 1:12		

2015 Ant-Man Autographed Memorabilia

COMMON AU MEM	100.00	200.00
STATED PRINT RUN 10 SER.#'d SETS		
AMCS Corey Stoll	100.00	200.00
AMEL Evangeline Lilly	250.00	500.00
AMMP Michael Pena	100.00	200.00

2015 Ant-Man Autographs

COMMON AUTO	10.00	25.00
RANDOMLY INSERTED INTO PACKS		
AACO Corey Stoll	50.00	100.00
AACS Corey Stoll	50.00	100.00
AAEL Evangeline Lilly	150.00	300.00
AAMP Michael Pena	50.00	100.00
AAPE Michael Pena	50.00	100.00

2015 Ant-Man Behind-the-Lens

COMPLETE SET (16)	6.00	15.00
COMMON CARD (BTL1-BTL16)	.75	2.00
STATED ODDS 1:4		

2015 Ant-Man Bite-Sized Team-Ups

COMPLETE SET (10)	10.00	25.00
COMMON CARD (BS1-BS10)	1.50	4.00
STATED ODDS 1:12		

2015 Ant-Man Pym Particles Dual Memorabilia

COMMON MEM	3.00	8.00
STATED OVERALL MEM ODDS 1:10		
PT2A S.Lang/Ant-Man	12.00	30.00
PT2A Ant-Man	12.00	30.00
PT2C Darren Cross	8.00	20.00
PT2L Luis	6.00	15.00
PT2P Paxton	6.00	15.00
PT2AC D.Cross/Ant-Man	10.00	25.00
PT2AL Luis/Ant-Man	6.00	15.00
PT2CL D.Cross/S.Lang	6.00	15.00
PT2DA Dave/Ant-Man	5.00	12.00
PT2DK Kurt/Dave	6.00	15.00
PT2HA H.Van Dyne/Ant-Man	10.00	25.00
PT2KH H.Van Dyne/Kurt	6.00	15.00
PT2KL Kurt/Luis	4.00	10.00
PT2LD Luis/Dave	6.00	15.00
PT2LL Kurt/S.Lang	4.00	10.00
PT2LP Paxton/S.Lang	6.00	15.00
PT2LS S.Lang/Luis	5.00	12.00
PT2LV Luis/H.Van Dyne	8.00	20.00
PT2PL Luis/Paxton	5.00	12.00
PT2SD S.Lang/Dave	5.00	12.00
PT2VC D.Cross/H.Van Dyne	10.00	25.00
PT2VD H.Van Dyne/Dave	5.00	12.00
PT2VL H. Van Dyne S.Lang	15.00	40.00

2015 Ant-Man Pym Particles Memorabilia

COMPLETE SET (16)	75.00	150.00
COMMON MEM	2.50	6.00
STATED OVERALL MEM ODDS 1:10		
PTAM Ant-Man	6.00	15.00
PTAT Ant-Man	15.00	40.00
PTCR Darren Cross	6.00	15.00
PTDC Darren Cross	4.00	10.00
PTHV Hope Van Dyne	10.00	25.00
PTLA Scott Lang	8.00	20.00
PTLU Luis	4.00	10.00
PTLV Luis	4.00	10.00
PTPA Paxton	3.00	8.00
PTPV Paxton	3.00	8.00
PTSL Scott Lang	6.00	15.00
PTVA Hope Van Dyne	8.00	20.00

2015 Ant-Man Movie Posters

COMPLETE SET (2)	6.00	15.00
COMMON CARD (MP1-MP2)	4.00	10.00
STATED ODDS 1:24		

2015 Ant-Man Professionals

COMPLETE SET (10)	6.00	15.00
COMMON CARD (P1-P10)	1.00	2.50
STATED ODDS 1:6		

2015 Ant-Man Pym Particles Triple Memorabila

COMMON MEM	6.00	15.00
STATED OVERALL MEM ODDS 1:10		
PT3K Kurt	15.00	40.00
PT3L S.Lang/Ant-Man	15.00	40.00
PT3ACL Ant-Man/D.Cross/Luis	10.00	25.00
PT3HDA Cross/Van Dyne/Ant-Man	15.00	40.00
PT3KDA Ant-Man/Cross/Kurt	8.00	20.00
PT3KPL Kurt/Luis/Paxton	8.00	20.00
PT3LDK Dave/Luis/Kurt	20.00	50.00
PT3LHK Kurt/Luis/Van Dyne	8.00	20.00
PT3LLD Lang/Luis/Dave	8.00	20.00
PT3PHA Paxton/Van Dyne/Ant-Man	12.00	30.00
PT3VCL Lang/Van Dyne/Cross	10.00	25.00

2015 Ant-Man Dog Tags

COMPLETE SET (24)	25.00	60.00
UNOPENED BOX (24 PACKS)	65.00	80.00
UNOPENED PACK (1 TAG+1 STICKER)	3.50	4.00
COMMON TAG (1-24)	2.00	5.00
COMMON FOIL TAG (25-48)	4.00	10.00

2015 Ant-Man Dog Tags Stickers

COMPLETE SET (48)	5.00	12.00
COMMON STICKER (1-24)	.40	1.00
COMMON FOIL STICKER (25-48)	1.25	3.00
STATED ODDS 1:1		

2018 Ant-Man and the Wasp

COMPLETE SET (100)	10.00	25.00
UNOPENED BOX (15 PACKS)	75.00	125.00
UNOPENED PACK (5 CARDS)	5.00	8.00
COMMON CARD (1-100)	.20	.50
*MINI (1-100): 1.2X TO 3X BASIC CARDS		
P.P.BLACK/1: UNPRICED DUE TO SCARCITY		
P.P.CYAN/1: UNPRICED DUE TO SCARCITY		
P.P.MAGENTA/1: UNPRICED DUE TO SCARCITY		
P.P.YELLOW/1: UNPRICED DUE TO SCARCITY		

2018 Ant-Man and the Wasp Minis

*MINI: 1.2X TO 3X BASIC CARDS		
COMMON SP	2.00	5.00

2018 Ant-Man and the Wasp 28-Piece Micro Swatch Relic

MSR Ghost/Wasp/Scott Lang/Luis/Dave Kurt/Anitolov/Ant-Man/Sonny Burch#{Uzman/Bill Foster/Ava#{Cassie Lang/Hope Van Dyne#{Ghost/Wasp/Scott Lang/Luis/Dave#{Kurt/Anitolov/Ant-Man/Sonny Burch#{Uzman/Bill Foster/Ava#{Cassie Lang/Hope Van Dyne	150.00	300.00

2018 Ant-Man and the Wasp Behind-the-Lens

COMPLETE SET (15)	6.00	15.00
COMMON CARD (BTL1-BTL15)	.75	2.00
STATED ODDS 1:2		

2018 Ant-Man and the Wasp Mini Giants Autographs

COMMON AUTO	20.00	50.00
STATED ODDS 1:480		
MGEL Evangeline Lilly	150.00	300.00
MGHK Hannah John-Kamen	60.00	120.00
MGJG Judy Greer	30.00	75.00

2018 Ant-Man and the Wasp Quantum Anomaly Autographed Relics

COMMON AUTO	20.00	50.00
STATED ODDS 1:480		
QMAG Hannah John-Kamen	125.00	250.00

Ghost Cost.
QMEL Evangeline Lilly 150.00 300.00
QMHD Evangeline Lilly 150.00 300.00
QMHK Hannah John-Kamen 120.00 250.00

2018 Ant-Man and the Wasp Quantum Anomaly Dual Relics

COMMON MEM 3.00 8.00
GROUP A ODDS 1:283
GROUP B ODDS 1:63
STATED OVERALL ODDS 1:45
QMD1 Ghost/Wasp 20.00 50.00
Ghost Cost./Wasp Cost. A
QMD2 Ant-Man/Wasp B 12.00 30.00
QMD3 S.Burch/Luis B 5.00 12.00
QMD6 S.Lang/Luis B 5.00 12.00
QMD8 Cassie & Scott Lang A 8.00 20.00
QMD10 Ant-Man/Dave B 5.00 12.00
QMD11 Ant-Man/Kurt B 6.00 15.00
QMD12 Ghost/B.Foster B 8.00 20.00
QMD13 Ant-Man/Ghost B 12.00 30.00
QMD14 Luis/Ghost 5.00 12.00
Jeans/Ghost Cost. A

2018 Ant-Man and the Wasp Quantum Anomaly Relics

COMMON MEM 2.50 6.00
GROUP A ODDS 1:71
GROUP B ODDS 1:25
STATED OVERALL ODDS 1:15
QM1 Ghost 6.00 15.00
Ghost Cost. B
QM2 Wasp B 8.00 20.00
QM3 Scott Lang B 6.00 15.00
QM4 Luis A 3.00 8.00
QM8 Ant-Man B 5.00 12.00
QM9 Sonny Burch B 3.00 8.00
QM11 Bill Foster B 8.00 20.00
QM12 Ava A 6.00 15.00
QM14 Hope B 5.00 12.00
QM15 Ghost B 4.00 10.00
QM16 Wasp B 8.00 20.00
QM18 Scott Lang B 6.00 15.00

2018 Ant-Man and the Wasp Quantum Anomaly Triple Relics

COMMON MEM (QMT1-QMT9) 10.00 25.00
GROUP A ODDS 1:275
GROUP B ODDS 1:136
STATED OVERALL ODDS 1:90
QMT1 Ghost/Wasp/Ant-Man 20.00 50.00
Ghost Cost./Ant-Man Cost. A
QMT2 Scott/Cassie/Van Dyne A 30.00 75.00
QMT6 Wasp/Van Dyne/Ant-Man B 12.00 30.00
QMT8 Uzman/Dave/Kurt B 12.00 30.00
QMT9 Ghost/Ant-Man/Wasp B 25.00 60.00

2018 Ant-Man and the Wasp Quantum Stars Full Body Autographs

COMMON AUTO 12.00 30.00
GROUP A ODDS 1:945
GROUP B ODDS 1:493
STATED OVERALL ODDS 1:640
QSFEL Evangeline Lilly A 125.00 250.00
QSFHK Hannah John-Kamen A 75.00 150.00
QSFJG Judy Greer A 50.00 100.00
QSFSB Walton Goggins B 15.00 40.00
QSFTG Hannah John-Kamen A 75.00 150.00
QSFTW Evangeline Lilly A 125.00 250.00
QSFWG Walton Goggins B 15.00 40.00

2018 Ant-Man and the Wasp Quantum Stars Portrait Autographs

COMMON AUTO 15.00 40.00
GROUP A ODDS 1:536
GROUP B ODDS 1:182
STATED OVERALL ODDS 1:160
QSEL Evangeline Lilly B 100.00 200.00
QSHK Hannah John-Kamen A 125.00 200.00
QSJG Judy Greer B 50.00 100.00
QSTG Hannah John-Kamen A 125.00 200.00
QSTW Evangeline Lilly B 100.00 200.00
QSWG Walton Goggins A 20.00 50.00

2018 Ant-Man and the Wasp Quantum Stars Torso Autographs

COMMON AUTO 12.00 30.00
GROUP A ODDS 1:1,720
GROUP B ODDS 1:516
STATED OVERALL ODDS 1:320
QSTEL Evangeline Lilly B 100.00 200.00
QSTHK Hannah John-Kamen A 60.00 120.00
QSTJG Judy Greer B 30.00 75.00
QSTTG Hannah John-Kamen A 75.00 150.00
QSTTW Evangeline Lilly B 100.00 200.00
QSTWG Walton Goggins A 25.00 60.00

2018 Ant-Man and the Wasp Tiny Tech

COMPLETE SET (15) 8.00 20.00
COMMON CARD (TT1-TT15) 1.00 2.50
STATED ODDS 1:2

2018 Ant-Man and the Wasp Wasp Wing

COMPLETE SET (18) 50.00 100.00
COMMON CARD (WW1-WW18) 3.00 8.00
STATED ODDS 1:15

2018 Ant-Man and the Wasp X-Con Background Check

COMPLETE SET (10) 12.00 30.00
COMMON CARD (XCB1-XCB10) 2.50 6.00
STATED ODDS 1:10

2012 Avengers Assemble

COMPLETE SET (176) 10.00 25.00
UNOPENED BOX (24 PACKS) 250.00 300.00
UNOPENED PACK (7 CARDS) 10.00 12.00
COMMON CARD (1-176) .15 .40
UM23 STATED PRINT RUN 84
UM23 Avengers #1 CBP/84 60.00 120.00

2012 Avengers Assemble Autographs

CH Chris Hemsworth 200.00 350.00
CS Cobie Smulders 75.00 150.00
JR Jeremy Renner 75.00 150.00

2012 Avengers Assemble Classic Covers

COMPLETE SET (36) 10.00 20.00
COMMON CARD (A1-A36) .60 1.50
STATED ODDS 1:2.5

2012 Avengers Assemble Concept Series

COMPLETE SET (9) 15.00 30.00
COMMON CARD (CS1-CS9) 2.50 6.00
STATED ODDS 1:10

2012 Avengers Assemble Dual Memorabilia

COMMON CARD (AD1-AD25) 8.00 20.00
RANDOM INSERTS IN PACKS
AD1 Black Widow/Black Widow 60.00 120.00
AD2 Justin Hammer/Tony Stark 10.00 25.00
AD3 Ivan Vanko/Justin Hammer 10.00 25.00
AD4 Ivan Vanko/Tony Stark 12.00 30.00
AD6 Black Widow/Nick Fury 15.00 40.00
AD7 Thor/Loki 12.00 30.00
AD9 Jane Foster/Thor 15.00 40.00
AD10 Thor/Frigga 10.00 25.00
AD11 Capt America/Nick Fury 12.00 30.00
AD12 Capt America/Tony Stark 15.00 40.00
AD16 Hawkeye/Thor 10.00 25.00
AD17 Thor/Tony Stark 10.00 25.00
AD19 Nick Fury/Maria Hill 12.00 30.00
AD20 Hawkeye/Agent Coulson 10.00 25.00
AD22 Thor/Loki 15.00 40.00
AD23 Loki/Captain America 15.00 40.00
AD24 Capt America/Hawkeye 12.00 30.00
AD25 Hawkeye/Loki 10.00 25.00

2012 Avengers Assemble Heroes-Villains Evolve

COMPLETE SET (60) 20.00 40.00
COMMON CARD (E1-E60) .60 1.50
STATED ODDS 1:2

2012 Avengers Assemble Memorabilia

COMMON CARD (AS1-AS11) 6.00 15.00
RANDOM INSERTS IN PACKS
AS1 Thor 10.00 25.00
AS2 Captain America 20.00 50.00
AS3 Tony Stark 10.00 25.00
AS4 Bruce Banner 12.00 30.00
AS5 Steve Rogers 12.00 30.00
AS6 Loki 12.00 30.00
AS9 Black Widow 50.00 100.00
AS10 Hawkeye 10.00 25.00
AS11 Maria Hill 20.00 50.00

2012 Avengers Assemble Quad Memorabilia

COMMON CARD (AQ1-AQ7) 20.00 50.00
RANDOM INSERTS IN PACKS
AQ2 Thor/Cap/Hawk/Stark 25.00 60.00
AQ6 Fury/Widow/Hawk/Couls. 25.00 60.00
AQ7 Banner/Stark/Thor/Cap 40.00 80.00

2012 Avengers Assemble Stickers

COMPLETE SET (30) 12.00 30.00
COMMON CARD (S1-S30) .75 2.00
RANDOM INSERTS IN RETAIL PACKS

2012 Avengers Assemble Triple Memorabilia

COMMON CARD (AT1-AT14) 8.00 20.00
RANDOM INSERTS IN PACKS
AT1 Hammer/Stark/Vanko 12.00 30.00
AT2 Hogun/Fandral /Volstagg 12.00 30.00
AT3 Thor/Jane Foster/Loki 15.00 40.00
AT4 Loki/Thor/Frigga 12.00 30.00
AT5 Captain America X3 15.00 40.00
AT6 Cap/Thor/Banner 12.00 30.00
AT8 Nick Fury/Thor/Loki 12.00 30.00
AT9 Thor/Cap/Stark 15.00 40.00
AT10 Banner/Rogers/Hill 15.00 40.00
AT11 M.Hill/Hawkeye/N.Fury 12.00 30.00
AT12 Fury/Widow/Hill 12.00 30.00
AT13 Widow/Hawkeye/Fury 15.00 40.00
AT14 Fury/Cap/Hawkeye 15.00 40.00

2012 Avengers 3-D Philippines 7-11

COMPLETE SET (8) 10.00 25.00
COMMON CARD 1.50 4.00
NNO Avengers Logo 3.00 8.00
NNO Captain America 2.50 6.00
NNO Iron Man 3.00 8.00
NNO Thor 2.50 6.00

2015 Avengers Age of Ultron

COMPLETE SET (90) 8.00 20.00
UNOPENED BOX (20 PACKS) 300.00 500.00
UNOPENED PACK (5 CARDS) 15.00 25.00
COMMON CARD (1-90) .20 .50
*SILVER: 1.2X TO 3X BASIC CARDS
*AOU BLUE/199: 6X TO 15X BASIC CARDS

2015 Avengers Age of Ultron Age of Autographs

COMMON AUTO 15.00 40.00
AACH Chris Hemsworth 150.00 300.00
AACO Cobie Smulders 60.00 120.00
AACR Cobie Smulders 60.00 120.00
AACS Cobie Smulders 60.00 120.00
AACV Cobie Smulders 60.00 120.00
AAHC Chris Hemsworth 150.00 300.00
AAHE Chris Hemsworth 150.00 300.00
AAJE Jeremy Renner 125.00 250.00
AAJR Jeremy Renner 125.00 250.00
AAJV Jeremy Renner 125.00 250.00
AAJY Jeremy Renner 125.00 250.00

2015 Avengers Age of Ultron Age of Autographs Double

COMMON AUTO 125.00 250.00
AA2HR Chris Hemsworth 200.00 400.00
Jeremy Renner
AA2HS C.Smulders/C.Hemsworth 150.00 300.00

2015 Avengers Age of Ultron Age of Autographs Double Memorabilia

DMADH J.Renner/C.Hemsworth 300.00 450.00

2015 Avengers Age of Ultron Age of Autographs Memorabilia

COMMON AUTO 20.00 50.00
AMCH Chris Hemsworth 200.00 350.00
AMJR Jeremy Renner 120.00 200.00

2015 Avengers Age of Ultron Age of Autographs Triple

AA3HRS Hemsworth/Renner/Smulders 400.00 750.00

2015 Avengers Age of Ultron AVENGERS Connection Bronze

COMPLETE SET (8) 12.00 30.00
COMMON CARD (ACB1-ACB8) 1.50 4.00
RANDOMLY INSERTED INTO PACKS
ACB1 Captain America 3.00 8.00
ACB4 Hulk 2.50 6.00
ACB5 Black Widow 5.00 12.00
ACB6 Hawkeye 5.00 12.00
ACB7 Vision 4.00 10.00

2015 Avengers Age of Ultron AVENGERS Connection Silver

COMPLETE SET (8) 15.00 40.00
COMMON CARD (ACB1-ACB8) 2.50 6.00
RANDOMLY INSERTED INTO PACKS
ACB1 Captain America 5.00 12.00
ACB4 Hulk 4.00 10.00
ACB5 Black Widow 8.00 20.00
ACB6 Hawkeye 8.00 20.00
ACB7 Vision 6.00 15.00

2015 Avengers Age of Ultron AVENGERS Connection Theatrical

COMPLETE SET (8) 25.00 60.00
COMMON CARD (ACB1-ACB8) 3.00 8.00
RANDOMLY INSERTED INTO PACKS
ACB1 Captain America 6.00 15.00
ACB4 Hulk 5.00 12.00
ACB5 Black Widow 10.00 25.00
ACB6 Hawkeye 10.00 25.00
ACB7 Vision 8.00 20.00

2015 Avengers Age of Ultron Avengers' Database

COMPLETE SET (15) 8.00 20.00
COMMON CARD .75 2.00
RANDOMLY INSERTED INTO PACKS
ADB Black Widow 1.50 4.00
ADH Hulk 1.25 3.00
ADI Iron Man 2.00 5.00
ADT Thor 1.50 4.00
ADCA Captain America 2.00 5.00
ADNF Nick Fury 1.25 3.00

2015 Avengers Age of Ultron Avengers' Locker

COMMON CARD 5.00 12.00
STATED ODDS 1:20
ALB Black Widow SP 80.00 150.00
ALC Captain America 10.00 25.00
ALH Hulk SP 25.00 60.00
ALT Thor 8.00 20.00
ALW Scarlet Witch 12.00 30.00
ALCR Captain America SP 30.00 80.00
ALCV Captain America 8.00 20.00
ALHA Hawkeye 6.00 15.00
ALHR Hawkeye SP 10.00 25.00
ALHV Hawkeye 8.00 20.00
ALPV Quicksilver SP 20.00 50.00
ALTR Thor SP 10.00 25.00
ALTS Tony Stark SP 15.00 40.00
ALTV Thor 8.00 20.00

ALWR Scarlet Witch SP	30.00	80.00
ALWV Scarlet Witch SP	20.00	50.00

2015 Avengers Age of Ultron Avengers' Locker Dual

COMMON CARD	5.00	12.00
STATED ODDS 1:20		
AL2BC Cap/Widow	12.00	30.00
AL2BW Widow/Witch SP	12.00	30.00
AL2CP Quick/Cap	6.00	15.00
AL2CT Cap/Thor SP	30.00	80.00
AL2HB Hulk/Widow SP	25.00	60.00
AL2HC Hulk/Cap	8.00	20.00
AL2NB Fury/Widow	15.00	40.00
AL2NC Fury/Cap	6.00	15.00
AL2PW Quick/Witch	8.00	20.00
AL2SW Scarlet Witch/B.Strucker	6.00	15.00
AL2TC Stark/Cap	8.00	20.00
AL2TH Hulk/Thor	8.00	20.00
AL2TP Thor/Quicksilver	6.00	15.00
AL2WC Witch/Cap	12.00	30.00
AL2HAB Hawkeye/Widow SP	30.00	80.00
AL2TSH Stark/Hulk SP	15.00	40.00
AL2TTS Thor/Stark SP	150.00	300.00

2015 Avengers Age of Ultron Avengers' Locker Quad

COMMON CARD	12.00	30.00
AL4C Captain America SP	150.00	300.00
AL4P Quicksilver SP	120.00	250.00
AL4BTWC B.Widow/Thor/S.Witch/Cap SP	50.00	100.00
AL4CBTH Cap/Widow/Thor/Hulk	15.00	40.00
AL4HCTH Hulk/Cap/Thor/Hawkeye SP		
AL4PHWT Quick/Hawkeye/Witch/Thor	20.00	50.00
AL4SCTH Strucker/Cap/Thor/Hawkeye SP		
AL4TCHT Stark/Cap/Hawkeye/Thor SP		
AL4TPWH Thor/Quick/Witch/Hulk	25.00	60.00
AL4WPBC Witch/Quick/Widow/Cap SP	150.00	300.00

2015 Avengers Age of Ultron Avengers' Locker Triple

COMMON CARD	8.00	20.00
STATED ODDS 1:20		
AL3T Thor SP	20.00	50.00
AL3W Scarlet Witch SP	25.00	60.00
AL3BCN Cap/Fury/Widow SP	30.00	80.00
AL3BHN Widow/Fury/Hawkeye	15.00	40.00
AL3BTW Thor/Witch/Widow	20.00	50.00
AL3CHT Cap/Thor/Hulk	25.00	60.00
AL3HBT Widow/Stark/Hulk SP	30.00	80.00
AL3HWP Hawkeye/Quick/Witch	15.00	40.00
AL3PTW Quick/Thor/Witch SP	20.00	50.00
AL3TTC Thor/Cap/Stark SP	25.00	60.00
AL3WCP Cap/Witch/Quick	15.00	40.00
AL3WPS Quicks/Witch/Strucker	15.00	40.00

2015 Avengers Age of Ultron Behind-the-Lens

COMPLETE SET (15)	6.00	15.00
COMMON CARD (BTL1-BTL15)	.75	2.00
RANDOMLY INSERTED INTO PACKS		

2015 Avengers Age of Ultron Character Shots

COMPLETE SET (15)	8.00	20.00
COMMON CARD (CS1-CS15)	.75	2.00
RANDOMLY INSERTED INTO PACKS		
CS1 Captain America	1.50	4.00
CS3 Iron Man	1.00	2.50
CS5 Black Widow	2.00	5.00
CS6 Hawkeye	1.25	3.00
CS7 Scarlet Witch	1.25	3.00
CS8 Quicksilver	1.25	3.00
CS12 Ultron	1.50	4.00
CS15 Vision	1.25	3.00

2015 Avengers Age of Ultron Comic Cover Autographs

AOUAP T.Palmer	12.00	30.00
N.Adams		
AOUBB B.Bendis/A.Briclot	12.00	30.00
AOUBF B.Bendis/D.Finch	15.00	40.00
AOUBP G.Perez/K.Busiek	25.00	60.00
AOUFB D.Finch/B.Bendis	8.00	20.00
AOUKH L.Kaminski/K.Hopgood	6.00	15.00
AOULB S.Buscema/S.Lee		
AOULE Stan Lee	200.00	500.00
AOUMG M.McKone/C.Gage	6.00	15.00
AOUPB G.Perez/K.Busiek	8.00	20.00
AOUPC G.Conway/G.Perez	8.00	20.00
AOUPK N.Klein/T.Palmer	8.00	20.00
AOUPP C.Pacheco/J.Ponsor	5.00	12.00
AOUSL Stan Lee	200.00	500.00
AOUTP R.Thomas/T.Palmer	10.00	25.00
AOUTS R.Thomas/J.Sinnott	8.00	20.00
AOUWP M.Waid	5.00	12.00
T.Palmer		

2015 Avengers Age of Ultron Concept Series

COMPLETE SET (15)	6.00	15.00
COMMON CARD (C1-C15)	.75	2.00
RANDOMLY INSERTED INTO PACKS		

2015 Avengers Age of Ultron Multiple Metallics

COMMON CARD (MM1-MM11)	1.50	4.00
RANDOMLY INSERTED INTO PACKS		
MM1 Black Widow	5.00	12.00
MM2 Iron Man	6.00	15.00
MM3 Thor	4.00	10.00
MM6 Captain America	4.00	10.00
MM7 Hawkeye	4.00	10.00
MM9 Scarlet Witch	4.00	10.00
MM11 Iron Man	6.00	15.00

2015 Avengers Age of Ultron Multiple Metallics Double

COMMON CARD (MD1-MD12)	3.00	8.00
RANDOMLY INSERTED INTO PACKS		
MD2 B.Widow/Capt.America	5.00	12.00
MD5 Thor/Iron Man	4.00	10.00

2015 Avengers Age of Ultron Multiple Metallics Team

COMMON CARD (MT1-MT6)	2.00	5.00
RANDOMLY INSERTED INTO PACKS		
MT3 Quick/Witch/Vision	2.50	6.00
MT4 Vision/Iron Man/Ultron	2.50	6.00
MT5 Hulk/Widow/Hawkeye	5.00	12.00
MT6 Hawkeye/Thor/Widow	4.00	10.00

2015 Avengers Age of Ultron Dog Tags

COMPLETE SET (18)	25.00	60.00
UNOPENED BOX (24 PACKS)		
UNOPENED PACK (1 TAG+1 STICKER)		
COMMON TAG (1-18)	2.00	5.00
AVENGERS METAL DOG TAG 1:1	.75	2.00

2015 Avengers Age of Ultron Dog Tags Film Cels

COMPLETE SET (6)	25.00	60.00
COMMON TAG (FT1-FT6)	6.00	15.00
RANDOMLY INSERTED INTO PACKS		

2015 Avengers Age of Ultron Dog Tags Foil

COMPLETE SET (6)	20.00	50.00
COMMON TAG (1-6)	4.00	10.00
RANDOMLY INSERTED INTO PACKS		

2015 Avengers Age of Ultron Dog Tags Stickers

COMPLETE SET (48)	12.00	30.00
COMMON STICKER (1-24)	.40	1.00
COMMON FOIL (25-48)	1.00	2.50

2015 Avengers Age of Ultron Magnets

COMPLETE SET (24)	12.00	30.00
COMMON MAGNET	.75	2.00
1 Age of Ultron	1.00	2.50
8 Behold the Vision	1.00	2.50
9 Black Widow	1.25	3.00
10 Black Widow and Hawkeye	1.25	3.00
11 Captain America (throwing shield)	1.50	4.00
12 Captain America The First Avenger	1.50	4.00
17 Hulk vs. Hulkbuster Iron Man	2.00	5.00
18 Iron Man	1.50	4.00
19 Iron Man (close-up mask)	1.50	4.00
20 Thor (raising hammer)	1.00	2.50
21 Thor (swinging hammer)	1.00	2.50
24 Vision (fighting Ultron army)	1.00	2.50

2015 Avengers Age of Ultron Subway Canada

COMPLETE SET (6)	8.00	20.00
COMMON CARD	1.50	4.00
*FRENCH: SAME VALUE		
NNO Black Widow	3.00	8.00
NNO Hawkeye	2.00	5.00
NNO Iron Man	3.00	8.00
NNO Thor	3.00	8.00

2018 Avengers Infinity War

COMPLETE SET W/O SP (50)	125.00	250.00
UNOPENED BOX (9 PACKS)	600.00	1000.00
UNOPENED PACK (3 CARDS)	75.00	125.00
TIER 1 (1-50)	3.00	8.00
TIER 2 (51-80)	5.00	12.00
TIER 3 (81-90)	8.00	20.00
STATED ODDS TIER 1 1:1		
STATED ODDS TIER 2 1:2		
STATED ODDS TIER 3 1:15		

2018 Avengers Infinity War Autographed Film Cels

STATED PRINT RUN 100 SER.#'d SETS		
FCADB Dave Bautista	50.00	100.00
FCAEO Elizabeth Olsen	250.00	500.00
FCAJB Josh Brolin EXCH		
FCAKG Karen Gillan	60.00	120.00
FCATH Tom Holland	400.00	750.00

2018 Avengers Infinity War Behind-the-Scenes

COMPLETE SET (6)	50.00	100.00
COMMON CARD (BTS1-BTS6)	8.00	20.00
STATED ODDS 1:72		

2018 Avengers Infinity War Film Cels

COMMON CEL	5.00	12.00
COMMON SP	10.00	25.00
STATED ODDS 1:12		
STATED ODDS SP 1:108		

2018 Avengers Infinity War Infinite Impressions Autographs

GROUP A ODDS 1:2,495		
GROUP B ODDS 1:624		
GROUP C ODDS 1:169		
GROUP D ODDS 1:238		
GROUP E ODDS 1:85		
STATED OVERALL ODDS 1:42		
IIBW Benedict Wong E	15.00	40.00
IICE Chris Evans B	475.00	750.00
IICH Chris Hemsworth B	125.00	250.00
IIDB Dave Batista C	30.00	75.00
IIEM Tom Vaughan-Lawlor E	15.00	40.00
IIEO Elizabeth Olsen C	300.00	500.00
IIJB Josh Brolin A	400.00	600.00
IIKG Karen Gillan C	60.00	120.00
IIMG Pom Klementieff D	20.00	50.00
IIPK Pom Klementieff D	20.00	50.00
IISW Elizabeth Olsen C	150.00	300.00
IITH Tom Holland A	600.00	1200.00
IIWS Benedict Wong E	15.00	40.00

2018 Avengers Infinity War Infinite Impressions Dual Autographs

COMMON AUTO	75.00	150.00
STATED ODDS 1:648		
IIDBK D.Bautista/P.Klementieff	100.00	200.00
IIDCE C.Evans/E.Olsen	600.00	1500.00

2018 Avengers Infinity War Infinite Impressions Inscriptions

COMMON AUTO	60.00	120.00
GROUP A ODDS 1:7,200		
GROUP B ODDS 1:1,800		
GROUP C ODDS 1:900		
STATED OVERALL ODDS 1:554		
IICE Chris Evans/CAP C	400.00	750.00
IIEO Elizabeth Olsen/Scarlett Witch B	400.00	800.00
IIKG Karen Gillan/Nebula C	100.00	200.00
IIPK Pom Klementieff/Mantis A	250.00	500.00
IISW Elizabeth Olsen/Scarlett Witch A	800.00	1300.00

2018 Avengers Infinity War Infinity Crusade

COMPLETE SET (10)	30.00	75.00
COMMON CARD (IC1-IC10)	5.00	12.00
STATED ODDS 1:8		

2018 Avengers Infinity War Infinity Stones Mind Stone Die-Cuts

COMPLETE SET W/EP (8)		
COMPLETE SET (7)	75.00	150.00
COMMON CARD (YM1-YM7)	6.00	15.00
STATED ODDS 1:240		
YM8 IS E-PACK ACHIEVEMENT		
YM1 Steve Rogers	25.00	60.00
YM2 Falcon	12.00	30.00
YM3 Natasha Romanova	20.00	50.00
YM5 Shuri	10.00	25.00
YM6 Wanda Maximoff	15.00	40.00
YM7 Vision	15.00	40.00
YM8 Loki/E-Pack	50.00	100.00

2018 Avengers Infinity War Infinity Stones Power Stone Die-Cuts

COMPLETE SET W/EP (8)		
COMPLETE SET (7)	10.00	25.00
COMMON CARD (PP1-PP10)	2.00	5.00
STATED ODDS 1:9		
PP8 IS E-PACK ACHIEVEMENT		
PP1 Loki	4.00	10.00
PP2 Steve Rogers	4.00	10.00
PP6 Doctor Strange	2.50	6.00
PP7 Thor	3.00	8.00
PP8 Star-Lord/E-Pack	12.00	30.00

2018 Avengers Infinity War Infinity Stones Reality Stone Die-Cuts

COMPLETE SET W/EP (8)		
COMPLETE SET (7)	12.00	30.00
COMMON CARD (RR1-RR7)	2.00	5.00
STATED ODDS 1:20		
RR8 IS E-PACK ACHIEVEMENT		
RR1 Gamora	3.00	8.00
RR2 Doctor Strange	5.00	12.00
RR3 Iron Man	4.00	10.00
RR6 Star-Lord	3.00	8.00
RR7 Thanos	5.00	12.00
RR8 Rocket/E-Pack	20.00	50.00

2018 Avengers Infinity War Infinity Stones Soul Stone Die-Cuts

COMPLETE SET W/EP (8)		
COMPLETE SET (7)	20.00	50.00
COMMON CARD (OS1-OS7)	2.50	6.00
STATED ODDS 1:60		
OS8 IS E-PACK ACHIEVEMENT		
OS1 Thanos	5.00	12.00
OS2 Gamora	6.00	15.00
OS3 Doctor Strange	6.00	15.00
OS4 Star-Lord	4.00	10.00
OS6 Black Panther	6.00	15.00
OS7 Spider-Man	8.00	20.00
OS8 Iron Man/E-Pack	30.00	75.00

2018 Avengers Infinity War Infinity Stones Space Stone Die-Cuts

COMPLETE SET W/EP (8)		
COMPLETE SET (7)	60.00	120.00
COMMON CARD (BS1-BS10)	8.00	20.00

STATED ODDS 1:128		
BS8 IS E-PACK ACHIEVEMENT		
BS1 Iron Man	15.00	40.00
BS2 Gamora	10.00	25.00
BS5 Thor	15.00	40.00
BS7 Doctor Strange	12.00	30.00
BS8 Steve Rogers/E-Pack	50.00	100.00

2018 Avengers Infinity War Infinity Stones Time Stone Die-Cuts

COMPLETE SET W/EP (8)		
COMPLETE SET (7)	12.00	30.00
COMMON CARD (GT1-GT7)	2.00	5.00
STATED ODDS 1:20		
GT8 IS E-PACK ACHIEVEMENT		
GT1 Wanda Maximoff	3.00	8.00
GT4 Iron Spider	4.00	10.00
GT5 Iron Man	3.00	8.00
GT6 Bruce Banner	2.50	6.00
GT7 Doctor Strange	3.00	8.00
GT8 Vision/E-Pack	20.00	50.00

2018 Avengers Infinity War Infinity Gauntlet

COMPLETE SET (10)	30.00	75.00
COMMON CARD (IG1-IG10)	5.00	12.00
STATED ODDS 1:8		

2018 Avengers Infinity War Infinity War Inserts

COMPLETE SET (10)	30.00	75.00
COMMON CARD (IW1-IW10)	5.00	12.00
STATED ODDS 1:8		

2018 Avengers Infinity War Mad Titan

COMPLETE SET (10)	30.00	75.00
COMMON CARD (MT1-MT10)	5.00	12.00
STATED ODDS 1:8		

2018 Avengers Infinity War Precious Stone Mind Stone Relics

COMMON CARD (YM1-YM7)	10.00	25.00
STATED PRINT RUN 49 SER.#'d SETS		
YM1 Steve Rogers	25.00	60.00
YM2 Falcon	12.00	30.00
YM5 Shuri	12.00	30.00
YM6 Wanda Maximoff	15.00	40.00
YM7 Vision	12.00	30.00

2018 Avengers Infinity War Precious Stone Power Stone Relics

COMMON CARD (PP1-PP7)	10.00	25.00
STATED PRINT RUN 49 SER.#'d SETS		
PP1 Loki	12.00	30.00
PP2 Steve Rogers	25.00	60.00
PP3 Bucky Barnes	15.00	40.00
PP6 Doctor Strange	20.00	50.00
PP7 Thor	15.00	40.00

2018 Avengers Infinity War Precious Stone Reality Stone Relics

COMMON CARD (RR1-RR7)	10.00	25.00
STATED PRINT RUN 49 SER.#'d SETS		
RR1 Gamora	12.00	30.00
RR2 Doctor Strange	20.00	50.00
RR3 Iron Man	20.00	50.00
RR6 Star-Lord	12.00	30.00
RR7 Thanos	15.00	40.00

2018 Avengers Infinity War Precious Stone Soul Stone Relics

COMMON CARD (OS1-OS7)	10.00	25.00
STATED PRINT RUN 49 SER.#'d SETS		
OS1 Thanos	15.00	40.00
OS2 Gamora	12.00	30.00
OS3 Doctor Strange	20.00	50.00
OS4 Star-Lord	12.00	30.00
OS6 Black Panther	15.00	40.00
OS7 Spider-Man	20.00	50.00

2018 Avengers Infinity War Precious Stone Space Stone Relics

COMMON CARD (BS1-BS7)	12.00	30.00
STATED PRINT RUN 49 SER.#'d SETS		
BS1 Iron Man	20.00	50.00
BS2 Gamora	12.00	30.00
BS3 Bruce Banner	12.00	30.00
BS4 Rhodey	12.00	30.00
BS5 Thor	15.00	40.00
BS6 Loki	12.00	30.00
BS7 Doctor Strange	20.00	50.00

2018 Avengers Infinity War Precious Stone Time Stone Relics

COMMON CARD (GT1-GT7)	10.00	25.00
STATED PRINT RUN 49 SER.#'d SETS		
GT1 Wanda Maximoff	15.00	40.00
GT4 Iron Spider	20.00	50.00
GT5 Iron Man	20.00	50.00
GT6 Bruce Banner	12.00	30.00
GT7 Doctor Strange	20.00	50.00

2018 Avengers Infinity War Remarkable People

COMPLETE SET (20)	20.00	50.00
COMMON CARD (RP1-RP20)	2.50	6.00
STATED ODDS 1:4		

2018 Avengers Infinity War Road to Infinity War

COMPLETE SET (40)	30.00	75.00
COMMON CARD (RTW1-RTW40)	2.00	5.00
STATED ODDS 1:2		

2018 Avengers Infinity War Strip Mined Metals

COMPLETE SET W/O SP (15)	60.00	120.00
COMMON CARD (SMM1-SMM15)	4.00	10.00
COMMON SP (SMM16-SMM35)	10.00	25.00
STATED ODDS 1:12		
STATED ODDS SP (SMM1-SMM25) 1:54		
STATED ODDS SP (SMM26-SMM35) 1:108		

2018 Avengers Infinity War Hero Tags

COMPLETE SET (24)	50.00	100.00
UNOPENED BOX (24 PACKS)		
UNOPENED PACK (1 TAG+1 STICKER)		
COMMON CARD (1-24)	2.00	5.00

2018 Avengers Infinity War Hero Tags Icon Tags

COMPLETE SET (6)	20.00	50.00
COMMON TAG (UNNUMBERED)	5.00	12.00
STATED ODDS 1:12		

2018 Avengers Infinity War Hero Tags Infinity Stone Tags

COMPLETE SET (6)	15.00	40.00
COMMON TAG (1-6)	3.00	8.00
STATED ODDS 1:4		

2020 Upper Deck Avengers Endgame and Captain Marvel

COMPLETE SET W/SP (97)	75.00	150.00
COMPLETE SET W/O SP (50)	10.00	25.00
UNOPENED BOX (9 PACKS)	250.00	400.00
UNOPENED PACK (4 CARDS)	30.00	45.00
TIER 1 (1-50)	.40	1.00
TIER 2 (51-80)	.75	2.00
TIER 3 (81-90)	2.00	5.00
TIER 4 (91-97)	4.00	10.00
TIER 1 ODDS 1:1		
TIER 2 ODDS 1:2		
TIER 3 ODDS 1:14		
TIER 4 ODDS 1:76		
90 After His Mission... SP	4.00	10.00
CM1 Captain Marvel SP	20.00	50.00
CM2 Nick Fury SP	6.00	15.00

2020 Upper Deck Avengers Endgame and Captain Marvel Avenge the Fallen

COMPLETE SET (10)	5.00	12.00
COMMON CARD (ATF1-ATF10)	.75	2.00
STATED ODDS 1:1		
ATF1 Iron Man	1.25	3.00
ATF2 Captain America	1.25	3.00

2020 Upper Deck Avengers Endgame and Captain Marvel Avengers Assemble

COMPLETE SET (10)	6.00	15.00
COMMON CARD (AA1-AA10)	1.00	2.50
STATED ODDS 1:3		
AA1 Captain America	1.50	4.00
AA2 Iron Man	1.50	4.00

2020 Upper Deck Avengers Endgame and Captain Marvel Captain Marvel

COMPLETE SET (41)	30.00	75.00
COMMON CARD (1-41)	2.00	5.00
*SILVER/125: .6X TO 1.5X BASIC CARDS		
*GOLD/25: 1.2X TO 3X BASIC CARDS		
STATED ODDS 1:2		

2020 Upper Deck Avengers Endgame and Captain Marvel Captain Marvel Binary Autographs

COMMON AUTO	6.00	15.00
STATED ODDS 1:875		
BADH Djimon Hounsou	15.00	40.00
BAKO Djimon Hounsou	15.00	40.00

2020 Upper Deck Avengers Endgame and Captain Marvel Captain Marvel Higher Further Faster

COMPLETE SET (5)	6.00	15.00
COMMON CARD (HFF1-HFF5)	2.50	6.00
*SILVER/125: .6X TO 1.5X BASIC CARDS		
*GOLD/25: 1.2X TO 3X BASIC CARDS		
STATED ODDS 1:22		

2020 Upper Deck Avengers Endgame and Captain Marvel Captain Marvel Not What It Seems

COMPLETE SET (5)	8.00	20.00
COMMON CARD (NW1-NW5)	2.50	6.00
*SILVER/125: .5X TO 1.2X BASIC CARDS		
*GOLD/25: 1.2X TO 3X BASIC CARDS		
STATED ODDS 1:22		

2020 Upper Deck Avengers Endgame and Captain Marvel Captain Marvel Supreme Intelligence

COMPLETE SET (10)	8.00	20.00
COMMON CARD (SI1-SI10)	1.50	4.00
*SILVER/125: .5X TO 1.2X BASIC CARDS		
*GOLD/25: 2X TO 5X BASIC CARDS		
STATED ODDS 1:10		

2020 Upper Deck Avengers Endgame and Captain Marvel Captain Marvel Supreme Intelligence Gold Foil

COMPLETE SET (10)		
*GOLD: 2X TO 5X BASIC CARDS		
STATED PRINT RUN 25 SER.#'d SETS		

2020 Upper Deck Avengers Endgame and Captain Marvel Exquisite Collection Autographed Diamond Relics

COMMON AUTO		
STATED PRINT RUN 25 SER.#'d SETS		
EVANS, HEMSWORTH & HOLLAND ARE		
SERIAL NUMBERED TO 5		
DABB Sebastian Stan/25		
DACE Chris Evans/5		
DACH Chris Hemsworth/5		
DAEO Elizabeth Olsen/25		
DAEV Chris Evans/25		
DAHS Hiroyuki Sanada/25		
DAJB Josh Brolin/25		
DAJR Jeremy Renner/25		
DAJS John Slattery/25		
DARM Ross Marquand/25		
DATH Tom Holland/5		
DATS Tilda Swinton/25		

2020 Upper Deck Avengers Endgame and Captain Marvel Exquisite Collection Diamond Relics

SERIAL NUMBERED TO 25 OR 49		
D1 Chris Hemsworth/25		
D2 Robert Downey Jr./25	1200.00	2000.00
D3 Chris Evans/25	400.00	800.00
D4 Jeremy Renner/49	50.00	100.00
D5 Paul Rudd/49	75.00	150.00
D6 Bradley Cooper/49	60.00	120.00
D7 Karen Gillan/49	50.00	100.00
D8 Mark Ruffalo/49	75.00	150.00
D9 Scarlett Johansson/25	300.00	600.00
D10 Don Cheadle/49	60.00	120.00
D11 Brie Larson/49	200.00	350.00
D12 Tessa Thompson/49	50.00	100.00
D13 Elizabeth Olsen/49		
D14 Benedict Cumberbatch/49	200.00	400.00
D15 Chadwick Boseman/49	75.00	150.00
D16 Anthony Mackie/49	50.00	100.00
D17 Sebastian Stan/49	50.00	100.00
D18 Tom Holland/25	300.00	600.00
D19 Zoe Saldana/49	75.00	150.00
D20 Josh Brolin/49	75.00	150.00

2020 Upper Deck Avengers Endgame and Captain Marvel Legends Never Die Avengers Autographs

COMMON AUTO	75.00	150.00
GROUP A ODDS 1:2,288		
GROUP B ODDS 1:391		
GROUP C ODDS 1:220		
GROUP D ODDS 1:408		
STATED OVERALL ODDS 1:100		
LNDACE Chris Evans B	500.00	800.00
LNDACH Chris Hemsworth A	400.00	800.00
LNDAHA Hayley Atwell D	100.00	200.00
LNDAJB Josh Brolin B	300.00	500.00
LNDATH Tom Holland C	500.00	800.00

2020 Upper Deck Avengers Endgame and Captain Marvel Legends Never Die Avengers White Autographs

GROUP A ODDS 1:997		
GROUP B ODDS 1:837		
GROUP C ODDS 1:419		
STATED OVERALL ODDS 1:218		
LNDWCE Chris Evans A	750.00	1500.00
LNDWCH Chris Hemsworth A		
LNDWEO Elizabeth Olsen C	150.00	300.00
LNDWHA Hayley Atwell B	100.00	200.00
LNDWJR Jeremy Renner A	75.00	150.00
LNDWTH Tom Holland A		

2020 Upper Deck Avengers Endgame and Captain Marvel Legends Never Die Avengers White Inscription

LNDWEO Elizabeth Olsen/"You Will"	300.00	500.00

2020 Upper Deck Avengers Endgame and Captain Marvel Legends Never Die Casual Autographs

COMMON AUTO	12.00	30.00
GROUP A ODDS 1:6,556		
GROUP B ODDS 1:887		
GROUP C ODDS 1:284		
GROUP D ODDS 1:130		
STATED OVERALL ODDS 1:80		
LNDCCE Chris Evans B	400.00	750.00
LNDCCH Chris Hemsworth A	600.00	1000.00
LNDCHA Hayley Atwell C	75.00	200.00
LNDCJB Josh Brolin B	600.00	1200.00
LNDCJR Jeremy Renner C	75.00	200.00

LNDCJS John Slattery D 15.00 40.00
LNDCSS Sebastian Stan C 100.00 250.00
LNDCTH Tom Holland B 250.00 600.00
LNDCTS Tilda Swinton C 40.00 100.00

2020 Upper Deck Avengers Endgame and Captain Marvel Legends Never Die Casual Inscriptions

LNDCJS John Slattery/"Stark" 30.00 75.00
LNDCRM Ross Marquand/"Red Skull" 60.00 150.00

2020 Upper Deck Avengers Endgame and Captain Marvel One Shot

COMPLETE SET W/SP (21)
COMPLETE SET W/O SP (15) 100.00 200.00
COMMON CARD (OS1-OS15) 3.00 8.00
COMMON SP (OS16-OS21) 15.00 40.00
STATED ODDS 1:60
SP STATED ODDS 1:576
OS1 Tom Holland 6.00 15.00
OS3 Josh Brolin 10.00 25.00
OS4 Chris Hemsworth 8.00 20.00
OS5 Chris Evans 10.00 25.00
OS7 Brie Larson 6.00 15.00
OS8 Scarlett Johansson 15.00 40.00
OS9 Paul Rudd 6.00 15.00
OS10 Elizabeth Olsen 6.00 15.00
OS11 Mark Ruffalo 5.00 12.00
OS12 Benedict Cumberbatch 5.00 12.00
OS13 Chadwick Boseman 8.00 20.00
OS14 Zoe Saldana 5.00 12.00
OS17 Robert Downey Jr. SP 75.00 150.00
OS18 Tessa Thompson SP 50.00 100.00
OS19 Anthony Mackie SP 30.00 75.00
OS20 Sebastian Stan SP 50.00 100.00
OS21 Bradley Cooper SP 30.00 75.00

2020 Upper Deck Avengers Endgame and Captain Marvel One Shot Autograph

OSEO Elizabeth Olsen/49 400.00 800.00

2020 Upper Deck Avengers Endgame and Captain Marvel Shadowbox

COMPLETE SET W/SP (20) 150.00 300.00
COMPLETE SET W/O SP (14) 75.00 150.00
COMMON CARD (SB1-SB14) 2.50 6.00
COMMON SP (SB15-SB20) 8.00 20.00
STATED ODDS 1:32
SP STATED ODDS 1:288
SB2 Karen Gillan 3.00 8.00
SB3 Zoe Saldana 6.00 15.00
SB4 Chadwick Boseman 5.00 12.00
SB5 Evangeline Lilly 6.00 15.00
SB7 Josh Brolin 8.00 20.00
SB8 Tom Holland 5.00 12.00
SB9 Benedict Cumberbatch 6.00 15.00
SB10 Tessa Thompson 5.00 12.00
SB11 Bradley Cooper 5.00 12.00
SB12 Don Cheadle 6.00 15.00
SB15 Robert Downey Jr. SP 12.00 30.00
SB16 Chris Evans SP 12.00 30.00
SB17 Chris Hemsworth SP 10.00 25.00
SB19 Scarlett Johansson SP 10.00 25.00

2020 Upper Deck Avengers Endgame and Captain Marvel Shadowbox Autograph

STATED PRINT RUN 25 SER.#'d SETS
SBAEO Elizabeth Olsen/25 300.00 500.00

2019 Avengers Endgame Combo Set Challenge Coins

COMPLETE SET (10) 12.00 30.00
COMMON COIN 2.00 5.00
STATED ODDS 1:1
2 Captain America 3.00 8.00
3 Iron Man 3.00 8.00
5 Black Widow 2.50 6.00
9 Thor 3.00 8.00
10 Thanos 4.00 10.00

2019 Avengers Endgame Combo Set Mission Patches

COMPLETE SET (10) 8.00 20.00
COMMON PATCH 1.00 2.50
NNO Avengers Logo 2.00 5.00
NNO Black Widow Logo 1.25 3.00
NNO Captain America Shield 1.50 4.00
NNO Infinity Gauntlet 2.00 5.00
NNO Iron Man Logo 1.50 4.00
NNO Thor Logo 1.50 4.00

2019 Avengers Endgame Funko Pop Vinyl Collector Cards

COMPLETE SET (11) 15.00 40.00
COMMON CARD (449-459) 2.50 6.00
*FOIL: 1X TO 2.5X BASIC CARDS
STATED ODDS 1:POP BOX
449 Tony Stark 5.00 12.00
450 Captain America 3.00 8.00
451 Hulk 2.50 6.00
452 Thor 3.00 8.00
453 Thanos 4.00 10.00
454 Black Widow 2.50 6.00
459 Captain Marvel 2.50 6.00

2018 Black Panther

COMPLETE SET (90) 8.00 20.00
UNOPENED BOX (20 PACKS) 125.00 200.00
UNOPENED PACK (5 CARDS) 6.00 10.00
COMMON CARD (1-90) .20 .50
*SILVER: .6X TO 1.5X BASIC CARDS .30 .75
*ACETATE: 4X TO 10X BASIC CARDS 2.00 5.00
*BLACK/149: 2.5X TO 6X BASIC CARDS 1.25 3.00
*INDIGO/50: 6X TO 15X BASIC CARDS 3.00 8.00
*ACETATE GOLD/10: 20X TO 50X BASIC CARDS 10.00 25.00

2018 Black Panther Behind-the-Lens

COMPLETE SET W/EP (15)
COMPLETE SET (14) 8.00 20.00
COMMON CARD (BTL1-BTL14) 1.50 3.00
STATED ODDS 1:8
BTL0 IS E-PACK ACHIEVEMENT
BTL0 Break in the Action/E-Pack 8.00 20.00

2018 Black Panther The King's Mantle Autographed Memorabilia

COMMON AU MEM 60.00 120.00
STATED ODDS 1:300

2018 Black Panther The King's Mantle Dual Memorabilia

COMMON MEM 6.00 15.00
STATED ODDS 1:30
KDBK Black Panther/Erik Killmonger 12.00 30.00
KDEN E.Ross/Nakia 10.00 25.00
KDET E.Ross/T'Challa 10.00 25.00
KDEU E.Killmonger/U.Klaue 8.00 20.00
KDMK M'Baku/E.Killmonger 10.00 25.00
KDNT Nakia/T'Challa 10.00 25.00
KDON Okoye/Nakia 15.00 40.00
KDRT Ramonda/T'Challa 10.00 25.00
KDRZ Ramonda/Zuri 8.00 20.00
KDST Shuri/T'Challa 12.00 30.00
KDTW T'Challa/W'Kabi 8.00 20.00
KDZN Zuri/Nakia 8.00 20.00

2018 Black Panther The King's Mantle Memorabilia

COMMON MEM 6.00 15.00
GROUP A ODDS 1:149
GROUP B ODDS 1:47
GROUP C ODDS 1:45
STATED OVERALL ODDS 1:20
KMBP Black Panther C 12.00 30.00
KMEK Erik Killmonger B 10.00 25.00
KMKI Erik Killmonger A 8.00 20.00
KMMB M'Baku C 6.00 15.00
KMNA Nakia B 12.00 30.00
KMOK Okoye A 10.00 25.00
KMRA Ramonda A 10.00 25.00
KMSH Shuri B 10.00 25.00
KMSI Shuri B 10.00 25.00
KMTC T'Challa C 8.00 20.00

2018 Black Panther The King's Mantle Quad Memorabilia

COMMON MEM 10.00 25.00
STATED ODDS 1:240
KQBKEK Black Panther/Ulysses Klaue/Erik Killmonger/Everett K. Ross 30.00 75.00
Tunic-Suit-Camo-Jacket
KQBRNZ B.Panther/Ramonda/Nakia/Zuri 50.00 100.00
KQKMKB Klaue/M'Baku/Killmonger/B.Panther15.00 40.00
KQNSRT Nakia/Shuri/Ross/T'Challa 20.00 50.00
KQOSNT Okoye/Shuri/Nakia/T'Challa 25.00 60.00
KQRRNS Ross/Ramonda/Nakia/Shuri
KQSNOW Shuri/Nakia/Okoye/W'Kabi 25.00 60.00
KQSRTN Shuri/Ramonda/T'Challa/Nakia 50.00 100.00
KQTNOR T'Challa/Nakia/Okoye/Ross 25.00 60.00
KQTSRZ T'Challa/Shuri/Ramonda/Zuri 60.00 120.00
KQTWKZ T'Challa/W'Kabi/Killmonger/Zuri20.00 50.00
KQWMBK W'Kabi/M'Baku B.Panther/Killmonger 12.00 30.00
KQWTKR W'Kabi/T'Challa Killmonger/Ramonda 12.00 30.00

2018 Black Panther The King's Mantle Triple Memorabilia

COMMON MEM 8.00 20.00
STATED ODDS 1:80
KTBKK Black Panther/Erik Killmonger Ulysses Klaue 12.00 30.00
KTKRZ Killmonger/Ramonda/Zuri 10.00 25.00
KTKSN Killmonger/Shuri/Nakia 12.00 30.00
KTNMT Nakia/M'Baku/T'Challa 10.00 25.00
KTNSO Nakia/Shuri/Okoye 12.00 30.00
KTONK Okoye/Nakia/Klaue 12.00 30.00
KTRKT Ross/Klaue/T'Challa 10.00 25.00
KTRSR Ross/Shuri/Ramonda 12.00 30.00
KTTZR T'Challa/Zuri/Ramonda 10.00 25.00

2018 Black Panther Language of the People

COMPLETE SET W/EP (9)
COMPLETE SET (8) 8.00 20.00
COMMON CARD (LOTP1-LOTP8) 1.50 4.00
STATED ODDS 1:12
LOTP0 IS E-PACK ACHIEVEMENT
LOTP0 Black Panther/E-Pack

2018 Black Panther Streets of Wakanda

COMPLETE SET W/EP (15)
COMPLETE SET (14) 12.00 30.00
COMMON CARD (SW1-SW14) 1.50 4.00
SW0 IS E-PACK ACHIEVEMENT

2018 Black Panther Wakanda Forever

COMPLETE SET W/EP (15)
COMPLETE SET (14) 15.00 40.00
COMMON CARD (WF1-WF14) 2.00 5.00
STATED ODDS 1:8
WF0 IS E-PACK ACHIEVEMENT
WF0 Black Panther/E-Pack

2018 Black Panther Wakandan Tech

COMPLETE SET W/EP (5)
COMPLETE SET (4) 10.00 25.00
COMMON CARD (WT1-WT4) 3.00 8.00
STATED ODDS 1:28
WT0 IS E-PACK ACHIEVEMENT
WT0 Black Panther Suit/E-Pack

2018 Black Panther Wakandan Vibranium

COMPLETE SET (20) 150.00 300.00
COMMON CARD (WV1-WV20) 6.00 15.00
STATED ODDS 1:80
WV1 Black Panther 10.00 25.00
WV2 Shuri 12.00 30.00
WV3 Okoye 12.00 30.00
WV4 Everett K. Ross 10.00 25.00
WV5 Black Panther 10.00 25.00
WV6 Erik Killmonger 8.00 20.00
WV7 Shuri 10.00 25.00
WV8 Black Panther 12.00 30.00
WV10 M'Baku 8.00 20.00
WV12 Nakia 12.00 30.00
WV13 T'Challa 8.00 20.00
WV14 Okoye 8.00 20.00
WV15 Erik Killmonger 12.00 30.00
WV16 Black Panther 8.00 20.00
WV17 Nakia 8.00 20.00
WV19 Black Panther 8.00 20.00
WV20 Erik Killmonger 8.00 20.00

2018 Black Panther Wakandan Writings Autographs

COMMON AUTO 10.00 25.00
GROUP A ODDS 1:2,090
GROUP B ODDS 1:479
GROUP C ODDS 1:182
GROUP D ODDS 1:116
STATED OVERALL ODDS 1:60
WWAB Angela Bassett B 50.00 100.00
WWER Martin Freeman B 50.00 100.00
WWMF Martin Freeman A 75.00 150.00
WWRA Angela Bassett C 50.00 100.00

2018 Black Panther Wakandan Writings Dual Autographs

COMMON AUTO 50.00 100.00
GROUP A ODDS 1:900
GROUP B ODDS 1:720
GROUP C ODDS 1:600
STATED OVERALL ODDS 1:240
WWDRR A.Bassett/M.Freeman A 75.00 150.00

2011 Captain America The First Avenger

COMPLETE SET (99) 8.00 20.00
UNOPENED BOX (24 PACKS) 200.00 300.00
UNOPENED PACK (7 CARDS) 8.00 12.00
COMMON CARD (1-99) .15 .40
UM14 STATED PRINT RUN 78
UM14 The Avengers No.4/78 (Comic Panel) 50.00 100.00

2011 Captain America The First Avenger Autographs

COMMON CARD 20.00 40.00
STATED ODDS 1:288 HOBBY, 1:2,500 RETAIL
BR ISSUED IN 2012 AVENGERS ASSEMBLE
BR Bruno Ricci AVENGERS 30.00 60.00
JO Toby Jones 30.00 60.00
NM Neal McDonough 30.00 60.00
ST Stanley Tucci 125.00 300.00

2011 Captain America The First Avenger Costumes

COMMON CARD (M1-M13) 15.00 30.00
STATED ODDS 1:12 HOBBY, 1:36 RETAIL
M1 Golden Age Capt. America 50.00 100.00
M2 Bucky Barnes 75.00 150.00
M4 Dr. Erskine 35.00 70.00
M6 Red Skull 20.00 40.00
M8 Heinz Kruger 50.00 100.00
M9 Dum Dum Dugan 20.00 40.00
M12 Steve Rogers 50.00 100.00
M13 Captain America 75.00 150.00

2011 Captain America The First Avenger Covers

COMPLETE SET (13) 6.00 15.00
COMMON CARD (C1-C13) .60 1.50
STATED ODDS 1:2
C1 Capt. America Issue 1 1.50 4.00
C2 Tales of Suspense Issue 59 1.00 2.50
C12 Capt. America Issue 1 1.00 2.50

2011 Captain America The First Avenger Insignia Patches

COMPLETE SET (6) 40.00 80.00
COMMON CARD (I1-I6) 8.00 20.00
STATED ODDS 1:16 HOBBY, 1:96 RETAIL

2011 Captain America The First Avenger Posters

COMPLETE SET (12) 8.00 20.00
COMMON CARD (P1-P12) .75 2.00
STATED ODDS 1:2
P1 Victory 2.00 5.00
P4 Super Soldier 1.25 3.00
P7 Sock Evil in the Jaw 4.00 10.00

2014 Captain America The Winter Soldier

COMPLETE SET (100) 12.00 30.00
UNOPENED BOX (20 PACKS) 225.00 350.00
UNOPENED PACK (6 CARDS) 10.00 15.00
COMMON CARD (1-90) .25 .60
COMMON ROLL CALL SP (91-100) .60 1.50
*SILVER: .8X TO 2X BASIC CARDS .50 1.25
*SILVER SP: .3X TO .75X BASIC CARDS .50 1.25
*RED/99: 3X TO 8X BASIC CARDS 2.00 5.00
*RED SP/99: 1.2X TO 3X BASIC CARDS 2.00 5.00
*BLUE/25: 5X TO 12X BASIC CARDS 3.00 8.00
*BLUE SP/25: 2X TO 5X BASIC CARDS 3.00 8.00

2014 Captain America The Winter Soldier Autographs

COMMON AUTO 20.00 50.00
STATED ODDS 1:20
AT Hayley Atwell 100.00 200.00
CS Cobie Smulders 125.00 250.00
DC Dominic Cooper 125.00 250.00
HA Hayley Atwell 100.00 200.00
ST Sebastian Stan 125.00 250.00

2014 Captain America The Winter Soldier Badges

COMMON CARD (B1-B14) 6.00 15.00
STATED ODDS 1:80
B1 Captain America 15.00 40.00
B2 Nick Fury 100.00 200.00
B3 Captain America 10.00 25.00
B4 Captain America 10.00 25.00
B5 Captain America 10.00 25.00
B6 Black Widow 100.00 200.00
B8 Captain America 15.00 40.00
B9 Steve Rogers 12.00 30.00
B10 Captain America 15.00 40.00
B11 Captain America 15.00 40.00
B12 Black Widow 50.00 100.00
B14 Black Widow 30.00 75.00

2014 Captain America The Winter Soldier Behind-the-Lens

COMPLETE SET (6) 4.00 10.00
COMMON CARD (BTL1-BTL6) 1.25 3.00
STATED ODDS 1:8

2014 Captain America The Winter Soldier Cap's Legacy

COMPLETE SET (9) 6.00 15.00
COMMON CARD (CL1-CL9) 1.25 3.00
STATED ODDS 1:5

2014 Captain America The Winter Soldier Comic Autographs

COMPLETE SET (15)
COMMON AUTO 10.00 25.00
STATED OVERALL ODDS 1:20 W/SKETCHES
CAGW R. Garney/M. Waid 15.00 40.00
CALE S. Lee 300.00 800.00
CALS J. Sinnott/S. Lee 300.00 800.00
CASJ J. Sinnott/S. Lee 300.00 800.00
CASL S. Lee 300.00 800.00
CASS S. Lee/J. Sinnott 300.00 800.00
CAST S. Lee 300.00 800.00

2014 Captain America The Winter Soldier Concept Series

COMPLETE SET (27) 12.00 30.00
COMMON CARD (CS1-CS27) .75 2.00
STATED ODDS 1:2

2014 Captain America The Winter Soldier Dual Autographs

COMMON AUTO 75.00 150.00
STATED OVERALL ODDS 1:20 W/SKETCHES
AC D. Cooper/H. Atwell 125.00 250.00
AS H. Atwell/C. Smulders 100.00 200.00
PS G. St-Pierre/C. Smulders 100.00 200.00
SP S. Stan/G. St-Pierre 125.00 250.00
SS S. Stan/C. Smulders 125.00 250.00

2014 Captain America The Winter Soldier Dual Fatigues

COMMON CARD (FD1-FD17) 6.00 15.00
STATED ODDS 1:10
FD1 C. America/B. Widow 8.00 20.00
FD3 Falcon/B. Widow 10.00 25.00
FD4 B. Widow/M. Hill 8.00 20.00
FD7 C. America/Falcon 8.00 20.00
FD8 Falcon/B. Widow 8.00 20.00
FD9 B. Widow/C. America 10.00 25.00
FD11 M. Hill/B. Widow 12.00 30.00
FD13 C. America/C. America 30.00 75.00
FD14 C. America/C. America 15.00 40.00
FD15 B. Widow/B. Widow 100.00 200.00
FD17 M. Hill/M. Hill 12.00 30.00

2014 Captain America The Winter Soldier Fatigues

COMMON CARD (F1-F9) 6.00 15.00
STATED ODDS 1:10
COBIE SMULDERS FATIGUES AU 1:480
F1 Captain America 8.00 20.00
F2 Captain America 8.00 20.00
F3 Captain America 8.00 20.00
F4 Black Widow 75.00 150.00
F5 Black Widow 75.00 150.00
F6 Maria Hill 8.00 20.00
FACS C.Smulders AU MEM 150.00 300.00

2014 Captain America The Winter Soldier Movie Posters

COMPLETE SET (3) 3.00 8.00
COMMON CARD (MP1-MP3) 1.50 4.00
STATED ODDS 1:5

2014 Captain America The Winter Soldier Triple Fatigues

COMMON CARD (FT1-FT10) 10.00 25.00
STATED ODDS 1:10
FT1 Falcon/Cap/B. Widow 15.00 40.00
FT2 B. Widow/Cap/Falcon 20.00 50.00
FT3 M. Hill/Cap/B. Widow 15.00 40.00
FT4 B. Widow/M. Hill/Falcon 12.00 30.00
FT7 Cap 50.00 100.00
FT8 Black Widow 125.00 250.00
FT9 Falcon 25.00 50.00
FT10 Maria Hill 20.00 50.00

2016 Captain America Civil War

COMPLETE SET (60) 10.00 25.00
UNOPENED BOX (10 PACKS) 70.00 100.00
UNOPENED PACK (8 CARDS) 7.00 10.00
COMMON CARD (1-60) .30 .75
*BLUE: 6X TO 8X BASIC CARDS 2.50 6.00
*RED/100: 5X TO 12X BASIC CARDS 4.00 10.00
*GOLD/10: 10X TO 25X BASIC CARDS 8.00 20.00

2016 Captain America Civil War Autographed Memorabilia

COMMON AUTO 60.00 120.00
STATED ODDS 1:BOX WITH SKETCHES
AND OTHER PREMIUM INSERTS
WTCE Chris Evans SP 600.00 1200.00
WTEV Emily VanCamp 150.00 300.00
WTSS Sebastian Stan 125.00 250.00

2016 Captain America Civil War Autographs

COMMON AUTO 15.00 40.00
STATED ODDS 1:BOX WITH SKETCHES
AND OTHER PREMIUM INSERTS
SACE Chris Evans 500.00 1000.00
SACH Chris Evans 500.00 1000.00
SAEV Emily VanCamp 125.00 250.00
SAJR Jeremy Renner 60.00 120.00
SARV Jeremy Renner 60.00 120.00
SASS Sebastian Stan 125.00 250.00
SAVC Emily VanCamp 125.00 250.00
SASV Sebastian Stan 125.00 250.00

2016 Captain America Civil War Broken Bonds Dual Team Captain America Relics

COMMON CARD 6.00 15.00
OVERALL RELIC ODDS 1:5 PACKS
BBCAB Captain America/Winter Soldier 10.00 25.00
BBCAC Captain America/Agent 13 10.00 25.00
BBCAW Captain America/Sam Wilson 10.00 25.00
BBCBC Winter Soldier/Agent 13 10.00 25.00
BBCBM Winter Soldier/Scarlet Witch 8.00 20.00
BBCCM Agent 13/Scarlet Witch 10.00 25.00
BBCMW Scarlet Witch/Sam Wilson 8.00 20.00
BBCRB Steve Rogers/Winter Soldier 8.00 20.00
BBCRC Steve Rogers/Agent 13 10.00 25.00
BBCRF Steve Rogers/Falcon SP 10.00 25.00
BBCRM Steve Rogers/Scarlet Witch 8.00 20.00
BBCRW Steve Rogers/Sam Wilson 8.00 20.00
BBCSW Sam Wilson/Falcon SP 25.00 60.00

2016 Captain America Civil War Broken Bonds Dual Team Iron Man Relics

COMMON CARD 8.00 20.00
OVERALL RELIC ODDS 1:5 PACKS
BBIBB Black Panther/Black Widow 15.00 40.00
BBIBP Black Panther/T'Challa SP 25.00 60.00
BBIBT Black Panther/Tony Stark 10.00 25.00
BBITW Black Widow/Tony Stark 12.00 30.00

2016 Captain America Civil War Broken Bonds Dual Vs. Relics

COMMON CARD 6.00 15.00
OVERALL RELIC ODDS 1:5 PACKS
BBVBB Black Widow/Winter Soldier 8.00 20.00
BBVBS Agent 13/Black Widow 10.00 25.00
BBVCB B.Panther/Cap 100.00 200.00
BBVCT Agent 13/T'Challa 8.00 20.00
BBVCW B.Widow/Captain 10.00 25.00
BBVRS T.Stark/S.Rogers 10.00 25.00
BBVTC T.Stark/Cap 10.00 25.00
BBVWB S.Witch/B.Widow SP 80.00 150.00

2016 Captain America Civil War Broken Bonds Quad Vs. Relics

OVERALL RELIC ODDS 1:5 PACKS
BBCFTB Stark/Cap/Falcon/B.Panther SP 20.00 50.00
BBCJBT Cap/Stark/W.Soldier/B.Widow SP50.00 100.00
BBCJTT W.Soldier/Stark/Cap/T'Challa 20.00 50.00
BBCSTB Cap/Stark/A13/B.Widow
BBJSTB B.Widow/W.Soldier/Rogers/T'Challa20.00 50.00
BBJSTT T'Challa/A13/W.Soldier/Stark 10.00 25.00
BBSCTB Rogers/B.Panther/Cap/T'Challa SP
BBSWTB T'Challa/S.Witch/A13/B.Widow 15.00 40.00
BBSWTT A13/Stark/S.Witch/T'Challa 30.00 80.00
BBWCTT T'Challa/S.Witch/Cap/Stark 15.00 40.00

2016 Captain America Civil War Broken Bonds Relics

COMMON CARD 6.00 15.00
OVERALL RELIC ODDS 1:5 PACKS
BBAM Captain America 8.00 20.00
BBBL Black Panther SP 90.00 175.00
BBBW Black Widow SP 20.00 50.00
BBCA Agent 13 10.00 25.00
BBCT Captain America 8.00 20.00
BBJB Winter Soldier 8.00 20.00
BBSC Agent 13 SP 15.00 40.00
BBSR Steve Rogers 8.00 20.00
BBTS Tony Stark 8.00 20.00
BBWA Scarlet Witch 25.00 60.00
BBWD Black Widow 15.00 40.00
BBWM Scarlet Witch 15.00 40.00

2016 Captain America Civil War Broken Bonds Triple Relics

COMMON CARD 6.00 15.00
OVERALL RELICS ODDS 1:5 PACKS
BBBCC Black Widow/Crossbones/Cap 10.00 25.00
BBBCT Cap/B.Panther/Stark 25.00 60.00
BBBJC B.Panther/W.Soldier/Cap 175.00 225.00
BBBSC Cap/A13/B.Widow 12.00 30.00
BBCCS Crossbones/A13/Cap 10.00 25.00
BBSBW S.Witch/A13/B.Widow SP 50.00 100.00
BBSCS S.Rogers/Cap SP 250.00 500.00
BBSCW Cap/S.Witch/A13 20.00 50.00
BBSTT Stark/Rogers/T'Challa 8.00 20.00
BBTBJ T'Challa/W.Soldier/B.Widow 15.00 40.00
BBTBT B.Widow/Stark/T'Challa 12.00 30.00
BBTSW T'Challa/A13/S.Witch 12.00 30.00
BBWCB S.Witch/Cap/B.Widow 12.00 30.00

2016 Captain America Civil War Captain America's 75 Best Moments

COMPLETE SET (75) 250.00 500.00
COMMON CARD (BM1-BM75) 5.00 12.00
STATED ODDS 1:30 PACKS

2016 Captain America Civil War Captain America's Best Moments Autographs

COMMON CARD 6.00 15.00
RANDOMLY INSERTED INTO HOBBY PACKS
BMBU Sal Buscema 15.00 40.00
BMEM Ed McGuinness 8.00 20.00
BMEP Steve Epting 10.00 25.00
BMLE Stan Lee 150.00 400.00
BMLS Stan Lee 150.00 400.00
BMMI Mike Zeck 8.00 20.00
BMMZ Mike Zeck 8.00 20.00
BMRF Ron Frenz 8.00 20.00
BMSA Sal Buscema 15.00 40.00
BMSB Sal Buscema 15.00 40.00
BMSE Steve Epting 10.00 25.00
BMSL Stan Lee 150.00 400.00
BMST Stan Lee 150.00 400.00
BMZE Mike Zeck 8.00 20.00

2016 Captain America Civil War Dual Autographs

STATED ODDS 1:BOX WITH SKETCHES
AND OTHER PREMIUM INSERTS
CAEE VanCamp/Evans 400.00 800.00
CAER Renner/Evans 400.00 800.00
CAES Stan/Evans 400.00 800.00
CARV Renner/VanCamp 125.00 250.00
CASR Renner/Stan 150.00 300.00
CASV Sebastian Stan/Emily VanCamp 150.00 300.00

2016 Captain America Civil War Hollywood Magic

COMPLETE SET (15) 10.00 25.00
COMMON CARD (HM1-HM15) 1.00 2.50
STATED ODDS 1:3 PACKS

2016 Captain America Civil War Strained Relationships

COMPLETE SET (10) 20.00 50.00
COMMON CARD (SR1-SR10) 3.00 8.00
STATED ODDS 1:9
SR1 Avengers 5.00 12.00
SR2 Avengers 5.00 12.00
SR3 Avengers 5.00 12.00
SR4 Avengers 5.00 12.00
SR5 Avengers 5.00 12.00
SR6 Avengers 5.00 12.00

2016 Captain America Civil War Team Bio Off the Grid

OGB1 Crossbones 3.00 8.00

2016 Captain America Civil War Team Building

COMPLETE SET (10) 12.00 30.00
COMMON CARD (TB1-TB10) 1.50 4.00
STATED ODDS 1:4
TB1 Captain America 3.00 8.00
TB2 Iron Man 3.00 8.00
TB6 Black Panther 2.00 5.00
TB9 Agent 13 2.00 5.00
TB10 Black Widow 2.50 6.00

2016 Captain America Civil War Team Captain America Bios

COMPLETE SET (7) 8.00 20.00
COMMON CARD (CAB1-CAB7) 1.25 3.00
STATED ODDS 1:6
CAB1 Captain America 4.00 10.00
CAB5 Ant-Man 1.50 4.00
CAB6 Scarlet Witch 2.00 5.00
CAB7 Agent 13 2.00 5.00

2016 Captain America Civil War Team Iron Man Bios

COMPLETE SET (7 8.00 20.00
COMMON CARD (IMB1-IMB7) 1.25 3.00
STATED ODDS 1:5 PACKS
IMB1 Iron Man 4.00 10.00
IMB4 Black Panther 2.00 5.00
IMB5 Black Widow 2.00 5.00
IMB7 Tony Stark 3.00 8.00

2016 Captain America Civil War Walmart Exclusives

COMMON CARD (CW1-CW50) .20 .50
*BLUE: SAME VALUE AS BASIC CARDS
*FOIL: 2.5X TO 6X BASIC CARDS
*BLUE FOIL: 2.5X TO 6X BASIC CARDS

2016 Captain America Civil War Walmart Exclusives Known Heroes

COMMON MEM 5.00 12.00
STATED ODDS 1:6 WALMART PACKS
KHBL Black Widow 15.00 40.00
KHBW Black Widow 20.00 50.00
KHCA Captain America 6.00 15.00
KHCM Captain America 6.00 15.00
KHCT Captain America 6.00 15.00
KHTO Tony Stark 8.00 20.00
KHTS Tony Stark 8.00 20.00
KHWM Wanda Maximoff 12.00 30.00
PKHCA Captain America 10.00 25.00
PKHCM Captain America 8.00 20.00
PKHCT Captain America 8.00 20.00

2016 Captain America Civil War Walmart Exclusives Necklace Tags

COMMON CARD (1-5) 2.00 5.00
RANDOMLY INSERTED INTO PACKS
1 Captain America 4.00 10.00
2 Iron Man 4.00 10.00
5 Black Panther 3.00 8.00
12 Captain America 4.00 10.00
13 Iron Man 4.00 10.00
15 Black Panther 3.00 8.00

2016 Captain America Civil War Dog Tags

COMPLETE SET W/O FOIL (24) 15.00 40.00
COMPLETE SET W/FOIL (48) 50.00 100.00
UNOPENED BOX (24 PACKS) 80.00 100.00
UNOPENED PACK (1 DOG TAG+STICKER) 4.00 5.00
COMMON DOG TAG (1-24) 1.25 3.00
COMMON DOG TAG FOIL (25-48) 2.00 5.00

2016 Captain America Civil War Dog Tags Embossed Tags

COMPLETE SET (4) 15.00 40.00
COMMON TAG 5.00 12.00
1 Cap's Shield 6.00 15.00
3 Team Cap 6.00 15.00

2016 Captain America Civil War Dog Tags Stickers

COMPLETE SET (12) 3.00 8.00
COMMON CARD (1-12) .40 1.00
*3-D: .75X TO 2X BASIC STICKERS
OVERALL ODDS 1:1

2016 Captain America Civil War Polish

COMPLETE SET (150) 12.00 30.00
UNOPENED BOX (24 PACKS) 25.00 40.00
UNOPENED PACK (6 CARDS) 1.75 2.00
COMMON CARD (1-150) .12 .30

2019 Captain Marvel Combo Set Challenge Coins

COMPLETE SET (8) 10.00 25.00
COMMON COIN (1-8) 2.50 6.00
STATED ODDS 1:1

2019 Captain Marvel Combo Set Mission Patches

COMPLETE SET (8) 6.00 15.00
COMMON PATCH 1.25 3.00

2018 Daredevil Seasons 1 and 2

COMPLETE SET (100) 10.00 25.00
UNOPENED BOX (20 PACKS) 200.00 300.00
UNOPENED PACK (5 CARDS) 10.00 15.00
COMMON CARD (1-100) .20 .50
*DAREDEVIL RED/299: 2.5X TO 6X BASIC CARDS 3.00
*PUNISHER WHITE/99: 5X TO 12X BASIC CARDS 2.50 6.00
*ELEKTRA BLACK/49: 8X TO 20X BASIC CARDS 4.00 10.00

2018 Daredevil Seasons 1 and 2 Autographed Film Cels

COMMON AUTO 15.00 40.00
GROUP A ODDS 1:827
GROUP B ODDS 1:298
GROUP C ODDS 1:266
COMBINED AUTO AND SKETCH ODDS 1:20
FCEN Elodie Yung C 75.00 150.00
FCFC Jon Bernthal A 75.00 150.00
FCKP Deborah Ann Woll B 60.00 120.00
FCMM Charlie Cox B 125.00 250.00
FCPU Jon Bernthal A 100.00 200.00
FCVM Ayelet Zurer B 25.00 60.00

2018 Daredevil Seasons 1 and 2 Dual Autographed Film Cel

E-PACK ACHIEVEMENT
FCDA Charlie Cox/Elodie Yung 400.00 600.00

2018 Daredevil Seasons 1 and 2 Episodic Art

COMPLETE SET (27) 15.00 40.00
COMMON CARD (EA1-EA27) 1.25 3.00
STATED ODDS 1:5

2018 Daredevil Seasons 1 and 2 Episodic Art Canvas Artist Autographs

COMMON AUTO (EA1-EA27) 8.00 20.00
STATED PRINT RUN 49 SER.#'d SETS

2018 Daredevil Seasons 1 and 2 Film Cels

COMPLETE SET W/O SP (26) 150.00 300.00
COMMON CEL (FC1-FC29) 6.00 15.00
*RED TINT: SAME VALUE AS BASIC CELS
STATED ODDS 1:18
STATED SP ODDS 1:480
FC0-FC000 ARE E-PACK ACHIEVEMENTS
FC0 Nobu's Daggers/E-Pack 6.00 15.00
FC00 Dodging Bullets/E-Pack 15.00 40.00
FC000 Hallway Brawl/E-Pack 60.00 120.00
FC27 Confronting the Russians SP
FC28 Chasing Turk SP
FC29 Young Love SP

2018 Daredevil Seasons 1 and 2 Hell's Kitchen Headlines

COMPLETE SET (10) 12.00 30.00
COMMON CARD (HKH1-HKH10) 2.50 6.00
STATED ODDS 1:11

2018 Daredevil Seasons 1 and 2 Life Lessons from Stick

COMPLETE SET (5) 10.00 25.00
COMMON CARD (LL1-LL5) 3.00 8.00
STATED ODDS 1:22

2018 Daredevil Seasons 1 and 2 Memorable Moments

COMPLETE SET (15) 12.00 30.00
COMMON CARD (DB1-DB15) 1.50 4.00
STATED ODDS 1:7

2018 Daredevil Seasons 1 and 2 Rabbit in a Snowstorm Autographs

COMMON AUTO 6.00 15.00
GROUP A ODDS 1:2,964
GROUP B ODDS 1:1,744
GROUP C ODDS 1:212
GROUP D ODDS 1:203
GROUP E ODDS 1:148
GROUP F ODDS 1:62
COMBINED AUTO AND SKETCH ODDS 1:20
SSAZ Ayelet Zurer C 25.00 60.00
SSBG Bob Gunton C 15.00 40.00
SSCH Vondie Curtis-Hall E 10.00 25.00
SSDD Charlie Cox D 100.00 200.00
SSDW Deborah Ann Woll C 30.00 75.00
SSEH Elden Henson C 20.00 50.00
SSEN Elodie Yung D 50.00 100.00
SSEY Elodie Yung C 75.00 150.00
SSFC Jon Bernthal D 50.00 100.00
SSFN Elden Henson E 12.00 30.00
SSJB Jon Bernthal A 100.00 200.00
SSKP Deborah Ann Woll D 25.00 60.00
SSLM Toby Leonard Moore F 12.00 30.00
SSLO Bob Gunton F 10.00 25.00
SSMM Charlie Cox C 100.00 200.00
SSOW Bob Gunton F 10.00 25.00
SSPN Jon Bernthal B 75.00 150.00
SSVC Vondie Curtis-Hall C 15.00 40.00
SSVM Ayelet Zurer E 25.00 60.00

2018 Daredevil Seasons 1 and 2 Rabbit in a Snowstorm Dual Autographs

COMMON AUTO 25.00 60.00
STATED ODDS 1:480
COMBINED AUTO AND SKETCH ODDS 1:20
SSDAW A.Zurer/T.L.Moore 30.00 75.00
SSDBK S.Rider/D.A.Woll 50.00 100.00
SSDED E.Yung/C.Cox 250.00 450.00
SSDFK E.Henson/D.A.Woll 75.00 150.00
SSDKB D.A.Woll/V. Curtis-Hall 50.00 100.00
SSDLV B.Gunton/A.Zurer 50.00 100.00
SSDLW B.Gunton/T.L.Moore 30.00 75.00
SSDMF C.Cox/E.Henson 125.00 250.00
SSDPD J.Bernthal/C.Cox 150.00 300.00
SSDPK J.Bernthal/D.A.Woll 200.00 400.00
SSDWK T.L.Moore/D.A.Woll 50.00 100.00

2018 Daredevil Seasons 1 and 2 Rabbit in a Snowstorm Quad Autograph

E-PACK ACHIEVEMENT
SSQ Charlie Cox/Elden Henson
Jon Bernthal/Elodie Yung

2018 Daredevil Seasons 1 and 2 Speak the Language

COMPLETE SET (15) 15.00 40.00
COMMON CARD (STL1-STL15) 2.00 5.00
STATED ODDS 1:7

2018 The Defenders

COMPLETE SET W/SP (130) 60.00 120.00
COMPLETE SET W/O SP (100) 12.00 30.00
UNOPENED BOX (20 PACKS)
UNOPENED PACK (5 CARDS)
COMMON CARD (1-100) .30 .75
COMMON SP (101-130) 2.00 5.00
*ACETATE: 1.5X TO 4X BASIC CARDS

2018 The Defenders Autographed Connecting Manufactured Patches

STATED PRINT RUN 25 SER.#'d SETS
DCACC Charlie Cox 150.00 400.00
DCAFJ Finn Jones 40.00 100.00
DCAKR Krysten Ritter 100.00 250.00

2018 The Defenders Back from the Dead

COMMON CARD (BFD1-BFD15) 12.00 30.00
STATED ODDS 1:240

2018 The Defenders Back from the Dead Autographs

COMMON AUTO 10.00 25.00
STATED PRINT RUN 25 SER.#'d SETS
BFDCC Charlie Cox 150.00 400.00
BFDEY Elodie Yung 40.00 100.00
BFDFJ Finn Jones 40.00 100.00

2018 The Defenders Collateral Damage

COMPLETE SET (7) 30.00 75.00
COMMON CARD (CD1-CD7) 6.00 15.00
E-PACK ACHIEVEMENT SET

2018 The Defenders Connecting Manufactured Patches

COMMON MEM 10.00 25.00
STATED ODDS 1:83
DCJJ1 Jessica Jones 15.00 40.00
DCJJ2 Jessica Jones 15.00 40.00
DCJJ3 Jessica Jones 15.00 40.00
DCJJ4 Jessica Jones 15.00 40.00
DCJJ5 Jessica Jones 15.00 40.00
DCJJ6 Jessica Jones 15.00 40.00
DCJJ7 Jessica Jones 15.00 40.00
DCJJ8 Jessica Jones 15.00 40.00

2018 The Defenders Header Cards

COMMON CARD (HC1-HC4) 50.00 100.00
STATED ODDS 1:480

2018 The Defenders Heroes Daredevil

COMPLETE SET (15) 12.00 30.00
COMMON CARD (THDD1-THDD15) 1.50 4.00
STATED OVERALL ODDS 1:8

2018 The Defenders Heroes Iron Fist

COMPLETE SET (15) 12.00 30.00
COMMON CARD (THIF1-THIF15) 1.50 4.00
STATED OVERALL ODDS 1:8

2018 The Defenders Heroes Jessica Jones

COMPLETE SET (15) 12.00 30.00
COMMON CARD (THJJ1-THJJ15) 1.50 4.00
STATED OVERALL ODDS 1:8

2018 The Defenders Heroes Luke Cage

COMPLETE SET (15) 12.00 30.00
COMMON CARD (THLC1-THLC15) 1.50 4.00
STATED OVERALL ODDS 1:8

2018 The Defenders Manufactured Logo Patches

COMMON MEM 30.00 75.00
STATED ODDS 1:1,920
CLDD Daredevil 75.00 150.00
CLIF Iron Fist 75.00 150.00

2018 The Defenders Markings of the Royal Dragon Autographs

COMMON AUTO	6.00	15.00
GROUP A ODDS 1:215		
GROUP B ODDS 1:164		
GROUP C ODDS 1:102		
GROUP D ODDS 1:51		
STATED OVERALL ODDS 1:25		
RDCC Charlie Cox B	100.00	200.00
RDCL Chloe Levine D	12.00	30.00
RDDD Charlie Cox B	100.00	200.00
RDDW Deborah Ann Woll B	20.00	50.00
RDEH Elden Henson A	15.00	40.00
RDEY Elodie Yung B	60.00	120.00
RDFJ Finn Jones A	50.00	100.00
RDIF Finn Jones A	50.00	100.00
RDKR Krysten Ritter C	60.00	120.00
RDMK Simone Missick A	15.00	40.00
RDSM Simone Missick A	15.00	40.00
RDWH Wai Ching Ho C	8.00	20.00

2018 The Defenders The Black Sky

COMPLETE SET (9)	75.00	150.00
COMMON CARD (BS1-BS9)	8.00	20.00
STATED ODDS 1:120		

2018 The Defenders The Hand

COMMON CARD (TH1-TH5)	10.00	25.00
STATED ODDS 1:240		

2016 Doctor Strange

COMPLETE SET W/O SP (50)	200.00	400.00
COMPLETE SET W/SP (60)	250.00	500.00
UNOPENED BOX (7 MINIBOXES)	75.00	100.00
UNOPENED MINIBOX (1 CARD)	15.00	20.00
COMMON CARD (1-50)	4.00	10.00
COMMON SP/50 (51-60)	6.00	15.00
*SILVER LTFX/50: .5X TO 1.2X BASIC CARDS		
*GOLD LTFX/25: .6X TO 1.5X BASIC CARDS		
STATED PRINT RUN 150 SER.#'d SETS		
52 Christine Palmer SP	10.00	25.00
59 Movie Poster SP	12.00	30.00
60 Movie Poster SP	12.00	30.00

2016 Doctor Strange Autographs

COMMON AUTO	8.00	20.00
STATED ODDS 1:14		
SSBC Benedict Cumberbatch	500.00	750.00
SSSW Tilda Swinton	30.00	75.00
SSTS Tilda Swinton	30.00	75.00

2016 Doctor Strange Behind-the-Lens

COMPLETE SET W/EP (22)		
COMPLETE SET (20)	120.00	250.00
COMMON CARD (BTL1-BTL20)	6.00	15.00
STATED PRINT RUN 49 SER.#'d SETS		
BTL0-BTL00 ARE E-PACK ACHIEVEMENTS		
BTL0 Behind-the-Lens/E-Pack		
BTL00 Behind-the-Lens/E-Pack		

2016 Doctor Strange Book of Cagliostro

COMPLETE SET (10)	80.00	150.00
COMMON CARD (BC1-BC10)	5.00	12.00
STATED PRINT RUN 99 SER.#'d SETS		
BC1 Dr. Stephen Strange	10.00	25.00
BC2 Christine Palmer	15.00	40.00
BC3 Ancient One	6.00	15.00
BC4 Baron Mordo	6.00	15.00
BC5 Kaecilius	6.00	15.00
BC9 Doctor Strange	10.00	25.00
BC10 Ancient One	6.00	15.00

2016 Doctor Strange Enchanted Arsenal

COMPLETE SET (10)	30.00	80.00
COMMON CARD (MA1-MA10)	4.00	10.00
STATED PRINT RUN 99 SER.#'d SETS		
MA0 Cloak of Levitation/E-Pack		
MA4 Mordo's Staff	6.00	15.00
MA6 Daniel Drumm's Staff	5.00	12.00
MA7 Curved Staff	5.00	12.00

2016 Doctor Strange Letterman Patches

COMPLETE SET (39)	250.00	400.00
COMMON CUMBERBATCH	10.00	25.00
COMMON MIKKELSON	4.00	10.00
COMMON SWINTON	6.00	15.00
STATED ODDS 1:60		

2016 Doctor Strange Sanctum Stars

SS0 Doctor Strange

2016 Doctor Strange Shadowbox Master Autograph

DS1 Benedict Cumberbatch

2016 Doctor Strange Strange Change

COMPLETE SET (18)	120.00	250.00
COMMON CARD (SC1-SC18)	6.00	15.00
STATED ODDS 1:42		
SC1 Strange Tales Vol 1 #110	12.00	30.00
SC7 Strange Tales Vol 1 #150	15.00	40.00

2016 Doctor Strange Strange Moments

COMPLETE SET (15)	80.00	150.00
COMMON CARD (SM1-SM15)	5.00	12.00
STATED PRINT RUN 99 SER.#'d SETS		
SM0 Last Days of Magic/E-Pack		

2016 Doctor Strange Vishanti's Vestments

COMPLETE SET (10)	60.00	120.00
COMMON CARD	4.00	10.00
STATED ODDS 1:7		
VHAO Ancient One	6.00	15.00
VHAV Ancient One	6.00	15.00
VHDS Doctor Strange	8.00	20.00
VHDV Doctor Strange	8.00	20.00

2016 Doctor Strange Vishanti's Vestments Autographs

STATED ODDS 1:176		
VHABC Benedict Cumberbatch	600.00	1000.00
VHATS Tilda Swinton	75.00	150.00

2016 Doctor Strange Vishanti's Vestments Dual

COMMON CARD	6.00	15.00
STATED ODDS 1:9		
VHDKD D.Strange/Kaecilius	10.00	25.00

2016 Doctor Strange Vishanti's Vestments Triple

COMMON CARD	8.00	20.00
STATED ODDS 1:28		
VHTA Ancient One/Ancient One/Ancient One	10.00	25.00
VHTD Doctor Strange	10.00	25.00
VHTAKB Mordo/Ancient1/Kaecilius	10.00	25.00
VHTDAB Strange/Mordo/Ancient1	25.00	50.00
VHTDBK Strange/Mordo/Kaecilius	12.00	30.00
VHTDKA Strange/Ancient1/Kaecilius	12.00	30.00
VHTKBW Mordo/Wong/Kaecilius	20.00	50.00
VHTWBA Mordo/Ancient1/Wong	15.00	40.00

2016 Doctor Strange Dog Tags

COMPLETE SET (24)	50.00	100.00
UNOPENED BOX (24 PACKS)	70.00	80.00
UNOPENED PACK (1 TAG+1 STICKER)	3.50	4.00
COMMON TAG (1-24))	2.00	5.00
COMMON FOIL (25-48)	3.00	8.00

2016 Doctor Strange Dog Tags 3-D Tags

COMPLETE SET (4)	12.00	30.00
COMMON TAG (1-4)	5.00	12.00
3 Doctor Strange	6.00	15.00

2016 Doctor Strange Dog Tags Stickers

COMPLETE SET (24)	6.00	15.00
COMMON CARD (1-24)	.40	1.00
COMMON FOIL (25-48)	1.25	3.00
STATED OVERALL ODDS 1:1		

2022 Upper Deck The Falcon and the Winter Soldier

COMPLETE SET (90)	15.00	40.00
UNOPENED BOX (15 PACKS)	75.00	100.00
UNOPENED PACK (6 CARDS)	5.00	6.00
COMMON CARD (1-90)	.40	1.00
*BLUE: .6X TO 1.5X BASIC CARDS		
*RED: .75X TO 2X BASIC CARDS		
*YELLOW: 1.25X TO 3X BASIC CARDS		
*BLACK&RED/225: 2.5X TO 6X BASIC CARDS		
*PURPLE/99: 3X TO 8X BASIC CARDS		

2022 Upper Deck The Falcon and the Winter Soldier Autographed Film Cels

COMMON AUTO	30.00	75.00
GROUP A ODDS 1:45,563		
GROUP B ODDS 1:12,150		
GROUP C ODDS 1:11,391		
GROUP D ODDS 1:2,025		
GROUP E ODDS 1:651		
STATED ODDS 1:450 HOBBY/EPACK		
FCAAM Anthony Mackie B	125.00	300.00
FCADC Don Cheadle A		
FCADR Danny Ramirez D	40.00	100.00
FCAEK Erin Kellyman E	60.00	150.00
FCAEV Emily VanCamp C	75.00	200.00
FCAGS Georges St. Pierre A		
FCAKE Erin Kellyman E	60.00	150.00
FCAMA Anthony Mackie C	150.00	400.00
FCARA Danny Ramirez D	40.00	100.00
FCASS Sebastian Stan B	150.00	400.00
FCAST Sebastian Stan B	150.00	400.00

2022 Upper Deck The Falcon and the Winter Soldier Autographs

COMMON AUTO	15.00	40.00
GROUP A ODDS 1:16,069		
GROUP B ODDS 1:6,939		
GROUP C ODDS 1:1,590		
GROUP D ODDS 1:1,339		
GROUP E ODDS 1:1,018		
GROUP F ODDS 1:761		
GROUP G ODDS 1:198		
STATED ODDS 1:112 HOBBY/EPACK		
STATED ODDS 1:1,800 BLASTER		
AAM Anthony Mackie D	125.00	300.00
AAN Anthony Mackie D	125.00	300.00
AAO Adepero Oduye G	20.00	50.00
ACA Anthony Mackie D	200.00	500.00
ADC Don Cheadle A		
ADR Danny Ramirez G	30.00	75.00
AEK Erin Kellyman F	30.00	75.00
AER Erin Kellyman E	30.00	75.00
AEV Emily VanCamp C	60.00	150.00
AGS Georges St. Pierre A		
AKE Erin Kellyman F	30.00	75.00
AMA Anthony Mackie C	125.00	300.00
ASE Sebastian Stan E	125.00	300.00
ASS Sebastian Stan E	125.00	300.00
AST Sebastian Stan B	125.00	300.00
AVA Emily VanCamp C	60.00	150.00

2022 Upper Deck The Falcon and the Winter Soldier Behind-the-Scenes

COMPLETE SET (15)	10.00	25.00
COMMON CARD (BS1-BS15)	1.25	3.00
STATED ODDS 1:3 HOBBY/EPACK/BLASTER		

2022 Upper Deck The Falcon and the Winter Soldier Character Profiles

COMPLETE SET (10)	12.00	30.00
COMMON CARD (P1-P10)	2.50	6.00
STATED ODDS 1:10 HOBBY/EPACK/BLASTER		

2022 Upper Deck The Falcon and the Winter Soldier Film Cels

COMMON TIER 1 (FC1-FC6)	6.00	15.00
COMMON TIER 2 (FC7-FC12)	6.00	15.00
COMMON TIER 3 (FC13-FC18)	6.00	15.00
COMMON TIER 4 (FC19-FC24)	6.00	15.00
COMMON TIER 5 (FC25-FC30)	12.00	30.00
COMMON TIER 6 (FC31-FC36)	12.00	30.00
TIER 1 ODDS 1:60 HOBBY/EPACK		
TIER 1 ODDS 1:125 BLASTER		
TIER 2 ODDS 1:60 HOBBY/EPACK		
TIER 2 ODDS 1:125 BLASTER		
TIER 3 ODDS 1:60 HOBBY/EPACK		
TIER 3 ODDS 1:125 BLASTER		
TIER 4 ODDS 1:60 HOBBY/EPACK		
TIER 4 ODDS 1:125 BLASTER		
TIER 5 ODDS 1:120 HOBBY/EPACK		
TIER 5 ODDS 1:250 BLASTER		
TIER 6 ODDS 1:120 HOBBY/EPACK		
TIER 6 ODDS 1:250 BLASTER		

2022 Upper Deck The Falcon and the Winter Soldier Forged Vibranium Dual Metal

COMPLETE SET (8)	60.00	150.00
COMMON CARD (DFV1-DFV8)	12.00	30.00
STATED ODDS 1:60 HOBBY/EPACK		
DFV1 Anthony Mackie/Sebastian Stan	20.00	50.00
DFV2 Anthony Mackie/Daniel Bruhl	15.00	40.00
DFV5 Florence Kasumba/Sebastian Stan	15.00	40.00
DFV6 Anthony Mackie/Wyatt Russell	20.00	50.00

2022 Upper Deck The Falcon and the Winter Soldier Forged Vibranium Metal

COMMON CARD (FV1-FV16)	5.00	12.00
STATED ODDS 1:60 HOBBY/EPACK		
FV1 Anthony Mackie	12.00	30.00
FV2 Sebastian Stan	10.00	25.00
FV3 Julia Louis Dreyfus	6.00	15.00
FV4 Daniel Bruhl	6.00	15.00
FV5 Wyatt Russell	6.00	15.00
FV7 Erin Kellyman	6.00	15.00
FV11 Don Cheadle	6.00	15.00
FV13 Anthony Mackie	12.00	30.00
FV14 Sebastian Stan	10.00	25.00
FV15 Wyatt Russell	6.00	15.00
FV16 Daniel Bruhl	6.00	15.00

2022 Upper Deck The Falcon and the Winter Soldier Horizontal Autographs

COMMON AUTO	40.00	100.00
GROUP A ODDS 1:5,004		
GROUP B ODDS 1:2,406		
GROUP C ODDS 1:809		
STATED ODDS 1:540 HOBBY/EPACK		
AM Anthony Mackie B	250.00	600.00
DR Danny Ramirez C	60.00	150.00
EK Erin Kellyman C	75.00	200.00
EV Emily VanCamp B	125.00	300.00
MA Anthony Mackie A	300.00	800.00
SS Sebastian Stan A	200.00	500.00
ST Sebastian Stan A	200.00	500.00
VA Emily VanCamp B	125.00	300.00

2022 Upper Deck The Falcon and the Winter Soldier Inscriptions

STATED PRINT RUN 250 SER.#'d SETS		
AFK Florence Kasumba "Wakanda Forever"	75.00	200.00

2022 Upper Deck The Falcon and the Winter Soldier Lineup

COMPLETE SET (18)	12.00	30.00
COMMON CARD (LU1-LU18)	1.50	4.00
STATED ODDS 1:5 BLASTER ONLY		

2022 Upper Deck The Falcon and the Winter Soldier Mission Briefing

COMPLETE SET (6)	8.00	20.00
COMMON CARD (MB1-MB6)	2.00	5.00
STATED ODDS 1:17 HOBBY/EPACK/BLASTER		

2022 Upper Deck The Falcon and the Winter Soldier The Power to Do Better Acetate

COMPLETE SET (10)	40.00	100.00

COMMON CARD (DB1-DB10) 6.00 15.00
STATED ODDS 1:180 HOBBY/EPACK

2022 Upper Deck The Falcon and the Winter Soldier Quad Autographs

COMPLETE SET (2)
STATED PRINT RUN 10 SER.#'d SETS
UNPRICED DUE TO SCARCITY
DASMKR Mackie/Stan/Ramirez/Kellyman
DASSVM Mackie/Stan/St-Pierre/VanCamp

2022 Upper Deck The Falcon and the Winter Soldier Villainous Measures Acetate

COMPLETE SET (10) 40.00 100.00
COMMON CARD (VM1-VM10) 6.00 15.00
STATED ODDS 1:180 HOBBY/EPACK

2022 Upper Deck The Falcon and the Winter Soldier Who Will Wield the Shield?

COMPLETE SET (18) 8.00 20.00
COMMON CARD (WWW1-WWW18) 1.00 2.50
STATED ODDS 1:2 HOBBY/EPACK/BLASTER

2014 Guardians of the Galaxy

COMPLETE SET (90) 8.00 20.00
COMPLETE SET w/SP (135) 25.00 60.00
UNOPENED BOX (10 PACKS) 90.00 110.00
UNOPENED PACK (8 CARDS) 10.00 12.00
COMMON CARD (1-90) .15 .40
COMMON SP (91-135) 1.25 3.00
*BRONZE: 2X TO 5X BASIC CARDS
*PURPLE/25: 12X TO 30X BASIC CARDS
103 Movie Poster SP 5.00 12.00

2014 Guardians of the Galaxy Autographs

COMMON AUTO 50.00 100.00
STATED ODDS 1:80
CP Chris Pratt 500.00 800.00
DB Dave Bautista 75.00 150.00
GC Glenn Close 250.00 400.00
MR Michael Rooker 100.00 200.00
ZS Zoe Saldana 300.00 600.00

2014 Guardians of the Galaxy BOOM

COMPLETE SET (13) 15.00 40.00
COMMON CARD (BOOM1-BOOM13) 2.50 6.00
STATED ODDS 1:10

2014 Guardians of the Galaxy Box-Toppers

COMPLETE SET (22) 50.00 100.00
COMMON CARD (G1-G22) 3.00 8.00
STATED ODDS 1:HOBBY BOX
G3 Rocket Raises Weapon 4.00 10.00

2014 Guardians of the Galaxy Classic Covers Autographs

COMMON AUTO 5.00 12.00
STATED ODDS 1:60
GGAB B.Walker/A.Garner 10.00 25.00
GGAG A.Garner/D.Abnett 8.00 20.00
GGAL D.Abnett/C.Langley 6.00 15.00
GGAW B.Walker/D.Abnett 10.00 25.00
GGDA D.Abnett/A.Lanning 6.00 15.00
GGDJ T.DeFalco/J.Valentino 10.00 25.00
GGDV J.Valentino/T.DeFalco 10.00 25.00
GGGC Gerry Conway 8.00 20.00
GGJT T.DeFalco/J.Valentino 10.00 25.00
GGLW B.Walker/A.Lanning 12.00 30.00
GGMW A.Milgrom/B.Wiacek 10.00 25.00
GGSL Stan Lee 250.00 600.00
GGTJ T.DeFalco/J.Valentino 8.00 20.00
GGTV T.DeFalco/J.Valentino 8.00 20.00
GGWG B.Walker/A.Garner 6.00 15.00

2014 Guardians of the Galaxy Cosmic Strings

COMMON CARD (CS1-CS11) 4.00 10.00
STATED ODDS 1:10
CS1 Star-Lord 6.00 15.00
CS3 Gamora 5.00 12.00
CS4 Rocket Raccoon 10.00 25.00
CS6 Nebula 8.00 20.00
CS8 Korath 6.00 15.00
CS11 Gamora 5.00 12.00

2014 Guardians of the Galaxy Cosmic Strings Autographed Memorabilia

COMMON AUTO (CSA1-CSA8) 60.00 150.00
STATED ODDS 1:480
CSA1 Chris Pratt 1200.00 2500.00
CSA2 Karen Gillan 125.00 300.00
CSA7 Glenn Close 250.00 400.00
CSA8 Zoe Saldana 225.00 450.00

2014 Guardians of the Galaxy Cosmic Strings Dual

COMMON CARD (CSD1-CSD19) 4.00 10.00
STATED ODDS 1:22
CSD1 Star-Lord 5.00 12.00
Gamora
CSD2 Gamora/Nebula 8.00 20.00
CSD3 Rocket/Drax 5.00 12.00
CSD5 Ronan/Nebula 6.00 15.00
CSD7 Rocket/Gamora 5.00 12.00
CSD8 Ronan/Korath 5.00 12.00
CSD9 Korath/Nebula 10.00 25.00
CSD14 Ronan/Drax 5.00 12.00
CSD15 Star-Lord 5.00 12.00
CSD17 Drax 12.00 30.00

2014 Guardians of the Galaxy Cosmic Strings Max

STATED ODDS 1:2400
GOTG1 S.Lord/Gamora/Drax/Rocket/Yondu150.00 300.00
Ronan/Korath/Nebula/N.Prime

2014 Guardians of the Galaxy Cosmic Strings Oversized

COMMON CARD (CSO1-CSO14) 4.00 10.00
STATED ODDS 1:BOX
CSO1 Star-Lord 6.00 15.00
CSO3 Gamora 8.00 20.00
CSO4 Rocket Raccoon 10.00 25.00
CSO5 Nebula 50.00 100.00
CSO6 Ronan 10.00 25.00
CSO7 Yondu 5.00 12.00
CSO8 Korath 10.00 25.00
CSO11 Star-Lord 12.00 30.00
CSO12 Gamora 15.00 40.00
CSO13 Drax The Destroyer 5.00 12.00
CSO14 Gamora 100.00 200.00

2014 Guardians of the Galaxy Cosmic Strings Quad

COMMON CARD (CSQ1-CSQ12) 15.00 40.00
STATED ODDS 1:120
CSQ1 Gamora/Nebula 12.00 30.00
Star-Lord/Ronan
CSQ3 S.Lord/Yondu/Gamora/Drax 10.00 25.00
CSQ4 Yondu/Ronan/Rocket/Korath 12.00 30.00
CSQ7 Rocket/S.Lord/Drax/Gamora 10.00 25.00
CSQ8 Gamora 100.00 200.00
CSQ9 Drax 25.00 60.00
CSQ10 Star-Lord 150.00 300.00
CSQ11 Ronan/Nebula/Korath/Gamora 25.00 60.00
CSQ12 Gamora/Nebula 120.00 250.00
N.Prime/Star-Lord

2014 Guardians of the Galaxy Cosmic Strings Team

STATED ODDS 1:2400
TEAM1 S.Lord/Gamora/Rocket/Drax 150.00 300.00

2014 Guardians of the Galaxy Cosmic Strings Trio

COMMON CARD (CST1-CST15) 5.00 12.00
STATED ODDS 1:50
CST1 S.Lord/Drax/Gamora 6.00 15.00
CST2 Ronan/Nebula/Korath 10.00 25.00
CST6 Gamora/Ronan/Nebula 6.00 15.00
CST7 Rocket/S.Lord/Gamora 12.00 20.00
CST8 S.Lord/Ronan/Yondu 6.00 15.00
CST11 S.Lord/Ronan/Rocket 12.00 15.00
CST12 S.Lord 25.00 60.00
CST13 Drax 20.00 50.00
CST14 Ronan 15.00 60.00
CST15 S.Lord/Nebula/Gamora 20.00 50.00

2014 Guardians of the Galaxy Dual Autographs

COMMON AUTO 100.00 200.00
STATED ODDS 1:480
PC C.Pratt/G.Close 300.00 500.00
PG K.Gillian/C.Pratt 300.00 500.00
SG K.Gillian/Z.Saldana 250.00 500.00

2014 Guardians of the Galaxy Galactic Residents

COMPLETE SET (12) 8.00 20.00
COMMON CARD (GR1-GR12) .75 2.00
STATED ODDS 1:7
GR2 Drax 2.00 5.00
GR4 Groot 2.00 5.00
GR5 Rocket Raccoon 2.00 5.00
GR9 Gamora 2.00 5.00

2014 Guardians of the Galaxy The Sights

COMPLETE SET (8) 10.00 25.00
COMMON CARD (S1-S8) 2.50 6.00
STATED ODDS 1:10

2014 Guardians of the Galaxy Zero Gravity

COMPLETE SET (9) 6.00 15.00
COMMON CARD (ZG1-ZG9) 1.25 3.00
STATED ODDS 1:7

2014 Guardians of the Galaxy Dog Tags

COMPLETE SET (24) 25.00 60.00
UNOPENED BOX (24 PACKS) 65.00 80.00
UNOPENED PACK (1 TAG+1 STICKER) 3.50 4.00
COMMON TAG (1-24) 2.00 5.00
*FOIL: 1X TO 2X BASIC TAGS 4.00 10.00

2017 Guardians of the Galaxy Vol. 2

COMPLETE SET W/O SP (80) 12.00 30.00
COMPLETE SET W/SP (90) 20.00 50.00
UNOPENED BOX (10 PACKS) 100.00 120.00
UNOPENED PACK (8 CARDS) 10.00 12.00
COMMON CARD (1-80) .30 .75
COMMON SP (81-90) 2.00 5.00
*BRONZE: .5X TO 1.2X BASIC CARDS .40 1.00
*BRONZE SP: .08X TO .2X BASIC CARDS .40 1.00
*BLUE/199: 1.5X TO 4X BASIC CARDS 1.25 3.00
*BLUE SP/199: .25X TO .6X BASIC CARDS1.25 3.00
*PURPLE/99: 2.5X TO 6X BASIC CARDS 2.00 5.00
*PURPLE SP/99: SAME
VALUE AS BASIC CARDS 2.00 5.00
*RED/49: 4X TO 10X BASIC CARDS 3.00 8.00
*RED SP/49: .6X TO 1.5X BASIC CARDS 3.00 8.00
*PINK/10: 8 TO 20X BASIC CARDS 6.00 15.00
*PINK SP/10: 1.2X TO 3X BASIC CARDS 6.00 15.00

2017 Guardians of the Galaxy Vol. 2 Behind-the-Lens

COMPLETE SET (15) 8.00 20.00
COMMON CARD (BTL1-BTL5) 1.00 2.50
STATED ODDS 1:2

2017 Guardians of the Galaxy Vol. 2 Family of Oddballs

COMPLETE SET (12) 15.00 40.00
COMMON CARD (F1-F12) 2.00 5.00
STATED ODDS 1:5

2017 Guardians of the Galaxy Vol. 2 Galactic Garb

COMMON CARD (SM1-SM25) 6.00 15.00
STATED ODDS 1:10
SM2 Gamora 80.00 150.00
SM4 Yondu 25.00 60.00
SM6 Mantis 30.00 80.00
SM7 Ego 8.00 20.00
SM8 Ayesha 10.00 25.00
SM9 Star-Lord 20.00 50.00
SM10 Gamora 10.00 25.00
SM14 Mantis 30.00 80.00
SM17 Star-Lord 20.00 50.00
SM18 Gamora 25.00 60.00
SM20 Yondu 12.00 30.00
SM22 Rocket 10.00 25.00
SM23 Ego 8.00 20.00
SM24 Ayesha 12.00 30.00
SM25 Rocket 10.00 25.00

2017 Guardians of the Galaxy Vol. 2 Galactic Garb Autographs

COMMON AUTO (SMA1-SMA5) 65.00 125.00
STATED ODDS 1:195
SMA1 Zoe Saldana 125.00 250.00
SMA3 Pom Klementieff 100.00 200.00
SMA5 Zoe Saldana 125.00 250.00

2017 Guardians of the Galaxy Vol. 2 Galactic Garb Dual

COMMON CARD (DM1-DM15) 6.00 15.00
STATED ODDS 1:24
DM1 Star-Lord/Gamora 8.00 20.00
DM2 Nebula/Drax 10.00 25.00
DM4 Star-Lord/Ego 15.00 40.00
DM5 Star-Lord/Mantis 15.00 40.00
DM7 Star-Lord/Rocket 8.00 20.00
DM8 Gamora/Nebula 10.00 25.00
DM9 Gamora/Drax 12.00 30.00
DM10 Mantis/Drax 12.00 30.00

2017 Guardians of the Galaxy Vol. 2 Galactic Garb Dual Autographs

COMMON AUTO (DMA1-DMA5) 150.00 300.00
STATED ODDS 1:1200
DMA1 Saldana/Bautista 200.00 400.00
DMA2 Saldana/Gillian 400.00 600.00
DMA5 Saldana/Klementieff 300.00 500.00

2017 Guardians of the Galaxy Vol. 2 Galactic Garb Quad

COMMON CARD (QM1-QM10) 8.00 20.00
STATED ODDS 1:48
QM3 Ego/Mantis/Ayesha/Rocket 25.00 60.00
QM4 Gamora/Rocket/Nebula/Drax 12.00 30.00
QM6 Star-Lord/Yondu/Mantis/Drax 15.00 40.00
QM7 Star-Lord/Rocket/Drax/Yondu 15.00 40.00
QM8 Star-Lord/Yondu/Ego/Mantis 25.00 60.00
QM10 Star-Lord/Gamora/Drax/Yondu 15.00 40.00

2017 Guardians of the Galaxy Vol. 2 Galactic Garb Triple

COMMON CARD (TM1-TM15) 8.00 20.00
STATED ODDS 1:30
TM2 Yondu/Nebula/Rocket 12.00 30.00
TM3 Gamora/Nebula/Mantis 25.00 60.00
TM4 Ego/Mantis/Ayesha 12.00 30.00
TM6 Drax/Mantis/Rocket 15.00 40.00
TM10 Star-Lord/Gamora/Drax 12.00 30.00
TM11 Gamora/Drax/Yondu 20.00 50.00
TM12 Star-Lord/Gamora/Ego 15.00 40.00

2017 Guardians of the Galaxy Vol. 2 Groot's Roots

COMPLETE SET (10) 120.00 250.00
COMMON CARD (GR1-GR10) 12.00 30.00
STATED ODDS 1:65

2017 Guardians of the Galaxy Vol. 2 Mix Tape Autographs

COMMON AUTO (MT1-MT15) 10.00 25.00
STATED ODDS 1:43
MT1 Dave Bautista 30.00 75.00
MT2 Zoe Saldana 100.00 200.00
MT3 Karen Gillan 50.00 100.00
MT4 Tommy Flanagan 30.00 75.00

MT5 Sean Gunn 15.00 40.00
MT7 Pom Klementieff 30.00 75.00
MT8 Dave Bautista 30.00 75.00
MT9 Zoe Saldana 100.00 200.00
MT10 Karen Gillan 30.00 75.00
MT11 Tommy Flanagan 30.00 75.00
MT12 Sean Gunn 15.00 40.00
MT14 Pom Klementieff 30.00 75.00
MT15 Zoe Saldana 100.00 200.00

2017 Guardians of the Galaxy Vol. 2 Mix Tape Dual Autographs

COMMON AUTO (DMT1-DMT10) 50.00 100.00
STATED ODDS 1:325
DMT1 Saldana/Gillan 200.00 350.00
DMT2 Saldana/Bautista 125.00 250.00
DMT3 Bautista/Klementieff 100.00 200.00
DMT4 Bautista/Gillan 100.00 200.00
DMT6 Saldana/Klementieff 125.00 250.00
DMT7 Gillan/Klementieff 100.00 200.00
DMT9 Gillan/Flanagan 80.00 150.00

2017 Guardians of the Galaxy Vol. 2 Oversized Art

COMPLETE SET (12) 30.00 75.00
COMMON CARD (OS1-OS12) 3.00 8.00
STATED ODDS 1:1

2017 Guardians of the Galaxy Vol. 2 Space Ships

COMPLETE SET (7) 10.00 25.00
COMMON CARD (SS1-SS7) 2.00 5.00
STATED ODDS 1:3

2017 Guardians of the Galaxy Vol. 2 AMC Promos

COMPLETE SET (10) 12.00 30.00
COMMON CARD (UNNUMBERED) 1.25 3.00
AMC THEATER EXCLUSIVES
NNO Baby Groot 2.50 6.00
NNO Drax 2.00 5.00
NNO Ego CL 2.50 6.00
NNO Gamora 2.00 5.00
NNO Mantis 1.50 4.00
NNO Star-Lord 2.50 6.00
NNO Yondu 1.50 4.00

2017 Guardians of the Galaxy Vol. 2 Dog Tags

COMPLETE SET W/O FOIL (24) 50.00 100.00
COMPLETE SET W/FOIL (48) 120.00 250.00
UNOPENED BOX (24 PACKS)
UNOPENED PACK (1 TAG+1 STICKER)
COMMON CARD (1-24) 2.00 5.00
COMMON FOIL SP (25-48) 3.00 8.00

2017 Guardians of the Galaxy Vol. 2 Dog Tags 3-D Tags

COMPLETE SET (4) 15.00 40.00
COMMON CARD 5.00 12.00
STATED ODDS 1:

2017 Guardians of the Galaxy Vol. 2 Dog Tags Stickers

COMPLETE SET (24) 6.00 15.00
COMMON CARD (1-24) .40 1.00
*FOIL: 1X TO 2.5X BASIC CARDS
STATED ODDS 1:1

2017 Guardians of the Galaxy Vol. 2 German

COMPLETE SET (125) 8.00 20.00
UNOPENED BOX (24 PACKS) 25.00 40.00
UNOPENED PACK (6 CARDS) 1.50 1.75
COMMON CARD (1-125) .15 .40

2017 Guardians of the Galaxy Vol. 2 Walmart Exclusives

COMPLETE SET (50) 6.00 15.00
UNOPENED BOX (10 PACKS)
UNOPENED PACK (4 CARDS) 4.00 5.00
COMMON CARD (WP1-WP50) .20 .50
*BLUE FOIL: 1.25X TO 3X BASIC CARDS 1.25 3.00
*RED FOIL: 2X TO 5X BASIC CARDS 4.00 10.00

2017 Guardians of the Galaxy Vol. 2 Walmart Exclusives Character Die-Cuts

COMPLETE SET (10) 12.00 30.00
COMMON CARD (DC1-DC10) 1.50 4.00
RANDOMLY INSERTED INTO PACKS

2017 Guardians of the Galaxy Vol. 2 Walmart Exclusives Chrome Cuts

COMMON CARD (CC1-CC10) 10.00 20.00
RANDOMLY INSERTED INTO PACKS

2017 Guardians of the Galaxy Vol. 2 Walmart Exclusives Silver Comic Characters

COMMON CARD (CO1-CO15) 6.00 15.00
RANDOMLY INSERTED INTO PACKS
CO9 Thanos 8.00 20.00

2017 Guardians of the Galaxy Vol. 2 Walmart Exclusives Throwback Memorabilia

COMMON MEM (RT1-RT10) 5.00 12.00
STATED ODDS 1:8
RT2 Gamora 12.00 30.00
RT3 Drax 8.00 20.00
RT6 Star-Lord 6.00 15.00
RT7 Gamora 12.00 30.00
RT8 Drax 8.00 20.00

2008 Incredible Hulk Previews

COMPLETE SET (6) 6.00 15.00
COMMON CARD (H1-H6) 2.00 5.00
STATED PRINT RUN 999 SER. #'d SETS

2008 Incredible Hulk Movie Expansion

CL Incredible Hulk Header/Checklist 2.50 6.00
CC1 Bruce Banner MEM 12.00 30.00
CC2 Betty Ross MEM 12.00 30.00
CC3 Emil Blonsky MEM 8.00 20.00
CC4 Samuel Sterns MEM 10.00 25.00
CC5 Leonard MEM 10.00 25.00
CC6 General Ross MEM 6.00 15.00
EN1 Edward Norton AU 120.00 250.00
EN2 Edward Norton/HulkAU 3SI 150.00 300.00
LF1 Lou Ferrigno AU 30.00 80.00
LF2 Lou Ferrigno/Hulk AU 3SI 100.00 200.00

2008 Iron Man

COMPLETE SET (70) 4.00 10.00
UNOPENED BOX (24 PACKS) 800.00 1200.00
UNOPENED PACK (5 CARDS) 35.00 50.00
COMMON CARD (1-70) .10 .30

2008 Iron Man Armored Hero

COMPLETE SET (9) 6.00 15.00
COMMON CARD (H1-H9) 1.25 3.00
STATED ODDS 1:24

2008 Iron Man Autographs

COMMON AUTO 12.00 30.00
OVERALL AUTO/MEM/SKETCH ODDS 1:12
LEIBER AU ISSUED AS CASE TOPPER 10.00 25.00
1 Clark Gregg 125.00 250.00
3 Jeff Bridges VL 400.00 700.00
4 Jon Favreau 300.00 750.00
5 Larry Lieber CT 15.00 40.00
6A Robert Downey Jr./Tony Stark VL 2500.00 4000.00
6B Robert Downey Jr./Iron Man VL 3000.00 6000.00
8A Terrence Howard 150.00 300.00
(normal signature)
8B Terrence Howard
(backward signature)

2008 Iron Man Casting Call

COMPLETE SET (9) 6.00 15.00
COMMON CARD (CC1-CC9) .75 2.00
STATED ODDS 1:12
CC1 Robert Downey Jr. 2.00 5.00
CC2 Terrence Howard 1.25 3.00
CC3 Jeff Bridges 1.50 4.00
CC4 Gwyneth Paltrow 1.50 4.00
CC8 Clark Gregg 1.25 3.00

2008 Iron Man Costumes

COMMON CARD 3.00 8.00
OVERALL AUTO/MEM/SKETCH ODDS 1:12
ARMOR PROPS ISSUED AS 2-CASE INCENTIVES
L (LIMITED): 300-500 COPIES
VL (VERY LIMITED): 200-300 COPIES
UNNUMBERED SET LISTED ALPHABETICALLY
NNO Iron Man Mark I 2CI 75.00 150.00
NNO Iron Man Mark III 2CI 200.00 350.00
NNO Iron Monger 2CI 300.00 500.00
NNO Obadiah Stane/Tie VL 30.00 60.00
NNO Pepper Potts/Bustier L 12.00 30.00
NNO Pepper Potts/Jacket 10.00 25.00
NNO Pepper Potts/Skirt 10.00 25.00
NNO Tony Stark/Jacket 8.00 20.00
NNO Tony Stark/Pants 8.00 20.00
NNO Tony Stark 8.00 20.00
Shirt

2008 Iron Man Iron Man Archives

COMPLETE SET (9) 6.00 15.00
COMMON CARD (AR1-AR9) 1.25 3.00
STATED ODDS 1:8

2008 Iron Man Promos

COMPLETE SET (3) 4.00 10.00
COMMON CARD (P1-P3) .75 2.00
P3 Iron Man ALB 3.00 8.00

2010 Iron Man 2

COMPLETE SET (75) 6.00 15.00
UNOPENED BOX (24 PACKS) 350.00 500.00
UNOPENED PACK (7 CARDS) 15.00 20.00
COMMON CARD (1-75) .15 .40

2010 Iron Man 2 Actor Gallery Die-Cuts

COMPLETE SET (9) 8.00 20.00
COMMON CARD (AH1-AH9) 1.25 3.00
RANDOMLY INSERTED INTO PACKS
AH1 Tony Stark 2.00 5.00
AH2 Pepper Potts 2.50 6.00
AH3 Jim Rhodey Rhodes 1.50 4.00
AH4 Natasha Romanoff 2.50 6.00
AH7 Nick Fury 1.50 4.00

2010 Iron Man 2 Armored

COMPLETE SET (9) 8.00 20.00
COMMON CARD (AC1-AC9) 1.50 4.00
AC2 Iron Man Mark V 3.00 8.00
AC7 Black Widow 2.00 5.00

2010 Iron Man 2 Autographs

COMMON AUTO (A1-A4) 20.00 50.00
AUTO/MEM/SKETCH ODDS 3:BOX
A1 Jon Favreau 150.00 400.00
A2 Mickey Rourke 100.00 250.00
A4 Don Cheadle 50.00 100.00

2010 Iron Man 2 Classic Covers

COMPLETE SET (9) 5.00 12.00
COMMON CARD (CC1-CC9) .75 2.00

2010 Iron Man 2 Memorabilia

COMPLETE SET W/O SP (11) 150.00 200.00
COMMON CARD 6.00 15.00
AUTO/MEM/SKETCH ODDS 3 PER BOX
IMC1 Tony Stark 10.00 25.00
IMC3 Natasha Romanoff 20.00 50.00
IMC4 Natasha Romanoff 20.00 50.00
IMC5 Pepper Potts 12.00 30.00
IMC9 Tony Stark 8.00 20.00
IMC12 Armored Card SP 350.00 500.00

2013 Iron Man 3

COMPLETE SET (60) 6.00 15.00
UNOPENED HOBBY BOX (24 PACKS) 200.00 300.00
UNOPENED HOBBY PACK (5 CARDS) 8.00 12.00
UNOPENED RETAIL BOX (36 PACKS)
UNOPENED RETAIL PACK (5 CARDS)
COMMON CARD (1-60) .20 .50
*FOIL: .8X TO 2X BASIC CARDS

2013 Iron Man 3 Actor Autographs

COMMON CARD 12.00 30.00
STATED ODDS 1:144 H, 1:14,400 R
FA Jon Favreau 15.00 40.00
JF Jon Favreau 15.00 40.00
RH Rebecca Hall 75.00 200.00
SA William Sadler 15.00 40.00
SB Shane Black 12.00 30.00
WS William Sadler 15.00 40.00

2013 Iron Man 3 Comic Artist Autographs

COMMON CARD 8.00 20.00
STATED ODDS 1:144 H, 1:14,400 R
IM3AG Adi Granov 15.00 40.00
IM3DA David Michelinie 30.00 60.00
IM3DM David Michelinie 30.00 60.00
IM3HO Kevin Hopgood 15.00 40.00
IM3LE Stan Lee 300.00 800.00
IM3LK Len Kaminski 20.00 50.00
IM3MD David Michelinie 30.00 60.00
IM3MG Manuel Garcia 20.00 50.00
IM3MI David Michelinie 30.00 60.00
IM3ML David Michelinie 30.00 60.00
IM3SG Manuel Garcia 20.00 50.00
IM3SL Stan Lee 300.00 800.00

2013 Iron Man 3 Hall of Armor

COMPLETE SET (22) 175.00 300.00
COMMON CARD (HOA1-HOA22) 8.00 20.00
STATED ODDS 1:36

2013 Iron Man 3 Heroic Threads

COMMON CARD (HT1-HT12) 6.00 15.00
OVERALL THREADS ODDS 1:12
HT1 Tony Stark 8.00 20.00
HT2 Tony Stark 8.00 20.00
HT3 Savin 15.00 40.00
HT4 Rhodey Rhodes 8.00 20.00
HT5 Rhodey Rhodes 8.00 20.00
HT6 Pepper Potts 25.00 60.00
HT7 Maya Hansen 25.00 60.00
HT9 Killian 8.00 20.00
HT10 Happy Hogan 8.00 20.00
HTP1 Tony Stark PATCH

2013 Iron Man 3 Heroic Threads Autographs

COMMON CARD (HTA2-HTA3) 30.00 75.00
HTA2 Maya Hansen 100.00 200.00

2013 Iron Man 3 Heroic Threads Dual

COMMON CARD (HTD1-HTD16) 8.00 20.00
OVERALL THREADS ODDS 1:12
HTD2 Rhodes/Stark 12.00 30.00
HTD3 Stark/Potts 15.00 40.00
HTD4 Stark/Hansen 12.00 30.00
HTD5 Mandarin/Stark 10.00 25.00
HTD6 Stark/Killian 12.00 30.00
HTD7 Hogan/Stark 10.00 25.00
HTD8 Rhodes/Mandarin 10.00 25.00
HTD9 Killian/Rhodes 12.00 30.00
HTD10 Potts/Hansen 10.00 25.00
HTD12 Killian/Mandarin 30.00 60.00
HTD13 Savin/Killian 10.00 25.00
HTD14 Killian/Potts 12.00 30.00
HTD15 Hogan/Savin 10.00 25.00

2013 Iron Man 3 Heroic Threads Quad

COMMON CARD (HTQ1-HTQ5) 8.00 20.00
OVERALL THREADS ODDS 1:12
HTQ3 Rhodes/Stark/Potts/Hogan 10.00 25.00
HTQ4 Killian/Hansen/Potts/Stark 12.00 30.00
HTQ5 Stark/Potts/Rhodes/Killian 12.00 30.00

2013 Iron Man 3 Heroic Threads Triple

COMMON CARD (HTT1-HTT15)	8.00	20.00
OVERALL THREADS ODDS 1:12		
HTT5 Rhodes/Stark/Hogan	12.00	30.00
HTT6 Stark/Potts/Rhodes	12.00	30.00
HTT7 Stark/Potts/Hogan	20.00	50.00
HTT8 Hansen/Stark/Potts	30.00	60.00
HTT9 Hansen/Stark/Killian	20.00	50.00
HTT11 Hansen/Potts/Killian	30.00	60.00
HTT14 Hogan/Potts/Rhodes	10.00	25.00
HTT15 Hogan/Potts/Killian	15.00	40.00

2013 Iron Man 3 Stickers

COMPLETE SET (50)	15.00	40.00
COMMON CARD (IM31-IM350)	.75	2.00
RANDOMLY INSERTED INTO PACKS		

2019 Marvel Studios The First Ten Years

COMPLETE SET W/SP (150)	75.00	150.00
COMPLETE SET W/O SP (100)	10.00	25.00
UNOPENED BOX (15 PACKS)	200.00	350.00
UNOPENED PACK (5 CARDS)	20.00	30.00
COMMON CARD (1-100)	.20	.50
COMMON SP (101-150)	1.50	4.00

2019 Marvel Studios The First Ten Years Autographed Film Cels

GROUP A ODDS 1:7,344		
GROUP B ODDS 1:3,672		
GROUP C ODDS 1:525		
STATED OVERALL ODDS 1:432		
FCACH Chris Hemsworth A		
FCACS Cobie Smulders C	150.00	300.00
FCAJB Josh Brolin B	500.00	700.00
FCAJR Jeremy Renner C	150.00	300.00

2019 Marvel Studios The First Ten Years Eclectic Collection Autographed Memorabilia

ECTH Tom Holland

2019 Marvel Studios The First Ten Years Eclectic Collection Relics

COMMON CARD (EC1-EC35)	5.00	12.00
COMMON SP (EC36-EC45)	12.00	30.00
BASE ODDS 1:30		
SP ODDS 1:288		
RANDOMLY INSERTED INTO PACKS		
EC1 Ant-Man/Fabric	10.00	25.00
EC2 Bruce Banner/Suit	8.00	20.00
EC3 Black Panther/Fabric	15.00	40.00
EC4 Black Widow/Jacket	25.00	60.00
EC5 Bucky Barnes/Jacket	6.00	15.00
EC6 Captain America/Fabric	20.00	50.00
EC7 Thor/Cape	15.00	40.00
EC8 Doctor Strange/Fabric	25.00	60.00
EC11 Gamora/Fabric	15.00	40.00
EC12 Valkyrie/Fabric	10.00	25.00
EC13 Grandmaster/Robe	6.00	15.00
EC14 Shuri/Vest	6.00	15.00
EC15 Hawkeye/Coat	10.00	25.00
EC16 Heimdall/Skirt	6.00	15.00
EC17 Hela/Fabric	15.00	40.00
EC18 Wasp/Suit	6.00	15.00
EC19 Iron Man/Jersey	12.00	30.00
EC20 Yondu/Fabric	10.00	25.00
EC21 Rocket/Fabric	8.00	20.00
EC24 Loki/Pants	15.00	40.00
EC25 Mandarin/Robe	8.00	20.00
EC26 Nova Corps/Fabric	6.00	15.00
EC27 Pepper Potts/Fabric	20.00	50.00
EC28 Nebula/Fabric	8.00	20.00
EC29 Ancient One/Silk	6.00	15.00
EC30 Quicksilver/Top	6.00	15.00
EC31 Rhodey/Fabric	8.00	20.00
EC33 Scarlet Witch/Shirt	15.00	40.00
EC34 Spider-Man/Fabric	25.00	60.00
EC35 Star-Lord/Flight Suit	15.00	40.00
EC36 Iron Man/Vest SP	50.00	100.00
EC37 Ant-Man/Fabric SP	25.00	60.00
EC38 Black Panther/Tunic SP		
EC41 Captain America/Collar SP	50.00	100.00
EC42 Mantis/Fabric SP	15.00	40.00
EC43 Odin/Fabric SP	15.00	40.00
EC44 Thor/Fabric SP	30.00	75.00
EC45 Black Widow/Fabric SP	30.00	75.00

2019 Marvel Studios The First Ten Years Film Cels

COMMON MEM (FC1-FC20)	5.00	12.00
COMMON SP (FC21-FC28)	8.00	20.00
COMMON SP (FC29-FC33)	8.00	20.00
BASE ODDS 1:20		
SP (FC21-FC28) ODDS 1:72		
SP (FC29-FC33) ODDS 1:360		
RANDOMLY INSERTED INTO PACKS		
FC1 Tony Stark	10.00	25.00
FC2 Iron Man	10.00	25.00
FC3 Thor	8.00	20.00
FC4 Steve Rogers	12.00	30.00
FC5 Loki	10.00	25.00
FC7 Jane Foster	8.00	20.00
FC8 The Winter Soldier	12.00	30.00
FC11 Ant-Man	6.00	15.00
FC13 Doctor Strange	10.00	25.00
FC15 Grandmaster	6.00	15.00
FC16 Black Panther	8.00	20.00
FC17 Thanos	12.00	30.00
FC18 Captain America	15.00	40.00
FC19 Iron Man	10.00	25.00
FC20 Wasp	6.00	15.00
FC22 Odin SP	12.00	30.00
FC25 Drax SP	10.00	25.00
FC26 Yellowjacket SP	10.00	25.00
FC28 Killmonger SP	12.00	30.00
FC30 Whiplash SP	12.00	30.00
FC32 Vision SP	15.00	40.00
FC33 Black Widow SP	20.00	50.00

2019 Marvel Studios The First Ten Years Legendary Scripts Autographs

COMMON AUTO	12.00	30.00
GROUP A ODDS 1:3,008		
GROUP B ODDS 1:412		
GROUP C ODDS 1:120		
STATED OVERALL ODDS 1:90		
LSAH Cobie Smulders C	75.00	150.00
LSCA Chris Evans B	350.00	500.00
LSCH Chris Hemsworth A	500.00	700.00
LSCS Cobie Smulders C	75.00	150.00
LSHE Jeremy Renner C	50.00	100.00
LSHK Jeremy Renner B	75.00	150.00
LSJB Josh Brolin A	400.00	800.00
LSJR Jeremy Renner B	75.00	150.00
LSKG Karen Gillan C	75.00	150.00
LSMH Cobie Smulders B	100.00	200.00
LSRJ Jeremy Renner B	75.00	150.00
LSTH Tom Holland A	1000.00	1500.00
LSTO Chris Hemsworth A	500.00	700.00

2019 Marvel Studios The First Ten Years The Marvel Cinematic Universe

COMPLETE SET (32)	15.00	40.00
COMMON CARD (TU1-TU32)	1.00	2.50
STATED ODDS 1:5		
TU1 Captain America	2.00	5.00
TU3 Iron Man	2.00	5.00
TU4 Hulk	1.25	3.00
TU5 Black Widow	1.25	3.00
TU6 Black Panther	1.25	3.00
TU8 Thor	1.50	4.00
TU10 Groot	1.25	3.00
TU15 Doctor Strange	1.50	4.00
TU21 Spider-Man	2.50	6.00
TU22 Ant-Man	1.25	3.00
TU27 Hawkeye	1.25	3.00

2019 Marvel Studios The First Ten Years Roman Numerals

COMPLETE SET (90)		
COMMON RN I (RN1-RN9)	.75	2.00
COMMON RN II (RN10-RN18)	1.25	3.00
COMMON RN III (RN19-RN27)	1.50	4.00
COMMON RN IV (RN28-RN36)	2.00	5.00
COMMON RN V (RN37-RN45)	2.50	6.00
COMMON RN VI (RN46-RN54)	3.00	8.00
COMMON RN VII (RN55-RN63)	3.00	8.00
COMMON RN VIII (RN64-RN72)	4.00	10.00
COMMON RN IX (RN73-RN81)	4.00	10.00
COMMON RN X (RN82-RN90)		
STATED RN I ODDS 1:18		
STATED RN II ODDS 1:21		
STATED RN III ODDS 1:24		
STATED RN IV ODDS 1:30		
STATED RN V ODDS 1:36		
STATED RN VI ODDS 1:48		
STATED RN VII ODDS 1:64		
STATED RN VIII ODDS 1:90		
STATED RN IX ODDS 1:120		
STATED RN X ODDS 1:208		
RN1 Tony Stark	2.00	5.00
RN2 Iron Man	2.50	6.00
RN3 Mark 1	1.50	4.00
RN6 Agent Coulson	1.25	3.00
RN10 Iron Man	2.50	6.00
RN13 Natasha Romanova	2.00	5.00
RN16 Nick	1.50	4.00
RN18 Pepper Potts	1.50	4.00
RN19 Thor	2.00	5.00
RN20 Loki	3.00	8.00
RN21 Heimdall	2.50	6.00
RN23 Steve Rogers	4.00	10.00
RN24 Red Skull	5.00	12.00
RN27 Bucky Barnes	3.00	8.00
RN28 Tony Stark	6.00	15.00
RN29 Captain America	5.00	12.00
RN30 Bruce Banner	4.00	10.00
RN32 Thor	5.00	12.00
RN33 Black Widow	4.00	10.00
RN34 Hawkeye	6.00	15.00
RN36 Loki	6.00	15.00
RN37 Iron Man	3.00	8.00
RN38 Pepper Potts	4.00	10.00
RN39 Iron Patriot	3.00	8.00
RN42 Thor	4.00	10.00
RN45 Loki	4.00	10.00
RN46 The Winter Soldier	5.00	12.00
RN51 Gamora	6.00	15.00
RN54 Rocket	8.00	20.00
RN55 Quicksilver	6.00	15.00
RN60 Hope Van Dyne	8.00	20.00
RN61 Yellowjacket	4.00	10.00
RN63 Scott Lang	8.00	20.00
RN64 T'Challa	6.00	15.00
RN65 Thunderbolt Ross	5.00	12.00
RN66 Spider-Man	10.00	25.00
RN68 Doctor Stephen Strange	6.00	15.00
RN70 Ancient One	5.00	12.00
RN71 Mordo	5.00	12.00
RN73 Baby Groot	8.00	20.00
RN77 Hela	8.00	20.00
RN78 Odin	10.00	25.00
RN79 Grandmaster	10.00	25.00
RN80 Valkyrie	8.00	20.00
RN81 Hulk	6.00	15.00
RN82 Black Panther	6.00	15.00
RN84 Shuri	10.00	25.00
RN86 Eitri	12.00	30.00
RN87 Wasp	8.00	20.00
RN88 Killmonger	12.00	30.00
RN89 Thanos	15.00	40.00
RN90 Ghost	8.00	20.00

2019 Marvel Studios The First Ten Years Story of the MCU

COMPLETE SET (16)	10.00	25.00
COMMON CARD (MCU1-MCU16)	1.25	3.00
STATED ODDS 1:8		

2018 Marvel Studios The First Ten Years SDCC Promos

COMPLETE SET (18)	15.00	40.00
COMMON CARD (1-18)	2.00	5.00
STATED PRINT RUN 500 SETS		

2022 Upper Deck Marvel Studios SDCC Special Edition Set

COMPLETE FACTORY SET (16)	20.00	50.00
COMPLETE SET (15)	10.00	25.00
COMMON CARD (1-15)	1.25	3.00
*FOIL: 3X TO 8X BASIC CARDS		
3 T'Challa Star-Lord	3.00	8.00
6 Zombie Captain America	2.00	5.00
8 Post-Apocalyptic Black Widow	1.50	4.00
11 Hailee Steinfeld as Kate Bishop	3.00	8.00
12 Florence Pugh as Yelena Belova	2.50	6.00
14 Oscar Isaac as Moon Knight	3.00	8.00
15 Oscar Isaac as Mr. Knight	4.00	10.00

2022 Upper Deck Marvel Studios SDCC Special Edition Set Rainbow Foil

COMPLETE SET (15)		
*FOIL: 3X TO 8X BASIC CARDS		
STATED ODDS 1:SET		
3 T'Challa Star-Lord	25.00	60.00
6 Zombie Captain America	15.00	40.00
8 Post-Apocalyptic Black Widow	12.00	30.00
11 Hailee Steinfeld as Kate Bishop	25.00	60.00
12 Florence Pugh as Yelena Belova	20.00	50.00
14 Oscar Isaac as Moon Knight	25.00	60.00
15 Oscar Isaac as Mr. Knight	30.00	75.00

2020 Upper Deck Marvel's Runaways Staff of One Autographs

COMMON AUTO	5.00	12.00
STATED ODDS 1:3		
SOOAW Annie Wersching	20.00	50.00
SOOGS Gregg Sulkin	6.00	15.00
SOOLO Lyrica Okano	8.00	20.00

2020 Upper Deck Marvel's Runaways Number 1 Photo Variant Autographs

STATED PRINT RUN 50 SER.#'d SETS		
R1AB Ariela Barer		
R1AP Angel Parker		
R1AW Annie Wersching		
R1BB Brigid Brannagh		
R1BI Brittany Ishibashi		
R1GS Gregg Sulkin	10.00	25.00
R1JY James Yaegashi		
R1KW Kevin Weisman		
R1LO Lyrica Okano	15.00	40.00
R1RS Ryan Sands		
R1VG Virginia Gardner	40.00	100.00

2020 Upper Deck Marvel's Runaways Wanted Autographs

COMMON AUTO	5.00	12.00
STATED ODDS 1:3		
WDC Danielle Campbell	12.00	30.00
WLO Lyrica Okano	10.00	25.00

2020 Upper Deck The Punisher Season 1

COMPLETE SET (100)	10.00	25.00
UNOPENED BOX (15 PACKS)	100.00	150.00
UNOPENED PACK (8 CARDS)	10.00	15.00
COMMON CARD (1-100)	.15	.40
*A.ORANGE (1-50): 2X TO 5X BASIC CARDS		
*A.ORANGE (51-85): 5X TO 12X BASIC CARDS		
*A.ORANGE (86-100): 20X TO 50X BASIC CARDS		

2020 Upper Deck The Punisher Season 1 Castle Crash Course

COMPLETE SET (17)	10.00	25.00
COMMON CARD (CC1-CC17)	1.25	3.00
STATED ODDS 1:9 HOBBY/ePACK		

2020 Upper Deck The Punisher Season 1 Cerberus

COMPLETE SET (10)	6.00	15.00

COMMON CARD (C1-C10) 1.25 3.00
STATED ODDS 1:8 HOBBY/ePACK

2020 Upper Deck The Punisher Season 1 Episodic Art

COMPLETE SET (14) 12.00 30.00
COMMON CARD (EA1-EA14) 1.50 4.00
STATED ODDS 1:11 HOBBY/ePACKS

2020 Upper Deck The Punisher Season 1 For the Corps Autographs

COMMON AUTO 8.00 20.00
GROUP A 1:1,471
GROUP B 1:892
GROUP C 1:213
GROUP D 1:31
STATED ODDS 1:26 HOBBY/ePACK
FTCEM Ebon Moss-Bachrach C 20.00 50.00
FTCJB Jon Bernthal B 100.00 200.00
FTCJN Jaime Ray Newman D 20.00 50.00
FTCKF Kobi Frumer D 10.00 25.00
FTCME Ebon Moss-Bachrach C 20.00 50.00
FTCMN Michael Nathanson D 10.00 25.00
FTCPR Jon Bernthal A 100.00 200.00
FTCTP Tony Plana
(E-Pack Achievement)

2020 Upper Deck The Punisher Season 1 For the Corps Dual Autographs

COMMON AUTO
STATED ODDS 1:460 HOBBY/ePACK
FTCEJ Ebon Moss-Bachrach/Jaime Ray Newman
(E-Pack Achievement)
FTCFW Paul Schulze/Jon Bernthal
FTCJE Jon Bernthal/Ebon Moss-Bachrach
FTCKE Ebon Moss-Bachrach/Kobi Frumer
FTCTN Tony Plana/Michael Nathanson
(E-Pack Achievement)

2020 Upper Deck The Punisher Season 1 For the Corps Plexiglass Autographs

COMMON AUTO
STATED PRINT RUN 50 SER.#'d SETS
FTPEM Ebon Moss-Bachrach
FTPJB Jon Bernthal
FTPJM Jordan Mahome
FTPKF Kobi Frumer
FTPME Ebon Moss-Bachrach
FTPMN Michael Nathanson
FTPPS Paul Schulze
FTPRH Rick Holmes
FTPSS Michael Nathanson
FTPTP Tony Plana
(E-Pack Achievement)

2020 Upper Deck The Punisher Season 1 For the Corps Variant Autographs

GROUP A 1:9,984
GROUP B 1:4,279
GROUP C(a) 1:632
GROUP C(b) 1:444
STATED ODDS 1:240 HOBBY/ePACK
FCVEM Ebon Moss-Bachrach C 8.00 20.00
FCVJB Jon Bernthal A
FCVJM Jordan Mahome C 10.00 25.00
FCVJR Jaime Ray Newman C 30.00 75.00
FCVKF Kobi Frumer B
FCVMN Michael Nathanson C 12.00 30.00
FCVPS Paul Schulze C 20.00 50.00
FCVRH Rick Holmes C
FCVTP Tony Plana 15.00 40.00
(E-Pack Achievement)

2020 Upper Deck The Punisher Season 1 Gun Metal Grey

COMMON CARD 10.00 25.00
COMMON SP (GG9-GG13) 15.00 40.00
COMMON SP (GG14-GG15)
STATED ODDS (GG1-GG8) 1:90
STATED ODDS (GG9-GG13) 1:210
STATED ODDS (GG14-GG15) 1:1,080

2020 Upper Deck The Punisher Season 1 Memento Mori

COMPLETE SET (10) 6.00 15.00
COMMON CARD (MM1-MM10) 1.25 3.00
STATED ODDS 1:8

2020 Upper Deck The Punisher Season 1 Micro Tech

COMPLETE SET (12) 8.00 20.00
COMMON CARD (MT1-MT12) 1.00 2.50
STATED ODDS 1:6 HOBBY/ePACK

2020 Upper Deck The Punisher Season 1 Patch-Work

STATED ODDS 1:75 HOBBY/ePACK
PW1 Frank Castle 8.00 20.00
PW2 Punisher
PW3 Billy Russo
PW4 David Lieberman 4.00 10.00
PW5 Lewis Wilson 6.00 15.00
PW6 Curtis Hoyle 8.00 20.00
PW7 Sam Stein 6.00 15.00
PW8 Karen Page
PW9 Dinah Madani 8.00 20.00
PW10 Ray Schoonover 10.00 25.00
PW11 Brett Mahoney 10.00 25.00
PW12 Carson Wolf

2020 Upper Deck The Punisher Season 1 Patch-Work Autographs

COMMON AUTO
STATED PRINT RUN 10 SER.#'d SETS
PWEM Ebon Moss-Bachrach
PWJB Jon Bernthal
PWPS Paul Schulze
PWRH Rick Holmes
PWTP Tony Plana

2020 Upper Deck The Punisher Season 1 Patch-Work Puzzles

COMMON MEM (PWP1-PWP15) 5.00 12.00
STATED ODDS 1:20 HOBBY/ePACK
PWP1 Frank Castle 12.00 30.00
PWP2 Gunner Henderson 6.00 15.00
PWP3 Billy Russo 8.00 20.00
PWP5 Ray Schoonover 6.00 15.00
PWP7 Micro 6.00 15.00
PWP8 Dinah Madani 10.00 25.00
PWP11 Lewis Wilson 8.00 20.00
PWP13 Karen Page 6.00 15.00

2020 Upper Deck The Punisher Season 1 Spec Ops

COMPLETE SET (5) 8.00 20.00
COMMON CARD (SO1-SO5) 2.50 6.00
STATED ODDS 1:30 HOBBY/ePack
SO1 Kandahar 2.50 6.00
SO2 Resupply 2.50 6.00
SO3 Crosshairs 2.50 6.00
SO4 Fron Toward Enemy 2.50 6.00
SO5 Danger Close 2.50 6.00

2017 Spider-Man Homecoming

COMPLETE SET (100) 10.00 25.00
UNOPENED BOX (10 PACKS) 100.00 150.00
UNOPENED PACK (8 CARDS) 10.00 15.00
COMMON CARD (1-100) .25 .60
*SILVER: 1.2X TO 3X BASIC CARDS
*RED/199: 4X TO 10X BASIC CARDS
*BLUE/99: 6X TO 15X BASIC CARDS
*BLACK/49: 5X TO 12X BASIC CARDS

2017 Spider-Man Homecoming Autographed Booklets

COMMON AUTO (BS1-BS10) 12.00 30.00
STATED OVERALL ODDS 1:10
STATED PRINT RUN 100 SER.#'d SETS
BS1 Michael Chernus 30.00 75.00
BS3 Bokeem Woodbine 30.00 75.00
BS4 Michael Mando 30.00 80.00
BS5 Michael Keaton 300.00 600.00
BS6 Laura Harrier 30.00 75.00
BS7 Jacob Batalon 25.00 60.00
BS9 Angourie Rice 120.00 250.00

2017 Spider-Man Homecoming Behind-the-Lens

COMPLETE SET (7) 8.00 20.00
COMMON CARD (BTL1-BTL7) 1.50 4.00
STATED ODDS 1:8
BTL0 Happy/Peter/Tony and Action!/E-Pack

2017 Spider-Man Homecoming Civil War Images

COMPLETE SET (11) 12.00 30.00
COMMON CARD (CW1-CW11) 2.00 5.00
STATED ODDS 1:8 HOBBY; 1:3 WALMART
CW0 Shield Staring Glare/E-Pack

2017 Spider-Man Homecoming Decathlon

COMPLETE SET (24) 15.00 40.00
COMMON CARD (SD1-SD24) 1.00 2.50
STATED ODDS 1:3 HOBBY; 1:1 WALMART
SD0 Kraven's Last Hunt/E-Pack

2017 Spider-Man Homecoming Friend or Foe

COMPLETE SET (9) 10.00 25.00
COMMON CARD (FF1-FF9) 1.50 4.00
STATED ODDS 1:8
FF0 Tony Stark/E-Pack

2017 Spider-Man Homecoming Queens to Screen Autographs

COMMON CARD (SS1-SS17) 8.00 20.00
GROUP A ODDS 1:155
GROUP B ODDS 1:120
GROUP C ODDS 1:75
GROUP D ODDS 1:21
STATED OVERALL ODDS 1:13
SS1 Bokeem Woodbine A 20.00 50.00
SS2 Michael Chernus C 12.00 30.00
SS3 Logan Marshall-Green C 10.00 25.00
SS4 Laura Harrier D 15.00 40.00
SS5 Jacob Batalon C 10.00 25.00
SS6 Tony Revolori B 10.00 25.00
SS7 Michael Mando B 30.00 75.00
SS8 Hannibal Buress D 12.00 30.00
SS10 Martin Starr A 25.00 60.00
SS11 Abraham Attah D 10.00 25.00
SS13 Garcelle Beauvais D 10.00 25.00
SS15 JJ Totah D 12.00 30.00
SS16 Angourie Rice B 75.00 150.00
SS17 Michael Keaton A 250.00 400.00

2017 Spider-Man Homecoming Queens to Screen Dual Autographs

STATED ODDS 1:960
SSD1 Woodbine/Chernus
SSD2 S.Leyva/A.Attah
SSD3 L.Marshall-Green/M.Chernus 50.00 100.00
SSD4 T.Revolori/J.Batalon
SSD5 M.Keaton/B.Woodbine 600.00 1000.00
SSD6 JJ Totah/A.Attah 15.00 40.00
SSD7 G.Beauvais/L.Harrier
SSD8 K.Choi/M.Starr 60.00 120.00
SSD9 K.Choi/H.Buress 50.00 100.00
SSD10 M.Starr/H.Buress

2017 Spider-Man Homecoming Spider-Men

COMPLETE SET (9) 10.00 25.00
COMMON CARD (SM1-SM9) 1.50 4.00
STATED ODDS 1:8 HOBBY; 1:2 WALMART

2017 Spider-Man Homecoming Spider Tech

COMPLETE SET (7) 8.00 20.00
COMMON CARD (ST1-ST7) 1.50 4.00
STATED ODDS 1:8

2017 Spider-Man Homecoming Webbed Threads Autographed Memorabilia

GROUP A ODDS 1:5,326
GROUP B ODDS 1:165
STATED OVERALL ODDS 1:160
WTA1 Woodbine/Jacket B 20.00 50.00
WTA2 Batalon/Sweatshirt B 12.00 30.00
WTA3 Starr/Blazer B 20.00 50.00
WTA4 Mando/Hoodie B 20.00 50.00
WTA5 Marshall-Green/Cap B

2017 Spider-Man Homecoming Webbed Threads Dual Autographed Memorabilia

GROUP A ODDS 1:12,480
GROUP B ODDS 1:499
STATED OVERALL ODDS 1:480
WTAD1 Starr/Batalon 30.00 75.00
Blazer/Sweatshirt B
WTAD2 B.Woodbine/M.Mando B 75.00 150.00
WTAD3 B.Woodbine/L.Marshall-Green A
WTAD4 J.Batalon/T.Revolori B 15.00 40.00
WTAD5 M.Starr/T.Revolori B 30.00 75.00

2017 Spider-Man Homecoming Webbed Threads Dual Memorabilia

COMMON CARD (WTD1-WTD10) 6.00 15.00
GROUP A ODDS 1:3,736
GROUP B ODDS 1:111
GROUP C ODDS 1:62
GROUP D ODDS 1:41
STATED OVERALL ODDS 1:20
WTD1 Spidey Homemade Hood/Stark Hood D12.00 30.00
WTD2 Liz/Michelle A 125.00 250.00
WTD7 Spidey Homemade/1st Shocker A 60.00 120.00

2017 Spider-Man Homecoming Webbed Threads Memorabilia

GROUP A ODDS 1:4,148
GROUP B ODDS 1:1,131
GROUP C ODDS 1:190
GROUP D ODDS 1:111
GROUP E ODDS 1:12
STATED OVERALL ODDS 1:5
WTS1 Spider-Man Homemade Torso E 6.00 15.00
WTS2 The Second Shocker D 5.00 12.00
WTS3 Spider-Man Stark Torso E 6.00 15.00
WTS4 Ned Leeds C 6.00 15.00
WTS5 Spider-Man Stark Legs E 6.00 15.00
WTS6 Michelle D 20.00 50.00
WTS7 Spider-Man Stark Eyes E 6.00 15.00
WTS8 Mr. Harrington C 5.00 12.00
WTS9 Abraham A 15.00 40.00
WTS10 Spider-Man Stark Torso E 6.00 15.00
WTS11 Liz Allan B 30.00 75.00
WTS12 Flash Thompson C 12.00 30.00
WTS13 Spider-Man Stark Torso E 12.00 30.00
WTS14 Mac Gargan D 8.00 20.00
WTS15 Spider-Man Stark Torso E 10.00 25.00

2017 Spider-Man Homecoming Webbed Threads Quad Memorabilia

GROUP A ODDS 1:1,337
GROUP B ODDS 1:121
GROUP C ODDS 1:131
STATED OVERALL ODDS 1:60
WTQ1 Spidey Homemade Hood
Legs-Mask-Torso C 12.00 30.00
WTQ2 Ned/Liz/Michelle/Mr. Harrington A 75.00 150.00
WTQ3 2nd & 1st Shocker/Gargan/Flash A
WTQ4 Spidey Homemade/Spidey Stark Suit B10.00 25.00
WTQ5 Spidey/Stark Legs/Liz/Michelle A
WTQ6 Spidey Stark/Homemade
Ned/2nd Shocker A 100.00 200.00
WTQ7 Spidey Stark & Red Torso-Legs B 12.00 30.00

2017 Spider-Man Homecoming Webbed Threads Triple Memorabilia

GROUP A ODDS 1:3,756
GROUP B ODDS 1:2,087

GROUP C ODDS 1:963
GROUP D ODDS 1:43
STATED OVERALL ODDS 1:40
WTT1 1st & 2nd Shocker/Mac Gargan A 60.00 120.00
WTT2 Spider-Man Homemade Suit D 10.00 25.00
WTT3 Ned/L.Allan/Michelle A 60.00 120.00
WTT4 Spider-Man Stark Suit D 10.00 25.00
WTT5 Mr. Harrington/Flash/Ned C 25.00 60.00
WTT6 Spider-Man Homemade/Stark Suit D12.00 30.00
WTT7 Ned/Flash/Spider-Man B 75.00 150.00
WTT8 L.Allan/Spider-Man/Michelle B 50.00 100.00

2017 Spider-Man Homecoming Walmart Exclusives

COMPLETE SET (50) 5.00 12.00
UNOPENED PACK (10 CARDS)
COMMON CARD (RB1-RB50) .20 .50
*BLUE: 1X TO 2.5X BASIC CARDS
*RED: 1X TO 2.5X BASIC CARDS

2019 Spider-Man Far from Home

COMPLETE SET (100) 10.00 25.00
UNOPENED BOX (15 PACKS) 125.00 250.00
UNOPENED PACK (5 CARDS) 10.00 15.00
COMMON CARD (1-100) .25 .60

2019 Spider-Man Far from Home Autographed Obsidian Diamond Relics

COMMON AUTO 50.00 100.00
STATED PRINT RUN 25-49 SER.#'d SETS
BDTH UNPRICED DUE TO SCARCITY
BDCS Cobie Smulders/49 150.00 300.00
BDJG Jake Gyllenhaal/49 300.00 600.00
BDPP Tom Holland/25 600.00 1200.00
BDTH Tom Holland/10

2019 Spider-Man Far from Home Behind-the-Lens

COMPLETE SET (10) 6.00 15.00
COMMON CARD (BTL1-BTL10) 1.00 2.50
STATED ODDS 1:3

2019 Spider-Man Far from Home Flash Mob Autographs

COMMON AUTO 15.00 40.00
GROUP A ODDS 1:2,340
GROUP B ODDS 1:691
GROUP C ODDS 1:220
STATED OVERALL ODDS 1:120
FMCS Cobie Smulders C 30.00 75.00
FMGJ Jake Gyllenhaal C 150.00 300.00
FMHT Tom Holland A 600.00 1200.00
FMJG Jake Gyllenhaal A 300.00 500.00
FMMH Cobie Smulders B 60.00 120.00
FMSC Cobie Smulders B 60.00 120.00
FMTH Tom Holland C 300.00 500.00

2019 Spider-Man Far from Home Greetings from Abroad

COMPLETE SET (15) 6.00 15.00
COMMON CARD (GFA1-GFA15) .75 2.00
STATED ODDS 1:3

2019 Spider-Man Far from Home Mysterio

COMPLETE SET W/SP (42)
COMPLETE SET W/O SP (20) 30.00 75.00
COMMON CARD (M1-M20) 2.50 6.00
COMMON SP (M21-M35) 6.00 15.00
COMMON SP (M36-M42) 12.00 30.00
STATED ODDS 1:50
STATED ODDS (M21-M35) 1:180
STATED ODDS (M36-M42) 1:450

2019 Spider-Man Far from Home Mysterious Markings Autographs

COMMON AUTO 15.00 40.00
GROUP A ODDS 1:2,340
GROUP B ODDS 1:751
GROUP C ODDS 1:252
STATED OVERALL ODDS 1:160
MMCS Cobie Smulders C 30.00 75.00
MMGJ Jake Gyllenhaal C 250.00 400.00
MMHT Tom Holland B 300.00 600.00
MMJG Jake Gyllenhaal B 250.00 400.00
MMQB Jake Gyllenhaal A 300.00 600.00
MMSC Cobie Smulders B 75.00 150.00
MMTH Tom Holland A 600.00 1200.00

2019 Spider-Man Far from Home Obsidian Diamond Relics

COMMON MEM (BD1-BD8) 30.00 75.00
STATED ODDS 1:183

2019 Spider-Man Far from Home Primary Elements

COMPLETE SET (5) 5.00 12.00
COMMON CARD (E1-E5) 1.50 4.00
STATED ODDS 1:10

2019 Spider-Man Far from Home Road Trip

COMPLETE SET W/SP (30) 100.00 200.00
COMPLETE SET W/O SP (15) 12.00 30.00
COMMON CARD (RT1-RT15) 1.00 2.50
COMMON SP (RT16-RT25) 6.00 15.00
COMMON SP (RT26-RT30) 12.00 30.00
STATED ODDS 1:25
STATED ODDS (RT16-RT25) 1:45
STATED ODDS (RT26-RT30) 1:180

2019 Spider-Man Far from Home Sights and Sounds

COMPLETE SET (5) 8.00 20.00
COMMON CARD (SS1-SS5) 2.50 6.00
EPACK ACHIEVEMENT

2019 Spider-Man Far from Home Travel Passports

COMPLETE SET (10) 8.00 20.00
COMMON CARD (PP1-PP10) 1.25 3.00
STATED ODDS 1:3

2011 Thor Movie

COMPLETE SET (81) 6.00 15.00
UNOPENED BOX (24 PACKS) 100.00 150.00
UNOPENED PACK (7 CARDS) 4.00 6.00
COMMON CARD (1-81) .15 .40

2011 Thor Movie Autographs

COMMON AUTO 30.00 75.00
STATED ODDS 1:288 H, 1:2,500 R
CF Colm Feore AVENGERS 60.00 120.00
CH Chris Hemsworth 200.00 400.00
IE Idris Elba AVENGERS 200.00 350.00
JA J.Alexander AVENGERS 150.00 300.00
KD Kat Dennings AVENGERS 150.00 300.00
TH Tom Hiddleston 200.00 400.00

2011 Thor Movie Classic Covers

COMPLETE SET (12) 5.00 12.00
COMMON CARD (T1-T12) .75 2.00
RANDOM INSERT IN PACKS

2011 Thor Movie Concept Art

COMPLETE SET (13) 3.00 8.00
COMMON CARD (C1-C13) .50 1.25
RANDOM INSERT IN PACKS

2011 Thor Movie Film Cels

COMPLETE SET (41) 120.00 250.00
COMMON CARD (M1-M41) 4.00 10.00
STATED ODDS 1:16

2011 Thor Movie Memorabilia

COMMON CARD (F1-F13) 5.00 12.00
STATED ODDS 1:12 H, 1:48 R
F1 Thor 10.00 25.00
F2 Jane Foster 15.00 40.00
F4 Loki 8.00 20.00
F12 Jane Foster 8.00 20.00
F13 Thor 6.00 15.00

2013 Thor The Dark World

COMPLETE SET (100) 8.00 20.00
COMMON CARD (1-100) .20 .50
*AETHER: 8X TO 20X BASIC CARDS 4.00 10.00
*AETHER RED/10: 25X TO 60X BASIC CARDS12.00 30.00

2013 Thor The Dark World Artist Autographs

COMMON CARD 5.00 12.00
OVERALL AUTO/SKETCH ODDS 1:24

2013 Thor The Dark World Dual Artist Autographs

COMMON CARD 8.00 20.00
OVERALL AUTO/SKETCH ODDS 1:24
CASL S.Lee/M.Hebb 200.00 500.00

2013 Thor The Dark World Autographs

COMMON CARD 80.00 150.00
OVERALL AUTO/SKETCH ODDS 1:24
CH Chris Hemsworth 200.00 350.00
JA Jaimie Alexander 100.00 200.00
KD Kat Dennings 150.00 300.00
TH Chris Hemsworth 200.00 350.00
TO Tom Hiddleston 120.00 250.00

2013 Thor The Dark World Dual Autographs

COMMON AUTO 200.00 350.00
OVERALL AUTO/SKETCH ODDS 1:24
AD J.Alexander/K.Dennings 250.00 500.00
HA J.Alexander/C.Hemsworth 250.00 400.00
HH C.Hemsworth/T.Hiddleston 300.00 600.00

2013 Thor The Dark World Dark Materials

COMMON CARD (DM1-DM10) 6.00 15.00
OVERALL MEM ODDS 1:12
DM1 Darcy Lewis 12.00 30.00
DM3 Jane Foster 12.00 30.00
DM4 Loki 8.00 20.00
DM8 Thor 10.00 25.00
DMP1 Jane Foster

2013 Thor The Dark World Dark Materials Autographs

COMMON AU MEM 100.00 200.00
OVERALL AUTO/SKETCH ODDS 1:24
MACH Chris Hemsworth 200.00 400.00
MAKD Kat Dennings 200.00 350.00
MATH Tom Hiddleston 250.00 500.00

2013 Thor The Dark World Dark Materials Dual

COMMON MEM (DMD1-DMD15) 8.00 20.00
OVERALL MEM ODDS 1:12
DMD2 J.Foster/E.Selvig 10.00 25.00
DMD3 J.Foster/Sif 15.00 40.00
DMD4 Thor/D.Lewis 15.00 40.00
DMD5 D.Lewis/E.Selvig 15.00 40.00
DMD6 E.Selvig/Loki 10.00 25.00
DMD7 J.Foster/D.Lewis 15.00 40.00
DMD8 J.Foster/Thor 25.00 60.00
DMD9 Thor/Sif 12.00 30.00
DMD10 Thor/Loki 40.00 80.00
DMD12 Thor/E.Selvig 10.00 25.00
DMD14 J.Foster/Odin 12.00 30.00
DMD15 Sif/D.Lewis 20.00 50.00

2013 Thor The Dark World Dark Materials Quad

COMMON CARD (DMQ1-DMQ4) 50.00 100.00
OVERALL MEM ODDS 1:12
DMQ1 Fost/Odin/Thor/Loki 60.00 120.00
DMQ2 Loki/Fand/Thor/Volst 60.00 120.00
DMQ3 Fost/Lewis/Thor/Sif 60.00 120.00

2013 Thor The Dark World Dark Materials Triple

COMMON MEM (DMT1-DMT8) 15.00 40.00
OVERALL MEM ODDS 1:12
DMT2 Fandral/Volstagg/Sif 40.00 80.00
DMT3 Thor/Odin/Loki 30.00 60.00
DMT4 Thor/Foster/Loki 20.00 50.00

2013 Thor The Dark World Stickers

COMPLETE SET (50) .50 12.00
COMMON CARD (1-50) .20 .50
STATED ODDS 1:2

2018 Thor Ragnarok

COMPLETE SET (50) 8.00 20.00
UNOPENED BOX (15 PACKS) 90.00 110.00
UNOPENED PACK (4 CARDS) 6.00 8.00
COMMON CARD (0-49) .30 .75
*RED LTFX: 1.5X TO 4X BASIC CARDS 2.00 5.00
*BLUE LTFX/199: 2X TO 5X BASIC CARDS3.00 8.00

2018 Thor Ragnarok Armory Autographed Memorabilia

COMMON CARD (ASA1-ASA5) 20.00 50.00
STATED ODDS 1:480 HOBBY/EPACK
ASA1 Chris Hemsworth 200.00 400.00
Cape
ASA3 Tessa Thompson 100.00 200.00
ASA4 Chris Hemsworth 150.00 300.00

2018 Thor Ragnarok Armory Dual Autographed Memorabilia

STATED ODDS 1:1,440 HOBBY/EPACK
ADA1 Chris Hemsworth/Tessa Thompson
Cape-Cape
ADA2 T.Thompson/R.House
ADA3 C.Hemsworth/R.House 150.00 300.00

2018 Thor Ragnarok Armory Dual Memorabilia

COMMON MEM 6.00 15.00
GROUP A ODDS 1:294
GROUP B ODDS 1:147
GROUP C ODDS 1:68
STATED ODDS 1:40 HOBBY/EPACK
AD1 Thor/Loki 12.00 30.00
Cape-Leather C
AD6 Grandmaster/Topaz B 12.00 30.00
AD7 Heimdall/Hela A 10.00 25.00
AD8 Thor/B.Banner B 8.00 20.00
AD9 Grandmaster/Loki B 12.00 30.00

2018 Thor Ragnarok Armory Memorabilia

COMPLETE SET (20) 120.00 250.00
COMMON MEM (AS1-AS20) 6.00 15.00
STATED ODDS 1:16 HOBBY/EPACK
AS1 Thor 12.00 30.00
Cape
AS3 Loki 10.00 25.00
AS5 Loki 10.00 25.00
AS6 Valkyrie 10.00 25.00
AS7 Bruce Banner 8.00 20.00
AS8 Loki 10.00 25.00
AS10 Valkyrie 8.00 20.00
AS12 Loki 10.00 25.00
AS14 Hela 20.00 50.00
AS15 Bruce Banner 10.00 25.00
AS16 Loki 10.00 25.00
AS17 Topaz 8.00 20.00
AS20 Loki 8.00 20.00

2018 Thor Ragnarok Armory Triple Memorabilia

COMMON MEM (AT1-AT5) 8.00 20.00
STATED ODDS 1:80 HOBBY/EPACK
AT1 Thor/Heimdall/Valkyrie 10.00 25.00
Cape-Pants-Body Suit
AT3 Thor/Loki/Hela 15.00 40.00
AT4 Hela/Valkyrie/Topaz 25.00 60.00
AT5 Thor/Banner/Grandmaster 12.00 30.00

2018 Thor Ragnarok Behind-the-Lens

COMPLETE SET (20) 10.00 25.00
COMMON CARD (BTL1-BTL20) 1.50 4.00
STATED ODDS 1:4 HOBBY/EPACK

2018 Thor Ragnarok Dyson Rip

COMMON CARD (D1-D40)	10.00	25.00
STATED ODDS 1:15 HOBBY/EPACK		

2018 Thor Ragnarok Dyson Rip Short Prints

COMMON CARD (DS1-DS10)	12.00	30.00
STATED PRINT RUN 15 SER.#'d SETS		

2018 Thor Ragnarok Grandmaster's Contenders

COMPLETE SET (5)	8.00	20.00
COMMON CARD (GC1-GC5)	2.00	5.00
STATED ODDS 1:30 HOBBY/EPACK		

2018 Thor Ragnarok Grandmaster's Prized Possessions Autographed Chain

COMMON AUTO (GP1-GP5)	30.00	75.00
RANDOMLY INSERTED INTO PACKS		
STATED PRINT RUN 100 SER.#'d SETS		
GP1 Chris Hemsworth	175.00	350.00
GP2 Tessa Thompson	125.00	250.00
GP3 Taika Waititi	60.00	120.00
GP5 Taika Waititi	60.00	120.00

2018 Thor Ragnarok Mini Comics

COMMON CARD (C1-C30)	1.25	3.00
*ACETATE: 1X TO 2.5X BASIC CARDS	3.00	8.00
RANDOMLY INSERTED INTO DYSON RIP		

2018 Thor Ragnarok Mini Comics Actor Autographs

COMMON AUTO (CAA1-CAA5)	15.00	40.00
RANDOMLY INSERTED INTO DYSON RIP		
CAA1 Chris Hemsworth	120.00	250.00
CAA3 Taika Waititi	60.00	120.00
CAA4 Tessa Thompson	60.00	120.00
CAA5 Taika Waititi	30.00	75.00

2018 Thor Ragnarok Mini Comics Creator Autographs

COMMON AUTO	5.00	12.00
*ACETATE: .6X TO 1.5X BASIC AUTOS		
RANDOMLY INSERTED INTO DYSON RIP		
CCA1 Walt Simonson	10.00	25.00
CCA2 Carlo Pagulayan	8.00	20.00
CCA3 Esad Ribic	6.00	15.00
CCA4 Gerry Conway	6.00	15.00
CCA5 Robert Rodi	6.00	15.00
CCA6 Jim Starlin	12.00	30.00
CCA7 Aaron Lopresti	6.00	15.00
CCA9 Chris Samnee	6.00	15.00
CCA11 Gerry Conway	6.00	15.00
CCA13 Ron Garney	6.00	15.00
CCA14 Sal Buscema	6.00	15.00
CCA15 Chris Samnee	8.00	20.00
CCA16 Ron Garney	6.00	15.00
CCA17 Aaron Lopresti	10.00	25.00
CCA18 Gerry Conway	6.00	15.00
CCA20 Robert Rodi	10.00	25.00
CCA21 Esad Ribic	6.00	15.00
CCA23 Michael Avon Oeming	6.00	15.00
CCA24 Sal Buscema	8.00	20.00
CCA25 Jim Starlin	8.00	20.00

2018 Thor Ragnarok Mistress of Death

COMPLETE SET (5)	8.00	20.00
COMMON CARD (MD1-MD5)	2.00	5.00
STATED ODDS 1:30 HOBBY/EPACK		

2018 Thor Ragnarok Stars of Sakaar Autographs

COMMON CARD (SS1-SS8)	20.00	50.00
STATED ODDS 1:120 HOBBY AND EPACK		
SS1 Chris Hemsworth B	150.00	300.00
SS3 Taika Waititi D	30.00	75.00
SS4 Tessa Thompson B	100.00	200.00
SS5 Chris Hemsworth A	250.00	500.00
SS6 Taika Waititi C	50.00	100.00
SS8 Tessa Thompson A	175.00	350.00

2018 Thor Ragnarok Stars of Sakaar Dual Autographs

COMMON CARD (SSD1-SSD6)		
STATED ODDS 1:2,000 HOBBY AND EPACK		
SSD1 Chris Hemsworth/Tessa Thompson	250.00	500.00
SSD2 R.House/T.Waititi	30.00	75.00
SSD3 R.House/T.Thompson	100.00	200.00
SSD4 C.Hemsworth/R.House		
SSD5 T.Waititi/C.Hemsworth	200.00	350.00
SSD6 T.Thompson/T.Waititi	125.00	250.00

2022 Upper Deck WandaVision

COMPLETE SET (90)	15.00	40.00
COMMON CARD (1-90)	.30	.75
*PURPLE SPELL: 1.5X TO 4X BASIC CARDS		
*MIND STONE YELLOW: 2.5X TO 6X BASIC CARDS		
*SCARLET RED: 2.5X TO 6X BASIC CARDS		
*GREEN VISION/225: 4X TO 10X BASIC CARDS		
*WHITE VISION/99: 6X TO 15X BASIC CARDS		

2022 Upper Deck WandaVision Agatha All Along Acetate

COMPLETE SET (10)	100.00	250.00
COMMON CARD (AAA1-AAA10)	15.00	40.00
STATED ODDS 1:180 HOBBY/EPACK		

2022 Upper Deck WandaVision Classic Sitcom Signatures

GROUP A ODDS 1:5,248		
GROUP B ODDS 1:1,687		
GROUP C ODDS 1:945		
GROUP D ODDS 1:430		
STATED ODDS 1:240 HOBBY/EPACK		
CS20EO Elizabeth Olsen B		
CS20EP Evan Peters B		
CS20KH Kathryn Hahn D	125.00	300.00
CS20PB Paul Bettany B	150.00	400.00
CS20RP Randall Park D	75.00	200.00
CS50EO Elizabeth Olsen A		
CS50FH Fred Melamed B		
CS50KD Kat Dennings C	200.00	500.00
CS50KH Kathryn Hahn D	125.00	300.00
CS50PB Paul Bettany B	150.00	400.00
CS60EO Elizabeth Olsen A		
CS60KH Kathryn Hahn D	125.00	300.00
CS60PB Paul Bettany B	150.00	400.00
CS60TP Teyonah Parris B		
CS70EO Elizabeth Olsen A		
CS70KH Kathryn Hahn D	125.00	300.00
CS70PB Paul Bettany B	150.00	400.00
CS70TP Teyonah Parris B		
CS80EO Elizabeth Olsen A		
CS80KD Kat Dennings C	200.00	500.00
CS80KH Kathryn Hahn D	125.00	300.00
CS80RP Randall Park C	75.00	200.00
CS90EO Elizabeth Olsen A		
CS90KD Kat Dennings C	200.00	500.00
CS90KH Kathryn Hahn D	125.00	300.00
CS90PB Paul Bettany B	150.00	400.00
CS60EO2 Elizabeth Olsen A		
CS70PB2 Paul Bettany B	150.00	400.00
CS80KD2 Kat Dennings C	200.00	500.00

2022 Upper Deck WandaVision One Lifetime or Another Autographed Film Cels

GROUP A ODDS 1:11,174		
GROUP B ODDS 1:5,587		
GROUP C ODDS 1:2,483		
GROUP D ODDS 1:1,126		
GROUP E ODDS 1:383		
STATED ODDS 1:240 HOBBY/EPACK		
FCAEO Elizabeth Olsen B	600.00	1500.00
FCAEP Evan Peters E	150.00	400.00
FCAFM Fred Melamed E	12.00	30.00
FCAKH Kathryn Hahn C	100.00	250.00
FCAPB Paul Bettany A		
FCARP Randall Park C		
FCATP Teyonah Parris D	125.00	300.00
FCADJR Debra Jo Rupp E	25.00	60.00
FCAEO2 Elizabeth Olsen B	600.00	1500.00
FCAPB2 Paul Bettany A		
FCATP2 Teyonah Parris D	125.00	300.00
FCADJR2 Debra Jo Rupp E	25.00	60.00

2022 Upper Deck WandaVision One Lifetime or Another Film Cels 1950s

COMMON CARD	4.00	10.00
STATED ODDS 1:60 HOBBY/EPACK		
19501 Elizabeth Olsen as Wanda Maximoff	20.00	50.00
19502 Paul Bettany as Vision	12.00	30.00
19503 Kathryn Hahn as Agnes	6.00	15.00
19504 Debra Jo Rupp as Mrs. Hart	5.00	12.00
19506 Kat Dennings as Darcy Lewis	8.00	20.00

2022 Upper Deck WandaVision One Lifetime or Another Film Cels 1960s

COMMON CARD	5.00	12.00
STATED ODDS 1:60 HOBBY/EPACK		
STATED ODDS 1:180 BLASTER		
19602 Paul Bettany as Vision	12.00	30.00
19603 Kathryn Hahn as Agnes	6.00	15.00
19604 Teyonah Parris as Geraldine	6.00	15.00
19605 Elizabeth Olsen as Wanda Maximoff	20.00	50.00
19606 Paul Bettany as Vision	12.00	30.00

2022 Upper Deck WandaVision One Lifetime or Another Film Cels 1970s

COMMON CARD	6.00	15.00
STATED ODDS 1:60 HOBBY/EPACK		
STATED ODDS 1:180 BLASTER		
19701 Elizabeth Olsen as Wanda Maximoff	20.00	50.00
19702 Paul Bettany as Vision	12.00	30.00
19705 Elizabeth Olsen as Wanda Maximoff	20.00	50.00

2022 Upper Deck WandaVision One Lifetime or Another Film Cels 1980s

COMMON CARD	4.00	10.00
STATED ODDS 1:60 HOBBY/EPACK		
STATED ODDS 1:180 BLASTER		
19801 Elizabeth Olsen as Wanda Maximoff	20.00	50.00
19802 Paul Bettany as Vision	12.00	30.00
19803 Kat Dennings as Darcy Lewis	8.00	20.00
19805 Teyonah Parris as Monica Rambeau	6.00	15.00
19806 Elizabeth Olsen as Wanda Maximoff	20.00	50.00

2022 Upper Deck WandaVision One Lifetime or Another Film Cels 1990s

COMMON CARD	4.00	10.00
STATED ODDS 1:90 HOBBY/EPACK		
STATED ODDS 1:270 BLASTER		
19901 Elizabeth Olsen as Wanda Maximoff	20.00	50.00
19902 Paul Bettany as Vision	12.00	30.00
19903 Kathryn Hahn as Agatha Harkness	10.00	25.00
19905 Kat Dennings as Darcy Lewis	8.00	20.00
19906 Paul Bettany as Vision	12.00	30.00

2022 Upper Deck WandaVision One Lifetime or Another Film Cels 2000s

COMMON CARD	4.00	10.00
STATED ODDS 1:180 HOBBY/EPACK		
STATED ODDS 1:360 BLASTER		
20001 Elizabeth Olsen as Wanda Maximoff	20.00	50.00
20002 Paul Bettany as Vision	12.00	30.00
20003 Evan Peters as Pietro	12.00	30.00
20004 Kat Dennings as Darcy Lewis	8.00	20.00
20006 Elizabeth Olsen as Scarlet Witch	30.00	75.00

2022 Upper Deck WandaVision Picturesque Signatures

GROUP A ODDS 1:46,536		
GROUP B ODDS 1:9,307		
GROUP C ODDS 1:7,843		
GROUP D ODDS 1:1,939		
GROUP E ODDS 1:997		
GROUP F ODDS 1:997		
STATED OVERALL ODDS 1:360 HOBBY/EPACK		
STATED OVERALL ODDS 1:1,800 BLASTER		
PSEO Elizabeth Olsen C	750.00	2000.00
PSEP Evan Peters E	150.00	400.00
PSFM Fred Melamed F	20.00	50.00
PSKD Kat Dennings D	200.00	500.00
PSKH Kathryn Hahn E	150.00	400.00
PSPB Paul Bettany B	200.00	500.00
PSRP Randall Park E	75.00	200.00
PSTP Teyonah Parris D	100.00	250.00
PSDJR Debra Jo Rupp F	40.00	100.00
PSEO2 Elizabeth Olsen A		
PSEP2 Evan Peters C		
PSFM2 Fred Melamed B	25.00	60.00
PSKH2 Kathryn Hahn E	150.00	400.00
PSPB2 Paul Bettany B	200.00	500.00
PSTP2 Teyonah Parris D	100.00	250.00

2022 Upper Deck WandaVision S.W.O.R.D. Profiles

COMPLETE SET (10)	10.00	25.00
COMMON CARD (SP1-SP10)	1.50	4.00
STATED ODDS 1:10 HOBBY/EPACK/BLASTER		
SP1 Elizabeth Olsen as Scarlet Witch	3.00	8.00

2022 Upper Deck WandaVision Suburban Synthezoid

COMPLETE SET (6)	6.00	15.00
COMMON CARD (WS1-WS6)	1.50	4.00
STATED ODDS 1:17 HOBBY/EPACK/BLASTER		

2022 Upper Deck WandaVision Warped Reality Autographs

GROUP A ODDS 1:39,216		
GROUP B ODDS 1:6,920		
GROUP C ODDS 1:6,536		
GROUP D ODDS 1:1,569		
GROUP E ODDS 1:550		
STATED OVERALL ODDS 1:360 HOBBY/EPACK		
STATED OVERALL ODDS 1:1,800 BLASTER		
WRAEO Elizabeth Olsen C		
WRAEP Evan Peters E	100.00	250.00
WRAFM Fred Melamed E	30.00	75.00
WRAKD Kat Dennings D		
WRAKH Kathryn Hahn C		
WRAPB Paul Bettany B	300.00	800.00
WRARP Randall Park E	75.00	200.00
WRATP Teyonah Parris D		
WRADJR Debra Jo Rupp E	30.00	75.00
WRAEO2 Elizabeth Olsen A		
WRAEP2 Evan Peters E	100.00	250.00
WRAKD2 Kat Dennings D		
WRAKH2 Kathryn Hahn B		
WRAPB2 Paul Bettany B	300.00	800.00
WRATP2 Teyonah Parris D		

2022 Upper Deck WandaVision Warped Reality Dual Autographs

COMMON AUTO		
STATED PRINT RUN 10-25		
WRDMR F.Melamed/D.Rupp/25		
WRDOB E.Olsen/P.Bettany/10		
WRDOH E.Olsen/K.Hahn/25		
WRDOP E.Olsen/T.Parris/25		
WRDPH E.Peters/K.Hahn/25		

2022 Upper Deck WandaVision We Are an Unusual Couple

COMPLETE SET (18)	10.00	25.00
COMMON CARD (WV1-WV18)	1.25	3.00
STATED ODDS 1:2 HOBBY/EPACK/BLASTER		

2022 Upper Deck WandaVision Welcome to Westview

COMPLETE SET (15)	10.00	25.00
COMMON CARD (PR1-PR15)	1.25	3.00
STATED ODDS 1:3 HOBBY/EPACK/BLASTER		

1996 Authentic Images Marvel Classic Characters 24K Gold

COMMON CARD (1-4)	30.00	75.00
STATED PRINT RUN 1996 SER.#'d SETS		
NNO Spider-Man	50.00	100.00
NNO Captain America Prototype		

1987 Comic Images Marvel Colossal Conflicts

COMPLETE SET (90) 6.00 15.00
UNOPENED BOX (50 PACKS)
UNOPENED PACK (5 CARDS)
COMMON CARD (1-90) .12 .30

1998 Marvel Comics Jumbo Postcards

NNO1 Wolverine Unleashed 2.00 5.00
NNO2 Wolverine Unleashed (Jean Grey) 2.00 5.00

1992 Marvel Comics Annuals

COMPLETE SET (6) 4.00 10.00
COMMON CARD (1-6) 1.25 3.00

1993 Marvel Comics Annuals

COMPLETE SET (27) 4.00 10.00
COMMON CARD (1-27) .30 .75

1992 Marvel Comics Bi-Weeklies

COMPLETE SET (8) 8.00 20.00
COMMON CARD (1-8) 1.25 3.00
1 The Punisher 2.00 5.00
3 Captain America 2.00 5.00
4 Wolverine 2.00 5.00
7 The Mighty Thor 2.00 5.00
8 Spider-Man 2.00 5.00

2019 Marvel Contest of Champions Dave and Busters

COMPLETE SET (75) 25.00 60.00
COMMON CARD (1-75) .60 1.50
*HOLOFOIL: 1.5X TO 4X BASIC CARDS

1998 Fleer SkyBox Marvel Creator's Collection

COMPLETE SET (73) 20.00 50.00
UNOPENED BOX (36 PACKS) 600.00 1000.00
UNOPENED PACK (9 CARDS) 15.00 30.00
COMMON CARD (1-72+CL) .40 1.00
1 Spider-Man 2.00 5.00
3 Punisher 1.25 3.00
7 Hulk .75 2.00
10 Deadpool 1.50 4.00
12 Deadpool 1.50 4.00
13 Spider-Man 2.00 5.00
32 Thor 1.25 3.00
33 Loki .75 2.00
34 Wolverine 2.00 5.00
37 Captain America 1.25 3.00
46 Daredevil 1.00 2.50
47 Black Widow 1.00 2.50
52 Spider-Man 2.00 5.00
55 Cable 1.00 2.50
59 Carnage 1.50 4.00
64 Silver Surfer 1.25 3.00
70 Iron Man 1.25 3.00
CL Checklist 2.00 5.00

1998 Fleer SkyBox Marvel Creator's Collection Autographs

COMMON CARD (A1-A19) 10.00 25.00
STATED ODDS 1:36
A1 George Perez 40.00 100.00
A4 John K. Snyder 12.00 30.00
A6 Larry Hama 15.00 40.00
A7 Todd Dezago 15.00 40.00
A10 Luke Ross 30.00 75.00
A12 Dan Jurgens 15.00 40.00
A13 Marc Sasso 15.00 40.00
A14 Kurt Busiek 12.00 30.00
A18 Walt McDaniel 12.00 30.00
NNO Stan Lee/Mike Wieringo 250.00 500.00

1998 Fleer SkyBox Marvel Creator's Collection Editor's Choice

COMPLETE SET (12) 15.00 40.00
COMMON CARD (1-12) 1.00 2.50
STATED ODDS 1:3
1 Avengers 2.00 5.00
2 Cable 1.25 3.00
3 Captain America 1.50 4.00
4 Deadpool 5.00 12.00
5 Fantastic Four 1.25 3.00
8 Iron Man 3.00 8.00
9 Spider-Man 5.00 12.00
11 Wolverine 4.00 10.00
12 X-Men 2.00 5.00

1998 Fleer SkyBox Marvel Creator's Collection Marvel Gold

COMMON CARD (1-4) 5.00 12.00
STATED ODDS 1:9
1 Spider-Man 20.00 50.00
2 Wolverine 10.00 25.00

2016 Marvel Dossier

COMPLETE SET (55) 20.00 35.00
UNOPENED BOX (36 PACKS)
UNOPENED PACK (3 CARDS+1 TAG)
COMMON CARD (1-55) .50 1.25
*FOIL: .75X TO 2X BASIC CARDS 1.00 2.50
5 Spider-Man 2.00 5.00
7 Wolverine 1.00 2.50
10 Deadpool 1.50 4.00
41 Mystique .75 2.00

2016 Marvel Dossier Dog Tags

COMPLETE SET W/O SP (40) 60.00 120.00
COMPLETE SET W/SP (55) 100.00 200.00
COMMON CARD (1-40) 1.25 3.00
COMMON SP (41-55); INSERTED 1:7 PACKS2.50 6.00
STATED ODDS 1:1
4 Thanos 2.00 5.00
5 Spider-Man 5.00 12.00
7 Wolverine 3.00 8.00
8 Agent Venom 2.00 5.00
10 Deadpool 3.00 8.00
41 Mystique SP 4.00 10.00
43 She-Hulk SP 3.00 8.00
50 Spider-Woman SP 3.00 8.00

1991 Marvel Editor Autographs Series I

COMPLETE SET (32)
COMMON AUTO (1-32)
1 Terry Stewart
2 Tom DeFalco 15.00 40.00
3 Mark Gruenwald
4 Carl Potts
5 Craig Anderson 12.00 30.00
6 Bob Budiansky
7 Bobbie Chase
8 Don Dailey
9 Danny Fingeroth 15.00 40.00
10 Bob Harras
11 Glenn Herdling
12 Marie Javins 25.00 60.00
13 Terry Kavanagh
14 Ralph Macchio
15 Marc McLaurin 15.00 40.00
16 Fabian Nicieza
17 Mike Rockwitz 12.00 30.00
18 Jim Salicrup
19 Rob Tokar 20.00 50.00
20 Renee Witterstaetter
21 Nel Yomtov 30.00 75.00
22 Tammy Brown
23 Dana Moreshead
24 Mariano Nicieza 12.00 30.00
25 Steve Saffel 12.00 30.00
26 Lou Bank
27 Bruce G. Costa 12.00 30.00
28 Dave Kosinski
29 Sven Larsen 12.00 30.00
30 Mike Martin
31 Tom Brevoort
32 Kelly Corvese 20.00 50.00

1966 Topps Marvel Flyers

COMPLETE SET (12) 900.00 1800.00
UNOPENED PACK (1 FLYER) 250.00 300.00
COMMON FLYER (UNNUMBERED) 50.00 100.00
NNO The Angel 75.00 150.00
NNO Dare Devil 60.00 120.00
NNO Dr. Doom 60.00 120.00
NNO Human Torch 75.00 150.00
NNO Iron Man 75.00 150.00
NNO Spider-Man 100.00 200.00

2016 Marvel Gems

COMPLETE SET (60) 200.00 400.00
UNOPENED BOX (2 PACKS) 400.00 600.00
UNOPENED PACK (5 CARDS) 200.00 300.00
COMMON CARD (1-60) 3.00 8.00
*RUBY/99: .75X TO 1.2X BASIC CARDS
*SAPPHIRE/25: .75X TO 2X BASIC CARDS
*TOPAZ/10: 4X TO 10X BASIC CARDS
1 Captain Marvel 8.00 20.00
2 Kitty Pryde 4.00 10.00
5 Tigra 4.00 10.00
6 Black Widow 6.00 15.00
7 Magik 6.00 15.00
8 Dazzler 4.00 10.00
9 Madame Hydra 4.00 10.00
10 Storm 5.00 12.00
12 Hellcat 4.00 10.00
13 Mystique 8.00 20.00
14 Blink 4.00 10.00
16 Valkyrie 4.00 10.00
17 Scarlet Witch 6.00 15.00
18 Psylocke 4.00 10.00
19 Gamora 4.00 10.00
20 Elektra 6.00 15.00
22 Misty Knight 5.00 12.00
23 Wasp 4.00 10.00
25 She-Hulk 4.00 10.00
30 Nebula 5.00 12.00
34 Spider-Woman 5.00 12.00
36 Jocasta 4.00 10.00
38 Hawkeye 6.00 15.00
40 Spider-Gwen 12.00 30.00
41 Silk 4.00 10.00
44 Maria Hill 4.00 10.00
45 Moondragon 6.00 15.00
46 Lady Deadpool 5.00 12.00
47 Ms. Marvel 12.00 30.00
51 Dagger 4.00 10.00
54 Red She-Hulk 4.00 10.00
56 Jean Grey 4.00 10.00
58 Squirrel Girl 5.00 12.00
60 Thor 6.00 15.00

2016 Marvel Gems Battling Beauties

COMPLETE SET (15) 50.00 100.00
COMMON CARD (BB1-BB15) 3.00 8.00
STATED ODDS 1:4
BB1 Black Cat/Silk 5.00 12.00
BB5 Black Widow/Ms. Marvel 5.00 12.00
BB7 Storm/Emma Frost 6.00 15.00
BB10 Sera/Angela 6.00 15.00
BB12 Scarlet Witch/Magik 4.00 10.00

2016 Marvel Gems Crystal Clear

COMPLETE SET (20) 80.00 150.00
COMMON CARD (CC1-CC20) 3.00 8.00
*RED: .5X TO 1.2X BASIC CARDS 4.00 10.00
*BLUE: .6X TO 1.5X BASIC CARDS 5.00 12.00
*GREEN: 1.2X TO 3X BASIC CARDS 10.00 25.00
*PURPLE: 2X TO 5X BASIC CARDS 15.00 40.00
STATED ODDS 1:2
CC5 She-Hulk 5.00 12.00
CC9 Black Cat 4.00 10.00
CC11 Mystique 5.00 12.00
CC16 Black Widow 6.00 15.00
CC17 X-23 6.00 15.00
CC19 Scarlet Witch 5.00 12.00

2016 Marvel Gems Diamond Cut

COMPLETE SET (50) 200.00 400.00
COMMON PEAR (DCP1-DCP20) 2.50 6.00
PEAR ODDS 1:4
COMMON TRILLION (DCT1-DCT15) 3.00 8.00
TRILLION ODDS 1:6
COMMON ROUND (DCR1-DCR10) 4.00 10.00
ROUND ODDS 1:8
COMMON HEART (DCH1-DCH5) 6.00 15.00
HEART ODDS 1:24
DCP1 Hellcat 12.00 30.00
DCP2 Armor 3.00 8.00
DCP5 Madame Masque 5.00 12.00
DCP6 Squirrel Girl 10.00 25.00
DCP9 Mercury 5.00 12.00
DCP10 Spectrum 5.00 12.00
DCP14 Ko-Rel 3.00 8.00
DCP15 Ruby Summers 6.00 15.00
DCP16 Darkstar 3.00 8.00
DCT1 Black Panther 5.00 12.00
DCT2 Valkyrie 5.00 12.00
DCT3 Psylocke 6.00 12.00
DCT4 Lady Sif 6.00 15.00
DCT5 X-23 8.00 20.00
DCT6 Satana 6.00 15.00
DCT7 Medusa 6.00 15.00
DCT8 Mantis 6.00 12.00
DCT9 Ms. Marvel 6.00 15.00
DCT13 Blink 10.00 25.00
DCT14 Spider-Girl 6.00 12.00
DCR1 Spider-Woman 6.00 12.00
DCR2 Mystique 12.00 30.00
DCR5 Storm 6.00 12.00
DCR7 Mockingbird 6.00 12.00
DCR8 Kitty Pryde 6.00 15.00
DCR10 Thor 8.00 20.00
DCH2 Scarlet Witch 10.00 25.00
DCH3 Black Widow 8.00 20.00
DCH4 Jean Grey 15.00 40.00

2016 Marvel Gems Diamond Mine

COMMON CARD 30.00 75.00
SINGLE (SDM1-SDM12)
DOUBLE (DDM1-DDM10)
TRIPLE (TDM1-TDM5)
QUAD (QDM1-QDM3)
SDM1 Spider-Gwen 1000.00 2500.00
SDM2 Thor 1200.00 3000.00
SDM4 Quake 100.00 250.00
SDM6 Magik 150.00 400.00
SDM7 Lady Deadpool 50.00 100.00
SDM8 Snowbird 75.00 200.00
SDM9 Diamondback 100.00 250.00
SDM10 Dagger 250.00 600.00
SDM11 Black Panther 400.00 1000.00
DDM1 Silk 50.00 100.00
DDM2 Mystique 100.00 250.00
DDM4 Elektra 500.00 1200.00
DDM5 Misty Knight 60.00 150.00
DDM7 Enchantress 125.00 300.00
DDM8 Psylocke 300.00 750.00
DDM10 Medusa 150.00 400.00
TDM1 She-Hulk 125.00 300.00
TDM2 Jean Grey 125.00 300.00
TDM3 Scarlet Witch 200.00 500.00
TDM4 Black Cat 100.00 250.00
TDM5 Wasp 60.00 150.00
QDM1 Black Widow 30.00 250.00
QDM2 Storm 300.00 800.00
QDM3 Captain Marvel 400.00 1000.00

2016 Marvel Gems Exquisite Emma Frost Collection

COMPLETE SET (15) 100.00 200.00
COMMON CARD (EFC1-EFC15) 6.00 15.00
*DIAM.SKIN: 1.5X TO 4X BASIC CARDS
STATED ODDS 1:3

2016 Marvel Gems Exquisite

COMMON (1-19)/199 20.00 50.00
COMMON (20-35)/99 30.00 75.00
COMMON (36-45)/50 100.00 250.00
COMMON (46-50)/30 400.00 1000.00
STATED ODDS 1:EX.PACK PER BOX
2 Gladiator 30.00 75.00
3 Diamondback 25.00 60.00

4 Baron Zemo 30.00 75.00
5 Viper 30.00 75.00
6 Colossus 40.00 100.00
7 Enchantress 60.00 150.00
8 Bullseye 25.00 60.00
10 Namor 50.00 125.00
11 Black Bolt 30.00 75.00
12 Psylocke 60.00 150.00
13 Doctor Octopus 40.00 100.00
14 Emma Frost 40.00 100.00
17 Ultron 25.00 60.00
18 Winter Soldier 50.00 125.00
19 Spider-Woman 40.00 100.00
20 Punisher 60.00 150.00
22 Doctor Strange 75.00 200.00
23 Green Goblin 125.00 300.00
24 Mystique 50.00 125.00
25 Red Skull 40.00 100.00
26 Blade 75.00 200.00
29 Ghost Rider 60.00 150.00
30 Jean Grey 50.00 125.00
31 Loki 60.00 150.00
32 Storm 40.00 100.00
33 She-Hulk 60.00 150.00
34 Beast 50.00 125.00
35 Scarlet Witch 100.00 250.00
36 Black Widow 400.00 1000.00
37 Cyclops 150.00 400.00
39 Captain America 150.00 400.00
40 Black Panther 125.00 300.00
41 Magneto 150.00 400.00
42 Kitty Pryde 200.00 500.00
43 Hulk 125.00 300.00
44 Venom 400.00 1000.00
45 Thor 300.00 750.00
46 Iron Man 500.00 1200.00
47 Deadpool 1200.00 3000.00
49 Wolverine 1000.00 2500.00
50 Spider-Man 3000.00 7500.00

2016 Marvel Gems Focus Frames

COMPLETE SET (15) 80.00 150.00
COMMON CARD (FF1-FF15) 4.00 10.00
STATED ODDS 1:8
FF2 Arachne 5.00 12.00
FF3 Elsa Bloodstone 6.00 15.00
FF6 Gwenpool 15.00 40.00
FF8 Captain Marvel 6.00 15.00
FF10 Firebird 6.00 15.00
FF11 Kitty Pryde 5.00 12.00
FF13 Black Panther 5.00 12.00
FF15 Thor 8.00 20.00

2016 Marvel Gems Gem-Balaya

COMMON CARD (GB1-GB20) 30.00 75.00
STATED ODDS 1:10
GB1 Spider-Woman 125.00 300.00
GB2 Black Widow 100.00 250.00
GB3 Mystique 75.00 200.00
GB4 Scarlet Witch 200.00 500.00
GB5 Gamora 60.00 150.00
GB7 Thor 75.00 200.00
GB9 She-Hulk 150.00 400.00
GB10 Kitty Pryde 75.00 200.00
GB11 Madame Hydra 40.00 100.00
GB15 Jean Grey 40.00 100.00
GB17 Ms. Marvel 75.00 200.00
GB18 Spider-Gwen 150.00 400.00
GB19 Storm 125.00 300.00
GB20 Captain Marvel 100.00 250.00

2016 Marvel Gems No Boys Allowed

COMPLETE SET (20) 60.00 120.00
COMMON CARD (NBA1-NBA20) 3.00 8.00
STATED ODDS 1:5
NBA1 Lady Bullseye/Daredevil 6.00 15.00
NBA3 Black Cat/Spider-Man 8.00 20.00
NBA4 Black Widow/Deadpool 6.00 15.00
NBA9 Red She-Hulk/Red Hulk 4.00 10.00
NBA10 Lady Deathstrike/Wolverine 4.00 10.00

2016 Marvel Gems Shadowbox

COMPLETE SET (10) 60.00 120.00
COMMON CARD (SB1-SB10) 5.00 12.00
STATED ODDS 1:10
SB2 Storm 12.00 30.00
SB8 Spider-Gwen 15.00 40.00
SB10 Silver Sable 8.00 20.00

2016 Marvel Gems XOXO

COMPLETE SET (30) 150.00 300.00
COMMON CARD (XO1-XO30) 4.00 10.00
STATED ODDS 1:2
XO2 Mockingbird 5.00 12.00
XO10 Clea 5.00 12.00
XO13 Gwen Stacey 6.00 15.00
XO20 Black Cat 5.00 12.00
XO21 Black Widow 6.00 15.00
XO22 Storm 5.00 12.00
XO23 Mystique 5.00 12.00
XO30 Shanna The She-Devil 6.00 15.00

1993-94 Marvel UK Gene Cards

COMPLETE SET (16) 10.00 25.00
COMMON CARD (1-16) 1.00 2.50

1999 Marvel Got Milk?

COMPLETE SET (9) 10.00 25.00
COMMON CARD (1-9) 1.50 4.00
1 Venom 2.00 5.00
2 Spider-Man 2.00 5.00
7 Hulk 2.00 5.00
8 Captain America 2.00 5.00

1999 Marvel Got Milk? 4-Card Panels

COMPLETE SET (3) 10.00 25.00
COMMON CARD (1-3) 4.00 10.00

1999 Marvel Got Milk? Triptych

COMPLETE SET (3) 8.00 20.00
COMMON CARD (1-3) 3.00 8.00

2013 Marvel Greatest Battles

COMPLETE SET (90) 15.00 40.00
UNOPENED BOX (24 PACKS) 400.00 600.00
UNOPENED PACK (5 CARDS) 15.00 25.00
COMMON CARD (1-90) .40 1.00
*RED: 1.2X TO 3X BASIC CARDS
*GOLD/75: 12X TO 30X BASIC CARDS

2013 Marvel Greatest Battles Avengers vs. X-Men

COMPLETE SET (18) 15.00 40.00
COMMON CARD (VS1-VS18) 1.00 2.50
STATED ODDS 1:12
VS1 Captain America vs. Cyclops 1.25 3.00
VS4 Spider-Man vs. Iceman 1.50 4.00
VS5 Thing vs. Colossus 1.25 3.00
VS9 Daredevil vs. Archangel 1.25 3.00
VS11 Black Widow vs. Psylocke 1.25 3.00
VS12 Iron Man vs. Magneto 2.00 5.00
VS14 Captain America vs. Wolverine 4.00 10.00

2013 Marvel Greatest Battles Battle Scars

COMPLETE SET (9) 20.00 50.00
COMMON CARD (BS1-BS9) 3.00 8.00
STATED ODDS 1:12
BS1 Spider-Man 8.00 20.00
BS2 Iron Man 5.00 12.00
BS3 Thor 5.00 12.00
BS4 Captain America 6.00 15.00
BS5 Hulk 5.00 12.00
BS6 Wolverine 10.00 25.00

2013 Marvel Greatest Battles Gold Covers

COMPLETE SET W/RR (10) 40.00 100.00
COMPLETE SET W/O RR ((9) 25.00 60.00
COMMON CARD (GC1-GC9) 2.50 6.00
STATED ODDS 1:24
GC10 ISSUED AS RITTENHOUSE REWARD
GC1 Captain America 6.00 15.00
GC4 Iron Man 6.00 15.00
GC5 Spider-Man 8.00 20.00
GC7 Wolverine 8.00 20.00
GC10 Nova RR 15.00 40.00

2013 Marvel Greatest Battles Secret Warriors Case-Toppers

COMPLETE SET (2) 20.00 50.00
COMMON CARD (CT1-CT2) 12.00 30.00
STATED ODDS 1:CASE

2013 Marvel Greatest Battles Promos

P1 Spider-Man GEN .75 2.00
P2 Wolverine ALB 3.00 8.00

2012 Marvel Greatest Heroes

COMPLETE SET (81) 15.00 40.00
UNOPENED BOX (24 PACKS) 300.00 450.00
UNOPENED PACK (5 CARDS) 12.00 20.00
COMMON CARD (1-81) .15 .40
*SILVER FOIL: 1.25X TO 3X BASIC CARDS .60 1.25

2012 Marvel Greatest Heroes Avengers Case-Toppers

COMPLETE SET (5) 40.00 80.00
COMMON CARD (CT1-CT5) 10.00 25.00
STATED ODDS 1:CASE

2012 Marvel Greatest Heroes I Am an Avenger

COMPLETE SET (18) 12.00 30.00
COMPLETE SET W/SP (19) 20.00 50.00
COMMON CARD (IAM1-IAM18) 1.00 2.50
STATED ODDS 1:12
IAM19 ISSUED AS RITTENHOUSE REWARD
IAM6 Captain America 2.50 6.00
IAM7 Hawkeye 1.25 3.00
IAM9 Thor 1.50 4.00
IAM16 Spider-Man 3.00 8.00
IAM18 Wolverine 3.00 8.00
IAM19 Luke Cage SP RR 12.00 30.00

2012 Marvel Greatest Heroes Icons Shadowbox

COMPLETE SET (6) 30.00 60.00
COMMON CARD (S1-S6) 6.00 15.00
STATED ODDS 1:72

2012 Marvel Greatest Heroes Ultimate Heroes

COMPLETE SET (9) 75.00 200.00
COMMON CARD (UH11-UH19) 4.00 10.00
STATED ODDS 1:36
UH11 Captain America 6.00 15.00
UH13 Iron Man 6.00 15.00
UH15 Scarlet Witch 10.00 25.00
UH16 Spider-Man 60.00 150.00
UH17 Thor 6.00 15.00
UH18 Valkyrie 5.00 12.00

2012 Marvel Greatest Heroes Villains

COMPLETE SET (18) 12.00 30.00
COMMON CARD (V1-V18) 1.25 3.00
STATED ODDS 1:6

2012 Marvel Greatest Heroes Promos

P1 Spider-Man .75 2.00
Iron Man GEN
P2 Steve Rogers/Cap NSU .75 2.00
P3 Thor/Valkyrie ALB 4.00 10.00
P4 Black Widow/Black Panther 8.00 20.00

2010 Marvel Heroes and Villains

COMPLETE SET (81) 10.00 25.00
UNOPENED BOX (24 PACKS) 150.00 250.00
UNOPENED PACK (5 CARDS) 6.00 10.00
COMMON CARD (1-81) .25 .60
*FOIL: 1.2X TO 3X BASIC CARDS

2010 Marvel Heroes and Villains Alliances

COMPLETE SET (18) 15.00 40.00
COMMON CARD (A1-A18) 1.50 4.00
STATED ODDS 1:12

2010 Marvel Heroes and Villains Case-Toppers

COMPLETE SET (5) 50.00 100.00
COMMON CARD (CT1-CT5) 12.00 30.00
STATED ODDS 1:CASE
STATED PRINT RUN 175 SER. #'d SETS
CT1 Spider-Man 15.00 40.00
CT3 Captain America 15.00 40.00
CT5 Black Pather 15.00 40.00

2010 Marvel Heroes and Villains Lenticular Flip

COMPLETE SET (6) 15.00 40.00
COMMON CARD (L1-L6) 3.00 8.00
STATED ODDS 1:48
L1 Hulk 5.00 12.00
Red Hulk
L2 Thor/Destroyer 4.00 10.00
L5 Punisher/Bullseye 5.00 12.00
L6 Ms. Marvel 4.00 10.00
Ms. Marvel

2010 Marvel Heroes and Villains Marvel's Most Wanted

COMPLETE SET W/SP (10) 25.00 60.00
COMPLETE SET W/O SP (9) 10.00 25.00
COMMON CARD (M1-M9) 1.00 2.50
STATED ODDS 1:8
M10 ISSUED AS RITTENHOUSE REDEMPTION
M2 Red Hulk 4.00 10.00
M4 M.O.D.O.K 1.50 4.00
M7 Red Skull 1.25 3.00
M9 Mystique 1.50 4.00
M10 Magneto SP 12.00 30.00

2010 Marvel Heroes and Villains Posters

COMPLETE SET (6) 10.00 25.00
COMMON CARD (PC1-PC6) 2.50 6.00
STATED ODDS 1:48

2010 Marvel Heroes and Villains Promos

COMMON CARD 1.50 4.00
P2 Wolverine/Sabretooth NSU 1.25 3.00
P3 Hulk/Abomination ALB 10.00 25.00
CP1 Black Panther/Sabretooth SDCC 3.00 8.00
PNSCS1 Capt.America/Red Skull PHILLY 4.00 10.00
PNSCS2 Green Hulk/Red Hulk PHILLY 5.00 12.00

2021 Marvel Heroes Reborn Promos

COMPLETE SET (10) 3.00 8.00
COMMON CARD (1-9, NNO) .40 1.00
2 Thor 1.25 3.00
4 Blade .75 2.00
5 Mephisto .50 1.25
8 Captain America 1.50 4.00

2008 Marvel Heroes Stickers

COMPLETE SET (100) 12.00 30.00
COMMON CARD (1-100) .30 .75

1990 Marvel Keepsake Collection Ghost Rider

COMPLETE SET (6) 12.00 30.00
COMMON CARD 3.00 8.00

1991 Marvel Keepsake Collection Infinity Gauntlet

COMPLETE SET (7) 8.00 20.00
COMMON CARD 2.00 5.00
NNO 6-Card Panel (color)

1994 Marvel Kids Month Universal Studios

COMPLETE SET (3)	5.00	12.00
COMMON CARD (1-3)	1.50	4.00
2 Spider-Man	3.00	8.00
Daredevil#{Captain America		
3 Storm	4.00	10.00
Wolverine#{Cyclops		

1998 Marvel Comics Marvel Knights

NNO Four Marvel Icons

2001 Marvel Legends

COMPLETE SET (72)	20.00	50.00
UNOPENED HOBBY BOX (36 PACKS)	300.00	350.00
UNOPENED HOBBY PACK (8 CARDS)	8.00	10.00
UNOPENED RETAIL BOX (36 PACKS)	40.00	50.00
UNOPENED RETAIL PACK (8 CARDS)	1.25	1.50
COMMON CARD (1-72)	.40	1.00
*FOIL: 4X TO 10X	.75	2.00
1 Spider-Man	3.00	8.00
7 Captain America	1.50	4.00
11 Iron Man	1.50	4.00
12 Black Panther	2.00	5.00
13 Black Widow	1.50	4.00
14 Ant-Man	1.00	2.50
16 Giant Man	1.00	2.50
19 The Vision	1.25	3.00
20 Scarlet Witch	2.00	5.00
21 Cyclops	2.50	6.00
28 Wolverine	2.50	6.00
30 Gambit	2.00	5.00
36 Daredevil	1.25	3.00
38 The Punisher	1.25	3.00
41 Doctor Strange	1.25	3.00
42 Deadpool	1.50	4.00
43 Apocalypse	1.25	3.00
50 Venom	2.50	6.00
60 Loki	1.25	3.00
68 Thanos	1.50	4.00

2001 Marvel Legends Costume Change

COMPLETE SET (18)	15.00	40.00
COMMON A CARD (CC1-CC9)	.75	2.00
COMMON B CARD (CC10-CC18)	1.25	3.00
STATED ODDS 1:8		
CC1 Spider-Man	2.00	5.00
CC3 Iron Man	1.50	4.00
CC4 Cyclops	1.50	4.00
CC5 Marvel Girl	4.00	10.00
CC7 Wolverine	2.00	5.00
CC10 Spider-Man	2.00	5.00
CC11 The Captain	1.50	4.00
CC16 Ultimate Wolverine	2.50	6.00

2001 Marvel Legends Secret Identity

COMPLETE SET (5)	5.00	12.00
COMMON CARD (1-5)	1.25	3.00
STATED ODDS 1:6		
1 Wolverine/Logan	2.00	5.00
3 Spider-Man/Peter Parker	2.50	6.00

2001 Marvel Legends Ultimate Spider-Man

COMPLETE SET (4)	15.00	40.00
COMMON CARD (1-4)	6.00	15.00
STATED ODDS 1:BOX		

2001 Marvel Legends Oversized Dealer Promos

1 Secret Identity Cards	.75	2.00
2 Custom Cover Cards	.75	2.00
3 Costume Change Cards	.75	2.00
4 Own an Original Legend	.75	2.00

2001 Marvel Legends Promos

COMPLETE SET (3)	4.00	10.00
COMMON CARD (P1-P3)	1.00	2.50
P1 Spider-Man	4.00	10.00
P2 Human Torch WIZARD	1.25	3.00

2021 Upper Deck Marvel Legends Series Promos

COMMON WAVE 1 (1-15)	1.25	3.00
COMMON WAVE 2 (16-30)	1.25	3.00
COMMON WAVE 3 (31-45)	1.25	3.00
*FOIL: X TO X BASIC CARDS		
ONE PACK PER ACTION FIGURE PURCHASE		
30 Thanos	3.00	8.00
35 Captain America	2.00	5.00
36 Iron Man	2.00	5.00

2001 Marvel Master Prints Series One

COMPLETE SET (12)	10.00	25.00
COMMON CARD (1-12)	1.50	4.00

2001 Marvel Master Prints Series Two

COMPLETE SET (12)	10.00	25.00
COMMON CARD	1.50	4.00

1992 SkyBox Marvel Masterpieces

COMPLETE SET (100)	60.00	120.00
UNOPENED BOX (36 PACKS)	500.00	800.00
UNOPENED PACK (6 CARDS)	15.00	25.00
COMMON CARD (1-100)	.40	1.00
1 Blob	.75	2.00
3 Black Widow	4.00	10.00
4 Black Panther	3.00	8.00
5 Black Cat	1.25	3.00
7 Beast	2.00	5.00
9 Apocalypse	1.25	3.00
10 Adam Warlock	1.00	2.50
12 Daredevil	1.50	4.00
13 Cyclops	1.50	4.00
14 Colossus	1.00	2.50
16 Captain America	2.50	6.00
24 Dr. Strange	1.50	4.00
25 Dr. Octopus	.75	2.00
26 Dr. Doom	1.25	3.00
27 Dormammu	1.00	2.50
29 Gambit	3.00	8.00
30 Galactus	2.50	6.00
31 Human Torch	1.25	3.00
32 Hulk	3.00	8.00
36 Green Goblin	4.00	10.00
37 Ghost Rider	1.50	4.00
38 Iron Man	2.00	5.00
39 Invisible Woman	1.25	3.00
46 Jean Grey	1.25	3.00
49 Magneto	1.25	3.00
50 Loki	2.00	5.00
57 Namor	.75	2.00
58 Mr. Sinister	.75	2.00
59 Mr. Fantastic	.75	2.00
60 Morbius	1.25	3.00
64 Nick Fury	1.25	3.00
65 Psylocke	2.00	5.00
66 Professor X	.60	1.50
67 Phoenix	1.25	3.00
73 Punisher	1.50	4.00
78 Sabretooth	1.50	4.00
79 Rogue	1.50	4.00
80 Red Skull	1.00	2.50
83 Thanos	2.00	5.00
86 Storm	1.50	4.00
87 Spider-Man	5.00	12.00
90 Silver Surfer	1.25	3.00
91 Thing	1.50	4.00
92 Thor	1.50	4.00
94 Wolverine	4.00	10.00
97 Venom	2.50	6.00
100 Checklist	1.25	3.00

1992 SkyBox Marvel Masterpieces Battle Spectra

COMPLETE SET (5)	30.00	75.00
COMMON CARD (1D-5D)	8.00	20.00
2D Silver Surfer vs. Thanos	10.00	25.00
3D Wolverine vs. Sabretooth	12.00	30.00
4D Spider-Man vs. Venom	12.00	30.00

1992 SkyBox Marvel Masterpieces Lost Marvel Bonus

COMPLETE SET (5)	60.00	120.00
COMMON CARD (LM1-LM5)	12.00	30.00
LM1 Scarlet Witch	15.00	40.00
LM3 Deathbird	25.00	50.00
LM4 Typhoid Mary	15.00	40.00

1992 SkyBox Marvel Masterpieces Promos

1 Captain America	10.00	25.00
2 Hulk	5.00	12.00
3 Psylocke	4.00	10.00
4 Silver Surfer	8.00	20.00
5 Spider-Man	3.00	8.00
6 Wolverine	30.00	75.00

1992 SkyBox Marvel Masterpieces Prototypes

36 Hulk	3.00	8.00
86 Spider-Man	4.00	10.00
98 Wolverine	10.00	25.00

1993 SkyBox Marvel Masterpieces

COMPLETE SET (90)	20.00	50.00
UNOPENED BOX (36 PACKS)	200.00	300.00
UNOPENED PACK (6 CARDS)	6.00	8.00
COMMON CARD (1-90)	.50	1.25

1993 SkyBox Marvel Masterpieces Spectra Etch

COMPLETE SET (8)	30.00	75.00
COMMON CARD (S1-S8)	3.00	8.00
S3 Krystalin	4.00	10.00
S4 Metalhead	6.00	15.00
S6 Bloodhawk	4.00	10.00
S7 Skullfire	6.00	15.00
S8 Xi'an	5.00	12.00

1993 SkyBox Marvel Masterpieces Promos

30 She-Hulk	3.00	8.00
(prototype)		
P8 Venom (gray print)		
NNO Daredevil	2.50	6.00
(Hero magazine)		
NNO Hulk 2099	6.00	15.00
NNO Venom (black print)	15.00	40.00
(SDCC)		

1994 Fleer Marvel Masterpieces

COMPLETE SET (140)	10.00	25.00
UNOPENED HOBBY BOX (36 PACKS)	250.00	400.00
UNOPENED HOBBY PACK (10 CARDS)	7.00	12.00
UNOPENED JUMBO BOX (36 PACKS)	800.00	1200.00
UNOPENED JUMBO PACK (14 CARDS)	25.00	35.00
UNOPENED WALMART BOX (20 PACKS)	1000.00	1500.00
UNOPENED WALMART PACK (11 CARDS)	50.00	75.00
COMMON CARD (1-140)	.30	.75
*GOLD SIG.: .75X TO 2X BASIC CARDS	.60	1.50
1 Apocalypse	.50	1.25
8 Black Panther	3.00	8.00
9 Black Widow	.60	1.50
12 Blade	.75	2.00
18 Captain America	2.00	5.00
20 Carnage	.50	1.25
25 Cyclops	.40	1.00
26 Daredevil	.75	2.00
28 Deadpool	2.50	6.00
41 Gambit	.60	1.50
42 Ghost Rider	.50	1.25
49 Hawkeye	.40	1.00
50 Hulk	.75	2.00
56 Iron Man	1.25	3.00
70 Magneto	.40	1.00
81 Namor	.40	1.00
94 Punisher	1.50	4.00
111 Silver Surfer	.50	1.25
115 Spider-Man	2.00	5.00
116 Spider-Man 2099	1.25	3.00
117 Spider-Woman	.75	2.00
118 Storm	.75	2.00
124 Thor	.75	2.00
131 Venom (copyright 1944)	2.50	6.00
137 Wolverine	2.50	6.00

1994 Fleer Marvel Masterpieces Holofoil Silver

COMPLETE SET (10)	20.00	50.00
COMMON CARD (1-10)	2.50	6.00
*GOLD: 2X TO 5X BASIC CARDS		
*BRONZE: 2.5X TO 6X BASIC CARDS		
1 Captain America	4.00	10.00
2 Carnage	3.00	8.00
5 Iron Man	3.00	8.00
6 Punisher	3.00	8.00
7 Scarlet Witch	4.00	10.00
8 Spider-Man	8.00	20.00
9 Venom	6.00	15.00

1994 Fleer Marvel Masterpieces Masterprints

COMPLETE SET (10)	20.00	50.00
COMMON CARD	2.50	6.00
1 Capt. America	4.00	10.00
4 Psylocke	4.00	10.00
6 Silver Surfer	4.00	10.00
8 Venom	5.00	12.00
10 Wolverine	4.00	10.00

1994 Fleer Marvel Masterpieces PowerBlast

COMPLETE SET (9)	12.00	30.00
COMMON CARD (PB1-PB9)	1.50	4.00
PB1 Apocalypse	2.00	5.00
PB3 Cable	2.00	5.00
PB5 Gambit	2.00	5.00
PB6 Magneto	2.50	6.00
PB7 Rogue	2.50	6.00
PB8 Sabretooth	2.00	5.00
PB9 Wolverine	5.00	12.00

1995 Fleer Marvel Masterpieces

COMPLETE SET (151)	125.00	250.00
UNOPENED BOX (36 PACKS)	2000.00	4000.00
UNOPENED PACK (10 CARDS)	60.00	125.00
UNOPENED JUMBO BOX	1250.00	2500.00
COMMON CARD (1-151)	1.00	2.50
*EMOTION: 1.5X TO 4X BASIC CARDS		
NO #151 ISSUED IN EMOTION		

1995 Fleer Marvel Masterpieces Canvas

COMPLETE SET (22)	30.00	75.00
COMMON CARD (1-22)	1.25	3.00
STATED ODDS 1:2		
2 Beast	2.50	6.00
3 Bishop	3.00	8.00
4 Cable	5.00	12.00
5 Daredevil	3.00	8.00
7 Gambit	4.00	10.00
8 Ghost Rider	2.50	6.00
9 Human Torch	3.00	8.00
11 Invisible Woman	2.00	5.00
12 Jubilee	1.50	4.00
13 Magneto	2.00	5.00
14 Namor	1.50	4.00
16 Psylocke	3.00	8.00
17 Punisher	3.00	8.00
18 Rogue	2.50	6.00
19 Silver Surfer	4.00	10.00
20 Spider-Man	4.00	12.00
21 Thing	2.50	6.00

1995 Fleer Marvel Masterpieces Holoflash

COMPLETE SET (8)	125.00	250.00
COMMON CARD (1-8)	10.00	25.00
STATED ODDS 1:12		
2 Carnage	50.00	100.00
3 Dr. Doom	15.00	40.00

5 Mr. Sinister	30.00	75.00
6 Sabretooth	15.00	40.00
7 Thanos	20.00	50.00
8 Venom	30.00	75.00

1995 Fleer Marvel Masterpieces Mirage

COMPLETE SET (2)	500.00	1000.00
STATED ODDS 1:360		

1995 Fleer Marvel Masterpieces Promo Panel

NNO Wolverine Dare to Compare	1.25	3.00
NNO Wolverine Dare to Compare Herb Trimpe AU		
NNO Wolverine Dare to Compare Herb Trimpe AU#(Certificate of Authenticity		

1996 Fleer SkyBox Marvel Masterpieces

COMPLETE SET (100)	2000.00	4000.00
UNOPENED BOX (18 PACKS)	6000.00	0000.00
UNOPENED PACK (7 CARDS)	350.00	600.00
COMMON CARD (1-54; 100)	15.00	40.00
COMMON DUELS/LEGACY (55-84)	12.00	30.00
COMMON GENESIS (85-99)	12.00	30.00
1 Archangel	25.00	60.00
3 Bishop	30.00	75.00
4 Black Cat	25.00	60.00
5 Black Widow	30.00	75.00
7 Captain America	20.00	50.00
8 Carnage	40.00	100.00
9 Crystal	25.00	60.00
10 Cyclops	25.00	60.00
12 Dr. Doom	30.00	75.00
13 Dr. Strange	20.00	50.00
15 Gambit	50.00	125.00
16 Ghost Rider	20.00	50.00
20 Hulk	20.00	50.00
21 Human Torch	20.00	50.00
23 Invisible Woman	20.00	50.00
24 Iron Man	20.00	50.00
26 Jean Grey	50.00	125.00
29 Mystique	50.00	125.00
31 Omega Red	20.00	50.00
35 Psylocke	100.00	250.00
37 Quicksilver	20.00	50.00
38 Rogue	40.00	100.00
40 Scarlet Witch	30.00	75.00
42 She-Hulk	30.00	75.00
43 Silver Sable	20.00	50.00
44 Silver Surfer	20.00	50.00
45 Spider-Man	60.00	150.00
46 Spider-Woman	20.00	50.00
47 Storm	20.00	50.00
48 Thanos	40.00	100.00
50 Thor	20.00	50.00
51 Venom	50.00	125.00
54 White Queen	20.00	50.00
61 Apocalypse	30.00	75.00
64 Spider-Man	25.00	60.00
69 War Machine	15.00	40.00
70 Phoenix	30.00	75.00
71 Magneto	15.00	40.00
72 Phoenix	40.00	100.00
73 Captain America	30.00	75.00
76 Ghost Rider	15.00	40.00
79 Venom	40.00	100.00
80 Spider-Man	20.00	50.00
81 Carnage	25.00	60.00
82 Thor	15.00	40.00
83 Loki	15.00	40.00
84 Thunderstrike	15.00	40.00
85 Spider-Man GEN	25.00	60.00
87 Spider-Man GEN	30.00	75.00
88 Ant-Man GEN	12.00	30.00
91 Weapon X GEN	25.00	60.00
92 Wolverine GEN	40.00	100.00
93 Wolverine GEN	30.00	75.00
94 Daredevil GEN	15.00	40.00
95 Daredevil GEN	15.00	40.00
96 Daredevil GEN	30.00	75.00
97 Hulk GEN	20.00	50.00
98 Hulk GEN	15.00	40.00
99 Hulk GEN	15.00	40.00
100 Checklist	50.00	125.00

1996 Fleer SkyBox Marvel Masterpieces Double Impact

COMPLETE SET (6)	800.00	2000.00
COMMON CARD (1-6)	100.00	250.00
STATED ODDS 1:4		
1 Bishop Beast	200.00	500.00
2 Punisher Psylocke	250.00	600.00
3 Rogue Human Torch	250.00	600.00
4 Silver Surfer Captain America	300.00	750.00
6 Wolverine Venom	125.00	300.00

1996 Fleer SkyBox Marvel Masterpieces Gallery

COMPLETE SET (6)	200.00	500.00
COMMON CARD (1-6)	40.00	100.00
STATED ODDS 1:3		
2 Hulk	50.00	125.00
5 Spider-Man	100.00	250.00
6 Wolverine	60.00	150.00

1996 Fleer SkyBox Marvel Masterpieces Power Pop-Ups

COMPLETE SET (27)	60.00	120.00
COMMON CARD (1-27)	3.00	8.00

1996 Fleer SkyBox Marvel Masterpieces Promos

COMPLETE SET (6)	75.00	150.00
COMMON CARD	12.00	30.00
1 Cyclops	15.00	40.00
2 Hulk	15.00	40.00
4 Sabretooth	25.00	60.00
5 Spider-Man	30.00	75.00
6 Wolverine	20.00	50.00

2007 Marvel Masterpieces

COMPLETE SET (90)	15.00	40.00
UNOPENED BOX (36 PACKS)	800.00	1200.00
UNOPENED PACK (7 CARDS)	25.00	35.00
COMMON CARD (1-90)	.40	1.00
*FOIL: 1X TO 2.5X BASIC CARDS	.60	1.50
*GOLD: 2.5X TO 6X BASIC CARDS	1.00	2.25
4 Apocalypse	.75	2.00
10 Black Panther	1.25	3.00
11 Black Widow	1.25	3.00
15 Cable	1.25	3.00
16 Captain America	1.50	4.00
20 Cyclops	.50	1.25
22 Daredevil	1.00	2.50
31 Gambit	.75	2.00
43 Iron Man	1.50	4.00
61 Mystique	1.25	3.00
66 Punisher	1.50	4.00
72 Scarlet Witch	1.25	2.00
77 The Silver Surfer	.50	1.25
79 Spider-Man	1.50	4.00
81 Storm	1.25	3.00
86 Thor	1.25	3.00
88 Venom	1.50	4.00
90 Wolverine	2.00	5.00

2007 Marvel Masterpieces Spider-Man

COMPLETE SET (9)	8.00	20.00
COMMON CARD (S1-S9)	1.50	4.00
*FOIL: .6X TO 1.5X BASIC CARD		
STATED ODDS 1:4		

2007 Marvel Masterpieces Splash Page Alex Ross

COMPLETE SET (3)	3.00	8.00
COMMON CARD (1-3)	1.50	4.00
*ASH CAN: .6X TO 1.5X BASIC CARD		
STATED ODDS 1:6		

2007 Marvel Masterpieces Splash Page Art Adams

COMPLETE SET (3)	3.00	8.00
COMMON CARD (1-3)	1.50	4.00
*ASH CAN: 4X TO 10X BASIC CARDS		
STATED ODDS 1:6		

2007 Marvel Masterpieces Splash Page Drew Struzan

COMPLETE SET (3)	3.00	8.00
COMMON CARD (1-3)	1.50	4.00
STATED ODDS 1:6		

2007 Marvel Masterpieces Subcasts

COMPLETE SET (5)	.75	2.00
COMMON CARD (1-5)	.25	.60
STATED ODDS ONE PER PACK		

2007 Marvel Masterpieces X-Men

COMPLETE SET (9)	8.00	20.00
COMMON CARD (X1-X9)	1.50	4.00
*FOIL: .75X TO 2X BASIC CARD		
STATED ODDS 1:4		
X2 Wolverine	3.00	8.00
X4 Cyclops	2.00	5.00

2007 Marvel Masterpieces Promos

COMMON CARD (P1-P5)	2.00	5.00
P1 Magneto SDCC	2.50	6.00
P4 Wolverine SDCC	3.00	8.00
P5 Wolverine NSU	5.00	12.00

2008 Marvel Masterpieces 2

COMPLETE SET (90)	12.00	30.00
UNOPENED BOX (36 PACKS)	250.00	400.00
UNOPENED PACK (7 CARDS)	8.00	12.00
COMMON CARD (1-90)	.25	.60
1 Marvel Masterpieces 2	.40	1.00
8 Captain America	1.50	4.00
9 Captain Marvel	1.25	3.00
13 Cyclops	1.25	3.00
14 Daredevil	1.50	4.00
15 Dazzler	.75	2.00
18 Dr. Doom	2.00	5.00
19 Dr. Octopus	.40	1.00
21 Dr. Strange	.75	2.00
27 Galactus	1.25	3.00
28 Ghost Rider	.75	2.00
34 The Hulk	1.25	3.00
38 Iron Man	1.50	4.00
42 Kang	.60	1.50
48 Magneto	1.00	2.50
62 The Punisher	1.25	3.00
72 Scarlet Witch	1.25	3.00
79 Silver Surfer	1.00	2.50
80 Spider-Man	2.00	5.00
81 Spider-Woman	.75	2.00
82 Storm	.40	1.00
85 Thor	1.00	2.50
87 Venom	2.50	6.00
90 Wolverine	3.00	8.00

2008 Marvel Masterpieces 2 Avengers

COMPLETE SET (9)	8.00	20.00
COMMON CARD (A1-A9)	1.25	3.00
STATED ODDS 2:9		
A2 Captain America	2.00	5.00
A4 The Hulk	1.50	4.00
A5 Iron Man	2.00	5.00
A6 Scarlet Witch	1.50	4.00
A7 Thor	1.50	4.00
A8 The Vision	1.50	4.00

2008 Marvel Masterpieces 2 Fantastic Four Memorabilia

COMMON MEM (FF1-FF5)	6.00	15.00
STATED ODDS 1:36		
FF1 Mr. Fantastic	8.00	20.00
FF2 Invisible Woman	30.00	75.00
FF5 Dr. Doom	8.00	20.00

2008 Marvel Masterpieces 2 Hulk Die-Cuts

COMPLETE SET (3)	60.00	120.00
COMMON CARD (A-C)	5.00	10.00
CARD A STATED ODDS 1:18 HOBBY		
CARDS B AND C RANDOM INSERT IN RETAIL PACKS		
B Hulk R	30.00	75.00
C Hulk R	50.00	100.00

2008 Marvel Masterpieces 2 Iron Man Die-Cuts

COMPLETE SET (3)	50.00	100.00
COMMON CARD (A-C)	3.00	8.00
CARD A STATED ODDS 1:18 HOBBY		
CARDS B AND C RANDOM INSERT IN RETAIL PACKS		
B Iron Man R	20.00	50.00
C Iron Man R	30.00	75.00

2008 Marvel Masterpieces 2 Jumbo Box-Toppers

COMPLETE SET (5)	8.00	20.00
COMMON CARD (1-5)	2.00	5.00
STATED ODDS ONE PER BOX		
1 Dr. Strange	2.50	6.00
2 Scarlet Witch	3.00	8.00
3 Spider-Woman	2.50	6.00

2008 Marvel Masterpieces 2 Marvel Heroines

COMPLETE SET (9)	6.00	15.00
COMMON CARD (MH1-MH9)	.60	1.50
STATED ODDS 2:9		
MH1 Elektra	1.25	3.00
MH3 Jean Grey	2.00	5.00
MH4 Ms. Marvel	2.50	6.00
MH5 Mystique	1.50	4.00
MH6 She-Hulk	1.50	4.00
MH9 Storm	1.25	3.00

2008 Marvel Masterpieces 2 Promos

COMPLETE SET (5)	12.00	30.00
COMMON CARD (P6-P10)	3.00	8.00
P7 Spider-Woman SDCC	4.00	10.00
P8 Venom SDCC	6.00	15.00
P10 The Hulk SDCC	4.00	10.00

2008 Marvel Masterpieces 3

COMPLETE SET (90)	15.00	40.00
UNOPENED BOX (36 PACKS)	250.00	400.00
UNOPENED PACK (7 CARDS)	8.00	12.00
COMMON CARD (1-90)	.30	.75
3 Baron Zemo	.40	1.00
7 Dark Phoenix	.40	1.00
9 Dormammu and Umar	.40	1.00
10 Dr. Doom	1.00	2.50
12 Elektra	.40	1.00
14 Fin Fang Foom	.60	1.25
15 Green Goblin	1.00	2.50
20 Kang	.75	2.00
21 The Kingpin	.75	2.00
44 Venom	4.00	10.00
53 Death of Elektra	.75	2.00
68 To Court Death	1.25	3.00
70 To Save the Earth	1.50	4.00
74 Doc Ock Mug Shot 1	.60	1.50
75 Doc Ock Mug Shot 2	.60	1.50
77 Electro Mug Shot 1	.60	1.50
78 Electro Mug Shot 2	.60	1.50
80 Kraven Mug Shot 1	.60	1.50
81 Kraven Mug Shot 2	.60	1.50
83 Mysterio Mug Shot 1	.60	1.50
84 Mysterio Mug Shot 2	.60	1.50
86 Sandman Mug Shot 1	.60	1.50
87 Sandman Mug Shot 2	.60	1.50
89 Vulture Mug Shot 1	.60	1.50
90 Vulture Mug Shot 2	.60	1.50

2008 Marvel Masterpieces 3 Marvel Knights

COMPLETE SET (9)	4.00	10.00
COMMON CARD (MK1-MK9)	.50	1.25
MK1 Blade	.75	2.00
MK5 Dr. Strange	1.25	3.00
MK7 Moon Knight	1.25	3.00
MK9 The Punisher	1.50	4.00

2008 Marvel Masterpieces 3 Marvel Moments

COMPLETE SET (9)	25.00	60.00
COMMON CARD (MM1-MM9)	4.00	10.00

2008 Marvel Masterpieces 3 Writer Autographs

COMMON AUTO	5.00	12.00
STATED ODDS 1:108		
AL Andy Lanning	10.00	25.00
GP Greg Pak	6.00	15.00
HM Howard Mackie	8.00	20.00
JL Jeph Loeb	15.00	40.00
JS Jim Salicrup	10.00	25.00
LH Larry Hama	12.00	30.00
MB Mike Baron	8.00	20.00
MO Mike Avon Oeming	8.00	20.00
PJ Paul Jenkins	10.00	25.00
PT Paul Tobin	6.00	15.00
RS Roger Stern	8.00	20.00
RT Roy Thomas	6.00	15.00
WS Walt Simonson	12.00	30.00
BKV Brian K. Vaughan	10.00	25.00
CBC C. B. Cebulski	12.00	30.00
DM1 David Mack	10.00	25.00
DM2 Dwayne McDuffie	6.00	15.00
FVL Fred Van Lente	10.00	25.00
JP1 Jeff Parker	8.00	20.00
JP2 Jimmy Palmiotti	6.00	15.00
TD1 Todd Dezago	6.00	15.00
TD2 Tom DeFalco	12.00	30.00

2008 Marvel Masterpieces 3 X-Men Secret Identities

COMPLETE SET (9)	10.00	25.00
COMMON CARD (XM1-XM9)	2.00	5.00

2016 Marvel Masterpieces

COMPLETE SET W/O SP (81)	250.00	500.00
COMPLETE SET W/SP (90)	1250.00	2500.00
UNOPENED BOX (12 PACKS)	200.00	250.00
UNOPENED PACK (3 CARDS)	20.00	25.00
COMMON/1999 (1-36)	3.00	8.00
COMMON/1499 (37-63)	5.00	12.00
COMMON/999 (64-81)	6.00	15.00
COMMON/99 (82-90)	100.00	200.00
*EPIC PURPLE/199 (1-36): 1X TO 2.5X BASIC CARDS		
*EPIC PURPLE/199 (37-63): .6X TO 1.5X BASIC CARDS		
*EPIC PURPLE/199 (64-81): .5X TO 1.2X BASIC CARDS		
*EPIC PURPLE/199 (82-90): .15X TO .40X BASIC CARDS		
*LEG.ORANGE/99 (1-36): 2X TO 5X BASIC CARDS		
*LEG.ORANGE/99 (37-63): 1.2X TO 3X BASIC CARDS		
*LEG.ORANGE/99 (64-81): 1X TO 2.5X BASIC CARDS		
*LEG.ORANGE/99 (82-90): .25X TO .60X BASIC CARDS		

2016 Marvel Masterpieces Battle Spectra

COMPLETE SET (16)	200.00	500.00
COMMON CARD (BS1-BS16)	12.00	30.00
BS2 Wolverine/Sabretooth	40.00	100.00
BS3 Iron Man/Fin Fang Foom	15.00	40.00
BS4 Spider-Man/Morlun	20.00	50.00
BS5 Carnage/Venom	100.00	250.00
BS7 Bushman/Moon Knight	20.00	50.00
BS9 Iron Man/Captain	25.00	60.00
BS10 Iron Man/Thor	15.00	40.00
BS11 Taskmaster/Deadpool	30.00	75.00
BS12 Hulk/Sentry	20.00	50.00
BS15 Hulk/Red Hulk	15.00	40.00
BS16 Bullseye Daredevil	15.00	40.00

2016 Marvel Masterpieces Battle Spectra Gems

COMPLETE SET (16)		
COMMON CARD	150.00	400.00
STATED PRINT RUN 99 SER.#'d SETS		
BS2 Wolverine/Sabretooth	800.00	2000.00
BS3 Iron Man/Fin Fang Foom	200.00	500.00
BS4 Spider-Man/Morlun	600.00	1500.00
BS5 Carnage/Venom	800.00	2000.00
BS7 Bushman/Moon Knight	300.00	800.00
BS8 Drax/Thanos	200.00	500.00
BS9 Iron Man/Captain	600.00	1500.00
BS10 Iron Man/Thor	400.00	1000.00
BS11 Taskmaster/Deadpool	500.00	1200.00
BS12 Hulk/Sentry	200.00	500.00
BS15 Hulk/Red Hulk	250.00	600.00
BS16 Bullseye/Daredevil	300.00	750.00

2016 Marvel Masterpieces Canvas

COMPLETE SET (10)	100.00	200.00
COMMON CARD (91-100)	6.00	15.00
*GALLERY/99: 2.5X TO 6X BASIC CARDS		
*GALLERY RED/25: 4X TO 10X BASIC CARDS		
91 Spider-Man	10.00	25.00
92 Wolverine	15.00	40.00
96 Iron Man	10.00	25.00
97 Daredevil	10.00	25.00
100 Venom	8.00	20.00

2016 Marvel Masterpieces Canvas Gallery

COMMON CARD	75.00	200.00
STATED PRINT RUN 99 SER.#'d SETS		

2016 Marvel Masterpieces Holofoil

COMPLETE SET (17)	200.00	500.00
COMMON CARD (1-17)	12.00	30.00
1 Spider-Man	60.00	150.00
2 Wolverine	60.00	150.00
3 Hulk	15.00	40.00
5 Iron Man	15.00	40.00
11 Jean Grey	15.00	40.00
12 Deadpool	20.00	50.00
14 Professor X	15.00	40.00
15 Doctor Strange	20.00	50.00
17 Captain America	15.00	40.00

2016 Marvel Masterpieces Holofoil Speckle

COMMON CARD	60.00	150.00
STATED PRINT RUN 99 SER.#'d SETS		
1 Spider-Man	300.00	750.00
2 Wolverine	300.00	750.00
3 Hulk	100.00	250.00
4 Thor	100.00	250.00
5 Iron Man	75.00	200.00
8 Daredevil	100.00	250.00
10 Magneto	100.00	250.00
11 Jean Grey	125.00	300.00
12 Deadpool	200.00	500.00
13 Scarlet Witch	75.00	200.00
14 Professor X	125.00	300.00
15 Doctor Strange	75.00	200.00
16 Black Panther	150.00	400.00
17 Captain America	100.00	250.00

2016 Marvel Masterpieces Joe Jusko Commemorative Buybacks

COMMON CARD	10.00	25.00
RANDOMLY INSERTED INTO PACKS		

2016 Marvel Masterpieces Mirage

COMPLETE SET (9)		
COMMON CARD	75.00	200.00
1 Iron Man	100.00	250.00
Captain America#{Thor#{Hulk/Avengers		
4 Defenders	125.00	300.00
5 Illuminati	100.00	250.00
6 Lady Liberators	125.00	300.00
7 Secret Avengers	100.00	250.00
8 Thunderbolts	200.00	500.00

2016 Marvel Masterpieces What If

COMMON CARD/1,499 (1-36)	2.50	6.00
COMMON CARD/999 (37-63)	4.00	10.00
COMMON CARD/499 (64-81)	8.00	20.00
COMMON CARD/50 (82-90)	100.00	250.00
82 Doctor Doom	125.00	300.00
Amazing Spider-Man Vol 1 #5/50		
84 Deadpool	150.00	400.00
New Mutants #98/50		
85 Hulk	125.00	300.00
86 Venom	150.00	400.00
Amazing Spider-Man #299/50		
87 Iron Man	125.00	300.00
Tales of Suspense #39/50		
88 Silver Surfer	125.00	300.00
89 Wolverine	150.00	400.00
Incredible Hulk Vol 1 #181/50		
90 Spider-Man	150.00	400.00
Amazing Fantasy #15/50		

2018 Marvel Masterpieces

COMPLETE SET W/SP (90)		
COMPLETE SET W/O SP (36)		
UNOPENED BOX (12 PACKS)		
UNOPENED PACK (3 CARDS)		
COMMON CARD (1-36)	2.00	5.00
COMMON CARD (37-63)	3.00	8.00
COMMON CARD (64-81)	6.00	15.00
COMMON CARD (82-90)	75.00	200.00
COMMON CANVAS (91-100)	6.00	15.00
*GOLD (1-81): SAME VALUE AS BASIC		
*GOLD (82-90): .30X TO .80X BASIC CARDS		
*GOLD (91-100): 1.5X TO 4X BASIC CARDS		
*WHAT IF/1499 (1-81): SAME VALUE AS BASIC		
*WHAT IF/1499 (82-90): .5X TO 1.2X BASIC CARDS		
*PURPLE/199 (1-81): .6X TO 1.5X BASIC CARDS		
*PURPLE/199 (82-90): .2X TO .5X BASIC CARDS		
*ORANGE/99 (1-81): .75X TO 2X BASIC CARDS		
*ORANGE/99 (82-90): .25X TO .6X BASIC CARDS		
TIER ONE (1-36)/1999		
TIER TWO (37-63)/1499		
TIER THREE (64-81)/999		
TIER FOUR (82-90)		
CANVAS GALLERY (91-100)		
83 Phoenix	150.00	400.00
84 Thor	125.00	300.00
87 Wolverine	300.00	800.00
88 Captain America	125.00	300.00
89 Iron Man	125.00	300.00
90 Spider-Man	300.00	750.00
91 Loki CG	12.00	30.00
92 Phoenix CG	8.00	20.00
96 Wolverine CG	10.00	25.00
97 Captain America CG	8.00	20.00
98 Iron Man CG	8.00	20.00
99 Spider-Man CG	15.00	40.00

2018 Marvel Masterpieces Battle Spectra

COMPLETE SET (15)	75.00	200.00
COMMON CARD (BS1-BS15)	6.00	15.00
STATED ODDS 1:14		
BS1 Captain America vs. Crossbones	10.00	25.00
BS2 Thanos vs. Nova and Star-Lord	8.00	20.00
BS4 Agent Venom vs. Spider-Queen	10.00	25.00
BS5 Thor Odinson vs. Thor (Jane Foster)	10.00	25.00
BS7 Spider-Man vs. The New Jackal	10.00	25.00
BS8 Silk vs. Black Cat	8.00	20.00
BS9 Cyclops vs. Wolverine	10.00	25.00
BS11 Spider-Man vs. Doctor Octopus	12.00	30.00
BS13 Iron Man vs. Captain Marvel	8.00	20.00

2018 Marvel Masterpieces Battle Spectra Gems

COMMON CARD	75.00	200.00
STATED PRINT RUN 99 SER.#'d SETS		
BS2 Thanos vs. Nova and Star-Lord	200.00	500.00
BS5 Thor Odinson vs. Thor (Jane Foster)	125.00	300.00
BS7 Spider-Man vs. The New Jackal	100.00	250.00
BS8 Silk vs. Black Cat	100.00	250.00
BS9 Cyclops vs. Wolverine	200.00	500.00
BS11 Spider-Man vs. Doctor Octopus	200.00	500.00
BS12 Hulk vs. Doctor Strange (Zom)	150.00	400.00

2018 Marvel Masterpieces E-Pack Master Achievement Rainbow

COMMON CARD (RFB1-RFB5)	20.00	50.00
RFB3 Storm	25.00	60.00
RFB4 Captain Marvel	25.00	60.00
RFB5 Spider-Man	2000.00	5000.00

2018 Marvel Masterpieces Holofoil

COMPLETE SET (20)	75.00	200.00
COMMON CARD (1-20)	4.00	10.00
STATED ODDS 1:14		
1 Vision	5.00	12.00
2 X-23	12.00	30.00
3 Radioactive Man	5.00	12.00
4 Quasar	6.00	15.00
6 Thanos	12.00	30.00
8 Drax	5.00	12.00
9 Star-Lord	6.00	15.00
10 Rocket Raccoon	10.00	25.00
11 Groot	6.00	15.00
12 Ultron	5.00	12.00
13 Punisher	8.00	20.00
14 She-Hulk	10.00	25.00
16 Namor	5.00	12.00
17 Taskmaster	8.00	20.00
18 Ant-Man	5.00	12.00
19 Enchantress	5.00	12.00
20 Deadpool	12.00	30.00

2018 Marvel Masterpieces Holofoil Kaleidoscope

COMMON CARD	40.00	100.00
STATED PRINT RUN 25 SER.#'d SETS		
1 Vision	60.00	150.00
2 X-23	200.00	500.00
5 Elektra	100.00	250.00
6 Thanos	300.00	750.00
7 Gamora	75.00	200.00
8 Drax	50.00	125.00
9 Star-Lord	125.00	300.00
10 Rocket Raccoon	75.00	200.00
11 Groot	60.00	150.00
12 Ultron	60.00	150.00
13 Punisher	100.00	250.00
14 She-Hulk	60.00	150.00
16 Namor	75.00	200.00
17 Taskmaster	50.00	125.00
18 Ant-Man	75.00	200.00
19 Enchantress	50.00	125.00
20 Deadpool	600.00	1500.00

2018 Marvel Masterpieces Holofoil Speckle

COMMON CARD	25.00	60.00
STATED PRINT RUN 99 SER.#'d SETS		
2 X-23	50.00	125.00
3 Radioactive Man	30.00	75.00
5 Elektra	60.00	150.00
6 Thanos	50.00	125.00
7 Gamora	60.00	150.00
8 Drax	30.00	75.00
9 Star-Lord	50.00	125.00
10 Rocket Raccoon	50.00	150.00
11 Groot	40.00	100.00
12 Ultron	30.00	75.00
13 Punisher	40.00	100.00
14 She-Hulk	30.00	75.00
16 Namor	40.00	100.00
17 Taskmaster	30.00	75.00
20 Deadpool	100.00	250.00

2018 Marvel Masterpieces Mirage

COMPLETE SET (9)	400.00	1000.00
COMMON CARD (1-9)	60.00	150.00
STATED ODDS 1:144		
3 Daredevil/Iron Fist/Luke Cage/Jessica Jones	100.00	250.00
4 Doc Ock/Kraven/Electro/Mysterio	125.00	300.00
5 Black Bolt/Medusa/Karnak/Gorgon	100.00	250.00

7 Spider-Woman/Spidey Wolverine/Luke Cage	125.00	300.00

2018 Marvel Masterpieces Preliminary Art

COMMON CARD (PA1-PA90)	2.50	6.00
STATED ODDS 1:12		
PA1 Vision	3.00	8.00
PA2 Punisher	5.00	12.00
PA3 Deadpool	8.00	20.00
PA4 Venom	6.00	15.00
PA5 Hellcat	3.00	8.00
PA8 Nova	3.00	8.00
PA10 Hercules vs. Amatsu-Mikaboshi	4.00	10.00
PA11 Elektra	5.00	12.00
PA12 Hyperion vs. Namor	6.00	15.00
PA13 Hulk	4.00	10.00
PA14 Wonder Man	3.00	8.00
PA16 Falcon	5.00	12.00
PA17 Absorbing Man	8.00	20.00
PA18 Madame Masque	3.00	8.00
PA20 Ant-Man	3.00	8.00
PA21 Maria Hill	5.00	12.00
PA22 Gorgon	3.00	8.00
PA23 Hercules	3.00	8.00
PA25 Adam Warlock	6.00	15.00
PA26 Wasp	3.00	8.00
PA27 Spider-Man	10.00	25.00
PA29 Leader	4.00	10.00
PA30 War Machine	8.00	20.00
PA31 Taskmaster	4.00	10.00
PA33 Winter Soldier	4.00	10.00
PA34 Sabretooth	3.00	8.00
PA36 Spider-Woman	5.00	12.00
PA38 Yellowjacket	6.00	15.00
PA40 Deathlok	3.00	8.00
PA41 Kitty Pryde	4.00	10.00
PA42 Beast	5.00	12.00
PA43 Psylocke	5.00	12.00
PA44 Magik	4.00	10.00
PA45 Mockingbird	6.00	15.00
PA48 Colossus	5.00	12.00
PA52 Beta Ray Bill	5.00	12.00
PA53 Iron Fist	3.00	8.00
PA54 Jessica Jones	3.00	8.00
PA56 Mephisto	3.00	8.00
PA57 Professor X	3.00	8.00
PA58 Thanos	8.00	20.00
PA59 Spider-Man vs. Doctor Octopus	6.00	15.00
PA60 Daredevil	6.00	15.00
PA61 Red Hulk	3.00	8.00
PA62 Agent Venom vs. Spider-Queen	8.00	20.00
PA63 Hulk vs. Doctor Strange	6.00	15.00
PA64 Lady Sif	4.00	10.00
PA66 Emma Frost	10.00	25.00
PA67 Thanos vs. Nova and Star-Lord	10.00	25.00
PA68 Thor Odinson vs. Thor (Jane Foster)	6.00	15.00
PA69 Havok	5.00	12.00
PA73 Carnage	6.00	15.00
PA74 Iron Fist vs. Daredevil	5.00	12.00
PA75 Captain Marvel	6.00	15.00
PA76 Iceman	6.00	15.00
PA78 Drax	3.00	8.00
PA79 Cyclops	4.00	10.00
PA80 Thor	5.00	12.00
PA81 Spider-Gwen	8.00	20.00
PA82 Phoenix	12.00	30.00
PA83 Magneto	3.00	8.00
PA84 Cyclops vs. Wolverine	12.00	30.00
PA85 Crossbones	3.00	8.00
PA86 Loki	4.00	10.00
PA87 Ultron	8.00	20.00
PA88 Crystal	5.00	12.00
PA89 Man-Thing	5.00	12.00
PA90 Spider-Man vs. The New Jackal	10.00	25.00

2018 Marvel Masterpieces Silver Spectrum Foil Autographs

COMMON AUTO	75.00	200.00
STATED PRINT RUN 10 SER.#'d SETS		

2018 Marvel Masterpieces What If?

COMPLETE SET (90)		
COMMON CARD/1,499 (WI1-WI36)	2.00	5.00
COMMON CARD/999 (WI37-WI63)	3.00	8.00
COMMON CARD/499 (WI64-WI81)	6.00	15.00
COMMON CARD/50 (WI82-WI90)	75.00	200.00

2020 Upper Deck Marvel Masterpieces

UNOPENED BOX (12 PACKS)	800.00	1200.00
UNOPENED PACK (3 CARDS)	65.00	100.00
COMMON LEVEL 1 (1-36)	1.00	2.50
COMMON LEVEL 2 (37-63)	1.50	4.00
COMMON LEVEL 3 (64-81)	3.00	8.00
COMMON LEVEL 4 (82-90)	75.00	150.00
COMMON SP (91-100)	4.00	10.00
*GOLD: .5X TO 1.2X BASIC CARDS		
*PRELIM.ART: X TO X BASIC CARDS		
*WHAT IF?: X TO X BASIC CARDS		
*EPIC PURPLE/199: .6X TO 1.5X BASIC CARDS		
*LEG.ORANGE/99: .75X TO 2X BASIC CARDS		
*METALLURGY/25: 4X TO 10X BASIC CARDS		
LEVEL 1 PRINT RUN 1999 SER.#'d SETS		
LEVEL 2 PRINT RUN 1499 SER.#'d SETS		
LEVEL 3 PRINT RUN 999 SER.#'d SETS		
LEVEL 4 PRINT RUN 99 SER.#'d SETS		
64 Groot/999	5.00	12.00
66 Rogue/999	4.00	10.00
68 Graviton/999	5.00	12.00
70 Ultron/999	5.00	12.00
71 Howard The Duck/999	4.00	10.00
72 Cyclops/999	6.00	15.00
73 Sentinels/999	4.00	10.00
74 Colossus/999	6.00	15.00
76 Captain Marvel/999	8.00	20.00
77 Man-Thing/999	5.00	12.00
78 Boom Boom/999	4.00	10.00
82 Wolverine/99	100.00	200.00
83 Skaar/99	125.00	250.00
84 Red Skull/99	125.00	250.00
85 Grey Gargoyle/99	150.00	300.00
86 Ego The Living Planet/99	100.00	200.00
88 Martinex/99	100.00	200.00
89 Kraven/99	125.00	250.00
90 Emma Frost/99	100.00	200.00
92 Gambit SP	6.00	15.00
93 Spider-Man SP	8.00	20.00
94 Hulk SP	6.00	15.00
95 Mysterio SP	5.00	12.00
96 Black Panther SP	8.00	20.00
97 Thor SP	8.00	20.00
98 Thanos SP	10.00	25.00
99 Black Widow SP	10.00	25.00
100 Taskmaster SP	5.00	12.00

2020 Upper Deck Marvel Masterpieces Battle Spectra

COMPLETE SET (15)	75.00	200.00
COMMON CARD (BS1-BS15)	5.00	12.00
STATED ODDS 1:12		
BS1 Black Knight vs. Swordsman	8.00	20.00
BS4 Hulk vs. Thanos	8.00	20.00
BS9 Cyclops vs. Mr. Sinister	8.00	20.00
BS10 Captain America vs. Arnim Zola	10.00	25.00
BS11 Thor vs. Gorr the God Butcher	8.00	20.00
BS12 Black Panther vs. Killmonger	8.00	20.00
BS13 Ultron vs. Vision	8.00	20.00
BS15 Doctor Strange vs. Mr. Misery	8.00	15.00

2020 Upper Deck Marvel Masterpieces Battle Spectra Gems

COMMON CARD	50.00	125.00
STATED PRINT RUN 99 SER.#'d SETS		
BS1 Black Knight vs. Swordsman	125.00	300.00
BS2 Legion vs. Shadow King	75.00	200.00
BS3 Spider-Man vs. Mysterio	200.00	500.00
BS4 Hulk vs. Thanos	150.00	400.00
BS6 Old Man Logan vs. Scarlet Samurai	75.00	200.00
BS7 Hercules V Thor	60.00	150.00
BS8 Hawkeye vs. Bullseye	75.00	200.00
BS9 Cyclops vs. Mr. Sinister	125.00	300.00
BS10 Captain America vs. Arnim Zola	100.00	250.00
BS11 Thor vs. Gorr the God Butcher	200.00	500.00
BS12 Black Panther vs. Killmonger	200.00	500.00
BS14 Daredevil vs. Typhoid Mary	100.00	250.00
BS15 Doctor Strange vs. Mr. Misery	200.00	400.00

2020 Upper Deck Marvel Masterpieces Holofoil

COMPLETE SET (20)		
*SPECKLE/99: .75X TO 2X BASIC CARDS		
STATED ODDS 1:12		
HF1 Star-Lord	8.00	20.00
HF2 Deadpool	10.00	25.00
HF3 Cable	6.00	15.00
HF6 Nova	5.00	12.00
HF7 Beast	6.00	15.00
HF8 Doctor Strange	6.00	15.00
HF10 Wolverine	12.00	30.00
HF13 Colossus	6.00	15.00
HF14 Emma Frost	5.00	12.00
HF15 Dormammu	5.00	12.00
HF16 Mystique	6.00	15.00
HF17 Punisher	10.00	25.00
HF18 Venom	8.00	20.00
HF19 Captain America	10.00	25.00

2020 Upper Deck Marvel Masterpieces Mirage

COMMON CARD (1-9)	75.00	150.00
STATED ODDS 1:144		
2 Cyclops/Wolverine/Storm	100.00	200.00
3 Thor/Black Widow/Vision	125.00	250.00
4 Black Knight/Black Panther/Spider-Man	125.00	250.00
5 Iron Man/Doctor Strange/Captain Marvel	150.00	300.00
6 Captain America/Nick Fury/Hulk	150.00	300.00
7 Green Goblin/Kingpin/Venom	125.00	250.00
8 Thanos/Magneto/Red Skull	150.00	300.00
9 Ultron/Bullseye/Mysterio	125.00	200.00

2020 Upper Deck Marvel Masterpieces Promo

NNO Wolverine NSU	6.00	15.00

1995 Fleer Metal Marvel

COMPLETE SET (138)	25.00	60.00
UNOPENED BOX (36 PACKS)	1250.00	2000.00
UNOPENED PACK (8 CARDS)	40.00	60.00
UNOPENED JUMBO BOX (24 PACKS)		
UNOPENED JUMBO PACK (10 CARDS)		
COMMON CARD (1-138)	.30	.75
*SILVER FLASHER: .5X TO 1.2X BASIC CARDS	.40	1.00
NO #138 ISSUED IN SILVER		
NNO1 Magneto	4.00	10.00
Venom#{Wolverine#{Iron Man 5X7 Promo		

1995 Fleer Metal Marvel Blaster

COMPLETE SET (18)	10.00	25.00
COMMON CARD (1-18)	.75	2.00
*GOLD: .6X TO 1.5X BASIC BLASTER		
STATED ODDS 1:2 HOBBY, 2:3 JUMBO		

1995 Fleer Metal Marvel Prints

COMPLETE SET (10)	12.00	30.00
COMMON CARD (1-10)	1.50	4.00
STATED ODDS 1:CASE		

1996 Fleer SkyBox Marvel Motion

COMPLETE SET (30)	30.00	75.00
UNOPENED BOX (35 PACKS)	125.00	200.00
UNOPENED PACK (2 CARDS)	4.00	6.00
COMMON CARD (1-30)	.75	2.00
3 Colossus	2.00	5.00
5 Gambit	1.50	4.00
6 Human Torch	1.25	3.00
7 Iceman	1.00	2.50
8 Iron Man	5.00	12.00
9 Phoenix	1.25	3.00
10 Mr. Fantastic	1.00	2.50
11 Rogue	4.00	10.00
12 Sabretooth	1.00	2.50
13 Silver Surfer	1.50	4.00
14 Spider-Man	10.00	25.00
16 Thing	1.50	4.00
18 Wolverine	3.00	8.00
19 Ghost Rider	2.50	6.00
20 Hulk	1.25	3.00
21 Mystique	2.00	5.00
22 Venom	6.00	15.00
23 Human Torch	1.50	4.00
24 Remy LeBeau - Gambit	2.00	5.00
25 Steve Rogers - Captain America	1.50	4.00
26 Robert Bruce Banner - Hulk	1.25	3.00
27 Rogue	1.25	3.00
28 Peter Parker - Spider-Man	1.50	4.00
29 Logan - Wolverine	2.00	5.00
30 Remy LeBeau - Gambit	2.00	5.00

1996 Fleer SkyBox Marvel Motion VirtualVision

COMPLETE SET (4)	25.00	60.00
COMMON CARD (1-4)	6.00	15.00
STATED ODDS 1:18		
1 Captain America	10.00	25.00
3 Spider-Man	15.00	40.00
4 Wolverine	12.00	30.00

1996 Fleer SkyBox Marvel Motion Promos

1 Spider-Man	4.00	10.00
2 Spider-Man	4.00	10.00
3 Wolverine	2.00	5.00
4 Wolverine	2.00	5.00
BB Wolverine (w/Spider-Man) (blank back)		
NNO Hobgoblin	12.00	30.00
NNO Venom	12.00	30.00

2014 Marvel Movies Vudu Pizza Promos

COMPLETE SET (4)	5.00	12.00
COMMON CARD	1.50	4.00
NNO Captain America	2.00	5.00
NNO Thor	2.00	5.00

2014 Marvel Now

COMPLETE SET W/O SP (100)	8.00	20.00
COMPLETE SET W/SP (150)	200.00	400.00
UNOPENED BOX (24 PACKS)		
UNOPENED PACK (6 CARDS)		
COMMON CARD (1-100)	.20	.50
COMMON CARD (101-130)	3.00	8.00
COMMON SP (131-150)	6.00	15.00
*SILVER: .8X TO 2X BASIC CARDS		
*RED: 8X TO 20X BASIC CARDS		
101-130 STATED ODDS 1:6		
131-150 STATED ODDS 1:24		
25 Deadpool	.40	1.00

2014 Marvel Now Autographs

COMMON AUTO	6.00	15.00
STATED ODDS 1:24		
8A Stuart Immonen	8.00	20.00
9A Stuart Immonen	8.00	20.00
15A Jorge Molina	8.00	20.00
23A Stuart Immonen	8.00	20.00
30A Stuart Immonen	8.00	20.00
31A Ed McGuinness	8.00	20.00
40A Mark Bagley	8.00	20.00
42A Stuart Immonen	8.00	20.00
44A Mark Bagley	8.00	20.00
48A Stuart Immonen	8.00	20.00
62A Giuseppe Camuncoli	8.00	20.00
68A Mark Bagley	8.00	20.00
76A Ed McGuinness	8.00	20.00
82A Ed McGuinness	8.00	20.00
91A Giuseppe Camuncoli	8.00	20.00
92A Simone Bianchi	8.00	20.00
93A Mark Bagley	8.00	20.00
97A Mark Bagley	8.00	20.00

2014 Marvel Now Cutting Edge Autographs

COMMON AUTO	6.00	15.00
OVERALL CUTTING EDGE AUTO ODDS 1:72		
101 John Cassaday	8.00	20.00

103A Brian Michael Bendis	10.00	25.00
103B Stuart Immonen	8.00	20.00
105 Tony Moore	8.00	20.00
107B Mike Allred	10.00	25.00
113 Steve Epting	8.00	20.00
117A Joe Keatinge	8.00	20.00
119A Ryan Stegman	8.00	20.00
119B Dan Slott	8.00	20.00
123A Brian Michael Bendis	10.00	25.00
126A Brian Michael Bendis	10.00	25.00
126B Chris Bachalo	8.00	20.00

2014 Marvel Now Cutting Edge Covers

COMPLETE SET (30)	10.00	25.00
COMMON CARD (101-130)	.50	1.25
STATED ODDS 1:1		

2014 Marvel Now Cutting Edge Dual Autographs

COMMON AUTO	12.00	30.00
OVERALL CUTTING EDGE AUTO ODDS 1:72		
103 Brian Michael Bendis Stuart Immonen	20.00	50.00
106 M.Fraction/M.Bagley	20.00	50.00
107 M.Fraction/M.Allred	25.00	50.00
108 M.Waid/L.Yu	15.00	40.00
117 J.Keating/R.Elson	15.00	40.00
124 J.Leob/E.McGuinness	15.00	40.00
107T Laura Allred Matt Fraction#{Mike Allred	75.00	150.00

2014 Marvel Now Cutting Edge Variant Covers Autographs

COMMON AUTO	6.00	15.00
OVERALL CUTTING EDGE AUTO ODDS 1:72		
102MD Mike Deodato Jr.	8.00	20.00
102SY Skottie Young	10.00	25.00
103SY Skottie Young	10.00	25.00
105CB Chris Bachalo	8.00	20.00
105SY Skottie Young	10.00	25.00
105TM Tony Moore	10.00	25.00
106SY Skottie Young	10.00	25.00
107SY Skottie Young	10.00	25.00
109HA Carlo Pagulayan	10.00	25.00
109SY Skottie Young	10.00	25.00
110ER Esad Ribic	10.00	25.00
110SY Skottie Young	10.00	25.00
111SY Skottie Young	10.00	25.00
112ER Esad Ribic	10.00	25.00
113SY Skottie Young	10.00	25.00
114SY Skottie Young	10.00	25.00
115MD Mike Deodato Jr.	8.00	20.00
115SY Skottie Young	10.00	25.00
116SY Skottie Young	10.00	25.00
117SY Skottie Young	10.00	25.00
118SY Skottie Young	10.00	25.00
119GC Giuseppe Camuncoli	8.00	20.00
119SY Skottie Young	10.00	25.00
120SY Skottie Young	10.00	25.00
122MD Mike Deodato Jr.	8.00	20.00
122SY Skottie Young	10.00	25.00
123MD Mike Deodato Jr.	8.00	20.00
124SY Skottie Young	10.00	25.00
125SY Skottie Young	10.00	25.00
126SY Skottie Young	10.00	25.00
127SY Skottie Young	10.00	25.00
129MD Mike Deodato Jr.	8.00	20.00
130SY Skottie Young	10.00	25.00

2014 Marvel Now Holograms

COMMON CARD (FX1-FX42)	12.00	30.00
STATED ODDS 1:72		
FX6 Captain America	15.00	40.00
FX11 Deadpool	20.00	50.00
FX18 Hulk	15.00	40.00
FX20 Iron Man	15.00	40.00
FX36 Superior Spider-Man	15.00	40.00
FX42 Wolverine	20.00	50.00

2014 Marvel Now Then and Now

COMPLETE SET (10)	15.00	40.00
COMMON CARD	3.00	8.00
STATED ODDS 1:38		

2014 Marvel Now Then and Now Dual Autographs

COMMON AUTO	125.00	250.00
STATED ODDS 1:24 WITH ALL AUTOGRAPHS		
TNLA Stan Lee	300.00	750.00
TNLE Stan Lee	300.00	750.00
TNLR Stan Lee	300.00	750.00
TNLS Ryan Stegman	300.00	750.00
TNSD Dan Slott	300.00	750.00

2014 Marvel Now Variant Covers

COMMON CARD	2.50	6.00
STATED ODDS 1:3.5		

1996 Fleer SkyBox Marvel Ultra Onslaught Previews

COMPLETE SET (9)	20.00	50.00
COMMON CARD (1-9)	2.50	6.00
INSERTED IN SPIDER-MAN '96 PACKS		
1 Cable	4.00	10.00
2 Hulk	4.00	10.00
3 Magneto	10.00	25.00
9 Captain America	6.00	15.00

1996 Fleer SkyBox Marvel Ultra Onslaught

COMPLETE SET (100)	30.00	75.00
UNOPENED BOX (36 PACKS)	200.00	400.00
UNOPENED PACK (8 CARDS)	6.00	12.00
COMMON CARD (1-100)	.75	2.00
6 Gambit	1.50	4.00
10 Rogue	1.25	3.00
11 Storm	1.25	3.00
12 Wolverine	2.00	5.00
22 Captain America	1.50	4.00
28 Scarlet Witch	1.25	3.00
29 Thor	1.25	3.00
32 Cable	1.25	3.00
41 Human Torch	1.00	2.50
42 Invisible Woman	1.00	2.50
43 Mr. Fantastic	1.00	2.50
44 Thing	1.00	2.50
60 Black Panther	1.50	4.00
61 Daredevil	1.00	2.50
62 Dr. Strange	1.25	3.00
65 Hulk	1.00	2.50
80 Black Bolt	1.00	2.50
81 Black Panther	1.25	3.00
90 Iron Man	1.50	4.00
93 Namor	1.25	3.00
95 Scarlet Witch	1.50	4.00

1996 Fleer SkyBox Marvel Ultra Onslaught Autographs

COMMON AUTO	15.00	40.00
STATED ODDS 1:4500		
2 Rob Liefeld	75.00	200.00
3 Stan Lee	200.00	500.00
4 Stan Lee	200.00	500.00

1996 Fleer SkyBox Marvel Ultra Onslaught Mirage

COMPLETE SET (3)	60.00	150.00
COMMON CARD (1-3)	30.00	75.00
STATED ODDS 1:36		
2 Fantastic Four	40.00	100.00

1996 Fleer SkyBox Marvel Ultra Onslaught Promos

COMMON CARD	.75	2.00
P1 Mr. Fantastic	1.50	4.00
P2 Iron Man	1.50	4.00

1992 Marvel Overkill Promos

COMPLETE SET (12)	20.00	50.00
COMMON CARD (1-12)	2.50	6.00

1994 Marvel Pepsi Mexico

COMPLETE SET (100)	25.00	60.00
UNOPENED BOX (50 PACKS)	300.00	500.00
UNOPENED PACK (5 CARDS)	6.00	10.00
COMMON CARD (1-100)	.25	.60
3 Con Gran Poder (Spider-Man Peter Parker)	.40	1.00
5 Hombre AraÃ±a (Spider-Man)	.40	1.00
6 Hombre de Acero (Iron Man)	.40	1.00
8 Buitre vs. Hombre AraÃ±a (Vulture vs. Spider-Man)	.30	.75
13 CapitÃ¡n AmÃ©rica	.30	.75
16 Hombre AraÃ±a vs. Duende Verde (Spider-Man vs. Green Goblin)	.30	.75
17 Rhino vs. Hombre AraÃ±a (Rhino vs. Spider-Man)	.30	.75
22 El Original Ghost Rider	.30	.75
24 The Punisher	.40	1.00
25 Wolverine vs. Hulk	.75	2.00
34 Puma vs. Spidey	.30	.75
45 Venom	.30	.75
48 Hombre AraÃ±a CÃ³smico (Cosmic Spider-Man)	.40	1.00
50 El Nuevo Ghost Rider	.30	.75
59 Omega Red vs. Wolverine	.40	1.00
61 Hombre AraÃ±a 2099 (Spider-Man 2099)	.40	1.00
66 Punisher 2099	.40	1.00
74 Wolverine Derrotado	.40	1.00
87 Venom	.30	.75
98 Wolverine	.75	2.00
NNO1 4UP Panel Wolverine Bloodhawk#{Hulk#{Jean Grey	4.00	10.00

1994 Marvel Pepsi Mexico Holograms

COMPLETE SET (4)	15.00	40.00
2 Spider-Man	10.00	25.00

1994 Marvel Pepsi Mexico Prisms Circular

COMPLETE SET (9)	15.00	40.00
COMMON CARD (1-9)	2.00	5.00
*TRIANGULAR: SAME VALUE		
2 Punisher	4.00	10.00
4 Gambit	4.00	10.00
5 Hombre Arana (Spider-Man)	5.00	12.00
6 Ghost Rider	3.00	8.00
9 Hombre de Acero (Iron Man)	3.00	10.00

1994 Marvel Pizza Hut Public Service

COMPLETE SET (4)	10.00	25.00
COMMON CARD	2.50	6.00
1 Captain America Falcon#{Daredevil#{Wasp	3.00	8.00
4 Spider-Man Iron Man#{Firestar#{Human Torch	4.00	10.00

2012 Marvel Premier

UNOPENED BOX (5 CARDS)	2000.00	4000.00
COMMON CARD (1-50)	8.00	20.00
STATED PRINT RUN 199 SER. #'d SETS		
5 Spider-Man	40.00	100.00
7 Captain America	12.00	30.00
8 Thor	10.00	25.00
11 Wasp	12.00	30.00
19 Scarlet Witch	12.00	30.00
20 Wolverine	20.00	50.00
21 Emma Frost	15.00	40.00
22 Cyclops	12.00	30.00
25 Rogue	20.00	50.00
27 Nightcrawler	10.00	25.00
28 Storm	15.00	40.00
30 Psylocke	25.00	60.00
31 Professor X	25.00	60.00
37 Ghost Rider	12.00	30.00
39 Doctor Doom	25.00	60.00
43 Loki	15.00	40.00
47 Thanos	20.00	50.00
48 Mystique	10.00	25.00
50 Galactus	15.00	40.00

2012 Marvel Premier Classic Corners

COMMON CARD (CC1-CC50)	12.00	30.00
STATED ODDS 1:2.3		
GROUP A ODDS 1:33.3		
GROUP B ODDS 1:10.4		
GROUP C ODDS 1:5.7		
GROUP D ODDS 1:3.2		
CC4 Secret Wars #1 A	125.00	300.00
CC5 Am. Spider-man #252 A	150.00	400.00
CC9 Daredevil #1 D	15.00	40.00
CC14 Defenders (vol. 1) #1 C	30.00	60.00
CC25 Am. Spider-Man #279 A	200.00	500.00
CC27 Am. Spider-Man #250 B	20.00	40.00
CC28 Guard of Galaxy #3 B	40.00	80.00
CC29 Am. Spider-Man #32 A	75.00	200.00
CC30 Am. Spider-Man #200 B	20.00	40.00
CC35 Wolverine Vol. 2 #1 C	30.00	60.00
CC37 Black Goliath #2 B	20.00	40.00
CC38 Nova #1 B	40.00	100.00
CC40 Night Rider #1 B	20.00	40.00
CC43 Howard The Duck #33 A	250.00	600.00
CC44 Invaders (vol 1) #1 B	40.00	80.00
CC46 Marvel Two-in-One #22 B	20.00	40.00
CC49 Mar.Spot. Warriors 3 B	20.00	50.00
CC50 Mar.Spot. Deathlok #33 B	20.00	40.00

2012 Marvel Premier Emotion Jason Adams Sketches

COMMON CARD	15.00	40.00
STATED PRINT RUN 50 SER. #'d SETS		
E2 Responsibility - Spider-Man	35.00	70.00
E4 Patriotism - Captain America	30.00	60.00
E9 Ferocity - Sabertooth	30.00	60.00
E12 Torment - Wolverine	60.00	120.00
E14 Anxiety - Rogue	40.00	80.00
E16 Turmoil - Psylocke	30.00	60.00
E17 Horror - Venom	30.00	60.00
E18 Insanity - Deadpool	40.00	80.00

2012 Marvel Premier Shadowbox

COMMON CARD (S1-S42)	12.00	30.00
STATED ODDS 1:2.7		
GROUP A ODDS 1:41.7		
GROUP B ODDS 1:13		
GROUP C ODDS 1:6.1		
GROUP D ODDS 1:3.2		
S3 Punisher/Spider-Man A	150.00	400.00
S5 Wolverine/Magneto B	50.00	125.00
S9 Dark Aveng/Aveng A	150.00	400.00
S11 Ult.Wolverine/Ult.Hulk A	250.00	600.00
S14 Venom/Spid/Carn/Anti C	75.00	200.00
S20 X-Men/Sentinels D	15.00	40.00
S21 Deadpool/Taskmaster D	15.00	40.00
S27 Thanos/Earth's Heroes C	15.00	40.00
S29 Iron Fist/Hydra Soldiers B	15.00	40.00
S30 Moon Knight/Bushman A	60.00	150.00
S35 Brotherhood/X-Men B	15.00	40.00
S36 Hulk/Namor B	15.00	40.00
S37 Lizard/Spider-Man B	15.00	40.00
S38 Iron Man/Mandarin B	15.00	40.00
S39 Firelord/Spider-Man B	20.00	50.00
S40 The Avengers/X-Men C	15.00	40.00
S41 Sabretooth/Wolverine D	20.00	50.00
S42 Professor X/Magneto B	20.00	50.00

2014 Marvel Premier

UNOPENED BOX (5 CARDS)	1500.00	2000.00
COMMON CARD (1-61)	10.00	25.00
*GOLD SPEC: 1.2X TO 3X BASIC CARDS		
P1 Spider-Man Power (NSU)	6.00	15.00

2014 Marvel Premier Classic Covers Shadow Box

COMMON CARD (CSB1-CSB42)	15.00	40.00
GROUP A STATED ODDS 1:4 (1-23)		
GROUP B STATED ODDS 1:9 (24-36)		
GROUP C STATED ODDS 1:35 (37-42)		
CSB1 Incredible Hulk #1	20.00	50.00
CSB2 Journey...Mystery #83/Thor	20.00	50.00
CSB3 Amazing Fantasy #15 Spider-Man	25.00	60.00

DC/MARVEL

CSB4 Tales of Sus.#39/Iron Man 25.00 60.00
CSB5 Am.Spider-Man #1 30.00 80.00
CSB7 X-Men #1 20.00 50.00
CSB8 Avengers #1 40.00 100.00
CSB12 Avengers #4 25.00 60.00
CSB13 X-Men #4 20.00 50.00
CSB14 Daredevil #1 20.00 50.00
CSB15 Am.Spider-Man #14 20.00 50.00
CSB16 Am.Spider-Man #33 20.00 50.00
CSB19 Avengers #57 20.00 50.00
CSB20 Captain America #109 25.00 60.00
CSB22 Am.Spider-Man #121 25.00 60.00
CSB23 Am.Spider-Man #122 25.00 60.00
CSB24 Incredible Hulk #181 40.00 100.00
CSB25 Giant Size X-Men #1 25.00 60.00
CSB26 X-Men #95 40.00 100.00
CSB27 X-Men #137 30.00 80.00
CSB28 Daredevil #181 30.00 80.00
CSB29 Wolverine #1 60.00 150.00
CSB30 Wolverine #4 60.00 150.00
CSB31 Secret Wars #1 80.00 200.00
CSB32 Am.Spider-Man #252 80.00 200.00
CSB33 Daredevil #227 40.00 100.00
CSB34 Cap.America Annual #8 40.00 100.00
CSB35 Incredible Hulk #340 40.00 100.00
CSB36 Wolverine #1 50.00 120.00
CSB37 Spider-Man #1 (1990) 100.00 250.00
CSB38 X-Men Vol. 2 #1 80.00 200.00
CSB39 Uncanny X-Men #350 50.00 120.00
CSB40 Wolverine #145 125.00 300.00
CSB41 Ultimate Spider-Man #1 150.00 400.00
CSB42 Ultimate X-Men #1 60.00 150.00

2014 Marvel Premier Code Name

COMMON SPIDEY 20.00 50.00
COMMON THOR 15.00 40.00
COMMON HULK 15.00 40.00
COMMON CAP.AMERICA 12.00 30.00
COMMON HAWKEYE 12.00 30.00
COMMON IRON MAN 15.00 40.00
COMMON BLACK WIDOW 12.00 30.00
COMMON FALCON 12.00 30.00
COMMON BLACK PANTHER 12.00 30.00
COMMON IRON FIST 8.00 20.00
COMMON SHE-HULK 12.00 30.00
COMMON STORM 12.00 30.00
COMMON NIGHTCRAWLER 12.00 30.00
COMMON GAMBIT 15.00 40.00
COMMON WOLVERINE 30.00 80.00
COMMON SHADOWCAT 10.00 25.00
COMMON WHITE QUEEN 10.00 25.00
COMMON SCARLET WITCH 10.00 25.00
COMMON ROGUE 15.00 40.00
COMMON ICEMAN 12.00 30.00
COMMON PSYLOCKE 15.00 40.00
COMMON CYCLOPS 10.00 25.00
COMMON DEADPOOL 30.00 80.00
COMMON CABLE 10.00 25.00
COMMON DAREDEVIL 10.00 25.00
COMMON MOON KNIGHT 15.00 40.00
COMMON LUKE CAGE 8.00 20.00
COMMON PUNISHER 25.00 60.00
COMMON NOVA 12.00 30.00
COMMON STAR-LORD 20.00 50.00
COMMON ROCKET RACCOON 15.00 40.00

2014 Marvel Premier Emotion Booklets

COMMON CARD (E1-E18) 15.00 40.00
E1 Punisher 30.00 80.00
Vengeance
E2 Daredevil 25.00 60.00
E3 Black Panther 20.00 50.00
E4 Iron Fist 20.00 50.00
E5 Gambit 20.00 50.00
E6 Cable 30.00 80.00
E7 Spider-Man 40.00 100.00
E9 Phoenix 25.00 60.00
E11 Star-Lord 25.00 60.00
E12 Rocket Raccoon 20.00 50.00
E13 Thanos 25.00 60.00
E14 Wolverine 40.00 100.00
E16 Apocalypse 20.00 50.00
E18 Havok 20.00 50.00
Frustration

2017 Marvel Premier

COMPLETE SET (55) 600.00 1000.00
UNOPENED BOX (1 PACK/5 CARDS) 225.00 275.00
COMMON CARD (1-55) 10.00 25.00
*BLUE/50: .6X TO 1.5X BASIC CARDS 15.00 40.00
*GOLD/10: .75X TO 2X BASIC CARDS 20.00 50.00
STATED PRINT RUN 125 SER.#'d SETS
1 Black Panther 12.00 30.00
3 Deadpool 15.00 40.00
12 Punisher 12.00 30.00
21 Rocket Raccoon 12.00 30.00
36 Wolverine 15.00 40.00
38 Spider-Man 15.00 40.00
47 Hulk 12.00 30.00
49 Iron Man 12.00 30.00

2017 Marvel Premier Busts

COMMON CARD (BL1-BL25) 8.00 20.00
STATED ODDS 1:2
BL1 Thanos 15.00 40.00
BL4 Punisher 12.00 30.00
BL8 Spider-Man 12.00 30.00
BL17 Iron Man 10.00 25.00
BL18 Deadpool 12.00 30.00
BL24 Thor 10.00 25.00

2017 Marvel Premier Classic Art Shadowbox

COMMON CARD (CA1-CA25) 20.00 50.00
STATED ODDS 1:3
CA3 Thor 25.00 60.00
CA6 Black Panther 30.00 80.00
CA7 Hawkeye 30.00 80.00
CA9 Spider-Man 25.00 60.00
CA10 Captain Marvel 25.00 60.00
CA13 Scarlet Witch 25.00 60.00
CA15 Iceman 25.00 60.00
CA16 Ghost Rider 30.00 80.00
CA17 Storm 25.00 60.00
CA21 Gamora 30.00 80.00
CA22 Thanos 30.00 75.00

2017 Marvel Premier E-Pack Achievement

COMPLETE SET (5) 100.00 200.00
COMMON CARD (A1-A5) 20.00 50.00
*BLACK: .5X TO 1.2X BASIC CARDS
*BLUE: .75X TO 2X BASIC CARDS
*GOLD: 1X TO 2.5X BASIC CARDS
A1 Thanos 25.00 60.00
A3 Thor 25.00 60.00

2019 Marvel Premier

COMPLETE SET (50)
UNOPENED BOX (1 PACK) 600.00 1000.00
COMMON CARD (1-50) 8.00 20.00
*BLUE/50: .5X TO 1.2X BASIC CARDS
*RED/30: .6X TO 1.5X BASIC CARDS
0 Deadpool EPACK
00 Luke Cage EPACK
000 X-23 EPACK
0000 Moon Knight EPACK
00000 Old Man Hawkeye EPACK

2019 Marvel Premier Color Box

COMMON CARD (CB1-CB20) 6.00 15.00
COMMON CARD (CB21-CB35) 8.00 20.00
COMMON CARD (CB36-CB45) 12.00 30.00
STATED ODDS (CB1-CB20) 1:3
STATED ODDS (CB21-CB35) 1:8
STATED ODDS (CB36-CB45) 1:15
CB0 Hela EPACK 60.00 120.00
CB00 Shang-Chi EPACK
CB000 Dazzler EPACK
CB3 Colossus 12.00 30.00
CB5 Doctor Strange 8.00 20.00
CB9 Mantis 8.00 20.00
CB11 Mystique 8.00 20.00
CB14 Rogue 10.00 25.00
CB15 Sabretooth 8.00 20.00
CB18 Ultron 10.00 25.00
CB24 Morbius SP 10.00 25.00
CB25 Rage SP 10.00 25.00
CB28 Black Cat SP 10.00 25.00
CB37 Scarlet Witch SP 15.00 40.00
CB38 Gwen Stacy SP 20.00 50.00
CB39 Dormammu SP 15.00 40.00
CB41 Yondu SP 15.00 40.00

2019 Marvel Premier Written in the Stars

COMMON CARD (WIS1-WIS15) 5.00 12.00
COMMON CARD (WIS16-WIS25) 8.00 20.00
COMMON CARD (WIS26-WIS30) 12.00 30.00
STATED ODDS (WIS1-WIS15) 1:3
STATED ODDS (WIS16-WIS25) 1:8
STATED ODDS (WIS26-WIS30) 1:25
WIS0 Nick Fury EPACK
WIS00 White Wolf EPACK
WIS000 Red Skull EPACK
WIS1 Falcon 6.00 15.00
WIS3 Beta Ray Bill 8.00 20.00
WIS8 Wasp 6.00 15.00
WIS12 Captain America 10.00 25.00
WIS13 Valkyrie 6.00 15.00
WIS16 Iron Man SP 12.00 30.00
WIS18 Vision SP 12.00 30.00
WIS19 Archangel SP 10.00 25.00
WIS22 Daredevil SP 10.00 25.00
WIS25 Thanos SP 15.00 40.00
WIS26 Deadpool SP 15.00 40.00
WIS27 Wolverine SP 20.00 50.00
WIS29 Captain Marvel SP 15.00 40.00

1997 Fleer SkyBox Marvel Premium QFX

COMPLETE SET (72) 15.00 40.00
UNOPENED BOX (24 PACKS) 150.00 250.00
UNOPENED PACK (5 CARDS) 6.00 10.00
COMMON CARD (1-72) .30 .75
3 Silver Surfer .75 2.00
5 Captain America 1.25 3.00
6 Carnage 1.25 3.00
8 Daredevil 1.25 3.00
12 Ghost Rider 1.25 3.00
14 Hulk 1.00 2.50
15 Human Torch .40 1.00
17 Invisible Woman .40 1.00
18 Iron Man 1.25 3.00
20 Kingpin .40 1.00
22 Magneto .75 2.00
23 Namor .40 1.00
24 Punisher 1.25 3.00
26 Thor 1.25 3.00
27 Venom 1.50 4.00
28 Wolverine 2.00 5.00
30 Black Panther 1.50 4.00
31 Black Widow 1.00 2.50
34 Dr. Strange 1.25 3.00
39 Moon Knight 1.25 3.00
43 Storm 1.00 2.50
44 Thanos 1.50 4.00
46 Ant-Man 1.00 2.50
55 Gambit 1.25 3.00
57 Mr. Fantastic .40 1.00
60 Scarlet Witch 1.50 4.00
61 Spider-Man 3.00 8.00
62 Thing .40 1.00
63 Wolverine 2.00 5.00
72 Maximum Carnage .75 2.00

1997 Fleer SkyBox Marvel Premium QFX LazerBlast

COMPLETE SET (4) 20.00 50.00
COMMON CARD (1-4) 5.00 12.00
STATED ODDS 1:9
1 Wolverine 8.00 20.00
2 Spider-Man 15.00 40.00

1997 Fleer SkyBox Marvel Premium QFX PhotoGrafix

COMPLETE SET (9) 12.00 30.00
COMMON CARD (1-9) 1.50 4.00
STATED ODDS 1:6
2 Captain America 5.00 12.00
3 Hulk 2.50 6.00
6 Iron Man 4.00 10.00
9 Thor 3.00 8.00

2010 Marvel 70th Anniversary

COMPLETE SET (72) 10.00 25.00
UNOPENED BOX (24 PACKS) 200.00 350.00
UNOPENED PACK (5 CARDS) 8.00 15.00
COMMON CARD (1-72) .25 .60
*FOIL: 2X TO 5X BASIC CARDS

2010 Marvel 70th Anniversary Case-Toppers

COMPLETE SET (3) 25.00 60.00
COMMON CARD (CT1-CT3) 10.00 25.00
STATED ODDS 1:CASE
STATED PRINT RUN 333 SER.#'d SETS

2010 Marvel 70th Anniversary Characters

COMPLETE SET W/RR (10) 20.00 50.00
COMPLETE SET W/O RR (9) 8.00 20.00
COMMON CARD (C1-C9) 1.25 3.00
STATED ODDS 1:12
ALT ISSUED AS RITTENHOUSE REWARD
C1 Captain America 2.00 5.00
C2 Cyclops 1.25 3.00
C4 Iron Man 1.50 4.00
C6 Spider-Man 2.00 5.00
C9 Wolverine 2.00 5.00
ALT Power Man SP (RR) 15.00 40.00

2010 Marvel 70th Anniversary Clearly Heroic

COMPLETE SET (6) 12.00 30.00
COMMON CARD (PC1-PC6) 2.50 6.00
STATED ODDS 1:24
PC1 Captain America 3.00 8.00
PC3 Iron Man 5.00 12.00
PC4 Spider-Man 5.00 12.00
PC6 Wolverine 6.00 15.00

2010 Marvel 70th Anniversary Stickers

COMPLETE SET (18) 12.00 30.00
COMMON CARD (S1-S18) 1.00 2.50
STATED ODDS 1:8
S1 Spider-Man 2.00 5.00
S2 Captain America 1.50 4.00
S4 Iron Man 1.50 4.00
S5 Thor 1.25 3.00
S14 Daredevil 1.25 3.00
S18 Wolverine 2.00 5.00

2010 Marvel 70th Anniversary Tribute

COMPLETE SET (9) 2.50 6.00
COMMON CARD (T1-T9) .40 1.00
*FOIL: 1.2X TO 3X BASIC CARDS
RANDOMLY INSERTED INTO PACKS
T1 Captain America .60 1.50
T2 Captain America .60 1.50
T3 Captain America .60 1.50

2010 Marvel 70th Anniversary Promos

COMMON CARD (P1-P3) .75 2.00
P2 Thor NSU 2.50 6.00
P3 Spider-Man Archives ALB 10.00 25.00

2014 Marvel 75th Anniversary

COMPLETE SET (90) 8.00 20.00
UNOPENED BOX (24 PACKS) 250.00 400.00
UNOPENED PACK (5 CARDS) 10.00 15.00
COMMON CARD (1-90) .20 .50
*SAPPHIRE: 1.2X TO 3X BASIC CARDS .60 1.50
*EMERALD/100: 8X TO 20X BASIC CARDS4.00 10.00

*RUBY/50: 12X TO 25X BASIC CARDS	5.00	12.00
*DIAMOND/10: 20X TO 50X BASIC CARDS	10.00	25.00

2014 Marvel 75th Anniversary 75th Anniversary

COMMON CARD (SKIP #'d)	8.00	20.00
STATED ODDS 1:144		
2 Archangel	15.00	40.00
5 Nick Fury	12.00	30.00
8 Hulk	20.00	50.00
14 Human Torch	12.00	30.00
17 Dr. Doom	12.00	30.00
20 Iron Man	25.00	60.00
23 DarkHawk	12.00	30.00
26 Deadpool	20.00	50.00
29 Nightcrawler	15.00	40.00
38 Morbius	12.00	30.00
44 Wolverine	25.00	60.00
53 Odin	10.00	25.00
56 Mr. Fantastic	12.00	30.00
59 Spider-Man	25.00	60.00
62 Loki	12.00	30.00
65 Gambit	15.00	40.00
71 Hawkeye	15.00	40.00
74 Green Goblin	12.00	30.00

2014 Marvel 75th Anniversary Bronze Age Cut Comic Panels

COMMON CARD (BA1-BA17)	15.00	40.00
STATED ODDS 1:288		

2014 Marvel 75th Anniversary Case-Topper Art Deco Posters

COMPLETE SET (5)	20.00	50.00
COMMON CARD (D1-D5)	5.00	12.00
STATED ODDS 1:CASE		
D1 Spider-Man	8.00	20.00
D3 Captain America	8.00	20.00
D5 Iron Man	12.00	30.00

2014 Marvel 75th Anniversary Die-Cut Panel Bursts

COMPLETE SET (9)	25.00	60.00
COMMON CARD (PB1-PB9)	1.25	3.00
STATED ODDS 1:24		

2014 Marvel 75th Anniversary Golden Age Cut Comic Panels

COMMON CARD (GA1-GA9)	15.00	40.00
STATED ODDS 1:288		

2014 Marvel 75th Anniversary Silver Age Cut Comic Panels

COMMON CARD (SA1-SA18)	15.00	40.00
STATED ODDS 1:288		

2014 Marvel 75th Anniversary Stickers

COMPLETE SET (18)	15.00	40.00
COMMON CARD (S19-S36)	2.00	5.00
STATED ODDS 1:24		

2014 Marvel 75th Anniversary X-Men Evolution

COMPLETE SET (13)	8.00	20.00
COMMON CARD (XE1-XE13)	1.25	3.00
*GOLD: 1.2X TO 3X BASIC CARDS		
STATED ODDS 1:24		
XE08 Wolverine	2.00	5.00

2014 Marvel 75th Anniversary Promos

COMPLETE SET (2)	2.50	6.00
COMMON CARD (P1-P2)	.75	2.00
P2 Hulk ALB	3.00	8.00

1998 SkyBox Marvel Silver Age

COMPLETE SET (100)	15.00	40.00
UNOPENED BOX (36 PACKS)	500.00	750.00
UNOPENED PACK (9 CARDS)	15.00	20.00
COMMON CARD (1-100)	.40	1.00

1998 SkyBox Marvel Silver Age Alex Ross Salutes the Silver Age

COMPLETE SET (9)	30.00	75.00
COMMON CARD (AR1-AR9)	5.00	12.00

1998 SkyBox Marvel Silver Age Autographs

COMMON CARD (A1-A11)	8.00	20.00
STATED ODDS 1:36		
A1 Stan Lee	300.00	750.00
A2 Jazzy John Romita, Sr.	10.00	25.00
A3 Tom Palmer	20.00	50.00
A4 Dick Ayers	12.00	30.00
A5A Sal Buscema blue ink	40.00	100.00
A5B Sal Buscema black ink	30.00	75.00
A6 John Buscema	50.00	125.00
A11 George Tuska	15.00	40.00

1998 SkyBox Marvel Silver Age Heroes

COMPLETE SET (9)	50.00	125.00
COMMON CARD (1S-9S)	4.00	10.00
1S Spider-Man	12.00	30.00
5S Thor	8.00	20.00
6S Captain America	10.00	25.00
7S Silver Surfer	8.00	20.00
8S Hulk	6.00	15.00
9S Iron Man	8.00	20.00

1998 SkyBox Marvel Silver Age Tribute to Jack Kirby

COMPLETE SET (6)	20.00	50.00
COMMON CARD (JK1-JK6)	5.00	12.00

2014 Marvel Super Hero Month Vudu Pizza Promos

COMPLETE SET (4)		
COMMON CARD		
NNO Captain America	2.50	6.00
NNO Hulk	2.50	6.00
NNO Spider-Man	2.50	6.00
NNO Star-Lord and Rocket Raccoon	2.50	6.00

1966 Donruss Marvel Super Heroes

COMPLETE SET (66)	500.00	1000.00
UNOPENED BOX (24 PACKS)		
UNOPENED PACK		
COMMON CARD (1-66)	.75	2.00
1 I Love These Class Parties!	60.00	120.00
34 Next Time I'll Fly the Kite!	125.00	250.00

1993 Crunch 'n Munch Marvel Super Heroes Series One

COMPLETE SET (6)	6.00	15.00
COMMON CARD (1-6)	.75	2.00
4 Spider-Man	2.00	5.00
6A Wolverine (red font on back)	2.00	5.00
6B Wolverine (white font on back)	2.00	5.00
NNO Wolverine sticker	2.00	5.00

1994 Crunch 'n Munch Marvel Super Heroes Series Two

COMPLETE SET (6)	5.00	12.00
COMMON CARD (1-6)	.75	2.00
1 Cable	1.25	3.00
3 Gambit	1.25	3.00
5 Spider-Man	2.00	5.00
6 Wolverine	2.00	5.00

1996 Marvel Super Heroes Pro Magnets

COMPLETE SET (51)	12.00	30.00
UNOPENED BOX (24 PACKS)		
UNOPENED PACK (5 MAGNETS)		
COMMON CARD (1-50; CL)	.40	1.00
11 Captain America	.75	2.00
27 Iron Man	1.25	3.00
43 Spider-Man	2.00	5.00
48 Venom	.75	2.00
50 Wolverine	2.00	5.00

1967 Philadelphia Gum Marvel Super Heroes Stickers

COMPLETE SET (55)	175.00	350.00
COMMON CARD (1-55)	1.50	4.00
*CANADIAN: SAME VALUE		
3 Daredevil	2.00	5.00
10 Iron Man	2.50	6.00
11 Daredevil	2.00	5.00
12 Spider-Man	4.00	10.00
18 Daredevil	2.00	5.00
21 Spider-Man	4.00	10.00
23 Daredevil	2.00	5.00
27 Daredevil	2.00	5.00
28 Iron Man	2.50	6.00
29 Spider-Man	4.00	10.00
33 Iron Man	2.50	6.00
35 Captain America	2.50	6.00
37 Iron Man	2.50	6.00
39 Spider-Man	4.00	10.00
40 Iron Man	2.50	6.00
42 Spider-Man	4.00	10.00
43 Spider-Man	4.00	10.00
44 Iron Man	2.50	6.00
49 Spider-Man	4.00	10.00
50 Captain America	2.50	6.00
53 Captain America	2.50	6.00
54 Captain America	2.50	6.00

1976 Topps Marvel Super Heroes Stickers

COMPLETE SET W/CL (55)	150.00	300.00
COMPLETE SET W/O CL (46)	150.00	300.00
COMPLETE CL SET (9)	6.00	15.00
UNOPENED BOX (36 PACKS)	1800.00	3000.00
UNOPENED PACK (CARDS)	40.00	75.00
COMMON CARD (1-46)	2.00	5.00
COMMON CL (1-9)	1.25	3.00
2 Blade	6.00	15.00
3 Bucky	5.00	12.00
4 Captain America	10.00	25.00
5 Conan Hold the Pickle Or Else!	6.00	15.00
6 Conan Shall We Dance?	10.00	25.00
7 Cyclops	5.00	12.00
8 Daredevil	6.00	15.00
10 Dr. Doom	8.00	20.00
11 Dr. Strange	6.00	15.00
12 Dracula	3.00	8.00
13 Galactus	6.00	15.00
15 Hercules Like My Nail Polish?	4.00	10.00
16 Hercules Look, I Have a Hang Nail!	6.00	15.00
17 Howard the Duck	5.00	12.00
18 Ice Man	3.00	8.00
19 Invisible Girl	3.00	8.00
20 Iron Man	8.00	20.00
23 Loki What an Awful Case of Ear Wax!	12.00	30.00
24 Loki Who Says I'm Bull-Headed?	8.00	20.00
25 Luke Cage Like My Denture Work?	6.00	15.00
26 Luke Cage Two All Beef Patties Please	5.00	12.00
27 Peter Parker	4.00	10.00
28 Red Skull	2.50	6.00
31 Silver Surfer	10.00	25.00
33 Spider-Man	15.00	40.00
35 The Hulk Can Anyone Make Cuffs Right?	6.00	15.00
36 The Hulk Help Cure Athlete's Feet	8.00	20.00
37 The Human Torch	2.50	6.00
38 The Punisher	10.00	25.00
39 The Thing	2.50	6.00
40 The Vision	3.00	8.00
42 Thor	5.00	12.00
43 Tigra	2.50	6.00

1984 FTCC Marvel Superheroes First Issue Covers

COMPLETE SET (60)	10.00	25.00
COMMON CARD	.30	.75

2015 Marvel 3-D

COMPLETE SET (72)	15.00	40.00
UNOPENED BOX (20 PACKS)	60.00	100.00
UNOPENED PACK (6 CARDS)	4.00	5.00
COMMON CARD (1-72)	.40	1.00
*VARIANT: .6X TO 1.5X BASIC CARD	.60	1.50
*FRAMEWORK: 2X TO 5X BASIC CARD	2.00	5.00
3 Black Widow	.75	2.00
4 Captain America	1.50	4.00
8 Hawkeye	.75	2.00
9 Hulk	1.50	4.00
10 Iron Man	1.50	4.00
13 Loki	1.25	3.00
17 Nick Fury	1.25	3.00
21 Thor	1.50	4.00
23 Ultron	1.25	3.00
29 Doctor Octopus	1.25	3.00
30 Green Goblin	1.25	3.00
31 Spider-Man	1.50	4.00
32 Venom	1.25	3.00
35 Deadpool	1.50	4.00
37 Gambit	1.50	4.00
38 Magneto	1.25	3.00
41 Storm	.75	2.00
42 Wolverine	1.50	4.00
45 Daredevil	1.50	4.00
48 Punisher	1.50	4.00
49 Blade	.75	2.00
50 Daredevil	1.50	4.00
52 Ghost Rider	.75	2.00
54 Punisher	1.50	4.00
55 Blade	.75	2.00
56 Daredevil	1.50	4.00
57 Ghost Rider	.75	2.00
59 Punisher	1.50	4.00
63 Bishop	.75	2.00

2015 Marvel 3-D Affinity Lenticular Quads

COMMON CARD (A1 - A24)	12.00	30.00
STATED ODDS 1:30		
A1 Wolverine/Punisher Deadpool/Hulk	30.00	80.00
A3 Thor/Hulk/Iron Man/Cap	25.00	60.00
A4 Zemo/Supreme Hydra/Red Skull/M.Hydra	15.00	40.00
A7 Ymir/Destroyer/Enchantress/Frost Giant	15.00	40.00
A8 Egghead/Doc Ock/Leader/Mister Sinister	20.00	50.00
A9 Lilith/Elektra/Enchantress/Black Widow	20.00	50.00
A10 Cap/Daredevil/Iron Fist/Spidey	20.00	50.00
A11 Sentinels/Mutates/The Hand/Phalanx	25.00	60.00
A13 Blade/Daredevil/Ghost Rider/Elektra	20.00	50.00
A14 Stryfe/Red Skull/Magneto/Loki	25.00	60.00
A17 Bullseye/Daredevil/Elektra/The Hand	15.00	40.00
A18 Shield Agent/Maria Hill/Fury/Black Widow	15.00	40.00
A19 Hammerhead/Kingpin/Jigsaw/Tombstone	20.00	50.00
A20 Punisher/Iron Fist/Elektra/Daredevil	25.00	60.00
A21 Domino/Forge/Hawkeye/Nick Fury	20.00	50.00
A22 Melter/Punisher/Ghost Rider/Blade	25.00	60.00
A23 Angel/Cyclops/Iceman/Jean Grey	25.00	60.00
A24 Master Strike/Wound Scheme Twist/Bystander	20.00	50.00

2015 Marvel 3-D Legendary

COMPLETE SET (26)	25.00	60.00
COMMON CARD	1.25	3.00
STATED ODDS 2:1		
1 Bulldozer Driver	5.00	12.00
2 B.Widow Covert Operation U	1.50	4.00
5 Black Widow R	2.50	6.00
9 Deadpool U	2.50	6.00
10 Deadpool R	3.00	8.00
13 Hulk R	4.00	10.00
15 Howard The Duck R	4.00	10.00
16 Howard The Duck C	1.50	4.00

17 Howard The Duck U	2.00	5.00
18 Howard The Duck C	1.50	4.00
19 Fortune Teller	6.00	15.00
20 Double Agent of S.H.I.E.L.D.	5.00	12.00
21 Stan Lee	2.00	5.00
22 Photographer	5.00	12.00
24 Man-Thing R	4.00	10.00
26 Man-Thing U	1.50	4.00

2015 Marvel 3-D Lenticular Comic Covers

COMPLETE SET (23)	80.00	150.00
COMMON CARD (3D1 - 3D23)	5.00	12.00
RANDOMLY INSERTED INTO PACKS		
3D3 Amazing Fantasy #15	6.00	15.00
3D5 The Amazing Spider-Man #1	6.00	15.00
3D7 The Avengers #1	6.00	15.00
3D10 Daredevil #1	6.00	15.00
3D12 The Avengers #57	6.00	15.00
3D14 Amazing Spider-Man #121	6.00	15.00
3D18 Secret Wars #1	6.00	15.00
3D23 X-Men (vol. 2) #1	6.00	15.00
3D24 Wolverine #145	6.00	15.00

2015 Marvel 3-D Promos

COMPLETE SET (2)	8.00	20.00
COMMON CARD	6.00	15.00

2021 Upper Deck Marvel Unbound

COMPLETE SET (52)	100.00	250.00
COMMON CARD (1-52)	2.00	5.00
STATED PRINT RUN 999 SER.#'d SETS		
3 Black Widow	3.00	8.00
7 Doctor Strange	4.00	10.00
11 Gambit	6.00	15.00
13 Hulk	3.00	8.00
14 Iron Man	3.00	8.00
15 Jean Grey	10.00	25.00
17 Loki	3.00	8.00
20 Ms. Marvel	4.00	10.00
24 Scarlet Witch	5.00	12.00
25 Squirrel Girl	6.00	15.00
26 Mystique	8.00	20.00
28 Captain America	5.00	12.00
29 Cosmic Ghost Rider	4.00	10.00
30 Domino	2.50	6.00
31 Gamora	4.00	10.00
34 Ironheart	3.00	8.00
36 Moon Knight	8.00	20.00
38 Nick Fury Jr.	2.50	6.00
39 Nova	3.00	8.00
42 Sentry	2.50	6.00
43 Spider-Man	20.00	50.00
44 Spider-Woman	6.00	15.00
45 Storm	3.00	8.00
48 Thor	4.00	10.00
49 Venom	12.00	30.00
52 Wolverine	12.00	30.00

2021 Upper Deck Marvel Unbound Character Quarterly

COMPLETE SET (4)	40.00	100.00
COMMON CARD (CQC1-CQC4)	12.00	30.00
STATED PRINT RUN 999 SER.#'d SETS		
CQC1 Spider-Man/Green Goblin	15.00	40.00
CQC2 Hulk/Wolverine	20.00	50.00
CQC4 Iron Man/Captain America	15.00	40.00

2021 Upper Deck Marvel Unbound Gold Autographs

COMMON AUTO	60.00	150.00
STATED PRINT RUN 50 SER.#'d SETS		
AUTOGRAPHS OF FRED IAN		

2011 Marvel Universe

COMPLETE SET (90)	10.00	25.00
UNOPENED BOX (24 PACKS)	200.00	300.00
UNOPENED PACK (5 CARDS)	15.00	12.00
COMMON CARD (1-90)	.20	.50
*CLEAR: 1.25X TO 3X BASIC CARDS		

2011 Marvel Universe Artist Draft

COMPLETE SET (9)	15.00	40.00
COMMON CARD (AD1-AD9)	3.00	8.00
STATED ODDS 1:8		

2011 Marvel Universe Case-Toppers

COMPLETE SET (3)	30.00	75.00
COMMON CARD (CT1-CT3)	10.00	25.00
STATED ODDS 1:CASE		

2011 Marvel Universe Marvel Originals

COMPLETE SET (9)	15.00	40.00
COMMON CARD (MO1-MO9)	2.50	6.00
STATED ODDS 1:12		
MO1 Marvel Universe	5.00	12.00
MO3 Spider-Man	12.00	30.00
MO5 Iron Man	3.00	8.00
MO6 Wolverine/Psylocke	6.00	15.00
MO7 Wolverine/Sabretooth	5.00	12.00
MO8 Fantastic Four	3.00	8.00
MO9 Fantastic Four	3.00	8.00

2011 Marvel Universe Ultimate Heroes

COMPLETE SET W/RR (10)	20.00	50.00
COMPLETE SET W/O RR (9)	10.00	25.00
COMMON CARD (UH1-UH9)	1.50	4.00
STATED ODDS 1:24		
UH10 ISSUED AS RITTENHOUSE REWARD		
UH1 Wolverine	4.00	10.00
UH3 Storm	2.00	5.00
UH4 Cyclops	3.00	8.00
UH8 Gambit	2.50	6.00
UH9 Jean Grey	2.00	5.00
UH10 Polaris SP RR	15.00	40.00

2011 Marvel Universe Promos

COMMON CARD	1.00	2.50
P3 Cap/Hulk/Medusa ALB	8.00	20.00
P4 Daredevil/Hulk/Cap PHILLY	1.50	4.00

2011 Marvel Universe SDCC Promos

COMPLETE SET (9)	15.00	40.00
COMMON CARD (SD1-SD9)	2.00	5.00
SD1 Iron Man	4.00	10.00
SD2 Captain America	4.00	10.00
SD5 Hulk	2.50	6.00
SD6 Thor	2.50	6.00

2014 Marvel Universe

COMPLETE SET (90)	8.00	20.00
UNOPENED BOX (24 PACKS)	200.00	350.00
UNOPENED PACK (5 CARDS)	8.00	15.00
COMMON CARD (1-90)	.20	.50
*SAPPHIRE: 1X TO 2.5X BASIC CARDS	.50	1.25
*EMERALD/100: 4X TO 10X BASIC CARDS	2.00	5.00
*RUBY/50: 8X TO 20X BASIC CARDS	4.00	10.00
*DIAMOND/10: 40X TO 100X BASIC CARDS	20.00	50.00

2014 Marvel Universe 75th Anniversary

COMPLETE SET (25)	150.00	400.00
COMMON CARD (SKIP #'d)	10.00	25.00
STATED ODDS 1:144		
1 Captain America	20.00	50.00
4 Ghost Rider	15.00	40.00
7 Starlord	12.00	30.00
10 Doctor Strange	12.00	30.00
13 Galactus	15.00	40.00
22 Winter Soldier	15.00	40.00
25 Daredevil	15.00	40.00
28 Ant-Man	12.00	30.00
34 Red Hulk	12.00	30.00
43 Deathlok	12.00	30.00
46 Silver Surfer	15.00	40.00
52 Black Panther	15.00	40.00
61 Thor	20.00	50.00
64 Punisher	15.00	40.00
67 Doctor Voodoo	12.00	30.00
73 Thing	12.00	30.00

2014 Marvel Universe Artist Draft

COMPLETE SET (9)	8.00	20.00
COMMON CARD (AD10-AD18)	1.50	4.00
STATED ODDS 1:12		
AD13 Nova #7	2.00	5.00
AD15 Nova #4	2.00	5.00
AD16 Chaos War #1	2.50	6.00
AD17 Dark Avengers #11	2.00	5.00
AD18 Dark Avengers #12	2.00	5.00
AD19 Dark Avengers #1 RR		

2014 Marvel Universe Avengers Origins

COMPLETE SET (5)	4.00	10.00
COMMON CARD (AO1-AO5)	1.25	3.00
STATED ODDS 1:48		
AO3 Scarlet Witch/Quicksilver	1.50	4.00
AO4 Thor	2.00	5.00

2014 Marvel Universe Case-Toppers

L7 Bishop vs. Apocalypse Lent.	5.00	12.00

2014 Marvel Universe Heroes and Villains Expansion

COMPLETE SET (9)	8.00	20.00
COMMON CARD (82-90)	1.50	4.00
STATED ODDS 1:48		

2014 Marvel Universe Marvel Greatest Battles Expansion

COMPLETE SET (18)	12.00	30.00
COMMON THOR (91-99)	1.50	4.00
COMMON CAP. AMERICA (100-108)	1.50	4.00
STATED ODDS 1:24		

2014 Marvel Universe Shadowbox

COMPLETE SET (6)	15.00	40.00
COMMON CARD (S7-S12)	4.00	10.00
STATED ODDS 1:48		
S7 Wolverine	6.00	15.00
S9 Spider-Man	8.00	20.00
S11 Daredevil	5.00	12.00

2014 Marvel Universe Promos

COMPLETE SET (2)	5.00	12.00
COMMON CARD (P1-P2)	2.00	5.00
P2 Album Exclusive	4.00	10.00

1990 Impel Marvel Universe I

COMPLETE SET (162)	75.00	200.00
COLLECTIBLE TIN SET (167)	20.00	500.00
UNOPENED BOX (36 PACKS)	600.00	1000.00
UNOPENED PACK (12 CARDS)	15.00	30.00
COMMON CARD (1-162)	.40	1.00
1 Captain America	1.50	4.00
2 Spider-Man	6.00	15.00
3 Hulk	1.50	4.00
4 Daredevil	2.50	6.00
5 Nick Fury	1.25	3.00
6 Thing	1.50	4.00
7 Professor X	1.25	3.00
8 Cyclops	1.50	4.00
9 Marvel Girl	2.00	5.00
10 Wolverine	4.00	10.00
11 Phoenix	1.25	3.00
13 Dazzler	.50	1.25
17 Hulk	2.00	5.00
18 Thor	2.00	5.00
19 Mister Fantastic	1.25	3.00
20 Black Panther	6.00	15.00
21 Archangel	.75	2.00
23 Wolverine	4.00	10.00
24 Storm	.75	2.00
26 Moon Knight	6.00	15.00
28 Aunt May	1.25	3.00
29 Spider-Man	10.00	25.00
30 Cosmic Spider-Man	8.00	20.00
31 Captain America	1.50	4.00
32 Silver Surfer	2.50	6.00
33 Human Torch	.50	1.25
34 Doctor Strange	1.25	3.00
39 She-Hulk	2.50	6.00
54 Loki	2.00	5.00
73 Venom	5.00	12.00
74 Green Goblin	1.25	3.00
75 Galactus	1.50	4.00
79 Thanos	2.50	6.00
82 Ghost Rider	2.00	5.00
90 Fantastic Four vs. Doctor Doom	2.50	6.00
93 Spider-Man vs. Dr. Octopus	2.50	6.00
97 Captain America vs. Red Skull	1.50	4.00
106 Spider-Man vs. Venom	3.00	8.00
111 Spider-Man vs. Green Goblin	2.00	5.00
112 Spider-Man vs. Hobgoblin	1.50	4.00
113 Hulk vs. Wolverine	2.50	6.00
114 Hulk vs. Spider-Man	2.00	5.00
115 Captain America vs. Wolverine	2.00	5.00
116 Silver Surfer vs. Thanos	1.00	2.50
117 X-Factor vs. Apocalypse	1.50	4.00
119 Wolverine vs. Sabretooth	1.25	3.00
120 X-Men in the Savage Land	.75	2.00
121 Iron Man vs. Titanium Man	1.25	3.00
122 Thor vs. Loki	1.25	3.00
125 X-Men #1	2.00	5.00
129 Amazing Spider-Man #129	2.50	6.00
130 Avengers #1	2.50	6.00
131 Amazing Spider-Man #1	2.50	6.00
132 Giant-Size X-Men #1	1.50	4.00
133 Wolverine Limited Series #1	5.00	12.00
149 Spider-Man	5.00	12.00
150 Doctor Doom	1.50	4.00
152 The Hulk	1.50	4.00
153 Silver Surfer	1.50	4.00
154 Thor	1.50	4.00
156 Magneto	1.25	3.00
157 Captain America	4.00	10.00
158 Doctor Strange	4.00	10.00
159 Iron Man	1.50	4.00
160 Wolverine	1.50	4.00
161 Stan Lee: Mr. Marvel	15.00	40.00
162 Marvel 1990 Checklist	5.00	12.00

1990 Impel Marvel Universe I Holograms

COMPLETE SET (5)	60.00	150.00
COMMON CARD (MH1-MH5)	12.00	30.00
RANDOMLY INSERTED INTO PACKS		
MH1 Cosmic Spider-Man	25.00	60.00
MH2 Magneto	15.00	40.00
MH4 Wolverine	25.00	60.00
MH5 Spider-Man vs. Green Goblin	25.00	60.00

1991 Impel Marvel Universe II Diamond Previews

COMPLETE SET (6)	8.00	20.00
COMMON CARD (SKIP #'d)	1.25	3.00
UNC 6-Card Panel of all 5	6.00	15.00

1991 Impel Marvel Universe II

COMPLETE SET (162)	50.00	100.00
UNOPENED BOX (36 PACKS)	250.00	400.00
UNOPENED PACK (12 CARDS)	4.00	12.00
COMMON CARD (1-162)	.40	1.00
1 Spider-Man	2.50	6.00
2 Daredevil	1.50	4.00
3 Thing	.60	1.50
4 Marvel Girl	.50	1.25
5 Phoenix	.60	1.50
7 Mister Fantastic	.75	2.00
8 Iceman	.60	1.50
9 Shadowcat	.60	1.50
10 Human Torch	.60	1.50
11 Nightcrawler	.75	2.00
12 Captain Britain	.75	2.00
13 Iron Man	2.00	5.00
14 Punisher	1.50	4.00
15 Cable	.60	1.50
16 Deathlok	1.00	2.50
17 Gambit	1.50	4.00
18 Psylocke	1.00	2.50
19 Vision	.75	2.00
20 Hawkeye	.60	1.50
21 Silver Sable	.50	1.25

22 Night Thrasher .50 1.25
23 Puck 1.00 2.50
25 Quicksilver .60 1.50
26 Scarlet Witch 2.00 5.00
27 Havok .60 1.50
28 Iron Fist .50 1.25
29 Adam Warlock .60 1.50
31 Sasquatch .50 1.25
32 Firestar .60 1.50
33 Death's Head .60 1.50
34 Speedball .60 1.50
35 US Agent 1.25 3.00
37 Meggan .75 2.00
38 Jubilee .50 1.25
39 Ghost Rider .75 2.00
40 Beast .75 2.00
41 Invisible Woman .75 2.00
42 Rogue 1.00 2.50
43 She-Hulk 1.00 2.50
44 Dr. Strange 1.25 3.00
45 Silver Surfer 1.25 3.00
46 Storm .75 2.00
47 Archangel .75 2.00
48 Thor 1.25 3.00
50 Wolverine 2.50 6.00
51 Cyclops .75 2.00
52 Nick Fury .60 1.50
53 Hulk 1.25 3.00
54 Captain America 2.00 5.00
55 Kingpin .60 1.50
56 Sabretooth 1.00 2.50
57 Magneto .75 2.00
58 Venom 1.50 4.00
59 Galactus .75 2.00
60 Mandarin .60 1.50
62 Super Skrull .50 1.25
64 Mojo .60 1.50
67 Tombstone .60 1.50
69 Baron Strucker .75 2.00
70 Mysterio 1.00 2.50
72 Annihilus .75 2.00
73 Rhino .60 1.50
74 Absorbing Man .60 1.50
75 Doctor Octopus .75 2.00
76 Baron Mordo .60 1.50
77 Saracen .60 1.50
78 Nebula .60 1.50
79 Puma .50 1.25
81 Kang .75 2.00
82 Blackout .75 2.00
83 Calypso .60 1.50
84 Ultron .75 2.00
85 Thanos 3.00 8.00
88 Doctor Doom .75 2.00
89 Loki .60 1.50
90 Red Skull .75 1.50
91 Spider-Man vs. Venom 1.50 4.00
92 Fantastic Four vs. Skrulls .50 1.25
93 Wolverine vs. Sabretooth 1.50 4.00
94 Silver Surfer vs. Galactus .75 2.00
95 Daredevil vs. Elektra .60 1.50
96 Avengers vs. Kang 1.00 2.50
97 Human Torch vs. Sub-Mariner .75 2.00
98 Spider-Man vs. Hobgoblin 1.25 3.00
99 Captain America vs. Baron Zemo .75 2.00
100 Punisher vs. Jigsaw 1.25 3.00
101 X-Factor vs. Apocalypse .50 1.25
102 Punisher vs. Kingpin 1.50 4.00
103 Thing vs. Hulk .60 1.50
104 Daredevil vs. Bullseye .75 2.00
105 Spider-Man vs. Doctor Octopus 1.00 2.50
106 X-Men vs. Sentinels .60 1.50
108 Wolverine vs. Hulk 2.00 5.00
110 Dr. Strange vs. Baron Mordo .60 1.50
111 Nick Fury vs. Baron Strucker .60 1.50
113 Silver Surfer vs. Thanos .60 1.50
115 Captain America vs. Red Skull 1.25 3.00
116 Daredevil vs. Punisher .60 1.50
123 Silver Surfer vs. Mephisto 1.25 3.00
124 Fantastic Four vs. Doctor Doom 1.50 4.00
125 X-Men vs. Magneto 1.50 4.00
126 Daredevil vs. Kingpin 1.00 2.50
127 Captain America's Shield 1.00 2.50
128 Thor's Hammer .75 2.00
131 Spider-Man's Web-Shooters 1.50 4.00
132 Punisher's Arsenal .60 1.50
133 Iron Man's Armor .60 1.50
134 Infinity Gauntlet 2.00 5.00
138 Wolverine's Claws 1.50 4.00
139 Captain Marvel 1.00 2.50
141 Green Goblin .60 1.50
142 Original Ghost Rider .60 1.50
143 Kraven .75 2.00
144 Dark Phoenix .60 1.50
145 Darkhawk .50 1.25
148 X-Force 1.25 3.00
149 New Fantastic Four .75 2.00
150 Fantastic Four .60 1.50
151 Avengers .75 2.00
153 X-Men 1.00 2.50
154 X-Factor .60 1.50
155 Excalibur .60 1.50
162 Marvel 1991 Checklist 2.00 5.00

1991 Impel Marvel Universe II Holograms

COMPLETE SET (5) 20.00 50.00
COMMON CARD (H1-H5) 5.00 12.00
H1 Spider-Man 10.00 25.00
H4 Doctor Doom 6.00 15.00
H5 Fantastic Four and the Mole Man 8.00 20.00
H1AU Spider-Man and Stan Lee AU

1991 Impel Marvel Universe II Toy Biz Promos

COMPLETE SET (9) 20.00 50.00
COMMON CARD 2.50 6.00
STATED ODDS 1:ACTION FIGURE
1 Apocalypse 3.00 8.00
6 Magneto 4.00 10.00
8 Storm 4.00 10.00
9 Wolverine 6.00 15.00

1992 Impel Marvel Universe III

COMPLETE SET (200) 25.00 60.00
UNOPENED BOX (36 PACKS) 125.00 200.00
UNOPENED PACK (12 CARDS) 4.00 6.00
COMMON CARD (1-200) .25 .60
200B Checklist (border) 20.00 50.00

1992 Impel Marvel Universe III Holograms

COMPLETE SET (5) 15.00 40.00
COMMON CARD 2.50 6.00
H3A Wolverine (cyan) 6.00 15.00
H4A Venom (blue) 5.00 12.00
H4B Venom (purple) 5.00 12.00

1992 Impel Marvel Universe III Promos

1P Spider-Man 1.25 3.00
(Comic Buyer's Guide)
57P Human Torch 1.25 3.00
(Comic Buyer's Guide)
NNO Venom hologram 1.50 4.00
(Advance Comics)
NNO Silver Surfer/Thanos
Spider-Man/Human Torch#(Diamond Previews)
NNO Silver Surfer/Thanos
Spider-Man/Human Torch#(Diamond Previews wide)
NNO Silver Surfer/Thanos 4.00 10.00
Spider-Man/Human Torch/30,000#(Impel Logo)
NNO Silver Surfer/Thanos
Spider-Man/Human Torch#(Comic Buyer's Price Guide logo)

1992 Impel Marvel Universe III Prototypes

1 Spider-Man PROTO 1.25 3.00
34 Invisible Woman PROTO 1.25 3.00
37 Captain America PROTO 1.25 3.00

1993 SkyBox Marvel Universe IV

COMPLETE SET (180) 10.00 25.00
UNOPENED BOX (36 PACKS) 125.00 200.00
UNOPENED PACK (10 CARDS) 4.00 6.00
COMMON CARD (1-180) .12 .30
HIV Spider-Man vs. Venom HOLO 50.00 120.00

1993 SkyBox Marvel Universe IV Red Foil

COMPLETE SET (9) 12.00 30.00
COMMON CARD (1-9) 1.50 4.00

1993 SkyBox Marvel Universe IV Promos

0 Deathlok .75 2.00
3UP Specialist/Dethstryk/Tiger Wylde
(1993 Capital City Conference Exclusive Panel)
NNO Silver Sable .40 1.00

1994 Fleer Marvel Universe V

COMPLETE SET (200) 30.00 75.00
UNOPENED HOBBY BOX (36 PACKS) 250.00 400.00
UNOPENED HOBBY PACK (9 CARDS) 8.00 12.00
UNOPENED JUMBO BOX (36 PACKS) 300.00 500.00
UNOPENED JUMBO PACK (12 CARDS) 10.00 15.00
UNOPENED WALMART BOX (20 PACKS)500.00 750.00
UNOPENED WALMART PACK (11 CARDS)25.00 40.00
COMMON CARD (1-200) .30 .75
1 Spider-Man 1.50 4.00
8 Iron Man .50 1.25
75 Iron Man and Hulkbuster 2.00 5.00
98 Deadpool 2.00 5.00
100 Gambit 1.00 2.50
124 Wolverine 1.50 4.00
130 Spider-Man 2.50 6.00
131 Venom 2.00 5.00
134 Punisher 1.00 2.50
145 Captain America 1.50 4.00

1994 Fleer Marvel Universe V Holograms

COMPLETE SET (4) 30.00 75.00
COMMON CARD (1-4) 8.00 20.00
1 Spider-Man 12.00 30.00
2 Wolverine 12.00 30.00

1994 Fleer Marvel Universe V Power Blast Rainbow

COMPLETE SET (9) 12.00 30.00
COMMON CARD (1-9) 2.00 5.00
*SILVER: SAME VALUE
*GOLD: .75X TO 2X BASIC CARDS
HOBBY PACK EXCLUSIVE

1994 Fleer Marvel Universe V Suspended Animation

COMPLETE SET (10) 12.00 30.00
COMMON CARD 1.50 4.00
1 Gambit 2.50 6.00
2 Human Torch 2.00 5.00
4 Iron Man 2.00 5.00
6 Spider-Man 2.50 6.00
8 Venom 3.00 8.00
10 Wolverine 3.00 8.00

1994 Fleer Marvel Universe V Suspended Animation Jumbo

COMPLETE SET (6) 12.00 30.00
COMMON CARD 2.50 6.00

1994 Fleer Marvel Universe V Promos

COMMON CARD .60 1.50
NNO Pro Action 2-Card Panel 1.50 4.00
Cards 98 and 130
NNO Spider-Man Magazine 4-Card Panel 2.00 5.00
Cards 130-92-124-155
NNO Wolverine/Iron Man 1.50 4.00
Spider-Man/Cable 4-Card Panel

1986 Comic Images Marvel Universe Stickers

COMPLETE SET (77) 15.00 40.00
COMMON CARD (1-77) .40 1.00

2015 Marvel Vibranium

COMPLETE SET (90) 100.00 200.00
UNOPENED BOX (20 PACKS) 1500.00 3000.00
UNOPENED PACK (5 CARDS) 75.00 150.00
COMMON CARD (1-90) .75 2.00
1 Captain America 2.00 5.00
2 Captain Marvel 1.50 4.00
3 Colossus 1.25 3.00
5 Daredevil 1.25 3.00
6 Hulk 1.25 3.00
9 Rocket Raccoon 1.25 3.00
12 Scarlet Witch 2.00 5.00
13 Star-Lord 1.25 3.00
15 Thanos 3.00 8.00
16 Ultimate Iron Man 2.50 6.00
17 Spider-Woman 1.50 4.00
18 Vision 1.00 2.50
19 Wolverine 8.00 20.00
20 War Machine 1.00 2.50
21 Nightcrawler 1.25 3.00
24 Doctor Strange 1.50 4.00
25 Cable 1.00 2.50
26 Black Panther 2.50 6.00
28 Gamora 1.25 3.00
30 Iron Man 5.00 12.00
31 Thor 1.25 3.00
34 Beast 1.25 3.00
36 Black Widow 1.50 4.00
37 Spider-Gwen 10.00 25.00
38 Psylocke 2.00 5.00
40 Winter Soldier 1.25 3.00
44 Punisher 2.50 6.00
45 Bishop 1.25 3.00
47 Green Goblin 1.25 3.00
48 Iceman 1.25 3.00
50 Namor 1.00 2.50
52 She-Hulk 1.50 4.00
56 Magik 1.25 3.00
58 Moon Knight 6.00 15.00
60 Black Cat 1.50 4.00
61 Drax The Destroyer 1.25 3.00
63 Rogue 1.00 2.50
67 White Tiger 1.00 2.50
68 Loki 1.25 3.00
69 Luke Cage 1.00 2.50
71 Groot 1.00 2.50
73 Magneto 1.25 3.00
76 Hawkeye 1.25 3.00
78 Storm 1.50 4.00
79 Ultimate Spider-Man 15.00 40.00
80 Ultimate Venom 6.00 15.00
85 Valkyrie 1.50 4.00
90 Deadpool 5.00 12.00

2015 Marvel Vibranium Molten

COMMON CARD 8.00 20.00
STATED PRINT RUN 299 SER.#'d SETS
1 Captain America 30.00 75.00
2 Captain Marvel 30.00 75.00
3 Colossus 25.00 60.00
4 Cyclops 50.00 100.00
5 Daredevil 60.00 120.00
6 Hulk 50.00 100.00
7 Kitty Pryde 12.00 30.00
8 Lockheed 10.00 25.00
9 Rocket Raccoon 30.00 75.00
10 Ronin 10.00 25.00
11 Sabretooth 20.00 50.00
12 Scarlet Witch 100.00 200.00
13 Star-Lord 25.00 60.00
14 Taskmaster 12.00 30.00
15 Thanos 100.00 200.00
16 Ultimate Iron Man 60.00 120.00
17 Spider-Woman 60.00 120.00
18 Vision 25.00 60.00
19 Wolverine 300.00 600.00

Card	Low	High
20 War Machine	15.00	40.00
21 Nightcrawler	15.00	40.00
22 Emma Frost	20.00	50.00
24 Doctor Strange	100.00	200.00
25 Cable	20.00	50.00
26 Black Panther	100.00	200.00
28 Gamora	20.00	50.00
29 Iron Fist	15.00	40.00
30 Iron Man	150.00	300.00
31 Thor	50.00	100.00
33 Black Bolt	12.00	30.00
34 Beast	20.00	50.00
36 Black Widow	30.00	75.00
37 Spider-Gwen	200.00	400.00
38 Psylocke	25.00	60.00
40 Winter Soldier	25.00	60.00
41 Enchantress	12.00	30.00
42 Leader	10.00	25.00
44 Punisher	30.00	75.00
45 Bishop	12.00	30.00
46 Hela	15.00	40.00
47 Green Goblin	30.00	75.00
48 Iceman	10.00	25.00
49 Nick Fury	15.00	40.00
50 Namor	20.00	50.00
52 She-Hulk	30.00	75.00
53 Black Swan	12.00	30.00
55 Darkhawk	20.00	50.00
56 Magik	30.00	75.00
58 Moon Knight	150.00	300.00
60 Black Cat	30.00	75.00
61 Drax The Destroyer	12.00	30.00
63 Rogue	30.00	75.00
65 Shroud	10.00	25.00
67 White Tiger	10.00	25.00
68 Loki	25.00	60.00
69 Luke Cage	12.00	30.00
71 Groot	30.00	75.00
73 Magneto	75.00	150.00
74 Mockingbird	10.00	25.00
75 Red Hulk	30.00	75.00
76 Hawkeye	20.00	50.00
77 Nova	10.00	25.00
78 Storm	60.00	120.00
79 Ultimate Spider-Man	400.00	800.00
80 Ultimate Venom	125.00	250.00
81 Sentry	10.00	25.00
82 Gladiator	12.00	30.00
85 Valkyrie	15.00	40.00
89 Warpath	10.00	25.00
90 Deadpool	200.00	400.00

2015 Marvel Vibranium Radiance

Card	Low	High
COMMON CARD	30.00	75.00
STATED PRINT RUN 50 SER.#'d SETS		
1 Captain America	250.00	500.00
2 Captain Marvel	125.00	250.00
3 Colossus		
4 Cyclops	200.00	400.00
5 Daredevil	150.00	300.00
6 Hulk	500.00	1000.00
7 Kitty Pryde	100.00	200.00
9 Rocket Raccoon	150.00	300.00
10 Ronin	125.00	250.00
11 Sabretooth	200.00	400.00
12 Scarlet Witch	150.00	300.00
13 Star-Lord	100.00	200.00
14 Taskmaster	150.00	300.00
15 Thanos	200.00	400.00
16 Ultimate Iron Man	150.00	300.00
17 Spider-Woman	125.00	250.00
18 Vision	75.00	150.00
19 Wolverine	2000.00	4000.00
20 War Machine	75.00	150.00
21 Nightcrawler	100.00	200.00
22 Emma Frost	100.00	200.00
24 Doctor Strange	300.00	600.00
25 Cable	125.00	250.00
26 Black Panther	250.00	500.00
28 Gamora	125.00	250.00
29 Iron Fist	50.00	100.00
30 Iron Man	750.00	1500.00
31 Thor	150.00	300.00
33 Black Bolt	125.00	250.00
34 Beast	200.00	400.00
35 Baron Zemo	125.00	250.00
36 Black Widow	150.00	300.00
37 Spider-Gwen	200.00	400.00
38 Psylocke	200.00	400.00
39 Angel	50.00	100.00
40 Winter Soldier	125.00	250.00
41 Enchantress		
42 Leader		
43 Chamber	60.00	120.00
44 Punisher	150.00	300.00
45 Bishop		
46 Hela	75.00	150.00
47 Green Goblin	150.00	300.00
48 Iceman	175.00	350.00
49 Nick Fury	125.00	250.00
50 Namor	100.00	200.00
51 Quicksilver		
52 She-Hulk	150.00	300.00
53 Black Swan		
54 Blindfold	100.00	200.00
55 Darkhawk	125.00	250.00
56 Magik	150.00	300.00
57 Nightmask		
58 Moon Knight	400.00	800.00
60 Black Cat	125.00	250.00
61 Drax The Destroyer	150.00	300.00
63 Rogue	100.00	200.00
65 Shroud		
66 Speedball		
67 White Tiger		
68 Loki	200.00	400.00
69 Luke Cage	200.00	400.00
70 Havok		
71 Groot	125.00	250.00
72 Amadeus Cho		
73 Magneto	250.00	500.00
74 Mockingbird		
75 Red Hulk	125.00	250.00
76 Hawkeye	100.00	200.00
77 Nova		
78 Storm	100.00	200.00
79 Ultimate Spider-Man		
80 Ultimate Venom		
82 Gladiator		
84 Manifold		
85 Valkyrie		
86 Hope		
87 Whirlwind		
88 Ulysses Klaw		
90 Deadpool	1000.00	2000.00

2015 Marvel Vibranium Raw

Card	Low	High
COMMON CARD	3.00	8.00
STATED ODDS 1:1		
1 Captain America	12.00	30.00
2 Captain Marvel	12.00	30.00
3 Colossus	8.00	20.00
4 Cyclops	6.00	15.00
5 Daredevil	12.00	30.00
6 Hulk	20.00	50.00
7 Kitty Pryde	10.00	25.00
9 Rocket Raccoon	6.00	15.00
11 Sabretooth	8.00	20.00
12 Scarlet Witch	25.00	60.00
13 Star-Lord	10.00	25.00
14 Taskmaster	8.00	20.00
15 Thanos	20.00	50.00
16 Ultimate Iron Man	20.00	50.00
17 Spider-Woman	8.00	20.00
18 Vision	6.00	15.00
19 Wolverine	75.00	150.00
20 War Machine	8.00	20.00
21 Nightcrawler	10.00	25.00
22 Emma Frost	8.00	20.00
24 Doctor Strange	15.00	40.00
25 Cable	6.00	15.00
26 Black Panther	50.00	100.00
28 Gamora	8.00	20.00
29 Iron Fist	6.00	15.00
30 Iron Man	30.00	75.00
31 Thor	12.00	30.00
33 Black Bolt	4.00	10.00
34 Beast	4.00	10.00
36 Black Widow	5.00	12.00
37 Spider-Gwen	75.00	150.00
38 Psylocke	12.00	30.00
40 Winter Soldier	4.00	10.00
42 Leader	5.00	12.00
44 Punisher	20.00	50.00
45 Bishop	6.00	15.00
46 Hela	4.00	10.00
47 Green Goblin	12.00	30.00
48 Iceman	4.00	10.00
49 Nick Fury	6.00	15.00
50 Namor	6.00	15.00
51 Quicksilver	4.00	10.00
52 She-Hulk	50.00	100.00
55 Darkhawk	5.00	12.00
56 Magik	6.00	15.00
58 Moon Knight	30.00	75.00
60 Black Cat	15.00	40.00
61 Drax The Destroyer	4.00	10.00
63 Rogue	6.00	15.00
65 Shroud	4.00	10.00
68 Loki	8.00	20.00
69 Luke Cage	6.00	15.00
71 Groot	8.00	20.00
73 Magneto	12.00	30.00
74 Mockingbird	5.00	12.00
75 Red Hulk	15.00	40.00
76 Hawkeye	4.00	10.00
77 Nova	4.00	10.00
78 Storm	20.00	50.00
79 Ultimate Spider-Man	150.00	300.00
80 Ultimate Venom	30.00	75.00
81 Sentry	4.00	10.00
85 Valkyrie	6.00	15.00
86 Hope	5.00	12.00
89 Warpath	4.00	10.00
90 Deadpool	50.00	100.00

2015 Marvel Vibranium Refined

Card	Low	High
COMMON CARD	12.00	30.00
STATED PRINT RUN 99 SER.#'d SETS		
1 Captain America	100.00	200.00
2 Captain Marvel	75.00	150.00
3 Colossus	50.00	100.00
4 Cyclops	100.00	200.00
5 Daredevil	60.00	120.00
6 Hulk	100.00	200.00
7 Kitty Pryde	20.00	50.00
9 Rocket Raccoon	50.00	100.00
10 Ronin	30.00	75.00
11 Sabretooth	75.00	150.00
12 Scarlet Witch	150.00	300.00
13 Star-Lord	60.00	120.00
14 Taskmaster	20.00	50.00
15 Thanos	75.00	150.00
16 Ultimate Iron Man	250.00	500.00
17 Spider-Woman	50.00	100.00
18 Vision	50.00	100.00
19 Wolverine	600.00	1200.00
20 War Machine	60.00	120.00
21 Nightcrawler	50.00	100.00
22 Emma Frost	60.00	120.00
23 Cannonball	15.00	40.00
24 Doctor Strange	100.00	200.00
25 Cable	15.00	40.00
26 Black Panther	175.00	350.00
28 Gamora	60.00	120.00
29 Iron Fist	20.00	50.00
30 Iron Man	150.00	300.00
31 Thor	125.00	250.00
33 Black Bolt	20.00	50.00
34 Beast	50.00	100.00
36 Black Widow	125.00	250.00
37 Spider-Gwen	250.00	500.00
38 Psylocke	30.00	75.00
40 Winter Soldier	60.00	120.00
41 Enchantress	25.00	60.00
44 Punisher	30.00	75.00
45 Bishop	50.00	100.00
46 Hela	60.00	120.00
47 Green Goblin	75.00	150.00
48 Iceman	75.00	150.00
49 Nick Fury	30.00	75.00
50 Namor	50.00	100.00
51 Quicksilver	15.00	40.00
52 She-Hulk	75.00	150.00
56 Magik	50.00	100.00
58 Moon Knight	200.00	400.00
60 Black Cat	200.00	400.00
61 Drax The Destroyer	30.00	75.00
63 Rogue	125.00	250.00
64 Misty Knight	25.00	60.00
65 Shroud	15.00	40.00
67 White Tiger	15.00	40.00
68 Loki	75.00	150.00
69 Luke Cage	25.00	60.00
70 Havok	20.00	50.00
71 Groot	20.00	50.00
72 Amadeus Cho	25.00	60.00
73 Magneto	200.00	400.00
74 Mockingbird	20.00	50.00
75 Red Hulk	75.00	150.00
76 Hawkeye	30.00	75.00
77 Nova	30.00	75.00
78 Storm	50.00	100.00
79 Ultimate Spider-Man	1500.00	3000.00
80 Ultimate Venom	200.00	400.00
85 Valkyrie	30.00	75.00
90 Deadpool	375.00	750.00

2015 Marvel Vibranium Double Patches

Card	Low	High
COMMON CARD	6.00	15.00
P21 Groot	15.00	40.00
Rocket Raccoon		
P22 Lockheed/Kitty Pryde	10.00	25.00
P24 Iron Fist/Daredevil	15.00	40.00
P25 Cyclops/Jean Grey	8.00	20.00
P26 Gamora/Star-Lord	8.00	20.00
P27 Spider-Man/Spider-Gwen	20.00	50.00
P28 Thor/Cap	8.00	20.00
P210 Cable/Cyclops	8.00	20.00
P211 Captain Marvel/Luke Cage	12.00	30.00
P213 Ult.Venom/Ult.Spider-Man	20.00	50.00
P214 Ronin/Mockingbird	10.00	25.00
P215 Cyclops/Emma Frost	10.00	25.00
P217 Taskmaster/Cap	10.00	25.00
P219 Nightcrawler/Beast	15.00	40.00
P221 Wolverine/Sabretooth SP	175.00	350.00
P222 Spider-Woman/Ult.Spider-Man SP	80.00	150.00
P223 Ult.Iron Man/Iron Man SP	100.00	200.00
P224 Vision/Scarlet Witch SP	15.00	40.00
P225 Lockjaw/Black Bolt SP	50.00	100.00

2015 Marvel Vibranium Hero PowOre

Card	Low	High
COMPLETE SET (20)	25.00	60.00
COMMON CARD (HP1-HP20)	1.50	4.00
STATED ODDS 1:13		
HP2 Thanos	2.00	5.00
HP3 Hulk	3.00	8.00
HP4 Ultron	2.00	5.00
HP5 Doctor Strange	2.50	6.00
HP6 Magneto	2.50	6.00
HP8 Black Panther	2.00	5.00
HP9 Wolverine	8.00	20.00
HP10 Spider-Man	4.00	10.00
HP11 Daredevil	3.00	8.00
HP12 Scarlet Witch	2.50	6.00
HP14 Storm	2.50	6.00
HP16 Squirrel Girl	2.00	5.00
HP17 Ultimate Venom	2.50	6.00
HP18 Spider-Gwen	3.00	8.00
HP19 Moon Knight	2.00	5.00
HP20 Captain America	2.50	6.00

2015 Marvel Vibranium In Memoriam

COMPLETE SET (20)	15.00	40.00
COMMON CARD (IM1-IM20)	1.00	2.50
STATED ODDS 1:13		
IM1 Wolverine	6.00	15.00
IM2 Black Widow	1.50	4.00
IM7 Thor	1.50	4.00
IM8 Superior Spider-Man	3.00	8.00
IM10 Black Panther	1.50	4.00
IM15 Ultimate Captain America	2.00	5.00
IM18 Nova	1.25	3.00
IM20 Deadpool	3.00	8.00

2015 Marvel Vibranium Patches

COMMON CARD (P1-P25)	6.00	15.00
STATED ODDS 1:24		
P2 Deadpool	15.00	40.00
P3 Ultimate Iron Man	15.00	40.00
P4 Thor	12.00	30.00
P5 Magneto	12.00	30.00
P8 Ultimate Spider-Man	8.00	20.00
P12 Colossus	8.00	20.00
P13 Namor	10.00	25.00
P14 Scarlet Witch	8.00	40.00
P16 Jean Grey	12.00	30.00
P19 Ghost Rider	8.00	20.00
P20 Daredevil	10.00	25.00
P21 Spider-Gwen SP	30.00	80.00
P22 Nightcrawler SP	25.00	60.00
P23 Iron Man SP	25.00	60.00
P24 Wolverine SP	30.00	80.00
P25 Captain America SP	30.00	80.00

2015 Marvel Vibranium Rookie Heroes

COMPLETE SET (10)	20.00	50.00
COMMON CARD (RH1-RH10)	3.00	8.00
STATED ODDS 1:27		
RH3 Silk	4.00	10.00
RH4 Thor	5.00	12.00
RH7 Sun Girl	5.00	12.00
RH8 Water Snake	6.00	15.00

2015 Marvel Vibranium Universal Heroes

COMPLETE SET (20)	30.00	80.00
COMMON CARD (UH1-UH20)	2.00	5.00
UH1 Wolverine	2.50	6.00
UH3 Spider-Man	3.00	8.00
UH4 Cyclops	3.00	8.00
UH6 Thor	3.00	8.00
UH8 Deadpool	5.00	12.00
UH9 Daredevil	3.00	8.00
UH13 Punisher	4.00	10.00
UH20 Hawkeye	2.50	6.00

2015 Marvel Vibranium When Worlds Collide

COMPLETE SET (20)	30.00	80.00
COMMON CARD (WC1-WC20)	1.50	4.00
WC2 Thanos	2.00	5.00
Nova		
WC3 Spidey 2099	8.00	20.00
Sup.Spidey		
WC4 Thor	5.00	12.00
Wolverine		
WC5 Thanos	3.00	8.00
Hulk		
WC6 Sup.Spidey	6.00	15.00
Spidey		
WC7 X-23	5.00	12.00
Xavier		
WC9 Beast	3.00	8.00
Hulk		
WC10 Hammer of God	2.50	6.00
Black Widow		
WC11 Cap	3.00	8.00
Iron Nail		
WC12 Hulk	2.00	5.00
Zoran		
WC13 Nick Fury	2.50	6.00
Cap		
WC15 Hulk	2.00	5.00
Captain Marvel		
WC16 Malekith	2.00	5.00
Thor		
WC17 Spider-Man	2.50	6.00
Medusa		
WC18 Cap	3.00	8.00
Batroc		
WC19 Spider-Man	2.50	6.00
Vulture		
WC20 Deadpool	4.00	10.00
Hawkeye		

1996 Fleer SkyBox Marvel Vision

COMPLETE SET (100)	10.00	25.00
UNOPENED BOX (48 PACKS)	125.00	200.00
UNOPENED PACK (7 CARDS)	3.00	4.00
COMMON CARD (1-100)	.20	.50
1 Spider-Man	.40	1.00
2 Spider-Man Alien Costume	.40	1.00
3 Spider-Man Six Arms	.40	1.00
4 Blade Spider-Man Team-Up	.30	.75
5 Punisher Spider-Man Team-Up	.50	1.25
6 Wolverine Spider-Man Team-Up	.40	1.00
21 Spider-Man vs. Doctor Octopus	.30	.75
22 Spider-Man vs. Lizard	.30	.75
23 Spider-Man vs. Mysterio	.30	.75
24 Spider-Man vs. Rhino	.30	.75
25 Spider-Man vs. Venom	.30	.75
31 Gambit	.30	.75
40 Wolverine	.40	1.00
41 Apocalypse	.30	.75
44 Mr. Sinister	.30	.75
51 Gambit vs. Bishop	.30	.75
54 Wolverine vs. Sabretooth	.30	.75
68 Daredevil	.40	1.00
78 Iron Man	.40	1.00
79 Iron Man Exo Battle Armor	.30	.75
80 Iron Man Deep Space Armor	.30	.75
81 Iron Man Hydro Armor	.30	.75
95 Iron Man vs. Blacklash	.30	.75
96 Iron Man vs. Crimson Dynamo	.30	.75
97 Iron Man vs. Fin Fang Foom	.30	.75
98 Iron Man vs. Mandarin	.30	.75
99 Iron Man vs. Titanium Man	.30	.75
NNO Decode Answer	.40	1.00

1996 Fleer SkyBox Marvel Vision Mini-Mags

COMPLETE SET (4)	5.00	12.00
COMMON CARD (1-4)	.75	2.00
STATED ODDS 1:1		
2 Iron Man	2.50	6.00
3 Spider-Man	3.00	8.00

1996 Fleer SkyBox Marvel Vision Temporary Tattoos

COMPLETE SET (16)	5.00	15.00
COMMON CARD (1-16)	.60	1.50
STATED ODDS 1:3		
7 Wolverine	1.25	3.00
10 Iron Man Yellow	.75	2.00
11 Iron Man	.75	2.00
15 Spider-Man	1.25	3.00

1997 Fleer SkyBox Marvel vs. WildStorm

COMPLETE SET (90)	12.00	30.00
UNOPENED BOX (24 PACKS)	100.00	150.00
UNOPENED PACK (5 CARDS)	4.00	6.00
COMMON CARD (1-90)	.25	.60
*REFRACTORS: 1.2X TO 3X BASIC CARDS	.75	2.00
NNO1 Fairchild vs. She-Hulk PROMO	3.00	8.00

1997 Fleer SkyBox Marvel vs. WildStorm Clearchrome

COMPLETE SET (9)	4.00	10.00
COMMON CARD (A1-A9)	.40	1.00
STATED ODDS 1:6		
A1 Silver Surfer	3.00	8.00
A2 Captain America	.75	2.00
A5 Backlash vs. Captain America	.75	2.00

1987 Comic Images Marvel's Magic Moments Stickers

COMPLETE SET (80)	10.00	25.00
COMMON CARD (1-80)	.25	.60

1987 Comic Images Mutant Hall of Fame Stickers

COMPLETE SET (80)	25.00	60.00
COMMON CARD (1-80)	.60	1.50

1988 Marvel Comics Nick Fury vs. SHIELD Promo

NNO SHIELD ID Card	5.00	12.00
Art by Paul Neary		

1983 Ovaltine Marvel Super Heroes Round Stickers

COMPLETE SET (10)	8.00	20.00
COMMON CARD	.40	1.00
1 Captain America	2.00	5.00
5 Spider-Man	4.00	10.00
7 The Hulk	1.50	4.00
9 Thor	2.00	5.00
10 Wolverine	4.00	10.00

1988 Comic Images The Punisher

COMPLETE SET (50)	6.00	15.00
UNOPENED BOX (50 PACKS)	100.00	150.00
UNOPENED PACK (5 CARDS)	2.00	3.00
COMMON CARD (1-50)	.30	.75

1992 Comic Images The Punisher Guts and Gunpowder

COMPLETE SET (90)	4.00	10.00
UNOPENED BOX (48 PACKS)	50.00	75.00
UNOPENED PACK (10 CARDS)	1.50	2.00
COMMON CARD (1-90)	.10	.25

1992 Comic Images The Punisher Guts and Gunpowder Prisms

COMPLETE SET (3)	8.00	20.00
COMMON CARD (1-3)	3.00	8.00
STATED ODDS 1:48		

1992 Comic Images The Punisher Guts and Gunpowder Promos

NNO Promo 1	.75	2.00
NNO Promo 2 Prism Oversized	1.50	4.00
NNO 4-Card Panel		

1992 Comic Images The Punisher Guts and Gunpowder Scratch and Sniff

COMPLETE SET (3)	6.00	15.00
COMMON CARD (1-3)	2.00	5.00
STATED ODDS 1:24		
1 Preparation	4.00	10.00

1990 Comic Images The Punisher Papers Stickers

COMPLETE SET (75)	20.00	50.00
COMMON CARD (1-75)	.50	1.25

1992 Comic Images Silver Surfer

COMPLETE SET (72)	10.00	25.00
UNOPENED BOX (36 PACKS)	175.00	300.00
UNOPENED PACK (7 CARDS)	5.00	8.00
COMMON CARD (1-72)	.25	.60
NNO Silver Surfer PROMO	2.50	6.00

Spider-Man

1994 Fleer The Amazing Spider-Man

COMPLETE SET (150)	25.00	60.00
UNOPENED HOBBY BOX (36 PACKS)	200.00	350.00
UNOPENED HOBBY PACK (8 CARDS)	6.00	10.00
UNOPENED JUMBO BOX (36 PACKS)	200.00	350.00
UNOPENED JUMBO PACK (12 CARDS)	6.00	10.00
UNOPENED WALMART BOX (20 PACKS)	600.00	1200.00
UNOPENED WALMART PACK (11 CARDS)	30.00	60.00
COMMON CARD (1-150)	.30	.75

1994 Fleer The Amazing Spider-Man Gold-Web

COMPLETE SET (6)	60.00	120.00
COMMON CARD (1-6)	10.00	25.00
RANDOMLY INSERTED INTO JUMBO PACKS		
1 Venom	15.00	40.00
3 Spider-Man	15.00	40.00
5 Hobgoblin	12.00	30.00
6 Carnage	15.00	40.00

1994 Fleer The Amazing Spider-Man Gold-Web Wal-Mart

COMPLETE SET (6)	100.00	200.00
COMMON CARD (1-6)	15.00	40.00
STATED ODDS 1:7 WAL-MART PACKS		
1 Spider-Man	20.00	50.00
3 Black Cat	25.00	60.00
4 Vulture	30.00	75.00
6 Spider-Man	25.00	60.00

1994 Fleer The Amazing Spider-Man Holograms

COMPLETE SET (4)	50.00	100.00
COMMON CARD (1-4)	10.00	25.00
STATED ODDS 1:18		
1 Carnage	25.00	60.00
3a Venom (green)	15.00	40.00
3b Venom (red)		

1994 Fleer The Amazing Spider-Man Masterprints

COMPLETE SET (9)	15.00	40.00
COMMON CARD (1-9)	3.00	8.00
STATED ODDS 1:CASE		

1994 Fleer The Amazing Spider-Man Suspended Animation

COMPLETE SET (12)	30.00	75.00
COMMON CARD (1-12)	4.00	10.00
STATED ODDS 1:4 HOBBY		

1992 Impel Amazing Spider-Man 1962-1992 Comic Dealer Promos

COMPLETE SET (5)	8.00	20.00
COMMON CARD (1-5)	2.50	6.00

2012 Amazing Spider-Man Movie

COMPLETE SET (9)	10.00	25.00
COMMON CARD	1.50	4.00
COMMON MEM	8.00	20.00
ONE AUTO WITH EVERY SET PURCHASED		
AUR1 ISSUED AS 4-SET INCENTIVE		
CC1 Spider-Man MEM	25.00	60.00
CC3 Gwen Stacy MEM	25.00	60.00
CC5 Gwen Stacy MEM	25.00	60.00
NNO A. Garfield AU	1000.00	2000.00
NNO A. Garfield AU FB	1000.00	2000.00
NNO A. Garfield AU MEM	750.00	1500.00

2014 Amazing Spider-Man 2 McDonald's

COMPLETE SET (4)	2.50	6.00
COMMON CARD (1-4)	.75	2.00
1 Spider-Man	1.25	3.00
3 Spider-Man vs. Electro	1.00	2.50

2014 Amazing Spider-Man 2 McDonald's Boy Toys

COMPLETE SET (8)	8.00	20.00
COMMON TOY (1-8)	1.50	4.00
1 Spider-Man Light-Up Figure	2.50	6.00
3 Spider-Man Light-Up Vehicle	2.00	5.00

5 Wind-Up Spider 2.50 6.00
7 Spider-Man Specs 3.00 8.00

2014 Amazing Spider-Man 2 McDonald's Girl Toys

COMPLETE SET (8) 6.00 15.00
COMMON TOY (1-8) 1.25 3.00
3 Comb and Mirror Set 1.50 4.00
6 Note Card Set 1.50 4.00

1995 Fleer Ultra Spider-Man Premiere

COMPLETE SET (150) 25.00 60.00
UNOPENED BOX (36 PACKS) 500.00 750.00
UNOPENED PACK (11 CARDS) 15.00 25.00
UNOPENED JUMBO BOX (24 PACKS) 350.00 500.00
UNOPENED JUMBO PACK 15.00 20.00
COMMON CARD (1-150) .30 .75
*GOLD FOIL SIG: 2X TO 5X BASIC CARDS

1995 Fleer Ultra Spider-Man Premiere Gold Foil Signature

*GOLD FOIL SIG: 2X TO 5X BASIC CARDS
STATED ODDS 1:1

1995 Fleer Ultra Spider-Man Premiere ClearChrome

COMPLETE SET (10) 50.00 100.00
COMMON CARD (1-10) 2.50 6.00
STATED ODDS 1:7
1 Dr. Octopus 4.00 10.00
2 Green Goblin 5.00 12.00
3 Hobgoblin 4.00 10.00
5 Lizard 3.00 8.00
7 Scorpion 5.00 12.00
9 Spider-Man 15.00 40.00
10 Venom 12.00 30.00

1995 Fleer Ultra Spider-Man Premiere Golden Web

COMPLETE SET (9) 12.00 30.00
COMMON CARD (1-9) 1.25 3.00
STATED ODDS 1:3
1 Black Cat 2.00 5.00
2 Carnage 3.00 8.00
5 Lizard 2.50 6.00
6 Scorpion 1.50 4.00
7 Spider-Man 4.00 10.00
8 Venom 8.00 20.00

1995 Fleer Ultra Spider-Man Premiere Holoblast

COMPLETE SET (6) 15.00 40.00
COMMON CARD (1-6) 4.00 10.00
STATED ODDS 1:9

1995 Fleer Ultra Spider-Man Premiere Masterpieces

COMPLETE SET (9) 20.00 50.00
COMMON CARD (1-9) 4.00 10.00
1 Carnage 5.00 12.00
2 Carnage 5.00 12.00
3 Carnage 5.00 12.00

1995 Fleer Ultra Spider-Man Premiere Ultraprints

COMPLETE SET (10) 30.00 75.00
COMMON CARD (1-10) 5.00 12.00
STATED ODDS 1:CASE

1995 Fleer Ultra Spider-Man Premiere Promo Panels

COMMON CARD 1.50 4.00
NNO Black Cat/Hobgoblin/Venom/Spider-Man2.00 5.00
(4-Card Panel)

1995 Fleer Ultra Ralston Spider-Man Premiere Cereal

COMPLETE SET (6) 6.00 15.00
COMPLETE MAIL-IN SET (6) 6.00 15.00
COMPLETE MASTER SET (12) 10.00 25.00
COMMON CARD 1.50 4.00
INSERTED IN BOXES OF COOKIE CRISP
5 Spider-Man 4.00 10.00

1997 Fleer Ultra Spider-Man

COMPLETE SET (81) 8.00 20.00
UNOPENED BOX (24 PACKS) 300.00 500.00
UNOPENED PACK (8 CARDS) 12.00 20.00
COMMON CARD (1-81) .20 .50
*BLUE FOIL: 1X TO 2.5X BASIC CARDS
*RED FOIL: 1.5X TO 4X BASIC CARDS

2017 Fleer Ultra Spider-Man

COMPLETE SET (100) 30.00 80.00
UNOPENED BOX (12 PACKS) 6000.00 7500.00
UNOPENED PACK (5 CARDS) 500.00 625.00
COMMON CARD (1-100) 1.00 2.50
*SILVER FOIL: 1.2X TO 3X BASIC CARDS

2017 Fleer Ultra Spider-Man Gold Foil Autographs

COMMON AUTO (1-100) 15.00 40.00
STATED PRINT RUN 49 SER.#'d SETS

2017 Fleer Ultra Spider-Man 1995 Buybacks

COMMON CARD (1-149) 8.00 20.00
STATED PRINT RUN 29-30 SER.#'d SETS

2017 Fleer Ultra Spider-Man Coin Cards

COMMON CARD (CC1-CC25) 25.00 60.00
STATED ODDS 1:600

2017 Fleer Ultra Spider-Man Comic and Coin Autographs

COMMON CARD (CCP1-CCP25) 15.00 40.00
STATED ODDS 1:600
CCP1 Sal Buscema 30.00 75.00
CCP2 Sal Buscema 30.00 75.00
CCP3 Sal Buscema 30.00 75.00
CCP4 Sal Buscema 30.00 75.00
CCP5 Sal Buscema 30.00 75.00
CCP6 Gerry Conway 25.00 60.00
CCP7 Gerry Conway 25.00 60.00
CCP8 Gerry Conway 25.00 60.00
CCP15 Glynis Oliver Marsh 20.00 50.00
CCP16 Glynis Oliver Marsh 20.00 50.00
CCP17 Glynis Oliver Marsh 20.00 50.00
CCP18 Glynis Oliver Marsh 20.00 50.00
CCP19 Glynis Oliver Marsh 20.00 50.00
CCP20 Walt Simonson 25.00 60.00
CCP21 Walt Simonson 25.00 60.00
CCP22 Jim Starlin 20.00 50.00
CCP23 Jim Starlin 20.00 50.00
CCP24 Jim Starlin 20.00 50.00
CCP25 Jim Starlin 20.00 50.00

2017 Fleer Ultra Spider-Man Comic Cut Panels

COMMON CARD (CP1-CP25) 20.00 50.00
STATED ODDS 1:160

2017 Fleer Ultra Spider-Man Deadpool Across America

COMPLETE SET (10) 12.00 30.00
COMMON CARD (DA1-DA10) 2.50 6.00
*SILVER FOIL: .75X TO 2X BASIC CARDS
STATED ODDS 1:6

2017 Fleer Ultra Spider-Man Deadpool Across America Gold Foil Autographs

COMMON AUTO (DA1-DA10) 15.00 40.00
STATED PRINT RUN 49 SER.#'d SETS

2017 Fleer Ultra Spider-Man Dual Comic Cut Panels

COMMON CARD (DCP1-DCP25) 30.00 75.00
STATED ODDS 1:1,200

2017 Fleer Ultra Spider-Man E-X Century

COMMON CARD (EX1-EX42)) 8.00 20.00
STATED ODDS 1:12
EX1 Venom 60.00 150.00
EX3 Shang-Chi 40.00 100.00
EX4 Gwen Stacy 50.00 125.00
EX6 Mysterio 20.00 50.00
EX7 Scarlet Spider 15.00 40.00
EX8 Iron Patriot 15.00 40.00
EX11 Carnage 40.00 100.00
EX14 Hobgoblin 12.00 30.00
EX18 Iron Man 30.00 75.00
EX19 Spider-Man Noir 20.00 50.00
EX23 Silk 15.00 40.00
EX24 Madame Web 12.00 30.00
EX25 Moon Knight 40.00 100.00
EX26 J. Jonah Jameson 25.00 60.00
EX28 Spider-Girl 15.00 40.00
EX31 Black Cat 15.00 40.00
EX34 Morbius 12.00 30.00
EX41 Punisher 15.00 40.00
EX42 Spider-Man 100.00 250.00

2017 Fleer Ultra Spider-Man Holoblast

COMMON CARD (HH1-HH21) 40.00 100.00
STATED ODDS 1:72
HH1 Spider-Man/Venom 100.00 250.00
HH2 Deadpool/Carnage 200.00 500.00
HH4 Spider-Man/Lizard 60.00 150.00
HH6 Spider-Man/Carnage 150.00 400.00
HH9 Spider-Man/Scarlet Spider 60.00 150.00
HH10 Spider-Man/Punisher 50.00 125.00
HH11 Spider-Man/Doctor Octopus 75.00 200.00
HH13 Spider-Man/Iron Man 100.00 250.00
HH14 Agent Venom/Toxin 50.00 125.00
HH15 Spider-Man/Green Goblin 60.00 150.00
HH16 Spider-Man/Captain America 75.00 200.00
HH17 Spider-Man/Morlun 75.00 200.00
HH19 Spider-Man/Morbius 50.00 125.00
HH20 Spider-Man/Dagger/Cloak 50.00 125.00
HH21 Green Goblin/Hobgoblin 50.00 125.00

2017 Fleer Ultra Spider-Man Jambalaya

COMMON CARD (1-30) 40.00 100.00
STATED ODDS 1:72
1 Spider-Woman 125.00 300.00
2 Shocker 50.00 125.00
3 Spider-Man 1200.00 3000.00
4 Wolverine 500.00 1200.00
6 Spider-Man 2099 600.00 1500.00
7 Daredevil 250.00 600.00
8 Mary Jane Parker 100.00 250.00
9 Punisher 200.00 500.00
10 Mysterio 75.00 200.00
11 Arachne 100.00 250.00
13 Spider-Gwen 400.00 1000.00
14 Hobgoblin 125.00 300.00
16 Venom 600.00 1500.00
17 Carnage 200.00 500.00
18 Electro 125.00 300.00
19 Iron Fist 125.00 300.00
20 Chameleon 60.00 150.00
21 Kingpin 125.00 300.00
22 Spider-Man 400.00 1000.00
23 Silver Sable 75.00 200.00
24 Deadpool 600.00 1500.00
25 Doctor Octopus 150.00 400.00
26 Kraven 100.00 250.00
27 Doctor Strange 500.00 1200.00
28 Scorpion 60.00 150.00
29 Lizard 100.00 250.00
30 Black Cat 125.00 300.00

2017 Fleer Ultra Spider-Man Legacy

COMPLETE SET (12) 10.00 25.00
COMMON CARD (L1-L12) 2.00 5.00
*SILVER FOIL: .6X TO 1.5X BASIC CARDS 3.00 8.00
STATED ODDS 1:2

2017 Fleer Ultra Spider-Man Legacy Gold Foil Autographs

COMMON CARD (L1-L12) 10.00 25.00
STATED PRINT RUN 49 SER.#'d SETS
L1 Symbiote Spider-Man 15.00 40.00
Greg Hildebrandt
L2 Venom 15.00 40.00
Greg Hildebrandt
L3 Carnage 15.00 40.00
Greg Hildebrandt

2017 Fleer Ultra Spider-Man Manufactured Webbing

COMMON CARD (WEB1-WEB32)
SPIDER-MAN 49 SER.#'d SETS 30.00 75.00
VENOM 25 SER.#'d SETS 100.00 200.00
CARNAGE 10 SER.#'d SETS 200.00 400.00

2017 Fleer Ultra Spider-Man Marvel Metal

COMMON CARD (MM1-MM50) 4.00 10.00
MM0 E-PACK ACHIEVEMENT EXCLUSIVE
RANDOMLY INSERTED INTO PACKS
MM0 Spider-Man 300.00 750.00
(E-Pack Achivement Exclusive)
MM1 Spider-Man 125.00 300.00
MM2 Shocker 12.00 30.00
MM3 Madame Web 30.00 75.00
MM4 Agent Venom 20.00 50.00
MM6 Black Cat 15.00 40.00
MM8 Iron Man 15.00 40.00
MM9 Spider-Woman 10.00 25.00
MM10 Luke Cage 6.00 15.00
MM11 Black Widow 15.00 40.00
MM12 Deadpool 40.00 100.00
MM13 Iron Fist 6.00 15.00
MM14 Carnage 25.00 60.00
MM19 Hulk 12.00 30.00
MM20 Green Goblin 8.00 20.00
MM21 Moon Knight 30.00 75.00
MM22 Spider-Gwen 50.00 125.00
MM23 Venom 50.00 125.00
MM24 Lizard 6.00 15.00
MM25 Mary Jane Watson 6.00 15.00
MM26 Spider-Girl 12.00 30.00
MM29 Punisher 10.00 25.00
MM30 Anti-Venom 10.00 25.00
MM32 Kraven 5.00 12.00
MM33 Wolverine 20.00 50.00
MM34 Silver Sable 5.00 12.00
MM35 Spider-Man 2099 15.00 40.00
MM37 Scarlet Spider 12.00 30.00
MM38 Kingpin 6.00 15.00
MM40 Electro 5.00 12.00
MM43 Silk 10.00 25.00
MM45 Captain America 12.00 30.00
MM48 Daredevil 10.00 25.00
MM50 Spider-Man 100.00 250.00

2017 Fleer Ultra Spider-Man Marvel Metal PMG Blue

COMMON CARD (MM1-MM50) 125.00 300.00
STATED PRINT RUN 49 SER.#'d SETS
MM1 Spider-Man 2500.00 6000.00
MM2 Shocker 250.00 600.00
MM3 Madame Web 150.00 400.00
MM4 Agent Venom 300.00 800.00
MM6 Black Cat 400.00 1000.00
MM7 Doctor Octopus 250.00 600.00
MM8 Iron Man 750.00 1500.00
MM9 Spider-Woman 250.00 600.00
MM10 Luke Cage 150.00 400.00
MM11 Black Widow 200.00 500.00
MM12 Deadpool 1200.00 3000.00
MM14 Carnage 1200.00 3000.00
MM15 Sandman 150.00 400.00
MM19 Hulk 1200.00 3000.00
MM20 Green Goblin 300.00 800.00

MM21 Moon Knight	600.00	1500.00
MM22 Spider-Gwen	1500.00	4000.00
MM23 Venom	1500.00	4000.00
MM24 Lizard	200.00	500.00
MM25 Mary Jane Watson	200.00	500.00
MM26 Spider-Girl	300.00	800.00
MM27 White Tiger	150.00	400.00
MM28 Morbius	300.00	750.00
MM29 Punisher	400.00	1000.00
MM30 Anti-Venom	300.00	800.00
MM31 Nick Fury Jr.	150.00	400.00
MM32 Kraven	250.00	600.00
MM33 Wolverine	2500.00	6000.00
MM34 Silver Sable	300.00	750.00
MM35 Spider-Man 2099	150.00	400.00
MM36 Jack O'Lantern	150.00	400.00
MM37 Scarlet Spider	750.00	2000.00
MM38 Kingpin	250.00	600.00
MM39 Mysterio	150.00	400.00
MM41 Nova	150.00	400.00
MM42 Vulture	250.00	600.00
MM43 Silk	600.00	1500.00
MM44 Scorpion	200.00	500.00
MM45 Captain America	1200.00	3000.00
MM46 Kitty Pryde	150.00	400.00
MM47 Prowler	200.00	500.00
MM48 Daredevil	400.00	1000.00
MM49 Jackal	500.00	1200.00
MM50 Spider-Man	2000.00	4500.00

2017 Fleer Ultra Spider-Man Marvel Metal PMG Bronze

COMMON CARD (MM1-MM50)	50.00	125.00
STATED PRINT RUN 199 SER.#'d SETS		
MM1 Spider-Man	500.00	1200.00
MM2 Shocker	75.00	200.00
MM3 Madame Web	100.00	250.00
MM5 Rhino	75.00	200.00
MM6 Black Cat	150.00	400.00
MM7 Doctor Octopus	125.00	300.00
MM8 Iron Man	250.00	600.00
MM9 Spider-Woman	100.00	250.00
MM10 Luke Cage	60.00	150.00
MM11 Black Widow	125.00	300.00
MM12 Deadpool	150.00	400.00
MM13 Iron Fist	60.00	150.00
MM14 Carnage	150.00	400.00
MM19 Hulk	200.00	500.00
MM20 Green Goblin	100.00	250.00
MM21 Moon Knight	200.00	500.00
MM22 Spider-Gwen	300.00	750.00
MM23 Venom	200.00	500.00
MM24 Lizard	60.00	150.00
MM25 Mary Jane Watson	60.00	150.00
MM26 Spider-Girl	100.00	250.00
MM28 Morbius	125.00	300.00
MM29 Punisher	125.00	300.00
MM30 Anti-Venom	100.00	250.00
MM31 Nick Fury Jr.	60.00	150.00
MM32 Kraven	100.00	250.00
MM33 Wolverine	250.00	600.00
MM35 Spider-Man 2099	200.00	500.00
MM36 Jack O'Lantern	100.00	250.00
MM37 Scarlet Spider	125.00	300.00
MM38 Kingpin	100.00	250.00
MM39 Mysterio	75.00	200.00
MM41 Nova	75.00	200.00
MM43 Silk	200.00	500.00
MM44 Scorpion	100.00	250.00
MM45 Captain America	300.00	750.00
MM46 Kitty Pryde	75.00	200.00
MM47 Prowler	125.00	300.00
MM48 Daredevil	200.00	500.00
MM50 Spider-Man	300.00	750.00

2017 Fleer Ultra Spider-Man Marvel Metal PMG Green

COMPLETE SET (50)		
STATED PRINT RUN 10 SER.#'d SETS		
MM3 Madame Web	1500.00	4000.00
MM4 Agent Venom	750.00	2000.00
MM6 Black Cat	1500.00	4000.00
MM9 Spider-Woman	600.00	1500.00
MM11 Black Widow	1200.00	3000.00
MM12 Deadpool	2000.00	5000.00
MM13 Iron Fist	1000.00	2500.00
MM17 Cloak	300.00	800.00
MM18 Morlun	150.00	400.00
MM20 Green Goblin	1200.00	3000.00
MM23 Venom	1000.00	2500.00
MM24 Lizard	600.00	1500.00
MM27 White Tiger	250.00	600.00
MM39 Mysterio	600.00	1500.00
MM40 Electro	750.00	2000.00
MM42 Vulture	600.00	1500.00
MM43 Silk	1500.00	4000.00
MM44 Scorpion	400.00	1000.00
MM46 Kitty Pryde	1200.00	3000.00
MM48 Daredevil	1000.00	2500.00
MM49 Jackal	1200.00	3000.00

2017 Fleer Ultra Spider-Man Marvel Metal PMG Red

COMMON CARD (MM1-MM50)	75.00	200.00
STATED PRINT RUN 99 SER.#'d SETS		
MM1 Spider-Man	3000.00	5000.00
MM2 Shocker	100.00	250.00
MM3 Madame Web	150.00	400.00
MM4 Agent Venom	200.00	500.00
MM6 Black Cat	200.00	500.00
MM7 Doctor Octopus	150.00	400.00
MM8 Iron Man	600.00	1500.00
MM9 Spider-Woman	150.00	400.00
MM10 Luke Cage	125.00	300.00
MM11 Black Widow	150.00	400.00
MM12 Deadpool	600.00	1500.00
MM14 Carnage	500.00	1200.00
MM18 Morlun	100.00	250.00
MM19 Hulk	300.00	800.00
MM20 Green Goblin	250.00	600.00
MM21 Moon Knight	400.00	1000.00
MM22 Spider-Gwen	600.00	1500.00
MM23 Venom	1200.00	3000.00
MM25 Mary Jane Watson	100.00	250.00
MM26 Spider-Girl	100.00	250.00
MM28 Morbius	200.00	500.00
MM29 Punisher	500.00	1200.00
MM30 Anti-Venom	125.00	300.00
MM31 Nick Fury Jr.	100.00	250.00
MM32 Kraven	125.00	300.00
MM33 Wolverine	1200.00	3000.00
MM34 Silver Sable	100.00	250.00
MM35 Spider-Man 2099	300.00	800.00
MM37 Scarlet Spider	600.00	1500.00
MM38 Kingpin	250.00	600.00
MM39 Mysterio	100.00	250.00
MM40 Electro	126.00	300.00
MM41 Nova	100.00	250.00
MM43 Silk	200.00	500.00
MM45 Captain America	750.00	2000.00
MM47 Prowler	100.00	250.00
MM48 Daredevil	250.00	600.00
MM50 Spider-Man	2500.00	6000.00

2017 Fleer Ultra Spider-Man Milestones

COMPLETE SET (12)	8.00	20.00
COMMON CARD (M1-M12)	1.50	4.00
*SILVER FOIL: .75X TO 2X BASIC CARDS	3.00	8.00
STATED ODDS 1:5		
M2 Spider-Man: No More!	2.50	6.00
M3 Death of Gwen Stacy	2.00	5.00
M7 Maximum Carnage	2.00	5.00
M8 Civil War	2.00	5.00

2017 Fleer Ultra Spider-Man Milestones Gold Foil Autographs

COMMON AUTO (M1-M12)	15.00	40.00
STATED PRINT RUN 49 SER.#'d SETS		

2017 Fleer Ultra Spider-Man Preserved Amber Black and White

COMMON CARD (PA1-PA30)	6.00	15.00
STATED PRINT RUN 175 SER.#'d SETS		
PA1 Venom	75.00	200.00
PA2 Jackpot	10.00	25.00
PA3 Jackal	8.00	20.00
PA4 Tinkerer	10.00	25.00
PA5 Vulture	12.00	30.00
PA6 Doctor Strange	100.00	250.00
PA7 Green Goblin	30.00	75.00
PA8 Kaine	8.00	20.00
PA11 Kingpin	15.00	40.00
PA12 Sandman	10.00	25.00
PA13 Mr. Negative	10.00	25.00
PA14 Boomerang	8.00	20.00
PA15 Morbius	15.00	40.00
PA16 Rhino	10.00	25.00
PA17 Punisher	40.00	100.00
PA18 Daredevil	30.00	75.00
PA19 Spider-Woman	12.00	30.00
PA21 Luke Cage	10.00	25.00
PA22 Black Cat	20.00	50.00
PA25 Deadpool	50.00	125.00
PA26 Carnage	50.00	125.00
PA27 Hobgoblin	8.00	20.00
PA29 Deathlok	15.00	40.00
PA30 Spider-Man	125.00	300.00

2017 Fleer Ultra Spider-Man Royal Foil

COMMON CARD (GC1-GC30)	60.00	150.00
STATED PRINT RUN 99 SER.#'d SETS		
GC1 Black Cat	200.00	500.00
GC2 Arachne	100.00	250.00
GC3 Silk	150.00	400.00
GC5 Deathlok	100.00	250.00
GC6 Deadpool	250.00	600.00
GC7 Black Widow	150.00	400.00
GC8 Spider-Woman	75.00	200.00
GC10 Wolverine	400.00	1000.00
GC11 Kraven	75.00	200.00
GC12 Anti-Venom	100.00	250.00
GC13 Doctor Octopus	125.00	300.00
GC14 Ultimate Spider-Man	750.00	2000.00
GC15 Venom	400.00	1000.00
GC16 Shriek	100.00	250.00
GC17 Captain America	200.00	500.00
GC18 Shocker	100.00	250.00
GC19 Spider-Man	2000.00	4000.00
GC22 Spider-Man 2099	150.00	400.00
GC23 Doppelganger	125.00	300.00
GC24 Gwen Stacy	75.00	200.00
GC25 Electro	75.00	200.00
GC26 Hobgoblin	100.00	250.00
GC27 Agent Venom	150.00	400.00
GC28 Scarlet Spider	200.00	500.00
GC29 Hawkeye	75.00	200.00
GC30 Carnage	150.00	400.00

2017 Fleer Ultra Spider-Man Team-Ups

COMPLETE SET (11)	15.00	40.00
COMMON CARD (TU1-TU11)	2.00	5.00
*SILVER FOIL: .75X TO 2X BASIC CARDS	4.00	10.00
STATED ODDS 1:12		
TU2 Captain America	3.00	8.00
TU3 Punisher	3.00	8.00
TU6 Iron Man	2.50	6.00
TU9 Wolverine	3.00	8.00
TU11 Deadpool	4.00	10.00

2017 Fleer Ultra Spider-Man Team-Ups Gold Foil Autographs

COMMON AUTO (TU1-TU11)	15.00	40.00
STATED PRINT RUN 49 SER.#'d SETS		

2014 Legends of Marvel Spider-Man

COMPLETE SET (9)	12.00	30.00
COMMON CARD (L1-L9)	2.00	5.00
STATED PRINT RUN 1939 SER.#'d SETS		

2002 Spider-Man

COMPLETE SET (100)	20.00	50.00
UNOPENED BOX (24 PACKS)	75.00	125.00
UNOPENED PACK (7 CARDS)	3.00	5.00
COMMON CARD (1-100)	.40	1.00

2002 Spider-Man Spider-Sense Glow Puzzle Stickers

COMPLETE SET (10)	5.00	12.00
COMMON CARD (1-10)	.75	2.00
STATED ODDS 1:3		

2002 Spider-Man Spidey Holograms

COMPLETE SET (5)	3.00	8.00
COMMON CARD (H1-H5)	1.00	2.50
STATED ODDS 1:6		

2002 Spider-Man Web-Shooter

COMPLETE SET (5)	6.00	15.00
COMMON CARD (C1-C5)	2.00	5.00
STATED ODDS 1:6		

2002 Spider-Man Web-Tech Foil

COMPLETE SET (5)	5.00	12.00
COMMON CARD (F1-F5)	1.50	4.00
STATED ODDS 1:6		

2002 Spider-Man Promos

COMPLETE SET (3)	3.00	8.00
COMMON CARD	1.25	3.00
P1 In Theatres Everywhere May 3	1.50	4.00
P2 Wizard Magazine	2.00	5.00

1997 Fleer SkyBox Spider-Man .99

COMPLETE SET (50)	5.00	12.00
UNOPENED HOBBY BOX (48 PACKS)	75.00	125.00
UNOPENED HOBBY PACK (8 CARDS)	2.00	3.00
UNOPENED RETAIL BOX (18 PACKS)		
UNOPENED RETAIL PACK (8 CARDS)		
COMMON CARD (1-50)	.15	.40

1992 Comic Images Spider-Man II 30th Anniversary

COMPLETE SET (90)	10.00	25.00
UNOPENED BOX (48 PACKS)	75.00	125.00
UNOPENED PACK (10 CARDS)	2.00	3.00
COMMON CARD (1-90)	.20	.50

1992 Comic Images Spider-Man II 30th Anniversary Prisms

COMPLETE SET (6)	15.00	40.00
COMMON CARD (P7-P12)	4.00	10.00
STATED ODDS 1:16		

2004 Spider-Man 2

COMPLETE SET (70)	8.00	20.00
UNOPENED BOX (24 PACKS)	60.00	100.00
UNOPENED PACK (5 CARDS)	3.00	5.00
COMMON CARD (SMC1-SMC70)	.20	.50

2004 Spider-Man 2 Lenticular

COMPLETE SET (3)	3.00	8.00
COMMON CARD (L1-L3)	1.25	3.00
STATED ODDS 1:4		

2004 Spider-Man 2 Reel Action

COMPLETE SET (2)	8.00	20.00
COMMON CARD (1-2)	6.00	15.00
STATED ODDS 1:24		

2007 Spider-Man 3

COMPLETE SET (79)	10.00	25.00
UNOPENED BOX (40 PACKS)	500.00	750.00
UNOPENED PACK (5 CARDS)	12.00	20.00
COMMON CARD (1-70)	.25	.60
BEHIND-THE-SCENES (BTS1-BTS8)	.40	1.00
CHECKLIST (C1)	.30	.75

2007 Spider-Man 3 Autographs

COMMON AUTO	6.00	15.00
STATED ODDS 1:20		
L (LIMITED): 300-500 COPIES		
VL (VERY LIMITED): 200-300 COPIES		
NNO Aasif Madvi	10.00	25.00

NNO Avi Arad VL	25.00	60.00
NNO Bill Nunn	10.00	25.00
NNO Bruce Campbell L	60.00	150.00
NNO Dylan Baker	15.00	40.00
NNO Elizabeth Banks L	125.00	300.00
NNO Elyse Dinh	8.00	20.00
NNO Hal Sparks	12.00	30.00
NNO J.K. Simmons	75.00	200.00
NNO James Franco L	200.00	500.00
NNO Joe Manganiello	20.00	50.00
NNO Lucy Lawless VL	60.00	150.00
NNO Mageina Tovah	20.00	50.00
NNO Stan Lee	500.00	1200.00
NNO Tobey Maguire VL	600.00	1500.00
NNO Willem Dafoe L	250.00	600.00

2007 Spider-Man 3 Black Costume

COMPLETE SET (6)	8.00	20.00
COMMON CARD (B1-B6)	2.50	6.00
STATED ODDS 1:40		

2007 Spider-Man 3 Memorabilia

COMMON CARD	20.00	40.00
STATED ODDS 1:CASE		
AUTO MEM IS 2-CASE INCENTIVE		
NNO J.K. Simmons Tie AU	100.00	250.00

2007 Spider-Man 3 Red and Blue

COMPLETE SET (6)	6.00	15.00
COMMON CARD (R1-R6)	2.00	5.00
STATED ODDS 1:40		

2007 Spider-Man 3 The Goblin

COMPLETE SET (5)	5.00	12.00
COMMON CARD (G1-G5)	1.50	4.00
STATED ODDS 1:40		

2007 Spider-Man 3 The Sandman

COMPLETE SET (5)	5.00	12.00
COMMON CARD (S1-S5)	1.50	4.00
STATED ODDS 1:40		

2007 Spider-Man 3 Venom

COMPLETE SET (5)	6.00	15.00
COMMON CARD (V1-V5)	2.00	5.00
STATED ODDS 1:40		

2007 Spider-Man 3 Promos

COMPLETE SET (3)	5.00	12.00
COMMON CARD	1.50	4.00
P2 Black Spider-Man ALB	2.50	6.00
SD07 Peter Parker SDCC	3.00	8.00

2008 Spider-Man 3 Expansion A

NNO Tobey Maguire AU	600.00	1000.00
NNO Peter Parker Pants	25.00	60.00
NNO Peter Parker Shirt	25.00	60.00

2013 Spider-Man 1967 Original Animated Series Lenticular

COMPLETE SET (9)	10.00	25.00
COMMON CARD (L1-L9)	2.00	5.00

2013 Spider-Man 1967 Original Animated Series Lenticular Autographs

COMMON AUTO	60.00	150.00
STATED PRINT RUN 250 SER.#'d SETS		

1996 Team Metal Spider-Man All Metal

COMPLETE SET (4)	6.00	15.00
COMMON CARD (1-4)	2.00	5.00
1 Spider-Man	4.00	10.00
2 Venom	3.00	8.00

2009 Spider-Man Archives

COMPLETE SET (72)	10.00	25.00
UNOPENED BOX (24 PACKS)	100.00	150.00
UNOPENED PACK (5 CARDS)	4.00	5.00
COMMON CARD (1-72)	.30	.75
*FOIL: 1.2X TO 3X BASIC CARDS		

2009 Spider-Man Archives Allies

COMPLETE SET (9)	12.00	30.00
COMMON CARD (A1-A9)	2.50	6.00
STATED ODDS 1:8		

2009 Spider-Man Archives Case-Toppers

COMPLETE SET (3)	30.00	75.00
COMMON CARD (CT1-CT3)	12.00	30.00
STATED ODDS ONE PER CASE		

2009 Spider-Man Archives Rogues Gallery

COMPLETE SET (9)	10.00	25.00
COMMON CARD (R1-R9)	1.50	4.00
STATED ODDS 1:12		

2009 Spider-Man Archives Swinging into Action

COMPLETE SET W/E10 (10)	30.00	75.00
COMPLETE SET (9)	25.00	60.00
COMMON CARD (E1-E9)	4.00	10.00
STATED ODDS 1:24		
E10 ISSUED AS RITTENHOUSE REWARD		
E10 Spider-Man SP RR	10.00	25.00

1995 Cookie Crisp Spider-Man

COMPLETE SET (12)	15.00	40.00
COMMON CARD (UNNUMBERED)	2.50	6.00

2002 Spider-Man Filmcardz

COMPLETE SET (72)	4.00	10.00
UNOPENED HOBBY BOX (24 PACKS)		
UNOPENED HOBBY PACK (5 CARDS)		
UNOPENED MASS MARKET BOX (24 PACKS)		
UNOPENED MASS MARKET PACK (5 CARDS)		
COMMON CARD (1-72)	.12	.30

2002 Spider-Man Filmcardz Chase One

COMPLETE SET (9)	2.50	6.00
COMMON CARD (Ph1-Ph9)	.40	1.00
STATED ODDS 1:1		
HOBBY EXCLUSIVE		

2002 Spider-Man Filmcardz Chase Rare

COMPLETE SET (6)	8.00	20.00
COMMON CARD (R1-R6)	2.00	5.00
STATED ODDS 1:8		

2002 Spider-Man Filmcardz Chase Two

COMPLETE SET (9)	2.50	6.00
COMMON CARD (Pm1-Pm9)	.40	1.00
STATED ODDS 1:1		
RETAIL EXCLUSIVE		

2002 Spider-Man Filmcardz Chase Ultra Rare

COMPLETE SET (3)	6.00	15.00
COMMON CARD (UR1-UR3)	2.50	6.00
STATED ODDS 1:12		

2002 Spider-Man Filmcardz Promos

COMPLETE SET (5)	4.00	10.00
COMMON CARD (P1-P5)	.75	2.00
P1 Peter Parker	2.00	5.00

1997 Fleer SkyBox Spider-Man International

COMPLETE SET (50)	5.00	12.00
UNOPENED BOX (36 PACKS)	100.00	150.00
UNOPENED PACK (5 CARDS)	3.00	5.00
COMMON CARD (1-50)	.20	.50

2022 Upper Deck Spider-Man Into the Spider-Verse

COMPLETE SET (90)	15.00	40.00
UNOPENED BOX (15 PACKS)	65.00	90.00
UNOPENED PACK (7 CARDS)	5.00	6.00
COMMON CARD (1-90)	.40	1.00
*PETER PARKER RED: .6X TO 1.5X BASIC CARDS		
*GWEN STACY WHITE: 1X TO 2.5X BASIC CARDS		
*SPIDER PI: 1.5X TO 4X BASIC CARDS		
*CANVAS: 6X TO 15X BASIC CARDS		
*SPECTRAL SPIDER/25: 15X TO 40X BASIC CARDS		

2022 Upper Deck Spider-Man Into the Spider-Verse Amazing Stickers

COMPLETE SET (20)	15.00	40.00
COMMON CARD (AS01-AS20)	1.25	3.00
STATED ODDS 1:5		

2022 Upper Deck Spider-Man Into the Spider-Verse Dimensions Collide Lenticular

COMPLETE SET (30)	75.00	200.00
COMMON CARD (DC01-DC30)	4.00	10.00
*COLORS COLLIDE: 1X TO 2.5X BASIC CARDS		
STATED ODDS 1:15		

2022 Upper Deck Spider-Man Into the Spider-Verse Everything's Relative Stickers

COMPLETE SET (10)	12.00	30.00
COMMON CARD (ER01-ER10)	2.00	5.00
STATED ODDS 1:8		

2022 Upper Deck Spider-Man Into the Spider-Verse In the Vault Character Manufactured Patches

COMMON MEM (VCP1-VCP12)	10.00	25.00
STATED ODDS 1:80 HOBBY/EPACK		
VCP1 Peter B. Parker	15.00	40.00
VCP2 Miles Morales	20.00	50.00
VCP3 Spider-Gwen	25.00	60.00
VCP4 Spider-Man Noir	12.00	30.00
VCP5 Spider-Ham	12.00	30.00
VCP9 Miles Morales	20.00	50.00

2022 Upper Deck Spider-Man Into the Spider-Verse In the Vault Letterman Manufactured Patches

COMMON AUNT MAY	8.00	20.00
COMMON DOC OCK	8.00	20.00
COMMON GREEN GOBLIN	8.00	20.00
COMMON JEFFERSON DAVIS	8.00	20.00
COMMON KINGPIN	8.00	20.00
COMMON MILES MORALES	15.00	40.00
COMMON PENI PARKER	8.00	20.00
COMMON PETER B. PARKER	20.00	50.00
COMMON PROWLER	10.00	25.00
COMMON SPIDER-GWEN	12.00	30.00
COMMON SPIDER-HAM	8.00	20.00
COMMON SPIDER-MAN NOIR	12.00	30.00
STATED PRINT RUN 125 SER.#'d SETS		

2022 Upper Deck Spider-Man Into the Spider-Verse In the Vault Mask Manufactured Patches

COMMON MEM (VMP1-VMP12)	10.00	25.00
STATED ODDS 1:80 HOBBY/EPACK		
VMP1 Peter B. Parker	15.00	40.00
VMP2 Miles Morales	25.00	60.00
VMP3 Spider-Gwen	20.00	50.00
VMP6 Spider-Ham	20.00	50.00
VMP7 Kingpin	15.00	40.00
VMP8 Green Goblin	12.00	30.00
VMP9 Jefferson Davis	12.00	30.00
VMP10 Doc Ock	12.00	30.00
VMP11 Aunt May	12.00	30.00

2022 Upper Deck Spider-Man Into the Spider-Verse It's Proprietary

COMPLETE SET (10)	6.00	15.00
COMMON CARD (IP1-IP10)	1.00	2.50
*PETER PARKER RED: .75X TO 2X BASIC CARDS		
*GWEN STACY WHITE: 1X TO 2.5X BASIC CARDS		
*SPIDER PI: 1.2X TO 3X BASIC CARDS		
*CANVAS: 2X TO 5X BASIC CARDS		
STATED ODDS 1:2 HOBBY/EPACK		

2022 Upper Deck Spider-Man Into the Spider-Verse My Story

COMPLETE SET W/SP (20)	40.00	100.00
COMPLETE SET W/O SP (15)	25.00	60.00
COMMON CARD (MS01-MS215)	2.00	5.00
COMMON SP (MS16-MS20)	4.00	10.00
*RED: 1.5X TO 4X BASIC CARDS		
*RED SP: 1.2X TO 3X BASIC CARDS		
STATED ODDS 1:4 HOBBY/EPACK		
STATED SP ODDS 1:38 HOBBY/EPACK		
MS17 Miles Morales SP	6.00	15.00
MS18 Spider-Gwen SP	8.00	20.00
MS19 Spider-Man Noir SP	5.00	12.00

2022 Upper Deck Spider-Man Into the Spider-Verse Spider-Sigs Action

COMMON AUTO	20.00	50.00
GROUP A ODDS 1:8,823		
GROUP B ODDS 1:1,1357		
GROUP C ODDS 1:671		
GROUP D ODDS 1:253		
GROUP E ODDS 1:233		
STATED ODDS 1:60 HOBBY/EPACK		
SSAKG Kimiko Glenn D	50.00	125.00
SSAKH Kathryn Hahn B	75.00	200.00
SSALB Lake Bell E	30.00	75.00
SSASM Shameik Moore D	125.00	300.00
SSABTH Brian Tyree Henry B	75.00	200.00
SSAHS2 Hailee Steinfeld C	400.00	1000.00
SSAKG2 Kimiko Glenn D	50.00	125.00
SSAKH2 Kathryn Hahn B	75.00	200.00
SSASM2 Shameik Moore B	150.00	400.00
SSABTH2 Brian Tyree Henry A	125.00	300.00

2022 Upper Deck Spider-Man Into the Spider-Verse Spider-Sigs Portraits

COMMON AUTO		
GROUP A ODDS 1:8,823		
GROUP B ODDS 1:1,1357		
GROUP C ODDS 1:671		
GROUP D ODDS 1:253		
GROUP E ODDS 1:233		
GROUP F ODDS 1:162		
STATED ODDS 1:60 HOBBY/EPACK		
SSPKG Kimiko Glenn F	50.00	125.00
SSPKH Kathryn Hahn D	75.00	200.00
SSPLB Lake Bell F	30.00	75.00
SSPSM Shameik Moore F	100.00	250.00
SSPBTH Brian Tyree Henry B	75.00	200.00
SSPHS2 Hailee Steinfeld D	400.00	1000.00
SSPKG2 Kimiko Glenn C	50.00	125.00
SSPKH2 Kathryn Hahn C	75.00	200.00
SSPSM2 Shameik Moore E	100.00	250.00
SSPBTH2 Brian Tyree Henry A	125.00	300.00

2022 Upper Deck Spider-Man Into the Spider-Verse Spider-Sigs Torso

COMMON AUTO	20.00	50.00
GROUP A ODDS 1:8,823		
GROUP B ODDS 1:1,1357		
GROUP C ODDS 1:671		
GROUP D ODDS 1:253		
GROUP E ODDS 1:233		
GROUP F ODDS 1:162		
STATED ODDS 1:60 HOBBY/EPACK		
SSTKG Kimiko Glenn E	50.00	125.00
SSTKH Kathryn Hahn C	75.00	200.00
SSTLB Lake Bell F	30.00	75.00
SSTSM Shameik Moore E	100.00	250.00
SSTBTH Brian Tyree Henry B	75.00	200.00
SSTHS2 Hailee Steinfeld D	400.00	1000.00
SSTKG2 Kimiko Glenn D	50.00	125.00
SSTKH2 Kathryn Hahn C	75.00	200.00
SSTSM2 Shameik Moore B	150.00	400.00
SSTBTH2 Brian Tyree Henry A	125.00	300.00

2022 Upper Deck Spider-Man Into the Spider-Verse Triple Autographs

TASMKGJJ Moore/Glenn/Steinfeld
TASMKGKH Moore/Glenn/Hahn

2018 Spider-Man Into the Spider-Verse AMC Theater Promos

COMPLETE SET (12)	12.00	30.00
COMMON CARD	1.50	4.00

2018 Spider-Man Into the Spider-Verse General Mills Decals

COMPLETE SET (6)	5.00	12.00
COMMON CARD	1.25	3.00

1995 Kool-Aid Spider-Man First Encounters

COMPLETE SET (6)	20.00	50.00
COMMON CARD (1-6)	5.00	12.00

2022 SkyBox Marvel Metal Universe Spider-Man

COMPLETE SET W/SP (200)	150.00	400.00
COMPLETE SET W/O SP (100)	40.00	100.00
UNOPENED BOX (12 PACKS)	350.00	500.00
UNOPENED PACK (6 CARDS)	30.00	45.00
UNOPENED BLASTER BOX (6 PACKS)	40.00	60.00
UNOPENED BLASTER PACK (6 CARDS)	8.00	10.00
COMMON CARD (1-200)	1.00	2.50
COMMON HI SERIES (101-200)	1.50	4.00
*YELLOW: .5X TO 1.2X BASIC CARDS		
*GOLD: .6X TO 1.5X BASIC CARDS		
*GRANDIOSE: 1.2X TO 3X BASIC CARDS		
*PINK/75: 12X TO 30X BASIC CARDS		
*TURQUOISE/50: 20X TO 50X BASIC CARDS		
4 Ant-Man	1.25	3.00
7 Beast	1.25	3.00
10 Black Cat	1.50	4.00
11 Black Panther	2.00	5.00
13 Black Widow	2.50	6.00
15 Cosmic Spider-Man	1.50	4.00
16 Captain America	2.00	5.00
17 Captain Marvel	2.50	6.00
18 Carnage	2.50	6.00
21 Daredevil	1.25	3.00
28 Ghost-Spider	3.00	8.00
36 Iron Man	2.50	6.00
38 Ironheart	1.50	4.00
42 Knull	1.25	3.00
44 Lizard	1.25	3.00
49 Mary Jane Watson	1.50	4.00
52 Miles Morales	2.50	6.00
55 Moon Knight	1.25	3.00
56 Morbius	1.25	3.00
59 Ms. Marvel	1.50	4.00
60 Mysterio	1.25	3.00
64 Spider-Man	2.50	6.00
65 Peter Porker	1.50	4.00
72 Scarlet Witch	2.50	6.00
77 She-Hulk	1.25	3.00
80 Silk	1.50	4.00
84 Spider-Man 2099	3.00	8.00
85 Spider-Man Noir	1.25	3.00
86 Spider-Punk	2.00	5.00
89 Thor	1.50	4.00
93 Venom	5.00	12.00
100 Wolverine	6.00	15.00
101 Agent Venom SP	3.00	8.00
104 Ant-Man SP	2.00	5.00
107 Beast SP	2.00	5.00
110 Black Cat SP	2.50	6.00
111 Black Panther SP	3.00	8.00
113 Black Widow SP	4.00	10.00
115 Calypso SP	2.50	6.00
116 Captain America SP	3.00	8.00
117 Captain Marvel SP	4.00	10.00
118 Carnage SP	4.00	10.00
121 Daredevil SP	2.00	5.00
128 Ghost-Spider SP	5.00	12.00
129 Green Goblin SP	2.00	5.00
136 Iron Man SP	4.00	10.00
138 Ironheart SP	2.50	6.00
142 Knull SP	2.00	5.00
144 Lizard SP	2.00	5.00
149 Mary Jane Watson SP	2.50	6.00
152 Miles Morales SP	4.00	10.00
155 Moon Knight SP	2.00	5.00
156 Morbius SP	2.00	5.00
159 Ms. Marvel SP	2.50	6.00
160 Mysterio SP	2.00	5.00
164 Spider-Man SP	4.00	10.00
165 Peter Porker SP	2.50	6.00
171 Scarlet Spider SP	2.00	5.00
172 Scarlet Witch SP	4.00	10.00
177 She-Hulk SP	2.00	5.00
180 Silk SP	2.50	6.00
184 Spider-Man 2099 SP	5.00	12.00
185 Spider-Man Noir SP	2.00	5.00
186 Spider-Punk SP	3.00	8.00
189 Thor SP	2.50	6.00
193 Venom SP	8.00	20.00
200 Wolverine SP	10.00	25.00

2022 SkyBox Marvel Metal Universe Spider-Man Comic Cuts Clippings

STATED PRINT RUN 35-55		
CCASM1 Amazing Spider-Man #1/40	125.00	300.00
CCASM2 Amazing Spider-Man #2/40		
CCASM3 Amazing Spider-Man #3/40	125.00	250.00
CCASM5 Amazing Spider-Man #5/40		
CCASM6 Amazing Spider-Man #6/40		
CCASM7 Amazing Spider-Man #7/40		
CCASM11 Amazing Spider-Man #11/40	30.00	75.00
CCASM12 Amazing Spider-Man #12/40		
CCASM13 Amazing Spider-Man #13/40		
CCASM14 Amazing Spider-Man #14/40	250.00	600.00
CCASM15 Amazing Spider-Man #15/40		
CCASM17 Amazing Spider-Man #17/40		
CCASM18 Amazing Spider-Man #18/40	25.00	60.00
CCASM20 Amazing Spider-Man #20/40		
CCASM21 Amazing Spider-Man #21/40		
CCASM22 Amazing Spider-Man #22/40		
CCASM23 Amazing Spider-Man #23/40		
CCASM24 Amazing Spider-Man #24/40		
CCASM25 Amazing Spider-Man #25/40		
CCASM26 Amazing Spider-Man #26/40		
CCASM28 Amazing Spider-Man #28/40		
CCASM29 Amazing Spider-Man #29/40		
CCASM31 Amazing Spider-Man #31/40		
CCASM32 Amazing Spider-Man #32/40		
CCASM33 Amazing Spider-Man #33/40		
CCASM34 Amazing Spider-Man #34/40		
CCASM35 Amazing Spider-Man #35/40		
CCASM37 Amazing Spider-Man #37/40		
CCASM38 Amazing Spider-Man #38/40		
CCASM39 Amazing Spider-Man #39/40		
CCASM40 Amazing Spider-Man #40/40		
CCASM41 Amazing Spider-Man #41/40		
CCASM42 Amazing Spider-Man #42/40		
CCASM43 Amazing Spider-Man #43/40		
CCASM44 Amazing Spider-Man #44/40		
CCASM46 Amazing Spider-Man #46/40		
CCASM50 Amazing Spider-Man #50/40		
CCASM51 Amazing Spider-Man #51/40		
CCASM59 Amazing Spider-Man #59/40		
CCASM62 Amazing Spider-Man #62/40		
CCASM68 Amazing Spider-Man #68/40		
CCASM75 Amazing Spider-Man #75/40		
CCASM78 Amazing Spider-Man #78/40		
CCASM82 Amazing Spider-Man #82/40		
CCASM86 Amazing Spider-Man #86/40		
CCASM89 Amazing Spider-Man #89/40		
CCASM92 Amazing Spider-Man #92/40		
CCASM94 Amazing Spider-Man #94/40		
CCASM96 Amazing Spider-Man #96/40		
CCASM97 Amazing Spider-Man #97/40		
CCASM98 Amazing Spider-Man #98/40		
CCASMA1 Amazing Spider-Man Annual #1/40		
CCASM100 Amazing Spider-Man #100/40		
CCASM101 Amazing Spider-Man #101/40	60.00	150.00
CCASM102 Amazing Spider-Man #102/40	60.00	150.00
CCASM111 Amazing Spider-Man #111/40	60.00	150.00
CCASM113 Amazing Spider-Man #113/40	30.00	75.00
CCASM114 Amazing Spider-Man #114/30		
CCASM119 Amazing Spider-Man #119/40	100.00	250.00
CCASM120 Amazing Spider-Man #120/40	100.00	250.00
CCASM121 Amazing Spider-Man #121/40		
CCASM122 Amazing Spider-Man #122/40		
CCASM123 Amazing Spider-Man #123/40	125.00	300.00
CCASM124 Amazing Spider-Man #124/40	100.00	250.00
CCASM125 Amazing Spider-Man #125/40		
CCASM131 Amazing Spider-Man #131/35		
CCASM133 Amazing Spider-Man #133/40		
CCASM134 Amazing Spider-Man #134/40		
CCASM136 Amazing Spider-Man #136/40	125.00	300.00
CCASM137 Amazing Spider-Man #137/40		
CCASM144 Amazing Spider-Man #144/40		
CCASM149 Amazing Spider-Man #149/40		
CCASM194 Amazing Spider-Man #194/40		
CCASM195 Amazing Spider-Man #195/40		
CCASM210 Amazing Spider-Man #210/40		
CCASM212 Amazing Spider-Man #212/40		
CCASM238 Amazing Spider-Man #238/40		
CCASM252 Amazing Spider-Man #252/40		
CCASM256 Amazing Spider-Man #256/40		
CCASM265 Amazing Spider-Man #265/40		
CCASM293 Amazing Spider-Man #293/40		
CCASM294 Amazing Spider-Man #294/40		
CCASM298 Amazing Spider-Man #298/40		
CCASM299 Amazing Spider-Man #299/40		
CCASM300 Amazing Spider-Man #300/40		
CCASM316 Amazing Spider-Man #316/40		
CCASM337 Amazing Spider-Man #337/30		
CCASM345 Amazing Spider-Man #345/40		
CCASM346 Amazing Spider-Man #346/35		
CCASM360 Amazing Spider-Man #360/45		
CCASM361 Amazing Spider-Man #361/45		
CCASM362 Amazing Spider-Man #362/30		
CCASM363 Amazing Spider-Man #363/40		
CCASM375 Amazing Spider-Man #375/55		
CCASM400 Amazing Spider-Man #400/50		
CCASM410 Amazing Spider-Man #410/35		
CCASM415 Amazing Spider-Man #415/30		
CCASMA16 Amazing Spider-Man Annual #16/45		
CCASMA21 Amazing Spider-Man Annual #21/55		

2022 SkyBox Marvel Metal Universe Spider-Man Daily Bugle Headlines

COMMON CARD (DB1-DB25))	6.00	15.00
COMMON SP	10.00	25.00
STATED ODDS 1:64 HOBBY/EPACK		
STATED ODDS 1:192 BLASTER		
STATED SP ODDS 1:192 HOBBY/EPACK		
STATED SP ODDS 1:384 BLASTER		
DB1 Scarlet Spider	15.00	40.00
DB2 Black Cat	20.00	50.00
DB3 Carnage	25.00	60.00
DB4 Daredevil	8.00	20.00
DB6 Electro SP	20.00	50.00
DB8 Iron Man	15.00	40.00
DB9 Iron Spider	12.00	30.00
DB11 Mysterio	8.00	20.00
DB12 SP//dr	12.00	30.00
DB13 Sandman	8.00	20.00
DB14 Silk	8.00	20.00
DB15 Scorpion	10.00	25.00
DB17 Ghost-Spider SP	25.00	60.00
DB18 Miles Morales SP	60.00	150.00
DB19 Spider-Man SP	60.00	150.00
DB20 Spider-Man Noir SP	20.00	50.00
DB21 Venom SP	40.00	100.00
DB22 Lizard SP	10.00	25.00
DB24 Wilson Fisk SP	15.00	40.00

2022 SkyBox Marvel Metal Universe Spider-Man Palladium

COMMON CARD (1-50)	5.00	12.00
STATED ODDS 1:12 HOBBY/EPACK		
STATED ODDS 1:120 BLASTER		
1 Aunt May	6.00	15.00
3 Black Cat	15.00	40.00
4 Black Tarantula	6.00	15.00
5 Carnage	20.00	50.00
7 Daredevil	12.00	30.00
8 Doctor Octopus	10.00	25.00
9 Doctor Strange	15.00	40.00
10 Electro	8.00	20.00
11 Ghost-Spider	30.00	75.00
14 Hobgoblin	8.00	20.00
16 Iron Fist	8.00	20.00
17 Iron Man	15.00	40.00
19 Knull	10.00	25.00
20 Kraven	6.00	15.00
21 Lizard	8.00	20.00
22 Luke Cage	6.00	15.00
25 Miles Morales	15.00	40.00
27 Morbius	8.00	20.00
29 Ms. Marvel	12.00	30.00
30 Mysterio	8.00	20.00
33 Captain America	15.00	40.00
36 Scarlet Spider	15.00	40.00
38 Scream	6.00	15.00
39 Silver Sable	6.00	15.00
41 Spider-Man	50.00	125.00
42 Spider-Man 2099	12.00	30.00
43 Spider-Woman	10.00	25.00
46 Venom	40.00	100.00
48 Wilson Fisk	6.00	15.00
49 Wolverine	20.00	50.00
50 Green Goblin	10.00	25.00

2022 SkyBox Marvel Metal Universe Spider-Man Planet Metal

COMMON CARD (1-20)	12.00	30.00
*COPPER/99: 1X TO 2.5X BASIC CARDS		
*PLATINUM/49: 1.2X TO 3X BASIC CARDS		
STATED ODDS 1:48 HOBBY/EPACK		
1 Carnage	50.00	125.00
2 Doctor Octopus	15.00	40.00
4 Green Goblin	20.00	50.00
5 Hobgoblin	15.00	40.00
6 Knull	20.00	50.00
7 Kraven	15.00	40.00
8 Lizard	20.00	50.00
10 Mysterio	15.00	40.00
11 Miles Morales	60.00	150.00
16 Venom	60.00	150.00
19 Spider-Man	60.00	150.00
20 Ghost-Spider	60.00	150.00

2022 SkyBox Marvel Metal Universe Spider-Man Platinum Portraits

COMMON CARD (1-15)	200.00	500.00
STATED ODDS 1:864 HOBBY/EPACK		
STATED ODDS 1:8,640 BLASTER		
1 Carnage	750.00	2000.00
2 Doctor Octopus	400.00	1000.00
3 Green Goblin	500.00	1200.00
4 Knull	400.00	1000.00
8 Ghost-Spider	750.00	2000.00
12 Venom	1000.00	2500.00
15 Spider-Man	3000.00	6000.00

2022 SkyBox Marvel Metal Universe Spider-Man Precious Metal Gems Red

COMMON CARD (1-200)	25.00	60.00
STATED PRINT RUN 90 SER.#'d SETS		
1 Agent Venom	125.00	300.00
2 Ai Apaec	60.00	150.00
4 Ant-Man	125.00	300.00
5 Anya Corazon	60.00	150.00
6 Aunt May	30.00	75.00
7 Beast	50.00	125.00
8 Ben Parker	30.00	75.00
9 Black Bolt	100.00	250.00
10 Black Cat	150.00	400.00
11 Black Panther	300.00	750.00
13 Black Widow	500.00	1200.00
15 Cosmic Spider-Man	150.00	400.00
16 Captain America	125.00	300.00
17 Captain Marvel	125.00	300.00
18 Carnage	800.00	2000.00
20 Crime Master	50.00	125.00
21 Daredevil	150.00	400.00
22 Doctor Octopus	75.00	200.00

23 Doctor Strange 100.00 250.00
24 Doppleganger 125.00 300.00
25 Electro 40.00 100.00
26 Falcon 100.00 250.00
28 Ghost-Spider 1000.00 2500.00
29 Green Goblin 125.00 300.00
31 Hawkeye 40.00 100.00
32 Hobgoblin 40.00 100.00
33 Hulk 150.00 400.00
35 Iron Fist 50.00 125.00
36 Iron Man 800.00 2000.00
37 Iron Spider 150.00 400.00
38 Ironheart 150.00 400.00
39 J. Jonah Jameson 40.00 100.00
40 Jessica Jones 50.00 125.00
41 Kangaroo 40.00 100.00
42 Knull 200.00 500.00
43 Kraven 30.00 75.00
44 Lizard 40.00 125.00
45 Luke Cage 40.00 100.00
46 Madame Web 30.00 75.00
47 Magneto 250.00 600.00
48 Maria Hill 30.00 75.00
49 Mary Jane Watson 100.00 250.00
50 Mayday Parker 75.00 200.00
51 Medusa 30.00 75.00
52 Miles Morales 300.00 750.00
53 Mister Sinister 40.00 100.00
54 Molten Man 40.00 100.00
55 Moon Knight 125.00 300.00
56 Morbius 60.00 150.00
57 Morlun 30.00 75.00
58 Mr. Negative 60.00 150.00
59 Ms. Marvel 100.00 250.00
60 Mysterio 100.00 250.00
62 Nova 75.00 200.00
63 SP//dr 60.00 150.00
64 Spider-Man 1000.00 2500.00
65 Peter Porker 150.00 400.00
66 Prowler 30.00 75.00
67 Jackal 30.00 75.00
68 Rhino 40.00 100.00
69 Ronin 50.00 125.00
70 Sandman 50.00 125.00
71 Scarlet Spider 150.00 400.00
72 Scarlet Witch 125.00 300.00
73 Scorpion 50.00 125.00
74 Scream 60.00 150.00
75 Sentry 60.00 150.00
76 Spider-Man
77 She-Hulk 75.00 200.00
79 Shriek 40.00 100.00
80 Silk 250.00 600.00
81 Silver Sable 40.00 100.00
82 Silvermane 30.00 75.00
84 Spider-Man 2099 150.00 400.00
85 Spider-Man Noir 125.00 300.00
86 Spider-Punk 150.00 400.00
87 Spider-Woman 75.00 200.00
88 Superior Spider-Man 300.00 750.00
89 Thor 150.00 400.00
91 Tombstone 30.00 75.00
92 Toxin 100.00 250.00
93 Venom 750.00 2000.00
94 Vision 100.00 250.00
95 Vulture 40.00 100.00
96 War Machine 75.00 200.00
98 Wilson Fisk 50.00 125.00
99 Winter Soldier 50.00 125.00
100 Wolverine 600.00 1500.00
101 Agent Venom 125.00 300.00
102 Ai Apaec 60.00 150.00
104 Ant-Man 125.00 300.00
105 Anya Corazon 60.00 150.00
106 Aunt May 60.00 150.00
107 Beast 50.00 125.00
108 Ben Parker 30.00 75.00
109 Black Bolt 100.00 250.00
110 Black Cat 150.00 400.00
111 Black Panther 300.00 750.00
113 Black Widow 500.00 1200.00
115 Calypso 75.00 200.00
116 Captain America 125.00 300.00
117 Captain Marvel 125.00 300.00
118 Carnage 800.00 2000.00
120 Crime Master 50.00 125.00
121 Daredevil 150.00 400.00
122 Doctor Octopus 75.00 200.00
123 Doctor Strange 100.00 250.00
124 Doppleganger 125.00 300.00
125 Electro 40.00 100.00
126 Falcon 100.00 250.00
128 Ghost-Spider 1000.00 2500.00
129 Green Goblin 125.00 300.00
131 Hawkeye 40.00 100.00
132 Hobgoblin 40.00 100.00
133 Hulk 150.00 400.00
135 Iron Fist 50.00 125.00
136 Iron Man 250.00 600.00
137 Iron Spider 150.00 400.00
138 Ironheart 150.00 400.00
139 J. Jonah Jameson 40.00 100.00
140 Jessica Jones 50.00 125.00
141 Kangaroo 40.00 100.00
142 Knull 200.00 500.00
143 Kraven 30.00 75.00
144 Lizard 40.00 125.00
145 Luke Cage 40.00 100.00
146 Madame Web 30.00 75.00
147 Magneto 250.00 600.00
148 Maria Hill 30.00 75.00
149 Mary Jane Watson 100.00 250.00
150 Mayday Parker 75.00 200.00
151 Medusa 30.00 75.00
152 Miles Morales 300.00 750.00
153 Mister Sinister 40.00 100.00
154 Molten Man 40.00 100.00
155 Moon Knight 125.00 300.00
156 Morbius 60.00 150.00
157 Morlun 30.00 75.00
158 Mr. Negative 60.00 150.00
159 Ms. Marvel 100.00 250.00
160 Mysterio 100.00 250.00
162 Nova 75.00 200.00
163 SP//dr 60.00 150.00
164 Spider-Man 1000.00 2500.00
165 Peter Porker 150.00 400.00
166 Prowler 30.00 75.00
167 Jackal 30.00 75.00
168 Rhino 40.00 100.00
169 Ronin 50.00 125.00
170 Sandman 50.00 125.00
171 Scarlet Spider 150.00 400.00
172 Scarlet Witch 125.00 300.00
173 Scorpion 50.00 125.00
174 Scream 60.00 150.00
175 Sentry 60.00 150.00
176 Spider-Man
177 She-Hulk 75.00 200.00
179 Shriek 40.00 100.00
180 Silk 250.00 600.00
181 Silver Sable 40.00 100.00
182 Silvermane 30.00 75.00
184 Spider-Man 2099 150.00 400.00
185 Spider-Man Noir 125.00 300.00
186 Spider-Punk 150.00 400.00
187 Spider-Woman 75.00 200.00
188 Superior Spider-Man 300.00 750.00
189 Thor 150.00 400.00
191 Tombstone 30.00 75.00
192 Toxin 100.00 250.00
193 Venom 750.00 2000.00
194 Vision 100.00 250.00
195 Vulture 40.00 100.00
196 War Machine 75.00 200.00
198 Wilson Fisk 50.00 125.00
199 Winter Soldier 50.00 125.00
200 Wolverine 300.00 750.00

2022 SkyBox Marvel Metal Universe Spider-Man Rogues Gallery

COMMON CARD (RG1-RG24) 10.00 25.00
STATED ODDS 1:144
RG2 Carnage 75.00 200.00
RG3 Chameleon 15.00 40.00
RG5 Doctor Octopus 25.00 60.00
RG6 Doppleganger 75.00 200.00
RG7 Electro 20.00 50.00
RG9 Green Goblin 50.00 125.00
RG10 Hammerhead 12.00 30.00
RG11 Hobgoblin 40.00 100.00
RG13 Wilson Fisk 20.00 50.00
RG14 Knull 30.00 75.00
RG15 Kraven 12.00 30.00
RG16 Lizard 15.00 40.00
RG17 Mr. Negative 15.00 40.00
RG18 Morbius 12.00 30.00
RG19 Mysterio 20.00 50.00
RG20 Prowler 15.00 40.00
RG21 Rhino 40.00 100.00
RG22 Scorpion 15.00 40.00
RG24 Venom 100.00 250.00

2022 SkyBox Marvel Metal Universe Spider-Man Skyscraper Shadow Box

COMMON CARD (SS1-SS18) 10.00 25.00
COMMON SP (SS19-SS24) 20.00 50.00
COMMON SSP (SS25-SS30)
STATED ODDS 1:96
STATED SP ODDS 1:408
STATED SSP ODDS 1:936
SS1 Agent Venom 20.00 50.00
SS2 Anya Corazon 12.00 30.00
SS3 Carnage 40.00 100.00
SS4 Daredevil 20.00 50.00
SS5 Doctor Octopus 15.00 40.00
SS6 Doppleganger 12.00 30.00
SS8 Green Goblin 15.00 40.00
SS10 Black Cat 30.00 75.00
SS11 Iron Man 30.00 75.00
SS12 Ironheart 15.00 40.00
SS13 Knull 25.00 60.00
SS14 Mysterio 30.00 75.00
SS15 Peni Parker 12.00 30.00
SS16 Sandman 12.00 30.00
SS17 Silk 30.00 75.00
SS19 Spider-Man 2099 SP 40.00 100.00
SS20 Spider-Woman SP 30.00 75.00
SS22 Doctor Strange SP 25.00 60.00
SS24 Venom SP 60.00 150.00
SS25 Miles Morales SSP 125.00 300.00
SS26 Peter Porker SSP 60.00 150.00
SS27 Ghost-Spider SSP 100.00 250.00
SS28 Peter Parker SSP 75.00 200.00
SS29 Spider-Man Noir SSP
SS30 Spider-Punk SSP

2022 SkyBox Marvel Metal Universe Spider-Man Z-Force Rave

COMMON CARD (Z1-Z50) 25.00 60.00
*AMAZING/62: X TO X BASIC CARDS
STATED PRINT RUN 100 SER.#'d SETS
Z1 Agent Venom 100.00 250.00
Z2 Anya Corazon 30.00 75.00
Z3 Aunt May 30.00 75.00
Z5 Black Cat 75.00 200.00
Z6 Carnage 125.00 300.00
Z7 Chameleon 30.00 75.00
Z9 Daredevil 75.00 200.00
Z10 Doctor Octopus 30.00 75.00
Z11 Electro 30.00 75.00
Z12 Green Goblin 75.00 200.00
Z14 Hobgoblin 60.00 150.00
Z15 Iron Spider 50.00 125.00
Z16 Knull 40.00 100.00
Z17 Kraven 50.00 125.00
Z18 Lizard 30.00 75.00
Z19 Mary Jane Watson 75.00 200.00
Z20 Miles Morales 300.00 750.00
Z21 Mister Sinister 40.00 100.00
Z22 Moon Knight 75.00 200.00
Z23 Morbius 60.00 150.00
Z24 SP//dr 60.00 150.00
Z25 Peter Porker 50.00 125.00
Z26 Prowler 40.00 100.00
Z27 Captain America 150.00 400.00
Z28 Rhino 40.00 100.00
Z29 Sandman 30.00 75.00
Z30 Scarlet Spider 100.00 250.00
Z31 Scorpion 40.00 100.00
Z32 Scream 30.00 75.00
Z33 Shocker 30.00 75.00
Z34 Shriek 40.00 100.00
Z35 Silk 100.00 250.00
Z36 She-Hulk 60.00 150.00
Z37 Mayday Parker 60.00 150.00
Z38 Ghost-Spider 300.00 750.00
Z39 Spider-Man 400.00 1000.00
Z40 Spider-Man 2099 100.00 250.00
Z41 Spider-Man Noir 50.00 125.00
Z42 Spider-Punk 150.00 400.00
Z43 Spider-Woman 40.00 100.00
Z44 Superior Spider-Man 60.00 150.00
Z46 Venom 150.00 400.00
Z48 White Tiger 30.00 75.00
Z50 Mysterio 60.00 150.00

1996 Fleer SkyBox Spider-Man Premium

COMPLETE SET (100) 8.00 20.00
UNOPENED BOX (36 PACKS) 50.00 60.00
UNOPENED PACK (8 CARDS) 1.75 2.00
COMMON CARD (1-100) .15 .40

1996 Fleer SkyBox Spider-Man Premium Canvas

COMPLETE SET (6) 4.00 10.00
COMMON CARD (1-6) .75 2.00
STATED ODDS 1:6

1996 Fleer SkyBox Spider-Man Premium Holomotion

COMPLETE SET (3) 15.00 40.00
COMMON CARD (1-3) 6.00 15.00
STATED ODDS 1:36

1990 Comic Images Spider-Man Team-Up

COMPLETE SET (46) 8.00 20.00
UNOPENED BOX (50 PACKS) 35.00 50.00
UNOPENED PACK (5 CARDS) .75 1.25
COMMON CARD (1-46) .40 1.00

1995 Eskimo Pies Spider-Man Timeline

COMPLETE SET (24) 30.00 80.00
COMMON CARD (1-24) 2.00 5.00

1992 Comic Images Spider-Man Todd McFarlane Era

COMPLETE SET (90) 8.00 20.00
UNOPENED BOX (48 PACKS) 200.00 300.00
UNOPENED PACK (10 CARDS) 4.00 6.00
COMMON CARD (1-90) .20 .50
P Spider-Man Todd McFarlane Era PROMO3.00 8.00
(unnumbered)

1992 Comic Images Spider-Man Todd McFarlane Era Prisms

COMPLETE SET (6) 50.00 100.00
COMMON CARD (P1-P6) 10.00 25.00
STATED ODDS 1:16

2011 Stussy Marvel Series

COMPLETE SET (17) 250.00 500.00
UNOPENED BOX (16 SETS)
COMMON CARD 20.00 50.00
1 Wolverine 60.00 150.00
2 Captain America 30.00 75.00
6 Dr. Doom 25.00 60.00
7 Ghost Rider 30.00 75.00
8 The Incredible Hulk 25.00 60.00
10 Spider-Man 125.00 300.00

13 Dr. Strange 60.00 150.00
14 Thor 40.00 100.00

1979 Wimpy's Super Heroes and Super Villains

COMPLETE SET (20) 25.00 60.00
COMMON CARD (1-20) 2.00 5.00
1 Spider-Man 4.00 10.00
2 The Incredible Hulk 2.50 6.00
5 Thor 2.50 6.00
6 Iron Man 3.00 8.00
7 Captain America 3.00 8.00
12 Daredevil 2.50 6.00
15 The Vision 2.50 6.00
18 Hawkeye 2.50 6.00

1989 Comic Images Todd McFarlane Series I

COMPLETE SET (46) 6.00 15.00
UNOPENED BOX (50 PACKS) 40.00 50.00
UNOPENED PACK (5 CARDS) 1.00 1.25
COMMON CARD (1-45) .25 .60

1990 Comic Images Todd McFarlane Series II

COMPLETE SET (45) 25.00 60.00
UNOPENED BOX (50 PACKS) 40.00 50.00
UNOPENED PACK (5 CARDS) 1.00 1.25
COMMON CARD (1-45) 1.00 2.50

X-Men

1995 Chef Boyardee X-Men Mystery Super Villains

COMPLETE SET (5) 10.00 25.00
COMMON CARD 4.00 10.00

2018 Fleer Ultra X-Men

COMPLETE SET W/O SP (75) 50.00 100.00
UNOPENED BOX (12 PACKS) 1000.00 1500.00
UNOPENED PACK (6 CARDS) 85.00 125.00
COMMON CARD (1-75) 1.00 2.50
COMMON SP (76-150) 1.50 4.00
*SILVER FOIL: .75X TO 2X BASIC CARDS 2.00 5.00
*GOLD FOIL/99: 2.5X TO 6X BASIC CARDS 15.00
CARDS 1-75 INSERTED 3:2
CARDS 76-100 INSERTED 1:2
CARDS 101-150 INSERTED 1:1
0 Pixie/E-Pack
000 Negasonic Teenage Warhead/E-Pack
00 Daken/E-Pack
81 Mikhail Rasputin SP 2.50 6.00
84 Wendigo SP 2.50 6.00
96 Graydon Creed SP 2.50 6.00
104 Callisto SP 2.50 6.00
107 Stryfe SP 2.50 6.00
113 Dark Phoenix SP 3.00 8.00
138 Master Mold SP 2.50 6.00
140 Mystique SP 2.00 5.00

2018 Fleer Ultra X-Men Artist Autographs

COMMON AUTO 10.00 25.00
STATED PRINT RUN 50 SER.#'d SETS
1 German Ponce 12.00 30.00
2 Caio Cacau
3 Meghan Hetrick 15.00 40.00
4 Ray Lago 15.00 40.00
5 John Stanko 175.00 350.00
6 Jason Juta 12.00 30.00
7 Tom Fleming 50.00 100.00
9 Joe Corroney 20.00 50.00
10 Agustin Alessio 15.00 40.00
11 Alessandra Pisano 20.00 50.00
12 Jason Juta 20.00 50.00
13 J.P. Targete 15.00 40.00
14 German Ponce 15.00 40.00
15 Kathryn Steele 20.00 50.00
16 Ray Lago 60.00 120.00
18 J.P. Targete 15.00 40.00
19 J.P. Targete 12.00 30.00
20 Crystal Graziano 60.00 120.00
22 Ray Lago 20.00 50.00
23 J.P. Targete 15.00 40.00
26 Jason Juta 20.00 50.00
28 Dave DeVries 30.00 75.00
29 Joe Slucher 25.00 60.00
30 J.P. Targete 15.00 40.00
33 Crystal Graziano 15.00 40.00
36 J.P. Targete 15.00 40.00
38 Jason Juta 20.00 50.00
39 Kate Laird 15.00 40.00
41 Brian Rood 20.00 50.00
43 John Grello 30.00 75.00
44 Bob MacNeil 25.00 60.00
48 Mark Evans 15.00 40.00
49 John Stanko 20.00 50.00
50 (Jason Juta 15.00 40.00
52 Mark Evans 12.00 30.00
55 Brian Rood 15.00 40.00
59 Ariel Olivetti 15.00 40.00
61 John Grello 15.00 40.00
62 Jason Juta 12.00 30.00
65 Bob MacNeil 15.00 40.00
67 Caio Cacau
69 Crystal Graziano 15.00 40.00
72 Christopher Mangum 15.00 40.00
73 Moonstar 15.00 40.00
Brian Rood
74 Joe Corroney 12.00 30.00
77 Mark Evans
78 Jason Juta 25.00 60.00
81 Kate Laird 15.00 40.00
83 Meghan Hetrick 15.00 40.00
84 Dave DeVries 20.00 50.00
87 Crystal Graziano 12.00 30.00
88 Mark Evans 12.00 30.00
90 Mark Evans 15.00 40.00
91 J.P. Targete 15.00 40.00
93 Ariel Olivetti 12.00 30.00
94 J.P. Targete 20.00 50.00
98 Agustin Alessio 15.00 40.00
99 German Ponce 20.00 50.00
101 German Ponce 20.00 50.00
102 J.P. Targete 20.00 50.00
108 German Ponce 15.00 40.00
109 Mike Thompson 15.00 40.00
111 Nicholas Gregory 15.00 40.00
113 John Stanko 25.00 60.00
114 J.P. Targete 20.00 50.00
118 Jason Juta 12.00 30.00
125 German Ponce 12.00 30.00
126 Ariel Olivetti 15.00 40.00
129 Christopher Mangum
130 Ariel Olivetti 15.00 40.00
131 J.P. Targete 12.00 30.00
132 Agustin Alessio 12.00 30.00
133 Ariel Olivetti 20.00 50.00
134 Ariel Olivetti 15.00 40.00
135 Agustin Alessio 12.00 30.00
136 Ariel Olivetti 15.00 40.00
138 Agustin Alessio 12.00 30.00
139 Agustin Alessio 15.00 40.00
140 Crystal Graziano 20.00 50.00
142 Mark Evans 12.00 30.00
144 Ariel Olivetti 12.00 30.00
146 Joe Slucher 30.00 75.00
147 J.P. Targete 12.00 30.00
148 Meghan Hetrick 30.00 75.00
149 Jason Juta 30.00 75.00
150 Ariel Olivetti 15.00 40.00

2018 Fleer Ultra X-Men '94 Buybacks Gold Foil

COMMON CARD (1-149) 10.00 25.00
STATED PRINT RUN 50 SER.#'d SETS
6 Wolverine 12.00 30.00
57 Deadpool 15.00 40.00
100 Beast 12.00 30.00
104 Fall of the Mutants 12.00 30.00
111 Bishop, Jean Grey 12.00 30.00
114 Cyclops, Rogue 12.00 30.00
124 It was boy meets girlâ•¦ 12.00 30.00
134 Dark Phoenix 25.00 60.00
137 Wolverine vs. Sabretooth 15.00 40.00
140 Wolverine vs. Hulk 12.00 30.00
145 Wolverine vs. Cable 12.00 30.00
146 Wolverine vs. Sauron 12.00 30.00

2018 Fleer Ultra X-Men Comic Cut Panels

STATED PRINT RUN VARIES
SCUX1 Uncanny X-Men #1 60.00 120.00
SCUX2 Uncanny X-Men #2/119 30.00 75.00
SCUX3 Uncanny X-Men #3/85 20.00 50.00
SCUX4 Uncanny X-Men #4/85 15.00 40.00
SCUX8 Uncanny X-Men #8/137 15.00 40.00
SCUX9 Uncanny X-Men #9/70 15.00 40.00
SCAA11 Amazing Adventures #11/109 25.00 60.00
SCGSX1 Giant-Size X-Men Vol 1 #1/137 15.00 40.00
SCIF14 Iron Fist #14/78 20.00 50.00
SCMM18 Ms. Marvel #18/95 15.00 40.00
SCUX10 Uncanny X-Men #10/109 20.00 50.00
SCUX11 Uncanny X-Men #11/117 15.00 40.00
SCUX12 Uncanny X-Men #12/72 15.00 40.00
SCUX14 Uncanny X-Men #14/113 15.00 40.00
SCUX15 Uncanny X-Men #15/110 25.00 60.00
SCUX16 Uncanny X-Men #16/68 50.00 100.00
SCUX35 Uncanny X-Men #35/101 20.00 50.00
SCUX49 Uncanny X-Men #49/74 30.00 75.00
SCUX53 Uncanny X-Men #53/91 20.00 50.00
SCUX60 Uncanny X-Men #60/89 15.00 40.00
SCUX64 Uncanny X-Men #64/85 15.00 40.00
SCUX66 Uncanny X-Men #66/107 15.00 40.00
SCUX94 Uncanny X-Men #94/68 15.00 40.00
SCUX95 Uncanny X-Men #95/85 15.00 40.00
SCUX97 Uncanny X-Men #97/98 15.00 40.00
SCIH181 Incredible Hulk Vol 1 #181/74 20.00 50.00
SCUX101 Uncanny X-Men #101/69 60.00 120.00
SCUX102 Uncanny X-Men #102/80 15.00 40.00
SCUX108 Uncanny X-Men #108/84 15.00 40.00
SCUX109 Uncanny X-Men #109/95 15.00 40.00
SCUX110 Uncanny X-Men #110/90 15.00 40.00
SCUX129 Uncanny X-Men #129/85 15.00 40.00
SCUX130 Uncanny X-Men #130/93 20.00 50.00
SCUX137 Uncanny X-Men #137/151 15.00 40.00
SCUX139 Uncanny X-Men #139/88 15.00 40.00

2018 Fleer Ultra X-Men Connected Images

COMPLETE SET (9) 50.00 100.00
COMMON CARD (1-9) 6.00 15.00
STATED ODDS 1:12
2 Storm 8.00 20.00
3 Rogue/Iceman 8.00 20.00
6 Wolverine 10.00 25.00
8 Beast/Professor X 8.00 20.00

2018 Fleer Ultra X-Men Dead and Gone

COMPLETE SET (10) 10.00 25.00
COMMON CARD (DG1-DG10) 1.50 4.00
*SILVER FOIL: .6X TO 1.5X BASIC CARDS 2.50 6.00
*GOLD FOIL/99: 1.5X TO 4X BASIC CARDS6.00 15.00
STATED ODDS 1:5

2018 Fleer Ultra X-Men Dead and Gone Artist Autographs

COMMON AUTO 15.00 40.00
STATED PRINT RUN 50 SER.#'d SETS
ALL AUTOS BY ERIC WILKERSON

2018 Fleer Ultra X-Men Deadpool Around the World

COMPLETE SET (10) 12.00 30.00
COMMON CARD (DAW1-DAW10) 2.00 5.00
*SILVER FOIL: .6X TO 1.5X BASIC CARDS 3.00 8.00
*GOLD FOIL/99: 1.2X TO 3X BASIC CARDS6.00 15.00
STATED ODDS 1:5

2018 Fleer Ultra X-Men Dual Comic Cut Panels

STATED PRINT RUN VARIES
DCW1 Wolverine Vol 1 #1 25.00 60.00
DCNM1 New Mutants Vol 1 #1/46 12.00 30.00
DCXF6 X-Factor Vol 1 #6/49 20.00 50.00
DCXF8 X-Force Vol 1 #8/42 15.00 40.00
DCMGN4 Marvel Graphic Novel Vol 1 #4/9715.00 40.00
DCNM14 New Mutants Vol 1 #14/43
DCNM87 New Mutants Vol 1 #87/43 15.00 40.00
DCUX99 Uncanny X-Men #99 15.00 40.00
DCXF24 X-Factor Vol 1 #24/53 15.00 40.00
DCXV21 X-Men Vol 2 #1/66 30.00 75.00
DCUX100 Uncanny X-Men #100/38 15.00 40.00
DCUX107 Uncanny X-Men #107/50 25.00 60.00
DCUX120 Uncanny X-Men #120/36 15.00 40.00
DCUX121 Uncanny X-Men #121/47 15.00 40.00
DCUX133 Uncanny X-Men #133/43 15.00 40.00
DCUX141 Uncanny X-Men #141/66 15.00 40.00
DCUX142 Uncanny X-Men #142/48 12.00 30.00
DCUX158 Uncanny X-Men #158/58 15.00 40.00
DCUX168 Uncanny X-Men #168/47 15.00 40.00
DCUX184 Uncanny X-Men #184/45 15.00 40.00
DCUX200 Uncanny X-Men #200/96 15.00 40.00
DCUX201 Uncanny X-Men #201/52 15.00 40.00
DCUX218 Uncanny X-Men #218/57 15.00 40.00
DCUX219 Uncanny X-Men #219/70 15.00 40.00
DCUX244 Uncanny X-Men #244/66 15.00 40.00
DCUX248 Uncanny X-Men #248/46
DCUX256 Uncanny X-Men #256/30 50.00 100.00
DCUX282 Uncanny X-Men #282/24 60.00 120.00
DCUX287 Uncanny X-Men #287/51
DCUX290 Uncanny X-Men #290/31 12.00 30.00
DCUX390 Uncanny X-Men #390/42 25.00 60.00
DCUX401 Uncanny X-Men #401/38 30.00 75.00
DCXV230 X-Men Vol 2 #30/53 15.00 40.00

2018 Fleer Ultra X-Men Greatest Battles

COMPLETE SET (10) 10.00 25.00
COMMON CARD (GB1-GB10) 1.50 4.00
*SILVER FOIL: .6X TO 1.5X BASIC CARDS 2.50 6.00
*GOLD FOIL/99: 1.5X TO 4X BASIC CARDS6.00 15.00
STATED ODDS 1:5

2018 Fleer Ultra X-Men Jambalaya

COMMON CARD (1-30) 40.00 100.00
STATED ODDS 1:48
1 Cyclops 250.00 600.00
2 Colossus 200.00 500.00
3 Namor 150.00 400.00
4 Magik 125.00 300.00
5 Emma Frost 300.00 800.00
6 Beast 75.00 200.00
7 Angel 60.00 150.00
8 Iceman 150.00 400.00
9 Jean Grey 150.00 400.00
10 Havok 200.00 500.00
11 Scarlet Witch 600.00 1500.00
12 Rogue 200.00 500.00
14 Sunfire 75.00 200.00
16 Kitty Pryde 150.00 400.00
18 Dazzler Thor 60.00 150.00
19 Moonstar 50.00 125.00
20 Doop 50.00 125.00
22 Madelyne Pryor 60.00 125.00
23 Juggernaut 200.00 500.00
24 Mister Sinister 150.00 400.00
26 Toad 150.00 400.00
28 Quentin Quire 50.00 125.00
30 Weapon X 600.00 1500.00

2018 Fleer Ultra X-Men Master of Magnetism

COMPLETE SET (15) 100.00 200.00
COMMON CARD (MM1-MM15) 6.00 15.00
STATED ODDS 1:36

2018 Fleer Ultra X-Men Metal Blasters

COMMON CARD (MB1-MB49) 2.00 5.00
STATED ODDS 1:2
MB0 Old Man Logan/E-Pack 100.00 200.00
MB1 Cyclops 2.50 6.00
MB2 Iceman 4.00 10.00

DC/MARVEL

MB4 Beast	3.00	8.00
MB5 Phoenix	5.00	12.00
MB10 Banshee	4.00	10.00
MB11 Storm	5.00	12.00
MB14 Psylocke	3.00	8.00
MB16 Mystique	5.00	12.00
MB18 Emma Frost	2.50	6.00
MB19 Kitty Pryde	3.00	8.00
MB20 Dazzler	4.00	10.00
MB21 Phoenix II	3.00	8.00
MB22 Rogue	6.00	15.00
MB23 Cannonball	3.00	8.00
MB26 Forge	3.00	8.00
MB28 Legion	2.50	6.00
MB31 Mister Sinister	2.50	6.00
MB32 Jubilee	4.00	10.00
MB34 Bishop	2.50	6.00
MB35 Domino	4.00	10.00
MB37 Marrow	4.00	10.00
MB39 M	4.00	10.00
MB40 Stepford Cuckoos	2.50	6.00
MB42 X-23	10.00	25.00
MB43 Armor	3.00	8.00
MB46 Deathlok Prime	3.00	8.00
MB47 Warbird	3.00	8.00
MB48 Tempus	3.00	8.00
MB49 Red Onslaught	2.50	6.00

2018 Fleer Ultra X-Men Precious Metal Gems Blue

COMMON CARD	8.00	20.00
STATED PRINT RUN 49 SER.#'d SETS		
MB1 Cyclops	30.00	75.00
MB2 Iceman	10.00	25.00
MB4 Beast	12.00	30.00
MB5 Phoenix	12.00	30.00
MB6 Magneto	12.00	30.00
MB10 Banshee	15.00	40.00
MB11 Storm	150.00	300.00
MB12 Magik	12.00	30.00
MB13 Colossus	20.00	50.00
MB14 Psylocke	15.00	40.00
MB15 Sabretooth	20.00	50.00
MB16 Mystique	25.00	60.00
MB18 Emma Frost	50.00	100.00
MB19 Kitty Pryde	15.00	40.00
MB20 Dazzler	12.00	30.00
MB21 Phoenix II	12.00	30.00
MB22 Rogue	20.00	50.00
MB30 Cable	15.00	40.00
MB31 Mister Sinister	125.00	250.00
MB32 Jubilee	12.00	30.00
MB35 Domino	12.00	30.00
MB42 X-23	125.00	250.00

2018 Fleer Ultra X-Men Precious Metal Gems Bronze

COMMON CARD (MB1-MB49)	20.00	50.00
STATED PRINT RUN 199 SER.#'d SETS		
MB0 Old Man Logan/E-Pack	1500.00	4000.00
MB1 Cyclops	75.00	200.00
MB2 Iceman	60.00	150.00
MB3 Archangel	50.00	125.00
MB4 Beast	60.00	150.00
MB5 Phoenix	50.00	125.00
MB6 Magneto	75.00	200.00
MB7 Blob	40.00	100.00
MB8 Juggernaut	75.00	200.00
MB9 Sentinels	50.00	125.00
MB10 Banshee	40.00	100.00
MB11 Storm	100.00	250.00
MB12 Magik	75.00	200.00
MB13 Colossus	60.00	150.00
MB14 Psylocke	50.00	125.00
MB15 Sabretooth	60.00	150.00
MB16 Mystique	50.00	125.00
MB18 Emma Frost	40.00	100.00
MB20 Dazzler	60.00	150.00
MB21 Phoenix II	50.00	75.00
MB22 Rogue	40.00	100.00
MB23 Cannonball	30.00	75.00
MB24 Puck	30.00	75.00
MB25 Warlock	30.00	75.00
MB26 Forge	40.00	100.00
MB27 Adversary	30.00	75.00
MB30 Cable	60.00	150.00
MB31 Mister Sinister	60.00	150.00
MB32 Jubilee	75.00	200.00
MB33 Alchemy	30.00	75.00
MB34 Bishop	50.00	125.00
MB35 Domino	40.00	100.00
MB36 Dr. Nemesis	30.00	75.00
MB38 Blink	60.00	150.00
MB42 X-23	100.00	250.00
MB49 Red Onslaught	30.00	75.00

2018 Fleer Ultra X-Men Precious Metal Gems Red

COMPLETE SET (50)		
COMMON CARD	4.00	10.00
STATED PRINT RUN 99 SER.#'d SETS		
MB0 Old Man Logan/E-Pack	250.00	500.00
MB1 Cyclops	20.00	50.00
MB3 Archangel	25.00	60.00
MB4 Beast	8.00	20.00
MB5 Phoenix	15.00	40.00
MB6 Magneto	15.00	40.00
MB10 Banshee	8.00	20.00
MB11 Storm	10.00	25.00
MB13 Colossus	10.00	25.00
MB14 Psylocke	12.00	30.00
MB15 Sabretooth	10.00	25.00
MB16 Mystique	15.00	40.00
MB18 Emma Frost	10.00	25.00
MB19 Kitty Pryde	10.00	25.00
MB20 Dazzler	8.00	20.00
MB22 Rogue	8.00	20.00
MB30 Cable	25.00	60.00
MB31 Mister Sinister	30.00	75.00
MB32 Jubilee	10.00	25.00
MB34 Bishop	5.00	12.00
MB35 Domino	25.00	60.00
MB38 Blink	8.00	20.00
MB42 X-23	20.00	50.00

2018 Fleer Ultra X-Men Stax Bottom Layer

COMMON CARD (1C-25C)	4.00	10.00
COMMON SP (26C-30C)	15.00	40.00
STATED ODDS 1:19		
STATED ODDS SP 1:432		
1C Cyclops	8.00	20.00
3C Dark Phoenix	5.00	12.00
4C Beast	5.00	12.00
6C Magneto	8.00	20.00
7C Northstar	5.00	12.00
9C Sentinels	5.00	12.00
10C Master Mold	5.00	12.00
11C Banshee	5.00	12.00
15C Storm	5.00	12.00
16C Wolverine	10.00	25.00
17C Colossus	6.00	15.00
18C Kitty Pryde	5.00	12.00
19C Guardian	6.00	15.00
20C Dazzler	5.00	12.00
23C Brood	5.00	12.00
24C Mister Sinister	5.00	12.00
26C Cable SP	20.00	50.00
27C Exodus SP	30.00	75.00
28C Onslaught SP	30.00	75.00
30C X-23 SP	50.00	100.00

2018 Fleer Ultra X-Men Stax Middle Layer

COMMON CARD (1B-25B)	4.00	10.00
COMMON SP (26B-30B)	15.00	40.00
STATED ODDS 1:19		
STATED ODDS SP 1:432		
1B Cyclops	8.00	20.00
2B Mimic	6.00	15.00
3B Dark Phoenix	5.00	12.00
4B Beast	5.00	12.00
6B Magneto	12.00	30.00
7B Northstar	5.00	12.00
8B Juggernaut	6.00	15.00
9B Sentinels	8.00	20.00
10B Master Mold	5.00	12.00
12B Polaris	5.00	12.00
14B Sauron	6.00	15.00
15B Storm	6.00	15.00
16B Wolverine	8.00	20.00
17B Colossus	6.00	15.00
18B Kitty Pryde	8.00	20.00
19B Guardian	6.00	15.00
20B Dazzler	6.00	15.00
21B Corsair	5.00	12.00
24B Mister Sinister	6.00	15.00
26B Cable SP	20.00	50.00
27B Exodus SP	25.00	60.00
30B X-23 SP	50.00	100.00

2018 Fleer Ultra X-Men Stax Top Layer

COMMON CARD (1A-25A)	4.00	10.00
COMMON SP (26A-30A)	20.00	50.00
STATED ODDS 1:19		
STATED ODDS SP 1:432		
1A Cyclops	6.00	15.00
3A Dark Phoenix	6.00	15.00
5A Archangel	5.00	12.00
6A Magneto	6.00	15.00
9A Sentinels	6.00	15.00
11A Banshee	6.00	15.00
12A Polaris	5.00	12.00
14A Sauron	6.00	15.00
15A Storm	8.00	20.00
16A Wolverine	8.00	20.00
17A Colossus	6.00	15.00
18A Kitty Pryde	5.00	12.00
19A Guardian	5.00	12.00
20A Dazzler	6.00	15.00
24A Mister Sinister	5.00	12.00
26A Cable SP	25.00	60.00
27A Exodus SP	25.00	60.00
29A Multiple Man SP	30.00	75.00
30A X-23 SP	50.00	100.00

2018 Fleer Ultra X-Men The Originals

COMPLETE SET (10)	12.00	25.00
COMMON CARD (O1-O10)	1.50	4.00
*SILVER FOIL: .6X TO 1.5X BASIC CARDS	2.50	6.00
*GOLD FOIL/99: 1.2X TO 3X BASIC CARDS	5.00	12.00
STATED ODDS 1:5		

2018 Fleer Ultra X-Men The Originals Artist Autographs

COMMON AUTO	15.00	40.00
STATED PRINT RUN 50 SER.#'d SETS		
ALL AUTOS ARE TOM FLEMING		
O10 Scarlet Witch	120.00	250.00
Tom Fleming		

2018 Fleer Ultra X-Men X-Cuts

COMMON CARD (XC1-XC42)	3.00	8.00
*RED/99: .6X TO 1.5X BASIC CARDS		
*YELLOW/50: .75X TO 2X BASIC CARDS		
*BLUE/25: 1X TO 2.5X BASIC CARDS		
STATED ODDS 1:20		
XC1 Wolverine	8.00	20.00
XC2 X-23	5.00	12.00
XC3 Vanisher	4.00	10.00
XC4 Warpath	8.00	20.00
XC5 Archangel	6.00	15.00
XC6 Psylocke	6.00	15.00
XC13 Cyclops	6.00	15.00
XC14 Namor	5.00	12.00
XC15 Emma Frost	4.00	10.00
XC16 Stepford Cuckoos	4.00	10.00
XC18 Magneto	6.00	15.00
XC19 Storm	4.00	10.00
XC20 Cable	6.00	15.00
XC22 Magik	5.00	12.00
XC24 Rogue	8.00	20.00
XC27 Pixie	4.00	10.00
XC30 Sunspot	4.00	10.00
XC31 Warlock	5.00	12.00
XC36 Darwin	5.00	12.00
XC37 Vulcan	4.00	10.00
XC38 Bishop	6.00	15.00
XC40 Lady Deathstrike	6.00	15.00
XC42 Bastion	8.00	20.00

2018 Fleer Ultra X-Men X-Men '92

COMPLETE SET (10)	10.00	25.00
COMMON CARD (X1-X10)	2.00	5.00
*SILVER FOIL: .6X TO 1.5X BASIC CARDS	3.00	8.00
*GOLD FOIL/99: 1.2X TO 3X BASIC CARDS	6.00	15.00
STATED ODDS 1:5		

2018 Fleer Ultra X-Men X-Men '92 Artist Autographs

COMMON AUTO (X1-X10)	60.00	150.00
STATED PRINT RUN 50 SER.#'d SETS		
X1 David Nakayama	60.00	150.00
X2 David Nakayama	60.00	150.00
X3 David Nakayama	60.00	150.00
X4 David Nakayama	60.00	150.00
X5 David Nakayama	60.00	150.00
X6 David Nakayama	60.00	150.00
X7 David Nakayama	60.00	150.00
X8 David Nakayama	60.00	150.00
X9 David Nakayama	60.00	150.00
X10 David Nakayama	60.00	150.00

2011 Legends of Marvel Wolverine

COMPLETE SET (9)	10.00	25.00
COMMON CARD (L1-L9)	2.00	5.00
STATED PRINT RUN 1939 SER.#'d SETS		

2012 Legends of Marvel Storm

COMPLETE SET (9)	6.00	15.00
COMMON CARD (L1-L9)	1.25	3.00
STATED PRINT RUN 1939 SER.#'d SETS		

1994 Marvel Comics X-Men Phone Cards

COMPLETE SET (5)	12.00	30.00
COMMON CARD (1-5)	3.00	8.00
3 Professor X vs. Magneto	4.00	10.00
5 Wolverine vs. Omega Red	6.00	15.00

1988 Comic Images Marvel Wolverine Trivia

COMPLETE SET (50)	15.00	40.00
COMMON CARD (1-50)	.60	1.50
NNO Wolverine Mutant Trivia PROMO	2.50	6.00

1993 Hanes Marvel X-Men

COMPLETE SET (3)	5.00	12.00
COMMON CARD (1-3)	1.50	4.00
3 Wolverine	4.00	10.00

1995 Hardee's Marvel X-Men

COMPLETE SET (5)	5.00	12.00
COMMON CARD (1-5)	1.50	4.00

1995 Hardee's Marvel X-Men Figurine Cards

COMPLETE SET (4)	8.00	20.00

COMMON CARD (1-4)	2.00	5.00
COMMON CHECKLIST	.75	2.00

2020 SkyBox Marvel Metal Universe X-Men

UNOPENED BOX (12 PACKS)	600.00	1000.00
UNOPENED PACK (6 CARDS)	50.00	85.00
COMMON CARD (1-100)	.60	1.50
COMMON SP (101-200)	1.50	4.00
*GOLD: .5X TO 1.2X BASIC CARDS		
*GRANDIOSE: .6X TO 1.5X BASIC CARDS		
*PINK/75: .75X TO 2X BASIC CARDS		
13 Cable	3.00	8.00
23 Deadpool	5.00	12.00
31 Gambit	1.25	3.00
36 Iceman	.75	2.00
37 Jean Grey	1.25	3.00
50 Professor X	1.25	3.00
56 Rogue	1.00	2.50
60 Storm	1.25	3.00
65 Ultimate Wolverine	2.00	5.00
69 Wolverine	6.00	15.00
70 X-23	2.00	5.00
77 Scarlet Witch	2.50	6.00
84 Magneto	1.00	2.50
86 Mister Sinister	.75	2.00
87 Mystique	1.25	3.00
101 Angel SP	2.00	5.00
102 Armor SP	2.00	5.00
105 Beast SP	2.50	6.00
107 Bishop SP	2.50	6.00
113 Cable SP	6.00	15.00
117 Colossus SP	2.50	6.00
119 Cyclops SP	3.00	8.00
122 Dazzler SP	4.00	10.00
123 Deadpool SP	10.00	25.00
124 Domino SP	2.50	6.00
131 Gambit SP	3.00	8.00
136 Iceman SP	2.50	6.00
137 Jean Grey SP	2.50	6.00
150 Professor X SP	2.00	5.00
156 Rogue SP	2.50	6.00
160 Storm SP	2.00	5.00
165 Ultimate Wolverine SP	3.00	8.00
169 Wolverine SP	6.00	15.00
170 X-23 SP	4.00	10.00
173 Dark Phoenix SP	5.00	12.00
174 Emma Frost SP	2.50	6.00
177 Scarlet Witch SP	5.00	12.00
184 Magneto SP	3.00	8.00
186 Mister Sinister SP	2.00	5.00
187 Mystique SP	4.00	10.00
192 Sabretooth SP	2.50	6.00

2020 SkyBox Marvel Metal Universe X-Men '95 Marvel Metal Buybacks

COMPLETE SET (118)		
STATED PRINT RUN 10 SER.#'d SETS		
2 Bishop	60.00	150.00
3 Cyclops	125.00	300.00
4 Gambit	200.00	500.00
8 Sunfire	30.00	75.00
9 Weapon X	100.00	250.00
12 Giant Man	25.00	60.00
21 Warlock	25.00	60.00
22 Hawkeye	75.00	200.00
25 Scarlet Witch	100.00	250.00
26 Spider-Woman	75.00	200.00
28 Daredevil	60.00	150.00
31 Hulk	150.00	400.00
39 She-Hulk	125.00	300.00
44 Brimstone Love	30.00	75.00
46 Ghost Rider 2099	100.00	250.00
47 Hulk 2099	30.00	75.00
49 Meanstreak	20.00	50.00
51 Ravage 2099	125.00	300.00
62 Vengeance	30.00	75.00
64 Justice	20.00	50.00
66 Night Thrasher	30.00	75.00
70 Black Cat	40.00	100.00
76 Scorpion	30.00	75.00
77 Shocker	30.00	75.00
78 Spider-Man	1200.00	2000.00
79 Stunner	20.00	50.00
87 Boomer	30.00	75.00
88 Cable	125.00	300.00
96 Iceman	30.00	75.00
102 Longshot	30.00	75.00
105 Mondo	25.00	60.00
109 Penance	60.00	150.00
110 Phoenix	100.00	250.00
111 Professor X	50.00	120.00
112 Psylocke	100.00	250.00
113 Random	20.00	50.00
119 Storm	200.00	350.00
123 Warpath	30.00	75.00
125 Wolverine	300.00	800.00
126 Beast (Alternate)	40.00	100.00
131 Kraven (Alternate)	40.00	100.00
132 Rogue (Alternate)	60.00	150.00
136 Venom (Alternate)	500.00	1000.00

2020 SkyBox Marvel Metal Universe X-Men Arc Weld

COMPLETE SET W/O SP (22)	150.00	300.00
COMMON CARD (AW1-AW22)	6.00	15.00
COMMON SP (AW23-AW28)	12.00	30.00
STATED ODDS 1:48 HOBBY/RETAIL		
STATED SP ODDS 1:576 HOBBY/RETAIL		
AW1 Angel	12.00	30.00
AW2 Banshee	10.00	25.00
AW3 Beast	10.00	25.00
AW4 Blob	8.00	20.00
AW5 Dark Phoenix	12.00	30.00
AW6 Dazzler	15.00	40.00
AW7 Domino	20.00	50.00
AW8 Iceman	12.00	30.00
AW10 Legion	8.00	20.00
AW11 Mister Sinister	8.00	20.00
AW13 Namor	10.00	25.00
AW14 Omega Red	15.00	40.00
AW17 Sebastian Shaw	10.00	25.00
AW18 Sentinels	12.00	30.00
AW19 Silver Samurai	10.00	25.00
AW20 Sunpyre	15.00	40.00
AW24 Gambit SP	100.00	200.00
AW25 Jean Grey SP	75.00	150.00
AW26 Rogue SP	100.00	200.00
AW27 Storm SP	75.00	150.00
AW28 Wolverine SP	300.00	600.00

2020 SkyBox Marvel Metal Universe X-Men Blast Furnace

COMPLETE SET W/O SP (22)	250.00	500.00
COMMON CARD (B1-B22)	6.00	15.00
COMMON SP (B23-B28)	60.00	120.00
STATED ODDS 1:48 HOBBY/RETAIL		
STATED SP ODDS 1:576 HOBBY/RETAIL		
B1 Avalanche	10.00	25.00
B2 Bishop	10.00	25.00
B3 Blink	10.00	25.00
B4 Cable	12.00	30.00
B5 Colossus	15.00	40.00
B6 Copycat	10.00	25.00
B7 Emma Frost	10.00	25.00
B8 Gladiator	8.00	20.00
B9 Havok	10.00	25.00
B10 Hope Summers	10.00	25.00
B11 Jubilee	8.00	20.00
B12 Juggernaut	15.00	40.00
B13 Kitty Pryde	15.00	40.00
B14 Magik	12.00	30.00
B15 Phoenix	30.00	75.00
B16 Psylocke	30.00	75.00
B18 Rachel Summers	15.00	40.00
B19 Scarlet Witch	15.00	40.00
B21 Wolverine	60.00	120.00
B22 X-23	20.00	50.00
B23 Deadpool SP	200.00	400.00
B24 Magneto SP	150.00	300.00
B26 Old Man Logan SP	200.00	400.00
B28 Sabretooth SP	75.00	150.00

2020 SkyBox Marvel Metal Universe X-Men Comic Cut Clippings

COMMON MEM	25.00	60.00
STATED PRINT RUN 45-50		

2020 SkyBox Marvel Metal Universe X-Men Comic Cuts Masterworks Clipping Autographs

COMMON AUTO	125.00	250.00
STATED PRINT RUN 10 SER.#'d SETS		

2020 SkyBox Marvel Metal Universe X-Men Geodes

COMMON CARD (G1-G15)	12.00	30.00
COMMON SP (G16-G21)	40.00	100.00
COMMON SP (G22-G24)	125.00	300.00
ODDS (G1-G15) 1:96 HOBBY/RETAIL		
ODDS (G16-G21) 1:360 HOBBY/RETAIL		
ODDS (G22-G24) 1:1,440 HOBBY/RETAIL		
G1 Angel	20.00	50.00
G2 Banshee	15.00	40.00
G3 Beast	20.00	50.00
G4 Cyclops	20.00	50.00
G5 Emma Frost	25.00	60.00
G7 Gambit	30.00	75.00
G10 Jean Grey	30.00	75.00
G12 Kitty Pryde	15.00	40.00
G13 Professor X	15.00	40.00
G14 Quicksilver	15.00	40.00
G18 Psylocke SP	50.00	120.00
G21 Deadpool SP	75.00	200.00
G22 Magneto SP	400.00	800.00
G24 Wolverine SP	350.00	600.00

2020 SkyBox Marvel Metal Universe X-Men Palladium

COMPLETE SET (50)	250.00	600.00
COMMON CARD (1-50)	6.00	15.00
STATED ODDS 1:12 HOBBY/EPACK		
1 Angel	8.00	20.00
3 Banshee	8.00	20.00
5 Bishop	8.00	20.00
7 Cable	10.00	25.00
8 Cannonball	8.00	20.00
11 Cyclops	8.00	20.00
12 Dark Phoenix	15.00	40.00
13 Deadpool	25.00	60.00
14 Domino	20.00	50.00
15 Emma Frost	20.00	50.00
16 Gambit	12.00	30.00
17 Havok	8.00	20.00
18 Iceman	10.00	25.00
19 Jean Grey	15.00	40.00
20 Jubilee	8.00	20.00
21 Kitty Pryde	12.00	30.00
23 Magik	12.00	30.00
24 Magma	10.00	25.00
25 Magneto	15.00	40.00
27 Mister Sinister	12.00	30.00
28 Mystique	10.00	25.00
29 Namor	10.00	25.00
30 Noriko Ashida	8.00	20.00
31 Omega Red	12.00	30.00
32 Onslaught	10.00	25.00
34 Polaris	8.00	20.00
35 Professor X	10.00	25.00
38 Rogue	15.00	40.00
39 Sabretooth	10.00	25.00
40 Sauron	10.00	25.00
41 Sebastian Shaw	8.00	20.00
42 Storm	12.00	30.00
43 Stryfe	10.00	25.00
48 Wolfsbane	8.00	20.00
49 Wolverine	100.00	200.00
50 X-23	30.00	75.00

2020 SkyBox Marvel Metal Universe X-Men Planet Metal

COMMON CARD (1PM-20PM)	6.00	15.00
*COPPER/85: SAME VALUE AS BASIC		
*PLATINUM/49: .75X TO 2X BASIC CARDS		
STATED OVERALL ODDS 1:72 HOBBY/RETAIL		
1PM Archangel	10.00	25.00
4PM Cyclops	8.00	20.00
5PM Dark Phoenix	12.00	30.00
6PM Deadpool	20.00	50.00
8PM Juggernaut	8.00	20.00
10PM Magneto	15.00	40.00
12PM Omega Red	10.00	25.00
15PM Storm	12.00	30.00
18PM Warlock	12.00	30.00
19PM Wolverine	40.00	100.00
20PM X-23	12.00	30.00

2020 SkyBox Marvel Metal Universe X-Men Platinum Portraits

COMMON CARD (1-25)	150.00	300.00
STATED ODDS 1:600 HOBBY/EPACK		
1 Archangel	200.00	350.00
3 Bishop	200.00	350.00
4 Cable	500.00	1000.00
5 Colossus	300.00	600.00
6 Cyclops	500.00	1000.00
7 Dark Phoenix	750.00	1500.00
8 Deadpool	1000.00	2000.00
9 Domino	200.00	350.00
10 Gambit	400.00	800.00
11 Havok	200.00	400.00
12 Juggernaut	200.00	400.00
14 Magneto	750.00	1500.00
15 Marvel Girl	400.00	750.00
17 Mystique	250.00	500.00
18 Quicksilver	250.00	500.00
19 Sabretooth	200.00	400.00
20 Scarlet Witch	400.00	800.00
22 Storm	400.00	800.00
24 Wolverine	2000.00	4000.00
25 X-23	600.00	1200.00

2020 SkyBox Marvel Metal Universe X-Men Precious Metal Gems Green

COMMON CARD	250.00	500.00
STATED PRINT RUN 10 SER.#'d SETS		
2 Armor	400.00	800.00
3 Aurora	400.00	800.00
4 Banshee	450.00	900.00
6 Bedlam	500.00	1000.00
7 Bishop	600.00	1200.00
8 Blindfold	400.00	800.00
9 Bling!	400.00	800.00
13 Cable	1000.00	2000.00
14 Cannonball	400.00	800.00
16 Chamber	400.00	800.00
19 Cyclops	400.00	800.00
20 Cypher	375.00	750.00
21 Danger	600.00	1200.00
22 Dazzler	500.00	1000.00
23 Deadpool	2500.00	5000.00
24 Domino	600.00	1200.00
26 Eye-Boy	500.00	1000.00
27 Fantomex	400.00	800.00
28 Firestar	600.00	1200.00
30 Frenzy	375.00	700.00
32 Gateway	600.00	1200.00
33 Havok	500.00	1000.00
34 Hope Summers	300.00	600.00
36 Iceman	300.00	600.00
37 Jean Grey	750.00	1500.00

DC/MARVEL

38 Jubilee	450.00	900.00
41 Kitty Pryde	300.00	600.00
42 Legion	400.00	800.00
46 Multiple Man	450.00	900.00
47 Namor	450.00	900.00
48 Northstar	400.00	750.00
49 Polaris	750.00	1500.00
50 Professor X	1500.00	3000.00
53 Rachel Summers	400.00	800.00
55 Rictor	400.00	750.00
56 Rogue	750.00	1500.00
57 Sage	500.00	1000.00
58 Shatterstar	300.00	600.00
59 Stepford Cuckoos	500.00	1000.00
60 Storm	300.00	600.00
61 Sunfire	300.00	600.00
63 Sunspot	400.00	750.00
65 Ultimate Wolverine	2000.00	4000.00
67 Warpath	400.00	800.00
69 Wolverine	5000.00	10000.00
73 Dark Phoenix	750.00	1500.00
74 Emma Frost		
76 Quicksilver	450.00	900.00
77 Scarlet Witch	3000.00	6000.00
79 Blob	600.00	1200.00
80 Deathbird	400.00	800.00
81 Exodus	400.00	800.00
82 Juggernaut	450.00	900.00
84 Magneto	1500.00	3000.00
85 Master Mold	300.00	600.00
86 Mister Sinister	500.00	1000.00
87 Mystique	1000.00	2000.00
88 Nimrod	400.00	750.00
89 Omega Red	500.00	1000.00
90 Onslaught	600.00	1200.00
91 Pyro	450.00	900.00
93 Sebastian Shaw	300.00	600.00
94 Sentinels	600.00	1200.00
95 Shadow King	400.00	800.00
96 Silver Samurai	600.00	1200.00
99 Vanisher	300.00	600.00
102 Armor	400.00	800.00
103 Aurora	400.00	800.00
104 Banshee	450.00	900.00
106 Bedlam	500.00	1000.00
107 Bishop	600.00	1200.00
108 Blindfold	400.00	800.00
109 Bling!	400.00	800.00
113 Cable	1000.00	2000.00
114 Cannonball	400.00	800.00
116 Chamber	400.00	800.00
119 Cyclops	400.00	800.00
120 Cypher	375.00	750.00
121 Danger	600.00	1200.00
122 Dazzler	500.00	1000.00
123 Deadpool	2500.00	5000.00
124 Domino	600.00	1200.00
126 Eye-Boy	500.00	1000.00
127 Fantomex	400.00	800.00
128 Firestar	600.00	1200.00
130 Frenzy	375.00	700.00
132 Gateway	600.00	1200.00
133 Havok	500.00	1000.00
134 Hope Summers	300.00	600.00
136 Iceman	300.00	600.00
137 Jean Grey	750.00	1500.00
138 Jubilee	450.00	900.00
141 Kitty Pryde	300.00	600.00
142 Legion	400.00	800.00
146 Multiple Man	450.00	900.00
147 Namor	450.00	900.00
148 Northstar	400.00	750.00
149 Polaris	750.00	1500.00
150 Professor X	1500.00	3000.00
153 Rachel Summers	400.00	800.00
155 Rictor	400.00	750.00
156 Rogue	750.00	1500.00
157 Sage	500.00	1000.00
158 Shatterstar	300.00	600.00
159 Stepford Cuckoos	500.00	1000.00
160 Storm	300.00	600.00
161 Sunfire	300.00	600.00
163 Sunspot	400.00	750.00
165 Ultimate Wolverine	2000.00	4000.00
167 Warpath	400.00	800.00
169 Wolverine	5000.00	10000.00
173 Dark Phoenix	750.00	1500.00
174 Emma Frost		
176 Quicksilver	450.00	900.00
177 Scarlet Witch	3000.00	6000.00
179 Blob	600.00	1200.00
180 Deathbird	400.00	800.00
181 Exodus	400.00	800.00
182 Juggernaut	450.00	900.00
184 Magneto	1500.00	3000.00
185 Master Mold	300.00	600.00
186 Mister Sinister	500.00	1000.00
187 Mystique	1000.00	2000.00
188 Nimrod	400.00	750.00
189 Omega Red	500.00	1000.00
190 Onslaught	600.00	1200.00
191 Pyro	450.00	900.00
193 Sebastian Shaw	300.00	600.00
194 Sentinels	600.00	1200.00
195 Shadow King	400.00	800.00
196 Silver Samurai	600.00	1200.00
199 Vanisher	300.00	600.00

2020 SkyBox Marvel Metal Universe X-Men Precious Metal Gems Red

COMMON CARD (1-200)	15.00	40.00
STATED PRINT RUN 100 SER.#'d SETS		
1 Angel	30.00	75.00
2 Armor	25.00	60.00
3 Aurora	30.00	75.00
4 Banshee	20.00	50.00
5 Beast	75.00	200.00
7 Bishop	75.00	200.00
8 Blindfold	30.00	75.00
9 Bling!	25.00	60.00
10 Blink	25.00	60.00
11 Boom-Boom	20.00	50.00
12 Broo	20.00	50.00
13 Cable	75.00	200.00
14 Cannonball	20.00	50.00
16 Chamber	20.00	50.00
17 Colossus	75.00	200.00
19 Cyclops	100.00	250.00
22 Dazzler	30.00	75.00
23 Deadpool	500.00	1200.00
24 Domino	60.00	150.00
25 Elixir	20.00	50.00
27 Fantomex	25.00	60.00
28 Firestar	30.00	75.00
31 Gambit	150.00	400.00
33 Havok	25.00	60.00
34 Hope Summers	50.00	120.00
36 Iceman	100.00	250.00
37 Jean Grey	50.00	120.00
38 Jubilee	60.00	150.00
39 Karma	25.00	60.00
41 Kitty Pryde	40.00	100.00
42 Legion	20.00	50.00
45 Magik	100.00	250.00
47 Namor	60.00	150.00
49 Polaris	30.00	75.00
50 Professor X	100.00	250.00
52 Psylocke	100.00	250.00
53 Rachel Summers	30.00	75.00
56 Rogue	100.00	250.00
58 Shatterstar	30.00	75.00
60 Storm	100.00	250.00
61 Sunfire	20.00	50.00
64 Thunderbird	30.00	75.00
65 Ultimate Wolverine	200.00	500.00
69 Wolverine	1200.00	3000.00
70 X-23	150.00	400.00
72 Daken	25.00	60.00
73 Dark Phoenix	100.00	250.00
74 Emma Frost	40.00	100.00
76 Quicksilver	60.00	150.00
77 Scarlet Witch	150.00	400.00
78 Arcade	20.00	50.00
79 Blob	30.00	75.00
82 Juggernaut	75.00	200.00
83 Lady Deathstrike	30.00	75.00
84 Magneto	125.00	300.00
86 Mister Sinister	75.00	200.00
87 Mystique	125.00	300.00
89 Omega Red	75.00	200.00
90 Onslaught	40.00	100.00
92 Sabretooth	125.00	300.00
96 Silver Samurai	25.00	60.00
98 Toad	30.00	75.00
100 Wendigo	20.00	50.00
101 Angel	30.00	75.00
102 Armor	25.00	60.00
103 Aurora	30.00	75.00
104 Banshee	20.00	50.00
105 Beast	75.00	200.00
107 Bishop	75.00	200.00
108 Blindfold	30.00	75.00
109 Bling!	25.00	60.00
110 Blink	25.00	60.00
111 Boom-Boom	20.00	50.00
112 Broo	20.00	50.00
113 Cable	75.00	200.00
114 Cannonball	20.00	50.00
116 Chamber	20.00	50.00
117 Colossus	75.00	200.00
119 Cyclops	100.00	250.00
122 Dazzler	30.00	75.00
123 Deadpool	500.00	1200.00
124 Domino	60.00	150.00
125 Elixir	20.00	50.00
127 Fantomex	25.00	60.00
128 Firestar	30.00	75.00
131 Gambit	150.00	400.00
133 Havok	25.00	60.00
134 Hope Summers	50.00	120.00
136 Iceman	100.00	250.00
137 Jean Grey	50.00	120.00
138 Jubilee	60.00	150.00
139 Karma	25.00	60.00
141 Kitty Pryde	40.00	100.00
142 Legion	20.00	50.00
145 Magik	100.00	250.00
147 Namor	60.00	150.00
149 Polaris	30.00	75.00
150 Professor X	100.00	250.00
152 Psylocke	100.00	250.00
153 Rachel Summers	30.00	75.00
156 Rogue	100.00	250.00
158 Shatterstar	30.00	75.00
160 Storm	100.00	250.00
161 Sunfire	20.00	50.00
164 Thunderbird	30.00	75.00
165 Ultimate Wolverine	200.00	500.00
169 Wolverine	1200.00	3000.00
170 X-23	150.00	400.00
172 Daken	25.00	60.00
173 Dark Phoenix	100.00	250.00
174 Emma Frost	40.00	100.00
176 Quicksilver	60.00	150.00
177 Scarlet Witch	150.00	400.00
178 Arcade	20.00	50.00
179 Blob	30.00	75.00
182 Juggernaut	75.00	200.00
183 Lady Deathstrike	30.00	75.00
184 Magneto	125.00	300.00
186 Mister Sinister	75.00	200.00
187 Mystique	125.00	300.00
189 Omega Red	75.00	200.00
190 Onslaught	40.00	100.00
192 Sabretooth	125.00	300.00
196 Silver Samurai	25.00	60.00
198 Toad	30.00	75.00
200 Wendigo	20.00	50.00

2020 SkyBox Marvel Metal Universe X-Men Purely Periodic

PUP1 Angel/3		
PUP2 Armor/4		
PUP3 Aurora/11		
PUP4 Avalanche/12		
PUP5 Banshee/13		
PUP6 Beast/19		
PUP7 Bedlam/20	20.00	50.00
PUP8 Black Tom/21	75.00	150.00
PUP9 Blindfold/22	25.00	60.00
PUP10 Blink/23	60.00	120.00
PUP11 Blob/24	60.00	150.00
PUP12 Boom-Boom/25	100.00	250.00
PUP13 Broo/26	25.00	60.00
PUP14 Cable/27	75.00	20.00
PUP15 Caliban/28	30.00	75.00
PUP16 Cannonball/29	100.00	250.00
PUP17 Chamber/30	30.00	75.00
PUP18 Colossus/31	100.00	250.00
PUP19 Cyclops/37	60.00	150.00
PUP20 Daken/38	30.00	75.00
PUP21 Danger/39	8.00	20.00
PUP22 Dark Phoenix/40	60.00	150.00
PUP23 Darwin/41	25.00	60.00
PUP24 Dazzler/42	50.00	120.00
PUP25 Deathbird/43	25.00	60.00
PUP26 Deadpool/44	250.00	500.00
PUP27 Domino/45	50.00	120.00
PUP28 Emma Frost/46	50.00	100.00
PUP29 Exodus/47	25.00	60.00
PUP30 Fantomex/48	25.00	60.00
PUP31 Firestar/49	40.00	100.00
PUP32 Forge/50	10.00	25.00
PUP33 Frenzy/55	30.00	75.00
PUP34 Gambit/56	125.00	250.00
PUP35 Gateway/57	10.00	25.00
PUP36 Gladiator/58	15.00	40.00
PUP37 Havok/59	15.00	40.00
PUP38 Hope/60	20.00	50.00
PUP39 Hope Summers/61	25.00	50.00
PUP40 Husk/62	12.00	30.00
PUP41 Iceman/63	30.00	75.00
PUP42 Ink/64	12.00	30.00
PUP43 Jean Grey/65	50.00	100.00
PUP44 Jubilee/66	20.00	50.00
PUP45 Juggernaut/67	40.00	100.00
PUP46 Karma/68	15.00	40.00
PUP47 Kid Omega/69	12.00	30.00
PUP48 Kitty Pryde/70	25.00	60.00
PUP49 Lady Deathstrike/71	20.00	50.00
PUP50 Legion/72	25.00	60.00
PUP51 Magik/73	25.00	60.00
PUP52 Magneto/74	60.00	150.00
PUP53 Master Mold/75	12.00	30.00
PUP54 Mister Sinister/76	20.00	50.00
PUP55 Mystique/77	30.00	75.00
PUP56 Namor/78	15.00	40.00
PUP57 Northstar/79	12.00	30.00
PUP58 Omega Red/80	20.00	50.00
PUP59 Onslaught/81	20.00	50.00
PUP60 Polaris/82	10.00	25.00
PUP61 Professor X/83	20.00	50.00
PUP62 Psylocke/84	75.00	150.00
PUP63 Pyro/87	15.00	40.00
PUP64 Quicksilver/88	15.00	40.00
PUP65 Rachel Summers/89	15.00	40.00
PUP66 Sabretooth/90	20.00	50.00
PUP67 Scarlet Witch/91	20.00	50.00
PUP68 Sebastian Shaw/92	15.00	40.00
PUP69 Sentinels/93	20.00	50.00
PUP70 Shadow King/94	8.00	20.00

PUP71 Silver Samurai/95	12.00	30.00
PUP72 Storm/96	40.00	100.00
PUP73 Stryfe/97	15.00	40.00
PUP74 Sunfire/98	10.00	25.00
PUP75 Sunpyre/99	10.00	25.00
PUP76 Sunspot/100	10.00	25.00
PUP77 Thunderbird/101	15.00	40.00
PUP78 Toad/102	8.00	20.00
PUP79 Warlock/103	12.00	30.00
PUP80 Warpath/104	10.00	25.00
PUP81 Wolfsbane/105	10.00	25.00
PUP82 Wolverine/106	125.00	250.00
PUP83 X-23/107	30.00	75.00
PUP84 X-Man/108	12.00	30.00
PUP85 Xorn/112	10.00	25.00

1995 Nerds Marvel X-Men Series I

COMPLETE SET (8)	30.00	80.00
COMMON CARD (1-8)	3.00	8.00
ENTIRE SET FORMS A PUZZLE OF THE X-MEN BATTLING SENTINELS		
2 Storm	6.00	15.00
3 Cyclops	4.00	10.00
4 Beast	4.00	10.00
6 Jean Grey	4.00	10.00
7 Wolverine	10.00	25.00

1993 Pizza Hut Marvel X-Men

COMPLETE SET (3)	3.00	8.00
COMMON CARD (1-3)	1.50	4.00

1992 Impel Uncanny X-Men

COMPLETE SET (100)	15.00	40.00
UNOPENED BOX (36 PACKS)	150.00	250.00
UNOPENED PACK (6 CARDS)	5.00	8.00
COMMON CARD (1-100)	.30	.75
*NELSONIC: 10X TO 25X BASIC CARDS		
1 Beast	.40	1.00
2 Wolverine	2.00	5.00
4 Iceman	.40	1.00
12 Psylocke	.50	1.25
17 Cyclops	.50	1.25
18 Gambit	.50	1.25
19 Cable	.75	2.00
24 Jean Grey	.50	1.25
41 Magneto	1.00	2.50
43 Deadpool	4.00	10.00
51 Apocalypse	1.50	4.00
62 Mystique	1.25	3.00
93 Storm	.50	1.25
95 Wolverine	2.00	5.00

1992 Impel Uncanny X-Men Holograms

COMPLETE SET (5)	15.00	40.00
COMMON CARD (XH1-XH5)	3.00	8.00
XH1 Wolverine	10.00	25.00
XH2 Cable	5.00	12.00
XH3 Gambit	4.00	10.00

1992 Impel Uncanny X-Men Jim Lee Autographs

COMMON CARD (8)	30.00	80.00
2 Wolverine	50.00	100.00

1992 Impel Uncanny X-Men Promos

COMPLETE SET (6)	8.00	20.00
COMMON CARD (SKIP #'d)	.75	2.00
NNO1 Magneto (Gold Hologram) (Advance Comics Magazine Exclusive)	6.00	15.00

1990 Comic Images Uncanny X-Men Covers Series I

COMPLETE SET (90)	12.00	30.00
UNOPENED BOX (48 PACKS)	200.00	300.00
UNOPENED PACK (5 CARDS)	4.00	6.00
COMMON CARD (1-90)	.25	.60
NNO Header	.40	1.00

1990 Comic Images Uncanny X-Men Covers Series II

COMPLETE SET (45)	8.00	20.00
UNOPENED BOX (36 PACKS)		
UNOPENED PACK (6 CARDS)		
COMMON CARD (1-45)	.30	.75
NNO Header Card	.40	1.00

1993 SkyBox Uncanny X-Men Series II

COMP.SET (100)	8.00	20.00
BOX (36 PACKS)	200.00	300.00
PACK (6 CARDS)	6.00	10.00
COM.CARD (1-100)	.15	.40

1993 SkyBox Uncanny X-Men Series II Gold Foil

COMPLETE SET (9)	10.00	25.00
COMMON CARD (G1-G9)	1.50	4.00
RANDOMLY INSERTED INTO PACKS		
G1 Cable	2.00	5.00
G8 Storm	2.00	5.00
G9 Wolverine	4.00	10.00

1993 SkyBox Uncanny X-Men Series II Holithograms

COMPLETE SET (3)	12.00	30.00
COMMON CARD	6.00	15.00
RANDOMLY INSERTED INTO PACKS		
HXa Wolverine 3-D (blue-green)	12.00	30.00
HXb Wolverine 3-D (orange)	15.00	40.00
HXc Wolverine 3-D (blue)	15.00	40.00

1993 SkyBox Uncanny X-Men Series II Promos

65a Juggernaut	.75	2.00
65b Juggernaut (Comic Book Collector)	1.25	3.00

1991 Comic Images X-Men

COMP.SET (90)	8.00	20.00
BOX (48 PACKS)	200.00	300.00
PACK (10 CARDS)	4.00	6.00
COM.CARD (1-90)	.20	.50
NNO Jim Lee AUTO	150.00	300.00

1997 Fleer SkyBox X-Men '97

COMP.SET (50)	4.00	10.00
BOX (48 PACKS)	125.00	200.00
PACK (8 CARDS)	3.00	4.00
COM.CARD (1-50)	.15	.40

1997 Fleer SkyBox X-Men 2099 Oasis

COMP.SET (90)	8.00	20.00
BOX (36 PACKS)	200.00	400.00
PACK (8 CARDS)	6.00	12.00
COM.CARD (1-90)	.15	.40
BT1 X-Men 2099 (BT)	2.00	5.00
NNO The Oasis Hildebrandt AU/500	20.00	50.00
NNO X-Men 2099 Promo	2.00	5.00

1997 Fleer SkyBox X-Men 2099 Oasis Chromium

COMPLETE SET (9)	12.00	30.00
COMMON CARD (1-9)	2.50	6.00
STATED ODDS 1:12		

2009 Rittenhouse X-Men Archives

COMPLETE SET (72)	5.00	12.00
UNOPENED BOX (24 PACKS)	100.00	150.00
UNOPENED PACK (5 CARDS)	4.00	5.00
UNOPENED ARCHIVE BOX	1200.00	2000.00
COMMON CARD (1-72)	.15	.40

2009 Rittenhouse X-Men Archives Case-Toppers

COMPLETE SET (3)	40.00	100.00
COMMON CARD (CT1-CT3)	15.00	40.00
STATED ODDS 1:CASE		

2009 Rittenhouse X-Men Archives Cover Gallery

COMPLETE SET (9)	8.00	20.00
COMMON CARD (CA1-CA9)	1.50	4.00
STATED ODDS 1:12		

2009 Rittenhouse X-Men Archives Legendary Heroes

COMPLETE SET (9)	20.00	50.00
COMMON CARD (LH1-LH9)	4.00	10.00
STATED ODDS 1:24		
LH10 ISSUED AS RITTENHOUSE REWARD		
LH10 Shadowcat SP RR	12.00	30.00

2009 Rittenhouse X-Men Archives Nemesis

COMPLETE SET (9)	6.00	15.00
COMMON CARD (N1-N9)	1.25	3.00
STATED ODDS 1:8		

2009 Rittenhouse X-Men Archives Promos

COMPLETE SET (5)	6.00	15.00
COMMON CARD	.75	2.00
P3 Album Exclusive	3.00	8.00
CP1 Emerald City Comic Con	1.50	4.00
CP2 Philly Non-Sport Show	3.00	8.00

2014 X-Men Blu-Ray Experience Collection

COMPLETE SET (13)	30.00	80.00
COMMON CARD (1-13))	2.00	5.00
SABRETOOTH IS CANADIAN EXCLUSIVE		
1 Beast	3.00	8.00
2 Cyclops	2.50	6.00
4 Magneto	6.00	12.00
5 Mystique	4.00	10.00
7 Professor X	6.00	12.00
8 Rogue	2.50	6.00
9 Sabretooth (Canadian excl.)	3.00	8.00
11 Storm	3.00	8.00
13 Wolverine	8.00	20.00

2019 X-Men Cards of X

COMPLETE SET (6)	2.50	6.00
COMMON CARD	.60	1.50

1997 Fleer SkyBox X-Men International

COMPLETE SET (100)	6.00	15.00
UNOPENED BOX (36 PACKS)	100.00	150.00
UNOPENED PACK (5 CARDS)	3.00	4.00
COMMON CARD (1-100)	.12	.30

2000 Topps X-Men Movie

COMPLETE SET (72)	5.00	12.00
UNOPENED HOBBY BOX (36 PACKS)	150.00	200.00
UNOPENED HOBBY PACK (8 CARDS)	5.00	6.00
UNOPENED RETAIL BOX (24 PACKS)		
UNOPENED RETAIL PACK (8 CARDS)		
COMMON CARD (1-72)	.15	.40

2000 Topps X-Men Movie Autographs

COMMON AUTO	10.00	25.00
STATED ODDS 1:36 HOBBY		
PAQUIN AND ROMIJN-STAMOS OFFERED AS#(DIA-MOND DISTRIBUTORS INCENTIVE		
PARK INSERTED WITH 2001 MARVEL LEGENDS		
NNO Anna Paquin (Diamond Distributors incentive) SP	200.00	500.00
NNO Bryan Singer	400.00	800.00
NNO Famke Janssen	150.00	400.00
NNO Halle Berry (unsigned) SP		
NNO Hugh Jackman	400.00	1000.00
NNO James Marsden	40.00	100.00
NNO Patrick Stewart	150.00	400.00
NNO Ray Park	40.00	100.00
NNO Rebecca Romijn-Stamos	125.00	300.00
NNO Sir Ian McKellen	250.00	600.00

2000 Topps X-Men Movie Chromium

COMPLETE SET (10)	12.50	30.00
COMMON CARD	1.50	4.00
RANDOMLY INSERTED INTO PACKS		

2000 Topps X-Men Movie Cling

COMPLETE SET (12)	10.00	25.00
COMMON CARD (CL1-CL12)	1.25	3.00
STATED ODDS 1:3 RETAIL		

2000 Topps X-Men Movie Memorabilia

COMPLETE SET (4)	25.00	60.00
COMMON CARD	6.00	15.00
STATED ODDS 1:36 HOBBY		
1 Famke Janssen	8.00	20.00
3 Hugh Jackman	10.00	25.00

2000 Topps X-Men Movie X-Foil

COMPLETE SET (10)	12.50	30.00
COMMON CARD (1-10)	1.50	4.00
STATED ODDS 1:6 RETAIL		

2000 Topps X-Men Movie Promos

COMPLETE SET (5)	4.00	10.00
COMMON CARD	1.25	3.00

2003 X2 X-Men United

COMPLETE SET (72)	5.00	12.00
UNOPENED HOBBY BOX (36 PACKS)	50.00	60.00
UNOPENED HOBBY PACK (7 CARDS)	1.50	2.00
UNOPENED RETAIL BOX (24 PACKS)		
UNOPENED RETAIL PACK (7 CARDS)		
COMMON CARD (1-72)	.15	.40
2 Wolverine	.40	1.00

2003 X2 X-Men United Autographs

COMMON AUTO	6.00	15.00
STATED ODDS 1:36 HOBBY		
NNO Aaron Stanford	20.00	50.00
NNO Alan Cumming	60.00	150.00
NNO Bryan Singer	300.00	500.00
NNO James Marsden	30.00	75.00
NNO Katie Stuart	15.00	40.00
NNO Kea Wong	12.00	30.00
NNO Michael Reid Mackay	10.00	25.00
NNO Shawn Ashmore	20.00	50.00

2003 X2 X-Men United Clear

COMPLETE SET (5)	6.00	15.00
COMMON CARD (C1-C5)	1.50	4.00
STATED ODDS 1:12 RETAIL		

2003 X2 X-Men United Foil

COMPLETE SET (10)	12.50	30.00
COMMON CARD (1-10)	1.50	4.00
STATED ODDS 1:6 RETAIL		

2003 X2 X-Men United Memorabilia

COMPLETE SET (3)	30.00	80.00
COMMON CARD (UNNUMBERED)	12.00	30.00
STATED ODDS 1:64 HOBBY		

2003 X2 X-Men United Promos

P1 Wolverine	.75	2.00
P2 Wolverine	.75	2.00
P3 Nightcrawler	.75	2.00

2006 X-Men The Last Stand

COMPLETE SET (72)	5.00	12.00
UNOPENED BOX (40 PACKS)	150.00	250.00
UNOPENED PACK (5 CARDS)	4.00	8.00
COMMON CARD (1-72)	.15	.40

2006 X-Men The Last Stand Art and Images of the X-Men

COMPLETE SET (9)	40.00	80.00
COMMON CARD (ART1-ART9)	4.00	10.00
STATED ODDS 1:20		
ART10 ISSUED AS A RITTENHOUSE REWARD		
ART10 Iceman RR	10.00	25.00

2006 X-Men The Last Stand Autographs

COMMON AUTO	6.00	15.00
STATED ODDS 1:40		
RATNER AUTO ISSUED AS CASE TOPPER		
AGHDASHLOO AU ISSUED AS ALBUM EXCLUSIVE		
LEE AU ISSUED AS 2-CASE INCENTIVE		
JACKMAN AU ISSUED AS 6-CASE INCENTIVE		
L (LIMITED): 300-500 COPIES		
VL (VERY LIMITED): 200-300 COPIES		
NNO Aaron Stanford	20.00	50.00
NNO Anna Paquin SP	100.00	200.00
NNO Bill Duke SP	8.00	20.00
NNO Brett Ratner CT	15.00	40.00
NNO Cayden Boyd	8.00	20.00
NNO Dania Ramirez	25.00	50.00
NNO Daniel Cudmore SP	10.00	25.00
NNO Haley Ramm	8.00	20.00
NNO Hugh Jackman 6CI	400.00	1000.00
NNO James Marsden SP	30.00	75.00
NNO Kelsey Grammer SP	150.00	400.00
NNO Michael Murphy	8.00	20.00
NNO Olivia Williams	10.00	25.00
NNO Patrick Stewart SP	300.00	750.00
NNO Shawn Ashmore	15.00	40.00
NNO Shohreh Aghdashloo ALB	10.00	25.00
NNO Stan Lee 2CI	300.00	750.00
NNO Vinnie Jones SP	30.00	75.00

2006 X-Men The Last Stand Casting Call

COMPLETE SET (16)	20.00	40.00
COMMON CARD (CC1-CC16)	1.50	4.00
STATED ODDS 1:20		
CARD CC3 WAS NOT ISSUED		

2006 X-Men The Last Stand Take a Stand

COMPLETE SET (6)	25.00	50.00
COMMON CARD (MP1-MP6)	4.00	10.00
STATED ODDS 1:80		

2006 X-Men The Last Stand Wolverine Portraits of a Hero

COMPLETE SET (9)	8.00	20.00
COMMON CARD (W1-W9)	1.00	2.50
STATED ODDS 1:13		

2009 Rittenhouse X-Men Origins Wolverine

COMPLETE SET (72)	6.00	15.00
UNOPENED BOX (24 PACKS)	150.00	250.00
UNOPENED PACK (5 CARDS)	6.00	10.00
COMMON CARD (1-72)	.15	.40
MOVIE POSTER CARD INSERTED ONE PER CASE		
MOVIE POSTER CARD SER. #'d TO 600		
NNO Movie Poster/600	10.00	25.00

2009 Rittenhouse X-Men Origins Wolverine Archives

COMPLETE SET (9)	4.00	10.00
COMMON CARD (A1-A9)	.75	2.00
STATED ODDS 1:8		

2009 Rittenhouse X-Men Origins Wolverine Autographs

COMMON AUTO	6.00	15.00
STATED AUTO/SKETCH ODDS 1:12		
will.i.am AUTO 2-CASE INCENTIVE		
NNO Hugh Jackman	400.00	1000.00
NNO Hugh Jackman	500.00	1200.00
NNO Kevin Durand	8.00	20.00
NNO Liev Schreiber	60.00	150.00
NNO Lynn Collins	75.00	200.00
NNO Ryan Reynolds	600.00	1500.00
NNO Taylor Kitsch	60.00	150.00
NNO Troye Sivan	12.00	30.00
NNO will.i.am 2CI	60.00	150.00

2009 Rittenhouse X-Men Origins Wolverine Casting Call

COMPLETE SET (9)	4.00	10.00
COMMON CARD (C1-C9)	.75	2.00
STATED ODDS 1:8		
C1 Wolverine	1.25	3.00
C2 Ryan Reynolds as Wade Wilson	1.25	3.00
C5 Gambit	1.25	3.00

2009 Rittenhouse X-Men Origins Wolverine Classic Confrontations

COMPLETE SET (6)	5.00	12.00
COMMON CARD (G1-G6)	1.25	3.00
STATED ODDS 1:12		

2009 Rittenhouse X-Men Origins Wolverine Promos

COMPLETE SET (3)	5.00	12.00
COMMON CARD	.75	2.00
P3 Remy LeBeau ALB	3.00	8.00
CP1 Spring 2009 Philly Show Exclusive	3.00	8.00

2009 X-Men Origins Wolverine London Expo Promos

COMPLETE SET (8)	60.00	120.00
COMMON CARD	4.00	10.00
NNO Gambit	10.00	25.00
NNO Sabretooth	6.00	15.00
NNO Wade Wilson	10.00	25.00
NNO Wolverine	15.00	40.00

2014 X-Men Days of Future Past Carl's Jr. Promos

COMPLETE SET (9)	8.00	12.00
COMMON CARD (1-9)	.75	2.00
KID'S MEAL EXCLUSIVE		
6 Mystique	2.00	5.00

2014 X-Men Days of Future Past Wyndham Rewards Hotel Key Cards

COMPLETE SET (6)	8.00	20.00
COMMON CARD	1.50	4.00
NNO Mystique	3.00	8.00
NNO Quicksilver	2.50	6.00
NNO Wolverine	4.00	10.00

1996 Team Metal X-Men

COMPLETE SET (4)	6.00	15.00
COMMON CARD (1-4)		5.00
4 Wolverine	4.00	10.00

1997 Fleer SkyBox X-Men Timelines

COMPLETE SET (82)	8.00	20.00
UNOPENED BOX (24 PACKS)	200.00	350.00
UNOPENED PACK (8 CARDS)	10.00	15.00
COMMON CARD (1-82)	.20	.50

1997 Fleer SkyBox X-Men Timelines Deadpool Party

COMPLETE SET (9)	10.00	25.00
COMMON CARD (1-9)	1.50	4.00
STATED ODDS 1:5		
1 Deadpool	4.00	10.00
4 Hulk	2.50	6.00

1997 Fleer SkyBox X-Men Timelines New Recruits

COMPLETE SET (8)	6.00	15.00
COMMON CARD (1-8)	1.25	3.00
STATED ODDS 1:3		

1997 Fleer SkyBox X-Men Timelines Wanted Posters

COMMON CARD (1-4)	4.00	10.00
STATED ODDS 1:12		
1 Logan	8.00	20.00
2 Charles Xavier SP	100.00	200.00

1994 Fleer Ultra X-Men

COMPLETE SET (150)	25.00	60.00
UNOPENED HOBBY BOX (36 PACKS)	250.00	400.00
UNOPENED HOBBY PACK (10 CARDS)	8.00	12.00
UNOPENED JUMBO BOX (36 PACKS)	500.00	750.00
UNOPENED JUMBO PACK (14 CARDS)	15.00	20.00
UNOPENED WALMART BOX (20 PACKS)	400.00	600.00
UNOPENED WALMART PACK (12 CARDS)	20.00	30.00
COMMON CARD (1-150)	.15	.40
4 Gambit	1.00	2.50
6 Wolverine	1.25	3.00
43 Weapon X (Wolverine)	1.25	3.00
57 Deadpool	1.00	2.50
98B Iceman (NNO)	.75	2.00
137 Wolverine vs. Sabretooth	.60	1.50
138 Wolverine vs. Cyber	.60	1.50
139 Wolverine vs. Omega Red	.75	2.00
140 Wolverine vs. Hulk	.75	2.00
141 Wolverine vs. The Thing	.60	1.50
142 Wolverine vs. Spider-Man	1.50	4.00
143 Wolverine vs. Silver Samurai	.60	1.50
144 Wolverine vs. Hellfire Club	.60	1.50
145 Wolverine vs. Cable	.60	1.50
146 Wolverine vs. Sauron	.60	1.50
147 Wolverine vs. Punisher	1.25	3.00
148 Wolverine vs. Lord Shingen	.60	1.50
149 Wolverine vs. Lady Deathstrike	.60	1.50

1994 Fleer Ultra X-Men Fatal Attractions

COMPLETE SET (6)	8.00	20.00
COMMON CARD (1-6)	2.00	5.00
STATED ODDS 1:7		
JUMBO PACK AND HOBBY EXCLUSIVE		
6B Exit: Wolverine!	10.00	25.00
(ERR - Behold Avalon! Foil Stamp)		

1994 Fleer Ultra X-Men Greatest Battles

COMPLETE SET (6)	6.00	15.00
COMMON CARD (1-6)	.75	2.00
STATED ODDS 1:3		
JUMBO PACK EXCLUSIVE		
3 Gambit vs. Mystique	2.50	6.00
4 Wolverine vs. Sentinels	5.00	12.00
6 Gambit vs. Bishop	2.50	6.00

1994 Fleer Ultra X-Men Promos

COMMON CARD	2.00	5.00

1994 Fleer Ultra X-Men Sega Game Gear

COMPLETE SET (5)	6.00	15.00
COMMON CARD (1-5)	1.00	2.50
STORM ISSUED AS VIDEO GAME EXCLUSIVE		
6 Storm Video Game Excl.	2.00	5.00

1994 Fleer Ultra X-Men Silver X-Over

COMPLETE SET (6)	150.00	300.00
COMMON CARD (1-6)	30.00	75.00
STATED ODDS 1:12 OR 1:11		
INSERTED IN BOTH 12-CARD AND 11-CARD PACKS		
WAL-MART EXCLUSIVE		
6 Fatal Attractions	50.00	100.00

1994 Fleer Ultra X-Men Team Portraits

COMPLETE SET (9)	6.00	15.00
COMMON CARD (1-9)	1.25	3.00
STATED ODDS 1:5		
WAL-MART AND HOBBY EXCLUSIVE		
1 Storm	1.50	4.00
5 Wolverine	2.50	6.00
8 Gambit, Bishop	2.00	5.00

1994 Fleer Ultra X-Men Team Triptych

COMPLETE SET (6)	8.00	20.00
COMMON CARD (1-6)	2.50	6.00
STATED ODDS 1:1		
WAL-MART EXCLUSIVE		

1994 Fleer Ultra X-Men Ultraprints

COMPLETE SET (5)	12.00	30.00
COMMON CARD (UNNUMBERED)	3.00	8.00
STATED ODDS 1:CASE		

1995 Fleer Ultra X-Men

COMPLETE SET (150)	10.00	25.00
UNOPENED BOX (36 PACKS)	300.00	500.00
UNOPENED PACK (10 CARDS)	8.00	15.00
UNOPENED JUMBO BOX (36 PACKS)	350.00	600.00
UNOPENED JUMBO PACK (14 CARDS)	10.00	20.00
UNOPENED WALMART BOX (20 PACKS)	300.00	500.00
UNOPENED WALMART PACK (11 CARDS)	12.00	15.00
COMMON CARD (1-150)	.10	.25
NO.39 AND NO.61 HAVE VARIANTS		
2 Apocalypse	.30	.75
14 Cyclops	.40	1.00
20 Gambit	.75	2.00
25 Jean Grey	.50	1.25
28 Magneto	.75	2.00
32 Mr. Sinister	.40	1.00
33 Mystique	.50	1.25
38 Psylocke	.50	1.25
39A Redd & Slym (flying)	1.25	3.00
40 Rogue	.40	1.00
41 Sabretooth	.50	1.25
47 Storm	.75	2.00
52 Wolverine	1.50	4.00
61B Sauron (facing right)	2.00	5.00
63 Sabretooth	.50	1.25
89 Beast	.60	1.50
90 Cyclops	.40	1.00
91 Iceman	.40	1.00
93 Professor X	.60	1.50
94 Beast	.60	1.50
95 Cyclops	.40	1.00
96 Gambit	.75	2.00
97 Psylocke	.50	1.25
98 Rogue	.40	1.00
99 Wolverine	1.50	4.00
102 Jean Grey	.50	1.25
104 Storm	.75	2.00
105 Professor X	.60	1.50
113 Cable	1.25	3.00
127 Cable vs Deadpool	2.00	5.00
129 Cable vs Wolverine	2.00	5.00
130 Cyber vs Wolverine	1.25	3.00
133 Magneto vs Professor X	1.50	4.00
134 Magneto vs Wolverine	2.00	5.00
135 Omega Red vs Wolverine	1.25	3.00
139 Sabretooth vs Wolverine	1.50	4.00
140 Sauron vs Wolverine	.10	3.00
146 Rogue	.40	1.00
148 Storm	.75	2.00
149 Wolverine	1.50	4.00

1995 Fleer Ultra X-Men Hunters and Stalkers Rainbow

COMPLETE SET (9)	8.00	20.00
COMMON CARD (1-9)	.60	1.50
*GOLD: SAME VALUE AS RAINBOW		
*SILVER: .6X TO 1.5X BASIC CARDS		
RANDOMLY INSERTED IN HOBBY PACKS		
1 Apocalypse	1.50	4.00
3 Deadpool	3.00	8.00
5 Bishop	1.50	4.00
6 Sabretooth	1.25	3.00
7 Wolverine	3.00	8.00
8 Magneto	1.25	3.00

1995 Fleer Ultra X-Men Oversized Ultra-Prints

COMPLETE SET (10)	15.00	40.00
COMMON CARD (UNNUMBERED)	2.00	5.00
STATED ODDS 1 SET PER CASE		
NNO Bishop	2.50	6.00
NNO Cable	4.00	10.00
NNO Cyclops	3.00	8.00
NNO Gambit	4.00	10.00
NNO Jean Grey	2.50	6.00
NNO Wolverine	6.00	15.00

1995 Fleer Ultra X-Men Sinister Observations

COMPLETE SET (10)	25.00	60.00
COMMON CARD 1-10	2.50	6.00
RANDOMLY INSERTED INTO PACKS		
1 Archangel	3.00	8.00
4 Gambit	4.00	10.00
6 Jean Grey	4.00	10.00
7 Psylocke	4.00	10.00
8 Rogue	4.00	10.00
9 Storm	5.00	12.00
10 Wolverine	6.00	15.00

1995 Fleer Ultra X-Men Suspended Animation

COMPLETE SET (10)	10.00	25.00
COMMON CARD (1-10)	1.25	3.00
*TOY BIZ: .75X TO 2X BASIC CARDS		
RANDOMLY INSERTED INTO PACKS		
2 Cyclops	1.50	4.00
3 Gambit	2.00	5.00
4 Jean Grey	1.50	4.00
6 Magneto	1.50	4.00
8 Professor X	1.50	4.00
9 Storm	2.00	5.00
10 Wolverine	3.00	8.00

1995 Fleer Ultra X-Men All-Chromium

COMP.SET (100)	12.00	30.00
HOBBY BOX (36 PACKS)	300.00	500.00
HOBBY PACK (8 CARDS)	10.00	15.00
RETAIL BOX (20 PACKS)		
RETAIL PACK (8 CARDS)		
JUMBO BOX (36 PACKS)	300.00	600.00
JUMBO PACK (10 CARDS)	10.00	15.00
COM.CARD (1-100)	.20	.50
*GOLD SIG.: .75 TO 2X		
2 Beast	.40	1.00
5 Cyclops	.50	1.25
6 Gambit	.75	2.00
12 Storm	.60	1.50
13 Wolverine	1.25	3.00
16 Mystique	.50	1.25
21 Cable	.75	2.00
51 Deadpool	1.25	3.00
55 Magneto	.75	2.00
59 Apocalypse	.40	1.00
71 Mr. Sinister	.40	1.00
80 Logan	.60	1.50
92 Cyclops as The King	.30	.75
93 Gambit as The Cajun Cowboy	.40	1.00
99 Wolverine as Captain Claw	.40	1.00

1995 Fleer Ultra X-Men All-Chromium Alternate X

COMPLETE SET (20)	15.00	40.00
COMMON CARD (1-20)	1.25	3.00
STATED ODDS 1:2		
3 Bishop	2.00	5.00
4 Bishop	2.00	5.00
7 Cyclops	1.50	4.00
8 Cyclops	1.50	4.00
17 Storm	1.50	4.00
18 Storm	1.50	4.00
19 Wolverine	4.00	10.00

1995 Fleer Ultra X-Men All-Chromium Lethal Weapons Holo-Flash

COMPLETE SET (9)	15.00	40.00
COMMON CARD (1-9)	2.00	5.00
STATED ODDS 1:6		
2 Bishop	3.00	8.00
3 Cable	3.00	8.00
5 Gambit	4.00	10.00
9 Wolverine	8.00	20.00

1995 Fleer Ultra X-Men All-Chromium Promos

P1 Cyclops Wizard #51	1.25	3.00
P2 Wolverine Dealer Excl.	2.00	5.00
P3 3UP Promo	1.25	3.00

1996 Fleer Ultra X-Men Wolverine

COMPLETE SET (100)	12.00	30.00
UNOPENED BOX (36 PACKS)	500.00	750.00
UNOPENED PACK (8 CARDS)	15.00	20.00
COMMON CARD (1-100)	.30	.75
5 Wolverine vs. Shiva	.75	2.00
7 Deadpool	.75	2.00
10 Wolverine	.75	2.00
14 Wolverine vs. Hulk	1.25	3.00
18 Wolverine & Weapon Alpha	.75	2.00
19 Wolverine	.75	2.00
23 Wolverine vs. Krakoa	.75	2.00
27 Wolverine & Colossus	.75	2.00
28 Wolverine	.75	2.00
32 Wolverine vs. Lord Shingen	.75	2.00
36 Wolverine & Shadowcat	.75	2.00
37 Wolverine	.75	2.00
41 Wolverine vs. Thing	.75	2.00
43 Punisher	.60	1.50
45 Wolverine & Spider-Man	1.25	3.00
46 Wolverine	.75	2.00
50 Wolverine vs. Cyber	.75	2.00
54 Wolverine & Hulk	1.25	3.00
59 Wolverine vs. Spiral	.75	2.00
63 Wolverine & Longshot	.75	2.00
64 Wolverine	.75	2.00
68 Wolverine vs. Sabretooth	.75	2.00
72 Wolverine & Typhoid Mary	.75	2.00
73 Wolverine	.75	2.00
75 Gambit	.75	2.00
77 Wolverine vs. Magneto	.75	2.00
81 Wolverine & Jubilee	.75	2.00
91 Wolverine	.75	2.00
95 Wolverine vs. Genesis	.75	2.00

1996 Fleer Ultra X-Men Wolverine Holo-Flash

COMPLETE SET (9)	12.00	30.00
COMMON CARD (1-9)	2.00	5.00
RANDOMLY INSERTED INTO PACKS		
2 Gambit	3.00	8.00
4 Wolverine	4.00	10.00

1996 Fleer Ultra X-Men Wolverine Mirage

COMPLETE SET (3)	25.00	60.00
COMMON CARD (1-3)	10.00	25.00
RANDOMLY INSERTED INTO PACKS		

1996 Fleer Ultra X-Men Wolverine Promos

P1 Wolverine Bone Claws Dealer Excl.	.75	2.00
NNO1 4UP Panel (19-37-73-82) 5X7	1.25	3.00

1992 SkyBox X-Men X-Cutioner's Song

COMPLETE SET (12)	3.00	8.00
COMMON CARD (1-12)	.50	1.25

1991 Comic Images Wolverine From Then 'Til Now

COMPLETE SET (45)	4.00	10.00
UNOPENED BOX (50 PACKS)	30.00	40.00
UNOPENED PACK (5 CARDS)	.75	1.00
COMMONS (1-45)	.15	.40

1992 Comic Images Wolverine From Then 'Til Now II

COMPLETE SET (90)	5.00	12.00
UNOPENED BOX (48 PACKS)	30.00	40.00
UNOPENED PACK (10 CARDS)	.75	1.00
COMMON CARD (1-90)	.15	.40
NNO Wolverine Promo (prism)	1.25	3.00
NNO Wolverine Promo (non-prism)	.75	2.00
NNO Prisms Set (6-card panel)		

1992 Comic Images Wolverine From Then 'Til Now II Prisms

COMPLETE SET (6)	12.00	30.00
COMMON CARD (P1-P6)	3.00	8.00
STATED ODDS 1:16		

1990 Comic Images Wolverine Untamed Stickers

COMPLETE SET (76)	8.00	20.00
COMMON CARD	.20	.50
NNO1 Wolverine Untamed Header Card	1.00	2.50

2008 Women of Marvel

COMPLETE SET (81)	20.00	50.00
UNOPENED BOX (24 PACKS)	200.00	300.00
UNOPENED PACK (5 CARDS)	8.00	12.00
COMMON CARD (1-81)	.50	1.25
HUGHES AU ISSUED AS CASE TOPPER		
5 Black Cat	1.50	4.00
6 Black Widow	2.50	6.00
9 Callisto	.75	2.00
11 Dark Phoenix	1.25	3.00
12 Dazzler	.75	2.00
14 Domino	1.25	3.00
16 Elektra	1.00	2.50
17 Emma Frost	1.25	3.00
20 Hawkeye (Kate Bishop)	1.00	2.50
25 Invisible Woman	.75	2.00
26 Jean Grey	1.00	2.50
37 Magik	1.25	3.00
40 Marvel Girl	.75	2.00
41 Mary Jane Watson-Parker	1.25	3.00
44 Mystique	1.50	4.00
51 Psylocke	1.25	3.00
53 Rogue	1.00	2.50
55 Scarlet Witch	2.00	5.00
65 Spider Woman	1.00	2.50
66 Spider-Girl	1.25	3.00
69 Storm 1	1.50	4.00
76 Ultron	.75	2.00
81 X-23	2.00	5.00
NNO Adam Hughes AU CT	15.00	40.00

2008 Women of Marvel Embossed

COMPLETE SET W/O SP (9)	12.00	30.00
COMMON CARD (T1-T9)	2.00	5.00
STATED ODDS 1:12		
T10 ISSUED AS RITTENHOUSE REWARDS		
T2 Black Widow	2.50	6.00
T4 Ms. Marvel	4.00	10.00
T5 Mystique	3.00	8.00
T6 Rogue	4.00	10.00
T8 She-Hulk	3.00	8.00
T9 Spider Woman	2.50	6.00
T10 Ms. Marvel/Spider-Woman SP RR	12.00	30.00

2008 Women of Marvel Embrace

COMPLETE SET (9)	50.00	100.00
COMMON CARD (E1-E9)	4.00	10.00
STATED ODDS 1:24		
E2 Captain America and Scarlet Witch	10.00	25.00
E3 Colossus and Shadowcat	8.00	20.00
E4 Daredevil and Elektra	6.00	15.00
E5 Cyclops and Emma Frost	6.00	15.00
E6 Phoenix and Wolverine	12.00	30.00
E7 Mr. Fantastic and Invisible Woman	8.00	20.00
E8 Wolverine and Rogue	10.00	25.00

2008 Women of Marvel Swimsuit

COMPLETE SET (18)	50.00	100.00
COMMON CARD (S1-S18)	2.00	5.00
STATED ODDS 1:6		
S2 Black Widow	4.00	10.00
S3 Domino and Val Cooper	3.00	8.00
S5 Emma Frost	2.50	6.00
S6 Jean Grey	6.00	15.00
S7 Mary Jane Watson-Parker	5.00	12.00
S10 Polaris	3.00	8.00
S11 Psylocke	6.00	15.00
S12 Rogue	5.00	12.00
S14 She Hulk	4.00	10.00
S17 Storm	2.50	6.00

2008 Women of Marvel Promos

P3 Ms. Marvel ALB	4.00	10.00
CP1 Black Widow WonderCon	6.00	15.00

2013 Women of Marvel Series Two

COMPLETE SET (90)	50.00	120.00
UNOPENED BOX (24 PACKS)	150.00	300.00
UNOPENED PACK (5 CARDS)	6.00	12.00
COMMON CARD (1-90)	1.25	3.00
*SAPPHIRE: 2.5X TO 6X BASIC CARDS		
*EMERALD/100: 4X TO 10X BASIC CARDS		
*RUBY/50: 10X TO 25X BASIC CARDS		

2013 Women of Marvel Series Two ArtiFEX

COMPLETE SET (9)	8.00	20.00
COMMON CARD (01-09)	2.00	5.00
STATED ODDS 1:12		

2013 Women of Marvel Series Two ArtiFEX Rhiannon Owens Autographs

COMMON CARD	12.00	30.00
STATED ODDS 1:CASE		

2013 Women of Marvel Series Two Embrace

COMPLETE SET (18)	12.00	30.00
COMMON CARD (E20-E37)	1.50	4.00
STATED ODDS 1:8		

2013 Women of Marvel Series Two Framed

COMPLETE SET (9)	12.00	30.00
COMMON CARD (F1-F9)	2.50	6.00
STATED ODDS 1:24		

2013 Women of Marvel Series Two Jean Grey Case-Toppers

COMPLETE SET (3)	30.00	70.00
COMMON CARD (CT1-CT3)	12.00	30.00
STATED ODDS 1:CASE		

2013 Women of Marvel Series Two Ultimate Heroes

COMPLETE SET (9)	12.00	30.00
COMMON CARD (UH20-UH28)	2.50	6.00
STATED ODDS 1:24		
UH29 ISSUED AS RITTENHOUSE REWARD		
UH29 Psylocke RR	15.00	40.00

2013 Women of Marvel Series Two Promos

P1 Black Cat plus 2 GEN	1.25	3.00
P2 Storm plus 5 NSU	2.00	5.00
P3 Psylocke plus 2 PHILLY	3.00	8.00
P4 Invisible Woman plus 2 SDCC	2.00	5.00
P5 Emma Frost plus 6 ALB	3.00	8.00

1991 Comic Images X-Force

COMPLETE SET (90)	15.00	40.00
UNOPENED BOX (48 PACKS)	100.00	150.00
UNOPENED PACK (10 CARDS)	2.50	4.00
COMMON CARD (1-90)	.25	.60
60 Deadpool	8.00	20.00
NNO Rob Liefield AU/1000		100.00

1991 Impel X-Force Comic Book Promos

COMMON CARD (1-5)		
1 Cable	2.50	6.00
2 Shatterstar	2.50	6.00
3 Deadpool	15.00	40.00
4 Sunspot and Gideon	3.00	8.00
5 X-Force	2.00	5.00

1995 Ziploc Marvel Team-Ups

COMPLETE SET (3)	4.00	10.00
1 Hulk and The Thing	1.25	3.00
2 Captain America and Iron Man	2.00	5.00
3 Spider-Man and Wolverine	3.00	8.00

Garbage Pail Kids

Vintage GPK

1985 Topps Garbage Pail Kids

COMPLETE SERIES 1 SET (82)	1200.00	2500.00
COMPLETE SERIES 2 SET (84)	250.00	600.00
UNOPENED SER.1 BOX (48 PACKS)	12000.00	20000.00
UNOPENED SER.1 PACK (5 CARDS)	300.00	400.00
UNOPENED SER.2 BOX (48 PACKS)	2500.00	4000.00
UNOPENED SER.2 PACK (5 CARDS)	75.00	100.00
COMMON CARD (1a-41b)	3.00	8.00
COMMON CARD (42a-83b)	1.25	3.00
1a Nasty Nick	150.00	400.00
1b Evil Eddie	60.00	150.00
2a Junkfood John	8.00	20.00
2b Ray Decay	6.00	15.00
3a Up Chuck	6.00	15.00
3b Heavin' Steven	6.00	15.00
4a Fryin' Brian	10.00	25.00
4b Electric Bill	8.00	20.00
5a Dead Ted (Stupid Student)	12.00	30.00
5a Dead Ted (checklist)	12.00	30.00
5b Jay Decay (Stupid Student)	8.00	20.00
5b Jay Decay (checklist)	12.00	30.00
6a Art Apart	5.00	12.00
6b Busted Bob	5.00	12.00
7a Stormy Heather	5.00	12.00
7b April Showers	4.00	10.00
8a Adam Bomb (Cheater's License)	100.00	250.00
8a Adam Bomb (checklist)	125.00	300.00
8b Blasted Billy (Cheater's License)	75.00	150.00
8b Blasted Billy (checklist)	50.00	100.00
9a Boozin' Bruce	6.00	15.00
9b Drunk Ken	6.00	15.00
10a Tee-Vee Stevie	6.00	15.00
10b Geeky Gary	5.00	12.00
11a Itchy Ritchie	5.00	12.00
11b Bugged Bert	5.00	12.00
12a Furry Fran	8.00	20.00
12b Hairy Mary	4.00	10.00
13a Ashcan Andy	8.00	20.00
13b Spacey Stacy	5.00	12.00
14a Potty Scotty	6.00	15.00
14b Jason Basin	8.00	20.00
15a Ailin' Al	5.00	12.00
15b Mauled Paul	5.00	12.00
16a Weird Wendy	8.00	20.00
16b Haggy Maggie	6.00	15.00
17a Wacky Jackie	4.00	10.00
18a Cranky Frankie	5.00	12.00
18b Bad Brad	6.00	15.00
19a Corroded Carl	5.00	10.00
19b Crater Chris	5.00	10.00
20a Swell Mel	5.00	10.00
20b Dressy Jesse	4.00	10.00
21a Virus Iris	5.00	12.00
22a Junky Jeff	5.00	12.00
22b Stinky Stan	5.00	12.00
23a Drippy Dan	6.00	15.00
23b Leaky Lou	4.00	10.00
24a Nervous Rex	6.00	15.00
24b Nerdy Norm	6.00	15.00
25b Scary Carrie	4.00	10.00
26a Slobby Robbie	5.00	12.00
26b Fat Matt	6.00	15.00
27a Brainy Janie	5.00	12.00
27b Jenny Genius	5.00	12.00
28a Oozy Suzy	5.00	12.00
28b Meltin' Melissa	5.00	12.00
29a Bony Joanie (Reform School)	8.00	20.00
29a Bony Joanie (checklist)	6.00	15.00
29b Thin Lynn (Reform School)	5.00	12.00
29b Thin Lynn (checklist)	8.00	20.00
30a New Wave Dave	25.00	60.00
30b Graffiti Petey	20.00	50.00
31a Run Down Rhoda	5.00	12.00
31b Flat Pat	6.00	15.00
32a Frigid Bridget	8.00	20.00
32b Chilly Millie	5.00	12.00
33a Mad Mike	6.00	15.00
33b Savage Stuart	5.00	12.00
34a Kim Kong	6.00	15.00
34b Anna Banana	6.00	15.00
35a Wrinkly Randy	4.00	10.00
35b Rockin' Robert	5.00	12.00
36a Wrappin' Ruth	5.00	12.00
36b Tommy Tomb	5.00	12.00
37a Guillo Tina	4.00	10.00
37b Cindy Lopper	4.00	10.00
38a Slimy Sam	5.00	12.00
38b Lizard Liz	6.00	15.00
39a Buggy Betty	6.00	15.00
39b Green Jean	5.00	12.00
40a Unstitched Mitch	4.00	10.00
41a Mean Gene	10.00	25.00
41b Joltin' Joe	6.00	15.00
42a Patty Putty	2.50	6.00
42b Muggin' Megan	2.00	5.00
43a Smelly Kelly	2.50	6.00
43b Doug Plug	1.50	4.00
44b One-Eyed Jack	2.50	6.00
45a Leaky Lindsay	2.00	5.00
45b Messy Tessie	1.50	4.00
46a Rappin' Ron	6.00	15.00
46b Ray Gun	5.00	12.00
47a Disgustin' Justin	5.00	12.00
47b Vile Kyle	4.00	10.00
48a Tongue Tied Tim	2.50	6.00
49a Double Heather	2.50	6.00
49b Fran Fran	6.00	15.00
49b Schizo Fran	15.00	40.00
50a Mad Donna	1.50	4.00
51b Brett Sweat	1.50	4.00
52a Dirty Harry	1.50	4.00
53a Jolted Joel	4.00	10.00
53b Live Mike	12.00	30.00
54a Fryin' Ryan	3.00	8.00
54b Charred Chad	1.50	4.00
55b Brutal Brad	2.50	6.00
56a Hairy Carrie	1.50	4.00
57a Tommy Gun	2.50	6.00
57b Dead Fred	2.50	6.00
58a Cracked Jack	1.50	4.00
60a Prickly Rick	2.00	5.00
60b Cactus Carol	1.50	4.00
61a Jolly Roger	2.50	6.00
61b Pegleg Peter	2.00	5.00
62a Greaser Greg	4.00	10.00
62b Chris Hiss	5.00	12.00
63a Spacey Stacy	5.00	12.00
63b Janet Planet	3.00	8.00
64a Hot Scott	1.50	4.00
64b Luke Warm	1.50	4.00
66b Rachel Rodent	1.50	4.00
67a Phony Lisa	2.00	5.00
67b Mona Loser	1.50	4.00
68a Oliver Twisted	1.50	4.00
69a Jenny Jelly	1.50	4.00
70a Bad Breath Seth	3.00	8.00
70b Foul Phil	2.00	5.00
71a Odd Todd	2.00	5.00
72b Brainy Brian	2.00	5.00
73a Gorgeous George	2.00	5.00
73b Dollar Bill	3.00	8.00
74a Mark Bark	1.50	4.00
75a Off-The-Wall Paul	4.00	10.00
75b Zach Plaque	1.50	4.00
76a Bonnie Bunnie	1.25	3.00
76b Pourin' Lauren	2.00	5.00
77b Acne Amy	2.50	6.00
78a Wrinkled Rita	1.50	4.00
78b Ancient Annie	1.50	4.00
79a Sewer Sue	2.50	6.00
79b Michelle Muck	2.50	6.00
80a Tattoo Lou	2.00	5.00
80b Art Gallery	1.50	4.00
81b Mixed-Up Mitch	1.50	4.00
82a Slain Wayne	2.00	5.00
82b Ventilated Vinnie	2.00	5.00
83a Ugh Lee	2.50	6.00
83b Sumo Sid	2.50	6.00

1986 Topps Garbage Pail Kids

COMPLETE SERIES 3 SET (82)	60.00	150.00
COMPLETE SERIES 4 SET (84)	50.00	125.00
COMPLETE SERIES 5 SET (80)	40.00	100.00
COMPLETE SERIES 6 SET (88)	50.00	125.00
UNOPENED SER.3 BOX (48 PACKS)	400.00	600.00
UNOPENED SER.3 PACK (5 CARDS)	8.00	12.00
UNOPENED SER.4 BOX (48 PACKS)	200.00	400.00
UNOPENED SER.4 PACK (5 CARDS)	4.00	8.00
UNOPENED SER.5 BOX (48 PACKS)	200.00	400.00
UNOPENED SER.5 PACK (5 CARDS)	4.00	8.00
UNOPENED SER.6 BOX (48 PACKS)	200.00	300.00
UNOPENED SER.6 PACK (5 CARDS)	4.00	6.00
COMMON SERIES 3 CARD (84a-124b)	.75	2.00
COMMON SERIES 4 CARD (125a-166b)	.75	2.00
COMMON SERIES 5 CARD (167a-206b)	.60	1.50
COMMON SERIES 6 CARD (207a-250b)	.60	1.50
84a Joe Blow	1.50	4.00
85a Stuck Chuck	1.50	4.00
85b Pinned Lynn	1.00	2.50
86a Horsey Henry	1.25	3.00
86b Galloping Glen	1.25	3.00

87a Hot Head Harvey	4.00	10.00
87b Roy Bot	2.50	6.00
88a Dinah Saur	2.00	5.00
88b Farrah Fossil	1.25	3.00
89a Hurt Curt	1.25	3.00
90a Stoned Sean	1.25	3.00
90b Thick Vic	1.00	2.50
91b Hippie Skippy	1.50	4.00
92a Marvin Gardens	1.25	3.00
92b Spittin' Spencer	1.50	4.00
93a Drew Blood	1.25	3.00
93b Bustin' Dustin	.75	2.00
94a Bruised Lee	1.50	4.00
94b Karate Kate	1.25	3.00
95a Grim Jim	1.25	3.00
95b Beth Death	1.00	2.50
96a Distorted Dot	1.00	2.50
96b Mirror Imogene	1.00	2.50
97a Punchy Perry	1.25	3.00
97b Creamed Keith	1.25	3.00
98a Charlotte Web	1.00	2.50
99a Beaky Becky	1.00	2.50
99b Picky Mickey	1.00	2.50
100a Ali Gator	2.00	5.00
100b Marshy Marshall	1.25	3.00
101a Mushy Marsha	1.00	2.50
101b Basking Robin	1.00	2.50
102a Mugged Marcus	1.00	2.50
102b Kayo'd Cody	1.25	3.00
103b Curly Carla	1.50	4.00
104a Silent Sandy	1.00	2.50
104b Barren Aaron	1.25	3.00
105a Juicy Jessica	1.25	3.00
105b Green Dean	2.00	5.00
106b Mack Quack	1.00	2.50
107a Totem Paula	1.25	3.00
107b Tatum Pole	1.00	2.50
108a Smelly Sally	1.25	3.00
108b Fishy Phyllis	1.00	2.50
109b Croakin' Colin	1.00	2.50
110a Snooty Sam	1.50	4.00
110b U.S. Arnie	1.50	4.00
111a Target Margaret	1.25	3.00
111b Bullseye Barry	2.00	5.00
112a Frank N. Stein	1.00	2.50
112b Undead Jed	1.50	4.00
113a Alice Island	1.25	3.00
114a Starin' Darren	2.50	6.00
114b Peepin' Tom	1.50	4.00
115a Warmin' Norman	1.25	3.00
115b Well Done Sheldon	1.00	2.50
116a Eerie Eric	1.25	3.00
116b Berserk Kirk	1.50	4.00
117a Rocky N. Roll	1.25	3.00
117b Les Vegas	1.25	3.00
119b Still Jill	1.50	4.00
120a Babbling Brooke	1.00	2.50
120b Jelly Kelly	1.25	3.00
121a Apple Cory	1.00	2.50
122b Large Marge	1.00	2.50
123a Glooey Gabe	1.25	3.00
123b Sticky Rick	1.00	2.50
124a Hugh Mungous	1.00	2.50
124b King-Size Kevin	2.50	6.00
125a Holly Wood	2.00	5.00
125b Woody Alan (1st Print Run)	1.50	4.00
125b Oak Kay (2nd Print Run)	4.00	10.00
126a Armpit Britt	1.25	3.00
126b Shaggy Aggie	1.25	3.00
127a Travellin' Travis	1.00	2.50
127b Flat Tyler	1.25	3.00
128a Sloshed Josh	1.00	2.50
128b Low Cal	1.25	3.00
129a Second Hand Rose	1.50	4.00

129b Trashed Tracy	1.00	2.50
131a Stuffed Stephen	1.00	2.50
132a Bony Tony	1.50	4.00
132b Unzipped Zack	1.50	4.00
133b Foxy Francis	1.25	3.00
134a Hip Kip	1.25	3.00
135a Rock E. Horror	1.25	3.00
135b Marty Gras	1.00	2.50
136a Swollen Sue Ellen	1.00	2.50
137a Max Axe	1.25	3.00
138a Alien Ian	1.50	4.00
138b Outerspace Chase	3.00	8.00
139a Double Iris	1.25	3.00
139b 4-Eyed Ida	1.00	2.50
140a Mouth Phil	2.00	5.00
140b Tooth Les	1.50	4.00
141a Ashley Can	1.25	3.00
141b Greta Garbage	1.25	3.00
142a Bruce Moose	1.00	2.50
142b Hunted Hunter	1.00	2.50
143a Melba Toast	1.00	2.50
143b Hy Rye	1.25	3.00
144a Horny Hal	1.00	2.50
144b Rudy Toot	1.50	4.00
145a Dale Snail	1.00	2.50
145b Crushed Shelly	2.00	5.00
146a Baked Jake	1.25	3.00
146b Dry Guy	1.25	3.00
147a Amazin' Grace	1.25	3.00
147b Muscular Molly	1.25	3.00
148a Turned-On Tara	1.25	3.00
148b Tiffany Lamp	1.25	3.00
149a Reese Pieces (1st Print Run)	1.25	3.00
149a Puzzled Paul (2nd Print Run)	2.50	6.00
149b Incomplete Pete	1.25	3.00
153b Duncan Pumpkin ERR (pink swirl)	12.00	30.00
154a Basket Casey	1.25	3.00
155b Nailed Neil	1.00	2.50
156a Warrin' Warren	1.50	4.00
156b Brett Vet	1.25	3.00
158a Meltin' Elton	2.50	6.00
158b Crystal Gale (1st Print Run)	1.50	4.00
158b Ig Lou (2nd Print Run)	3.00	8.00
159b Kitty Litter	1.25	3.00
160a Decapitated Hedy	1.00	2.50
160b Formalde Heidi	1.25	3.00
161a Shorned Sean	1.00	2.50
163b Ruby Cube	1.25	3.00
164a Teddy Bear	1.25	3.00
164b Salvatore Dolly (1st Print Run)	1.25	3.00
164b Battered Brad (2nd Print Run)	2.50	6.00
165b Flakey Fay	1.00	2.50
166a Gored Gordon	1.25	3.00
166b No Way Jose	1.25	3.00
167b Slayed Slade	1.50	4.00
168a Handy Randy	.75	2.00
168b Jordan Nuts	1.25	3.00
169a Dee Faced	1.25	3.00
170b Luke Puke	1.25	3.00
171b Spencer Dispenser	1.25	3.00
172a Nat Nerd	2.00	5.00
172b Clark Can't	1.25	3.00
173b Wormy Shermy	1.25	3.00
174a Fred Thread	1.25	3.00
174b Repaired Rex	1.00	2.50
175b Johnny One-Note	.75	2.00
176b Bill Ding	1.00	2.50
177a Meltin' Milton	1.00	2.50
177b Lazy Louie	.75	2.00
178a Earl Painting	1.50	4.00
178b Blue-Boy George	1.50	4.00
180a Haunted Hollis	.75	2.00
180b Batty Barney	1.00	2.50
182a Sprayed Wade	1.25	3.00

182b Tagged Tad	1.00	2.50
183a Diaper Dan	1.25	3.00
183b Pinned Penny	.75	2.00
184a Upside Down Donald	.75	2.00
184b Hugh Turn	1.00	2.50
185b Hot Doug	1.50	4.00
188a Mel Meal	1.00	2.50
188b Ross Roast	1.50	4.00
189a Brenda Blender	1.00	2.50
190b Gil Grill	1.00	2.50
191a Ben Bolt	1.00	2.50
192b Hamburger Pattie	.75	2.00
193a Shattered Shelby	.75	2.00
193b Cracked Craig	1.25	3.00
194a Nasty Nancy	1.00	2.50
196b Surreal Neal	1.50	4.00
197a Doughy Joey	1.00	2.50
197b Starchy Archie	1.25	3.00
200b Dental Daniel	1.00	2.50
201a Michael Mutant	.75	2.00
201b Zeke Freak	1.25	3.00
202a Ultra Violet	.75	2.00
202b Tanya Hide	.75	2.00
204a Jules Drools	1.25	3.00
205a Hot Rod	1.25	3.00
205b Bud Buggy	1.25	3.00
206b Audio Augie	1.25	3.00
207a Over Flo	.75	2.00
207b Moist Joyce	1.50	4.00
209a Whacked-Up Wally	.75	2.00
209b Paddlin' Madeline	1.25	3.00
210a Intense Payne	1.25	3.00
211a See More Seymour	1.00	2.50
212a Upliftin' Clifton	.75	2.00
213a Otto Whack	1.00	2.50
213b Elliot Mess	.75	2.00
214a Off-Color Clara	.75	2.00
214b Brushed-Off Brends	1.25	3.00
215a Gnawing Nora	1.25	3.00
216b Small Saul	.75	2.00
218a Tom Thumb	1.00	2.50
218b Bridget Digit	1.00	2.50
219a George Washingdone	1.00	2.50
220a Joan Clone	1.50	4.00
221a Cracked Crystal	.75	2.00
222b Loose Spring	1.00	2.50
223a Lolly Poppy	.75	2.00
223b Lily Popped	1.00	2.50
224a Monte Zuma	.75	2.00
224b Pagan Megan	1.00	2.50
225a Nasal Hazel	.75	2.00
226a Pierced Pearl	.75	2.00
228b Uncool Carl	1.00	2.50
229a Clair Stare	1.00	2.50
230a Manuel Labor	.75	2.00
230b Handy Andy	.75	2.00
231b Bernie Burns	.75	2.00
232a Pam Hame	1.00	2.50
232b Cole Cut	2.00	5.00
233a Wes Mess	2.00	5.00
233b Trash-Can Ken	.75	2.00
234a Harry Canary	1.00	2.50
234b Burt Cage	1.00	2.50
236a Trina Cleaner	1.25	3.00
237a Totaled Todd	.75	2.00
237b Towin' Owen	.75	2.00
238a Marc Spark	.75	2.00
238b Cherry Bomb	1.00	2.50
239a Jerry Atric	1.00	2.50
239b Abraham Wrinklin'	.75	2.00
240a Radar Ray	.75	2.00
241a Old Gloria Checklist	1.00	2.50
242a Clean Maureen	1.00	2.50
243a Lee Tree	1.00	2.50

243b Sherwood Forest	.75	2.00
244a Welcome Matt	.75	2.00
244b Muddy Maude	.75	2.00
245a Shish K. Bob	.75	2.00
246a John John	1.00	2.50
246b Flushing Floyd	.75	2.00
247b Rustin' Justin	1.00	2.50
249a Many Lenny	.75	2.00
250a Newly-Dead Ed	1.25	3.00
250b Dyna Mike	1.00	2.50

1987 Topps Garbage Pail Kids

COMPLETE SERIES 7 SET (84)	40.00	100.00
COMPLETE SERIES 8 SET (84)	50.00	125.00
COMPLETE SERIES 9 SET (88)	40.00	100.00
COMPLETE SERIES 10 SET (78)	40.00	100.00
COMPLETE SERIES 11 SET (84)	40.00	100.00
UNOPENED SER.7 BOX (48 PACKS)	250.00	400.00
UNOPENED SER.7 PACK (5 CARDS)	6.00	8.00
UNOPENED SER.8 BOX (48 PACKS)	250.00	400.00
UNOPENED SER.10 PACK (5 CARDS)	6.00	8.00
UNOPENED SER.9 BOX (48 PACKS)	250.00	400.00
UNOPENED SER.8 PACK (5 CARDS)	6.00	8.00
UNOPENED SER.10 BOX (48 PACKS)	200.00	400.00
UNOPENED SER.11 PACK (5 CARDS)	6.00	8.00
UNOPENED SER.11 BOX (48 PACKS)	200.00	400.00
UNOPENED SER.9 PACK (5 CARDS)	6.00	8.00
COMMON SERIES 7 CARD (251a-292b)	.40	1.00
COMMON SERIES 8 CARD (293a-334b)	.40	1.00
COMMON SERIES 9 CARD (335a-378b)	.40	1.00
COMMON SERIES 10 CARD (379a-417b)	.40	1.00
COMMON SERIES 11 CARD (418a-459b)	.40	1.00
251a Barfin' Barbara	.75	2.00
252b Dairy Cari	.75	2.00
253a Russ Pus (puzzle center back)	1.25	3.00
253b Louise Squeeze (puzzle center back)	1.25	3.00
254a Chris Mess	1.25	3.00
254b Sandy Clod	.75	2.00
255a On The Mark	1.00	2.50
256a Jack Pot	.75	2.00
256b Monte Carlo	1.25	3.00
258b Oral Laurel	1.00	2.50
259a Grilled Gil	.60	1.50
259b Well Don	.60	1.50
260a Adam Boom	2.50	6.00
260b Blasted Billy II (blue header)	2.50	6.00
260b Blasted Billy II (purple header)	6.00	15.00
261a Gooey Huey	.75	2.00
261b Bobbi Booger (blue header)	2.00	5.00
261b Bobbi Booger (purple header)	5.00	12.00
262a Brainless Bryan	1.00	2.50
262b Jughead Ted	.75	2.00
263a Vincent Van Gone	1.25	3.00
263b Modern Art	.75	2.00
264a Pete Seat	.75	2.00
264b Noel Bowl	1.00	2.50
265a Curly Shirley (puzzle side back)	.75	2.00
265b Blown Joan (puzzle center back)	.75	2.00
265b Blown Joan (puzzle side back)	2.00	5.00
266a Roy L. Flush	.75	2.00
266b Shuffled Sherman	.75	2.00
267a Tongue Tied Tina	.50	1.25
267b Braided Brandy	.50	1.25
268b William Penned	1.00	2.50
269a Sharpened Sheena	.75	2.00
269b Cranky Kristin	1.00	2.50
270b Brewin' Bruno	.50	1.25
271a Bratty Maddy	1.25	3.00
273a Haunted Forrest	1.00	2.50
273b Sappy Sarah	1.00	2.50
274a Reptilian Lillian	.75	2.00
274b Jay Prey	.75	2.00
275b Rollin' Roland	1.00	2.50
276a Vanessa Undresser	1.25	3.00
276b Banana Anna	1.00	2.50
278a Have A Nice Dave	2.00	5.00
278b Miles Smiles	.50	1.25
279b Noah Body	1.00	2.50
280b Filled Up Philip	.60	1.50
281b Paul Bunion	1.00	2.50
282b Bent Brent	.75	2.00
283a Alien Alan	.75	2.00
283b Martian Marcia	.75	2.00
284a Manny Heads	1.00	2.50
285a Wind Sheila	.75	2.00
285b Hit N' Ronni	.75	2.00
286a Haley Comet	1.50	4.00
286b June Moon	2.50	6.00
287a Christine Vaccine	.75	2.00
287b Medi Kate	1.25	3.00
288a Grant Ant	.75	2.00
288b Sticky Nikki	1.25	3.00
289a Stair Casey	.75	2.00
289b Alexander The Grate (black card number)	3.00	8.00
289b Alexander The Grate (white card number)	6.00	15.00
290a Busted Armand	.75	2.00
290b Jim Nauseum	.75	2.00
291a Homer Runt	.75	2.00
291b Screwball Lew	1.00	2.50
292a Staple Gunther	1.50	4.00
292b Clipped Claude	1.00	2.50
293a Explorin' Norman	.60	1.50
293b Drillin' Dylan	1.00	2.50
295a Charlie Horse	1.00	2.50
295b Amusement Parker	.75	2.00
296a Plucked Daisy	1.25	3.00
296b Wiltin' Milton	.50	1.25
298a Bloody Mary (puzzle center back)	1.25	3.00
298b Donna Donor (puzzle center back)	.60	1.50
298b Donna Donor (puzzle corner back)	.75	2.00
299a Buck Puck	.75	2.00
299b Lowell Goal	.75	2.00
300a Corrina Corona	.75	2.00
300b Smokey Joe	1.25	3.00
301b Mike Strike	.60	1.50
302a Mixed-Up Mick	1.00	2.50
303b Coat Rack Zack	1.00	2.50
304a Rubbin' Robyn	1.00	2.50
304b Soapy Opie	.75	2.00
305a Grate Scott	1.00	2.50
305b Reggie Veggie	.75	2.00
306a Midge Fridge	1.00	2.50
306b Leftover Grover ERR/Slime	6.00	15.00
307a Divin' Ivan	1.00	2.50
307b Walter Sport	1.50	4.00
308a Fritz Spritz	2.50	6.00
308b Ella P. Record	1.25	3.00
309b Bowen Arrow	1.00	2.50
310a Stinkin' Stella	1.00	2.50
310b Smellin' Helen	1.00	2.50
311a Stu Spew	.75	2.00
311b Slimin' Simon	.75	2.00
312a Moe Bile	2.00	5.00
312b Dang Len	.75	2.00
313b Death Nell	1.00	2.50
314a Shifting Sandy	1.00	2.50
315b Unclean Helene	.75	2.00
316a Flowin' Owen	.75	2.00
316b Russell Spout	1.00	2.50
317a James Flames	1.00	2.50
317b Burnin' Vernon	.75	2.00
318a Haley's Vomit (puzzle center back)	1.00	2.50
318a Haley's Vomit (puzzle side back)	1.00	2.50
318b Inter Stella (puzzle center back)	1.00	2.50
318b Inter Stella (puzzle side back)	1.00	2.50
319a Chopped Susie	.75	2.00
320a Pumping Aaron	.75	2.00
320b Will Explode	1.00	2.50
321a Squashed Josh	1.25	3.00
322a K.O.'d Karl	.60	1.50
323b Wedding Bella	.75	2.00
325a Marcel Parcel	1.25	3.00
326a Leather Heather	2.00	5.00
326b Chained Shane	1.25	3.00
327a Needled Nina	.75	2.00
327b Knittin' Brittany	1.00	2.50
328a Glowing Amber	1.00	2.50
328b Bright Dwight	1.00	2.50
330a Lotta Lotta	1.00	2.50
331a Page Cage	1.00	2.50
331b Tommy Ache	.75	2.00
332a Sling Scott	.75	2.00
332b Teddy Aim Fire	1.00	2.50
333a Ortho Donny	.75	2.00
333b Ruth Canal	.50	1.25
334a Ashley To Ashes	1.00	2.50
334b Dustin To Dust	.75	2.00
335b Waxy Wendy	1.25	3.00
336a Laser Ray	1.00	2.50
336b Sizzlin' Sid	1.25	3.00
338b Teeter Todd	1.25	3.00
339b Drippy Debbie	1.00	2.50
340b Rollin' Rolanda	1.00	2.50
342a Jim Equipment	1.00	2.50
342b Buddy Builder	1.50	4.00
343b Al Catraz	.75	2.00
346a Peeled Paul	1.25	3.00
346b Skin Les	1.00	2.50
349a Polluted Percy	.75	2.00
349b Barnacle Bill	1.00	2.50
350a Misty Suds	1.00	2.50
350b Amelia Airhead	1.00	2.50
351a Cheryl Peril	.75	2.00
351b Deflatin' Nathan	.75	2.00
352a Herman Hormone	.60	1.50
352b Turned-On Ron	.75	2.00
354a Clark Shark	1.00	2.50
354b Manny Eater	1.25	3.00
355a Beasty Boyd	.75	2.00
355b Semi Colin	1.25	3.00
355b Semi Colin ERR NNO	100.00	200.00
356b Electric Shari	.75	2.00
358b Wade Blade	1.50	4.00
359a Kerosene Kerry	1.00	2.50
359b Blazin' Blake	.50	1.25
361a Diced Brice	1.00	2.50
361b Chopped Chet	.60	1.50
362a Doug Food	.75	2.00
362b Nick Yick	.50	1.25
364a Sticky Ricky	1.25	3.00
364b Gooey Louie	1.50	4.00
365a Shrap Nell	1.50	4.00
365b Hanna Grenade	1.25	3.00
366a Low-Life Lola	1.00	2.50
366b Sis Pool	.75	2.00
370a Cementin' Quentin	1.00	2.50
370b Minus Hans	.75	2.00
371a Grippin' Griffin	.75	2.00
371b Ren Wrench	1.00	2.50
372a Jack Frost	1.00	2.50
372b Window Payne	.75	2.00
373a Desi Island	.75	2.00
373b Marooned Maureen	.75	2.00
374a Swiss Kris	1.25	3.00
374b Cheesy Chandra	.75	2.00
375b Rear View Myra	.75	2.00
377b Hooked Howie	1.25	3.00
378a Empty Emmy	.60	1.50
379a Locked Dorian (puzzle preview back)	.75	2.00
379a Locked Dorian	1.00	2.50

GARBAGE PAIL KIDS

Card		
(blue Garbage Gang header)		
379a Locked Dorian	1.00	2.50
(red Garbage Gang header)		
379b Sidney Kidney	1.25	3.00
(red Garbage Gang header)		
380a Vermin Herman	2.00	5.00
380b Gullivered Travis	1.25	3.00
381a Ground Chuck	.60	1.50
382b Farewell Mel	1.00	2.50
384a Flamin' Raymond	.75	2.00
(white square under banner)		
384b Hot Toddy	1.50	4.00
(white square under banner)		
385a Phil 'Er Up	3.00	8.00
(red Garbage Gang header, die-cut runs through "PEEL HERE")		
385a Phil 'Er Up	1.25	3.00
(red Garbage Gang header, correct die-cut)		
385b Chuckin' Charlie	1.25	3.00
(blue Garbage Gang header)		
385b Chuckin' Charlie	4.00	10.00
(red Garbage Gang header, die-cut runs through "PEEL HERE"		
385b Chuckin' Charlie	1.00	2.50
(red Garbage Gang header, correct die-cut)		
388b Heads Upton	1.00	2.50
389b Overflow Joe	1.00	2.50
391a Glass Isaac	1.25	3.00
391b False Iris	.50	1.25
392b Sardine Candice	.75	2.00
393a Jess Express	1.00	2.50
393b Choo-Choo Trina	.75	2.00
395a Paved Dave	1.25	3.00
395b Run-Over Grover	.60	1.50
397a Cleaned Up Clint	1.25	3.00
398a Skiin' Ian	.60	1.50
399a Dirty Flora	2.00	5.00
399b Gina Cleaner	2.00	3.00
401a Viv E. Section	1.50	4.00
401b Disect Ed	1.25	3.00
402a Lunchpail Gail ERR	1.25	6.00
(die-cut runs through "PEEL HERE")		
402a Lunchpail Gail COR	.40	3.00
402b Lunchbox Stu ERR	2.50	6.00
(die-cut runs through "PEEL HERE")		
402b Lunchbox Stu COR	1.25	3.00
403a Hunter Punter	.75	2.00
404a Airy Mary	1.00	2.50
407b Wally Walnut	1.25	3.00
408a Lickin' Leon	.60	1.50
(blue Garbage Gang header)		
408a Lickin' Leon	.60	1.50
(red Garbage Gang header)		
409a Tiltin' Milton	1.00	2.50
410a Scratching Pole Paul	1.00	2.50
410b Clawed Claude	.75	2.00
411b Bud Sucker	.75	2.00
413a Barnyard Barney	1.25	3.00
413b Dick Hick	1.00	2.50
414a Umbilical Courtney	.75	2.00
419a Meg-A-Volt	1.00	2.50
419b Charged Marge	1.25	3.00
420a Spanked Hank	1.25	3.00
421a Groovy Greg	.75	2.00
425a Denny Saur	.75	2.00
425b Rip Tile	1.50	4.00
427a Ripped Fletch	.75	2.00
428b Garbage Mouth Gilbert	.75	2.00
429a Laundry Matt	1.25	3.00
432b Sue Case	1.00	2.50
433a Porcelain Lynn	1.00	2.50
433b Arlene Latrine	.75	2.00
434a Holly Daze	.75	2.00
434b Joyous Noel	.50	1.25
435a London Bridget	2.00	5.00
435b Toxic Wes	.75	2.00
438b Trick Or Tricia	1.00	2.50
439a Jack Splat	.75	2.00
439b Abstract Art	.60	1.50
443b Wee-Wee Willie	.60	1.50
444a Fairy Tale Dale	1.00	2.50
444b Nose Drip Skip	.75	2.00
445b Ellie Deli	.75	2.00
447a Gushing Garfield	.75	2.00
448a Touch Toni	1.00	2.50
448b Phoney Joni	1.00	2.50
449a Bert Food	1.00	2.50
450b Mason Mace	.60	1.50
453a Dead End Kit	1.25	3.00
454b Bruce Noose	.75	2.00
455a Charred Cole	2.00	5.00
455b Deviled Egbert	.75	2.00
458a Dental Hy Gene	1.25	3.00
(w/green bar)		
458a Dental Hy Gene	1.25	3.00
(w/o green bar)		
459a Vomited (light yellow checklist)	.75	2.00
459b Juicy Jules (light yellow checklist)	1.00	2.50

1988 Topps Garbage Pail Kids

Card		
COMPLETE SERIES 12 (82)	40.00	100.00
COMPLETE SERIES 13 (80)	30.00	75.00
COMPLETE SERIES 14 (80)	60.00	150.00
COMPLETE SERIES 15 (80)	200.00	500.00
UNOPENED SER.12 BOX (48 PACKS)	250.00	400.00
UNOPENED SER.12 PACK (5 CARDS)	6.00	8.00
UNOPENED SER.13 BOX (48 PACKS)	250.00	500.00
UNOPENED SER.13 PACK (5 CARDS)	8.00	12.00
UNOPENED SER.14 BOX (48 PACKS)	300.00	600.00
UNOPENED SER.14 PACK (5 CARDS)	8.00	12.00
UNOPENED SER.15 BOX (48 PACKS)	800.00	1200.00
UNOPENED SER.15 PACK (5 CARDS)	15.00	25.00
COMMON SERIES 12 CARD (460a-500b)	.40	1.00
COMMON SERIES 13 CARD (501a-540b)	.60	1.50
COMMON SERIES 14 CARD (541a-580b)	.60	1.50
COMMON SERIES 15 CARD (581a-620b)	.75	2.00
461a Mara Thon	.75	2.00
461b Racy Lacey	.75	2.00
465a Upsy Daisys	.75	2.00
467a Tongue In Chico	.75	2.00
469a Upset Tommy (checklist)	.75	2.00
469b Tub O' Lars (checklist)	.75	2.00
473b One-Night Stan	.75	2.00
475a Road-Kill Will	1.00	2.50
477a Ingrid Inc.	1.00	2.50
477b Smokestack Zach	.75	2.00
480b Garbage Pail Kitty	.75	2.00
482a Lickin' Leo	.75	2.00
483a Seedy Sydney	1.00	2.50
484a Tim Can	.75	2.00
486b Julius Sneezer	.75	2.00
490a Kinky Kristine	.75	2.00
490b Knot The Norm	.75	2.00
492a Cory On The Cob	1.00	2.50
494a Mitch Match	.75	2.00
496b Jon Pond	.75	2.00
498a Rolls Royce	1.00	2.50
499a Abandoned Amanda	1.25	3.00
501a Missing Marcia	.75	2.00
501b Hidden Heidi	.75	2.00
502b Undead Ned	1.00	2.50
504a Cooper Scooper	1.00	2.50
505a Sucked Chuck	.75	2.00
507a Target Prentice (puzzle preview)	1.25	3.00
508a Barry Bomber	.75	2.00
508b Hi-Flyin' Brian	.75	2.00
509a Misfortune Cookie	1.00	2.50
510a Grim Kim	1.00	2.50
510b Taffy Pull	.75	2.00
514a Ampu-Ted	.75	2.00
517b Natty Dresser	.75	2.00
518a Barfin' Marvin	1.25	3.00
(blue Garbage Gang header)		
518a Barfin' Marvin	1.25	3.00
(yellow Garbage Gang header)		
518b Over Etan	1.25	3.00
(blue Garbage Gang header)		
518b Over Etan	1.25	3.00
(yellow Garbage Gang header)		
519a Paddlin' Adeline	1.25	3.00
520b Jay Spray	.75	2.00
521a Dee Odorant	.75	2.00
522b Juan For The Road	.75	2.00
524a Pop Connie	.75	2.00
525a Cocktail Dale	.75	2.00
527b Butt-Bit Brandon	1.00	2.50
528a Daniel Prune	.75	2.00
529a Corkscrewed Drew	1.50	4.00
529b Champ-Pain Dwayne	1.00	2.50
530a Fun Gus	.75	2.00
531a Stormy Skye	.75	2.00
533a Jiggley Jennifer	1.50	4.00
534a Jayne Drain (checklist)	.75	2.00
534b Eda Mouthful (checklist)	.75	2.00
535a Howie Hanging	.75	2.00
538a Cat-Cradled Cathy (Garbage Gang)	.75	2.00
538a Cat-Cradled Cathy (puzzle preview)	.75	2.00
538b Gooey Gwen (puzzle preview)	1.25	3.00
539a John John	1.00	2.50
541a Rocco Socko (puzzle preview)	1.25	3.00
541b Destroyed Boyd (Garbage Gang)	.75	2.00
541b Destroyed Boyd (puzzle preview)	.75	2.00
542b Up In The Aaron	.75	2.00
543a Undersea Lee	.75	2.00
543b Sailin' Waylon	1.00	2.50
544b Jack Tracks	.75	2.00
545a Artie Party	.75	2.00
545b Driftin' Clifton	1.00	2.50
546b Abstract Abby	.75	2.00
547a Cuckoo Clark	.75	2.00
547b Bile Lyle	1.00	2.50
548a Walt To Wall (checklist)	2.00	5.00
548a Walt To Wall (Garbage Gang)	.75	2.00
548b Nailed Noel (checklist)	1.00	2.50
549b Bomb Shelly	1.00	2.50
553b Kissy Missy	1.25	3.00
554a Rufus Refuse	1.00	2.50
555a Alien Ed	1.50	4.00
555b Phone Homer	2.50	6.00
556b Nailed Natalie	1.25	3.00
557a Stu Brew	.75	2.00
558b Numb Nate	1.25	3.00
560a Lappin' Larry	.75	2.00
560b Guzzlin' Guy	1.25	3.00
561a Marsh Room	1.00	2.50
562a Post No Bill	2.00	5.00
(blue Garbage Gang header)		
562a Post No Bill	1.25	3.00
(yellow Garbage Gang header)		
562b Bulletin Boris	.75	2.00
(blue Garbage Gang header)		
562b Bulletin Boris	.75	2.00
(yellow Garbage Gang header)		
564b Asa Rule	.75	2.00
565a Easter Bonnie	1.25	3.00
565b Hard-Boiled Meg	1.25	3.00
566b Infested Lester	1.00	2.50
567b A-Bomb Tom	1.00	2.50
568a Glut Tony	.75	2.00
570a Ava Shaver	1.00	2.50
570b Holly Hormone	.75	2.00
571a Rubber Robert	1.00	2.50
573a Snotwich Sandra (Garbage Gang)	1.25	3.00
573a Snotwich Sandra (puzzle preview)	1.25	3.00
573b Hedda Spreader (Garbage Gang)	1.00	2.50

573b Hedda Spreader (puzzle preview)	1.25	3.00
574b Fractured Frank	.75	2.00
575a Brain Drain Brian	.75	2.00
575b Pick A Winnie	1.00	2.50
577b Stitchin' Tyne	.75	2.00
579a Judd Cud	1.00	2.50
579b Spearmint Mindy	1.25	3.00
580b Burne Toast	1.25	3.00
581a Shel Game (checklist)	2.00	5.00
581b 3-Card Monte (checklist)	1.25	3.00
582a Take-Out Dinah (Garbage Gang)	1.00	2.50
582b Chow Mame (puzzle)	2.00	5.00
583a Lyle Tile (puzzle preview)	1.25	3.00
583b Harry Glyph (puzzle preview)	1.25	3.00
584a Slimy Hymie (puzzle piece)	1.00	2.50
584a Slimy Hymie (puzzle preview)	1.25	3.00
584b Crawlin' Rollin (puzzle piece)	1.25	3.00
584b Crawlin' Rollin (puzzle preview)	2.00	5.00
585a Picky Nick	1.50	4.00
585b Beulah Ghoul	1.00	2.50
586a Peter Cheater	1.00	2.50
586b Dean List (w/eyelash on name)	10.00	25.00
586b Dean List (w/o eyelash on name)	1.25	3.00
587a Cornelia Flake	1.25	3.00
587b Mala Nutrition	1.00	2.50
588a Yo! Gert	1.50	4.00
588b Ice Cream Connie	1.25	3.00
589a Ecch Benedict	1.50	4.00
589b Brain Les	1.25	3.00
590a Little Leak Len	2.00	5.00
591a Frank Footer	1.25	3.00
591b Dog Bites Boyd	1.50	4.00
592a Extra Dexter	1.25	3.00
592b Flabby Abby	1.50	4.00
593a Footloose Fred	1.50	4.00
593b Lucky Lew	2.50	6.00
594a Tied Di	1.25	3.00
594a Tied Di (black line error)	8.00	20.00
594b Knotty Lottie	1.00	2.50
595a Mal Practice	1.00	2.50
595b Intensive Carrie	1.00	2.50
596a Sani Klaus	1.50	4.00
596b Sick Nick	2.00	5.00
597a Harry Armpits	1.50	4.00
597b Under Arnie	2.00	5.00
598a Vise Guy	2.00	5.00
598b Hugh Fix-It	1.25	3.00
599a Bern-Out	1.00	2.50
599b Dim-Bulb Bob	1.50	4.00
600a Vendo-Matt	1.00	2.50
600b Doug Slug	1.50	4.00
601a Losin' Wade	1.25	3.00
601b Hy Cholesterol	1.25	3.00
602a Upside Donna	1.25	3.00
602b Two-Fer Juan	1.00	2.50
603a Mitch Mitt	1.25	3.00
603b Foul Bill	1.25	3.00
604a Sandi Box	1.00	2.50
604b Cat Litter	1.50	4.00
605a Windy Mindy	1.25	3.00
605b Birthday Kate	1.25	3.00
606a Foul-Towel Raoul	2.00	5.00
606b Muddy Buddy	1.50	4.00
607a Kit Video	1.00	2.50
608a Fairy Mary	1.25	3.00
608b Stinker Belle	4.00	10.00
609a Dewy Dewey	1.25	3.00
609b Dank Frank	1.50	4.00
610a Beau Constricted	1.25	3.00
611a Acid Wayne	1.00	2.50
611b Polluted Paul	1.50	4.00
612b Weird Walker	1.25	3.00
613a Bag Piper	1.50	4.00
613b Great Scott	2.50	6.00
614a Fillin' Dylan	1.25	3.00
614b Cutting Juan	1.50	4.00
615a Preston Change-O	1.00	2.50
615b Sleight Of Hans	1.25	3.00
616a Alec Gator	2.50	6.00
616b Croco-Dale	2.00	5.00
617a Claude Flesh	6.00	15.00
617b Slasher Asher	8.00	20.00
618a Paper Dolly	1.25	3.00
619a V.C. Arnie	1.25	3.00
619b Cassette Casey	1.25	3.00
620a Ada Bomb	4.00	10.00
620b Blasted Betty (w/eyelash on top border)	12.00	30.00
620b Blasted Betty (w/o eyelash on top border)	6.00	15.00

Modern GPK

2020 Topps Garbage Pail Kids Adam Bomb Autograph Toy Fair Exclusive

NNO Adam Bomb	75.00	150.00

2017 Garbage Pail Kids Adam-Geddon

COMPLETE SET (180)	10.00	25.00
UNOPENED BOX (24 PACKS)	45.00	60.00
UNOPENED PACK (8 CARDS)	2.50	3.00
COMMON CARD	.20	.50
*BRUISED: 1.2X TO 3X BASIC CARDS	.60	1.50
*PUKE: 1.5X TO 4X BASIC CARDS	.75	2.00
*PEE: 2X TO 5X BASIC CARDS	1.00	2.50
*SPIT/99: 4X TO 10X BASIC CARDS	2.00	5.00
*BLOODY NOSE/75: 6X TO 15X BASIC CARDS	3.00	8.00
*FOOL'S GOLD/50: 8X TO 20X BASIC CARDS	4.00	10.00

2017 Garbage Pail Kids Adam-Geddon Artist Autographs

COMMON CAMERA	12.00	30.00
COMMON ENGSTROM	6.00	15.00
COMMON GROSS	5.00	12.00
COMMON IM	10.00	25.00
COMMON PINGITORE		
COMMON SIMKO		
COMMON WHEATON	6.00	15.00
STATED ODDS 1:168 ALL PACKS		
STATED PRINT RUN 25 SER.#'d SETS		

2017 Garbage Pail Kids Adam-Geddon Bathroom Buddies

COMPLETE SET (6)	5.00	12.00
COMMON CARD (7a-9b)	1.00	2.50
STATED ODDS 3:TARGET VALUE BOX		

2017 Garbage Pail Kids Adam-Geddon Best of the 2016 U.S. Presidential Election

COMPLETE SET (10)	100.00	200.00
COMMON CARD (1a-5b)	10.00	25.00
STATED ODDS 1:24 HOBBY/COLLECTOR		

2017 Garbage Pail Kids Adam-Geddon Classic Adam-Geddon

COMPLETE SET (20)	8.00	20.00
COMMON CARD (1a-10b)	1.00	2.50
STATED ODDS 2:1 JUMBO EXCLUSIVE		

2017 Garbage Pail Kids Adam-Geddon Gross Bears

COMPLETE SET (6)	5.00	12.00
COMMON CARD (11-15, L3)	1.25	3.00
STATED ODDS 3:WALMART VALUE BOX		

2017 Garbage Pail Kids Adam-Geddon Patches

COMPLETE SET (20)	300.00	600.00
COMMON CARD (1a-10b)	15.00	40.00
STATED ODDS 1:36 HOBBY AND COLLECTOR PACKS		
STATED PRINT RUN 50 SER.#'d SETS		
2a Adam Bomb	20.00	50.00
2b Blasted Billy	20.00	50.00

2003 Garbage Pail Kids All-New Series 1

COMPLETE SET (80)	8.00	20.00
UNOPENED BOX (24 PACKS)	100.00	200.00
UNOPENED PACK (6 STICKERS)	4.00	8.00
COMMON CARD (1a-40b)	.12	.30

2003 Garbage Pail Kids All-New Series 1 Foil Silver Glossy Back

COMPLETE SET (50)	15.00	40.00
COMMON CARD (1a-25b)	1.00	2.50
*GOLD: SAME AS GLOSSY BACK		
*MATTE BACK: SAME AS GLOSSY BACK		
STATED ODDS ONE PER FIRST PRINTING PACK		

2003 Garbage Pail Kids All-New Series 1 Gum Wraps

COMPLETE SET (60)	5.00	12.00
COMMON CARD (1a-30b)	.10	.25
STATED ODDS FOUR PER PACK		

2004 Garbage Pail Kids All-New Series 2

COMPLETE SET (80)	6.00	15.00
UNOPENED BOX (24 PACKS)	125.00	200.00
UNOPENED PACK (6 CARDS)	3.00	5.00
COMMON CARD (1a-40b)	.10	.25

2004 Garbage Pail Kids All-New Series 2 Bonus

COMPLETE SET (2)	30.00	75.00
STATED ODDS ONE PER RETAIL BONUS BOX		
B1 On Camera Cameron	30.00	60.00
B2 Paintball Paul	10.00	20.00

2004 Garbage Pail Kids All-New Series 2 Foil

COMPLETE SET (50)	15.00	40.00
COMMON CARD (F1a-F25b)	.40	1.00
STATED ODDS ONE PER PACK		

2004 Garbage Pail Kids All-New Series 2 Scratch 'n Stink

COMPLETE SET (12)	4.00	10.00
COMMON CARD (S1a-S6b)	.75	2.00
STATED ODDS 1:6		

2004 Garbage Pail Kids All-New Series 3

COMPLETE SET (80)	6.00	15.00
UNOPENED BOX (24 PACKS)		
UNOPENED PACK (6 CARDS)		
COMMON CARD (1a-40b)	.10	.25

2004 Garbage Pail Kids All-New Series 3 Bonus

COMPLETE SET (3)	80.00	150.00
COMMON CARD (B3-B5)	4.00	10.00
B3 STATED ODDS ONE PER WALMART BONUS BOX		
B4 STATED ODDS ONE PER TARGET BONUS BOX		
B5 STATED ODDS ONE PER TOYS R US/KMART BONUS BOX		
B4 Hill Billy	30.00	60.00
B5 Cole Gate	60.00	120.00

2004 Garbage Pail Kids All-New Series 3 Foil

COMPLETE SET (50)	12.00	30.00
COMMON CARD (1a-25b)	.40	1.00
STATED ODDS ONE PER PACK		

2004 Garbage Pail Kids All-New Series 3 Pop-Ups

COMPLETE SET (10)	4.00	10.00
COMMON CARD (1-10)	.60	1.50
STATED ODDS 1:6		

2004 Garbage Pail Kids All-New Series 3 Scratch 'n Stink

COMPLETE SET (24)	10.00	25.00
COMMON CARD (S1a-S12b)	.75	2.00
STATED ODDS 1:6		

2004 Garbage Pail Kids All-New Series 3 Promo

P1 Christina Ugliera SDCC	2.50	6.00

GARBAGE PAIL KIDS

2005 Garbage Pail Kids All-New Series 4

COMPLETE SET (80)	6.00	15.00
UNOPENED BOX (36 PACKS)	250.00	400.00
UNOPENED PACK (5 CARDS)	8.00	12.00
COMMON CARD (1a-40b)	.10	.25

2005 Garbage Pail Kids All-New Series 4 Bonus

COMPLETE SET (4)	10.00	25.00
COMMON CARD (B6-B9)	1.25	3.00
B6 ODDS 1:WALMART BONUS BOX		
B7 ODDS 1:TOYS R US/KMART BONUS BOX		
B8 ODDS 1:TARGET BONUS BOX		
B9 ODDS 1:TWO-PACK BLISTER		
B6 Doug Sledding	6.00	15.00
B7 Propelled Miguel	6.00	15.00
B8 Swarmed Norm	4.00	10.00

2005 Garbage Pail Kids All-New Series 4 Game

COMPLETE SET (36)	25.00	50.00
COMP.SET w/o SP's (33)	4.00	10.00
STATED ODDS ONE PER PACK		
SP STATED ODDS 1:72		
GPK10 Fartin' Martin FOIL SP	10.00	20.00
GPK14 Richie Retch FOIL SP	10.00	20.00
GPK31 Adam Bomb FOIL SP	10.00	20.00

2005 Garbage Pail Kids All-New Series 4 Scratch 'n Stink

COMPLETE SET (12)	6.00	15.00
COMMON CARD (S1a-S6b)	.75	2.00
STATED ODDS 1:6		

2005 Garbage Pail Kids All-New Series 4 Tattoos

COMPLETE SET (10)	2.50	6.00
COMMON CARD (1-10)	.30	.75
STATED ODDS 1:4		

2005 Garbage Pail Kids All-New Series 4 Promo

NNO Batty Brad SDCC	1.50	4.00

2006 Garbage Pail Kids All-New Series 5

COMPLETE SET (80)	6.00	15.00
COMMON CARD (1a-40b)	.10	.25

2006 Garbage Pail Kids All-New Series 5 Bonus

COMPLETE SET (5)	12.00	30.00
COMMON CARD (B10-B14)	1.25	3.00
B10 STATED ODDS 1:WALMART BONUS BOX		
B11 STATED ODDS 1:TARGET/KB BONUS BOX		
B12, B13, B14 STATED ODDS 1:BLISTER PACK		
B10 Bruce Brush	6.00	15.00
B11 Opera Ursula	6.00	15.00

2006 Garbage Pail Kids All-New Series 5 Letters

COMPLETE SET (15)	2.00	5.00
COMMON CARD (1-15)	.15	.40
STATED ODDS 1:2		

2006 Garbage Pail Kids All-New Series 5 Magnets

COMPLETE SET (9)	6.00	15.00
COMMON CARD (1-9)	.75	2.00
STATED ODDS 1:6		

2007 Garbage Pail Kids All-New Series 6

COMPLETE SET (80)	6.00	15.00
UNOPENED BOX (36 PACKS)	250.00	400.00
UNOPENED PACK (5 CARDS)	8.00	12.00
COMMON CARD (1a-40b)	.10	.25
P2 ISSUED AS SDCC EXCLUSIVE		

2007 Garbage Pail Kids All-New Series 6 Action Punch-Outs

COMPLETE SET (12)	2.00	5.00
COMMON CARD (1-12)	.20	.50
STATED ODDS 1:3		

2007 Garbage Pail Kids All-New Series 6 Bonus

COMPLETE SET (5)	30.00	80.00
COMMON CARD (B15-B19)	6.00	15.00
B15-B17 ODDS 1:BLISTER PACK		
B18 ODDS 1:WALMART BONUS BOX		
B19 ODDS 1:TARGET/KB BONUS BOX		
B19 Scrapped Brooke	20.00	50.00

2007 Garbage Pail Kids All-New Series 6 Magnets

COMPLETE SET (9)	5.00	12.00
COMMON CARD (1-9)	.75	2.00
STATED ODDS 1:6		

2007 Garbage Pail Kids All-New Series 6 Promo

P2 Alien Alan SDCC	2.50	6.00

2007 Garbage Pail Kids All-New Series 7

COMPLETE SET (110)	8.00	20.00
UNOPENED BOX (24 PACKS)	250.00	400.00
UNOPENED PACK (10 CARDS)	8.00	12.00
COMMON CARD (1a-55b)	.10	.25
P1 ISSUED AS SDCC EXCLUSIVE		

2007 Garbage Pail Kids All-New Series 7 Action Punch-Outs

COMPLETE SET (10)	5.00	12.00
COMMON CARD (1-10)	.60	1.50
STATED ODDS 1:4		

2007 Garbage Pail Kids All-New Series 7 Bonus

COMPLETE SET (6)	5.00	12.00
COMMON CARD (B1-B6)	1.50	4.00
B1 ODDS 1:WALMART/KB BONUS BOX		
B2 ODDS 1:TARGET BONUS BOX		
B3-B5 ODDS 1:BLISTER PACK		
B6 ODDS 1:KMART/TOYS R US BONUS BOX		

2007 Garbage Pail Kids All-New Series 7 Loco-Motion

COMPLETE SET (5)	8.00	20.00
COMMON CARD (1-5)	2.00	5.00
STATED ODDS 1:8		

2007 Garbage Pail Kids All-New Series 7 Pop-Ups

COMPLETE SET (10)	4.00	10.00
COMMON CARD (1-10)	.60	1.50
STATED ODDS 1:6		

2007 Garbage Pail Kids All-New Series 7 Puzzle

COMPLETE SET (10)	3.00	8.00
COMMON CARD (1-10)	.50	1.25
STATED ODDS 1:6		

2007 Garbage Pail Kids All-New Series 7 Promos

P1 Dough Boyd SDCC	1.00	2.50
P1 Rock 'Em O-Sock 'Em NYCC	15.00	40.00
P2 Drum Kit PHILLY	2.00	5.00

2017 Garbage Pail Kids and Wacky Packages 4th of July

COMPLETE SET (9)	30.00	75.00
COMMON CARD (1a-3b, 7-9)	6.00	15.00

2018 Garbage Pail Kids and Wacky Packages Easter

COMPLETE SET (7)	25.00	60.00
COMMON CARD (1a-7)	6.00	15.00
STATED PRINT RUN 195 SER.#'d SETS		

2017 Garbage Pail Kids and Wacky Packages Holiday

COMPLETE SET (15)	60.00	120.00
COMMON CARD (1a-10)	4.00	10.00
1a Christmas Tory	15.00	40.00
6 Kringles	5.00	12.00
8 Orna-mentos	6.00	15.00

2017 Garbage Pail Kids and Wacky Packages Jay Lynch Tribute

COMPLETE SET (11)	75.00	150.00
COMMON CARD (1-11)	8.00	20.00

2018 Garbage Pail Kids and Wacky Packages The Not-Scars

COMPLETE SET (8)	30.00	75.00
COMMON CARD	3.00	8.00
STATED PRINT RUN 172 SETS		

2017 Garbage Pail Kids and Wacky Packages Philly Non-Sports Card Show Promos

COMPLETE SET (9)	30.00	80.00
COMMON CARD (1a-6)	5.00	12.00

2017 Garbage Pail Kids and Wacky Packages Summer Comic Convention

COMPLETE SET (10)	60.00	120.00
COMMON CARD (1a-6)	6.00	15.00

2017 Garbage Pail Kids and Wacky Packages Summer Time TV

COMPLETE SET (10)	75.00	150.00
COMMON CARD (1a-7)	10.00	25.00
STATED PRINT RUN 126 SETS		
1a Casino Copper	10.00	25.00
1b Jackpot Jones	10.00	25.00
2a Prisoner Piper	10.00	25.00
2b Chain Gang Chapman	10.00	25.00
3a Ripped Ruth	10.00	25.00
3b Wild Ahir Wilder	10.00	25.00
4 Twin Freaks	10.00	25.00
5 Shame of Thrones	10.00	25.00
6 Sharknada	10.00	25.00
7 Big Bother	10.00	25.00

2017 Garbage Pail Kids and Wacky Packages Thanksgiving

COMPLETE SET (15)	50.00	100.00
COMMON CARD (1a-10)	4.00	10.00

2018 Garbage Pail Kids and Wacky Packages Valentine's Day

COMPLETE SET (9)	50.00	100.00
COMMON CARD	5.00	12.00
STATED PRINT RUN 170 SETS		
1a Adam Bomb	6.00	15.00
1b Ada Bomb	6.00	15.00

2016 Garbage Pail Kids Apple Pie

COMPLETE SET (220)	15.00	40.00
COMMON CARD	.20	.50
*BRUISED: 1.2X TO 3X BASIC CARDS		
*PUKE SPLATTER: 1.5X TO 4X BASIC CARDS		
*PEE: 2X TO 5X BASIC CARDS		
*SPIT SPLATTER/99: 4X TO 10X BASIC CARDS		
*BLOODY NOSE/75: 6X TO 15X BASIC CARDS		
*GOLD DUST/50: 8X TO 20X BASIC CARDS		
THIS HEADER REPRESENTS ALL SUBSETS		

2016 Garbage Pail Kids Apple Pie 4th of July

COMPLETE SET (8)	20.00	50.00
COMMON CARD (1a-4b)	3.00	8.00
TOPPS.COM EXCLUSIVE		

2016 Garbage Pail Kids Apple Pie Adam Bomb Americana

COMPLETE SET (2)	3.00	8.00
COMMON CARD (1a-1b))	2.00	5.00
BLISTER PACK EXCLUSIVES		

2016 Garbage Pail Kids Apple Pie Adam Boom Americana

COMPLETE SET (2)	3.00	8.00
COMMON CARD (1a-1b)	2.00	5.00
BLISTER PACK EXCLUSIVES		

2016 Garbage Pail Kids Apple Pie April Primaries

COMPLETE SET (10)	50.00	100.00
COMMON CARD (1a-5b)	2.50	6.00
TOPPS.COM 24-HOUR EXCLUSIVE		
1a Dirty Donald/288*	8.00	20.00
1b Tawdry Trump/288*	8.00	20.00
4a Hoodwinking Hillary/276*	4.00	10.00
4b Cagey Clinton/276*	4.00	10.00

GARBAGE PAIL KIDS

5a Birdbrain Bernie/270* 4.00 10.00
5b Birdie Sanders/270* 4.00 10.00

2016 Garbage Pail Kids Apple Pie Artist Relics

COMMON CARD 6.00 15.00
STATED PRINT RUN 99 SER.#'d SETS
1 Brent Engstrom 10.00 25.00
3 Joe Simko 8.00 20.00
5 Mark Pingitore 8.00 20.00

2016 Garbage Pail Kids Apple Pie Bathroom Buddies

COMPLETE SET (6) 4.00 10.00
COMMON CARD (1a-3b) 1.00 2.50
STATED ODDS 3:1 TARGET VALUE BOX

2016 Garbage Pail Kids Apple Pie Best of the Fest

COMPLETE SET (20) 75.00 150.00
COMMON CARD (1a-10b) 5.00 12.00

2016 Garbage Pail Kids Apple Pie Christmas

COMPLETE SET (13) 20.00 50.00
COMMON CARD (1a-7) 2.50 6.00

2016 Garbage Pail Kids Apple Pie Classic Patriots

COMPLETE SET (18) 8.00 20.00
COMMON CARD (1a-9b) .75 2.00

2016 Garbage Pail Kids Apple Pie Comic Covers

COMPLETE SET (8) 30.00 80.00
COMMON CARD (1a-4b) 6.00 15.00
STATED ODDS 1:24 HOBBY PACKS
1a Over Killian 8.00 20.00
1b Blasted Bob 10.00 25.00
2a Alien Ian 10.00 25.00
2b Outerspace Chase 12.00 30.00
4a Adam Bomb 12.00 30.00

2016 Garbage Pail Kids Apple Pie Democratic National Convention

COMPLETE SET (10) 30.00 80.00
COMMON CARD (1a-5b) 2.00 5.00
TOPPS.COM 24-HOUR EXCLUSIVE
1a Dollar Billary/283* 4.00 10.00
1b Cash Clinton/283* 4.00 10.00
3a Bye Bye Barack/288* 3.00 8.00
3b Obama Out/288* 3.00 8.00
4b Strong-Armed Sanders/285* 12.00 30.00

2016 Garbage Pail Kids Apple Pie Gross Bears

COMPLETE SET (6) 4.00 10.00
COMMON CARD 1.00 2.50
STATED ODDS 3:1 WALMART VALUE BOX

2016 Garbage Pail Kids Apple Pie Halloween

COMPLETE SET (16) 25.00 60.00
COMMON CARD (1a-8b) 3.00 8.00

2016 Garbage Pail Kids Apple Pie Horror Stickers

COMPLETE SET (8) 30.00 80.00
COMMON CARD (1a-4b) 5.00 12.00
STATED ODDS 1:24 HOBBY PACKS

2016 Garbage Pail Kids Apple Pie Iowa Caucus Special Edition

COMPLETE SET (10) 25.00 60.00
COMMON CARD (1a-5b) 2.00 5.00
TOPPS.COM 24-HOUR EXCLUSIVE
1a Hounded Hilary/1084* 3.00 8.00
1b Cyber Clinton/1084* 3.00 8.00
2a Berserk Bernie/1082* 3.00 8.00
2b Savage Sanders/1082* 3.00 8.00
3a Donald Dump/1174* 15.00 40.00
3b Tumultuous Trump/1174* 8.00 20.00

2016 Garbage Pail Kids Apple Pie Mega Tuesday

COMPLETE SET (16) 50.00 100.00
COMMON CARD (1a-8b) 2.00 5.00
TOPPS.COM 24-HOUR EXCLUSIVE
1a Dinky Donald/377* 4.00 10.00
1b Teeny Tiny Trump/377* 4.00 10.00
2a Dodgy Donald/353* 4.00 10.00
2b Trickster Trump/353* 4.00 10.00
3b Chews Cruz/337* 4.00 10.00
5a Hollering Hillary/338* 4.00 10.00
5b Shrillary Clinton/338* 4.00 10.00
6a Replica Rodham Clinton/339* 4.00 10.00
6b Copycat Clinton/339* 4.00 10.00

2016 Garbage Pail Kids Apple Pie New Hampshire Primaries

COMPLETE SET (18) 25.00 60.00
COMMON CARD (1a-9a) 1.50 4.00
TOPPS.COM 24-HOUR EXCLUSIVE
1a Donald Dumpty/758* 3.00 8.00
1b Humpty Trumpty/758* 3.00 8.00
8a Billary Hillary/729* 2.00 5.00
8b Coattails Clinton/729* 2.00 5.00
9a Batty Bernie/722* 2.00 5.00
9b Psycho Sanders/722* 2.00 5.00

2016 Garbage Pail Kids Apple Pie The Not-Scars

COMPLETE SET (18) 50.00 100.00
COMMON CARD (1a-9b) 2.50 6.00
TOPPS.COM 24-HOUR EXCLUSIVE
2a Last Chance Leonardo/280* 6.00 15.00
2b Desperate DiCaprio/280* 6.00 15.00
5a Joyful Jennifer/253* 5.00 12.00
5b Low Rinse Lawrence/253* 5.00 12.00
7a Confused Chris/252* 3.00 8.00
7b Rattled Rock/252* 3.00 8.00

2016 Garbage Pail Kids Apple Pie Patches

COMPLETE SET (10) 150.00 300.00
COMMON CARD (1-10) 12.00 30.00
STATED PRINT RUN 50 SER.#'d SETS
1 Snooty Sam 15.00 40.00
3 Alice Island 15.00 40.00
4 Marc Spark 20.00 50.00
5 Ben Bolt 20.00 50.00
7 Baby Abie 20.00 50.00
9 Barnyard Barney 15.00 40.00

2016 Garbage Pail Kids Apple Pie Presidential Candidates Oversized SDCC Promos

COMPLETE SET (10) 50.00 100.00
COMMON CARD (1-10) 6.00 15.00
10 Donald Dump 20.00 50.00

2016 Garbage Pail Kids Apple Pie Presidential Losers

COMPLETE SET (20) 60.00 120.00
COMMON CARD (1a-10b) 3.00 8.00
TOPPS.COM 24-HOUR EXCLUSIVE

2016 Garbage Pail Kids Apple Pie Republican National Convention

COMPLETE SET (10) 50.00 100.00
COMMON CARD (1a-5b) 2.00 5.00
TOPPS.COM 24-HOUR EXCLUSIVE
1a Donald Dictator/293* 25.00 60.00
1b Tyrant Trump/293* 15.00 40.00

2016 Garbage Pail Kids Apple Pie Rock and Roll Hall of Lame

COMPLETE SET (20) 100.00 200.00
COMMON CARD (1a-10b) 6.00 15.00
TOPPS.COM 24-HOUR EXCLUSIVE

2016 Garbage Pail Kids Apple Pie The Shammy Awards

COMPLETE SET (18) 50.00 100.00
COMMON CARD (1a-9b) 2.50 6.00
TOPPS.COM 24-HOUR EXCLUSIVE
4a Loony Lady/257* 8.00 20.00
4b Gooty Gaga/257* 8.00 20.00
7a Kanye Pest/281* 5.00 12.00
7b Welcome West/281* 5.00 12.00
8a Jilted Justin/262* 3.00 8.00
8b Booted Bieber/262* 3.00 8.00

2016 Garbage Pail Kids Apple Pie Super Tuesday

COMPLETE SET (10) 30.00 80.00
COMMON CARD (1a-5b) 2.50 6.00
TOPPS.COM 24-HOUR EXCLUSIVE
1a Distressed Donald/508* 8.00 20.00
1b Terrified Trump/508* 8.00 20.00
4a Hand Puppet Hillary/477* 4.00 10.00
4b Crony Clinton/477* 4.00 10.00
5a Basket Bernie/475* 3.00 8.00
5b Slam Dunk Sanders/475* 3.00 8.00

2016 Garbage Pail Kids Apple Pie Thanksgiving

COMPLETE SET (11) 50.00 100.00
COMMON CARD (1a-6) 5.00 12.00
TOPPS 24-HOUR EXCLUSIVE
1b Turned Back Trump 8.00 20.00
6 Duck and Hide Pie Flinging Mix WP 12.00 30.00

2017 Garbage Pail Kids Apple Pie Presidential Inaug-Hurl Ceremony

COMPLETE SET (19) 50.00 100.00
COMMON CARD (1a-8b) 3.00 8.00
9 Melania's Jackie-Oh No! WP 8.00 20.00
10 Trump Scouts Cookies WP 8.00 20.00

2017 Garbage Pail Kids Battle of the Bands

COMPLETE SET (180) 8.00 20.00
UNOPENED BOX (24 PACKS)
UNOPENED PACK (8 CARDS)
COMMON CARD .20 .50
*PUKE: .75X TO 2.5X BASIC CARDS .50 1.25
*BRUISED: 1.2X TO 3X BASIC CARDS .60 1.50
*PEE: 2X TO 5X BASIC CARDS 2.00 5.00
*SPIT/99: 4X TO 10X BASIC CARDS 3.00 8.00
*BLOODY NOSE/75: 6X TO 15X BASIC CARDS 5.00 12.00
*FOOL'S GOLD/50: 10X TO 25X BASIC CARDS

2017 Garbage Pail Kids Battle of the Bands Artist Autographs

COMMON CAMERA 12.00 30.00
COMMON ENGSTROM 15.00 40.00
COMMON GROSS 15.00 40.00
COMMON IM 10.00 25.00
COMMON SIMKO 10.00 25.00
COMMON SMOKIN' JOE 12.00 30.00
STATED PRINT RUN 25 SER.#'d SETS

2017 Garbage Pail Kids Battle of the Bands Bathroom Buddies

COMPLETE SET (6) 4.00 10.00
COMMON CARD (10a-12b) 1.00 2.50

2017 Garbage Pail Kids Battle of the Bands GPK Album Covers and Concert Posters

COMPLETE SET (10) 120.00 200.00
COMMON CARD (1-10) 10.00 25.00

2017 Garbage Pail Kids Battle of the Bands Gross Bears

COMPLETE SET (6) 4.00 10.00
COMMON CARD (16-20, L4) 1.00 2.50

2017 Garbage Pail Kids Battle of the Bands Patches

COMMON CARD (1a-10b) 15.00 40.00
STATED PRINT RUN 50 SER.#'d SETS

2017 Garbage Pail Kids Battle of the Bands Promo

NNO Krazy Katy NYCC 5.00 12.00

2017 Garbage Pail Kids Best of the Fest

COMPLETE SET (18) 60.00 120.00
COMMON CARD (1a-9b) 5.00 12.00

GARBAGE PAIL KIDS

2020 Topps Garbage Pail Kids Beyond the Streets

COMPLETE SET W/SP (98)	125.00	250.00
COMPLETE SET W/O SP (96)	75.00	150.00
UNOPENED BOX (24 PACKS)	150.00	250.00
UNOPENED PACK (8 CARDS)	6.00	10.00
COMMON CARD (1a-48b)	1.25	3.00
00a Adam Bomb SP	30.00	75.00
00b Blasted Billy SP	20.00	50.00
28a Adam Bomb	15.00	40.00
28b Blasted Billy	10.00	25.00

2021 Topps Garbage Pail Kids Beyond the Streets Series 2

COMPLETE SET (82)	50.00	125.00
UNOPENED BOX (20 PACKS)	100.00	150.00
UNOPENED PACK (8 CARDS)	5.00	8.00
COMMON CARD (1a-31b)	1.00	2.50
EXCLUSIVE TO NTWRK APP		
31a Adam Bomb	10.00	25.00
31b Blasted Billy	8.00	20.00

2020 Topps Garbage Pail Kids Bizarre Holidays April

COMPLETE SET (40)	30.00	75.00
COMPLETE WK 1 SET (10)	12.00	30.00
COMPLETE WK 2 SET (10)	12.00	30.00
COMPLETE WK 3 SET (10)	15.00	40.00
COMPLETE WK 4 SET (10)	10.00	25.00
COMMON WK 1 (1a-5b)	2.50	6.00
COMMON WK 2 (6a-10b)	2.50	6.00
COMMON WK 3 (11a-15b)	3.00	8.00
COMMON WK 4 (16a-20b)	2.00	5.00
WK 1 PRINT RUN 582 SETS		
WK 2 PRINT RUN 469 SETS		
WK 3 PRINT RUN 474 SETS		
WK 4 PRINT RUN 440 SETS		

2020 Topps Garbage Pail Kids Bizarre Holidays May

COMPLETE SET (40)	50.00	100.00
COMPLETE WK 1 SET (10)	12.00	30.00
COMPLETE WK 2 SET (10)	12.00	30.00
COMPLETE WK 3 SET (10)	12.00	30.00
COMPLETE WK 4 SET (10)	12.00	30.00
COMPLETE WK 5 SET (10)	12.00	30.00
COMMON WK 1 (1a-5b)	2.50	6.00
COMMON WK 2 (6a-10b)	2.50	6.00
COMMON WK 3 (11a-15b)	2.50	6.00
COMMON WK 4 (16a-20b)	2.50	6.00
COMMON WK 5 (21a-25b)	2.50	6.00
*GREEN: .75X TO 2X BASIC CARDS		
WK 1 PRINT RUN 449 SETS		
WK 2 PRINT RUN 456 SETS		
WK 3 PRINT RUN 479 SETS		
WK 4 PRINT RUN 562 SETS		
WK 5 PRINT RUN 449 SETS		

2020 Topps Garbage Pail Kids Bizarre Holidays June

COMPLETE SET (40)	30.00	75.00
COMPLETE WK1 SET (10)	10.00	25.00
COMPLETE WK 2 SET (10)	12.00	30.00
COMPLETE WK 3 SET (10)	8.00	20.00
COMPLETE WK 4 SET (10)	15.00	40.00
COMMON WK 1 (1a-5b)	2.00	5.00
COMMON WK 2 (6a-10b)	2.50	6.00
COMMON WK 3 (11a-15b)	1.50	4.00
COMMON WK 4 (16a-20b)	3.00	8.00
*PURPLE: .75X TO 2X BASIC CARDS		
WK 1 PRINT RUN 478 SETS		
WK 2 PRINT RUN 492 SETS		
WK 3 PRINT RUN 502 SETS		
WK 4 PRINT RUN 650 SETS		

2020 Topps Garbage Pail Kids Bizarre Holidays July

COMPLETE SET (50)	50.00	100.00
COMPLETE WK 1 SET (10)	12.00	30.00
COMPLETE WK 2 SET (10)	12.00	30.00
COMPLETE WK 3 SET (10)	10.00	25.00
COMPLETE WK 4 SET (10)	12.00	30.00
COMPLETE WK 5 SET (10)	12.00	30.00
COMMON WK 1 (1a-5b)	2.50	6.00
COMMON WK 2 (6a-10b)	2.50	6.00
COMMON WK 3 (11a-15b)	2.00	5.00
COMMON WK 4 1 (16a-20b)	2.50	6.00
COMMON WK 5 (21a-25b)	2.50	6.00
*RED: .75X TO 2X BASIC CARDS		
WK 1 PRINT RUN 514 SETS		
WK 2 PRINT RUN 474 SETS		
WK 3 PRINT RUN 457 SETS		
WK 4 PRINT RUN 466 SETS		
WK 5 PRINT RUN 578 SETS		

2020 Topps Garbage Pail Kids Bizarre Holidays August

COMPLETE SET (40)	30.00	75.00
COMPLETE WK 1 SET (10)	10.00	25.00
COMPLETE WK 2 SET (10)	10.00	25.00
COMPLETE WK 3 SET (10)	8.00	20.00
COMPLETE WK 4 SET (10)	8.00	20.00
COMMON WK 1 (1a-5b)	2.00	5.00
COMMON WK 2 (6a-10b)	2.00	5.00
COMMON WK 3 (11a-15b)	1.50	4.00
COMMON WK 4 (16a-20b)	1.50	4.00
*LT.GREEN: .75X TO 2X BASIC CARDS		
WK 1 PRINT RUN 489 SETS		
WK 2 PRINT RUN 629 SETS		
WK 3 PRINT RUN 449 SETS		
WK 4 PRINT RUN 516 SETS		
10a Adam Bomb/629*	4.00	10.00

2020 Topps Garbage Pail Kids Bizarre Holidays September

COMPLETE SET (40)	50.00	100.00
COMPLETE WK 1 SET (10)	15.00	40.00
COMPLETE WK 2 SET (10)	12.00	30.00
COMPLETE WK 3 SET (10)	8.00	20.00
COMPLETE WK 4 SET (10)	12.00	30.00
COMMON WK 1 (1a-5b)	3.00	8.00
COMMON WK 2 (6a-10b)	2.50	6.00
COMMON WK 3 (11a-15b)	1.50	4.00
COMMON WK 4 (16a-20b)	2.50	6.00
*DEEP BLUE: .75X TO 2X BASIC CARDS		
WK 1 PRINT RUN 460 SETS		
WK 2 PRINT RUN 420 SETS		
WK 3 PRINT RUN 498 SETS		
WK 4 PRINT RUN 423 SETS		

2020 Topps Garbage Pail Kids Bizarre Holidays October

COMPLETE SET (50)	50.00	100.00
COMPLETE WK 1 SET (10)	12.00	30.00
COMPLETE WK 2 SET (10)	12.00	30.00
COMPLETE WK 3 SET (10)	10.00	25.00
COMPLETE WK 4 SET (10)	10.00	25.00
COMPLETE WK 5 SET (10)	12.00	30.00
COMMON WK 1 (1a-5b)	2.50	6.00
COMMON WK 2 (6a-10b)	2.50	6.00
COMMON WK 3 (11a-15b)	2.00	5.00
COMMON WK 4 (16a-20b)	2.00	5.00
COMMON WK 5 (21a-25b)	2.50	6.00
*PINK: .75X TO 2X BASIC CARDS		
WK 1 PRINT RUN 471 SETS		
WK 2 PRINT RUN 480 SETS		
WK 3 PRINT RUN 446 SETS		
WK 4 PRINT RUN 504 SETS		
WK 5 PRINT RUN 474 SETS		

2020 Topps Garbage Pail Kids Bizarre Holidays November

COMPLETE SET (40)	30.00	75.00
COMPLETE WK 1 SET (10)	12.00	30.00
COMPLETE WK 2 SET (10)	12.00	30.00
COMPLETE WK 3 SET (10)	12.00	30.00
COMPLETE WK 4 SET (10)	12.00	30.00
COMMON WK 1 (1a-5b)	2.50	6.00
COMMON WK 2 (6a-10b)	2.50	6.00
COMMON WK 3 (11a-15b)	2.50	6.00
COMMON WK 4 (16a-20b)	2.50	6.00
*YELLOW: .75X TO 2X BASIC CARDS		
WK 1 PRINT RUN 472 SETS		
WK 2 PRINT RUN 403 SETS		
WK 3 PRINT RUN 630 SETS		
WK 4 PRINT RUN 460 SETS		

2020 Topps Garbage Pail Kids Bizarre Holidays December

COMPLETE SET (40)	30.00	75.00
COMPLETE WK 1 SET (10)	10.00	25.00
COMPLETE WK 2 SET (10)	8.00	20.00
COMPLETE WK 3 SET (10)	12.00	30.00
COMPLETE WK 4 SET (10)	12.00	30.00
COMMON WK 1 (1a-5b)	2.00	5.00
COMMON WK 2 (6a-10b)	1.50	4.00
COMMON WK 3 (11a-15b)	2.50	6.00
COMMON WK 4 (16a-20b)	2.50	6.00
*BLUE: 1.2X TO 3X BASIC CARDS		
WK 1 PRINT RUN 556 SETS		
WK 2 PRINT RUN 465 SETS		
WK 3 PRINT RUN 432 SETS		
WK 4 PRINT RUN 507 SETS		

2021 Topps Garbage Pail Kids Bizarre Holidays January

COMPLETE SET (50)	50.00	100.00
COMPLETE WK 1 SET (10)	10.00	25.00
COMPLETE WK 2 SET (10)	10.00	25.00
COMPLETE WK 3 SET (10)	10.00	25.00
COMPLETE WK 4 SET (10)	10.00	25.00
COMPLETE WK 5 SET (10)	10.00	25.00
COMMON WK 1 (1a-5b)	1.50	4.00
COMMON WK 2 (6a-10b)	1.50	4.00
COMMON WK 3 (11a-15b)	1.50	4.00
COMMON WK 4 (16a-20b)	1.50	4.00
COMMON WK 5 (21a-25b)	1.50	4.00
*DEEP RED: 2X TO 5X BASIC CARDS		
WK 1 PRINT RUN 429 SETS		
WK 2 PRINT RUN 450 SETS		
WK 3 PRINT RUN 491 SETS		
WK 4 PRINT RUN 736 SETS		
WK 5 PRINT RUN 703 SETS		
1a Dover Slept/429*	1.50	4.00
1b Tired Tim/429*	1.50	4.00
20a Adam Bomb/736*	3.00	8.00

2021 Topps Garbage Pail Kids Bizarre Holidays February

COMPLETE SET (40)	50.00	100.00
COMPLETE WK 1 SET (10)	12.00	30.00
COMPLETE WK 2 SET (10)	10.00	25.00
COMPLETE WK 3 SET (10)	10.00	25.00
COMPLETE WK 4 SET (10)	15.00	40.00
COMMON WK 1 (1a-5b)	2.50	6.00
COMMON WK 2 (6a-10b)	2.00	5.00
COMMON WK 3 (11a-15b)	2.00	5.00
COMMON WK 4 (16a-20b)	2.50	6.00
*PURPLE: 1.2X TO 3X BASIC CARDS		
WK 1 PRINT RUN 505 SETS		
WK 2 PRINT RUN 509 SETS		
WK 3 PRINT RUN 555 SETS		
WK 4 PRINT RUN 652 SETS		
19a Adam Bomb/652*	8.00	20.00

2021 Topps Garbage Pail Kids Bizarre Holidays March

COMPLETE SET (40)	50.00	100.00
COMPLETE WK 1 SET (10)	10.00	25.00
COMPLETE WK 2 SET (10)	12.00	30.00
COMPLETE WK 3 SET (10)	12.00	30.00
COMPLETE WK 4 SET (10)	12.00	30.00
COMMON WK1 (1a-5b)	2.00	5.00
COMMON WK2 (6a-10b)	2.50	6.00
COMMON WK3 (11a-15b)	2.50	6.00
COMMON WK4 (16a-20b)	2.50	6.00
*LT.BLUE: 1.2X TO 3X BASIC CARDS		
WK1 PRINT RUN 529 SETS		
WK2 PRINT RUN 547 SETS		
WK3 PRINT RUN 511 SETS		
WK4 PRINT RUN 542 SETS		

2022 Topps Garbage Pail Kids Book Worms

COMPLETE SET (200)	25.00	60.00
UNOPENED BOX (24 PACKS)	40.00	50.00
UNOPENED PACK (8 CARDS)	2.00	3.00
UNOPENED COLL.BOX (24 PACKS)	60.00	80.00
UNOPENED COLL.PACK (8 CARDS)	3.00	4.00
UNOPENED MEGA BOX (17 PACKS)	20.00	35.00
COMMON CARD (1-200)	.40	1.00
*GREEN: .75X TO 2X BASIC CARDS		
*BLACK: 1X TO 2.5X BASIC CARDS		
*GRAY/199: 1.5X TO 4X BASIC CARDS		
*BLUE/99: 5X TO 12X BASIC CARDS		
*RED/75: 6X TO 15X BASIC CARDS		
*GOLD/50: 12X TO 30X BASIC CARDS		

2022 Topps Garbage Pail Kids Book Worms Authors of Their Own Misfortune

COMPLETE SET (10)	10.00	25.00
COMMON CARD (1a-5b)	1.50	4.00
STATED ODDS 1:3 DISPLAY BOX		

2022 Topps Garbage Pail Kids Book Worms Book Marked

COMPLETE SET (5)	30.00	75.00
COMMON CARD (BM1-BM5)	8.00	20.00
STATED ODDS 1:24 COLLECTOR BOX		

2022 Topps Garbage Pail Kids Book Worms GPK Patches

COMMON MEM	15.00	40.00
*BLUE/99: .5X TO 1.2X BASIC MEM		
*RED/75: .6X TO 1.5X BASIC MEM		
*GOLD/50: .75X TO 2X BASIC MEM		
STATED PRINT RUN 199 SER.#'d SETS		
2a Nasty Nick	40.00	100.00
2b Evil Eddie	30.00	75.00
4a Sy Clops	25.00	60.00
5a Buggy Betty	25.00	60.00

2022 Topps Garbage Pail Kids Book Worms Gross Adaptations

COMPLETE SET (25)	25.00	60.00
COMMON CARD (1-25)	2.00	5.00
RANDOMLY INSERTED INTO PACKS		

2022 Topps Garbage Pail Kids Book Worms Wacky Package Prose

COMPLETE SET (8)	60.00	150.00
COMMON CARD (WP1-WP8)	10.00	25.00
STATED ODDS 1:24 COLLECTOR BOX		

2012 Garbage Pail Kids Brand New Series One

COMPLETE SET (110)	10.00	25.00
UNOPENED BOX (24 PACKS)	250.00	400.00
UNOPENED PACK (8 CARDS)	10.00	15.00
COMMON CARD (1a-55b)	.15	.40
*GREEN: 1X TO 2.5X BASIC CARDS	.40	1.00
*SILVER: 2X TO 5X BASIC CARDS	.75	2.00
*BLACK: 10X TO 25X BASIC CARDS	4.00	10.00
*GOLD: 40X TO 100X BASIC CARDS	15.00	40.00

2012 Garbage Pail Kids Brand New Series One Adam Bomb Through History

COMPLETE SET (10)	4.00	10.00
COMMON CARD (1-10)	.75	2.00
*GREEN: .8X TO 2X BASIC CARDS		
*SILVER: 2X TO 5X BASIC CARDS		
*GOLD: 50X TO 100X BASIC CARDS		
STATED ODDS 1:2		

2012 Garbage Pail Kids Brand New Series One Bonus

COMPLETE SET (12)	60.00	120.00
COMP.SET HOBBY (8)	50.00	100.00
COMP.SET RETAIL (4)	15.00	40.00
COMMON HOBBY BONUS (B1a-B4b)	4.00	10.00
COMMON RETAIL BONUS (B5a-B6b)	4.00	10.00
B1a Mountain Dewey	10.00	25.00
B3a Morbid Mort	12.00	30.00
B4b Barbarian Brian	12.00	30.00

2012 Garbage Pail Kids Brand New Series One Loco-Motion

COMPLETE SET (10)	10.00	25.00
COMMON CARD (1-10)	2.00	5.00
STATED ODDS 1:12		
2 Adam Bomb	4.00	10.00

2012 Garbage Pail Kids Brand New Series One Magnets

COMPLETE SET (16)	10.00	20.00
COMMON CARD (1-16)	.75	2.00
1 Adam Bomb	1.25	3.00

2012 Garbage Pail Kids Brand New Series One Mix 'n Match

COMPLETE SET (10)	8.00	20.00
COMMON CARD (1-10)	1.50	4.00
STATED ODDS 1:12		
1 Adam Bomb	2.50	6.00

2012 Garbage Pail Kids Brand New Series One Posters

COMPLETE SET (6)	10.00	20.00
COMMON CARD	2.00	5.00
ONE POSTER PER RACK PACK		

2013 Garbage Pail Kids Brand New Series Two

COMP.SET W/O SP's (146)	10.00	25.00
UNOPENED BOX (24 PACKS)	40.00	50.00
UNOPENED PACK (10 CARDS)	2.00	2.50
COMMON CARD (56a-128b)	.20	.50
COMMON SP (101c-128c)	100.00	175.00
*BLACK: 2.5X TO 6X BASIC CARDS	1.25	3.00
*SILVER: 10X TO 25X BASIC CARDS	5.00	12.00
*GOLD: 30X TO 80X BASIC CARDS	15.00	40.00
101c Evil Eddie SP	125.00	250.00
123c G.P. Kay SP	125.00	250.00
125c Retchin' Gretchen SP	125.00	250.00
128a Adam Bomb	.60	1.50
128c Blasted Billy SP	125.00	250.00

2013 Garbage Pail Kids Brand New Series Two 3-D Motion

COMPLETE SET (10)	12.00	30.00
COMMON CARD (1-10)	2.00	5.00
STATED ODDS 1:12		

2013 Garbage Pail Kids Brand New Series Two Bonus

COMPLETE SET (18)	100.00	200.00
COMMON CARD (B7a-B15b)	4.00	10.00
STATED ODDS 1:24 HOBBY		
B7a Bridget Bride	8.00	20.00
B7b Just Mary	8.00	20.00
B8a Albert Alien	8.00	20.00
B8b Spacey Scott	8.00	20.00
B9a Son of Manny	8.00	20.00
B9b Ripe Rene	8.00	20.00
B10a Riveting Rosie	8.00	20.00
B10b Propaganda Paula	8.00	20.00
B13a Ike Berg	6.00	15.00
B13b Icy Ian	6.00	15.00
B14a Taser Frasier	6.00	15.00
B14b Shocked Sol	6.00	15.00
B15a Dayna the Dead	6.00	15.00
B15b Mia de los Muertos	6.00	15.00

2013 Garbage Pail Kids Brand New Series Two Foldees

COMPLETE SET (10)	5.00	12.00
COMMON CARD (1-10)	1.00	2.50
STATED ODDS 1:4		

2013 Garbage Pail Kids Brand New Series Two Glow-in-the-Dark

COMPLETE SET (10)	8.00	20.00
COMMON CARD (1-10)	1.50	4.00
STATED ODDS 1:6		
1 Adam Bomb	2.00	5.00

2013 Garbage Pail Kids Brand New Series Three

COMP.SET w/o SP's (132)	8.00	20.00
COMMON CARD (129a-194b)	.20	.50
COMMON SP	40.00	80.00
*BLACK: 1.5X TO 4X BASIC CARDS		
*SILVER: 4X TO 10X BASIC CARDS		
*GOLD: 25X TO 60X BASIC CARDS		

2013 Garbage Pail Kids Brand New Series Three 3-D Motion

COMPLETE SET (10)	12.00	30.00
COMMON CARD (1-10)	2.50	6.00
STATED ODDS 1:12		

2013 Garbage Pail Kids Brand New Series Three Adam Bombing

COMPLETE SET (10)	5.00	12.00
COMMON CARD (1-10)	1.00	2.50
*BLACK: 1X TO 2.5X BASIC CARDS		
*SILVER: 4X TO 10X BASIC CARDS		
*GOLD: 10X TO 25X BASIC CARDS		
STATED ODDS 1:4		

2013 Garbage Pail Kids Brand New Series Three Artist Autographs

COMMON DEJARNETTE	25.00	60.00
COMMON ENGSTROM	20.00	50.00
COMMON GROSS	25.00	60.00
COMMON IM	20.00	50.00
COMMON PINGITORE	25.00	60.00
COMMON SIMKO	25.00	60.00

2013 Garbage Pail Kids Brand New Series Three Bonus

COMPLETE SET (18)	100.00	175.00
COMP.HOBBY BOX SET (8)	60.00	120.00
COMP.BLASTER BOX SET (4)	10.00	25.00
COMP.JUMBO PACK SET (6)	12.00	30.00
COMMON CARD (B16a-B19b)	6.00	15.00
COMMON CARD (B20a-B21b)	3.00	8.00
COMMON CARD (B22a-B24b)	3.00	8.00

2013 Garbage Pail Kids Brand New Series Three Sticker Scenes

COMPLETE SET (10)	6.00	15.00
COMMON CARD (1-10)	1.25	3.00
STATED ODDS 1:6		

2013 Garbage Pail Kids Brand New Series Three Promo

P1 Hoodie Harlan PHILLY	12.00	30.00

2013 Garbage Pail Kids Brand New Series Three Oversized Promo

B21a Volt Ron WW	6.00	15.00

1986 Topps Garbage Pail Kids Buttons

COMPLETE SET (24)	30.00	75.00
COMMON BUTTON	2.00	5.00

2019 Garbage Pail Kids Cereal

COMPLETE SET (4)	15.00	40.00
COMMON CARD (1f-4f)	6.00	15.00
STATED ODDS 2:GPK CEREAL BOX		
1f Adam Bomb	8.00	20.00

2013 Topps Chrome Garbage Pail Kids Series One

COMPLETE SET W/SP (119)	250.00	600.00
COMP.SET W/O SP (110)	75.00	200.00
UNOPENED BOX (24 PACKS)	800.00	1200.00
UNOPENED PACK (4 CARDS)	35.00	50.00
COMMON CARD	1.50	4.00
COMMON SP	50.00	125.00
*REFRACTOR: .6X TO 1.5X BASIC CARDS		
*ATOM.REF.: 1.2X TO 3X BASIC CARDS		
*X-FRACTOR: 2X TO 5X BASIC CARDS		
*PRISM REF.: 3X TO 8X BASIC CARDS		
*GOLD REF.: 8X TO 20X BASIC CARDS		
1a Nasty Nick	10.00	25.00
1b Evil Eddie	6.00	15.00
8a Adam Bomb	20.00	50.00
8b Blasted Billy	8.00	20.00
19c Kit Zit SP	100.00	200.00

2013 Topps Chrome Garbage Pail Kids Series One Artist Autographs

COMMON BUNK	200.00	500.00
COMMON POUND	300.00	750.00
STATED PRINT RUN 10 SER.#'d SETS		
1a Nasty Nick	300.00	750.00
1b Evil Eddie	300.00	750.00
8a Adam Bomb	300.00	750.00
8b Blasted Billy	300.00	750.00

2013 Topps Chrome Garbage Pail Kids Series One Pencil Art

COMPLETE SET (82)	75.00	200.00
COMMON CARD	1.50	4.00
STATED ODDS 1:6		
1a Nasty Nick	10.00	25.00
1b Evil Eddie	6.00	15.00
8a Adam Bomb	20.00	50.00
8b Blasted Billy	8.00	20.00

2014 Topps Chrome Garbage Pail Kids Series Two

COMPLETE SET W/SP (130)	250.00	600.00
COMPLETE SET W/O SP (110)	100.00	250.00
UNOPENED BOX (24 PACKS)	400.00	800.00
UNOPENED PACK (4 CARDS)	20.00	35.00
COMMON CARD	1.50	4.00
COMMON SP	25.00	60.00
*PENCIL ART: SAME VALUE AS BASIC		
*REF.: SAME VALUE AS BASIC		
*ATOM.REF.: .75X TO 2X BASIC CARDS		
*X-FRACT.: 1.2X TO 3X BASIC CARDS		
*PRISM REF/199: 2X TO 5X BASIC CARDS		
*BLACK REF/99: 2.5X TO 6X BASIC CARDS		
*GOLD REF/50: 5X TO 12X BASIC CARDS		

2014 Topps Chrome Garbage Pail Kids Series Two John Pound Autographs

COMMON AUTO (42A-83B)	250.00	600.00
STATED ODDS 1:305		

2020 Topps Chrome Garbage Pail Kids Series 3

COMPLETE SET W/O SP (100)	20.00	50.00
UNOPENED BOX (24 PACKS)	200.00	300.00
UNOPENED BLASTER BOX (5 PACKS)	25.00	40.00
UNOPENED PACK (4 CARDS)	8.00	12.00
COMMON CARD (84a-AN9b)	.75	2.00
COMMON SP (84c-AN9c)	25.00	60.00
*REFRACTOR: .6X TO 1.5X BASIC CARDS		
*ATOMIC REF: .75X TO 2X BASIC CARDS		
*GREEN/299: .75X TO 2X BASIC CARDS		
*GREEN WAVE/299: .75X TO 2X BASIC CARDS		
*PURPLE/250: 1X TO 2.5X BASIC CARDS		
*PURPLE WAVE/250: 1X TO 2.5X BASIC CARDS		
*PRISM/199: 1.5X TO 4X BASIC CARDS		
*XFRACTOR/150: 2X TO 5X BASIC CARDS		
*BLACK/99: 2X TO 5X BASIC CARDS		
*BLACK WAVE/99: 2.5X TO 6X BASIC CARDS		
*ORANGE/75: 6X TO 15X BASIC CARDS		
*GOLD/50: 12X TO 30X BASIC CARDS		
SP C-VARIATION ODDS 1:101		
85c Voodoo Drew SP	30.00	75.00
86c Oat Bran SP	30.00	75.00
87c Android Boyd SP	50.00	100.00
93c Kay O'd SP	30.00	75.00
95c Tim Reaper SP	50.00	100.00
98c Spidey Heidi SP	50.00	100.00
100c Croco Lyle SP	30.00	75.00
104c Mythical Myra SP	50.00	100.00
105c Feed Me Seymour SP	50.00	100.00
107c Carved Karen SP	30.00	75.00
108c Sar-Dina SP	60.00	120.00
110c We Want Hugh SP	60.00	120.00
113c Katie Liberty SP	30.00	75.00
114c Looky Lou SP	50.00	100.00
115c Toasted Tom SP	50.00	100.00
116c Scary Harry SP	30.00	75.00
117c Jailhouse Brock SP	50.00	100.00
119c Shrunk Ken SP	30.00	75.00
120c Phoebe & J SP	30.00	75.00
AN5c Got A Dwight SP	100.00	200.00
AN6c Buy George SP	50.00	100.00
AN8c Albie Back SP	50.00	100.00

2022 Topps Chrome Garbage Pail Kids Series 4

COMPLETE SET W/O SP (100)	20.00	50.00
UNOPENED BOX (24 PACKS)	60.00	80.00
UNOPENED PACK (4 CARDS)	3.00	4.00
UNOPENED BLASTER BOX (5 PACKS)		
COMMON CARD (125a-AN6b))	.40	1.00
COMMON SP	15.00	40.00
*REF: .6X TO 1.5X BASIC CARDS		
*ATOMIC: 2.5X TO 6X BASIC CARDS		
*GREEN/299: 3X TO 8X BASIC CARDS		
*GREEN WAVE/299: 3X TO 8X BASIC CARDS		
*YELLOW/275: 8X TO 20X BASIC CARDS		
*YELLOW WAVE/275: 8X TO 20X BASIC CARDS		
*PURPLE/250: 6X TO 15X BASIC CARDS		
*PURPLE WAVE/250: 6X TO 15X BASIC CARDS		
*PRISM/199: 10X TO 25X BASIC CARDS		
*AQUA PRISM/199: 10X TO 25X BASIC CARDS		
*X-FRAC/150: 12X TO 30X BASIC CARDS		
*BLACK WAVE/99: 25X TO 60X BASIC CARDS		
*ORANGE/75: 30X TO 80X BASIC CARDS		
*ROSE GOLD/25: 100X TO 250X BASIC CARDS		
125c May-Hogany SP	20.00	50.00
128c Carbon Nate SP	25.00	60.00
130c Phil-Landerer SP	25.00	60.00
131c Scary Gary SP	20.00	50.00
132c Leonard Skinner SP	20.00	50.00
135c Butch Quinn SP	20.00	50.00
137c Head Les SP	40.00	100.00
138c Marv Attacks SP	60.00	150.00
139c Sally Specs SP	30.00	75.00
141c Home Lesley SP	30.00	75.00
143c Bread Bernie SP	25.00	60.00
144c Toney Tony SP	20.00	50.00
146c Jerky Joey SP	25.00	60.00
147c Brolic Beth SP	30.00	75.00
148c Issa Lit SP	25.00	60.00
149c Jesse Jigsaw SP	25.00	60.00
150c Growing Gerda SP	20.00	50.00
151c Falling Coleen SP	40.00	100.00
153c Hal Oween SP	40.00	100.00
154c Hedy Hooper SP	30.00	75.00
155c Al Q. Puncture SP	30.00	75.00
156c Combat Pat SP	20.00	50.00
158c Cole Weathers SP	40.00	100.00
159c Tubby Tabby SP	25.00	60.00
160c Al Core SP	25.00	60.00
163c Dense Denise SP	20.00	50.00
164c Fallon Apart SP	30.00	75.00
165c Shedding Sheila SP	30.00	75.00
166c Hole In Juan SP	20.00	50.00
AN1c Ward Winner SP	40.00	100.00
AN2c Carpenter Carl SP	20.00	50.00
AN3c Bad Ash SP	25.00	60.00
AN4c Shiny Sean SP	30.00	75.00
AN5c Sherm-Minator SP	30.00	75.00
AN6c Dez-Troyer SP	40.00	100.00

2022 Topps Chrome Garbage Pail Kids Series 4 Autographs

COMMON BUNK	150.00	400.00
COMMON BURKE		
STATED PRINT RUN 50 SER.#'d SETS		

2022 Topps Chrome Garbage Pail Kids Series 5

COMPLETE SET (150)		
COMPLETE SET W/O SP (100)	20.00	50.00
UNOPENED BOX (24 PACKS)	60.00	80.00
UNOPENED PACK (4 CARDS)	3.00	4.00
COMMON CARD (167a-216b)	.50	1.25
COMMON C-VARIANT SP	15.00	40.00
*REF: .75X TO 2X BASIC CARDS		
*ATOMIC: 2.5X TO 6X BASIC CARDS		
*GREEN/299: 6X TO 15X BASIC CARDS		
*GREEN WAVE/299: 8X TO 20X BASIC CARDS		
*YELLOW/275: 8X TO 20X BASIC CARDS		
*YELLOW WAVE/275: 10X TO 25X BASIC CARDS		
*PURPLE/250: 12X TO 30X BASIC CARDS		
*PURPLE WAVE/250: 12X TO 30X BASIC CARDS		
*PRISM/199: 15X TO 40X BASIC CARDS		
*AQUA/199: 15X TO 40X BASIC CARDS		
*X-FRAC/150: 20X TO 50X BASIC CARDS		
*BLACK/99: 25X TO 60X BASIC CARDS		
*BLACK WAVE/99: 25X TO 60X BASIC CARDS		
*ORANGE/75: 30X TO 75X BASIC CARDS		
*GOLD/50: 40X TO 100X BASIC CARDS		
167c Sliced Dice SP	25.00	60.00
169c Fay Soff SP	20.00	50.00
172c Zeke Geek SP	20.00	50.00
174c Patched-Up Pat SP	25.00	60.00
175c Gassy Massey SP	25.00	60.00
176c Wrecked Ralph SP	20.00	50.00
178c Classy Camille SP	20.00	50.00
180c Scary Terry SP	20.00	50.00
183c Pierced Brosnan SP	20.00	50.00
185c Hot Link SP	20.00	50.00
188c Im-Paul-Sible Meat SP	25.00	60.00
189c Milkshake Blake SP	20.00	50.00
191c Zapped Saunders SP	20.00	50.00
196c Hanging Channing SP	20.00	50.00
198c Snotty Dotty SP	20.00	50.00
201c Monster Mack SP	30.00	75.00
202c Sunburn Verne SP	25.00	60.00
205c Weird Wheeler SP	30.00	75.00
206c Max Volume SP	30.00	75.00
208c Stuck Buck SP	20.00	50.00
209c Tilted Tommy SP	40.00	100.00
210c Board Walker SP	25.00	60.00
211c Charlie Sheen SP	20.00	50.00

213c Fly Guy SP 30.00 75.00
214c Remy Rem SP 20.00 50.00
215c Liquid Louie SP 20.00 50.00

2022 Topps Chrome Garbage Pail Kids Series 5 Artist Autographs

COMMON BUNK 250.00 600.00
COMMON CAMERA 150.00 400.00
COMMON GROSS 100.00 250.00
COMMON SIMKO 75.00 200.00
STATED ODDS 1:1,392
STATED PRINT RUN 50 SER.#'d SETS

2022 Topps Chrome Garbage Pail Kids Series 5 No Blue Ink Variations

COMMON CARD (BI167-BI216) 150.00 400.00
STATED ODDS 1:1,986

2022 Topps Garbage Pail Kids Clash of Clans

COMPLETE SET (20) 12.00 30.00
COMMON CARD (1a-10b) 1.00 2.50
*GOLD COIN: 2.5X TO 6X BASIC CARDS
*GREEN GEM: 5X TO 12X BASIC CARDS
STATED PRINT RUN 2,176 SETS

2017 Garbage Pail Kids Comedy of Comey

COMPLETE SET (10) 40.00 80.00
COMMON CARD (1a-5b) 5.00 12.00
STATED PRINT RUN 113-126

2021 Topps Garbage Pail Kids ComplexCon

COMPLETE SET (12) 12.00 30.00
COMMON CARD (1a-6b) 3.00 8.00
*RED BACKS: .5X TO 1.5X BASIC CARDS
STATED PRINT RUN 1,233 ANNCD SETS

2021 Topps Garbage Pail Kids ComplexLand

COMPLETE SET (10)
COMMON CARD (1a-5b) 2.00 5.00
STATED PRINT RUN 1,071 ANNCD SETS

2014-15 Topps Garbage Pail Kids Convention Exclusives

COMPLETE SET (4) 30.00 75.00
COMMON CARD (P1-P4) 4.00 10.00
P1 Comic Conner SDCC 5.00 12.00
P2 Fan Boyd NYCC 10.00 25.00
P4 Smilin' Stan Comikaze 20.00 50.00

2020 Topps Garbage Pail Kids Crash Gordon 40th Anniversary

COMPLETE SET (10) 12.00 30.00
COMMON CARD (1a-5b) 2.00 5.00
STATED PRINT RUN 538 SETS

2016-17 Topps Garbage Pail Kids Disg-Race to the White House

COMPLETE SET (152) 1200.00 2000.00
COMMON CARD (1-152) 4.00 10.00
TOPPS 24-HOUR EXCLUSIVE
1 Disg-Race to the White House/1196* 6.00 15.00
2 Drippy Donald/399* 60.00 120.00
3 Desperado Donald/391* 15.00 40.00
4 400 LB. Hack Earl/345* 15.00 40.00
5 Chucklin' Clinton/410* 5.00 12.00
6 Dueling Donald/291* 10.00 25.00
7 Hated Hillary/287* 12.00 30.00
8 2nd Aleppo Gaffe Gary/286* 12.00 30.00
9 Dumpy Donald/301* 8.00 20.00
10 Tax-Dodgin' Donald/507* 5.00 12.00
13 Tiring Tim and Monotonous Mike/300* 6.00 15.00
14 Rushmore of Dictators/266* 15.00 40.00
15 Russ-Ian Dolls/255* 12.00 30.00
16 Eyebrow's Insane Kaine/255* 10.00 25.00
17 Criminal Al-Ian/256* 12.00 30.00
20 Tissue Issue Trump/379* 6.00 15.00
22 Locker Room Talk Trump/535* 5.00 12.00
23 Undead Donald/400* 6.00 15.00
24 Marionette Melee/371* 6.00 15.00
27 Discount Donald/344* 6.00 15.00
28 Rootin' for Putin/383* 6.00 15.00
29 Toupee Trump/398* 5.00 12.00
30 Disastrous Donald/259* 6.00 15.00
31 Human Hillary/258* 5.00 12.00
32 Toddler Trump/263* 5.00 12.00
33 Battlin' Biden/310* 60.00 120.00
34 Hackin' Hillary/307* 5.00 12.00
35 Dispensed Pence/289* 5.00 12.00
36 Coaxed Comey/407* 5.00 12.00
37 Combed Over Clinton/407* 5.00 12.00
38 Treasurer Trump/396* 5.00 12.00
39 Double-Dealing Donald/349* 5.00 12.00
40 Hit Job Hillary/310* 6.00 15.00
41 Taco Trump/365* 5.00 12.00
42 Ill Hill/354* 5.00 12.00
43 Downloaded Donald/349* 6.00 15.00
44 Compu-Clinton & Taxes Trump/310* 5.00 12.00
45 Assaultin' Assange/281* 8.00 20.00
46 Tardy Trump/280* 6.00 15.00
47 Rehearsed Rodham Clinton/285* 6.00 15.00
52 Temperamental Trump/337* 6.00 15.00
53 Contribution Clinton/288* 8.00 20.00
54 Trump Takeoff/307* 6.00 15.00
55 Nasty Hillary/301* 8.00 20.00
56 Contradicted Conway/286* 8.00 20.00
57 Misappropriating Melania/286* 6.00 15.00
59 Check Collectin' Clinton/391* 6.00 15.00
60 Threatening Trump/382* 5.00 12.00
61 Cashin' In Clinton/381* 6.00 15.00
62 Trump Television/426* 6.00 15.00
63 Kellyanne Con Job/375* 6.00 15.00
64 Towering Trump/729* 6.00 15.00
65 Refugee Rodham Clinton/496* 6.00 15.00
66 Deplorable Donald/566* 6.00 15.00
67 Begrudging Barack/554* 20.00 50.00
69 Tan-Trump/401* 6.00 15.00
70 Demonstration Donald/622* 6.00 15.00
71 Divided Donald/417* 6.00 15.00
72 Troll Trump/389* 6.00 15.00
73 Bad Bannon/403* 20.00 50.00
74 Priebus & Butt-Head/488* 6.00 15.00
75 De-Fence Donald/331* 6.00 15.00
77 Trump Tribe/289* 8.00 20.00
78 Drain the Swamp Donald/361* 6.00 15.00
79 The Trouble with Trump/372* 5.00 12.00
80 Rudolph Ghouliani/349* 5.00 12.00
82 Jewelry You'll Wantka... WP/447* 6.00 15.00
85 Scorched Steve/279* 8.00 20.00
86 Trumpbucks Coffee WP/410* 6.00 15.00
87 Roped In Romney/321* 8.00 20.00
88 Countin' Clinton/316* 6.00 15.00
89 Tantrum Trump/341* 6.00 15.00
90 Jill Stein Recount Calculator WP/375* 10.00 25.00
91 Double Chin Donald/343* 5.00 12.00
92 Double Standard Donald/351* 6.00 15.00
95 Mad Dog Mattis/300* 8.00 20.00
96 Two-Faced Trump/304* 6.00 15.00
98 Bigly Chew WP/407* 10.00 25.00
99 Tag Sale Trump/308* 5.00 12.00
100 Construction Carson/277* 8.00 20.00
101 Trump Thank Me Tour Ticker WP/441* 6.00 15.00
102 Trump Time/758* 200.00 400.00
103 Dealer Dole/305* 6.00 15.00
104 Honey-Combover WP/405* 6.00 15.00
105 Terminator Trump/316* 5.00 12.00
108 GOP Pail Kids WP/581* 6.00 15.00
109 Voter Duping Donald/292* 8.00 20.00
111 Very Bigly Thank You...WP/419* 15.00 40.00
112 Two-Timer Trump/276* 6.00 15.00
113 Cuckoo Kanye/327* 6.00 15.00
114 Red Rex/296* 5.00 12.00
116 Tangerine Dream Spray On Tan (Wacky Packages)/391* 6.00 15.00
117 Happy New Fears!/358* 5.00 12.00
118 Dangerous Donald/287* 6.00 15.00
119 Tormented Trump/298* 6.00 15.00
120 Cheapa Pet/393* 5.00 12.00
122 Trumped Donald/305* 6.00 15.00
125 Trump Talking Hand Puppet WP/484* 20.00 50.00
126 Disapproving Donald/277* 5.00 12.00
127 Hit Job Holder/297* 5.00 12.00
128 Duped Donald/303* 6.00 15.00
129 Presidency for Donalds WP/441* 6.00 15.00
130 Thieving Trump/286* 5.00 12.00
131 Terse Trump/291* 6.00 15.00
132 Joker's Trump Card/353* 5.00 12.00
133 Coronation Trump-et WP/363* 6.00 15.00
134 Toil and Trouble Trump/267* 6.00 15.00
135 Assange's Trump-et/266* 6.00 15.00
136 Grow (up) Joe/281* 5.00 12.00
137 DNC Pail Kids WP/446* 8.00 20.00
138 Deceiver Donald/285* 5.00 12.00
139 Blubbering Barack/316* 20.00 50.00
140 Truthiness Trump/297* 5.00 12.00
141 Gifted Jared/288* 5.00 12.00
142 Swamp Draino WP/438* 6.00 15.00
143 Dogfight Donald/248* 5.00 12.00
144 Detached Donald/275* 5.00 12.00
145 Cross-Examined Comey/257* 5.00 12.00
146 L.L. Green$ WP/291* 6.00 15.00
147 Dirty-Dealing Donald/269* 5.00 12.00
148 Steve Hardly/262* 5.00 12.00
149 Hack 'Em Blackmail 'Em WP/342* 6.00 15.00
150 Neopalpa Donaldtrumpi/277* 6.00 15.00
151 Donald Grump/339* 6.00 15.00
152 The Real WhiteHousewives... WP/370* 6.00 15.00

2020 Topps Garbage Pail Kids Disg-Race to the White House

COMPLETE SET (94) 150.00 300.00
COMPLETE SET 1 (12) 30.00 75.00
COMPLETE SET 2 (10) 15.00 40.00
COMPLETE SET 3 (12) 15.00 40.00
COMPLETE SET 4 (12) 20.00 50.00
COMPLETE SET 5 (10) 12.00 30.00
COMPLETE SET 6 (12) 20.00 50.00
COMPLETE SET 7 (10) 12.00 30.00
COMPLETE SET 8 (16) 20.00 50.00
COMMON SET 1 (1a-6b) 4.00 10.00
COMMON SET 2 (7a-11b) 3.00 8.00
COMMON SET 3 (12a-17b) 3.00 8.00
COMMON SET 4 (18a-23b) 4.00 10.00
COMMON SET 5 (24a-28b) 2.50 6.00
COMMON SET 6 (29a-34b) 3.00 8.00
COMMON SET 7 (35a-39b) 2.50 6.00
COMMON SET 8 (40a-48b) 2.50 6.00
SET 1 PRINT RUN 1,870 SETS
SET 2 PRINT RUN 1,351 SETS
SET 3 PRINT RUN 1,689 SETS
SET 4 PRINT RUN 1,357 SETS
SET 5 PRINT RUN 1,687 SETS
SET 6 PRINT RUN 1,062 SETS
SET 7 PRINT RUN 1,307 SETS
SET 8 PRINT RUN 1,199 SETS

2020 Topps Garbage Pail Kids eBay

COMPLETE SET (10) 10.00 25.00
COMMON CARD (1a-5b) 1.50 4.00
STATED PRINT RUN 1,937 SETS

2017 Garbage Pail Kids Empty-V Awards

COMPLETE SET (12) 50.00 100.00
COMMON CARD (1a-6b) 6.00 15.00

2017 Garbage Pail Kids Fall Comic Convention Promos

COMPLETE SET (12) 100.00 200.00
COMMON CARD (1a-6b) 8.00 20.00
STATED PRINT RUN 187 SETS
TOPPS.COM EXCLUSIVE

2010 Topps Garbage Pail Kids Flashback

COMPLETE SET (160) 20.00 40.00
UNOPENED BOX (24 PACKS) 200.00 300.00
UNOPENED PACK (10 CARDS) 8.00 12.00
COMMON CARD .20 .50
*GREEN: 2X TO 5X BASIC CARDS
*PINK: 3X TO 8X BASIC CARDS
*SILVER: 6X TO 15X BASIC CARDS
*GOLD: 30X TO 80X BASIC CARDS
1a Nasty Nick .40 1.00
1b Evil Eddie .40 1.00
3a Adam Bomb .75 2.00
3b Blasted Billy .40 1.00
71a Nasty Nick .30 .75
71b Evil Eddie .30 .75
72a Adam Bomb .30 .75
72b Blasted Billy .30 .75

2010 Topps Garbage Pail Kids Flashback Bonus Stickers

COMPLETE SET (4) 10.00 25.00
COMMON CARD (B1-B4) 2.00 5.00
B1-B3 INSERTED IN BONUS BOXES
B4 INSERTED IN BLISTER PACKS
B4 Mixed-Up Trixie 5.00 12.00

2010 Topps Garbage Pail Kids Flashback Loco Motion

COMPLETE SET (10) 20.00 40.00
COMMON CARD (1-10) 2.50 6.00
STATED ODDS 1:8

2011 Garbage Pail Kids Flashback Series Two

COMPLETE SET (160) 12.00 30.00
UNOPENED BOX (24 PACKS) 150.00 250.00
UNOPENED PACK (10 CARDS) 6.00 10.00
COMMON CARD (1a-80b) .15 .40
*GREEN: .8X TO 2X BASIC CARDS
*PINK: 1.5X TO 4X BASIC CARDS
*SILVER: 6X TO 15X BASIC CARDS
*GOLD: 40X TO 100X BASIC CARDS

2011 Garbage Pail Kids Flashback Series Two 3-D

COMPLETE SET (5) 10.00 25.00
COMMON CARD (3D1-3D4) 3.00 8.00
STATED ODDS 1:12
SP STATED ODDS 1:85
3D5 Adam Bomb SP 6.00 15.00

2011 Garbage Pail Kids Flashback Series Two Adam Mania

COMPLETE SET (10) 12.00 30.00
COMMON CARD (1-10) 2.50 6.00
*GREEN: .5X TO 1.2X BASIC CARDS
*PINK: .8X TO 2X BASIC CARDS
*SILVER: 1.5X TO 4X BASIC CARDS
*GOLD: 15X TO 30X BASIC CARDS
STATED ODDS 1:8

2011 Garbage Pail Kids Flashback Series Two Posters

COMPLETE SET (5) 10.00 25.00
COMMON POSTER 3.00 8.00
STATED ODDS 1:RACK PACK
1 Adam Bomb 4.00 10.00

2011 Garbage Pail Kids Flashback Series Two Retail Bonus

COMPLETE SET (4) 8.00 20.00
COMMON CARD (B1-B4) 3.00 8.00
B1-B3 STATED ODDS ONE PER BLISTER PACK
B4 STATED ODDS ONE PER BLASTER BOX
B4 Cleaned Up Clint 4.00 10.00

2011 Garbage Pail Kids Flashback Series Three

COMPLETE SET (160) 12.00 30.00
UNOPENED BOX (24 PACKS) 300.00 500.00
UNOPENED PACK (10 CARDS) 12.00 20.00
COMMON CARD (1a-80b) .15 .40
*GREEN: .8X TO 2X BASIC CARDS
*PINK: 1.5X TO 4X BASIC CARDS
*SILVER: 6X TO 15X BASIC CARDS
*GOLD: 40X TO 100X BASIC CARDS
S1 STATED ODDS 1:7,700
S1 John Pound AUTO 350.00 700.00

2011 Garbage Pail Kids Flashback Series Three 3-D

COMPLETE SET (5) 10.00 25.00
COMMON CARD (3D1-3D5) 3.00 8.00
STATED ODDS 1:12
SP STATED ODDS 1:85
3D5 Adam Boom SP 6.00 15.00

2011 Garbage Pail Kids Flashback Series Three Adam Mania

COMPLETE SET (10) 12.00 30.00
COMMON CARD (1-10) 2.50 6.00
*GREEN: .5X TO 1.2X BASIC CARDS
*PINK: .8X TO 2X BASIC CARDS
*SILVER: 1.5X TO 4X BASIC CARDS
*GOLD: 15X TO 30X BASIC CARDS
STATED ODDS 1:8

2011 Garbage Pail Kids Flashback Series Three Posters

COMPLETE SET (5) 5.00 20.00
COMMON CARD 2.00 5.00

2011 Garbage Pail Kids Flashback Series Three Retail Bonus

COMPLETE SET (5) 8.00 20.00
COMMON CARD 3.00 8.00
B1-B3 STATED ODDS ONE PER BLISTER PACK

2021 Topps Garbage Pail Kids Food Fight

COMPLETE SET (200) 15.00 40.00
UNOPENED HOBBY BOX (24 PACKS) 60.00 100.00
UNOPENED HOBBY PACK (8 CARDS) 3.00 4.00
UNOPENED H.COLLECTOR BOX (24 PACKS)
UNOPENED H.COLLECTOR PACK (8 CARDS)
COMMON CARD (1a-100b) .20 .50
*BLACK: 1.2X TO 3X BASIC CARDS
*GREEN: 2X TO 5X BASIC CARDS
*YELLOW: 4X TO 10X BASIC CARDS
*BLUE/99: 8X TO 20X BASIC CARDS
*RED/75: 12X TO 30X BASIC CARDS
*GOLD/50: 15X TO 40X BASIC CARDS

2021 Topps Garbage Pail Kids Food Fight Artist Autographs

COMMON ENGSTROM 12.00 30.00
COMMON GROSS 15.00 40.00
COMMON SIMKO 20.00 50.00
COMMON SMOKIN' JOE 15.00 40.00
RANDOMLY INSERTED INTO PACKS
STATED PRINT RUN 80 SER.#'d SETS
58 Smokin' Joe 50.00 100.00

2021 Topps Garbage Pail Kids Food Fight Celebrity Chefs

COMPLETE SET (16) 10.00 25.00
COMMON CARD (1a-8b) 1.25 3.00
STATED ODDS 3:1 BOX
BLASTER BOX EXCLUSIVE

2021 Topps Garbage Pail Kids Food Fight The Cereal Aisle

COMPLETE SET (24) 25.00 60.00
COMMON CARD (1a-12b) 1.50 4.00
RANDOMLY INSERTED INTO PACKS

2021 Topps Garbage Pail Kids Food Fight GPK Food Wacky Packages

COMPLETE SET (10) 100.00 200.00
COMMON CARD (WP1-WP10) 10.00 25.00
STATED ODDS 1:1
HOBBY COLLECTOR BOX EXCLUSIVE
WP2 Orville Red-Blockers 12.00 30.00
WP3 Moonbeam Hippie Bread 12.00 30.00
WP5 Kool Ache 20.00 50.00
WP6 Twit Kat 15.00 40.00
WP7 Morbid Salt 12.00 30.00
WP9 Boogzooka 25.00 60.00
WP10 Kentucky Fried Garbage 15.00 40.00

2021 Topps Garbage Pail Kids Food Fight Mini Refrigerator Magnets

COMPLETE SET (12) 75.00 150.00
COMMON CARD (M1-M12) 8.00 20.00
STATED ODDS 2:HOBBY COLLECTOR BONUS PACK

2021 Topps Garbage Pail Kids Food Fight Wacky Packages Patches

COMMON MEM 10.00 25.00
HOBBY COLLECTOR EXCLUSIVE
STATED PRINT RUN 199 SER.#'d SETS
WPG Gadzooka 12.00 30.00
WPBB Hurtz Baked Bears 15.00 40.00
WPBR Baby Runt 15.00 40.00
WPGM Glutton Sloppy Brown Mustard 12.00 30.00
WPSB Soggy Babies 15.00 40.00
WPTC Taster's Choke 15.00 40.00
WPOFQ Old Fashioned Quacker Oats 12.00 30.00

2021 Topps Garbage Pail Kids Food Fight You Are What You Eat

COMPLETE SET (10) 10.00 25.00
COMMON CARD (1a-5b) 1.50 4.00
DISPLAY BOX EXCLUSIVE

2021 Topps Garbage Pail Kids Gamestonk

COMPLETE SET (12) 20.00 50.00
COMMON CARD (1a-6b) 2.00 5.00
STATED PRINT RUN 1070 ANNCD SETS
1a Big Screen Bernie 5.00 12.00
1b Sanders Cinema 4.00 10.00
2a Adam Bomb 2.00 8.00
4a Electic Elon 4.00 10.00
4b U. Musk Invest 4.00 10.00

2019 Garbage Pail Kids Geeki Tiki Promos

COMPLETE SET (3) 25.00 60.00
COMMON CARD (1-3) 10.00 25.00
3 Luau Lindsay 12.00 30.00

1986 Topps Garbage Pail Kids Giant Series One

COMPLETE SET (39) 75.00 150.00
UNOPENED BOX (36 PACKS) 250.00 300.00
UNOPENED PACK (3 CARDS) 7.00 10.00
COMMON CARD (1-39) 1.00 2.50
1 Nasty Nick 12.00 30.00
2 Junkfood John 3.00 8.00
6 Art Apart 2.50 6.00
7 Stormy Heather 5.00 12.00
8A Adam Bomb/Succeed 15.00 40.00
8B Adam Bomb/Student Award 20.00 50.00
9 Unstitched Mitch 2.50 6.00
10 Tee-Vee Stevie 3.00 8.00
11 Itchy Richie 2.50 6.00

13 Ashcan Andy	2.50	6.00
16 Weird Wendy	2.50	6.00
17 Mean Gene	2.50	6.00
19 Corroded Carl	2.50	6.00
22 Junky Jeff	3.00	8.00
25 Creepy Carol	2.50	6.00
29 Bony Joanie	3.00	8.00
30 New Wave Dave	5.00	12.00
39 Buggy Betty	6.00	15.00

1986 Topps Garbage Pail Kids Giant Series Two

COMPLETE SET (15)	10.00	25.00
UNOPENED BOX (36 PACKS)	20.00	30.00
UNOPENED PACK (3 CARDS)	1.00	1.25
COMMON CARD (1-15)	1.25	3.00
1 Bazooka Jerk	2.50	6.00
2 Bony Joanie	1.50	4.00
15 Garbage Pail School Senior Class	2.00	5.00

2023 Topps Garbage Pail Kids Go on Vacation

COMPLETE SET (200)	15.00	40.00
UNOPENED BOX (24 PACKS)	40.00	60.00
UNOPENED PACK (8 CARDS)	2.00	3.00
UNOPENED COLL BOX (24 PACKS)	100.00	125.00
UNOPENED COLL PACKS (8 CARDS)	5.00	6.00
COMMON CARD (1a-100b)	.20	.50
*BLACK: .75X TO 2X BASIC CARDS		
*GREEN: 1.5X TO 4X BASIC CARDS		
*YELLOW: 1.5X TO 4X BASIC CARDS		
*BLUE/99: 4X TO 10X BASIC CARDS		
*RED/75: 10X TO 25X BASIC CARDS		
*ASPHALT/66: 10X TO 25X BASIC CARDS		
*GOLD/50: 30X TO 75X BASIC CARDS		

2023 Topps Garbage Pail Kids Go on Vacation Artist Autographs

COMMON ENGSTROM	20.00	50.00
COMMON GROSS	20.00	50.00
COMMON SIMKO	15.00	40.00
COMMON SMOKIN' JOE	15.00	40.00
STATED PRINT RUN 75 SER.#'d SETS		

2023 Topps Garbage Pail Kids Go on Vacation Bumper Stickers

COMPLETE SET (10)	5.00	12.00
COMMON CARD (1-10)	1.25	3.00
STATED ODDS 1:4 BLASTER EXCLUSIVE		

2023 Topps Garbage Pail Kids Go on Vacation Don't Make Me Pull This Car Over

COMPLETE SET (20)	12.00	30.00
COMMON CARD (1a-10b)	1.25	3.00
STATED ODDS 1:3		

2023 Topps Garbage Pail Kids Go on Vacation Famous Landmarks

COMPLETE SET (10)	6.00	15.00
COMMON CARD (1a-5b)	1.25	3.00
STATED ODDS 1:3 DISPLAY BOX		

2023 Topps Garbage Pail Kids Go on Vacation Pack Your Bag Wacky Packages

COMPLETE SET (10)	50.00	125.00
COMMON CARD (WP1-WP10)	8.00	20.00
STATED ODDS 1:1 COLLECTOR'S TIN		

2023 Topps Garbage Pail Kids Go on Vacation Short-Printed Variants

COMMON CARD (SP1-SP9)	60.00	150.00
RANDOMLY INSERTED INTO PACKS		
SP1 Cluttered Clay	100.00	250.00
SP3 Magnificent Mark	100.00	250.00
SP5 Jackie of All Trades	75.00	200.00
SP7 Neil Camera	75.00	200.00
SP8 Tom Junk	100.00	250.00

2023 Topps Garbage Pail Kids Go on Vacation State Quarter Relics

COMMON MEM	30.00	75.00
STATED PRINT RUN 99 SER.#'d SETS		
COLLECTOR'S TIN EXCLUSIVE		

2017 Garbage Pail Kids Golden Groan Awards

COMPLETE SET (10)	25.00	60.00
COMMON CARD (1a-5b)	5.00	12.00

2018 Garbage Pail Kids Golden Groan Awards

COMPLETE SET (12)	25.00	60.00
COMMON CARD (1a-6b)	3.00	8.00
STATED PRINT RUN 147 SETS		
TOPPS.COM EXCLUSIVE		

2020 Topps Garbage Pail Kids Gone Exotic

COMPLETE SET (30)	30.00	75.00
COMPLETE S1 SET (10)	12.00	30.00
COMPLETE S2 SET (10)	15.00	40.00
COMPLETE S3 SET (10)	12.00	30.00
COMMON CARD (1a-5b)	2.50	6.00
COMMON CARD (6a-10b)	3.00	8.00
COMMON CARD (11a-15b)	2.00	5.00
SERIES 1 SET PRINT RUN 3,285 SETS		
SERIES 2 SET PRINT RUN 1,378 SETS		
SERIES 3 SET PRINT RUN 1,193 SETS		

2019 Garbage Pail Kids Greenlight Collectibles Series 1

COMPLETE SET (6)	15.00	40.00
COMMON CARD	4.00	10.00

2019 Garbage Pail Kids Greenlight Collectibles Series 2

COMPLETE SET (6)	10.00	40.00
COMMON CARD	4.00	10.00

2020 Topps Garbage Pail Kids Gross Greetings

COMPLETE SET (10)	12.00	30.00
COMMON CARD (1a-5b)	2.00	5.00
STATED PRINT RUN 535 SETS		

2017 Garbage Pail Kids Halloween

COMPLETE SET (20)	60.00	120.00
COMMON CARD (1a-10b)	5.00	12.00

2020 Topps Garbage Pail Kids Halloween Stories

COMPLETE SET (63)	60.00	120.00
COMMON CARD (1-63)	1.25	3.00
STATED PRINT RUN 2099 SETS		

2020 Topps Garbage Pail Kids Halloween Stories GPK Cover Story

COMPLETE SET (5)	12.00	30.00
COMMON CARD (1-5)	4.00	10.00

2013 Garbage Pail Kids Holiday Greeting Cards Box A

COMPLETE SET (10)	20.00	50.00
COMMON CARD (1-10)	2.50	6.00
TOPPS.COM EXCLUSIVE		

2013 Garbage Pail Kids Holiday Greeting Cards Box B

COMPLETE SET (10)	20.00	50.00
COMMON CARD (1-10)	2.50	6.00
TOPPS.COM EXCLUSIVE		

2022 Topps Garbage Pail Kids International Trading Card Day

COMPLETE SET (15)	12.00	30.00
COMMON CARD (GPKB1-GPKB15)	1.50	4.00

2022 Topps Garbage Pail Kids International Trading Card Day Autographs

COMMON ENGSTROM	12.00	30.00
COMMON GROSS	15.00	40.00
COMMON SIMKO	12.00	30.00
COMMON SMOKIN' JOE	25.00	60.00
GPKAAA Brent Engstrom	12.00	30.00
GPKAAU Brent Engstrom	12.00	30.00
GPKABM Brent Engstrom	12.00	30.00
GPKACP Brent Engstrom	12.00	30.00
GPKAFF Brent Engstrom	12.00	30.00
GPKAHH David Gross	15.00	40.00
GPKARR Smokin' Joe	25.00	60.00
GPKASB Joe Simko	12.00	30.00
GPKASJ Brent Engstrom	12.00	30.00
GPKASK Joe Simko	12.00	30.00
GPKASS Smokin' Joe	25.00	60.00
GPKATT Joe Simko	12.00	30.00
GPKAWW Smokin' Joe	25.00	60.00
GPKAAAR Smokin' Joe	25.00	60.00
GPKASSL Joe Simko	12.00	30.00

2022 Topps Garbage Pail Kids International Trading Card Day Original Series

COMPLETE SET (15)	20.00	50.00
COMMON CARD (GPKOS11-GPKOS115)	1.00	2.50
GPKOS11 Nasty Nick	2.50	6.00
GPKOS13 Up Chuck	2.00	5.00
GPKOS14 Dead Ted	2.50	6.00
GPKOS15 Stormy Heather	1.50	4.00
GPKOS16 Adam Bomb	12.00	30.00
GPKOS17 Tee-Vee Stevie	2.00	5.00
GPKOS18 Potty Scotty	1.50	4.00
GPKOS19 Junky Jeff	2.00	5.00
GPKOS113 New Wave Dave	2.00	5.00

2020 Topps Garbage Pail Kids Kitchen

COMPLETE A SET (10)	10.00	25.00
COMPLETE B SET (10)	150.00	300.00
COMMON A CARD	1.50	4.00
COMMON B CARD	15.00	40.00
A SET PRINT RUN 725 SETS		
1b Pete Slice SP	25.00	60.00
3b Jilly Donut SP	20.00	50.00
4b Rhett Delicious SP	20.00	50.00

2020 Topps Garbage Pail Kids Late to School

COMPLETE SET (200)	10.00	25.00
UNOPENED BOX (24 PACKS)		
UNOPENED PACK (8 CARDS)		
COMMON CARD (1-200)	.20	.50
*BOOGER: 2X TO 5X BASIC CARDS		
*BRUISED: 2X TO 5X BASIC CARDS		
*JELLY: 2.5X TO 6X BASIC CARDS		
*PHLEGM: 5X TO 12X BASIC CARDS		
*SPIT/99: 6X TO 15X BASIC CARDS		
*BLOODY NOSE/75: 8X TO 20X BASIC CARDS		
*FOOL'S GOLD/50: 12X TO 30X BASIC CARDS		

2020 Topps Garbage Pail Kids Late to School Artist Autographs

COMMON ENGSTROM	20.00	50.00
COMMON GROSS	15.00	40.00
COMMON SIMKO	15.00	40.00
COMMON SMOKIN' JOE	25.00	60.00
STATED ODDS 1:260		
COLLECTOR BOX ODDS 1:61		

2020 Topps Garbage Pail Kids Late to School Class Superlatives

COMPLETE SET (10)	5.00	12.00
COMMON CARD (1a-5b)	.75	2.00
STATED ODDS 1:		

2020 Topps Garbage Pail Kids Late to School Faculty Lounge

COMPLETE SET (20)	8.00	20.00
COMMON CARD (1a-10b)	.75	2.00
FAT PACKS EXCLUSIVE		
1a Adam Bomb	2.50	6.00

2020 Topps Garbage Pail Kids Late to School GPK Mascots

COMPLETE SET (10)	8.00	20.00
COMMON CARD (1a-5b)	1.25	3.00
STATED ODDS 1:		

2020 Topps Garbage Pail Kids Late to School Pennant Patches

COMMON MEM (SP1-SP10)	15.00	40.00
STATED PRINT RUN 100 SER.#'d SETS		
SP1 Fartmouth	20.00	50.00
SP2 Puke	20.00	50.00
SP3 Gorgetown	20.00	50.00
SP5 Notre Lame	20.00	50.00
SP6 Mini Soda	20.00	50.00
SP8 GoneGaga	20.00	50.00

2020 Topps Garbage Pail Kids Late to School Wacky Packages Parodies

COMPLETE SET (10)	50.00	100.00
COMMON CARD (1-10)	6.00	15.00
STATED ODDS 1:24		
COLLECTOR BOX EXCLUSIVE		

2020 Topps Garbage Pail Kids Late to School Promo

WM1 Cubby Colby WM	8.00	20.00

2017 Garbage Pail Kids Lord of the Flyes Festival

COMPLETE SET (6)	20.00	50.00
COMMON CARD	5.00	12.00
STATED PRINT RUN 109 SETS		

2018 Garbage Pail Kids Memes

COMPLETE SET W/C (30)	125.00	250.00
COMPLETE SET W/O C (20)	25.00	60.00
COMMON CARD (1a-10b)	2.00	5.00
COMMON C (1c-10c)	10.00	25.00
*GREEN/75: .75X TO 2X BASIC CARDS		
*PINK/25: 3X TO 8X BASIC CARDS		
STATED PRINT RUN 500 SER.#'d SETS		
STATED C PRINT RUN 50 SER.#'d SETS		
1a Nasty Nick	2.50	6.00
1b Evil Eddie	2.50	6.00
1c Season Al	30.00	75.00
2a Adam Bomb	6.00	15.00
2b Blasted Billy	4.00	10.00
2c Mind Blown Mike	30.00	75.00
3c Ancient Allen	12.00	30.00
4c Disaster Pearl	12.00	30.00
6c Success Les	12.00	30.00

2017 Garbage Pail Kids Network Spews

COMPLETE SET (94)	600.00	1200.00
COMMON CARD (1-94)	5.00	12.00
TOPPS.COM EXCLUSIVES		
2 Emissions-Scandal Emmanuel/270*	8.00	20.00
4 Hawaiian Punk/238*	6.00	15.00
5 TV Snide Hillary's One View WP/243*	6.00	15.00
6 Riled Up Ryder/198*	6.00	15.00
7 Human/Pig Hy-brid/165*	6.00	15.00
8 Gagging Guthrie/194*	8.00	20.00
9 Lunatic Lady/195*	8.00	20.00
12 Bowen Arrow/148*	8.00	20.00
13 Desparate Don/147*	8.00	20.00
14 Orange Ali Gator/179*	8.00	20.00
15 Aster-Oid/143*	8.00	20.00
16 The Leggo Bootman Movie WP/285*	6.00	15.00
17 Split Ice Shel/164*	8.00	20.00
18 Careless Cullinan/144*	8.00	20.00
19 The Charo Mister E./163*	6.00	15.00
20 Kid-Crashed Kelly/213*	5.00	12.00
21 Texas Teeth Tacos/226*	6.00	15.00
22 'Bot Bezos/153*	6.00	15.00
23 Trudeau Canadian Cut-Out WP/183*	6.00	15.00
26 Homemade Slime Science Kit WP/192*	6.00	15.00
28 Neurafink WP/175*	6.00	15.00
29 $1 Million Gold Coin WP/181*	6.00	15.00
30 Turfs BG Massacre WP/216*	6.00	15.00
33 Fuma WP/168*	6.00	15.00
34 Fan Down Ticket WP/168*	6.00	15.00
37 Ousted O'Reilly/185*	6.00	15.00
46 Diet Mountain De-Mentia WP/210*	8.00	20.00
49 Smokin' Haute Wheels WP/232*	10.00	25.00
63 Poisoned Penny/136*	8.00	20.00
68 Fidgety Finn/103*	6.00	15.00
73 Wrinkling and Boring Bros. WP/116*	6.00	15.00
75 Mowin' Rowan/137*	8.00	20.00
88 The Wolf of Vine Street WP/127*	10.00	25.00
91 Ceiling-Destorying Diana/185*	8.00	20.00

2017 Garbage Pail Kids The Not-Scars

COMPLETE SET (18)	30.00	80.00
COMMON CARD (1a-8b)		
9 Oscar of Mired Wieners (Wacky Packages)	6.00	15.00
10 Harlequin Puddin' (Wacky Packages)	6.00	15.00
1a Warren Batty	6.00	15.00
1b Baiting Beatty	6.00	15.00
2a Rhythmic Ryan	6.00	15.00
2b Ensemble Emma	6.00	15.00
3a Losing Lin	6.00	15.00
3b Missed Out Manuel	6.00	15.00
4a Cracked Quinn	6.00	15.00
4b Hurtin' Harley	6.00	15.00
5a Eaten Eddie	6.00	15.00
5b Ravaged Redmayne	6.00	15.00
6a Amy Arrived	6.00	15.00
6b Alien Adams	6.00	15.00
7a Monster Michael	6.00	15.00
7b Swipin' Shannon	6.00	15.00
8a Viggo Mortified	6.00	15.00
8b Misappropriatin' Mortensen	6.00	15.00

2019 Garbage Pail Kids The Not-Scars

COMPLETE SET (12)	15.00	40.00
COMMON CARD (1a-6b)	2.50	6.00
TOPPS.COM EXCLUSIVE		

2020 Topps Garbage Pail Kids The Not-Scars

COMPLETE SET (10)	20.00	50.00
COMMON CARD (1a-5b)	2.50	6.00
STATED PRINT RUN 494 SETS		
1a Joe King	4.00	10.00
1b Wacky Joaquin	4.00	10.00

2023 Topps Garbage Pail Kids The Not-Scars

COMPLETE SET (10)	12.00	30.00
COMMON CARD (1a-5b)	2.00	5.00
STATED PRINT RUN 2,066 ANNCD SETS		

2018 Garbage Pail Kids NYCC Exclusives

COMPLETE SET (2)	6.00	15.00
COMMON CARD	4.00	10.00

2022 Topps Garbage Pail Kids NYCC Misfortune Teller Set

COMPLETE SET (10)	50.00	125.00
COMMON CARD (1-10)	8.00	20.00
1 Adam Bomb	12.00	30.00
2 Nasty Nick	10.00	25.00
4 New Wave Dave	10.00	25.00
8 Dead Ted	10.00	25.00

2017 Garbage Pail Kids NYCC Oversized Exclusive

NNO Hazardous Hand	15.00	40.00

2019 Garbage Pail Kids NYCC Promos

COMPLETE SET (2)	15.00	40.00
COMMON CARD	3.00	8.00
NNO Comic Puketacular #1 (Nat Nerd)	15.00	40.00

2022 Topps Garbage Pail Kids NYCC Promos

COMMON CARD	20.00	50.00
NNO Adam Book	30.00	75.00

2022 Topps Garbage Pail Kids NYCC Scavenger Hunt Set

COMPLETE SET (9)	30.00	75.00
COMMON CARD (1-9)	5.00	12.00

2018 Garbage Pail Kids Oh The Horror-ible!

COMPLETE SET (200)	10.00	25.00
UNOPENED BOX (24 PACKS)		
UNOPENED PACK (8 CARDS)		
COMMON CARD	.20	.50
*BRUISED: .5X TO 1.2X BASIC CARDS		
*JELLY: .6X TO 1.5X BASIC CARDS		
*PHLEGM: .75X TO 2X BASIC CARDS		
*PUKE: 1X TO 2.5X BASIC CARDS		
*SPIT/99: 2.5X TO 6X BASIC CARDS		
BLOODY NOSE/75: 3X TO 8X BASIC CARDS		
*FOOL'S GOLD/50: 4X TO 10X BASIC CARDS		

2018 Garbage Pail Kids Oh The Horror-ible! Artist Autographs

COMMON CAMERA	15.00	40.00
COMMON DEJARNETTE	10.00	25.00
COMMON ENGSTROM	15.00	40.00
COMMON GROSS	12.00	30.00
COMMON IM	8.00	20.00
COMMON KIM	10.00	25.00
COMMON SIMKO	10.00	25.00
COMMON SMOKIN JOE	12.00	30.00
STATED ODDS 1:103		
STATED PRINT RUN 25 SER.#'d SETS		

2018 Garbage Pail Kids Oh The Horror-ible! Bathroom Buddies

COMPLETE SET (6)	3.00	8.00
COMMON CARD (16a-18b)	.75	2.00
BLASTER BOX EXCLUSIVE		

2018 Garbage Pail Kids Oh The Horror-ible! Classic Monsters

COMPLETE SET (20)	12.00	30.00
COMMON CARD (1a-10B)	1.00	2.50
FAT PACK EXCLUSIVE		

2018 Garbage Pail Kids Oh The Horror-ible! Horror Film Poster Parodies

COMPLETE SET (10)	60.00	120.00
COMMON CARD (1-10)	6.00	15.00
COLLECTOR BOX EXCLUSIVE		
1 The Cabinet of Dr. Calamari	8.00	20.00
2 Slight-ly Intelligent Zombie	6.00	15.00
3 Bacteria	6.00	15.00
4 Dawn in the Bed	10.00	25.00
5 The Whining	8.00	20.00
6 The Fowling	10.00	25.00
7 The Dancing	10.00	25.00
8 The Wrong Stuff	8.00	20.00
9 The Silence of the Lame	6.00	15.00
10 Fad Alive	6.00	15.00

2018 Garbage Pail Kids Oh The Horror-ible! Manufactured Patches

COMPLETE SET (20)	300.00	500.00

COMMON PATCH	12.00	30.00
STATED PRINT RUN 50 SER.#'d SETS		
COLLECTOR BOX EXCLUSIVE		
1a Nasty Nick	30.00	75.00
1b Evil Eddie	25.00	60.00
2a Dead Ted	25.00	60.00
2b Jay Decay	30.00	75.00
6a Spacey Stacy	15.00	40.00
6b Janet Planet	15.00	40.00
7a Hot Scott	15.00	40.00
7b Luke Warm	15.00	40.00
9a Frank N. Stein	15.00	40.00
10a Eerie Eric	20.00	50.00

2018 Garbage Pail Kids Oh The Horror-ible! Trick or Treats

COMPLETE SET (10)	10.00	25.00
COMMON CARD (1-10)	1.50	4.00
STATED ODDS 1:3		

2021 Topps Garbage Pail Kids Oh the Horror-ible! Expansion Set

COMPLETE SET (10)	20.00	50.00
COMMON CARD (1a-5b)	3.00	8.00
*SEPIA: 1.2X TO 3X BASIC CARDS		
STATED PRINT RUN 1,289 ANNCD SETS		

2022 Topps Garbage Pail Kids Oh the Horror-ible Expansion

COMPLETE SET (60)	75.00	200.00
COMPLETE W1 SET (10)	15.00	40.00
COMPLETE W2 SET (10)	15.00	40.00
COMPLETE W3 SET (10)	15.00	40.00
COMPLETE W4 SET (10)	15.00	40.00
COMPLETE W5 SET (10)	15.00	40.00
COMPLETE W6 SET (10)	15.00	40.00
COMMON W1 (1a-5b)	4.00	10.00
COMMON W2 (6a-10b)	4.00	10.00
COMMON W2 (11a-15b)	4.00	10.00
COMMON W2 (16a-20b)	4.00	10.00
COMMON W2 (21a-25b)	4.00	10.00
COMMON W2 (26a-30b)	4.00	10.00
*SEPIA: .75X TO 2X BASIC CARDS		
STATED W1 PRINT RUN 1,383 SETS		
STATED W2 PRINT RUN 2,144 SETS		
STATED W3 PRINT RUN 1,406 SETS		
STATED W4 PRINT RUN 1,212 SETS		
STATED W5 PRINT RUN 1,380 SETS		
STATED W6 PRINT RUN 1,269 SETS		

2022 Topps Garbage Pail Kids Oh the Horror-ible NYCC Set

COMPLETE SET (12)	30.00	75.00
COMMON CARD (1a-6b)	2.50	6.00
*SEPIA: .75X TO 2X BASIC CARDS		
STATED PRINT RUN 2,127 SETS		
6a Addy Adams	10.00	25.00
6b Wicked Wednesday	12.00	30.00

2021 Topps On-Demand Garbage Pail Kids Funny Valentines

COMPLETE SET (21)	5.00	12.00
COMMON CARD (1a-10b+CL)	.60	1.50
*RED: 2.5X TO 6X BASIC CARDS		
*BLACK: 4X TO 10X BASIC CARDS		
STATED PRINT RUN 1,700 ANNCD SETS		

2021 Topps On-Demand Garbage Pail Kids Funny Valentines Character Valentines

COMPLETE SET (10)	20.00	50.00
COMMON CARD (1-10)	3.00	8.00
STATED ODDS 2:1		

2020 Topps On-Demand Garbage Pail Kids Garbage Pail Krashers

COMPLETE SET (21)	6.00	15.00
COMMON CARD (1-20, NNO)	.75	2.00
*LICENSE PLATE: .75X TO 2X BASIC CARDS		
*ROUGH ART: 1X TO 2.5X BASIC CARDS		
STATED PRINT RUN 1,800 SETS		

2020 Topps On-Demand Garbage Pail Kids Garbage Pail Krashers 5x7 Posters

COMPLETE SET (10)	50.00	100.00
COMMON CARD (1-10)	6.00	15.00
STATED ODDS 1:1		

2021 Topps On-Demand Garbage Pail Kids Garbage Pail Krashers Series 2

COMPLETE SET (21)	8.00	20.00
COMMON CARD (1-20;HEADER)	1.00	2.50
*LICENSE: .75X TO 2X BASIC CARDS		
*GOLD/50: 4X TO 10X BASIC CARDS		
*RAINBOW/25: 6X TO 15X BASIC CARDS		
STATED PRINT RUN 2,504 ANNCD SETS		
1 Mad Mike	1.00	2.50
2 Buggy Betty	1.00	2.50
3 Cracked Jack	1.00	2.50
4 Junk Food John	1.00	2.50
5 Windy Winston	1.00	2.50
6 Joe Blow	1.00	2.50
7 Oozy Suzy	1.00	2.50
8 Starrin Darren	1.00	2.50
9 Weird Wendy	1.00	2.50
10 Jolted Joel	1.00	2.50
11 Grime Buggy	1.00	2.50
12 Bug Bug	1.00	2.50
13 Egg CARton	1.00	2.50
14 Food Junker	1.00	2.50
15 Gas Breaker	1.00	2.50
16 Gum Runner	1.00	2.50
17 Oozer Cruiser	1.00	2.50
18 Sight Seer	1.00	2.50
19 Weird Wheeler	1.00	2.50
20 Volt Vette	1.00	2.50
NNO Header	1.00	2.50

2022 Topps On-Demand Garbage Pail Kids Garbage Pail Krashers Series 3

COMPLETE SET (21)	6.00	15.00
COMMON CARD (1-20; HEADER)	.50	1.25
*GOLD/50: 8X TO 20X BASIC CARDS		
*RAINBOW/25: X TO X BASIC CARDS		
STATED PRINT RUN 2,447 ANNCD SETS		

2022 Topps On-Demand Garbage Pail Kids Garbage Pail Krashers Series 3 License Plate Backs

COMPLETE SET (10)	15.00	40.00
COMMON CARD (1-10)	2.50	6.00
STATED ODDS 3:1		

2022 Topps On-Demand Garbage Pail Kids Garbage Pail Krashers Series 3 Pop Culture Krashers

COMPLETE SET (5)	20.00	50.00
COMMON CARD (1-5)	6.00	15.00
STATED ODDS 1:1		

2017 Garbage Pail Kids On-Demand GPK Classic

COMPLETE BOXED SET (41)	60.00	120.00
COMPLETE SET (40)	25.00	60.00
COMMON CARD (1a-20b)	1.25	3.00
RELEASED 9/28/2017		

2020 Topps On-Demand Garbage Pail Kids GPK Mr. and Mrs.

COMPLETE SET (20)	15.00	40.00
UNOPENED SET (26 CARDS)		
COMMON CARD (1a-10b)	1.50	4.00
*GREEN: .5X TO 1.2X BASIC CARDS		
*RED: .75X TO 2X BASIC CARDS		
*BLACK: 2X TO 5X BASIC CARDS		
STATED PRINT RUN 1,474 SETS		
2a Adam Bomb	2.50	6.00
2b Addy Bomb	2.50	6.00

2019 Garbage Pail Kids On-Demand Scratch and Stink

COMPLETE SET (20)	8.00	20.00
COMMON CARD (1a-10b)	1.00	2.50
*GREEN: .75X TO 2X BASIC CARDS		
*PINK: 1.2X TO 3X BASIC CARDS		

2020 Topps On-Demand Garbage Pail Kids 35 Years of Untold Stories

COMPLETE SET (90)	30.00	75.00
COMMON CARD (1-90)	.60	1.50
STATED PRINT RUN 2,015 SETS		
1 Adam Bomb	1.25	3.00
2 Adam Bomb	1.25	3.00
3 Adam Bomb	1.25	3.00
4 Adam Bomb	1.25	3.00
5 Adam Bomb	1.25	3.00
6 Adam Bomb	1.25	3.00
7 Adam Bomb	1.25	3.00
8 Adam Bomb	1.25	3.00
9 Adam Bomb	1.25	3.00

2020 Topps On-Demand Garbage Pail Kids 35 Years of Untold Stories Cover Story

COMPLETE SET (7)	50.00	100.00
COMMON CARD (1-7)	8.00	20.00
STATED ODDS 1:1		

2020 Topps On-Demand Garbage Pail Kids 35 Years of Untold Stories Skateboard Deck Stickers

COMPLETE SET (5)	20.00	50.00
COMMON CARD (1-5)	6.00	15.00
1 Alien Ian	6.00	15.00
2 Varicose Wayne	6.00	15.00
3 Spacey Stacy	6.00	15.00
4 Bony Joanie	6.00	15.00
5 Haley's Vomit	6.00	15.00

2019 Garbage Pail Kids On-Demand Valentine's Day Set

COMPLETE SET (20)	10.00	25.00
COMMON CARD (1a-10b)	.75	2.00
COMMON C VARIANT (1c-10c)	8.00	20.00
*GREEN: 1.2X TO 3X BASIC CARDS		
*PINK: 2.5X TO 6X BASIC CARDS		
TOPPS.COM EXCLUSIVE		
1a Adam Bomb	.75	10.00
1b Blasted Billy	.75	8.00
1c I Love Hugh	30.00	75.00
2c Love Sick Nick	8.00	20.00
3c Vino Vince	8.00	20.00
4c Chocolate Chip	10.00	25.00
5c Regurgitatin' Ray	8.00	20.00
6c Faux Fur Freddy	10.00	25.00
7c Art Attack	8.00	20.00
8c Love Loren	12.00	30.00
9c Grover Stuffed	8.00	20.00
10c Last Meal Neil	15.00	40.00

2019 Garbage Pail Kids On-Demand We Hate the Holidays

COMPLETE SET (20)	12.00	30.00
UNOPENED SET (26 CARDS+1 POSTER)		
COMMON CARD (1a-10b)	1.00	2.50
*GREEN: .75X TO 2X BASIC CARDS		
*RED: 1.2X TO 3X BASIC CARDS		
*SNOWFLAKE: 2.5X TO 6X BASIC CARDS		
STATED PRINT RUN 1304 ANNCD SETS		
6a Nasty Nick	2.50	6.00
9a Adam Bomb	4.00	10.00
9b Blasted Billy	1.50	4.00

2019 Garbage Pail Kids On-Demand We Hate the Holidays 5x7 Foldable Posters

COMPLETE SET (10)	50.00	100.00
COMMON POSTER	4.00	10.00
STATED ODDS 1:SET		
NNO Cranky Frankie	6.00	15.00
NNO Ailin' Al	5.00	12.00
NNO New Wave Dave	8.00	20.00
NNO Nasty Nick	10.00	25.00
NNO Adam Bomb	12.00	30.00

2019 Garbage Pail Kids On-Demand X NYC Takeover

COMPLETE SET W/SP (30)		
COMPLETE SET W/O SP (20)	10.00	25.00
COMMON CARD (1a-10b)	1.25	3.00
COMMON SP "C" VARIANT (1c-10c)	5.00	12.00
*GREEN: .5X TO 1.2X BASIC CARDS		
*PINK: .6X TO 1.5X BASIC CARDS		
2c Coney Connie SP	8.00	20.00
4c Sub Wayne SP	6.00	15.00
5c Construction Conner SP	10.00	25.00
6c Liberty Lily SP	10.00	25.00
7c Scalper Sal SP	8.00	20.00
8c Taxi Cab Caleb SP	8.00	20.00
9c Central Park Mark SP	6.00	15.00
10c Pizza Rat Pat SP	8.00	20.00

2019 Garbage Pail Kids On-Demand X NYC Takeover Promo

NNO Nat Nerd	12.00	30.00

1986 Topps Garbage Pail Kids Posters

COMPLETE SET (18)	25.00	60.00
UNOPENED BOX (36 PACKS)	200.00	300.00
UNOPENED PACK (1 POSTER)	4.00	6.00
COMMON POSTER (1-18)	2.00	5.00
5 Visit Garbage Pail Land	4.00	10.00
7 Eat My Face!	3.00	8.00
9 Miss Dumpster	5.00	12.00
13 Beauty Is Only Skin Deep	6.00	15.00
17 Garbage Pail Kids Want You!	4.00	10.00
18 Busted!	3.00	8.00

2017 Garbage Pail Kids Prime Slime Awards

COMPLETE SET (12)	60.00	120.00
COMMON CARD (1a-6b)	6.00	15.00
STATED PRINT RUN 87 SETS		

2016 Garbage Pail Kids Prime Slime Trashy TV

COMPLETE SET (220)	15.00	40.00
COMMON CARD	.20	.50
*BRUISED: 1.2X TO 3X BASIC CARDS		
*PUKE: 1.5X TO 4X BASIC CARDS		
*PEE: 2X TO 5X BASIC CARDS		
*SPIT: 4X TO 10X BASIC CARDS		
*BLOODY NOSE/75: 6X TO 15X BASIC CARDS		
*FOOL'S GOLD/50: 8X TO 20X BASIC CARDS		

2016 Garbage Pail Kids Prime Slime Trashy TV Artist Autographs

COMMON CAMERA	12.00	30.00
COMMON ENGSTROM	12.00	30.00
COMMON GROSS	8.00	20.00
COMMON IM	8.00	20.00
COMMON KIM	8.00	20.00
COMMON PINGITORE	10.00	25.00
COMMON SIMKO	10.00	25.00
STATED PRINT RUN 25 SER.#'d SETS		

2016 Garbage Pail Kids Prime Slime Trashy TV Adam Bomb Your TV

COMPLETE SET (4)	10.00	25.00
COMMON CARD (1a-2b)	3.00	8.00
STATED ODDS 2:1 BLISTER PACK		

2016 Garbage Pail Kids Prime Slime Trashy TV Artist Relics

COMMON CARD	15.00	40.00
STATED PRINT RUN 50 SER.#'d SETS		

2016 Garbage Pail Kids Prime Slime Trashy TV Bathroom Buddies

COMPLETE SET (6)	5.00	12.00
COMMON CARD (4a-6b)	1.00	2.50
STATED ODDS 3:1 EA BLASTER BOX		

2016 Garbage Pail Kids Prime Slime Trashy TV Classic Re-Runs

COMPLETE SET (20)	10.00	25.00
COMMON CARD (1a-10b)	.60	1.50
STATED ODDS 2:1 JUMBO EXCLUSIVE		

2016 Garbage Pail Kids Prime Slime Trashy TV Fall TV Previews

COMPLETE SET (10)	20.00	50.00
COMMON CARD (1a-5b)	2.50	6.00
TOPPS ONLINE STORE EXCLUSIVE		

2016 Garbage Pail Kids Prime Slime Trashy TV Garbage Pail Wacky Packages

COMPLETE SET (8)	50.00	100.00
COMMON CARD	4.00	10.00
STATED ODDS 1:24 HOBBY/COLLECTOR PACKS		
3 Gadzooka	8.00	20.00
4 Cover Ghoul	8.00	20.00
5 Duzn't	8.00	20.00
6 Quacker Oats	5.00	12.00
7 Commie Cleanser	6.00	15.00
8 Beanball	5.00	12.00

2016 Garbage Pail Kids Prime Slime Trashy TV Gross Bears

COMPLETE SET (6)	6.00	15.00
COMMON CARD	1.25	3.00
STATED ODDS 3:1 SE BLASTER BOX		

2016 Garbage Pail Kids Prime Slime Trashy TV Patches

COMMON CARD	15.00	40.00
STATED ODDS 1:35		
STATED PRINT RUN 99 SER.#'d SETS		
1 Roy Bot	20.00	50.00
2 Catty Kathy	25.00	60.00
4 Lisa Loser	20.00	50.00
5 On Camera Cameron	20.00	50.00
6 Clay Achin'	20.00	50.00
8 Matt Mobile	20.00	50.00
10 Leonard Nimrod	25.00	60.00

2016 Garbage Pail Kids Prime Slime Trashy TV Summer TV Previews

COMPLETE SET (10)	20.00	50.00
COMMON CARD (1a-5b)	2.00	5.00
TOPPS ONLINE STORE EXCLUSIVE		

2016 Garbage Pail Kids Prime Slime Trashy TV Oversized SDCC Promos

COMPLETE SET (10)	25.00	60.00
COMMON CARD (1a-5b)	4.00	10.00

2016 Garbage Pail Kids Prime Slime Trashy TV Prime Slime Awards

COMPLETE SET (20)	30.00	80.00
COMMON CARD (1a-10b)	2.50	6.00

2019 Garbage Pail Kids Revenge of Oh The Horror-ible!

COMPLETE SET (200)	10.00	25.00
UNOPENED BOX (24 PACKS)	100.00	200.00
UNOPENED PACK (8 CARDS)	6.00	8.00
COMMON CARD	.20	.50
*GREEN: 1X TO 2.5X BASIC CARDS		
*BLACK LIGHT: 1.5X TO 4X BASIC CARDS		
*PURPLE: 2.5X TO 6X BASIC CARDS		
*YELLOW: 4X TO 10X BASIC CARDS		
*BLUE/99: 4X TO 10X BASIC CARDS		
*RED/75: 5X TO 12X BASIC CARDS		
*GOLD/50: 6X TO 15X BASIC CARDS		

2019 Garbage Pail Kids Revenge of Oh The Horror-ible! Artist Autographs

COMMON ENGSTROM	15.00	40.00
COMMON GROSS	15.00	40.00
COMMON SIMKO	20.00	50.00
STATED ODDS 1:409 BLASTER; HOBBY 1:410		
STATED PRINT RUN 25 SER.#'d SETS		

2019 Garbage Pail Kids Revenge of Oh The Horror-ible! Classic Monsters

COMPLETE SET (20)	8.00	20.00
COMMON CARD (1a-10b)	.60	1.50
RANDOMLY INSERTED INTO PACKS		

2019 Garbage Pail Kids Revenge of Oh The Horror-ible! Faux Character Relics

COMMON MEM	15.00	40.00
RANDOMLY INSERTED INTO PACKS		

2019 Garbage Pail Kids Revenge of Oh The Horror-ible! GPK Horror Victims

COMPLETE SET (10)	6.00	15.00
COMMON CARD (1a-5b)	1.00	2.50
BLASTER BOX EXCLUSIVE		

2019 Garbage Pail Kids Revenge of Oh The Horror-ible! Horror Film Poster Parodies

COMMON CARD (1-9)	6.00	15.00
COLLECTOR BOX EXCLUSIVE		
1 Yackula	8.00	20.00
5 Village of the Adamed	10.00	25.00

2019 Garbage Pail Kids Revenge of Oh The Horror-ible! Trick or Treats

COMPLETE SET (10)	10.00	25.00
COMMON CARD (1-10)	2.00	5.00
STATED ODDS 1:3		
HOBBY EXCLUSIVE		

2019 Garbage Pail Kids Revenge of Oh The Horror-ible! Promo

NYCC2019 Village of the Adamed	15.00	40.00

2016 Garbage Pail Kids Riot Fest

COMPLETE SET (8)	60.00	120.00
COMMON CARD (1-8)	10.00	25.00

2017 Garbage Pail Kids Riot Fest

COMPLETE SET (10)	30.00	75.00
COMMON CARD (1-10)	5.00	12.00

2017 Garbage Pail Kids Rock and Roll Hall of Lame

COMPLETE SET (17)	50.00	100.00
COMMON CARD (1a-6b)	5.00	12.00

2018 Garbage Pail Kids Rock and Roll Hall of Lame

COMPLETE SET (10)	25.00	60.00
COMMON CARD (1a-5b)	5.00	12.00
STATED PRINT RUN 171 SER.#'d SETS		
TOPPS ONLINE EXCLUSIVE		

2022 Topps Garbage Pail Kids Rock and Roll Hall of Lame

COMPLETE SET (10)	15.00	40.00
COMMON CARD (1a-5b)	3.00	8.00
*NOTES: .75X TO 2X BASIC CARDS		
STATED PRINT RUN 1,517 SETS		

2020 Topps Garbage Pail Kids Sapphire Edition

COMPLETE SET (166)	750.00	1500.00
UNOPENED BOX (8 BLANK PACKS)	800.00	1200.00
UNOPENED PACK (4 CARDS)	100.00	150.00

COMMON CARD (1a-84b)	3.00	8.00
*BLUE/99: .5X TO 1.2X BASIC CARDS		
*GREEN/50: .75X TO 2X BASIC CARDS		
1a Nasty Nick	50.00	100.00
1b Evil Eddie	25.00	60.00
2a Junkfood John	6.00	15.00
2b Ray Decay	4.00	10.00
3a Up Chuck	6.00	15.00
3b Heavin' Steven	4.00	10.00
5a Dead Ted	12.00	30.00
5b Jay Decay	10.00	25.00
8a Adam Bomb	75.00	150.00
8b Blasted Billy	30.00	75.00
10a Tee-Vee Stevie	4.00	10.00
11a Itchy Richie	5.00	12.00
12b Hairy Mary	5.00	12.00
13a Ashcan Andy	6.00	15.00
14b Jason Basin	4.00	10.00
16a Weird Wendy	4.00	10.00
17a Wacky Jackie	4.00	10.00
17b Loony Lenny	4.00	10.00
19a Corroded Carl	5.00	12.00
19b Crater Chris	4.00	10.00
21a Virus Iris	5.00	12.00
21b Sicky Vicky	4.00	10.00
22a Junky Jeff	5.00	12.00
27a Brainy Janie	4.00	10.00
27b Jenny Genius	4.00	10.00
29a Bony Joanie	5.00	12.00
30a New Wave Dave	6.00	15.00
30b Graffiti Petey	5.00	12.00
33a Mad Mike	8.00	20.00
41a Mean Gene	6.00	15.00
41b Joltin' Joe	5.00	12.00
45a Leaky Lindsay	5.00	12.00
45b Messy Tessie	4.00	10.00
46a Rappin' Ron	5.00	12.00
46b Ray Gun	4.00	10.00
49a Double Heather	5.00	12.00
49b Fran Fran	4.00	10.00
54a Fryin' Ryan	15.00	40.00
54b Charred Chad	6.00	15.00
63a Spacey Stacy	5.00	12.00
66a Matt Ratt	6.00	15.00

2021 Topps Garbage Pail Kids Sapphire Edition

COMPLETE SET (170)	250.00	600.00
UNOPENED BOX (8 PACKS)		
UNOPENED PACK (4 CARDS)		
COMMON CARD (84a-166b)	2.00	5.00
*AQUA/99: 4X TO 10X BASIC CARDS		
*FUCHSIA/75: 12X TO 30X BASIC CARDS		
*GREEN/50: 15X TO 40X BASIC CARDS		

2022 Topps Garbage Pail Kids SDCC Scavenger Hunt Set

COMPLETE SET (9)	25.00	60.00
COMMON CARD (1-9)	4.00	10.00
STATED PRINT RUN 500 SETS		

2014 Garbage Pail Kids Series One

COMP.SET W/O SP (132)	10.00	25.00
UNOPENED HOBBY BOX (24 PACKS)	200.00	300.00
UNOPENED HOBBY PACK (10 CARDS)	8.00	12.00
UNOPENED COLLECTOR BOX (24 PACKS)	450.00	600.00
UNOPENED COLLECTOR PACK (6 CARDS)	20.00	25.00
COMMON CARD (1a-66b)	.20	.50
COMMON PHOTO VARIATION	50.00	90.00
COMMON "C" VARIATION	20.00	50.00
*BLACK: 2X TO 5X BASIC CARDS	1.00	2.50
*CANVAS: 2X TO 5X BASIC CARDS	1.00	2.50
*RED METALLIC: 2X TO 5X BASIC CARDS	1.00	2.50
*BLANK BACK: 6X TO 15X BASIC CARDS	3.00	8.00
*SILVER: 6X TO 15X BASIC CARDS	3.00	8.00
*CLOTH: 12X TO 30X BASIC CARDS	6.00	15.00
*SEPIA: 12X TO 30X BASIC CARDS	6.00	15.00
*GOLD: 15X TO 40X BASIC CARDS	8.00	20.00
65a2 Bony Joanie w/rider SP	25.00	60.00
66a Adam Bomb	.60	1.50
66b Bobsled Ned	.60	1.50
66c Blasted Billy SP	30.00	60.00

2014 Garbage Pail Kids Series One Artist Autographs

COMMON BUNK	15.00	40.00
COMMON DEJARNETTE	15.00	40.00
COMMON ENGSTROM	15.00	40.00
COMMON GROSS	15.00	40.00
COMMON IM	15.00	40.00
COMMON PINGITORE	25.00	60.00
COMMON SIMKO	15.00	40.00
RANDOMLY INSERTED INTO PACKS		

2014 Garbage Pail Kids Series One Bonus

COMP. HOBBY BOX SET (8)	75.00	150.00
COMP. BLASTER BOX SET (4)	15.00	40.00
COMP. JUMBO PACK SET (6)	8.00	20.00
COMMON CARD (B1a-B4b)	10.00	25.00
COMMON CARD (B5a-B6b)	6.00	15.00
COMMON CARD (B7a-B9b)	3.00	8.00
B3a Adam Boom	12.00	30.00
B3b Mischievous Michelangelo	12.00	30.00

2014 Garbage Pail Kids Series One Olym-Picks 3-D Motion

COMPLETE SET (10)	12.00	30.00
COMMON CARD (1-10)	2.50	6.00
STATED ODDS 1:12		

2014 Garbage Pail Kids Series One Olym-Picks Medals Bronze

COMPLETE SET (10)	6.00	15.00
COMMON CARD (1-10)	1.25	3.00
*SILVER: .5X TO 1.2X BASIC CARDS		
*GOLD: 1.5X TO 4X BASIC CARDS		
STATED ODDS 1:4		

2014 Garbage Pail Kids Series One Texture Relics

COMPLETE SET (10)	250.00	350.00
COMMON CARD (1-10)	15.00	40.00
STATED ODDS 1:48 COLLECTORS PACKS		
1 Adam Bomb	50.00	100.00

2014 Garbage Pail Kids Series Two

COMP.SET w/o SPs (132)	10.00	25.00
UNOPENED HOBBY BOX (24 PACKS)		
UNOPENED HOBBY PACK (10 CARDS)		
UNOPENED COLLECTOR BOX (24 PACKS)		
UNOPENED COLLECTOR BOX (6 CARDS)		
COMMON CARD (67a-132b)	.20	.50
COMMON "C" VARIATION	8.00	20.00
*GREEN: .75X TO 2X BASIC CARDS		
*BLACK: 2X TO 5X BASIC CARDS		
*CANVAS: 2X TO 5X BASIC CARDS		
*RED METALLIC: 2X TO 5X BASIC CARDS		
*SILVER: 3X TO 8X BASIC CARDS		
*CHARACTER: 6X TO 15X BASIC CARDS		
*SEPIA: 12X TO 30X BASIC CARDS		
*GOLD: 15X TO 40X BASIC CARDS		
122c Howlin' James SP	12.00	30.00
128c Wrecked Rupert SP	12.00	30.00
129c Itchy Eric SP	10.00	25.00
132c Ben Really? SP	20.00	50.00

2014 Garbage Pail Kids Series Two Artist Autographs

COMMON DEJARNETTE	8.00	20.00
COMMON ENGSTROM	12.00	30.00
COMMON GROSS	12.00	30.00
COMMON IM	10.00	25.00
COMMON PINGITORE	10.00	25.00
COMMON SIMKO	10.00	25.00
RANDOMLY INSERTED INTO PACKS		

2014 Garbage Pail Kids Series Two Art Variants

COMMON CARD	40.00	100.00
STATED ODDS 1:CASE		

2014 Garbage Pail Kids Series Two Battles

COMPLETE SET (4)	3.00	8.00
COMMON CARD (1-4)	1.25	3.00
STATED ODDS 1:3		

2014 Garbage Pail Kids Series Two Bonus

COMPLETE SET (18)	120.00	250.00
COMMON CARD	2.00	5.00
B10a Clark Work Orange	15.00	40.00
B10b Drew Droog	10.00	25.00
B11a Pop Eyal	8.00	20.00
B11b Ah Gu Guy	8.00	20.00
B12a Bad Bruce	10.00	25.00
B12b Boomer Stick	8.00	20.00
B13a Frightening Freddy	12.00	30.00
B13b Maniac Mike	10.00	25.00
B14a Costumed June	3.00	8.00
B15a Sunny Roof	4.00	10.00

2014 Garbage Pail Kids Series Two Full Comic

COMPLETE SET (4)	3.00	8.00
COMMON CARD (1-4)	1.25	3.00

2014 Garbage Pail Kids Series Two Patch Relics

COMPLETE SET (10)	200.00	400.00
COMMON CARD (1-10)	15.00	40.00
STATED ODDS 1:48		
1 Swiss Arnie	20.00	50.00
5 Rust Ty	20.00	50.00
7 One Ivan	20.00	50.00
8 Airsick Vick	30.00	80.00
9 Eight Armand	20.00	50.00
10 Steve Rotters	20.00	50.00

2015 Garbage Pail Kids Series One

COMPLETE SET w/o SP (132)	12.00	30.00
UNOPENED HOBBY BOX (24 PACKS)	300.00	500.00
UNOPENED HOBBY PACK (10 CARDS)	12.00	20.00
UNOPENED COLLECTOR BOX (24 PACKS)	500.00	800.00
UNOPENED COLLECTOR PACK (6 CARDS)	20.00	35.00
COMMON CARD (1a-66b)	.20	.50
COMMON SP	6.00	15.00
*GREEN: .75X TO 2X BASIC CARDS		
*BLACK: 2X TO 5X BASIC CARDS		
*CANVAS: 2X TO 5X BASIC CARDS		
*MET. RED: 2X TO 5X BASIC CARDS		
*SILVER: 3X TO 8X BASIC CARDS		
*CHARACTER: 6X TO 15X BASIC CARDS		
*SEPIA: 12X TO 30X BASIC CARDS		
*GOLD: 15X TO 40X BASIC CARDS		
56c Look Out Luke SP	8.00	20.00
57c Plate Paul SP	8.00	20.00
58c Fanatic Floyd SP	8.00	20.00
59c Broken Ken SP	8.00	20.00
60c Unnatur Al SP	8.00	20.00
61c Safe Sal SP	8.00	20.00
62c Hit Whit SP	8.00	20.00
64c Chomping Chad SP	8.00	20.00
66c Autograph Raph SP	8.00	20.00

2015 Garbage Pail Kids Series One All-Star Stickers

COMPLETE SET (10)	8.00	20.00
COMMON CARD (1-10)	1.25	3.00
STATED ODDS 1:12		
1 Double Heather	2.00	5.00
3 Semi Colin	1.50	4.00
5 Oliver Twisted	1.50	4.00
10 Nasty Nick	2.50	6.00

2015 Garbage Pail Kids Series One Artist Autographs

COMMON DEJARNETTE	6.00	15.00
COMMON ENGSTROM	10.00	25.00
COMMON GROSS	8.00	20.00
COMMON IM	10.00	25.00
COMMON PINGITORE	8.00	20.00
COMMON SIMKO	10.00	25.00
RANDOMLY INSERTED INTO PACKS		

2015 Garbage Pail Kids Series One Baseball Cards

COMPLETE SET (10)	6.00	15.00
COMMON CARD (1-10)	1.25	3.00
STATED ODDS 1:4		

2015 Garbage Pail Kids Series One Baseball Cards Variants

COMPLETE SET (10)	150.00	300.00
COMMON CARD (1-10)	15.00	40.00
STATED ODDS 1:CASE		
1 Foul Bill	25.00	60.00
4 Snot-Ball Saul	25.00	60.00
5 Mitch Mitt	20.00	50.00
7 Busted Wally	20.00	50.00
8 Stitched Steve	25.00	60.00
10 Calvin Catcher	30.00	80.00

2015 Garbage Pail Kids Series One Baseball Character Autographs

COMMON CARD	25.00	60.00
STATED ODDS 1:76 COLLECTOR'S PACKS		
JD Josh Donaldson	30.00	80.00
MM Manny Machado	80.00	150.00
MP Mike Piazza	60.00	120.00

2015 Garbage Pail Kids Series One Bonus Stickers

COMPLETE SET (18)	80.00	150.00
COMMON CARD (B1a-B9b)	6.00	15.00
STATED ODDS 1:24		

2015 Garbage Pail Kids Series One Mascot Stickers

COMPLETE SET (10)	6.00	15.00
COMMON CARD (1-10)	1.25	3.00
STATED ODDS 1:6		

2015 Garbage Pail Kids Series One Patches

COMPLETE SET (10)	120.00	250.00
COMMON CARD (1-10)	12.00	30.00
1 Double Heather	15.00	40.00
2 Max Axe	15.00	40.00
3 Semi Colin	15.00	40.00
5 Oliver Twisted	15.00	40.00
6 Dead Ted	20.00	50.00
7 Joe Blow	15.00	40.00
9 Fat Matt	15.00	40.00
10 Nasty Nick	20.00	50.00

2017 Garbage Pail Kids The Shammy Awards

COMPLETE SET (19)	50.00	100.00
COMMON CARD (1a-11)	3.00	8.00

2018 Garbage Pail Kids The Shammy Awards

COMPLETE SET (10)	30.00	75.00
COMMON CARD (1a-5b)	4.00	10.00
STATED PRINT RUN 120 SETS		
TOPPS.COM EXCLUSIVE		

2020 Topps Garbage Pail Kids The Shammy Awards

COMPLETE SET (10)	15.00	40.00
COMMON CARD (1a-5b)	3.00	8.00
STATED PRINT RUN 466 SETS		

2021 Topps Garbage Pail Kids The Shammy Awards

COMPLETE SET (10)	10.00	25.00
COMMON CARD (1a-5b)	1.50	4.00
STATED PRINT RUN 1426 ANNCD SETS		
1a Tree-Swift	2.50	6.00
1b Taylor Turf	2.50	6.00
3a Buoyant Billie	2.00	5.00
3b Island Eilish	2.00	5.00

2020 Topps Garbage Pail Kids Skateboard Stickers

COMPLETE SET (10)	12.00	30.00
COMMON CARD (1-10)	2.00	5.00
STATED PRINT RUN 1,025 SETS		
1 Adam Bomb	2.00	5.00
2 Tee-Vee Stevie	2.00	5.00
3 Beasty Boyd	2.00	5.00
4 New Wave Dave	2.00	5.00
5 Gutsy Gabriel	2.00	5.00
6 Junk Food John	2.00	5.00
7 Creepy Carol	2.00	5.00
8 Dead Ted	2.00	5.00
9 Hot Rod	2.00	5.00
10 Max Axe	2.00	5.00

2015 Garbage Pail Kids 30th Anniversary

COMPLETE SET (220)	15.00	40.00
UNOPENED HOBBY BOX (24 PACKS)	1000.00	1500.00
UNOPENED HOBBY PACK (6 CARDS)	40.00	65.00
UNOPENED COLLECTOR BOX (24 PACKS)	1200.00	2000.00
UNOPENED COLLECTOR BOX (6 CARDS)	50.00	85.00
UNOPENED RETAIL BOX (5 PACKS)		
UNOPENED RETAIL PACK (10 CARDS)		
COMMON CARD	.20	.50
*GREEN: .5X TO 1.2X BASIC CARDS		
*BLACK: .6X TO 1.5X BASIC CARDS		
*RED MET.: .6X TO 1.5X BASIC CARDS		
*BROWN: .75X TO 2X BASIC CARDS		
*SILVER: 1.2X TO 2.5X BASIC CARDS		
*CH. BACK: 1.5X TO 3X BASIC CARDS		
*SEPIA: 2X TO 4X BASIC CARDS		
*GOLD/85: 4X TO 10X BASIC CARDS		
*PINK: 4X TO 10X BASIC CARDS		
80S7a Mad Michael	30.00	75.00
80S7b Jumpin' Jordan	25.00	60.00

2015 Garbage Pail Kids 30th Anniversary Artist Relics

COMMON CARD (1-5)	4.00	10.00
RANDOM INSERT IN PACKS		
COLLECTOR PACK EXCLUSIVE		
1 Adam Goldberg	12.00	30.00
2 Brent Engstrom	6.00	15.00
4 Joe Simko	5.00	12.00

2015 Garbage Pail Kids 30th Anniversary Autographs

COMMON AUTO	6.00	15.00
RANDOM INSERTS IN PACKS		
NNO Adam Goldberg	15.00	40.00
NNO Art Spiegelman	12.00	30.00
NNO Fred Wheaton	10.00	25.00
NNO Jay Lynch	8.00	20.00
NNO Joe Simko	8.00	20.00
NNO John Pound	25.00	60.00
NNO Katie Cook	10.00	25.00
NNO Layron DeJarnette	8.00	20.00
NNO Len Brown	10.00	25.00
NNO Mark Pingitore	8.00	20.00
NNO Miran Kim	10.00	25.00
NNO Pat Barrett	8.00	20.00
NNO Tom Bunk	10.00	25.00

2015 Garbage Pail Kids 30th Anniversary Barf Bags

COMPLETE SET (10)	30.00	80.00
COMMON CARD (1-10)	5.00	12.00
STATED ODDS 1:HOBBY BOX		

2015 Garbage Pail Kids 30th Anniversary Bonus Box Posters

COMPLETE SET (18)	50.00	100.00
COMMON CARD (1-18)	3.00	8.00
STATED ODDS 1:BOX		

2015 Garbage Pail Kids 30th Anniversary Dual Autographs

COMMON AUTO	50.00	125.00
1 J.Pound/T.Bunk	200.00	500.00
2 A.Spiegelman/L.Brown	125.00	300.00

2015 Garbage Pail Kids 30th Anniversary Famous Movie Scenes

COMPLETE SET (15)	10.00	25.00
COMMON CARD (1-15)	1.25	3.00
STATED ODDS 1:4		

2015 Garbage Pail Kids 30th Anniversary Foreign Legion

COMPLETE SET (10)	50.00	100.00
COMMON CARD (1-10)	5.00	12.00
STATED ODDS 1:24		
HOBBY EXCLUSIVE		
1 Alex Plosivo	10.00	25.00
Basuritas		
2 Hedda Offa/Garbage Gang	6.00	15.00
3 Ike Nojo/Gang Do Lixo	6.00	15.00
7 Pat Splat/Bukimi Kun	6.00	15.00

2015 Garbage Pail Kids 30th Anniversary Foreign Legion Oversized SDCC Exclusives Adam Bomb

COMPLETE SET (10)	60.00	120.00
COMMON CARD (1-10)	10.00	25.00
2015 SDCC EXCLUSIVE		

2015 Garbage Pail Kids 30th Anniversary Foreign Legion Oversized SDCC Exclusives Ashcan Andy

COMPLETE SET (10)	25.00	60.00
COMMON CARD (1-10)	4.00	10.00
2015 SDCC EXCLUSIVE		

2015 Garbage Pail Kids 30th Anniversary Foreign Legion Oversized SDCC Exclusives Nasty Nick

COMPLETE SET (10)	25.00	60.00
COMMON CARD (1-10)	4.00	10.00
2015 SDCC EXCLUSIVE		

2015 Garbage Pail Kids 30th Anniversary Foreign Legion Oversized SDCC Exclusives New Wave Dave

COMPLETE SET (10)	25.00	60.00
COMMON CARD (1-10)	4.00	10.00
2015 SDCC EXCLUSIVE		

2015 Garbage Pail Kids 30th Anniversary Foreign Legion Oversized SDCC Exclusives Potty Scotty

COMPLETE SET (10)	25.00	60.00
COMMON CARD (1-10)	4.00	10.00
2015 SDCC EXCLUSIVE		

2015 Garbage Pail Kids 30th Anniversary Horror Films

COMPLETE SET (5)	4.00	10.00
COMMON CARD (1-5)	1.25	3.00
RANDOM INSERTS IN PACKS		

2015 Garbage Pail Kids 30th Anniversary Medallions

COMPLETE SET (6)	80.00	150.00
COMMON CARD (1-6)	12.00	30.00
RANDOM INSERTS IN PACKS		
COLLECTOR PACK EXCLUSIVE		
1 Nasty Nick	20.00	50.00
2 Potty Scotty	20.00	50.00
3 Bad Brad	15.00	40.00
6 New Wave Dave	20.00	50.00

2015 Garbage Pail Kids 30th Anniversary Mini Giant Stickers

COMPLETE SET (15)	8.00	20.00
COMMON CARD (1-15)	1.00	2.50
RANDOM INSERTS IN PACKS		

2015 Garbage Pail Kids 30th Anniversary Super Fan Tattoo

COMPLETE SET (5)	4.00	10.00
COMMON CARD (1-5)	1.50	4.00
STATED ODDS 1:4		

2020 Topps Garbage Pail Kids 35th Anniversary

COMPLETE SET (200)	15.00	40.00
UNOPENED BOX (24 PACKS)	60.00	100.00
UNOPENED PACK (8 CARDS)	3.00	4.00
COMMON CARD (1a-100b)	.20	.50
*BOOGER: 1.2X TO 3X BASIC CARDS		
*BRUISED: 2.5X TO 6X BASIC CARDS		
*SPIT/99: 4X TO 10X BASIC CARDS		
*BLOODY/75: 6X TO 15X BASIC CARDS		
*FOOL'S GOLD/35: 12X TO 30X BASIC CARDS		

2020 Topps Garbage Pail Kids 35th Anniversary Fan Favorites

COMPLETE SET (20)	15.00	40.00
COMMON CARD (FV1a-FV10b)	1.25	3.00
RANDOMLY INSERTED INTO PACKS		
FV1a Adam Bomb	3.00	8.00
FV3a New Wave Cave	2.00	5.00
FV6a Tee-Vee Stevie	1.50	4.00
FV9a Nasty Nick	3.00	8.00
FV10a Dead Ted	2.00	5.00

2020 Topps Garbage Pail Kids 35th Anniversary GPK Wacky Packages

COMPLETE SET (10)	100.00	200.00
COMMON CARD (WP1-WP10)	10.00	25.00
STATED ODDS 1:1		
HOBBY COLLECTOR BOX EXCLUSIVE		
WP4 Sicko Cereal	15.00	40.00
WP5 Low Energy Snooze Inducing Drink	12.00	30.00
WP8 Plop!	12.00	30.00

2020 Topps Garbage Pail Kids 35th Anniversary Location Relics

COMMON MEM	20.00	50.00
RANDOMLY INSERTED INTO PACKS		
LRFR Dead Ted	30.00	75.00
LRRD Spacey Stacy	25.00	60.00
LRRH Brain Freeze Brian	30.00	75.00
LRSU Gored Gordon	25.00	60.00
LRTG Wrinkled Rita	25.00	60.00

2020 Topps Garbage Pail Kids 35th Anniversary Midlife Crisis

COMPLETE SET (20)	15.00	40.00
COMMON CARD (1a-10b)	1.25	3.00
RANDOMLY INSERTED INTO PACKS		
2a Adam Bomb	2.00	5.00

2020 Topps Garbage Pail Kids 35th Anniversary No Ragerts Temporary Tattoos

COMPLETE SET (10)	6.00	15.00
COMMON CARD (1-10)	1.00	2.50
HOBBY DISPLAY BOX EXCLUSIVE		

2020 Topps Garbage Pail Kids Trashy Treasures Series 1 Trading Card Inserts

COMPLETE SET (5)	15.00	40.00
COMMON CARD	5.00	12.00
STATED ODDS 1:FIGURE		
NNO Adam Bomb	10.00	25.00

2017 Garbage Pail Kids Trumpocracy

COMPLETE SET (38)	150.00	300.00
COMMON CARD (1-38)	5.00	12.00
1 100 Days Donald/346*	15.00	40.00
2 Colin Alien Hotline/176*	6.00	15.00
3 Tough Cookie Trump/151*	6.00	15.00
11 Sneaky Sean/108*	10.00	25.00
12 Displeased Donald/114*	10.00	25.00
14 Take Away Trump/110*	8.00	20.00
16 Curtains Comey/70*	10.00	25.00
17 No Hugs Hillary/68*	8.00	20.00
19 Nut Job James/238*	6.00	15.00
20 Me! Me! Me! Mix WP/246*	6.00	15.00
21 Global Domination Donald/144*	10.00	25.00
22 Mean Melania/126*	8.00	20.00
23 Mar-A-Lucifer/115*	6.00	15.00
27 Decapitated Kathy/164*	6.00	15.00
30 Trashed Trump/160*	6.00	15.00

2017 Garbage Pail Kids Trumpocracy The First 100 Days

COMPLETE SET (166)	1000.00	2000.00
COMMON CARD (1-166)	5.00	12.00
TOPPS 24-HOUR EXCLUSIVE		
2 Mad Donna/425*	8.00	20.00
4 Storyteller Spicer/281*	6.00	15.00
5 Tasteless Trump/237*	6.00	15.00
6 Masked Melania/226*	6.00	15.00
7 Treasury Trump/193*	6.00	15.00
8 Pricey Tom/193*	8.00	20.00
9 Defunding Donald/216*	6.00	15.00
10 Discarding Donald/214*	8.00	20.00
11 Devastation DeVos/196*	8.00	20.00
12 Take-A-Me & Go WP/254*	8.00	20.00
13 Trump's Duplicake Mix WP/272*	6.00	15.00
16 Dead Voter Ted/231*	8.00	20.00
19 Dystopian Donald/204*	6.00	15.00
20 Oil Drilling Donald/197*	6.00	15.00
21 Throttling Trump/187*	6.00	15.00
22 Job Decreasing Donald/192*	6.00	15.00
23 Dastardly Donald/200*	6.00	15.00
25 Ballot Bernhard/185*	6.00	15.00
26 Deserted Donald/198*	6.00	15.00
28 Fracky Packages WP/328*	6.00	15.00
33 Reality Show Schwarzenegger/232*	6.00	15.00
37 We Are Devos! WP/292*	6.00	15.00
41 Deal Breakers WP/262*	6.00	15.00
42 Pampered WP/301*	6.00	15.00
43 Disapproval Donald/178*	8.00	20.00
45 Tramplin' Trump/189*	8.00	20.00
46 My Way WP/246*	6.00	15.00
51 Fruit of the Loon WP/302*	6.00	15.00
52 Trumpocracy Dominos WP/298*	6.00	15.00
53 No-Strom WP/292*	6.00	15.00
54 Dining Donald/180*	8.00	20.00
58 Colonel Bernie Sanders WP/290*	8.00	20.00
60 Thieving Trump/156*	6.00	15.00
61 Stop-A-Leak WP/262*	6.00	15.00
62 Al Franken Berry WP/277*	6.00	15.00
63 Trump's Map of America WP/251*	6.00	15.00
75 White House Confidential WP/210*	8.00	20.00
77 Hardly Donaldson/168*	6.00	15.00
79 Deregulatin' Donald/158*	6.00	15.00
86 Bread Crum Barack/184*	6.00	15.00
93 Hair Tonic Trump/143*	8.00	20.00
94 Uninsure-Ed/153*	6.00	15.00
95 Silly Rabbit Spicer/143*	6.00	15.00
98 Obama-Ear Spy Gear WP/233*	6.00	15.00
101 Drowning Donald/191*	6.00	15.00
106 Tricky Dicky/154*	8.00	20.00
108 Don't Care Donald/162*	6.00	15.00
117 Dissenting Dogg/141*	6.00	15.00
126 Donald Truck/161*	8.00	20.00
131 Kim/Don Duel/224*	6.00	15.00
141 Bye-Bye Bannon/156*	8.00	20.00
149 Deference Donald/173*	6.00	15.00
150 Touring Trump/182*	6.00	15.00
153 Detracted Donald/151*	8.00	20.00

2021 Topps Garbage Pail Kids 2021 Was the Worst

COMPLETE SET (10)	15.00	40.00
COMMON CARD (1a-5b)	3.00	8.00
*FROWN: 1.5X TO 4X BASIC CARDS		
STATED PRINT RUN 1,876 ANNCD SETS		

2022 Topps Garbage Pail Kids 2022 Was the Worst

COMPLETE SET (10)	15.00	40.00
COMMON CARD (1-10)	2.00	5.00
*FROWN: 1X TO 2.5X BASIC CARDS		
1 Eaton Elon/3,593*	8.00	20.00

2019 Garbage Pail Kids Universal Monsters

COMPLETE SET (24)	50.00	100.00
COMMON CARD (1a-12b)	2.50	6.00

2014 Garbage Pail Kids Valentine's Day Box A

COMPLETE SET (10)	20.00	50.00
COMMON CARD	2.50	6.00

2014 Garbage Pail Kids Valentine's Day Box B

COMPLETE SET (10)	20.00	50.00
COMMON CARD	2.50	6.00

2022 Topps Garbage Pail Kids Valentine's Day Disgusting Dating

COMPLETE SET (10)	10.00	25.00
COMMON CARD (1a-10b)	1.50	4.00
*RED HEART: .75X TO 2X BASIC CARDS		
*BLACK HEART: 2X TO 5X BASIC CARDS		
*GOLD/50: 4X TO 10X BASIC CARDS		
*RAINBOW/25: 6X TO 15X BASIC CARDS		

2022 Topps Garbage Pail Kids Valentine's Day Disgusting Dating Profiles

COMPLETE SET (10)	10.00	25.00
COMMON CARD (1-10)	2.00	5.00
STATED ODDS 2:SET		

2023 Topps Garbage Pail Kids Valentine's Day Is Canceled

COMPLETE SET W/O SP (20)	6.00	15.00
UNOPENED BOX (PACKS)	100.00	150.00
COMMON CARD (1a-10b)	.75	2.00
COMMON SP	8.00	20.00
*RED: 1.5X TO 4X BASIC CARDS		
*BLACK: 4X TO 10X BASIC CARDS		
*GOLD/50: 12X TO 30X BASIC CARDS		
*RAINBOW/25: 15X TO 40X BASIC CARDS		
1c Love Able SP	12.00	30.00
3c Matt Fink SP	10.00	25.00
4c Romantic Rodney SP	10.00	25.00
5c Fancy Clancy SP	10.00	25.00
10c Fat Chance SP	10.00	25.00

2023 Topps Garbage Pail Kids Valentine's Day Is Canceled Dating Profiles

COMPLETE SET (10)	15.00	40.00
COMMON CARD (1-10)	3.00	8.00
STATED ODDS 2:1		

2023 Topps Garbage Pail Kids Valentine's Day Is Canceled Ermsy

NNO Deaf Geoff	20.00	50.00

GARBAGE PAIL KIDS

2023 Topps Garbage Pail Kids Valentine's Day Is Canceled Variant Box

NNO Lovely Lea	25.00	60.00

2020 Topps Garbage Pail Kids Video Series

COMPLETE SET (15)	25.00	60.00
COMPLETE SET 1 (5)	10.00	25.00
COMPLETE SET 2 (5)	10.00	25.00
COMPLETE SET 3 (5)	15.00	40.00
SET 1 COMMON (1-5)	2.50	6.00
SET 2 COMMON (6-10)	3.00	8.00
SET 3 COMMON (11-15)	5.00	12.00
SET 1 PRINT RUN 556 SETS		
SET 2 PRINT RUN 493 SETS		
SET 3 PRINT RUN 348 SETS		

2018 Garbage Pail Kids We Hate the '80s

COMPLETE SET (180)	8.00	20.00
UNOPENED BOX (24 PACKS)	200.00	300.00
UNOPENED PACK (8 CARDS)	8.00	12.00
COMMON CARD	.20	.50
*PUKE: 1.2X TO 3X BASIC CARDS	.60	1.50
*BRUISED: 1.5X TO 4X BASIC CARDS	.75	2.00
*PHLEGM: 2X TO 5X BASIC CARDS	1.00	2.50
*SPIT/99: 2.5X TO 6X BASIC CARDS	1.25	3.00
*BLOODY NOSE/75: 6X TO 15X BASIC CARDS	3.00	8.00
*FOOL'S GOLD/50: 12X TO 30X BASIC CARDS	6.00	15.00

2018 Garbage Pail Kids We Hate the '80s Artist Autographs

COMMON CAMERA	15.00	30.00
COMMON DEJARNETTE	12.00	30.00
COMMON ENGSTROM	15.00	40.00
COMMON GROSS	15.00	40.00
COMMON IM	10.00	25.00
COMMON KIM	12.00	30.00
COMMON SIMKO	12.00	30.00
COMMON SMOKIN' JOE	15.00	40.00
COMMON WHEATON	10.00	25.00
STATED PRINT RUN 25 SER.#'d SETS		

2018 Garbage Pail Kids We Hate the '80s Bathroom Buddies

COMPLETE SET (6)	4.00	10.00
COMMON CARD (13a-15b)	1.00	2.50
RANDOMLY INSERTED INTO PACKS		

2018 Garbage Pail Kids We Hate the '80s Classic Stickers

COMPLETE SET (20)	10.00	25.00
COMMON CARD (1a-10b)	1.00	2.50
RANDOMLY INSERTED INTO PACKS		

2018 Garbage Pail Kids We Hate the '80s The Goldbergs Sitcom Autographs

COMMON AUTO	100.00	200.00
RANDOMLY INSERTED INTO PACKS		
NNO Adam F. Goldberg	150.00	300.00
NNO George Segal	120.00	250.00
NNO Hayley Orrantia	150.00	300.00
NNO Jeff Garlin	200.00	400.00
NNO Sean Giambrone	120.00	250.00
NNO Troy Gentile	150.00	300.00
NNO Wendi McLendon-Covey	250.00	500.00

2018 Garbage Pail Kids We Hate the '80s Gross Bears

COMPLETE SET (8)	5.00	12.00
COMMON CARD (21-28)	1.25	3.00
RANDOMLY INSERTED INTO PACKS		

2018 Garbage Pail Kids We Hate the '80s Manufactured Patches

COMMON PATCH (1a-10b)	10.00	25.00
RANDOMLY INSERTED INTO PACKS		
1a New Wave Dave	20.00	50.00
1b Graffiti Petey	15.00	40.00
2a Rappin' Ron	15.00	40.00
2b Ray Gun	12.00	30.00
3a Hot Head Harvey	15.00	40.00
3b Roy Bot	15.00	40.00
4b Brett Vet	12.00	30.00
5a Catty Kathy	12.00	30.00
5b Kitty Litter	12.00	30.00
6a Sprayed Wade	15.00	40.00
7a Reuben Cube	12.00	30.00
8a Kit Video	15.00	40.00
8b Ham Actor	12.00	30.00
9b Croco-Dale	12.00	30.00
10b Cassette Casey	12.00	30.00

2018 Garbage Pail Kids We Hate the '80s Wax Pack Parodies

COMPLETE SET (10)	120.00	200.00
COMMON CARD (1-10)	10.00	25.00
HOBBY AND COLLECTOR PACK EXCLUSIVE		

2022 Topps Garbage Pail Kids We Hate the '80s Expansion Set

COMPLETE SET (60)	100.00	250.00
COMPLETE SET 1 (10)	20.00	50.00
COMPLETE SET 2 (10)	20.00	50.00
COMPLETE SET 3 (10)	20.00	50.00
COMPLETE SET 4 (10)	20.00	50.00
COMPLETE SET 5 (10)	20.00	50.00
COMPLETE SET 6 (10)	20.00	50.00
COMMON S1 (1a-5b)	3.00	8.00
COMMON S2 (6a-10b)	3.00	8.00
COMMON S3 (11a-15b)	3.00	8.00
COMMON S4 (16a-20b)	3.00	8.00
COMMON S5 (21a-25b)	3.00	8.00
COMMON S6 (26a-30b)	3.00	8.00
*SEPIA: .75X TO 2X BASIC CARDS		
SET 1 ANNCD PRINT RUN 1,309 SETS		
SET 2 ANNCD PRINT RUN 2,176 SETS		
SET 3 ANNCD PRINT RUN 1,172 SETS		
SET 4 ANNCD PRINT RUN 1,406 SETS		
SET 5 ANNCD PRINT RUN 1,229 SETS		
SET 6 ANNCD PRINT RUN 1,133 SETS		

2019 Garbage Pail Kids We Hate the '90s

COMPLETE SET (220)	10.00	25.00
UNOPENED BOX (24 PACKS)	100.00	150.00
UNOPENED PACK (8 CARDS)	3.00	6.00
UNOPENED COLLECTOR BOX	200.00	300.00
UNOPENED COLLECTOR PACK	8.00	12.00
COMMON CARD	.20	.50
*PUKE: .75X TO 2X BASIC CARDS		
*BRUISED: 2.5X TO 6X BASIC CARDS		
*JELLY: 3X TO 8X BASIC CARDS		
*SPIT/99: 5X TO 12X BASIC CARDS		
*BLOODY NOSE/75: 6X TO 15X BASIC CARDS		
*FOOL'S GOLD/50: 10X TO 25X BASIC CARDS		

2019 Garbage Pail Kids We Hate the '90s Artist Autographs

COMMON CAMERA	15.00	40.00
COMMON DEJARNETTE	15.00	40.00
COMMON ENGSTROM	12.00	30.00
COMMON GROSS	12.00	30.00
COMMON IM	10.00	25.00
COMMON KIM	12.00	30.00
COMMON SIMKO	15.00	40.00
COMMON SMOKIN JOE	15.00	40.00
COMMON WHEATON	15.00	40.00
STATED ODDS 1:103		
STATED PRINT RUN 25 SER.#'d SETS		

2019 Garbage Pail Kids We Hate the '90s Bathroom Buddies

COMPLETE SET (8)	5.00	12.00
COMMON CARD (19a-22b)	1.00	2.50
RANDOMLY INSERTED INTO BLASTER PACKS		

2019 Garbage Pail Kids We Hate the '90s Classic '90s

COMPLETE SET (20)	10.00	25.00
COMMON CARD (1a-10b)	1.25	3.00
RANDOMLY INSERTED INTO PACKS		

2019 Garbage Pail Kids We Hate the '90s Manufactured Patches

COMMON CARD (1a-10b)	10.00	25.00
RANDOMLY INSERTED INTO COLLECTOR PACKS		
1a Bad Bart	15.00	40.00
1b Mad Matt	15.00	40.00
2a Cruel Cal	12.00	30.00
2b Brutal Bill	12.00	30.00
3a Legendary Lincoln	20.00	50.00
3b Heart Les	15.00	40.00
4a Mega Manny	12.00	30.00
5a Limber Luigi	15.00	40.00
5b Messy Mario	20.00	50.00
6a Battle Tod	15.00	40.00
6b Rash Ash	15.00	40.00
7a Booger Manny	12.00	30.00
9a Super Manuel	15.00	40.00
9b Charged Clark	15.00	40.00
10b Grim Tim	15.00	40.00

2019 Garbage Pail Kids We Hate the '90s Wacky Pails

COMPLETE SET (20)	6.00	15.00
COMMON CARD (1-20)	.75	2.00
RANDOMLY INSERTED INTO FAT PACKS		

2019 Garbage Pail Kids We Hate the '90s Wax Pack Parodies

COMPLETE SET (10)	75.00	150.00
COMMON CARD (1-10)	10.00	25.00
RANDOMLY INSERTED INTO COLLECTOR PACKS		

2020 Topps Garbage Pail Kids Welcome to Smellville

COMPLETE SET (4)	4.00	10.00
COMMON CARD (1-4)	1.50	4.00

2021 Topps Garbage Pail Kids Zoom Mishaps

COMPLETE SET (12)	20.00	50.00
COMMON CARD (1a-6b)	3.00	8.00
STATED PRINT RUN 776 ANNCD SETS		
1a I'm Nate a Cat	4.00	10.00

2018 Stranger Kids

COMPLETE SET (40)	75.00	150.00
COMMON CARD (1a-20b)	3.00	8.00
*GREEN: X TO X BASIC CARDS		
*PINK: X TO X BASIC CARDS		

2018 Stranger Kids NYCC Promos

COMPLETE SET (4)	60.00	120.00
COMMON CARD	15.00	40.00

2019 Topps WWE Garbage Pail Kids

COMPLETE SET (13)	200.00	500.00
STATED PRINT RUN 1,028 ANNCD SETS		
1 Gigantic Andre	25.00	60.00
2 Breakin' Becky	15.00	40.00
3 C-Thru Cena	30.00	75.00
4 Savage Randy	25.00	60.00
5 Mixed-Up Mick	20.00	50.00
6 Mouthy Miz & Maryse	15.00	40.00
7 Slick Ric	30.00	75.00
8 Rowdy Ronda	20.00	50.00
9 Brawlin' Rollins	25.00	60.00
10 Seething Steve	40.00	100.00
11 Chipped Rock	40.00	100.00
12 Unravelled Warrior	25.00	60.00
13 Undead Taker	30.00	75.00

Star Trek

STAR TREK

The Original Series

1967 Leaf Star Trek

COMPLETE SET (72) 1200.00 2000.00
UNOPENED PACK 250.00 500.00
COMMON CARD (1-72) 8.00 20.00
1 No Time for Escape 12.00 30.00
72 Raspberries 15.00 40.00

1969 A&BC Star Trek

COMPLETE SET (55) 400.00 800.00
COMMON CARD (1-55) 5.00 12.00

1971 Primrose Star Trek

COMPLETE SET (12) 10.00 25.00
COMMON CARD (1-12) 1.25 3.00

1976 Topps Star Trek

COMPLETE SET W/STICKERS (110) 100.00 200.00
COMPLETE SET (83) 75.00 150.00
UNOPENED BOX (36 PACKS) 6000.00 7000.00
UNOPENED PACK (5 CARDS+1 STICKER) 150.00 200.00
COMMON CARD (1-88) .75 2.00
1 The U.S.S. Enterprise 1.50 4.00
88 Star Trek Lives 1.50 4.00

1976 Topps Star Trek Stickers

COMPLETE SET (22) 60.00 120.00
COMMON CARD (1-22) 2.00 5.00
1 James Kirk 3.00 8.00

1978 Weetabix Star Trek

COMPLETE SET (18) 12.00 30.00
COMMON CARD (1-18) 1.00 2.50

1997 SkyBox Star Trek The Original Series Season 1

COMPLETE SET (148) 5.00 12.00
UNOPENED BOX (36 PACKS) 250.00 400.00
UNOPENED PACK (9 CARDS) 8.00 12.00
COMMON CARD (1-90; C1-C58) .15 .40

1997 SkyBox Star Trek The Original Series Season 1 Autograph Challenge

COMP.SET W/O SP (11) 4.00 10.00
COMMON CARD .75 2.00
STATED ODDS 1:1
I Insignia SP 1000.00 1800.00

1997 SkyBox Star Trek The Original Series Season 1 Autographs

COMMON CARD (A1-A26) 8.00 20.00
STATED ODDS 1:36
A1 William Shatner SP 450.00 800.00
A2 James Doohan 90.00 175.00
A3 Nichelle Nichols 60.00 120.00
A4 George Takei 30.00 80.00
A5 Grace Lee Whitney 25.00 60.00
A7 Barbara Anderson 15.00 40.00
A9 Robert Brown 20.00 50.00
A10 Paul Carr 12.00 30.00
A11 Kim Darby 15.00 40.00
A12 Gene Dynarski 12.00 30.00
A13 Clint Howard 30.00 75.00
A14 Bruce Hyde 12.00 30.00
A15 William Campbell 10.00 25.00
A16 Gary Lockwood 15.00 40.00
A17 Ricardo Montalban 150.00 300.00
A19 Madlyn Rhue 50.00 100.00
A21 Morgan Woodward 10.00 25.00
A22 Meg Wyllie 25.00 60.00
A23 Joan Collins SP 125.00 250.00
A25 Majel Barrett SP 225.00 450.00
A26 Sherry Jackson 30.00 75.00

1997 SkyBox Star Trek The Original Series Season 1 Behind-the-Scenes

COMPLETE SET (58) 15.00 40.00
COMMON CARD (B1-B58) .40 1.00
STATED ODDS 1:2

1997 SkyBox Star Trek The Original Series Season 1 Gold Plaques

COMPLETE SET (29) 100.00 200.00
COMMON CARD (G1-G29) 3.00 8.00
STATED ODDS 1:12

1997 SkyBox Star Trek The Original Series Season 1 Profiles

COMPLETE SET (29) 12.00 30.00
COMMON CARD (P1-P29) .60 1.50
STATED ODDS 1:4

1998 SkyBox Star Trek The Original Series Season 2

COMPLETE SET (133) 5.00 25.00
UNOPENED BOX (36 PACKS) 125.00 200.00
UNOPENED PACK (9 CARDS) 4.00 6.00
COMMON CARD (91-171; C59-C110) .15 .40

1998 SkyBox Star Trek The Original Series Season 2 Autograph Challenge

COMPLETE SET W/O SP (11) 1.50 4.00
COMPLETE SET W/SP (12)
COMMON CARD .20 .50
STATED ODDS ONE PER PACK
V Spock SP 60.00 120.00

1998 SkyBox Star Trek The Original Series Season 2 Autographs

COMPLETE SET (33)
COMMON CARD 6.00 15.00
STATED ODDS 1:36
A27 DeForest Kelley SP 500.00 1200.00
A28 Walter Koenig 25.00 60.00
A29 Dorothy Fontana 10.00 25.00
A30 Majel Barrett 75.00 150.00
A31 William Shatner SP 300.00 800.00
A32 James Doohan SP 75.00 200.00
A33 George Takei 30.00 80.00
A34 Nichelle Nichols 30.00 80.00
A35 Antoinette Bower 10.00 25.00
A36 Tige Andrews 12.00 30.00
A37 Michael Forest 15.00 40.00
A38A Tasha Martel 12.00 30.00
A38B Tasha Martel 20.00 50.00
A39 William Windom 20.00 50.00
A40 John Fiedler 10.00 25.00
A41 Charles Macaulay 10.00 25.00
A42 Keith Andes 8.00 20.00
A43 BarBara Luna 15.00 40.00
A45 William Campbell 20.00 50.00
A46 William Schallert 10.00 25.00
A47 William O'Connell 12.00 30.00
A48 John Wheeler 12.00 30.00
A49 Nancy Kovack 15.00 40.00
A51 Stephen Brooks 8.00 20.00
A52 Anthony Caruso 15.00 40.00
A54 Barbara Bouchet 25.00 60.00
A55 Warren Stevens 10.00 25.00
A56 William Marshall 30.00 80.00
A57 Roy Jenson 10.00 25.00
A58 Teri Garr SP 50.00 125.00

1998 SkyBox Star Trek The Original Series Season 2 Behind-the-Scenes

COMPLETE SET (52) 12.00 30.00
COMMON CARD (B59-B110) .40 1.00
STATED ODDS 1:2

1998 SkyBox Star Trek The Original Series Season 2 Gold Plaques

COMPLETE SET (26) 50.00 100.00
COMMON CARD (G30-G55) 2.50 6.00
STATED ODDS 1:12

1998 SkyBox Star Trek The Original Series Season 2 Mirror Mirror

COMMON CARD (M1-M7) 200.00 400.00
STATED ODDS 1:720
STATED PRINT RUN 200 SER.#'d SETS
M1 Captain Kirk 400.00 800.00
M2 Mr. Spock 400.00 800.00
M5 Sulu 300.00 600.00

1998 SkyBox Star Trek The Original Series Season 2 Profiles

COMPLETE SET (26) 15.00 40.00
COMMON CARD (P30-P55) .75 2.00
STATED ODDS 1:4

1999 SkyBox Star Trek The Original Series Season 3

COMPLETE SET (123) 10.00 25.00
UNOPENED BOX (36 PACKS) 100.00 150.00
UNOPENED PACK (9 CARDS) 2.00 5.00
COMMON CARD (172-246; C111-C158) .15 .40

1999 SkyBox Star Trek The Original Series Season 3 Autographs

COMMON CARD (A59-A85) 6.00 15.00
STATED ODDS 1:36
A59 Leonard Nimoy 250.00 400.00
A60 James Doohan 75.00 150.00
A61 DeForest Kelley 500.00 1200.00
A62 Walter Koenig 20.00 50.00
A63 John Winston 10.00 25.00
A64 Herb Solow 15.00 30.00
A68 Jay Robinson 20.00 50.00
A69 Jack Donner 12.00 25.00
A70 Diana Muldaur 15.00 40.00
A71 Alan Bergmann 12.00 30.00
A72 Michael Ansara 20.00 40.00
A73 Susan Howard 12.00 30.00
A74 Barbara Babcock 15.00 40.00
A75 Jason Evers 8.00 20.00
A76 Lee Meriwether 25.00 60.00
A77 Frank Gorshin 75.00 150.00
A78 Yvonne Craig 30.00 75.00
A79 Sharon Acker 20.00 40.00
A80 Gene Dynarski 15.00 30.00
A81 Charles Napier 15.00 30.00
A82 Victor Brandt 12.00 25.00
A83 Phillip Pine 12.00 25.00
A84 Nathan Jung 12.00 25.00
A85 Mariette Hartley 20.00 40.00

1999 SkyBox Star Trek The Original Series Season 3 Behind-the-Scenes

COMPLETE SET (48) 6.00 15.00
COMMON CARD (111-158) .20 .50
STATED ODDS 1:2

1999 SkyBox Star Trek The Original Series Season 3 Gold Plaques

COMPLETE SET (24) 40.00 100.00
COMMON CARD (56-79) 2.50 6.00
STATED ODDS 1:12

1999 SkyBox Star Trek The Original Series Season 3 Profiles

COMPLETE SET (24) 7.50 20.00
COMMON CARD (56-79) .60 1.50
STATED ODDS 1:4

2006 Star Trek The Original Series 40th Anniversary

COMPLETE SET (110) 6.00 15.00
UNOPENED BOX (40 PACKS) 60.00 70.00
UNOPENED PACK (5 CARDS) 3.00 3.50
UNOPENED ARCHIVE BOX 1500.00 2000.00
COMMON CARD (1-110) .15 .40

2006 Star Trek The Original Series 40th Anniversary 1967 Expansion

COMPLETE SET (18) 60.00 120.00
COMMON CARD (73-90) 3.00 8.00
STATED ODDS 1:40

2006 Star Trek The Original Series 40th Anniversary Autographs

COMMON CARD	6.00	15.00
STATED ODDS 1:20		
A126 ISSUED AS ALBUM EXCLUSIVE		
QA8 ISSUED AS 2-CASE INCENTIVE		
E.RODDENBERRY AU #'D TO 225		
G.RODDENBERRY AU #'D TO 25		
NIMOY AU/MEM ISSUED AS 6-CASE INCENTIVE		
L (LIMITED): 300-500 COPIES		
VL (VERY LIMITED): 200-300 COPIES		
A106 Jason Wingreen	12.00	30.00
A107 Lawrence Montaigne	8.00	20.00
A109 Robert Walker Jr. VL	100.00	200.00
A110 Kathryn Hays L	8.00	20.00
A111 France Nuyen VL	60.00	120.00
A112 Joan Collins L	60.00	120.00
A113 Brian Tochi	12.00	30.00
A114 Sheldon Collins	15.00	40.00
A115 David Soul	20.00	50.00
A116 John Crawford L	30.00	80.00
A117 Ned Romero	12.00	30.00
A119 Leonard Nimoy VL	250.00	500.00
A120 Majel Barrett VL	150.00	300.00
A121 Laurel Goodwin	12.00	30.00
A122 Bobby Clark L	10.00	25.00
A123 Bruce Hyde	10.00	25.00
A125 Malachi Throne	10.00	25.00
A126 Walter Koenig ALB	15.00	40.00
A128 Marianne Hill	15.00	40.00
A129 Emily Banks	12.00	30.00
A131 Garrison True	20.00	50.00
A133 Kate Woodville	15.00	40.00
A134 Mary Rice	12.00	30.00
A135A George Takei L	30.00	80.00
A135B Richard Compton	8.00	20.00
A137 Rhodes Reason	8.00	20.00
QA8 Grace Lee Whitney CI	60.00	120.00
NNO Eugene Roddenberry Jr. CUT/220	100.00	200.00
NNO Gene Roddenberry CUT/25	3000.00	5000.00
NNO Leonard Nimoy AU/MEM CI	150.00	300.00

2006 Star Trek The Original Series 40th Anniversary Bridge Crew Delta Shield Patches

COMPLETE SET (7)	150.00	300.00
COMMON PATCH (DS1-DS7)	15.00	40.00
STATED ODDS 1:200		
DS1 Captain James T. Kirk	20.00	50.00
DS2 Commander Spock	20.00	50.00
DS3 Dr. Leonard McCoy	25.00	60.00
DS7 Lieutenant Uhura	25.00	60.00

2006 Star Trek The Original Series 40th Anniversary Captain Pike

COMPLETE SET (9)	10.00	25.00
COMMON CARD (CP1-CP9)	1.25	3.00
STATED ODDS 1:14		

2006 Star Trek The Original Series 40th Anniversary Portraits

COMPLETE SET (18)	60.00	120.00
COMMON CARD (PT1-PT18)	3.00	8.00
STATED ODDS 1:40		
PT1 Captain Kirk	6.00	15.00
PT2 Spock	5.00	12.00

2006 Star Trek The Original Series 40th Anniversary Faces of Vina

COMPLETE SET (6)	6.00	15.00
COMMON CARD (FV1-FV6)	1.25	3.00
STATED ODDS 1:20		

2006 Star Trek The Original Series 40th Anniversary Star Trek Expansion Quotables

COMPLETE SET (18)	30.00	60.00
COMMON CARD (111-128)	1.50	4.00
STATED ODDS 1:10		

2006 Star Trek The Original Series 40th Anniversary TV Guide Covers

COMPLETE SET (2)	6.00	15.00
COMMON CARD (TV8-TV9)	4.00	10.00
STATED ODDS 1:CASE		

2006 Star Trek The Original Series 40th Anniversary Promos

COMMON CARD	.75	2.00
P3 Kirk	3.00	8.00
Spock ALB		
UK Kirk (UK)	2.00	5.00
CP1 Kirk CON	1.25	3.00

2008 Star Trek The Original Series 40th Anniversary Series 2

COMPLETE SET (110)	6.00	15.00
UNOPENED BOX (24 PACKS)	60.00	100.00
UNOPENED PACK (5 CARDS)	3.00	4.00
COMMON CARD (111-220)	.15	.40

2008 Star Trek The Original Series 40th Anniversary Series 2 1967 Expansion

COMPLETE SET (18)	20.00	50.00
COMMON CARD (91-108)	1.50	4.00
STATED ODDS 1:12		

2008 Star Trek The Original Series 40th Anniversary Series 2 Autographs

COMMON CARD	5.00	12.00
STATED ODDS 1:8		
A136 STATED ODDS ONE PER CASE		
A187 ISSUED AS ALBUM EXCLUSIVE		
TAKEI AU/MEM STATED ODDS ONE PER 3 CASE PURCHASE		
DOOHAN AU STATED ODDS ONE PER 6 CASE PURCHASE		
L (LIMITED): 300-500 COPIES		
VL (VERY LIMITED): 200-300 COPIES		
A132 James X. Mitchell	6.00	15.00
A136 Joanne Linville CT	25.00	60.00
A141 Lou Antonio	8.00	20.00
A142 Felix Silla	8.00	20.00
A143 Billy Blackburn	12.00	30.00
A144 Billy Blackburn	20.00	50.00
A145 Julie Cobb	10.00	25.00
A147 Deborah Downey	8.00	20.00
A149b Barbara Baldavin TI	15.00	40.00
A150 William Shatner VL	150.00	300.00
A152 Bob Herron	6.00	15.00
A153 Sean Morgan	10.00	25.00
A154 Sean Kenney	8.00	20.00
A155a Majel Barrett Voice VL	80.00	150.00
A155b Majel Barrett TI VL	60.00	120.00
A157 Win De Lugo	12.00	30.00
A159 Michael Dante	10.00	25.00
A161 Grace Lee Whitney VL	30.00	80.00
A162 BarBara Luna	12.00	30.00
A163 Jan Shutan	8.00	20.00
A164 Stewart Moss	6.00	15.00
A165 Celeste Yarnall	12.00	30.00
A166 Yvonne Craig VL	30.00	75.00
A170 Richard Evans	8.00	20.00
A171 Pamelyn Ferdin	12.00	30.00
A173 Sid Haig	10.00	25.00
A174 Andrea Dromm	15.00	40.00
A176 Venita Wolf	12.00	30.00
A178 Craig Huxley L	20.00	50.00
A179 Craig Huxley L	20.00	50.00
A180 Irene Kelly	8.00	20.00
A181 Steve Marlo	8.00	20.00
A182 Erik Holland	6.00	15.00
A185 Jerry Ayres	6.00	15.00
A187 Ralph Maurer ALB	12.00	30.00
NNO George Takei MEM CI	50.00	100.00
NNO James Doohan CI	150.00	300.00

2008 Star Trek The Original Series 40th Anniversary Series 2 Charlie X

COMPLETE SET (9)	10.00	25.00
COMMON CARD	1.50	4.00
STATED ODDS 1:24		

2008 Star Trek The Original Series 40th Anniversary Series 2 Portraits

COMPLETE SET (27)	15.00	40.00
COMMON CARD (PT19-PT45)	1.00	2.50
STATED ODDS 1:8		

2008 Star Trek The Original Series 40th Anniversary Series 2 Stickers

COMPLETE SET (18)	20.00	50.00
COMMON CARD (S1-S18)	1.25	3.00
STATED ODDS 1:12		
S1 Captain Kirk	2.50	6.00
S2 Spock	2.00	5.00

2008 Star Trek The Original Series 40th Anniversary Series 2 Promos

COMMON CARD (P1-P4)	.75	2.00
P3 Kirk ALB	3.00	8.00
P4 Group Shot CON	1.50	4.00

2009 Star Trek The Original Series 40th Anniversary Series 3

COMPLETE SET (110)	6.00	15.00
UNOPENED BOX (24 PACKS)	55.00	65.00
UNOPENED PACK (5 CARDS)	2.50	3.00
UNOPENED ARCHIVE BOX	1000.00	2000.00
COMMON CARD (221-330)	.15	.40

2009 Star Trek The Original Series 40th Anniversary Series 3 Autographs

COMMON CARD	6.00	15.00
STATED ODDS 1:8		
KOENIG AUTO ONE PER 3 CASE PURCHASE		
SHATNER/NICHOLS AUTO ONE PER 6 CASE PURCHASE		
A140 Lisabeth Shatner	40.00	80.00
A160 Leslie Shatner	40.00	80.00
A168 Leslie Parrish	40.00	80.00
A193 Leonard Nimoy	150.00	250.00
A199 William Shatner	150.00	250.00
A203 Sandra Smith	8.00	20.00
A205 William Wintersole	40.00	80.00
A206 Lee Meriwether	15.00	30.00
A207 Sabrina Scharf	8.00	20.00
A208 Mariette Hartley	25.00	50.00
A214 John Winston	40.00	80.00
A219 Roger Perry	8.00	20.00
A220 Kim Darby	8.00	20.00
A228 Gary Combs	8.00	20.00
A229 Gary Combs	8.00	20.00
A231 Shirley Bonne	10.00	25.00
A232 Barbara Bouchet	30.00	75.00
NNO Walter Koenig MEM 3CI	50.00	100.00
DA4 W.Shatner/N.Nichols 6CI	200.00	300.00

2009 Star Trek The Original Series 40th Anniversary Series 3 In Motion

COMPLETE SET (2)	15.00	40.00
COMMON CARD (M7-M8)	10.00	25.00
STATED ODDS 1:CASE		
COMPLETE SET (18)	8.00	20.00
COMMON CARD (L1-L18)	1.00	2.50
STATED ODDS 1:6		

2009 Star Trek The Original Series 40th Anniversary Series 3 Portraits

COMPLETE SET (18)	10.00	25.00
COMMON CARD (M46-M63)	1.25	3.00
STATED ODDS 1:8		

2009 Star Trek The Original Series 40th Anniversary Series 3 Tribute

COMPLETE SET (18)	25.00	60.00
COMMON CARD (T1-T18)	2.00	5.00
STATED ODDS 1:12		

2009 Star Trek The Original Series 40th Anniversary Series 3 Promos

COMMON CARD (P1-P4)	.75	2.00
P3 Kirk/Spock	3.00	8.00
P4 Spock/Romulan Commander	2.00	5.00

2016 Star Trek The Original Series 50th Anniversary

COMPLETE SET (80)	6.00	15.00
UNOPENED BOX (24 PACKS)	65.00	80.00
UNOPENED PACK (5 CARDS)	3.00	3.50
COMMON CARD (1-80)	.12	.30

2016 Star Trek The Original Series 50th Anniversary Black Autographs

COMMON CARD	5.00	12.00
STATED ODDS 1:12 W/SILVER AUTOS		
NNO Anthony Call	6.00	15.00
NNO Barbara Babcock	10.00	25.00
NNO Barbara Bouchet	12.00	30.00
NNO BarBara Luna	6.00	15.00
NNO Clint Howard	10.00	25.00
NNO Elinor Donahue	10.00	25.00
NNO Emily Banks	6.00	15.00
NNO Gene Dynarski	6.00	15.00
NNO Kathryn Hays	20.00	50.00
NNO Laurel Goodwin	10.00	25.00
NNO Lee Meriweather	12.00	30.00
NNO Lou Antonio	20.00	50.00
NNO Maggie Thrett	8.00	20.00
NNO Mariette Hartley	8.00	20.00
NNO Michael Forest	6.00	15.00
NNO Michael J. Pollard	8.00	20.00
NNO Nancy Kovack	6.00	15.00
NNO Pamelyn Ferdin	10.00	25.00
NNO Sabrina Scharf	6.00	15.00
NNO Sally Kellerman	10.00	25.00
NNO Sandy Gimpel	10.00	25.00
NNO Sherry Jackson	10.00	25.00
NNO Shirley Bonne	8.00	20.00
NNO Skip Homeier	15.00	40.00
NNO Teri Garr	25.00	60.00

2016 Star Trek The Original Series 50th Anniversary Bridge Crew Heroes

COMPLETE SET (9)	15.00	40.00
COMMON CARD (P1-P9)	2.50	6.00
STATED ODDS 1:96		
P1 Captain Kirk	4.00	10.00
P2 Spock	5.00	12.00
P3 Dr. McCoy	4.00	10.00
P6 Sulu	3.00	8.00

2016 Star Trek The Original Series 50th Anniversary Case Incentive Autographs

6CI Leonard Nimoy as Mirror Spock Silver AU 6CI	125.00	250.00
DA35 William Shatner and Leonard Nimoy Dual AU 9CI	300.00	500.00

2016 Star Trek The Original Series 50th Anniversary Cut Signatures

1 Jeffrey Hunter/12		
2 Jill Ireland/35	2000.00	3000.00
3 Susan Oliver/13	5000.00	7500.00

2016 Star Trek The Original Series 50th Anniversary Enterprise Concept Art

COMPLETE SET (9)	20.00	50.00
COMMON CARD (E1-E9)	4.00	10.00
STATED ODDS 1:96		

2016 Star Trek The Original Series 50th Anniversary Leonard Nimoy In Memoriam

COMPLETE SET (9)	200.00	350.00
COMMON CARD (M1-M9)	30.00	75.00
STATED ODDS 1:288		
STATED PRINT RUN 125 SER.#'d SETS		

2016 Star Trek The Original Series 50th Anniversary Mirror Mirror Heroes

COMPLETE SET (9)	120.00	200.00
COMMON CARD (MM1-MM9)	12.00	30.00
STATED ODDS 1:288		
MM1 Captain Kirk	15.00	40.00
MM2 Spock	15.00	40.00
MM3 Dr. McCoy	20.00	50.00
MM8 Marlena	20.00	50.00

2016 Star Trek The Original Series 50th Anniversary Mirror Mirror Uncut

COMPLETE SET (50)	25.00	60.00
COMMON CARD (MM1-MM50)	1.00	2.50
STATED ODDS 1:12		

2016 Star Trek The Original Series 50th Anniversary Silver Autographs

COMMON CARD	5.00	12.00
STATED ODDS 1:12 W/BLACK AUTOS		
NNO Charlie Brill	8.00	20.00
NNO Clint Howard	10.00	25.00
NNO Diana Muldaur	15.00	40.00
NNO Gary Lockwood	6.00	15.00
NNO Geoffrey Binney	6.00	15.00
NNO George Takei	25.00	60.00
NNO Grace Lee Whitney	25.00	60.00
NNO Joan Collins	30.00	80.00
NNO John Wheeler	8.00	20.00
NNO Lou Antonio	15.00	40.00
NNO Maggie Thrett	10.00	25.00
NNO Mariette Hartley	12.00	30.00
NNO Michael J. Pollard	8.00	20.00
NNO Morgan Woodward	6.00	15.00
NNO Nichelle Nichols	25.00	60.00
NNO Pamelyn Ferdin	10.00	25.00
NNO Robert Walker	6.00	15.00
NNO Skip Homeier	15.00	40.00
NNO Walter Koenig	25.00	60.00
NNO William O'Connell	6.00	15.00
NNO William Shatner	120.00	250.00
NNO Yvonne Craig	30.00	80.00

2016 Star Trek The Original Series 50th Anniversary The Cage Uncut

COMPLETE SET (70)	30.00	80.00
COMMON CARD (1-70)	1.00	2.50
STATED ODDS 1:12		

2016 Star Trek The Original Series 50th Anniversary Promos

P1 General Distribution	2.00	5.00
P2 Album Exclusive	12.00	30.00

2020 Rittenhouse Star Trek The Original Series Archives and Inscriptions

COMPLETE SET W/VAR. (2,023)	200.00	400.00
COMPLETE SET W/O VAR. (98)	6.00	15.00
UNOPENED BOX (24 PACKS)	125.00	200.00
UNOPENED PACK (5 CARDS)	5.00	8.00
COMMON CARD (1-98)	.12	.30

2020 Rittenhouse Star Trek The Original Series Archives and Inscriptions Autograph Inscriptions

COMMON ANTONIO	10.00	25.00
COMMON BABCOCK	10.00	25.00
COMMON BANKS	10.00	25.00
COMMON BEECHER	10.00	25.00
COMMON BONNE	10.00	25.00
COMMON BRILL	8.00	20.00
COMMON CALL	20.00	50.00
COMMON DANTE	8.00	20.00
COMMON DONAHUE	12.00	30.00
COMMON DONNER	6.00	15.00
COMMON DOWNEY	8.00	20.00
COMMON FRANKHAM	6.00	15.00
COMMON GOODWIN	6.00	15.00
COMMON KOENIG	25.00	60.00
COMMON MARS	10.00	25.00
COMMON MAURER	15.00	40.00
COMMON MERIWETHER	10.00	25.00
COMMON NICHOLS	25.00	60.00
COMMON POLLARD	6.00	15.00
COMMON RAPELYE	10.00	25.00
COMMON SCHARF	10.00	25.00
COMMON SHATNER	250.00	400.00
COMMON TAKEI	30.00	75.00
COMMON WASHBURN	8.00	20.00
COMMON WHEELER	6.00	15.00
L = 300-500 COPIES		
VL = 200-300 COPIES		
EL = 100-200 COPIES		
S = 100 OR FEWER		
OVERALL ODDS 1:24		

2020 Rittenhouse Star Trek The Original Series Archives and Inscriptions Black Border Autographs

COMMON AUTO	10.00	25.00
L = 300-500 COPIES		
VL = 200-300 COPIES		
EL = 100-200 COPIES		
S = 100 OR FEWER		
OVERALL ODDS 1:24		
NNO April Tatro EL	25.00	60.00
NNO Joan Collins 9CI	75.00	150.00
NNO Louise Sorel EL	20.00	50.00
NNO Skip Homeier EL	12.00	30.00

2020 Rittenhouse Star Trek The Original Series Archives and Inscriptions Classic TOS Autographs

COMMON AUTO	6.00	15.00
L = 300-500 COPIES		
VL = 200-300 COPIES		
EL = 100-200 COPIES		
S = 100 OR FEWER		
OVERALL ODDS 1:24		
A278 William Shatner EL	125.00	250.00
A309 April Tatro EL	50.00	100.00
A310 Ralph Maurer EL	8.00	20.00

2020 Rittenhouse Star Trek The Original Series Archives and Inscriptions Dual Autograph

DA39 W.Koenig/B.Beecher	30.00	75.00

2020 Rittenhouse Star Trek The Original Series Archives and Inscriptions Laser Cut Villains

COMPLETE SET (18)
COMMON CARD (L25-L42)
STATED ODDS 1:24.
L25 The Keeper from The Cage
L26 Harry Mudd from Mudd's Women/I, Mudd
L27 Romulan Commander from Balance of Terror
L28 Charlie Evans from Charlie X
L29 Roger Korby from What Are Little Girls Made Of?
L30 Tristan Adams from Dagger of the Mind
L31 Finnegan from Shore Leave
L32 Trelane from The Squire of Gothos
L33 Gorn Captain from Arena
L34 Sylvia from Catspaw
L35 Kras from Friday's Child
L36 Apollo from Who Mourns for Adonais?
L37 Romulan Commander from The Enterprise Incident
L38 Parmen from Plato's Stepchildren
L39 Bele from Let That Be Your Last Battlefield
L40 Garth from Whom Gods Destroy
L41 Dr. Sevrin from The Way to Eden
L42 Dr. Janice Lester from Turnabout Intruder
NNO Congratulations! Redemption Card

2020 Rittenhouse Star Trek The Original Series Archives and Inscriptions Legends Autograph

L = 300-500 COPIES		
VL = 200-300 COPIES		
EL = 100-200 COPIES		
S = 100 OR FEWER		
OVERALL ODDS 1:24		
NNO Sean Kenney VL	10.00	25.00

2020 Rittenhouse Star Trek The Original Series Archives and Inscriptions Metal Case Topper

CT1 The City on the Edge of Forever	5.00	12.00

2020 Rittenhouse Star Trek The Original Series Archives and Inscriptions Silver Signature Autographs

COMMON AUTO	8.00	20.00
L = 300-500 COPIES		
VL = 200-300 COPIES		
EL = 100-200 COPIES		
S = 100 OR FEWER		
OVERALL ODDS 1:24		
NNO April Tatro EL	25.00	60.00
NNO Barbara Babcock VL	10.00	25.00
NNO Celeste Yarnall EL	12.00	30.00
NNO Nancy Kovack VL	12.00	30.00
NNO Sherry Jackson L	10.00	25.00

2020 Rittenhouse Star Trek The Original Series Archives and Inscriptions Uncut The City on the Edge

COMPLETE SET (44)	15.00	40.00
COMMON CARD (1-44)	.75	2.00
STATED ODDS 1:12		

2020 Rittenhouse Star Trek The Original Series Archives and Inscriptions Promos

COMPLETE SET (3)		
COMMON CARD (P1-P3)		
P1 Captain James T. Kirk (General Distribution)	1.50	4.00
P2 Spock (NSU Exclusive)	2.50	6.00
P3 Dr. McCoy (Album Exclusive)	6.00	15.00

2005 Star Trek The Original Series Art and Images

COMPLETE SET (81)	4.00	10.00
UNOPENED BOX (24 PACKS)	55.00	65.00
UNOPENED PACK (5 CARDS)	2.50	3.00
COMMON CARD (1-81)	.10	.30

2005 Star Trek The Original Series Art and Images Animated Series Expanded Universe

COMPLETE SET (39)	8.00	20.00
COMMON CARD (AS1-AS39)	.20	.50
STATED ODDS 1:8		

2005 Star Trek The Original Series Art and Images ArtiFEX

COMPLETE SET (9)	30.00	80.00
COMMON CARD (CZ1-CZ9)	4.00	10.00
STATED ODDS 1:24		

2005 Star Trek The Original Series Art and Images Autographs

COMMON CARD (A11-A42;LA3)	8.00	20.00
STATED ODDS 1:12		
A15 ISSUED AS ALBUM EXCLUSIVE		
LA3 STATED ODDS ONE PER 6 CASE PURCHASE		
L (LIMITED): 300-500 COPIES		
VL (VERY LIMITED): 200-300 COPIES		
A11 Walter Koenig L	20.00	50.00
A12 Grace Lee Whitney L	30.00	80.00
A13 Bobby Clark L	15.00	30.00
A14 Joan Collins VL	50.00	100.00
A15 Arlene Martel ALB	10.00	25.00
A16 Ricardo Montalban VL	150.00	300.00
A17 Leonard Nimoy VL	150.00	250.00
A18 George Takei VL	30.00	80.00
A19 BarBara Luna	10.00	25.00
A22 Sherry Jackson	10.00	25.00
A23 William Windom L	10.00	25.00
A26 Michael Ansara L	20.00	40.00
A27 Lee Meriwether L	10.00	25.00
A30 Laurel Goodwin VL	20.00	40.00
A32 Majel Barrett VL	50.00	100.00
A34 Joanne Linville L	10.00	25.00
A39 Yvonne Craig VL	25.00	50.00
A42 Charles Napier	10.00	25.00
LA3 William Shatner CI	150.00	250.00

2005 Star Trek The Original Series Art and Images Comic Book Art

COMPLETE SET (61)	30.00	60.00
COMMON CARD (GK1-GK61)	.60	1.50
STATED ODDS 1:4		

2005 Star Trek The Original Series Art and Images SketchaFEX

COMMON CARD	12.00	30.00
STATED ODDS 1:48		
U.S.S. ENTERPRISE STATED ODDS ONE PER 2 CASE PURCHASE		
UNNUMBERED SET		

2005 Star Trek The Original Series Art and Images SketchaFEX Case-Toppers

COMPLETE SET (3)	30.00	80.00
COMMON CARD	12.00	30.00
STATED ODDS 1:CASE		
UNNUMBERED SET		

2005 Star Trek The Original Series Art and Images Promos

COMPLETE SET (6)	6.00	15.00
COMMON CARD	.75	2.00
P3 Talosian ALB	3.00	8.00
UK Spock UK	1.25	3.00
CE2005 Uhura/Kirk CNE	1.25	3.00
CP2005 Gorn CON	1.25	3.00

2018 Star Trek The Original Series Captain's Collection

COMPLETE SET (80)	8.00	20.00
UNOPENED BOX (24 PACKS)		
UNOPENED PACK (5 CARDS)		
COMMON CARD (1-80)	.20	.50
*THROWBACK: 4X TO 10X BASIC CARDS		

2018 Star Trek The Original Series Captain's Collection 50th Anniversary Canada Stamps

COMMON CARD	10.00	25.00
STATED ODDS 1:288		
L1 Transporter	75.00	150.00
L2 Guardian of Forever	75.00	150.00
S1 Captain Kirk	12.00	30.00
SS1 U.S.S. Enterprise	90.00	175.00
SS2 Klingon Battlecruiser	30.00	75.00

2018 Star Trek The Original Series Captain's Collection Autographs

COMMON AUTO	6.00	15.00
STATED OVERALL ODDS 1:12		
L (LIMITED) = 300-500		
VL (VERY LIMITED) = 200-300		
EL (EXTREMELY LIMITED) = 100-200		
A270 William Shatner EL	120.00	250.00
A280 Leonard Nimoy EL	150.00	300.00
A281 Walter Koenig EL	30.00	75.00
A282 Nichelle Nichols EL	50.00	100.00
A283 George Takei EL	30.00	75.00
A284 Morgan Woodward VL	12.00	30.00
A286 Michael J. Pollard EL	20.00	50.00
A288 Nancy Kovack EL	25.00	60.00
A289 John Wheeler EL	20.00	50.00
A290 Sandy Gimpel EL	20.00	50.00
A292 Barbara Babcock EL	20.00	50.00
A293 Phil Adams EL	15.00	40.00
A295 Virginia Aldridge L	8.00	20.00
A296 John Bellah EL	20.00	50.00
A298 Sandy Gimpel EL	20.00	50.00
A299 Phil Adams EL	15.00	40.00

2018 Star Trek The Original Series Captain's Collection Black Autographs

STATED OVERALL ODDS 1:12		
L (LIMITED) = 300-500		
VL (VERY LIMITED) = 200-300		
EL (EXTREMELY LIMITED) = 100-200		
NNO Celeste Yarnall L	8.00	20.00
NNO John Bellah EL	15.00	40.00

2018 Star Trek The Original Series Captain's Collection Bridge Crew Duals

COMMON CARD (D1-D7)	6.00	15.00
STATED ODDS 1:144		

2018 Star Trek The Original Series Captain's Collection Case-Toppers

16a The Menagerie, Part 1 (Pike's Log)	3.00	8.00
17a The Menagerie, Part 2 (Pike's Log)	3.00	8.00
40a Mirror, Mirror (Mirror Kirk's Log)	30.00	75.00

2018 Star Trek The Original Series Captain's Collection Dual Autographs

DA36 W.Shatner/L.Sorel	200.00	350.00
DA37 W.Koenig/C.Yarnall	60.00	120.00

2018 Star Trek The Original Series Captain's Collection Inscriptions

COMMON CARD	10.00	25.00
STATED OVERALL ODDS 1:12		
L (LIMITED) = 300-500		
VL (VERY LIMITED) = 200-300		
EL (EXTREMELY LIMITED) = 100-200		
A2 BarBara Luna L	12.00	30.00
A3 Clint Howard L	15.00	40.00
A4 Robert Walker Jr. L	12.00	30.00
A5 Joan Collins EL	50.00	100.00
A7 Michael Forest VL	15.00	40.00
A8 Louise Sorel EL	25.00	60.00
A10 Antoinette Bower	12.00	30.00
A12 Mariette Hartley L	12.00	30.00
A15 Joanne Linville L	15.00	40.00
A16 Gary Lockwood L	12.00	30.00

2018 Star Trek The Original Series Captain's Collection Inside the Enterprise

COMPLETE SET W/O RR (9)	12.00	30.00
COMMON CARD (E1-E9)	2.50	6.00
STATED ODDS 1:48		
E10 IS A RITTENHOUSE REWARD		
E10 Recreation Room (Rittenhouse Reward)	30.00	75.00

2018 Star Trek The Original Series Captain's Collection Juan Ortiz Lobby Cards

COMPLETE SET (80)	50.00	100.00
COMMON CARD (1-80)	1.00	2.50
STATED ODDS 1:12		

2018 Star Trek The Original Series Captain's Collection Relic

NNO Susan Oliver	200.00	400.00

2018 Star Trek The Original Series Captain's Collection Silver Signature Autographs

COMMON AUTO	8.00	20.00
STATED OVERALL ODDS 1:12		
L (LIMITED) = 300-500		
VL (VERY LIMITED) = 200-300		
EL (EXTREMELY LIMITED) = 100-200		
NNO Barbara Bouchet EL	15.00	40.00
NNO Elinor Donahue EL	12.00	30.00
NNO Kathryn Hays EL	25.00	60.00
NNO Laurel Goodwin EL	12.00	30.00
NNO Lee Meriwether EL	15.00	40.00
NNO Sally Kellerman EL	20.00	50.00
NNO Shirley Bonne EL	15.00	40.00

2018 Star Trek The Original Series Captain's Collection Star Trek Discovery Preview

COMPLETE SET (4)	20.00	50.00
COMMON CARD (DP1-DP4)	8.00	20.00
STATED ODDS 1:288		

2018 Star Trek The Original Series Captain's Collection Star Trek Movies

COMPLETE SET (7)	50.00	100.00
COMMON CARD (M1-M7)	8.00	20.00
STATED ODDS 1:288		

2018 Star Trek The Original Series Captain's Collection Where No Man Has Gone Before Uncut

COMPLETE SET (70)	12.00	30.00
COMMON CARD (W1-W70)	.40	1.00
STATED ODDS 1:8		

2018 Star Trek The Original Series Captain's Collection Promos

COMPLETE SET (3)	8.00	20.00
COMMON CARD (P1-P3)	2.00	5.00
P2 Non-Sport Update Magazine	2.50	6.00
P3 Album Exclusive	6.00	15.00

2013 Star Trek The Original Series Heroes and Villains

COMPLETE SET (100)	5.00	12.00
UNOPENED BOX (24 PACKS)	65.00	80.00
UNOPENED PACK (5 CARDS)	3.00	4.00
COMMON CARD (1-100)	.15	.40
*RETRO: 2X TO 5X BASIC CARDS	.75	2.00

2013 Star Trek The Original Series Heroes and Villains Autographs

COMMON CARD	6.00	15.00
STATED ODDS ONE PER BOX		
A202 Maggie Thrett L	10.00	25.00
A236 Victor Brandt L	8.00	20.00
A242 Arlene Martel L	12.00	30.00
A255 Garth Pillsbury L	8.00	20.00
A257 Brioni Farrell	8.00	20.00
A258 Sean Morgan L	8.00	20.00
A260 Michael Barrier L	10.00	25.00
A262 David L. Ross L	10.00	25.00
A264 Diana Muldaur VL	30.00	75.00
A268 Nichelle Nichols EL	75.00	150.00
A269 William Shatner EL	125.00	250.00
LN Leonard Nimoy 6CI	175.00	300.00
NN Nichelle Nichols MEM 3CI	75.00	150.00

2013 Star Trek The Original Series Heroes and Villains Dual Autographs

COMMON CARD	10.00	25.00
STATED ODDS 1:BOX		
DA5 Shatner/Shatner EL	100.00	200.00
DA7 Shatner/Collins EL	350.00	500.00
DA8 Whitney/Walker L	15.00	40.00
DA14 Nichols/Koenig VL	75.00	150.00
DA20 Wolf/Campbell L	15.00	40.00
DA26 Napier/Brandt VL	30.00	60.00
DA27 Brandt/Downey VL	40.00	80.00
DA28 Napier/Downey L	12.00	30.00
DA29 Howard/Ansara L	25.00	60.00
DA30 Combs/Clark L	12.00	30.00
DA31 Forest/Parrish L	12.00	30.00
DA33 Muldaur/Frankham VL	50.00	100.00

2013 Star Trek The Original Series Heroes and Villains Kirk's Battles

COMPLETE SET (9)	6.00	15.00
COMMON CARD (GB1-GB9)	1.25	3.00
STATED ODDS 1:12		

2013 Star Trek The Original Series Heroes and Villains Mirror Mirror

COMPLETE SET (9)	12.00	30.00
COMMON CARD (MM1-MM9)	2.50	6.00
STATED ODDS 1:24		

2013 Star Trek The Original Series Heroes and Villains Montage Case-Toppers

COMPLETE SET (2)	20.00	40.00
COMMON CARD (CT1-CT2)	10.00	25.00
STATED ODDS 1:CASE		

2013 Star Trek The Original Series Heroes and Villains Shadowbox

COMPLETE SET (7)	25.00	50.00
COMMON CARD (S1-S7)	5.00	12.00
STATED ODDS 1:41		
S1 Captain Kirk	6.00	15.00
S2 Spock	6.00	15.00

2013 Star Trek The Original Series Heroes and Villains Tribute

COMPLETE SET W/RR (13)	25.00	60.00
COMPLETE SET (12)	5.00	12.00
COMMON CARD (T38-T49)	.75	2.00
STATED ODDS 1:6		
T50 ISSUED AS RITTENHOUSE REWARD		
T50 Harry Mudd RR SP	20.00	50.00

2013 Star Trek The Original Series Heroes and Villains Promos

P1 Khan/Kirk GEN	.75	2.00
P2 Spock/Kor NSU	2.00	5.00
P3 Keeper/Pike ALB	10.00	25.00

1999 Rittenhouse Star Trek The Original Series In Motion

COMPLETE SET (24)	15.00	40.00
UNOPENED BOX (20 PACKS)	50.00	75.00
UNOPENED PACK (3 CARDS)	2.00	3.00
COMMON CARD (1-24)	.75	2.00

1999 Rittenhouse Star Trek The Original Series In Motion DeForest Kelley Memoriam

COMPLETE SET (3)	100.00	200.00
COMMON CARD (M1-M3)	40.00	80.00
STATED ODDS 1:120		

1999 Rittenhouse Star Trek The Original Series In Motion Promos

COMPLETE SET (24)	30.00	60.00
COMMON CARD (1-24)	1.25	3.00

1999 Rittenhouse Star Trek The Original Series In Motion Sound in Motion

COMPLETE SET (6)	50.00	100.00
COMMON CARD (S1-S6)	8.00	20.00
STATED ODDS 1:BOX		
BS1 ISSUED AS ALBUM EXCLUSIVE		
CS1 ISSUED AS CASE TOPPER		

2014 Star Trek The Original Series Portfolio Prints

COMPLETE SET (80)	5.00	12.00
UNOPENED BOX (24 PACKS)	60.00	100.00
UNOPENED PACK (5 CARDS)	3.00	4.00
UNOPENED ARCHIVE BOX	1250.00	1500.00
COMMON CARD (1-80)	.20	.50
*GOLD SIG/150: 5X TO 12X BASIC CARDS	2.50	6.00
*JUAN ORTIZ: 10X TO 25X BASIC CARDS	5.00	12.00

2014 Star Trek The Original Series Portfolio Prints Animated Series

COMPLETE SET (22)	15.00	40.00
COMMON CARD (TAS1-TAS22)	1.50	4.00
STATED ODDS 1:12		

2014 Star Trek The Original Series Portfolio Prints Autographs

COMMON AUTO	6.00	15.00
STATED ODDS 1:24		
REGULAR = >500		
L = 300-499		
VL = 200-299		
EL = <200		
A263 David L. Ross L	8.00	20.00
A265 Ralph Senensky	8.00	20.00
A274 William O'Connell VL	15.00	40.00
A275 Yvonne Craig EL	50.00	120.00
NNO William Shatner EL	300.00	500.00
NNO Leonard Nimoy VL	300.00	500.00
NNO Walter Koenig VL	25.00	60.00
NNO Nichelle Nichols VL	40.00	100.00
NNO George Takei VL	30.00	75.00
NNO Grace Lee Whitney VL	30.00	75.00

2014 Star Trek The Original Series Portfolio Prints Bridge Crew Abstracts

COMPLETE SET (9)	12.00	30.00
COMMON CARD (U1-U9)	2.00	5.00
STATED PRINT RUN 250 SER.#'d SETS		

2014 Star Trek The Original Series Portfolio Prints Bridge Crew Portraits

COMPLETE SET (7)	10.00	25.00
COMMON CARD (RA1-RA7)	2.50	6.00
*ALT GOLD: 1.2X TO 3X		
STATED ODDS 1:24		

2014 Star Trek The Original Series Portfolio Prints Case-Toppers

COMPLETE SET (2)	10.00	25.00
COMMON CARD (CT1-CT2)	6.00	15.00
STATED PRINT RUN 400 SETS		

2014 Star Trek The Original Series Portfolio Prints Incentives

DA32 OFFERED AS 9-CASE INCENTIVE		
C6 Mick and Matt Glebe Painted Art Card		
DA32 Mirror Mirror AU2 Shatner L.Nimoy	750.00	1500.00

2014 Star Trek The Original Series Portfolio Prints Promos

COMPLETE SET (4)	4.00	10.00
COMMON CARD (P1-P4)	.75	2.00
P2 Spock (Non-Sport Update)	1.25	3.00
P3 Dr. McCoy (Album Exclusive)	2.00	5.00
P4 USS Enterprise NCC1701 (Philly Non-Sport Show)	2.00	5.00

2004 Quotable Star Trek Original Series

COMPLETE SET (110)	3.00	8.00
UNOPENED BOX (40 PACKS)	50.00	60.00
UNOPENED PACK (7 CARDS)	2.50	3.00
UNOPENED ARCHIVE BOX	800.00	1200.00
COMMON CARD (1-110)	.10	.25

2004 Quotable Star Trek Original Series Animated Series

COMPLETE SET (18)	8.00	20.00
COMMON CARD (Q1-Q18)	.50	1.25
STATED ODDS 1:5		

2004 Quotable Star Trek Original Series Autographs

COMMON CARD	12.00	25.00
STATED ODDS 1:20		
L (LIMITED): 300-500 COPIES		
A87 Sally Kellerman SP	25.00	60.00
A89 Morgan Woodward	12.00	30.00
A93 Phyllis Douglas	12.00	30.00
A94 Tanya Lemani	12.00	30.00
A99 Julie Newmar SP	20.00	50.00
A100 Lois Jewell	12.00	30.00

2004 Quotable Star Trek Original Series Comic Books

COMPLETE SET (9)	15.00	40.00
COMMON CARD (GK1-GK9)	2.00	5.00
STATED ODDS 1:10		

2004 Quotable Star Trek Original Series From the Archives Costumes

C1 STATED ODDS ONE PER U.S. CASE		
C2 STATED ODDS ONE PER COLLECTOR'S ALBUM		
C3 STATED ODDS ONE PER INTERNATIONAL CASE		
C1 Captain Kirk US CT	20.00	50.00
C2 Scotty ALB	12.00	30.00
C3 Yeoman Rand UK CT	60.00	120.00

2004 Quotable Star Trek Original Series Quotable Autographs

COMMON CARD	12.00	30.00
STATED ODDS 1:20		
DQA1 STATED ODDS ONE PER MULTI CASE PURCHASE		
L (LIMITED): 300-500 COPIES		
VL (VERY LIMITED): 200-300 COPIES		
QA1A William Shatner I'm a Soldier L	200.00	500.00
QA1B William Shatner Only a Fool L	200.00	500.00
QA1C William Shatner Space L	300.00	400.00
QA2A Leonard Nimoy Fascinating VL	250.00	600.00
QA2B Leonard Nimoy Live Long VL	250.00	600.00
QA3A George Takei May the Great Bird L	40.00	80.00
QA3B George Takei Phasers Locked L	40.00	80.00
QA4A Walter Koenig Cossackel L	40.00	80.00
QA4B Walter Koenig Invented By L	40.00	80.00
QA5 Nichelle Nichols L	30.00	75.00
QA6 Majel Barrett L	40.00	80.00
QA7A James Doohan I Can't Change L	125.00	300.00
QA7B James Doohan The Haggie L	125.00	300.00
DQA1 Sally Kelleman/Gary Lockwood MCI	40.00	100.00

2004 Quotable Star Trek Original Series Starfleet's Finest

COMPLETE SET (9)	300.00	600.00
COMMON CARD (F1-F9)	30.00	80.00
STATED ODDS 1:120		
STATED PRINT RUN 399 SER.#'d SETS		

2004 Quotable Star Trek Original Series Captain's Women

COMPLETE SET (6)	40.00	80.00
COMMON CARD (W1-W6)	6.00	15.00
STATED ODDS 1:40 INTERNATIONAL PACKS		

2004 Quotable Star Trek Original Series The Final Frontier

COMPLETE SET (9)	4.00	10.00
COMMON CARD (ST1-ST9)	.50	1.25
STATED ODDS 1:5		

2004 Quotable Star Trek Original Series TV Guide Covers

COMPLETE SET (7)	30.00	60.00
COMMON CARD (TV1-TV7)	4.00	10.00
STATED ODDS 1:40 U.S. PACKS		

2004 Quotable Star Trek Original Series Promos

COMPLETE SET (3)	4.00	10.00
COMMON CARD (P1-P3)	.75	2.00
P2 Spock NSU	1.25	3.00
P3 Dr. McCoy ALB	3.00	8.00

2010 Star Trek Remastered Original Series

COMPLETE SET (81)	4.00	10.00
UNOPENED BOX (24 PACKS)	75.00	80.00
UNOPENED PACK (5 CARDS)	3.50	4.00
COMMON CARD (1-81)	.12	.30
*GOLD: 2.5X TO 6X BASIC CARDS		

2010 Star Trek Remastered Original Series Autographs

COMMON CARD	8.00	20.00
STATED ODDS 1:BOX		
L (LIMITED): 300-500 COPIES		
VL (VERY LIMITED): 200-300 COPIES		
NICHOLS AUTO ISSUED AS 3-CASE INCENTIVE		
NIMOY AUTO ISSUED AS 6-CASE INCENTIVE		
A200 Leonard Nimoy 6CI	150.00	300.00
A202 Maggie Thrett L	20.00	40.00
A214 John Winston VL	30.00	75.00
A230 George Takei VL	60.00	120.00
A248 Nichelle Nichols 3CI	75.00	150.00
A252 Tom LeGarde VL	15.00	30.00

2010 Star Trek Remastered Original Series Creatures

COMPLETE SET (9)	6.00	15.00
COMMON CARD (AE1-AE9)	1.00	2.50
STATED ODDS 1:12		

2010 Star Trek Remastered Original Series Dual Autographs

COMMON CARD	12.00	30.00
STATED ODDS 1:BOX		
L (LIMITED): 300-500 COPIES		
VL (VERY LIMITED): 200-300 COPIES		
DA1 W.Shatner/B.Luna VL	250.00	400.00
DA2 C.Huxley/P.Ferdin VL	30.00	60.00
DA3 W.Campbell/M.Pataki VL	60.00	120.00
DA6 L.Nimoy/M.Barrett VL	250.00	400.00
DA10 S.Smith/H.Landers L	25.00	60.00
DA13 G.Takei/W.Koenig VL	75.00	125.00
DA23 W.Stevens/S.Moss VL	15.00	40.00

2010 Star Trek Remastered Original Series Elaan of Troyius Revised

COMPLETE SET (9)	5.00	12.00
COMMON CARD	.75	2.00
STATED ODDS 1:24		

2010 Star Trek Remastered Original Series Ships in Motion

COMPLETE SET w/o SP (9)	20.00	50.00
COMPLETE SET W/SP (11)	30.00	75.00
COMMON CARD (L1-L9)	3.00	8.00
STATED ODDS 1:24		
RL10 ISSUED AS CASE TOPPER		
RL11 ISSUED AS RITTENHOUSE REWARD		
RL10 Doomsday Machine CT	10.00	25.00
RL11 U.S.S. Enterprise SP RR	12.00	30.00

2010 Star Trek Remastered Original Series Tribute

COMPLETE SET (18)	10.00	25.00
COMPLETE SET W/RR (19)	20.00	50.00
COMMON CARD (T19-T36)	.75	2.00
STATED ODDS 1:6		
T37 ISSUED AS RITTENHOUSE REWARD		
T37 Trelane SP RR	12.00	30.00

2010 Star Trek Remastered Original Series Promos

COMPLETE SET (4)	6.00	15.00
COMMON CARD	2.00	5.00

The Next Generation

1992 SkyBox Star Trek The Next Generation

COMPLETE SET (120)	5.00	12.00
UNOPENED BOX (36 PACKS)	20.00	25.00
UNOPENED PACK (10 CARDS)	.75	1.00
COMMON CARD (1-120)	.15	.40
1B Where No One Has... - Japanese	.60	1.50
1C Where No One Has... - Spanish	.60	1.50
1D Where No One Has... - German	.60	1.50
1E Where No One Has... - French	.60	1.50
1F Where No One Has... - Russian	.60	1.50

2022 Rittenhouse Star Trek The Next Generation Archives and Inscriptions

COMPLETE SET W/VARIANTS (612)	60.00	150.00
COMPLETE SET (60)	8.00	20.00
UNOPENED BOX (24 PACKS)	50.00	75.00
UNOPENED PACK (5 CARDS)	2.50	4.00
ARCHIVE BOX	1500.00	2000.00
COMMON CARD (1-60)	.15	.40

2022 Rittenhouse Star Trek The Next Generation Archives and Inscriptions Aliens Autographs

COMMON AUTO	4.00	10.00
L = 300-500 COPIES		
VL = 200-300 COPIES		
EL = 100-200 COPIES		
S = 100 OR FEWER COPIES		
STATED OVERALL ODDS 1:12		
NNO Daniel Riordan L	6.00	15.00
NNO John de Mita L	5.00	12.00
NNO Leonard John Crofoot VL	12.00	30.00
NNO Richard Cox EL	25.00	60.00
NNO Rudolph Willrich L	5.00	12.00
NNO Spencer Garrett L	6.00	15.00

2022 Rittenhouse Star Trek The Next Generation Archives and Inscriptions Autograph Inscriptions

COMMON ALLPORT	12.00	30.00
COMMON ASTAR	15.00	40.00
COMMON BERMAN		
COMMON BERRYMAN	10.00	25.00
COMMON BONSALL	15.00	40.00
COMMON BRANDY	15.00	40.00
COMMON BROPHY	15.00	40.00
COMMON BROWN	12.00	30.00

COMMON BRYANT 12.00 30.00
COMMON CROSBY 40.00 100.00
COMMON CULEA 8.00 20.00
COMMON CURTIS 12.00 30.00
COMMON D'ABO 30.00 75.00
COMMON DAVIS 25.00 60.00
COMMON DE LANCIE 60.00 150.00
COMMON DEL ARCO 20.00 50.00
COMMON DENNEHY 25.00 60.00
COMMON DIOL 12.00 30.00
COMMON FORBES 20.00 50.00
COMMON FRAKES 75.00 200.00
COMMON GARRETT 10.00 25.00
COMMON GIBNEY 30.00 75.00
COMMON GUNTON 15.00 40.00
COMMON HETRICK 15.00 40.00
COMMON JACOBSON 10.00 25.00
COMMON JUDD 100.00 250.00
COMMON KEANE 12.00 30.00
COMMON KUSATSU 10.00 25.00
COMMON MCBROOM 15.00 40.00
COMMON MCCOY 10.00 25.00
COMMON MCDONALD 15.00 40.00
COMMON MCFADDEN 75.00 200.00
COMMON MENYUK 15.00 40.00
COMMON NOGULICH 15.00 40.00
COMMON O'REILLY 12.00 30.00
COMMON PLAKSON 20.00 50.00
COMMON REED 12.00 30.00
COMMON SCARABELLI 12.00 30.00
COMMON SEELEY 20.00 50.00
COMMON SELMON 12.00 30.00
COMMON SEYMOUR 15.00 40.00
COMMON SIRTIS 100.00 250.00
COMMON SPINER 75.00 200.00
COMMON STRUYCKEN 10.00 25.00
COMMON TODD 15.00 40.00
COMMON WILCOX 15.00 40.00
COMMON WILLIAMS 15.00 40.00
STATED OVERALL ODDS 1:12

2022 Rittenhouse Star Trek The Next Generation Archives and Inscriptions Case-Toppers

COMPLETE SET (2) 15.00 40.00
COMMON CARD (CT1-CT2) 10.00 25.00
STATED ODDS 1:CASE

2022 Rittenhouse Star Trek The Next Generation Archives and Inscriptions Infinite Possibilities

COMPLETE SET (9) 12.00 30.00
COMMON CARD (IP1-IP9) 2.00 5.00
STATED ODDS 1:24

2022 Rittenhouse Star Trek The Next Generation Archives and Inscriptions Laser-Cut Villains

COMPLETE SET (18) 20.00 50.00
COMMON CARD (L43-L60) 2.50 6.00
STATED ODDS 1:24

2022 Rittenhouse Star Trek The Next Generation Archives and Inscriptions Legends Autographs

NNO Marina Sirtis VL 150.00 400.00

2022 Rittenhouse Star Trek The Next Generation Archives and Inscriptions Lower Decks Characters

COMPLETE SET (22) 25.00 60.00
COMMON CARD (LDC01-LDC22) 2.00 5.00
STATED ODDS 1:24

2022 Rittenhouse Star Trek The Next Generation Archives and Inscriptions Lower Decks Episodes

COMPLETE SET (20) 10.00 25.00
COMMON CARD (LDE01-LDE20) 1.25 3.00
STATED ODDS 1:12

2022 Rittenhouse Star Trek The Next Generation Archives and Inscriptions Relics

COMPLETE SET (3)
COMMON MEM
RANDOMLY INSERTED INTO PACKS
NNO Dr. Tolian Soran RR
NNO Jean-Luc Picard 6CI 125.00 300.00
NNO Lt. Commander Data 125.00 300.00

2022 Rittenhouse Star Trek The Next Generation Archives and Inscriptions Stamps

COMPLETE SET (2) 125.00 300.00
COMMON CARD (S1-S2) 75.00 200.00
STATED ODDS 1:864

2022 Rittenhouse Star Trek The Next Generation Archives and Inscriptions TNG Classic Autographs

COMMON AUTO 5.00 12.00
L = 300-500 COPIES
VL = 200-300 COPIES
EL = 100-200 COPIES
S = 100 OR FEWER COPIES
STATED OVERALL ODDS 1:12
NNO Alan Scarfe L 6.00 15.00
NNO Ben Vereen L 10.00 25.00
NNO Carolyn Allport VL 10.00 25.00
NNO Cary-Hiroyuki Tarawa VL 12.00 30.00
NNO Dick Miller VL 15.00 40.00
NNO Eileen Seeley VL 12.00 30.00
NNO Estee Chandler VL 12.00 30.00
NNO Evelyn Guerrero VL 15.00 40.00
NNO Harvey Jason L 6.00 15.00
NNO Jimmy Ortega L 6.00 15.00
NNO Kim Braden L 6.00 15.00
NNO Marc Alaimo EL 50.00 125.00
NNO Marco Rodriguez L 6.00 15.00
NNO Melinda Culea VL 10.00 25.00
NNO Richard Cox L 6.00 15.00
NNO Robert O'Reilly L 6.00 15.00
NNO Sherman Howard L 6.00 15.00

2022 Rittenhouse Star Trek The Next Generation Archives and Inscriptions The Uncut Best of Both Worl

COMPLETE SET (53) 20.00 50.00
COMMON CARD (1-53) 1.00 2.50
STATED ODDS 1:12
1 Best of Both Worlds 1.00 2.50
2 Best of Both Worlds 1.00 2.50
3 Best of Both Worlds 1.00 2.50
4 Best of Both Worlds 1.00 2.50
5 Best of Both Worlds 1.00 2.50
6 Best of Both Worlds 1.00 2.50
7 Best of Both Worlds 1.00 2.50
8 Best of Both Worlds 1.00 2.50
9 Best of Both Worlds 1.00 2.50
10 Best of Both Worlds 1.00 2.50
11 Best of Both Worlds 1.00 2.50
12 Best of Both Worlds 1.00 2.50
13 Best of Both Worlds 1.00 2.50
14 Best of Both Worlds 1.00 2.50
15 Best of Both Worlds 1.00 2.50
16 Best of Both Worlds 1.00 2.50
17 Best of Both Worlds 1.00 2.50
18 Best of Both Worlds 1.00 2.50
19 Best of Both Worlds 1.00 2.50
20 Best of Both Worlds 1.00 2.50
21 Best of Both Worlds 1.00 2.50
22 Best of Both Worlds 1.00 2.50
23 Best of Both Worlds 1.00 2.50
24 Best of Both Worlds 1.00 2.50
25 Best of Both Worlds 1.00 2.50
26 Best of Both Worlds 1.00 2.50
27 Best of Both Worlds 1.00 2.50
28 Best of Both Worlds 1.00 2.50
29 Best of Both Worlds 1.00 2.50
30 Best of Both Worlds 1.00 2.50
31 Best of Both Worlds 1.00 2.50
32 Best of Both Worlds 1.00 2.50
33 Best of Both Worlds 1.00 2.50
34 Best of Both Worlds 1.00 2.50
35 Best of Both Worlds 1.00 2.50
36 Best of Both Worlds 1.00 2.50
37 Best of Both Worlds 1.00 2.50
38 Best of Both Worlds 1.00 2.50
39 Best of Both Worlds 1.00 2.50
40 Best of Both Worlds 1.00 2.50
41 Best of Both Worlds 1.00 2.50
42 Best of Both Worlds 1.00 2.50
43 Best of Both Worlds 1.00 2.50
44 Best of Both Worlds 1.00 2.50
45 Best of Both Worlds 1.00 2.50
46 Best of Both Worlds 1.00 2.50
47 Best of Both Worlds 1.00 2.50
48 Best of Both Worlds 1.00 2.50
49 Best of Both Worlds 1.00 2.50
50 Best of Both Worlds 1.00 2.50
51 Best of Both Worlds 1.00 2.50
52 Best of Both Worlds 1.00 2.50
53 Best of Both Worlds 1.00 2.50

2022 Rittenhouse Star Trek The Next Generation Archives and Inscriptions The Uncut Encounter at Farp

COMPLETE SET (46) 20.00 50.00
COMMON CARD (1-46) 1.00 2.50
STATED ODDS 1:12

2022 Rittenhouse Star Trek The Next Generation Archives and Inscriptions Promos

COMPLETE SET (2)
COMMON CARD (P1-P2)
P1 Captain Picard GEN 1.50 4.00
P2 Enterprise D ALB 2.00 5.00

1993 SkyBox Star Trek The Next Generation Behind-the-Scenes

COMPLETE BOXED SET (39) 5.00 12.00
COMMON CARD (1-39) .25 .60

2011 Complete Star Trek The Next Generation

COMPLETE SET (180) 12.00 30.00
COMPLETE SERIES 1 SET (90) 6.00 15.00
COMPLETE SERIES 2 SET (90) 6.00 15.00
UNOPENED SERIES 1 BOX (24 PACKS) 100.00 150.00
UNOPENED SERIES 1 PACK (5 CARDS) 4.00 6.00
UNOPENED SERIES 1 ARCHIVE BOX 750.00 900.00
UNOPENED SERIES 2 BOX (24 PACKS) 100.00 150.00
UNOPENED SERIES 2 PACK (5 CARDS) 4.00 6.00
UNOPENED SERIES 2 ARCHIVE BOX 900.00 1200.00
COMMON SERIES 1 CARD (1-90) .15 .40
COMMON SERIES 2 CARD (91-180) .15 .40
*FOIL: 2.5X TO 6X BASIC CARDS 1.00 2.50
RODDENBERRY BUSINESS CARD
ISSUED AS 3-CASE INCENTIVE
GR G.Rodenberry BC/350 3CI 75.00 125.00

2011 Complete Star Trek The Next Generation Aliens

COMPLETE SET (13) 8.00 20.00
COMMON CARD (A1-A13) 1.25 3.00
STATED ODDS 1:8

2011 Complete Star Trek The Next Generation Autographs

COMMON AUTO 5.00 12.00
UNLISTED L (LIMITED) 6.00 15.00
STATED ODDS 1:6
YEAGER ISSUED AS SER. 1 CASE TOPPER
STEWART ISSUED AS SER. 1 6-CASE INCENTIVE
BOEN ISSUED AS SER. 2 CASE TOPPER
SPINER/SOONG ISSUED AS SER. 2 3-CASE INCENTIVE
NIMOY ISSUED AS SER. 2 6-CASE INCENTIVE
L (LIMITED): 300-500 COPIES
VL (VERY LIMITED): 200-300 COPIES
EL (EXTREMELY LIMITED): 200 OR FEWER COPIES
NNO Armin Shimerman L 8.00 20.00
NNO Ashley Judd VL 75.00 150.00
NNO Biff Yeager CT 15.00 40.00
NNO Brent Spiner VL 75.00 125.00
NNO Brent Spiner 3CI 60.00 120.00
NNO Colm Meaney VL 25.00 60.00
NNO Daniel Benzali VL 30.00 60.00
NNO David Ogden Stiers EL 100.00 200.00
NNO Denise Crosby EL 20.00 50.00
NNO Dwight Schultz VL 25.00 50.00
NNO Earl Boen CT 10.00 25.00
NNO Elizabeth Dennehy VL 20.00 40.00
NNO Gates McFadden QUOT VL 40.00 80.00
NNO Gene Roddenberry/30 CUT 1800.00 3000.00
NNO James Doohan CUT/50 500.00 1000.00
NNO Joe Piscopo L 15.00 30.00
NNO John Delancie EL 60.00 120.00
NNO John Tesh L 12.00 25.00
NNO Jonathan Del Arco L 8.00 20.00
NNO Jonathan Frakes EL 60.00 120.00
NNO Kelsey Grammer VL 50.00 100.00
NNO Leonard Nimoy 6CI 200.00 300.00
NNO LeVar Burton QUOT VL 60.00 120.00
NNO Marina Sirtis EL 50.00 100.00
NNO Matt Frewer EL 35.00 70.00
NNO Matt McCoy L 10.00 25.00
NNO Michelle Phillips L 12.00 30.00
NNO Nicole Orth-Pallavicini L 8.00 20.00
NNO Patrick Stewart 6CI 250.00 350.00
NNO Robert O'Reilly VL 25.00 50.00
NNO Susan Diol VL 25.00 50.00
NNO Tony Todd EL 40.00 80.00

2011 Complete Star Trek The Next Generation Best of the Holodeck

COMPLETE SET (9) 6.00 15.00
COMPLETE SET W/RR (10) 25.00 60.00
COMMON CARD (H1-H9) 1.25 3.00
STATED ODDS 1:8
H10 ISSUED AS RITTENHOUSE REWARD
H10 Relics SP RR 20.00 50.00

2011 Complete Star Trek The Next Generation Communicator Pins

COMPLETE SET (10) 225.00 450.00
COMMON CARD (CP1-CP10) 30.00 60.00
STATED ODDS 1:200
STATED PRINT RUN 300 SER.#'d SETS

2011 Complete Star Trek The Next Generation Tribute

COMPLETE SET (36) 20.00 40.00
COMMON CARD (T1-T36) 1.00 2.50
STATED ODDS 1:6

2011 Complete Star Trek The Next Generation USS Enterprise

COMPLETE SET (18) 10.00 25.00
COMMON CARD (E1-E18) 1.50 4.00
STATED ODDS 1:12

2011 Complete Star Trek The Next Generation Promos

COMPLETE SET (4) 8.00 20.00
COMMON CARD (P1-P4) .75 2.00
P2 Locutus/Worf/Yar NSU 2.00 5.00
P3 Data/Picard/Riker ALB 10.00 20.00
P4 Picard/Riker PHILLY 2.00 5.00

1994-99 SkyBox Star Trek The Next Generation Episode Collection

COMPLETE SET (740) 50.00 100.00
SEASON ONE SET (108) 8.00 20.00
SEASON TWO SET (96) 6.00 15.00
SEASON THREE SET (108) 6.00 15.00
SEASON FOUR SET (108) 6.00 15.00
SEASON FIVE SET (108) 6.00 15.00
SEASON SIX SET (108) 5.00 12.00
SEASON SEVEN SET (103) 6.00 15.00
UNOPENED S.ONE BOX (36 PACKS) 65.00 80.00
UNOPENED S.ONE PACK (8 CARDS) 2.00 2.50
UNOPENED S.TWO BOX (36 PACKS) 15.00 25.00
UNOPENED S.TWO PACK (8 CARDS) .75 1.00
UNOPENED S.THREE BOX (36 PACKS) 15.00 25.00
UNOPENED S.THREE PACK (8 CARDS) .75 1.00
UNOPENED S.FOUR BOX (36 PACKS) 15.00 25.00
UNOPENED S.FOUR PACK (8 CARDS) .75 1.00
UNOPENED S.FIVE BOX (36 PACKS) 15.00 25.00
UNOPENED S.FIVE PACK (8 CARDS) .75 1.00
UNOPENED S.SIX HOBBY BOX (24 PACKS) 20.00 30.00
UNOPENED S.SIX HOBBY PACK (11 CARDS) 1.00 1.25
UNOPENED S.SIX RETAIL BOX (18 PACKS) 20.00 30.00
UNOPENED S.SIX RETAIL PACK (11 CARDS) 1.00 1.25
UNOPENED S.SEVEN BOX (36 PACKS) 65.00 80.00
UNOPENED S.SEVEN PACK (9 CARDS) 2.00 2.50
S.ONE COMMON (1-108) .15 .40
S.TWO COMMON (109-204) .12 .30
S.THREE COMMON (205-312) .12 .30
S.FOUR COMMON (313-420) .12 .30
S.FIVE COMMON (421-528) .12 .30
S.SIX COMMON (529-636) .10 .25
S.SEVEN COMMON (637-739) .12 .30
C2 STATED PRINT RUN 1200 SER.#'d CARDS
C2 Jean-Luc Picard/1200 50.00 100.00

1994-99 SkyBox Star Trek The Next Generation Episode Collection Autographs

COMMON CARD (A1-A19) 8.00 20.00
STATED ODDS 1:36
ONLY INSERTED IN SEASON SEVEN PACKS
A1 Patrick Stewart 80.00 150.00
A2 Jonathan Frakes 30.00 80.00
A3 Brent Spiner 60.00 120.00
A4 Gates McFadden 25.00 60.00
A5 Marina Sirtis 50.00 100.00
A6 Levar Burton 60.00 120.00
A7 Patti Yasutake 10.00 25.00
A8 John Delancie 15.00 40.00
A9 Dwight Schultz 25.00 60.00
A10 Jonathan Del Arco 20.00 50.00
A12 Eric Menyuk 10.00 25.00

1994-99 SkyBox Star Trek The Next Generation Episode Collection Holograms

COMPLETE SET (14) 250.00 500.00
SEASON ONE SET (2) 50.00 100.00
SEASON TWO SET (2) 50.00 100.00
SEASON THREE SET (2) 30.00 80.00
SEASON FOUR SET (2) 30.00 80.00
SEASON FIVE SET (2) 30.00 80.00
SEASON SIX SET (2) 50.00 100.00
SEASON SEVEN SET (2) 15.00 40.00
S.ONE COMMON (HG1-HG2; 1:180) 20.00 50.00
S.TWO COMMON (HG3-HG4; 1:180) 20.00 50.00
S.THREE COMMON (HG5-HG6; 1:180H, 1:96J) 15.00 40.00
S.FOUR COMMON (HG7-HG8; 1:180) 15.00 40.00
S.FIVE COMMON (H9-H10; 1:180) 15.00 40.00
S.SIX COMMON (H11-H12; 1:90) 20.00 50.00
S.SEVEN COMMON (H13-H14; 1:90) 8.00 20.00

1994-99 SkyBox Star Trek The Next Generation Episode Collection Klingon-Embossed Characters

COMPLETE SET (42) 125.00 250.00
SEASON ONE SET (6) 15.00 40.00
SEASON TWO SET (6) 15.00 40.00
SEASON THREE SET (6) 15.00 40.00
SEASON FOUR SET (6) 15.00 40.00
SEASON FIVE SET (6) 12.00 30.00
SEASON SIX SET (6) 15.00 40.00
SEASON SEVEN SET (6) 15.00 40.00
S.ONE COMMON (SP1-SP6; 1:12) 3.00 8.00
S.TWO COMMON (S7-S12; 1:24) 3.00 8.00
S.THREE COMMON (S13-S18; 1:12H, 1:6J) 3.00 8.00
S.FOUR COMMON (S19-S24; 1:12) 3.00 8.00
S.FIVE COMMON (S25-S30; 1:12) 2.50 6.00
S.SIX COMMON (S31-S36; 1:12) 3.00 8.00
S.SEVEN COMMON (S37-S42; 1:12) 3.00 8.00

1994-99 SkyBox Star Trek The Next Generation Episode Collection Promos

COMMON CARD .75 2.00
NNO 3-Card Strip (13, 14, 15) 1.50 4.00
(Star Trek Communicator Fan Club Exclusive)
NNO 2-Card Strip (118, 132) 2.00 5.00
(Season Two Exclusive)
NNO 2-Card Strip (122, 127) 2.00 5.00
(Season Two Exclusive)
NNO 2-Card Strip (130, 126) 2.00 5.00
(Season Two Exclusive)
NNO 2-Card Strip (128, 124) 2.00 5.00
(Season Two Exclusive)
NNO 2-Card Strip (119, 133) 2.00 5.00
(Season Two Exclusive)
NNO 2-Card Strip (120, 134) 2.00 5.00
(Season Two Exclusive)
NNO 2-Card Strip (121, 135) 2.00 5.00
(Season Two Exclusive)
NNO 2-Card Strip (131, 123) 2.00 5.00
(Season Two Exclusive)
NNO Star Trek The Next Generation Season Seven 1.25 3.00
(General Distribution)
NNO All Good Things... 3.00 8.00
(Season One Exclusive)
NNO All Good Things... (crew playing poker)/10,000 15.00 40.00
(QVC Exclusive)
3P1 9-Card Promo Sheet 2.00 5.00
(Season Three Exclusive)
4P1 9-Card Promo Sheet 3.00 8.00
(Season Four Exclusive)
PAN2 Season Two 96-Card Uncut Sheet
PAN3 Season Three 108-Card Uncut Sheet
PAN4 Season Four 108-Card Uncut Sheet
PAN5 Season Five 108-Card Uncut Sheet
PAN6 Season Six 108-Card Uncut Sheet
PAN7 Season Seven 103-Card Uncut Sheet

1994-99 SkyBox Star Trek The Next Generation Episode Collection Ships

COMPLETE SET (3) 8.00 20.00
COMMON CARD (1-3) 3.00 8.00
K-MART AND SAM'S CLUB EXCLUSIVE

1994-99 SkyBox Star Trek The Next Generation Episode Collection Skymotion

COMMON CARD (SM1-SM2) 2.00 5.00
SM1 Amanda Rogers CT 4.00 10.00

2013 Star Trek The Next Generation Heroes and Villains

COMPLETE SET (100) 5.00 12.00
UNOPENED BOX (24 PACKS) 60.00 100.00
UNOPENED PACK (5 CARDS) 2.50 4.00
COMMON CARD (1-100) .10 .25
*RETRO: 1.25X TO 3X BASIC CARDS

2013 Star Trek The Next Generation Heroes and Villains Autographs

COMMON CARD 4.00 10.00
STATED ODDS 4:BOX
NNO Armin Shimerman EL 15.00 40.00
NNO Bebe Neuwirth VL 15.00 40.00
NNO Brenda Strong 6.00 15.00
NNO Brian Markinson VL 8.00 20.00
NNO Brian Thompson 5.00 12.00
NNO Carolyn Seymour L 6.00 15.00
NNO Christopher McDonald 6.00 15.00
NNO Cristine Rose VL 10.00 25.00
NNO Daniel Stewart L 6.00 15.00
NNO Eric Pierpoint VL 12.00 30.00
NNO Gates McFadden EL 50.00 100.00
NNO Harry Groener VL 8.00 20.00
NNO Howie Seago L 5.00 12.00
NNO James Horan EL 20.00 50.00
NNO James Horan EL 20.00 50.00
NNO Jerry Hardin EL 30.00 60.00
NNO Kathryn Leigh Scott L 5.00 12.00
NNO Lee Arenberg L 5.00 12.00
NNO LeVar Burton EL 40.00 80.00
NNO Linda Thorson VL 12.00 30.00
NNO Margot Rose VL 10.00 25.00
NNO Marie Marshall L 5.00 12.00
NNO Mark Rolston L 6.00 15.00
NNO Maryann Plunkett L 5.00 12.00
NNO Michael Dorn EL 40.00 80.00
NNO Michelle Forbes EL 30.00 60.00
NNO Michelle Forbes EL 30.00 60.00
NNO Olivia d'Abo EL 40.00 80.00
NNO Patrick Massett L 5.00 12.00
NNO Patrick Stewart EL 75.00 150.00
NNO Paul Sorvino L 8.00 20.00
NNO Penny Johnson Jerald VL 12.00 30.00
NNO Richard Herd L 6.00 15.00
NNO Robert Duncan McNeill EL 15.00 40.00
NNO Robin Curtis EL 12.00 30.00
NNO Robin Gammell EL 12.00 30.00
NNO Ronny Cox 6.00 15.00
NNO Scott MacDonald EL 15.00 40.00
NNO Shay Astar 5.00 12.00
NNO Terry O'Quinn EL 20.00 50.00
NNO Tim DeZarn VL 10.00 25.00
NNO Tim Russ EL 35.00 70.00
NNO Tricia O'Neil EL 30.00 60.00
NNO Tricia O'Neil EL 30.00 60.00
NNO Denise Crosby QUOT 3CI 40.00 80.00
NNO Brent Spiner MEM/275 75.00 150.00

2013 Star Trek The Next Generation Heroes and Villains Montage Case-Toppers

COMPLETE SET (2) 15.00 30.00
COMMON CARD (CT1-CT2) 8.00 20.00
STATED ODDS 1:CASE

2013 Star Trek The Next Generation Heroes and Villains Posters

COMPLETE SET (5) 10.00 25.00
COMMON CARD (PC1-PC5) 3.00 8.00
STATED ODDS 1:48

2013 Star Trek The Next Generation Heroes and Villains Relics

COMPLETE SET (8) 120.00 250.00
COMMON CARD (C10-C17) 15.00 40.00
STATED ODDS 1:96

2013 Star Trek The Next Generation Heroes and Villains Remastered

COMPLETE SET (18) 10.00 25.00
COMMON CARD (R1-R18) 1.00 2.50
STATED ODDS 1:12

2013 Star Trek The Next Generation Heroes and Villains Romance

COMPLETE SET (18) 8.00 20.00
COMMON CARD (L1-L18) .75 2.00
STATED ODDS 1:12

2013 Star Trek The Next Generation Heroes and Villains Undercover Heroes

COMPLETE SET (9) 8.00 20.00
COMPLETE SET W/RR (10) 25.00 60.00
COMMON CARD (H1-H9) 1.50 4.00
STATED ODDS 1:24
H10 ISSUED AS RITTENHOUSE REWARD
H10 Commander Riker RR SP 20.00 40.00

2013 Star Trek The Next Generation Heroes and Villains Promos

P3 Picard ALB 5.00 12.00
P4 Data SDCC 2.00 5.00

1994 SkyBox Making of Star Trek The Next Generation

COMPLETE COLLECTOR'S SET (100) 15.00 40.00
COMPLETE GOLD SET (100) 20.00 50.00
COMPLETE PLATINUM SET (100) 30.00 75.00
COMMON CARD (1-100) .30 .75
NNO Lucite Encased Enterprise 1701-D
(Platinum Bonus Exclusive)
NNO Brass Collector's Pin
(Gold Bonus Exclusive)
PAN 100-Card Uncut Sheet

1994 SkyBox Making of Star Trek The Next Generation SkyVision

COMPLETE SET (5) 4.00 10.00
COMMON CARD (SV1-SV5) 1.25 3.00
STATED ODDS 1:COLLECTOR'S EDITION SET

2015 Star Trek The Next Generation Portfolio Prints

COMPLETE SET (89)	8.00	20.00
COMMON CARD (1-89)	.20	.50
*GOLD SIG/125: 5X TO 12X BASIC CARDS		
*GOLD SIG ORTIZ: 10X TO 25X BASIC CARDS		

2015 Star Trek The Next Generation Portfolio Prints Autographs

COMMON AUTO	6.00	15.00
STATED ODDS 1:8		
L (LIMITED) 300-500 COPIES		
VL (VERY LIMITED) 200-300		
EL (EXTREMELY LIMITED) 200 OR FEWER		
NNO Brent Spiner VL	25.00	60.00
NNO Daniel Davis VL	12.00	30.00
NNO Jonathan Frakes VL	25.00	60.00
NNO Marina Sirtis VL	25.00	60.00
NNO Whoopi Goldberg EL	50.00	100.00
NNO Sirtis/Frakes CI Dual	125.00	250.00

2015 Star Trek The Next Generation Portfolio Prints Case-Toppers

COMPLETE SET (2)	8.00	20.00
COMMON CARD	5.00	12.00
STATED ODDS 1:CASE		

2015 Star Trek The Next Generation Portfolio Prints Comic Archive Cuts

COMPLETE SET (40)	100.00	200.00
COMMON CARD	4.00	10.00
STATED ODDS 1:48		
SERIAL NUMBERS VARY		

2015 Star Trek The Next Generation Portfolio Prints Comic Book Inserts

COMPLETE SET (40)	20.00	50.00
COMMON CARD	1.00	2.50
STATED ODDS 1:24		
SKIP-NUMBERED SET		

2015 Star Trek The Next Generation Portfolio Prints Rendered Art Metal

COMPLETE SET (6)	100.00	200.00
COMMON CARD (SKIP #'d)	12.00	30.00
STATED ODDS 1:576		
STATED PRINT RUN 100 SER.#'d SETS		
R1 Commander William T. Riker	15.00	40.00
R7 Borg	15.00	40.00
R11 USS Enterprise NCC1701-D (Archive Box excl)	80.00	150.00

2015 Star Trek The Next Generation Portfolio Prints Ships of the Line

COMPLETE SET (9)	15.00	40.00
COMMON CARD (SL1-SL9)	3.00	8.00
STATED ODDS 1:48		

2015 Star Trek The Next Generation Portfolio Prints Silhouette Gallery Metal

COMPLETE SET (5)	50.00	100.00
COMMON CARD (SKIP #'d)	10.00	25.00
STATED ODDS 1:576		
STATED PRINT RUN 100 SER.#'d SETS		
SG1 Captain Jean-Luc Picard	12.00	30.00
SG3 Counselor Deanna Troi	15.00	40.00
SG5 Lt. Cmdrr Geordi La Forge	12.00	30.00
SG7 Lt. Worf	15.00	40.00

2015 Star Trek The Next Generation Portfolio Prints Universe Gallery

COMPLETE SET (9)	10.00	25.00
STATED ODDS 1:24		
SKIP-NUMBERED SET		

2015 Star Trek The Next Generation Portfolio Prints Promos

COMPLETE SET (3)	6.00	15.00
COMMON CARD (P1-P3)	1.50	4.00
P2 NSU	2.50	6.00
P3 Album excl Borg Cube	5.00	12.00

2016 Star Trek The Next Generation Portfolio Prints Series 2

COMPLETE SET (88)	8.00	20.00
UNOPENED BOX (24 PACKS)	45.00	60.00
UNOPENED PACK (5 CARDS)	2.50	3.00
COMMON CARD (SKIP #'d)	.20	.50
*GOLD SIG/125: 4X TO 10X BASIC CARDS	2.00	5.00
*GOLD SIG ORTIZ: 8X TO 20X BASIC CARDS	4.00	10.00

2016 Star Trek The Next Generation Portfolio Prints Series 2 Bordered Autographs

COMMON CARD	4.00	10.00
ALL AUTOS STATED ODDS 1:8		
2 Dennis Cockrum L	6.00	15.00
3 Diedrich Bader L	10.00	25.00
4 Doug Wert L	5.00	12.00
5 Erich Anderson VL	6.00	15.00
7 Glenn Morshower VL	10.00	25.00
8 James Sloyan VL	10.00	25.00
9 Jennifer Nash VL	8.00	20.00
11 Lanai Chapman L	5.00	12.00
12 Leonard John Crofoot VL	6.00	15.00
14 Madchen Amick EL	20.00	50.00
16 Marnie Mosiman L	5.00	12.00
18 Michael Champion L	6.00	15.00
19 Mick Fleetwood VL	15.00	40.00
20 Mitchell Ryan L	8.00	20.00
23 Patricia Tallman L	8.00	20.00
24 Peter Parros VL	12.00	30.00
25 Robert Costanzo	6.00	15.00
27 Rosalind Allen	6.00	15.00
28 Samantha Eggar	10.00	25.00
29 Saxon Trainor	15.00	40.00
31 Spencer Garrett L	5.00	12.00
32 Stephanie Beacham L	5.00	12.00
33 Tracee Cocco	8.00	20.00
35 Wayne Grace L	6.00	15.00

2016 Star Trek The Next Generation Portfolio Prints Series 2 Case-Incentives

NNO Spiner/Crosby DUAL AU/6CI	100.00	200.00
NNO Q Metal Art Card/18CI	50.00	100.00

2016 Star Trek The Next Generation Portfolio Prints Series 2 Case-Toppers

COMPLETE SET (2)	10.00	25.00
COMMON CARD (CT2, CT4)	6.00	15.00
CT2 I Am Locutus of Borg	6.00	15.00
CT4 Q	6.00	15.00

2016 Star Trek The Next Generation Portfolio Prints Series 2 Comic Archive Cuts

COMMON CARD (SKIP #'d)	4.00	10.00
STATED ODDS 1:48		

2016 Star Trek The Next Generation Portfolio Prints Series 2 Comic Book Cards

COMPLETE SET (39)	100.00	200.00
COMMON CARD (SKIP #'d)	3.00	8.00
STATED ODDS 1:24		

2016 Star Trek The Next Generation Portfolio Prints Series 2 Rendered Art Metal

COMPLETE SET W/O R11 (5)	100.00	200.00
COMPLETE SET W/R11 (6)	200.00	400.00
COMMON CARD (SKIP #'d)	20.00	50.00
STATED ODDS 1:576		
R11 ISSUED AS ARCHIVE BOX EXCLUSIVE		
R11 Q (Archive Box Exclusive)	120.00	200.00

2016 Star Trek The Next Generation Portfolio Prints Series 2 Ships of the Line

COMPLETE SET (9)	8.00	20.00
COMMON CARD (SL10-SL18)	1.25	3.00
STATED ODDS 1:48		

2016 Star Trek The Next Generation Portfolio Prints Series 2 Silhouette Gallery Metal

COMPLETE SET (5)	100.00	175.00
COMMON CARD (SKIP #'d)	15.00	40.00
STATED ODDS 1:576		

2016 Star Trek The Next Generation Portfolio Prints Series 2 Silver Autographs

ALL AUTOS STATED ODDS 1:8		
1 Denise Crosby EL	15.00	40.00
2 Gates McFadden EL	20.00	50.00
3 Michael Dorn EL	20.00	50.00
4 Patrick Stewart EL	80.00	150.00

2016 Star Trek The Next Generation Portfolio Prints Series 2 Promos

COMPLETE SET (3)		
COMMON CARD (P1-P3)		
P1 General Distribution	.75	2.00
P2 Non-Sport Update Magazine	1.50	4.00
P3 Convention Exclusive	1.25	3.00

2016 Star Trek The Next Generation Portfolio Prints Series 2 Universe Gallery

COMPLETE SET (9)	8.00	20.00
COMMON CARD (SKIP #'d)	1.25	3.00
STATED ODDS 1:24		

2000 Star Trek The Next Generation Profiles

COMPLETE SET (82)	4.00	10.00
UNOPENED BOX (36 PACKS)	40.00	50.00
UNOPENED PACK (10 CARDS)	1.50	1.75
COMMON CARD (1-82)	.10	.25
STAR THREADS STATED ODDS 1:360		
CAPTAIN'S SERIES STATED ODDS 1:720		
NNO Picard Captain's Series/1200		
NNO Jean-Luc Picard/2500 MEM	25.00	60.00

2000 Star Trek The Next Generation Profiles Alter Ego

COMPLETE SET (9)	5.00	12.00
COMMON CARD (AE1-AE9)	1.00	2.50
STATED ODDS 1:6		

2000 Star Trek The Next Generation Profiles Autographs

COMMON CARD (A1-A19)	8.00	20.00
STATED ODDS 1:40		
A1 Patrick Stewart	100.00	200.00
A2 Jonathan Frakes	30.00	80.00
A3 Denise Crosby	10.00	25.00
A4 Wil Wheaton	10.00	25.00
A5 John de Lancie	30.00	75.00
A7 James Doohan	80.00	150.00
A8 Walter Koenig	150.00	300.00
A9 William Shatner	125.00	250.00
A10 Gates McFadden	80.00	150.00
A11 Majel Barrett	60.00	120.00
A13 Marina Sirtis	60.00	120.00
A14 Brent Spiner	250.00	500.00
A16 Dwight Schultz	10.00	25.00
A19 Corbin Bernsen	100.00	200.00

2000 Star Trek The Next Generation Profiles Crossover Characters

COMPLETE SET (9)	6.00	15.00
COMMON CARD (C1-C9)	1.25	3.00
STATED ODDS 1:8		

2000 Star Trek The Next Generation Profiles First Contacts

COMPLETE SET (9)	2.00	5.00
COMMON CARD (F1-F9)	.40	1.00
STATED ODDS 1:4		

2000 Star Trek The Next Generation Profiles Q's Quips

COMPLETE SET (9)	30.00	80.00
COMMON CARD (Q1-Q9)	4.00	10.00
STATED ODDS 1:36		

2005 Quotable Star Trek The Next Generation

COMPLETE SET (110)	6.00	15.00
UNOPENED BOX (40 PACKS)	50.00	60.00
UNOPENED PACK (5 CARDS)	1.50	2.00
COMMON CARD (1-110)	.08	.20

2005 Quotable Star Trek The Next Generation Autographs

COMMON CARD	8.00	20.00
STATED ODDS ONE PER BOX		
MD ISSUED AS ALBUM EXCLUSIVE		
PSBS ISSUED AS 6-CASE INCENTIVE		
L (LIMITED): 300-500 CARDS		
VL (VERY LIMITED): 200-300 CARDS		
NNO Brent Spiner VL	50.00	100.00
NNO Denise Crosby L	15.00	30.00
NNO Diana Muldaur L	20.00	40.00
NNO Famke Janssen VL	60.00	120.00
NNO John de Lancie L	20.00	40.00
NNO Majel Barrett VL	60.00	120.00
NNO Marta DuBoise ALB	15.00	40.00
NNO Michelle Forbes	15.00	30.00
NNO Patrick Stewart VL	75.00	150.00
NNO Wil Wheaton L	25.00	50.00
QA1 Patrick Stewart VL	100.00	200.00
QA2 Brent Spiner VL	50.00	100.00
QA3 Jonathan Frakes VL	50.00	100.00
QA4 Marina Sirtis VL	40.00	80.00
QA5 Michael Dorn VL	40.00	80.00
NNO J.Frakes/M.Sirtis VL	60.00	120.00
NNO M.Barrett/C.Struycken VL	60.00	120.00
NNO M.Dorn/S.Plakson VL	60.00	120.00
NNO M.Sirtis/M.Barrett VL	125.00	200.00
NNO P.Stewart/B.Spiner 6CI	150.00	300.00

2005 Quotable Star Trek The Next Generation Comic Book Covers

COMPLETE SET (6)	10.00	25.00
COMMON CARD (CB1-CB6)	2.00	5.00
STATED ODDS 1:14		

2005 Quotable Star Trek The Next Generation From the Archives Costumes

COMPLETE SET (9)	120.00	250.00
COMMON CARD (C1-C9)	8.00	20.00
STATED ODDS 1:BOX		
C1 Captain Jean-Luc Picard	30.00	60.00
C2 Lt. Commander Data	20.00	40.00
C3 Commander William Riker	20.00	40.00
C4 Counselor Deanna Troi	20.00	40.00
C6 Dr. Beverly Crusher	15.00	30.00

2005 Quotable Star Trek The Next Generation Starfleet's Finest

COMPLETE SET (9)	100.00	200.00
COMMON CARD (F1-F9)	12.00	30.00
STATED ODDS 1:120		

2005 Quotable Star Trek The Next Generation Captain's Women

COMPLETE SET (9)	25.00	60.00
COMMON CARD (W1-W9)	3.00	8.00
STATED ODDS 1:40 INT'L PACKS		

2005 Quotable Star Trek The Next Generation The Final Frontier

COMPLETE SET (9)	6.00	15.00
COMMON CARD (ST1-ST9)	1.00	2.50
STATED ODDS 1:5		

2005 Quotable Star Trek The Next Generation TV Guide Covers

COMPLETE SET (9)	30.00	75.00
COMMON CARD (TV1-TV9)	4.00	10.00
STATED ODDS 1:40 U.S. PACKS		
SIRTIS AUTO ONE PER TWO-CASE PURCHASE		
MS Marina Sirtis AU 2CI	30.00	80.00

2005 Quotable Star Trek The Next Generation Promos

COMPLETE SET (4)	5.00	12.00
COMMON CARD	.75	2.00
BP Picard ALB	4.00	10.00
P3 Borg UK	1.50	4.00

1997 SkyBox Star Trek The Next Generation Season Six

COMPLETE SET (108)	8.00	20.00
COMMON CARD (529-636)	.12	.30

1997 SkyBox Star Trek The Next Generation Season Six Embossed Characters

COMPLETE SET (3)	10.00	20.00
COMMON CARD (S34-S36)	4.00	10.00
STATED ODDS 1:24		

1997 SkyBox Star Trek The Next Generation Season Six Holograms

COMPLETE SET (2)	20.00	40.00
COMMON CARD (H11-H12)	12.00	30.00
STATED ODDS 1:90		

1997 SkyBox Star Trek The Next Generation Season Six Klingon

COMPLETE SET (3)	10.00	20.00
COMMON CARD (S31-S33)	4.00	10.00
STATED ODDS 1:24		

1997 SkyBox Star Trek The Next Generation Season Six Skymotion

COMPLETE SET (2)	8.00	20.00
SM1 Amanda Rogers CT	8.00	20.00
SM2 Timescape BT	4.00	10.00

1990 Fleer Star Trek The Next Generation Stickers West Germany

COMPLETE SET (32)	60.00	120.00
COMMON STICKER (1-32)	2.00	5.00

1994 Weetabix Star Trek The Next Generation

COMPLETE SET (10)	15.00	40.00
COMMON CARD (UNNUMBERED)	2.00	5.00

Deep Space Nine

1993 SkyBox Star Trek Deep Space Nine

COMPLETE BOXED SET (52)	6.00	15.00
COMMON CARD (1-48)	.12	.30

1994 SkyBox Star Trek Deep Space Nine

COMPLETE SET (100)	6.00	15.00
UNOPENED BOX (36 PACKS)	30.00	40.00
UNOPENED PACK (8 CARDS)	1.00	1.25
COMMON CARD (1-100)	.12	.30

1994 SkyBox Star Trek Deep Space Nine Redemption

COMPLETE SET (1-10)	30.00	80.00
COMMON CARD (R-10)	4.00	10.00
AVAILABLE VIA REDEMPTION OFFER		
REDEMPTION CARD 1:180		
NNO Redemption Card		

1994 SkyBox Star Trek Deep Space Nine Spectra

COMPLETE SET (4)	10.00	25.00
COMMON CARD (SP1-SP4)	3.00	8.00
STATED ODDS 1:18		
SPG STATED ODDS 1:72		
SPG The Wormhole SP	5.00	12.00

1994 SkyBox Star Trek Deep Space Nine Promos

NNO Beaming to Retail November 1993	.75	2.00
NNO Beaming to Retail Fall 1993 (gold stamp)	.75	2.00
NNO Beaming to Retail Fall 1993 (orange stamp)	.75	2.00
NNO Commander Benjamin Sisko (DS9 #2 Comic Exclusive)	.75	2.00
S2 Personal Phasers	.75	2.00
6UP 6UP Panel Holograms		

2003 Complete Star Trek Deep Space Nine

COMPLETE SET (189)	4.00	10.00
UNOPENED BOX (40 PACKS)	75.00	125.00
UNOPENED PACK (9 CARDS)	2.50	4.00
UNOPENED ARCHIVE BOX	500.00	1000.00
COMMON CARD (1-189)	.08	.25

2003 Complete Star Trek Deep Space Nine Allies and Enemies

COMPLETE SET (27)	8.00	20.00
COMMON CARD (B1-B27)	.40	1.00
STATED ODDS 1:3		

2003 Complete Star Trek Deep Space Nine Alternate Realities

COMPLETE SET (7)	30.00	80.00
COMMON CARD (AR1-AR7)	6.00	15.00
STATED ODDS 1:80		

2003 Complete Star Trek Deep Space Nine Autographs

COMMON CARD (A1-A26)	8.00	20.00
STATED ODDS 1:20		
DA2 ISSUED AS CASE TOPPER		
L (LIMITED): 300-500 CARDS		
A1 Avery Brooks L	30.00	80.00
A2 Colm Meaney L	20.00	50.00
A3 Michael Dorn L	15.00	40.00
A4 Armin Shimerman	10.00	25.00
A5 Nana Visitor L	25.00	60.00
A9 Wallace Shawn	15.00	40.00
A10 Rene Auberjonois L	12.00	30.00
A11 Alexander Siddig L	25.00	50.00
A13 Terry Farrell L	15.00	40.00
A14 Jeffrey Combs L	12.00	30.00
A15 Nicole DeBoer L	20.00	50.00
A21 Tony Todd L	12.00	30.00
DA1 Michael Dorn/Terry Farrell L	50.00	100.00
DA2 Barbara March/Gwynyth Walsh	15.00	40.00

2003 Complete Star Trek Deep Space Nine From the Archives Costumes

COMPLETE SET (5)	30.00	80.00
COMPLETE SET W/VARIANTS (10)	80.00	150.00
COMMON CARD (CC1-CC5)	8.00	20.00
STATED ODDS 1:100		
CC4a Intendant Kira/Shiny Silver and Black	10.00	25.00
CC4b Intendant Kira/Dull Silver	10.00	25.00

2003 Complete Star Trek Deep Space Nine Gallery

COMPLETE SET (10)	15.00	40.00
COMMON CARD (G1-G10)	2.00	5.00
STATED ODDS 1:40		

2003 Complete Star Trek Deep Space Nine Ships of the Dominion War

COMPLETE SET (9)	2.50	6.00
COMMON CARD (S1-S9)	.40	1.00
STATED ODDS 1:8		

2003 Complete Star Trek Deep Space Nine Promos

COMMON CARD (P1-P3)	1.25	3.00
P3 Defiant ALB	3.00	8.00
RAUKDS9 Sisko/Dax/500 UK	15.00	40.00

2018 Star Trek Deep Space Nine Heroes and Villains

COMPLETE SET (100)	8.00	20.00
UNOPENED BOX (24 PACKS)	55.00	65.00
UNOPENED PACK (5 CARDS)	2.50	3.00
COMMON CARD (1-100)	.15	.40
*METAL/100: 6X TO 15X BASIC CARDS	2.50	6.00

2018 Star Trek Deep Space Nine Heroes and Villains Aliens of Star Trek DS9

COMPLETE SET (9)	15.00	40.00
COMMON CARD (A1-A9)	3.00	8.00
STATED ODDS 1:24		

2018 Star Trek Deep Space Nine Heroes and Villains Autographs

COMMON AUTO	5.00	12.00
L = 300-500 COPIES		
VL = 200-300 COPIES		
EL = 100-200 COPIES		
STATED ODDS 1:8		
NNO Andrea Martin L	6.00	15.00
NNO Andrew Robinson EL	15.00	40.00
NNO Andrew Robinson Mirror AB	25.00	60.00
NNO Avery Brooks Legend CI	60.00	120.00
NNO Barbara Bosson VL	6.00	15.00
NNO Bernie Casey Variant AB	20.00	50.00
NNO Bernie Casey VL	15.00	40.00
NNO Bertila Damas VL	8.00	20.00
NNO Bill Smitrovich L	6.00	15.00
NNO Bill Smitrovich AB	15.00	40.00
NNO Bill Mumy EL	20.00	50.00
NNO Bill Mumy Variant AB	20.00	50.00
NNO Brett Cullen VL	6.00	15.00
NNO Bridget Ann White VL	10.00	25.00
NNO Camille Saviola VL	6.00	15.00
NNO Chase Masterson EL	25.00	60.00
NNO Chase Masterson Variant AB	30.00	75.00
NNO Courtney Peldon VL	8.00	20.00
NNO Cyia Batten VL	6.00	15.00
NNO Daphne Ashbrook VL	6.00	15.00
NNO Deborah Lacey EL	12.00	30.00
NNO Deborah Lacey Variant AB	20.00	50.00
NNO Deborah Van Valkenburgh EL	15.00	40.00
NNO Deirdre L. Imershein VL	8.00	20.00
NNO Dick Miller VL	6.00	15.00
NNO Felecia Bell Jennifer Sisko EL	10.00	25.00
NNO Felecia Bell Mirror Jennifer Sisko VL	8.00	20.00
NNO Fionnula Flanagan VL	6.00	15.00
NNO Harris Yulin VL	8.00	20.00
NNO Heidi Swedberg VL	6.00	15.00
NNO Helene Udy VL	6.00	15.00
NNO Hilary Shepard Hoya VL	8.00	20.00
NNO Hilary Shepard Lauren VL	8.00	20.00
NNO Iggy Pop Aliens Variant AB	60.00	120.00
NNO Iggy Pop EL	25.00	60.00
NNO Jill Jacobson VL	6.00	15.00
NNO Jim Metzler Variant AB	12.00	30.00
NNO Joel Swetow VL	6.00	15.00
NNO Kaitlin Hopkins VL	8.00	20.00
NNO Leland Crooke L	6.00	15.00
NNO Marc Alaimo Anjohl Tennan EL	15.00	40.00
NNO Marc Alaimo Gul Dukat EL	15.00	40.00
NNO Mark Allen Shepherd L	10.00	25.00
NNO Melanie Smith VL	8.00	20.00
NNO Michael Canavan VL	6.00	15.00
NNO Molly Hagan VL	6.00	15.00
NNO Nana Visitor Mirror AB	60.00	120.00
NNO Patricia Tallman L	8.00	20.00
NNO Paul Popowich L	6.00	15.00
NNO Salome Jens VL	8.00	20.00
NNO Shannon Cochran Sirella VL	6.00	15.00
NNO Stephen Macht VL	6.00	15.00
NNO Steven Weber VL	12.00	30.00
NNO Susan Bay Nimoy VL	12.00	30.00
NNO Susanna Thompson L	8.00	20.00
NNO Tracy Scoggins VL	8.00	20.00
NNO Vanessa Williams EL	25.00	60.00
NNO Wallace Shawn VL	10.00	25.00
NNO Wayne Grace VL	6.00	15.00
NNO Wendy Robie EL	12.00	30.00

2018 Star Trek Deep Space Nine Heroes and Villains Case-Toppers

COMPLETE SET (2) 12.00 30.00
COMMON CARD (CT1-CT2) 8.00 20.00
STATED ODDS 1:CASE

2018 Star Trek Deep Space Nine Heroes and Villains Comic Cuts

COMPLETE SET (15) 125.00 250.00
COMMON CARD (CC1-CC15) 12.00 30.00
STATED ODDS 1:144

2018 Star Trek Deep Space Nine Heroes and Villains Communicator Pins

STATED ODDS 1:864
NNO Captain Sisko 50.00 100.00
NNO Kira Nerys 60.00 120.00

2018 Star Trek Deep Space Nine Heroes and Villains Dual Autographs

COMMON AUTO 15.00 40.00
NNO A.Shimerman/W.Shawn EL 50.00 100.00
NNO A.Shimerman/M.Grodenchik VL 20.00 50.00
NNO M.Grodenchik/C.Masterson EL 30.00 75.00
NNO R.Auberjonois/N.Visitor EL 50.00 100.00
NNO T.Farrell/N.Visitor 60.00 120.00

2018 Star Trek Deep Space Nine Heroes and Villains DVD Character Cover Art

COMPLETE SET (7) 20.00 50.00
COMMON CARD (D1-D7) 4.00 10.00
*METAL: 1.5X TO 4X BASIC CARDS 15.00 40.00
STATED ODDS 1:48

2018 Star Trek Deep Space Nine Heroes and Villains Niners Baseball Patches

COMPLETE SET (12) 100.00 175.00
COMMON PATCH (BP1-BP12) 8.00 20.00
STATED ODDS 1:144

2018 Star Trek Deep Space Nine Heroes and Villains Relationships

COMPLETE SET (18) 75.00 150.00
COMMON CARD (R1-R18) 5.00 12.00
STATED ODDS 1:144

2018 Star Trek Deep Space Nine Heroes and Villains Relic

RC1 Routines and Duty Roster Display Panel25.00 60.00

2018 Star Trek Deep Space Nine Heroes and Villains Rules of Acquisition

COMPLETE SET (36) 12.00 30.00
COMMON CARD (RA1-RA36) .75 2.00
STATED ODDS 1:8

2018 Star Trek Deep Space Nine Heroes and Villains Ships of the Line

COMPLETE SET (9) 10.00 25.00
COMMON CARD (SL28-SL36) 2.00 5.00
STATED ODDS 1:48

2018 Star Trek Deep Space Nine Heroes and Villains Silver Signature Autographs

COMMON AUTO 15.00 40.00
STATED OVERALL ODDS 1:8
NNO Alexander Siddig EL 20.00 50.00
NNO Avery Brooks VL 20.00 50.00
NNO Michael Dorn EL 20.00 50.00
NNO Rene Auberjonois EL 20.00 50.00
NNO Terry Farrell EL 30.00 75.00

2018 Star Trek Deep Space Nine Heroes and Villains Promos

COMPLETE SET (3) 5.00 12.00
COMMON CARD (P1-P3) 1.00 2.50
P2 Kira Nerys/Kai Winn Adami 1.50 4.00
P3 Odo/Female Changling 4.00 10.00

1999 SkyBox Star Trek Deep Space Nine Memories from the Future

COMPLETE SET (100) 6.00 15.00
UNOPENED BOX (36 PACKS) 60.00 100.00
UNOPENED PACK (9 CARDS) 2.00 3.00
COMMON CARD (1-100) .12 .30

1999 SkyBox Star Trek Deep Space Nine Memories from the Future Autographs

COMMON CARD (1-20) 10.00 25.00
STATED ODDS 1:BOX
1 Alexander Siddig 30.00 75.00
2 Armin Shimerman 15.00 40.00
3 Cirroc Lofton 12.00 30.00
4 Nana Visitor 20.00 50.00
5 Rene Auberjonois 20.00 50.00
6 Terry Farrell 20.00 50.00
7 Nicole DeBoer 25.00 60.00
9 Aron Eisenberg 12.00 30.00
10 William Campbell 12.00 30.00
11 Robert O'Reilly 20.00 50.00
12 Jennifer Hetrick 12.00 30.00
13 John de Lancie 20.00 50.00
15 Majel Barrett 50.00 100.00
17 Max Grodenchik 12.00 30.00
18 Avery Brooks 30.00 75.00
19 Rick Berman 250.00 500.00
20 Chase Masterson 12.00 30.00

1999 SkyBox Star Trek Deep Space Nine Memories from the Future Greatest Alien Races

COMPLETE SET (9) 4.00 10.00
COMMON CARD (AR1-AR9) .60 1.50

1999 SkyBox Star Trek Deep Space Nine Memories from the Future Greatest Legends

COMPLETE SET (9) 6.00 15.00
COMMON CARD (L1-L9) 1.00 2.50

1999 SkyBox Star Trek Deep Space Nine Memories from the Future Greatest Space Battles

COMPLETE SET (6) 4.00 10.00
COMMON CARD (B1-B6) 1.00 2.50

1997 SkyBox Star Trek Deep Space Nine Profiles

COMPLETE SET (82) 5.00 12.00
UNOPENED BOX (36 PACKS) 125.00 200.00
UNOPENED PACK (8 CARDS) 4.00 6.00
COMMON CARD (1-82) .10 .25

1997 SkyBox Star Trek Deep Space Nine Profiles Autographs

COMPLETE SET (3) 200.00 350.00
COMMON CARD (UNNUMBERED) 60.00 120.00
STATED ODDS 1:216
1 Armin Shimerman 75.00 150.00

1997 SkyBox Star Trek Deep Space Nine Profiles Latinum

COMPLETE SET (9) 25.00 60.00
COMMON CARD (1-9) 3.00 8.00
STATED ODDS 1:6

1997 SkyBox Star Trek Deep Space Nine Profiles Quark's Bar

COMPLETE SET (9) 7.50 20.00
COMMON CARD (QB1-QB9) 1.25 3.00
STATED ODDS 1:3

1997 SkyBox Star Trek Deep Space Nine Profiles Trials and Tribbleations

COMPLETE SET (9) 10.00 25.00
COMMON CARD (TT1-TT9) 1.50 4.00
STATED ODDS 1:6

2007 Quotable Star Trek Deep Space Nine

COMPLETE SET (108) 6.00 15.00
UNOPENED BOX (40 PACKS) 60.00 100.00
UNOPENED PACK (5 CARDS) 2.00 3.00
COMMON CARD (1-108) .12 .30

2007 Quotable Star Trek Deep Space Nine Autographs

COMMON CARD 10.00 25.00
STATED ODDS 1:BOX
BERMAN ISSUED AS 3-CASE INCENTIVE
L (LIMITED): 300-500 CARDS
VL (VERY LIMITED): 200-300 CARDS
A18 Cirroc Lofton L 15.00 40.00
NNO Armin Shimerman L 20.00 50.00
NNO Avery Brooks VL 50.00 100.00
NNO James Darren L 15.00 40.00
NNO Jennifer Hetrick VL 12.00 30.00
NNO John de Lancie VL 12.00 30.00
NNO Max Grodenchik L 15.00 40.00
NNO Nana Visitor L 30.00 75.00
NNO Rene Auberjonois L 15.00 40.00
NNO Rick Berman CI 100.00 200.00
NNO Terry Farrell VL 25.00 60.00

2007 Quotable Star Trek Deep Space Nine Comic Books

COMPLETE SET (9) 12.00 30.00
COMMON CARD (CB1-CB9) 2.50 6.00
STATED ODDS 1:35

2007 Quotable Star Trek Deep Space Nine Costumes

COMPLETE SET (22) 100.00 200.00
COMMON CARD (C1-C22) 4.00 10.00
STATED ODDS 2:BOX
C22 ODDS 1:ALBUM
AC1 OFFERED AS 6-CASE INCENTIVE
C1 Capt. Benjamin Sisko 8.00 20.00
C3 Security Chief Odo 8.00 20.00
C4 Lt. Comm. Jadzia Dax 15.00 40.00
C5 Lt. Commander Worf 6.00 15.00
C8 Lt. Ezri Dax 6.00 15.00
C9 Capt. Benjamin Sisko 8.00 20.00
C11 Capt. Benjamin Sisko 8.00 20.00
C16 Security Chief Odo 8.00 20.00
C20 Promenade Banner 8.00 20.00
C21 Promenade Banner 8.00 20.00
C22 Grand Nagus Zek ALB 5.00 12.00

2007 Quotable Star Trek Deep Space Nine Starfleet's Finest

COMPLETE SET (9) 120.00 250.00
COMPLETE SET W/RR (10) 150.00 275.00
COMMON CARD (F1-F9) 12.00 30.00
STATED ODDS 1:120
STATED PRINT RUN 399 SER. #'d SETS
F10 ISSUED AS RITTENHOUSE REWARD

2007 Quotable Star Trek Deep Space Nine The Final Frontier

COMPLETE SET (9) 6.00 15.00
COMMON CARD (DSN1-DSN9) 1.25 3.00
STATED ODDS 1:8

2007 Quotable Star Trek Deep Space Nine TV Guide Covers

COMPLETE SET (9) 12.00 30.00
COMMON CARD (TV1-TV9) 2.00 5.00
STATED ODDS 1:20

2007 Quotable Star Trek Deep Space Nine Promos

COMPLETE SET (6) 8.00 20.00
COMMON CARD 1.25 3.00
P1 Sisko GEN 2.00 5.00
P2 Jadzia Dax NSU 2.00 5.00
P3 Sisko ALB 4.00 10.00
SD07 Bashir/Sisko SDCC 1.50 4.00
DST07 DS9 Action Figure Promo 2.00 5.00

Voyager

1999 SkyBox Star Trek Voyager Closer to Home

COMPLETE SET (100) 8.00 20.00
UNOPENED BOX (36 PACKS) 35.00 50.00
UNOPENED PACK (9 CARDS) 1.50 2.50
COMMON CARD (178-277) .15 .40
NNO1 Stardate 11.17.99 Cast Shot NSU

1999 SkyBox Star Trek Voyager Closer to Home Advanced Technology Foil

COMPLETE SET (9) 5.00 12.00
COMMON CARD (AT1-AT9) .60 1.50
STATED ODDS 1:4

1999 SkyBox Star Trek Voyager Closer to Home Adventures of Captain Proton Foil

COMPLETE SET (9) 6.00 15.00
COMMON CARD (CP1-CP9) 1.00 2.50
STATED ODDS 1:8

1999 SkyBox Star Trek Voyager Closer to Home Autographs

COMMON CARD (A1-A9) 15.00 40.00
STATED ODDS 1:72
A1 Kate Mulgrew 30.00 80.00
A2 Robert Beltran 25.00 60.00
A7 Jeri Ryan 50.00 100.00
A8 Roxanne Dawson 25.00 60.00

1999 SkyBox Star Trek Voyager Closer to Home Command Crew Lenticular

COMPLETE SET (9) 80.00 150.00
COMMON CARD (CC1-CC9) 8.00 20.00
STATED ODDS 1:18
CC1 Capt. Kathyrn Janeway 15.00 40.00
CC3 Neelix 15.00 40.00
CC6 Lt. Cmdr. Tuvok 20.00 50.00
CC7 Seven of Nine 15.00 40.00
CC8 Lt. B'Elanna Torres 10.00 25.00
CC9 Ens. Kim 12.00 30.00

1999 SkyBox Star Trek Voyager Closer to Home Interstellar Species Glow Green

COMPLETE SET (9) 15.00 40.00
COMMON CARD (IS1-IS9) 2.50 6.00
*ORANGE: 2X TO 5X BASIC CARDS
STATED ODDS 1:12

2002 Complete Star Trek Voyager

COMPLETE SET (180) 5.00 12.00
UNOPENED BOX (40 PACKS) 50.00 75.00
UNOPENED PACK (9 CARDS) 2.00 2.50
COMMON CARD (1-180) .15 .20
P1 Complete Star Trek Voyager PROMO 1.00 2.50

2002 Complete Star Trek Voyager Adventures in the Holodeck

COMPLETE SET (9) 2.50 6.00
COMMON CARD (H1-H9) .40 1.00
STATED ODDS 1:4

2002 Complete Star Trek Voyager Autographs

COMMON CARD 6.00 15.00
STATED ODDS 1:20
CA1 ODDS 1:CASE
A4 Kurtwood Smith 8.00 20.00
A5 Bruce McGill 8.00 20.00
A7 Joseph Campanella 12.00 30.00
CA1 Jeri Ryan 30.00 80.00
DA1 Robert Duncan McNeill/Roxann Dawson 50.00 100.00
DA2 Ethan Phillips/Jennifer Lien 30.00 80.00
DA3 Tim Russ/Marva Hicks 30.00 80.00
PA1 Robert Duncan McNeill 15.00 40.00
PA2 Martin Rayner 10.00 25.00
PA3 Kate Mulgrew 25.00 60.00
PA4 Garrett Wang 30.00 80.00
PA5 Robert Picardo 30.00 75.00
PA6 Nicholas Worth 10.00 25.00
PA7 Jim Krestalude 8.00 20.00
PA8 Heidi Kramer 8.00 20.00
PA9 Alissa Kramer 10.00 25.00
PA11 Kirsten Turner 10.00 25.00

2002 Complete Star Trek Voyager Checklists

COMPLETE SET (3) 1.50 4.00
COMMON CARD (C1-C3) .60 1.50
STATED ODDS 1:10

2002 Complete Star Trek Voyager Costumes

COMPLETE SET (3) 60.00 120.00
COMMON COSTUME (CC1-CC3) 12.00 30.00
STATED ODDS 1:480
CC1 Seven of Nine 50.00 100.00
CC2 B'Elanna Torres 15.00 40.00

2002 Complete Star Trek Voyager Formidable Foes

COMPLETE SET (9) 4.00 10.00
COMMON CARD (F1-F9) .60 1.50
STATED ODDS 1:8

2002 Complete Star Trek Voyager Gallery Cels

COMPLETE SET (9) 30.00 80.00
COMMON CARD (G1-G9) 4.00 10.00
STATED ODDS 1:40

2015 Star Trek Voyager Heroes and Villains

COMPLETE SET (99) 3.00 8.00
UNOPENED BOX (24 PACKS) 60.00 100.00
UNOPENED PACK (5 CARDS) 2.50 4.00
COMMON CARD (1-99) .10 .25
*GOLD/100: 6X TO 15X BASIC CARDS 1.50 4.00

2015 Star Trek Voyager Heroes and Villains Aliens

COMPLETE SET (11) 10.00 25.00
COMMON CARD (A1-A11) 1.25 3.00
STATED ODDS 1:24

2015 Star Trek Voyager Heroes and Villains Autographs

COMMON AUTO 4.00 10.00
STATED ODDS 1:8
L (LIMITED): 300-500 COPIES
VL (VERY LIMITED): 200-300 COPIES
EL (EXTREMELY LIMITED): 200 OR LESS
UNNUMBERED SET LISTED ALPHABETICALLY
NNO Armin Shimerman EL 10.00 25.00
NNO Bertila Damas EL 5.00 12.00
NNO Brad Dourif EL 10.00 25.00
NNO Brian Markinson (Lt. Durst) VL 5.00 12.00
NNO Brian Markinson (Sulan) VL 5.00 12.00
NNO Cari Shayne EL 5.00 12.00
NNO Dan Shor EL 8.00 20.00
NNO David Clennon EL 8.00 20.00
NNO Ed Begley Jr. EL 6.00 15.00
NNO Ethan Phillips EL 12.00 30.00
NNO Fintan McKeown EL 5.00 12.00
NNO Garrett Wang EL 15.00 40.00
NNO Gary Graham EL 8.00 20.00
NNO Gerrit Graham VL 6.00 15.00
NNO J. Paul Boehmer EL 8.00 20.00
NNO Jad Moger EL 6.00 15.00
NNO James Horan EL 8.00 20.00
NNO Jason Alexander EL 30.00 75.00
NNO Jennifer Lien EL 15.00 40.00
NNO Jeri Ryan EL 50.00 100.00
NNO Jerry Hardin EL 5.00 12.00
NNO Joel Grey EL 6.00 15.00
NNO John Rhys-Davies EL 12.00 30.00
NNO Johnathan Frakes EL 20.00 50.00
NNO Judy Geeson L 5.00 12.00
NNO Kate Mulgrew EL 25.00 60.00
NNO Kim Rhodes (Jhet'leya) EL 10.00 25.00
NNO K.Rhodes (Lyndsay Ballard) EL 12.00 30.00
NNO Lee Arenberg EL 6.00 15.00
NNO Len Cariou EL 8.00 20.00
NNO Lindsay Ridgeway L 5.00 12.00
NNO Lisa Kaminir EL 10.00 25.00
NNO Lori Petty EL 10.00 25.00
NNO Marina Sirtis EL 20.00 50.00
NNO Mary Elizabeth McGlynn EL 10.00 25.00
NNO Michael Horton EL 8.00 20.00
NNO Robert Beltran EL 15.00 40.00
NNO Robert Duncan McNeill EL 20.00 50.00
NNO Robert Knepper EL 12.00 30.00
NNO Robert Picardo EL 25.00 60.00
NNO Roxann Dawson EL 15.00 40.00
NNO Sandra Nelson EL 8.00 20.00
NNO Scott Lawrence VL 6.00 15.00
NNO Scott MacDonald EL 6.00 15.00
NNO Tim Russ EL 15.00 40.00
NNO Wayne Thomas L 5.00 12.00
NNO Zoe McLellan EL 8.00 20.00

2015 Star Trek Voyager Heroes and Villains Black Gallery

COMPLETE SET (9) 10.00 25.00
COMMON CARD (BG1-BG9) 2.00 5.00
*GOLD/100: 5X TO 12X BASIC CARDS
STATED ODDS 1:24

2015 Star Trek Voyager Heroes and Villains Case-Incentives

COMPLETE SET (4)
COMMON CARD
NNO J.Alexander Alt. AU 18CI 120.00 200.00
NNO Jeri Ryan Alt. Black Gallery 18CI 50.00 100.00
NNO Jeri Ryan Silver AU 6CI 60.00 120.00
NNO J.Ryan/K.Mulgrew Dual AU 9CI 120.00 200.00

2015 Star Trek Voyager Heroes and Villains Case-Toppers

COMPLETE SET (2) 10.00 25.00
COMMON CARD (CT1-CT2) 6.00 15.00
STATED ODDS 1:CASE

2015 Star Trek Voyager Heroes and Villains Relationships

COMPLETE SET (24) 15.00 40.00
COMMON CARD (R1-R24) 1.25 3.00
*GOLD/100: 2X TO 5X BASIC CARDS
STATED ODDS 1:12

2015 Star Trek Voyager Heroes and Villains Promos

COMPLETE SET (4) 5.00 12.00
COMMON CARD (P1-P4) 1.25 3.00
P3 Philly Non-Sport Show 2.00 5.00
P4 Album Exclusive 3.00 8.00

1998 SkyBox Star Trek Voyager Profiles

COMPLETE SET (90) 6.00 15.00
UNOPENED BOX (36 PACKS) 50.00 75.00
UNOPENED PACK (9 CARDS) 2.00 3.00
COMMON CARD (1-90) .15 .40
C4 Captain Janeway/1200 80.00 150.00

1998 SkyBox Star Trek Voyager Profiles Alien Technology

COMPLETE SET (9) 3.00 8.00
COMMON CARD (AT1-AT9) .40 1.00
STATED ODDS 1:6

1998 SkyBox Star Trek Voyager Profiles Autograph Challenge

COMPLETE SET W/O SP (9) 2.50 6.00
COMMON CARD 4.00 1.00
Y Seven of Nine SP 40.00 80.00

1998 SkyBox Star Trek Voyager Profiles Autographs

COMMON CARD 10.00 25.00
STATED ODDS 1:36
A1 Kate Mulgrew 30.00 75.00
A2 Robert Beltran 30.00 75.00
A3 Garrett Wang 25.00 60.00
A4 Tim Russ 20.00 50.00
A5 Roxann Dawson 25.00 60.00
A6 Robert Duncan McNeill 25.00 60.00
A7 Jeri Ryan 60.00 120.00
A8 Robert Picardo 25.00 60.00
A9 Ethan Phillips 20.00 50.00
A10 Jennifer Lien 25.00 60.00
A11 John De Lancie 25.00 60.00
A12 Dwight Schultz 20.00 50.00
A13 Henry Darrow 20.00 50.00
A14 Alexander Enberg 15.00 40.00
A15 Tony Todd 12.00 30.00
A17b M.McKean WHITE 20.00 50.00
A18 Josh Clark 15.00 40.00
A19 John Rhys-Davies 25.00 60.00
A20 George Takei 30.00 80.00

1998 SkyBox Star Trek Voyager Profiles Makeup with Michael Westmore

COMPLETE SET (9) 5.00 12.00
COMMON CARD (MW1-MW9) 1.00 2.50
STATED ODDS 1:4

1998 SkyBox Star Trek Voyager Profiles Seven of Nine

COMPLETE SET (8) 8.00 20.00
COMPLETE SET W/SP (9) 12.00 30.00
COMMON CARD (1-9) 2.00 5.00
STATED ODDS 1:8
SP STATED ODDS 1:144
7 Duty Assignment I SP 8.00 20.00

2012 Quotable Star Trek Voyager

COMPLETE SET (72) 4.00 10.00
UNOPENED BOX (24 PACKS) 75.00 125.00
UNOPENED PACK (5 CARDS) 3.00 5.00
UNOPENED ARCHIVE BOX 1200.00 1400.00
COMMON CARD (1-72) .12 .30
CC45 ISSUED AS CASE TOPPER
DF ISSUED AS 3-CASE INCENTIVE
KM AU MEM ISSUED AS 6-CASE INCENTIVE
DF Delta Flyer MEM 60.00 120.00
KM Kate Mulgrew AU MEM 120.00 200.00
CC45 Capt. Janeway MEM 12.00 30.00

2012 Quotable Star Trek Voyager Autographs

COMMON CARD 4.00 10.00
STATED ODDS 1:8
L (LIMITED): 300-500 COPIES
VL (VERY LIMITED): 200-300 COPIES
EL (EXTREMELY LIMITED): LESS THAN 200
NNO Andy Dick L 5.00 12.00
NNO Don Most L 5.00 12.00
NNO Ed Begley, Jr. VL 8.00 20.00
NNO Eric Pierpoint VL 8.00 20.00
NNO Estelle Harris EL 12.00 30.00
NNO Ethan Phillips EL 15.00 40.00
NNO Garrett Wang EL 15.00 40.00
NNO Harry Groener VL 6.00 15.00
NNO Jeffrey Combs L 5.00 12.00
NNO Jennifer Lien EL 15.00 40.00
NNO Jeri Ryan EL 60.00 120.00
NNO John DeLancie EL 15.00 40.00
NNO John Rhys-Davies EL 25.00 60.00
NNO John Savage L 5.00 12.00
NNO Karen Austin VL 8.00 20.00
NNO Kate Mulgrew EL 30.00 80.00
NNO Kevin Tighe 6.00 15.00
NNO Kristanna Loken EL 35.00 70.00
NNO Leigh McCloskey VL 8.00 20.00
NNO Martha Hackett VL 8.00 20.00
NNO Robert Beltran EL 25.00 60.00
NNO Robert Duncan McNeill EL 25.00 50.00
NNO Robert Picardo EL 25.00 50.00
NNO Roxann Dawson EL 20.00 50.00
NNO Scarlett Pomers VL 12.00 30.00
NNO Sharon Lawrence L 5.00 12.00
NNO Susanna Thompson VL 12.00 30.00
NNO Tim Russ EL 25.00 50.00
NNO Virgina Madsen VL 12.00 30.00

2012 Quotable Star Trek Voyager Best of the Holodeck

COMPLETE SET (9) 5.00 12.00
COMMON CARD (H1-H9) .75 2.00
STATED ODDS 1:12

2012 Quotable Star Trek Voyager Communicator Pins

COMPLETE SET (9) 120.00 250.00
COMMON CARD (1-9) 20.00 40.00
STATED ODDS 1:96
STATED PRINT RUN 225 SER. #'d SETS
1 Captain Janeway 25.00 50.00
7 Seven of Nine 25.00 50.00

2012 Quotable Star Trek Voyager Starfleet's Finest

COMPLETE SET (10) 60.00 120.00
COMMON CARD (F1-F10) 6.00 15.00
STATED ODDS 1:48
STATED PRINT RUN 399 SER. #'d SETS
F2 Seven of Nine 8.00 20.00

2012 Quotable Star Trek Voyager USS Voyager

COMPLETE SET (9) 5.00 12.00
COMMON CARD (V1-V9) .75 2.00
STATED ODDS 1:12

2012 Quotable Star Trek Voyager Promos

COMPLETE SET (4) 4.00 10.00
COMMON CARD (P1-P4) .75 2.00
P3 Captain Janeway ALB 3.00 8.00

1995 SkyBox Star Trek Voyager Series 1

COMPLETE SET (98) 6.00 15.00
UNOPENED BOX (36 PACKS) 30.00 50.00
UNOPENED PACK (8 CARDS) 2.00 2.50
COMMON CARD (1-98) .15 .40
T1 Title Card 1.25 3.00
NNO1 Skymotion EXCH
NNO2 Skymotion Card 15.00 40.00
NNO3 Emergency Holographic Doctor HOLO20.00 50.00

1995 SkyBox Star Trek Voyager Series 1 Blueprint Expand-A-Cards

COMPLETE SET (3) 8.00 20.00
COMMON CARD (X1-X3) 3.00 8.00
STATED ODDS 1:18H, 1:9J

1995 SkyBox Star Trek Voyager Series 1 Crew

COMPLETE SET (9) 8.00 20.00
COMMON CARD (1-9) 1.25 3.00
STATED ODDS 1:12H, 1:9J

1995 SkyBox Star Trek Voyager Series 1 Promos

C1 Cards Illustrated 3.00 8.00
N1 Non-Sport Update 3.00 8.00
P1 Sneak Peek 1.25 3.00
Series Two
NNO1 4-Up Panel 3.00 8.00
NNO2 9-Up Panel 4.00 10.00

1995 SkyBox Star Trek Voyager Series 2

COMPLETE SET (90) 6.00 15.00
UNOPENED BOX (36 PACKS) 30.00 50.00
UNOPENED PACK (8 CARDS+1 TATTOO) 2.00 2.50
COMMON CARD (1-90) .12 .30
CHAKOTAY TATTOO ISSUED ONE PER WALMART PACK
NNO Chakotay Temporary Tattoo .20 .50
NNO Small Skymotion 20.00 50.00
NNO Supersized Skymotion 15.00 40.00
NNO Skymotion EXCH
NNO Survey Card .75 2.00

1995 SkyBox Star Trek Voyager Series 2 Crew

COMPLETE SET (9) 12.00 30.00
COMMON CARD (E1-E9) 1.50 4.00
STATED ODDS 1:1 WALMART PACK

1995 SkyBox Star Trek Voyager Series 2 Pop-Outs

COMPLETE SET (9) 8.00 20.00
COMMON CARD (P1-P2) 1.25 3.00
STATED ODDS 1:1
INSERTED INTO BLOCKBUSTER PACKS

1995 SkyBox Star Trek Voyager Series 2 Recipes

COMPLETE SET (6) 8.00 20.00
COMMON CARD (R1-R6) 1.50 4.00
STATED ODDS 1:18

1995 SkyBox Star Trek Voyager Series 2 Xenobio

COMPLETE SET (9) 20.00 50.00
COMMON CARD (S1-S9) 3.00 8.00
STATED ODDS 1:12

1995 SkyBox Star Trek Voyager Series 2 Promos

0 Trek Credit Card exclusive/10000 30.00 80.00
NNO1 NSU 1995 Gummies/1000 6.00 15.00
NNO2 6-Up Panel 1.50 4.00

1997 SkyBox Star Trek Voyager Season Two

COMPLETE SET W/O SP (100) 5.00 12.00
COMPLETE SET W/SP (112) 20.00 50.00
UNOPENED BOX (48 PACKS) 30.00 40.00
UNOPENED PACK (8 CARDS) 1.00 1.25
COMMON CARD (91-202) .15 .40
XENOBIO SKETCHES (191-193) 1:12 1.25 3.00
24TH CEN.TECH (194-196) 1:12 1.25 3.00
STRANGE NEW WORLDS (197-199) 1:18 1.25 3.00
HOLODECK (200-202) 1:48 5.00 12.00

2000 Star Trek Voyager Tsunkatse Archive Collection

COMPLETE SET (5) 10.00 25.00
COMMON CARD (T1-T5) 2.50 6.00

2001 Women of Star Trek Voyager HoloFEX

COMPLETE SET (70) 4.00 10.00
UNOPENED BOX (20 PACKS) 60.00 70.00
UNOPENED PACK (6 CARDS) 3.00 4.00
COMMON CARD (1-70) .10 .30
*PROOF: 1.2X TO 3X BASIC CARDS .40 1.00
*P.P.BLACK/25: 4X TO 10X BASIC CARDS 1.25 3.00
*P.P.CYAN/25: 4X TO 10X BASIC CARDS 1.25 3.00
*P.P.MAGENTA/25: 4X TO 10X BASIC CARDS1.25 3.00
*P.P.YELLOW/25: 4X TO 10X BASIC CARDS 1.25 3.00

2001 Women of Star Trek Voyager HoloFEX ArtiFEX

COMPLETE SET (2) 15.00 40.00
COMMON CARD (AR1-AR2) 10.00 25.00
STATED ODDS 1:CASE

2001 Women of Star Trek Voyager HoloFEX Autographs

COMPLETE SET (22) 200.00 400.00
COMMON CARD 6.00 15.00
STATED ODDS TWO PER BOX
A2 ISSUED AS ALBUM EXCLUSIVE
A3 ISSUED AS CASE TOPPER
A2 Nancy Hower ALB 12.00 30.00
A3 Vanessa Branch CT 10.00 25.00
SA1 Jeri Ryan 50.00 100.00

2001 Women of Star Trek Voyager HoloFEX From the Archives Costumes

COMPLETE SET (2) 50.00 100.00
COMMON CARD (F1-F2) 20.00 50.00
STATED ODDS 1:120

2001 Women of Star Trek Voyager HoloFEX MorFEX

COMPLETE SET (9) 6.00 15.00
COMMON CARD (M1-M9) .75 2.00
STATED ODDS 1:4

2001 Women of Star Trek Voyager HoloFEX ReflectFEX

COMPLETE SET (9) 8.00 20.00
COMMON CARD (R1-R9) 1.00 2.50
STATED ODDS 1:10

2001 Women of Star Trek Voyager HoloFEX SpaceFEX

COMPLETE SET (6) 12.00 30.00
COMMON CARD (SF1-SF6) 2.50 6.00
STATED ODDS 1:20

2001 Women of Star Trek Voyager HoloFEX Promos

COMPLETE SET (3) 2.50 6.00
COMMON CARD 1.00 2.50

Enterprise

2002 Enterprise Previews

COMPLETE SET (9) 6.00 15.00
COMMON CARD (1-9) 1.00 2.50
STATED PRINT RUN 2151 SER.#'d SETS

2002 Enterprise Season One

COMPLETE SET (81) 4.00 10.00
UNOPENED BOX (40 PACKS) 75.00 125.00
UNOPENED PACK (9 CARDS) 2.00 3.00
COMMON CARD (1-81) .10 .25
BOLSON SKETCH ODDS ONE PER CASE
ZC1 STATED ODDS 1:480
CB Cris Bolson SKETCH 25.00 50.00
P1 Capt. Archer PROMO 1.00 2.50
ZC1 Enterprise: To Boldly Go/999 20.00 40.00

2002 Enterprise Season One 22nd Century Technology

COMPLETE SET (9) 5.00 12.00
COMMON CARD (T1-T9) .75 2.00
STATED ODDS 1:4

2002 Enterprise Season One Aliens of Enterprise Autographs

COMMON CARD 6.00 15.00
OVERALL AUTO ODDS 2:BOX
AA1 ISSUED AS ALBUM EXCLUSIVE
AA1 Clint Howard ALB 10.00 25.00
AA2 Ethan Phillips 30.00 60.00
AA3 Dean Stockwell 30.00 60.00

2002 Enterprise Season One Autographs

COMMON CARD (A1-A3) 15.00 30.00
OVERALL AUTO ODDS 2:BOX
A1 Dominic Keating 30.00 60.00
A2 John Billingsley 25.00 50.00
A3 Erick Avari 15.00 30.00

2002 Enterprise Season One Broken Bow Autographs

COMMON CARD (BBA1-BBA13) 6.00 15.00
OVERALL AUTO ODDS 2:BOX
BBA2 Vaughn Armstrong 8.00 25.00

2002 Enterprise Season One First Contact

COMPLETE SET (12) 8.00 20.00
COMMON CARD (F1-F12) .75 2.00
STATED ODDS 1:10

2002 Enterprise Season One Star Trek Nemesis Previews

COMPLETE SET (5) 10.00 25.00
COMMON CARD (N1-N5) 2.50 6.00
STATED ODDS 1:BOX

2003 Enterprise Season Two

COMPLETE SET (81) 4.00 10.00
UNOPENED BOX (40 PACKS) 100.00 150.00
UNOPENED PACK (8 CARDS) 3.00 4.00
UNOPENED ARCHIVE BOX 700.00 800.00
COMMON CARD (82-162) .12 .30
*SILVER: 1.5X TO 4X BASIC CARDS
C1 ISSUED AS ALBUM EXCLUSIVE
T1 ISSUED AS MULTI-CASE INCENTIVE
C1 T'Pol MEM ALB 15.00 30.00
T1 T'Pol MCI/333 50.00 100.00

2003 Enterprise Season Two 22nd Century Vessels

COMPLETE SET (12) 8.00 20.00
COMMON CARD (V1-V12) .75 2.00
STATED ODDS 1:5

2003 Enterprise Season Two Autographs

COMMON CARD 6.00 15.00
STATED ODDS 2:BOX
L (LIMITED): 300-500 COPIES
VL (VERY LIMITED): 200-300 COPIES
A4 Anthony Montgomery L 25.00 60.00
A5 Linda Park L 25.00 60.00
A6 Scott Bakula VL 120.00 250.00
A13 Daniel Riordan L 10.00 25.00
A14 Brigid Brannagh 25.00 60.00
A15 Ed O'Ross L 8.00 20.00
A17 Kellie Waymire 8.00 20.00
A18 Matt Winston L 12.00 30.00
A20 Bruce Davison L 12.00 30.00
AA14 Jeffrey Combs VL 30.00 80.00

2003 Enterprise Season Two Enterprise Gallery

COMPLETE SET (7) 30.00 60.00
COMMON CARD (G1-G7) 5.00 12.00
STATED ODDS 1:40

2003 Enterprise Season Two First Contact

COMPLETE SET (9) 10.00 25.00
COMMON CARD (F13-F21) 1.25 3.00
STATED ODDS 1:10

2003 Enterprise Season Two In Motion Case-Toppers

COMPLETE SET (2)	15.00	40.00
COMMON CARD (CT1-CT2)	10.00	25.00
STATED ODDS ONE SET PER CASE		

2003 Enterprise Season Two Promos

COMPLETE SET (5)	4.00	10.00
COMMON CARD	1.00	2.50
MNCE2003 ISSUED AT MID-WEST NONSPORTS EXPO		
C2003 The Borg CON	1.50	4.00
MNCE2003 Mayweather/Archer MWNSCE	1.50	4.00

2004 Enterprise Season Three

COMPLETE SET (72)	3.00	8.00
UNOPENED BOX (40 PACKS)	125.00	200.00
UNOPENED PACK (5 CARDS)	3.00	5.00
UNOPENED ARCHIVE BOX	500.00	600.00
COMMON CARD (163-234)	.10	.25
C2 ISSUED AS ALBUM EXCLUSIVE		
LA1 ISSUED AS MULTI-CASE INCENTIVE		
C2 Captain Archer MEM ALBUM	20.00	50.00
LA1 Scott Bakula AU MCI	80.00	150.00

2004 Enterprise Season Three Autographs

COMMON CARD	6.00	15.00
OVERALL AUTO ODDS TWO PER BOX		
L (LIMITED): 300-500 COPIES		
VL (VERY LIMITED): 200-300 COPIES		
A7 Connor Trinneer L	30.00	80.00
A23 Jolene Blalock VL	150.00	300.00

2004 Enterprise Season Three Checklists

COMPLETE SET (3)	3.00	8.00
COMMON CARD (CK1-CK3)	1.25	3.00
STATED ODDS 1:16		

2004 Enterprise Season Three Enterprise Crew

COMPLETE SET (7)	25.00	50.00
COMMON CARD (CC1-CC7)	4.00	10.00
STATED ODDS 1:40		

2004 Enterprise Season Three First Contact

COMPLETE SET (9)	10.00	25.00
COMMON CARD (F22-F30)	1.25	3.00
STATED ODDS 1:20		

2004 Enterprise Season Three MACO Autographs

COMPLETE SET (7)	30.00	80.00
COMMON CARD (MACO1-MACO7)	6.00	15.00
OVERALL AUTO ODDS TWO PER BOX		
MACO3 Daniel Dae Kim	8.00	20.00

2004 Enterprise Season Three MACO in Action

COMPLETE SET (9)	6.00	15.00
COMMON CARD (M1-M9)	1.25	3.00
STATED ODDS 1:10		

2004 Enterprise Season Three Ultimate Jolene

COMPLETE SET (9)	25.00	60.00
COMMON CARD (J1-J9)	3.00	8.00
STATED ODDS 1:40		

2004 Enterprise Season Three Promos

COMPLETE SET (3)	4.00	10.00
COMMON CARD (P1-P3)	.75	2.00
P3 T'Pol ALB	3.00	8.00

2005 Enterprise Season Four

COMPLETE SET (72)	4.00	10.00
UNOPENED BOX (40 PACKS)	125.00	200.00
UNOPENED PACK (5 CARDS)	3.00	5.00
UNOPENED ARCHIVE BOX	600.00	650.00
COMMON CARD (235-306)	.10	.30

2005 Enterprise Season Four Archer in Action

COMPLETE SET (9)	15.00	40.00
COMMON CARD (AIA1-AIA9)	2.50	6.00

2005 Enterprise Season Four Autographs

COMMON CARD	8.00	20.00
STATED ODDS 2:BOX		
ARENBERG AU ISSUED AS ALBUM EXCLUSIVE		
L (LIMITED): 300-500 COPIES		
VL (VERY LIMITED): 200-300 COPIES		
4 Anthony Montgomery VL	20.00	40.00
6 Bobbi Sue Luther	15.00	30.00
7 Brent Spiner L	75.00	150.00
10 Crystal Allen	15.00	30.00
12 Gary Graham L	10.00	25.00
14 Jeffrey Combs	15.00	30.00
17 Jolene Blalock L	200.00	300.00
22 Linda Park L	30.00	80.00
23 Menina Fortunato	10.00	25.00
24 Richard Riehle	10.00	25.00
25 Steve Schirripa VL	15.00	30.00
26 Vaughn Armstrong VL	10.00	25.00

2005 Enterprise Season Four Costume Autographs

PARK AU ISSUED AS 2-CASE INCENTIVE		
BLALOCK AU ISSUED AS 6-CASE INCENTIVE		
1 Linda Park 2CI	30.00	80.00
2 Jolene Blalock 6CI	150.00	400.00

2005 Enterprise Season Four From the Archives Costumes

COMPLETE SET (14)	150.00	300.00
COMMON CARD (C3-C16)	6.00	15.00
STATED ODDS 1:BOX		
DC1 ISSUED AS CASE TOPPER		
C3 T'Pol	20.00	40.00
C4 T'Pol	20.00	40.00
C5 T'Pol (Mirror Universe)	20.00	40.00
C7 Archer (Mirror Universe)	15.00	30.00
C10 Daniels	10.00	25.00
C14 Persis	8.00	20.00
C16 Soval	8.00	20.00
DC1 Dr. Arik Soong DUAL CT	25.00	50.00

2005 Enterprise Season Four Genesis

COMPLETE SET (9)	15.00	40.00
COMMON CARD (G1-G9)	2.00	5.00
STATED ODDS 1:20		

2005 Enterprise Season Four In a Mirror

COMPLETE SET (9)	10.00	25.00
COMMON CARD (M1-M9)	1.25	3.00
STATED ODDS 1:10		

2005 Enterprise Season Four Promos

COMPLETE SET	4.00	10.00
COMMON CARD	.75	2.00
P3 T'Pol/Ambassador Soval ALB	2.00	5.00
UK T'Pol UK	1.50	4.00
CP1 Three Orion Slave Girls CON	1.25	3.00

2018 Star Trek Enterprise Archives Series 1

COMPLETE SET (50)	12.00	30.00
COMMON CARD (1-50)	.50	1.25

2018 Star Trek Enterprise Archives Series 1 Ships of the Line

COMPLETE SET (9)	15.00	40.00
COMMON CARD (SL37-SL45)	3.00	8.00
STATED ODDS 1 SET:FACTORY SET		

2018 Star Trek Enterprise Archives Series 1 Silver Signature Autographs

COMMON AUTO	20.00	50.00
STATED ODDS 3:FACTORY SET		
NNO Connor Trinneer	25.00	60.00
NNO John Billingsley	25.00	60.00
NNO Linda Park	30.00	75.00
NNO Scott Bakula	50.00	100.00

2019 Star Trek Enterprise Archives Series 2

COMPLETE SET (50)	10.00	25.00
UNOPENED BOX SET (66 CARDS)		
COMMON CARD (1-50)	.30	.75

2019 Star Trek Enterprise Archives Series 2 Autographed Relics

COMMON AUTO	12.00	30.00
STATED ODDS 3:BOX SET		
NNO Connor Trinneer	15.00	40.00
NNO Dominic Keating	15.00	40.00

2019 Star Trek Enterprise Archives Series 2 Autographs

COMMON AUTO	15.00	40.00
STATED ODDS 1:BOX SET		
NNO Brian Thompson	20.00	50.00

2019 Star Trek Enterprise Archives Series 2 Relationships

COMPLETE SET (12)	10.00	25.00
COMMON CARD (R1-R12)	1.25	3.00
STATED ODDS 1 SET:BOX		

Discovery

2019 Star Trek Discovery Season One

COMPLETE SET (90)	8.00	20.00
UNOPENED BOX (24 PACKS)	60.00	100.00
UNOPENED PACK (5 CARDS)	2.50	4.00
COMMON CARD (1-90)	.15	.40

2019 Star Trek Discovery Season One Autographed Relic

NNO Mary Wiseman 6CI	50.00	100.00

2019 Star Trek Discovery Season One Behind-the-Scenes

COMPLETE SET (18)	5.00	12.00
COMMON CARD (BTS1-BTS18)	.50	1.25
STATED ODDS 1:12		

2019 Star Trek Discovery Season One Bordered Autographs

COMMON AUTO	5.00	12.00
L = 300-500 COPIES		
VL = 200-300 COPIES		
EL = 100-200 COPIES		
STATED ODDS 1:12		
NNO Katherine Barrell VL	10.00	25.00
NNO Rekha Sharma L	6.00	15.00
NNO Sonequa Martin-Green AB	100.00	200.00
NNO Wilson Cruz AB	20.00	50.00

2019 Star Trek Discovery Season One Case-Toppers

COMPLETE SET (2)	8.00	20.00
COMMON CARD (CT1-CT2)	6.00	15.00
STATED ODDS 1:CASE		

2019 Star Trek Discovery Season One Characters

COMPLETE SET (11)	10.00	25.00
COMMON CARD (E1-E11)	1.50	4.00
STATED ODDS 1:24		

2019 Star Trek Discovery Season One Dual Autographs

COMMON AUTO	20.00	50.00
VL = 200-300 COPIES		
EL = 100-200 COPIES		
STATED OVERALL ODDS 1:12		
NNO J.Isaacs/J.Brook EL	30.00	75.00
NNO A.Rapp/W.Cruz EL	75.00	150.00
NNO R.Wilson/K.Barrell EL	50.00	100.00
NNO S.Martin-Green/J.Isaacs 9CI	75.00	150.00

2019 Star Trek Discovery Season One Full-Bleed Autographs

COMMON AUTO	5.00	12.00
L = 300-500 COPIES		
VL = 200-300 COPIES		
EL = 100-200 COPIES		
STATED OVERALL ODDS 1:12		
NNO Conrad Coates L	6.00	15.00
NNO Doug Jones VL	15.00	40.00
NNO Emily Coutts VL	12.00	30.00
NNO James Frain VL	10.00	25.00
NNO Jason Isaacs EL	30.00	75.00
NNO Jayne Brooke L	10.00	25.00
NNO Jeremy Crittenden L	6.00	15.00
NNO Katherine Barrell VL	12.00	30.00
NNO Kenneth Mitchell EL	12.00	30.00
NNO Mary Chieffo VL	12.00	30.00
NNO Michelle Yeoh VL	75.00	200.00
NNO Oyin Oladejo VL	10.00	25.00
NNO Rainn Wilson EL	30.00	75.00
NNO Riley Gilchrist L	6.00	15.00
NNO Ronnie Rowe Jr. L	6.00	15.00
NNO Sam Vartholomeos/Mirror Connor L	6.00	15.00
NNO Shazad Latif/Ash Tyler/Voq EL	30.00	75.00
NNO Shazad Latif/Mirror Voq AB	30.00	75.00
NNO Sonequa Martin-Green EL	150.00	300.00
NNO Terry Serpico L	6.00	15.00
NNO Wilson Cruz EL	75.00	150.00

2019 Star Trek Discovery Season One Mirror Mirror

COMPLETE SET (8)	75.00	150.00
COMMON CARD (M1-M8)	12.00	30.00
STATED ODDS 1:288		

2019 Star Trek Discovery Season One Opening Sequence Artwork

COMPLETE SET (9)	6.00	15.00
COMMON CARD (01-09)	1.25	3.00
STATED ODDS 1:24		

2019 Star Trek Discovery Season One Relics

COMMON RELIC 12.00 30.00
RANDOMLY INSERTED INTO PACKS
RC1 Commander Michael Burnham 20.00 50.00
RC2 Specialist Michael Burnham 20.00 50.00
RC3 Captain Philippa Georgiou 20.00 50.00
RC4 Captain Gabriel Lorca 20.00 50.00
RC5 Commander Saru 15.00 40.00
RC6 Commander Saru 15.00 40.00
RC9 Lt. Paul Stamets 15.00 40.00
RC10 Dr. Hugh Culber 15.00 40.00
RC11 Admiral Katrina Cornwell 15.00 40.00

2019 Star Trek Discovery Season One Rittenhouse Reward

DP5 Captain Philippa Georgiou 8.00 20.00

2019 Star Trek Discovery Season One Promos

COMPLETE SET (4)
COMMON CARD (P1-P4)
P1 General Distribution 1.25 3.00
P2 Non-Sport Update Magazine 1.50 4.00
P3 Album Exclusive 8.00 20.00
P4 Facebook Exclusive 8.00 20.00

2020 Rittenhouse Star Trek Discovery Season Two

COMPLETE SET (84) 6.00 15.00
UNOPENED BOX (24 PACKS) 60.00 100.00
UNOPENED PACK (5 CARDS) 3.00 5.00
COMMON CARD (1-84) .15 .40

2020 Rittenhouse Star Trek Discovery Season Two Autographed Relics

COMMON AUTO 50.00 100.00
STATED ODDS 1:576
NNO Ethan Peck 75.00 150.00
NNO Hannah Cheesman 75.00 150.00
NNO Michelle Yeoh 125.00 300.00
NNO Sonequa Martin-Green 6CI 150.00 300.00

2020 Rittenhouse Star Trek Discovery Season Two Bordered Autographs

COMMON AUTO 6.00 15.00
STATED OVERALL ODDS 1:12
NNO Alan van Sprang EL 8.00 20.00
NNO Avaah Blackwell EL 8.00 20.00
NNO Bahia Watson as May Ahearn S AB 15.00 40.00
NNO Doug Jones VL 20.00 50.00
NNO Emily Coutts VL 12.00 30.00
NNO Ethan Peck as Spock S AB 100.00 200.00
NNO Hannah Cheesman as Lt. Airiam S AB 30.00 75.00
NNO Hannah Spear as Siranna S AB 15.00 40.00
NNO Jayne Brooke EL 15.00 40.00
NNO Kenneth Mitchell EL 15.00 40.00
NNO Kenneth Mitchell VL 12.00 30.00
NNO Kenric Green as Mike Burnham S AB 8.00 20.00
NNO Mary Chieffo VL 10.00 25.00
NNO Mia Kirschner VL 12.00 30.00
NNO Patrick Kwok-Choon L 8.00 20.00
NNO Rachael Ancheril as Commander Nhan S AB 15.00 40.00
NNO Rainn Wilson EL 30.00 75.00
NNO Rob Brownstein as The Keeper S AB
NNO Shazad Latif S 50.00 100.00
NNO Yadira Guevara-Prip L 8.00 20.00

2020 Rittenhouse Star Trek Discovery Season Two Case-Toppers

COMPLETE SET (2) 6.00 15.00
COMMON CARD (CT1-CT2) 5.00 12.00
STATED ODDS 1:CASE

2020 Rittenhouse Star Trek Discovery Season Two Character Quotes

COMPLETE SET (9) 12.00 30.00
COMMON CARD (CQ01-CQ09) 2.50 6.00
STATED ODDS 1:24

2020 Rittenhouse Star Trek Discovery Season Two Characters

COMPLETE SET W/RR (12)
COMPLETE SET W/O RR (11) 25.00 60.00
COMMON CARD (CC01-CC12) 4.00 10.00
STATED ODDS 1:24
CC12 Spock in Starfleet Uniform RR

2020 Rittenhouse Star Trek Discovery Season Two Dual Autographs

COMMON AUTO 20.00 50.00
STATED OVERALL ODDS 1:12
NNO Ethan Peck/Mia Kirschner EL 75.00 150.00
NNO Mary Wiseman/Bahia Watson 6CI 75.00 150.00
NNO Mary Wiseman/Hannah Cheesman S 100.00 200.00
NNO Sonequa Martin-Green/Ethan Peck S 150.00 300.00
NNO Sonequa Martin-Green/Sonja Sohn S100.00 200.00

2020 Rittenhouse Star Trek Discovery Season Two Expressions of Heroism

COMPLETE SET (9) 50.00 100.00
COMMON CARD (44-52) 6.00 15.00
STATED ODDS 1:144
STATED PRINT RUN 150 SER.#'d SETS
44 Michael Burnham 6.00 15.00
45 Philippa Georgiou 6.00 15.00
46 Sylvia Tilly 6.00 15.00
47 Saru 6.00 15.00
48 Paul Stamets 6.00 15.00
49 Sarek 6.00 15.00
50 Ash Tyler 6.00 15.00
51 Hugh Culber 6.00 15.00
52 Christopher Pike 6.00 15.00

2020 Rittenhouse Star Trek Discovery Season Two Full Bleed Autographs

COMMON AUTO 6.00 15.00
STATED OVERALL ODDS 1:12
NNO Alan van Sprang VL 8.00 20.00
NNO Anthony Rapp EL 25.00 60.00
NNO Avaah Blackwell L 8.00 20.00
NNO Dee Pelletier L 8.00 20.00
NNO Emily Coutts VL 15.00 40.00
NNO Ethan Peck S 125.00 250.00
NNO Hannah Cheesman EL 30.00 75.00
NNO Hannah Spear VL 8.00 20.00
NNO Kenric Green VL 10.00 25.00
NNO Mary Wiseman EL 60.00 120.00
NNO Mia Kirschner VL 12.00 30.00
NNO Oyin Oladejo VL 12.00 30.00
NNO Rachael Ancheril VL 15.00 40.00
NNO Ronnie Rowe Jr. L 8.00 20.00
NNO Sheila McCarthy VL 10.00 25.00
NNO Sonja Sohn S 30.00 75.00
NNO Yadira Guevara-Prip L 10.00 25.00

2020 Rittenhouse Star Trek Discovery Season Two Full Bleed Inscription Autographs

COMMON AUTO 30.00 75.00
STATED OVERALL ODDS 1:12
NNO Rob Brownstein 50.00 100.00
Welcome back to Talos IV

2020 Rittenhouse Star Trek Discovery Season Two Inscription Autographs

COMMON ANCHERIL 25.00 60.00
COMMON BROWNSTEIN 30.00 75.00
COMMON MOMEN 25.00 60.00
COMMON NOTARO 25.00 60.00
COMMON SOHN 30.00 75.00
COMMON SPEAR 30.00 75.00
COMMON TOMLINSON 15.00 40.00
COMMON VAN SPRANG 30.00 75.00
COMMON WATSON 25.00 60.00
STATED OVERALL ODDS 1:12

2020 Rittenhouse Star Trek Discovery Season Two Opening Sequence Artwork Expansion

COMPLETE SET (3) 10.00 25.00
COMMON CARD (Q11-Q13) 5.00 12.00
STATED ODDS 1:96

2020 Rittenhouse Star Trek Discovery Season Two Relics

COMMON MEM (RC13-RC37) 10.00 25.00
STATED ODDS 1:24
RC13 Captain Christopher Pike 25.00 60.00
RC14 Spock 20.00 50.00
RC15 Number One 20.00 50.00
RC16 Commander Nhan 12.00 30.00
RC17 Captain Christopher Pike 15.00 40.00
RC18 Commander Nhan 15.00 40.00
RC19 Commander Michael Burnham 12.00 30.00
RC20 Spock 15.00 40.00
RC21 Lt. Cmdr. Airiam 12.00 30.00
RC22 Philippa Georgiou 15.00 40.00
RC23 Lt. Cmdr. Paul Stamets 12.00 30.00
RC24 Dr. Culber 12.00 30.00
RC27 Commander Jett Reno 12.00 30.00
RC29 Captain Christopher Pike 15.00 40.00
RC34 Commander Michael Burnham 25.00 60.00
RC35 L'Rell 20.00 50.00
RC36 Philippa Georgiou 12.00 30.00
RC37 Commander Michael Burnham 20.00 50.00

2020 Rittenhouse Star Trek Discovery Season Two Short Trek

COMPLETE SET (27) 15.00 40.00
COMMON CARD (SS01-SS27) 1.00 2.50
STATED ODDS 1:8

2020 Rittenhouse Star Trek Discovery Season Two Starfleet's Finest Painted Portrait Metal

COMPLETE SET (10) 500.00 800.00
COMMON CARD (AC50-AC59) 75.00 150.00
STATED ODDS 1:432
STATED PRINT RUN 50 SER.#'d SETS

2020 Rittenhouse Star Trek Discovery Season Two Stickers

COMPLETE SET (9) 20.00 50.00
COMMON CARD (S1-S9) 4.00 10.00
STATED ODDS 1:144

2020 Rittenhouse Star Trek Discovery Season Two Storyboard Artwork

COMPLETE SET (27) 15.00 40.00
COMMON CARD (SB01-SB27) 1.00 2.50
STATED ODDS 1:12

2020 Rittenhouse Star Trek Discovery Season Two Triple Relic

ARCHIVE BOX EXCLUSIVE
TRC1 Pike/Burnham/Nhan 200.00 350.00

2020 Rittenhouse Star Trek Discovery Season Two Promos

P1 General Distribution 3.00 8.00
P2 Non-Sport Update 2.50 6.00
P3 Album Exclusive 12.00 30.00
P4 Social Media

2022 Rittenhouse Star Trek Discovery Season Three

COMPLETE SET (78) 8.00 20.00
UNOPENED BOX (24 PACKS) 60.00 100.00
UNOPENED PACK (5 CARDS) 3.00 5.00
COMMON CARD (1-78) .20 .50
*GOLD: .75X TO 2X BASIC CARDS
*RED: 6X TO 15X BASIC CARDS

2022 Rittenhouse Star Trek Discovery Season Three 32nd Century Technology

COMPLETE SET (9) 12.00 30.00
COMMON CARD (T1-T9) 2.00 5.00
STATED ODDS 1:24

2022 Rittenhouse Star Trek Discovery Season Three Autographed Relics

COMMON AUTO 15.00 40.00
L = 300-500 COPIES
VL = 200-300 COPIES
EL = 100-200 COPIES
S = 100 OR FEWER
STATED OVERALL ODDS 1:12
NNO Doug Jones EL 50.00 100.00
NNO Emily Coutts VL 25.00 60.00
NNO Oyin Oladejo VL 20.00 50.00
NNO Rachael Ancheril EL 60.00 120.00
NNO Sara Mitich VL 25.00 60.00
NNO Sonequa Martin-Green S 150.00 300.00

2022 Rittenhouse Star Trek Discovery Season Three Bordered Autographs

COMMON AUTO 8.00 20.00
L = 300-500 COPIES
VL = 200-300 COPIES
EL = 100-200 COPIES
S = 100 OR FEWER
STATED OVERALL ODDS 1:12
NNO Andrew Shaver AB 10.00 25.00
NNO Avaah Blackwell VL 15.00 40.00
NNO Brendan Beiser AB 10.00 25.00
NNO Christopher Heyerdahl AB 12.00 30.00
NNO Dorren Lee AB 15.00 40.00
NNO Emmanuel Kabongo AB 12.00 30.00
NNO Ian Lake AB 12.00 30.00
NNO Jake Epstein AB 10.00 25.00
NNO Jake Weber VL 12.00 30.00
NNO Javier Botet VL 10.00 25.00
NNO Karen Robinson AB 10.00 25.00
NNO Kenneth Welsh AB 15.00 40.00
NNO Lindsay Owen Pierre AB 12.00 30.00
NNO Oded Fehr VL 10.00 25.00
NNO Oliver Becker AB 10.00 25.00
NNO Riley Gilchrist AB 12.00 30.00
NNO Tara Rosling AB 15.00 40.00
NNO Tig Notaro AB 20.00 50.00
NNO Vanessa Jackson AB 12.00 30.00

2022 Rittenhouse Star Trek Discovery Season Three Characters

COMPLETE SET (8) 12.00 30.00
COMMON CARD (CC1-CC8) 2.50 6.00
STATED ODDS 1:24

2022 Rittenhouse Star Trek Discovery Season Three Costume Design

COMPLETE SET (27) 15.00 40.00
COMMON CARD (CD01-CD27) 1.25 3.00
STATED ODDS 1:8

2022 Rittenhouse Star Trek Discovery Season Three Dual Autographs

COMMON AUTO 60.00 120.00
L = 300-500 COPIES
VL = 200-300 COPIES
EL = 100-200 COPIES
S = 100 OR FEWER
STATED OVERALL ODDS 1:12
NNO S.Martin-Green/M.Yeoh EL 150.00 400.00
NNO S.Martin-Green/M.Wiseman S 75.00 150.00
NNO S.Martin-Green/D.Jones 9CI 125.00 250.00

2022 Rittenhouse Star Trek Discovery Season Three Full Bleed Autographs

COMMON AUTO 5.00 12.00
L = 300-500 COPIES
VL = 200-300 COPIES
EL = 100-200 COPIES
S = 100 OR FEWER
STATED OVERALL ODDS 1:12
NNO Adil Hussain L 8.00 20.00
NNO Ana Sani L 6.00 15.00
NNO Anthony Rapp EL 30.00 75.00
NNO Christopher Heyerdahl L 6.00 15.00
NNO David Ajala VL 25.00 60.00
NNO David Benjamin Tomlinson VL 12.00 30.00
NNO David Benjamin Tomlinson VL 12.00 30.00
NNO Dorren Lee L 6.00 15.00
NNO Doug Jones AB 30.00 75.00
NNO Doug Jones EL 20.00 50.00
NNO Ian Alexander VL 8.00 20.00
NNO Jake Weber VL 12.00 30.00
NNO Janet Kidder VL 15.00 40.00
NNO Javier Botet VL 10.00 25.00
NNO Mary Wiseman EL 30.00 75.00
NNO Michelle Yeoh VL 75.00 200.00
NNO Oded Fehr VL 20.00 50.00
NNO Vanessa Jackson L 8.00 20.00
NNO Wilson Cruz S 100.00 200.00

2022 Rittenhouse Star Trek Discovery Season Three Inscriptions

COMMON ALEXANDER 30.00 75.00
COMMON BLACKWELL 25.00 60.00
COMMON COUTTS 50.00 100.00
COMMON CRUZ 75.00 150.00
COMMON FEHR 25.00 60.00
COMMON JONES 30.00 75.00
COMMON KIDDER 20.00 50.00
COMMON KWOK-CHOON 20.00 50.00
COMMON MITICH 20.00 50.00
COMMON OLADEJO 30.00 75.00
COMMON ROSLING 30.00 75.00
COMMON ROWE JR. 20.00 50.00
COMMON WEBER 20.00 50.00
COMMON WISEMAN 60.00 120.00
STATED OVERALL ODDS 1:12

2022 Rittenhouse Star Trek Discovery Season Three Kelpien-Ba'ul Booklets

COMPLETE SET (8) 12.00 30.00
COMMON CARD (KB1-KB8) 3.00 8.00
*ENGLISH: .5X TO 1.2X BASIC CARDS
STATED ODDS 1:96

2022 Rittenhouse Star Trek Discovery Season Three Metal Case Toppers

COMMON CARD (CT1-CT2)) 8.00 20.00
STATED ODDS 1:CASE

2022 Rittenhouse Star Trek Discovery Season Three Opening Sequence Expansion

COMPLETE SET (4) 12.00 30.00
COMMON CARD (014-017) 4.00 10.00
STATED ODDS 1:72

2022 Rittenhouse Star Trek Discovery Season Three Relics

COMMON MEM (RC38-RC64) 6.00 15.00
STATED ODDS 1:24 W/AUTO RELICS
RC65 IS RITTENHOUSE REWARD
RC38 Emperor Philippa Georgiou 12.00 30.00
RC39 Captain Michael Burnham 15.00 40.00
RC40 Ensign Sylvia Tilly 10.00 25.00
RC41 Lieutenant Paul Stamets 12.00 30.00
RC42 Lt. Audrey Willa 8.00 20.00
RC44 Lieutenant Keyla Detmer 15.00 40.00
RC45 Lieutenant junior grade Joann Owosekun10.0025.00
RC47 Captain Saru 12.00 30.00
RC48 Cleveland Booker 8.00 20.00
RC49 Me Hani Ika Hali Ka Po 10.00 25.00
RC50 Captain Christopher Pike 8.00 20.00
RC58 Commander Michael Burnham 10.00 25.00
RC60 Lieutenant Spock 8.00 20.00
RC65 Ensign Adira Tal RR 75.00 150.00

2022 Rittenhouse Star Trek Discovery Season Three Storyboard Artwork

COMPLETE SET (14) 6.00 15.00
COMMON CARD (SB28-SB41) .75 2.00
STATED ODDS 1:12

2022 Rittenhouse Star Trek Discovery Season Three Promos

COMPLETE SET (3)
COMMON CARD (P1-P3)
P1 General Distribution 2.50 6.00
P2 Philly Non-Sport Show Fall 2021 3.00 8.00
P3 Album Exclusive 8.00 20.00

Picard

2021 Rittenhouse Star Trek Picard Season One

COMPLETE SET (60) 5.00 12.00
UNOPENED BOX (24 PACKS) 60.00 100.00
UNOPENED PACK (5 CARDS) 3.00 4.00
ARCHIVE BOX (118 CARDS)
COMMON CARD (1-60) .15 .40

2021 Rittenhouse Star Trek Picard Season One Bordered Autographs

COMMON AUTO 12.00 30.00
L = 300-500 COPIES
VL = 200-300 COPIES
EL = 100-200 COPIES
S = 100 OR FEWER
STATED OVERALL ODDS 1:12
NNO Alex Diehl S 20.00 50.00
NNO Amirah Vann EL 25.00 60.00
NNO Brent Spiner EL 60.00 120.00
NNO Dominic Burgess S 20.00 50.00
NNO Evan Evagora EL 50.00 100.00
NNO Harry Treadaway S 60.00 120.00
NNO Harry Treadaway S AB
NNO Ian Nunney S 25.00 60.00
NNO Isa Briones S AB 125.00 250.00
NNO Jade Ramsey S 30.00 75.00
NNO Jamie McShane S 25.00 60.00
NNO Jeri Ryan EL 75.00 150.00
NNO John Ales S 20.00 50.00
NNO Jonathan Del Arco EL 30.00 75.00
NNO Jonathan Frakes S AB 100.00 200.00
NNO Lulu Wilson S 30.00 75.00
NNO Marina Sirtis S AB 75.00 150.00
NNO Matt Perfetuo S 25.00 60.00
NNO Maya Eshet S 20.00 50.00
NNO Nikita Ramsey S 30.00 75.00
NNO Patrick Stewart S AB 250.00 500.00
NNO Peyton List S AB
NNO Peyton List S 50.00 100.00
NNO Rebecca Wisocky S 25.00 60.00
NNO Santiago Cabrera EL 30.00 75.00
NNO Sumalee Montano EL 15.00 40.00
NNO Tamlyn Tomita S 30.00 75.00
NNO Tamlyn Tomita S AB

2021 Rittenhouse Star Trek Picard Season One Case Topper

NNO Data's Painting Called "Daughter" 6.00 15.00

2021 Rittenhouse Star Trek Picard Season One Cast of Picard

COMPLETE SET W/RR (10)
COMPLETE SET W/O RR (9) 50.00 100.00
COMMON CARD (CP01-CP10) 6.00 15.00
STATED ODDS 1:96
CP10 Isa Briones RR

2021 Rittenhouse Star Trek Picard Season One Characters

COMPLETE SET (22) 20.00 50.00
COMMON CARD (C01-C22) 1.50 4.00
STATED ODDS 1:12

2021 Rittenhouse Star Trek Picard Season One Dual Autographs

COMMON AUTO
L = 300-500 COPIES
VL = 200-300 COPIES
EL = 100-200 COPIES
S = 100 OR FEWER
STATED OVERALL ODDS 1:12
NNO H.Treadaway/I.Briones S 125.00 250.00
NNO I.Briones/J.Del Arco S 75.00 150.00
NNO J.Ramsey/N.Ramsey EL 30.00 75.00
NNO J.Ryan/E.Evagora 6CI 100.00 200.00
NNO M.Sirtis/J.Frakes S 100.00 200.00
NNO P.Stewart/M.Sirtis 9CI 250.00 500.00
NNO P.List/H.Treadaway EL 50.00 100.00
NNO S.Cabrera/D.Burgess EL 25.00 60.00

2021 Rittenhouse Star Trek Picard Season One Full Bleed Autographs

COMMON AUTO 5.00 12.00
L = 300-500 COPIES
VL = 200-300 COPIES
EL = 100-200 COPIES
S = 100 OR FEWER
STATED OVERALL ODDS 1:12
A01 Patrick Stewart S 200.00 400.00
A03 Isa Briones S 125.00 250.00
A04 Jeri Ryan EL 75.00 150.00
A05 Jonathan Del Arco EL 20.00 50.00
A06 Isa Briones S 125.00 250.00
A07 Marina Sirtis EL 75.00 150.00
A08 Jonathan Frakes EL 60.00 120.00
A11 Santiago Cabrera EL 20.00 50.00
A12 Harry Treadaway EL 30.00 75.00
A13 Evan Evagora EL 25.00 60.00
A14 Peyton List S 75.00 150.00
A17 Tamlyn Tomita EL 25.00 60.00
A19 Sumalee Montano L 6.00 15.00
A21 Brent Spiner EL 60.00 120.00
A24 Merrin Dungey L 6.00 15.00
A30 Dominic Burgess VL 10.00 25.00
A31 John Ales L 8.00 20.00
A32 Ayushi Chhabra VL 8.00 20.00
A34 Jane Hae Kim L 6.00 15.00
A36 Jade Ramsey EL 15.00 40.00
A37 Nikita Ramsey EL 12.00 30.00
A38 Matt Perfetuo EL 10.00 25.00
A40 Lulu Wilson L 10.00 25.00
A42 Harry Treadaway EL 30.00 75.00
A43 Jamie McShane VL 12.00 30.00
A49 Amirah Vann L 6.00 15.00

2021 Rittenhouse Star Trek Picard Season One Holocrew of La Sirena

COMPLETE SET (5) 12.00 30.00
COMMON CARD (H1-H5) 5.00 12.00
STATED ODDS 1:48

2021 Rittenhouse Star Trek Picard Season One Promotional Travel Posters

COMPLETE SET (9) 8.00 20.00
COMMON CARD (T1-T9) 1.50 4.00
STATED ODDS 1:24

2021 Rittenhouse Star Trek Picard Season One Romulan Tarot Cards

COMPLETE SET (32) 15.00 40.00
COMMON CARD 1.25 3.00
STATED ODDS 1:6

2021 Rittenhouse Star Trek Picard Season One Promos

P1 General Distribution 1.50 4.00
P2 Social Media 30.00 75.00
P3 Album Exclusive

Movies

1979 Topps Star Trek The Motion Picture

COMPLETE SET (88) 10.00 25.00
COMPLETE SET W/STICKERS (110) 15.00 40.00
UNOPENED BOX (36 PACKS) 100.00 200.00
UNOPENED PACK (10 CARDS+1 STICKER) 3.00 6.00
COMMON CARD (1-88) .10 .25

1979 Topps Star Trek The Motion Picture Stickers

COMPLETE SET (22) 3.00 8.00
COMMON STICKER (1-22) .20 .50

1979 Topps Star Trek Colonial Bread Backs

COMPLETE SET (33) 6.00 15.00
COMMON CARD (1-33) .40 1.00

1979 Topps Star Trek Kilpatrick Bread Backs

COMPLETE SET (33) 8.00 20.00
COMMON CARD (1-33) .50 1.25

1979 Lyons Maid Star Trek

COMPLETE SET (25) 15.00 40.00
COMMON CARD (1-25) 1.00 2.50

1979 Topps Star Trek Manor Bread Backs

COMPLETE SET (33)	4.00	10.00
COMMON CARD (1-33)	.20	.50

1979 Star Trek Rainbo Bread

COMPLETE SET (33)	4.00	10.00
COMMON CARD (1-33)	.40	.50

1982 FTCC Star Trek II The Wrath of Khan

COMPLETE SET (30)	20.00	50.00
UNOPENED BOX (30 PACKS)	60.00	100.00
UNOPENED PACK (2 CARDS)	3.00	5.00
COMMON CARD (1-30)	.75	2.00

1982 Monty Gum Star Trek II The Wrath of Khan

COMPLETE SET (100)	20.00	50.00
COMMON CARD (1-100)	.40	1.00

1984 FTCC Star Trek III The Search for Spock

COMPLETE SET (60)	15.00	40.00
UNOPENED BOX (36 PACKS)	40.00	75.00
UNOPENED PACK (5 CARDS)	2.00	3.00
COMMON CARD (1-60)	.30	.75

1987 FTCC Star Trek The Voyage Home

COMPLETE SET (60)	12.00	30.00
UNOPENED BOX (36 PACKS)	40.00	50.00
UNOPENED PACK (5 CARDS)	1.50	2.00
COMMON CARD (1-60)	.25	.60

1995 SkyBox Star Trek Generations

COMPLETE SET (72)	6.00	15.00
UNOPENED BOX (36 PACKS)	20.00	30.00
UNOPENED PACK (6 CARDS)	1.25	1.50
COMMON CARD (1-72)	.15	.40

1995 SkyBox Star Trek Generations Foil

COMPLETE SET (3)	10.00	25.00
COMMON CARD (F1-F3)	4.00	10.00
STATED ODDS 1:18		

1995 SkyBox Star Trek Generations SkyMotion

1 Redemption Card		
2 SkyMotion	30.00	80.00
3 SkyMotion Oversized	15.00	40.00

1995 SkyBox Star Trek Generations Spectra-Etch

COMPLETE SET (3)	15.00	40.00
COMMON CARD (S1-S3)	6.00	15.00
STATED ODDS 1:36		

1995 SkyBox Star Trek Generations Promos

0 MNBA MasterCard/1000*	12.00	30.00
S1a Prototpye (sic)	1.25	3.00
S1b Prototype New Zealand Edition	1.25	3.00

1996 Fleer SkyBox Star Trek First Contact

COMPLETE SET (60)	5.00	12.00
UNOPENED BOX (36 PACKS)	50.00	60.00
UNOPENED PACK (9 CARDS)	1.50	2.00
COMMON CARD (1-60)	.15	.40
SPINER AUTO ODDS 1:3,600		
NNO Brent Spiner AU	500.00	800.00

1996 Fleer SkyBox Star Trek First Contact Behind-the-Scenes

COMPLETE SET (10)	12.00	30.00
COMMON CARD (BS1-BS10)	1.50	4.00
STATED ODDS 1:6		

1996 Fleer SkyBox Star Trek First Contact Blueprint Posters

COMPLETE SET (3)	15.00	40.00
COMMON CARD (S1-S3)	6.00	15.00
STATED ODDS 1:36		

1996 Fleer SkyBox Star Trek First Contact Characters

COMPLETE SET (10)	25.00	60.00
COMMON CARD (C1-C10)	3.00	8.00
STATED ODDS 1:9		

1996 Fleer SkyBox Star Trek First Contact Enterprise

COMPLETE SET (6)	15.00	40.00
COMMON CARD (E1-E6)	3.00	8.00
STATED ODDS 1:8		

1996 Fleer SkyBox Star Trek First Contact Techno-Cel Borg

COMPLETE SET (12)	10.00	25.00
COMMON CARD (B1-B12)	2.00	5.00
STATED ODDS 1:8		

1998 SkyBox Star Trek Insurrection

COMPLETE SET (72)	6.00	15.00
UNOPENED BOX (36 PACKS)	50.00	75.00
UNOPENED PACK (9 CARDS)	2.00	3.00
COMMON CARD (1-72)	.15	.40

1998 SkyBox Star Trek Insurrection Gold

COMPLETE SET (7)	500.00	800.00
COMMON CARD (G1-G7)	80.00	150.00
STATED PRINT RUN 400 SER.#'d SETS		

1998 SkyBox Star Trek Insurrection Autographs

COMMON CARD (A1-A19)	6.00	15.00
STATED ODDS 1:36		
A1 Patrick Stewart	100.00	250.00
A2 Jonathan Frakes	50.00	125.00
A3 Brent Spiner	60.00	150.00
A4 Marina Sirtis	50.00	125.00
A5 LeVar Burton	30.00	75.00
A6 Gates McFadden	30.00	75.00
A10 Anthony Zerbe	12.00	30.00
A19 Donna Murphy	25.00	60.00

1998 SkyBox Star Trek Insurrection Okudagrams

COMPLETE SET (9)	6.00	15.00
COMMON CARD (OK1-OK9)	.75	2.00
STATED ODDS 1:8		

1998 SkyBox Star Trek Insurrection Relationships

COMPLETE SET (9)	8.00	20.00
COMMON CARD (R1-R9)	1.25	3.00
STATED ODDS 1:8		

1998 SkyBox Star Trek Insurrection Schematics

COMPLETE SET (9)	2.00	5.00
COMMON CARD (S1-S9)	.40	1.00
STATED ODDS 1:4		

1998 SkyBox Star Trek Insurrection Wardrobes

COMPLETE SET (9)	2.00	5.00
COMMON CARD (W1-W9)	.40	1.00
STATED ODDS 1:4		

2002 Star Trek Nemesis

COMPLETE SET (72)	4.00	10.00
UNOPENED BOX (40 PACKS)	100.00	150.00
UNOPENED PACK (9 CARDS)	2.50	4.00
COMMON CARD (1-72)	.12	.30
RC1 STATED ODDS ONE PER CASE		
RC1 Romulan Costume	12.50	30.00

2002 Star Trek Nemesis Autographs

COMPLETE SET (12)	400.00	750.00
COMMON CARD (NA1-NA12)	10.00	25.00
STATED ODDS 1:20		
NA11 (BRYAN SINGER) ISSUED IN EXPANSION SET		
NA1 Michael Dorn SP	30.00	75.00
NA2 Ron Perlman	20.00	50.00
NA3 Tom Hardy	300.00	750.00
NA5 Kate Mulgrew	30.00	75.00
NA6a Brent Spiner B-4 SP	60.00	150.00
NA6b Brent Spiner Data SP	60.00	150.00
NA10 Marina Sirtis	25.00	60.00
NA12 Patrick Stewart SP	100.00	200.00

2002 Star Trek Nemesis Casting Call

COMPLETE SET (7)	20.00	50.00
COMMON CARD (CC1-CC7)	3.00	8.00
STATED ODDS 1:40		

2002 Star Trek Nemesis Romulan History

COMPLETE SET (27)	7.50	20.00
COMMON CARD (R1-R27)	.40	1.00
STATED ODDS 1:3		

2002 Star Trek Nemesis Romulan History Autographs

COMPLETE SET (14)	150.00	300.00
COMMON CARD (RA1-RA14)	10.00	25.00
STATED ODDS 1:20		
RA4 ISSUED AS ALBUM EXCLUSIVE		
RA4 Lawrence Montaigne ALB	15.00	30.00
RA12 Andreas Katsulas SP	20.00	40.00
RA14 Joanne Linville SP	30.00	75.00

2002 Star Trek Nemesis Technology

COMPLETE SET (8)	4.00	10.00
COMMON CARD (T1-T8)	.60	1.50
STATED ODDS 1:8		

2002 Star Trek Nemesis Promos

P3 Riker/Troi ALB	2.00	5.00

2003 Star Trek Nemesis Expansion

COMPLETE SET (19)	20.00	50.00
COMMON CARD (NE1-NE18)	.75	2.00
STATED PRINT RUN 999 SER. #'d SETS		
NA11 STATED ODDS ONE PER 5 SET PURCHASE		
CC1 Commander William Riker MEM	15.00	30.00
NA11 Bryan Singer AU	90.00	150.00

2002 Star Trek Nemesis Wallace Theater Promos

COMPLETE SET (6)	20.00	50.00
COMMON CARD (PT1-PT6)	5.00	12.00

2009 Star Trek Movie

COMPLETE SET (81)	8.00	20.00
UNOPENED BOX (24 PACKS)	200.00	300.00
UNOPENED PACK (5 CARDS)	8.00	12.00
COMMON CARD (1-81)	.15	.40

2009 Star Trek Movie Autographs

COMMON CARD (UNNUMBERED)	12.00	30.00
AUTO/MEM COMBINED ODDS 2:BOX		
NNO Alex Kurtzman	30.00	80.00
NNO Anton Yelchin	120.00	250.00
NNO Bruce Greenwood	20.00	50.00
NNO Chris Hemsworth	50.00	100.00
NNO Chris Pine	250.00	400.00
NNO Eric Bana	60.00	120.00
NNO J.J. Abrams	150.00	300.00
NNO John Cho	50.00	100.00
NNO Karl Urban	30.00	80.00
NNO Roberto Orci	75.00	150.00
NNO Simon Pegg	60.00	120.00
NNO Zachary Quinto	50.00	100.00
NNO Zoe Saldana	150.00	300.00

2009 Star Trek Movie Behind-the-Scenes

COMPLETE SET (6)	4.00	10.00
COMMON CARD (1-6)	.75	2.00
STATED ODDS 1:9		

2009 Star Trek Movie Case-Topper Posters

COMPLETE SET (2)	10.00	25.00
COMMON POSTER (UNNUMBERED)	6.00	15.00
STATED ODDS ONE PER CASE		

2009 Star Trek Movie Costumes

COMPLETE SET (11)	120.00	225.00
COMMON CARD	8.00	20.00
AUTO/MEM COMBINED ODDS TWO PER BOX		
CC1 Kirk	15.00	40.00
CC2 Spock	15.00	40.00
CC3 Uhura	12.00	30.00
CC4 Sulu	12.00	30.00
CC5 Chekov	12.00	30.00
CC6 Spock	15.00	40.00
CC7 Bones	15.00	40.00
CC8 Captain Pike	12.00	30.00
CC9 Nero	15.00	40.00

2009 Star Trek Movie Relics

RC1 STATED ODDS ONE PER 3 CASE PURCHASE		
RC2,RC3 STATED ODDS ONE PER 6 CASE PURCHASE		
RC1 Secure Order Attache 3CI	30.00	80.00
RC2 Starfleet Cadet Badge 6CI	500.00	800.00
RC3 Starfleet Badge 6CI	1000.00	1500.00

2009 Star Trek Movie Stars

COMPLETE SET (9)	5.00	12.00
COMPLETE SET W/RR (10)	12.00	30.00
COMMON CARD (S1-S9)	.75	2.00
STATED ODDS 1:6		
SP10 ISSUED AS RITTENHOUSE REWARD		
S10 Spock SP (Rittenhouse Reward)	10.00	25.00

2009 Star Trek Movie USS Enterprise

COMPLETE SET (6)	4.00	10.00
COMMON CARD (E1-E6)	.60	1.50
STATED ODDS 1:9		

2009 Star Trek Movie Promos

COMPLETE SET (4)	6.00	15.00
COMMON CARD	.75	2.00
P3 U.S.S. Enterprise ALB	3.00	8.00
CP1 Uhura/(Spring Philly)	4.00	10.00

2009 Star Trek Movie Kellogg's

COMPLETE SET (12)	30.00	80.00
COMMON CARD (1-12)	4.00	10.00
INSERTED IN SPECIALLY MARKED		
PACKAGES OF KELLOGG'S CEREAL		

2013 Star Trek Into Darkness

COMPLETE SET (11)	350.00	500.00
COMMON CARD	3.00	8.00
CP Chris Pine AU MEM	150.00	250.00
ZQ Zachary Quinto AU MEM	120.00	200.00

2017 Star Trek Beyond

COMPLETE SET (85)	5.00	12.00
UNOPENED BOX (24 PACKS)		
UNOPENED PACK (5 CARDS)		
COMMON CARD (1-85)	.12	.30
*METAL: 6X TO 15X BASIC CARDS	2.00	5.00
MP11 Star Trek (2009) Movie Poster Clear Plastic Card		

2017 Star Trek Beyond Anton Yelchin In Memoriam

COMPLETE SET (9)	200.00	400.00
COMMON CARD (M1-M9)	20.00	50.00
STATED ODDS 1:288		

2017 Star Trek Beyond Autographed Relics

COMMON CARD	25.00	60.00
STATED ODDS OVERALL 1:12		
NNO Alice Eve VL	60.00	120.00
NNO Chris Pine EL 9CI	100.00	200.00
NNO Sofia Boutella VL	60.00	120.00
NNO Zoe Saldana EL 6CI	125.00	250.00

2017 Star Trek Beyond Autographs

COMMON CARD (UNNUMBERED)	5.00	12.00
STATED ODDS OVERALL 1:12		
NNO Ben Cross L	8.00	20.00
NNO Chris Pine VL	75.00	150.00
NNO Danny Puci VL	8.00	20.00
NNO Doug Jung VL	6.00	15.00
NNO Faran Tahir VL	6.00	15.00
NNO Fiona Vroom VL	8.00	20.00
NNO Fraser Aitcheson VL	6.00	15.00
NNO Jacob Kogan VL	6.00	15.00
NNO Jeremy Raymond/Nibiran Leader VL	6.00	15.00
NNO Jeremy Raymond/Shazeer VL	6.00	15.00
NNO Justin Lin/Director EL	20.00	50.00
NNO Karl Urban VL	20.00	50.00
NNO Lorenzo James Henrie VL	6.00	15.00
NNO Lydia Wilson L	6.00	15.00
NNO Melissa Roxburgh VL	6.00	15.00
NNO Nazheen Contractor	10.00	25.00
NNO Sofia Boutella VL	30.00	75.00
NNO Zachary Quinto VL	30.00	75.00

2017 Star Trek Beyond Classic Movie Design Autographs

COMMON CARD (UNNUMBERED)	5.00	12.00
STATED ODDS OVERALL 1:12		
NNO Alice Eve L	25.00	60.00
NNO Bruce Greenwood L	10.00	25.00
NNO Danny Pudi EL	10.00	25.00
NNO Doug Jung VL	6.00	15.00
NNO Faran Tahir VL	6.00	15.00
NNO Fiona Vroom VL	8.00	20.00
NNO Fraser Aitcheson VL	6.00	15.00
NNO Jacob Kogan VL	6.00	15.00
NNO Jeremy Raymond L	6.00	15.00
NNO Karl Urban VL	20.00	50.00
NNO Lorenzo James Henrie VL	6.00	15.00
NNO Lydia Wilson VL	6.00	15.00
NNO Melissa Roxburgh VL	6.00	15.00
NNO Noel Clarke L	6.00	15.00
NNO Peter Weller L	15.00	40.00
NNO Simon Pegg EL	120.00	250.00
NNO Sofia Boutella VL	30.00	75.00
NNO Zoe Saldana EL	100.00	200.00

2017 Star Trek Beyond Dual Character Relics

COMPLETE SET (5)	60.00	120.00
COMMON CARD (DC1-DC5)	10.00	25.00
STATED ODDS OVERALL 1:24		
DC1 Kirk and Spock VL	15.00	40.00
DC3 Kirk and Scotty VL	12.00	30.00
DC4 Kirk and Krall EL	15.00	40.00

2017 Star Trek Beyond Dual Relics

COMPLETE SET (4)	30.00	75.00
COMMON CARD (DR1-DR4)	8.00	20.00
STATED ODDS OVERALL 1:24		
DR1 Captain Kirk	12.00	30.00
DR2 Spock	10.00	25.00
DR4 Jaylah	10.00	25.00

2017 Star Trek Beyond Expansion Relics

COMMON CARD (SKIP #'d)	8.00	20.00
STATED ODDS OVERALL 1:24		
RC4 Starfleet Academy Chair	15.00	40.00
RC5 Shuttlecraft Interior	50.00	100.00
RC13 Kirk and Khan Spacejump Suit	15.00	40.00
RC14 Klingon Shoulder Armor	20.00	50.00
RC16 Admiral Pike Uniform	200.00	300.00

2017 Star Trek Beyond Leonard Nimoy In Memoriam Expansion

COMPLETE SET (6)	150.00	300.00
COMMON CARD (M10-M15)	25.00	60.00
STATED ODDS 1:288		

2017 Star Trek Beyond Metal Posters

COMPLETE SET (9)	60.00	120.00
COMMON CARD (MC1-MC9)	5.00	12.00
STATED ODDS 1:144		
MC1 Kirk	8.00	20.00
MC3 Uhura	6.00	15.00
MC4 Spock	6.00	15.00
MC6 Sulu	6.00	15.00
MC7 Scotty	6.00	15.00
MC8 Chekov	6.00	15.00
MC9 McCoy	8.00	20.00

2017 Star Trek Beyond Patches

COMMON CARD (BP1-BP9)	5.00	12.00
STATED ODDS 1:144		
BP1 Spock (U.S.S. Franklin)	10.00	25.00
BP2 Scotty (U.S.S. Franklin)	8.00	20.00
BP3 Kirk (Yorktown Military)	12.00	30.00
BP4 Commander Finnegan (Yorktown Military)	6.00	15.00
BP6 Kirk (Starfleet Flight Suit)	10.00	25.00
BP7 Chekov (Starfleet Flight Suit)	8.00	20.00
BP8 McCoy (Starfleet Flight Suit - STID)	10.00	25.00
BP9 Carol Marcus (Starfleet Flight Suit - STID)	8.00	20.00

2017 Star Trek Beyond Quotables

COMPLETE SET (15)	12.00	30.00
COMMON CARD (Q1-Q15)	1.00	2.50
STATED ODDS 1:18		

2017 Star Trek Beyond Relics

COMPLETE SET (2)	75.00	150.00
COMMON CARD (BRC1-BRC2)	30.00	75.00
STATED ODDS OVERALL 1:24		
BRC1 Enterprise Interior VL	30.00	75.00
BRC2 Swarm Ship EL	50.00	100.00

2017 Star Trek Beyond Seven-Piece Bridge Crew Relic

ARCHIVE BOX EXCLUSIVE		
BC1 Chekov/McCoy/Uhura Kirk/Spock/Scotty/Sulu AB	300.00	500.00

2017 Star Trek Beyond Single Relics

COMMON CARD	6.00	15.00
STATED ODDS OVERALL 1:24		
SR1 Captain Kirk L	10.00	25.00
SR2 Spock L	8.00	20.00
SR3 Uhura L	10.00	25.00
SR4 Scotty L	8.00	20.00
SR6 Krall EL	15.00	40.00
SR7 Jaylah L	8.00	20.00
SR8a Chekov (Rittenhouse Reward)		

2017 Star Trek Beyond Uniform Pins

COMMON CARD	6.00	15.00
STATED ODDS OVERALL 1:24		
UB1 Kirk	10.00	25.00
UB6 Chekov	8.00	20.00
UB6a Chekov (command badge) (Archive Box Exclusive)	60.00	120.00
UB8 Kirk	8.00	20.00

2017 Star Trek Beyond Promos

COMMON CARD (P1-P3)	1.50	4.00
P2 Non-Sport Update Magazine	2.00	5.00
P3 Album Exclusive	12.00	30.00

Expanded Universe

1995-96 SkyBox 30 Years of Star Trek

COMPLETE SET (300)	15.00	40.00
PHASE ONE SET (100)	6.00	15.00
PHASE TWO SET (100)	6.00	15.00
PHASE THREE SET (100)	6.00	15.00
UNOPENED PH.ONE BOX (36 PACKS)	40.00	50.00
UNOPENED PH.ONE PACK (8 CARDS)	1.25	1.50
UNOPENED PH.TWO BOX (36 PACKS)	40.00	50.00
UNOPENED PH.TWO PACK (8 CARDS)	1.25	1.50
UNOPENED PH.THREE BOX (36 PACKS)	40.00	50.00
UNOPENED PH.THREE PACK (8 CARDS)	1.25	1.50
PHASE ONE (1-100)	.12	.30
PHASE TWO (101-200)	.12	.30
PHASE THREE (201-300)	.12	.30

1995-96 SkyBox 30 Years of Star Trek 3-D Motion

COMPLETE SET (3)	10.00	25.00
COMMON CARD (M1-M3)	4.00	10.00
STATED ODDS 1:18		

1995-96 SkyBox 30 Years of Star Trek Die-Cut Technology

COMPLETE SET (3)	15.00	40.00
COMMON CARD (D1-D3)	6.00	15.00
STATED ODDS 1:36		
INSERTED INTO PHASE ONE PACKS		

1995-96 SkyBox 30 Years of Star Trek Dopplegangers

COMPLETE SET (9)	20.00	50.00
COMMON CARD (F1-F9)	3.00	8.00
STATED ODDS 1:12		
INSERTED INTO PHASE TWO PACKS		

1995-96 SkyBox 30 Years of Star Trek Evolution of Technology

COMPLETE SET (9)	20.00	50.00
COMMON CARD (E1-E9)	3.00	8.00
STATED ODDS 1:12		
INSERTED INTO PHASE ONE PACKS		

1995-96 SkyBox 30 Years of Star Trek Game Cards

COMPLETE SET (6)	2.00	5.00
COMMON CARD	.40	1.00
STATED ODDS 1:6		
INSERTED INTO PHASE THREE PACKS		
UNNUMBERED SET		

1995-96 SkyBox 30 Years of Star Trek Poster Order Cards

COMPLETE SET (9)	10.00	25.00
COMMON CARD (1-9)	2.50	6.00
STATED ODDS 1:5		

1995-96 SkyBox 30 Years of Star Trek Registry Plaques

COMPLETE SET (9)	100.00	200.00
COMMON CARD (R1-R9)	12.00	30.00
STATED ODDS 1:72		
INSERTED INTO PHASE ONE PACKS		

1995-96 SkyBox 30 Years of Star Trek Space Mural Foil

COMPLETE SET (9)	25.00	60.00
COMMON CARD (S1-S9)	4.00	10.00
STATED ODDS 1:12		
INSERTED INTO PHASE THREE PACKS		

1995-96 SkyBox 30 Years of Star Trek Undercover

COMPLETE SET (9)	50.00	100.00
COMMON CARD (L1-L9)	6.00	15.00
STATED ODDS 1:18		
INSERTED INTO PHASE TWO PACKS		

1995-96 SkyBox 30 Years of Star Trek Promos

PROMOS ARE UNNUMBERED		
1 NCC-1701, tricorder; 2-card panel		
2 NCC-1701 Non-Sport Update	2.00	5.00
3 MBNA bank		
4 Kirk and Alien 2-card panel		
5 Unreleased 2-card panel		

2003 Complete Star Trek Animated Adventures

COMPLETE SET (198)	4.00	10.00
UNOPENED BOX (40 PACKS)	50.00	60.00
UNOPENED PACK (8 CARDS)	1.50	2.00
COMMON CARD (1-198)	.08	.25
CHECKLIST STATED ODDS 1:20		

2003 Complete Star Trek Animated Adventures Autographs

COMMON CARD	8.00	20.00
STATED ODDS 1:40		

A3 ISSUED AS ALBUM EXCLUSIVE		
A1 William Shatner	150.00	300.00
A2 Leonard Nimoy	250.00	500.00
A3 George Takei ALB	30.00	80.00
A4 Nichelle Nichols	15.00	40.00
A5a Majel Barrett (Lt. M'Ress)	50.00	100.00
A5b Majel Barrett (Nurse Chapel)	60.00	120.00
A6a James Doohan (Lt. Cmdr. Scott)	60.00	120.00
A6b James Doohan (Lt. Arex)	50.00	100.00
A7 Dorothy Fontana	15.00	40.00

2003 Complete Star Trek Animated Adventures Captain Kirk in Motion

COMPLETE SET (9)	12.50	30.00
COMMON CARD (K1-K9)	1.50	4.00
STATED ODDS 1:20		

2003 Complete Star Trek Animated Adventures Die-Cut CD-ROMs

COMPLETE SET (5)	10.00	25.00
COMMON CARD	2.50	6.00
STATED ODDS 1:BOX		
UNNUMBERED SET		

2003 Complete Star Trek Animated Adventures James Doohan Tribute

COMPLETE SET (9)	2.50	6.00
COMMON CARD (JD1-JD9)	.40	1.00
STATED ODDS 1:4		

2003 Complete Star Trek Animated Adventures Star Trek Micro-Cels

COMPLETE SET (22)	40.00	100.00
COMMON CARD (MC1-MC22)	2.50	6.00
STATED ODDS 1:20		

2003 Complete Star Trek Animated Adventures Enterprise Bridge Crew

COMPLETE SET (9)	7.50	20.00
COMMON CARD (BC1-BC9)	1.25	3.00
STATED ODDS 1:8		

2003 Complete Star Trek Animated Adventures Promos

COMPLETE SET (3)	2.50	6.00
COMMON CARD (P1-P3)	.75	2.00
P3 McCoy/Kirk/Spock ALB	2.00	5.00

2007 Complete Star Trek Movies

COMPLETE SET (90)	4.00	10.00
UNOPENED BOX (24 PACKS)	50.00	75.00
UNOPENED PACK (9 CARDS)	3.00	4.00
UNOPENED ARCHIVE BOX	1600.00	2000.00
COMMON CARD (1-90)	.10	.25

2007 Complete Star Trek Movies Autographs

COMMON CARD	6.00	15.00
STATED ODDS 1:12		
A20 ISSUED AS 2-CASE INCENTIVE		
A40 ISSUED AS ALBUM EXCLUSIVE		
A50 ISSUED AS 6-CASE INCENTIVE		
L (LIMITED): 300-500 CARDS		
VL (VERY LIMITED): 200-300 CARDS		
A1 Ricardo Montalban VL	200.00	300.00
A2 Stephen Collins VL	50.00	100.00
A3 Malcolm McDowell VL	60.00	120.00
A6 Robin Curtis	10.00	25.00
A7 George Murdock	8.00	20.00
A9 Harve Bennett VL	75.00	150.00
A10 Michele Ameen Billy	8.00	20.00
A11 Phil Morris L	15.00	40.00
A12 Ike Eisenmann	8.00	20.00
A13 Cathie Shirriff	8.00	20.00
A14 Christopher Lloyd VL	90.00	175.00
A15 Todd Bryant	8.00	20.00
A16 Charles Cooper	8.00	20.00
A17 Spice Williams	8.00	20.00
A19 Jenette Goldstein	8.00	20.00
A20 George Takei CI	30.00	80.00
A25 Cynthia Gouw	8.00	20.00
A26 Neal McDonough L	10.00	25.00
A28 Robert Picardo VL	60.00	120.00
A30 Walter Koenig L	30.00	60.00
A33 F. Murray Abraham L	20.00	50.00
A34 W. Morgan Sheppard L	10.00	25.00
A38 Rene Auberjonois VL	30.00	80.00
A39 Judson Scott	8.00	20.00
A40 Miguel Ferrer ALB	15.00	40.00
A49 Catherine Hicks L	20.00	50.00
A50 William Shatner 6CI	200.00	300.00

2007 Complete Star Trek Movies Behind-the-Scenes

COMPLETE SET (10)	12.00	30.00
COMMON CARD (B1-B10)	1.50	4.00
STATED ODDS 1:24		

2007 Complete Star Trek Movies Camp Khitomer Banners

COMPLETE SET (4)	75.00	150.00
COMMON CARD (KB1-KB4)	25.00	50.00
STATED ODDS 1:120		
STATED PRINT RUN 575 SER.#'d SETS		

2007 Complete Star Trek Movies Character Logs

COMPLETE SET (10)	15.00	40.00
COMMON CARD (C1-C10)	2.50	6.00
STATED ODDS 1:24		

2007 Complete Star Trek Movies Costumes

COMPLETE SET (16)	100.00	200.00
COMMON CARD	5.00	12.00
STATED ODDS 1:12		
STATED PRINT RUN 701-1701		
MC1 Captain Kirk	25.00	50.00
MC2 Spock	10.00	25.00
MC3 Lt. Sulu	8.00	20.00
MC4 Lt. Chekov	8.00	20.00
MC5 Scotty	8.00	20.00
MC9 Lt. Uhura	6.00	15.00
MC11 Dr. McCoy	8.00	20.00
MC13 Lt. Chekov	6.00	15.00
MC14 Dr. McCoy	8.00	20.00
MC15 Data	6.00	15.00
MC16 Commander Riker	6.00	15.00

2007 Complete Star Trek Movies Gold Plaque

COMPLETE SET (10)	20.00	50.00
COMMON CARD (G1-G10)	3.00	8.00
STATED ODDS 1:24		

2007 Complete Star Trek Movies In Motion

COMPLETE SET (10)	15.00	40.00
COMMON CARD (L1-L10)	3.00	8.00
STATED ODDS 1:24		

2007 Complete Star Trek Movies Movie Posters

COMPLETE SET (2)	20.00	50.00
COMMON CARD (MP1-MP2)	12.00	30.00
STATED ODDS 1:CASE		

2007 Complete Star Trek Movies Plot Synopses

COMPLETE SET (30)	15.00	40.00
COMMON CARD (S1-S30)	.75	2.00
STATED ODDS 1:8		

2007 Complete Star Trek Movies Profiles

COMPLETE SET (20)	15.00	40.00
COMMON CARD (P1-P20)	1.25	3.00
STATED ODDS 1:12		

2007 Complete Star Trek Movies Promos

COMMON CARD	.75	2.00
P3 Album Exclusive	3.00	8.00
CP1 Convention	1.25	3.00
CP2 NSU Allentown	1.25	3.00
FX1 Canadian Fan Expo	6.00	15.00

2003 Legends of Star Trek Captain Kirk

COMPLETE SET (9)	12.00	30.00
COMMON CARD (L1-L9)	2.50	6.00
STATED PRINT RUN 1,701 SER. #'d SETS		

2004 Legends of Star Trek Dr. McCoy

COMPLETE SET (9)	10.00	20.00
COMMON CARD (L1-L9)	1.00	2.50
STATED PRINT RUN 1,701 SER. #'d SETS		

2004 Legends of Star Trek Scotty Uhura Sulu

COMPLETE SET (9)	10.00	20.00
COMMON CARD (L1-L9)	1.00	2.50
STATED PRINT RUN 1,701 SER. #'d SETS		

2004 Legends of Star Trek Spock

COMPLETE SET (9)	10.00	20.00
COMMON CARD (L1-L9)	1.00	2.50
STATED PRINT RUN 1,701 SER. #'d SETS		

2005 Legends of Star Trek Chekov Rand Chapel

COMPLETE SET (9)	8.00	20.00
COMMON CARD (L1-L9)	1.00	2.50
STATED PRINT RUN 1,701 SER. #'d SETS		

2006 Legends of Star Trek Captain Picard

COMPLETE SET (9)	10.00	20.00
COMMON CARD (L1-L9)	1.00	2.50
STATED PRINT RUN 1,701 SER. #'d SETS		

2006 Legends of Star Trek Commander William T. Riker

COMPLETE SET (9)	10.00	20.00
COMMON CARD (L1-L9)	1.00	2.50
STATED PRINT RUN 1,701 SER. #'d SETS		

2006 Legends of Star Trek Counselor Deanna Troi

COMPLETE SET (9)	10.00	20.00
COMMON CARD (L1-L9)	1.00	2.50
STATED PRINT RUN 1,701 SER. #'d SETS		

2006 Legends of Star Trek Lt. Commander Data

COMPLETE SET (9)	10.00	20.00
COMMON CARD (L1-L9)	1.00	2.50
STATED PRINT RUN 1,701 SER. #'d SETS		

2007 Legends of Star Trek Dr. Beverly Crusher

COMPLETE SET (9)	8.00	20.00
COMMON CARD (L1-L9)	1.50	4.00
STATED PRINT RUN 1,701 SER.#'d SETS		

2007 Legends of Star Trek LaForge Yar Wesley Crusher

COMPLETE SET (9)	8.00	20.00
COMMON CARD (L1-L9)	1.50	4.00
STATED PRINT RUN 1,701 SER. #'d SETS		

2007 Legends of Star Trek Lt. Commander Worf

COMPLETE SET (9)	10.00	20.00
COMMON CARD (L1-L9)	1.50	4.00
STATED PRINT RUN 1,701 SER.#'d SETS		

2008 Legends of Star Trek Lt. Commander Jadzia Dax

COMPLETE SET (9)	6.00	15.00
COMMON CARD (L1-L9)	1.25	3.00
STATED PRINT RUN 1,701 SER.#'d SETS		

2008 Legends of Star Trek Seven of Nine

COMPLETE SET (9)	6.00	15.00
COMMON CARD (L1-L9)	1.25	3.00
STATED PRINT RUN 1,701 SER.#'d SETS		

2008 Legends of Star Trek T'Pol

COMPLETE SET (9)	6.00	15.00
COMMON CARD (L1-L9)	1.25	3.00
STATED PRINT RUN 1,701 SER. #'d SETS		

2009 Legends of Star Trek Captain Benjamin Sisko

COMPLETE SET (9)	7.50	20.00
COMMON CARD (L1-L9)	1.25	3.00
STATED PRINT RUN 1,701 SER.#'d SETS		

2009 Legends of Star Trek Captain Jonathan Archer

COMPLETE SET (9)	7.50	20.00
COMMON CARD (L1-L9)	1.25	3.00
STATED PRINT RUN 1,701 SER.#'d SETS		

2009 Legends of Star Trek Captain Kathryn Janeway

COMPLETE SET (9)	7.50	20.00
COMMON CARD (L1-L9)	1.25	3.00
STATED PRINT RUN 1,701 SER.#'d SETS		

2009 Legends of Star Trek Lt. B'Elaana Torres

COMPLETE SET (9)	7.50	20.00
COMMON CARD (L1-L9)	1.25	3.00
STATED PRINT RUN 1,701 SER.#'d SETS		

2009 Legends of Star Trek Lt. Hoshi Sato

COMPLETE SET (9)	7.50	20.00

COMMON CARD (L1-L9)	1.25	3.00
STATED PRINT RUN 1,701 SER.#'d SETS		

2009 Legends of Star Trek Quark

COMPLETE SET (9)	7.50	20.00
COMMON CARD (L1-L9)	1.25	3.00
STATED PRINT RUN 1,701 SER.#'d SETS		

2010 Legends of Star Trek Dr. Julian Bashir

COMPLETE SET (9)	6.00	15.00
COMMON CARD (L1-L9)	1.25	3.00
STATED PRINT RUN 1701 SER. #'d SETS		

2010 Legends of Star Trek Dr. Phlox

COMPLETE SET (9)	6.00	15.00
COMMON CARD (I1-I9)	1.25	3.00
STATED PRINT RUN 1701 SER. #'d SETS		

2010 Legends of Star Trek Harry Kim

COMPLETE SET (9)	6.00	15.00
COMMON CARD (L1-L9)	1.25	3.00
STATED PRINT RUN 1701 SER.#'d SETS		

2010 Legends of Star Trek Odo

COMPLETE SET (9)	6.00	15.00
COMMON CARD (L1-L9)	1.25	3.00
STATED PRINT RUN 1701 SER.#'d SETS		

2010 Legends of Star Trek The Doctor

COMPLETE SET (9)	6.00	15.00
COMMON CARD (L1-L9)	1.25	3.00
STATED PRINT RUN 1701 SER.#'d SETS		

2010 Legends of Star Trek Trip Tucker

COMPLETE SET (9)	6.00	15.00
COMMON CARD (L1-L9)	1.25	3.00
STATED PRINT RUN 1701 SER. #'d SETS		

2011 Legends of Star Trek Chief O'Brien

COMPLETE SET (9)	6.00	15.00
COMMON CARD (L1-L9)	1.25	3.00
STATED PRINT RUN 1701 SER.#'d SETS		

2011 Legends of Star Trek Kira Nerys

COMPLETE SET (9)	6.00	15.00
COMMON CARD (L1-L9)	1.25	3.00
STATED PRINT RUN 1701 SER.#'d SETS		

2011 Legends of Star Trek Tuvok

COMPLETE SET (9)	6.00	15.00
COMMON CARD (L1-L9)	1.25	3.00
STATED PRINT RUN 1701 SER.#'d SETS		

2013 Legends of Star Trek Expansion Chapel

COMPLETE SET (6)	4.00	10.00
COMMON CARD (L1-L6)	1.25	3.00
STATED PRINT RUN 1,701 SER.#'d SETS		

2013 Legends of Star Trek Expansion Chekov

COMPLETE SET (6)	4.00	10.00
COMMON CARD (L4-L9))	1.25	3.00
STATED PRINT RUN 1,701 SER.#'d SETS		

2013 Legends of Star Trek Expansion Rand

COMPLETE SET (6)	4.00	10.00
COMMON CARD (L1-3, L7-9)	1.25	3.00
STATED PRINT RUN 1,701 SER.#'d SETS		

2013 Legends of Star Trek Expansion Scotty

COMPLETE SET (6)	4.00	10.00
COMMON CARD (L4-L9))	1.25	3.00
STATED PRINT RUN 1,701 SER.#'d SETS		

2013 Legends of Star Trek Expansion Sulu

COMPLETE SET (6)	4.00	10.00
COMMON CARD (L1-3, L7-9))	1.25	3.00
STATED PRINT RUN 1,701 SER.#'d SETS		

2013 Legends of Star Trek Expansion Uhura

COMPLETE SET (6)	4.00	10.00
COMMON CARD (L1-L6))	1.25	3.00
STATED PRINT RUN 1,701 SER. #'d SETS		

2015 Legends of Star Trek Geordi LaForge

COMPLETE SET (6)	6.00	15.00
COMMON CARD (L4-L9)	1.25	3.00
STATED PRINT RUN 1,701 SER.#'d SETS		

2015 Legends of Star Trek Kes

COMPLETE SET (9)	8.00	20.00
COMMON CARD (L1-L9)	1.25	3.00
STATED PRINT RUN 1,701 SER.#'d SETS		

2015 Legends of Star Trek Neelix

COMPLETE SET (9)	8.00	20.00
COMMON CARD (L1-L9)	1.25	3.00
STATED PRINT RUN 1,701 SER.#'d SETS		

2015 Legends of Star Trek Tasha Yar

COMPLETE SET (6)	5.00	12.00
COMMON CARD (L1-L6)	1.25	3.00
STATED PRINT RUN 1,701 SER.#'d SETS		

2015 Legends of Star Trek Wesley Crusher

COMPLETE SET (6)	5.00	12.00
COMMON CARD (L1-L6)	1.25	3.00
STATED PRINT RUN 1,701 SER.#'d SETS		

2011-13 The Danbury Mint Star Trek 22kt Gold Card Collection

COMPLETE SET (60)	150.00	300.00
COMMON CARD (22KT1-22KT60)	3.00	8.00

1991 Impel Star Trek 25th Anniversary

COMPLETE SET (310)	15.00	40.00
UNOPENED S1 BOX (36 PACKS)	15.00	20.00
UNOPENED S1 PACK (12 CARDS)	.50	.75
UNOPENED S2 BOX (36 PACKS)	15.00	20.00
UNOPENED S2 PACK (12 CARDS)	.50	.75
SERIES ONE COMMON (1-160)	.10	.25
SERIES TWO COMMON (161-310)	.10	.25

1991 Impel Star Trek 25th Anniversary Holograms

COMPLETE SET (4)	20.00	50.00
COMMON CARD (H1-H4)	6.00	15.00
SERIES ONE (H1-H2)		
SERIES TWO (H3-H4)		

1991 Impel Star Trek 25th Anniversary Tin Exclusives

COMPLETE SET (2)	20.00	50.00
COMMON CARD (B1-B2)	12.00	30.00
COLLECTIBLE TIN SET EXCLUSIVE		

2001 Star Trek 35th Anniversary HoloFEX

COMPLETE SET (72)	5.00	12.00
UNOPENED BOX (20 PACKS)	200.00	300.00
UNOPENED PACK (6 CARDS)	10.00	15.00
COMMON CARD (1-72)	.12	.30
*PP BLACK/25: 1.2X TO 3X BASIC CARDS		
*PP CYAN/25: 1.2X TO 3X BASIC CARDS		
*PP MAGENTA/25: 1.2X TO 3X BASIC CARDS		
*PP YELLOW/25: 1.2X TO 3X BASIC CARDS		

2001 Star Trek 35th Anniversary HoloFEX Autographs

COMMON CARD	6.00	15.00
STATED ODDS THREE PER BOX		
A33 ISSUED AS CASE TOPPER		
A34 ISSUED AS ALBUM EXCLUSIVE		
DA1 STATED ODDS 1:480		
A1 Joanne Linville	20.00	50.00
A3 Julie Newmar	20.00	50.00
A5 Sally Kellerman	12.00	30.00
A7 Jane Wyatt	15.00	40.00
A13 Michael Pataki	12.00	30.00
A14 Emily Banks	10.00	25.00
A18 Deborah Downey	10.00	25.00
A24 Elinor Donahue	10.00	25.00
A26 Barbara Baldavin	10.00	25.00
A27 William Smithers	10.00	25.00
A28 Louise Sorel	10.00	25.00
A29 Jan Shutan	10.00	25.00
A30 Pamelyn Ferdin	10.00	25.00
A31 Alexander Courage	20.00	50.00
A33 Marianne Hill CT	15.00	40.00
A34 Kate Woodville ALB	10.00	25.00
DA1 William Shatner	400.00	700.00
Leonard Nimoy		

2001 Star Trek 35th Anniversary HoloFEX Federation Foes

COMPLETE SET (6)	12.50	30.00
COMMON CARD (FF1-FF6)	2.50	6.00
STATED ODDS 1:20		

2001 Star Trek 35th Anniversary HoloFEX From the Archives Costumes

COMPLETE SET (3)		
COMMON CARD (CC1-CC3)	25.00	60.00
STATED ODDS ONE PER CASE		
CC1 Captain James T. Kirk	50.00	100.00
CC2 Spock	50.00	100.00

2001 Star Trek 35th Anniversary HoloFEX MorFEX

COMPLETE SET (9)	6.00	15.00
COMMON CARD (M1-M9)	.75	2.00
STATED ODDS 1:5		

2001 Star Trek 35th Anniversary HoloFEX Best of Bones

COMPLETE SET (9)	8.00	20.00
COMMON CARD (BB1-BB9)	1.25	3.00
STATED ODDS 1:10		

2001 Star Trek 35th Anniversary HoloFEX Promos

COMPLETE SET (3)	2.50	6.00
COMMON CARD (P1-P3)	.75	2.00
P3 Dr. McCoy	2.00	5.00
(Album Exclusive)		

2006 Star Trek 40th Anniversary

COMPLETE SET (90)	4.00	10.00
UNOPENED BOX (40 PACKS)	60.00	70.00
UNOPENED PACK (5 CARDS)	2.00	2.50
COMMON CARD (1-90)	.15	.40
LA2 ISSUED AS A 6-CASE INCENTIVE		
LA2 Patrick Stewart AU 6CI	150.00	300.00

2006 Star Trek 40th Anniversary ArtiFEX Box-Toppers

COMPLETE SET (5)	10.00	25.00
COMMON CARD (BT1-BT5)	2.50	6.00
STATED ODDS 1:BOX		

2006 Star Trek 40th Anniversary ArtiFEX Bridge Crew Portraits

COMPLETE SET (43)	12.00	30.00
COMMON CARD (FP1-FP43)	.40	1.00
STATED ODDS 1:10		

2006 Star Trek 40th Anniversary ArtiFEX Villains Portraits

COMPLETE SET (9)	25.00	60.00
COMMON CARD (VP1-VP9)	3.00	8.00
STATED ODDS 1:40 UK PACKS		

2006 Star Trek 40th Anniversary Autographed Costumes

COMMON CARD	60.00	120.00
STATED ODDS 1:240		
C1 Jeri Ryan	80.00	150.00
NNO William Shatner	120.00	250.00

2006 Star Trek 40th Anniversary First Officers

COMPLETE SET (6)	15.00	40.00
COMMON CARD (N1-N6)	3.00	8.00
STATED ODDS 1:40		

2006 Star Trek 40th Anniversary From the Archives Costumes

COMMON CARD (C4-C44;DC1)	8.00	20.00
STATED ODDS 1:20		
DC1 2-CASE INCENTIVE		
C11 Deanna Troi	12.00	30.00
C12 Seven of Nine	12.00	30.00
C15 Leeta	10.00	25.00
C18 T'Pol	12.00	30.00
C24 Major Kira Nerys	10.00	25.00
C25 Seven of Nine	15.00	40.00
C34 Seven of Nine	12.00	30.00
C35 T'Pol	12.00	30.00
C40 Captain Benjamin Sisko	10.00	25.00

C43 T'Pol	12.00	30.00
DC1 Captain Kirk	30.00	80.00
Captain Picard DUAL		

2006 Star Trek 40th Anniversary In Motion

COMPLETE SET (5)	80.00	150.00
COMMON CARD (M1-M5)	15.00	40.00
STATED ODDS 1:240		

2006 Star Trek 40th Anniversary James Doohan In Memoriam

COMPLETE SET (3)	30.00	80.00
COMMON CARD (M4-M6)	12.00	30.00
STATED ODDS 1:CASE		
CARDS MEASURE 5 X 7		
STATED PRINT RUN 300 SER.#'d SETS		

2006 Star Trek 40th Anniversary TV Guide Covers

COMPLETE SET (17)	25.00	60.00
COMMON CARD (TV1-TV17)	1.50	4.00
STATED ODDS 1:20 US PACKS		

2006 Star Trek 40th Anniversary Promos

COMPLETE SET (5)	5.00	12.00
COMMON CARD	.75	2.00
P3 Capt. Sisko ALB	3.00	8.00
UK Capt. Janeway UK	1.50	4.00
CP1 Capt. Archer CON	1.25	3.00

2017 Star Trek 50th Anniversary

COMPLETE SET (100)	8.00	20.00
UNOPENED BOX (24 PACKS)	80.00	100.00
UNOPENED PACK (5 CARDS)	3.00	4.00
COMMON CARD (1-100)	.15	.40
ARCHER CASE-TOPPER 1:CASE		
CT Captain Jonathan Archer (Case-Topper)	10.00	25.00

2017 Star Trek 50th Anniversary Aliens Expansion Autographs

COMPLETE SET (60)	300.00	500.00
COMMON CARD	6.00	15.00
L = 300-500 COPIES		
VL = 200-300 COPIES		
STATED ODDS 1:12		
NNO Christopher Carroll VL	8.00	20.00
NNO Fintan McKeown VL	8.00	20.00
NNO Gerrit Graham L	8.00	20.00
NNO Gina Hecht L	8.00	20.00
NNO Jaime Hubbard VL	8.00	20.00
NNO James Horan VL	8.00	20.00
NNO Jonathan Frakes (Rivas Jakara) VL	12.00	30.00
NNO Kaitlin Hopkins L	8.00	20.00
NNO Kim Rhodes VL	10.00	25.00
NNO Lawrence Montaigne VL	8.00	20.00
NNO Lee Meriwether L	20.00	50.00
NNO Madchen Amick VL	15.00	40.00
NNO Melanie Smith VL	8.00	20.00
NNO Michael Nouri VL	8.00	20.00
NNO Mike Genovese VL	10.00	25.00
NNO Sandy Gimpel VL	10.00	25.00
NNO Scott MacDonald VL	8.00	20,00
NNO Wayne Thomas Yorke L	12.00	30.00

2017 Star Trek 50th Anniversary ArtiFEX

COMPLETE SET (50)	20.00	50.00
COMMON CARD (1-50)	1.50	4.00
STATED ODDS 1:12		

2017 Star Trek 50th Anniversary Captains Autographs

STATED ODDS 1:288		
SHATNER/PICARD IS 9-CASE INCENTIVE		
NNO Avery Brooks	30.00	75.00
NNO Kate Mulgrew	50.00	100.00
NNO Patrick Stewart	60.00	120.00
NNO Scott Bakula	60.00	120.00
NNO William Shatner	100.00	200.00
NNO Shatner/Stewart DUAL AU 9CI	150.00	300.00

2017 Star Trek 50th Anniversary Commemorative Stamps

COMPLETE SET (4)	60.00	120.00
COMMON CARD (S1-S4)	15.00	40.00
STATED ODDS 1:576		

2017 Star Trek 50th Anniversary Cut Signatures

COMMON CARD	500.00	800.00
NNO DeForest Kelley/50	500.00	800.00
NNO Gene Roddenberry/30	2000.00	4500.00
NNO Mark Lenard/33	500.00	800.00

2017 Star Trek 50th Anniversary Dual Relics

COMMON CARD (DRC1-DRC6)	10.00	25.00
STATED ODDS 1:24		
ERC1 IS A 6-CASE INCENTIVE		
DRC3 Archer & T'Pol	15.00	40.00
DRC4 Tucker & Archer	12.00	30.00
DRC5 Sisko & Solok	12.00	30.00
DRC6 Phlox & T'Pol	12.00	30.00
ERC1 Piece of the Enterprise NCC1701-E 6CI	60.00	120.00

2017 Star Trek 50th Anniversary Metal

COMMON CARD (1-50)	10.00	25.00
STATED ODDS 1:24		

2017 Star Trek 50th Anniversary Phaser Cuts

COMPLETE SET (10)	100.00	200.00
COMMON CARD (PC1-PC10)	8.00	20.00
STATED ODDS 1:288		
PC1 Captain Kirk	15.00	40.00
PC2 Spock	12.00	30.00
PC3 Captain Picard	12.00	30.00
PC4 Commander Riker	10.00	25.00
PC6 Major Kira	10.00	25.00
PC7 Captain Janeway	12.00	30.00
PC9 Captain Archer	12.00	30.00
PC10 Commander T'Pol	12.00	30.00

2017 Star Trek 50th Anniversary Relic Booklets

COMMON CARD (RC1-RC54)	6.00	15.00
STATED ODDS 1:24		
RC1 Kirk	20.00	50.00
RC2 Spock	15.00	40.00
RC3 Uhura	8.00	20.00
RC4 Carol Marcus	8.00	20.00
RC5 McCoy	12.00	30.00
RC6 Saavik	10.00	25.00
RC7 Spock	12.00	30.00
RC8 Chekov	8.00	20.00
RC9 Scotty	12.00	30.00
RC10 McCoy	10.00	25.00
RC11 Picard	12.00	30.00
RC12 Riker	8.00	20.00
RC13 Beverly Crusher	12.00	30.00
RC15 Guinan	10.00	25.00
RC16 Picard	8.00	20.00
RC17 Data	10.00	25.00
RC18 Borg Queen	8.00	20.00
RC19 Riker	8.00	20.00
RC20 Picard	12.00	30.00
RC21 Data	8.00	20.00
RC22 Sisko	8.00	20.00
RC23 Kira	10.00	25.00
RC24 Worf	10.00	25.00
RC25 Jadzia Dax	8.00	20.00
RC26 Odo	8.00	20.00
RC27 Bashir	8.00	20.00
RC29 Ezri Dax	8.00	20.00
RC31 Janeway	10.00	25.00
RC32 Seven of Nine	12.00	30.00
RC34 Seven of Nine	10.00	25.00
RC35 Neelix	10.00	25.00
RC36 Kes	8.00	20.00
RC37 Seven of Nine	12.00	30.00
RC38 Kes	8.00	20.00
RC39 Archer	10.00	25.00
RC40 T'Pol	8.00	20.00
RC41 Phlox	10.00	25.00
RC42 Reed	8.00	20.00
RC43 Archer	10.00	25.00
RC44 T'Pol	10.00	25.00
RC45 Tucker	10.00	25.00
RC47 Phlox	8.00	20.00
RC48 T'Pol	8.00	20.00
RC49 Phlox	8.00	20.00
RC50 Mayweather	8.00	20.00

2017 Star Trek 50th Anniversary Ships of the Line

COMPLETE SET (9)	60.00	120.00
COMMON CARD (SL19-SL27)	6.00	15.00
STATED ODDS 1:96		

2017 Star Trek 50th Anniversary Star Trek Tech Evolution

COMPLETE SET W/RR (10)	25.00	60.00
COMPLETE SET W/O RR (9)	12.00	30.00
COMMON CARD (E1-E9)	2.00	5.00
STATED ODDS 1:96		
E10 IS A RITTENHOUSE REWARD		
E10 Dress Uniform (Rittenhouse Rewards Exclusive)	15.00	40.00

2017 Star Trek 50th Anniversary Starfleet Captains

COMMON CARD (C1-C18)	8.00	20.00
STATED ODDS 1:48		

2017 Star Trek 50th Anniversary Promos

P1 Album Exclusive		
P2 50th Anniversary		
P3 Live Long and Prosper (Album Exclusive)		
P4 Enterprise-D		

2016 Star Trek 50 for 50

COMPLETE FACTORY SET (100)	25.00	60.00
COMMON CARD (1-100)	.30	.75

1981 Leaf Star Trek '67 Reprints

COMPLETE SET (72)	6.00	15.00
COMMON CARD (1-72)	.20	.50

2014 Star Trek Aliens

COMPLETE SET (100)	4.00	10.00
UNOPENED BOX (24 PACKS)	55.00	60.00
UNOPENED PACK (5 CARDS)	3.00	4.00
COMMON CARD (1-100)	.08	.20
*GOLD: 4X TO 10X BASIC CARDS	.75	2.00

2014 Star Trek Aliens Alien Ships

COMPLETE SET (10)	10.00	25.00
COMMON CARD (S01-S10)	1.50	4.00
STATED ODDS 1:24		

2014 Star Trek Aliens Alien Stickers

COMPLETE SET (18)	15.00	40.00
COMMON CARD (S01-S18)	1.25	3.00
STATED ODDS 1:16		

2014 Star Trek Aliens Autographs

COMMON AUTO	4.00	10.00
STATED ODDS 1:8		
L = 300-500		
VL = 200-300		
EL = 100-200		
NNO Adrienne Barbeau L	6.00	15.00
NNO Antoinette Bower L	5.00	12.00
NNO Armin Shimerman VL	12.00	30.00
NNO Bruce Gray VL	8.00	20.00
NNO Cari Shayne VL	5.00	12.00
NNO Chris Sarandon VL	15.00	40.00
NNO Cristine Rose L	5.00	12.00
NNO Daniel Davis EL	25.00	60.00
NNO Dennis Christopher (Borath) L	5.00	12.00
NNO Dennis Christopher (Danik) L	5.00	12.00
NNO Estelle Harris VL	8.00	20.00
NNO James Horan VL	8.00	20.00
NNO Jeffrey Combs L	6.00	15.00
NNO Jeri Ryan EL	50.00	100.00
NNO John de Lancie VL	12.00	30.00
NNO Jonathan Del Arco L	5.00	12.00
NNO Karen Austin L	5.00	12.00
NNO Kristanna Loken VL	10.00	25.00
NNO Lawrence Montaigne VL	8.00	20.00
NNO Lee Arenberg VL	6.00	15.00
NNO Leonard Nimoy EL	125.00	250.00
NNO Linda Thorson L	5.00	12.00
NNO Malcolm McDowell L	20.00	50.00
NNO Margot Rose L	5.00	12.00
NNO Marina Sirtis VL	25.00	60.00
NNO Martha Hackett L	5.00	12.00
NNO Meg Foster L	5.00	12.00
NNO Michael Dorn VL	12.00	30.00
NNO Michael Westmore	5.00	12.00
NNO Olivia d'Abo VL	15.00	40.00
NNO Penny Johnson L	5.00	12.00
NNO Robert O'Reilly L	5.00	12.00
NNO Robin Curtis as Saavik VL	12.00	30.00
NNO Scarlett Pomers L	5.00	12.00
NNO Scott MacDonald (Cmdr Dolim) VL	8.00	20.00
NNO Scott MacDonald (N'Vek) VL	6.00	15.00
NNO Spice Williams L	8.00	20.00
NNO Tim Russ VL	15.00	40.00
NNO Tony Todd VL	10.00	25.00
NNO Tricia O'Neil VL	10.00	25.00
NNO Virginia Madsen L	6.00	15.00
NNO Whoopi Goldberg EL	75.00	150.00
NNO William O'Connell VL	8.00	20.00
NNO Yvonne Craig EL	50.00	100.00

2014 Star Trek Aliens Badges

COMPLETE SET (6)	120.00	250.00
COMMON AUTO (B1-B5;GL5)	15.00	40.00
STATED ODDS 1:288		
STATED PRINT RUN 200 SER.#'d SETS		
B1 Vulcan IDIC Badge	20.00	50.00
B2 Klingon Comm Badge	20.00	50.00

B4 Borg Badge	20.00	50.00
GL1 Gold Pressed Latinum	30.00	75.00

2014 Star Trek Aliens Case-Incentives

1 Mick and Matt Glebe Sketch	250.00	500.00
2 Warren Martineck Sketch	150.00	300.00

2014 Star Trek Aliens Case-Toppers

COMPLETE SET (2)	6.00	15.00
COMMON CARD (CT1-CT2)	4.00	10.00

2014 Star Trek Aliens First Appearances

COMPLETE SET (9)	6.00	15.00
COMMON CARD (FA1-FA9)	.75	2.00
STATED ODDS 1:24		

2014 Star Trek Aliens Klingon Quotables

COMPLETE SET (9)	5.00	12.00
COMMON CARD (K1-K9)	.60	1.50
STATED ODDS 1:24		

2014 Star Trek Aliens Promos

COMMON CARD (P1-P4)	.75	2.00
P2 Spock (2014 Fall Philly)	1.50	4.00
P3 Troi (Album Exclusive)	3.00	8.00
P4 Quark (Card Collective Exclusive)	8.00	20.00

1996 Blockbuster Video Star Trek Captains

COMPLETE SET (4)	12.00	30.00
COMMON CARD	4.00	10.00

1976 Phoenix Candy Star Trek Candy Boxes

COMPLETE SET (8)	75.00	150.00
COMMON BOX (1-8)	10.00	25.00

2000 Star Trek Cinema 2000

COMPLETE SET (82)	4.00	10.00
UNOPENED BOX (24 PACKS)	60.00	100.00
UNOPENED PACK (8 CARDS)	3.00	5.00
COMMON CARD (1-82)	.10	.25
*FOIL: .6X TO 1.5X BASIC CARDS		

2000 Star Trek Cinema 2000 Alien Worlds

COMPLETE SET (9)	2.50	6.00
COMMON CARD (AW1-AW9)	.40	1.00
STATED ODDS 1:3		

2000 Star Trek Cinema 2000 Autographs

COMMON CARD (A1-A25)	6.00	15.00
STATED ODDS 1:24		
A1 Patrick Stewart	80.00	150.00
A2 Nichelle Nichols	25.00	60.00
A3 George Takei	25.00	60.00
A4 Alfre Woodard	25.00	60.00
A5 Jonathan Frakes	50.00	100.00
A6 Daniel Hugh Kelly	10.00	25.00
A7 Grace Lee Whitney	25.00	60.00
A8 Alice Krige	20.00	50.00
A8R Alice Krige (red.)		
A10 Laurence Luckinbill	12.00	30.00
A11 Donna Murphy	20.00	50.00
A12 Dwight Schultz	10.00	25.00
A12R Dwight Schultz (red.)		
A13 Jane Wyatt	10.00	25.00
A14 Alan Ruck	15.00	40.00
A15 Catherine Hicks	25.00	60.00
A16R Anthony Zerbe (red.)		
A17 Paul Winfield	12.00	30.00
A22 Patti Yasutake	12.00	30.00
A24 Spice Williams	8.00	20.00
A25 Robert Hooks	8.00	20.00

2000 Star Trek Cinema 2000 Dr. McCoy Tribute

COMPLETE SET (9)	12.00	30.00
COMMON CARD (M1-M9)	2.50	6.00
STATED ODDS 1:12		

2000 Star Trek Cinema 2000 Female Guest Stars

COMPLETE SET (9)	10.00	25.00
COMMON CARD (F1-F9)	2.00	5.00
*FOIL: .6X TO 1.5X BASIC CARDS		

2000 Star Trek Cinema 2000 Galactic Conflix Silver

COMPLETE SET (9)	25.00	60.00
COMMON CARD (GC1-GC9)	5.00	12.00
*BLACK/750: .75X TO 2X BASIC CARDS		
*BLUE/250: 2X TO 5X BASIC CARDS		
STATED PRINT RUN 1,000 SER. #'d SETS		

2000 Star Trek Cinema 2000 Movie Posters

COMPLETE SET (9)	4.00	10.00
COMMON CARD (P1-P9)	.60	1.50
STATED ODDS 1:2		

2000 Star Trek Cinema 2000 Saluting the Captains

COMPLETE SET (9)	5.00	12.00
COMMON CARD (SC1-SC9)	.75	2.00
STATED ODDS 1:6		

2000 Star Trek Cinema 2000 The Dark Side

COMPLETE SET (9)	4.00	10.00
COMMON CARD (1-9)	.75	2.00
*FOIL: .6X TO 1.5X BASIC CARDS		

1994 SkyBox Star Trek Cinema Collection The Motion Picture

COMPLETE BOX SET (72)	10.00	25.00
COMMON CARD (1-72)	.20	.50
ST II SET (72)	10.00	25.00
ST II COMMON CARD (1-72)	.20	.50
ST III SET (72)	10.00	25.00
ST III COMMON CARD (1-72)	.20	.50
ST IV SET (72)	10.00	25.00
ST IV COMMON CARD (1-72)	.20	.50
ST V SET (72)	10.00	25.00
ST V COMMON CARD (1-72)	.20	.50
ST VI SET (72)	10.00	25.00
ST VI COMMON CARD (1-72)	.20	.50

1994 SkyBox Star Trek Cinema Collection The Voyage Home

COMPLETE BOX SET (72)	10.00	25.00
COMMON CARD (1-72)	.20	.50

1994 SkyBox Star Trek Cinema Collection The Wrath of Khan

COMPLETE BOXED SET (72)	10.00	25.00
COMMON CARD (1-72)	.20	.50

1997 Fritt Star Trek Stickers

COMPLETE SET (33)	50.00	100.00
COMMON CARD (1-33)	2.00	5.00

1998 Fritt Star Trek Stickers

COMPLETE SET (33)	25.00	60.00
COMMON CARD (1-33)	1.25	3.00

1993 Hostess Star Trek Minis

COMPLETE SET (38)	60.00	120.00
COMMON TNG CARD (1-38)	1.25	3.00
COMMON DS9 CARD (D1-D10)	1.25	3.00
ALB Star Trek Hostess Minis Album	150.00	300.00

1993 Hostess Star Trek Minis Posters

COMPLETE SET (10)	12.00	30.00
COMMON CARD (1-10)	1.50	4.00

2019 Star Trek Inflexions

COMPLETE SET (100)	10.00	25.00
UNOPENED BOX (3 PACKS)	200.00	300.00
UNOPENED PACK (6 CARDS)	70.00	100.00
COMMON CARD (1-100)	.20	.50
*WHITE/150: 2X TO 5X BASIC CARDS		
*HOLO/75: 6X TO 15X BASIC CARDS		
*ONYX/40: 10X TO 25X BASIC CARDS		

2019 Star Trek Inflexions 50th Anniversary Stamps

COMMON MEM	5.00	12.00
STATED PRINT RUN 125 SER.#'d SETS		
CS1 Captain Kirk	10.00	25.00
CS2 Captain Picard	8.00	20.00

2019 Star Trek Inflexions Aliens Autographs

COMMON AUTO	6.00	15.00
STATED OVERALL ODDS 1:BOX		
NNO Andrew Robinson VL	12.00	30.00
NNO Carel Struycken EL	8.00	20.00
NNO Chase Masterson EL	12.00	30.00
NNO David Warner S	50.00	100.00
NNO Mark Alaimo EL	15.00	40.00

2019 Star Trek Inflexions Autographed Booklets

COMMON AUTO	100.00	200.00
STATED OVERALL ODDS 1:BOX		
ACB1 W.Shatner/A.Brooks	200.00	400.00
ACB3 B.Cumberbatch/R.Montalban	600.00	1200.00

2019 Star Trek Inflexions Autographed Relics

COMMON AUTO	25.00	60.00
STATED OVERALL ODDS 1:BOX		
NNO Jolene Blalock S	250.00	400.00
NNO Malcolm McDowell EL	30.00	75.00

2019 Star Trek Inflexions Bridge Crew Autographs

COMMON AUTO	6.00	15.00
STATED ODDS 1:BOX		
NNO Alexander Siddig EL	12.00	30.00
NNO Armin Shimerman EL	15.00	40.00
NNO Brent Spiner VL	20.00	50.00
NNO Colm Meaney VL	12.00	30.00
NNO Connor Trinneer EL	20.00	50.00
NNO Dominic Keating EL	12.00	30.00
NNO Ethan Phillips VL	8.00	20.00
NNO Gates McFadden VL	20.00	50.00
NNO George Takei VL	25.00	60.00
NNO Grace Lee Whitney VL	25.00	60.00
NNO Jeri Ryan VL	50.00	100.00
NNO John Billingsley EL	15.00	40.00
NNO Jonathan Frakes VL	15.00	40.00
NNO Leonard Nimoy VL	150.00	300.00
NNO Linda Park EL	20.00	50.00
NNO Marina Sirtis VL	20.00	50.00
NNO Michael Dorn EL	15.00	40.00
NNO Nana Visitor EL	12.00	30.00
NNO Nichelle Nichols VL	30.00	75.00
NNO Rene Auberjonois EL	25.00	60.00
NNO Robert Picardo L	8.00	20.00
NNO Terry Farrell EL	25.00	60.00
NNO Tim Russ L	8.00	20.00
NNO Walter Koenig VL	20.00	50.00

2019 Star Trek Inflexions Dynamic Duos Mirror

COMPLETE SET (10)	20.00	50.00
COMMON CARD (DD1-DD10)	4.00	10.00
RANDOMLY INSERTED INTO PACKS		

2019 Star Trek Inflexions Expressions of Heroism

COMPLETE SET (43)	100.00	250.00
COMMON CARD (E1-E43)	3.00	8.00
STATED PRINT RUN 150 SER.#'d SETS		

2019 Star Trek Inflexions Laser-Cut Villains

COMPLETE SET (24)	100.00	200.00
COMMON CARD (L1-L24)	6.00	15.00
STATED PRINT RUN 100 SER.#'d SETS		

2019 Star Trek Inflexions Legends Autograph

NNO Kate Mulgrew	20.00	50.00

2019 Star Trek Inflexions Movie Art of Star Trek Autograph

NNO Christopher Plummer L	25.00	60.00

2019 Star Trek Inflexions Movie Autographs

COMMON AUTO	5.00	12.00
STATED ODDS 1:BOX		
A133 Patrick Stewart VL	60.00	120.00
A135 LeVar Burton VL	30.00	75.00
A136 Gates McFadden VL	15.00	40.00
A137 Branscombe Richmond L	6.00	15.00
A138 Whoopi Goldberg EL	60.00	120.00
A140 Julie Morgan L	6.00	15.00
A142 Momo Yashima L	6.00	15.00
A143 Nicholas Meyer VL	15.00	40.00
A145 David Warner VL	20.00	50.00
A146 Sharon Thomas L	8.00	20.00
A147 Walter Koenig VL	25.00	60.00
A148 Ethan Phillips VL	10.00	25.00

2019 Star Trek Inflexions Movie Full-Bleed Autographs

STATED OVERALL ODDS 1:BOX		
NNO Zoe Saldana EL	125.00	250.00
NNO Benedict Cumberbatch EL	200.00	400.00

2019 Star Trek Inflexions The Next Generation Autographs

COMMON AUTO	6.00	15.00
STATED OVERALL ODDS 1:BOX		
NNO Brent Spiner VL	25.00	60.00
NNO David Warner S	50.00	100.00
NNO Denise Crosby VL	12.00	30.00
NNO Gates McFadden VL	12.00	30.00
NNO Jonathan Frakes VL	20.00	50.00
NNO Michael Dorn EL	25.00	60.00

2019 Star Trek Inflexions Phaser-Cut Bridge Crew

COMPLETE SET (24) 125.00 250.00
COMMON CARD (PC11-PC34) 8.00 20.00
STATED PRINT RUN 100 SER.#'d SETS

2019 Star Trek Inflexions Quintuple Captains Costume Relic

STATED PRINT RUN 200 SER.#'d SETS
NNO Kirk/Picard/Sisko/Janeway/Archer 75.00 150.00

2019 Star Trek Inflexions Quotable Autographs

COMMON AUTO 15.00 40.00
STATED OVERALL ODDS 1:BOX
NNO Jason Alexander VL 25.00 60.00

2019 Star Trek Inflexions Seven-Piece Deep Space Nine Costume Relic

NNO Seven-Piece Deep Space Nine Swatch 125.00 250.00

2019 Star Trek Inflexions Silver Signature Autographs

COMMON AUTO 12.00 30.00
STATED OVERALL ODDS 1:BOX
NNO Kate Mulgrew VL 25.00 60.00

2019 Star Trek Inflexions Starfleet's Finest Painted Portraits Metal

COMPLETE SET (49) 400.00 650.00
COMMON CARD (AC1-AC49) 12.00 30.00
RANDOMLY INSERTED INTO PACKS
STATED PRINT RUN 50 SER.#'d SETS

2019 Star Trek Inflexions Throwback Stickers

COMPLETE SET (45) 75.00 150.00
COMMON STICKER (S1-S45) 2.50 6.00
RANDOMLY INSERTED INTO PACKS

2019 Star Trek Inflexions Promos

PT1 Picard Metal ALB 6.00 15.00

2010 Star Trek Live Long and Prosper Autograph

Twitter Exclusive
NNO Leonard Nimoy 300.00 600.00

1993 SkyBox Star Trek Master Series

COMPLETE SET (90) 5.00 12.00
UNOPENED BOX (36 PACKS) 20.00 30.00
UNOPENED PACK (6 CARDS) 1.25 1.50
COMMON CARD (1-90) .10 .25

1993 SkyBox Star Trek Master Series Promos

1 6-Card Panel NSCC 50.00 100.00
2 Excelsior Leaves Spacedock .75 2.00
3 Uhura .75 2.00
4 Worf NSU 6.00 15.00

1993 SkyBox Star Trek Master Series Spectra

COMPLETE SET (5) 12.00 30.00
COMMON CARD (S1-S5) 3.00 8.00

1994 SkyBox Star Trek Master Series

COMPLETE SET (100) 5.00 12.00
UNOPENED BOX (36 PACKS) 30.00 40.00
UNOPENED PACK (6 CARDS) 1.25 1.50
COMMON CARD (1-100) .10 .25

1994 SkyBox Star Trek Master Series Crew Triptychs

COMPLETE SET (9) 20.00 50.00
COMMON CARD (F1-F9) 4.00 10.00
STATED ODDS 1:10

1994 SkyBox Star Trek Master Series Proscenium Holograms

COMPLETE SET (4) 12.00 30.00
COMMON CARD (HG1-HG4) 4.00 10.00

1994 SkyBox Star Trek Master Series Promos

COMMON CARD 1.25 3.00
S2 Gowron (dealers) 1.50 4.00

2014 Star Trek Movies

COMPLETE SET (110) 5.00 12.00
UNOPENED BOX (24 PACKS)
UNOPENED PACKS (5 CARDS)
COMMON CARD (1-110) .20 .50
*SILVER/200: 4X TO 10X BASIC CARDS
*GOLD/100: 10X TO 25X BASIC CARDS

2014 Star Trek Movies 2009 Star Trek Movie

COMPLETE SET (110) 20.00 50.00
COMMON CARD (1-110) .75 2.00
*SILVER/200: 1X TO 2.5X BASIC CARDS
*GOLD/100: 2.5X TO 6X BASIC CARDS
STATED ODDS 1:3

2014 Star Trek Movies Autographs

COMMON AUTO 5.00 12.00
STATED ODDS 1:12
REGULAR = >500
L = 300-500
VL = 200-300
EL = <201
CUMBERBATCH AU ISSUED AS 9-CASE INCENTIVE
NNO Aisha Hinds L 6.00 15.00
NNO Alice Eve VL 60.00 120.00
NNO Ben Cross EL 20.00 50.00
NNO Benedict Cumberbatch ID 9CI 400.00 800.00
NNO Bruce Greenwood L 12.00 30.00
NNO Chris Pine EL 250.00 500.00
NNO Clifton Collins, Jr. 6.00 15.00
NNO Deep Roy 8.00 20.00
NNO Jennifer Morrison 12.00 30.00
NNO Joseph Gatt L 10.00 25.00
NNO Joseph Gatt ID L 10.00 25.00
NNO Kasia Kowalczyk 6.00 15.00
NNO Leonard Nimoy EL 400.00 600.00
NNO Nick Tarabay ID VL 12.00 30.00
NNO Nick Tarabay VL 12.00 30.00
NNO Noel Clarke L 12.00 30.00
NNO Nolan North 6.00 15.00
NNO Peter Weller VL 50.00 125.00
NNO Rachel Nichols VL 30.00 80.00
NNO Scott Lawrence VL 15.00 40.00
NNO Scottie Thompson L 8.00 20.00
NNO Simon Pegg EL 200.00 400.00
NNO Zachary Quinto EL 250.00 500.00

2014 Star Trek Movies Final Frontier Case-Toppers

COMPLETE SET (2) 12.00 30.00
COMMON CARD (CT1-CT2) 8.00 20.00
STATED ODDS 1:CASE

2014 Star Trek Movies Foldouts

COMPLETE SET (9) 12.00 30.00
COMPLETE SET W/RR (10) 25.00 60.00
COMMON CARD (F1-F9) 2.50 6.00
STATED ODDS 1:24
F10 ISSUED AS RITTENHOUSE REWARD
F10 Chekov RR SP 15.00 40.00

2014 Star Trek Movies Uniform Badges

COMMON MEM (B1-B24) 12.00 30.00
STATED ODDS 1:60
STATED PRINT RUN 250 SER. #'d SETS
B1 Captain Kirk 20.00 50.00
B2 Captain Kirk 20.00 50.00
B3 Captain Kirk 20.00 50.00
B4 Spock 15.00 40.00
B5 Spock 15.00 40.00
B6 Spock 15.00 40.00
B7 Admiral Marcus 15.00 40.00
B8 Admiral Pike 15.00 40.00
B9 McCoy 15.00 40.00
B13 Captain Kirk 20.00 50.00
B14 Spock 15.00 40.00
B15 McCoy 15.00 40.00
B20 Carol Marcus 15.00 40.00
B22 McCoy 15.00 40.00

2014 Star Trek Movies Uniform Relics

COMMON MEM (RC1-RC12) 12.00 30.00
STATED ODDS 1:96
STATED PRINT RUN 300 SER. #'d SETS
PEGG AU ISSUED AS 6-CASE INCENTIVE
RC1 Captain Kirk (Starship) 20.00 50.00
RC2 Spock (Starship) 15.00 40.00
RC3 Uhura (Starship) 15.00 40.00
RC4 McCoy (Starship) 15.00 40.00
RC8 Carol Marcus (Starship) 20.00 50.00
RC9 Spock (Away Team Jacket) 15.00 40.00
RC10 Kirk (Formal) 20.00 50.00
RC11 Spock (Formal) 15.00 40.00
RC12 Uhura (Formal) 15.00 40.00
NNO Simon Pegg AU 6CI 100.00 200.00

2014 Star Trek Movies Promos

P1 Capt. Kirk GEN .75 2.00
P2 Spock NSU 2.00 5.00
P3 Khan ALB 6.00 15.00

2011 Star Trek Movies Heroes and Villains

COMPLETE SET (54) 25.00 60.00
COMPLETE SET W/RR (55) 40.00 80.00
COMMON CARD (1-54) 1.25 3.00
STATED PRINT RUN 550 SER. #'d SETS
CARD 55 ISSUED AS RITTENHOUSE REWARD
55 Capt. James T. Kirk SP RR 12.00 30.00

2011 Star Trek Movies Heroes and Villains Autographs

COMMON AUTO 4.00 10.00
STATED ODDS 2:1
L (LIMITED): 300-500 COPIES
VL (VERY LIMITED): 200-300 COPIES
EL (EXTREMELY LTD): UNDER 200 COPIES
NICHOLS AUTO ISSUED AS 4-BOX INCENTIVE
A107 Donna Murphy L 12.00 30.00
A111 Patti Yasutake VL 10.00 25.00
A113 Anthony Zerbe VL 30.00 75.00
A119 Brent Spiner VL 75.00 150.00
A120 William Shatner VL 200.00 350.00
A121 Christian Slater L 50.00 100.00
A122 Nichelle Nichols EL 4BI 150.00 300.00
A124 Joseph Ruskin EL 60.00 120.00
A126 Leonard Nimoy VL 175.00 250.00
A127 David Orange L 6.00 15.00

2011 Star Trek Movies Heroes and Villains Bridge Crew Patches

COMPLETE SET (2) 20.00 50.00
COMMON CARD (PC10-PC11) 12.00 30.00
STATED ODDS 1:CASE
STATED PRINT RUN 250 SER.#'d SETS

2011 Star Trek Movies Heroes and Villains Die-Cut Gold Plaques

COMPLETE SET (14) 25.00 60.00
COMMON CARD (H1-H14) 3.00 8.00
STATED ODDS 1:1
STATED PRINT RUN 425 SER. #'d SETS
H1 Kirk 5.00 12.00
H2 Spock 4.00 10.00

2011 Star Trek Movies Heroes and Villains Tribute

COMPLETE SET (12) 15.00 40.00
COMMON CARD (T1-T12) 2.50 6.00
STATED ODDS 1:1
STATED PRINT RUN 475 SER.#'d SETS

2011 Star Trek Movies Heroes and Villains Promos

COMMON CARD (P1-P4) .75 2.00
P3 Data ALB 6.00 15.00
P4 Data PHILLY 1.50 4.00

2008 Star Trek Movies In Motion

COMPLETE SET (60) 4.00 10.00
UNOPENED BOX (24 PACKS) 75.00 125.00
UNOPENED PACK (4 CARDS) 3.00 5.00
UNOPENED ARCHIVE BOX 850.00 1000.00
COMMON CARD (1-60) .12 .30

2008 Star Trek Movies In Motion Autographs

COMMON CARD (A41-A76) 5.00 12.00
STATED ODDS 1:8
L (LIMITED): 300-500 COPIES
VL (VERY LIMITED): 200-300 COPIES
A41 James Cromwell L 15.00 40.00
A42 James B. Sikking 10.00 25.00
A43 Majel Barrett VL 60.00 120.00
A44 Patrick Stewart VL 120.00 200.00
A45 David Warner L 30.00 75.00
A46 Kirstie Alley L 60.00 120.00
A47 Alice Krige L 15.00 40.00
A48 Laurence Luckinbill L 12.00 30.00
A51 Grace Lee Whitney CI 50.00 100.00
A57 Christopher Plummer 20.00 50.00
A57 Robert Easton 30.00 75.00
A60 Nichelle Nichols VL 30.00 75.00
A62 Stephen Liska 6.00 15.00
A63 Leonard Nimoy CI 150.00 300.00
A66 Marina Sirtis VL 50.00 100.00
A70 Gwyneth Walsh 6.00 15.00
A71 Stephanie Niznik 6.00 15.00
A72 Jacqueline Kim 8.00 20.00
A73 Tim Russ VL 25.00 60.00
A74 Alfre Woodard CT 15.00 40.00
A75 Rif Hutton L 6.00 15.00

2008 Star Trek Movies In Motion Movie Stars

COMPLETE SET (12)	3.00	8.00
COMMON CARD (C1-C12)	.40	1.00
STATED ODDS 1:2		

2008 Star Trek Movies In Motion Portraits

COMPLETE SET (16)	10.00	25.00
COMMON CARD (POR1-POR16)	1.00	2.50
STATED ODDS 1:8		

2008 Star Trek Movies In Motion Quotables

COMPLETE SET (10)	5.00	12.00
COMMON CARD (Q1-Q10)	.60	1.50
STATED ODDS 1:12		

2008 Star Trek Movies In Motion Promos

COMPLETE SET (4)		
COMMON CARD (P1a-P3)		
P1a Logo (Non-Lenticular) GEN	.75	2.00
P1b Khan GEN	.75	2.00
P2 U.S.S. Enterprise NSU	1.25	3.00
P3 Shapeshifter ALB	3.00	8.00

2010 Quotable Star Trek Movies

COMPLETE SET (90)	3.00	8.00
UNOPENED BOX (24 PACKS)	125.00	250.00
UNOPENED PACK (5 CARDS)	6.00	10.00
UNOPENED ARCHIVE BOX	1000.00	1500.00
COMMON CARD (1-90)	.15	.20

2010 Quotable Star Trek Movies Autographs

COMMON CARD (SKIP #'d)	4.00	10.00
STATED ODDS 3:BOX		
A96 ISSUED AS 3-CASE INCENTIVE		
L (LIMITED): 300-500 COPIES		
VL (VERY LIMITED): 200-300 COPIES		
A56 Kurtwood Smith L	12.00	30.00
A59 Kim Cattrall L	50.00	100.00
A77 Glenn Morshower	5.00	12.00
A78 Brian Thompson	5.00	12.00
A80 Marcy Lafferty	6.00	15.00
A81 Gates McFadden VL	40.00	80.00
A83b Alan Ruck	10.00	25.00
A87 Paul Rossilli	5.00	12.00
A88 John Larroquette L	20.00	50.00
A90 Jon Kamal Rashad	5.00	12.00
A91 Rex Holman VL	25.00	60.00
A93 Levar Burton VL	50.00	100.00
A94 John Winston L	6.00	15.00
A95 Michael Dorn VL	25.00	60.00
A96 Michael Dorn 3CI	30.00	75.00
A97 Jonathan Frakes VL	30.00	75.00
A99 Breon Gorman	5.00	12.00
A100 Brent Spiner VL	60.00	120.00
A101 Daniel Hugh Kelly L	10.00	25.00
A103 Peggy Miley	5.00	12.00
A104 Dina Meyer	10.00	25.00
A105 Dwight Schultz VL	12.00	30.00
A112 Jude Ciccolella	5.00	12.00

2010 Quotable Star Trek Movies Bridge Crew Patches

COMPLETE SET (9)	350.00	650.00
COMMON CARD (PC1-PC9)	40.00	80.00
STATED ODDS 1:110		
STATED PRINT RUN 250 SER.#'d SETS		
PC1 Admiral Kirk	50.00	100.00
PC2 Spock	50.00	100.00
PC3 Dr. McCoy	50.00	100.00
PC5 Lt. Commander Uhura	50.00	100.00

2010 Quotable Star Trek Movies Costumes

BS ISSUED AS 6-CASE INCENTIVE		
MC17 ISSUED AS CASE TOPPER		
BS Brent Spiner AU 6CI/200	120.00	200.00
MC17 Data suit CT/775	10.00	25.00

2010 Quotable Star Trek Movies Movie Posters

COMPLETE SET (10)	10.00	25.00
COMMON CARD (MP1-MP10)	1.25	3.00
STATED ODDS 1:12		

2010 Quotable Star Trek Movies Transitions

COMPLETE SET (9)	8.00	20.00
COMPLETE SET W/RR (10)	15.00	40.00
COMMON CARD (T1-T9)	1.00	2.50
STATED ODDS 1:12		
T10 ISSUED AS RITTENHOUSE REWARD		
T1 Kirk	1.50	4.00
T2 Spock	1.50	4.00
T10 USS Enterprise NCC-1701 SP RR	10.00	25.00

2010 Quotable Star Trek Movies Promos

COMMON CARD (P1-P4)	.75	2.00
P3 Enterprise ALB	3.00	8.00
P4 Borg Queen FACEBOOK	1.25	3.00

2010 Women of Star Trek

COMPLETE SET (81)	5.00	12.00
COMPLETE SET W/SP (90)	8.00	20.00
UNOPENED BOX (24 PACKS)	75.00	125.00
UNOPENED PACK (5 CARDS)	4.00	6.00
COMMON CARD (1-81)	.12	.30
EXPANSION CARD (82-90)	.75	2.00

2010 Women of Star Trek ArtiFex

COMPLETE SET (10)	8.00	20.00
COMMON CARD (1-10)	1.25	3.00
STATED ODDS 1:8		

2010 Women of Star Trek Autographs

COMMON AUTO	4.00	10.00
STATED ODDS 1:8		
L (LIMITED): 300-500 COPIES		
VL (VERY LIMITED): 200-300 COPIES		
BARRETT AUTO ISSUED AS 6-CASE INCENTIVE		
NNO Andrea Martin VL	12.00	30.00
NNO Antoinette Bower	10.00	25.00
NNO BarBara Luna	10.00	25.00
NNO Barbara Williams	5.00	12.00
NNO Carolyn Seymour	6.00	15.00
NNO Chase Masterson	15.00	40.00
NNO Claire Rankin	5.00	12.00
NNO Denise Crosby	20.00	50.00
NNO Elizabeth Dennehy VL	25.00	60.00
NNO Emily Banks	10.00	25.00
NNO Famke Janssen VL	125.00	250.00
NNO France Nuyen VL	60.00	120.00
NNO Gates McFadden VL	25.00	60.00
NNO Grace Lee Whitney L	25.00	60.00
NNO Gwynyth Walsh	5.00	12.00
NNO Jennifer Lien VL	20.00	50.00
NNO Jeri Ryan VL	60.00	120.00
NNO Joan Collins VL	125.00	250.00
NNO Julie Caitlin Brown	6.00	15.00
NNO Kate Mulgrew VL	50.00	100.00
NNO Lee Meriwether L	15.00	40.00
NNO Lisa Wilcox	5.00	12.00
NNO Louise Fletcher	8.00	20.00
NNO Majel Barrett 6CI	100.00	200.00
NNO Mariette Hartley L	12.00	30.00
NNO Marina Sirtis VL	50.00	100.00
NNO Megan Gallagher	6.00	15.00
NNO Michele Scarabelli	5.00	12.00
NNO Michelle Forbes L	15.00	40.00
NNO Musetta Vander	6.00	15.00
NNO Nana Visitor VL	30.00	75.00
NNO Nana Visitor/Terry Farrell	50.00	100.00
NNO Natalija Nogulich L	10.00	25.00
NNO Nichelle Nichols VL	50.00	100.00
NNO Penny Johnson Jerald	8.00	20.00
NNO Rhonda Aldrich L	10.00	25.00
NNO Robin Curtis	6.00	15.00
NNO Sabrian Scarf CT	10.00	25.00
NNO Sally Kellerman	12.00	30.00
NNO Sherry Jackson	25.00	60.00
NNO Susan Gibney	6.00	15.00
NNO Suzie Plakson	6.00	15.00
NNO Terry Farrell VL	30.00	75.00
NNO Tina Lifford	6.00	15.00

2010 Women of Star Trek Costumes

COMPLETE SET (23)	150.00	300.00
COMPLETE SET W/SP (25)	225.00	450.00
COMMON CARD (WCC1-WCC25)	8.00	20.00
STATED ODDS 1:12		
WCC1 Kathryn Janeway	10.00	25.00
WCC3 Kathryn Janeway	10.00	25.00
WCC5 Beverly Crusher	15.00	40.00
WCC7 Seven of Nine	10.00	25.00
WCC8 Seven of Nine	10.00	25.00
WCC9 T'Pol	12.00	30.00
WCC10 T'Pol	10.00	25.00
WCC11 T'Pol	10.00	25.00
WCC15 Deanna Troi SP	125.00	200.00
WCC17 Kes	10.00	25.00
WCC22 Seven of Nine SP	50.00	100.00
WCC23 Seven of Nine	12.00	30.00

2010 Women of Star Trek Leading Ladies

COMPLETE SET (9)	12.00	30.00
COMMON CARD (LL1-LL9)	2.00	5.00
STATED ODDS 1:24		

2010 Women of Star Trek Romantic Relationships

COMPLETE SET (9)	12.00	30.00
COMMON CARD (RR1-RR9)	1.50	4.00
STATED ODDS 1:24		

2010 Women of Star Trek Promos

COMMON CARD (P1-P4)	.75	2.00
P3 Dax ALB	3.00	8.00
P4 Deanna Troi SDCC	15.00	40.00

2021 Rittenhouse Women of Star Trek Art and Images

COMPLETE SET (72)	8.00	20.00
UNOPENED BOX (24 PACKS)	60.00	90.00
UNOPENED PACK (5 CARDS)	2.50	4.00
COMMON CARD (1-72)	.25	.60
*BLUE/99: 4X TO 10X BASIC CARDS		
*RED/50: 20X TO 50X BASIC CARDS		
P.PLATES ARE ARCHIVES BOX EXCLUSIVE		

2021 Rittenhouse Women of Star Trek Art and Images '10 Expansion

COMPLETE SET (18)	12.00	30.00
COMMON CARD (91-108)	1.00	2.50
STATED ODDS 1:24		

2021 Rittenhouse Women of Star Trek Art and Images 20th Anniversary Archive Collection

COMPLETE SET (12)	150.00	300.00
COMMON CARD (AC17-AC28)	15.00	40.00
STATED PRINT RUN 99 SER.#'d SETS		

2021 Rittenhouse Women of Star Trek Art and Images Artist Rendition

COMPLETE SET (24)	10.00	25.00
COMMON CARD (AR01-AR24)	1.25	3.00
*RED/50: 6X TO 15X BASIC CARDS		
STATED ODDS 1:12		

2021 Rittenhouse Women of Star Trek Art and Images Autographed Relic

NNO Mary Chieffo EL	50.00	100.00

2021 Rittenhouse Women of Star Trek Art and Images Autographs

COMMON AUTO	6.00	15.00
STATED OVERALL ODDS 1:18		
L = 300-500 COPIES		
VL = 200-300 COPIES		
EL = 100-200 COPIES		
S = 100 OR FEWER COPIES		
NNO Alice Eve VL	60.00	120.00
NNO April Tatro VL	15.00	40.00
NNO Ashley Judd EL	75.00	150.00
NNO Barbara Anderson VL	15.00	40.00
NNO Beth Toussiant VL	10.00	25.00
NNO Camille Saviola VL	10.00	25.00
NNO Carolyn Allport VL	10.00	25.00
NNO Catherine Hicks L	12.00	30.00
NNO Courtney Peldon VL	8.00	20.00
NNO Daphne Asbrook VL	8.00	20.00
NNO Deborah Lacey EL	20.00	50.00
NNO Deborah Van Valkenburgh AB	30.00	75.00
NNO Eileen Seeley VL	10.00	25.00
NNO Estee Chandler VL	12.00	30.00
NNO Helen Udy VL	8.00	20.00
NNO Jandi Swanson VL	8.00	20.00
NNO Judith Jones VL	12.00	30.00
NNO Karole Selmon VL	8.00	20.00
NNO Kirstie Alley VL	30.00	75.00
NNO Linda Park EL	30.00	75.00
NNO Louise Sorel EL	30.00	75.00
NNO Lucy Boryer VL	10.00	25.00
NNO Majel Barrett VL	50.00	100.00
NNO Margaret Reed VL	8.00	20.00
NNO Marina Sirtis EL	60.00	120.00
NNO Mary Chieffo	8.00	20.00
NNO Mary Wiseman EL	30.00	75.00
NNO Nichelle Nichols EL	50.00	100.00
NNO Nicole De Boer VL	30.00	75.00
NNO Oyin Oladejo VL	10.00	25.00
NNO Peyton List AB	100.00	200.00

NNO Sara Mitich VL	8.00	20.00
NNO Sofia Boutella EL	30.00	75.00
NNO Sonequa Martin-Green S	100.00	200.00
NNO Tamilyn Tomita VL	12.00	30.00
NNO Tracy Scoggins VL	10.00	25.00
NNO Walker Brandt VL	10.00	25.00
NNO Wendy Robie EL	10.00	25.00

2021 Rittenhouse Women of Star Trek Art and Images Classic Autographs

COMMON AUTO	6.00	15.00
STATED OVERALL ODDS 1:18		
L = 300-500 COPIES		
VL = 200-300 COPIES		
EL = 100-200 COPIES		
S = 100 OR FEWER COPIES		
NNO Judith Jones TNG VL	12.00	30.00
NNO Julie Warner TNG L	8.00	20.00
NNO Karole Selmon TNG VL	10.00	25.00
NNO Lucy Boryer TNG VL	10.00	25.00
NNO Margaret Reed TNG VL	8.00	20.00
NNO Victoria George TOS VL	15.00	40.00
NNO Walker Brandt TNG VL	10.00	25.00
A314 Barbara Anderson TOS VL	10.00	25.00
A315 Barbara Baldavin TOS VL	12.00	30.00

2021 Rittenhouse Women of Star Trek Art and Images Dual Autograph

NNO S.Martin-Green/M.Kirshner	125.00	250.00

2021 Rittenhouse Women of Star Trek Art and Images Quotables

COMPLETE SET (18)	8.00	20.00
COMMON CARD (Q19-Q36)	1.00	2.50
STATED ODDS 1:24		

2021 Rittenhouse Women of Star Trek Art and Images Relic

RC51 T'Pol	50.00	100.00

2021 Rittenhouse Women of Star Trek Art and Images Rendered Art Metal Toppers

COMMON CARD (CT1-CT2)		
STATED ODDS 1:CASE		
CT2 Seven of Nine	12.00	30.00

2021 Rittenhouse Women of Star Trek Art and Images Starfleet's Finest Painted Potrait Metal

COMMON CARD (AC60-AC77)	25.00	60.00
STATED PRINT RUN 50 SER.#'d SETS		
AC60 Lt. Commander Uhura	30.00	75.00
AC61 Dr. Chapel	50.00	100.00
AC62 Chief Petty Officer Rand	30.00	75.00
AC63 Lieutenant Ilia	30.00	75.00
AC64 Dr. Carol Marcus	50.00	100.00
AC65 Lieutenant Saavik	30.00	75.00
AC66 Dr. Gillian Taylor	50.00	100.00
AC70 Number One	50.00	100.00
AC74 Lt. Junior Grade Joann Owosekun	30.00	75.00
AC75 Lt. Commander Airiam	30.00	75.00
AC76 Uhura	50.00	100.00
AC77 Carol Marcus	50.00	100.00

2021 Rittenhouse Women of Star Trek Art and Images Various Autographs

COMMON AUTO	6.00	15.00
STATED OVERALL ODDS 1:18		
L = 300-500 COPIES		
VL = 200-300 COPIES		
EL = 100-200 COPIES		
S = 100 OR FEWER COPIES		
LA18 Alice Eve LEGENDS VL	50.00	100.00
NNO Barbara Anderson SILVER SIG VL	15.00	40.00
NNO Barbara Anderson TOS BLACK VL	12.00	30.00
NNO Barbara Anderson TOS INS L	60.00	120.00
NNO Bertila Damas ALIENS VL	10.00	25.00
LA19 Catherine Hicks LEGENDS L	15.00	40.00
NNO Daphne Ashbrook ALIENS VL	10.00	25.00
NNO Felicia Bell AB	75.00	150.00
NNO Grace Lee Whitney LEGENDS EL	30.00	75.00
NNO Isa Briones PICARD EL	60.00	120.00
NNO Jeri Ryan AB	200.00	400.00
NNO Kirstie Alley LEGENDS VL	50.00	100.00
NNO Michelle Yeoh DISCOVERY VL	50.00	100.00
NNO Nana Visitor 6CI	30.00	75.00
NNO Nicole De Boer DS9 VL	15.00	40.00
NNO Nicole De Boer DS9Q VL	20.00	50.00
NNO Nicole De Boer SILVER SIG VL	20.00	50.00
NNO Robin Curtis LEGENDS	10.00	25.00
NNO Sofia Boutella LEGENDS EL	30.00	75.00
NNO Tig Notaro DISCOVERY VL	15.00	40.00
NNO Tracy Scoggins ALIENS VL	10.00	25.00
NNO Victoria George TOS BLACK VL	15.00	40.00
NNO Whoopi Goldberg TNGQ EL	75.00	150.00
NNO Zoe Saldana MOVIES S	200.00	400.00

2021 Rittenhouse Women of Star Trek Art and Images Women of Star Trek Universe Gallery

COMPLETE SET W/O RR (17)	6.00	15.00
COMMON CARD (U19-U34)	.60	1.50
STATED ODDS 1:12		
U35 IS A RITTENHOUSE REWARD		
U35 L'Rell (Rittenhouse Reward)	25.00	60.00

2021 Rittenhouse Women of Star Trek Art and Images Promos

P1 Album Exclusive	4.00	10.00

2017 Women of Star Trek 50th Anniversary

COMPLETE SET (100)	6.00	15.00
UNOPENED BOX (24 PACKS)	60.00	75.00
UNOPENED PACK (5 CARDS)	3.00	4.00
COMMON CARD (1-100)	.15	.40
*METAL: 12X TO 30X BASIC CARDS	5.00	12.00

2017 Women of Star Trek 50th Anniversary Autographs

COMMON CARD (UNNUMBERED)	5.00	12.00
L = 300-500 COPIES		
VL = 200-300 COPIES		
EL = 100-200 COPIES		
STATED ODDS 1:8		
NNO Adrienne Barbeau L	6.00	15.00
NNO Annette Helde VL	6.00	15.00
NNO Barbara Babcock VL	8.00	20.00
NNO Barbara Bouchet L	6.00	15.00
NNO Bridget Anne White VL	10.00	25.00
NNO Cari Shayne VL	8.00	20.00
NNO Cyia Batten VL	6.00	15.00
NNO Deirdre Imershein as Joval VL	6.00	15.00
NNO Deirdre Imershein as Lt. Watley VL	8.00	20.00
NNO Elinor Donahue L	6.00	15.00
NNO Fionnula Flanagan VL	6.00	15.00
NNO Galyn Gorg L	6.00	15.00
NNO Heidi Swedberg VL	10.00	25.00
NNO Jennifer Nash VL	6.00	15.00
NNO Jeri Ryan VL	30.00	80.00
NNO Jill Jacobson VL	6.00	15.00
NNO Julie Warner VL	8.00	20.00
NNO Kathryn Hays EL	30.00	80.00
NNO Kim Rhodes VL	6.00	15.00
NNO Linda Thorson VL	10.00	25.00
NNO Lori Petty VL	8.00	20.00
NNO Madchen Amick L	6.00	15.00
NNO Maggie Thrett L	6.00	15.00
NNO Margot Rose VL	6.00	15.00
NNO Marina Sirtis VL	25.00	60.00
NNO Martha Hackett VL	8.00	20.00
NNO Melanie Smith VL	6.00	15.00
NNO Molly Hagan VL	6.00	15.00
NNO Nichelle Nichols 6CI	60.00	120.00
NNO Pamelyn Ferdin L	6.00	15.00
NNO Robin Curtis VL	6.00	15.00
NNO Roxann Dawson L	12.00	30.00
NNO Salome Jens VL	6.00	15.00
NNO Scarlett Pomers VL	8.00	20.00
NNO Shannon Cochrane VL	6.00	15.00
NNO Sharon Lawrence VL	10.00	25.00
NNO Susanna Thompson VL	10.00	25.00
NNO Tasia Valenza VL	6.00	15.00
NNO Teri Garr AB	250.00	400.00
NNO Tricia O'Neil VL	8.00	20.00
NNO Vanessa Williams EL	75.00	150.00
NNO Virginia Madsen VL	8.00	20.00
NNO Whoopi Goldberg EL	50.00	100.00
NNO Yvonne Craig EL	30.00	80.00
NNO Zoe McLellan VL	6.00	15.00

2017 Women of Star Trek 50th Anniversary Costumes

COMMON CARD (RC1-RC15)	5.00	12.00
STATED ODDS 1:24		
WCC27 IS ARCHIVE BOX EXCLUSIVE		
RC3 Anij	6.00	15.00
RC4 Anij	6.00	15.00
RC5 Anij	6.00	15.00
RC6 Guinan	6.00	15.00
RC10 T'Pol	8.00	20.00
RC14 Keiko O'Brien	6.00	15.00
WCC16 Yeoman Rand	60.00	120.00
WCC27 Seven of Nine AB	120.00	200.00

2017 Women of Star Trek 50th Anniversary Gold Metal

COMPLETE SET (19)	200.00	400.00
COMMON CARD (WS1-WS19)	10.00	25.00
STATED ODDS 1:96		
WS1 Majel Barrett as Number One	12.00	30.00
WS4 Grace Lee Whitney as Janice Rand	15.00	40.00
WS5 Gates McFadden as Beverly Crusher	12.00	30.00
WS6 Marina Sirtis as Deanna Troi	15.00	40.00
WS7 Whoopi Goldberg as Guinan	12.00	30.00
WS8 Denise Crosby as Tasha Yar	12.00	30.00
WS11 Nana Visitor as Kira Nerys	12.00	30.00
WS13 Nicole de Boer as Ezri Dax	12.00	30.00
WS16 Jeri Ryan as Seven of Nine	20.00	50.00

2017 Women of Star Trek 50th Anniversary Quotables

COMPLETE SET (18)	10.00	25.00
COMMON CARD (QW1-QW18)	1.50	4.00
STATED ODDS 1:24		

2017 Women of Star Trek 50th Anniversary Women in Command

COMPLETE SET (10)	10.00	25.00
COMMON CARD (WC1-WC10)	2.00	5.00
STATED ODDS 1:12		
WC10 Erika Hernandez RR	4.00	10.00

2017 Women of Star Trek 50th Anniversary Promos

COMMON CARD (P1-P2)	2.50	6.00
*METAL: .75X TO 2X BASIC CARDS		
P2 Seven of Nine ALB	3.00	8.00

2000 Women of Star Trek In Motion

COMPLETE SET (32)	12.50	30.00
UNOPENED BOX (20 PACKS)	150.00	250.00
UNOPENED PACK (3 CARDS)		12.00
COMMON CARD (1-32)	.40	1.00

2000 Women of Star Trek In Motion Archive Collection

COMPLETE SET (16)	80.00	150.00
COMMON CARD (AC1-AC16)	4.00	10.00
STATED ODDS 3:BOX		

2000 Women of Star Trek In Motion Archive Collection Gold

COMPLETE SET (4)	80.00	150.00
COMMON CARD (1-4)	20.00	50.00
STATED PRINT RUN 500 SER. #'d SETS		

2000 Women of Star Trek In Motion Autographs

COMPLETE SET (5)	75.00	150.00
COMMON CARD (A1-A5)	15.00	40.00
STATED ODDS 1:BOX		
A1 Denise Crosby	20.00	50.00
A4 Alice Krige	12.00	30.00
A5 Terry Farrell	15.00	40.00

2000 Women of Star Trek In Motion Extension

COMPLETE SET (5)	30.00	75.00
COMMON CARD (G1-G5)	8.00	20.00
STATED PRINT RUN 999 SER. #'d SETS		

2000 Women of Star Trek In Motion Heroines of Star Trek

COMPLETE SET (4)	3.00	8.00
COMMON CARD (H1-H4)	1.00	2.50
STATED ODDS 1:8		

2000 Women of Star Trek In Motion Seven of Nine Extension

COMPLETE SET (5)	20.00	50.00
COMMON CARD (S1-S5)	5.00	12.00

2000 Women of Star Trek In Motion Sound in Motion

COMPLETE SET (6)	40.00	100.00
COMMON CARD (S1-S6)	8.00	20.00
STATED ODDS 1:BOX		
BS1 ISSUED AS ALBUM EXCLUSIVE		
CS1 ISSUED AS CASE TOPPER		

2000 Women of Star Trek In Motion Villainesses of Star Trek

COMPLETE SET (4)	3.00	8.00
COMMON CARD (V1-V4)	1.00	2.50
STATED ODDS 1:5		

2000 Women of Star Trek In Motion Promos

COMPLETE SET (40)	75.00	150.00
COMMON CARD	1.50	4.00
ANNOUNCED PRINT RUN 300 SETS		

Star Wars

A New Hope

1977 Topps Star Wars

COMPLETE SET W/STICKERS (330)	500.00	1000.00
COMP.SER.1 SET W/STICKERS (66)	300.00	600.00
COMP.SER.2 SET W/STICKERS (66)	150.00	300.00
COMP.SER.3 SET W/STICKERS (66)	125.00	250.00
COMP.SER.4 SET W/STICKERS (66)	125.00	250.00
COMP.SER.5 SET W/STICKERS (66)	100.00	200.00
SER.1 BOX (36 PACKS)	8000.00	15000.00
SER.1 PACK (7 CARDS+1 STICKER)	150.00	300.00
SER.2 BOX (36 PACKS)	2000.00	3500.00
SER.2 PACK (7 CARDS+1 STICKER)	75.00	125.00
SER.3 BOX (36 PACKS)	1750.00	3000.00
SER.3 PACK (7 CARDS+1 STICKER)	60.00	100.00
SER.4 BOX (36 PACKS)	1750.00	3000.00
SER.4 PACK (7 CARDS+1 STICKER)	50.00	100.00
SER.5 BOX (36 PACKS)	1500.00	3000.00
SER.5 PACK (7 CARDS+1 STICKER)	50.00	100.00
COMMON BLUE (1-66)	1.25	3.00
COMMON RED (67-132)	.75	2.00
COMMON YELLOW (133-198)	.75	2.00
COMMON GREEN (199-264)	.75	2.00
COMMON ORANGE (265-330)	1.25	3.00
1 Luke Skywalker	25.00	60.00
2 C-3PO and R2-D2	4.00	10.00
3 The Little Droid R2-D2	6.00	15.00
4 Space pirate Han Solo	10.00	25.00
5 Princess Leia Organa	12.00	30.00
6 Ben Kenobi	4.00	10.00
7 The villainous Darth Vader	12.00	30.00
8 Grand Moff Tarkin	2.50	6.00
10 Princess Leia captured!	1.00	5.00
207A C-3PO A.Daniels ERR Obscene	75.00	150.00
207B C-3PO A.Daniels COR Airbrushed	15.00	40.00

1977 Topps Star Wars Stickers

COMPLETE SET (55)	100.00	200.00
COMPLETE SERIES 1 (11)	50.00	100.00
COMPLETE SERIES 2 (11)	15.00	40.00
COMPLETE SERIES 3 (11)	15.00	40.00
COMPLETE SERIES 4 (11)	12.00	30.00
COMPLETE SERIES 5 (11)	12.00	30.00
COMMON STICKER (1-11)	3.00	8.00
COMMON STICKER (12-22)	2.00	5.00
COMMON STICKER (23-33)	1.50	4.00
COMMON STICKER (34-44)	1.25	3.00
COMMON STICKER (45-55)	1.25	3.00
1 Luke Skywalker	12.00	30.00
2 Princess Leia Organa	6.00	15.00
3 Han Solo	6.00	15.00
4 Chewbacca the Wookiee	5.00	12.00
5 See-Threepio	4.00	10.00
6 Artoo-Detoo	8.00	20.00
7 Lord Darth Vader	20.00	50.00
8 Grand Moff Tarkin	4.00	10.00
9 Ben (Obi-Wan) Kenobi	4.00	10.00
12 Han and Chewbacca	5.00	12.00
13 Alec Guinness as Ben	3.00	8.00
14 The Tusken Raider	2.50	6.00
15 See-Threepio	3.00	8.00
16 Chewbacca	3.00	8.00
18 The Rebel Fleet	2.50	6.00
19 The Wookiee Chewbacca	4.00	10.00
20 R2-D2 and C-3PO	2.50	6.00
23 Dave Prowse as Darth Vader	5.00	12.00
28 Peter Cushing as Grand Moff Tarkin	2.50	6.00
29 Han Solo Hero Or Mercenary?	4.00	10.00
30 Stormtroopers	3.00	8.00
31 Princess Leia Comforts Luke	3.00	8.00
32 Preparing for the Raid	2.00	5.00
34 The Star Warriors Aim for Action!	1.50	4.00
35 Han Solo (Harrison Ford)	5.00	12.00
36 Star Pilot Luke Skywalker	2.50	6.00
37 The Marvelous Droid See-Threepio!	2.00	5.00
38 R2-D2 (Kenny Baker)	2.50	6.00
40 Darth Vader (David Prowse)	12.00	30.00
42 Luke Poses with His Weapon	4.00	10.00
45 A Crucial Moment for Luke Skywalker	2.50	6.00
46 Chewie Aims for Danger!	1.50	4.00
48 Inside the Sandcrawler	1.50	4.00
50 George Lucas and Greedo	1.50	4.00
51 Technicians Ready C-3PO for the Cameras	1.50	4.00

1977 Topps Mexican Star Wars

COMPLETE SET (66)	300.00	600.00
UNOPENED PACK (2 CARDS)	35.00	40.00
COMMON CARD (1-66)	5.00	12.00

1977 O-Pee-Chee Star Wars

COMPLETE SET (264)	200.00	400.00
COMPLETE SERIES 1 SET (66)	100.00	200.00
COMPLETE SERIES 2 SET (66)	60.00	120.00
COMPLETE SERIES 3 SET (132)	50.00	100.00
UNOPENED SERIES 1 BOX (36 PACKS)		
UNOPENED SERIES 1 PACK (7 CARDS+1 STICKER)		
UNOPENED SERIES 2 BOX (36 PACKS)		
UNOPENED SERIES 2 PACK (7 CARDS+1 STICKER)		
UNOPENED SERIES 3 BOX (36 PACKS)		
UNOPENED SERIES 3 PACK (7 CARDS+1 STICKER)		
COMMON BLUE (1-66)	2.50	5.00
COMMON RED (67-132)	1.25	3.00
COMMON ORANGE (133-264)	.50	1.25

1978 General Mills Star Wars

COMPLETE SET (18)	12.00	30.00
COMMON CARD (1-18)	1.00	2.50

1977 Tip Top Ice Cream Star Wars

COMPLETE SET (15)	150.00	300.00
COMMON CARD	15.00	40.00

ALSO KNOWN AS R2-D2 SPACE ICE

1977 Wonder Bread Star Wars

COMPLETE SET (16)	100.00	200.00
COMMON CARD (1-16)	5.00	12.00
1 Luke Skywalker	10.00	25.00
3 Princess Leia Organa	8.00	20.00
4 Han Solo	10.00	25.00
5 Darth Vader	20.00	50.00
9 Chewbacca	6.00	15.00
10 Jawas	6.00	15.00
11 Tusken Raiders	6.00	15.00
13 Millenium Falcon	8.00	20.00
15 X-Wing	6.00	15.00
16 Tie-Vader's Ship	6.00	15.00

1995 Topps Widevision Star Wars

COMPLETE SET (120)	15.00	40.00
UNOPENED BOX (36 PACKS)	60.00	100.00
UNOPENED PACK (10 CARDS)	2.50	3.00
COMMON CARD (1-120)	.20	.50

1995 Topps Widevision Star Wars Finest

COMPLETE SET (10)	40.00	100.00
COMMON CARD (1-10)	5.00	12.00

STATED ODDS 1:11

2007 Star Wars 30th Anniversary

COMPLETE SET (120)	5.00	12.00
UNOPENED HOBBY BOX (24 PACKS)	500.00	800.00
UNOPENED HOBBY PACK (7 CARDS)	20.00	35.00
UNOPENED RETAIL BOX (24 PACKS)		
UNOPENED RETAIL PACK (7 CARDS)		
COMMON CARD (1-120)	.15	.40
*BLUE: 4X TO 10X BASIC CARDS		
*RED: 8X TO 20X BASIC CARDS		
*GOLD/30: 80X TO 150X BASIC CARDS		

2007 Star Wars 30th Anniversary Animation Cels

COMPLETE SET (9)	6.00	15.00
COMMON CARD (1-9)	1.50	4.00

STATED ODDS 1:6 RETAIL

2007 Star Wars 30th Anniversary Autographs

COMMON AUTO (UNNUMBERED)	10.00	20.00
STATED ODDS 1:43 HOBBY		
NNO Anthony Daniels	300.00	800.00
NNO Carrie Fisher	600.00	1200.00
NNO Christine Hewett	25.00	60.00
NNO Colin Higgins	40.00	100.00
NNO David Prowse	300.00	750.00
NNO Gary Kurtz	30.00	75.00
NNO George Roubichek	12.00	30.00
NNO Harrison Ford	3000.00	7500.00
NNO Joe Viskocil	15.00	40.00
NNO John Dykstra	20.00	50.00
NNO John Williams	2500.00	5000.00
NNO Jon Berg	12.00	30.00
NNO Ken Ralston	15.00	40.00
NNO Kenny Baker	250.00	600.00
NNO Lorne Peterson	12.00	30.00
NNO Maria De Aragon	15.00	40.00
NNO Norman Reynolds	25.00	60.00
NNO Peter Mayhew	150.00	400.00
NNO Phil Tippet	30.00	75.00
NNO Richard Edlund	15.00	40.00
NNO Richard LeParmentier	8.00	20.00
NNO Rusty Goffe	20.00	50.00

2007 Star Wars 30th Anniversary Blister Bonus

COMPLETE SET (3)	3.00	8.00
COMMON CARD (1-3)	1.25	3.00

STATED ODDS 1:BLISTER PACK

2007 Star Wars 30th Anniversary Magnets

COMPLETE SET (9)	12.00	30.00
COMMON CARD (UNNUMBERED)	1.50	4.00

STATED ODDS 1:8 RETAIL

2007 Star Wars 30th Anniversary Original Series Box-Toppers

SERIES 1 (1-66) BLUE	12.00	30.00
SERIES 2 (67-132) RED	12.00	30.00
SERIES 3 (133-198) YELLOW	12.00	30.00
SERIES 4 (199-264) GREEN	12.00	30.00
SERIES 5 (265-330) ORANGE SP	30.00	80.00

STATED ODDS 1:BOX

2007 Star Wars 30th Anniversary Triptych Puzzle

COMPLETE SET (27)	12.00	25.00
COMMON CARD (1-27)	.75	2.00

STATED ODDS 1:3

2017 Star Wars 40th Anniversary

COMPLETE SET (200)	10.00	25.00
UNOPENED BOX (24 PACKS)	120.00	150.00
UNOPENED PACK (8 CARDS)	5.00	6.50
COMMON CARD (1-200)	.20	.50
*GREEN: .5X TO 1.2X BASIC CARDS	.40	1.00
*BLUE: .6X TO 1.5X BASIC CARDS	.50	1.25
*PURPLE/100: 3X TO 8X BASIC CARDS	2.50	6.00
*GOLD/40: 6X TO 15X BASIC CARDS	5.00	12.00

2017 Star Wars 40th Anniversary Autographs

COMMON AUTO	6.00	15.00
*PURPLE/40: .6X TO 1.5X BASIC AUTOS		
*GOLD/10: 1X TO 2.5X BASIC AUTOS		
RANDOMLY INSERTED INTO PACKS		
AAAH Alan Harris	6.00	15.00
AAAL Al Lampert	10.00	20.00
AABF Barbara Frankland	10.00	25.00
AABL Bai Ling	8.00	20.00
AACR Clive Revill	10.00	25.00
AADL Denis Lawson	10.00	25.00
AADR Deep Roy	10.00	25.00
AAFF Femi Taylor	8.00	20.00
AAGB Glyn Baker	8.00	20.00
AAGH Garrick Hagon	8.00	20.00
AAGR George Roubicek	10.00	25.00
AAHQ Hugh Quarshie	10.00	25.00
AAIL Ian Liston	10.00	25.00
AAJB Jeremy Bulloch	15.00	40.00
AAJK Jack Klaff	10.00	25.00
AAKC Kenneth Colley	8.00	20.00
AAKR Kipsang Rotich	10.00	25.00
AAMC Michael Carter	12.00	30.00
AAMW Matthew Wood	10.00	25.00
AAPS Paul Springer	8.00	20.00
AARO Richard Oldfield	10.00	25.00
AASC Stephen Costantino	8.00	20.00
AATR Tim Rose	8.00	20.00
AACDW Corey Dee Williams	8.00	20.00
AAPBL Paul Blake	10.00	25.00
AAPBR Paul Brooke	8.00	20.00

2017 Star Wars 40th Anniversary Celebration Orlando Promos

COMPLETE SET (4)	225.00	450.00
COMMON CARD (C1-C4)	50.00	100.00
C1 Luke Skywalker	80.00	150.00
C2 Princess Leia	80.00	150.00
C3 Han Solo	60.00	120.00

2017 Star Wars 40th Anniversary Classic Stickers

COMMON CARD	12.00	30.00
STATED PRINT RUN 100 SER.#'d SETS		

2017 Star Wars 40th Anniversary Medallions

COMMON MEDALLION	6.00	15.00
MILLENNIUM FALCON (1-12)		
DEATH STAR (13-23)		
*BLUE/40: .5X TO 1.2X BASIC MEDALLIONS	8.00	20.00
*PURPLE/25: .6X TO 1.5X BASIC MEDALLIONS	10.00	25.00
*GOLD/10: 1.2X TO 3X BASIC MEDALLIONS	20.00	50.00

2017 Star Wars 40th Anniversary Patches

COMMON CARD (1-20)	5.00	12.00
*BLUE/40: 6X TO 1.5X BASIC CARDS	8.00	20.00
*PURPLE/25: 1X TO 2.5X BASIC CARDS	12.00	30.00
*GOLD/10: 1.5X TO 4X BASIC CARDS	20.00	50.00
RANDOMLY INSERTED INTO PACKS		
TARGET EXCLUSIVE		

2017 Star Wars 1978 Sugar Free Wrappers Set

COMPLETE SET (49)	10.00	25.00
COMPLETE FACTORY SET (51)		
COMMON CARD (1-49)	.30	.75
*BLUE/75: 2X TO 5X BASIC CARDS	1.50	4.00
*GREEN/40: 4X TO 10X BASIC CARDS	3.00	8.00
*GOLD/10: 6X TO 15X BASIC CARDS	5.00	12.00

2017 Star Wars 1978 Sugar Free Wrappers Set Autographs

COMMON AUTO	8.00	20.00
STATED ODDS 2:SET		
NNO Alan Harris/199	15.00	40.00
NNO Angus MacInnes/99	10.00	25.00
NNO Barbara Frankland/50	10.00	25.00
NNO Clive Revill/99	12.00	30.00
NNO Corey Dee Williams/50	10.00	25.00
NNO David Ankrum/45	25.00	60.00
NNO Deep Roy/50	12.00	30.00
NNO Denis Lawson/99	15.00	40.00
NNO Dickey Beer/Barada/99	12.00	30.00
NNO Dickey Beer/Boba Fett/99	15.00	40.00
NNO Dickey Beer/Scout Trooper/99	10.00	25.00
NNO Femi Taylor/99	10.00	25.00
NNO Garrick Hagon/199	10.00	25.00
NNO Jeremy Bulloch/99	20.00	50.00
NNO John Morton/45	10.00	25.00
NNO John Ratzenberger/135	10.00	25.00
NNO Julian Glover/99	12.00	30.00
NNO Mark Dodson/199	12.00	30.00
NNO Michael Carter/99	10.00	25.00
NNO Mike Quinn/Nien Nunb/99	12.00	30.00
NNO Mike Quinn/Sy Snootles/99	15.00	40.00
NNO Paul Blake/199	10.00	25.00
NNO Tim Rose/99	12.00	30.00
NNO Toby Philpott/199	10.00	25.00
NNO Warwick Davis/99	15.00	40.00

2013 Star Wars Illustrated A New Hope

COMPLETE SET (100)	8.00	20.00
COMMON CARD (1-100)	.20	.50
*PURPLE: 2.5X TO 6X BASIC CARDS		
*BRONZE: 5X TO 12X BASIC CARDS		
*GOLD/10: 50X TO 120X BASIC CARDS		

2013 Star Wars Illustrated A New Hope Film Cels

COMPLETE SET (20)	250.00	500.00
COMMON CARD (FR1-FR20)	12.00	30.00
FR8 Greedo's Bounty	15.00	40.00
FR14 The Final Encounter	60.00	120.00

2013 Star Wars Illustrated A New Hope Movie Poster Reinterpretations

COMPLETE SET (9)	5.00	12.00
COMMON CARD (MP1-MP9)	1.25	3.00
STATED ODDS 1:3		

2013 Star Wars Illustrated A New Hope One Year Earlier

COMPLETE SET (18)	5.00	12.00
COMMON CARD (OY1-OY18)	.60	1.50
STATED ODDS 1:2		

2013 Star Wars Illustrated A New Hope Radio Drama Puzzle

COMPLETE SET (6)	5.00	12.00
COMMON CARD (1-6)	1.50	4.00
STATED ODDS 1:8		

2013 Star Wars Illustrated A New Hope The Mission Destroy the Death Star

COMPLETE SET (12)	30.00	60.00
COMMON CARD (1-12)	3.00	8.00
STATED ODDS 1:12		

2013 Star Wars Illustrated A New Hope Promos

COMPLETE SET (4)	5.00	12.00

2018 Star Wars A New Hope Black and White

COMPLETE SET (140)	15.00	40.00
UNOPENED BOX (7 PACKS)		
UNOPENED PACK (8 CARDS)		
COMMON CARD (1-140)	.25	.60
*SEPIA: .75X TO 2X BASIC CARDS	.50	1.25
*BLUE: 1X TO 2.5X BASIC CARDS	.60	1.50
*GREEN/99: 3X TO 8X BASIC CARDS	2.00	5.00
*PURPLE/25: 8X TO 20X BASIC CARDS	5.00	12.00

2018 Star Wars A New Hope Black and White Autographs

COMMON AUTO	6.00	15.00
*BLUE/99: .5X TO 1.2X BASIC AUTOS		
*GREEN/25: .6X TO 1.5X BASIC AUTOS		
STATED ODDS 1:18		
NNO Al Lampert	8.00	20.00
NNO Annette Jones	8.00	20.00
NNO Barbara Frankland	8.00	20.00
NNO Denis Lawson	12.00	30.00
NNO Garrick Hagon	8.00	20.00
NNO Paul Blake	10.00	25.00

2018 Star Wars A New Hope Black and White Autographs Blue

*BLUE: .5X TO 1.2X BASIC AUTOS		
STATED ODDS 1:62		
STATED PRINT RUN 99 SER.#'d SETS		
NNO Peter Mayhew	30.00	75.00

2018 Star Wars A New Hope Black and White Autographs Green

*GREEN: .6X TO 1.5X BASIC AUTOS		
STATED ODDS 1:202		
STATED PRINT RUN 25 SER.#'d SETS		
NNO Anthony Daniels	75.00	150.00
NNO Kenny Baker	60.00	120.00

2018 Star Wars A New Hope Black and White Behind-the-Scenes

COMPLETE SET (41)	20.00	50.00
COMMON CARD (BTS1-BTS41)	2.00	5.00
STATED ODDS 1:2		

2018 Star Wars A New Hope Black and White Concept Art

COMPLETE SET (12)	10.00	25.00
COMMON CARD (CA1-CA12)	1.50	4.00
STATED ODDS 1:4		

2018 Star Wars A New Hope Black and White Iconic Characters

COMPLETE SET (12)	15.00	40.00
COMMON CARD (IC1-IC12)	2.00	5.00
STATED ODDS 1:12		
IC1 Luke Skywalker	4.00	10.00
IC2 Han Solo	5.00	12.00
IC3 Princess Leia Organa	4.00	10.00
IC4 Chewbacca	2.50	6.00
IC5 Ben (Obi-Wan) Kenobi	4.00	10.00
IC7 R2-D2	2.50	6.00
IC8 Darth Vader	5.00	12.00

2018 Star Wars A New Hope Black and White Posters

COMPLETE SET (12)	12.00	30.00
COMMON CARD (PO1-PO12)	1.50	4.00
STATED ODDS 1:6		

Empire Strikes Back

1980 Topps Star Wars Empire Strikes Back

COMPLETE SET W/STICKERS (440)	125.00	250.00
COMPLETE SET (352)	100.00	200.00
COM.SERIES 1 SET W/STICKERS (165)	75.00	150.00
COM.SERIES 1 SET (132)	50.00	100.00
COM.SERIES 2 SET W/STICKERS (165)	50.00	100.00
COM.SERIES 2 SET (132)	30.00	75.00
COM.SERIES 3 SET W/STICKERS (110)	30.00	75.00
COM.SERIES 3 SET (88)	25.00	60.00
SERIES 1 BOX (36 PACKS)	1000.00	2000.00
SERIES 1 PACK (12 CARDS+1 STICKER)	30.00	60.00
SERIES 1 COL.BOX (80 CARDS+COL.BOX)	100.00	200.00
SERIES 1 RACK BOX (24 PACKS)		
SERIES 1 RACK PACK (51 CARDS)	75.00	150.00
SERIES 2 BOX (36 PACKS)	600.00	800.00
SERIES 2 PACK (12 CARDS+1 STICKER)	15.00	25.00
SERIES 3 BOX (36 PACKS)	500.00	1000.00
SERIES 3 PACK (12 CARDS+1 STICKER)	15.00	30.00
COMMON SERIES 1 CARD (1-132)	.60	1.50
COMMON SERIES 2 CARD (133-264)	.50	1.25
COMMON SERIES 3 CARD (265-352)	.60	1.50
210 The Captor, Boba Fett	2.00	5.00
220 Bounty Hunter Boba Fett	2.50	6.00
272 Boba Fett	8.00	20.00

1980 Topps Star Wars Empire Strikes Back Stickers

COMPLETE SET (88)	60.00	150.00
COMPLETE SERIES 1 SET (33)	50.00	100.00
COMPLETE SERIES 2 SET (33)	15.00	40.00
COMPLETE SERIES 3 SET (22)	12.00	30.00
COMMON CARD (1-33)	2.50	6.00
COMMON CARD (34-66)	1.00	2.50
COMMON CARD (67-88)	1.50	4.00
27 Stormtrooper, Luke, Yoda	3.00	8.00
56 Darth Vader	3.00	8.00
57 Boba Fett	6.00	15.00
58 Probot	2.50	6.00
59 Luke Skywalker	2.50	6.00
60 Princess Leia	3.00	8.00
61 Han Solo	2.50	6.00
62 Lando Calrissian	3.00	8.00
63 Chewbacca	3.00	8.00
64 R2-D2	2.50	6.00
65 C-3PO	4.00	10.00
66 Yoda	2.00	5.00

1980 Topps Star Wars Empire Strikes Back 5X7 Photos

COMPLETE SET (30)	25.00	50.00
UNOPENED BOX (36 PACKS)		
UNOPENED PACK (1 CARD)		
COMMON CARD (1-30)	1.50	4.00

1980 Topps Star Wars Empire Strikes Back 5X7 Photos Test Series

COMPLETE SET (30)	100.00	200.00
COMMON CARD (1-30)	3.00	8.00

1980 Hershey's Star Wars Empire Strikes Back

COMPLETE SET (5)	12.00	30.00
COMMON CARD	4.00	10.00
1 Boba Fett	5.00	12.00

1980 Twinkies Star Wars Empire Strikes Back New Zealandic

COMPLETE SET (6)	15.00	40.00
COMMON CARD	4.00	10.00

1980 York Peanut Butter Star Wars Empire Strikes Back Discs

COMPLETE SET (6)	12.00	30.00
COMMON CARD (1-6)	3.00	8.00

1995 Topps Widevision Star Wars Empire Strikes Back

COMPLETE SET (144)	12.00	30.00
UNOPENED BOX (36 PACKS)	50.00	75.00
UNOPENED PACK (9 CARDS)	2.00	3.00
COMMON CARD (1-144)	.25	.60

1995 Topps Widevision Star Wars Empire Strikes Back Finest

COMPLETE SET (10)	40.00	100.00
COMMON CARD (C1-C10)	4.00	10.00
STATED ODDS 1:12		

1995 Topps Widevision Star Wars Empire Strikes Back Mini Posters

COMPLETE SET (6)	40.00	80.00
COMMON CARD (1-6)	6.00	15.00
STATED ODDS 1:BOX		

1995 Topps Widevision Star Wars Empire Strikes Back Promos

COMMON CARD	2.00	5.00
NNO 3-Card Sheet	5.00	12.00
P1-P3		

2010 Star Wars Empire Strikes Back 3-D Widevision

COMPLETE SET (48)	10.00	25.00
UNOPENED BOX (24 PACKS)		
UNOPENED PACK (3 CARDS)		
COMMON CARD (1-48)	.40	1.00
P1 Luke Skywalker PROMO	8.00	20.00

2010 Star Wars Empire Strikes Back 3-D Widevision Autographs

COMMON AUTO	125.00	300.00
STATED ODDS 1:1,055		
1 Irvin Kershner	600.00	1500.00
2 Ralph McQuarrie	2000.00	4000.00
4 David Prowse	150.00	400.00
6 Carrie Fisher	750.00	2000.00
8 Mark Hamill	1500.00	4000.00

1996 Topps Star Wars Empire Strikes Back 3-Di

P1 AT-ATs	2.00	5.00

2019 Star Wars Empire Strikes Back Black and White

COMPLETE SET (150)	20.00	50.00
UNOPENED BOX (7 PACKS)	200.00	300.00
UNOPENED PACK (8 CARDS)	30.00	40.00

COMMON CARD (1-150) .30 .75
*SEPIA: 1X TO 2.5X BASIC CARDS
*BLUE HUE: 2.5X TO 6X BASIC CARDS
*GREEN HUE/99: 4X TO 10X BASIC CARDS
*PURPLE HUE/25: 6X TO 15X BASIC CARDS

2019 Star Wars Empire Strikes Back Black and White Autographs

*BLUE HUE/99: .5X TO 1.2X BASIC AUTOS
*GREEN HUE/25: .6X TO 1.5X BASIC AUTOS
STATED ODDS 1:22
AAH Alan Harris 15.00 40.00
ACM Cathy Munro 8.00 20.00
ACP Chris Parsons 8.00 20.00
ACR Clive Revill 6.00 15.00
AHW Howie Weed 8.00 20.00
AJB Jeremy Bulloch 40.00 100.00
AJM John Morton 8.00 20.00
AJR John Ratzenberger 15.00 40.00
AKC Kenneth Colley 8.00 20.00
AMC Mark Capri 6.00 15.00
AMJ Milton Johns 10.00 25.00
ARO Richarc Oldfield 8.00 20.00
AJMB John Morton 10.00 25.00

2019 Star Wars Empire Strikes Back Black and White Behind-the-Scenes

COMPLETE SET (40) 25.00 60.00
COMMON CARD (BTS1-BTS40) 1.25 3.00
STATED ODDS 1:2

2019 Star Wars Empire Strikes Back Black and White Concept Art

COMPLETE SET (10) 12.00 30.00
COMMON CARD (CA1-CA10) 2.00 5.00
STATED ODDS 1:4

2019 Star Wars Empire Strikes Back Black and White Iconic Characters

COMMON CARD (IC1-IC20) 5.00 12.00
STATED ODDS 1:12

2019 Star Wars Empire Strikes Back Black and White Posters

COMPLETE SET (10) 12.00 30.00
COMMON CARD (P01-P010) 2.00 5.00
STATED ODDS 1:6

2015 Star Wars Illustrated Empire Strikes Back

COMPLETE SET (100) 10.00 25.00
UNOPENED BOX (24 PACKS) 200.00 300.00
UNOPENED PACK (6 CARDS) 8.00 12.00
COMMON CARD (1-100) .20 .50
*PURPLE: 5X TO 12X BASIC CARDS 2.50 6.00
*BRONZE: 8X TO 20X BASIC CARDS 4.00 10.00
*GOLD/10: 20X TO 50X BASIC CARDS 10.00 25.00

2015 Star Wars Illustrated Empire Strikes Back Celebration VII Promos

COMPLETE SET (10) 10.00 25.00
COMMON CARD (1-10) 1.50 4.00

2015 Star Wars Illustrated Empire Strikes Back Artist Autographs

COMMON BUSCH (EVEN #'s) 5.00 12.00
COMMON MARTINEZ (ODD #'s) 5.00 12.00

2015 Star Wars Illustrated Empire Strikes Back Film Cel Relics

COMPLETE SET (25) 100.00 200.00
COMMON CARD (SKIP #'d) 6.00 15.00
FR2 Back at Echo Base 8.00 20.00
FR3 Monster in the Snow 8.00 20.00
FR6 The Imperial Walkers 10.00 25.00
FR7 Luke Vs. the AT-AT 8.00 20.00
FR8 Imperial Pursuit 10.00 25.00
FR9 Asteroid Field 8.00 20.00
FR10 Dagobah Landing 8.00 20.00
FR13 Message From the Emperor 12.00 30.00
FR15 Bounty Hunters Assemble 8.00 20.00
FR16 Failure at the Cave 10.00 25.00
FR20 A Most Gracious Host 10.00 25.00
FR25 You Are not a Jedi Yet 10.00 25.00
FR26 Lando's Redeption 8.00 20.00
FR27 Battle in the Gantry 10.00 25.00
FR28 The Truth Revealed 8.00 20.00
FR29 Rescuing Luke 15.00 40.00
FR30 Saying Farewell 8.00 20.00

2015 Star Wars Illustrated Empire Strikes Back Movie Poster Reinterpretations

COMPLETE SET (10) 8.00 20.00
COMMON CARD (MP1-MP10) 1.50 4.00
STATED ODDS 1:3

2015 Star Wars Illustrated Empire Strikes Back One Year Earlier

COMPLETE SET (18) 15.00 40.00
COMMON CARD (OY1-OY18) 1.50 4.00
STATED ODDS 1:2

2015 Star Wars Illustrated Empire Strikes Back The Force Awakens Inserts

COMPLETE SET (4) 20.00 50.00
COMMON CARD (SKIP #'d) 8.00 20.00

2015 Star Wars Illustrated Empire Strikes Back The Mission Capture Skywalker

COMPLETE SET (10) 12.00 30.00
COMMON CARD (1-10) 2.50 6.00
STATED ODDS 1:8
3 Han Solo 3.00 8.00
9 Boba Fett 4.00 10.00

2016 Topps Throwback Thursday Star Wars Empire Strikes Back

COMPLETE SET (6) 60.00 150.00
COMMON CARD (SW1-SW6) 15.00 40.00
STATED PRINT RUN 989 ANNCD SETS

2016 Star Wars Empire Strikes Back Bonus Abrams

COMPLETE SET (4) 5.00 12.00
COMMON CARD (1-4) 2.50 6.00

Return of the Jedi

1983 Topps Star Wars Return of the Jedi

COM.SET W/STICKERS (308)
COM.SET W/OSTICKERS (275) 75.00 150.00
COMPLETE SET (220) 60.00 120.00
COM.SERIES 1 SET W/STICKERS (165)
COM.SERIES 1 SET (132) 30.00 75.00
COM.SERIES 2 SET W/STICKERS (110)
COM.SERIES 2 SET (88) 20.00 50.00
SERIES 1 BOX (36 PACKS) 200.00 400.00
SERIES 1 PACK (12 CARDS+1 STICKER) 8.00 12.00
SERIES 2 BOX (36 PACKS) 150.00 300.00
SERIES 2 PACK (12 CARDS+1 STICKER) 6.00 10.00
COMMON SERIES 1 CARD (1-132) .50 1.25
COMMON SERIES 2 CARD (133-264) .50 1.25

1983 Topps Star Wars Return of the Jedi Stickers

COMPLETE SET W/VARIANTS (88) 50.00 100.00
COMPLETE SET W/O VARIANTS (55) 30.00 75.00
COMPLETE S1 SET A&B (66) 25.00 60.00
COMPLETE S1 SET (33) 8.00 20.00
COMPLETE S2 SET (22) 25.00 60.00
COMMON S1 PURPLE (1-11) .40 1.00
COMMON S1 YELLOW (1-11) .60 1.50
COMMON S1 RED (12-22) .75 2.00
COMMON S1 TURQUOISE (12-22) .40 1.00
COMMON S1 GREEN (23-33) .60 1.50
COMMON S1 ORANGE (23-33) .40 1.00
COMMON S2 (34-55) 1.50 4.00
STATED ODDS 1:1

2014 Star Wars Return of the Jedi 3-D Widevision

COMPLETE SET (44) 12.00 30.00
COMMON CARD (1-44) .50 1.25
TOPPS WEBSITE EXCLUSIVE SET

2014 Star Wars Return of the Jedi 3-D Widevision Autographs

COMMON AUTO (UNNUMBERED) 10.00 25.00
STATED ODDS 1:SET
NNO Carrie Fisher 600.00 1000.00
NNO Femi Taylor 15.00 40.00
NNO Jeremy Bulloch 50.00 100.00
NNO Kenneth Colley 15.00 40.00
NNO Mark Hamill 500.00 800.00
NNO Mike Quinn 20.00 50.00
NNO Peter Mayhew 75.00 150.00
NNO Tim Rose 20.00 50.00

2014 Star Wars Return of the Jedi 3-D Widevision Manufactured Patches

COMPLETE SET (4) 50.00 100.00
COMMON CARD 10.00 25.00
STATED ODDS ONE PATCH/SKETCH PER SET

2020 Topps Star Wars Return of the Jedi Black and White

COMPLETE SET (133) 12.00 30.00
UNOPENED BOX (7 PACKS) 100.00 150.00
UNOPENED PACK (8 CARDS) 15.00 20.00
COMMON CARD (1-133) .25 .60
*SEPIA: .5X TO 1.2X BASIC CARDS
*BLUE: .75X TO 2X BASIC CARDS
*GREEN/99: 2X TO 5X BASIC CARDS
*PURPLE/25: 3X TO 8X BASIC CARDS

2020 Topps Star Wars Return of the Jedi Black and White Autographs

COMMON AUTO 5.00 12.00
RANDOMLY INSERTED INTO PACKS
ACB Caroline Blakiston 6.00 15.00
ADR Deep Roy 8.00 20.00
AFT Femi Taylor 6.00 15.00
AJB Jeremy Bulloch 15.00 40.00
AMC Michael Carter 6.00 15.00
APB Paul Brooke 6.00 15.00
ATR Tim Rose 6.00 15.00
ADBB Dickey Beer 10.00 25.00
AMQS Mike Quinn 6.00 15.00

2020 Topps Star Wars Return of the Jedi Black and White Behind-the-Scenes

COMPLETE SET (24) 12.00 30.00
COMMON CARD (BTS1-BTS24) 1.00 2.50
RANDOMLY INSERTED INTO PACKS

2020 Topps Star Wars Return of the Jedi Black and White Concept Art

COMPLETE SET (19) 15.00 40.00
COMMON CARD (CA1-CA19) 1.25 3.00
RANDOMLY INSERTED INTO PACKS

2020 Topps Star Wars Return of the Jedi Black and White Iconic Characters

COMPLETE SET (15) 12.00 30.00
COMMON CARD (IC1-IC15) 1.50 4.00
RANDOMLY INSERTED INTO PACKS

2020 Topps Star Wars Return of the Jedi Black and White Posters

COMPLETE SET (6) 5.00 12.00
COMMON CARD (P1-P6) 1.00 2.50
RANDOMLY INSERTED INTO PACKS

1983 Kellogg's Star Wars Return of the Jedi Stick'R

COMPLETE SET (10) 12.00 30.00
COMMON CARD (1-10) 2.00 5.00

1983 O-Pee-Chee Star Wars Return of the Jedi

COMPLETE SET (132) 25.00 60.00
UNOPENED BOX (36 PACKS) 125.00 150.00
UNOPENED PACK 4.00 5.00
COMMON CARD (1-132) .30 .75

1997 Lucasfilm Star Wars Return of the Jedi Special Edition

NNO Crescent City Con XII

1996 Topps Widevision Star Wars Return of the Jedi

COMPLETE SET (144) 10.00 25.00
UNOPENED BOX (24 PACKS) 50.00 100.00
UNOPENED PACK (9 CARDS) 2.50 4.00
COMMON CARD (1-144) .20 .50
DIII Admiral Akbar

1996 Topps Widevision Star Wars Return of the Jedi Finest

COMPLETE SET (10) 40.00 80.00
COMMON CARD (C1-C10) 4.00 10.00
STATED ODDS 1:12

1996 Topps Widevision Star Wars Return of the Jedi Mini Posters

COMPLETE SET (6) 40.00 80.00
COMMON CARD (1-6) 6.00 15.00
STATED ODDS 1:BOX

1996 Topps Widevision Star Wars Return of the Jedi Promos

COMMON CARD 2.00 5.00
P6 Luke, Han, & Chewbacca in Jabba's Palace 25.00 60.00
NNO 1-Card Sheet
Complete the Trilogy

The Phantom Menace

1999 Topps Widevision Star Wars Episode I Series One

COMPLETE SET (80) 8.00 20.00
UNOPENED HOBBY BOX (36 PACKS) 50.00 75.00
UNOPENED HOBBY PACK (8 CARDS) 2.00 3.00
UNOPENED RETAIL BOX (11 PACKS) 30.00 45.00
UNOPENED RETAIL PACK (8 CARDS) 2.75 4.00
COMMON CARD (1-80) .25 .60

1999 Topps Widevision Star Wars Episode I Series One Chrome

COMPLETE SET (8) 30.00 60.00
COMMON CARD (C1-C8) 4.00 10.00
STATED ODDS 1:12

1999 Topps Widevision Star Wars Episode I Series One Expansion

COMPLETE SET (40) 30.00 60.00
COMMON CARD (X1-X40) 1.00 2.50
STATED ODDS 1:2

1999 Topps Widevision Star Wars Episode I Series One Foil

COMPLETE SET (10) 30.00 60.00
COMMON CARD (F1-F10) 3.00 8.00

1999 Topps Widevision Star Wars Episode I Series One Stickers

COMPLETE SET (16) 8.00 20.00
COMMON CARD (S1-S16) .60 1.50

1999 Topps Widevision Star Wars Episode I Series One Tin Inserts

COMPLETE SET (5) 12.00 30.00

COMMON CARD (1-5) 4.00 10.00
STATED ODDS ONE PER RETAIL TIN
2 Darth Maul 5.00 12.00

1999 Topps Widevision Star Wars Episode I Series Two

COMPLETE SET (80) 8.00 20.00
UNOPENED HOBBY BOX (36 PACKS) 50.00 75.00
UNOPENED HOBBY PACK (8 CARDS) 2.00 3.00
UNOPENED RETAIL BOX (24 PACKS) 35.00 45.00
UNOPENED RETAIL PACK (8 CARDS) 1.50 1.75
COMMON CARD (1-80) .25 .60

1999 Topps Widevision Star Wars Episode I Series Two Box-Toppers

COMPLETE SET (3) 10.00 20.00
COMMON CARD (1-3) 4.00 10.00
STATED ODDS 1:HOBBY BOX

1999 Topps Widevision Star Wars Episode I Series Two Chrome Hobby

COMPLETE SET (4) 12.00 25.00
COMMON CARD (HC1-HC4) 4.00 10.00
STATED ODDS 1:18 HOBBY

1999 Topps Widevision Star Wars Episode I Series Two Chrome Retail

COMPLETE SET (4) 20.00 40.00
COMMON CARD (C1-C4) 6.00 15.00
STATED ODDS 1:18 RETAIL

1999 Topps Widevision Star Wars Episode I Series Two Embossed Hobby

COMPLETE SET (6) 8.00 20.00
COMMON CARD (HE1-HE6) 2.50 6.00
STATED ODDS 1:12 HOBBY

1999 Topps Widevision Star Wars Episode I Series Two Embossed Retail

COMPLETE SET (6) 20.00 40.00
COMMON CARD (E1-E6) 4.00 10.00
STATED ODDS 1:12 RETAIL

1999 Topps Widevision Star Wars Episode I Series Two Promos

COMPLETE SET (2) 3.00 8.00
COMMON CARD (P1-P2) 2.00 5.00

2000 Star Wars Episode One 3-D

COMPLETE SET (46) 20.00 40.00
UNOPENED BOX (36 PACKS) 45.00 60.00
UNOPENED PACK (2 CARDS) 1.50 2.00
COMMON CARD (1-46) .50 1.25

2000 Star Wars Episode One 3-D Multi-Motion

COMPLETE SET (2) 10.00 25.00
COMMON CARD (1-2) 6.00 15.00

1999 Bluebird Star Wars Episode I The Phantom Menace

COMPLETE SET (30) 10.00 25.00
COMMON CARD (1-30) .60 1.50

1999 Family Toy Star Wars Episode I

COMPLETE SET (3) 8.00 20.00
COMMON CARD 4.00 10.00

1999 Flip Images Star Wars Episode I

COMPLETE SET (6) 5.00 12.00
COMMON CARD 1.25 3.00

1999 iKon Star Wars Episode I

COMPLETE SET (60) 6.00 15.00
UNOPENED BOX (36 PACKS)
UNOPENED PACK (6 CARDS)
COMMON CARD (1-60) .20 .50
*SILVER: 1.5X TO 4X BASIC CARDS
*GOLD: 2.5X TO 6X BASIC CARDS

1999 KFC Star Wars Episode I Australian

COMPLETE SET (10) 3.00 8.00
COMMON CARD (1-10) .50 1.25

1999 KFC Star Wars Episode I UK

COMPLETE SET (20) 8.00 20.00
COMMON CARD (1-20) .60 1.50
STATED ODDS 1:

1999 Lay's Star Wars Episode I Minis

COMPLETE SET (12) 6.00 15.00
COMMON CARD (1-12) .75 2.00

1999 Pepsi Star Wars Episode I Collector Can Contest Cards

COMPLETE SET (24) 15.00 40.00
COMMON CARD (1-24) 1.25 3.00

1999 Harmony Foods Star Wars Episode I The Phantom Menace

COMPLETE SET (24) 50.00 100.00
COMMON CARD (1-24) 2.00 5.00

1999 KFC Star Wars Episode I The Phantom Menace Employee Stickers

COMPLETE SET (5) 6.00 15.00
COMMON CARD (UNNUMBERED) 2.00 5.00

1999 Lucasfilm Star Wars Episode I The Phantom Menace Show Promo

NNO DLP Exclusive Presentation 5.00 12.00

2001 Star Wars Episode I The Phantom Menace Walmart DVD Promos

COMPLETE SET (4) 3.00 8.00
COMMON CARD 1.25 3.00

2019 Star Wars On-Demand Phantom Menace 20th Anniversary

COMPLETE SET (25) 8.00 20.00
COMMON CARD (1-25 .60 1.50
*SILVER: 1.2X TO 3X BASIC CARDS

2019 Star Wars On-Demand Phantom Menace 20th Anniversary Autographs

COMMON AUTO 8.00 20.00
STATED OVERALL ODDS 1:SET
2 Samuel L. Jackson
3 Ray Park 50.00 125.00
4 Oliver Ford Davies 10.00 25.00
6 Kenny Baker 100.00 250.00
7 Hugh Quarshie 15.00 40.00
8 Andy Secombe 12.00 30.00
10 Michonne Bourriague 10.00 25.00
12 Silas Carson 12.00 30.00

2019 Star Wars On-Demand Phantom Menace 20th Anniversary Jedi Council

COMPLETE SET (12) 150.00 300.00
COMMON CARD (1-12) 10.00 25.00
STATED ODDS 1:2

Attack of the Clones

2002 Star Wars Attack of the Clones

COMPLETE SET (100) 5.00 12.00
UNOPENED BOX (36 PACKS) 125.00 200.00
UNOPENED PACK (7 CARDS) 4.00 6.00
COMMON CARD (1-100) .15 .40

2002 Star Wars Attack of the Clones Foil

COMPLETE SET (10) 6.00 15.00
COMMON CARD (1-10) .75 2.00

2002 Star Wars Attack of the Clones Panoramic Fold-Outs

COMPLETE SET (5) 12.00 30.00
COMMON CARD (1-5) 3.00 8.00
STATED ODDS 1:12

2002 Star Wars Attack of the Clones Prisms

COMPLETE SET (8) 8.00 20.00
COMMON CARD (1-8) 1.25 3.00

2002 Star Wars Attack of the Clones Promos

COMMON CARD 1.25 3.00
B1 UK ALB 2.50 6.00
P4 Star Wars Insider/Gamer 3.00 8.00
P6 Star Wars Celebration II Exclusive 3.00 8.00
NNO Best Buy Soundtrack Exclusive 3.00 8.00

2002 Star Wars Attack of the Clones Widevision

COMPLETE SET (80) 5.00 12.00
COMMON CARD (1-80) .15 .40

2002 Star Wars Attack of the Clones Widevision Autographs

COMMON AUTO 12.00 30.00
STATED ODDS 1:24
NNO Ahmed Best 40.00 100.00
NNO Alethea McGrath 60.00 150.00
NNO Amy Allen 25.00 60.00
NNO Andrew Secombe 15.00 40.00
NNO Ayesha Dharker 50.00 125.00
NNO Bodie Taylor 15.00 40.00
NNO Bonnie Piesse 50.00 125.00
NNO Daniel Logan 25.00 60.00
NNO David Bowers 15.00 40.00
NNO Frank Oz 1000.00 2500.00
NNO Jay Laga'aia 40.00 100.00
NNO Joel Edgerton 100.00 250.00
NNO Kenny Baker 100.00 250.00
NNO Leeanna Walsman 15.00 40.00
NNO Mary Oyaya 20.00 50.00
NNO Matt Doran 15.00 40.00
NNO Nalini Krishan 15.00 40.00
NNO Rena Owen 15.00 40.00
NNO Ronald Falk 50.00 100.00
NNO Silas Carson/Ki-Adi-Mundi 40.00 100.00
NNO Silas Carson/Nute Gunray 40.00 100.00

2002 Star Wars Attack of the Clones Widevision Promos

P1 Spider Droid NSU .60 1.50
S1 Spider Droid UK

2002 Star Wars Attack of the Clones Widevision DVD Promos

COMPLETE SET (5) 3.00 8.00
COMMON CARD (W1-W5) 1.00 2.50

2016 Star Wars Attack of the Clones 3-D Widevision

COMPLETE SET (44) 12.00 30.00
COMMON CARD (1-44) .50 1.25

2016 Star Wars Attack of the Clones 3-D Widevision Autographs

COMMON AUTO 12.00 30.00
STATED ODDS 1:SET
NNO Alan Ruscoe 15.00 40.00
NNO Amy Allen 12.00 30.00
NNO Daniel Logan 15.00 40.00
NNO Jesse Jensen 15.00 40.00
NNO Jett Lucas 15.00 40.00
NNO Kenny Baker 80.00 150.00
NNO Matthew Wood/Magaloof 25.00 60.00
NNO Oliver Ford 15.00 40.00

2016 Star Wars Attack of the Clones 3-D Widevision Medallions

COMPLETE SET (10) 175.00 350.00
COMMON CARD (MC1-MC10) 15.00 40.00
STATED ODDS PATCH OR MEDALLION 1:1

2016 Star Wars Attack of the Clones 3-D Widevision Patches

COMPLETE SET (12) 200.00 350.00
COMMON CARD (MP1-MP12) 15.00 40.00
STATED ODDS PATCH OR MEDALLION 1:1

2002 Star Wars Episode II Instant Win

COMPLETE SET (5) 5.00 12.00
COMMON CARD 1.50 4.00

2002 Star Wars Episode II Jedi Fruit Rolls

COMPLETE SET (6) 5.00 12.00
1 Luke vs. Darth Vader 3.00 8.00
2 Luke vs. Darth Vader 3.00 8.00
3 Obi-Wan vs. Count Dooku .75 2.00
4 Obi-Wan vs. Darth Vader 2.00 5.00
5 Obi-Wan vs. Jango Fett .75 2.00
6 Qui-Gon Jinn vs. Darth Maul 1.25 3.00

Revenge of the Sith

2005 Star Wars Revenge of the Sith

COMPLETE SET (90) 5.00 12.00
UNOPENED HOBBY BOX (36 PACKS) 150.00 250.00
UNOPENED HOBBY PACK (7 CARDS) 5.00 8.00
UNOPENED RETAIL BOX (24 PACKS) 30.00 40.00
UNOPENED RETAIL PACK (7 CARDS) 1.50 1.75
COMMON CARD (1-90) .15 .40

2005 Star Wars Revenge of the Sith Blister Bonus

COMPLETE SET (3) 6.00 15.00
COMMON CARD (B1-B3) 2.50 6.00
STATED ODDS ONE PER BLISTER PACK

2005 Star Wars Revenge of the Sith Embossed Foil

COMPLETE SET (10) 20.00 50.00
COMMON CARD (1-10) 2.50 6.00
STATED ODDS 1:6 RETAIL

2005 Star Wars Revenge of the Sith Etched Foil Puzzle

COMPLETE SET (6) 12.00 30.00
COMMON CARD (1-6) 2.50 6.00
STATED ODDS 1:6

2005 Star Wars Revenge of the Sith Flix-Pix

COMPLETE SET (68) 50.00 100.00
UNOPENED BOX (36 PACKS) 100.00 150.00
UNOPENED PACK 3.00 5.00
COMMON CARD (1-68) 1.00 2.50
CL (TRI-FOLD INSERT) .40 1.00

2005 Star Wars Revenge of the Sith Holograms

COMPLETE SET (3)	5.00	12.00
COMMON CARD (1-3)	2.00	5.00
STATED ODDS 1:14 RETAIL		

2005 Star Wars Revenge of the Sith Lenticular Morph Hobby

COMPLETE SET (2)	5.00	12.00
COMMON CARD (1-2)	3.00	8.00
STATED ODDS 1:24 HOBBY		

2005 Star Wars Revenge of the Sith Lenticular Morph Retail

COMPLETE SET (2)	5.00	12.00
COMMON CARD (1-2)	3.00	8.00
STATED ODDS 1:24 RETAIL		

2005 Star Wars Revenge of the Sith Stickers

COMPLETE SET (10)	2.50	6.00
COMMON CARD (1-10)	.40	1.00
STATED ODDS 1:3 RETAIL		

2005 Star Wars Revenge of the Sith Tattoos

COMPLETE SET (10)	4.00	10.00
COMMON CARD (1-10)	1.00	2.50
STATED ODDS 1:3 RETAIL		

2005 Star Wars Revenge of the Sith Tin Gold

COMPLETE SET (6)	5.00	12.00
COMMON CARD (A-F)	1.00	2.50
STATED ODDS ONE PER TIN		

2005 Star Wars Revenge of the Sith Tin Story

COMPLETE SET (6)	5.00	12.00
COMMON CARD (1-6)	1.00	2.50
STATED ODDS ONE PER TIN		

2005 Star Wars Revenge of the Sith Promos

COMMON CARD (P1-P5)	1.00	2.50
P3 The Circle is Complete SW Shop	15.00	40.00

2005 Star Wars Revenge of the Sith Medalionz

COMPLETE SET (24)	15.00	40.00
COMMON CARD (1-24)	1.00	2.50
*GOLD: .8X TO 2X BASIC MED.		
CL Checklist	.20	.50

2005 Star Wars Revenge of the Sith Widevision

COMPLETE SET (80)	5.00	12.00
UNOPENED HOBBY BOX (24 PACKS)	150.00	250.00
UNOPENED HOBBY PACK (6 CARDS)	6.00	10.00
UNOPENED RETAIL BOX (24 PACKS)	25.00	40.00
UNOPENED RETAIL PACK (6 CARDS)	1.50	2.00
COMMON CARD (1-80)	.15	.40

2005 Star Wars Revenge of the Sith Widevision Autographs

COMMON CARD	12.00	30.00
STATED ODDS 1:48 HOBBY		
NNO Matthew Wood	75.00	150.00
NNO Peter Mayhew	100.00	200.00
NNO Samuel L. Jackson	750.00	1500.00

2005 Star Wars Revenge of the Sith Widevision Chrome Hobby

COMPLETE SET (10)	12.50	30.00
COMMON CARD (H1-H10)	1.50	4.00
STATED ODDS 1:6 HOBBY		

2005 Star Wars Revenge of the Sith Widevision Chrome Retail

COMPLETE SET (10)	15.00	40.00
COMMON CARD (R1-R10)	2.00	5.00
STATED ODDS 1:60 RETAIL		

2005 Star Wars Revenge of the Sith Widevision Flix-Pix

COMPLETE SET (10)	15.00	40.00
COMMON CARD (1-10)	2.00	5.00
STATED ODDS 1:6		

2015 Star Wars Revenge of the Sith 3-D Widevision

COMPLETE SET (44)	10.00	25.00
COMPLETE FACTORY SET (46)	60.00	120.00
COMMON CARD (1-44)	.40	1.00

2015 Star Wars Revenge of the Sith 3-D Widevision Autographs

COMMON AUTO	15.00	40.00
NNO Peter Mayhew	60.00	120.00
NNO Jeremy Bulloch	25.00	60.00
NNO Bai Ling	30.00	80.00

2015 Star Wars Revenge of the Sith 3-D Widevision Medallions

COMPLETE SET (8)	100.00	200.00
COMMON MEM	15.00	40.00
*SILVER/30: .6X TO 1.5X BASIC MEM		
STATED PRINT RUN 60 SER.#'d SETS		

2015 Star Wars Revenge of the Sith 3-D Widevision Patches

COMPLETE SET (4)	50.00	100.00
COMMON MEM	15.00	40.00
*SILVER/30: .6X TO 1.5X BASIC MEM		
STATED PRINT RUN 60 SER.#'d SETS		

The Force Awakens

2017 Star Wars The Force Awakens 3-D Widevision

COMPLETE SET (44)	12.00	30.00
COMPLETE BOXED SET (46)		
COMMON CARD (1-44)	.40	1.00

2017 Star Wars The Force Awakens 3-D Widevision Autographs

COMMON AUTO	6.00	15.00
STATED ODDS 2:SET		
WVAAJ Andrew Jack	6.00	15.00
WVAASH Arti Shah	8.00	20.00
WVABH Brian Herring	10.00	25.00
WVABV Brian Vernel	6.00	15.00
WVACC Crystal Clarke	8.00	20.00
WVAEE Emun Elliott	6.00	15.00
WVAHW Harriet Walter	6.00	15.00
WVAIU Iko Uwais	10.00	25.00
WVAJH Jessica Henwick	10.00	25.00
WVAKF Kate Fleetwood	6.00	15.00
WVAPW Paul Warren	6.00	15.00
WVATC Tosin Cole	6.00	15.00
WVAYR Yayan Ruhian	6.00	15.00

2016 Star Wars The Force Awakens Chrome

COMPLETE SET (100)	8.00	20.00
UNOPENED BOX (24 PACKS)	50.00	70.00
UNOPENED PACK (6 CARDS)	3.00	3.50
COMMON CARD (1-100)	.25	.60
*REFRACTOR: 1.2X TO 3X BASIC CARDS	.60	1.50
*PRISM REF./99: 5X TO 12X BASIC CARDS	3.00	8.00
*SHIMMER REF./50: 10X TO 25X BASIC CARDS	6.00	15.00
*PULSAR REF./10: 15X TO 40X BASIC CARDS	10.00	25.00

2016 Star Wars The Force Awakens Chrome Autographs

COMMON CARD	5.00	12.00
*ATOMIC/99: .5X TO 1.2X BASIC CARDS		
*PRISM/50: .6X TO 1.5X BASIC CARDS		
*X-FRACTOR/25: .75X TO 2X BASIC CARDS		
OVERALL AUTO ODDS 1:24		
CAAB Anna Brewster	8.00	20.00
CABV Brian Vernel	10.00	25.00
CAGG Greg Grunberg	10.00	25.00
CAJS Joonas Suotamo	10.00	25.00
CAKS Kipsang Rotich	8.00	20.00
CAMD Mark Dodson	10.00	25.00
CAMQ Mike Quinn	8.00	20.00
CAPM Peter Mayhew	20.00	50.00
CASA Sebastian Armesto	8.00	20.00
CAYR Yayan Ruhian	10.00	25.00
CAMWG Matthew Wood	8.00	20.00

2016 Star Wars The Force Awakens Chrome Autographs Atomic Refractors

*ATOMIC/99: .5X TO 1.2X BASIC CARDS		
CAJB John Boyega	120.00	200.00
CAWD Warwick Davis	12.00	30.00

2016 Star Wars The Force Awakens Chrome Autographs Prism Refractors

*PRISM/50: .6X TO 1.5X BASIC CARDS		
CAAD Anthony Daniels		
CAAS Andy Serkis	120.00	200.00

2016 Star Wars The Force Awakens Chrome Autographs X-fractors

*X-FRACTORS: .75X TO 2X BASIC CARDS		
CACF Carrie Fisher	120.00	250.00
CADR Daisy Ridley	600.00	1200.00
CAEB Erik Bauersfeld		
CAKB Kenny Baker	150.00	300.00
CAMWU Matthew Wood		

2016 Star Wars The Force Awakens Chrome Behind-the-Scenes

COMPLETE SET (12)	10.00	25.00
COMMON CARD (1-12)	1.25	3.00
*SHIMMER REF./50: 1X TO 2.5X BASIC CARDS	3.00	8.00
STATED ODDS 1:4		

2016 Star Wars The Force Awakens Chrome Heroes of the Resistance

COMPLETE SET (18)	10.00	25.00
COMMON CARD (1-18)	.75	2.00
*SHIMMER REF./50: 1X TO 2.5X BASIC CARDS	2.00	5.00
STATED ODDS 1:2		
1 Finn	1.25	3.00
2 Rey	1.25	3.00
3 Poe Dameron	1.00	2.50
9 BB-8	1.50	4.00
10 C-3PO	1.00	2.50
11 R2-D2	1.00	2.50
13 Han Solo	1.50	4.00
14 Chewbacca	1.00	2.50
18 General Leia Organa	1.00	2.50

2016 Star Wars The Force Awakens Chrome Medallions

COMPLETE SET (25)	200.00	400.00
COMMON CARD	3.00	8.00
*SILVER/25: .5X TO 1.2X BASIC CARDS		
M1 Han Solo	12.00	30.00
M2 General Leia Organa	12.00	30.00
M3 Admiral Ackbar	5.00	12.00
M4 Chewbacca	6.00	15.00
M5 Admiral Statura	5.00	12.00
M6 Snap Wexley	8.00	20.00
M7 Jess Testor Pava	8.00	20.00
M10 Poe Dameron	8.00	20.00
M11 Rey	20.00	50.00
M12 Finn	10.00	25.00
M13 BB-8	10.00	25.00
M14 Riot Control Stormtrooper	8.00	20.00
M16 Colonel Datoo	6.00	15.00
M17 Supreme Leader Snoke	6.00	15.00
M18 Flametrooper	5.00	12.00
M19 Kylo Ren	8.00	20.00
M20 Kylo Ren	8.00	20.00
M21 General Hux	5.00	12.00
M22 Captain Phasma	8.00	20.00
M23 FN-2187	10.00	25.00

2016 Star Wars The Force Awakens Chrome Patches

COMPLETE SET (27)	175.00	350.00
COMMON CARD (P1-P27)	5.00	12.00
*SHIMMER/199: .5X TO 1.2X BASIC CARDS		
*PULSAR/99: .6X TO 1.5X BASIC CARDS		
P1 Rey/686	15.00	40.00
P2 Han Solo/299	8.00	20.00
P4 Finn/686	8.00	20.00
P7 Kylo Ren/401	6.00	15.00
P11 General Leia Organa/755	8.00	20.00
P15 BB-8/686	6.00	15.00
P16 Poe Dameron & BB-8/686	6.00	15.00
P17 Rey & BB-8/686	12.00	30.00
P18 R2-D2/686	6.00	15.00
P19 Rey/299	10.00	25.00
P20 Rey/686	10.00	25.00
P23 Han Solo & Chewbacca/737	10.00	25.00

2016 Star Wars The Force Awakens Chrome Power of the First Order

COMPLETE SET (9)	6.00	15.00
COMMON CARD (1-9)	.75	2.00
*SHIMMER REF./50: 1X TO 2.5X BASIC CARDS		
STATED ODDS 1:12		
1 Supreme Leader Snoke	1.50	4.00
2 Kylo Ren	1.50	4.00
3 General Hux	1.25	3.00
4 Captain Phasma	1.25	3.00

2016 Star Wars The Force Awakens Chrome Ships and Vehicles

COMPLETE SET (11)	6.00	15.00
COMMON CARD (1-11)	1.00	2.50
*SHIMMER REF./50: 1X TO 2.5X BASIC CARDS	2.50	6.00
STATED ODDS 1:8		

2015 Star Wars The Force Awakens Dog Tags

COMPLETE SET (16)	15.00	40.00
COMMON CARD (1-16)	1.25	3.00
*GOLD: 1X TO 2.5X BASIC TAGS		
1 Kylo Ren	2.00	5.00
2 Rey	2.00	5.00
3 Finn	1.50	4.00
5 Captain Phasma	1.50	4.00
10 BB-8	2.50	6.00
11 Rey	2.00	5.00
12 Finn	1.50	4.00
13 Kylo Ren	2.00	5.00

2015 Star Wars The Force Awakens Dog Tags Target Exclusives

COMPLETE SET (2)	10.00	25.00
COMMON CARD (T1-T2)	5.00	12.00
*GOLD: .75X TO 2X BASIC TAGS		
EXCLUSIVE TO TARGET		
T2 BB-8	8.00	20.00

2015 Star Wars The Force Awakens Dog Tags Toys 'R' Us Exclusives

COMPLETE SET (2)	10.00	25.00
COMMON CARD (TR1-TR2)	6.00	15.00
*GOLD: 1X TO 2.5X BASIC TAGS		
EXCLUSIVE TO TOYS 'R' US		

2015 Star Wars The Force Awakens Dog Tags Walmart Exclusives

COMPLETE SET (2)	6.00	15.00
COMMON CARD (W1-W2)	4.00	10.00
*GOLD: 1X TO 2.5X BASIC TAGS		
EXCLUSIVE TO WALMART		

2016 Star Wars The Force Awakens Factory Set

COMPLETE FACTORY SET (310) 40.00 80.00
COMMON CARD .15 .40
JOURNEY TO TFA (1-110)
TFA SERIES ONE (1-100)
TFA SERIES TWO (1-100)
*LIM.ED./100: 6X TO 15X BASIC CARDS 2.50 6.00

2015 Star Wars The Force Awakens Glow-in-the-Dark Decals

COMPLETE SET (7) 10.00 25.00
COMMON CARD 1.25 3.00
STATED ODDS 1:CEREAL BOX
INSERTED IN BOXES OF GENERAL MILLS CEREAL
MILLENNIUM FALCON IS KROGER EXCLUSIVE
1 BB-8 2.50 6.00
2 C-3PO and R2-D2 1.50 4.00
3 Captain Phasma 2.00 5.00
5 Kylo Ren 2.00 5.00
6 Millennium Falcon SP 5.00 12.00
Kroger Exclusive

2015 Star Wars The Force Awakens Series One

COMPLETE SET w/o SP (100) 10.00 25.00
COMMON CARD (1-100) .20 .50
*LTSBR GREEN: .5X TO 1.2X BASIC CARDS
*LTSBR BLUE: .6X TO 1.5X BASIC CARDS
*LTSBR PURPLE: .75X TO 2X BASIC CARDS
*FOIL/250: 4X TO 10X BASIC CARDS
*GOLD/100: 6X TO 15X BASIC CARDS
TARGET EXCLUSIVES SP 101-103
100 Han Solo & Chewbacca return home .75 2.00
101 Maz Kanata SP 3.00 8.00
102 Wollivan SP 3.00 8.00
103 Grummgar SP 3.00 8.00

2015 Star Wars The Force Awakens Series One Autographs

COMMON AUTO 15.00 40.00
STATED ODDS 1:106 H; 1:12,334 R
NNO Anthony Daniels 100.00 200.00
NNO Carrie Fisher 600.00 1500.00
NNO Daisy Ridley 400.00 1000.00
NNO John Boyega 75.00 200.00
NNO Peter Mayhew 50.00 100.00

2015 Star Wars The Force Awakens Series One Behind-the-Scenes

COMPLETE SET (7) 5.00 12.00
COMMON CARD (1-7) 1.00 2.50
*LTSBR GREEN: .5X TO 1.2X BASIC CARDS
*LTSBR BLUE: .6X TO 1.5X BASIC CARDS
*LTSBR PURPLE: .75X TO 2X BASIC CARDS
*FOIL/250: 4X TO 10X BASIC CARDS
*GOLD/100: 6X TO 15X BASIC CARDS
STATED ODDS 1:8 H; 1:5 R

2015 Star Wars The Force Awakens Series One Character Montages

COMPLETE SET (8) 4.00 10.00
COMMON CARD (1-8) .75 2.00
*LTSBR GREEN: .5X TO 1.2X BASIC CARDS
*LTSBR BLUE: .6X TO 1.5X BASIC CARDS
*LTSBR PURPLE: .75X TO 2X BASIC CARDS
*FOIL/250: 4X TO 10X BASIC CARDS
*GOLD/100: 6X TO 15X BASIC CARDS
STATED ODDS 1:7 H; 1:4 R
1 Rey 1.50 4.00
5 Captain Phasma 1.25 3.00
7 BB-8 1.50 4.00

2015 Star Wars The Force Awakens Series One Character Stickers

COMPLETE SET (18) 6.00 15.00
COMMON CARD (1-18) .60 1.50
*LTSBR GREEN: .5X TO 1.2X BASIC CARDS
*LTSBR BLUE: .6X TO 1.5X BASIC CARDS
*LTSBR PURPLE: .75X TO 2X BASIC CARDS
*FOIL/250: 4X TO 10X BASIC CARDS
*GOLD/100: 6X TO 15X BASIC CARDS
STATED ODDS 1:3 H; 1:2 R
1 Rey 1.25 3.00
5 Captain Phasma 1.00 2.50
8 BB-8 1.25 3.00
12 Rey 1.25 3.00

2015 Star Wars The Force Awakens Series One Concept Art

COMPLETE SET (20) 8.00 20.00
COMMON CARD (1-20) .75 2.00
*LTSBR GREEN: .5X TO 1.2X BASIC CARDS
*LTSBR BLUE: .6X TO 1.5X BASIC CARDS
*LTSBR PURPLE: .75X TO 2X BASIC CARDS
*FOIL/250: 4X TO 10X BASIC CARDS
*GOLD/100: 6X TO 15X BASIC CARDS
STATED ODDS 1:3 H; 1:2 R

2015 Star Wars The Force Awakens Series One First Order Rises

COMPLETE SET (9) 6.00 15.00
COMMON CARD (1-9) 1.25 3.00
*LTSBR GREEN: .5X TO 1.2X BASIC CARDS
*LTSBR BLUE: .6X TO 1.5X BASIC CARDS
*LTSBR PURPLE: .75X TO 2X BASIC CARDS
*FOIL/250: 4X TO 10X BASIC CARDS
*GOLD/100: 6X TO 15X BASIC CARDS
STATED ODDS 1:6 H; 1:4 R
2 Captain Phasma 1.50 4.00

2015 Star Wars The Force Awakens Series One First Order Stormtrooper Costume Relics

COMMON CARD 12.00 30.00
*BRONZE/99: .75X TO 2X BASIC CARDS
*SILVER/50: 1.2X TO 3X BASIC CARDS
*GOLD/10: 2X TO 5X BASIC CARDS

2015 Star Wars The Force Awakens Series One Locations

COMPLETE SET (9) 3.00 8.00
COMMON CARD (1-9) .60 1.50
*LTSBR GREEN: .5X TO 1.2X BASIC CARDS
*LTSBR BLUE: .6X TO 1.5X BASIC CARDS
*LTSBR PURPLE: .75X TO 2X BASIC CARDS
*FOIL/250: 4X TO 10X BASIC CARDS
*GOLD/100: 6X TO 15X BASIC CARDS
STATED ODDS 1:6 H; 1:4 R

2015 Star Wars The Force Awakens Series One Medallions

COMMON CARD (M1-M66) 8.00 20.00
STATED ODDS 1:BOX

2015 Star Wars The Force Awakens Series One Movie Scenes

COMPLETE SET (20) 5.00 12.00
COMMON CARD (1-20) .50 1.25
*LTSBR GREEN: .5X TO 1.2X BASIC CARDS
*LTSBR BLUE: .60X TO 1.5X BASIC CARDS
*LTSBR PURPLE: .75X TO 2X BASIC CARDS
*FOIL/250: 4X TO 10X BASIC CARDS
*GOLD/100: 6X TO 15X BASIC CARDS
STATED ODDS 1:3 H; 1:2 R

2015 Star Wars The Force Awakens Series One Weapons

COMPLETE SET (10) 4.00 10.00
COMMON CARD (1-10) .60 1.50
*LTSBR GREEN: .5X TO 1.2X BASIC CARDS
*LTSBR BLUE: .6X TO 1.5X BASIC CARDS
*LTSBR PURPLE: .75X TO 2X BASIC CARDS
*FOIL/250: 4X TO 10X BASIC CARDS
*GOLD/100: 6X TO 15X BASIC CARDS
STATED ODDS 1:6 H; 1:3 R
1 Kylo Ren's lightsaber 1.25 3.00
9 Han Solo's Blaster .75 2.00

2016 Star Wars The Force Awakens Series Two

COMPLETE SET W/O SP (100) 10.00 25.00
COMPLETE SET W/SP (102) 20.00 50.00
UNOPENED HOBBY BOX (24 PACKS) 60.00 100.00
UNOPENED HOBBY PACK (8 CARDS) 2.50 4.00
COMMON CARD (1-100) .20 .50
*LTSBR GREEN: .5X TO 1.2X BASIC CARDS
*LTSBR BLUE: .6X TO 1.5X BASIC CARDS
*LTSBR PURPLE: .75X TO 2X BASIC CARDS
*FOIL: 4X TO 10X BASIC CARDS
*GOLD/100: 6X TO 15X BASIC CARDS
101 Finding Luke Skywalker SP 6.00 15.00
102 The Lightsaber Returned SP 10.00 25.00

2016 Star Wars The Force Awakens Series Two Autographs

COMMON CARD 8.00 20.00
*LTSBR PURPLE/50: .5X TO 1.2X BASIC AUTOS
*FOIL/25: .75X TO 2X BASIC AUTOS
1 David Acord/FN-2199 20.00 50.00
2 David Acord/Teedo 15.00 40.00
4 Kenny Baker 50.00 100.00
6 John Boyega 150.00 300.00
7 Anna Brewster 12.00 30.00
8 Dante Briggins 12.00 30.00
9 Thomas Brodie-Sangster 10.00 25.00
10 Aidan Cook 12.00 30.00
11 Anthony Daniels 50.00 100.00
12 Warrick Davis 10.00 25.00
13 Harrison Ford
14 Greg Grunberg 15.00 40.00
17 Jessica Henwick 15.00 40.00
18 Brian Herring 60.00 120.00
19 Andrew Jack 10.00 25.00
20 Billie Lourd 15.00 40.00
21 Rocky Marshall 10.00 25.00
22 Peter Mayhew 25.00 60.00
25 Arti Shah 12.00 30.00
26 Kiran Shah 10.00 25.00
27 Joonas Suotamo 15.00 40.00
28 Brian Vernel 10.00 25.00
29 Dame Harriet Walter 12.00 30.00
30 Paul Warren 10.00 25.00

2016 Star Wars The Force Awakens Series Two Card Trader Characters

COMMON CARD (1-9) 50.00 100.00
STATED PRINT RUN 100 SER.#'d SETS
1 BB-8 60.00 120.00
3 Finn 60.00 120.00
5 Kylo Ren 80.00 150.00
6 Captain Phasma 80.00 150.00
7 Poe Dameron 60.00 120.00
8 Rey 120.00 200.00

2016 Star Wars The Force Awakens Series Two Character Poster Inserts

COMPLETE SET (5) 5.00 12.00
COMMON CARD (1-5) 1.50 4.00
STATED ODDS 1:24
1 Rey 2.50 6.00
2 Finn 2.50 6.00
5 Han Solo 2.00 5.00

2016 Star Wars The Force Awakens Series Two Character Stickers

COMPLETE SET (18) 6.00 15.00
COMMON CARD (1-18) .50 1.25
1 Finn .75 2.00
2 Rey 1.00 2.50
5 Han Solo 1.00 2.50
6 Leia Organa .75 2.00
8 Poe Dameron 1.25 3.00
11 BB-8 1.25 3.00
12 Unkar Plutt .60 1.50
13 General Hux .75 2.00
15 Admiral Ackbar .60 1.50
16 Stormtrooper .75 2.00
18 Maz Kanata .60 1.50

2016 Star Wars The Force Awakens Series Two Concept Art

COMPLETE SET (9) 5.00 12.00
COMMON CARD (1-9) 1.00 2.50

2016 Star Wars The Force Awakens Series Two Galactic Connexions

COMPLETE SET (5) 120.00 250.00
COMMON CARD (1-5) 30.00 80.00
STATED PRINT RUN 100 ANNCD SETS
WALMART EXCLUSIVE
3 BB-8 50.00 100.00

2016 Star Wars The Force Awakens Series Two Heroes of the Resistance

COMPLETE SET (16) 8.00 20.00
COMMON CARD (1-16) .75 2.00
2 Poe Dameron 1.00 2.50
3 Finn 1.00 2.50
4 Rey 1.25 3.00
5 Han Solo 1.50 4.00
16 BB-8 1.50 4.00

2016 Star Wars The Force Awakens Series Two Maz's Castle

COMPLETE SET (9) 5.00 12.00
COMMON CARD (1-9) .75 2.00

2016 Star Wars The Force Awakens Series Two Medallions

COMMON CARD 4.00 10.00
*SILVER p/r 244-399: .5X TO 1.2X BASIC MEDALLIONS
*SILVER p/r 120-199: .6X TO 1.5X BASIC MEDALLIONS
*SILVER p/r 50-99: 1X TO 2.5X BASIC MEDALLIONS
*GOLD p/r 120-199: .6X TO 1.5X BASIC MEDALLIONS
*GOLD p/r 74-100: .75X TO 2X BASIC MEDALLIONS
*GOLD p/r 25-50: 1.2X TO 3X BASIC MEDALLIONS
1 Kylo Ren 6.00 15.00
2 General Hux 5.00 12.00
3 Captain Phasma 5.00 12.00
4 FN-2187 5.00 12.00
6 Kylo Ren 6.00 15.00
12 Kylo Ren 6.00 15.00
13 Maz Kanata 5.00 12.00
14 Rey 6.00 15.00
15 BB-8 5.00 12.00
16 Han Solo 8.00 20.00
17 Chewbacca 5.00 12.00
18 Finn 6.00 15.00
19 Rey 6.00 15.00
22 Colonel Datoo 6.00 15.00
23 Captain Phasma 5.00 12.00
24 Finn 5.00 12.00
27 BB-8 5.00 12.00
28 Resistance X-Wing Fighter 5.00 12.00
29 Nien Nunb 6.00 15.00
30 C-3PO 6.00 15.00
31 R2-D2 8.00 20.00
32 Jess Testor Pava 10.00 25.00
33 Snap Wexley 6.00 15.00
34 Admiral Statura 6.00 15.00
35 Admiral Ackbar 6.00 15.00
36 Major Brance 5.00 12.00

2016 Star Wars The Force Awakens Series Two Power of the First Order

COMPLETE SET (11) 5.00 12.00
COMMON CARD (1-11) .40 1.00
1 Kylo Ren 1.25 3.00
2 General Hux 1.00 2.50
3 Captain Phasma 1.25 3.00
11 Supreme Leader Snoke 1.00 2.50

Rogue One

2016 Star Wars Rogue One Series One

COMPLETE SET (90) 8.00 20.00
UNOPENED BOX (24 PACKS) 80.00 100.00
UNOPENED PACK (8 CARDS) 3.00 4.00
COMMON CARD (1-90) .25 .60
*DEATH STAR BL.: .6X TO 1.5X BASIC CARDS
*GREEN SQ.: .75X TO 2X BASIC CARDS
*BLUE SQ.: 1X TO 2.5X BASIC CARDS
*GRAY SQ./100: 4X TO 10X BASIC CARDS
*GOLD SQ./50: 6X TO 15X BASIC CARDS

2016 Star Wars Rogue One Series One Autographs

COMMON CARD 10.00 25.00
*BLACK/50: .6X TO 1.5X BASIC CARDS
RANDOMLY INSERTED INTO PACKS
1 Donnie Yen 100.00 200.00
2 Felicity Jones 300.00 600.00
3 Forest Whitaker 100.00 200.00
4 Genevieve O'Reilly 15.00 40.00

2016 Star Wars Rogue One Series One Blueprints of Ships and Vehicles

COMPLETE SET (8) 5.00 12.00
COMMON CARD (BP1-BP8) 1.00 2.50
RANDOMLY INSERTED INTO PACKS

2016 Star Wars Rogue One Series One Character Icons

COMPLETE SET (11) 8.00 20.00
COMMON CARD (CI1-CI11) 1.25 3.00
RANDOMLY INSERTED INTO PACKS

2016 Star Wars Rogue One Series One Character Stickers

COMPLETE SET (18) 10.00 25.00
COMMON CARD (CS1-CS18) .75 2.00
RANDOMLY INSERTED INTO PACKS

2016 Star Wars Rogue One Series One Gallery

COMPLETE SET (10) 4.00 10.00
COMMON CARD (G1-G10) .50 1.25
RANDOMLY INSERTED INTO PACKS
G1 Jyn Erso .75 2.00
G2 Jyn Erso .75 2.00
G3 Jyn Erso .75 2.00
G4 Jyn Erso .75 2.00
G5 Jyn Erso .75 2.00
G6 Jyn Erso .75 2.00
G7 Jyn Erso .75 2.00

2016 Star Wars Rogue One Series One Heroes of the Rebel Alliance

COMPLETE SET (14) 8.00 20.00
COMMON CARD (HR1-HR14) 1.00 2.50
RANDOMLY INSERTED INTO PACKS
HR1 Jyn Erso 1.50 4.00
HR4 Chirrut IMWE 1.25 3.00

2016 Star Wars Rogue One Series One Medallions

COMMON CARD 4.00 10.00
*BRONZE: SAME VALUE AS BASIC
*SILVER/99: .5X TO 1.2X BASIC CARDS
*GOLD/50: .6X TO 1.5X BASIC CARDS
RANDOMLY INSERTED INTO PACKS
5 Captain Cassian Andor with X-Wing 6.00 15.00
6 Captain Cassian Andor with U-Wing 6.00 15.00
7 Chirrut Imwe with Y-Wing 6.00 15.00
8 Darth Vader with Death Star 6.00 15.00
9 Darth Vader with Imperial Star Destroyer 6.00 15.00
10 Death Trooper with Imperial Star Destroyer 6.00 15.00
14 Edrio Two Tubes with U-Wing 6.00 15.00
15 Jyn Erso with X-Wing 8.00 20.00
16 Jyn Erso with U-Wing 8.00 20.00
17 Jyn Erso with Death Star 8.00 20.00
18 K-2SO with X-Wing 5.00 12.00
20 Moroff with U-Wing 5.00 12.00
24 Shoretrooper with AT-ACT 5.00 12.00
25 Stormtrooper with AT-ST 5.00 12.00
27 TIE Fighter Pilot with TIE Striker 5.00 12.00

2016 Star Wars Rogue One Series One Montages

COMPLETE SET (9) 5.00 12.00
COMMON CARD (M1-M9) 1.00 2.50

2016 Star Wars Rogue One Series One Villains of the Galactic Empire

COMPLETE SET (8) 6.00 15.00
COMMON CARD (VE1-VE8) 1.00 2.50

2017 Star Wars Rogue One Series Two

COMPLETE SET (100) 6.00 15.00
UNOPENED BOX (24 PACKS) 110.00 120.00
UNOPENED PACK (8 CARDS) 5.00 6.00
COMMON CARD (1-100) .20 .50
*DTHSTR BLACK: .6X TO 1.5X BASIC CARDS
*GREEN SQ: .75X TO 2X BASIC CARDS
*BLUE SQ: 1X TO 2.5X BASIC CARDS
*GRAY SQ/100: 5X TO 12X BASIC CARDS
*GOLD SQ/50: 10X TO 25X BASIC CARDS

2017 Star Wars Rogue One Series Two Autographs

COMMON AUTO 10.00 25.00
*BLACK/50: .6X TO 1.5X BASIC AUTOS
*GOLD/10: 1.2X TO 3X BASIC AUTOS
STATED ODDS 1:36
JONES, WHITAKER, AND KELLINGTON DO NOT HAVE BASE AUTOGRAPHS
DA Derek Arnold 12.00 30.00
DY Donnie Yen 80.00 150.00
GO Genevieve O'Reilly 8.00 20.00
RA Riz Ahmed 120.00 200.00
WD Warwick Davis 12.00 30.00
AC1 Aidan Cook/Benthic 2 Tubes 10.00 25.00
AC2 Aidan Cook/Caitken 10.00 25.00

2017 Star Wars Rogue One Series Two Autographs Black

*BLACK/50: .6X TO 1.5X BASIC AUTOS
STATED ODDS 1:163
STATED PRINT RUN 50 SER.#'d SETS
FJ Felicity Jones 300.00 600.00
FW Forest Whitaker 100.00 200.00
NK Nick Kellington 20.00 50.00

2017 Star Wars Rogue One Series Two Character Stickers

COMPLETE SET (18) 30.00 80.00
COMMON CARD (CS1-CS18) 2.50 6.00
STATED ODDS 1:12
CS1 Jyn Erso 5.00 12.00
CS8 Director Krennic 3.00 8.00
CS9 Darth Vader 4.00 10.00
CS10 K-2SO 3.00 8.00
CS14 Chirrut Imwe 4.00 10.00
CS18 Admiral Raddus 3.00 8.00

2017 Star Wars Rogue One Series Two Heroes of the Rebel Alliance

COMPLETE SET (10) 6.00 15.00
COMMON CARD (HR1-HR10) 1.00 2.50
STATED ODDS 1:7

2017 Star Wars Rogue One Series Two Movie Posters

COMPLETE SET (10) 30.00 80.00
COMMON CARD (1-10) 3.00 8.00
STATED ODDS 1:24
1 United States Theatrical Poster 6.00 15.00
5 Cassian Andor Character Poster 4.00 10.00
6 Bodhi Rook Character Poster 5.00 12.00
7 Chirrut Imwe Character Poster 6.00 15.00
9 K-2SO Character Poster 6.00 15.00

2017 Star Wars Rogue One Series Two Patches

COMMON CARD 5.00 12.00
*SILVER/100: .5X TO 1.2X BASIC CARDS
*GOLD/50: .6X TO 1.5X BASIC CARDS
*RED/10: 1.2X TO 3X BASIC CARDS

2017 Star Wars Rogue One Series Two Prime Forces

COMPLETE SET (10) 8.00 20.00
COMMON CARD (PF1-PF10) 1.50 4.00
STATED ODDS 1:2

2017 Star Wars Rogue One Series Two Troopers

COMPLETE SET (10) 8.00 20.00
COMMON CARD (TR1-TR10) 1.50 4.00
STATED ODDS 1:2

2017 Star Wars Rogue One Series Two Villains of the Galactic Empire

COMPLETE SET (10) 12.00 30.00
COMMON CARD (VG1-VG10) 2.50 6.00
STATED ODDS 1:7

2016-17 Topps Star Wars Rogue One Darth Vader Continuity

COMPLETE SET (15) 20.00 50.00
COMMON CARD (1-15) 2.50 6.00
MISSION BRIEFING (1-5)
SERIES ONE (6-10)
SERIES TWO (11-15)
STATED ODDS 1:12

The Last Jedi

2017 Star Wars The Last Jedi Disney Movie Reward Oversized Theater Promos

COMPLETE SET (9) 15.00 40.00
COMMON CARD 2.00 5.00
THEATER PROMOTION EXCLUSIVE

2017 Star Wars The Last Jedi Series One

COMPLETE SET (100) 6.00 15.00
UNOPENED BOX (24 PACKS) 75.00 100.00
UNOPENED PACK (8 CARDS) 4.00 5.00
COMMON CARD (1-100) .12 .30
*BLUE: 2X TO 5X BASIC CARDS .60 1.50
*GREEN: 2.5X TO 6X BASIC CARDS .75 2.00
*PURPLE: 3X TO 8X BASIC CARDS 1.00 2.50
*RED: 4X TO 10X BASIC CARDS 1.25 3.00
*SILVER/99: 10X TO 25X BASIC CARDS 3.00 8.00
*GOLD/25: 20X TO 50X BASIC CARDS 6.00 15.00

2017 Star Wars The Last Jedi Series One Autographs

COMMON AUTO 6.00 15.00
*RED/99: .5X TO 1.2X BASIC AUTOS
*SILVER/25: .6X TO 1.5X BASIC AUTOS
RANDOMLY INSERTED INTO PACKS
NNO Aidan Cook 8.00 20.00
NNO Andy Serkis TFA AU 60.00 120.00
NNO Billie Lourd 60.00 120.00
NNO Brian Herring 12.00 30.00
NNO Crystal Clarke 10.00 25.00
NNO Dave Chapman 12.00 30.00
NNO Ian Whyte 8.00 20.00
NNO Jimmy Vee 15.00 40.00
NNO Mike Quinn 8.00 20.00
NNO Paul Kasey 10.00 25.00
NNO Tom Kane 8.00 20.00
NNO Veronica Ngo 15.00 40.00

2017 Star Wars The Last Jedi Series One Autographs Red

*RED: .5X TO 1.2X BASIC AUTOS
STATED PRINT RUN 99 SER.#'d SETS
NNO John Boyega 120.00
NNO Joonas Suotamo 75.00

2017 Star Wars The Last Jedi Series One Autographs Silver

STATED PRINT RUN 25 SER.#'d SETS
NNO Gwendoline Christie 100.00 200.00

2017 Star Wars The Last Jedi Series One Blueprints and Schematics

COMPLETE SET (8) 6.00 15.00
COMMON CARD (BP1-BP8) 1.25 3.00
*PURPLE/250: .6X TO 1.5X BASIC CARDS 2.00 5.00
*RED/199: .75X TO 2X BASIC CARDS 2.50 6.00
*SILVER/99: 1X TO 2.5X BASIC CARDS 3.00 8.00
RANDOMLY INSERTED INTO PACKS

2017 Star Wars The Last Jedi Series One Character Portraits

COMPLETE SET (16) 12.00 30.00
COMMON CARD (CP1-CP16) 1.50 4.00
*PURPLE/250: .6X TO 1.5X BASIC CARDS 2.50 6.00
*RED/199: .75X TO 2X BASIC CARDS 3.00 8.00
*SILVER/99: 1X TO 2.5X BASIC CARDS 4.00 10.00
RANDOMLY INSERTED INTO PACKS

2017 Star Wars The Last Jedi Series One Character Stickers

COMPLETE SET (6) 8.00 20.00
COMMON CARD (DS1-DS6) 1.25 3.00
RANDOMLY INSERTED INTO PACKS
DS1 Kylo Ren 1.50 4.00
DS4 Rey 3.00 8.00
DS5 Finn 2.50 6.00
DS6 Poe Dameron 2.00 5.00

2017 Star Wars The Last Jedi Series One Illustrated

COMPLETE SET (11) 8.00 20.00
COMMON CARD (SWI1-SWI11) 1.25 3.00
*PURPLE/250: .6X TO 1.5X BASIC CARDS 2.00 5.00
*RED/199: .75X TO 2X BASIC CARDS 2.50 6.00
*SILVER/99: 1X TO 2.5X BASIC CARDS 3.00 8.00
RANDOMLY INSERTED INTO PACKS

2017 Star Wars The Last Jedi Series One Medallions

COMMON MEDALLION 4.00 10.00
*PURPLE/99: .5X TO 1.2X BASIC MEDALLIONS 5.00 12.00
*RED/25: 1.2X TO 3X BASIC MEDALLIONS 12.00 30.00
RANDOMLY INSERTED INTO PACKS
NNO BB-8 / BB-8 5.00 12.00
NNO BB-8 / Resistance 6.00 15.00
NNO C-3PO / R2-D2 5.00 12.00
NNO Chewbacca / R2-D2 8.00 20.00
NNO Executioner Stormtrooper / First Order 5.00 12.00
NNO Finn / BB-8 5.00 12.00
NNO Finn / Resistance 6.00 15.00
NNO General Hux / First Order 5.00 12.00
NNO General Leia Organa / Resistance 6.00 15.00
NNO Kylo Ren / First Order 6.00 15.00
NNO Luke Skywalker / Millennium Falcon 10.00 25.00
NNO Poe Dameron / BB-8 5.00 12.00
NNO Poe Dameron / Resistance 6.00 15.00
NNO Porg / Millennium Falcon 6.00 15.00
NNO Porg / R2-D2 6.00 15.00
NNO Praetorian Guard / First Order 5.00 12.00
NNO R2-D2 / Resistance 5.00 12.00
NNO Rey / BB-8 8.00 20.00
NNO Rey / Millennium Falcon 8.00 20.00
NNO Rey / Resistance 8.00 20.00
NNO Rose / Resistance 5.00 12.00

2017 Star Wars The Last Jedi Series One Red Character Illustrations

COMPLETE SET (8) 8.00 20.00
COMMON CARD (RL1-RL8) 1.50 4.00
*PURPLE/250: .6X TO 1.5X BASIC CARDS 2.50 6.00

*RED/199: .75X TO 2X BASIC CARDS 3.00 8.00
*SILVER/99: 1X TO 2.5X BASIC CARDS 4.00 10.00
RANDOMLY INSERTED INTO PACKS

2017 Star Wars The Last Jedi Series One Resist!

COMPLETE SET (8) 5.00 12.00
COMMON CARD (R1-R8) 1.00 2.50
*PURPLE/250: .6X TO 1.5X BASIC CARDS 1.50 4.00
*RED/199: .75X TO 2X BASIC CARDS 2.00 5.00
*SILVER/99: 1X TO 2.5X BASIC CARDS 2.50 6.00
RANDOMLY INSERTED INTO PACKS

2017 Star Wars The Last Jedi Series One Source Material Fabric Relics

COMMON RELIC 12.00 30.00
*SILVER/99: .5X TO 1.2X BASIC RELICS 15.00 40.00
RANDOMLY INSERTED INTO PACKS

2018 Star Wars The Last Jedi Series Two

COMPLETE SET (100) 6.00 15.00
UNOPENED BOX (24 PACKS)
UNOPENED PACK (8 CARDS)
COMMON CARD (1-100) .12 .30
*BLUE: 2X TO 5X BASIC CARDS .60 1.50
*PURPLE: 3X TO 8X BASIC CARDS 1.00 2.50
*RED/199: 4X TO 10X BASIC CARDS 1.25 3.00
*BRONZE/99: 10X TO 25X BASIC CARDS 3.00 8.00
*SILVER/25: 20X TO 50X BASIC CARDS 6.00 15.00

2018 Star Wars The Last Jedi Series Two Autographs

COMMON AUTO 6.00 15.00
*RED/99: .5X TO 1.2X BASIC AUTOS
*SILVER/25: .75X TO 2X BASIC AUTOS
STATED ODDS 1:36
AAE Adrian Edmondson 10.00 25.00
AAL Amanda Lawrence 12.00 30.00
ABL Billie Lourd 30.00 75.00
ABH Brian Herring 8.00 20.00
ACC Crystal Clarke 8.00 20.00
AHC Hermione Corfield 20.00 50.00
AJV Jimmy Vee 10.00 25.00
AJB John Boyega 50.00 100.00
AKS Kiran Shah 8.00 20.00
AMQ Mike Quinn 10.00 25.00
AVN Veronica Ngo 15.00 40.00

2018 Star Wars The Last Jedi Series Two Autographs Red

*RED: .5X TO 1.2X BASIC AUTOS
STATED ODDS 1:127
STATED PRINT RUN 99 SER.#'d SETS
ALD Laura Dern 75.00 150.00

2018 Star Wars The Last Jedi Series Two Autographs Silver

STATED ODDS 1:350
STATED PRINT RUN 25 SER.#'d SETS
NNO Adam Driver 300.00 500.00
AAS Andy Serkis 60.00 120.00
AADC Anthony Daniels 100.00 200.00
AJS Joonas Suotamo 50.00 100.00

2018 Star Wars The Last Jedi Series Two Character Stickers

COMPLETE SET (10) 15.00 40.00
COMMON STICKER (CS1-CS10) 1.25 3.00
STATED ODDS 1:16
CS1 Rey 3.00 8.00
CS2 Kylo Ren 1.50 4.00
CS3 Finn 2.00 5.00
CS4 Poe Dameron 5.00 12.00
CS5 Supreme Leader Snoke 1.50 4.00
CS6 Captain Phasma 2.00 5.00
CS8 General Leia Organa 2.00 5.00
CS10 Luke Skywalker 2.50 6.00

2018 Star Wars The Last Jedi Series Two Commemorative Patches

COMMON PATCH 3.00 8.00
STATED ODDS 1:67
MEC Chewbacca 4.00 10.00
MEAH Vice Admiral Holdo 5.00 12.00
MEBB BB-8 5.00 12.00
MECB Chewbacca 4.00 10.00
MECP Captain Phasma 6.00 15.00
MECT C'ai Threnalli 5.00 12.00
MEDR Rey 6.00 15.00
MEFA Finn 6.00 15.00
MEFB Finn 6.00 15.00
MEGE General Ematt 5.00 12.00
MEJB Finn 6.00 15.00
MEKR Kylo Ren 6.00 15.00
MELO General Leia Organa 8.00 20.00
MELS Luke Skywalker 8.00 20.00
MENG Ensign Pamich Nerro Goode 5.00 12.00
MEPD Poe Dameron 5.00 12.00
MEPG Praetorian Guard 6.00 15.00
MEPT Resistance Gunner Paige Tico 5.00 12.00
MER2 R2-D2 5.00 12.00
MERA Rey 6.00 15.00
MERB Rey 6.00 15.00
MERT Rose Tico 5.00 12.00
MESE Stormtrooper Executioner 4.00 10.00
MEBB8 BB-8 5.00 12.00
MEBBR BB-8 5.00 12.00
MEC3B C-3PO 4.00 10.00
MEC3P C-3PO 4.00 10.00
MECPB Captain Phasma 6.00 15.00
MEGEA General Ematt 5.00 12.00
MEKCA Kaydel Ko Connix 6.00 15.00
MEKKC Kaydel Ko Connix 6.00 15.00
MEKRB Kylo Ren 6.00 15.00
MELOR General Leia Organa 8.00 20.00
MELSB Luke Skywalker 8.00 20.00
MENGA Ensign Pamich Nerro Goode 5.00 12.00
MEPDA Poe Dameron 5.00 12.00
MEPDB Poe Dameron 5.00 12.00
MEPDP Poe Dameron 5.00 12.00
MEPGB Praetorian Guard 6.00 15.00
MER2B R2-D2 5.00 12.00
MER2R R2-D2 5.00 12.00
MESLB Supreme Leader Snoke 5.00 12.00
MESLS Supreme Leader Snoke 5.00 12.00

2018 Star Wars The Last Jedi Series Two Items and Artifacts

COMPLETE SET (20) 10.00 25.00
COMMON CARD (IA1-IA20) .75 2.00
*RED/99: .5X TO 1.2X BASIC CARDS
*BRONZE/50: .75X TO 2X BASIC CARDS
STATED ODDS 1:1
IA1 Skywalker's Lightsaber 2.00 5.00
IA2 Luke Skywalker's Compass 2.00 5.00
IA4 Proton Bomb 1.25 3.00
IA14 Kylo Ren's Lightsaber 3.00 8.00

2018 Star Wars The Last Jedi Series Two Leaders of the Resistance

COMPLETE SET (10) 5.00 12.00
COMMON CARD (RS1-RS10) .75 2.00
*RED/99: .5X TO 1.2X BASIC CARDS
*BRONZE/50: .75X TO 2X BASIC CARDS
STATED ODDS 1:2

2018 Star Wars The Last Jedi Series Two Patrons of Canto Bight

COMPLETE SET (10) 6.00 15.00
COMMON CARD (CB1-CB10) 1.25 3.00
*RED/99: .5X TO 1.2X BASIC CARDS 1.50 4.00
*BRONZE/50: .75X TO 2X BASIC CARDS 2.50 6.00
STATED ODDS 1:6

2018 Star Wars The Last Jedi Series Two Ships and Vehicles

COMPLETE SET (10) 8.00 20.00
COMMON CARD (SV1-SV10) 1.50 4.00
*RED/99: .5X TO 1.2X BASIC CARDS 2.00 5.00
*BRONZE/50: .75X TO 2X BASIC CARDS 3.00 8.00
STATED ODDS 1:8

2018 Star Wars The Last Jedi Series Two Soldiers of the First Order

COMPLETE SET (10) 6.00 15.00
COMMON CARD (FO1-FO10) 1.25 3.00
*RED/99: .5X TO 1.2X BASIC CARDS 1.50 4.00
*BRONZE/50: .75X TO 2X BASIC CARDS 2.50 6.00
STATED ODDS 1:4

2018 Star Wars The Last Jedi Series Two Source Material Fabric Swatches

COMMON MEM 20.00 50.00
STATED ODDS 1:360
STATED PRINT RUN 99 SER.#'d SETS
MR1 Caretaker's Smock 60.00 120.00
MR3 Praetorian Guard's Ceremonial Battle Skirt 50.00 100.00
MR4 Captain Peavy's First Order Uniform 25.00 60.00

2018 Star Wars The Last Jedi Series Two Teaser Posters

COMPLETE SET (6) 8.00 20.00
COMMON CARD (TP1-TP6) 2.00 5.00
STATED ODDS 1:24
TP1 Rey 2.50 6.00
TP5 General Leia Organa 2.50 6.00

2018 Star Wars On-Demand The Last Jedi

COMPLETE SET (20) 15.00 40.00
COMMON CARD (1-20) 1.25 3.00
*PURPLE: .75X TO 2X BASIC CARDS 2.50 6.00

2018 Star Wars On-Demand The Last Jedi Autographs

STATED OVERALL ODDS 1:SET
1A Daisy Ridley
4A John Boyega 50.00 100.00
5A Adam Driver
9A Gwendoline Christie
11A Billie Lourd
14AA Dave Chapman 8.00 20.00
14BA Brian Herring 8.00 20.00
15AA Tim Rose 15.00 40.00
15BA Tom Kane 8.00 20.00
16A Jimmy Vee 10.00 25.00
17A Anthony Daniels
19A Andy Serkis
21A Andrew Jack 10.00 25.00
22A Paul Kasey 8.00 20.00
23A Mike Quinn 15.00 40.00

Solo

2018 Countdown to Solo A Star Wars Story

COMPLETE SET (25) 60.00 120.00
COMMON CARD (1-25) 4.00 10.00

2018 Solo A Star Wars Story

COMPLETE SET (100) 8.00 20.00
UNOPENED BOX (24 PACKS) 50.00 60.00
UNOPENED PACK (8 CARDS) 2.50 3.00
COMMON CARD (1-100) .15 .40
*YELLOW: .6X TO 1.5X BASIC CARDS .25 .60
*BLACK: .75X TO 2X BASIC CARDS .30 .75
*SILVER: 1.5X TO 4X BASIC CARDS .60 1.50
*PINK/99: 6X TO 15X BASIC CARDS 2.50 6.00
*ORANGE/25: 15X TO 40X BASIC CARDS 6.00 15.00

2018 Solo A Star Wars Story Autographs

COMMON AUTO 8.00 20.00
*PINK/99: .5X TO 1.2X BASIC AUTOS
*ORANGE/25: .6X TO 1.5X BASIC AUTOS
STATED ODDS 1:33
AAF Anna Francolini 12.00 30.00
AAJ Andrew Jack 10.00 25.00
AAW Andrew Woodall 12.00 30.00
ADA Derek Arnold 12.00 30.00
ADT Dee Tails 10.00 25.00
AIK Ian Kenny 10.00 25.00

2018 Solo A Star Wars Story Autographs Pink

STATED ODDS 1:231
STATED PRINT RUN 99 SER.#'d SETS
AJS Joonas Suotamo 50.00 100.00
AWD Warwick Davis 20.00 50.00
AJSC Joonas Suotamo 50.00 100.00

2018 Solo A Star Wars Story Character Stickers

COMPLETE SET (7) 8.00 20.00
COMMON CARD (CS1-CS7) 2.00 5.00
STATED ODDS 1:12

2018 Solo A Star Wars Story Icons

COMPLETE SET (7) 5.00 12.00
COMMON CARD (I1-I7) 1.00 2.50
STATED ODDS 1:8

2018 Solo A Star Wars Story Manufactured Patches

COMMON PATCH 3.00 8.00
*PINK/99: .5X TO 1.2X BASIC PATCHES
*ORANGE/25: .6X TO 1.5X BASIC PATCHES
STATED ODDS 1:32
MPCC Chewbacca 5.00 12.00
MPCH Chewbacca 5.00 12.00
MPHM Han Solo 6.00 15.00
MPIS Imperial Fleet Trooper 4.00 10.00
MPLH L3-37 5.00 12.00
MPLM Lando Calrissian 6.00 15.00
MPME Enfys Nest 5.00 12.00
MPMS Mimban Stormtrooper 6.00 15.00
MPQC Qi'ra 8.00 20.00
MPQH Qi'ra 8.00 20.00
MPRS R5-PHT 4.00 10.00
MPSS Stormtrooper 4.00 10.00
MPTS TIE Fighter Pilot 6.00 15.00
MPENH Enfys Nest 5.00 12.00
MPHSC Han Solo 6.00 15.00
MPHSH Han Solo 6.00 15.00
MPLCH Lando Calrissian 6.00 15.00

2018 Solo A Star Wars Story Ships and Vehicles

COMPLETE SET (9) 4.00 10.00
COMMON CARD (SV1-SV9) .60 1.50
STATED ODDS 1:4

2018 Solo A Star Wars Story Silhouettes

COMPLETE SET (11) 6.00 15.00
COMMON CARD (SL1-SL11) 1.00 2.50
STATED ODDS 1:2

2018 Solo A Star Wars Story Smooth Sayings

COMPLETE SET (8) 8.00 20.00
COMMON CARD (SS1-SS8) 1.50 4.00
STATED ODDS 1:6
SS1 I Got This 1.50 4.00
SS2 Chewie Is My Copilot 1.50 4.00
SS3 Just Be Charming 1.50 4.00
SS4 We're Doing This My Way 1.50 4.00
SS5 Kessel Crew 1.50 4.00
SS6 Just Trust Us 1.50 4.00
SS7 Smooth & Sophisticated 1.50 4.00
SS8 Double-Crossing No-Good Swindler 1.50 4.00

2018 Solo A Star Wars Story Target Exclusive Manufactured Patches

COMMON PATCH 5.00 12.00
*PINK/99: .5X TO 1.2X BASIC PATCHES 6.00 15.00
*ORANGE/25: .6X TO 1.5X BASIC PATCHES8.00 20.00
STATED ODDS 1:TARGET BLASTER BOX

2018 Solo A Star Wars Story Promo

P1 Han Solo 4.00 10.00

2018 Solo A Star Wars Story Denny's

COMPLETE SET (12) 20.00 50.00
UNOPENED PACK (2 CARDS+1 COUPON) 3.00 8.00
COMMON CARD 2.00 5.00
*FOIL: 6X TO 15X BASIC CARDS 30.00 75.00

2018 Solo A Star Wars Story Odeon Cinemas

COMPLETE SET (4) 3.00 8.00
COMMON CARD 1.00 2.50

The Rise of Skywalker

2019 Star Wars The Rise of Skywalker General Mills Interactive Tattoos

COMPLETE SET (6) 5.00 12.00
COMMON CARD .75 2.00
NNO BB-8 1.25 3.00
NNO Kylo Ren 2.00 5.00
NNO Rey 2.00 5.00

2019 Star Wars The Rise of Skywalker Series One

COMPLETE SET (99) 10.00 25.00
UNOPENED BOX (24 PACKS) 60.00 100.00
UNOPENED PACK (8 CARDS) 2.50 4.00
COMMON CARD (1-99) .20 .50
*RED: .75X TO 2X BASIC CARDS
*BLUE: 1X TO 2.5X BASIC CARDS
GREEN: 1.2X TO 3X BASIC CARDS
*PURPLE: 1.5X TO 4X BASIC CARDS
*ORANGE/99: 4X TO 10X BASIC CARDS
*GOLD/25: 6X TO 15X BASIC CARDS

2019 Star Wars The Rise of Skywalker Series One Autographs

COMMON AUTO 6.00 15.00
RANDOMLY INSERTED INTO PACKS
AAH Amanda Hale 10.00 25.00
AAL Amanda Lawrence 8.00 20.00
ABB Brian Herring 6.00 15.00
ADB Dave Chapman 6.00 15.00
ADM Dominic Monaghan 50.00 100.00
AGF Geff Francis 10.00 25.00
AGG Greg Grunberg 12.00 30.00
AJA Josef Altin 10.00 25.00
AVR Vinette Robinson 12.00 30.00
ASPD Simon Paisley 10.00 25.00

2019 Star Wars The Rise of Skywalker Series One Autographs Blue

STATED PRINT RUN 99 SER.#'d SETS
AJB John Boyega 25.00 60.00
ANA Naomi Ackie 25.00 60.00

2019 Star Wars The Rise of Skywalker Series One Character Stickers

COMPLETE SET (19) 15.00 40.00
COMMON CARD (CS1-CS19) 1.25 3.00
RANDOMLY INSERTED INTO PACKS
CS1 Rey 3.00 8.00
CS2 Kylo Ren 2.00 5.00

2019 Star Wars The Rise of Skywalker Series One Commemorative Medallions

COMMON MEM 4.00 10.00
*PURPLE/99: .5X TO 1.2X BASIC MEM
*ORANGE/50: .6X TO 1.5X BASIC MEM
*GOLD/25: .75X TO 2X BASIC MEM
RANDOMLY INSERTED INTO PACKS
MCBD D-O 6.00 15.00
MCBF Finn 6.00 15.00
MCBP Poe Dameron 6.00 15.00
MCC3 C-3PO 5.00 12.00
MCCC Chewbacca 5.00 12.00
MCCL Lando Calrissian 6.00 15.00
MCCR R2-D2 5.00 12.00
MCD0 D-O 8.00 20.00
MCDB BB-8 5.00 12.00
MCDR R2-D2 5.00 12.00
MCKY Kylo Ren 8.00 20.00
MCR2 R2-D2 6.00 15.00
MCRP Poe Dameron 5.00 12.00
MCRR Rey 10.00 25.00
MCTK Kylo Ren 6.00 15.00
MCBB8 BB-8 6.00 15.00
MCDC3 C-3PO 6.00 15.00
MCRC3 C-3PO 5.00 12.00

2019 Star Wars The Rise of Skywalker Series One Costume Relics

RANDOMLY INSERTED INTO PACKS
CRF Finn
CRJ Jannah/62 30.00 75.00
CRR Rey/99
CRGP Allegiant General Pryde
CRKR Kylo Ren/99
CRLC Lando Calrissian
CRPD Poe Dameron
CRZB Zorii Bliss

2019 Star Wars The Rise of Skywalker Series One Crush the Resistance

COMPLETE SET (8) 5.00 12.00
COMMON CARD (CR1-CR8) 1.00 2.50
*GREEN/299: .6X TO 1.5X BASIC CARDS
*PURPLE/199: 1X TO 2.5X BASIC CARDS
*RED/149: 1.2X TO 3X BASIC CARDS
*ORANGE/99: 1.5X TO 4X BASIC CARDS
*GOLD/25: 2.5X TO 6X BASIC CARDS
RANDOMLY INSERTED INTO PACKS

2019 Star Wars The Rise of Skywalker Series One Illustrated Characters

COMMON CARD (IC1-IC19) 2.00 5.00
*GREEN/299: SAME VALUE AS BASIC
*PURPLE/199: .5X TO 1.25X BASIC CARDS
*RED/149: .6X TO 1.5X BASIC CARDS
*ORANGE/99: 1X TO 2.5X BASIC CARDS
*GOLD/25: 1.2X TO 3X BASIC CARDS
RANDOMLY INSERTED INTO PACKS

2019 Star Wars The Rise of Skywalker Series One Long Live the Resistance

COMPLETE SET (8) 4.00 10.00
COMMON CARD (RB1-RB8) .75 2.00
*GREEN/299: .75X TO 2X BASIC CARDS
*PURPLE/199: 1X TO 2.5X BASIC CARDS
*RED/149: 1.2X TO 3X BASIC CARDS
*ORANGE/99: 2X TO 5X BASIC CARDS
*GOLD/25: 3X TO 8X BASIC CARDS
RANDOMLY INSERTED INTO PACKS

2019 Star Wars The Rise of Skywalker Series One May the Force Be with You

COMPLETE SET (5) 5.00 12.00
COMMON CARD (FWY1-FWY5) 1.50 4.00
*GREEN/299: SAME VALUE AS BASIC
*PURPLE/199: .6X TO 1.5X BASIC CARDS
*RED/149: .75X TO 2X BASIC CARDS
*ORANGE/99: 1X TO 2.5X BASIC CARDS
*GOLD/25: 1.5X TO 4X BASIC CARDS
RANDOMLY INSERTED INTO PACKS

2019 Star Wars The Rise of Skywalker Series One Ships and Vehicles

COMPLETE SET (7) 4.00 10.00
COMMON CARD (SV1-SV7) 1.00 2.50
*GREEN/299: .6X TO 1.5X BASIC CARDS
*PURPLE/199: .75X TO 2X BASIC CARDS
*RED/149: X TO X BASIC CARDS
*ORANGE/99: 1.2X TO 3X BASIC CARDS
*GOLD/25: X TO X BASIC CARDS
RANDOMLY INSERTED INTO PACKS

2019 Star Wars The Rise of Skywalker Series One CineWorld UK Promos

COMPLETE SET (2) 2.00 5.00
COMMON CARD 1.25 3.00
CWD Be a Hero (Droids) 1.25 3.00
CWK Darkness Rises (Kylo Ren) 1.25 3.00

2020 Topps Star Wars The Rise of Skywalker Series Two

COMPLETE SET (100) 6.00 15.00
UNOPENED BOX (24 PACKS) 100.00 150.00
UNOPENED PACK (8 CARDS) 4.00 6.00
COMMON CARD (1-100) .12 .30
*BLUE: 1X TO 2.5X BASIC CARDS
*PURPLE: 2X TO 5X BASIC CARDS
*RED/199: 10X TO 25X BASIC CARDS
*BRONZE/99: 12X TO 30X BASIC CARDS
*SILVER/25: 20X TO 50X BASIC CARDS

2020 Topps Star Wars The Rise of Skywalker Series Two Autographs

*RED/99: .5X TO 1.2X BASIC AUTOS
RANDOMLY INSERTED INTO PACKS
AAC Aidan Cook 6.00 15.00
AAL Amanda Lawrence 5.00 12.00
ABH Brian Herring 10.00 25.00
ADB Dave Chapman 10.00 25.00
ADW Debra Wilson 6.00 15.00
AGF Geff Francis 6.00 15.00
AKS Kiran Shah 10.00 25.00
AMQ Mike Quinn 8.00 20.00
AMW Matthew Wood 6.00 15.00
ANK Nick Kellington 8.00 20.00
APK Paul Kasey 6.00 15.00
ATW Tom Wilton 5.00 12.00
AKMT Kelly Marie Tran
AKRN Kipsang Rotich 8.00 20.00
ASPD Simon Paisley Day 5.00 12.00

2020 Topps Star Wars The Rise of Skywalker Series Two Character Posters

COMPLETE SET (6) 12.00 30.00
COMMON CARD (TP1-TP6) 2.50 6.00
RANDOMLY INSERTED INTO PACKS
TP1 Rey 4.00 10.00
TP2 Finn 2.50 6.00
TP3 Poe Dameron 2.50 6.00
TP4 Lando Calrissian 2.50 6.00
TP5 Chewbacca 2.50 6.00
TP6 Kylo Ren 3.00 8.00

2020 Topps Star Wars The Rise of Skywalker Series Two Commemorative Vehicle Medallions

*SILVER/50: .6X TO 1.5X BASIC MEM
RANDOMLY INSERTED INTO PACKS
MVMCF C-3PO 6.00 15.00
MVMCX C'ai Threnalli 6.00 15.00
MVMFF Finn 5.00 12.00
MVMJF Jannah 8.00 20.00
MVMKF Kaydel Ko Connix 8.00 20.00
MVMKT Kylo Ren 6.00 15.00
MVMLF Lando Calrissian 5.00 12.00
MVMPF Poe Dameron 6.00 15.00
MVMPX Poe Dameron 6.00 15.00
MVMRF Rey 15.00 40.00
MVMRX R2-D2 5.00 12.00
MVMWX Wedge Antilles 6.00 15.00
MVMBKF Beaumont Kin 5.00 12.00
MVMRDF R2-D2 6.00 15.00

2020 Topps Star Wars The Rise of Skywalker Series Two Costume Relics

COMMON MEM 12.00 30.00
RANDOMLY INSERTED INTO PACKS
CRKC Kylo Ren/Cloak Hood Lining 30.00 75.00
CRKU Kylo Ren/Undershirt 30.00 75.00
CRLC Lando Calrissian/Cloak Lining 40.00 100.00
CRRH Rey/Hood 125.00 300.00
CRRT Rey/Trousers 75.00 200.00
CRZJ Zorii Bliss/Jumpsuit Sleeve 30.00 75.00

2020 Topps Star Wars The Rise of Skywalker Series Two Foil Puzzle

COMPLETE SET (9) 30.00 75.00
COMMON CARD (1-9) 5.00 12.00
RANDOMLY INSERTED INTO PACKS

2020 Topps Star Wars The Rise of Skywalker Series Two Heroes of the Resistance

COMPLETE SET (11) 6.00 15.00
COMMON CARD (HR1-HR11) 1.00 2.50
*RED/99: .75X TO 2X BASIC CARDS
*BRONZE/50: 1.2X TO 3X BASIC CARDS
RANDOMLY INSERTED INTO PACKS
HR1 Rey 4.00 10.00

2020 Topps Star Wars The Rise of Skywalker Series Two Image Variation Autographs

RANDOMLY INSERTED INTO PACKS
AAD2 Adam Driver
ADG2 Domhnall Gleeson
ADR2 Daisy Ridley
AJB2 John Boyega
ANA2 Naomi Ackie 25.00 60.00
ABDW2 Billy Dee Williams

2020 Topps Star Wars The Rise of Skywalker Series Two The Knights of Ren

COMPLETE SET (10) 5.00 12.00
COMMON CARD (KR1-KR10) .75 2.00
*RED/99: .75X TO 2X BASIC CARDS
*BRONZE/50: 1.2X TO 3X BASIC CARDS
RANDOMLY INSERTED INTO PACKS

2020 Topps Star Wars The Rise of Skywalker Series Two Villains of the First Order

COMPLETE SET (9)
COMMON CARD (VF1-VF9) 1.00 2.50
*RED/99: .6X TO 1.5X BASIC CARDS
*BRONZE/50: 1X TO 2.5X BASIC CARDS
VF1 Kylo Ren 1.50 4.00

2020 Topps Star Wars The Rise of Skywalker Series Two Weapons

COMPLETE SET (10) 5.00 12.00
COMMON CARD (W1-W10) .75 2.00
*RED/99: .75X TO 2X BASIC CARDS
*BRONZE/50: 1X TO 2.5X BASIC CARDS
RANDOMLY INSERTED INTO PACKS
W1 Skywalker Lightsaber 2.00 5.00

2019 Star Wars The Rise of Skywalker Trailer

COMPLETE SET (20)
COMPLETE SET 1 (1-10) 10.00 25.00
COMPLETE SET 2 (11-20)
COMMON CARD (1-10) 1.50 4.00
COMMON CARD (11-20)
TOPPS ONLINE EXCLUSIVE

2009 Art of Star Wars Comics Postcards
COMPLETE SET (100) 12.00 30.00
COMMON CARD (1-100) .25 .60

2014 Disney Store Star Wars North America
COMPLETE SET (9) 10.00 25.00
COMMON CARD (1-10) .75 2.00
US/CANADA EXCLUSIVE
1 Luke Skywalker 2.00 5.00
4 Darth Vader 2.00 5.00
7 Princess Leia 2.00 5.00
9 Han Solo 2.00 5.00

2014 Disney Store Star Wars United Kingdom
COMPLETE SET (12) 15.00 40.00
COMMON CARD (1-12) 1.00 2.50
UK EXCLUSIVE
1 Chewbacca 1.25 3.00
2 Darth Vader 4.00 10.00
4 Han Solo 4.00 10.00
6 Luke Skywalker 3.00 8.00
8 Obi-Wan Kenobi 1.25 3.00
9 Princess Leia Organa 3.00 8.00
10 R2-D2 and C-3PO 1.25 3.00
11 Stormtrooper 1.25 3.00

2008 Family Guy Episode IV A New Hope
COMPLETE SET (50) 5.00 12.00
UNOPENED BOX (36 PACKS)
UNOPENED PACK (6 CARDS)
COMMON CARD (1-50) .15 .40
CL1 ISSUED AS CASE EXCLUSIVE
CL1 Evil Empire Cl 12.00 25.00

2008 Family Guy Episode IV A New Hope Droid Chat
COMPLETE SET (3) 5.00 12.00
COMMON CARD (DC1-DC3) 2.00 5.00
STATED ODDS 1:23

2008 Family Guy Episode IV A New Hope Promos
P1 Left half w/Han 1.00 2.50
Pi Right half w/Leia 1.00 2.50

2008 Family Guy Episode IV A New Hope Puzzle
COMPLETE SET (9) 4.00 10.00
COMMON CARD (NH1-NH9) .75 2.00
STATED ODDS 1:7

2008 Family Guy Episode IV A New Hope Scenes from Space
COMPLETE SET (6) 4.00 10.00
COMMON CARD (S1-S6) 1.25 3.00
STATED ODDS 1:11

2008 Family Guy Episode IV A New Hope Spaceships and Transports
COMPLETE SET (9) 4.00 10.00
COMMON CARD (ST1-ST9) 1.00 2.50
STATED ODDS 1:9

2008 Family Guy Episode IV A New Hope What Happens Next?
COMPLETE SET (6) 4.00 10.00
COMMON CARD (WN1-WN6) 1.25 3.00
STATED ODDS 1:11

2017 Funko Pop Buttons Star Wars
COMMON CARD 1.25 3.00
NNO Darth Vader 3.00 8.00
NNO Han Solo HT 2.00 5.00
NNO Jabba/vaping HT 2.00 5.00
NNO Luke Skywalker HT 2.00 5.00
NNO Princess Leia 3.00 8.00

2017 Funko Pop Flair Star Wars
NNO Chewbacca 1.50 4.00
NNO Darth Vader 2.50 6.00
NNO Greedo 1.25 3.00
NNO Han Solo 2.50 6.00
NNO Princess Leia 1.50 4.00
NNO Stormtrooper 1.25 3.00
NNO Yoda 1.50 4.00

2015-17 Funko Star Wars Smuggler's Bounty Patches
COMMON PATCH 2.00 5.00
SMUGGLER'S BOUNTY EXCLUSIVE
NNO BB-8 2.50 6.00
NNO Boba Fett 2.00 5.00
NNO Boushh 2.00 5.00
NNO Cassian Andor 2.00 5.00
NNO Darth Vader 2.50 6.00
NNO Greedo 2.00 5.00
NNO TIE Fighter Pilot 2.00 5.00
NNO X-Wing Pilot 2.00 5.00
NNO Yoda 2.00 5.00
NNO Zeb 2.00 5.00

2015 Star Wars Original Trilogy Series Bikkuriman Stickers
COMPLETE SET (24) 30.00 80.00
COMMON CARD 2.00 5.00

2015 Star Wars Prequel Trilogy Series Bikkuriman Stickers
COMPLETE SET (24) 25.00 60.00
COMMON CARD 1.25 3.00

1996 Topps Widevision Star Wars 3-Di
COMPLETE SET (63) 30.00 60.00
COMMON CARD (1-63) .60 1.50
1M STATED ODDS 1:24
1M Death Star Explosion 6.00 15.00

1996 Topps Widevision Star Wars 3-Di Promos
3Di1 Darth Vader 2.50 6.00
3Di2 Luke Skywalker 12.00 30.00
Darth Vader/1000*

2015 Star Wars Abrams Promos
COMPLETE SET (4) 6.00 15.00
COMMON CARD (1-4) 2.50 6.00
STATED ODDS 1:SET PER BOOK

2022 Topps Now Star Wars Andor Episodes
COMPLETE SET (60) 100.00 250.00
EP. 1 SET (5) 5.00 12.00
EP. 2 SET (5) 5.00 12.00
EP. 3 SET (5) 5.00 12.00
EP. 4 SET (5) 10.00 25.00
EP. 5 SET (5) 10.00 25.00
EP. 6 SET (5) 10.00 25.00
EP. 7 SET (5) 15.00 40.00
EP. 8 SET (5) 15.00 40.00
EP. 9 SET (5) 15.00 40.00
EP. 10 SET (5) 15.00 40.00
EP. 11 SET (5) 15.00 40.00
EP. 12 SET (5) 12.00 30.00
EP. 1 COMMON (1-5) 1.50 4.00
EP. 2 COMMON (6-10) 1.50 4.00
EP. 3 COMMON (11-15) 1.50 4.00
EP. 4 COMMON (16-20) 3.00 8.00
EP. 5 COMMON (21-25) 3.00 8.00
EP. 6 COMMON (26-30) 3.00 8.00
EP. 7 COMMON (31-35) 5.00 12.00
EP. 8 COMMON (36-40) 5.00 12.00
EP. 9 COMMON (41-45) 5.00 12.00
EP. 10 COMMON (46-50) 5.00 12.00
EP. 11 COMMON (51-55) 5.00 12.00
EP. 12 COMMON (56-60) 4.00 10.00
*BLUE/49: 1.2X TO 3X BASIC CARDS
EP.1 STATED PRINT RUN 914 SETS
EP.2 STATED PRINT RUN 914 SETS
EP.3 STATED PRINT RUN 914 SETS
EP.4 STATED PRINT RUN 740 SETS
EP.5 STATED PRINT RUN 670 SETS
EP.6 STATED PRINT RUN 699 SETS
EP.7 STATED PRINT RUN 687 SETS
EP.8 STATED PRINT RUN 718 SETS
EP.9 STATED PRINT RUN 663 SETS
EP.10 STATED PRINT RUN 679 SETS
EP.11 STATED PRINT RUN 657 SETS
EP.12 STATED PRINT RUN 703 SETS

2022 Topps Star Wars Andor Trailer Set
COMPLETE SET (5) 15.00 40.00
COMMON CARD (1-5) 4.00 10.00
*BLUE/49: 1.2X TO 3X BASIC CARDS
STATED PRINT RUN 1,075 ANNCD SETS

2019 Star Wars Authentics
COMPLETE SET (25) 150.00 300.00
UNOPENED BOX (1 CARD+1 AUTO'd 8X10)
COMMON CARD (1-25) 4.00 10.00
*BLUE/25: .6X TO 1.5X BASIC CARDS
STATED PRINT RUN 75 SER.#'d SETS
1 Ahsoka Tano 10.00 25.00
2 Anakin Skywalker 8.00 20.00
3 BB-8 12.00 30.00
5 Captain Tarkin 6.00 15.00
6 Chancellor Palpatine 10.00 25.00
7 Chirrut ÃŽmwe 5.00 12.00
8 Darth Maul 10.00 25.00
9 Director Krennic 6.00 15.00
10 Dryden Vos 6.00 15.00
11 Finn 6.00 15.00
12 Han Solo 8.00 20.00
13 Jango Fett 5.00 12.00
14 Jyn Erso 6.00 15.00
15 K-2SO 5.00 12.00
16 Kanan Jarrus 6.00 15.00
17 Kylo Ren 10.00 25.00
18 Lando Calrissian 10.00 25.00
19 Maul (Sam Witwer) 8.00 20.00
20 Obi-Wan Kenobi 5.00 12.00
21 Rey 15.00 40.00
23 Seventh Sister 5.00 12.00
24 Vice Admiral Holdo 15.00 40.00

2019 Star Wars Authentics Series Two
COMPLETE SET (29) 100.00 200.00
UNOPENED BOX (1 CARD+1 AUTO'd 8X10)
COMMON CARD (1-29) 3.00 8.00
*BLUE/25: .5X TO 1.2X BASIC CARDS
STATED PRINT RUN 99 SER.#'d SETS
1 Boba Fett 4.00 10.00
3 C'ai Threnalli 10.00 25.00
9 Han Solo 6.00 15.00
10 Hera Syndulla 6.00 15.00
16 Kazuda Xiono 10.00 25.00
19 Obi-Wan Kenobi 6.00 15.00
21 Padmé Amidala 5.00 12.00
23 Sabine Wren 5.00 12.00
25 Tallie Lintra 10.00 25.00
27 The Grand Inquisitor 5.00 12.00
29 Wicket 4.00 10.00

2020 Topps Star Wars Authentics 8x10
UNOPENED BOX (1 AUTO+1 CARD)
COMMON CARD 6.00 15.00
*BLUE/25: SAME VALUE AS BASIC CARDS
ADRR Rey 10.00 25.00
AGCC Cara Dune 8.00 20.00
AHFH Han Solo 10.00 25.00

2020 Topps Star Wars Authentics 11x14
UNOPENED BOX (1 AUTO+1 CARD)
COMMON CARD 6.00 15.00
*BLUE/25: SAME VALUE AS BASIC CARDS
AGC Cara Dune 8.00 20.00
ADRRS Rey 10.00 25.00
AHCRS Darth Vader 10.00 25.00

2021 Topps Star Wars The Bad Batch Exclusive Set
COMPLETE SET (10) 12.00 30.00
COMMON CARD (1-10) 2.00 5.00
STATED PRINT RUN 2,504 SETS
EXCLUSIVE TO EBAY
9 Omega 4.00 10.00

2021 Topps Star Wars Battle Plans
COMPLETE SET (100) 10.00 25.00
UNOPENED BOX (24 PACKS) 100.00 150.00
UNOPENED PACK (8 CARDS) 5.00 6.00
COMMON CARD (1-100) .20 .50
*FOILBOARD: .75X TO 2X BASIC CARDS
*BLUE: 1.5X TO 4X BASIC CARDS
*GREEN/99: 5X TO 12X BASIC CARDS
*ORANGE/50: 6X TO 15X BASIC CARDS
*PURPLE/25: 12X TO 30X BASIC CARDS

2021 Topps Star Wars Battle Plans Autographs
COMMON AUTO 6.00 15.00
*BLUE/149: .5X TO 1.2X BASIC AUTOS
*GREEN/99: .6X TO 1.5X BASIC AUTOS
*ORANGE/50: .75X TO 2X BASIC AUTOS
*PURPLE/25: 1X TO 2.5X BASIC AUTOS
STATED ODDS 1:45
AAE Ashley Eckstein 75.00 150.00
AAH Alan Harris 20.00 50.00
AAM Angus MacInnes 8.00 20.00
ACL Charlotte Louise 10.00 25.00
ACO Candice Orwell 20.00 50.00
ADB Dee Bradley Baker 25.00 60.00
ADM Dominic Monaghan 12.00 30.00
ADY Donnie Yen 125.00 300.00
AGH Gerald Home 15.00 40.00
AJA Jeremy Bulloch 60.00 120.00
AJK Jaime King 8.00 20.00
AJM John Morton 10.00 25.00
ALL Lex Lang 10.00 25.00
AMJ Mark Lewis Jones 8.00 20.00
AML Matt Lanter 25.00 60.00
AMM Mary Elizabeth McGlynn 10.00 25.00
ANA Naomi Ackie 10.00 25.00
ANF Nika Futterman 30.00 75.00
AOD Oliver Ford Davies 8.00 20.00
ARA Riz Ahmed 25.00 60.00
ARO Rena Owen 8.00 20.00
ARP Ray Park 60.00 120.00
ATG Taylor Gray 12.00 30.00
ATR Tim Rose 10.00 25.00

2021 Topps Star Wars Battle Plans Autographs Blue
STATED PRINT RUN 149 SER.#'d SETS
AED Adrian Edmondson 8.00 20.00

2021 Topps Star Wars Battle Plans Galactic Adversaries
COMMON CARD (GA1-GA30) .75 2.00

*GREEN/99: .5X TO 1.2X BASIC CARDS
*ORANGE/50: .75X TO 2X BASIC CARDS
*PURPLE/25: 1.5X TO 4X BASIC CARDS
STATED ODDS 1:2
GA1 Princess Leia Organa 1.50 4.00
GA2 Luke Skywalker 1.50 4.00
GA3 Han Solo 1.50 4.00
GA4 Chewbacca 1.00 2.50
GA5 R2-D2 1.00 2.50
GA6 C-3PO 1.00 2.50
GA7 Jyn Erso 1.25 3.00
GA9 Yoda 1.50 4.00
GA10 Mace Windu 1.00 2.50
GA12 Obi-Wan Kenobi 1.00 3.00
GA13 Rey 2.50 6.00
GA14 Poe Dameron 1.00 2.50
GA15 Finn 1.00 2.50
GA16 Darth Vader 2.00 5.00
GA17 Kylo Ren 1.50 4.00
GA18 Emperor Palpatine 1.00 2.50
GA20 Boba Fett 2.00 5.00
GA26 Captain Phasma 1.00 2.50
GA29 Asajj Ventress 1.00 3.00
GA30 Aurra Sing 1.00 2.50

2021 Topps Star Wars Battle Plans Manufactured Helmet Medallion Relics

COMMON MEM 4.00 10.00
*BLUE/149: .6X TO 1.2X BASIC MEM
*GREEN/99: .75X TO 2X BASIC MEM
*ORANGE/50: 1.2X TO 3X BASIC MEM
*PURPLE/25: 2X TO 5X BASIC MEM
HMAV Anakin Skywalker 6.00 15.00
HMCS Chewbacca 5.00 12.00
HMHS Han Solo 15.00 40.00
HMKV Kylo Ren 8.00 20.00
HMLS Luke Skywalker 10.00 25.00
HMLV Luke Skywalker 10.00 25.00
HMOV Obi-Wan Kenobi 5.00 12.00
HMPV Padmé Amidala 12.00 30.00
HMVS Darth Vader 10.00 25.00
HMVT Darth Vader 10.00 25.00
HMVV Darth Vader 10.00 25.00
HMC3S C-3PO 6.00 15.00
HMCST Chewbacca 5.00 12.00
HMHST Han Solo 15.00 40.00
HMLAT Luke Skywalker 10.00 25.00
HMLST Princess Leia Organa 8.00 20.00
HMMST Luke Skywalker 10.00 25.00
HMOAT Princess Leia Organa 8.00 20.00
HMPLS Princess Leia Organa 8.00 20.00
HMPLV Princess Leia Organa 8.00 20.00
HMWST Wicket W. Warrick 5.00 12.00

2021 Topps Star Wars Battle Plans Sourced Fabric Relics

COMMON MEM 15.00 40.00
*GREEN/99: SAME VALUE AS BASIC
*ORANGE/50: .5X TO 1.2X BASIC MEM
*PURPLE/25: .6X TO 1.5X BASIC MEM
STATED ODDS 1:87
STATED PRINT RUN 149 SER.#'d SETS
FRF Finn/149 20.00 50.00
FRL Luke Skywalker/149 75.00 150.00
FRP Poe Dameron/149 25.00 60.00
FRQ Qi'ra/149 75.00 150.00
FRR Rey/149 75.00 150.00
FRDV Dryden Vos/149 25.00 60.00
FREN Enfys Nest/135 30.00 75.00
FRGE Galen Erso/149 25.00 60.00
FRJE Jyn Erso/149 50.00 100.00
FRLC Lando Calrissian/85 50.00 100.00
FRLS Luke Skywalker/149 50.00 100.00
FRPD Poe Dameron/149 25.00 60.00
FRRT Rose Tico/149 50.00 100.00
FRRY Rey/149 100.00 200.00

2021 Topps Star Wars Battle Plans Tools of Warfare

COMPLETE SET (10) 6.00 15.00
COMMON CARD (TW1-TW10) 1.00 2.50
*GREEN/99: .6X TO 1.5X BASIC CARDS
*ORANGE/50: .75X TO 2X BASIC CARDS
*PURPLE/25: 1.5X TO 4X BASIC CARDS
STATED ODDS 1:4

2021 Topps Star Wars Battle Plans Ultimate Showdowns

COMPLETE SET (10) 8.00 20.00
COMMON CARD (US1-US10) 1.25 3.00
*GREEN/99: .6X TO 1.5X BASIC CARDS
*ORANGE/50: .75X TO 2X BASIC CARDS
*PURPLE/25: 1.5X TO 4X BASIC CARDS
STATED ODDS 1:4
US1 Luke Skywalker vs. Darth Vader 2.50 6.00
US2 Qui-Gon Jinn & Obi-Wan Kenobi vs. Darth Maul 2.00 5.00
US4 Luke Skywalker vs. Darth Vader 2.50 6.00
US6 Rey vs. Kylo Ren 3.00 8.00
US8 Yoda vs. Emperor Palpatine 1.50 4.00
US10 Kylo Ren & Rey vs. Praetorian Guards 2.50 6.00

2022 Topps Now Star Wars The Book of Boba Fett

COMPLETE SET (35) 60.00 150.00
COMPLETE CH.1 SET (5) 10.00 25.00
COMPLETE CH.2 SET (5) 10.00 25.00
COMPLETE CH.3 SET (5) 10.00 25.00
COMPLETE CH.4 SET (5) 10.00 25.00
COMPLETE CH.5 SET (5) 10.00 25.00
COMPLETE CH.6 SET (5) 10.00 25.00
COMPLETE CH.7 SET (5) 10.00 25.00
CH.1 COMMON (1-5) 3.00 8.00
CH.2 COMMON (6-10) 3.00 8.00
CH.3 COMMON (11-15) 3.00 8.00
CH.4 COMMON (16-20) 3.00 8.00
CH.5 COMMON (21-25) 3.00 8.00
CH.6 COMMON (26-30) 3.00 8.00
CH.7 COMMON (31-35) 3.00 8.00
CH.1 PRINT RUN 2,623 SETS
CH.2 PRINT RUN 1,630 SETS
CH.3 PRINT RUN 1,510 SETS
CH.4 PRINT RUN 1,453 SETS
CH.5 PRINT RUN 1,769 SETS
CH.6 PRINT RUN 2,005 SETS
CH.7 PRINT RUN 1,920 SETS
29 Cad Bane/2,005* 10.00 25.00

2021 Topps Star Wars The Book of Boba Fett Trailer Set

COMPLETE SET (6) 12.00 30.00
COMMON CARD (1-6) 3.00 8.00
STATED PRINT RUN 1,279 ANNCD SETS

2021 Topps Star Wars Bounty Hunters

COMPLETE SET (300) 100.00 250.00
COMPLETE L1 SET (100) 10.00 25.00
COMPLETE L2 SET (100) 20.00 50.00
COMPLETE L3 SET (100) 75.00 200.00
UNOPENED BOX (24 PACKS)
UNOPENED PACK (8 CARDS)
COMMON L1 (B11-B1100) .20 .50
COMMON L2 (B21-B2100) .40 1.00
COMMON L3 (B31-B3100) 1.50 4.00
*BLUE L1: .5X TO 1.2X BASIC CARDS
*BLUE L2: .75X TO 2X BASIC CARDS
*BLUE L3: 1.5X TO 4X BASIC CARDS
*GREEN L1/150: 3X TO 8X BASIC CARDS
*GREEN L2/99: 4X TO 10X BASIC CARDS
*GREEN L3/50: 5X TO 12X BASIC CARDS
*PURPLE L1/99: 5X TO 12X BASIC CARDS
*PURPLE L2/75: 6X TO 15X BASIC CARDS
*PURPLE L3/35: 8X TO 20X BASIC CARDS
*RED L1/75: 5X TO 12X BASIC CARDS
*RED L2/50: 6X TO 15X BASIC CARDS
*RED L3/25: 10X TO 25X BASIC CARDS

2021 Topps Star Wars Bounty Hunters Autographs

*BLUE/99: .5X TO 1.2X BASIC AUTOS
*GREEN/75: .6X TO 1.5X BASIC AUTOS
*PURPLE/50: .75X TO 2X BASIC AUTOS
RANDOMLY INSERTED INTO PACKS
AAB Anna Brewster 6.00 15.00
AAG Anna Graves 8.00 20.00
ABW Billy Dee Williams
ACM Cathy Munro
ACP Chris Parsons
ACT Catherine Taber 10.00 25.00
ACW Carl Weathers
ADB Dee Bradley Baker 10.00 25.00
ADE Dee Bradley Baker 20.00 50.00
ADL Daniel Logan 20.00 50.00
AES Emily Swallow
AGE Giancarlo Esposito
AHC Hayden Christensen
AHF Harrison Ford
AIM Ian McDiarmid
AJB Jeremy Bulloch
AJD Julie Dolan 10.00 25.00
AJT James Arnold Taylor
AKB Kenny Baker
ALM Lars Mikkelsen
ALW Leanna Walsman 15.00 40.00
AMB Michonne Bourriague 10.00 25.00
AME Mike Edmonds 8.00 20.00
AML Matt Lanter
AMM Mary Elizabeth McGlynn 6.00 15.00
ANF Nika Futterman 12.00 30.00
ANN Nick Nolte
AOA Omid Abtahi
APB Paul Blake 6.00 15.00
APM Peter Mayhew
ASK Simon Kassianides 10.00 25.00
ATE Temuera Morrison
ATG Taylor Gray 10.00 25.00
ATM Temuera Morrison
ATW Taika Waititi
AWH Werner Herzog

2021 Topps Star Wars Bounty Hunters Feared Mercenaries Aurra Sing

COMPLETE SET (10) 5.00 12.00
COMMON CARD (IA1-IA10) 1.00 2.50
STATED ODDS 1:6

2021 Topps Star Wars Bounty Hunters Feared Mercenaries Boba Fett

COMPLETE SET (10) 5.00 12.00
COMMON CARD (IB1-IB10) 1.00 2.50
STATED ODDS 1:4

2021 Topps Star Wars Bounty Hunters Feared Mercenaries Cad Bane

COMPLETE SET (10) 8.00 20.00
COMMON CARD (IC1-IC10) 1.50 4.00
STATED ODDS 1:12

2021 Topps Star Wars Bounty Hunters Feared Mercenaries Die-Cuts

COMPLETE SET (5) 30.00 75.00
COMMON CARD 6.00 15.00
STATED ODDS 1:12
DC4 Bossk 10.00 25.00
DCD Dengar 10.00 25.00
DCZ IG-88 8.00 20.00

2021 Topps Star Wars Bounty Hunters Feared Mercenaries Jango Fett

COMPLETE SET (10) 5.00 12.00
COMMON CARD (IJ1-IJ10) .75 2.00
STATED ODDS 1:4

2021 Topps Star Wars Bounty Hunters Feared Mercenaries The Mandalorian

COMPLETE SET (10) 6.00 15.00
COMMON CARD (IM1-IM10) 1.25 3.00
RANDOMLY INSERTED INTO PACKS

2021 Topps Star Wars Bounty Hunters Manufactured Bounty Hunter Patch Relics

COMMON MEM 4.00 10.00
*ORANGE/250: SAME VALUE AS BASIC
*BLUE/199: .5X TO 1.2X BASIC MEM
*GREEN/99: .6X TO 1.5X BASIC MEM
*PURPLE/50: .75X TO 2X BASIC MEM
*GOLD/25: 1X TO 2.5X BASIC MEM
STATED ODDS 1:BLASTER BOX
BLASTER BOX EXCLUSIVE
PBHB Bossk 8.00 20.00
PBHD Dengar 6.00 15.00
PBHZ Zam Wesell 5.00 12.00
PBHAS Aurra Sing 6.00 15.00
PBHAV Asajj Ventress 6.00 15.00
PBHBF Boba Fett 12.00 30.00
PBHCB Cad Bane 12.00 30.00
PBHIG IG-88 8.00 20.00
PBHJF Jango Fett 8.00 20.00

2021 Topps Star Wars Bounty Hunters Manufactured Bounty Patch Relics

COMMON MEM 4.00 10.00
*GREEN/99: .5X TO 1.2X BASIC MEM
*PURPLE/50: .6X TO 1.5X BASIC MEM
*GOLD/25: .75X TO 2X BASIC MEM
STATED PRINT RUN 199 SER.#'d SETS
PBHC Han Solo in Carbonite 12.00 30.00
PBHS Han Solo 10.00 25.00
PBPA Padme Amidala 8.00 20.00
PBSP Padme Amidala 6.00 15.00
PBZH Ziro the Hutt 8.00 20.00
PBSCP Supreme Chancellor Palpatine 5.00 12.00

2021 Topps Star Wars Bounty Hunters Star Wars '77 Buybacks

COMMON CARD 150.00 400.00
STATED ODDS 1:1,122

1984 Kellogg's Star Wars C-3PO's Cereal Masks

COMPLETE SET (6) 150.00 300.00
COMMON CARD 12.00 30.00
STATED ODDS 1:CEREAL BOX
1 C-3PO 60.00 120.00
2 Chewbacca 25.00 60.00
5 Stormtrooper 15.00 40.00
6 Yoda 15.00 40.00

2016 Star Wars Card Trader

COMPLETE SET (100) 6.00 15.00
UNOPENED BOX (24 PACKS) 35.00 50.00
UNOPENED PACK (6 CARDS) 2.00 3.00
COMMON CARD (1-100) .12 .30
*BLUE: .6X TO 1.5X BASIC CARDS .20 .50
*RED: 1.2X TO 3X BASIC CARDS .40 1.00
*GREEN/99: 6X TO 15X BASIC CARDS 2.00 5.00
*ORANGE/50: 12X TO 30X BASIC CARDS 4.00 10.00
*BAT.DAM./10: 30X TO 80X BASIC CARDS 10.00 25.00

2016 Star Wars Card Trader Actor Digital Autographs

COMPLETE SET (20) 150.00 300.00
COMMON CARD (DA1-DA20) 8.00 20.00
STATED ODDS 1:788
STATED PRINT RUN 25 SER.#'d SETS

2016 Star Wars Card Trader Bounty

COMPLETE SET (20) 15.00 40.00
COMMON CARD (B1-B20) 1.25 3.00
STATED ODDS 1:5

2016 Star Wars Card Trader Classic Artwork

COMPLETE SET (20)	15.00	40.00
COMMON CARD (CA1-CA20))	1.25	3.00
STATED ODDS 1:5		

2016 Star Wars Card Trader Film Quotes

COMPLETE SET (20)	10.00	25.00
COMMON CARD (FQ1-FQ20)	1.00	2.50
STATED ODDS 1:4		

2016 Star Wars Card Trader Galactic Moments

COMPLETE SET (20)	15.00	40.00
COMMON CARD (GM1-GM20)	1.25	3.00
STATED ODDS 1:5		

2016 Star Wars Card Trader Reflections

COMPLETE SET (7)	12.00	30.00
COMMON CARD (R1-R7)	2.50	6.00
STATED ODDS 1:8		

2016 Star Wars Card Trader Topps Choice

COMPLETE SET (13)	15.00	40.00
COMMON CARD (TC1-TC13)	2.00	5.00
STATED ODDS 1:16		
TC4 Kabe	8.00	20.00
TC7 Lak Sivrak	3.00	8.00
TC10 Bo-Katan Kryze	3.00	8.00
TC13 Todo 360	2.50	6.00

2015 Star Wars Celebration VII Oversized Vintage Wrappers

COMPLETE SET (16)	50.00	100.00
COMMON CARD	3.00	8.00

1999 Topps Chrome Archives Star Wars

COMPLETE SET (90)	10.00	25.00
UNOPENED BOX (36 PACKS)	250.00	400.00
UNOPENED PACK (5 CARDS)	8.00	12.00
COMMON CARD (1-90)	.20	.50

1999 Topps Chrome Archives Star Wars Clearzone

COMPLETE SET (4)	7.50	20.00
COMMON CARD (C1-C4)	2.50	6.00

1999 Topps Chrome Archives Star Wars Double Sided

COMPLETE SET (9)	40.00	100.00
COMMON CARD (C1-C9)	6.00	15.00

1999 Topps Chrome Archives Star Wars Promos

P1 Hate me, Luke! Destroy me!	1.00	2.50
P2 Welcome, young Luke	1.00	2.50

2022 Topps Chrome Black Star Wars

COMPLETE SET (100)	150.00	400.00
UNOPENED BOX (1 PACK)	100.00	150.00
UNOPENED PACK (4 CARDS)		
COMMON CARD (1-100)	3.00	8.00
*REF./199: .75X TO 2X BASIC CARDS		
*GREEN/99: 1.2X TO 3X BASIC CARDS		
*BLUE/75: 1.5X TO 4X BASIC CARDS		
*GOLD/50: 2X TO 5X BASIC CARDS		

2022 Topps Chrome Black Star Wars Autographs

RANDOMLY INSERTED INTO PACKS		
AAK Andrew Kishino	8.00	20.00
ABD Ben Diskin	10.00	25.00
ACS Christopher Sean	6.00	15.00
ADC Dave Chapman	6.00	15.00
AGE Giancarlo Esposito	30.00	75.00
AJB John Boyega	40.00	100.00
AJC Jim Cummings	10.00	25.00
AJD Julie Dolan	8.00	20.00
AJK Jaime King	10.00	25.00
AMW Matthew Wood	20.00	50.00
ANF Nika Futterman	10.00	25.00
APK Paul Kasey	8.00	20.00
APL Phil LaMarr	6.00	15.00
ASB Steve Blum	15.00	40.00
ATG Taylor Gray	15.00	40.00
ATS Tiya Sircar	20.00	50.00
AAEH Alden Ehrenreich	75.00	200.00
AASE Amy Sedaris	15.00	40.00
ABED Ben Daniels	6.00	15.00
ADBB Dee Bradley Baker	15.00	40.00
ADBC Dee Bradley Baker	15.00	40.00
ADBE Dee Bradley Baker	15.00	40.00
ADBH Dee Bradley Baker	15.00	40.00
ADBT Dee Bradley Baker	15.00	40.00
ADBW Dee Bradley Baker	15.00	40.00
AKSH Kiran Shah	6.00	15.00
AMIB Michonne Bourriague	8.00	20.00
ARAD Robin Atkin Downes	10.00	25.00
ASLJ Samuel L. Jackson		

2022 Topps Chrome Black Star Wars B Design Autographs

RANDOMLY INSERTED INTO PACKS		
ABAL Amanda Lawrence	6.00	15.00
ABBD Ben Diskin	8.00	20.00
ABBH Brian Herring	12.00	30.00
ABBL Billie Lourd	30.00	75.00
ABCF Carrie Fisher		
ABCH Clint Howard	10.00	25.00
ABCS Christopher Sean	6.00	15.00
ABHC Hayden Christensen	250.00	600.00
ABJC Jim Cummings	12.00	30.00
ABJI Jason Isaacs	25.00	60.00
ABKS Kiran Shah	6.00	15.00
ABMR Misty Rosas	10.00	25.00
ABMW Matthew Wood	10.00	25.00
ABNF Nika Futterman	10.00	25.00
ABPK Paul Kasey	6.00	15.00
ABPL Phil LaMarr	6.00	15.00
ABRB Ralph Brown	6.00	15.00
ABTS Tiya Sircar	15.00	40.00
ABADA Annabelle Davis	8.00	20.00
ABASE Amy Sedaris	10.00	25.00
ABLBR Lynn Robertson Bruce	12.00	30.00
ABMBJ Mark Boone Jr.	10.00	25.00

2022 Topps Chrome Black Star Wars Dark Side Autographs

COMMON AUTO	10.00	25.00
RANDOMLY INSERTED INTO PACKS		
DSAB Anna Brewster	15.00	40.00
DSAS Andy Serkis	40.00	100.00
DSGE Giancarlo Esposito	50.00	125.00
DSHC Hayden Christensen	300.00	750.00
DSJI Jason Isaacs	20.00	50.00
DSPB Paul Bettany	75.00	200.00
DSIMC Ian McDiarmid	150.00	400.00

2022 Topps Chrome Black Star Wars Galactic Black Autographs

RANDOMLY INSERTED INTO PACKS		
GBAE Alden Ehrenreich	75.00	200.00
GBCW Carl Weathers	100.00	250.00
GBJB John Boyega	50.00	125.00

2022 Topps Star Wars The Book of Boba Fett

COMPLETE SET (100)	10.00	25.00
UNOPENED BOX (7 PACKS)	50.00	75.00
UNOPENED PACK (8 CARDS)	8.00	10.00
UNOPENED BLASTER BOX (10 PACKS)	20.00	30.00
UNOPENED BLASTER PACK (6 CARDS)	2.00	3.00
COMMON CARD (1-100)	.20	.50
*BLUE: .5X TO 1.2X BASIC CARDS		
*PURPLE: .6X TO 1.5X BASIC CARDS		
*RED/99: 2.5X TO 6X BASIC CARDS		
*GREEN/75: 5X TO 12X BASIC CARDS		
*BRONZE/50: 6X TO 15X BASIC CARDS		

2022 Topps Star Wars The Book of Boba Fett Aliens and Creatures

COMPLETE SET (10)	6.00	15.00
COMMON CARD (AC1-AC10)	1.25	3.00
*RED/99: .6X TO 1.5X BASIC CARDS		
STATED ODDS 1:7		

2022 Topps Star Wars The Book of Boba Fett Autographs

COMMON AUTO	8.00	20.00
*RED/99: .5X TO 1.2X BASIC AUTOS		
*GREEN/75: .6X TO 1.5X BASIC AUTOS		
*BRONZE/50: .75X TO 2X BASIC AUTOS		
STATED ODDS 1:16		
AAB Andrea Bartlow	15.00	40.00
AAG Allan Graf	10.00	25.00
AAS Amy Sedaris	12.00	30.00
ABL Barry Lowin	10.00	25.00
ACJ Carey Jones	30.00	75.00
ADK Dorian Kingi	40.00	100.00
ADP David Pasquesi	15.00	40.00
AES Emily Swallow	30.00	75.00
AJR John Rosengrant	10.00	25.00
AMB Matt Berry	30.00	75.00
APL Phil LaMarr EXCH	12.00	30.00
ASK Skyler Bible	10.00	25.00
ACB1 Chris Bartlett	10.00	25.00
APSL Paul Sun-Hyung Lee	12.00	30.00

2022 Topps Star Wars The Book of Boba Fett Boba Fett's Arsenal

COMPLETE SET (10)	6.00	15.00
COMMON CARD (BA1-BA10)	1.00	2.50
*RED/99: 1.2X TO 3X BASIC CARDS		
STATED ODDS 1:7		

2022 Topps Star Wars The Book of Boba Fett Characters

COMPLETE SET (15)	10.00	25.00
COMMON CARD (C1-C15)	1.25	3.00
*RED/99: .6X TO 1.5X BASIC CARDS		
STATED ODDS 1:3		

2022 Topps Star Wars The Book of Boba Fett Concept Art

COMPLETE SET (15)	12.00	30.00
COMMON CARD (CA1-CA15)	1.50	4.00
*RED/99: .75X TO 2X BASIC CARDS		
STATED ODDS 1:4		

2022 Topps Star Wars The Book of Boba Fett Manufactured Patches

COMMON MEM	6.00	15.00
*RED/99: .5X TO 1.2X BASIC MEM		
*BRONZE/50: 1.2X TO 3X BASIC MEM		
STATED ODDS 1:1 BLASTER BOX EXCLUSIVE		
MP1 Boba Fett	15.00	40.00
MP2 Boba Fett	10.00	25.00
MP3 Boba Fett	8.00	20.00
MP4 Boba Fett	8.00	20.00
MP5 Boba Fett	12.00	30.00
MP6 Boba Fett	8.00	20.00
MP7 Boba Fett	8.00	20.00
MP8 Boba Fett	10.00	25.00
MP10 Boba Fett	10.00	25.00
MP11 Fennec Shand	8.00	20.00
MP12 Fennec Shand	8.00	20.00
MP13 Fennec Shand	8.00	20.00
MP14 Fennec Shand	12.00	30.00
MP15 Fennec Shand	15.00	40.00
MP20 Fennec Shand	8.00	20.00

2022 Topps Star Wars The Book of Boba Fett Prop Relics

STATED PRINT RUN 50 SER.#'d SETS		
PR1 Boba Fett		
PR2 Fennec Shand	125.00	300.00
PR3 Twi'lek Majordomo	50.00	125.00
PR4 Drash		
PR5 Skad	75.00	200.00

2022 Topps Star Wars The Book of Boba Fett Sourced Fabric Relics

COMMON MEM	40.00	100.00
*BRONZE/50: .5X TO 1.2X BASIC MEM		
STATED PRINT RUN 99 SER.#'d SETS		
FR3 The Armorer	60.00	150.00

2019 Star Wars Chrome Legacy

COMPLETE SET (200)	75.00	150.00
UNOPENED BOX (12 PACKS)		
UNOPENED PACK (5 CARDS)		
COMMON CARD (1-200)	.60	1.50
*REFRACTOR: .75X TO 2X BASIC CARDS		
*BLUE/99: 1.2X TO 3X BASIC CARDS		
*GREEN/50: 1.5X TO 4X BASIC CARDS		
*ORANGE/25: 2X TO 5X BASIC CARDS		
*BLACK/10: 4X TO 10X BASIC CARDS		

2019 Star Wars Chrome Legacy Classic Trilogy Autographs

STATED ODDS 1:113		
CAAD Anthony Daniels		
CACB Caroline Blakiston	6.00	15.00
CACF Carrie Fisher		
CACR Clive Revill	6.00	15.00
CADB David Barclay	8.00	20.00
CAHF Harrison Ford		
CAJB Jeremy Bulloch		
CAKB Kenny Baker		
CAMQ Mike Quinn	5.00	12.00
CARG Rusty Goffe	5.00	12.00
CAWD Warwick Davis		
CABDW Billy Dee Williams		
CAIME Ian McDiarmid		

2019 Star Wars Chrome Legacy Concept Art

COMPLETE SET (20)	12.00	30.00
COMMON CARD (CA1-CA20)	1.00	2.50
*GREEN/50: .5X TO 1.2X BASIC CARDS		
*ORANGE/25: .6X TO 1.5X BASIC CARDS		
STATED ODDS 1:3		

2019 Star Wars Chrome Legacy Droid Medallions

COMMON MEM	5.00	12.00
*GREEN/50: .6X TO 1.5X BASIC MEM		
*ORANGE/25: .75X TO 2X BASIC MEM		
STATED ODDS 1:23		

2019 Star Wars Chrome Legacy Marvel Comic Book Covers

COMPLETE SET (25)	15.00	40.00
COMMON CARD (MC1-MC25)	1.25	3.00
*GREEN/50: .6X TO 1.5X BASIC CARDS		
*ORANGE/25: .75X TO 2X BASIC CARDS		
STATED ODDS 1:3		

2019 Star Wars Chrome Legacy New Trilogy Autographs

STATED ODDS 1:225		
NAAD Adam Driver		
NAAL Amanda Lawrence	5.00	12.00
NAAS Andy Serkis		
NABH Brian Herring	6.00	15.00
NABL Billie Lourd		
NADG Domhnall Gleeson		
NADR Daisy Ridley		
NAJS Joonas Suotamo		
NALD Laura Dern		
NAJBF John Boyega		
NAKMT Kelly Marie Tran		

2019 Star Wars Chrome Legacy Posters

COMPLETE SET (25) 15.00 40.00
COMMON CARD (PC1-PC25) 1.25 3.00
*GREEN/50: .6X TO 1.5X BASIC CARDS
*ORANGE/25: .75X TO 2X BASIC CARDS
STATED ODDS 1:6

2019 Star Wars Chrome Legacy Prequel Trilogy Autographs

STATED ODDS 1:229
PAEM Ewan McGregor
PAGP Greg Proops
PAHC Hayden Christensen
PAHQ Hugh Quarshie
PAJB Jerome Blake 5.00 12.00
PALM Lewis MacLeod
PAMW Matthew Wood 6.00 15.00
PARP Ray Park
PATM Temuera Morrison
PASLJ Samuel L. Jackson

2021 Topps Chrome Star Wars Legacy

COMPLETE SET (200) 100.00 200.00
UNOPENED BOX (12 PACKS) 250.00 400.00
UNOPENED PACK (5 CARDS) 20.00 35.00
COMMON CARD (1-200) .60 1.50
*REFRACTORS: .5X TO 1.2X BASIC CARDS
*BLUE/99: .6X TO 1.5X BASIC CARDS
*GREEN/50: 1.2X TO 3X BASIC CARDS

2021 Topps Chrome Star Wars Legacy Age of Rebellion Autographs

ARBAT Alan Tudyk 50.00 100.00
ARBBM Ben Mendelsohn 100.00 200.00
ARBDC Dermot Crowley 8.00 20.00
ARBDY Donnie Yen 75.00 150.00
ARBFJ Felicity Jones 500.00 1000.00
ARBFW Forest Whitaker 75.00 150.00
ARBGE Giancarlo Esposito 75.00 150.00
ARBHF Harrison Ford
ARBIM Ian McDiarmid
ARBJB Jeremy Bulloch
ARBJM John Morton
ARBKB Ben Burtt 20.00 50.00
ARBMB Mark Boone Jr.
ARBMC Michael Carter
ARBMM Mads Mikkelsen
ARBMP Michael Pennington
ARBMQ Mike Quinn
ARBNN Nick Nolte
ARBPM Peter Mayhew
ARBPR Pam Rose
ARBRA Riz Ahmed
ARBRD Rosario Dawson
ARBTW Taika Waititi
ARBWH Werner Herzog
ARBBDW Billy Dee Williams

2021 Topps Chrome Star Wars Legacy Age of Republic Autographs

ARPAB Ahmed Best 30.00 75.00
ARPAE Ashley Eckstein 60.00 150.00
ARPDL Daniel Logan 12.00 30.00
ARPDT David Tennant 15.00 40.00
ARPEM Ewan McGregor
ARPHC Hayden Christensen
ARPLM Lewis Macleod
ARPRP Ron Perlman
ARPJAT James Arnold Taylor
ARPSLJ Samuel L. Jackson

2021 Topps Chrome Star Wars Legacy Age of Resistance Autographs

ARSAD Adam Driver 300.00 500.00
ARSAS Andy Serkis
ARSCF Carrie Fisher
ARSDC Dave Chapman 10.00 25.00
ARSDG Domhnall Gleeson
ARSDM Dominic Monaghan 20.00 50.00
ARSDR Daisy Ridley
ARSEE Emun Elliott 8.00 20.00
ARSGC Gwendoline Christie 125.00 250.00
ARSGG Greg Grunberg 10.00 25.00
ARSHF Harrison Ford
ARSJB John Boyega
ARSKB Kenny Baker
ARSKL Ken Leung
ARSMQ Mike Quinn
ARSNA Naomi Ackie
ARSTW Tom Wilton
ARSBDW Billy Dee Williams

2021 Topps Chrome Star Wars Legacy Commemorative Ship Medallion Relics

COMMON MEM 3.00 8.00
*GREEN/50: .6X TO 1.5X BASIC MEM
STATED PRINT RUN 99 SER.#'d SETS
SMC Chewbacca 6.00 15.00
SMBM Baze Malbus 5.00 12.00
SMBR Bodhi Rook 4.00 10.00
SMC3 C-3PO 6.00 15.00
SMCA Captain Cassian Andor 5.00 12.00
SMCI Chirrut Imwe 6.00 15.00
SMDV Darth Vader 15.00 40.00
SMFT Finn 5.00 12.00
SMGE Galen Erso 6.00 15.00
SMHS Han Solo 12.00 30.00
SMJE Jyn Erso 15.00 40.00
SMK2 K-2SO 8.00 20.00
SMLC Lando Calrissian 5.00 12.00
SMLO Princess Leia Organa 12.00 30.00
SMLS Luke Skywalker 15.00 40.00
SMR2 R2-D2 5.00 12.00
SMRT Rey 10.00 25.00
SMSD Stormtrooper 6.00 15.00
SMSG Saw Gerrera 6.00 15.00
SMBBT BB-8 6.00 15.00
SMBKT Biggs Darklighter 8.00 20.00
SMDVD Darth Vader 15.00 40.00
SMDVT Darth Vader 15.00 40.00
SMEAX Ello Asty 4.00 10.00
SMKRT Kylo Ren 6.00 15.00
SMLST Luke Skywalker 15.00 40.00
SMLSX Luke Skywalker 15.00 40.00
SMPDT Poe Dameron 6.00 15.00
SMPDX Poe Dameron 6.00 15.00
SMTIE TIE Fighter Pilot 5.00 12.00
SMTLX Tallie Lintra 6.00 15.00

2021 Topps Chrome Star Wars Legacy Mandalorian Concept Art

COMPLETE SET (15) 30.00 75.00
COMMON CARD (MCA1-MCA15) 3.00 8.00
*GREEN/50: .75X TO 2X BASIC CARDS

2021 Topps Chrome Star Wars Legacy Visions Concept Art

COMPLETE SET (15) 20.00 50.00
COMMON CARD (MCA1-MCA15) 2.50 6.00
*GREEN/50: .75X TO 2X BASIC CARDS

2021 Topps Chrome Star Wars Legacy Wielders of the Lightsaber

COMPLETE SET (15) 50.00 100.00
COMMON CARD (MCA1-MCA15) 2.00 5.00
*GREEN/50: .75X TO 2X BASIC CARDS
WL1 Luke Skywalker 6.00 15.00
WL2 Anakin Skywalker 3.00 8.00
WL3 Darth Vader 4.00 10.00
WL4 Darth Sidious 2.50 6.00
WL7 Kylo Ren 4.00 10.00
WL8 Rey 4.00 10.00
WL10 Ahsoka Tano 8.00 20.00
WL13 Yoda 5.00 12.00
WL14 Mace Windu 3.00 8.00
WL15 Obi-Wan Kenobi 3.00 8.00
WL16 Qui-Gon Jinn 2.50 6.00
WL19 The Grand Inquisitor 2.50 6.00
WL20 Seventh Sister 2.50 6.00

2014 Star Wars Chrome Perspectives

COMPLETE SET (100) 30.00 60.00
UNOPENED BOX (24 PACKS) 300.00 500.00
UNOPENED PACK (6 CARDS) 12.00 20.00
COMMON CARD (1E-50E) .40 1.00
COMMON CARD (1R-50R) .40 1.00
*REFRACTOR: 1.2X TO 3X BASIC CARDS
*PRISM: 1.5X TO 4X BASIC CARDS
*X-FRACTOR/99: 3X TO 8X BASIC CARDS
*GOLD REF./50: 6X TO 15X BASIC CARDS

2014 Star Wars Chrome Perspectives Autographs

COMMON AUTO 6.00 15.00
STATED ODDS 1 PER BOX W/SKETCHES
NNO Angus MacInnes 12.00 30.00
NNO Anthony Daniels 125.00 250.00
NNO Billy Dee Williams 60.00 120.00
NNO Carrie Fisher 400.00 800.00
NNO Harrison Ford 1500.00 3000.00
NNO James Earl Jones 200.00 400.00
NNO Jeremy Bulloch 30.00 75.00
NNO John Ratzenberger 10.00 20.00
NNO Kenneth Colley 12.00 25.00
NNO Mark Capri 12.00 25.00
NNO Mark Hamill 800.00 1500.00
NNO Paul Blake 12.00 30.00

2014 Star Wars Chrome Perspectives Empire Priority Targets

COMPLETE SET (10) 8.00 20.00
COMMON CARD (1-10) 1.25 3.00
STATED ODDS 1:4

2014 Star Wars Chrome Perspectives Empire Propaganda

COMPLETE SET (10) 15.00 40.00
COMMON CARD (1-10) 3.00 8.00
STATED ODDS 1:24

2014 Star Wars Chrome Perspectives Helmet Medallions

COMPLETE SET (30) 75.00 200.00
COMMON CARD (1-30) 5.00 12.00
*GOLD/50: 1.2X TO 3X BASIC MEDALLIONS
STATED ODDS 1:24

2014 Star Wars Chrome Perspectives Rebel Propaganda

COMPLETE SET (10) 12.00 30.00
COMMON CARD (1-10) 2.00 5.00
STATED ODDS 1:12

2014 Star Wars Chrome Perspectives Rebel Training

COMPLETE SET (10) 6.00 15.00
COMMON CARD (1-10) 1.25 3.00
STATED ODDS 1:8

2014 Star Wars Chrome Perspectives Triple Autograph

1 Ford/Hamill/Fisher EXCH

2014 Star Wars Chrome Perspectives Wanted Posters Rebellion

COMPLETE SET (10) 5.00 12.00
COMMON CARD (1-10) .75 2.00
STATED ODDS 1:2

2015 Star Wars Chrome Perspectives Jedi vs. Sith

COMPLETE SET (100) 25.00 60.00
UNOPENED BOX (24 PACKS) 200.00 400.00
UNOPENED PACK (6 CARDS) 8.00 15.00
COMMON CARD .40 1.00
*REFRACTOR: 1.2X TO 3X BASIC CARDS
*PRISM REF/199: 1.5X TO 4X BASIC CARDS
*X-FRACTOR/99: 3X TO 8X BASIC CARDS
*GOLD REF/50: 6X TO 15X BASIC CARDS

2015 Star Wars Chrome Perspectives Jedi vs. Sith Autographs

COMMON AUTO 6.00 15.00
*PRISM REF./50: .5X TO 1.2X BASIC AUTOS
* X-FRACTORS/25: .6X TO 1.5X BASIC AUTOS
NNO Ashley Eckstein 40.00 100.00
NNO Barbara Goodson 10.00 25.00
NNO Carrie Fisher 400.00 600.00
NNO David Prowse 50.00 100.00
NNO Jerome Blake 10.00 25.00
NNO Matthew Wood 10.00 25.00
NNO Michaela Cottrell 10.00 25.00
NNO Nalini Krishan 12.00 30.00
NNO Olivia D'Abo 10.00 25.00
NNO Peter Mayhew 25.00 60.00
NNO Ray Park 20.00 50.00
NNO Sam Witwer 10.00 25.00

2015 Star Wars Chrome Perspectives Jedi vs. Sith Jedi Hunt

COMPLETE SET (10) 10.00 25.00
COMMON CARD (1-10) 2.00 5.00
STATED ODDS 1:4

2015 Star Wars Chrome Perspectives Jedi vs. Sith Jedi Information Guide

COMPLETE SET (10) 20.00 50.00
COMMON CARD (1-10) 4.00 10.00
STATED ODDS 1:12

2015 Star Wars Chrome Perspectives Jedi vs. Sith Jedi Training

COMPLETE SET (10) 12.00 30.00
COMMON CARD (1-10) 2.50 6.00
STATED ODDS 1:24

2015 Star Wars Chrome Perspectives Jedi vs. Sith Medallions

COMPLETE SET (36) 120.00 250.00
COMMON MEDALLION (1-36) 5.00 10.00
*SILVER/150: .6X TO 1.5X
BASIC MEDALLIONS 6.00 15.00
*GOLD/50: .75X TO 2X BASIC MEDALLIONS8.00 20.00
OVERALL MEDALLION ODDS 1:BOX

2015 Star Wars Chrome Perspectives Jedi vs. Sith Rare Dual Autographs

COMMON AUTO 25.00 60.00
STATED PRINT RUN 200 SER.#'d SETS
NNO A.Allen/O.Shoshan 50.00 100.00
NNO A.Eckstein/N.Futterman 30.00 75.00
NNO A.Eckstein/O.D'Abo 50.00 100.00
NNO M.Cottrell/Z.Jensen 50.00 100.00

2015 Star Wars Chrome Perspectives Jedi vs. Sith Sith Fugitives

COMPLETE SET (10) 8.00 20.00
COMMON CARD (1-10) 1.50 4.00
STATED ODDS 1:2

2015 Star Wars Chrome Perspectives Jedi vs. Sith Sith Propaganda

COMPLETE SET (10) 12.00 30.00
COMMON CARD (1-10) 2.50 6.00
STATED ODDS 1:8

2015 Star Wars Chrome Perspectives Jedi vs. Sith The Force Awakens

COMPLETE SET (8) 20.00 50.00
COMMON CARD 4.00 10.00
*MATTE BACK: .6X TO1.5X BASIC CARDS
STATED ODDS 1:24

2020 Topps Star Wars Chrome Perspectives Resistance vs. First Order

COMPLETE SET (100) 15.00 40.00
UNOPENED BOX (18 PACKS) 100.00 150.00
UNOPENED PACK (6 CARDS) 6.00 8.00

COMMON CARD .40 1.00
*REFRACTOR: .75X TO 2X BASIC CARDS
*PRISM REF/299: 1.2X TO 3X BASIC CARDS
*BLUE REF/150: 2X TO 5X BASIC CARDS
*XFRAC/99: 3X TO 8X BASIC CARDS
*GOLD REF/50: 4X TO 10X BASIC CARDS

2020 Topps Star Wars Chrome Perspectives Resistance vs. First Order Choose Your Allegiance First Ord

COMPLETE SET (15) 8.00 20.00
COMMON CARD (CF1-CF15) 1.00 2.50
RANDOMLY INSERTED INTO PACKS

2020 Topps Star Wars Chrome Perspectives Resistance vs. First Order Choose Your Allegiance Resistanc

COMPLETE SET (15) 8.00 20.00
COMMON CARD (CR1-CR15) 1.00 2.50
RANDOMLY INSERTED INTO PACKS

2020 Topps Star Wars Chrome Perspectives Resistance vs. First Order Empire at War

COMPLETE SET (20) 10.00 25.00
COMMON CARD (EW1-EW20) 1.25 3.00
RANDOMLY INSERTED INTO PACKS

2020 Topps Star Wars Chrome Perspectives Resistance vs. First Order First Order Autographs

COMMON AUTO 8.00 12.00
RANDOMLY INSERTED INTO PACKS
AAE Adrian Edmondson 6.00 15.00
AMJ Michael Jibson 6.00 15.00
AMLJ Mark Lewis Jones 8.00 20.00

2020 Topps Star Wars Chrome Perspectives Resistance vs. First Order Resistance Autographs

COMMON AUTO 5.00 12.00
RANDOMLY INSERTED INTO PACKS
ABH Brian Herring 10.00 25.00
ACC Crystal Clarke 6.00 15.00
ADB Dave Chapman 6.00 15.00
AIW Ian Whyte 8.00 20.00
ANC Nathalie Cuzner 8.00 20.00
ATK Tom Kane 6.00 15.00

2022 Topps Chrome Sapphire Edition Star Wars

COMPLETE SET (132) 500.00 1200.00
UNOPENED BOX (8 PACKS) 300.00 400.00
UNOPENED PACK (4 CARDS) 40.00 50.00
COMMON CARD (1-132) 5.00 12.00
*AQUA/99: 1.5X TO 4X BASIC CARDS
*PERIDOT/75: 2X TO 5X BASIC CARDS
*GREEN/50: 2.5X TO 6X BASIC CARDS
*ORANGE/25: 6X TO 15X BASIC CARDS
1 Luke Skywalker 150.00 400.00
2 See-Threepio and Artoo-Detoo 15.00 40.00
3 The Little Droid, Artoo-Detoo 15.00 40.00
4 Space Pirate Han Solo 20.00 50.00
5 Princess Leia Organa 40.00 100.00
6 Ben (Obi-Wan) Kenobi 15.00 40.00
7 The Villainous Darth Vader 60.00 150.00
8 Grand Moff Tarkin 10.00 25.00
10 Princess Leia - Captured! 12.00 30.00
13 A Sale on Droids 8.00 20.00
17 Lord Vader Threatens Princess Leia! 8.00 20.00
20 Hunted by the Sandpeople! 8.00 20.00
24 Stormtroopers Seek the Droids! 12.00 30.00
26 A Horrified Luke Sees His Family Killed10.00 25.00
27 Some Repairs for See-Threepio 8.00 20.00
31 Sighting the Death Star 12.00 30.00
34 See-Threepio Diverts the Guards 8.00 20.00
43 Luke Prepares to Swing Across the Chasm10.00 25.00
44 Han and Chewie Shoot it Out! 12.00 30.00
45 The Lightsaber 15.00 40.00
46 A Desperate Moment for Ben 8.00 20.00
47 Luke Prepares for the Battle 10.00 25.00
53 Battle in Outer Space! 8.00 20.00
54 The Victors Receive Their Reward 12.00 30.00
55 Han, Chewie and Luke 10.00 25.00
57 Mark Hamill as Luke Skywalker 20.00 50.00
58 Harrison Ford as Han Solo 30.00 75.00
59 Alec Guinness as Ben Kenobi 10.00 25.00
60 Peter Cushing as Grand Moff Tarkin 8.00 20.00
62 Lord Vader's Stormtroopers 8.00 20.00
63 May the Force be With You! 12.00 30.00
65 Carrie Fisher and Mark Hamill 10.00 25.00
66 Amazing Robot See-Threepio 8.00 20.00
68 The Millennium Falcon 8.00 20.00
71 The Incredible See-Threepio 12.00 30.00
76 Artoo-Detoo on the Rebel Starship! 8.00 20.00
86 A Mighty Explosion! 8.00 20.00
87 The Droids Try to Rescue Luke! 10.00 25.00
89 The Imprisoned Princess Leia 15.00 40.00
96 The Droids on Tatooine 8.00 20.00
98 See-Threepio 10.00 25.00
99 Ben with the Lightsaber! 15.00 40.00
100 Our Heroes at the Spaceport 8.00 20.00
101 The Wookiee Chewbacca 12.00 30.00
106 A Message From Princess Leia! 8.00 20.00
108 Princess Leia Observes the Battle 10.00 25.00
111 Chewie and Han Solo! 15.00 40.00
118 R2-D2 and C-3P0 8.00 20.00
121 Han Solo and Chewbacca 12.00 30.00
122 Millennium Falcon Speeds Through Space! 8.00 20.00
124 Threepio Searches for R2-D2 8.00 20.00
125 Luke in Disguise! 15.00 40.00
129 May the Force be With You! 8.00 20.00
132 Lord Vader and a Soldier 10.00 25.00

2022 Topps Chrome Sapphire Edition Star Wars Aqua

*AQUA: 1.5X TO 4X BASIC CARDS
STATED PRINT RUN 99 SER.#'d SETS
1 Luke Skywalker 750.00 2000.00
2 See-Threepio and Artoo-Detoo 50.00 125.00
4 Space Pirate Han Solo 125.00 300.00
5 Princess Leia Organa 200.00 500.00
6 Ben (Obi-Wan) Kenobi 75.00 200.00
7 The Villainous Darth Vader 200.00 500.00
8 Grand Moff Tarkin 40.00 100.00
10 Princess Leia - Captured! 50.00 120.00
19 Searching for the Little Droid 30.00 75.00
20 Hunted by the Sandpeople! 30.00 75.00

2022 Topps Chrome Sapphire Edition Star Wars Green

*GREEN: 2.5X TO 6X BASIC CARDS
STATED PRINT RUN 50 SER.#'d SETS
1 Luke Skywalker 2000.00 5000.00
3 The Little Droid, Artoo-Detoo 75.00 200.00
4 Space Pirate Han Solo 200.00 500.00
5 Princess Leia Organa 300.00 800.00
6 Ben (Obi-Wan) Kenobi 250.00 600.00
7 The Villainous Darth Vader 300.00 800.00

2022 Topps Chrome Sapphire Edition Star Wars Orange

*ORANGE: 6X TO 15X BASIC CARDS
STATED PRINT RUN 25 SER.#'d SETS
1 Luke Skywalker 3000.00 8000.00
4 Space Pirate Han Solo 250.00 600.00
5 Princess Leia Organa 500.00 1200.00
6 Ben (Obi-Wan) Kenobi 300.00 750.00
7 The Villainous Darth Vader 600.00 1500.00

2022 Topps Chrome Sapphire Edition Star Wars Peridot

*PERIDOT: 2X TO 5X BASIC CARDS
STATED PRINT RUN 75 SER.#'d SETS
1 Luke Skywalker 1200.00 3000.00
2 See-Threepio and Artoo-Detoo 50.00 125.00
3 The Little Droid, Artoo-Detoo 150.00 400.00
4 Space Pirate Han Solo 150.00 400.00
5 Princess Leia Organa 250.00 600.00
6 Ben (Obi-Wan) Kenobi 150.00 400.00
7 The Villainous Darth Vader 250.00 600.00

2004 Star Wars Clone Wars Cartoon

COMPLETE SET (90) 5.00 12.00
UNOPENED HOBBY BOX (36 PACKS) 50.00 60.00
UNOPENED HOBBY PACK (7 CARDS) 1.50 2.00
UNOPENED RETAIL BOX (36 PACKS) 55.00 65.00
UNOPENED RETAIL PACK (7 CARDS) 1.75 2.25
COMMON CARD (1-90) .15 .40

2004 Star Wars Clone Wars Cartoon Autographs

COMMON AUTO 12.00 30.00

2004 Star Wars Clone Wars Cartoon Battle Motion

COMPLETE SET (10) 15.00 40.00
COMMON CARD (B1-B10) 2.00 5.00

2004 Star Wars Clone Wars Cartoon Stickers

COMPLETE SET (10) 3.00 8.00
COMMON CARD (1-10) .40 1.00

2008 Star Wars Clone Wars

COMPLETE SET (90) 5.00 12.00
UNOPENED BOX (36 PACKS) 100.00 150.00
UNOPENED PACK (7 CARDS) 2.50 4.00
COMMON CARD (1-90) .15 .40
*GOLD: 8X TO 20X BASIC CARD

2008 Star Wars Clone Wars Foil

COMPLETE SET (10) 12.00 25.00
COMMON CARD (1-10) 2.00 5.00
STATED ODDS 1:3 RETAIL

2008 Star Wars Clone Wars Animation Cels

COMPLETE SET (10) 7.50 15.00
COMMON CARD (1-10) 1.25 3.00
STATED ODDS 1:6
ALSO KNOWN AS THE WHITE CELS

2008 Star Wars Clone Wars Blue Animation Cels

COMPLETE SET (5) 15.00 40.00
COMMON CARD 4.00 10.00
STATED ODDS 1:6 WALMART PACKS

2008 Star Wars Clone Wars Red Animation Cels

COMPLETE SET (5) 20.00 50.00
COMMON CARD 5.00 12.00
STATED ODDS 1:6 TARGET PACKS

2008 Star Wars Clone Wars Coins Purple

COMPLETE SET (12) 15.00 40.00
COMMON CARD (1-12) 2.50 6.00
*RED: SAME VALUE
*YELLOW: SAME VALUE
PURPLE ODDS 2:WALMART/MEIER BONUS BOX
RED ODDS 2:TARGET BONUS BOX
YELLOW ODDS 2:TRU BONUS BOX

2008 Star Wars Clone Wars Motion

COMPLETE SET (5) 4.00 8.00
COMMON CARD (1-5) 1.25 3.00
STATED ODDS 1:8 RETAIL

2008 Star Wars Clone Wars Promos

COMPLETE SET (2) 2.50 6.00
COMMON CARD (P1-P2) 1.50 4.00

2008 Star Wars Clone Wars Stickers

COMPLETE SET (90) 15.00 40.00
COMMON CARD (1-90) .40 1.00

2008 Star Wars Clone Wars Stickers Die-Cut Magnets

COMPLETE SET (9) 10.00 25.00
COMMON CARD (1-9) 2.00 5.00
STATED ODDS 1:12

2008 Star Wars Clone Wars Stickers Die-Cut Pop-Ups

COMPLETE SET (10) 3.00 8.00
COMMON CARD (1-10) .60 1.50
STATED ODDS 1:3

2008 Star Wars Clone Wars Stickers Foil

COMPLETE SET (10) 5.00 12.00
COMMON CARD (1-10) .75 2.00
STATED ODDS 1:3

2008 Star Wars Clone Wars Stickers Temporary Tattoos

COMPLETE SET (10) 6.00 15.00
COMMON CARD (1-10) 1.00 2.50
STATED ODDS 1:4

2008 Star Wars Clone Wars Stickers Tin Lid Stickers

COMPLETE SET (6) 12.00 30.00
STATED ODDS 1 PER TIN
1 Anakin 3.00 8.00
2 Obi-Wan 3.00 8.00
3 Anakin and Obi-Wan 3.00 8.00
4 Clone Troopers 3.00 8.00
5 Yoda 3.00 8.00
6 Anakin and Ahsoka 3.00 8.00

2010 Star Wars Clone Wars Rise of the Bounty Hunters

COMPLETE SET (90) 4.00 10.00
UNOPENED BOX (24 PACKS) 100.00 200.00
UNOPENED PACK (7 CARDS) 4.00 8.00
COMMON CARD (1-90) .10 .30
*SILVER/100: 20X TO 50X BASIC CARDS

2010 Star Wars Clone Wars Rise of the Bounty Hunters Cels Red

COMPLETE SET (5) 8.00 20.00
COMMON CARD (1-5) 3.00 8.00

2010 Star Wars Clone Wars Rise of the Bounty Hunters Cels Yellow

COMPLETE SET (5) 6.00 15.00
COMMON CARD (1-5) 2.50 6.00

2010 Star Wars Clone Wars Rise of the Bounty Hunters Foil

COMPLETE SET (20) 8.00 20.00
COMMON CARD (1-20) .60 1.50
STATED ODDS 1:3

2010 Star Wars Clone Wars Rise of the Bounty Hunters Motion

COMPLETE SET (5) 6.00 15.00
COMMON CARD (1-5) 1.50 4.00
STATED ODDS 1:6

2010 Star Wars Clone Wars Rise of the Bounty Hunters Promos

P1 Cad Bane and Others 1.25 3.00
P3 Pre Vizsla and Mandalorian Death Watch1.25 3.00

2018 Star Wars Clone Wars 10th Anniversary

COMPLETE SET (25) 15.00 40.00
COMMON CARD (1-25) 1.00 2.50
*PURPLE: .75X TO 2X BASIC CARDS

2018 Star Wars Clone Wars 10th Anniversary Autographs

STATED OVERALL ODDS 1:SET
1A Matt Lanter
2A Ashley Eckstein
3A James Arnold Taylor 8.00 20.00
4A Tom Kane

STAR WARS

6A Tim Curry
7A Catherine Taber
8A Phil Lamarr
9A Nika Futterman
10A Meredith Salenger
12A Stephen Stanton
13A Daniel Logan
14A Sam Witwer
15A Anna Graves
16A Anthony Daniels
18A Dee Bradley Baker
20A Matthew Wood
21A David Tennant
22A Blair Bess
23A Cas Anvar
24A Kathleen Gati
25A George Takei

2009 Star Wars Clone Wars Widevision

COMPLETE SET (80)	5.00	12.00
UNOPENED BOX (24 PACKS)	60.00	70.00
UNOPENED PACK (7 CARDS)	2.50	3.00
COMMON CARD (1-80)	.15	.40
*SILVER: 5X TO 12X BASIC CARDS		

2009 Star Wars Clone Wars Widevision Animation Cels

COMPLETE SET (10)	6.00	15.00
COMMON CARD (1-10)	.75	2.00
STATED ODDS 1:4		

2009 Star Wars Clone Wars Widevision Autographs

COMMON AUTO	8.00	20.00
STATED ODDS 1:67 HOBBY; 1:174 RETAIL		
NNO Ian Abercrombie	75.00	200.00
NNO James Arnold Taylor	40.00	100.00
NNO Matt Lanter	15.00	40.00
NNO Matthew Wood/Droids	15.00	40.00
NNO Matthew Wood/Grievous	15.00	40.00
NNO Nika Futterman	12.00	30.00
NNO Tom Kane	12.00	30.00

2009 Star Wars Clone Wars Widevision Foil Characters

COMPLETE SET (20)	15.00	40.00
COMMON CARD (1-20)	1.00	2.50
STATED ODDS 1:3		

2009 Star Wars Clone Wars Widevision Motion

COMPLETE SET (5)	6.00	15.00
COMMON CARD (1-5)	1.50	4.00
STATED ODDS 1:8		

2009 Star Wars Clone Wars Widevision Season Two Previews

COMPLETE SET (8)	3.00	8.00
COMMON CARD (PV1-PV8)	.50	1.25
STATED ODDS 1:2		

2019 Star Wars Comic Convention Exclusives

1 Darth Vader SWC	75.00	150.00
2 Luke Skywalker SWC		
3 Princess Leia Organa SWC	25.00	60.00
4 Han Solo SWC	30.00	75.00
5 Chewbacca SWC	30.00	75.00
6 Anakin Skywalker SDCC	12.00	30.00
7 Obi-Wan Kenobi SDCC	12.00	30.00
8 Padme Amidala SDCC	10.00	25.00
9 Qui-Gon Jinn SDCC	10.00	25.00
10 Darth Maul SDCC	20.00	50.00
11 Rey NYCC	60.00	120.00
12 Kylo Ren NYCC	20.00	50.00
13 Finn NYCC	15.00	40.00
14 Poe Dameron NYCC	25.00	60.00
15 General Hux NYCC	20.00	50.00

2017 Star Wars Countdown to The Last Jedi

COMPLETE SET (20)	75.00	150.00
COMMON CARD (1-20)	5.00	12.00
1 Rey Encounters Luke Skywalker/775*	8.00	20.00

1994 Topps Star Wars Day

COMPLETE SET (2)	6.00	15.00
COMMON CARD (SD1-SD2)	4.00	10.00

1995 Topps Star Wars Day

NNO Millennium Falcon w/X-Wings and TIE Fighters	5.00	12.00

1999 Lucasfilm Star Wars Defeat the Dark Side and Win Medallions

COMPLETE SET W/O SP (16)	12.00	30.00
COMMON MEDALLION	1.00	2.50
2 Daultay Dofine/50*		
4 Yoda/1500*		
10 Shmi Skywalker/1*		
13 Battle Droid/1*		
20 Chancellor Valorum/1*		

2015 Star Wars Disney Pixar Cars Promos

COMPLETE SET (5)	30.00	80.00
COMMON CARD	10.00	25.00

2015 Star Wars Disney Store The Force Awakens Promos

COMPLETE SET (8)	20.00	50.00
COMMON CARD (SKIP #'d)	4.00	10.00
11 BB-8 on the move!	6.00	15.00
67 Kylo Ren ignites his Lightsaber!	5.00	12.00
96 The Millennium Falcon	5.00	12.00

2011 Star Wars Dog Tags

COMPLETE SET (24)	25.00	60.00
UNOPENED BOX (PACKS)		
UNOPENED PACK (1 TAG+1 CARD)		
COMMON TAG (1-24)	2.00	5.00
*SILVER: .5X TO 1.2X BASIC TAGS	2.50	6.00
*RAINBOW: 1.2X TO 3X BASIC TAGS	6.00	15.00

2001 Topps Star Wars Evolution

COMPLETE SET (93)	5.00	12.00
UNOPENED BOX (36 PACKS)		
UNOPENED PACK (8 CARDS)		
COMMON CARD (1-93)	.15	.40

2001 Topps Star Wars Evolution Autographs

COMMON AUTO	15.00	40.00
GROUP A/1000* STATED ODDS 1:37		
GROUP B/400* STATED ODDS 1:919		
GROUP C/300* STATED ODDS 1:2450		
GROUP D/100* STATED ODDS 1:3677		
NNO Anthony Daniels/100*	750.00	2000.00
NNO Billy Dee Williams/300*	150.00	400.00
NNO Carrie Fisher/100*	1250.00	3000.00
NNO Dalyn Chew/1000*	30.00	75.00
NNO Dermot Crowley/1000*	20.00	50.00
NNO Femi Taylor/1000*	40.00	100.00
NNO Ian McDiarmid/400*	250.00	600.00
NNO James Earl Jones/1000*	500.00	1200.00
NNO Jeremy Bulloch/1000*	125.00	300.00
NNO Kenneth Colley/1000*	30.00	75.00
NNO Kenny Baker/1000*	150.00	400.00
NNO Lewis MacLeod/1000*	25.00	60.00
NNO Michael Culver/1000*	40.00	100.00
NNO Michael Pennington/1000*	25.00	60.00
NNO Michael Sheard/1000*	60.00	150.00
NNO Michonne Bourriague/1000*	20.00	50.00
NNO Peter Mayhew/400*	125.00	300.00
NNO Phil Brown/1000*	75.00	200.00
NNO Tim Rose/1000*	25.00	60.00
NNO Warwick Davis/1000*	60.00	150.00

2001 Topps Star Wars Evolution Insert A

COMPLETE SET (12)	15.00	30.00
COMMON CARD (1A-12A)	1.50	4.00
STATED ODDS 1:6		

2001 Topps Star Wars Evolution Insert B

COMPLETE SET (8)	20.00	40.00
COMMON CARD (1B-8B)	2.50	6.00
STATED ODDS 1:12		

2001 Topps Star Wars Evolution Promos

COMMON CARD	1.00	2.50
P3 Nien Nunb ALPHA CON	3.00	8.00
P4 Anakin Skywalker SDCC	2.00	5.00

2006 Star Wars Evolution Update

COMPLETE SET (90)	5.00	12.00
UNOPENED BOX (24 PACKS)	150.00	250.00
UNOPENED PACK (6 CARDS)	8.00	12.00
COMMON CARD (1-90)	.15	.40
1D ISSUED AS DAMAGED AUTO REPLACEMENT		
CL1 Luke Connections CL	.40	1.00
CL2 Leia Connections CL	.40	1.00
1D Luke Skywalker SP	2.00	5.00
P1 Obi-Wan Kenobi PROMO	1.00	2.50
P2 Darth Vader PROMO	1.00	2.50

2006 Star Wars Evolution Update Autographs

COMMON AUTO	6.00	15.00
STATED ODDS 1:24 HOBBY		
GROUP A ODDS 1:2,005		
GROUP B ODDS 1:231		
GROUP C ODDS 1:81		
GROUP D ODDS 1:259		
GROUP E ODDS 1:48		
NNO Alec Guinness		
NNO Bob Keen B	60.00	150.00
NNO David Barclay B	20.00	50.00
NNO Garrick Hagon E	10.00	25.00
NNO George Lucas		
NNO Hayden Christensen A	600.00	1500.00
NNO James Earl Jones A	200.00	400.00
NNO John Coppinger B	15.00	40.00
NNO Maria De Aragon C	10.00	25.00
NNO Matt Sloan E	8.00	20.00
NNO Michonne Bourriague C	10.00	25.00
NNO Mike Edmonds B	15.00	40.00
NNO Mike Quinn B	20.00	50.00
NNO Nalini Krishan D	8.00	20.00
NNO Peter Cushing		
NNO Richard LeParmentier C	10.00	25.00
NNO Sandi Finlay C	8.00	20.00
NNO Toby Philpott B	20.00	50.00
NNO Wayne Pygram B	50.00	100.00

2006 Star Wars Evolution Update Etched Foil Puzzle

COMPLETE SET (6)	6.00	15.00
COMMON CARD (1-6)	1.25	3.00
STATED ODDS 1:6		

2006 Star Wars Evolution Update Galaxy Crystals

COMPLETE SET (10)	12.50	30.00
COMMON CARD (G1-G10)	1.50	4.00
STATED ODDS 1:4 RETAIL		

2006 Star Wars Evolution Update Insert A

COMPLETE SET (20)	20.00	40.00
COMMON CARD (1A-20A)	1.50	4.00
STATED ODDS 1:6		

2006 Star Wars Evolution Update Insert B

COMPLETE SET (15)	20.00	40.00
COMMON CARD (1B-15B)	2.00	5.00
STATED ODDS 1:12		

2006 Star Wars Evolution Update Luke and Leia

COMPLETE SET (2)	1000.00	2000.00
COMMON CARD (1-2)	600.00	1200.00
STATED ODDS 1:1975 HOBBY		
STATED PRINT RUN 100 SER. #'d SETS		

2016 Star Wars Evolution

COMPLETE SET (100)	8.00	20.00
UNOPENED BOX (24 PACKS)	60.00	75.00
UNOPENED PACK (8 CARDS)	2.50	3.00
COMMON CARD (1-100)	.15	.40
*LTSBR BLUE: 4X TO 10X BASIC CARDS		
*LTSBR PURPLE: 8X TO 20X BASIC CARDS		
*GOLD/50: 15X TO 40X BASIC CARDS		

2016 Star Wars Evolution Autographs

COMMON AUTO	6.00	15.00
*PURPLE/25: .6X TO 1.5X BASIC AUTOS		
RANDOMLY INSERTED INTO PACKS		
NNO Alan Harris	8.00	20.00
NNO Amy Allen	10.00	25.00
NNO Andy Serkis	100.00	200.00
NNO Angus MacInnes	12.00	30.00
NNO Ashley Eckstein	40.00	100.00
NNO Clive Revill	25.00	60.00
NNO Dee Bradley Baker	8.00	20.00
NNO Deep Roy	10.00	25.00
NNO Denis Lawson	15.00	40.00
NNO Dickey Beer	12.00	30.00
NNO Freddie Prinze Jr.	60.00	120.00
NNO George Takei	15.00	40.00
NNO Greg Grunberg	15.00	40.00
NNO Harriet Walter	12.00	30.00
NNO Hugh Quarshie	20.00	50.00
NNO Jeremy Bulloch	15.00	40.00
NNO Jerome Blake	10.00	25.00
NNO John Boyega	75.00	150.00
NNO John Ratzenberger	8.00	20.00
NNO Keisha Castle-Hughes	10.00	25.00
NNO Kenneth Colley	12.00	30.00
NNO Matthew Wood	12.00	30.00
NNO Mercedes Ngoh	20.00	50.00
NNO Michael Carter	20.00	50.00
NNO Mike Quinn	8.00	20.00
NNO Orli Shoshan	8.00	20.00
NNO Paul Blake	8.00	20.00
NNO Phil Lamarr	15.00	40.00
NNO Ray Park	25.00	60.00
NNO Sam Witwer	8.00	20.00
NNO Stephen Stanton	10.00	25.00
NNO Taylor Gray	10.00	25.00
NNO Tim Dry	12.00	30.00
NNO Tiya Sircar	8.00	20.00
NNO Tom Kane	10.00	25.00
NNO Vanessa Marshall	8.00	20.00
NNO Warwick Davis	12.00	30.00

2016 Star Wars Evolution Evolution of the Lightsaber

COMPLETE SET (9)	12.00	30.00
COMMON CARD (EL1-EL9)	2.00	5.00
STATED ODDS 1:8		

2016 Star Wars Evolution Evolution of Vehicles and Ships

COMPLETE SET (18)	8.00	20.00
COMMON CARD (EV1-EV18)	.75	2.00
STATED ODDS 1:2		

2016 Star Wars Evolution Lenticular Morph

COMPLETE SET (9)	60.00	120.00
COMMON CARD (1-9)	6.00	15.00

STATED ODDS 1:72
1 Darth Vader 10.00 25.00
2 Luke Skywalker 10.00 25.00
3 Leia Organa 8.00 20.00
4 Han Solo 10.00 25.00
9 Chewbacca 8.00 20.00

2016 Star Wars Evolution Marvel Star Wars Comics

COMPLETE SET (17) 12.00 30.00
COMMON CARD (EC1-EC17) 1.50 4.00
STATED ODDS 1:4

2016 Star Wars Evolution Patches

COMMON CARD 5.00 12.00
*SILVER/50: 5X TO 1.2X BASIC CARDS
*GOLD/25: .6X TO 1.5X BASIC CARDS
NNO Admiral Ackbar 6.00 15.00
NNO Ahsoka Tano 6.00 15.00
NNO BB-8 8.00 20.00
NNO Chancellor Palpatine 6.00 15.00
NNO Clone Trooper 6.00 15.00
NNO Darth Vader 6.00 15.00
NNO Ezra Bridger 6.00 15.00
NNO General Hux 6.00 15.00
NNO Grand Moff Tarkin 8.00 20.00
NNO Han Solo 8.00 20.00
NNO Kylo Ren 8.00 20.00
NNO Luke Skywalker 6.00 15.00
NNO Mon Mothma 6.00 15.00
NNO Poe Dameron 6.00 15.00
NNO Princess Leia Organa 6.00 15.00
NNO Qui-Gon Jinn 6.00 15.00
NNO Rey 10.00 25.00
NNO Senator Amidala 6.00 15.00
NNO Supreme Leader Snoke 6.00 15.00

2016 Star Wars Evolution SP Inserts

COMPLETE SET (9) 250.00 500.00
COMMON CARD (1-9) 25.00 60.00
STATED PRINT RUN 100 SER.#'d SETS
1 Luke/Stormtrooper 30.00 80.00
2 Leia/Boussh 30.00 80.00
5 Darth Vader 50.00 100.00
6 Boba Fett 30.00 80.00

2016 Star Wars Evolution Stained Glass Pairings

COMPLETE SET (9) 20.00 50.00
COMMON CARD (1-9) 2.50 6.00
STATED ODDS 1:24
1 Luke/Leia 5.00 12.00
2 Han/Lando 4.00 10.00
4 Sidious/Maul 4.00 10.00
5 Vader/Tarkin 3.00 8.00
6 Kylo/Phasma 3.00 8.00
7 Chewbacca/C-3PO 3.00 8.00
9 Rey/Finn 6.00 15.00

2007 Star Wars Family Guy Blue Harvest DVD Promos

COMPLETE SET (12) 3.00 8.00
COMMON CARD .60 1.50
*GERMAN: SAME VALUE AS ENGLISH
*ITALIAN: SAME VALUE AS ENGLISH
*SPANISH: SAME VALUE AS ENGLISH

1996 Finest Star Wars

COMPLETE SET (90) 10.00 25.00
UNOPENED BOX (36 PACKS) 300.00 500.00
UNOPENED PACK (5 CARDS) 10.00 15.00
COMMON CARD (1-90) .20 .50
*REF.: 5X TO 12X BASIC CARDS

1996 Finest Star Wars Embossed

COMPLETE SET (6) 10.00 25.00
COMMON CARD (F1-F6) 2.00 5.00

1996 Finest Star Wars Matrix

COMPLETE SET (4) 6.00 15.00
COMMON CARD (M1-M4) 2.00 5.00
NNO Exchange Card

1996 Finest Star Wars Promos

COMPLETE SET (3) 2.50 6.00
COMMON CARD (SWF1-SWF3) 1.00 2.50
B1 Han Solo & Chewbacca 3.00 8.00
(Album Exclusive)
NNO 1-Card Sheet
NNO 1-Card Sheet Refractor
NNO Star Wars Goes Split Level 200.00 400.00

2018 Star Wars Finest

COMPLETE SET W/SP (120) 75.00 150.00
COMPLETE SET W/O SP (100) 20.00 50.00
UNOPENED BOX (12 PACKS)
UNOPENED PACK (5 CARDS)
COMMON CARD (1-100) .40 1.00
COMMON SP (101-120) 3.00 8.00
*REF.: 1.25X TO 3X BASIC CARDS
*BLUE/150: 2X TO 5X BASIC CARDS
*GREEN/99: 3X TO 8X BASIC CARDS
*GOLD/50: 4X TO 10X BASIC CARDS
*GOLD SP/50: .5X TO 1.2X BASIC CARDS

2018 Star Wars Finest Autographs

FAAL Amanda Lawrence
FADBB Dee Bradley Baker 8.00 20.00
FAHCT Hermione Corfield 10.00 25.00
FAJAT James Arnold Taylor
FAJBM Jerome Blake 5.00 12.00
FAMEM Mary Elizabeth McGlynn 6.00 15.00
FAJZ Zac Jensen

2018 Star Wars Finest Droids and Vehicles

COMPLETE SET (20) 12.00 30.00
COMMON CARD (DV1-DV20) 1.50 4.00
*GOLD/50: .75X TO 2X BASIC CARDS

2018 Star Wars Finest Lightsaber Hilt Medallions

COMMON MEM 5.00 12.00
*GOLD/50: .5X TO 1.2X BASIC MEM
LMAV Asajj Ventress 6.00 15.00
LMBO Barriss Offee 6.00 15.00
LMSF Finn 6.00 15.00
LMSR Rey 15.00 40.00
LMST Shaak Ti 6.00 15.00
LMY2 Yoda 8.00 20.00
LMYC Yoda 6.00 15.00
LMA22 Anakin Skywalker 12.00 30.00
LMAS1 Anakin Skywalker 6.00 15.00
LMAS2 Ahsoka Tano 6.00 15.00
LMAS3 Ahsoka Tano 6.00 15.00
LMASC Ahsoka Tano 6.00 15.00
LMDM1 Darth Maul 10.00 25.00
LMDS3 Darth Sidious 6.00 15.00
LMDV4 Darth Vader 8.00 20.00
LMDV5 Darth Vader 10.00 25.00
LMDVR Darth Vader 10.00 25.00
LMGIR The Grand Inquisitor 8.00 20.00
LMKR7 Kylo Ren 12.00 30.00
LMKR8 Kylo Ren 12.00 30.00
LML24 Luke Skywalker 10.00 25.00
LML25 Luke Skywalker 8.00 20.00
LML28 Luke Skywalker 10.00 25.00
LMLS6 Luke Skywalker 10.00 25.00
LMLS8 Luke Skywalker 10.00 25.00
LMMW2 Mace Windu 8.00 20.00
LMO22 Obi-Wan Kenobi 6.00 15.00
LMR27 Rey 15.00 40.00
LMSAS Anakin Skywalker 10.00 25.00
LMSLS Luke Skywalker 10.00 25.00

2018 Star Wars Finest Rogue One

COMPLETE SET (20) 20.00 50.00
COMMON CARD (RO1-RO20) 2.00 5.00
*GOLD/50: .6X TO 1.5X BASIC CARDS

2018 Star Wars Finest Rogue One Autographs

RAAP Alistair Petrie
RAAT Alan Tudyk
RABD Ben Daniels
RABM Ben Mendelsohn
RADA Derek Arnold
RADY Donnie Yen
RAFJ Felicity Jones
RAFW Forest Whitaker
RAGO Genevieve O'Reilly
RAIM Ian McElhinney 6.00 15.00
RAMM Mads Mikkelsen
RARA Riz Ahmed

2018 Star Wars Finest Solo A Star Wars Story

COMPLETE SET (20) 15.00 40.00
COMMON CARD (SO1-SO20) 1.25 3.00
*GOLD/50: .75X TO 2X BASIC CARDS

2022 Finest Star Wars

COMPLETE SET W/O SP (100) 30.00 75.00
COMMON CARD (1-100) .60 1.50
COMMON SP (101-120) 4.00 12.00
*REF.: .6X TO 1.5X BASIC CARDS
*BLUE:/150: 1.2X TO 3X BASIC CARDS
*GREEN/99: 2X TO 5X BASIC CARDS
*GOLD/50: 3X TO 8X BASIC CARDS
101 Ahsoka Tano SP 25.00 60.00
102 Anakin Skywalker SP 10.00 25.00
104 C-3PO SP 6.00 15.00
108 Maul SP 10.00 25.00
109 Darth Vader SP 15.00 40.00
110 Fennec Shand SP 6.00 15.00
111 Grogu SP 30.00 75.00
112 Han Solo SP 10.00 25.00
113 Kylo Ren SP 10.00 25.00
114 General Leia Organa SP 8.00 20.00
115 Obi-Wan Kenobi SP 10.00 25.00
116 R2-D2 SP 8.00 20.00
117 Rey SP 12.00 30.00
118 The Mandalorian SP 12.00 30.00
119 Finn SP 6.00 15.00
120 Yoda SP 15.00 40.00

2022 Finest Star Wars Autographs

COMMON AUTO 5.00 12.00
*PURPLE/299: .5X TO 1.2X BASIC AUTOS
*BLUE/199: .6X TO 1.5X BASIC AUTOS
*AQUA/199: .6X TO 1.5X BASIC AUTOS
*GREEN/99: .75X TO 2X BASIC AUTOS
*GOLD/50: 1.2X TO 3X BASIC AUTOS
STATED ODDS 1 AUTO OR SKETCH PER BOX
FAAP Angelique Perrin 6.00 15.00
FACB Caroline Blakiston 6.00 15.00
FAJD Julie Dolan 10.00 25.00
FAJS Jason Spisak 8.00 20.00
FAMC Michaela Cottrell 6.00 15.00
FAPW Paul Warren 6.00 15.00
FARB Richard Brake 12.00 30.00
FATR Tim Rose 12.00 30.00
FAVK Valene Kane 10.00 25.00
FAAPE Alistair Petrie 6.00 15.00

2022 Finest Star Wars The Bad Batch

COMPLETE SET (20) 20.00 50.00
COMMON CARD (BB1-BB20) 2.50 6.00
*GOLD/50: 2X TO 5X BASIC CARDS
RANDOMLY INSERTED INTO PACKS

2022 Finest Star Wars The Book of Boba Fett

COMPLETE SET (2) 5.00 12.00
COMMON CARD (BF1-BF2) 3.00 8.00
*GOLD/50: 6X TO 15X BASIC CARDS

2022 Finest Star Wars Galaxy's Finest Heroes Die-Cuts

COMMON CARD (GF1-GF20) 10.00 25.00
GF1 Luke Skywalker 15.00 40.00
GF2 Han Solo 30.00 75.00
GF3 Yoda 25.00 60.00
GF4 Leia Organa 15.00 40.00
GF5 The Mandalorian 20.00 50.00
GF6 Chewbacca 15.00 40.00
GF7 Rey 50.00 125.00
GF9 R2-D2 12.00 30.00
GF10 Obi-Wan Kenobi 20.00 50.00
GF11 Lando Calrissian 25.00 60.00
GF13 Poe Dameron 30.00 75.00
GF14 Chirrut Imwe 15.00 40.00
GF15 Ahsoka Tano 50.00 125.00
GF17 Qui-Gon Jinn 20.00 50.00
GF18 Mace Windu 30.00 75.00
GF20 Padme Amidala 40.00 100.00

2022 Finest Star Wars The High Republic Concept Art

COMPLETE SET (20) 15.00 40.00
COMMON CARD (HR1-HR20) 2.00 5.00
*GOLD/50: 3X TO 8X BASIC CARDS
RANDOMLY INSERTED INTO PACKS

2022 Finest Star Wars The Mandalorian

COMPLETE SET (20) 40.00 100.00
COMMON CARD (MD1-MD20) 2.50 6.00
*GOLD/50: .75X TO 2X BASIC CARDS
RANDOMLY INSERTED INTO PACKS
MD1 Grogu 8.00 20.00
MD2 The Mandalorian 6.00 15.00
MD3 Koska Reeves 3.00 8.00
MD5 IG-11 4.00 10.00
MD6 Boba Fett 3.00 8.00
MD7 Fennec Shand 3.00 8.00
MD9 Ahsoka Tano 6.00 15.00
MD10 Moff Gideon 4.00 10.00
MD12 Mayfeld 3.00 8.00
MD13 Cobb Vanth 3.00 8.00
MD14 Peli Motto 5.00 12.00
MD15 Bo-Katan Kryze 5.00 12.00
MD17 The Client 3.00 8.00
MD19 Valin Hess 3.00 8.00
MD20 Luke Skywalker 5.00 12.00

2022 Finest Star Wars Promo

NNO Grogu NYCC 12.00 30.00

2012 Star Wars Galactic Files

COMPLETE SET (350) 25.00 50.00
UNOPENED BOX (24 PACKS) 250.00 400.00
UNOPENED PACK (12 CARDS) 10.00 15.00
COMMON CARD (1-350) .15 .40
*BLUE: 8X TO 20X BASIC CARDS 3.00 8.00
*RED: 20X TO 50X BASIC CARDS 8.00 20.00
76 Darth Vader (Jedi Purge) SP 12.00 30.00
96 Luke Skywalker (Stormtrooper) SP 12.00 30.00
125B Princess Leia (Despair) SP 12.00 30.00

2012 Star Wars Galactic Files Autographs

COMMON AUTO 8.00 20.00
STATED ODDS ONE AUTO OR PATCH PER HOBBY BOX
NNO Amy Allen 12.00 30.00
NNO Carrie Fisher 750.00 2000.00
NNO Felix Silla 25.00 60.00
NNO Harrison Ford 2000.00 3000.00
NNO Irvin Kershner 600.00 1000.00
NNO Jake Lloyd 150.00 400.00
NNO James Earl Jones 400.00 1000.00
NNO Jeremy Bulloch 20.00 50.00
NNO Mark Hamill 2000.00 5000.00
NNO Matthew Wood 15.00 40.00
NNO Peter Mayhew 125.00 250.00
NNO Ray Park 30.00 75.00
NNO Richard LeParmentier 15.00 40.00

2012 Star Wars Galactic Files Classic Lines

COMPLETE SET (10)	3.00	8.00
COMMON CARD (CL1-CL10)	.75	2.00
STATED ODDS 1:4		

2012 Star Wars Galactic Files Duels of Fate

COMPLETE SET (10)	4.00	10.00
COMMON CARD (DF1-DF10)	1.00	2.50
STATED ODDS 1:6		

2012 Star Wars Galactic Files Galactic Moments

COMPLETE SET (20)	20.00	40.00
COMMON CARD (GM1-GM20)	1.50	4.00
STATED ODDS 1:6		

2012 Star Wars Galactic Files Heroes on Both Sides

COMPLETE SET (10)	4.00	10.00
COMMON CARD (HB1-HB10)	1.00	2.50
STATED ODDS 1:6		

2012 Star Wars Galactic Files I Have a Bad Feeling About This

COMPLETE SET (8)	3.00	8.00
COMMON CARD (BF1-BF8)	.75	2.00
STATED ODDS 1:4		

2012 Star Wars Galactic Files Patches

COMMON MEM	8.00	20.00
STATED ODDS ONE AUTO OR PATCH PER HOBBY BOX		
PR1 Garven Dreis	40.00	100.00
PR2 Wedge Antilles	40.00	100.00
PR3 Biggs Darklighter	40.00	100.00
PR4 John D. Branon	40.00	100.00
PR5 Luke Skywalker	75.00	200.00
PR6 Jek Porkins	40.00	100.00
PR12 Obi-Wan Kenobi	12.00	30.00
PR13 Anakin Skywalker	15.00	40.00
PR14 Plo Koon	12.00	30.00
PR17 Luke Skywalker	60.00	150.00
PR18 Zev Senesca	30.00	75.00
PR19 Wedge Antilles	30.00	75.00
PR20 Derek Hobbie Kuvian	25.00	60.00
PR21 Dak Ralter	25.00	60.00
PR23 Grand Moff Tarkin	15.00	40.00
PR24 Darth Vader	15.00	40.00
PR25 Han Solo	30.00	75.00
PR26 Chewbacca	15.00	40.00
PR27 Lando Calrissian	20.00	50.00
PR28 Nien Numb	15.00	40.00

2013 Star Wars Galactic Files 2

COMPLETE SET (353)	20.00	50.00
COMP.SET W/O SP (350)	12.00	30.00
UNOPENED BOX (24 PACKS)	200.00	300.00
UNOPENED PACK (12 CARDS)	8.00	12.00
COMMON CARD (351-699)	.15	.40
COMMON SP	4.00	10.00
*BLUE/350: 2X TO 5X BASIC CARDS		
*RED/35: 15X TO 40X BASIC CARDS		
*GOLD/10: 50X TO 120X BASIC CARDS		
463b Han Solo Stormtrooper SP	4.00	10.00
481b Luke Skywalker Bacta Tank SP	4.00	10.00
510b Princess Leia Slave Girl SP	4.00	10.00

2013 Star Wars Galactic Files 2 Autographs

COMMON AUTO	12.00	30.00
STATED ODDS 1:55		
NNO Alan Harris	30.00	75.00
NNO Ashley Eckstein	75.00	200.00
NNO Billy Dee Williams	100.00	250.00
NNO Carrie Fisher	750.00	2000.00
NNO Ian McDiarmid	400.00	600.00
NNO James Earl Jones	300.00	750.00
NNO Jeremy Bulloch	30.00	75.00
NNO Mark Hamill	1500.00	4000.00
NNO Peter Mayhew	60.00	150.00

2013 Star Wars Galactic Files 2 Dual Autographs

ANNOUNCED COMBINED PRINT RUN 200		
NNO A.Eckstein/T.Kane	125.00	300.00
NNO J.Bulloch/A.Harris	100.00	250.00
NNO J.E.Jones/I.McDiarmid	750.00	2000.00
NNO C.Fisher/M.Hamill	2500.00	6000.00
NNO H.Ford/P.Mayhew		

2013 Star Wars Galactic Files 2 Classic Lines

COMPLETE SET (10)	3.00	8.00
COMMON CARD (CL1-CL10)	.60	1.50
STATED ODDS 1:4		

2013 Star Wars Galactic Files 2 Galactic Moments

COMPLETE SET (20)	30.00	60.00
COMMON CARD (GM1-GM20)	2.00	5.00
STATED ODDS 1:12		

2013 Star Wars Galactic Files 2 Honor the Fallen

COMPLETE SET (10)	4.00	10.00
COMMON CARD (HF1-HF10)	.75	2.00
STATED ODDS 1:6		

2013 Star Wars Galactic Files 2 Medallions

COMMON MEDALLION (MD1-MD30)	8.00	20.00
STATED ODDS 1:55		
MD1 Luke Skywalker	12.00	30.00
MD3 Han Solo	20.00	50.00
MD5 Lando Calrissian	12.00	30.00
MD6 Han Solo	150.00	250.00
MD7 Boba Fett	30.00	75.00
MD9 Princess Leia Organa	15.00	40.00
MD10 Bail Organa	10.00	25.00
MD12 General Veers	20.00	50.00
MD13 Jawa	20.00	50.00
MD14 C-3PO	30.00	75.00
MD15 R2-D2	15.00	40.00
MD16 R5-D4	12.00	30.00
MD19 Luke Skywalker	30.00	75.00
MD20 Obi-Wan Kenobi	12.00	30.00
MD21 C-3PO & R2-D2	30.00	75.00
MD22 TIE Fighter Pilot	10.00	25.00
MD23 Darth Vader	15.00	40.00
MD24 Stormtrooper	12.00	30.00
MD25 Obi-Wan Kenobi	12.00	30.00
MD26 Plo Koon	12.00	30.00
MD27 Captain Panaka	12.00	30.00
MD28 Qui-Gon Jinn	12.00	30.00
MD29 Obi-Wan Kenobi	15.00	40.00
MD30 Queen Amidala	50.00	100.00

2013 Star Wars Galactic Files 2 Ripples in the Galaxy

COMPLETE SET (10)	4.00	10.00
COMMON CARD (RG1-RG10)	.75	2.00
STATED ODDS 1:6		

2013 Star Wars Galactic Files 2 The Weak Minded

COMPLETE SET (7)	2.50	6.00
COMMON CARD (WM1-WM7)	.60	1.50
STATED ODDS 1:3		

2017 Star Wars Galactic Files Reborn

COMPLETE SET (200)	10.00	25.00
UNOPENED BOX (24 PACKS)	80.00	100.00
UNOPENED PACK (6 CARDS)	4.00	5.00
COMMON CARD	.15	.40
*ORANGE: .75X TO 2X BASIC CARDS		
*BLUE: 1.2X TO 3X BASIC CARDS		
*GREEN/199: 4X TO 10X BASIC CARDS		
*PURPLE/99: 8X TO 20X BASIC CARDS		
*GOLD/10: 20X TO 50X BASIC CARDS		

2017 Star Wars Galactic Files Reborn Autographs

COMMON AUTO	5.00	12.00
NNO Adrienne Wilkinson	6.00	15.00
NNO Alan Tudyk	100.00	200.00
NNO Anna Graves	8.00	20.00
NNO Ashley Eckstein	50.00	125.00
NNO Bruce Spence	5.00	12.00
NNO Catherine Taber	15.00	40.00
NNO Dave Barclay	10.00	25.00
NNO David Bowers	6.00	15.00
NNO Dee Bradley	12.00	30.00
NNO Denis Lawson	10.00	25.00
NNO Freddie Prinze		
NNO George Takei	12.00	30.00
NNO Hassani Shapi	8.00	20.00
NNO Jeremy Bulloch	20.00	50.00
NNO Jerome Blake	6.00	15.00
NNO Jesse Jensen	6.00	15.00
NNO Jim Cummings	6.00	15.00
NNO Julian Glover	6.00	15.00
NNO Kath Soucie	8.00	20.00
NNO Keone Young	20.00	50.00
NNO Lewis MacLeod	5.00	12.00
NNO Mary Oyaya	12.00	30.00
NNO Megan Udall	6.00	15.00
NNO Michael Carter	8.00	20.00
NNO Michonne Bourriague	6.00	15.00
NNO Nika Futterman	12.00	30.00
NNO Oliver Ford	8.00	20.00
NNO Oliver Walpole	10.00	25.00
NNO Olivia D'Abo	8.00	20.00
NNO Phil Eason	6.00	15.00
NNO Phil LaMarr	10.00	25.00
NNO Rajia Baroudi	8.00	20.00
NNO Rena Owen	6.00	15.00
NNO Rohan Nichol	10.00	25.00
NNO Sam Witwer	15.00	40.00
NNO Stephen Stanton	25.00	60.00
NNO Tom Kenny	6.00	15.00
NNO Wayne Pygram	8.00	20.00
NNO Zac Jensen	8.00	20.00

2017 Star Wars Galactic Files Reborn Dual Autographs

COMMON CARD	15.00	40.00
STATED PRINT RUN 5-50 SER.#'d SETS		
NNO C.Blakiston/T.Rose/50	20.00	50.00
NNO C.Fisher/C.Blakiston/5		
NNO I.McDiarmid/S.Carson/5		

2017 Star Wars Galactic Files Reborn Famous Quotes

COMPLETE SET (15)	8.00	20.00
COMMON CARD (MQ1-MQ15)	1.00	2.50

2017 Star Wars Galactic Files Reborn Galactic Moments

COMPLETE SET (9)	8.00	20.00
COMMON CARD (GM1-GM9)	1.25	3.00

2017 Star Wars Galactic Files Reborn Locations

COMPLETE SET (10)	6.00	15.00
COMMON CARD (L1-L10)	1.00	2.50

2017 Star Wars Galactic Files Reborn Vehicle Medallions

COMMON MEM	5.00	12.00
*SILVER/99: .6X TO 1.5X BASIC MEM		
*GOLD/25: 1.2X TO 3X BASIC MEM		

2017 Star Wars Galactic Files Reborn Vehicles

COMPLETE SET (20)	10.00	25.00
COMMON CARD (V1-V20)	.75	2.00
*PURPLE/99: 1.5X TO 4X BASIC CARDS		

2017 Star Wars Galactic Files Reborn Weapons

COMPLETE SET (10)	6.00	15.00
COMMON CARD (W1-W10)	1.00	2.50
*PURPLE/99: 1.2X TO 3X BASIC CARDS		

2018 Star Wars Galactic Files

COMPLETE SET (200)	12.00	30.00
UNOPENED BOX (24 PACKS)	60.00	90.00
UNOPENED PACK (8 CARDS)	3.00	4.00
COMMON CARD (R09-ROTS23)	.20	.50
*ORANGE: .6X TO 1.5X BASIC CARDS		
*BLUE: .75X TO 2X BASIC CARDS		
*GREEN/199: 4X TO 10X BASIC CARDS		
*PURPLE/99: 6X TO 15X BASIC CARDS		

2018 Star Wars Galactic Files Autographs

AAB Ariyon Bakare	6.00	15.00
AAD Adam Driver		
AAG Anna Graves	5.00	12.00
AAP Alistair Petrie		
AAT Alan Tudyk		
ABG Barbara Goodson		
ABP Bonnie Piesse	5.00	12.00
ACA Cas Anvar	10.00	25.00
ACF Carrie Fisher		
ACR Clive Revill		
ADM Daniel Mays	6.00	15.00
ADR Daisy Ridley		
ADT David Tennant		
ADY Donnie Yen		
AFJ Felicity Jones		
AFW Forest Whitaker		
AGC Gwendoline Christie		
AGG Greg Grunberg		
AGT George Takei		
AHC Hayden Christensen		
AHF Harrison Ford		
AHS Hugh Skinner	8.00	20.00
AIM Ian McDiarmid		
AJB John Boyega		
AJL Jett Lucas	6.00	15.00
AKB Kenny Baker		
AKF Kate Fleetwood	5.00	12.00
AKR Kipsang Rotich	5.00	12.00
ALD Laura Dern		
AMS Meredith Salenger	6.00	15.00
ARA Riz Ahmed		
ARD Robbie Daymond	5.00	12.00
ARN Robert Nairne	10.00	25.00
ARP Ray Park		
ATM Temuera Morrison		
AVK Valene Kane	6.00	15.00
AADT Andy De La Tour	12.00	30.00
AAEK Ashley Eckstein		
AAND Anthony Daniels		
ABDW Billy Dee Williams		
AFPJ Freddie Prinze Jr.		
AJSC Jordan Stephens	5.00	12.00
AMSA Marc Silk	5.00	12.00
ASMG Sarah Michelle Gellar		

2018 Star Wars Galactic Files Band of Heroes

COMPLETE SET (7)	5.00	12.00
COMMON CARD (BH1-BH7)	1.25	3.00
*PURPLE/99: .6X TO 1.5X BASIC CARDS		

2018 Star Wars Galactic Files Galactic Moments

COMPLETE SET (10)	6.00	15.00
COMMON CARD (GM1-GM10)	1.00	2.50
*PURPLE/99: .75X TO 2X BASIC CARDS		

2018 Star Wars Galactic Files Locations

COMPLETE SET (10)	8.00	20.00
COMMON CARD (L1-L10)	1.25	3.00
*PURPLE/99: .75X TO 2X BASIC CARDS		

2018 Star Wars Galactic Files Manufactured Movie Poster Patches

COMPLETE SET (56) 300.00 750.00
COMMON MEM 10.00 25.00
*BLUE/99: .5X TO 1.2X BASIC PATCHES
*GREEN/50: .6X TO 1.5X BASIC PATCHES
*PURPLE/25: .75X TO 2X BASIC PATCHES

2018 Star Wars Galactic Files Memorable Quotes

COMPLETE SET (10) 6.00 15.00
COMMON CARD (MQ1-MQ10) 1.00 2.50
*PURPLE/99: .75X TO 2X BASIC CARDS

2018 Star Wars Galactic Files Sinister Syndicates

COMPLETE SET (15) 10.00 25.00
COMMON CARD (SS1-SS15) 1.25 3.00
*PURPLE/99: .75X TO 2X BASIC CARDS

2018 Star Wars Galactic Files Source Material Fabric Swatches

COMMON SWATCH 20.00 50.00
CRGE Galen Erso's Jacket 25.00 60.00
CRJE Jyn Erso's Poncho 50.00 100.00
CRPD Poe Dameron's Shirt 25.00 60.00
CRPG Praetorian Guard's Uniform 30.00 75.00
CRRH Rey's Head Wrap 60.00 120.00
CRRJ Rey's Jacket 100.00 200.00

2018 Star Wars Galactic Files Vehicles

COMPLETE SET (10) 6.00 15.00
COMMON CARD (V1-V10) 1.00 2.50
*NO FOIL: .5X TO 1.2X BASIC CARDS
*PURPLE/99: .75X TO 2X BASIC CARDS

2018 Star Wars Galactic Files Weapons

COMPLETE SET (10) 6.00 15.00
COMMON CARD (W1-W10) 1.00 2.50
*PURPLE/99: .75X TO 2X BASIC CARDS

2018-19 Topps Star Wars Galactic Moments Countdown to Episode 9

COMPLETE SET (157) 400.00 1000.00
ANH COMMON (1-18) 5.00 12.00
ESB COMMON (19-36) 5.00 12.00
ROTJ COMMON (37-54) 5.00 12.00
TPM COMMON (55-69) 5.00 12.00
AOTC COMMON (70-87) 5.00 12.00
ROTS COMMON (88-105) 5.00 12.00
TFA COMMON (106-126) 5.00 12.00
TLJ COMMON (127-141) 5.00 12.00
TROS COMMON (142-156) 5.00 12.00
PRINT RUN VARIES FROM CARD TO CARD

1993-95 Topps Star Wars Galaxy

COMPLETE SET (365) 15.00 40.00
COMP.SER 1 SET (140) 6.00 15.00
COMP.SER 2 SET (135) 6.00 15.00
COMP.SER 3 SET (90) 6.00 15.00
UNOPENED SER.1 BOX (36 PACKS) 30.00 40.00
UNOPENED SER.1 PACK (8 CARDS) 1.00 1.25
UNOPENED SER.2 BOX (36 PACKS) 20.00 30.00
UNOPENED SER.2 PACK (8 CARDS) .75 1.00
UNOPENED SER.3 BOX (36 PACKS) 20.00 30.00
UNOPENED SER.3 PACK (7 CARDS) .75 1.00
COMMON CARD (1-365) .15 .40
*MIL.FALCON FOIL: .8X TO 2X BASIC CARDS
*FIRST DAY: 1X TO 2.5X BASIC CARDS
DARTH VADER FOIL UNNUMBERED 4.00 10.00

1993-95 Topps Star Wars Galaxy Clearzone

COMPLETE SET (6) 15.00 40.00
COMMON CARD (E1-E6) 3.00 8.00

1993-95 Topps Star Wars Galaxy Etched Foil

COMPLETE SET (18) 60.00 120.00
COMMON CARD (1-18) 3.00 8.00

1993-95 Topps Star Wars Galaxy LucasArts

COMPLETE SET (12) 6.00 15.00
COMMON CARD (L1-L12) .60 1.50

1993-95 Topps Star Wars Galaxy Promos

0 Ralph McQuarrie (Darth Vader) 2.50 6.00
0 Drew Sturzan artwork (SW Galaxy Magazine)1.25 3.00
0 Ken Steacy Art
P1 Jae Lee/Rancor Monster(dealer cello pack)1.25 4.00
P1 Jae Lee/Rancor Monster/AT-AT
P1 Rancor Card
AT-AT/Yoda 5X7
P2 Chris Sprouse
Luke building lightsaber (NSU) 2.00 5.00
P2 Snowtrooper (Convention exclusive) 1.50 4.00
P3 Yoda Shrine SP 250.00 400.00
P3 Darth Vader on Hoth (NSU) 1.25 3.00
P4 Dave Gibbons/C-3PO and Jawas (SW Galaxy 1 Tin Set)
P4 Luke on Dagobah/Art Suydam .60 1.50
P5 Joe Phillips/Han and Chewbacca
(Cards Illustrated) 2.00 5.00
P5 AT-AT .75 2.00
P6 Tom Taggart/Boba Fett (Hero) 2.50 6.00
P6 Luke with lightsaber (SW Galaxy Magazine)
P7 Leia with Jacen and Jania
(Wizard Magazine) 2.00 5.00
P8 Boba Fett and Darth Vader
(Cards Illustrated) 4.00 10.00
140 Look for Series Two (Bend Ems Toys)
DH2 Cam Kennedy artwork/BobaFett 2.00 5.00
DH3 Cam Kennedy artwork/Millennium Falcon2.00 5.00
NNO Jim Starlin/Stormtrooper and Ewoks
(Triton #3) 1.50 4.00
NNO Tim Truman/Tuskan Raiders 3.00 8.00
NNO Boba Fett 3.00 8.00
NNO AT-AT 5 x 7 (Previews)
NNO Boba Fett/Dengar (Classic Star Wars) 2.00 5.00
NNO Jabba the Hutt (NSU/Starlog/Wizard) 1.25 3.00
NNO Princess Leia (NSU) 1.50 4.00
NNO Sandtrooper (Wizard Magazine) 1.50 4.00
NNO Truce at Bakura (Bantam exclusive) 4.00 10.00
NNO Princess Leia/Sandtrooper 2-Card Panel (Advance exclusive)
NNO Jabba the Hutt, Obi-Wan/Darth Vader 5X7 (Previews exclusive)
DH1A Cam Kennedy artwork/Battling Robots
(Dark Lords of the Sith comic) 2.00 5.00
Series at line 8
DH1B Cam Kennedy artwork/Battling Robots
(Dark Lords of the Sith comic) 2.00 5.00
Series at line 9
SWB1 Grand Moff Tarkin (album exclusive)4.00 10.00

2016 Star Wars Galaxy Bonus Abrams

COMPLETE SET (4) 5.00 12.00
COMMON CARD (1-4) 2.50 6.00

2023 Topps Star Wars Galaxy Celebration Edition

COMMON VOL I (1-10) 5.00 12.00
COMMON VOL II (11-20) 5.00 12.00
COMMON VOL III (21-30) 5.00 12.00
COMMON VOL IV (31-40) 5.00 12.00
*PURPLE/299: .6X TO 1.5X BASIC CARDS
*YELLOW/150: .75X TO 2X BASIC CARDS
*BLUE/99: 1.2X TO 3X BASIC CARDS
*GREEN/50: 2X TO 5X BASIC CARDS
1 Luke Skywalker 8.00 20.00
2 Darth Vader 12.00 30.00
3 Han Solo 8.00 20.00
4 Princess Leia UER/No Logo 10.00 25.00
5 C-3PO 6.00 15.00
6 Yoda 6.00 15.00
7 Lando Calrissian 6.00 15.00
9 Chewbacca 6.00 15.00
10 R2-D2 8.00 20.00
12 Darth Maul 15.00 40.00
15 Padme 20.00 50.00
16 Jango Fett 6.00 15.00
17 Mace Windu 6.00 15.00
20 Anakin Skywalker UER/No Logo 12.00 30.00
21 Poe Dameron 8.00 20.00
22 BB-8 8.00 20.00
23 Supreme Leader Snoke UER/No Logo 6.00 15.00
26 Rey 10.00 25.00
27 Captain Phasma 6.00 15.00
29 Kylo Ren 10.00 25.00
30 Palpatine 6.00 15.00
31 The Mandalorian 15.00 40.00
32 Moff Gideon UER/No Logo 6.00 15.00
33 Grogu 15.00 40.00
35 Ahsoka Tano 20.00 50.00
36 Boba Fett 8.00 20.00
37 Cad Bane 10.00 25.00
39 Obi-Wan Kenobi 12.00 30.00
40 Cassian Andor 6.00 15.00

1999 Topps Star Wars Galaxy Collector

COMPLETE SET W/O SP (9) 6.00 15.00
COMMON CARD (SW0-SW9) 1.25 3.00
SW0 Episode I 30.00 75.00
(Non-Sport Update Gummie Award Exclusive)

1996 Topps Star Wars Galaxy Magazine Cover Gallery

COMPLETE SET (4) 3.00 8.00
COMMON CARD (C1-C4) 1.00 2.50

1995 Topps Star Wars Galaxy Magazine Finest Promos

COMPLETE SET (4) 3.00 8.00
COMMON CARD (SWGM1-SWGM4) 1.50 4.00

2009 Star Wars Galaxy Series 4

COMPLETE SET (120) 5.00 12.00
UNOPENED BOX (24 PACKS) 75.00 125.00
UNOPENED PACK (7 CARDS) 3.00 5.00
COMMON CARD (1-120) .15 .40

2009 Star Wars Galaxy Series 4 Silver Foil

COMPLETE SET (15) 5.00 12.00
COMMON CARD (1-15) .60 1.50
*BRONZE: 2X TO 5X BASIC CARDS
*GOLD: .8X TO 2X BASIC CARDS
STATED ODDS 1:3

2009 Star Wars Galaxy Series 4 Etched Foil

COMPLETE SET (6) 6.00 12.00
COMMON CARD (1-6) 1.50 4.00
STATED ODDS 1:6

2009 Star Wars Galaxy Series 4 Galaxy Evolutions

COMPLETE SET (6) 30.00 80.00
COMMON CARD (1-6) 8.00 20.00
STATED ODDS 1:24 RETAIL

2009 Star Wars Galaxy Series 4 Lost Galaxy

COMPLETE SET (5) 12.00 25.00
COMMON CARD (1-5) 3.00 8.00
STATED ODDS 1:24
YODA'S WORLD/999 STATED ODDS 1:277
JOHN RHEAUME AUTO STATED ODDS 1:2,789
NNO Yoda's World/999 15.00 30.00
NNOAU Yoda's World
Rheaume AU

2009 Star Wars Galaxy Series 4 Promos

COMPLETE SET (4) 8.00 20.00
COMMON CARD (P1A-P3) .75 2.00
P1A Ventress 1.50 4.00
Dooku GEN
P1B Starcruiser crash/ (Fan Club Excl.) 6.00 15.00
P3 Group shot WW 2.00 5.00

2010 Star Wars Galaxy Series 5

COMPLETE SET (120) 8.00 20.00
UNOPENED BOX (24 PACKS)
UNOPENED PACK (7 CARDS)
COMMON CARD (1-120) .15 .40

2010 Star Wars Galaxy Series 5 Etched Foil

COMPLETE SET (6) 4.00 10.00
COMMON CARD (1-6) 1.25 3.00
STATED ODDS 1:6 H/R

2010 Star Wars Galaxy Series 5 Silver Foil

COMPLETE SET (15) 6.00 15.00
COMMON CARD (1-15) .60 1.50
*BRONZE FOIL: 1.2X TO 3X BASIC CARDS
*GOLD FOIL/770: 6X TO 15X BASIC CARDS
STATED ODDS 1:3 H/R

2010 Star Wars Galaxy Series 5 Autographs

COMMON AUTO 75.00 150.00
STATED ODDS 1:274 HOBBY
DP David Prowse 100.00 200.00
JJ James Earl Jones 150.00 300.00
MH Mark Hamill 600.00 1200.00
PM Peter Mayhew 100.00 200.00

2010 Star Wars Galaxy Series 5 Lost Galaxy

COMPLETE SET (5) 10.00 25.00
COMMON CARD (1-5) 3.00 8.00
STATED ODDS 1:24 HOBBY

2011 Star Wars Galaxy Series 6

COMPLETE SET (120) 8.00 20.00
UNOPENED BOX (24 PACKS) 225.00 350.00
UNOPENED PACK (7 CARDS) 10.00 15.00
COMMON CARD (1-120) .15 .40

2011 Star Wars Galaxy Series 6 Silver Foil

COMPLETE SET (10) 6.00 15.00
COMMON CARD (1-10) 1.00 2.50
*BRONZE: 1.2X TO 3X BASIC CARDS
*GOLD/600: 4X TO 10X BASIC CARDS
UNPRICED REFR. PRINT RUN 1
STATED ODDS 1:3

2011 Star Wars Galaxy Series 6 Animation Cels

COMPLETE SET (9) 20.00 40.00
COMMON CARD (1-9) 3.00 8.00
STATED ODDS 1:4 RETAIL

2011 Star Wars Galaxy Series 6 Etched Foil

COMPLETE SET (6) 5.00 12.00
COMMON CARD (1-6) 1.25 3.00
STATED ODDS 1:6

2012 Star Wars Galaxy Series 7

COMPLETE SET (110) 8.00 20.00
UNOPENED BOX (24 PACKS) 250.00 400.00
UNOPENED PACK (7 CARDS) 10.00 15.00
COMMON CARD (1-110) .15 .40

STAR WARS

2012 Star Wars Galaxy Series 7 Silver Foil

COMPLETE SET (15) 6.00 15.00
COMMON CARD (1-15) .75 2.00
*BRONZE: 1.5X TO 4X SILVER
*GOLD: 3X TO 8X SILVER
STATED ODDS 1:3

2012 Star Wars Galaxy Series 7 Cels

COMPLETE SET (9) 35.00 70.00
COMMON CARD (1-9) 4.00 10.00

2012 Star Wars Galaxy Series 7 Etched Foil

COMPLETE SET (6) 5.00 12.00
COMMON CARD (1-6) 1.50 4.00
STATED ODDS 1:6

2018 Star Wars Galaxy

COMPLETE SET (100) 15.00 40.00
UNOPENED BOX (24 PACKS) 65.00 80.00
UNOPENED PACK (8 CARDS) 3.00 4.00
COMMON CARD (1-100) .40 1.00
*BLUE: .6X TO 1.5X BASIC CARDS
*GREEN: 1.2X TO 3X BASIC CARDS
*PURPLE/99: 2.5X TO 6X BASIC CARDS
*ORANGE/25: 6X TO 15X BASIC CARDS

2018 Star Wars Galaxy Art Patches

*BLUE/199: SAME VALUE AS BASIC
*GREEN/150: .5X TO 1.2X BASIC MEM
*PURPLE/99: .6X TO 1.5X BASIC MEM
*ORANGE/25: .75X TO 2X BASIC MEM
MD Droids 8.00 20.00
MDV Darth Vader 8.00 20.00
MHL Han and Leia 10.00 25.00
MJW Jawas 6.00 15.00
MLL Luke and Leia 10.00 25.00
MLS Luke Skywalker 8.00 20.00
MPL Princess Leia 8.00 20.00
MSC Salacious B. Crumb 6.00 15.00
MTR Tusken Raider 8.00 20.00
MWT Wilhuff Tarkin 6.00 15.00
MWW Wicket W. Warrick 6.00 15.00
MXW X-Wings 8.00 20.00

2018 Star Wars Galaxy Autographs

RANDOMLY INSERTED INTO PACKS
GAAA Amy Allen 8.00 20.00
GAAD Anthony Daniels
GAAE Ashley Eckstein
GAAS Andrew Secombe
GAAT Alan Tudyk
GABL Bai Ling 6.00 15.00
GACF Carrie Fisher
GACR Clive Revill
GADL Daniel Logan 12.00 30.00
GADR Daisy Ridley
GADT David Tennant
GADY Donnie Yen
GAEL Eric Lopez 6.00 15.00
GAFJ Felicity Jones
GAFP Freddie Prinze Jr.
GAFW Forest Whitaker
GAGC Gwendoline Christie
GAGT George Takei
GAHC Hayden Christensen
GAHF Harrison Ford
GAHQ Hugh Quarshie
GAIM Ian McDiarmid
GAJB John Boyega
GAJC Jim Cummings 6.00 15.00
GAJI Jason Isaacs
GAKB Kenny Baker
GALS Lloyd Sherr
GAMC Michaela Cottrell 6.00 15.00
GAMK Michael Kingma
GAMO Mary Oyaya 5.00 12.00
GANF Nika Futterman
GANK Nalini Krishan 6.00 15.00
GAOD Olivia d'Abo
GAPM Peter Mayhew
GAPW Paul Warren 5.00 12.00
GARA Riz Ahmed
GARB Raija Baroudi 6.00 15.00
GARN Rohan Nichol 5.00 12.00
GARP Ray Park
GASB Steven Blum 5.00 12.00
GASS Stephen Stanton
GASW Sam Witwer
GATB Tom Baker
GATK Tom Kenny
GAADK Adam Driver
GABDW Billy Dee Williams
GADRY Deep Roy
GAGAT James Arnold Taylor
GAJCW John Coppinger 8.00 20.00
GAKCH Keisha Castle-Hughes
GAPAR Philip Anthony-Rodriguez 5.00 12.00
GARWB Ralph Brown 8.00 20.00
GASMG Sarah Michelle Gellar
GATCB Tosin Cole 5.00 12.00

2018 Star Wars Galaxy Dual Autographs

STATED PRINT RUN 25 SER.#'d SETS
DABD J.Boyega/A.Driver
DABH D.Barclay/G.Home 15.00 40.00
DABW J.Boyega/M.Wood
DADS A.Driver/A.Serkis
DAFD N.Futterman/A.Ventress
DAGR G.Grunberg/K.Rotich
DAJA F.Jones/R.Ahmed
DATE G.Takei/A.Eckstein
DAVR B.Vernel/Y.Ruhian 15.00 40.00
DAWU O.Walpole/M.Udall 12.00 30.00

2018 Star Wars Galaxy Etched Foil Galaxy Puzzle

COMPLETE SET (6) 15.00 40.00
COMMON CARD (GP1-GP6) 4.00 10.00
RANDOMLY INSERTED INTO PACKS

2018 Star Wars Galaxy Ghost Crew Wanted Posters

COMPLETE SET (6) 5.00 12.00
COMMON CARD (P1-P6) 1.25 3.00
RANDOMLY INSERTED INTO PACKS

2018 Star Wars Galaxy Journey of Ahsoka

COMPLETE SET (10) 6.00 15.00
COMMON CARD (1-10) 1.00 2.50
*PURPLE/99: .6X TO 1.5X BASIC CARDS
*ORANGE/25: 1.2X TO 3X BASIC CARDS
RANDOMLY INSERTED INTO PACKS

2018 Star Wars Galaxy Legends

COMPLETE SET (5) 10.00 25.00
COMMON CARD (C1-C5) 3.00 8.00
*PURPLE/99: .6X TO 1.5X BASIC CARDS
RANDOMLY INSERTED INTO PACKS

2018 Star Wars Galaxy New Trilogy Propaganda

COMPLETE SET (6) 5.00 10.00
COMMON CARD (TP1-TP6) 1.00 2.50
RANDOMLY INSERTED INTO PACKS

2018 Star Wars Galaxy Rogue One Propaganda

COMPLETE SET (9) 6.00 15.00
COMMON CARD (RP1-RP9) 1.25 3.00
RANDOMLY INSERTED INTO PACKS

2022 Topps Star Wars Galaxy Promo

NNO Vader vs. Obi-Wan NYCC 10.00 25.00

2021 Topps Chrome Star Wars Galaxy

COMPLETE SET (100) 20.00 50.00
UNOPENED BOX (24 PACKS) 350.00 500.00
UNOPENED PACK (8 CARDS) 15.00 20.00
COMMON CARD (1-100) .40 1.00
*REF./: .75X TO 2X BASIC CARDS
*ATOMIC/150: 3X TO 8X BASIC CARDS
*WAVE/99: 4X TO 10X BASIC CARDS
*PRISM/75: 5X TO 12X BASIC CARDS
*MOJO/50: 6X TO 15X BASIC CARDS
*PURPLE/25: 8X TO 20X BASIC CARDS

2021 Topps Chrome Star Wars Galaxy Autographs

STATED ODDS 1:35

2021 Topps Chrome Star Wars Galaxy Mandalorian Visions

COMPLETE SET (10) 20.00 50.00
COMMON CARD (MN1-MN10) 3.00 8.00
*GREEN/99: .6X TO 1.5X BASIC CARDS
*PURPLE/50: .75X TO 2X BASIC CARDS
*ORANGE/25: 2X TO 5X BASIC CARDS
STATED ODDS 1:9

2021 Topps Chrome Star Wars Galaxy Star Wars Global Posters

COMPLETE SET (20) 15.00 40.00
COMMON CARD (GP1-GP20) 2.00 5.00
*GREEN/99: .5X TO 1.2X BASIC CARDS
*PURPLE/50: .6X TO 1.5X BASIC CARDS
*ORANGE/25: .75X TO 2X BASIC CARDS
STATED ODDS 1:9

2021 Topps Chrome Star Wars Galaxy Vintage Star Wars Posters

COMPLETE SET (15) 15.00 40.00
COMMON CARD (V1-V15) 2.50 6.00
*GREEN/99: .5X TO 1.2X BASIC CARDS
*PURPLE/50: .6X TO 1.5X BASIC CARDS
*ORANGE/25: .75X TO 2X BASIC CARDS
STATED ODDS 1:9

2022 Topps Chrome Star Wars Galaxy

COMPLETE SET (104) 20.00 50.00
UNOPENED BOX (24 PACKS) 200.00 300.00
UNOPENED PACK (8 CARDS) 10.00 12.50
COMMON CARD (1-100;P1-P4) .40 1.00
*REF: 1X TO 2.5X BASIC CARDS
*WAVE/99: 25X TO 60X BASIC CARDS
*ATOMIC/150: 30X TO 75X BASIC CARDS
*PRISM:/75: 40X TO 100X BASIC CARDS
*MOJO/50: 50X TO 125X BASIC CARDS

2022 Topps Chrome Star Wars Galaxy Autographs

STATED ODDS 1:43
GAAK Andrew Kishino 10.00 25.00
GABD Ben Diskin
GABH Brian Herring 10.00 25.00
GACH Clint Howard 8.00 20.00
GACJ Carey Jones 12.00 30.00
GADP David Pasquesi 6.00 15.00

2022 Topps Chrome Star Wars Galaxy Gameplay Galaxy

COMPLETE SET (25) 60.00 150.00
COMMON CARD (GG1-GG25) 5.00 12.00
*GREEN/99: 1.2X TO 3X BASIC CARDS
*PURPLE/50: 2X TO 5X BASIC CARDS
STATED ODDS 1:9

2022 Topps Chrome Star Wars Galaxy Original Trilogy Concept Art

COMPLETE SET (10) 20.00 50.00
COMMON CARD (OT1-OT10) 3.00 8.00
*GREEN/99: 2X TO 5X BASIC CARDS
*PURPLE/50: 3X TO 8X BASIC CARDS
STATED ODDS 1:9

2022 Topps Chrome Star Wars Galaxy Retro Rewind

COMPLETE SET (15) 15.00 40.00
COMMON CARD (V1-V15) 2.50 6.00
*GREEN/99: 1.2X TO 3X BASIC CARDS
*PURPLE/50: 1.5X TO 4X BASIC CARDS
STATED ODDS 1:9

2022 Topps Star Wars The Galaxy's Most Powerful Women

COMPLETE SET (12) 12.00 30.00
COMMON CARD (1-12) 1.50 4.00
*RED/25: 8X TO 20X BASIC CARDS
ANNCD PRINT RUN SER.#'d SETS
1 Leia Organa 2.50 6.00
2 Rey 3.00 8.00
4 Padme Amidala 3.00 8.00
5 Ahsoka Tano 2.00 5.00
9 Jyn Erso 2.00 5.00
11 Omega 2.50 6.00
12 Fennec Shand 3.00 8.00

2022 Topps Star Wars The Galaxy's Most Powerful Women Red

COMPLETE SET (12)
*RED: 8X TO 20X BASIC CARDS
STATED PRINT RUN 25 SER.#'d SETS
1 Leia Organa 50.00 125.00
2 Rey 60.00 150.00
4 Padme Amidala 40.00 100.00
5 Ahsoka Tano 60.00 150.00
9 Jyn Erso 40.00 100.00
12 Fennec Shand 50.00 125.00

2004 Star Wars Heritage

COMPLETE SET (120) 8.00 20.00
UNOPENED BOX (36 PACKS) 300.00 600.00
UNOPENED PACK (5 CARDS) 2.00 2.50
COMMON CARD (1-120) .15 .40

2004 Star Wars Heritage Alphabet Stickers

COMPLETE SET (30) 12.00 30.00
STATED ODDS 1:3 RETAIL

2004 Star Wars Heritage Autographs

STATED ODDS 1:578
NNO Carrie Fisher 1200.00 3000.00
NNO James Earl Jones 750.00 1500.00
NNO Mark Hamill 1500.00 4000.00

2004 Star Wars Heritage Etched Wave One

COMPLETE SET (6) 6.00 15.00
COMMON CARD (1-6) 1.25 3.00
STATED ODDS 1:9

2004 Star Wars Heritage Etched Wave Two

COMPLETE SET (6) 6.00 15.00
COMMON CARD (1-6) 1.25 3.00
STATED ODDS 1:9

2004 Star Wars Heritage Promos

COMMON CARD (P1-P6, S1) .75 2.00
P1 The Phantom Menace 2.00 5.00
P2 Attack of the Clones 6.00 15.00
P6 Return of the Jedi 2.00 5.00
S1 Empire Strikes Back CT UK 2.50 6.00

2015 Star Wars High Tek

COMPLETE SET w/o SP (112) 60.00 120.00
COMPLETE SET w/SP (127) 250.00 500.00
UNOPENED BOX (8 CARDS) 150.00 250.00
COMMON CARD (1-112) .40 1.00
*DS CORE: .5X TO 1.2X BASIC CARDS
*HOTH TAC.: .5X TO 1.2X BASIC CARDS
*TIE FRONT: .6X TO 1.5X BASIC CARDS
*VADER TIE: .6X TO 1.5X BASIC CARDS
*MIL.FALCON: .75X TO 2X BASIC CARDS

*STAR DEST.: .75X TO 2X BASIC CARDS
*CARBON: 1X TO 2.5X BASIC CARDS
*EMP.THRONE: 1X TO 2.5X BASIC CARDS
*DS EXT.: 2X TO 5X BASIC CARDS
*TIE WING: 2X TO 5X BASIC CARDS
TIDAL/99: 1.2X TO 3X BASIC CARDS
GOLD RAINBOW/50: 1.5X TO 4X BASIC CARDS
CLOUDS/25: 2X TO 5X BASIC CARDS

1A Luke/lightsaber	3.00	8.00
1B Luke/blaster SP	10.00	25.00
1C Luke/Jedi Knight SP	12.00	30.00
2A Leia/A New Hope	3.00	8.00
2B Leia/Bespin uniform SP	15.00	40.00
2C Leia/Slave SP	120.00	200.00
3A Han Solo/blaster	4.00	10.00
3B Han Solo/Bespin SP	20.00	50.00
3C Han Solo/Endor SP	12.00	30.00
4 Darth Vader	5.00	12.00
5A The Emperor	2.00	5.00
5B Sheev Palpatine SP	4.00	10.00
5C Darth Sidious SP	12.00	30.00
6 Yoda	1.25	3.00
7A C-3PO/shiny chrome	4.00	10.00
7B C-3PO/dirty chrome SP	8.00	20.00
8 R2-D2	1.25	3.00
9 Chewbacca	1.25	3.00
10A Lando/cape	2.00	5.00
10B Lando/blaster SP	8.00	20.00
11 Boba Fett	2.00	5.00
36A Anakin Skywalker	1.25	3.00
36B Anakin/two lightsabers SP	6.00	15.00
37A Obi-Wan Kenobi	1.25	3.00
37B Obi-Wan/young SP	12.00	30.00
37C Obi-Wan/old SP	8.00	20.00
40A Padme/dark dress	1.25	3.00
40B Padme/white outfit SP	10.00	25.00
42 Darth Maul	1.25	3.00
44B Boba Fett/armor SP	25.00	60.00
88 Anakin Skywalker	1.25	3.00
94 The Inquisitor	.75	2.00
106 Finn	3.00	8.00
107 Kylo Ren	3.00	8.00
108 Rey	5.00	12.00
109 Poe Dameron	3.00	8.00
110 BB-8	4.00	10.00
111 Captain Phasma	3.00	8.00
112 Flametrooper	2.00	5.00

2015 Star Wars High Tek Armor Tek

COMPLETE SET (10)	120.00	250.00
COMMON CARD (AT1-AT10)	8.00	20.00
STATED PRINT RUN 50 SER.#'d SETS		
AT1 Boba Fett	15.00	40.00
AT3 Commander Cody	15.00	40.00
AT4 Darth Vader	20.00	50.00
AT5 Jango Fett	12.00	30.00
AT7 Luke Skywalker	12.00	30.00
AT8 Sabine Wren	10.00	25.00
AT9 Poe Dameron	15.00	40.00
AT10 Kylo Ren	15.00	40.00

2015 Star Wars High Tek Autographs

COMMON AUTO	6.00	15.00
*TIDAL/75: .5X TO 1.2X BASIC AUTOS		
*GOLD RAINBOW/50: .6X TO 1.5X BASIC AUTOS		
*CLOUDS/25: .75X TO 2X BASIC AUTOS		
2 Carrie Fisher	200.00	400.00
4 David Prowse	120.00	250.00
6 Deep Roy	20.00	50.00
7 Anthony Daniels	80.00	150.00
9 Peter Mayhew	25.00	60.00
11 Jeremy Bulloch	15.00	40.00
12 Paul Blake	10.00	25.00
14 Alan Harris	8.00	20.00
16 Tim Rose	10.00	25.00
20 Warwick Davis	12.00	30.00
23 Dickey Beer	10.00	25.00
27 John Ratzenberger	10.00	25.00
28 Pam Rose	30.00	80.00
29 Dickey Beer	15.00	40.00
30 Paul Brooke	10.00	25.00
42 Ray Park	20.00	50.00
49 Bai Ling	8.00	20.00
57 Amy Allen	10.00	25.00
61 Silas Carson	10.00	25.00
78 Bruce Spence	8.00	20.00
79 Wayne Pygram	10.00	25.00
80 Silas Carson	10.00	25.00
90 Andy Secombe	8.00	20.00
96 Taylor Gray	10.00	25.00
97 Vanessa Marshall	8.00	20.00
100 Tiya Sircar	12.00	30.00
102 Ashley Eckstein	40.00	100.00
104 George Takei	20.00	50.00
105 Dee Bradley Baker	12.00	30.00

2015 Star Wars High Tek Moments of Power

COMPLETE SET (15)	175.00	350.00
COMMON CARD (MP1-MP15)	8.00	20.00
STATED PRINT RUN 50 SER.#'d SETS		
MP1 Anakin Skywalker	10.00	25.00
MP2 Darth Maul	12.00	30.00
MP3 Obi-Wan Kenobi	15.00	40.00
MP4 Padme Amidala	12.00	30.00
MP6 Yoda	12.00	30.00
MP7 The Emperor	10.00	25.00
MP8 Han Solo	20.00	50.00
MP9 Luke Skywalker	15.00	40.00
MP10 Boba Fett	15.00	40.00
MP11 Chewbacca	10.00	25.00
MP13 Princess Leia Organa	15.00	40.00
MP15 Darth Vader	20.00	50.00

2015 Star Wars High Tek Tek Heads

COMPLETE SET (15)	150.00	275.00
COMMON CARD (TH1-TH15)	6.00	15.00
STATED PRINT RUN 50 SER.#'d SETS		
TH1 Darth Vader	20.00	50.00
TH2 C-3PO	10.00	25.00
TH3 Luke Skywalker	10.00	25.00
TH4 R2-D2	8.00	20.00
TH5 IG-88	8.00	20.00
TH7 BB-8	12.00	30.00
TH8 FX-7	8.00	20.00
TH10 2-1B	10.00	25.00
TH12 R7-A7	10.00	25.00
TH13 General Grievous	8.00	20.00
TH14 Chopper	10.00	25.00

2016 Star Wars High Tek

COMPLETE SET W/O SP (112)	100.00	200.00
COMPLETE SET W/SP (127)	300.00	600.00
UNOPENED BOX (1 PACK/8 CARDS)	50.00	60.00
COMMON CARD (SW1-SW112)	1.25	3.00
*F1P1: SAME VALUE AS BASIC		
*F1P2: SAME VALUE AS BASIC		
*F1P3: .75X TO 2X BASIC CARDS		
*F1P4: .75X TO 2X BASIC CARDS		
*F1P5: 1.5X TO 4X BASIC CARDS		
*F2P1: SAME VALUE AS BASIC		
*F2P2: SAME VALUE AS BASIC		
*F2P3: .75X TO 2X BASIC CARDS		
*F2P4: 1X TO 2.5X BASIC CARDS		
*F2P5: 1.50X TO 4X BASIC CARDS		
*BLUE RAIN/99: .75X TO 2X BASIC CARDS		
*GOLD RAIN/50: 1.5X TO 4X BASIC CARDS		
*ORANGE MAGMA/25: 3X TO 6X BASIC CARDS		
*GREEN CUBE/10: 4X TO 10X BASIC CARDS		
*RED ORBIT/5: 6X TO 15X BASIC CARDS		
SW60A Kylo Ren/Dark Side Disciple SP	15.00	40.00
SW72A General Leia/Resistance Leader SP	25.00	60.00
SW75A Rey/Jakku Scavenger SP	15.00	40.00
SW75B Rey/Force Sensitive SP	80.00	150.00
SW75C Rey/Starkiller Base Duel SP	60.00	120.00
SW76A FN-2187/F.O.Stormtrooper SP	30.00	80.00
SW76B Flametrooper/F.O.Infantry SP	12.00	30.00
SW76C Snowtrooper/F.O.Infantry SP	12.00	30.00
SW76D TIE Pilot/F.O.Pilot SP	12.00	30.00
SW84A Han Solo/Smuggler SP	50.00	100.00
SW87A Finn/Resistance Warrior SP	30.00	80.00
SW87B Finn/Resistance Fighter SP	20.00	50.00
SW88A Chewbacca/M.Falcon Co-Pilot SP	30.00	80.00
SW100A Poe/Resistance Messenger SP	25.00	60.00
SW100B Poe/Resistance Pilot SP	15.00	40.00

2016 Star Wars High Tek Armor Tek

COMMON CARD (AT1-AT11)	8.00	20.00
STATED PRINT RUN 50 SER.#'d SETS		
AT1 Kylo Ren	15.00	40.00
AT2 Captain Phasma	12.00	30.00
AT3 Poe Dameron	10.00	25.00
AT6 First Order Tie Fighter Pilot	12.00	30.00
AT7 First Order Stormtrooper	12.00	30.00
AT8 Rey	20.00	50.00
AT9 Stormtrooper (Heavy Gunner)	10.00	25.00
AT11 Sidon Ithano	12.00	30.00

2016 Star Wars High Tek Autographs

COMMON CARD	5.00	12.00
*BLUE RAIN/75: .5X TO 1.2X BASIC CARDS		
*GOLD RAIN/50: .6X TO 1.5X BASIC CARDS		
*ORANGE MAGMA/25: .75X TO 2X BASIC CARDS		
STATED ODDS 1:		
3 Aidan Cook/Cookie Tuggs	8.00	20.00
4 Alan Ruscoe/Bib Fortuna	6.00	15.00
6 Amy Allen	8.00	20.00
8 Anna Brewster	8.00	20.00
10 Ashley Eckstein	50.00	120.00
13 Brian Vernel	6.00	15.00
15 Catherine Taber	6.00	15.00
17 Cristina da Silva	8.00	20.00
20 Dave Barclay	8.00	20.00
21 David Acord/Med.Droid	6.00	15.00
22 David Acord/Voiceover	6.00	15.00
23 David Bowers	6.00	15.00
24 Dee Bradley Baker	6.00	15.00
26 Dickey Beer		
30 Harriet Walter	6.00	15.00
33 Jeremy Bulloch	12.00	30.00
38 Julie Dolan	8.00	20.00
39 Kiran Shah	6.00	15.00
40 Marc Silk	6.00	15.00
42 Mark Dodson/S.Crumb	6.00	15.00
45 Michael Kingma	6.00	15.00
47 Mike Edmonds	6.00	15.00
48 Mike Quinn	8.00	20.00
50 Paul Blake	6.00	15.00
51 Paul Springer	6.00	15.00
57 Sam Witwer	8.00	20.00
59 Sebastian Armesto	6.00	15.00
60 Silas Carson	8.00	20.00
62 Taylor Gray	6.00	15.00
63 Tim Rose	6.00	15.00
64 Tiya Sircar	6.00	15.00
66 Tosin Cole	10.00	25.00

2016 Star Wars High Tek Autographs Gold Rainbow

*GOLD RAINBOW/50: .6X TO 1.5X BASIC CARDS		
12 Brian Herring	25.00	60.00
25 Denis Lawson	15.00	40.00
67 Warwick Davis	12.00	30.00

2016 Star Wars High Tek Autographs Orange Magma Diffractor

*ORANGE MAGMA/25: .75X TO 2X BASIC CARDS		
14 Carrie Fisher	250.00	500.00
28 Freddie Prinze Jr.	30.00	80.00
37 John Boyega	120.00	250.00

2016 Star Wars High Tek Living Tek

COMMON CARD (LT1-LT13)	6.00	15.00
STATED PRINT RUN 50 SER.#'d SETS		
LT1 Crusher Roodown	10.00	25.00
LT2 Luke Skywalker	15.00	40.00
LT3 C-3PO	8.00	20.00
LT4 BB-8	12.00	30.00
LT5 GA-97	8.00	20.00
LT6 Luggabeast	8.00	20.00
LT7 PZ-4CO	8.00	20.00
LT9 B-U4D	12.00	30.00
LT11 Sidon Ithano	12.00	30.00
LT12 HURID-327	8.00	20.00
LT13 R2-D2	8.00	20.00

2017 Star Wars High Tek

UNOPENED BOX (1 PACK OF 8 CARDS)	50.00	80.00
COMMON FORM 1 (1-56)	1.00	2.50
COMMON FORM 2 (57-112)	1.50	4.00
*F1P1: .75X TO 2X BASIC CARDS	2.00	5.00
*F1P2: .75X TO 2X BASIC CARDS	2.00	5.00
*F1P3: 1X TO 2.5X BASIC CARDS	2.50	6.00
*F2P1: .6X TO 1.5X BASIC CARDS	2.50	6.00
*F2P3: .6X TO 1.5X BASIC CARDS	2.50	6.00
*TIDAL DIFF./99: 1X TO 2.5X BASIC CARDS	2.50	6.00
*F2P2: .75X TO 2X BASIC CARDS	3.00	8.00
*GOLD R.F./50: 1.2X TO 3X BASIC CARDS	3.00	8.00
*F1P4: 2X TO 5X BASIC CARDS	5.00	12.00
*F2P4: 1.2X TO 3X BASIC CARDS	5.00	12.00
*F1P5: 3X TO 8X BASIC CARDS	8.00	20.00
7 Rey	2.50	6.00
14 Han Solo	1.50	4.00
15 Luke Skywalker	1.50	4.00
16 Princess Leia Organa	3.00	8.00
20 Jango Fett	2.00	5.00
36 Boba Fett	1.50	4.00
53 Kylo Ren	1.25	3.00
56 Yoda	1.25	3.00
57 Jyn Erso	4.00	10.00
62 Chirrut Imwe	2.00	5.00
68 Darth Vader	2.00	5.00

2017 Star Wars High Tek Autographs

RANDOMLY INSERTED INTO PACKS		
NNO Adrienne Wilkinson	6.00	15.00
NNO Alistair Petrie	6.00	15.00
NNO Angus MacInnes	6.00	15.00
NNO Anthony Forest	6.00	15.00
NNO Ariyon Bakare	10.00	25.00
NNO Ashley Eckstein	40.00	100.00
NNO Ben Daniels	6.00	15.00
NNO Brian Herring	15.00	40.00
NNO Cathy Munroe	12.00	30.00
NNO Chris Parsons	8.00	20.00
NNO Daniel Mays	15.00	40.00
NNO David Acord	6.00	15.00
NNO Derek Arnold	6.00	15.00
NNO Duncan Pow	6.00	15.00
NNO Guy Henry	20.00	50.00
NNO Ian McElhinney	6.00	15.00
NNO Ian Whyte	6.00	15.00
NNO Jeremy Bulloch	15.00	40.00
NNO Jordan Stephens	10.00	25.00
NNO Lars Mikkelsen	10.00	25.00
NNO Lloyd Sherr	6.00	15.00
NNO Matthew Wood	6.00	15.00
NNO Olivia d'Abo	6.00	15.00
NNO Stephen Stanton		
NNO Valene Kane	10.00	25.00
NNO Zarene Dallas	6.00	15.00

2017 Star Wars High Tek Heroes and Villains of The Force Awakens

COMPLETE SET (20)	150.00	300.00
COMMON CARD (HV1-HV20)	6.00	15.00
STATED PRINT RUN 50 SER.#'d SETS		
HV1 Han Solo	10.00	25.00
HV2 Luke Skywalker	10.00	25.00
HV4 Kylo Ren	8.00	20.00
HV5 Rey	20.00	50.00
HV6 Finn	12.00	30.00
HV8 Supreme Leader Snoke	8.00	20.00
HV9 R2-D2	10.00	25.00
HV12 Snap Wexley	10.00	25.00
HV13 Captain Phasma	8.00	20.00
HV14 General Hux	8.00	20.00

HV17 Ello Asty	8.00	20.00
HV18 Unkar Plutt	8.00	20.00
HV19 Chewbacca	10.00	25.00
HV20 Riot Control Stormtrooper	12.00	30.00

2017 Star Wars High Tek A More Elegant Weapon

COMMON CARD (MW1-MW10)	10.00	25.00
STATED PRINT RUN 50 SER.#'d SETS		
MW1 Yoda	15.00	40.00
MW2 Ahsoka Tano	12.00	30.00
MW3 Anakin Skywalker	12.00	30.00
MW5 Rey	30.00	75.00
MW6 Luke Skywalker	15.00	40.00
MW7 Darth Vader	15.00	40.00
MW8 Obi-Wan Kenobi	12.00	30.00
MW10 Mace Windu	12.00	30.00

2017 Star Wars High Tek Rogue One Vehicles

STATED PRINT RUN 50 SER.#'d SETS		
RV1 Jyn Erso/U-wing	10.00	25.00
RV2 Gunner/Death Star	6.00	15.00
RV3 Krennic/Krennic's Shuttle	12.00	30.00
RV4 Tank Commander/Combat Assault Tank	6.00	15.00
RV5 Tarkin/Imperial Star Destroyer	8.00	20.00
RV6 Merrick/X-wing	12.00	30.00
RV7 TIE Striker Pilot/TIE Striker		
RV8 Cassian Andor/U-wing		
RV9 K-2SO/U-wing		
RV10 Bohdi Rook		
Imperial Zeta-Class Transport	6.00	15.00

2017 Star Wars High Tek Troopers

COMMON CARD (TR1-TR16)	6.00	15.00
STATED PRINT RUN 50 SER.#'d SETS		
TR1 First Order TIE Fighter Pilot	10.00	25.00
TR2 First Order Stormtrooper	8.00	20.00
TR3 First Order Riot Control Stormtrooper	10.00	25.00
TR9 Imperial Death Trooper	15.00	40.00
TR12 Imperial Sandtrooper	10.00	25.00
TR14 Imperial TIE Fighter Pilot	8.00	20.00
TR15 Galactic Republic Clone Trooper	8.00	20.00
TR16 Galactic Marine	10.00	25.00

2020 Topps Star Wars Holocron

COMPLETE SET W/SP (225)	200.00	400.00
COMPLETE SET W/O SP (200)	15.00	40.00
UNOPENED BOX (18 PACKS)	100.00	200.00
UNOPENED PACK (8 CARDS)	6.00	10.00
COMMON CARD	.20	.50
COMMON SP	10.00	25.00
*FOILBOARD: .75X TO 2X BASIC CARDS		
*GREEN: 1.5X TO 4X BASIC CARDS		
*ORANGE/99: 3X TO 8X BASIC CARDS		
N21 The Child	4.00	10.00
PX7 Ahsoka Tano	2.00	5.00
BH14 Boba Fett	1.25	3.00
BH15 The Mandalorian	2.00	5.00
BH2S Boba Fett SP	20.00	50.00
CD1S Qi'Ra SP	25.00	60.00
FO1S Kylo Ren SP	15.00	40.00
N21S The Child SP	50.00	100.00
BH15S The Mandalorian SP	15.00	40.00
EMP1S Darth Vader SP	15.00	40.00
REB1S Luke Skywalker SP	12.00	30.00
REB2S Princess Leia Organa SP	12.00	30.00
REB33 Cara Dune	6.00	15.00
REB3S Han Solo SP	12.00	30.00
REP6S Padme Amidala SP	20.00	50.00
REP8S C-3PO SP	12.00	30.00
REP9S R2-D2 SP	12.00	30.00
RES1S Rey SP	15.00	40.00
JEDI15 Ahsoka Tano	2.00	5.00
JEDI1S Obi-Wan Kenobi SP	12.00	30.00
JEDI3S Yoda SP	15.00	40.00
REB23S Jyn Erso SP	15.00	40.00
SITH1S Darth Maul SP	12.00	30.00
JEDI15S Ahsoka Tano SP	20.00	50.00

2020 Topps Star Wars Holocron The Adventures of Han Solo

COMPLETE SET (20)	10.00	25.00
COMMON CARD (AH1-AH20)	1.25	3.00
*ORANGE/99: .6X TO 1.5X BASIC CARDS		
STATED ODDS 1:3		

2020 Topps Star Wars Holocron Autographs

COMMON AUTO	6.00	15.00
*GREEN/99: .5X TO 1.2X BASIC AUTOS		
*BLUE/50: .6X TO 1.5X BASIC AUTOS		
STATED ODDS 1:859		
MANY OF THE KEY SIGNERS		
DO NOT HAVE BASE AUTOGRAPHS		
AAV Attila Vajda	8.00	20.00
ADA David Ankrum	8.00	20.00
AHD Harley Durst	8.00	20.00

2020 Topps Star Wars Holocron Autographs Green

STATED ODDS 1:3,258		
STATED PRINT RUN 99 SER.#'d SETS		
ACR Clive Revill	12.00	30.00

2020 Topps Star Wars Holocron Charting the Galaxy

COMPLETE SET (20)	12.00	30.00
COMMON CARD (CG1-CG20)	1.00	2.50
*ORANGE/99: .5X TO 1.2X BASIC CARDS		
STATED ODDS 1:3		

2020 Topps Star Wars Holocron Commemorative Creature Patches

COMMON MEM	3.00	8.00
*GREEN/99: .5X TO 1.2X BASIC MEM		
STATED ODDS 1:RETAIL BOX		
PCB The Child	10.00	25.00
PCE Chewbacca	5.00	12.00
PCJ The Child	10.00	25.00
PCP Chewbacca	5.00	12.00
PHE Han Solo	8.00	20.00
PHT Han Solo	8.00	20.00
PKB Kuiil	4.00	10.00
PKJ Kuiil	4.00	10.00
PLJ Luke Skywalker	6.00	15.00
PLP Luke Skywalker	6.00	15.00
PLT Luke Skywalker	6.00	15.00
PMJ Mudhorn	4.00	10.00
PPP Paploo	5.00	12.00
PRP Rey	8.00	20.00
PSJ Stormtrooper	4.00	10.00
PTE Teebo	4.00	10.00
PTT Tauntaun	5.00	12.00
PLOE Princess Leia Organa	6.00	15.00
POWJ Obi-Wan Kenobi	4.00	10.00
PPGP Porg	4.00	10.00
PTKE Tokkat	5.00	12.00
PTMB The Mandalorian	6.00	15.00
PTMJ The Mandalorian	6.00	15.00

2020 Topps Star Wars Holocron Lightsabers of the Jedi

COMPLETE SET (10)	6.00	15.00
COMMON CARD (LJ1-LJ10)	1.00	2.50
*ORANGE/99: 1.5X TO 4X BASIC CARDS		
STATED ODDS 1:3		

2015 Star Wars Honey Maid

COMPLETE SET (12)	3.00	8.00
COMMON CARD	.40	1.00

2020 Topps Star Wars I Am Your Father's Day

COMPLETE SET (10)	12.00	30.00
COMMON CARD (1-10)	2.50	6.00
STATED PRINT RUN 896 SETS		

2021 Topps Star Wars I Am Your Father's Day

COMPLETE SET (10)	15.00	40.00
COMMON CARD (1-10)	2.00	5.00
STATED PRINT RUN 896 SETS		
1 The Mandalorian / Grogu	6.00	15.00
2 Darth Vader / Luke Skywalker	3.00	8.00

2013 Star Wars Jedi Legacy

COMPLETE SET (90)	6.00	15.00
UNOPENED BOX (24 PACKS)	250.00	400.00
UNOPENED PACK (8 CARDS)	12.00	20.00
COMMON CARD (1A-45L)	.20	.50
*BLUE: 1.2X TO 3X BASIC CARDS		
*MAGENTA: 4X TO 10X BASIC CARDS		
*GREEN: 5X TO 12X BASIC CARDS		
*GOLD/10: 50X TO 120X BASIC CARDS		

2013 Star Wars Jedi Legacy Autographs

COMMON AUTO	10.00	25.00
STATED ODDS 1:72		
NNO Alan Harris	20.00	50.00
NNO Anthony Daniels	150.00	400.00
NNO Billy Dee Williams	125.00	300.00
NNO Carrie Fisher	750.00	2000.00
NNO Harrison Ford	1250.00	3000.00
NNO Ian McDiarmid	150.00	400.00
NNO James Earl Jones	250.00	600.00
NNO Jeremy Bulloch	50.00	125.00
NNO Kenny Baker	125.00	250.00
NNO Mark Hamill	1250.00	3000.00

2013 Star Wars Jedi Legacy Chewbacca Fur Relics

COMPLETE SET (4)	400.00	1000.00
COMMON MEM (CR1-CR4)	150.00	400.00
STATED ODDS 1:720		

2013 Star Wars Jedi Legacy Connections

COMPLETE SET (15)	5.00	12.00
COMMON CARD (C1-C15)	.60	1.50
STATED ODDS 1:2		

2013 Star Wars Jedi Legacy Ewok Fur Relics

COMPLETE SET (8)	125.00	300.00
COMMON MEM (ER1-ER8)	30.00	75.00
STATED ODDS 1:120		

2013 Star Wars Jedi Legacy Film Cels

COMMON CARD (FR1-FR30)	10.00	25.00
STATED ODDS 1:BOX		
FR6 Darth Vader	20.00	50.00

2013 Star Wars Jedi Legacy Dual Film Cels

COMPLETE SET (6)	120.00	250.00
COMMON CARD (DFR1-DFR6)	20.00	50.00
STATED ODDS 1:144		
DFR1 Darth Vader/Luke Skywalker	30.00	60.00

2013 Star Wars Jedi Legacy Triple Film Cels

COMPLETE SET (10)	250.00	500.00
COMMON CARD (TFR1-TFR10)	30.00	60.00
STATED ODDS 1:144		

2013 Star Wars Jedi Legacy Influencers

COMPLETE SET (18)	5.00	12.00
COMMON CARD (I1-I18)	.50	1.25
STATED ODDS 1:2		

2013 Star Wars Jedi Legacy Jabba's Sail Barge Relics

COMPLETE SET (5)	150.00	400.00
COMMON MEM (JR1-JR5)	60.00	150.00
STATED ODDS 1:336		

2013 Star Wars Jedi Legacy The Circle is Now Complete

COMPLETE SET (12)	35.00	70.00
COMMON CARD (CC1-CC12)	4.00	10.00
STATED ODDS 1:12		
NNO1 Luke Skywalker PROMO		

2013 Star Wars Jedi Legacy Promos

COMMON CARD	3.00	8.00
P1 Battle Through Blood/Vader	8.00	20.00
P2 Battle Through Blood/Luke	8.00	20.00
P3 Fallen Jedi/Anakin vs. Count Dooku	8.00	20.00
P4 Fallen Jedi/Luke vs. Vader	8.00	20.00
P5 Death of a Mentor PHILLY	3.00	8.00
NNO Darth Vader Disc	1.50	4.00
NNO Luke Skywalker Disc	1.50	4.00
NNO Two Paths/Two Journeys/One Desitny 5x7		

2015 Star Wars Journey to The Force Awakens

COMPLETE SET (110)	10.00	25.00
UNOPENED HOBBY BOX (24 PACKS)		
UNOPENED HOBBY PACK (6 CARDS)		
UNOPENED RETAIL BOX (24 PACKS)		
UNOPENED RETAIL PACK (6 CARDS)		
UNOPENED BLASTER BOX (10 PACKS)		
UNOPENED BLASTER PACK (6 CARDS)		
UNOPENED JUMBO PACK (14 CARDS)		
COMMON CARD (1-110)	.20	.50
*JABBA SLIME GREEN: .5X TO 1.2X BASIC CARDS		
*BLACK: .6X TO 1.5X BASIC CARDS		
*DEATH STAR SILVER: .75X TO 2X BASIC CARDS		
*LTSBR. NEON PINK: 1.5X TO 4X BASIC CARDS		
*PURPLE: 4X TO 10X BASIC CARDS		
*HOTH ICE/150: 6X TO 15X BASIC CARDS		
*GOLD/50: 10X TO 25X BASIC CARDS		
*HOLOGRAM/25: 15X TO 40X BASIC CARDS		

2015 Star Wars Journey to The Force Awakens Autographs

COMMON AUTO	8.00	20.00
*SILVER/50: .75X TO 2X BASIC AUTOS		
NNO Alan Harris	10.00	25.00
NNO Amy Allen	12.00	30.00
NNO Anthony Daniels	200.00	400.00
NNO Ashley Eckstein	40.00	100.00
NNO Bai Ling	15.00	40.00
NNO Billy Dee Williams	50.00	100.00
NNO Caroline Blakiston	10.00	25.00
NNO Carrie Fisher	120.00	250.00
NNO David Prowse	80.00	150.00
NNO Dickey Beer	10.00	25.00
NNO Femi Taylor	12.00	30.00
NNO Hassani Shapi	12.00	30.00
NNO Jeremy Bulloch	25.00	60.00
NNO Jerome Blake	10.00	25.00
NNO John Ratzenberger	12.00	30.00
NNO Kenji Oates	10.00	25.00
NNO Kenneth Colley	10.00	25.00
NNO Kenny Baker	100.00	200.00
NNO Mark Hamill	225.00	350.00
NNO Michonne Bourriague	12.00	30.00
NNO Mike Quinn	25.00	60.00
NNO Nika Futterman	10.00	25.00
NNO Olivia d'Abo	80.00	150.00
NNO Orli Shoshan	10.00	25.00
NNO Pam Rose	10.00	25.00
NNO Peter Mayhew	50.00	100.00
NNO Ray Park	25.00	60.00
NNO Rohan Nichol	12.00	30.00
NNO Steven Blum	10.00	25.00
NNO Taylor Gray	12.00	30.00
NNO Tiya Sircar	25.00	60.00
NNO Vanessa Marshall	15.00	40.00
NNO Wayne Pygram	12.00	30.00

2015 Star Wars Journey to The Force Awakens Behind-the-Scenes

COMPLETE SET (9)	5.00	12.00
COMMON CARD (BTS1-BTS9)	1.00	2.50

2015 Star Wars Journey to The Force Awakens Blueprints

COMPLETE SET (8) 15.00 40.00
COMMON CARD (BP1-BP8) 3.00 8.00
BP1 BB-8 6.00 15.00
BP3 Millennium Falcon 5.00 12.00
BP4 X-Wing Fighter 4.00 10.00

2015 Star Wars Journey to The Force Awakens Character Stickers

COMPLETE SET (18) 15.00 40.00
COMMON CARD (S1-S18) 1.25 3.00
S1 Luke Skywalker 1.50 4.00
S2 Han Solo 2.00 5.00
S9 BB-8 2.50 6.00
S10 Captain Phasma 1.50 4.00
S11 Kylo Ren 2.00 5.00
S14 Darth Vader 2.00 5.00
S15 Boba Fett 1.50 4.00
S17 Kylo Ren 2.00 5.00
S18 Yoda 1.50 4.00

2015 Star Wars Journey to The Force Awakens Choose Your Destiny

COMPLETE SET (9) 12.00 30.00
COMMON CARD (CD1-CD9) 2.50 6.00

2015 Star Wars Journey to The Force Awakens Classic Captions

COMPLETE SET (8) 15.00 40.00
COMMON CARD (CC1-CC8) 4.00 10.00

2015 Star Wars Journey to The Force Awakens Cloth Stickers

COMPLETE SET (9) 8.00 20.00
COMMON CARD (CS1-CS9) 1.50 4.00
CS6 Kylo Ren 2.00 5.00
CS9 Kylo Ren (w/TIE Fighters) 2.00 5.00

2015 Star Wars Journey to The Force Awakens Concept Art

COMPLETE SET (9) 5.00 12.00
COMMON CARD (CA1-CA9) 1.00 2.50

2015 Star Wars Journey to The Force Awakens Family Legacy Matte Backs

COMPLETE SET (8) 10.00 25.00
COMMON CARD (FL1-FL8) 1.50 4.00
*GLOSSY: .5X TO 1.2X BASIC CARDS
FL1 Boba Fett and Jango Fett 2.00 5.00
FL2 Anakin Skywalker and Luke Skywalker 2.00 5.00
FL3 Padme Amidala and Leia Organa 2.00 5.00

2015 Star Wars Journey to The Force Awakens Heroes of the Resistance

COMPLETE SET (9) 6.00 15.00
COMMON CARD (R1-R9) 1.25 3.00
R4 BB-8 2.00 5.00
R8 The Millennium Falcon 1.50 4.00

2015 Star Wars Journey to The Force Awakens Patches

COMPLETE SET (20) 150.00 300.00
COMMON CARD (P1-P20) 8.00 20.00
P1 Kylo Ren 12.00 30.00
P3 Captain Phasma 12.00 30.00
P9 BB-8 12.00 30.00
P18 BB-8 12.00 30.00

2015 Star Wars Journey to The Force Awakens Power of the First Order

COMPLETE SET (8) 6.00 15.00
COMMON CARD (FD1-FD8) 1.25 3.00
FD1 Kylo Ren 2.00 5.00
FD2 Captain Phasma 1.50 4.00

2015 Star Wars Journey to The Force Awakens Silhouette Foil

COMPLETE SET (8) 4.00 10.00
COMMON CARD (1-8) .75 2.00
ERRONEOUSLY LISTED AS A 9-CARD SET
ON THE CARD BACKS

5 Kylo Ren 1.50 4.00
7 Captain Phasma 1.25 3.00

2015 Star Wars Journey to The Force Awakens Promos

COMPLETE SET (6) 10.00 25.00
COMMON CARD (P1-P6) 2.00 5.00
P1 Luke Skywalker 6.00 15.00
(SDCC Marvel Star Wars Lando exclusive)
P6 Kanan Jarrus 5.00 12.00
(NYCC exclusive)

2015 Star Wars Journey to The Force Awakens UK

COMPLETE SET (208) 30.00 80.00
COMMON CARD .30 .75
LEY Yoda
LEBF Boba Fett
LECH Chewbacca
LEHS Han Solo
LELC Lando Calrissian
LELS Luke Skywalker
LEPL Princess Leia
LER2 R2-D2
LEST Stormtrooper
LETE The Emperor

2017 Star Wars Journey to The Last Jedi

COMPLETE SET (110) 12.00 30.00
UNOPENED BOX (24 PACKS) 85.00 100.00
UNOPENED PACK (8 CARDS) 3.00 4.00
COMMON CARD (1-110) .20 .50
*GREEN STAR.: .5X TO 1.2X BASIC CARDS .25 .60
*PINK STAR.: .6X TO 1.5X BASIC CARDS .30 .75
*BLACK STAR.: .75X TO 2X BASIC CARDS .40 1.00
*SILVER STAR.: 1.2X TO 3X BASIC CARDS .60 1.50
*PURPLE STAR.: 2X TO 5X BASIC CARDS 1.00 2.50
*WHITE STAR./199: 12X TO
30X BASIC CARDS 6.00 15.00
*ORANGE STAR./50: 15X TO
40X BASIC CARDS 8.00 20.00
*GOLD STAR./25: 25X TO
60X BASIC CARDS 12.00 30.00

2017 Star Wars Journey to The Last Jedi Allies

COMPLETE SET (5) 50.00 100.00
COMMON CARD (1-5) 10.00 25.00
GAMESTOP EXCLUSIVE

2017 Star Wars Journey to The Last Jedi Autographs

AAD Adam Driver
AAE Ashley Eckstein
AAP Alistair Petrie
AAS Andy Serkis
AAT Alan Tudyk
ABD Ben Daniels 20.00 50.00
ABH Brian Herring 12.00 30.00
ABL Billie Lourd
ABW Billy Dee Williams
ACD Cristina da Silva 12.00 30.00
ACF Carrie Fisher
ACR Clive Revill
ACT Catherine Taber 15.00 40.00
ADB Dee Bradley Baker 12.00 30.00
ADC Dave Champman 20.00 50.00
ADL Daniel Logan 12.00 30.00
ADP Duncan Pow 8.00 20.00
ADR Daisy Ridley
ADY Donnie Yen
AFJ Felicity Jones
AFP Freddie Prinze Jr.
AFW Forest Whitaker
AGC Gwendoline Christie
AGT George Takei
AHC Hayden Christensen
AHF Harrison Ford
AIU Iko Uwais
AIW Ian Whyte 10.00 25.00
AJB John Boyega
AJC Jim Cummings 10.00 25.00
AJD Julie Dolan 10.00 25.00
AJI Jason Isaacs
AKB Kenny Baker
AKF Kate Fleetwood
AKY Keone Young 15.00 40.00
AMH Mark Hamill
APB Paul Blake 15.00 40.00
APM Peter Mayhew
APW Paul Warren 10.00 25.00
ARA Riz Ahmed
ARC Richard Cunningham 12.00 30.00
ARP Ray Park
ASG Stefan Grube 12.00 30.00
ASR Scott Richardson 15.00 40.00
ASW Sam Witwer
ATB Thomas Brodie-Sangster
ATC Tosin Cole
ATK Tom Kane
ATW Tom Wilton 12.00 30.00
AWP Wayne Pygram 10.00 25.00
AYR Yayan Ruhian
AZD Zarene Dallas 12.00 30.00
AADA Anthony Daniels
AADX Adam Driver Unmasked
ACAR Cecp Arif Rahman 15.00 40.00
ADAR Derek Arnold
ADBA Dave Barclay 10.00 25.00
ADRX Daisy Ridley Scavenger
AGGA Gloria Garcia 12.00 30.00
AGGA Greg Grunberg
AIMD Ian McDiarmid
AIME Ian McElhinney 12.00 30.00
AJBL Jerome Blake 10.00 25.00
AJBU Jeremy Bulloch
ASDB Sharon Duncan-Brewster 15.00 40.00

2017 Star Wars Journey to The Last Jedi Blueprints

COMPLETE SET (7) 8.00 20.00
COMMON CARD (1-7) 2.00 5.00

2017 Star Wars Journey to The Last Jedi Character Retro Stickers

COMPLETE SET (18) 100.00 200.00
COMMON CARD (1-18) 6.00 15.00

2017 Star Wars Journey to The Last Jedi Characters

COMPLETE SET (16) 12.00 30.00
COMMON CARD (1-16) 1.25 3.00

2017 Star Wars Journey to The Last Jedi Choose Your Destiny

COMPLETE SET (10) 8.00 20.00
COMMON CARD (1-10) 1.25 3.00

2017 Star Wars Journey to The Last Jedi Darkness Rises

COMPLETE SET (6) 6.00 15.00
COMMON CARD (1-6) 1.50 4.00

2017 Star Wars Journey to The Last Jedi Family Legacy

COMPLETE SET (6) 5.00 12.00
COMMON CARD (1-6) 1.25 3.00

2017 Star Wars Journey to The Last Jedi Illustrated Characters

COMPLETE SET (14) 10.00 25.00
COMMON CARD (1-14) 1.00 2.50

2017 Star Wars Journey to The Last Jedi Patches

COMMON CARD (UNNUMBERED) 5.00 12.00
*ORANGE/99: .75X TO 2X BASIC CARDS 10.00 25.00
*GOLD/25: 1.2X TO 3X BASIC CARDS 15.00 40.00

2017 Star Wars Journey to The Last Jedi Rey Continuity

COMPLETE SET (10) 12.00 30.00
COMMON CARD (1-5) 1.25 3.00
COMMON CARD (6-10) 2.00 5.00
RANDOMLY INSERTED INTO PACKS
1-5 JOURNEY TO THE LAST JEDI EXCLUSIVE
6-10 THE LAST JEDI SER.1 EXCLUSIVE
11-15 THE LAST JEDI SER.2 EXCLUSIVE

2019 Star Wars Journey to The Rise of Skywalker

COMPLETE SET (110) 10.00 25.00
UNOPENED BOX (24 PACKS) 60.00 100.00
UNOPENED PACK (8 CARDS) 2.50 4.00
COMMON CARD (1-110) .20 .50
*RED: X TO X BASIC CARDS
*GREEN: .75X TO 2X BASIC CARDS
*SILVER: 1.2X TO 3X BASIC CARDS
*BLACK/199: 3X TO 8X BASIC CARDS
*ORANGE/50: 6X TO 15X BASIC CARDS
*GOLD/25: 12X TO 30X BASIC CARDS

2019 Star Wars Journey to The Rise of Skywalker Autographs

COMMON AUTO 5.00 12.00
RANDOMLY INSERTED INTO PACKS
AAD Adam Driver
AAD Anthony Daniels
AAE Adrian Edmondson 5.00 12.00
AAJ Andrew Jack 5.00 12.00
AAL Amanda Lawrence 5.00 12.00
AAS Andy Serkis 1
AAS Andy Serkis 2
AAS Arti Shah 6.00 15.00
ABL Billie Lourd
ABV Brian Vernel
ACC Cavin Cornwall 8.00 20.00
ACC Crystal Clarke
ACF Carrie Fisher
ADA David Acord
ADC Dave Chapman
ADG Domhnall Gleeson
ADR Daisy Ridley
AEE Emun Elliott
AGG Greg Grunberg
AHC Hermione Corfield 12.00 30.00
AHF Harrison Ford
AHS Hugh Skinner 6.00 15.00
AIU Iko Uwais 5.00 12.00
AIW Ian Whyte 6.00 15.00
AJB John Boyega 1
AJB John Boyega 2
AJS Joonas Suotamo
AJV Jimmy Vee 8.00 20.00
AKB Kenny Baker
AKS Kiran Shah 5.00 12.00
ALC Lily Cole 6.00 15.00
ALD Laura Dern
AMQ Mike Quinn 6.00 15.00
ANC Nathalie Cuzner 5.00 12.00
APK Paul Kasey 5.00 12.00
APW Paul Warren 5.00 12.00
ARM Rocky Marshall
ASA Sebastian Armesto
ASG Stefan Grube 5.00 12.00
ATK Tom Kane 6.00 15.00
ATR Tim Rose
ATW Tom Wilton 6.00 15.00
AWD Warwick Davis
ACAR Cecep Arif Rahman
ADAV Derek Arnold
AGGJ Gloria Garcia 6.00 15.00
AKMT Kelly Marie Tran
ATBS Thomas Brodie-Sangster

2019 Star Wars Journey to The Rise of Skywalker Battle Lines

COMPLETE SET (10) 25.00 60.00

COMMON CARD (BL1-BL10) 4.00 10.00
RANDOMLY INSERTED IN PACKS

2019 Star Wars Journey to The Rise of Skywalker Character Foil

COMPLETE SET (8) 6.00 15.00
COMMON CARD (FC1-FC8) 1.00 2.50
RANDOMLY INSERTED INTO PACKS

2019 Star Wars Journey to The Rise of Skywalker Character Stickers

COMPLETE SET (19) 10.00 25.00
COMMON CARD (CS1-CS19) 1.25 3.00
RANDOMLY INSERTED INTO PACKS

2019 Star Wars Journey to The Rise of Skywalker Choose Your Destiny

COMPLETE SET (10) 12.00 30.00
COMMON CARD (CD1-CD10) 2.00 5.00
RANDOMLY INSERTED INTO PACKS

2019 Star Wars Journey to The Rise of Skywalker Commemorative Jumbo Patches

COMMON MEM 3.00 8.00
*BLACK/99: .5X TO 1.2X BASIC MEM
*ORANGE/50: .6X TO 1.5X BASIC MEM
RANDOMLY INSERTED INTO PACKS
JPF Finn 5.00 12.00
JPR Rey 6.00 15.00
JPAH Vice Admiral Holdo 4.00 10.00
JPBB BB-8 4.00 10.00
JPC3 C-3PO 4.00 10.00
JPCT C'ai Threnalli 4.00 10.00
JPHS Han Solo 6.00 15.00
JPKC Lieutenant Connix 5.00 12.00
JPLC Lando Calrissian 4.00 10.00
JPLO General Leia Organa 5.00 12.00
JPLS Luke Skywalker 5.00 12.00
JPPA Padmé Amidala 5.00 12.00
JPPD Poe Dameron 4.00 10.00
JPR2 R2-D2 4.00 10.00

2019 Star Wars Journey to The Rise of Skywalker Commemorative Patches

COMMON MEM 3.00 8.00
*BLACK/99: .5X TO 1.2X BASIC MEM
*ORANGE/50: .6X TO 1.5X BASIC MEM
RANDOMLY INSERTED INTO PACKS
PCCR Chewbacca 5.00 12.00
PCFR Finn 4.00 10.00
PCRR Rey 6.00 15.00
PCCPK Captain Phasma 4.00 10.00
PCHSR Han Solo 8.00 20.00
PCKFO Kylo Ren 5.00 12.00
PCKRK Kylo Ren 5.00 12.00
PCKRT Kylo Ren 6.00 15.00
PCLOR General Leia Organa 5.00 12.00
PCLSR Luke Skywalker 5.00 12.00
PCPDX Poe Dameron 5.00 12.00
PCPFO Captain Phasma 4.00 10.00
PCPXP Poe Dameron 5.00 12.00
PCSFO Supreme Leader Snoke 4.00 10.00
PCSLK Supreme Leader Snoke 4.00 10.00

2019 Star Wars Journey to The Rise of Skywalker Illustrated Characters

COMPLETE SET (16) 12.00 30.00
COMMON CARD (IC1-IC16) 1.25 3.00
RANDOMLY INSERTED INTO PACKS

2019 Star Wars Journey to The Rise of Skywalker Schematics

COMPLETE SET (10) 5.00 12.00
COMMON CARD (S1-S10) .75 2.00
RANDOMLY INSERTED INTO PACKS

2019 Star Wars Kylo Ren Continuity

COMPLETE SET (15) 15.00 40.00
JOURNEY TO TROS (1-5) 2.00 5.00
TROS S1 (6-10) 2.00 5.00
TROS S2 (11-15) 2.00 5.00
JOURNEY STATED ODDS 1:24
TROS S1 STATED ODDS 1:24
TROS S2 STATED ODDS 1:24

1996 Topps Star Wars Laser

0 Star Wars 20th Anniversary Commemorative Magazine 3.00 8.00

2016 Star Wars LEGO Droid Tales

COMPLETE SET (9) 15.00 40.00
UNOPENED PACK (3 CARDS) 6.00 8.00
COMMON CARD (DT1-DT9)
ONE PACK INSERTED INTO
STAR WARS LEGO DROID TALES DVD

2019-23 Topps Living Star Wars Set

COMMON CARD 3.00 8.00
TOPPS ONLINE EXCLUSIVE
1 Darth Vader/3,909* 25.00 60.00
2 Nien Nunb/2,888* 10.00 25.00
3 R2-D2/2,710* 10.00 20.00
4 Stormtrooper/2,601* 15.00 30.00
5 Bossk/2,205* 10.00 20.00
6 Val/2,161* 6.00 15.00
7 Queen Amidala/2,038* 10.00 20.00
8 Death Star Gunner/1,922* 5.00 12.00
9 Grand Admiral Thrawn/1,760* 40.00 100.00
10 Uncle Owen Lars/1,721* 10.00 20.00
11 Wedge Antilles/1,662* 6.00 15.00
12 Dengar/1,641* 6.00 15.00
13 Jar Jar Binks/1,692* 12.00 30.00
14 Moloch/1,565* 8.00 20.00
15 Orson Krennic/1,385* 15.00 40.00
16 Jawa/1,441* 15.00 40.00
17 Lando Calrissian/1,427* 20.00 50.00
18 Rancor/1,405* 12.00 30.00
19 Ezra Bridger/1,375* 15.00 40.00
20 Admiral Piett/1,378* 10.00 25.00
21 Han Solo/2,376* 15.00 40.00
22 Tasu Leech/1,501* 8.00 20.00
23 Mon Mothma/1,435* 10.00 25.00
24 Wampa/1,454* 8.00 20.00
25 Darth Maul/1,739* 25.00 60.00
26 Tallie Lintra/1,493* 12.00 30.00
27 Shaak Ti/1,311* 20.00 50.00
28 Quay Tolsite/1,307* 12.00 30.00
29 4-LOM/1,356* 15.00 40.00
30 BB-8/1,502* 12.00 30.00
31 Aurra Sing/1,343* 10.00 25.00
32 Tobias Beckett/1,395* 10.00 25.00
33 Wicket W. Warrick/1,390* 40.00 100.00
34 Scout Trooper/1,283* 12.00 30.00
35 General Hux/1,170* 30.00 75.00
36 Dak Ralter/1,164* 20.00 50.00
37 Bail Organa/1,124 15.00 40.00
38 Gamorrean Guard/1,161* 25.00 60.00
39 Sebulba/1,101* 12.00 30.00
40 Kanan Jarrus/1,086* 30.00 75.00
41 K-2SO/1,151* 30.00 75.00
42 Echo Base Trooper/1,136* 15.00 40.00
43 Maz Kanata/1,122* 10.00 25.00
44 Captain Needa/1,108* 10.00 25.00
45 Salacious B. Crumb/1,090* 20.00 50.00
46 Chirrut Imwe/1,102* 25.00 60.00
47 Rey/1,503* 40.00 100.00
48 Savage Opress/1,114* 30.00 75.00
49 Captain Phasma/1,011 20.00 50.00
50 Cliegg Lars/938* 25.00 60.00
51 L3-37/902* 60.00 150.00
52 Nute Gunray/985* 60.00 150.00
53 General Grievous/1,007* 50.00 125.00
54 Saw Gerrera/967* 60.00 150.00
55 Finn/1,079* 25.00 60.00
56 Imperial Pilots/1,021* 30.00 75.00
57 Dorme/2,021* 8.00 20.00
58 The Child/9,663* 20.00 50.00
59 Supreme Leader Snoke/942* 60.00 150.00
60 Plo Koon/887* 100.00 250.00
61 Greedo/1,178* 15.00 40.00
62 Young Anakin Skywalker/1,207* 10.00 25.00
63 Poe Dameron/1,301 12.00 30.00
64 Mother Talzin/1,203 25.00 60.00
65 Watto/1,259* 15.00 40.00
66 Darth Sidious/1,422* 15.00 40.00
67 Jyn Erso/1,425* 20.00 50.00
68 BB-9E/1,068* 12.00 30.00
69 Max Rebo/956* 25.00 60.00
70 Count Dooku/946* 25.00 50.00
71 Admiral Ackbar/1,041* 25.00 60.00
72 Young Boba Fett/1,158* 50.00 125.00
73 C-3PO/1,156* 20.00 50.00
74 Lady Proxima/959* 40.00 100.00
75 Kylo Ren/1,187* 20.00 50.00
76 Kit Fisto/960* 20.00 50.00
77 Princess Leia/2,093* 15.00 40.00
78 Lieutenant Connix/1,351* 12.00 30.00
79 Emperor Palpatine/1,103* 15.00 40.00
80 Porg/1,130* 15.00 40.00
81 Ahsoka Tano/1,293* 60.00 150.00
82 Bala Tik/992* 15.00 40.00
83 Boba Fett/1,913* 60.00 120.00
84 Tauntaun/1,190* 12.00 30.00
85 Kuiil/1,068* 20.00 50.00
86 Elite Praetorian Guard/1,038* 12.00 30.00
87 Dryden Vos/1,003* 30.00 75.00
88 Bistan/996* 30.00 75.00
89 Paige Tico/996* 15.00 40.00
90 Rose Tico/901* 50.00 100.00
91 Grand Moff Tarkin/1,042* 30.00 75.00
92 Galen Erso/1,005* 20.00 50.00
93 Vice Admiral Holdo/1,079* 15.00 40.00
94 General Veers/979* 25.00 60.00
95 Jango Fett/1,252* 12.00 30.00
96 Jannah/1,074* 8.00 20.00
97 Hera Syndulla/1,131* 25.00 60.00
98 Jabba the Hutt/1,395* 10.00 20.00
99 Obi-Wan Kenobi/2,656* 6.00 15.00
100 Luke Skywalker/2,833* 8.00 20.00
101 Royal Guard/1,255* 10.00 25.00
102 Captain Rex/1,259* 12.00 30.00
103 Babu Frik/1,279* 6.00 15.00
104 Mas Amedda/1,105* 6.00 15.00
105 Fennec Shand/1,217* 30.00 75.00
106 Zorri Bliss/1,244* 6.00 15.00
107 Cassian Andor/1,246* 8.00 20.00
108 Clone Trooper/1,257* 8.00 20.00
109 Kazuda "Kaz" Xiono/1,241* 6.00 15.00
110 Aayla Secura/1,286* 10.00 25.00
111 Peli Motto/1,305* 12.00 30.00
112 Yaddle/1,328* 6.00 15.00
113 Sabine Wren/1,480* 15.00 40.00
114 Allegiant General Pryde/1,222* 6.00 15.00
115 Baze Malbus/1,268* 6.00 15.00
116 The Grand Inquisitor/1,228* 10.00 25.00
117 Ben Solo/2,304* 12.00 30.00
118 Rio Durant/1,325* 6.00 15.00
119 Bodhi Rook/1,277* 10.00 25.00
120 Mythrol/1,265* 8.00 20.00
121 Logray/1,303* 6.00 15.00
122 Chancellor Valorum/* 5.00 12.00
123 Qi'Ra/1,737* 8.00 20.00
124 Battle Droid/1,376* 10.00 25.00
125 Snap Wexley/1,191* 6.00 15.00
126 Bendu/1,114* 8.00 20.00
127 Cara Dune/2,316* 20.00 50.00
128 Klaud/1,421* 6.00 15.00
129 Reboltt/1,259* 6.00 15.00
130 Zam Wesell/1,293* 6.00 15.00
131 Moff Gideon/1,411* 15.00 40.00
132 Torra Doza/1,184* 5.00 12.00
133 Jan Dodonna/1,209* 5.00 12.00
134 Zuckuss/1,227* 6.00 15.00
135 Beaumont Kin/1,184* 6.00 15.00
136 Pre Vizsla/1,317* 8.00 20.00
137 Cal Kestis/1,278* 6.00 15.00
138 Lobot/1,252* 5.00 12.00
139 Ello Asty/1,242* 6.00 15.00
140 First Order TIE Fighter Pilot/1,319* 5.00 12.00
141 D-O/1,283* 6.00 15.00
142 Bazine Netal/1,023* 8.00 20.00
143 Tam Ryvora/1,130* 6.00 15.00
144 Second Sister/1,215* 6.00 15.00
145 The Mandalorian/4,283* 20.00 50.00
146 Bo-Katan Kryze/1,352* 10.00 25.00
147 WG-22/1,186* 6.00 15.00
148 The Client/1,291* 8.00 20.00
149 Gardulla the Hutt/1,240* 4.00 10.00
150 Master Codebreaker/1,215* 6.00 15.00
151 Bo Keevil/1,139* 6.00 15.00
152 Blurrg/1,250* 5.00 12.00
153 Vulptex/1,142* 8.00 20.00
154 IG-88/1,298* 6.00 15.00
155 Stass Allie/1,192* 8.00 20.00
156 Xi'an/1,296* 5.00 12.00
157 General Leia Organa/1,740* 6.00 15.00
158 Queen Breha Organa/1,328* 6.00 15.00
159 Chopper/1,332* 6.00 15.00
160 Toro Calican/1,269* 6.00 15.00
161 Even Piell/1,131* 4.00 10.00
162 2-1B Droid/1,148* 6.00 15.00
163 Iden Versio/1,286* 6.00 15.00
164 Ap'lek/1,251* 5.00 12.00
165 Bo-Katan Kryze/2,171* 8.00 20.00
166 Commander Cody/1,541* 6.00 15.00
167 Yoda/5,157* 8.00 20.00
168 Mace Windu/2,985* 5.00 12.00
169 Shmi Skywalker/1,236* 4.00 10.00
170 Gasgano/1,217* 4.00 10.00
171 Han Solo/1,838* 5.00 12.00
172 Dark Trooper/1,945* 5.00 12.00
173 DJ/1,334* 4.00 10.00
174 Greez/1,309* 4.00 10.00
175 Bantha/1,667* 4.00 10.00
176 Tusken Raider/1,811* 6.00 15.00
177 The Armorer/2,277* 8.00 20.00
178 Slowen Lo/1,388* 5.00 12.00
179 Loth-cat/1,544* 8.00 20.00
180 Beru Lars/1,435* 5.00 12.00
181 Therm Scissorpunch/1,519* 6.00 15.00
182 Seventh Sister/1,586* 8.00 20.00
183 Greef Karga/2,112* 4.00 10.00
184 Aftab Ackbar/1,576* 4.00 10.00
185 Aurodia Ventafoli/1,731* 8.00 20.00
186 Darth Bane/2,548* 6.00 15.00
187 Alexsandr Kallus/1,504* 6.00 15.00
188 Malakili/1,466* 6.00 15.00
189 Lando Calrissian/1,786* 4.00 10.00
190 Neeku Vozo/1,416* 5.00 12.00
191 Cobb Vanth/2,048* 5.00 12.00
192 Sagwa/1,504* 5.00 12.00
193 Lyra Erso/1,441* 4.00 10.00
194 Admiral Motti/1,428* 4.00 10.00
195 Axe Woves/2,155* 6.00 15.00
196 General Quinn/1,372* 4.00 10.00
197 Wes Janson/1,437* 5.00 12.00
198 Emir Wat Tambor/1,376* 5.00 12.00
199 Zeb Orrelios/2,153* 4.00 10.00
200 Chewbacca/4,903* 4.00 10.00
201 Zero/1,589* 4.00 10.00
202 Hunter/1,873* 8.00 20.00
203 Caretakers/1,303* 5.00 12.00
204 Sidon Ithano/1,363* 6.00 15.00
205 Boolio/1,296* 5.00 12.00
206 Dr. Pershing/1,440* 4.00 10.00
207 Barriss Offee/1,363* 6.00 15.00
208 FN-2199/1,430* 8.00 20.00
209 General Rieekan/1,252* 4.00 10.00
210 Boussh/1,435* 4.00 10.00
211 Pamich Nerro Goode/1,160* 5.00 12.00

212 Tion Medon/1,210* 4.00 10.00
213 Chief Chirpa/1,505* 4.00 10.00
214 Luminara Unduli/1,340* 6.00 15.00
215 Koska Reeves/2,637* 12.00 30.00
216 Sith Jet Troopers/1,519* 4.00 10.00
217 Mon Mothma/1,154* 4.00 10.00
218 EV-9D9/1,162* 4.00 10.00
219 Dexster Jettster/1,102 6.00 15.00
220 Sarlacc/1,146* 6.00 15.00
221 C-3PO/2,676* 4.00 10.00
222 Mouse Droid/1,412* 4.00 10.00
223 Commander Pyre/1,345* 6.00 15.00
224 Padme Amidala/3,356* 5.00 12.00
225 Captain Panaka/1,246* 4.00 10.00
226 Clone Commander Bly/1,343* 4.00 10.00
227 Enfys Nest/1,514* 6.00 15.00
228 Tank Trooper/1,443* 6.00 15.00
229 Sy Snootles/1,299* 6.00 15.00
230 GA-97/1,290* 5.00 12.00
231 Biggs Darklighter/1,266* 5.00 12.00
232 Lor San Tekka/1,211* 6.00 15.00
233 Bib Fortuna/1,621* 4.00 10.00
234 Boba Fett/3,700* 5.00 12.00
243 Crosshair/2,137* 4.00 10.00
246 Derek "Hobbie" Klivia/1,173* 4.00 10.00
248 Qui-Gonn Jinn/2,470* 5.00 12.00
255 Echo/1,487* 6.00 15.00
256 Omega/1,606* 8.00 20.00
261 Major Bren Derlin/1,192* 5.00 12.00
263 Momaw Nadon/1,321* 5.00 12.00
268 R5-D4/1,363* 4.00 10.00
270 Obi-Wan Kenobi/2,813* 4.00 10.00
275 Migs Mayfield/1,797* 5.00 12.00
278 Darth Vader/3,449* 4.00 10.00
280 Weeteef Cyu-Bee/1,244* 10.00 25.00
282 Garsa Fwip/1,811* 5.00 12.00
285 Rancor/2,044* 4.00 10.00
286 Krrsantan/2,625* 5.00 12.00
290 Cad Bane/2,975* 6.00 15.00
294 Jek Lawquane/1,189* 4.00 10.00
300 Ahsoka Tano/4,649* 6.00 15.00
303 Fennec Shand/1,863* 4.00 10.00
309 Tarfful/1,346* 5.00 12.00
312 Tiplee/1,296* 4.00 10.00

2021 Topps Star Wars Lucasfilm 50th Anniversary

COMPLETE SET (25) 60.00 150.00
COMMON CARD (1-25) 3.00 8.00

2020 Topps Star Wars The Mandalorian Art eBay Exclusive Set

COMPLETE SET (10) 20.00 50.00
COMMON CARD (1-10) 3.00 8.00
EBAY EXCLUSIVE

2022 Topps Chrome Star Wars The Mandalorian Beskar Edition

COMPLETE SET (100) 15.00 40.00
UNOPENED BOX (18 PACKS) 60.00 100.00
UNOPENED PACK (4 CARDS) 4.00 6.00
COMMON CARD .40 1.00
*REF: 1.2X TO 3X BASIC CARDS
*BLUE/99: 1.5X TO 4X BASIC CARDS
*PURPLE/75: 2X TO 5X BASIC CARDS
*GREEN/50: 2.5X TO 6X BASIC CARDS

2022 Topps Chrome Star Wars The Mandalorian Beskar Edition Armored and Ready

COMPLETE SET (10) 10.00 25.00
COMMON CARD (AR1-AR10) 1.50 4.00
*BLUE/99: .6X TO 1.5X BASIC CARDS
*GREEN/50: .75X TO 2X BASIC CARDS
STATED ODDS 1:6
AR1 The Mandalorian 1.50 4.00
AR2 Boba Fett 1.50 4.00
AR3 The Armorer 1.50 4.00
AR4 Clan Kryze 1.50 4.00
AR5 Cobb Vanth 1.50 4.00
AR6 Dark Trooper 1.50 4.00
AR7 Paz Vizsla 1.50 4.00
AR8 IG-11 1.50 4.00
AR9 The Mandalorian 1.50 4.00
AR10 Fennec Shand 1.50 4.00

2022 Topps Chrome Star Wars The Mandalorian Beskar Edition Autographs

COMMON AUTO 5.00 12.00
*BLUE/150: .5X TO 1.2X BASIC AUTOS
*GREEN/99: .6X TO 1.5X BASIC AUTOS
*PURPLE/50: .75X TO 2X BASIC AUTOS
STATED ODDS 1:33
AAW Alexander Wraith 6.00 15.00
ACB Chris Bartlett 10.00 25.00
ADB Dmitrious Bistrevsky 8.00 20.00
AIS Isaac Singleton Jr. 15.00 40.00
AJJ Julia Jones 12.00 30.00
ALS Leilani Shiu 8.00 20.00
AMR Misty Rosas 10.00 25.00
AMV Mercedes Varnado 30.00 75.00
AMW Matthew Wood 12.00 30.00
AOA Omid Abtahi 8.00 20.00
APL Paul Sun-Hyung Lee 10.00 25.00
ARB Richard Brake 6.00 15.00
ASK Simon Kassianides 15.00 40.00
ATF Tait Fletcher 6.00 15.00
ACBT Chris Bartlett 10.00 25.00
ACHB Chris Bartlett 10.00 25.00
ADLI Diana Lee Inosanto 8.00 20.00
AISF Isla Farris 10.00 25.00
AJKC Jake Cannavale 15.00 40.00
AMBJ Mark Boone Jr. 12.00 30.00
AMRK Misty Rosas 10.00 25.00
AWEB W. Earl Brown 15.00 40.00

2022 Topps Chrome Star Wars The Mandalorian Beskar Edition Comic Covers

COMPLETE SET (5) 6.00 15.00
COMMON CARD (CC1-CC5) 2.00 5.00
*BLUE/99: .5X TO 1.2X BASIC CARDS
*GREEN/50: .75X TO 2X BASIC CARDS
STATED ODDS 1:3

2022 Topps Chrome Star Wars The Mandalorian Beskar Edition Illustrated Characters

COMPLETE SET (25) 25.00 60.00
COMMON CARD (IC1-IC25) 1.00 4.00
*BLUE/99: .5X TO 1.2X BASIC CARDS
*GREEN/50: .75X TO 2X BASIC CARDS
STATED ODDS 1:6

2022 Topps Chrome Star Wars The Mandalorian Beskar Edition Legends Die-Cuts

COMMON CARD (ML1-ML10) 20.00 50.00
RANDOMLY INSERTED INTO PACKS
ML1 Grogu 40.00 100.00
ML2 The Mandalorian 30.00 75.00
ML4 IG-11 25.00 60.00
ML5 Boba Fett 40.00 100.00
ML7 Ahsoka Tano 50.00 125.00
ML8 Fennec Shand 25.00 60.00

2020 Topps Star Wars The Mandalorian Journey of the Child

COMPLETE SET (25) 5.00 12.00
UNOPENED BOX (32 CARDS) 15.00 25.00
COMMON CARD (1-25) .20 .50
*GREEN: .6X TO 1.5X BASIC CARDS
*RED/99: 1X TO 2.5X BASIC CARDS
*BLUE/50: 1.5X TO 4X BASIC CARDS

2020 Topps Star Wars The Mandalorian Journey of the Child Illustrated

COMPLETE SET (5) 2.50 6.00
COMMON CARD (1-5) .75 2.00
*GREEN: .6X TO 1.5X BASIC CARDS
*RED/99: 1X TO 2.5X BASIC CARDS
*BLUE/50: 1.5X TO 4X BASIC CARDS
STATED ODDS 1 SET PER BOX

2019 Star Wars The Mandalorian Season 1

COMPLETE SET (40) 50.00 125.00
COMPLETE CH.1 SET (5) 10.00 25.00
COMPLETE CH.2 SET (5) 10.00 25.00
COMPLETE CH.3 SET (5) 8.00 20.00
COMPLETE CH.4 SET (5) 8.00 20.00
COMPLETE CH.5 SET (5) 8.00 20.00
COMPLETE CH.6 SET (5) 10.00 25.00
COMPLETE CH.7 SET (5) 10.00 25.00
COMPLETE CH.8 SET (5) 6.00 15.00
CHAPTER 1 COMMON (1-5) 3.00 8.00
CHAPTER 2 COMMON (6-10) 3.00 8.00
CHAPTER 3 COMMON (11-15) 2.50 6.00
CHAPTER 4 COMMON (16-20) 2.50 6.00
CHAPTER 5 COMMON (21-25) 2.50 6.00
CHAPTER 6 COMMON (26-30) 3.00 8.00
CHAPTER 7 COMMON (31-35) 3.00 8.00
CHAPTER 8 COMMON (36-40) 2.00 5.00
CHAPTER 1 PRINT RUN 714 SETS
CHAPTER 2 PRINT RUN 553 SETS
CHAPTER 3 PRINT RUN 1,315 SETS
CHAPTER 4 PRINT RUN 1,004 SETS
CHAPTER 5 PRINT RUN 1,179 SETS
CHAPTER 6 PRINT RUN 998 SETS
CHAPTER 7 PRINT RUN 884 SETS
CHAPTER 8 PRINT RUN 2,219 SETS

2019 Star Wars The Mandalorian Season 1 Autographs

COMMON AUTO 40.00 100.00
STATED PRINT RUN 49 SER.#'d SETS
GCAE Gina Carano 400.00 800.00
GEAE Giancarlo Esposito 75.00 200.00

2019 Star Wars The Mandalorian Season 1 Trailer Set

COMPLETE SET (10) 10.00 25.00
COMMON CARD (1-10) 2.00 5.00
STATED PRINT RUN 1,425 SER.#'d SETS

2020 Topps Star Wars The Mandalorian Season 1

COMPLETE SET (100) 15.00 40.00
UNOPENED BOX (7 PACKS) 125.00 250.00
UNOPENED PACK (8 CARDS) 15.00 40.00
COMMON CARD (1-100) .40 1.00
*BLUE: .5X TO 1.2X BASIC CARDS
*PURPLE: .75X TO 2X BASIC CARDS
*BRONZE/50: 3X TO 8X BASIC CARDS
*SILVER/25: 5X TO 12X BASIC CARDS

2020 Topps Star Wars The Mandalorian Season 1 Aliens and Creatures

COMPLETE SET (10) 8.00 20.00
COMMON CARD (AC1-AC10) 1.25 3.00
*RED/99: .5X TO 1.2X BASIC CARDS
*BRONZE/50: .75X TO 2X BASIC CARDS
STATED ODDS 1:7

2020 Topps Star Wars The Mandalorian Season 1 Autographs

COMMON AUTO 8.00 20.00
*RED/99: .5X TO 1.2X BASIC AUTOS
*BRONZE/50: .6X TO 1.5X BASIC AUTOS
STATED ODDS 1:19 HOBBY
STATED ODDS 1:372 RETAIL BLASTER
ADB Dmitrious Bistrevsky 10.00 25.00
AGC Gina Carano 100.00 200.00
AGE Giancarlo Esposito 50.00 100.00
AML Matt Lanter 10.00 25.00
AMR Misty Rosas 15.00 40.00
AOA Omid Abtahi 12.00 30.00
ATF Tait Fletcher 12.00 30.00
ACBF Chris Bartlett as Ferryman 10.00 25.00
ACBZ Chris Bartlett as Zero 12.00 30.00

2020 Topps Star Wars The Mandalorian Season 1 Autographs Bronze

STATED PRINT RUN 50 SER.#'d SETS
ACW Carl Weathers EXCH 125.00 250.00

2020 Topps Star Wars The Mandalorian Season 1 Autographs Red

AES Emily Swallow 100.00 200.00
AHS Horatio Sanz 25.00 60.00

2020 Topps Star Wars The Mandalorian Season 1 Characters

COMPLETE SET (18) 10.00 25.00
COMMON CARD (C1-C18) 1.25 3.00
*RED/99: .75X TO 2X BASIC CARDS
*BRONZE/50: 1X TO 2.5X BASIC CARDS
STATED ODDS 1:2 HOBBY & RETAIL BLASTER

2020 Topps Star Wars The Mandalorian Season 1 Commemorative Medallions

COMMON MEM 6.00 15.00
*RED/99: .5X TO 1.2X BASIC MEM
*BRONZE/50: .6X TO 1.5X BASIC MEM
STATED ODDS 1:98 HOBBY
STATED ODDS 1:1 RET.BLASTER BOXES
MAH The Armorer 12.00 30.00
MBM Blurrg 10.00 25.00
MCC The Child 15.00 40.00
MCH The Child 15.00 40.00
MCM The Child 15.00 40.00
MGC Greef Karga 8.00 20.00
MMC The Mandalorian 12.00 30.00
MMH The Mandalorian 12.00 30.00
MMM The Mandalorian 12.00 30.00
MOH Omera 8.00 20.00
MTC Toro Calican 10.00 25.00
MCDC Cara Dune 10.00 25.00
MCDH Cara Dune 10.00 25.00
MIGC IG-11 12.00 30.00
MMGC Moff Gideon 8.00 20.00

2020 Topps Star Wars The Mandalorian Season 1 Concept Art

COMPLETE SET (10) 8.00 20.00
COMMON CARD (CA1-CA10) 1.25 3.00
*RED/99: .75X TO 2X BASIC CARDS
*BRONZE/50: 1X TO 2.5X BASIC CARDS
STATED ODDS 1:7 HOBBY & RETAIL BLASTER

2020 Topps Star Wars The Mandalorian Season 1 Sourced Fabric Relics

COMMON MEM 30.00 75.00
*BRONZE/50: .5X TO 1.2X BASIC MEM
STATED ODDS 1:175 HOBBY EXCLUSIVE

2020 Topps Star Wars The Mandalorian Season 1 Tools of the Bounty Hunter

COMPLETE SET (10) 10.00 25.00
COMMON CARD (TB1-TB10) 1.50 4.00
*RED/99: .5X TO 1.2X BASIC CARDS
*BRONZE/50: .6X TO 1.5X BASIC CARDS
STATED ODDS 1:7 HOBBY & RETAIL BLASTER

2020 Topps Now Star Wars The Mandalorian Season 2

COMPLETE SET (40) 40.00 100.00

COMPLETE CH.9 SET (5) 8.00 20.00
COMPLETE CH.10 SET (5) 8.00 20.00
COMPLETE CH.11 SET (5) 8.00 20.00
COMPLETE CH.12 SET (5) 8.00 20.00
COMPLETE CH.13 SET (5) 8.00 20.00
COMPLETE CH.14 SET (5) 8.00 20.00
COMPLETE CH.15 SET (5) 8.00 20.00
COMPLETE CH.16 SET (5) 6.00 15.00
CHAPTER 9 COMMON (1-5) 2.50 6.00
CHAPTER 10 COMMON (6-10) 2.50 6.00
CHAPTER 11 COMMON (11-15) 2.50 6.00
CHAPTER 12 COMMON (16-20) 2.50 6.00
CHAPTER 13 COMMON (21-25) 2.50 6.00
CHAPTER 14 COMMON (26-30) 2.50 6.00
CHAPTER 15 COMMON (31-35) 2.50 6.00
CHAPTER 16 COMMON (36-40) 2.00 5.00
CHAPTER 9 PRINT RUN 1,527 SETS
CHAPTER 10 PRINT RUN 1,540 SETS
CHAPTER 11 PRINT RUN 1,459 SETS
CHAPTER 12 PRINT RUN 1,468 SETS
CHAPTER 13 PRINT RUN 1,982 SETS
CHAPTER 14 PRINT RUN 1,844 SETS
CHAPTER 15 PRINT RUN 1,582 SETS
CHAPTER 16 PRINT RUN 2,172 SETS
21 In Search of Information/1,982* 5.00 12.00
24 Ahsoka vs. the Magistrate/1,982* 4.00 10.00

2021 Topps Star Wars The Mandalorian Season 2

COMPLETE SET (100) 12.00 30.00
UNOPENED BOX (7 PACKS) 100.00 150.00
UNOPENED PACK (8 CARDS) 15.00 20.00
COMMON CARD (1-100) .25 .60
*BLUE: 1.2X TO 3X BASIC CARDS
*PURPLE: 2.5X TO 6X BASIC CARDS
*BRONZE/50: 8X TO 20X BASIC CARDS
*SILVER/25: 15X TO 40X BASIC CARDS

2021 Topps Star Wars The Mandalorian Season 2 Autographs

COMMON AUTO 10.00 25.00
*RED/99: SAME VALUE AS BASIC
*BRONZE/50: .5X TO 1.2X BASIC AUTOS
*SILVER/25: .6X TO 1.5X BASIC AUTOS
RANDOMLY INSERTED INTO PACKS
ACB Chris Bartlett 12.00 30.00
ACW Carl Weathers 150.00 300.00
AGE Giancarlo Esposito 60.00 120.00
AHS Horatio Sanz 30.00 75.00
ALS Leilani Shiu 15.00 40.00
AMR Misty Rosas 20.00 50.00
APA Philip Alexander 12.00 30.00
APL Paul Sun-Hyung Lee 30.00 75.00
APP Pedro Pascal 600.00 1200.00
ASK Simon Kassianides 30.00 75.00
ATM Temuera Morrison 150.00 300.00
ADLI Diana Lee Inosanto 20.00 50.00

2021 Topps Star Wars The Mandalorian Season 2 Characters

COMPLETE SET (14) 25.00
COMMON CARD (C1-C14) .75 2.00
*BRONZE/50: 3X TO 8X BASIC CARDS
*SILVER/25: 2X TO 5X BASIC CARDS
RANDOMLY INSERTED INTO PACKS
C1 The Mandalorian 1.50 4.00
C2 The Child 2.00 5.00
C4 Moff Gideon 1.25 3.00
C8 Cobb Vanth 1.50 4.00
C9 Dark Trooper 1.25 3.00
C11 Bo-Katan Kryze 1.50 4.00
C12 Koska Reeves 1.50 4.00
C13 Ahsoka Tano 3.00 8.00
C14 Boba Fett 1.50 4.00

2021 Topps Star Wars The Mandalorian Season 2 The Child

COMPLETE SET (12) 15.00 40.00
COMMON CARD (TC1-TC12) 2.00 5.00
*BRONZE/50: 2X TO 5X BASIC CARDS
*SILVER/25: 5X TO 12X BASIC CARDS
RANDOMLY INSERTED INTO PACKS

2021 Topps Star Wars The Mandalorian Season 2 Comic Covers

COMPLETE SET (7) 15.00 40.00
COMMON CARD (CC1-CC7) 3.00 8.00
*BRONZE/50: 2X TO 5X BASIC CARDS
*SILVER/25: 3X TO 8X BASIC CARDS
RANDOMLY INSERTED INTO PACKS

2021 Topps Star Wars The Mandalorian Season 2 Commemorative Metal Buttons

COMMON MEM 5.00 12.00
*RED/99: SAME VALUE AS BASIC
*BRONZE/50: .5X TO 1.2X BASIC CARDS
*SILVER/25: .6X TO 1.5X BASIC CARDS
RANDOMLY INSERTED INTO PACKS
MCCB The Child 10.00 25.00
MCCF The Child 10.00 25.00
MCMB The Mandalorian 12.00 30.00
MCMC The Mandalorian 12.00 30.00
MCMF The Mandalorian 12.00 30.00
MCBHW Bo-Katan Kryze 8.00 20.00
MCBMF Bo-Katan Kryze 8.00 20.00
MCBTW Bo-Katan Kryze 8.00 20.00
MCCCC The Child 10.00 25.00
MCCGC The Child 10.00 25.00
MCCMC The Child 10.00 25.00
MCCMF The Child 10.00 25.00
MCKHW Koska Reeves 10.00 25.00
MCKTW Koska Reeves 10.00 25.00
MCMGC The Mandalorian 12.00 30.00
MCMHW The Mandalorian 12.00 30.00
MCMMC The Mandalorian 12.00 30.00
MCMMF The Mandalorian 12.00 30.00
MCMTW The Mandalorian 12.00 30.00
MCPMF Ahsoka Tano 15.00 40.00

2021 Topps Star Wars The Mandalorian Season 2 Concept Art

COMPLETE SET (16) 20.00 50.00
COMMON CARD (CA1-CA16) 2.50 6.00
*BRONZE/50: .6X TO 1.5X BASIC CARDS
*SILVER/25: 2X TO 5X BASIC CARDS
RANDOMLY INSERTED INTO PACKS

2021 Topps Star Wars The Mandalorian Season 2 Prop Relics

STATED PRINT RUN 50 SER.#'d SETS
PRAF The Armorer/Razor Crest 200.00 400.00
PRCR The Child/Razor Crest 350.00 700.00
PRKR Kuiil/Razor Crest
PRMF The Mandalorian/Chimney 250.00 500.00
PRMR The Mandalorian/Chimney 250.00 500.00

2021 Topps Star Wars The Mandalorian Season 2 Sourced Fabric Relics

COMMON MEM 50.00 100.00
*BRONZE/50: .5X TO 1.2X BASIC MEM
*SILVER/25: .6X TO 1.5 BASIC MEM
STATED PRINT RUN 99 SER.#'d SETS
FRM Mythrol/Jacket 50.00 100.00
FRAA Ahsoka Tano/Pants 100.00 200.00
FRAB Ahsoka Tano/Arm Wraps 125.00 250.00
FRAC Ahsoka Tano/Body Suit 125.00 250.00
FRGG Gamorrean Guard/Shirt 50.00 100.00
FRMG Magistrate Morgan Elsbeth/Body Suit 60.00 120.00

2020 Topps Star Wars The Mandalorian Season 2 Trailer Set

COMPLETE SET (7) 15.00 40.00
COMMON CARD (1-7) 4.00 10.00
STATED PRINT RUN 1,482 SETS
NNO A Curious Figure Watches 4.00 10.00
NNO A Tusken Raider Spots Razor Crest 4.00 10.00
NNO Landing on a Mysterious Planet 4.00 10.00
NNO Scout Trooper in Pursuit 4.00 10.00
NNO So I've Heard 4.00 10.00
NNO The Child Surveys the Situation 4.00 10.00
NNO Mandalorian
The Child Inspect the Location 4.00 10.00

2023 Topps Now Star Wars The Mandalorian Season 3

COMPLETE SET (40)
COMPLETE CH.17 SET (5) 10.00 25.00
COMPLETE CH.18 SET (5) 10.00 25.00
COMPLETE CH.19 SET (5) 10.00 25.00
COMPLETE CH.20 SET (5) 10.00 25.00
COMPLETE CH.21 SET (5) 10.00 25.00
COMPLETE CH.22 SET (5) 10.00 25.00
COMPLETE CH.23 SET (5) 10.00 25.00
COMPLETE CH.24 SET (5) 10.00 25.00
COMMON CH.17 (1-5) 3.00 8.00
COMMON CH.18 (6-10) 3.00 8.00
COMMON CH.19 (11-15) 3.00 8.00
COMMON CH.20 (16-20) 3.00 8.00
COMMON CH.21 (21-25) 3.00 8.00
COMMON CH.22 (26-30) 3.00 8.00
COMMON CH.23 (31-35) 3.00 8.00
COMMON CH.24 (36-40) 3.00 8.00
*BLUE/49: .6X TO 1.5X BASIC CARDS
CHAPTER 17 PRINT RUN 901 SETS
CHAPTER 18 PRINT RUN 829 SETS
CHAPTER 19 PRINT RUN 802 SETS
CHAPTER 20 PRINT RUN 806 SETS
CHAPTER 21 PRINT RUN 703 SETS
CHAPTER 22 PRINT RUN 899 SETS
CHAPTER 23 PRINT RUN
CHAPTER 24 PRINT RUN

2023 Topps Star Wars The Mandalorian Season 3 Trailer Set

COMPLETE SET (5) 12.00 30.00
COMMON CARD (1-5) 4.00 10.00
*BLUE/49: 1.2X TO 3X BASIC CARDS

2021 Topps UK Star Wars The Mandalorian Seasons 1 and 2

COMPLETE SET (156) 15.00 40.00
UNOPENED PREMIUM BOX (1 PACK)
UNOPENED PREMIUM PACK (100 CARDS)
UNOPENED DISPLAY BOX (10 PACKS)
UNOPENED DISPLAY PACK (24 CARDS)
COMMON S1 CARD (1-78) .20 .50
COMMON S2 CARD (79-156) .20 .50

2021 Topps UK Star Wars The Mandalorian Seasons 1 and 2 Aliens and Creatures

COMPLETE SET (10) 5.00 12.00
COMMON CARD (AC1-AC10) .75 2.00
RANDOMLY INSERTED INTO PACKS

2021 Topps UK Star Wars The Mandalorian Seasons 1 and 2 Characters

COMPLETE SET (25) 15.00 40.00
COMMON CARD (C1-C25) .75 2.00
*YELLOW: .5X TO 1.2X BASIC CARDS
*GREEN/299: .6X TO 1.5X BASIC CARDS
*BLUE/99: 1.2X TO 3X BASIC CARDS
*PURPLE/50: 2X TO 5X BASIC CARDS
STATED ODDS 1:4
C1 The Mandalorian 1.50 4.00
C2 The Child 2.00 5.00
C15 The Mandalorian 1.50 4.00
C16 The Child 2.00 5.00
C22 Bo-Katan Kryze 1.25 3.00
C24 Ahsoka Tano 2.00 5.00
C25 Boba Fett 1.25 3.00

2021 Topps UK Star Wars The Mandalorian Seasons 1 and 2 Comic Covers

COMPLETE SET (6) 4.00 10.00
COMMON CARD (CC1-CC6) 1.00 2.50
RANDOMLY INSERTED INTO PACKS

2021 Topps UK Star Wars The Mandalorian Seasons 1 and 2 Concept Art

COMPLETE SET (18) 10.00 25.00
COMMON CARD (CA1-CA18) 1.25 3.00
RANDOMLY INSERTED INTO PACKS

2021 Topps UK Star Wars The Mandalorian Seasons 1 and 2 Crystal Cards

COMPLETE SET (6) 40.00 100.00
COMMON CARD (CR1-CR6) 6.00 15.00
STATED ODDS 1:12
CR1 Bo-Katan Kryze 10.00 25.00
CR2 The Mandalorian 12.00 30.00
CR3 The Child 15.00 40.00
CR5 Ahsoka Tano 15.00 40.00

2021 Topps UK Star Wars The Mandalorian Seasons 1 and 2 Tools of the Bounty Hunter

COMPLETE SET (10) 5.00 12.00
COMMON CARD (TB1-TB10) .75 2.00
RANDOMLY INSERTED INTO PACKS

1995 Topps Star Wars Mastervisions

COMPLETE BOXED SET (36) 10.00 25.00
COMMON CARD (1-36) .30 .75

1995 Topps Star Wars Mastervisions Promos

COMMON CARD .75 2.00
P2 Luke on Hoth 1.25 3.00
(Star Wars Galaxy Magazine Exclusive)

2015 Star Wars Masterwork

COMPLETE SET w/o SP (50) 60.00 120.00
UNOPENED BOX (4 MINIBOXES)
UNOPENED MINIBOX (5 CARDS)
COMMON CARD (1-50) 2.00 5.00
COMMON CARD (51-75) 5.00 12.00
*BLUE/299: .5X TO 1.2X BASIC CARDS
*BLUE SP/299: .2X TO .50X BASIC CARDS
*SILVER/99: .75X TO 2X BASIC CARDS
*SILVER SP/99: .3X TO .80X BASIC CARDS
*GREEN/50: 1.2X TO 3X BASIC CARDS
*GREEN SP/50: .5X TO 1.2X BASIC CARDS

2015 Star Wars Masterwork Autographs

COMMON AUTO 8.00 20.00
STATED ODDS 1:4
NNO Alan Harris 10.00 25.00
NNO Amy Allen 12.00 30.00
NNO Angus MacInnes 10.00 25.00
NNO Anthony Daniels 120.00 250.00
NNO Ashley Eckstein 50.00 125.00
NNO Billy Dee Williams 100.00 200.00
NNO Carrie Fisher 600.00 1000.00
NNO Chris Parsons 10.00 25.00
NNO Dermot Crowley 10.00 25.00
NNO Dickey Beer 8.00 20.00
NNO Gerald Home 10.00 25.00
NNO Harrison Ford 1800.00 3000.00
NNO James Earl Jones 300.00 450.00
NNO Jeremy Bulloch 20.00 50.00
NNO Jesse Jensen 10.00 25.00
NNO John Morton 15.00 40.00
NNO John Ratzenberger 12.00 30.00
NNO Julian Glover 12.00 30.00
NNO Kenneth Colley 10.00 25.00
NNO Kenny Baker 150.00 300.00

NNO Mark Hamill 400.00 750.00
NNO Michonne Bourriague 10.00 25.00
NNO Mike Quinn 12.00 30.00
NNO Oliver Ford Davies 10.00 25.00
NNO Orli Shoshan 10.00 25.00
NNO Pam Rose 10.00 25.00
NNO Paul Brooke 12.00 30.00
NNO Peter Mayhew 75.00 150.00
NNO Phil Eason 10.00 25.00
NNO Rusty Goffe 12.00 30.00
NNO Tim Rose 15.00 40.00
NNO Wayne Pygram 10.00 25.00

2015 Star Wars Masterwork Companions

COMPLETE SET (10) 25.00 60.00
COMMON CARD (C1-C10) 10.00 10.00
*RAINBOW/299: .6X TO 1.5X BASIC CARDS
*CANVAS/99: 1X TO 2.5X BASIC CARDS
*WOOD/50: 1.2X TO 3X BASIC CARDS
*CLEAR ACE./25: 1.5X TO 4X BASIC CARDS
C1 Han Solo and Chewbacca 6.00 15.00
C2 Luke and Leia 6.00 15.00
C3 Vader and Palpatine 5.00 12.00
C5 C-3PO and R2-D2 5.00 12.00
C8 R2-D2 and Luke Skywalker 5.00 12.00
C10 Boba Fett and Jango Fett 5.00 12.00

2015 Star Wars Masterwork Defining Moments

COMPLETE SET (10) 25.00 60.00
COMMON CARD (DM1-DM10) 4.00 10.00
*RAINBOW/299: .6X TO 1.5X BASIC CARDS
*CANVAS/99: 1X TO 2.5X BASIC CARDS
*WOOD/50: 1.2X TO 3X BASIC CARDS
*CLEAR ACE./25: 1.5X TO 4X BASIC CARDS
DM1 Darth Vader 5.00 12.00
DM2 Luke Skywalker 5.00 12.00
DM3 Han Solo 8.00 20.00
DM4 Princess Leia Organa 5.00 12.00
DM7 Anakin Skywalker 5.00 12.00
DM8 Obi-Wan Kenobi 5.00 12.00
DM10 Chewbacca 5.00 12.00

2015 Star Wars Masterwork Return of the Jedi Bunker Relics Bronze

COMMON CARD 12.00 30.00
*SILVER/77: .75X TO 2X BASIC CARDS
CARDS 1, 2, 3, 4, 10, 12 SER.#'d TO 155
CARDS 5, 6, 7, 8, 9, 11 SER.#'d TO 255
1 Han Solo/155 20.00 50.00
2 Princess Leia Organa/155 20.00 50.00
3 Chewbacca/155 15.00 40.00
4 Luke Skywalker/155 25.00 60.00
10 Ewok (frame)/155 15.00 40.00
12 Han, Leia & Luke/155 20.00 50.00

2015 Star Wars Masterwork Scum and Villainy

COMPLETE SET (10) 25.00 60.00
COMMON CARD (SV1-SV10) 4.00 10.00
*RAINBOW/299: 1.5X TO 6X BASIC CARDS
*CANVAS/99: 1X TO 2.5X BASIC CARDS
*WOOD/50: 1.2X TO 3X BASIC CARDS
*CLEAR ACE./25: 1.5X TO 4X BASIC CARDS
SV1 Boba Fett 6.00 15.00
SV2 Jabba the Hutt 5.00 12.00
SV4 General Grievous 6.00 15.00
SV5 Jango Fett 5.00 12.00
SV8 Ponda Baba 6.00 15.00
SV9 Bossk 5.00 12.00
SV10 Tusken Raider 6.00 15.00

2015 Star Wars Masterwork Stamp Relics

COMMON CARD 20.00 50.00
STATED ODDS 1:CASE
NNO Anakin vs. Obi-Wan 50.00 100.00
NNO Ben (Obi-Wan) Kenobi 30.00 80.00
NNO Boba Fett 60.00 120.00
NNO C-3PO 25.00 60.00
NNO Darth Maul 50.00 100.00
NNO Darth Vader 30.00 80.00
NNO Emperor Palpatine 30.00 80.00
NNO Han Solo and Chewbacca 50.00 100.00
NNO Luke Skywalker 30.00 80.00
NNO The Millennium Falcon 50.00 100.00
NNO X-Wing Fighter 30.00 80.00

2015 Star Wars Masterwork Weapons Lineage Medallions

COMPLETE SET (30) 250.00 500.00
COMMON CARD 8.00 20.00
*SILVER/50: 1.2X TO 3X BASIC CARDS
STATED ODDS 1:6
NNO Anakin Skywalker 10.00 25.00
Mace Windu's Lightsaber
NNO Anakin Skywalker 12.00 30.00
Anakin Skywalker's Lightsaber
NNO B. Fett's Blaster 10.00 25.00
NNO B. Fett's Blaster 12.00 30.00
NNO Darth Maul's Lightsaber 10.00 25.00
NNO Vader 10.00 25.00
Vader's Lightsaber
NNO Vader 10.00 25.00
Vader's Lightsaber
NNO Vader 10.00 25.00
Vader's Lightsaber
NNO Vader Solo's Blaster 12.00 30.00
NNO Darth Vader 15.00 40.00
Luke Skywalker's Lightsaber
NNO Han Solo 12.00 30.00
Han Solo's Blaster
NNO Han Solo 12.00 30.00
Han Solo's Blaster
NNO Han Solo 15.00 40.00
Luke Skywalker's Lightsaber
NNO Luke Skywalker 10.00 25.00
Luke Skywalker's Lightsaber
NNO Luke Skywalker 10.00 25.00
Luke Skywalker's Lightsaber
NNO Mace Windu 10.00 25.00
Mace Windu's Lightsaber
NNO Princess Leia Organa 10.00 25.00
Stormtrooper Blaster Rifle
NNO Leia 12.00 30.00
Leia's Blaster
NNO R2-D2 10.00 25.00
Luke's Lightsaber
NNO Stormtrooper 12.00 30.00
Stormtrooper Blaster Rifle
NNO Yoda 15.00 40.00
Yoda's Lightsaber

2016 Star Wars Masterwork

COMPLETE SET W/SP (75) 200.00 400.00
COMPLETE SET W/O SP (50) 30.00 80.00
UNOPENED BOX (4 PACKS) 150.00 200.00
UNOPENED PACK (5 CARDS) 50.00 60.00
COMMON CARD (1-75) 2.00 5.00
COMMON SP (51-75) 4.00 10.00
*BLUE MET.: SAME VALUE 2.00 5.00
*BLUE MET.SP: SAME VALUE 4.00 10.00
*SILVER MET./99: .75X TO 1.5X BASIC CARDS3.00 8.00
*SILVER MET.SP/99: .30X TO .75X BASIC CARDS 3.00 8.00
*GREEN MET./50: 1.2X TO 3X BASIC CARDS6.00 15.00
*GREEN MET.SP/50: .6X TO 1.5X BASIC CARDS 6.00 15.00
*LTSBR PURP./25: 1.5X TO 4X BASIC CARDS8.00 20.00
*LTSBR PURP.SP/25: .75X TO 2X BASIC CARDS 8.00 20.00
66 Han Solo SP 6.00 15.00
71 Rey SP 8.00 20.00

2016 Star Wars Masterwork Alien Identification Guide

COMPLETE SET (10) 20.00 50.00
COMMON CARD (AI1-AI10) 2.50 6.00
*FOIL/299: .6X TO 1.5X BASIC CARDS 3.00 8.00
*CANVAS/99: .75X TO 2X BASIC CARDS 5.00 12.00
*WOOD/50: 1X TO 2.5X BASIC CARDS 6.00 15.00
STATED ODDS 1:4

2016 Star Wars Masterwork Autographs

COMMON CARD 6.00 15.00
*FOIL/50: .6X TO 1.5X BASIC CARDS
*CANVAS/25: .75X TO 2X BASIC CARDS
5 Andy Serkis 80.00 150.00
8 Ashley Eckstein 75.00 200.00
11 Caroline Blakiston 8.00 20.00
14 Clive Revill 12.00 30.00
15 Corey Dee Williams 8.00 20.00
19 David Ankrum 8.00 20.00
20 David Barclay 8.00 20.00
24 Dickey Beer 10.00 25.00
34 Jeremy Bulloch 15.00 40.00
39 John Coppinger 8.00 20.00
47 Mark Dodson 10.00 25.00
50 Matthew Wood 8.00 20.00
55 Mike Edmonds 8.00 20.00
56 Mike Quinn 8.00 20.00
65 Sam Witwer 8.00 20.00
73 Tim Dry 8.00 20.00
74 Tim Rose 8.00 20.00
75 Tiya Sircar 8.00 20.00

2016 Star Wars Masterwork Autographs Canvas

*CANVAS/25: .75X TO 2X BASIC CARDS
STATED ODDS 1:25
STATED PRINT RUN 25 SER.#'d SETS
1 Adam Driver 400.00 800.00
5 Andy Serkis 150.00 300.00
7 Anthony Daniels 80.00 150.00
10 Billy Dee Williams
12 Carrie Fisher 300.00 600.00
16 Daisy Ridley 1200.00 2000.00
23 Denis Lawson 25.00 60.00
26 Freddie Prinze Jr. 30.00 80.00
29 Greg Grunberg 12.00 30.00
31 Harrison Ford/1
32 Hugh Quarshie
38 John Boyega
42 Julian Glover
43 Keisha Castle-Hughes
48 Mark Hamill 250.00 500.00
52 Michael Carter 12.00 30.00
60 Peter Mayhew
61 Ray Park
79 Warwick Davis 15.00 40.00

2016 Star Wars Masterwork Autographs Foil

*FOIL/50: .6X TO 1.5X BASIC CARDS
STATED ODDS 1:30
STATED PRINT RUN 50 SER.#'d SETS
3 Alan Harris
7 Anthony Daniels 50.00 100.00
12 Carrie Fisher
14 Clive Revill
15 Corey Dee Williams
19 David Ankrum
20 David Barclay
23 Denis Lawson
25 Femi Taylor
26 Freddie Prinze Jr.
27 Garrick Hagon
28 George Takei 15.00 40.00
29 Greg Grunberg 10.00 25.00
32 Hugh Quarshie 10.00 25.00
33 Jack Klaff
38 John Boyega 120.00 250.00
40 John Morton
41 John Ratzenberger
43 Keisha Castle-Hughes
44 Kenneth Colley
47 Mark Dodson
51 Mercedes Ngoh
52 Michael Carter
59 Paul Blake
60 Peter Mayhew 30.00 80.00
61 Ray Park
67 Sean Crawford
76 Toby Philpott
79 Warwick Davis

2016 Star Wars Masterwork Dual Autographs

STATED ODDS 1:4,658
NNO C.Fisher/K.Baker
NNO D.Barclay/T.Philpott 25.00 60.00
NNO I.McDiarmid/C.Revill
NNO J.Blake/D.Bowers 20.00 50.00
NNO M.Hamill/D.Ridley
NNO M.Hamill/K.Baker
NNO W.Pygram/S.Stanton 15.00 40.00

2016 Star Wars Masterwork Great Rivalries

COMPLETE SET (10) 15.00 40.00
COMMON CARD (GR1-GR10) 2.50 6.00
*FOIL/299: .6X TO 1.5X BASIC CARDS
*CANVAS/99: .75X TO 2X BASIC CARDS
*WOOD/50: 1X TO 2.5X BASIC CARDS
STATED ODDS 1:2

2016 Star Wars Masterwork Medallion Relics

COMMON CARD 5.00 12.00
*SILVER/99: .6X TO 1.5X BASIC CARDS 8.00 20.00
*GOLD/10: 1.5X TO 4X BASIC CARDS 20.00 50.00
STATED ODDS 1:7
NNO Han Solo 6.00 15.00
Hoth
NNO Han Solo 6.00 15.00
Starkiller Base
NNO Han Solo 6.00 15.00
Yavin
NNO Kylo Ren
Starkiller Base
NNO Rey 6.00 15.00
Starkiller Base

2016 Star Wars Masterwork Show of Force

COMPLETE SET (10) 25.00 60.00
COMMON CARD (SF1-SF10) 3.00 8.00
*FOIL/299: .6X TO 1.5X BASIC CARDS 5.00 12.00
*CANVAS/99: .75X TO 2X BASIC CARDS 6.00 15.00
*WOOD/50: 1X TO 2.5X BASIC CARDS 8.00 20.00
STATED ODDS 1:4
SF10 Rey 4.00 10.00

2016 Star Wars Masterwork Stamp Relics

COMPLETE SET (12) 100.00 200.00
COMMON CARD 8.00 20.00
*BRONZE/99: .6X TO 1.5X BASIC CARDS12.00 30.00
*SILVER/50: .75X TO 2X BASIC CARDS 15.00 40.00
STATED ODDS 1:13
STATED PRINT RUN 249 SER.#'d SETS
NNO Han Solo 10.00 25.00
NNO Rey 12.00 30.00

2017 Star Wars Masterwork

COMMON CARD (1-75) 2.50 6.00
COMMON SP (76-100) 5.00 12.00
*BLUE: .5X TO 1.25X BASIC CARDS 3.00 8.00
*GREEN/99: .6X TO 1.5X BASIC CARDS 4.00 10.00
*PURPLE/50: .75X TO 2X BASIC CARDS 5.00 12.00
*GOLD/25: 1X TO 2.5X BASIC CARDS 6.00 15.00

2017 Star Wars Masterwork Adventures of R2-D2

COMMON CARD (AR1-AR10) 2.50 6.00
*RAINBOW FOIL: .5X TO 1.25X BASIC CARDS3.00 8.00
*CANVAS: .6X TO 1.5X BASIC CARDS 4.00 10.00
*WOOD/50: .75X TO 2X BASIC CARDS 5.00 12.00

STAR WARS

STAR WARS

2017 Star Wars Masterwork Autographs

COMMON CARD	6.00	15.00
SILVER FRAMED/10>: UNPRICED DUE TO SCARCITY		
NNO Adam Driver (horizontal)		
NNO Adam Driver (vertical)		
NNO Alan Tudyk	50.00	100.00
NNO Andy Serkis		
NNO Ashley Eckstein	40.00	100.00
NNO Ben Daniels	8.00	20.00
NNO Billy Dee Williams		
NNO Brian Herring	15.00	40.00
NNO Clive Revill	8.00	20.00
NNO Daisy Ridley		
NNO Dee Bradley Baker	10.00	25.00
NNO Derek Arnold	8.00	20.00
NNO Donnie Yen	60.00	120.00
NNO Felicity Jones (horizontal)		
NNO Felicity Jones (vertical)		
NNO Forest Whitaker (horizontal)		
NNO Forest Whitaker (vertical)		
NNO Freddie Prinze Jr.		
NNO Gwendoline Christie		
NNO Harrison Ford		
NNO Hayden Christensen	150.00	300.00
NNO Ian McDiarmid		
NNO Ian Whyte	10.00	25.00
NNO Jeremy Bulloch	15.00	40.00
NNO John Boyega (horizontal)		
NNO John Boyega (vertical)	60.00	120.00
NNO Julian Glover	12.00	30.00
NNO Lars Mikkelsen	25.00	60.00
NNO Mark Hamill		
NNO Mary Elizabeth McGlynn	12.00	30.00
NNO Matt Lanter	15.00	40.00
NNO Matthew Wood		
NNO Phil LaMarr	8.00	20.00
NNO Ray Park		
NNO Riz Ahmed		
NNO Robbie Daymond	10.00	25.00
NNO Sam Witwer	10.00	25.00
NNO Sarah Michelle Gellar		
NNO Temuera Morrison	25.00	60.00
NNO Tiya Sircar	8.00	20.00
NNO Tom Baker		
NNO Valene Kane	25.00	60.00
NNO Warwick Davis	10.00	25.00
NNO Zarene Dallas	8.00	20.00

2017 Star Wars Masterwork Droid Medallion Relics

COMMON CARD	5.00	12.00
*SILVER/40: .5X TO 1.2X BASIC RELICS	6.00	15.00
*GOLD/25: .6X TO 1.5X BASIC RELICS	8.00	20.00
STATED PRINT RUN 150 SER.#'d SETS		

2017 Star Wars Masterwork Dual Autographs

NNO A.Graves/C.Taber	20.00	50.00
NNO A.Daniels/K.Baker		
NNO B.Herring/K.Baker		
NNO C.Fisher/K.Baker		
NNO D.Barclay/F.Taylor	15.00	40.00
NNO F.Jones/A.Tudyk		
NNO F.Whitaker/R.Ahmed		
NNO F.Prinze Jr./S.M.Gellar		
NNO G.Christie/J.Boyega		
NNO H.Christensen/K.Baker		
NNO H.Christensen/M.Wood		
NNO I.McDiarmid/H.Christensen		
NNO I.Uwais/C.Rahman	12.00	30.00
NNO J.Isaacs/T.Gray	20.00	50.00
NNO J.Ratzenberger/A.MacInnes	12.00	30.00
NNO M.Hamill/H.Christensen		
NNO M.Hamill/K.Baker		
NNO M.Salenger/N.Futterman	12.00	30.00
NNO P.Kasey/S.Stanton	12.00	30.00
NNO R.Marshall/K.Fleetwood		
NNO S.Witwer/A.Wilkinson	15.00	40.00
NNO T.Morrison/D.Logan	20.00	50.00
NNO T.Cole/S.Grube		

2017 Star Wars Masterwork Evolution of the Rebel Alliance

COMMON CARD (LP1-LP10)	2.50	6.00
*RAINBOW FOIL/249: .5X TO 1.25X BASIC CARDS	3.00	8.00
*CANVAS/99: .6X TO 1.5X BASIC CARDS	4.00	10.00
*WOOD/50: .75X TO 2X BASIC CARDS	5.00	12.00

2017 Star Wars Masterwork Film Strips

COMMON CARD (FCR1-FCR40)	10.00	25.00

2017 Star Wars Masterwork Hall of Heroes

COMPLETE SET (10)	12.00	30.00
COMMON CARD (HH1-HH10)	3.00	8.00
*RAINBOW FOIL: .5X TO 1.2X BASIC CARDS	4.00	10.00
*CANVAS: .6X TO 1.5X BASIC CARDS	5.00	12.00

2017 Star Wars Masterwork Source Material Jumbo Swatch Relics

COMMON CARD	25.00	60.00
JRCAR Admiral Ackbar Resistance Uniform	30.00	75.00
JRCGE Galen Erso Farmer Disguise	60.00	120.00
JRCGF General Hux First Order Uniform	50.00	100.00
JRCRD Rey Desert Tunic	200.00	400.00
JRCRO Rey Outer Garment	150.00	300.00

2018 Star Wars Masterwork

COMPLETE SET W/SP (125)		
COMPLETE SET W/O SP (100)		
UNOPENED BOX (4 PACKS)	150.00	200.00
UNOPENED PACK (5 CARDS)	40.00	50.00
COMMON CARD (1-100)	2.50	6.00
COMMON SP (101-125)	6.00	15.00
*BLUE: .5X TO 1.2X BASIC CARDS		
*GREEN/99: .6X TO 1.5X BASIC CARDS		
*PURPLE/50: .75X TO 2X BASIC CARDS		
101 Luke Skywalker SP	8.00	20.00
102 Princess Leia Organa SP	12.00	30.00
103 Rey SP	15.00	40.00
104 Finn SP	10.00	25.00
105 Obi-Wan Kenobi SP	10.00	25.00
106 Anakin Skywalker SP	10.00	25.00
108 Darth Vader SP	8.00	20.00
109 Darth Maul SP	8.00	20.00
110 Boba Fett SP	12.00	30.00
111 Han Solo SP	12.00	30.00
113 Lando Calrissian SP	10.00	25.00
114 Saw Gerrera SP	10.00	25.00
115 Jyn Erso SP	12.00	30.00
116 Captain Cassian Andor SP	10.00	25.00
119 Kylo Ren SP	10.00	25.00
121 Ahsoka Tano SP	8.00	20.00
124 Bo-Katan Kryze SP	8.00	20.00

2018 Star Wars Masterwork Autographs

COMMON AUTO	6.00	15.00
*BLUE FOIL/99: .5X TO 1.2X BASIC AUTOS		
AAE Ashley Eckstein	40.00	100.00
AAK Andrew Kishino	8.00	20.00
ABS Brent Spiner	12.00	30.00
ACC Cavin Cornwall	12.00	30.00
ADB David Barclay	10.00	25.00
ADL Denis Lawson	8.00	20.00
ADM Daniel Mays	8.00	20.00
AGH Guy Henry	8.00	20.00
AHW Howie Weed	12.00	30.00
AJB Jeremy Bulloch	15.00	40.00
AJV Jimmy Vee	10.00	25.00
ALD Laura Dern	100.00	200.00
ALM Lars Mikkelsen	10.00	25.00
AML Matt Lanter	8.00	20.00
AMW Matthew Wood	10.00	25.00
ANC Nathalie Cuzner	8.00	20.00
ARN Robert Nairne	8.00	20.00
ASW Simon Williamson	12.00	30.00
ATW Tom Wilton	8.00	20.00
AJAT James Arnold Taylor	10.00	25.00
AJSP Jason Spisak	8.00	20.00
ASWT Sam Witwer	12.00	30.00

2018 Star Wars Masterwork Commemorative Vehicle Patches

COMMON PATCH	4.00	10.00
*PURPLE/50: .6X TO 1.5X BASIC PATCHES		
STATED PRINT RUN 175 SER.#'d SETS		
MPBHF Slave I/Boba Fett	8.00	20.00
MPGEA Chimaera/Grand Admiral Thrawn	6.00	15.00
MPGEK Chimaera/Kassius Konstantine	6.00	15.00
MPGEM Krennic's Shuttle/Grand Moff Tarkin	6.00	15.00
MPGEP Chimaera/Governor Arihnda Pryce	5.00	12.00
MPGEV Star Destroyer/Darth Vader	5.00	12.00
MPGRB Radiant VII/Bail Organa	6.00	15.00
MPGRP Radiant VII/Padmé Amidala	8.00	20.00
MPJOA Anakin's Fighter/Anakin Skywalker	5.00	12.00
MPJOO Anakin's Fighter/Obi-Wan Kenobi	6.00	15.00
MPJOQ Anakin's Fighter/Qui-Gon Jinn	5.00	12.00
MPPSA The Ghost/Ahsoka Tano	5.00	12.00
MPPSE The Ghost/Ezra Bridger	5.00	12.00
MPPSH The Ghost/Hera Syndulla	5.00	12.00
MPPSZ The Ghost/Zeb Orrelios	6.00	15.00
MPRAB U-Wing/Bodhi Rook	5.00	12.00
MPRAH Y-Wing/Han Solo	12.00	30.00
MPRAJ U-Wing/Jyn Erso	5.00	12.00
MPRAK U-Wing/K-2SO	5.00	12.00
MPRAM U-Wing/Baze Malbus	6.00	15.00
MPRAP Y-Wing/Princess Leia Organa	8.00	20.00
MPRAR Y-Wing/R2-D2	5.00	12.00
MPRAS Y-Wing/Luke Skywalker	6.00	15.00
MPRMH The Millennium Falcon/Han Solo	10.00	25.00
MPRML The Millennium Falcon Lando Calrissian	5.00	12.00
MPRMN The Millennium Falcon/Nien Nunb	5.00	12.00
MPRMP The Millennium Falcon Princess Leia Organa	8.00	20.00
MPRMS The Millennium Falcon Luke Skywalker	6.00	15.00
MPTRF Black One/Finn	6.00	15.00
MPTRL Black One/General Leia Organa	8.00	20.00
MPTRR Black One/Rey	8.00	20.00

2018 Star Wars Masterwork Dual Autographs

DAAT R.Ahmed/A.Tudyk		
DABB K.Baker/D.Barclay		
DABH J.Boyega/B.Herring	75.00	150.00
DABO C.Blakiston/G.O'Reilly		
DABR E.Bauersfeld/K.Rotich	20.00	50.00
DABS J.Boyega/J.Suotamo	75.00	150.00
DACP H.Christensen/R.Park		
DACW A.Cook/I.Whyte		
DAGA S.M.Gellar/P.Anthony-Rodriguez		
DAGM G.Takei/M.Lanter		
DAJM F.Jones/B.Mendelsohn		
DALG K.Leung/G.Grunberg	15.00	40.00
DAMH B.Mendelsohn/G.Henry		
DAMM L.Mikkelsen/M.McGlynn	20.00	50.00
DAPW R.Park/M.Wood		
DARB D.Ridley/J.Boyega		
DASD M.Salenger/O.D'Abo	30.00	75.00
DATF J.A.Taylor/N.Futterman		
DAWQ B.D.Williams/M.Quinn		
DAWS S.Witwer/S.Stanton		

2018 Star Wars Masterwork History of the Jedi

COMPLETE SET (10)	10.00	25.00
COMMON CARD (HJ1-HJ10)	1.50	4.00
*RAINBOW/299: SAME VALUE AS BASIC		
*CANVAS/25: 1.2X TO 3X BASIC CARDS		
HJ1 Yoda	2.50	6.00
HJ2 Mace Windu	2.50	6.00
HJ4 Qui-Gon Jinn	2.00	5.00
HJ5 Obi-Wan Kenobi	2.00	5.00
HJ6 Anakin Skywalker	2.00	5.00
HJ9 Luke Skywalker	2.00	5.00
HJ10 Rey	3.00	8.00

2018 Star Wars Masterwork Powerful Partners

COMPLETE SET (8)	10.00	25.00
COMMON CARD (PP1-PP8)	1.50	4.00
*RAINBOW/299: SAME VALUE AS BASIC		
PP1 Han Solo & Chewbacca	2.50	6.00
PP3 Luke Skywalker & Princess Leia Organa	2.50	6.00
PP4 Darth Vader & Grand Moff Tarkin	2.50	6.00
PP6 Jyn Erso & Captain Cassian Andor	3.00	8.00
PP7 Rey & Finn	3.00	8.00
PP8 Finn & Rose Tico	2.00	5.00

2018 Star Wars Masterwork Source Material Fabric Swatches

JRGH General Hux Jacket Lining		
JRLP Luke Skywalker Pants		
JRLT Luke Skywalker Tunic	75.00	150.00
JRPD Poe Dameron Jacket Lining	100.00	200.00
JRRG Poe Dameron Shirt	50.00	100.00
JRRS Jyn Erso Poncho		
JRRT Rey Desert Tunic Sleeves	150.00	300.00
JRCRT Rose Tico Ground Crew Flightsuit Lining	100.00	200.00

2018 Star Wars Masterwork Stamp Relics

COMMON MEM	6.00	15.00
RANDOMLY INSERTED INTO PACKS		
SBF Finn	8.00	20.00
SBP Poe Dameron	8.00	20.00
SBR Rey	10.00	25.00
SCC Chewbacca	8.00	20.00
SCH Han Solo	8.00	20.00
SCP Princess Leia Organa	12.00	30.00
SKJ Jyn Erso	10.00	25.00
SKK K-2SO	12.00	30.00
SMH Han Solo	8.00	20.00
SMR Rey	8.00	20.00
SPR Rey	12.00	30.00
SRO Obi-Wan Kenobi	8.00	20.00
SRP Padmé Amidala	8.00	20.00
SSK Kylo Ren	10.00	25.00

2018 Star Wars Masterwork Super Weapons

COMPLETE SET (7)	8.00	20.00
COMMON CARD (SW1-SW7)	2.00	5.00
*RAINBOW/299: .5X TO 1.2X BASIC CARDS		
*CANVAS/25: 1.2X TO 3X BASIC CARDS		

2019 Star Wars Masterwork Promo

NYCC2019 Darth Maul	6.00	15.00

2019 Star Wars Masterwork

COMPLETE SET (100)	15.00	40.00
UNOPENED BOX (4 MINI BOXES)	300.00	450.00
UNOPENED MINI BOX (5 CARDS)	75.00	125.00
COMMON CARD (1-100)	.60	1.50
*BLUE: .75X TO 2X BASIC CARDS		
*GREEN/99: 1.5X TO 4X BASIC CARDS		
*PURPLE/50: 2.5X TO 6X BASIC CARDS		

2019 Star Wars Masterwork Autographs

COMMON AUTO	6.00	15.00
*BLUE/99: .5X TO 1.2X BASIC AUTOS		
*RAINBOW/50: .6X TO 1.5X BASIC AUTOS		
RANDOMLY INSERTED INTO PACKS		
AAE Ashley Eckstein	15.00	40.00
ACR Clive Revill	8.00	20.00
ACS Christopher Sean	10.00	25.00
ADT David Tennant	20.00	50.00
AFT Fred Tatasciore	8.00	20.00
AKK Katy Kartwheel	10.00	25.00
AKS Katee Sackhoff	15.00	40.00
ALL Lex Lang	10.00	25.00

ALM Lars Mikkelsen	8.00	20.00
AMA Mark Austin	20.00	50.00
AMP Michael Pennington	10.00	25.00
AMV Myrna Velasco	10.00	25.00
ANC Nazneen Contractor	8.00	20.00
ASL Scott Lawrence	12.00	30.00
AJAT James Arnold Taylor	8.00	20.00
AJBR Josh Brener	8.00	20.00
AJVM Jimmy Vee	8.00	20.00
ASIL Stephanie Silva	8.00	20.00

2019 Star Wars Masterwork Commemorative Artifact Medallions

COMMON MEM	3.00	8.00
*PURPLE/50: .5X TO 1.2X BASIC MEM		
RANDOMLY INSERTED INTO PACKS		
MCFR Finn	5.00	12.00
MCJK Jyn Erso	6.00	15.00
MCPR Paige Tico	4.00	10.00
MCRR Rose Tico	4.00	10.00
MCSD Han Solo	6.00	15.00
MCYN Yoda	6.00	15.00
MCASB Anakin Skywalker	5.00	12.00
MCGJK Galen Erso	5.00	12.00
MCHBH Han Solo	6.00	15.00
MCKSR Kylo Ren	6.00	15.00
MCLBH Luke Skywalker	8.00	20.00
MCLJK Lyra Erso	4.00	10.00
MCLSC Luke Skywalker	10.00	25.00
MCLSY Luke Skywalker	8.00	20.00
MCMRB Grand Moff Tarkin	4.00	10.00
MCMSC Darth Maul	5.00	12.00
MCOBH Obi-Wan Kenobi	5.00	12.00
MCPDN Poe Dameron	4.00	10.00
MCQAB Queen Amidala	6.00	15.00
MCR2C R2-D2	5.00	12.00
MCR2Y R2-D2	5.00	12.00
MCRLC Rey	8.00	20.00
MCRSR Rey	8.00	20.00
MCSSB Sabe	5.00	12.00
MCVSC Darth Vader	6.00	15.00

2019 Star Wars Masterwork The Dark Side

COMPLETE SET (10)	8.00	20.00
COMMON CARD (DS1-DS10)	1.25	3.00
*RAINBOW/299: .6X TO 1.5X BASIC CARDS		
*CANVAS/25: 1X TO 2.5X BASIC CARDS		
RANDOMLY INSERTED INTO PACKS		

2019 Star Wars Masterwork Defining Moments

COMPLETE SET (25)	12.00	30.00
COMMON CARD (DM1-DM25))	1.00	2.50
*RAINBOW/299: 1X TO 2.5X BASIC CARDS		
*CANVAS/25: 2.5X TO 6X BASIC CARDS		
RANDOMLY INSERTED INTO PACKS		

2019 Star Wars Masterwork Heroes of the Rebellion

COMPLETE SET (15)	8.00	20.00
COMMON CARD (HR1-HR15)	1.00	2.50
*RAINBOW/299: .75X TO 2X BASIC CARDS		
*CANVAS/25: 1.5X TO 4X BASIC CARDS		
RANDOMLY INSERTED INTO PACKS		

2020 Topps Star Wars Masterwork

COMPLETE SET (100)	15.00	40.00
UNOPENED BOX (4 MINIBOXES)	300.00	450.00
UNOPENED MINIBOX (5 CARDS)	75.00	110.00
COMMON CARD (1-100)	.60	1.50
*BLUE: .75X TO 2X BASIC CARDS		
*GREEN/99: 1.5X TO 4X BASIC CARDS		
*PURPLE/50: 2.5X TO 6X BASIC CARDS		

2020 Topps Star Wars Masterwork Autographs

COMMON AUTO	6.00	15.00
*BLUE/99: .5X TO 1.2X BASIC AUTOS		
*RAINBOW/50: .6X TO 1.5X BASIC AUTOS		
AAB Ahmed Best	20.00	50.00
AAH Amanda Hale	8.00	20.00
ACM Cameron Monaghan	20.00	50.00
ADL Denis Lawson	10.00	25.00
ADW Debra Wilson	8.00	20.00
AEK Erin Kellyman	20.00	50.00
AES Emily Swallow	50.00	100.00
AGE Giancarlo Esposito	75.00	150.00
AGG Greg Grunberg	10.00	25.00
AJG Janina Gavankar	15.00	40.00
AJT John Tui	8.00	20.00
ALW Leeanna Walsman	12.00	30.00
AML Misty Lee	10.00	25.00
AMW Matthew Wood	20.00	50.00
ANA Naomi Ackie	15.00	40.00
AOA Omid Abtahi	12.00	30.00
APB Paul Blake	10.00	25.00
AVK Valene Kane	10.00	25.00
AADW Annabelle Davis EXCH	10.00	25.00
AAEA Ashley Eckstein	50.00	125.00
ADBB Dee Bradley Baker	12.00	30.00
AHCT Hermione Corfield	15.00	40.00
ALRB Lynn Robertson Bruce	10.00	25.00

2020 Topps Star Wars Masterwork Autographs Blue Foil

STATED PRINT RUN 99 SER.#'d SETS		
ADY Donnie Yen	60.00	120.00
ASW Sam Witwer	20.00	50.00
ADMB Dominic Monaghan	15.00	40.00

2020 Topps Star Wars Masterwork Autographs Rainbow Foil

STATED PRINT RUN 50 SER.#'d SETS		
AWH Werner Herzog	100.00	200.00

2020 Topps Star Wars Masterwork Behind-the-Scenes Autographed Pen Relics

NNO Ben Burtt
NNO Jake Lunt Davies
NNO Neal Scanlan
NNO Lee Towersey

2020 Topps Star Wars Masterwork Behind-the-Scenes Autographs

COMMON AUTO	15.00	40.00
*RAINBOW/50: .5X TO 1.2X BASIC AUTOS		
STATED PRINT RUN 99 SER.#'d SETS		
BSABB Ben Burtt	30.00	75.00
BSALT Lee Towersey	25.00	60.00
BSANS Neal Scanlan	25.00	60.00

2020 Topps Star Wars Masterwork Commemorative Dog Tag Medallions

COMMON MEM	4.00	10.00
*PURPLE/50: .5X TO 1.2X BASIC MEM		
STATED PRINT RUN 99 SER.#'d SETS		
DTEB Sandtrooper	5.00	12.00
DTED Commander Daine Jir	5.00	12.00
DTES Stormtrooper	6.00	15.00
DTET Grand Moff Tarkin	6.00	15.00
DTEV Darth Vader	10.00	25.00
DTEX Death Star Trooper	8.00	20.00
DTFB Biggs Darklighter	5.00	12.00
DTFD Biggs Darklighter	5.00	12.00
DTFW Wedge Antilles	8.00	20.00
DTJC Chewbacca	6.00	15.00
DTJH Han Solo	10.00	25.00
DTJL Luke Skywalker	12.00	30.00
DTJP Princess Leia Organa	10.00	25.00
DTJR R2-D2	6.00	15.00
DTRD Garven Dreis	6.00	15.00
DTRJ John D. Branon	5.00	12.00
DTRW Wedge Antilles	8.00	20.00
DTSD Darth Vader	10.00	25.00
DTSG Greedo	5.00	12.00
DTST Stormtrooper	6.00	15.00
DTSV Jon "Dutch" Vander	5.00	12.00
DTXL Luke Skywalker	12.00	30.00
DTXW Wedge Antilles	8.00	20.00

2020 Topps Star Wars Masterwork Dual Autographs

STATED PRINT RUN 50 SER.#'d SETS		
DADA H.Durst/D.Arnold	15.00	40.00
DADK H.Durst/I.Kenny	15.00	40.00
DADM R.Downes/V.Marshall	30.00	75.00
DAHP A.Harris/C.Parsons	60.00	120.00
DAMW T.Morrison/L.Walsman	150.00	400.00
DASL S.Smart/C.Louise	12.00	30.00

2020 Topps Star Wars Masterwork Empire Strikes Back 40th Anniversary

COMPLETE SET (25)	30.00	75.00
COMMON CARD (ESB1-ESB25)	2.00	5.00
*RAINBOW/299: .5X TO 1.2X BASIC CARDS		

2020 Topps Star Wars Masterwork Sourced Fabric Dual Relics

COMPLETE SET (16)		
COMMON MEM	30.00	75.00
DCBD Beckett/Dryden Vos	100.00	200.00
DCBQ Beckett/Qi'ra	100.00	200.00
DCDQ Dryden Vos/Qi'ra	125.00	250.00
DCFR Finn/Rose Tico	50.00	100.00
DCJB Jyn Erso/Bodhi Rook	75.00	150.00
DCJG Jyn Erso/Galen Erso	100.00	200.00
DCJM Jyn Erso/General Merrick	75.00	150.00
DCLF Luke Skywalker/Finn	50.00	100.00
DCLP Luke Skywalker/Poe Dameron	100.00	200.00
DCPG Poe Dameron/General Hux	60.00	120.00
DCRP Rey/Poe Dameron	125.00	250.00
DCRPJ Rey/Poe Dameron	125.00	250.00
DCRPW Rey/Poe Dameron	125.00	250.00

2020 Topps Star Wars Masterwork Stamps

COMMON MEM	6.00	15.00
*GREEN/99: .5X TO 1.2X BASIC MEM		
*PURPLE/50: .6X TO 1.5X BASIC MEM		
SCAA Anakin Skywalker/Queen Amidala	8.00	20.00
SCCD Count Dooku/Count Dooku	10.00	25.00
SCCJ Chewbacca/Jannah	8.00	20.00
SCDM Darth Maul/Darth Maul	10.00	25.00
SCFP Finn/Poe Dameron	8.00	20.00
SCKS Kylo Ren/Sith Trooper	8.00	20.00
SCLC Lando Calrissian/Lando Calrissian	10.00	25.00
SCLL Lobot/Lando Calrissian	8.00	20.00
SCLW Logray/Wicket W. Warrick	8.00	20.00
SCOM Obi-Wan Kenobi/Darth Maul	10.00	25.00
SCPZ Poe Dameron/Zorii Bliss	10.00	25.00
SCQA Queen Amidala/Queen Amidala	8.00	20.00
SCQM Qui-Gon Jinn/Darth Maul	10.00	25.00
SCSS Sith Trooper/Sith Trooper	8.00	20.00
SCVM Darth Vader/Grand Moff Tarkin	10.00	25.00
SCYD Yoda/Count Dooku	8.00	20.00
SCPLW Princess Leia Organa Wicket W. Warrick	10.00	25.00

2020 Topps Star Wars Masterwork Troopers of the Galactic Empire

COMPLETE SET (15)	15.00	40.00
COMMON CARD (TE1-TE15)	2.00	5.00
*RAINBOW/299: .5X TO 1.2X BASIC CARDS		

2020 Topps Star Wars Masterwork The Wisdom of Yoda

COMPLETE SET (10)	20.00	50.00
COMMON CARD (WY1-WY10)	3.00	8.00
*RAINBOW/299: .5X TO 1.2X BASIC CARDS		

2021 Topps Star Wars Masterwork

COMPLETE SET (100)	100.00	250.00
UNOPENED BOX (4 MINIBOXES)	300.00	500.00
UNOPENED MINIBOX (5 CARDS)	75.00	125.00
COMMON CARD (1-100)	1.50	4.00
*BLUE: .5X TO 1.2X BASIC CARDS		
*GREEN/99: .6X TO 1.5X BASIC CARDS		
*PURPLE/50: .75X TO 2X BASIC CARDS		
4 Ahsoka Tano	6.00	15.00
11 BB-8	2.00	5.00
15 Boba Fett	5.00	12.00
17 Bo-Katan Kryze	2.50	6.00
21 Cad Bane	2.50	6.00
28 Darth Maul	3.00	8.00
41 Grand Admiral Thrawn	4.00	10.00
45 Grogu	10.00	25.00
46 Han Solo	4.00	10.00
55 Jedi Master Yoda	3.00	8.00
64 Kylo Ren	2.50	6.00
69 Luke Skywalker	3.00	8.00
70 Mandalorian	4.00	10.00
74 Koska Reeves	2.50	6.00
84 Rey	6.00	15.00

2021 Topps Star Wars Masterwork Autographs

COMMON AUTO	6.00	15.00
*BLUE/99: SAME VALUE AS BASIC		
*RAINBOW/50: .75X TO 2X BASIC AUTOS		
*CANVAS/25: 1.2X TO 3X BASIC AUTOS		
RANDOMLY INSERTED INTO PACKS		
MWAAB Ahmed Best	30.00	75.00
MWAAE Ashley Eckstein	60.00	150.00
MWAAL Amanda Lawrence	8.00	20.00
MWAAS Amy Sedaris	30.00	75.00
MWAAW Alexander Wraith	10.00	25.00
MWABH Brian Herring	10.00	25.00
MWACG Clare Grant	15.00	40.00
MWADI Diana Lee Inosanto	12.00	30.00
MWAES Emily Swallow	25.00	60.00
MWAGE Giancarlo Esposito	60.00	150.00
MWAGG Greg Grunberg	8.00	20.00
MWAIM Ian McDiarmid	125.00	300.00
MWAJG Janina Gavankar	10.00	25.00
MWAJL John Leguizamo	75.00	200.00
MWAKO Katy O'Brian	10.00	25.00
MWALM Lars Mikkelsen	40.00	100.00
MWALS Leilani Shiu	12.00	30.00
MWAMM Mary Elizabeth McGlynn	10.00	25.00
MWAMV Mercedes Varnado	75.00	200.00
MWANF Nika Futterman	12.00	30.00
MWAOA Omid Abtahi	10.00	25.00
MWAPA Philip Anthony-Rodriguez	10.00	25.00
MWAPL Paul Sun-Hyung Lee	25.00	60.00
MWARB Richard Brake	12.00	30.00
MWARG Richard Grant	40.00	100.00
MWASK Simon Kassianides	12.00	30.00
MWASS Stephen Stanton	10.00	25.00
MWASW Sam Witwer	40.00	100.00
MWATG Taylor Gray	20.00	50.00
MWATR Tim Rose	20.00	50.00
MWAADA Annabelle Davis	10.00	25.00
MWADBC Dee Bradley Baker	30.00	75.00
MWADBE Dee Bradley Baker	30.00	75.00
MWADBH Dee Bradley Baker	30.00	75.00
MWADBR Dee Bradley Baker	30.00	75.00
MWADBT Dee Bradley Baker	30.00	75.00
MWADBW Dee Bradley Baker	30.00	75.00
MWAMBO Mark Boone Junior	12.00	30.00
MWAMIB Michonne Bourriague	10.00	25.00
MWAPAL Philip Alexander	10.00	25.00

2021 Topps Star Wars Masterwork Commemorative Character Medallion Relics

COMMON MEM	5.00	12.00
*GREEN/99: .6X TO 1.5X BASIC MEM		
*PURPLE/50: .75X TO 2X BASIC MEM		
RANDOMLY INSERTED INTO PACKS		
CMCC Chewbacca	6.00	15.00
CMCR Chewbacca	6.00	15.00
CMLC Luke Skywalker	10.00	25.00
CMLR Luke Skywalker	10.00	25.00
CMLS Luke Skywalker	10.00	25.00
CMLV Luke Skywalker	10.00	25.00
CMRC R2-D2	8.00	20.00

CMRR R2-D2 8.00 20.00
CMVS Darth Vader 12.00 30.00
CMVV Darth Vader 12.00 30.00
CMC3C C-3PO 6.00 15.00
CMC3R C-3PO 6.00 15.00
CMLOR Princess Leia Organa 12.00 30.00
CMPLC Princess Leia Organa 12.00 30.00
CMPLV Princess Leia Organa 12.00 30.00

2021 Topps Star Wars Masterwork Jumbo Sourced Fabric Costume Relics

COMMON MEM 30.00 75.00
RANDOMLY INSERTED INTO PACKS
JCRAT Ahsoka Tano 100.00 250.00
JCRBE Tobias Beckett 40.00 100.00
JCRBF Boba Fett 150.00 400.00
JCRBR Bodhi Rook 40.00 100.00
JCRFN Finn 40.00 100.00
JCRGE Galen Erso 40.00 100.00
JCRJE Jyn Erso 60.00 150.00
JCRLS Luke Skywalker 150.00 400.00
JCRLU Luke Skywalker 150.00 400.00
JCRMC The Mandalorian 60.00 150.00
JCRPO Poe Dameron 40.00 100.00
JCRQI Qi'ra 100.00 250.00
JCRRE Rey 125.00 300.00
JCRTMA The Mandalorian 60.00 150.00

2021 Topps Star Wars Masterwork Lucasfilm 50th Anniversary

COMPLETE SET (14) 20.00 50.00
COMMON CARD (LFA1-LFA14) 2.50 6.00
*RAINBOW/299: 1.5X TO 4X BASIC CARDS
RANDOMLY INSERTED INTO PACKS

2021 Topps Star Wars Masterwork Out of the Box

COMPLETE SET (25) 12.00 30.00
COMMON CARD (OTB1-OTB25) 1.25 3.00
*RAINBOW/299: .75X TO 2X BASIC CARDS
RANDOMLY INSERTED INTO PACKS

2021 Topps Star Wars Masterwork Postage Stamp Relics

COMMON MEM 3.00 8.00
*GREEN/99: .6X TO 1.5X BASIC MEM
*PURPLE/50: .75X TO 2X BASIC MEM
RANDOMLY INSERTED INTO PACKS
SCAN Anakin Skywalker 8.00 20.00
SCAS Anakin Skywalker 8.00 20.00
SCBB BB-8 5.00 12.00
SCFB Fode and Beed 4.00 10.00
SCFN Finn 6.00 15.00
SCKR Kylo Ren 8.00 20.00
SCLO Leia Organa 10.00 25.00
SCLS Luke Skywalker 10.00 25.00
SCPD Poe Dameron 6.00 15.00
SCQG Qui Gon Jin 4.00 10.00
SCR2 R2-D2 6.00 15.00
SCCHW Chewbacca 8.00 20.00
SCPDA Poe Dameron 6.00 15.00

2021 Topps Star Wars Masterwork Welcome to the Dark Side

COMPLETE SET (10) 10.00 25.00
COMMON CARD (WDS1-WDS10) .75 2.00
*RAINBOW/299: 1.2X TO 3X BASIC CARDS
RANDOMLY INSERTED INTO PACKS

2017 Star Wars May the 4th Be with You

COMPLETE SET (20) 12.00 30.00
COMPLETE FACTORY SET (21) 40.00 80.00
COMMON CARD (1-20) 1.00 2.50
*SILVER/10: 6X TO 15X BASIC CARDS 15.00 40.00
RELEASED 5/4/2017

2017 Star Wars May the 4th Be with You Autographs

COMMON CARD 10.00 25.00
*SILVER/10: .6X TO 1.5X BASIC AUTOS
STATED ODDS 1:SET
1A Harrison Ford
2A Mark Hamill 400.00 600.00
3A Carrie Fisher
4A Kenny Baker
5A Anthony Daniels 175.00 300.00
7A Jeremy Bulloch 25.00 60.00
8A Ian McDiarmid 250.00 400.00
10A Billy Dee Williams
14A Kenneth Colley 12.00 30.00
16A Erik Bauersfeld 25.00 60.00
16A Tim Rose 15.00 40.00
19A Paul Blake

2022 Topps Star Wars May the 4th Wrapper Art

COMPLETE SET (8) 75.00 200.00
COMMON CARD (1-8) 12.00 30.00
*RAINBOW/99: 1.5X TO 4X BASIC CARDS
*SILVER/49: 2.5X TO 6X BASIC CARDS
4 Boba Fett by Blake Jamieson/1,378* 15.00 40.00
6 The Mandalorian by Blake Jamieson/1,302*15.00 40.00
7 Obi-Wan & Luke Skywalker
by Blake Jamieson/1,102* 15.00 40.00

1997-98 Topps Star Wars Men Behind the Masks

P1 Darth Vader & Boba Fett 10.00 25.00
(Given to Auction Seat Holders)
P2 Darth Vader & Boba Fett 10.00 25.00
(Given as Admission Ticket)
P3 Peter Mayhew as Chewbacca 8.00 20.00
(Given to Auction Reserve Seat Holders)/1000*
P4 Maria de Aragon as Greedo 10.00 25.00
(Show Exclusive)/800*

1997-98 Topps Star Wars Men Behind the Masks Test Issue

NNO Chewbacca 125.00 250.00
(prismatic foil/triangles)
NNO Chewbacca 125.00 250.00
(prismatic foil/vertical lines)
NNO Chewbacca 125.00 250.00
(refractor foil)
NNO Greedo 125.00 250.00
(prismatic foil/spotted)
NNO Greedo 125.00 250.00
(prismatic foil/traingles)
NNO Greedo 125.00 250.00
(prismatic foil/vertical lines)
NNO Greedo 125.00 250.00
(refractor foil)

1994-96 Metallic Impressions Star Wars Metal

COMPLETE SET (60) 30.00 75.00
COMMON CARD (1-60) 1.00 2.50

1994-96 Metallic Impressions Star Wars Metal Promos

COMPLETE SET (3) 12.00 30.00
COMMON CARD (P1-P3) 6.00 15.00
P1 Star Wars Episode IV 6.00 15.00
P2 The Empire Strikes Back 6.00 15.00
P3 Return of the Jedi 6.00 15.00

1996 Metallic Impressions Star Wars Metal Art of Ralph McQuarrie

COMPLETE SET (20) 10.00 25.00
COMMON CARD (1-20) 1.00 2.50
COA Certificate of Authenticity

1998 Metallic Impressions Star Wars Metal Bounty Hunters

COMPLETE SET (5) 2.50 6.00
COMMON CARD (1-5) 1.00 2.50
HSJH Han Solo and Jabba the Hutt SE

1995 Metallic Impressions Star Wars Metal Dark Empire I

COMPLETE SET (6) 3.00 8.00
COMMON CARD (1-6) 1.00 2.50

1996 Metallic Impressions Star Wars Metal Dark Empire II

COMPLETE SET (6) 3.00 8.00
COMMON CARD (1-6) 1.00 2.50

1998 Metallic Impressions Star Wars Metal Jedi Knights

COMPLETE SET (5) 3.00 8.00
COMMON CARD (1-5) 1.00 2.50
MES Mos Eisley Spaceport SE 1.50 4.00

1998 Metallic Impressions Star Wars Metal Jedi Knights Avon

COMPLETE SET (4) 3.00 8.00
COMMON CARD (1-4) 1.00 2.50
WIC Wampa Ice Creature SE 1.50 4.00

1997 Metallic Impressions Star Wars Metal Shadows of the Empire

COMPLETE SET (6) 4.00 10.00
COMMON CARD (1-6) 1.00 2.50

2015 Star Wars Micro Collector Packs

COMPLETE SET (36) 60.00 120.00
COMMON CARD (1-36) 1.50 4.00
NNO 3-D Glasses .40 1.00

2015 Star Wars Micro Collector Packs 3-D Posters

COMPLETE SET (6) 3.00 8.00
COMMON CARD .60 1.50
STATED ODDS 1:1

2015 Star Wars Micro Collector Packs Micro-Comics

COMPLETE SET (6) 4.00 10.00
COMMON CARD .75 2.00
STATED ODDS 1:1

1996 Topps Star Wars Multimotion

2M Star Wars 20th Anniversary
Commemorative Magazine 2.50 6.00

1999 Del Rey Books Star Wars The New Jedi Order

NNO SDCC Exclusive 2.00 5.00

2018 Star Wars Nickel City Con Promos

COMPLETE SET (3) 3.00 8.00
COMMON CARD (P1-P3) 1.25 3.00
NNO Darth Vader 2.00 5.00
NNO Luke Skywalker 1.50 4.00

2015 Star Wars NYCC Oversized Exclusives

COMPLETE SET (70) 75.00 150.00
COMMON CARD (1-70) 2.00 5.00

2022 Topps Now Star Wars Obi-Wan Kenobi Set

COMPLETE SET (30) 50.00 125.00
COMPLETE EP.I SET (5) 10.00 25.00
COMPLETE EP.II SET (5) 10.00 25.00
COMPLETE EP.III SET (5) 10.00 25.00
COMPLETE EP.IV SET (5) 10.00 25.00
COMPLETE EP.V SET (5) 10.00 25.00
COMPLETE EP.VI SET (5) 10.00 25.00
COMMON EP.I (1-5) 3.00 8.00
COMMON EP.II (6-10) 3.00 8.00
COMMON EP.III (11-15) 3.00 8.00
COMMON EP.IV (16-20) 3.00 8.00
COMMON EP.V (21-25) 3.00 8.00
COMMON EP.VI (26-30) 3.00 8.00
*BLUE/49: 1X TO 2.5X BASIC CARDS
EP.I SET PRINT RUN 1,221 SETS
EP.II SET PRINT RUN 1,161 SETS
EP.III SET PRINT RUN 1,330 SETS
EP.IV SET PRINT RUN 1,019 SETS
EP.V SET PRINT RUN
EP.VI SET PRINT RUN

2020 Topps On-Demand Star Wars 3-D Lenticular

COMPLETE SET (100) 125.00 300.00
UNOPENED PACK (8 CARDS)
COMMON CARD (3D1-3D100) 2.00 5.00
STATED PRINT RUN 720 SETS

2021 Topps On-Demand Star Wars The High Republic

COMPLETE SET (20) 15.00 40.00
UNOPENED PACK (21 CARDS)
COMMON CARD (1-20)
*BLACK/25: 4X TO 10X BASIC CARDS
ANNCD PRINT RUN 1,180 SETS

2021 Topps On-Demand Star Wars The High Republic Cover Art

COMPLETE SET (5) 200.00 350.00
COMMON CARD (1-5) 50.00 100.00
STATED ODDS 1:1 W/ PARALLELS
3 A Test of Courage 75.00 150.00
5 Marvel #1 60.00 120.00

2019 Star Wars On-Demand The Power of the Dark Side

COMPLETE SET W/EXCL. (26) 15.00 40.00
COMPLETE SET W/O EXCL. (25) 10.00 25.00
COMMON CARD (1-26) 1.25 3.00
*BLUE: 1X TO 2.5X BASIC CARDS
STATED PRINT RUN 700 SETS
SDCC SITH TROOPER PRINT RUN 300 CARDS
26 Sith Trooper/300* 8.00 20.00
(SDCC Exclusive)

2019 Star Wars On-Demand The Power of the Dark Side Galactic Battles

COMPLETE SET (6) 15.00 40.00
COMMON CARD (G1-G6) 4.00 10.00
STATED ODDS 1:SET

2019 Star Wars On-Demand The Power of the Light Side

COMPLETE SET W/EXCL. (26) 15.00 40.00
COMPLETE SET W/O EXCL.(25) 10.00 25.00
COMMON CARD (1-25) 1.25 3.00
*BLUE: 1X TO 2.5X BASIC CARDS
26 Luke Skywalker 12.00 30.00
(NYCC Exclusive)

2019 Star Wars On-Demand The Power of the Light Side Galactic Battles

COMPLETE SET (6) 25.00 60.00
COMMON CARD (G1-G6) 4.00 10.00
STATED ODDS 1:SET

2019 Star Wars On-Demand Women of Star Wars

COMPLETE SET (25) 12.00 30.00
COMMON CARD (1-25) .75 2.00
*PURPLE: 2X TO 5X BASIC CARDS

2019 Star Wars On-Demand Women of Star Wars Autographs

COMMON AUTO 8.00 20.00
STATED OVERALL ODDS 1:SET

1 Carrie Fisher
2 Daisy Ridley 300.00 500.00
3 Felicity Jones 125.00 250.00
4 Genevieve O'Reilly 10.00 25.00
5 Ashley Eckstein 15.00 40.00
6 Sarah Michelle Gellar 75.00 150.00
7 Vanessa Marshall 12.00 30.00
8 Tiya Sircar 10.00 25.00
9 Nika Futterman 10.00 25.00
10 Laura Dern
12 Tovah Feldshuh 15.00 40.00
13 Orli Shoshan 12.00 30.00
15 Billie Lourd 60.00 120.00
16 Gwendoline Christie

2019 Star Wars On-Demand Women of Star Wars Evolution of Leia

COMPLETE SET (8) 75.00 150.00
COMMON CARD (EL1-EL8) 12.00 30.00

2019 Star Wars On-Demand Women of Star Wars Women of the Galaxy

COMPLETE SET (10) 75.00 150.00
COMMON CARD (WG1-WG10) 10.00 25.00
RANDOMLY INSERTED INTO SETS

1995 Kenner Star Wars The Power of the Force

NNO Luke Skywalker 2.00 5.00

2011 Star Wars Power Plates

COMPLETE SET W/SP (30) 75.00 150.00
COMP.SET W/O SP (24) 50.00 100.00
UNOPENED BOX (48 PACKS) 120.00 150.00
UNOPENED PACK (1 PLATE) 2.50 3.00
COMMON PLATE 3.00 8.00
COMMON PLATE SP 5.00 12.00
SP STATED ODDS 1:8

1999 Orange County Register Star Wars Preview Guide

NNO Pod Racers 5.00
(Orange County Register Exclusive)

1997 Quality Bakers Star Wars

COMPLETE SET (10) 12.00 30.00
COMMON CARD (1-10) 2.00 5.00

2016 Star Wars Rancho Obi-Wan Little Debbie

COMPLETE SET (12) 20.00 50.00
COMMON CARD (1-12) 2.50 6.00
STATED ODDS 1:1 BOXES OF STAR CRUNCH

2018 Star Wars On-Demand Rebels Series Finale

COMPLETE SET (20) 15.00 40.00
COMMON CARD (1-20) 1.25 3.00
*BLUE: 1X TO 2.5X BASIC CARDS
STATED PRINT RUN 461 SETS

2018 Star Wars On-Demand Rebels Series Finale Autographs

STATED OVERALL ODDS 1:SET
NNO Ashley Eckstein
NNO Dee Bradley Baker 12.00 30.00
NNO Forest Whitaker
NNO Freddie Prinze Jr.
NNO Genevieve O'Reilly 10.00 25.00
NNO Ian McDiarmid 60.00 120.00
NNO Lars Mikkelsen 30.00 75.00
NNO Mary Elizabeth McGlynn 15.00 40.00
NNO Stephen Stanton 12.00 30.00
NNO Steve Blum 15.00 40.00
NNO Taylor Gray
NNO Tom Baker
NNO Vanessa Marshall
NNO Warwick Davis

2015 Star Wars Rebels

COMPLETE SET (100) 6.00 15.00
UNOPENED BOX (24 PACKS) 50.00 75.00
UNOPENED PACK (6 CARDS) 2.00 3.00
COMMON CARD (1-100) .12 .30
*FOIL: 2X TO 5X BASIC CARDS

2015 Star Wars Rebels Stickers

COMPLETE SET (20) 5.00 12.00
COMMON CARD (1-20) .40 1.00

2015 Star Wars Rebels Tattoos

COMPLETE SET (10) 6.00 15.00
COMMON CARD (1-10) 1.00 2.50
STATED ODDS 1:8

2017 Star Wars Rebels Season 4 Preview Set

COMPLETE SET (25) 30.00 80.00
UNOPENED BOXED SET (27 CARDS)
COMMON CARD 2.00 5.00
*PURPLE/25: 1.2X TO 3X BASIC CARDS 6.00 15.00
RELEASED 10/17/2017

2017 Star Wars Rebels Season 4 Preview Set Autographs

STATED ODDS 1:1 PER BOX SET
NNO Freddie Prinze Jr.
NNO Taylor Gray
NNO Vanessa Marshall
NNO Tiya Sircar
NNO Steve Blum
NNO Ashley Eckstein
NNO Sam Witwer
NNO Jason Isaacs
NNO Philip Anthony Rodriguez
NNO Sarah Michelle Gellar
NNO Stephen Stanton 12.00 30.00
NNO Billy Dee Williams
NNO Forest Whitaker
NNO Stephen Stanton
NNO Genevieve O'Reilly
NNO Mary Elizabeth McGlynn 12.00 30.00
NNO Phil Lamarr
NNO Tom Baker
NNO Jim Cummings

2014 Star Wars Rebels Subway Promos

COMPLETE SET (6) 6.00 15.00
COMMON CARD 1.50 4.00

2019 Star Wars Resistance Surprise Packs

COMPLETE SET (100) 12.00 30.00
UNOPENED BOX (24 PACKS)
UNOPENED PACK (6 CARDS)
COMMON CARD (1-100) .25 .60
*BRONZE/50: 4X TO 10X BASIC CARDS
*SILVER/25: 6X TO 15X BASIC CARDS

2019 Star Wars Resistance Surprise Packs Character Foil

COMPLETE SET (25) 12.00 30.00
COMMON CARD (1-25) .75 2.00

2019 Star Wars Resistance Surprise Packs Danglers

COMPLETE SET (12) 12.00 30.00
COMMON CARD (1-12) 2.50 6.00

2019 Star Wars Resistance Surprise Packs Mini Albums

COMPLETE SET (4) 12.00 30.00
COMMON ALBUM 4.00 10.00

2019 Star Wars Resistance Surprise Packs Pop-Ups

COMPLETE SET (10) 6.00 15.00
COMMON CARD (1-10) 1.00 2.50

2019 Star Wars Resistance Surprise Packs Temporary Tattoos

COMPLETE SET (10) 8.00 20.00
COMMON CARD (1-10) 1.25 3.00

2016 Star Wars Rogue One Mission Briefing

COMPLETE SET (110) 8.00 20.00
UNOPENED BOX (24 PACKS) 85.00 100.00
UNOPENED PACK (8 CARDS) 4.00 5.00
COMMON CARD (1-110) .20 .50
*BLACK: .75X TO 2X BASIC CARDS .40 1.00
*GREEN: 1.2X TO 3X BASIC CARDS .60 1.50
*BLUE: 1.5X TO 4X BASIC CARDS .75 2.00
*GRAY/100: 8X TO 20X BASIC CARDS 4.00 10.00
*GOLD/50: 12X TO 30X BASIC CARDS 6.00 15.00

2016 Star Wars Rogue One Mission Briefing Autographs

COMMON CARD 6.00 15.00
*BLACK/50: .6X TO 1.5X BASIC AUTOS
*BLUE/25: 1.2X TO 3X BASIC AUTOS
RANDOMLY INSERTED INTO PACKS
NNO Adrienne Wilkinson 12.00 30.00
NNO Al Lampert 10.00 25.00
NNO Anna Graves 15.00 40.00
NNO Barbara Frankland 10.00 25.00
NNO Brian Blessed 8.00 20.00
NNO Candice Orwell 12.00 30.00
NNO Catherine Taber
NNO Clive Revill 12.00 30.00
NNO Corey Dee Williams 10.00 25.00
NNO Dave Barclay
NNO David Ankrum 10.00 25.00
NNO Eric Lopez 10.00 25.00
NNO Femi Taylor 8.00 20.00
NNO Garrick Hagon 10.00 25.00
NNO George Roubicek 10.00 25.00
NNO Glyn Baker 10.00 25.00
NNO Ian Liston 10.00 25.00
NNO Jack Klaff 8.00 20.00
NNO Jim Cummings 12.00 30.00
NNO John Coppinger 15.00 40.00
NNO Kenneth Colley 8.00 20.00
NNO Lloyd Sherr 10.00 25.00
NNO Megan Udall 10.00 25.00
NNO Mercedes Ngoh 8.00 20.00
NNO Michaela Cottrell 8.00 20.00
NNO Mike Edmonds 12.00 30.00
NNO Oliver Walpole 10.00 25.00
NNO Paul Springer 12.00 30.00
NNO Rajia Baroudi 12.00 30.00
NNO Rich Oldfield 15.00 40.00
NNO Rusty Goffe 10.00 25.00
NNO Sam Witwer 15.00 40.00
NNO Scott Capurro 12.00 30.00
NNO Sean Crawford 10.00 25.00
NNO Stephen Stanton 8.00 20.00
NNO Tom Kane 8.00 20.00
NNO Wayne Pygram 10.00 25.00

2016 Star Wars Rogue One Mission Briefing Character Foil

COMPLETE SET (9) 12.00 20.00
COMMON CARD (1-9) 2.00 5.00
STATED ODDS 1:8

2016 Star Wars Rogue One Mission Briefing Comic Strips Inserts

COMPLETE SET (12) 8.00 20.00
COMMON CARD (1-12) 1.25 3.00

2016 Star Wars Rogue One Mission Briefing The Death Star

COMPLETE SET (9) 6.00 15.00
COMMON CARD (1-9) .75 2.00
STATED ODDS 1:4

2016 Star Wars Rogue One Mission Briefing Heroes of the Rebel Alliance

COMPLETE SET (9) 10.00 25.00
COMMON CARD (1-9) 1.50 3.00
STATED ODDS 1:8
1 Luke Skywalker 2.00 5.00
2 Princess Leia 2.00 5.00
3 Han Solo 2.00 5.00
4 Chewbacca 1.50 4.00
6 Obi-Wan Kenobi 1.50 4.00
7 R2-D2 1.50 4.00

2016 Star Wars Rogue One Mission Briefing Mission Briefing Monday

COMPLETE SET (36) 150.00 300.00
COMMON CARD 6.00 15.00
NOV.7, 2016 (MBME1-MBME6)/206*
NOV.14, 2016 (MBM1-MBM5)/226*
NOV.21, 2016 (MBM6-MBM10)/218*
NOV.28, 2016 (MBM11-MBM15)/212*
DEC.5, 2016 (MBM16-MBM20)/224*
DEC.12, 2016 (MBM21-MBM25)/234*
DEC.19, 2016 (MBM26-MBM30)/252*

2016 Star Wars Rogue One Mission Briefing Montages

COMPLETE SET (9) 15.00 40.00
COMMON CARD (1-9) 3.00 8.00
STATED ODDS 1:24
1 Storming the Beach 3.00 8.00
2 Imperial Assault 3.00 8.00
3 Jyn Erso 5.00 12.00
4 Within Rebel Base 3.00 8.00
5 Patrol of the Empire 3.00 8.00
6 Fearsome Death Trooper 3.00 8.00
7 Director Krennic 3.00 8.00
8 In Flames 3.00 8.00
9 Rebel Ensemble 3.00 8.00

2016 Star Wars Rogue One Mission Briefing NYCC Exclusives

COMPLETE SET (10) 12.00 30.00
COMMON CARD (E1-E10) 2.00 5.00
2016 NYCC EXCLUSIVE

2016 Star Wars Rogue One Mission Briefing Patches

COMPLETE SET (12) 50.00 100.00
COMMON CARD (M1-M12) 3.00 8.00
*GRAY/100: .75X TO 2X BASIC CARDS
*GOLD/50: 1.5X TO 4X BASIC CARDS
*RED/10: 3X TO 8X BASIC CARDS
STATED ODDS 1:26
1 Jyn Erso 6.00 15.00
3 L-1 Droid 5.00 12.00
4 Admiral Raddus 4.00 10.00
6 TIE Fighter Pilot 4.00 10.00
7 Shoretrooper 4.00 10.00
10 Captain Cassian Andor 5.00 12.00
11 Bistan 4.00 10.00

2016 Star Wars Rogue One Mission Briefing Stickers

COMPLETE SET (18) 10.00 25.00
COMMON CARD (1-18) 1.00 2.50
STATED ODDS 1:12
1 Jyn Erso 1.50 4.00
13 Darth Vader 2.00 5.00

2016 Star Wars Rogue One Mission Briefing Villains of the Galactic Empire

COMPLETE SET (8) 8.00 20.00
COMMON CARD (1-8) 1.25 3.00
STATED ODDS 1:8
1 Darth Vader 1.25 5.00

1999 Sci-Fi Expo Star Wars Celebrity Promos

P1 Garrick Hagon 8.00 20.00
(Biggs Darklighter)

P2 Peter Mayhew 8.00 20.00
(Chewbacca)

2015 Star Wars SDCC Oversized Exclusives

COMPLETE SET (100) 120.00 250.00
COMMON CARD (1-100) 2.00 5.00

1997 Doritos Star Wars SE Trilogy 3-D Discs

COMPLETE SET (20) 5.00 12.00
COMMON CARD .40 1.00

1997 Doritos-Cheetos Star Wars SE Trilogy 3-D

COMPLETE SET (6) 3.00 8.00
COMMON CARD (1-6) .75 2.00

1996 Topps Star Wars Shadows of the Empire

COMPLETE SET (100) 15.00 40.00
UNOPENED BOX (36 PACKS) 75.00 125.00
UNOPENED PACK (9 CARDS) 2.50 4.00
COMMON CARD (1-72, 83-100) .15 .40
COMMON ETCHED (73-78) 2.00 5.00
COMMON EMBOSSED (79-82) 3.00 8.00
73-78 STATED ODDS 1:9
79-82 STATED ODDS 1:18

1996 Topps Star Wars Shadows of the Empire Promos

COMMON CARD 1.00 2.50
SOTE1 Xizor 2.00 5.00
SOTE2 Darth Vader 2.00 5.00
SOTE3 Luke Skywalker 2.00 5.00
SOTE4 Dash Rendar & Leebo 2.00 5.00
SOTE5 Boba Fett 8.00 15.00
(Convention Exclusive)
SOTE6 Guri 2.00 5.00
SOTE7 C-3PO & R2-D2 2.00 5.00
NNO SOTE3-SOTE1 (Luke Skywalker/Darth Vader)

2021 Topps Star Wars Signature Series Autographs

UNOPENED BOX (1 CARD) 100.00 150.00
AA Annabelle Davis 10.00 25.00
AS Stephen Stanton
AA2 Annabelle Davis 10.00 25.00
AAF Anthony Forrest 6.00 15.00
AAG Anna Graves 6.00 15.00
AAH Alden Ehrenreich
AAS Andy Serkis
ABB Ben Burtt
ABL Billie Lourd
ABM Ben Mendelsohn
ABW Billy Dee Williams
ACC Cavin Cornwall 6.00 15.00
ACF Carrie Fisher
ACH Clint Howard
ACM Cameron Monaghan 15.00 40.00
ACW Carl Weathers
ADA Derek Arnold 6.00 15.00
ADB Dee Bradley Baker 15.00 40.00
ADC Dave Chapman 8.00 20.00
ADF Donald Faison
ADG Domhnall Gleeson
ADL Daniel Logan 8.00 20.00
ADM Dominic Monaghan
ADR Daisy Ridley
ADT Dee Tails
ADW Debra Wilson 10.00 25.00
ADY Donnie Yen
AES Emily Swallow
AEW Ewan McGregor
AFJ Felicity Jones
AFP Freddie Prinze Jr.
AFW Forest Whitaker
AGC Gwendoline Christie
AGE Giancarlo Esposito 50.00 100.00
AGG Greg Grunberg 12.00 30.00
AGO Genevieve O'Reilly
AGP Greg Proops 6.00 15.00
AHC Hayden Christensen
AHD Harley Durst 6.00 15.00
AHF Harrison Ford
AHS Horatio Sanz 15.00 40.00
AIM Ian McDiarmid
AIR Ian Ruskin 6.00 15.00
AIW Ian Whyte 10.00 25.00
AJB John Boyega 30.00 75.00
AJK Jaime King 10.00 25.00
AJR Jerome Blake 8.00 20.00
AJS Joonas Suotamo 60.00 120.00
AJT James Arnold Taylor 15.00 40.00
AKB Kenny Baker
AKT Kelly Marie Tran
ALT Lee Towersey 15.00 40.00
AMD Matt Doran 6.00 15.00
AMM Mads Mikkelsen
ANF Nika Futterman 10.00 25.00
ANK Nick Kellington 6.00 15.00
ANN Nick Nolte
APA Philip Anthony-Rodriguez 10.00 25.00
APB Paul Bettany
APM Peter Mayhew
APP Pedro Pascal
ARA Riz Ahmed
ARD Robin Atkin Downes 6.00 15.00
ARP Ray Park
AS2 Stephen Stanton
AS3 Stephen Stanton
ASJ Samuel L. Jackson
ASW Sam Witwer 15.00 40.00
ATD Tim Dry 6.00 15.00
ATF Tovah Feldshuh 6.00 15.00
ATG Taylor Gray
ATK Tom Kenny 8.00 20.00
ATM Temuera Morrison 50.00 100.00
ATR Tim Rose
ATW Taika Waititi
AWA Denis Lawson 12.00 30.00
AWD Warwick Davis 30.00 75.00
AWH Werner Herzog
AAB2 Ahmed Best
AAB3 Ahmed Best
AAD2 Adam Driver
AAD3 Adam Driver
AAE2 Ashley Eckstein
AAE3 Ashley Eckstein
AAF2 Anthony Forrest 6.00 15.00
AAG2 Anna Graves 6.00 15.00
AAH2 Alden Ehrenreich
AAS2 Andy Serkis
AASG Arti Shah 5.00 12.00
ABB2 Ben Burtt
ABBE Blair Bess 8.00 20.00
ABL2 Billie Lourd
ABL3 Billie Lourd
ABMR Bobby Moynihan 6.00 15.00
ABW2 Billy Dee Williams
ABW3 Billy Dee Williams
ACC2 Cavin Cornwall 6.00 15.00
ACDW Corey Dee Williams 12.00 30.00
ACF2 Carrie Fisher
ADA2 Derek Arnold
ADA3 Derek Arnold
ADB2 Dee Bradley Baker 5.00 12.00
ADB3 Dee Bradley Baker 6.00 15.00
ADC2 Dave Chapman 12.00 30.00
ADG2 Domhnall Gleeson
ADG3 Domhnall Gleeson
ADL2 Daniel Logan 8.00 20.00
ADR2 Daisy Ridley
ADR3 Daisy Ridley
ADT2 Dee Tails
ADT3 Dee Tails
AEW2 Ewan McGregor
AEW3 Ewan McGregor
AFJ2 Felicity Jones
AFJ3 Felicity Jones
AFP2 Freddie Prinze Jr.
AGC2 Gwendoline Christie
AGCM Gina Carano
AGG2 Greg Grunberg 12.00 30.00
AHC2 Hayden Christensen
AHC3 Hayden Christensen
AHF2 Harrison Ford
AHF3 Harrison Ford
AIM2 Ian McDiarmid
AIM3 Ian McDiarmid
AIW2 Ian Whyte 8.00 20.00
AJB2 John Boyega 30.00 75.00
AJB3 John Boyega 30.00 75.00
AJR2 Jerome Blake
AJS2 Joonas Suotamo 60.00 120.00
AJT2 James Arnold Taylor 15.00 40.00
AJT3 James Arnold Taylor 12.00 30.00
AJTS John Tui 8.00 20.00
AKB2 Kenny Baker
AKB3 Kenny Baker
AKT2 Kelly Marie Tran
ANF2 Nika Futterman 10.00 25.00
ANF3 Nika Futterman 10.00 25.00
ANK2 Nick Kellington 8.00 20.00
APM2 Peter Mayhew
APM3 Peter Mayhew
ARD2 Robin Atkin Downes 8.00 20.00
ARP2 Ray Park
ARP3 Ray Park
ARPC Ron Perlman
ASJ2 Samuel L. Jackson
ASJ3 Samuel L. Jackson
ASW2 Sam Witwer 25.00 60.00
ASW3 Sam Witwer
ATBS Thomas Brodie-Sangster 5.00 12.00
ATG2 Taylor Gray
ATK2 Tom Kenny 10.00 25.00
ATK3 Tom Kenny 10.00 25.00
ATM2 Temuera Morrison 75.00 150.00
ATR2 Tim Rose
ATR3 Tim Rose
AWA2 Denis Lawson 12.00 30.00
AWA3 Denis Lawson 12.00 30.00
AWD2 Warwick Davis
AWD3 Warwick Davis

2022 Topps Star Wars Signature Series

UNOPENED BOX (1 AUTO) 75.00 100.00
COMMON AUTO 6.00 15.00
*BLUE/50: .5X TO 1.2X BASIC AUTOS
*GREEN/25: .6X TO 1.5X BASIC AUTOS
AAB Ahmed Best 30.00 75.00
AAE Ashley Eckstein 125.00 250.00
AAG Anna Graves 10.00 25.00
AAR Alan Ruscoe 10.00 25.00
AAW Andrew Woodall 8.00 20.00
ABS Bruce Spence 10.00 25.00
ACA Cas Anvar 10.00 25.00
ACB Chris Bartlett 15.00 40.00
ACE Chris Edgerly 10.00 25.00
ACH Clint Howard 20.00 50.00
ACO Candice Orwell 12.00 30.00
ACR Clive Revill 20.00 50.00
ADB Dee Bradley Baker 25.00 60.00
ADC Dave Chapman 15.00 40.00
ADI Diana Lee Inosanto 12.00 30.00
ADT David Tennant 30.00 75.00
AES Emily Swallow 30.00 75.00
AGE Giancarlo Esposito 60.00 125.00
AGG Greg Grunberg 10.00 25.00
AGH Garrick Hagon 12.00 30.00
AHD Harley Durst 8.00 20.00
AHQ Hugh Quarshie 10.00 25.00
AIR Ian Ruskin 8.00 20.00
AJB John Boyega 25.00 60.00
AJG Janina Gavankar 12.00 30.00
AJI Jason Isaacs 50.00 125.00
AJK Jack Klaff 8.00 20.00
AKL Ken Leung 10.00 25.00
AKM Cathy Munroe 15.00 40.00
AKO Katy O'Brian 15.00 40.00
ALC Lily Cole 8.00 20.00
ALM Lewis MacLeod 20.00 50.00
ALS Leilani Shiu 25.00 60.00
ALT Lee Towersey 15.00 40.00
ALW Leeanna Walsman 8.00 20.00
AMA Mark Austin 50.00 100.00
AMB Mark Boone Jr. 15.00 40.00
AMD Mark Dodson 15.00 40.00
AMW Matthew Wood 30.00 75.00
ANA Naomi Ackie 15.00 40.00
ANF Nika Futterman 20.00 50.00
AOA Omid Abtahi 10.00 25.00
AOD Oliver Ford Davies 10.00 25.00
AOW Oliver Walpole 8.00 20.00
APA Philip Alexander 8.00 20.00
APK Paul Kasey 8.00 20.00
APL Paul Sun-Hyung Lee 15.00 40.00
APR Paul Reubens 60.00 120.00
ARO Rena Owen 10.00 25.00
ASC Scott Capurro 15.00 40.00
ASK Simon Kassianides 15.00 40.00
ASL Scott Lawrence 8.00 20.00
ASS Stephanie Silva 12.00 30.00
ATD Tim Dry 8.00 20.00
ATG Taylor Gray 30.00 75.00
AVK Valene Kane 10.00 25.00
AAD1 Annabelle Davis 10.00 25.00
AAE2 Ashley Eckstein 125.00 250.00
AAG1 Anna Graves 10.00 25.00
AAH1 Amanda Hale 12.00 30.00
ADB2 Dee Bradley Baker 25.00 60.00
ADT1 Dee Tails 10.00 25.00
AJB2 Jeremy Bulloch 50.00 100.00
AKS1 Kath Soucie 15.00 40.00
ALM1 Lars Mikkelsen 60.00 120.00
AMB1 Michonne Bourriague 10.00 25.00
ANK1 Nick Kellington 8.00 20.00
ANK2 Nick Kellington 8.00 20.00
APB1 Paul Brooke 15.00 40.00
APB2 Paul Blake 12.00 30.00
ARB1 Richard Brake 12.00 30.00

2019 Star Wars Skywalker Saga

COMPLETE SET (100) 8.00 20.00
UNOPENED BOX (24 PACKS) 100.00 150.00
UNOPENED PACK (8 CARDS) 4.00 6.00
COMMON CARD (1-100) .20 .50
*ORANGE: .6X TO 1.5X BASIC CARDS
*BLUE: .75X TO 2X BASIC CARDS
*GREEN/99: 2.5X TO 6X BASIC CARDS
*PURPLE/25: 6X TO 15X BASIC CARDS

2019 Star Wars Skywalker Saga Allies

COMPLETE SET (10) 6.00 15.00
COMMON CARD (A1-A10) .75 2.00
*GREEN/99: 1X TO 2.5X BASIC CARDS
*PURPLE/25: 3X TO 8X BASIC CARDS
STATED ODDS 1:12 HOBBY & BLASTER

2019 Star Wars Skywalker Saga Autographs

STATED ODDS 1:39 HOBBY; 1:826 BLASTER
AAB Ahmed Best
AAD Anthony Daniels
AAS Andy Serkis
AAT Alan Tudyk
ABH Brian Herring 6.00 15.00
ABL Billie Lourd
ABM Ben Mendelsohn
ACF Carrie Fisher

ADB David Barclay	6.00	15.00
ADG Domhnall Gleeson		
ADL Daniel Logan	5.00	12.00
ADR Daisy Ridley		
ADY Donnie Yen		
AEK Erin Kellyman	30.00	75.00
AEM Ewan McGregor		
AFJ Felicity Jones		
AFW Forest Whitaker		
AGH Garrick Hagon	6.00	15.00
AGO Genevieve O'Reilly		
AHC Hayden Christensen		
AHF Harrison Ford		
AIM Ian McDiarmid		
AJB Jerome Blake	5.00	12.00
AKB Kenny Baker		
AKK Katy Kartwheel	12.00	30.00
AML Matt Lanter		
AMM Mads Mikkelsen		
ANF Nika Futterman	5.00	12.00
APB Paul Bettany		
APL Phil LaMarr	6.00	15.00
APM Peter Mayhew		
ARA Riz Ahmed		
ARP Ray Park		
ASC Silas Carson	5.00	12.00
ATM Temuera Morrison		
AWD Warwick Davis		
AADK Adam Driver		
AAEH Alden Ehrenreich		
AASW Andy Secombe	5.00	12.00
ABDW Billy Dee Williams		
AHCV Hayden Christensen		
AIMS Ian McDiarmid		
AJAT James Arnold Taylor		
AJBF John Boyega		
AJSC Joonas Suotamo		
ASLJ Samuel L. Jackson		
ATKY Tom Kane	6.00	15.00

2019 Star Wars Skywalker Saga Commemorative Blueprint Relics

COMMON MEM	5.00	12.00
*ORANGE/99: SAME VALUE AS BASIC		
*BLUE/50: .5X TO 1.2X BASIC MEM		
*GREEN/25: .75X TO 2X BASIC MEM		
STATED ODDS 1:64 HOBBY; 1:218 BLASTER		
BPIS Imperial Speeder Bike	6.00	15.00
BPMF Millennium Falcon	8.00	20.00
BPSI Slave I	6.00	15.00
BPST AT-ST	6.00	15.00
BPTI Tie Interceptor	6.00	15.00
BPXW X-wing Fighter	6.00	15.00

2019 Star Wars Skywalker Saga Commemorative Nameplate Patches

COMMON ANAKIN	3.00	8.00
COMMON KYLO	4.00	10.00
COMMON LEIA	4.00	10.00
COMMON LUKE	5.00	12.00
*ORANGE/99: SAME VALUE AS BASIC		
*BLUE/50: .5X TO 1.2X BASIC MEM		
*GREEN/25: .75X TO 2X BASIC MEM		
STATED ODDS 1:1 BLASTER		

2019 Star Wars Skywalker Saga Enemies

COMPLETE SET (10)	6.00	15.00
COMMON CARD (E1-E10)	.75	2.00
*GREEN/99: 1X TO 2.5X BASIC CARDS		
*PURPLE/25: 3X TO 8X BASIC CARDS		
STATED ODDS 1:12 HOBBY; 1:12 BLASTER		

2019 Star Wars Skywalker Saga Iconic Looks

COMPLETE SET (10)	6.00	15.00
COMMON CARD (IL1-IL10)	.75	2.00
*GREEN/99: 1X TO 2.5X BASIC CARDS		
*PURPLE/25: 3X TO 8X BASIC CARDS		
STATED ODDS 1:4 HOBBY & BLASTER		

2019 Star Wars Skywalker Saga Path of the Jedi

COMPLETE SET (10)	6.00	15.00
COMMON CARD (PJ1-PJ10)	.75	2.00
*GREEN/99: 1X TO 2.5X BASIC CARDS		
*PURPLE/25: 3X TO 8X BASIC CARDS		
STATED ODDS 1:2 HOBBY & BLASTER		

2019 Star Wars Skywalker Saga Skywalker Legacy

COMPLETE SET (11)	6.00	15.00
COMMON CARD (FT1-FT11)	1.00	2.50
*GREEN/99: 1.5X TO 4X BASIC CARDS		
*PURPLE/25: 2.5X TO 6X BASIC CARDS		
STATED ODDS 1:12 HOBBY & BLASTER		

1978 General Mills Star Wars Spaceship Hang Gliders

COMPLETE SET (4)	75.00	150.00
COMMON CARD	20.00	50.00

2022 Topps Star Wars Star File NYCC Set

COMPLETE SET (10)	8.00	20.00
COMMON CARD (1-10)	1.25	3.00

2017 Star Wars Stellar Signatures

COMMON AUTOS	25.00	60.00
*BLUE/25: .5X TO 1.2X BASIC AUTOS	30.00	75.00
STATED PRINT RUN 40 SER.#'d SETS		
100 TOTAL BOXES PRODUCED		
NNO Adam Driver	300.00	750.00
NNO Alan Tudyk	75.00	200.00
NNO Andy Serkis	60.00	150.00
NNO Ashley Eckstein	50.00	125.00
NNO Ben Mendelsohn EXCH		
NNO Billy Dee Williams	60.00	150.00
NNO Brian Herring	30.00	75.00
NNO Carrie Fisher	200.00	500.00
NNO Daisy Ridley	500.00	1200.00
NNO Donnie Yen	60.00	150.00
NNO Felicity Jones	200.00	500.00
NNO Forest Whitaker	60.00	150.00
NNO Freddie Prinze Jr.	40.00	100.00
NNO Genevieve O'Reilly	40.00	100.00
NNO Gwendoline Christie	150.00	400.00
NNO Harrison Ford	1500.00	4000.00
NNO Hayden Christensen	150.00	400.00
NNO Ian McDiarmid	150.00	400.00
NNO Jeremy Bulloch	30.00	75.00
NNO John Boyega	100.00	250.00
NNO Joonas Suotamo	30.00	75.00
NNO Kenny Baker	60.00	150.00
NNO Lars Mikkelsen	60.00	150.00
NNO Mark Hamill EXCH		
NNO Matthew Wood	30.00	75.00
NNO Peter Mayhew	60.00	150.00
NNO Ray Park	50.00	125.00
NNO Riz Ahmed	40.00	100.00
NNO Sarah Michelle Gellar	100.00	250.00
NNO Stephen Stanton EXCH		
NNO Temuera Morrison	30.00	75.00
NNO Tim Curry	100.00	200.00
NNO Tom Baker	75.00	200.00
NNO Warwick Davis	40.00	100.00

2018 Star Wars Stellar Signatures

COMMON AUTO	20.00	50.00
*BLUE/25: SAME VALUE AS BASIC AUTOS		
AAD Anthony Daniels	125.00	250.00
AAE Ashley Eckstein	30.00	75.00
AAS Andy Serkis	50.00	100.00
AAT Alan Tudyk	50.00	100.00
ABH Brian Herring	25.00	60.00
ACB Caroline Blakiston	25.00	60.00
ADG Domhnall Gleeson	125.00	250.00
ADR Daisy Ridley	400.00	600.00
AEB Erik Bauersfeld	50.00	100.00
AEK Erin Kellyman	125.00	250.00
AFW Forest Whitaker	60.00	120.00
AGG Greg Grunberg	25.00	60.00
AHC Hayden Christensen	125.00	250.00
AHF Harrison Ford	800.00	1400.00
AIM Ian McDiarmid	100.00	200.00
AJB Jeremy Bulloch	30.00	75.00
AJI Jason Isaacs	30.00	75.00
AJS Joonas Suotamo	50.00	100.00
AKB Kenny Baker	100.00	200.00
ALD Laura Dern	60.00	120.00
AMM Mads Mikkelsen	125.00	250.00
APR Paul Reubens	75.00	150.00
ARA Riz Ahmed	30.00	75.00
ARP Ray Park	50.00	100.00
ATC Tim Curry	50.00	100.00
AADR Adam Driver	200.00	350.00
ABDW Billy Dee Williams	75.00	150.00
ASLJ Samuel L. Jackson	600.00	800.00

2018 Star Wars Stellar Signatures Autographed Relics

COMMON AUTO	60.00	120.00
*BLUE/25: SAME VALUE AS BASIC AUTOS		
ARD Paul Bettany	150.00	300.00
ARJ Felicity Jones	200.00	350.00

2019 Star Wars Stellar Signatures

COMPLETE SET (100)	750.00	1500.00
COMMON CARD (1-100)	10.00	25.00
STATED ODDS 1:SET PER BOXED SET		

2019 Star Wars Stellar Signatures Autographs

COMMON AUTO	15.00	40.00
AADR Adam Driver	125.00	250.00
AAB Ahmed Best	50.00	100.00
AAT Alan Tudyk	30.00	75.00
AAE Alden Ehrenreich	200.00	400.00
AAS Andy Serkis	30.00	75.00
ABL Billie Lourd	60.00	120.00
ABDW Billy Dee Williams	60.00	120.00
ABMY Bobby Moynihan	25.00	60.00
ADR Daisy Ridley	300.00	500.00
ADB David Barclay		
ADT David Tennant EXCH		
ADGL Domhnall Gleeson	100.00	200.00
ADFA Donald Faison	25.00	60.00
ADY Donnie Yen	50.00	100.00
AEK Erin Kellyman	50.00	100.00
AEM Ewan McGregor	500.00	1000.00
AFW Forest Whitaker	30.00	75.00
AFPJ Freddie Prinze Jr.	25.00	60.00
AHF Harrison Ford	600.00	1200.00
AHC Hayden Christensen	125.00	250.00
AHCO Hermione Corfield	25.00	60.00
AIM Ian McDiarmid	100.00	200.00
AJB Jeremy Bulloch	30.00	75.00
AKMT Kelly Marie Tran	75.00	150.00
AKB Kenny Baker	60.00	120.00
ALM Lars Mikkelsen	50.00	100.00
ALD Laura Dern	30.00	75.00
AMM Mads Mikkelsen	75.00	150.00
APB Paul Bettany	75.00	150.00
APR Paul Reubens	50.00	100.00
ARP Ray Park	25.00	60.00
ARA Riz Ahmed	20.00	50.00
ATC Tim Curry	20.00	50.00
AWD Warwick Davis	20.00	50.00

2019 Star Wars Stellar Signatures Dual Autographs

COMMON AUTO		
STATED ODDS 4:BOXED SET		
STATED PRINT RUN 25 SER.#'d SETS		
DALC A.Lawrence/H.Corfield		
DAES A.Eckstein/T.Sircar	75.00	200.00
DABW B.Williams/J.Bulloch		
DAMW B.Williams/P.Mayhew		
DARD D.Ridley/A.Driver		
DAKD E.Kellyman/W.Davis	60.00	120.00
DAMC E.McGregor/H.Christensen		
DAFD H.Ford/A.Driver		
DAMC I.McDiarmid/H.Christensen		
DATL J.A.Taylor/M.Lanter	25.00	60.00
DAIG J.Isaacs/T.Gray	25.00	60.00
DAMD L.Mikkelsen/W.Davis	50.00	100.00
DAFT N.Futterman/J.A.Taylor	25.00	60.00
DAPB R.Park/P.Bettany		
DAPW R.Park/S.Witwer	50.00	100.00
DAWB S.Witwer/P.Bettany		

2020 Topps Star Wars Stellar Signatures

COMPLETE SET (100)	500.00	750.00
COMMON CARD (1-100)	6.00	15.00
STATED ODDS 1 SET PER BOX		

2020 Topps Star Wars Stellar Signatures Autographs

UNOPENED BOX (141 CARDS)		
COMMON AUTO	25.00	60.00
100 TOTAL BOXES WERE PRODUCED		
AAB Ahmed Best	25.00	60.00
AAD Adam Driver	200.00	400.00
ABB Ben Burtt	60.00	120.00
ABL Billie Lourd	60.00	120.00
ACM Cameron Monaghan	25.00	60.00
ACW Carl Weathers	200.00	400.00
ADL Denis Lawson	50.00	100.00
ADM Dominic Monaghan	25.00	60.00
ADR Daisy Ridley	500.00	1000.00
ADW Debra Wilson	25.00	60.00
ADY Donnie Yen	75.00	150.00
AEM Ewan McGregor	500.00	1000.00
AES Emily Swallow	125.00	250.00
AGC Gina Carano	250.00	500.00
AGE Giancarlo Esposito	75.00	150.00
AGG Greg Grunberg	25.00	60.00
AHC Hayden Christensen	100.00	200.00
AHF Harrison Ford	1000.00	2000.00
AIM Ian McDiarmid	100.00	200.00
AJG Janina Gavankar	500.00	100.00
AKB Kenny Baker	75.00	150.00
ALD Laura Dern EXCH	30.00	75.00
ANA Naomi Ackie	50.00	100.00
ANN Nick Nolte	200.00	350.00
AOA Omid Abtahi	50.00	100.00
APP Pedro Pascal	750.00	1500.00
ASW Sam Witwer	50.00	100.00
ATM Temuera Morrison EXCH	25.00	60.00
ATW Taika Waititi	200.00	400.00
AWH Werner Herzog	100.00	200.00
AAE1 Alden Ehrenreich	150.00	300.00
AAE2 Ashley Eckstein	100.00	200.00
AASL Andy Serkis	50.00	100.00
ABDW Billy Dee Williams	75.00	150.00
AJBF Jeremy Bulloch	100.00	200.00
AJSC Joonas Suotamo	60.00	120.00

2021 Topps Star Wars Stellar Signatures

COMPLETE SET (100)	600.00	1200.00
COMMON CARD (1-100)	5.00	12.00
STATED PRINT RUN 100 SER.#'d SETS		
3 Omega	8.00	20.00
11 Qi'ra	30.00	75.00
14 Captian Cassian Andor	6.00	15.00
17 Crosshair	10.00	25.00
27 Cad Bane	15.00	40.00
28 General Leia Organa	6.00	15.00
29 Jyn Erso	15.00	40.00
31 Obi-Wan Kenobi	25.00	60.00
32 Captain Rex	20.00	50.00
35 C-3PO	6.00	15.00
36 Jango Fett	12.00	30.00

40 R2-D2 8.00 20.00
44 Greedo 6.00 15.00
45 Darth Vader 8.00 20.00
47 Ahsoka Tano 30.00 75.00
48 Hera Syndulla 10.00 25.00
53 Kanan Jarras 12.00 30.00
58 The Grand Inquisitor 8.00 20.00
59 Chewbacca 8.00 20.00
63 Zeb Orrelios 8.00 20.00
64 Darth Maul 8.00 20.00
67 Ezra Bridger 15.00 40.00
68 The Mandalorian 25.00 60.00
69 Darth Sidious 10.00 25.00
70 The Armorer 12.00 30.00
71 Wicket W. Warrick 12.00 30.00
72 Grand Admiral Thrawn 15.00 40.00
79 Jar Jar Binks 8.00 20.00
82 Rey 12.00 30.00
83 Moff Gideon 8.00 20.00
85 Boba Fett's Ship 8.00 20.00
88 Bo-Katan Kryze 10.00 25.00
89 Queen Amidala 12.00 30.00
91 Grogu 30.00 75.00
92 Ahsoka Tano 12.00 30.00
95 The Razor Crest 15.00 40.00
97 Boba Fett 10.00 25.00
98 Fennec Shand 12.00 30.00
99 Boba Fett 20.00 50.00

2021 Topps Star Wars Stellar Signatures Autographs

COMMON AUTO 15.00 40.00
*BLUE/25: .5X TO 1.2X BASIC AUTOS
STATED PRINT RUN 40 SER.#'d SETS
AAB Ahmed Best 30.00 75.00
AAD Adam Driver 300.00 600.00
AAE Ashley Eckstein 100.00 200.00
AAS Andy Serkis 60.00 120.00
ABL Billie Lourd 75.00 150.00
ACH Clint Howard 50.00 100.00
ACW Carl Weathers 125.00 250.00
ADR Daisy Ridley 400.00 800.00
AEC Emilia Clarke 1500.00 3000.00
AEK Erin Kellyman 30.00 75.00
AES Emily Swallow 75.00 150.00
AFJ Felicity Jones 450.00 900.00
AGE Giancarlo Esposito 60.00 120.00
AHC Hayden Christensen 300.00 600.00
AHF Harrison Ford EXCH 1500.00 3000.00
AHQ Hugh Quarshie 25.00 60.00
AKB Kenny Baker 100.00 200.00
ALM Lars Mikkelsen 60.00 150.00
AML Matt Lanter 30.00 75.00
AMP Michael Pennington 20.00 50.00
AMV Mercedes Varnado (Sasha Banks) 175.00 350.00
AMW Matthew Wood 50.00 100.00
ANA Naomi Ackie 20.00 50.00
ANP Natalie Portman 4000.00 6500.00
ARD Rosario Dawson 1000.00 2000.00
ASK Simon Kassianides 20.00 50.00
ATG Taylor Gray 25.00 60.00
ATW Taika Waititi 200.00 400.00
AWD Warwick Davis EXCH 30.00 75.00
AASP Amy Sedaris 75.00 150.00
ABDW Billy Dee Williams 100.00 200.00
ADLI Diana Lee Inosanto 25.00 60.00
AJAT James Arnold Taylor 50.00 100.00
AKMT Kelly Marie Tran 50.00 125.00

2021 Topps Star Wars Stellar Signatures Dual Autographs

STATED PRINT RUN 25 SER.#'d SETS
DABG T.Gray/D.Baker 100.00 200.00
DADD H.Davis/W.Davis EXCH
DAEB D.Baker/A.Eckstein 150.00 300.00
DAFD A.Driver/H.Ford EXCH
DALE M.Lanter/A.Eckstein 125.00 300.00
DARD D.Ridley/A.Driver 600.00 1200.00
DARW B.D.Williams/D.Ridley 500.00 1000.00
DAVK S.Kassianides/M.Vernado EXCH 150.00 300.00

2021 Topps Star Wars Stellar Signatures Quad Autographs

*BLUE/25: X TO X BASIC AUTOS
STATED PRINT RUN 40 SER.#'d SETS
QDCW Baker/Lanter 300.00 500.00
Taylor/Eckstein

1997 Panini Star Wars Stickers

COMPLETE SET (66) 7.50 20.00
COMMON CARD (1-66) .20 .50
PRODUCED BY PANINI

2022 Topps 206 Star Wars Wave 1

COMPLETE SET W/SP (60)
COMPLETE SET W/O SP (50) 30.00 75.00
COMMON CARD (1-50) 1.00 2.50
COMMON SP 25.00 60.00
*BLUE: .6X TO 1.5X BASIC CARDS
*LOGO BACKS: .75X TO 2X BASIC CARDS
*ORANGE/101: 4X TO 10X BASIC CARDS
*GREEN/51: 2X TO 5X BASIC CARDS
*YELLOW/34: 3X TO 8X BASIC CARDS
FINAL PRINT RUN 25,102 BOXES
1 Luke Skywalker SP 60.00 150.00
2 Leia Organa SP 40.00 100.00
3 C-3PO SP 30.00 75.00
6 Lando Calrissian SP 40.00 100.00
7 Han Solo in Carbonite SP 75.00 200.00
14 Qui-Gon Jinn SP 50.00 125.00
23 Jyn Erso SP 60.00 150.00
38 Finn SP 30.00 75.00

2022 Topps 206 Star Wars Wave 1 Homeworld

COMMON CARD 12.00 30.00
STATED ODDS 1:30
1 Luke Skywalker 75.00 200.00
5 Jawas 15.00 40.00
8 Sheev Palpatine 20.00 50.00
9 Nien Nunb 15.00 40.00
10 Jabba the Hutt 30.00 75.00
23 Jyn Erso 60.00 150.00
25 Bail Organa 15.00 40.00

2022 Topps 206 Star Wars Wave 2

COMPLETE SET W/SP (60)
COMPLETE SET W/O SP (50) 30.00 75.00
COMMON CARD (1-50) 1.00 2.50
COMMON SP 20.00 50.00
*BLUE: .6X TO 1.5X BASIC CARDS
*LOGO BACKS: .75X TO 2X BASIC CARDS
*ORANGE/56: 4X TO 10X BASIC CARDS
FINAL PRINT RUN 14,009 BOXES
1IV Darth Vader SP 150.00 400.00
2IV Yoda SP 125.00 300.00
3IV Chewbacca SP 50.00 125.00
5IV Mace Windu SP 40.00 100.00
6IV Jango Fett SP 50.00 125.00
14IV Poe Dameron SP 25.00 60.00
20IV Captain Cassian Andor SP 60.00 150.00
39IV Darth Sidious SP 30.00 75.00

2022 Topps 206 Star Wars Wave 2 Autographs

COMMON AUTO 40.00 100.00
RANDOMLY INSERTED INTO PACKS
NNO Ahmed Best 100.00 250.00
NNO Carey Jones 60.00 150.00
NNO Hugh Quarshie 60.00 150.00

2022 Topps 206 Star Wars Wave 2 Homeworld

COMMON CARD 15.00 40.00
STATED ODDS 1:30
2 Yoda 75.00 200.00
4 R2-D2 60.00 150.00
9 Queen Jamillia 30.00 75.00
10 Tusken Raider 40.00 100.00
11 Grand Moff Tarkin 25.00 60.00
16 Captain Phasma 50.00 125.00
39 Darth Sidious 25.00 60.00

2022 Topps 206 Star Wars Wave 2 Planets

COMMON CARD (P1-P10) 12.00 30.00
STATED ODDS 1:10
P1 Tatooine 15.00 40.00
P9 Kamino 15.00 40.00
P10 Pasaana 15.00 40.00

2022 Topps 206 Star Wars Wave 3

COMPLETE SET W/SP (60)
COMPLETE SET W/O SP (50) 30.00 75.00
COMMON CARD (1-60) 1.00 2.50
COMMON SP 25.00 60.00
*BLUE: .6X TO 1.5X BASIC CARDS
*LOGO BACKS: .75X TO 2X BASIC CARDS
*ORANGE/54: 4X TO 10X BASIC CARDS
FINAL PRINT RUN 13,318 BOXES
4A Grogu SP 60.00 150.00
5A Darth Maul SP 50.00 125.00
12A Chirrut Imwe SP 40.00 100.00
13A Bo-Katan Kryze SP 50.00 125.00
1A The Mandalorian SP 100.00 250.00
26A Plo Koon SP 40.00 100.00
2A Boba Fett SP 50.00 125.00
3A Rey SP 60.00 150.00

2022 Topps 206 Star Wars Wave 3 Autographs

COMMON AUTO 50.00 125.00
RANDOMLY INSERTED INTO PACKS
NNO Amy Sedaris 100.00 250.00
NNO Richard Brake 75.00 200.00

2022 Topps 206 Star Wars Wave 3 Homeworld

COMMON CARD 25.00 60.00
STATED ODDS 1:30
2 Boba Fett 60.00 150.00
5 Darth Maul 60.00 150.00
9 Wicket W. Warrick 50.00 125.00
10 Admiral Piett 40.00 100.00
12 Chirrut Imwe 40.00 100.00
15 BB-8 40.00 100.00

2022 Topps 206 Star Wars Wave 3 Vehicles

COMMON CARD (V1-V10) 15.00 40.00
STATED ODDS 1:10
V1 Millennium Falcon 30.00 75.00
V2 Death Star 20.00 50.00
V5 Star Destroyer 25.00 60.00
V6 Slave I

2022 Topps 206 Star Wars Wave 4

COMPLETE SET W/SP (60)
COMPLETE SET W/O SP (50) 30.00 75.00
COMMON CARD (1-60) 1.00 2.50
COMMON SP 50.00 125.00
*BLUE: .6X TO 1.5X BASIC CARDS
*LOGO BACKS: .75X TO 2X BASIC CARDS
*ORANGE/56: 4X TO 10X BASIC CARDS
FINAL PRINT RUN 11,097 BOXES
1 Obi-Wan Kenobi SP 75.00 200.00
2 Kylo Ren SP 75.00 200.00
3 Anakin Skywalker SP 60.00 150.00
4 Ahsoka Tano SP 75.00 200.00
5 Fennec Shand SP 60.00 150.00
6 Padme Amidala SP 125.00 300.00
46 Tala Durith SP
47 Haja Estre SP

2022 Topps 206 Star Wars Wave 4 Autographs

COMMON AUTO 40.00 100.00
RANDOMLY INSERTED INTO PACKS
NNO Caroline Blakiston 60.00 150.00
NNO Giancarlo Esposito 125.00 300.00

2022 Topps 206 Star Wars Wave 4 Crests

COMPLETE SET (8)
COMMON CARD (C1-C8)
STATED ODDS 1:10
C1 Rebel Alliance 15.00 40.00
C2 Galactic Empire 20.00 50.00
C3 Mandalorian 10.00 25.00
C4 Boba Fett 10.00 25.00
C5 Galactic Republic
C6 General Grievous 15.00 40.00
C7 Jedi Order 10.00 25.00
V6 Slave I

2022 Topps 206 Star Wars Wave 4 Homeworld

COMMON CARD (10) 15.00 40.00
STATED ODDS 1:30
1 Obi-Wan Kenobi 60.00 150.00
4 Ahsoka Tano 60.00 150.00
8 Admiral Ackbar 40.00 100.00
11 Mon Mothma 50.00 125.00
19 Qi'ra 30.00 75.00
21 Ponda Baba 40.00 100.00
25 Val 25.00 60.00

2023 Topps Throwback Thursday Star Wars

COMMON CARD 3.00 8.00
COMMON SP 40.00 100.00
SET 1-4 IN '52 TOPPS BB DESIGN
SET 5-8 IN '84 TOPPS BB DESIGN
SET 9-12 IN '58 TOPPS FB DESIGN
SET 13-16 IN '71 TOPPS BB DESIGN
SET 1 PRINT RUN 4,521 SETS
SET 2 PRINT RUN 2,934 SETS
SET 3 PRINT RUN 4,283 SETS
SET 4 PRINT RUN 3,039 SETS
SET 5 PRINT RUN 2,034 SETS
SET 6 PRINT RUN 1,704 SETS
SET 7 PRINT RUN 1,380 SETS
SET 8 PRINT RUN 1,566 SETS
SET 9 PRINT RUN 1,428 SETS
SET 10 PRINT RUN 1,576 SETS
SET 11 PRINT RUN 1,913 SETS
SET 12 PRINT RUN
SET 13 PRINT RUN
SET 14 PRINT RUN
SET 15 PRINT RUN
1 Princess Leia 4.00 10.00
2 Darth Vader 5.00 12.00
2A Darth Vader VAR SP 50.00 125.00
3 Luke Skywalker 4.00 10.00
5 Boba Fett 6.00 15.00
5A Boba Fett VAR SP 60.00 150.00
8 Yoda 4.00 10.00
8A Yoda VAR SP 75.00 200.00
11 Ahsoka Tano 8.00 20.00
11A Ahsoka Tano VAR SP 100.00 250.00
13 Darth Maul 5.00 12.00
14 Padme Amidala 6.00 15.00
14A Padme Amidala VAR SP 75.00 200.00
15 Jyn Erso 5.00 12.00
17 Han Solo 6.00 15.00
17A Han Solo VAR SP 75.00 200.00
20 Kylo Ren 5.00 12.00
20A Kylo Ren VAR SP 60.00 150.00
23A Chewbacca VAR SP 40.00 100.00
26A Cassian Andor VAR SP 50.00 125.00

27 Ahsoka Tano 8.00 20.00
28 Cobb Vanth
29 The Mandalorian
29A The Mandalorian VAR SP
30 Moff Gideon
31 Mon Mothma
32 Grogu
32A Grogu VAR SP
33 Krrsantan
34 Vel Sartha
35 Boba Fett
35A Boba Fett VAR SP
36 Peli Motto
37 Luminara Unduli
38 Obi-Wan Kenobi
38A Obi-Wan Kenobi VAR SP
39 Chirrut Imwe
40 Rancor
41 Rey
41A Rey VAR SP
42 Wicket W. Warrick
43 Poe Dameron
44 Anakin Skywalker
44A Anakin Skywalker VAR SP
45 Captain Phasma

1997 Topps Star Wars Trilogy The Complete Story

COMPLETE SET (72) 6.00 15.00
COMMON CARD (1-72) .25 .60
0 Promo 1.00 2.00

1997 Topps Star Wars Trilogy The Complete Story Laser

COMPLETE SET (6) 6.00 15.00
COMMON CARD (LC1-LC6) 1.25 3.00
STATED ODDS 1:9

1997 Merlin Star Wars Trilogy

COMPLETE SET (125) 10.00 25.00
UNOPENED BOX (48 PACKS) 25.00 40.00
UNOPENED PACK (5 CARDS) 1.00 1.25
COMMON CARD (1-125) .15 .40

1997 Merlin Star Wars Trilogy Case-Toppers

COMPLETE SET (3) 20.00 50.00
COMMON CARD (P1-P3) 8.00 20.00
STATED ODDS 1:CASE

1997 Topps Star Wars Trilogy Special Edition

COMPLETE SET (72) 6.00 15.00
UNOPENED BOX (36 PACKS) 100.00 200.00
UNOPENED PACK (9 CARDS) 3.00 6.00
COMMON CARD (1-72) .15 .40
13D ISSUED AS BOX TOPPER
13D X-Wings Departing 6.00 15.00

1997 Topps Star Wars Trilogy Special Edition Holograms

COMPLETE SET (2) 10.00 25.00
COMMON CARD (1-2) 6.00 15.00
STATED ODDS 1:18

1997 Topps Star Wars Trilogy Special Edition Laser

COMPLETE SET (6) 6.00 15.00
COMMON CARD (LC1-LC6) 1.25 3.00
STATED ODDS 1:9

1997 Topps Star Wars Trilogy Special Edition Promos

COMPLETE SET (8) 10.00 25.00
COMMON CARD (P1-P8) 1.25 3.00
P1 Three Stormtroopers 4.00 10.00
P4 Sandcrawler 3.00 8.00
P5 Jawa and Landspeeder 3.00 8.00
P6 Millennium Falcon 3.00 8.00

1997 Kenner Star Wars Trilogy Special Edition Promos

COMPLETE SET (4) 10.00 25.00
COMMON CARD (H1-H4) 4.00 10.00

1997 MicroMachines Star Wars Trilogy Special Edition Promos

COMPLETE SET (5) 12.00 30.00
COMMON CARD (G1-G5) 4.00 10.00

1997 Kenner Star Wars Vehicles

COMPLETE SET (72) 5.00 12.00
UNOPENED BOX (36 PACKS) 40.00 60.00
UNOPENED PACK (5 CARDS) 1.50 2.50
COMMON CARD (1-72) .15 .40

1997 Topps Star Wars Vehicles 3-D

COMPLETE SET (3) 25.00 60.00
COMMON CARD 8.00 20.00
STATED ODDS 1:36
3 Princess Leia 15.00 40.00
Luke Skywalker

1997 Topps Star Wars Vehicles Cut-Away

COMPLETE SET (4) 7.50 20.00
COMMON CARD (C1-C4) 2.50 6.00
STATED ODDS 1:18

1997 Topps Star Wars Vehicles Promos

P1A Darth Vader & Stormtroopers on Speeder Bikes 12.00 30.00
chromium)/3200*
P1B Darth Vader & Stormtroopers on Speeder Bikes 30.00 75.00
(refractor)/320*
P2A Stormtroopers on Speeder Bikes 20.00 50.00
(chromium)/1600*
P2B Stormtroopers on Speeder Bikes 50.00 100.00
(refractor)/160*
NNO 2-Card Sheet

2021 Topps Now Star Wars Visions Episode 1 The Duel

COMPLETE SET (5) 8.00 20.00
COMMON CARD (1-5) 2.50 6.00
STATED PRINT RUN 665 ANNCD SETS

2021 Topps Now Star Wars Visions Episode 2 Tatooine Rhapsody

COMPLETE SET (5) 8.00 20.00
COMMON CARD (1-5) 2.50 6.00
STATED PRINT RUN 501 ANNCD SETS

2021 Topps Now Star Wars Visions Episode 3 The Twins

COMPLETE SET (5) 8.00 20.00
COMMON CARD (1-5) 2.50 6.00
STATED PRINT RUN 461 ANNCD SETS

2021 Topps Now Star Wars Visions Episode 4 The Elder

COMPLETE SET (5) 8.00 20.00
COMMON CARD (1-5) 2.50 6.00
STATED PRINT RUN 539 ANNCD SETS

2021 Topps Now Star Wars Visions Episode 5 The Village Bride

COMPLETE SET (5) 8.00 20.00
COMMON CARD (1-5) 2.50 6.00
STATED PRINT RUN 463 ANNCD SETS

2021 Topps Now Star Wars Visions Episode 6 Akakiri

COMPLETE SET (5) 8.00 20.00
COMMON CARD (1-5) 2.50 6.00
STATED PRINT RUN 484 ANNCD SETS

2021 Topps Now Star Wars Visions Episode 7 T0-B1

COMPLETE SET (5) 8.00 20.00
COMMON CARD (1-5) 2.50 6.00
STATED PRINT RUN 517 ANNCD SETS

2021 Topps Now Star Wars Visions Episode 8 The Ninth Jedi

COMPLETE SET (5) 8.00 20.00
COMMON CARD (1-5) 2.50 6.00
STATED PRINT RUN 474 ANNCD SETS

2021 Topps Now Star Wars Visions Episode 9 Lop and Ocho

COMPLETE SET (5) 8.00 20.00
COMMON CARD (1-5) 2.50 6.00
STATED PRINT RUN 466 ANNCD SETS

2017 Star Wars Widevision Bonus Abrams

COMPLETE SET (4) 5.00 12.00
COMMON CARD (1-4) 2.50 6.00

2022-23 Topps Star Wars Wrapper Art Collection Set

COMPLETE SET (28) 150.00 400.00
WAVE 1 SET (4) 25.00 60.00
WAVE 2 SET (4) 20.00 50.00
WAVE 3 SET (4) 15.00 40.00
WAVE 4 SET (4) 20.00 50.00
WAVE 5 SET (4) 15.00 40.00
WAVE 6 SET (4) 15.00 40.00
WAVE 7 SET (4) 25.00 60.00
COMMON CARD (1-28) 6.00 15.00
*RAINBOW/99: .75X TO 2X BASIC CARDS
*SILVER FR./49: 1.2X TO 3X BASIC CARDS
STATED PRINT RUN VARIES PER CARD
1 Rey/632* 12.00 30.00
2 Kylo Ren/536* 12.00 30.00
3 BB-8/572* 10.00 25.00
4 Finn/473* 10.00 25.00
5 Darth Maul/614* 12.00 30.00
6 Qui-Gon Jinn/536* 10.00 25.00
7 Anakin Skywalker/500* 10.00 25.00
8 Queen Amidala/556* 8.00 20.00
9 Obi-Wan Kenobi/422* 12.00 30.00
13 Ahsoka Tano/461* 12.00 30.00
15 Krrsantan/400* 10.00 25.00
16 Cad Bane/437* 10.00 25.00
18 K-2SO/285* 10.00 25.00
19 Hunter/266* 10.00 25.00
20 Omega/279* 8.00 20.00
25 Luke Skywalker/399* 10.00 25.00
26 Yoda/535* 12.00 30.00
27 General Leia Organa/387* 12.00 30.00
28 Han Solo/404* 10.00 25.00

1999 Dark Horse Comics Star Wars X-Wing Rogue Squadron

COMMON CARD 2.50 6.00

2020 Topps Women of Star Wars

COMPLETE SET (100) 8.00 20.00
UNOPENED BOX (7 PACKS) 125.00 200.00
UNOPENED PACK (8 CARDS) 20.00 30.00
COMMON CARD (1-100) .20 .50
*ORANGE: .5X TO 1.2X BASIC CARDS
*BLUE: .6X TO 1.5X BASIC CARDS
*GREEN/99: 4X TO 10X BASIC CARDS
*PURPLE/25: 8X TO 20X BASIC CARDS

2020 Topps Women of Star Wars Autographs

COMMON AUTO 4.00 10.00
*ORANGE/99: .5X TO 1.2X BASIC AUTOS
*BLUE/50: .6X TO 1.5X BASIC AUTOS
*PURPLE/25: .75X TO 2X BASIC AUTOS
STATED ODDS 1:14
AAA Amy Allen 10.00 25.00
AAF Anna Francolini 5.00 12.00
AAG Anna Graves 5.00 12.00
AAP Angelique Perrin 6.00 15.00
ACC Crystal Clarke 5.00 12.00
ACL Charlotte Louise 5.00 12.00
ACT Catherine Taber 5.00 12.00
AJD Julie Dolan 5.00 12.00
AJK Jaime King 8.00 20.00
ALC Lily Cole 5.00 12.00
ALW Leeanna Walsman 8.00 20.00
AML Misty Lee 6.00 15.00
AMV Myrna Velasco 6.00 15.00
ANC Nazneen Contractor 5.00 12.00
AOS Orli Shoshan 8.00 20.00
ATS Tiya Sircar 10.00 25.00

2020 Topps Women of Star Wars Autographs Blue

STATED PRINT RUN 50 SER.#'d SETS
AAH Amanda Hale 8.00 20.00
AJH Jessica Henwick 12.00 30.00
AMB Michonne Bourriague 12.00 30.00
ANF Nika Futterman 15.00 40.00
ASM Suzie McGrath 6.00 15.00
AVR Vinette Robinson 10.00 25.00

2020 Topps Women of Star Wars Autographs Orange

STATED PRINT RUN 99 SER.#'d SETS
AAB Anna Brewster 6.00 15.00
ADW Debra Wilson 10.00 25.00
AEK Erin Kellyman 15.00 40.00
AHC Hermione Corfield 12.00 30.00
AJG Janina Gavankar 15.00 40.00
AVM Vanessa Marshall 10.00 25.00

2020 Topps Women of Star Wars Autographs Purple

STATED PRINT RUN 25 SER.#'d SETS
AAE Ashley Eckstein 50.00 100.00
ACB Caroline Blakiston 20.00 50.00
ANA Naomi Ackie 60.00 120.00
AGCM Gina Carano 200.00 400.00
AKCH Keisha Castle-Hughes 25.00 60.00

2020 Topps Women of Star Wars Iconic Moments

COMPLETE SET (22) 12.00 30.00
COMMON CARD (IM1-IM22) 1.25 3.00
*GREEN/99: .6X TO 1.5X BASIC CARDS
*PURPLE/25: 1.2X TO 3X BASIC CARDS

2020 Topps Women of Star Wars Journey of Leia Organa

COMPLETE SET (8) 10.00 25.00
COMMON CARD (JL1-JL8) 1.50 4.00
STATED ODDS 1:7

2020 Topps Women of Star Wars Powerful Pairs

COMPLETE SET (28) 15.00 40.00
COMMON CARD (PP1-PP28) .75 2.00
*GREEN/99: .6X TO 1.5X BASIC CARDS
*PURPLE/25: 1.2X TO 3X BASIC CARDS
STATED ODDS 1:3

2020 Topps Women of Star Wars Weapon of Choice

COMPLETE SET (24) 12.00 30.00
COMMON CARD (WC1-WC24) 1.00 2.50
*GREEN/99: .6X TO 1.5X BASIC CARDS
*PURPLE/25: 1.5X TO 4X BASIC CARDS

Wacky Packages

WACKY PACKAGES

Vintage Wackys

1980 Topps Wacky Packages Can Labels

COMPLETE SET (12)	50.00	100.00
COMMON LABEL	5.00	12.00

1973 Topps Wacky Packages Cloth Series

COMPLETE SET (30)	120.00	250.00
COMMON CARD	4.00	10.00
2 Band-Ache Strips SP	10.00	25.00
17 Lavirus Mouthwash SP	8.00	20.00
22 Mutt's Apple Juice SP	8.00	20.00
23 Paul Maul SP	8.00	20.00

1967-68 Topps Wacky Packages Die-Cuts

COMPLETE SET W/O SP (44)	1500.00	2500.00
COMPLETE SET W/SP (56)	4000.00	7500.00
UNOPENED PACK (5 CARDS)	1000.00	1300.00
COMMON CARD	8.00	20.00
1 Boredom's Coffee	12.00	30.00
2A Duzn't Do Nuthin'	15.00	40.00
2B Fearstone Tires	15.00	40.00
3 Vicejoy Cigarettes	8.00	20.00
4 Camals Cigarettes	8.00	20.00
5A Campy Spider Soup	30.00	75.00
5B Chock Full O' Nuts and Bolts	60.00	120.00
6A Grave Train	100.00	200.00
6B Slum-Maid Raisins	25.00	60.00
7 Spray Nit	8.00	20.00
8 Lavirus Mouthwash	12.00	30.00
9 Paul Maul Cigarettes	10.00	25.00
10 Dopey Whip	8.00	20.00
11 Cracked Jerk	15.00	40.00
12 Crust Toothpaste	8.00	20.00
13 Kook-Aid	8.00	20.00
14 Alcohol Seltzer	15.00	40.00
15A De-Mented Tomatoes	20.00	50.00
15B Skimpy	25.00	60.00
16 Pure Hex Bleach	8.00	20.00
17 Weakies	8.00	20.00
18A Quacker Oats	25.00	60.00
18B Schmutz Beer	50.00	100.00
19 Minute Lice	8.00	20.00
20 Gadzooka Gum	12.00	30.00
21A Jolly Mean Giant SP	1000.00	1500.00
21B Maddie Boy	80.00	150.00
21C Moron Salt	30.00	80.00
22 Liptorn Molten Lava Soup	8.00	20.00
23A 6 Up SP	100.00	200.00
23B Muller Low Life	50.00	100.00
24 Band-Ache Strips	12.00	30.00
25 Chock Full O' Nuts and Bolts	8.00	20.00
26 Tied Detergent	8.00	20.00
27 Mrs. Klean	8.00	20.00
28 Breadcrust Corned Beef Hash	20.00	50.00
29 Cover Ghoul	8.00	20.00
30 Horrid Deodorant	8.00	20.00
31 Jail-O	8.00	20.00
32A Ratz Crackers SP	1250.00	2500.00
32B Weakies	8.00	20.00
33 Grave Train	8.00	20.00
34 Duzn't Do Nuthin'	8.00	20.00
35 Canada Wet Fink	8.00	20.00
36 Maddie Boy	12.00	30.00
37A Breadcrust Corned Beef Hash	20.00	50.00
37B Coronation Milk	30.00	80.00
38A Cracked Animals SP	1200.00	2000.00
38B Cracked Jerk	20.00	50.00
39 Hostage Cupcakes	8.00	20.00
40 Mutt's Apple Juice	10.00	25.00
41 6 Up	8.00	20.00
42 Skimpy	8.00	20.00
43A Jolly Mean Giant	50.00	100.00
43B Maddie Boy	100.00	175.00
44 Quacker Oats	8.00	20.00

1975 Topps Wacky Packages Hostess Double Wackys

COMMON CARD	50.00	100.00
2 Ajerx/Hawaiian Punks SP	200.00	400.00
5 Blecch/Neveready SP	200.00	400.00
7 Botch/Rice-a-Phoni SP	200.00	400.00
9 Crust/Liptorn SP	200.00	400.00
11 Gyppy Pop/Motorzola SP	200.00	400.00
16 Mutt's/Rabid Shave SP	200.00	400.00
17 Nertz/Sledge SP	200.00	400.00

1973 Topps Wacky Packages Posters

COMPLETE SET W/SP (24)	375.00	750.00
COMPLETE SET W/O SP (24)	200.00	400.00
COMMON CARD (1-24)	6.00	15.00
1 Log Cave-In Syrup	8.00	20.00
2 Koduck Photos	10.00	25.00
3 Blast Blew Ribbon Beer	8.00	20.00
4 Nevereaady Battery	12.00	30.00
5 Toadal SP	150.00	300.00
6 Hipton Tea Bags	10.00	25.00
8 Gadzooka Gum	10.00	25.00
9 Crakola Crayons	10.00	25.00
10 Milk-Foam	10.00	25.00
11 Ivery Snow	10.00	25.00
13 Wacky Garbage	15.00	40.00
14 Burpsi-Cola	8.00	20.00
15 Mex-Pax Coffee	12.00	30.00
16 Hurtz Tomato Ketchup	12.00	30.00
17 Jail-O Dessert	10.00	25.00
18 STD Oil Shortage	10.00	25.00
20 Slopicana Juice	12.00	30.00
21 Cheapios SP	75.00	150.00
22 Fang	8.00	20.00
23 Weakies SP	120.00	250.00
24 Glutton	10.00	25.00

1974 Topps Wacky Packages Posters

COMPLETE SET (24)	150.00	300.00
COMMON POSTER (1-24)	6.00	15.00

1979-80 Topps Wacky Packages Rerun Complete Series

COMPLETE SET (264)	80.00	150.00
COMP.SET SERIES I (66)	200.00	40.00
COMP.SET SERIES II (66)	30.00	80.00
COMP.SET SERIES III (66)	10.00	25.00
COMP.SET SERIES IV (66)	15.00	40.00
UNOPENED BOX SER.I (36 PACKS)	200.00	300.00
UNOPENED PACK SER.I (6 CARDS)	6.00	8.00
UNOPENED BOX SER.II (36 PACKS)	500.00	1000.00
UNOPENED PACK SER.II (6 CARDS)	15.00	25.00
UNOPENED BOX SER.III (36 PACKS)	200.00	300.00
UNOPENED PACK SER.III (6 CARDS)	6.00	8.00
UNOPENED BOX SER.IV (36 PACKS)	150.00	250.00
UNOPENED PACK SER.IV (6 CARDS)	4.00	6.00
COMMON SERIES I (1-66)	.15	.40
COMMON SERIES II (67-132)	.50	1.25
COMMON SERIES III (133-198)	.15	.40
COMMON SERIES IV (199-264)	.30	.75

1973 Topps Wacky Packages Series 1 White Backs

COMPLETE SET (30)	300.00	600.00
Common 6X Print	1.50	4.00
Common 4X Print	3.00	8.00
Common 3X Print	5.00	12.00
Common 2X Print	6.00	15.00
2 Band-Ache Strips SP (1)	80.00	150.00
17 Lavirus Mouthwash SP (1)	50.00	100.00
22 Mutt's Apple Juice SP (1)	30.00	80.00
23 Paul Maul SP (1)	30.00	80.00

1973 Topps Wacky Packages Series 1 Black Ludlow Backs

COMPLETE SET (30)	1500.00	2500.00
Common 6X Print	12.00	30.00
Common 4X Print	20.00	50.00
Common 3X Print	30.00	60.00
Common 2X Print	50.00	100.00

1973 Topps Wacky Packages Series 1 Red Ludlow Backs

COMPLETE SET (30)	3000.00	5000.00
Common 6X Print	20.00	50.00
Common 4X Print	20.00	50.00
Common 3X Print	30.00	80.00
Common 2X Print	60.00	120.00
2 Band-Ache Strips SP (1)	1800.00	2200.00
17 Lavirus Mouthwash SP (1)	200.00	400.00
22 Mutt's Apple Juice SP (1)	150.00	300.00
23 Paul Maul SP (1)	150.00	300.00

1973 Topps Wacky Packages Series 1 Tan Backs

2 Band-Ache Strips SP (1)	450.00	800.00
17 Lavirus Mouthwash SP (1)	100.00	200.00
22 Mutt's Apple Juice SP (1)	100.00	200.00
23 Paul Maul SP (1)	80.00	150.00

1973 Topps Wacky Packages Series 1 Puzzle

COMPLETE SET (9)	12.00	30.00
COMMON CARD	2.00	5.00

1973 Topps Wacky Packages Series 2 White Backs

COMPLETE SET (33)	60.00	120.00
COMMON CARD	1.50	4.00
2 Ajerx	2.50	6.00
3 Awful Bits	4.00	10.00

4 Blecch Shampoo 2.50 6.00
5 Blunder Bread 2.00 5.00
6 Boo-Hoo Drink 3.00 8.00
11 Commie Cleanser 2.00 5.00
13 Dull Pineapple 2.00 5.00
14 Exceedrin 2.50 6.00
15 Fish Bone Dressing 2.50 6.00
16 Gloom 2.50 6.00
17 Gurgle Baby Food 2.50 6.00
18 Gyppy Pop Corn 2.50 6.00
19 Hurts Tomatoes 2.00 5.00
20 Kook Cigarettes 2.00 5.00
21 Kooloff's All-Brain Crereal 2.50 6.00
22 Log Cave-In Syrup 2.50 6.00
23 Minute Mud 2.00 5.00
24 Nertz 5.00 12.00
25 Plastered Peanuts 2.00 5.00
26 Poopsie 2.50 6.00
27 Putrid Cat Chow 2.00 5.00
28 Run Tony Shells SP 15.00 40.00
29 Sailem 2.00 5.00
31 Sugarmess Bubble Gum 2.50 6.00

1973 Topps Wacky Packages Series 2 Black Ludlow Backs

COMPLETE SET (33) 600.00 1100.00
COMMON CARD 12.00 30.00
28 Run Tony Shells SP 50.00 100.00

1973 Topps Wacky Packages Series 2 Red Ludlow Backs

COMPLETE SET (33) 1000.00 2000.00
COMMON CARD 20.00 50.00
3 Awful Bits 80.00 150.00
4 Blecch Shampoo 80.00 150.00
5 Blunder Bread 80.00 150.00
28 Run Tony Shells SP 120.00 250.00
29 Sailem 80.00 150.00

1973 Topps Wacky Packages Series 2 Tan Backs

COMPLETE SET (33) 60.00 120.00
COMMON CARD 1.50 4.00
2 Ajerx 2.50 6.00
3 Awful Bits 4.00 10.00
4 Blecch Shampoo 2.50 6.00
5 Blunder Bread 2.00 5.00
6 Boo-Hoo Drink 3.00 8.00
11 Commie Cleanser 2.00 5.00
13 Dull Pineapple 2.00 5.00
14 Exceedrin 2.50 6.00
15 Fish Bone Dressing 2.50 6.00
16 Gloom 2.50 6.00
17 Gurgle Baby Food 2.50 6.00
18 Gyppy Pop Corn 2.50 6.00
19 Hurts Tomatoes 2.00 5.00
20 Kook Cigarettes 2.00 5.00
21 Kooloff's All-Brain Crereal 2.50 6.00
22 Log Cave-In Syrup 2.50 6.00
23 Minute Mud 2.00 5.00
24 Nertz 5.00 12.00
25 Plastered Peanuts 2.00 5.00
26 Poopsie 2.50 6.00
27 Putrid Cat Chow 2.00 5.00
28 Run Tony Shells SP 15.00 40.00
29 Sailem 2.00 5.00
31 Sugarmess Bubble Gum 2.50 6.00

1973 Topps Wacky Packages Series 2 Puzzle

COMPLETE SET (9) 8.00 20.00
COMMON CARD 1.25 3.00

1973 Topps Wacky Packages Series 3 White Backs

COMPLETE SET (30)
1 1-A Sauce
2 Argh
3 Beanball Gum
4 Busted Finger Candy
5 Choke King
6 Crakola Crayons
7 Dr. Ono
8 Drowny
9 Foolball
10 Harm and Hammer
11 Hawaiian Punks Juice
12 Hired Root Beer
13 Hungry Jerk
14 Hurtz Crazy Canary Food
15 Killette Fright Guard
16 Koduck Photos
17 Lova Soap
18 Lucky Stride Cigarettes
19 Moonshine Wheez-It
20 Motorzola
21 Neveready Battery
22 No Tips
23 Rabid Shave
24 Raw Leaves Cigarettes
25 Rice-A-Phoni
26 Sledge
27 Snatch-A-Pack
28 Spit and Spill UER
(Spic and Span)
29 Sweat Hard Soap
30 Windchester

1973 Topps Wacky Packages Series 3 Tan Backs

1 1-A Sauce 1.50 4.00
2 Argh 2.00 5.00
3 Beanball Gum 1.50 4.00
5 Choke King 1.25 3.00
7 Dr. Ono 2.50 6.00
8 Drowny 1.25 3.00
10 Harm and Hammer 1.50 4.00
11 Hawaiian Punks Juice 2.50 6.00
12 Hired Root Beer 4.00 10.00
13 Hungry Jerk 2.50 6.00
15 Killette Fright Guard 1.25 3.00
16 Koduck Photos 1.50 4.00
17 Lova Soap 2.00 5.00
18 Lucky Stride Cigarettes 1.50 4.00
20 Motorzola 1.25 3.00
21 Neveready Battery 2.00 5.00
22 No Tips 1.25 3.00
23 Rabid Shave 1.50 4.00
25 Rice-A-Phoni 1.50 4.00
26 Sledge 1.25 3.00
28A Spit and Spill 2.50 6.00
28B Spit and Spill ERR 30.00 75.00
(Spic and Span Logo)
29 Sweat Hard Soap 1.25 3.00
30 Windchester 1.50 4.00

1973 Topps Wacky Packages Series 3 Puzzle

COMPLETE SET (9) 8.00 20.00
1 Beanball Gum Bottom Left 1.25 3.00
2 Beanball Gum Bottom Middle 1.25 3.00
3 Beanball Gum Bottom Right 1.25 3.00
4 Beanball Gum Center Left 1.25 3.00
5 Beanball Gum Center Middle 1.25 3.00
6 Beanball Gum Center Right 1.25 3.00
7 Beanball Gum Top Left 1.25 3.00
8 Beanball Gum Top Middle 1.25 3.00
9 Beanball Gum Top Right 1.25 3.00

1973 Topps Wacky Packages Series 4

COMPLETE SET w/SP (32) 80.00 150.00
COMMON CARD 1.00 2.50
1 Armor Hot Dogs 2.00 5.00
5 Brute 88 2.00 5.00
6 Bum Chex SP 25.00 60.00
8 Chef Girl-Ar-Dee 2.00 5.00
9 Choke Wagon SP 30.00 80.00
10 Dampers 2.50 6.00
11 Escuire Foot Polish 1.50 4.00
12 Fang 1.50 4.00
13 Freetoes 2.50 6.00
14 Gatoraid 6.00 15.00
18 Hipton Tea Bags 2.50 6.00
22 Mess Clairoil 2.50 6.00
24 Mustard Charge 1.50 4.00
25 Nestree 1.50 4.00
26 Nutlee's Quit 1.50 4.00
27 Quake N' Ache 2.50 6.00
28 Raw Goo Sauce 1.50 4.00
29 Rinkled Wrap 2.50 6.00
30 Taster's Choke 1.50 4.00
31 Windhex 3.00 8.00
32 Wormy Packages 2.00 5.00

1973 Topps Wacky Packages Series 4 Puzzle

COMPLETE SET (18) 30.00 75.00
COMPLETE BUM CHEX SET (9) 8.00 20.00
COMPLETE MESS CLAIROL SET (9) 25.00 60.00
COMMON BUM CHEX 1.25 3.00
COMMON MESS CLAIROL 4.00 10.00

1974 Topps Wacky Packages Series 5

COMPLETE SET (32) 50.00 100.00
COMMON CARD 1.50 4.00

1974 Topps Wacky Packages Series 5 Puzzle

COMPLETE SET (9) 8.00 20.00
COMMON CARD 1.25 3.00

1974 Topps Wacky Packages Series 6

COMPLETE SET (33) 30.00 80.00
COMMON CARD 1.25 3.00

1974 Topps Wacky Packages Series 6 Puzzle

COMPLETE SET (18) 12.00 30.00
COMPLETE SPILLS BAD SET (9) 8.00 20.00
COMPLETE SPILLS BROS. SET (9) 8.00 20.00
COMMON SPILLS BAD 1.25 3.00
COMMON SPILLS BROS. 1.25 3.00

1974 Topps Wacky Packages Series 7

COMPLETE SET w/o SP (33) 30.00 80.00
COMPLETE SET w/SP (34) 100.00 200.00
COMMON CARD 1.25 3.00
16B Grime Dog Chow - Heavy SP 50.00 100.00

1974 Topps Wacky Packages Series 7 Puzzle

COMPLETE SET (9) 8.00 20.00
COMMON CARD 1.25 3.00

1974 Topps Wacky Packages Series 8

COMPLETE SET (30) 30.00 80.00
COMMON CARD 1.25 3.00
CHECKLIST VARIANTS ARE UNNUMBERED

1974 Topps Wacky Packages Series 8 Puzzle

COMPLETE SET (9) 6.00 15.00
COMMON CARD .75 2.00

1974 Topps Wacky Packages Series 9

COMPLETE SET (29) 50.00 100.00
COMMON CARD 1.50 4.00

1974 Topps Wacky Packages Series 9 Puzzle

COMPLETE SET (9) 8.00 20.00
COMMON CARD 1.25 3.00

1974 Topps Wacky Packages Series 10

COMPLETE SET w/SP (30) 60.00 120.00
COMPLETE SET w/o SP (29) 30.00 80.00
COMMON CARD 1.00 2.50
1 Badzooka Gum 1.50 4.00
2 Bigtumi Spaghetti Sauce 1.50 4.00
3 Bum Baked Beans 2.00 5.00
4 Caraid Bandages 2.50 6.00
5 Casket Soap 2.50 6.00
6 Clunky Candy 2.00 5.00
7 Coffin-Mate 3.00 8.00
10 Greaseline 3.00 8.00
11 Hairy Lee Brownies 2.00 5.00
12 Heavy Trash Bags 2.00 5.00

14 Lox Soap	2.50	6.00
15 Milk of Amnesia	3.00	8.00
16 Mold Power	2.50	6.00
17 Mountain Goo	5.00	12.00
19 Oscar Moron Bacon	2.00	5.00
20 Painters Peanuts	2.00	5.00
21 Pepto Dismal	2.00	5.00
22 Poopedridge Farm	2.50	6.00
23 Pupsi-Cola SP	30.00	80.00
24 Ruden's Cough Drops	2.00	5.00
26 Stove Glop	2.50	6.00
27 Sunsweat Prune Juice	2.50	6.00
28 Tic-Toc Candy	2.00	5.00
29 Uncle Bum's Rice	2.50	6.00

1974 Topps Wacky Packages Series 10 Puzzle

COMPLETE SET w/o SP (9)	12.00	30.00
COMMON CARD	2.00	5.00
COMMON SP	3.00	8.00

1974 Topps Wacky Packages Series 11

COMPLETE SET (30)	50.00	100.00
COMMON CARD	1.50	4.00
3 Bash Detergent	2.00	5.00
5 Chaffed and Sunburn Coffee	3.00	8.00
8 Cult 45	4.00	10.00
9 Decay Toothpaste	3.00	8.00
10 Dizzie Cups	2.00	5.00
11 Easy Cuss-Words	3.00	8.00
12 Family Circuit	3.00	8.00
14 Gulp Oil	2.50	6.00
16 Moron Chicken Dinner	3.00	8.00
17 Mr. Bog Wet Bread	3.00	8.00
19 Muler's Dregg Noodles	2.50	5.00
20 National Geografink	3.00	8.00
21 Planet of The Grapes	2.50	6.00
22 Progreaso Raw Clammy Sauce	3.00	8.00
23 Saparin Coffee	3.00	8.00
26 Sleepy	6.00	15.00
27 Stinkertoy	2.50	6.00
28 Swiss Fright Cheese	3.00	8.00
29 TV Garbage	3.00	8.00
30 Unpopular Mechanics	3.00	8.00

1974 Topps Wacky Packages Series 11 Puzzle

COMPLETE SET (9)	8.00	20.00
COMMON CARD	1.25	3.00

1975 Topps Wacky Packages Series 12

COMPLETE SET (27)	50.00	100.00
COMMON CARD	1.50	4.00

1975 Topps Wacky Packages Series 12 Puzzle

COMPLETE SET (9)	8.00	20.00
COMMON CARD	1.25	3.00

1975 Topps Wacky Packages Series 13 Tan Backs

1 Ale Detergent
2 Ape Green Beans
3 Bathless Ribbons
4 Battle Ball
5 Beastball Bubble Gum
6 Brain Power
7 Bug Wally
8 Bum's Life Magazine
9 Crocked Magazine
10 Doesn't Delight
11 Don't-Touch-Mee Tea
12 Doomed Matches
13 Drainola Cereal
14 Dumb and Crazy Salt
15 Hazel Mishap Lipstuck
16 Icicle Playing Cards
17 Jerk in Jail Magazine
18 Le Rage's
19 National Spittoon Mag.
20 Nooseweek Magazine
21 Playskull
22 Rowdy Gelatine
23 Scream Sicle
24 Screech Tape
25 Shorts Illustrated Mag.
26 Shrunken Donuts
27 Sneezer Dressing
28 Sore Deodorant
29 Umbrella Magazine
30 Windaxe

1975 Topps Wacky Packages Series 13 White Backs

1 Ale Detergent
2 Ape Green Beans
3 Bathless Ribbons
4 Battle Ball
5 Beastball Bubble Gum
6 Brain Power
7 Bug Wally
8 Bum's Life Magazine
9 Crocked Magazine
10 Doesn't Delight
11 Don't-Touch-Mee Tea
12 Doomed Matches
13 Drainola Cereal
14 Dumb and Crazy Salt
15 Hazel Mishap Lipstuck
16 Icicle Playing Cards
17 Jerk in Jail Magazine
18 Le Rage's
19 National Spittoon Mag.
20 Nooseweek Magazine
21 Playskull
22 Rowdy Gelatine
23 Scream Sicle
24 Screech Tape
25 Shorts Illustrated Mag.
26 Shrunken Donuts
27 Sneezer Dressing
28 Sore Deodorant
29 Umbrella Magazine
30 Windaxe

1975 Topps Wacky Packages Series 13 Puzzle

1 Beastball Bubble Gum Puzzle Bottom Left
2 Beastball Bubble Gum Puzzle Bottom Middle
3 Beastball Bubble Gum Puzzle Bottom Right
4 Beastball Bubble Gum Puzzle Center Left
5 Beastball Bubble Gum Puzzle Center Middle
6 Beastball Bubble Gum Puzzle Center Right
7 Beastball Bubble Gum Puzzle Top Left
8 Beastball Bubble Gum Puzzle Top Middle
9 Beastball Bubble Gum Puzzle Top Right

1975 Topps Wacky Packages Series 14 White Backs

COMPLETE SET (30)	60.00	120.00
COMMON CARD	2.00	5.00

*TAN BACKS: .5X TO 1.2X WHITE BACKS

1975 Topps Wacky Packages Series 14 Tan Backs

COMPLETE SET (30)	80.00	150.00
COMMON CARD	2.50	6.00

1975 Topps Wacky Packages Series 14 Puzzle

COMPLETE SET (9)	15.00	40.00
COMMON CARD	2.00	5.00

1975 Topps Wacky Packages Series 15

COMPLETE SET (30)	200.00	400.00
COMP.SET W/PUZZLE (39)	225.00	450.00
UNOPENED BOX (48 PACKS)	2000.00	4000.00
UNOPENED PACK	60.00	100.00
COMMON CARD	4.00	10.00
3 Bloodweiser	6.00	15.00

1975 Topps Wacky Packages Series 15 Puzzle

COMPLETE SET (9)	20.00	50.00
COMMON CARD	3.00	8.00

1977 Topps Wacky Packages Series 16

COMPLETE SET (30)	1000.00	2200.00
COMPLETE SET W/PUZZLE (39)	1200.00	2400.00
UNOPENED BOX (48 PACKS)	2500.00	4000.00
UNOPENED PACK (3 STICKERS+1 CHECKLIST)	8.00	10.00
COMMON CARD	15.00	40.00
1 Arise Cream	50.00	100.00
2 Bleed's Candy	25.00	60.00
3 Clubbed Canadian	30.00	80.00
4 Copperbone Lotion	30.00	80.00
5 Cracked Lighter	80.00	150.00
6 Dirtycell Battery	30.00	80.00
7 Dr.Nest's Toothbrush	50.00	100.00
8 Earth Bum Shampoo	20.00	50.00
9 Fling 'Ems Candy	50.00	100.00
10 Floral Cigarettes	50.00	100.00
11 Fool Guard	30.00	80.00
12 Ghoul Humor	25.00	60.00
13 Gillo Port	60.00	120.00
14 Horsey Feed Bags	60.00	120.00
16 Krummies Diapers	50.00	100.00
17 Old Grand-Mom Whiskey	60.00	120.00
18 Prowl Shampoo	25.00	60.00
19 Ram-A-Liar Syrup	25.00	60.00
21 Regal Clown	60.00	120.00
22B Scoot Mouthwash No Copyright	100.00	200.00
23 Seven Spies	30.00	80.00
24 Smartz Collar	30.00	80.00
25 Similecch Squid	30.00	80.00
26 Sucker Twin	25.00	60.00
27 Sufferin Coffee	30.00	80.00
28 Suspect Deodorant	25.00	60.00
29 Tipsy Roll Pop	30.00	80.00
30 Yichs Sign-X	25.00	60.00

1977 Topps Wacky Packages Series 16 Puzzle

COMPLETE SET (9)	150.00	300.00
COMMON CARD	15.00	40.00

1977 Topps Wacky Packages Shedd's Peanut Butter

COMPLETE SET (22)	1000.00	1800.00
COMMON CARD	30.00	80.00
9 Fright Guard Deodorant	100.00	200.00
13 Hawaiian Punks	100.00	200.00

1979 Topps Wacky Packages Test Issue

1 6-Up	20.00	50.00
2 Ajerx		
3 Botch Tape		
4 Breadcrust Hash	25.00	60.00
5 Camals	75.00	200.00
6 Chock Full O'Nuts	30.00	75.00
7 Cover Ghoul		
8 Crust		
9 Ditch Masters	50.00	125.00
10 Dopey Whip		
11 Duzn't	20.00	50.00
12 Fink		
13 Gadzooka	30.00	75.00
14 Grave Train	15.00	40.00

15 Gurgle	60.00	150.00
16 Horrid		
17 Hostage Cupcakes		
18 Jail-O	25.00	60.00
19 Lavirus	100.00	250.00
20 Liptorn	30.00	75.00
21 Minute Lice	15.00	40.00
22 Mrs. Klean	25.00	60.00
23 Mutts		
24 Paul Maul		
25 Plastered Peanuts		
26 Pure Hex		
27 Sail'em		
28 Spray Nit		
29 Sugarmess		
30 Tied		
31 Ultra Blight		
32 Vicejoy		
33 Weakies		

1973 Topps Wacky Packages Wonder Bread Series 1

COMPLETE SET (23)	30.00	80.00
COMMON CARD	1.50	4.00

1974 Topps Wacky Packages Wonder Bread Series 2

COMPLETE SET (32)	50.00	100.00
COMMON CARD	1.50	4.00

1975 Topps Wacky Packages Wonder Bread Series 3

COMPLETE SET (16)	25.00	60.00
COMMON CARD	1.50	4.00

1974 Topps Wacky Patches

COMPLETE SET (12)	12.00	40.00
COMMON PATCH	1.25	3.00

Modern Wackys

2011 Wacky Erasers Series 1

COMPLETE SET (24)	12.00	30.00
UNOPENED BOX (24 PACKS)		
UNOPENED PACK (3 ERASERS+3 STICKERS)		
COMMON ERASER (UNNUMBERED)	.75	2.00
COMMON R (UNNUMBERED)	1.50	4.00

2011 Wacky Erasers Series 1 Stickers

COMPLETE SET (24)	8.00	20.00
COMMON STICKER (1-24)	.60	1.50

2011 Wacky Erasers Series 2

COMPLETE SET (24)	12.00	30.00
UNOPENED BOX (24 PACKS)		
UNOPENED PACK (3 ERASERS+3 STICKERS)		
COMMON ERASER (UNNUMBERED)	.75	2.00
COMMON R (UNNUMBERED)	1.50	4.00

2011 Wacky Erasers Series 2 Stickers

COMPLETE SET (24)	8.00	20.00
COMMON STICKER (1-24)	.60	1.50

2008 Wacky Pack Flashback

COMPLETE SET (72)	5.00	12.00
UNOPENED BOX (24 PACKS)	50.00	75.00
UNOPENED PACK (10 CARDS)	2.00	3.00
COMMON CARD (1-72)	.12	.30
*GREEN: 1.2X TO 3X BASIC CARDS	.40	1.00
*HOT PINK: 2.5X TO 6X BASIC CARDS	.75	2.00
*SILVER: 4X TO 10X BASIC CARDS	1.25	3.00
*GOLD: 30X TO 80X BASIC CARDS	10.00	25.00

2008 Wacky Pack Flashback Bonus

COMPLETE SET (2)	3.00	8.00
COMMON CARD (B1-B2)	2.00	5.00
STATED ODDS 1:6 RETAIL		

2008 Wacky Pack Flashback Motion Lenticular

COMPLETE SET (10)	5.00	12.00
COMMON CARD (1-10)	1.00	2.50
STATED ODDS 1:12		

2008 Wacky Pack Flashback Series 2

COMPLETE SET (72)	5.00	12.00
UNOPENED BOX (24 PACKS)		
UNOPENED PACK (10 CARDS)		
COMMON CARD (1-72)	.12	.30
*GREEN: 1.2X TO 3X BASIC CARDS		
*HOT PINK: 2.5X TO 6X BASIC CARDS		
*SILVER: 4X TO 10X BASIC CARDS		
*GOLD: 15X TO 40X BASIC CARDS		

2008 Wacky Pack Flashback Series 2 Bonus

COMPLETE SET (4)	5.00	12.00
COMMON CARD (B1-B4)	1.50	4.00
RANDOMLY INSERTED INTO PACKS		

2008 Wacky Pack Flashback Series 2 Motion Lenticular

COMPLETE SET (10)	5.00	12.00
COMMON CARD (1-10)	1.00	2.50
STATED ODDS 1:12		

2008 Wacky Pack Flashback Series 2 Promos

P1 Commie Cleanser	2.00	5.00

1985 Topps Wacky Packages

COMPLETE SET (44)	12.00	30.00
UNOPENED BOX	65.00	80.00
UNOPENED PACK	1.50	2.00
COMMON CARD (1-44)	.40	1.00
1 T.V. Ghoul	.75	2.00
31 Dr. Pooper	.50	1.25
32 Ghost Soap	.50	1.25
33 Velaphants	.50	1.25
34 Peter Panic Peanut Butter	.50	1.25
35 Bananacin	.50	1.25
36 Lazy Goo	.50	1.25
37 Hamel Cigarettes	.50	1.25
38 Snoot Powder	.50	1.25
39 Beastball Bubble Gum Cards	.50	1.25
40 Chimpwich Ice Cream	.50	1.25
41 Batzooka Bubble Gum	.50	1.25
42 Kid Kudd	.50	1.25
43 Go Bums	.50	1.25
44 Everdeady Battery	.50	1.25

1985 Topps Ireland Wacky Packages

COMPLETE SET (30)	80.00	150.00
UNOPENED PACK	8.00	20.00
COMMON CARD (1-30)	1.25	3.00
5 Gadzooka Gum	4.00	10.00
6 Chump Dog Food	2.50	6.00
7 Eviltime	3.00	8.00
8 Android Bath Tissue	5.00	12.00
10 Nurd's Custard	5.00	12.00
12 Fisto Gravy	6.00	15.00
13 Downhill Cigarettes	2.00	5.00
14 Kick Kat	2.50	6.00
17 Neveready Batteries	2.00	5.00
18 Koduck Film	2.00	5.00
19 Fright Guard	2.00	5.00
20 Botch Tape	4.00	10.00
22 Toad Detergent	2.00	5.00
23 Muleburro Cigarettes	6.00	15.00
24 Kleenaxe Tissue	2.00	5.00
29 Crust Toothpaste	2.00	5.00
30 Mashbox Toys	2.00	5.00

1991 Topps Wacky Packages

COMPLETE SET (55)	6.00	15.00
COMPLETE SET w/VARIATIONS (1-67)	10.00	25.00
UNOPENED BOX (24 PACKS)	50.00	75.00
UNOPENED PACK (5 CARDS)	2.50	3.00
COMMON CARD (1-55)	.30	.75
26B Barf's Root Beer SP	5.00	12.00

2023 Topps Wacky Packages All-New Series

COMPLETE SET (50)	50.00	125.00
UNOPENED BOX (12 CARDS)		
COMMON CARD (1-50)	1.50	4.00
*SILVER: .75X TO 2X BASIC CARDS		
*COUPON:1.5X TO 4X BASIC CARDS		
*RAINBOW/25: 10X TO 25X BASIC CARDS		

2023 Topps Wacky Packages All-New Series Comics

COMPLETE SET (5)	50.00	125.00
COMMON CARD	15.00	40.00
RANDOMLY INSERTED INTO BOXES		
1 Wacky Pals!/Boo Hoo Drink	15.00	40.00
2 Wacky Pals!/Ditch Boy Paint	25.00	60.00
3 Wacky Pals!/Goonman's Noodles	20.00	50.00

2017 Wacky Packages Alternative Facts

COMPLETE SET (7)	30.00	75.00
COMMON CARD (1-7)	5.00	12.00
1 Alternative Tally Counter/354*	8.00	20.00
2 Pumpkin Lie Pie/247*	6.00	15.00
3 Fiction Facts/258*	8.00	20.00
4 Lies Potato Chips/288*	6.00	15.00
5 Swedish Fist/284*	5.00	12.00
6 Baffleship/201*	5.00	12.00
7 Botz/184*	6.00	15.00

2015 Wacky Packages Art Prints

COMPLETE SET (10)	25.00	60.00
COMMON CARD (1-10)	5.00	12.00

2015 Wacky Packages Cereal Postcards SDCC Promos

COMPLETE SET (5)	20.00	50.00
COMMON CARD (C1-C5)	6.00	15.00
STATED PRINT RUN 200 SETS		

1982 Topps Wacky Packages Ralston Purina Cereal Stickers

COMPLETE SET (8)	50.00	100.00
COMMON CARD	6.00	15.00

2014 Wacky Packages Chrome

COMPLETE SET (110)	15.00	40.00
UNOPENED BOX (24 PACKS)	150.00	250.00
UNOPENED PACK (5 CARDS)	6.00	10.00
COMMON CARD (1-107; CL1-CL3)	.40	1.00
*XFRACTOR: .5X TO 1.2X BASIC CARDS	.50	1.25
*REFRACTOR: 1.2X TO 2X BASIC CARDS	.75	2.00
*BLUE REF/50: 4X TO 10X BASIC CARDS	4.00	10.00
*GOLD REF/25: 10X TO 25X BASIC CARDS	10.00	25.00

2014 Wacky Packages Chrome Cutting Room Floor Wackys

COMPLETE SET (20)	25.00	60.00
COMMON CARD (1-20)	2.00	5.00
STATED ODDS 1:4		

2014 Wacky Packages Chrome Lost Wackys

COMPLETE SET (10)	8.00	20.00
COMMON CARD (1-10)	1.00	2.50
STATED ODDS 1:6		

2014 Wacky Packages Chrome Wacky Ads

COMPLETE SET (35)	25.00	60.00
COMMON CARD (1-35)	1.25	3.00
STATED ODDS 1:3		

2014 Wacky Packages Chrome Where Are They Now

COMPLETE SET (5)	12.00	30.00
COMMON CARD (1-5)	4.00	10.00
STATED ODDS 1:8		

2017 Wacky Packages Fall TV Preview

COMPLETE SET (7)	25.00	60.00
COMMON CARD (1-7)	5.00	12.00
STATED PRINT RUN 154 SETS		
1 Bar Trek	5.00	12.00
2 The Overkill	5.00	12.00
3 The Flush	5.00	12.00
4 Riverjail	5.00	12.00
5 Young Shell-don	5.00	12.00
6 Will & Grapes	5.00	12.00
7 The Vice	5.00	12.00

2017 Wacky Packages 50th Anniversary

COMPLETE SET (90)	6.00	15.00
UNOPENED HOBBY BOX (24 PACKS)	40.00	60.00
UNOPENED HOBBY PACK (8 CARDS)	2.50	3.00
UNOPENED COLLECTOR BOX (24 PACKS)	80.00	100.00
UNOPENED COLLECTOR PACK (8 CARDS)	4.00	5.00
COMMON CARD	.20	.50
*BLUE: .75X TO 2X BASIC CARDS	.40	1.00
*SEPIA: 1.5X TO 4X BASIC CARDS	.75	2.00
*YELLOW: 2.5X TO 6X BASIC CARDS	1.25	3.00
*BRONZE: 2.5X TO 6X BASIC CARDS	1.25	3.00
*BLACK LUDLOW/99: 10X TO 25X BASIC CARDS	5.00	12.00
*SILVER/50: 12X TO 30X BASIC CARDS	6.00	15.00
*RED LUDLOW/25: 20X TO 50X BASIC CARDS	10.00	25.00
*RED/10: 30X TO 80X BASIC CARDS	15.00	40.00

2017 Wacky Packages 50th Anniversary Artist Autographs

COMMON CAMERA	12.00	30.00
COMMON ENGSTROM	25.00	60.00
COMMON GROSS	15.00	40.00
COMMON GROSSBERG	25.00	60.00
COMMON IM	15.00	40.00
COMMON SIMKO	20.00	50.00
COMMON SMOKIN' JOE	15.00	40.00
COMMON WHEATON	12.00	30.00
STATED PRINT RUN 25 SER.#'d SETS		

2017 Wacky Packages 50th Anniversary Best of the 00's

COMPLETE SET (10)	10.00	25.00
COMMON CARD (1-10)	1.50	4.00

2017 Wacky Packages 50th Anniversary Best of the 80's

COMPLETE SET (10)	5.00	12.00
COMMON CARD (1-10)	.75	2.00

2017 Wacky Packages 50th Anniversary Best of the 90's

COMPLETE SET (10)	6.00	15.00
COMMON CARD (1-10)	1.25	3.00

2017 Wacky Packages 50th Anniversary Box-Toppers

COMPLETE SET (10)	25.00	60.00
COMMON CARD (1-10)	4.00	10.00
STATED ODDS 1 PER COLLECTOR BOX		

2017 Wacky Packages 50th Anniversary Medallions

COMMON MEDALLION	8.00	20.00
*SILVER/50: .5X TO 1.5X BASIC MEDALLIONS	12.00	30.00
*RED/10: 1.2X TO 3X BASIC MEDALLIONS	25.00	60.00
STATED PRINT RUN 99 SER.#'d SETS		

2017 Wacky Packages 50th Anniversary Old School

COMPLETE SET (10)	10.00	25.00
COMMON CARD (1-10)	2.50	6.00
STATED ODDS 1:		

2018 Wacky Packages Go to the Movies

COMPLETE SET (90)	8.00	20.00
UNOPENED BOX (24 PACKS)	40.00	50.00
UNOPENED PACK (8 CARDS)	2.50	3.00
COLLECTOR BOX (24 PACKS)	70.00	80.00
COLLECTOR PACK (8 CARDS)	3.00	4.00
COMMON CARD (1-90)	.20	.50
*BLUE: .6X TO 1.5X BASIC CARDS		
*SEPIA: .6X TO 1.5X BASIC CARDS		
*ORANGE: .75X TO 2X BASIC CARDS		
*BRONZE: 1X TO 2.5X BASIC CARDS		
*YELLOW: 1X TO 2.5X BASIC CARDS		
*BLACK LUD/99: 3X TO 8X BASIC CARDS		
*SILVER/50: 6X TO 15X BASIC CARDS		
*RED LUD/25: 15X TO 40X BASIC CARDS		
*RED/10: 100X TO 200X BASIC CARDS		

2018 Wacky Packages Go to the Movies Artist Autographs

COMMON CAMERA	15.00	40.00
COMMON ENGSTROM	12.00	30.00
COMMON GROSS	12.00	30.00
COMMON IM	12.00	30.00
COMMON JIMENEZ	15.00	40.00
COMMON SCHERES		
COMMON SIMKO	15.00	40.00
COMMON SMOKIN JOE	12.00	30.00
COMMON WHEATON	20.00	50.00
COMMON ZELEZNIK	12.00	30.00
STATED ODDS 1:99		
STATED PRINT RUN 25 SER.#'d SETS		

2018 Wacky Packages Go to the Movies Box-Toppers

COMPLETE SET (10)	60.00	120.00
COMMON CARD (1-10)	8.00	20.00
STATED ODDS 1:COLLECTOR BOX		

2018 Wacky Packages Go to the Movies Classic Film

COMPLETE SET (20)	8.00	20.00
COMMON CARD (1-20)	1.00	2.50
STATED ODDS 1:2		

2018 Wacky Packages Go to the Movies Concession Stand

COMPLETE SET (20)	6.00	15.00
COMMON CARD (1-20)	.75	2.00
STATED ODDS 5:1 BLASTER BOX		

2018 Wacky Packages Go to the Movies Horror Film Inserts

COMPLETE SET (10)	120.00	250.00
COMMON CARD (1-10)	15.00	40.00
RANDOMLY INSERTED INTO COLLECTOR PACKS		

2018 Wacky Packages Go to the Movies Manufactured Patches

COMMON PATCH (MP1-MP10)	12.00	30.00
*SILVER/50: .5X TO 1.2X BASIC PATCHES	15.00	40.00
STATED PRINT RUN 99 SER.#'d SETS		

2018 Wacky Packages Go to the Movies Small Screen

COMPLETE SET (20)	10.00	25.00
COMMON CARD (1-20)	1.25	3.00
STATED ODDS 1:1 HOBBY		

2020 Topps Wacky Packages Halloween Postcards

COMPLETE SET (3)	8.00	20.00
COMMON CARD	4.00	10.00

2020 Topps Wacky Packages Halloween Postcards Bios

COMPLETE SET (3)	20.00	50.00
COMMON CARD	10.00	25.00
NNO Jeff Dionise	10.00	25.00
NNO Matthew Kirscht	10.00	25.00
NNO Pat Chaimuang	10.00	25.00

2020 Topps Wacky Packages Halloween Postcards Glow-in-the-Dark

COMPLETE SET (3)	20.00	50.00
COMMON CARD	10.00	25.00

2020 Topps Wacky Packages Halloween Postcards Masks

COMPLETE SET (3)	20.00	50.00
COMMON CARD	10.00	25.00

2008 Wacky Packages Lost Abrams Promos

COMPLETE SET (8)	12.00	30.00
COMMON CARD (1-8)	2.00	5.00

2010 Wacky Packages Lost Abrams Promos

COMPLETE SET (4)	8.00	20.00
COMMON CARD	3.00	8.00

2021 Topps Wacky Packages Monthly Series January

COMPLETE SET (21)	15.00	40.00
COMMON CARD (1-20, CL)	1.50	4.00
*COUPON: 1.2X TO 3X BASIC CARDS		
STATED PRINT RUN 554 ANNCD SETS		

2021 Topps Wacky Packages Monthly Series January Wacky Playing Cards

COMPLETE SET (4)	10.00	25.00
COMMON CARD	4.00	10.00
STATED ODDS 2:1		

2021 Topps Wacky Packages Monthly Series January Wonky Packages

COMPLETE SET (4)	25.00	60.00
COMMON CARD (WP1-WP4)	10.00	25.00
STATED ODDS 1:1		

2021 Topps Wacky Packages Monthly Series February

COMPLETE SET (21)	15.00	40.00
COMMON CARD (1-20, CL)	1.50	4.00
*COUPON: 1.2X TO 3X BASIC CARDS		
STATED PRINT RUN 546 ANNCD SETS		

2021 Topps Wacky Packages Monthly Series February Wacky Playing Cards

COMPLETE SET (4)	10.00	25.00
COMMON CARD	4.00	10.00
STATED ODDS 2:1		

2021 Topps Wacky Packages Monthly Series February Wonky Packages

COMPLETE SET (4)	25.00	60.00
COMMON CARD (WP1-WP4)	10.00	25.00
STATED ODDS 1:1		

2021 Topps Wacky Packages Monthly Series March

COMPLETE SET (21)	15.00	40.00
COMMON CARD (1-20, CL)	1.50	4.00
*COUPON: 1.2X TO 3X BASIC CARDS		
STATED PRINT RUN 625 ANNCD SETS		

2021 Topps Wacky Packages Monthly Series March Wacky Playing Cards

COMPLETE SET (4)	10.00	25.00
COMMON CARD	4.00	10.00
STATED ODDS 2:1		

2021 Topps Wacky Packages Monthly Series March Wonky Packages

COMPLETE SET (4)	25.00	60.00
COMMON CARD (WP1-WP4)	10.00	25.00
STATED ODDS 1:1		

2021 Topps Wacky Packages Monthly Series April

COMPLETE SET (21)	15.00	40.00

COMMON CARD (1-20, CL) 1.50 4.00
*COUPON: 1.2X TO 3X BASIC CARDS
STATED PRINT RUN 592 ANNCD SETS

2021 Topps Wacky Packages Monthly Series April Wacky Playing Cards

COMPLETE SET (4) 10.00 25.00
COMMON CARD 4.00 10.00
STATED ODDS 2:1

2021 Topps Wacky Packages Monthly Series April Wonky Packages

COMPLETE SET (4) 25.00 60.00
COMMON CARD (WP1-WP4) 10.00 25.00
STATED ODDS 1:1

2021 Topps Wacky Packages Monthly Series May

COMPLETE SET (21) 15.00 40.00
COMMON CARD (1-20, CL) 1.50 4.00
*COUPON: 1.2X TO 3X BASIC CARDS
STATED PRINT RUN 532 ANNCD SETS

2021 Topps Wacky Packages Monthly Series May Wacky Playing Cards

COMPLETE SET (4) 10.00 25.00
COMMON CARD 4.00 10.00
STATED ODDS 2:1

2021 Topps Wacky Packages Monthly Series May Wonky Packages

COMPLETE SET (4) 25.00 60.00
COMMON CARD (WP1-WP4) 10.00 25.00
STATED ODDS 1:1

2021 Topps Wacky Packages Monthly Series June

COMPLETE SET (21) 15.00 40.00
COMMON CARD (1-20, CL) 1.50 4.00
*COUPON: 1.2X TO 3X BASIC CARDS
STATED PRINT RUN 565 ANNCD SETS

2021 Topps Wacky Packages Monthly Series June Wacky Playing Cards

COMPLETE SET (4) 10.00 25.00
COMMON CARD 4.00 10.00
STATED ODDS 2:1

2021 Topps Wacky Packages Monthly Series June Wonky Packages

COMPLETE SET (4) 25.00 60.00
COMMON CARD (WP1-WP4) 10.00 25.00
STATED ODDS 1:1

2021 Topps Wacky Packages Monthly Series July

COMPLETE SET (21) 15.00 40.00
COMMON CARD (1-20, CL) 1.50 4.00
*COUPON: 1.2X TO 3X BASIC CARDS
STATED PRINT RUN 550 ANNCD SETS

2021 Topps Wacky Packages Monthly Series July Wacky Playing Cards

COMPLETE SET (4) 10.00 25.00
COMMON CARD 4.00 10.00
STATED ODDS 2:1

2021 Topps Wacky Packages Monthly Series July Wonky Packages

COMPLETE SET (4) 25.00 60.00
COMMON CARD (WP1-WP4) 10.00 25.00
STATED ODDS 1:1

2021 Topps Wacky Packages Monthly Series August

COMPLETE SET (21) 15.00 40.00
COMMON CARD (1-20, CL) 1.50 4.00
*COUPON: 1.2X TO 3X BASIC CARDS
STATED PRINT RUN 570 ANNCD SETS

2021 Topps Wacky Packages Monthly Series August Wacky Playing Cards

COMPLETE SET (4) 10.00 25.00
COMMON CARD 4.00 10.00
STATED ODDS 2:1

2021 Topps Wacky Packages Monthly Series August Wonky Packages

COMPLETE SET (4) 25.00 60.00
COMMON CARD (WP1-WP4) 10.00 25.00
STATED ODDS 1:1

2021 Topps Wacky Packages Monthly Series September

COMPLETE SET (21)
COMMON CARD (1-20, CL)
*COUPON: 1.2X TO 3X BASIC CARDS
STATED PRINT RUN 632 ANNCD SETS

2021 Topps Wacky Packages Monthly Series September Wacky Playing Cards

COMPLETE SET (5) 12.00 30.00
COMMON CARD 4.00 10.00
STATED ODDS 2:1

2021 Topps Wacky Packages Monthly Series September Wonky Packages

COMPLETE SET (4) 25.00 60.00
COMMON CARD (WP1-WP4) 10.00 25.00
STATED ODDS 1:1

2021 Topps Wacky Packages Monthly Series October

COMPLETE SET (21)
COMMON CARD (1-20, CL)
*COUPON: 1.2X TO 3X BASIC CARDS
STATED PRINT RUN 698 ANNCD SETS

2021 Topps Wacky Packages Monthly Series October Wacky Playing Cards

COMPLETE SET (5) 12.00 30.00
COMMON CARD 4.00 10.00
STATED ODDS 2:1

2021 Topps Wacky Packages Monthly Series October Wonky Packages

COMPLETE SET (4) 25.00 60.00
COMMON CARD (WP1-WP4) 10.00 25.00
STATED ODDS 1:1

2021 Topps Wacky Packages Monthly Series November

COMPLETE SET (21) 15.00 40.00
COMMON CARD (1-20, CL) 1.50 4.00
*COUPON: 1.2X TO 3X BASIC CARDS
STATED PRINT RUN 630 ANNCD SETS

2021 Topps Wacky Packages Monthly Series November Wacky Playing Cards

COMPLETE SET (5) 12.00 30.00
COMMON CARD 4.00 10.00
STATED ODDS 2:1

2021 Topps Wacky Packages Monthly Series November Wonky Packages

COMPLETE SET (4) 25.00 60.00
COMMON CARD (WP1-WP4) 10.00 25.00
STATED ODDS 1:1

2021 Topps Wacky Packages Monthly Series December

COMPLETE SET (21) 15.00 40.00
COMMON CARD (1-20, CL) 1.50 4.00
*COUPON: 1.2X TO 3X BASIC CARDS
STATED PRINT RUN 747 ANNCD SETS

2021 Topps Wacky Packages Monthly Series December Wacky Playing Cards

COMPLETE SET (5) 12.00 30.00
COMMON CARD 4.00 10.00
STATED ODDS 2:1

2021 Topps Wacky Packages Monthly Series December Wonky Packages

COMPLETE SET (4) 25.00 60.00
COMMON CARD (WP1-WP4) 10.00 25.00
STATED ODDS 1:1

2022 Topps Wacky Packages Monthly Series January

COMPLETE SET (21) 15.00 40.00
COMMON CARD (1-20: CL) 1.25 3.00
*COUPON: 1.2X TO 3X BASIC CARDS
STATED PRINT RUN 505 ANNCD SETS

2022 Topps Wacky Packages Monthly Series January Wacky Portraits

COMPLETE SET (4) 15.00 40.00
COMMON CARD 6.00 15.00
STATED ODDS 2:1

2022 Topps Wacky Packages Monthly Series January Wonky Packages

COMPLETE SET (4) 25.00 60.00
COMMON CARD (1-4) 8.00 20.00
STATED ODDS 1:1

2022 Topps Wacky Packages Monthly Series February

COMPLETE SET (21) 15.00 40.00
COMMON CARD (1-20: CL) 1.25 3.00
*COUPON: 1.2X TO 3X BASIC CARDS
STATED PRINT RUN ANNCD SETS

2022 Topps Wacky Packages Monthly Series February Wacky Portraits

COMPLETE SET (4) 15.00 40.00
COMMON CARD 6.00 15.00
STATED ODDS 2:1

2022 Topps Wacky Packages Monthly Series February Wonky Packages

COMPLETE SET (4) 25.00 60.00
COMMON CARD (1-4) 8.00 20.00
STATED ODDS 1:1

2022 Topps Wacky Packages Monthly Series March

COMPLETE SET (21) 15.00 40.00
COMMON CARD (1-20: CL) 1.25 3.00
*COUPON: 1.2X TO 3X BASIC CARDS
STATED PRINT RUN 501 ANNCD SETS

2022 Topps Wacky Packages Monthly Series March Wacky Portraits

COMPLETE SET (4) 15.00 40.00
COMMON CARD 6.00 15.00
STATED ODDS 2:1

2022 Topps Wacky Packages Monthly Series March Wonky Packages

COMPLETE SET (4) 25.00 60.00
COMMON CARD (1-4) 8.00 20.00
STATED ODDS 1:1

2022 Topps Wacky Packages Monthly Series April

COMPLETE SET (21) 15.00 40.00
COMMON CARD (1-20: CL) 1.25 3.00
*COUPON: 1.2X TO 3X BASIC CARDS
STATED PRINT RUN 493 ANNCD SETS

2022 Topps Wacky Packages Monthly Series April Wacky Portraits

COMPLETE SET (4) 15.00 40.00
COMMON CARD 6.00 15.00
STATED ODDS 2:1

2022 Topps Wacky Packages Monthly Series April Wonky Packages

COMPLETE SET (4) 25.00 60.00
COMMON CARD (1-4) 8.00 20.00
STATED ODDS 1:1

2022 Topps Wacky Packages Monthly Series May

COMPLETE SET (21) 15.00 40.00
COMMON CARD (1-20: CL) 1.25 3.00
*COUPON: 1.2X TO 3X BASIC CARDS
STATED PRINT RUN 489 ANNCD SETS

2022 Topps Wacky Packages Monthly Series May Wacky Portraits

COMPLETE SET (4) 15.00 40.00
COMMON CARD 6.00 15.00
STATED ODDS 2:1

2022 Topps Wacky Packages Monthly Series May Wonky Packages

COMPLETE SET (4) 25.00 60.00
COMMON CARD (1-4) 8.00 20.00
STATED ODDS 1:1

2022 Topps Wacky Packages Monthly Series June

COMPLETE SET (21) 15.00 40.00
COMMON CARD (1-20; CL) 1.25 3.00
*COUPON: 1.2X TO 3X BASIC CARDS
STATED PRINT RUN 499 ANNCD SETS

2022 Topps Wacky Packages Monthly Series June Wacky Pals Comics

COMPLETE SET (4) 15.00 40.00
COMMON CARD 6.00 15.00
STATED ODDS 2:1

2022 Topps Wacky Packages Monthly Series June Wonky Packages

COMPLETE SET (4) 25.00 60.00
COMMON CARD (1-4) 8.00 20.00
STATED ODDS 1:1

2022 Topps Wacky Packages Monthly Series July

COMPLETE SET (21) 15.00 40.00
COMMON CARD (1-20; CL) 1.25 3.00
*COUPON: 1.2X TO 3X BASIC CARDS
STATED PRINT RUN ANNCD SETS

2022 Topps Wacky Packages Monthly Series July Wacky Pals Comics

COMPLETE SET (4) 15.00 40.00
COMMON CARD 6.00 15.00
STATED ODDS 2:1

2022 Topps Wacky Packages Monthly Series July Wonky Packages

COMPLETE SET (4) 25.00 60.00
COMMON CARD (1-4) 8.00 20.00
STATED ODDS 1:1

2022 Topps Wacky Packages Monthly Series August

COMPLETE SET (21) 15.00 40.00
COMMON CARD (1-20; CL) 1.25 3.00
*COUPON: 1.2X TO 3X BASIC CARDS
STATED PRINT RUN 447 ANNCD SETS

2022 Topps Wacky Packages Monthly Series August Wacky Pals Comics

COMPLETE SET (4) 15.00 40.00
COMMON CARD 6.00 15.00
STATED ODDS 2:1

2022 Topps Wacky Packages Monthly Series August Wonky Packages

COMPLETE SET (4) 25.00 60.00
COMMON CARD (1-4) 8.00 20.00
STATED ODDS 1:1

2022 Topps Wacky Packages Monthly Series September

COMPLETE SET (21) 15.00 40.00
COMMON CARD (1-20, CL) 1.25 3.00
*COUPON: 1.2X TO 3X BASIC CARDS
STATED PRINT RUN 567 ANNCD SETS

2022 Topps Wacky Packages Monthly Series September Wacky Pals Comics

COMPLETE SET (4) 15.00 40.00
COMMON CARD (1-4) 6.00 15.00
STATED ODDS 2:1

2022 Topps Wacky Packages Monthly Series September Wonky Packages

COMPLETE SET (4) 25.00 60.00
COMMON CARD (1-4) 8.00 20.00
STATED ODDS 1:1

2022 Topps Wacky Packages Monthly Series October

COMPLETE SET (21) 15.00 40.00
COMMON CARD (1-20, CL) 1.25 3.00
*COUPON: 1.2X TO 3X BASIC CARDS
STATED PRINT RUN 466 ANNCD SETS

2022 Topps Wacky Packages Monthly Series October Wacky Pals Comics

COMPLETE SET (4) 15.00 40.00
COMMON CARD (1-4) 6.00 15.00
STATED ODDS 2:1

2022 Topps Wacky Packages Monthly Series October Wonky Packages

COMPLETE SET (4) 25.00 60.00
COMMON CARD (1-4) 8.00 20.00
STATED ODDS 1:1

2022 Topps Wacky Packages Monthly Series November

COMPLETE SET (21) 15.00 40.00
COMMON CARD (1-20, CL) 1.25 3.00
*COUPON: 1.2X TO 3X BASIC CARDS
STATED PRINT RUN 435 ANNCD SETS

2022 Topps Wacky Packages Monthly Series November Wacky Pals Comics

COMPLETE SET (4) 15.00 40.00
COMMON CARD (1-4) 6.00 15.00
STATED ODDS 2:1

2022 Topps Wacky Packages Monthly Series November Wonky Packages

COMPLETE SET (4) 25.00 60.00
COMMON CARD (1-4) 8.00 20.00
STATED ODDS 1:1

2022 Topps Wacky Packages Monthly Series December

COMPLETE SET (21) 15.00 40.00
COMMON CARD (1-20, CL) 1.25 3.00
*COUPON: 1.2X TO 3X BASIC CARDS
STATED PRINT RUN 513 ANNCD SETS

2022 Topps Wacky Packages Monthly Series December Wacky Pals Comics

COMPLETE SET (4) 15.00 40.00
COMMON CARD (1-4) 6.00 15.00
STATED ODDS 2:1

2022 Topps Wacky Packages Monthly Series December Wonky Packages

COMPLETE SET (4) 25.00 60.00
COMMON CARD (1-4) 8.00 20.00
STATED ODDS 1:1

2010 Wacky Packages Old School Series 1

COMPLETE SET (33) 5.00 12.00
UNOPENED BOX (24 PACKS) 100.00 150.00
UNOPENED PACK (5 CARDS) 4.00 6.00
COMMON CARD (1-33) .25 .60
*LARGE: 1X TO 2.5X BASIC CARDS .60 1.50
JL Jay Lynch (sketch)
P1 BC (Before Culture) Cola Promo .75 2.00
NNO1 Wacky Packages Old School Logo Sticker
NNO2 Series 2 Promo Sticker

2010 Wacky Packages Old School Series 1 Puzzle Checklists

COMPLETE SET (9) 1.50 4.00
COMMON CARD .20 .50

2011 Wacky Packages Old School Series 2

COMPLETE SET (33) 5.00 12.00
UNOPENED BOX (24 PACKS)
UNOPENED PACK (CARDS)
COMMON CARD (1-33) .25 .60
NNO1 Wacky Packages Old School Promo 1.50 4.00

2011 Wacky Packages Old School Series 2 Jay Lynch

COMPLETE SET (9) 10.00 25.00
COMMON CARD (1-9) 1.25 3.00
STATED ODDS 1:

2011 Wacky Packages Old School Series 2 Puzzle Checklists

COMPLETE SET (9) 1.50 4.00
COMMON CARD (1-9) .20 .50

2011-12 Topps Wacky Packages Old School Series 3

COMPLETE SET (33) 10.00 25.00
COMMON CARD (1-33) .40 1.00
NNO1 Um & Um's Promo 1.25 3.00

2011-12 Topps Wacky Packages Old School Series 3 Hippy Days

COMPLETE SET (9) 2.50 6.00
COMMON CARD (1-9) .40 1.00

2012 Wacky Packages Old School Series 4

COMPLETE SET (33) 3.00 8.00
COMMON CARD .20 .50

2012 Wacky Packages Old School Series 4 Walla Walla Wackys Old School All-Stars

COMPLETE SET (9) 2.50 6.00
COMMON CARD (1-9) .40 1.00
STATED ODDS 1:
6B Weakies (green)
6C Weakies (orange)
6D Weakies (red; rare)

2012 Wacky Packages Old School Series 4 Wrapper Stickers

COMPLETE SET (16) 6.00 15.00
COMMON CARD .75 2.00

2012 Wacky Packages Old School Series 4 Yackety Package Poems

COMPLETE SET (9) 2.50 6.00
COMMON CARD (1-9) .40 1.00

2012 Wacky Packages Old School Series 4 Promos

COMPLETE SET (2) 2.00 5.00
COMMON CARD (P1-P2) 1.50 4.00

2014 Wacky Packages Old School Series 5

COMPLETE SET (33) 2.50 6.00
UNOPENED BOX (24 PACKS) 40.00 50.00
UNOPENED PACK (5 CARDS) 2.00 2.50
COMMON CARD (1-33) .12 .30

2014 Wacky Packages Old School Series 5 Presidolts Puzzle Checklists

COMPLETE SET (9) 8.00 20.00
COMMON CARD (1-9) 1.25 3.00

2014 Wacky Packages Old School Series 5 Tattoos

COMPLETE SET (18) 25.00 60.00
COMMON CARD (1-18) 1.50 4.00

2017 Wacky Packages Old School Series 6

COMPLETE SET (30)	30.00	75.00
UNOPENED BOX (3 PACKS)		
UNOPENED PACK (21 CARDS)		
COMMON CARD	1.50	4.00
*BLACK LUDLOW: X TO X BASIC CARDS		
*RED LUDLOW: X TO X BASIC CARDS		
*TAN BACKS: X TO X BASIC CARDS		

2017 Wacky Packages Old School Series 6 Pencil Roughs

COMPLETE SET (30)	60.00	120.00
COMMON CARD	3.00	8.00
STATED ODDS 5:1		

2018 Wacky Packages Old School Series 7

COMPLETE SET (30)	6.00	15.00
UNOPENED A SET (21 CARDS)		
UNOPENED B SET (63 CARDS)		
COMMON CARD (1-30)	.60	1.50
*TAN: .5X TO 1.2X BASIC CARDS		
*BLACK: .6X TO 1.5X BASIC CARDS		
*RED: .6X TO 1.5X BASIC CARDS		
*PENCIL: .75X TO 2X BASIC CARDS		
STATED PRINT RUN 955 ANNCD SETS		

2019 Wacky Packages Old School Series 8

COMPLETE SET (31)	30.00	75.00
UNOPENED SET (63 CARDS)		
COMMON CARD (1-30)	1.50	4.00
*TAN: .5X TO 1.2X BASIC CARDS		
*BLACK: .6X TO 1.5X BASIC CARDS		
*RED: .6X TO 1.5X BASIC CARDS		
*PENCIL: .75X TO 2X BASIC CARDS		
STATED PRINT RUN 477 ANNCD SETS		

2020 Topps Wacky Packages Old School Series 9

COMPLETE SET (31)	10.00	25.00
COMMON CARD (1-30, NNO)	.75	2.00
*TAN BACKS: .5X TO 1.2X BASIC CARDS		
*RED LUDLOW: .75X TO 2X BASIC CARDS		

2020 Topps Wacky Packages Old School Series 9 Graduation Photos

COMPLETE SET (20)	15.00	40.00
COMMON CARD (1-20)	1.25	3.00
STATED ODDS 8:PACK		

2022 Topps Wacky Packages Old School 10

COMPLETE SET (31)	12.00	30.00
COMMON CARD (1-30; CL)	.75	2.00
*RED LUDLOW: 1.2X TO 3X BASIC CARDS		

2022 Topps Wacky Packages Old School 10 Graduation Photos

COMPLETE SET (15)	15.00	40.00
COMMON CARD (GP1-GP15)	2.00	5.00
STATED ODDS 8:1		

2022 Topps Wacky Packages Old School 10 Mad Caps

COMPLETE SET (15)	20.00	50.00
COMMON CARD (MC1-MC15)	2.50	6.00
STATED ODDS 5:1		

2020 Topps On-Demand Wacky Packages April Fools Limited Edition Postcard Set

COMPLETE SET (6)	8.00	20.00
COMMON CARD (1-6)	2.00	5.00
STATED PRINT RUN 566 SETS		

2020 Topps On-Demand Wacky Packages April Fools Limited Edition Postcard Set Artist Autographs

1 Neil Camera		
2 Matthew Kirscht		
3 Smokin' Joe	6.00	15.00
4 Jon Gregory	6.00	15.00
5 Pat Chaimuang	6.00	15.00
6 Brent Engstrom		

2020 Topps On-Demand Wacky Packages April Fools Limited Edition Postcard Set Artist Bios

COMPLETE SET (6)	15.00	40.00
COMMON CARD	3.00	8.00

2020 Topps On-Demand Wacky Packages April Fools Limited Edition Postcard Set Bonus

COMPLETE SET (2)	6.00	15.00
COMMON CARD (TS22-TS23)	3.00	8.00
TS23 Sweattios Odorous Rings	5.00	12.00

2020 Topps On-Demand Wacky Packages April Fools Limited Edition Postcard Set Souvenir Stamp Sticker

NNO Wacky Packages Postcards	2.50	6.00

2021 Topps On-Demand Wacky Packages Wonky Ads

COMPLETE SET (8)	8.00	20.00
UNOPENED BOX (9 CARDS)		
COMMON CARD (1-7, CL)	1.50	4.00
*VAR: X TO X BASIC CARDS		

2021 Topps On-Demand Wacky Packages Wonky Ads Black Panel Die-Cuts

COMPLETE SET (4)	25.00	60.00
COMMON CARD	10.00	25.00
STATED ODDS 1:SET		

2022 Topps On-Demand Wacky Packages Wonky Ads Series 2

COMPLETE SET (7)	5.00	12.00
UNOPENED BOX (9 CARDS)		
COMMON CARD (1-7)	1.25	3.00
*VAR: 4X TO 10X BASIC CARDS		

2022 Topps On-Demand Wacky Packages Wonky Ads Series 2 Black Panel Die-Cuts

COMPLETE SET (4)	25.00	60.00
COMMON CARD	8.00	20.00
STATED ODDS 1:1		

2022 Topps On-Demand Wacky Packages Wonky Ads Series 2 Puzzle Back Checklists

COMPLETE SET (4)	4.00	10.00
COMMON CARD	1.50	4.00
STATED ODDS 1:1		
NNO Bottom Left		
NNO Bottom Right		
NNO Top Left		
NNO Top Right		

1992 O-Pee-Chee Wacky Packages

COMPLETE SET (48)	6.00	15.00
COMPLETE SET w/VARIATIONS (1-66)	10.00	25.00
UNOPENED BOX (36 PACKS)	25.00	40.00
UNOPENED PACK (5 STICKERS)	1.25	1.50
COMMON CARD (1-66)	.30	.75

2012 Wacky Packages Posters Series 1

COMPLETE SET (24)	25.00	60.00
COMMON CARD	1.25	3.00

2012 Wacky Packages Posters Series 1 Promos

COMMON CARD (PP1-PP3)	4.00	10.00
SHOPTOPPS.COM EXCLUSIVE		
PP1 Panther	10.00	25.00
PP2 Wriggling Gum	6.00	15.00

2004 Wacky Packages Series 1

COMPLETE SET (55)	8.00	20.00
UNOPENED BOX (24 PACKS)	50.00	75.00
UNOPENED PACK (6 CARDS)	2.50	3.00
COMMON CARD (1-55)	.25	.60

2004 Wacky Packages Series 1 Bonus Retail Box-Toppers

COMPLETE SET (2)	3.00	8.00
COMMON CARD (B1-B2)	2.00	5.00
STATED ODDS 1:BOX		

2004 Wacky Packages Series 1 Clear-Cling

COMPLETE SET (9)	6.00	15.00
COMMON CARD (1-9)	.75	2.00
STATED ODDS 1:4		

2004 Wacky Packages Series 1 Temporary Tattoos

COMPLETE SET (10)	8.00	20.00
COMMON CARD (1-10)	1.25	3.00
STATED ODDS 1:6		

2004 Wacky Packages Series 1 Promos

COMPLETE SET (3)	1.50	4.00
COMMON CARD (1-3)	.75	2.00

2005 Wacky Packages Series 2

COMPLETE SET (55)	6.00	15.00
UNOPENED HOBBY BOX (24 PACKS)	50.00	75.00
UNOPENED HOBBY PACK (6 CARDS)	2.00	3.00
UNOPENED RETAIL BOX (18 PACKS)	15.00	25.00
UNOPENED RETAIL PACK (6 CARDS)	1.00	1.25
COMMON CARD (1-55)	.20	.50

2005 Wacky Packages Series 2 Bonus

COMPLETE SET (5)	8.00	20.00
COMMON CARD (B3-B7)	2.00	5.00

2005 Wacky Packages Series 2 Clear-Cling

COMPLETE SET (9)	5.00	12.00
COMMON CARD (1-9)	.75	2.00
STATED ODDS 1:4		

2005 Wacky Packages Series 2 Magnets

COMPLETE SET (9)	6.00	15.00
COMMON CARD (1-9)	1.00	2.50
STATED ODDS 1:4		

2005 Wacky Packages Series 2 Temporary Tattoos

COMPLETE SET (10)	8.00	20.00
COMMON CARD (1-10)	1.25	3.00
STATED ODDS 1:6		

2005 Wacky Packages Series 2 Promo

P1 Goodbye Kitty SDCC	3.00	8.00

2006 Wacky Packages Series 3

COMPLETE SET (55)	5.00	12.00
UNOPENED HOBBY BOX (36 PACKS)	75.00	125.00
UNOPENED HOBBY PACK (6 CARDS)	2.50	4.00
UNOPENED RETAIL BOX (24 PACKS)	15.00	25.00
UNOPENED RETAIL PACK (6 CARDS)	1.00	1.25
UNOPENED BONUS BOX (11 PACKS)	8.00	10.00
UNOPENED BONUS PACK (6 CARDS)	1.00	1.25
UNOPENED BLISTER PACK (2 PACKS)	1.00	2.00
COMMON CARD (1-55)	.15	.40
NNO Annoying Spitter-Man Promo	6.00	15.00

2006 Wacky Packages Series 3 Bonus

COMPLETE SET (6)	4.00	10.00
COMMON CARD (B1-B6)	.75	2.00
B1-B3 STATED ODDS 1:BOX		
B4-B6 STATED ODDS 1:BLISTER PACK		

2006 Wacky Packages Series 3 Magnets

COMPLETE SET (9)	6.00	15.00
COMMON CARD (1-9)	1.00	2.50
STATED ODDS 1:6		

2006 Wacky Packages Series 3 Rainbow Foil

COMPLETE SET (10)	6.00	15.00
COMMON CARD (F1-F10)	.75	2.00
STATED ODDS 1:3		

2006 Wacky Packages Series 4

COMPLETE SET (55)	4.00	10.00
UNOPENED HOBBY BOX (36 PACKS)	30.00	40.00
UNOPENED HOBBY PACK (5 CARDS)	1.25	1.50
UNOPENED RETAIL BOX (24 PACKS)	15.00	25.00
UNOPENED RETAIL PACK (5 CARDS)	1.00	1.25
UNOPENED BONUS BOX (11 PACKS)	8.00	10.00
UNOPENED BONUS PACK (5 CARDS)	1.00	1.25
UNOPENED BLISTER PACK (2 PACKS)	1.00	2.00
COMMON CARD (1-55)	.15	.40
P1 Superham SDCC Promo	2.00	5.00

2006 Wacky Packages Series 4 Bonus

COMPLETE SET (6)	5.00	12.00
COMMON CARD (B1-B6)	.75	2.00
B6 Sic Blood Stic	2.50	6.00

2006 Wacky Packages Series 4 Classic Wacky Foil

COMPLETE SET (10)	3.00	8.00
COMMON CARD (F1-F10)	.40	1.00
STATED ODDS 1:3		

2006 Wacky Packages Series 4 Magnets

COMPLETE SET (9)	5.00	12.00
COMMON CARD (1-9)	1.00	2.50
STATED ODDS 1:6		

2007 Wacky Packages Series 5

COMPLETE SET (55)	5.00	12.00
UNOPENED BOX (24 PACKS)	60.00	100.00
UNOPENED PACK (5 CARDS)	3.00	4.00
COMMON CARD (1-55)	.15	.40

2007 Wacky Packages Series 5 Bonus

COMPLETE SET (5)	3.00	8.00
COMMON CARD (B1-B5)	.75	2.00

2007 Wacky Packages Series 5 Foil

COMPLETE SET (10)	4.00	10.00
COMMON CARD (F1-F10)	.60	1.50
STATED ODDS 1:3		

2007 Wacky Packages Series 5 Magnets

COMPLETE SET (9)	5.00	12.00
COMMON CARD (1-9)	.75	2.00
STATED ODDS 1:6		

2007 Wacky Packages Series 6

COMPLETE SET (80)	8.00	20.00
UNOPENED BOX (24 PACKS)	50.00	75.00
UNOPENED PACK (10 CARDS)	2.00	3.00
COMMON CARD (1-80)	.15	.40
P1 Quiet Pupsi PROMO SDCC		2.50

2007 Wacky Packages Series 6 Bonus

COMPLETE SET (5)	5.00	12.00
COMMON CARD (B1-B5)	1.25	3.00

2007 Wacky Packages Series 6 Foil

COMPLETE SET (10)	25.00	60.00
COMMON CARD (F1-F10)	3.00	8.00
STATED ODDS 1:8		

2007 Wacky Packages Series 6 Make Your Own Wacky Packs

COMPLETE SET (10)	5.00	12.00
COMMON CARD (1-10)	.75	2.00
STATED ODDS 1:3		

2007 Wacky Packages Series 6 What's in the Box?

COMPLETE SET (10)	6.00	15.00
COMMON CARD (1-10)	1.00	2.50
STATED ODDS 1:4		

2010 Wacky Packages Series 7

COMPLETE SET (55)	6.00	15.00
UNOPENED BOX (24 PACKS)	75.00	125.00
UNOPENED PACK (10 CARDS)	3.00	5.00
COMMON CARD (1-55)	.15	.40
POLIGRIPE ISSUED AS ALBUM EXCLUSIVE		
NNO Poligripe ALBUM	8.00	20.00

2010 Wacky Packages Series 7 Blister Bonus

COMPLETE SET (4)	4.00	10.00
COMMON CARD (B1-B4)	1.25	3.00
STATED ODDS 1:1 BLISTER PACK		

2010 Wacky Packages Series 7 Cereal Box Bonus

COMPLETE SET (6)	8.00	20.00
COMMON CARD (C1-C6)	2.00	5.00
STATED ODDS THREE PER 3-BOX CEREAL PACKAGE		

2010 Wacky Packages Series 7 Classic Foil

COMPLETE SET (10)	12.00	30.00
COMMON CARD (F1-F10)	2.00	5.00
STATED ODDS 1:4		

2010 Wacky Packages Series 7 Classic Foil Jay Lynch Autographs

COMMON CARD	75.00	150.00
STATED ODDS 1:701		

2010 Wacky Packages Series 7 Wack-O-Mercials

COMPLETE SET (20)	8.00	20.00
COMMON CARD (1-20)	.60	1.50
*RED: 1.2X TO 3X BASIC CARDS		
*FLASH FOIL: 4X TO 10X BASIC CARDS		
*GOLD FLASH: 60X TO 120X BASIC CARDS		
STATED ODDS 1:1		

2010 Wacky Packages Series 7 Web Bonus

COMPLETE SET (3)	3.00	8.00
COMMON CARD (1-3)	1.50	4.00
STATED ODDS THREE PER 3-BOX CEREAL PACKAGE		

2011 Wacky Packages Series 8

COMPLETE SET (55)	5.00	12.00
UNOPENED BOX (24 PACKS)	50.00	75.00
UNOPENED PACK (10 CARDS)	2.00	3.00
COMMON CARD (1-55)	.15	.40
*PINK: 1X TO 2.5X BASIC CARDS		
*FLASH FOIL: 6X TO 15X BASIC CARDS		
*FLASH GOLD: 200X TO 500X BASIC CARDS		

2011 Wacky Packages Series 8 Bonus

COMPLETE SET (5)	12.00	25.00
COMMON CARD (B1-B5)	2.00	5.00
CARDS B1-B3 ODDS 1:BLISTER PACK		
CARDS B4,B5 ODDS 1:BLASTER BOX		
B4 Maximum	6.00	15.00
B5 Oct	5.00	12.00

2011 Wacky Packages Series 8 Go to the Movies

COMPLETE SET (8)	5.00	12.00
COMMON CARD (1-8)	1.25	3.00
STATED ODDS 1:3		

2011 Wacky Packages Series 8 Magnets

COMPLETE SET (10)	15.00	30.00
COMMON CARD (1-10)	2.50	6.00
STATED ODDS 1:6		

2011 Wacky Packages Series 8 Motion Luggage Tags

COMPLETE SET (10)	10.00	25.00
COMMON CARD (1-10)	2.00	5.00
STATED ODDS 1:6		

2011 Wacky Packages Series 8 Pack to the Future

COMPLETE SET (10)	6.00	15.00
COMMON CARD (1-10)	1.25	3.00
STATED ODDS 1:3		

2012 Wacky Packages Series 9

COMPLETE SET (55)	6.00	15.00
UNOPENED BOX (24 PACKS)	40.00	60.00
UNOPENED PACK (10 CARDS)	2.00	3.00
COMMON CARD (1-55)	.15	.40
*PINK: 1X TO 2.5X BASIC CARDS		
*FLASH FOIL: 6X TO 15X BASIC CARDS		
*FLASH GOLD: 200X TO 500X BASIC CARDS		

2012 Wacky Packages Series 9 Awful Apps

COMPLETE SET (10)	4.00	10.00
COMMON CARD (1-10)	.60	1.50
STATED ODDS 1:3		

2012 Wacky Packages Series 9 Lame Games

COMPLETE SET (10)	4.00	10.00
COMMON CARD (1-10)	.60	1.50
STATED ODDS 1:3		

2012 Wacky Packages Series 9 Magnets

COMPLETE SET (10)	12.00	25.00
COMMON CARD (1-10)	2.00	5.00
STATED ODDS 1:6		

2012 Wacky Packages Series 9 Motion Luggage Tags

COMPLETE SET (9)	10.00	25.00
COMMON CARD (1-9)	2.00	5.00
STATED ODDS 1:6		

2013 Wacky Packages Series 10

COMPLETE SET (55)	6.00	15.00
UNOPENED HOBBY BOX (24 PACKS)	75.00	125.00
UNOPENED HOBBY PACK (6 CARDS)	4.00	6.00
UNOPENED RETAIL BOX (24 PACKS)	40.00	50.00
UNOPENED RETAIL PACK (10 CARDS)	2.00	2.50
COMMON CARD (1-55)	.25	.60
*BLUE: 1.5X TO 4X BASIC CARDS		
*RED: 1.5X TO 4X BASIC CARDS		
*BLACK: 2X TO 5X BASIC CARDS		
*SILVER: 3X TO 8X BASIC CARDS		
*LUDLOW BLACK: 25X TO 70X BASIC CARDS		
*CLOTH: 30X TO 80X BASIC CARDS		
*GOLD: 60X TO 150X BASIC CARDS		
*LUDLOW RED: 100X TO 200X BASIC CARDS		

2013 Wacky Packages Series 10 Artist Autographs

COMMON CAMERA	30.00	75.00
COMMON CHAIMUANG		
COMMON ENGSTROM	40.00	100.00
COMMON GAMBINO	25.00	60.00
COMMON GROSS		
COMMON IM	25.00	60.00
COMMON KIRSCHT	25.00	60.00
COMMON PINGITORE		
COMMON SIMKO	30.00	80.00
COMMON SMOKIN' JOE	25.00	60.00
COMMON ST. AUBIN		
COMMON WHEATON	30.00	80.00
COMMON ZELEZNIK		
STATED PRINT RUN 15 SER.#'d SETS		

2013 Wacky Packages Series 10 As Screamed on TV

COMPLETE SET (10)	6.00	15.00
COMMON CARD (1-10)	1.00	2.50
*CLOTH: 1X TO 2.5X BASIC CARDS		
STATED ODDS 1:2 HOBBY		

2013 Wacky Packages Series 10 Awful Apps

COMPLETE SET (10)	5.00	12.00
COMMON CARD (1-10)	.75	2.00
*CLOTH: 1.2X TO 3X BASIC CARDS		
STATED ODDS 1:2 HOBBY		

2013 Wacky Packages Series 10 Billboards

COMPLETE SET (6)	20.00	50.00
COMMON CARD (1-6)	5.00	12.00
ONE PER COLLECTOR EDITION BOX		

2013 Wacky Packages Series 10 Bonus

COMPLETE SET (14)	15.00	40.00
COMMON CARD (B1-B4)	2.00	5.00
COMMON CARD (B5-B14)	2.00	5.00
COMMON CARD (B5-B14)	2.00	5.00
B7-B14 ODDS 1:14 COLLECTOR EDITION PACK		

2013 Wacky Packages Series 10 Cereal Box Bonus

COMPLETE SET (9)	15.00	40.00
COMMON CARD (C1-C9)	3.00	8.00
TOPPS.COM EXCLUSIVE		

2013 Wacky Packages Series 10 Commercial Star Autographs

COMPLETE SET (5)	30.00	80.00
COMMON CARD	6.00	15.00
1 Jimmy Nelson	8.00	20.00

2 John Gilchrist	12.00	30.00
4 Matt Frewer	10.00	25.00

2013 Wacky Packages Series 10 Lost Wackys

COMMON CARD (L1-L3)	40.00	100.00
STATED ODDS 1:84 COLLECTOR EDITION PACK		

2013 Wacky Packages Series 10 Magnets

COMPLETE SET (10)	30.00	70.00
COMMON CARD (1-10)	4.00	10.00
STATED ODDS 1:12		

2013 Wacky Packages Series 10 Tattoos

COMPLETE SET (10)	12.00	30.00
COMMON CARD (1-10)	2.00	5.00
STATED ODDS 1:6		

2013 Wacky Packages Series 11

COMPLETE SET (110)	8.00	20.00
UNOPENED BOX (24 PACKS)	600.00	1000.00
UNOPENED PACK (10 CARDS)	25.00	40.00
COMMON CARD (1a-55b)	.20	.50
*CANVAS: 1.2X TO 3X BASIC CARDS		
*BLUE: 1.2X TO 3X BASIC CARDS		
*RED: 1.2X TO 3X BASIC CARDS		
*DIE-CUT: 5X TO 12X BASIC CARDS		
*PENCIL: 5X TO 12X BASIC CARDS		
*SILVER: 5X TO 12X BASIC CARDS		
*LUDLOW BLACK: 6X TO 15X BASIC CARDS		
*CLOTH: 12X TO 30X BASIC CARDS		
*GOLD: 30X TO 80X BASIC CARDS		
*LUDLOW RED: 50X TO 120X BASIC CARDS		
9c SurReal Friends CL SP	30.00	60.00
19c My Little Bony SP	30.00	60.00
25c Horderlands 2 SP	30.00	60.00
P1 Fruit of the Moon PROMO	2.00	5.00

2013 Wacky Packages Series 11 Artist Autographs

COMMON CAMERA		
COMMON CHAIMUANG		
COMMON EDMISTON	20.00	50.00
COMMON ENGSTROM	20.00	50.00
COMMON GAMBINO		
COMMON GROSS	20.00	50.00
COMMON IM	20.00	50.00
COMMON KIRSCHT		
COMMON SIMKO	20.00	50.00
COMMON SMOKIN' JOE		
COMMON WHEATON	25.00	60.00
COMMON ZELEZNIK		
STATED ODDS 1:14 COLLECTORS PACKS		
STATED PRINT RUN 15 SER. #'d SETS		

2013 Wacky Packages Series 11 Billboard Box-Toppers

COMPLETE SET (6)	8.00	20.00
COMMON CARD (1-6)	2.50	6.00
STATED ODDS 1:BOX		

2013 Wacky Packages Series 11 Bonus

COMP.SET (JUMBO PACK) (6)	20.00	50.00
COMP.SET (COLL.PACK) (8)	25.00	60.00
COMMON CARD	6.00	15.00
COLL. PACK ODDS 1:14 COLLECTORS PACKS		
JUMBO PACK ODDS 1:PACK		

2013 Wacky Packages Series 11 Coloring Cards

COMPLETE SET (10)	8.00	20.00
COMMON CARD (1-10)	1.50	4.00
STATED ODDS 1:6		

2013 Wacky Packages Series 11 Comedian Autographs

COMPLETE SET (2)	8.00	20.00
OVERALL AUTO ODDS 1:14 COLLECTORS PACKS		
1 Jay Mohr	5.00	12.00
2 Jim Breuer	5.00	12.00

2013 Wacky Packages Series 11 Coming Distractions

COMPLETE SET (9)	3.00	8.00
COMMON CARD (1-9)	.60	1.50
*RED: .8X TO 2X BASIC CARDS		
*BLUE: 1X TO 2.5 BASIC CARDS		
*SILVER: 1.5X TO 4X BASIC CARDS		
*CLOTH: 4X TO 10X BASIC CARDS		
*GOLD: 25X TO 50X BASIC CARDS		
STATED ODDS ONE PER PACK		

2013 Wacky Packages Series 11 Lost Wackys

COMPLETE SET (3)	40.00	100.00
COMMON CARD (L1-L3)	15.00	40.00
STATED ODDS 1:144 COLLECTORS PACKS		

2013 Wacky Packages Series 11 Magnets

COMPLETE SET (10)	35.00	70.00
COMMON CARD (1-10)	5.00	12.00
STATED ODDS 1:12		

2013 Wacky Packages Series 11 Patches

COMMON CARD	30.00	60.00

2013 Wacky Packages Series 11 Rude Food

COMPLETE SET (9)	3.00	8.00
COMMON CARD (1-9)	.60	1.50
*RED: .8X TO 2X BASIC CARDS		
*BLUE: 1X TO 2.5X BASIC CARDS		
*SILVER: 1.5X TO 4X BASIC CARDS		
*CLOTH: 4X TO 10X BASIC CARDS		
*GOLD: 25X TO 50X BASIC CARDS		
STATED ODDS ONE PER PACK		

2014 Wacky Packages Series One

COMPLETE SET (55)	6.00	15.00
UNOPENED BOX (24 PACKS)	40.00	50.00
UNOPENED PACK (10 CARDS)	2.00	2.50
COMMON CARD (1a-55b)	.20	.50
*RED MET.: 3X TO 8X BASIC CARDS	1.50	4.00
*GOLD: 12X TO 30X BASIC CARDS	6.00	15.00
*SILVER: 3X TO 8X BASIC CARDS	1.50	4.00
*LUDLOW BLACK: 8X TO 20X BASIC CARDS	4.00	10.00
*LUDLOW RED: 20X TO 50X BASIC CARDS	10.00	25.00
*PENCIL DRAWING: 4X TO 10X BASIC CARDS	2.00	5.00

2014 Wacky Packages Series One Hobby Bonus

COMPLETE SET (12)	25.00	60.00
COMMON CARD (B1-B12)	2.00	5.00
STATED ODDS 1:24		
COLLECTOR EDITION EXCLUSIVE		
B5 Chucky	4.00	10.00
B7 Dronestrike	4.00	10.00
B9 Unkist	4.00	10.00
B10 Soul Patch	4.00	10.00
B12 Bum Pop	5.00	12.00

2014 Wacky Packages Series One Lost Wackys

COMPLETE SET (3)	25.00	60.00
COMMON CARD (L1-L3)	10.00	25.00
STATED ODDS 1:CASE		
L2 Twits	12.00	30.00
L3 Snore-Caps	15.00	40.00

2014 Wacky Packages Series One Medallions

COMPLETE SET (12)	125.00	300.00
COMMON CARD	15.00	40.00
COLLECTOR EDITION EXCLUSIVE		

2014 Wacky Packages Series One Patch Relics

COMMON CARD (1-8)	12.00	30.00
COLLECTOR EDITION EXCLUSIVE		
1 Apple Jerks	15.00	40.00
2 Band-Ache	20.00	50.00
3 Garbage Pail Geezers	15.00	40.00
6 Ratz	15.00	40.00

2014 Wacky Packages Series One Ridiculous Reads

COMPLETE SET (10)	6.00	15.00
COMMON CARD (1-10)	1.25	3.00
*SILVER: .8X TO 1.5X BASIC CARDS		
*GOLD: 3X TO 8X BASIC CARDS		

2014 Wacky Packages Series One Terrible TV

COMPLETE SET (10)	6.00	15.00
COMMON CARD (1-10)	1.25	3.00
*SILVER: .8X TO 1.5X BASIC CARDS		
*GOLD: 3X TO 8X BASIC CARDS		

2015 Wacky Packages Series One

COMPLETE SET (110)	10.00	25.00
UNOPENED BOX (24 PACKS)	50.00	75.00
UNOPENED PACK (10 CARDS)	2.00	3.00
COMMON CARD (1-110)	.20	.50
*PATTERN: 1.5X TO 4X BASIC CARDS		
*RED METALLIC: 2X TO 5X BASIC CARDS		
*PURPLE: 2.5X TO 6X BASIC CARDS		
*PENCIL: 3X TO 8X BASIC CARDS		
*LUDLOW BLACK: 4X TO 10X BASIC CARDS		
*SILVER: 5X TO 12X BASIC CARDS		
*GOLD/25: 12X TO 30X BASIC CARDS		
*LUDLOW GREEN: 25X TO 60X BASIC CARDS		
*LUDLOW RED: 30X TO 80X BASIC CARDS		

2015 Wacky Packages Series One Artist Autographs

COMMON CAMERA	10.00	25.00
COMMON ENGSTROM	8.00	20.00
COMMON GAMBINO	10.00	25.00
COMMON GREGORY	6.00	15.00
COMMON GROSS	12.00	30.00
COMMON GROSSBERG	6.00	15.00
COMMON IM	8.00	20.00
COMMON KIRSCHT	12.00	30.00
COMMON PINGITORE	10.00	25.00
COMMON SIMKO	12.00	30.00
COMMON SMOKIN' JOE	12.00	30.00
COMMON TAYLOR	8.00	20.00
COMMON WHEATON	8.00	20.00
COMMON ZELEZNIK	10.00	25.00
STATED PRINT RUN 15 SER.#'d SETS		

2015 Wacky Packages Series One Box-Loaders

COMPLETE SET (4)	8.00	20.00
COMMON CARD	3.00	8.00
STATED ODDS 1:BOX		

2015 Wacky Packages Series One Patch Relics

COMPLETE SET (6)	120.00	250.00
COMMON CARD	30.00	80.00
*SP: 1.2X TO 3X BASIC CARDS		

2015 Wacky Packages Series One Patch Relics SP

*SP: 1.2X TO 3X BASIC CARDS		
STATED ODDS 1:		

2015 Wacky Packages Series One Tattoos

COMPLETE SET (10)	8.00	20.00
COMMON CARD	1.50	4.00
STATED ODDS 1:4		

2015 Wacky Packages Series One Wardrobes

COMMON CARD	20.00	50.00
*BLUE: .6X TO 1.5X BASIC CARDS		
*RED: .75X TO 2X BASIC CARDS		
1 Barf Wimpson	30.00	80.00
2 Blue Beanie	50.00	100.00
5 Fruit of the Tomb	30.00	80.00
6 Mold Rush	30.00	80.00
7 Pure Hex	25.00	60.00
8 Shorts Illustrated	30.00	80.00
9 Tied	25.00	60.00
10 Wash'N Fly	25.00	60.00

2020 Topps Wacky Packages Weekly Series May

COMPLETE SET (20)	25.00	60.00
COMPLETE WK 1 SET (5)	8.00	20.00
COMPLETE WK 2 SET (5)	8.00	20.00
COMPLETE WK 3 SET (5)	8.00	20.00
COMPLETE WK 4 SET (5)	8.00	20.00
COMMON WK 1 (1-5)	2.50	6.00
COMMON WK 2 (6-10)	2.50	6.00
COMMON WK 3 (11-15)	2.50	6.00
COMMON WK 4 (16-20)	2.50	6.00
*COUPON: .5X TO 1.2X BASIC CARDS		
*RED LUDLOW: .6X TO 1.5X BASIC CARDS		
WK 1 PRINT RUN 886 SETS		

WK 2 PRINT RUN 745 SETS
WK 3 PRINT RUN 739 SETS
WK 4 PRINT RUN 740 SETS

2020 Topps Wacky Packages Weekly Series May Wonky Packages

COMMON CARD (WP1-WP4)	25.00	60.00
STATED ODDS 1:SET		
WP1 Baby Rant	30.00	75.00
WP2 Crumbs	75.00	150.00
WP3 Clumsy	100.00	200.00

2020 Topps Wacky Packages Weekly Series June

COMPLETE SET (20)	12.00	30.00
COMPLETE WK 1 SET (5)	4.00	10.00
COMPLETE WK 2 SET (5)	4.00	10.00
COMPLETE WK 3 SET (5)	4.00	10.00
COMPLETE WK 4 SET (5)	4.00	10.00
COMMON WK 1 (1-5)	1.25	3.00
COMMON WK 2 (6-10)	1.25	3.00
COMMON WK 3 (11-15)	1.25	3.00
COMMON WK 4 (16-20)	1.25	3.00

*COUPON BACKS: .6X TO 1.5X BASIC CARDS
*RED LUDLOW: .75X TO 2X BASIC CARDS
WK 1 PRINT RUN 1000 SETS
WK 2 PRINT RUN 952 SETS
WK 3 PRINT RUN 891 SETS
WK 4 PRINT RUN 935 SETS

2020 Topps Wacky Packages Weekly Series June Guest Artists

COMPLETE SET (4)	10.00	25.00
COMMON CARD (GA1-GA4)	4.00	10.00
STATED OVERALL ODDS 1:1 W/WONKY PACKAGES		
GA1 Pezzimist by Robert Jimenez	4.00	10.00
GA2 Old Lice by Chad Scheres	4.00	10.00
GA3 Paesan Cheese by Chenduz	4.00	10.00
GA4 Slim by Jon Gregory	4.00	10.00

2020 Topps Wacky Packages Weekly Series June Wonky Packages

COMPLETE SET (4)	10.00	25.00
COMMON CARD (WP1-WP4)	4.00	10.00
STATED OVERALL ODDS 1:1 W/GUEST ARTISTS		
WP1 Gatorage	5.00	12.00

2020 Topps Wacky Packages Weekly Series July

COMPLETE SET (25)	20.00	50.00
COMPLETE WK 1 SET (5)	6.00	15.00
COMPLETE WK 2 SET (5)	6.00	15.00
COMPLETE WK 3 SET (5)	6.00	15.00
COMPLETE WK 4 SET (5)	6.00	15.00
COMPLETE WK 5 SET (5)	6.00	15.00
COMMON WK 1 (1-5)	1.50	4.00
COMMON WK 2 (6-10)	1.50	4.00
COMMON WK 3 (11-15)	1.50	4.00
COMMON WK 4 (16-20)	1.50	4.00
COMMON WK 5 (21-25)	1.50	4.00

*COUPON BACKS: .5X TO 1.2X BASIC CARDS
*RED LUDLOW: .75X TO 2X BASIC CARDS
WK 1 PRINT RUN 944 SETS
WK 2 PRINT RUN 909 SETS
WK 3 PRINT RUN 901 SETS
WK 4 PRINT RUN 755 SETS
WK 5 PRINT RUN 784 SETS

2020 Topps Wacky Packages Weekly Series July Guest Artists

COMPLETE SET (5)	12.00	30.00
COMMON CARD (GA7-GA11)	4.00	10.00
STATED OVERALL ODDS 1:1 W/WONKY PACKAGES		

2020 Topps Wacky Packages Weekly Series July Wonky Packages

COMPLETE SET (5)	10.00	25.00
COMMON CARD (WP1-WP5)	2.50	6.00
STATED OVERALL ODDS 1:1 W/GUEST ARTISTS		
WP2 Aged	3.00	8.00
WP4 Crypt	3.00	8.00

2020 Topps Wacky Packages Weekly Series August

COMPLETE SET (20)	12.00	30.00
COMPLETE WK 1 SET (5)	4.00	10.00
COMPLETE WK 2 SET (5)	4.00	10.00
COMPLETE WK 3 SET (5)	4.00	10.00
COMPLETE WK 4 SET (5)	4.00	10.00
COMMON WK 1 (1-5)	1.25	3.00
COMMON WK 2 (6-10)	1.25	3.00
COMMON WK 3 (11-15)	1.25	3.00
COMMON WK 4 (16-20)	1.25	3.00

*RED LUDLOW: 1.5X TO 4X BASIC CARDS
*COUPON BACKS: 3X TO 8X BASIC CARDS
WK 1 PRINT RUN 715 SETS
WK 2 PRINT RUN 734 SETS
WK 3 PRINT RUN 699 SETS
WK 4 PRINT RUN 688 SETS

2020 Topps Wacky Packages Weekly Series August Guest Artists

COMPLETE SET (4)	12.00	30.00
COMMON CARD (GA1-GA4)	4.00	10.00
STATED OVERALL ODDS 1:1 W/WACKY INITIALS		

2020 Topps Wacky Packages Weekly Series August Wacky Initials

COMPLETE SET (4)	15.00	40.00
COMMON CARD (WI1-WI4)	6.00	15.00
STATED OVERALL ODDS 1:1 W/GUEST ARTISTS		

2020 Topps Wacky Packages Weekly Series September

COMPLETE SET (25)	25.00	60.00
COMPLETE WK 1 SET (5)	6.00	15.00
COMPLETE WK 2 SET (5)	6.00	15.00
COMPLETE WK 3 SET (5)	6.00	15.00
COMPLETE WK 4 SET (5)	6.00	15.00
COMPLETE WK 5 SET (5)	6.00	15.00
COMMON WK 1 (1-5)	1.50	4.00
COMMON WK 2 (6-10)	1.50	4.00
COMMON WK 3 (11-15)	1.50	4.00
COMMON WK 4 (16-20)	1.50	4.00
COMMON WK 5 (21-25)	1.50	4.00

*RED LUDLOW: 1.2X TO 3X BASIC CARDS
*COUPON BACKS: 1.5X TO 4X BASIC CARDS
WK 1 PRINT RUN 714 SETS
WK 2 PRINT RUN 677 SETS
WK 3 PRINT RUN 701 SETS
WK 4 PRINT RUN 716 SETS
WK 5 PRINT RUN 718 SETS

2020 Topps Wacky Packages Weekly Series September Guest Artists

COMPLETE SET (5)	10.00	25.00
COMMON CARD (GA1-GA5)	3.00	8.00
STATED OVERALL ODDS 1:1 W/WONKY PACKAGES		
GA2 Wide by Paul Harris	4.00	10.00

2020 Topps Wacky Packages Weekly Series September Wonky Packages

COMPLETE SET (5)	15.00	40.00
COMMON CARD (WP1-WP5)	5.00	12.00
STATED OVERALL ODDS 1:1 W/GUEST ARTISTS		

2020 Topps Wacky Packages Weekly Series October

COMPLETE SET (20)	20.00	50.00
COMPLETE WK 1 SET (5)	6.00	15.00
COMPLETE WK 2 SET (5)	6.00	15.00
COMPLETE WK 3 SET (5)	6.00	15.00
COMPLETE WK 4 SET (5)	6.00	15.00
COMMON WK 1 (1-5)	1.50	4.00
COMMON WK 2 (6-10)	1.50	4.00
COMMON WK 3 (11-15)	1.50	4.00
COMMON WK 4 (16-20)	1.50	4.00

*RED LUDLOW: 1X TO 2.5X BASIC CARDS
*COUPON BACKS: 1.2X TO 3X BASIC CARDS
WK 1 PRINT RUN 730 SETS
WK 2 PRINT RUN 754 SETS
WK 3 PRINT RUN 756 SETS
WK 4 PRINT RUN 723 SETS

2020 Topps Wacky Packages Weekly Series October Guest Artists

COMPLETE SET (4)	12.00	30.00
COMMON CARD (GA1-GA4)	4.00	10.00
STATED OVERALL ODDS 1:1 W/WONKY PACKAGES		

2020 Topps Wacky Packages Weekly Series October Wonky Packages

COMPLETE SET (4)	8.00	20.00
COMMON CARD (WP1-WP4)	3.00	8.00
STATED OVERALL ODDS 1:1 W/GUEST ARTISTS		

2020 Topps Wacky Packages Weekly Series November

COMPLETE SET (20)	20.00	50.00
COMPLETE WK 1 SET (5)	6.00	15.00
COMPLETE WK 2 SET (5)	6.00	15.00
COMPLETE WK 3 SET (5)	6.00	15.00
COMPLETE WK 4 SET (5)	6.00	15.00
COMMON WK 1 (1-5)	1.50	4.00
COMMON WK 2 (6-10)	1.50	4.00
COMMON WK 3 (11-15)	1.50	4.00
COMMON WK 4 (16-20)	1.50	4.00

*RED LUDLOW: .5X TO 1.2X BASIC CARDS
*COUPON BACKS: .6X TO 1.5X BASIC CARDS
WK 1 PRINT RUN 644 SETS
WK 2 PRINT RUN 665 SETS
WK 3 PRINT RUN 709 SETS
WK 4 PRINT RUN 700 SETS

2020 Topps Wacky Packages Weekly Series November Guest Artists

COMPLETE SET (4)	12.00	30.00
COMMON CARD (GA1-GA4)	4.00	10.00
STATED OVERALL ODDS 1:1 W/WONKY PACKAGES		
GA1 Criminal Critters by Greg13	4.00	10.00
GA2 Asphalt by Jason Chalker	4.00	10.00
GA3 Among Us Beans by Mike McHugh	4.00	10.00
GA4 Scooty Snacks by Patrick Giles	4.00	10.00

2020 Topps Wacky Packages Weekly Series November Wonky Packages

COMPLETE SET (4)	12.00	30.00
COMMON CARD (WP1-WP4)	5.00	12.00
STATED OVERALL ODDS 1:1 W/GUEST ARTISTS		

2020 Topps Wacky Packages Weekly Series December

COMPLETE SET (20)	12.00	30.00
COMPLETE WK 1 SET (5)	4.00	10.00
COMPLETE WK 2 SET (5)	4.00	10.00
COMPLETE WK 3 SET (5)	4.00	10.00
COMPLETE WK 4 SET (5)	4.00	10.00
COMMON WK 1 (1-5)	1.25	3.00
COMMON WK 2 (6-10)	1.25	3.00
COMMON WK 3 (11-15)	1.25	3.00
COMMON WK 4 (16-20)	1.25	3.00

*RED LUDLOW: 1X TO 2.5X BASIC CARDS
*COUPON BACKS: 2X TO 5X BASIC CARDS
WK 1 PRINT RUN 654 SETS
WK 2 PRINT RUN 605 SETS
WK 3 PRINT RUN 680 SETS
WK 4 PRINT RUN 658 SETS

NNO Thank You to Our Fans! SP	2.50	6.00

2020 Topps Wacky Packages Weekly Series December Guest Artists

COMPLETE SET (3)		
COMMON CARD (GA1-GA3)	5.00	12.00
STATED OVERALL ODDS 1:1 W/GUEST ARTISTS		

2020 Topps Wacky Packages Weekly Series December Wonky Packages

COMPLETE SET (3)	12.00	30.00
COMMON CARD (WP1-WP3)	6.00	15.00
STATED OVERALL ODDS 1:1 W/WONKY PACKAGES		